CRANIAL MRI AND CT

Notice

CRANIAL MRI AND CT

THIRD EDITION

Editors

S. HOWARD LEE, M.D.

Clinical Professor of Radiology
University of Medicine and Dentistry of New Jersey and Temple University School of Medicine
Director of Neurosciences Center
Muhlenberg Regional Medical Center
Plainfield, New Jersey, and
Somerset Medical Center
Somerset, New Jersey

KRISHNA C. V. G. RAO, M.D.

Clinical Professor of Radiology
University of Maryland School of Medicine and Uniformed Services University of Health Sciences
Consultant Neuroradiologist
Bethesda Naval Hospital
Bethesda, Maryland

ROBERT A. ZIMMERMAN, M.D.

Professor of Radiology
University of Pennsylvania School of Medicine
Chief, Neuroradiology and MR
Children's Hospital of Philadelphia
Philadelphia, Pennsylvania

Health Professions Division
New York St. Louis San Francisco Auckland
Bogotá Caracas Lisbon London Madrid Mexico
Milan Montreal New Delhi Paris San Juan
Singapore Sydney Tokyo Toronto

CRANIAL MRI AND CT

1234567890 HALHAL 987654321

ISBN 0-07-037508-9

This book was set in Garamond by Compset, Inc.
The editors were Edward M. Bolger, Roger Kasunic, and Lester A. Sheinis;
the production supervisor was Richard C. Ruzycka;
the book and cover designer was Judy Allan / The Designing Woman Concepts;
the page layout was done by José Fonfrias and Judy Allan;
the indexer was Barbara Littlewood.
Arcata Graphics/Halliday was printer and binder.

Library of Congress Cataloging-in-Publication Data

Cranial MRI and CT / [edited by] S. Howard Lee, Krishna C.V.G. Rao,
Robert A. Zimmerman. — 3d ed.
p. cm.
Rev. ed. of: Cranial computed tomography and MRI. 2d ed. c1987.
Includes bibliographical references and index.
ISBN 0-07-037508-9
1. Cranium—Magnetic resonance imaging. 2. Cranium—Tomography.
I. Lee, Seungho Howard. II. Rao, Krishna C. V. G. III. Zimmerman,
Robert A.
[DNLM: 1. Brain Diseases—diagnosis. 2. Magnetic Resonance
Imaging. 3. Skull—radiography. 4. Tomography, X-ray Computed.
WE 705 C8893]
RC936.C73 1992
617.5′107548—dc20
DNLM/DLC
for Library of Congress 91–37930
CIP

DEDICATED TO OUR TEACHERS, WHO TAUGHT US THAT LEARNING IS A LIFE-LONG PROCESS.

CONTENTS

CONTRIBUTORS

Scott W. Atlas, M.D. [5]
Assistant Professor of Radiology
University of Pennsylvania School of Medicine and Hospital
Philadelphia, Pennsylvania

Jacqueline A. Bello, M.D. [16]
Associate Professor of Radiology
Director of Neuroradiology
Albert Einstein College of Medicine
Montefiore Medical Center
Bronx, New York

Larissa T. Bilaniuk, M.D. [5]
Professor of Radiology
University of Pennsylvania School of Medicine
Children's Hospital of Philadelphia
Philadelphia, Pennsylvania

Andrew R. Bogdan, Ph.D. [3]
Assistant Professor of Radiology Oncology
New England Medical Center
Boston, Massachusetts

T. Linda Chi, M.D. [16]
Assistant Professor of Radiology and Neurosurgery
Chief, Interventional Neuroradiology Section
Albert Einstein College of Medicine
Montefiore Medical Center
Bronx, New York

David L. Daniels, M.D. [11]
Professor of Radiology
Medical College of Wisconsin
Froedtort Memorial Lutheran Hospital
Milwaukee, Wisconsin

Herbert I. Goldberg, M.D. [15]
Professor of Radiology
University of Pennsylvania School of Medicine and Hospital
Philadelphia, Pennsylvania

The numbers in brackets following the contributors' names refer to the chapters written or co-written by the contributors.

Debra A. Gusnard, M.D. [6]
Radiologist
Christian Hospital–North East/North West
St. Louis, Missouri

Victor M. Haughton, M.D. [11]
Professor of Radiology
Chief of Magnetic Resonance Imaging
Medical College of Wisconsin
Milwaukee, Wisconsin

Carl E. Johnson, M.D. [10]
Clinical Assistant Professor of Radiology
SUNY-Health Science Center at Brooklyn
Attending Neuroradiologist
The Long Island College Hospital
Brooklyn, New York

S. Howard Lee, M.D. [8, 13, 15]
Clinical Professor of Radiology
University of Medicine and Dentistry of New Jersey
and Temple University School of Medicine
Director of Neurosciences Center
Muhlenberg Regional Medical Center
Plainfield, New Jersey, and Somerset Medical Center,
Somerset, New Jersey

Krishna C. V. G. Rao, M.D. [4, 7, 14]
Clinical Professor of Radiology
University of Maryland School of Medicine and Uniformed
Services University of Health Sciences
Consultant Neuroradiologist
Bethesda Naval Hospital
Bethesda, Maryland

Katherine A. Shaffer, M.D. [11]
Associate Professor of Radiology
Medical College of Wisconsin
Milwaukee, Wisconsin

James G. Smirniotopoulos, M.D. [8]
Assistant Chairman and Chief of Neuroradiology
Armed Forces Institute of Pathology
Washington, D.C.
Assistant Professor of Radiology and Nuclear Medicine
Uniformed Services University of Health Sciences
Bethesda, Maryland
Clinical Professor of Radiology and Neurology
Georgetown University
Washington, D.C.

Gordon Sze, M.D. [10, 13]
Associate Professor of Radiology
and Chief of Neuroradiology
Yale University School of Medicine
New Haven, Connecticut

Karel G. TerBrugge, M.D., F.R.C.P. [14]
Associate Professor of Radiology
University of Toronto Medical School
Head, Division of Diagnostic and Therapeutic Neuroradiology
The Toronto Hospital
Toronto, Ontario

Theodore Villafana, Ph.D. [1, 2]
Professor of Radiology
Temple University School of Medicine
Director of Diagnostic Physics
Temple University School of Medicine and Hospital
Philadelphia, Pennsylvania

Robert A. Zimmerman, M.D. [5, 9, 12]
Professor of Radiology
University of Pennsylvania School of Medicine
Chief, Neuroradiology and MR
Children's Hospital of Philadelphia
Philadelphia, Pennsylvania

PREFACE

Neuroimaging was revolutionized by the introduction of computed tomography (CT) in the early 1970s. Without doubt, CT drastically improved our approach to neurodiagnosis, which continued until the introduction of magnetic resonance imaging (MRI) in the early 1980s. The last few years have seen significant changes in the evolution of neuroradiology as it is practiced today. MRI has clearly established itself as an imaging modality, providing the most precise depiction of the normal and pathological anatomy as it relates to the head and spine, surpassing any available imaging techniques in vivo.

Since the last edition of this book, there has been an explosion of knowledge both in the technical aspect relating to the software and hardware of the MRI scanner and our own body of knowledge on the clinical imaging aspects in neuroradiology. This is reflected in the numerous excellent MRI textbooks that are presently available.

We believe that CT is still the foundation for the evaluation of many neurologic diseases and continues to play a significant role alongside MRI. Therefore, we made every effort to integrate and present these two modalities equally in all the chapters. Also, attempt was made to avoid much of the redundancy that can occur so easily in a multi-authored work. Certainly, the fact that neuroimaging is a complex and rapidly developing field is reflected by the rewriting of most of the chapters in the third edition. New information requires new images and new thoughts. However, the overall goal of the text has not changed. It is not a comprehensive reference textbook but is still the representation of relevant information in a concise and readable fashion for practical clinical matters. As before, the audience for this text will be primarily trainees in radiology, neurology, neurosurgery, and ophthalmology and radiologists and neuroscientists in clinical practice.

We would like to thank, first of all, the outstanding group of contributors who made this book a reality. Special thanks go to all the individuals who have helped us in preparation of this book: Michele Lee, Jennifer Lee, Valerie Tsafos, Christine Harris, Ann Rismondo, Kim Kaiser, Frank Trojanowski, Lauris Beam, Fredric Okun, Warren Vroom, Juanita James, and Steve Strommer. We also acknowledge Dr. Jeff Rutledge, Dr. John Sherman, Dr. Roger Countee, Dr. R. K. Gupta, Dr. Robert K. Coates, Dr. Adrian Doyle, Dr. Kee Hyun Chang, Dr. Barry Pollock, Dr. Youn K. Oh, and Dr. William F. Cunningham for allowing us to use their clinical material.

No textbook is perfect unless there has been a team effort with the publishers. We would like to thank McGraw-Hill and its staff involved with this book: Edward M. Bolger, Roger Kasunic, Lester A. Sheinis, Anna Ferrera, John M. Farrell, and Richard C. Ruzycka.

Lastly, we are deeply indebted to our families who have endured the aggravations inherent in the never-ending quest of publishing a book.

CRANIAL MRI AND CT

1 PHYSICS AND INSTRUMENTATION: COMPUTED TOMOGRAPHY

Theodore Villafana

INTRODUCTION

A wealth of radiological information was overlooked in classical radiology and tomography (Ter-Pogossian 1974). In fact, even now, CT and MRI as we know them are probably just the beginning of what will come. Radiologists, of course, have been caught up in this imaging revolution. They must become increasingly familiar with the physical principles, instrumentation, and technical limitations of these modalities in order to make accurate and precise diagnostic interpretations. The purpose of this chapter and Chap. 2 is to provide a fuller understanding of the basic CT and MRI scanning principles of direct importance to the clinician. The presentation consists first of a brief overview of the basis and the limitations of classical radiographic imaging. Second, the use of classical tomography as an attempt to overcome some of the problems of classical radiography is also briefly discussed. Finally, computed tomography and its limitations are discussed fully. Chapter 2 will address MRI.

Basic X-Ray Image Formation

The basic aim of diagnostic radiology is to record on a film (or display on a monitor) a pattern of densities (or illumination levels on a monitor) which corresponds to and conveys diagnostic information about the size, shape, and distribution of the anatomic tissues within a patient. For instance, Fig. 1-1 shows a beam of x-rays penetrating a "simplified patient" consisting simply of a square block of tissue surrounded by a different but uniform tissue background. As the x-rays pass through the patient, they are attenuated; that is, they are both absorbed and scattered within the patient. Attenuation will depend on the type of tissues present and the x-ray beam energy. Finally, the x-rays emerge from the patient and arrive at the image receptor level, where they are detected or recorded.

Figure 1-1 depicts one particular x-ray intensity profile. It is important to realize that this profile is the sum total of the transmitted primary beam and the scattered radiation reaching the receptor level. Each point along the final profile thus depends on the x-ray attenuation that occurred along each ray path within the patient as well as the scatter generated. Note also that the final two-dimensional image is composed of the collection of all such intensity profiles within the patient for the entire exposed field.

Let us study further the representation of radiographic images by intensity profiles, as this is the key to understanding CT technology. Referring again to Fig. 1-1, we see that this profile exhibits a certain depth (subject shadow) as well as a certain edge character. It should be clear that if the anatomic square structure under study had been more similar in atomic number and density to the background medium, the pattern depth or shadow

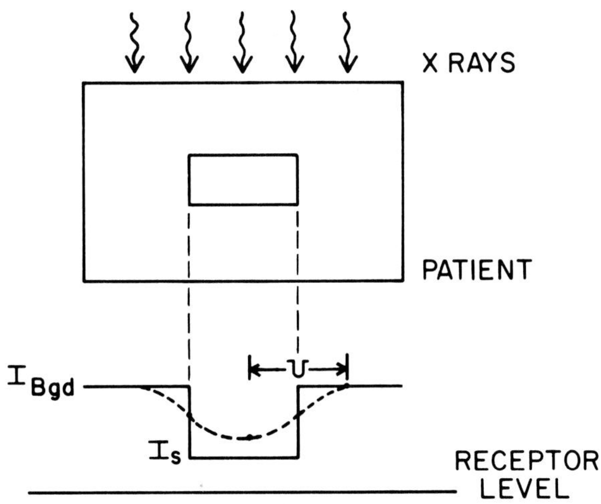

Figure 1-1 An intensity profile of the x-ray beam as it emerges from the patient. Here a hypothetical square-edged anatomic structure ideally casts a shadow (I_s) relative to the adjoining background tissue (I_{Bgd}). The relative depth of the shadow or subject contrast, C_s, depends on the difference in attenuation between the two areas. Factors such as scatter, motion, and focal spot size tend to degrade both subject contrast and the edge character of the pattern (dashed curve). U is the resulting unsharpness or distance over which edge is blurred.

would have been diminished and visualization would have been poorer. The relative x-ray intensity difference between the background and the anatomic structure of interest is referred to as the *subject contrast* (C_s).

$$C_s = \frac{I_{Bgd} - I_s}{I_{Bgd}} \qquad (1)$$

Subject contrast (also referred to as tissue contrast) depends on a number of factors, of which the beam energy is one of the most important. Beam energy in turn is governed by the operating kilovoltage and the beam filtration present in the beam. The second factor is the atomic number difference between the background and the anatomic structure in question. Figure 1-2 plots subject contrast as a function of beam energy for various combinations of anatomic tissues. Note that subject contrast diminishes as beam energy increases and as tissues become more similar. The practical importance of the C_s measure and how it limits routine radiography can be illustrated by the case of blood vessels within soft tissue surrounds. Visualization of brain vasculature in radiography, for instance, is essentially impossible. However, introduction of contrast media into the blood vessel drastically increases its attenuation properties compared to the surrounding tissues, and the blood vessels "light up." Visualization is markedly improved.

In addition to subject contrast, a second important aspect of the x-ray image is its edge character. Figure 1-1 shows the ideal case, in which the x-ray image has exactly the same well-defined edges as the structure itself. In practice, this is not the case in that unsharp edges usually

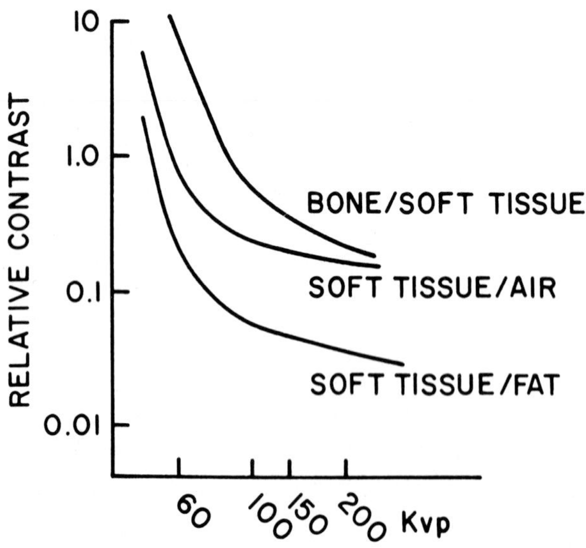

Figure 1-2 Plot of subject contrast between typical tissues as a function of energy. Note how subject contrast diminishes with increasing energy and increasing similarity in tissue densities. (*Adapted from Meredith and Massey 1972.*)

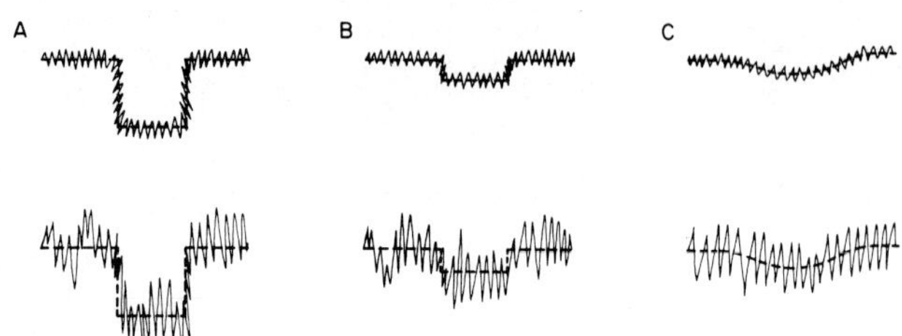

Figure 1-3 The effects of x-ray noise (quantum mottle) on x-ray intensity profiles. **A.** Ideal intensity profile with relatively high subject contrast (deep shadow). Increasing amounts of noise mask the x-ray image, but it may still be detected. **B.** Ideal profile with relatively low subject contrast. Increasing amounts of noise readily obscure pattern. **C.** Unsharp and low subject contrast pattern is also readily obscured by noise.

appear. Deviation from a well-defined edge is quantitated with the concept of *unsharpness* (or *blur*). Unsharpness represents the smear around the edge and is simply expressed as the distance from the point of maximum intensity to the point of minimum intensity. A number of factors affect unsharpness in the x-ray image. The most important are anatomic and patient motion, focal-spot size, and the relative geometry of the patient and the x-ray source. The concept of unsharpness can be applied not only to the x-ray image but also to the final recorded and visible image by incorporating the recording-system image-degrading effects.

In addition to subject contrast and unsharpness, a third aspect of the x-ray image is *quantum mottle* (or *x-ray image noise*). Quantum mottle can be simply defined as the relative fluctuation in photon number arriving at the image plane. Figure 1-3 illustrates how quantum mottle can seriously obscure both the edge character and the depth character of a given image, especially for low subject contrast and small object sizes. Quantum mottle arises from the fact that there are random fluctuations in the x-ray emission spectrum of the x-ray source as well as in the interactions the x-rays undergo within the patient.

To minimize the effect of quantum mottle in the x-ray image, the overall number of photons utilized at the image plane must be increased. This can be accomplished by increases in x-ray tube current, or kilovoltage, or by a decrease in distance from the x-ray source to the image receptor. Attempts to decrease quantum mottle in such a manner, however, may result in an increased radiation dose to the patient.

CLASSICAL RADIOGRAPHY

In classical radiography, one attempts to record directly the x-ray intensity profiles in the form of a density distribution on a film. This process, though simple and direct, forms the major limitation for classical radiography. The reason for this limitation is clear when one considers the fact that the patient is made up of a complex distribution of different tissues and structures. Any particular x-ray intensity profile emerging from the patient is thus the compounded sum of the attenuation which occurred in the patient along a particular ray path (the superimposition effect). Under these conditions contour can interfere with contour and shadow with shadow. What will finally be most prominent in the recorded image is the anatomic structure with the greatest absorption. Thus lesions can be "lost" behind the ribs or the heart shadow or, in the skull, behind the fossa as well as along the base of the calvarium. In practice, this information loss is compensated for in part by obtaining two views perpendicular to each other, such as anterior-posterior and lateral views, or by obtaining oblique views.

Other limitations in classical radiography include the presence of scatter and the use of nonlinear receptors. Scatter is a major source of image degradation; hence, scatter-eliminating grids are generally used. It is true that the use of high-ratio grids reduces scatter as much as 95 to 98 percent, depending on patient thickness and grid ratio. However, it is also true that the difference in subject contrast between such structures as gray matter and white matter is of the order of 0.5 percent. As a result, even a small percentage of scatter can obscure visualization of subtle tissue differences.

In the case of nonlinear receptors, the basic problem is the fact that low subject contrast structures may have densities falling in the nonlinear response region of the receptor. These nonlinear regions yield less film contrast and, consequently, low image contrast. This can be seen in the H&D response curve and the corresponding film contrast curve illustrated in Fig. 1-4. Here, film contrast is merely the slope of the H&D response curve and determines the actual density differences seen on the film. Note that the point of maximum film contrast occurs at about the middle of the linear region. This means that slight exposure or x-ray intensity differences at this level of the H&D curve result in the greatest displayed density differences. Film contrast progressively falls toward both the high-density and low-density sides of the linear region. Final displayed density difference (ΔB) is referred to as *image, radiographic,* or *broad-area contrast.*

Figure 1-4 illustrates these ideas graphically. Here a given slight exposure difference along *B* is finally displayed with a density difference ΔB. If exposures had been such that tissue structures of interest were in the low-density region, i.e., along *A*, then final displayed contrast would be ΔA and the observed density difference would be less than that obtained along the center of the H&D curve. Radiographically, this can be seen in Fig. 1-5*A*, where a bullet is not visible in an approximately correctly exposed chest film, which usually leaves the mediastinum area at relatively low densities and thus low display contrast. Figure 1-5*B* shows the same patient but

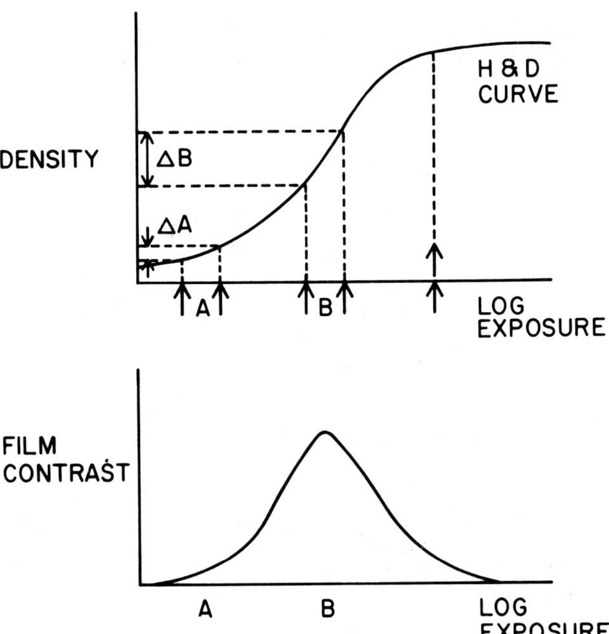

Figure 1-4 Typical H&D curve plotting log exposure versus resulting optical density. Nonlinearity of this curve results in a variable film contrast as seen in the lower figure, where the film contrast at any point of the curve is plotted as merely the slope of the H&D curve at each point. Slight differences in exposure along *B* lying on the linear portion of the H&D curve are displayed with the greatest difference in densities or image contrast (ΔB) and thus are better visualized. Exposures at the lower densities (*A*) are visualized at lower image contrast (ΔA). This is also true for exposures at higher densities.

with exposures sufficiently high so that structures of interest are displayed at higher densities and thus higher display contrast; the presence of the bullet then becomes obvious.

One last observation should be made here: Even if the exposure factors (kilovoltage and milliamperage) are selected optimally for a given tissue or subject contrast, one may still be limited by a relatively small final display contrast (difference in illumination on the display monitor). In CT scanning using linear detectors under computer control, one can increase and optimize the display contrast, utilizing the full black-and-white capability of modern cathode ray tube (CRT) monitors. This is referred to as *windowing.* For instance, exposures along *B* in Fig. 1-4, rather than being displayed with display contrast ΔB, can be windowed in such a way that one can arbitrarily assign them any desired gray-scale values, including the full range of white to black. This important feature is discussed further in a subsequent section.

The following limiting factors of classical radiography as seen in this section can be summarized as follows:

1. Superimposition of three-dimensional information onto two dimensions causes the loss of low-tissue-contrast anatomic structures.

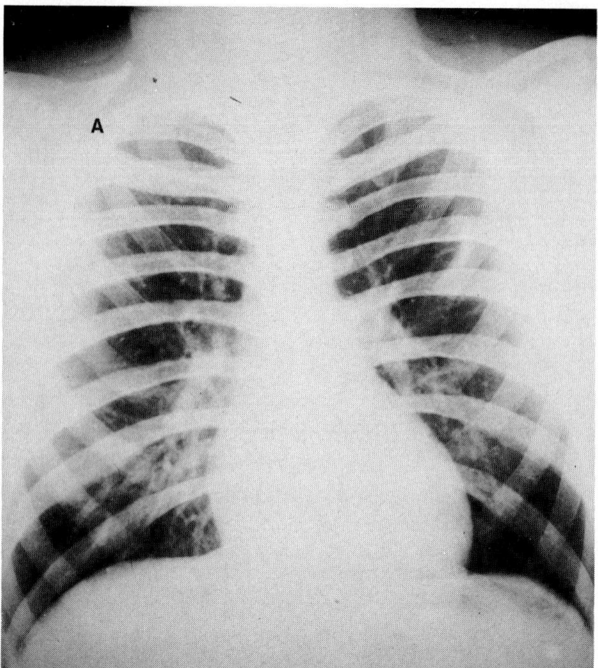

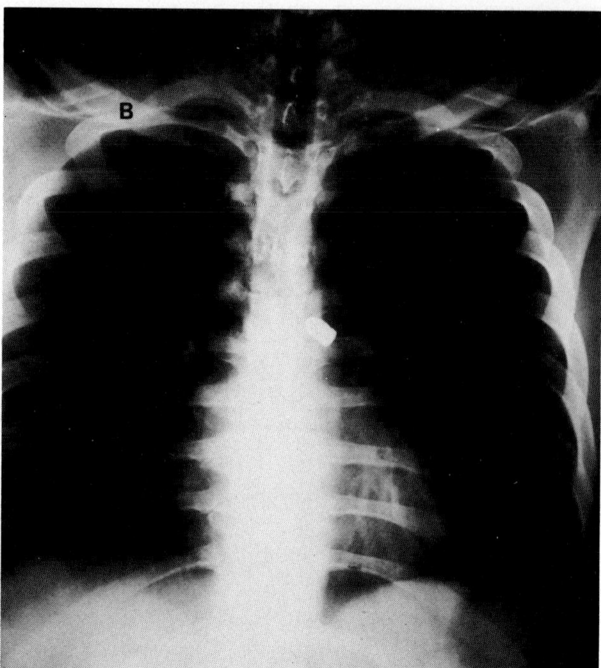

Figure 1-5 Example of loss of important image details in classical radiography as a function of density on the film. **A.** Correctly exposed chest film leaving heart shadow and mediastinum at low density and thus low image contrast. **B.** Bullet obviously present when film is exposed to higher density levels where image contrast is higher. However, note the loss of details in lung areas.

2. Presence of scatter obscures low-tissue-contrast anatomic structures.
3. Presence of nonlinear film receptors limits display contrast at high and low densities; furthermore, display contrast is not adjustable on film by the observer.

CLASSICAL TOMOGRAPHY

Classical tomography was formulated in an attempt to minimize the problem of the superimposition of three-dimensional information onto two dimensions. It is based on moving the x-ray source and film cassette relative to each other in such a way that the recorded images of anatomic structures within the patient are blurred. However, one anatomic layer (referred to as the *focal, fulcrum,* or *pivot plane*) within the patient remains stationary relative to the film and is recorded unblurred. Thus the third dimension (patient thickness, or depth) is removed, and presumably only the specified or pivot layer is recorded at full contrast and sharpness. It is clear, however, that the scatter problem is still present, as are the limitations of nonlinear film and screen systems.

Classical tomography has been reviewed in depth (Littleton 1976), and the reader is referred to the literature already available. What must be emphasized here is that tomography has certain inherent limitations that result in less than optimal information acquisition. These limitations can be summarized as follows:

1. There is incomplete tomographic blurring of the nonfocused planes. This means that obscuring anatomy is never completely and totally removed. The degree of blurring depends on distance from the focal plane. Therefore, structures near the focal plane affect the image to a greater extent than do structures far from the focal plane. Likewise, structures nearer to the film side produce less of a tomographic effect than do structures on the far side of the pivot level.
2. Some blur occurs within the focal plane itself, obscuring the anatomy one desires to visualize, since theoretically only an infinitesimally thin plane is truly in focus. This may be overcome in part by scanning over wide-arc angles (thin-section tomography). Finally, some blur also may occur within the focal plane because of mechanical vibration of the moving apparatus.
3. Tomographic blur is dependent on the direction of motion relative to the shape of the anatomy to be blurred. For example, linear tomography does not blur structures whose boundaries are parallel to the direction of arc motion; rather, only structures whose margins are at an angle to the arc motion are blurred.
4. Even though unwanted structures are blurred, they contribute fog background density to the film, which lowers the relative contrast of the structures within the pivot plane.
5. Since the whole body section is irradiated, large amounts of image-degrading scatter are generated.

COMPUTED TOMOGRAPHY

We now come to computed tomography (CT). CT has in great measure overcome the various limitations of both classical radiography and classical tomography. This has been accomplished by

1. Scanning only a thin, well-defined volume of interest, which serves to minimize the superimposition effect
2. Minimizing scatter by collimating down to relatively thin volumes
3. Using linear detectors with computerized windowing functions

The final success of the diagnostic task hinges on how well the image displays or conveys diagnostic information on the distribution of anatomic structures within the patient. In classical radiography the emerging x-ray beam is recorded directly, with an intensifying screen/film combination. The emerging beam, however, represents the total attenuation which occurred within the patient cross section, and as discussed previously, the superimposition effect is present. Ideally, one would like to have displayed a point-by-point characterization of the anatomic cross section under study. The characterization currently most useful is that of x-ray attenuation in tissue. A host of other characterizations and different radiation types have been proposed and studied with varying degrees of success. These include the atomic number and electron density (Phelps 1975; Rutherford 1976; Latchaw 1978), ultrasound acoustic impedance (Carson 1977; Kak 1979), microwaves (Kak 1979; Maini 1980), neutrons (Koeppe 1981), protons (Cormack 1976), and isotopic emission (Emission Computed Tomography I 1980; Emission Computed Tomography II 1981). CT reconstructions based on fluoroscopic techniques have also been developed (Baily 1976; Kak 1977). Finally, we have proton magnetic resonance, which has been extremely successful and will be discussed in Chap. 2.

The computed tomography approach consists in isolating a specific planar volume within the patient. This plane, or slice, has a thickness z, as seen in Fig. 1-6. The x-ray beam to be utilized passes through only this volume; thus superimposition and scatter effects are greatly minimized but not totally eliminated. Final characterization of tissues within the scanned volume will be expressed and displayed for each element area given by x and y, as seen in Fig. 1-6. This element area is referred to as a *pixel* (*pic*ture *el*ement). The volume formed by virtue of the slice having some thickness z is referred to as a *voxel* (*vo*lume *el*ement). In practice, the whole patient part is arbitrarily broken down into a matrix array of such pixels. The pioneer EMI Mark I unit consisted of an 80 × 80 array in which each pixel corresponded to a 3 mm × 3 mm area within the patient and had a slice thickness of 13 mm. Matrix sizes of modern units are 256 × 256 or 512 × 512. Pixel sizes can now correspond to less than 1 mm by 1 mm within the patient. Different CT units have different pixel configurations. In most cases, however, the critical parameter is not the number of pixels but the area and volume they correspond to within the patient. This in turn depends on the field of view employed for a particular scan protocol.

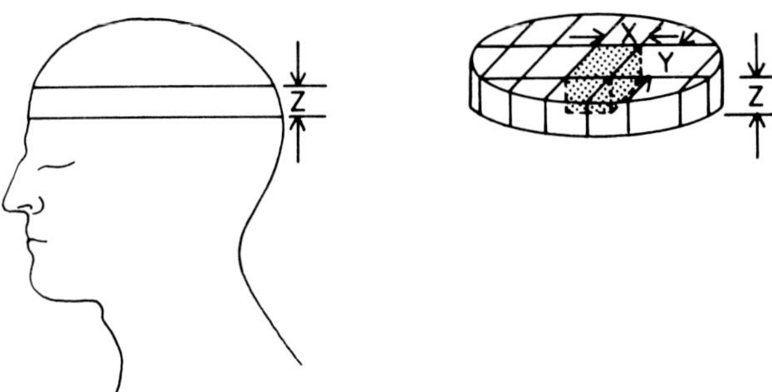

Figure 1-6 Cross-sectional slice across patient. The expanded view shows arrangement of pixels (or picture elements) of dimensions x by y in a grid array. Volume element (or voxel) is formed in a third dimension due to the finite slice thickness.

Attenuation Coefficients and Algorithms

The tissue type within each pixel is characterized by the tissue's ability to attenuate x-rays. Attenuation is defined simply as the removal of x-ray photons from the beam. This removal can be accomplished either by absorption (energy deposited at or near the site of photon interaction) or scatter events (energy removed from the site of photon interaction). Tissues in general have different attenuation properties, depending on their atomic number and physical density and the incident photon energy. One can describe the attenuation of a material in terms of the *attenuation coefficient,* usually symbolized by the Greek letter μ and having units of cm^{-1}. The attenuation coefficient is quite familiar to radiological scientists and, with the advent of CT scanning, has taken on special importance to the clinical radiologist. Table 1-1 lists typical biological tissues of interest and their corresponding attenuation coefficients. Also shown is their representation on an arbitrary scale on which bone is specified as +1000, air as −1000, and water as zero. This scale is referred to as the *Hounsfield scale* in honor of the inventor of computed tomography, Godfrey N. Hounsfield (1972). More commonly, the numbers are simply referred to as *CT numbers.* (For extensive tabulation of attenuation coefficients and CT numbers, see Phelps 1975*b*, Rao 1975, and McCullough 1975.)

The decision to characterize tissue types by CT numbers still leaves the problem of actually determining the value of the CT number for each pixel within that patient. Figure 1-7 shows a simplified 3 × 3 matrix array containing nine pixels, each having specific but unknown values

Table 1-1 Attenuation Coefficients and CT Numbers for Biological Tissues at 60 keV

TISSUE	ATTENUATION COEFFICIENT μ (CM⁻¹)	CT NUMBER
Bone	0.400	+ 1000
Blood	0.215	+ 100 (approx.)
Brain matter	0.210	+ 30 (approx.)
CSF	0.207	+ 5 (approx.)
Water	0.203	0
Fat	0.185	− 100 (approx.)
Air	0.0002	− 1000

Adapted from Phelps 1975b.

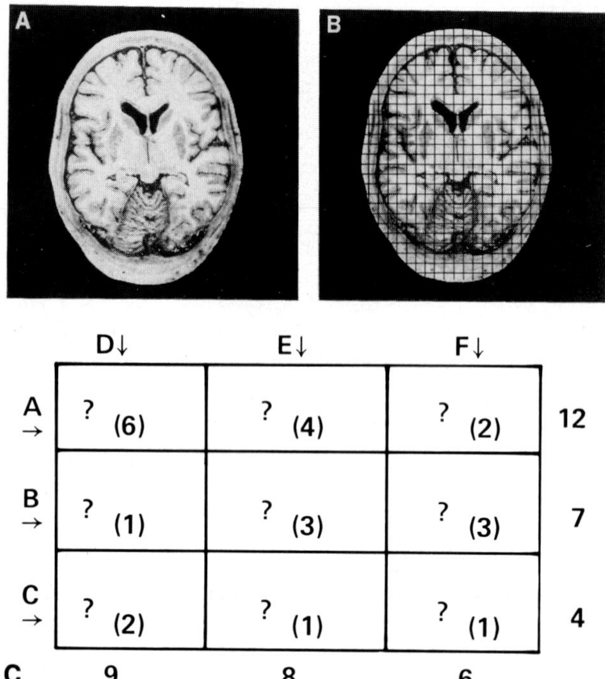

Figure 1-7 **A.** Cross-sectional slice of brain showing structures to be imaged. **B.** Grid array of pixels superimposed over brain slice. The task in CT scanning is to determine tissue type within each pixel. **C.** As an example of how pixel values are determined, here is an unknown 3 × 3 array of pixels. Each pixel has some number value. Even though the interior values are unknown, the total exterior sums along the horizontal paths *A, B,* and *C* and vertical paths *D, E,* and *F* as well as along various angles can be determined (transmission values when using x-rays). Mathematical techniques (algorithms) are available to reconstruct the true interior values from this type of exterior data even for a very large number of pixels. (Solutions to pixel values are shown in parentheses.)

of attenuation. The task is to determine the attenuation for each pixel. If x-rays are passed through ray path *A,* a total attenuation corresponding to, for instance, 12 units is determined. This value is referred to as a *ray sum* and represents the total attenuation occurring from the sum of the attenuation in all the pixels along that ray. Likewise, ray paths *B* and *C* yield totals of 7 and 4, respectively. The process is repeated from another angle perpendicular to the first (ray-paths *D, E,* and *F*), and ray sums of 9, 8, and 6 are found. Now the task is to assign or reconstruct values for each pixel which will conform with ray sums experimentally found from the two angles used. One may in fact "play" with the numbers and finally arrive at the correct distribution, such as that indicated in parentheses in Fig. 1-6. In practice, ray sums also have to be taken at various angles to assure unique and accurate reconstructions.

In the case of matrix arrays which are, for instance, 512 × 512 in extent, one must determine ray scans over a complete contour of the patient and the amount of data to be collected is formidable—so much so that a computer is necessary to keep track of the data and perform the actual calculations necessary for a successful reconstruction. The model, or calculation scheme used for reconstruction, is referred to as an *algorithm.* The most popular algorithm for commercial scanners is the filtered back-projection algorithm. In this algorithm the ray sum for each row of pixels for a first approximation is assigned to each pixel along that row (this is called *back projection*). As each new set of data corresponding to a new angle of scan is determined, it is also back-projected and averaged into each pixel. Such a procedure, though not directly intuitive, does in fact, as seen in Fig. 1-8, result in a successful image reconstruction. Note in Fig. 1-8 that back projection is accomplished by linearly smearing (back-projecting) the image for a number of different angles, and the sum, or superimposition, of all

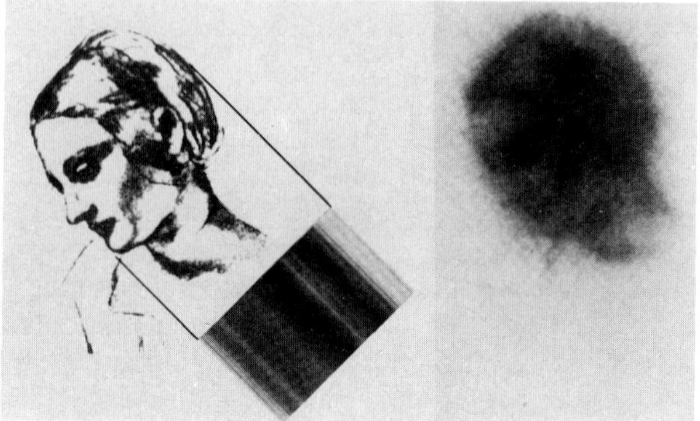

Figure 1-8 Example of back-projection technique using a pictorial view of a face. The value of the density along each line is given by the average along each line. In this case the average is obtained via a smearing motion (equivalent to back projection). When all such projections are summed, the original face is, surprisingly enough, reconstructed. (*After Gordon 1975.*)

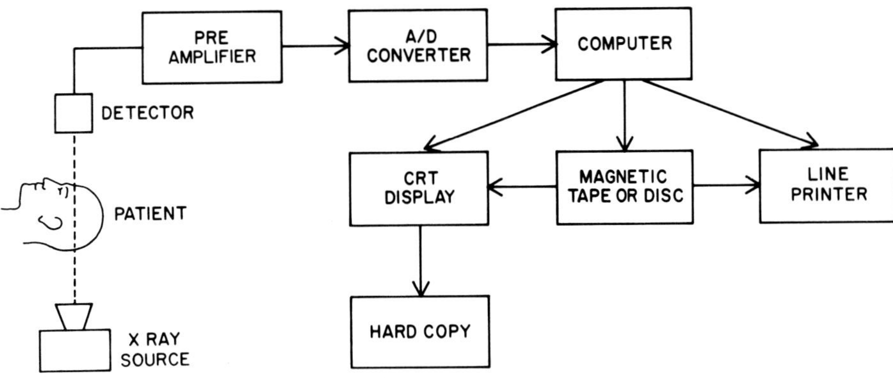

Figure 1-9 Block diagram of a typical CT system. After x-rays emerge from the patient, they are detected, amplified, and digitized with an analog-to-digital (A/D) converter. After computer processing, the reconstruction results are assigned a gray scale and displayed on a CRT video monitor from which hard-copy views may be obtained. Since CRTs are analog devices, the image data must be converted from digital form back to analog form. CT number data can also be outputed to a line printer for quantitative analysis. Normally a tape or disk system is also used for storage of data for later redisplay and/or image manipulation.

the views represents a reconstruction of the original image.

In practice, before back projection is implemented, each intensity profile is modified or filtered to minimize starlike artifacts caused by the use of a finite set of angular images made to correspond to a square pixel. A number of *filter functions* are incorporated in the algorithms that have been used or proposed, and the reader is referred to various reviews (Gordon 1974; Brooks 1975). These filter functions, which are sometimes called *kernels,* can also incorporate varying degrees of *smoothing* and edge enhancement. Smoothing may sometimes be of value when noise limits the detail visible in the image (Joseph 1978*a*). Many CT units have a number of filter functions available, and the user should be aware of possible improvements in the images and the possibility of decreasing patient dose with their use. It should, however, also be realized that the smoothing operation degrades image resolution and thus limits the smallest sizes that can be displayed. It should be considered only as a noise suppressant in imaging relatively large structures.

Data-Collection Geometry

It is worth repeating that the reconstruction process involves the collection of x-ray transmission values outside the patient. These transmission values are an index of how much the radiation was attenuated in passage through the patient. The collection of such data from a number of different angles around the patient is used to calculate the attenuation occurring at each picture element within the patient. Various data-collection schemes have been employed for the acquisition of x-ray transmission data. All schemes involve some geometrical pattern of scanning around the patient coupled with use of a suitable radiation detector. The signal from the radiation detector is digitized by the use of an analog-to-digital (A/D) converter and passed onto the computer for processing. After the reconstruction is completed, the results are displayed on a video monitor. The images can be preserved for long-term storage either on disks or on magnetic tape. The overall layout is illustrated in Fig. 1-9.

Translate/Rotate Geometry

The first successful clinical CT scanner was based on a translate/rotate gantry geometry. Although this technology is now obsolete, it will be discussed since it illustrates the basic principles of CT scanning.

In this type of system the x-ray beam is collimated down to the desired slice thickness and to a narrow slit. The resulting x-ray pattern is referred to as a *pencil beam.* The pencil beam is then passed through the patient and is incident on a radiation detector, as seen in Fig. 1-10. The quantity of radiation arriving at the detector for each ray path will depend on the total attenuation that occurred along the ray path for each volume element (voxel) traversed.

In order to determine the ray-attenuation sums for each row of voxels, the pencil beam is made to linearly scan, or translate, across the patient. During the translate motion the detector, being rigidly connected to the x-ray tube, moves in such a manner that it always intercepts the x-ray pencil beam. The signals detected during the translation motion form a profile representing the ray sums along all voxel rows.

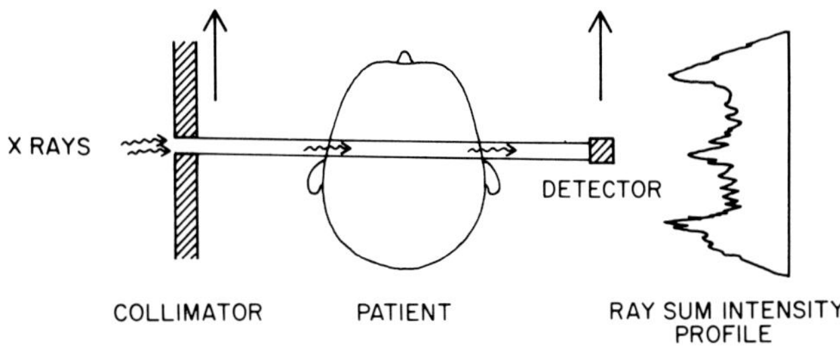

Figure 1-10 First-generation CT configuration. A pencil beam is formed with a collimator and passed through the patient at a particular angle onto a detector traversing the patient along with the x-ray pencil beam. A ray sum intensity profile is thus detected and channeled to the computer for processing. The process is repeated at 1° intervals for 180°.

To determine the ray-sum profiles at different angles, the unit must sequentially rotate and perform a translation movement across the patient for each angle of rotation. The original EMI Mark I system rotated a total of 180° one degree at a time (the configuration usually referred to as *first-generation geometry*). These movements required a total of 5½ to 6 minutes to complete. Unfortunately, patient motion and resulting mismatch between patient position and pixel position resulted in severe image streaks. To reduce overall patient examination time, two detectors were placed side by side in the z (or slice thickness) direction and the x-ray beam was made wide enough to include both detectors. This had the effect of providing two image slices simultaneously and shortening the overall time needed to obtain all the slices desired as well as minimizing patient motion between slices.

Individual slice scan times can be reduced significantly by providing for multiple pencil beams, with each beam directed at its own detector. This has the effect of obtaining ray sums from different angles on one translation (the configuration referred to as *second-generation geometry*). This is illustrated in Fig. 1-11 for a three-pencil-beam system. Here the pencil beams are configured to be at a 1° angle to one another. Consequently, during one translation data are collected for three different angles, and the unit can be rotated 3° instead of 1° as needed for a single-pencil-beam configuration. Scan times can thus be reduced approximately by three since the unit has to complete only one-third the number of rotations and translations. (Sixty rotations at 3° increments will still provide for 180° around the patient and 180 ray-sum profiles.) Additionally, one may again provide for a second bank of detectors identical to the first to detect and process two slices simultaneously. To further reduce scan times one may incorporate even more pencil beams, each with its own detector. Thus 10 beams will require 10 detectors and only 18 rotations, 20 beams will require 9 rotations, etc. In fact, given sufficient beams and detectors, scan times can be effectively reduced to a few seconds. In this latter case, since scan times are relatively short, the second bank of detectors may be eliminated for a considerable cost saving.

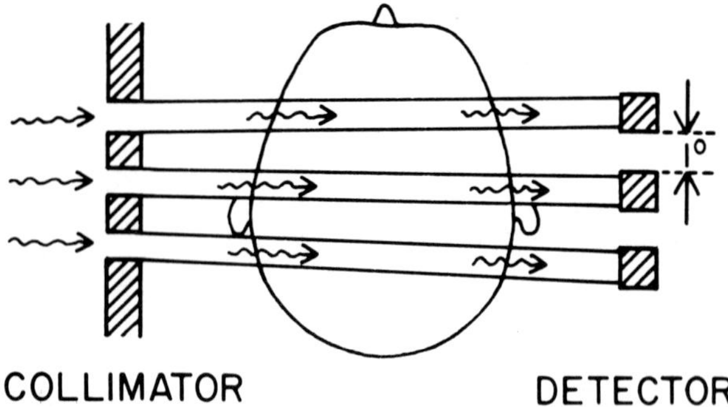

Figure 1-11 Configuration for second-generation gantry systems. A series of pencil beams pass through the patient at an angle, for instance, of 1° to one another. To obtain 180° of information, the number of translations across the patient is then reduced to 180/N, where N is the number of detectors. When possible, another row of detectors is added to obtain a second slice simultaneously with the first.

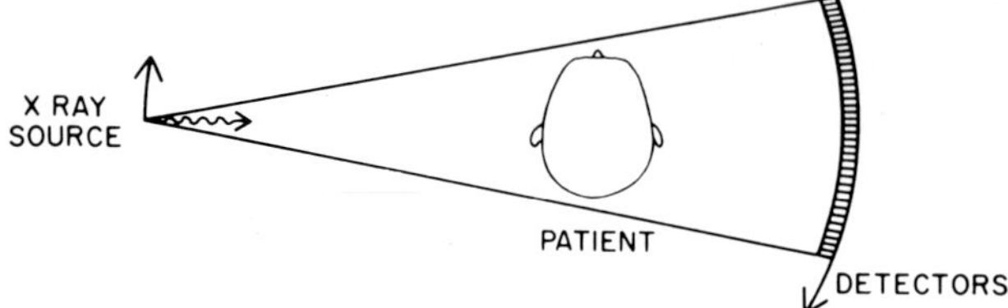

Figure 1-12 Configuration for a third-generation gantry system. Here an entire fan of x-rays is passed through the patient onto the array of detectors. Since all portions of the patient are viewed, translation motion across the patient is eliminated entirely.

Rotate-Only Geometry

The logical extension of using more and more pencil beams is to open up the x-ray beam in the transverse plane to produce a fan beam large enough to encompass the entire patient. This is the so-called *third-generation geometry*. This fan beam is incident on a whole array of detectors which move along with the fan, as in Fig. 1-12. In this process one eliminates entirely the time-consuming translation motion. Note that not only must detectors number at least 180 (one for each of the 180° of view), but actually one needs even more detectors, since the array must be large enough to include a wide range of patient diameters. It is also necessary to include additional detectors to serve as monitoring chambers to correct for any variations in x-ray output. Modern third-generation units use up to 600 or more detectors, with subsecond scan times possible. At these scanning times it is not necessary to have a second array of detectors for simultaneous two-plane scanning, as was common with single-pencil and some multiple-pencil systems. This reduces the cost and complexity of the equipment considerably.

One problem, however, with third-generation configuration is related to the detector calibration problem. The reconstruction process requires extremely high precision, and slight variations (even less than 1 percent) in x-ray output or in detector electronics must be corrected for. Each individual detector must then be calibrated to assure constancy and uniformity of response as compared to adjacent detectors. In first- and second-generation systems, because of the translation motion, the detectors were out from behind the patient and were directly exposed through air to the x-ray beam at the extreme ends of their travel during each scan motion. They could thus be easily calibrated in air before traversing the

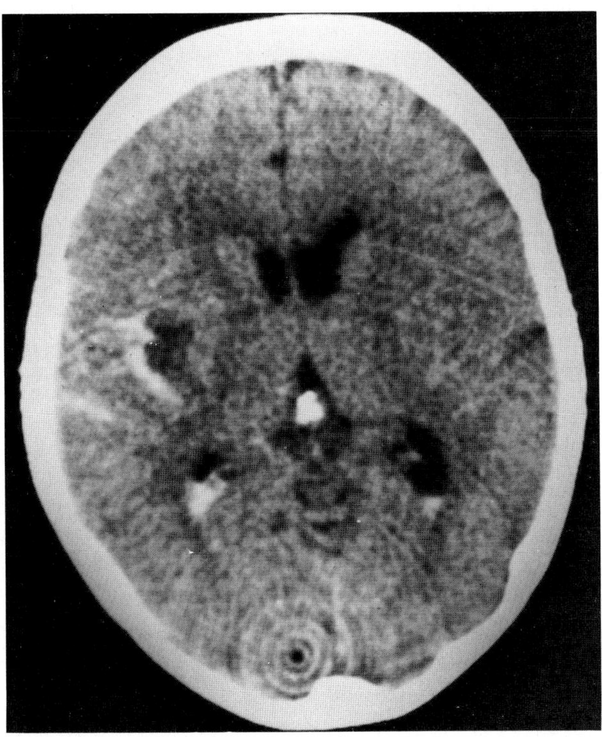

Figure 1-13 Demonstration of typical third-generation ring artifacts. These ring structures are caused by slight detector calibration drifts (typically less than 1 percent).

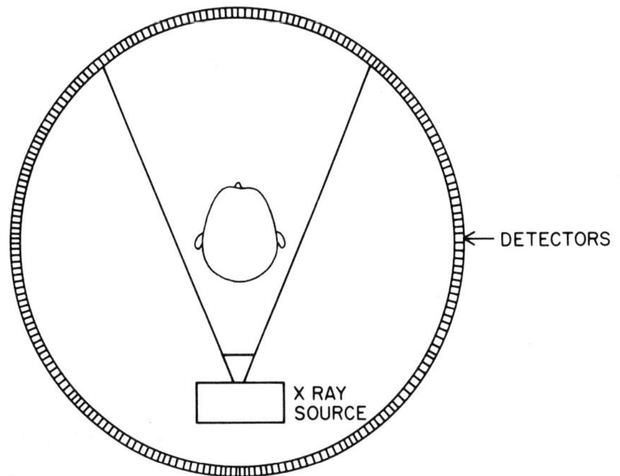

Figure 1-14 Configuration for a fourth-generation gantry system. Detectors are fixed around the entire gantry, and the x-ray tube rotates around the patient.

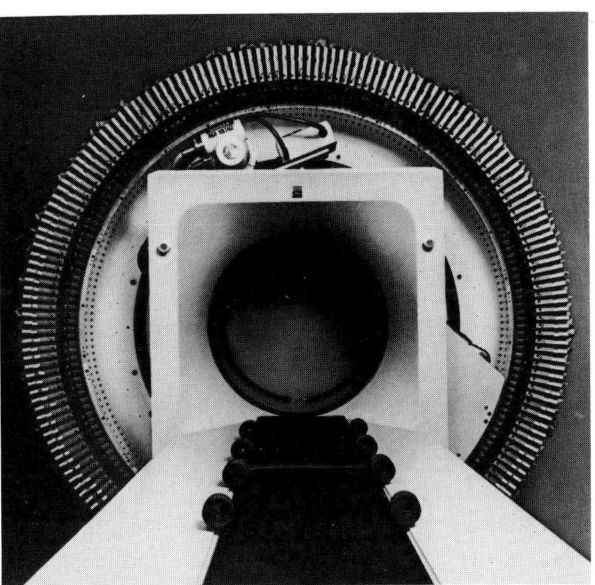

Figure 1-15 Photograph of detector configuration for a fourth-generation gantry system.

patient. Third-generation systems preclude the possibility of frequent calibrations in that detectors are always behind the patient and cannot be calibrated between individual scans. The result is the formation of artifactual ring structures, with each ring corresponding to a drift in one or more detectors, as seen in Fig. 1-13. Ring artifacts can be minimized with certain algorithm corrections; however, stability in the detector system and uniformity of detector response are crucial. In fact, detector drifts of much less than 1 percent can cause visible artifacts (Shepp 1977).

One possible method of avoiding detector-calibration problems, as found in third-generation configurations, is to use a ring of detectors fixed around the entire periphery of the gantry (*fourth-generation geometry*). This configuration is seen in Figs. 1-14 and 1-15. In such an arrangement the x-ray beam rotates around the patient and always radiates a freshly calibrated detector. The added complexity and cost of fixing detectors around the entire gantry periphery and the associated electronics are obvious. Recently, some modern CT designs have reverted back to third-generation configurations, especially in view of the fact that algorithms to minimize ring-artifact formation have been greatly improved. Variations on the fourth-generation configuration include putting the x-ray tube outside the detector array. This allows the use of a smaller detector ring as well as more closely packed smaller detectors, which result in enhanced resolution. In this configuration (which was pioneered by the EMI Corporation), provision is made for continuously moving the detector ring out of the direct x-ray beam path. The reader is referred to a number of review papers for further discussion of geometries and CT scanning in general (Gordon 1975; Ter-Pogossian 1977; Brooks 1976*b*; Kak 1979).

ELECTRON SCAN GEOMETRY

One gantry configuration that is being called by some a fifth-generation system consists of a stationary gantry/detector system with a moving electron beam sweeping across an extended anode target arranged semicircularly around the patient (Boyd 1982; Lipton 1985, 1986). In this approach there are actually multiple target layers so that electrons sequentially sweeping across each result in the formation of multiple successive fan beams of x-rays. The result of all this is that one can acquire multiple image slices within a very short period of time. This high-speed image acquisition (about 50 milliseconds per image) allows for cine-type scan sequences. Additionally, flow phenomena can also be studied. Applications of the scanning concept have been limited to cardiac imaging until recently (Brundage 1985; Lipton 1986; Villafana 1991). For general CT use it is commercially available under the name Fastrack.

Detectors

Let us now look at the various radiation detector types commonly used in CT scanning. Three general types of detection system have emerged: the scintillation detector/photomultiplier, the scintillation detector/photodiode multiplier, and the pressurized ionization chamber. Each of these is briefly discussed in turn.

SCINTILLATION DETECTOR/PHOTOMULTIPLIER

Now obsolete, this is the original type of detector package utilized for CT scanning and is most familiar to the clinician in that it is the type commonly used for nuclear medicine scans. It consists of a solid scintillation crystal such as NaI (TI), which has the property of emitting light when x-ray or gamma photons are incident upon it. This emitted light falls upon a photocathode surface that converts the light to an electronic signal, which in turn is amplified within a photomultiplier. In CT scanning the signal is then digitized and transmitted to the computer for processing. Examples of typical scintillation crystals used in such configurations are seen in Table 1-2. Scintillation crystal/photomultiplier technology is well established and was used extensively in first- and second-generation CT units.

Photo multipliers are notorious for drifting and afterglow. These properties, which result in reconstruction inaccuracies and image degradation, preclude their use in modern CT scanners.

SCINTILLATION CRYSTAL/PHOTODIODE MULTIPLER

At present it is most common to use solid-state photodiode-multiplier scintillation-crystal systems. Here, instead of coupling the emitted scintillation light to a photomultiplier, it is coupled to a silicon photodiode. Advantages include high stability, small size, and possible cost savings.

PRESSURIZED IONIZATION CHAMBERS

One of the requirements for CT detectors is that they be small and capable of being configured very close to one another to provide for full capture of the incident radiation. The ionization chamber approach comes very close to providing these features. Such a chamber consists of one large assembly having very thin walls defining each small collection region, as in Fig. 1-16. This configuration yields a very high packing density of these small detectors. Additionally, xenon gas is perfused evenly throughout the assembly to assure uniformity of response. Some disadvantages include the fact that xenon, being a gas, does not provide for as much absorption efficiency as do solid-state detectors. To compensate for these losses, ionization chambers are pressurized at 10 to 30 atm (providing more gas molecules for absorbing the x-ray beam) and are constructed with relatively great depths (providing greater path length for x-ray photons to be absorbed). Some attenuation loss is experienced within the relatively thick face plate needed to withstand the relatively high xenon gas pressure, and this serves to attenuate the x-ray beam.

DETECTOR REQUIREMENTS

To be effective in CT scanning applications, detectors should have the characteristics listed in Table 1-3. The need for *high absorption efficiency* is self-evident. This provides for maximum utilization of the photons incident on the face of the detector. Here the important factors

Table 1-2 CT Detectors

DETECTOR TYPES	CHEMICAL FORM
Scintillation crystals + photomultiplier	Sodium iodide NaI (TI)
	Calcium fluoride CaF_2
	Bismuth germanate $BI_4Ge_3O_{12}$ (BGO)
Scintillation crystals + photodiode	Cadmium tungstate $CdWO_4$
	Cesium iodide CsI (Na)
Ionization chamber	Xenon (under pressure)

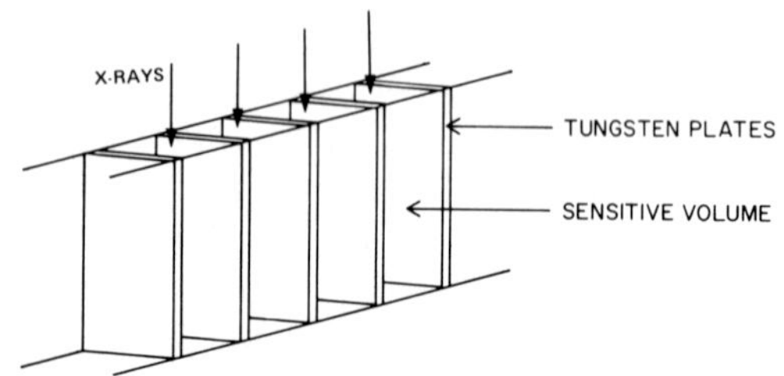

Figure 1-16 Close-up view of adjacent plates within a pressurized xenon gas detector. The small size of these detectors allows for very small data-sampling distances; also, there is minimal information loss between detector cells (high capture ratio).

Table 1-3 Favorable Detector Characteristics

High absorption efficiency
High conversion efficiency
High capture efficiency
Good temporal response (little afterglow)
Wide dynamic range
High reproducibility and stability

are the physical density, atomic number, size, and thickness of the detector. *Conversion efficiency* relates to the ability of the detector to convert the absorbed x-ray energy to a usable electronic signal. *Capture efficiency* means that the size of the detector and the distance to adjacent detectors should be such that as many as possible of the photons passing through the patient are incident on (or captured by) the detector face. The total detector efficiency is merely the running product of these three individual efficiencies. Total detector efficiency is also referred to as *dose efficiency*. Typical dose efficiencies fall between 50 and 70 percent. The *temporal response* of a detector should be as fast as possible in that in a scanning configuration each detector sees the radiation for a relatively short time measured in milliseconds. Within this time, the signal must be processed and the detector must be ready for the next measurement. It is clear that the performance of a unit would be severely degraded if the detector had a significantly delayed response, sometimes referred to as *phosphorescence* or *afterglow*. With significant afterglow, correlation between the specific voxel the x-ray beam is traversing and the signal received by the computer would be lost. Afterglow would be especially limiting for fast, dynamic scanning. Because of the relatively poor temporal response of NaI (TI) and CaF_2, these crystals are no longer used in modern scanners. *Wide dynamic range* refers to the ability of the detector to respond linearly to a wide range of x-ray intensities. When scanning patients, the x-ray beam is sometimes passing through air having negligible attenuation and consequently forming a very intense signal at the detector. On the other hand, the beam may then traverse a thick patient or body part having a high beam attenuation. The x-ray signal formed at the detector would then be very low. Ideally a detector should respond linearly between these two extremes; a dynamic range of 10,000 to 1 should be minimal. Finally, *high reproducibility and stability* are required to avoid drift and resultant detector fluctuation or noise.

CT Image Display and Recording

What the computer understands to be an image consists merely of an array of CT numbers, one number corresponding to each pixel. In order for the viewer to see a "real" image, this array of numbers must be displayed on a suitable medium such as a video monitor. Three considerations must be taken into account for the proper display and storage of CT images:

1. Adjustment of the video monitor display characteristics of brightness and display contrast, i.e., the video gray scale
2. Selection of settings (center and window) to optimize the display of anatomic tissues of interest within the given video gray scale
3. Recording of the image for long-term storage

VIDEO GRAY SCALE

Every video device has its own gray scale. The gray scale refers to the manner in which the device goes from its darkest to its brightest illumination. The gray scale usually is displayed as a graded series of steps, at one end representing the darkest and at the other end the brightest illumination. Steps in between, therefore, have intermediate values of gray, and the rapidity with which they go from light to dark is the video monitor contrast. Rather than steps, some units have a continuous illumination strip. In any case, the result is the same, namely, that one can observe the actual display brightness and contrast of the monitor. Adjustments can be made exactly as one controls monitor display characteristics during image-intensified fluoroscopy, ultrasound video, or home video viewing. These settings are usually chosen initially and remain fixed thereafter. The basis for actual settings varies with the individual viewer. Usually, however, the final gray scale should display both the very darkest and the very brightest that the monitor can display as well as a relatively uniform gradation of gray between these two extremes. All installations have a monitor for direct viewing and a monitor to obtain hard-copy films. In the latter case, the gray scale should be adjusted to match the needs of the film which will be used to record the image. Selection of film and the monitor brightness and contrast used to record the film are not trivial matters, and care must be taken to assure the best possible film image (Schwenker 1979).

Variations in window and center settings reported between CT sites are usually due in part to differences in initial gray-scale settings and differences in video monitor display characteristics.

CENTER AND WINDOW SETTINGS

One of the biggest differences between radiographic film viewing and CT viewing is the ability in the latter to *window* the anatomic tissues of interest. By this is meant that one can optimize the viewing of particular tissues of interest by assigning to them the full range of blacks and whites available on the CRT monitor. For example, the center setting assigns the video midgray value to the CT number (or tissue) desired; the window setting defines the CT number range which will occupy the scale from black to white. To illustrate, consider a head CT scan viewed at a center of +50 and a window of 200 CT units. The +50 corresponds to the approximate CT number of gray and white matter, and it is these tissues that will be displayed with the midgray illumination. A window of 200 CT units implies that the range will be from +150 (100 above 50) to −50 (100 below 50). Consequently all tissues having CT numbers of 150 or above will be displayed as white, while all tissues at −50 and below will be displayed as black. On these settings, bone calcifications and blood pools will appear light and ventricular volumes will appear darker. The above settings may be ideal for a head scan, but different settings are needed for body scanning, since body scanning involves a greater range of tissue types, so that a greater window must be selected.

The power of the windowing function will be appreciated when it is recalled that in film radiography one must accept whatever exposure was made and is limited to what is seen on the film. Film, however, is nonlinear and thus results in different image contrast, depending on the density. Additionally, films may be underexposed or overexposed. In either case, as discussed previously, information is lost at both the low- and high-density regions of the film. Figure 1-17 illustrates the role of windowing using linear detectors. If the full tissue range of −1000 to +1000 is displayed, note that the particular tissues of interest in the previous example (−50 to +150) would be limited to a relatively small range of grays, and visualization would be poor. However, with windowing as in Fig. 1-17*B*, the full black-and-white range is assigned between the −50 and +150 CT values, and visualization of these particular tissues is optimal in that the greatest illumination difference results.

LONG-TERM STORAGE MEDIA

It has always been necessary to record the final image for patient records and subsequent comparisons and for referring physicians. Such recording can be done on film as for classical radiography. However, it is advantageous to record the actual computer image consisting of all the pixel values since pixel values, if available, can allow for subsequent windowing and redisplay and for computer manipulations such as magnification, CT number, or tissue identification and various image-enhancement routines. Thus magnetic tape and magnetic disk systems are usually incorporated into the basic CT instrumentation. In fact, the basic image-recording configuration of a clinical scanner may consist of some or all of the items listed in Table 1-4.

Table 1-4 Storage Media

MEDIUM	PIXELS RECOVERABLE?	COMMENTS
Film	No	Convenient, various sizes available
Polaroid film	No	Relatively expensive; relatively poor contrast scale
Magnetic tape	Yes	Access time long, good for long-term storage
Floppy disk	Yes	Convenient size and format; relatively expensive; limited capacity
Magnetic disks	Yes	Expensive but fast
Optical disks	Yes	Greatly expanded storage capacity

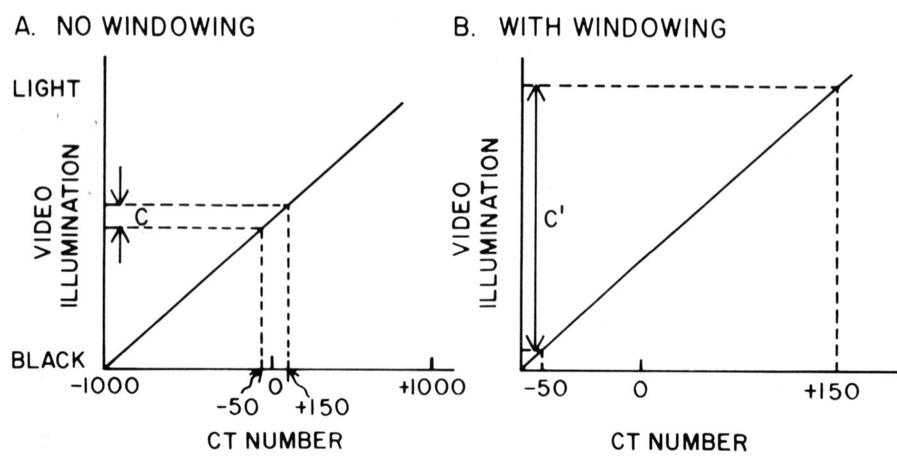

Figure 1-17 On a scale of −1000 to +1000, if no windowing is available, a given CT number difference such as −50 to +150 is displayed with only a limited range of gray values (low image contrast *C*). With windowing invoked, the same CT number range can be displayed with up to the maximum video range from white to black (high image contrast *C*'); that is, −50 can be assigned full dark and +150 is assigned full light.

Film

Film continues to be the most popular and economic long-term storage medium. It should be realized that the films used in CT imaging are quite different from the films used in radiography inasmuch as one is recording an image off a video monitor. Consequently, the film usually consists of a single emulsion sensitive to the light-emission spectrum of the video-screen phosphor. Additionally, these nonscreen films tend to be linear. To facilitate film recording, multi-image-format cameras have been developed, consisting of a self-enclosed video monitor with independent access to the computer pixel image information. The arrangement is such that the camera exposes the film to the particular size format desired. For instance, four views (or image slices) on an 8 × 10 film and nine views on a 14 × 17 film are quite popular. The laser camera is the latest improvement. Here, the data are recorded via laser on film directly from the computer, bypassing the video system entirely.

Polaroid film originally had three drawbacks: limited film contrast range, expense, and the need for mounting for permanent records. To a lesser extent there was also the nuisance of paper wrappers, the wait for development, and the need for coating. Newer Polaroid film emulsions have extended film contrast range and do not need coating. This form of image recording, however, will probably still remain limited to relatively low patient-volume sites where the capital cost of multi-image cameras or tape recorders is a factor and sites where rapid film processing equipment is not available. In addition, CT numbers are not recoverable because original pixel data are not available.

Magnetic Tape

Magnetic tape recording of computer outputs is a well-established technology. Pixel values as well as patient identification data can be readily recorded in relatively short times. This means that images can be redisplayed at any subsequent time, and different computer manipulations of the images, including windowing, are possible. Additionally, the fidelity of the images is excellent. A number of drawbacks exist, however. For example, storage space is limited to around 300 images per tape, depending on the number of pixels on the image. A 256 × 256 pixel array demands 4 times less tape space than a 512 × 512 pixel array. A few hundred images, in the case of a busy site, means that only one or two days' worth of patient images may be stored on one tape. In practice, this is a severe limitation because accessing patient images on different tapes requires an inordinate amount of time, because of the need for loading and reloading tapes, and because of the relatively slow search times characteristic of magnetic tape systems. Finally, the number of tapes accumulated and the required floor storage space have dictated the recycling of tapes. Thus it is not uncommon to find tapes covering only 6 to 12 months or even less at a particular site.

Disk-Based Systems

Three basic approaches to disk imaging have evolved. One approach uses so-called floppy disks. These disks are relatively small and flexible. In many cases a full patient examination or more can be recorded on one disk and can be conveniently transported to another room or site for image review at an independent viewing station. Disk search time is essentially negligible. However, the cost of each disk is such that many sites rely on magnetic tape recording for long-term storage and use floppy disks only for recent patients or for particularly interesting cases.

Another disk-based system consists of a bank of large disks capable of storing thousands of images. These are random-access devices, so that stepping through every image in the file to find the required one is not necessary and search and access times are minimal. Viewing at remote consoles is possible only via direct data-link connection to the computer. The overall costs of such a system are relatively high. Every CT scanner, however, is outfitted with disks for short-term storage of image data.

The third disk system is the optical disk. The optical disk expands storage capability to many thousands of images. It is now emerging as a cost-effective long-term archival modality. Image information is stored on these disks by producing a computer-coded pattern of micron-sized holes with a laser beam.

Artifacts in CT Scanning

CT scanning, like any imaging modality, has artifacts unique to it. Many artifacts have multiple causes, and their description requires rigorous mathematical techniques. Here we present a number of the more significant artifacts that the clinician should be aware of. Artifacts can manifest themselves either visibly in the form of streaks or quantitatively in the form of inaccurate CT numbers.

Streaks arise in general because there is an inconsistency in a particular ray path through the patient. This inconsistency can be due either to an error along the ray or to inconsistencies between rays. Table 1-5 summarizes the various sources of artifacts. Classification of artifacts has been troublesome (Joseph 1981). For our purposes here, we have classified artifacts according to what is happening to the data. Each of the artifacts listed in Table 1-5 is discussed in turn.

DATA FORMATION

In this section we are concerned with how data are formed as x-rays pass through the patient. As previously

Table 1-5 Sources of CT Artifacts

SOURCE AREA	CAUSE
Data formation	Patient motion
	Polychromatic effects
	Equipment misalignment
	Faulty x-ray source
Data acquisition	Slice geometry
	Profile sampling
	Angular sampling
Data measurement	Detector imbalance
	Detector nonlinearity
	Scatter collimation
Data processing	Algorithm effects

discussed, the transmitted x-ray beam detected in CT scanning is an index of the degree of attenuation that has occurred as the beam passed through the patient. Reference to Fig. 1-6 shows that the patient contour is arbitrarily divided up into pixels. To accomplish the CT scan process, ray paths along different angles around the patient are obtained. Thus data are collected for the attenuation at each point in the field from different angles. If such ray-path data are inconsistent—that is, if the pixel does not contribute the same attenuation regardless of the particular angle of view—then streaks result. The most familiar example of data inconsistency is that caused by patient motion.

Patient Motion

Motion has plagued CT scanning from the beginning (Alfidi 1976). The original CT scan units took up to 6 minutes of scan time. The inordinate amount of time allowed for considerable patient motion during the course of the examination. When such motion occurs during the scanning process, the computer has no means of keeping track of where the pixels are in space and which ray-path sums belong to which row and column. This inconsistency results in severe streaking and is especially aggravated by the presence of high-density structures. In early CT units, the relatively long scanning time necessary was so limited that it provided the impetus to develop faster and faster scanners. Modern scanners can routinely perform scans in a few seconds.

It should be clear that motion not only introduces artifactual steaks but, as in classical radiography, may cause both a loss of *spatial resolution* (the ability to visualize fine spatial detail) and a loss of *tissue resolution* or low-contrast resolution (the ability to visualize small differences in tissue densities). These losses are usually minimal compared to the presence of streaks. To minimize motion artifacts one may, in addition to scanning faster, provide for immobilization of the patient. Another approach used in earlier scanners involves overscanning. Here the patient was typically scanned 40° to 60° beyond the normal 180° or 360°, the rationale being that one is then collecting repeat, or redundant, views. For instance, if the patient has moved between the beginning of the scan and the end, there will be a discrepancy between the data collected on the 0° pass and the 180° pass. If the patient has not moved during the scan, these two views should be identical; any difference detected is entirely due to patient motion. Under computer control these differences can be averaged (or feathered) out. One obvious drawback to overscanning is the fact that scan times are longer, introducing the possibility of further motion artifacts. In spite of this, however, overscanning was shown to be useful in slower scanners.

Polychromatic Effects

Probably the best-known polychromatic artifact referred to in clinical practice is the beam-hardening artifact. The basis for this artifact is the fact that in the reconstruction process one attempts to assign an attenuation coefficient value to each voxel within the patient. However, attenuation coefficients are highly dependent on x-ray beam energy. Photons in x-ray beams do not have a unique energy but rather are polychromatic; that is, they are made up of photons having a wide distribution of energy. As the beam passes through the patient, the lower-energy photons are preferentially absorbed, and we say that the beam becomes harder. (This is similar to the rationale for the use of filters in diagnostic radiology to reduce the patient dose.) Any given voxel within the patient is, however, viewed along different ray paths for each different angular projection. Consequently, the x-ray beam, having experienced different degrees of beam hardening, will have a different energy as it passes any particular voxel along these different ray-paths (Fig. 1-18). The overall result will be a general decrease in the CT numbers, since higher energies imply lower attenuation coefficients. This effect is most notable along ray paths containing thicker and denser bony structures, as along the orbit-base views. The visual result is dark streaks, since higher energies result in the display of CT numbers denoting less dense tissues. The best example of this effect is the interpetrous bone hypodensity streaks seen in Fig. 1-19. This particular artifact is also caused in part by the nonlinear partial volume effect (Glover 1980).

Beam hardening also leads to a spillover effect near the interface of bony structures with adjoining softer tissues. This is evident at the edge of the skull and was originally interpreted as the cerebral cortex (Ambrose 1973). Its artifactual nature was demonstrated by Gado and Phelps (1975), and it is now referred to as the *pseudocortex*. The basis for this effect, which is also referred to as *cupping*, is illustrated in Fig. 1-18: rays passing through the periph-

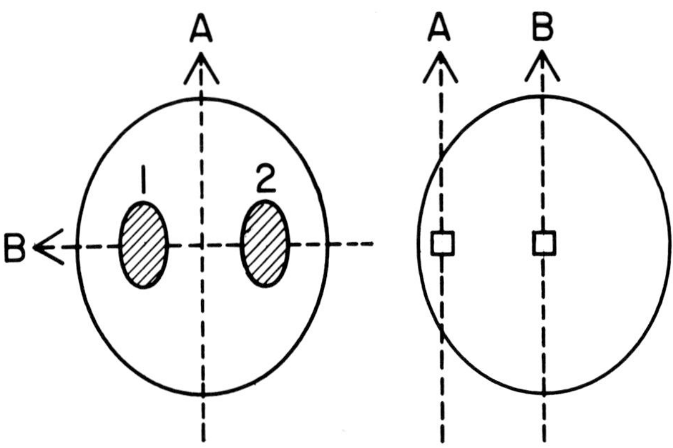

Figure 1-18 Demonstration of beam hardening in CT scanning. *Left:* Interpetrous bone hypodensity artifact. Ray *A* suffers a different degree of beam hardening from ray *B*, which travels through bony structures 1 and 2. The result is an inconsistency in the CT numbers calculated, and streaks result between the bony structures. *Right:* Cupping artifact. Rays such as *A*, passing through the periphery of a uniform structure, suffer less attenuation than do rays such as *B*, passing through the center of that structure. The result is an apparent cupping, or increase in tissue density toward the periphery.

ery of a structure suffer less hardening than do rays passing through the center of that structure. The central regions thus are displayed as having lower CT numbers and appear darker. A similar effect is seen in the apical artifact discussed in the CT number accuracy section and illustrated in Fig. 1-26. The original water-bag systems circumvented many of these problems by providing for an essentially equal path length for all rays in all projections. Another approach to minimize beam-hardening effects is to add filtration to the beam or to add specially shaped compensating attenuators to the beam. These approaches

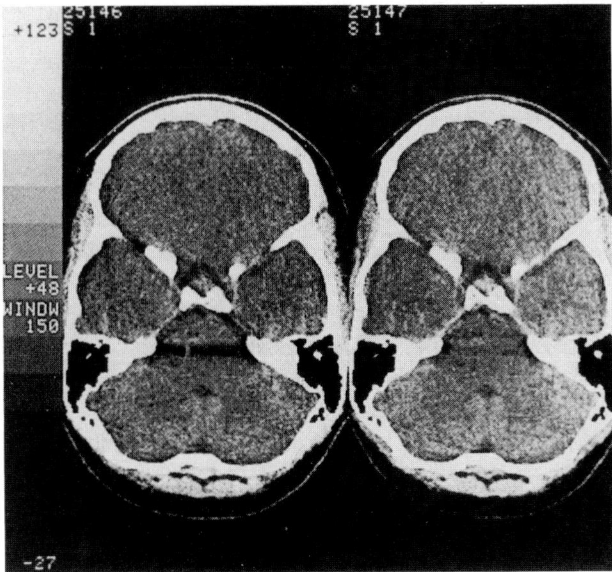

Figure 1-19 *Left:* Interpetrous bone artifact. *Right:* Same view after bone corrections are performed.

will be discussed further in the section on CT number variations.

Beam hardening has been discussed at length, and a number of algorithms have been proposed to correct for the beam-hardening artifact (Brooks 1976*a;* Duerinckx 1978; McDavid 1977*a;* Joseph 1978*b;* Hermon 1978; Nalcioglu 1979). Typical CT scanners include within their reconstruction algorithm a so-called water correction based on the linearization of the data collected. However, a more complete correction may involve off-line processing which may take from seconds to minutes per image to perform. Algorithms of this kind are referred to as *bone* or *calcium correction algorithms* and, because of the necessity of off-line processing, are often implemented only for specially selected cases.

Equipment Misalignment

Mechanical misalignment of the x-ray source and radiation detectors may lead to artifactual streak formation. The basic problem is that of isocenter location (Shepp 1977). If an aluminum pin is placed at the isocenter and scanned, its position will be isocentric for all views and projections. If a misalignment is present, an inconsistency results between angular views, and streaks sometimes referred to as "tuning fork" streaks result.

Another misalignment problem occurred for early 180° dual-slice scanners. Hounsfield (1977) has described what happens when the central ray of the x-ray beam is not aligned perpendicular to the axis of the patient's head. Under these conditions a bony structure may be included within the collimated x-ray field in the z direction for the 0° view but excluded from the 180° view. The result is a vertical streak along the edges of the bony object. This problem is limited to early dual slice, 180° rotating units.

Faulty X-ray Source

If the x-ray output varies during the scan process, an obvious inconsistency in data immediately arises, since detectors cannot distinguish between increases or decreases in radiation level due to increases or decreases in x-ray output and those due to increased or decreased absorption along the ray path. All CT units include reference detectors to detect output variations for the purpose of correcting for such changes. These corrections, however, are for data from a single angular view. If variations are present between angular views, streaks crisscrossing the image field and forming moiré patterns result (Joseph 1981; Stockham 1979). These are assumed to be most likely related to the speed of anode rotation, which is also called *anode wobble.* Other possible x-ray source problems include momentary high-voltage arcing and fluctuations, which may reduce or increase instantaneous x-ray output. Again, such changes, though detected by reference chambers, still may result in inconsistencies between angular views, and streaks result.

Data Acquisition

In this section, artifactual effects resulting from the manner in which the data are collected are studied.

Slice Geometry

The thickness of the slice scanned determines a very significant though nonvisible artifact: the partial volume effect. To understand this effect and its significance in practice, remember that the pixel displayed represents a volume in the patient given by both the area size and the slice thickness (the voxel). The voxel representing some finite patient volume may contain more than one tissue type. What happens is that if tissues are relatively similar (small CT number differences), the total contents of the voxel are in effect linearly averaged. It is this average CT number value that is assigned to the voxel. Figure 1-20 illustrates this effect. For instance, if half the pixel is filled with a tissue having a CT number of 100 and the other half with a tissue having a CT number of 200, the average of the two is 150, and this voxel will be displayed as if it were filled with a tissue type of CT number 150 which in fact is not present within the voxel.

This effect is significant for relatively small anatomic structure sizes or for tissue volumes which are rapidly changing in size. Examples are the orbital base level and regions near the calvarium. Additionally, vascular structures, blood clots (Lim 1977), and thin flat structures, as well as optic nerve visualization (Salvolini 1978), are subject to the partial volume effect. The result of the partial volume effect is the loss of tissue and spatial resolution and not necessarily streaks. In many instances, however, volume averaging is nonlinear in that tissue types within the voxel have widely different CT numbers. This in turn results in large exponential, nonlinear absorption differences. An example of this would be the bony structures of the petrous ridges and the adjacent brain matter. The result is the interpetrous ridge lucency artifact which has been discussed previously. At first this artifact was thought to be entirely due to beam-hardening effects.

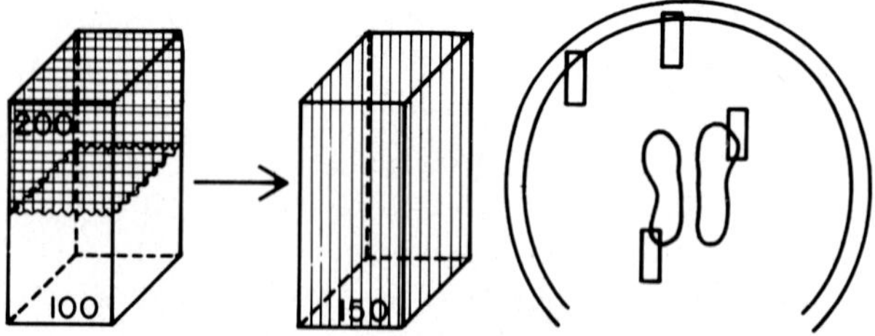

Figure 1-20 *Left:* Example of the partial volume artifact. Here, if a particular voxel contains different tissues, the final computed value will be characterized by the average CT number. If the CT numbers are very different from each other, the summing average process is exponential and therefore nonlinear, and streaks may result. *Right:* Cross-sectional view of voxel positions at various levels within the skull, showing a varying degree of partial volume averaging for different tissue-structure boundaries.

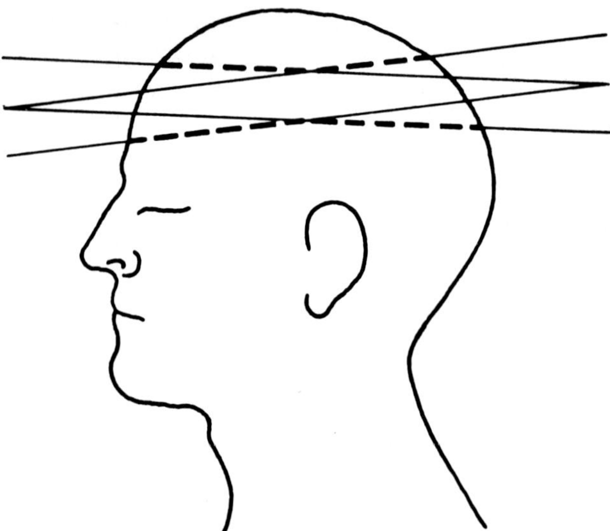

Figure 1-21 Beam diverges as it passes through patient. As beam rotates around patient, it forms not a parallel-sided slice but a concave slice (given by dashed lines) with the center thinner than the periphery.

However, these artifacts were subsequently shown to be partly due to the nonlinear partial volume effect, which in turn is related to the sampling slice thickness (Glover 1980). Thus this artifact can be minimized by diminishing the slice thickness, although it cannot be eliminated entirely unless beam hardness is also corrected for.

The basis for the nonlinear partial volume effect is that the detector response varies nonlinearly with the degree of bony intrusion into any given volume element; that is, the net signal at the detectors depends on the relative amount of soft tissue and bony tissue within the voxel. However, this dependence does not vary linearly, since attenuation in each material is an exponential function. These nonlinearities result in an inconsistency in the data collected as the volume element is viewed from various angles around the patient, and it is this inconsistency that creates the streaks observed. These streaks appear not only across the petrous bones but also from the occipital protuberance and wherever there are relatively large, abrupt variations in tissue or structure densities such as air-liquid interfaces and metallic objects. To minimize this artifact, one merely reduces the slice thickness, in which case one must contend with more image noise because of fewer photons being detected. Alternatively, x-ray tube factors may be adjusted upward, resulting in a greater patient dose for the thinner slices.

Another slice-geometry artifact is that associated with the fact that the x-ray beam is diverging as it passes through the patient. This causes some interesting effects. For instance, where is the slice thickness indicated? Figure 1-21 shows that there is no unique slice thickness; thickness varies throughout the scanned volume! By convention, we specify the thickness at the center of rotation (isocenter) of the CT unit. If the scan is completely around the patient (360°), the volume actually being imaged is symmetrically depressed in the center. The consequences of this effect are as follows.

1. Partial volume effects are then a function of position in the field as well as whether 180° or 360° scans are obtained. As a result, greater spatial and tissue resolution will be found in the center than at the periphery.
2. A missed volume may occur between slices (Goodenough 1975). These effects are minimized when patient scan volumes are relatively far from the x-ray source (less beam divergence) and when slices are exactly juxtaposed (or overlapped) at the center. Overlapping, of course, results in an increase in patient dose. The effect depends on exposure geometry; that is, there is less beam divergence for greater source to patient distance.

Profile Sampling

Figure 1-22 shows an intensity profile of the x-ray beam after it has emerged from the patient. This profile, together with all the other profiles taken at different angles or views around the patient, represents the total ray-sum information necessary for the reconstruction process. In third- and fourth-generation systems, this intensity profile is sampled by the detector array. Each detector intercepts and averages that portion of the profile that is incident over its face. This constitutes a sampling process. The sampled profile as it is transmitted to the computer is then seen to be not the exact replica of the incident profile but only a representation of it, and in fact it generally is degraded (dashed curve in Fig. 1-22). This degradation takes the final form of decreased tissue and spatial resolution (note that valleys and peaks tend to flatten or smooth out). Additionally, information is lost between detectors. These effects are a function of how large the detectors are as well as the space between them. As either of these dimensions increases, progressive degradation occurs. First- and second-generation systems provide for continuous sampling along the scans, and no interdetector dead spaces exist.

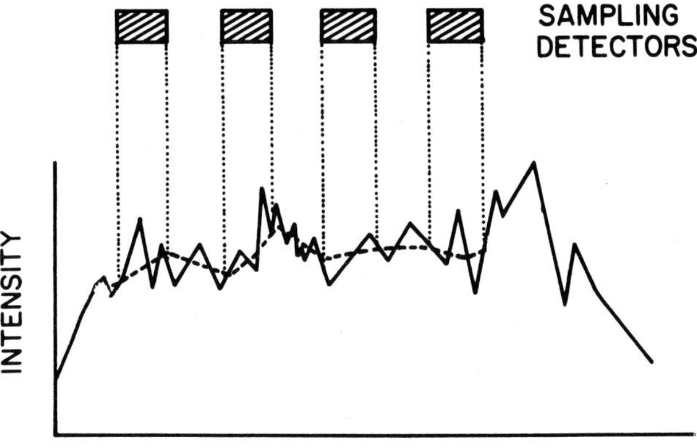

Figure 1-22 Demonstration of how a series of finite-sized detectors sample an x-ray intensity profile as it emerges from the patient. Each detector responds in proportion to the average intensity sampled. The discrete distribution processed by the computer is then given by the dashed curve. Note the loss of information at the peaks and valleys as well as in the voids between the detectors.

From Fig. 1-22 it can be seen that the sampled image has features in it that may not be present in the original profile. These bogus features consist of valleys and peaks that do not match the original profiles. In general, low-frequency details* not present in the original image are introduced into the resulting data. This effect is referred to as *aliasing* and is characteristic of all digitizing and sampling systems. The aliasing effect is further illustrated in Fig. 1-23. Here we have an elementary sinusoidal-type profile having some particular frequency. It is seen that if the profile is sampled over very short intervals (Fig. 1-23*A*), that profile is completely and accurately determined both in frequency and in amplitude. However, if sampling distances are relatively long, as in Fig. 1-23*D*, the pattern resulting has totally different amplitudes and has a lower frequency than the original pattern. Thus, a poorly sampled profile introduces patterns in the final result not present in the original.

If the pattern is sampled only once within each cycle, the response is flat, as in Fig. 1-23*C*. Figure 1-23*B* shows that when the pattern is sampled at least twice in a cycle, the frequency recorded is identical to that of the original pattern. We refer to this sampling frequency as the *Nyquist frequency* (f_n). The Nyquist frequency is seen to be merely twice the maximum frequency (f_m) present in the x-ray profile:

$$f_n = 2f_m \tag{2}$$

The maximum frequency associated with a structure of dimension d is $1/d$. Thus, to sample at the Nyquist frequency, the profile must be sampled at

$$f_n = \frac{2}{d} \tag{3}$$

When sharp discontinuities are present in the scanned image, Equation (3) does not hold and aliasing artifacts appear in the reconstructed image.

Visually, aliasing artifacts for a complete reconstruction appear as shown for a computer simulation in Fig. 1-24. Aliasing patterns serve to mask details in the clinical reconstruction. However, in practice their visibility may at

*By frequency we mean the rapidity with which profiles change; thus high frequency implies sharp edges or relatively small structures.

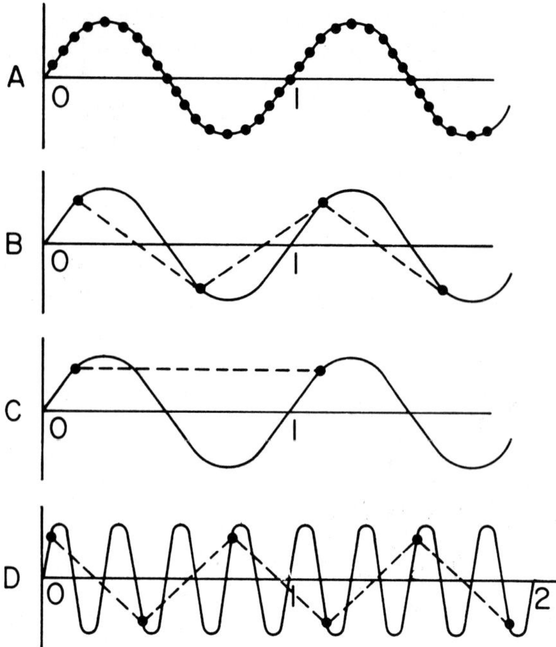

Figure 1-23 Demonstration of the aliasing effect with a pure sinusoidal profile distribution. *Curve A:* If samples are taken at rates much greater than the frequency of the information distribution being sampled, all the frequency as well as all the amplitude information is saved. *Curve B:* If samples are taken at twice the frequency of the distribution, as shown here, all the frequency information is saved (this is the Nyquist frequency). Note, however, that some amplitude information is still lost. *Curve C:* If samples are taken at a rate equal to the frequency of the information distribution, all the frequency and amplitude information will be lost: that is, a flat response results. *Curve D:* Aliasing occurs if sampling rate is less than twice the frequency of the information distribution. Information *not* present in the original is then produced. For example, if time distribution is 4 cycles per millimeter and a sample is obtained every 1½ cycles, as shown here, then the apparent frequency detected is approximately ¾ cycle per millimeter. In general, aliasing results in lower frequencies appearing. The result is streaks in the image.

times be suppressed by noise present in the image (Stockham 1979). Aliasing streaks can be serious. Examples are clip or star artifacts, which usually consist of streaks emanating from small high-density structures within the patient such as a surgical clip or any metallic object. Similar artifacts can also be seen coming from tooth fillings, gas/liquid interfaces in the stomach, and bony protuberances in the skull. It should also be noted that these streaks are also partly due to nonlinear partial volume effects, detector nonlinearity, and angular undersampling. One final artifact related to the presence of small or sharp high-contrast structure is that related to the presence of opaque markers such as catheters on the surface of patients. It has been shown that the use of such opaque catheters and markers does indeed generate artifacts (Villafana 1978*b*).

Since aliasing is due to insufficient sampling, an obvious solution is to sample at higher rates, taking readings closer together or using smaller detectors packed closer. The minimum rate to avoid aliasing effects as discussed above is the Nyquist rate, which is a function of anatomic structure sizes and the presence of sharp discontinuities. Another method which can be used to minimize aliasing is to purposely smooth or eliminate sharp discontinuities in the profiles before they are sampled. This is accomplished by having a relatively wide sampling aperture. One drawback of this approach is that spatial and tissue resolution are sacrificed as well.

A third method to suppress aliasing, which has the advantage of not degrading resolution, is the one-quarter detector shift technique. This technique, which has been successfully applied to fan-beam third-generation geometry (Peters 1977; Brooks 1979), consists of offsetting the central detector by one-fourth of the detector dimensions. As a result, as the scanner obtains views around the

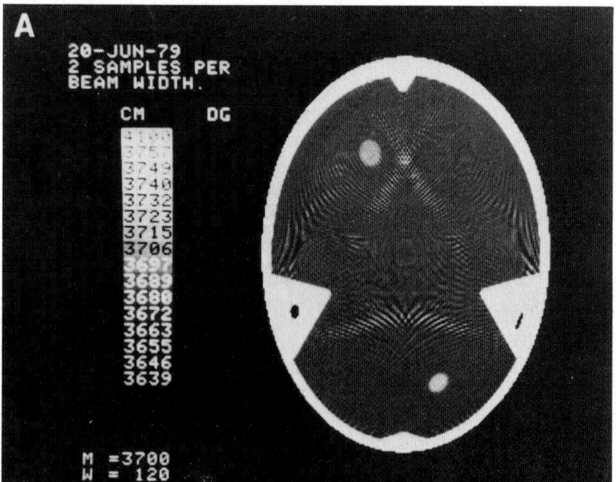

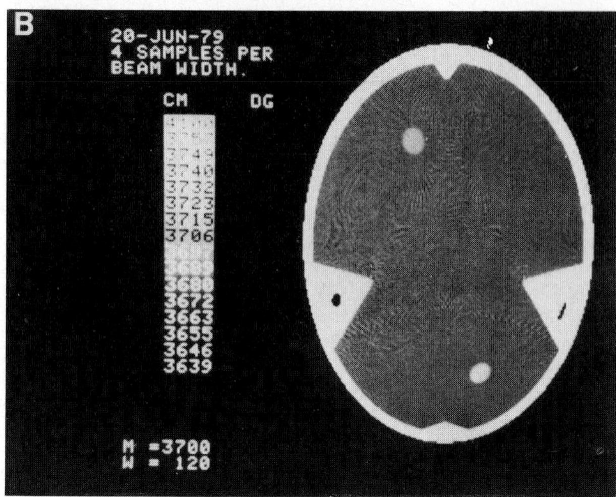

Figure 1-24 Aliasing streaks due to undersampling. Overlapping streaks emanating over the periphery of the skull result in a moiré pattern. The lower figure shows a phantom simulation sampled at a rate twice that of the upper figure: 0.96 mm sample spacing versus 0.48 mm. (*After Stockham 1979 and Joseph 1981.*)

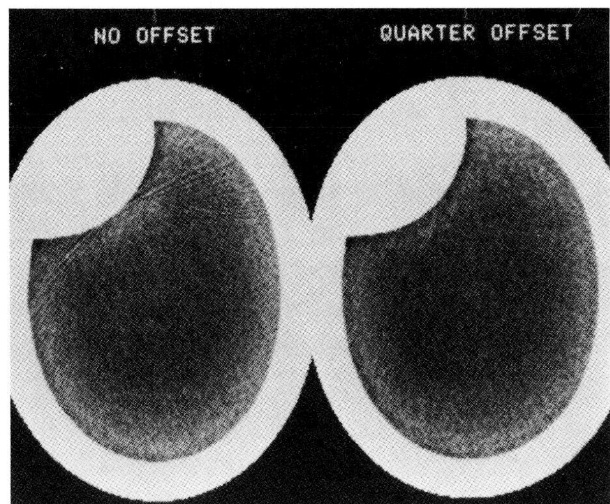

Figure 1-25 Verification of the removal of aliasing streaks, seen on the left, by quarter offset or shift of the central detector in a third-generation geometry array. (*After Brooks 1979.*)

patient, all the views from 180° to 360° are exactly interleaved with the views from 0° to 179°; that is, the view at 180° is interleaved with that from 0° and the 360° view is interleaved with that from 180°. The result is that each view is offset by one-half of the detector dimensions. The significance of this is that the highest frequency available at the detector is determined by the detector dimensions, and we thus need, according to Equation (3), to obtain two samples per detector width d (a frequency of 2/d); the quarter offset provides exactly this sampling interval, and aliasing streaks are markedly reduced, as seen in Fig. 1-25. Finally, undersampling in the z direction can be reduced by using thinner slices.

Angular Sampling

Just as a particular profile can be undersampled as discussed above, the number of profiles or angular view samples around the patient can be deficient. Such angular undersampling also leads to the formation of streak artifacts. However, these streaks, although radiating from small, dense objects, always occur at some distance from the object. It has been shown that undersampling along the profile is more important and leads to more severe aliasing streaks compared to undersampling the number of angular views around the patient (Brooks 1979; Schulz 1977). Streaks due to view undersampling usually lead to artifacts in the image emanating from the undersampled structure but first appear at some distance from that structure.

To summarize this section, data acquisition or sampling schemes play a key role in the quality and accuracy of the final image. Sampling includes the thickness of the slice, the sampling along each profile, and the number of views around the patient. Effects can range from simple inaccuracies in the CT number to severe streaks obliterating the desired diagnostic information. Some of the ways to minimize aliasing streaks include thinner slices, closely packed small detectors, and quarter-shifted detector geometry.

DATA MEASUREMENT

Detector Imbalance

We have already emphasized that detectors should have high efficiency and high reproducibility. Of importance also is that each detector in an array of detectors be matched in response compared to the other detectors in the array. When an imbalance occurs, for instance, in a third-generation system, ring artifacts such as those in Fig. 1-13 result. Imbalance may result from individual detector gain shifts. Shepp (1977) has shown that shifts as low as 0.1 percent can result in visible streaks. Furthermore, the appearance of streaks is more severe if detector error affects only one ray path or a small group of ray paths, as in first-, second-, and third-generation systems. Fourth-generation system detector errors affect the whole view (each detector sees the whole patient), and as a result, inconsistency is smoothed over the whole image and detector matching is not as critical.

When shifts occur, they can be calibrated out. This calibration is performed whenever the detector is out from behind the patient. Calibration is automatic for first-, second-, and fourth-generation systems. Third-generation systems, however, present a problem in that the detectors are behind the patient throughout the examination. The resulting ring artifacts (Fig. 1-13) are particularly troublesome. To minimize these ring artifacts, these units must be calibrated between patients—typically every few hours, especially for solid-state detector systems.

Detector Nonlinearities

Ideally, the response of a detector should be directly proportional to the quantity of radiation incident on it. In CT scanning, the range of x-ray intensities may be as high as 10,000 to 1 or even higher. The detector should have a dynamic range at least this high. Some factors contributing to detector nonlinearity (Joseph 1981) are dark current or leakage (current flow in the absence of radiation), saturation (detector output is at its maximum and higher intensities do not evoke higher output), and hysteresis (detector continues to respond after irradiation ends). One form of hysteresis is the afterglow of scintillation detectors. All these may lead to inconsistency in data and can result in streaks. The severity of these streaks is related to the contrast of the structure as well as the presence of abrupt discontinuities in its shape. One way to minimize the detector nonlinearity problem is to reduce the range of intensities arriving at the detector. This was accomplished by placing the patient within a water box to provide equal ray paths in the original EMI Mark I system. More commonly, a compensating wedge filter can be used (Fig. 1-27).

Scatter Collimation

Scatter present at the detector plane is similar to that from leakage in the detector. This can be appreciated by considering a very dense object. The primary x-ray intensity behind this object is expected to be low; however, small amounts of scatter at the detector will indicate a higher than actual transmission. The resulting data are inconsistent with data from ray paths not traversing the high-contrast object, and streaks can result. Scatter is less of a problem in first-, second-, and third-generation systems, where scatter-rejecting collimation can be incorporated into detectors. In fourth-generation systems, unlike the others, stationary detectors must accept radiation from a wide range of angles, and collimation cannot be used. Consequently, these latter systems are more susceptible to scatter effects.

DATA PROCESSING

The final step to be considered here is how the data are processed within the computer. The specific algorithm used may introduce artifacts into the final image that are not due to sampling or measurement factors. Examples of this are the use of an edge-enhancement algorithm, which can result in a false subarachnoid space. Another example is that described by Hounsfield (1977), Stockham (1979), and Joseph (1981) involving scanning long, straight-edged, bony, or high-contrast structures. Approximations normally used in algorithms lead to the formation of streaks along the edge of such structures. These streaks can be minimized by using narrower collimators for first- and second-generation units and smaller detectors for third- and fourth-generation units. The use of hardened (filtered) x-ray beams also helps. Needless to say, algorithm-induced artifacts are mathematically complex, and further discussion is beyond our scope here.

CT Number Accuracy

In the previous section the factors resulting in mainly visible streak artifacts were studied. In this section the factors affecting actual accuracy of the CT numbers are considered.

A number of factors limiting the absolute accuracy of CT numbers are listed in Table 1-6. As discussed in an earlier section, the CT reconstruction process computes a value for the linear attenuation coefficient of each volume element within the patient scanned. In all CT designs, the computer then assigns to the attenuation coefficient a value based on the arbitrary −1000 for air to +1000 for bone scale. (Modern units are capable of accurately computing and displaying values up to +3000 and above.) These values (CT numbers, or Hounsfield numbers) represent quantitative data from which tissue identification can be made. In general, they are related to the attenuation coefficient of water (μ_w) as follows:

Table 1-6 Factors Affecting CT Number Accuracy

X-ray beam kilovoltage and filtration
Patient thickness and shape
Tissue type and location
Partial volume effect
Algorithm and calibration shifts
Field calibration accuracy

$$\text{CT no.} = \frac{\mu - \mu_w}{\mu_w} \times 1000 \qquad (4)$$

where μ = the attenuation coefficient of the material the CT number is specified for. Table 1-1 gives a short list of CT numbers for typical tissues. All CT scanners have provisions for determining the CT number for any specified point or region of points in the image field either by direct interaction with the video display, using a region-of-interest (ROI) indicator, or by direct printout on a line printer.

Since CT numbers characterize the tissue or its chemical composition, it is no wonder that considerable effort has been expended to use these quantitative data. This involves not only identifying gross tissue type but, among other more sophisticated applications, the determination of bone mineral content (Weissberger 1978; Exner 1979; Revak 1980; Genant 1985) and the identification of calcified versus noncalcified pulmonary nodules (Siegelman 1980; Checkley 1984; Zerhouni 1982). In fact, CT scanning can be configured to determine directly the effective atomic numbers or electron densities (tomochemistry) instead of the attenuation coefficients (McDavid 1977*b*; Latchaw 1978).

The question of validity must be posed before undue reliance is placed on CT numbers. A number of factors affect the validity of correlating directly the CT number obtained from a particular CT machine and the tissue it is supposed to characterize (McCullough 1977; Levi 1982). Specific factors to be considered are given in Table 1-6, from which it is easy to see that one cannot in fact expect the CT numbers from one machine to match those from another exactly. One reason is that CT numbers are dependent on x-ray beam energy. Thus correlation cannot be rigorously expected between units operated at different kilovoltage (Ruegsegger 1978) or even between similar units operated at the same nominal kilovoltage because of kilovoltage calibration inaccuracies. CT number anomalies can also occur for the same unit whenever the kilovoltage shifts. In general, the CT number of any material will shift as a function of the difference between the atomic number of that material and the atomic number of water: it will increase for materials with an atomic number less than water and decrease for materials with an atomic number greater than water (Zatz 1976). A tight quality-assurance program monitoring the constancy of CT numbers for a given unit is necessary as well as frequent system calibration by service engineers.

Beam filtration also affects the energy distribution of the x-ray beam. In general, the greater the filtration, the harder the beam (or the greater the effective beam energy); also, the beam becomes more monochromatic and therefore less subject to further hardening. This means that CT numbers are subject to variation between units depending on the degree of beam filtration incorporated in each unit as well as the calibration and shift effects discussed above. It is also interesting to note that some CT units provide for two filtration modes—one for head scans and a relatively thicker filtration for body scans—the rationale being that the greater tissue-path lengths in bodies would produce greater beam hardening. Greater initial filtration would then reduce this effect in that the beam is prehardened via the additional filter and is closer to a monochromatic beam before it enters the patient. Patient thickness is crucial in determining the CT numbers finally computed. Again, beam hardening is involved in that different patient thicknesses yield different beam paths and different degrees of beam hardening. This is illustrated in Fig. 1-26. It can also be seen that results will depend on the shape of the body parts. Figure 1-26 also illustrates the so-called apical artifact (DiChiro 1978), in which CT number variations occur between the slice levels scanned owing to varying head thickness and thus different degrees of beam hardening.

It has already been noted that the original EMI Mark I unit provided a water box surrounding the patient's head. This meant that all ray-paths were more nearly equal, as seen in Fig. 1-27, for any orientation around the head. With such a configuration, beam hardening is minimal. Figure 1-27 also shows one attempt to provide for a fixed path length by providing for a "bow tie" compensating filter. Here added filter thickness toward the periphery of the bow tie presumably compensates for decreased peripheral patient thickness. Patient centering here will obviously be important, and the configuration will not be as effective as a water box, though it is certainly simpler. Some advanced designs provide for varying the shape of this bow tie as a function of reconstruction field size to more accurately accomplish equalization of the ray paths. Figure 1-27 also shows how the presence of dense structures adds to the beam-hardening problem. Discrepancies for ray paths close to the tangent of the edges of the structure in fact result in severe image streaking.

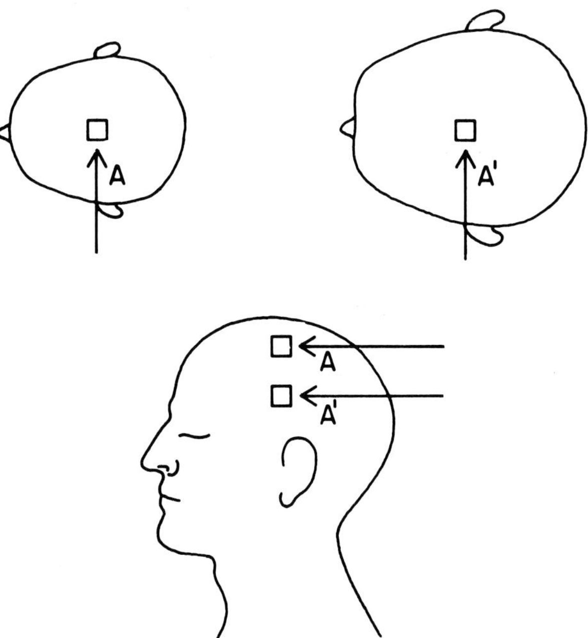

Figure 1-26 Different degrees of beam hardening yielded by different patient thicknesses and the effect on CT number accuracy. Ray path *A* to any particular pixel is shorter in the smaller patient on the left than ray path *A'* in the larger patient on the right. As shown in the lower figure, even in the same patient path length to any given pixel can differ depending on slice level (apical artifact). All these effects are further compounded when the beam rotates around the patient and path length is a function of ray angle.

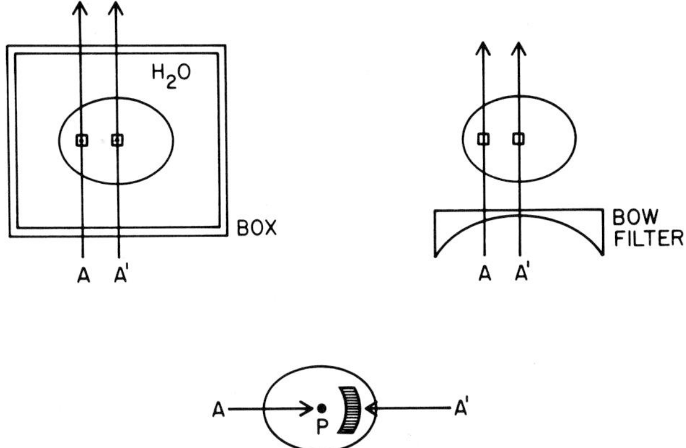

Figure 1-27 *Left:* In original CT units a water bath providing a fixed path length for any and all ray paths, such as *A* and *A'*, resulted in minimal beam-hardening effects on CT numbers. *Right:* In an attempt to equalize ray paths *A* and *A'* without a water bath one can provide for a "bow tie" filter arrangement. Here varying filter thickness results in attenuation matching the curvature of the patient. *Bottom:* Presence of dense structures (shaded region) aggravates the beam-hardening problem between ray paths *A* and *A'*, since the beam through a point such as *P* suffers different beam hardening along the two paths indicated. This is particularly severe for ray paths falling along the edges of the structures, and image streaks are usually formed.

The partial volume effect also strongly influences CT number accuracy. This was discussed in the previous section.

Finally, the question of algorithms must be addressed. Each CT manufacturer attempts to minimize the beam-hardening problem and to calibrate its CT number scale to maximize accuracy. Such algorithms vary between manufacturers, and the actual field calibrations on any given unit at any given time vary.

An additional application of the quantitative use of CT number data is in dynamic scanning. In this approach the absolute value of the CT number is unimportant; rather, it is the relative change in the CT numbers at a point which is observed. Here a given tissue slice is repeatedly scanned while contrast is being administered. A region of interest (ROI) is defined, and a plot of the average CT number within that ROI versus time is obtained. Note that beam hardening is not a problem since measurements are made within the same region. Presumably, the CT number variation here is proportional to the time concentration of contrast within the ROI, which in turn is a function of the blood flow and vascularization properties of the tissue within that ROI (Michael 1985; Som 1985).

To accomplish dynamic scanning the CT x-ray tube must be capable of withstanding high heat loads because of the need for rapid successive scan acquisition. One software approach which extends capability for obtaining data at short time intervals is that of segmental scanning. That is, the data from a 360° scan, which normally produces only one image, are divided and reallocated into a multiple number of overlapping shorter angular segment scans. Thus, for instance, one 360° scan can be reconstructed as three images (or more) at shorter intervals of time, with data from one angular interval overlapping the other. Finally, the accuracy and frequency of system calibration plays an important role in CT number accuracy.

This section can be summarized simply by stating that great caution must be exercised in using CT numbers, not only between and within different manufacturers' models but also for one's own unit, as a function of the factors listed in Table 1-6. When quantitative CT number data are desired, it is best to scan a phantom with calibrated CT number materials.

CT Reconstruction Performance

As already seen, CT performance is a complex area of study. A number of different aspects of it require discussion (Table 1-7). The interested reader is also referred to a number of articles reviewing CT performance and comparisons between specific CT units (Weaver 1975; McCollough 1976, 1980; Bassano 1977; Cohen 1979*b*). Attention is also drawn to a very comprehensive but somewhat mathematical and technical text (Newton and Potts, 1981).

Table 1-7 Aspects of CT Reconstruction Performance

CT number performance
- CT number accuracy
- CT number linearity
- Spatial independence of CT numbers
- Sensitivity to artifactual effects
- Contrast scale

Geometric and mechanical factors
- Divergence of beam
- Focal-spot penumbra
- Source and detector collimation and alignment
- Dual-slice effects
- Slice location and table incrementation
- Mechanical vibration

Imaging performance
- Spatial resolution
- Tissue resolution
- Noise characteristics
- Pixel sizes and zoom
- Data sampling

Patient dose
- Single-slice dose
- Multiple-slice dose
- Dose profile

CT NUMBER PERFORMANCE

CT Number Accuracy

CT numbers have been discussed at length in previous sections, especially as they relate to factors causing artifactual variations in their reproducibility and accuracy. To quantitate the accuracy of CT numbers, one merely scans a collection of plastics having known attenuation coefficients (or CT numbers) in a water bath. The CT numbers computed are then compared with the known values. In addition, these data when plotted should form a straight line (CT number linearity). There is no generally accepted performance standard covering day-to-day variations in CT numbers; each site should set its own limits, taking into account the manufacturer's recommendations. Generally these variations should not exceed 10 to 20 percent. It should again be noted that CT numbers vary with beam energy. Thus kilovoltage and beam filtration as well as size of the phantom used affect the CT number. Proper field service calibration of the unit, however, will assure that water gives a CT number of zero for a given reconstruction scan circle or field size and that the known plastics scanned also display their correct CT numbers.

Spatial Independence of CT Numbers

Clearly it is desirable for computed CT numbers to be independent of spatial position in the reconstruction field. Spatial independence or uniformity is readily measured by scanning a uniform water bath. Variations in CT numbers can be quantitated by computing the standard deviation. This computation is readily available on all commercial scanners, as is the selection of the region of interest over which such determinations are made. In general, for a water bath, the standard deviation in CT numbers in particular regions over the field should not be greater than a factor of 2 compared to the central region (McCullough 1976).

Contrast Scale

Reference is often made to the contrast scale, defined as the change in the linear attenuation coefficient per CT number (McCullough 1976). It specifies the range of attenuation coefficients which will appear as one CT number. Thus, if the manufacturer's specified performance is 0.5 percent accuracy, the contrast scale should be at least 0.5 percent per CT number. In general, the contrast scale is used to compare results between different CT units. It is necessary because different CT number normalizations may be incorporated in individual CT units. Examples of this would be, for instance, a scale of −500 to +500 as in early CT units compared to the current −1000 to +1000 scale. Even if two units have the same nominal scale, there may still be differences. Thus, to make one's results independent of one's particular unit, one should specify the contrast scale. This would particularly apply in making statements pertaining to CT numbers and noise performance values.

It is relatively simple to determine the contrast scale (CS). It may be done by simply scanning Plexiglas in a water bath and using the following equation:

$$\mathrm{CS} = \frac{\mu_{\text{plex}} - \mu_{\mathrm{H_2O}}}{(\text{CT no.})_{\text{plex}} - (\text{CT no.})_{\mathrm{H_2O}}} \; \frac{\text{cm}^{-1}}{\text{CT no.}} \qquad (5)$$

In this equation the average linear attenuation coefficient difference between Plexiglas and water ($\mu_{\text{plex}} - \mu_{\mathrm{H_2O}}$) is constant and is equal to 0.001 cm^{-1} for the range of 100 to 150 kV and for moderate beam filtration (AAPM 1978). $(\text{CT no.})_{\text{plex}} - (\text{CT no.})_{\mathrm{H_2O}}$ is the actual measured CT number difference.

GEOMETRIC AND MECHANICAL FACTORS

A number of geometric and mechanical factors affect the performance of CT scanners. We have already discussed, for instance, the fact that the slice is not necessarily uniformly thick throughout the patient volume; also, all points within the defined slice volume do not contribute equally to the image (Goodenough 1977; Brooks 1977). Some reasons for this effect are discussed in the following paragraphs.

Divergence of Beam

The x-ray beam is not parallel but rather diverges as it passes through the patient (Fig. 1-21). If the beam is then made to rotate 180° or 360° around the patient, the actual volume scanned is depressed in the center. Slice width is defined at the center of rotation; therefore, this results in volume elements at the center contributing more to the CT response than do those off the center. This is shown in Fig. 1-28 (top), where a theoretical slice is shown. When the x-ray beam is superimposed, the voxels at the periphery intercept fewer x-rays than those at the center do.

Focal-Spot Penumbra

As is true for classical radiography, finite-sized focal spots are utilized for CT scanning x-ray tubes; thus focal-spot effects are also expected. These effects take the form of the expected decrease in overall resolution as the focal spot size increases. Probably more important, however, is the fact that the focal spot contributes to nonuniformity of the slice along the z direction. This nonuniformity in turn results in a nonuniform sensitivity response of the detector. This effect was particularly true for early dual-slice units utilizing relatively large focal-spot dimensions extending along the z direction.

Source and Detector Collimation

A focal spot of any given size will form some penumbral region at the detector. To reduce unnecessary dose to the patient, efforts at collimation or increasing detector size may be made. These efforts, however, add to the nonuniformity of the CT response, since the beam will then be even more divergent, because tighter source collimation provides for a smaller effective focal-spot size and there is more divergence from a point source than from an extended source. Also, larger detector sizes result in larger beam diameter, which in turn results in more divergence; that is, the beam is parallel along the central ray and becomes less so for peripheral rays as the beam diameter increases.

Since it affects x-ray beam field size, collimation obviously affects scatter degradation of the image and also contributes to the patient dose. First-, second-, and third-generation CT systems can easily incorporate collimation, but fourth-generation systems cannot, since detectors must view x-rays emerging from the patient from different angles. Self-collimation can be incorporated in xenon ionization chamber detector systems. Here the chamber walls, though thin, are made up of a highly absorbent material like tungsten arranged in relatively long channels. As a result, image scatter degradation is minimized.

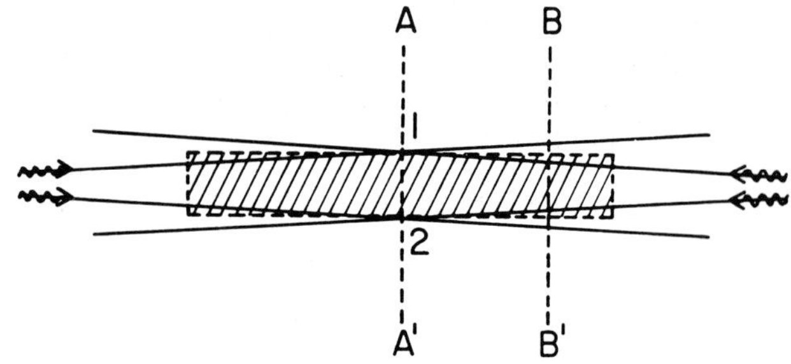

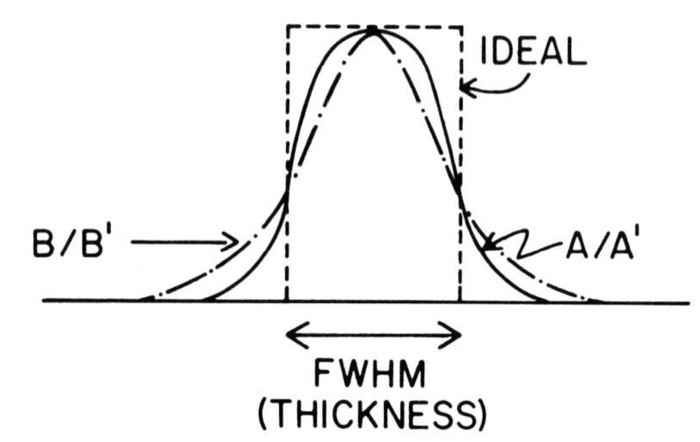

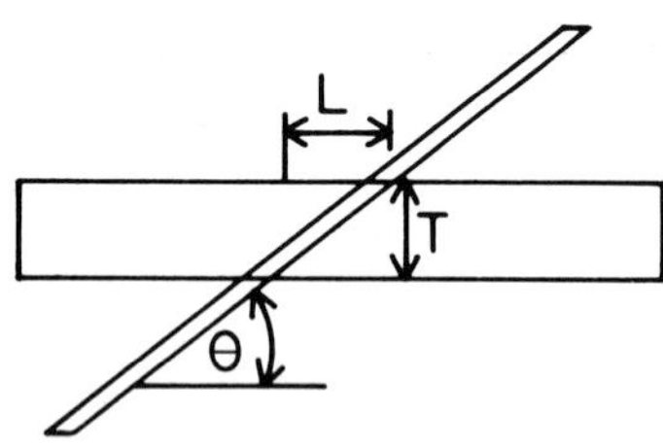

Figure 1-28 Determination of sensitivity profiles. *Top:* CT response varies along lines perpendicular to the slice plane such as *AA′* and *BB′* because of the divergent nature of beam. *Middle:* Curve *AA′*: sensitivity profile along the center defines the slice thickness as the full width at half maximum (*FWHM*). Curve *BB′*: sensitivity profile along a line closer to the periphery. Note the greater degree of flaring out in the tails and the decreased response within the slice thickness borders. The ideal sensitivity curve should be uniform within the confines of the slice and drop to zero response just outside the slice (this corresponds to the ideal slice). *Bottom:* Slice thickness and sensitivity profiles may be determined by scanning an inclined ramp (usually made of a thin slice of aluminum). Thickness (T) is determined from length L measured on the CT scan, knowledge of the ramp angle (Θ), and simple trigonometry (e.g., $T = L$ tangent Θ).

Detector collimator alignment also presents a possible source of problems. This effect, as well as how to measure it on dual-slice units, has been described by Goodenough (1977).

Dual-Slice Effects

Older units that scan two slices simultaneously inherently produce two partially overlapped and inclined beams. This effect may lead to asymmetric slice profiles. Hounsfield (1977) has described the consequence of this: the possibility of just including an object at the 0° view (clipping it) and missing it at the 180° view; the resulting inconsistency in the data would lead to streaking, especially if the object was very dense, like bone.

To illustrate the consequences of having nonuniform slice thickness and resulting nonuniform response sensitivity, refer to Fig. 1-28. Imagine a dense, high-contrast point placed at different levels along a line perpendicular to the slice plane at the center of the slice (along line AA′ in Fig. 1-28). Ideally, the response of the CT unit should be rectangular (dashed curve), in that the test point will be detected with equal response as long as it is within the slice thickness (between points 1 and 2) and will not be detected at all if it falls outside the slice. In practice, the situation does not follow the ideal; rather, a loss of response occurs inside the slice width borders and some response occurs beyond the borders of the slice due to the effects discussed above and to the focal-spot penumbra and collimation effects discussed earlier. The final response is as shown in Fig. 1-28 (solid line). If a similar test had been conducted along a line closer to the periphery, such as BB′, a broader response would have occurred (alternating dash-circle curve). These curves are termed *sensitivity profiles.* By convention, the slice thickness is defined as the full width at half maximum of the sensitivity profile through the center of the slice.

A number of methods to measure the slice thickness have been proposed, including the use of small beads on a 45° ramp (Goodenough 1975) and inclined cylinders (Sorenson 1979) or wires, but the most popular is the use of an aluminum ramp (AAPM 1978; Brooks 1977). All these methods are based on the fact that projection of the inclined objects will demonstrate different lengths, as seen in Fig. 1-28 (bottom). Here, with knowledge of the angle of inclination, one can calculate the slice thickness directly from simple trigonometric considerations. Phantoms can be made up with such inclines at various positions in the field to test for variations in slice thickness. Sensitivity profiles can be approximated by plotting out the CT numbers along the inclination.

Slice Location and Table Incrementation

CT scanners normally have a number of light alignment devices to locate and align the patient. In addition, provision is usually made for automatic incrementation of the table to move the patient into position for consecutive scans. The most recent CT scanners, in fact, provide for both automatic incrementation of the table and inclination of the gantry. These features are indeed convenient and time-saving and offer potentially more accuracy than does manual incrementation. Their benefit, however, is clearly compromised if they themselves lack accuracy. The accuracy of all alignments and incrementation features should be verified at regular intervals.

Mechanical Vibration

Inherent to the CT scan process is mechanical motion. Such motion may and usually does create some degree of vibration, which in turn may induce image-degrading effects. The best example of this is the problem of microphonics for third-generation xenon ionization chamber systems. The term *microphonics* refers to the vibrations induced in relatively thin ionization chamber walls by the various gantry motions. These vibrations induce fluctuations in output signals, which result in additive CT image noise. To minimize microphonics, thicker chamber walls with smaller overall area must be used. However, this then affects image quality since ideally walls should be as thin as possible and placed as close to each other as possible. Because of the relatively inefficient quantum absorption of the gas, long chamber walls are required to maintain low patient dosage. This in turn may make the chamber susceptible to further vibration.

CT Imaging Performance

In addition to the problem of artifact sensitivity, as discussed previously, there are three basic descriptors of CT imaging performance: spatial (or high-contrast) resolution, image noise, and tissue (or low-contrast) resolution.

SPATIAL RESOLUTION

Spatial resolution is the ability of a CT scanner to record fine, high-contrast detail. Various measures of spatial resolution are available (Table 1-8). What they all have in common is essentially 100 percent contrast and noise-free conditions. These measures do not necessarily predict the actual performance of a CT unit when imaging tissues having similar attenuation coefficients. The resolution-bar pattern is probably the most familiar test object used in general radiology. It can be configured for CT scanning (Goodenough 1977; Maue-Dickson 1979), for instance, with a series of Plexiglas strips (or similar material) in a water bath in such a manner that equal widths of Plexiglas alternate with equal spaces of water. These Plexiglas widths form a *line pair* with the adjoining water space, and each line pair is made progressively narrower; that is, a greater number of line pairs per millimeter (higher line-pair frequency) is formed. The resolving power of the system is that line-pair frequency which is just barely visible on the image.

A variation of the basic resolution bar pattern is the sunburst phantom (Goodenough 1977), in which alternate radial strips and spaces are arranged in a tapered manner around a circle like wheel spokes to provide for continuously varying frequencies (Fig. 1-29, top). Resolution is given by the distinctly visible tapered pattern

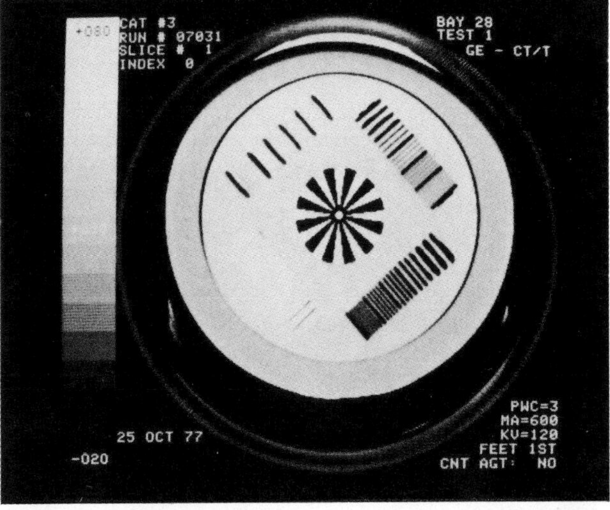

A

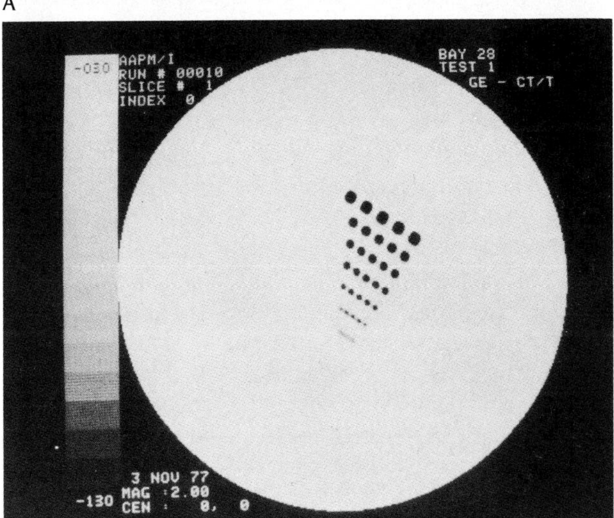

B

Figure 1-29 Examples of spatial resolution test-scan results for two popular phantom configurations. **A.** Starburst and bar pattern scans. Four different bar patterns of differing subject contrast can be displayed on the Catphan phantom (Goodenough 1977). **B.** Phantom made up of Plexiglas with different-diameter holes in each row (AAPM phantom; AAPM 1978). Both of these phantoms have a variety of test objects in addition to those shown here for evaluating the full range of CT system performance as well as for ongoing quality control tests.

Table 1-8 Spatial Resolution Measures (100 Percent Contrast and Noise-Free Conditions)

MEASURE	MATHEMATICAL EQUIVALENT
Resolution bar and pin pattern	Zero cutoff of MTF
Sunburst pattern	Zero cutoff of MTF
Point-spread function (PSF)	Basic response function
Line-spread function (LSF)	Integral of PSF along line
Edge-response function (ERF)	Integral of LSF along line (slope of ERF = LSF)
Modulation transfer function (MTF)	Fourier transform of LSF

closest to the center. This approach was actually used to approximate the modulation-transfer function of early CT systems (MacIntyre 1976). Instead of repetitive bar patterns, a series of varying-diameter Plexiglas, high-contrast pins in a water bath can be used to assess spatial resolution. Alternatively, one can have holes of varying diameters in Plexiglas. Figure 1-29 shows the results for two popular phantoms incorporating various spatial-resolution patterns.

A number of other spatial-resolution descriptors are shown in Table 1-8. Though each is distinct, they are all interrelated. The *point-spread function* (PSF) is the most fundamental measure and is defined as the response of a system to a point object. The PSF can be measured by scanning a high-contrast wire pin which is perpendicular to the long axis of the slice. The *line-spread function* (LSF) is the response of the system to a line object lying within or along the long axis of the slice plane. Mathematically, the LSF can be obtained from the PSF by integrating the PSF along a line. The *edge-response function* (ERF) in turn is merely the mathematical integration of the LSF along a plane. Experimentally, the ERF may be obtained directly by scanning an edge object.

In addition to the resolution-bar and pin patterns, the *modulation-transfer function* (Villafana 1978*a*) approach is probably the most commonly cited descriptor of spatial resolution. The MTF is defined as the response of the system to a sinusoidally varying object. Because of the difficulty of constructing objects with sinusoidally varying CT numbers, usually the PSF (Weaver 1975; Goodenough 1977), LSF (Bishop 1977; Judy 1976), or ERF (Judy 1976) is measured and then mathematically converted to the MTF. For instance, the LSF may be subjected to a Fourier transform operation and converted to an MTF. For the interested reader, Jones (1954) has reviewed in depth the various mathematical relationships between these various measures.

The point at which the MTF goes to zero can be used as a single number description of overall resolution. However, due to the presence of noise and the difficulty of locating the zero cutoff, the resolution measure is many times specified at the 10 percent or 20 percent MTF response.

To illustrate the use of MTFs, Fig. 1-30 shows for comparison purposes the MTF for the early GE CT/T 7800 and 8800 systems as well as the more recent 9800 system. The 8800 system has a detector aperture nearly one-half the size of the 7800. As a result, the MTF of the 8800 system is correspondingly better (about twice as good). This can be seen from the fact that the MTF response of the 8800 system drops at higher frequencies than the drop for the 7800 system.

The ideal MTF would correspond to a unit (MTF = 1) response regardless of frequency. Such comparisons can

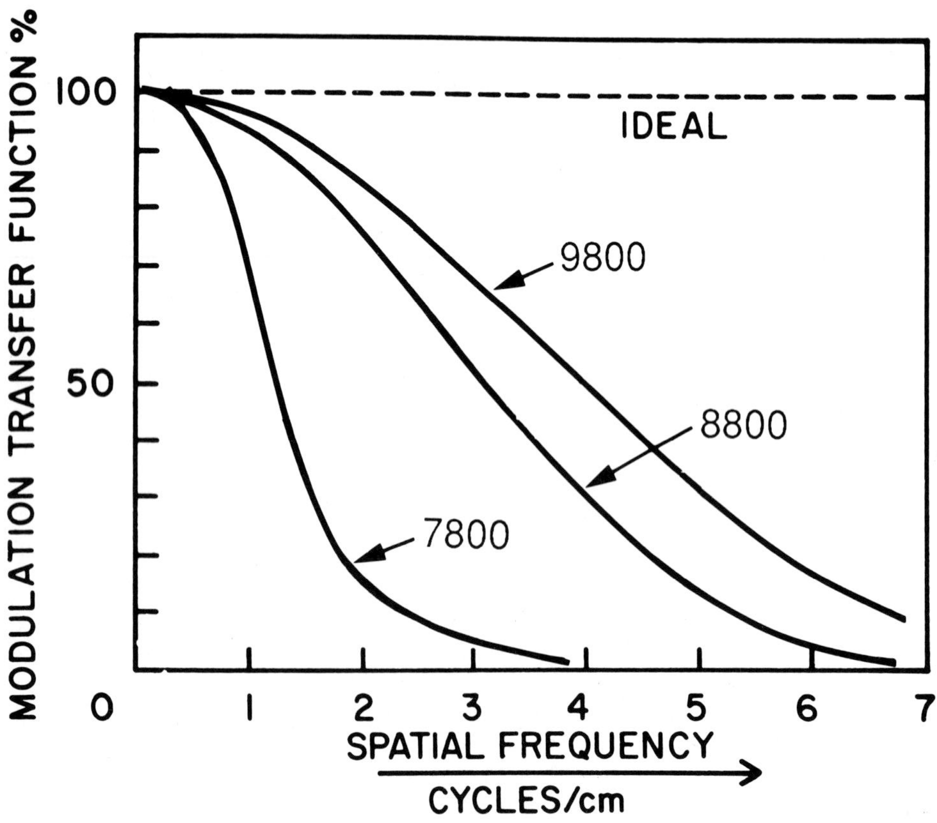

Figure 1-30 The modulation-transfer functions (MTF) for the GE CT T 7800, 8800, and 9800 systems. The GE 8800 system has a detector aperture size nearly half as large as the 7800, and the detectors are correspondingly more closely spaced. The improvement in the MTF is significant (nearly two times). Further reduction in detector size yields even greater improvement for the 9800 system. The ideal curve represents the situation in which the system response is unity regardless of how high the frequency is. (*Adapted from GE brochures.*)

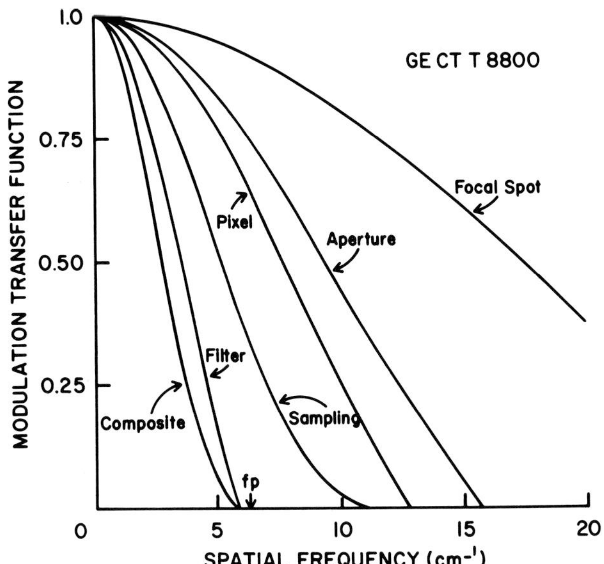

Figure 1-31 Comparison of individual-component MTFs for a given CT system. System shown is the GE CT/T8800 for a 24-cm-diameter patient circle, 0.78-mm pixel size. (Adapted from Barnes 1979.) Here the sampling and the algorithm filter function would be the limiting component, while the focal spot would be the least limiting. Also shown is the composite or total MTF curve, which is the product of all the component curves. Note that the composite is poorer than any individual component.

be of great value in assessing performance. Comparisons can also be made between different manufacturers' models and even between subcomponents of a given model CT. This latter application has been admirably demonstrated by Barnes (1979), as shown in Fig. 1-31, where it is seen that for the particular CT unit under study, the algorithm (or filter function) represents the limiting system component, since its MTF drops to zero the most quickly, and the focal spot is the component least limiting CT performance. The overall total or composite curve is obtained from the product of the MTFs of all the system components at each frequency; that is, in the general case,

$$MTF_{TOT} = MTF_1 \times MTF_2 \times MTF_3 \times \ldots \qquad (6)$$

Note that the composite MTF is in general lower than, and at most equal to, the lowest MTF response component in the system. Attempts to improve the spatial resolution of a system should be directed toward improving the lowest-response link in the system. In the specific case shown in Fig. 1-31, the sampling MTF would be the next most advantageous component to improve after the filter function.

As previously seen, insufficient sampling results in aliasing and artifactual streak formation. Even if algorithms are available to remove such artifacts, a generalized loss of spatial resolution will still be present as predicted by the sampling MTF in Fig. 1-31. The pixel MTF refers to the fact that choice of pixel size or pixel matrix will affect the resolution of the final image. For instance, a smaller patient or reconstruction circle results in a smaller effective pixel size and higher resolution. This relation is given by

$$\text{Pixel size} = \frac{\text{reconstruction diameter}}{\text{matrix size}} \qquad (7)$$

For example, a 256 × 256 matrix applied over a 400-mm reconstruction diameter results in a pixel size of 400 mm/256 = 1.56 mm. Likewise, a 512 × 512 matrix for the some diameter results in a pixel size of 400 mm/512 = 0.78 mm, or half the pixel size of a 256 matrix. Finally, the aperture (or collimator) MTF in Fig. 1-31 refers to the physical opening at the detector.

It should be noted that some systems with relatively large detectors provide for an absorbing pin which can be placed in front of the detector to reduce its effective size and thus improve its MTF or resolution response. Here again, component MTF curves can predict the possible success of such a maneuver. For instance, such an absorbing pin would be essentially futile for all third-generation xenon ionization chamber systems, since such systems can be configured with small detector face area and the aperture MTF is not limiting.

Finally, we again caution that MTF data do not of themselves predict actual clinical performance, since they are defined for 100 percent contrast and for essentially noise-free conditions. Consequently, they should be used for comparative purposes only and for the imaging of high-contrast structures.

NOISE

In detecting low-contrast tissue structures (tissues of similar CT numbers), noise plays a dominant role; it is in general the limiting factor in CT scanning, since in many applications diagnosis hinges on the visualization of tissue structures with very similar CT numbers. For instance, gray- and white-matter tissues are separated by only 5 to 10 CT numbers. Noise can be defined as the standard deviation in CT numbers in a scanned uniform water bath. All CT scanners provide for an ROI selector where one can read out automatically the standard deviation of the CT numbers falling within the selected area (usually about 25 pixels in size). To make the noise measure independent of the particular CT unit and contrast scale (CS) [Equation (5)], the following expression is used:

$$\text{Noise} = \frac{CS \times \sigma_w}{\mu_w} \times 100 \qquad (8)$$

where μ_w = the linear attenuation coefficient of water ($0.195\ cm^{-1}$ for 70 keV) and σ_w is the observed standard deviation for a uniform water-bath region.

It is crucial to note that image noise is directly related to the number of photons received and processed at the detectors. Consequently, to decrease CT noise, one must increase the number of photons passing through the patient and available at the detectors. This, of course, increases the patient dose. The statistical variation in the photon number in a uniform beam that is finally detected is given by the standard deviation of that photon number as follows:

$$\sigma_N = \sqrt{N} \tag{9}$$

σ_N above, as the fluctuation in the photon number N (which is related to patient dose), must be distinguished from σ_w as specified for the standard deviation in CT numbers of the final reconstructed uniform water field, the difference between these two being the contribution of algorithm noise (Joseph 1978*a*).

From Equation (9) emerges an underlying and crucial conclusion: *CT imaging performance depends on patient radiation dose.* This is true because the number of photons at the detector is directly related to the number of photons passing through the patient, which in turn determines patient dose. Because of the dependence of image quality on patient dose, one must specify the patient dose associated with any image performance specification. Stated another way, an image may be of very high quality but may have been obtained at the cost of an unacceptably high radiation dose to the patient. Haaga et al. (1981) have illustrated how photon levels of different milliamperage affect actual visualization.

Brooks (1976*c*) has shown that the statistical noise σ_N, pixel size w (representing the limiting resolution measure), slice thickness h, dose D, and the fractional attenuation of the patient B are related as follows:

$$\sigma_N = \left(\frac{KB}{w^3hD}\right)^{1/2} \tag{10}$$

where K is a proportionality constant for any given CT unit. Equation (10) reveals that in general, as the slice thickness decreases, the noise value increases. This is evident, since less thickness h implies a narrower beam and consequently the delivery of fewer photons to the detector. A similar statement is true for the patient-dose factor D in that a lower dose to the patient (for instance, less tube milliamperage or scan time) results in fewer photons at the detector. Both these factors vary as the square root, which means that halving either one results in a $\sqrt{2}$ times greater noise level. The noise dependence on pixel size, on the other hand, is as the third power. Thus halving the pixel size (which may result in doubling the resolution) results in an eightfold increase in dose to maintain the same level of noise! Not only does CT image performance depend on noise, but attempts at increasing performance by reducing noise may result in a very considerable dose increase to the patient.

If noise is in fact limiting CT performance and not spatial resolution, one may opt, for instance, to increase pixel size. Such a move would reduce noise and might improve visualization of large but low-contrast structures, but care must be taken since a net reduction of spatial resolution would also result. As discussed above in Equation (10), noise dependence varies with slice thickness to the 1/2 power. Thus increases in slice thickness also reduce noise, but not nearly to the same degree as increases in pixel width, which vary to the 3/2 power. The rationale for the noise dependence on pixel width and slice thickness is simply that reduction in these sizes causes a reduction in the number of photons available to make up the image for each pixel. A reduced number of photons in turn creates greater statistical variation, and image noise is increased.

An interesting approach to reducing final noise without increase in dose to the patient is by mathematical smoothing. Algorithms can be configured to include various smoothing routines (referred to as *kernels* or algorithm filters). Such smoothing, however, usually results in blurring and thus a loss of spatial resolution. However, if accomplishment of a particular task is limited by the presence of noise, smoothing may in some circumstances yield significant results, as reported by Joseph (1978*a*).

Finally, it should be stated that other descriptors of noise even more complete and general are available. For instance, noise power spectra can be constructed (Riederer 1978). These describe noise as a function of spatial frequency; hence, they are similar to and can be combined with the MTF descriptor. For further details, the reader is referred to the literature (Barnes 1979; Riederer 1978; Rossman 1972).

TISSUE RESOLUTION

Tissue, or low-contrast, resolution may be defined as the smallest object or pin size detectable under low-contrast conditions. Low contrast is considered to exist when scanning CT number differences of less than 0.5 percent or 5 CT numbers. (For a −1000 to +1000 CT system, each CT number represents 0.1 percent difference.) Phantoms used are similar to the bar and pin object types already discussed. Recent CT units have a tissue resolution of 4 to 5 mm, compared to a spatial high-contrast resolution of 0.5 mm or less. Tissue resolution is also called *low-contrast detectivity* or *low-contrast sensitivity*.

The tissue-resolution measure is more accurate in predicting clinically expected performance, since low-contrast conditions are more clinically relevant. Also, since low-contrast conditions are specified, the influence of

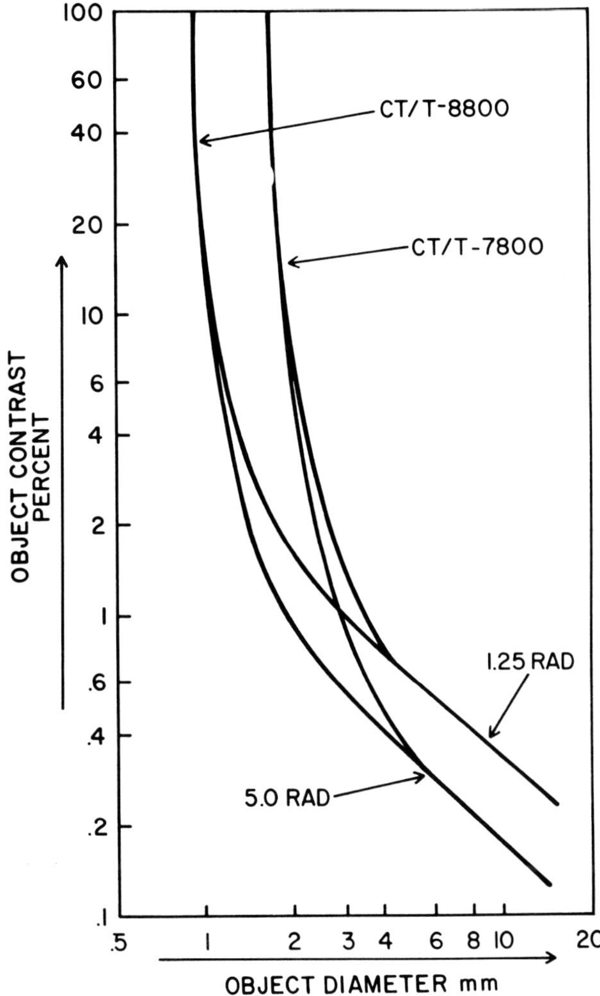

Figure 1-32 Detail-contrast curves. Plot of object diameter visible on both the GE 7800 and the GE 8800 versus object contrast for two different dose levels. At high contrast the smallest possible object diameter is visible (the resolution limit) independent of dose or noise. At low contrast, noise becomes a significant factor and results are highly dependent on dose. (*Adapted from Cohen 1979a,b.*)

noise is incorporated. Because of crucial interplay among noise, performance, and patient dose, tissue-resolution specifications must be accompanied by statements of pixel size, patient dose, phantom diameter, kilovoltage or filter, and other reconstruction details (McCullough 1980).

Another approach describing system resolution has been introduced which uses so-called contrast-detail curves (Cohen 1979*a,b*). In this approach both the low-contrast and high-contrast resolution responses of a system are specified. Figure 1-32 shows a contrast-detail curve for two levels of radiation dose and two different CT systems. In general, spatial resolution is relatively good for both units at high contrast and is independent of dose (noise). Note that in both cases spatial resolution still does not get better than a certain minimum detectable size (called the *resolution limit* and occurring at 100 percent contrast). As contrast decreases, resolution falls. At low-contrast levels, curves tend to flatten out (this is referred to as the *noise limit*). Note from Fig. 1-32 that if noise levels are reduced (dose increased), detectable size decreases at low-contrast levels but not at high-contrast levels.

Finally, mention should be made of still another approach to quantitating the performance of CT equipment. This consists in using receiver- (or reader) operator-characteristic (ROC) curves. Here, an attempt is made to compare the numbers of false-positive and false-negative detection rates as a function of reader bias and decision criteria. The interested reader is referred elsewhere for further details (Weaver 1975; Goodenough 1974*a,b;* Rossmann 1972).

PIXEL SIZES, ZOOM, AND CT PERFORMANCE

Various aspects of pixels have been previously discussed. Since much discussion concerning CT units centers on statements of pixel sizes, we now summarize some pertinent facts. (1) Pixels are the basic building blocks of the CT image. They represent an element or area of the view over which the reconstruction process has calculated a CT number. (2) Pixels represent a weighted nonlinear average CT number of the various tissues which fall within a given volume element (voxel) within the patient (volume-averaging or partial volume effect) and as a result may be artifactual, especially in regions of the patient where tissue type and structure are rapidly changing. (3) The original EMI Mark I pixel sizes were relatively large in that they represented a $3 \times 3 \times 13$ mm volume (80×80 array). Currently, pixel sizes can be configured to less than 1 mm on a side. (4) Changing pixel sizes can indeed improve CT images in that the partial volume effect is reduced and, consequently, both spatial and low-contrast tissue resolution can improve. Improvement, however, is dependent on whether there is a corresponding increase in photon levels to overcome the greater noise levels inherent with smaller pixels (that is, smaller pixel sizes imply a greater number of pixels and thus fewer photons per pixel) and whether the imaging limitation was in fact the pixel size. It is clear that other components, such as motion, focal-spot size, and detector-aperture size, may be limitations, in which case pixel-size reduction may result only in either image degradation due to noise or an increase in patient dose if photon levels are increased to overcome the higher noise levels for smaller pixel sizes.

Other features that affect pixel size and imaging performance are magnification and zoom. There are a variety of ways in which magnification and zoom can be accomplished. These are referred to as geometric zoom, interpolated zoom, and reconstructed zoom.

Geometric Zoom

Geometric zoom refers to image enlargement accomplished by varying geometric factors such as sampling distances, number of detectors used for the reconstruction process, and mechanical configuration of the gantry. For instance, if a smaller reconstruction area is chosen and if the number of pixels is the same, the patient volume size corresponding to each pixel decreases, and the size of the image increases. This results in an increase in system performance. For instance, if a particular system is configured for displaying 256 × 256 pixels for a reconstruction circle of 400 mm, each pixel represents 400/256 = 1.56 mm. If the reconstruction circle is reduced to 200 mm, each pixel represents 200/256 = 0.78 mm. To exploit this, CT units have selectable lengths or reconstruction circles over which data can be collected, selection being based on the size of the patient. One must be careful to distinguish between the gantry opening (or patient window), which is the physical opening within which the patient is placed, and the reconstruction circle, which is that region within the gantry opening over which the data are collected and processed. For the best images, the CT operator should select the smallest possible reconstruction circle. Actually, in some applications where resolution is critical, a reconstruction circle even smaller than the patient size is selected and is centered on a particular region of interest, as in scanning the cervical spine.

Sometimes this latter approach is also referred to as *region-of-interest* scanning (still a form of geometric zoom). In ROI scanning, caution must be observed in interpreting the resulting CT numbers, since inaccuracies may be introduced by the contribution of patient volumes outside the ROI. As already stated, the pixel size for small reconstruction circles represents a smaller volume in the patient. As a consequence, the actual size of the patient image on the display screen is enlarged. Furthermore, this represents a true zoom in that enlargement of the image is accomplished with each pixel still representing actual patient data.

In third- and fourth-generation systems, the detectors see the full patient contour, and the millimeters of patient per pixel and thus data sampling distances are fixed; thus the use of small detectors is especially necessary. These units, however, still have a selectable reconstruction circle and different possible degrees of final display magnification in that the smaller regions scanned can still be imaged over the full display with the total pixels available. Image quality is again usually improved, but such improvement will depend on the relative role of the sampling and pixel size MTFs.

One interesting variation of geometric zoom is a configuration providing for variable magnification within the gantry. For example, the detector array, along with the x-ray source, can be moved closer to or farther away from the patient in such a manner that the full array of detectors is always used. When the x-ray source is closer to the patient (and detectors far), a smaller patient diameter is viewed. For larger patient diameter, the source is placed farther away. In either case, all the detectors are utilized. With this arrangement, the sampling distances and therefore the image quality can always be optimized in addition to having images with variable magnification.

Interpolated Zoom

This is quite different from geometric zoom. Interpolated zoom enlarges the image of a relatively small region of interest within an already processed image and, under computer control, expands it to fill the entire display by averaging the CT numbers in each particular pixel over the neighboring pixels. Therefore, while the final pixels represent a smaller patient volume, they do not represent unique and true patient data but arithmetic averages (or interpolations) over adjacent pixels. It is always performed on a finished image without a reconstruction routine. As the ROI decreases, the image appears larger but spatial resolution is progressively degraded.

Reconstructed Zoom

This type of zoom depends on original data being available to allow reconstruction over a smaller area. Typically, reconstructed zoom can be performed with optimal results when scan sampling distances are smaller than the pixel display sizes. For example, if a scanner is used with a 512 × 512 calculation matrix but final reconstruction results are condensed and displayed on a 256 × 256 pixel array, then if original data are still available, a reconstructed zoom of at least two times can be invoked on the original image. This is a true zoom in that original patient data are reconstructed and displayed.

In summary, it can be stated that pixel size is indeed an important parameter determining CT imaging performance. A statement of array size by itself is not, however, sufficient. Rather, it is important to state what size (or volume) the pixel actually represents in the patient. There are various ways to enlarge or magnify the image which correspond to decreasing the volume each pixel represents. Such zooming may or may not lead to an increase in perceived image quality.

Data Sampling

We have seen that detector size and sampling frequency are important parameters. Some recent CT designs incorporate various features to enhance the imaging performance of CT scanners by affecting these two parameters. The two most notable of these are dynamic focal spots and asymmetric scanning. Both are illustrated in Fig. 1-33.

The dynamic focal spot feature provides for focal spots to fall on two different regions of the x-ray target. One

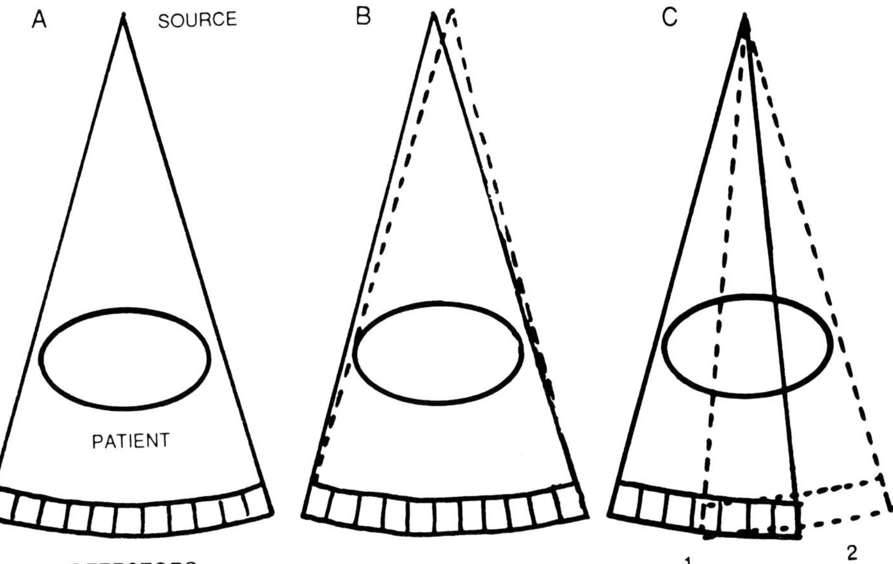

Figure 1-33 Schemes to increase the sampling frequency. **A.** Normal configuration: one fan beam, one focal spot, one view of patient. **B.** Dynamic focal spots: two fan beams, two focal spots, two views of patient. **C.** Shifting gantry: one focal spot, two fan beams array, views half the patient at position 1; after shifting to position 2, detectors view the other half of patient. The result is more efficient use of available detectors.

therefore has two fan x-ray beams slightly offset one from the other and essentially doubling the image-sampling frequency. That is, the same detector sees two separate fans through the patient with two separate sets of information.

In asymmetric scanning, the detector bank is shifted under computer control so that it is asymmetrically aligned with respect to the central axis of the beam on either side of the patient. Using data from both asymmetric scans, one can effectively double the sampling frequency for the same detector size and number.

In both of these approaches, the spatial resolution can be theoretically doubled. If both approaches are used simultaneously, a four-times increase in spatial resolution is theoretically possible. On the other hand, these techniques can also be used to allow for a reduction in the number of detectors needed to accomplish the scan.

Scan Speed and Spiral Scanning

As discussed earlier, the main impetus for improvements in CT instrumentation was the need for shorter scan times to minimize motion streaks, improve image quality, and increase patient throughput.

The various generations that evolved provided such shorter scan times. This, in combination with improvements in spatial and tissue resolution, has resulted in modern high-performance scanners. The electron scan beam geometry is the fastest of the modern scanners; however, this is accomplished at the expense of spatial resolution. Recently, scanners utilizing slip ring technology have become commercially available. This technology provides for the continuous one-way rotation of the x-ray tube and detector assembly without the need for rewinding the x-ray tube and its cables. If the patient is simultaneously moved through the gantry, obtaining data over a whole patient volume in a single breath holding becomes possible. This process is referred to as *spiral scanning* (Kalender 1990; Villafana 1991). Its advantages include minimizing problems due to motion streaks, inconsistent scan-to-scan levels of inspiration, and the resulting missed anatomic levels due to patient motion. The problems of prolonged examination times due to interscan delays and respiration between scans resulting in noncompletion of extended volume contrast-enhanced studies during the vascular enhancement phase in dynamic scanning will also be alleviated. In addition to dynamic scanning, other applications of spiral scanning include quantitative CT number studies such as for bone mineral density and lung nodule quantification.

Patient Radiation Dose

We have already discussed the fact that CT scanning is noise-limited in that image quality increases as the number of x-ray photons utilized increases. A greater number of photons, however, results in greater patient dose. Fortunately, radiation dosimetry in general is an established technology. Even though there are some unique aspects to the dose problem in CT scanning, such as highly collimated scanning fields, they can be taken into account.

The radiological units of roentgens and rads are familiar to all. The *roentgen* is a measure of the ionization occurring in air. The International Commission on Radiological Units (ICRU) has recommended dropping this unit, and the clinician will be seeing less and less of it. The *rad* is a measure of the absorbed energy per unit mass, or absorbed dose (1 rad = 2.58×10^{-4} joules per kilogram). Given the roentgen exposure, the rad dose

Table 1-9 Factors Affecting Patient Dose

Patient thickness
Generator and tube factors
  Kilovoltage and filtration
  Tube current (milliamperage) and scan on time
  Focal-spot size (penumbral spread)
Gantry factors
  Beam collimation
  Slice width and overlap
  Scan orientation
  Detector efficiency
Image quality desired

may be obtained by multiplication by a suitable factor (0.91 for diagnostic x-ray energies and soft tissue). The ICRU has also recommended the use of the unit *gray* as a replacement for absorbed dose (1 gray = 1 joule per kilogram) as a replacement for the rad. Most dose information currently is available in rads, but this is expected to shift toward the gray in the future (1 gray = 100 rads).

Table 1-9 summarizes the various factors affecting patient dose. The factors most familiar to the clinician are patient thickness, beam filtration, and the radiographic factors of kilovoltage and milliamperage. To these must be added a number of factors unique to CT scanning such as beam collimation, detector efficiency, slice-width effects, and image quality desired.

Patient Thickness

It stands to reason that as patient thickness increases, so does the attenuation of the x-ray beam and the amount of radiation which must pass through the patient to provide the required number of photons at the detector level. As a consequence, more total energy is absorbed in the patient. The fact that larger patients have their entry skin surface closer to the x-ray source also results in greater patient skin dose.

Kilovoltage

Kilovoltage affects the dose in two possible ways. If kilovoltage is increased, more photons are produced and patient dose is also increased (this is the usual case for CT). Dose is decreased on increasing kilovoltage only if this allows a greater proportional decrease in the milliamperage. This relative decrease comes about because the number of photons arriving at the detector is greater owing to the higher penetrating ability of the higher-kilovoltage beam.

Filtration

Added beam filtration always leads to lower patient doses. The reason for this is the same as in clinical radiography: Filtration removes the softer, low-energy photons that are readily absorbed in the patient and have little probability of penetrating through to the detectors. Selection of filters on CT scanners, however, is not to provide for dose saving but rather to harden the beam to avoid beam-hardening effects within the patient. Typically, such added filtration is selected for scanning large body parts, compared to scanning heads. (The filtration referred to here should not be confused with software filters incorporated in an algorithm, which are part of the mathematical reconstruction process.)

Tube Current and Scan on Time

Tube current represents the flow of electrons across the x-ray tube, and it controls the final quantity of x-rays emitted. By convention it is measured in milliamperes. Scan "on time" refers to the period of time milliamperes are actually flowing and x-rays are actually on or not shuttered. Most CT units provide for continuous x-ray production throughout the scan. Pulsing units are configured to fire or turn on for x-ray pulses or various intervals of time (pulse length). These pulses are repeated at various angles as the x-ray tube rotates around the patient. This is the product of the tube current and the "on time" (the milliamperage product) which is the important dose-determining factor. Many CT units offer a fast scan at low image quality and a slower scan at higher image quality (if patient motion is not limiting). Typically, the faster scans are accomplished by pulsing at fewer intervals around the patient or by an overall reduction in scan times. Likewise, a partial scan (less than 360° rotation) may be provided. Since the milliamperes product will be lower for such fast scans, the dose also will be lower.

Focal Spot Spread

Figure 1-28 illustrates the fact that there is a spread of radiation across the slice. This spread affects the dose overlapping from one slice into another slice, which then affects the overall dose to the patient. The smaller the focal spot, the less the penumbral spread beyond slice borders and the better the dose characteristics of the scanner. Remember, however, that smaller focal spots unfortunately also result in diminished x-ray tube capacity.

Beam Collimation

Typically, CT scanning involves the use of highly collimated beams. Fan beams, as used in third- and fourth-generation systems, are opened up along the horizontal direction. As far as dose is concerned, the important idea is that the x-ray beam should be collimated down to yield a field incident on the patient which corresponds to the desired slice thickness. Figure 1-34 shows examples of a poorly collimated beam and a well-collimated beam. Note that for poor collimation the region which extends beyond the active area dimensions of the detector un-

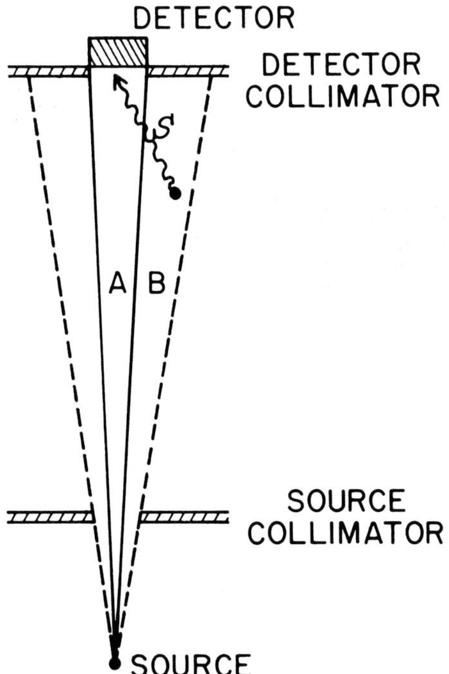

Figure 1-34 **A.** Well-collimated beam along slice direction confined to the dimensions of the detector. **B.** Poorly collimated beam. Radiation passing through the patient is not utilized at the detector. Additionally, scatter (*S*) from the patient may degrade image quality.

necessarily adds to the patient dose and forms a region of overlapping dose when the adjacent slice is scanned. To study this in more detail, dose profiles are usually obtained across the patient in a direction perpendicular to the slice plane (along the z axis). These can be obtained by the use of thermoluminescent dosimeters (TLD),* for instance, placed on tissue-equivalent phantoms or on patients directly. Alternatively, ionization chambers on phantoms can also be used.

One of the prime means of evaluating the dose characteristics of a CT scanner is to compare the dose profiles with the sensitivity profiles. It will be recalled that the sensitivity profile is the response of the CT system along the perpendicular (z direction) to the scan plane. The dose profile is the radiation distribution along the same direction. Ideally, the dose profile should be identical to the sensitivity profile for a particular set of scan parameters when both are compared at the patient level. Thus the ratio of the two should be 1.0, or 100 percent. This ratio is referred to as *dose utilization*. The practitioner is cautioned that a particular CT unit may have a high dose utilization yet also result in a relatively high dose to the patient, since dose utilization indicates how efficiently the radiation was detected but does not yield the magnitude of the actual dose received.

Slice Width and Overlap

As slice width decreases, the penumbral region of the field becomes relatively more important, because the tails of the dose profiles then represent a proportionately larger fraction of the dose distribution, and overlapping on multiple scans becomes correspondingly more serious. Additionally, some degree of slice overlap may be incorporated into the scan sequence. Thus a 1.5-mm slice width being scanned may be incremented, for instance, by a 1.6-mm distance. This results in a 1-mm scan overlap, which drives the patient dose even higher. Figure 1-35 shows how total dose distribution for a series of consecutive scans can be obtained by summation of a single-scan dose profile incremented by a known amount; it also shows the case in which peaks may appear in dose distribution, depending on the extent of the tails in the dose profile and the degree of overlap incorporated in the scan sequence.

Scan Orientation

A number of factors associated with scan orientation should be noted. For instance, in a 180° head scanner the x-ray tube should rotate over the posterior of the patient, sparing the eye lens a considerable dose (Villafana 1978c; Batter 1977) (a factor of about 10!). Third- and fourth-generation scanners typically rotate 360° around the patient periphery. Some units may incorporate an overscan feature for patient-motion and streak correction. In this case, more than 360° is scanned and the dose is greater in the region of overscan. Such a case requires particular attention to avoid having the scan both begin and end over a critical organ such as the eye lens.

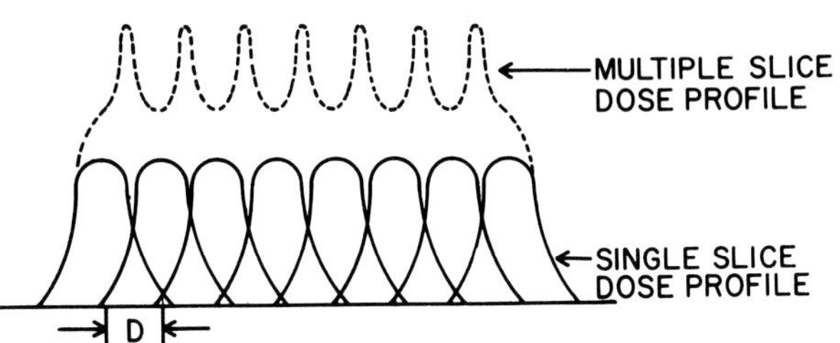

Figure 1-35 Determination of dose distribution over an extended body part when multiple scans are obtained. Appropriate summation of the dose profiles is accomplished by superimposing the dose profiles with incrementation distance *D*. Because of the tailing off of the dose profiles and the degree of overlap in incrementation, dose peaks may appear in the distribution.

*TLD detectors usually consist of a small lithium fluoride chip (typically about 1.0 mm × 3 mm × 3 mm), which has the advantage of being small and tissue-equivalent; however, it has a low-energy dependency and must be calibrated very carefully. The TLD detector is based on the principle that electrons liberated by the incident radiation are trapped at certain impurity centers, or electron traps, within the crystal. When the crystal is heated, the electron traps are emptied and light is emitted as the electrons fall back to the ground state. This emitted light is proportional to the original incident radiation.

Detector Efficiency

We have already discussed the various factors influencing overall detector efficiency (capture, quantum, and conversion efficiency). It stands to reason that as the efficiency of the detector gets lower, fewer photons will be utilized for the image. As a result, a higher dose will have to be given to the patient to maintain acceptable noise levels. In general, solid-state detectors have a higher overall efficiency than do gas detectors and result in a somewhat lower dose.

Image Quality Desired

Image quality for CT is directly related to the noise present in the image. Therefore, better image quality may be obtained at higher dose levels (see Fig. 1-32). Likewise, to reduce artifactual streaks, thinner slices may be invoked that in turn require a greater dose. Finally, we have also seen that pixel size reduction leads to greater image quality, but again, this will be at the expense of greater patient dose to overcome loss of photons in smaller pixel volumes. When one is evaluating image quality or comparing systems, the patient dose should always be taken into account.

EXPRESSING DOSE

There are a number of ways to express patient dose. For instance, average or maximum skin dose, or dose at the middepth of the patient, or even the dose at some critical organ such as the eye lens or gonads has been used (Villafana 1978*c;* Isherwood 1978; Shrivastava 1977; Gyldensted 1977; McCullough 1974; Perry 1973). Other measures include total integrated energy absorbed in the body (integral dose). Since image quality depends on dose and dose in turn depends on many factors (Table 1-9), care must be exercised in interpreting dose data; for example, depending on the extent of the dose profile tails, very high dose regions may exist which may be masked by the statement of a simple average. The simplest adequately descriptive measures of patient dose are the single-slice dose profile and the multiple-slice dose factor (typical values = 1.2 to 2.0). These should be known to the user for the various operating modes of the equipment used. For example, if the single-slice skin dose is 2 rads and the multiple slice dose factor is 1.5, what would the total dose be for 10 slices? The answer is 3 rads—that is, the product of the single-slice dose with the multiple-slice factor. The multiple-slice dose factor represents the spread in dose beyond the slice due to scatter and penumbral effects. Along with the dose profiles, a plot of dose distribution along the total body part, similar to that in Fig. 1-35, should be available. In general, the dose in CT scanning falls between 2 and 10 rads to the skin.

The most complete description of the patient dose is that using isodose curves (Perry 1973; Agarwal 1979; Jucius 1977; Wall 1979). From these the relative dose at any point or level can readily be picked out, since each isodose curve represents the points having the same dose within the patient, and the points falling between the curves can easily be interpolated.

One way of expressing CT dose is the "computed tomography dose index"(CTDI). The CTDI is obtained at a particular measurement site by integrating the single-slice dose profile and dividing by the nominal slice thickness (Shope 1981). This is equal to the average dose at the measurement site which would result from scanning a series of contiguous slices as in a typical procedure. The CTDI is usually measured with a special long and thin ionization chamber.

Gonad Dose

When the head or upper torso is scanned, the gonads receive a relatively low dose (typically 10 mrad or less). The gonads are exposed to both scattered radiation produced within the patient and leakage radiation from the x-ray tube. Scatter in general must pass through and be extensively attenuated by whatever tissue thickness exists between the region scanned and the position of the gonads. Gonad dose increases as the distance to the irradiated region decreases. Tube-leakage levels are limited by law to a maximum of 100 mR/h at 1 meter. As with any diagnostic x-ray tube, most CT tubes have leakage rates well within this maximum because of the lead lining usually placed inside the tube housing. In addition to internally scattered and leakage radiation, there is the possibility of radiation scattering from various portions of the gantry components, which also can contribute to patient dose. Each unit should be evaluated as to gonad doses as well as radiation dosages to persons remaining in the scan room to hold or calm patients.

In summary, then, it is recognized that CT scanning-image quality is noise-limited. Noise in turn is dependent on the number of photons utilized to make up the image. Therefore, patient dose, noise, and image quality are all intimately related. When evaluating the performance of a CT scanner, the dose must be explicitly stated for the conditions under which the image was obtained.

References

AAPM: *Phantoms for Performance Evaluation and Quality Assurance of CT Scanners,* Report Number 1. New York, AAPM, 1978.

AGARWAL SK, FRIESEN EJ, BHADURI D, COURLAS G: Dose distribution from a delta 25 head scanner. *Med Phys* 6:302–304, 1979.

ALFIDI RJ, MACINTYRE WJ, HAAGA JR: The effects of biological motion on CT resolution. *Am J Roentgenol* 127:11–15, 1976.

AMBROSE J: Computerized transverse axial scanning (tomography): II. Clinical application. *Br J Radiol* 46:1023–1047, 1973.

BAILY NA, KELLER RA, JAKOWATZ CV, KAK AC: The capability of fluoroscopic systems for the production of computerized axial tomograms. *Invest Radiol* 11:434–439, 1976.

BARNES G, YESTER MV, KING MA: Optimizing computed tomography (CT) scanner geometry. *Proc Soc Photo-Opt Eng* 173:(Med VII)225–237, 1979.

BASSANO DA, CHAMBERLAIN CC, MOSLEY JM, KIEFFER SA: Physical performance and dosimetric characteristics of the delta 50 whole body/brain scanner. *Radiology* 123:455–462, 1977.

BATTER S: A philosophy of dose specification for computed tomography. *Med Mundi* 22:11–12, 1977.

BISHOP CJ, EHRHARDT JC: Modulation transfer function of the EMI head scanner. *Med Phys* 4:163–167, 1977.

BOYD DP, HERMANNEFELDT WB, QUINN JR, SPARKS RA: Xray transmission scanning system and method and electron beam Xray scan tube. U.S. Patent 435202-1, September 28, 1982.

BROOKS RA, DICHIRO G: Theory of image reconstruction in computed tomography. *Radiology* 117:561–572, 1975.

BROOKS RA, DICHIRO G: Beam hardening in x-ray reconstructive tomography. *Phys Med Biol* 21:390–398, 1976*a*.

BROOKS RA, DICHIRO G: Principles of computer assisted tomography (CAT) in radiographic and radiosotopic imaging. *Phys Med Biol* 21:689–732, 1976*b*.

BROOKS RA, DICHIRO G: Statistical limitations in x-ray reconstructive tomography. *Med Phys* 3:237–240, 1976*c*.

BROOKS RA, DICHIRO G: Slice geometry in computer assisted tomography. *J Comput Assist Tomogr* 1:191–199, 1977.

BROOKS RA, GLOVER AJ, TOLBERT RL, EISNER FA, DIBIANCA FA: Aliasing, a source of streaks in computed tomograms. *J Comput Assist Tomogr* 3:511–518, 1979.

BRUNDAGE BH, CHOMKE E: Clinical applications of cardiac CT imaging. *Modern Concepts of Cardiovascular Disease* 8:39–43, 1985.

CARSON PL, OUGHTON TV, HENDEE WR, AHIYA AS: Imaging soft tissue through bone with ultrasound transmission tomography by reconstruction. *Med Phys* 4:302–309, 1977.

CHECKLEY DR, ZHU XP, ANTOUN N, CHEN SZ, ISHERWOOD I: An investigation into the problems of attenuation and area measurements made from CT images of pulmonary modules. *J Comput Assist Tomogr* 8:237–243, 1984.

COHEN G, DIBIANCA FA: The use of contrast-detail-dose evaluation of image quality in a computed tomographic scanner. *J Comput Assist Tomogr* 3:189–195, 1979*a*.

COHEN G: Contrast-detail dose analysis of six different computed tomographic scanners. *J Comput Assist Tomogr* 3:197–203, 1979*b*.

CORMACK AM, KOEHLER AM: Quantitative proton tomography: Preliminary experiments. *Phys Med Biol* 21:560–569, 1976.

DICHIRO G, BROOKS RA, DUBAL L, CHEN E: The apical artifact: Elevated attenuation values toward the apex of the skull. *J Comput Assist Tomogr* 2:65–70, 1978.

DUERINCKX AJ, MACOVSKI A: Polychromatic streak artefacts in computed tomography images. *J Comput Assist Tomogr* 2:481–487, 1978.

Emission computed tomography I. *Semin Nucl Med,* vol 10, 1980.

Emission computed tomography II. *Semin Nucl Med,* vol 11, 1981.

EXNER GU, ELSASSER U, RUEGSEGGER P, ANLIKER M: Bone densimetry using computer tomography: I and II: *Br J Radiol* 52:14–28, 1979.

GADO M, PHELPS M: Peripheral zone of increased density in computed tomography. *Radiology* 117:71–74, 1975.

GENANT HK, ETTINGER B, CANN CE, REISERU, GORDON GS, KOLB FO. Osteoporosis: Assessment by quantitative computed tomography. *Orthop Clin North Am* 16(3):557–568, 1985.

GLOVER GN, PELC NJ: Nonlinear volume artefacts in x-ray computed tomography: *Med Phys* 7:238–248, 1980.

GOODENOUGH DJ, ROSSMAN K, LUSTED LB: Radiographic applications of receiver operating characteristic curves. *Radiology* 110:89–95, 1974*a*.

GOODENOUGH DJ, ROSSMAN K, LUSTED LB: Factors affecting the detectability of a simulated radiographic signal. *Invest Radiol* 8:339–344, 1974*b*.

GOODENOUGH DJ, WEAVER KE, DAVIS DO: Potential artefacts associated with the scanning pattern of the EMI scanner. *Radiology* 117:615–619, 1975.

GOODENOUGH DJ, WEAVER KE, DAVIS DO: Development of a phantom for evaluation and assurance of image quality in CT scanning. *Opt Eng* 16:52–65, 1977.

GORDON R, HERMAN GT: Three dimensional reconstructions from projections: A review of algorithms. *Int Rev Cytol* 38:111–151, 1974.

GORDON R, HERMAN GT, JOHNSON SA: Image reconstruction from projections. *Sci Am* October 1975, pp 56–68.

GLYDENSTED C: Gonadal thermoluminescence dosimetry in cranial computed tomography with the EMI scanner. *Neuroradiology* 14:111–112, 1977.

HAAGA J, MIRALDI F, MACINTYRE W, LIPUMA JP, BRYAN PS, WIESEN E: The effect of mAs variation upon computed tomography image quality as evaluated by invivo and invitro studies. *Radiology* 138:449–454, 1981.

HERMON G: Demonstration of beam hardening correction in computerized tomography of the head. *J Comput Assist Tomogr* 3:373–378, 1978.

HOUNSFIELD N: A Method of and Apparatus for Examination of a Body Part by Radiation such as X-ray or Gamma Radiation. British Patent 1283915, 1972.

HOUNSFIELD N: Some practical problems in computerized tomography scanning, in Ter-Pogossian MM et al (eds): *Reconstruction Tomography in Diagnostic Radiology and Nuclear Medicine.* Baltimore, University Park Press, 1977.

ISHERWOOD I, PULLON BR, RITCHINGS RT: Radiation dose in neuroradiological procedures. *Neuroradiology* 16:477–481, 1978.

JONES RC: On the point and line spread functions of photographic images. *J Opt Soc Am* 44:468, 1954.

JOSEPH PM: Image noise and smoothing in computed tomography (CT) scanners. *Opt Eng* 17:396–399, 1978*a.*

JOSEPH PM, SPITAL RD: A method for correcting bone induced artefacts in computed tomography scanners. *J Comput Assist Tomogr* 2:100–108, 1978*b.*

JOSEPH PM: Artefacts in computed tomography, in *Radiology of the Skull and Brain: Technical Aspects of Computed Tomography,* vol 5. St. Louis, Mosby, 1981.

JUCIUS RA, KAMBIC GX: Radiation dosimetry in computed tomography. *Proc Soc Photo-Opt Instrument Eng* 127(Med IV):286–295, 1977.

JUDY PF: The line spread function and modulation transfer function of a computed tomographic scanner. *Med Phys* 3:233, 1976.

KAK AC, JAKOWATZ CV, BAILY NA, KELLER RA: Computerized tomography using video recorded fluoroscopic images. *IEEE Trans BioMed Eng BME* 24:157–169, 1977.

KAK AC: Computerized tomography with x-ray emission and ultrasound sources. *Proc IEEE* 67:1245–1272, 1979.

KALENDER VA, SEISSLER W, KLOTZ E, VOCK P: Spiral volumetric CT with single breath-hold technique, continuous transport, and continuous scanner rotation. *Radiology* 176:183–191, 1990.

KOEPPE RA, BRIGGER RM, SCHLAPPER GA, LARSEN GN, JOST RJ: Neutron computed tomography. *J Comput Assist Tomogr* 5:79–88, 1981.

LATCHAW RE, PAYNE JT, GOLD LHA: Effective atomic number and electron density as measured with a computed tomography scanner: Computation and correlation with brain tumor histology. *J Comput Assist Tomogr* 2:199–208, 1978.

LEVI C, GRAY JE, MCCULLOUGH EC, HATTERY RR: The unreliability of CT numbers as absolute values. *Am J Radiol* 139:443–447, 1982.

LIM ST, SAGE DJ: Detection of subarachnoid blood clot and other flat thin structures by computed tomography. *Radiology* 123:79–84, 1977.

LIPTON MJ, HIGGINS CB, BOYD DP: Computed tomography of heart: Evaluation of anatomy and function. *J Am Coll Cardiol* 5:55S–69S, 1985.

LIPTON MJ, BRUNDAGE BH, HIGGINS CH, BOYD DP: Clinical applications of dynamic computed tomography. *Prog Cardiovasc Dis* 28:349–366, 1986.

LITTLETON JT, DURIZCH ML, CROSBY EH, GEORY JC: Tomography: Physical principles and clinical applications, in Robbins LL (ed): *Golden's Diagnostic Radiology,* Sec. 17. Baltimore, Williams & Wilkins, 1976.

MACINTYRE WJ, ALFIDE RJ, HAAGA J, CHERNAK E, MEANY TF: Comparative modulation transfer functions of the EMI and delta scanners. *Radiology* 120:189–191, 1976.

MAINI R, ISKANDER MF, DURNEY CH: On electro-magnetic imaging using linear reconstruction techniques. *Proc IEEE* 68:1550–1552, 1980.

MAUE-DICKSON W, TREFLER M, DICKSON DR: Comparison of dosimetry and image quality in computed and conventional tomography. *Radiology* 131:509–514, 1979.

MCCULLOUGH EC et al: On evaluation of the quantitative and radiation features of a scanning x-ray transverse axial tomograph: The EMI scanner. *Radiology* 111:709–715, 1974.

MCCULLOUGH EC: Photon attenuation in computed tomography. *Med Phys* 2:307–320, 1975.

MCCULLOUGH EC, PAYNE JT, BAKER HL, HATTERY RR, SHEEDY PF, STEPHENS DH, GEDGAUDUS E: Performance evaluation and quality assurance of computed tomography scanners with illustrations from the EMI, acta, and delta scanners. *Radiology* 120:173–188, 1976.

MCCULLOUGH EC: Factors affecting the use of quantitative information from a CT scanner. *Radiology* 124:99–107, 1977.

MCCULLOUGH EC: Specifying and evaluating the performance of computed tomography (CT) scanners. *Med Phys* 7:291–296, 1980.

MCDAVID WD, WAGGENER RG, PAYNE WH, DENNIS MJ: Correction for spectral artefacts in cross sectional reconstruction from x-rays. *Med Phys* 4:54–57, 1977*a*.

MCDAVID WD, WAGGENER RG, DENNIS MJ, SANK VS, PAYNE WH: Estimation of chemical composition and density from computed tomography carried out at a number of energies. *Invest Radiol* 12:189–194, 1977*b*.

MEREDITH WJ, MASSEY JB: The effect of x-ray absorption on the radiographic image, in *Fundamental Physics of Radiology,* 2d ed, chap 19. Baltimore, Williams & Wilkins, 1972.

MICHAEL AS, MAFFEE MF, VALVASSORI GE, TAN WS: Dynamic computed tomography of the head and neck: Differential diagnostic value. *Radiology* 154:413–419, 1985.

NALCIOGLU O, LOU RY: Post reconstruction method of beam hardening in computerized tomography. *Phys Med Biol* 24:330–340, 1979.

NEWTON TH, POTTS DG: *Radiology of the Skull and Brain,* Vol 5: *Technical Aspects of Computed Tomography.* St. Louis, Mosby, 1981.

PERRY BJ, BRIDGES C: Computerized transverse and axial scanning (tomography): Part III. Radiation dose considerations. *Br J Radiol* 46:1048–1051, 1973.

PETERS JM, LEWITT RM: Computed tomography with fan beam geometry. *J Comput Assist Tomogr* 1:429–436, 1977.

PHELPS ME, GADO MH, HOFFMAN EJ: Correlation of effective atomic number and electron density with attenuation coefficients. *Radiology* 117:585–588, 1975*a*.

PHELPS ME, HOFFMAN EJ, TER-POGOSSIAN MM: Attenuation coefficients of various body tissues, fluids and lesions at photon energies 18 to 136 Kev. *Radiology* 117:573–583, 1975*b*.

RAO PS, GREGG EC: Attenuation of monoenergic gamma rays in tissues. *Am J Roentgenol* 123:631–637, 1975.

RAO PS, SANTOSH K, GREGG EC: Computed tomography with microwaves. *Radiology* 135:769–770, 1980.

REVAK CS: Mineral content of cortical bone measured by computed tomography. *J Comput Assist Tomogr* 4:342–350, 1980.

RIEDERER SJ, PELC NJ, CHESTER DA: The noise power spectrum in computed x-ray tomography. *Phys Med Biol* 23:446–454, 1978.

ROSSMAN K: Image quality and patient exposure. *Curr Probl Radiol* 22:2–34, 1972.

RUEGSEGGER P, HANGARTNER TH, KELLER HU, HINDERLING TH: Standardization of computed tomography images by means of a material-selective beam hardening correction. *J Comput Assist Tomogr* 2:184–188, 1978.

RUTHERFORD RA, PULLAN BR, ISHERWOOD I: Measurement of effective atomic number and electron density using an EMI scanner. *Neuroradiology* 11:15–21, 1976.

SALVOLINI U, CABANIS EA, RODOLLEE A, MENICHELLI F, POSQUINI FU, IBA-ZIZEN MT: Computed tomography of the optic nerve: I. Normal results. *J Comput Assist Tomogr* 2:141–149, 1978.

SCHULZ RA, OLSON EC, HON KS: A comparison of the number of rays versus the number of views in reconstruction tomography. *Proc SPIE* 127:25–27, 1977.

SCHWENKER RP: Film selection considerations for computed tomography and ultrasound video photography. *Proc Soc Photo-Opt Instrum Eng* 173 (Med VII):75–80, 1979.

SHEPP LA, STEIN JA: Simulated reconstruction artifacts in computerized x-ray tomography, in Ter-Pogossian M, Phelps M, Brownell GL, Cox JR, Davis DO, Evans RG (eds): *Reconstruction Tomography in Diagnostic Radiology and Nuclear Medicine,* University Park Press, 1977.

SHOPE T, GAGNE R, JOHNSON G: A method for describing the doses delivered by transmission x-ray computed tomography. *Med Phys* 8:488–495, 1981.

SHRIVASTAVA PN, LYNN SL, TING JY: Exposures to patient and personnel in computed axial tomography. *Radiology* 125: 411–415, 1977.

SIEGELMAN SS, ZERHOUNI EA, LEO FP, KHOURI NF, STITIK FP: CT of the solitary pulmonary nodule. *Am J Radiol* 135:1–13, 1980.

SOM PM, LANZIERI CF, SACHER M, LAWSON W, BILLER HF: Extracranial tumor vascularity: Determination by dynamic CT scanning. *Radiology* 154:401–405, 1985.

SORENSON JA: Technique for evaluating radiation beam and image slice parameters of CT scanners. *Med Phys* 6:68–69, 1979.

STOCKHAM CD: A simulated study of aliasing in computed tomography. *Radiology* 132:721–726, 1979.

TER-POGOSSIAN MM, PHELPS ME, HOFFMAN EJ, EICHLING JO: The extraction of the yet unused wealth of information in diagnostic radiology. *Radiology* 113:515–520, 1974.

TER-POGOSSIAN MM: Computerized cranial tomography. *Semin Roentgenol* 12:13–25, 1977.

VILLAFANA T: Advantage of limitations and significance of the modulation transfer function in radiologic practice. *Curr Probl Diagn Radiol* 7:10, 1978*a*.

VILLAFANA T, LEE SH, LAPAYOWKER MS: A device to indicate anatomical level in computed tomography. *J Comput Assist Tomogr* 2:368–371, 1978*b*.

VILLAFANA T, SCOURAS J, KIRKLAND L, MCELROY N, PARAS P: Health physics aspects of the EMI computerized tomography brain scanner. *Health Phys J* 34:71–83, 1978*c*.

VILLAFANA T: Technological advances in computed tomography. *Curr Op Radiol* 3:275–283, 1991.

WALL BF, GREEN DAC: Radiation dose to patients from EMI brain and body scanners. *Br J Radiol* 52:189–196, 1979.

WEAVER KE, GOODENOUGH DJ, DAVIS DO: Physical measurements of the EMI computerized axial tomographic imaging system. *Proc Soc Photo-Opt Instrum Eng* 70:299–309, 1975.

WEISSBERGER MA, ZOMENHOF RG, ARANON S, NEER RM: Computed tomography scanning for the measurement of bone mineral in the human spine. *J Comput Assist Tomogr* 2:253–262, 1978.

ZATZ LM: The effect of the kVp level on EMI values. *Radiology* 119:683–688, 1976.

ZERHOUNI EA, SPIVEY IF, MORGAN RH, LEO FP, STITIK FP, SIEGELMAN SS: Factors influencing quantitative CT measurements of solitary pulmonary nodules. *J Comput Assist Tomogr* 6:1075–1087, 1982.

2 PHYSICS AND INSTRUMENTATION: MAGNETIC RESONANCE IMAGING

Theodore Villafana

PHYSICS AND INSTRUMENTATION: MAGNETIC RESONANCE IMAGING

Magnetic resonance imaging (MRI) is based on totally different physical principles than computerized tomography (CT). MRI, however, does share with CT the fact that radiant energy is beamed into the patient and in turn is detected as it emerges from the patient. In MRI this radiant energy is in the form of radio-frequency waves rather than x-rays, as in CT. Like CT, the radiant energy detected correlates with various parameters characteristic of tissue properties. What is important, however, is the fact that MRI allows us to image much smaller contrast differences between tissues. Just as CT represented a significant increase in tissue contrast sensitivity compared with classical tomography, MRI represents an even greater contrast sensitivity step beyond CT. To understand why this is so we will look at the MR process and the instrumentation necessary for its implementation in this chapter. The MR process can be broken up into four distinct phases: a preparatory alignment, excitation, signal detection, and image generation. Let us look at each of these in turn.

Preparatory Alignment

All matter, of course, is composed of molecules and atoms. Atoms in turn contain nuclei that have different numbers of protons and neutrons. What may not be realized is the fact that nuclei have an inherent spin that is due to the spins associated with the individual component protons and neutrons. If charged particles spin or move in any way, a magnetic field is generated around them. Thus, the nucleus in fact has a magnetic field or magnetic moment associated with it as a result of the fundamental spin properties of its component nucleons. Even the neutrons, which are uncharged, contribute to the spin properties of the nucleus since they are made up of charged particles. The magnitude of the magnetic field associated with any particular nucleus depends on the degree to which the magnetic fields of the individual nucleons add to or cancel each other. In general, nuclei with an even number of protons and an even number of neutrons ("even-even" nuclei) have zero spin magnetic moment. Examples of these are ^{12}C, ^{16}O, ^{32}S, and ^{40}Ca. Odd-atomic-numbered nuclei with an odd number of protons have much stronger magnetic fields associated with them. These "odd-odd" nuclei are most amenable for imaging. Examples include ^{1}H, ^{13}C, ^{19}F, and ^{31}P. Odd-even and even-odd nuclei tend to have intermediate-strength magnetic fields.

The magnetic resonance process depends critically on the net magnetic moment of the nucleus. Of the biologically important nuclei, the hydrogen nucleus provides the greatest overall sensitivity to the MR process (Table 2-1). This is because of both its large magnetic moment and its great abundance in the body in the form of water and other biologically important molecules. Though much research is certainly going on in sodium imaging as well as imaging of other biologically important nuclei, all practical clinical MR imaging is currently done with hydrogen nuclei. We can understand why MRI is so much more sensitive than CT scanning when we realize that the differences in water content (and thus hydrogen content) of biological tissues are much greater than the corresponding differences in x-ray attenuation upon which CT depends.

We have established that a magnetic field may exist around any given nucleus. The particular configuration of this magnetic field is always of the dipole type; that is, there is a distinct north pole and south pole. The alignment of the north and south poles defines what is referred to as a magnetic vector. Thus, if a nucleus has a magnetic vector, that vector will always have some magnitude and will be aligned in some particular direction in space. In the case of a spinning nucleus, the vector is aligned perpendicular to the plane of spin, as seen in Fig. 2-1*A*. In an extended medium all the various nuclei, because of random interactions with neighboring nuclei and with thermal environments, have their magnetic vec-

Table 2-1 MR Properties of Certain Nuclei

NUCLEUS	SPIN QUANTUM NUMBER	NATURAL ABUNDANCE, %	GYROMAGNETIC RATIO (MHZ/ TESLA)	RELATIVE SENSITIVITY FOR EQUAL NUMBER OF NUCLEI AT CONSTANT FIELD (RELATIVE TO ^{1}H), %
^{1}H	½	100	42.56	100
^{13}C	½	1.1	10.7	0.25
^{14}N	1	99.6	3.1	0.20
^{15}N	½	0.36	4.3	0.10
^{19}F	½	100	40.1	0.94
^{31}P	½	100	17.2	0.41

Adapted from House 1983.

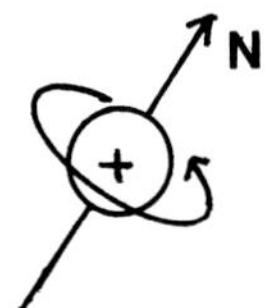

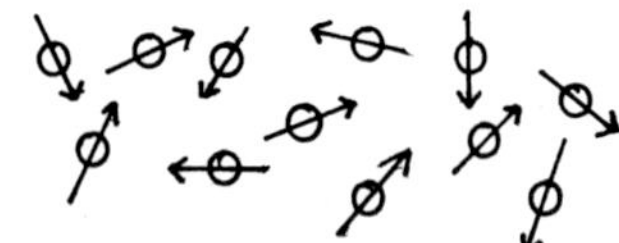

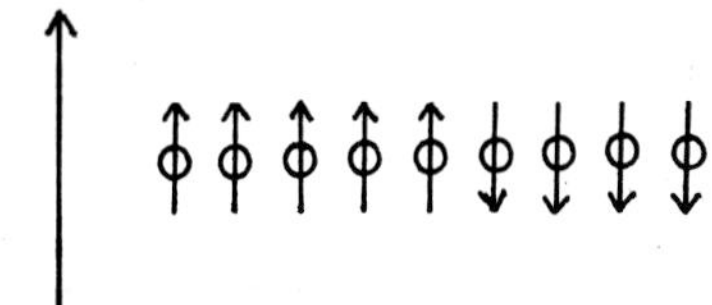

Figure 2-1 **A.** Individual nucleus possessing spin manifests a magnetic field directed perpendicular to the plane of spin. This defines a magnetic dipole with north and south poles, and we say the nucleus has a magnetic moment or vector. **B.** In a medium, individual nuclei with their individual magnetic vectors align randomly. There is no net external magnetic field since they will all cancel each other out. **C.** When an external magnetic field (B_0) is present, the nuclei of hydrogen, for instance, line up either in the same direction as B_0 (parallel) or in the opposite direction of B_0 (antiparallel). There is only a slight excess aligned in the parallel direction.

tors aligned at random in all directions throughout the medium. These vectors add to or cancel each other (Fig. 2-1*B*). As a result, the overall medium does not have an external magnetic field because all the nuclei cancel each other within that medium. Such is the case for biological tissues, which do not normally have externally detectable magnetic fields. Yet the potential for magnetic effects is there since tissues in fact contain nuclei that have magnetic vectors which, if properly manipulated, can be made to be externally detected.

If the medium is placed in a strong external magnetic field (usually referred to as the B_0 field), the magnetic vectors of the individual nuclei will tend to align with this external magnetic field. Hydrogen, for instance, has two possible alignments: one for the magnetic vector lining up in the same direction as the external magnetic field (referred to as a parallel alignment) and the other for the magnetic vector aligning in the direction opposite to the magnetic field (antiparallel alignment), as seen in Fig. 2-1*C*. The parallel direction is a lower-energy state, and as a result a slight excess number of protons are aligned in this direction compared with the antiparallel direction. Since these two vectors are in opposite directions, they tend to cancel out. Because of the slight excess in the parallel directions, however, some net magnetization will remain in the parallel direction. The magnitude of this net magnetization varies with the strength of the B_0 field, but in general it is due to only about one to three excess parallel aligned protons for every million protons in the medium. Only these relatively few protons enter into the MR process.

One additional very important phenomenon occurs when the nuclear magnetic vectors are under the influence of an external magnetic field: The magnetic vectors will not line up exactly parallel or antiparallel but rather will precess around that magnetic field. That is, the vector will circle around the B_0 direction, as seen in Fig. 2-2*A*. This precession occurs with a particular frequency. Equation (1) shows the relationship between the frequency of precession and the applied external magnetic field.

$$F = KB_0 \tag{1}$$

In this equation, B_0 is the magnitude of the external magnetic field and K is a constant for each different nucleus

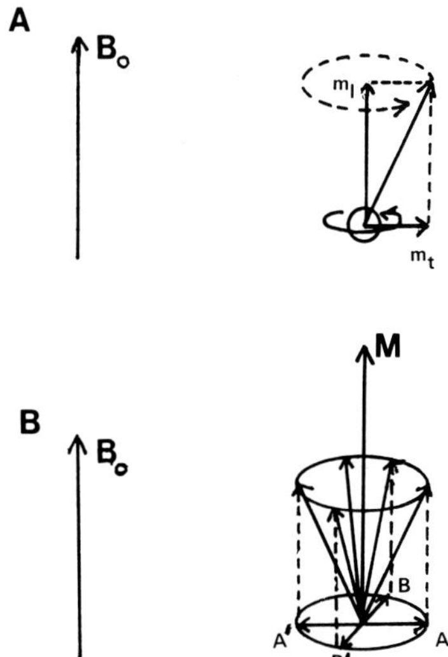

Figure 2-2 **A.** Individual nuclear magnetic vector precessing around the B_0 field. There will be only a couple of protons out of every million whose magnetic field will remain uncanceled and precessing parallel to the external field. Each of these nuclei will have a transverse (m_t) and a longitudinal (m_l) component to the precessing magnetic vector at any instant. **B.** When the ensemble of all nuclei in a particular region of space is considered, each is in a random position in its precessional cycle. As a result, all the transverse components will cancel out (A cancels with A', B with B', etc.). There will, however, be a net longitudinal component since vectors all add up in this direction. This resulting longitudinal component is called the bulk magnetization vector (M).

called the gyromagnetic ratio constant. For hydrogen the gyromagnetic constant equals 42.56 megahertz (MHz) per tesla. Equation (1), also referred to as the Larmor equation, is a fundamental relationship governing the MR process. The tesla is a unit of magnetic field strength and is numerically equal to 10,000 gauss. The gauss is also a measure of magnetic field strength. To give a sense of magnitude for this unit, the natural magnetic field around the earth is approximately 0.5 gauss.

Table 2-1 shows the constant K as well as other physical data for various isotopes of interest in medical practice. Note the relatively large sensitivity for hydrogen nuclei.

Figure 2-2B shows that the magnetic vectors for the ensemble of all participating nuclei at any one region in space precessing around the static external magnetic field essentially form a cone of vectors. These randomly rotate around the external field. If we look at the projections of each of these vectors onto the transverse plane (the horizontal plane), we see that each vector precesses in a random orientation relative to every other vector, and since there are no preferred directions in space, there are just as many vectors in one direction as there are in any other direction. In this case, then, all these vectors cancel out in the transverse plane. (In Fig. 2-2B, A cancels with A', B with B', etc.) As a result, for any point in the medium, at equilibrium no net magnetic vector exists in the transverse plane. However, when one looks at the projections of the vectors on the longitudinal (up and down or vertical) axis, one sees that each vector in fact adds to every other vector along this longitudinal axis and that a large net longitudinal vector results, composed of the sum of all the various precessing vectors. This net magnetization, also called the bulk magnetization vector (M), is seen to lie entirely in the longitudinal direction. At this point we say that the system is in dynamic equilibrium and is relaxed.

We will discuss at length the detection of signals in another section, but suffice it to say here that a signal will be generated whenever there is a net transverse component. In the equilibrium condition just described there is no net transverse component to the bulk magnetization and no net signal is detected. However, any displacement away from equilibrium will shift some magnetization away from the longitudinal direction onto the transverse plane and then a signal will be generated. All these steps are summarized in Table 2-2.

The next step in the MR process is to excite the nuclei, purposely cause a displacement away from the longitudinal alignment, and thus increase transverse magnetization.

Table 2-2 Summary of the MR Preparatory Phase

1. Each nucleus in the medium possesses a magnetic moment caused by the inherent spin of its nucleus.
2. The medium possesses no overall externally detectable magnetization since all the individual nuclei are aligned randomly and cancel each other's magnetic fields.
3. When placed in a strong external magnetic field, the nuclear magnetic moments align themselves in either the parallel or the antiparallel direction and in addition precess around the external field direction with frequency given by the Larmor equation ($F = KB_0$).
4. A slight excess population of nuclear magnetic vectors aligned in parallel direction do not cancel out with antiparallel vectors. This yields a net magnetization in the parallel direction (direction of the magnetic field).
5. The magnetic vectors will have their transverse plane projections all cancel out at each point in space because of their random motions. The vectors, however, add up in the longitudinal direction, giving the medium a bulk magnetization along the applied external magnetic field direction. This is the equilibrium or relaxed state.
6. No signal will be detected when the system is in the equilibrium state since no transverse magnetic component exists. However, a signal will be produced when the system is disturbed away from the equilibrium state.

The Excitation Process

We have already seen that under equilibrium conditions no net signal is detected since the net bulk magnetization vector (from now on we will call it the magnetization vector) is entirely along the longitudinal direction. A signal will be detected only if there is some net magnetization along the transverse axis. In the MR process, the intent is to purposely excite nuclei away from the longitudinal alignment into the transverse plane and thus create a signal. As the nuclei relax (return to equilibrium), this signal decays at a time rate characteristic of the particular chemical and tissue milieu of the hydrogen nuclei and will convey information about the tissue properties at each point in the medium.

What form of energy can be utilized to excite these hydrogen nuclei and their magnetic vectors as they precess around the direction of the external field? Radio-frequency electromagnetic waves are capable of doing just that. The reason for this can be understood by going back to Equation (1), the Larmor relationship. The precessional frequency in megahertz specified there is the key to exciting the nucleus. That is, if one comes in with magnetic energy varying at exactly the Larmor frequency, a resonance absorption effect occurs in which energy is transferred to the nucleus and the nucleus becomes excited. The frequency expressed in the Larmor relationship in fact falls in the electromagnetic radio-frequency (RF) range for nuclei of clinical interest. To further understand this resonance effect we remember that electromagnetic radiation does in fact have electric and magnetic properties. The magnetic component of these waves having magnitude that we call B_1 is of interest here. Additionally, we know that this magnetic component varies sinusoidally. If the frequency of the RF sinusoidally varying B_1 field exactly matches the Larmor frequency, resonance absorption of RF energy occurs. The net effect is that the bulk magnetization vector is tipped in space away from the longitudinal alignment and into the transverse plane. Additionally, where before all the individual vectors were randomly precessing around the B_0 direction, they now become coherently bundled together so that not only are they tipped toward the transverse plane but they are all spinning in phase relative to each other (phase coherence). Therefore, instead of many vectors randomly precessing, the vectors are spinning together as one. This means that the individual vectors no longer cancel out in the transverse plane. Rather, there is now a very large net transverse plane magnetization. Depending on how long the exciting RF energy is on, the tip angle will increase. Thus, one can tip the vector to any angle such as 90°, 180°, or 270°, as seen in Fig. 2-3*A*. The actual manner in which the magnetization vector is displaced is also seen in this figure. Essentially what occurs is that the RF wave provides a torque on the bulk vector such that the angle with respect to the longitudinal axis increases, resulting in a spiraling precessional motion of the vector away from the original longitudinal alignment. This motion traces out the surface of a sphere as the vector is rotated from equilibrium (0°) to the desired tip angle. As the magnetization vector spirals down, the longitudinal magnetization is reduced. For instance, as seen in Fig. 2-3*A*, at equilibrium (position 1) full magnetization (vector height *A*) exists. At positions 2 and 3 there is only a partial longitudinal magnetization projection (vector heights *B* and *C*). Notice that we now also have some signal-producing transverse magnetization present (vector lengths B_2 and C_3). At position 4 (90° tip angle) there is zero longitudinal and maximum transverse magnetization (vector length D_4). For simplicity's sake, it is common to depict this spiraling precessional motion as viewed from a moving frame of reference, that is, as if

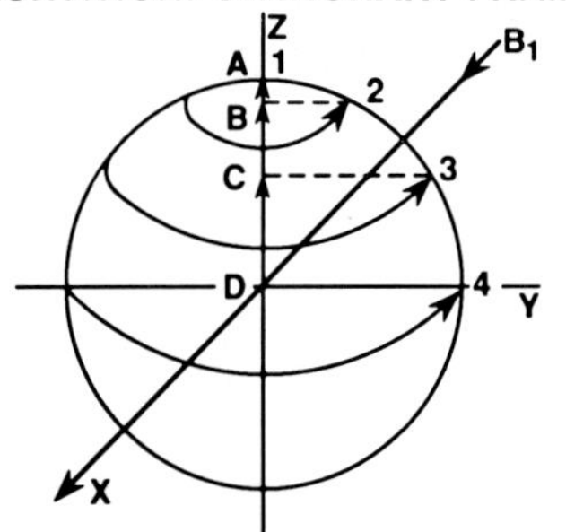

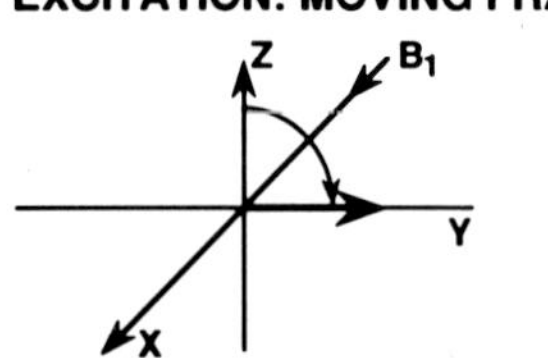

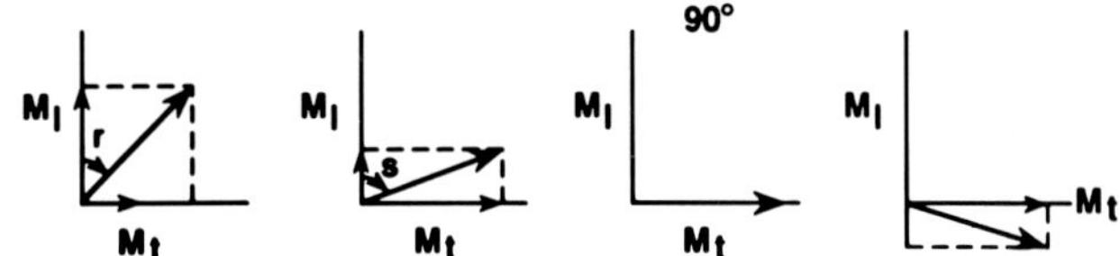

Figure 2-3 **A.** When a radio-frequency wave of appropriate frequency is incident on the nuclei at equilibrium, the magnetic field component B_1 of that RF wave provides a torque such that the magnetization vector precesses in spiral fashion away from the original longitudinal alignment. Longitudinal magnetization goes from maximum (position 1, tip angle 0°) to zero (position 4, tip angle 90°). At intermediate positions (2 and 3) longitudinal magnetization is of intermediate value. Corresponding to each position, the transverse magnetization builds up from zero at position 1 to maximum at position 4. **B.** It is common to use the moving frame representation of excitation by which the original magnetization vector is tipped directly from the original longitudinal alignment to any tip angle. Here we have a tip angle of 90°. **C.** During excitation over any angle (*r* or *s*, for instance) m_l steadily decreases while m_t steadily increases. At 90°, m_l is zero and m_t is maximum. Beyond 90°, m_l assumes negative values while m_t begins to decrease.

one were riding on the vector. In such a frame of reference the magnetic vector is represented as directly rotating from the longitudinal z axis to the transverse axis y, as seen in Fig. 2-3*B*.

What is important to realize in this section is that RF energy can in fact excite the nuclei of interest and that such excitation results in the perturbation of the equilibrium longitudinal alignment to create a transverse component. This transverse component can generate a detectable electrical signal. It should also be noted that the RF energy incident on the tissues is of such low energy and frequency that it does not disturb the electrostatic bonds of the constituent atoms and molecules within the tissues, so there are no other effects perturbing the MR process.

When the RF field is turned off, the hydrogen protons will be at some given state of excitation manifested by the magnetic vector at some angle relative to the longitudinal axis and generating some signal from the transverse magnetization induced. Individual nuclei will gradually revert to the longitudinal alignment by losing excitational energy to the overall thermal environment. We call such interactions spin-lattice interactions. Nuclei can also exchange energy between themselves and the immediately neighboring nuclei. These interactions cause a dephasing of the individual spinning vectors; that is, nuclear spins which were originally in phase immediately after excitation interact with each other and rapidly lose their phase coherence. These we call spin-spin interactions. The time constant associated with recovery of the longitudinal magnetization (spin-lattice interactions) is given by T_1, and the time constant associated with loss of phase coherence (spin-spin interactions) is given by T_2. Both of these processes lead to the loss of transverse magnetization and a consequent loss in the detected signal. Table 2-3 summarizes the MR excitation phase.

Table 2-3 Summary of the MR Excitation Phase

1. Magnetic component (B_1) of an RF wave with frequency exactly matching the Larmor precessional frequency provides a torque on the longitudinal magnetization vector.
2. Magnetization vector begins to precess in a spiraling motion away from the longitudinal alignment. As a result, the longitudinal magnetization is reduced and the transverse magnetization increases.
3. Nuclei will return to the relaxed original state (longitudinal alignment) with relaxation times (T_1 and T_2) characteristic of the particular tissue milieu nuclei sit in.
4. Transverse magnetization component provides a detectable signal allowing the determination of spin relaxation rates as the system returns to the equilibrium state.

Signal Detection and Signal Decay Processes

We have already seen that RF energy can excite the nuclear spin system, causing the magnetization vector to reorient in space, and thus create some transverse magnetization and consequently a detectable signal. But just how is this signal detected? Figure 2-3*C* shows the magnetization vector M at some intermediate tip angle (r). Note that the vector has projections in both the longitudinal axis (m_l) and transverse axis (m_t). At a greater tip angle (s), m_t is larger and m_l smaller. At the 90° angle m_t is at a maximum while m_l is zero. If M is tipped beyond 90° then m_t decreases while m_l starts assuming negative values. One can determine the relative amount of transverse magnetization by providing a coil of wire nearby. As the magnetization vector precesses, it induces an electrical signal in the wire coil. This is merely the phenomenon of electromagnetic induction that governs, for instance, the operation of electrical transformers and other devices familiar in x-ray instrumentation. The magnitude of the induced signal is dependent on the angle that exists at a particular moment between the vector and the wires in the coil. A maximum signal will be induced when the vector is cutting across the coil at 90°, which corresponds to the situation when transverse magnetization is maximum. As the magnetization angle decreases, the transverse component (m_t) decreases and consequently the signal decreases. It is crucial to emphasize that *the signal detected in MR always depends entirely on the amount of transverse magnetization present.* This therefore forms the basis for signal detection and provides the means of determining m_t and m_l, as will be seen shortly. As the nuclei return to the ground state by losing energy to the thermal lattice environment (via spin-lattice interactions), the magnetic vector gradually returns to the original longitudinal alignment. But as this occurs, the projection on the transverse axis would be expected to gradually diminish and the signal detected would also gradually diminish. The actual manner in which the signal is expected to diminish is exponential.

We define T_1 relaxation in terms of the longitudinal magnetization recovery; specifically, T_1 is defined for 63.2 percent recovery, as seen in Fig. 2-4*A*. This figure also shows the different T_1 recovery times expected for a solid compared with a liquid. In a solid, molecules are closer and are more directly coupled to each other; as a result, their energy loss due to spin-lattice interactions is more rapid and T_1 will be correspondingly shorter. Different biological tissues also exhibit different T_1's.

In addition to spin-lattice interactions, the nuclei immediately start undergoing spin-spin interactions. These involve individual spins interacting with other spins in their immediate local neighborhood. In this process, energy is transferred back and forth between nuclei, speeding up some and slowing down others. As a result, the

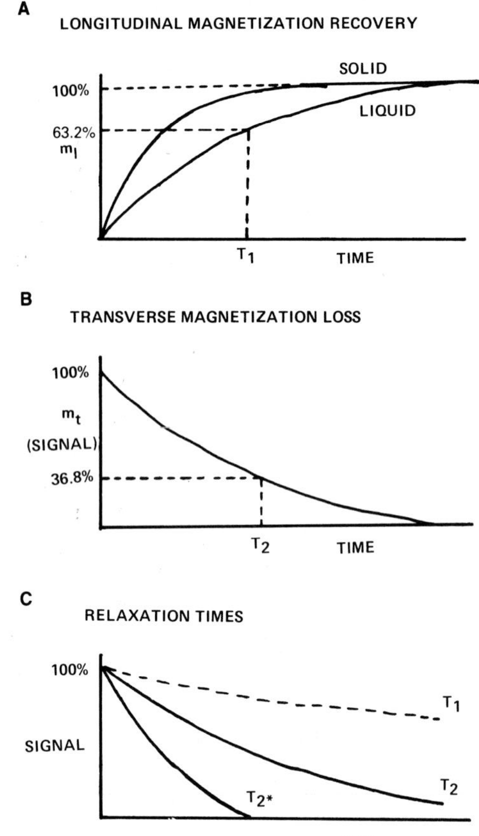

Figure 2-4 **A.** After a 90° RF excitation pulse the longitudinal magnetization begins to recover. T_1 represents the time constant of this recovery and is defined for 63.2 percent recovery. Also shown is the expected elongation in T_1 for a liquid compared with a solid. **B.** Loss of transverse magnetization (the signal) is principally due to dephasing and is usually very rapid compared with recovery of the longitudinal magnetization. T_2 is the time necessary for signal to decay to 36.8 percent of its original value. **C.** T_2* decay rate is due mainly to local nonhomogeneities of the magnet. It is the dominant dephasing mechanism and drives the detected signal to zero very quickly. True T_2 signal is shown for the case where T_2* is absent. T_1 (dashed curve) is relatively long, and its signal would normally not be seen.

initial phase coherence (i.e., vectors precessing in phase) that existed immediately after excitation is degraded. This dephasing drives the MR signal to zero since the individual vectors revert to their random dephased orientations with subsequent cancellation of each other, and as a result the transverse magnetization goes to zero independently of longitudinal recovery. The rate at which the vectors dephase, and thus the rate at which the signal decays, is given by a second time constant, the T_2 relaxation time. Figure 2-4*B* shows the signal diminishing to zero as dephasing progresses. T_2 is defined in a manner similar to but not exactly like that of T_1. T_2 represents the time necessary for signal to be reduced down to 36.8 percent of its original value. The choice of 36.8 percent signal remaining is not entirely arbitrary—36.8 percent is merely the reciprocal of the exponential number (2.718). This particular percentage (and its complement, 63.2 percent) is chosen since it simplifies the mathematical equations related to exponential phenomena. In general, T_2 values are roughly one-tenth the values of T_1 for biological tissues, T_1 being in hundreds of milliseconds and T_2 in tens of milliseconds.

One more level of complication beyond the two relaxation mechanisms given by T_1 and T_2 must be described. An additional mechanism that contributes to spin-spin interactions is due to the fact that the external magnetic field is not totally uniform. It does have local nonhomogeneities. In general, these local nonhomogeneities enhance spin-spin interactions and speed the dephasing process and consequently the signal decay. Thus in a simple MR experiment what one would principally measure after excitation is usually the loss of signal due to dephasing as a result of local magnetic field nonhomogeneities. This dephasing is so rapid that it masks all the T_2 and T_1 signal information. This relaxation time is referred to as T_2*, and as mentioned previously, it is related to the quality of the magnets and its homogeneity. For the usual MR procedures, one must eliminate the influence of T_2* and thus get at the more interesting T_1 and T_2 rates.

We now can illustrate the simplest of MR experiments, referred to as the free induction decay (FID) process (Fig. 2-5*A*). The FID process also illustrates the T_2 behavior just discussed and is described as follows: A 90° RF pulse is given. This tips the magnetization entirely onto the transverse plane, with a correspondingly large signal detected. Notice that the initial magnitude of this signal is dependent on the number of nuclei (spin density) participating in this process and will be characteristic of the tissue properties at a given point. After cessation of the excitation pulse, all the individual nuclei are in phase with each other. But these rapidly lose their phase coherence owing to spin-spin interactions induced by local magnetic field nonhomogeneities as well as to a lesser extent the true T_2 interactions, and m_t rapidly goes to zero. This loss is due to the fact that individual vectors again revert to their random precessional motion and start to cancel out in the transverse plane. Figure 2-4*C* shows the resulting loss of signal that occurs. The T_2* relaxation dominates the signal in that it quickly drives it to zero. If T_2* were absent, the signal would follow the T_2 curve. However, T_2 in turn masks the relatively long T_1 relaxation signal. How to unravel T_1 from T_2 from T_2* is the subject of the next section. Notice in Fig. 2-5*A* that longitudinal magnetization continues to grow and eventually reaches maximum value. If the original tip angle was 180° instead of 90°, an inversion occurs and longitudinal magnetization is maximum in the negative direction (Fig. 2-5*B*). After the cessation of the pulse, as was true of the FID, dephasing proceeds and m_t goes to zero. However, m_l steadily diminishes to zero and then continues growing (recovering) until it becomes a maximum in the positive direction.

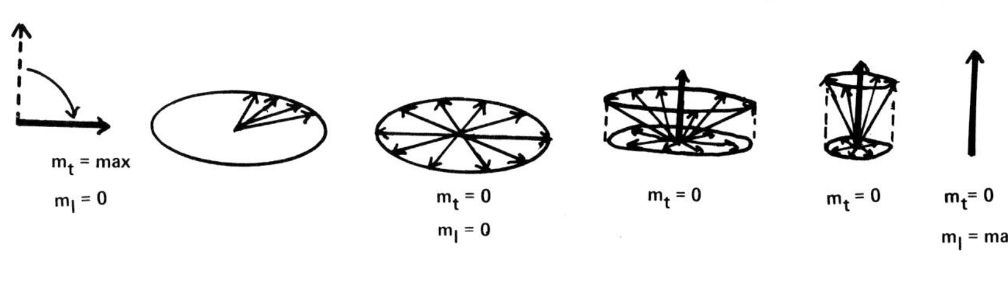

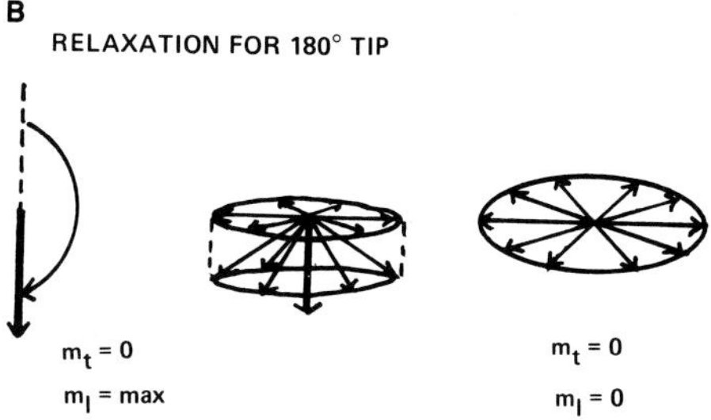

Figure 2-5 Dephasing of vectors. **A.** After a 90° tip angle, the vector rapidly dephases (FID) until $m_t = 0$ and $m_l = 0$. No signal is possible after this; however, longitudinal magnetization continues to recover until equilibrium is attained ($m_t = 0$, $m_l =$ max). **B.** If a 180° tip angle is used, the longitudinal magnetization is maximum but negative. No signal is possible since $m_t = 0$. As time goes on, the vectors dephase and m_l assumes smaller negative values. Since vectors are dephased, no signal is possible. When vectors arrive at the transverse plane, $m_t = 0$, $m_l = 0$. Progress after this is the same as for the FID response.

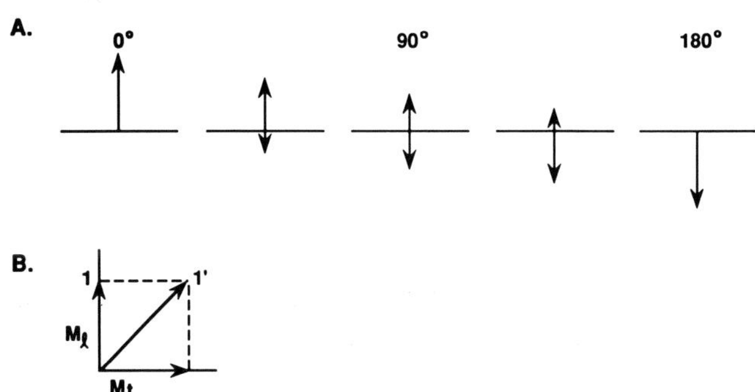

Figure 2-6 **A.** In the quantum mechanical description, an individual nucleus can be either in the low-energy or high-energy state. Therefore, individual nuclei invert from the low-energy parallel state to the higher-energy antiparallel state upon absorbing a quantum of RF energy. For a 90° flip half the nuclei have been inverted, while at 180° they all have. In the relaxation process, events are exactly reversed. **B.** Correlation with the classical description is seen by the fact that m_l at some particular height (1) and at some particular angle corresponds to a particular transverse component m_t.

In the preceding discussion, a "classical" description was invoked. The quantum mechanical approach views the excitation process as individual nuclei absorbing quanta of RF energy. Each nucleus reverts from the low-energy, parallel-alignment state to the higher-energy antiparallel state. A 90° flip, for instance, corresponds to half the nuclei inverting, as seen in Fig. 2-6*A*. As a consequence, no net longitudinal magnetization exists. As flip angle increases, more magnetization is continuously inverted to a point where it is all aligned at 180°. Notice in Fig. 2-6*B* that an intermediate m_l corresponds to the classical description using tilted vectors. For instance, intermediate m_l at position 1 corresponds to tilted vector 1′, which in turn corresponds to some intermediate m_t.

Upon relaxation, the individual nuclei emit RF energy and each reverts to the original low-energy state. Though the quantum mechanical description is the more rigorous one, we will use the classical description because of its simplicity.

SATURATION RECOVERY

To determine T_1 or T_2, T_2^* effects must be suppressed. Various pulse sequences have been designed to accomplish this. One of these is the saturation recovery pulse sequence. This sequence, though not generally used, illustrates nicely the MR process and will be discussed here.

The saturation recovery pulse sequence is merely a repeated FID sequence; i.e., a series of 90° RF pulses is given separated by repetition time TR, as shown in Fig. 2-7*A*. Remember that after each 90° pulse, all the magnetic vectors are in phase and immediately start to dephase as well as spiraling back to the longitudinal position. (We will indicate the ensemble of dephased vectors as dashed and the in-phase signal-producing vectors as solid throughout this chapter.) Since the 90° pulses are repeated, the second 90°, for instance, will catch the vectors at some intermediate position before they have completely recovered to their longitudinal alignment and will project them 90° into the next quadrant, as seen in Fig. 2-7*B*. Here there is a net vector projection onto the transverse axis, and a signal results. The magnitude of this signal depends on the degree of longitudinal recovery or T_1 relaxation that had occurred at each point. Therefore, we have a way of distinguishing between different T_1's and the different tissue they represent. For instance, if the longitudinal magnetization has recovered to position 1 and the second 90° pulse is given, these dephased vectors are

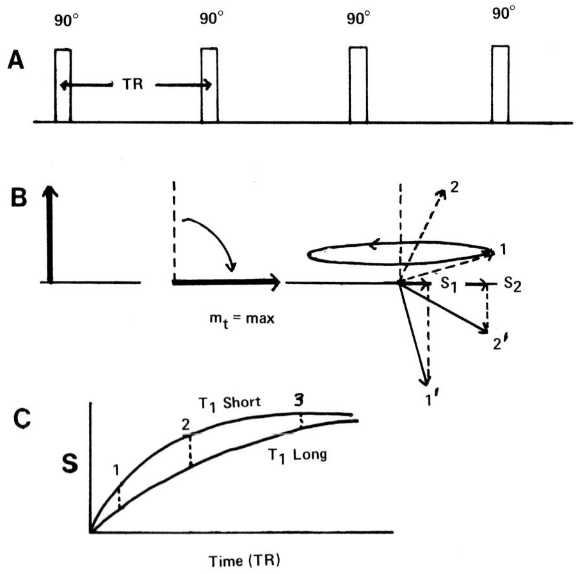

Figure 2-7 **A.** Saturation recovery. Saturation recovery pulse sequence consisting of a series of 90° pulses separated by some repetition time (TR). A signal whose magnitude correlates with spin density and whose fall-off is governed mainly by T_2* is detectable after each pulse. **B.** T_1 can be determined from the saturation recovery sequence by repeating the sequence so that only partial longitudinal recovery has occurred for subsequent pulses. For instance, dephased vectors (dashed) at position 1 yield no signal; however, when they are projected 90° to position 1′ they once again are coherent (all add up) and yield a signal (S_1). A shorter T_1 tissue would have recovered to position 2 and be projected 90° so that signal S_2 is higher. **C.** Plot of signal magnitude as a function of TR. Contrast is given by the relative T_1 differences between the differing tissues. At long TR (point 3), relatively little contrast results. Higher contrast is found at intermediate and lower TR values (points 1 and 2).

rephased and are projected 90° into the next quadrant, yielding a signal corresponding to the transverse magnetization signal S_1. If T_1 is short, vectors have recovered to position 2 and will project to a larger signal S_2 after the 90° pulse. If a period of time greater than the T_1 values of the tissues in question elapses before the 90° pulse is repeated, the spin system recovers closer to the full longitudinal magnetization value and subsequent pulses will not distinguish between the different T_1 values as well (point 3 in Fig. 2-7*C*). In all cases, however, the initial signal measured is devoid of T_2* influence.

If repetition times are short relative to T_1, longitudinal magnetization has only partially recovered and subsequent 90° pulses will yield relatively low signals yet relatively high signal differences and consequently better contrast. This is seen at level 1 in Fig. 2-7*C*. Note that the image contrast is merely the difference between the two recovery curves. Obviously, we must configure an optimal TR timing to achieve both large signal strengths and greater T_1 contrast differences. Sometimes we refer to the above pulse sequence as "partial saturation" in the sense that usually TR is sufficiently short that the system recovers only partially before the next pulse is applied.

Equation (2) shows the magnitude of the signal as a function of the various timing parameters:

$$S_{ps} = N[1 - \exp(-\ TR/T_1)] \qquad (2)$$

where *N* is a constant dependent on the number of protons present (spin density) and *exp* represents the exponential function which all MR signal decay processes follow. From Equation (2) it is seen that the signal depends on the ratio TR/T_1 or the fraction that TR represents relative to T_1. It is this fraction that determines the degree of longitudinal recovery occurring between the different tisues (or T_1 weighting) and thus the contrast between them.

The saturation recovery sequence is also applicable in determining proton-weighted images. In Equation (2), if TR is sufficiently long to allow full recovery, the exponential term goes to zero and the initial signal is related only to proton density. The saturation recovery sequence is quite sensitive to irregularities in tip angle accuracy and consistency as well as having a relatively low contrast scale available compared, for instance, with inversion recovery. As a result, the latter is usually invoked to obtain T_1-weighted images (T_1WI).

INVERSION RECOVERY

Inversion recovery is a two-pulse sequence used to produce T_1WI. Specifically, a pulse is given that inverts the magnetization vector into the 180° antiparallel direction. Immediately after cessation of the pulse, even though all the vectors are in phase, there is no signal since there is no net transverse magnetization. As time proceeds and vectors recover to longitudinal position, dephasing occurs that prevents a signal from developing. After some appropriate interval of time, called the inversion time TI, the different vectors have recovered to varying decrees according to their T_1 values and a 90° pulse is given. This pulse has the effect of placing the magnetization vector into the next quadrant and rephasing the spins and thus providing a measurable signal. This signal will depend on T_1, as shown in Fig. 2-8. We see that inversion recovery is very similar to saturation recovery, with the exception that vectors have a greater distance over which to recover (180° instead of 90°) and greater differentiation between them is possible.

What occurs is that during the interval TI the magnetization vector reverts to its original longitudinal alignment; at any given time it has recovered some fractional amount, as at position 1 in Fig. 2-8*B*. When the 90° pulse is given, the spins are rephased and shifted 90° to position 1′. At that instant, they have a projection along the transverse axis that constitutes the signal S. The signals generated are dependent on the inversion time TI and magnitude of the T_1 of the tissues, as can be seen in Fig.

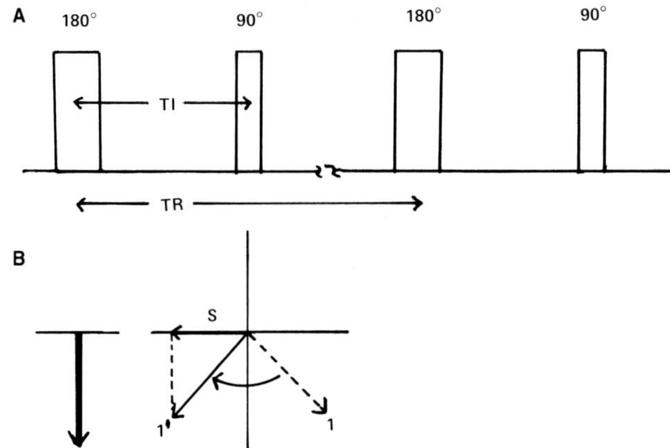

Figure 2-8 **A.** Inversion recovery pulse sequence consisting of a 180° pulse followed by a 90° pulse after inversion time interval TI. The 90° pulse rephases the spins and allows for a signal readout that depends on the amount of relaxation or recovery that has occurred. **B.** After inversion, if dephased vector has progressed to position 1, then after 90° tip it will be at position 1′ and in phase, yielding some signal S.

2-9*A*. Correspondingly, the image contrast between long and short T_1 tissues is determined by differences in transverse magnetization for any particular TI. For instance, it can be seen in Fig. 2-9*A* that if the magnetization vector is at position 1, a 90° pulse will drive the magnetization to position 1′ and a signal S_1 on the negative side results. If the magnetization vector is at position 2 when the 90° pulse is given, no signal is generated since the vector would be projected totally onto the negative longitudinal axis (position 2′), where no transverse magnetization exists. If it is at position 3, a positive signal S_3 results. If we plot the values of the signal as a function of TI, curves similar to Fig. 2-9*B* (solid curve) result. It is, however, usual to work with the absolute values of the signal (dashed portion) at all times to avoid phase effects. Figure 2-9*C* illustrates how image contrast is generated between two tissues having different T_1 times when plotting absolute values of the signal with varying TI. Image contrast generated at any TI is just the difference in the magnitude of signals produced by the different T_1 tissues. One notes that contrast is relatively low at both short TI (point 1) and long TI (point 4). This is true since at short TI little time has been given to allow a separation in magnetization vectors; at longer TI almost full longitudinal recovery of the different TI tissues has occurred, and therefore there is very little difference between them.

One interesting aspect of MR imaging is the fact that relative contrast can be inverted; that is, under one set of timing conditions a particular tissue may appear light, and under other timing conditions that tissue may appear dark. This can be seen in Fig. 2-9*C,* where short T_1 (white matter) and long T_1 (gray matter) are plotted. At short TI (region 1 to 2), gray matter, for instance, may have a higher signal and thus appear lighter than the shorter T_1 white matter. At longer T_1 (regions 4 to 6) the shorter T_1 white matter will have a greater signal and thus will appear lighter than the gray matter. Notice also that at point 3, both tissues yield the same signal; therefore, there will be no contrast and one could not distinguish between them.

Figure 2-9*D* shows the more general case when spin densities are different. In this case, initial signals will be different and contrast obviously will depend on a complex interplay between TI, TR, and the T_1's of the tissues under study.

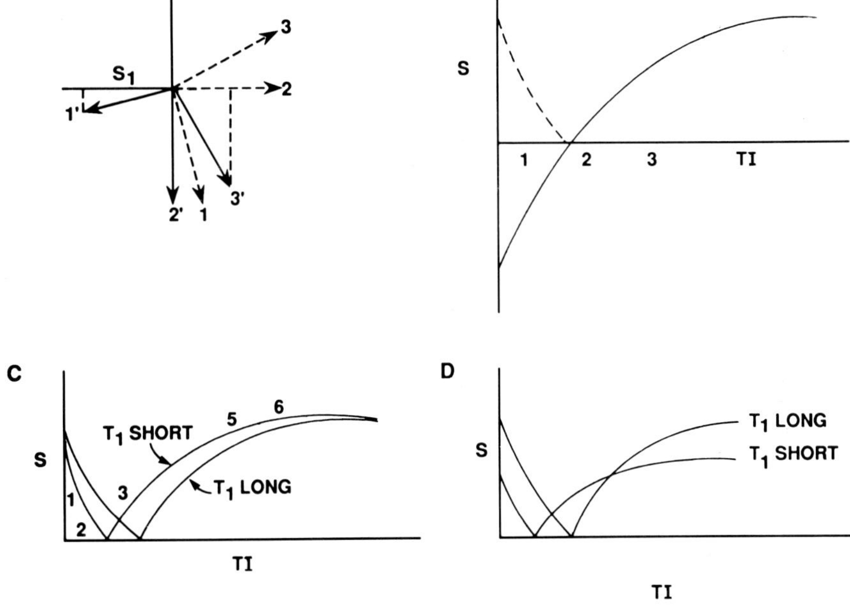

Figure 2-9 In inversion recovery, the magnitude of the signal detected depends not only on the spin density but also on the time interval TI and the magnitude of T_1 for the tissues. **A.** A signal S_1 resulting from a TI such that the dephased vector is arrested at position 1 and which after a 90° pulse is projected to position 1′. Position 2 when projected 90° gives zero signal at 2′ (no transverse magnetization), and signal S_3 is gotten when vector 3 is projected 90° to 3′. **B.** Plot of signals resulting as function of TI. Solid curve shows both negative (region 1) and positive signals (regions 2 and 3). In practice, only the absolute values are plotted for region 1 (dashed curve). **C.** Contrast between different tissues having different T_1 values as a function of TI. For instance, at long TI (position 6) there is less contrast than at shorter TI (position 1). Notice the inversion of contrast that occurs after position 3, where the shorter T_1 tissues appear brighter in the image (because of large signal) compared with regions 1 to 3, where longer T_1 tissues have higher signal and appear brighter. **D.** More general case for when different spin densities are also present. Here long TI also has higher spin density.

The TR dependency can be seen because TR determines how much longitudinal magnetization recovery has occurred, which in turn determines signal strength available upon applying the 90° pulse. For instance, in Fig. 2-9*C* for inversion recovery at level 2, signal is low for short T_1 but larger for the long T_1; contrast is therefore larger. At positions 5 and 6, though, signal strength is large for both short and long T_1 tissues; the contrast is low.

SPIN-ECHO PULSE SEQUENCE

To obtain a T_2WI we must remove the influence of the T_2* relaxation time. This is done in a unique way, as seen in Fig. 2-10. One first gives a 90° pulse, which will align the bulk magnetization vector in the transverse plane. Of course, immediately thereafter, dephasing begins to occur. This dephasing, as explained previously, is due to both true T_2 spin-spin interactions and spin-spin interactions due to the local nonhomogeneities of the external magnetic field. As discussed previously, with time the faster precessing vectors separate away from the slower precessing vectors, causing the transverse magnetization and consequently the signal to go to zero. At an appropriate time interval (TE/2), we add an additional 180° pulse. This 180° pulse is designed to drive the vectors around to the opposite side of the transverse plane (a pancake flip) such that the precessing vectors are now moving toward the original starting point and consequently the vectors are rephasing. That is, the faster ones are catching up to the slower ones. It can be seen that both the slow and the fast will arrive back at the starting line at the same time and be back in phase at time TE. As soon as the vectors begin rephasing, a signal is detectable (the echo signal). This echo signal increases and finally reaches a maximum when the vectors are totally in phase at time interval TE, as seen in Fig. 2-10*A* and *B*. In actuality, this rephasing occurs only for dephasing resulting from the local magnet nonhomogeneities. This is true since these nonhomogeneities are fixed in space and the dephasing they cause is reversible. On the other hand, dephasing due to true T_2 is random and irreversible and will not be affected by rephasing. The signal, in fact, builds up to that corresponding to whatever T_2 dephasing would have been expected if T_2* had not been present, as seen in Fig. 2-10*B*. Also of interest is that if TE is lengthened, more time is given for vectors to dephase, and thus the final image is more T_2-weighted.

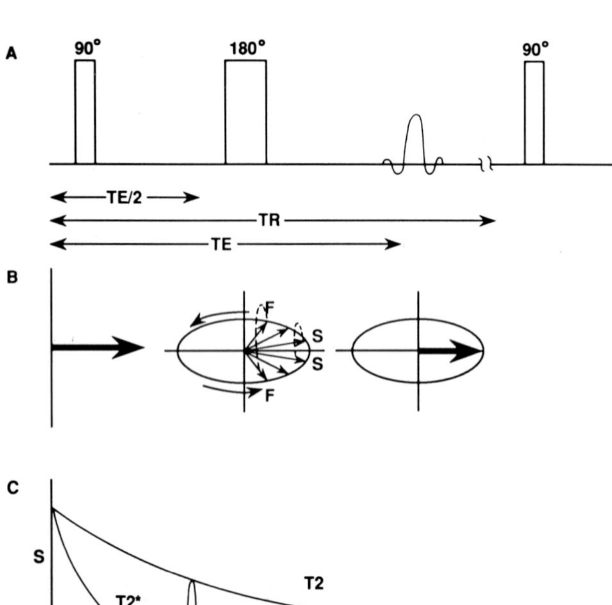

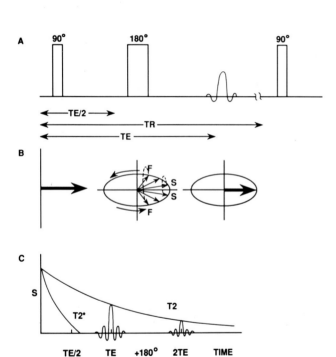

Figure 2-10 The spin-echo pulse sequence. **A.** After the magnetization vector is tipped 90° into the transverse plane, the individual faster (F) and slower (S) vectors start separating out via spin-spin interactions. This process is dominated by interactions due to local magnet nonhomogeneities (T_2*). After a time interval TE/2, vectors are flipped 180° onto the opposite side of the transverse plane and rephasing begins till vectors are again in phase coherence at starting point (at time TE). Only the T_2* interactions are reversible and rephaseable since they are fixed in space. Thus at interval TE the signal obtained is due to the remaining true T_2 interactions. **B.** Graph of signals decaying from T_2* and T_2 if T_2* is absent. As the effeccts of T_2* are removed, echo signal increases to the signal value expected if only true T_2 dephasing had been occurring for the period of time TE. Multiple 180° rephasing pulses may be given to collect additional echoes at different echo times. These occur, for instance, at 2TE, 3TE, etc., until the T_2 signal is irretrievably dephased away and lost.

If TE is very short, very little dephasing occurs and the sequence in fact approximates the partial saturation sequence yielding T_1 information. This can also be appreciated from the spin-echo signal strength equation as follows:

$$S = N \exp(-\text{TE}/T_2)\,[1 - \exp(-\text{TR}/T_1)] \qquad (3)$$

Here $\exp(-\text{TE}/T_2)$ goes to unity as TE goes to zero (exp of 0 = 1) and the partial saturation equation (2) depending only on TR and T_1 results. It can also be seen that signal intensity increases as TE or T_1 decreases and TR or T_2 increases (Table 2-4). As is true for the inversion recovery sequence, contrast reversal is also found in the spin-echo sequence. Often, multiple echo sampling is done; that is, the spin system is continually rephased, producing successive echoes. Each succeeding echo is of lower magnitude and is located at 2TE, 3TE, etc., as is seen in Fig. 2-10*C*; each results in a different image.

It should finally be noted that in clinical practice, because of mathematically favorable processing of the echo envelope signal, both saturation recovery and inversion recovery are in fact implemented with a final 180° rephasing pulse. TEs used, however, are so short that final images are essentially T_2-independent.

It is interesting to consider an analogy from a foot race that explains the separation of T_2 from T_2* and features of the spin-echo sequence discussed above. Imagine a foot

Table 2-4 Signal Strength Variation as a Function of Time Parameters

PARAMETER INCREASED	SATURATION RECOVERY	INVERSION RECOVERY	SPIN ECHO
T	———	Increases	Decreases
TR	Increases	Decreases 180° to 90° Increases 90° to 0°	Increases
T_1	Decreases	Increases for long T_1 180° to 90° Decreases for short T_1 90° to 0°	Decreases
T_2	———	———	Increases

Note: T = the interpulse time; TI = inversion recovery; TE = spin-echo pulse sequence. Angles cited refer to position of the vector as they return to equilibrium after initial 180° flip.

race with runners lined up at the starting line. Unfortunately, along with the proper runners (analogous to T_2) there are some unwanted runners (analogous to T_2*). Some of these unwanted runners are very fast and will easily win the race and mask the performance of the proper runners. To eliminate these unwanted runners, we issue them orders that at the signal (corresponding to time TE/2) they are to turn around and run back to the starting line. As soon as the race begins, the field is filled with slow and fast runners. At the appropriate time, the unwanted runners turn around and run back toward the starting line. They run at exactly the same velocity that they came out with (the magnetic field nonhomogeneity at a point in space is unchanging). As the faster unwanted runners race off the field, they catch up with the slower unwanted runners back at the starting line; the performance of the appropriate runners who are still racing out on the field becomes more and more apparent. At time TE, all the unwanted runners are at the starting line and the field is clear of them (the signal is dependent on T_2 only). Notice that if TE is very short in this analogy, the appropriate runners have not had enough chance to separate out clearly which are faster and which are slower. Thus, as we lengthen TE, differences between runners (tissue T_2) become more and more pronounced.

As discussed previously, the contrast between two tissues is merely the difference in signal strengths emanating from these tissues. Signal strength in turn depends on the specific combinations of TI, TR, and TE involved in the pulse sequence.

Let us look more closely at the relative role of TR and TE as applied to the spin-echo process. The recovery time TR determines how much m_l has recovered for a specific tissue. If little recovery is allowed, a subsequent 90° or 180° pulse will flip little onto the transverse plane and a small signal results from that specific tissue. Contrast against any other tissue may be small or great, depending on signal strength from that tissue.

We have already seen that TR determines the degree to which m_l can recover. For instance, Fig. 2-11*A* shows the resulting initial signals as a function of TR and the more general case where one of the tissues also has different spin densities. Short TR yields some intermediate recovery (m_l height 1) and will result in small m_t and a low signal. Long TR allows for more complete m_l recovery (m_l height 2), and subsequent signal upon 90° flip will always be larger. Signal contrast at any TR is merely the difference between signals such as at levels 1 or 2 in Fig. 2-11*B*. This, however, is not the only consideration in that before the signal is sampled, a delay TE/2 occurs. This is seen in Fig. 2-11*C*, where we see that each tissue will dephase with its own T_2 time parameter and final image contrast is the difference in signals at the given TE. Contrast depending on TR is seen in this figure. For instance, if a TR at level 1 is chosen, the resulting signals vary as a function of TE as shown. For that TR, a shorter TE gives contrast difference at a; for longer TE, the contrast difference is obtained at b (note gray scale inversion). For longer TR, such as position 2, both short and long T_2 tissues have nearly fully recovered and the signals at levels a and b are quite different (Fig. 2-11*D*). We say that at long TR, differences observed do not depend on T_1 and depend more on T_2 differences. From this we see that one can vary the relative contributions or weighting of T_1 and T_2 in the image with appropriate selection of TR and TE (Bradley 1984).

In general, TR affects T_1 weighting and TE affects T_2 weighting. Tables 2-5 and 2-6 summarize these as well as proton weighting schemes. The proton density weighting in general is obtained whenever one suppresses both T_1 and T_2 weighting.

Table 2-5 Weighting as a Function of Pulse Parameters

	SHORT TR	LONG TR
Short TE	TI	Proton density
Long TE	—	T_2

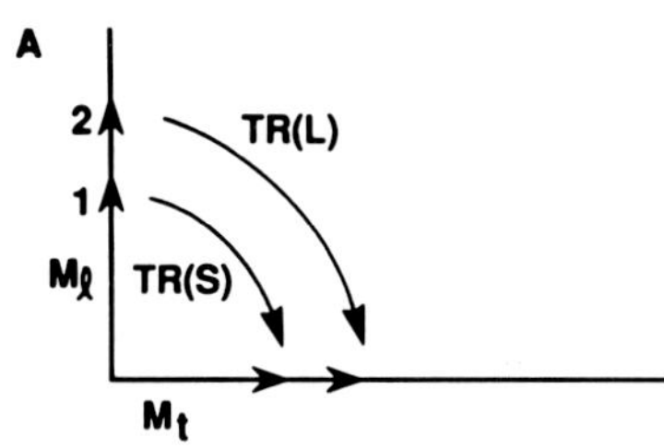

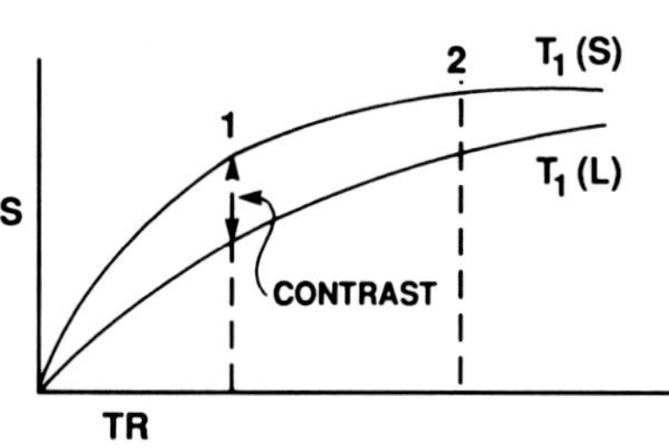

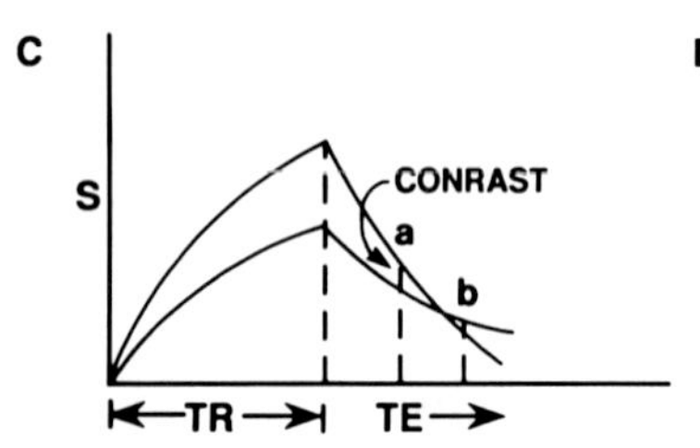

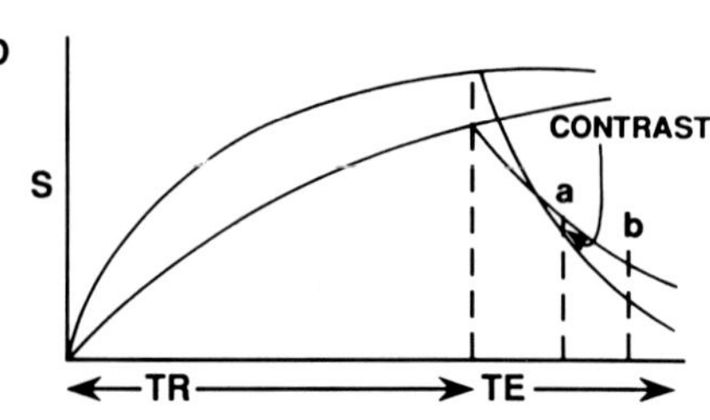

Figure 2-11 The effect of short (s) or long (l) TR and TE on image contrast. **A.** As TR gets larger, the signal increases (m_l larger) for both short and long T_1 tissues, since a greater amount of m_l recovers and more magnetization is available for flipping into transverse planes. **B.** Signal and contrast as function of TR. Signal contrast (difference in signal magnitude) is less at larger TR (level 2) compared to short TR (level 1). Lower signal (m_l) results from incomplete m_l recovery obtained at shorter TR. However, contrast is greater compared to a longer TR (level 1) in spite of the lower signal available. **C.** Any signal at a given TR will depend on the subsequent TE chosen. For short TR (level 1), there is a larger difference in signal magnitude, but this difference is greatly influenced by the initial T_1 differences in tissue. This initial contrast mechanism (T_1 weighting) diminishes with large TE (levels a and b), where the image becomes more T_2-weighted. **D.** At long TR for almost full m_l recovery for the various tissues, signal is high and again varies as TE but now is less dependent on T_1 differences. This is true since initial T_1 contrast differences are small and do not influence the signal at subsequent TE.

Table 2-6 Pulse Sequences

APPROACH	PULSE SEQUENCE	WEIGHTING
Partial saturation	Repeated 90° pulses	T_1 at short TR Proton density at long TR
Inversion recovery	180° pulse followed by 90°	T_1 at short TR Same as for partial saturation
Spin echo	90° pulse followed by 180° pulse	T_2 or proton density at long TR, long TE.

Table 2-7 Summary of MR Signal Detection

1. Signal detected always corresponds to the magnitude of the in-phase transverse magnetization.
2. In the original unexcited state, all the magnetization is longitudinal, none transverse, and no signal is available.
3. When the RF wave excites the nuclear spin system, the magnetization vector is tipped away from the longitudinal alignment and a transverse component is formed with a resulting MR signal.
4. Detected signal rapidly goes to zero as magnetization vector is dephased by T_2 and by T_2* spin-spin interactions. To determine T_2, the effects of T_2* local magnet nonhomogeneities must be removed.
5. Special pulse sequences are designed to obtain images weighted to proton density, T_1, and T_2 of the biological tissues.

To obtain T_1 weighting, one chooses short TE (reduces T_2 weighting) and long TR (enhances T_1 weighting). Likewise, for T_2 weighting, one chooses the opposite, i.e., long TE, to enhance T_2 and long TR to remove T_1 dependency.

Up to this point we have established that given appropriate pulse sequences and timing parameters, MR signals weighted for T_1, T_2, or spin density can be generated and detected (see Table 2-7 for summary). MR experiments in this area go back a number of years. What is new for medical imaging is the ability to create two-dimensional images from these parameters; this will now be discussed.

Image Generation

To generate an image from the MR signals, one must be able to spatially localize the origin of those signals. To do this, as first suggested by Laturbur (1973), a gradient mag-

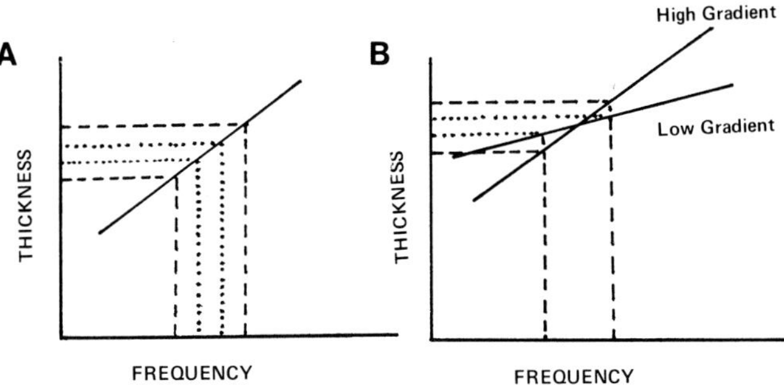

Figure 2-12 Slice thickness dependence on the range of frequencies present and on strength (or slope) of the gradient. **A.** When a wider range of RF frequencies (dashes) is used, a thicker slice results. **B.** When a gradient of greater magnitude is used (steeper gradient slope), the thickness that will encompass the fixed frequency range is greater (dashes).

netic field is superimposed upon the external magnetic field. The gradient field is just a linear variation of magnetic intensity across the magnetic field. This means that every point along a given direction experiences a different magnetic field. This, however, would then correspond to a different Lamor frequency [Equation (1)]. Thus, in the presence of the gradient each point in the image precesses at its own particular frequency, which then corresponds to a particular spatial position. When the signals along a gradient are detected, they represent the grand sum of all the frequencies present. A means must be had to analyze and separate the various frequencies detected and to determine the amplitude of the signal originating from each particular point along that gradient direction. The mathematical method used to accomplish this is called the Fourier transformation. The Fourier transformation has the unique property that it can transfrom frequency data into spatial position data, and thus it plays a key role in MRI. In an earlier reconstruction approach, one gradient is provided to define a slice and a second gradient is rotated at 1° intervals to obtain 180 projections around the patient. Data collected are then subjected to conventional back-projection algorithms as in the CT approach (Laturbur 1973). The Fourier approach is less susceptible to motion artifacts and magnetic field nonhomogeneities as well as having more favorable signal to noise characteristics (Crooks 1983). It is referred to as the two-dimensional Fourier transform (2DFT) approach since the Fourier transform has to be done in two directions (Kumar 1975).

To accomplish MR imaging via the 2DFT approach, three gradients must be activated: the slice selection, phase encoding, and readout gradients. These are now discussed.

SLICE SELECTION GRADIENT

This gradient sets the variation of frequency across the magnetic field (the z direction) such that a slice may be defined. When the slice selection gradient (G_z) is activated, only spins in a particular slice, corresponding to the specific range of RF frequencies used, are excited. Subsequent MR signals must come from this slice. The slice selection gradient can be oriented to yield transverse, coronal, or sagittal views. By increasing the range of frequencies (bandwidth), one in effect increases the slice thickness, as seen in Fig. 2-12. Notice in this figure that slice thickness can also be varied by increasing the magnitude (or slope) of the gradient. This approach has the effect of encompassing a greater range of frequencies and thus increasing the slice thickness. In practice, the magnitude of the gradients is a small fraction of the overall magnetic field strength.

PHASE ENCODING GRADIENT

Having excited the spins in the z plane with a position defining frequency, one must proceed to selectively excite spins to define the x-y coordinates. It has been found that rather than varying frequency in all three axes, a phase variation in one of the directions is more advantageous (Kumar 1975). This direction is called the y direction. In effect, after the spins are excited within a slice, the phase gradient (G_y) alters the phase slightly along each y column direction. When the phase gradient is turned off, each spin reverts to precessing at its original frequency. The net effect is that each position within a given y direction has a slightly different phase angle. That is, each one is slightly ahead of the preceding one. The phase gradient must be repeated for each x position in the matrix array, e.g., 256 times for a 256 × 256 matrix.

READOUT GRADIENT

Finally, after the application of the z and simultaneously with the y gradients, we apply a final x axis frequency gradient for reading out the signal. G_x must be applied for each value of G_y. This process essentially goes through the selected slice, interrogating each line defined by the x-y gradient combination until MR signals from the entire slice are accumulated. Figure 2-13 illustrates the process of gradient application in the specific case of a spin-echo pulse sequence.

It is also interesting to note that the only noise heard by the patient during an MRI scan is from the electric

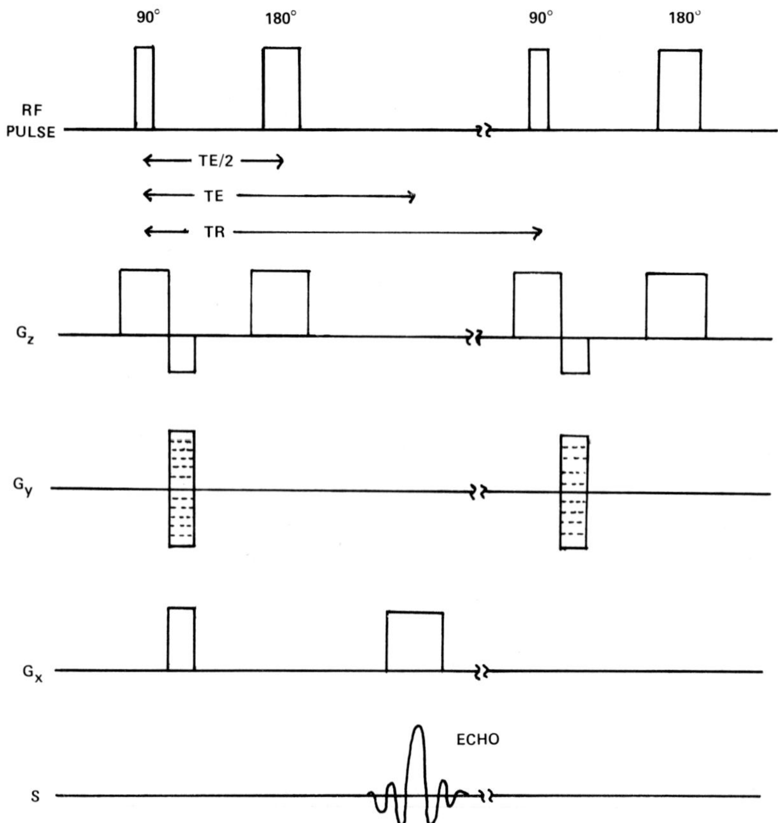

Figure 2-13 Depiction of events occurring in a two-dimensional FT spin-echo pulse sequence. The initial 90° pulse is given in the presence of a slice selection gradient G_z. (Only those spins within this particular slice will be flipped 90°.) The G_z gradient is followed by the phase encoding gradient G_y and a frequency encoded gradient G_x. G_x defines the spatial position of each row in terms of frequency, and G_y defines the position along each column in terms of phase. These are followed by a reapplication of G_z when the 180° pulse is given. (This will flip 180° those spins within the slice that had been defined originally by G_z.) Finally G_x is applied as a readout gradient, and the spin-echo signal is collected. The whole sequence is repeated for a different value of the phase encoding gradient G_y (dashed lines) for the number of times equal to the matrix size (e.g., 256 times for a 256 × 256 matrix).

current flowing through the gradient coils, where it experiences a force in the presence of the external magnetic field. As a result, the gradient coils "thump" back and forth as they are turned on and off. The magnitude of this noise is proportional to the square of the external field strength.

The possibilities of three-dimensional FT techniques are much discussed. In this approach, rather than a narrow (slice-selective) bandwidth range of frequencies, a broad (nonselective) band of frequencies is beamed into the patient. This broad frequency range essentially excites the entire volume. Then two variable-phase encoding gradients are applied simultaneously. The data are collected after the readout gradient. Three Fourier transformations must be performed, first along the readout gradient and then along the other two directions. One can reformat these data to yield any combination of planes, including oblique ones. Optimal resolution is achieved in 3DFT reformatted images if all the gradient slopes are the same, yielding isotropic resolution voxel elements. Anisotropic imaging results if resolution elements are not the same (i.e., if the voxel shape is not a cube).

There is a distinct signal to noise ratio advantage from the three-dimensional approach in that signals are collected from a larger volume. On the other hand, the penalty paid is increased scan times, especially for isotropic imaging. Compromises can be made to speed up the

Table 2-8 Summary of MR Image Generation

1. Signals detected must be localized in space. Gradients in three directions are utilized for this task.
2. A gradient is a linear variation of the magnetic field such that each point in space is defined by a unique frequency (or phase) given by the Larmor equation ($F = KB_0$).
3. Detected signals, even though spatially localized, still have contributions from T_2^*, T_2, and T_1 processes. T_2^* is due to both tissue T_2 and the presence of local nonhomogeneities present in magnet and has by far the shortest time. It generally drives the signal to zero very rapidly.
4. To unfold T_2 or T_1 from T_2^*, special pulse sequences are needed: saturation recovery, inversion recovery, and the spin-echo sequence.
5. For a given pulse sequence, one can weight the image for protons (spin density), T_1, or T_2 by varying the time parameters TR, TE, and TI.
6. Image contrast between tissues depends critically on the time parameters selected. Gray scale inversions are possible.

three-dimensional approach, such as anisotropic imaging, less than 90° flip angles, and shorter TR times. The former affects resolution and the latter two affect signal strength and contrast. See Table 2-8 for a summary of this information.

Multiplanar and Multiecho Imaging Acquisition

In general, T_1 relaxation time is relatively long (in hundreds of milliseconds) and determines how short a TR can be used. Additionally, the required interpulse delay times (TI or TE) can add up to a considerable sum in repeating sequences for each point. To efficiently use the inherent TR and delay times, a multiplanar approach can be used. Here one can utilize the TR interval to excite other planes. The result is the acquisition of a multiple number of planar images at the end of the pulse sequence. To illustrate the timing considerations in MR, let us look at acquisition times.

Equation (4) can be used to calculate the image acquisition time for a single slice.

$$\text{Time} = \text{matrix size} \times \text{number of excitations} \times \text{TR} \tag{4}$$

Notice that this includes not only matrix size and TR but also the number of times the sequence or excitation is repeated (number of data acquisitions) for purposes of signal averaging to gain an improvement in the signal to noise ratio. For a simple example, consider a matrix size of 256 × 256 (implies 256 phase steps), and the number of acquisitions = 2, and TR = 1000 millisec (1 sec). Then acquisition time is 512 secs (256 × 2 × 1), or 8.53 min. For a 10-slice procedure we would, for instance, need 10 × 8.53, or 85.3 min. This would be an inordinately long time, and the multiplanar approach becomes very attractive in that rather than repeat time necessary for each individual slice, multiple slices are acquired utilizing the waiting times between pulses.

The thickness of each slice produced is not rectangular but rather trails off in a gaussian manner (similar to CT slices). One must then be careful of how each plane is excited. The planes are usually acquired in interleaved fashion to avoid cross-talk effects between planes. With interleaving one essentially allows a little more time for recovery before giving the readout pulse to any particular slice level. One can also minimize gaussian tail-off of the slice by custom tailoring the frequency distribution of the RF pulse such that slice profile is more rectangular in shape.

The multiplanar technique allows not only for the acquisition of multiple planes but for different pulse timing sequences. One can thus, in a particular sequence, obtain two separate and different TE-weighted images. This then can provide additional clinical information to differentiate between different disease states, as illustrated in Fig. 2-10*C*.

Fast Imaging

As in any imaging technique, one would like to reduce the imaging time and therefore reduce image-degrading patient motion as well as optimizing patient throughput. In addition, faster scan times reduce patient discomfort as well as allowing for new imaging possibilities such as dynamic scanning, MR angiography, cine, and 3D imaging. Equation (4) specified the three major factors determining imaging time. Specifically, it is the product of the number of acquisitions, matrix array size, and repetition time TR. To reduce scan time, one or more of these must be reduced.

Number of Excitations (NEX)

Many times, if signal to noise is relatively low, the MR process is repeated for each image point and an average is obtained. This obviously extends scan times. Improvements in instrumentation and magnetic field uniformity over the years have allowed a reduction in the number of acquisitions necessary to achieve current levels of 1 or 2. To go even lower, one approach is referred to as half NEX acquisition (Feinberg 1986). To understand this approach, one must remember that normally one steps through the full range of phase encoding steps once for each array step (256 times for a 256 × 256 array). However, there is a certain symmetry here in that half these steps are complex conjugates of the other half. This means that we can sample only half the field and mathematically calculate the other half. For instance, we can obtain an image with 128 phase steps in half the time that 256 would have required. In practice, rather than half the data, about 60 percent is sampled. Notice also that half NEX acquisition results in lower signal to noise since less signal is actually being sampled. Theory predicts a reduction to $1/\sqrt{2}$ of SNR if 50 percent of phase space is sampled. Rather than calling this approach half NEX, it is more appropriate to call it fractional Fourier sampling. Fractional Fourier sampling that results in fractional phase encoding information is not to be confused with fractional echo sampling that results in fractional frequency encoding information. Fractional echo sampling is directed toward reducing susceptibility artifacts common in gradient echo imaging, where echo times have to be as short as possible to reduce phase dispersion effects (Wehrli 1990). Unfortunately, fractional echo and fractional Fourier are not possible at the same time. This is to be expected, since only a small fraction of total signal would be collected, and signal to noise ratio would suffer significantly.

Matrix Array Size

Matrix array size ultimately determines the possible resolution available in the system. Reduction here would not be totally productive. More specifically, the matrix array refers to the number of phase encoding and frequency encoding steps. There is no time penalty in keeping the number of frequency encoding steps high, while the opposite is true for the phase encoding steps. Accordingly, time reductions are accomplished by using fewer phase encoding steps. Anisotropic matrices (in which vertical and horizontal matrix sizes are not equal) of 128 × 256 would cut the scan time by 50 percent compared to a 256 × 256 matrix. This, however, results in loss of resolution in the phase encoding direction unless one invokes complex conjugate symmetry interpolation as in half NEX acquisition.

Reduced Repetition Time (Gradient Echoes)

The remaining parameter is TR. TR in fact is the longest period of time in the pulse sequence, and it is here that the greatest time savings can be obtained. Of course, we take advantage of the TR interval to excite additional slices to accomplish multislice acquisition. The real reason, however, that TR is relatively long is that we need to reestablish longitudinal magnetization after the 90° flip in spin-echo imaging. This full, or near-full, magnetization assures high signal strength on subsequent excitations. Remember also that reduction of TR in a standard spin-echo sequence introduces T_1 weighting and less T_2 weighting, as seen in Table 2-5. Also, there would be a decrease in the number of tissue slices one could image during multislice acquisition schemes. If one uses a partial flip angle, the time for the longitudinal magnetization to recover is less and a net reduction of scan time is possible (Fig. 2-14).

As seen in Fig. 2-14*A*, a normal spin-echo sequence flips m_l (vector 1) to the transverse plane (vector 2). A partial flip angle is seen to reduce the longitudinal magnetization only minimally (vector 3 versus full height vector 1). Yet the transverse magnetization vector 4, though not at full possible magnitude as vector 2, is still appreciable. This means that a relatively large gain in transverse magnetization (signal) is possible at a relatively small loss in longitudinal magnetization at small flip angles. Though subsequent excitations will yield less signal and signal to noise will not be optimal, one has here the mechanism for reducing scan times significantly.

The actual signal obtainable as a function of the flip angle is depicted in Fig. 2-14*B*. Signal magnitude will depend on tissue T_1 and TR. The angle at which maximum signal is obtained is called the Ernst angle. It should be noted that the Ernst angle need not give the maximum contrast between any two tissues. One must distinguish between high contrast to noise ratio (CNR), yielding large signal differences, and high signal to noise ratio, yielding large signals.

One major problem immediately comes into play when one is using reduced flip angles: The normal 180°-RF pancake flip inverts m_l, as seen in Fig. 2-14*C*. This inverted m_l yields an unstable situation in that it proceeds to recover back to the longitudinal position and subsequent excitations yield much lower signal strengths. This problem is avoided by not using RF to rephase spins. Instead, one can reverse the gradients and recover a gradient echo.

That is, rather than following up the initial 90° RF pulse with a 180° RF pulse, a negative gradient in the readout direction is applied instead. This is immediately followed by a positive gradient. This gradient reversal rephases the spins and provides an echo for signal detection. Gradient echo techniques have been dubbed with acronyms such as GRASS, FISP, and FLASH (Haase 1986). These techniques are particularly advantageous for short-TR, small-angle techniques because of the shorter time necessary for gradient reversals compared to 180° magnetization flips.

Gradient echoes represent the rephasing of spins that were dephased by the presence of the gradient. This does not, however, reverse the dephasing caused by magnetic nonhomogeneities. As a result, the signal returned is T_2*-weighted. Current magnet technology and the ability to achieve very uniform fields by shimming* have reduced the nonhomogeneity dephasing contribution considerably.

In fact, gradient echo techniques were proposed much earlier but were not implemented till recently, due in part to their high sensitivity to magnetic field nonhomogeneities. This limitation has been relaxed due to ad-

*Shimming is accomplished by incorporating various coils (called *shim coils*) within the gantry. These coils produce small magnetic fields that can be adjusted to make the overall magnetic field distribution more uniform.

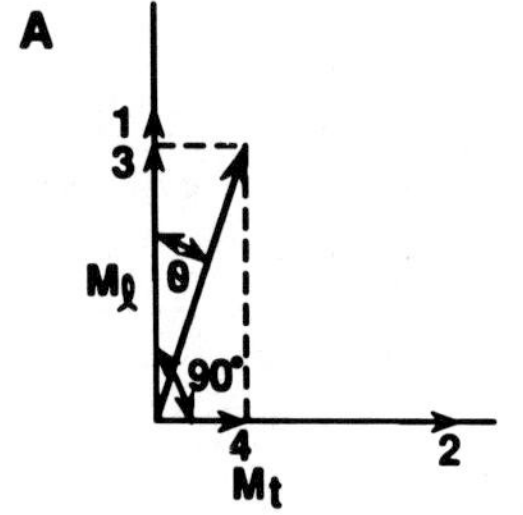

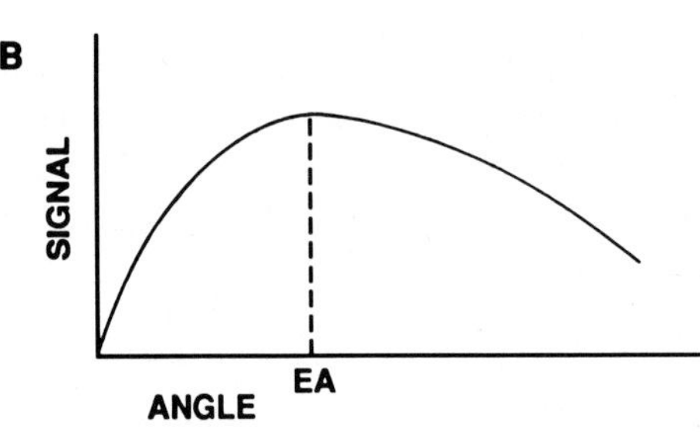

Figure 2-14 **A.** A 90° flip of the longitudinal magnetization (vector 1) yields full signal along m_t (vector 2). Partial flip, however, hardly affects m_l (vector 3 is almost the same as the original m_l vector). There is, however, still an appreciable signal along m_t (vector 4). **B.** Signal obtainable as a function of flip angle will vary with tissue T_1 and TR set. Shown here is maximum response at the flip angle referred to as the Ernst angle (EA).

vances in magnetic field shimming technique. The gradient echo approach is also very sensitive to RF field nonhomogeneities (Mills 1987). One important consideration when using gradient echoes is the associated sensitivity to magnetic susceptibility and flow artifacts. This is particularly apparent in the vicinity of air cavities (sinuses, mastoids, bowel) and near ferromagnetic implants. Another problem is that water and fat signals are not rephased, as occurs with RF pulses. This results in the possibility of imaging low-intensity borders at fat/water interfaces. This would also suppress tumor contrast in the fatty liver and bone marrow tumor imaging. The fat/water cancellation disadvantages of the gradient echo approach are much reduced for lower magnetic field strength units. As in spin-echo imaging, gradient echo imaging allows for multiecho acquisition. This is accomplished by reversing the readout gradient repeatedly.

An additional advantage of gradient echoes is that much less overall RF power is deposited in the patient by eliminating the 180° RF rephasing flip. There is no RF power deposition for gradient reversals, while 180° rephasing pulses deposit up to four times more energy in patients compared to the initial 90° excitation pulses. Additionally, if partial flips are employed, there is an additional reduction in RF power. This reduction factor is $(\theta/90)^2$. Thus, at 45° the RF power is reduced by $(45/90)^2$, or one-fourth. This has particular importance in scanning at high magnetic field strengths, where RF power deposition becomes limiting (Winkler 1988).

In summary, scan times and RF power deposition are significantly reduced using a combination of partial flip and gradient echoes. TRs of 10 to 50 msec, TEs less than 10 msec, and overall scanning times of a few seconds per image are now possible.

FLOW EFFECTS

In the previous discussions, the protons being excited were assumed to be stationary. If, in fact, the protons are moving, one can easily see that signals may be altered significantly. For instance, moving protons may not receive both the 90° and the 180° pulse in a spin-echo sequence and thus cannot be rephased. Interestingly, flow effects lead to signals that can be either enhanced or suppressed. Signal suppression resulting in a flow void can result from losses due to time of flight (TOF) effects, turbulence loss, and odd echo dephasing effects. Signal enhancement can come about from even echo rephasing, flow-related enhancement, and diastolic pseudogating (Table 2-9).

Table 2-9 MR Flow Effects

Flow signal suppressed via:
- Time of flight (TOF) losses
- Turbulence losses
- Odd echo dephasing

Flow signal enhanced via:
- Even echo rephasing
- Flow-related enhancement
- Diastolic pseudogating

Time of Flight (TOF) Effects

In TOF high-velocity losses, the protons acquire an initial 90° pulse in the standard spin-echo sequence, then flow out of slice before acquiring the 180° rephasing pulse. A subsequent signal loss will thus occur since protons need to experience both the 90° and 180° pulses to return an echo signal. The degree of TOF losses depends wholly on flow velocity, thickness of the slice, and timing sequence. The faster the flow, the greater the reduction in protons able to participate in both the 90° and 180° pulses. This is a linear function governed by the ratio of protons receiving both pulses and thus also depends on slice thickness and timing sequence. In a similar manner, view to view velocity variations during the cardiac cycle also affect the flow signal (Bradley 1984; Axel 1984).

It is interesting to note that velocity profiles across a vessel tend to be parabolic, with the highest velocity at the center. This is referred to as laminar flow, which is just the opposite of plug flow, where the whole fluid volume moves at the same velocity. In the presence of laminar flow, one may observe a flow void in the center of a vessel that will suffer the greater TOF loss since flow velocity is greater there, along with a stronger signal from the outer rim of the vessel, where velocity flow is lower and fewer TOF effects occur. Laminar flow, i.e., undisturbed flow but with a velocity gradient, tends to occur at higher flow velocities and smaller vessel diameters.

Turbulence

Turbulence loss occurs whenever flow is disturbed, for instance, slower protons moving over rough atherosclerotic vessel walls, at points of vascular branching, at stenotic constrictions, and for acceleration and deceleration associated with arterial flow. Flow disturbance tends to induce random fluctuations in velocity components, which in turn induce phase loss in spins that finally result in signal loss. Under laminar flow conditions, there will be no signal loss resulting from turbulence. There will, however, still be TOF loss effects.

The velocity at which turbulence occurs is directly proportional to the product of the vessel diameter, fluid velocity, and fluid density and inversely proportional to fluid viscosity (Bradley 1984).

In general, turbulence losses are more severe for slow flow in large vessels and may be present in vessels at any diameter at regions of transition between a high flow center and the slow flow region near the vessel wall.

Odd Echo Dephasing

The third flow mechanism by which the MR signal is suppressed is odd echo dephasing (Valk 1981; Waluch 1984). This effect and its companion even echo rephasing, yielding an enhanced signal, occur for laminar flow and are due to the fact that flowing protons experience different magnetic field gradients as they flow into the plane (weaker gradients are used for slice selection) or flow within the plane (readout and phase encoding gradients are stronger). Additionally, the flow velocity profile across the vessel is important. The greater this profile, the greater the dephasing that will occur. To understand this dephasing mechanism, remember that in a spin-echo sequence, the spins, after experiencing the 90° pulse, dephase relative to each other. When the 180° pulse is given at TE/2 time, these same spins rephase until they zero out at time TE. However, if these spins, for instance, are moving into a magnetic gradient, they experience a phase advance; to the extent to which they are out of phase at the time of the spin, the echo signal will be reduced. A similar effect occurs if spins are moving into a lesser gradient, in which case spin phases are retarded; this also yields a relative dephasing effect.

The degree of dephasing depends on both the magnetic field gradient strength and its flow velocity. It can be shown (Bradley 1988) that the net result will be a signal loss in echo in every other (odd) slice in a multiecho sequence. However, dephasing is totally rephased on every other (even) echo. Such rephasing returns an enhanced image signal. TE is important as well, since it determines the time given the spins to interact with the gradients. As TE increases, dephasing increases and greater signal loss occurs.

There are three modes by which signals can be enhanced: even echo rephasing, flow-related enhancement, and diastolic pseudogating.

Even Echo Rephasing

Even echo rephasing results from the fact that the dephasing that occurred for the entry first slice (odd echo) cyclically rephases to reestablish coherence at the time of the second echo (even echo). This rephasing, however, occurs only for uniform velocity into linear gradients with no acceleration or deceleration effects (Waluch 1984). Additionally, this phenomenon holds only for symmetric echoes. The reader is referred to the literature for clinical examples of this flow phenomenon (Bradley 1988).

Flow Related Enhancement

Flow related enhancement (FRE) occurs under conditions of slow laminar flow when fully magnetized spins move into a slice and displace saturated spins (spins that have experienced an initial 90° pulse but have not yet fully recovered). These fully magnetized spins return a higher signal upon applying a 90° pulse if a saturation recovery pulse sequence is used. In the more usual spin-echo case, the signal depends on whether spins experience both the 90° and the 180° pulses, in which case FRE competes with TOF signal suppression effects. For sufficiently low velocities enhancement may still occur, since signal loss due to TOF effects is then offset by signal gain from unsaturated spins that experience both the 90° and 180° pulses. Even echo rephasing also depends on flow characteristics being much more prominent for laminar than for more random turbulent flow. Maximum signal in the entry slice occurs when the flow rate is such that all the blood in the slice is replaced in the time interval TR (true for venous flow for 1 cm/sec for a 1 cm slice and a TR of 1000 msec). For higher velocities, in-flowing spins can avoid the 90° pulse until arriving at an inner slice, in which case enhanced signals can arise from these inner slices. In general, flow-related enhancement increases for longer T_1 (as is characteristic of unclotted blood) and shorter TR (less longitudinal recovery of the spins) as well as for higher magnetic field systems. The latter is true since field strength determines the degree of magnetization that spins begin with. The position of the slice is important when one is utilizing multislice acquisitions. Enhancement is greatest in the first slice, where the inflow of fully magnetized spins is greatest. Notice that FRE can be eliminated by applying a presaturation pulse to tissue volume just outside the imaging volume. Spins flowing into the first slice would therefore be just as saturated as stationary spins within that slice.

FRE is more prominent at high magnetic field strength, since the degree of magnetization is greater. Also, it is more prominent for short TR, since this determines the fraction of the stationary spins relative to inflowing spins. Likewise, stationary tissues with greater T_1 relaxation times will be more saturated and will return lower signal than will inflowing spins.

With the exception of the entry slices, signals in general are suppressed within tissue volume due to flow effects. One can exploit FRE to visualize lesions by using single slice acquisitions with the anatomy of interest at the entry slice (Kucharczyk 1986). This aids in determining vascularity and allows more confident separation of tumor from surrounding edema.

Diastolic Pseudogating

Diastolic pseudogating can occur whenever the cardiac and MRI cycles become synchronized. If synchronization occurs in diastole, the signal is enhanced since flow is slower. If synchronization occurs in diastole, signal is suppressed due to faster, more turbulent flow. Synchronization in fact is more likely during diastole, since this phase occupies the major time of the heartbeat cycle. Whenever diastolic pseudogating occurs, the resulting enhanced signal can be erroneously mistaken for a thrombus or tumor. In this case, a gating technique may be needed to eliminate the possibility of pseudogating. Note that one could exploit the enhanced signal character of slow flow by purposely gating to the R wave and therefore introducing enhanced flow signals.

All the above effects work in combination and may or may not compete with each other. At very low flow velocities, FRE dominates at entry slices. As velocities increase, FRE will be noticed for the inner slices as a function of distance from the entry slice. Concurrently, signal begins to diminish at the entry slice as TOF and odd echo dephasing begin. Likewise, to the extent that there is odd echo dephasing, even echo rephasing will also kick in, and as a result, the second echo as well as succeeding even echoes will begin to show enhanced signals. This signal, however, will be offset by the losses due to TOF effects, since higher velocity allows more spins to flow out of the slice before it receives the second 180° pulse. Simultaneously, we have the possibility of pseudogating effects.

Finally, it should be mentioned that the flow effects described above are also associated with CSF flow. The reader is referred to the literature (Thomas 1989; Bradley 1988; Enzmann 1986) for more on this, as well as for applications in angiography (Edelman 1990; Nishimura 1990).

Other Imaging Features

Like CT scanning, MR allows for a number of additional imaging features.

1. *Projected scanning.* A projected scan is merely a quick scan similar to a "Scoutview" or "Topogram." That is, it is a two-dimensional image in which all structures are superimposed one on the other. To accomplish this, a broadband RF (non-slice-selective) input is used.
2. *True zoom imaging.* One can produce a true zoom image by supplying the full gradient not over the entire patient but rather over a limited region of the patient. This has the effect of increasing the gradient over the region of interest. Furthermore, one then applies the full number of available pixels to the desired region. The result is that image is magnified and spatial resolution improves (since each pixel now corresponds to a smaller region of space). In the zoom approach, one must limit the excitation pulses to the specific region of interest to avoid artifacts.
3. *Image manipulation.* As in CT scanning, a number of gray scale and image quality manipulations can be performed. Examples are window width and window level selection. Also available are the usual range of different filtering kernels for such operations as image smoothing and edge enhancement. Essentially all software functions available to CT can be made available for MRI (distance and angle calculations, histogram analysis, etc.)

INSTRUMENTATION

Figure 2-15 shows a block diagram of a typical MRI system. The major components consist of a large magnet providing the strong magnetic field, the radio-frequency generator and coil, a set of gradient coils with its power supply, and finally the computer, which serves as the control center along with its peripherals. As in CT, there is also a facility for storage and multiformat filming. Given these features, excitational RF energy is generated and made incident on the patient, the signal is detected, and the MR image is finally generated. The analog to digital converter (ADC) converts the analog RF signal to a digital form for computer processing. Since the video display is analog, the final image data must go through the digital to analog converter (DAC). Let us look closely at some of these instrument components.

MAGNETS

Magnets are of three general types as currently configured for magnetic resonance imaging: permanent, resistive, and superconducting magnets. They are quite distinct in their features (Table 2-10) and result in significant differences in possible field strengths, stability, and uniformity as well as expense in their purchase and operation. In all cases, however, a relatively strong, uniform, and temporally stable magnetic field must be produced.

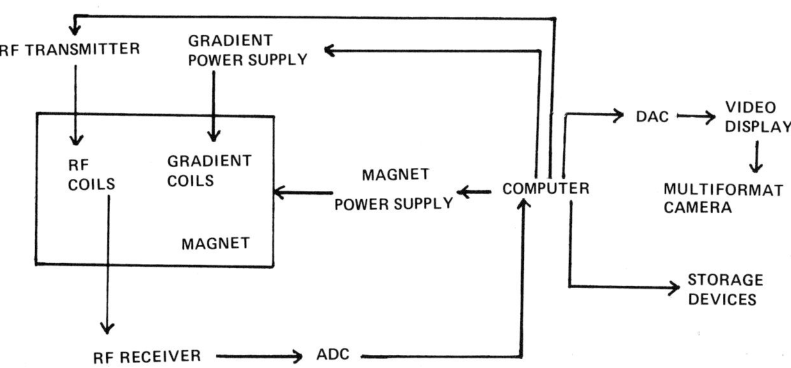

Figure 2-15 Block diagram of MRI imager.

Table 2-10 Major Advantages and Disadvantages of Various Magnet Types

TYPE	ADVANTAGES	DISADVANTAGES
Permanent	Low fringe fields Relatively inexpensive upkeep No cryogens Transverse field (enhanced SNR coils)	Limited field strength Relatively heavy Temperature-sensitive
Resistive (iron core)	Good field uniformity Relatively inexpensive No cryogens Transverse field possible	Limited field strength (up to 0.6T) Field not as stable Electrical costs higher
Superconducting	Very high fields possible High field uniformity Very stable field	Expensive to buy and maintain Expensive site preparation Cryogens needed Quenchable Fringe field problem

To help establish magnetic field uniformity and counteract the presence of magnetic field warping due to ferrous structures in the environment, small coils (called shim coils) are usually incorporated into the magnet.

The direction of the magnetic field can be aligned either across the bore (transverse), as in the permanent as well as iron core resistive magnet types, or parallel to the bore (longitudinal), i.e., from head to foot on the patient, as in superconducting magnets and certain earlier designs of air resistive magnets. These magnet types are now discussed.

Permanent Magnets

Permanent magnets usually consist of two opposing north and south poles within which the patient may be placed. Two possible configurations are shown in Fig. 2-16; these are the C and H types. The magnetic field in such configurations is confined between the two poles. These north and south poles are connected via the body of the magnet, creating a return path for the magnetic field lines. Because the magnetic field is directed and confined between the poles, the permanent magnet configuration will result in only minimal magnetic field levels outside and around the magnet. These stray magnetic fields are referred to as fringe fields. The lack of fringe fields greatly facilitates the operation of the MR scanner and the expenses related to its installation. This is true since the presence of fringe fields not only affects nearby instrumentation but can also pose a hazard, for instance, to persons wearing cardiac pacemakers. In addition, the interaction of the fringe fields with stationary ferrous structures (structural girders, ducts, etc.) and moving ferrous structures (vehicular traffic, elevators, etc.) warps the magnetic field within the magnet gantry, with resulting detrimental effects on MR image quality. The continuing upkeep costs for permanent magnets, however, are expected to be relatively low since no field driving electrical power is necessary nor are cryogen replacement costs necessary, as is true for superconducting systems.

One possible disadvantage of the permanent magnet approach is its relatively large weight (up to and beyond 100,000 pounds). One saving grace, however, concerning weight is that these magnets can usually be shipped and installed in smaller pieces. Another factor is temperature sensitivity; the magnet must be kept under controlled temperature conditions.

Permanent magnets can be made from ceramic materials or rare earth materials. The latter, however, tend to be more costly and weigh more. Alnico magnets are not used because of possible gradual loss of their field strength. Using permanent magnets, one need not worry about magnetic field quenching. The quenching phenomenon is characteristically possible for superconducting systems whereby the superconducting state suddenly ceases and there is a sudden reduction and collapse of the magnetic field. Quenching may result in damage to the magnet as well as significant amounts of downtime. A very serious drawback of permanent magnet systems

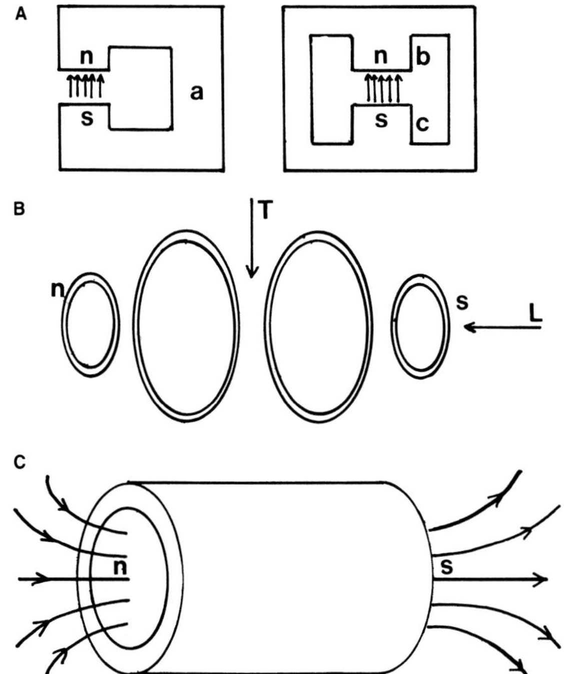

Figure 2-16 **A.** Permanent magnet of either the C (*left*) or H (*right*) type of pole configurations. These confine the magnetic field between the pole faces. The return path for the magnetic flux is through the body of the magnet, and very little fringe magnetic field is produced. To obtain an iron-core resistive magnet a coil of wire is placed either at **a** or at **b** and **c** for nonpermanent magnet poles. **B.** Air-resistive magnets are configured with air core Helmholtz coils (two central coils) or a four-coil arrangement as seen above. These coils are arranged around the gantry, and flowing current through these coils generates the desired magnetic field. If the patient is placed along T, a transverse field results. If the patient is placed along L, a longitudinal field results. **C.** Fringe fields produced by air-core resistive and superconducting systems. There is no internal magnetic field line return path. Such a path must be established outside the gantry. Superconducting magnets have coil configured solenoidally around gantry. Magnetic field is maintained without need for continuing electrical current or power. Patient is placed within bore of magnet, and magnetic field is longitudinal (along long axis of patient). Significant fringe fields are produced in both superconducting and air-core resistive magnets.

are the limited magnetic fields possible. Such systems at present operate at a maximum of 0.3 to 0.4 tesla.

One additional very important feature of permanent magnets is the fact that since the magnetic field is confined within and directed between the pole faces, simple cylindrical RF coils can be designed that provide greater inherent signal to noise characteristics (two to three times better) and correspondingly better image quality. This serves to offset somewhat the inherent advantages in signal to noise ratio obtainable at higher field strengths characteristic of superconducting systems.

Resistive Magnets

Air-core resistive magnets are configured with a series of wire coils. These coils are referred to as Helmholtz coils. They are arranged as seen in Fig. 2-16*B*. What occurs is that as an electric current flows through the coils, a magnetic field is produced whose direction is perpendicular to the plane of the coils. For optimal field uniformity, the coils should be arranged such that their diameters fall on the surfaces of a sphere. At least four coils in air (air core) are used as a sufficient approximation to produce a homogeneous field. These four coils consist of two large-diameter coils and two of smaller diameter. For clinical scanning, the complete spherical coil arrangement cannot be utilized, as there must be at least an opening for the patient. We refer to magnets produced by passing electrical current through wire coils as resistive since copper from which the coil wires are made provides for a small but not insignificant amount of electrical resistance and therefore power consumption. The magnitude of the magnetic field is proportional to the magnitude of the current. The electrical power consumption, however, varies as the square of the current. Thus doubling the magnetic field strength would require quadrupling the electrical power needed to drive the magnets. In addition, considerable heat is produced. The wire coils may in fact be made of hollow copper tubing that allows cooling water to run through to carry off the heat generated. Because of the electrical and heat production problems, resistive magnets are typically limited to field strengths of only up to 0.15 to 0.20 tesla.

Resistive magnets can be configured such that the magnetic field can be either longitudinal (along the length of the patient) or transverse (perpendicular to the patient). The transverse arrangement is obtained by placing the patient at the center of the coils perpendicular to the field lines. To obtain the longitudinal arrangement, the patient is placed down through the bore of the coils parallel to the field lines.

One important concern with air-core magnets is that fringe fields are produced. There is no internal path for magnetic field lines, and such a path is established outside the gantry.

To date, many consider that air-core resistive magnet technology provides only a lower-cost, lower-performance alternative to superconducting systems. Iron core systems, on the other hand, have become more and more popular because of their lower costs and relatively good imaging performance.

Iron-core resistive magnets are accomplished by placing solenoidal coils at region *a* for a C arrangement and at regions *b* and *c* for an H arrangement, as seen in Fig. 2-16*A*. These iron-core resistive magnets have the advantage of providing a return path for the magnetic field lines and thus have minimal fringe fields beyond the gantry. Additionally, the advantages of these are relatively uniform and stable fields. At present, though, these are not as optimal as those found in superconducting systems. The magnetic field alignment between the pole faces provides for greater signal to noise RF coil design, as is true for permanent magnets.

Superconducting Magnets

Superconducting magnet systems operate at very low temperature (near absolute zero). At these temperatures, some metals lose all electrical resistance and flow without additional energy being expended. Under these conditions, very large currents can flow and therefore very large magnetic fields can be produced. Typical units can operate between 0.5 and 2.0 tesla, but there are prototype imaging units operating up to 4.0 tesla. The fringe field problem is present in superconductive systems and is even more critical as these systems operate at much higher magnetic field levels. Unlike air-core Helmholtz coil pair resistive systems, the main field coils are configured in the much simpler solenoidal fashion. This is necessary because of the considerable forces which individual coils would experience. This could result in warping of the coils and the magnetic field. In any case, because of the high currents possible with superconducting systems, the efficiency of Helmholtz coil pairs is not needed. Additionally, for human lengths and for large bores, the solenoidal configuration is sufficient (Crooks 1984; Kaufman 1981). Superconducting systems must be provided with a cryogenic environment to maintain the low temperatures necessary. The coils are thus immersed in liquid helium and surrounded by a vacuum and then a bath of liquid nitrogen. Nitrogen serves to absorb the heat from the environment and maintain the necessary low temperatures. If there is a loss of helium or loss of the vacuum, the system rises in temperature and the superconducting state is eventually lost, with a resultant collapse of the magnetic field. This is referred to as a "quench," and large electric currents can flow through the conductor, which would then revert to operating in the resistive mode. Meltdown of the conductor is then possible and must be prevented. The material used for the superconductor is NbTi embedded in a copper matrix. In the superconductor state, the copper serves as a heat conductor. When superconductivity is lost, the excess currents flow through the copper and damage to NbTi is avoided.

In addition to high field strengths, another advantage of superconducting systems is the high stability and very high uniformity of the field.

Among the disadvantages is the relatively high cost of purchase and the continuing high cost of operating the system due to cryogen replacement expenses. Because of the large fringe fields produced, siting is also a problem, though this has been minimized recently by using magnetic field containment systems around the magnet gantry or around the room. These field containment systems consist of steel structures that soak up the magnetic fields and greatly reduce the fringe field beyond the containment area. The need for magnetic field steel shielding should not be confused with the need for RF field shielding. Because of the high sensitivity to RF fields necessary in MR scanning, one must shield the gantry from external RF energy such as from radio and TV broadcasts and power lines. RF shielding is simply accomplished with copper plates.

Table 2-11 Summary of Coil Types in MRI

COIL	CONFIGURATION
Resistive coils	
Air core	Either 1 coil pair (2 coils) (Helmholtz pair) or 2 pairs (4 coils) whose diameters describe surface of a sphere. Resulting field is either longitudinal or transverse.
Iron core	Coil windings are directly around poles of the electromagnet (either C or H configuration). Resulting field is always transverse.
Superconducting coils	Windings are solenoidal (around gantry). Conductors are of NbTi filaments in a copper matrix. Resulting fields are always longitudinal.
RF coils	
For transverse fields	Solenoidal configuration. Approximately 2 times the SNR advantage over comparable size saddle-shaped coils.
For longitudinal fields	Saddle-shaped coils.
Surface coil	Circular loop coils placed directly over the anatomic region of interest. Serves as the RF signal receiver.
Gradient coils	
Maxwell pair	Pair of coils with current flowing in opposite directions. Used for the slice-selection gradient in the direction of the main field axis.
Golay coils	Opposing parallel side coils, curved over the cylindrical surface of the gantry bore. There are 2 sets arranged at a 90° rotation to each other in order to define the two x and y gradient axes.
Shim coils	Additional small coils incorporated within gantry to make magnetic field more uniform.

GRADIENT COILS

As previously discussed, three gradients, one in each of three directions, must be available to perform MR imaging. These gradients are produced with special additional coils that produce a linearly varying magnetic field superimposed upon the uniform main magnetic field. The magnitude of this gradient field is relatively low and is usually between 0.5 and 1 gauss/cm. A linear gradient can be sufficiently approximated in the magnetic field direction with a Maxwell coil pair. This coil pair is similar to a Helmholtz coil arrangement except that the electric current is flowing in opposite directions. The other two gradients are produced using two Golay coils (Golay 1971). Golay coils consist of opposing coil loops with parallel sides wrapped around the gantry. These coils are displaced one from another by 90° to provide gradients for the two remaining directions.

Since the gradients define spatial position, it is important that they be very linear and uniform to within a few percent (Pickett 1983). Their strength must be such that they ride above any nonhomogeneities in the main field magnets. Gradients, along with the bandwidth of the RF pulse, define the slice thickness (Fig. 2-12) and consequently affect spatial resolution as well as the contrast sensitivity of the system.

RADIO-FREQUENCY COIL SYSTEM

We have seen that to excite the nuclear spin system, RF waves must be generated and beamed into the patient. The RF coils used to accomplish this are the so-called head and body coils within which the patient is placed. These coils typically serve as both the transmitter and the receiver of the MRI signal. The design of the coil is of either the saddle shape or the solenoidal type. The choice depends on whether the main magnetic field is transverse (perpendicular to the long axis of the patient) or longitudinal (along the long axis of the patient). In the transverse case, we use solenoidal coils. These are simple circularly wound wire loops. If the magnetic field is longitudinal, we must use saddle-shaped coils, which are somewhat more complexly configured. The solenoidal RF coils in general provide a signal to noise ratio (SNR) approximately two times that of the saddle-shaped coil of comparable size (Hoult 1976). This enhanced signal to noise ratio can allow for a reduction in imaging time (a factor of 4), or it can allow for an increase in the spatial resolution for the same scan time. This enhanced SNR serves to offset somewhat the disadvantage in loss of SNR for the lower field systems.

RF field nonuniformities lead to image intensity variations and consequently can also produce artifacts. In all cases, the best RF field uniformity is expected at the center of the coil.

Surface coils have recently gained popularity as a means of significantly increasing the SNR and consequently enhancing spatial resolution and contrast sensitivity. Essentially, a surface coil is merely a coil loop of wire that is placed directly onto the anatomic area to be imaged and usually serves as the RF receiver coil. The increased SNR of such a surface coil is due to its proximity to the region of interest, which allows for enhanced signal reception. The fact that it looks at a relatively small anatomic area enhances spatial resolution. One probably minor drawback with surface coils is the possible limited depth response and the consequent variability in gray scale shading. All the various coils are summarized in Table 2-11.

References

AXEL L: Blood flow effects in magnetic resonance imaging. *AJR* 143:1157–1166, 1984.

BRADLEY WG: Effect of relaxation times on magnetic resonance image interpretation. *Noninvasive Med Imag* 1:193–204, 1984.

BRADLEY WG, WALUCH, V, LAI KS, et al: The appearance of rapidly flowing blood on magnetic resonance images. *AJR* 43:1167–1174, 1984.

BRADLEY WG: Flow phenomena, in Stark DD, Bradley WG, (eds): *Magnetic Resonance Imaging*. St. Louis, Mosby, 1988.

CROOKS LE, ORTENDAHL D, KAUFMAN L: Clinical efficiency of nuclear magnetic resonance imaging. *Radiology* 146:123, 1983.

CROOKS LE, KAUFMAN L: Imaging methodology, in James TJ, Margulis AR (eds): *Bio Medical Magnetic Resonance*. Radiology Research and Education Foundation, 1984.

EDELMAN RR, MATTLE HP, ATKINSON DJ, HOOGEWOOD HM: MR angiography. *AJR* 154:937–946, 1990.

ENZMANN DR, RUBIN JB, DELAPAZ R, et al: Cerebrospinal fluid pulsation: Benefits and pitfalls in MR imaging. *Radiology* 161:773–778, 1986.

FEINBERG DA, NOLE JD, WALLS TC, KAUFMAN L, MARK A: Halfing MR imaging time by conjugation: Demonstration at 3.5KG. *Radiology* 161:527–531, 1986.

GOLAY MJE: U.S. Patents Nos. 3569523 and 3622869, 1971.

HAASE A, FRAHM J, MATHAEI D, et al: Flash imaging: Rapid NMR imaging using low flip angle pulses. *J Mag Reson* 67:258–266, 1986.

HOULT DI, RICHARDS RE: The signal to noise ratio in the nuclear magnetic resonance experiment. *J Mag Res* 24:71–85, 1976.

HOUSE WV: Theoretical basis for NMR imaging, in Partain CL, James AE, Rollo FD, Price RR (eds): *Nuclear Magnetic Resonance (NMR) Imaging.* Philadelphia, Saunders 1983, pp 60–72.

KAUFMAN SL, CROOKS LE: Hardware for NMR imaging, in Kaufman L, Crooks LE, Margulis AR: *Nuclear Magnetic Resource Imaging in Medicine.* Igaku-Shoin, 1981, pp 53–67.

KUCHARCZYK W, KELLEY WN, DAVIS DO: Intracranial lesions: Flow related enhancement on MR images using time of flight effects. *Radiology* 161:767–772, 1986.

KUMAR A, WELTI D, ERNST RR: NMR Fourier zeugmatography. *J Magn Res* 18:69–83, 1975.

LATURBUR PC: Image formation by induced local interactions: Example employing nuclear magnetic resonance. *Nature* 242:190–191, 1973.

NISHIMURA DG: Time of flight angiography. *Mag Reson Med* 14:194–201, 1990.

PICKETT IL: Instrumentation for nuclear magnetic resonance imaging. *Semin Nucl Med* 13:319–328, 1983.

THOMAS SR, POMERANZ SJ: Flow effects in magnetic resonance, in Pomeranz SJ (ed): *Craniospinal MRI.* Philadelphia, Saunders, 1989.

VALK PE, HALE JJ, CROOKS LE, et al: MRI of blood flow: correlation of image appearance with spin-echo phase shift and signal intensity. *AJR* 146:931–939, 1981.

WALUCH V, BRADLEY WG: NMR even echo rephasing in slow laminar flow. *J Comput Assist Tomog* 8:594–598, 1984.

WEHRLI FW: Fast-scan magnetic resonance: Principles and applications. *Mag Reson Q* 6(3):165–236, 1990.

WINKLER ML, ORTENDAHL DA, MILLS TC: Characteristics of partial flip angle and gradient reversed MR imaging. *Radiology* 166:17–26, 1988.

3 MRI ARTIFACTS AND SAFETY

Andrew R. Bogdan

SECTION A: MRI ARTIFACTS

INTRODUCTION

This chapter discusses artifacts in magnetic resonance imaging (MRI). An *artifact* can be defined as any deviation of an MR image from a purely anatomic representation. These artifacts can be classified into several groups. Following a review of some basic aspects of MRI necessary for an understanding of the origin of artifacts, the most common artifacts are discussed, accompanied by clinical examples. The purpose is to provide a more thorough understanding of MRI, the ability to recognize artifacts, and the know-how to reduce or eliminate their presence.

MRI artifacts can be broken down into four basic categories, depending on the cause:

1. Intrinsic
2. Motion
3. Chemistry and physics
4. Equipment fault

The first group refers to artifacts based on limitations of the MRI process and can be explained on a mathematical basis. These artifacts are known as (1) aliasing, (2) Gibbs or truncation, (3) cross talk, and (4) partial volume averaging.

The second group refers to artifacts that occur as a result of (1) patient motion and (2) flow. Patient motion may be either voluntary or involuntary. Flow, although involuntary, is treated separately and is usually considered to be either steady or pulsatile.

The third group refers to artifacts known as (1) chemical shift, (2) fat/water phasing, or multiple spectral components, (3) magnetic susceptibility, and (4) transverse coherence. These artifacts can be understood by using the tools of chemistry and physics as they apply to nuclear magnetic resonance (NMR) and MRI.

The fourth group refers to artifacts due to improper adjustment or functioning of the receiver, transmitter, magnetic field gradients, or analog-to-digital converter (ADC); improper electrical shielding of the MRI room or equipment; computer malfunction; and eddy currents. These artifacts can be avoided or corrected. Examples are ghosts, unusual image contrast, faint parallel stripes throughout the image, and bright vertical or horizontal lines through the image.

Only the artifacts in the first three groups will be discussed in this chapter, as they occur in a properly functioning MRI unit. Their possible presence in clinical images should be recognized and understood.

BASICS OF MRI

The detected signal that makes MRI possible is based on the phenomenon known as *nuclear magnetic resonance*. The Nobel Prize in physics was awarded in 1952 to Purcell and Bloch for their pioneering work in NMR. Twenty years would pass before Lauterbur (1973) showed that spatial information can be encoded in an NMR signal. However, the ability to make homogeneous high-field superconducting magnets, low-noise radio frequency (RF) amplifiers, and high-speed computers was necessary to make imaging a clinically accepted tool.

Definition of Terms

In the presence of an external magnetic field, an atomic nucleus with nonzero spin, and hence a nonzero magnetic dipole moment, has its energy levels modified, allowing it to absorb magnetic dipole radiation (Abragam 1961; Farrar 1971; Harris 1986; Thomas 1986). The nucleus of the hydrogen atom has two energy states, usually referred to as *spin-up* and *spin-down* in reference to its orientation with respect to the magnetic field. The energy difference between these two states is given by the Larmor equation as

$$\Delta E = \hbar\,\omega_0 = \gamma B_0 \hbar \quad \text{or } \omega_0 = \gamma B_0 \qquad (1)$$

where ω_0 = NMR or Larmor frequency
γ = gyromagnetic ratio, which depends on the type of nucleus ($\gamma/2\pi$ = 42.6 MHz/Tesla for the proton)
B_o = magnetic field in Tesla

The presence of hydrogen nuclei (approximately 10^{22}/cm^3) in the human body gives rise to a small but detectable NMR signal when the nuclei are irradiated at the Larmor frequency. Typically, in the nuclei that give rise to the signal, the difference between spin-up and spin-down is only about 1 part in 10^6 of the total number present.

The NMR signal is the net effect of nuclei at many different positions, each contributing its own frequency and having its own amplitude, which depends on the number of nuclei (density) present at that location as well as how much they have relaxed via T_1, T_2, or T_2^* processes. A local group of nuclei are treated mathematically as if they were a single *macroscopic spin* known as an *isochromat.* The signal intensity is related to the *flip* or *tip angle.* This is a measure of how much the macroscopic spin is tipped away from its equilibrium value.

Spatial information is encoded in MRI through the use of specially designed coils which produce linear magnetic field gradients (Thomas 1986) when an electrical current is passed through them. The coils' magnetic field is superimposed on the main magnetic field. These gradients are necessary to encode information in either the x, y, or z direction (orthogonal planes—sagittal, coronal, or transverse) or another direction (oblique). When present, the gradient causes a linear variation in the frequency (or energy levels) of the nucleus of interest (usually ^1H) (Hinshaw 1983):

$$\omega_i = \omega_0 + \gamma g_i x_i \tag{2}$$

where g_i, the gradient amplitude in the i direction, is typically 100 to 1000 times smaller than B_o

This variation of frequency with position has given rise to the term *frequency-encoding gradient.* This gradient, also referred to as the *readout gradient,* is turned on while the NMR signal is digitized and recorded.

To understand how spatial information is encoded in a second orthogonal direction, the term *phase* must be introduced. After an RF pulse, all the macroscopic spins are considered to be coaligned and rotating at a frequency given by Equation (1). In the presence of a gradient g_y, these spins rotate at frequencies different from ω_0 [Equation (2)]. When the gradient is turned off, after a time interval T, these spins resume precessing at ω_0 but are no longer coaligned. The difference in angular position is referred to as *phase,* which is given by

$$\phi_y = \gamma g_y y T \tag{3}$$

The direction in which the phase of the spins is modified is known as the *phase-encoding direction.* The details of how this phase information is detected and decoded are beyond the scope of this chapter.

The third direction is referred to as the *slice-selection direction.* It has already been shown [Equations (1) and (2)] that the presence of magnetic field gradients gives rise to a spatial variation in resonance frequency. To image a particular anatomic plane using the tools of phase and frequency encoding, spins must first be excited with an RF pulse. A careful choice of the shape of the RF pulse gives rise to a spread in frequencies $\Delta\omega$ known as the bandwidth of the RF pulse, centered at some frequency ω_{rf}. In the presence of a magnetic field gradient, only a certain spatial region will be excited, that is, the region whose resonant frequencies correspond to those present in the RF pulse. If one controls the shape and duration of the RF pulse and the amplitude of the slice-selection gradient, a plane of known position and thickness can be selectively excited.

Dephasing and Rephasing

The NMR signal used for imaging is present immediately after the RF pulse and is known as *free induction decay* (FID). This signal decays with a time constant characteristic of the nucleus and its environment (chemical, physical, and magnetic). In order to have time to spatially encode the MRI signal, the FID must be delayed from the RF pulse. This is done by creating an echo. Two types of echoes are used for MRI: a gradient echo and a spin echo (Fig. 3-1).

GRADIENT ECHO

It was shown in the section on phase encoding that a magnetic field gradient causes a spatial variation in the phase of the local spins or isochromats. If a second gradient of the opposite sign is applied, the spins rephase, giving rise to a detectable signal. This signal is known as a *gradient echo.* However, the signal intensity will have been somewhat reduced from the initial FID intensity as a result of any source of inhomogeneity in the magnetic field as well as interactions between neighboring spins. If the echo delay t_e from the initial RF pulse is varied, an exponential decrease in signal intensity is observed with a time constant T_2^* [i.e., $\exp(-t_e/T_2^*)$].

The technique of a dephasing (or prephasing) gradient followed by a rephasing gradient is applied in the frequency-encoding direction (Fig. 1*A*). It is used to move the signal away from the RF pulse and to allow the data to range over both negative and positive values of spatial frequencies in a single data acquisition (see Spatial Frequency Representation below). At the same time the dephasing frequency-encoding gradient is applied, the phase-encoding gradient is turned on to encode information in the orthogonal direction.

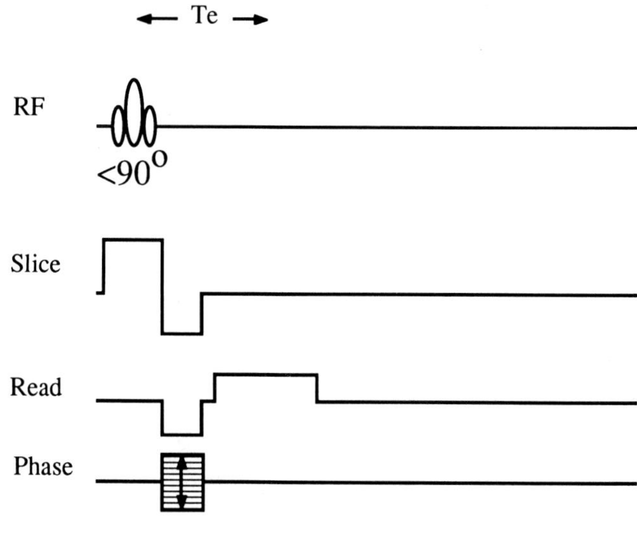

A

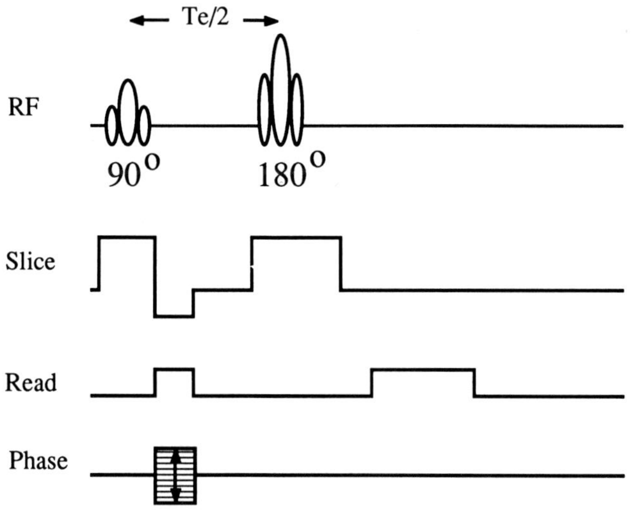

B

Figure 3-1 **A.** Gradient-echo pulse sequence. **B.** Spin-echo pulse sequence.

SPIN ECHO

The addition of a 180° RF pulse to the FID from a 90° pulse causes a *spin echo.* As the spins start to dephase in the presence of magnetic field inhomogeneities and the natural spin-spin interaction, a 180° pulse is applied at time $t_e/2$, causing them to rephase. At a time t_e after the 90° pulse, the spins will have rephased maximally. The signal caused by this rephasing is the spin echo. The inhomogeneities in the static magnetic field are corrected, and the signal intensity decays exponentially as $\exp(-t_e/T_2)$, where $T_2 > T_2^*$. The relaxation process that occurs with a time constant T_2 is primarily due to spin-spin interaction.

However, a 90 to 180° pulse sequence does not spatially encode information; both frequency- and phase-encoding gradients must also be present, increasing the minimum achievable echo time. These gradients may be placed either before or after the 180° pulse. Additionally, slice-selection gradients must be applied to define the imaging plane.

The presence of these pulsed gradients gives rise to *eddy currents* in the metallic structures of the magnet housing. According to Lenz's law, a changing magnetic field gives rise to currents in conducting structures. The direction of the induced current creates a magnetic field that opposes the change. This effect can cause degradation of image quality and lower signal intensities because of their time-varying nature, which cannot be compensated for by a spin echo. However, it is possible to reduce the cause of the eddy currents by modifying the currents that flow through the gradient coils (eddy current compensation) or by using actively shielded gradient coils.

Spatial Frequency Representation

To create an MR image, one repeats the experiment of (1) an RF pulse in the presence of a slice-selection gradient, followed by (2) a phase-encoding (y) gradient and a dephasing frequency-encoding (x) gradient, and then (3) signal detection in the presence of the rephasing frequency-encoding gradient. During each repetition of the experiment, only the phase-encoding gradient is incremented. In effect, a signal is being built up in the y direction analogous to the x direction in order to have a matrix of data which is Fourier-transformed (see Fourier Transformation below) into a two-dimensional (2D) image. Figure 3-1 depicts this series of events for spin echo and gradient echo imaging sequences.

To tie together the x and y spatial information, the concept of *spatial frequency* (Twieg 1983) can be used. High spatial frequencies contain information about the fine detail of the image, whereas low spatial frequencies contain information about the larger structures. Consider an image with vertical lines with a spacing d. The spatial frequency is $k = 1/d$, that is, one line per unit distance. As d decreases, k increases. Thus, by definition, smaller spacing implies higher spatial frequency.

It can be shown that the signal detected as a function of time during the frequency-encoding gradient is also a function of spatial frequency. During the sampling time, the negative high spatial frequencies are collected, followed by lower frequencies, the zero spatial frequency, and finally positive high spatial frequencies. The signal in the x direction as a function of time is related to spatial frequency as follows:

$$k(t) = \gamma[G_x - g_x t]x \tag{4}$$

This can be written as

$$[K_x - k_x]x \quad (5)$$

where $K_x = \gamma G_x$ (G_x is the area of the prephasing or dephasing gradient) and $k_x = \gamma g_x t$ are known as spatial frequencies. k_x ranges from 0 to $2K_x$, and thus spatial frequency $(K_x - k_x)$ ranges from $-K_x$ to $+K_x$. Thus, as the signal is detected as a function of time, one is learning about its spatial frequency content. Because the range of high spatial frequencies sampled is limited, it follows that there is a limit to the fine detail which can be revealed.

It can be shown that the spatial frequency of phase-encoded information as a function of the phase-encoding step is given by

$$k_y = (n/2)\gamma g_y T \quad (6)$$

where g_y = gradient necessary to cause a phase shift of 2π across the field of view (FOV)
$n = -N/2$ to $+N/2$ in steps of 1 where
N = number of phase-encoding steps

As the phase-encoding gradient value changes, the range covered is $-K_y$ to $+K_y$ ($K_y = \gamma g_y TN/2$). For a square matrix with the same field of view in the x and y directions, $K_x = K_y$. Thus, although the x and y data are collected differently—the x data in a matter of milliseconds and the y data over the course of seconds or minutes—both represent spatial frequency information. As data are acquired, "k space" is being filled up. The number of points acquired and their range determine the x and y FOVs and the pixel dimensions.

Fourier Transformation

A Fourier transformation is a mathematical tool that is used to link two conjugate representations of the same data (Brigham 1988). When one listens to a violin being played, one's ear senses a temporal variation in air pressure but one hears different tones. Two different notes sound different because of their different temporal waveforms. The brain is actually performing a Fourier transformation. If the pressure variation were recorded, it could be Fourier-transformed to determine what frequency was being played.

The MRI signal is more like the complex variation due to an entire orchestra. However, if it is recorded (or digitized), this temporal information can be transformed into frequency information and, using Equation (2), can be transformed into spatial information. Thus, frequency and time are conjugate Fourier variables. Similarly, spatial frequency and position are also conjugate Fourier variables. Which representation is used in MRI is a matter of preference. However, the spatial frequency representation is useful in the discussion of several artifacts.

Slice Profile

In MRI it is desirable to excite a thin slab of matter uniformly so that if density is uniform, an equal number of spins will be excited as a function of position. When a linear gradient is applied, a linear variation in excitation frequency is imposed [Equation (2)]. To select a slice, it is necessary to produce an RF pulse with equal amplitudes over a desired frequency range, or *bandwidth*, $\Delta\omega = \gamma g_z \Delta z$ (Fig. 3-2). This will produce an equal probability of excitation across the slice thickness.

As stated above, the Fourier transform links a frequency distribution to the temporal waveform necessary to produce it. In the above case of a rectangular frequency distribution, it can be shown that a sinc-shaped $[\sin(x)/x]$ temporal distribution is necessary to produce it (modulated at the RF frequency ω_0). Also, to have a perfect distribution, as shown in Fig. 3-2, the temporal waveform must last forever. As the RF pulse must be applied in a finite amount of time, the resultant profile cannot be perfect, leading to some variation in flip angle with position. The consequences of this are discussed below, under Cross Talk. Many analyses have been done to study this phenomenon and optimize slice profiles (Connolly 1989; Hoult 1979; Joseph 1984; Locher 1980; Pauly 1989; Runge 1988; Silver 1984).

Consider what can happen in a T_1-weighted gradient echo image as a result of an imperfect profile (Hanicke 1988). The Ernst angle (Ernst 1966) is the flip angle which gives maximum signal intensity for a given T_1 and repetition time TR. An actual RF excitation pulse gives

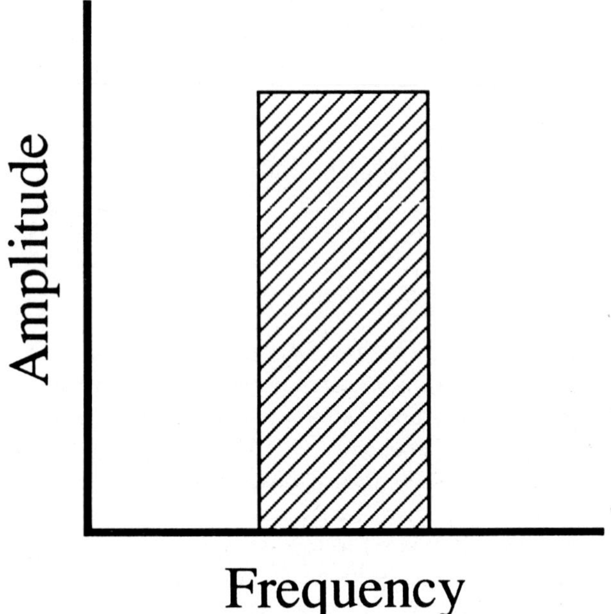

Figure 3-2 Ideal frequency distribution.

rise to a spatial distribution of flip angles ranging from 0 to θ°. In regions where the local flip angle either exceeds or is less than the Ernst angle, a lower signal intensity will be produced. Hence, the total signal from the excited slice does not arise uniformly from all regions.

ARTIFACTS

Aliasing

Aliasing, also referred to as *wrap-around,* is a phenomenon that is known to occur in digital signal processing (Brigham 1988). According to the Nyquist sampling theorem, a temporal waveform must be sampled at greater than twice the frequency of the highest frequency present to reproduce the information present in that waveform properly. If this condition is not met—that is, if the sampling is not done frequently enough—this high-frequency component masquerades as a lower frequency. Mathematically, it is stated that a waveform with a maximum frequency component f_{max} must be sampled at a rate greater than or equal to $2f_{max}$ to properly determine, by Fourier transformation, the amplitude of the frequencies present. If a frequency component $f_{max} + \Delta f$ is present, it will appear as if its frequency were really $-f_{max} + \Delta f$. This presents itself in imaging as follows.

READOUT DIRECTION

As was discussed earlier, the readout gradient causes a spatial variation of the NMR frequency. For a chosen imaging sequence, the sampling rate is normally fixed and the FOV is varied by increasing or decreasing the readout and phase-encoding gradient amplitudes. As the gradient amplitude increases, the deviation of the proton frequency at a fixed point in the body from that in the absence of a gradient also increases. As the sampling frequency is fixed, this means that the FOV decreases.

For example, an object of 300-mm extent, centered in the magnet with a gradient of 2 mTesla/m, gives rise to frequencies ranging from about −12.8 kHz to +12.8 kHz relative to the proton frequency in the absence of a magnetic field gradient. If one desires a FOV of 250 mm, corresponding to a range of −10.6 kHz to +10.6 kHz, the higher frequencies which are present will appear in the wrong position.

This effect can be eliminated by using two techniques. The first is a *low pass filter.* Ideally, such a filter placed in the receiver will pass frequencies below a cutoff frequency f_{lp} unattenuated and completely attenuate frequency components above f_{lp}. The second is *oversampling,* in which the data-sampling rate is doubled. This doubles the FOV and the number of pixels in the x direction, causing any aliasing to occur outside the desired FOV. After reconstruction of the image, only the central pixels corresponding to the desired FOV are displayed. This technique has little or no effect on the image signal-to-noise ratio (SNR). Oversampling also corrects the residual aliasing caused by the nonexistence of ideal low-pass filters.

PHASE-ENCODING DIRECTION

Aliasing in the phase-encoding direction (Fig. 3-3) is somewhat more difficult to comprehend. In the section on spatial frequency representation, Equations (4) through (6), it was shown that the signals as a function of the phase- and frequency-encoding directions are both representations of the imaged object in spatial frequency. In Equation (4) the x direction information is encoded for each phase-encoding value g_y by using t as the independent variable and k_x as the dependent variable ($k_x = \gamma g_x t$), while g_x remains constant. That is, as time increases, a range of spatial frequencies is swept through. For the phase-encoding direction, g_y is the independent variable which has discrete values $G_y/(n/2)$ (for a square pixel) and T is a constant. However, as only the product g_yT is used, the phase-encoding information can be thought of as a time variable with the same aliasing problems that occur in the x direction. It is more difficult to suppress the aliased information in the y direction, as there is no equivalent receiver low-pass filter for data which are gathered discretely and as oversampling adds time to the scan.

To get a more intuitive feel for aliasing in the phase-encoding direction, consider a distribution of spins (Fig. 3-4) to which no gradient has been applied. Next, consider the spins' transverse orientation after the increment

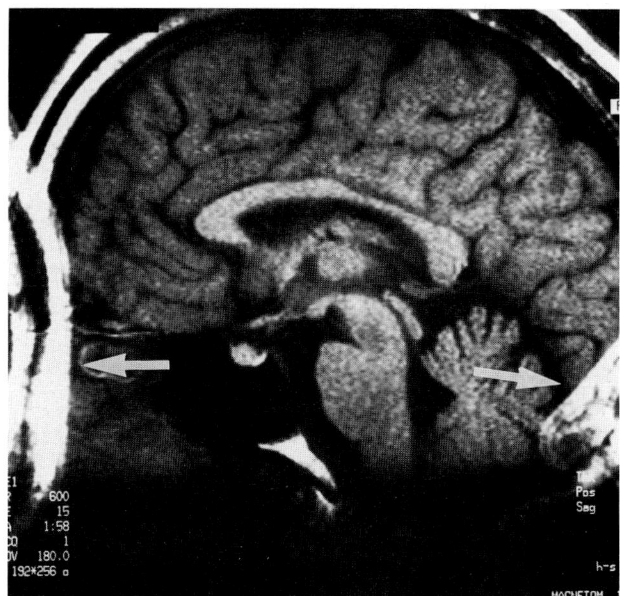

Figure 3-3 Wrap-around (arrows) in the phase-encoding direction resulting from the use of an FOV smaller than the size of the head.

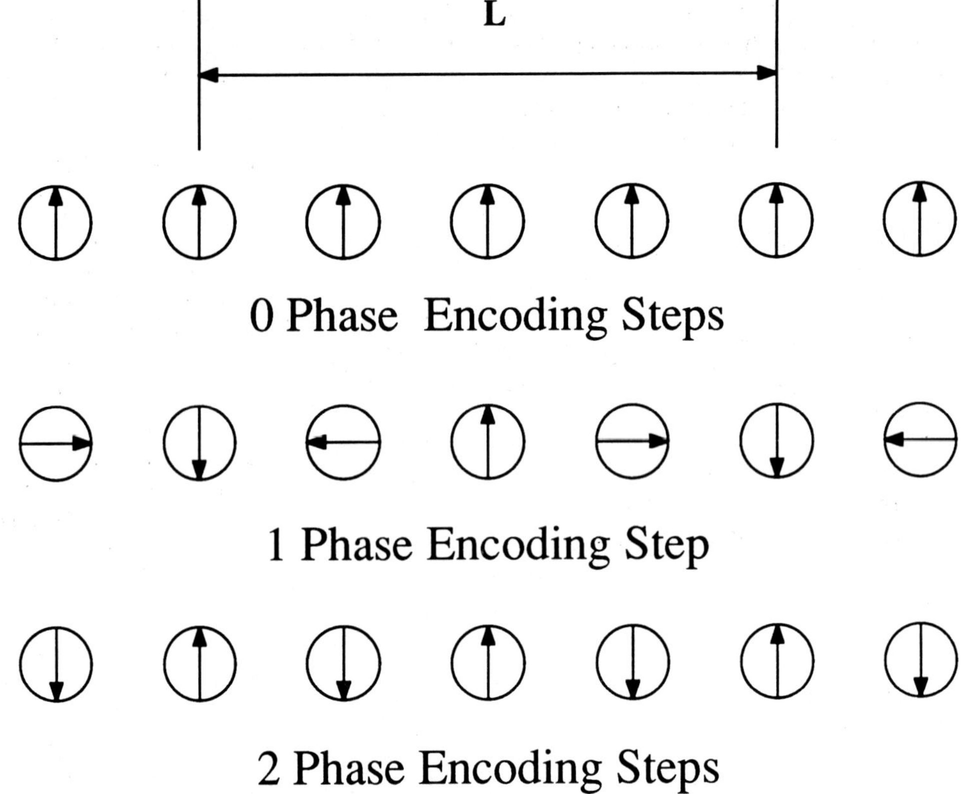

Figure 3-4 Schematic representation of incremental applications of the phase-encoding gradient. *Top.* Spins are initially aligned after an RF pulse and no phase encoding. *Middle.* The smallest phase-encoding increment is applied, causing a 2π variation in the phase angle across the FOV, L. *Bottom.* Two units of the phase-encoding gradient have been applied, causing a 4π rotation across L. Note that the spins outside L mimic the behavior of those inside. This effect gives rise to aliasing, or wrap-around.

$\gamma g_y T$ has been applied. g_y is chosen so that the variation in phase angle [Equation (3)] across the FOV is 2π, causing a $\pm\pi$ rotation at the two extremes and intermediate values for $|y| < L/2$. The next time $2\gamma g_y T$ is applied, causing a 4π rotation across the FOV. Note that the spins at $\pm L/2$ are changing their sign every step; that is, M_{xy} is oscillating at a frequency one-half that of the sampling rate. This is the highest frequency allowed by the Nyquist sampling theorem. However, the physical extent of the body may exceed $\pm L/2$. Note that these spins are indistinguishable from spins inside the FOV. That is, they oscillate at the same frequency and with the same phase and give rise to the familiar wrap-around in the phase-encoding direction if the FOV in the y direction is not great enough.

How can this be avoided? Either the FOV must be chosen to be larger than the object or the signal from those spins must be eliminated. The latter is accomplished through the application of *presaturation pulses* to regions outside the FOV (Edelman 1988). Presaturation pulses are slice-selective 90° pulses that are followed by strong gradients which crush, or scramble, the transverse magnetization so that its net value within a voxel is approximately zero. The imaging sequence immediately follows these pulses.

SLICE-SELECTION DIRECTION

In three-dimensional (3D) data acquisition, phase encoding is applied in the slice-selection direction. Thin contiguous slices are reconstructed by Fourier transformation in this direction. The use of a non-slice-selective RF pulse, which excites the whole volume, will lead to wrap-around if the dimension as determined by the 3D phase-encoding gradient is less than the physical extent of the object being imaged. It will appear (Fig. 3-5) as if two anatomic regions were superimposed in the same image.

This artifact can be eliminated by means of a careful choice of the slab thickness or minimized by using a slice-selective RF pulse to excite only the volume of interest. In the latter case some wrap-around may occur as a result of imperfect slice profiles (see the section on slice profile), but this is of concern only for a few outer slices.

Gibbs Phenomenon

A second artifact based on the mathematics of MRI reconstruction is the *Gibbs,* or *truncation, artifact* (Parker 1987). This artifact, which manifests itself as a "ringing" (periodic spatial intensity variation) appearance near edges or transition regions, is due to the fact that data are sampled for a finite amount of time (Fig. 3-6).

As was discussed previously, the MR image is reconstructed by performing a Fourier transform on data acquired as a function of time. As data are acquired for a finite time, mathematically they are treated as if they were *windowed,* or multiplied, by a rectangular function which is equal to 1.0 during data acquisition and 0.0

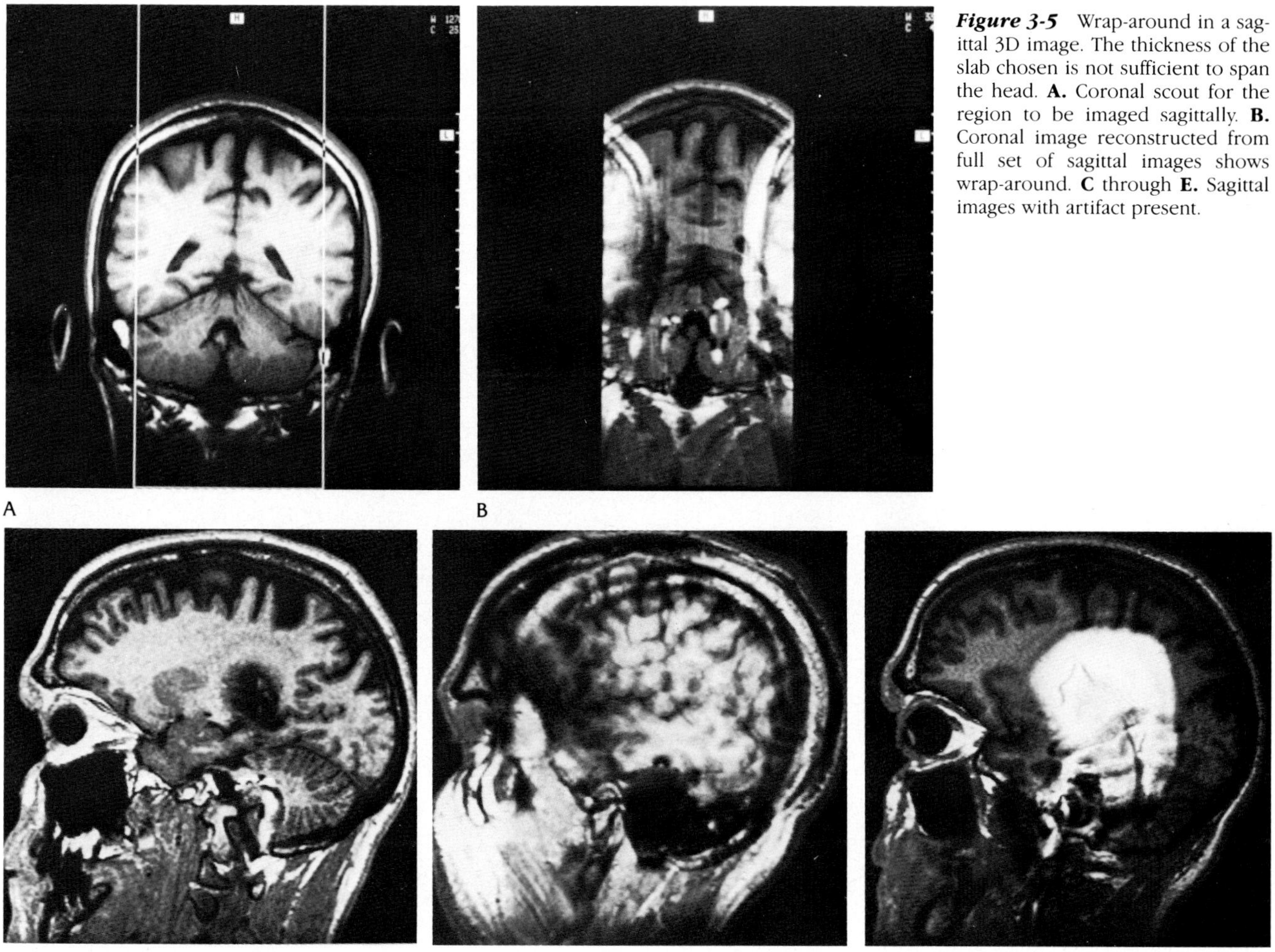

Figure 3-5 Wrap-around in a sagittal 3D image. The thickness of the slab chosen is not sufficient to span the head. **A.** Coronal scout for the region to be imaged sagittally. **B.** Coronal image reconstructed from full set of sagittal images shows wrap-around. **C** through **E.** Sagittal images with artifact present.

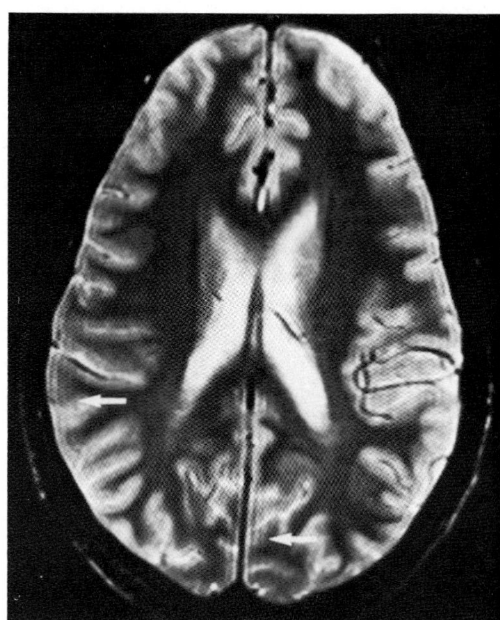

Figure 3-6 Gibbs artifact. This image was acquired with a 192 × 256 matrix. Note the "ringing" appearance (arrows) near the edge regions.

everywhere else. A rectangular function has as its Fourier transform a sinc(x), or sin(x)/x, form. This damped sinusoidal waveform gives rise to the ringing appearance.

A more intuitive understanding of this artifact can be reached by considering the spatial frequency representation (see the section on spatial frequency representation). Edges, or sharp transitions, in an object are represented by high-spatial-frequency components. It was shown, however, that the range of spatial frequencies sampled is limited. Therefore, the information necessary for edge definition is not collected. For a fixed FOV, the range of spatial frequencies sampled is proportional to N_r (or N_p), the number of data samples in the readout direction (the number of phase-encoding steps). Thus, an image with 512 pixels will reproduce an edge with less ringing than will one with 256 or 128 pixels.

How can this effect be reduced if it is troublesome? The simplest way is to apply a *filter,* or window, to the data. It was stated above that the data can be treated mathematically as if they were multiplied by a rectangular function. What is the effect of multiplying the data by a different function which is also equal to 1.0 in the center and approaches 0.0 at the edges of the sampling region, but in a smoother fashion? The effect is to convolve the data with a function other than a sinc function. In fact, the data are convolved with the Fourier transform of the smoother function, which is itself broader than the sinc function but has fewer or no oscillations. This has three effects:

1. Reduction or elimination of ringing at the edges.
2. Improved SNR. If the data are multiplied with a function that has an amplitude less than 1.0, the noise present in the data and the signal will both be reduced. However, most of the signal power is at lower spatial frequencies, whereas the noise is uniformly distributed. Thus, the noise is reduced more than the signal is.
3. Decreased resolution. The effect of convolving the image with a broader function spreads out information among pixels. Thus, there are trade-offs. Fortunately, it is possible to reduce the ringing without a substantial loss of resolution.

Cross Talk

Most MRI scans are acquired as multiple two-dimensional slices. From one slice to the next, only the RF frequency is changed (unless the slices are not parallel). Consider a scan of n slices with a repetition time TR. Although TR is the repetition time for any chosen slice, a new RF pulse is applied every TR/n seconds. As was discussed in the section on slice profile, the ideal rectangular profile is only approximated. Therefore, if slices are placed too closely, the tail of one RF slice excitation can partially excite the neighboring slice (Crawley 1987; Runge 1988). This effect can be reduced by *interleaving* the slice acquisitions. For example, six slices can be excited in the order 1, 3, 5, 2, 4, 6. In this case, an adjacent slice ($i - 1$) is not excited until a time $[(n/2) - 1]\text{TR}/n$ later (after slice i). During this time, the magnetization in the adjacent slice will recover toward the equilibrium value it would have if that were the only slice excited.

On a T_2-weighted image with a TR of 2500 to 3000 msec and about 15 to 25 slices, a new slice is excited every 100 to 150 msec. If the slices are not interleaved, the excess excitation of the adjacent slices will reduce the magnetization available. The magnitude of this effect depends on the T_1's of the tissues in the slices. Tissues with short T_1's will recover more than regions with a long T_1 (e.g., CSF) will. Thus, SNR will be reduced and some T_1 weighting will be added (Kucharczyk 1988). If the same slices are interleaved, adjacent slice excitation occurs at an interval about 10 times greater and the effects of cross talk are reduced.

On a T_1-weighted image, the TR is much shorter, typically in the range of 300 to 800 msec. However, because of the shorter echo times, one can still scan nearly as many slices. Therefore, adjacent slices are excited as much as 25 to 50 msec apart if they are not interleaved and about 100 to 400 msec apart if they are interleaved. In either case, this can lead to more T_1 weighting (i.e., a change in image contrast) and a reduction in the SNR.

In the case of gradient echo sequences which generally use flip angles less than 90°, excitation of the adjacent slices is done with an RF excitation well below 90°. In the case of spin-echo sequences, the use of one or two 180° pulses can lead to a higher degree of excitation in an adjacent slice. It is difficult to achieve a good slice profile for 180° pulses (Joseph 1984). However, much theoretical and experimental work has been done in optimizing pulse profiles for the purpose of achieving uniform excitation of the desired slice. That is, the flip angle should drop from the desired value to 0° over as short a region as possible and should maintain a nearly uniform value over the excited region.

While a radiologist has no influence over the pulse profiles that are provided with an MR system, it is important to understand the concept of cross talk and recognize how the slice profile can affect overall image quality. Clearly, the interleaving of slices is desirable in general, but how much of a gap should be left between slices can best be determined by comparing images.

Motion

The discussion of motion-related artifacts will be divided into two sections: (1) patient motion, either voluntary or involuntary, and (2) flow and its effect on images. The common aspect of ghosting will be discussed first.

Ghosts are images of lesser intensity displaced from the desired (or average) location. They always appear displaced in the phase-encoding direction (Axel 1986) and can lead to images which are difficult to interpret or are nondiagnostic.

Motion in the imaging plane generally is small during the few milliseconds of data acquisition. Thus, motion in the frequency-encoding direction leads to some blurring in that direction as information is encoded which represents the position of the patient at that moment in time. However, as motion is in general asynchronous between phase-encoding steps, image information is incorrectly encoded in that direction. It has been shown that periodic motion in any direction gives rise to a series of ghosts in the phase-encoding direction; separation of those ghosts is a function of the period of motion and the TR of the sequence (Wood 1986). It is not possible to deliberately displace the ghosts out of the FOV, because they fold back as a result of aliasing.

PATIENT MOTION

Artifacts due to patient motion can be ascribed to either voluntary or involuntary motion. Voluntary motion can often be reduced by making the patient comfortable and

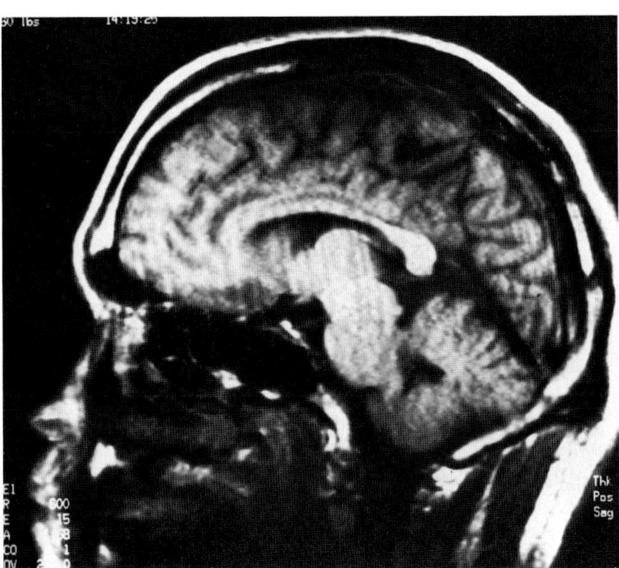

Figure 3-7 Motion artifact. Note the striated appearance superimposed on the brain.

restricting the range of motion (by padding the head, for example). Involuntary motion is due to respiration, cardiac motion, peristalsis, orbital motion, and swallowing (flow is involuntary but will be covered below). The effect of motion on a sagittal T_1-weighted head image is shown in Fig. 3-7.

Several techniques have been developed to minimize the effects of involuntary motion (Edelman 1988; Haacke 1986, 1987; Wood 1986). Only the techniques that are most commonly used for cranial imaging will be discussed here.

ECG or pulse triggering is useful in reducing CSF pulsation artifacts in cervical and thoracic spine imaging. Also of concern are motion artifacts due to respiration and swallowing. Two useful techniques for preventing ghosts from interfering with spinal images are (1) swapping the phase- and frequency-encoding directions and (2) using presaturation techniques to eliminate the signal from the moving tissue (Edelman 1988). In the former technique, motion of the spine is negligible, as the patient is lying on his or her back. However, when phase encoding is done along the magnet bore for sagittal images or from left to right for transverse images, the ghosts are rotated 90° and no longer interfere with the region of interest. The latter technique—presaturation—was described in the section on aliasing. In this context, the presaturation region is placed coronally and eliminates the ghosts from the throat for cervical imaging but does not interfere with the spinal region (Fig. 3-8).

For cranial imaging, swapping phase- and frequency-encoding directions will rotate the ghost artifacts from orbital motion so that they go from left to right rather than from anterior to posterior.

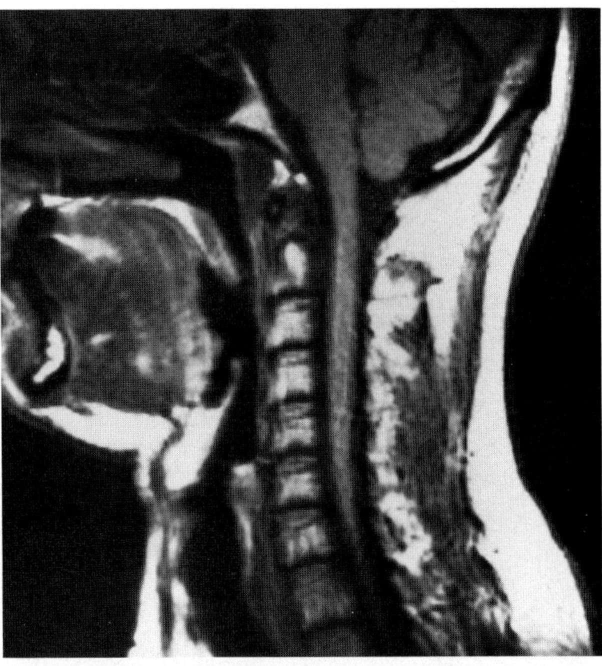

A

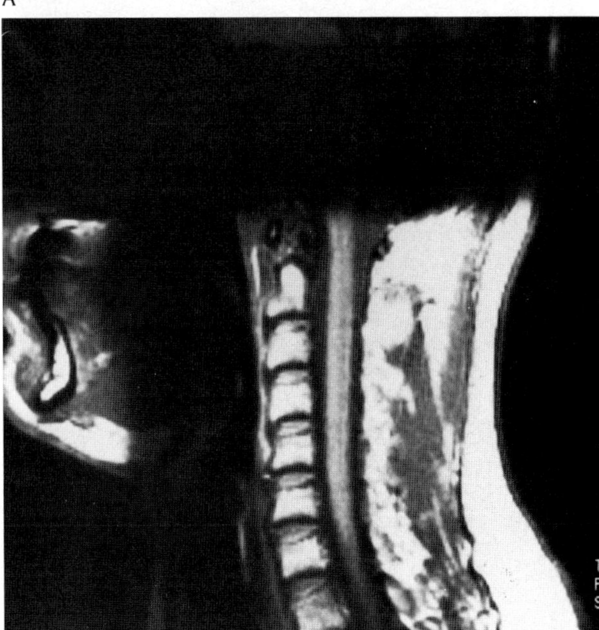

B

Figure 3-8 T_1-weighted, 4-mm-thick sagittal image of the cervical spine. **A.** Poor definition of anatomy caused by swallowing. **B.** With the use of presaturation regions, image appearance is greatly improved.

FLOW

Pulsatile flow can also give rise to ghost artifacts. Blood motion and CSF motion are periodic with the cardiac cycle, and unless the MRI scan is ECG- or pulse-triggered, artifacts arise (Figs. 3-9*A* and 3-10).

Because blood flows throughout the body, different spins constantly flow into and out of the imaging planes.

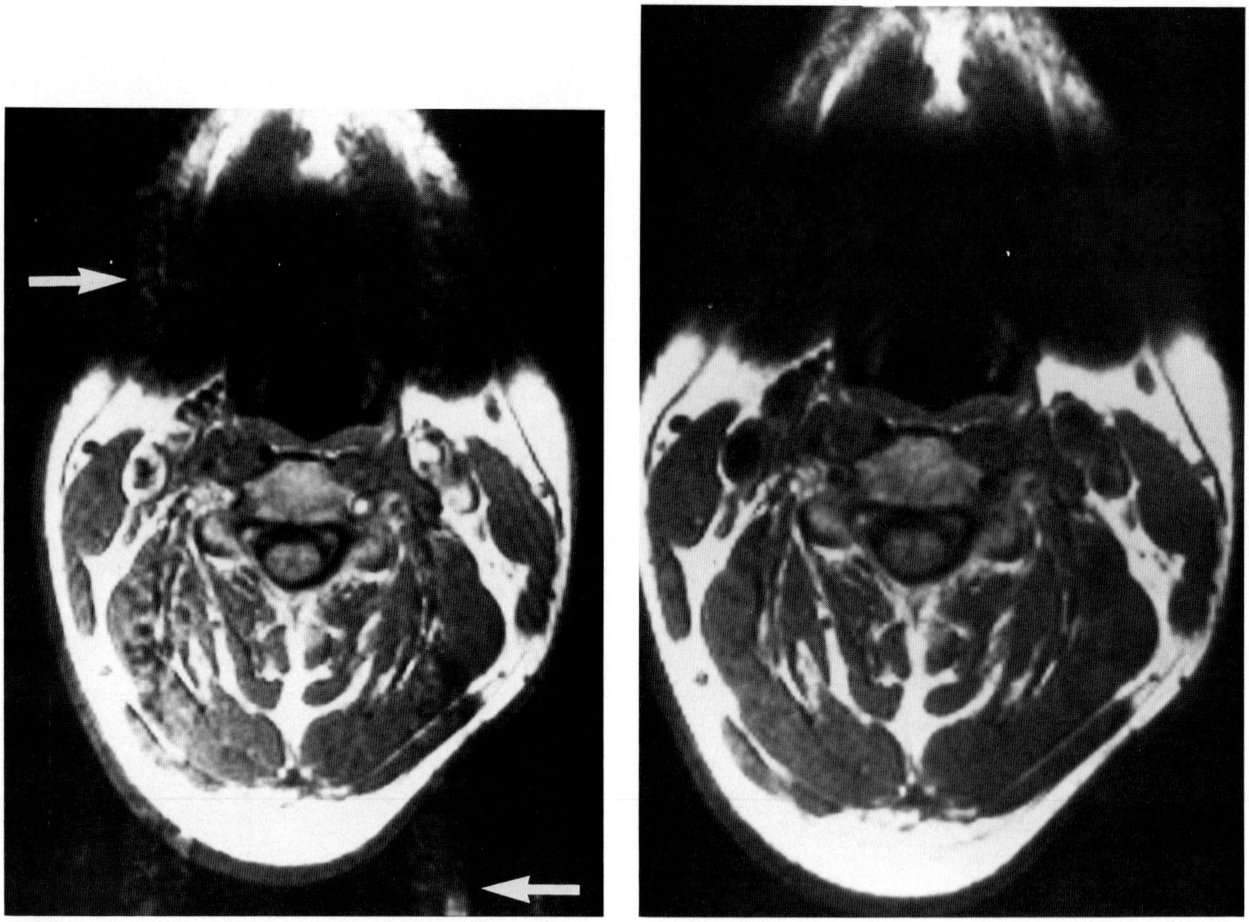

A B

Figure 3-9 T_1-weighted spin-echo images of the cervical spine. **A.** Note the ghost artifacts due to blood flow (arrows). **B.** Application of presaturation regions superiorly and inferiorly has eliminated the blood signal and the accompanying ghosts.

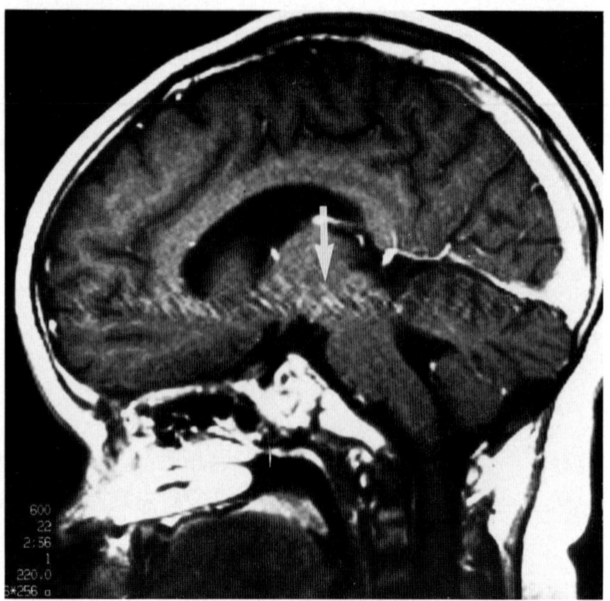

Figure 3-10 Flow artifact (arrow) due to CSF motion in a T_1-weighted spin-echo image after the administration of Gd-DTPA.

Depending on the imaging parameters, this effect can give rise to very different appearances of the intravascular signal (Axel 1984). Consider a single imaging plane. The tissue being imaged is considered to be stationary. However, blood is flowing into one side of the slab and out the other. In gradient echo imaging, TR is generally less than 500 msec. As the plane is repeatedly excited with RF pulse, the signal intensity of static spins is reduced by a factor $[1 - \exp(-TR/T_1)]$, which can be approximated by TR/T_1 if TR is much less than T_1. However, fully magnetized "blood spins" are constantly flowing into the slab. Thus, their signal is not reduced by the same factor. Relative to the surrounding tissue, the blood appears to be bright (Fig. 3-11*A*). This effect has been referred to as paradoxical enhancement, or the in-flow or wash-in effect. The actual magnitude of this effect depends on TR, the slice thickness TH, and the flow velocity V. The blood travels only a distance $V \times TR$ between RF pulses. If $V \times TR < TH$, some spins are fully magnetized and some are not.

In a multislice imaging sequence, this effect is complicated by the fact that blood in downstream slices has

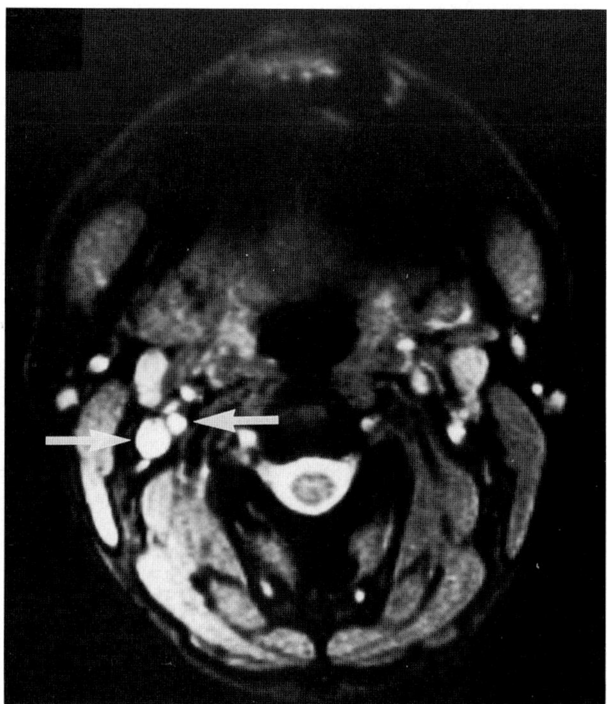

A

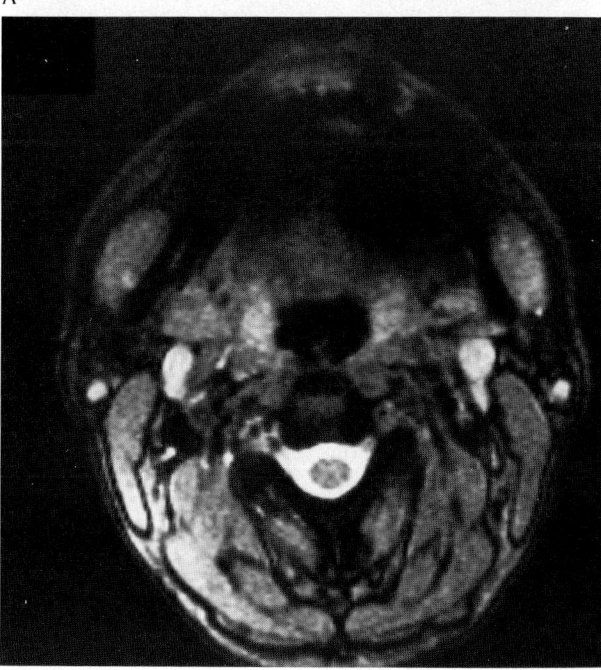

B

Figure 3-11 Gradient moment refocused FLASH images of the cervical spine (TR = 500, TE = 12, 15° flip angle). **A.** Note the bright appearance of the blood (arrows). **B.** Application of presaturation regions superiorly and inferiorly has eliminated the blood signal.

been excited by multiple RF pulses. It follows that the blood in these slices will appear relatively less intense.

These effects have been used to develop techniques for magnetic resonance angiography (MRA) (Alfidi 1987). It is important to note that the spread in velocities in laminar flow or in turbulence can lead to a reduction in signal intensity from flowing blood. It was shown in the section on dephasing and rephasing that dephasing and rephasing in gradient-echo and spin-echo imaging sequences are designed to rephase the signal from the static excited spins. However, flowing spins do not see a constant gradient amplitude, and at the time of the echo their phase is not 0. In laminar flow, where there is a parabolic flow profile across the lumen, a given voxel may contain a range of velocities, each with a different phase. Destructive interference between these components causes a reduction in signal intensity. This effect can be compensated for by using the technique known as *gradient moment nulling* or *rephasing* (GMR), or *flow compensation*. With the use of additional gradient pulses, it can be shown that it is possible to cause all constant velocity spins to rephase at the time of the echo, giving rise to an increased signal. Such sequences are also less sensitive to patient motion.

In the case of turbulent flow, in which the velocities at a given location vary randomly, the spins are still dephased. This can be seen in MRA images of the carotid bifurcation (Anderson 1990). In a normal carotid there is often a reduction of intensity in the internal carotid just superior to the bifurcation. In the case of stenosis an extended region of reduced signal intensity occurs until laminar flow is reestablished.

The appearance of blood in spin-echo imaging (Fig. 3-9*A*) is somewhat different from what it is in gradient-echo imaging (Fig. 3-11*A*) as a result of the use of the slice-selective 180° pulse. Blood that has been excited by the 90° pulse may not be excited by the 180° pulse because it has flowed out of the imaging plane. This effect causes a reduction in the blood signal. This can be referred to as a wash-out or outflow effect. In T_1-weighted imaging, in which the static spins become reduced in intensity by $[1 - \exp(-TR/T_1)]$, there remains the effect of wash-in of fresh spins to the imaging volume; this can partially counteract the above effects. In T_2-weighted imaging, with a much longer TR, the wash-in effect is of little consequence, as static spins are generally not reduced in intensity.

To remove the effects of flow on MR images, three techniques are useful.

1. *ECG or pulse triggering.* Imaging is synchronized with the cardiac cycle so that blood or CSF motion is nearly identical from one phase-encoding step to the next and ghosts are eliminated. The limitation is that one has less control over the TR, which can vary through the image acquisition and is limited to being a multiple of the R-R interval.
2. *Presaturation of blood.* The effect of presaturation (a slice-selective 90° pulse followed by strong gradients

to dephase the transverse magnetization) is to eliminate the signal from the blood. That is, if there is no blood signal, there is no ghost artifact. The elimination of ghosts and the blood signal are shown in Figs. 3-9*B* and 3-11*B*.

3. *Dephasing of moving spins.* This is the opposite of GMR. Instead of choosing the gradient amplitudes to rephase the transverse magnetization of the flowing spins, one deliberately chooses the amplitudes to dephase the magnetization of those spins. This technique is also used in MRA. Rephased and dephased images are acquired and subtracted from one another.

Even Echo Rephasing

There has been much discussion (Axel 1984; Waluch 1984; Katz 1987*a,b*) of the phenomenon known as *even echo rephasing,* which is related to GMR. It has been reported that in some circumstances of spin-echo imaging, the intensity of blood in the second echo of a double echo sequence is greater than it is in the first. It was necessary to have slow flow and for the second echo time to be equal to twice the first. Slow flow, or in-plane flow, is also necessary to avoid the wash-out effect.

The analyses done by Waluch (1984) and Axel (1984) do not represent the actual gradients used in an imaging sequence. Waluch analyzed the case of a constant magnetic field gradient. Axel considered this case as well as two 180° pulses with a slice-selection gradient applied.

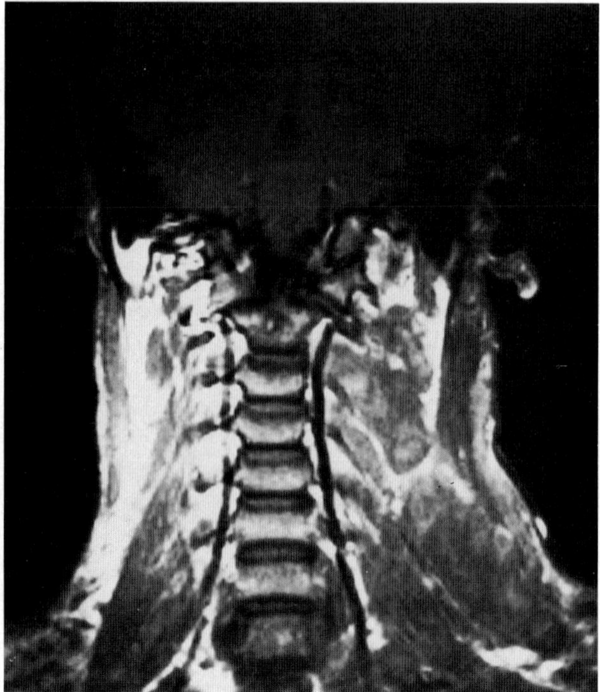

Figure 3-12 Note the outline of the vertebral arteries in this spin-echo image. The blood appears dark because of the effects discussed in this section.

However, imaging is not done with gradients applied constantly, nor is it proper to ignore the gradients applied to the slice-selective 90° pulse. A more complete theoretical analysis of even-echo rephasing has been done by Katz (1987*a,b*) for both constant velocity and pulsatile flow, showing that the conditions under which flow is rephased for the second echo are quite limited. There may be less dephasing in the second echo than in the first, but it does not follow a priori that flow will appear brighter in the second echo than it does in the first. Thus, one should be aware that this phenomenon may occur in some cases, but reduced intensity of blood in spin-echo imaging (Fig. 3-12) versus bright blood in gradient-echo imaging (Fig. 3-11*A*) is generally the rule.

Chemical Shift

The *chemical shift artifact* appears as a displacement of the fat signal along the frequency-encoding direction relative to other tissues. This occurs because the protons in fatty acids have a resonant frequency slightly different from that of protons in the water molecule. This difference is referred to as a chemical shift (Brateman 1986).

In NMR spectroscopy, this effect is represented by including an additional factor σ, which is known as the shielding constant (Harris 1986). It represents the shielding of the nucleus from the magnetic field and replaces the magnetic field B_0 with the effective field $B_0(1 - \sigma)$. When this factor is carried through to Equation (2), the frequency at a given position is changed. When a Fourier transform of the data is performed, this difference in frequency is transformed to a difference in spatial location by $\Delta x = -\sigma B_0/g$. For a given imaging sequence, the appearance of this shift depends on the readout gradient amplitude. As the readout gradient amplitude is proportional to the data-sampling frequency (or bandwidth) divided by the FOV, the shift is more apparent with lower bandwidth sequences. At 1.5 Tesla a chemical shift of 4 ppm corresponds to a frequency shift of about 250 Hz. For imaging parameters of 130 Hz per pixel, this corresponds to a 2-pixel shift.

To reduce the chemical shift artifact, a higher bandwidth sequence can be used. However, some trade-offs must be recognized. Increasing the bandwidth for a fixed TE also reduces the SNR by the square root of the bandwidth. That is, doubling the bandwidth reduces the SNR by $2^{1/2}$.

Two other techniques for reducing the chemical shift artifact are to (1) saturate the fat signal (Szumowski 1989) or (2) use a technique referred to as STIR. The former technique has already been described, but in this case a pulse must be applied which does not simultaneously suppress the water signal. The latter technique is an inversion recovery spin-echo sequence with the inversion time TI adjusted to give a null in the fat signal ($TI = T_{1,fat} \ln 2 = 0.7T_{1,fat} \sim 150$ msec at 1.5T).

Finally, if one works at a lower magnetic field strength, the chemical shift effect can be reduced. As the chemical shift is in ppm, working at 0.5T rather than 1.5T reduces the difference in resonance frequency by three times. However, the SNR is lower at 0.5T, and the choice of the imaging system to be used does not usually depend on the possible presence or absence of this artifact.

Fat/Water Phasing

Fat is known to contain more than one type of proton. The presence of multiple spectral components within the same voxel causes a different appearance of fat and fat/muscle boundaries in gradient-echo imaging and spin-echo imaging (Wehrli 1987). Because of the multiple closely spaced spectral components in fat, the signal from these components goes in and out of phase as a function of time in the manner of a beat frequency. If one acquires a gradient echo at different points in time, the fat intensity varies and does not have a simple monoexponential decay such as $\exp(-T_e/T_2^*)$. At the border of fat and muscle this effect is more pronounced because of the presence of water protons. The use of a spin-echo sequence eliminates the periodic variation in signal intensity with TE because the 180° pulse causes a rephasing of the different frequency components. However, the spatial shift between fat and muscle is still present.

Magnetic Susceptibility

Magnetic susceptibility is a physical property of a material which describes its ability to be magnetized by an external magnetic field. Depending on the magnitude and direction of this effect, materials are generally categorized as paramagnetic, diamagnetic, or ferromagnetic (Lorrain 1970). This property alters the magnetic field present in bone and soft tissue to make it differ from the magnetic field present in air. As these substances have different magnetic susceptibilities, there will be inhomogeneities in the local magnetic field. This effect is most pronounced at boundaries.

In cranial imaging, the effect is greatest at the bone/air interface in sinuses (Fig. 3-13) (Schick 1988). Because the inhomogeneities are static, their effect can be corrected by the 180° pulse present in a spin-echo image. However, in gradient-echo imaging the effect of a gradient in the local magnetic field causes dephasing of the spins (a T_2^* effect) within a voxel, leading to a loss of signal intensity (Czervionke 1988). This effect can be minimized by reducing the echo time and using thinner slices (as in 3D imaging) (Haacke 1989). In the former process, a shorter T_e indicates that the inhomogeneities have less time to play out their effect. In the latter case, thinner slices reduce the effect because MRI techniques are sensitive to the integrated effect over a voxel. However, both techniques may lead to a reduced SNR unless this is compensated for by additional signal averaging, which increases scan time.

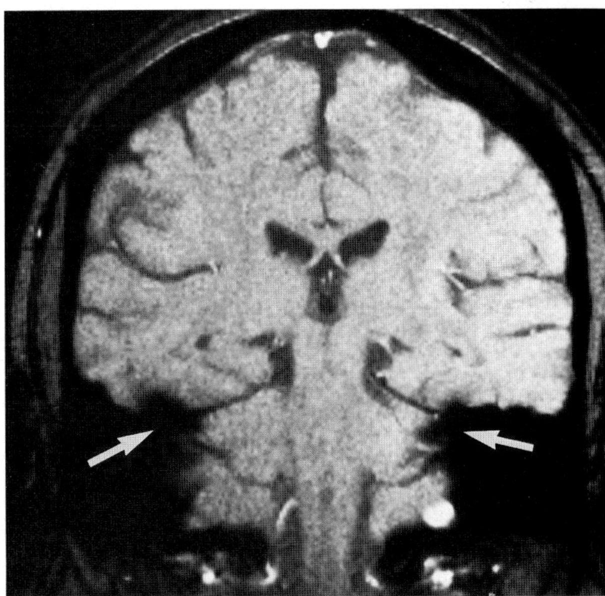

Figure 3-13 Magnetic susceptibility artifacts (arrows) in a gradient-echo image, caused by the bone-air interface.

The presence of foreign metal objects such as dental braces and fillings, aneurysm clips, and surgical staples also gives rise to local magnetic field distortion. If these materials are ferromagnetic, a large distortion in the magnetic field can actually distort the image appearance. This occurs if the local gradient is not negligible compared with the frequency-encoding gradient. This effect is shown in Fig. 3-14, a transverse T_1-weighted image of the cervical spine of a patient with braces.

Transverse Coherence

Transverse coherence is an effect that often causes artifacts in gradient-echo images that are used to give T_1 contrast (Frahm 1987). These artifacts appear as bright bands running along the phase-encoding direction. *Transverse coherence* refers to the presence of residual transverse magnetization from the *i*th RF pulse at the time of the $(i + 1)$th pulse. This occurs if T_2 is not much less than TR. This transverse magnetization affects the steady state that would have been reached by the longitudinal magnetization if the condition $T_2 << TR < T_1$ existed. The $(i + 1)$th pulse rotates the remaining transverse magnetization so that it affects the transverse magnetization during the data-sampling interval and the longitudinal magnetization present for the $(i + 2)$th RF pulse. The appearance of this effect is dependent on the flip angle and TR.

This effect is generally not apparent on multiple-slice gradient-echo images because of the presence of either

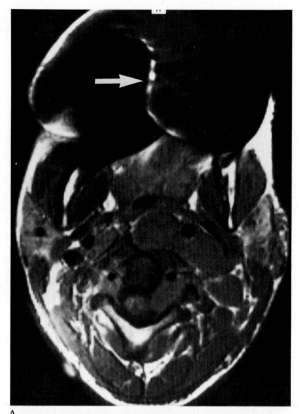

A

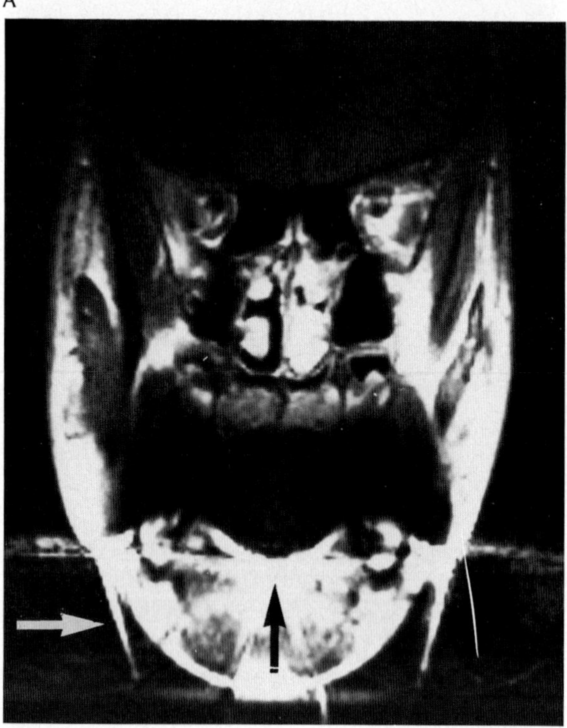

B

Figure 3-14 **A** and **B.** Magnetic susceptibility artifacts (arrows) caused by dental braces.

(1) *rephasing* of the phase-encoding gradient (that is, after data acquisition, a phase-encoding gradient of the opposite sign is applied, leading to a steady state for the transverse magnetization independent of position) or (2) *variable spoiling* (Crawley 1988). In the latter case, the slice-selection gradient is turned on with a great enough amplitude and for a long enough time to effectively disperse the remaining transverse magnetization so that its integrated value over a voxel is equal to zero. Additionally, the gradient strength is usually varied from one phase-encoding step to the next to guarantee that a steady state is not reached. Although the phase-encoding gradient varies in amplitude from pulse to pulse, it does not effectively spoil the transverse magnetization across the image. In fact, it leads to bright bands at predictable locations in the absence of either rephasing or variable spoiling (Wood 1987).

The rephasing technique is often referred to as SSFP (steady state free precession), FISP (fast imaging with steady state precession), or GRASS (gradient recalled acquisition in the steady state). Because a steady state is reached, its contrast is generally not T_1-weighted (Buxton 1987; van der Meulen 1988). In fact, the contrast is determined mainly by T_1/T_2.

The variable spoiling technique, often referred to as FLASH (fast low-angle shot) or spoiled-GRASS, is used for obtaining fast T_1-weighted images with reduced RF power deposition and a good SNR. Although this technique is successful in eliminating the transverse coherence artifact in 2D imaging, the artifact reappears in 3D imaging (Wood 1988). 3D imaging uses two phase-encoding directions. One is the same as in 2D imaging; the second is the slice-selection direction. When they are reconstructed normally, the images have a normal appearance (Fig. 3-15*A*). However, when the 3D data set is used to reconstruct an image in a different plane, the artifactual bands are present (Fig. 3-15*B*). Additional spoiler gradients in different directions do not eliminate this effect. 3D versions of the steady state sequences eliminate this effect, but at the expense of changing the image contrast.

Partial Volume Averaging

Although the MR image appears to be two-dimensional, it is important to realize that it is acquired with a finite thickness. All the information within the excited slice is averaged and contributes to the final image appearance. Thus, a tumor that is only partially contained within a slice will appear to be different from one that spans the slice. This effect is known as *partial volume averaging* and leads to reduced conspicuity within a slice containing a portion of the pathology. To avoid missing pathology as a result of the reduced contrast, it is customary to image the region of interest in more than one orientation (e.g., transversely and sagittally).

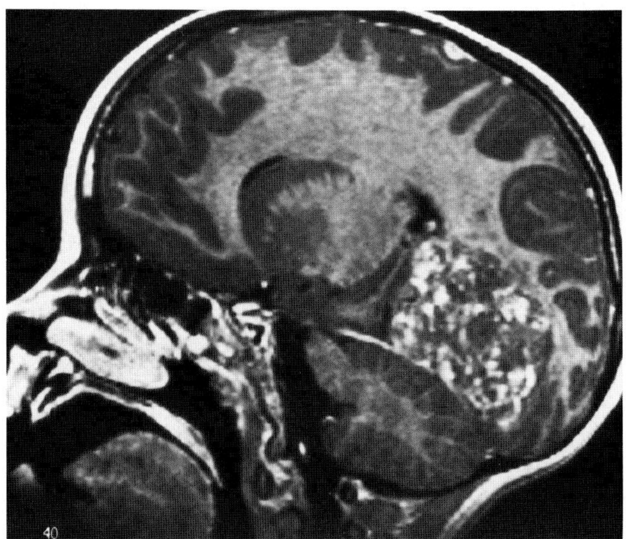

A

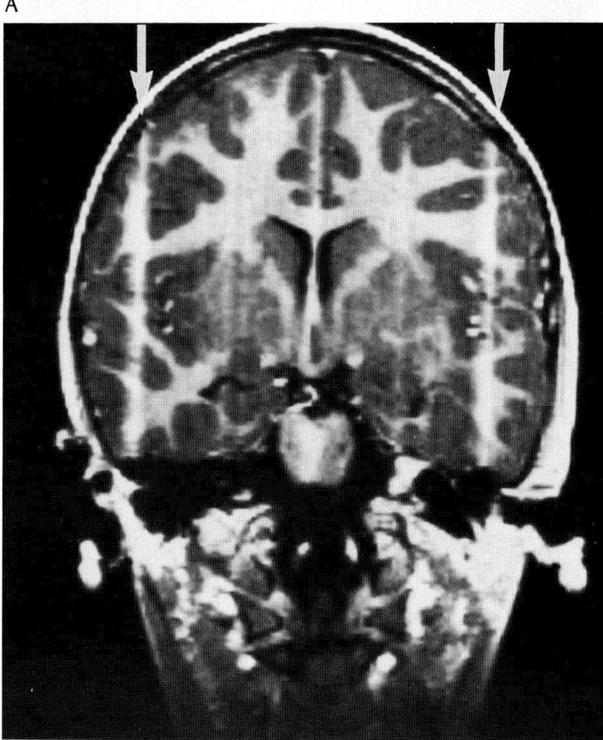

B

Figure 3-15 A 3D FLASH image (TR = 40, TE = 5, 40° flip angle, 1.3-mm effective slice thickness) after the administration of Gd-DTPA. **A.** Image as acquired in the sagittal plane. **B.** Image reformatted for display coronally. Note the artifactual bands caused by transverse coherence (arrows).

Additionally, for those regions, calculations of T_1 or T_2 are inaccurate and give values which lie between the shortest and longest components present.

CONCLUSION

This section has described and presented images of the major artifacts that are present in a properly adjusted clinical MRI unit. These artifacts are caused by limitations in the MRI process, patient motion or physiology, and the physics and chemistry of NMR. The appearance of these artifacts depends on the details of the chosen pulse sequence. In general, if a new artifact appears and persists, one should examine the possibility of a malfunction in the equipment.

MRI is a complex process which requires the proper functioning of many interacting elements to produce detailed images of internal anatomy and pathology. It has had a revolutionary impact on medical diagnosis. However, an understanding of its imperfections is necessary for its proper use.

SECTION B: SAFETY CONSIDERATIONS IN MRI

INTRODUCTION

Although MRI does not require the use of ionizing radiation, it is not totally risk-free. This section will discuss some of the potential risks and safety issues that one must be aware of to avoid the possibility of injuring the patient. One category of risks is due to the interaction of the electromagnetic fields of the MRI system components with the human body and their physicial and biological effects. These fields include the radio frequency (RF) magnetic fields, the static magnetic field, and the magnetic field gradients, all of which are necessary for imaging. A second set of concerns arises from the presence of foreign metallic objects that may be present in the patient's body and can interact with these magnetic fields. These objects may be introduced surgically or through injury. Interactions with these objects can present themselves as a strong attractive force on ferromagnetic materials or as induced electrical currents with concomitant local heating. Other concerns are auditory effects resulting from the pulsing of the magnetic field gradients, psychological effects such as claustrophobia and anxiety caused by the restrictive nature of the imaging procedure and the potential for learning about life-threatening pathology, and the potential risks of scanning pregnant women.

Much of the literature in this field has been extensively reviewed by Shellock and Kanal (Kanal 1990; Shellock 1989, 1991*a,b*). This section will give an overview of the findings. The focus will be on contraindications for MRI and on the concerns that arise in the everyday operation of an MRI center. Issues such as the biological effects of the static magnetic field and rapidly switched magnetic field gradients will not be discussed. For further information on specific topics, the reader should refer to the cited articles and the references contained therein.

INTERACTIONS WITH THE STATIC MAGNETIC FIELD

It is important that all patients be screened for the presence of foreign metallic objects before entering the scan room. Ferromagnetic objects will be subject to an attractive magnetic force that can increase rapidly when approaching the magnet. Such objects can become projectiles, moving with sufficient velocity to cause severe injury to anyone standing in the way. Similar care must be taken to ensure that monitoring equipment, wheelchairs, and stretchers are made of nonmagnetic materials or are excluded from the scan room.

If ferromagnetic objects are present within the patient's body, the patient must not be scanned or even brought near the magnet because of the potential for dislodgement of such objects. Patient histories must include the presence of a pacemaker; foreign objects such as bullets, shrapnel, or other metallic fragments (Teitlebaum, 1990); and any intraocular metallic foreign bodies. Patients with pacemakers should not be scanned. In fact, MRI is contraindicated for any patient with an electrically, magnetically, or mechanically activated implant. Patients with suspected intraocular foreign bodies should have anterior-posterior and lateral radiographs of their orbits to rule out the presence of such fragments (Shellock 1989, 1991*a*). Table 3-1 is a recently published list of metallic implants and materials that have been tested for attractive forces in the presence of different magnetic field strengths (Shellock 1988).

Alterations of electrocardiograph (ECG) patterns are also observed when a patient is placed in the magnet. It is often seen that the T-wave amplitude is increased, although the exact effect is dependent on the actual lead placement. Because of this, proper triggering is sometimes difficult to achieve. This effect increases with increasing magnetic field strength. The physical cause of this effect is the voltage induced by the interaction of the field with a flowing electrolytic substance (blood). The ECG signal returns to normal after the patient has been removed from the magnet. Thus, the alteration in the ECG signal is not believed to have any biological effect.

INTERACTIONS WITH THE RF MAGNETIC FIELD

The detected MR signal arises as a result of resonant absorption of RF energy by the protons in the human body. However, this energy is low and is primarily dissipated as an amount of heat that is of no clinical concern. However, the induced RF electrical currents (according to the laws of physics, a time-varying magnetic field gives rise to an electric field, and hence to currents) can give rise to heating of the patient's tissues because of their resistance to the flow of this current. This is analogous to the heat in a toaster or a light bulb when house current flows through it. These thermal effects are of major concern, and guidelines for acceptable exposure have been set by the U.S. Food and Drug Administration (U.S. FDA 1988). The quantity used to measure this exposure is known as the *specific absorption rate* (SAR). It is the mass normalized rate at which power is absorbed by biological tissues. Its units are watts per kilogram (W/kg), and its calculation is a complex function of the imaging parameters, the RF coil used, and the resistivity and configuration of the anatomic region imaged.

An additional concern is the possibility of burns caused by improper placement of monitoring leads (e.g., ECG and finger pulse monitors). Care should be taken to ensure that leads run directly out of the scanner, with no loops, and the leads should be kept away from the patient's body through careful placement or through the use of insulating material.

THE USE OF MRI IN PREGNANT PATIENTS

No definite association has been demonstrated between static magnetic fields and any deleterious biological effects to date (Kanal 1990). However, the safety of MR imaging during pregnancy has not been established by the FDA (U.S. FDA 1988). MR imaging may be used cautiously in pregnant women after a critical assessment of the relative risks versus the benefits of the examination (Shellock 1991*b*). Complete disclosure of the limited evidence and experience in this area and the patient's consent are required prior to MR imaging.

In Great Britain, the National Radiological Protection Board has specified that "it might be prudent to exclude pregnant women during the first three months of pregnancy" (National Radiological Protection Board 1983).

AUDITORY EFFECTS

The rapidly changing currents in the magnetic field gradient coils interact with the static magnetic field and give rise to acoustic vibrations of the coils. The amplitude and frequency of this noise are dependent on the static magnetic field strength, the imaging sequence repetition time, and the gradient rise time. Three-dimensional sequences, which are usually run with repetition times of less than 50 msec, are particularly noisy. The noise can be particularly annoying to some patients, and there have been reports of possible temporary and permanent hearing loss (Shellock 1991*b*).

The least expensive and easiest method of reducing the acoustic noise is through the use of disposable earplugs. Nonmagnetic headphones that use advances in noise cancellation technology are available at a much higher cost. However, the ability to listen to music may have a relaxing effect on some patients.

Table 3-1 Metallic Implants and Materials Tested for Deflection Forces: A Compilation of the Literature*

Metallic implant or material	Deflection	Highest field strength (T)[a]
Aneurysm and hemostatic clips		
Drake (DR14, DR24) (Edward Weck, Triangle Park, NJ)	Yes	1.44
Drake (DR16) (Edward Weck)	Yes	0.147
Drake (301 SS) (Edward Weck)	Yes	1.5
Downs multipositional (17-7PH)	Yes	1.44
Gastrointestinal anastomosis clip, Auto Suture SGIA (SS) (United States Surgical, Norwalk, CT)	No	1.5
Heifetz (17-7PH) (Edward Weck)	Yes	1.89
Heifetz (Elgiloy) (Edward Weck)	No	1.89
Hemoclip #10 (316L SS) (Edward Weck)	No	1.5
Hemoclip (tantalum) (Edward Weck)	No	1.5
Housepian	Yes	0.147
Kapp (405 SS) (V. Mueller)	Yes	1.89
Kapp curved (404 SS) (V. Mueller)	Yes	1.44
Kapp straight (404 SS) (V. Mueller)	Yes	1.44
Ligaclip #6 (316L SS) (Ethicon, Somerville, NJ)	No	1.5
Ligaclip (tantalum) (Ethicon)	No	1.5
Mayfield (301 SS) (Codman & Shurtleff, Randolph, MA)	Yes	1.5
Mayfield (304 SS) (Codman & Shurtleff)	Yes	1.89
McFadden (301 SS) (Codman & Shurtleff)	Yes	1.5
Olivecrona	No	1.44
Pivot (17-7PH) (V. Mueller)	Yes	1.89
Scoville (EN58J) (Downs Surgical, Decatur, GA)	Yes	1.89
Stevens (50-4190, silver alloy)	No	0.15
Sugita (Elgiloy) (Downs Surgical)	No	1.89
Sundt-Kees (301 SS) (Downs Surgical)	Yes	1.5
Sundt-Kees Multi-Angle (17-7PH) (Downs Surgical)	Yes	1.89
Surgiclip, Auto Suture M-9.5 (SS) (United States Surgical)	No	1.5
Vari-Angle (17-7PH) (Codman & Shurtleff)	Yes	1.89
Vari-Angle McFadden (MP35N) (Codman & Shurtleff)	No	1.89
Vari-Angle Micro (17-7PM SS) (Codman & Shurtleff)	Yes	0.15
Vari-Angle Spring (17-7PM SS) (Codman & Shurtleff)	Yes	0.15
Yasargil (316 SS) (Aesculap)	No	1.89
Yasargil (Phynox) (Aesculap)	No	1.89
Dental materials		
Brace Band (SS) (American Dental, Missoula, MT)	No	1.5
Brace Wire (chrome alloy) (Ormco, San Marcos, CA)	Yes[b]	1.5
Dental amalgam	No	1.44
Silver point (Union Broach, New York, NY)	No	1.5
Permanent crown (amalgam) (Ormco)	No	1.5
Intravascular coils, filters, and stents		
Amplatz IVC filter (Cook, Bloomington, IN)	No	4.7
Cragg nitinol spiral filter	No	4.7
Gianturco embolization coil (Cook)	Yes	1.5
Gianturco bird nest IVC filter (Cook)	Yes	1.5
Gianturco zig-zag stent (Cook)	Yes	1.5

(continued on next page)

Note: Names and locations of manufacturers are given if known. The location is given only once (the first time the manufacturer is mentioned); thereafter, only the name is given. SS = stainless steel; IVC = inferior vena cava.

[a]*Numbers in this column refer to the highest static magnetic field strength [expressed in Tesla (T)] at which the deflection force of an implant or material was evaluated.*

[b]*Considered safe for MR imaging even though it was deflected by the static magnetic fields. Certain prosthetic heart valves, for example, were deflected by the static magnetic fields, but the deflection forces were considered to be less than the force exerted on the valves by the beating heart.*

Source: From Shellock 1988, with permission.

Table 3-1 *(continued)*

METALLIC IMPLANT OR MATERIAL	DEFLECTION	HIGHEST FIELD STRENGTH (T)[a]
Intravascular coils, filters, and stents (*continued*)		
Greenfield vena caval filter (SS) (Medi-tech, Watertown, MA)	Yes[b]	1.5
Greenfield vena caval filter (titanium alloy) (Ormco, Glendora, CA)	No	1.5
Gunther IVC filter (William Cook Europe, Bjaeverskov, Denmark)	Yes	1.5
Maas helical IVC filter (Medinvent, Lausanne, Switzerland)	No	4.7
Maas helical endovascular stent (Medinvent)	No	4.7
Mobin-Uddin IVC/umbrella filter (American Edwards, Santa Ana, CA)	No	4.7
New retrievable IVC filter (Thomas Jefferson University, Philadelphia, PA)	Yes	1.5
Palmaz endovascular stent (Ethicon)	Yes	1.5
Prosthetic ear implants		
Cody tack	No	0.6
Cochlear implant (3M/House)	Yes	0.6
Cochlear implant (3M/Vienna)	Yes	0.6
House-type incus prosthesis	No	0.6
McGee stainless-steel piston	No	0.6
Reuter drain tube	No	0.6
Richards House-type wire loop (Richard's Company, Memphis, TN)	No	1.5
Richards-McGee piston (Richard's)	No	1.5
Richards Plasti-pore with Armstong-style platinum ribbon (Richard's)	No	1.5
Richards-Schuknecht Teflon wire (Richard's)	No	1.5
Richards Trapeze platinum ribbon (Richard's)	No	1.5
Schuknecht Gelfoam and wire prosthesis, Armstrong-style (Richard's)	No	1.5
Shea stainless-steel and Teflon wire prosthesis	No	1.5
Xomed stapes prosthesis, Robinson-style (Richard's)	No	1.5
Prosthetic heart valves		
Beall (Coratomic, Indiana, PA)	Yes[b]	2.35
Bjork-Shiley (convexo/concave) (Shiley, Irvine, CA)	No	1.5
Bjork-Shiley (universal/spherical) (Shiley)	Yes[b]	1.5
Bjork-Shiley, model MBC (Shiley)	Yes[b]	2.35
Bjork-Shiley, model 25 MBRC 11030 (Shiley)	Yes[b]	2.35
Carpentier-Edwards, model 2650 (American Edwards)	Yes[b]	2.35
Carpentier-Edwards (porcine) (American Edwards)	Yes[b]	2.35
Hall-Kaster, model A7700 (Medtronic, Minneapolis, MN)	Yes[b]	1.5
Hancock I (porcine) (Johnson & Johnson, Anaheim, CA)	Yes[b]	1.5
Hancock II (porcine) (Johnson & Johnson)	Yes[b]	1.5
Hancock extracorporeal, model 242R (Johnson & Johnson)	Yes[b]	2.35
Hancock extracorporeal, model M 4365-33 (Johnson & Johnson)	Yes[b]	2.35
Hancock Vascor, model 505 (Johnson & Johnson)	No	2.35
Ionescu-Shiley (Universal ISM)	Yes[b]	2.35
Lillehi-Kaster, model 300S (Medical, Inver Grove Heights, MN)	Yes[b]	2.35
Lillehi-Kaster, model 5009 (Medical)	Yes[b]	2.35
Medtronic-Hall (Medtronic)	Yes[b]	2.35
Medtronic-Hall, model A7700-D-16 (Medtronic)	Yes[b]	2.35
Omnicarbon, model 3523T029 (Medical)	Yes[b]	2.35
Omniscience, model 6522 (Medical)	Yes[b]	2.35
Smeloff-Cutter (Cutter Laboratories, Berkeley, CA)	Yes[b]	2.35
Starr-Edwards, model 1260 (American Edwards)	Yes[b]	2.35

Table 3-1 *(continued)*

METALLIC IMPLANT OR MATERIAL	DEFLECTION	HIGHEST FIELD STRENGTH (T)[a]
Prosthetic heart valves (*continued*)		
Starr-Edwards, model 2320 (American Edwards)	Yes[b]	2.35
Starr-Edwards, model 2400 (American Edwards)	No	1.5
Starr-Edwards, model Pre 6000 (American Edwards)	Yes	1.5
Starr-Edwards, model 6520 (American Edwards)	Yes[b]	2.35
St. Jude (St. Jude Medical, St. Paul, MN)	No	1.5
St. Jude, model A 101 (St. Jude Medical)	Yes[b]	2.35
St. Jude, model M 101 (St. Jude Medical)	Yes[b]	2.35
Orthopedic materials and devices		
AML femoral component, bipolar hip prosthesis (Zimmer, Warsaw, IN)	No	1.5
Harris hip prosthesis (Zimmer)	No	1.5
Jewett nail (Zimmer)	No	1.5
Kirschner intermedullary rod (Kirschner Medical, Timonium, MD)	No	1.5
Stainless-steel plate (Zimmer)	No	1.5
Stainless-steel screw (Zimmer)	No	1.5
Stainless-steel mesh (Zimmer)	No	1.5
Stainless-steel wire (Zimmer)	No	1.5
Penile implants		
Penile implant, AMS Malleable 600 (American Medical Systems, Minnetonka, MN)	No	1.5
Penile implant, AMS 700 CX Inflatable (American Medical Systems)	No	1.5
Penile implant, Flexi-Flate (Surgitek, Medical Engineering, Racine, WI)	No	1.5
Penile implant, Flexi-Rod (standard) (Surgitek, Medical Engineering)	No	1.5
Penile implant, Flexi-Rod II (firm) (Surgitek, Medical Engineering)	No	1.5
Penil implant, Jonas (Dacomed, Minneapolis, MN)	No	1.5
Penile implant, Mentor Flexible (Mentor, Minneapolis, MN)	No	1.5
Penil implant, Mentor Inflatable (Mentor)	No	1.5
Penile implant, OmniPhase (Dacomed)	Yes	1.5
Miscellaneous metallic implants and materials		
Artificial urinary sphincter, AMS 800 (American Medical Systems)	No	1.5
BB's (Daisy)	Yes	1.5
BB's (Crosman)	Yes	1.5
Cerebral ventricular shunt tube connector, Accu-Flow, straight (Codman & Shurtleff)	No	1.5
Cerebral ventricular shunt tube connector, Accu-Flow, right angle (Codman & Shurtleff)	No	1.5
Cerebral ventricular shunt tube connector, Accu-Flow, T-connector (Codman & Shurtleff)	No	1.5
Cerebral ventricular shunt tube connector (type unknown)	Yes	0.147
Contraceptive diaphragm, All Flex (Ortho Pharmaceutical, Raritan, NJ)	Yes[b]	1.5
Contraceptive diaphragm, flat spring (Ortho Pharmaceutical)	Yes[b]	1.5
Contraceptive diaphragm, Koroflex (Young Drug Products, Piscataway, NJ)	Yes[b]	1.5
Forceps (titanium)	No	1.44
Hakim valve and pump	No	1.44
Intraocular lens implant (Binkhorst, iridocapsular lens, platinum-iridium loop)	No	1.0
Intraocular lens implant (Binkhorst, iridocapsular lens, titanium loop)	No	1.0
Intraocular lens implant (Worst, platinum clip lens)	No	1.0
Intrauterine contraceptive device (IUD, Copper T) (Searle Pharmaceuticals, Chicago, IL)	No	1.5
Tantalum powder	No	1.44

PSYCHOLOGICAL EFFECTS

Because of the restrictive nature of the MRI system and the acoustic noise, claustrophobic or anxious patients may be unable to complete an MRI examination. A patient who has not been appropriately briefed on the nature of the examination may be unable or unwilling to be placed into the bore of the magnet. To reduce the incidence of such occurrences it is suggested (1) that patients be allowed to have a friend or relative present in the scan room, (2) that the technologist speak with the patient (through an intercom) after the completion of each scan, (3) that the patient be made as comfortable as possible because of the requirement to lie motionless for extended periods of time, and (4) that relaxation techniques be suggested to the patient. Such techniques could rely on controlled breathing or mental imagery (desensitization technique). Mirrors or a blindfold may help alleviate the feelings of "closed-in" surroundings. Occasionally, short-acting sedation or anesthesia may be required for adequate monitoring and scanning.

CONCLUSIONS

The risks associated with MRI are quite different from those inherent in all other radiological examinations. As this imaging modality has been used for only about 10 years, the long-term risks have not yet been evaluated. The purpose of current guidelines and regulations is to reduce the risks associated with the day-to-day use of MRI. However, the benefits of MRI are shown to be substantial, and new applications are still being developed that set MRI apart from other imaging modalities.

References

ABRAGAM A: *Principles of Nuclear Magnetism,* New York, Oxford University Press, 1961.

ALFIDI RJ, MASARYK TJ, HAACKE EM, et al: MR angiography of peripheral, carotid, and coronary arteries. *AJR* 149:1097, 1987.

ANDERSON CM, SALONER D, TSURUDA JS, et al: Artifacts in maximum-intensity-projection display of MR angiograms. *AJR* 154:623, 1990.

AXEL L: Blood flow effects in magnetic resonance imaging. *AJR* 143:1157, 1984.

AXEL L, SUMMERS RM, KRESSEL HY, et al: Respiratory effects in two-dimensional Fourier transform MR imaging. *Radiology* 160:795, 1986.

BRATEMAN L: Chemical shift imaging: A review. *AJR* 146:971, 1986.

BRIGHAM EO: *The Fast Fourier Transform and Its Applications,* Englewood Cliffs, N.J., Prentice-Hall, 1988.

BUXTON RB, EDELMAN RR, ROSEN BR, et al: Contrast in rapid MR imaging: T1- and T2- weighted imaging. *J Comput Assist Tomogr* 11:7, 1987.

CONNOLLY S, NISHIMURA D, MACOVSKI A: A selective adiabatic spin-echo pulse. *J Magn Reson* 83:324, 1989.

CRAWLEY AP, HENKELMAN RM: A stimulated echo artifact from slice interference in magnetic resonance imaging. *Med Phys* 14:842, 1987.

CRAWLEY AP, WOOD ML, HENKELMAN RM: Elimination of transverse coherences in FLASH MRI. *Magn Reson Med* 8:248, 1988.

CZERVIONKE LF, DANIELS DL, WEHRLI FW, et al: Magnetic susceptibility artifacts in gradient-recalled echo MR imaging. *AJNR* 9:1149, 1988.

EDELMAN RR, ATKINSON DJ, SILVER MS, et al: FRODO pulse sequences: A new means of eliminating motion, flow, and wraparound artifacts. *Radiology* 166:231, 1988.

ERNST RR, ANDERSON WA: Application of Fourier transform spectroscopy to magnetic resonance. *Rev Sci Inst* 37:93, 1966.

FARRAR TC, BECKER ED: *Pulse and Fourier Transform NMR: Introduction to Theory and Methods,* New York, Academic Press, 1971.

FRAHM J, HANICKE W, MERBOLDT K-D: Transverse coherence in rapid FLASH NMR imaging. *J Magn Reson* 72:307, 1987.

HAACKE EM, PATRICK JL: Reducing motion artifacts in two-dimensional Fourier transform imaging. *Magn Reson Imaging* 4:359, 1986.

HAACKE EM, LENZ GW: Improving MR image quality in the presence of motion by using rephasing gradients. *AJR* 148:1251, 1987.

HAACKE EM, TKACH J, PARRISH TB: Reduction of T_2^* dephasing in gradient field-echo imaging. *Radiology* 170:457, 1989.

HANICKE W, MERBOLDT K-D, FRAHM J: Slice selection and T_1 contrast in FLASH NMR imaging. *J Magn Reson* 77:64, 1988.

HARRIS RK: *Nuclear Magnetic Resonance Spectroscopy.* Essex, U.K., Longman, 1986.

HENKELMAN RM, BRONSKILL MJ: Artifacts in magnetic resonance imaging. *Rev Magn Reson Med* 2:1, 1987.

HINSHAW WS, LENT AH: An introduction to NMR imaging: From the Bloch equation to the imaging equation. *Proc IEEE* 71:338, 1983.

HOULT DI: The solution of the Bloch equation in the presence of a varying B1 field—An approach to selective pulse analysis. *J Magn Reson* 35:69, 1979.

JOSEPH PM, AXEL L, O'DONNELL M: Potential problems with selective pulses in NMR imaging systems. *Med Phys* 11:772, 1984.

KANAL, E, SHELLOCK FG, TALAGALA L: Safety considerations in MR imaging. *Radiology* 176:593, 1990.

KATZ J, PESHOCK RM, MALLOY CR: Even-echo rephasing and constant velocity flow. *Magn Reson Med* 4:422, 1987*a*.

KATZ J, PESHOCK RM, MCNAMEE P: Analysis of spin-echo rephasing with pulsatile flow in 2D FT magnetic resonance imaging. *Magn Reson Med* 4:307, 1987*b*.

KUCHARCZYK W, CRAWLEY AP, KELLY WM: Effect of multislice interference on image contrast in T2- and T1- weighted MR images. *AJNR* 9:443, 1988.

LAUTERBUR P: Image formation by induced local interactions: Examples employing nuclear magnetic resonance. *Nature* 242:190, 1973.

LOCHER PR: Computer simulation of selective excitation in NMR imaging. *Philos Trans R Soc Lond* [*Biol*]289:537, 1980.

LORRAIN P, CORSON D: *Electromagnetic Fields and Waves.* San Francisco, W H Freeman, 1970.

NATIONAL RADIOLOGICAL PROTECTION BOARD: Revised guidance on acceptable limits of exposure during nuclear magnetic clinical imaging. *Br J Radiol* 56:974, 1983.

PARKER DL, GULLBERG GT, FREDERICK PR: Gibbs artifact removal in magnetic resonance imaging. *Med Phys* 14:640, 1987.

PAULY J, NISHIMURA D, MACOVSKI A: A linear class of large-tip-angle selective excitation pulses. *J Magn Reson* 82:571, 1989.

RUNGE VM, WOOD ML, KAUFMAN DM, et al: MR imaging section profile optimization: Improved contrast and detection of lesions. *Radiology* 167:831, 1988.

SCHICK RM, WISMER GL, DAVIS KR: Magnetic susceptibility effects secondary to out-of-plane air in fast MR scanning. *AJNR* 9:439, 1988.

SHELLOCK FG: MR imaging of metallic implants and materials: A compilation of the literature. *AJR* 151:811, 1988.

SHELLOCK FG: Biological effects and safety aspects of magnetic resonance imaging. *Mag Reson Quart* 5:243, 1989.

SHELLOCK FG: Bioeffects and safety considerations, in Atlas SW (ed): *Magnetic Resonance Imaging of the Brain and Spine.* New York, Raven Press, 1991*a*, pp 87–107.

SHELLOCK FG, KANAL E: Policies, guidelines, and recommendations for MR imaging safety and patient management. *JMRI* 1:97, 1991*b*.

SILVER MS, JOSEPH RI, HOULT DI: Highly selective $\pi/2$ and π pulse generation. *J Magn Reson* 59:347, 1984.

SZUMOWSKI J, EISEN JK, VINITSKI S., et al: Hybrid methods of chemical shift imaging. *Magn Reson Med* 9:379, 1989.

TEITLEBAUM GP, YEE CA, VANHORN DD, et al: Metallic ballistic fragments: MR imaging safety and artifacts. *Radiology* 175:855, 1990.

THOMAS SR, DIXON RL (eds): *NMR in Medicine: The Instrumentation and Clinical Applications,* New York, AIP, 1986.

TWIEG DB: The k-trajectory formulation of the NMR imaging process with applications in analysis and synthesis of imaging methods. *Med Phys* 10:610, 1983.

U.S. FOOD AND DRUG ADMINISTRATION: Magnetic resonance diagnostic device: Panel recommendation and report on petitions for MR reclassification. *Federal Register* 53:7575, 1988.

VAN DER MEULEN P, GROEN JP, TINUS AMC, et al: Fast field echo imaging: An overview and contrast calculations. *Magn Reson Imaging* 6:355, 1988.

WALUCH V, BRADLEY WG: NMR even echo rephasing in slow laminar flow. *J Comput Assist Tomogr* 8:594, 1984.

WEHRLI FW, PERKINS TG, SHIMAKAWA A, et al: Chemical shift-induced amplitude modulations in images obtained with gradient refocussing. *Magn Reson Imaging* 5:157, 1987.

WOOD ML, HENKELMAN RM: Suppression of respiratory motion artifacts in magnetic resonance imaging. *Med Phys* 13:794, 1986.

WOOD ML, SILVER M, RUNGE VM: Optimization of spoiler gradients in FLASH MRI. *Magn Reson Imaging* 5:455, 1987.

WOOD ML, RUNGE VM: Artifacts due to residual magnetization in three-dimensional magnetic resonance imaging. *Med Phys* 15:825, 1988.

4 NORMAL ANATOMY

Krishna C. V. G. Rao

The anatomy of the head is evaluated on CT and MR by means of cross-sectional images. In CT these images are obtained in the axial plane, whereas in MR they can be obtained in any plane, although they are often viewed in the axial, sagittal, and coronal planes. This chapter deals with the components of the cranial vault when viewed in axial sections in both CT and MRI. Images in the coronal and sagittal planes are utilized where necessary to demonstrate an anatomic feature and its connecting link within the different components of the brain. On MRI both the morphological and, to a certain extent, the gross histology of the brain tissue can be evaluated. This is based on the relaxation parameters of the different tissues. This is achieved by viewing T_1WI (short TR/TE). T_2-WI consists of either long TR/short TE (spin-density-weighted, proton-density-weighted or balanced images) or long TR/long TE (pronounced T_2 effect). Although angiography is the ideal imaging modality for evaluating the vascular anatomy, the major cerebral arteries can be demonstrated on MRI and contrast-enhanced computed tomography (CECT). This provides a basis for establishing the regional distribution of the major vascular branches even though the actual branch vessels cannot be demonstrated. This information is also necessary when one is evaluating CT or MR in regard to occlusive vascular disease.

THE CRANIAL CAVITY

The cranial contents are enclosed within the cranial vault in a confined space. The vault is connected to the axial skeleton at the base of the cranium. The cranial contents exit or enter the vault through numerous foramina. The largest of these foramina is the foramen magnum, through which the hindbrain continues as the spinal cord. The skull base is best evaluated with CT in scan sections parallel to the skull base. Some of the neural foramina also can be evaluated with axial or coronal MR sections (Fig. 4-1).

The Dural Attachments

The inner table of the cranial vault and base is covered by the outer layer of the meninges, the dura mater. The dura is firmly attached to the inner table of the skull, except at the foraminal openings. The inner layer of the dura forms folds within the cranial vault. The two major folds of the dura, which separates the different components of the brain parenchyma, are the tentorium and the falx cerebri. These dural folds also provide protection to brain parenchyma as well as the large venous sinuses, which are located within the margins or attachment of these folds.

The *tentorium cerebelli* (Fig. 4-2) is a dural partition that overlies the superior surface of the cerebellum and separates it from the inferior surfaces of the cerebral hemispheres. The free margin of the tentorium has a U-shaped configuration, with the margins at each end attached to the posterior clinoid, the anterior clinoid, and the petrous apex, respectively. The resulting dural folds form small triangular shelves for the passage of the second to sixth cranial nerves in a portion of their exit through the skull base. The tentorium is kept taut and elevated by its attachment in the midline with the posterior part of the other dural fold, the falx cerebri.

The *falx cerebri* (Fig. 4-2) separates the two halves of the cerebral hemisphere. It is a midline sheet of dura that lies in the interhemispheric fissure. Anteriorly, the falx cerebri is attached to the bony spur and the midline surface of the cribriform plate of the frontal bone. Posteriorly, it is continuous with the dural fold of the tentorium. The straight venous sinus runs in the midline between the posterior attachment of the falx cerebri and the tentorium cerebelli. The free margin of the dural fold between its anterior and posterior attachments lies above the corpus callosum. The falx cerebri and tentorium cerebelli are best identified on CECT and MRI in the coronal plane.

With aging, calcification within the dural folds, especially at the sites of attachment to the calvarium, is not

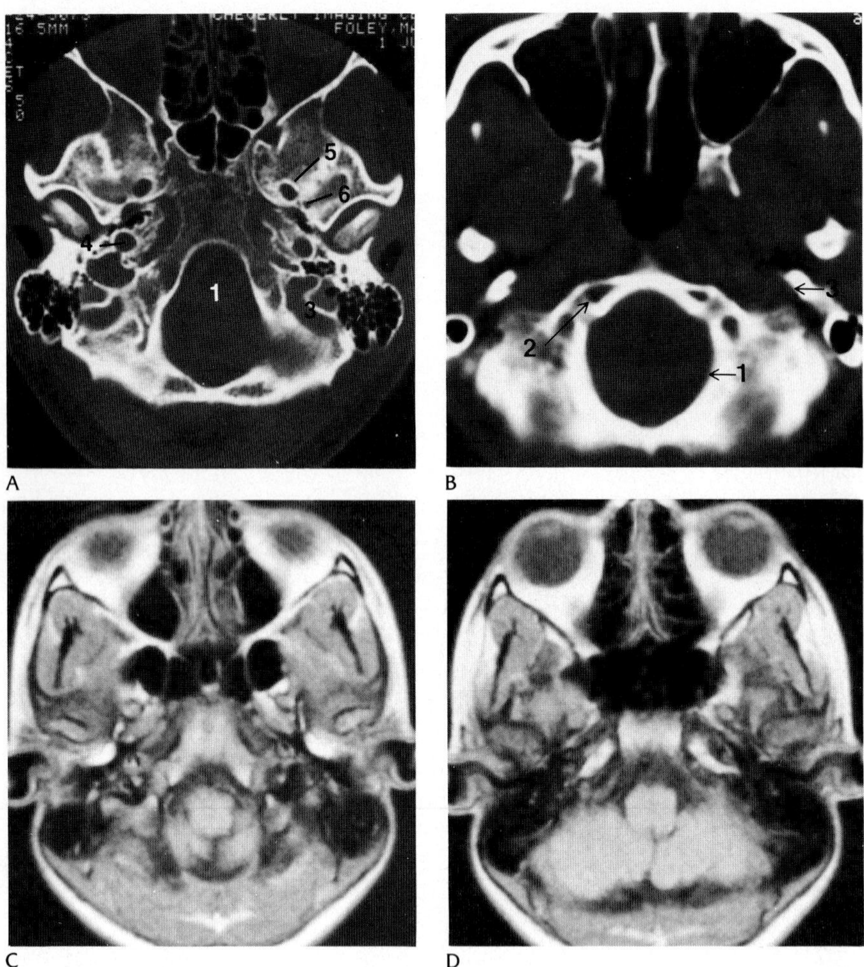

Figure 4-1 Neurovascular foramina of the skull base: axial CT (**A, B**) and axial MR (**C, D**) 1 = foramen magnum; 2 = hypoglossal canal; 3 = jugular foramen; 4 = foramen lacerum; 5 = foramen ovale, 6 = foramen spinosum.

unusual. Similar calcification also can be seen within the surface of the tentorium as well as within the falx.

THE CRANIAL CONTENTS

Within the confines of the cranium are the brain parenchyma, the cranial nerves, and the vascular structures surrounded by the cerebrospinal fluid (CSF).

The CSF Spaces

The CSF spaces consist of the ventricles within the brain parenchyma and the subarachnoid cisterns and sulci surrounding the brain. The CSF is produced within the ventricles by the choroid plexus. The largest volume of the choroid plexus is within the lateral ventricles and to a lesser extent within the third and fourth ventricles. The choroid plexuses lie along the ependymal surface and surround the major choroidal arteries. The glomera of the choroid plexus within the atrium of the lateral ventricle and occasionally within the fourth ventricle are seen as tissue hypodensity on CT. The size of the glomera varies between 3 and 22 mm (Hinshaw 1988). The size of the glomera and choroid plexuses generally is larger in infants, compared with their brain volume. On CECT there is homogeneous enhancement of the choroid plexuses. Heterogeneous enhancement with focal areas of hypodensity usually is secondary to small cysts or results from the deposition of lipid material. Asymmetry in the size of the glomera or in the extent of their calcification between the choroid plexuses of the two lateral ventricles is not uncommon (Fig. 4-3).

On MR, the glomera of the choroid plexus are hypointense as a result of their vascularity or the presence of calcium deposits. In T_2WI the glomera has variable signal intensity between low and bright signal components. The heterogeneous appearance in T_2WI is due to the flow void signal as well as cysts, lipid material, and calcification (Fig. 4-3).

Mild variation in the size of the ventricles or the subarachnoid cisterns and sulci within the same age group and sex is a common finding. The communication between the ventricles as well as that between the fourth

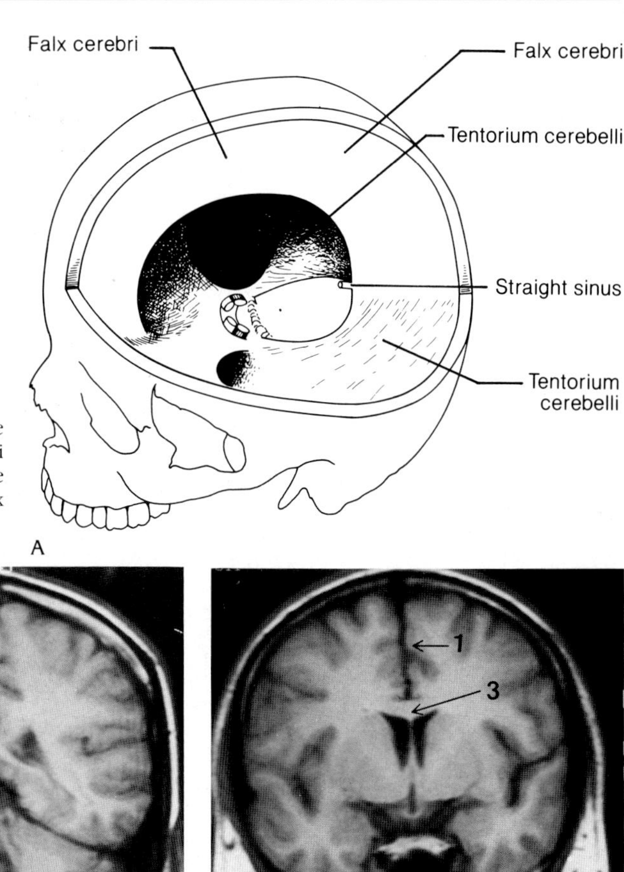

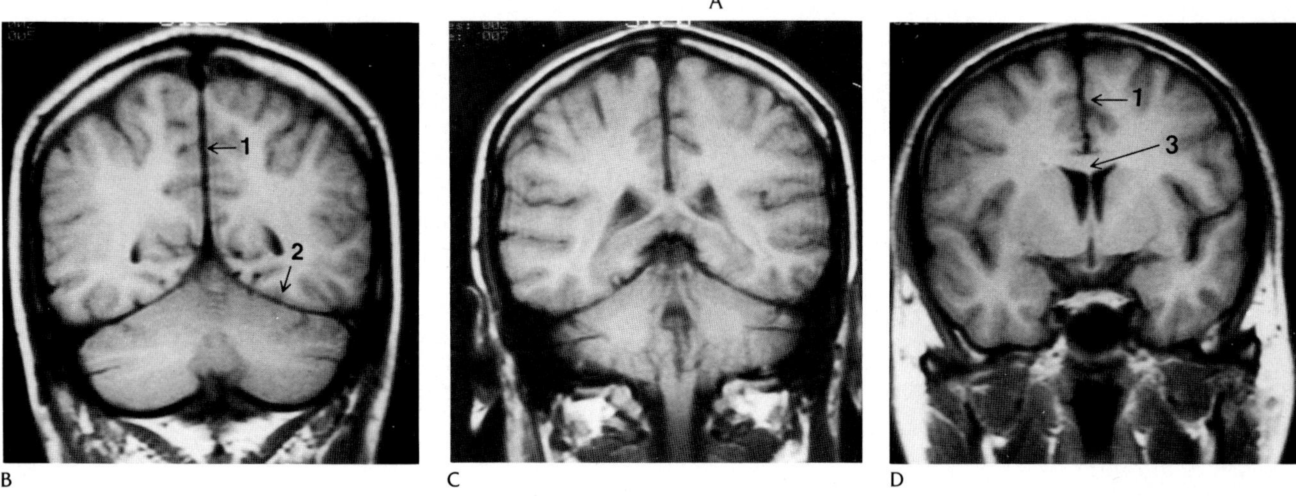

Figure 4-2 **A.** Superior lateral view of the cranium. The left half of the cranial vault has been removed to show the attachment of the falx cerebri and the tentorium cerebelli. **B–D.** Coronal MR sections demonstrating the dural folds separating the cerebral and cerebellar hemispheres. 1 = falx cerebri; 2 = tentorium cerebelli; 3 = corpus collosum.

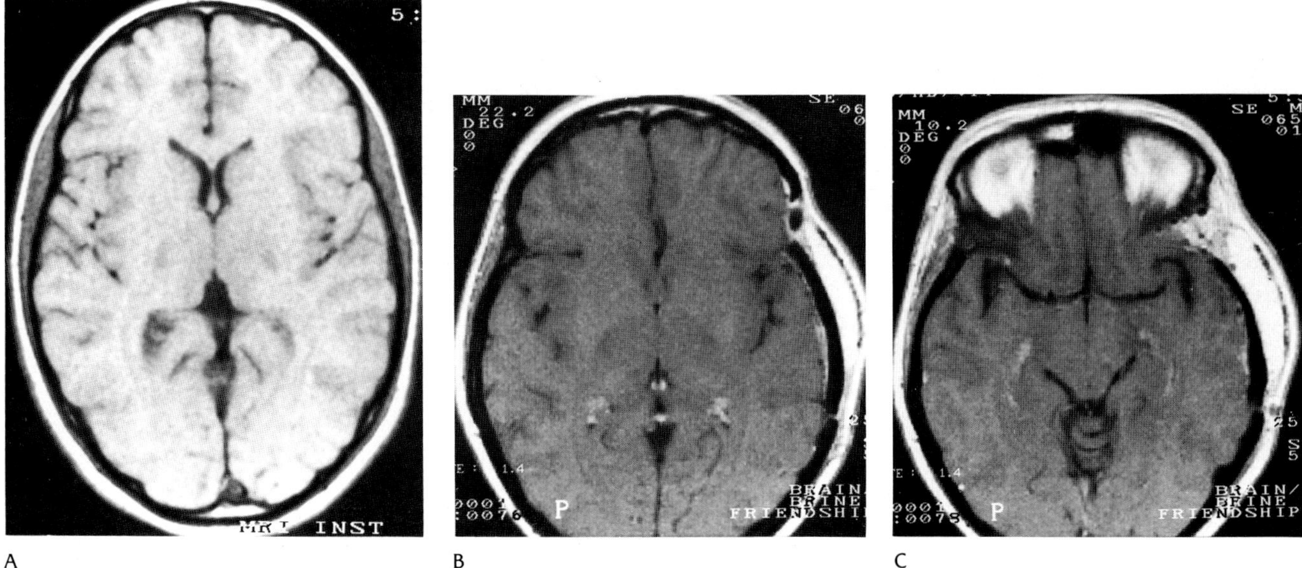

Figure 4-3 **A.** Noncontrast T_1WI MR. **B, C.** Contrast-enhanced axial MR section. The choroid plexus has a heterogeneous signal better evaluated on contrast studies.

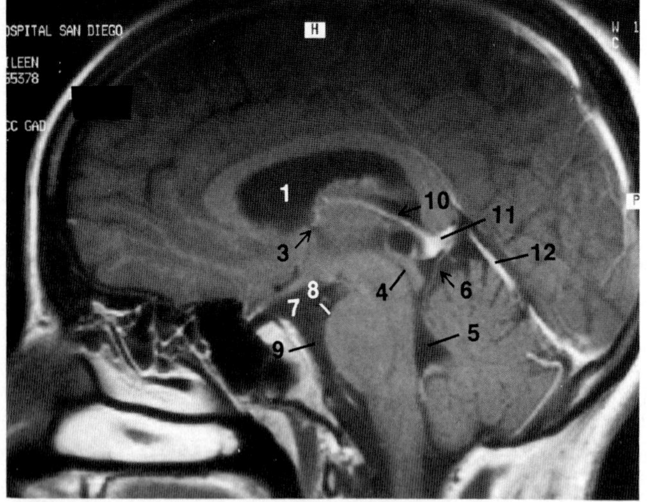

A

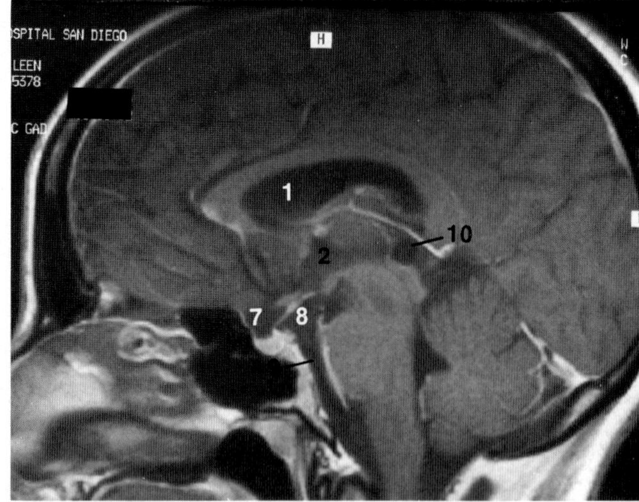

B

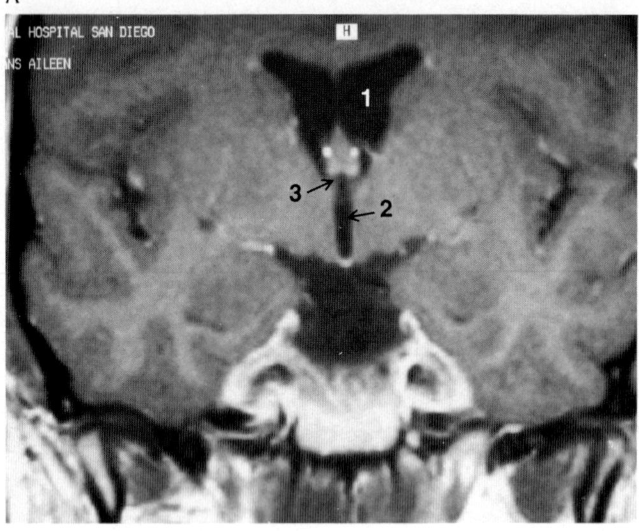

C

Figure 4-4 The CSF spaces. Contrast-enhanced MR. Parasagittal (**A**), midsagittal (**B**), and coronal (**C**) sections demonstrating the communication between the ventricular and subarachnoid CSF spaces. 1 = lateral ventricle; 2 = third ventricle; 3 = foramen of Monro; 4 = aqueduct of Sylvius; 5 = fourth ventricle; 6 = superior cerebellar cistern; 7 = suprasellar cistern; 8 = interpeduncular cistern; 9 = prepontine cistern; 10 = internal cerebral vein; 11 = vein of Galen; 12 = straight sinus.

ventricle and the medullary cistern can be identified in both high-resolution CT and MRI, utilizing the appropriate sections and orthogonal planes (Fig. 4-4). Sagittal and coronal T_1-weighted MRI provides an accurate assessment of the ventricular size and shape and any anomalies of the corpus callosum (Atlas 1986). The midsagittal section is particularly useful in evaluating the shape and configuration of the aqueduct (Fig. 4-4) (Kemp 1987).

The CSF within both the ventricles and the subarachnoid space is in constant motion. On MRI, its signal characteristics depend on several factors, including (1) the image acquisition time (TR/TE), (2) the relaxation time of the CSF and its constituents, and (3) physiological flow factors (Chap. 7). The CSF is hypointense on T_1WI and hyperintense on T_2WI. In long narrow sections of the ventricular system, such as the aqueduct of Sylvius, in addition to the above factors, turbulence is created at the orifice of the aqueduct. Thus, with longer acquisition time, loss of the normal CSF signal is common. This has been termed the *CSF or aqueductal flow void sign* (Bradley 1986; Sherman 1986). This is often seen in the first echo of a long TR sequence (SE 2000/30) (Fig. 4-5). When evaluating MRI in long TR sequences, one must be aware of several flow-related artifacts in the CSF spaces (Chap. 3). These include a bright signal in the periaqueductal region caused by flow-related enhancement in the first slice during volume acquisition (FRE) (Enzmann 1986) and pseudoaneurysms resulting from radial pulsation of large vessels within the CSF space (Burt 1987).

On CT, the CSF is hypodense, a state that is not affected by its motion. The CSF attenuation value is dependent on its protein content.

The cranial nerves and the major vascular channels lie within the subarachnoid spaces, surrounded by CSF. The location of the neurovascular structures in the CSF cisterns is identified in Table 4-1.

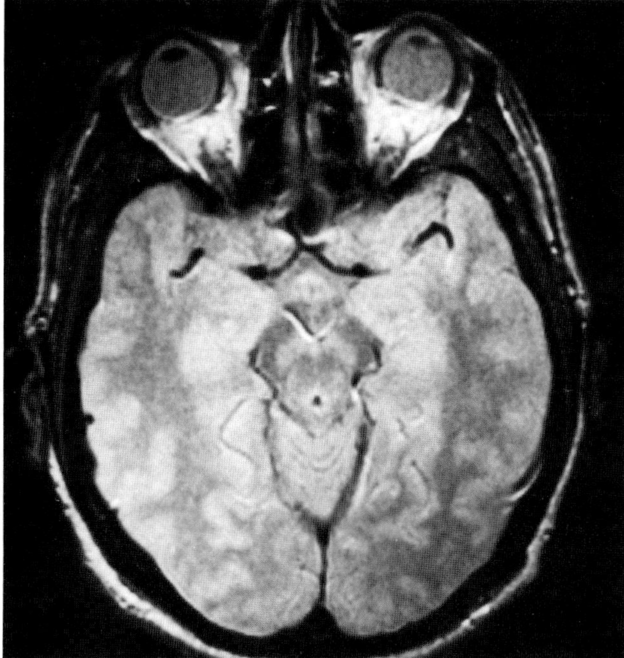

A

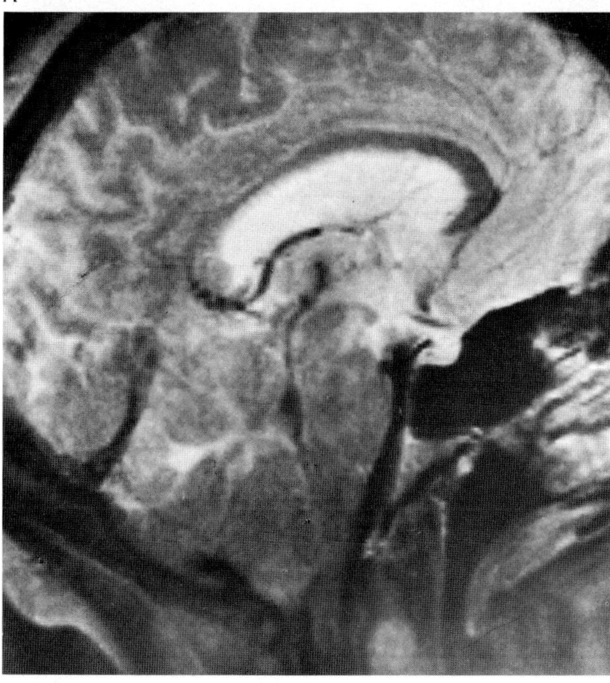

B

Figure 4-5 CSF flow void signal (CFVS). Axial (**A**) and sagittal (**B**) MR (SE 2000/40) demonstrating the normal flow void signal within the aqueduct of Sylvius (arrowhead).

Table 4-1 Contents of the Cisternal Spaces

CRANIAL COMPARTMENT	CISTERN	CONTENTS
Anterior fossa	Olfactory sulcus	Olfactory bulb and tract
Middle fossa	Suprasellar cistern	Optic nerve, chiasm, and tract Pituitary stalk Internal carotid arteries Origin of middle and anterior cerebral artery Posterior communicating artery
	Parasellar and sylvian cistern	Middle cerebral artery Meckel's cave Trigeminal nerve
Posterior fossa	Interpeduncular cistern	Oculomotor nerve Basilar artery Posterior cerebral artery Superior cerebellar artery
	Mesencephalic cistern	Choroidal arteries Basal vein of Rosenthal Trochlear nerve Abducens nerve
	Cerebellopontine angle cistern	Facial nerve Acoustic nerve
	Medullary cistern	Vertebral artery Glossopharyngeal nerve Vagus nerve Hypoglossal nerve

The Vascular Anatomy

CECT provides some information relating to the intracranial vascular anatomy. This is achieved because of the presence of iodinated contrast within the larger intracranial vessels. Similar evaluation can also be achieved on MRI but does not require the use of paramagnetic contrast. Since flowing blood results in loss of signal (Bradley 1985), this phenomenon is utilized to evaluate the vascular anatomy on spin-density-weighted MRI. Greater clarity and evaluation of normal vascular anatomy can be achieved on MR with special sequences (GRE, or gradient refocused echo) or MRA (magnetic resonance angiography).

The intracranial arterial supply is provided by the two internal carotid arteries and the vertebrobasilar artery.

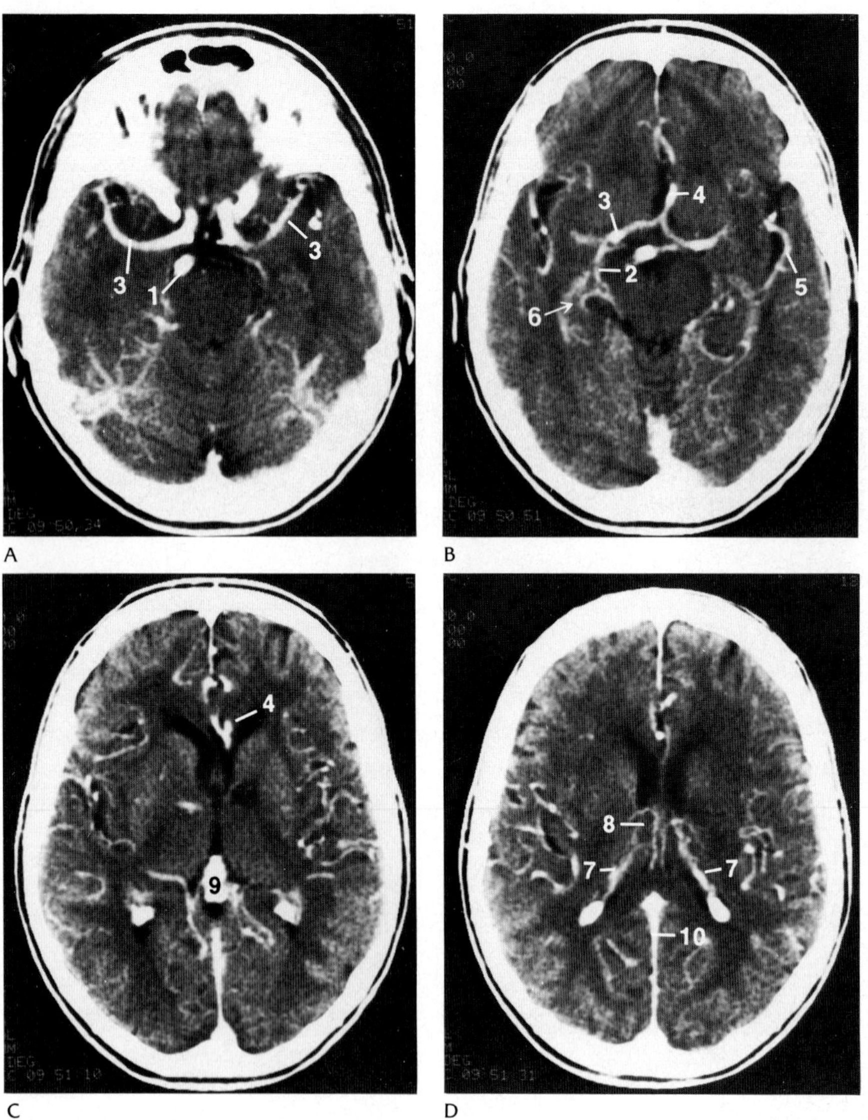

Figure 4-6 Contrast-enhanced CT demonstrating the vascular anatomy at the prepontine (**A**), interpeduncular (**B**), third ventricle (**C**), and lateral ventricle (**D**) levels. 1 = basilar artery; 2 = posterior cerebral artery; 3 = middle cerebral artery; 4 = anterior cerebral artery; 5 = middle cerebral branches; 6 = choroidal fissure; 7 = choroid plexus; 8 = internal cerebral vein; 9 = vein of Galen; 10 = straight venous sinus.

Within the cerebral hemispheres these arteries provide two types of branches: striate branches and cortical branches. The striate branches are end arteries that supply the diencephalic structures and some portions of the telencephalon. The cortical branches supply the cerebral and cerebellar hemispheres and the underlying white matter tracts. The internal carotid artery on each side pierces the dura to enter the subarachnoid space adjacent to the anterior clinoid process (Figs. 4-6 and 4-7). There is a short supraclinoid segment of the internal carotid artery. The posterior communicating artery and the anterior choroidal artery are the major branches of the supraclinoid segment of the internal carotid artery. They course posteriorly in the mesencephalic and suprasellar cisterns, respectively. The anterior choroidal artery supplies the choroid plexus of the lateral ventricles, the medial temporal pole, and some striate branches. The posterior communicating artery anastomoses with the posterior cerebral artery to form the posterior part of the circle of Willis. It gives rise to numerous striate branches that supply the deep ganglionic structures, including the thalamus. The internal carotid artery on each side bifurcates into the middle cerebral and anterior cerebral arteries. The two anterior cerebral arteries proceed medially to enter the interhemispheric fissure. Before the artery enters the fissure, a few striate branches (artery of Huebner) supply the anterior medial portions of the basal ganglia and the anterior commissure. Within the interhemispheric fissure, the anterior cerebral artery branches to supply the medial and superior surfaces of the individual cerebral hemispheres. They are separated from each other by the falx cerebri.

The two anterior cerebral arteries are connected to each other before they enter the interhemispheric fissure by the anterior communicating artery.

The middle cerebral arteries on each side are the largest cerebral vessels (Figs. 4-6 and 4-7). They run laterally in the subarachnoid space to enter the sylvian cistern.

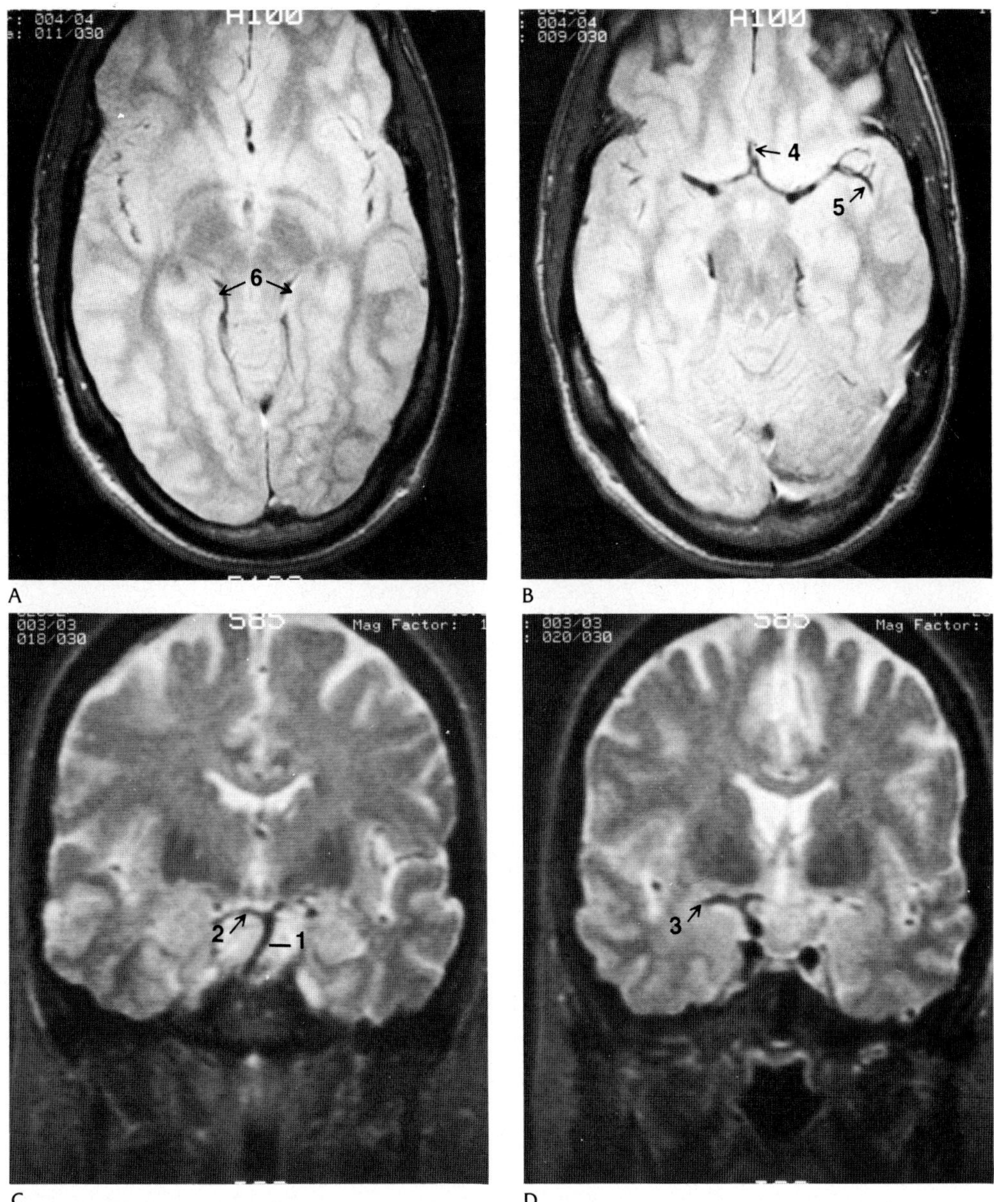

Figure 4-7 Axial (**A, B**) and coronal (**B, C**) T_2-weighted MR (SE 2500/40) demonstrating the vascular structures. 1 = anterior cerebral artery; 2 = middle cerebral artery; 3 = posterior cerebral artery; 4 = basilar artery; 5 = internal carotid artery; 6 = middle cerebral branches.

Before entering the cistern, five to six small striate arteries supply the basal ganglia. They enter through the anterior perforated substance. Although the striate arteries may not be seen on CT and MR, their locations or entry zones are identified on T_2WI as focal areas of bright signal intensity adjacent to the anterior commissure (Fig. 4-7). Within the cistern, the middle cerebral arteries on either side bifurcate or trifurcate. These branches further divide into named branches which supply the brain parenchyma forming the temporal lobe, the parietal lobe, and variable portions of the frontal and occipital lobes as well as the deeper portions of the brain parenchyma through the insular branches. These branches can be seen end-on on axial CT and MR sections and along part of their course on sagittal and coronal MRI (Figs. 4-6 and 4-7).

Similarly to the carotid arteries, the vertebral arteries on each side enter the cranial vault through the foramen magnum. Within the cranial vault, after giving rise to one major intracranial branch—the posterior inferior cerebellar artery—the two vertebral arteries join to form the basilar artery. This artery runs cephalad in the prepontine cistern of the subarachnoid space to terminate at the level of the interpeduncular cistern by dividing into the posterior cerebral arteries. These arteries proceed posterolaterally in the circummesencephalic cistern and give

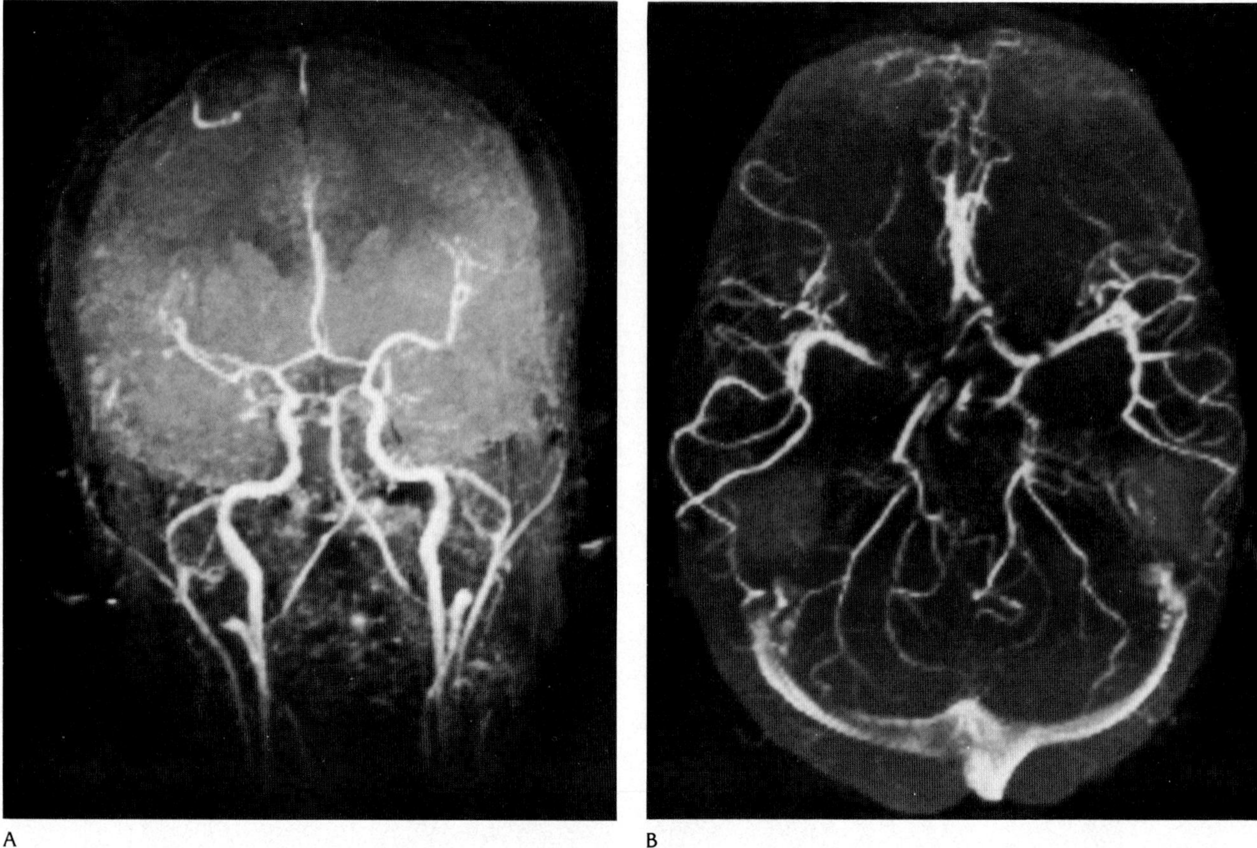

Figure 4-8 MR angiography. Coronal (**A**) and axial (**B**) planes demonstrating most of the major intracranial vasculature without the use of contrast. (*Courtesy of Seimens Medical.*)

off branches to the occipital lobe, portions of the temporal lobe, and the choroid plexuses within the roof of the third ventricle (medial posterior choroidal arteries) and the choroid plexuses within the two lateral ventricles (lateral posterior choroidal arteries). The choroidal fissure demarcates the site of entry of these arteries (Figs. 4-6 and 4-7).

In the interpeduncular cistern, the posterior cerebral artery on each side supplies the thalamus through numerous branches (thalamo-perforating arteries) that are similar to the striate branches of the middle cerebral arteries.

The communicating channels between the two anterior cerebral arteries as well as between the internal carotid and posterior cerebral arteries form the *circle of Willis,* which is located in the suprasellar cistern.

The intracranial vasculature is demonstrated as sectional images on both CECT and gradient-echo MRI. Recent technological advances in MR allow visualization of intracranial vasculature that is similar to that provided by angiography (Fig. 4-8).

The vascular distribution within the brain parenchyma is well defined. Collateral channels provide anastomoses at the border zones of the major vascular territories. These vascular territories and the border zones have been described in CT sectional anatomy (Hayman 1981; Berman 1980, 1984) (Fig. 4-29). This can be done equally well with MRI.

The venous system consists of the deep and superficial (cortical) veins which drain into the major dural venous sinuses. The dural venous sinuses can be identified on CECT and MRI. However, only a few of the recognized deep veins can be demonstrated on both CECT and MRI (Fig. 4-8).

When evaluating the vascular anatomy on MRI, one must be aware of flow-related artifacts, especially in long TR sequences (SE 2000/30) (Chap. 3).

The Cranial Nerves

Identification and anatomic localization of the cranial nerves are useful in evaluating imaging studies. On CT, except for the optic nerve, the cranial nerves are difficult to image. The neural foramina can be demonstrated in many instances in both coronal and axial planes (Fig. 4-1). With MRI, it is possible in many instances to identify the cisternal segment of the cranial nerves. The cranial nerves are seen best on T_1WI. The foraminal or extracranial segment of the nerve can be better appreciated on MRI after paramagnetic contrast (Barakos 1991).

There are 12 pairs of cranial nerves. They contain the motor, sensory, and special sensory fibers that serve the region of the head, face, and the upper part of the neck in addition to the senses of smell, vision, hearing, taste, and balance. The first and second cranial nerves carry special sensory fibers to the brain. The fifth, seventh, eighth, and ninth cranial nerves are mixed, having both motor and sensory components, whereas the third, fourth, sixth, tenth, eleventh, and twelfth cranial nerves are purely motor in function. Except for the intraorbital segment of the optic nerve, the remaining cranial nerves are not usually visualized on CT. On MR, utilizing an appropriate section thickness and orthogonal orientation, the intracranial cisternal segments of most of the cranial nerves can be identified, except that of the trochlear (CN4) nerve. The ninth, tenth, and eleventh cranial nerves are seen only as a common bundle rather than individually.

The *olfactory nerve* (first cranial nerve) is a special sensory nerve associated with the sense of smell and is the only cranial nerve that is not myelinated. Numerous fibers from the nasal mucosa penetrate through the cribriform plate to end in the paddle-shaped olfactory bulb. The olfactory tract runs posteriorly along the undersurface of the frontal lobes and divides above the anterior clinoid process and in front of the anterior perforated substance to form the medial and lateral stria, which end in the medial temporal lobe adjacent to the anterior perforated substance and the amygdaloid nuclei, respectively.

As a result of the location of the olfactory bulb and tract between the cribriform plate and the inferior surface of the frontal lobe, it is difficult to visualize these structures consistently on imaging studies.

The bulb and the tract have been shown on MR studies (Suzuki 1989). The bulb is best seen on sagittal and coronal T_1WI. More often the olfactory bulb can be visualized when there is an increase in CSF space, as is seen in atrophy of the frontal lobe (Fig. 4-9).

The *optic nerve* (second cranial nerve) is a special sensory nerve associated with the visual pathway. For imaging purposes it can be divided into the orbital segment, the cisternal segment, and the parenchymal segment.

The intraorbital segment originates from the optic disk within the globe, which emerges along the posterior, superior, and medial aspects of the globe, along with its meningeal sheath, to proceed to the apex of the orbit. It exits the orbit after passing through the optic canal.

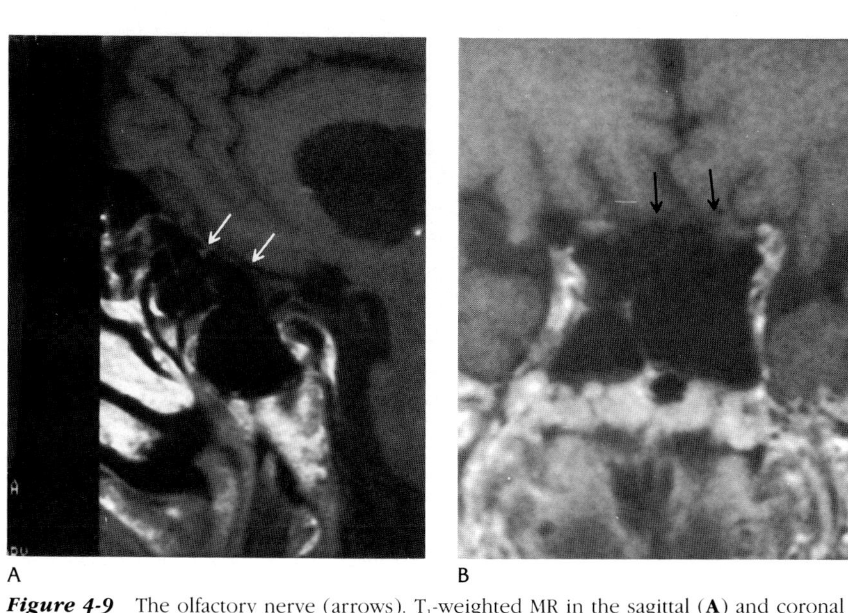

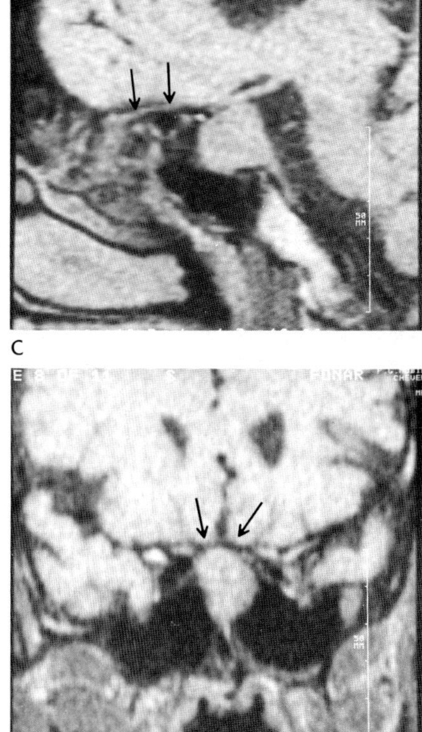

Figure 4-9 The olfactory nerve (arrows). T_1-weighted MR in the sagittal (**A**) and coronal (**B**) planes. Sagittal (**C**) and coronal (**D**) MR in another patient with frontal lobe atrophy demonstrating the nerve adjacent to the gyrus rectus.

Within the cranium, the optic nerve runs for a short distance within the suprasellar cistern in a superior and medial direction to decussate with the opposite optic nerve within the optic chiasm. The nerve continues posterolaterally as the optic tract. Within the brain the visual fibers enter the lateral geniculate body. From the geniculate body the visual fibers diverge in a fan-shaped pattern—the optic radiation—which eventually ends in the visual center located in the occipital lobe.

The intraorbital segment can be well visualized on both CT and MR when an appropriate section thickness and the correct pulse sequences, respectively, are utilized (Hilal 1977; Daniels 1984) (Chap. 5).

The intracanalicular and cisternal segments can often be visualized on CT but are always ideally visualized in MR studies, especially in the axial and sagittal planes, because the surrounding CSF provides contrast (Fig. 4-10). The optic chiasm is well visualized in coronal and axial views. On MR in T_1WI, the chiasm is isointense with the rest of the brain parenchyma. In the majority of cases the pituitary stalk and infundibulum are located behind the optic chiasm, although in about 10 percent of studies they may be situated anterior to the chiasm.

The anterior third of the optic tract runs lateral to the cerebral peduncles. The optic tracts are seen on MR in axial and coronal T_1WI. The optic radiation fibers are myelinated and merge with the white matter tracts in adults; however, during the process of myelination, this can be identified on MR in infants below the age of 12 months as a hyperintense signal on T_1WI (Fig. 4-32).

The *oculomotor* (third cranial nerve), *trochlear* (fourth cranial nerve), and *abducens* (sixth cranial nerve) are the nerves which innervate the extraocular muscles of the eye. The trochlear nerve innervates the superior oblique muscle, and the abducens innervates the lateral rectus muscle; the remaining extraocular muscles are innervated by the oculomotor nerve.

All three of these nerves are difficult to identify on CT, except in the intracavernous segment. On MRI, the cisternal segment of the third cranial nerve can be identified in most instances in the axial plane and occasionally in the sagittal and coronal planes (Fig. 4-11). In coronal sections the nerve is situated between the posterior cerebral and superior cerebellar arteries.

Because of the thin nerve bundle, the trochlear nerve is difficult to demonstrate. The abducens nerve can often be identified in the sagittal section in the mesencephalic cistern between the anterior belly of the pons and the posterolateral aspect of the dorsum sellae (Fig. 4-12). MR imaging in the evaluation of dysfunction in these cranial nerves has been described (Braffman 1987).

The *trigeminal nerve* (fifth cranial nerve) is associated with motor, sensory, and proprioceptive functions. Its sensory fibers innervate the scalp and face and the mucous membrane of the sinuses, nasal cavity, and mouth.

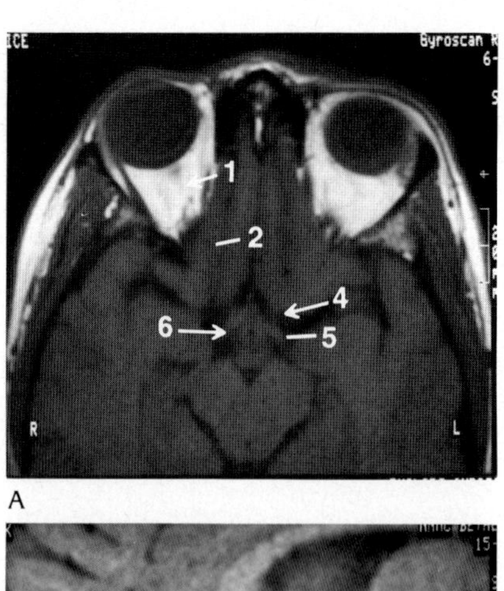

A

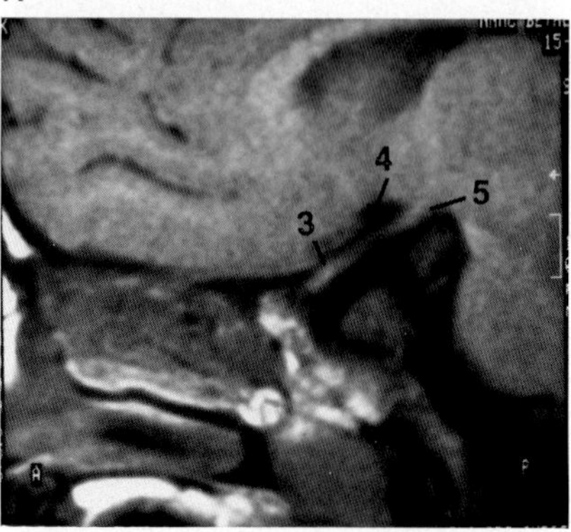

B

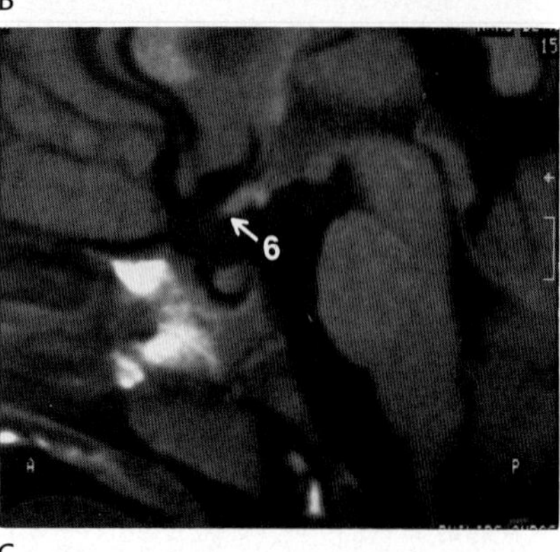

C

Figure 4-10 The optic nerve. Axial (**A**), sagittal (**B**), and coronal (**C**), MR demonstrating the cisternal and orbital segments of the nerve. 1 = orbital segment; 2 = intracanalicular segment; 3 = cisternal segment; 4 = optic chiasm; 5 = optic tract; 6 = pituitary stalk.

Its motor fibers innervate the muscles of mastication, the tensor muscles (palatine and tympani), and the digastric and mylohyoid muscles. It is one of the largest cranial nerves.

The nuclei of the trigeminal nerve extend in a longitudinal plane between the inferior colliculi and the second cervical segment of the spinal cord.

The cisternal segment of the trigeminal nerve extends from the anterolateral surface of the brainstem until its three divisions—the opthalmic (V1), maxillary (V2), and mandibular (V3) divisions—leave the skull base after piercing the dural attachments through the superior or-

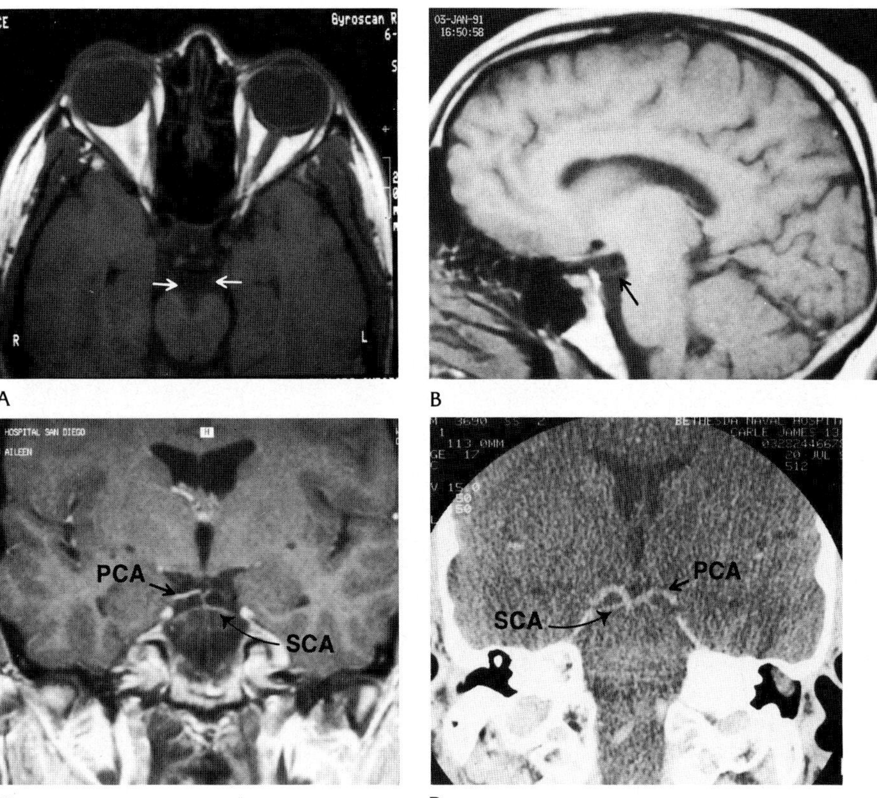

Figure 4-11 Oculomotor nerve. Axial (**A**) and sagittal (**B**) T_1-weighted MR through the midbrain level. Contrast-enhanced T_1-weighted coronal MR (**C**) and coronal CECT (**D**). The nerve (arrow) is between the posterior cerebral (PCA) and superior cerebellar (SCA) arteries in the coronal plane.

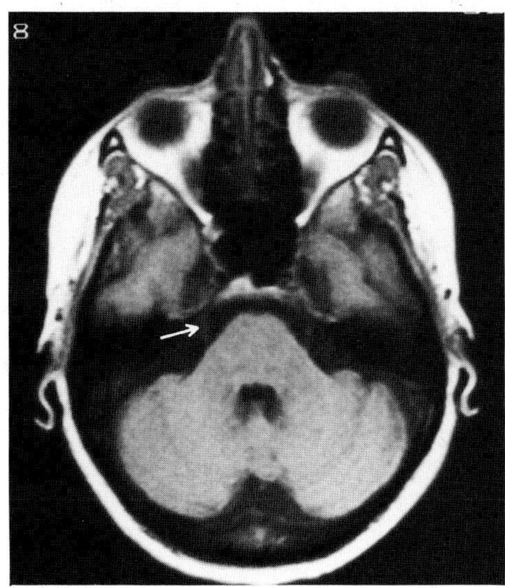

Figure 4-12 Abducens nerve. Axial T_1-weighted section. The nerve (arrow) is seen as a result of the prominent cisternal space and large section thickness.

bital fissure, the foramen rotundum, and the foramen ovale, respectively. The sensory and proprioceptive fibers join the nerve roots near the gasserian or semilunar ganglion, which is located in the trigeminal cistern, a CSF space within the dural folds also known as *Meckel's cave.* Meckel's cave is posterolateral to the sella, in close proximity to exit foramina of the trigeminal nerve branches.

In high-resolution thin-section CECT, Meckel's cave can be clearly seen as an oval hypodense region (Kapila 1984; Chui 1985). CT density within Meckel's cave depends on the amounts of CSF and fat. It is defined laterally by the dural attachment and the contained venous sinus, and medially by the petrous tip and the dural fold (Fig. 4-13). The trigeminal nerve is seen in T_1WI MR studies in axial sections through the level of the upper pons. Most of the time it can also be identified in coronal and sagittal sections. Meckel's cave in T_1WI is hypointense or isointense, and in T_2WI and T_2*WI it is hyperintense. These intensity characteristics are due to the contents of Meckel's cave, the volume-averaging effect, and the T_2 relaxation characteristics of the tissue contents. The extracranial pathways of the trigeminal nerve as seen on MRI have been dealt with extensively (Daniels 1986; Hardin 1987).

The *facial nerve* (seventh cranial nerve) is a mixed nerve consisting of motor, sensory, and special-function fibers. Its nuclei are situated anterolaterally within the pons, in front of the floor of the fourth ventricle. The nerve emerges at the lateral margin of the pons. A short segment runs in the cerebellopontine (CP) angle cistern between the brainstem and the internal auditory canal.

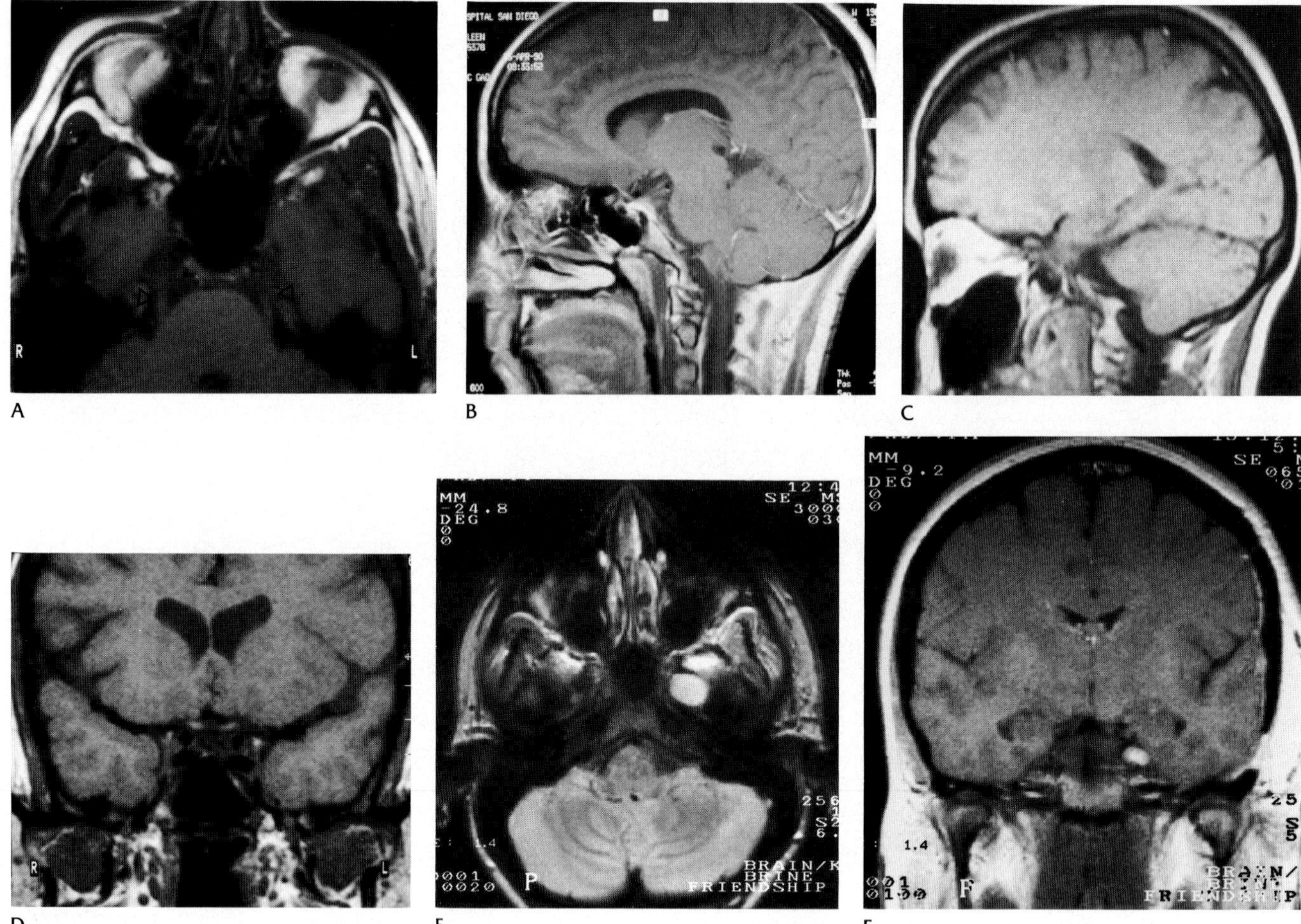

Figure 4-13 Trigeminal nerve (arrowhead) in axial (**A**), sagittal (**B, C**), and coronal (**D**) planes. The three divisions of the nerve can be occasionally identified (1 = ophthalmic; 2 = maxillary; 3 = mandibular). T_1-weighted contrast-enhanced MR is useful in demonstrating the cranial and extracranial segments of the nerve, as in this patient with a schwanomma (arrow) involving the mandibular division of the nerve or axial (**E**) and coronal (**F**) sections.

In the internal auditory canal the nerve is located in the superior outer quadrant. At the lateral end of the canal the nerve makes a loop, with the anterior end of the loop forming the labyrinthine segment and the posterior end forming the tympanic segment. The labyrinthine segment is connected to the geniculate ganglion. The tympanic segment passes under the lateral semicircular canal to form the vertical, or mastoid, portion of the facial nerve. The facial nerve leaves the cranial base through the stylomastoid foramen.

The facial nerve, along with the eighth cranial nerve, can be identified in CT studies when positive or negative intrathecal contrast is utilized and thin axial sections are obtained. The need for these studies has been obviated by the availability of high-resolution MRI. This nerve is isointense in both T_1WI and T_2WI. Within the internal auditory canal the facial nerve is separated from the acoustic nerve by the crista falciformis. On both CT and MRI the seventh and eighth nerves are difficult to separate within the internal auditory canal unless the crista falciformis can be identified (Fig. 4-14) (Teresi 1987; Daniels 1984*a*) (Chap. 11).

The *acoustic nerve* (eighth cranial nerve) consists of the cochlear component, which is associated with hearing, and the vestibular component, which is associated with the sense of position in space.

The cochlear nucleus is located in the lateral aspect of the inferior cerebellar peduncle. The vestibular nucleus is between the cerebellum and the inferior cerebellar peduncle.

The intratemporal and intracanalicular segments of the nerve are visualized on CT or MR in similar planes and pulse sequences, respectively, for the seventh cranial nerve (Fig. 4-14). The brainstem nuclei and connections are located in sections through the levels of the inferior cerebellar peduncles.

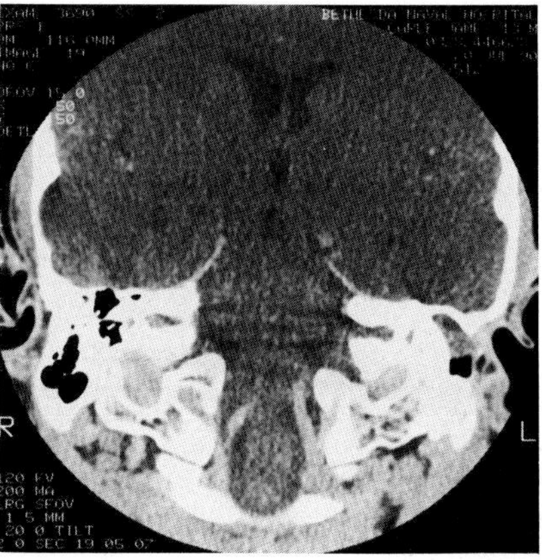
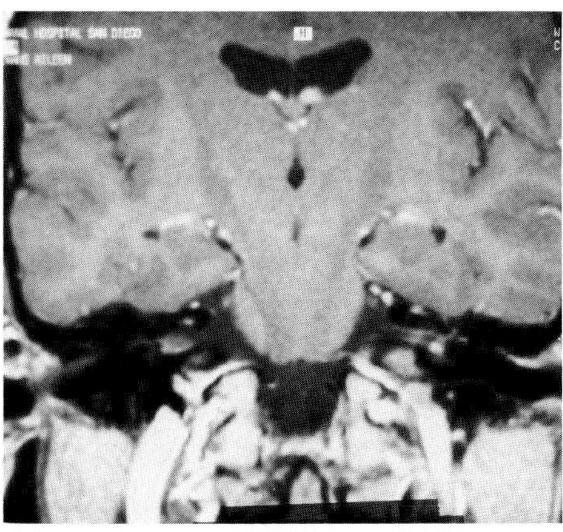
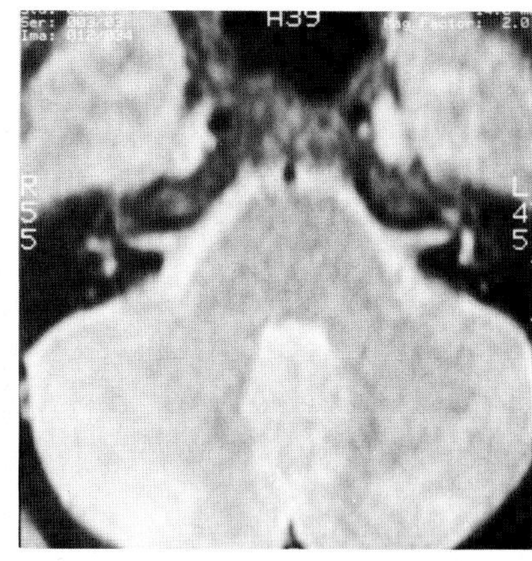

A B C

Figure 4-14 Coronal CECT (**A**) and axial T_2-weighted MR (**B**) (SE 2500/80) demonstrate the CSF within the internal auditory canal. The cranial nerves may be identified on MR. **C.** Gadolinium-enhanced coronal T_1-weighted MR allows better appreciation of the nerve.

The *glossopharyngeal nerve* (ninth cranial nerve) innervates the stylopharyngeal muscle. Its sensory component receives sensation from the posterior oropharynx and the soft palate. It has special sense fibers that are associated with taste sensation and discrimination in the posterior third of the tongue. It also has fibers that subserve parasympathetic functions and Jacobson's nerve, which is the sensory nerve to the middle ear. The *vagus nerve* (tenth cranial nerve) is also a mixed nerve that enters the skull base in the posterior compartment, along with the *accessory nerve* (eleventh cranial nerve). The vagus nerve carries motor fibers from the nucleus ambiguus and sensory and parasympathetic fibers to the tractus solitarius and dorsal motor nucleus. The accessory-spinal nerve, as the name suggests, has a spinal component. These three cranial nerves run a short course in the medullary cistern to enter the posterolateral compartment of the jugular foramen.

In the jugular foramen the ninth cranial nerve is located in the anterior compartment, along with the inferior petrosal sinus. A fibrous band separates the anterior compartment from the posterolateral compartment (Daniels 1985; Han 1984). The nuclei of the three nerves are in close proximity to each other.

The cisternal segment is difficult to visualize on CT but can be identified occasionally in axial and coronal MR studies (Fig. 4-15). The course of these nerves through the jugular foramen can be demonstrated on CT or MRI (Remley 1987).

The *hypoglossal nerve* (twelfth cranial nerve) is a pure motor nerve that primarily supplies the muscles of the tongue, both intrinsic and extrinsic. The nucleus of the

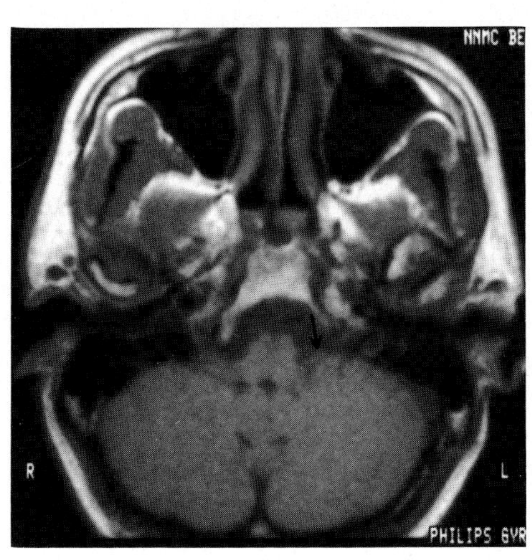
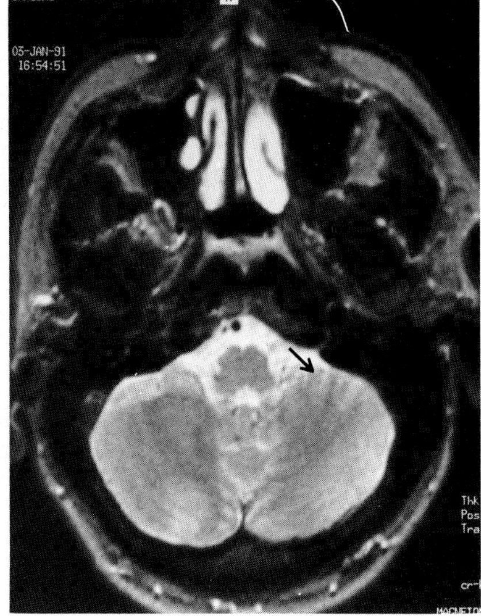

A B

Figure 4-15 Axial T_1-weighted (**A**) and T_2-weighted (**B**) MR through the inferior medullary cisterns identifying the cisternal segment of the ninth, tenth, and eleventh cranial nerves (arrows). (*Continued on p. 98*)

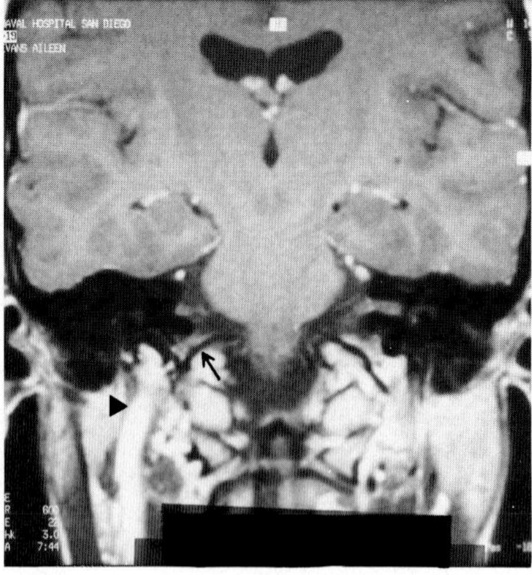
C

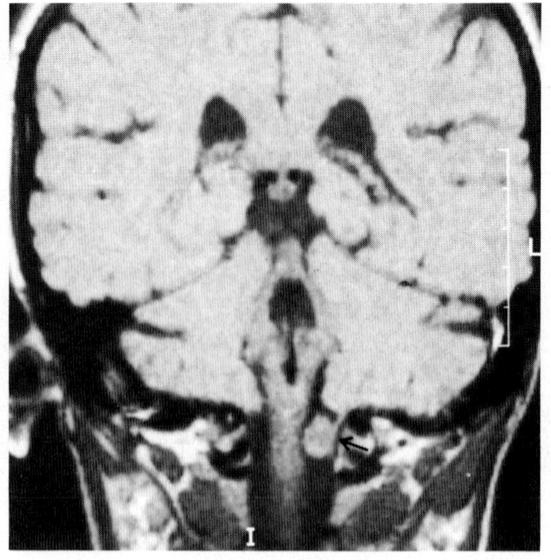
D

Figure 4-15 (continued) **C.** Coronal postcontrast T_1-weighted MR demonstrating the relationship with the jugular vein (arrowhead), the seventh and eighth CN, and IAC (arrow). **D.** Coronal T_1-weighted postcontrast MR in a patient with a schwanomma of the eleventh CN (arrow).

nerve has a bulbar and spinal extension. The bulbar nuclei lie in a paramedian location in the floor of the fourth ventricle. The fibers exit as rootlets between the inferior olivary nucleus and the pyramid (corticospinal tract). In the medullary cistern they fuse to form the hypoglossal nerve. The nerve has a very short cisternal segment, directed anterolaterally and downward, in which it enters the hypoglossal canal (anterior condylar foramen) of the occipital bone. The canal is posteromedial and inferior to the jugular foramen (Fig. 4-1).

The cisternal and canalicular segments of the hypoglossal nerve are demonstrated on MRI in both the axial and coronal planes (Smoker 1987). In the axial plane the nerve is seen in section parallel to the foramen magnum (Fig. 4-16).

Pathological processes that affect the cranial nerves in the cisternal or extracranial pathways are best evaluated with MRI after paramagnetic contrast (Barakos 1991).

The Brain Parenchyma

The brain parenchyma consists of three major components, each of which is composed of several parts.

- Forebrain (prosencephalon)
  - Telencephalon
  - Diencephalon
- Midbrain (mesencephalon)
- Hindbrain
  - Pons
  - Medulla

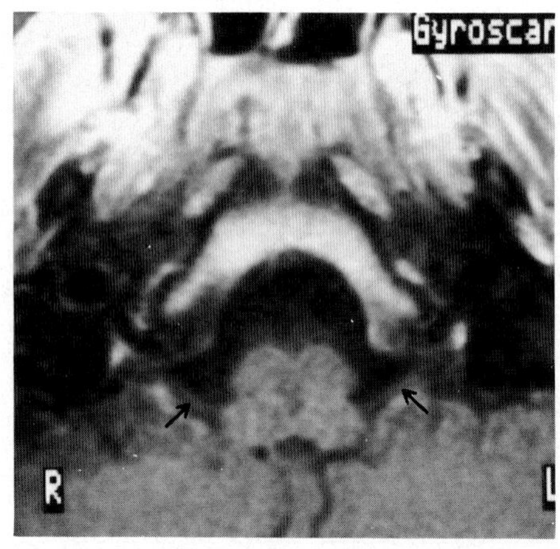

A

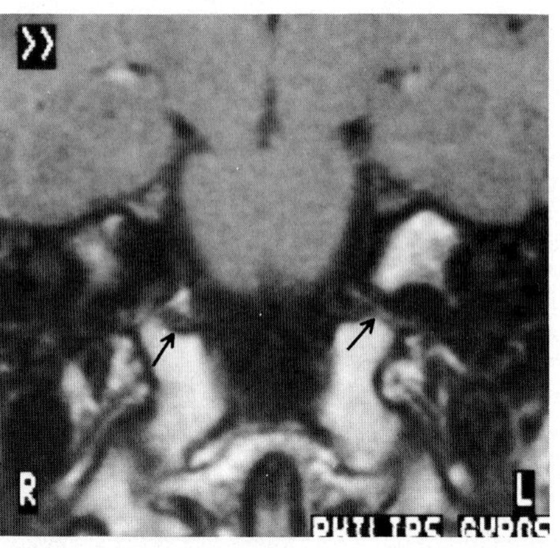

B

Figure 4-16 Hypoglossal nerve. Axial (**A**) and coronal (**B**) MR through region of the medullary cistern demonstrating the hypoglossal nerve (arrow).

COMPONENTS OF THE BRAIN

The different components of the brain are interconnected internally by a series of ependyma-lined CSF spaces. The lateral ventricles are located within the telencephalon, the third ventricle within the structures of the diencephalon, the aqueduct within the midbrain, and the fourth ventricle within the hindbrain.

CT and MR imaging of the brain is achieved through sectional imaging in the axial plane. In addition, MRI allows a three-dimensional approach by utilizing the coronal and sagittal imaging planes. On MR, T_1WI is similar to the CT image, since the gray-white contrast differentiation is minimal. The tissue contrast between gray and white matter is greater on spin-density-weighted (SDW or proton density) images, whereas heavily T_2WI shows greater contrast with CSF than between gray and white matter.

The forebrain, or prosencephalon, consists of the two cerebral hemispheres (telencephalon), which are connected to the midbrain by several structures consisting of fiber tracts (diencephalon). The anatomy of the cerebral hemisphere and midbrain is evaluated in sagittal and coronal T_1WI (Figs. 4-17 and 4-18), and the internal gray and white matter areas are seen in T_2WI (Figs. 4-19 through 4-23 and Fig. 4-26).

The Cerebral Hemispheres

The two cerebral hemispheres occupy the cranial cavity above the tentorium. They are separated from each other in the midline by the interhemispheric fissure, which extends anteriorly to the floor of the anterior cranial fossa. In its middle part the interhemispheric fissure stops at the corpus callosum, which connects the two cerebral hemispheres. Posteriorly, the interhemispheric fissure separates the two occipital lobes. The posterior inferior surfaces of the cerebral hemispheres are separated from the cerebellum by the tentorium cerebelli.

Each cerebral hemisphere consists of outer gray matter (the cerebral cortex) and underlying white matter (the centrum semiovale). Deeper in the white matter is the diencephalon (Figs. 4-17, 4-18, 4-20 through 4-23).

The *cerebral cortex* covers the surface of the cerebral hemisphere. There are three surfaces for each hemisphere, separated by three borders. The superior border separates the medial and lateral surfaces, the inferolateral border separates the inferior and lateral surfaces, and the inferomedial border separates the medial and inferior surfaces. The medial surfaces are straight and are situated in the midline, separated by the interhemispheric fissure and the falx cerebri. The lateral surface is convex and lies against the inner table of the cranial vault. The inferior surface on each side is divided into an anterior portion that lies against the floor of the anterior cranial fossa, which is formed by the roof of the orbits laterally and by the cribriform plate of the ethmoid bone and the planum sphenoidale medially. Posterior to this part, the inferior surface dips downward to occupy the hollow of the middle cranial fossa and thus lies against the inner table of the greater wings of the sphenoid bone and the anterior surfaces of the petrous bones. Farther posteriorly, this surface slants to fit the slope of the tentorium cerebelli.

The three surfaces of the cerebral hemisphere contain numerous sulci that separate the cerebral gyri. Four of these sulci are helpful in dividing the cerebral hemispheres into their constituent lobes (Figs. 4-17 and 4-18). The *lateral sulcus* (sylvian fissure) separates the greater part of the temporal lobe from the frontal lobe and the anterior part of the parietal lobe above. The *central sulcus* (rolandic fissure) begins on the medial surface of the hemisphere at about the middle of the superior border. It runs on the lateral surface of the hemisphere downward and forward and stops short of the lateral sulcus.

The *parietooccipital sulcus* lies on the medial surface of the cerebral hemisphere (Fig. 4-18). It starts at the superior margin about 5 cm from the occipital pole and extends downward and forward, where it meets the *calcarine sulcus* near the splenium of the corpus callosum. The calcarine sulcus extends from this point backward on the medial surface of the occipital lobe and ends at the occipital pole (Figs. 4-17 and 4-18).

Each cerebral hemisphere is divided into five lobes. The boundaries separating these lobes are formed in part by the sulci described above and in part by imaginary lines. The *frontal lobe* is the anterior part of the hemisphere. On the lateral surface it is limited posteriorly by the central sulcus (rolandic fissure) and inferiorly by the lateral sulcus (sylvian fissure). On the medial surface it is limited posteriorly by a line drawn downward and anteriorly from the end of the central sulcus to the corpus callosum (Fig. 4-18). The *occipital lobe* is the small posterior part of the hemisphere. On the medial surface it is limited anteriorly by the parietooccipital sulcus (Fig. 4-18). Its anterior border on the lateral surface is an imaginary line extending from the upper end of the parietooccipital sulcus at the superior border of the hemisphere to the preoccipital notch on the inferolateral border (Fig. 4-18). The *parietal lobe* lies between the frontal lobe anteriorly and the occipital lobe posteriorly. The inferior border of the parietal lobe on the lateral surface is formed by the posterior part of the lateral sulcus and by an arbitrary line extending from the lateral sulcus toward the arbitrary line which forms the anterior border of the occipital lobe (Fig. 4-18). The separation between the parietal, temporal, and occipital lobes on the lateral surface is formed by arbitrary lines and thus is ill defined. On the medial surface (Fig. 4-18) the posterior border of the parietal lobe is formed by the parietooccipital sulcus, which separates the parietal lobe from the occipital lobe. The *insula (central lobe)* is hidden in the

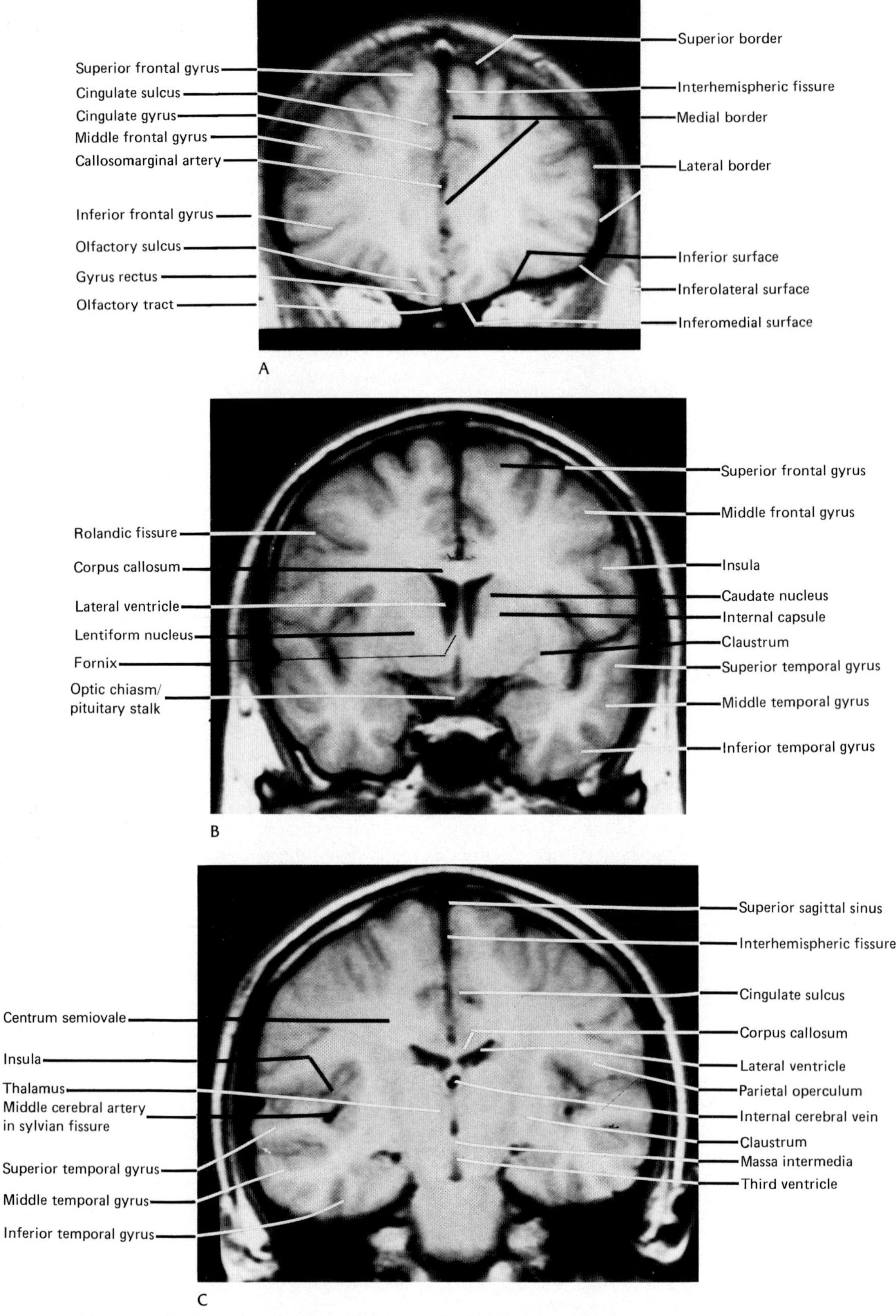

Figure 4-17 Coronal MR section of the brain. The levels of the sections correspond to: **A.** frontal lobe anterior to the frontal horn of the lateral ventricle; **B.** at the level of foramen of Monro; **C.** posterior aspect of third ventricle. (*Continued on p. 101.*)

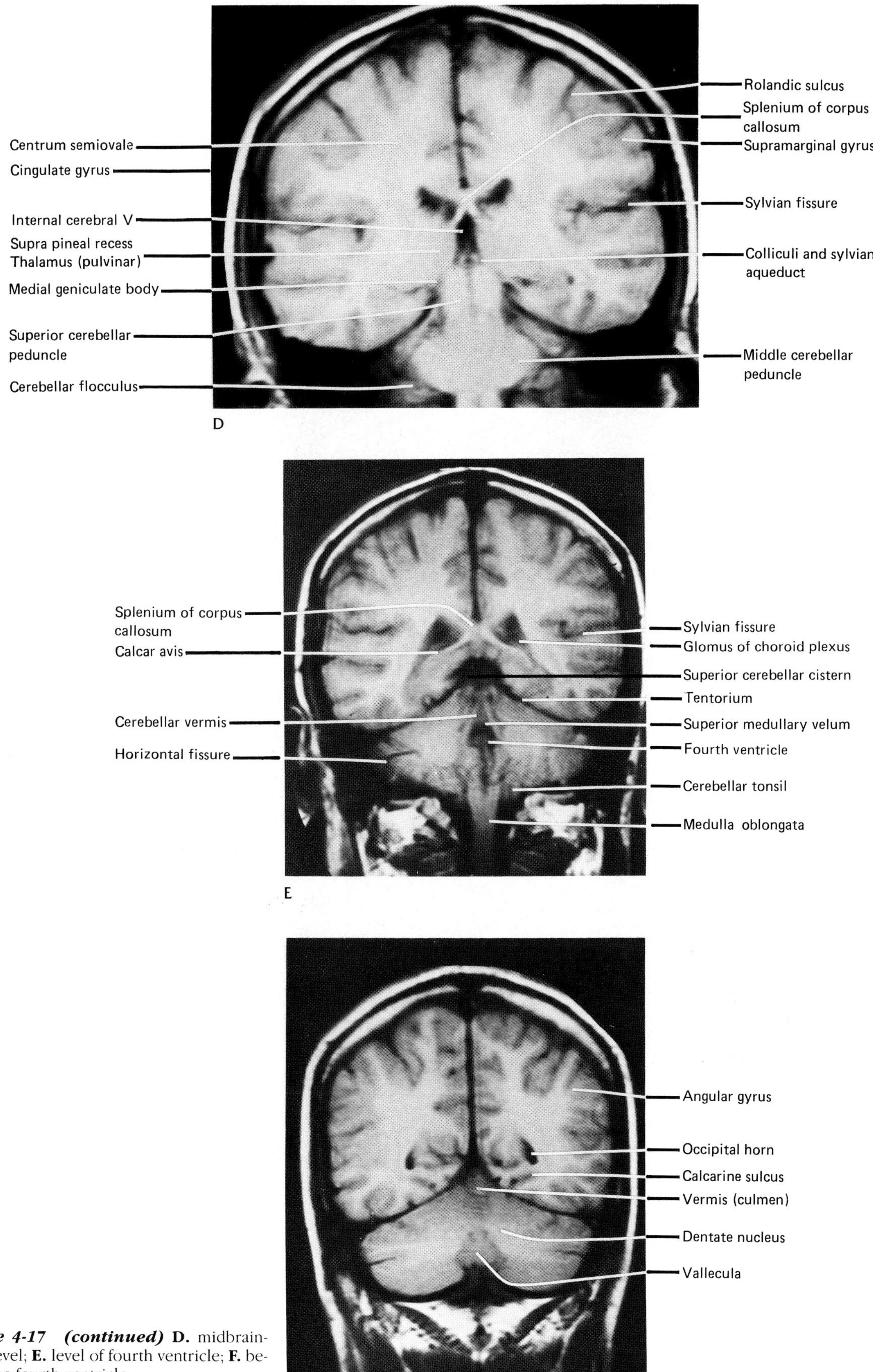

Figure 4-17 (continued) **D.** midbrain-stem level; **E.** level of fourth ventricle; **F.** behind the fourth ventricle.

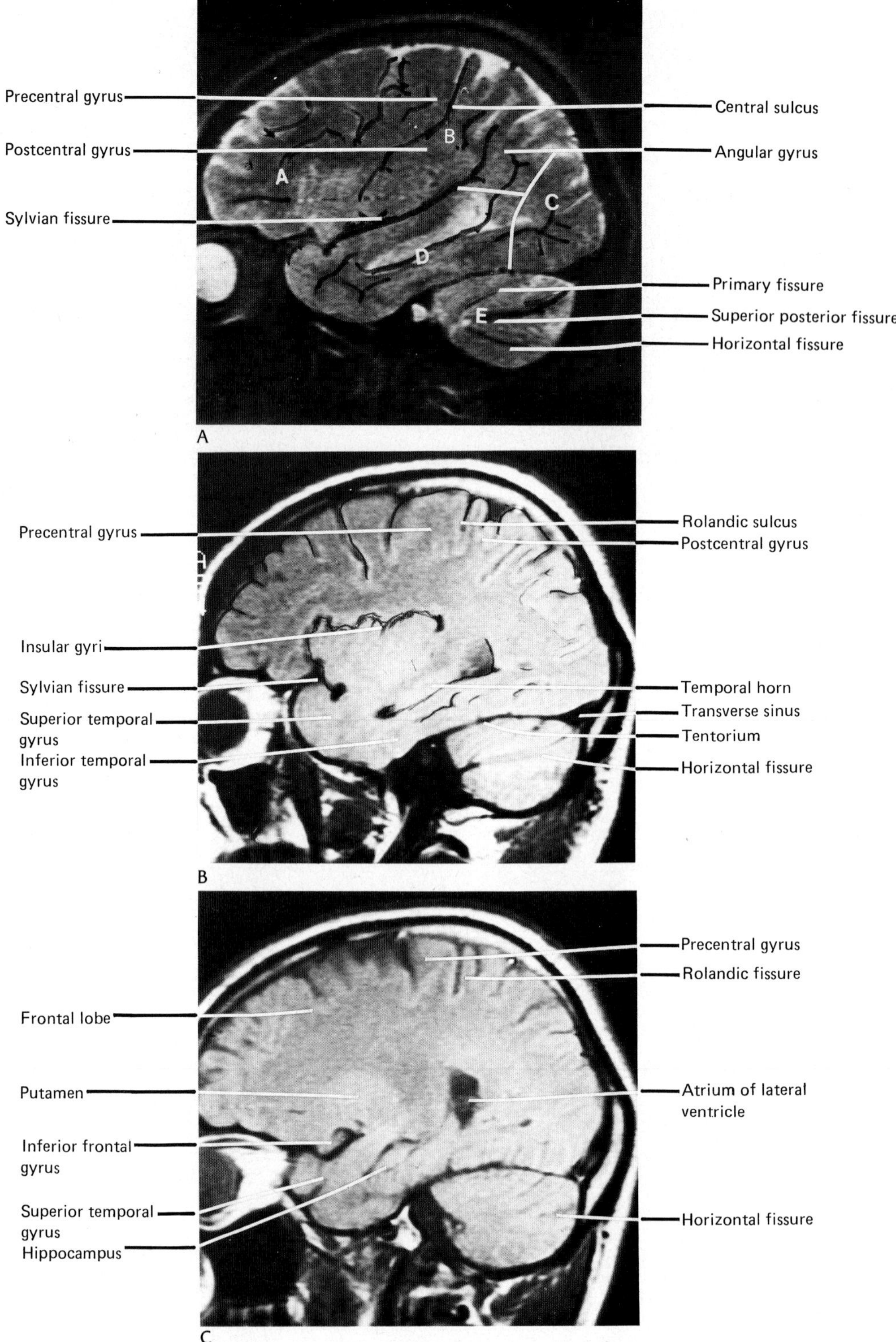

Figure 4-18 Sagittal MR section to identify the components of the brain parenchyma. (**A**) Extreme lateral, (**B**) atrial level, and (**C**) more medial. (*Continued on p. 103.*)

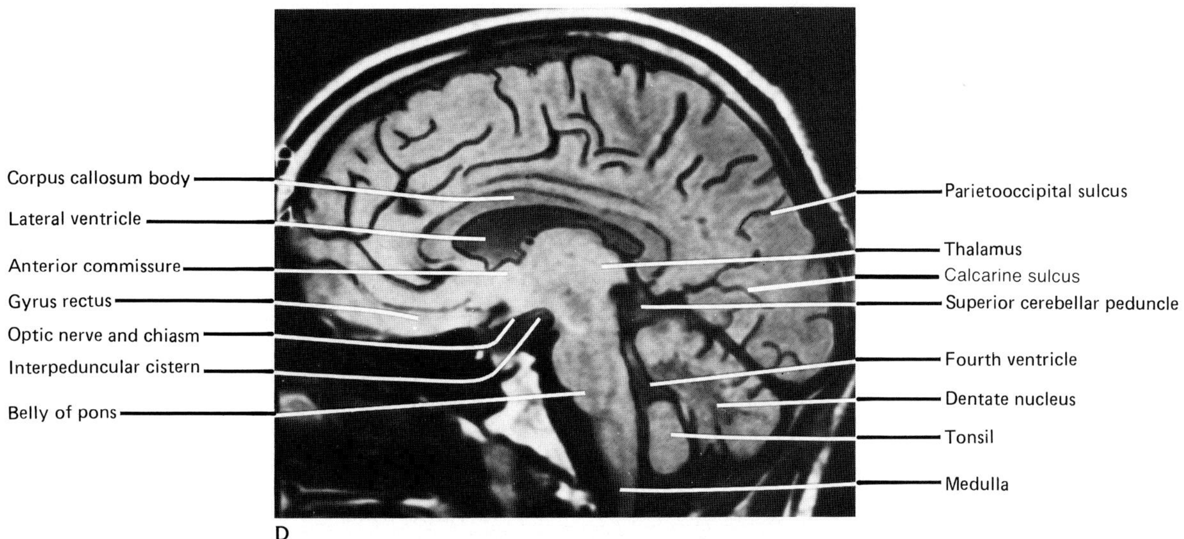

Figure 4-18 (continued) **(D)** Midsagittal plane demonstrating anatomical structures. (*Courtesy of Dr. Zimmerman, Hospital of University of Pennsylvania.*)

depth of the lateral sulcus, which is formed by portions of the frontal, parietal, and temporal lobes called the *operculum* (Figs. 4-17 and 4-18).

The *centrum semiovale* constitutes the white matter of the internal portion of the cerebral hemisphere. The *corpus callosum* is a band of central white matter that connects the two cerebral hemispheres and consists of an anterior bent portion, the *genu.* The body of the corpus callosum overlies the roof of the lateral ventricle but continues in the midline in a thick rounded free edge—the *splenium*—that overhangs the pineal body and the colliculi (Fig. 4-18). MRI studies have demonstrated that there is a slightly greater thickness in the body of the corpus callosum in men, whereas the splenium of the callosal bundle is thicker in women (Smoker 1987). The two lateral ventricles are large CSF-containing spaces that separate the two cerebral hemispheres. The roof in the midline is formed by the corpus callosum. The lateral ventricles extend anteriorly into the medial portions of the frontal lobe (frontal horn) and posteromedially into the occipital lobe (occipital horn). The body of the lateral ventricle continues inferolaterally into the temporal lobe (temporal horn). The junction where the occipital horn and the temporal horn meet the body of the lateral ventricle is called the *trigone* of the ventricle.

The choroidal arteries which supply the choroid plexus of the lateral ventricles penetrate along the medial surface of the trigone in the region of the choroidal fissure (Fig. 4-21). The frontal horns and the body of the two lateral ventricles are separated by the septum pellucidum. The two layers of the septum pellucidum containing CSF are consistently seen in infants. In the majority of instances they fuse. Nonfusion of the two layers results in the CSF-containing spaces identified as the *cavum septum pellucidum* and its posterior extension, the *cavum vergae.* The septum pellucidum is not an inert membrane separating the two lateral ventricles but has neural connections with the cerebral hemispheres (Sarwar 1989).

The *basal ganglia* represent the central gray matter of the telencephalon in the lower parts of each cerebral hemisphere. The basal ganglia consist of the *corpus striatum* (caudate nucleus and lentiform nucleus); the *claustrum,* a thin strip of gray matter lateral to the lentiform nucleus and separated by a band of white matter (Figs. 4-17 through 4-22); and the amygdala, which is located in the roof of the temporal horn and represents the tail of the caudate nucleus. The *caudate nucleus* has an enlarged anterior end, the head of which indents the lateral wall of the anterior horn of the lateral ventricle. It has a narrow posterior portion—the tail—which follows the superolateral border of the thalamus. The *lentiform nucleus* has a wedge-shaped appearance in the axial and coronal planes (Figs. 4-17, 4-21, and 4-22). It consists of the *globus pallidus* medially and the *putamen* laterally. The superior surface of the lentiform nucleus is covered by white matter tracts consisting of the corona radiata, association fibers, and the corpus callosum. The inferior surface of the lentiform nucleus is above the anterior perforated substance and the anterior commissure. The perforated substance is the site of entry zones of the striate vessels. In axial MR sections, as a result of CSF in the perivascular spaces, this appears as oval areas of bright signal intensity adjacent to the anterior commissure (Jungreis 1988).

The *internal capsule* consists of boomerang-shaped thick white matter bounded anteromedially by the caudate nucleus, posteromedially by the thalamus, and laterally by the lentiform nuclei (Figs. 4-21 through 4-23).

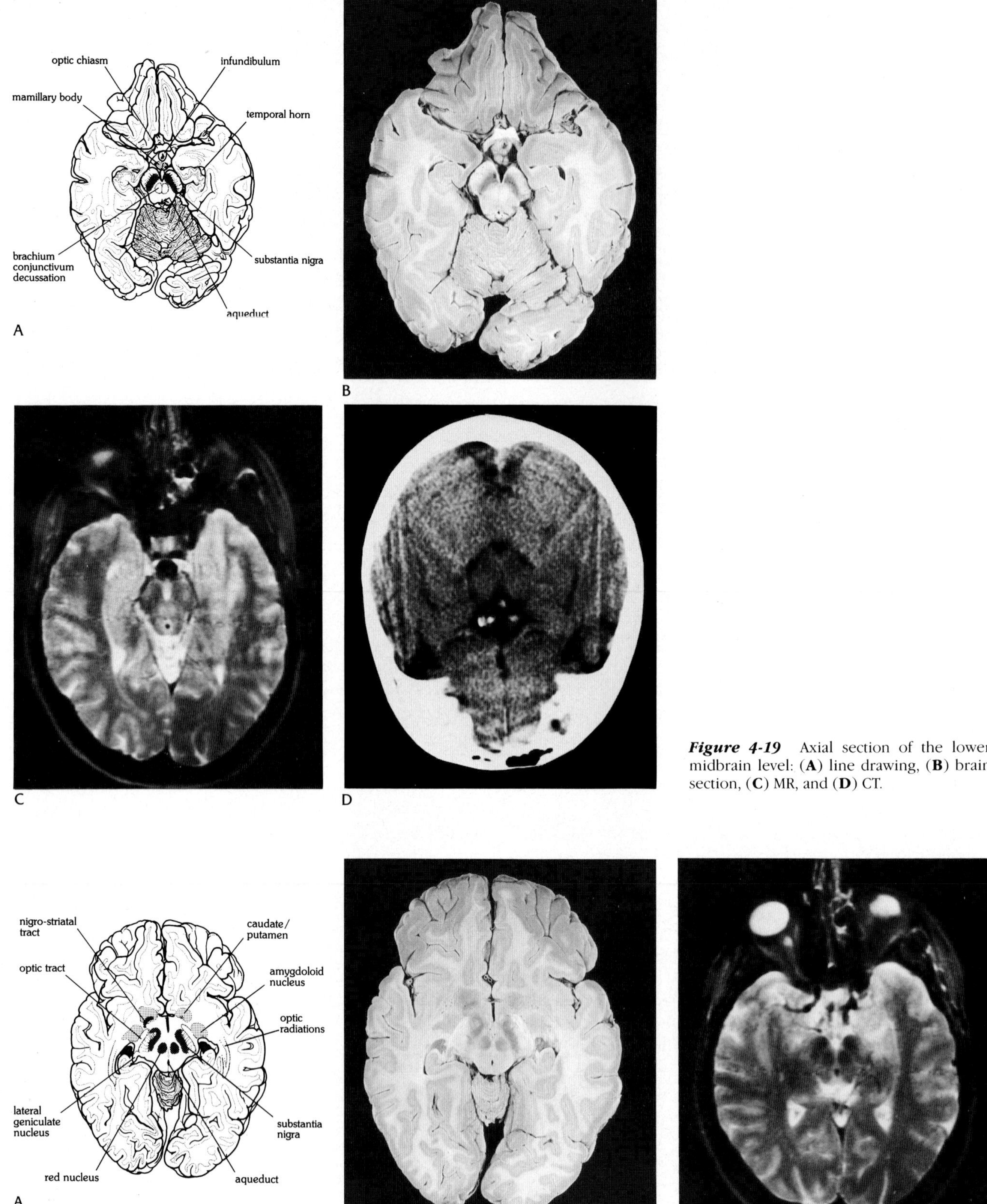

Figure 4-19 Axial section of the lower midbrain level: (**A**) line drawing, (**B**) brain section, (**C**) MR, and (**D**) CT.

Figure 4-20 Axial anatomy at the level of the cerebral peduncles: (**A**) line drawing; (**B**) brain section; (**C**) MR.

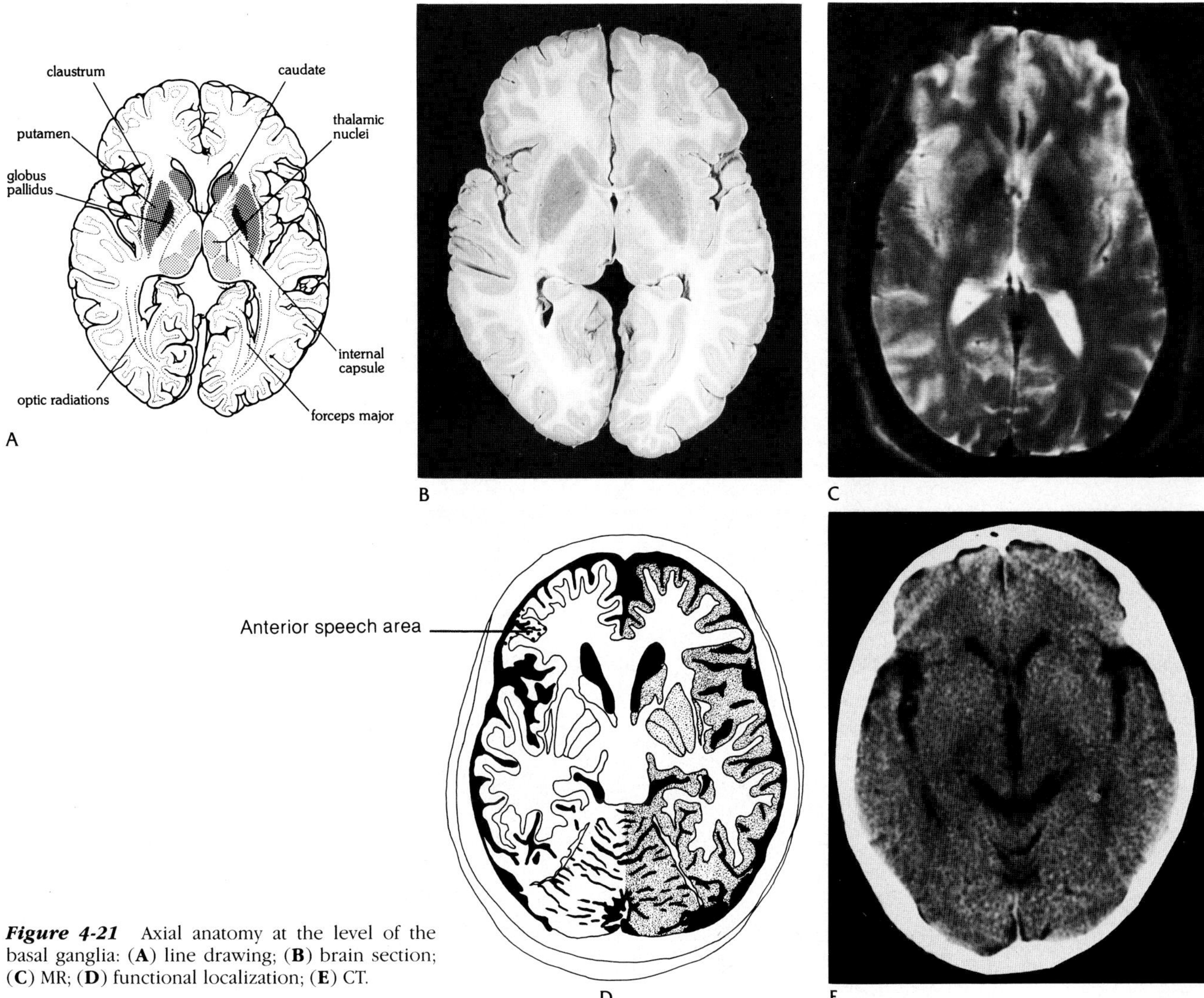

Figure 4-21 Axial anatomy at the level of the basal ganglia: (**A**) line drawing; (**B**) brain section; (**C**) MR; (**D**) functional localization; (**E**) CT.

Certain normal anatomic structures may be confused with pathological changes on T_2WI. These include the hyperintense signal in the posterior limb of the internal capsule, the entry zones of the vessel, and the perivascular spaces. Usually these are symmetrical, not associated with mass effect, and nonenhancing (Table 4-2).

The Diencephalon

The diencephalon is made up of several structures around the third ventricle, consisting of fiber tracts that connect the midbrain on one side to the cerebral hemispheres on the other side. It includes the thalami, the geniculate bodies, the epithalamus, the subthalamus, and the hypothalamus. Both the diencephalon and the midbrain structures are evaluated in axial section on CT and MR through the middle third of the cranial vault (Figs. 4-17, 4-21, and 4-22).

The *thalami* are two large ovoid masses that are small anteriorly and more voluminous posteriorly. Each thalamus is 4 cm long. Its medial surface forms the lateral wall of the third ventricle. Each thalamus is covered with ependyma and is separated from the opposite thalamus by the third ventricle (Figs. 4-17, 4-21, and 4-22). The superior surface forms part of the floor of the lateral ventricle on each side. The posteromedial part of the superior surface of the thalamus is covered with the fold of pia called the tela choroidea, which forms the *velum interpositum* in the roof of the third ventricle. The fornix lies on the superior surface of the thalamus, separating the lateral part from the medial part. The anterior end of the thalamus is small and forms the posterior boundary of the foramen of Monro, while the column of the fornix that overlies the thalamus forms the anterior border of this foramen. Each foramen of Monro forms the passageway between the third and lateral ventricles.

Table 4-2 Anatomic Regions of Normal Hyperintense Signal on T_2-Weighted, MRI

LOCATION	ANATOMIC/PATHOLOGICAL CORRELATION
Tips of frontal horns	Anterolateral aspects of frontal horns. Triangle-shaped. Related to decreased myelin. Fissures in ependymal lining with extracellular fluid. Astrocytic gliosis.
Posterior internal capsule	3 to 4 mm in size. Medial to distal putamen and anterolateral to thalamus. Usually seen beyond age 10. Probably related to decreased myelination or absent iron. Bilateral, symmetrical, not seen on T_1WI or in low-field-strength magnets.
Paratrigonal region	Located posterior and superior to the trigone. Usually seen before the second decade, often in high-field MR systems. Probably represent delayed myelination in association fiber tracts.
Anterior/posterior commisural regions	Perivascular spaces: seen on axial and coronal planes; represents perivascular CSF spaces around the striatal vessels. More prominent with aging.
Choroidal fissure	Perivascular spaces: seen on axial sections in medial temporal pole, adjacent to the quadrigeminal cistern. These focal bright regions represent entry zones of choroidal vessels.
Centrum semiovale	Perivascular spaces: small punctate foci, isointense to CSF, related to perivascular extracellular fluid. Becomes more visible with aging.

The voluminous posterior end of the thalamus is called the pulvinar. The pulvinar on each side extends beyond the posterior end of the third ventricle so that each pulvinar overlies a superior colliculus. The pineal gland lies in the midline, between the two pulvinars and above the superior colliculus. The inferior surface of the thalamus is continuous with the upper end of the tegmentum of the midbrain. The lateral surface forms the posteromedial boundary of the internal capsule. The two thalami are connected by the massa intermedia in the middle (Fig. 4-17).

The *geniculate bodies* (Fig. 4-20) constitute the metathalamus. On each side there are the lateral and medial geniculate bodies, which serve as relay stations. The lateral geniculate body is connected by the superior brachium to the superior colliculus and serves as part of the visual pathways that end in the visual cortex of the occipital lobe. The medial geniculate body on each side is connected by the inferior brachium to the inferior colliculus and serves as part of the auditory pathways that end in the auditory cortex of the superior temporal gyrus.

The *habenula,* the *pineal body,* and the *posterior commissure* constitute the epithalamus (Fig. 4-22). The pineal stalk has a superior lamina and an inferior lamina. The superior lamina is formed by the habenula, and the inferior lamina is formed by the posterior commissure. The space between the laminae forms the pineal recess of the third ventricle.

The subthalamus is the transition zone between the thalamus and the tegmentum of the midbrain.

The hypothalamus forms the wall of the anterior third ventricle. It consists of the mamillary bodies, the tuber cinereum, the infundibulum, the hypophysis, and the optic chiasm (Fig. 4-18).

The Midbrain, or Mesencephalon

The midbrain is a short segment of the brainstem that forms the connecting link between the forebrain and the hindbrain. Within the cranial vault the midbrain is situated at the level of the tentorial incisura. It is seen in the axial section through the middle portion of the cranial vault (Fig. 4-20).

The midbrain consists of a smaller dorsal portion—the tectum—and a larger ventral portion—the cerebral peduncles. Between the tectum and the cerebral peduncles, the central gray substance of the midbrain surrounds the aqueduct, which connects the third and fourth ventricles. In axial sections the aqueduct is seen as a focal area of hypodensity in front of the colliculi on CT and MRI. The entire length of the aqueduct can be identified on sagittal MRI (Fig. 4-18). The aqueduct is continuous superiorly with the posterior inferior aspect of the third ventricle and inferiorly with the superior aspect of the fourth ventricle. In axial and coronal planes the cerebral peduncles appear as two prominent ridges that diverge as they approach the cerebral hemispheres. The triangular space between the two peduncles forms the interpeduncular fossa, or cistern. The posterior perforated substance forms the floor of the fossa.

The tectum of the midbrain consists of four rounded prominences—the *colliculi,* or *corpora quadrigemina.* The superior colliculi on each side are continuous with the superior brachia. Each connects to the ipsilateral lateral geniculate body where the ipsilateral optic tract ends. Thus the fibers of the superior brachium connect

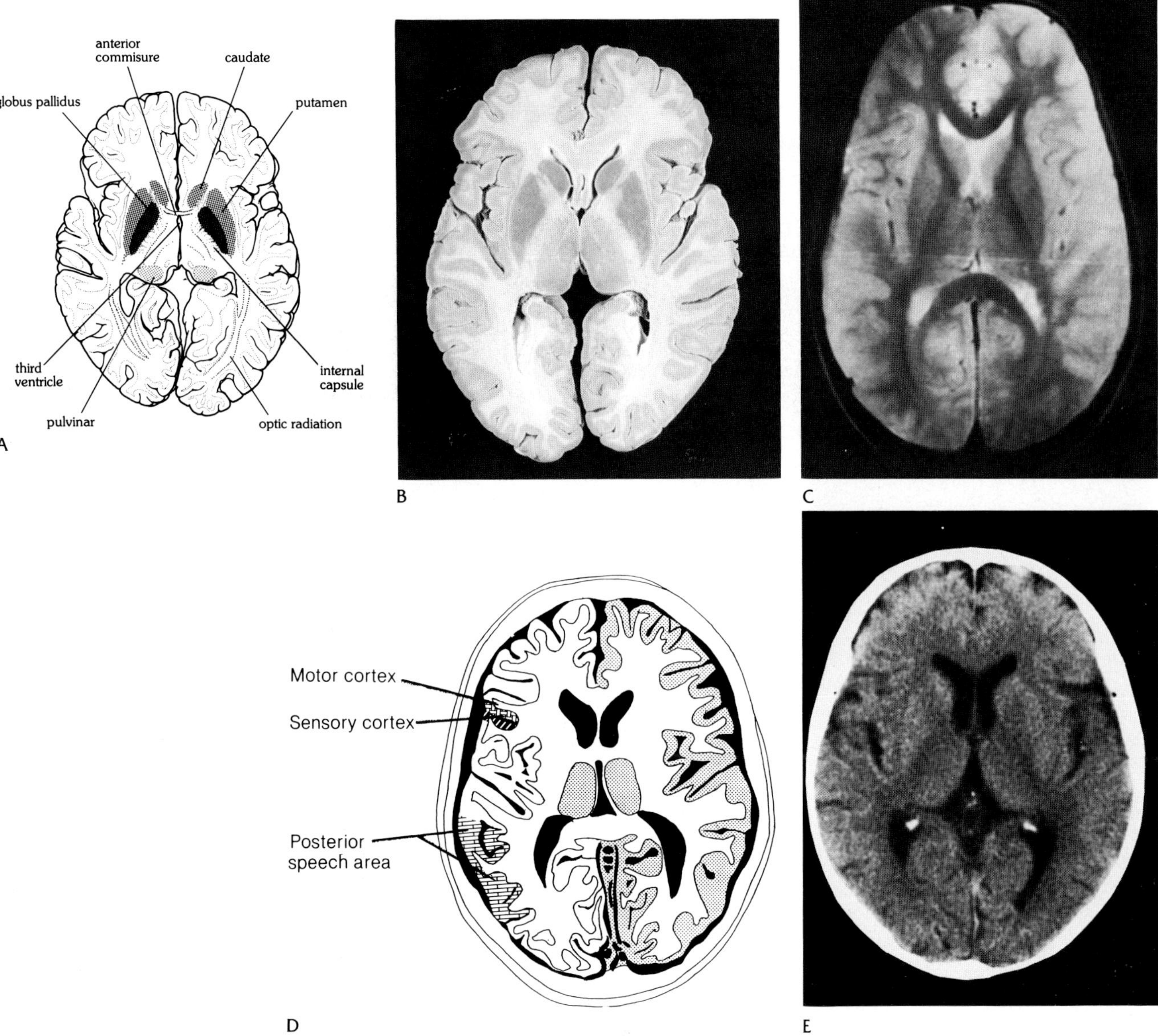

Figure 4-22 Axial section at the level of the foramen of Monro: (**A**) line drawing; (**B**) brain section; (**C**) MR; (**D**) functional localization; (**E**) CT.

the superior colliculi and the visual cortex. The inferior brachia extend from the inferior colliculi to the medial geniculate bodies, connecting the inferior colliculus with the auditory cortex. On sagittal MR, the superior and inferior colliculi form part of the roof of the aqueduct in its proximal portion. The width and height of each colliculus range between 3 and 6 mm. Their average diameter is 5 mm (Sherman 1986).

Each cerebral peduncle has a ventral part—the crus (basis pedunculi)—and a dorsal part—the tegmentum of the midbrain. The superior cerebellar peduncle (brachium conjunctivum) penetrates deeply into the tegmentum of the inferior part of the midbrain from the dorsal aspect on each side of the midline. The ventral and dorsal aspects of the cerebral peduncle are separated by the *substantia nigra,* a layer of pigmented gray matter that is semilunar in shape. Owing to the presence of iron pigment in the substantia nigra, it appears as a hypointense semilunar signal in T_2WI on MR studies (Figs. 4-19 and 4-20). Dorsomedial to the substantia nigra and slightly cephalad is another oval area of pigmented nuclei, the red nucleus, which is also seen as a hypointense signal similar to the substantia nigra (Fig. 4-20). Progressive increase in hypointensity of the corpus striatum, the substantia nigra, and the red nucleus with aging is presumed to be due to iron deposition (Drayer 1986). Other trace

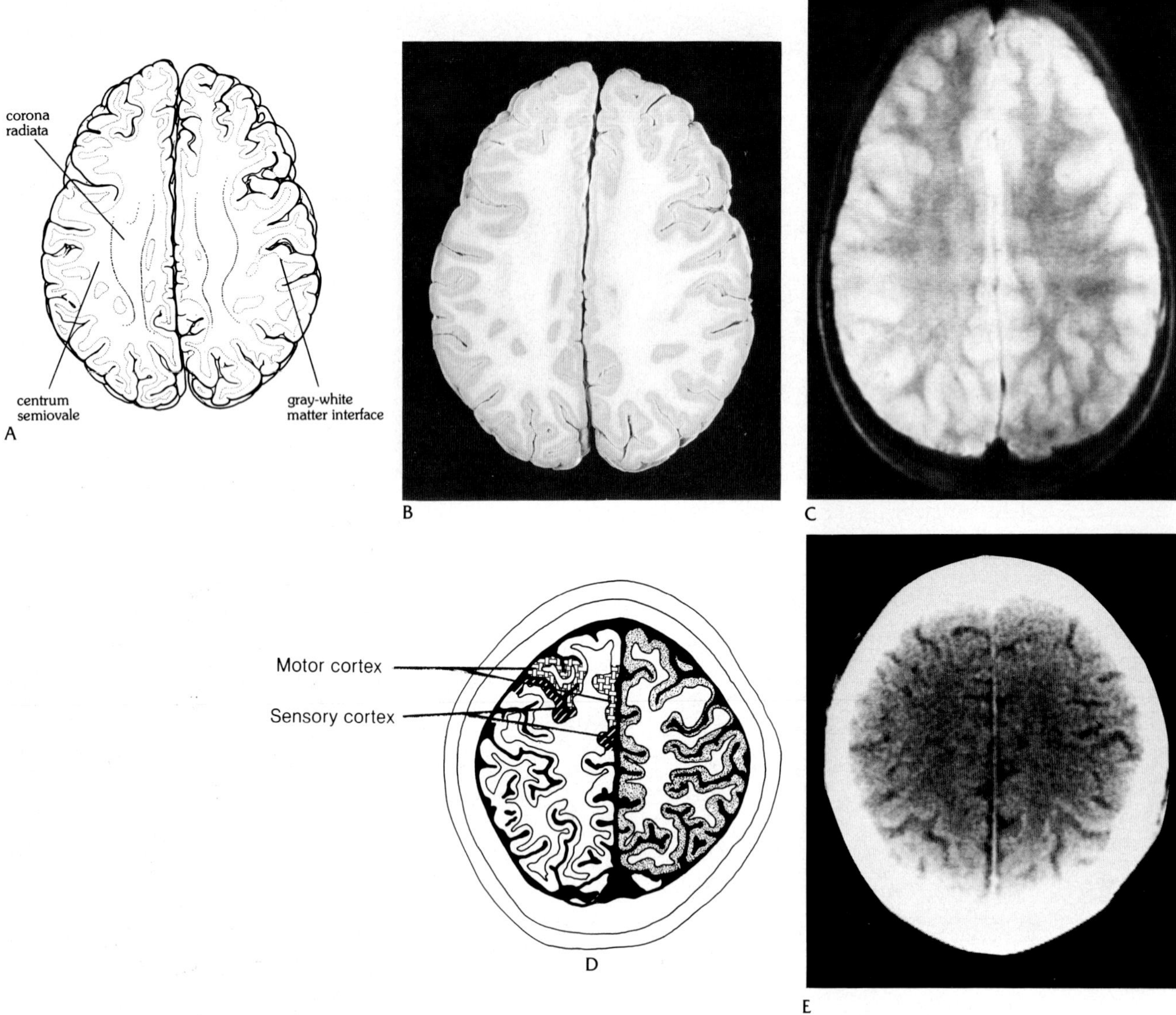

Figure 4-23 Axial section through the region of the centrum semiovale: (**A**) line drawing; (**B**) brain section; (**C**) MR; (**D**) functional localization; (**E**) CT.

elements, such as copper and manganese, and metabolic end products, such as neuromelanin, may also contribute to the hypointense signal in these nuclei. Neither of these nuclei can be identified on CT.

The Hindbrain

The hindbrain consists of the *pons* and the *medulla oblongata* anteriorly and the *cerebellum* posteriorly. The fourth ventricle is situated between the anterior and posterior portions of the hindbrain. This region is evaluated in axial CT and MRI sections through the lower half of the cranial vault (Figs. 4-24 through 4-27). High-resolution CT after intracisternal contrast has been suggested to evaluate this area (Mawad 1983). MRI has obviated the need for this invasive study, since the regional anatomy can be better evaluated with sections in the sagittal plane (Flannigan 1985; Press 1989; Courcheasne 1989).

The fourth ventricle is connected to the posterior aspect of the third ventricle through the aqueduct of Sylvius. It communicates with the subarachnoid cisterns through the foramen of Magendie, located in the midline posteriorly and anterolaterally through the foramina of Luschka, on either side of the brainstem. The floor of the fourth ventricle is formed by the dorsal aspect of the pons and the medulla. The roof of the fourth ventricle is formed by the superior and inferior vermis in its midportion and by the cerebellar hemispheres along its pos-

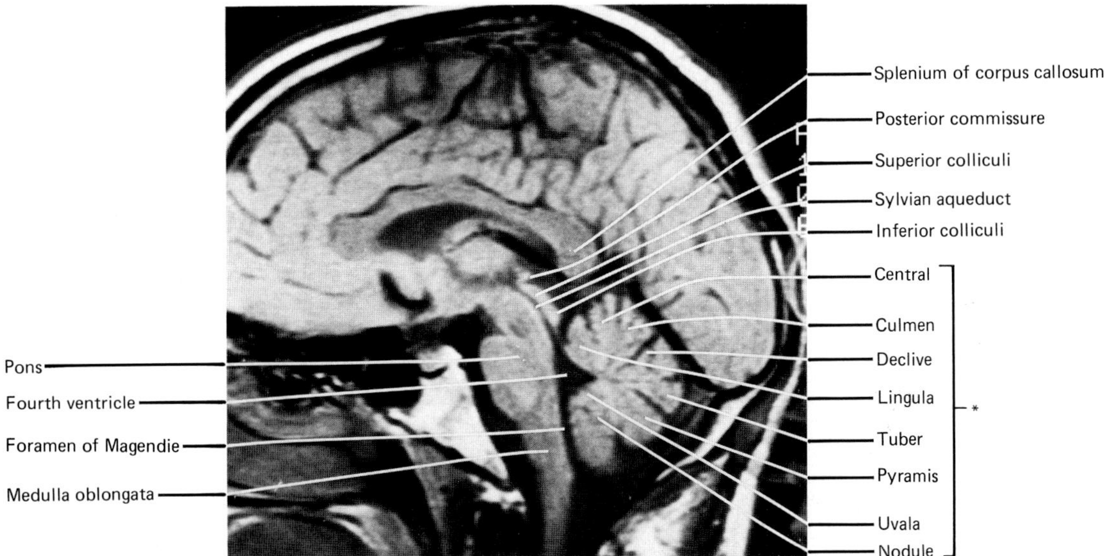

Figure 4-24 Midsagittal T_2-weighted MR through the hindbrain.

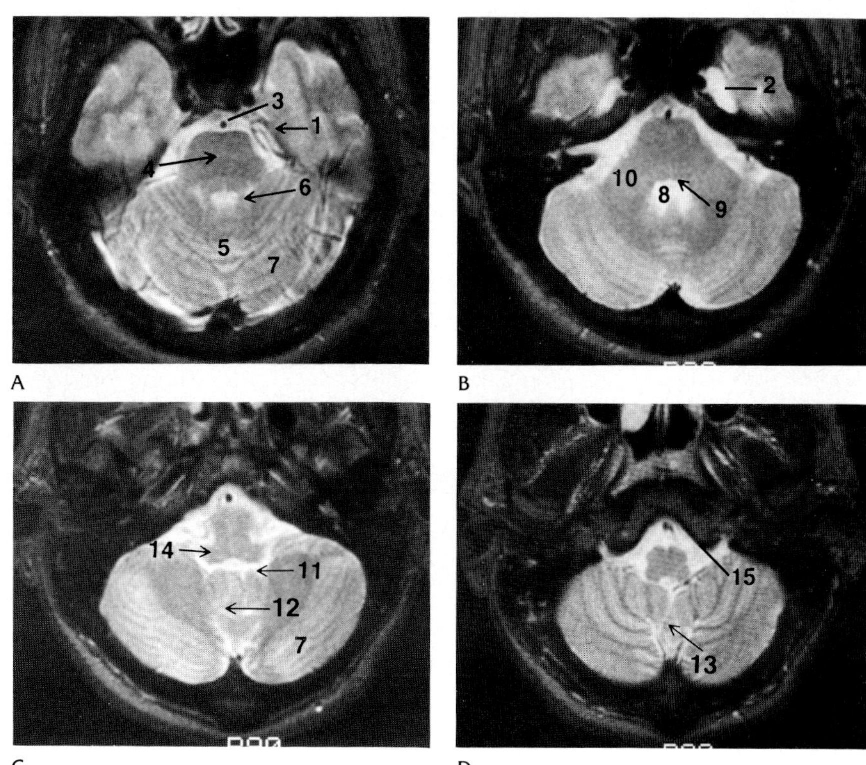

Figure 4-25 **A–D.** Axial MR through the hindbrain. 1 = petroclinoid ligament; 2 = Meckel's cave; 3 = basilar artery; 4 = pons; 5 = superior vermis; 6 = superior cerebellar peduncle; 7 = cerebellar folia; 8 = fourth ventricle; 9 = facial colliculus; 10 = middle cerebellar peduncle; 11 = nodulus; 12 = inferior vermis; 13 = pyramid; 14 = inferior cerebellar peduncle; 15 = olive.

terior and lateral surface. In the coronal plane the fourth ventricle has a rhomboid shape as a result of the connection of the cerebellar peduncles between the pons and medulla anteriorly and the cerebellar hemispheres posteriorly (Figs. 4-17 and 4-27).

THE PONS

The pons connects with the midbrain above and the medulla below. It forms a massive protuberance with well-defined borders on the ventral surface of the brainstem (Figs. 4-17 through 4-19). The ventral surface of the pons

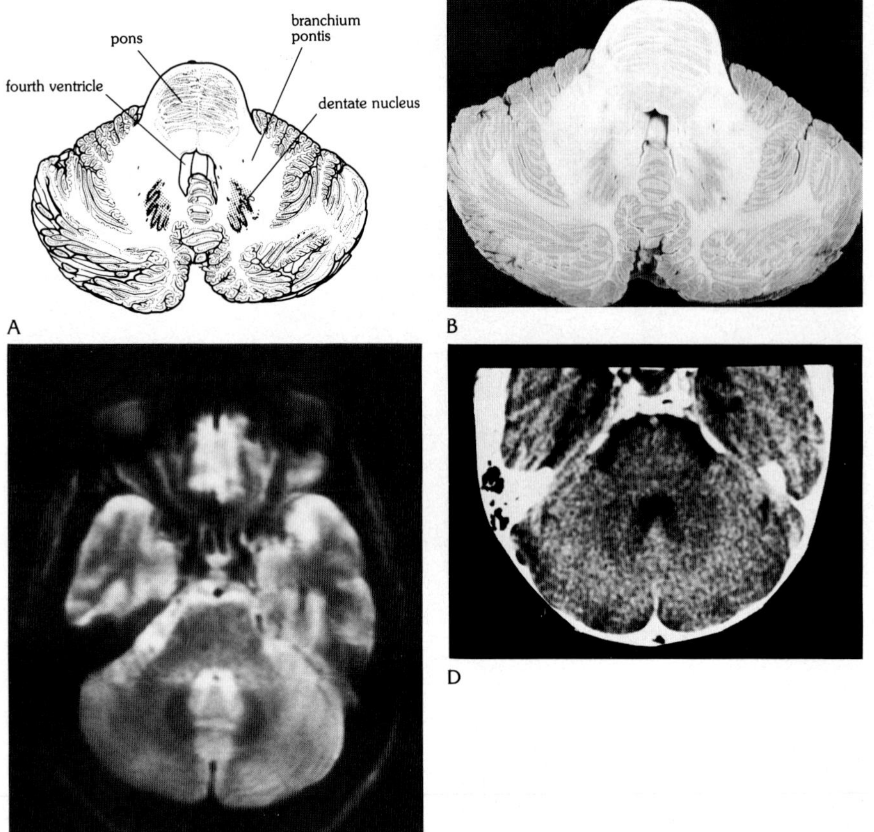

Figure 4-26 Anatomic correlation through the region of the middle cerebellar peduncle: (**A**) line drawing; (**B**) brain section; (**C**) MR; (**D**) CT.

is separated from the medulla by the inferior pontine sulcus, and from the cerebral peduncles by the superior pontine sulcus. The ventral prominence consists of transverse strands across the midline. On each side these strands form the middle cerebellar peduncle. The basilar sulcus, a shallow midline depression on the ventral surface of the pons, forms the depression for the basilar artery.

A smaller dorsal component—the tegmentum of the pons—forms the upper half of the floor of the fourth ventricle. Small projections in this portion of the floor on either side represent the sites of the facial colliculi (Fig. 4-25). The dorsal surface of the pons forms the upper half of the floor of the fourth ventricle.

THE MEDULLA OBLONGATA

The medulla oblongata is continuous inferiorly with the spinal cord and cephalad with the pons (Fig. 4-24). It measures 3 cm in length, its sagittal diameter is 1.25 cm, and in the coronal plane it measures 2 cm from side to side. There are two midline grooves along the anterior and posterior aspects. The anterior, or ventral, median fissure starts below at the pyramidal decussation and ends superiorly at the inferior border of the pons. The posterior median sulcus, or dorsal sulcus, is present only in the inferior half and ends where the dorsal surface of the medulla forms the floor of the fourth ventricle. The two midline grooves bisect the medulla. Each half has two additional grooves: the ventral lateral sulcus and the dorsal lateral sulcus (Fig. 4-25).

The lateral boundaries of the floor of the fourth ventricle are formed by the inferior cerebellar peduncles, which connect the dorsal surface of the medulla with the cerebellum.

The Cerebellum

The cerebellum occupies the greater part of the posterior cranial fossa. It is posterolateral to the pons and medulla and is separated from these two structures by the fourth ventricle (Fig. 4-26).

The surface contour of the cerebellum is defined by the cranial vault and the tentorium cerebelli. The highest point of the cerebellum is in the midline anteriorly. The posterior surface of the cerebellum lies against the inner table of the occipital bone, whereas the anterolateral surface is opposite the inner table of the temporal bone. The

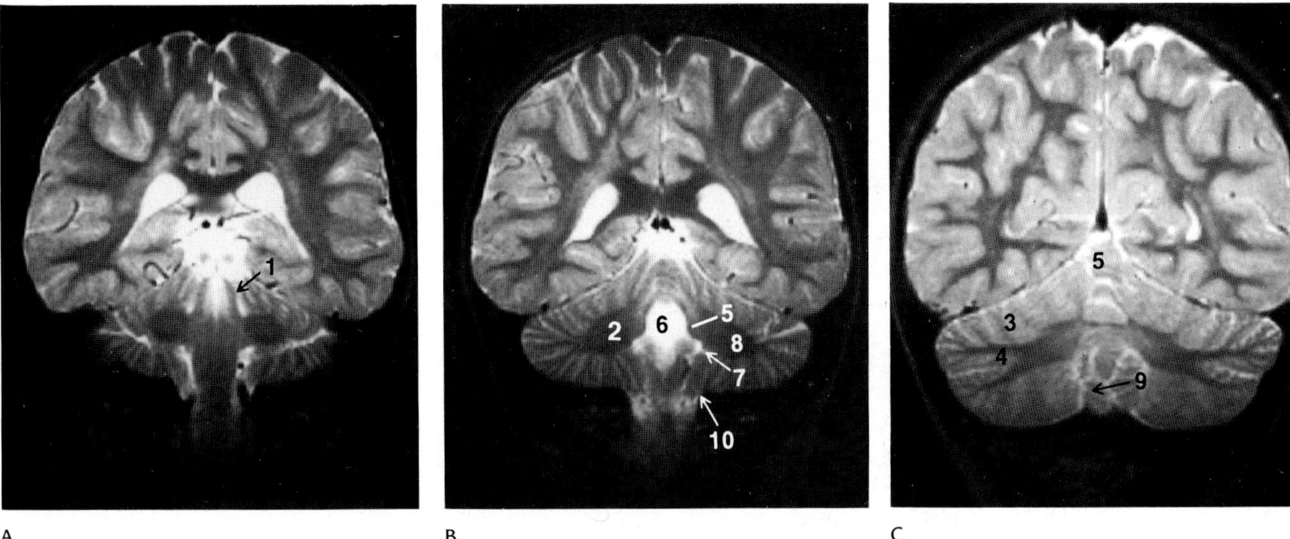

Figure 4-27 Coronal MR sections through the hindbrain: (**A**) level of cerebellar peduncles; (**B**) level of fourth ventricle; (**C**) posterior to the fourth ventricle. 1 = superior cerebellar peduncle; 2 = middle cerebellar peduncle; 3 = gray matter; 4 = white matter; 5 = superior vermis; 6 = fourth ventricle; 7 = foramen of Luschka; 8 = dentate nucleus; 9 = nodules; 10 = tonsil.

cerebellum is attached to the brainstem by three cerebellar peduncles: the superior (brachium conjunctivum), middle (brachium pontis), and inferior (restiform body) cerebellar peduncles, which are connected to the midbrain, pons, and medulla, respectively. The cerebellum consists of a narrow medial portion—the vermis—and two hemispheres that extend laterally and posteriorly (Fig. 4-25).

The different components of the cerebellar hemisphere and vermis seen in axial sections can be better defined when combined with images in the sagittal (Press 1989; Courcheasne 1989) and coronal planes (Fig. 4-27).

FUNCTIONAL ANATOMIC CORRELATION

This section deals with imaging correlation of some of the major functional areas within the brain (Gado 1979), including the motor, sensory, speech, and visual cortical areas.

Functional Localization in the Frontal Lobe

The anterior cortical speech area (Broca's speech area) is located in the dominant hemisphere. It occupies the posterior end of the inferior frontal gyrus on the lateral surface of the frontal lobe (Figs. 4-21, 4-28, and 4-29). The motor cortical area occupies the precentral gyrus. It starts inferiorly just posterior to the speech area and extends superiorly to the superior margin of the cerebral hemispheres, with an extension for a short distance downward along the medial surface that forms part of the paracentral lobule.

Functional Localization in the Temporal Lobe

The acoustic cortical area is located in the superior temporal gyrus. It is within the lateral surface of the temporal lobe at the posterior limit of the sylvian fissure (Figs. 4-28 and 4-29).

The posterior speech center occupies an extensive area of the posterior parts of the superior and middle temporal gyri and extends into the inferior part of the parietal lobe (Figs. 4-22, 4-28, and 4-29).

Functional Localization in the Parietal Lobe

The sensory cortex occupies the postcentral gyrus of the parietal lobe. The cortical area starts inferiorly in the parietal operculum and extends superiorly to the superior border of the cerebral hemisphere, with an extension in the medial surface forming part of the paracentral lobule (Figs. 4-22, 4-23, 4-28, and 4-29).

Functional Localization in the Occipital Lobe

The primary visual area, referred to as the *striate cortex*, occupies the upper and lower lips and the depth of the calcarine sulcus (Figs. 4-28 and 4-29). It lies mostly along

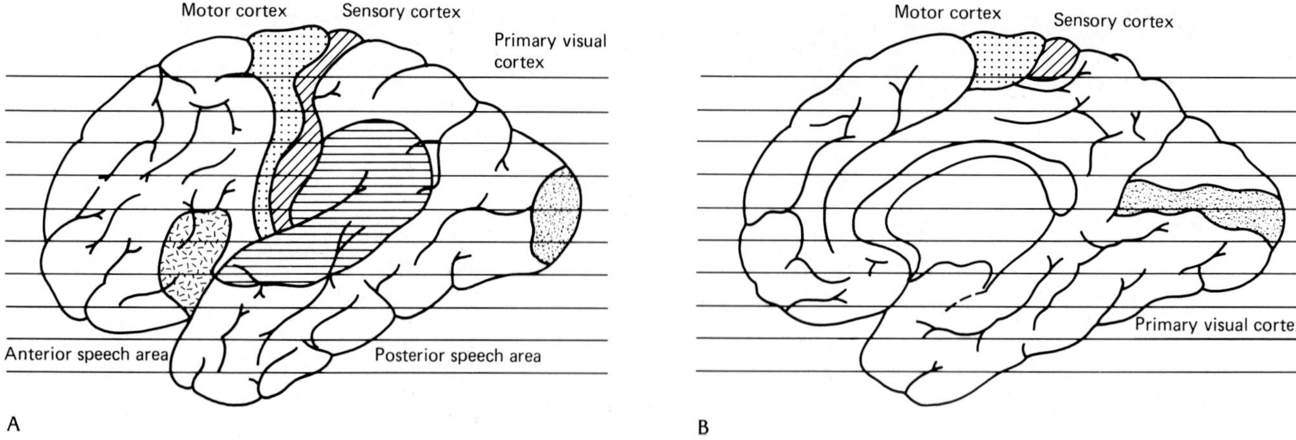

Figure 4-28 Diagramatic representation of the lateral (**A**) and medial (**B**) surfaces of the brain showing the motor, sensory, speech, and primary visual areas of the cortex.

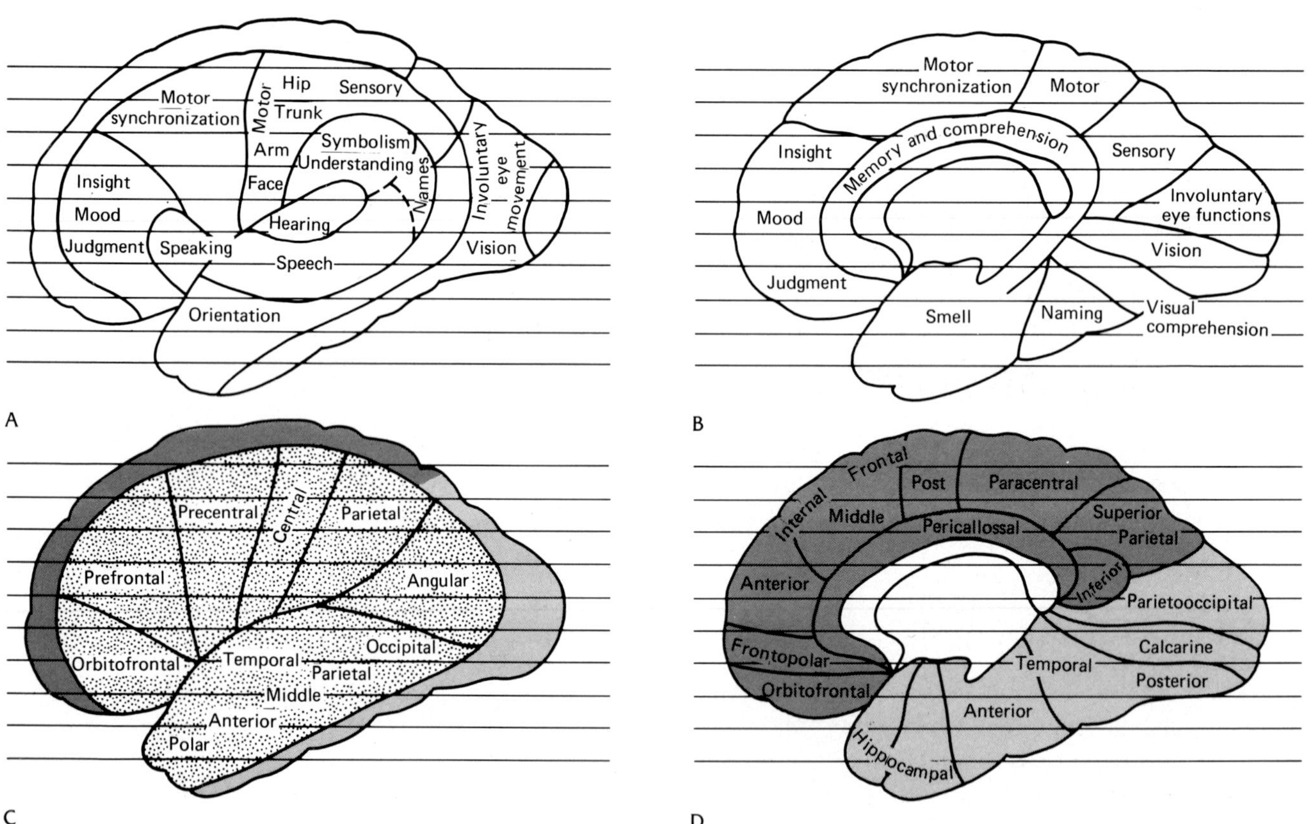

Figure 4-29 Diagramatic representation of the cerebral hemisphere showing the functional localization of the medial (**A**) and lateral (**B**) surfaces and surface demarcation (**C, D**) of the vascular territories to match the functional areas.

the medial surface of the occipital lobe, extending posteriorly into the occipital pole and limited laterally by the lunate sulcus. The primary visual center receives fibers of the optic radiation from the lateral geniculate body. The geniculate radiation spreads out through the white matter of the occipital lobe, terminating in the occipital cortex.

Functional Localization in the Diencephalon and Mesencephalon

The pyramidal and extrapyramidal tracts and the associated nuclei are best evaluated in the coronal plane (Fig. 4-30). These fiber tracts eventually end in the motor and sensory centers in the gray matter.

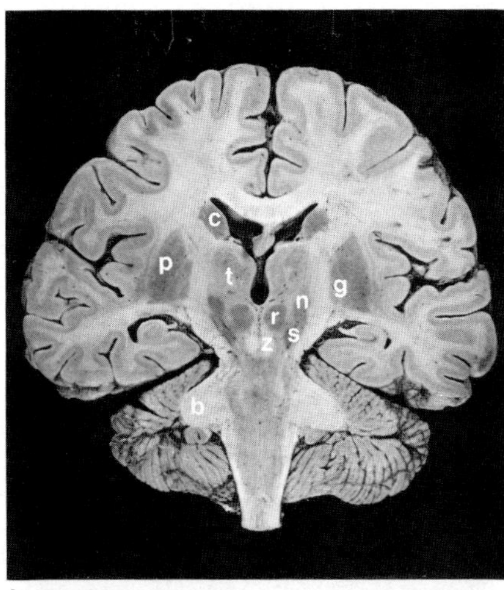

A

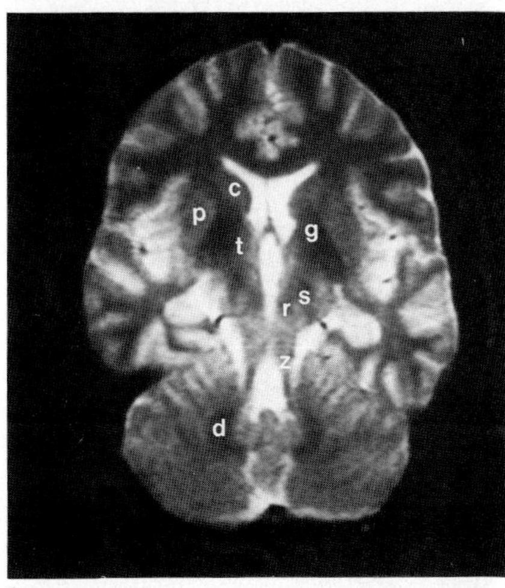

B

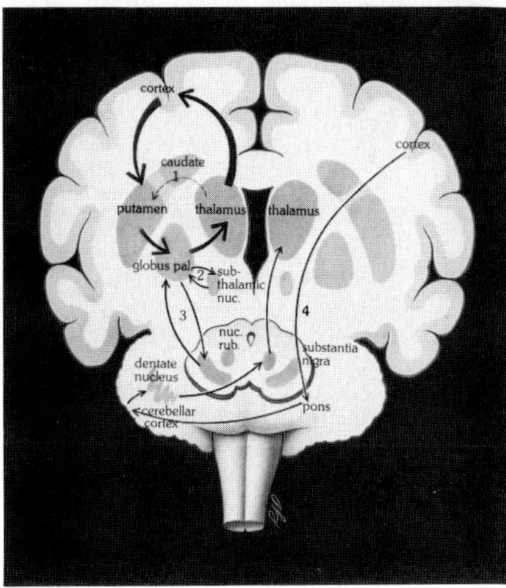

C

Figure 4-30 The extrapyramidal tracts and their localization on MRI: (**A**) line drawing; (**B**) semicoronal brain section; (**C**) T_2-weighted MR. c = caudate nucleus; p = putamen; g = globus pallidus; t = thalamus; s = substantia nigra; r = red nucleus; z = brachium conjunctivum; d = dentate nucleus.

CT AND MRI OF MATURING BRAIN

The morphological anatomy of the brain in a newborn full-term infant is similar to that of the adult brain in CT and MR imaging. However, from birth and up to 18 months to 2 years of age, the brain undergoes certain changes in ultrastructural organization (Table 4-3). These include myelination of the neural fibers in a centrifugal manner and an increase in the volume of neurons and glial cells. Both processes contribute to the maturation of the brain. Myelination is a continuous process that usually begins during the twenty-sixth week of gestation. The maximum spurt in myelination occurs during the neonatal period, extending up to 18 to 24 months. Myelination initially involves the cranial nerves, with the optic nerve being the first nerve demonstrating myelination.

Table 4-3A Brain Maturation Pattern (Based on Myelination in Full-term Infant)

AGE	WHITE MATTER SIGNAL INTENSITY ON T_1-WEIGHTED MRI	WHITE MATTER SIGNAL INTENSITY ON T_2-WEIGHTED MRI
Birth to 16 weeks	Hypointense	Hyperintense
16–40 weeks	Hyperintense	Hyperintense
Beyond 40 weeks	Hyperintense	Hypointense

Table 4-3B Chronological Pattern of Myelination Seen as Hyperintense Signal on Spin Echo T_1-Weighted MRI

AGE	STRUCTURES SHOWING HYPERINTENSE SIGNAL
At birth	Posterior limb of internal capsule
	Cerebellar peduncles
	Corona radiata close to central sulcus
4–20 weeks	Optic radiation fibers
20–40 weeks	Splenium of corpus callosum
	Anterior limb of internal capsule
40–52 weeks	Genu of corpus callosum
1–2 years	Body of corpus callosum
	Central white matter

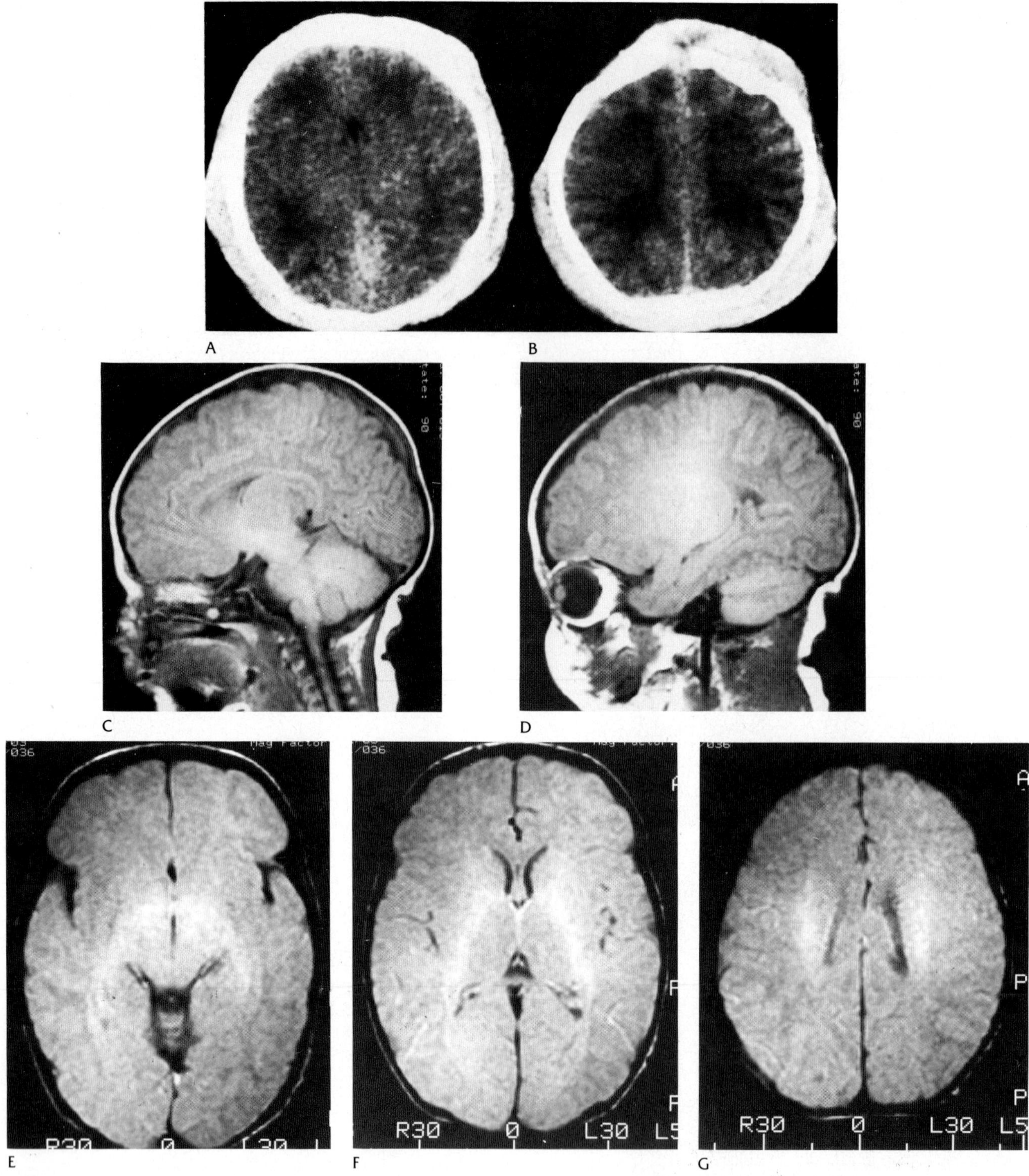

Figure 4-31 A 3-week-old infant. **A, B.** NCCT demonstrates relative hyperdensity of the brain parenchyma with patchy hypodensity in the white matter. Sagittal SE 600/20 (T_1WI) (**C, D**) and axial (**E–G**) SE 2800/30 MR. Hyperintense signal in the cerebellar peduncles, brainstem, optic radiation, and precentral cortical gyri.

CT and MRI (Holland 1986; Lee 1986; McArdle 1987; Barkovich 1988) of the normal maturation of the brain are based on histological studies by Yakovlev (1967). On CT, maturation and myelination result in the following appearance: During the first 3 months there is homogeneous intensity of both gray and white matter. The basal ganglia and the thalamus cannot be clearly separated from the rest of the brain parenchyma. From 3 months to 6 months a relative hypodensity is noted in the periventricular region, fading toward the cortical surface. The

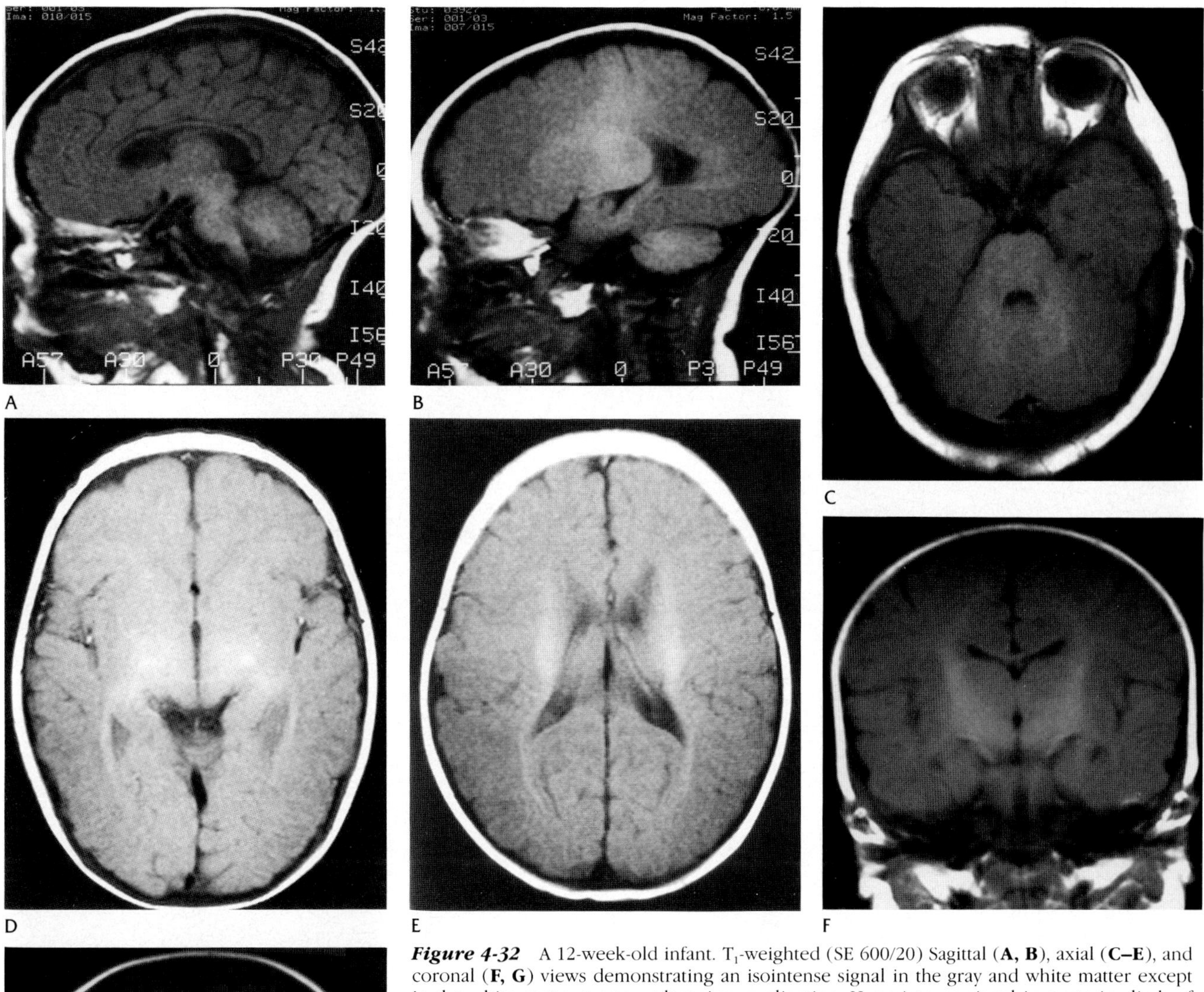

G

Figure 4-32 A 12-week-old infant. T_1-weighted (SE 600/20) Sagittal (**A, B**), axial (**C–E**), and coronal (**F, G**) views demonstrating an isointense signal in the gray and white matter except in the white matter tracts undergoing myelination. Hyperintense signal in posterior limb of internal capsule, corona radiata, and subcortical white matter of the paracentral gyri.

adult form of appearance is achieved between 6 months and 2 years.

MR is much more sensitive in demonstrating the myelination and maturation of the brain. The magnetic field strength influences the appearance of the tissue signal characteristics. This accounts for the minor differences described in the literature (Nowell 1987; McArdle 1987; Barkovich 1988). At higher field strength the T_1 relaxation time is prolonged (Barkovich 1988). Myelination of the white matter tracts is seen as a bright signal intensity on T_1WI and as a decreased signal intensity in T_2WI.

In the neonatal brain, on T_1WI the white matter is hypointense relative to the gray matter. The brainstem, cerebellar peduncles, optic tract, optic radiation, and posterior limb of the internal capsule have a hyperintense signal. In heavily T_2WI, the posterior limb of the internal capsule, the anterolateral thalamus, the dorsal brainstem, and the precentral cortical gyri have decreased signal intensity (Fig. 4-31). By age 3 months, in T_1WI, the middle cerebellar peduncle, the anterior aspect of the brainstem, the anterior limb of the internal capsule, and the optic radiation have a hyperintense signal. Since myelination occurs in a centrifugal as well as an anterior-to-posterior direction, the hyperintense signal is initially seen in the subcortical white matter of the paracentral gyri before this change occurs in the white matter of the postcentral gyrus (Fig. 4-32).

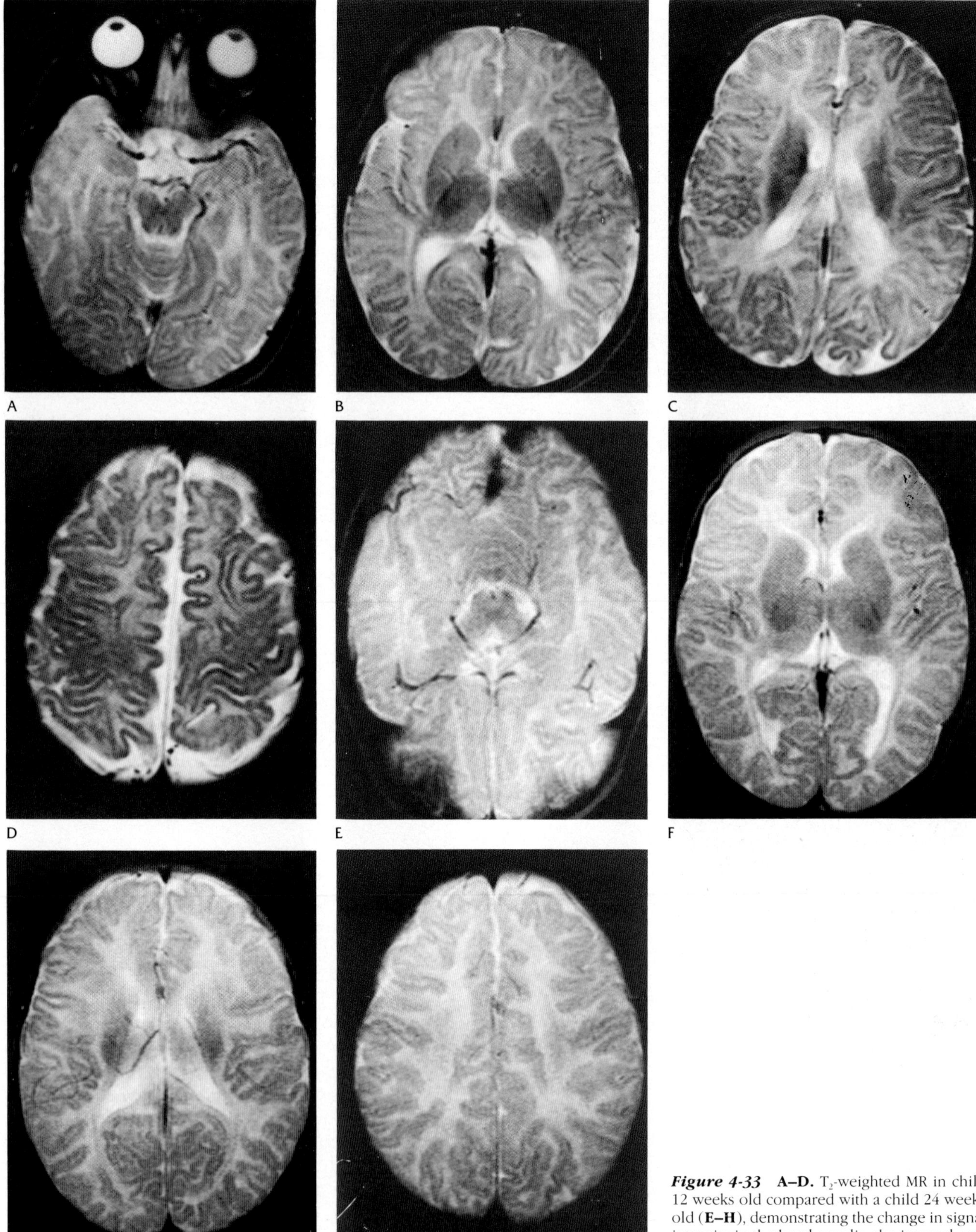

Figure 4-33 **A–D.** T_2-weighted MR in child 12 weeks old compared with a child 24 weeks old (**E–H**), demonstrating the change in signal intensity in the basal ganglia, the internal capsule, and the splenium of the corpus callosum.

Between 3 and 6 months there is a progressive decrease in signal intensity in the basal ganglia, the centrum semiovale, and the splenium of the corpus callosum (Fig. 4-33).

Between 6 and 12 months, the white matter signal changes toward the adult type, progressing from the subcortical white matter of the occipital lobe to the frontal lobe. During this period the signal intensity of the basal ganglia has an adult appearance. The change in signal intensity during the postnatal development of the brain on T_1WI and T_2WI is not completely understood. It is probably related to the decrease in water content over the first 2 years of life (Holland 1986). Other factors that influence the signal characteristics are probably due to the presence of phospholipids and myelin-based proteins.

Imaging of Trace Elements

Identification of normal physiological calcification is more easily achieved with CT than with MRI. Calcium deposition is seen as hyperdensity on CT studies. On MRI, calcium deposition is seen as a hypointense signal in all pulse sequences. Differentiation of calcium deposits from vascular structures requires gradient-echo sequences.

Macromolecular deposits of Fe(III) in the basal ganglia, substantia nigra, and red nucleus can be seen on MRI in T_2WI (Rutledge 1987; Drayer 1986).

Normal Variants

Minor variations in the anatomy of the brain or the CSF space should not be confused with pathological processes. These variations include the following:

1. Variation in the size of the cisterna magna and the superior cerebellar cistern.
2. The occipital horn on one side may extend farther posteriorly than does the opposite side.
3. Persistence of the cavum septum pellucidum beyond infancy.
4. A prominent cavum veli interpositum.
5. Prominent perivascular or Robin-Virchow spaces. These are often seen beyond the fifth decade but may be seen in younger patients.
6. Anomalous venous drainage patterns, especially around the torcular Herophili.
7. Calcification in the basal ganglia, falx cerebri, and tentorium cerebelli.
8. Variable amount of CSF within the sella, extending from the suprasellar cistern.
9. Variability in the amount of marrow within the petrous apex of the temporal bone.

REFERENCES

ATLAS SW, ZIMMERMAN RA, BILANIUK LT, et al: Corpus callosum and limbic system: Neuroanatomic MR evaluation of developmental anomalies. *Radiology* 160:355–358, 1986.

BARAKOS JA, DILLON WP, CHEW WM: Orbit, skull base and pharynx: Contrast enhanced fat suppression MR imaging. *Radiology* 179:191–198, 1991.

BARKOVICH AJ, KJOS BO, JACKSON DE, et al: Normal maturation of the neonatal and infant brain: MR imaging at 1.5 T. *Radiology* 166:173–180, 1988.

BERMAN SA, HAYMAN LA, HINCK VC: Correlation of cerebral vascular territories with cerebral function by computed tomography: I. Anterior cerebral artery. *AJNR* 1:259–263, 1980.

BERMAN SA, HAYMAN LA, HINCK VC: Correlation of CT cerebral vascular territories with function: III. Middle cerebral arteries. *AJNR* 1:161–166, 1984.

BRADLEY WG, WALUCH V: Bloodflow, magnetic resonance imaging. *Radiology* 154:443–450, 1985.

BRADLEY WG, KORTMAN KE, BURGOYNE B: Flowing cerebrospinal fluid in normal and hydrocephalic states: Appearance on MR images. *Radiology* 159:611–616, 1986.

BRAFFMAN BH, ZIMMERMAN RA, RABISSCHONG P: Cranial nerves III, IV, VI: A clinical approach to the evaluation of their dysfunction. *Semin US CT MR* 8:185–213, 1987.

BURT TB: MR of CSF flow phenomenon mimicking basilar artery aneurysm. *AJNR* 8:55–58, 1987.

CHUI M, TUCKER W, HUDSON A, et al: High resolution CT of Meckel's cave. *Neuroradiology* 27:403–409, 1985.

COURCHEASNE E, PRESS GA, MURAKAMI J, et al: Cerebellum in sagittal plane: Anatomic MR correlation: I. Vermis. *AJNR* 10:659–666, 1989.

DANIELS DL, WILLIAMS AL, HAUGHTON KVM: Jugular foramen: Anatomic and computed tomographic study. *AJR* 142:153–158, 1984*a*.

DANIELS DL, HERFKINS R, GAGER WE, et al: Magnetic resonance imaging of the optic nerves and chiasm. *Radiology* 152:79–83, 1984*b*.

DANIELS DL, HERFKINS R, GAGER WE, et al: Magnetic resonance imaging of the optic nerves and chiasm. *Radiology* 152:79–83, 1984*c*.

DANIELS DL, SCHENCK JF, FOSTER T, et al: Magnetic resonance imaging of the jugular foramen. *AJNR* 6:699–703, 1985.

DANIELS DL, PECH P, POJUNAS KW, et al: Magnetic resonance imaging of the trigeminal nerve. *Radiology* 159:577–583, 1986.

DRAYER B, BURGER P, DARWIN R, et al: Magnetic resonance imaging of brain iron. *AJNR* 7:373–378, 1986.

ENZMANN DR, RUBIN JB, DELAPAZ R, et al: Cerebrospinal fluid pulsation: Benefits and pitfalls in MR imaging. *Radiology* 161:773–778, 1986.

FLANNIGAN BD, BRADLEY WG, MAZZIOTTA JC, et al: Magnetic resonance imaging of the brainstem: Normal structure and basic functional anatomy. *Radiology* 154:375–383, 1985.

GADO M, HANAWAY J, FRANK R: Functional anatomy of the cerebral cortex by computed tomography. *J Comput Assist Tomogr* 3:1–19, 1979.

HAN JS, HUSS RG, BENSON JE, et al: MR imaging of the skull base. *J Comput Assist Tomgr* 8:944–952, 1984.

HARDIN CW, HARNSEBERGER HR: The radiographic evaluation of trigeminal neuropathy. *Semin US CT MR* 8:214–239, 1987.

HAYMAN LA, BERMAN SA, HINCK VC: Correlation of CT cerebral vascular territories with function: II. Posterior cerebral artery. *AJNR* 2:219–225, 1981.

HILAL SK, TROKEL SI: Computed tomography of the orbit using thin sections. *Semin Roentgenol* 12:137–147, 1977.

HINSHAW DB Jr, FAHMY JL, PECKHAM N, et al: The bright choroid plexus on MR: CT and pathologic correlation. *AJNR* 9:483–486, 1988.

HOLLAND BA, HAAS DK, NORMAN D, et al: MRI of normal brain maturation. *AJNR* 7:201–208, 1986.

JUNGREIS CA, KANAL E, HIRSCH WL, et al: Normal perivascular spaces mimicking lacunar infarction: MR imaging. *Radiology* 169:101–104, 1988.

KAPILA A, CHAKERAS DW, BLANCO E: The Meckel cave: Computed tomographic study. *Radiology* 152:425–433, 1984.

KEMP SS, ZIMMERMAN RA, BILANIUK LT, et al: Magnetic resonance imaging of the cerebral aqueduct. *Neuroradiology* 29:430–436, 1987.

LEE BCP, LIPPER E, NAAS R, et al: MRI of the central nervous system in neonates and young children. *AJNR* 7:605–616, 1986.

MAWAD ME, SILVER AJ, HILAL SK, et al: Computed tomography of the brainstem with intrathecal metrizamide: I. The normal brain stem. *AJNR* 4:553–563, 1983.

MCARDLE CB, RICHARDSON CJ, NICHOLAS DA, et al: Developmental features of the neonatal brain: MR imaging: I. Gray-white matter differentiation and myelination. *Radiology* 162:223–229, 1987.

NOWELL MA, HACKNEY DB, ZIMMERMAN RA, et al: Immature brain: Spin-echo pulse sequence parameters for high contrast MR imaging. *Radiology* 162:119–124, 1987.

PRESS GA, MURAKAMI J, COURCHEASNE E, et al: Cerebellum in sagittal plane—Anatomic MR correlation: II. The cerebellar hemispheres. *AJNR* 10:667–676, 1989.

REMLEY K, HARNSBERGER HR, SMOKER WRK, et al: CT and MR in the evaluation of glossopharyngeal, vagal and spinal accesory neuropathy. *Semin US CT MR* 8:284–300, 1987.

RUTLEDGE JN, HILAL SK, SILVER AJ, et al: Study of movement disorders and brain iron by MR. *AJNR* 8:397–411, 1987.

SARWAR M: The septum pellucidum: Normal and abnormal. *AJNR* 10:989–1006, 1989.

SHERMAN JL, CITRIN CM, BOWEN BJ, et al: MR demonstration of normal CSF flow. *AJNR* 7:3–6, 1986.

SMOKER WRK, HARNESBERGER HR, OSBORN AG: The hypoglossal nerve. *Semin US CT MR* 8:301–312, 1987.

SUZUKI M, TAKASHIMA T, KADOYA M, et al: MR imaging of olfactory bulbs and tracts. *AJNR* 10:955–957, 1989.

TERESI L, LUFKIN R, NITTA K, et al: MRI of the facial nerve: Normal anatomy and pathology. *Semin US CT MR* 8:240–255, 1987.

YAKOVLEV PL, LECOUR AR: The myelogenic cycles of regional maturation of the brain, in Mankowski A (ed): *Regional Development of the Brain in Early Life*. Philadelphia, W A Davis, 1967, pp 3–69.

5 THE ORBIT

Larissa T. Bilaniuk
Scott W. Atlas
Robert A. Zimmerman

INTRODUCTION

Major advances have been achieved in the diagnosis of orbital and visual pathway lesions, first with the application of computed tomography (CT) to the evaluation of the orbit (Forbes 1980, 1982; Trokel 1979; Jacobs 1980) and then with the application of magnetic resonance (MR) (Sullivan 1986; Bilaniuk 1987; Atlas 1987*a*) to the evaluation of the orbit. Both CT and MR provide excellent anatomic detail (Figs. 5-1 through 5-4) and information regarding the presence, location, and extent of intraorbital lesions as well as the involvement of the orbit by lesions arising in the adjacent bone and paranasal sinuses (Mancuso 1978; Weber 1978; Som 1985). Generally, CT is the first procedure performed, with MR playing a complementary role. CT of the orbit is a well-established technique. It is more widely available than MR, easier to perform and interpret, and less susceptible to motion artifacts, and it provides better bony detail. However, a tremendous upsurge in the number of MR scanners and new software and surface coil developments as well as the utilization of paramagnetic contrast agents have made MR a serious competitor of CT. Thin sections in multiple planes with high resolution can now be obtained with MR without the penalty of longer scanning times. In some categories of orbital disease MR shows clear advantages over CT. MR provides better characterization of ocular, vascular, and hemorrhagic lesions and more precisely delineates visual pathway lesions and other lesions with extraorbital extension. Familiarity with the advantages and disadvantages of each technique is important in deciding on the proper sequencing of diagnostic studies and leads to customized approach in the evaluation of orbital abnormalities.

TECHNIQUE

The examination of the orbit by CT or MR should be tailored to the clinical problem at hand but also should be anatomically complete. Thin sections are obtained routinely in at least two planes. The entire orbit is encompassed, along with the adjacent portions of the brain, the cavernous sinus, and portions of the paranasal sinus and facial and pharyngeal soft tissues. Familiarity with the history and clinical results leads to proper planning and thus a more efficient and successful imaging study. It is also important to anticipate sedation when children, retarded patients, or claustrophobic patients are being evaluated.

The adequacy of an imaging examination of the orbit can be assured only if the study is carefully monitored and if images that are marred by motion or artifacts are repeated. After completion of the examination, the study must be carefully reviewed. Such a review is best done on a diagnostic display console so that the sections can be examined for the osseous and soft tissue structures at a variety of window widths with different window levels. To obtain a permanent film record of a CT study, two settings are recommended: one for soft tissue and the other for bony detail. Unless a technique for fat suppression or surface coil correction is used, a similar window level and width manipulation may be necessary for MR images to optimally visualize both the superficial and deep structures of the orbit.

Computed Tomography

Contiguous thin sections, generally 3 mm thick in the transverse plane and 5 mm thick in the coronal plane, are obtained routinely (Baleriaux-Waha 1977; Hoyt 1979; Osborn 1980; Tadmor 1978; Unsold 1980*a;* Wing 1979) (Figs. 5-1*A–D* and 5-2*A–D*). The search for a small lesion may require 1- to 1.5-mm-thick sections. Provided that the patient has not moved during the examination, such thin sections also permit reformation in other planes, such as the sagittal, as well as three-dimensional reconstruction, which is useful in the evaluation of congenital or post-traumatic facial-orbital deformities (Vannier 1987). The authors' experience indicates that examination is necessary in the transverse plane, usually at an angulation of $-10°$ to the orbitomeatal baseline (Fig. 5-1*A–D*) and that

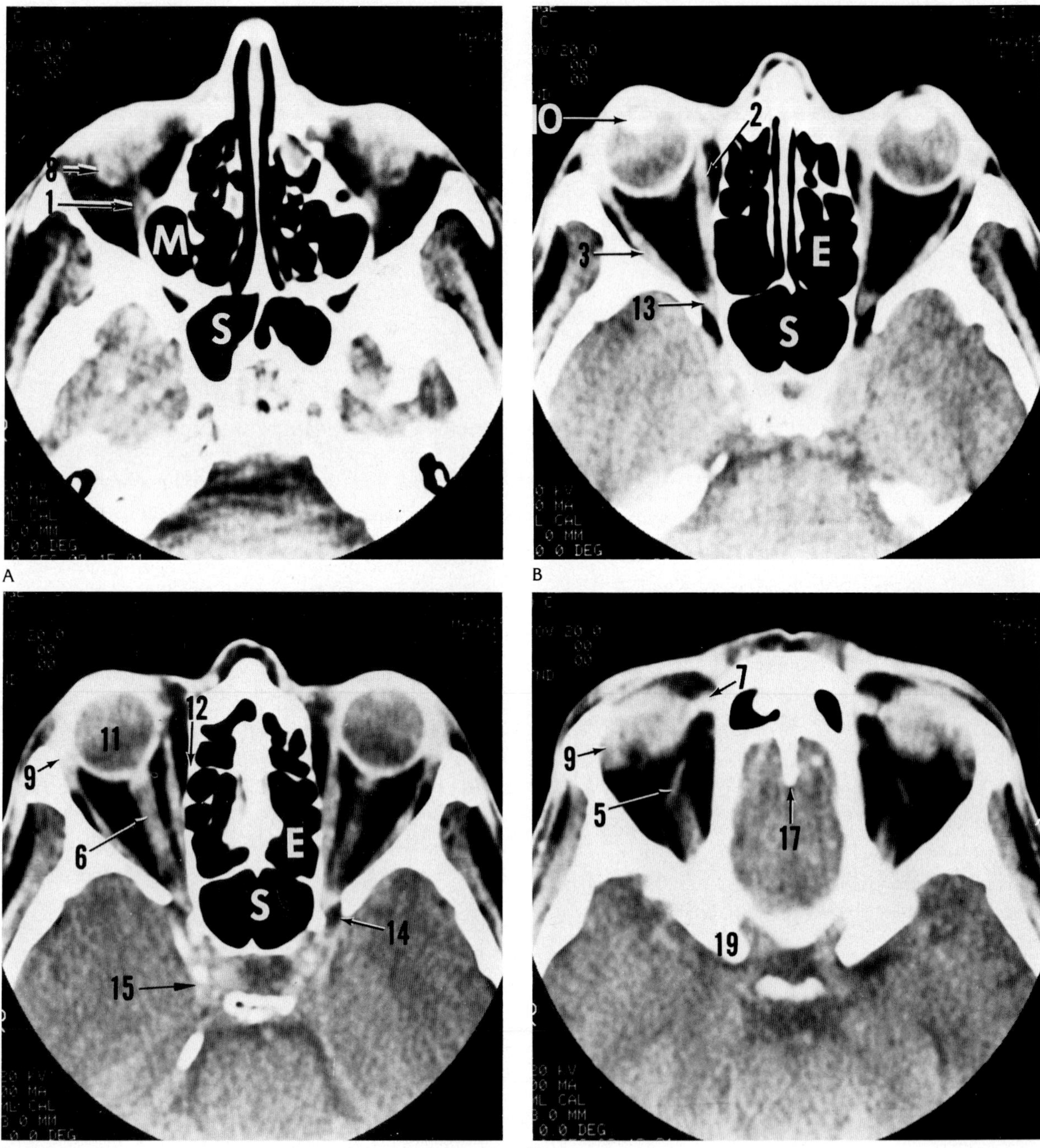

Figure 5-1 (CT: **A–D;** MR: **E–H**) Normal orbit, axial plane, inferior to superior. 1 = inferior rectus, 2 = medial rectus, 3 = lateral rectus, 4 = superior rectus, 5 = superior ophthalmic vein, 6 = optic nerve, 7 = superior oblique, 8 = inferior oblique, 9 = lacrimal gland, 10 = lens, 11 = vitreous, 12 = lamina papyracea, 13 = optic canal, 14 = superior orbital fissure, 15 = cavernous sinus, 16 = floor of orbit, 17 = crista galli, 18 = cribriform plate, 19 = anterior clinoid, 20 = planum sphenoidale, 21 = inferior orbital fissure, 22 = levator palpebrae superioris, 23 = ophthalmic artery, 24 = III, V^1, VI cranial nerves, 25 = V^2 and foramen rotundum. M = maxillary sinus; E = ethmoid sinus; S = sphenoid sinus; C = chiasm; CA = carotid artery; P = pituitary gland.

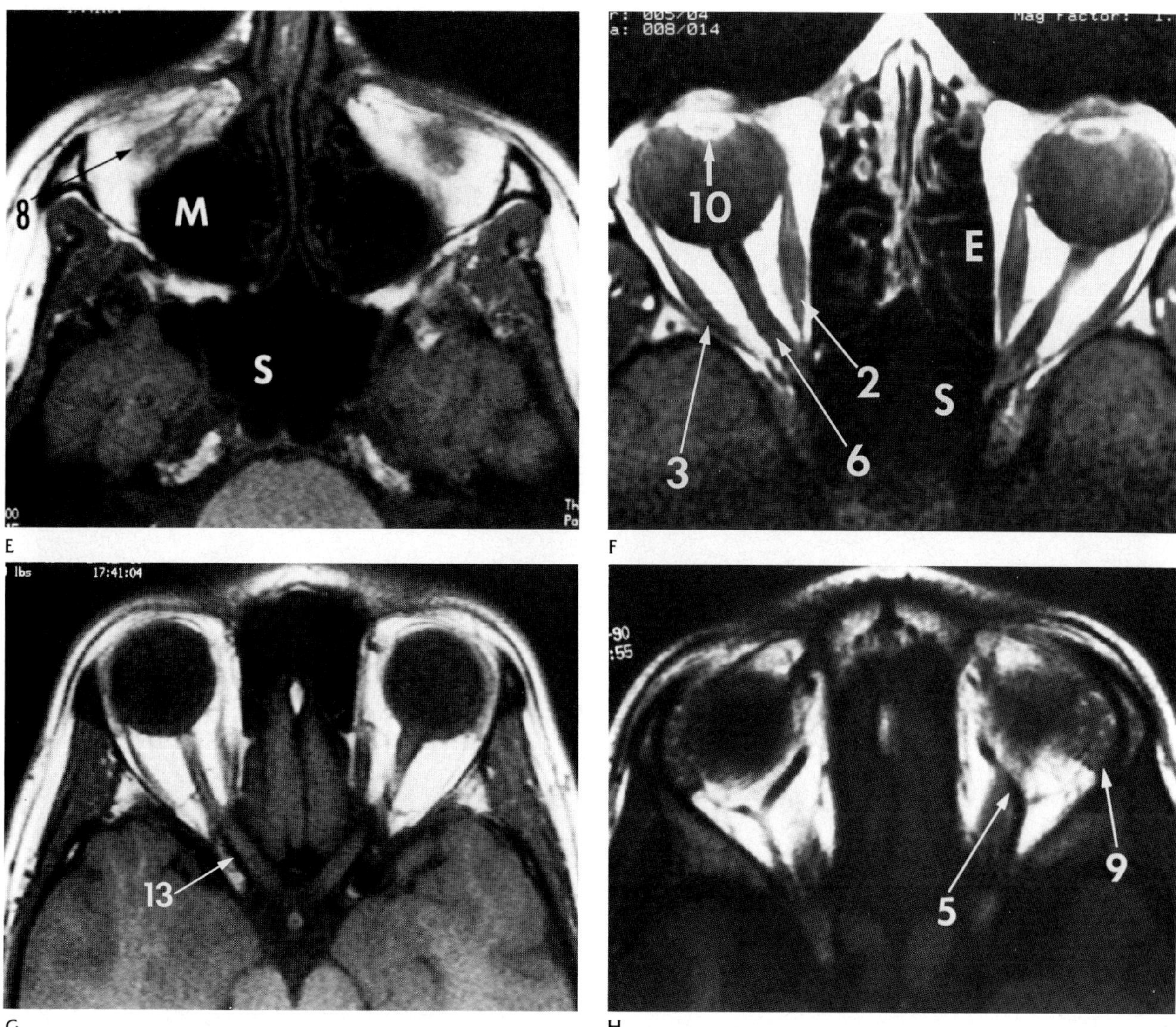

Figure 5-1 (continued)

the initial examination should be made both before and after the injection of an adequate amount of iodinated contrast material. Oblique reformation, which allows one to follow the plane of the optic nerve (Unsold 1980*a*) or that of the superior ophthalmic vein, may be of value in specific cases.

A recently developed CT technology, spiral CT, permits rapid volumetric data acquisition and reconstruction of images in any plane (Zimmerman 1991). This technique is faster than conventional CT, and so there is less likelihood of motion artifacts. The need for patient sedation is decreased, and it entails a lower radiation dose.

Because of its sinuous course in two places, the appearance and course of the optic nerve depend on the thickness and plane of the CT section as well as the direction of gaze (Unsold 1980*b*). Unsold recommends a negative angulation of $-20°$ to the orbitomeatal baseline with the eye in the upgaze position in order to stretch the nerves and have their course parallel to the plane of section.

Magnetic Resonance Imaging

Patients considered for MR scanning must be screened for ferromagnetic orbital foreign bodies (Kelly 1986), vascular clips, and prosthetic material as well as electronic devices (New 1983). Imaging centers generally have lists of devices and materials that are contraindicated for MR imaging. One such list has been published (Shellock 1988) (see Chap. 3).

Certain forms of eye makeup contain iron oxides and can produce artifacts on images (Fig. 5-5); they can also be attracted toward the magnet and accumulate on it (Wright 1985). Patients should be instructed not to wear any eye makeup on the day of the study or to remove it before the MR examination.

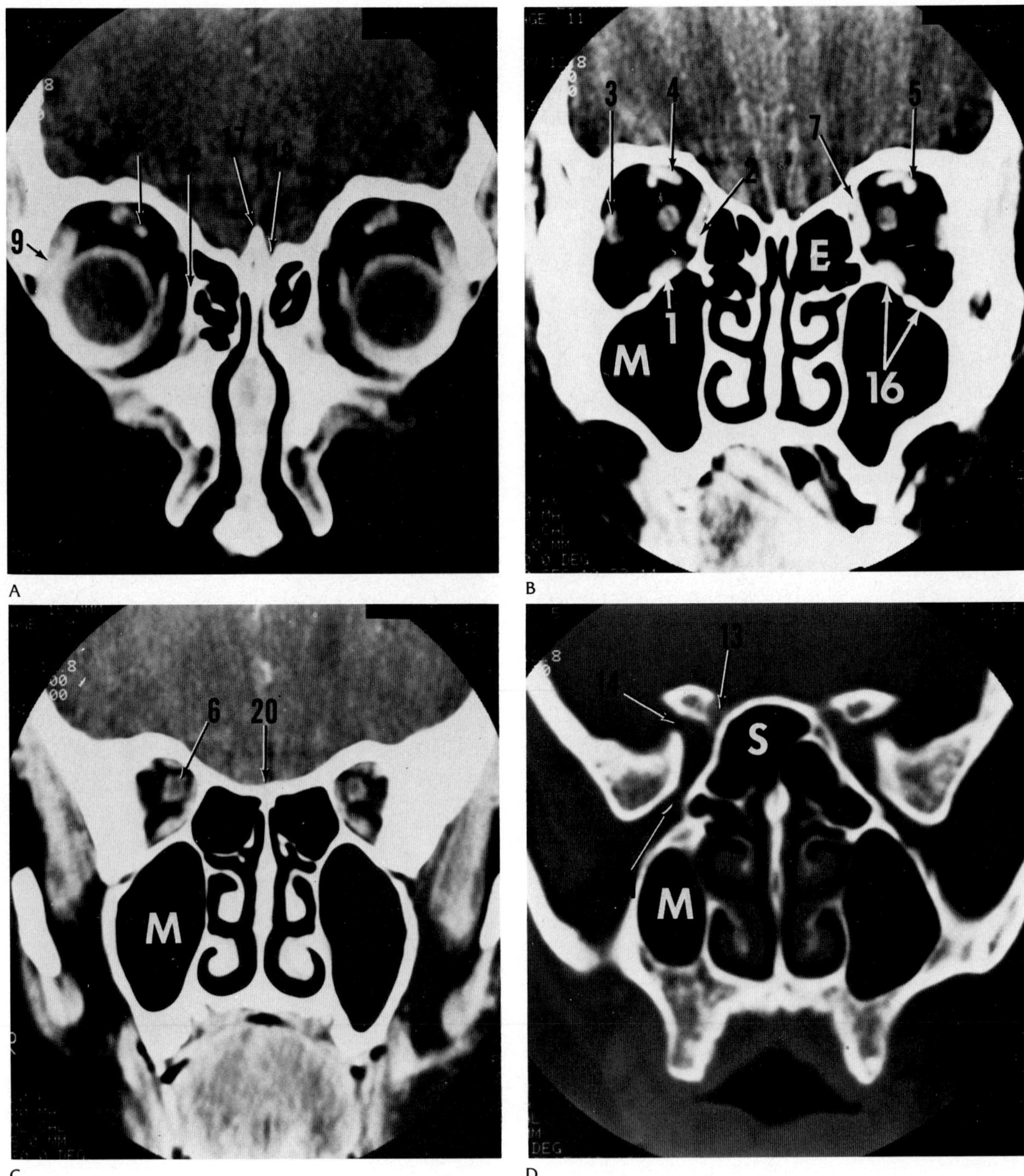

Figure 5-2 (CT: **A–D;** MR: **E–H**) Normal orbit, coronal plane, anterior to posterior. See legend for Fig. 5-1.

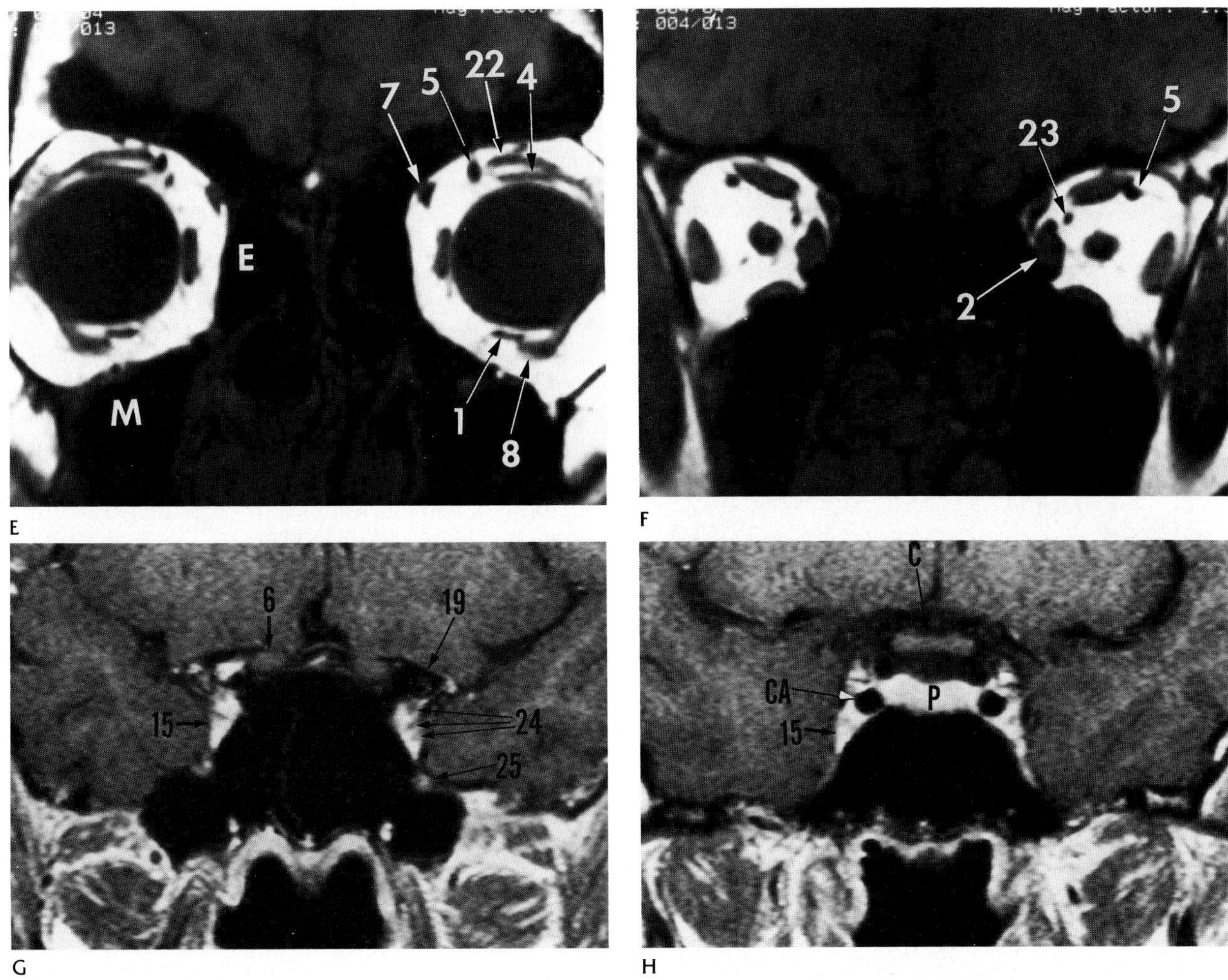

Figure 5-2 (continued)

Careful explanation of what the orbital MR study entails can ensure a successful examination. To avoid artifacts caused by globe motion in scans requiring shorter scanning times, the patient should be asked to relax but gaze in one direction. To avoid eye strain in longer scanning sequences, the patient should be asked to keep the eyes closed but consciously try not to wander with the globes. Children and retarded, uncooperative, or severely claustrophobic patients generally require sedation. Sedated patients should be carefully monitored while in the magnet. This is done with equipment specially designed for the magnetic environment.

MR scanning of the orbits involves the use of two coils: one for transmitting the imaging pulse sequence (whole body coil) and one for receiving the signals induced by the relaxing magnetization (generally a surface coil). To obtain thin sections with high spatial resolution in short scanning times, the surface coil should be of a size that allows it to primarily capture signal from the orbits (Shenck 1985). This is particularly important for short TR/TE spin-echo sequences, which provide the best morphological detail. The orbit has such good inherent soft tissue contrast that a short TR/TE sequence (T_1WI) with 3-mm-thick sections can be obtained in about 2 minutes of scanning time with the number of excitations being just one (NEX = 1). Long TR/short TE (PD-WI) and long TR/long TE spin-echo sequences (T_2WI) that provide information that helps characterize lesions take longer and may be obtained either with an orbital surface coil or a head receiving coil, preferably a quadrature head coil. Numerous pulse sequences other than the routine spin echo are available and may be utilized in special circumstances (Atlas 1987*b*,1988; Dixon 1984; Simon 1988; Keller 1987) (Table 5-1). Three-dimensional or time-of-flight acquisitions are utilized for the imaging of vessels. Magnetic resonance angiography permits excellent delineation of major vessels; even the ophthalmic artery can be demonstrated (Fig. 5-4).

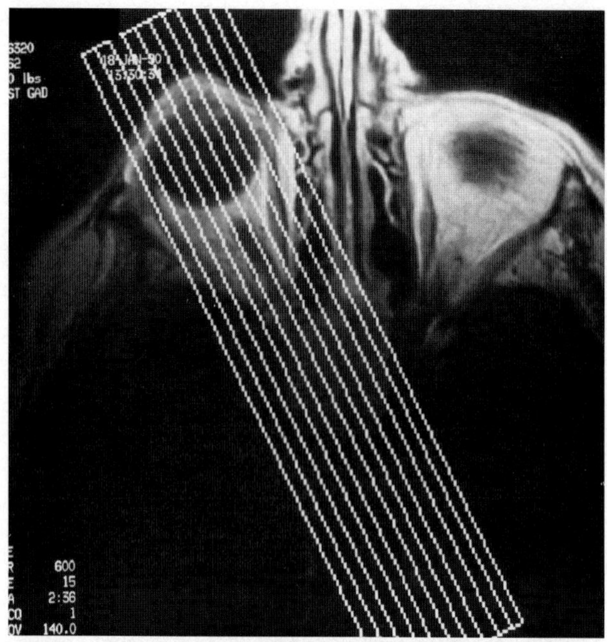

A

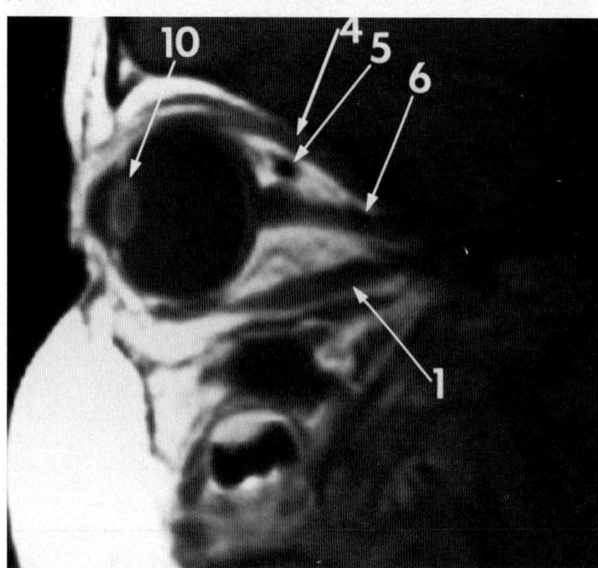

B

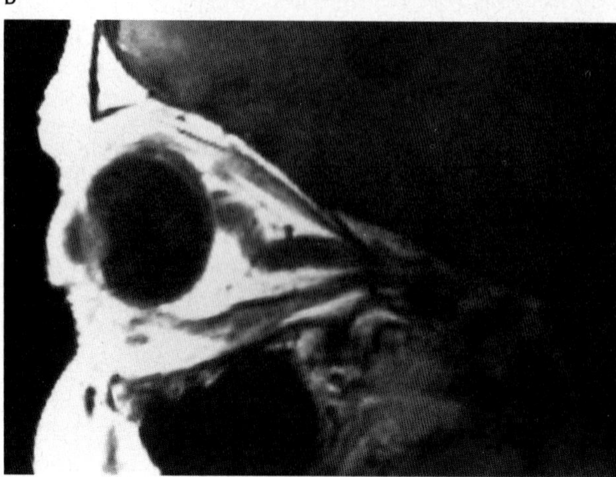
C

◄ ***Figure 5-3*** Normal orbit: MRI, sagittal plane. **A.** The position of the sagittal slices is indicated by white lines on an axial image of the orbits. **B.** Sagittal section, T_1WI (600/15; 3mm) obtained along the long axis of the orbit demonstrates the entire optic nerve, intraorbital, intracanalicular, and intracranial. See legend for Fig. 5-1. **C.** Sagittal section, T_1WI (600/15; 4 mm thick) shows a tortuous optic nerve which would have been difficult to demonstrate in its entirety on other planes. The superior and inferior rectus muscles are also well shown on this plane.

The rationale for the use of contrast material is the same as that for contrast-enhanced CT (CECT): to characterize and delineate ocular and orbital mass lesions and lesions that extend beyond or into the orbit. Because it may be difficult to delineate contrast-enhanced high-intensity orbital fat, some form of fat-suppression technique is required (Keller 1987).

Proper interpretation of MR images requires familiarity with numerous artifacts that can occur during scanning. These artifacts are listed and discussed in several publications (Pusey 1986; Hahn 1988; Clark 1988). The chemical shift artifact is of particular importance in orbital scanning because it can be misinterpreted as an anatomic structure or a pathological process, particularly in the case of optic nerve sheath complex or superior ophthalmic veins. The artifact, which consists of a black band on one side and a bright band on the other side of a structure (Fig. 5-6), results from the fact that fat and water protons are found in different electron environments and therefore resonate at slightly different frequencies (Babcock 1985).

NORMAL ANATOMY OF THE ORBIT

Orbital Walls

The orbit is a pyramidal bony compartment that houses the eyeball and its functional components (extraocular muscles, blood vessels, nerves, lacrimal gland, and fat) (Tadmor 1978; Last 1968). The orbital walls separate the intraorbital components from the surrounding brain and facial structures (Hesselink 1978).

The roof of the orbit (Fig. 5-2) is formed for the most part by the orbital plate of the frontal bone and separates the orbit from the anterior cranial fossa. The lacrimal gland (Figs. 5-1 and 5-2) forms the lacrimal fossa in the superolateral aspect of the orbit. Overall, the bone that forms the roof of the orbit is relatively thin. To a variable extent, the frontal sinus and sometimes the ethmoid sinuses extend into the roof of the orbit (Fig. 5-2E). The posterior component of the roof of the orbit that is formed by the lesser wing of the sphenoid may also contain air cells derived from either the posterior ethmoidal cells or the sphenoid sinus.

Table 5-1 Orbital MR Techniques

INDICATION	COIL	SEQUENCE	PLANE
Routine morphology (cong./trauma)	Surface coil	SE short TR, short TE TR 600 ± 100; TE 15 msec	Axial, coronal 3-mm-thick sec.
Morphology of orbital roof, floor and optic canal	Surface coil	SE short TR, short TE TR 600 ± 100; TE 15 msec	Sagittal along long axis of orbit; coronal
Tissue characterization	Head or surface coil	SE long TR/short TE long TR/long TE 2500–3000/20–90	Axial, coronal (3- to 5-mm-thick sections)
Contrast enhancement ocular, orbital, periorbital lesions	Surface coil	Fat suppression (if not available, careful wide window photography)	Axial, coronal and/or sagittal
Contrast enhancement if orbital lesion with intracranial extent	Head coil	Short TR/short TE; fat suppression for orbital component	Axial, coronal, and/or sagittal
Intravascular flow; thrombosis	Head coil	Gradient echo	Axial, coronal
Vascular malformation or vascular lesions	Head coil	MRA	Axial, coronal
Thin sections of optic nerve sheath complex	Head coil	3-dimensional acquisition	Reconstruct in any plane (1-mm-thick sections)
Avoid high intensity from orbital fat		STIR	Axial, coronal, and/or sagittal

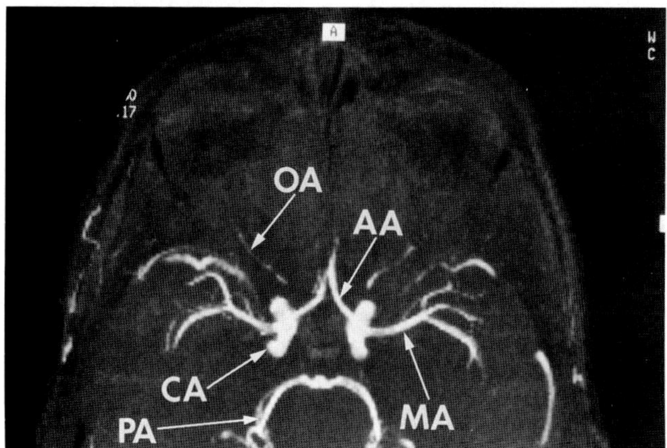

Figure 5-4 Magnetic resonance angiography, compressed image (3D acquisition; TR 35 msec, TE 7 msec, matrix 256 × 256). OA = ophthalmic artery; CA = carotid artery; MA = middle cerebral artery; AA = anterior cerebral artery; PA = posterior cerebral artery.

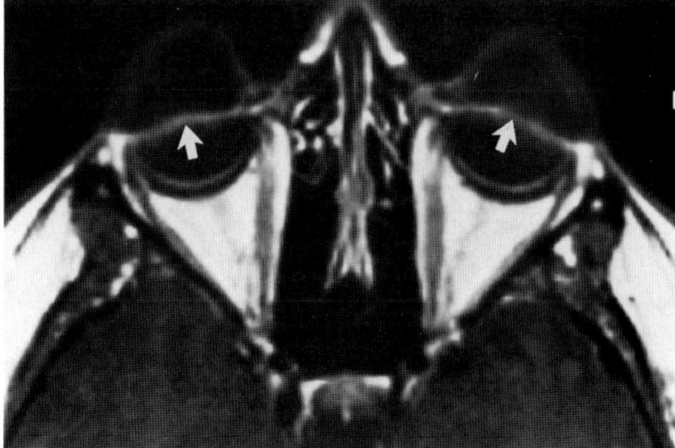

Figure 5-5 Artifact on MR created by eye makeup. An axial T_1WI (600/22) shows a prominent high-intensity line (arrows) crossing each globe and prominent distortion of the anterior aspect of the globes. This was caused by an eyeliner.

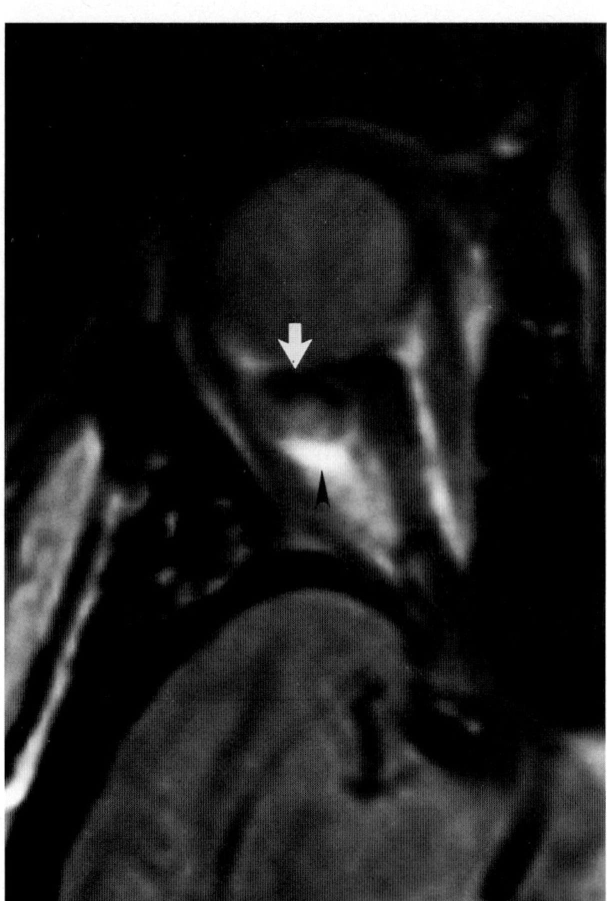

Figure 5-6 Chemical shift MR artifact demonstrated adjacent to a probable small hemangioma on an axial PD-WI. It consists of a black stripe (white arrow) anterior to the small mass and a bright stripe (arrowhead) posterior to the mass.

The floor of the orbit (Figs. 5-2 and 5-3) is composed primarily of the orbital plate of the maxilla. It has a triangular shape, with contributions from portions of the zygoma and the palatine bone. The infraorbital nerve and the infraorbital vessels course in the infraorbital groove and the infraorbital canal in the floor of the orbit. The orbital floor is thin, except at its most anterior margin, where the orbital rim is formed; the rim is a thicker osseous structure that is in continuity below with the anterior wall of the maxillary sinus. The floor of the orbit separates the intraorbital structures from the maxillary sinus (Fig. 5-2), which lies beneath.

The lateral wall of the orbit is formed by the zygoma (Figs. 5-1 and 5-2) anteriorly and the greater wing of the sphenoid posteriorly (Figs. 5-1 and 5-2). The lateral orbital wall is the thickest and strongest of the orbital walls. Lateral to this structure lies the temporal fossa, which contains the temporalis muscle.

The medial wall (Figs. 5-1 and 5-2) is the thinnest component of the orbital walls. It serves to separate the orbital contents from the ethmoid and sphenoid air cells. Contributions to the structure of the medial wall are made by the maxilla, the lacrimal bone, the ethmoid bone, and the body of the sphenoid. The largest component is the one contributed by the ethmoidal orbital plate (lamina papyracea).

Orbital Fissures and Canals

At the apex of the pyramidal structure of the orbit lie three openings that communicate with adjacent extraorbital areas.

The optic canal (Figs. 5-1 and 5-2) is formed by the sphenoid bone and serves to conduct the optic nerve and the ophthalmic artery between the orbit and the middle cranial fossa. The optic nerve is surrounded by a small subarachnoid space that contains cerebrospinal fluid (CSF) and is surrounded by the arachnoid. In the optic canal the ophthalmic artery lies beneath the optic nerve. The roof of the optic canal measures 10 to 12 mm in length and is formed by the lesser wing of the sphenoid. The medial wall of the optic canal is formed by the body of the sphenoid bone, while its inferior and lateral walls are formed by the roots of the lesser wing of the sphenoid (optic strut), which also separates the optic canal from the superior orbital fissure.

The superior orbital fissure (Fig. 5-2) is a space between the greater and lesser wings of the sphenoid. It is separated medially from the optic canal by the optic strut. Transmitted through the superior orbital fissure between the middle cranial fossa and the orbit are the ophthalmic veins; the third, fourth, and sixth cranial nerves; and the first division of the fifth cranial nerve.

The inferior orbital fissure (Fig. 5-2) permits communication between the orbit and the pterygopalatine and infratemporal fossae. Through it runs the zygomatic nerve and the communication between the inferior ophthalmic vein and the pterygoid venous plexus. The maxilla, the palatine bone, and the greater wing of the sphenoid bone contribute to its margins.

Periosteum

Periosteum, also referred to as *periorbita,* lines the bones of the orbit and is in communication with the periosteum (dura mater) covering the intracranial compartment through the various fissures. An intricate system of connective tissue septa exists throughout the orbital fat and provides support for the orbital structures (Koornneef 1979). The septum orbitale (Fig. 5-1) is a periosteal reflection from the anterior orbital margin that is continuous with the tarsal plates. It serves to separate the orbit into preseptal and postseptal components. The intraorbital fat is limited anteriorly by the orbital septum. The eyelids lie anterior to the orbital septum.

Orbital Soft Tissue

The wall of the globe consists of three layers. The innermost—the retina—contains the nerve elements that allow visual perception. The middle layer consists of the choroid, ciliary body, and iris. These three components are also referred to as the *uvea* and have vascular, nutritive, and temperature-regulating functions. The outermost layer is a fibrous protective coat that constitutes the sclera and, anteriorly, the transparent cornea. The lens (Figs. 5-1 and 5-3) is a transparent crystalline body approximately 1 cm in diameter that transmits and focuses light; it lies between the iris and the vitreous humor (Figs. 5-1 and 5-3). Between the cornea and the lens is a space containing the aqueous humor that is divided by the iris into an anterior chamber and a posterior chamber.

The optic nerve (Figs. 5-1 through 5-3), which is the second cranial nerve, extends from the papilla on the posterior surface of the globe to the optic chiasm. Its length is 35 to 50 mm, with the intraorbital component 20 to 30 mm, the intracanalicular portion 4 to 9 mm, and the intracranial portion 3 to 6 mm. The diameter of the optic nerve is approximately 3 to 4 mm. Running beneath the optic nerve as it enters the optic canal from the intracranial compartment is the ophthalmic artery, which remains beneath the optic nerve in its intracanalicular segment and initial intraorbital segment and then crosses medially, usually over (approximately 80 percent) the nerve. Surrounding the optic nerve sheath complex throughout its intraorbital course is the central orbital fat.

Six extraocular muscles (Figs. 5-1 through 5-3) insert on the sclera: the medial and lateral recti, the superior and inferior recti, and the superior and inferior oblique muscles. The superior rectus is the longest, 40 mm, with the medial, lateral, and inferior recti being of progressively shorter length. The medial rectus has the largest diameter of the ocular muscles. The superior oblique muscle is the thinnest muscle and lies in the superomedial aspect of the orbit. The levator palpebrae superioris muscle lies just under the roof of the orbit as a thin flat structure above the superior rectus. It attaches to the skin of the upper eyelid. Below the superior rectus muscle lies the superior ophthalmic vein, below which lies the optic nerve. The lateral rectus lies adjacent to the periosteum of the lateral orbital wall, and only anteriorly does a slight amount of fat intervene between the periosteum and the muscle. The medial rectus is separated from the lamina papyracea by some orbital fat. The posterior portion of the inferior rectus muscle lies in contact with the floor of the orbit, but its anterior portion is separated from the roof of the maxillary sinus by orbital fat.

Orbital fat (Figs. 5-1 through 5-3) fills the space that is not occupied by the globe, nerves, muscles, or vessels. It extends from the orbital septum anteriorly and from the optic nerve to the orbital walls. It is divided by an incomplete intermuscular membrane into a central portion and a more peripheral (extramuscular) portion. The peripheral fat lies between the periosteum of the orbital walls and the rectus muscles. The orbital fat is crossed by an extensive network of connective tissue septa (Koornneef 1977).

The superior ophthalmic vein (Figs. 5-1 through 5-3) forms at the root of the nose, at the juncture of the frontal and angular veins, and enters the orbit, passing around the trochlea for the superior oblique muscle. After coursing posterosuperiorly for a very short segment, it passes posterolaterally into the muscle cone and comes to lie adjacent to the inferior surface of the superior rectus muscle. It then turns posteromedially to course between the superior rectus and lateral rectus muscles. At the orbital apex, it is joined by the inferior ophthalmic vein and enters the superior orbital fissure (Bilaniuk 1977). After it passes through the superior orbital fissure, it joins the cavernous sinus. The diameter of the superior ophthalmic vein varies from 2 to 3.5 mm and can change with head position. Asymmetry may be present in a normal patient.

A small space filled with cerebrospinal fluid surrounds the optic nerve. The space lies within a meningeal sheath and extends from the optic canal forward to the papilla. The size of the space varies, and its degree of communication with the chiasmatic cistern also may vary (Haughton 1980). Entrance of both Pantopaque (Tabaddor 1973) and air (Tenner 1968) has been reported at the time of myelography and pneumocephalography. Radiographic visualization of the space has not been a regular phenomenon and has carried the risk of optic nerve injury (Tabaddor 1973). Water-soluble intrathecal contrast medium opacifies the intracranial subarachnoid space, putting into relief the structures which lie within, such as the optic chiasm. Opacification of the perioptic subarachnoid space has been recognized on CT after the intrathecal injection of metrizamide (Fox 1979; Manelfe 1978; Jinkins 1986). However, the subarachnoid space surrounding the optic nerve can be seen frequently on coronal T_2-weighted MR images without the injection of contrast material. The multiplanar capability of MR, particularly in sagittal scans along the long axis of the orbit, permits visualization of the optic nerve even when it is tortuous (Fig. 5-3) (Bilaniuk 1990*a*). High-resolution CT and MR, without and with intravenously injected contrast material, have obviated the need for intrathecal contrast instillation for the evaluation of possible optic nerve pathology.

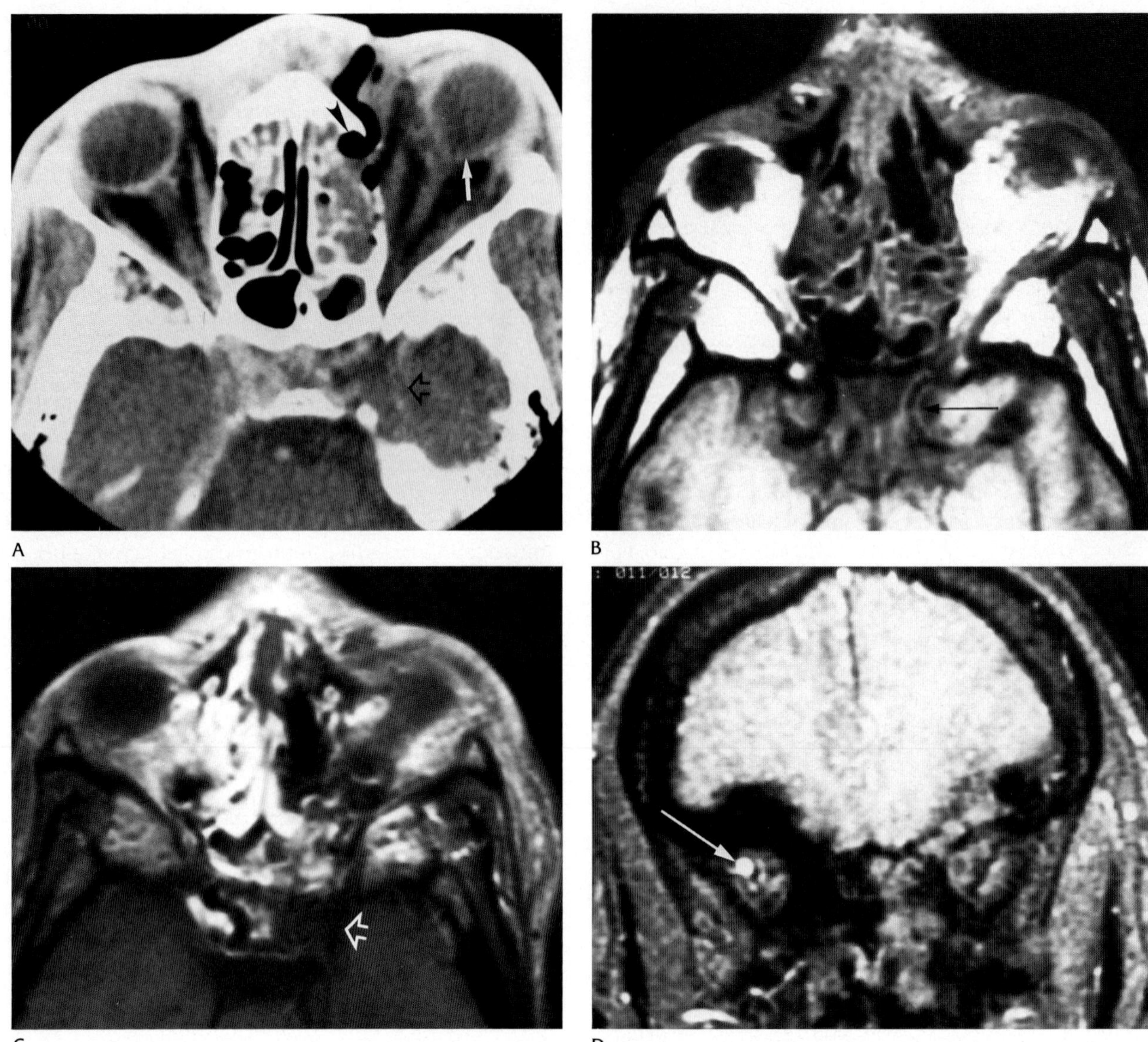

Figure 5-7 Paranasal sinus mucormycosis with extension into the orbit and cavernous sinus in a diabetic 19-year-old man. **A.** Axial CECT. Ethmoid sinuses are opacified, and there is air (arrowhead) escaping from the left ethmoid sinus because of destruction of the lamina papyracea. There is proptosis and tenting of the left globe (white arrow). Inflammatory process surrounds the globe and has produced irregularity of the rectus muscles. The left cavernous sinus (open arrow) has not opacified with contrast material. **B.** Axial MRI obtained 1 day later. The left intracavernous internal carotid artery (arrow) is of decreased caliber and has a thickened wall, indicating inflammation. **C.** CEMR shows lack of normal enhancement in the left cavernous sinus (arrow). There is swelling of the left facial tissues. **D.** Coronal gradient echo MRI (TR 150/TE 15, flip angle 50°) shows no evidence of flow in the left superior ophthalmic vein (compare with the normal right superior ophthalmic vein, arrow).

ORBITAL INFLAMMATION

Bacterial Infection

Bacterial infection of the orbit is most often due to sinus infection, a foreign body, skin infection, or bacteremia (Krohel 1982). Fungal infection, such as aspergillosis or mucormycosis, can produce extensive osteomyelitis and tends to occur in diabetic (Fig. 5-7) or immunocompromised patients. The orbital septum, the reflected periosteum from the anterior bony margin of the orbit, functions as a barrier that prevents preseptal cellulitis from

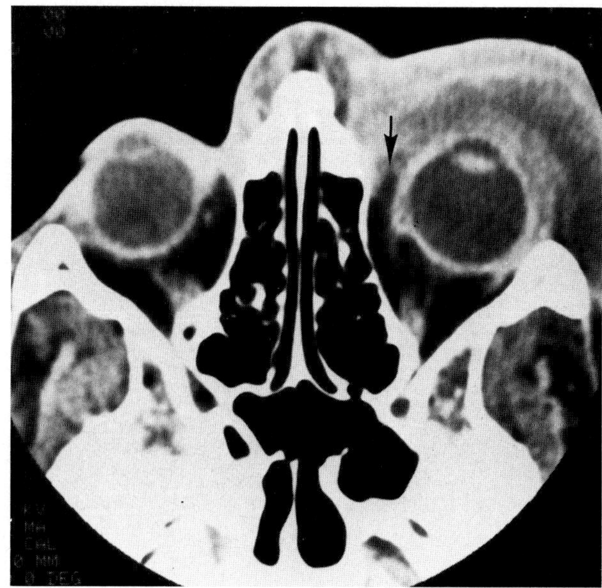

Figure 5-8 Preseptal cellulitis. CECT shows an enhancing mass anterior to orbital septum (arrow) with normal retrobulbar fat.

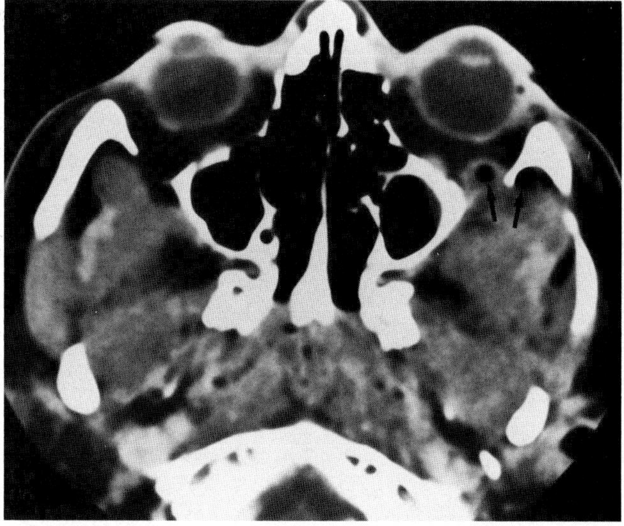

Figure 5-9 Orbital abscess secondary to maxillary sinus infection which resulted from tooth extraction. Transaxial CT demonstrates air entering the orbit posterolaterally. The air collection in the orbit is contained by soft tissue reaction. There is loss of tissue planes in the infratemporal fossa.

extending back into the orbital soft tissues (Fig. 5-8) (Kaplan 1976). The postseptal portion of the orbit may become involved by bacterial infection transmitted through the orbital septum. The infection may extend into the orbit proper along venous pathways, along fissures (Fig. 5-9), or through the orbital wall and then through the periosteum (Fig. 5-7).

The chief clinical manifestation of orbital infection is swelling and redness of the eyelids—either edematous swelling or actual cellulitis. In either situation, adequate physical examination of the eye is often difficult or impossible, and the extent of the infection cannot be delineated or its source determined clinically.

The absence of valves in the facial veins (including the orbit and the paranasal sinuses) leads to the free transmission of elevated pressure between the sinus and the orbit. In children and adolescents, orbital infection is most often a concomitant of sinusitis. Increased pressure in the sinus cavity is transmitted to the orbit and causes preseptal edema. Septic thrombophlebitis leads to cellulitis and may lead to orbital cellulitis. Direct extension of infection through congenital osseous dehiscences or involvement of the thin bony walls of the orbit by osteomyelitis can lead to the formation of a subperiosteal abscess (Fig. 5-10). The orbital periosteum is loosely attached except at the suture line, so that subperiosteal collections are easily formed. In a young child with ethmoid sinusitis, the subperiosteal collection forms along the medial orbital wall and produces lateral proptosis of the globe. In an adolescent or adult with frontal sinusitis, the subperiosteal collection is in the superior aspect of the orbit and produces anterior and downward displacement of the globe.

Both CT and MR show well the extent of involvement of soft tissues by infection; however, CT is more precise in demonstrating the bony changes (osteitis or erosion). Zimmerman (1980*a*) reported a series of 18 patients with orbital infection with or without cerebral complications who were studied with CT. All cases of acute periorbital cellulitis showed preseptal swelling, and the majority showed proptosis, scleral thickening, subperiosteal abscesses, and occasionally infection of the peripheral surgical space. Intracranial complications such as frontal lobe cerebritis and epidural inflammation are well shown by CT and MR. Soft tissue scarring of the retrobulbar space can be seen years after bacterial orbital cellulitis. In patients with trauma or a foreign body, CT not only localizes the radiodense foreign body but also demonstrates intraorbital, subperiosteal, and intracranial abscesses (Zimmerman 1980*a;* Bilaniuk 1984).

Infection within the orbit proper can be classified as (1) intraconic, within the muscle cone (central surgical space), (2) extraconic, extrinsic to the intermuscular fibrous septum (within the peripheral surgical space), or (3) subperiosteal, between the orbital wall and its periosteal covering. Most cases of postseptal cellulitis are limited to the extraconal space (Towbin 1986). Infection of the central surgical space obliterates the soft tissue planes that exist normally between the optic nerve, the orbital fat, and the rectus muscles. The intraconic fat shows abnormal density on CT and abnormal intensity on MR. In-

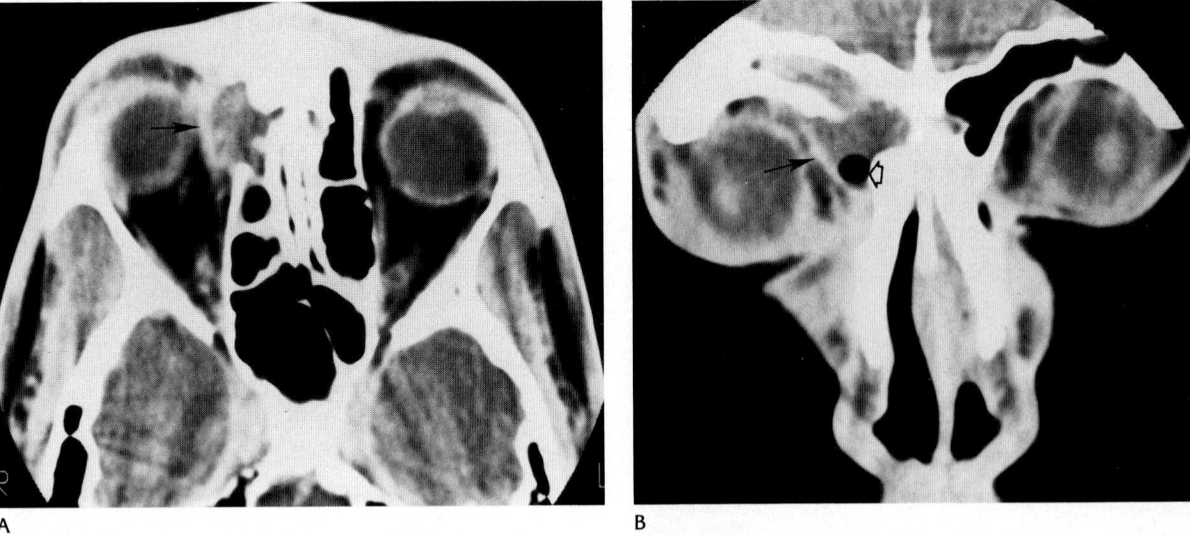

Figure 5-10 **A,B.** Subperiosteal abscess on CECT. Soft tissue density extending from the right frontoethmoid sinus into the orbit. Note focal defect in the nonexpanded sinus wall, enhancing the periosteal lining (arrow) and air within abscess (open arrow).

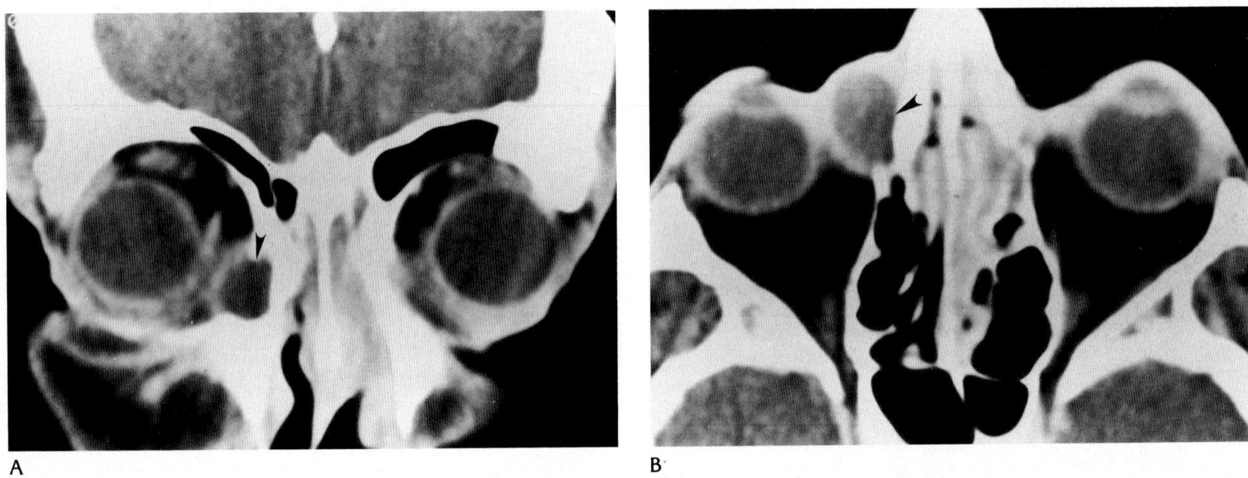

Figure 5-11 Dacryocystitis with pyocele formation. Coronal (**A**) and axial (**B**) CECT show marked dilatation of the right lacrimal sac (arrowhead).

fection in the peripheral surgical space obliterates the plane between the rectus muscles, the peripheral fat, and the wall of the orbit. Infection in the subperiosteal space is demonstrated by displacement of the contrast-enhanced periosteal membrane away from the orbital wall (Fig. 5-10). The infection may be limited to one structure of the orbit, such as the lacrimal sac, which can become markedly distended by pus (Fig. 5-11). The lacrimal sac can also become enlarged as a result of obstruction, which can be secondary to a tumor (Fig. 5-12).

Both CT and MR are very helpful in the evaluation of patients with orbital infection. Treatment of orbital infection, whether medical or surgical, must be timely, specific, and sufficient. It is imperative that the disease process be recognized quickly and treated aggressively and that operative drainage be carried out whenever indicated. A diffuse subperiosteal inflammatory process or small collections can be treated medically and followed with imaging studies. Larger subperiosteal abscesses must be drained, often along with the offending infected sinuses. The danger of cavernous sinus thrombosis is real and carries with it, even in the antibiotic era, significant morbidity and mortality. Once infection has extended into the cavernous sinus or beyond, MR is the procedure of choice. MR demonstrates and characterizes the cavernous sinus better and is more sensitive in showing a thrombosis (Fig. 5-7) and intracranial sites of inflammation. The consequences of inadequate treatment remain

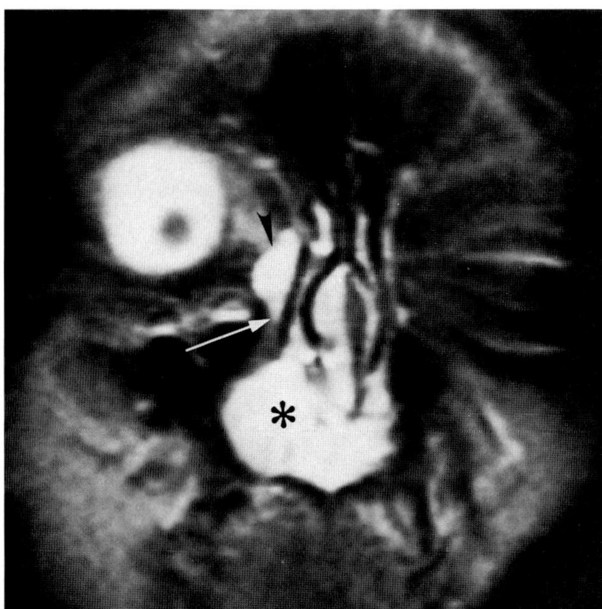

Figure 5-12 Obstruction of the nasolacrimal duct produced by a chondroid nasal tumor. A coronal MRI (3000/90; 5 mm) shows a dilated lacrimal sac (arrowhead), a dilated nasolacrimal duct (arrow) extending inferiorly from the sac, and an expansile nasal tumor (asterisk). On this T_2-WI both the tumor and the sac show increased intensity. On CEMR (not shown) the tumor enhanced, but not the lacrimal sac or the nasolacrimal duct.

potentially catastrophic because blindness and death may result. The consequences of cerebritis and cerebral abscess formation, even when the condition is adequately treated, may include seizures, motor weakness, and psychological aberrations.

Idiopathic Orbital Inflammation (Pseudotumor)

Between the ages of 10 and 40, the most common cause of an intraorbital mass is idiopathic orbital inflammation (orbital pseudotumor) (Bernardino 1977). The classic clinical triad includes proptosis, pain, and impaired ocular motility. To a variable degree there may also be diplopia, decreased vision, papillitis, and retinal striae. The symptomatology and clinical signs simulate those of an intraorbital tumor. Orbital pseudotumor is one of the most common causes of unilateral exophthalmos (Bernardino 1977), but bilaterality is common (Rothfus 1984; Dresner 1984).

The cause of orbital pseudotumor is not known, but experimental work has implicated an autoimmune response of the retrobulbar tissues to antigens (Wilner 1978). Pathologically, two categories of disease exist: (1) an acute form, in which the reaction is that of a vasculitis with vessel wall necrosis and fibrinoid changes, and (2) a chronic inflammatory process with diffuse infiltration of the affected tissues by lymphocytes, plasma cells, macrophages, and occasionally eosinophils (Jones 1979). The changes of orbital pseudotumor may be found in association with certain clinical conditions, including Wegener's midline granuloma (Vermess 1978), fibrosing mediastinitis, thyroiditis, and cholangitis (Bernardino 1978).

The classic CT finding originally described is that of contrast-enhancing uveal-scleral thickening (Bernardino 1977). Scleral-uveal thickening may obliterate both the sharply demarcated insertion of the optic nerve at the papilla and the insertion of the tendons of the rectus muscles into the sclera (Fig. 5-13). On CT, involved tissue

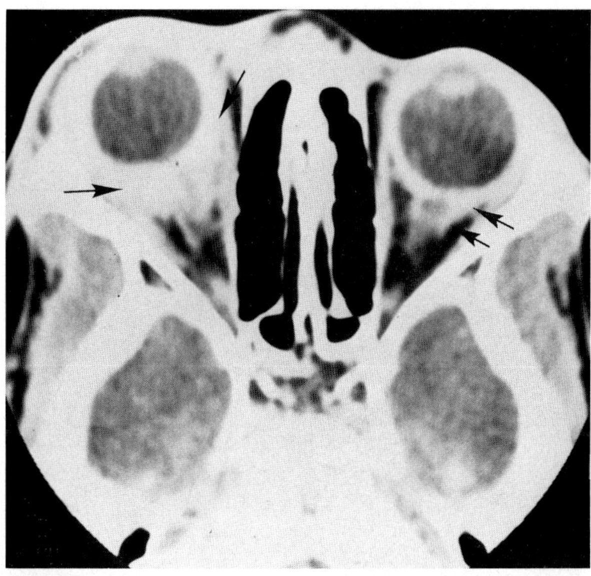

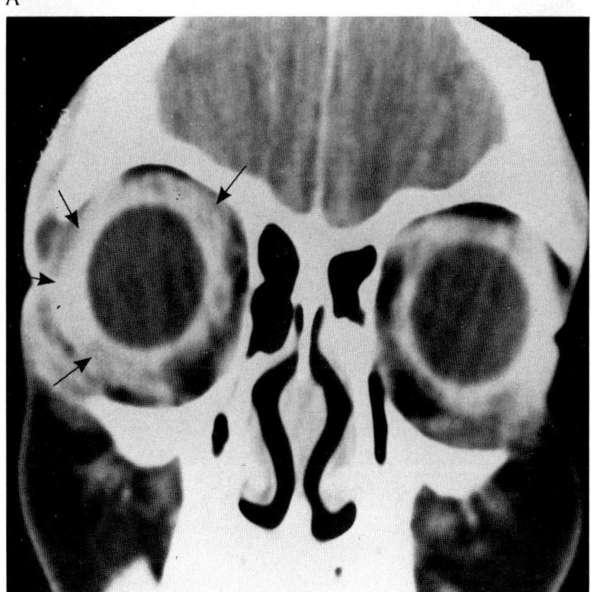

Figure 5-13 **A,B.** Bilateral pseudotumor. Axial (**A**) and coronal (**B**) CECT demonstrate marked bilateral irregular enhancement (worse on the right) involving the uveal-scleral regions (arrows) and extending posteriorly along the optic nerve sheath.

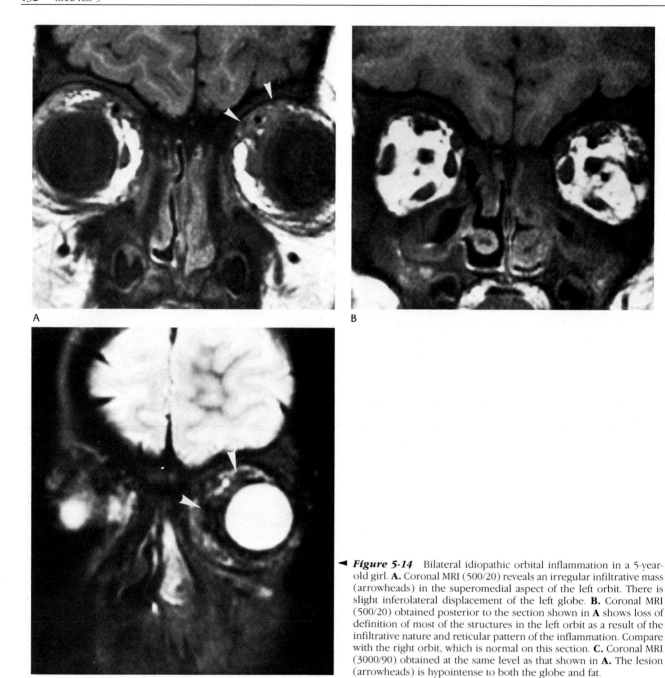

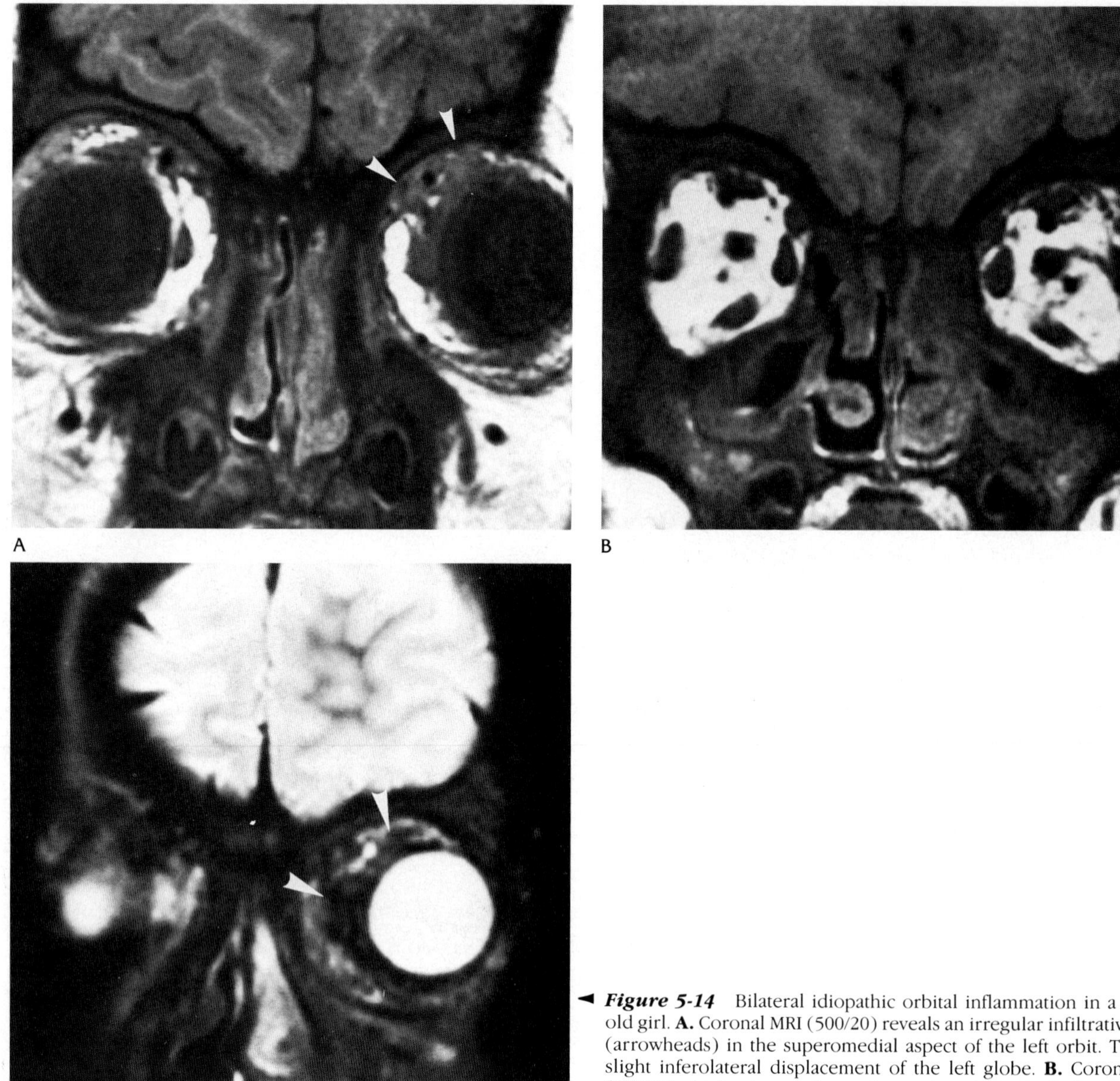

Figure 5-14 Bilateral idiopathic orbital inflammation in a 5-year-old girl. **A.** Coronal MRI (500/20) reveals an irregular infiltrative mass (arrowheads) in the superomedial aspect of the left orbit. There is slight inferolateral displacement of the left globe. **B.** Coronal MRI (500/20) obtained posterior to the section shown in **A** shows loss of definition of most of the structures in the left orbit as a result of the infiltrative nature and reticular pattern of the inflammation. Compare with the right orbit, which is normal on this section. **C.** Coronal MRI (3000/90) obtained at the same level as that shown in **A.** The lesion (arrowheads) is hypointense to both the globe and fat.

is usually isodense to slightly hyperdense compared with muscle before the injection of contrast. On nonenhanced MR, the lesions are usually isointense (Figs. 5-14 and 5-15) or slightly hyperintense to muscle on a short TR/short TE spin-echo sequence and isointense to minimally hyperintense to fat on a longer TR/TE sequence (Atlas 1987*a*). However, some idiopathic inflammations, particularly acute forms, may become prominently hyperintense on a long TR/long TE sequence (Fig. 5-15). On contrast-enhanced CT and MR, there is enhancement of the involved tissue. The disease process may present as uveal-scleral thickening (Fig. 5-13), a mass surrounding the optic nerve (Fig. 5-16), an obliteration of all retrobulbar soft tissue planes, a thickening of the rectus muscle(s) (Fig. 5-17), or a lacrimal mass (Fig. 5-18) (Nugent 1981). Occasionally, perioptic enhancement mimicking optic nerve sheath meningioma may be the sole manifestation of pseudotumor (Fig. 5-19). Single-muscle involvement in the form of a myositis is thought to be a variant in the manifestations of orbital pseudotumor. One muscle or multiple muscles may be involved. Although classically described as having muscle insertion involvement,

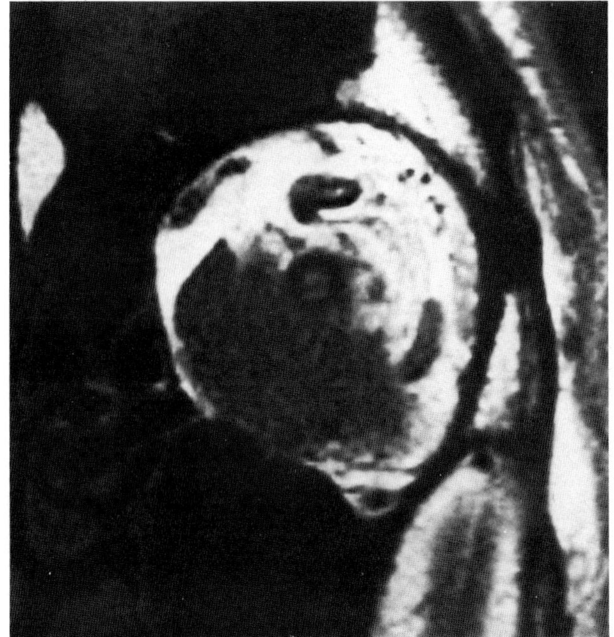

A

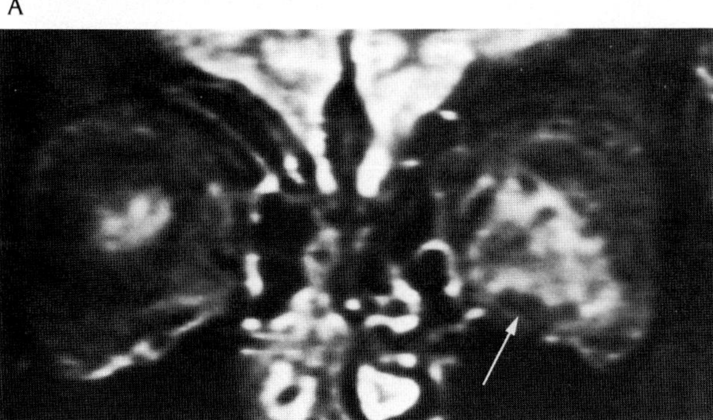

B

Figure 5-15 Idiopathic chronic orbital inflammation. **A.** Coronal MRI (600/20) shows an irregular soft tissue mass which has infiltrated a large portion of the orbital fat and obscured the inferior rectus muscle. **B.** Coronal MRI (2500/80) reveals the mass to be moderately hyperintense. Because the muscles are hypointense, the inferior rectus (arrow) can now be identified.

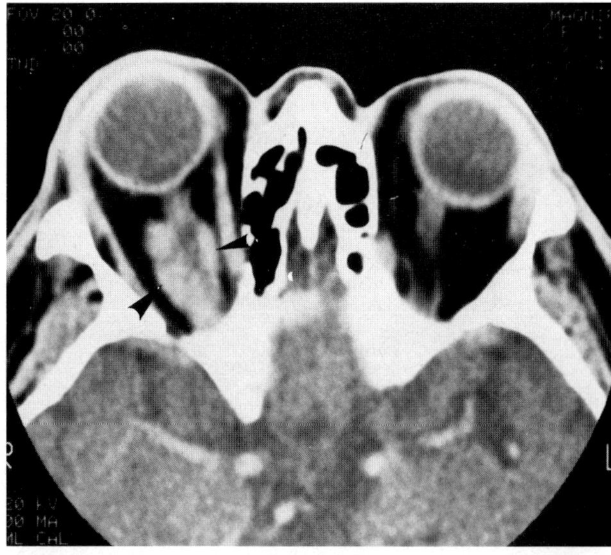

A

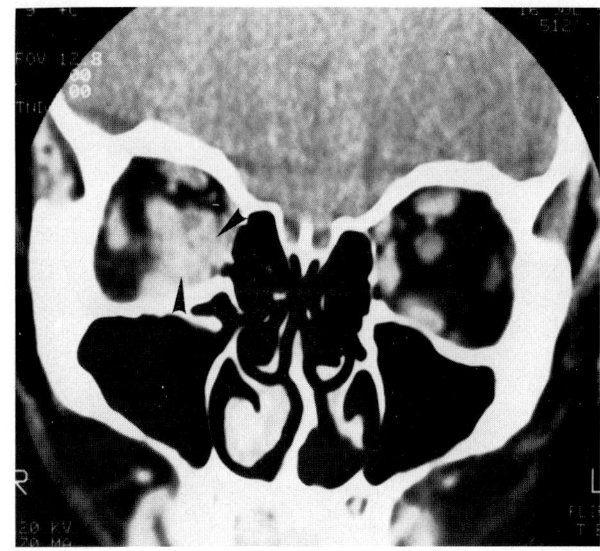

B

Figure 5-16 **A,B.** Pseudotumor on CECT. Enhancing irregular intraconal mass (arrowheads) surrounding the right optic nerve.

pseudotumor may involve any part of the muscle and often spares insertions. Therefore, if a muscle insertion is involved, pseudotumor is more likely than thyroid ophthalmopathy, but a normal muscle insertion with enlargement of the muscle belly has no differential utility (Dresner 1984). Lateral rectus muscle enlargement with extension into an enlarged lacrimal gland (Fig. 5-20) is a relatively common manifestation of this disease. Uveal-scleral thickening with enhancement may be seen in connection with other causes of intraorbital inflammation (Fig. 5-21) (trauma, surgery, and bacterial infection) and in connection with an infiltrating neoplasm (lymphoma or metastases).

Idiopathic orbital inflammation (pseudotumor) usually shows a dramatic clinical response to steroids, with evidence of improvement on an imaging study (Fig. 5-20). In fact, the diagnosis is confirmed on the basis of the patient's response to steroids. Biopsy is rarely indicated; it is reserved for the infrequent lesions that are steroid-unresponsive and therefore require radiation therapy (Sergott 1981; Leone 1985). Pseudotumor occasionally may be difficult to differentiate, both clinically and on the basis of imaging findings, from Graves' disease. Orbital pseudotumor may be mimicked clinically by other infiltrative disease processes, including lymphoma and metastatic carcinoma (breast), as well as retrobulbar hemor-

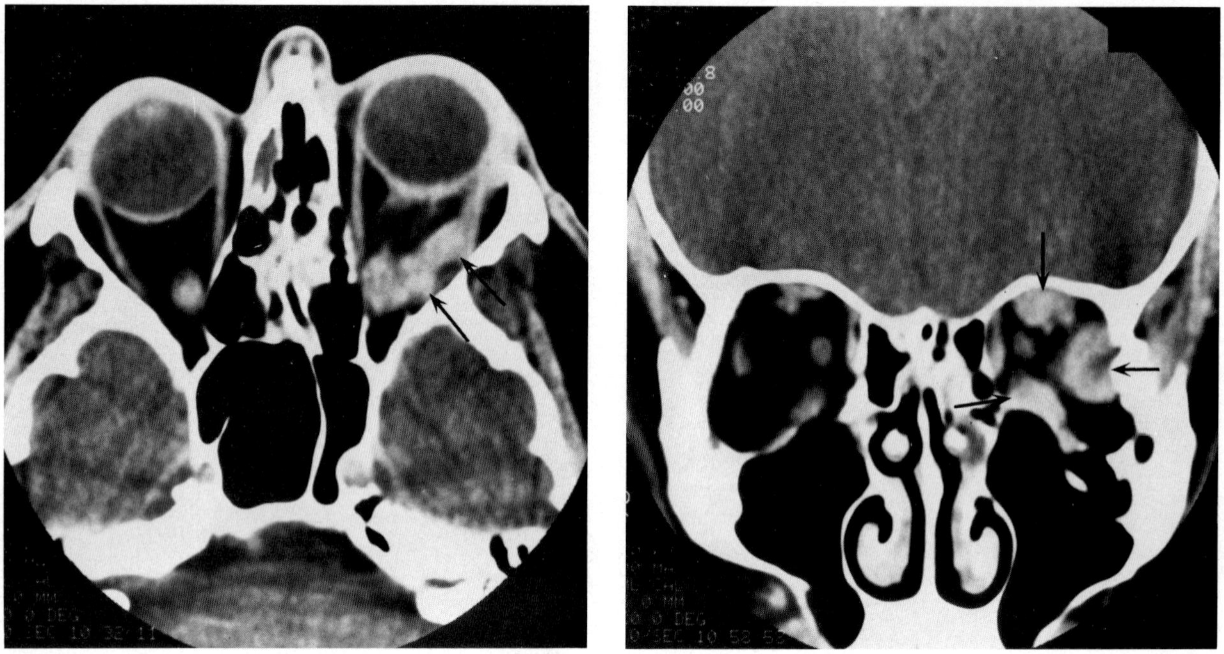

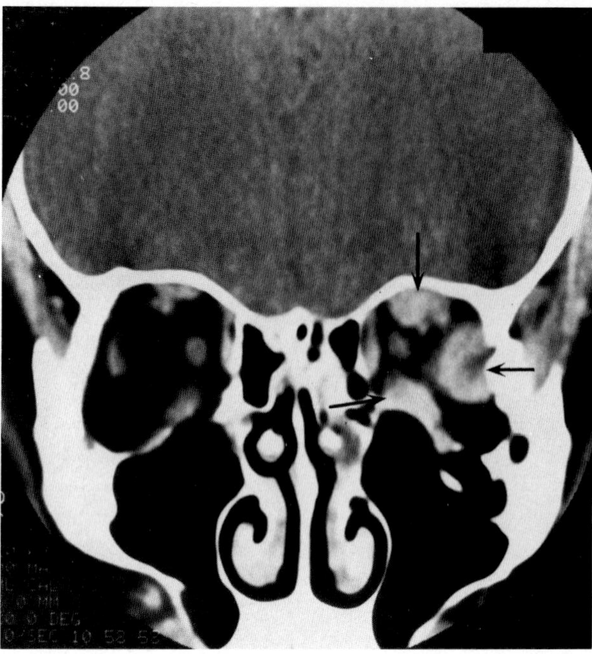

A B

Figure 5-17 Pseudotumor on CECT. Involvement of left superior, lateral, and inferior rectus muscles (arrows) demonstrated on a coronal image. Note sparing of the left medial rectus, in contrast to thyroid myositis.

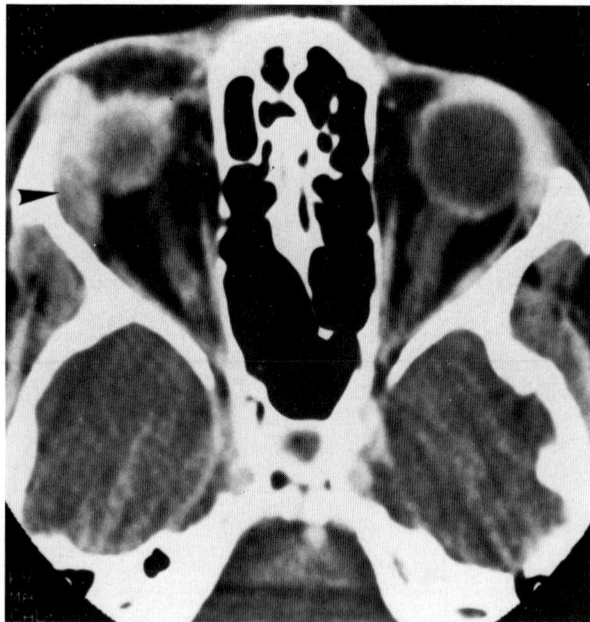

Figure 5-18 Pseudotumor on CECT. Mass in right lacrimal fossa (arrowhead) as the sole manifestation of pseudotumor.

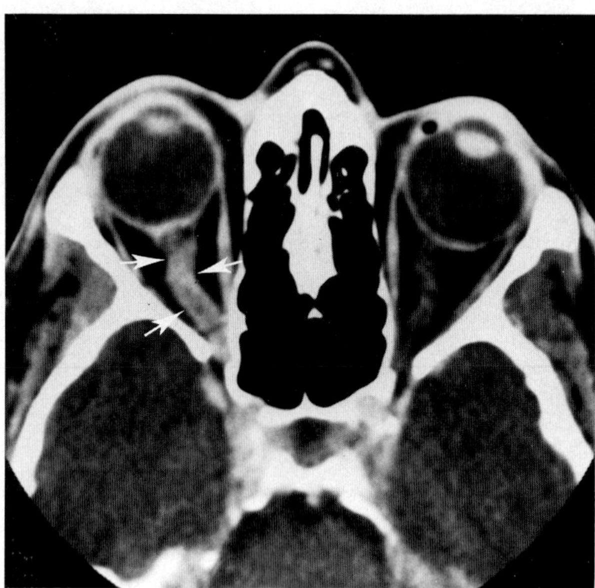

Figure 5-19 Pseudotumor on CECT. Enhancing thickening along the periphery of the right optic nerve/sheath complex ("tram-track" sign), mimicking optic nerve meningioma (arrows).

rhage. MR aids in the differential diagnosis by specifically identifying blood products. Also, metastatic breast carcinoma usually becomes hyperintense on T_2-weighted spin-echo images, while a pseudotumor is typically hypointense (Atlas 1987*a*).

Thyroid Exophthalmos

The exophthalmos of Graves' disease is of unknown etiology. Inflammatory infiltration and proliferation of connective tissue occur in the soft tissues of the orbit, especially the extraocular muscles (Alper 1977).

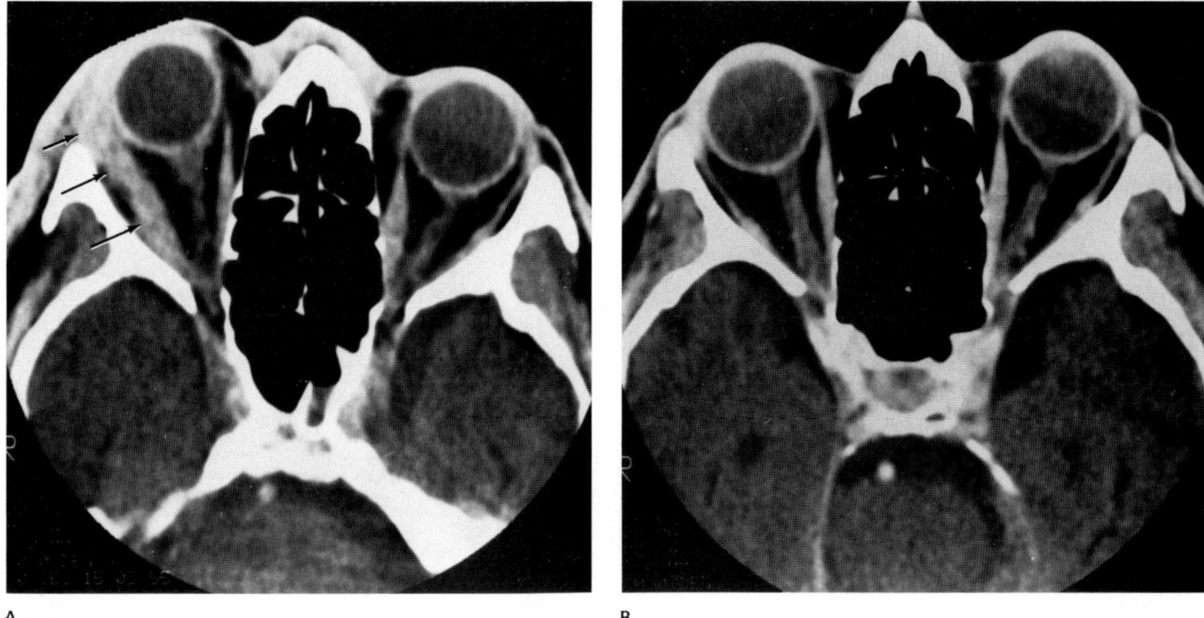

A B

Figure 5-20 Pseudotumor on CECT. **A.** Enlarged right lateral rectus with involvement of insertion and lacrimal gland (arrows), on presentation. **B.** After steroid therapy, there was total resolution.

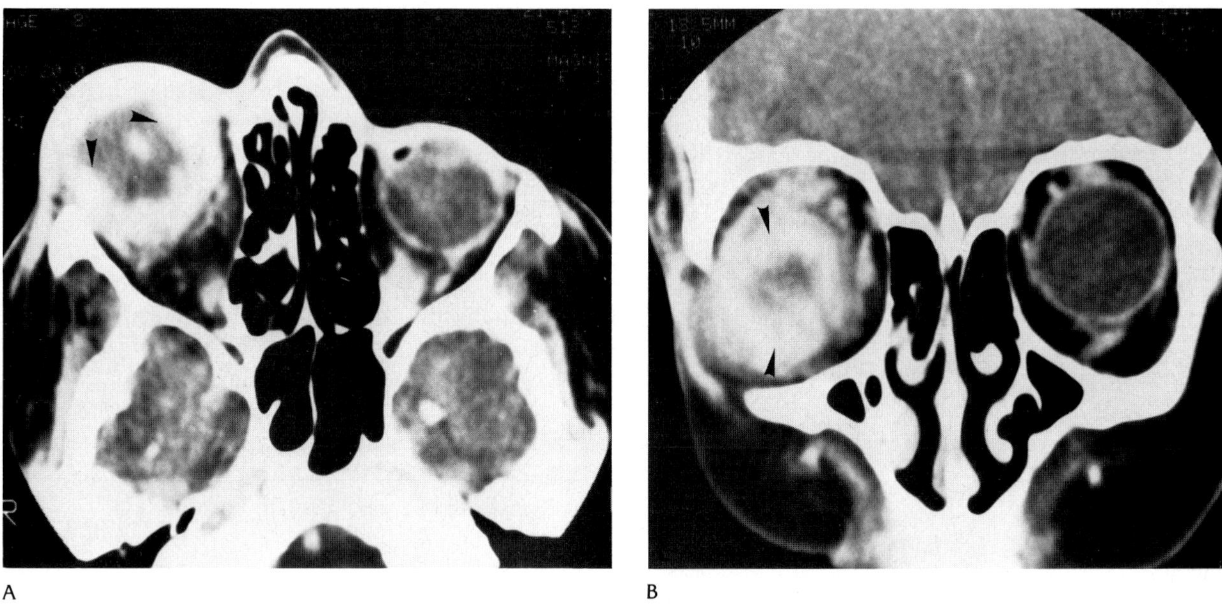

A B

Figure 5-21 **A,B.** Endophthalmitis-periophthalmitis. CECT shows markedly thickened, enhancing ill-defined sclera with streaky densities in retrobulbar fat. Lobulated thickened soft tissue within the peripheral vitreous (arrowheads) indicates endophthalmitis.

The histopathological picture of the muscles in Graves' disease is similar to that found in idiopathic orbital inflammation (Jones 1979). It is possible that autoimmune responses cause both the thyroid exophthalmos of Graves' disease and the changes associated with idiopathic orbital inflammation. Most easily recognized is the massive swelling of the extraocular muscles (Fig. 5-22), which may be enlarged volumetrically up to eight times their normal size. Infiltration of the muscles by lymphocytes, plasma cells, and mast cells and deposition of hydrophilic mucopolysaccharides account for their enlargement. When the condition occurs in association with thyrotoxicosis, the orbital fat content may be increased (Fig. 5-23) (Peyster 1986). However, increased orbital fat may also be seen in Cushing's disease or syndrome and in obesity (Cohen 1981; Carlson 1982). The increase in

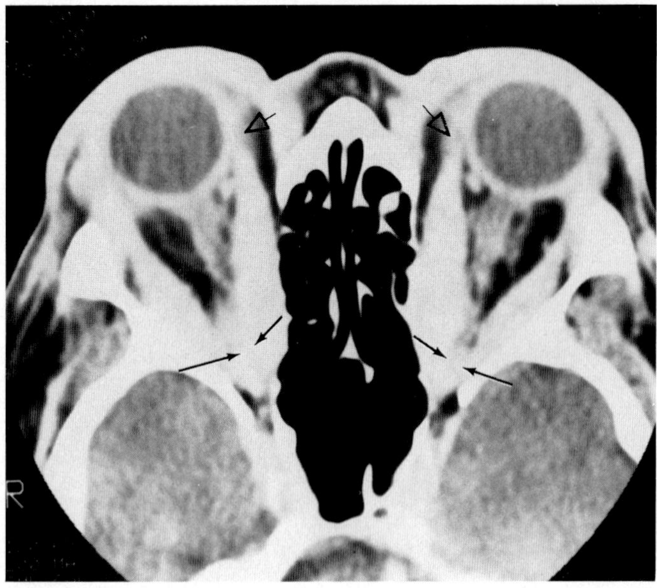

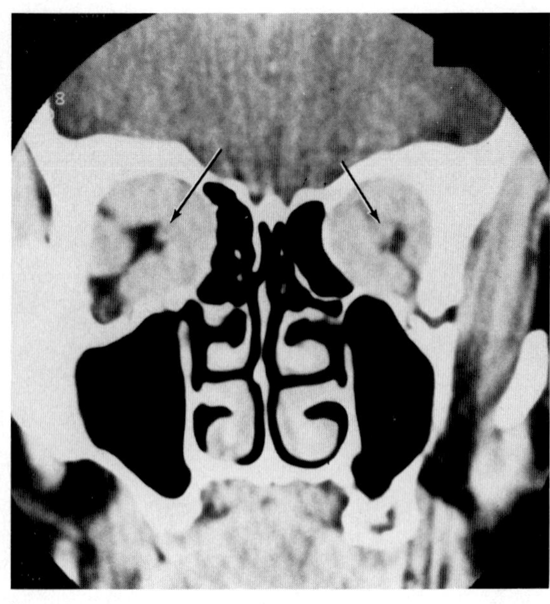

A B

Figure 5-22 **A,B.** Thyroid ophthalmopathy. Bilateral marked enlargement of all extraocular muscles with typical tapering at insertions (open arrowheads). Streaky increased densities in fat can be seen in severe thyroid ophthalmopathy as well as pseudotumor. Note compression of optic nerves at the orbital apex on axial (**A**) and coronal (**B**) CT (arrows).

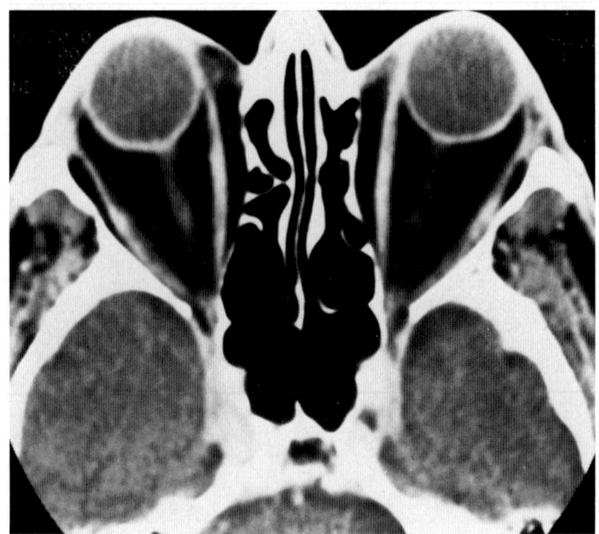

Figure 5-23 Thyroid ophthalmopathy. CT shows bilateral proptosis with a marked increase in orbital fat, bowing the orbital septum and separating the medial rectus from the medially bowed lamina papyracea.

volume of the orbital tissues produces proptosis. Ulceration of the cornea, occlusion of the central retinal vein or artery, and compressive optic neuropathy may be seen as a result. Muscle dysfunction occurs, and ocular motility is impaired. Pain is usually not a feature of thyroid ophthalmopathy.

The exact incidence of thyroid exophthalmos is not known. It occurs in both hyperthyroid and euthyroid patients. It may precede clinical hyperthyroidism. Its presentation is usually bilateral; it is unilateral in 5 to 10 percent of cases (Rothfus 1984; Peyster 1986). The classic, mild form is characterized clinically by a prominent stare, mild proptosis, eyelid retraction, and lid lag (Alper 1977). This is most frequently found associated with thyrotoxicosis in young females, and it is bilateral. Most often the patient is asymptomatic (Alper 1977). Typically, the more severe clinical form occurs in middle-aged patients and is associated with the gradual onset of severe proptosis and varying degrees of ophthalmoplegia. Thyrotoxicosis is usually present. Overall, women predominate in the incidence of both thyroid disease (4:1) and Graves' exophthalmos (Alper 1977). However, the female predominance decreases with age (Rootman 1988).

Soon after the introduction of CT, its efficacy in the study of Graves' disease was recognized (Brismar 1976; Enzmann 1976). This was followed by reports of studies correlating CT results with the pathological and clinical features of Graves' ophthalmopathy (Enzmann 1979; Trokel 1981). Eventually quantitative CT methods were developed for the evaluation of extraocular muscles and orbital fat (Feldon 1982; Forbes 1986). More recently Nugent (1990) reported the clinical and quantifiable nonvolumetric high-resolution CT data from 142 orbits of patients with Graves' orbitopathy and from 40 orbits of subjects without Graves' disease.

Graves' disease accounts for more cases of unilateral and bilateral exophthalmos in the adult than does any other single disease entity (Enzmann 1976; Jacobs 1980).

While an imaging study, either CT or MRI, is not always necessary for the diagnosis of Graves' disease, it is useful in indicating the degree of muscle involvement and its bilaterality is useful when there is ophthalmopathy without clinical or laboratory evidence or a history of thyroid disease (Enzmann 1979; Nugent 1990). CT is preferred to MR in presurgical evaluation, as it provides the greatest detail about the bony walls. CT or MR is useful for evaluating the results of orbital decompressive surgery. In the transverse section, the inferior and superior recti are cut tangentially (Fig. 5-1). These muscles are better evaluated either in the coronal projection (Fig. 5-2) or on reformed sagittal CT sections. In a direct sagittal CT section, the inferior and superior recti are visualized in their entire length, and so minimal changes of Graves' disease can be recognized (Wing 1979). The muscles can be demonstrated easily in multiple planes with MRI without having the patient assume an uncomfortable position, not the case with CT. The plane of sectioning can be optimized for each individual muscle or for the optic nerve sheath complex. Also, MR provides better resolution and the ability to identify the optic nerve sheath complex when there is crowding of structures at the orbital apex as a result of the enlarged muscles.

Enzmann (1979) reported the CT findings in 107 hyperthyroid and 9 euthyroid patients with thyroid ophthalmopathy. CT revealed bilateral involvement (Fig. 5-22) in 85 percent, unilateral involvement (Fig. 5-24) in 5 percent, and no abnormality in 10 percent. Seventy percent of Enzmann's patients with bilateral involvement had symmetrical muscle disease, whereas 30 percent had asymmetrical muscle involvement. Most commonly, all four of the recti mentioned above were involved (Fig. 5-22). The inferior and medial recti were involved in approximately three-fourths of the cases and had the most severe degree of enlargement, whereas the superior and lateral recti were involved in approximately half the cases and had a lesser degree of enlargement. Indeed, any or all extraocular muscles may be involved in nearly any combination. However, if isolated lateral rectus enlargement exists, another etiology is suggested. Enzmann (1979) found a rough linear parallel between the clinical assessment of the degree of ophthalmopathy and the severity of muscle enlargement. However, no correlation was found between the degree of muscle enlargement and the degree of abnormal thyroid function. Enzmann pointed out that in 6 of 12 patients who had given a clinical impression of unilateral disease, CT revealed the presence of bilateral disease.

Forbes (1986) found a higher frequency of abnormal changes on CT in hyperthyroid patients with Graves' disease without clinical ophthalmopathy than had previously been reported. He obtained pixel-calibrated measurements of muscle and fat in the orbits of 72 patients with Graves' disease and found abnormal measurements in 87 percent of those with clinically detectable ophthalmopathy and in 70 percent of hyperthyroid patients without clinical eye signs. Overall, the medial and inferior muscles were the most frequently involved. Among patients with ophthalmopathy, 46 percent had both muscle enlargement and fat increase and 8 percent had only an increase in fat. Among the seven patients with unilateral clinical ophthalmopathy, six were found to have abnormalities in the contralateral orbit.

In his study, Nugent (1990) obtained measurements directly from CT scans. He and his coworkers found muscle enlargement in all their patients with ophthalmopathy, but especially in those with optic neuropathy. In this

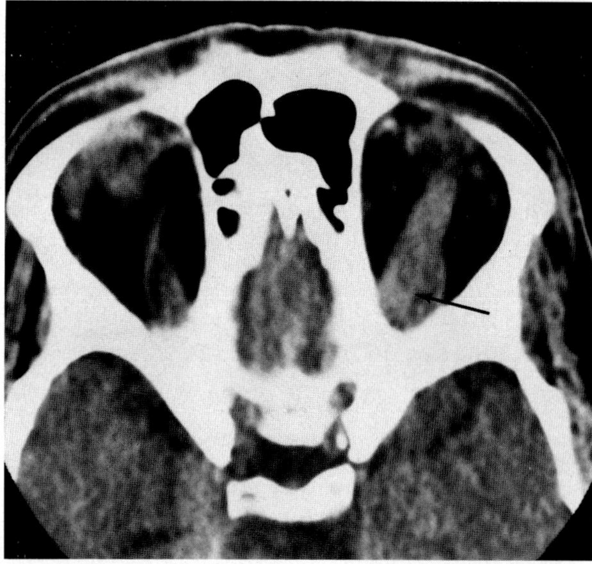

A

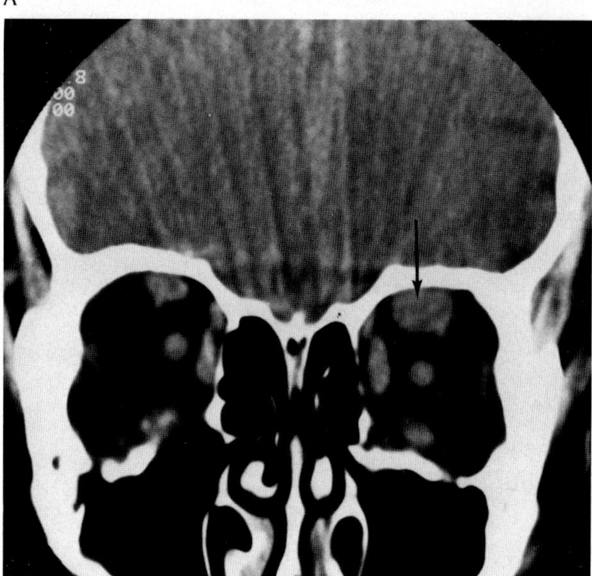

B

Figure 5-24 Thyroid ophthalmopathy. Isolated enlargement of the left superior rectus muscle (arrow) on axial (**A**) and coronal (**B**) CT.

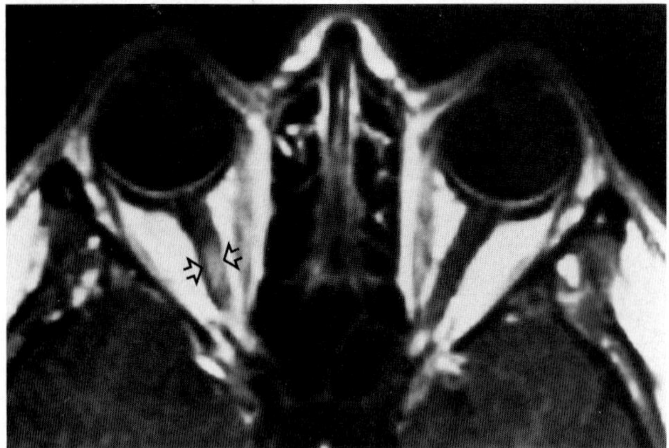

Figure 5-25 Right optic neuritis in a 26-year-old woman. Axial CEMR (600/22; Gd-DTPA) shows enhancement of the intraorbital optic nerve (arrows) on the right side.

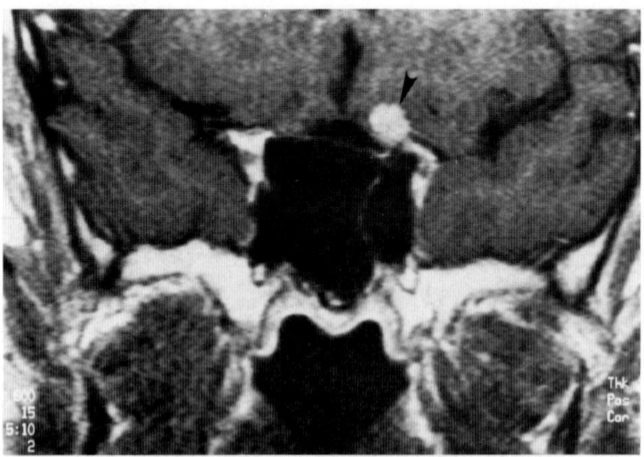

A

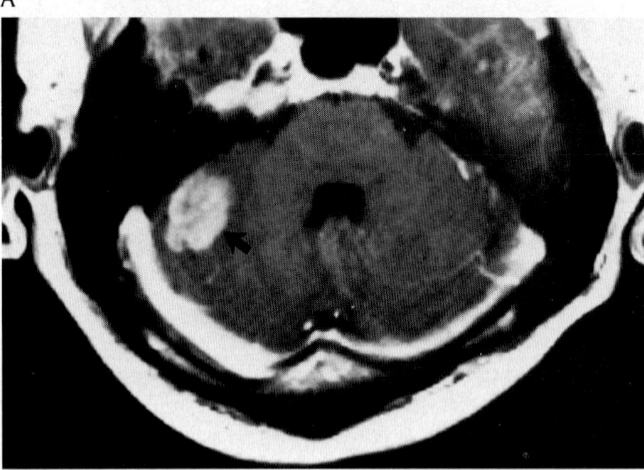

B

Figure 5-26 Left optic neuritis in a 38-year-old man with multiple sclerosis. **A.** CEMR (600/15; Gd-DTPA) shows enlarged prominently enhancing intracranial portion of the left optic nerve (arrowhead). **B.** CEMR of the posterior fossa reveals a large region (arrow) of abnormal contrast enhancement in the periphery of the right cerebellar hemisphere; it was thought to represent a demyelinating plaque.

study the superior muscle group was most frequently involved (63.4 percent), followed by medial (61.3 percent) and inferior (57 percent) recti. The most common pattern was involvement of all five muscles that were measured. Solitary involvement was most frequent in the superior muscle group (6.3 percent). Enlargement of the optic nerve sheath and the superior ophthalmic vein was noted in cases of optic neuropathy.

Optic Neuritis

Optic neuritis, an inflammatory process involving any part of the optic nerve, is clinically diagnosed on the basis of loss of visual acuity and visual field changes. It may be associated with inflammation in other portions of the visual pathway or more extensive intracranial inflammation. It may be a manifestation of multiple sclerosis (Sandberg-Wollheim 1990). High-resolution contrast-enhanced CT and particularly contrast-enhanced MR can demonstrate changes that are due to optic neuritis: swelling and contrast enhancement (Figs. 5-25 and 5-26). The process also can be shown to involve the chiasm.

ORBITAL TRAUMA

A blow to the face or head may result in injury to the osseous orbit and the orbital soft tissues. An overlying soft tissue hematoma may preclude adequate physical examination of the orbit. In such circumstances, CT is a useful adjunct in demonstrating the presence or absence of

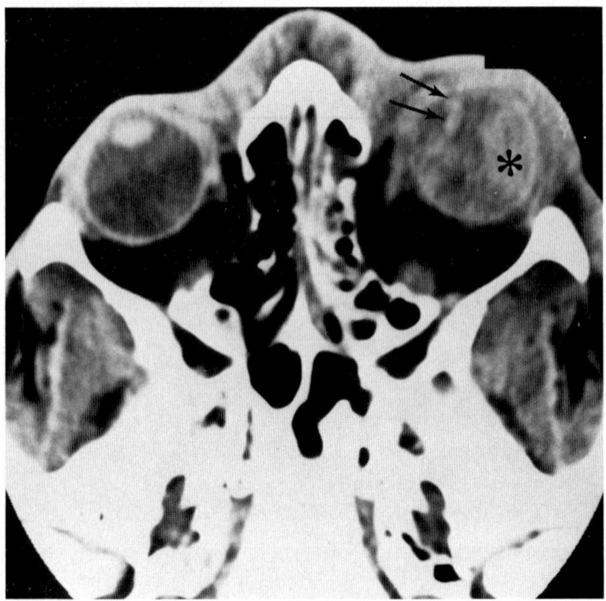

Figure 5-27 Blunt trauma on CT. Left globe is filled with hemorrhage (asterisk). Lens is disrupted (arrows). Note that a medial wall blowout fracture has opacified the left ethmoid sinus.

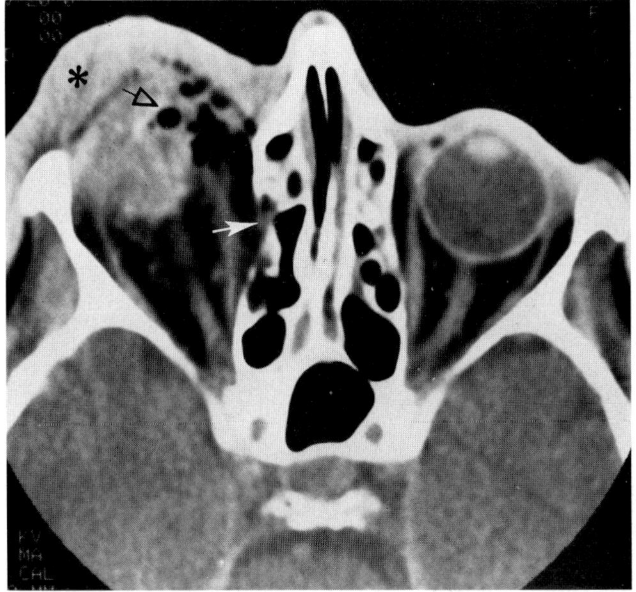

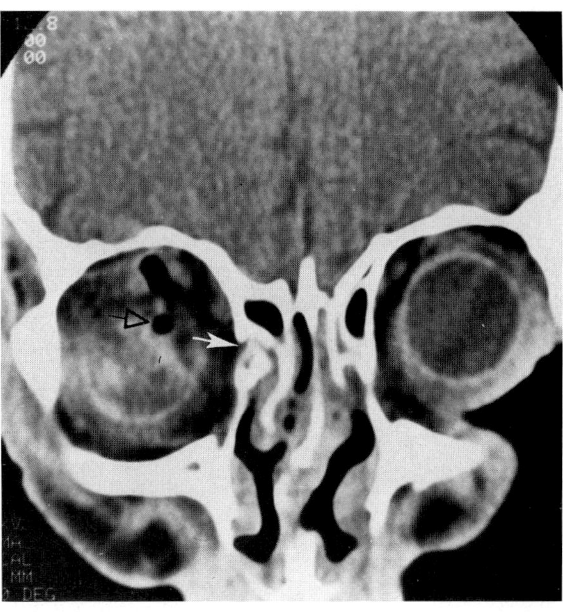

A B

Figure 5-28 **A,B.** Medial wall fracture with ruptured globe. Axial (**A**) and coronal (**B**) CT demonstrates right medial wall blowout fracture (arrow) and orbital emphysema. Signs of ruptured globe include distortion of normal shape with intravitreal hemorrhage and intraocular air (open arrow). The lens cannot be identified. Note extensive preseptal hemorrhage (asterisk).

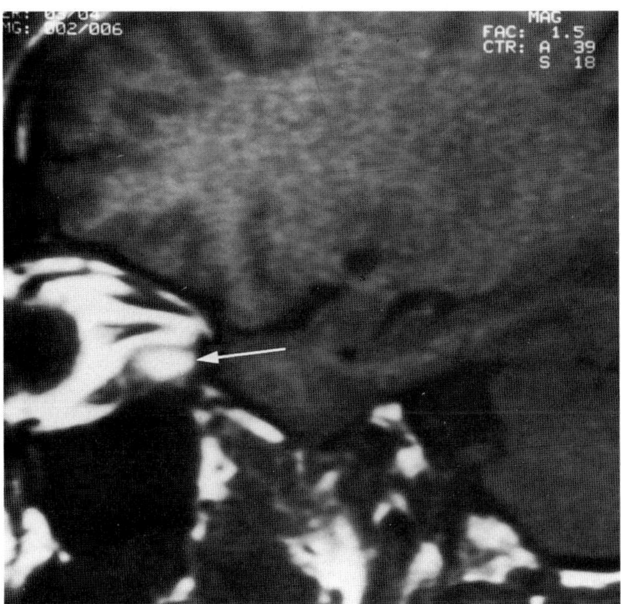

Figure 5-29 Hemorrhage in the left inferior rectus muscle. Sagittal MR T_1WI demonstrates the hemorrhage (arrow) within the inferior rectus muscle.

underlying osseous and soft tissue injury (Figs. 5-27 and 5-28). CT is the procedure of choice because of its ability to show bone detail and acute hemorrhage and demonstrate foreign bodies. MR is contraindicated whenever the mode of injury is uncertain and there is a possibility of a ferromagnetic foreign body. Also, on MR, acute orbital hemorrhage may be difficult to detect and differentiation between air bubbles and bone fragments may be difficult. However, MR can be a useful adjunct in the evaluation of orbital trauma by providing information on anatomic disruption in multiple planes as well as demonstrating associated intracranial traumatic lesions if they have occurred. Also, MR can demonstrate a chronic or subacute intramuscular hemorrhage (Fig. 5-29), which on CT may appear as a mass. Fractures of the orbit are classifiable as external (e.g., a tripod fracture of the zygoma and anterior orbital rim) (Fig. 5-30) or internal (a blowout fracture into the ethmoid or maxillary sinuses) (Figs. 5-28 and 5-31 through 5-34). In fractures of the orbital floor it is more often the tethering of the muscles caused by prolapsed orbital fat and the connective tissue (Fig. 5-32), rather than the actual entrapment of the muscles, that results in abnormalities of ocular motility (Koornneef 1977, 1979). Both CT and MR are able to demonstrate herniation of the soft tissue contents into the maxillary sinus (Grove 1978; Hammerschlag 1982; McArdle 1986). CT also may detect an unsuspected fracture of the orbital apex (Unger 1984).

In addition to damage to the bony orbit, trauma of sufficient force and direction can lead to damage to the globe and optic nerve. Rupture of the globe is most often associated with blows to the lateral aspect of the orbit that strike the globe just anterior to the lateral wall. CT and MR demonstrate the deformity of the eyeball and the presence of intraocular hemorrhage (Figs. 5-27, 5-28, 5-33, and 5-35). Direct damage to the optic nerve and peri-

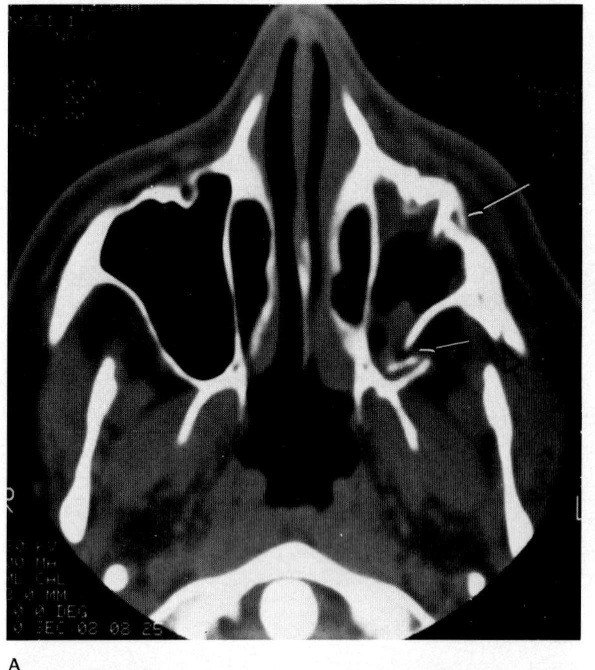

A

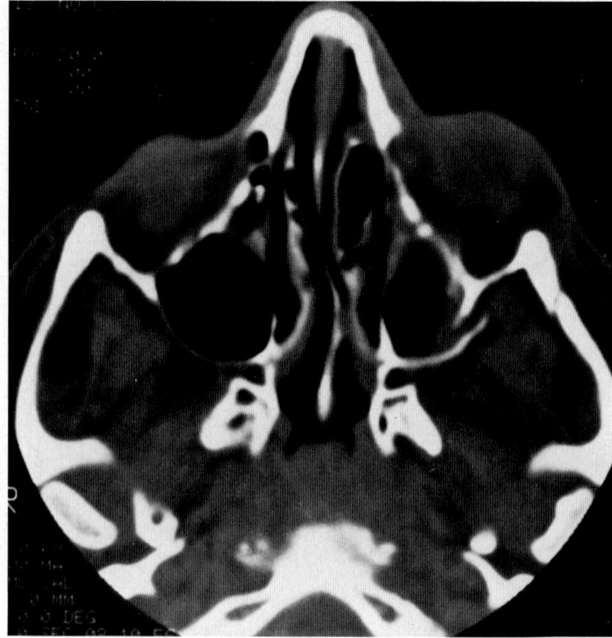

B

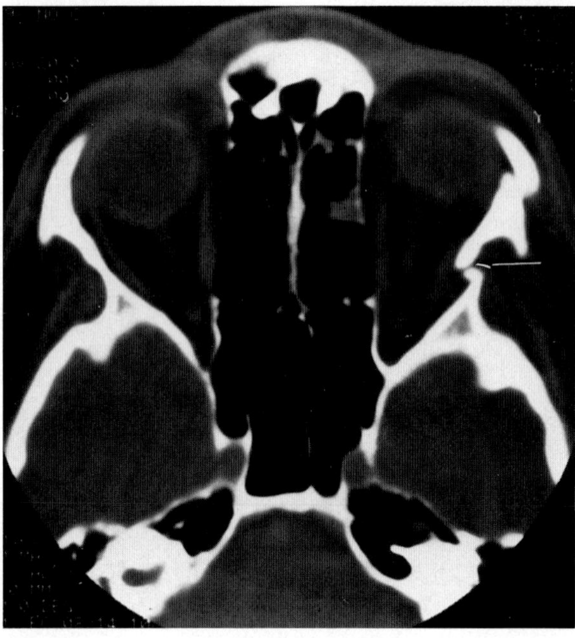

C

Figure 5-30 **A–C.** Tripod fracture. Axial CT demonstrates fractures involving anterior and lateral walls of the right maxillary sinus (arrows) and widening of the frontozygomatic suture (open arrow). Note intact pterygoids.

optic bleeding (Fig. 5-34) within the subarachnoid, subdural, and/or intradural spaces can lead to loss of vision as a result of either the primary optic nerve injury or secondary optic nerve injury by vascular compression or injury. Fractures in the vicinity of the optic foramen, especially those associated with local subperiosteal hemorrhage, may compress the optic nerve focally. This is an indication for emergency decompression. Intradural hemorrhage in the optic nerve sheath occurs most frequently at the apex of the orbit, where there is a close relationship between the tendinous ring of Zinn (the site of the origin of recti) and the dura mater which divides into the sheath of the optic nerve, the periorbita, and the orbital connective tissue system. The medial part of the tendinous ring is inserted into the cleft formed by the splitting of the dura into the periorbita and the perioptic sheath (Whitnall 1921). Intraneural optic nerve hemorrhage also occurs at the apex of the orbit. Subarachnoid and subdural hemorrhages occur more frequently just posterior to the papilla, where they are associated with subhyaloid retinal hemorrhages (Lindberg 1973) (Fig. 5-36).

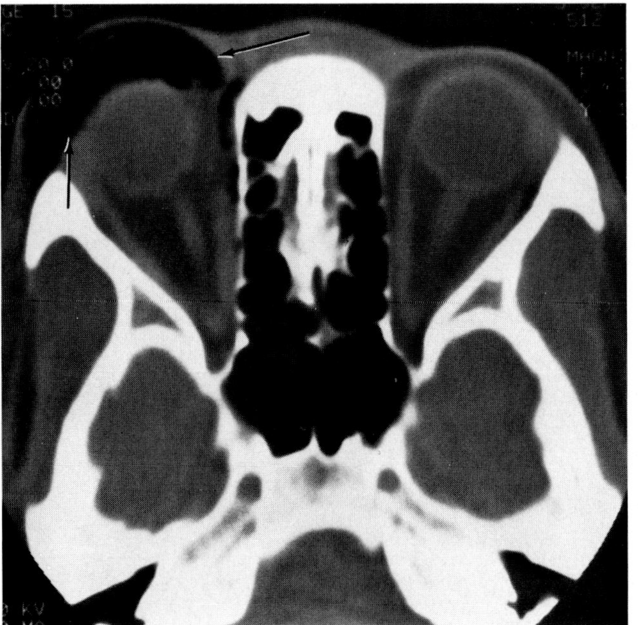

A

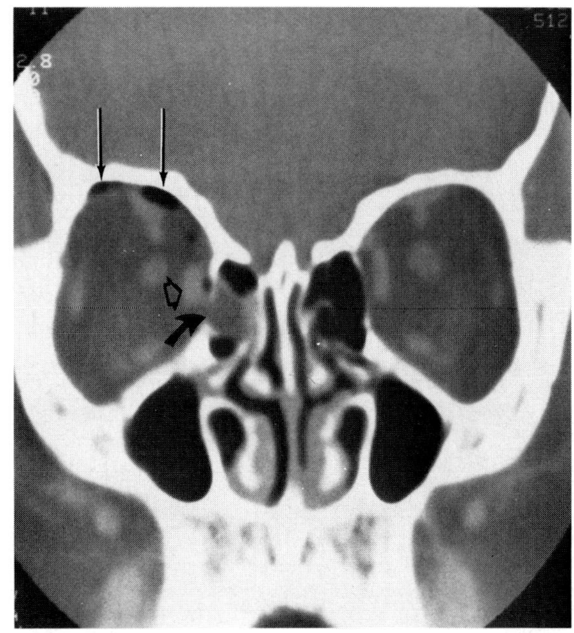

B

Figure 5-31 **A,B.** Medial wall fracture. Medial orbital wall fracture (curved arrow) is best demonstrated in coronal CT (**B**), with soft tissue and fat herniating into the right ethmoid. Medial rectus is in its normal position (open arrow). Extensive orbital emphysema is also present (straight arrows).

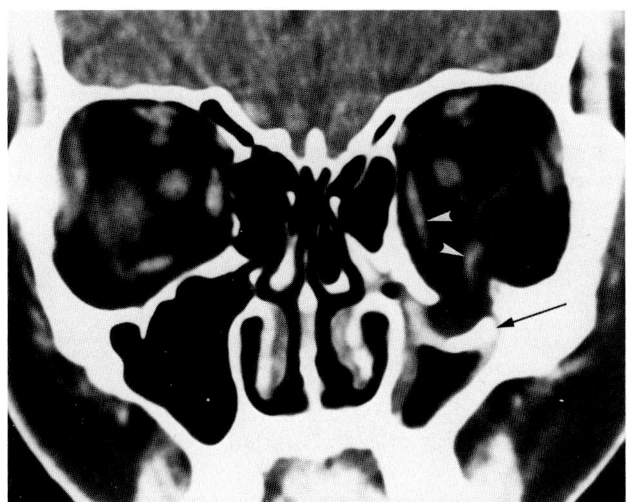

Figure 5-32 Blowout fracture of the left orbital floor. Coronal CT obtained just posterior to the globes reveals a blowout fracture on the left with inferior displacement of the fracture fragment (arrow). The orbital fat has prolapsed through the defect in the floor. There is rotation and tethering of the inferior rectus muscle (arrowhead) and the medial rectus muscle (arrowhead). Note the prominent elongation of the medial rectus muscle compared with the normal side.

Figure 5-33 Rupture of the left globe with avulsion of the optic nerve head. **A.** Coronal MRI (600/20) shows a smaller squared-off left globe filled with blood. The central irregular hypodensity (arrow) within the globe represents the avulsed optic nerve head. There is hemorrhage and swelling of the tissues lateral to the globe. **B.** Coronal MRI (600/20) posterior to that shown in **A** reveals bilateral medial blowout fractures (arrows), the old one on the right and the acute one on the left. Hemorrhage and edema obscure the left superior oblique and medial rectus muscles and produce an irregular reticular pattern in the orbital fat. As a result of the herniation of the fat through the fracture in the medial wall of the left orbit, the orbital structures are pulled toward the midline. Two fractures (arrows) are present in the lateral wall of the left orbit.

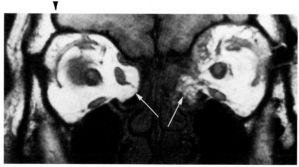

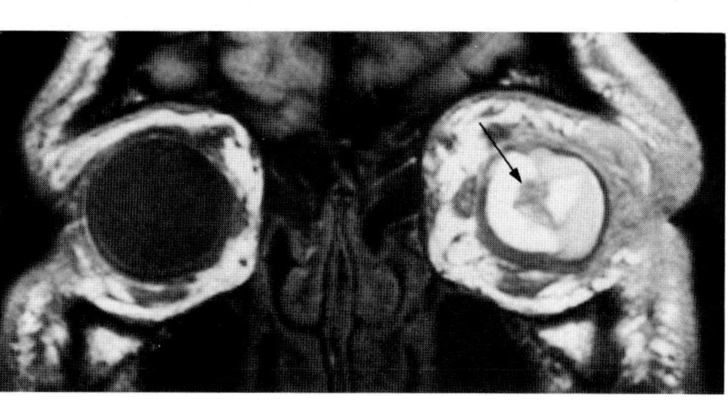

A

B

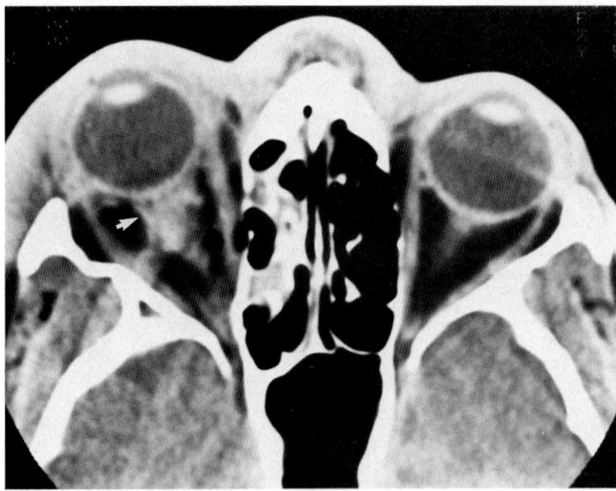
A

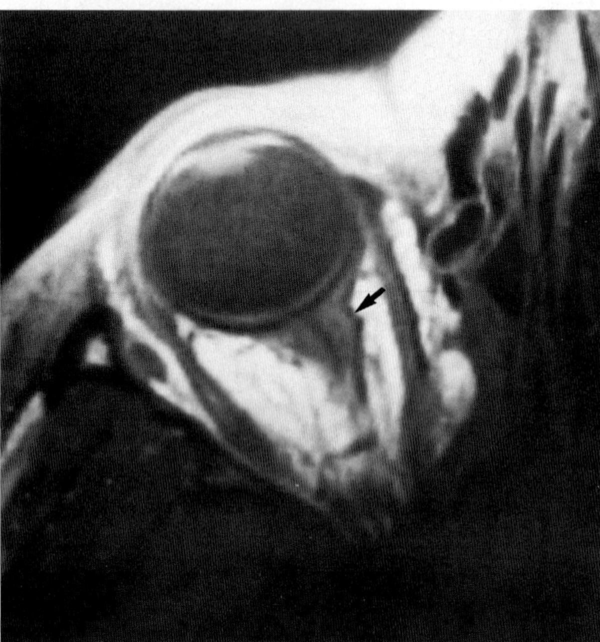
B

Figure 5-34 Orbital trauma with perioptic hemorrhage on the right. **A.** Axial CT shows an irregular retrobulbar hemorrhage (arrow) which obscures the optic nerve sheath complex. There is also proptosis of the right globe and swelling of the lids. There is soft tissue thickening at the insertions of the medial and lateral rectus muscles. A small amount of air has escaped into the medial extraconic space through a fracture in the medial wall of the right orbit. **B.** Axial MRI (600/20) reveals retrobulbar irregular hypodensity (arrow) which is consistent with recent hemorrhage. The optic nerve sheath complex is obscured by the hemorrhage.

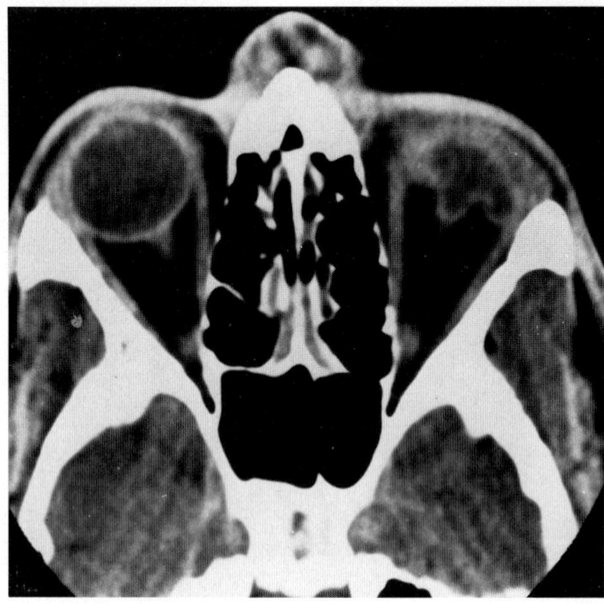

Figure 5-35 Perforated globe. Left globe on axial CT is markedly decreased in size and has an abnormal configuration after a perforating injury, indicating rupture.

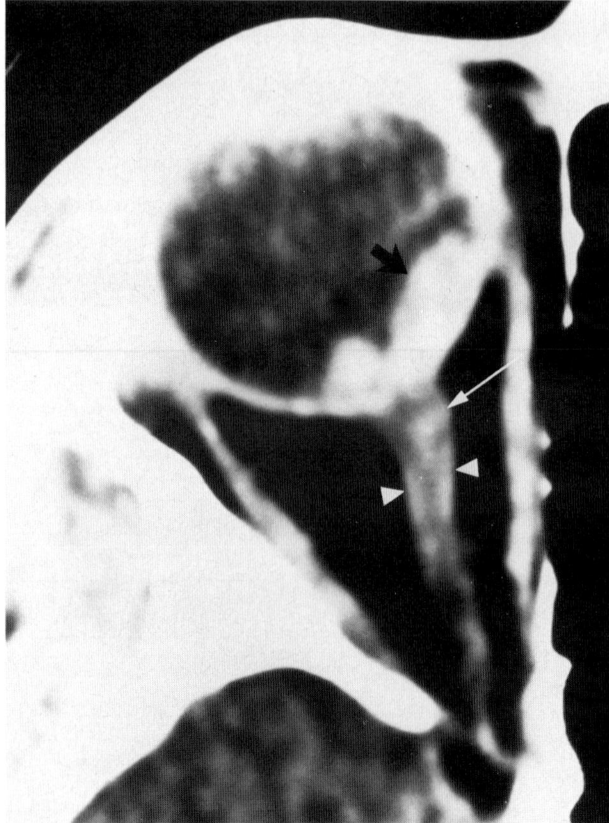

Figure 5-36 Posttraumatic hemorrhages. Axial CT shows retinal detachment (black arrow) and intraneural (white arrow) and perioptic (subarachnoid) hemorrhage (arrowheads).

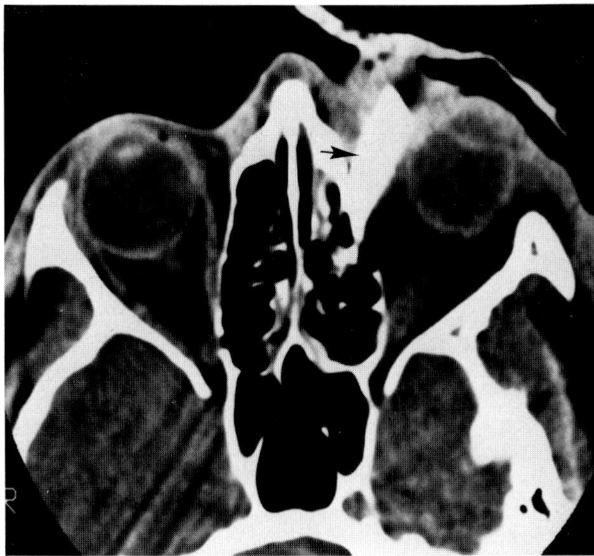

Figure 5-37 Glass foreign body. Axial CT demonstrates large high-attenuation glass foreign body (arrows) just medial to the left globe, leaving the globe intact.

A

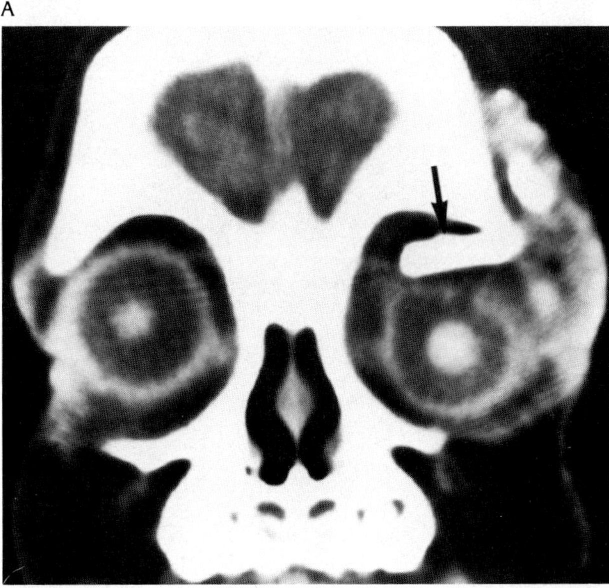
B

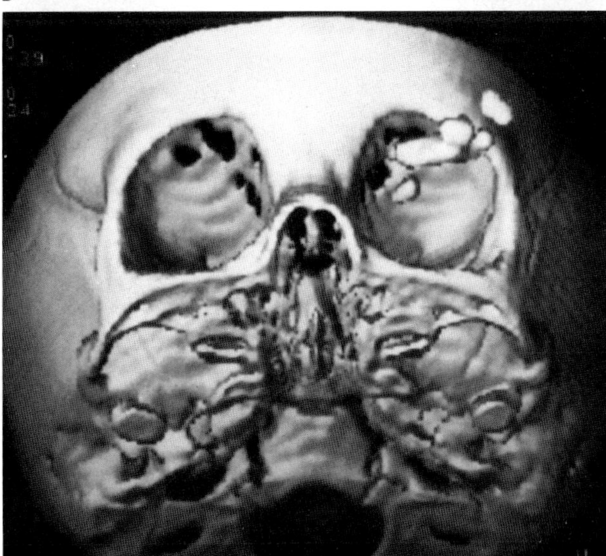
C

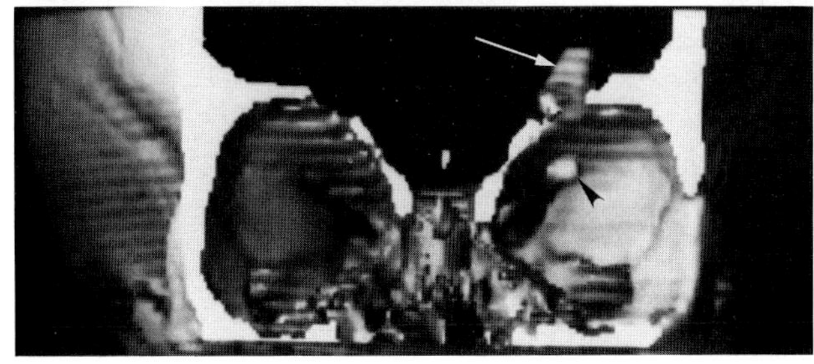
D

Foreign Bodies

Localization of an intraorbital foreign body by routine radiographic means may be difficult. To facilitate surgical planning for removal, it is necessary to localize the foreign body accurately. This is easier with radiodense foreign bodies, as they are well shown on routine x-rays and CT (Figs. 5-37 through 5-39). However, CT is clearly superior to conventional radiography in demonstrating the precise anatomic location of foreign bodies within the globe and their sequelae (ruptured globe, retinal detachment, lens disruption, or vitreal hemorrhage) in patients who may be difficult to examine clinically (Sevel 1983). In addition, unsuspected fragments, retrobulbar or intracranial in location, often are detected by CT. Three-dimensional CT reconstructions are particularly helpful in

Figure 5-38 Fracture and foreign body in the orbit and frontal lobe resulting from the fall of an 8-month-old child onto a shot glass. **A.** A 3D reconstruction of the soft tissues reveals prominent swelling of the left eyelid and a wound (arrow) in the supraorbital region. **B.** Coronal CT reveals a large linear foreign body (arrow) which was a large fragment of the shot glass. There is rupture of the globe (it has lost its normal round configuration), as can be seen on the right. Prominent soft tissue swelling, hemorrhage, and other foreign bodies are identified in the lateral aspect of the orbit. **C.** A 3D bony reconstruction demonstrates well the multiple foreign bodies in the left orbit. They were found to represent fragments of glass. **D.** A 3D reconstruction shows well the site of the orbital roof penetration and two foreign bodies, one representing a bony fragment and a larger one representing glass (arrow). In addition, a deeper foreign body (arrowhead) can be identified intraorbitally.

A

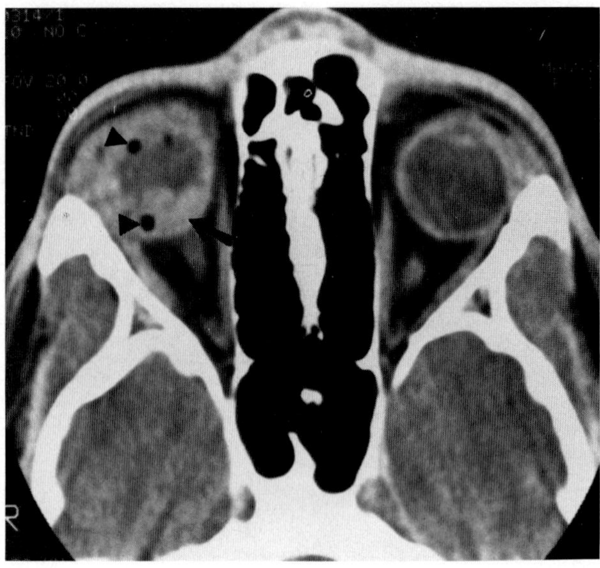

B

Figure 5-39 **A,B.** Intraocular foreign body. Metallic foreign body on coronal image (**A**) in vitreous, with secondary intraocular hemorrhage and air. Note subretinal hemorrhage (arrow) and air (arrowheads) on the axial CT (**B**).

the precise localization of fragments and foreign bodies (Fig. 5-38). Prognostic information may also be obtained by CT in penetrating injuries of the globe (Sternberg 1984; Brown 1985; Weisman 1983). Double penetration of the globe and optic nerve injury by foreign bodies are relevant to surgical planning and prognosis.

With a nonopaque foreign body (Fig. 5-40), such as a wood splinter, CT may show only the granulomatous reaction (Macrae 1979) or focal air density. In a patient who presents with proptosis or with evidence of a granulomatous reaction in the vicinity of the orbit, consideration should be given to a forgotten minor trauma produced by an intraorbital foreign body. In such a case, CT is capable of revealing metallic fragments and radiodense foreign bodies such as pencil lead and glass. MR is contraindicated in patients suspected of having a ferromagnetic ocular or orbital foreign body (Kelly 1986).

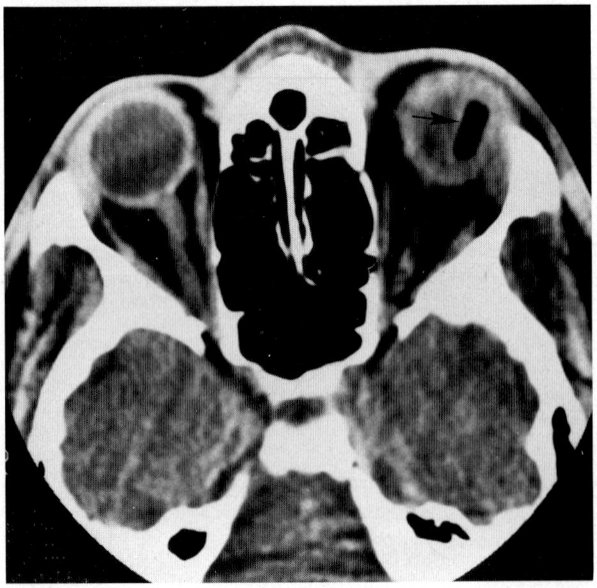

Figure 5-40 Intraocular sponge on CT. Intraocular air density (arrow) indicates a retained surgical sponge in the left globe.

VASCULAR LESIONS

Capillary Hemangiomas

Capillary hemangiomas are the most common vascular tumors of childhood, usually appearing within the first 2 weeks of life, with a female predominance. They are nonencapsulated infiltrative tumors that consist of abnormal blood vessels and endothelial cells (Plesner-Rasmussen 1983). They usually show a growth spurt during the first 6 months, reach a plateau within 1 to 2 years, and then involute by the sixth or seventh year (Flanagan 1979). The lesions can be very large and thus can produce prominent enlargement of the bony orbit. Because these lesions involute spontaneously and often do not require treatment, it is important to differentiate them from other lesions. MR is helpful in this regard, as it demonstrates the internal architecture of these lesions (Bilaniuk 1990*c*). On CT, the lesions have irregular margins and enhance prominently and at times may be difficult to differentiate from rhabdomyosarcomas. MR reveals hemangiomas to be heterogeneous and vascular. The lesions have slightly higher intensity than does muscle and contain signal voids as a result of vessels on T_1WI (Fig. 5-41).

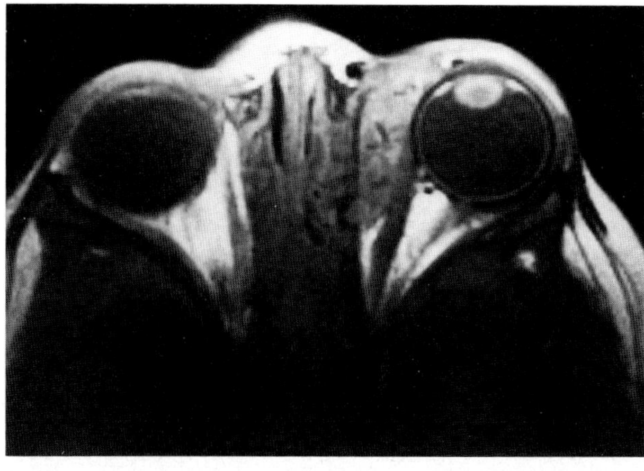

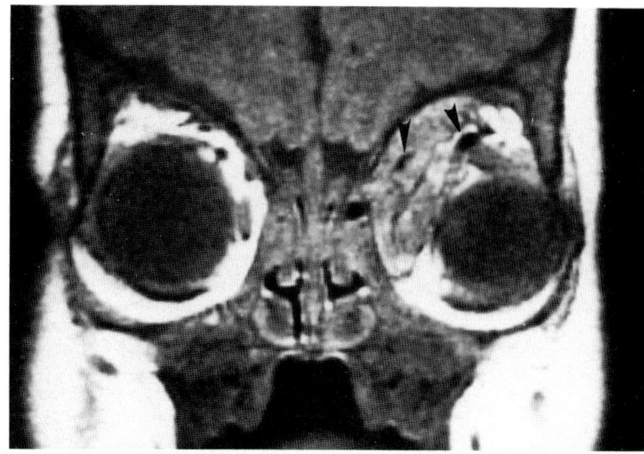

A B

Figure 5-41 Capillary hemangioma in the left orbit of an 11-week-old boy. **A.** Axial MRI (600/20) demonstrates a heterogeneous extraconic mass in the medial aspect of the left orbit. It contains linear signal voids within it, indicating vessels. **B.** Coronal MRI (600/20) shows a finely lobulated mass which has produced enlargement of the left bony orbit. Again demonstrated are signal voids (arrowheads) within the mass, indicating vessels.

They are hyperintense to fat on T_2WI and show contrast enhancement. By demonstrating vessels within the hemangioma, MR provides more specific information than does CT.

Cavernous Hemangioma

Cavernous hemangiomas show a female predominance and occur most frequently during the third and fourth decades of life (Harris 1978). They are characterized by a slowly progressive course. The symptoms consist of proptosis and difficulty with extraocular motility. Cavernous hemangioma is one of the most common benign intraorbital lesions (Forbes 1982) and is most often located within the muscle cone (Figs. 5-42 and 5-43), although extraconal hemangiomas are not uncommon (Fig. 5-44).

Cavernous hemangiomas consist of large, dilated endothelium-lined vascular channels. They are encompassed by a fibrous pseudocapsule. The arterial blood supply is not prominent, and blood flow is relatively stagnant. Thus, thrombosis is not uncommon. Spontaneous hemorrhage is not a feature of this lesion. Phlebolith formation with calcification is rare (Fig. 5-42).

Imaging studies demonstrate a cavernous hemangioma as a homogeneous mass, usually within the muscle cone, with smooth margins and generally uniform contrast enhancement (Figs. 5-42 and 5-44) (Davis 1980).

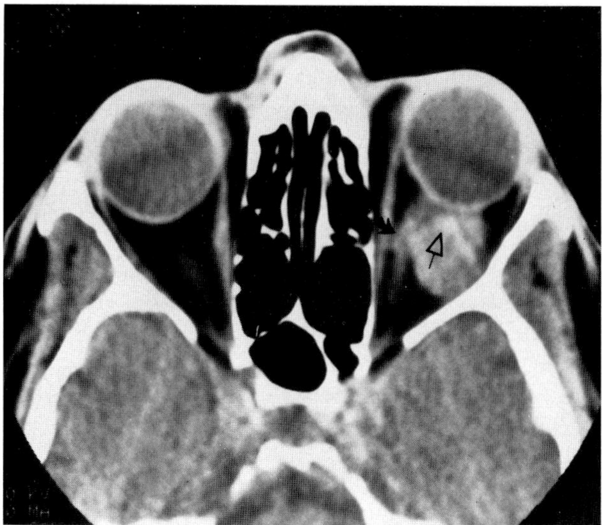

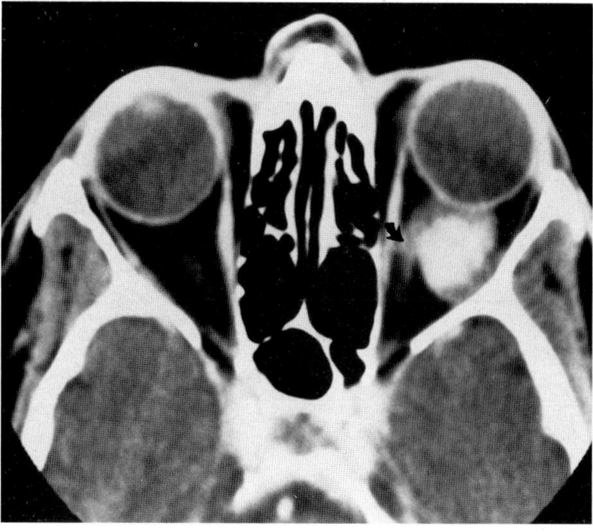

A B

Figure 5-42 **A,B.** Intraconal hemangioma. NCCT (**A**) demonstrates a well-circumscribed intraconal mass deviating the right optic nerve (curved arrow) medially. Note artifacts emanating from a calcified phlebolith (open arrow) within mass. Note absence of deformity of the posterior globe. Mass enhances homogeneously on CECT (**B**).

A

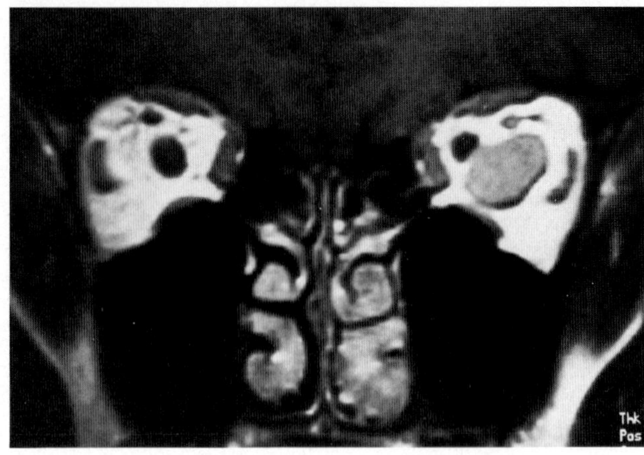

B

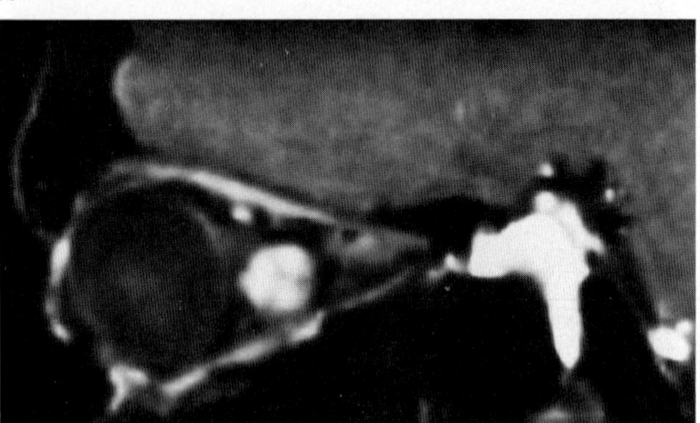

C

Figure 5-43 Presumed cavernous hemangioma. **A.** Axial CEMR (600/15) with Gd-DTPA. A well-marginated mass (asterisk) displaces the left optic nerve medially. It shows slight hypointensity in relationship to the fat. **B.** Coronal CEMR (600/15 with Gd-DTPA) shows the well-defined mass displacing the optic nerve superomedially. **C.** Contrast-enhanced fat-suppressed gradient-echo 3D acquisition reconstructed in the sagittal plane shows a slightly heterogeneous high-intensity mass inferior to the optic nerve.

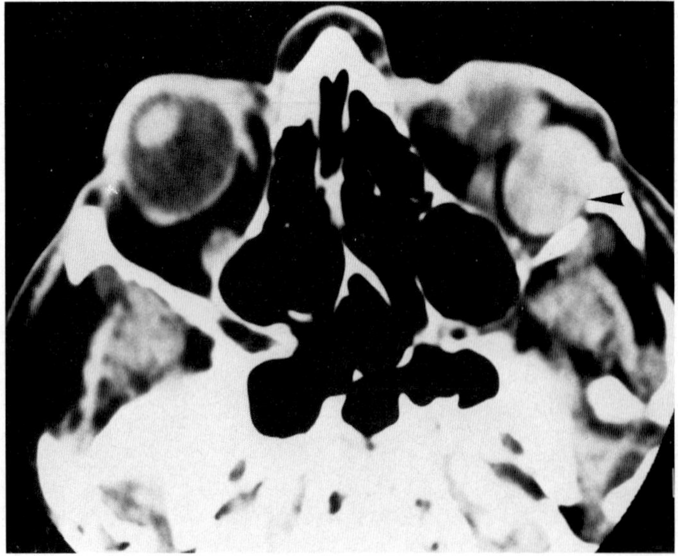

A

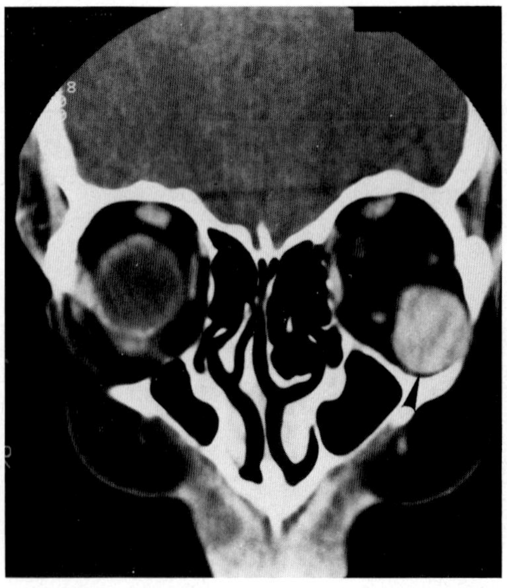

B

Figure 5-44 **A,B.** Extraconal hemangioma. Well-circumscribed, homogeneously enhancing mass (arrowhead) in the inferolateral aspect of the left orbit is outside the muscle cone on axial (**A**) and coronal (**B**) CT.

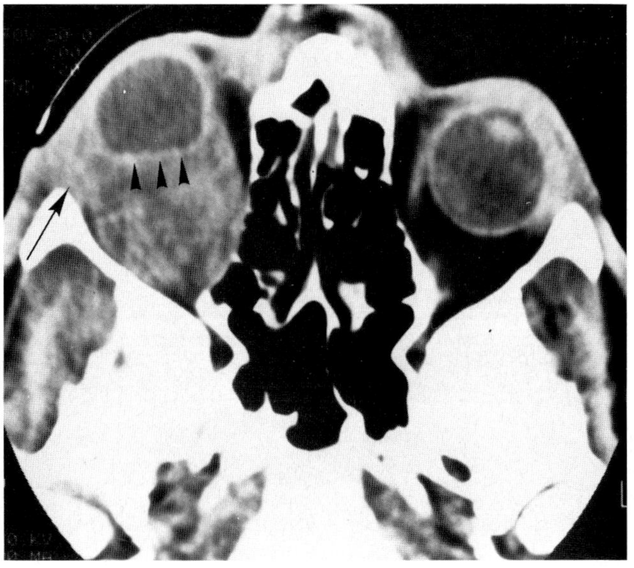

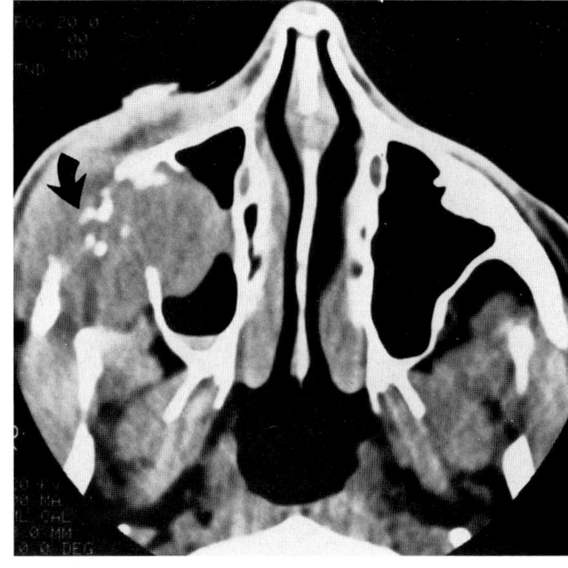

A B

Figure 5-45 Metastatic melanoma on CT. **A.** A slightly nonhomogeneous mass fills the right orbit, infiltrates the lacrimal gland (arrow), and deforms the posterior aspect of the globe (arrowheads). **B.** Mass destroys the right malar eminence (curved arrow) and erodes into the maxillary sinus.

However, a scan obtained during or immediately after the injection of contrast material may show heterogeneity caused by opacification of the large vascular channels within the lesion (Bilaniuk 1990*b*). On nonenhanced studies, the hemangioma appears as a dense mass on CT; on MR, it is isointense to muscle on T_1WI and hyperintense to muscle on T_2WI. These lesions often do not deform the globe when abutting it, distinguishing hemangioma from many retrobulbar metastases (Fig. 5-45). Lymphoma is similarly a soft mass which often does not deform the globe. Expansion of the adjacent orbital wall is common, but bone destruction does not occur and, if present, suggests a more aggressive lesion. The detection on CT of a calcified phlebolith is an infrequent but highly suggestive characteristic of this lesion. In Davis's series (1980), 83 percent of the cavernous hemangiomas were intraconic, with 67 percent being lateral to the optic nerve; 22 percent of his cases extended to the orbital apex. Even small hemangiomas, if located at the apex, may produce visual symptoms. On CT, but more so on MR, it is possible to demarcate a cavernous hemangioma from the adjacent optic nerve and muscles. This is important in planning for operative removal. Because a cavernous hemangioma is encapsulated, it is easily peeled off from the extraocular muscles and the optic nerve. These tumors show no tendency to recur or undergo malignant transformation (Jones 1979). It is important to differentiate hemangioma from lymphangioma of the orbit, a lesion that is not easily removed surgically, frequently recurs, and is more often extraconic, ill defined, and less homogeneous in its enhancement.

Lymphangioma

Lymphangiomas occur in the orbit in spite of the fact that there is no lymphatic tissue in the postseptal portions of the normal orbit. They most likely represent hamartomas (Jones 1979). Their histopathological spectrum includes dilated lymphatic vessels, clusters of dysplastic blood vessels, new and old blood products, lymphocytic aggregates, bundles of smooth muscle fibers, and loose connective tissue septa (Graeb 1990). The lesions are unencapsulated and often cross anatomic compartments. However, in Davis's series (1980) most of the lesions were extraconic. Lymphangiomas usually present during early childhood. In Graeb's (1990) series of 13 lymphangiomas, 11 occurred in children and 10 presented before age 6 years. Although lymphangiomas are relatively hemodynamically isolated, they show a great tendency for hemorrhage. The usual presentation of deep lesions is that of sudden proptosis caused by hemorrhage that can compress the optic nerve. In such situations emergency decompression is required. Imaging studies, particularly MR, are helpful in showing the relationship of the lesion to the optic nerve (Figs. 5-46 and 5-47). On CT and MR, the lymphangiomas appear as irregularly marginated, multilobulated, poorly defined lesions (Figs. 5-46 through 5-48) that may be heterogeneous and that enhance partially. The regions of enhancement correlate with the sites of the venous channels from which the hemorrhages originate (Graeb 1990). Localization of these sites is important for surgical planning. MR is more specific than CT in identifying old blood products and showing the various components of a lymphangioma. At

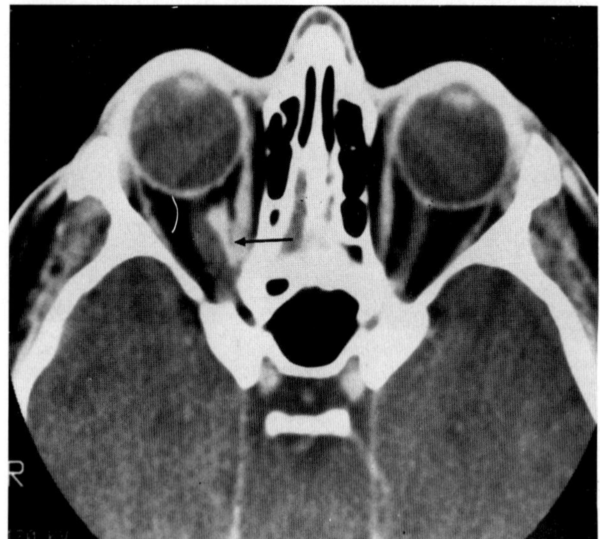

Figure 5-46 Lymphangioma. High-attenuation region of acute hemorrhage (arrow) in an ill-defined intraconal mass along the right optic nerve.

times the lesion may consist of a single giant cyst. Some lymphangiomas may be extensive, filling and expanding the bony orbit.

Varix

Vascular malformations of the venous system are infrequently occurring orbital lesions which include orbital varices and varicoceles. They are characterized by the production of intermittent exophthalmos, most often associated with activities that produce an increase in venous pressure (coughing, straining, the Valsalva maneuver). This type of response does not occur with lymphangiomas and helps to differentiate them clinically from varices. The lack of valves within the jugular vein allows back pressure to be transmitted to the orbital veins and the venous malformation. The distention of vascular spaces within the venous malformation produces the exophthalmos. Recurrent episodes of extreme proptosis have been reported to lead to blindness in up to 15 percent of patients with orbital varix. Some varices may hemorrhage (Fig. 5-49). Other causes of intermittent exophthalmos are bleeding into lymphangiomas, sinus infection with edema of the orbital soft tissue, and allergic edema. Venous varicocele formations associated with arteriovenous fistulas, carotid-cavernous in nature, are usually pulsatile and do not regress in size.

Routine skull radiographs are usually normal, although phleboliths may be present within the varix. Orbital venography was the most useful diagnostic modality (Bilaniuk 1977) before the advent of high-resolution CT. CT and MR clearly demonstrate the location of the soft tissue mass of a varix (Figs. 5-49 and 5-50) and characterize it

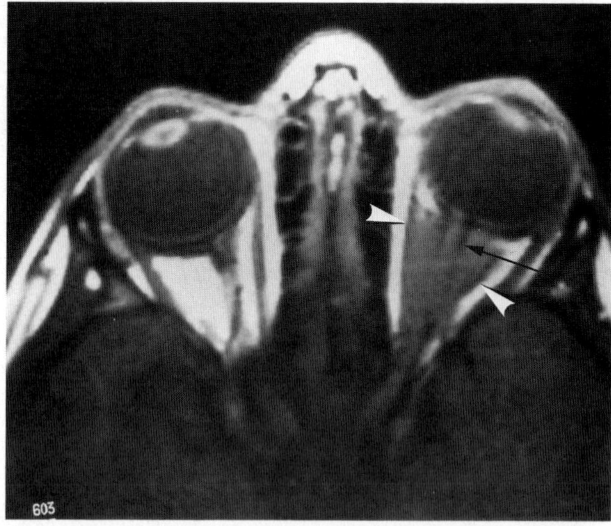

A

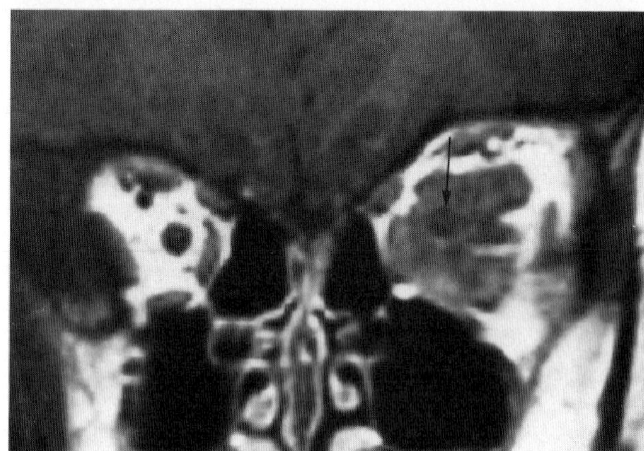

B

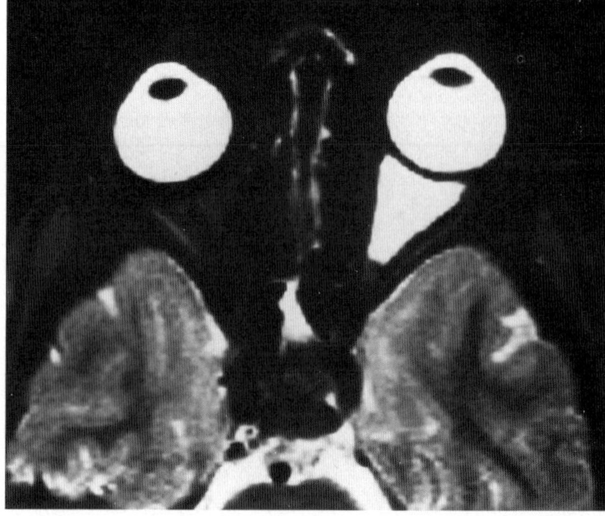

C

Figure 5-47 Extensive lymphangioma in the left orbit in a 4-year-old girl. **A.** An axial T_1WI (600/15) shows a conically shaped mass (arrowheads) encasing the left optic nerve (arrow). **B.** CEMR (600/15 with Gd-DTPA) reveals partial enhancement of the mass and shows well the lobulated nature of the lymphangioma. The nerve (arrow) can be identified. **C.** An axial T_2WI (3000/80) reveals the lesion to be of high intensity.

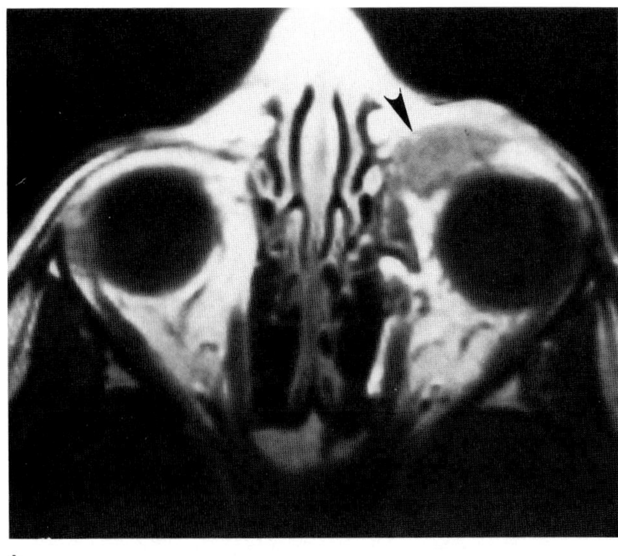

A

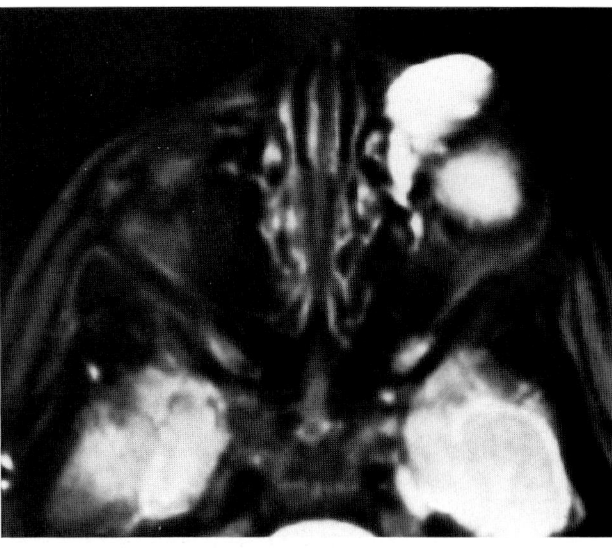

B

Figure 5-48 Lymphangioma in a 3-year-old boy. **A.** Axial CEMR (600/15 with Gd-DTPA) shows a somewhat irregular low-intensity mass (arrowhead) in the anteromedial aspect of the left orbit. **B.** Axial T_2WI (3000/90) shows increased intensity in the mass.

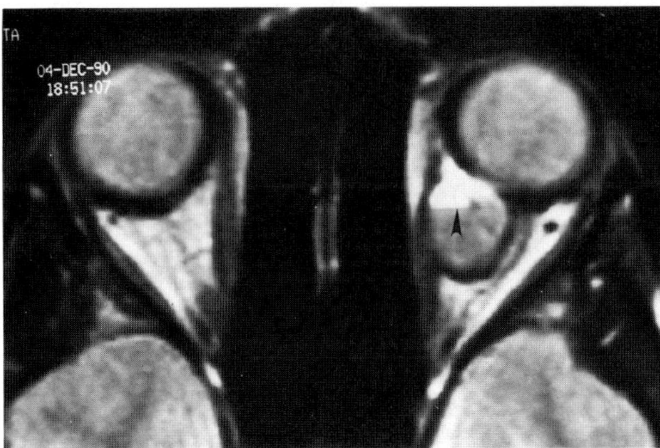

A

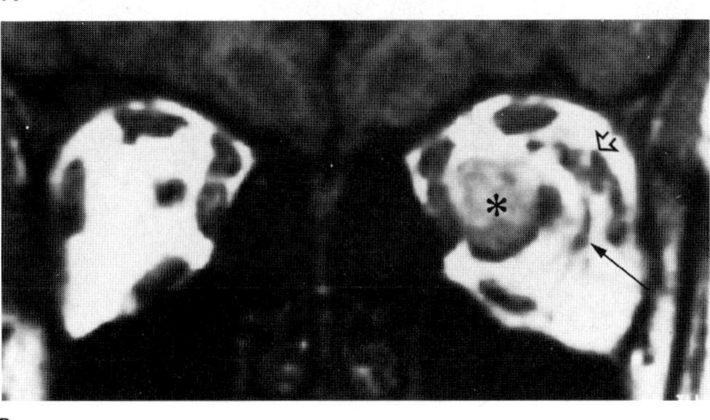

B

Figure 5-49 A 14-year-old girl with varix. **A.** Axial MRI (3000/30) shows a mass with a fluid level (arrowhead) between blood products. The mass displaces the left optic nerve laterally. **B.** A coronal T_1WI (600/15) reveals a somewhat lobulated heterogeneous mass (asterisk) which displaces the optic nerve laterally. The higher intensity within the mass is due to methemoglobin. An irregular portion of the varix (open arrow) is located in the lateral portion of the orbit and extends to the lateral rectus. There is also an enlarged lateral connecting vein (arrow).

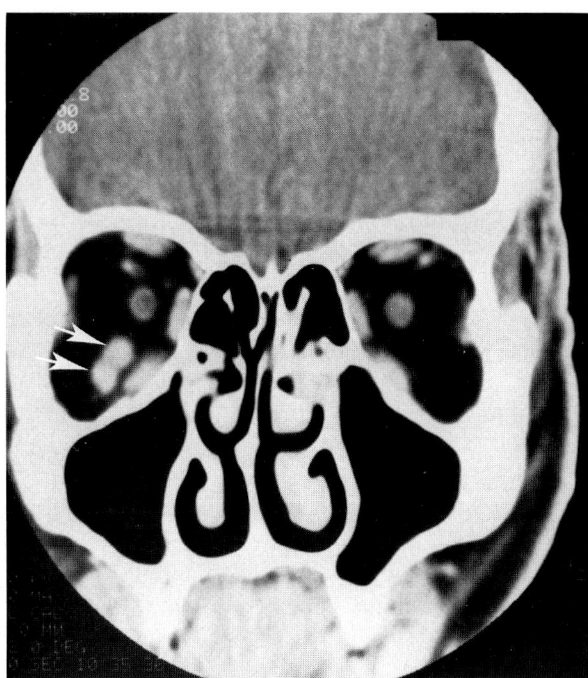

Figure 5-50 Varix, inferior ophthalmic vein. Coronal CECT demonstrates a "double-barrel" enlarged inferior ophthalmic vein (arrows), consistent with a tortuous venous varix.

by showing enlargement of the varix with the Valsalva maneuver and diminution in its size with the Muller maneuver. Alternatively, varix can be documented by its appearance and disappearance on CT with changes in head position. (Varix becomes evident when the neck is hyperextended to position the head for coronal scans.) By showing a signal void within the dilated veins, MR confirms the vascular nature of the lesion and helps differentiate it from morphologically similar lesions such as plexiform neurofibroma and orbital fibrosis.

Carotid-Cavernous Fistula

A communication between the internal carotid artery (or branches of the external carotid artery) and the cavernous sinus leads to the development of a fistula in which the veins are under arterial pressure. Valveless venous intercommunication between the cavernous sinus and the superior ophthalmic vein leads to a transmission of arterial pressure into the veins of the orbit. Proptosis, motility disturbances, pulsating exophthalmos (with a bruit), and suffusion of the globe, sclera, and conjunctiva are the hallmarks of a carotid-cavernous fistula. The etiology is most often trauma (Fig. 5-51), but fistulas may occur spontaneously, either secondary to atherosclerotic disease or from communications between the dural

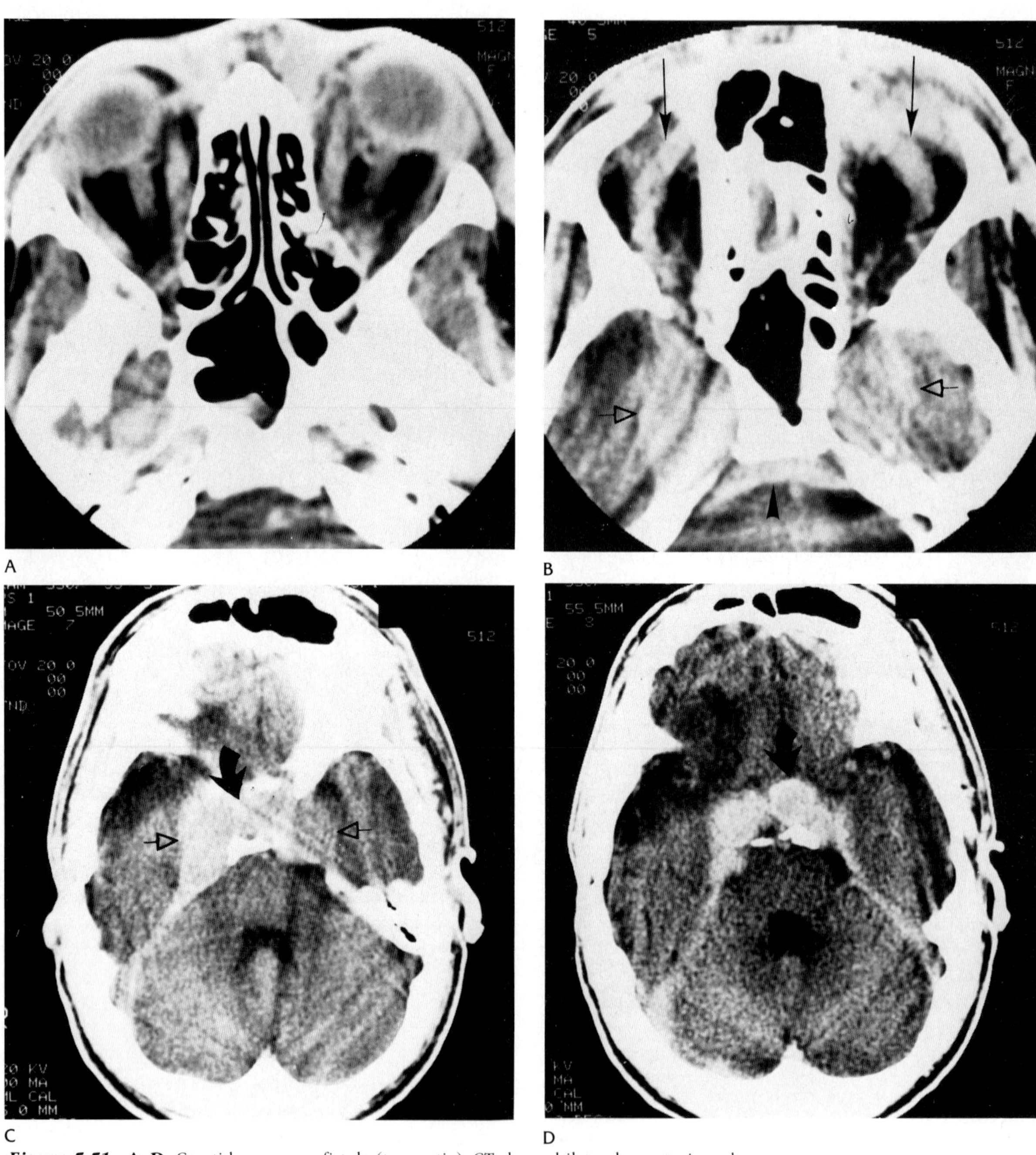

Figure 5-51 **A–D.** Carotid-cavernous fistula (traumatic). CT shows bilateral proptosis and engorgement of all muscles with markedly enlarged superior ophthalmic veins bilaterally (arrows). The cavernous sinuses are bulging (open arrows), and there appears to be an intrasellar and suprasellar mass (curved arrows). The basilar venous plexus is also engorged (arrowhead).

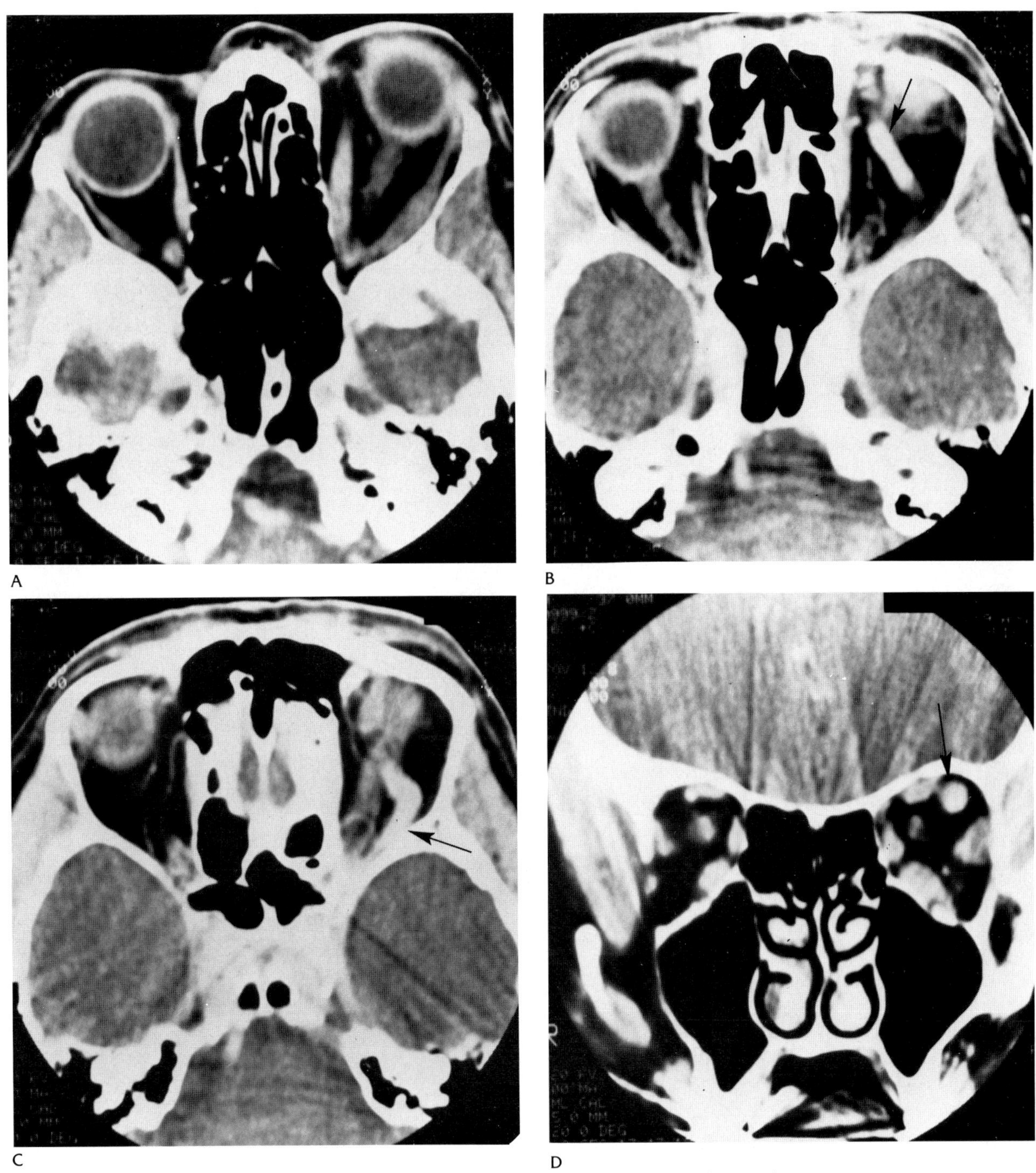

Figure 5-52 **A–D.** Dural cavernous fistula on CT. The left globe is proptotic, and extraocular muscles on the left are engorged. Note the enlarged left superior ophthalmic vein (arrow).

branches of the external carotid artery and the basilar venous plexus (dural arteriovenous malformations) (Figs. 5-52 and 5-53). The exophthalmos and ocular symptoms that accompany the fistula are usually ipsilateral to the site of the fistula but are contralateral in 10 percent and may be bilateral, as intercavernous sinus connections exist.

While carotid arteriography remains the definitive method for demonstrating the site of a fistula and its pattern of venous drainage (Zimmerman 1977), CT and MR are contributory in the initial diagnosis of cases that are not clinically obvious. Enlargement of the superior ophthalmic vein, engorgement of the rectus muscles, proptosis, and distention of the involved cavernous sinus

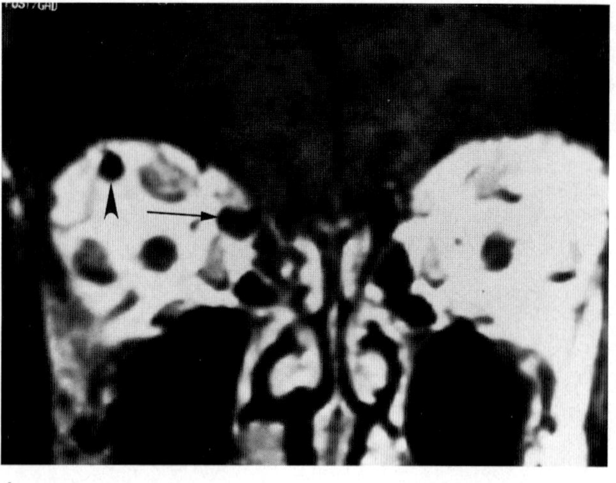

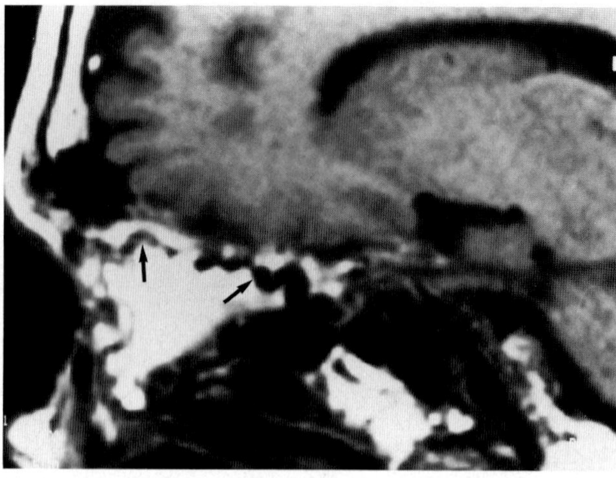

A B

Figure 5-53 Dural cavernous fistula with right orbital varix and enlargement of the right superior ophthalmic vein. **A.** Coronal CEMR (600/15 with Gd-DTPA). A prominent varix (arrow) is present in the medial extraconic space of the right orbit. The right superior ophthalmic vein (arrowhead) is prominently enlarged. Compare with the normal one on the left side. The rectus muscles show normal enhancement: **B.** A sagittal MRI (600/15) demonstrates the large varicose vein (arrows).

Table 5-2 Etiologies of Enlarged Superior Ophthalmic Vein

Carotid-cavernous fistula
- Traumatic
- Dural fistula (AVM)

Varix
Superior ophthalmic vein or cavernous sinus thrombosis
Orbital apex mass (compressing vein)
Thyroid opthalmopathy
Idiopathic orbital inflammation
Capillary hemangioma
Normal variant

can be demonstrated on CT (Figs. 5-51 and 5-52) and MR (Fig. 5-53). While traumatic fistulas require surgical or neurointerventional treatment, dural fistulas may thrombose spontaneously. The differential diagnosis of an enlarged superior ophthalmic vein is shown in Table 5-2.

OCULAR TUMORS

Ocular Melanoma

Both benign and malignant melanomas arise intraocularly from the uveal tract. Extraocular extension through the vortex veins occurs in approximately 13 percent of ocular melanomas (Starr 1962). Local recurrence of the melanoma after extenteration is extremely high if extraocular extension has already occurred. The diagnosis of melanoma as a primary tumor in the orbit requires the exclusion of a primary intraocular focus and an extracranial primary site (Jones 1979).

Malignant melanoma of the uveal tract (iris, choroid, ciliary body) is the most common intraocular malignancy in adults (Shields 1977), predominantly occurring in whites and rare in blacks (Shields 1977; Yanoff 1975). Primary malignant melanoma of the choroid is nearly always unilateral. Melanomas usually occur in older patients and are uncommon in the pediatric population. The clinical presentation varies from visual field defects or decreased visual acuity to pain or inflammation.

Table 5-3 Etiologies of Ocular Calcification

Optic nerve drusen
Phthisis bulbi
Neoplasm
- Retinoblastoma
- Choroidal osteoma
- Astrocytic hamartoma
  - Tuberous sclerosis
  - Neurofibromatosis
  - Isolated abnormality

Infection (congenital)
- Toxoplasmosis
- Cytomegalic virus
- Herpes
- Rubella

Metabolic
- Hyperparathyroidism
- Hypervitaminosis D
- Milk-alkali syndrome

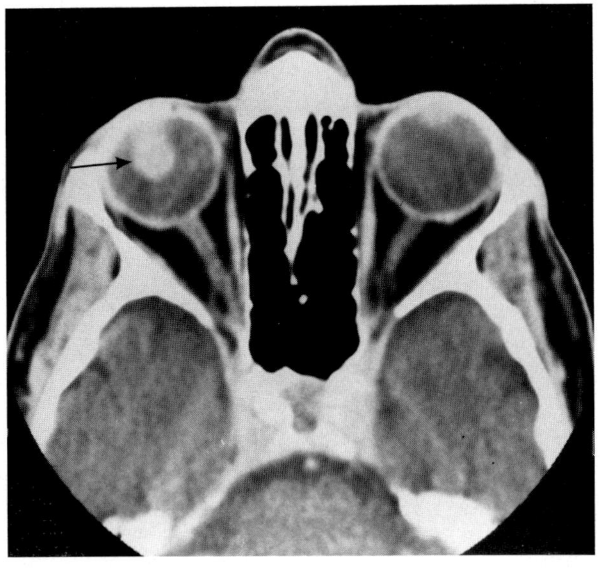

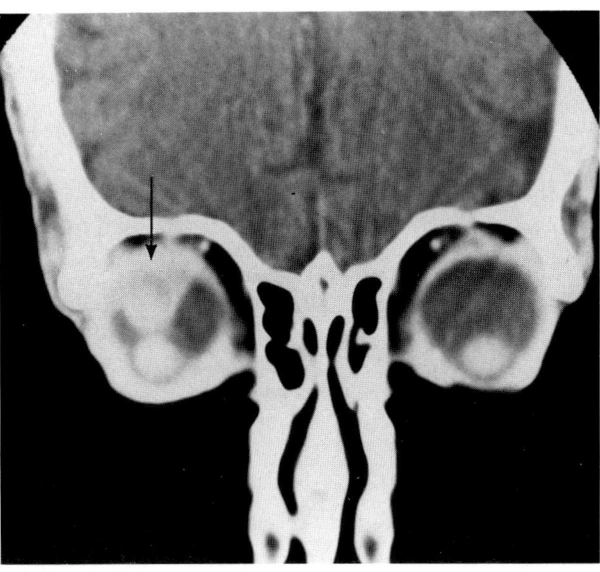

Figure 5-54 **A,B.** Melanoma. Large enhancing polypoid mass (arrow) projects from the superior choroid of the right globe. Its site of attachment is best appreciated on the coronal CT (**B**).

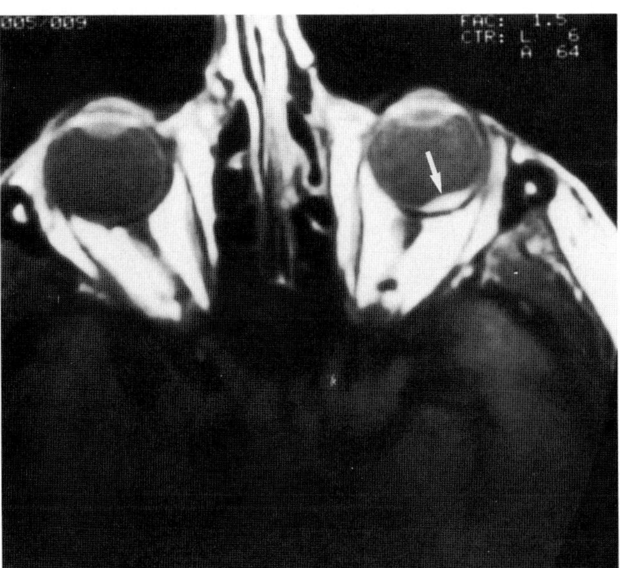

Figure 5-55 Melanotic melanoma in the left globe. Axial MRI (600/25) shows uveal melanoma (arrow) which is hyperintense to the vitreous.

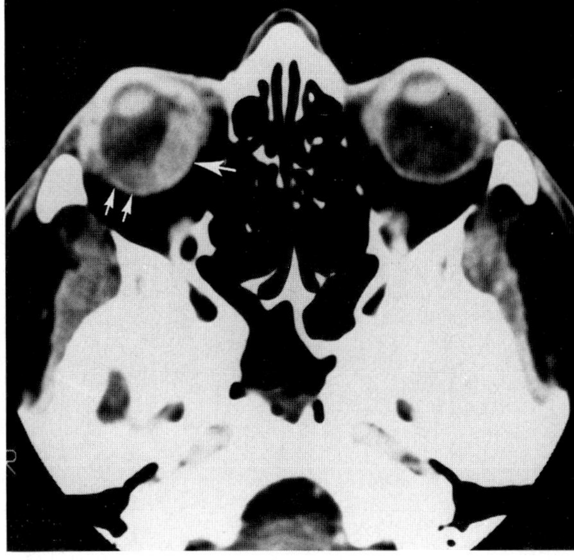

Figure 5-56 Ocular melanoma with retinal detachment. A large plaquelike melanoma enhances (single arrow) and is therefore distinguishable from the associated nonenhancing retinal detachment (double arrow) on CECT.

On CT, melanoma usually presents as a focal mass of slight hyperdensity which projects into the vitreous (Fig. 5-54). These tumors may show slight enhancement (Mafee 1985; Peyster 1985). The shape of the mass varies from polypoid (Fig. 5-54) to flat or crescentic (Fig. 5-55); associated retinal detachment is common and often requires intravenous contrast for CT differentiation (Fig. 5-56) or T_2WI for MR (Fig. 5-57). Rarely, choroidal melanoma can manifest as predominantly inflammatory (endophthalmitis, episcleritis, or iridocyclitis). Calcification in uveal melanomas has not been seen on CT (Table 5-3). The usefulness of CT and MR lies mainly in detecting episcleral extension and tumor recurrence and as an aid in the differential diagnosis (Figs. 5-58 through 5-60), as many benign and malignant lesions can simulate a melanoma funduscopically (Table 5-4). MR is particularly helpful because melanotic melanomas have a distinctive signal pattern due to paramagnetic properties of melanin and because MR is more sensitive than CT in distinguishing ocular tumors from fluid collections. Melanotic mel-

Table 5-4 Differential Diagnosis of Choroidal Melanoma

Malignant melanoma (melanotic or amelanotic)
Benign melanoma
Optic nerve melanocytoma
Choroidal hemangioma
Hemorrhage
Astrocytic hamartoma
Detached choroid
Choroidal metastasis (especially breast)
Inflammation (granuloma, endophthalmitis)
Retinal astrocytoma
Retinal cyst
Sarcoidosis
Arterial macroaneurysm (Brown 1985)

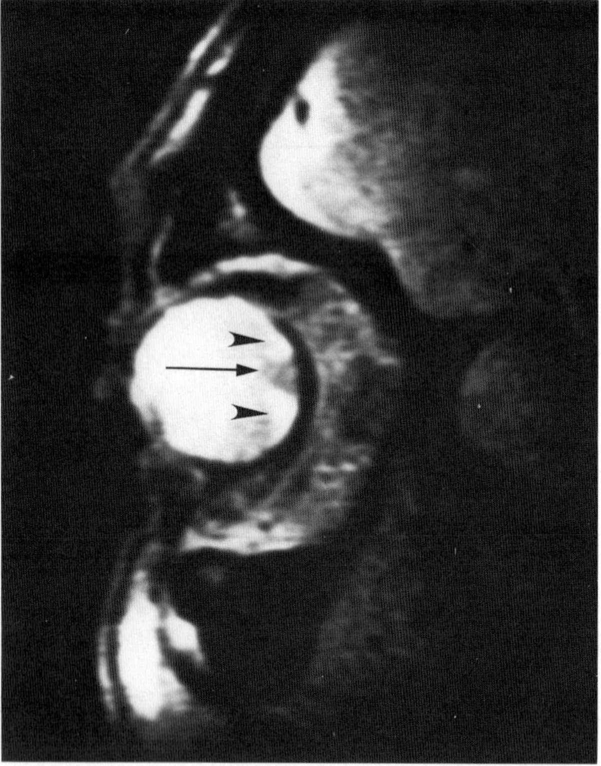

Figure 5-57 Ocular melanoma shown on a sagittal MRI (T_2WI). The cone-shaped melanoma (arrow) is hypointense, while the subretinal fluid (arrowheads) on either side of the melanoma is hyperintense.

anomas differ from most tumors by having short T_1 and T_2 values (Damadian 1973; Gomori 1986). On T_1WI melanotic melanomas are hyperintense to vitreous (Fig. 5-55), and on T_2WI they are slightly hypointense (Fig. 5-57). It is necessary to perform both T_1WI and T_2WI sequences

Figure 5-58 Left ocular metastatic disease in a 57-year-old woman. Axial MRI (700/25) reveals an irregular mass (arrowheads) filling the posterior half of the left globe.

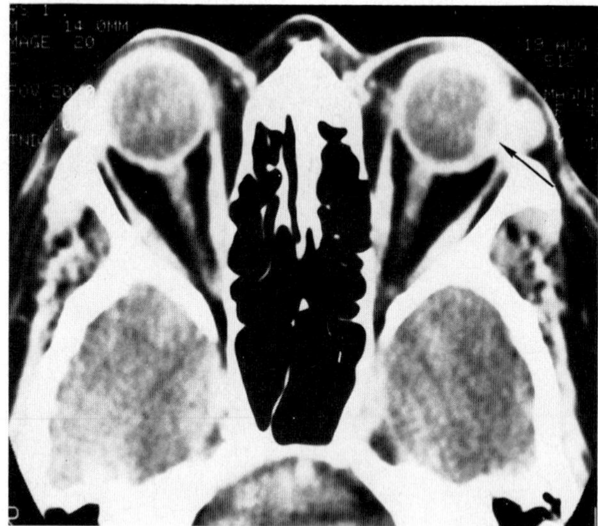

Figure 5-59 Choroidal metastases on CECT. An enhancing choroidal mass on the temporal aspect of the left globe (arrow), proven to be breast carcinoma metastases.

because on T_1WI melanotic melanomas may not be distinguishable from hemorrhagic or highly proteinaceous material or from choroidal hemangioma. On T_2WI, intracellular methemoglobin becomes more hypointense than melanoma and extracellular methemoglobin remains hyperintense. A choroidal hemangioma remains bright (hyperintense) on T_2WI.

Choroidal Hemangioma

Hemangiomas of the choroid are benign lesions that usually are detected in patients 10 to 20 years of age. Fifty percent of these patients have Sturge-Weber disease (Reese 1976). Histologically, these lesions are cavernous, and up to 90 percent have associated retinal detachments microscopically. CT demonstrates focal areas of intense contrast enhancement in the choroid (Fig. 5-60); indeed, the lesion may not be detected on nonenhanced CT (NCCT). These lesions can hemorrhage spontaneously. On MR, choroidal hemangiomas are hyperintense to vitreous on T_1WI and isointense to vitreous on T_2WI (Peyster 1988).

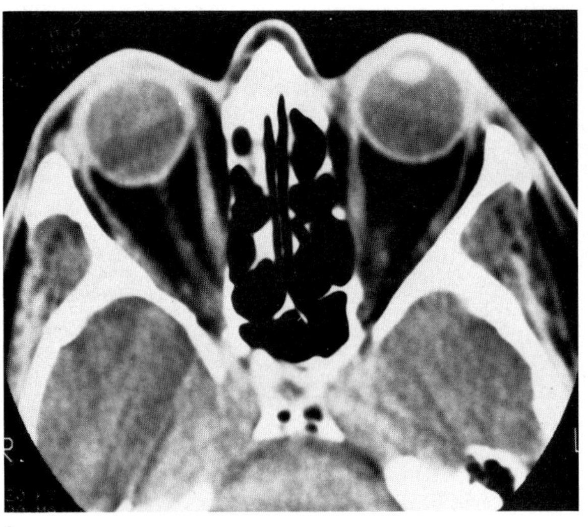

A

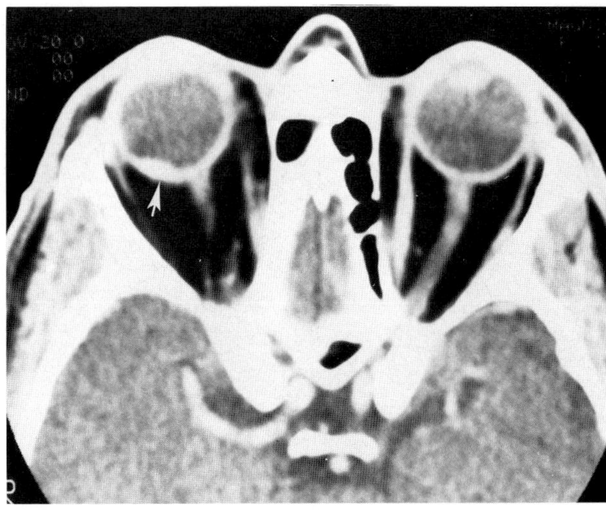

B

Figure 5-60 **A,B.** Choroidal hemangioma. NCCT (**A**) is normal. On CECT, there is marked enhancement of the mass posterotemporally (arrow), a typical appearance of this entity.

Retinoblastoma

Retinoblastoma, the most common intraocular malignancy of childhood, has an incidence between 1 in 15,000 and 1 in 30,000 (Zimmerman 1978). It accounts for 1 percent of early childhood deaths and 5 percent of childhood blindness (Zimmerman 1979). While this tumor is congenital, it is not necessarily recognized at birth. The average age at the time of diagnosis is 18 months (Reese 1976). In 25 to 33 percent of patients with retinoblastoma, the disease is bilateral and represents an autosomal dominant form of genetic transmission that has a variable penetrance (Zimmerman 1979); 50 percent of the offspring of an affected parent are at risk, and thus in bilateral cases there is a frequent familial history. Conversely, 60 percent of familial cases are bilateral. The typical presentation of leukokoria, strabismus, glaucoma, or vision loss occurs in 90 percent of cases, while the remaining 10 percent mimic a variety of illnesses, including orbital cellulitis, ophthalmitis, conjunctivitis, and systemic illness (Appelboom 1985).

Retinoblastoma arises in the nuclear layer of the retina as a primary malignant neuroectodermal neoplasm composed of small round or ovoid cells (Russell 1977). It is characterized by a multicentric origin, rapid growth, and the ability to invade adjacent tissues. As the tumor outgrows its blood supply, cell necrosis occurs and DNA is released that has a propensity to form a calcified complex. This calcified complex enables the tumor to be identified with confidence radiologically (Brant-Zawadzki 1979; Klintworth 1978; Zimmerman 1979). X-ray studies of enucleated eyes have shown a characteristic pattern of calcification consisting of closely packed discrete radiodensities (Klintworth 1978) 1 mm in diameter.

Intraocular spread of retinoblastoma occurs when the malignant cells disseminate throughout the eye and implant at other sites (choroid, retina, posterior surface of the cornea) (Reese 1976). Extension of the tumor along perineural and perivascular spaces results in intraorbital and optic nerve spread of the tumor. Enucleation as the sole treatment fails in such cases. Retinoblastoma usually recurs in the orbit within 1 year, on the average within 4 months, of enucleation and presents as a large mass extruding the prosthesis (Rootman 1978) (Fig. 5-61). Extension of the tumor into the subarachnoid space surrounding the optic nerve allows its dissemination by the CSF throughout the nervous system. Involvement of the intraorbital vascular system by tumor permits systemic extracranial spread to distant sites such as long bones, lymphatics, and viscera (Jones 1979).

The development of more sensitive diagnostic techniques, including CT, has led in recent years to better detection and earlier treatment. This has resulted in an increase in the survival of patients with retinoblastoma. However, spread beyond the globe carries a poor prognosis.

CT recognition of retinoblastomas is dependent on the identification of a soft tissue mass with calcification involving the retina (Figs. 5-61 through 5-63). The presence of calcification helps differentiate the tumor from other causes of retinal thickening, such as astrocytic hamartoma (Fig. 5-64) and retinal detachment. CT is particularly valuable in demonstrating the extension of the tumor to other sites within the globe (or multifocal origins) and bilaterality of the tumor (Fig. 5-63). Rarely, retinoblastoma can involve the entire globe, diffusely infiltrating the vitreous and aqueous humors (Fig. 5-65). In these cases calcification may be difficult to detect. In addition, the globe may be buphthalmic (Fig. 5-65).

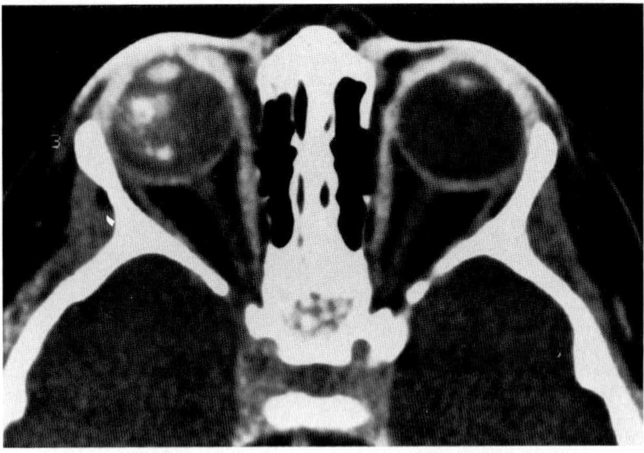

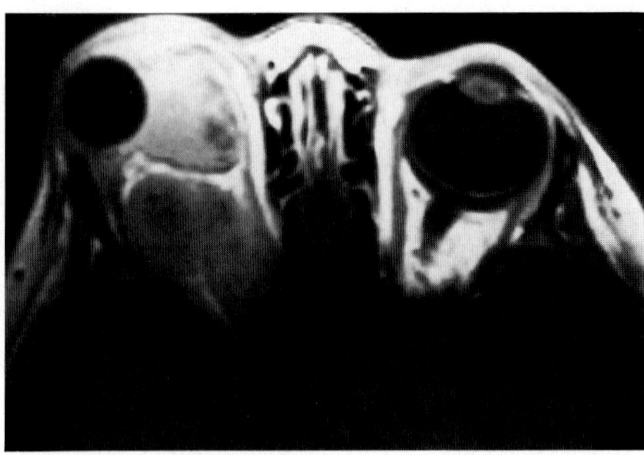

A B

Figure 5-61 Retinoblastoma with massive recurrence 3 months after enucleation. Choroidal invasion was noted at the time of surgery. **A.** Preoperative axial CECT reveals a calcified and enhancing tumor in the right globe with massive retinal detachment, producing slightly increased density in the medial half of the right globe (compare with the normal left globe). **B.** Axial MRI (600/15) obtained 3 months after enucleation demonstrates multiple lobules of the tumor filling the right orbit and encasing the prosthesis.

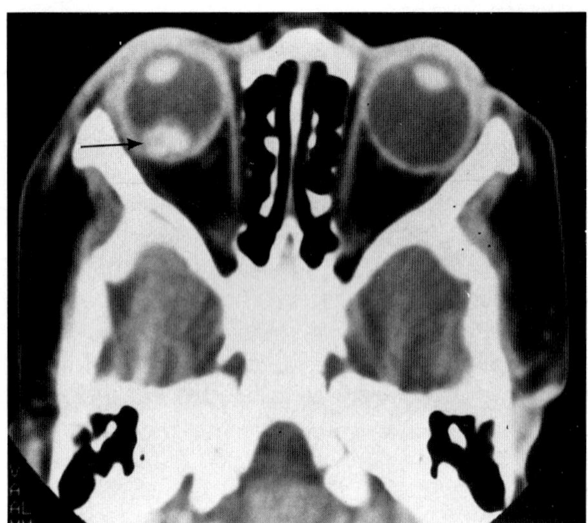

Figure 5-62 Unilateral retinoblastoma. Typical nodular calcification in right retinal mass (arrow) on NCCT.

Figure 5-63 Bilateral retinoblastoma. Large mass occupying most of the left globe with an irregular margin and nodular calcifications. Multiple calcifications in the right globe (open arrows) denote multifocal, bilateral retinoblastoma.

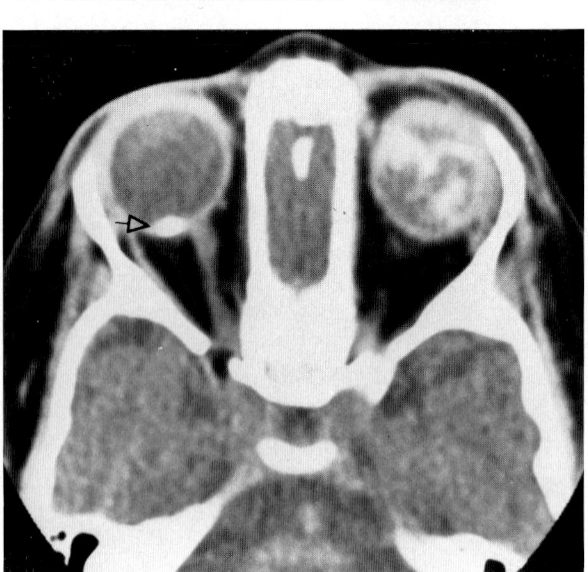

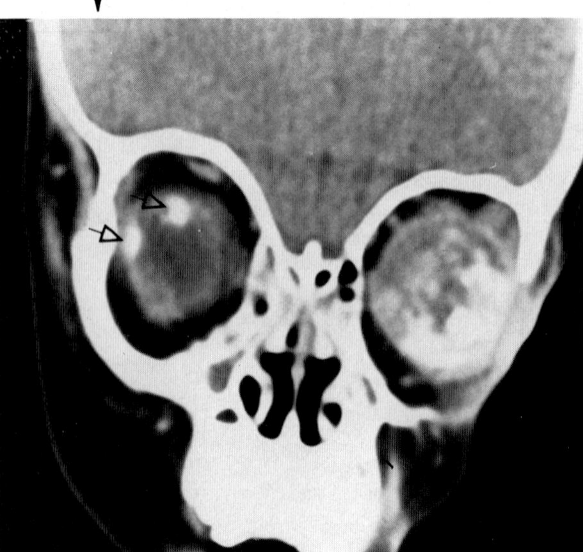

A B

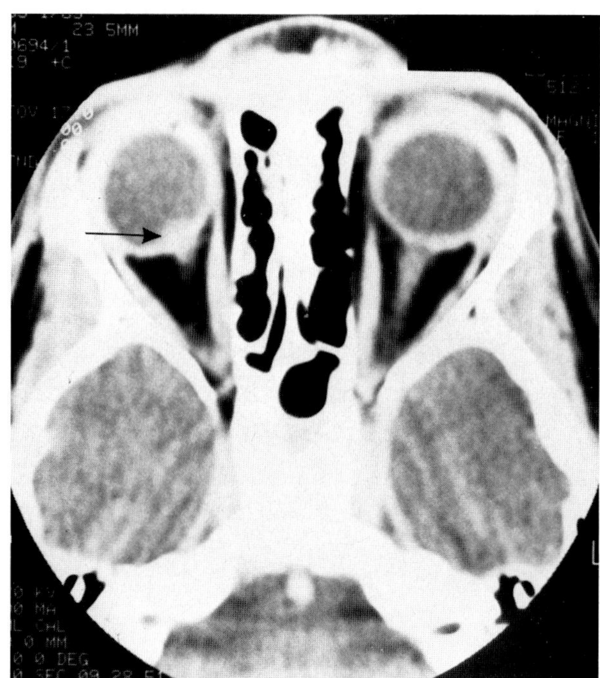

Figure 5-64 Astrocytic hamartoma on CT. Noncalcified mass at the right optic nerve head (arrow) in a patient without tuberous sclerosis.

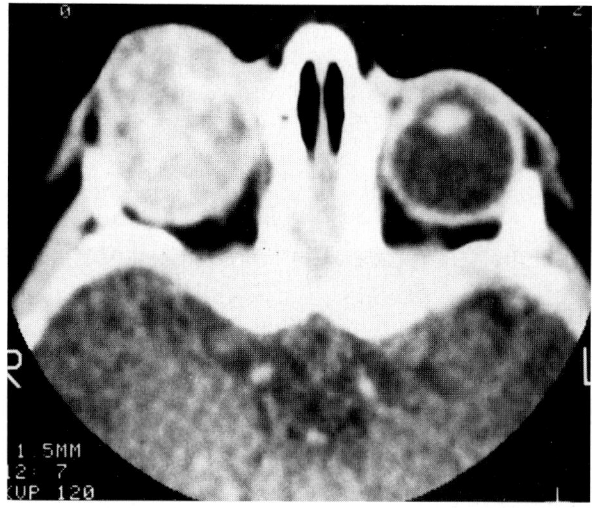

Figure 5-65 Infiltrative retinoblastoma. Enlarged right globe filled by a diffuse heterogeneous mass in the buphthalmic globe.

Although CT, because of its ability to detect calcification, is the imaging modality of choice for the evaluation of patients suspected of having a retinoblastoma, MR is a very useful adjunct study. The multiplanar capability and superior soft tissue discrimination make MR a valuable tool for the evaluation of the intraorbital and/or intracranial extent of a retinoblastoma. In addition, MR is more specific than CT for subretinal fluid, in detecting optic nerve involvement, and in differentiating the various causes of leukokoria (Mafee 1987, 1990). On MR, retinoblastomas are slightly to moderately hyperintense to the vitreous on T_1WI and PD-WI, contrast-enhance, and are moderately to markedly hypointense on T_2WI (Fig. 5-66). Regions of dense calcifications appear hypointense on both T_1WI and T_2WI.

Associated retinal detachment can be distinguished from the true tumor mass by MR or with CECT (Fig. 5-61), as most retinoblastomas with noncalcified portions enhance. Thickening of the optic nerve sheath complex may indicate extension of the tumor into the perineural subarachnoid space; this is a poor prognostic sign. This is best demonstrated with CECT or CEMR with fat suppression. The presence of tumor within the intracranial subarachnoid space can be demonstrated with contrast enhancement. In addition, intracerebral metastases and the rare "trilateral" retinoblastoma (bilateral retinoblastoma with an associated pineal tumor) can be detected with CT (Johnson 1985) or MR.

Concomitant with an improvement in the survival of patients with congenital bilateral retinoblastomas, there has been an appreciation that these patients have a predisposition to the development of radiation-induced neoplasm (Soloway 1966). This occurs in about one-fifth of survivors with bilateral retinoblastomas who have been irradiated. The site of secondary tumor is usually within the field of radiation. These tumors are most commonly manifested within 10 years of radiation therapy. The majority of them are of mesenchymal origin, in the form of sarcomas. However, carcinomas have also been reported (Zimmerman 1979). In addition, second malignancies apparently occur more frequently in nonirradiated patients than they do in the general population (Abramson 1984).

OTHER CAUSES OF LEUKOKORIA

Coat's Disease

This benign entity consists of unilateral retinal telangiectasia with associated massive subretinal exudative fluid accumulation causing retinal detachment. Males (80 percent) of ages 6 to 8 years are typically affected (Reese 1976). CT demonstrates relatively homogeneous hyperdensity involving the entire vitreous cavity (Fig. 5-67) secondary to lipoproteinaceous exudate underlying a (usually) total retinal detachment (Sherman 1983). Calcification is nearly always absent, although tiny foci of calcified cholesterol plaques may rarely be seen on funduscopy. Features distinguishing this entity from retinoblastoma include an older age at presentation, an exclusively unilateral occurrence, lack of calcification or enhancement, and absence of extraocular spread (Haik 1985). CT or MR can therefore obviate the need for globe

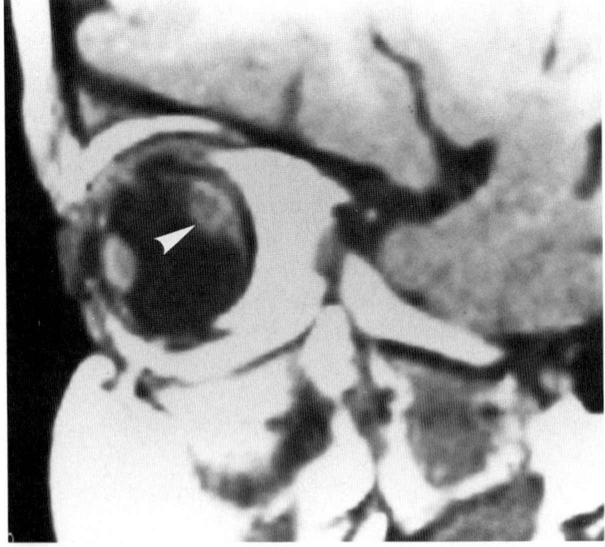
A

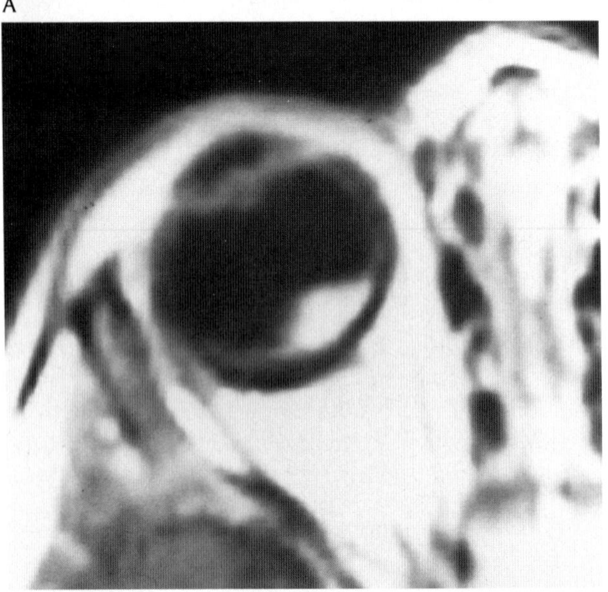
B

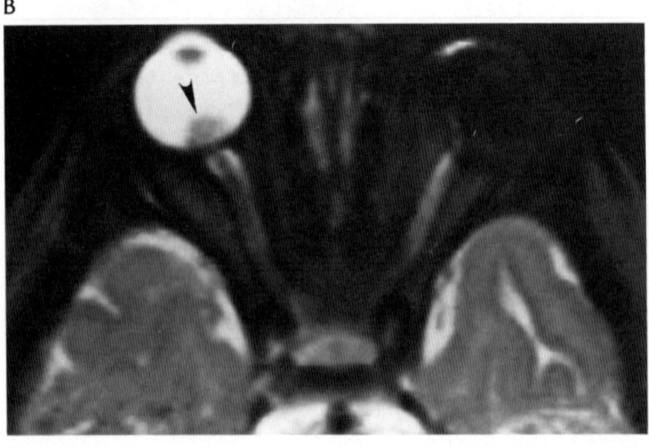
C

Figure 5-66 Retinoblastoma in a 1-year-old girl. **A.** Sagittal MR (600/15) shows a hyperintense mass (arrowhead) along the posterior pole of the globe. **B.** Axial MR (600/22 with Gd-DTPA) shows contrast enhancement of the tumor. **C.** Axial MR (3000/120) shows that the retinoblastoma (arrowhead) has become hypointense relative to the vitreous.

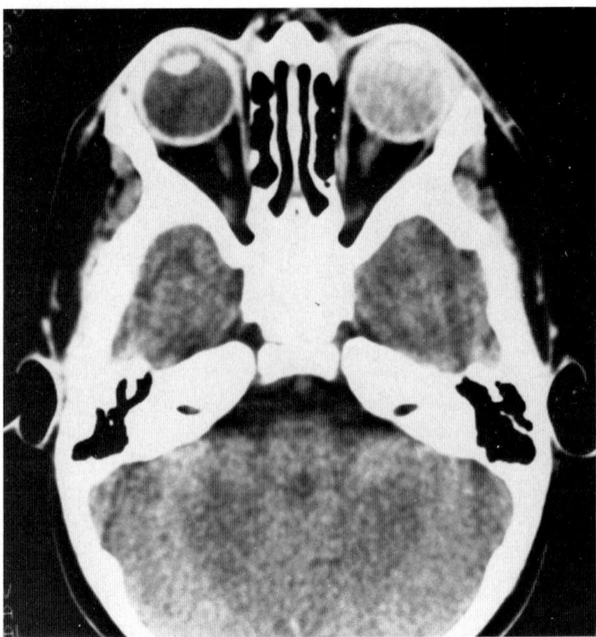

Figure 5-67 Coat's disease on CT. Uniformly hyperdense left globe presenting as leukokoria. Absence of calcifications helps distinguish this condition from retinoblastoma.

exenteration in these patients and instead lead to appropriate laser therapy. Coat's disease is the primary entity to distinguish from retinoblastoma in the differential diagnosis. MR is superior to CT in differentiating the two entities and in the case of Coat's disease demonstrates the lipoproteinaceous subretinal exudate which characteristically is hyperintense to the vitreous on both T_1WI and T_2WI (Mafee 1987, 1990).

Persistent Hyperplastic Primary Vitreous

Persistent hyperplastic primary vitreous (PHPV) results from failure of involution of the embryonic intraocular vascular system. Imaging studies demonstrate a linear or triangular density, the residual hyaloid vascular system with connective tissue, extending from the posterior aspect of the lens to the back of the globe (Fig. 5-68). There also may be associated retinal detachment as a result of recurrent hemorrhage. A hyaloid remnant may be difficult to differentiate from retinal detachment when it is complete. PHPV is unilateral and noncalcified. There usually is microphthalmos (Haik 1985), deformity of the globe and lens, increased density or intensity of the vitreous body, and enhancement of the band of tissue that extends between the lens and the posterior globe (Magill 1990). Without contrast enhancement the band of tissue may be difficult to detect on CT, but it is seen as a band of low intensity on MR images (Fig. 5-68). When PHPV is bilateral, it is usually part of optic dysplasia such as Norrie's disease (congenital progressive oculoacoustic cerebral degeneration).

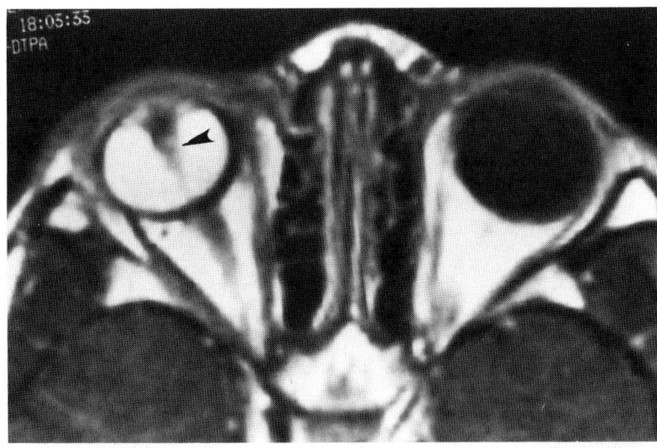

A

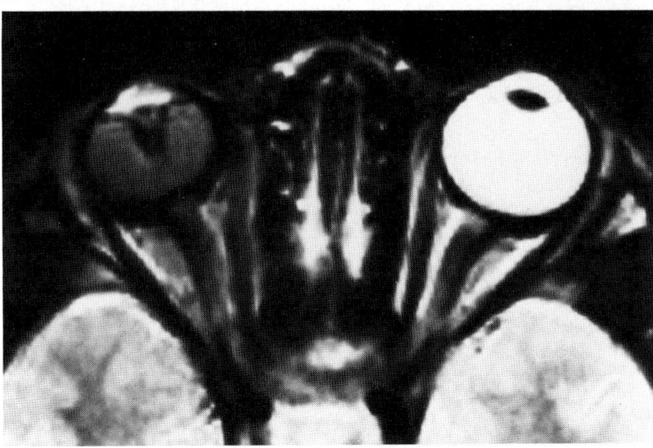

B

Figure 5-68 Persistent hyperplastic primary vitreous with microphthalmic globe. **A.** Axial MRI (600/20) reveals a smaller globe on the right with a shallow anterior chamber and an abnormal lens from which triangularly shaped tissue (arrowhead) extends posteriorly. This tissue represents persistence of the hyaloid vascular system. There is complete retinal detachment. The left globe appears normal. **B.** Axial T_2WI (3000/90) shows an abnormally deformed and small lens. The tissue extending posteriorly from the lens is of markedly decreased intensity. The probable subretinal fluid has decreased in intensity.

Norrie's Disease

Norrie's disease is a rare X-linked inherited disease that is transmitted by females but affects only males (Liberfarb 1985). The disease involves mental deterioration and progressive loss of vision and hearing. The eye abnormalities include retinal detachment with hemorrhage, retrolental mass, and lens abnormalities.

Retinopathy of Prematurity

Retinopathy of prematurity, or retrolental fibroplasia, is usually seen in premature infants who receive high oxygen concentrations. Recent literature suggests that the high oxygen concentration in inspired air is not a requisite for the development of this entity (Patz 1985). Bilateral retinal detachments with variable enhancement and occasional calcification may be seen. Microphthalmia has also been described (Haik 1985).

Ocular Toxicariasis

Toxocara canis infestation can present with leukokoria and retinal detachment secondary to endophthalmitis. "Pseudomicrophthalmia" (Haik 1985) from focally thickened sclera with enhancement is common. CT may also demonstrate a nonenhancing hyperdense mass occupying most of the vitreous cavity (Edwards 1985). MR may demonstrate the larval granuloma as a hyperintense mass on both T_1WI and T_2WI (Mafee 1990).

GLOBE SHAPE ABNORMALITIES

Coloboma

Colobomas are congenital defects in the retina, choroid, iris, optic nerve, and/or lens which result from deficient closure of the fetal optic fissure along the inferonasal aspect of the globe and optic nerve (Simmons 1983). The posterior globe and optic nerve are most commonly affected. The defect is transmitted as an autosomal dominant trait with variable penetrance, occurring bilaterally in 60 percent of cases. Visual field defects and decreased visual acuity are present. MR and CT (Fig. 5-69) demonstrate defects in the posterior globe extending into the optic nerve. Microphthalmia and retinal cysts may accompany optic nerve colobomas. CT and MR are useful in identifying retinal cysts posterior to the globe and in revealing any central nervous system (CNS) abnormality which can be associated with these lesions, such as encephalocele or callosal agenesis (Corbett 1980).

Staphyloma

Staphylomas are acquired defects in the wall of the globe that result in protrusion of either the cornea or the sclera. These defects are lined with iris or choroid tissue. In severe myopia, accompanying staphylomas typically are seen as focal bulges in the posterior surface of the globe, on the temporal side of the optic disk (Anderson 1983). Anterior staphylomas can be seen in inflammatory entities such as rheumatoid arthritis.

Axial Myopia

Axial myopia is characterized by an enlarged anteroposterior diameter of the globe (Fig. 5-70). Anterior protrusion may be noted and may result in proptosis (Brodey 1983). Axial myopia is distinguished from staphyloma by the absence of a focal bulge in an elongated globe. Retinal detachment and staphyloma may accompany the myopic globe.

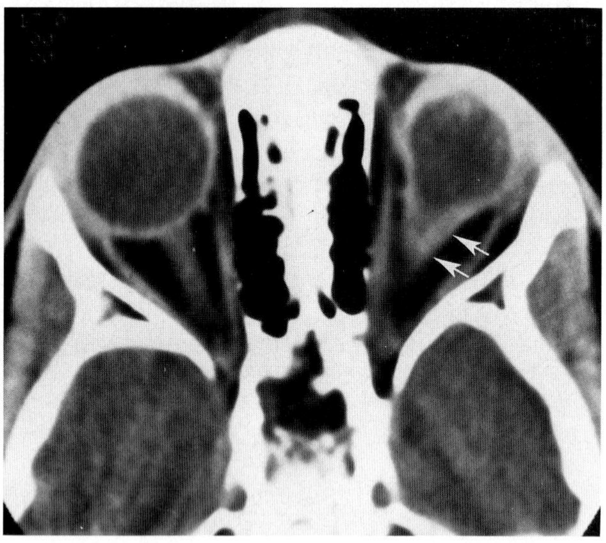

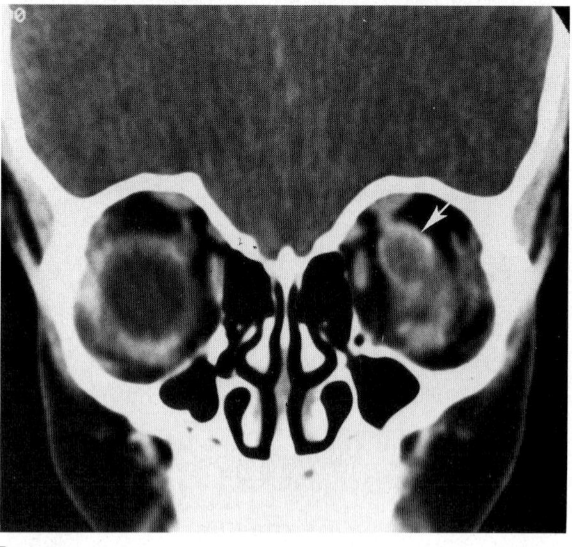

A B

Figure 5-69 **A,B.** Microphthalmos with coloboma. Conical defect in posterior globe extending into optic nerve (arrows) seen on axial (**A**) and coronal (**B**) CT in a microphthalmic globe.

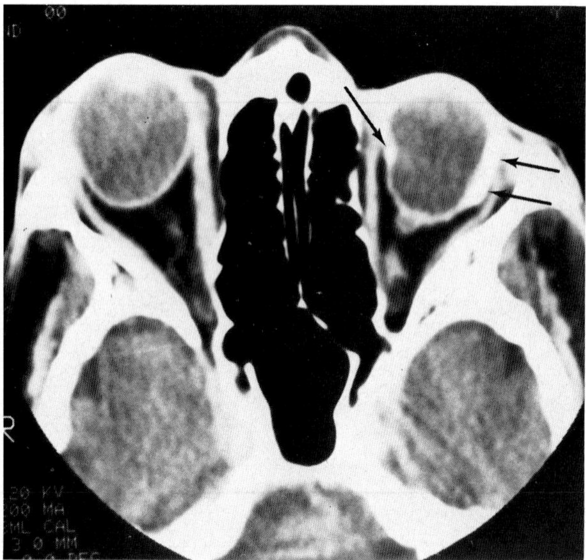

Figure 5-70 Myopia, status postscleral banding on CT. Both globes have a myopic configuration. High-density structures at the periphery of the left globe (arrows) with waistlike deformity represent scleral band placed for prior retinal detachment.

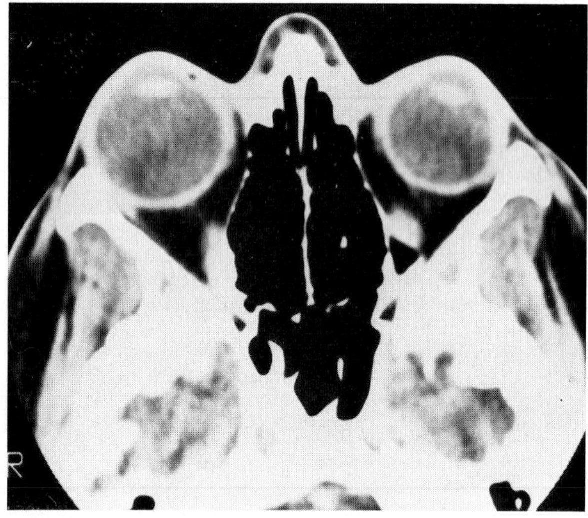

Figure 5-71 Buphthalmos. CT shows macrophthalmic right globe in a patient with glaucoma.

Buphthalmos

Buphthalmos, or congenital glaucoma, is usually detected because of clouding or enlargement of the cornea or because the child is insensitive to light (Gittinger 1984). It is unilateral in approximately 25 percent of cases and is caused by maldevelopment of aqueous humor outflow channels in the anterior chamber angle. Glaucoma in a child results in an enlarged globe (Fig. 5-71). Macrophthalmos may be unrelated to intraocular pressure, however, and can be seen as an isolated entity secondary to massive intraocular tumor or in association with neurofibromatosis.

Microphthalmos

Anophthalmia results when there is failure of the optic pit to deepen to form a vesicle or when an optic vesicle forms and then degenerates. Complete failure of eye development is extremely rare, and only a histological examination can differentiate between anophthalmia and microphthalmia. Microphthalmia (Fig. 5-72) may occur as an isolated finding, but much more often it is seen in association with other ocular (Fig. 5-69) and systemic abnormalities (Smith 1983). It is seen in 75 percent of pa-

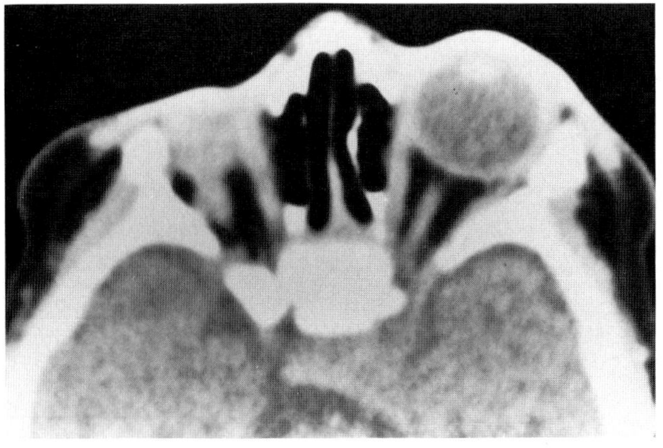

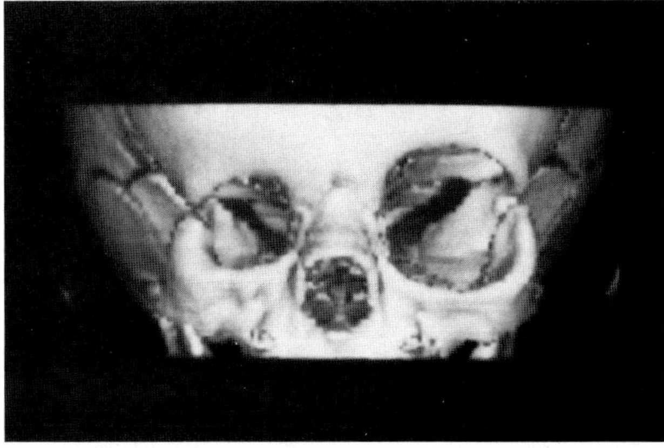

A B

Figure 5-72 Right microphthalmos in a 7-week-old girl. **A.** Axial CT fails to reveal a normal globe on the right. The right bony orbit is small. **B.** Three-dimensional CT reconstruction of the facial skeleton reveals marked hypoplasia of the right bony orbit.

tients with trisomy-13 syndrome and is commonly associated with mental retardation.

Microphthalmia with cyst results when there is malformation of the globe with incomplete closure of the fetal fissure. The disorganized cystic neuroectodermal tissue prolapses into the orbit and may be larger than the globe itself.

GLOBE CALCIFICATIONS

The etiology of calcification in the globe is varied (Hedges 1982; Turner 1983), and the differential diagnosis is highly dependent on the age of the patient (Table 5-3). In an infant or young child (up to 3 years of age), any focal calcification in the globe must be considered a retinoblastoma until proved otherwise. The contralateral eye must be examined thoroughly for calcification, as up to one-third of retinoblastomas are bilateral (Fig. 5-63). Calcification is seen in up to 95 percent of cases (Bullock 1977). Other etiologies of globe calcification in a child include astrocytic hamartoma, a nodular mass frequently associated with tuberous sclerosis (Fig. 5-64). Choroidal osteoma is a rare tumor that usually is seen in young women as a focal area of calcification near the optic disk (Hedges 1982).

In adults, the most common cause of focal calcification in the globe is optic nerve drusen. These lesions are commonly bilateral (Fig. 5-73) and represent benign ac-

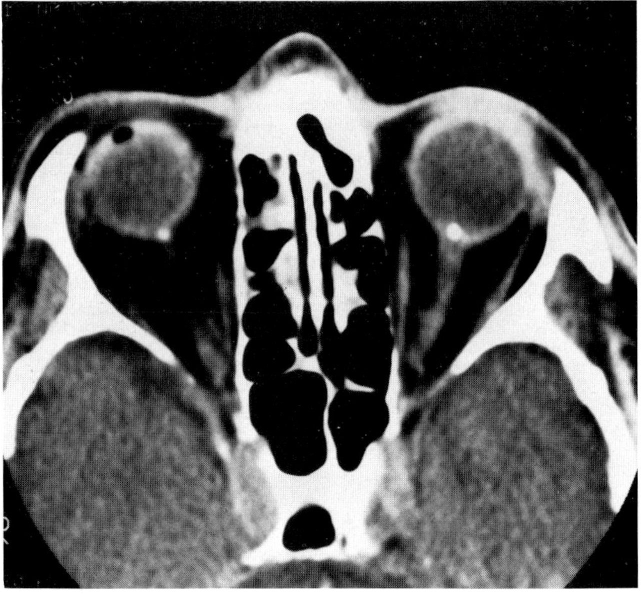

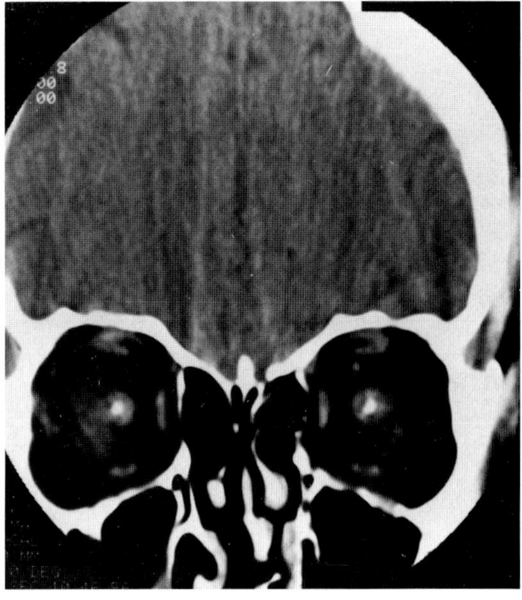

A B

Figure 5-73 **A,B.** Bilateral optic nerve drusen. Axial (**A**) and coronal (**B**) CT demonstrates round, focal calcification at the optic disks, diagnostic of optic nerve drusen.

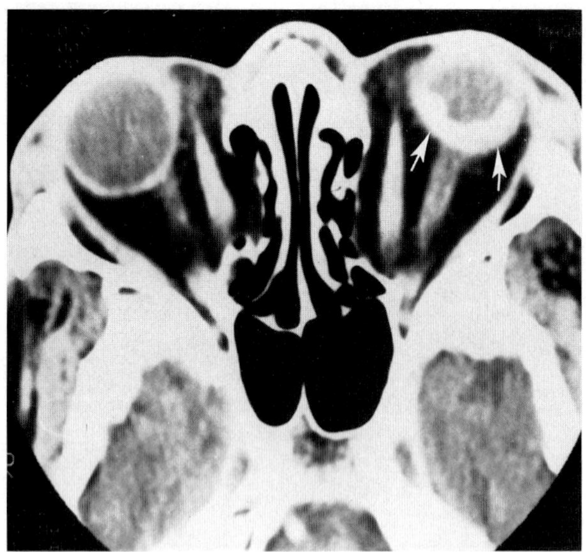

Figure 5-74 Phthisis bulbi on CT. Small left globe with extensive choroidal calcification (arrows) in a patient many years after trauma to the globe.

cumulations of hyalinelike material beneath the surface of the optic disk (Hedges 1982; Ramirez 1983). Funduscopically, drusen can masquerade as papilledema. Although frequently asymptomatic, optic nerve drusen can be associated with visual field defects in up to 80 percent of cases (Savage 1985). Interestingly, visual field defects typically occur in areas not corresponding to the funduscopic location of the drusen (Savage 1985). The etiology of optic nerve drusen is not clearly established, but drusen is considered to represent a developmental anomaly or degenerative process (Ramirez 1983). There is a familial tendency for the development of these lesions.

Phthisis bulbi is an end-stage calcified, shrunken globe which is blind. Extensive calcification is seen on CT in a small, irregularly shaped globe (Fig. 5-74). Etiologies include trauma, recurrent retinal hemorrhage, prior surgery, chronic ocular inflammation (Fig. 5-75), and radiation.

RETINAL DETACHMENT

When the retinal pigment epithelial layer is separated from the sensory retina by fluid, a retinal detachment is present (Figs. 5-36 and 5-76). A choroidal detachment can mimic a retinal detachment radiographically and often occurs after intraocular surgery. Detachments can be quite extensive and can meet in the midline to result in "kissing detachments." Retinal detachments can be classified as rhegmatogenous or nonrhegmatogenous, depending on whether a rhegma, or hole, exists in the sensory retina. Most detachments are rhegmatogeneous; retinal holes are secondary to retinal degeneration or vitreous traction from liquefaction of the vitreous. Spontaneous detachments occur in under 10 per 100,000 per year (Gittinger 1984). Predisposing factors include high myopia, surgical aphakia (lens absence), and a history of detachment in the contralateral eye. There may be no acute symptoms, but gradual vision loss may be noted.

Treatment of retinal detachment can be divided into two major techniques: scleral buckle (Fig. 5-70) and pars plana vitrectomy. In some cases temporary tamponade is obtained with intraocular silicone oil (Gonvers 1985) (Fig. 5-77).

Nonrhegmatogenous detachments are caused by subretinal fluid accumulation from abnormal vessels, most often in neoplastic tissues (choroidal melanoma, metastases, choroidal hemangioma, retinoblastoma). Nonneoplastic causes include Coat's disease and inflammation.

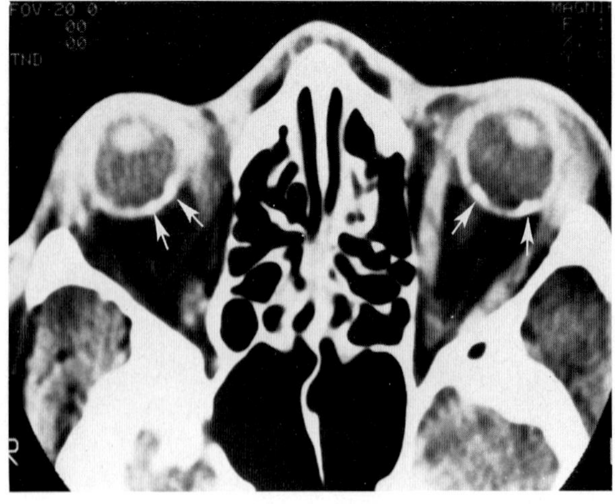

A

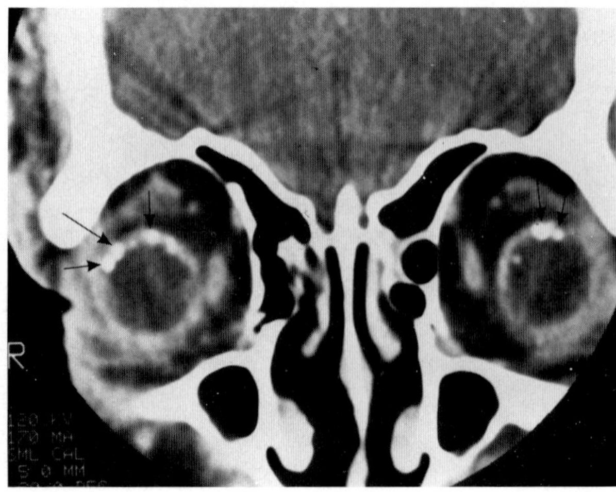

B

Figure 5-75 **A,B.** Congenital toxoplasmosis. Multiple associated foci of calcification bilaterally (arrows), consistent with chorioretinitis on CT.

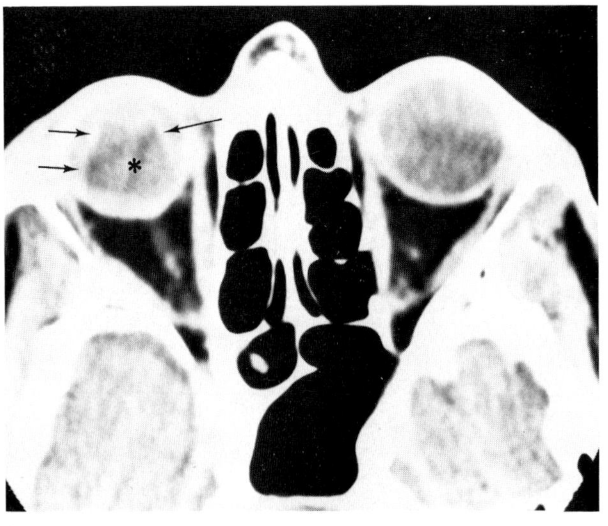

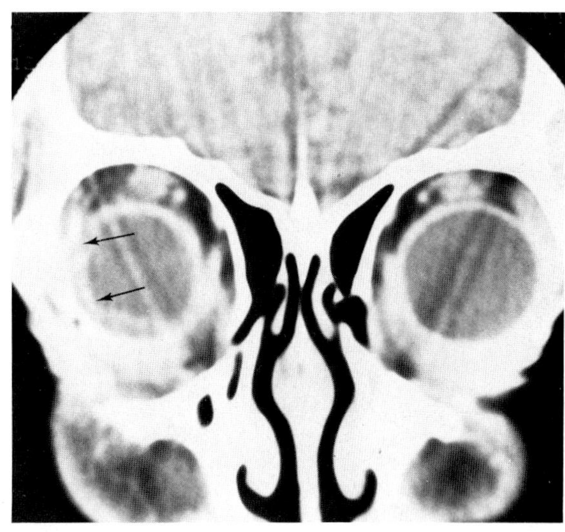

A B

Figure 5-76 Serous retinal detachment on CT. A thin line of high density (arrows) representing a detached retinal membrane separates the vitreous from subretinal fluid (asterisk).

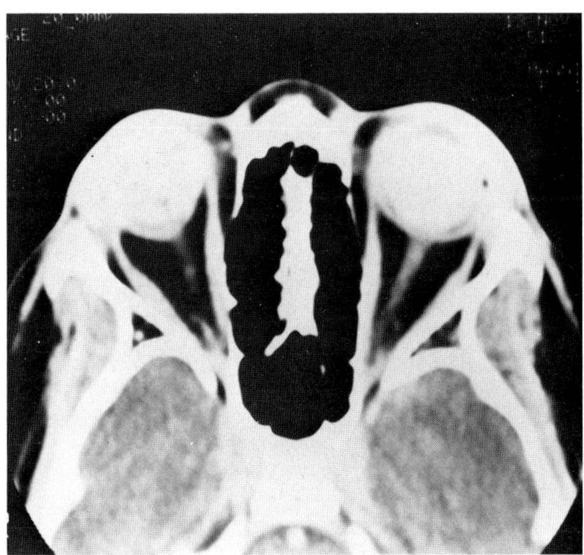

Figure 5-77 Silicone oil for retinal detachment. Intravitreal silicone appears as markedly high attenuation in this patient with recurrent retinal detachment on CT.

ORBITAL TUMORS

Optic Glioma

Optic gliomas are uncommon tumors of the orbit (1 in 100,000 eye complaints) (Jones 1979). However, they represent the most frequently occurring tumor of the optic nerve. The peak age for presentation is between 2 and 6 years, with 75 percent presenting by age 10 and 90 percent by age 20. There is an association with neurofibromatosis, and as the techniques for detection of the visual pathway gliomas have improved, so has the percentage of association, in some series reaching over 50 percent (Stern 1980). Aoki (1989) detected optic nerve glioma in 19 of 53 patients with neurofibromatosis type 1. The symptoms of an intraorbital optic glioma include progressive nonpulsatile exophthalmos, limitation of eye movement, optic atrophy, and papilledema. The proptosis precedes a decrease in vision and the onset of strabismus. Histologically, these lesions are low-grade astrocytomas.

CT represented a major breakthrough in the diagnostic evaluation of visual pathway gliomas (Byrd 1978; Peyster 1983; Rothfus 1984) because for the first time the tumors were directly visualized not only in the orbit but also intracranially. A significant number of optic gliomas are part of a more extensive disease process that involves the more posterior visual pathways, including not only the optic nerve but the optic chiasm, optic tract, lateral geniculate body, and optic radiations (Figs. 5-78 through 5-80). It has been the authors' experience that unsuspected involvement of the visual pathways can be present in a significant number of these patients (Bilaniuk 1989). In addition to better showing the extent of visual pathway gliomas, MR demonstrates the spectrum of brain abnormalities that can occur secondary to neurofibromatosis (Braffman 1988). Also, imaging modalities are helpful in the differential diagnosis of orbital lesions occurring in patients with neurofibromatosis. Plexiform neurofibroma, the most frequent orbital manifestation of neurofibromatosis, is well delineated and characterized by MR (Fig. 5-81).

Optic gliomas appear most often as nodular or fusiform enlargements of the optic nerve or as uniform enlargements (Fig. 5-82), most of which show contrast en-

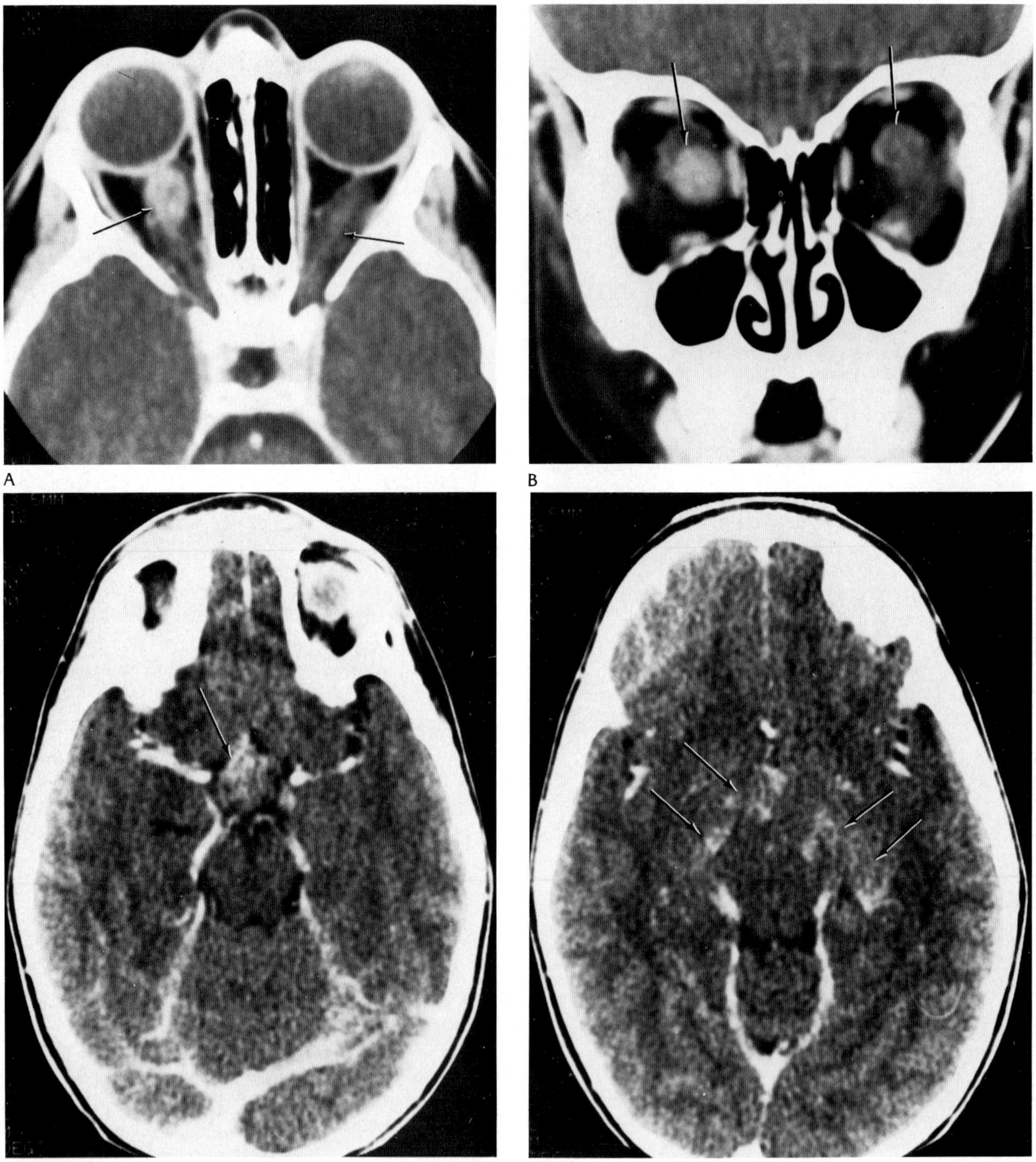

A B C D

Figure 5-78 **A–D.** Visual pathway glioma. Extensive optic pathway glioma involves the optic nerves, chiasm, and optic tracts bilaterally (arrows) on CECT.

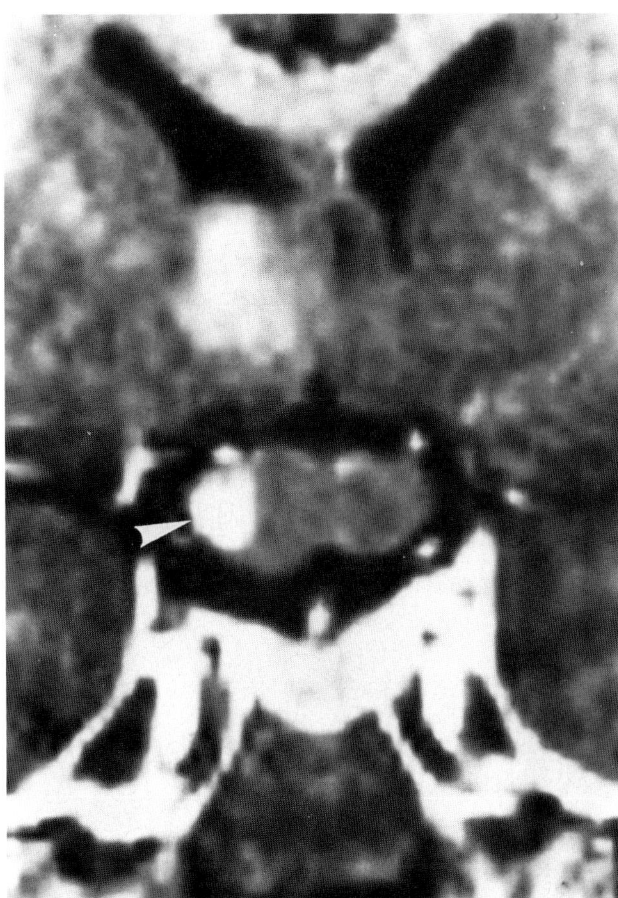

Figure 5-79 Extensive visual pathway glioma in a 14-year-old girl with neurofibromatosis. Coronal CEMR (600/15; Gd-DTPA) shows markedly enlarged chiasm that enhances (arrowhead) on the right. There is also a partially enhancing hypothalamic mass.

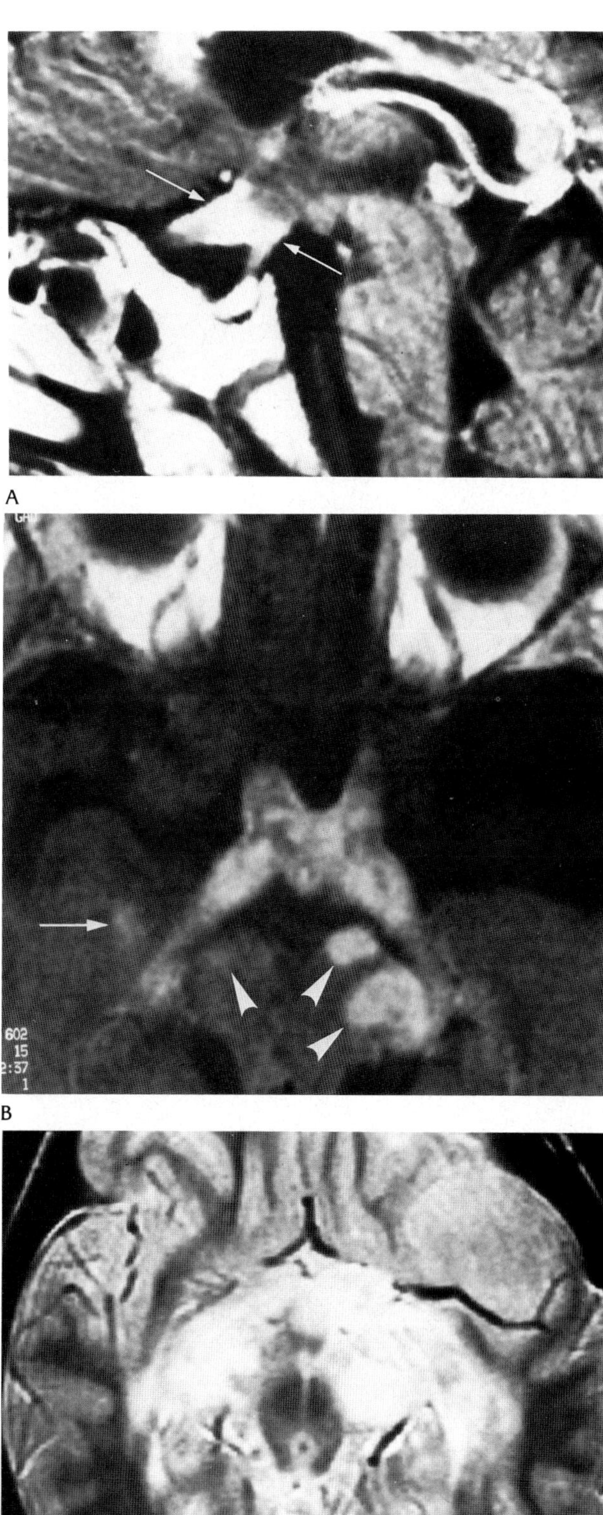

Figure 5-80 Extensive visual pathway glioma in a 5-year-old girl with neurofibromatosis. **A.** Sagittal CEMR shows a hyperintense enlarged chiasm (arrows). **B.** Axial CEMR (600/15; 3mm; Gd-DTPA) shows a glioma in both intracranial optic nerves, the chiasm, and the optic tracts, as well as sites of contrast enhancement in the medial right temporal lobe (arrow) and the midbrain (arrowheads). **C.** Axial T_2WI (3000/45) shows extensive abnormal hyperintensity in the region of the chiasm, optic tracts, and lateral geniculate bodies and in brain adjacent to these structures.

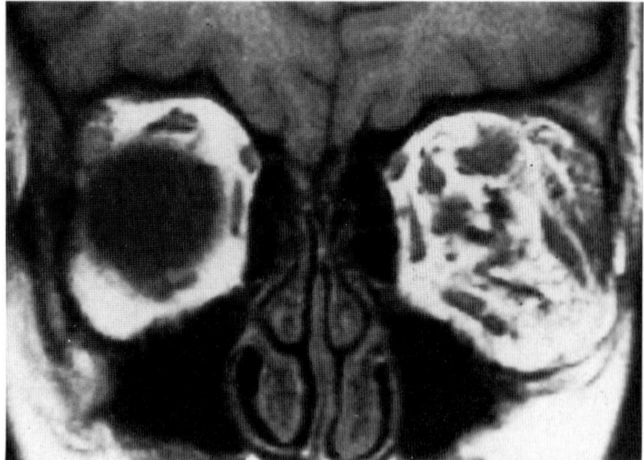

A

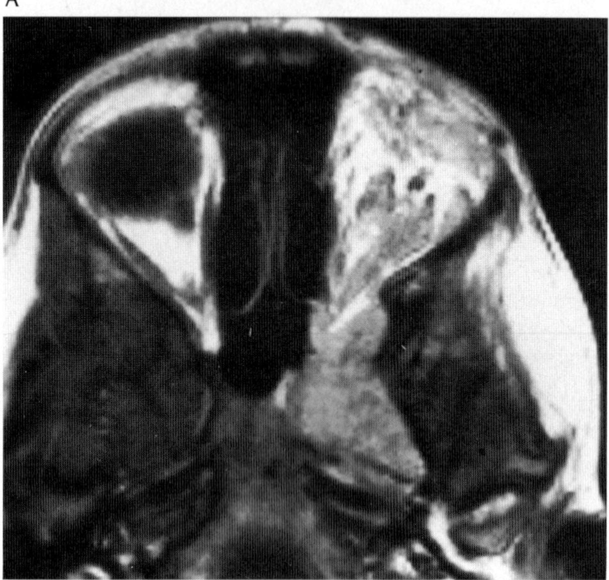

B

Figure 5-81 Extensive plexiform neurofibroma in an 11-year-old girl who had enucleation. **A.** Coronal MRI (600/15) reveals multiple small irregular masses throughout the fat of the left orbit. These are portions of a plexiform neurofibroma. **B.** Axial CEMR (600/15; Gd-DTPA) demonstrates the intraorbital as well as the cavernous sinus component of the plexiform neurofibroma.

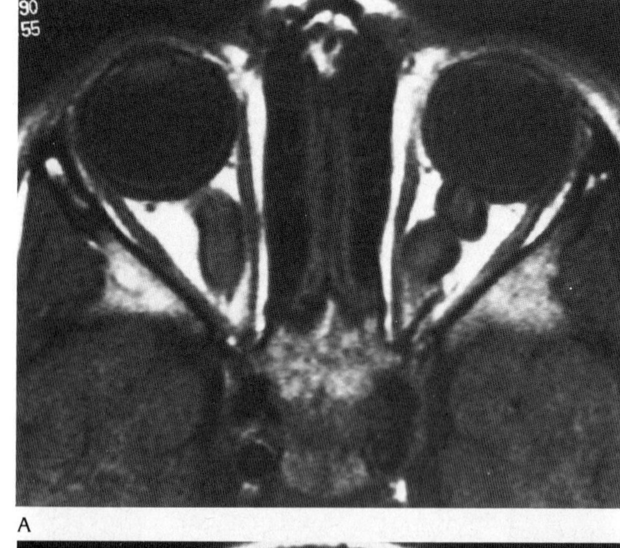

A

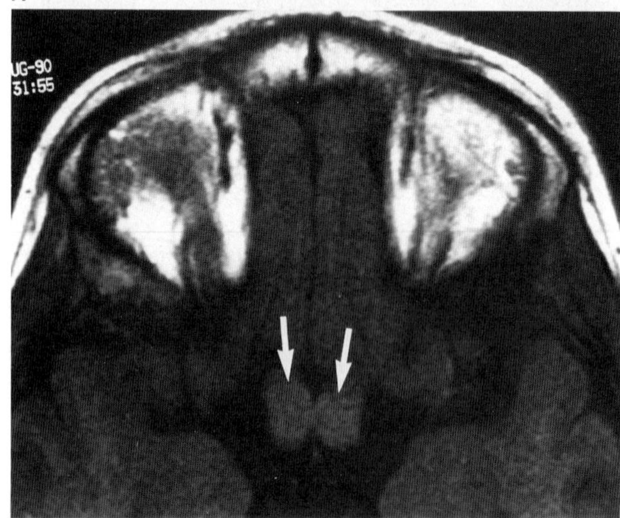

B

Figure 5-82 Bilateral optic nerve gliomas in a 4-year-old boy. **A.** Axial MRI (600/15; 3 mm) shows enlargement of both optic nerves. **B.** Axial MRI (600/15; 3 mm) obtained superior to that shown in **A** shows the two large optic nerves (arrows) joining to form the chiasm.

hancement (Figs. 5-78, 5-79, 5-80, 5-83, and 5-84). Optic nerve gliomas show a variable pattern on imaging, reflecting their different growth patterns. They may grow within the optic nerve, expanding it (Figs. 5-78, 5-82, and 5-83), or they may grow within the nerve as well as extraneurally, encircling the nerve (Fig. 5-84). In addition, these gliomas may be associated with arachnoidal hyperplasia, which may be confused with meningioma on biopsy (Cooling 1979). MR with the use of T_1- and T_2-weighted sequences and contrast enhancement is the best modality for the characterization of optic gliomas. Bilateral involvement (Figs. 5-78, 5-79, 5-80, and 5-82), which in some cases is clinically unsuspected, may be diagnostic of neurofibromatosis. Intracranially, visual pathway gliomas are better delineated with MR, showing increased intensity on proton density images (Fig. 5-80) and T_2WI. The intracranial components show variable contrast enhancement.

The management of visual pathway gliomas remains controversial. Generally, optic gliomas that are localized to the orbit are managed conservatively unless they produce marked proptosis, in which case they are resected. If more extensive tumors show progression, usually chemotherapy and/or radiotherapy are instituted.

Table 5-5 lists the causes of the enlarged optic nerve/sheath complex (Figs. 5-85 and 5-86).

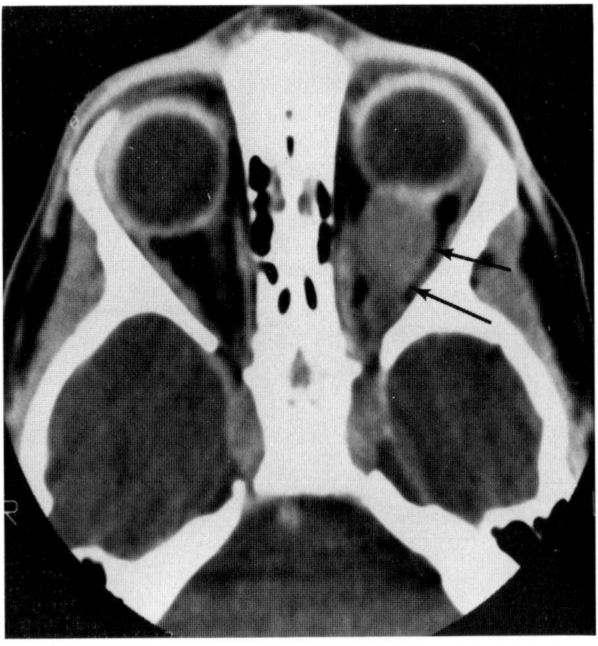

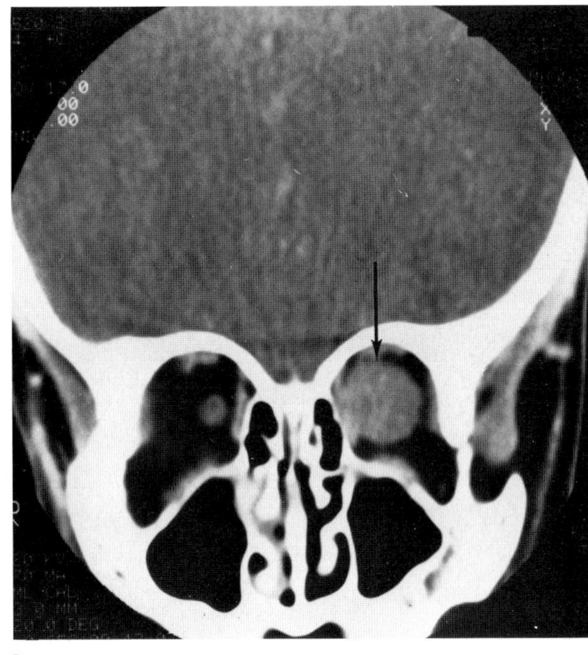

A B

Figure 5-83 **A,B.** Contrast-enhancing optic glioma. Massive lobulated enlargement of the left optic nerve (arrow) in axial (**A**) and coronal (**B**) CT. Note slight flattening of globe.

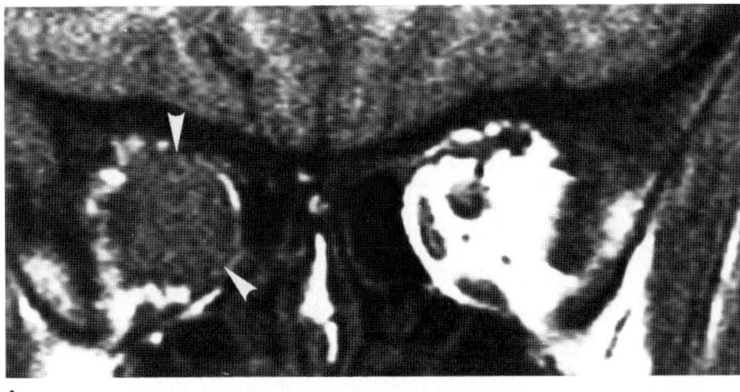

A

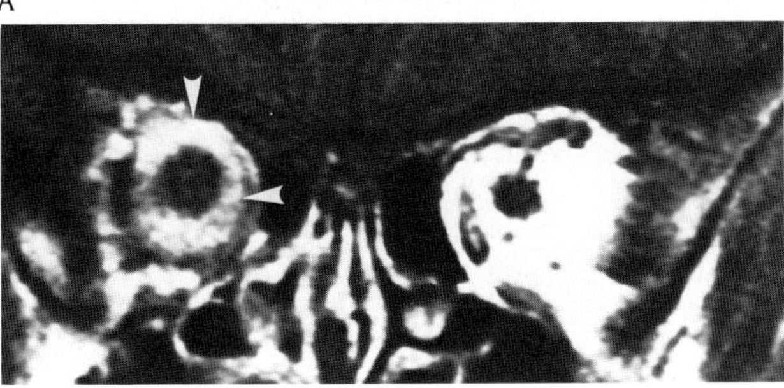

B

Figure 5-84 Right optic nerve glioma in a 6-year-old boy. **A.** Coronal MRI (600/15; 3 mm) shows a large mass (arrowheads) which occupies most of the right intraconic space. **B.** Coronal CEMR (600/15; 3 mm; Gd-DTPA) obtained at the same level shown in **A** shows that a thick rim of tumor (arrowheads) has enhanced but surrounds a central portion which does not show enhancement. The central portion is about three times as large as the normal optic nerve sheath complex on the left.

Table 5-5 Etiologies of Enlarged Optic Nerve/Sheath Complex

- Neoplasm
  - Optic nerve glioma
  - Meningioma
  - Hemangioblastoma (especially in von Hippel-Lindau disease)
  - Neuroma
  - Leukemia
  - Lymphoma
  - Metastases
- Other
  - Orbital pseudotumor
  - Optic neuritis
  - Distended subarachnoid space
  - Sarcoidosis
  - Perioptic hematoma
  - Thyroid ophthalmopathy
  - Tuberculosis
  - Toxoplasmosis

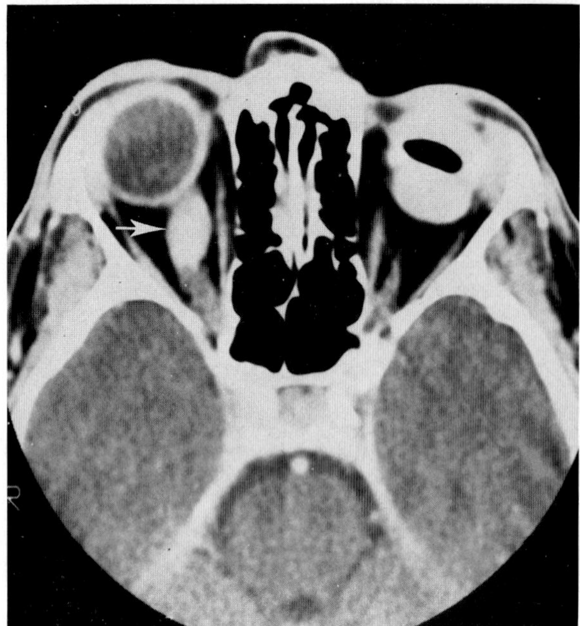

A

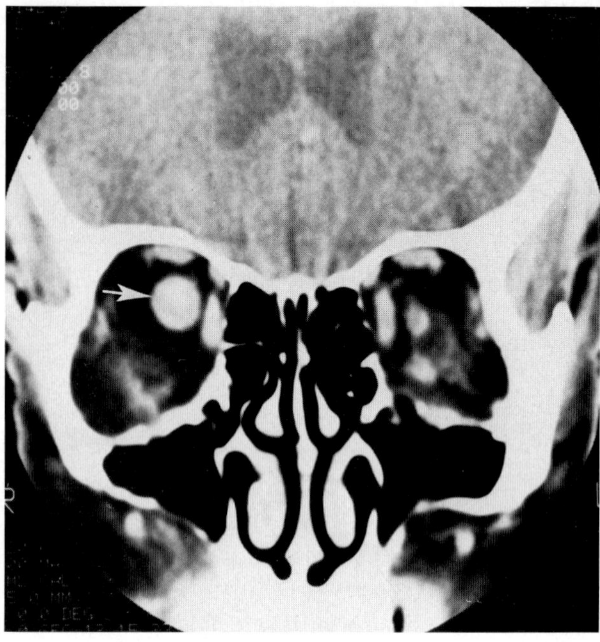

B

Figure 5-85 **A,B.** Hemangioblastoma of the optic nerve in von Hippel-Landau disease. In this patient, status/after left enucleation and prosthesis placement after multiple hemorrhages from retinal angiomas. Axial (**A**), and coronal (**B**) CT shows a markedly enhancing mass enlarging the right optic nerve (arrow).

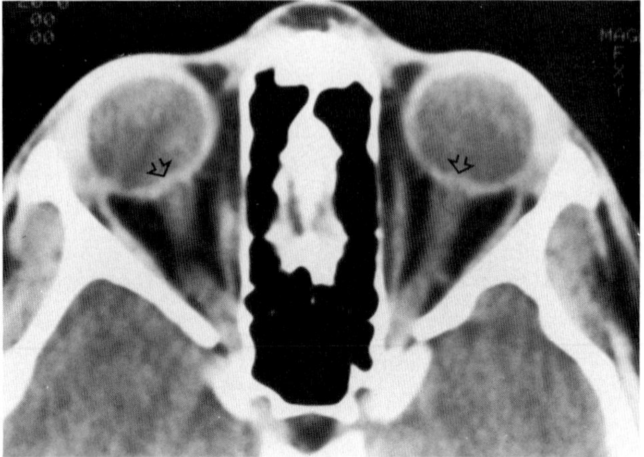

Figure 5-86 Papilledema in a 10-year-old girl. An axial CT (3 mm) reveals prominent optic nerve sheath complexes and elevation of the optic disks (arrows).

Meningioma

Meningiomas may originate within the orbit, most often from the optic nerve sheath (Figs. 5-87 and 5-88) and less frequently from the periosteum of the orbital wall or arachnoidal rests randomly located within the orbit. Meningiomas also secondarily involve the orbit by extension from a primary intracranial meningioma (Figs. 5-89 through 5-91). Primary intraorbital meningiomas (5 percent of primary orbital tumors) are less frequent than those which secondarily involve the orbit. If one considers only primary tumors of the optic nerve/sheath complex, optic nerve meningiomas account for one-third (Reese 1976). Bilateral lesions are often associated with neurofibromatosis.

Meningiomas that arise along the course of the optic nerve may do so intraorbitally (sheath meningioma) (Fig. 5-87), within the optic canal (intracanalicular meningioma), or at the intracranial opening of the optic canal (foraminal meningioma). Most commonly they occur in females (up to 80 percent) in the third, fourth, and fifth decades of life. The predominant feature of optic nerve sheath meningioma is early visual loss, with proptosis occurring later (Wright 1979). Papilledema and optic atrophy are common accompaniments.

High-resolution CT and MR accurately delineate the size of the optic nerve/sheath complex and its components: dura, subarachnoid space, and optic nerve. Significant enlargement of the nerve, subarachnoid space, or dural sheath is easily visualized. The problem lies in differentiating a perioptic meningioma from other lesions that occur at the same anatomic site. To a large extent, optic nerve gliomas occur in children and perioptic meningioma occurs in adults. The bilateral enlargement of the optic nerve/sheath complex caused by distention of the subarachnoid space by CSF (papilledema) (Fig. 5-86) usually can be differentiated from other causes of enlargement (optic glioma, perioptic meningioma). Tumor enlargement is more nodular and irregular or fusiform

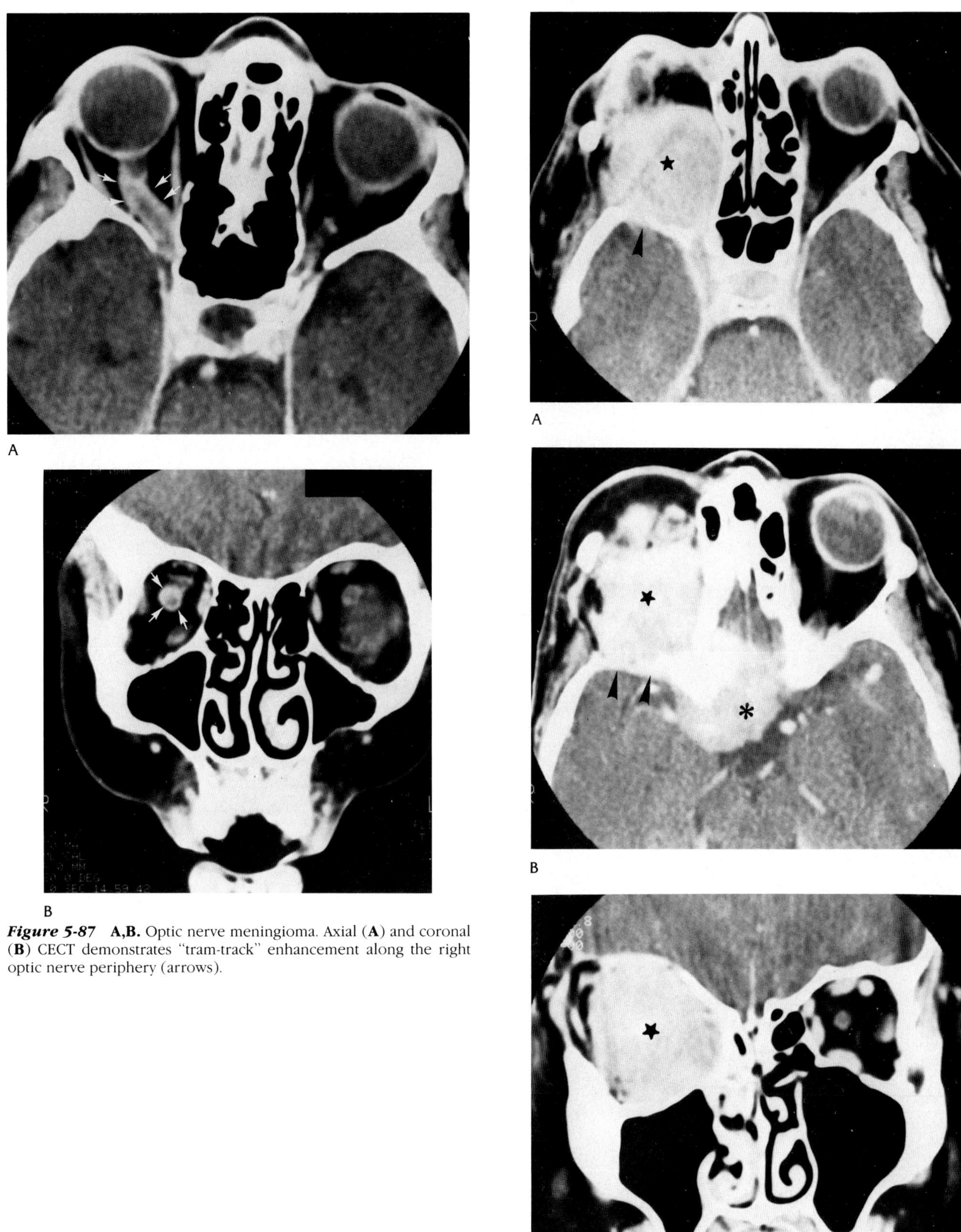

Figure 5-87 **A,B.** Optic nerve meningioma. Axial (**A**) and coronal (**B**) CECT demonstrates "tram-track" enhancement along the right optic nerve periphery (arrows).

Figure 5-88 Orbital meningioma. Homogeneously enhancing mass (star) filling the right orbit and extending into the suprasellar cistern, impinging on the right uncus. Destruction of the right sphenoid wing (arrowhead).

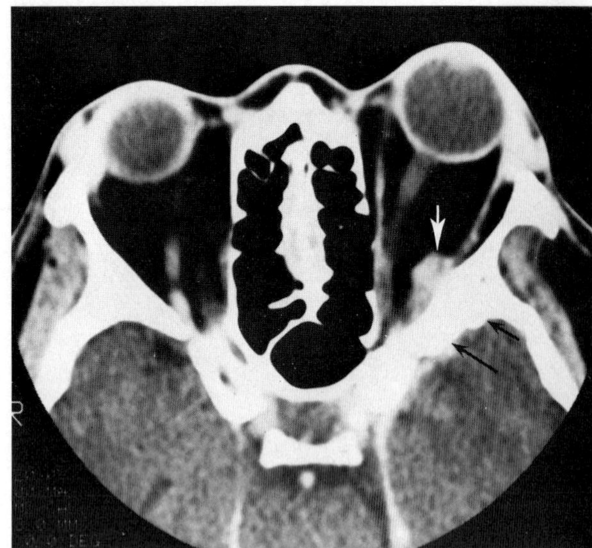

Figure 5-89 Orbital meningioma. Enhancing extraconal mass (white arrow) along the posterolateral aspect of the left orbit. Note the adjacent bony thickening of the left sphenoid wing (black arrows).

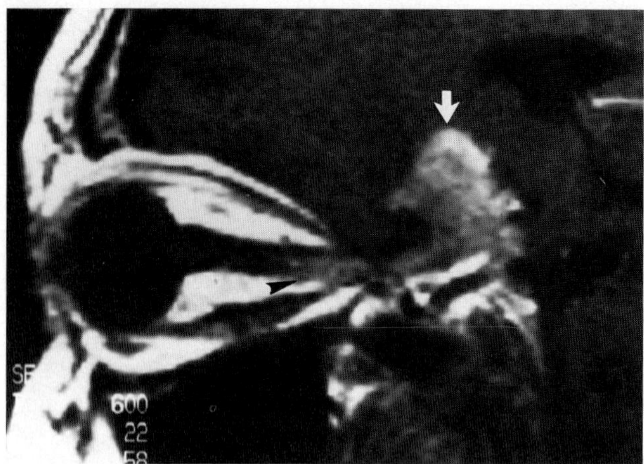

Figure 5-91 Parasellar and planum sphenoidale meningioma with perioptic extent. Sagittal CEMR (600/22; Gd-DTPA) obtained along the long axis of the orbit demonstrates the intracanalicular and intraorbital extent (arrowhead) of the meningioma. An arrow points to the large intracranial meningioma.

(Bilaniuk 1990*c*) than the smooth, parallel, symmetric enlargement that is seen in distention of the subarachnoid space (Cabanis 1978). The perineural location of a perioptic meningioma may actually be shown on CT or MR as a mass surrounding a relatively less dense center or a center of different intensity (compressed optic nerve). Contrast enhancement of an optic nerve sheath meningioma is usually present and marked, resulting in the "tram-track" appearance seen on axial and coronal views (Fig. 5-87). This finding distinguishes meningioma from optic nerve glioma or any other true nerve mass but is not specific (Table 5-6). Another differentiating point between meningiomas and optic gliomas is that, unlike gliomas, meningiomas invade the dural sheath and grow through it. Thus, meningiomas can have very irregular margins. Calcification, when present, helps confirm the diagnosis of meningioma. When a perioptic meningioma

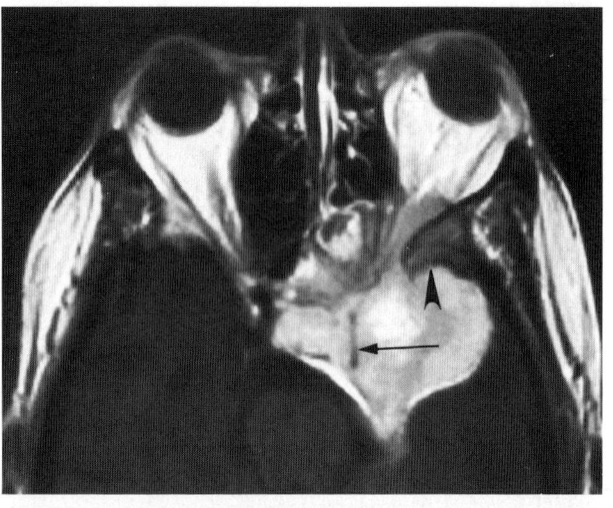

A

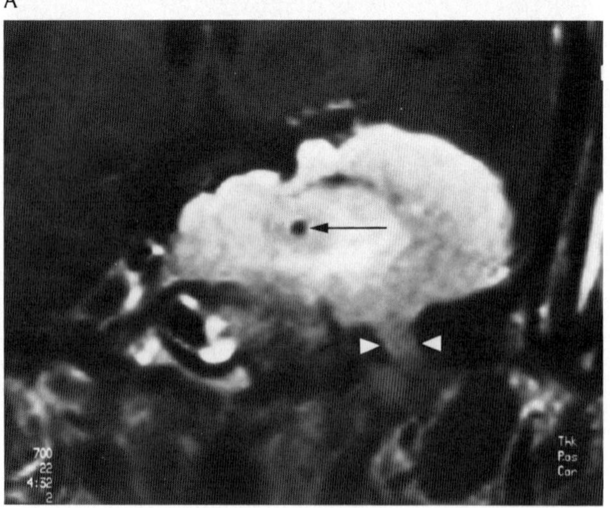

B

Figure 5-90 Extensive meningioma involving the sphenoid bone and left orbital apex in a 59-year-old woman. **A.** Axial CEMR (700/22; Gd-DTPA) demonstrates a large meningioma that has extended into the orbital apex, sphenoid sinus, and sella turcica. The greater wing of the left sphenoid (arrowhead) is thickened as a result of involvement by the meningioma. Compare with the normal sphenoid wing on the opposite side. There is prominent encasement of the left intracavernous carotid artery (arrow). The mass enhanced diffusely but somehow heterogeneously. **B.** Coronal CEMR (700/22; 3 mm; Gd-DTPA) shows the peripherally lobulated meningioma filling the left temporal fossa, the site of the left cavernous sinus, and the sella turcica. A small carotid artery (arrow) can be identified within the mass. Arrowheads indicate the extent of the meningioma into the foramen ovale. There is destruction of the floor of the cavernous sinus where the meningioma grows into the sphenoid bone.

Table 5-6 Etiologies of the "Tram-Track" Sign

Optic nerve meningioma
Orbital pseudotumor
Perioptic neuritis
Sarcoidosis
Leukemia
Lymphoma
Perioptic hemorrhage
Metastases
Normal variant

is thin, sheathlike, and calcified, it is better detected by CT, as the calcification cannot be detected with MR. However, when contrast material is given and fat suppression is used, MR can demonstrate even thin calcified meningiomas. Both CT and MR demonstrate optic canal or superior orbital fissure widening, hyperostosis, and an intracranial component of meningiomas (Figs. 5-89 through 5-91). However, MR is more sensitive than CT in detecting small intracanalicular meningiomas and is more effective in differentiating aneurysms from small meningiomas located at the intracranial opening of the optic canal.

Rhabdomyosarcoma

Orbital rhabdomyosarcoma is the most common primary malignant orbital tumor of childhood; it is rarely seen in adults. The tumor is composed of striated muscle cells and is thought to arise from undifferentiated mesenchymal elements that can differentiate into striated muscle. In the orbit, rhabdomyosarcomas appear to arise from the orbital soft tissues, not from the extraocular muscles. The most common clinical presentation is that of rapidly progressive exophthalmos over days to weeks, often mimicking orbital cellulitis. The superomedial aspect of the orbit is the most common site. In the authors' experience, rhabdomyosarcomas arising in the adjacent paranasal sinuses and extending into the orbit through the thin bony walls, thus presenting with orbital symptoms, have been almost as common.

CT and MR are excellent modalities for evaluating the location and extent of a sarcoma (Figs. 5-92 and 5-93); differentiation between primary orbital rhabdomyosarcoma and that arising from paranasal sinuses is usually possible (Zimmerman 1978). CT provides the best bony detail, while MR can better delineate tumor from fluid in an obstructed sinus. In one series of craniofacial sarcomas (Zimmerman 1978), there were six orbital rhabdomyosarcomas and none of them had CT evidence of bone destruction at the time of presentation; the tumors were all confined to the orbital soft tissues. In four paranasal sinus rhabdomyosarcomas which presented with orbital symptoms, CT showed a more extensive process within the paranasal sinus, with destruction of the sinus wall and intraorbital extension (Bilaniuk 1980). CT and MR are of further use in that they demonstrate intracranial epidural and subarachnoid extension of the tumor, which may be subclinical at the time of presentation (Zimmerman 1978;

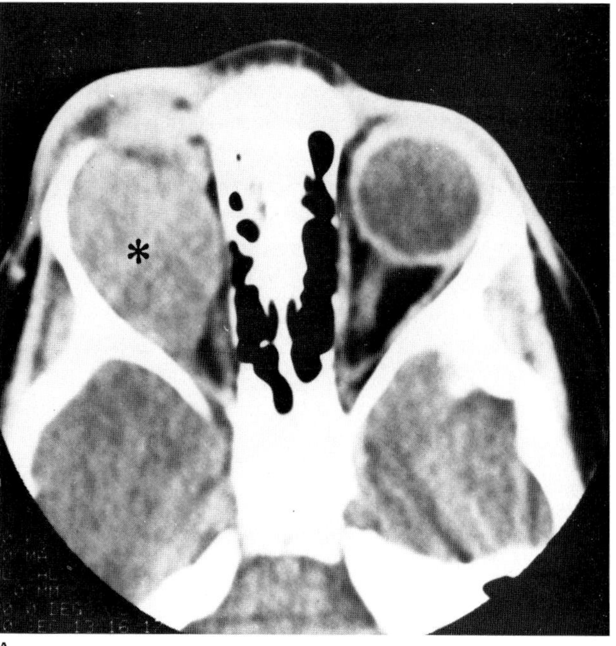

A

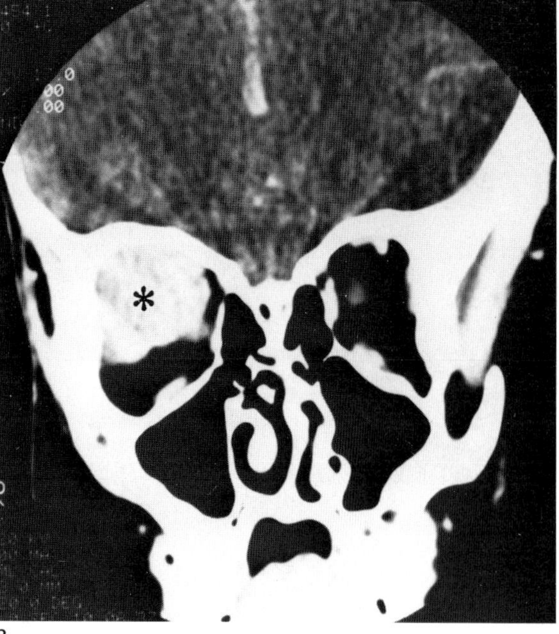

B

Figure 5-92 **A,B.** Rhabdomyosarcoma. A large homogeneous mass (asterisk) in the superolateral aspect of the right orbit is well circumscribed on an axial NCCT (**A**). Coronal CECT (**B**) shows marked enhancement in this mass, presenting as rapidly progressive proptosis.

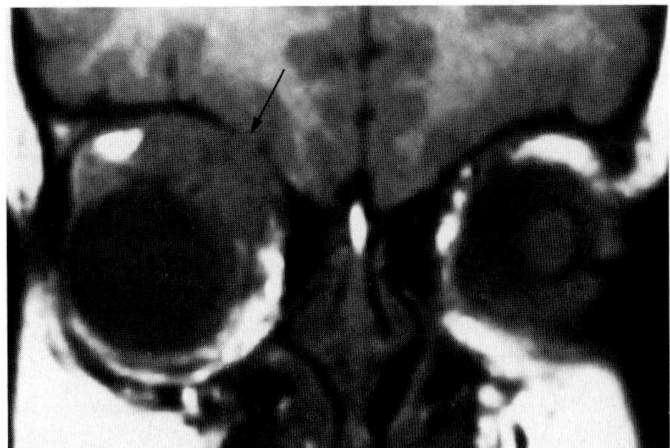

A

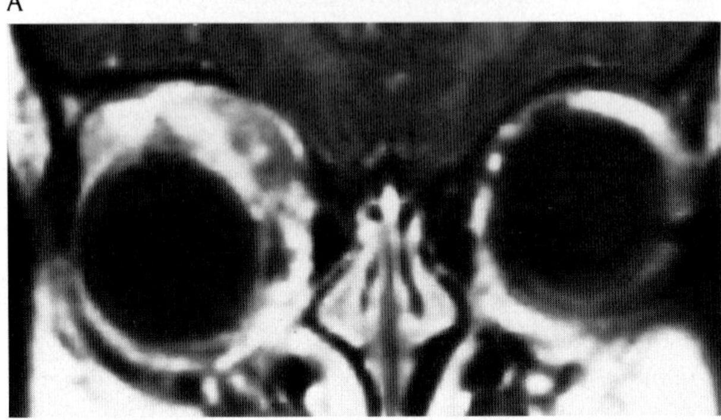

B

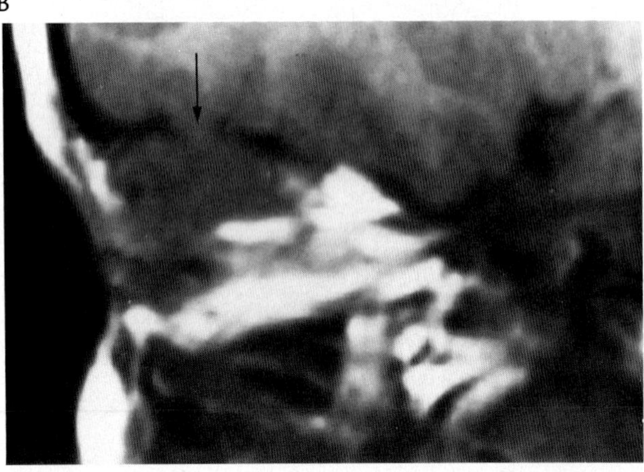

C

Figure 5-93 Right orbital rhabdomyosarcoma in a 3½-year-old girl. **A.** A coronal MRI (600/15) shows a poorly defined mass in the superomedial aspect of the left orbit, which has destroyed bone (arrows) and has slightly deformed the globe. **B.** Coronal CEMR (600/22; Gd-DTPA) shows heterogeneous enhancement of the mass. No gross intracranial extent is identified at the site of the bony destruction. Note that without fat suppression, it is more difficult to distinguish the enhanced mass from the adjacent fat. **C.** Sagittal NCMR shows the mass (arrowheads) and the destruction (arrow) in the orbital roof.

Yousem 1990). Contrast-enhanced multiplanar MR is the best method for demonstrating intracranial spread of a sarcoma. Intracranial spread into the subarachnoid or epidural space is a poor prognostic sign associated with a recurrence rate of almost 100 percent.

On CT, rhabdomyosarcoma appears as an enhancing isodense to slightly hyperdense mass which may infiltrate the retrobulbar fat and muscle planes and often involves the posterior aspect of the globe. However, at times the tumor may be expansile (Fig. 5-92) rather than infiltrative and thus may have a round margin and produce bone scalloping. The contrast enhancement of the tumor is often uniform.

On MR, typically rhabdomyosarcomas are isointense or nearly isointense to muscle on T_1WI (Fig. 5-93), are variable in signal intensity on proton density images, and are hyperintense on T_2WI (Yousem 1990). MR can easily differentiate rhabdomyosarcoma from the more vascular capillary hemangioma by demonstrating multiple vessels within the hemangioma (Bilaniuk 1990*a,b*). This is important because the two lesions can occur in patients of similar ages.

The local response to chemotherapy and radiotherapy is often dramatic, with almost complete disappearance of the tumor in 6 weeks (Jereb 1985).

Lacrimal Gland Tumors

The lacrimal fossa is located extraconically in the superolateral aspect of the orbit. The lacrimal gland, which has the size and shape of an almond, lies within the lacrimal fossa, adjacent to the tendons of the lateral and superior rectus muscles. Histologically, lacrimal gland tissue is similar to that of the salivary gland; pathologically, it is affected by similar disease processes. Among the masses that arise within the lacrimal gland, 50 percent are tumors of epithelial origin. Approximately half of these masses are benign mixed tumors, while the other half include a variety of carcinomas. The remaining 50 percent of masses arising in the lacrimal gland are either tumors of lymphomatous origin or inflammatory masses.

The correct surgical management of a benign mixed lacrimal gland tumor (pleomorphic adenoma) consists of the excision of the whole gland. This avoids the risk of seeding the tumor cells into the adjacent tissues and minimizes the possibility of recurrence (Wright 1979). Other lesions arising in the lacrimal fossa, such as inflammatory pseudotumor or lymphoma, are biopsied for tissue diagnosis. Thus, it is important to know the extent of the disease process and know whether the tumor is infiltrative or merely displaces adjacent soft tissues.

Benign mixed lacrimal gland tumors characteristically present in an age range that extends from the late twenties to the early sixties. They present as slowly progressive painless swellings beneath the upper eyelid, with the duration of symptoms usually over 12 months (Wright 1979). Carcinomas of the lacrimal gland characteristically have a rapidly worsening clinical course that usually lasts less than 9 months (Wright 1979). Adenoid cystic carcinoma is the most common malignant epithelial cell tumor of the lacrimal gland, accounting for 29 percent of all epithelial neoplasms of the gland (Lee 1985). These tumors present in adults, with a mean age of 45 years, and have a female preponderance. Approximately 50 percent of patients survive 2 1/2 years after diagnosis (Lee 1985). The tumor lacks a capsule and shows a propensity for perineural spread and muscle invasion.

Both benign and malignant tumors of the lacrimal gland expand and go on to produce unilateral exophthalmos. Because of their location in the superolateral aspect of the orbit, the globe is displaced inferomedially (Figs. 5-94 and 5-95). The mass tends to enlarge posteriorly so that the muscle cone and optic nerve are displaced along with the globe. The largest lesions extend to the orbital apex. Benign mixed adenomas do not invade the bone or the muscle cone. They are usually well-defined masses of the same density as brain tissue that erode and expand the adjacent lacrimal fossa. Contrast enhancement in benign mixed adenomas is variable,

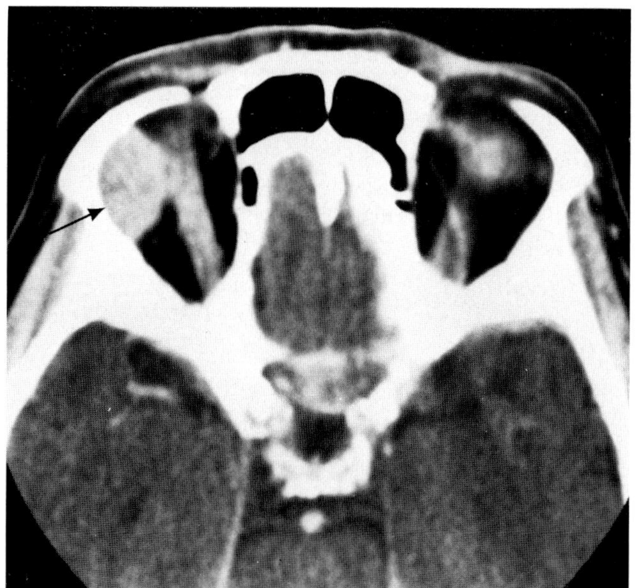
A

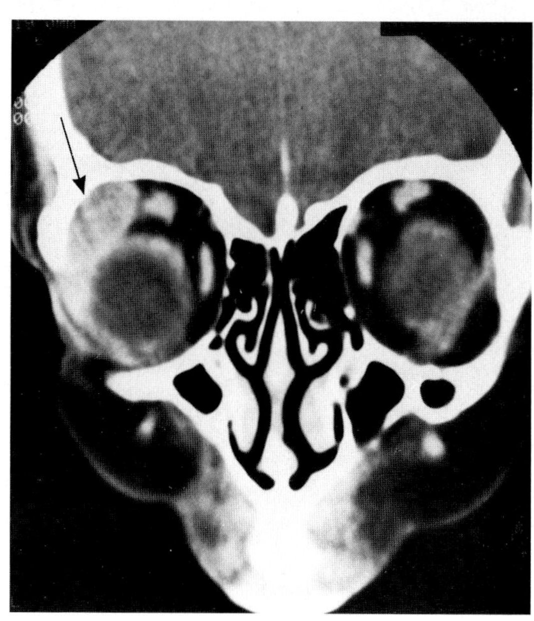
B

Figure 5-94 **A,B.** Lymphoma. Axial (**A**) and coronal (**B**) CECT show a well-circumscribed right lacrimal mass with peripheral rim enhancement (arrows).

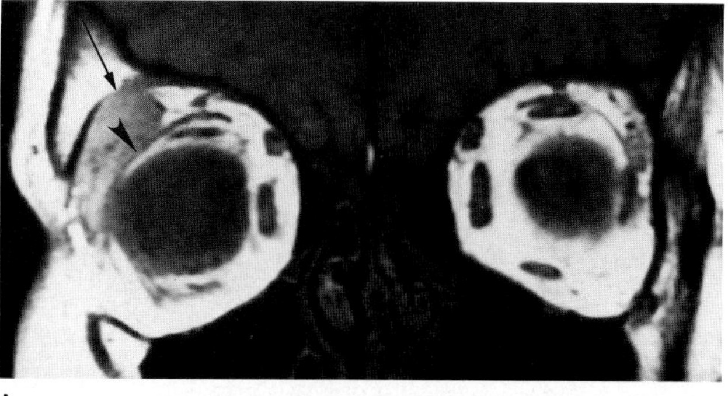
A

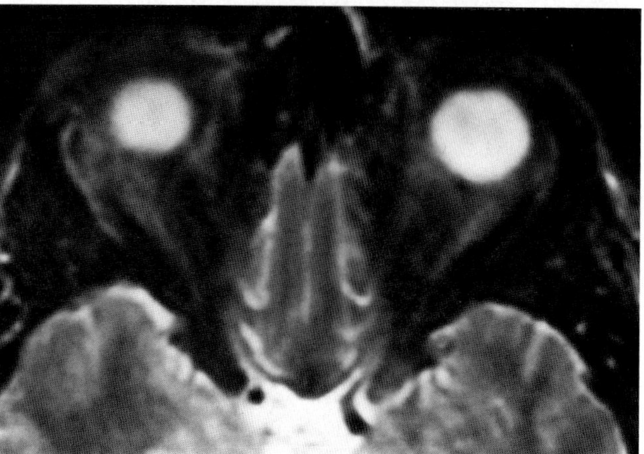
B

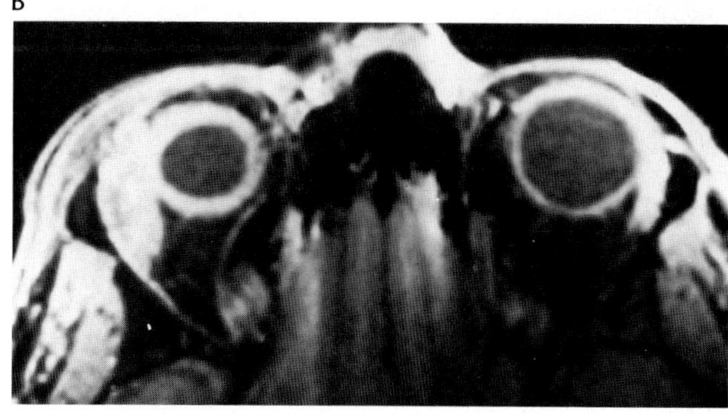
C

Figure 5-95 Lymphoma of the right lacrimal gland in a 26-year-old man. **A.** Coronal MRI (500/17; 3 mm thick). There is prominent enlargement of the right lacrimal gland. The intermuscular septum (arrowhead) is displaced medially. There is slight cortical erosion (arrow). **B.** Axial T_2WI (2700/90). With T_2 weighting, the lymphoma shows intensity similar to that of fat, and thus the tumor cannot be differentiated. There is only minimally higher intensity along the right orbital wall. **C.** Spoiled gradient-echo technique (SPGR with 30° flip angle; 46/6; 1 mm thick) is effective in delineating both abnormal and normal lacrimal glands from adjacent fat.

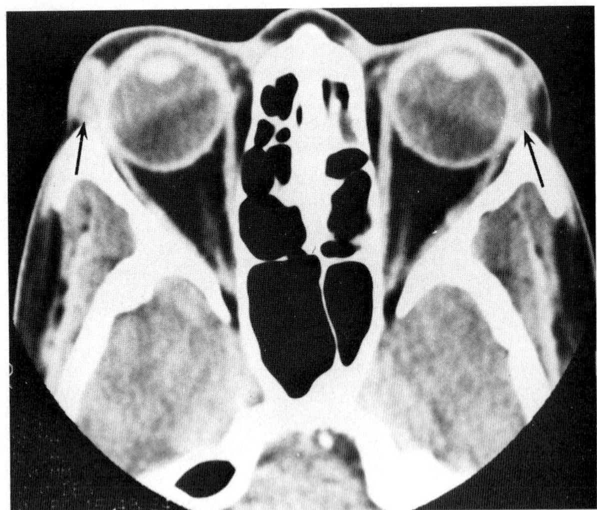

Figure 5-96 Sarcoid on CECT. Bilaterally prominent lacrimal glands (arrows) in a patient with sarcoid.

with only half enhancing (Forbes 1980). Hesselink (1979*b*) reported three cases of mucoepidermoid carcinoma of the lacrimal gland that were hyperdense and contrast-enhanced. Malignant neoplasms of the lacrimal gland have a tendency to invade the muscle cone and destroy adjacent margins of the orbital wall. They may also produce sclerosis of the adjacent bone and may contain calcifications. In general, however, although CT and MR can show the precise location and extent of lacrimal masses, specific etiologies are not differentiated in the majority of cases (Flanders 1987; Balchunas 1983) (Figs. 5-18, 5-94, 5-95, and 5-96). The irregular infiltrative pattern demonstrated by these imaging modalities supports the diagnosis of adenoid cystic carcinoma.

Lymphoma

The incidence of orbital involvement by lymphoma is approximately 1 percent (Jones 1979). The lacrimal gland is the most frequent site of lymphomatous disease within the orbit (Figs. 5-94 and 5-95). Lymphomas presenting in the lacrimal gland may be due to systemic disease or may indicate the primary site. Bilateral involvement of the lacrimal glands in patients with systemic lymphoma is not unusual. Undifferentiated lymphomas produce symptoms that last weeks to months, while the more differentiated ones often are associated with symptoms of longer duration. A patient with involvement of the lacrimal region presents with lid swelling and a palpable mass. The response to radiation therapy and chemotherapy may be dramatic, with a marked reduction in tumor size.

Lymphoma may also present as an infiltrative process in the retroconic space that obliterates the normal soft tissue planes. Thus, it may mimic idiopathic orbital inflammation (pseudotumor) and may be difficult to differentiate from that entity histologically, clinically, and with CT or MR. Most typically pseudotumors are hypointense on T_2WI (Atlas 1986), while the lymphomas more often are hyperintense. However, at times the two entities may have identical intensity patterns both on T_1WI and T_2WI (Fig. 5-95). On CT, lacrimal gland lymphoma appears as a mass in the lacrimal fossa of increased density that shows contrast enhancement and displaces the globe medially and forward (Fig. 5-94). Not infrequently there is extension of the lacrimal lymphomatous process into the eyelid and the fossa temporalis.

Orbital Metastases from Distant Sites

In a large series of orbital neoplasms, metastases from distant primary sites were relatively rare (5 percent) (Albert 1967). This may be a misleadingly low figure, because the orbital structures are rarely examined in patients who die with disseminated metastases. The patterns of orbital metastases differ between children and adults. The tumors that metastasize most frequently to the orbit in children are those which arise from embryonal tumors, neuroblastoma (Figs. 5-97 and 5-98), and Ewing's sarcoma (Jones 1979). Leukemia may also involve the orbit. In children, the orbit is more frequently involved and the globe is involved less often. In adults, metastases are most often from carcinomas of breast (Figs. 5-99 and 5-100) and lung and are more frequently linked to the globe (Hesselink 1980). In adults, 70 percent of metastases are ocular (Figs. 5-58 and 5-59) whereas only 30 percent are orbital (Jones 1979). In 50 percent of these orbital metastases, the primary is unknown. In such a sit-

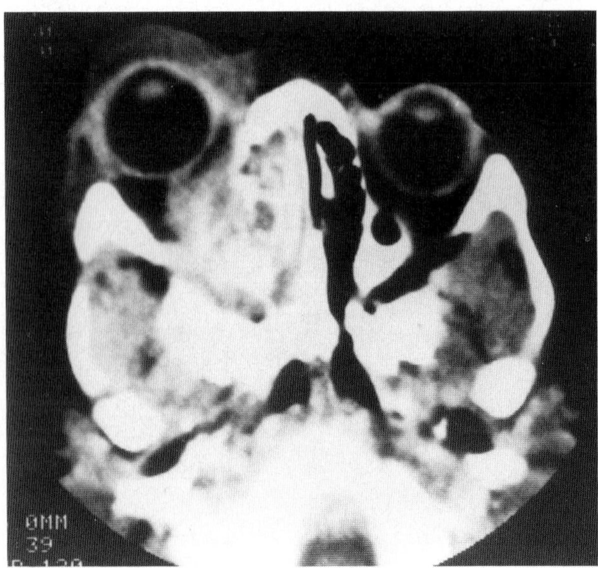

Figure 5-97 Neuroblastoma metastases. Destructive mass involving the right medial orbit and the ethmoid sinus causes proptosis on CECT.

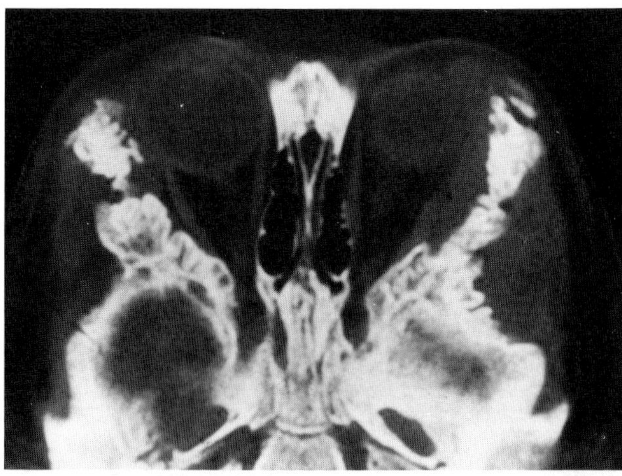

A

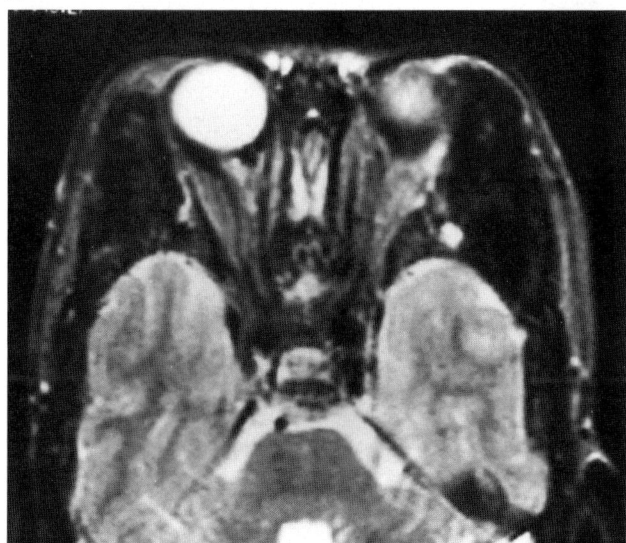

B

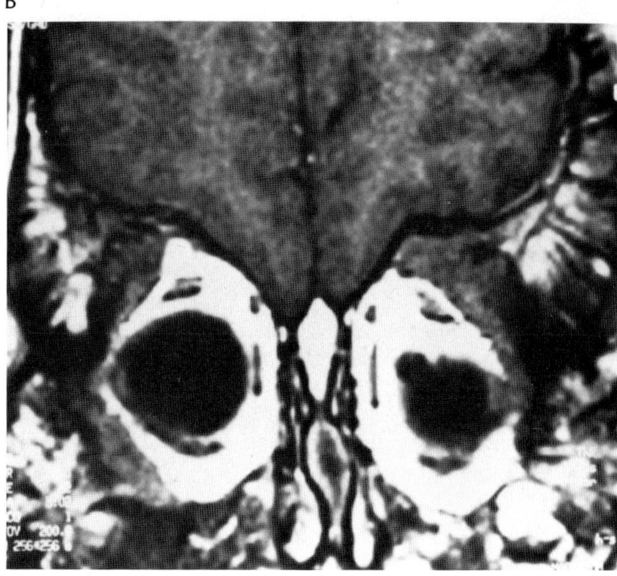

C

◄ ***Figure 5-98*** Extensive residual bony and soft tissue changes in a patient 5 years after treatment for metastatic neuroblastoma. The patient is 10 years old. **A.** An axial CT performed through the midportion of the orbits shows highly abnormal lateral orbital walls. It can also be faintly seen that there is increased soft tissue adjacent to the left lateral bony orbital wall. **B.** An axial MR (2500/90) shows that there is primarily hypointensity in the regions of the abnormal bones. **C.** A coronal MR (700/22) reveals markedly expanded bony orbital walls with multiple striations. In addition, there is prominent soft tissue in the superolateral extraconic portions of the orbits. The bony orbits themselves are deformed and show an increased vertical diameter. There also is hypotelorism.

uation, the site of the unknown primary is more likely to be the lung than the breast.

Symptoms of orbital metastatic disease include an abrupt onset of proptosis, external ophthalmoplegia, and orbital pain early in the course of the disease (Jones 1979).

Metastases to the orbit most often have indistinct boundaries and are diffusely infiltrating (Figs. 5-45 and 5-99 through 5-101). A minority of metastatic lesions are discrete and well circumscribed. Metastatic retrobulbar carcinoma from breast carcinoma has been relatively common in the authors' experience. This most often appears on CT or MR as a diffusely infiltrative contrast-enhancing mass lesion without clear-cut margins. At times metastases may have an appearance similar to that seen with extensive orbital pseudotumor. MR is of some help in differentiating these entities (Atlas 1986). Metastatic breast carcinoma shows increased intensity on T_2WI, while most pseudotumors are of decreased intensity (Atlas 1986). When the metastasis is from a scirrhous carcinoma, the fibrous response produces enophthalmos (Fig. 5-99).

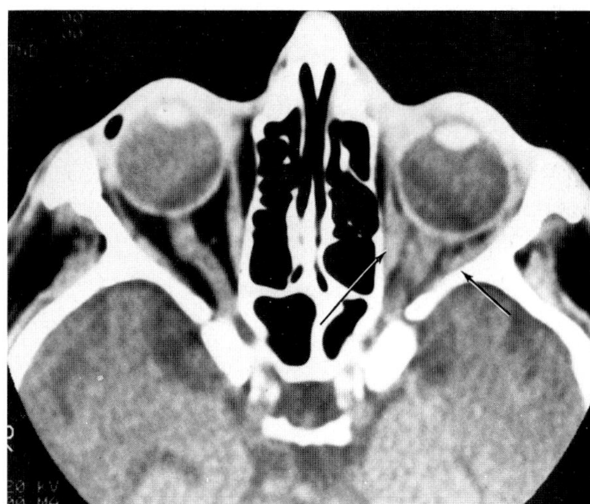

Figure 5-99 Metastatic breast carcinoma. CECT shows extraconal masses in the left orbit (arrows) with secondary enophthalmos, typical of scirrhous breast carcinoma metastasis.

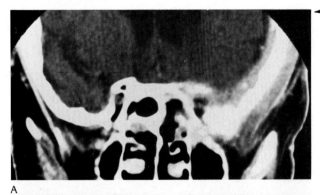

A

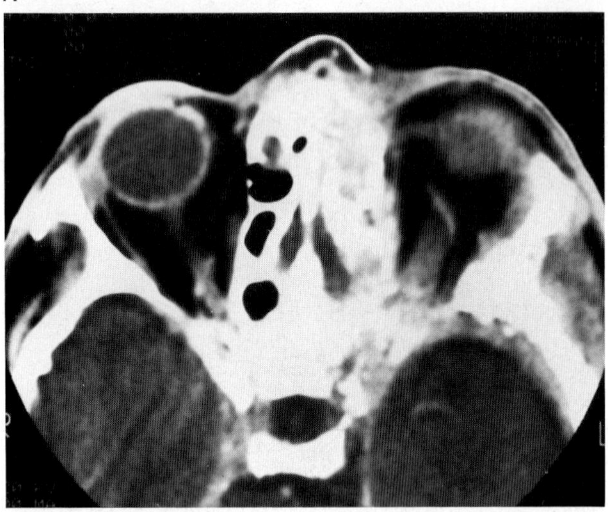

B

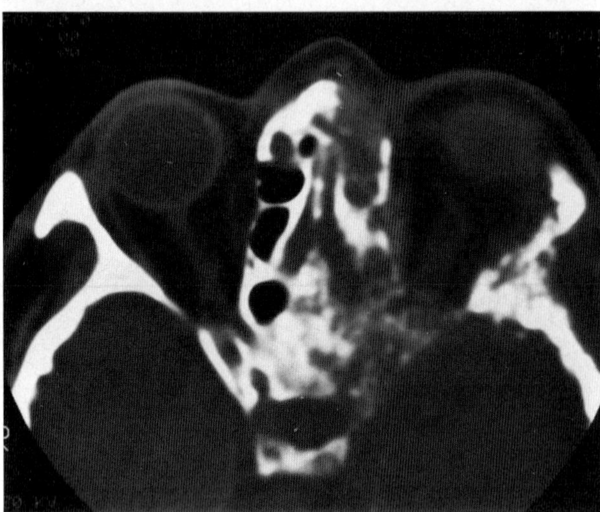

C

Figure 5-100 Metastatic breast carcinoma. **A.** Coronal CECT. Irregular bony destruction and contrast-enhanced tumor are present in the apex of the left orbit and in the lateral wall of the left middle cranial fossa. **B.** Axial CECT shows extensive tumor in the medial and lateral wall of the left orbit and in the anterior wall of the left middle cranial fossa. **C.** Axial CT with wide window setting shows the moth-eaten pattern of bony destruction in the left ethmoid sinus and left orbit.

In children, orbital metastases most often involve the walls of the orbit. The tumors extend subperiosteally into the orbital space. Neuroblastoma frequently presents with simultaneous metastases to both orbits (Rootman 1988) (Fig. 5-98) but often also presents as unilateral metastatic disease (Fig. 5-97). The bone is infiltrated, and the orbital periosteum is displaced (Zimmerman 1980*b;* Bilaniuk 1990*a*). Imaging studies show mixed lytic and hyperostotic bone changes, spiculated periosteal bone reaction, and obliteration of adjacent paranasal sinuses. These bone changes are different from those produced by histiocytosis, where there is sharply defined bone destruction. In addition to revealing the bone changes, CT and MR demonstrate the subperiosteal portion of the neuroblastoma, which shows contrast enhancement (Zimmerman 1980*b*). The orbital tumor in neuroblastoma may be hyperdense on NCCT because of hemorrhage within the tumor. MR is more specific in identifying the blood products within the tumor. There may be extensive residual bony changes even many years after treatment of a neuroblastoma (Fig. 5-98).

Distant metastases to the orbital bones and paranasal sinuses also occur in adults and may resemble pediatric neuroblastoma (Figs. 5-100 and 5-103). Metastatic prostate carcinoma is typified by its sclerotic bone reaction and subperiosteal extension, often presenting with large intraorbital soft tissue masses (Figs. 5-102 and 5-103).

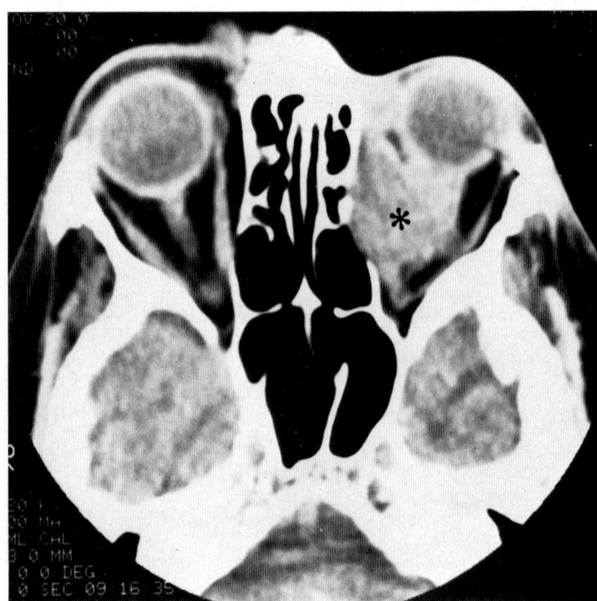

Figure 5-101 Metastatic melanoma. CECT shows an irregular, ill-defined mass (asterisk) in the left retrobulbar space from primary cutaneous malignant melanoma.

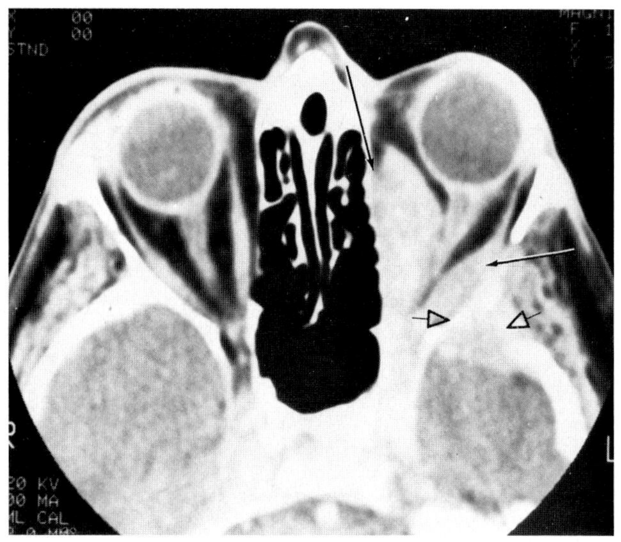

A

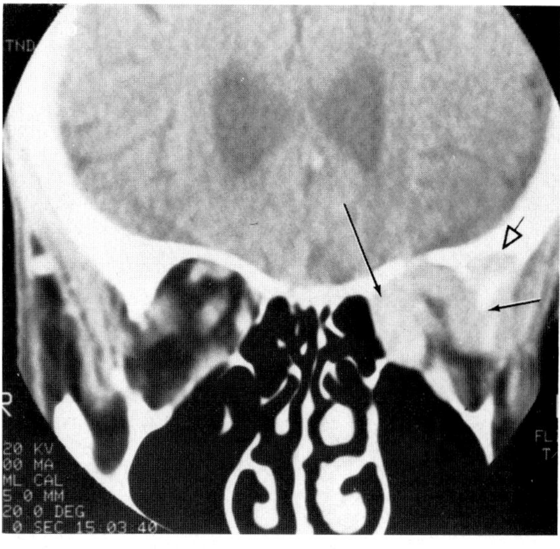

B

Figure 5-102 **A,B.** Metastatic prostate carcinoma. Axial (**A**) and coronal (**B**) CECT demonstrates an enhancing mass in the medial, superior, and lateral aspects of the left orbit (arrows) with destruction of the sphenoid wing (open arrow). Note extraaxial mass anterior to the left temporal lobe, a common site for metastasis.

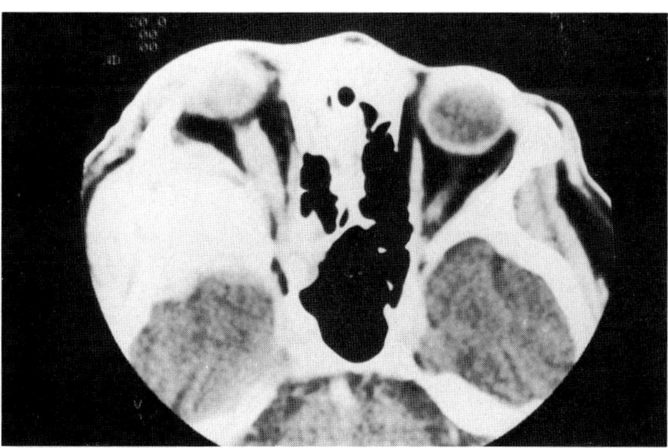

A

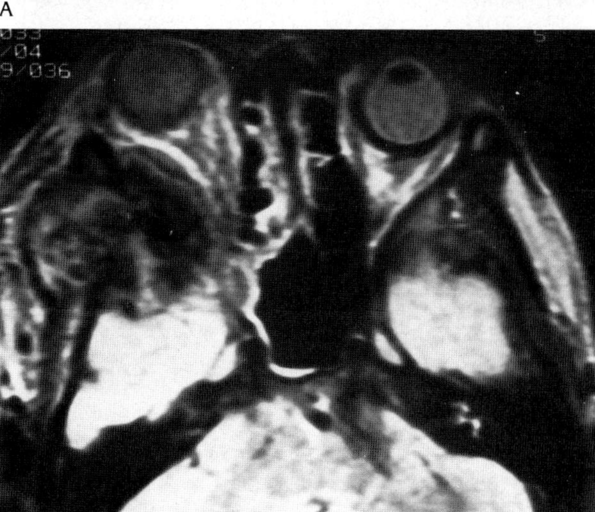

C

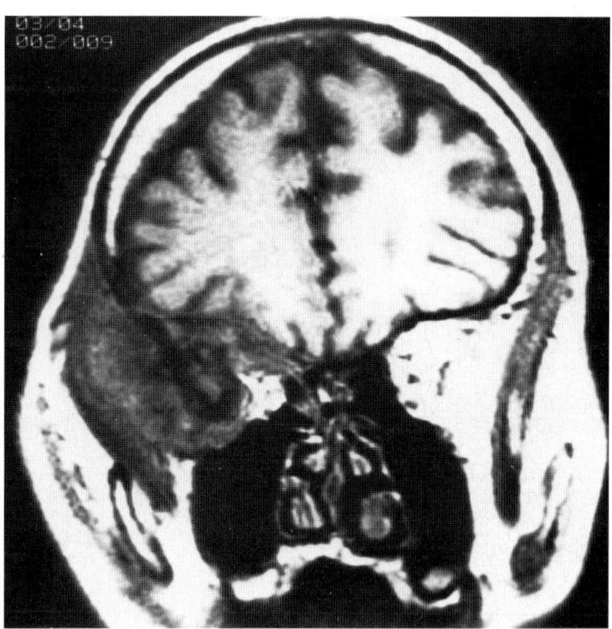

B

Figure 5-103 Metastatic prostate carcinoma. **A.** Axial CECT shows marked expansion of the right sphenoid wing with surrounding enhancing tumor. **B.** Coronal MR (600/25) shows a large mass in the superolateral right orbit and the temporalis fossa. Slight upward displacement of the frontal lobe is well shown. (*From Bilaniuk 1987 with permission*). **C.** Axial MR (2500/400) shows heterogeneous low intensity throughout the mass.

Langerhans Cell Histiocytosis (Histiocytosis X)

Langerhans cell histiocytosis is of unknown etiology, but it is thought to be related to an abnormal immune process. It is an uncommon cause of an orbital mass; however, it must be included in a differential diagnosis, particularly of superolateral orbital masses in children. It has been recommended that the traditional division of the histiocytosis X into eosinophilic granuloma, Hans-Schuller-Christian disease, and Letterer-Siewe disease be abandoned in favor of Langerhans cell histiocytosis, because the three entities cannot be distinguished on the basis of histopathological appearance and show considerable clinical overlap (Moore 1985). Electron microscopy of these lesions has revealed the presence of distinctive Langerhans cell (Birbeck's) granules in the cytoplasm (Jakobiec 1980). However, these granules are not identified in malignant histiocytosis. Langerhans cell histiocytosis generally presents with a rapidly progressive painful swelling. There typically is lid edema and erythema. In the orbit, Langerhans cell histiocytosis most often involves the lateral superior quadrant of the orbit, producing a soft tissue mass with sharply marginated bony destruction (Fig. 5-104). On CT, the mass is homogeneous and enhances homogeneously. On MR, the mass shows heterogeneity with regions of hypointensity on PD-WI and T_2WI, probably reflecting the pathologically

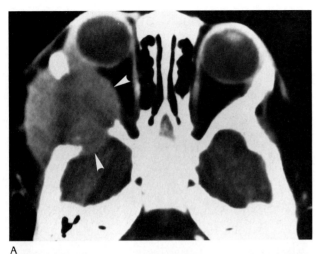

A

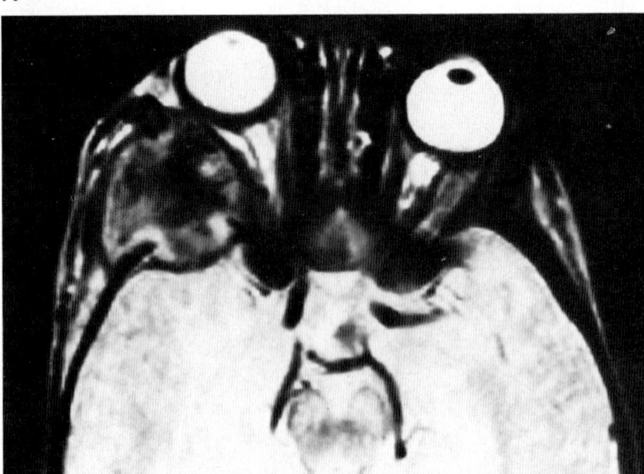

B

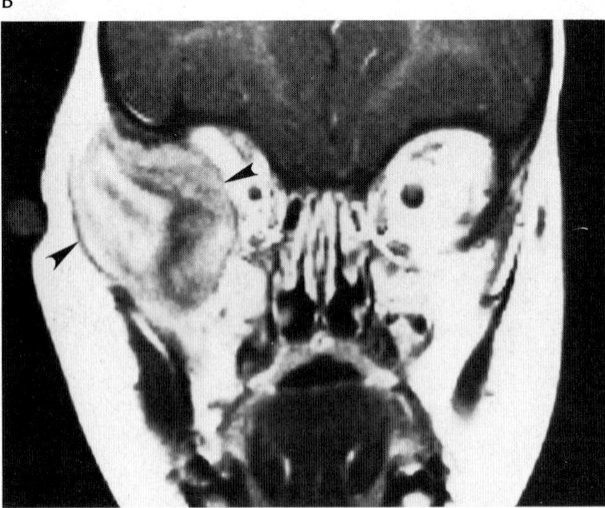

C

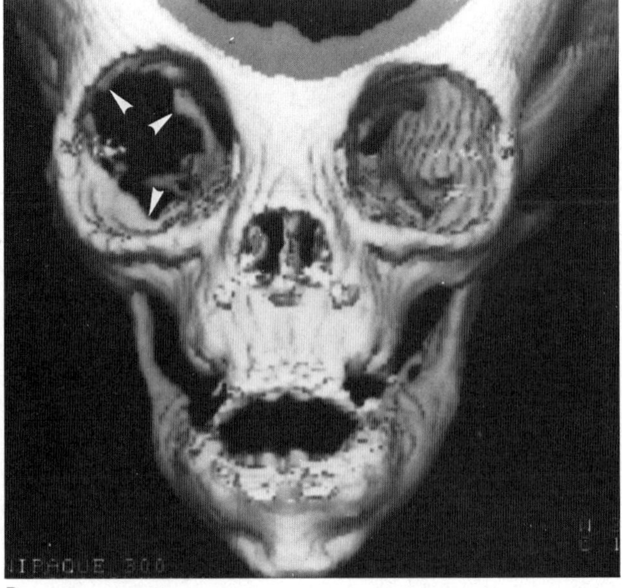

D

Figure 5-104 Histiocytosis X. **A.** Axial NCCT shows a large mass (arrowheads) destroying the lateral wall of the right orbit and the anterior wall of the right middle cranial fossa. **B.** The mass becomes heterogeneous and primarily hypointense on PD-WI (3000/45). **C.** Coronal CEMR (600/22, Gd-DTPA) shows heterogeneous enhancement of the well-delineated mass, which appears to have a thin wall (arrowheads). **D.** Three-dimensional reconstruction from CT sections shows a large defect (arrowheads) in the posterolateral wall of the right orbit.

reported presence of blood products and/or fibrosis. The mass shows prominent contrast enhancement on CE MR. The lesion may be localized to the orbit or may be part of a multifocal process. Identification of other sites leads to the correct diagnosis.

ORBITAL WALL AND PARANASAL SINUS TUMORS

Benign Tumors

FIBROUS DYSPLASIA

Fibrous dysplasia is probably a developmental mesodermal disorder that presents in either a monostotic or a polyostotic form. In its polyostotic form there may be an associated skin pigmentation abnormality and an endocrine disorder (Albright's syndrome). There is no sex predilection. The disease is most often encountered in children and young adolescents. The monostotic facial form presents clinically with headaches, facial asymmetry, and painless swelling of the cheek and periorbital region. When the craniofacial bones are involved, it is not unusual to find encroachment on the paranasal sinuses, the orbit, and the foramina that transmit nerves. This encroachment can produce visual loss, proptosis, diplopia, and epiphora (tearing) (Liakos 1979). Depending on the location of the fibrous dysplasia, the symptoms affecting the orbit differ. Fibrous dysplasia involving the cranial base may produce an extraocular palsy and fifth nerve neuralgia, whereas fibrous dysplasia involving the optic canal will produce visual loss and optic atrophy. Proptosis and bony prominence are common when there is involvement of the frontal bones (Moore 1985).

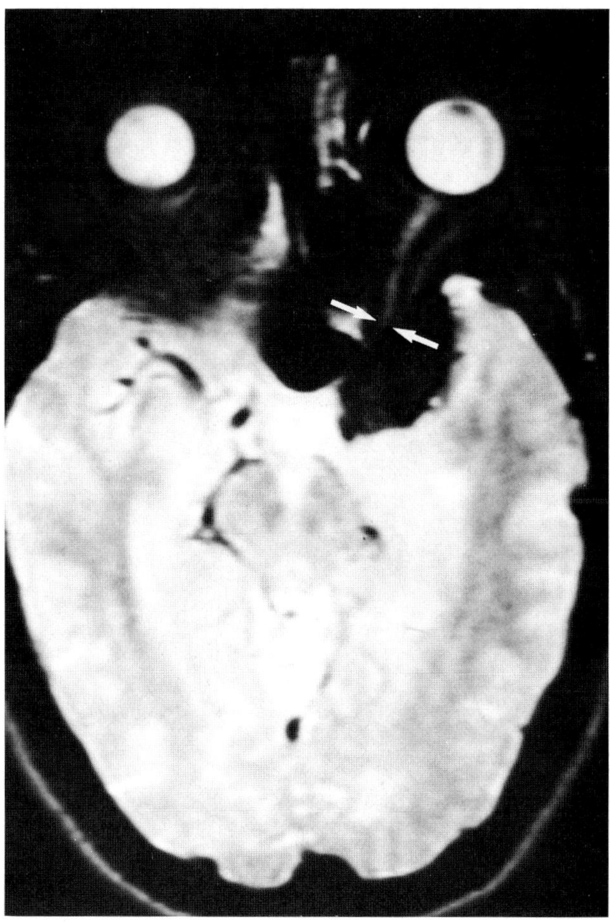

Figure 5-105 Fibrous dysplasia in a young adult male. An axial MRI (2500/80) reveals markedly expanded and hypointense left anterior clinoid and left sphenoid wing. The optic nerve sheath complex is identified because of the hyperintensity of the subarachnoid fluid. The left optic canal (arrows) is narrowed.

CT and MR, like skull radiography, reveal obliteration of the medullary canal by an expansile homogeneous matrix denser than that of the normal bone but occasionally containing focal sclerotic and lytic areas. Both CT and MR are excellent in defining the constrictive effect of an osteofibrous lesion on the orbit, the optic canal, and the adjacent paranasal sinuses. MR provides better delineation of the optic canal and the orbital apex (Fig. 5-105), while CT better demarcates fibrous dysplasia from adjacent air-containing sinuses. The treatment of fibrous dysplasia is surgical, with unroofing of the optic canal or cosmetic remodeling of the orbit to provide adequate room for the intraorbital contents. Radiation therapy is not advised because osteogenic sarcoma may develop as a result (Jones 1979).

Another process that produces markedly expanded abnormal bone which encroaches on the orbit is osteopetrosis (Fig. 5-106).

OSSIFYING FIBROMA

Ossifying fibromas are controversial lesions that often are linked to fibrous dysplasia. They are benign tumors which grow without regard to skeletal maturity and may occur in the mandible, maxilla, and paranasal sinuses, especially in the frontal and ethmoid sinuses (Margo 1985). They are found most often after 10 years of age and show no sex predilection. When they arise in the paranasal sinuses adjacent to the orbit, they most often present as exophthalmos. Histologically they are highly cellular, with a fibrous stroma, and osteoid, with a calcific matrix. Ossifying fibromas are more apt to show aggressive growth than is fibrous dysplasia.

The radiological picture of an ossifying fibroma reflects the variable composition of the lesion (fibrous tissue, osteoid, and calcific matrix). Conventional roentgenography shows opacification and expansion of the involved paranasal sinus. The lesion is relatively lucent compared with a typical case of fibrous dysplasia. CT demonstrates the expansion of the paranasal sinus, the homogeneous matrix which shows contrast enhancement, and the admixture of bone spicules within it.

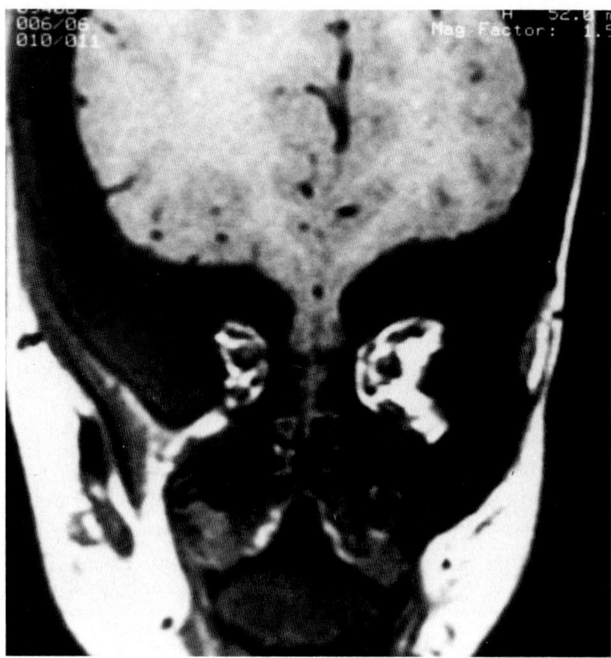

Figure 5-106 Osteopetrosis in a 2-year-old boy. Coronal MRI (1000/25) demonstrates markedly widened and hypointense calvarial and facial bones. As a result, the volume of the orbit and cranial cavity is decreased.

OSTEOMA

The incidence of osteomas on routine skull radiographs is on the order of 0.3 percent. They are found arising most often within the paranasal sinuses (Arger 1977) but on rare occasions may arise from the wall of the orbit. The most frequent location is within the frontal sinuses (40 to 80 percent), with the incidence decreasing in the ethmoid, maxillary, and sphenoid sinuses (2 percent). They are usually found after age 20 and are more common in males than in females. The lesion consists mainly of thick lamellar bone (Margo 1985).

The osteoma expands within, and conforms to, the shape of the sinus. As the osteoma grows, it may produce obstruction of the ostia, leading to infection or possibly the development of a mucocele. Pneumocephalus has been reported as a complication of ethmoidal and frontal osteomas that have eroded through the floor of the anterior cranial fossa.

Visual symptoms are due to encroachment on the orbit or compression of the optic nerve. Frontal osteomas may produce both facial asymmetry and downward displacement of the globe. Ethmoidal osteomas can produce lateral displacement of the globe. Sphenoidal osteomas may encroach on the optic canal and orbital apex (Jones 1979).

CT reveals an osteoma to be smoothly demarcated, frequently lobulated, homogeneously hyperdense (Fig. 5-107), and most often lying within the expanded paranasal sinuses. Encroachment on the orbit is graphically demonstrated in coronal and transverse CT sections. CT is the procedure of choice for the evaluation of osteomas, because on MR the signal void of osteoma is difficult to distinguish from the signal void of air within the sinuses.

INCLUSION CYST

Sequestration of ectoderm in the wall of the orbit or within the lids during embryogenesis leads to the formation of dermoid cysts. These cysts consist of an epi-

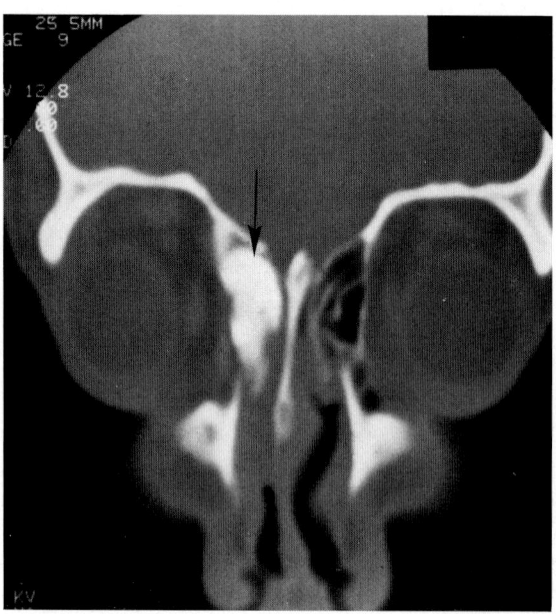

A

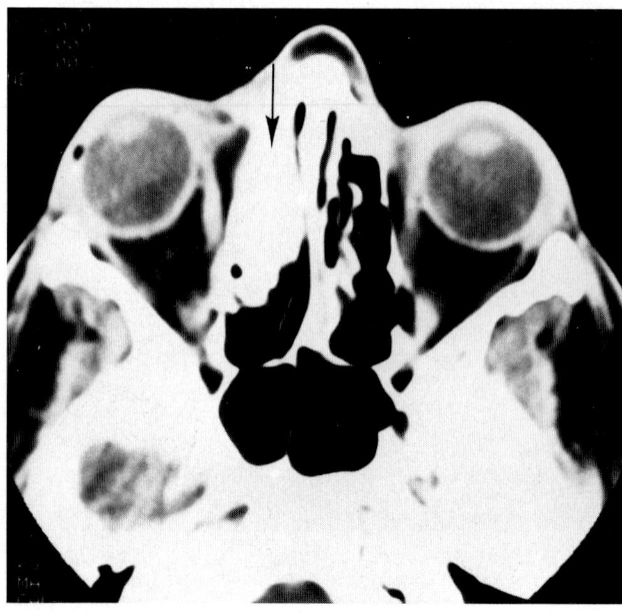

B

Figure 5-107 **A,B.** Osteoma. CT shows bone density within the right ethmoid sinus, involving the medial wall or right orbit (arrows).

dermal lining which contains dermal appendages and ectodermal material (sebaceous glands, hair follicles, and occasional sweat glands) sequestered during embryogenesis. The desquamated contents consist of laminated keratin and cholesterol crystals. Epidermoid cysts, which are less common than dermoid cysts, consist of a true epidermis and contain only desquamated keratin. Epithelial cysts also arise in the orbit and in the lacrimal gland as intrinsic lesions resulting from dilatation of the lacrimal ducts.

Dermoid cysts occur most often in the first decade of life, when they present with physical signs of proptosis or progressive swelling of the upper eyelid. A smooth mass may be palpable in the upper outer quadrant of the orbit.

Dermoid cysts are most often attached to the osseous structures surrounding the orbit. Most frequently they arise in the superolateral portion, in the vicinity of the lacrimal fossa. Extension through the bone, against the dura mater of the anterior cranial fossa, is not uncommon, nor is extension into the orbit with displacement of the orbital periosteum.

On CT or MR, dermoid cysts have well-defined margins and appear cystic, with the density or intensity of their center ranging from that of CSF to that of fat (Hesselink 1979*b;* Bilaniuk 1990*a*) (Figs. 5-108 through 5-110). The wall is noted to enhance, whereas the central portion remains the same in density. Imaging modalities are valuable in that they identify a relatively characteristic benign lesion and show both its intraorbital and intracranial extent. Surgical treatment is indicated for cosmetic purposes; total removal without dissemination of the contents is necessary. If ruptured, the contents may incite a granulomatous inflammatory reaction. Recurrences are unusual (Fig. 5-110).

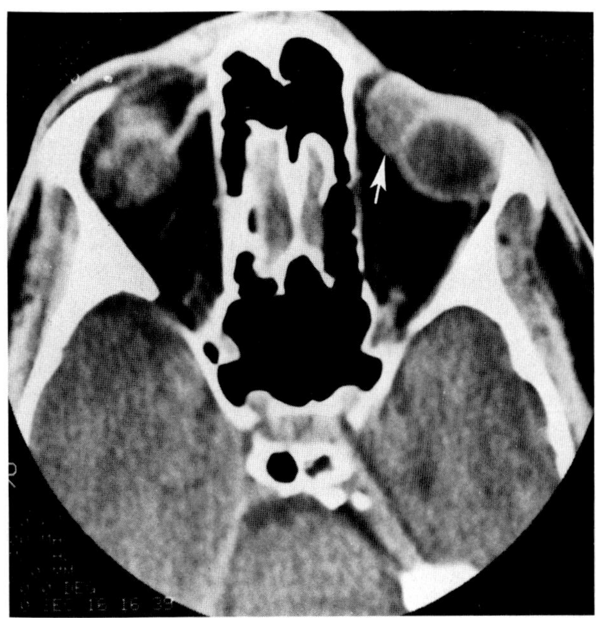

Figure 5-109 Dermoid. Soft-tissue density, well-circumscribed mass (arrow) medial to the left globe on axial CT.

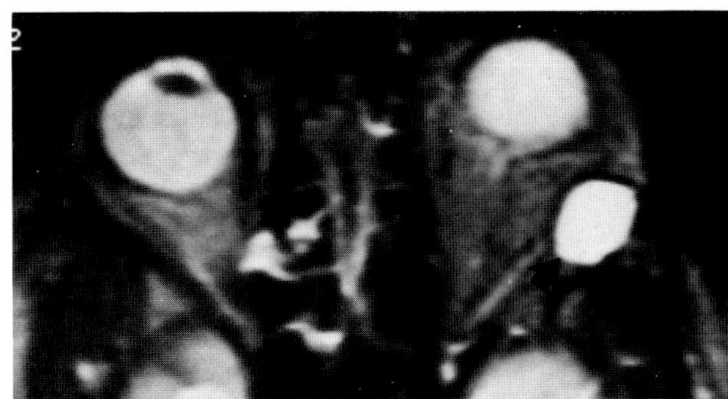

Figure 5-110 Recurrent dermoid cyst. Axial MR (2500/80) reveals marked hyperintensity in the residual dermoid cyst (arrow).

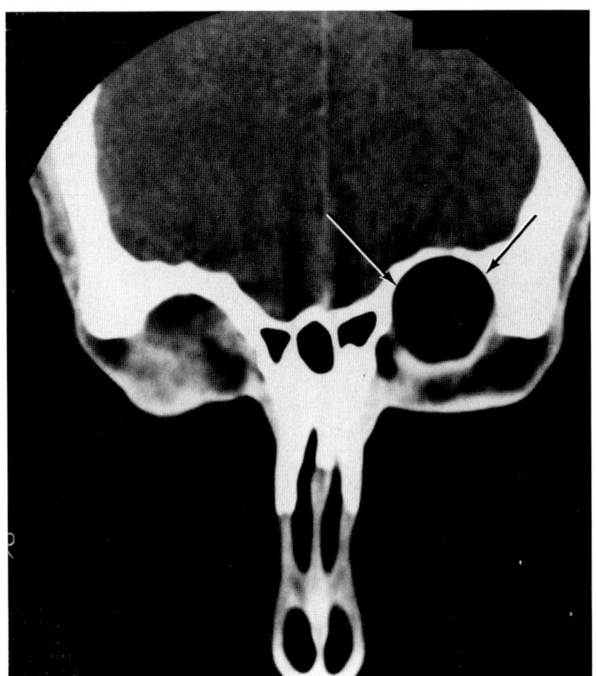

Figure 5-108 Dermoid. Extraconal mass of fat attenuation (arrows) with thinning of the adjacent left orbital roof on CT.

MUCOCELE

A mucocele consists of a sac lined by respiratory epithelium, often containing a thin serous fluid but at times showing evidence of hemorrhage or previous infection. There is a history of sinusitis in approximately half of patients with mucocele, a history of trauma in about one-quarter, and a history of allergy in one-eighth. The cause of the mucocele is blockage of the ostium of the involved sinus. The obstruction of the ostium may be due to inflammation, fibrosis, trauma, prior surgery, an anatomic abnormality, or osteoma. The developing mucocele produces an expansion of the sinus with thinning and remodeling of the sinus wall. The expanded sinus may protrude on the orbital contents or encroach on the optic canal or cavernous sinus. Mucoceles are uncommon before age 13, as the paranasal sinuses are in the process of developing during childhood. Those which occur in younger children usually result from problems in sinus drainage (cystic fibrosis). The most frequent location for mucoceles is the frontal sinus (60 percent); 30 percent occur in the ethmoid sinus. The sphenoid and maxillary sinuses are involved considerably less frequently (Som 1985). The type of symptoms depends on the location of the mucocele. Mucoceles that arise in the frontal and ethmoidal sinuses classically present as palpable masses in the superomedial aspect of the orbit. They produce proptosis and limitation of eye movement, resulting in diplopia. The swelling is usually painless but may be crepitant to palpation.

Skull radiography, CT, and MR all show the involved sinus to be opacified and expanded and the sinus wall to be thinned (Figs. 5-111 through 5-113). Because of its ability to show both bone and soft tissue, CT is an ideal method of evaluating the extent of a mucocele. However, because of its multiplanar capability, MR can show precisely the relationship of the mucocele to adjacent structures (Fig. 5-113). Lateral extension of a frontoethmoidal mucocele produces erosion of the lamina papyracea and lateral displacement of the medial rectus (Hesselink 1979*a*). There is preservation of the fat plane between the mucocele and the medial rectus muscle (Som 1980). Proptosis is often evident on CT and MR. Less commonly, there may be medial extension of the ethmoidal mucocele so that the medial wall of the ethmoid sinus is eroded, with the mucocele projecting into the nasal cavity and against the perpendicular plate of the ethmoid. Superior extension of frontal and ethmoidal mucoceles can occur through the roof of the ethmoid or the cribriform plate. The use of the term *frontoethmoidal mucocele* indicates the high incidence of contiguous sinus involvement (Figs. 5-111 through 5-113). The expanded sinus is most often isodense and rarely is calcified. On MR, mucoceles show a variable intensity pattern that is thought to be related to macromolecular protein concentration, the amount of free water, and the viscosity of the contents (Som 1989). Contrast enhancement is infrequent unless the mucocele is infected (mucopyocele) (Bilaniuk 1982; Som 1985) (Fig. 5-112).

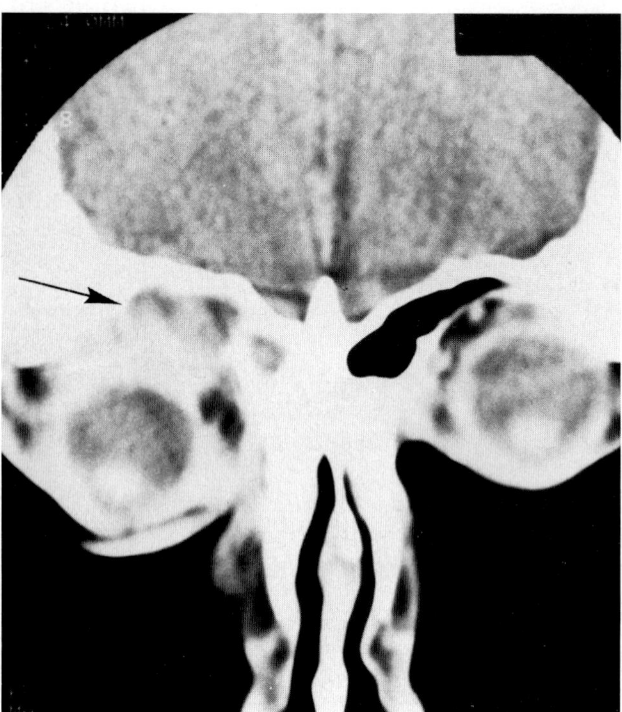

Figure 5-112 Mucopyelocele. Enhancing opacified right frontal sinus (arrow) which is slightly expanded on coronal CECT.

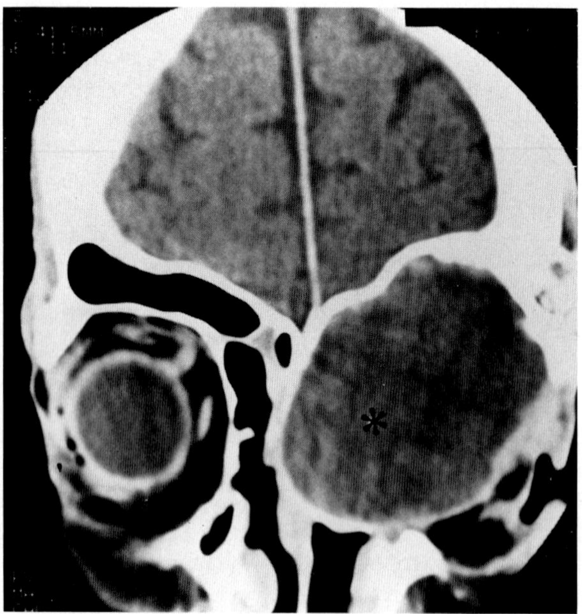

Figure 5-111 Mucocele. Markedly expanded left frontal and ethmoid sinuses secondary to a huge mucocele (asterisk) on coronal CT.

Mucoceles that arise in the sphenoid sinus can produce extraocular muscle palsies as a result of involvement of the cavernous sinus and can damage the optic nerve and chiasm by direct compression. They may also interfere with pituitary function and may mimic a primary intrasellar tumor. Both CT and MR show expansion and opacification of the sphenoid sinus and may show a soft tissue mass that extends out of the sphenoid sinus superiorly intracranially, inferiorly into the nasopharynx,

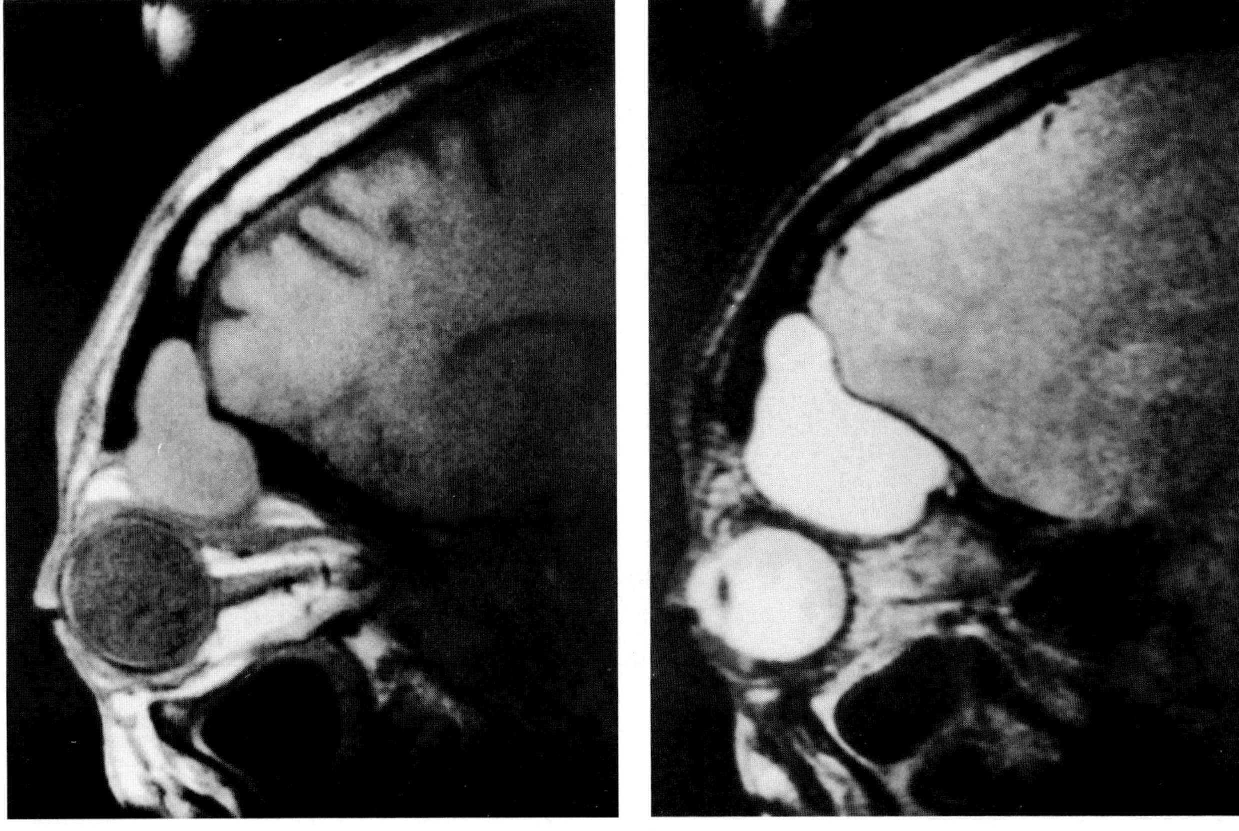

A B

Figure 5-113 Frontal sinus mucocele expanding into the superior orbit. **A.** Sagittal MRI (500/20) reveals the mucocele to be of slightly higher intensity than the vitreous of the globe. The mucocele depresses the superior rectus muscle and the globe. **B.** Sagittal MRI (1000/75) reveals the mucocele to be homogeneously hyperintense and minimally higher in intensity than the globe.

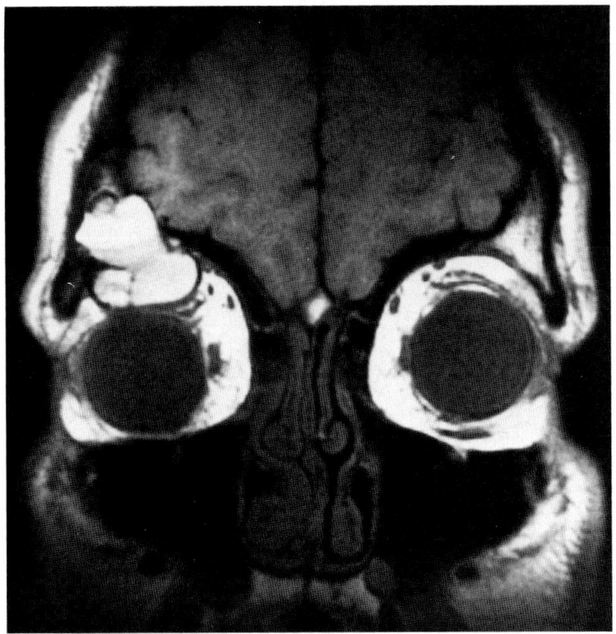

Figure 5-114 Cholesterol granuloma of the right orbit. Coronal MRI (600/20) reveals a lobulated hyperintense mass that has produced destruction of the roof of the right orbit. The mass remained hyperintense on T_2WI (not shown). Surgery revealed golden-colored oily fluid within the mass, and histological examination demonstrated cholesterol clefts and hematoidin crystals.

or laterally into the cavernous sinus. Destruction of the sellar floor, erosion of the optic canals, widening of the superior orbital fissure, and elevation of the anterior clinoid process are other manifestations of sphenoidal mucoceles. MR demonstrates better the effect on the adjacent structures. The clinical picture depends on the direction of expansion: There may be ophthalmoplegia and proptosis (anterolateral expansion into the orbit and cavernous sinus), chiasmal compression and pituitary dysfunction (with superior intracranial extension), airway obstruction (with expansion into the nasopharynx), and multiple cranial nerve (third, fifth, sixth) deficits (with posterolateral extension against the petrous apex) (Osborn 1979).

Cholesterol granuloma (chronic hematic cyst) is an expansile lesion that can occur in the roof of the orbit and should be differentiated from a mucocele. An orbital cholesterol granuloma does not originate from a paranasal sinus but is thought to arise from an intradiploic focus through recurrent hemorrhages. It is usually located in the superolateral aspect of the orbit (Parke 1982). MR is useful in the characterization of these lesions (Fig. 5-114).

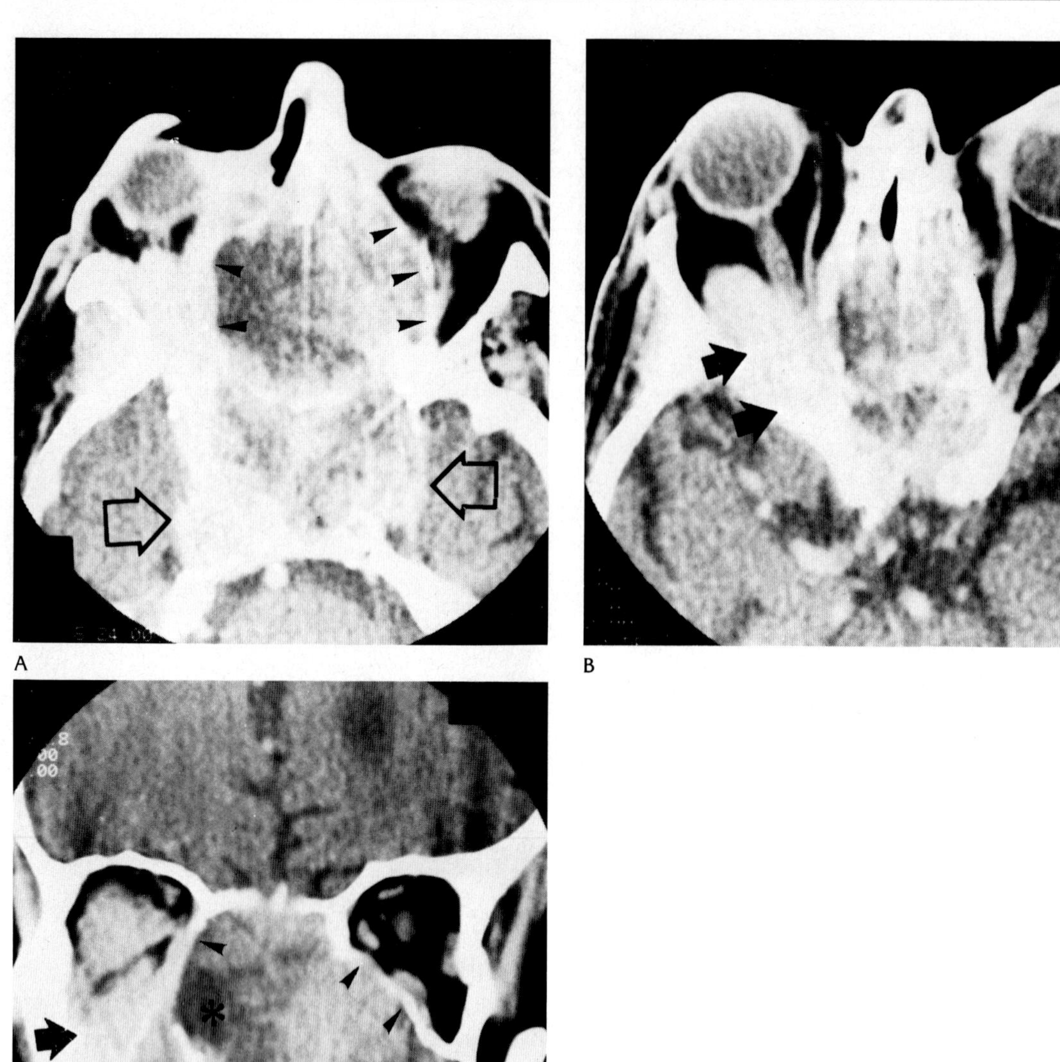

Figure 5-115 **A–C.** Adenocystic carcinoma. Axial CT (**A,B**) demonstrate a large mass replacing midline sinuses, extending into the right orbital apex (large arrows), bowing the medial orbital walls laterally (arrowheads), and invading the cavernous sinuses (open arrows). Coronal CT (**C**) defines the extent of the mass; destroyed bone fragments (small arrows) present within the mass, adjacent to necrotic area (asterisk).

Malignant Tumors

SINUS CARCINOMA

The thin osseous walls separating the orbit from the adjacent four paranasal sinuses offer little resistance to the direct spread of tumor. It has been estimated that in anywhere from 40 to 65 percent of paranasal sinus carcinomas the orbit is at risk. Preoperative management of these tumors necessitates an accurate evaluation of the extent of the malignancy and the presence or absence of orbital involvement. CT and MR have added a new dimension to the preoperative evaluation of and treatment planning for sinus carcinomas. With CT and MR, it is possible to identify osseous involvement of the orbital wall and extension of the tumor extraconically as well as intraconal extension (Bilaniuk 1982; Mancuso 1978) (Fig. 5-115). Any degree of orbital extension is particularly devastating because it necessitates either orbital exenteration or orbital reconstruction (Jones 1979). This information is also valuable in planning postoperative radiotherapy. Evaluation of the sinus and orbit should include both transverse sections and coronal sections. Sagittal sections, direct with MR or reformatted with CT, are also extremely valuable. The optimum plane depends on the site of the tumor. Three-dimensional reconstruction may also be useful.

Malignant tumors of the paranasal sinuses are relatively rare, constituting between 0.26 and 0.31 percent of cancers. The most frequent site of involvement is the maxillary sinus, with the ethmoid sinus coming next and the frontal or sphenoid sinus being relatively uncommon. The most common forms of paranasal sinus malignancy are squamous cell carcinomas and undifferentiated carcinomas. Less frequent is lymphoma, and relatively uncommon are melanoma, plasmocytoma, and various sarcomas. Squamous cell carcinoma represented over 50 percent of the lesions in the series reported by Weber (1978), constituting over half of those which arose in the maxillary antrum.

Not infrequently, the clinical diagnosis is delayed (over 50 percent of cases) and the tumor is advanced at the time of diagnosis. Often more than one of the paranasal sinuses is involved. The early symptoms are often trivial, and so the delay between the onset of symptoms and the histological diagnosis may be as long as a year. Presenting symptoms depend on the site of origin and the degree of extension of the tumor at the time of diagnosis. The most frequent locations of carcinomas of the maxillary sinus have been described by Baclesse (1952): (1) tumors arising within the inferior portion of the maxillary sinus—these do not involve the orbit; (2) tumors arising in the roof of the antrum—these not infrequently extend posteriorly and laterally to the infratemporal fossa and superiorly into the ethmoid sinuses and orbit; (3) a generalized growth arising from the mucosal surfaces of the antrum and tending not to involve the osseous wall but filling the sinus; (4) medial wall neoplasms that often extend from the maxillary sinuses into the nasal fossa; and (5) those that arise in the superior-medial angle at the ethmoidomaxillary septum—these classically have extensive involvement of the medial orbit.

Swelling of the face is the most common symptom with maxillary sinus carcinoma (40 percent). Involvement of the nasal cavity causing pain, unilateral obstruction, and nasal discharge is present in another 35 percent. The orbit is involved at the time of presentation in only 10 percent of cases. Ethmoidal carcinomas have a higher incidence of nasal involvement (55 percent) and a much higher incidence of orbital involvement (35 percent) at the time of initial presentation. The orbital signs are proptosis, diplopia, visual loss, paresthesias, and involvement of such structures as the infraorbital nerve.

The hallmark of sinus carcinoma detected by routine radiography, CT, and MR is the presence of a sinus soft tissue mass in association with extensive bone destruction (Fig. 5-74). Bone remodeling, as opposed to overt bone destruction, may be seen in malignant as well as benign lesions. Some of these malignancies (adenoid cystic carcinoma) have a worse 5-year survival than does squamous cell carcinoma, which is more destructive radiographically (Som 1985). Extension of the mass outside the sinus cavity into the face, the other paranasal sinuses, the adjacent orbit, or the intracranial contents is most typical of a carcinoma but can be seen with fungal infections or Wegener's granulomatosis (Vermess 1978) (Fig. 5-116) or even with benign but aggressive tumors such as juvenile angiofibroma (Fig. 5-117). It should be noted that opacification of adjacent paranasal sinuses does not necessarily indicate tumor involvement but may merely represent fluid retained within the sinus secondary to ostium obstruction. MR makes this distinction much better than CT by showing much greater hyperintensity in fluid than in tumor on T_2WI. Intravenous MR contrast enhancement may aid in this distinction.

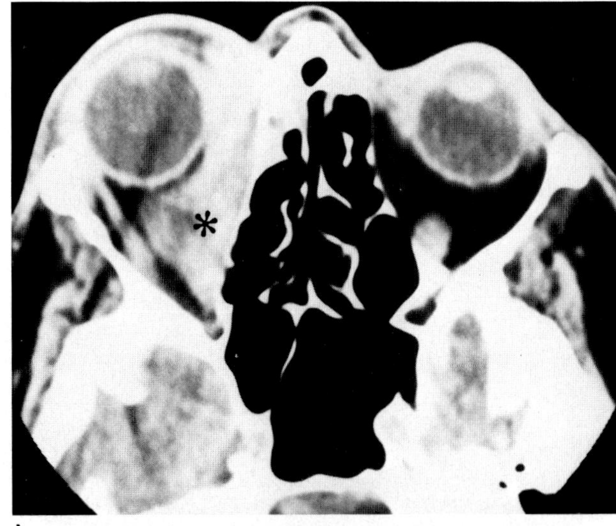

A

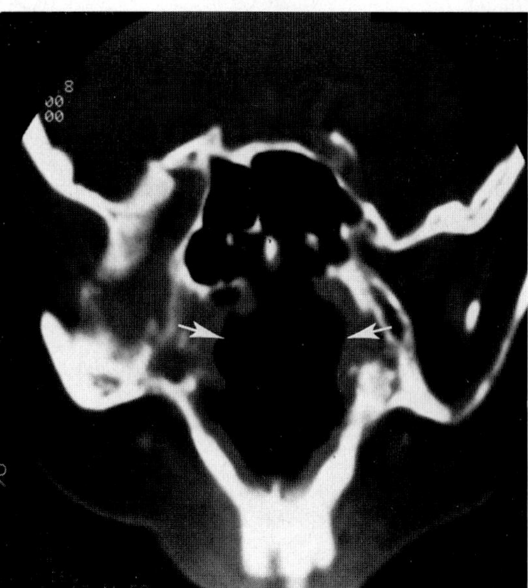

B

Figure 5-116 **A,B.** Wegener's granulomatosis on CT. **A.** Enhancing intraconal and extraconal mass extends along the medial aspect of the right orbit (asterisk). **B.** Destroyed nasal septa typical of a necrotizing aggressive process (arrows).

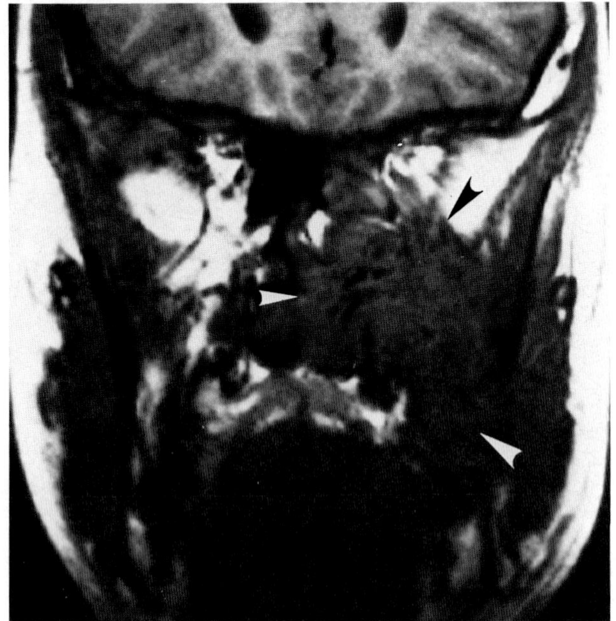

A

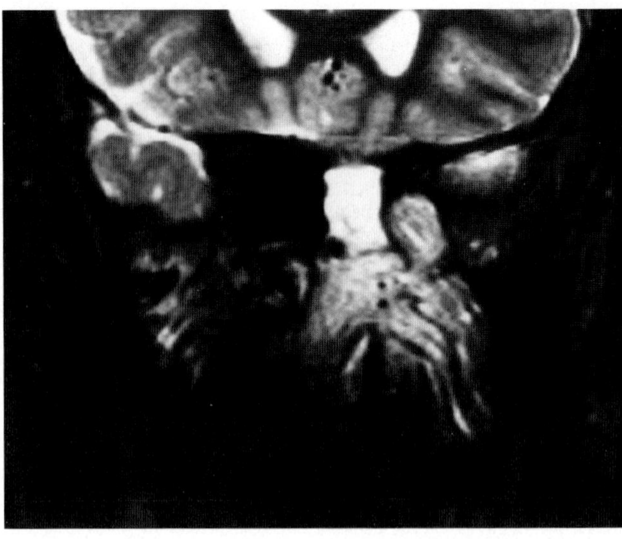

B

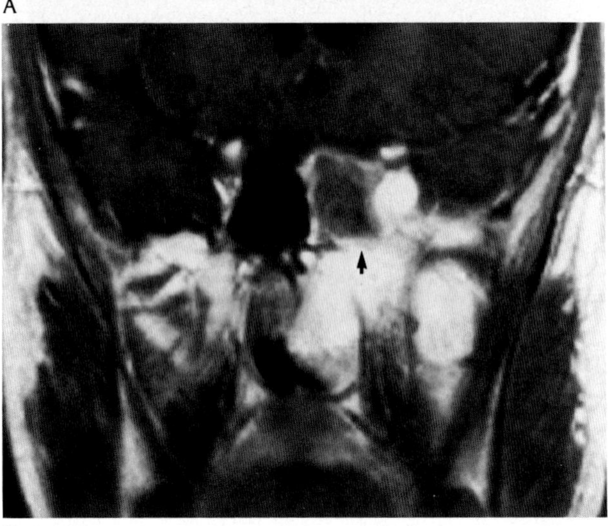

C

◄ ***Figure 5-117*** Juvenile angiofibroma extending into the orbital apex. **A.** Coronal MR (600/15). A large mass (arrowheads) with signal voids within it extends into the orbit through the inferior orbital fissure. The lateral wall of the left nasal cavity and the pterygoid processes have been destroyed by the mass. **B.** A coronal MR (3000/90) reveals a difference in intensity between the inflammatory process in the sphenoid sinus and the tumor mass (arrowheads). On this T_2WI the mass is of higher intensity than the adjacent muscles and can be delineated from them. **C.** Coronal CEMR (600/22 with Gd-DTPA). The mass shows contrast enhancement. The inflammatory process in the sphenoid sinus remains hypointense. There is a loss of the normal signal void of bone in the floor (arrow) of the sphenoid sinus. This indicates tumor invasion. A similar bony invasion is noted in the left pterygoid plates. Note that the normal fatty structures present on the right also have enhanced and show increased intensity. Therefore, it is necessary to compare this image with other pulse sequences to appreciate the tumor extent. A fat-suppressed image would have been helpful.

CHONDROSARCOMA

Among the chondrosarcomas occurring in the skeleton, approximately 9.4 percent occur in the bones of the face and cranium. Chondrosarcomas arise from cartilaginous rests in the walls of the orbit and paranasal sinuses. The bones of the base of the skull are preformed in cartilage, and rests from this formation give rise to tumors (Fig. 5-12), among them chondrosarcomas. Thus, the ethmoid region, maxilla, cribriform plate, and sphenoid bone are frequently involved. It is also possible for chondrosarcomas as well as other cartilaginous tumors to arise within the orbit from the cartilage of the trochlea (Jones 1979).

Chondrosarcomas of the craniofacial bones frequently are slowly progressive and form an expansile mass, most often in the maxilloethmoid region. One-third of patients are less than 20 years of age. Unlike osteogenic sarcomas of the facial bones, chondrosarcomas are not known to be painful during their initial growth. In contrast to chondrosarcomas, osteogenic sarcomas involving the orbit are rare. They occur predominantly in older patients (between 20 and 50 years of age), are painful, have a rapid onset of symptoms (less than 3 months), and are much more likely to occur in the mandible or alveolar ridge of the antrum than in the orbital region.

On CT, chondrosarcoma is a densely calcified mass, often showing a whorled pattern (with central hypodensity) and capped by a soft tissue mass that is not calcified. On MR, the tumor has heterogeneity as a result of the dense calcifications. Both calcified and noncalcified tumor components show contrast enhancement. Adjacent normal bone is destroyed, and the local soft tissue planes are obliterated as a result of invasion.

ACKNOWLEDGMENTS

It is a pleasure to express our sincere thanks to the ophthalmologists of the Wills Eye Hospital for sending us their patients. We also wish to thank Steven J. Strommer and Juanita James of Medical Photography, Department of Radiology, Hospital of the University of Pennsylvania, for their expert figure preparation. A special acknowledgment goes to Valerie Tsafos for her cheerful and tireless help and her exemplary efficiency in word processing this chapter.

REFERENCES

ABRAMSON DH, ELLSWORTH R, KITCHIN S: Second non-ocular tumors in retinoblastoma survivor. *Ophthalmol* 91:1351–1355, 1984.

ALBERT DM, RUBENSTEIN RA, SCHEIE HG: Tumor metastases to the eye: I. Incidence in 213 adult patients with generalized malignancy. *Am J Ophthalmol* 63:723–726, 1967.

ALPER MG: Endocrine orbital disease, in Arger PH (ed): *Orbit Roentgenology,* New York, Wiley, 1977, pp 69–72.

ANDERSON RL, EPSTEIN GA, DAUER EA: Computed tomographic diagnosis of posterior ocular staphyloma. *AJNR* 4:90–91, 1983.

AOKI S, BARKOVICH AJ, NISHIMURA K, KJOS BO, MACHIDA T, COGEN P, EDWARDS M, NORMAN D: Neurofibromatosis type 1 and 2: Cranial MR findings. *Radiology* 172:527–534, 1989.

APPELBOOM T, DURSO F: Retinoblastoma presenting as a total hyphema. *Ann Ophthalmol* 17:508–510, 1985.

ARGER PH: Tumor and tumor-like conditions, in Arger PH (ed): *Orbit Roentgenology,* New York, Wiley, 1977.

ATLAS SW, GROSSMAN RI, SAVINO PJ, SERGOTT RC, SCHATZ NJ, BOSLEY TM, HACKNEY DB, GOLDBERG HI, BILANIUK LT, ZIMMERMAN RA: Surface coil MR of orbital pseudotumor. *AJNR* 8:141–146, 1987*a*.

ATLAS SW, GROSSMAN RI, AXEL L, HACKNEY DB, BILANIUK LT, GOLDBERG HI, ZIMMERMAN RA: Orbital lesions: Proton spectroscopic phase dependent contrast MR imaging. *Radiology* 164:510–514, 1987*b*.

ATLAS SW, GROSSMAN RI, HACKNEY DB, GOLDBERG HI, BILANIUK LT, ZIMMERMAN RA: STIR MR imaging of the orbit. *AJNR* 9:969–974, 1988.

BABCOCK EE, BRATEMAN L, WEINREB JC, HORNER SD, NUNNALLY RL: Edge artifacts in MR images: Chemical shift effect. *J Comput Assist Tomogr* 9:252–257, 1985.

BACLESSE F: Les cancers du sinus maxillaire de l'ethmoide et des fosses nasales. *Ann Otolaryngol* 69:465, 1952.

BALCHUNAS WR, QUENCER RM, BYRNE SF: Lacrimal gland and fossa masses: Evaluation by computed tomography and A-mode echography. *Radiology* 149:751–758, 1983.

BALERIAUX-WAHA D, MORTELMANS LL, DUPONT MG, TERWINGHE G, JEANMART L: The use of coronal scans for computed tomography of the orbits. *Neuroradiology* 14:89–96, 1977.

BERNARDINO ME, ZIMMERMAN RD, CITRIN CM, DAVIS DO: Scleral thickening: A sign of orbital pseudo-tumor. *AJR* 129:703–706, 1977.

BERNARDINO ME, DANZIGER J, YOUNG SE, WALLACE S: Computed tomography in ocular neoplastic disease. *AJR* 131:111–113, 1978.

BILANIUK LT, VIGNAUD J, CLAY C: Orbital venography, in Arger PH (ed): *Orbit Roentgenology,* New York, Wiley, 1977, pp 171–193.

BILANIUK LT, ZIMMERMAN RA: Computer-assisted tomography: Sinus lesions with orbital involvement. *Head Neck Surg* 2:293–301, 1980.

BILANIUK LT, ATLAS SW, ZIMMERMAN RA: MRI of the orbit. *Radiol Clin North Am* 25:509–528, 1987.

BILANIUK LT, ZIMMERMAN RA: Computed tomography in evaluation of the paranasal sinuses. *Radiol Clin North Am* 20:51–66, 1982.

BILANIUK LT, ZIMMERMAN RA: Facial trauma, in Dalinka MK, Kaye JJ (eds): *Radiology in Emergency Medicine,* New York, Churchill Livingstone, 1984, pp 135–155.

BILANIUK LT, ZIMMERMAN RA, GUSNARD DA, PACKER RJ, SUTTON LN, ATLAS SW, HACKNEY DB, GOLDBERG HI, GROSSMAN RI, SCHUT L, RORKE LB: MR imaging of visual pathway gliomas. *Radiology* (RSNA '89 Abstracts) 173P:85, 1989.

BILANIUK LT: Magnetic resonance imaging: Orbital anatomy, in Newton TM, Bilaniuk LT (eds): *Radiology of the Eye and Orbit,* New York, Raven Press, 1990*a*, pp 4.1–4.12.

BILANIUK LT, ZIMMERMAN RA, NEWTON TH: Magnetic resonance imaging: Orbital pathology, in Newton TM, Bilaniuk LT (eds): *Radiology of the Eye and Orbit,* New York, Raven Press, 1990*b,* pp 5.1–5.84.

BILANIUK LT, ZIMMERMAN RA, GUSNARD DA: MR of head and neck hemangiomas. *Radiology* (RSNA '90 Abstracts) 177P: 256, 1990*c.*

BRAFFMAN BH, BILANIUK LT, ZIMMERMAN RA: The central nervous system manifestations of the phakomatosis on MR. *Radiol Clin North Am* 26:773–800, 1988.

BRANT-ZAWADZKI M, ENZMANN DR: Orbital computed tomography: Calcific densities of the posterior globe. *J Comput Assist Tomogr* 3:503–505, 1979.

BRISMAR J, DAVIS KR, DALLOW RL, BRISMAR G: Unilateral endocrine exophthalmos. Diagnostic problems in association with computed tomography. *Neuroradiology* 12:24, 1976.

BRODEY PA, RANDEL S, LANE B, FISCH AE: Computed tomography of axial myopia. *J Comput Assist Tomogr* 7:484–485, 1983.

BROWN GC, TASMAN WS, BENSON WE: BB-gun injuries to the eye. *Ophthal Surg* 16:505–508, 1985.

BROWN GC, WEINSTOCK F: Arterial macroaneurysm on the optic disk presenting as a mass lesion. *Ann Ophthalmol* 17:519–520, 1985.

BULLOCK JD, CAMPBELL RJ, WALKER RR: Calcification in retinoblastoma. *Invest Ophthalmol Vis Sci* 16:252–255, 1977.

BYRD SE, HARDWOOD-NASH DC, FITZ CR, BARRY JF, ROGOVITZ DM: Computed tomography of intraorbital optic nerve gliomas in children. *Radiology* 129:73–78, 1978.

CABANIS EA et al: Computed tomography of the optic nerve: II. Size and shape modifications in papilledema. *J Comput Assist Tomogr* 2:150–155, 1978.

CARLSON RE, SCHERIBEL KW, HERING PI, WOLIN L: Exophthalmos, global luxation, rapid weight gain: Differential diagnosis. *Ann Ophthalmol* 14:724–729, 1982.

CLARK JA, KELLY WM: Common artifacts encountered in magnetic resonance imaging. *Radiol Clin North Am* 26:893–920, 1988.

COHEN BA, SOM PM, HAFFNER PH, FRIEDMAN AH: Steroid exophthalmos. *J Comput Assist Tomogr* 5:907–908, 1981.

COOLING RJ, WRIGHT JE: Arachnoid hyperplasia in optic nerve glioma: Confusion with orgbital meningioma. *Br J Ophthalmol* 63:596–599, 1979.

CORBETT J, SAVINO PJ, SCHATZ NJ, ORR LS: Cavitary developmental defects of the optic disc. *Arch Neurol* 37:210–213, 1980.

DAMADIAN R, ZANER JK, HOR D: Human tumors by NMR. *Physiol Chem Phys* 5:381–402, 1973.

DAVIS KR, HESSELINK JR, DALLOW RL, GROVE AS Jr: CT and ultrasound in the diagnosis of cavernous hemangioma and lymphangioma of the orbit. *CT: J Comput Assist Tomogr* 4:98–104, 1980.

DIXON WT: Simple proton spectroscopic imaging. *Radiology* 153:189–194, 1984.

DRESNER SC, ROTHFUS WE, SLAMOVITZ TL, KENNERDELL JS, CURTIN HD: Computed tomography of orbital myositis. *AJR* 143:671–674, 1984.

EDWARDS MG, PORDELL GR: Ocular toxocariasis studied by CT scanning. *Radiology* 157:685–686, 1985.

ENZMANN D, DONALDSON SS, MARSHALL WH, KRISS JP: Computed tomography in orbital pseudotumor (idiopathic orbital inflammation). *Radiology* 120:597–601, 1976.

ENZMANN DR, DONALDSON SS, KRISS JP: Appearance of Graves' disease on orbital computed tomography. *J Comput Assist Tomogr* 3:815–819, 1979.

FELDON SE, WEINER JM: Clinical significance of extraocular muscle volumes in Graves' ophthalmopathy: A quantitative computed tomographic study. *Arch Ophthalmol* 100:1266–1269, 1982.

FLANAGAN JC: Vascular problems of the orbit. *Ophthalmology* 86:896–913, 1979.

FLANDERS AE, ESPINOSA GA, MARKIEWICZ DA, HOWELL DD: Orbital lymphoma: Role of CT and MR. *Radiol Clin North Am* 25:601–613, 1987.

FORBES GS, SHEEDY PF, WALLER RR: Orbital tumors evaluated by computed tomography. *Radiology* 136:101–111, 1980.

FORBES G: Computed tomography of the orbit. *Radiol Clin North Am* 20:37–49, 1982.

FORBES G, GORMAN CA, BRENNAN MD, GEHRING MD, ILSTRUP DM, EARNEST F IV: Ophthalmopathy of Graves disease: Computerized volume measurements of the orbital fat and muscle. *AJNR* 7:641–656, 1986.

FOX AJ, DEBRUN G, VINUELA F, ASSIS L, COATES R: Itrathecal metrizamide enhancement of the optic nerve sheath. *J Comput Assist Tomogr* 3:653–656, 1979.

GITTINGER JW: *Ophthalmology: A Clinical Introduction.* Boston, Little, Brown, 1984.

GOMORI JM, GROSSMAN RI, SHIELDS JA, AUGSBURGER JJ, JOSEPH PJH, DE SIMONE D: Choroidal melanomas: Correlation of NMR spectroscopy and MR imaging. *Radiology* 158:443–445, 1986.

GONVERS M: Temporary silicone oil tamponade in the management of retinal detachment with proliferative vitreoretinopathy. *Am J Ophthalmol* 100:239–245, 1985.

GRAEB DA, ROOTMAN J, ROBERTSON WD, LAPOINTE JS, NUGENT RA, HAY EJ: Orbital lymphangiomas: Clinical, radiologic, and pathologic characteristics. *Radiology* 175:417–421, 1990.

GROVE AS Jr, TADMOR R, NEW PFJ, MOMOSE KJ: Orbital fracture evaluation by coronal computed tomography. *Am J Ophthalmol* 85:679–685, 1978.

HAHN EJ, CHU WK, COLEMAN PE, ANDERSON JC, DOBRY CA, IMRAY TJ, HAHN PY, LEE SH: Artifacts and diagnostic pitfalls on magnetic resonance imaging: A clinical review. *Radiol Clin North Am* 26:717–735, 1988.

HAIK BG, SAINT LOUIS L, SMITH ME, ABRAMSON DH, ELLSWORTH RM: Computed tomography of the nonrhegmatogenous retinal detachment in the pediatric patient. *Ophthalmology* 92:1133–1142, 1985.

HAMMERSCHLAG SB, HUGHES S, O'REILLY GV, NAHEEDY MH, RUMBAUGH CL: Blow-out fractures of the orbit: A comparison of computed tomography and conventional radiography with anatomical correlation. *Radiology* 143:487–492, 1982.

HARRIS GJ, JAKOBIEC FA: Cavernous hemangioma of the orbit: A clinicopathologic analysis of ninty-six cases, in Jakobiec FA (ed): *Ocular and Adnexal Tumors,* Birmingham, Ala., Aesculapius, 1978, pp 741–781.

HAUGHTON VM, DAVIS JP, HARRIS GJ, HO KC: Metrizamide optic nerve sheath opacification. *Invest Radiol* 15:343–345, 1980.

HEDGES TR, POZZI-MUCELLI R, CHAR DH, NEWTON TH: Computed tomographic demonstration of ocular calcification: Correlations with clinical and pathologic findings. *Neuroradiology* 23:15–21, 1982.

HESSELINK JR et al: Computed tomography of the paranasal sinus and face. I. Normal anatomy. *J Comput Assist Tomogr* 2:559–567, 1978.

HESSELINK JR, WEBER AL, NEW PFJ, DAVIS KR, ROBERSON GH, TAVERAS JM: Evaluation of mucoceles of the paranasal sinuses with CT. *Radiology* 133:397–400, 1979*a*.

HESSELINK JR, DAVIS KR, DALLOW RL, ROBERSON GH, TAVERAS JM: Computed tomography of masses in the lacrimal gland region. *Radiology* 131:143–147, 1979*b*.

HESSELINK JR, DAVIS KR, WEBER AL, DAVIS JM, TAVERAS JM: Radiological evaluation of orbital metastases with emphasis on computed tomography. *Radiology* 137:363–366, 1980.

HOYT WF: Coronal sections in the diagnosis of orbital disease, in Thompson HS (ed): *Topics in Neuro-ophthalmology.* Baltimore, London, Williams & Wilkins, 1979, pp. 369–371.

JACOBS L, WEISBERG LA, KINKEL WR: *Computerized Tomography of the Orbit and Sella Turcica,* New York, Raven Press, 1980.

JAKOBIEC FA, TROKEL SL, ARON-ROSA D, IWAMOTO T, DOYON D: Localized eosinophilic granuloma (Langerhans' cell histiocytosis) of the orbital frontal bone. *Arch Ophthalmol* 98:1814–1820, 1980.

JEREB B, HAIK BG, ONG R, GHAVIMI F: Parameningeal rhabdomyosarcoma (including the orbit): Results of orbital irradiation. *Int J Radiat Oncol Biol Phys* 11:2057–2065, 1985.

JINKINS JR: Optic hydrops: Isolated nerve sheath dilation demonstrated by CT. *AJNR* 8:867–870, 1986.

JOHNSON DL, CHANDRA R, FISHER WS, HAMMOCK MK, MCKEOWN CA: Trilateral retinoblastoma: Ocular and pineal retinoblastomas. *J Neurosurg* 63:367–370, 1985.

JONES IS, JAKOBIEC FA: *Diseases of the Orbit.* Hagerstown, Md., Harper & Row, 1979.

KAPLAN RJ: Neurological complications of infections of the head and neck. *Otolaryngol Clin North Am* 9:729–749, 1976.

KELLER PJ, HUNTER WW Jr, SCHMALBROCK P: Multisection fat-watering imaging with chemical shift selective presaturation. *Radiology* 164:539–541, 1987.

KELLY WM, PAGLEN G, PEARSON JA, SAN DIEGO AG, SOLOMAN MA: Ferromagnetism of intraocular foreign body causes unilateral blindness after MR study. *AJNR* 7:243–245, 1986.

KLINTWORTH GK: Radiographic abnormalities in eyes with retinoblastoma and other disorders. *Br J Ophthalmol* 62:365–372, 1978.

KOORNNEEF L: New insights into human orbital connective tissue. *Arch Ophthalmol* 95:1269–1273, 1977.

KOORNNEEF L: Orbital septa: Anatomy and function. *Ophthalmology* 86:876–880, 1979.

KROHEL GB, KRAUSS HR, WINNICK J: Orbital abscess: Presentation, diagnosis, therapy and sequelae. *Ophthalmology* 85:492–498, 1982.

LAST RJ: *Eugene Wolff's Anatomy of the Eye and the Orbit,* Philadelphia, Saunders, 1968.

LEE DA, CAMPBELL RJ, WALLER RR, ILSTRUP OM: A clinicopathologic study of primary adenoid cystic carcinoma of the lacrimal gland. *Ophthalmology* 92:128–134, 1985.

LEONE CR, LLOYD WC: Treatment protocol for orbital inflammatory disease. *Ophthalmology* 92:1325–1331, 1985.

LIAKOS GM, WALKER CB, CARRUTH JAS: Ocular complications in craniofacial fibrous dysplasia. *Br J Ophthalmol* 63:611–616, 1979.

LIBERFARB RM, EAVEY RD, DE LONG GR, ALBERT DM, DIECKERT JP, HILROSE T: Norrie's disease: A study of two families. *Ophthalmology* 92:1445–1451, 1985.

LINDBERG R, WALSH FB, SACHS JG: *Neuropathology of Vision: An Atlas.* Philadelphia, Lea & Febiger, 1973.

MACRAE JA: Diagnosis and management of a wooden orbital foreign body: Case report. *Br J Ophthalmol* 63:848–851, 1979.

MAFEE MF, PEYMAN GA, MCKUSICK MA: Malignant uveal melanoma and similar lesions studied by computed tomography. *Radiology* 156:403–408, 1985.

MAFEE MF, GOLDBERG MF, GREENWALD MJ, SCHULMAN J, MALMED A, FLANDERS AE: Retinoblastoma and simulating lesions: Role of CT and MR imaging, in Mafee MF (ed): *Imaging in Ophthalmology,* Part II, *Radiol Clin North Am* 25:667–682, 1987.

MAFEE MF: Magnetic resonance imaging: Ocular pathology, in Newton TH, Bilaniuk LT (eds): *Radiology of the Eye and Orbit,* New York, Raven Press, 1990.

MAGILL HL, HANNA SL, BROOKS MT, JENKINS JJ, BURTON EW, BOULDEN TF, SEIDEL FG: Pediatric case of the day (persistent hyperplastic primary vitreous, PHPV). *Radiographics* 10:515–518, 1990.

MANCUSO AA, HANAFEE WN, WARD P: Extensions of paranasal sinus tumors and inflammatory disease as evaluated by CT and pluridirectional tomography. *Neuroradiology* 16:449–453, 1978.

MANELFE C, PASQUINI U, BONK WO: Metrizamide demonstration of the subarachnoid space surrounding the optic nerves. *J Comput Assist Tomogr* 2:545–548, 1978.

MARGO CE, RAGSDALE BD, PERMAN KI, ZIMMERMAN LE, SWEET DE: Psammomatoid (juvenile) ossifying fibroma of the orbit. *Ophthalmology* 92:150–159, 1985.

MCARDLE CB, AMPARO EG, MIRFAKHRAEE M: MR imaging of orbital blow-out fractures. *J Comput Assist Tomogr* 10:116–119, 1986.

MOORE AT, PRITCHARD J, TAYLOR DSI: Histiocytosis X: An ophthalmological review. *Br J Ophthalmol* 69:7–14, 1985.

NEW PFJ, ROSEN BR, BRADY TJ, BUONANNO FS, KISTLER JP, BURT CT, HINSHAW WS, NEWHOUSE JH, POHOST GM, TAVERAS JM: Potential hazards and artifacts of ferromagnetic and nonferromagnetic surgical and dental material and devices in nuclear magnetic resonance imaging. *Radiology* 147:139–148, 1983.

NUGENT RA, ROOTMAN J, ROBERTSON WD, LAPOINTE J, HARRISON PB: Acute orbital pseudotumors: Classification and CT features. *AJR* 137:957–962, 1981.

NUGENT RA, BELKIN RI, NEIGEL JM, ROOTMAN J, ROBERTSON WD, SPINELLI J, GRAEB DA: Graves orbitopathy: Correlation of CT and clinical findings. *Radiology* 177:675–682, 1990.

OSBORN AG, JOHNSON L, ROBERTS TS: Sphenoidal mucoceles with intracranial extension. *J Comput Assist Tomogr* 3:335–338, 1979.

OSBORN AG, ANDERSON RE, WING SD: Sagittal CT scans in the evaluation of deep facial and nasopharyngeal lesions. *CT: J Comput Tomogr* 4:19–24, 1980.

PARKE DW II, FONT RL, BONIUK M, MCCRARY JA: Cholesteatoma of the orbit. *Arch Ophthalmol* 100:612–616, 1982.

PATZ A: Observations on the retinopathy of prematurity. *Am J Ophthalmol* 100:164–168, 1985.

PEYSTER RG, HOOVER ED, HERSHEY BL, HASKIN ME: High-resolution CT of lesions of the optic nerve. *AJNR* 4:169–174, 1983.

PEYSTER RG, AUGSBERGER JJ, SHIELDS JA, SATCHELL TV, MARKOE AM, CLARKE K, HASKIN ME: Choroidal melanoma: Comparison of CT, funduscopy and US. *Radiology* 156:675–680, 1985.

PEYSTER RG, GINSBURG F, SILBER J, ADLER L: Exophthalmos caused by excessive fat: CT volumetric analysis and differential diagnosis. *AJNR* 7:35–40, 1986.

PEYSTER RG, AUGSBURGER JJ, SHIELDS JA, HERSHEY BL, EAGLE R JR, HASKIN ME: Intraocular tumors: Evaluation with MR imaging. *Radiology* 168:773–779, 1988.

PLESNER-RASMUSSEN H, MARUSHAK D, GOLSCHMIDT E: Capillary hamangiomas of the eyelids and orbit. *Acta Ophthalmol* 61:645–654, 1983.

PUSEY JE, LUFKIN RB, BROWN RKF, SOLOMON MA, STARK DD, TARR RW, HANAFEE WN: Magnetic resonance imaging artifacts: Mechanism and clinical significance. *Radiographics* 6:891–911, 1986.

RAMIREZ H, BLATT ES, HIBRI NS: Computed tomographic identification of calcified optic nerve drusen. *Radiology* 148:137–139, 1983.

REESE AB: *Tumors of the Eye.* New York, Harper & Row, 1976.

ROOTMAN J, ELLSWORTH M, HOFBAUER J, KITCHEN D: Orbital extension of retinoblastoma: A clinicopathologic study. *Can J Ophthalmol* 13:72–80, 1978.

ROOTMAN J, CHAN KW: Neuroblastoma, in Rootman J, *Diseases of the Orbit,* New York, Lippincott, 1988, p 425.

ROTHFUS WE, CURTIN HD, SLAMOVITZ TL, KENNERDELL JS: Optic nerve/sheath enlargement. *Radiology* 150:409–415, 1984.

ROTHFUS WE, CURTIN HD: Extraocular muscle enlargement: A CT review. *Radiology* 151:677–681, 1984.

RUSSELL DS, RUBENSTEIN LJ: *Pathology of Tumours of the Nervous System.* Baltimore, Williams & Wilkins, 1977.

SANDBERG-WOLLHEIM M, BYNK EH, CRONQUIST S, HOLTAS S, PLATZ P, RYDER LP: A long-term prospective study of optic neuritis: Evaluation of risk factors. *Ann Neurol* 27:386–393, 1990.

SAVAGE GL, CENTARO A, ENOCH JM, NEWMAN NM: Drusen of the optic nerve head: An important model. *Ophthalmology* 92:793–799, 1985.

SERGOTT RC, GLASER JS, CHARYULU K: Radiotherapy for idiopathic inflammatory pseudotumor: Indications and results. *Arch Ophthalmol* 99:853–856, 1981.

SEVEL D, KRAUSZ H, PONDER T, CENTENO R: Value of computed tomography for the diagnosis of a ruptured eye. *J Comput Assist Tomogr* 7:870–875, 1983.

SHELLOCK FG: MR imaging of metallic implants and materials: A compilation of the literature. *AJR* 151:811–814, 1988.

SHENCK JF, HART HR Jr, FOSTER TH, EDELSTEIN WA, BOTTOMLEY PA, REDINGTON RW, HARDY CJ, ZIMMERMAN RA, BILANIUK LT: Improved MR imaging of the orbit at 1.5 T with surface coils. *AJNR* 6:193–196, 1985.

SHERMAN JL, MCLEAN IW, BRAILLIER DR: Coat's disease: CT—pathologic correlation in two cases. *Radiology* 146:77–78, 1983.

SHIELDS JA: Current approaches to the diagnosis and management of choroidal melanomas. *Surv Ophthalmol* 21:443–463, 1977.

SIMMONS JD, LAMASTERS D, CHAR D: Computed tomography of ocular colobomas. *AJR* 141:1223–1226, 1983.

SIMON J, SZUMOSKI J, TOTTERMAN S, KIDO D, EKHOLM S, WICKS A, PLEWES D: Fat-suppression MR imaging of the orbit. *AJNR* 9:961–968, 1988.

SMITH CG, GALLIE BL, MORIN JD: Normal and abnormal development of the eye, in Crawford JS, Morin JD (eds): *The Eye in Childhood,* New York, Grune & Stratton, 1983.

SOLOWAY HB: Radiation-induced neoplasms following curative therapy for retinoblastoma. *Cancer* 12:1984–1988, 1966.

SOM PM, SHUGAR JMA: The CT classification of ethmoid mucoceles. *J Comput Assist Tomogr* 4:199–203, 1980.

SOM PM: CT of the paranasal sinuses. *Neuroradiology* 27:189–201, 1985.

SOM PM, DILLON WP, FULLERTON GD, ZIMMERMAN RA, RAJAGOPALAN B, MARON Z: Chronically obstructed sinonasal secretions: Observations on T1 and T2 shortening. *Radiology* 172:515–520, 1989.

STARR H, ZIMMERMAN L: Extrascleral extension and orbital recurrence of malignant melanomas of the choroid and ciliary body. *Int Ophthalmol Clin* 2:369, 1962.

STERN J, JACOBIEC FA, HOUSEPIAN EM: The architecture of optic nerve gliomas with and without neurofibromatosis. *Arch Ophthalmol* 98:505–511, 1980.

STERNBERG P, DE JUAN E, MICHELS RG, AUER C: Multivariate analysis of prognostic factors in penetrating ocular injuries. *Am J Ophthalmol* 98:467–472, 1984.

SULLIVAN JA, HARMS SE: Surface coil MR imaging of orbital neoplasms. *AJNR* 7:29–34, 1986.

TABADDOR K: Unusual complications of iophendylate injection myelography. *Arch Neurol* 29:435–436, 1973.

TADMOR R, NEW PFJ: Computed tomography of the orbit with special emphasis of coronal sections: 1. Normal anatomy. *J Comput Assist Tomogr* 2:24–34, 1978.

TENNER NS, TROKEL SL: Demonstration of the intraorbital portion of the optic nerves by pneumoencephalography. *Arch Ophthalmol* 79:572–573, 1968.

TOWBIN R, HAN BK, KAUFMAN RA, BURKE M: Post-septal cellulitis: CT in diagnosis and management. *Radiology* 158:735–737, 1986.

TROKEL SL, HILAL SK: CT scanning in orbital diagnosis, in Thompson HS (ed): *Topics in Neuro-ophthalmology.* Baltimore, Williams & Wilkins, 1979, pp 336–346.

TROKEL SL, JAKOBIEC FA: Correlation of CT scanning and pathologic features of ophthalmic Graves' disease. *Ophthalmology* 88:553–564, 1981.

TURNER RM, GUTMAN I, HILAL SK, BEHRENS M, ODEL J: CT of drusen bodies and other calcific lesions of the optic nerve: Case report and differential diagnosis. *AJNR* 4:175–178, 1983.

UNGER J: Orbital apex fractures: The contribution of computed tomography. *Radiology* 150:713–717, 1984.

UNSOLD R, NEWTON TH, HOYT WF: Technical note—CT examination of the optic nerve. *J Comput Assist Tomogr* 4:560–563, 1980*a*.

UNSOLD R, DEGROOT J, NEWTON TH: Images of the optic nerve: Anatomic CT correlation. *AJR* 135:767–773, 1980*b*.

VANNIER MW, MARSH JL, KNAPP RH: Three-dimensional reconstruction from CT scans: Disorders of the head. *Appl Radiol* 16:117–127, 1987.

VERMESS M, HAYNES BF, FANCI AS, WOLFF SM: Computed assisted tomography of orbital lesions in Wegener's granulomatosis. *J Comput Assist Tomogr* 2:45–48, 1978.

WEBER AL, TADMOR R, DAVIS R, ROBERSON G: Malignant tumors of the sinuses. *Neuroradiology* 16:443–448, 1978.

WEISMAN RA, SAVINO PJ, SCHUT L, SCHATZ NJ: Computed tomography in penetrating wounds of the orbit with retained foreign bodies. *Arch Otolaryngol* 109:265–268, 1983.

WHITNALL SE: *The Anatomy of the Human Orbit.* London, Frowder, Hodder and Stoughton, 1921.

WILNER HI, COHN EM, KLING G, JAMPEL RS: Computer assisted tomography in experimentally induced orbital pseudotumor. *J Comput Assist Tomogr* 2:431–455, 1978.

WING SD, HUNSAKER JN, ANDERSON RE, VANDYCK HJL, OSBORN AG: Direct sagittal computed tomography in Graves' ophthalmopathy. *J Comput Assist Tomogr* 3:820–824, 1979.

WRIGHT JE, STEWART WB, KROHEL GB: Clinical presentation and management of lacrimal gland tumors. *Br J Ophthalmol* 63:600–606, 1979.

WRIGHT RM, SWIETEK PA, SIMMONS ML: Eye artifacts from mascara in MRI. *AJNR* 6:652, 1985.

YANOFF M, FINE BS: *Ocular Pathology. A Text and Atlas.* Hagerstown, MD., Harper & Row, 1975.

YOUSEM DM, LEXA FJ, BILANIUK LT, ZIMMERMAN RA: Rhabdomyosarcomas in the head and neck: MR imaging evaluation. *Radiology* 177:683–686, 1990.

ZIMMERMAN RA, VIGNAUD J: Ophthalmic arteriography, in Arger PH (ed): *Orbit Roentgenology,* New York, Wiley, 1977, pp 135–169.

ZIMMERMAN RA, BILANIUK LT, LITTMAN P: Computed tomography of pediatric craniofacial sarcoma. *CT: J Comput Tomogr* 2:113–121, 1978.

ZIMMERMAN RA, BILANIUK LT: Computed tomography in the evaluation of patients with bilateral retinoblastomas. *CT: J Comput Tomogr* 3:251–257, 1979.

ZIMMERMAN RA, BILANIUK LT: CT of orbital infection and its cerebral complications. *Am J Roentgenol Radium Ther Nucl Med* 134:45–50, 1980*a*.

ZIMMERMAN RA, BILANIUK LT: Computed tomography of primary and secondary craniocerebral neuroblastoma. *AJNR* 1:431–434, 1980*b*.

ZIMMERMAN RA, GUSNARD DA, BILANIUK LT: Pediatric craniocervical spiral CT. To be published.

CRANIOCEREBRAL ANOMALIES

Debra A. Gusnard

Malformations of the central nervous system (CNS) are relatively common, constituting between 5 and 10 percent of all malformations (Myrianthopoulos 1977) and approximately one-third of those diagnosed after birth (Zimmerman 1988). These malformations vary in clinical severity. Some are lethal in utero or in early infancy or childhood, others are not incompatible with life but are associated with significant disability, and still others have minimal manifestations that are only hinted at on careful neuropsychological testing. Their clinical variability is matched by their morphological diversity, and both of these factors have prevented the establishment of an easily workable comprehensive classification.

The induction of a malformation is thought to depend on a specific insult to the developing brain. Only in this century have some of these insults (e.g., chromosomal aberrations, infectious agents, and toxins) been identified. Such potentially noxious influences are diverse, but the mechanisms by which specific patterns of malformation occur are thought to be limited (Poswillo 1976). The developing embryo (fetus) is believed to have a limited array of responses to noxious stimuli, with these responses depending on its gestational age. Consequently, while the cellular and organogenic mechanisms of malformation are still poorly understood, it is likely that the timing of an insult—its influence on a particular stage(s) of morphogenesis—is more critical in its influence on the ultimate pattern of malformation than is the inciting agent. Only a minority of CNS malformations involve specific chromosomal abnormalities or teratogens that can be shown to be a clearly pathogenetic factor. In most cases the pathogenesis is unknown. Many researchers believe that this process involves a complex interplay between environmental influences and the genetic susceptibility of the fetus.

Several attempts to classify anomalies have been made based on radiological findings. Harwood-Nash and Fitz (1976) proposed a classification based on the work of Yakovlev (1959) and DeMyer (1971), which distinguished disorders of so-called organogenesis from disorders of histogenesis. Disorders of organogenesis were regarded as those which result in an alteration in gross morphology while retaining some embryonal form of brain structure. Disorders were subdivided on the basis of a relatively crude conception of developmental stages (i.e., disorders of neural tube closure, diverticulation, sulcation and migration, brain size, and destructive lesions). By contrast, disorders of histogenesis (phakomatoses, neoplasia, and vascular lesions) were regarded as deriving primarily from differentiation of specific deviant cell lines. The greater contrast resolution and multiple planes of visualization provided by MRI have been used to further define and characterize certain malformations. With this information, some authors (Naidich 1987) have continued to emphasize classifications based on groups of disorders with morphologically similar features (i.e., disorders of neural tube closure, disorders of cerebral hemisphere organization, dysplasias of the cerebral cortex, dysplasias of cerebellar hemisphere organization, and dyshistogenesis [phakomatoses]), while others (Van der Knaap 1988; Zimmerman 1988) have proposed a classification derived from the work of Volpe (1977), which is based on an integration of morphological data with what is currently known about embryogenesis (i.e., categories based on stages of dorsal induction, ventral induction, neuronal proliferation, neuronal migration, organization, and myelination). In either scheme, some anomalies remain difficult to classify. This presumably reflects our incomplete understanding of the processes of malformation. Nonetheless, while current classification schemes are not necessarily complete, they provide useful starting points for understanding many anomalies and will be described in this chapter.

OVERVIEW OF THE DEVELOPMENT OF THE CNS

Six relatively well understood events provide an organizational framework for conceptualizing developmental stages in the formation of the CNS. Distinctions among many of the congenital brain anomalies can be regarded as being due to derangements that occur during these stages (Volpe 1977; Van der Knaap 1988; Zimmerman 1988) (Table 6-1). These stages are obviously not discrete, but there are peak time periods during which they occur. Maldevelopment at one stage can be anticipated to adversely influence development at subsequent stages.

Dorsal Induction

During the third and fourth weeks of gestation, the neural plate is induced to differentiate from the adjacent ectoderm by the underlying notochord and prechordal mesoderm. The neural plate proceeds to invaginate, with its lateral margins meeting dorsally first in the region of the future medulla and then rostrally and caudally, thus forming the complete neural tube. Interaction between the developing neural tube and the adjacent mesoderm stimulates the formation of meningeal structures (pia, arachnoid, and dura) and osseous structures (skull and spinal vertebrae).

Examples of failures of dorsal induction include Chiari II malformation and encephalocele.

Table 6-1 Stages of Development of the Central Nervous System and Corresponding Anomalies

EMBRYOLOGIC STAGE	GESTATIONAL AGE	ANOMALIES (NOT INCLUSIVE)
Dorsal induction	3–4 weeks	Chiari malformations Encephalocele (frontal-occipital)
Ventral induction	2 months	Holoprosencephaly Septo-optic dysplasia Encephalocele (basal) Dysgenesis of corpus callosum Dandy-Walker malformation Joubert's syndrome
Neuronal proliferation	3–5 months	Megalencephaly vera Micrencephaly vera Hemimegalencephaly Phakomatoses
Neuronal migration (and organization)	3–6 months	Schizencephaly Agyria-pachygyria Polymicrogyria Heterotopias
Myelination	7 months–2 years	Delayed myelination

Ventral Induction

Ventral induction refers to the interaction which takes place between the prechordal mesoderm and the neural tube at the rostral embryonic pole during the second month of gestation, particularly during the fifth and sixth weeks, resulting in the formation of the face and brain. During this period there is development of the three primary brain vesicles: the forebrain (prosencephalon), midbrain (mesencephalon), and hindbrain (rhombencephalon). During the fifth week, the forebrain initiates its division into the telencephalon and diencephalon and the hindbrain initiates its division into the metencephalon and myelencephalon. At the same time, the facial primordia and anlage of the cartilaginous skull base appear from the first two pairs of branchial arches. Between the fifth and eighth weeks, generally symmetrical lateral outgrowths develop into progressively distinct cerebral hemispheres with a lobar structure and the rudiments of a humanlike face. Accompanying the development of forebrain bilaterality is the development of templates of major commissures (e.g., the corpus callosum).

Examples of derangements of ventral induction include holoprosencephaly, septo-optic dysplasia, encephalocele (nasal, ethmoidal, and sphenoidal), and dysgenesis of the corpus callosum.

Though not referred to in the originally proposed term *ventral induction,* significant events also take place at this time along the dorsal aspect of the metencephalon. Thickenings occur on both sides of the midline forming the rhombic lips, which constitute the primordia of the cerebellar hemispheres. These structures fuse superiorly in the midline at the end of the second month, initiating the formation of the cerebellar vermis. Completion of the vermis occurs by the end of the fifteenth week. This process probably is closely related to development of the fourth ventricle, its roof (including the choroid plexus), and its outlets. The details of this process, however, are not well understood.

Examples of derangements of rhombic lip evolution include Dandy-Walker malformation and Joubert's syndrome.

Neuronal Proliferation

This developmental event is accelerated near the beginning of the third month of gestation and lasts until about the fifth month. After constitution of the rudimentary external form of the brain, significant growth based on primitive cellular proliferation takes place. This phenomenon occurs in the developing cerebral hemispheres and posterior fossa structures along the subependymal margins. The first postmitotic cells to differentiate are the neuronal cells; this occurs at approximately 10 to 18 weeks of gestation (significant glial cell differentiation associated with further cellular proliferation occurs between approximately 30 weeks of gestation and a year or more after birth).

Examples of derangements of cellular proliferation include megalencephaly (hemimegalencephaly), micrencephaly vera, and the phakomatoses (e.g., neurofibromatosis, tuberous sclerosis, and Sturge-Weber syndrome).

Neuronal Migration and Neuronal Organization

This developmental event overlaps with the phase of neuronal proliferation, occurring predominantly in the third to sixth months of gestation. Postmitotic cells destined to be neurons travel in patterned waves from their sites of origin along an intricate supporting network of glial cell processes to reach the developing cortex and deep nuclei (Berry 1965). This process takes place in both the cerebral hemispheres and the cerebellum, though some cells do migrate along the brain surface, such as the neurons destined to form the granular layer of the cerebellar cortex. Cellular migration is inseparable from some degree of organization within gray matter structures both at the level of cell pattern (e.g., the laminar architecture of the cerebral cortex) and at the level of gyral formation. This process influences the ultimate size, though not the essential configuration, of the commissures (e.g., the corpus callosum).

Examples of derangements of neuronal migration and organization that are visible on imaging studies include schizencephaly, agyria/pachygyria, polymicrogyria, and neuronal heterotopias.

Organization

Organization of neurons in regard to the elaboration of axonal and dendritic ramifications with the establishment of synaptic contacts is a process that is initiated in utero but is believed to continue for many years postnatally. Derangements of this process are likely to be present in at least some types of mental retardation. Most of these disorders of organization have no imaging manifestations with current technology.

Myelination

With the beginning of differentiation and proliferation of glial (specifically oligodendroglial) cells late in the second trimester, myelination becomes possible. Myelination begins in the third trimester and progresses rapidly after birth for the first 2 years, continuing at a progressively slower rate into adult life (Yakovlev 1967). Myelination begins in the peripheral nervous system (motor nerve roots before sensory nerve roots) and then extends to the central nervous system, progressing from the spinal cord to the brainstem and then to the cerebral hemispheres, where myelination of sensory pathways generally precedes that of motor pathways. The last pathways to myelinate are those involved in higher cortical functions, primarily in immediate subcortical locations.

MR imaging permits assessment of the postnatal progress of myelination (Fig. 6-1A–H). The pattern of changes in signal intensity on spin-echo images corresponding to this process has been described (Barkovich 1988*a;* Bird 1989; Deitrich 1988). Changes on T_1WI precede those on T_2WI. It has been suggested that this is due to an accumulation of the components of the myelin sheath (cholesterol and glycolipids) followed by the actual formation of the complete myelin sheath, a process that corresponds temporally to changes in the distribution of water that produce T_1 shortening before T_2 shortening (Barkovich 1988*a*). Myelinated pathways appear as high signal intensity on T_1WI and as low signal intensity on T_2WI. At birth, myelination is apparent in the medulla, the dorsal midbrain, the inferior and superior cerebellar peduncles, the ventrolateral nucleus of the thalamus, and the posterior limb of the internal capsule. These changes are somewhat more evident on T_1WI than on T_2WI. On T_1WI, a change in signal intensity is seen in the middle cerebellar peduncles by the end of the first month and throughout the deep cerebellar white matter by 3 months. On T_2WI, these changes are observed between approximately the second and third months of life and the eighth and eighteenth months of life, respectively. In the cerebral hemispheres, the pre- and postcentral gyri demonstrate changes in signal intensity on both T_1WI and T_2WI within the first month of life. At about the same time, changes in signal intensity are noted along the visual pathways from the optic chiasm through the optic radiations on T_1WI. On T_2WI changes progress along these portions of the visual pathway in the first 3 months of life. The anterior limb of the internal capsule appears to acquire myelin by about 3 months of age on T_1WI and between 7 and 11 months of age on T_2WI. Progressive thickening of the corpus callosum associated with changes in signal intensity corresponding to an increased bulk of myelinated axons proceeds from the splenium posteriorly to the genu anteriorly between 4 and 6 months on T_1WI and between 6 and 8 months on T_2WI. Areas of subcortical white matter, except in the rolandic and occipital regions, are the last to demonstrate myelination. Myelination proceeds from the occipital regions posteriorly to the frontal regions anteriorly; it is radiographically nearly complete by 8 months on T_1WI and by 18 to 24 months on T_2WI.

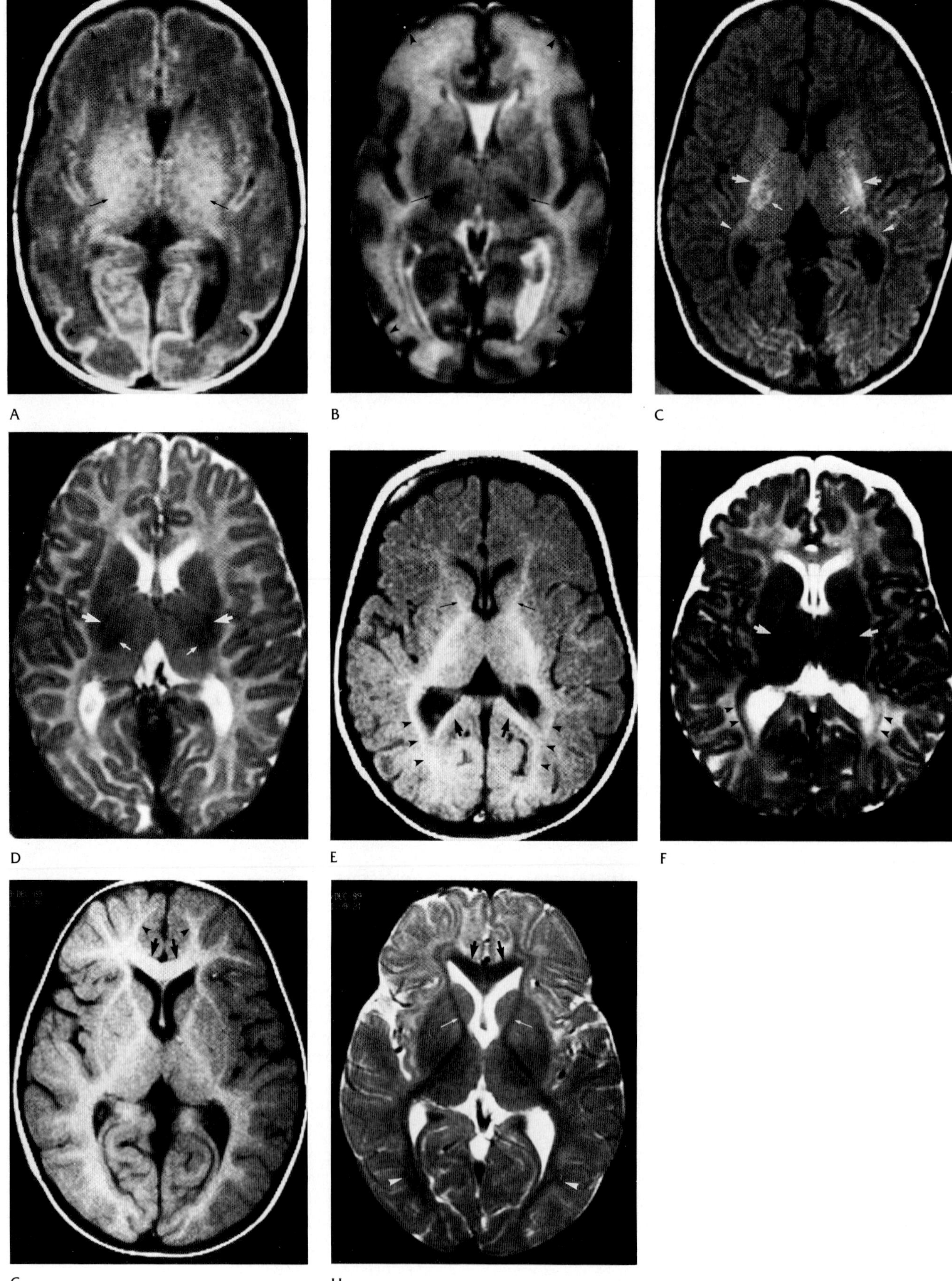
A
B
C
D
E
F
G
H

Derangements in myelination can be divided into those that are developmental and those that are "degenerative." Developmental derangements manifest delays in reaching the imaging milestones for myelination, which may be consequent to a variety of pre- and postnatal insults, including intrauterine infections and perinatal hypoxic events (Davison 1966; Naidich 1987). Degenerative derangements in myelination are a consequence of abnormalities of myelin metabolism or glial cell metabolism (Alexander's disease, Canavan's disease, Krabbe's disease, Pelizaeus-Merzbacher's disease, and metachromatic leukodystrophy). These entities are not truly congenital and will not be discussed further here.

In the following discussion, more detailed descriptions of some of the more common congenital anomalies and their MR and CT characteristics will be provided. It should be appreciated, however, that anomalies are just that—products of a disordering of normal formative processes to a greater or lesser degree, of which no two are exactly alike (Fig. 6-2A,B).

CONGENITAL ANOMALIES

Chiari Malformations

The Chiari malformations are the most common anomalies of the hindbrain. In 1891, Chiari reported a small group of cases in which he first described three types of hindbrain malformation (Chiari 1891) that have come to bear his name. In a more detailed publication 5 years later (Chiari 1896), he described the type I anomaly as an elongation of the cerebellar tonsils and the medial part of the inferior aspects of the cerebellar hemispheres into the cervical canal. He defined the type II anomaly as a displacement of part of the inferior vermis, the pons, and the medulla into the cervical canal and elongation of the fourth ventricle into the cervical canal. The rare type III anomaly has been described as a more severe variant of the type II anomaly, with an associated low occipital or high cervical (C1-C2) encephalocele. The relatively common type I malformation and type II (or Arnold-Chiari) malformation differ significantly in their clinical manifestations; this is consistent with their differences in regard to morphological abnormalities. These differences also suggest that the type I and type II anomalies are developmentally unrelated.

CHIARI I MALFORMATION

The type I malformation consists of a chronic tonsillar displacement below the foramen magnum. The malformation needs to be distinguished from acute tonsillar herniation secondary to increased intracranial pressure (pressure cones). The level to which the tonsils must descend in order to constitute the malformation has been debated. It has been suggested that more than 3 mm below a line joining the basion to the opisthion is sufficient

Figure 6-1 Normal morphological development and myelination. **A,B.** Axial T_1WI (600/15) and T_2WI (3000/120) images in a 31-week premature infant. Sylvian fissures and a few gyri and sulci, particularly in the parietooccipital region, have developed by this stage. Cortical gray matter (arrowheads) appears as a bright stripe and a dark stripe outlining the developing gyri on T_1WI and T_2WI, respectively. Note that the white matter appears diffusely hypointense on the T_1WI image and hyperintense on the T_2WI as a result of its relatively high water content except in a small portion of the posterior limb of the internal capsules and ventral portions of the thalami (arrows) on T_1WI and T_2WI, reflecting the beginning of the process of myelination in those areas. **C,D.** Normal 2-month-old infant. A nearly adult sulcal pattern is seen at this age. Cortical gray matter and underlying white matter are now nearly isointense on the T_1WI, while gray-white matter contrast has decreased to a lesser degree on the T_2WI, making the T_2WI more useful in the perception of structural detail at this age. On T_1WI, hyperintensity corresponding to progressing myelination is clearly evident in the posterior limb of the internal capsules (large arrows) and the ventral lateral nuclei of the thalami (small arrows), and beginning in the optic radiations (arrowheads). On T_2WI, relative hypointensity is becoming evident in most of the posterior limb of the internal capsules (large arrows) and the ventral lateral nuclei of the thalami (small arrows). **E,F.** Normal 4-month-old infant. In early infancy, signal intensity correlates to change in myelination first and most rapidly on T_1WI, as seen here. Progression to high signal intensity is clearly evident in the optic radiations proceeding into occipital subcortical white matter (arrowheads); progression has also occurred in the splenium of the corpus callosum (large arrows) and the anterior limb of the internal capsules (small arrows). On T_2WI, hypointensity is more evident throughout the posterior limb of the internal capsules (white arrows) and is seen in the optic radiations (black arrowheads) (more visible on the right as a result of asymmetry of ventricular trigones). Small bilateral subdural effusions are a consequence of recent uncomplicated meningitis. **G,H.** Normal 14-month-old. On T_1WI, nearly all changes in signal intensity in the white matter tracts have occurred by 8 months, so that a virtually adult appearance is seen at this age. Note the change in the genu of the corpus callosum (arrows) and arborization into the subcortical regions, including the frontal lobes (arrowheads). Changes are still occurring on T_2WI, which will be complete between approximately 18 and 24 months. At this patient's age, changes in signal intensity are complete in the corpus callosum (black arrows), the anterior limb of internal capsules (small white arrows), and the visual pathways, including the occipital subcortical tracts (white arrowheads). Note the difference in signal intensity between the latter and subcortical tracts in the frontal lobes, which remain incompletely myelinated.

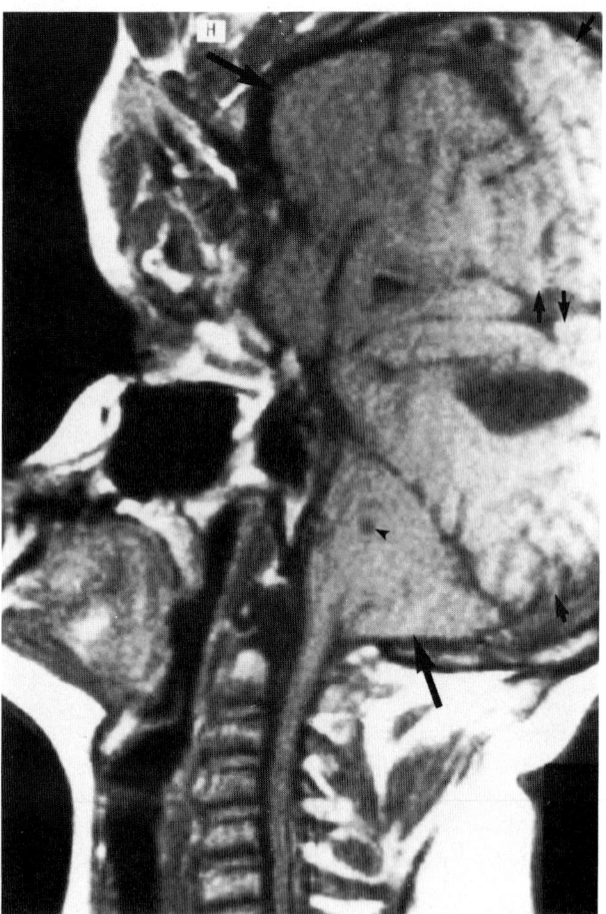

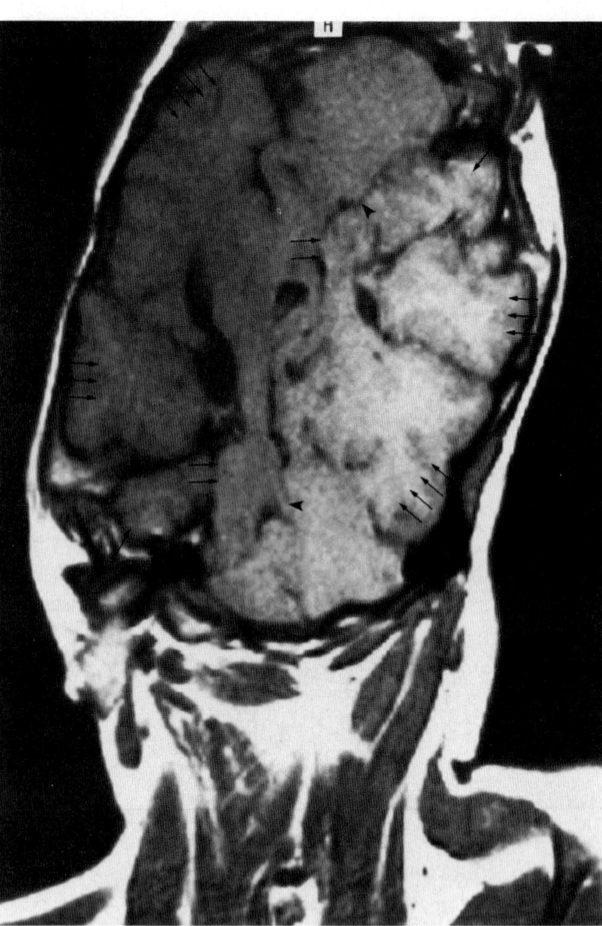

A B

Figure 6-2 Twins conjoined at the lateral aspect of the forehead (craniopagus). **A.** Sagittal T_1WI (600/15) demonstrates posterior fossa structures (large arrows) and portions of the occipital and parietal lobes (small arrows) of both twins. Posterior fossa structures are crowded in both twins; note virtual effacement of the fourth ventricle (arrowhead) in the larger twin (located more inferiorly). **B.** Coronal T_1WI (600/15) through the posterior aspects of the brains of both twins demonstrates contiguity and some interdigitation of structures of the two somewhat dysmorphic brains (arrowheads); no dural plane is identified between them. Portions of the twins' respective cerebellums (single arrows), brainstems (two arrows), temporal lobes (three arrows), and parietal lobes (four arrows) are seen.

(Barkovich 1986). Patients with tonsillar ectopia of this or a greater degree may or may not be symptomatic; it may be discovered incidentally at autopsy or on an MR scan obtained for unrelated reasons. When patients do present clinically, it is usually because of symptoms related to either brainstem compression at the foramen magnum or, more commonly, an associated syringohydromyelia. Most of these patients develop symptoms in the teenage or adult years, though symptomatic children as young as 2 years of age have been reported (Dauser 1988). The incidence of associated syringohydromyelia has been suggested to be as low as 20 percent (Banarji 1974) and, since the advent of MR, as high as 75 to 80 percent (Naidich 1987). There is no association of other brain anomalies with the type I malformation. Although the neural tissue involved in this anomaly is restricted to the cerebellum, the developmental origin appears to be variable. This is the case because associated pathology at the cervicomedullary junction, which in some cases appears fundamentally related to the anomaly, is variable. Some patients have craniocervical dysgenesis consisting of the Klippel-Feil anomaly, occipitalization of C1, or other anomalies, such as partial fusion of the cervical vertebrae. Others may have basiliar invagination, either congenital, as from anomalies of the clivus, or acquired. In many patients, no intrinsic bony abnormality is identified. Often the cerebellar tonsils themselves appear to be intrinsically abnormal, enlarged and peglike (Fig. 6-3A). The tonsils may be asymmetrical, with one extending more caudally than the other (Fig. 6-3B).

It is difficult to diagnose this malformation with certainty with plain CT. It may be suspected when images just below the level of the foramen magnum fail to demonstrate cerebrospinal fluid (CSF) density around the up-

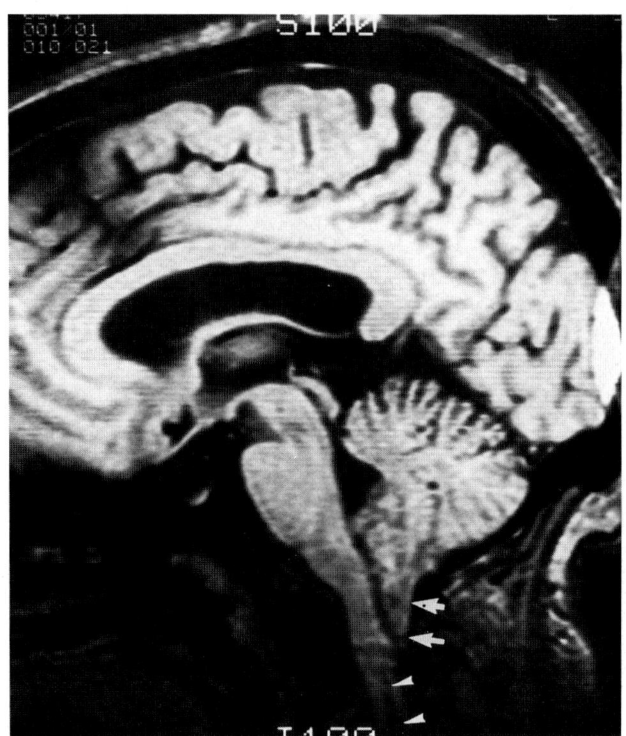

A

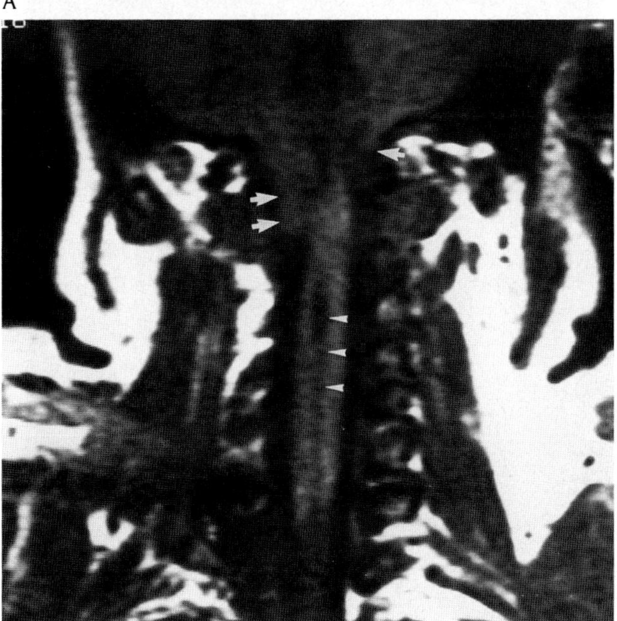

B

Figure 6-3 Chiari I malformation. **A.** Sagittal T_1WI (600/20) image reveals downward extension of peglike cerebellar tonsils through the foramen magnum to the level of C2 (arrows). The fourth ventricle is normally positioned. There is a hint of a syrinx in the cervical cord on this image (arrowheads). **B.** Coronal T_1WI (600/15) confirms the small syrinx cavity (arrowheads). There is asymmetry of the tonsillar displacement, with the right tonsil located more inferiorly than the left one (arrows).

per cervical cord. Before the advent of MR, confirmation depended on a demonstration of caudalization of the tonsils by myelography. An associated syringohydromyelia could be suggested when the spinal cord appeared widened and delayed postmyelogram CT demonstrated intramedullary high density resulting from entry of dye into the syrinx cavity within the widened cord. This means of diagnostic evaluation is no longer indicated unless the patient has a contraindication to obtaining an MR. MR is now the method of choice for evaluating abnormalities at the craniocervical junction and associated spinal cord pathology. Sagittal and coronal T_1WI most clearly demonstrate the normal to small posterior fossa and cerebellar tonsils that are low-lying relative to the foramen magnum. Syringohydromyelia is most commonly seen as a smoothly marginated elongated area of low density within the central portion of the cord (which may contain septations), beginning at the C2 level (Fig. 6-3A) and extending for a variable distance inferiorly (Fig. 6-3B); occasionally the upper margin of the syrinx cavity appears at a lower cervical level.

CHIARI II MALFORMATION

The Chiari II (or Arnold-Chiari) malformation is a morphologically more complex anomaly than the Chiari I malformation. By definition, it is characterized by cerebellar, brainstem, and fourth ventricular dysplasia (deformity) and caudal displacement (Fig. 6-4A). The severity of the characteristic hindbrain deformity covers a wide range so that in its milder forms in some patients, it may be difficult to distinguish radiographically from the Chiari I deformity (Fig. 6-4B). However, the greater spectrum of anomalies typically associated with the Chiari II malformation permits its proper identification in these cases. These other anomalies involve different elements of the neural axis, i.e., the midbrain, cerebral hemispheres, commissures, and ventricles, as well as mesodermal derivatives, i.e., the skull, intracranial dural partitions, and the spine, particularly in the lumbosacral and cervical regions. Several hypotheses have been proffered regarding the pathogenesis of the malformation (Barry 1957; Daniel 1958; Gardner 1959; McLone 1989). The tissue elements involved, however, suggest that the inciting influence and initiating maldevelopmental events occur during the phase of dorsal induction (3 to 4 weeks' gestation). Whether, for example, there is a primary dysgenetic process involving the hindbrain with faulty secondary bony development or a primary maldevelopment of bony structures (e.g., a small posterior fossa or a spinal dysraphic state) with secondary effects on the compartmentalization of the hindbrain structures is not yet known; nonetheless, maldevelopmental interaction at an early embryonic stage is apparent.

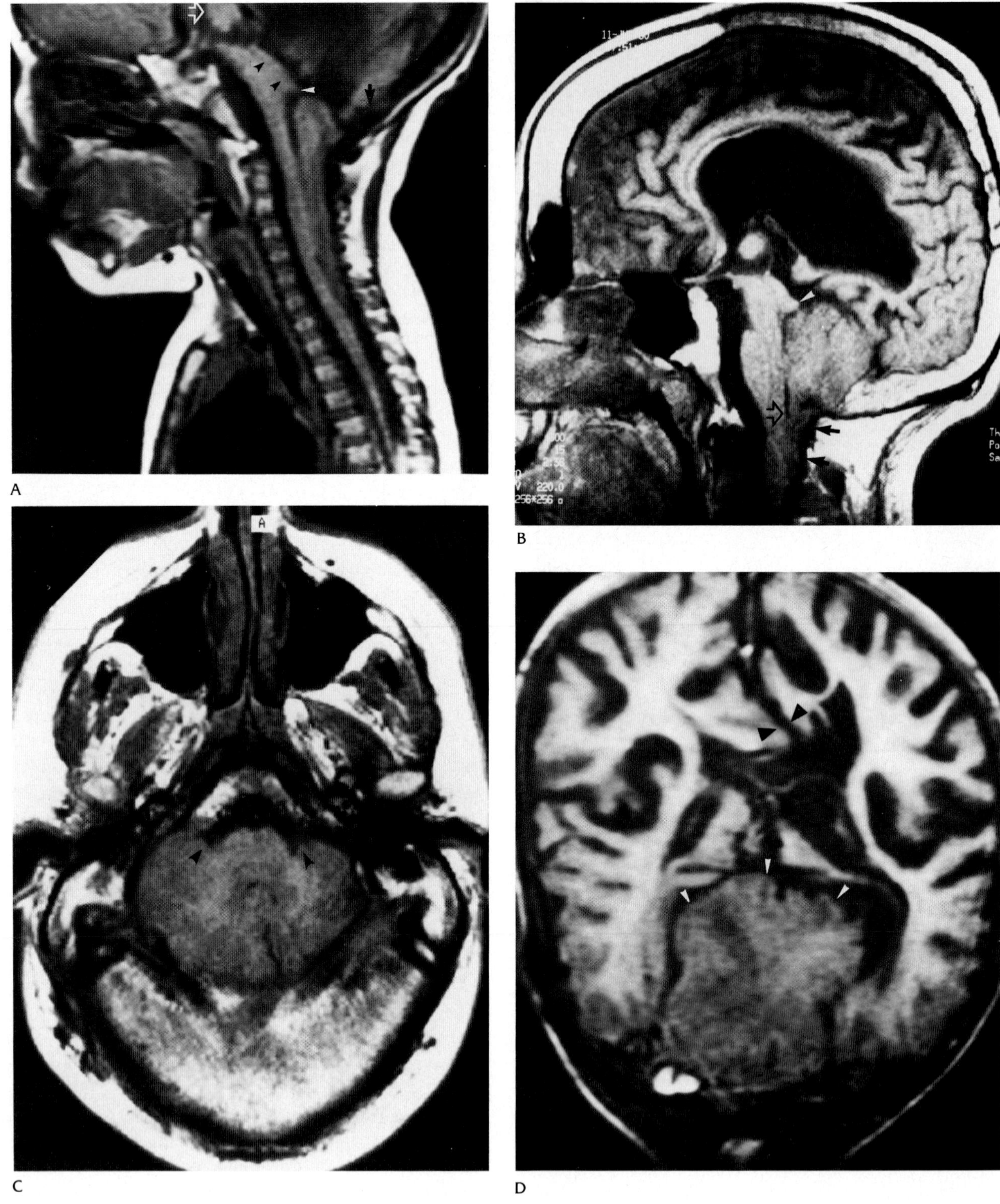

The Chiari II malformation is nearly always associated with a myelomeningocele (Ingraham 1943; Naidich 1983*b*); thus, all these patients present at birth, though not all are symptomatic in terms of the Chiari malformation at this time. Virtually all these patients develop hydrocephalus, the etiology of which has been speculated to be attributable to either aqueductal stenosis (primary or secondary to a hydrodynamic consequence of the repair of the myelomeningocele) or occlusion of CSF spaces at the level of the foramen magnum and upper

Figure 6-4 Chiari II malformation. **A.** Sagittal T_1WI (600/20) demonstrates the extremely small posterior fossa; note that the flow void of the torcula (black arrow) is nearly at the posterior lip of the foramen magnum. Deformed cerebellar vermis, cerebellar tonsils, and fourth ventricle extend downward into the spinal canal behind the cervical spinal cord to the T1 level. Other features of the malformation—the beaked tectum (white arrowhead), prominent massa intermedia (open white arrow), lack of flow void in the aqueduct (double black arrowheads) secondary to aqueductal stenosis, and the associated hydrocephalus—are evident. **B.** Sagittal T_1WI (600/15) demonstrates a less severe variant of the Chiari II malformation. In this case, more cerebellar tissue occupies the posterior fossa. Inferior vermis and cerebellar tonsils extend inferiorly only to the level of C2 (black arrows). Note, however, that the fourth ventricle extends below the foramen magnum (open black arrow). The midbrain appears somewhat elongated. The tectum is stubbier than in the previous case but is still beaked (white arrowhead). There is partial absence of the corpus callosum; there is thinning of the portion of the corpus callosum that formed secondary to hydrocephalus. Aqueductal stenosis is evident. The calvarium is thickened in this patient, who has been chronically shunted. **C.** Axial T_1WI (600/15) in the same patient at the level of the foramen magnum, which appears large, shows portions of the cerebellar hemispheres extending anteriorly, partially encircling the lower brainstem (arrowheads). Note the concavity of the clivus. **D.** Coronal T_1WI (600/20) demonstrates the "towering cerebellum" (white arrowheads) extending superiorly through the deficient tentorial incisura consequent to the small posterior fossa. Note absence of crossing commissural fibers in the expected location of the splenium of the corpus callosum (black arrowheads) as a result of partial agenesis of the corpus callosum. Also note the inferior parasagittal portions of the cerebral hemispheres in this region interdigitating and wandering off the midline as a result of falx hypoplasia. Cortical sulci are prominent in this shunted patient.

cervical canal. In contrast to the Chiari I malformation, because of the frequently associated anomalies in the Chiari II malformation, CT is often a useful modality in the initial characterization and follow-up of these chronically shunted patients. The CT signs of the Chiari II malformations have been described in detail (Zimmerman 1979; Naidich 1980*a–c,* 1983*b*). MR, however, demonstrates the parenchymal anomalies in greater detail and the craniocervical pathology more definitively.

Characteristically, there is a small posterior fossa and low tentorial attachment. In more severe cases, the attachment may approximate the foramen magnum (Fig. 6-4A). The cerebellar vermis, which may or may not be accompanied by the tonsils, impacts with the lower brainstem into the foramen magnum and upper cervical canal. These hindbrain structures appear variably elongated and dysplastic. The displaced pons is narrowed in its anteroposterior dimension, with the belly of the pons being imperceptible in some cases. The medulla extends below the foramen magnum; frequently, a posterior kinking occurs at the cervicomedullary junction. As the spinal cord may also be displaced downward, cervical and upper thoracic nerve roots commonly are angulated, ascending within the canal to exit at their intervertebral foramina. Scarring, gliosis, and parenchymal loss can affect the cerebellum so that folia may be poorly visualized and little cerebellar tissue may be present (Fig. 6-4A). Rather than gliosis, histologically the brainstem typically manifests distortion of its nuclei and fiber tracts. It has been postulated that this distortion, rather than the degree of brainstem herniation or the nature of the cervicomedullary deformity, accounts for the difficulties in breathing and swallowing experienced by some of these children (Wolpert 1988). The cerebellar hemisphere tissue that is present tends to crowd anterolaterally around the margins of the brainstem and may nearly encircle it (Fig. 6-4C). The inferiorly elongated fourth ventricle is typically narrowed in its anteroposterior dimension. There may be an associated syringohydromyelia; its incidence is lower than in the Chiari I malformation.

Like the hindbrain, the midbrain generally demonstrates vertical elongation. This may be recognized as an increased mamillopontine distance (Gammal 1987). The tectal plate appears to be posteroinferiorly pointed or "beaked," and this has been postulated to represent a secondary phenomenon consequent to temporal lobe compression from hydrocephalus or possibly a dysplasia (Friede 1989) with retention of the configuration of the early fetal tectum. The third ventricle is relatively small and often is associated with a large massa intermedia. Accessory massa intermedia with parasellar third ventricular pseudodiverticula and/or posterior third ventricular diverticula is noted occasionally (Gammal 1987).

Dysgenesis of the corpus callosum, consisting of the absence of the splenium more often than the absence of the entire commissure, is seen in the majority of these patients. The lateral ventricles appear dysmorphic and dilated posteriorly (colpocephaly), often asymmetrically, even after shunting. On coronal images, inferior pointing of the lateral ventricles near the foramen of Monro is frequently seen; this is due to prominence of the heads of the caudate nuclei (Naidich 1980*c*). Subependymal heterotopic gray matter is noted occasionally. Cerebral hemisphere sulci and the ambient and retropulvinar cisterns appear prominent after shunting, probably as an ex vacuo phenomenon consequent to dysplastic cerebral tissue. Redundant cortical gyri referred to as *stenogyria* or *polygyria* may be visible. These regions do not represent

Figure 6-5 Encephaloceles. **A.** Sagittal T_1WI (600/20) shows a large parietooccipital encephalocele containing a rim of compressed cortical tissue (arrowheads) around the expanded occipital horn of the lateral ventricle. **B.** Axial CT demonstrates a defect in the frontal bone at the level of its junction with the nasal bridge in this patient with a nasofrontal encephalocele (nasal "glioma"). Soft tissue density compatible with neural tissue (black arrowheads) is seen extending through this defect onto the midline of the face; lower density suggesting CSF is seen within the sac anteriorly (white arrowhead). **C,D.** Sagittal and coronal T_1WI (600/20) reveal a basal encephalocele extending downward through the sphenoid bone into the nasopharynx to the level of the hard palate (large white arrowheads). On the sagittal view (**C**), the thin stripe of lamina terminalis can be seen running anomalously to the bottom of the sac (small white arrowheads). As might be expected with this abnormality of the lamina terminalis, there is an associated agenesis of the corpus callosum. Note the radial orientation of the medial hemispheric sulci as they extend inferiorly to the margin of the third ventricle consequent to the lack of inversion of the cingulate gyrus and formation of the cingulate sulcus. On the coronal view (**D**), the inferior third ventricle (large white arrow), hypothalamus (small white arrows), and optic tracts (small white arrowheads) appear to be stretched inferiorly as they protrude into the sac. Note the characteristic configuration of the frontal horns secondary to agenesis of the corpus callosum.

polymicrogyria, since histologically they have a normal cortical laminar architecture.

In addition to the shallow posterior fossa, other mesodermal derivatives are frequently anomalous (Naidich 1980*a*). The foramen magnum is enlarged in a sagittal direction in approximately 70 percent of these patients. Scalloping or posterior concavity of the petrous bones is frequently seen; the internal auditory canals are consequently foreshortened. In most patients there is posterior concavity of the clivus, which involves the basiocciput (not the basisphenoid) (Fig. 6-4C).

Lückenschädel, or *craniolacunia,* refers to a dysplasia of the bones of the calvarium that is characterized by patches of irregularly shaped pitting along the inner table, which is visible on plain films and CT. They do not conform to the underlying cortical gyri. The anomaly is visible only in young infants, resolving radiographically within the first year of life.

The falx and tentorium are hypoplastic in virtually all these patients (Fig. 6-4D). An imaging correlate to hypoplasia or fenestration of the falx is interdigitation of gyri from the apposed surfaces of the cerebral hemispheres. The leaves of the caudally inserting tentorium are shallow and widely separated. Depending on the degree of crowding of posterior fossa structures, the resultant widened incisura may permit upward herniation or "towering" of the cerebellum (vermian pseudotumor) (Zimmerman 1979). The aforementioned mesodermal anomalies are not unique to the Chiari II malformation but in the aggregate are characteristic of it.

Encephaloceles

Developmental cranial defects may be of three types. Like spinal dysraphism, cranium bifidum may be occult, may be associated with extracranial extension of leptomeninges alone (meningocele), or may be associated with extracranial extension of leptomeninges and brain tissue (encephalocele). These defects are generally distinguished on the basis of their location in the skull: occipital (Fig. 6-5A), parietal, frontoethmoidal (Fig. 6-5B), and basal (sphenoidal) (Fig. 6-5C). Encephaloceles are much more common than are meningoceles and typically occur along the midline. The exceptions are defects in a parietal location, which are occasionally off the midline; in this location, meningoceles are reportedly more common than are encephaloceles (Friede 1989).

The relative incidence of types of encephaloceles varies with the population studied. In the western hemisphere the majority of encephaloceles are occipital, while in the Asian population those in a frontoethmoidal location are the most common. The rarest type occurs in a basal location; the bony defect in this case is transethmoidal, sphenoethmoidal, or transsphenoidal. It is postulated that the defect in development varies with the site: Those involving the membranous bones of the calvarium probably are consequent to an insult at a somewhat earlier stage (dorsal induction) than are those involving the endochondral skull base, which commonly are associated with facial clefts (stage of ventral induction) (e.g., frontonasal or intraorbital encephaloceles are commonly associated with nasal clefts, and basal encephaloceles with upper lip clefts) (Naidich 1983*a*).

CT is sensitive in the depiction of the bony defect (Fig. 6-5B) (Byrd 1978; Diebler 1983) but is much less sensitive in demonstrating the herniated sac's contents. MR demonstrates the sac's contents with much greater accuracy (Fig. 6-5A,C) (Curnes 1988); this can be critical when surgery is contemplated. Basal encephaloceles must be properly diagnosed and distinguished from other nasopharyngeal masses to obviate the catastrophic consequences of an attempted biopsy. Sagittal and coronal T_1WI are particularly useful for displaying the pathology and the commonly associated malformations (Fig. 6-5C,D). Knowledge of the position of major dural sinuses and the course of major cerebral arteries relative to the encephalocele's contents can influence neurosurgical planning, since repair of encephaloceles that contain

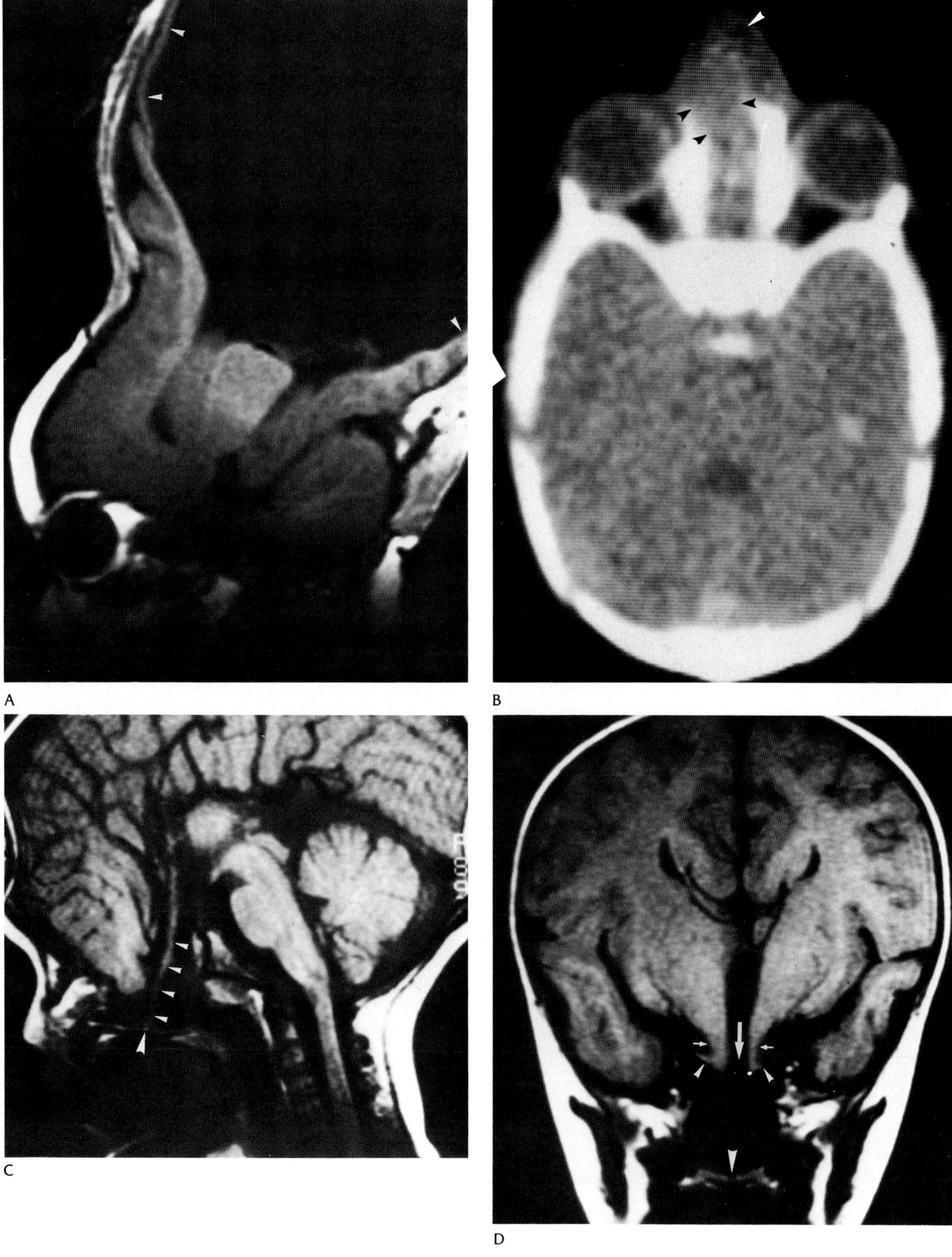
A
B
C
D

these structures can be hazardous. MR angiography will probably be a useful screening measure in this regard. The contents of an encephalocele may be more or less structurally organized. Formed cerebellar or cerebral tissue having a normal gyral pattern and containing portions of the ventricular system (which can become trapped and may distend if they contain choroid plexus) may herniate (Fig. 6-5A); in other cases, more disorganized islands of neuroectodermal tissue surrounded by highly vascularized (fetal) leptomeningeal tissue protrude through the defect into the sac. Other nervous system anomalies are frequently associated with encephaloceles, though they vary with the site: Dandy-Walker malformation and Chiari III malformation (occipital), dysgenesis of the corpus callosum (parietal), dysgenesis of the corpus callosum, callosal lipomas and globe anomalies such as microphthalmia/anophthalmia (frontoethmoidal), and agenesis of the corpus callosum and optic nerve dysplasias (basal). The prognosis depends on the nature of the contents of the cephalocele as well as the associated anomalies.

Holoprosencephaly

Holoprosencephaly refers to a spectrum of malformations consisting of midline anomalies of varying degrees of severity which affect the cerebrum and facial structures, leaving the brainstem and cerebellum intact. Although the details of their development are incompletely understood, these anomalies appear to derive from a disturbance of induction of the prosencephalon and premaxillary segments of the face, which takes place in the first 4 to 6 weeks of gestation, resulting in incomplete or absent cleavage of the prosencephalon into paired optic and cerebral vesicles and incomplete differentiation of the telencephalon from the diencephalon. Chromosomal abnormalities, including trisomy 13, deletion of the short arm of chromosome 18, and ring chromosome 18, and various forms of mosaicism are present in some cases of holoprosencephaly (Roach 1975). Patients with chromosomal abnormalities typically have associated visceral malformations (e.g., cardiac anomalies, syndactyly). A classification of the cerebral and facial anomalies into three subtypes corresponding to degrees of severity has been proposed (DeMyer 1977); these are referred to as the alobar, semilobar, and lobar types, respectively.

In alobar holoprosencephaly, the most severe manifestation of the anomaly, there is no detectable interhemispheric fissure. A horseshoe-shaped or crescent-shaped monoventricle spans the midline, communicating posteriorly with a dorsal cyst (Fig. 6-6). The thalami are fused. The olfactory tracts are absent or hypoplastic. Severe midline facial anomalies ranging from marked hypotelorism to cyclopia are frequently present. Those who are more severely affected typically are stillborn or fail to survive the neonatal period.

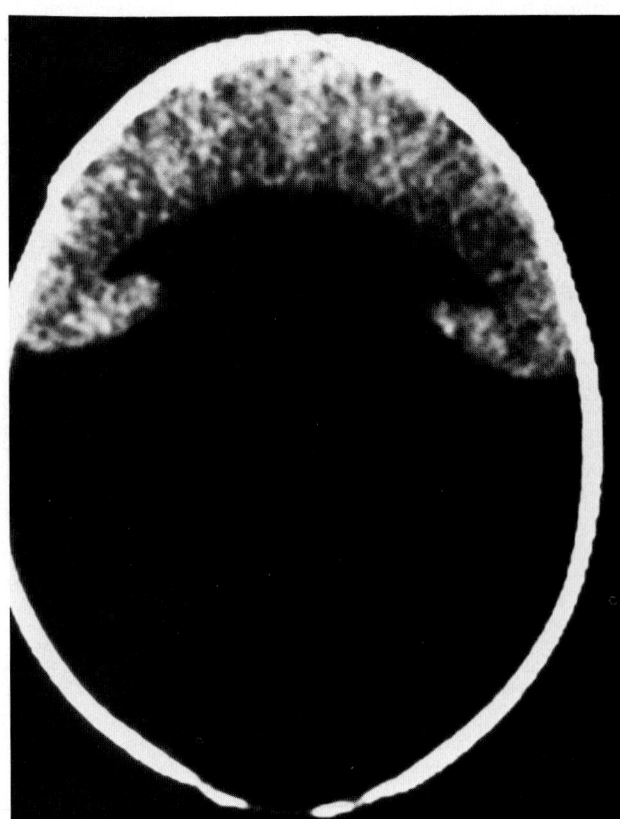

Figure 6-6 Alobar holoprosencephaly. On this axial CT at the level of the expected location of the bodies of the lateral ventricles, there is a crescent-shaped monoventricle which appears to be continuous with a large dorsal cyst. Characteristically, there is absence of an interhemispheric fissure and falx cerebri. The cerebrum forms a single curvilinear mass crossing the midline in the frontal region.

In semilobar holoprosencephaly, signs of partial cleavage of the primitive prosencephalon are present, consisting of varying degrees of development of an interhemispheric fissure and falx posteriorly. Discrete occipital lobes and atria of the lateral ventricles are seen, though incomplete separation of the hemispheres is noted more anteriorly (Fig. 6-7A). Incomplete separation of the thalami and only a rudimentary third ventricle and hippocampal formation are seen. A spleniumlike structure is present, but the rostral corpus callosum is not (Fig. 6-7B). The frontal lobes and rostral basal ganglia are not differentiated (Fig. 6-7C). There may be facial anomalies characterized by hypotelorism and cleft lip and palate.

While the alobar type and several of the features of the semilobar type of holoprosencephaly may be recognizable on CT (Fitz 1983; Altman 1984), more subtle manifestations of the anomaly may be appreciated only with the greater detail and multiplanar capability of MR. Lobar holoprosencephaly, for example, may have only a few features which distinguish it from a normal brain, such

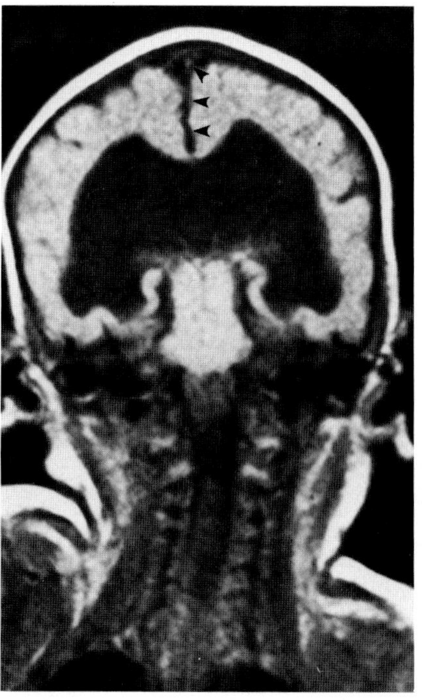
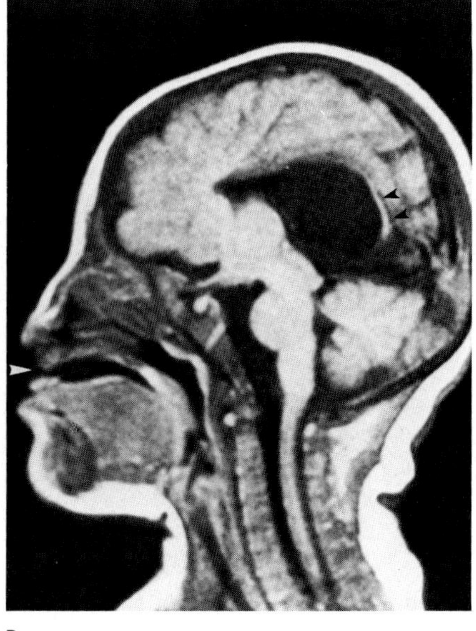
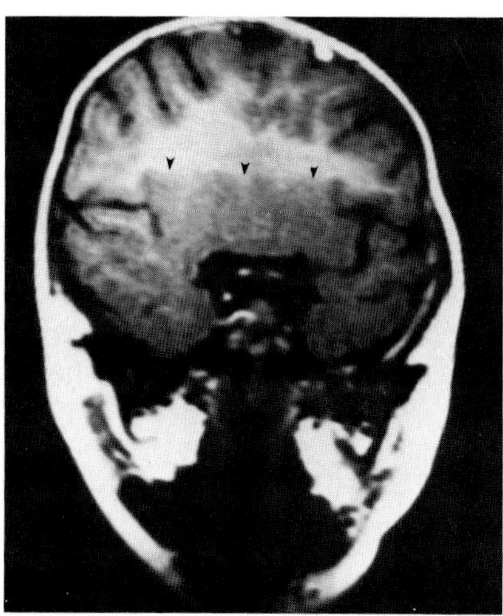

A B C

Figure 6-7 Semilobar holoprosencephaly. **A.** Coronal T_1WI (600/20) reveals an interhemispheric fissure and falx cerebri (arrowheads) between the parietal lobes posteriorly but absence of the interventricular septum and a single large horseshoe-shaped ventricle at this level. **B.** Sagittal T_1WI (600/20) demonstrates the dysmorphic lateral ventricular system prominent posteriorly and marginated posterosuperiorly by an attenuated spleniumlike structure (black arrowheads). There is no suggestion of callosal structure more anteriorly. Note the absence of a portion of the upper lip caused by clefting (white arrowhead); midline facial anomalies (e.g., clefts) are frequently associated with the more severe forms of holoprosencephaly. **C.** Coronal T_1WI (600/20) depicting structures anterior to those in **A.** Lack of separation of the anterior cerebrum into distinct frontal lobes is shown by the absence of interhemispheric fissure and falx cerebri and single malformed gray matter "basal ganglia complex" (arrowheads).

as the necessarily absent septum pellucidum and incomplete separation of the frontal lobes; in this case MR may actually be necessary for diagnosis.

Septo-Optic Dysplasia

Septo-optic dysplasia (DeMorsier's syndrome) is an anomaly of midline structures which in its fullest extent is characterized by the triad of (1) absence or hypoplasia of the septum pellucidum, (2) hypoplasia of the optic nerves, and (3) hypothalamic-pituitary dysfunction of a varying degree. The clinical manifestations are variable, but hypoplasia of the optic disks on ophthalmologic examination and growth retardation suggest the diagnosis. The findings on imaging studies may in fact be subtle. Small optic nerves and canals may be visible on CT (Manelfe 1979; O'Dwyer 1980), while small nerves and a small chiasm may be seen on MR (Fig. 6-8A,B), but determining whether these structures are hypoplastic is often difficult. Frequently, the more obvious finding is an absence of the septum pellucidum, which is associated with a boxlike appearance of the frontal horns on CT and MR (Fig. 6-8A). The anterior recesses of the third ventricle and the suprasellar cistern may appear prominent, while the hypothalamus appears diminutive. Schizencephaly has been reported to be associated in approximately half these cases (Barkovich 1988*d*).

Dysgenesis of the Corpus Callosum

Near the end of the phase of ventral induction, the dorsal portion of the thin rostral wall of the newly formed telencephalon—the lamina reunians—thickens and then invaginates and begins to elongate posteriorly along the midline cleft between the rudimentary cerebral hemispheres. Over the next 2 months this process leads to the formation of the massa commissuralis—the cellular framework for ingrowth of the commissural fibers of the corpus callosum. After the formation of the massa commissuralis there is immediate development of the corresponding portion of the corpus callosum. That is, the corpus callosum develops as neurons in the cerebral hemispheres are induced to send their axons into the

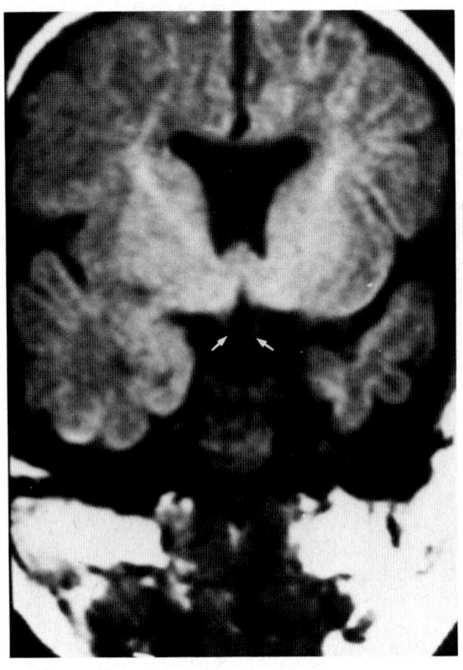

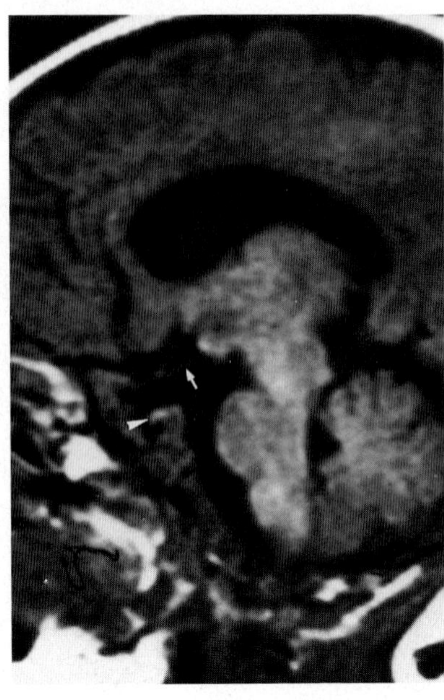

A B

Figure 6-8 Septo-optic dysplasia. **A.** Coronal T_1WI (600/15) demonstrates absence of the septum pellucidum and the relatively "boxlike" configuration of the frontal horns. The optic chiasm and tracts appear threadlike (arrows). **B.** Sagittal T_1WI (600/15) reveals a hypoplastic optic chiasm (arrow). The pituitary gland (arrowhead) may also be somewhat hypoplastic.

massa commissuralis (Rakic 1968) through the genu, then the body, then the splenium, and finally the rostrum. The rostrum, which is the short segment posteroinferior to the genu, is the exception to the otherwise anteroposterior trend in the development of the corpus callosum. When an insult interferes with the process of formation of the corpus callosum, it may lead to complete or partial absence of this structure. When there is only a partial absence, however, a predictable pattern results. The regions that normally form first are present, while those that form last are absent. Thus, with partial agenesis, the genu is always present. It may be present alone or may be associated with some portion of the body, with only the splenium and rostrum being absent.

Lack of formation of all or a portion of the corpus callosum is invariably accompanied by other alterations in brain morphology. These characteristic deformities may be useful signs in the identification of the callosal anomaly. However, on axial CT incomplete forms of agenesis may be difficult to recognize. By contrast, multiplanar MR permits ready identification of the anomaly and the segments of the corpus callosum which are involved (Fig. 6-5C,D) (Davidson 1985; Barkovich 1988*c*). In the absence of the corpus callosum, axons that otherwise would have crossed between the two hemispheres do reach the medial aspect of their respective cerebral hemispheres but then turn to run posteriorly, parallel to the interhemispheric fissure. These axonal fibers (Probst bundles) course longitudinally between the bodies of the lateral ventricles laterally and the cingulate gyri medially. These fiber bundles impress the medial walls of the ventricles, giving the frontal horns a characteristic crescent-shaped deformity on coronal images (Fig. 6-9A). There is a characteristic "straightening" or "paralleling" of the bodies of the lateral ventricles posteriorly, which is evident on axial images (Fig. 6-9B). The cingulate sulci do not form; consequently, the cingulate gyri do not become inverted but remain everted (Fig. 6-9A). Gyri dorsal to the cingulate gyri along the medial aspect of the hemispheres thus do not abut a cingulate sulcus but radiate unimpeded ventrally toward the third ventricle. This can be appreciated on sagittal MR images (Fig. 6-5C). In the absence of the capping effect of the corpus callosum, the third ventricle often protrudes superiorly between the two cerebral hemispheres, giving the impression that the interhemispheric fissure has been focally widened (Fig. 6-9A). An interhemispheric cyst, which may or may not communicate with the third ventricle, may be present in this location; it is usually distinguished by its larger size and mass effect. There is a characteristic irregular and often asymmetrical dilatation of the posterior portions of the bodies and trigones of the lateral ventricles. In the absence of the splenium of the corpus callosum, it is hypothesized that there is disorganization of the white matter that would have constituted crossing fibers in the parietooccipital regions, resulting in this altered ventricular appearance, which is known as *colpocephaly* (Fig. 6-9B).

In addition to malformation of the cingulate gyri, other limbic lobe anomalies are typically present (Atlas 1986). The cingulate gyri are continuous, via the cingulate isthmus, with the parahippocampal gyri. With dysgenesis of the corpus callosum, the parahippocampal gyri and more

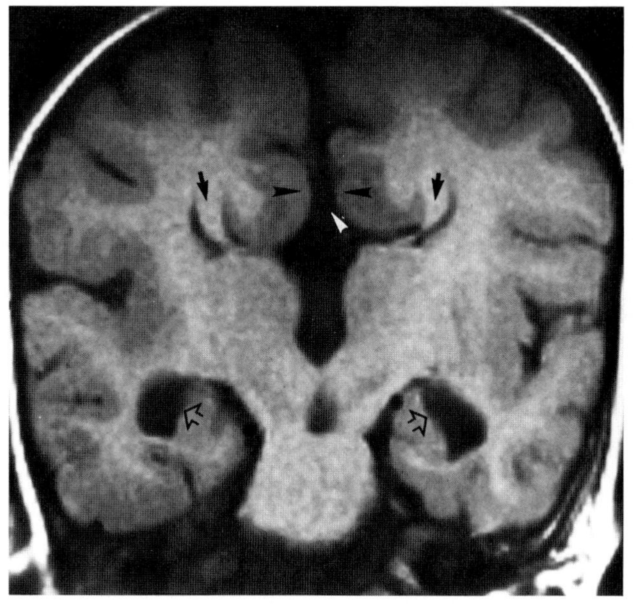

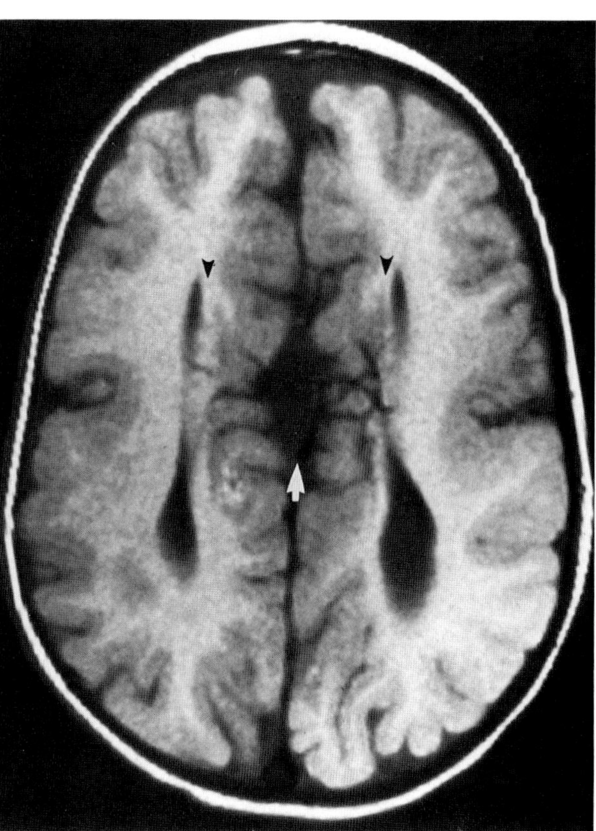

A B

Figure 6-9 Agenesis of the corpus callosum. **A.** Coronal T_1WI (600/20) demonstrates the persistently everted cingulate gyri (black arrowheads) and upward extension of the third ventricle (white arrowhead) above the level of the bodies of the lateral ventricles in continuity with the interhemispheric fissure. The frontal horns manifest a crescentic shape in this plane because of the impressions on their medial aspects made by the bundles of Probst (black arrows), which are white matter tracts normally destined to become crossing callosal fibers. Note the prominence (keyhole configuration) of the tips of the temporal horns as a result of underdeveloped Ammon's horns (open arrows). **B.** Axial T_1WI (600/20) demonstrates the high-riding third ventricle (white arrow) and characteristic parallel configuration of the bodies of the lateral ventricles, with the bundles of Probst running medially (black arrowheads). The flaring of the atria and occipital horns (referred to as *colpocephaly*) is due to the thinning of the Probst bundles posteriorly and associated disorganization of white matter tracts consequent to the absence of the corpus callosum.

medial hippocampal formations often appear underdeveloped, giving a patulous appearance to the temporal horns; this finding is best demonstrated on coronal images (Fig. 6-9A). The fornices are fiber bundles that normally arc posterosuperiorly from the hippocampal formations, run along the undersurface of the corpus callosum, pass anteriorly along the roof of the third ventricle, and subsequently run downward in the region of the foramina of Monro, terminating in the mamillary bodies. With complete agenesis of the corpus callosum, they appear to be widely separated anteriorly. They may appear to be hypoplastic, and their commissure (the hippocampal commissure) may be absent. With complete agenesis, the leaves of the septum pellucidum are divergent.

Other anomalies, though not typically associated with agenesis of the corpus callosum, occur more often with this anomaly than would be expected in a random association (Parrish 1979). These anomalies include interhemispheric lipomas, Chiari II malformations, Dandy-Walker malformations, basal encephaloceles, and heterotopias. Lipomas are relatively rare anomalies that may occur along the interhemispheric fissure in the presence or absence of the corpus callosum (Dean 1988). In its absence, interhemispheric lipomas are more commonly bulky midline masses, portions of which may insinuate into the bodies of the lateral ventricles on either side (Fig. 6-10A,B). On MR, these masses have the signal intensity of fat, appearing hyperintense on T_1WI and hypointense on T_2WI. Their characteristic fatty density is

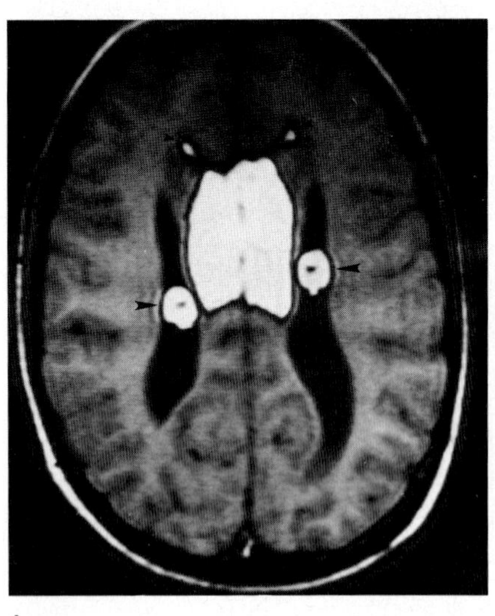

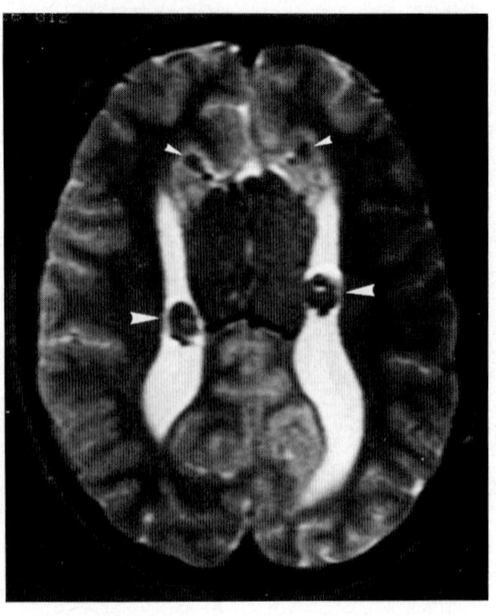

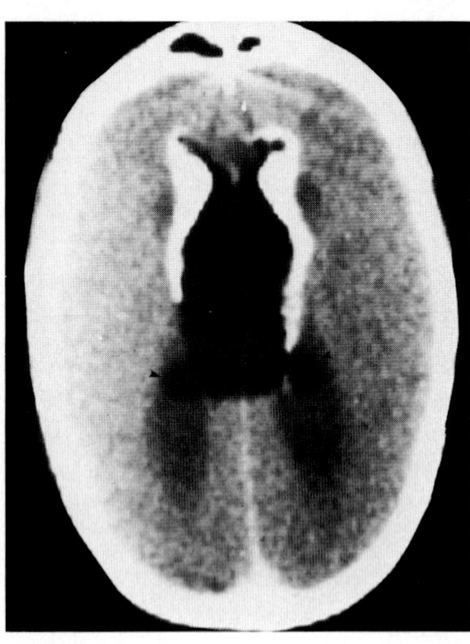

A B C

Figure 6-10 Agenesis of the corpus callosum associated with an interhemispheric lipoma. **A,B.** MRI: Axial T_1WI (600/20) and T_2WI (3000/80) reveal absence of the corpus callosum and a large lobulated mass following the signal intensity of fat along the interhemispheric fissure, insinuating into the adjacent cortical sulci (small arrowheads) and the bodies of both lateral ventricles (large arrowheads). Note the chemical shift artifact (black line) along the margins of the lipoma on these axial images. **C.** Axial CT demonstrates a bulky interhemispheric mass of fatty density extending into the bodies of the lateral ventricles (arrowheads); the mass is marginated bilaterally by dense calcification.

also readily detectable on CT (Fig. 6-10C); dystrophic calcification may appear along the margins of the lipoma. Traditionally, their pathogenesis has been ascribed to a faulty disjunction of cutaneous ectoderm from overlying mesoderm during the formation of the neural tube. More recently, faulty regression and maldifferentiation of the "meninx primitiva" (a neural crest derivative related in part to the primitive lamina reuniens, a source for the normal development of the subarachnoid cisterns) has been proposed (Truwit 1990). Agenesis of the corpus callosum is also a component of several syndromes, including Aicardi's syndrome (females with infantile spasms, mental retardation, and ocular and vertebral abnormalities as well as agenesis of the corpus callosum).

Patients with isolated agenesis of the corpus callosum may be asymptomatic. Careful neuropsychological testing may reveal a deficit in integrative capacities related to perceptual and language capabilities. Patients with other associated anomalies frequently have severe neurological disability, including mental retardation and seizures.

Posterior Fossa Cystic Malformations

Cystic malformations of the posterior fossa constitute a diverse group of anomalies that have been the subject of various attempts at classification. Controversy has centered primarily on cystic anomalies located posteriorly in the midline because of difficulties in distinguishing between normal and abnormal CSF collections in this region and in understanding the significance of the presence or absence of associated cerebellar, particularly vermian, dysmorphism. Classically, terminology has distinguished Dandy-Walker malformation, Dandy-Walker variant, mega cisterna magna, and retrocerebellar arachnoid cyst. Radiographic description, because it is based on in vivo information, has been particularly influential in establishing and modifying this terminology (Juhl 1966; Harwood-Nash 1976; Archer 1978; Raybaud 1982; Masdeu 1983). Pathological characterization of the "cysts" has been somewhat confounded by the inevitable loss of their intactness as a result of craniotomy at the time of autopsy. Imaging distinction among these anomalies depends on the CT and MR findings.

Since the original description by Dandy and Blackfan (1914) of a 13-year-old with obstructive hydrocephalus secondary to cystic dilatation of the fourth ventricle associated with hypoplasia of the vermis and absence of the foramina of Luschka and Magendie, most definitions of the Dandy-Walker malformation have included three features: dysgenesis of the vermis, cystic dilatation of the fourth ventricle, and enlargement of the posterior fossa with elevation of the tentorium/torcula. Dandy-Walker variant has been proposed (Harwood-Nash 1976) as a milder form of the malformation; it has been defined as a cystic outpouching from the inferior medullary velum with a more normal-appearing upper fourth ventricle, a lesser degree of vermian anomaly, and only mild posterior fossa enlargement. Although approximately 80 percent of these patients have hydrocephalus, this is said to be less common in patients with the variant. Likewise, patients with the variant are more likely to present in adulthood than are those with the malformation, who frequently present in infancy or childhood with rapidly increasing head size. The difficulty in clearly distinguishing subtypes of the Dandy-Walker complex on axial CT images is well recognized, however. Information derived from pathological data (Shaw 1977) and, more recently, from series of patients examined with MR (Gusnard 1988; Barkovich 1989*a*) suggests that rather than separate entities, there appears to be a continuum of cystic developmental anomalies that communicate with the fourth ventricle. On the basis of these data, it has been suggested that milder forms of the anomaly need not present gross evidence of vermian abnormality but simply a midline posterior cyst continuous with the fourth ventricle (through an attenuated posterior medullary velum). This would subsume under the term *Dandy-Walker complex* what in previous terminology had been referred to as a *mega cisterna magna*. Traditionally, a mega cisterna magna has been regarded as a benign developmental enlargement of the cisterna magna; it has been distinguished on imaging studies by its association with an apparently intact vermis (a vermis evident on axial images at least as inferiorly as the midportion of the fourth ventricle). MR imaging, however, has revealed that the vermis may be rotated upward along its axis, and so axial images alone may be misleading. This upward rotation has been recognized on sagittal T_1WI through the posterior fossa in some patients. In some cases the inferior lobules of the vermis appear to be hypoplastic, while in others they appear to be intact (Barkovich 1989*a*).

Thus, in the more severe malformations, the diagnosis is straightforward. Demonstration on either CT or MR of a large CSF collection expanding the posterior fossa, which is seen to be continuous with the fourth ventricle and to be associated with complete or nearly complete absence of the vermis (Fig. 6-11A,B), permits the diagnosis of a Dandy-Walker malformation. The torcula is elevated above the level of the lambdoid sutures. The tentorial leaves may appear splayed laterally and have an inverted V configuration. In these cases, there is frequently hydrocephalus, evidently as a result of aqueductal compression. Within the cerebellar hemispheres, the relative proportion of gray and white matter generally appears to be normal. In some cases the cerebellar hemispheres appear asymmetrical, suggesting dysplasia of the smaller hemisphere. This is further supported when, after shunting, the smaller hemisphere fails to grow to fill its portion of the decompressed posterior fossa as does the larger one.

In cases of milder degrees of "cystic malformation," it appears that MR can best define the relationships between the cyst and the fourth ventricle, the vermian rotation, and the presence or absence of signs of vermian dysgenesis (Fig. 6-11C–E). Distinction between the previously so-called Dandy-Walker variant and mega cisterna magna and the relevance of this distinction remain controversial. While traditionally the term *Dandy-Walker variant* implied more significant pathology than did *mega cisterna magna,* this has been challenged by reports of occasional symptomatic patients with the so-called mega cisterna magna. Further elucidation of the details of development of the roof of the fourth ventricle and cerebellar anlage may be helpful in this regard. However, the distinction may be of academic interest only, since it appears that the prognosis in these patients, even those with large posterior fossa cysts and vermian agenesis, does not correlate with the degree of the posterior fossa malformation but rather correlates (1) directly with the presence of associated supratentorial anomalies (e.g., agenesis of the corpus callosum, heterotopic gray matter) (Fig. 6-11C,F) and (2) inversely with the age at which the patient was treated for hydrocephalus (shunted) (Golden 1987; Maria 1987). Patients with the Dandy-Walker malformation may also have systemic anomalies, including syndactyly, polydactyly, cleft palate, Klippel-Feil syndrome, and Walker-Warburg syndrome. Treatment consists of shunting the posterior fossa cysts as well as the ventricles in cases where hydrocephalus is present. Shunting of only one compartment may result in transtentorial herniation in either an upward or a downward direction. Shunting of the cyst at an early age, before the end of the second year when most myelination has already taken place, typically permits more normal morphological development of the nonhypoplastic cerebellar hemispheres (Fig. 6-12A–C) (Gusnard 1988).

True retrocerebellar arachnoid cysts of developmental origin are uncommon (Shaw 1977). The distinction between a retrocerebellar arachnoid cyst with mild or moderate mass effect and a so-called mega cisterna magna (or a mild variant of the Dandy-Walker complex) may not be possible with current imaging techniques. Omnipaque cisternography can be useful if it shows a lack of filling of the cyst, but if there is delayed filling, the study may be inconclusive. Again, the distinction is clinically valuable only if the patient is symptomatic. Arachnoid cysts that are located elsewhere in the posterior fossa and have sufficient mass effect (Fig. 6-13) are commonly symptomatic, necessitating shunting and/or direct surgical decompression.

Finally, it is important to distinguish degenerative disorders involving posterior fossa structures from posterior fossa cystic malformations, as the prognosis is much different and shunting is not warranted. Enlargement of posterior fossa CSF spaces is only relative when there is a loss of hindbrain tissue (prominent cerebellar folia and/or small brainstem). No mass effect is seen.

Joubert's Syndrome

This is a rare familial disorder characterized by nearly total aplasia of the cerebellar vermis. Microscopically, it

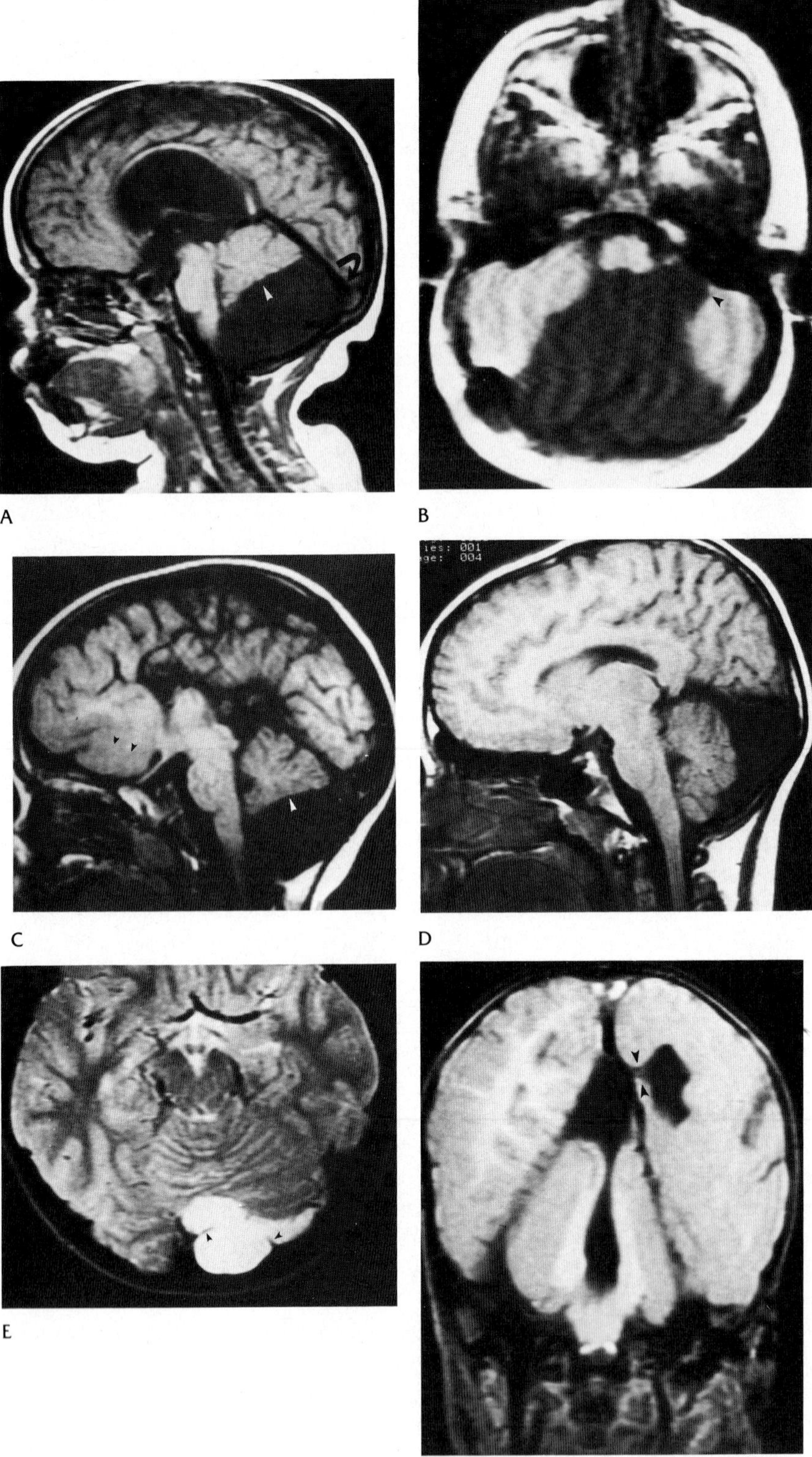

Figure 6-11 Dandy-Walker complex. **A.** Dandy-Walker malformation. Sagittal T_1WI (600/20) demonstrates absence of the inferior vermis (white arrowhead) and residual vermis being compressed by a posterior fossa cyst. The posterior fossa is enlarged, and the torcula (curved black arrow) is displaced superiorly. Hydrocephalus is present. **B.** Axial T_1WI (60/20) demonstrates continuity of the cyst with the fourth ventricle as well as distension of the left foramen of Luschka (arrowhead), the outlet of which is apparently obstructed. An artifact from the presence of a shunt catheter within the cyst is seen on the right margin of the cyst. **C.** Sagittal T_1WI (600/20) demonstrates malformation within the posterior fossa of lesser degree: A lesser amount of vermis is absent (white arrowhead) compared with **A,** the fourth ventricle is better formed, and the posterior fossa is not so enlarged (so-called Dandy-Walker variant). Hydrocephalus is not present. Of prognostic significance is the fact that there are associated supratentorial abnormalities in this case: agenesis of the corpus callosum and focal pachygyria along the inferior aspect of the frontal lobe (black arrowheads). **D.** Mega cisterna magna. Sagittal T_1WI (600/20) demonstrates a prominent CSF space continuous with the cisterna magna posterior to intact vermis. **E.** Axial T_2WI (2500/80) shows the mega cisterna magna extending asymmetrically to the left side behind the cerebellar hemisphere. Meningeal septa are seen extending through the cistern (arrowheads). **F.** Coronal T_1WI (600/20) is useful for demonstrating the total absence of vermis in this case. A posterior fossa cyst continuous with the fourth ventricle is seen extending well above the ventricle. There is an associated left paramedian schizencephalic cleft (arrowheads).

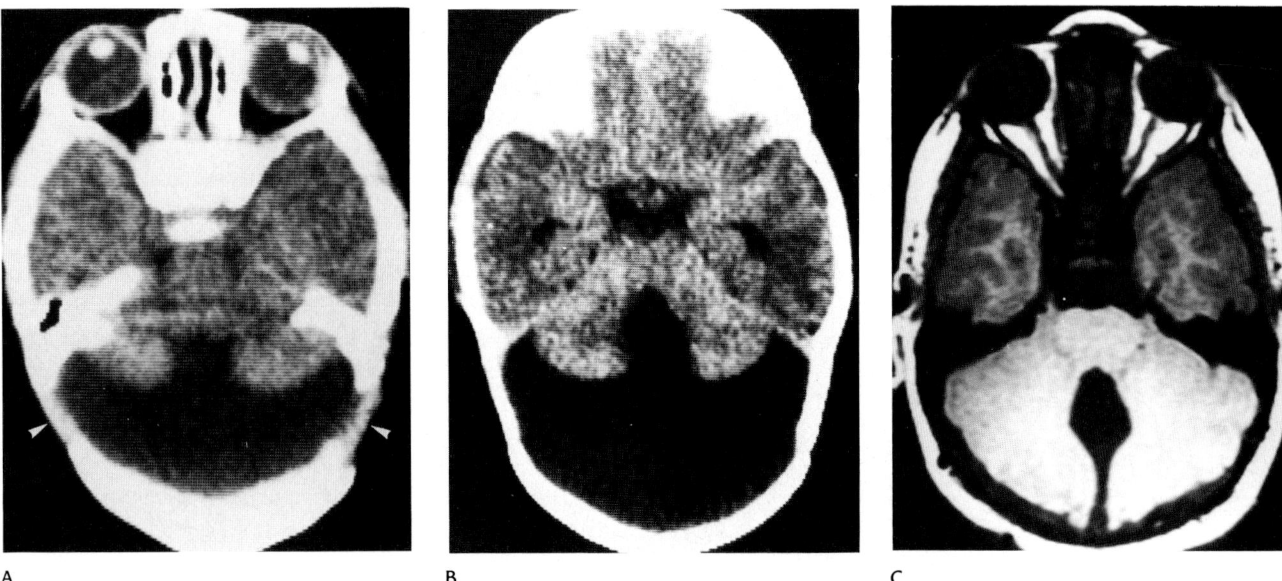

Figure 6-12 Dandy-Walker cyst before and after shunting. **A,B.** Axial CT images through the posterior fossa demonstrate complete absence of the vermis and "cyst" enlarging the posterior fossa; note widening of the lambdoid sutures, particularly inferiorly (arrowheads), in this 4-month-old infant. The patient underwent cyst-peritoneal shunting shortly after this scan was obtained. **C.** Axial T_1WI (600/20) from scan performed 1.5 years later demonstrates that the "cyst" has resolved and the cerebellar hemispheres have developed more normally within the decompressed posterior fossa compartment. Vermian absence is still evident.

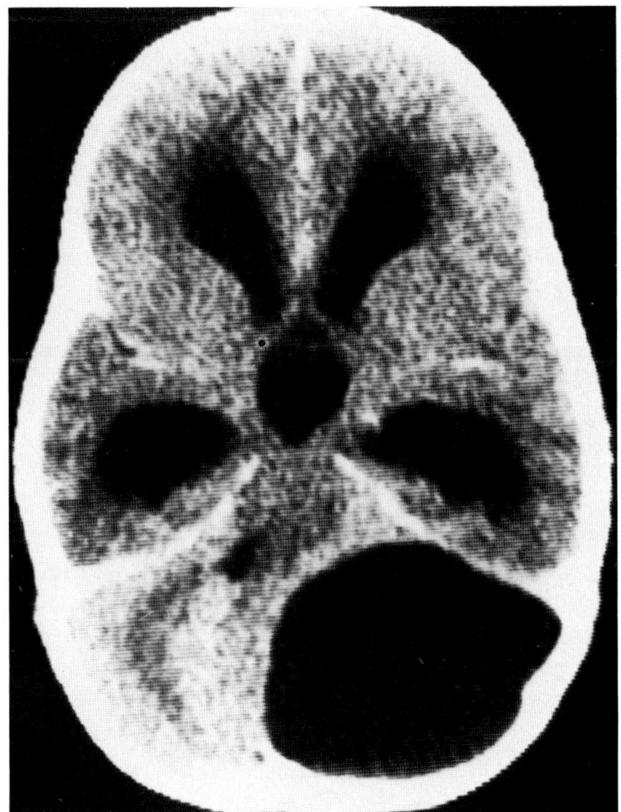

Figure 6-13 Arachnoid cyst. On this CECT image, a large posterolaterally located cyst is seen displacing and severely compressing the cerebellum and fourth ventricle. There is obstructive hydrocephalus.

is associated with cerebellar heterotopias and dysplasias of the cerebellar nuclei, inferior olives, trigeminal tract, and dorsal column nuclei as well as incomplete pyramidal decussation (Joubert 1969). Males are more commonly affected. Children with this disorder have abnormal eye movements, abnormal breathing patterns, and ataxia and are mentally retarded. They may have associated anomalies, including occipital encephaloceles, retinal dysplasia, syndactyly, and renal cystic disease (King 1984).

The CT and MR findings are characteristic. With absence of the cerebellar vermis, the cerebellar hemispheres appose each other directly in the midline. There is a distinctive "batwing" configuration to the fourth ventricle at the level of the upper pons and midbrain, and the superior cerebellar peduncles are unusually apparent (Fig. 6-14).

Anomalies of Neuronal Proliferation and Migration

DISTURBANCES OF BULK GROWTH

Micrencephaly refers to a primary hypoplasia of the brain and should be distinguished from *microcephaly,* which refers to a small cranial vault that may be due to a variety of causes (e.g., micrencephaly as well as a cavitated or atrophic brain secondary to vascular, infectious, or metabolic insults). Micrencephaly may manifest as an isolated

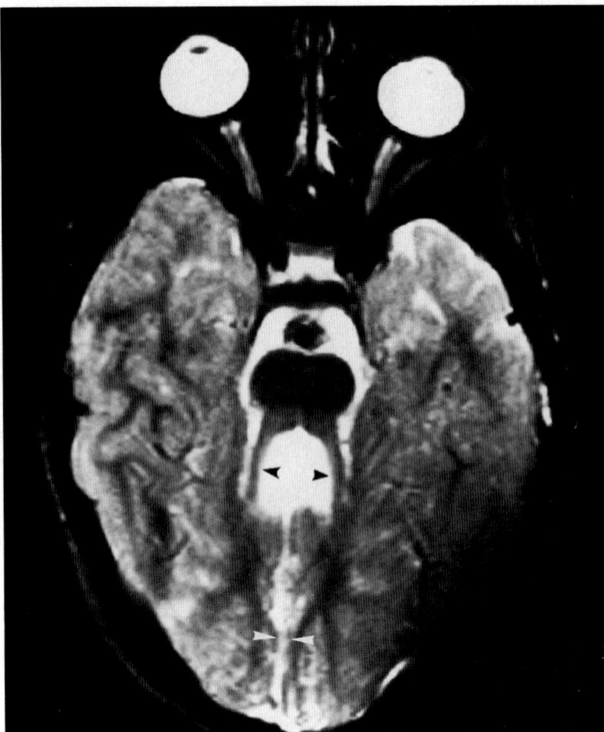

Figure 6-14 Joubert's syndrome. Axial T_2WI (2500/80) near the pontomesencephalic junction demonstrates the batwing configuration of the fourth ventricle and the unusual definition of the superior cerebellar peduncles (black arrowheads) at this level. The vermis is not seen, and the two cerebellar hemispheres (white arrowheads) appose each other in the midline.

phenomenon. That is, in some patients with micrencephaly, MR scanning reveals small cerebral hemispheres which appear to have nearly normal gross structural and relative gray-white matter proportions; commonly the convolutional pattern appears to be somewhat underdeveloped, however. The cerebellum is less affected, and so it appears relatively large. On the basis of experimental data (Dambska 1982; Hicks 1953), the anomaly is thought to be attributable to an interference with cellular proliferation of the germinal matrix. Patients are typically moderately to severely retarded. Micrencephaly may also accompany other pathological conditions, such as agyria, pachygyria, and holoprosencephaly.

Megalencephaly refers to a focal or diffuse enlargement of the cerebral hemispheres. It may be primary, occurring in isolation, or may be associated with a syndrome (e.g., achrondroplasia, Soto's syndrome) (DeMeyer 1972). Generally, the gross morphology of the cerebrum is unremarkable, with all the portions of the cerebrum enlarged in proportion to each other (Friede 1989). The pathogenesis of diffuse primary megalencephaly is uncertain. Although it is known that in normal brain development neurons are initially overproduced and that neurons which are unable to form synaptic connections are eliminated, the mechanisms which regulate this process and may be disturbed in megalencephaly are unknown.

Megalencephaly may also be secondary to an abnormal accumulation of metabolic products in brain tissue, as in the mucopolysaccharidoses, Alexander's disease, and Canavan's disease. These disorders typically demonstrate abnormalities of the brain parenchyma, particularly in the white matter.

Unilateral megalencephaly (hemimegalencephaly) is a rarer anomaly. There is significant variability in its manifestations. There may be enlargement of all brain structures on one side (cerebral hemisphere, ipsilateral brainstem, and cerebellar hemisphere) or, more commonly, enlargement of all or a part of one cerebral hemisphere alone (Fitz 1978). It may occur as an isolated lesion or occasionally with somatic ipsilateral hemihypertrophy. Radiographically and pathologically, at least two subtypes of anomaly have been suggested (Townsend 1975; Friede 1989; Barkovich 1990). In some cases, the overgrowth of the hemisphere is accompanied by signs of anomalous neuronal migration (e.g., pachygyria and/or polymicrogyria). Characteristically, the trigone of the ipsilateral lateral ventricle is enlarged; the frontal horn may appear narrowed and straightened. The relative proportion of white matter may be less than or much greater than normal, a finding which may depend on the severity of the migrational anomaly (Friede 1989). Its signal intensity on MR (density on CT) is often like that of the white matter in the contralateral hemisphere; however, heterotopic gray matter and foci of gliosis may be present. In other cases (Fig. 6-15A–C), the MR appearance of the affected hemisphere is more bizarre. In addition to a dysmorphic appearance which is not easily characterized in accordance with known forms of migration anomaly, the signal intensity of the parenchyma, particularly the white matter, appears to be grossly abnormal. Pathologically, these lesions may show signs suggestive of hamartomatous overgrowth (disorganized misshapen neurons and glial cells). Patients with unilateral megalencephaly typically have a severe seizure disorder which may require hemispherectomy.

Schizencephaly

Schizencephaly refers to gray-matter-lined full-thickness clefts involving one or both cerebral hemispheres. The gray matter bordering these clefts is abnormal, consisting of polymicrogyria which may be associated with underlying heterotopias. The pial covering over the adjacent brain surface extends inward along the margins of the cleft, fusing in its depths with the ventricular ependyma (pial-ependymal seam). The current terminology is intended to distinguish *schizencephaly* from *porencephaly,* which refers to parenchymal defects continuous with the ventricle that are not lined by gray matter and are thought

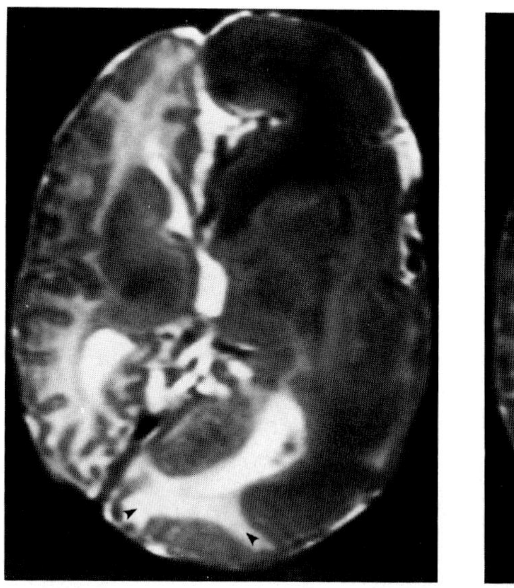

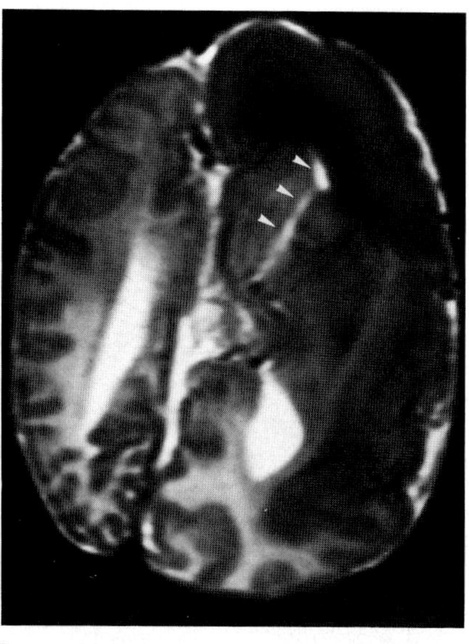

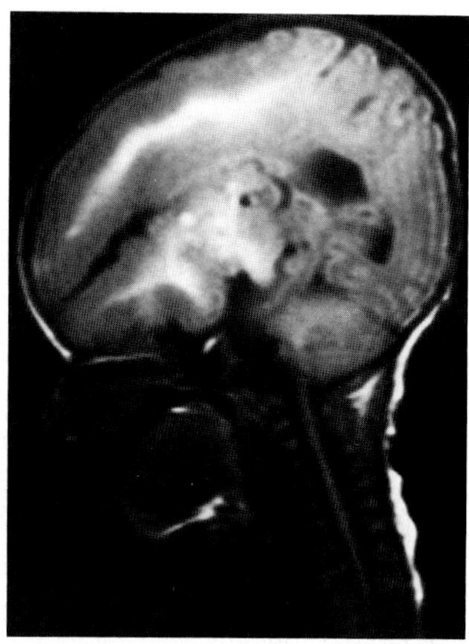

Figure 6-15 Hemimegalencephaly. **A,B.** Axial T_2WI (3000/120) in this newborn reveal marked asymmetry of the two cerebral hemispheres, with the right hemisphere appearing relatively normal. The left hemisphere is enlarged. There is thickening and disorganization of the cortical mantle, most marked in the frontal and temporal regions, associated with an abnormally smooth (lissencephalic/pachygyric) cortical surface. Almost no radiographically normal white matter is identifiable in the left hemisphere except in the occipital region (black arrowheads). Characteristically, the body (atria) of the ipsilateral ventricle is enlarged and the frontal horn is narrowed and pointed (white arrowheads). **C.** Sagittal T_1WI (600/15) shows the pachygyric cortex, anomalous sulcation in the midfrontal region, and abnormal signal intensity for age in the expected location of white matter in the frontal and temporal lobes. Posterior fossa structures are normal.

to be due to an in utero insult that destroys nearly fully formed brain tissue. By contrast, it has been postulated that schizencephalic clefts result from an insult to the germinal matrix at around the seventh week of gestation, resulting in the loss of cells that otherwise would have migrated outward along glial cell processes to populate the overlying targeted portion of cortical mantle (Barkovich 1988*b*). Most schizencephalic clefts are located laterally, involving the region of the pre- and postcentral gyri. Occasionally they are located elsewhere in the hemispheres, including parasagittally. A cleft may be very narrow, with its gray-matter-lined edges directly apposing each other (closed-lip type) (Fig. 6-16A), or it may be very wide (open-lip type) (Fig. 6-16B) (Yakovlev 1946*a,b*).

On CT, it is sometimes difficult to diagnose schizencephaly (Fig. 6-16C). The pathognomonic gray matter lining the cleft may or may not be discernible, compromising the distinction of this condition from porencephaly. The closed-lip type also may be difficult to distinguish from a focal irregularity along the margin of the ventricle, such as an irregularity due to periventricular leukomalacia. A thorough MR examination is usually definitive. Both T_1WI and T_2WI provide the necessary contrast resolution for discerning the anomalous gray matter along the cleft as well as the associated heterotopias (Barkovich 1988*b*; Osborne 1988). However, scanning along the plane of the cleft, particularly in instances of closed-lip schizencephaly, may obscure its relationship to the ventricular margin, confounding the diagnosis; thus, scanning is necessary in at least two planes. A helpful sign that aids in the detection of closed-lip schizencephaly is the focal ventricular irregularity that "points to" the cleft (Fig. 6-16A). The septum pellucidum is absent in the majority of patients with schizencephaly (Barkovich 1988*b*).

Patients with schizencephaly typically have a seizure disorder. The accompanying neurological symptoms may, however, range from minimal to severe depending on the amount of brain tissue which is absent as a consequence of the cleft(s). Thus, patients with unilateral closed-lip clefts are generally the least disabled, while those with bilateral open-lip clefts are the most severely disabled.

Agyria-Pachygyria

The terms *agyria* and *pachygyria* refer to a range of severity in the manifestation of a particular type of neuronal migrational anomaly. Agyria, or lissencephaly, is the most severe, implying a complete absence of cortical gyri. Pachygyria implies at least some gyral formation, although the gyri formed are abnormally broad and flat and are accompanied by shallow sulci. Complete agyria, or lissencephay, is rare; the brains of most patients have

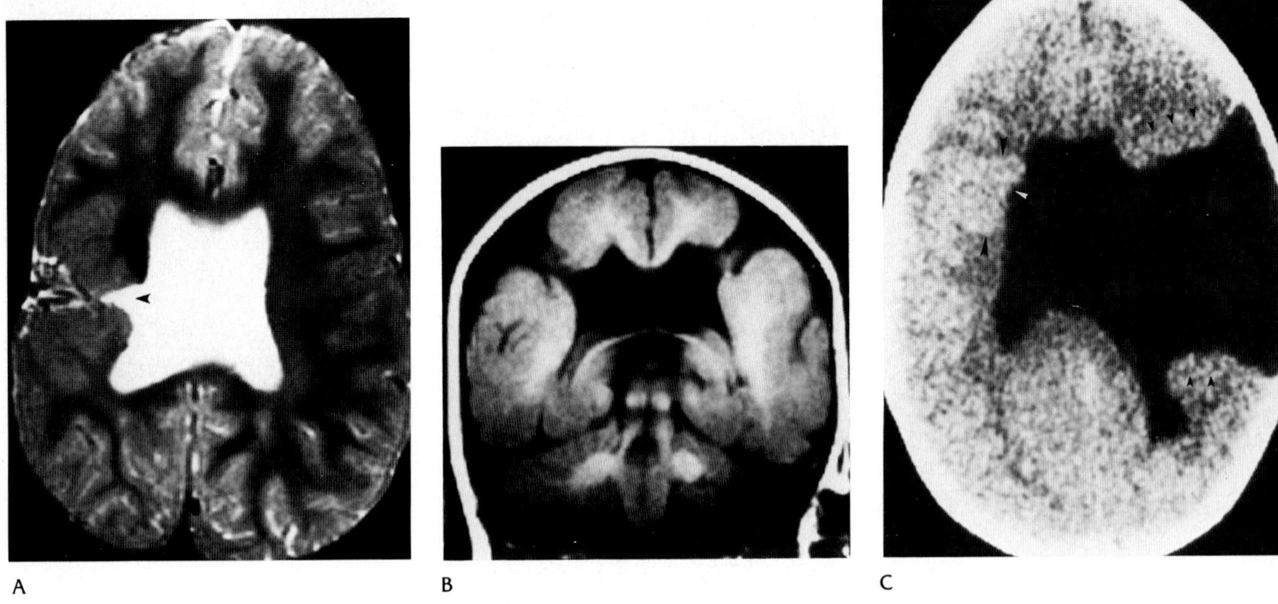

Figure 6-16 Schizencephaly. **A.** MRI. The excellent gray-white matter contrast definition on this T_2WI (2500/80) clearly distinguishes a closed-lip schizencephalic cleft. A ventricular "diverticulum" (arrowhead) characteristically defines the meeting of the closed-lip portion of the cleft with the margin of the ventricle. **B.** Coronal T_1WI (600/15) clearly depicts large bilateral schizencephalic clefts in this 8-month-old, who in addition to having seizures was severely delayed developmentally. **C.** Axial CT reveals a large CSF-filled cleft extending from the ventricle to the cortical surface. The parenchyma marginating the cleft (small black arrowheads) appears to have a relatively high density, like that of gray matter, consistent with a schizencephaly (open-lip type). There is the suggestion of a closed-lip schizencephaly on the contralateral side: irregularity along the edge of the body of the ventricle (white arrowhead) associated with apparent gray matter (large black arrowheads) extending inward to the ventricular margin at this point.

regions of both agyria and pachygyria. In these cases, there is typically a frontotemporal predominance to the pachygyria and a parietooccipital localization of the agyria (Byrd 1988; Titelbaum 1989). In other instances pachygyria is a very focal abnormality that affects only a small region of cortex that may be located anywhere in the cerebral hemispheres. The underlying pathology in all cases reflects an arrest in the radial migration of waves of neuroblasts from the germinal matrix to their cortical locations. This failure of migration is believed to occur between 8 and 16 weeks of gestation; there is then a subsequent lack of induction of formation of normal gyri, a process which begins after the fifth to sixth month of gestation. Microscopically, there is a derangement of the normal cortical architecture, with four abnormal layers instead of the normal six (Stewart 1975). The deepest of these four layers of neurons is the thickest and has been postulated to represent the region of halted neuronal migration. This abnormal cortex is actually broader in toto than is normal cortex, while the underlying white matter is thinned.

The more severe manifestations of the agyria-pachygyria complex can be appreciated on CT (Zimmerman 1983; Dobyns 1985*b;* Byrd 1988; Titelbaum 1989). In some cases, CT may in fact provide unique information, for example, when it reveals periventricular calcification in cases of cytomegalovirus (CMV) or toxoplasmosis-related malformations. In general, however, MR is the modality of choice for imaging these patients (Byrd 1988; Titelbaum 1989). Focal pachygyria frequently is discernible only with MR. In the most severe cases, the brain demonstrates a nearly completely smooth surface with an hourglass configuration as a result of shallow vertically oriented sylvian fissures (Fig. 6-17A–C). Less severe forms manifest some gyral formation (Fig. 6-17D,E). Pachygyria in the absence of agyria may be seen involving small or large areas anywhere, and so the multiplanar capability of MR is frequently useful in their detection (Fig. 6-11C). In all instances, the areas of involvement show thickening of the cortical mantle and a paucity of underlying white matter. The portions of the ventricular system that underlie regions of involvement typically are dilated, presumably secondary to the lack of formation of many white matter tracts. This also probably accounts for the small-appearing corpus callosum and brainstem in more severe cases. Pachygyria may also be seen in the brains of patients with other anomalies, such as hemimegalencephaly. The white matter that is present in the brains of more severely affected children may or may not appear normally myelinated; abnormal signal intensity in the

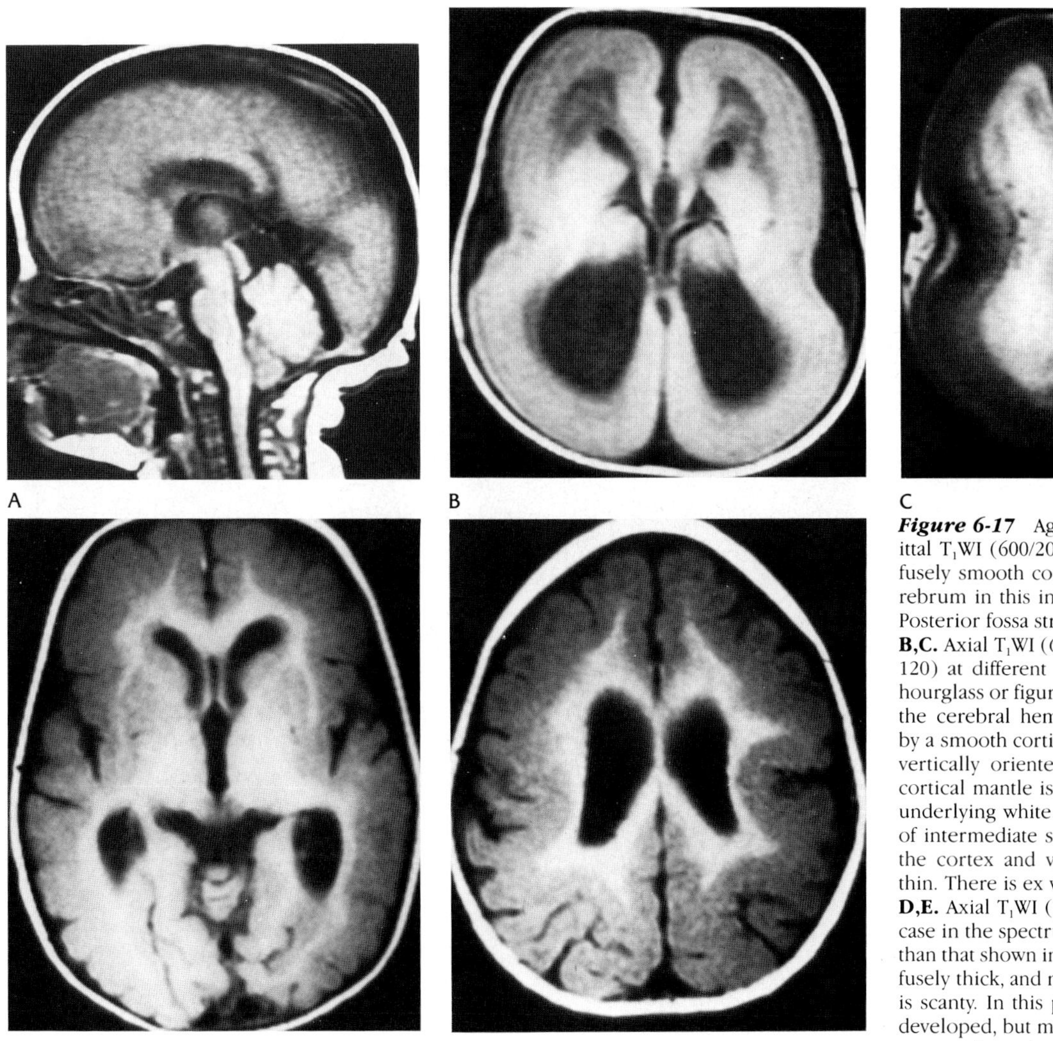

Figure 6-17 Agyria-pachygyria. **A.** Sagittal T_1WI (600/20) demonstrates the diffusely smooth cortical surface of the cerebrum in this infant with lissencephaly. Posterior fossa structures appear normal. **B,C.** Axial T_1WI (600/20) and T_2WI (3000/120) at different levels show the classic hourglass or figure-eight configuration of the cerebral hemispheres characterized by a smooth cortical surface and shallow, vertically oriented sylvian fissures. The cortical mantle is thick, while the rim of underlying white matter (seen as a band of intermediate signal intensity between the cortex and ventricles) is extremely thin. There is ex vacuo ventriculomegaly. **D,E.** Axial T_1WI (600/20) reveal a milder case in the spectrum of agyria/pachygyria than that shown in **A–C.** The cortex is diffusely thick, and myelinated white matter is scanty. In this patient, some gyri have developed, but most of those which have appeared are abnormally broad and flat.

white matter is frequently seen in patients with documented in utero infection (e.g., CMV).

Patients with the more severe forms of agyria-pachygyria have small brains (micrencephaly). They are frequently hypotonic and severely delayed developmentally. Those with agyria have a dismal prognosis; most do not survive beyond 2 years of age. Patients with pachygyria are less severely retarded. A seizure disorder is common. Some patients have agyria as a component of a syndrome (e.g., Miller-Dieker and Walker-Warburg syndromes); others have cardiac or ocular anomalies (Dobyns 1984, 1985*a*). Some patients are reported to have had in utero infections (CMV more commonly than toxoplasmosis) (Titelbaum 1989).

Polymicrogyria

Polymicrogyria consists of an anomalous region of cerebral cortex characterized by multiple small gyri with an abnormal cytoarchitecture. It represents a disturbance in neuronal migration that appears to date to the fifth month of gestation, which is the time of the onset of cortical gyral formation. Microscopically, there is typically a four-layered cortex that is thinner than normal cortex. On both gross pathological and radiographic inspection, however, it may be mistaken for pachygyria, since the small gyri have fused surfaces and superficially appear as regions of flat gyri and shallow sulci (Barkovich 1987). Occasionally on MR, the abnormally thin cortex may be perceptible and abnormal signal intensity in the subjacent white matter may be seen on T_2WI, allowing its distinction from pachygyria. Polymicrogyria also should be distinguished from stenogyria (polygyria), which consists of a region of redundant cortical gyri. Microscopically, stenogyria has a normal cortical architecture. It is most common in patients with a history of hydrocephalus as infants. Patients with polymicrogyria generally are afflicted with seizures.

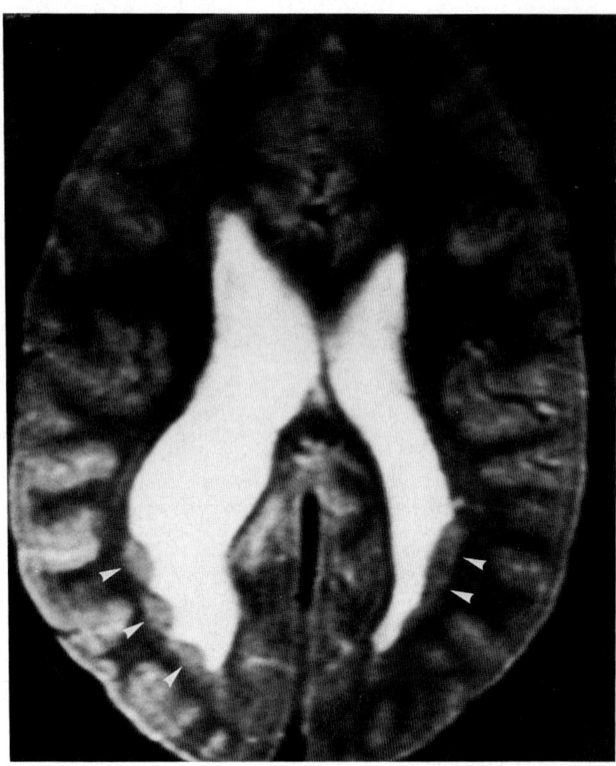

A

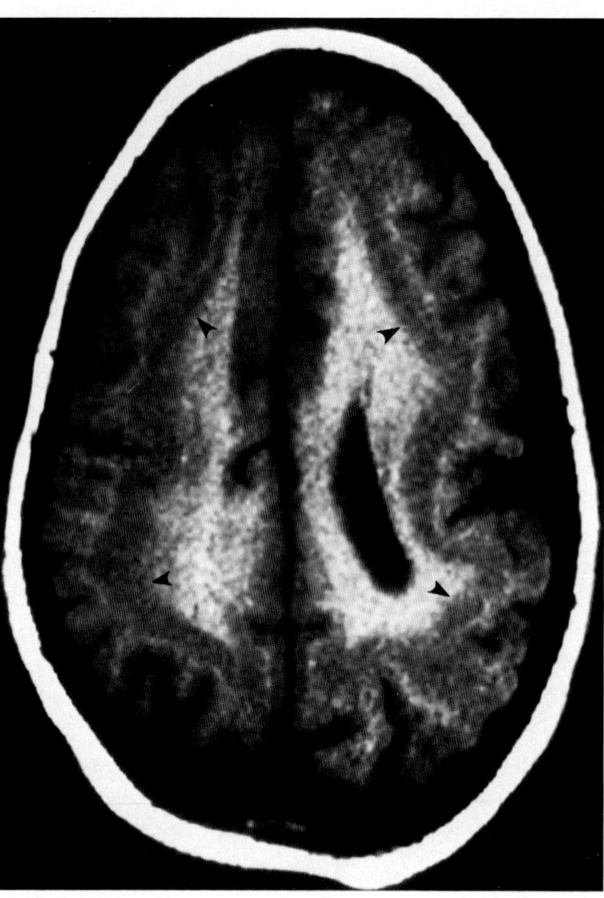

B

Figure 6-18 Heterotopias. **A.** Axial T_2WI (2500/80) demonstrates multiple small nodular foci along the margins of the posterolateral aspects of the bodies of both lateral ventricles (arrowheads). These foci have a signal intensity like that of the cortex, consistent with heterotopic gray matter. **B.** Axial T_1WI (600/15) in this 12-year-old with seizures reveals broad bands of ectopic gray matter (arrowheads) along the periphery of the centrum semiovale bilaterally. Note the normal high signal of the subcortical white matter between the ectopic gray matter and the overlying cortex.

Heterotopias

Heterotopias are nodular collections of neurons (and some glial tissue) anomalously located in the subependymal or periventricular regions, most commonly around the trigones. Their pathogenesis is believed to consist of an arrest of migration of a portion of a late "wave" of neuroblasts at approximately 5 months' gestation. They are frequently associated with other brain anomalies. The nodules may vary in size from punctate to large irregular clumps and may be single or numerous (Fig. 6-18A). Rarely, heterotopias may manifest as bilateral symmetrical bands of gray matter that run within the centrum semiovale between the ventricle and the overlying cortex (band heterotopias) (Fig. 6-18B). Pathologically, heterotopic gray matter may demonstrate rudimentary lamination.

Heterotopias are frequently not visible on CT. On MR, they are generally recognized as lesions in the subependymal region or periventricular white matter that are isointense to gray matter on all imaging sequences and do not enhance with contrast (Deeb 1985).

The incidence and severity of symptoms associated with isolated heterotopias are not known. Patients with or without associated anomalies may have a seizure disorder and developmental delay.

The Phakomatoses

The phakomatoses are congenital disorders characterized by disturbances of the development of primarily ectodermal structures, i.e., the skin, the eyes, and the central and peripheral nervous systems. Abnormalities may also affect mesodermal structures (bone and blood vessels) and endodermal structures (viscera). The most common of these childhood disorders are neurofibromatosis (NF), tuberous sclerosis (TS), and Sturge-Weber-Dimitri syndrome (SWD). Recent work has identified distinct chromosomal abnormalities in two subtypes of the most common of the phakomatoses, neurofibromatosis, though the actual gene products and their functional roles remain unknown. The developmental disturbances in phakomatoses appear to be associated with proliferative changes which may manifest as hamartomatous lesions or structural dysplasias. A propensity for neoplastic transformation of neural and other tissue types is also present in some of these disorders, particularly NF and, to a lesser degree, TS. Radiological imaging is particularly important in that it (1) aids in making the diagnosis when clinical features are not obvious, (2) provides an etiology in cases of seizures, and (3) allows detection of neoplasms at an earlier stage, often when patients are asymptomatic.

NEUROFIBROMATOSIS

Among the several subtypes of neurofibromatosis which have been proposed, the National Institutes of Health Consensus Development Conference has recognized two, which are referred to as NF 1 and NF 2 (Conference Statement 1988). They are genetically distinguishable: NF 1 is associated with an abnormality on chromosome 17, and NF 2 is associated with an abnormality on chromosome 22.

NF 1 is 10 times more common, affecting approximately 1 in 3000 to 5000 people in the population. It is more likely to be diagnosed in childhood than is NF 2 because of its greater association with multiple café-au-lait spots and deforming plexiform neurofibromas as well as the natural histories of the tumors which commonly afflict this group of patients, which are different from those that afflict NF 2 patients. NF 1 patients are at increased risk for the development of glial neoplasms, particularly optic gliomas (Fig. 6-19A) (Brown 1987; Aoki 1989). Estimates vary, but the incidence is probably between 5 and 20 percent.

Since the advent of MR, it has been recognized that over 50 percent of children with NF 1 also have foci of abnormal signal intensity within the brain parenchyma (Bognanno 1988; Braffman 1988; Hurst 1988), most commonly along the inferomedial aspects of the globus pallidus; within the thalami, midbrain, and middle cerebellar peduncles; and less commonly along the medial aspects of the temporal lobes and elsewhere in the brainstem (Fig. 6-19B–D). They may be isolated, multiple, unilateral, or bilateral. Little pathological correlation to these MR "lesions" currently exists, though some data suggest that they represent hamartomas containing disordered axons. The lesions appear hyperintense on T_2WI, are not visible on T_1WI, and are not associated with mass effect except for those in the globus pallidus, which commonly appear slightly hyperintense on T_1WI and may have mild mass effect (Fig. 6-19B,C) (Mirowitz 1989). They have been reported to disappear radiographically and generally are not seen in patients beyond the late teenage years. Rarely these lesions, most commonly those involving posterior fossa structures, have been observed to change character, become low in signal intensity on T_1WI, demonstrate mass effect, and/or contrast-enhance, suggesting malignant degeneration. Malignancy has been surgically proved in some of these cases.

In NF 1 patients with hydrocephalus, tectal gliomas must be distinguished from benign aqueductal stenosis, to which these patients may also be subject. This can be readily accomplished with sagittal T_1WI and T_2WI. Other intracranial manifestations of the disorder include intracranial extension of craniofacial plexiform neurofibromas and sphenoid wing dysplasia, an abnormality which permits herniation of the temporal lobe into the orbit, with resultant pulsatile exophthalmos. NF 1 accounts for approximately 50 percent of cases of buphthalmos, a congenital glaucoma which is secondary to maldevelopment of the angle of the anterior chamber of the eye. This maldevelopment results in obstruction of the outflow of aqueous humor, producing an enlarged globe on imaging studies.

Neurofibromatosis type 2 is only one-tenth as common as NF 1. Because of a relative absence of cutaneous and ocular manifestations, patients with NF 2 generally do not present with signs of the disease until the teenage or adult years. Frequently, the radiologist plays a significant role in establishing the diagnosis. Characteristically, patients with NF 2 develop bilateral acoustic schwannomas. Contrast-enhanced thin-section MR through the internal auditory canals is the method of choice for their detection, often revealing them at an early stage (Fig. 6-20). Other cranial nerves may be affected, with the trigeminal being next in frequency. Other neoplasms to which these patients are predisposed include intracranial and intraspinal meningiomas, which may be multiple (Aoki 1989), and, less commonly, ependymomas of the spinal cord and brainstem. NF 2 patients are not known to manifest foci of abnormal signal intensity within the brain like those seen in many children with NF 1 (Aoki 1989).

TUBEROUS SCLEROSIS

Tuberous sclerosis is a disorder classically characterized by the clinical triad of mental retardation, seizures, and a malar rash (angiofibromata) known as *adenoma sebaceum*. The clinical manifestations result from hamartomatous malformations that, in the brain, may be present in a subependymal location or more peripherally in the brain parenchyma. They are most common in the cerebral hemispheres, with cerebellar lesions being rare. It has been suggested that the clinical severity of the disorder correlates directly with the number of parenchymal lesions (Roach 1982).

The subependymal nodules appear as punctate to moderate-sized rounded structures which protrude from along the ependymal lining into the ventricle, marginated

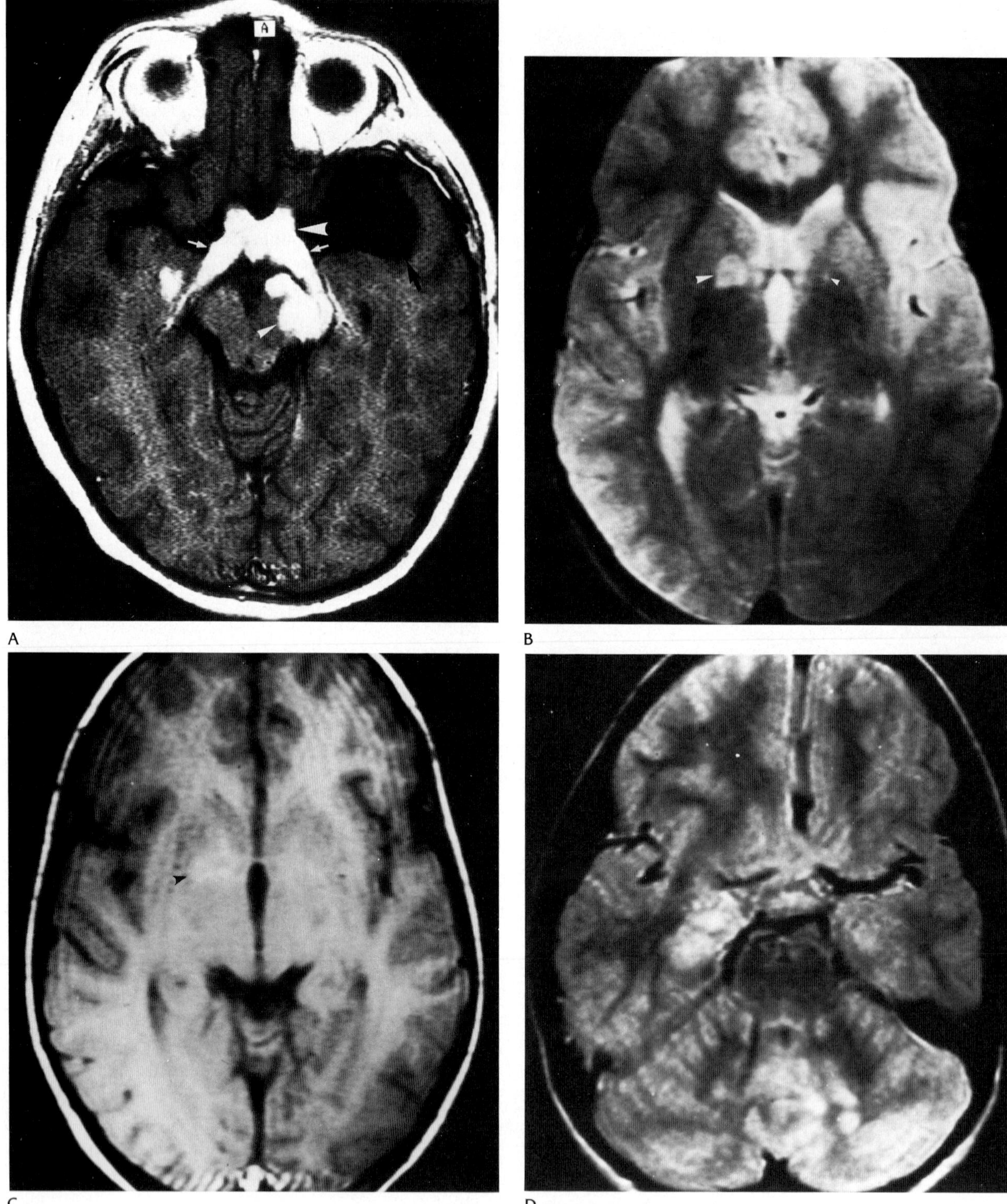

Figure 6-19 Neurofibromatosis type I. **A.** Axial T_1WI (600/22) CEMR reveals an enhancing chiasmatic mass (large white arrowhead) which extends posteriorly along both optic tracts (white arrows) and invades the left side of the midbrain (small white arrowhead). An arachnoid cyst is in the left middle cranial fossa (black arrow). **B,C.** Axial T_2WI (2500/80) in an 8-year-old female reveals a focus of hyperintensity in the right globus pallidus (large white arrowhead), which also appears slightly hyperintense on T_1WI (600/15) (black arrowhead in **C**). A more punctate focus is also seen in the left globus pallidus on the T_2WI (small white arrowhead in **B**). **D.** Other "hamartomatous" foci (arrowheads) are seen in the middle cerebellar peduncles, more extensively on the left, as well as along the medial aspect of the right temporal lobe. There was no evidence for optic nerve/chiasmatic glioma in this patient.

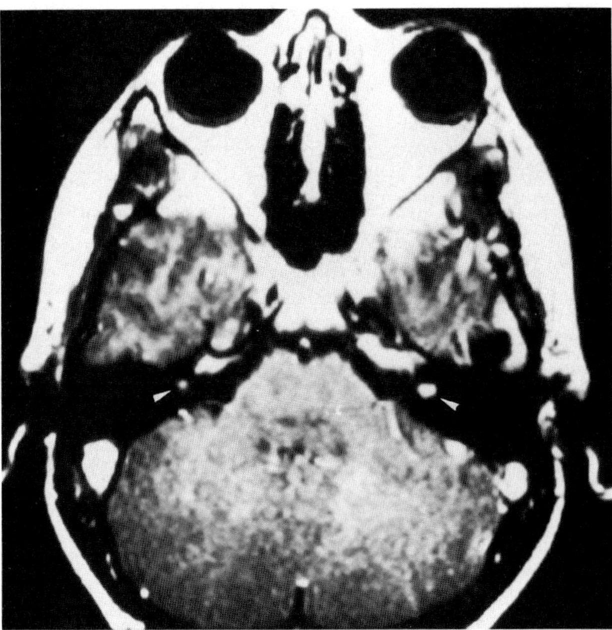

Figure 6-20 Neurofibromatosis type II. Axial T_1WI (600/20) CEMR reveals bilateral small enhancing eighth nerve (acoustic) schwannomas (arrowheads).

along their medial aspects by CSF. They may be so small as to be invisible on CT examination in the neonate, only to become visible as they calcify with time (Fig. 6-21A) (Altman 1988). On MR, they typically appear isointense to moderately hyperintense to white matter on T_1WI images and, depending on the degree of calcification, isointense to hypointense to white matter on T_2WI (Fig. 6-21B) (Vaghi 1987; Altman 1988). The cortical tubers, which pathologically are the most characteristic lesions of this disorder, appear in young children as focal hypodensities in the subcortical white matter associated with gyral broadening on CT (Fig. 6-21A). They are less visible in older children and adults. In young children, on T_1WI, the widened gyri appear hypointense; on T_2WI, they appear hyperintense to adjacent brain parenchyma (Fig. 6-21B). With aging, they become isointense on T_1WI but remain bright on T_2WI. In newborns, however, they may appear hyperintense on T_1WI and hypointense on T_2WI (Altman 1988). The deep white matter frequently contains clusters of heterotopic giant cells which are oriented in a radial distribution extending from the ventricular margin to either normal cortex or cortical tubers (Fig. 6-21B). These parenchymal hamartomas occasionally manifest calcification on CT (Fig. 6-21A). In approximately 10 percent of these patients, a subependymal nodule, most commonly in the region of the foramen of

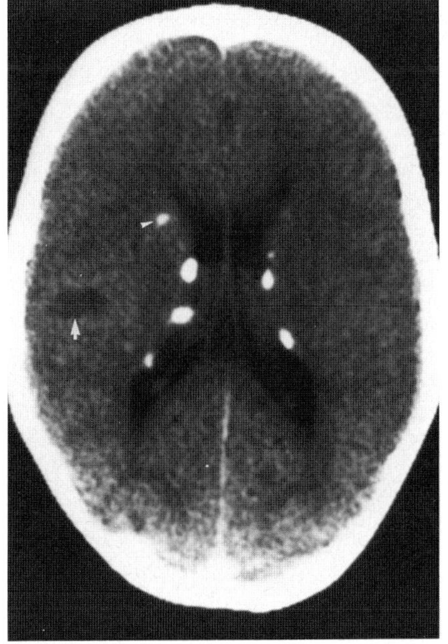

A

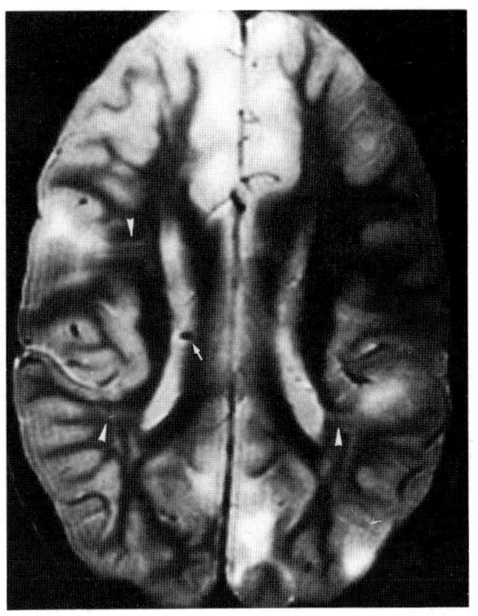

B

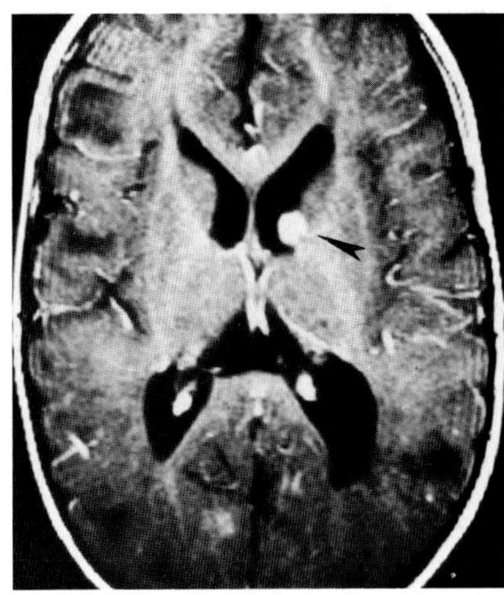

C

Figure 6-21 Tuberous sclerosis. **A.** Axial NCCT demonstrates multiple calcified subependymal nodules protruding into the ventricles. A focus of calcification is also seen somewhat more laterally (arrowhead) within a hamartomatous lesion in the parenchyma adjacent to the right frontal horn. A superficial ovoid hypodensity (arrow) consistent with a cortical tuber is also shown. **B.** Axial T_2WI (2500/80) NCMR image in another patient more clearly depicts multiple cortical tubers, which demonstrate high signal intensity and produce gyral broadening. Radially oriented parenchymal hamartomas are seen in the deep white matter (small arrowheads). A subependymal nodule along the margin of the right lateral ventricle (arrow) is seen as a small hypointense focus (presumably calcified). **C.** Axial T_1WI (600/20) CEMR reveals an enhancing nodule larger than most subependymal nodules (arrowhead) adjacent to the left foramen of Monro. Its appearance is consistent with a subependymal giant cell astrocytoma; it is not yet large enough to obstruct the foramen and produce hydrocephalus.

Monro, will demonstrate growth and contrast enhancement, indicating development of a subependymal giant cell astrocytoma (Fig. 6-21C). While these typically are slow-growing neoplasms, because of their location they may produce obstructive hydrocephalus at an early stage.

STURGE-WEBER SYNDROME

Sturge-Weber syndrome is characterized by cutaneous angiomatosis (port-wine nevus) in the distribution of the trigeminal nerve and a focal angiomatosis of the leptomeninges. Angiomatosis of the choroid of the eye, resulting in elevated intraocular pressure and buphthalmos and occasionally retinal detachment, occurs in a minority of cases.

Intracranial angiomatosis ordinarily is confined to the pia mater. Its effects account for the disorder's most significant clinical manifestations: seizures, mental retardation, hemiparesis, and hemianopia. It is typically located in the occipital lobe, though there may be extension to the posterior parietal and temporal lobes; rarely, the frontal lobes may be involved. It is most commonly unilateral and ipsilateral to the cutaneous nevus but may be bilateral and/or contralateral to the nevus. The angiomatosis associates with a focal absence of superficial cortical veins and underlying cerebral atrophy, though there are commonly prominent collaterals involving the deep venous system (Fig. 6-22C). Angiomatous malformation, manifesting as enlargement, of the ipsilateral choroid plexus may also be present. On plain film, "tram-track" calcification following the gyri of the involved portion of the cerebral hemisphere may be seen, though not commonly in the first year of life. On both CT and MR, the cerebral atrophy, the ipsilateral skull hypertrophy, and the deep venous and choroid anomalies are equally well visualized (Chamberlain 1989; Wasenko 1990). The gyral calcifications, which occur in a pericapillary distribution in the fourth layer of the chronically ischemic cortex, are more readily detectable on CT (Fig. 6-22A), though gradient-echo acquisitions may permit their detection on MR (Wasenko 1990). The damaged parenchyma is more readily appreciated on MR, often demonstrating abnormally high signal intensity in the involved white matter on T_2WI. Although gyriform enhancement may be seen in the region of the pial angioma on contrast-enhanced CT, contrast-enhanced MR is more sensitive in the detection and characterization of angiomas of the meninges (Fig. 6-22B) and retina (Elster 1990; Lipski 1990).

Aqueductal Stenosis

The cerebral aqueduct, which is the narrowest passage in the ventricular system, in the most common site of focal

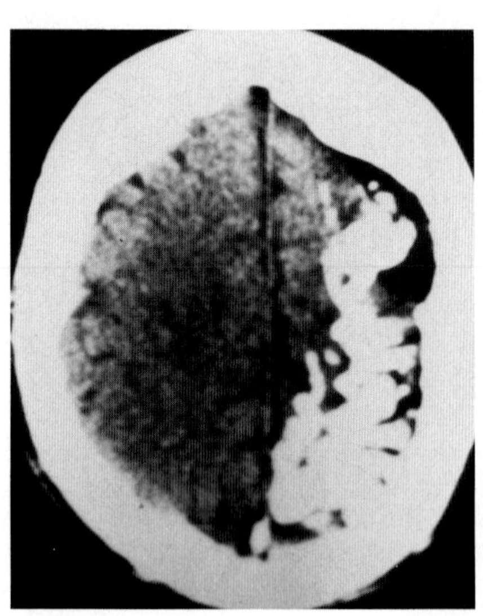
A

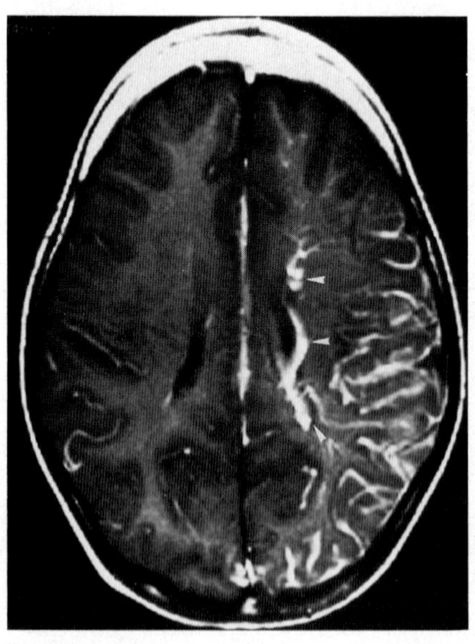
B

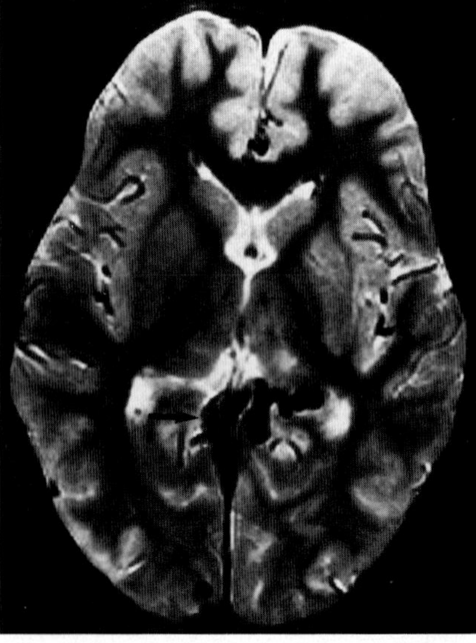
C

Figure 6-22 Sturge-Weber disease. **A.** NCCT through the vertex in this teenage male demonstrates dense calcification in a gyriform pattern along the left frontoparietal cortex. **B.** Axial T_1WI (600/20) CEMR in another patient demonstrates prominent leptomeningeal enhancement over the surface of the left posterior frontal and the parietooccipital regions following the course of the pial angiomatous malformation. Enhancement of prominent subependymal veins (arrowheads), presumably providing collateral venous drainage, is seen along the edge of the ipsilateral ventricle. **C.** In the same patient, at the level of the third ventricle, prominent subependymal veins demonstrating flow void on T_2WI (2500/80) are seen draining into a dilated vein of Galen (arrow) and straight sinus.

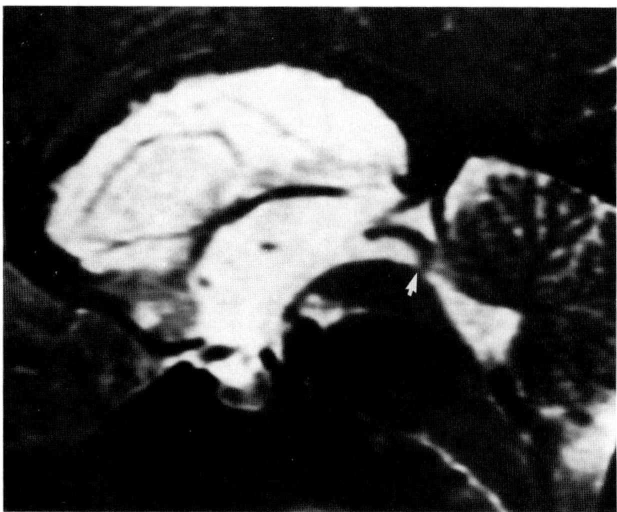

A

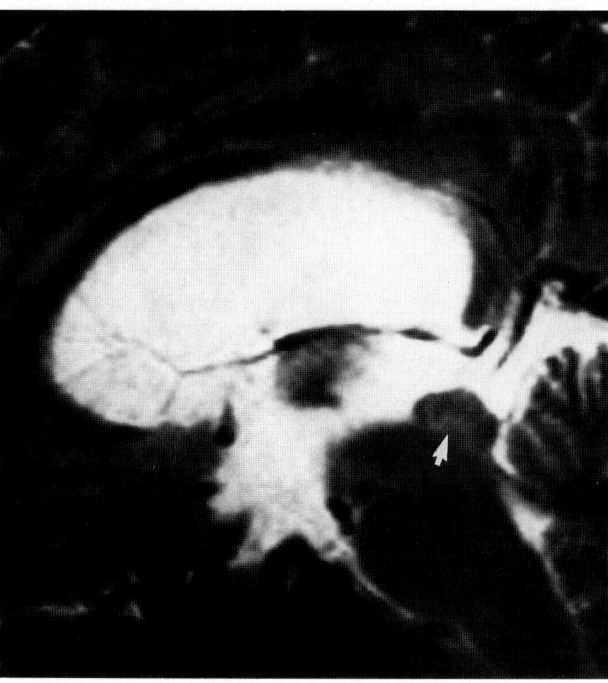

B

Figure 6-23 Aqueductal obstruction. **A.** Sagittal T_2WI (2500/80) reveals hydrocephalus secondary to obstruction at the posterior aspect of the cerebral aqueduct (arrow). The appearance is that of a benign aqueductal occlusion since there is no abnormal signal intensity or enlargement of the midbrain/tectum to suggest the presence of an obstructing neoplasm. **B.** Sagittal T_2WI (2500/80) reveals hydrocephalus, in this case secondary to a tectal mass (arrow). Note the enlarged tectal plate and the increased signal intensity within it. There is no visible CSF flow through the aqueduct.

obstruction to CSF flow. Aqueductal obstruction may occur in utero as well as postnatally and may be due to a variety of causes (Russell 1949; Turnbull 1966; Sovic 1977; Ho 1982). Clinically, and consequently radiographically, a critical distinction must be made between benign so-called aqueductal stenosis and neoplastic causes of obstruction.

Benign aqueductal narrowing or occlusion has variable histopathological correlates. The aqueduct may have an ependyma-lined lumen which is narrowed and slitlike in its long axis, as seen in the rare X-linked form of congenital aqueductal stenosis; there may be multiple ependymal nests or a network of ependymal channels referred to as "forking," or there may be a thin glial septum at the caudal end of the aqueduct. Maldevelopmental processes have been implicated in some instances, since it is known that in the fetus the aqueduct develops from a distended portion of the neural tube underneath the tectal plate, which gradually narrows to achieve its adult configuration later in gestation (Turkewitsch 1935). It has also been suggested that aqueductal narrowing may occur secondarily from hydrocephalus (Williams 1973; Nugent 1979), as in the Arnold-Chiari malformation, where it has been proposed that distention of the lateral ventricles induces tectal beaking and aqueductal compression. In some cases, postinflammatory changes that consist of denuded ependyma and overgrowth of glial tissue have been found microscopically, probably acquired from meningitis/ependymitis or perinatal intraventricular hemorrhage. Experimental data have shown that fetal viral infection is able to induce aqueductal occlusion without residual inflammatory changes (Nielsen 1972). Thus, even microscopically, the distinction between congenital and acquired lesions can be blurred (Drachman 1961). Distinction among the various forms of benign aqueductal stenosis is not possible radiographically (Barkovich 1989*b*).

On CT, the diagnosis of aqueductal stenosis is suggested when the lateral and third ventricles are dilated and the fourth ventricle is normal in size. Neoplastic forms of aqueductal obstruction, such as from a tectal glioma, may be difficult to distinguish on CT. Consequently, all patients with aqueductal obstruction should have an MR examination to more definitively evaluate the aqueduct and the tectal tissues. This is best performed with thin (3 mm or less) sagittal and axial images through the aqueduct. Both T_1WI and T_2WI are useful in characterizing aqueductal distortion (Fig. 6-23A), demonstrating total lack of or an incomplete aqueductal flow void (Kemp 1987), and detecting a mass in those with neoplasms (Fig. 6-23B).

References

ALTMAN NR, ALTMAN DH, SHELDON JJ, LEBORGNE J: Holoprosencephaly classified by computed tomography. *AJNR* 5:433–437, 1984.

ALTMAN NR, PURSER RK, POST MJD: Tuberous sclerosis: Characteristics at CT and MR imaging. *Radiology* 167:527–532, 1988.

AOKI S, BARKOVICH AJ, NISHIMURA K, KJOS BO, MACHIDA T, COGEN P, EDWARDS M, NORMAL D: Neurofibromatosis types 1 and 2: Cranial MR findings. *Radiology* 172:527–534, 1989.

ARCHER CR, DARWISH H, SMITH K JR: Enlarged cisternae magnae and posterior fossa cysts simulating Dandy-Walker syndrome on computed tomography. *Radiology* 127:681–686, 1978.

ATLAS SW, ZIMMERMAN RA, BILANIUK LT, RORKE L, HACKNEY DB, GOLDBERG HI, GROSSMAN RI: Corpus callosum and limbic system: Neuroanatomic MR evaluation of developmental anomalies. *Neuroradiology* 160:355–362, 1986.

BANERJI NK, MILLAR JHD: Chiari malformation presenting in adult life: Its relationship to syringomyelia. *Brain* 97:157–168, 1974.

BARKOVICH AJ, WIPPOLD FJ, SHERMAN JL, CITRIN CM: Significance of cerebellar tonsillar ectopia on MR. *AJNR* 7:795–799, 1986.

BARKOVICH AJ, CHUANG SH, NORMAN D: MR of neuronal migration anomalies. *AJNR* 8:1009–1017, 1987.

BARKOVICH AJ, KJOS BO, JACKSON DE Jr, NORMAN D: Normal maturation of the neonatal and infant brain: MR imaging at 1.5 T. *Radiology* 166;173–180, 1988*a*.

BARKOVICH AJ, NORMAN D: MR imaging of schizencephaly. *AJNR* 9:297–302, 1988*b*.

BARKOVICH AJ, NORMAN D: Anomalies of the corpus callosum: Correlation with further anomalies of the brain. *AJNR* 9:493–501, 1988*c*.

BARKOVICH AJ, NORMAN D: Absence of the septum pellucidum: A useful sign in the diagnosis of congenital brain malformations. *AJNR* 9:1107–1114, 1988*d*.

BARKOVICH AJ, KJOS BO, NORMAN D, EDWARDS MS: Revised classification of posterior fossa cysts and cystlike malformations based on the results of multiplanar MR imaging. *AJNR* 10:977–988, 1989*a*.

BARKOVICH AJ, NEWTON TH: MR of aqueductal stenosis: Evidence of a broad spectrum of tectal disorders. *AJNR* 10:471–476, 1989*b*.

BARKOVICH AJ, CHUANG SH: Unilateral megalencephaly: Correlation of MR imaging and pathologic characteristics. *AJNR* 11:523–531, 1990.

BARRY A, PATTEN BM, STEWART BH: Possible factors in the development of the Arnold-Chiari malformation. *J Neurosurg* 14:285–301, 1957.

BERRY M, ROGERS AW: The migration of neuroblasts in the developing neocortex. *J Anat* 99:691–709, 1965.

BIRD CR, HEDBERG M, DRAYER BP, KELLER PJ, FLOM RA, HODAK JA: MR assessment of myelination in infants and children: Usefulness of marker sites. *AJNR* 10:731–740, 1989.

BOGNANNO JR, EDWARDS MK, LEE TA, DUNN DW, ROOS KL, KLATTE EC: Cranial MR imaging in neurofibromatosis. *AJNR* 9:461–468, 1988.

BRAFFMAN BH, BILANIUK LT, ZIMMERMAN RA: The central nervous system manifestations of the phakomatoses on MR. *Radiol Clin North Am* 26(4):773–800, 1988.

BROWN EW, RICCARDI VM, MAWAD M, HANDEL S, GOLDMAN A, BRYAN RN: MR imaging of optic pathways in patients with neurofibromatosis. *AJNR* 8:1031–1036, 1987.

BYRD SE, HARWOOD-NASH DC, FITZ CR, ROGOVITZ DM: Computed tomography in the evaluation of encephaloceles in infants and children. *J Comput Assist Tomogr* 2:81–87, 1978.

BYRD SE, BOHAN TP, OSBORN RE, NAIDICH TP: The CT and MR evaluation of lissencephaly. *AJNR* 9:923–928, 1988.

CHAMBERLAIN MC, PRESS GA, HESSELINK JR: MR imaging and CT in three cases of Sturge-Weber syndrome: Prospective comparison. *AJNR* 10:491–496, 1989.

CHIARI H: Ueber Veranderungen des Kleinhirns infolge von Hydrocephalie des Grosshirns. *Dtsch Med Wochenschr* 17: 1172–75, 1891.

CHIARI H: Ueber Veranderungen des Kleinhirns, des Pons und der Medulla oblongata in Folge von genitaler Hydrocephalie des Grosshirns. *Denkschr Akad Wiss Wien* 63:71–116, 1896.

CONFERENCE STATEMENT: Neurofibromatosis: National Institutes of Health Consensus Development Conference. *Arch Neurol* 45:575–578, 1988.

CURNES JT, OAKES WJ: Parietal cephaloceles: Radiographic and magnetic resonance imaging evaluation. *Pediatr Neurosci* 14:71–76, 1988.

DAMBSKA M, HADDAD R, KOZLOWSKI PB, LEE MH, SHEK J: Telencephalic cytoarchitectonics in the brains of rats with graded degrees of micrencephaly. *Acta Neuropathol (Berl)* 58:203–209, 1982.

DANDY WE, BLACKFAN KD: Internal hydrocephalus: An experimental, clinical and pathological study. *Am J Dis Child* 8:406–482, 1914.

DANIEL PM, STRICH SJ: Some observations on the congenital deformity of the central nervous system known as the Arnold-Chiari malformation. *J Neuropathol Exp Neurol* 17:255–266, 1958.

DAUSER RC, DIPIETRO MA, VENES JL: Symptomatic Chiari I malformation in childhood: A report of 7 cases. *Pediatr Neurosci* 14:184–190, 1988.

DAVIDSON HD, ABRAHAM R, STEINER RE: Agenesis of the corpus callosum: Magnetic resonance imaging. *Radiology* 155:371–373, 1985.

DAVISON AN, DOBBING J, PATH MC: Myelination as a vulnerable period in brain development. *Br Med Bull* 22:40–44, 1966.

DEAN B, DRAYER BP, BERESINI DC, BIRD CR: MR imaging of pericallosal lipoma. *AJNR* 9:929–932, 1988.

DEEB ZL, ROTHFUS WE, MAROON JC: MR imaging of heterotopic gray matter. *J Comput Assist Tomogr* 9:1140–1141, 1985.

DEMYER W: Classification of cerebral malformations. *Birth Defects* 7:78–88, 1971.

DEMYER W: Megalencephaly in children: Clinical syndromes, genetic patterns and differential diagnosis from other causes of megalocephaly. *Neurology* 22:634–643, 1972.

DEMYER W: Holoprosencephaly (cyclopia-arhinencephaly), in Vinken PI, Bruyn GW (eds): *Handbook of Clinical Neurology,* vol 30, Amsterdam, Elsevier/North-Holland Biomedical, 1977, pp 431–478.

DIEBLER C, DULAC O: Cephaloceles: Clinical and neuroradiological appearance: Associated cerebral malformations. *Neuroradiology* 25:199–216, 1983.

DIETRICH RB, BRADLEY WG, ZAGAROZA EJ IV, OTTO RJ, TAIRA RK, WILSON GH, KANGARLOO H: MR evaluation of early myelination patterns in normal and developmentally delayed infants. *AJNR* 9:69–76, 1988.

DOBYNS WB, STRATTON RF, GREENBERG F: Syndromes with lissencephaly: I. Miller-Dieker and Norman-Roberts syndromes and isolated lissencephaly. *Am J Med Genet* 18:509–526, 1984.

DOBYNS WB, KIRKPATRICK JB, HITTNER HM, ROBERTS RM, KRETZER LF: Syndromes with lissencephaly: II. Walker-Warburg and cerebro-oculo-muscular syndromes and a new syndrome with type II lissencephaly. *Am J Med Genet* 22:157–195, 1985*a*.

DOBYNS WB, MCCLUGGAGE CW: Computed tomographic appearance of lissencephaly syndromes. *AJNR* 6:545–550, 1985*b*.

DRACHMAN DA, RICHARDSON EP Jr: Aqueductal narrowing, congenital and acquired: A critical view of the histologic criteria. *Arch Neurol* 5:106–113, 1961.

ELSTER AD, CHEN MYM: MR imaging of Sturge-Weber syndrome: Role of gadopentetate dimeglumine and gradient-echo techniques. *AJNR* 11:685–689, 1990.

FITZ CR, HARWOOD-NASH DC, BOLDT DW: The radiographic features of unilateral megalencephaly. *Neuroradiology* 15:145–148, 1978.

FITZ CR: Holoprosencephaly and related entities. *Neuroradiology* 25:225–238, 1983.

FRIEDE RL: *Developmental Neuropathology,* 2d ed, New York, Springer-Verlag, 1989.

GAMMAL TE, MARK EK, BROOKS BS: MR imaging of Chiari II malformation. *AJNR* 8:1037–1044, 1987.

GARDNER WJ: Anatomic features common to Arnold-Chiari and Dandy-Walker malformations suggest common origin. *Cleve Clin Q* 26:206–222, 1959.

GOLDEN JA, RORKE LB, BRUCE DA: Dandy-Walker syndrome and associated anomalies. *Pediatr Neurosci* 13:38–44, 1987.

GUSNARD DA, BILANIUK LT, ZIMMERMAN RA, et al: Imaging of posterior fossa cystic malformations: Pre- and post-shunting [Abstract]. *AJNR* 9:1015, 1988.

HARWOOD-NASH DC, FITZ CR: *Neuroradiology in Infants and Children,* vol 3, St. Louis, Mosby, 1976, pp 998–1053.

HICKS SP: Developmental malformations produced by radiation: A timetable of their development. *AJR* 69:272–293, 1953.

HO KL: Tumors of the cerebral aqueduct. *Cancer* 49:154–162, 1982.

HURST RW, NEWMAN SA, CAIL WS: Multifocal intracranial MR abnormalities in neurofibromatosis. *AJNR* 9:292–296, 1988.

INGRAHAM FD, SCOTT HW Jr: Spina bifida and cranium bifidum: V. The Arnold-Chiari malformation: A study of 20 cases. *N Engl J Med* 229:108–114, 1943.

JOUBERT M, EISENRING JJ, ROBB JP, ANDERMANN F: Familial agenesis of the cerebellar vermis. *Neurology* 19:813–825, 1969.

JUHL JH, WESENBERG RL: Radiological findings in congenital and acquired occlusions of the foramina of Magendie and Luschka. *Radiology* 86:801–813, 1966.

KEMP SS, ZIMMERMAN RA, BILANIUK LT, HACKNEY DB, GOLDBERG HI, GROSSMAN RI: Magnetic resonance imaging of the cerebral aqueduct. *Neuroradiology* 29:430–436, 1987.

KING MD, DUDGEON J, STEPHENSON JP: Joubert's syndrome with retinal dysplasia: Neonatal tachypnea as the clue to a genetic brain-eye malformation. *Arch Dis Child* 59:709–718, 1984.

LIPSKI S, BRUNELLE F, AICARDI J, HIRSCH JF, LALLEMAND D: Gd-DOTA-enhanced MR imaging in two cases of Sturge-Weber syndrome. *AJNR* 11:690–692, 1990.

MANELFE C, ROCHICCIOLI P: CT of septo-optic dysplasia. *AJR* 133:1157–1160, 1979.

MARIA BL, ZINREICH SJ, CARSON BC, ROSENBAUM AE, FREEMAN JM: Dandy-Walker syndrome revisited. *Pediatr Neurosci* 13:45–51, 1987.

MASDEU JC, DOBBEN GD, AZAR-KIA B: Dandy-Walker syndrome studied by computed tomography and pneumoencephalography. *Radiology* 147:109–114, 1983.

MCLONE DG, KNEPPER PA: The cause of Chiari II malformation: A unified theory. *Pediatr Neurosci* 15:1–12, 1989.

MIROWITZ ŞA, SARTOR K, GADO M: High-intensity basal ganglia lesions on T1-weighted MR images in neurofibromatosis. *AJNR* 10:1159–1163, 1989.

MYRIANTHOPOULOS NC: Concepts, definitions and classification of congenital and developmental malformations of the central nervous system and related structures, in Vinken PI, Bruyn GW (eds): *Handbook of Clinical Neurology,* vol 30, Amsterdam, Elsevier/North-Holland Biomedical, 1977, pp 1–13.

NAIDICH TP, PUDLOWSKI RM, NAIDICH JB, GORNISH M, RODRIGUEZ FJ: Computed tomographic signs of the Chiari II malformation: I. Skull and dural partitions. *Radiology* 134: 65–71, 1980*a*.

NAIDICH TP, PUDLOWSKI RM, NAIDICH JB: Computed tomographic signs of Chiari II malformation: II. Midbrain and cerebellum. *Radiology* 134:391–398, 1980*b*.

NAIDICH TP, PUDLOWSKI RM, NAIDICH JB: Computed tomographic signs of the Chiari II malformation: III. Ventricles and cisterns. *Radiology* 134:657–663, 1980*c*.

NAIDICH TP, MCLONE DG, BAUER BS, KERNAHAN DA, ZAPARACKAS ZG: Midline craniofacial dysraphism. *Concepts Pediatr Neurosurg* 4:186–207, 1983*a*.

NAIDICH TP, MCLONE DG, FULLING KH: The Chiari II malformation: IV. The hindbrain deformity. *Neuroradiology* 25: 179–197, 1983*b*.

NAIDICH TP, ZIMMERMAN RA: Common congenital malformations of the brain, in Brant-Zawadski M, Norman D (eds): *Magnetic Resonance Imaging of the Central Nervous System,* New York, Raven Press, 1987, pp 131–150.

NIELSEN SL, BARINGER JR: Reovirus-induced aqueductal stenosis in hamsters: Phase contrast electromicroscopic studies. *Lab Invest* 27:531–537, 1972.

NUGENT GR, AL-MEFTY O, CHOU S: Communicating hydrocephalus as a cause of aqueductal stenosis. *J Neurosurg* 51:812–818, 1979.

O'DWYER W, NEWTON TH, HOYT W: Radiologic features of septo-optic dysplasia: De Morsier syndrome. *AJNR* 1:443–447, 1980.

OSBORN RE, BYRD SE, NAIDICH TP, BOHAN TP, FRIEDMAN H: MR imaging of neuronal migrational disorders. *AJNR* 9:1101–1106, 1988.

PARRISH ML, ROESSMANN U, LEVINSOHN MW: Agenesis of the corpus callosum: A study of the frequency of associated malformations. *Ann Neurol* 6:349–354, 1979.

POSWILLO D: Mechanisms and pathogenesis of malformations. *Br Med Bull* 32:59–64, 1976.

RAKIC P, YAKOVLEV PI: Development of the corpus callosum and cavum septi in man. *J Comp Neurol* 132:45–72, 1968.

RAYBAUD C: Cystic malformations of the posterior fossa. *J Neuroradiol* 9:103–133, 1982.

ROACH E, DEMYER W, CONNEALLY P, et al: Holoprosencephaly: Birth data, genetic and demographic analyses of 30 families. *Birth Defects* 11:294–313, 1975.

ROACH ES, WILLIAMS DP, LASTER DW: Magnetic resonance imaging in tuberous sclerosis. *Arch Neurol* 44:301–303, 1982.

RUSSELL DS: Observations on the pathology of hydrocephalus, in Medical Research Council Special Report Series, No. 265, London. His Majesty's Stationery Office, 1949, pp 1–138.

SHAW CM, ALVORD EC: "Congenital arachnoid" cysts and their differential diagnosis, in Vinken PI, Bruyn GW (eds): *Handbook of Clinical Neurology,* vol 31, Amsterdam, Elsevier/North-Holland Biomedical, 1977, pp 75–135.

SOVIC O, VAN DER HAGEN CB, LOKEN AC: X-linked aqueductal stenosis. *Clin Genet* 11:416–420, 1977.

STEWART RM, RICHMAN DP, CAVINESS VS Jr: Lissencephaly and pachygyria: An architectonic and topographical analysis. *Acta Neuropathol (Berl)* 31:1–12, 1975.

TITELBAUM DS, HAYWARD JC, ZIMMERMAN RA: Pachygyriclike changes: Topographic appearance at MR imaging and CT and correlation with neurologic status. *Radiology* 173:663–667, 1989.

TOWNSEND JJ, NIELSEN SL, MALAMUD N: Unilateral megalencephaly: Hamartoma or neoplasm? *Neurology* 25:448–453, 1975.

TRUWIT CL, BARKOVICH AJ: Pathogenesis of intracranial lipoma: An MR study in 42 patients. *AJNR* 11:665–674, 1990.

TURKEWITSCH N: Die Entwicklung des Aquaeductus Cerebri des Menschen. *Morphol Jahrb* 76:421–477, 1935.

TURNBULL IM, DRAKE CG: Membranous occlusion of the aqueduct of Sylvius. *J Neurosurg* 24:24–33, 1966.

VAGHI M, VISCIANI A, TESTA D, BIVELLI S, PASSERNI A: Cerebral MR findings in tuberous sclerosis. *J Comput Assist Tomogr* 11:403–406, 1987.

VAN DER KNAAP MS, VALK J: Classification of congenital abnormalities of the CNS. *AJNR* 9:315–326, 1988.

VOLPE JJ: Normal and abnormal human brain development. *Clin Perinatol* 4:3–30, 1977.

WASENKO JJ, ROSENBLOOM SA, DUCHESNEAU PM, LANZIERI CF, WEINSTEIN MA: The Sturge-Weber syndrome: Comparison of MR and CT characteristics. *AJNR* 11:131–134, 1990.

WILLIAMS B: Is aqueduct stenosis the result of hydrocephalus? *Brain* 96:399–412, 1973.

WOLPERT SM, SCOTT RM, PLATENBERG C, RUNGE VM: The clinical significance of hindbrain herniation and deformity as shown on MR images of patients with Chiari II malformation. *AJNR* 9:1075–1078, 1988.

YAKOVLEV PI, WADSWORTH RC: Schizencephalies: A study of the congenital clefts in the cerebral mantle: I. Clefts with fused lips. *J Neuropathol Exp Neurol* 5:116–130, 1946*a*.

YAKOVLEV PI, WADSWORTH RC: Schizencephalies: A study of tne congenital clefts in the cerebral mantle: II. Clefts with hydrocephalus and lips separated. *J Neuropathol Exp Neurol* 5:169–206, 1946*b*.

YAKOVLEV PI: Pathoarchitectonic studies of cerebral malformations. *J Neuropathol Exp Neurol* 18:22–30, 1959.

YAKOVLEV PI, LECOURS AR: The myelogenetic cycles of regional maturation of the brain, in Minkowski A (ed): *Regional Development of the Brain in Early Life,* Philadelphia, Davis, 1967, pp 3–70.

ZIMMERMAN RD, BRECKBILL D, DENNIS MW, et al: Cranial CT findings in patients with meningomyelocele. *AJR* 132:623–629, 1979.

ZIMMERMAN RA, BILANIUK LT, GROSSMAN RI: Computed tomography in migratory disorders of human brain development. *Neuroradiology* 25:257–263, 1983.

ZIMMERMAN RD, BILANIUK LT: Pediatric central nervous system, in Stark DD, Bradley WG Jr (eds): *Magnetic Resonance Imaging,* St. Louis, Mosby, 1988, pp 683–714.

7 THE CSF SPACES (Hydrocephalus and Atrophy)

Krishna C.V.G. Rao

INTRODUCTION

Cerebrospinal fluid (CSF) in the cranial cavity is present within the ventricular and cisternal spaces as well as the interstitium of the brain parenchyma. CSF functions as an intermediary pathway between the neural tissue and the vascular capillaries, providing nutrients and metabolites to the brain parenchyma. Outside the ventricular system CSF flows between the pial membrane, covering the craniospinal surface, and the arachnoid membrane in the subarachnoid space. It is absorbed by the arachnoid villi in the walls of the cerebral venous sinuses.

A basic understanding of the normal CSF physiology and its direct and indirect effects on the brain parenchyma is essential in reviewing imaging studies. Pathological alterations within the constituents of CSF, its volume, and its flow dynamics may reflect pathological disease processes involving the brain parenchyma.

CSF PHYSIOLOGY

CSF is produced by the choroid plexus in the ventricular cavity and the ventricular ependyma (Milhorat 1975). The choroid plexus accounts for less than 0.25 percent of the weight of the adult human brain. The volume and weight of the choroid plexus relative to the brain are significantly greater in neonates than in adults. The choroid plexus is located primarily along the ependymal surfaces of the atrial walls of the lateral ventricles, in the roof of the third ventricle, and along the posterior inferior surface of the fourth ventricle. These sites are in close proximity to the vascular channels that penetrate the ependymal surfaces of the ventricular wall. The choroid plexus consists of a network of densely branched fronds composed of smaller arterioles and capillaries surrounded by a single layer of epithelial cells. The CSF is produced by a process of facilitated diffusion from the capillaries as well as active transportation of certain metabolites (Spector 1989).

CSF is produced continuously at a rate of 25 ml/h (0.35–0.40 ml/min) (Cutler 1968). In the normal physiological state, the total CSF volume at any given time amounts to 120 to 135 ml. Of this amount, about 25 to 35 ml is within the ventricular space and the rest is within the subarachnoid cisterns, with a small amount within the interstitial spaces of the brain parenchyma. CSF flows from the intracellular space to the ventricles in a centripetal manner. The flow from the ventricles to the subarachnoid cisterns is propagated by transmitted vascular pulsations within the CSF spaces (Marmarou 1975; Portnoy 1982) and the systolic expansion of the brain parenchyma. During its passage and turnover within the cellular spaces, it allows for exchange of metabolites and nutrients.

CT AND MRI OF CSF PATHWAYS

The in vivo demonstration of CSF pathways has come a long way since the description by Dandy (1919) utilizing pneumoencephalography. When CSF was replaced with air, pneumoencephalography could be used to provide anatomic correlation of the CSF spaces and indirect correlation of the structural or morphological anatomy of the brain parenchyma. Even though it provided some physiological information, the availability of noninvasive imaging studies has obviated the need for this imaging modality.

Both computed tomography (CT) and magnetic resonance imaging (MRI) allow noninvasive evaluation of the CSF spaces as well as the brain parenchyma. In most instances they have replaced earlier invasive studies.

On CT, the dynamics of CSF flow is determined by evaluating the size and configuration of the ventricles and sulcal spaces and the presence or absence of adjacent changes in parenchymal density. Imaging is based on attenuation values of the tissues and fluids within the cranial vault. Unlike MRI, imaging is not affected by the CSF or blood flow. CSF is hypodense relative to the brain parenchyma. An increase in density similar to (isointense) or higher than (hyperdense) brain parenchyma often is related to the presence of fresh blood products or appears after intrathecal contrast. Slight increases depending on the protein content of CSF are difficult to observe visually.

Direct imaging of the CSF flow and its dynamics is achieved with CT cisternography (Greitz 1974; Drayer 1977), a procedure similar to radionuclide cisternography (DiChiro 1964). In CT cisternography, a small amount (6 to 8 ml) of nonionic contrast is injected into the thecal space. CT studies are obtained at different time intervals to assess the rate of absorption of the contrast. As a result of the variable results and the need for repetitive scanning, CT cisternoraphy has not been popular. At the present time it has limited application and is used primarily in demonstrating CSF leaks in patients with suspected CSF rhinorrhoea and otorrhea (Ghoshhajra 1980).

The major drawbacks of CT are the inability to demonstrate the dynamics of CSF flow, the difficulty in demonstrating lesions within the CSF spaces with attenuation values similar to that of CSF, and the inability to demonstrate subtle changes in the white matter tracts within the brain parenchyma.

CSF Flow on MRI

MRI is better than CT in demonstrating not only the morphological changes associated with brain atrophy in neurodegenerative disorders and hydrocephalus but also the associated changes in the white matter. The CSF spaces can be evaluated in all three orthogonal planes. Routine spin-echo sequences provide some idea of CSF flow dynamics. With the availability of new and fast scanning techniques as well as data manipulation, CSF dynamics and flow in its natural state can be evaluated without the injection of any contrast or isotope (Jolesz 1987; Feinberg 1987; Enzmann 1991).

On MRI, CSF is hypointense on T_1WI, as it is on CT. On T_2WI, CSF is hyperintense except where it flows through narrow segments of the ventricular spaces, such as the aqueduct of Sylvius, the foramen of Monro, and the outlet foramina of the fourth ventricle. The varying intensity of the CSF signal on T_2WI within these regions in normal and pathological conditions is dependent on CSF flow dynamics.

On MRI, flowing blood creates a drop in signal, resulting in the flow-related artifact described as *flow void signal* (Bradley 1984, 1986; Mills 1983). A similar phenomenon is seen in the ventricular CSF pathways. This has been described as the *CSF flow void signal* (CFVS) or *aqueductal flow void signal* (Sherman 1986; Bradley 1986). This flow-related artifact is best appreciated in the first echo of T_2WI in sections through the aqueduct (Fig. 7-1). Occasionally CFVS may also be present in the region of the foramen of Monro and in sections through the outlet foramina of the fourth ventricle (Fig. 7-2).

The pulsatile flow of CSF from the ventricles to the subarachnoid cisterns and within the perivascular spaces is directly related to the state of the cardiovascular system, the transmitted vascular pulsations, and the tensile capacity of the brain parenchyma (Ohara 1988). During systole, CSF flows in a caudal direction from the ventricles. Within the subarachnoid cisterns, it moves in a cephalad direction during the diastolic phase (Enzmann 1991). The outward flow of CSF from the ventricles is aided by the compressive centrifugal pressure applied by

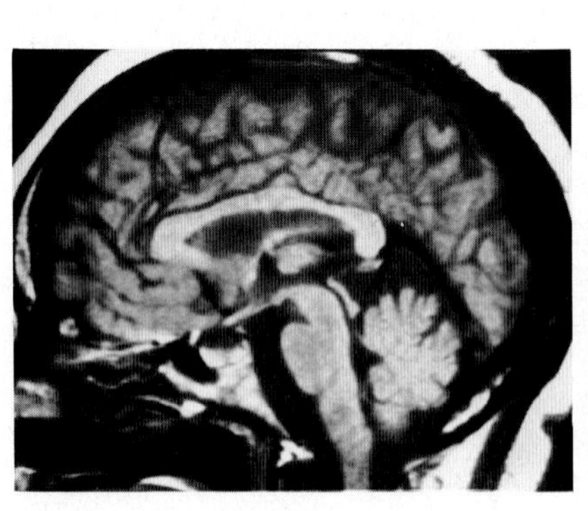
A

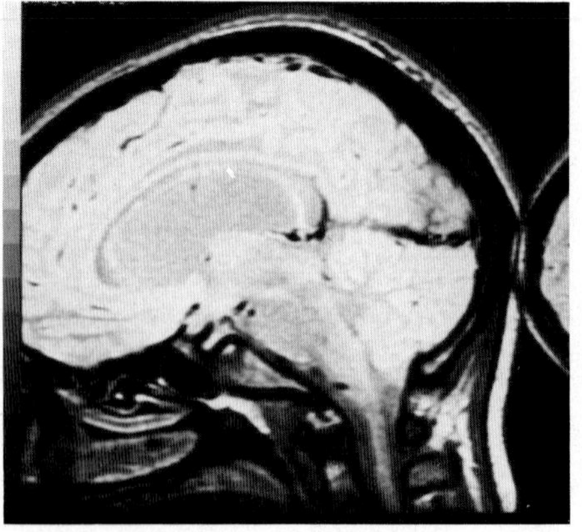
B

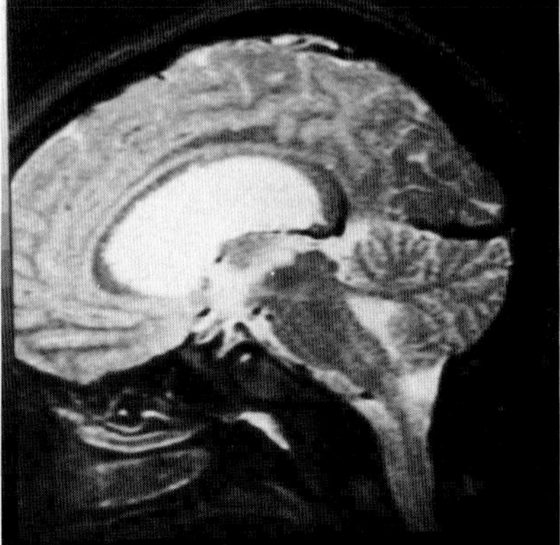
C

Figure 7-1 Appearance of CSF on MRI. Sagittal MR (**A**) SE 600/30 (T_1WI), (**B**) SE 2800/40 (T_2WI = proton density or spin density or balanced image) MR, (**C**) SE 2800/90 (T_2WI). On T_1WI the CSF is hypointense, similar to the hypodense appearance on CT. On T_2WI, the CSF is almost isointense in T_2-W short or first echo sequence (TE 20–40) and hyperintense in the longer or second echo sequence, except where it flows through narrow channels. This hypointensity is related to physiological factors (turbulence, eddy currents, pulsatory motion) and technical factors utilized in acquiring the image.

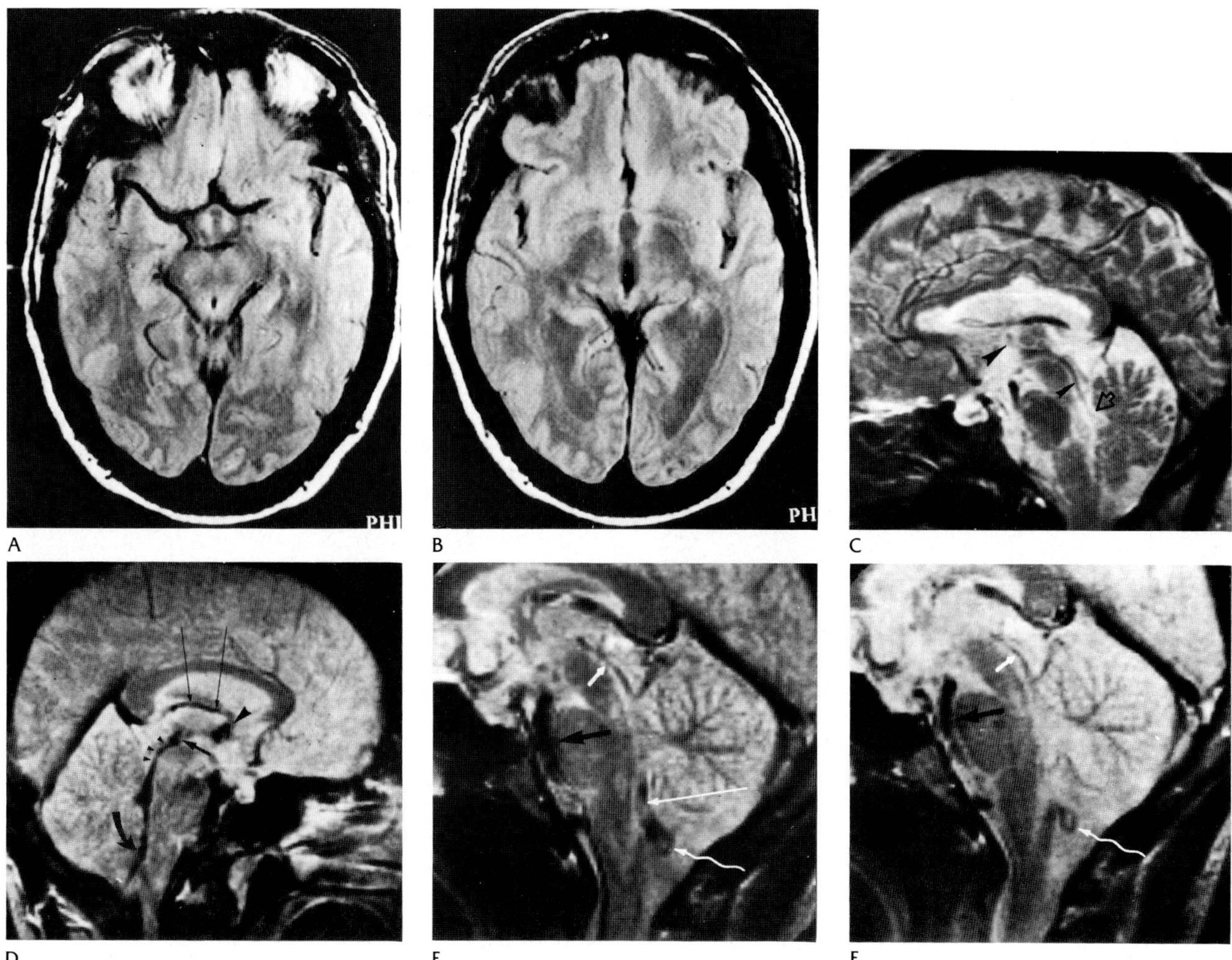

Figure 7-2 CSF flow void signal (CFVS). Axial T_2-W MR (SE 2500/30) in axial sections through the aqueduct (**A**) and the third ventricle (**B**). Sagittal T_2-W MR gradient-echo image (**C**) demonstrates CFVS in the interventricular foramen (large arrowhead), aqueduct (small arrowhead), and fourth ventricle (open arrow). **D.** Sagittal T_2-W MR (SE 2800/40) in a patient with atrophy and prominent CFVS in the foramen of Monro (arrowhead), third ventricle (long thin arrows), posterior third ventricle (small arrow), within the length of the aqueduct (small arrowheads), and midline outlet of the foramina of Magendie (curved arrow). Systolic (**E**) and diastolic (**F**) gated midsagittal MRI. Prominent CFVS within the aqueduct (short white arrow) in (**D**) compared to (**E**). Similar appearance in the basilar artery (black arrow) and the internal cerebral vein. Vascular loop (undulating white arrow) and foramen of Magendie (straight thin arrow) seen in a diastollic gated study.

the central portions of the brain (Feinberg 1987), such as the corpus callosum and the thalami (thalamic pump). These CSF dynamics have been demonstrated utilizing phase-contrast cine MR techniques (Enzmann 1991). These studies have demonstrated that the outward flow of CSF is accomplished by a slight delay in phase as well as time between the flow velocity within the ventricles and that in the subarachnoid CSF (Enzmann 1991; Feinberg 1987).

This physiological CSF pump creates turbulence at and within the orifice of the narrow channels, such as the aqueduct of Sylvius. The CFVS in the aqueduct thus results from turbulent nonlaminar flow of CSF as it pulsates between the narrow channel of the aqueduct and the larger ventricular space (Malko 1988). Cardiac pulsations affect the appearance of the CFVS, as shown on cardiac gated MRI studies (Citrin 1986). CFVS is more prominent in systolic gated MRI.

The absence of CFVS in the aqueduct of Sylvius in certain circumstances is indicative of an obstructive pathological condition (Sherman 1986*b*). The obstruction need not be at the aqueductal level but may be higher. In these circumstances, the absence of the signal is due to lack of bulk CSF flow and turbulence within the orifice of the aqueduct (Sherman 1986*b*).

Prominent CFVS is often seen in communicating hydrocephalus as a result of the patency of the aqueduct and increased turbulence and the to-and-fro motion of

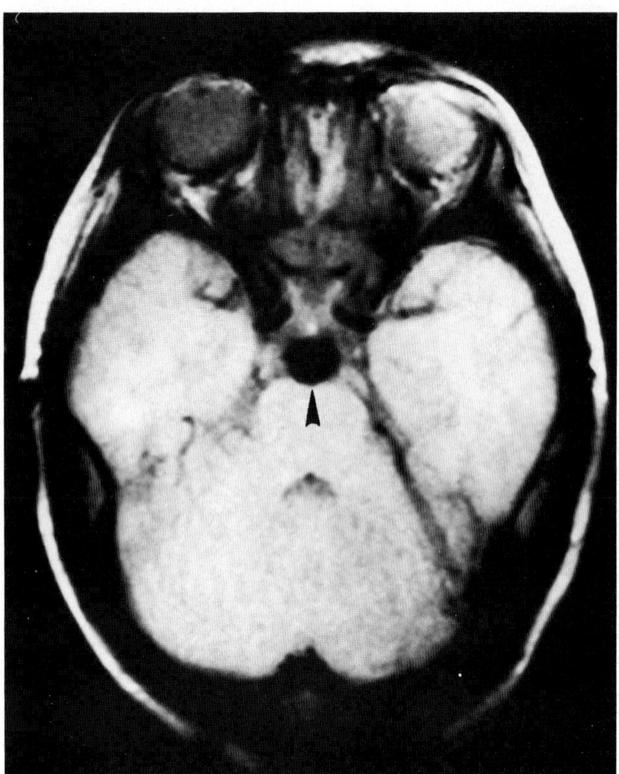

Figure 7-3 Pseudoaneurysm of the basilar artery (arrowhead) resulting from a combination of CSF flow and arterial pulsation. First echo of T_2WI (SE 2200/40).

CSF. Prominent CFVS may also be seen as a normal physiological phenomenon in infants resulting from their increased cardiac rate and the larger volume of the choroid plexus. In a similar manner, the combination of CSF flow and arterial pulsation may result in prominent arterial flow void signal. If not recognized, this may be mistaken for an aneurysm (Fig. 7-3) (Burt 1987).

Other factors may influence the appearance of CFVS. These factors are both operator- and equipment-dependent, such as field of view (FOV), echo time (TE), pulse sequence (spin echo versus gradient echo), slice thickness, cardiac gating, and field strength of the magnet (Malko 1988). CFVS is more prominent in a midfield strength magnet than in a higher-field-strength magnet (Jack 1987).

PARENCHYMAL CHANGES ON CT AND MRI

Morphological as well as histological alteration in the brain parenchyma as a consequence of an increase in CSF space or pulsatile pressure occurs when there is an obstruction to the flow of CSF between its site of production and its site of absorption. This is defined as *hydrocephalus.* When the apparent increase in the CSF space results from volume loss of the brain parenchyma caused by normal aging or a neurodegenerative process, it is defined as *atrophy.*

In hydrocephalus there is an increase in CSF volume proximal to the site of obstruction. In most instances this is associated with an increase in the CSF pressure above the site of obstruction, resulting in concentric enlargement of the ventricular cavity. This is also associated with effacement of the cortical sulci. Other features suggestive of ventricular enlargement due to increased CSF pressure include elevation and thinning of the corpus callosum and dilatation of the optic and infundibular recesses of the third ventricle anteriorly and the pineal and suprapineal recesses posteriorly. In acute communicating hydrocephalus or with obstruction at the outlet foramina of the fourth ventricle, all the ventricular compartments are dilated.

In the majority of imaging studies, differentiation between hydrocephalic and atrophic ventricular enlargement can be achieved easily. Diagnosis can be a problem when one is differentiating between diffuse cerebral atrophy and chronic communicating hydrocephalus (NPH) and when the communicating hydrocephalus is due to defective or delayed CSF absorption over the convexity (Maytal 1987; Gilles 1971). Several measurements or indexes have been utilized in differentiating atrophic ventricular enlargement from enlargement due to hydrocephalus (Fig. 7-3). These measurements include age-matched linear measurements of the ventricular spaces and sulci on CT (Barron 1976; Gyldensted 1977; Hahn 1976; Haug 1977; Pedersen 1979; Huckman 1975; Ramsay 1977). These measurements are subject to variability caused by operator- and equipment-related factors.

It is probably more reliable to use an index system (Heinz 1980). The most commonly used indexes are the frontal horn ratio and the ventricular span ratio. The frontal horn ratio is obtained by dividing the maximum width of the frontal horns by the transverse diameter of the inner table of the calvarium at the same level. The normal ratio is about 35 percent. In atrophic ventricular enlargement the ratio is between 45 and 50 percent, and in hydrocephalus it is usually above 45 percent and often exceeds 55 percent. These ratios must be combined with other morphological features.

The distention of the ventricular system in hydrocephalus is symmetrical and is characterized by concentric expansion. The ventricles bulge as if they were expanded by multiple vectors of force radiating from a central axis, resulting in a balloon-shaped appearance of the frontal horns (Fig. 7-4). In cerebral atrophy all parts of the ventricles may be affected equally, whereas in hydrocephalus the larger parts of the ventricular system distend first (frontal and occipital horns), to be followed by a distention of the smaller parts (temporal horns and fourth and third ventricles). Hydrocephalus should be suspected

Ventricular size index

$$\text{V.S.I.} = \frac{\text{Bifrontal diameter}}{\text{Frontal horn diameter}}$$

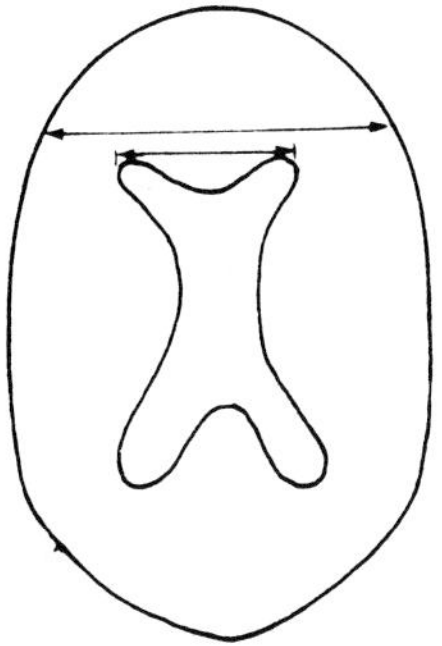

Normal	30%
Mild enlargement	30-39%
Moderate enlargement	40-46%
Severe enlargement	47%

	Atrophy		**Obstructive hydrocephalus**		**Remarks**
Angle of frontal horn	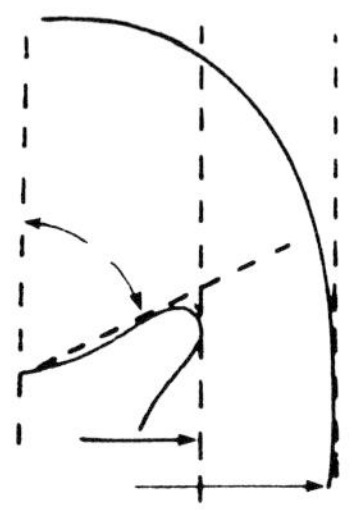	Obtuse	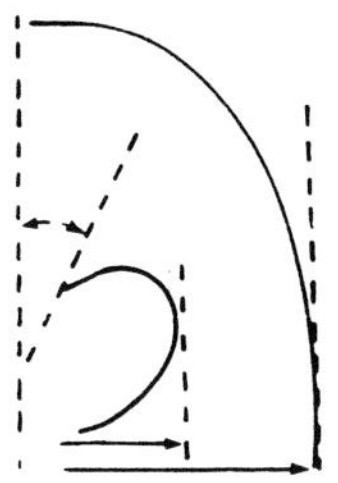	Acute	
Frontal horn ratio	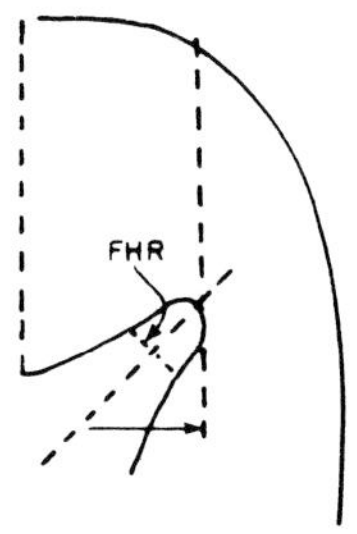	Small	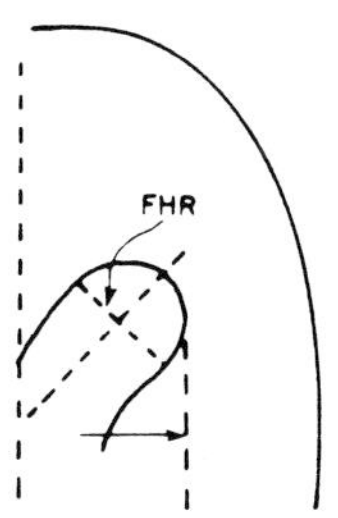	Wide	FHR: Measured at the widest part of the frontal horn perpendicular to the long axis of the frontal horn.
Temporal horn ratio	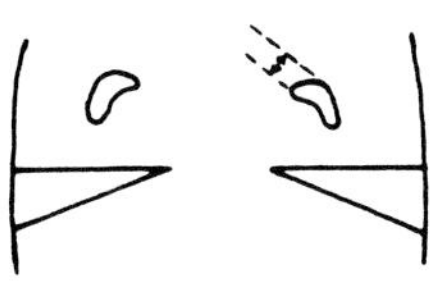	Not visible or small	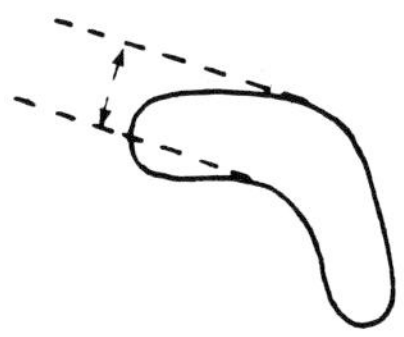	Wide	Width of temporal horn measured at the genu.
Sulci and cistern		Wide		Obliterated	

Figure 7-4 Differentiating features between atrophic and obstructive ventricular enlargement. These measurements can also be applied utilizing the different plane of imaging on MRI. (*Modified from Heinz 1980.*)

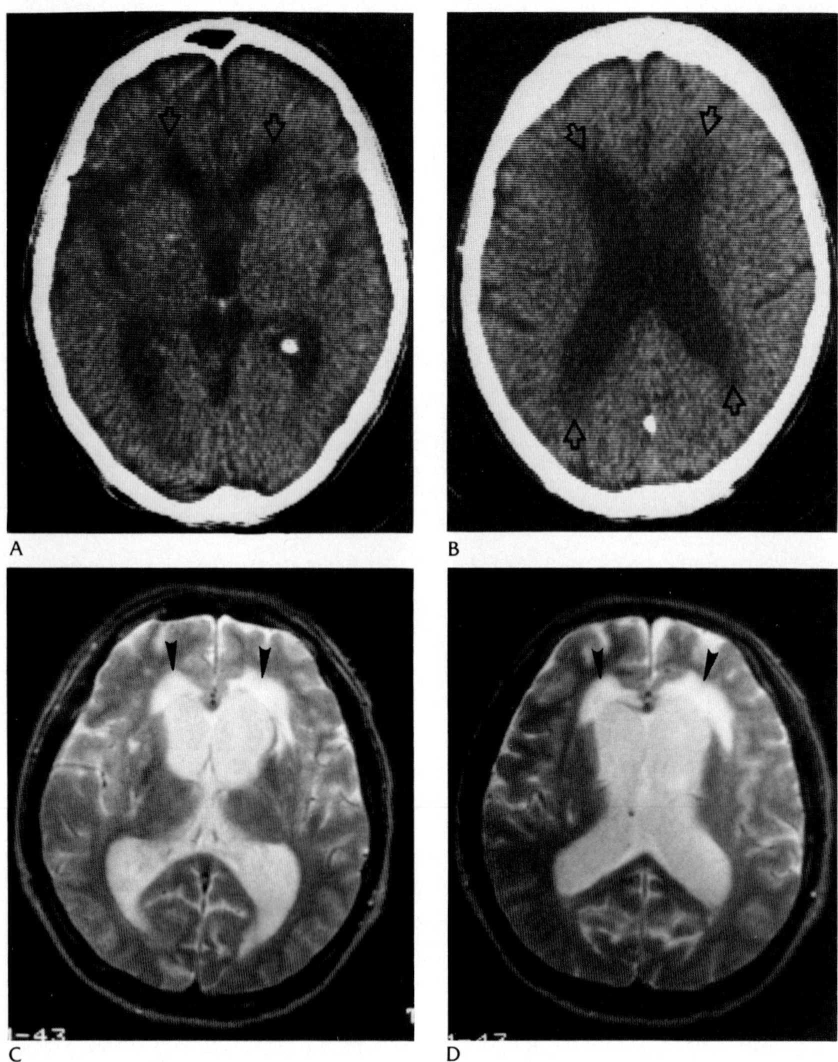

Figure 7-5 Periventricular parenchymal changes in hydrocephalus. **A, B**. Axial CT demonstrates periventricular hypodensity (arrow) that is distinct near the ventricular wall and less distinct peripherally. **C, D** Axial MR (SE 2500/80) demonstrates a similar hyperintense signal along the periventricular region. In addition, the ventricles are enlarged, with a decrease in the width of the sulci and cisterns.

when there is enlargement of the temporal horns and the sylvian and interhemispheric fissures are normal (Sjaastad 1969; LeMay 1970) or not visible (Fig. 7-4). These morphological changes are associated with changes in the parenchyma. On CT, periventricular hypodensity has been noted as a transient feature in the early stages of hydrocephalus (DiChiro 1979; Hiratsuka 1979; Mori 1980). This is often seen in acute noncommunicating hydrocephalus and in 40 percent of patients with communicating hydrocephalus. Periventricular hypodensity is best recognized along the dorsomedial and dorsolateral angle of the frontal horns of the lateral ventricles (Fig. 7-5). Periventricular hypodensity is also seen in elderly patients with cerebral atrophy, in patients with leukoencephalopathies (Mori 1980), and in association with hypertensive diseases (Hatazawa 1984). The pattern and extent as well as density measurements have been utilized in differentiating the various causes of periventricular hypodensity (DiChiro 1979). MRI and CT demonstrate similar features in the general differentiation of hydrocephalus from atrophy. The periventricular hypodensity seen on CT appears as a periventricular hyperintense (PVH) signal on T_2WI. As with CT, this is present not only in hydrocephalus but also in atrophic ventricular enlargement associated with a neurodegenerative process. Its significance and pathological correlation are discussed with the other white matter changes.

HYDROCEPHALUS

In hydrocephalus, the apparent increase in CSF is associated with an increase in the intracranial CSF pressure that is due to obstruction in the CSF pathways within the ventricles (obstructive or noncommunicating hydrocephalus) or outside the ventricles (communicating hydrocephalus). In a less common form of communicating hydrocephalus, it is associated with overproduction of CSF (Table 7-1).

Table 7-1 Hydrocephalus: Classification and Causative Factors

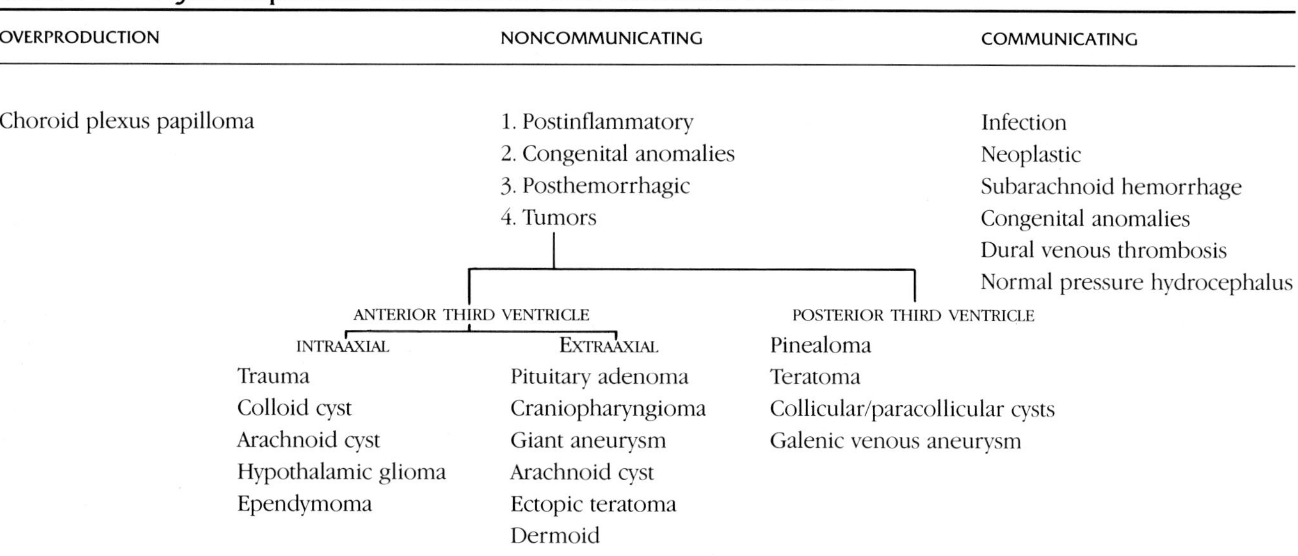

OVERPRODUCTION	NONCOMMUNICATING	COMMUNICATING
Choroid plexus papilloma	1. Postinflammatory	Infection
	2. Congenital anomalies	Neoplastic
	3. Posthemorrhagic	Subarachnoid hemorrhage
	4. Tumors	Congenital anomalies
		Dural venous thrombosis
		Normal pressure hydrocephalus

ANTERIOR THIRD VENTRICLE — INTRAAXIAL	ANTERIOR THIRD VENTRICLE — EXTRAAXIAL	POSTERIOR THIRD VENTRICLE
		Pinealoma
Trauma	Pituitary adenoma	Teratoma
Colloid cyst	Craniopharyngioma	Collicular/paracollicular cysts
Arachnoid cyst	Giant aneurysm	Galenic venous aneurysm
Hypothalamic glioma	Arachnoid cyst	
Ependymoma	Ectopic teratoma	
	Dermoid	

Noncommunicating Hydrocephalus

Noncommunicating hydrocephalus (obstructive hydrocephalus) is associated with an intrinsic (intraaxial) or extrinsic (extraaxial) lesion obstructing the flow of CSF in its passage through the ventricles. The ventricular chamber proximal to an obstructive lesion enlarges because of an increase in the volume and pulsatile pressure of the CSF. The ventricular chamber distal to the obstruction is normal or less than normal in its dimensions. The most common intraaxial lesion is a tumor (Fig. 7-6). Less often obstructive hydrocephalus is secondary to trauma, vascular anomaly, infection, and developmental anomalies (Fig. 7-7). Occasionally an intraaxial lesion involving the periaqueductal region can be missed on conventional CT and MR studies. Evaluation of the flow void signal within the aqueduct, the anatomic configuration of the aqueduct, and the appearance of the tectal plates may be helpful in arriving at a diagnosis. A tectal thickness greater than 7 mm is abnormal (Sherman 1987). In the absence of a congenital anomaly such as Chiari type II malformation, a tectal thickness greater than 7 mm or loss of the normal convexity of the aqueduct on sagittal MR should raise suspicion of an infiltrat-

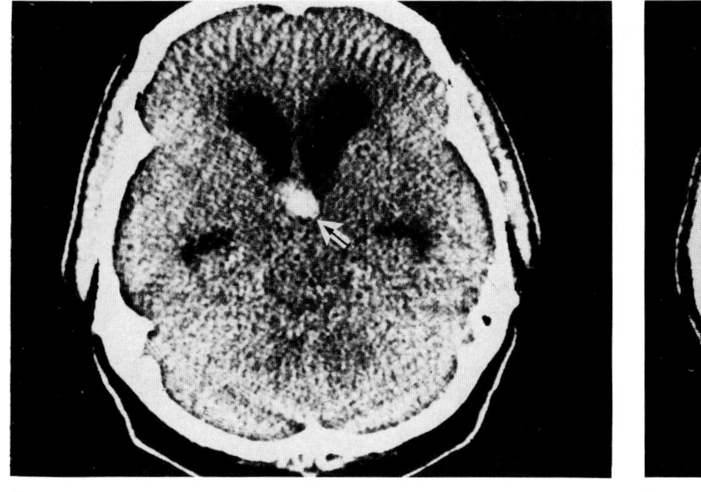

A

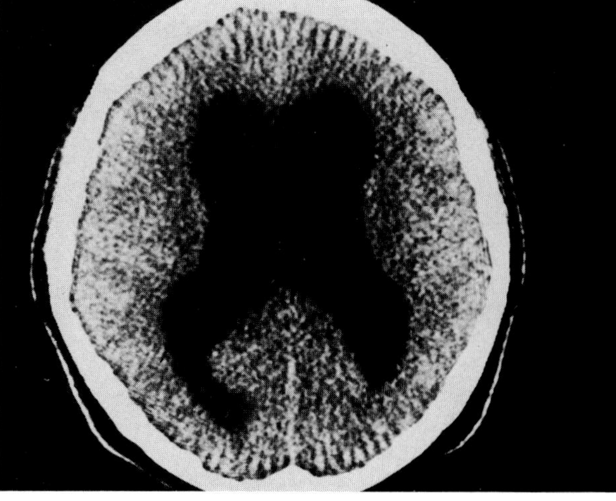

B

Figure 7-6 Obstructive hydrocephalus due to intraventricular mass. Axial NCCT (**A, B**) demonstrates hyperdense colloid cyst (arrow) blocking the foramen of Monro and resulting enlargement of the lateral ventricles. (*Continued on p. 234.*)

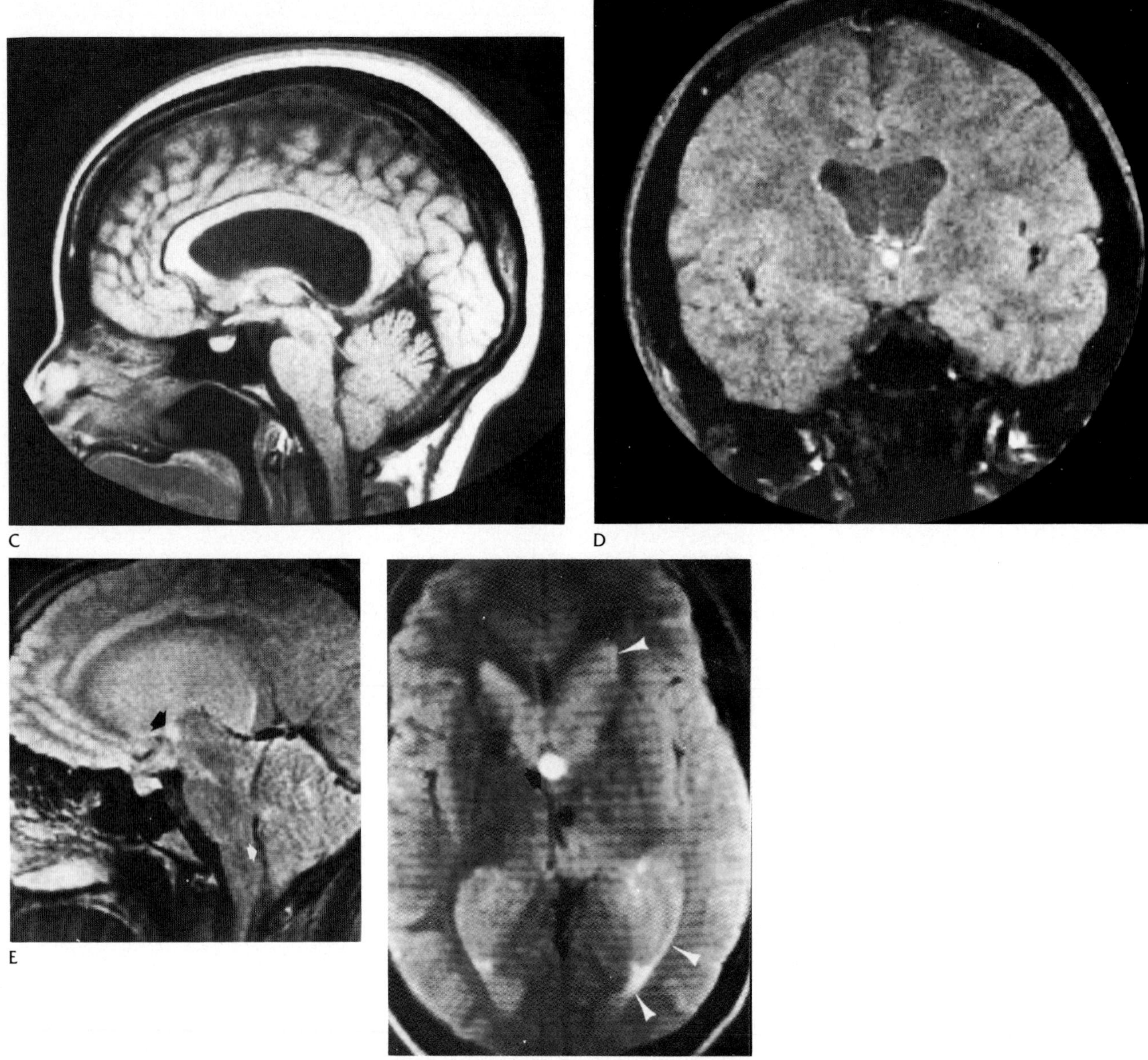

Figure 7-6 (continued) Sagittal (T_1WI) (**C**) and coronal (T_2-W) (**D**) MRI allows better appreciation of the cystic mass, its location, its effect on adjacent structures, and the CSF flow dynamics. Mild periventricular interstitial edema (arrowhead) is due to slow and intermittent obstruction. Another patient with hydrocephalus involving the lateral ventricle, resulting from obstruction of foramen of monro. Sagittal (**E**) and axial (**F**) T_2-weighted MR (SE 2800/40). Hyperintense colloid cyst (black arrow). The third ventricle is not enlarged. CFVS in the aqueduct is absent due to lack of bulk CSF flow and turbulence. CFVS is present in the caudal fourth ventricle and the foramen of Magendie (white arrows).

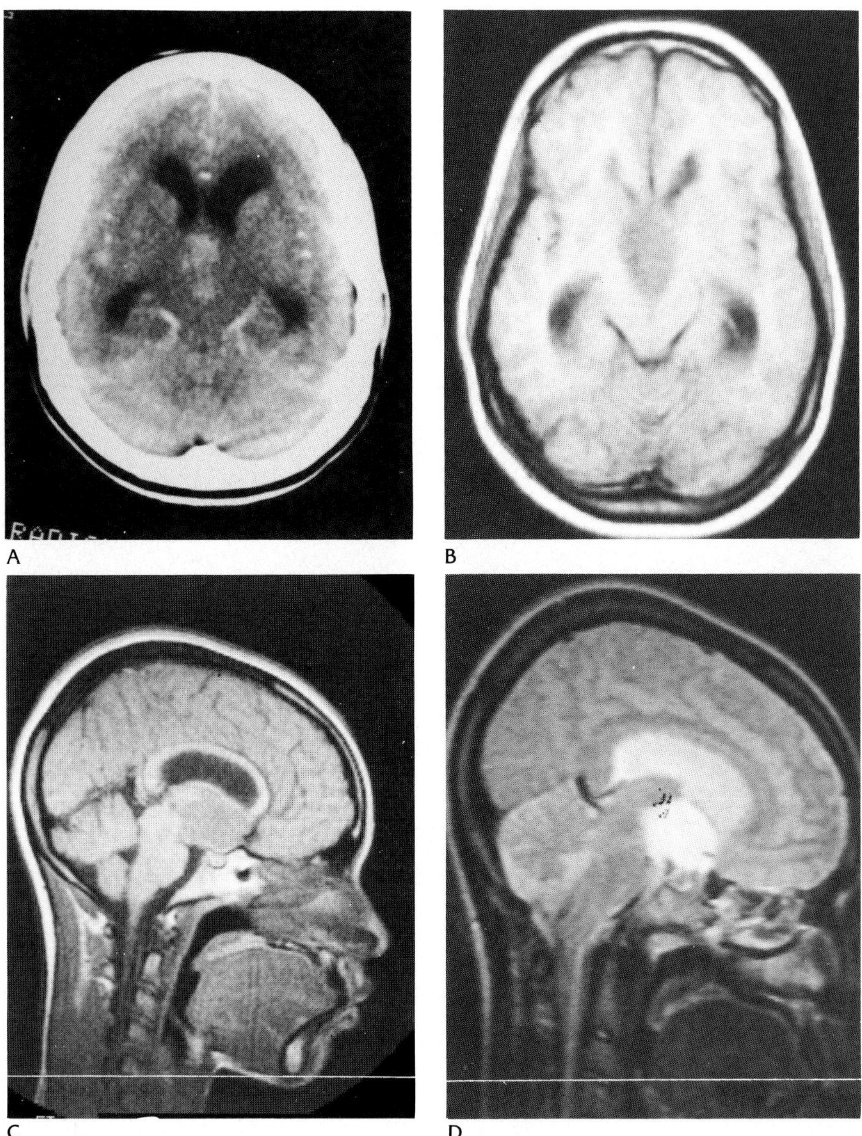

Figure 7-7 Hydrocephalus secondary to obstruction from an intraaxial mass. Histiocytosis X involving the hypothalamus. The lesion is hypodense on CT (**A**), hypointense on axial (**B**) and sagittal (**C**) T_1-weighted MR. The lateral ventricles are dilated. **D.** Sagittal T_2-weighted MR demonstrates the hyperintense signal mass and the absence of CFVS within the aqueduct.

ing glioma or granulomatous disease such as sarcoidosis. Extraaxial lesions resulting in obstructive hydrocephalus are usually located at sites where the walls of the ventricles are thin and inadequately protected by the brain parenchyma. Two such areas are the anterior and posterior regions of the third ventricle. Anteriorly, the common causes are tumors of the pituitary hypothalamic axis, large aneurysms from vessels forming the circle of Willis, epithelial cell rest tumors, arachnoid cysts, and less often meningiomas (Fig. 7-8). In a similar manner, extraaxial lesions in the posterior third ventricular region include pineal masses, cysts, and vascular anomalies (Fig. 7-9).

CT and especially MR are excellent in demonstrating not only the site of obstruction but also the tissue characteristics and extent of the lesion. In most instances MR provides all the presurgical information and diagnosis. Occasional patients may require conventional vascular studies, although these studies may not be necessary because of the availability of MR angiography.

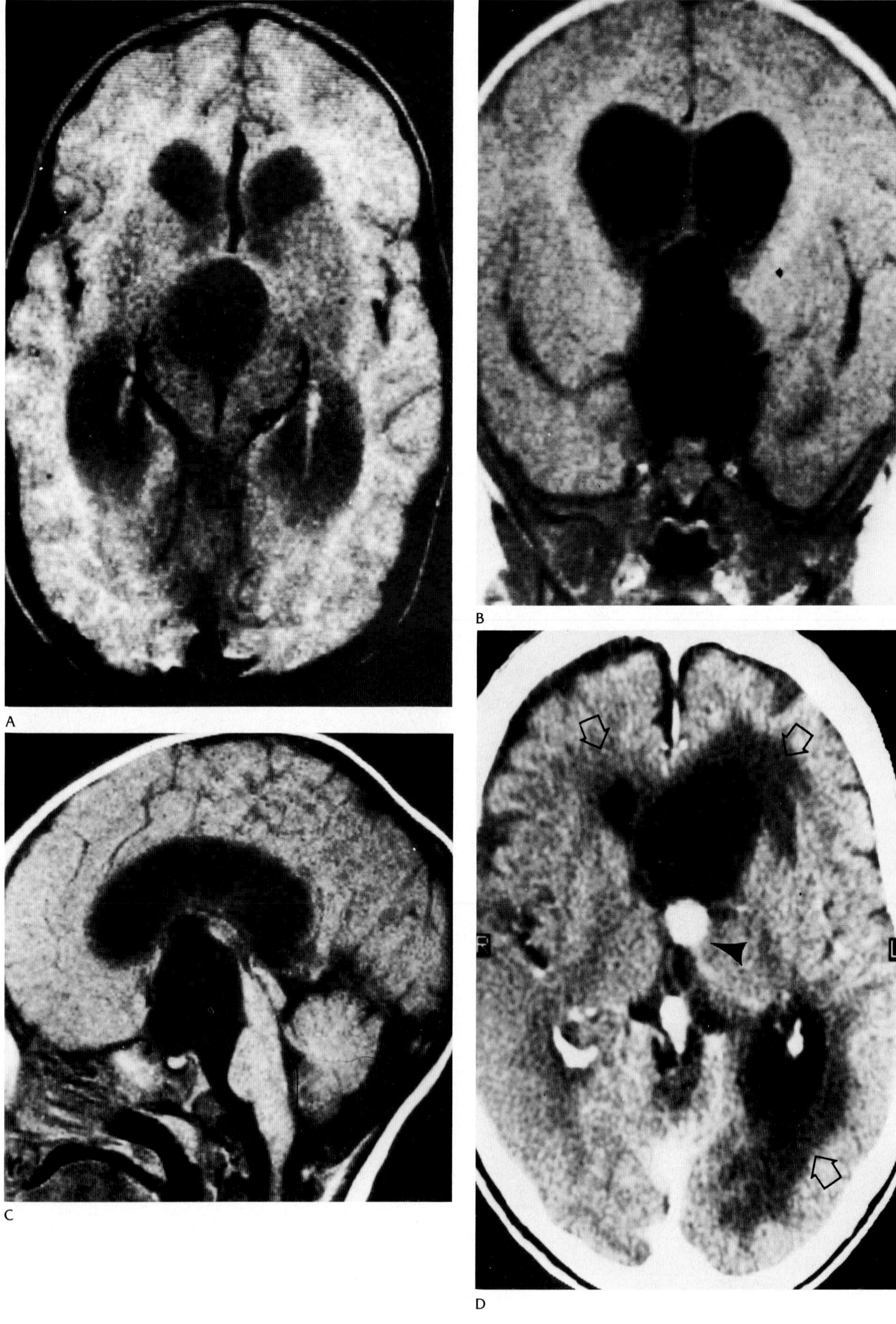
A
B
C
D
R
L

◄ ***Figure 7-8*** Obstructive hydrocephalus from extraaxial masses. Suprasellar arachnoid cyst: axial (**A**), coronal (**B**), and (**C**) sagittal T_1WI. The cystic mass has similar intensity to CSF. The lateral ventricles are enlarged, with compression of the third ventricle. The corpus callosum is thinned out. The ventricular walls are not sharply defined due to transependymal CSF absorption. **D.** Obstructive hydrocephalus in an elderly patient. Axial CECT demonstrates a large basilar tip aneurysm (arrowhead) causing unilateral ventricular obstruction. Extensive unilateral periventricular hypodensity (open arrow) is present due to interstitial edema and transependymal CSF absorption.

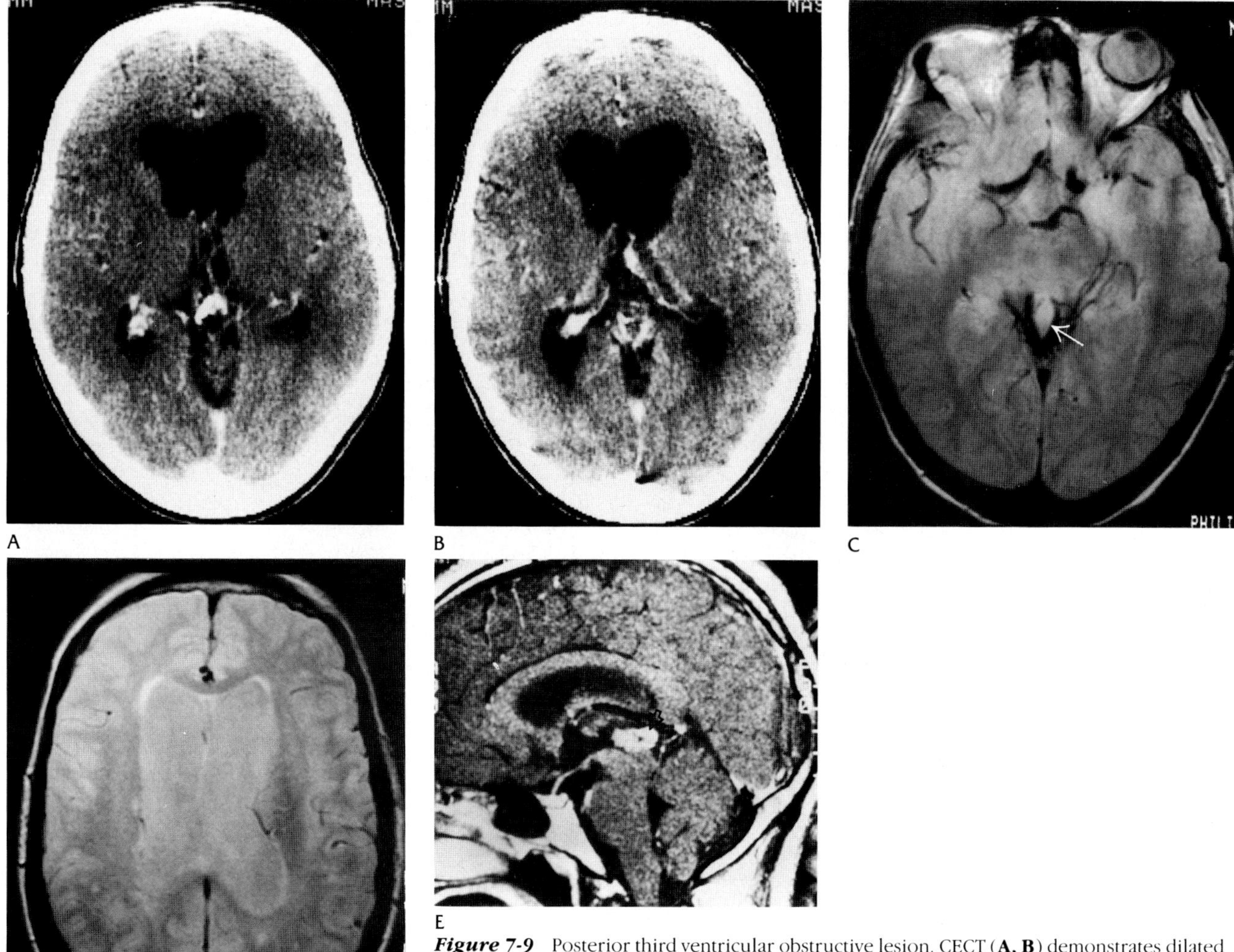

Figure 7-9 Posterior third ventricular obstructive lesion. CECT (**A, B**) demonstrates dilated lateral and third ventricles resulting from a mixed-density lesion in the pineal region in a young male. **C, D.** T_2-W MRI (SE 2500/40). A central hyperintense lesion resulting in obstruction (arrowhead). Sharply defined periventricular hyperintensity suggestive of noncompensated hydrocephalus. The aqueductal flow void signal (CFVS) is absent. The calcification seen on CT is masked by the blood flow void signal on MR. **E.** Sagittal postcontrast T_1-weighted MR demonstrates the enhancing pineal mass (open arrow) obstructing the CSF flow beyond the posterior third ventricle. Another patient with aqueductal obstruction. (*Continued on p. 238*)

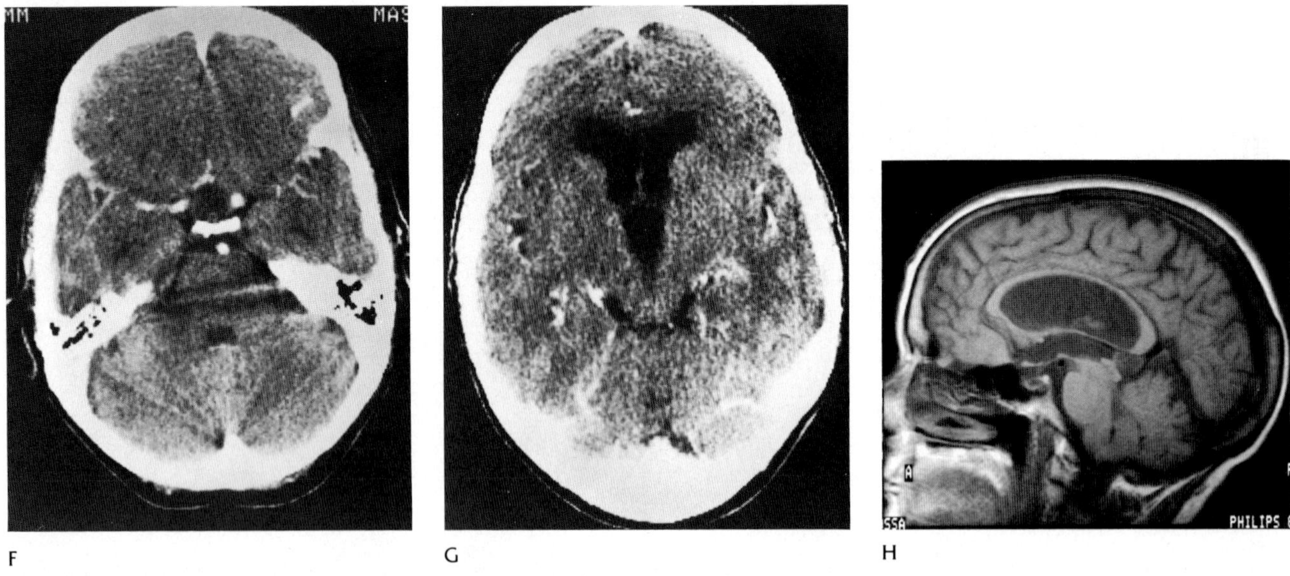

F G H

Figure 7-9 **(continued) F, G.** Axial CECT demonstrating enlarged lateral and third ventricles. Isodense mass in the pineal region. **H.** Midsagittal MR demonstrating a cystic pineal tumor compressing the aqueduct.

Aqueduct Stenosis

In infancy and childhood one of the nonneoplastic causes of obstructive hydrocephalus is obstruction at the level of the aqueduct. Most often it is due to narrowing, although rarely there may be complete occlusion. It may be an isolated anomaly, usually postulated to follow infection during the gestation period, with the formation of a web within the channel of the aqueduct. In children it is often seen after the repair of a myelomeningocele, in which case it is invariably associated with the Chiari II malformation. Infrequently it can be an inherited autosomal dominant trait. The clinical presentation consists of an enlarging head size with nonfusion of sutures and other clinical signs of increased intracranial pressure. Isolated aqueductal stenosis with resulting hydrocephalus is a specific entity seen in children between ages 8 and 11 years. The CT study should include contrast-enhanced studies to exclude enhancing masses. In the past, CT cisternography or ventriculography was necessary to demonstrate the stenosis or occlusion (Fitz 1978*a*). MR has eliminated the need for all these studies (Fig. 7-10).

In the majority of cases, the patency, narrowing, or occlusion of the aqueduct can be defined on spin-echo MR sequences in the sagittal and axial planes. If there is any

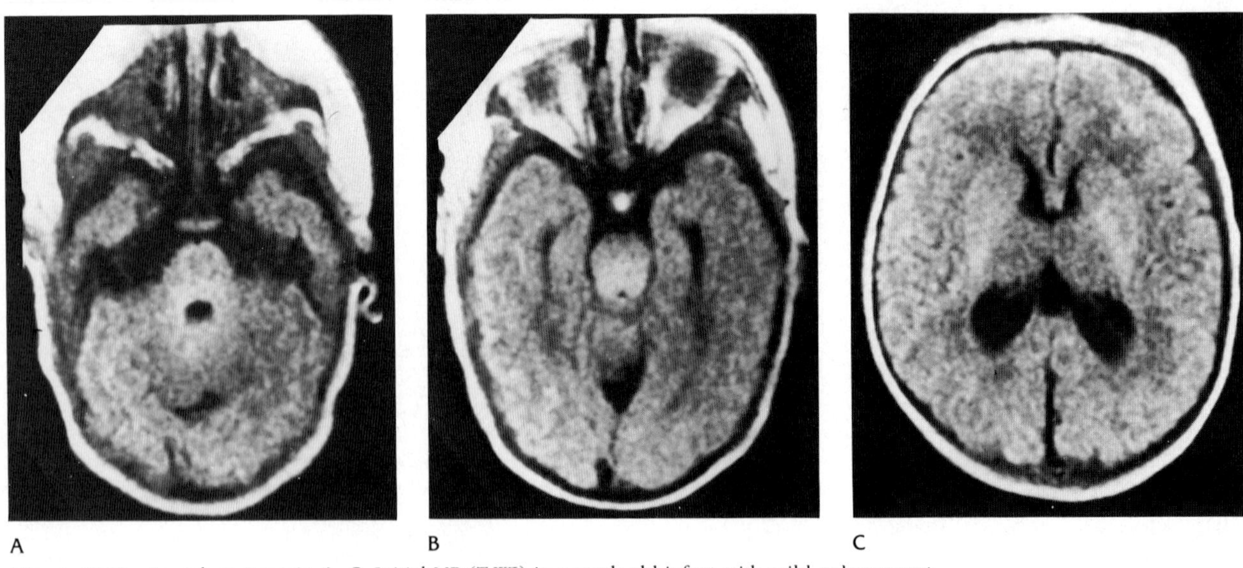

A B C

Figure 7-10 Aqueduct stenosis. **A–C.** Initial MR (T_1WI) in a week-old infant with mild enlargement of the head circumference. (*Continued on p. 239*)

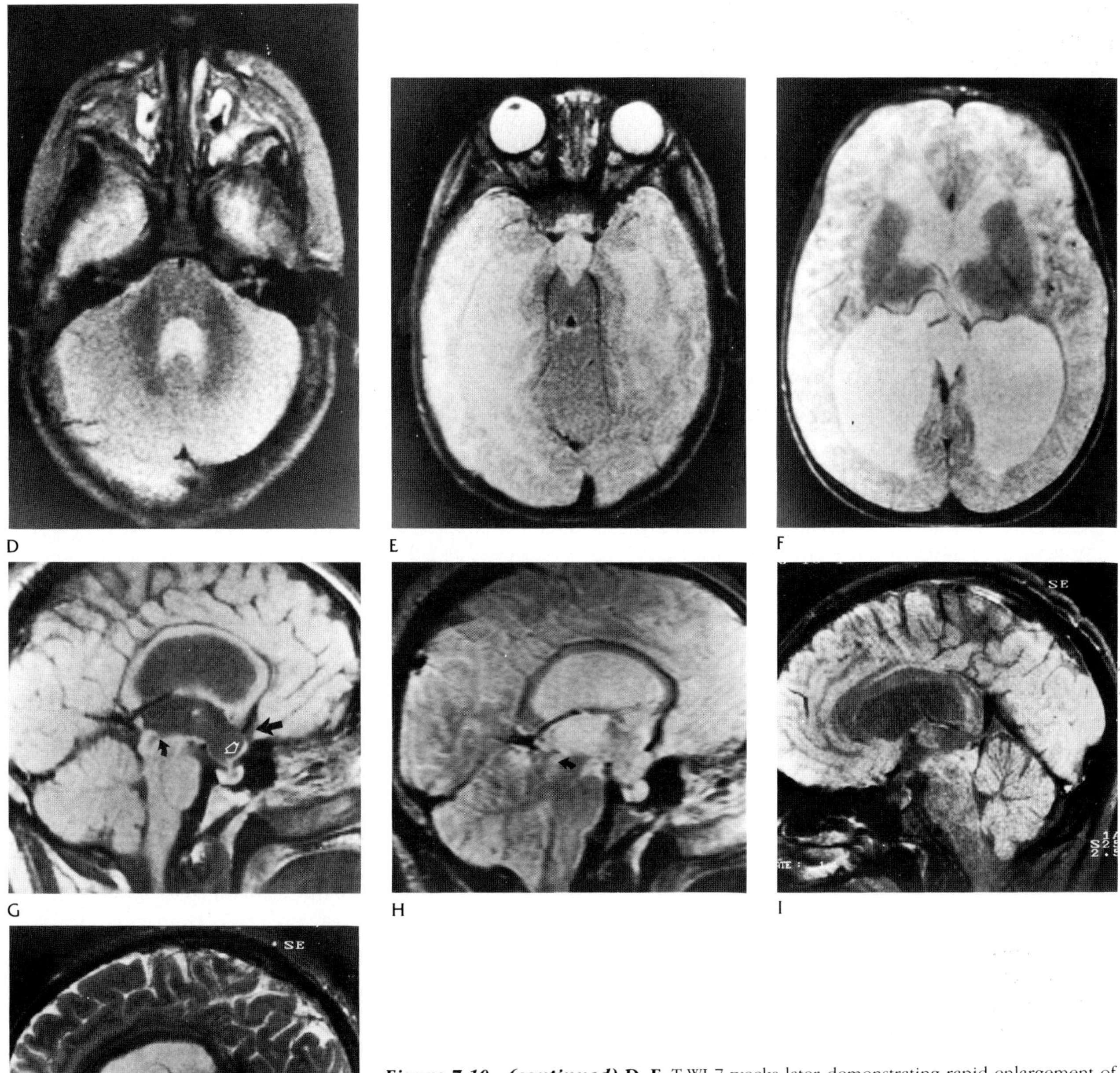

Figure 7-10 ***(continued)*** **D–F.** T_2WI 7 weeks later demonstrating rapid enlargement of third and lateral ventricles due to stenosis of the aqueduct. CFVS is present although not prominent. Sagittal (**G**) T_1-W and (**H**) T_2-W MRI in an older patient demonstrating suspected aqueductal stenosis with obstructive enlargement of the lateral and third ventricles. Note that the proximal segment of the aqueduct (arrow) is open with apparent lack of CSF signal in the distal third of the aqueduct in (**G**) and possibly throughout its extent in (**H**). Midsagittal GRASS study in another patient (**I, J**). This technique is useful in resolving the aqueductal patency; it demonstrates a patent but narrow aqueduct (arrowhead) with resulting hydrocephalus in a 27-year-old female.

doubt as a result of a flow-related artifact, MR utilizing gradient echo sequences has been advocated (Atlas 1988). This is indicated especially when stenosis in the distal portion of the aqueduct may result in a prominent CFVS within the dilated proximal segment of the aqueduct (Kemp 1987). MRI in the sagittal plane utilizing a gradient echo will demonstrate the patency or occlusion of the aqueduct along its entire length.

Outlet Obstruction of the Fourth Ventricle

Outlet obstruction of the foramina of Luschka and Magendie results in generalized enlargement of all portions of the ventricular CSF spaces. In both adults and children the common causes of obstruction are hemorrhage, infection, or tumors compressing the medullary cisterns.

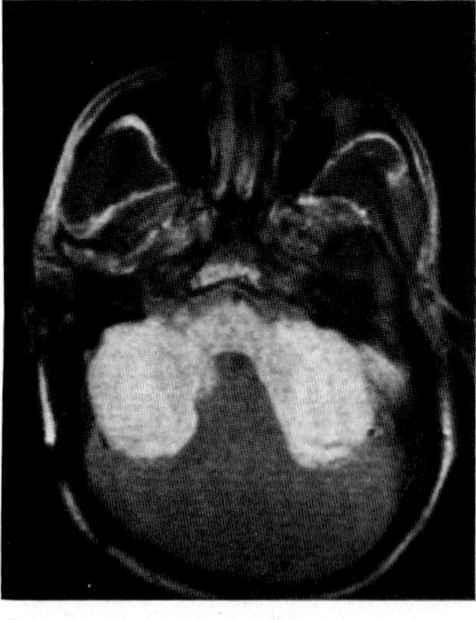

A

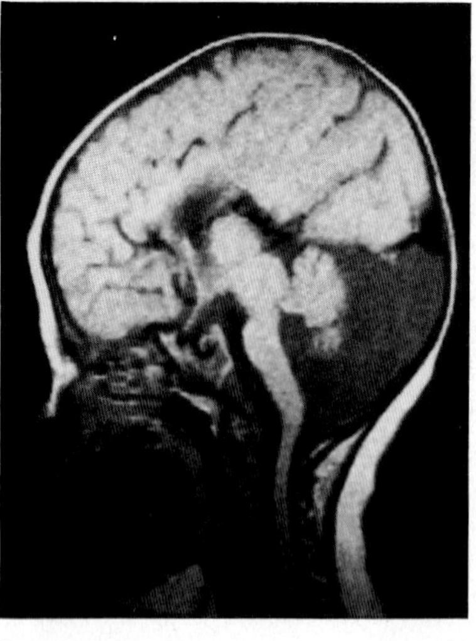

B

Figure 7-11 Extraaxial cyst mimicking a dilated fourth ventricle. (**A**). Axial, (**B**). Sagittal MR. The axial section demonstrates appearance of a markedly dilated fourth ventricle. The midline sagittal section demonstrates the fourth ventricle with dysgenesis of the inferior vermis.

The resulting appearance is similar to that of communicating hydrocephalus, except that the subarachnoid cisterns are completely obliterated. CECT may show cisternal enhancement if the occlusion is due to acute inflammation or in the presence of an enhancing mass. As with CT, pre- and postcontrast MR may help in identifying the pathological process.

In infants and children, extraaxial cystic masses may mimic a dilated fourth ventricle. In the past this required CT following intraventricular contrast (Archer 1978). These masses can often be differentiated on MRI (Fig. 7-11).

Communicating Hydrocephalus

In communicating hydrocephalus (EVOH, or extraventricular obstructive hydrocephalus), there is symmetrical enlargement of the entire ventricular system. The obstruction usually involves the subarachnoid cistern, most cistern, most often the basilar cisterns. Obstruction at a higher level may also involve the arachnoid villi along the parasagittal dural venous sinuses as well as following obstruction in the main venous drainage channels within the dural sinuses. Communicating hydrocephalus usually follows subarachnoid hemorrhage, meningeal carcinomatosis, meningeal infections, trauma, or intracranial surgery.

In the early or acute stage, the clinical presentation and the imaging features are similar to those of obstructive hydrocephalus. In addition, the aqueduct is dilated. On MRI (T_2WI), a prominent CFVS is seen not only within the aqueduct but extending proximally into the third ventricle and distally within the dilated fourth ventricle (Fig. 7-12). Enhancement of the cisternal space or pial surface is often seen on contrast-enhanced MRI (CEMR) and sometimes on CECT (Fig. 7-13). Sometimes the granulomatous foci, inflammatory adhesions, or nodular metastatic deposits can be well demonstrated. In communicating hydrocephalus due to a convexity block involving the arach-

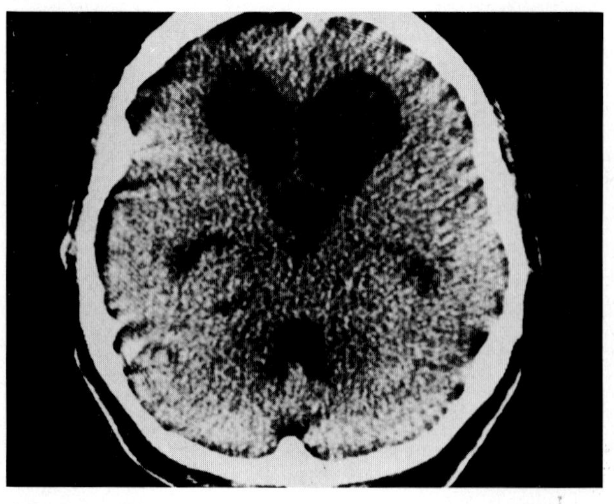

A

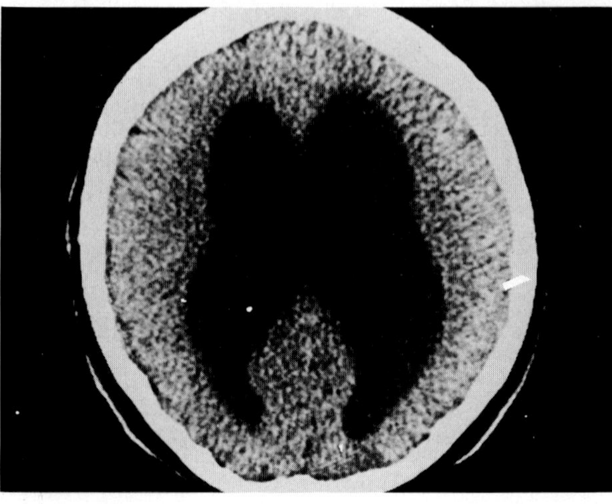

B

Figure 7-12 Communicating hydrocephalus (EVOH). Acute stage. **A, B.** On CT the ventricles are dilated. The margins of the lateral ventricles are not sharply defined. (*Continued on p. 241*)

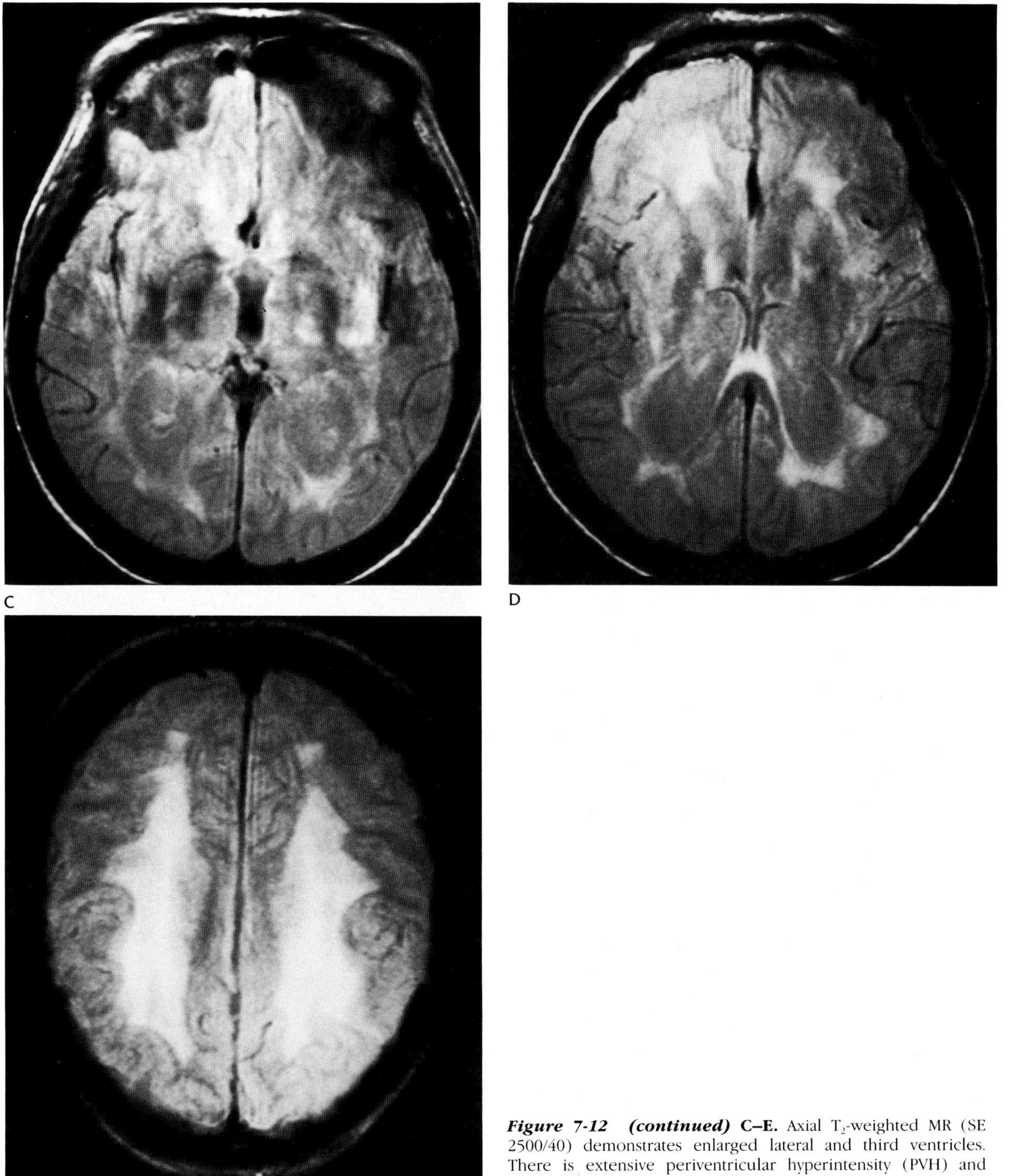

Figure 7-12 ***(continued)*** **C–E.** Axial T_2-weighted MR (SE 2500/40) demonstrates enlarged lateral and third ventricles. There is extensive periventricular hyperintensity (PVH) and prominent CFVS within the third ventricle (open arrow).

noid villi or the dural venous sinuses, CT and MRI may demonstrate dilated ventricles as well as prominent sulci that suggest an atrophic pattern. In these patients, increased CSF pressure on lumbar puncture, and occasionally dural enhancement along the convexity, may help in confirming the clinical diagnosis. In some cases magnetic resonance angiography (MRA) or vascular studies may be necessary to demonstrate the venous obstruction. These distinctions are useful since the subsequent surgical or medical management depends on the exact pathological process.

In children, although hydrocephalus is the most common cause of an enlarging head, other causes, such as megalencephaly and benign subdural effusions, must be excluded (Maytal 1987). These entities can be separated on the basis of CT and MR studies.

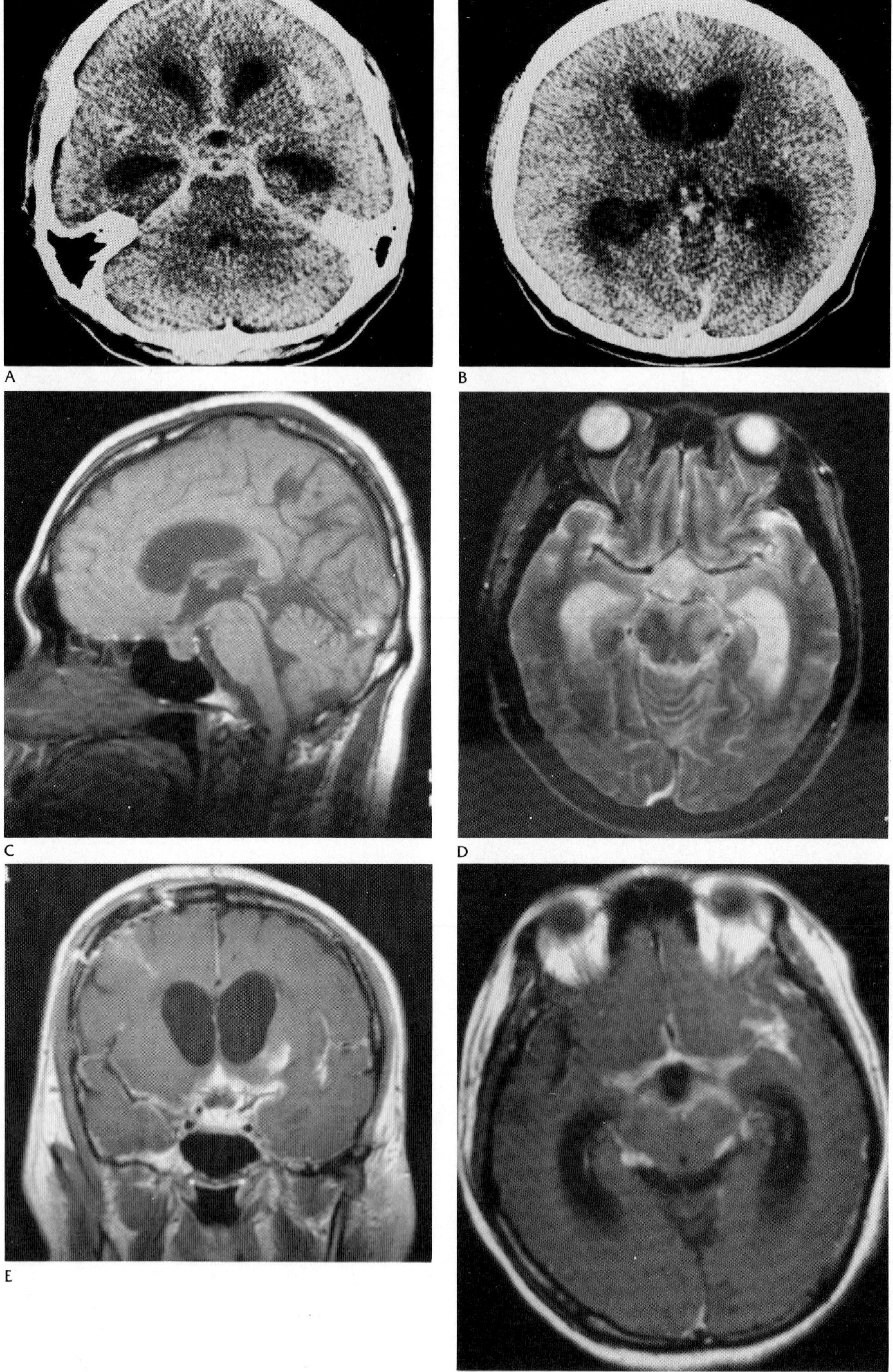
A
B
C
D
E
F

Normal Pressure Hydrocephalus

Adams (1965) and Hakim (1965) described a group of patients with the clinical features of dementia, gait apraxia, and urinary incontinence who on imaging studies (pneumoencephalography) demonstrated enlarged ventricles with variable prominence of the cortical sulci and marked delay in the absorption of the air within the intracranial CSF spaces (Benson 1970). On isotope cisternography, there was delayed clearance of the isotope from the ventricles. Both studies indicated a delay in or a decreased rate of CSF absorption. In spite of the "normal" craniospinal CSF pressure, these authors described clinical improvement after shunting of the ventricular CSF space.

The craniospinal CSF pressure in many of the patients was normal. In the majority of the patients clinical improvement was noted following CSF shunting. Since NPH is one of the treatable causes of dementia, there has been interest in defining the imaging characteristics and the clinical criteria for selecting patients who would benefit from the CSF diversionary procedure (Huckman 1981; Jensen 1979).

The causal relationship between the hydrocephalus and the clinical presentation has not been clearly established. NPH often presents in patients in the sixth decade. It is presumed that the clinical manifestations result from (1) pressure on critical areas within the cerebrum from the hydrocephalus (Fisher 1982) and (2) decreased vascular perfusion further compromised as a result of increased CSF pressure. Both of these factors are worsened by decreased compliance of the cerebral parenchyma caused by aging.

On the basis of currently utilized imaging studies (CT and MRI), one can only speculate about the morphological anatomy since these studies do not evaluate the dynamics of CSF flow. Most investigators have concentrated on morphological and histological correlation (see Dementia and Brain Atrophy, below).

Normal pressure hydrocephalus represents a combination of chronic communicating hydrocephalus and atrophic parenchymal changes. Although in some instances an earlier history of extraventricular obstructive hydrocephalus can be identified, in many cases such a history may not be available. The patients usually are in the sixth decade or beyond, with a history of worsening of the clinical triad of dementia, gait apraxia, and urinary incontinence. The exact pathogenesis of the dementia, gait disturbance, and urinary incontinence is not clear. Pathological correlations have shown tangential shearing of the paracentral fibers of the corona radiata (Hakim 1965; Fisher 1982). These findings probably correspond to some of the hyperintense signal changes seen on MR. Other pathological findings in patients with NPH consist of subcortical lesions and periventricular lesions (Awad 1986*b*; Fazekas 1991). These are not specifically related to NPH but represent arteriosclerotic changes in the microvasculature of the brain caused by aging, or result from ischemia or infarcts. Many of these patients have a history of hypertension or other metabolic disorders such as diabetes and are prone to arteriosclerotic vascular disease affecting both the extracranial and intracranial vasculature. The vascular element is further compromised, since hypotension from medication or cardiovascular causes may further decrease cerebral blood flow. Each of these factors probably has an impact on the clinical progression of the syndrome and on the results of the imaging studies.

Clinical studies have shown that the CSF pressure in NPH is not continuously normal. Prolonged intracranial pressure monitoring has shown peaks of high-pressure waves (Symon 1977; TerBrugge 1980). Patients who have had the best response to ventricular shunting have demonstrated variable CSF pressure on monitoring studies (Chawla 1974).

Several hypotheses have been postulated to explain this normal CSF pressure, which may be due to the following factors: (1) intermittent transependymal absorption of CSF allowing the CSF pressure to be normal till adequate volume and pressure are built up for the channels to reopen (Bannister 1967), (2) normal pressure due to decreased production of CSF and alteration in CSF absorption (Lorenzo 1974), and (3) a combination of the two factors in association with a decreased tensile capacity of the brain parenchyma (DiRocco 1977).

On imaging studies, generalized ventricular enlargement with absent sulci may not be seen in most of these patients. Depending on the severity of the atrophic process, the ventricular enlargement and the effect of CSF pressure may not obliterate the preexisting widened sulci (Fig. 7-14). In addition, if the obstruction is over the convexity involving the arachnoid villi or the venous sinuses, imaging studies will demonstrate an atrophic pattern (Fig. 7-15) or may even have the appearance of normal-

◄ ***Figure 7-13*** Communicating hydrocephalus. **A, B.** CECT following subarachnoid hemorrhage demonstrates enlarged ventricles with loss of sulcal spaces and enhancement of the cisternal space. Another patient with communicating hydrocephalus due to tuberculous meningitis. **C.** Sagittal T_1-weighted MR demonstrates ventricular enlargement. **D.** Axial T_2-weighted MR demonstrates enlarged temporal horns and absence of sulci indicative of communicating hydrocephalus. Coronal (**E**) and axial (**F**) T_1-weighted MR following contrast demonstrates communicating hydrocephalus with enhancing deposits throughout the cisternal spaces. Similar appearance may be seen in meningeal carcinomatosis.

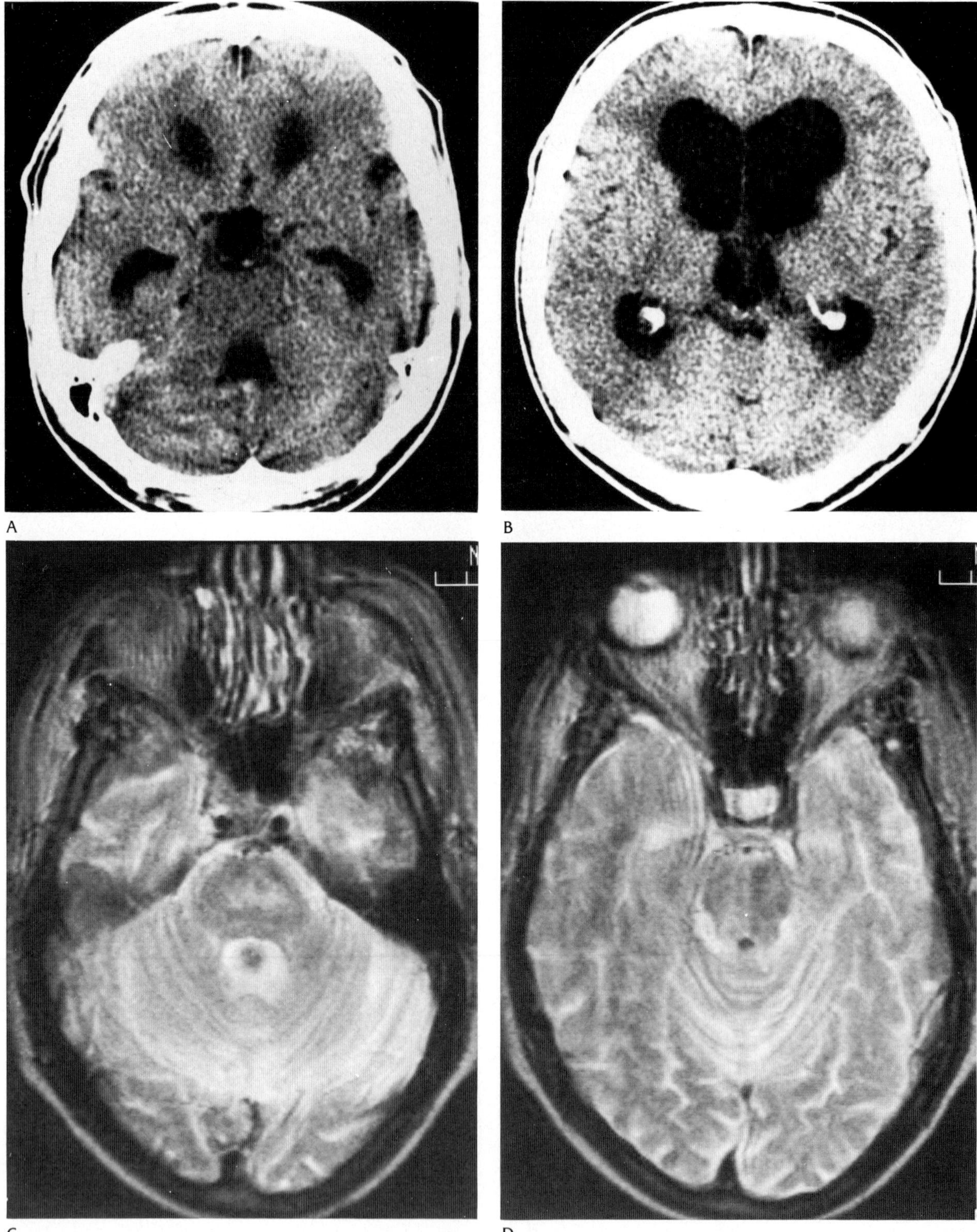

Figure 7-14 Normal pressure hydrocephalus. A 58-year-old male with a 5-month history of ataxia, urinary incontinence, and dementia. There was no antecedent history of trauma, infection, or hemorrhage. **A, B.** Axial CT demonstrates ventriculomegaly (lateral, third, and fourth ventricles) with normal sulci. MR in a 65-year-old male with similar symptoms. **C, D.** Coronal T_1WI demonstrating ventriculomegaly with mild cortical atrophy. Axial T_2WI MR (SE 2500/80). (*Continued on p. 245.*)

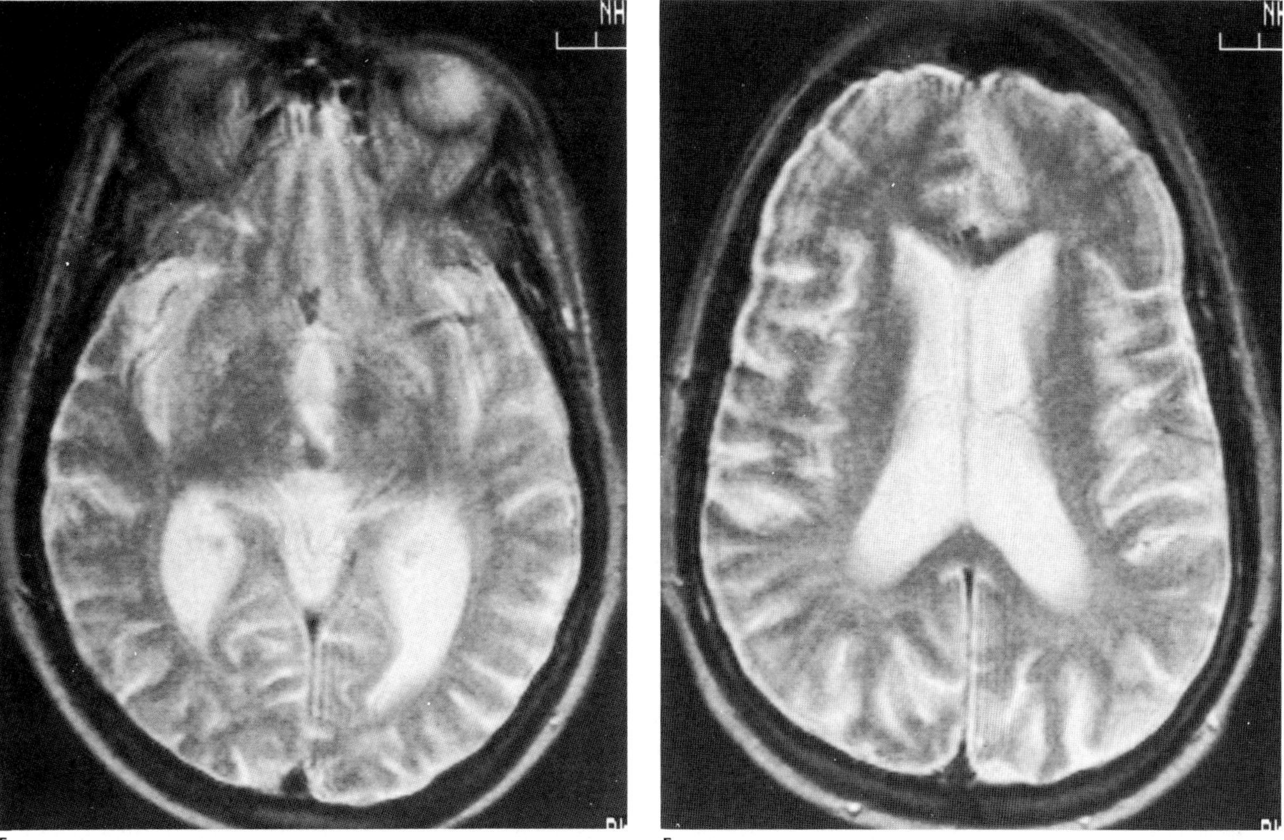

Figure 7-14 (continued) **E.** CFVS within the fourth ventricle (arrow). **F.** Section through lateral ventricles. Lateral ventricles are enlarged. There is no evidence of SCL or significant PVH.

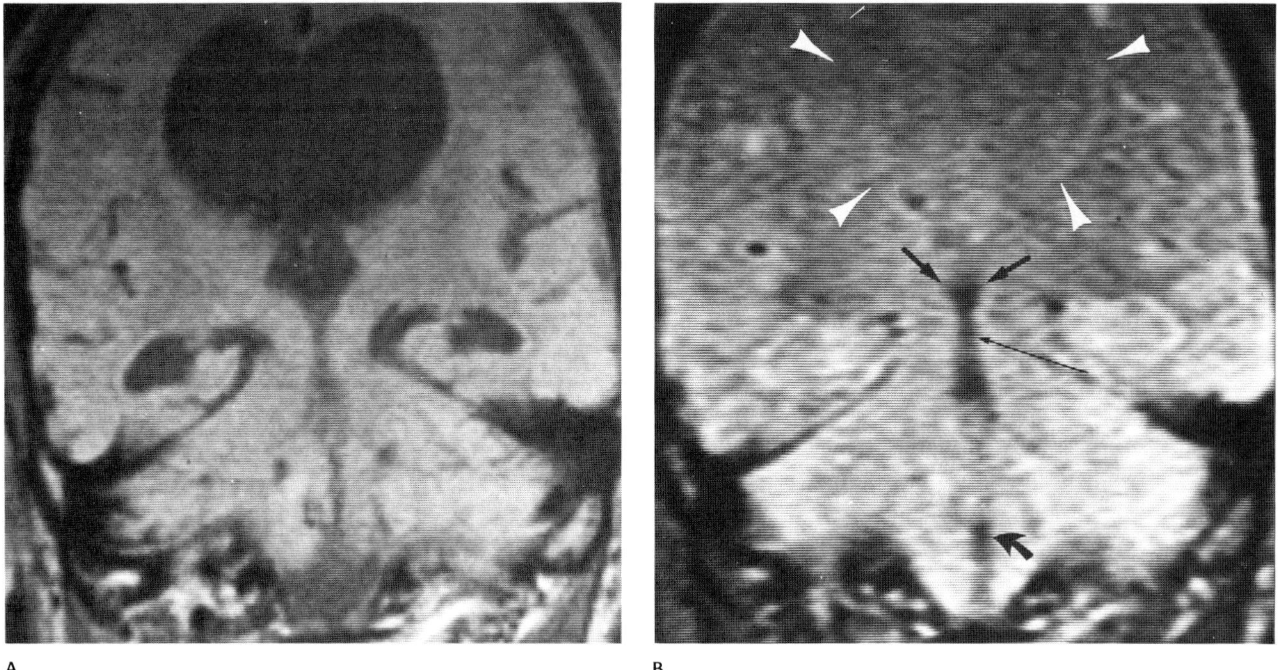

Figure 7-15 Normal pressure hydrocephalus. A 61-year-old male with NPH. T_2-W coronal MR: (**A**) SE 1500/40 and (**B**) SE 1600/100. The lateral and third ventricles are enlarged, and the fourth ventricle is normal. The CSF in the long TR sequence is isointense with the brain parenchyma (arrowheads). CFVS in the posterior third ventricle (short straight arrow), aqueduct (long straight arrow), and distal fourth ventricle adjacent to foramen of Magendie (curved arrow).

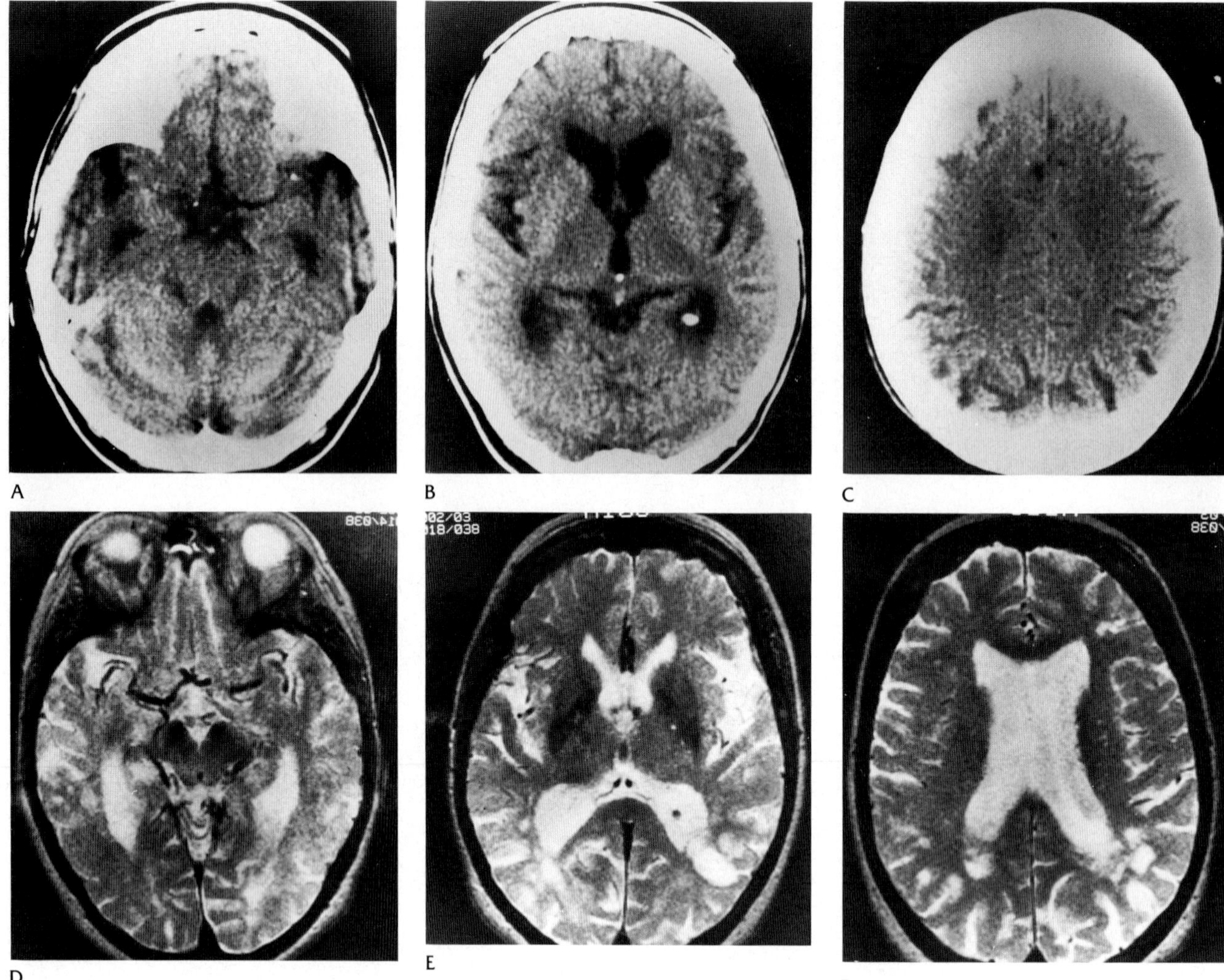

Figure 7-16 Normal pressure hydrocephalus. A 57-year-old patient with clinical features of dementia due to NPH. **A–C.** Axial CT sections demonstrating moderate ventricular enlargement and sulcal prominence suggestive of cerebral atrophy. **D–F.** Axial T_2-weighted MR demonstrates the enlarged ventricles with PVH and SCL. The basal cisterns are not enlarged, although the sulci over the convexity are mildly prominent. Mild CFVS is noted in the third ventricle and the aqueduct. None of the features are specific, although the patient's mental status improved following shunting.

size ventricles with prominent sulci and sylvian cisterns mimicking cortical atrophy. In these circumstances the interpretation of the dilated temporal horn as a sign of hydrocephalus (LeMay 1986) may not be valid. Periventricular hyperintense (PVH) signal and subcortical lesions in the white matter tracts are common findings in these patients; their significance in relation to NPH is not clear.

Although considered as deep white matter infarcts causing NPH (Bradley 1991*a*), these findings probably are age-related white matter changes or may even represent the appearance associated with Binswanger's disease (George 1991; Román 1991). The clinical presentation of NPH is very similar to that of Binswanger's disease. In both conditions there is a stepwise progression of the disease with periods of remission. A prominent CFVS, not only within the aqueduct but in the adjacent third and fourth ventricles, has been described as a sign indicative of NPH (Fig. 7-16) as opposed to a less prominent CFVS in diffuse cerebral atrophy (Bradley 1986, 1991*b*). When associated with other MR findings suggestive of communicating hydrocephalus, prominent CFVS is probably useful in the selection of patients who can benefit from ventricular CSF shunting. This sign should be evaluated in light of several factors which influence the appearance of CFVS (Malko 1986; Jack 1988). A prominent flow void sign may not be a consistent feature in all patients with NPH (Sherman 1986*b*).

At the present time the diagnosis of NPH depends on a combination of clinical and imaging findings. The di-

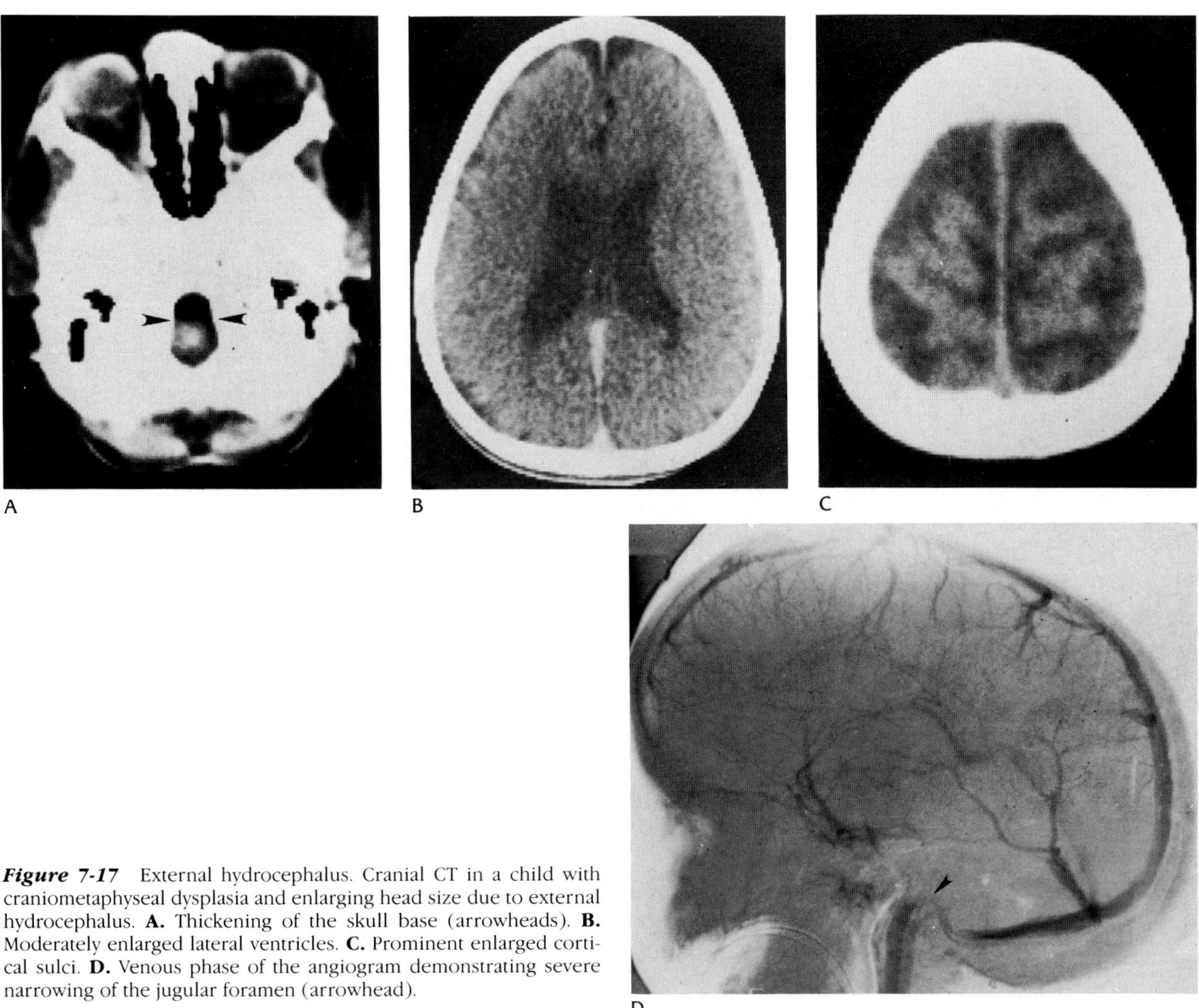

Figure 7-17 External hydrocephalus. Cranial CT in a child with craniometaphyseal dysplasia and enlarging head size due to external hydrocephalus. **A.** Thickening of the skull base (arrowheads). **B.** Moderately enlarged lateral ventricles. **C.** Prominent enlarged cortical sulci. **D.** Venous phase of the angiogram demonstrating severe narrowing of the jugular foramen (arrowhead).

agnosis should not be rejected because of a normal or atrophic pattern on imaging studies. In such cases the decision for surgical intervention may depend on the results of pressure monitoring studies and radionuclide cisternography. It is conceivable that a better understanding of the underlying pathology will be possible in the near future, utilizing physiological imaging such as phase contrast cine MR to evaluate the CSF flow, perfusion and diffusion MR (Moseley 1990; Rosen 1980) to determine the effect of cerebral blood flow, and PET scanning (George 1986*a,b,c*) to determine the neurotransmitters associated with the deteriorating intellectual functions.

Communicating Hydrocephalus in Children

Communicating hydrocephalus in children is often seen following infection during the gestation period or during infancy. Less common causes are tumor (leukemia, medulloblastoma, neuroblastoma) and trauma. On imaging studies, the findings are similar to those of the adult type. CECT or CEMR is essential in demonstrating cisternal or dural enhancement (Fig. 7-13).

A less common cause of communicating hydrocephalus described as *external hydrocephalus* is seen in children (Maytal 1987). In most of these children it is a benign process associated with macrocephaly and mild developmental delay during the first year. In some cases there may be a familial pattern. In other children the macrocephaly may be secondary to known genetic causes, including bone dysplasias resulting in obstruction of the dural venous sinuses (Yamada 1981; Allen 1982) and hypoplasia of the arachnoid granulation tissue (Gilles 1971).

On both CT and MR, the ventricles are mildly to moderately enlarged with a fluid collection over the surface of the brain, resulting in prominent sulci and a prominent interhemispheric fissure (Fig. 7-17). In most of these

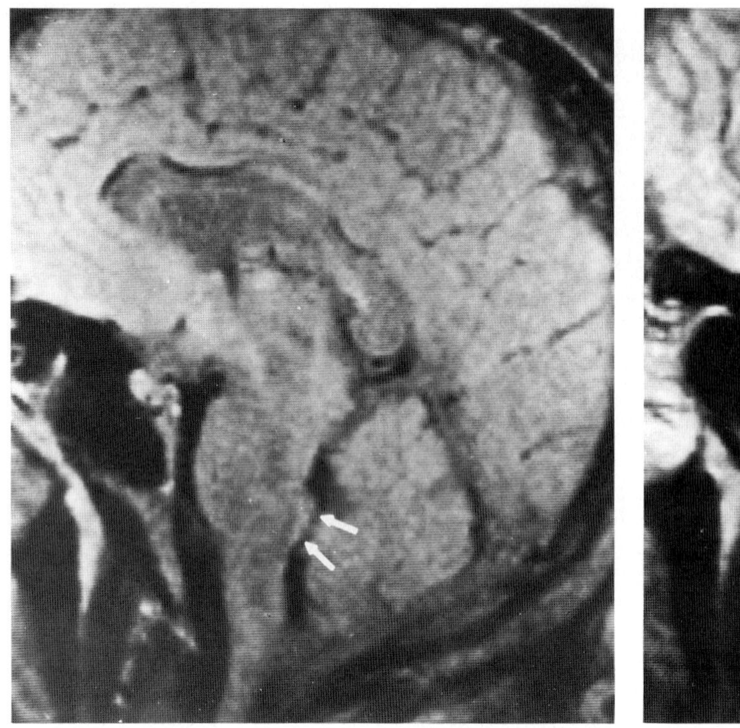

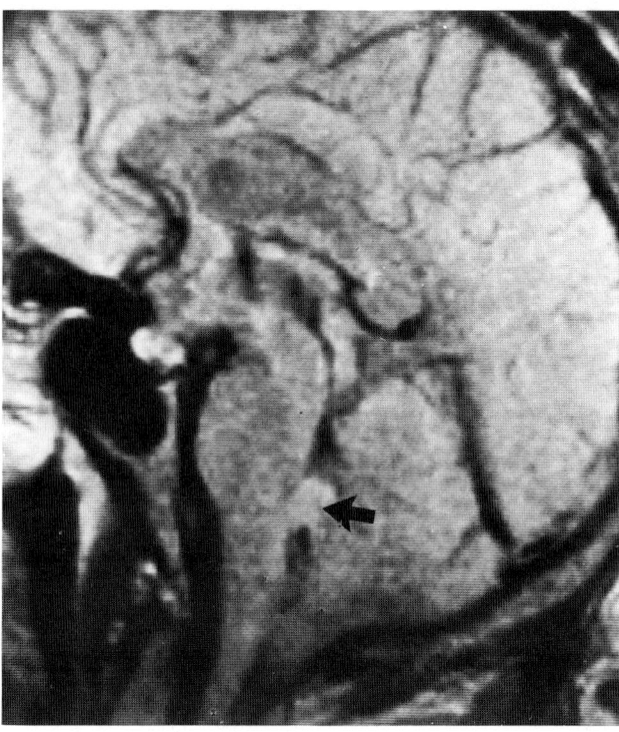

A B

Figure 7-18 Hydrocephalus due to increased CSF production. An elderly male with choroid plexus papilloma of the fourth ventricle. Midsagittal MR (**A**) demonstrates the mass in the floor of fourth ventricle (arrows). **B.** On T_2WI (SE 2500/40) the papilloma has a hyperintense signal (black arrow). Note the enlarged fourth ventricle with mild lateral and third ventricular enlargement.

children it is a self-limiting condition, with normal development and head size occurring before age 2 years. If there is a progressive increase in head size with clinical signs of increased CSF pressure, the diagnosis must be confirmed by evaluating CSF or venous sinus pressure as well as performing vascular studies.

Hydrocephalus Caused by Overproduction

Overproduction of CSF as a cause of hydrocephalus, although rare, is well recognized. This condition is often associated with benign or malignant neoplasms of the choroid plexus. The hydrocephalus is caused by the relative difference between the rate of CSF production and its absorption. In some cases the hydrocephalus is also related to a voluminous choroid plexus blocking the foramina (El Gammal 1987). In children the choroid plexus masses are often found in the lateral ventricles, whereas in adults they are often seen involving the choroid plexus of the fourth ventricle. Since the choroid plexus consists of fronds of vascular tissue, hemorrhage within the fronds may result in subsequent calcification. Choroid plexus papilloma or hemorrhage may even result in a trapped temporal horn or focal dilatation of the temporal horn proximal to the obstruction. This is more common in children. In adults, choroid plexus of the fourth ventricle or third ventricle may cause blockage of the outlet foramina of the fourth ventricle or the foramen of Monro (Schelahas 1988; Ford 1988; Hopper 1987).

In diagnosing hydrocephalus due to choroid plexus papilloma in children, one must be aware that asymmetry in the size of the glomera of the choroid plexus is not unusual and that the normal glomera can be as large as 23 mm (Hinshaw 1988). Calcification within the tumor is best assessed with CT. On MRI, choroid plexus papilloma has heterogenous signal intensity as a result of small cysts, an old hemorrhage, or lipid deposition (Zimmerman 1979; Hinshaw 1988) (Fig. 7-18).

In patients of all ages but more often in adults, choroid plexus tumors must be differentiated from intraventricular meningioma. Meningiomas usually have denser calcification and demonstrate intense enhancement, and the hydrocephalus, if present, is less severe.

Treated Hydrocephalus

Imaging studies are often necessary after the treatment of hydrocephalus to determine the position of the shunt catheter tip and to evaluate postsurgical complications, including improper placement of the shunt catheter tip and an intracerebral hematoma along the track of the

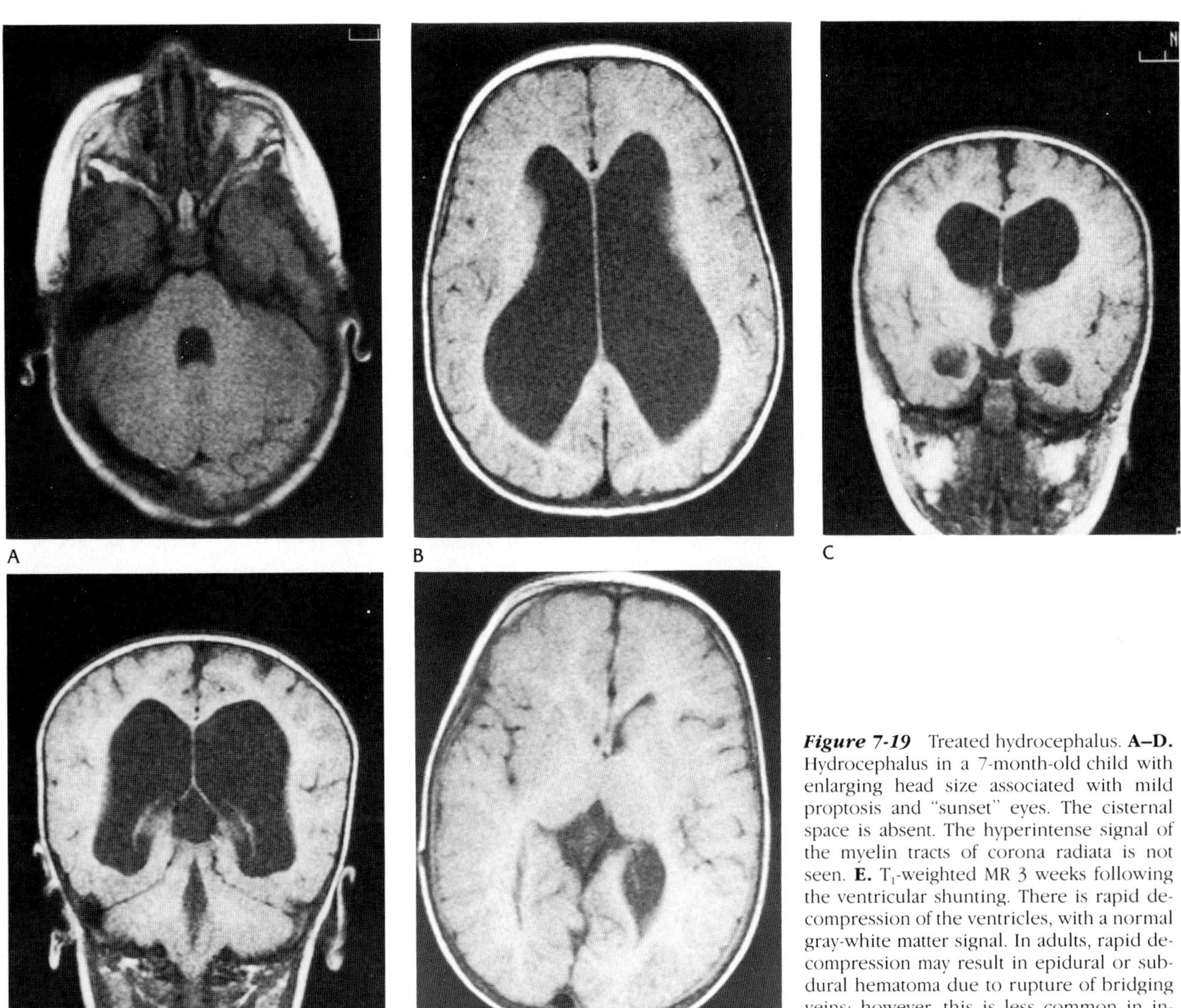

Figure 7-19 Treated hydrocephalus. **A–D.** Hydrocephalus in a 7-month-old child with enlarging head size associated with mild proptosis and "sunset" eyes. The cisternal space is absent. The hyperintense signal of the myelin tracts of corona radiata is not seen. **E.** T_1-weighted MR 3 weeks following the ventricular shunting. There is rapid decompression of the ventricles, with a normal gray-white matter signal. In adults, rapid decompression may result in epidural or subdural hematoma due to rupture of bridging veins; however, this is less common in infants due to their resilient brain parenchyma.

shunt tubing. A subdural hematoma may be due to a torn subdural vein or to rapid decompression of the ventricles (Fig. 7-19). In the later stages complications may result from infection, leading to isolated dilatation of the fourth ventricle, the slit ventricle syndrome, and porencephaly.

Trapped Fourth Ventricle

One of the complications of repeated infection, most often associated with shunt revision, is isolation of the fourth ventricle. This involves the aqueduct above and the outlet foramina of the fourth ventricle below. The CSF formed within the fourth ventricle increases in volume and protein concentration. The obstruction results in progressive enlargement of the fourth ventricle with the maximum expansion along the superior and inferior medullary velum, resulting in transtentorial (upward) and tonsillar (downward) herniation. Both CT and MR can demonstrate the pathological cystic mass in the posterior fossa (Fig. 7-20). CT studies may require ventriculography to demonstrate the obstruction and to differentiate the cystic dilatation of the fourth ventricle from the extraaxial cyst. Because of the expansile forces dilating the weaker portion of the ventricular wall, it has the appearance of a keyhole (Wolfson 1987). MRI demonstrates the same features. Sagittal sections and T_2WI on MRI demonstrate the intraaxial nature of the cystic lesion, the transtentorial and tonsillar herniation, and the higher protein content of the cystic fluid.

Slit Ventricles

Slit ventricles, or ventricles that are compressed, are seen in children in whom repeated shunt revision has been performed. The ventricles are small as a result of adhesions, ependymal scarring, or loss of tensile capacity. A combination of the above factors causes the ventricles to lose their compliance to expand. The child presents with

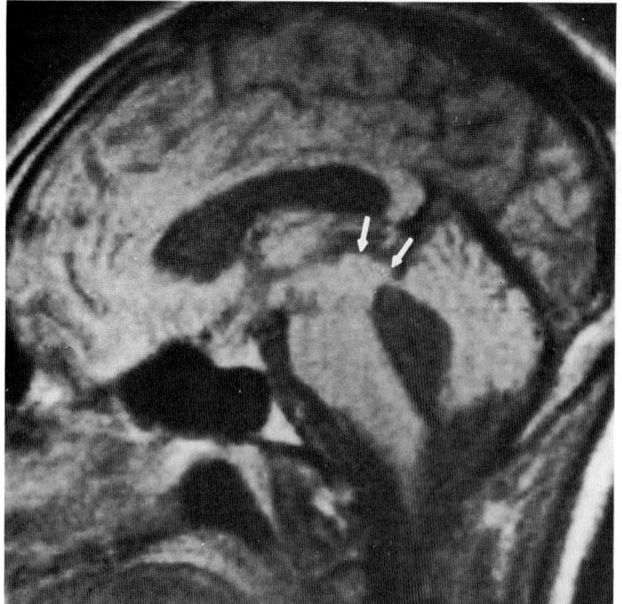

A

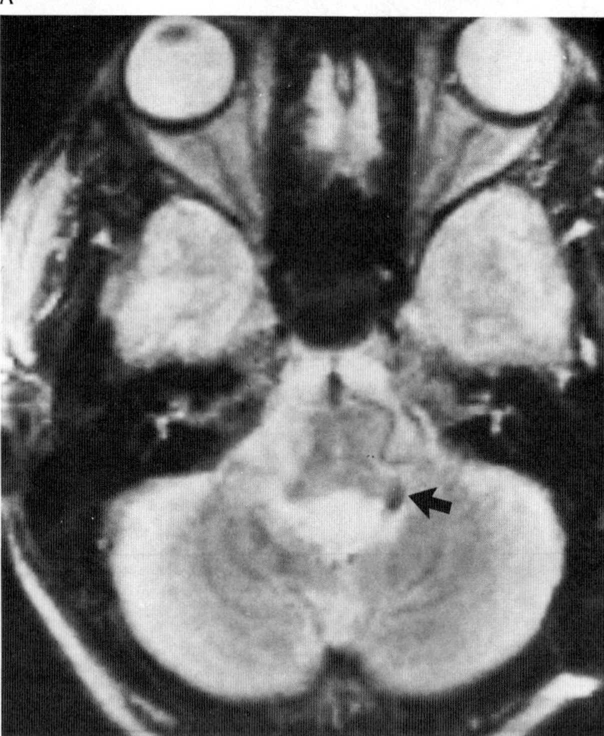

B

Figure 7-20 Trapped fourth ventricle in a 25-year-old female with repeated shunting for hydrocephalus due to aqueduct stenosis. **A.** Sagittal T_1WI. The lateral ventricles are mildly dilated. The aqueduct is not visualized. Quadrigeminal plate (arrows). The fourth ventricle is enlarged, as is the cervicomedullary cistern. **B.** Axial T_2WI demonstrates the enlarged fourth ventricle and CFVS in the foramen of Luschka (arrow).

features of a nonfunctioning shunt, but CT or MR may not show any characteristic features. The cisternal spaces are obliterated. Nonvisualization of the quadrigeminal cistern with slitlike lateral ventricles is suggestive of a blocked shunt (Johnson 1986) and is of ominous clinical significance. These findings may require an urgent decompressive procedure.

Porencephaly

Porencephaly is defined as a fluid-filled cavity (presumably CSF), usually secondary to infarction within the brain parenchyma. The cavity may communicate with the ventricle, in which case it is defined as porencephalic dilatation of the ventricle. A porencephalic cyst may be noncommunicating either de novo or from secondary infection (Fig. 7-21). The cyst can enlarge with time and act as a cystic mass, necessitating decompression.

Puncture porencephaly is the development of a cystic cavitation along the track of the ventricular needle. This becomes apparent with time, following nonfunctioning of the shunt and increased intracranial CSF pressure. The cysts develop when repeated ventricular punctures are performed and may be associated with small hemorrhages along the needle track. This condition has also been described following placement of a ventricular drainage catheter for prolonged periods.

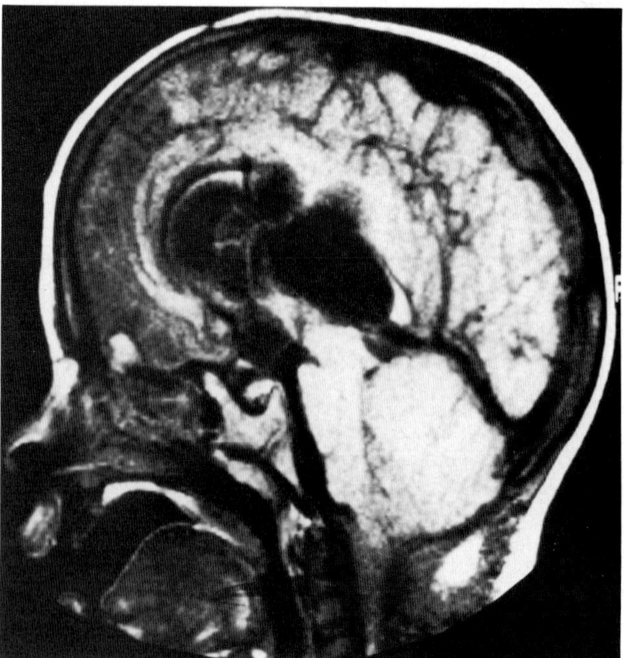

Figure 7-21 Porencephaly. Sagittal MR (T_1WI) in an 18-month-child with hydrocephalus following meningitis at the age of 3 months treated with repeated shunting. Porencephalic cavitation communicating with the dilated lateral ventricles. The aqueduct is not visualized. The fourth ventricle is of normal size. Apparent widening of the prepontine cistern.

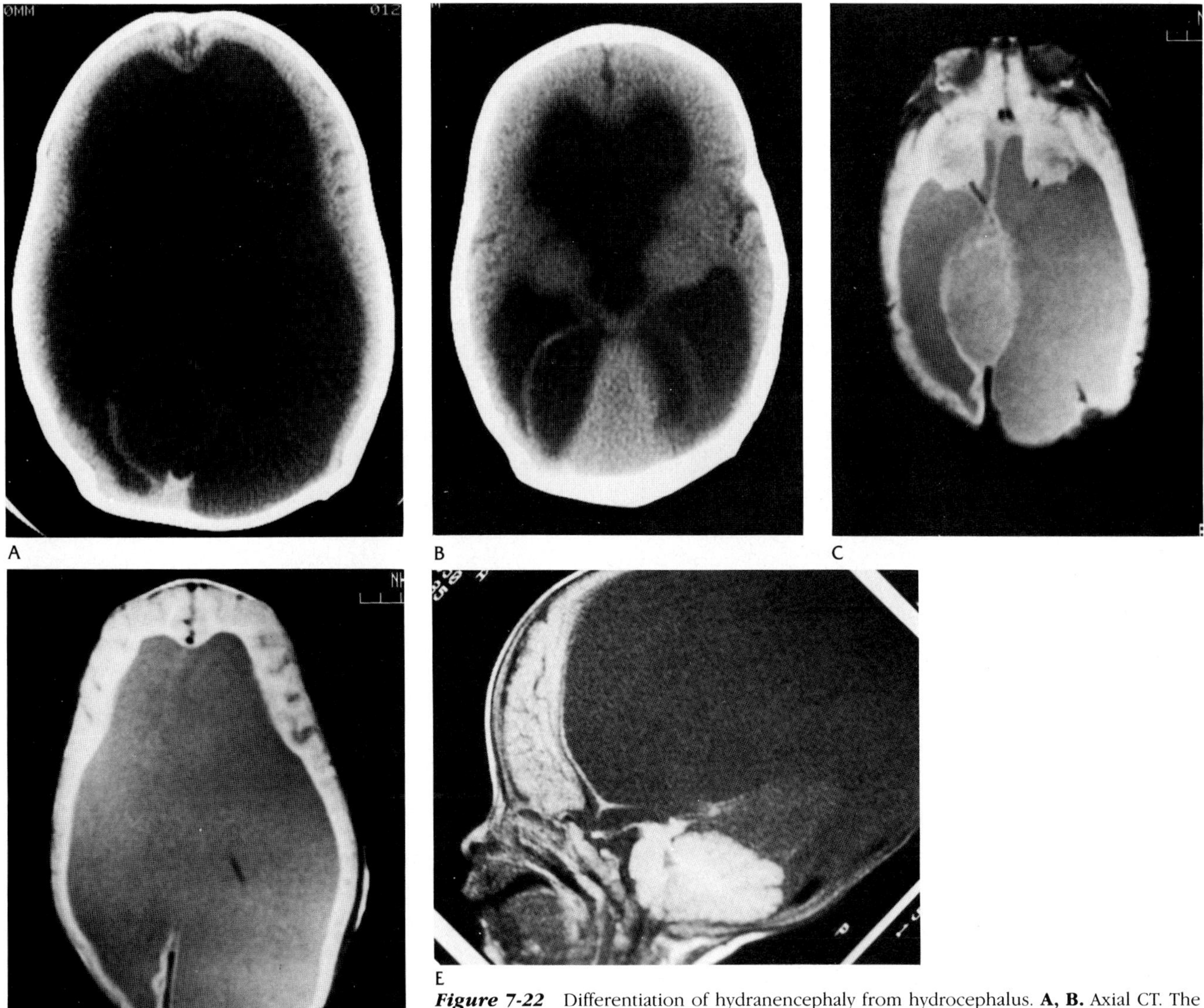

Figure 7-22 Differentiation of hydranencephaly from hydrocephalus. **A, B.** Axial CT. The ventricles are markedly dilated with a thin cortical mantle. **B.** Dilated third ventricle. **C, D.** Marked thinning of cortical mantle in a child suspected of hydrocephalus. **E.** Midsagittal T_1-weighted MR demonstrates some frontal cortical mantle. The brainstem and the posterior fossa structures are preserved. The aqueduct is patent. These features are indicative of hydranencephaly.

On CT, a porencephalic cyst has a density similar to that of CSF. Peripherally located porencephaly may produce scalloping of the inner table of the calvarium and be mistaken for an arachnoid cyst or a low-grade glioma. On MRI, the cyst fluid has the signal characteristics of CSF in all pulse sequences. On T_2WI (proton density), pericyst brightness represents either edema or glial scarring of the surrounding brain parenchyma.

HYDRANENCEPHALY

Hydranencephaly is a severe form of porencephaly resulting from occlusion or bilateral atresia of the carotid circulation (Crome 1972). Evidence of other malformations of the brain suggests that this condition may represent a developmental anomaly (Halsey 1971). Typically the basal ganglia is spared, with a strip of occipital lobe occasionally being visible adjacent to the tentorium (Fig. 7-22). The cranial cavity is filled with CSF without definite evidence of the third and lateral ventricles, except the fourth ventricle. Both CT and MR demonstrate the abnormality. Since in some cases the hydranencephaly may be associated with an enlarging head, MR is useful in differentiating hydranencephaly from hydrocephalus. In hydranencephaly vascular branches of the middle and anterior cerebral branches may not be present, whereas in hydrocephalus these cortical branches can be demonstrated.

CEREBRAL ATROPHY

In the process of normal aging, subtle changes of senescence are reflected, usually beyond the fifth decade, in a slight deterioration of intellectual capacity and cognitive function in most individuals. Paralleling these outward manifestations, there is a loss in the volume of the brain parenchyma or in the functioning neurons and a relative increase in CSF spaces (Creasy 1985; Dekaban 1978). In most parts of the world, because of improving living standards, longer survival of individuals is common, resulting in a larger population presenting with senility and its neurological manifestations. As the longevity of the individual increases, the loss in intellectual and cognitive functions becomes more noticeable and is described as dementia related to senility.

The imaging correlates of these changes are reflected in the apparent or absolute widening of the sulci and ventricles (LeMay 1984; Gomori 1984). This process is defined as brain atrophy. Atrophy of the brain may involve the gray matter, the white matter, or both (Tomlinson 1968). Pathological conditions may accelerate the process of senility both on clinical studies and on imaging studies. Depending on the etiology (Table 7-2), the atrophic or degenerative process may be focal or generalized. On CT and MRI, diffuse cerebral atrophy is diagnosed when there is enlargement of the ventricles as well as the subarachnoid spaces, such as the sulci and cisterns. In focal atrophy, there is focal enlargement of the cistern, sulci, and ventricles. These are general descriptive terms which provide an overall assessment of the morphological changes seen on CT and MRI.

Volumetric loss of brain parenchyma in diffuse cerebral atrophy involves, to varying degrees, both the gray matter and the white matter. Depending on the extent of gray matter loss or changes within the white matter, diffuse cerebral atrophy has also been classified as cortical atrophy or central atrophy, respectively. In central atrophy the ventricles enlarge out of proportion to the enlargement of the sulci. This is often associated with a pathological process involving the white matter. Cortical atrophy is suspected when the sulci and cisterns are wide, with a normal range in the size of the lateral ventricles. Cortical atrophy often represents the "normal" aging process (Fig. 7-23). Neuropathological studies have shown the progressive neuronal loss (Brody 1955) as well as a decrease in Betz cells (Scheibel 1975) as a natural process of aging, with a greater loss among patients with dementia (Tomlinson 1984).

Direct imaging of the intracranial contents with CT and better differentiation of the gray matter and white matter with MR have provided an impetus for numerous investigators to correlate the intellectual impairment assessed by clinical testing (Wechsler 1944) with the morphological features seen on CT and MRI (Earnest 1979; Jacoby

Table 7-2 Atrophy and Neurodegenerative Disorders

- Associated with dementia
  - Primary
    - Alzheimer's disease
    - Pick's disease
  - Secondary
    - Multi-infarct dementia
    - Binswanger's disease
    - Jakob-Creutzfeldt disease
    - Normal pressure hydrocephalus
    - Posttraumatic
    - Paraneoplastic
    - Infection (AIDS-related)
- Associated with movement disorders
  - Extrapyramidal nuclei
    - Primary
      - Parkinson's disease
      - Huntington's disease
      - Hallervorden-Spatz disease
      - Leigh's syndrome
    - Secondary
      - Wilson's disease
      - Zellweger's syndrome
      - Hypoxic-ischemic insult
      - Mitochondrial encephalopathy
  - Substantia nigra and related nuclei
    - Primary
      - Parkinson's disease
      - Striatonigral degeneration
      - Shy-Drager syndrome
      - Progressive supranuclear palsy
    - Secondary
      - Infarction
      - Infection
      - Trauma
      - Toxins
- Associated with ataxia involving cerebellum, brainstem, spinal cord
  - Primary
    - Olivopontocerebellar degeneration
    - Olivary-cerebellar degeneration
    - Friedreich's ataxia
    - Progressive bulbar palsy
    - Amyotrophic lateral sclerosis
  - Acquired
    - Alcohol
    - Drug toxicity
    - Infection
    - Toxins
  - Related disorders
    - Wallerian degeneration

Source: Modified from Adams 1989. Only those neurodegenerative disorders which have been demonstrated on imaging studies are included. The majority of these disorders demonstrate focal or diffuse atrophy.

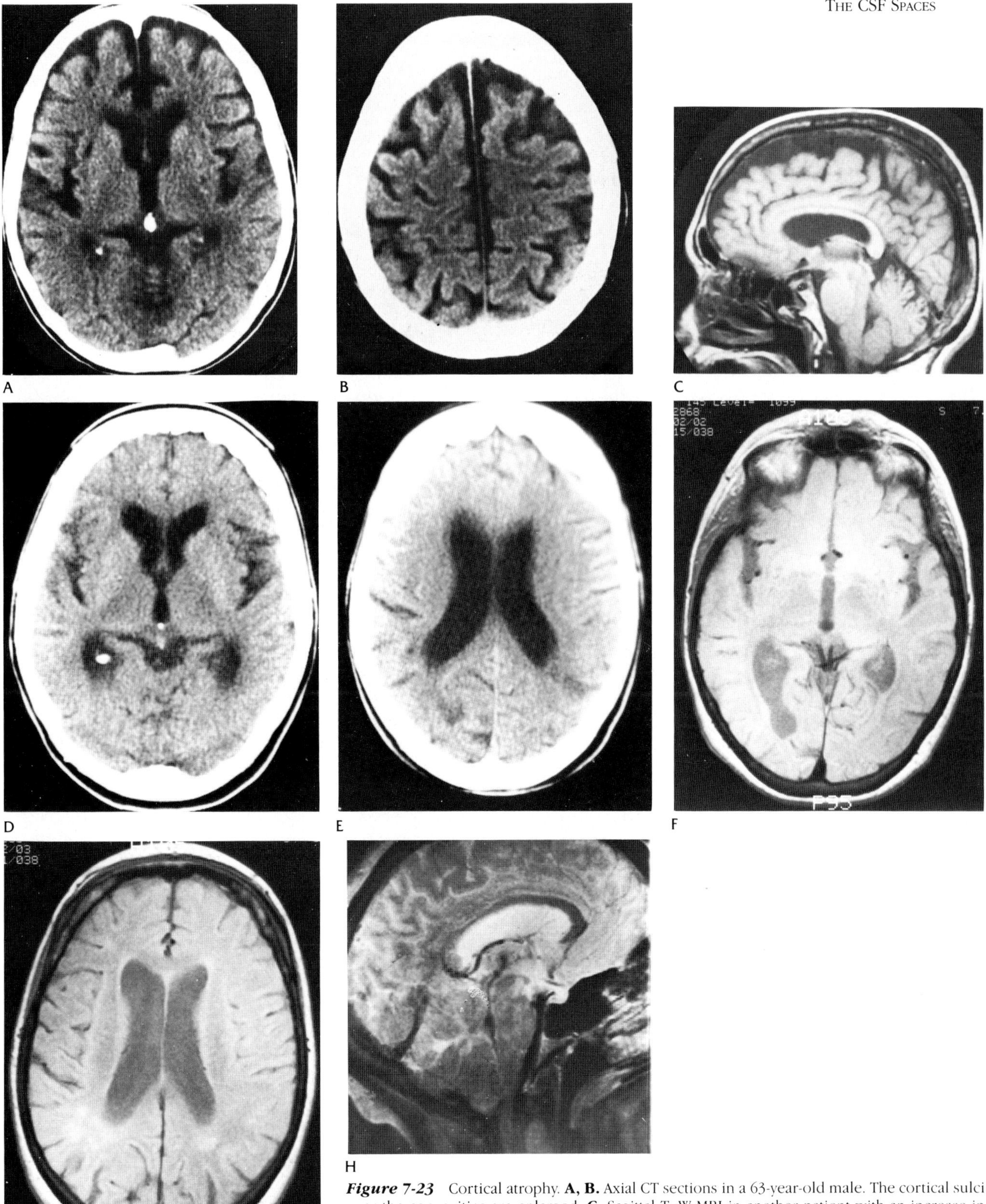

Figure 7-23 Cortical atrophy. **A, B.** Axial CT sections in a 63-year-old male. The cortical sulci over the convexities are enlarged. **C.** Sagittal T_1-W MRI in another patient with an increase in sulcal width and a large CSF space over the convexity. The ventricles in both patients are not enlarged. Cerebral atrophy. **D, E.** Axial CT demonstrates mild ventricular enlargement and slight prominence of the sylvian cisterns. **F, G.** Axial T_2-W (SE 2500/40) MR. In addition to the enlarged ventricles, there is mild periventricular hyperintensity (PVH) as well as a few subcortical hyperintense foci (arrowhead). **H.** Sagittal T_2-weighted MR demonstrates CFVS within the aqueduct and fourth ventricle.

1980; Johnson 1988; Erkinjutti 1984; LeMay 1986; Sandor 1988; Drayer 1988*a,b*; deLeon 1989; Bowen 1990; Wippold 1991). Other studies have dealt with the differentiation of the neurodegenerative process associated with normal aging from those seen with pathological aging. These studies have been based on age-matched, linear measurements (Barron 1976; Gyldensted 1977; Huckman 1975; Haug 1977; Laffey 1984), volumetric analysis (Yamaru 1980; Gado 1983*a,b*; Jack 1990; Khon 1991; Rusinek 1991; Tanna 1991), CT attenuation values (Naeser 1980; George 1981; Gado 1983*a,b*), and pathological correlation with CT and MRI (Awad 1986*a,b*; Brun 1986; Fazekas 1987; Kirkpatrick 1987; Braffman 1988*b*).

Although all these studies have demonstrated the differences between normal and pathological atrophic processes, their predictive value on an individual basis in patients beyond the sixth decade is subject to wide variability. The predictive value is more useful in patients below age 65 years (Sandor 1988). Similar attempts utilizing the signal characteristics of MR (Fazekas 1987; Brant-Zawadzki 1985*a,b*) have had similar results. At the present time, in patients beyond the sixth decade, no specific pattern can be determined which would be helpful in predicting the diagnosis of dementia from the normal aging process.

Age-Related Atrophy

The term *age-related atrophy* is used to describe the mild to moderate ventricular and sulcal prominence seen on CT and MRI in patients beyond the sixth decade (Fig. 7-23). The pathological correlation is due to neuronal loss and the accumulation of lipofuscin and ceroid. The neuronal loss predominately involves the superior frontal, temporal, and precentral gyri as well as the hippocampus, thalamus, and amygdaloid bodies. There is associated loss of neuronal synapses. At all ages the left lateral ventricle and left circular sulcus are larger than the right (LeMay 1984). This should not be considered as being due to infarction.

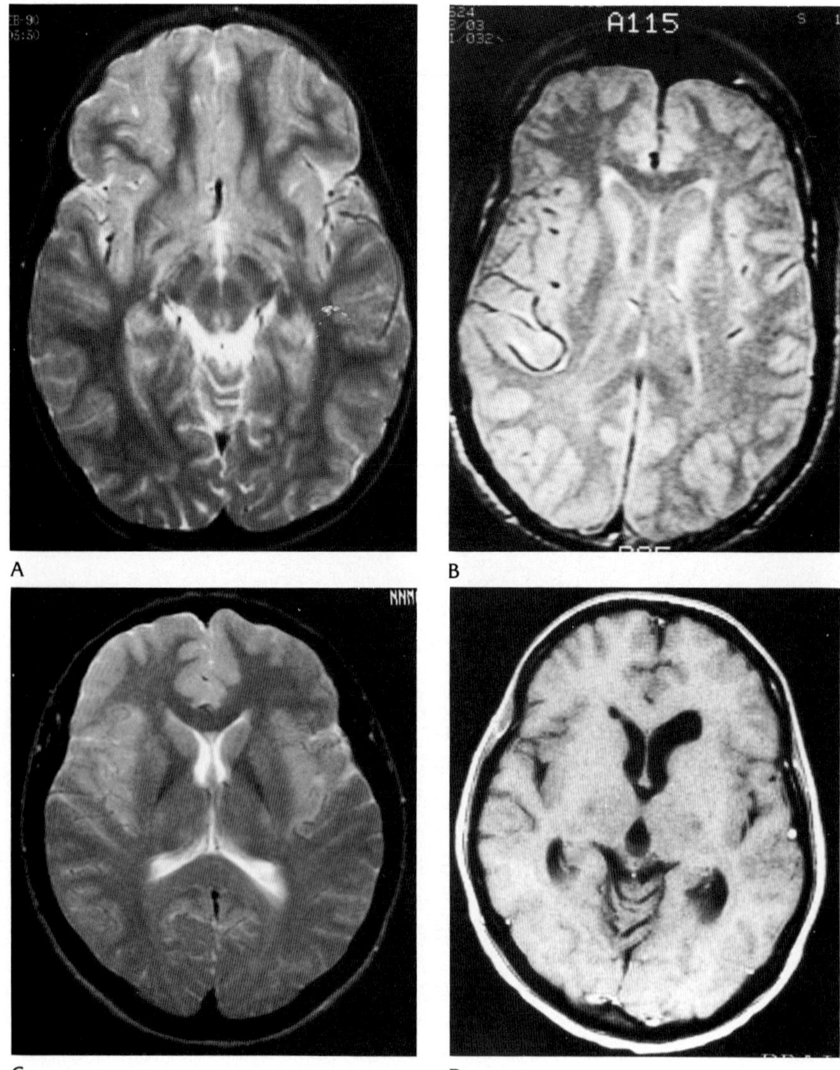

Figure 7-24 Normal focal hyperintense signal regions. **A–C.** Axial MR section (TR 2500/40). **A.** Hyperintense signal in the region of anterior commisure (arrowheads) due to anterior perforating arteries and in the region of the choroidal fissure (open arrows). **B.** Hyperintense signal capping the frontal horns. **C.** Hyperintense signal (arrowhead) adjacent to the posterior limb of the internal capsule. (**D**). This is seen as a hypointense signal (arrowhead) in a T_1-weighted sequence.

Table 7-3 Hyperintense Foci on T_2WI: Imaging Significance

LOCATION	HISTOLOGY	DIFFERENTIAL DIAGNOSIS
Normal		
Anterolateral margins of lateral ventricles	Usually bilateral Present beyond 1st dacade Related to fissures in the ependymal lining and gliosis and/or interstitial fluid	Demyelinating plaques
Posterior aspect of internal capsule	Usually symmetrical Usually beyond 1st decade Located posterior aspect of posterior limb of the internal capsule	Lacunar infarct; usually asymmetrical, large, irregular hypointense on T_1, may enhance with Gd-DTPA Demyelinating plaque
Perivascular spaces (Robin-Virchow spaces) Centrum semiovale Anterior commissure Adjacent to choroidal fissure	Less than 2 mm Is due to extension of CSF spaces along penetrating arteries Usually isointense with CSF in all pulse sequences	Lacunar infarcts Demyelinating plaques Subcortical lesions
Pathological		
Periventricular hyperintensity (PVH)	Along lateral walls of the lateral ventricles; irregular fading of peripheral margins; smooth inner margins	Age-related (most common) Severe cerebral atrophy Demyelinating (MS); usually scattered irregular inner margin; may involve corpus callosum Hydrocephalus; more prominent in acute stage; less prominent in NPH and compensated stage
Subcortical lesions (SCL) Centrum semiovale, corona radiata, basal ganglia, pons	Not clear; may represent ischemia or infarcts, vessel wall atherosclerosis, or myelination changes; of varying size, but not larger than 5 mm; cortex, medial portion of corpus callosum is spared; nonenhancing; not seen on T_1WI	Metastatic deposits; always enhances with Gd-DTPA Infarcts: may extend into cortical surface Multiple sclerosis: may involve corpus callosum

On MRI (T_2WI), focal bright signal lesions are often seen in the white matter, basal ganglia, and frontal periventricular region. Differentiation of the normal bright signal regions (posterior limb of the internal capsule (Mirowitz 1989), tips of the frontal horns [Sze 1986], perivascular spaces, vascular entry zones such as the anterior and posterior commissure, and medial trigonal region) (Fig. 7-24) (Chap. 4) from age-related neurodegenerative causes is important (Table 7-3).

With aging, focal or patchy areas of low attenuation in the white matter as well as in the pons and adjacent frontal horns are usually present on CT (George 1986*a,b*). On MRI these findings are seen as a hyperintense signal on T_2WI. The hyperintense signals are due to the following causes.

PROMINENT PERIVASCULAR SPACES

Perivascular spaces (PVS) are subarachnoid sleeves surrounding the penetrating vessels entering the brain parenchyma; they are also known as *Virchow-Robin spaces.* With aging and in neurodegenerative disorders, the perivascular spaces become prominent. On CT, PVS may appear as focal regions of hypodensity. They may not be visible unless the PVS are markedly prominent or confluent. On high-field MRI, apart from a dilated PVS, even a normal PVS can often be visualized (Braffman 1988*a*; Jungries 1988; Heier 1989). They are isointense with CSF on all pulse sequences, do not exhibit mass effect, and are best seen where the penetrating arteries enter the brain parenchyma (Fig. 7-25). On axial sections, they are adjacent to the anterior commissure and posteriorly adjacent to the choroidal fissure. Within the white matter in the centrum semiovale, PVS of less than 2 mm may occasionally be visible in the younger age group. Both smaller and larger PVS are routinely visible in the aging population (Jungries 1988; Heier 1989). The increase in the size and number of PVS in the centrum semiovale in both normal and pathological aging is related to the

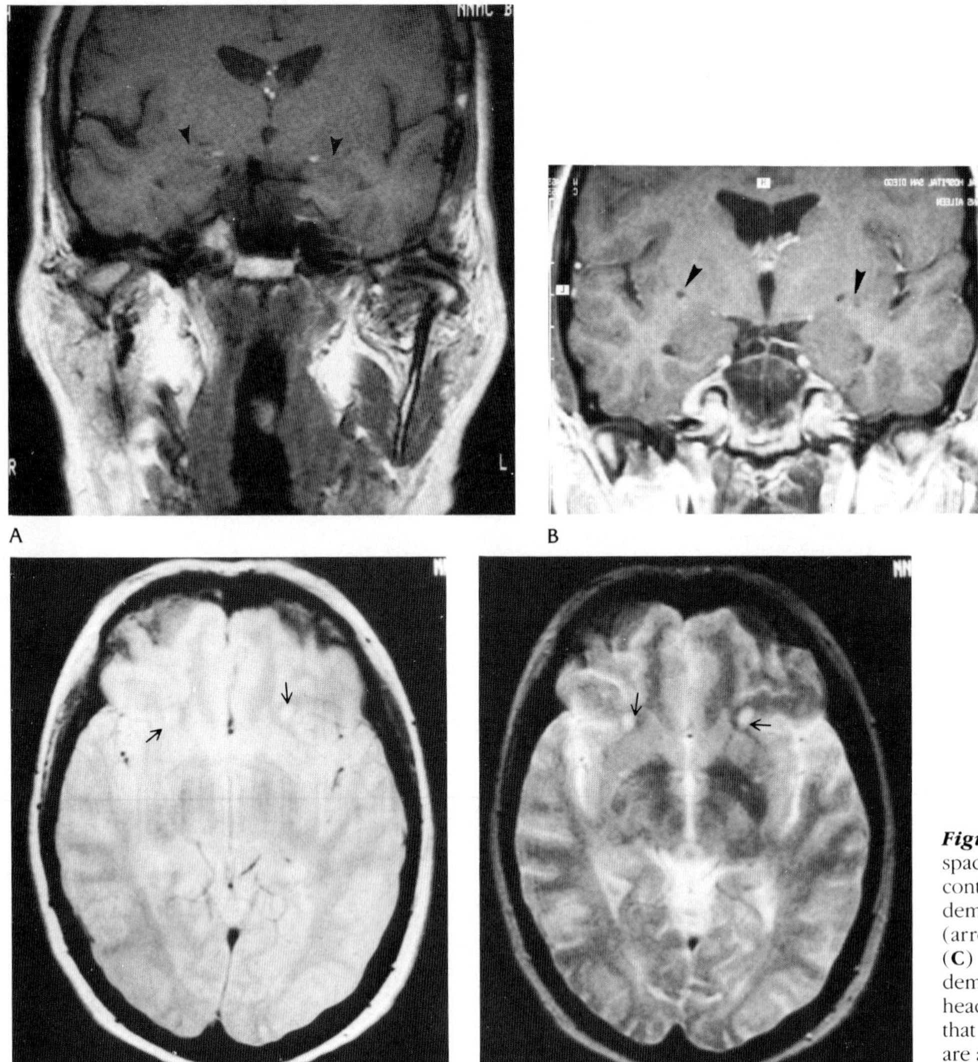

Figure 7-25 Prominent perivascular spaces (PVS). Coronal T_1-weighted precontrast (**A**) and postcontrast (**B**) MR demonstrates the perivascular spaces (arrowheads). Axial T_2-weighted MR (**C**) SE 2500/30 and (**D**) SE 2500/90 demonstrates bilateral PVS (arrowheads) with signal intensity similar to that of CSF. Common locations of PVS are adjacent to the anterior commisure, basal ganglia, and centrum semiovale.

atrophic brain associated with increased interstitial space and CSF, arteriosclerotic changes in the vessel, and hypertensive disease (Drayer 1988*a,b*). PVS need to be differentiated from lacunar infarcts, which are hyperintense on T_2WI and hypointense on T_1WI.

SUBCORTICAL HYPERINTENSE LESIONS

Unlike PVS, the exact histological nature of subcortical lesions (SCL) is not clear. These lesions probably represent ischemic foci or small infarcts (Awad 1986*a,b*; Marshall 1988). They may also represent perivascular atrophic demyelination (Kirkpatrick 1987), actual infarcts, or areas of gliosis (Braffman 1988*a,b*). These conditions are common in the aging population (Hendrie 1989), more often seen with hypertensive disease, multi-infarct dementia, and dementia associated with Binswanger's disease.

On CT, SCL appear as hypodense lesions from 2 to 5 mm in diameter, typically seen in sections through the centrum semiovale, as linear bands, and occasionally within the pons. Typically they do not enhance. On MRI, they are not visible on T_1WI. On T_2WI, they appear as hyperintense foci in the subcortical regions as well as in the basal ganglia, the central and upper pons, and the lateral aspect of the corpus callosum (Fig. 7-26) (Bowen 1990; Moody 1988; Salamon 1987), sparing the cortical and thin ribbon of adjacent subcortical white matter (arcuate 'U' fibers). The pathological basis of these lesions appears to be related to hypoperfusion and lack of autoregulation of the long penetrating arteries supplying these regions (Moody 1988). On T_2WI, SCL are sharply defined, measuring 1 to 10 mm. Larger lesions may have irregular ill-defined faded margins but do not have mass effect. The larger lesions may represent infarcts (Braffman 1988; Bradley 1990). The smaller lesions represent perivascular atrophic demyelination (Kirkpatrick 1987).

Depending on the age of the patient and the clinical presentation, these lesions may mimic demyelinating plaques of multiple sclerosis or even metastatic disease, and may require MR following paramagnetic contrast (Sze 1986). On T_1WI, SCL do not enhance or have mass effect. In some cases of multiple sclerosis the lesions may enhance, indicating active plaques of MS; in almost all cases of metastatic deposits the lesions will enhance and some may even show mass effect. Other causes of hyperintense lesions in the white matter include sarcoidosis, Lyme disease, vasculitis, and disseminated encephalomyelitis.

CORTICAL HEMORRHAGIC INFARCTS

Similar to degenerative changes in the parenchyma, the degenerative process also involves the cerebral vasculature in the form of amyloid deposition within the vessel walls. The vessel becomes friable and prone to rupture from minor trauma, an increase in blood pressure, and the use of anticoagulants. These changes are described as cerebral amyloid angiopathy. They present as incidental hemorrhages, usually superficial, within the cortical and subcortical regions. Cerebral amyloid angiopathy is commonly seen beyond the sixth or seventh decade, with the incidence increasing with age (Wagle 1984). Although they most often occur in the temporal and occipital lobes, other surface areas of the brain parenchyma may be in-

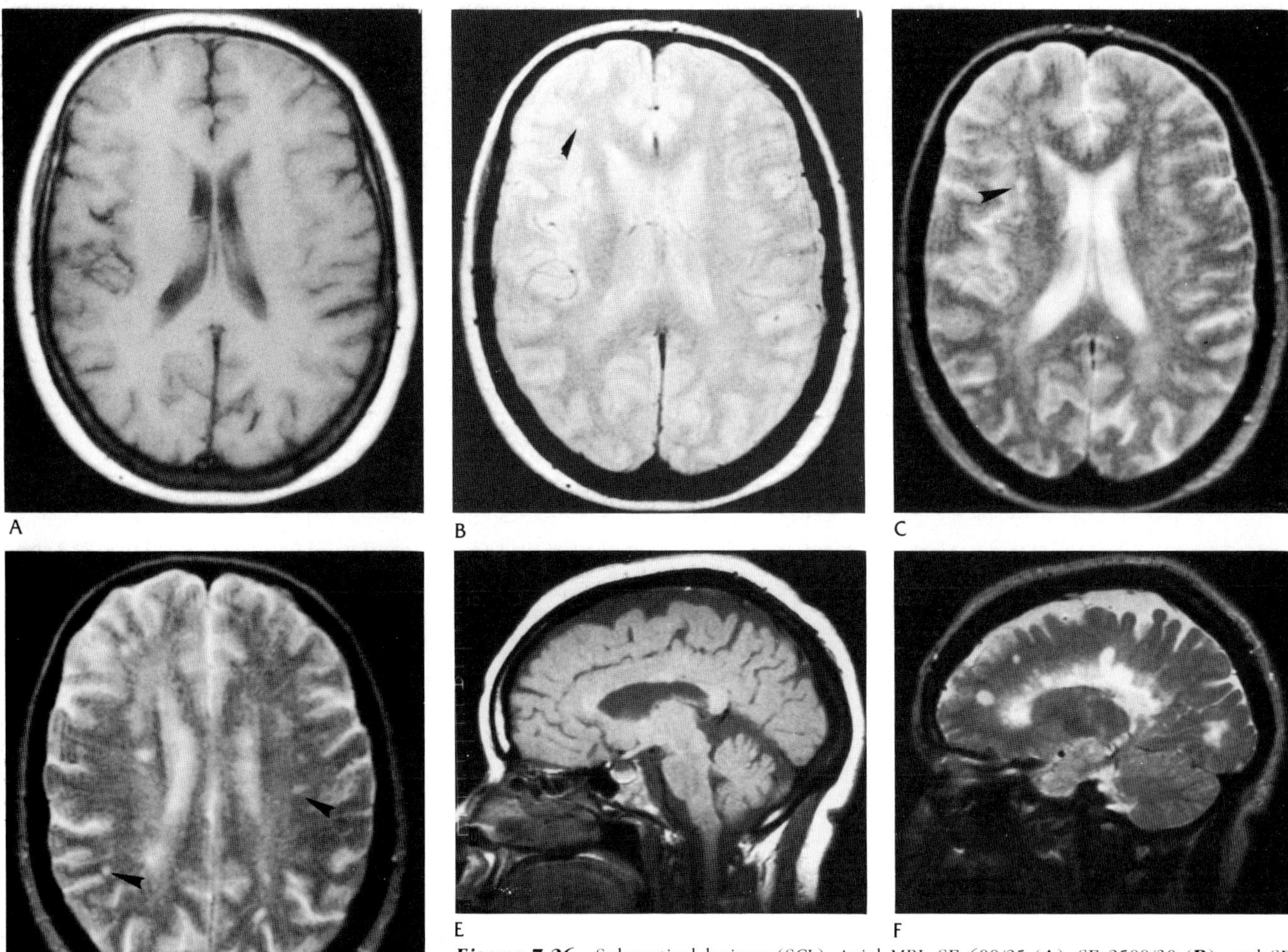

Figure 7-26 Subcortical lesions (SCL). Axial MRI: SE 600/25 (**A**), SE 2500/30 (**B**), and SE 2500/90 (**C, D**). Hyperintense focal signal intensity in the subcortical white matter (arrowheads) seen in the long TR sequence but not visualized in **A.** These are primarily located in the centrum semiovale, often adjacent to the gray matter. In the pons they are often in the upper pons, usually in the midline. Midsagittal (**E**) T_1-weighted and (**F**) T_2-weighted MR. T_1WI demonstrates cortical atrophy. Multiple hyperintense foci both in the white matter and in the corpus callosum on T_2WI in a patient with proven multiple sclerosis. SCL and infarcts spare the corpus callosum, unlike multiple sclerosis.

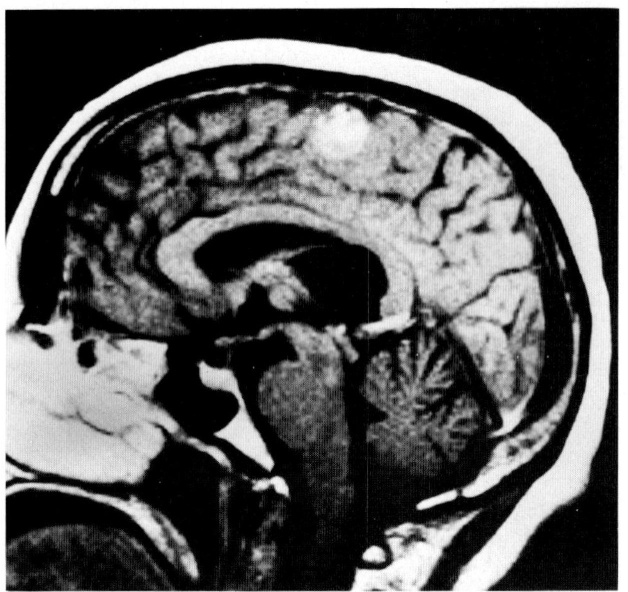
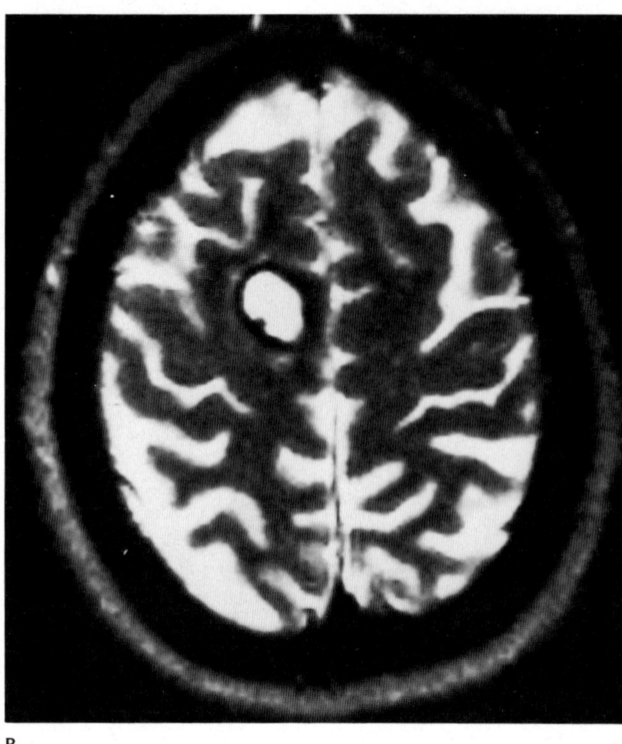

A B

Figure 7-27 Amyloid angiopathy. Sagittal (TR 600/30) (**A**) and axial (**B**) (TR 2500/80) MRI. Hyperintense foci in the cortical-subcortical region in the sagittal view and with a hypointense signal along its margin in the axial view in a patient suspected to have bled from amyloid angiopathy.

volved (Fig. 7-27). These hemorrhagic infarcts are not associated with hypertensive disease or arteriosclerotic disease. Sometimes the hematomas can be very large. Cerebral amyloid angiopathy, although a manifestation of normal aging, has a higher incidence in patients with Alzheimer's disease (Drayer 1988*a,b*; Esiri 1986; Patel 1984).

On CT and MRI, infarcts due to amyloid angiopathy are seen as focal areas of hyperdensity or hyperintensity, respectively, located in the cortical and subcortical regions, often in the temporal and occipital lobes. The hemorrhagic infarcts are due to rupture of cortical or leptomeningeal vessels, often sparing the white matter (Patel 1984; Wagle 1984).

PERIVENTRICULAR HYPERINTENSE LESIONS

Periventricular hyperintense lesions (PVH) are seen in patients with central atrophy and in normal aging but more often in pathological aging (Braffman 1988*c*; Drayer 1988*a*; George 1986*a,b*; Heier 1989; Fazekas 1987). On CT, PVH are seen as hypodense foci, most often adjacent to the frontal and occipital horns, and may extend along the lateral margins of the body of lateral ventricles. On MRI, PVH are seen as focal, or linear and bandlike, areas of hyperintense signal, with their medial margins contiguous to the lateral ventricles (Fig. 7-28). In the normal aging process they represent an accumulation of interstitial fluid in the periventricular region (Heier 1989) resulting from delayed absorption by the ependymal surface of the ventricles. A similar appearance is also seen with acute or chronic communicating hydrocephalus. On pathological studies, PVH has been associated with flattening, fissures, and thinning of the ependymal lining cells. As a result of the obstruction in CSF pathways, the fluid flows in a centrifugal manner. This may explain the hyperintense signal fading along its outer, lateral margins. Similar findings have been demonstrated on CT studies (DiChiro 1979). PVH is thus a nonspecific finding (Table 7-4) that can be seen with normal aging, various neurodegenerative processes, and hydrocephalus (Zimmerman 1986).

HYPOINTENSE SIGNAL

Hypointense signal on T_2W MRI is seen in younger patients in the compact heavily myelinated white matter tracts, such as the anterior commissure, optic radiation, inferior and superior frontooccipital fascicles, cingulum, internal capsule, fornix, brachium pontis, and corpus callosum. These fiber tracts cannot be clearly seen on CT (Curnes 1988). MRI demonstrates deposition of iron in the brain tissue, primarily within the extrapyramidal nuclei, including the corpus striatum and the dentate nucleus (Drayer 1986*a,b*). Hypointense signal due to iron

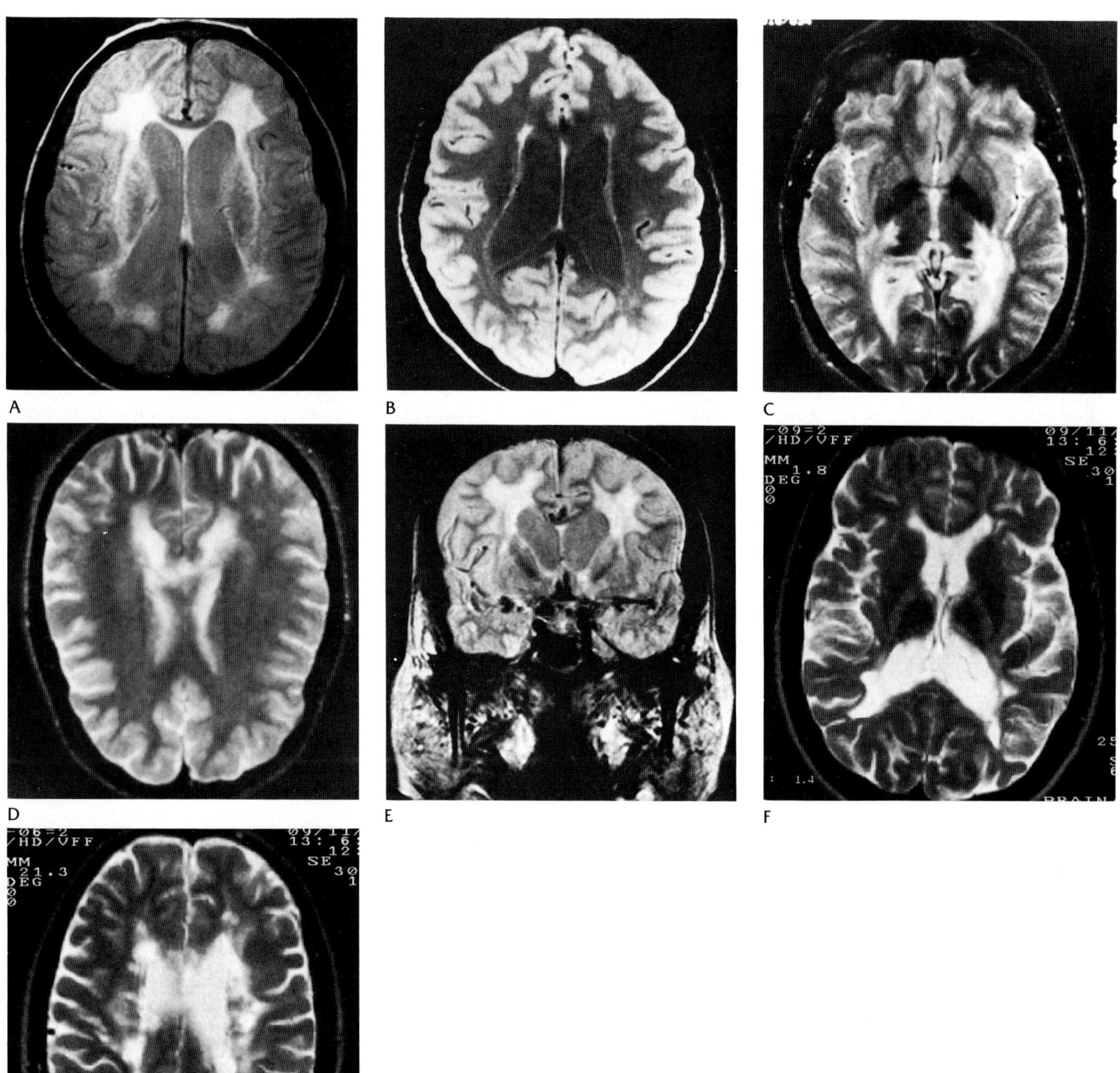

Figure 7-28 Periventricular hyperintensity (PVH). Axial T_2-weighted studies. **A.** Acute hydrocephalus. **B.** Compensated hydrocephalus. **C, D.** Atrophy in a patient with AIDS. Coronal T_2-weighted MR in acute communicating hydrocephalus (**E**). (**F**). Note the varying intensity and extent of the periventricular hyperintense signal. A 38-year-old female with multiple sclerosis. (**F**). Marked hypointense signal in the thalamus and basal ganglionic nuclei. (**G**). Periventricular and focal hyperintense signal extending into the corpus callosum.

deposition is also present in the subcortical U fibers (Drayer 1987). The iron is deposited in the form of ferritin, as can be demonstrated in histological studies with Perl's stain (Drayer 1986*a,b*; Rutledge 1987). These depositions are best visualized on high-field MRI (1.0 T and above) on T_2WI (Fig. 7-29). They appear as hypointense regions in the globus pallidus, substantia nigra, red nucleus, and, to a lesser extent, dentate nucleus, often occurring beyond the age of 25 years (Drayer 1986*a,b*; Rutledge 1987; Aoki 1989). The hypointensity increases in intensity and extends into the caudate nucleus and putamen. These changes are seen in normal aging beyond the sixth decade as well as in various neurodegenerative disorders. It is presumed that increased ferritin deposition

Table 7-4 Causes of Periventricular Hyperintensity

	DISEASE PROCESS	CHARACTERISTIC FEATURES
Normal	Often seen beyond 6th decade	Usually along lateral wall of ventricles Usually not prominent
Pathological	1. Alzheimer's disease	Usually prominent
	2. Multi-infarct dementia/ Binswanger's disease	Prominent; associated with SCL
	3. Hydrocephalus	Prominent in acute stage; associated with enlarged ventricles and narrow sulci
	4. Ventriculitis	Associated with ependymal enhancement
	5. Total brain radiation	Usually focal along frontal or occipital horns; ventricles may not be enlarged
	6. White matter Periventricular leukomalacia Multiple sclerosis	Usually focal; may be asymmetrical; often involves occipital horns

within the extrapyramidal nuclei as well as in other regions of the brain results from axonal disruption both during normal aging and in various pathological conditions (Drayer 1986*a,b*; Rutledge 1987). Increased hypointensity in the deep nuclei and compact white matter tracts, presumably caused by ferritin deposition, has also been described in certain demyelinating and dysmyelinating disorders, such as multiple sclerosis (Drayer 1987), Pelizaeus-Merzbacher disease (Penner 1987), and hemorrhagic infarct.

Dementia and Brain Atrophy

Dementia or memory loss associated with decreased intellectual and cognitive functions is a clinical diagnosis that is related to the aging process. However, when these changes are profound, rapidly progressive, and associated with other neurological changes, the neurodegenerative process has a pathological connotation. Its correlates on imaging studies are the volume loss and white matter changes that can be demonstrated better with MRI, although the morphological features can be demonstrated on CT.

The purpose of imaging studies in patients with dementia is not only to document the changes but, more important, to evaluate the severity and progression of the disease process. These studies are useful in identifying patients who may benefit from medical or surgical intervention and in preventing further progression of the disease process.

The importance of this finding can be understood when one realizes that because of increasing longevity, nearly 15 percent of the people in this country suffer from dementia-related syndromes (Fazekas 1987; Drayer 1988*b*). The percentage of the population with severe dementia increases from 1.5 percent at 65 years to 15 percent by age 85 years (Drayer 1988*b*). Since a fair number of these patients may suffer from dementia as a consequence of other risk factors, such as cardiovascular-related causes or metabolic causes, recognition of the effect of these factors on the brain parenchyma utilizing imaging studies may be important in developing preventive methods and improving the quality of life.

Imaging studies may demonstrate a neoplasm, other space-occupying mass, or chronic communicating hydrocephalus (NPH) as one of the curable causes of dementia. However, in a significant number of patients the memory loss is severe and is related to one of the following neurodegenerative pathological causes.

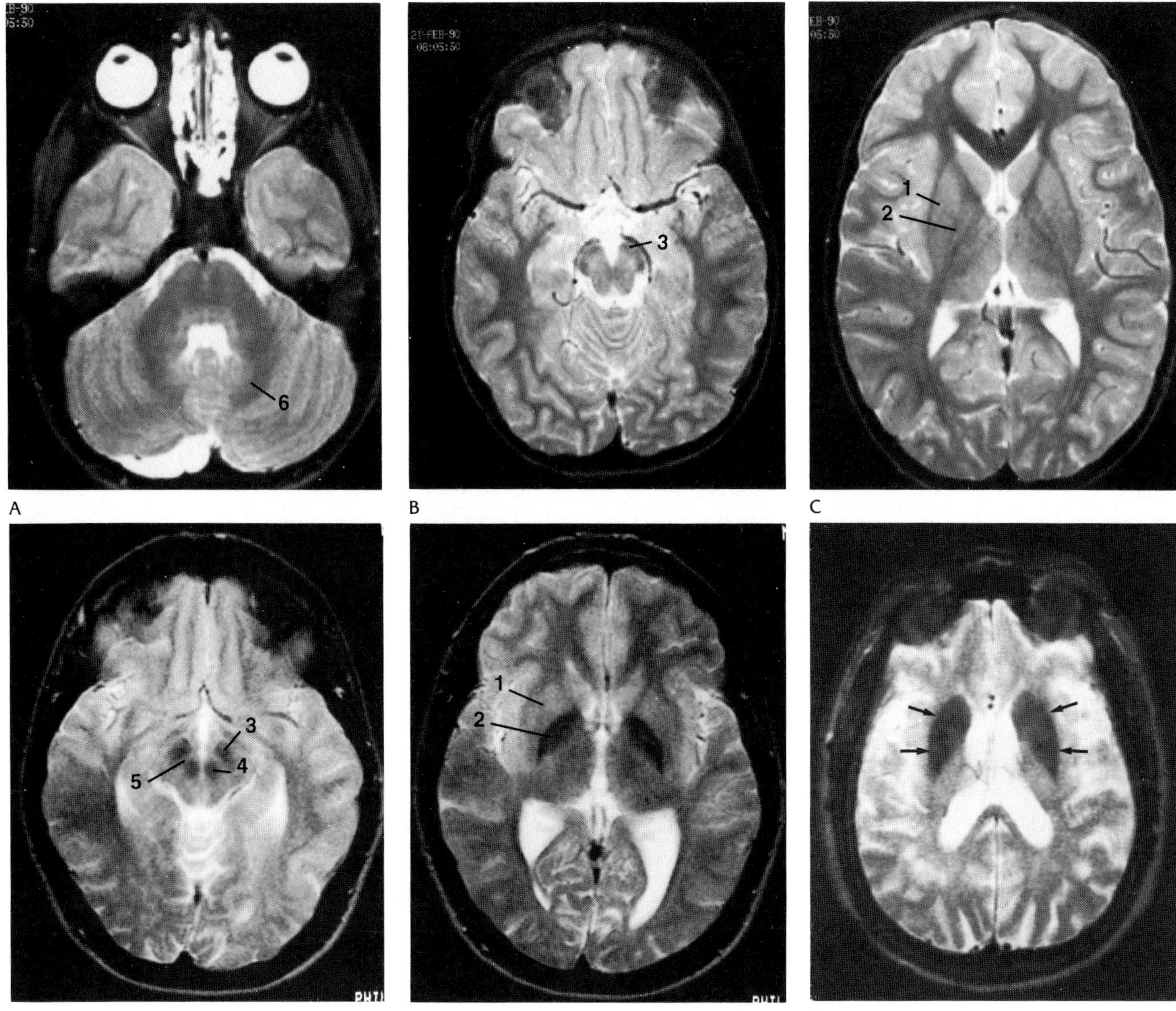

Figure 7-29 Normal regions of parenchymal hypointense signal on MR. Axial T_2-weighted MR. **A–C.** A 4-month-old infant. **D** and **E.** A 30-year-old adult. **F.** A 62-year-old adult. These nuclei are isointense or mildly hyperintense in infants. In normal aging beyond the sixth decade, the hypointensity can be pronounced and involve the putamen (arrows). 1 = putamen, 2 = globus pallidus, 3 = substantia nigra, 4 = red nucleus, 5 = pars reticulata, 6 = dentate nucleus.

ALZHEIMER'S DISEASE

This disease, a form of dementia seen as part of the aging process, is known as *senile dementia of the Alzheimer's type* (SDAT) when it presents after the sixth decade and as *presenile dementia* when it presents before the sixth decade. Both present with rapidly progressive memory loss (especially for recent events), confusion, gait apraxia, agnosia, and aphasia. The pathological features consist of generalized symmetrical gyral atrophy with enlargement of the cortical sulci and ventricles. The atrophic process predominantly involves the frontal and temporal lobes but may also involve the parietal and occipital lobes (Tomlinson 1970, 1984). The histological changes consist of an abundance of senile plaques, neurofibrillary tangles made up of thickened tortuous fibrils within neuronal cytoplasm, neuronal cell loss, and loss of dendritic spines and branching fibers. The exact cause of these changes has not been established. A combination of factors may

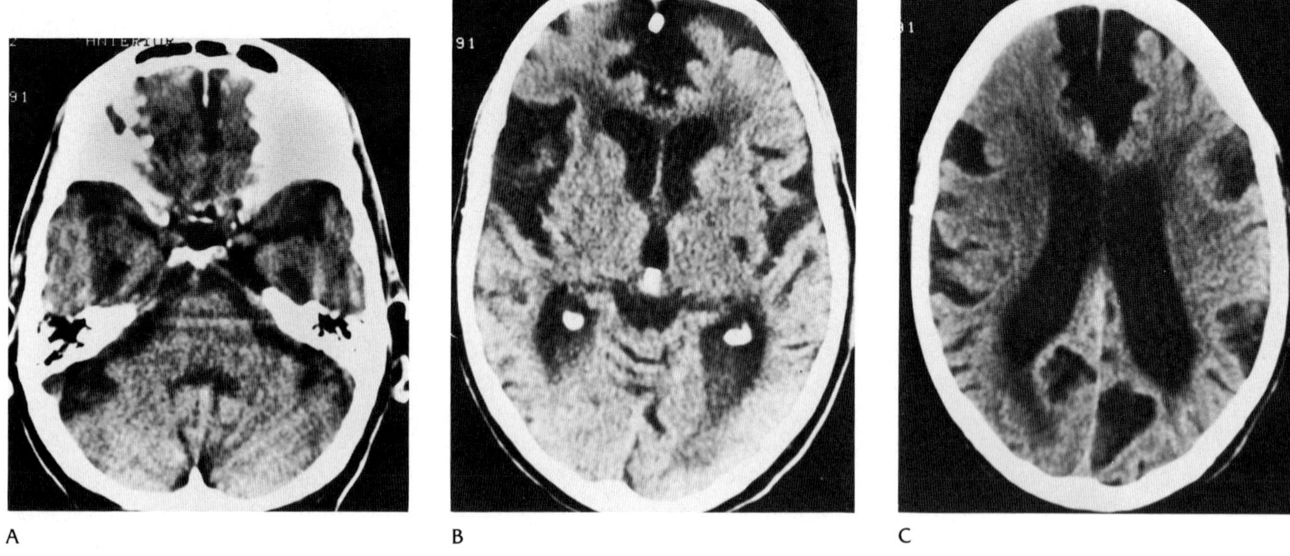

Figure 7-30 Alzheimer's disease. **A–C.** Axial CT sections demonstrate severe atrophy involving the frontal regions and temporal lobes with moderate enlaragement of the lateral and third ventricles.

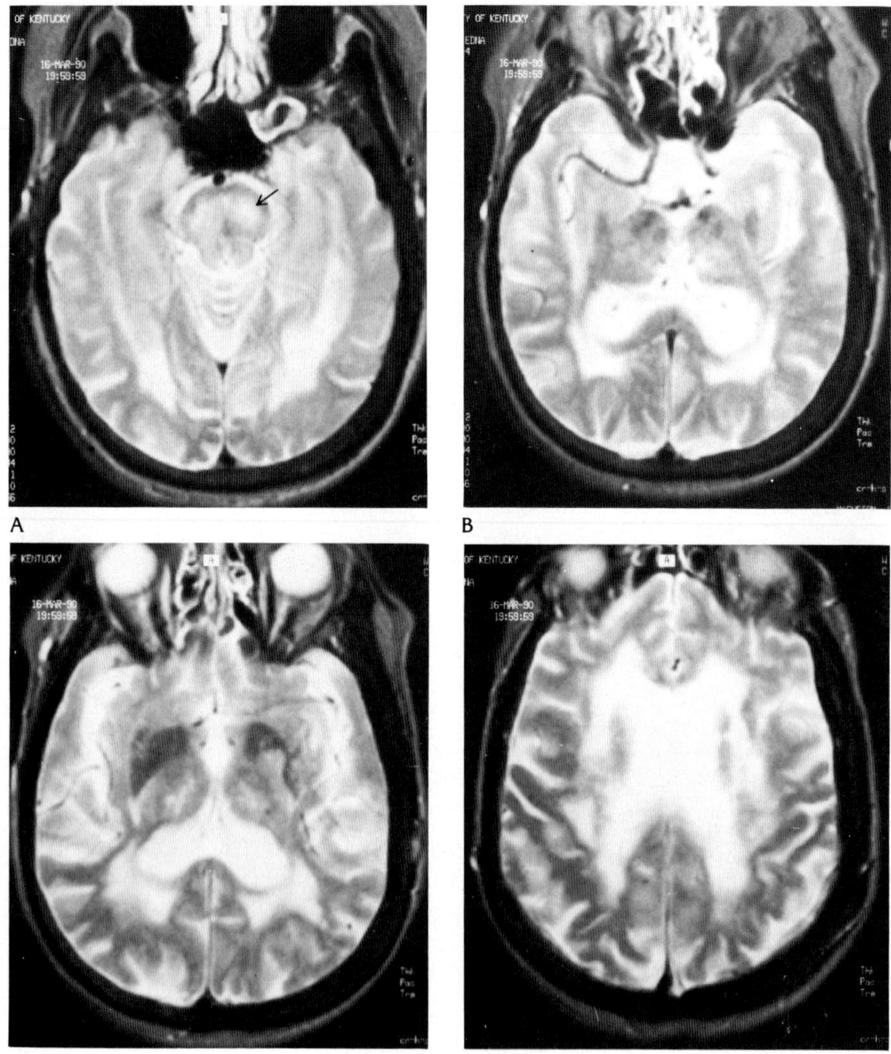

Figure 7-31 Alzheimer's disease in a 73-year-old male with a clinical diagnosis of dementia. **A–D.** Axial T_2-weighted MR demonstrates diffuse cerebral atrophy with predominant atrophy of the temporal lobe gyrus. There is some hyperintensity of the medial temporal pole and insula. The hyperintense signal within the pons could represent pontine myelinosis or SCL (arrowhead).

be involved, including multiple infarcts, mass lesions, low-grade or slow viral infections, and toxic or metabolic factors.

As previously mentioned, the value of imaging studies is to exclude (1) space-occupying lesions, (2) the presence of extensive infarcts, or (3) evidence of NPH. CT and MRI provide similar information, although MRI is more sensitive in demonstrating the associated white matter changes. CT findings consist of dilated ventricles and sulci (Fig. 7-30). Disproportionate enlargement of the third ventricle has been associated with an abnormal neuropsychological screening test indicative of Alzheimer's disease (Drayer 1988*b*). Other researchers have demonstrated loss of gray matter–white matter discrimination and hypodensity of the medial temporal lobe, indicative of hippocampal atrophy (Kido 1989; George 1981).

On MRI, apart from the enlarged ventricles and sulci similar to the appearance on CT, the coronal plane is useful in distinguishing the enlarged third ventricle and the focal temporal horn enlargement from hippocampal atrophy (Kido 1989) (Fig. 7-31). Hyperintensity along the medial temporal pole (matching the hypodense appearance on CT) on T_2WI probably represents interstitial fluid or gliosis of the hippocampal region. Gyral bands of hypodensity in axial sections through the convexity have been described on T_2WI (Drayer 1987). They are attributed to ferritin deposits and are seen in nearly 50 percent of patients with Alzheimer's disease. These findings are highly suggestive of Alzheimer's disease. Hyperintense lesions in the white matter (PVH, SCL, PVS) are a common finding. Several studies have shown an increased incidence of these hyperintense lesions in patients with a known clinical diagnosis of Alzheimer's disease compared with an age-matched normal population (Bowen 1990; Brant-Zawadzki 1985*a*; Fazekas 1987; George 1986*a,b*; Drayer 1988*a,b*). However, there has not been a good correlation between the severity of the dementia and the extent of the white matter changes (Erkinjuntti 1984; Bowen 1990). In fact, the diagnosis of Alzheimer's disease as the cause of dementia is more likely in the absence of these changes. A fair number of CT and MRI findings have been described, but none are specific for the diagnosis of the disease (Tables 7-5 and 7-6).

PICK'S DISEASE

Pick's disease (lobar atrophy, lobar sclerosis) is a form of primary dementia associated with severe frontal and tem-

Table 7-5 CT and MRI in Dementia: Imaging Characteristics

DISEASE ENTITY	CT FINDINGS	MRI FINDINGS
Alzheimer's disease	Atrophic pattern, predominantly frontal and temporal lobes; wide sulci; enlarged third ventricle; prominent mesencephalic cistern	Similar to CT; increased signal on T_2WI in medial temporal lobe; subcortical white matter, basal ganglia; hypointensity due to iron deposition in parietal gyri
Pick's disease	Similar to Alzheimer's disease but greater atrophy in caudate nucleus, frontal and inferior temporal gyrus	Similar to CT findings
Multi-infarct dementia	Atrophy with generalized widening of sulci and lateral ventricles; diffuse periventricular and subcortical hypodensity	Similar to CT; hyperintense signal foci throughout white matter, basal ganglia thalamus and pons; residual small hemorrhages due to amyloid angiopathy
Binswanger's disease	Vascular ectasia (hypertension); prominent sulcus; moderate ventricular enlargement; periventricular hypodensity	Bilateral symmetrical confluent regions of hyperintensity; sparing of subcortical arcuate fibers
Parkinsonian syndromes	Similar to Alzheimer's disease	In addition to findings under Alzheimer's disease, iso- or hyperintense signal in putamen, substantia nigra, and red nucleus
Normal pressure hydrocephalus	Ventricular dilatation out of proportion to sulcal widening; rounded frontal horn	In addition to CT findings may show periventricular hyperintensity; prominent aqueductal flow void signal

Table 7-6 CT and MRI Features in Dementias

DISORDER		CSF SPACES: VENTRICLES	CSF SPACES: SULCI	HYPERINTENSITY T_2WI: WHITE MATTER	HYPERINTENSITY T_2WI: BASAL GANGLIA	HYPERINTENSITY T_2WI: PONS THALAMUS	HYPOINTENSITY T_2WI: GP/SN RN/DN	HYPOINTENSITY T_2WI: PUTAMEN
Normal	Adult <50 yr	0	0	1	0	0	3	1
	Usual aging	1–2	½	2	1–2	0–1	3	1 or 2
Dementias	Alzheimer	2–3	3–4	3	2	1	3	2*
	Pick†	3†	4	3	2	1	3	2
	Binswanger	4	3	4	2–4	3	2	2 or 3
	NPH	3 or 4	1–3	2–3	1	1	2–3	2
	Wernicke's	3	3	2	2	2 or 3	2 or 3	2
Jacob-Creutzfeldt‡		2–4	2–4	1	0–2	0	1–2	0

Note: 0 = normal; 1 = equivocal; 2 = mild; 3 = moderate; 4 = severe or extensive.
**Abnormal gyral hypointensity in parietal cortex.*
†Predominant frontotemporal atrophy.
NPH = normal pressure hydrocephalus
GP = globus pallidus; RN = red nucleus; SN = substantia nigra; DN = dentate nucleus
‡ = rapidly progressive
Source: Modified from Drayer 1988.

poral lobe atrophy. It is rare compared with Alzheimer's disease and is clinically difficult to distinguish from that entity. The clinical diagnosis is based on progressive relentless loss of memory and concentration, with periods of apathy, agitation, unusual behavior, disorientation, and gait disturbance (Adams 1989; LeMay 1986). The disease is familial and probably is inherited. It is more common in females. Pathological studies demonstrate atrophy involving the medial and inferior surface of the frontal lobe and the anterior portions of the middle and inferior temporal gyrus, with possible involvement of the caudate lobe (Pick 1892). This results in enlarged frontal horns of the ventricles, an appearance similar to that of Huntington's disease. The atrophy is usually symmetrical, although it more often affects the left cerebral hemisphere. Pick's disease is a histological diagnosis, the main features of which consist of swollen neuronal cells with eccentric nuclei and globular cytoplasm with cytoplasmic filaments and tubules (Pick's body). There is loss of myelin in the white matter and gliosis of the adjacent cortex.

On CT, focal but extensive atrophy of the anterior inferior temporal lobe and focal atrophy of the frontal lobe with involvement of the caudate nucleus (Fig. 7-32) are suggestive (McGeachi 1979). Differentiation from Huntington's disease on the basis of imaging studies is difficult unless the caudate atrophy is shown to be asymmetrical. On MRI, a focal hyperintense signal within the atrophic cortex and adjacent white matter may be pres-

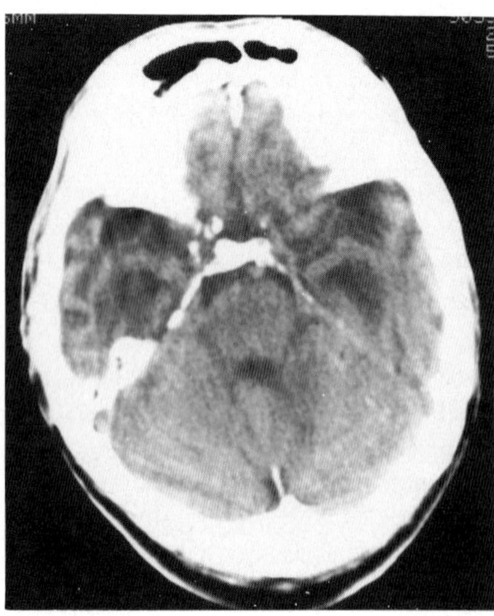

A

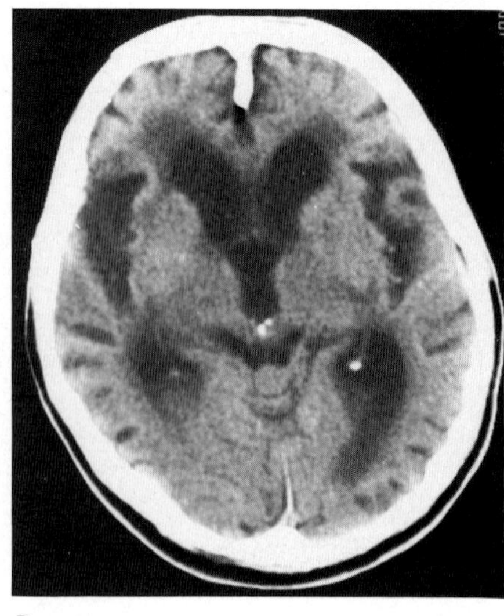

B

Figure 7-32 Pick's disease. CT (**A** and **B**) in a 67-year-old female with proven Pick's disease. Selective pronounced atrophy of the frontal and temporal lobes.

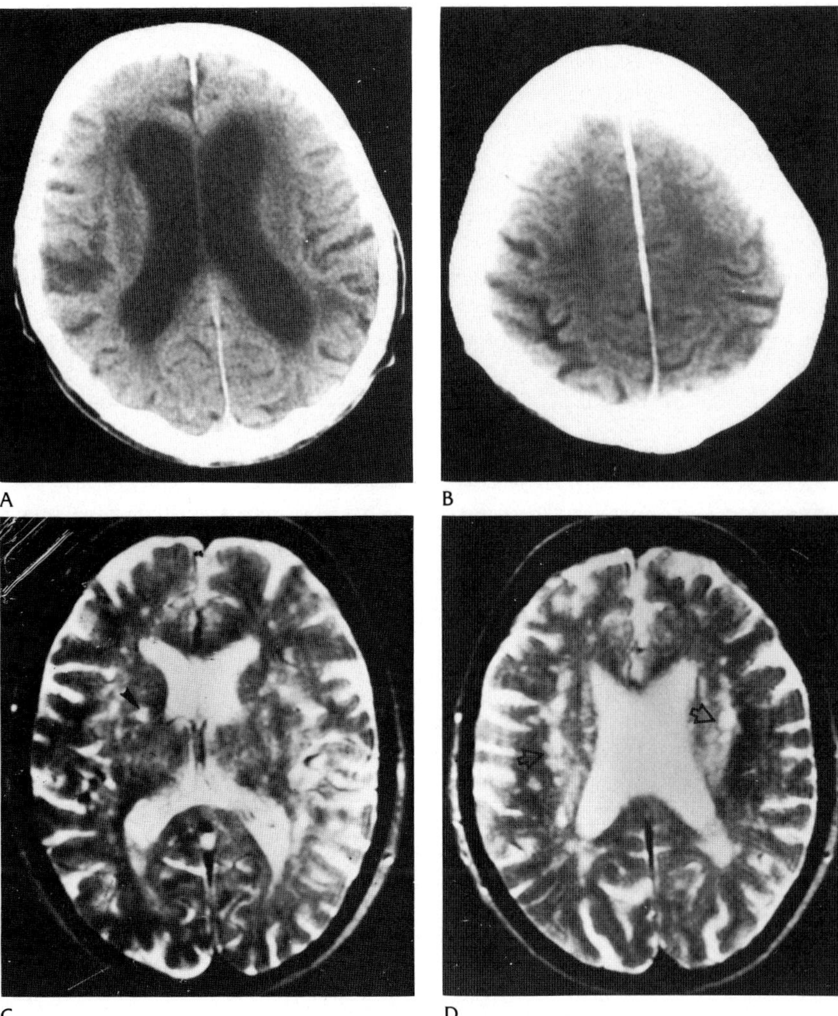

Figure 7-33 Multi-infarct dementia in a 62-year-old male with dementia and a history of hypertension controlled with medication. Axial CT (**A, B**) demonstrates moderate ventricular enlargement with periventricular hypodensity (arrows). **C, D.** T_2-weighted MR (SE 2700/80). Periventricular hyperintensity and multiple hyperintense signal foci of different sizes, with faded margins.

ent, with the histological basis being similar to that seen in Alzheimer's disease.

MULTI-INFARCT DEMENTIA

Arteriosclerotic change in the arterioles with resulting prominent perivascular spaces referred to as *état criblé* (sievelike) is a common feature in the aging brain after the sixth decade. In multi-infarct dementia these changes are prominent, although they do not represent ischemic changes but rather gliosis of the adjacent neuronal cells.

Dementia may be a manifestation when it is due to multiple infarcts over a period of time, with decreased blood flow to the brain. Multi-infarct dementia is usually associated with a systemic disease such as hypertension, cardiovascular disease, or diabetes mellitus. As a result of the primary disease itself or medical therapy, episodes of hypotension occur, resulting in decreased perfusion in the already compromised neuronal cells and arterioles, leading to ischemic episodes or an actual infarction. On CT, regions of low attenuation seen in multi-infarct dementia, although indicative of infarcts, can also be seen with several other neurodegenerative processes, including Alzheimer's disease. The usefulness of CT in the diagnosis of multi-infarct dementia is limited (Glatt 1983). Some investigators have combined the CT features with clinical scoring which measures cerebral blood flow (Hachinski 1988) to differentiate these two types of dementia (Glatt 1983; Rosen 1980). A diagnosis of dementia related to cerebrovascular causes may be suspected in the presence of multiple infarcts on CT and a Hachinski ischemic score above 5, whereas if the score is below 5, the dementia is more likely to be due to Alzheimer's disease. On MRI, a diffuse hyperintense signal is often present on T_2WI. The majority of these infarcts are usually subcortical, extensive, and asymmetrical. Their appearance and location are similar to subcortical lesions seen with normal aging, although they are more extensive.

Other hyperintense lesions represent lacunar infarcts, which are seen as hypointense lesions on T_1WI. These infarcts may involve the basal ganglia, the white matter, and the gray matter regions of the brain (Fig. 7-33). Unlike Alzheimer's disease, patients with multi-infarct dementia are in the younger age group and demonstrate a progressive stepwise decline in mental function. A history of multiple focal neurological deficits with recovery is suggestive of the etiology (LeMay 1986). In patients beyond the sixth decade in whom dementia is due to a combination of Alzheimer's disease and multi-infarct dementia, it is difficult to correlate the severity of the hyperintense lesions seen on MRI, their association with ischemic changes, and the severity of the dementia (Kirkpatrick 1987; Braffman 1988*a,b*; Kobari 1990; Bowen 1990).

BINSWANGER'S DISEASE

In this entity, which was first described by Binswanger (1894), patients present with progressive dementia with periods of remission and exacerbation caused by multifocal infarcts. On pathological studies, the infarcts involve the subcortical arterioles, resulting in microangiopathic leukoencephalopathy that usually involves both hemispheres symmetrically (Burger 1976).

On CT, the differentiation of Binswanger's disease from multi-infarct dementia is difficult unless purely symmetrical bilateral subcortical hypodense lesions that do not enhance with contrast can be demonstrated. More often

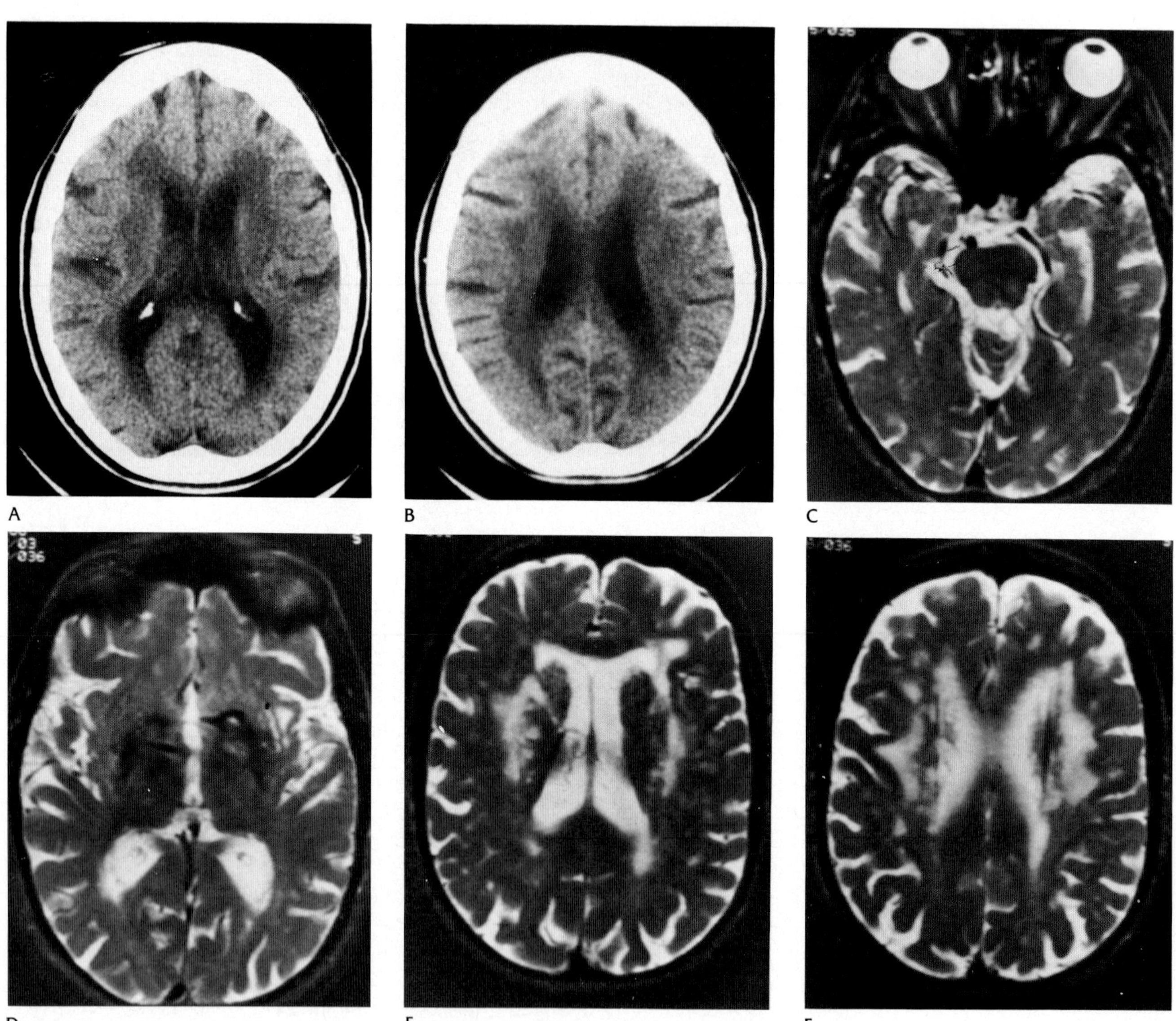

Figure 7-34 Binswanger's disease in a 59-year-old male with dementia. Axial CT. **A–B.** Mild ventricular enlargement with periventricular hypodensity and focal hypodensity in the centrum semiovale. **C–F.** MR demonstrates the typical linear hyperintense signal in the subcortical white matter, with sparing of the gray-white matter junction. In comparison to MID, there is more prominent PVH as well as mild ventricular enlargement.

the CT and MRI features are similar to those of multi-infarct dementia. On CT, hypodense lesions in the periventricular white matter, lacunar infarcts in the basal ganglia, and enlarged ventricles have been described (Zeumer 1980; Kinkel 1985; Lotz 1986; Rosenberg 1979) (Fig. 7-34). On MRI, these changes are best seen on T_2WI as symmetrical confluent regions of hyperintense foci involving the white matter, with sparing of the peripheral zone of white matter. Hyperintense foci are also present within the basal ganglia, thalamus, and pons. Increased deposition of iron seen as an abnormal hypointense signal in the putamen has been described (Drayer 1988*b*).

The clinical and imaging studies may mimic the dementia associated with NPH. It has been suggested that at least in a certain percentage of cases, NPH may actually be a result of these deep white matter infarcts, and the outcome of surgical results depends on the extent of these infarcts. The more extensive the subcortical and periventricular hyperintense signal changes, the lower the cerebral blood flow and thus the lower the response to ventricular shunting (Bradley 1991*b*).

JAKOB-CREUTZFELDT SYNDROME

Jakob-Creutzfeldt syndrome is a form of encephalopathy characterized by rapidly progressing dementia, presenting at an earlier age than other types of dementia. It is associated with altered perception, myoclonus, an increased response to startle stimulus, and cerebellar dysfunction. Initially believed to be caused by a specific viral strain similar to kuru (Gajdusek 1977), it is now thought to be caused by a slow infectious pathogen or prion, a transmissible protein substance. The disease may be familial in at least 15 percent of cases and has been explained on the basis of genetically inherited susceptibility (Kovanen 1985). The disease progresses to death, with an average course of less than 1 year from the time of diagnosis (LeMay 1986; Rao 1977). Pathological studies demonstrate atrophy of the gray matter with ventricular enlargement. Although rare, white matter changes have also been demonstrated (Macchi 1984). It is a form of encephalopathy with spongiform changes present in both the cerebral and cerebellar cortex, predominantly involving the temporal and occipital lobes (Masters 1978).

On imaging studies, the findings are nonspecific (Fig. 7-35). Progressive atrophic changes have been described on sequential imaging studies (Rao 1977; Kovanen 1985; LeMay 1986). In some instances hyperintense signal foci on T_2WI have been demonstrated in the corpus striatum, thalamus, cerebral cortex (Gertz 1988), and caudate nucleus (Pearl 1989).

The lack of hyperintense signal foci within the white matter, with rapid ventriculomegaly and dementia in a young person, is highly suggestive of this disease.

NEOPLASIA AND METABOLIC DISORDER

Diffuse brain atrophy is often present in patients with systemic neoplasia without metastatic brain involvement. The atrophic process is believed to be due to nutritional causes (Huckman 1975). A similar atrophic pattern is seen in patients with anorexia nervosa (Enzmann 1977; Kohlmeyer 1983), following the long-term use of steroids (Bentson 1978; Okuno 1980), in chronic alcoholics (Fox 1976; Schroth 1988), and in patients with chronic renal failure who are on dialysis (Kretzschmar 1983; Savazzi

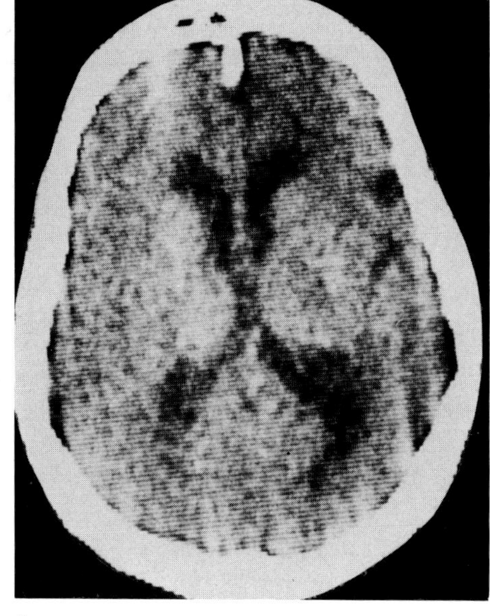
A

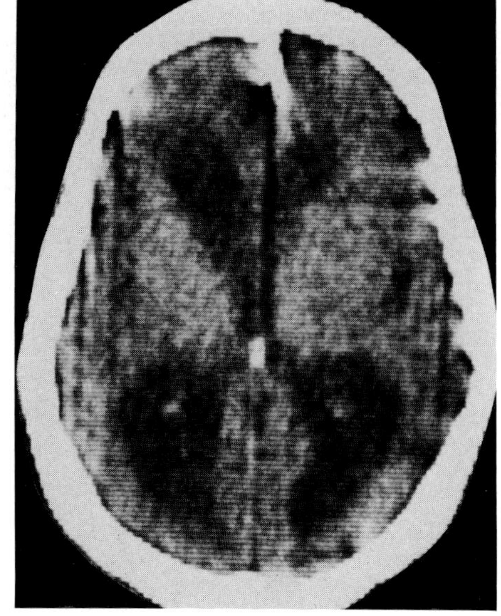
B

Figure 7-35 Jakob-Creutzfeldt disease. The rapid change in ventricular size is a characteristic feature in this disease. **A.** Initial CT. **B.** CT a few weeks later, demonstrating rapid progression of atrophic process. (*Continued on p. 268.*)

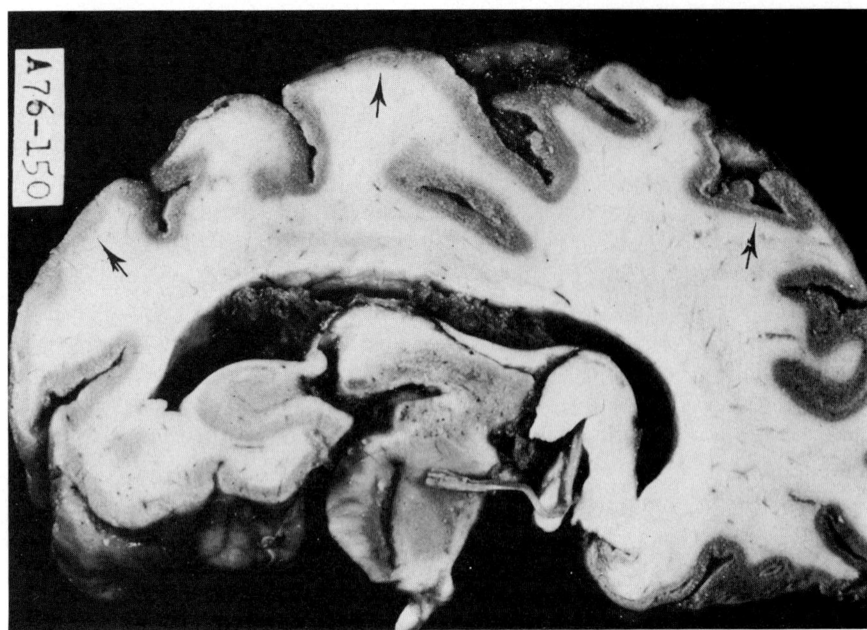

C

Figure 7-35 (continued) **C.** Significant loss of gray matter (arrows) characteristic of this disease at autopsy in the same patient.

1986; Komatsu 1988). In all these situations the atrophy is reversible after restoration of the proper nutrients or electrolytes.

Rapidly progressive diffuse cerebral atrophy in the younger age group is also seen in patients with acquired immune deficiency syndrome (AIDS) (Bursztyn 1984; Ekholm 1988; Chrysikopoulos 1990; Flowers 1990). On CT, these symptoms are associated with hypodense lesions; on MRI, they appear as hyperintense white matter lesions. They probably represent quiescent or active encephalitis from the virus infection, from secondary infection, or as a result of chemotherapy. The use of routine imaging studies in asymptomatic HIV-positive individuals as a screening test may, however, not be very useful (Post 1990).

POSTTRAUMATIC CEREBRAL ATROPHY

Diffuse cerebral atrophy as a result of trauma is rare but has been reported. It is most common in boxers, who get repeated injuries to the forehead, and is related to the

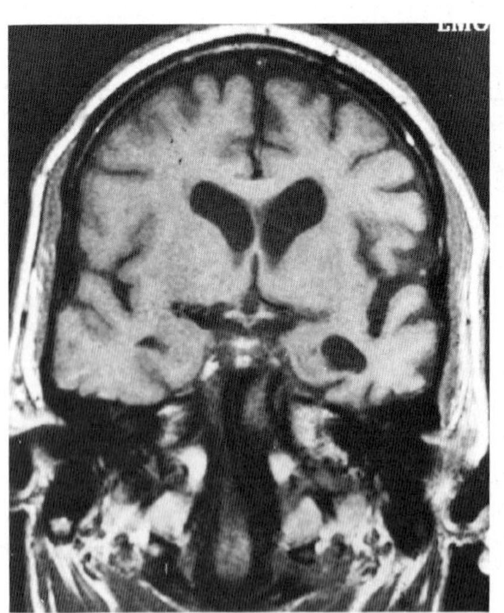

A

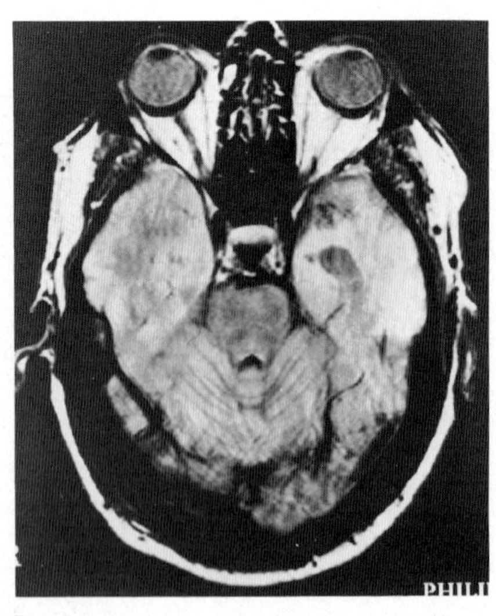

B

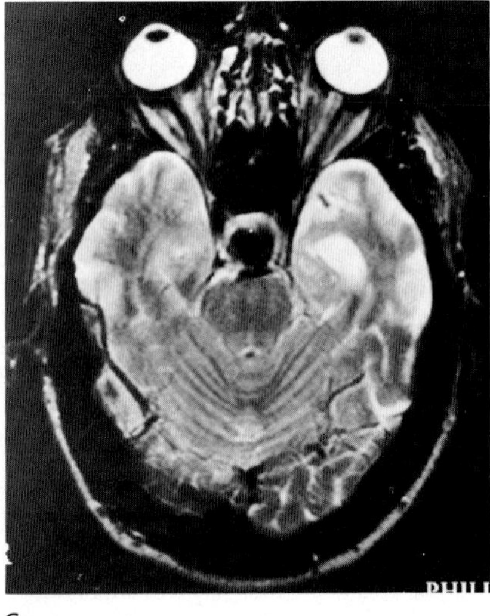

C

Figure 7-36 Focal cerebral atrophy. **A.** Coronal T_1-weighted MR demonstrates focal atrophy of the left temporal lobe with ipsilateral dilatation of the left temporal horn and lateral ventricle. **B.** Axial T_2-weighted MR (SE 2800/50) and (**C**) axial T_2-weighted MR (SE 2800/100) demonstrating focal atrophic enlargement of the temporal horn with surrounding gliosis.

length of their careers and evidence of brain damage during fights (Casson 1982). These individuals often present with dementia at an early age. Pathological features include dilated ventricles, thinning of the corpus callosum, and cysts of the septum pellucidum or cavum verge. On imaging studies the presence of frontal and temporal lobe atrophy and a prominent interhemispheric fissure in a young patient are suggestive of posttraumatic atrophy. In atrophy from boxer's injury, apart from these changes, cysts within the septum pellucidum have been described (LeMay 1986).

FOCAL ATROPHY

Unlike diffuse cerebral atrophy and dementia associated with aging, focal atrophy may be seen at any age. The most common clinical presentation is that of a focal neurological deficit or seizures. Focal atrophy usually is secondary to trauma, infection, infarction, or dysgenesis, or occurs after surgery. Depending on the preceding cause, the focal atrophic process may manifest as early as 3 months after the event or as late as years afterward. The pathogenesis of the atrophy is suggested by the location, although the clinical history is necessary for correlation with the imaging findings.

Posttraumatic focal atrophy follows cerebral contusion or cerebral hematoma after surgical evacuation or spontaneous resolution (Kishore 1980). Although atrophy may occur anywhere, the usual location is the frontal or temporal lobes (Fig. 7-36). Postinflammatory atrophy often follows brain abscess, herpes encephalitis, and chronic granulomatous disease. Focal atrophy secondary to vascular infarcts or vascular anomalies follows hemorrhages or infarction. These infarcts are usually confined to the vascular distribution, often involving the watershed areas of the major vascular channels. In long-standing cases focal prominence of the cortical sulci and/or ipsilateral ventricular enlargement may be the only findings.

Cerebral Hemiatrophy

Cerebral hemiatrophy (Davidoff-Dyke syndrome) is a form of focal cerebral atrophy which involves the whole cerebral hemisphere on one side. It is due to neonatal or gestational vascular occlusion primarily involving the middle cerebral vascular territory. Usually it manifests during adolescence. Imaging studies demonstrate unilateral atrophy of the cerebral hemisphere with ipsilateral shift of the ventricles. The sulci on the involved side are wide and often are replaced by gliotic brain tissue. On MRI (T_2WI), they are seen as hyperintensity of both the gray matter and white matter, with a thin rim of cortical gray matter. As a result of the remodeling process, osseous changes are seen in the adjacent calvarium. The calvarial bone is thickened, the roof of the orbit is elevated, and the adjacent air sinuses are prominent and enlarged (Fig. 7-37).

Focal or hemispherical atrophy associated with gyral calcification of the cortical layers is seen in Sturge-Weber syndrome. The cause of the atrophy is probably related to angioma and the associated venous thrombosis.

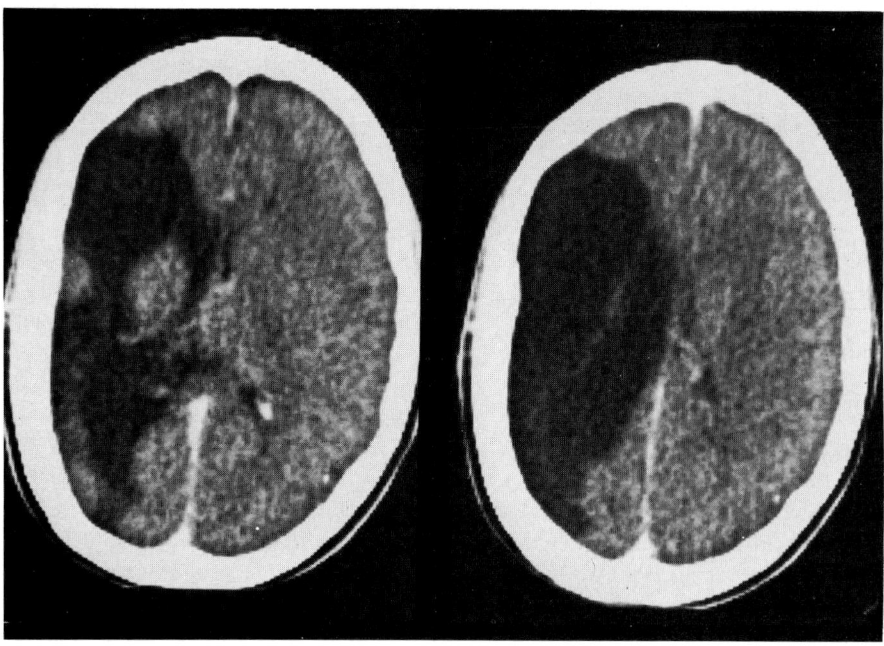

Figure 7-37 Cerebral hemiatrophy in a young male with uncontrolled seizures. **A, B.** Axial CECT. There is extensive loss of parenchyma in the right cerebral hemisphere. The volume loss is compensated by an apparent shift of the opposing cerebral hemisphere. Compensating thickness of the calvarium on the affected side. MR in another patient with similar changes on T_2WI (SE 2500/40) (*Continued on p. 270*)

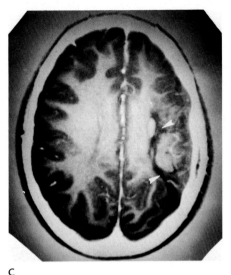

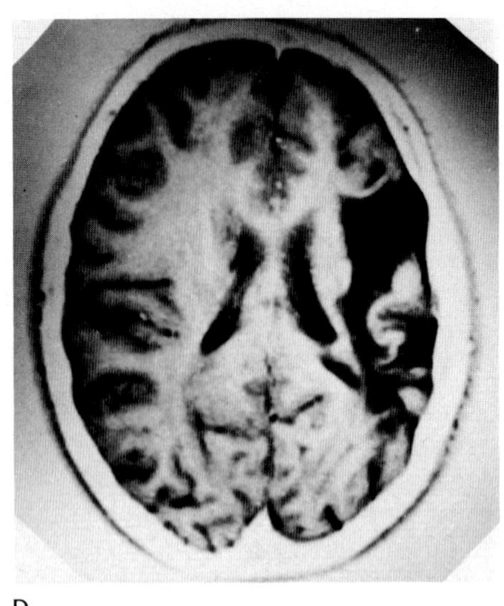

C D

Figure 7-37 ***(continued)*** (**C**) and T_2WI (SE 2500/80) (**D**). Note the glial scarring (arrowheads), not appreciated on CT and heavily T_2-weighted image.

REGIONAL ATROPHY

A pathological neurodegenerative process may involve specific regional areas more than the others and may result in a more defined clinical presentation. Examples include the extrapyramidal system associated with movement disorders, the hindbrain structures associated with ataxia, and the corticospinal tracts associated with motor neuron disease. These areas can be better evaluated with MRI because of greater tissue sensitivity, lack of bone artifact, and the ability to view in all orthogonal planes.

ATROPHY AND MOVEMENT DISORDERS

Neurological diseases associated with cerebral atrophy and movement disorders associated with the pyramidal and extrapyramidal tracts and nuclei result from a neurodegenerative process which involves these central nuclei in addition to the gray matter and white matter of the brain. The extrapyramidal system consists of the nuclei and fiber tracts connecting the corticospinal tract with the nuclei in the diencephalon (Fig. 7-38). The extrapyramidal nuclei consist of the basal ganglia (caudate nucleus, putamen, and globus pallidus) and the thalamus and subthalamic nuclei (substantia nigra, red nucleus, and dentate nucleus). Lesions or a disease process involving these nuclei result in a loss of control or mediation of the corticospinal tract (Table 7-7). Although CT can demonstrate some of the pathological changes, MRI (T_2WI) is better and more sensitive in visualizing tissue changes resulting from deposition or washout of paramagnetic substances, principally iron.

The movement disorders and the disease processes associated with them include tremor and rigidity associated with Parkinson's disease and syndrome; choreic disorders and hemiballismus associated with Sydenham's chorea, Huntington's disease, and choreoacanthocytosis; and dystonias associated with Wilson's disease or Leigh's disease. Since focal or generalized atrophy is a major manifestation of some of these movement disorders, they are considered in this chapter.

Parkinson's Disease and Syndrome

Parkinson's disease (paralysis agitans) is a movement disorder associated with cogwheel-type rigidity (Parkinson 1817). The rigidity is followed by tremor, akinesia, and postural deformities. The onset of the disease usually occurs in the fourth or fifth decade with progressive neurological deterioration and without remissions or exacerbations. The disease involves the cells and fibers of the substania nigra; in later stages, there is involvement of the corpus striatum and globus pallidus. There is a loss of neuromelanin-containing neurons in the pars compacta of the substantia nigra, the locus ceruleus, and the dorsal vagal nucleus with resulting gliosis. Other subtypes of Parkinson's disease have been described, such as striatonigral degeneration (Adams 1983) and Shy-Drager syndrome. In striatonigral degeneration, rigidity is the predominant feature. There is involvement of the putamen, and the patients respond poorly to antiparkinsonian medication (Adams 1983). In Shy-Drager syndrome, patients present with orthostatic hypotension, inability to sweat, and swallowing problems. This is due to a degenerative process not only in the substantia nigra but also the vagal nuclei. *Parkinson's syndrome* refers to rigidity similar to Parkinson's disease but usually secondary to encephalitis. It is less common these days. Parkinson's syndrome may be related to other types of infection, trauma, or vascular insult; it also may be drug-induced or related to toxic material.

Table 7-7 Imaging Features in Movement Disorders

DISEASE ENTITY	CEREBRAL ATROPHY	HYPERINTENSE SIGNAL ON T_2WI	MIDBRAIN ATROPHY	HINDBRAIN ATROPHY	HYPOINTENSE SIGNAL ON T_2WI
Parkinson's disease (tremor, rigidity, akinesia)	Mild to moderate Beyond 5th decade	White matter; lesser extent, BG/pons and thalamus	Normal to mild Pars compacta of SN	None	Moderate to marked SN/GP/RN/DN
Striatonigral degeneration (rigidity, akinesia)	Normal to mild Beyond 4th decade	On low and midfield MR: hyperintense putamen - ? gliosis	Pars compacta Atrophy of putamen	Present when part of multisystem atrophy	Putamen/SN Lesser extent, caudate
Shy-Drager syndrome (orthostatic hypotension, urinary incontinence, inability to sweat	Moderate Usually beyond 5th decade	Nonspecific, white matter	When associated with OPCA	When part of MSA	Primarily involves putamen
Progressive supranuclear palsy (rigidity, pseudobulbar palsy, ophthalmoplegia)	Mild to Moderate Usually beyond 5th decade	Periaqueductal region	Moderate to severe of mesencephalon	Moderate to severe	SN/RN Tectum
Hallervorden-Spatz disease (dystonia, dysphasia dysarthria, rigidity, gait disturbance)	Normal to mild Usually 2d decade 50% familial Progressive course	Occasional GP/pars reticularis of SN	Mild to moderate Mesencephalon	Not common	SN/GP
Huntington's disease (choreoathetosis, dementia)	Mild to moderate Involves caudate Beyond 4th decade	Occasionally present Caudate, putamen May represent gliosis	Usually none	None	Caudate and putamen: may represent iron
Wilson's disease (tremor, rigidity, dystonia, dysarthria, gait apraxia)	Mild to moderate Primarily lenticular nuclei Ceruloplasmin deficiency Between 1st and 5th decades	Putamen, GP On CT hypointense	Moderate	None	May be seen in putamen, GP
Leigh syndrome (SNE) (ataxia, dystonia, psychomotor regression, nystagmus)	Mild to moderate 1st and 2nd decades Progressive course	Extensive, patchy gray and white matter Putamen	Mild	None	Occasionally in thalamus, lentiform nuclei
Hypoxic-ischemic syndrome	Variable	Globus pallidus	Mild	None	Occasionally May represent iron deposition

(continued on next page)

Table 7-7 *continued*

DISEASE ENTITY	CEREBRAL ATROPHY	HYPERINTENSE SIGNAL ON T_2WI	MIDBRAIN ATROPHY	HINDBRAIN ATROPHY	HYPOINTENSE SIGNAL ON T_2WI
Olivopontocerebellar atrophy	Variable Beyond 3d decade	Normal unless part of MSA	Variable	Moderate to severe Pons, cerebellum, middle cerebellar peduncle	May be present in middle cerebellar peduncle, pons

GP = globus pallidus; SN = substantia nigra; RN = red nucleus; DN = dentate nucleus; OPCA = olivopontocerebellar atrophy; MSA = multisystem atrophy.
Source: Rutledge 1987; Savoiardo 1983, 1989, 1990; Braffman 1988; Drayer 1988.

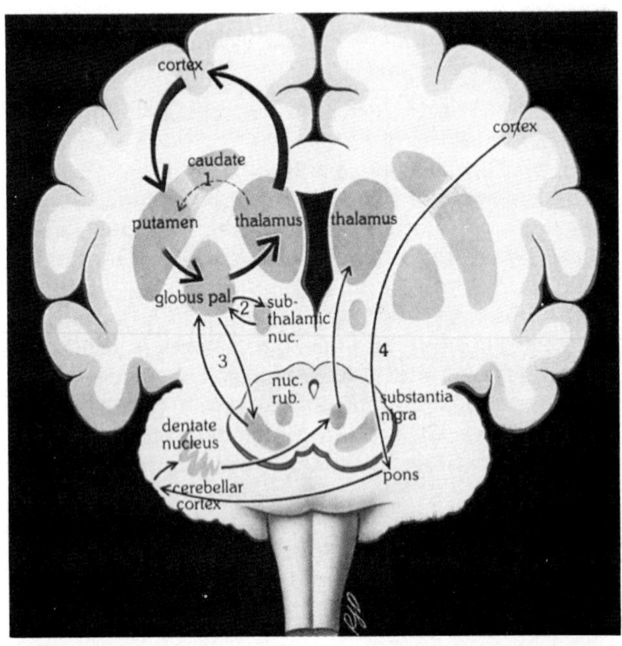

A

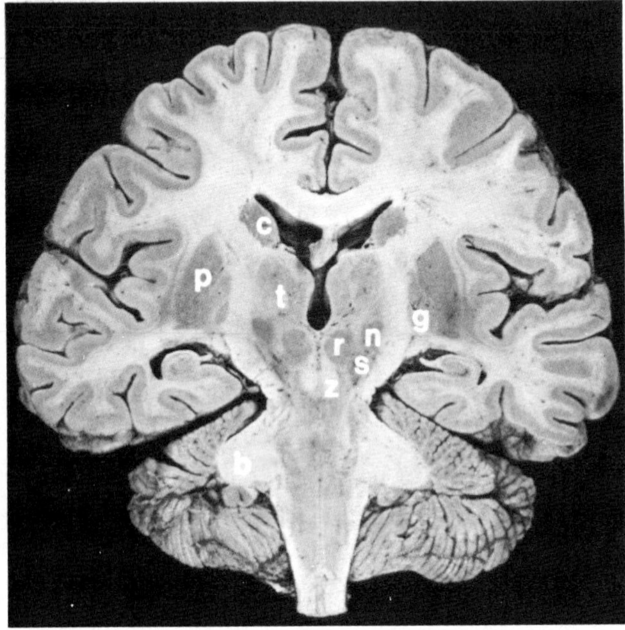

B

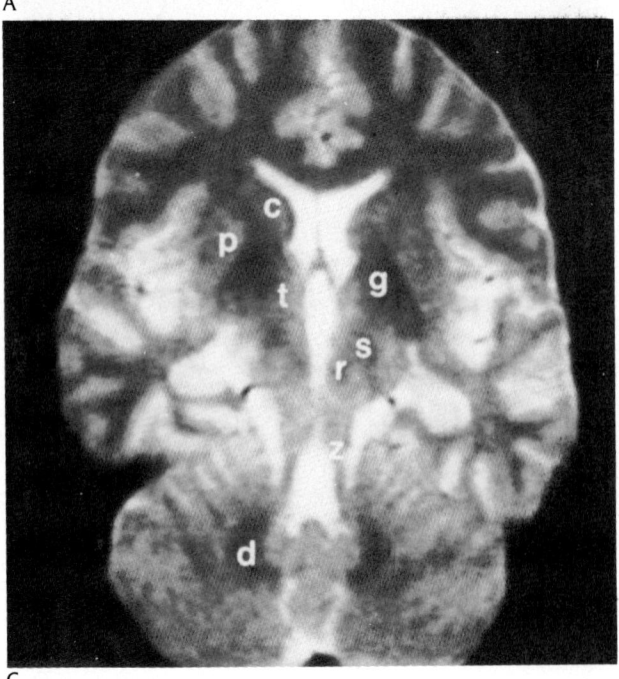

C

Figure 7-38 Extrapyramidal nuclei and pathways. **A.** The circuits frequently involved in movement disorders: dystonias and chorea (loop 1), hemiballismus (loop 2), and parkinsonisms (loops 3 and 4). **B.** Semicoronal section of normal brain. Pearl's stain to demonstrate the extrapyramidal nuclei. **C.** Semicoronal T_2-weighted MR demonstrating the normal hypointense signal of the extrapyramidal nuclei. c = caudate; p = putamen; g = globus pallidus; t = thalamus; n = subthalamic nucleus; r = red nucleus; s = substania nigra; z = brachium conjunctivum; b = brachium pontis; d = dentate nucleus. (*With permission from Rutledge et al, AJNR 8:397–411, 1987.*)

CT often demonstrates moderate to severe atrophy compared with age-matched groups. There is, however, no correlation between the severity of the atrophy seen on CT and the severity of the akinesia and tremor (Inzelberg 1987). In patients receiving L-dopa therapy, the presence of calcification in the basal ganglia has been associated with a poor medical response.

The characteristic MRI findings in Parkinson's disease and the parkinsonian syndrome consist of the following features, which are best evaluated on axial and coronal T_2WI:

1. A decrease in the width of the pars compacta resulting from loss of neuromelanin-containing cells and possible iron deposition (Duguid 1986; Braffman 1988*c*). Linear hyperintensity adjacent to the hypointense region is probably related to gliosis (Fig. 7-39).
2. The globus pallidus shows increased hypointensity. However, in Parkinson's disease there is a loss of normal hypointensity, and more frequently there is hyperintensity within the substantia nigra, possibly as a result of gliosis, neuronal loss (Braffman 1988*c*), or microvascular infarct. The putamen has a normal signal (Rutledge 1987).
3. In Shy-Drager syndrome and more often in striatonigral degeneration, the major change occurs in the putamen (Adams 1983). Compared to Parkinson's disease, apart from the atrophy of the striate nuclei, the putamen is markedly hypointense (Drayer 1986*b*; Pastakia 1986) (Fig. 7-40). The greater the severity of rigidity, the greater the hypointense signal of the putamen (Brown 1988; Rutledge 1987). This has been explained as being due to deposition of iron or other rare elements.
4. Focal or diffuse cerebral atrophy. The focal atrophy usually involves the frontal lobe (Adams 1983). A high association of Alzheimer's disease is associated with Parkinson's disease. Not all the findings are present in all parkinsonian patients. The MR findings also may not correlate with the progression of the disease.

Huntington's Disease

Huntington's disease is characterized by choreiform movements with a rapid onset of dementia. It is autoso-

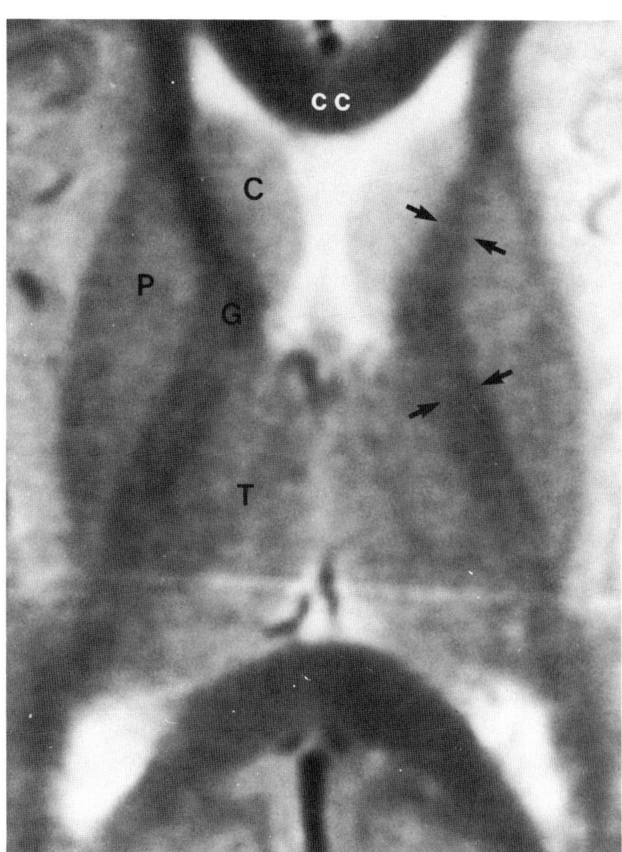

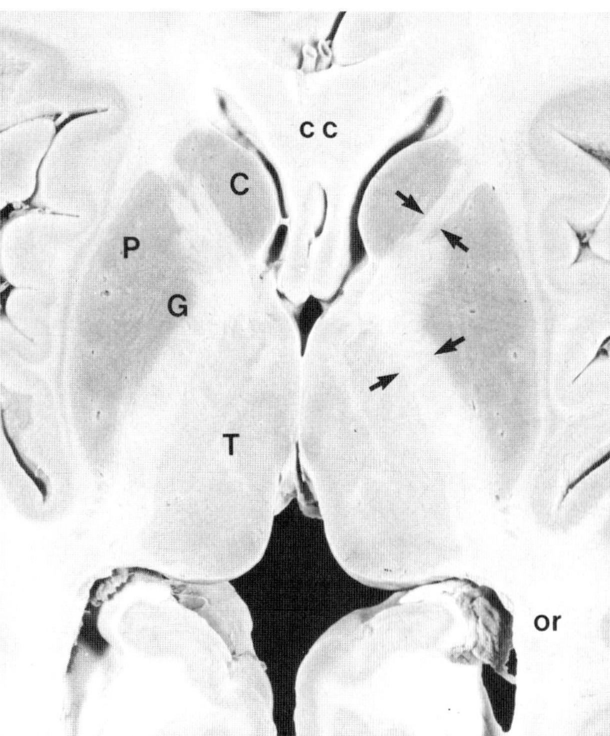

Figure 7-39 Parkinson's disease. Axial MR (**A**) and corresponding Pearl's-stained section (**B**) show comparison between the extent of ferric staining with hypointensity within the various nuclei. Caudate (C) and putamen (P) are stained without signal loss. Internal capsule (arrows) and corpus callosum (CC) show minimal staining and moderate signal loss. G = globus pallidus; T = thalamus. (*Continued on p. 274*)

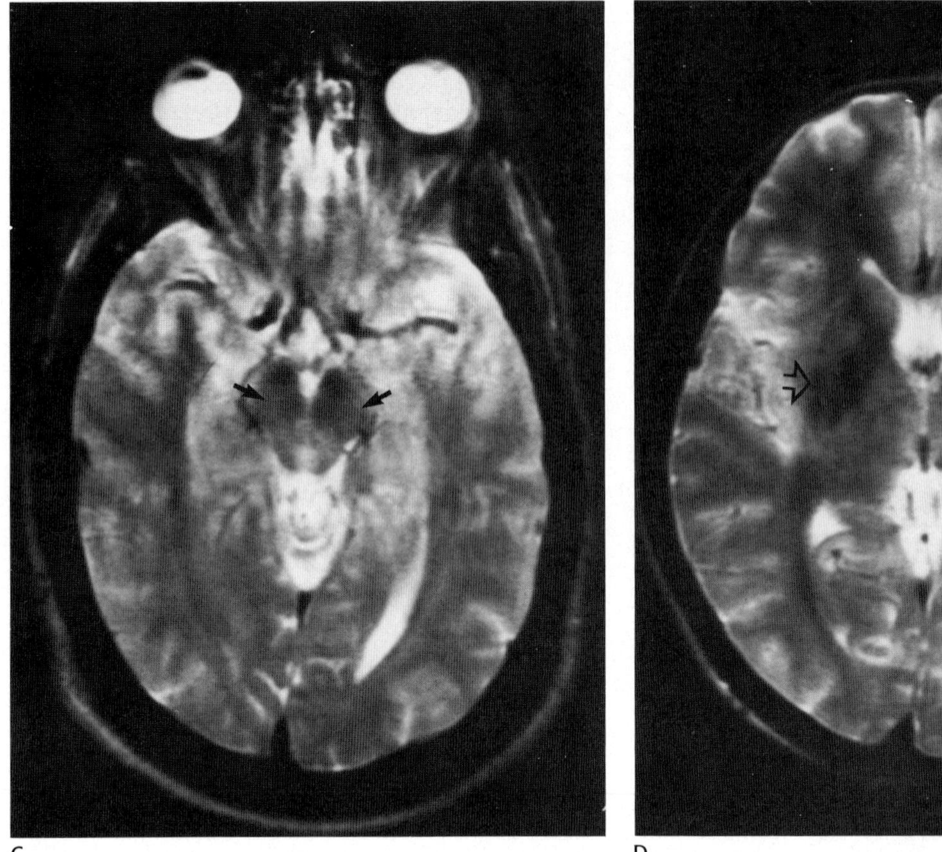

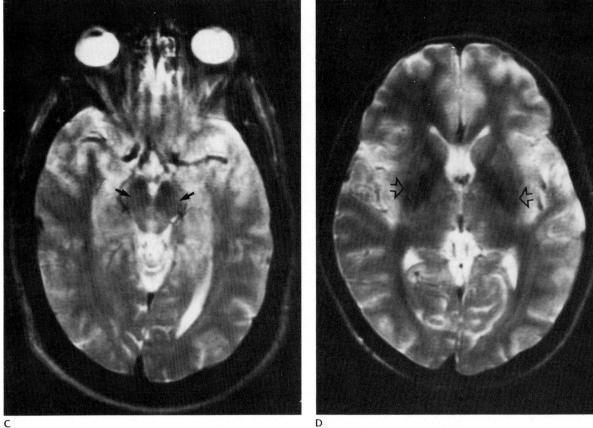

C D

Figure 7-39 (continued) **C, D.** T_2-weighted MR. The substantia nigra (arrow) is isointense to the rest of the brain parenchyma rather than showing the normal hypointensity. Hypointensity of the putamen (arrows) can be seen in both normal aging and with Parkinson's disease.

mal dominant, predominantly involving males, although some researchers have not found any sex predilection (Adams 1989). The choreiform movement manifests itself in the fourth decade or later. The genetic abnormality involves the short arm of the fourth chromosome, resulting in altered metabolic activity in the neostriatum (Schoene 1985). The disease starts with choreiform movement in the extremities, followed by dementia and personality changes. The hallmark in neuropathological studies is atrophy of the caudate nucleus and subsequently the putamen (Simmons 1986). In later stages atrophy involves the temporal and frontal lobes.

On CT, the caudate nucleus is atrophied, with a resulting increased bicaudate distance of the ventricles. With atrophy of the caudate nucleus, the normal convex wall of the frontal horn is flattened or becomes concave (Fig. 7-41). In addition to the above features on MRI, T_2WI may demonstrate a decreased signal in the neostriatum (caudate and putamen) (Rutledge 1987), probably as a result of iron deposition. Hyperintensity on T_2WI, when present, probably reflects neuronal loss or gliosis from vascular compromise. The role of CT and MRI is to demonstrate the extent of atrophic changes, since the diagnosis can be made by chromosomal studies. Choreoacanthocytosis is a metabolic disorder related to blood dyscrasia. It presents with choreiform movements which mimic Huntington's disease both clinically and on MR studies. It may be seen in the same age group. Diagnosis is achieved by demonstrating acanthocytes in the blood.

Wilson's Disease

Wilson's disease is an inherited disorder of copper metabolism caused by a deficiency of ceruloplasmin. It is an autosomal recessive trait, with the deficiency identified

Figure 7-40 Parkinsonian syndrome. Axial MR (SE 4300/80) in Shy-Drager syndrome (**A**). Reversal of the normal hypointense signal, seen as a hyperintense signal in the globus pallidus (arrows). Similar hypointense signal in the globus pallidus (bold arrow) is also seen in Hallervorden-Spatz disease. In (**B**) it is associated with a focal hyperintense signal (small arrow) or the more commonly seen pattern of uniform bilateral hypointense signal (**C, D**). (*Courtesy of Rutledge, AJNR 1987.*)

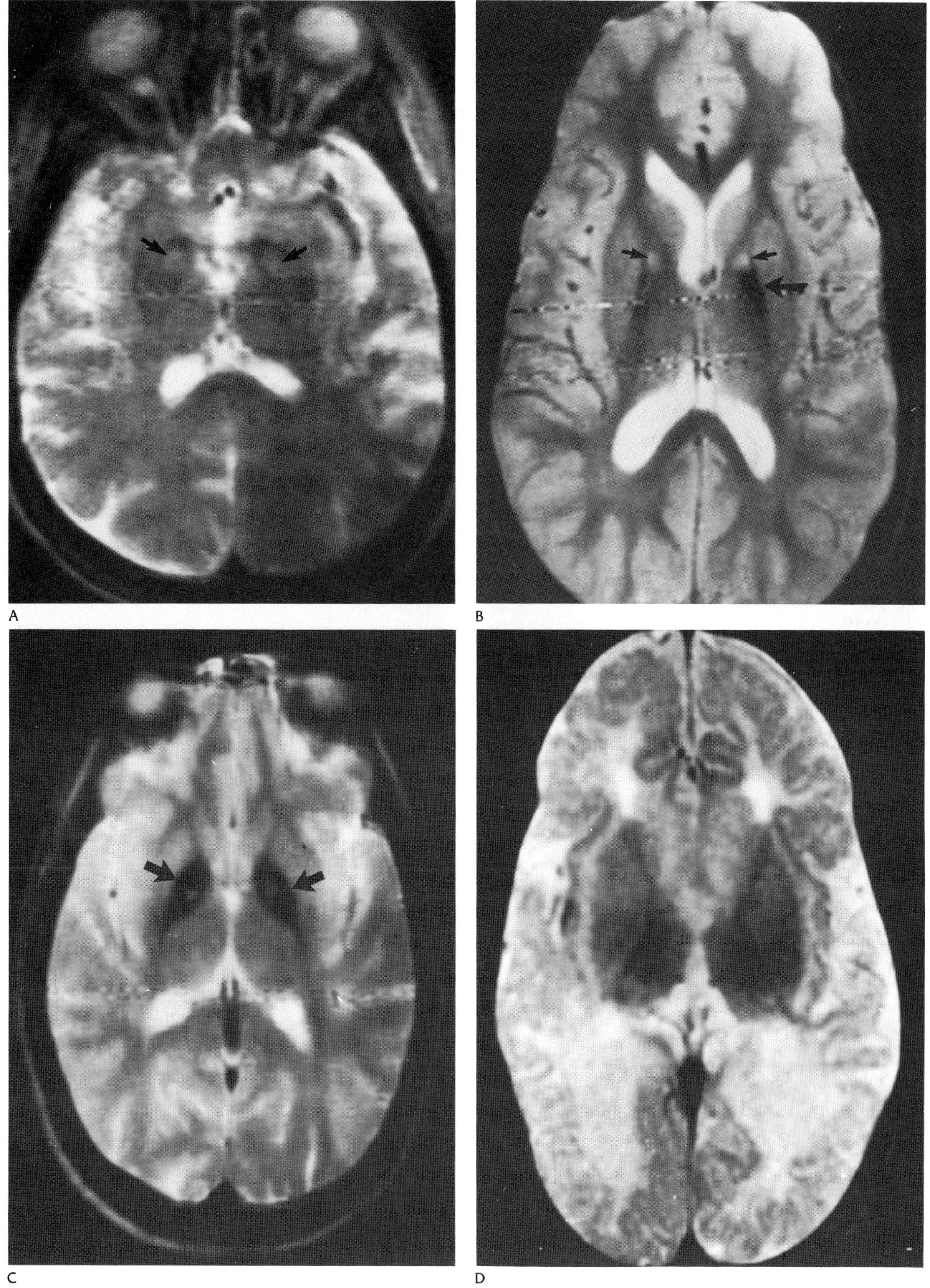
A
B
C
D

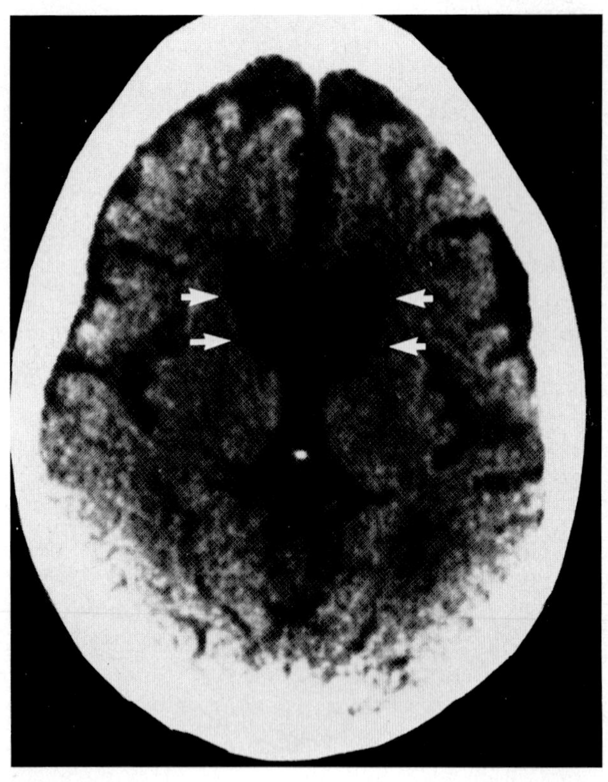

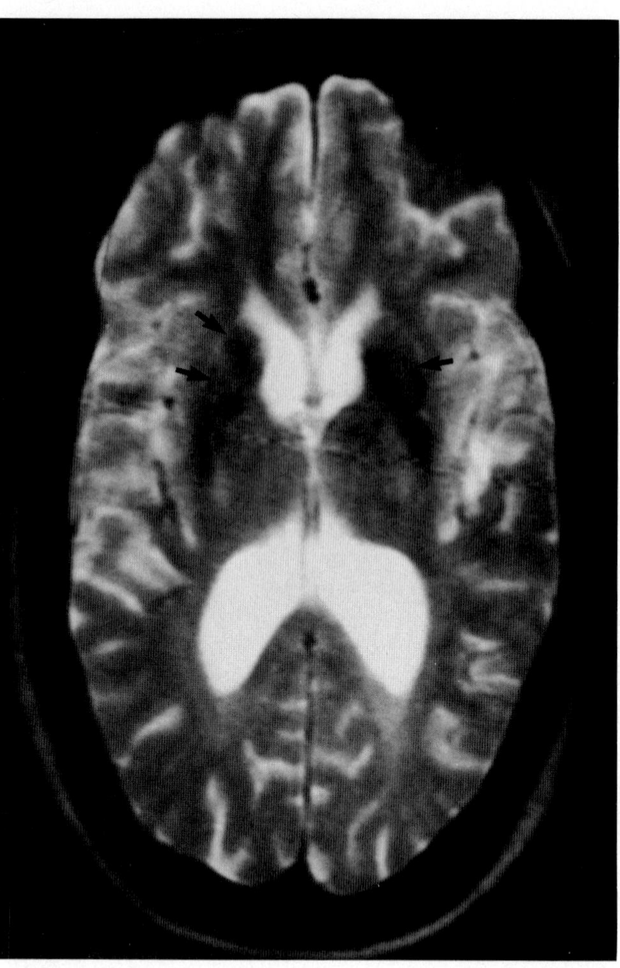

A B

Figure 7-41 Huntington's disease. **A.** NCCT demonstrates focal dilatation of the frontal horns, especially the lateral walls (arrows), due to atrophy of the caudate nucleus. **B.** Axial T_2-weighted MR (SE 4300/80) shows hypointense signal and atrophy of neostriatum, predominantly the caudate nucleus (arrows).

in chromosome 13. It is characterized by abnormal deposition of copper in various tissues, but primarily in the liver and the lentiform nucleus in the brain (hepatolenticular degeneration). Although the disease may manifest at any age, the peak period is between the first and second decades. Pathological changes in the brain consist of a loss of neurons and gliosis involving the basal ganglia, brainstem, and cerebellar nuclei.

CT findings consist of focal or generalized atrophy. There is atrophy of the caudate nuclei and/or the brainstem. Hypodensity within the caudate nuclei, brainstem, dentate nucleus, and cerebellar white matter is frequently present (Harik 1981; Ropper 1979) (Fig. 7-42). These lesions do not enhance on CECT (Kvicala 1983). In the majority of cases there is no correlation between the severity of dementia and the extent of atrophy seen on CT studies; however, the severity of the dystonia may match the CT abnormalities. These changes may persist in spite of clinical improvement following treatment with penicillamine. In general, CT is not helpful in establishing a prognosis.

MR is more sensitive in demonstrating pathological changes in the extrapyramidal system and the brain parenchyma. On T_2WI, focal areas of hyperintense signal can be present in the putamen, the caudate nucleus, the dentate nucleus, and the thalami and red nucleus of the midbrain. These changes are often symmetric and bilateral (Lawler 1983; Aisen 1985; DeHaan 1987). Putaminal lesions are associated with bradykinesia and dystonia. When both the putamen and the caudate nucleus are involved, there is also dysarthria. Frontal lobe involvement is associated with distractability of gaze fixation (Lennox 1989). Since the diagnosis is usually made on the basis of biochemical testing, the role of MRI or CT is probably to determine the response to therapy and the prognosis. Since MRI is more sensitive in demonstrating the pathological changes, it probably should be utilized in the diagnosis and evaluation of patients with dystonia.

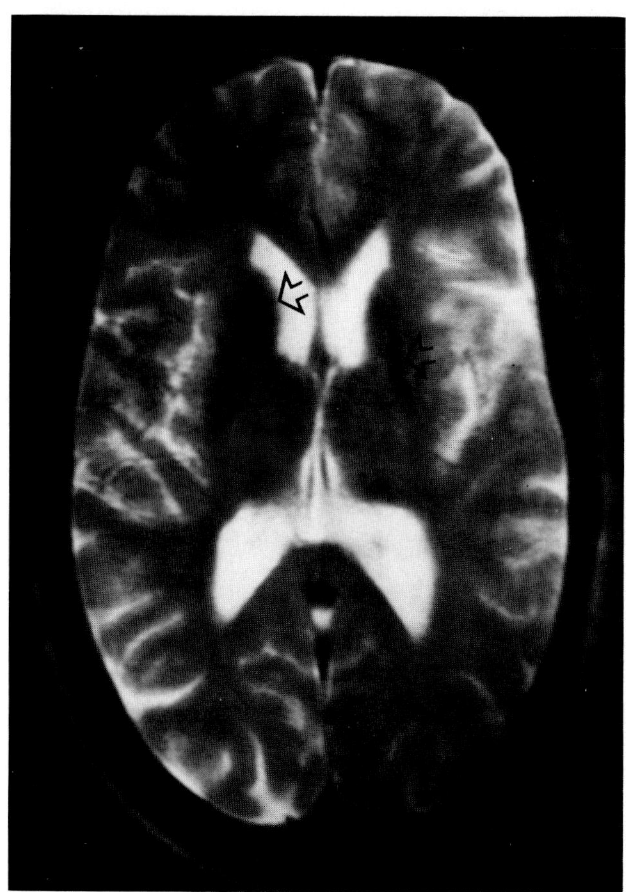

Figure 7-42 Wilson's disease. Axial T_2-weighted MR (SE 4300/80). Hypointense signal in the neostriatum (arrows) secondary to copper deposition.

Leigh's Syndrome

Leigh's syndrome is an uncommon neurodegenerative process that usually presents in infancy or childhood, although occasional cases may present at a later age. The clinical features and pathological changes are similar to those of Wernicke's encephalopathy associated with chronic ethanol use and nutritional encephalopathy. The encephalopathy in Leigh's disease is a result of metabolic acidosis caused by a biochemical defect. The enzyme defect leads to excessive accumulation of lactate and pyruvates in the blood and CSF.

Patients with Leigh's disease present with behavioral disorders, ataxia, dystonia, nystagmus, and visual disturbance. The disease runs a short clinical course, with death occurring within a year of respiratory failure. The pathological changes consist of subacute necrotizing encephalomyelitis characterized by necrosis with vascular proliferation in the gray and white matter, spongiform degeneration, and demyelination (Medina 1990; Geyer 1988). These changes are present in the brainstem (tegmentum), basal ganglia, optic pathways, and spinal cord.

On CT, these lesions appear as hypodense lesions that do not enhance on CECT. On MRI, the lesions are hypointense on T_1WI and hyperintense on T_2WI (Fig. 7-43) (Davis 1987). The lesions are symmetrical. Occasional hypointensity in the putaminal region on T_2WI probably represents iron deposition.

Atrophy Secondary to Anoxia

Cerebral atrophy following anoxia or hypoxia either from anoxic agents (carbon monoxide, cyanide, etc.) or from hypoperfusion at any age results in brain tissue infarction. The extent of the atrophic changes, as well as the neurological deficit, depends on numerous factors, including the age at the time of insult. Depending on the age of the patient at the time of the insult and the duration of the anoxic episode, the atrophic patterns are different. In general, there is edema followed by neuronal loss and gliosis. The end result of anoxia is diffuse cortical atrophy disproportionate to the dilatation of the ventricles.

In infants and children the atrophic process in those who survive depends on the gestational age when the anoxic episode occurred and whether the anoxic damage is due to partial prolonged asphyxiation or total cardiovascular collapse (Barkovich 1990). In the past CT was utilized in demonstrating the changes in infants who survived these episodes (Flodmark 1980). MR is useful in determining the gestational age at the time of insult based on the pattern of atrophic changes as well as the extent of periventricular leukomalacia (PVL) (Baker 1988). PVL is associated with a decrease in the amount of white matter, a hyperintense signal, and focal dilatation of the ventricle. MR also demonstrates the delayed myelination in these children (Johnson 1987).

Anoxic episodes occurring between 24 and 26 weeks of gestational age demonstrate an enlarged irregular trigone of the lateral ventricles without periventricular gliosis (Fig. 7-44). Patients between 26 and 34 weeks of gestation demonstrate not only enlarged ventricles but also show periventricular gliosis (Fig. 7-45). At about 36 weeks of gestation, since the cortical and subcortical parenchyma have developed, there is both cortical and deep white matter atrophy.

Full-term infants demonstrate an atrophy pattern associated with infarct in watershed areas with periventricular gliosis.

The CT and MR features in carbon monoxide or cyanide poisoning are similar in appearance to those of total circulatory collapse in children (Nardizzi 1979). The pathological process involves the basal ganglia, primarily the globus pallidus. It is often symmetrical (Sawa 1981; Kono 1983). In those who survive the acute episode, symmetrical hypodensity in the globus pallidus is seen on CT studies (Fig. 7-46). In later stages CT may show diffuse

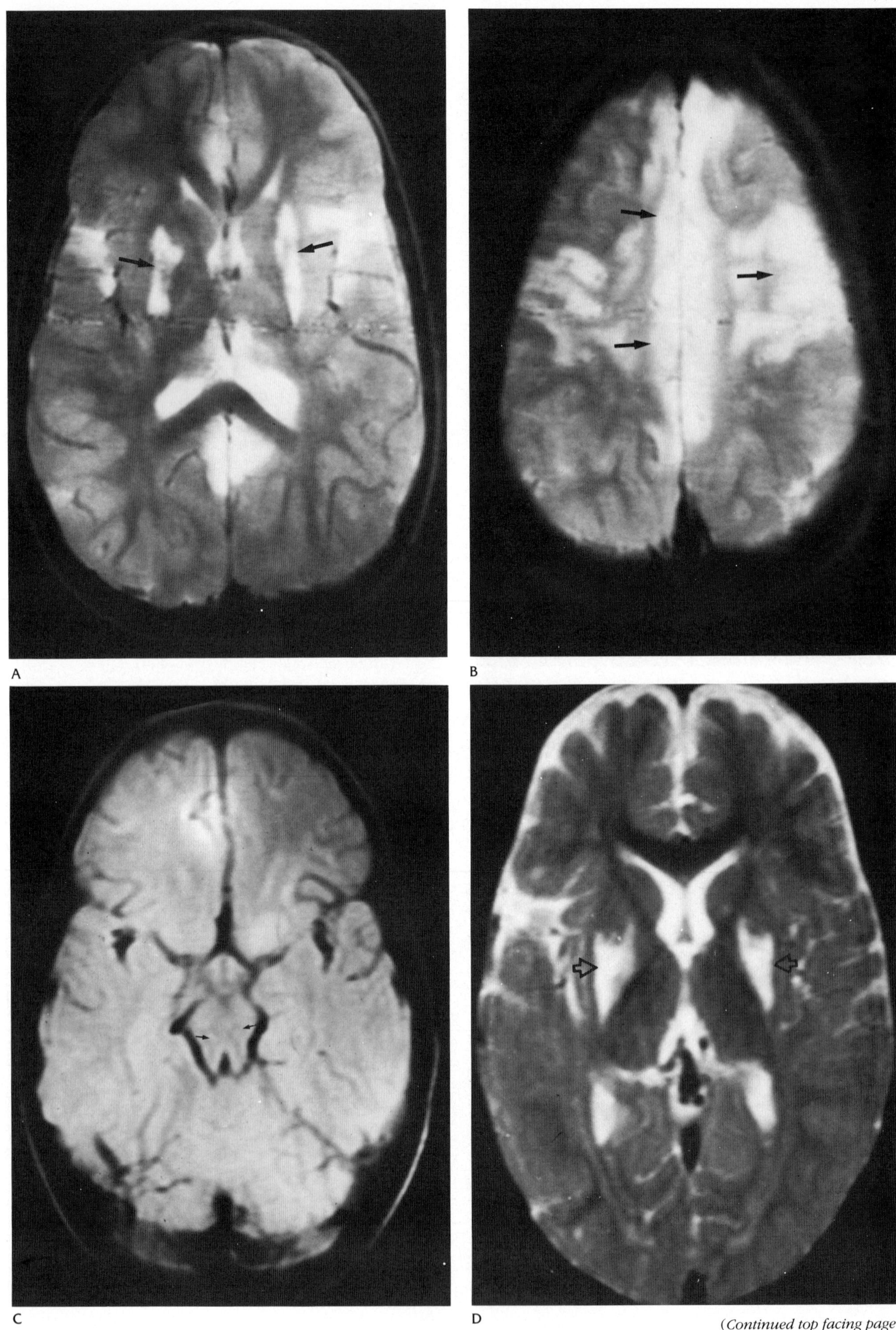

(*Continued top facing page*)

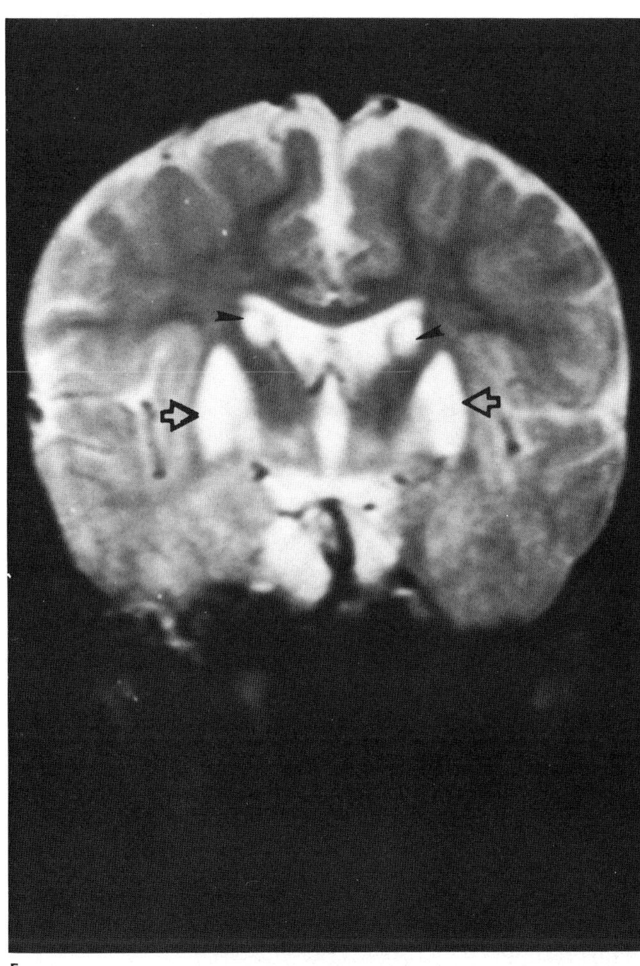
E

Figure 7-43 Leigh's syndrome. Axial MR SE 4300/80. **A.** Increased signal in both putamen (arrows) and (**B**) the cortical regions, indicative of the extensive subacute necrotizing form of disease. **C.** Axial MR (SE 2000/80). Typical butterfly pattern of periaqueductal increased signal (arrows). **D, E.** T_2-weighted (SE 3000/90) axial and coronal MR in another patient demonstrates the extensive involvement of the putamen and caudate nuclei.

Figure 7-44 Anoxic-hypoxia syndrome in a 13-year-old with a history of premature birth and anoxia presenting with cerebral diplegia. Axial T_2-weighted MR SE 2500/40 (**A**) and SE 2500/80 (**B**) demonstrates atrial enlargement with minimal periventricular hyperintensity due to gliosis.

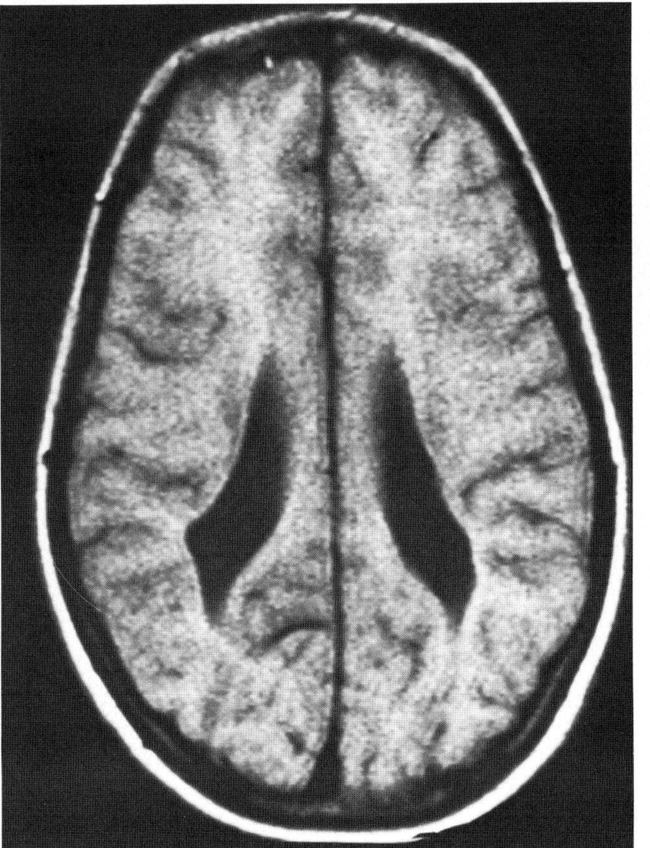
A

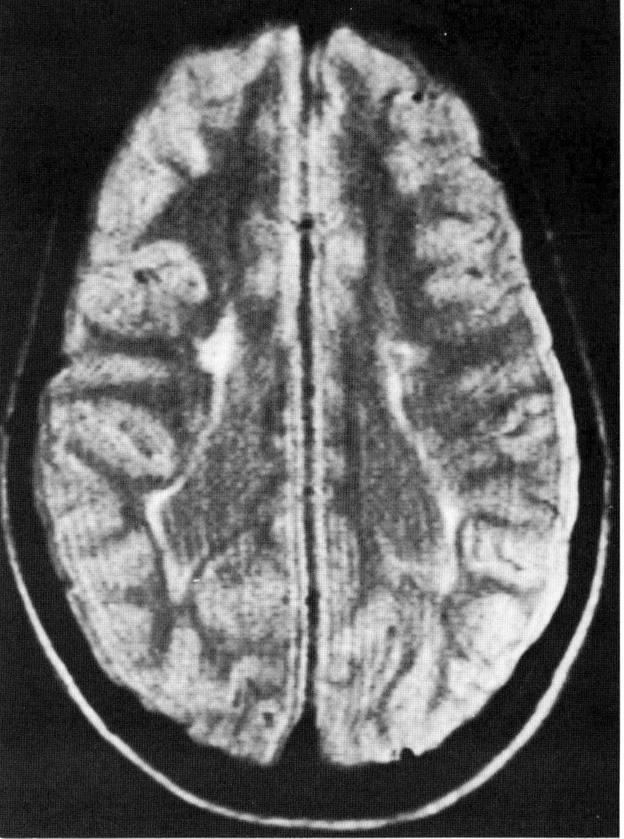
B

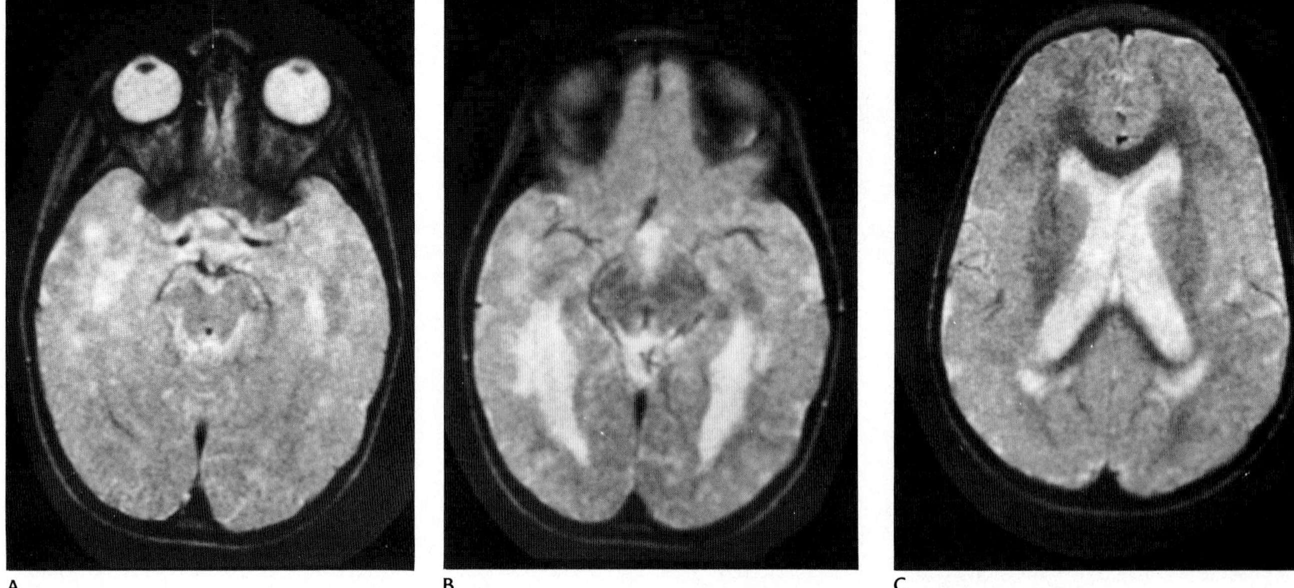

Figure 7-45 Anoxic-hypoxic syndrome. **A–C.** Axial T_2-weighted MR in a 26-month-old child born prematurely. Periatrial and periventricular symmetrical hyperintense signal associated with anoxia secondary to hypoperfusion. Ventricles are moderately enlarged.

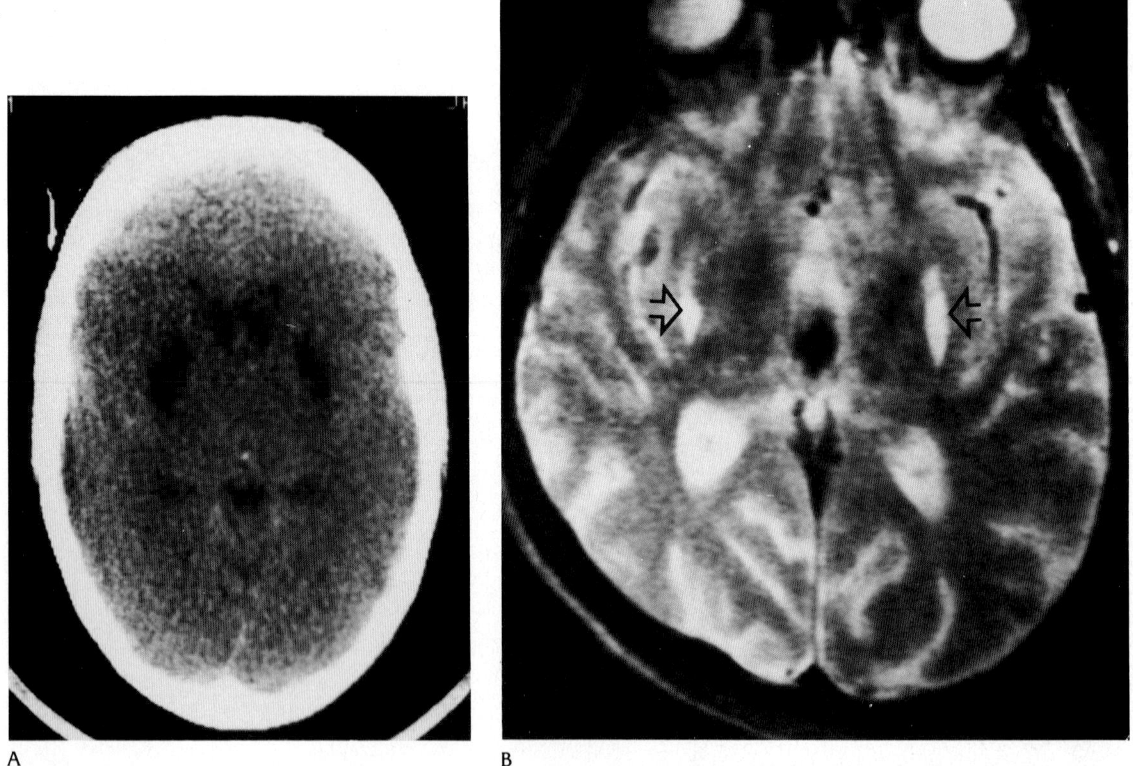

Figure 7-46 Anoxic-hypoxic syndrome. **A.** Axial NCCT in an adult following carbon monoxide poisoning. Bilateral, almost symmetrical hypodensity involving the putamen. **B.** Axial T_2-weighted MR (SE 4300/80) in another patient after anoxic infarct induced dystonia with a bilateral, almost symmetrical hyperintense lesion involving the putamen (arrows).

atrophy. The profound neurological deficit relative to the CT appearance of the lesion is a characteristic feature. MR demonstrates gliosis in the epicenter of the putamen. The gliotic changes may extend to other extrapyramidal nuclei. The presence of hemorrhage in the past or abnormal mineral deposition can be appreciated on MRI but not on CT (Dietrich 1988; Aoki 1989).

Progressive Supranuclear Palsy

Progressive supranuclear palsy (PSP) is associated with atrophy of the midbrain and the tectum, resulting in prominent perimesencephalic and quadrigeminal plate cisterns and dilatation of the aqueduct and the posterior third ventricle (Ambrosetto 1987). The disease usually manifests in an insidious manner with axial rigidity on neck extension, supranuclear opthalmoplegia with impaired vertical movement of the eye, and symptoms of extrapyramidal disease (Savoiardo 1989). Dementia is an associated finding. Although some of the atrophic changes have been demonstrated on CT studies (Ambrosetto 1987), MR is useful in demonstrating the focal atrophic change in the tectal region (Fig. 7-47). On T_2WI, periaqueductal gliosis is seen as a hyperintense signal. Occasionally MR may demonstrate atrophy of the supe-

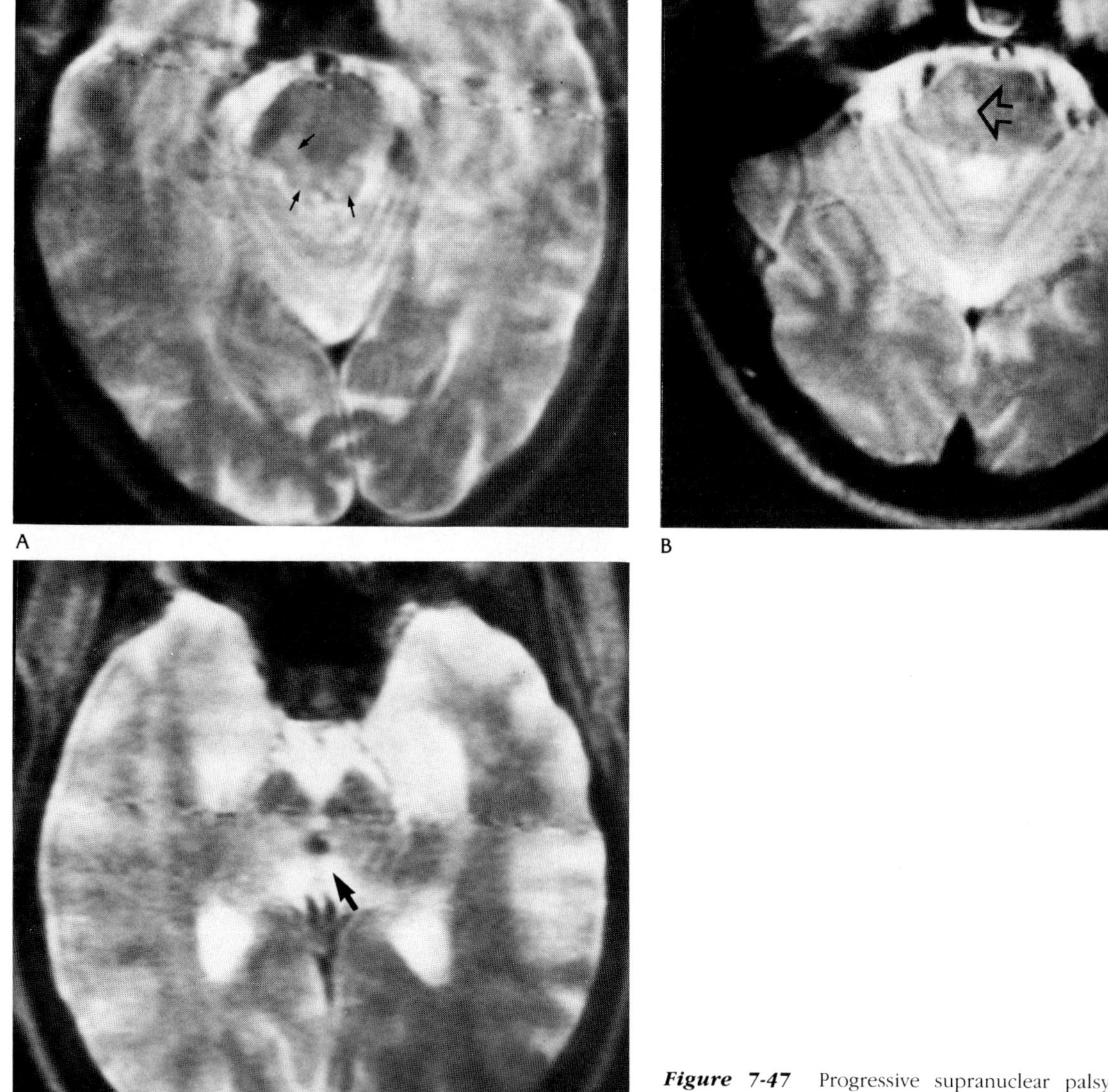

Figure 7-47 Progressive supranuclear palsy (PSP). Axial T_2-weighted MR (SE 4300/80). **A.** Patient with early progressive supranuclear palsy. Hyperintense signal (arrow) in tectum. **B.** Secondary parkinsonism due to midbrain infarct (arrow). **C.** Long-standing PSP with atrophy of the tectum (arrow).

rior colliculi, indicative of third nerve nucleus involvement. Focal hypodensity of the superior colliculi has also been observed (Savoiardo 1990), probably indicative of paramagnetic substance deposition. Differentiation from multisystem atrophy (MSA) is dependent on a lack of signal abnormalities in the subthalamic nuclei as well as in the putamen.

HINDBRAIN ATROPHY

Atrophy of the hindbrain (brainstem and cerebellar hemispheres) is associated with a variety of acquired and hereditary disorders (Table 7-7). The atrophic process, although predominantly involving the hindbrain structures, also involves in varying degrees the forebrain and

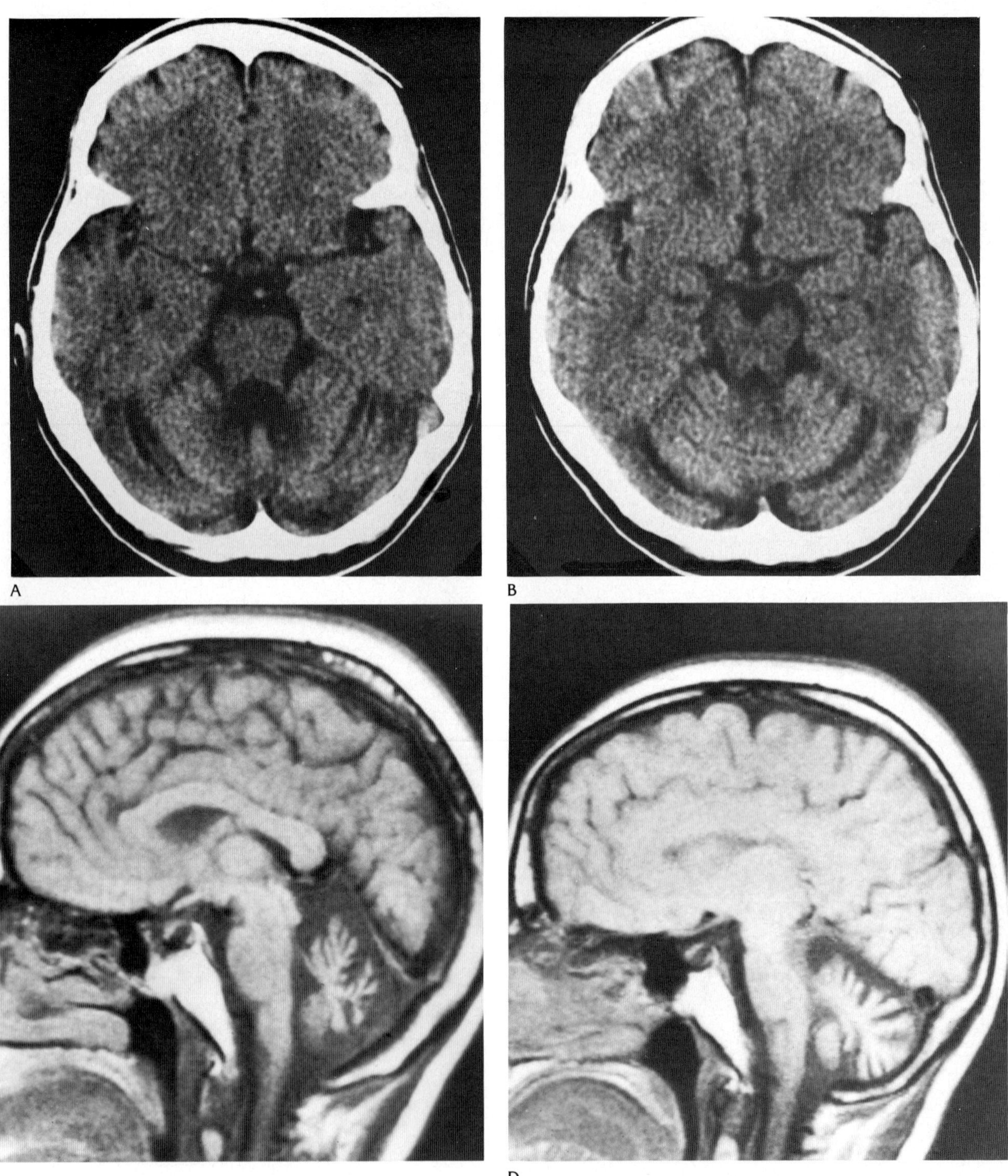

Figure 7-48 Cerebellar atrophy. **A, B.** NCCT demonstrating prominent cerebellar folia, enlarged fourth ventricle, and prominent pericerebellar cisterns. **C, D.** T_1-weighted sagittal MR demonstrates vermian atrophy and normal brainstem. (*Continued on p. 283*)

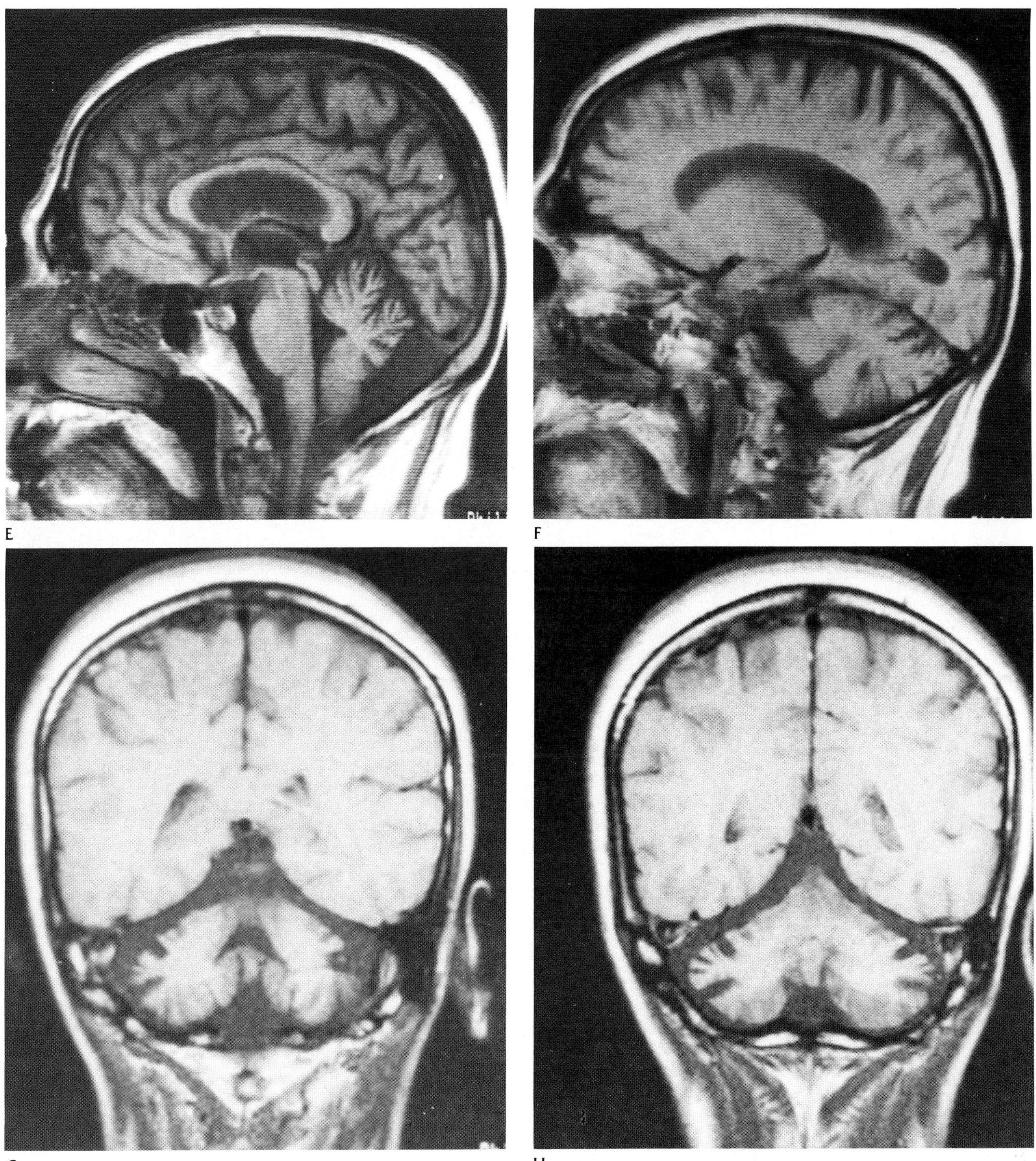

Figure 7-48 ***(continued)*** Sagittal (**E, F**) and coronal (**G, H**) T_1-weighted MR (SE 600/30) demonstrates cerebral atrophy with predominant atrophy of the vermis in a patient with a history of long-term alcohol abuse.

midbrain. Both CT and MRI are useful in evaluating the morphological changes (Rothman 1978; Ramos 1987; Savoiardo 1983; Savoiardo 1990). Degenerative and atrophic changes involving the brainstem and the cerebellum are evaluated better with MRI than with CT because of a lack of bone artifact, the ability to image in all orthogonal planes, and better discrimination between gray and white matter.

Isolated atrophy of the cerebellum is associated with a variety of degenerative disorders (Abe 1983; Andreula 1984) and may be secondary to toxic or prolonged use of ethanol and drugs such as diphenylhydantoin. In chronic ethanol toxicity, the cerebellar atrophy primarily involves the vermis and to a lesser extent the cerebellum (Allen 1979). Reversal of the atrophy has been reported after abstinence (Artmann 1981). Prolonged use of diphenylhydantoin results in degeneration of the Purkinje cells in animals. A similar mechanism is probably responsible for the cerebellar atrophy seen on CT, along with other systemic manifestations (McCrea 1980) (Fig. 7-48).

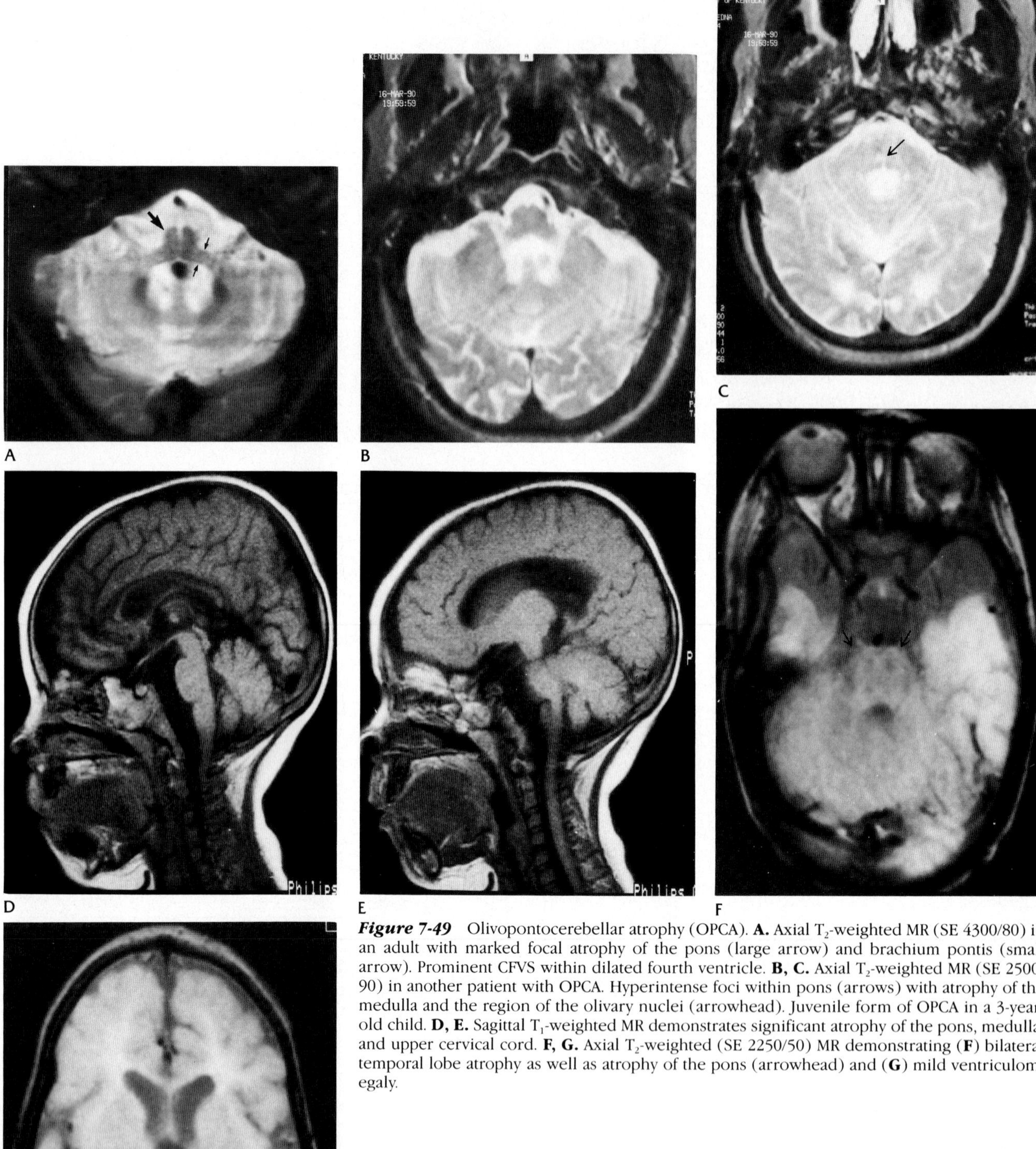

Figure 7-49 Olivopontocerebellar atrophy (OPCA). **A.** Axial T_2-weighted MR (SE 4300/80) in an adult with marked focal atrophy of the pons (large arrow) and brachium pontis (small arrow). Prominent CFVS within dilated fourth ventricle. **B, C.** Axial T_2-weighted MR (SE 2500/90) in another patient with OPCA. Hyperintense foci within pons (arrows) with atrophy of the medulla and the region of the olivary nuclei (arrowhead). Juvenile form of OPCA in a 3-year-old child. **D, E.** Sagittal T_1-weighted MR demonstrates significant atrophy of the pons, medulla, and upper cervical cord. **F, G.** Axial T_2-weighted (SE 2250/50) MR demonstrating (**F**) bilateral temporal lobe atrophy as well as atrophy of the pons (arrowhead) and (**G**) mild ventriculomegaly.

In olivopontocerebellar atrophy (OPCA) as initially described, the degenerative process involved the inferior olive, the pontine nuclei, the middle cerebellar peduncle, and the cerebellar hemisphere and vermis (Dejerine 1900). Depending on the subtype and the association with other regions of the brain, the clinical features and the age of onset may differ. In general, patients with OPCA present with ataxia, which usually progresses in the extremities and the bulbar musculature in a caudocephalad direction. The degenerative process usually manifests between the second and fifth decades. The pathological changes associated with OPCA consist of neuronal loss and gliosis of the pontocerebellar fibers which run through the pons in a transverse course into the middle cerebellar peduncle (resulting in atrophy of the pons and middle cerebellar peduncle), degenerative changes in the Purkinje cells and fibers in the dentate nuclei (resulting in a dilated fourth ventricle and vermian atrophy), and retrograde cell loss of the inferior olives as a result of cortical cerebellar lesions (resulting in atrophy of the olive and cerebellar hemisphere). Both CT and MR demonstrate these features (Fig. 7-49) (Nabatame 1988; Ramos 1987). MR not only demonstrates the morphological changes but on T_2WI demonstrates a hyperintense signal within these areas of degeneration. The importance of MR lies in its ability to differentiate OPCA from other multisystem atrophy (MSA), where ataxia may be a common clinical presentation. In OPCA, the cells of the dentate nuclei are preserved, as are their projection fibers to the red nuclei and thalami through the superior cerebellar peduncle. The demonstration of a normal superior cerebellar peduncle in the coronal plane (Savoiardo 1990) excludes degenerative disorders associated with MSA, such as Shy-Drager syndrome, striatonigral degeneration, and some cases of Leigh's syndrome. A combination of neurological examination with MR can be utilized in differentiating hindbrain atrophy (HBA) from MSA (Table 7-8).

ATROPHY OF THE CERVICOMEDULLARY REGION

Prior to the availability of MRI, evaluation of the cervicomedullary junction was difficult, even though intrathecal contrast was advocated. Subtle atrophic changes were easily missed. MR allows evaluation of this region in all orthogonal planes, without bone artifacts. In many instances the inferior brainstem atrophy is associated with atrophy of the pons and cerebellum (OPCA). Primary atrophy secondary to a neurodegenerative process may selectively involve the fiber tract in the lower brainstem and cord in motor neuron diseases. The motor neurons are fiber tracts that constitute the corticospinal tract between its origin from the precentral gyrus and its passage through the brainstem till it ends in the anterior and lateral horn cells of the spinal cord. In motor neuron disease, the upper or lower motor neurons are affected where they synapse either in the brainstem with the cranial nerve nuclei or in the cervical cord with the anterior horn cells.

Amyotrophic lateral sclerosis is the most common variety of motor neuron disease. It is usually detected in patients beyond the fifth decade and is usually sporadic. Although the exact pathogenesis is not known, the disease may be related to low-grade infection or toxic or

Table 7-8 CT and MR Features of Hindbrain Atrophy

DISEASE ENTITY	BRAINSTEM	FOURTH VENTRICLE	VERMIS	CEREBELLUM	MR SIGNAL CHANGES
Olivopontocerebellar atrophy	4	4	4	4	Mild hyperintense signal middle cerebellar peduncle and pons
Cerebellar atrophy	0	0–2	2–3	3–4	
Friedreich's ataxia	0	0	0	0–2	Atrophic spinal cord
Chronic alcoholism	0	0	2–4 Involves superior vermis	0–2	Associated cerebral atrophy
Phenytoin intoxication	0	0–2	0–2	1–3	
Occult neoplasm metabolic	0	0–2	1–2	0–2	Associated with cerebral atrophy

0 = normal; 1 = equivocal; 2 = mild; 3 = moderate; 4 = severe.

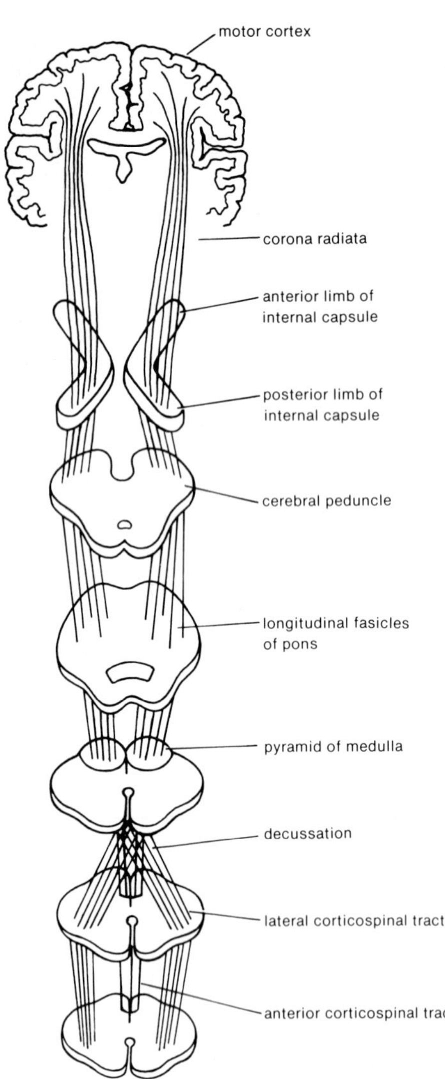

A

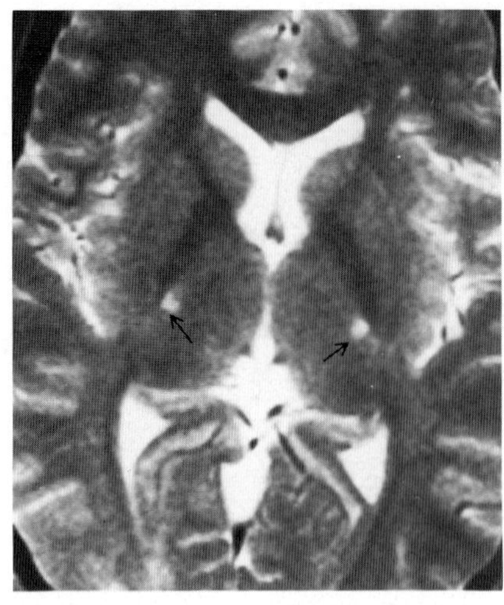

B

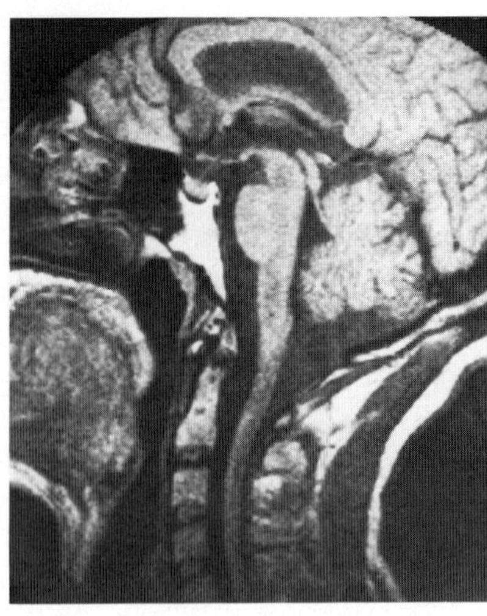

C

Figure 7-50 Amyotrophic lateral sclerosis. **A.** Diagrammatic representation of the corticospinal tracts. In amyotrophic lateral sclerosis, focal symmetrical lesions are identified in posterior limb of internal capsule as well as varying degrees of atrophy in the brainstem and spinal cord. In Wallerian degeneration, the atrophy is in an antegrade fashion and is always unilateral. **B.** Axial T_2-weighted MR (SE 3000/100). Bilateral hyperintense signal foci (arrowheads) in the posterior limb of internal capsule. These are anterior to the normal mildly hyperintense signal (arrow) normally seen in this region. **C.** Midsagittal MR demonstrating mild atrophy of the cervicomedullary region in another patient with a clinical diagnosis of ALS.

vascular causes. The clinical presentation consists of atrophy and weakness of the forearm and spasticity in the lower limbs. There is generalized hyperreflexia. The degenerative process can extend between the precentral gyrus to the level of the lower brainstem and spinal cord. On MRI, atrophy of the lower brainstem and, if the cord is imaged, atrophy of the cord can be demonstrated. The atrophy involves the anterior and lateral portion of the medulla and the spinal cord. On T_2WI, a focal hyperintense signal can be detected in the lower brainstem. This signal change reflects gliosis or myelin loss (Sherman 1987*b*; Biondi 1989). Occasionally the hyperintense signal may also be present at a higher level and may involve the posterior aspect of the posterior limb of the internal capsule, where the corticospinal tract is located (Sherman 1987*b*) (Fig. 7-50). The hyperintense signal is symmetrical, as is the cord or brainstem atrophy.

This is a useful differential from unilateral atrophy, as may be seen in *Wallerian degeneration.* Wallerian degeneration represents anterograde degeneration of the axon and its myelin sheath distal to the axonal cell injury. The histological changes in the fiber tracts within the brainstem and cerebral hemisphere are seen months to years after the initial injury. They involve the corticospinal, corticobulbar, and corticopontine fibers. There is shrinkage and asymmetrical atrophy of the cerebral peduncles, pons, and medullary pyramids following Wallerian degeneration of the corticospinal tract. These changes have been demonstrated on CT (Stovring 1983), although they are better appreciated on MR (Kuhn 1988). On MR there is asymmetrical atrophy of the cerebral peduncles, pons, and medulla. This is best appreciated on the axial and sagittal planes. In addition, on T_2WI, a hyperintense signal along the path of these tracts represents

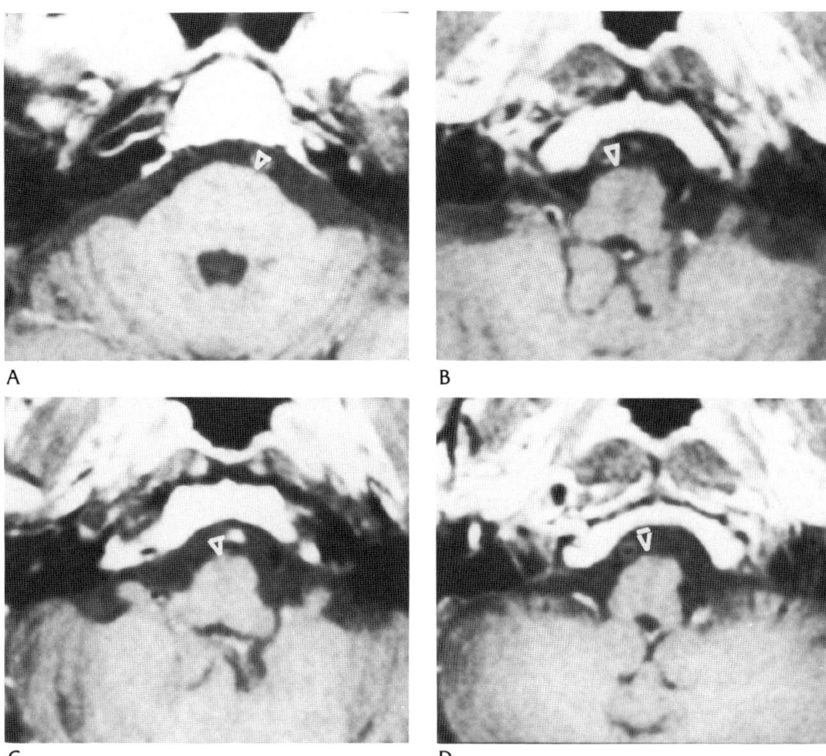

Figure 7-51 Wallerian degeneration. Axial T_1-weighted postcontrast MR. Level of the pons before decussation (**A**) and through the medulla after decussation of the pyramidal tract (**B–D**), demonstrating the unilateral atrophy (arrowhead) from a lesion involving the left corticospinal tract.

histological changes of increased water, loss of lipid, and derangement in the myelin protein; in later stages it is due to gliosis (Fig. 7-51).

Although CT played a major role in the in vivo demonstration of the intracranial contents, MR provides a more precise definition of the morphological changes. In addition, differentiation of gray and white matter changes in pathological disorders can be better appreciated. With the currently available improvements, MRI allows delineation of the vascular anatomy (MRA) and dynamic imaging of the CSF. It is conceivable that with further extension of its application, a more precise understanding of the metabolic pathways may allow us to detect as well as predict the various types of dementia.

ACKNOWLEDGMENTS

Extensive clinical material in this chapter, in the form of illustrations, was provided by Dr. Sherman and Dr. Rutledge from material previously published in *AJNR*. These consist of Figures 7-1, 7-9, 7-20, 7-38, 7-39, 7-41, 7-42, 7-47, and 7-49.

References

ABE S, MIYASAKA K, TAKEI H, et al: Evaluation of the brainstem with high resolution CT in cerebellar atrophic process. *AJNR* 4:446–449, 1983.

ADAMS P, FABRE N, GUELL A, et al: Cortical atrophy in Parkinsons disease: Correlation between clinical and CT findings with special emphasis on prefrontal atrophy. *AJNR* 4:442–445, 1983.

ADAMS RD, FISHER CM, HAKIM S, et al: Symptomatic occult hydrocephalus with "normal" cerebrospinal fluid pressure. *N Engl J Med* 273:117–126, 1965.

ADAMS RD, VICTOR M: *Principles of Neurology,* 4th ed., New York, McGraw-Hill, 1989.

AISEN AM, MARTEL W, GABRIELSON TO, et al: Wilson disease of the brain: MR imaging. *Radiology* 157:137–141, 1985.

ALLEN HA, HANEY P, RAO KCVG: Vascular involvement in cranial hyperostosis. *AJNR* 3:193–195, 1982.

ALLEN JH, MARTIN JT, MCLAIN LW: Computed tomography in cerebellar atrophic processes. *Radiology* 130:379–382, 1979.

AMBROSETTO P: CT in progressive supranuclear palsy. *AJNR* 8:849–851, 1987.

ANDREULA CF, CAMICIA M, LORUSSO A, et al: Clinical and CT parameters in degenerative cerebellar atrophy. *Neuroradiology* 26:29–30, 1984.

AOKI S, OKADA Y, NISHIMURA K, et al: Normal deposition of brain iron in childhood and adolescence: MR imaging at 1.5T. *Radiology* 172:381–385, 1989.

ARCHER S, DARWISH H, SMITH K, Jr: Enlarged cisterna magna and posterior cysts simulating Dandy Walker syndrome on computed tomography. *Radiology* 127:681–686, 1978.

ARTMANN H, GAIL MV, HACKER H, et al: Reversible enlargement of cerebral spinal fluid spaces in chronic alcoholics. *AJNR* 2:23–27, 1981.

ATLAS SW, MARK AS, FRAM EK: Aqueductal stenosis: Evaluation with gradient echo rapid MR imaging. *Radiology* 169:449–453, 1988.

AWAD IA, JOHNSON PC, SPETZLER RF, et al: Incidental subcortical lesions identified on magnetic resonance imaging in the elderly: I. Correlation with age and cerebrovascular risk factors. *Stroke* 17:1084–1089, 1986*a*.

AWAD IA, JOHNSON PC, SPETZLER RF, et al: Incidental subcortical lesions identified on magnetic resonance imaging in the elderly: II. Postmortem pathologic correlation. *Stroke* 17: 1090–1097, 1986*b*.

BAKER LL, STEVENSON DK, ENZMANN DR: End stage periventricular leukomalacia: MR evaluation. *Radiology* 168:809–813, 1988.

BANNISTER R, GILFORD E, KOCEN R: Isotope encephalography in the diagnosis of dementia due to communicating hydrocephalus. *Lancet* ii:1014–1017, 1967.

BARKOVICH AJ, NEWTON TH: MR of aqueductal stenosis: Evidence of a broad spectrum of tectal distortion. *AJNR* 10:471–476, 1989.

BARKOVICH AJ, TRUWIT CL: Brain damage from perinatal asphyxia: Correlation of MR findings with gestational age. *AJNR* 11:1087–1096, 1990.

BARRON SA, JACOBS L, KINKEL WR: Changes in size of normal lateral ventricles during aging determined by computerized tomography. *Neurology* 26:1011–1013, 1976.

BENSON DF, LEMAY M, PATTEN DH, et al: Diagnosis of normal pressure hydrocephalus. *N Engl J Med* 283:610–615, 1970.

BENTSON J, REZA M, WINTER J, et al: Steroids and apparent cerebral atrophy on computed tomography scans. *J Comput Assist Tomogr* 2:16–23, 1978.

BINSWANGER O: Die Abgrenzung der allgemeinen progressive Paralyse. *Berl Klin Wochenschr* 31:1103–1105, 1180–1186, 1894.

BIONDI A, DORMONT D, WEITZNER I Jr, et al: MR imaging of the cervical cord in juvenile amyotrophy of distal upper extremity. *AJNR* 10:263–268, 1989.

BOWEN BC, BARKER WW, LOEWENSTEIN DA, et al: MR signal abnormalities in memory disorder and dementia. *AJNR* 11:283–290, 1990.

BRADLEY WG, WALUCH V, LAI K, et al: Appearance of rapidly flowing blood on magnetic resonance imaging. *AJR* 143: 1167–1174, 1984.

BRADLEY WG, KORTMAN KE, BURGOYNE B: Flowing cerebrospinal fluid in normal and hydrocephalic states: Appearance on MR images. *Radiology* 159:611–616, 1986.

BRADLEY WG, WHITTEMORE AR, WATANABE AS, et al: Association of deep white matter infarction with chronic communicating hydrocephalus: Implication regarding the possible origin of normal-pressure hydrocephalus. *AJNR* 12:31–39, 1991*a*.

BRADLEY WG, WHITTEMORE AR, KORTMAN KE, et al: Marked cerebrospinal fluid void: Indicator of successful shunt in patients with suspected normal pressure hydrocephalus. *Radiology* 178:459–466, 1991*b*.

BRAFFMAN BH, ZIMMERMAN RA, TROJANOWSKI JQ, et al: Brain MR: Pathologic correlation with gross and histopathology: II. Hyperintense white matter foci in the elderly. *AJNR* 9:629–636, 1988*a*.

BRAFFMAN BH, ZIMMERMAN RA, TROJANOWSKI JQ, et al: Brain MR: Pathologic correlation with gross and histopathology: I. Lacunar infarction and Virchow-Robin spaces. *AJNR* 9:621–628, 1988*b*.

BRAFFMAN BH, GROSSMAN RI, GOLDBERG HI, et al: MR imaging of Parkinson disease with spin-echo and gradient-echo sequences. *AJNR* 9:1093–1099, 1988*c*.

BRANT-ZAWADZKI M, FEIN G, VAN DYKE C, et al: MR imaging of the aging brain: Patchy white matter lesions and dementia. *AJNR* 6:675–682, 1985*a*.

BRANT-ZAWADZKI M, KELLY W, KJOS B, et al: Magnetic resonance imaging and characterization of normal and abnormal intracranial cerebrospinal fluid (CSF) spaces. *Neuroradiology* 27:3–7, 1985*b*.

BRODY H: Organization of the human cerebral cortex: III. A study of aging in the human cerebral cortex. *J Comp Neurol* 102:511–556, 1955.

BROWN JJ, HESSELINK JR, ROTHROCK JF, et al: MR and CT of lacunar infarcts. *AJNR* 9:477–482, 1988.

BRUN A, ENGLUND E: A white matter disorder in dementia of the Alzheimer type: A pathoanatomical study. *Ann Neurol* 19:253–262, 1986.

BURGER PC, BURCH JG, KUNZE U: Subcortical arteriosclerotic encephalopathy (Binswanger disease): A vascular etiology of dementia. *Stroke* 12:626–631, 1976.

BURSZTYN EM, LEE BCP, BAUMAN J: CT of acquired immunodeficiency syndrome *AJNR* 5:711–714, 1984.

BURT TB: MR of CSF flow phenomenon mimicking basilar artery aneurysm. *AJNR* 8:55–58, 1987.

CASSON IR, SHAW R, CAMPBELL EA, et al: Neurological and CT evaluation of knocked-out boxers. *J Neurol Neurosurg Psychiatry* 45:170–174, 1982.

CHAWLA JC, HULME A, COOPER R: Intracranial pressure in patients with dementia and communicating hydrocephalus. *J Neurosurg* 40:376–380, 1974.

CHRYSKOPOULOS HS, PRESS GA, GRAFE MR, et al: Encephalitis caused by human immunodeficiency virus: CT and MR imaging manifestations with clinical and pathological correlation. *Radiology* 175:185–191, 1990.

CITRIN CM, SHERMAN JL, GANGAROSA RE, et al: Physiology of the CSF flow void sign: Modification by cardiac gating. *AJNR* 7:1021–1024, 1986.

CREASEY H, RAPOPORT SI: The aging human brain. *Ann Neurol* 17:2–10, 1985.

CROME L: Hydranencephaly. *Dev Med Child Neurol* 14:224–234, 1972.

CURNES JT, BURGER PC, DJANG WT, et al: MR imaging of the compact white matter pathways. *AJNR* 9:1061–1068, 1988.

CUTLER RW, PAGE L, GALICICH J, et al: Formation and absorption of cerebrospinal fluid in man. *Brain* 91:707–719, 1968.

DANDY WE: Roentgenography of the brain after the injection of air into the spinal canal. *Ann Surg* 70:397–403, 1919.

DAVIS PC, HOFFMAN JC Jr, BRAUN IF, et al: MR of Leigh's disease (subacute necrotising encephalomyelopathy). *AJNR* 8:71–75, 1987.

DEHAAN J, GROSSMAN RI, CIVITELLO L, et al: High field magnetic resonance imaging of Wilson's disease. *J Comput Assist Tomogr* 11:132–135, 1987.

DEJERINE J, THOMAS A: L'atrophie olivo-ponto-cerebelleuse. *Nouv Iconogr Salpet* 13:330–337, 1900.

DEKABAN AS, SADOWSKY D: Changes in brain weights during the span of human life: Relation of brain weights to body heights and body weights. *Ann Neurol* 4:345–356, 1978.

DELEON MJ, FERRIS SH, GEORGE AE, et al: Positron emission tomographic studies of aging and Alzheimer's disease. *AJNR* 4:568–571, 1983.

DELEON MJ, GEORGE AE, REISBERG B, et al: Alzheimer's disease: Longitudinal CT studies of ventricular change. *AJNR* 10:371–376, 1989.

DI CHIRO G, REAMES PM, MATHEWS WB: RISA ventriculography and RISA cisternography. *Neurology* 14:185–191, 1964.

DI CHIRO G, ARIMITSU T, BROOKS RA, et al: Computed tomography profiles of periventricular hypodensity in hydrocephalus and leukoencephalopathy. *Radiology* 130:661–666, 1979.

DIETRICH RB, BRADLEY WG: Iron accumulation in the basal ganglia following severe ischemic-anoxic insults in children. *Radiology* 168:203–206, 1988.

DIROCCO C, DITARPANI G, MAIRA G, et al: Anatomo-clinical correlations in normotensive hydrocephalus. *J Neurol Sci* 33:437–452, 1977.

DRAYER BP, ROSENBAUM AE, HIGMAN HB: Cerebrospinal fluid imaging using serial metrizamide CT cisternography. *Neuroradiology* 13:7–17, 1977.

DRAYER BP, BURGER P, DARWIN R, et al: Magnetic resonance imaging of brain iron. *AJNR* 7:373–380, 1986*a*.

DRAYER BP, OLANOW W, BURGER P, et al: Parkinson plus syndrome: Diagnosis using high field MR imaging of brain iron. *Radiology* 159:493–498, 1986*b*.

DRAYER BP, BURGER P, HURWITZ W, et al: Reduced signal intensity on MR images of thalamus and putamen in multiple sclerosis: Increased iron content? *AJNR* 8:413–419, 1987.

DRAYER BP: Imaging of the aging brain: I. Normal findings. *Radiology* 166:785–796, 1988*a*.

DRAYER BP: Imaging of the aging brain: II. Pathologic conditions. *Radiology* 166:797–806, 1988*b*.

DUGUID JR, DELA PAZ R, DEGROOT J: Magnetic resonance imaging of the midbrain in Parkinson's disease. *Ann Neurol* 25:744–747, 1986.

EARNEST MP, HEATON AK, WILKINSON WE, et al: Cortical atrophy, ventricular enlargement and intellectual impairment in the aged. *Neurology* 29:1138–1143, 1979.

EKHOLM S, SIMON JH: Magnetic resonance imaging and acquired immunodeficiency syndrome dementia complex. *Acta Radiol* 29:227–230, 1988.

EL GAMMAL T, ALLEN MB, BROOKS BS, et al: MR evaluation of hydrocephalus. *AJNR* 8:591–597, 1987.

ENZMANN DR, LANE B: Cranial computed tomography findings in anorexia nervosa. *J Comput Assist Tomogr* 1:410–414, 1977.

ENZMANN DR, NORBERT JP: Normal flow patterns of intracranial and spinal cerebrospinal fluid defined with phase-contrast cine MR imaging. *Radiology* 178:467–474, 1991.

ERKINJUNTTI T, SIPPONEN JT, LIVANAINEN M, et al: Cerebral NMR and CT imaging in dementia. *J Comput Assist Tomogr* 8:614–618, 1984.

ESIRI MM, WILCOCK GK: Cerebral amyloid angiopathy in dementia and old age. *J Neurol Neurosurg Psychiatry* 49:1221–1226, 1986.

FAZEKAS F, CHAWLUK JB, ALAVI A, et al: MR signal abnormalities at 1.5 T in Alzheimer's dementia and normal aging. *AJNR* 8:421–426, 1987.

FAZEKAS F, KLEINERT R, OFFENBACHER H, et al: The morphological correlate of incidental punctate white matter hyperintensities on MR images. *AJNR* 12:915–921, 1991.

FEINBERG DA, MARK AS: Human brain motion and cerebrospinal fluid circulation demonstrated with MR velocity imaging. *Radiology* 163:793–799, 1987.

FISHER CM: Hydrocephalus as a cause of disturbance of gait in the elderly. *Neurology* 32:1358–1363, 1982.

FITZ CR, HARWOOD-NASH DC: Computed tomography in hydrocephalus. *CT: Comput Tomogr* 2:91–108, 1978.

FLODMARK O, BECKER LE, HARWOOD-NASH DC, et al: Correlation between computed tomography and autopsy in premature and full term neonates that have suffered perinatal asphyxia. *Radiology* 137:93–103, 1980.

FLOWERS CH, MAFEE MF, CROWELL R, et al: Encephalopathy in AIDS patients: Evaluation with MR imaging. *AJNR* 11:1235–1245, 1990.

FORD WJ, BROOKS BS, EL GAMMAL T, et al: Adult cerebellopontine angle choroid plexus papilloma: MR evaluation. *AJNR* 9:611, 1988.

FOX JK, RAMSEY RG, HUCKMAN MS, et al: Cerebral ventricular enlargement: Chronic alcoholics examined by computed tomography. *JAMA* 236:365–368, 1976.

GADO MH, PATEL J, HUGHES CP, et al: Brain atrophy in dementia judged by CT scan ranking. *AJNR* 4:499–500, 1983*a*.

GADO MH, HUGHES CP, DANZIGER W, et al: Aging dementia and brain atrophy: A longitudinal computed tomographic study. *AJNR* 4:699–702, 1983*b*.

GAJDUSEK DC, GIBBS CJ, ASHER DM, et al: Precautions in medical care of, and in handling materials from, patients with transmissable virus dementia (Jacob-Creutzfeldt disease). *N Engl J Med* 297:1253–1258, 1977.

GEORGE AE, DELEON MJ, FERNS SH, et al: Parenchymal CT correlates of senile dementia (Alzheimer's disease)—loss of gray-white matter discriminability. *AJNR* 2:205–213, 1981.

GEORGE AE, DELEON MJ, GENTES CI, et al: Leukoencephalopathy in normal and pathologic aging: I. CT of brain lucencies. *AJNR* 7:561–566, 1986*a*.

GEORGE AE, DELEON MJ, KALNIN A, et al: Leukoencephalopathy in normal and pathologic aging: II. MRI of brain lucencies. *AJNR* 7:567–570, 1986*b*.

GEORGE AE, DELEON MJ, MILLER J, et al: Positron emission tomography of hydrocephalus. *Acta Radiol* 369:435–439, 1986*c*.

GEORGE AE: Chronic communicating hydrocephalus and periventricular white matter disease: A debate with regard to cause and effect. *AJNR* 12:42–44, 1991.

GERTZ HJ, HENKES H, CERVOS-NAVARRO J: Creutzfeldt-Jacob disease: Correlation of MRI and neuropathologic findings. *Neurology* 38:1481–1482, 1988.

GEYER CA, SARTOR KJ, PRENSKY AJ, et al: Leigh disease (subacute necrotising encephalomyelopathy) CT and MR in five cases. *J Comput Assist Tomogr* 12:40–46, 1988.

GILLES FH, DAVIDSON RI: Communicating hydrocephalus associated with deficient dysplastic parasagittal arachnoid granulations. *J Neurosurg* 35:421–426, 1971.

GLATT SL, GEORGE-LANTOS AD, et al: Efficacy of CT in the diagnosis of vascular dementia. *AJNR* 4:703–705, 1983.

GLYDENSTED C: Measurements of the normal ventricular system and hemispheric sulci of 100 adults with computed tomography. *Neuroradiology* 14:183–192, 1977.

GOMORI JM, STEINER I, MELAMED E, et al: The assessment of changes in brain volume using combined linear measurements: A CT-scan study. *Neuroradiology* 26:21–24, 1984.

GOSHHAJRA K: Metrizamide CT cisternography in CSF rhinorrhea. *J Comput Assist Tomogr* 4:306–310, 1980.

GREITZ T, HINDMARSH T: Computer assisted tomography of intracranial CSF circulation using a water soluble contrast medium. *Acta Radiol (Diagn) (Stockh)* 15:487–507, 1974.

HACHINSKI VC, ILIFF LD, ZILKHA E: Cerebral blood flow in dementia. *Arch Neurol* 7:486–488, 1988.

HAHN FJY, KEAN RIM: Frontal ventricular dimensions on normal computed tomography. *Am J Roentgenol Radium Ther Nucl Med* 126:593–596, 1976.

HAKIM S, ADAMS RD: The special clinical problem of symptomatic hydrocephalus with normal cerebrospinal fluid pressure. *J Neurol Sci* 2:307–327, 1965.

HALSEY JA, ALLEN N, CHAMBERLIN HR: The morphogenesis of hydranencephaly. *J Neurol Sci* 12:187–217, 1971.

HARIK SI, POST MJD: Computed tomography in Wilson's disease. *Neurology* 31:107–110, 1981.

HATAZAWA J, YAMAGUCHI T, ITO M, et al: Association of hypertension with increased atrophy of the brain matter in the elderly. *J Am Geriatr Soc* 32:370–374, 1984.

HAUG S: Age and sex dependence of the size of the normal ventricles on computed tomography. *Neuroradiology* 14: 201–204, 1977.

HEIER LA, BAUER CJ, SCHWARTZ J, et al: Large Virchow-Robin spaces: MR-clinical correlation. *AJNR* 10:929–936, 1989.

HEINZ ER, WARD A, DRAYER BP, et al: Distinction between obstructive and atrophic dilatation of ventricles in children. *J Comput Assist Tomogr.* 4:320–325, 1980.

HENDRIE HC, FARLOW MR, AUSTROM MG, et al: Foci of increased T2 signal intensity on brain MR scan of healthy elderly subjects. *AJNR* 10:703–707, 1989.

HINSHAW DB Jr, FAHMY JL, PECKHAM N, et al: Bright choroid plexus on MR: CT and pathologic correlation. *AJNR* 9:483–486, 1988.

HIRATSUKA A, FUJIWARA K, OKASA K, et al: Modification of periventricular hypodensity in hydrocephalus and ventricular reflux in metrizamide CT cisternography. *J Comput Assist Tomogr* 3:204–208, 1979.

HOPPER KD, FOLEY LC, NIEVES NL, et al: The intraventricular extension of choroid plexus papillomas. *AJNR* 8:469–472, 1987.

HUCKMAN MS, FOX J, TOPEL J: The validity of criteria for evaluation of cerebral atrophy by computed tomography. *Radiology* 116:85–92, 1975.

HUCKMAN MS: Normal pressure hydrocephalus: Evaluation of diagnostic and prognostic tests. *AJNR* 2:385–395, 1981.

INZELBERG R, TREVES T, REIDER I, et al: Computed tomography brain changes in Parkinsonian dementia. *Neuroradiology* 29:535–539, 1987.

JACK CR, MOKRI B, LAWS ER Jr, et al: MR findings in normal pressure hydrocephalus: Significance and comparison with other forms of dementia. *J Comput Assist Tomogr* 11:923–931, 1987.

JACK CR Jr, BENTLY MD, TWOMEY CK, et al: MR imaging-based volume measurements of the hippocampal formation and anterior temporal lobe: Validation studies. *Radiology* 176: 205–209, 1990.

JACOBY RJ, LEVY R: Computed tomography in the elderly: II. Senile dementia: Diagnosis and functional impairment. *Br J Psychiatry* 136:256–269, 1980.

JAMES AE, FLOR WJ, NOVAK GR, et al: The ultrastructural basis of periventricular edema: Preliminary studies. *Radiology* 135:757–760, 1980.

JENSEN F: Acquired hydrocephalus: III. A pathophysiological study correlated with neuropathological findings and clinical manifestations. *Acta Neurochir (Wien)* 47:91–104, 1979.

JINKINS JR: Cisternal ventricles. *AJNR* 9:111–113, 1988.

JOHNSON DL, FITZ CR, MCCULLOUGH DC, et al: Paramesencephalic cistern obliteration: A CT sign of life-threatening shunt failure. *J Neurosurg* 64:386–389, 1986.

JOHNSON KA, DAVIS KR, BUOANANO FS, et al: Comparison of MR and CT in dementia. *Radiology* 167:295, 1988.

JOHNSON MA, PENNOCK JM, BYDDER GM, et al: Serial MR imaging in neonatal cerebral injury. *AJNR* 8:83–92, 1987.

JOLESZ FA, PATZ S, HAWKES RC, et al: Fast imaging of CSF flow/motion patterns using steady-state free precession (SSFP). *Invest Radiol* 22:761–777, 1987.

JUNGREIS CA, KANAL E, HIRSCH WL, et al: Normal perivascular spaces mimicking lacunar infarction: MR imaging. *Radiology* 169:101–104, 1988.

KEMP SS, ZIMMERMAN RA, BILANIUK LT, et al: Magnetic resonance imaging of the cerebral aqueduct. *Neuroradiology* 29:430–436, 1987.

KIDO DK, CLAINE ED, LEMAY M, et al: Temporal lobe atrophy in patients with Alzheimer disease: A CT study. *AJNR* 10:551–557, 1989.

KINKEL WR, JACOBS L, POLACHINI I, et al: Subcortical arteriosclerotic encephalopathy (Binswanger's disease): Computed tomographic nuclear magnetic resonance and clinical correlation. *Arch Neurol* 42:951–959, 1985.

KIRKPATRICK JB, HAYMAN LA: White matter lesions in MRI imaging of clinically healthy brains of elderly subjects: Possible pathologic basis. *AJNR* 162:509–511, 1987.

KISHORE PRS, LIPPER MH, DASILVA AAD, et al: Delayed sequelae of head injury. *Comput Tomogr* 4:287–295, 1980.

KOBARI M, MEYER JS, ICHIJO M, et al: Leukokoriosis: Correlation of MR and CT findings with blood flow, atrophy, and cognition. *AJNR* 11:273–281, 1990.

KOHLMEYER K, LEHMKUHL G, POUTSKA F: Computed tomography of anorexia nervosa. *AJNR* 4(3):437–438, 1983.

KOHN MI, TANNA KN, HERMAN GT, et al: Analysis of brain and cerebrospinal fluid volumes with MR imaging: I. Methods, reliability, and validation. *Radiology* 178:115–122, 1991.

KOMATSU Y, SHINOHARA A, KUKITA C, et al: Reversible CT changes in uremic encephalopathy. *AJNR* 9:215, 1988.

KONO E, KONO R, SHIDA K: Computerized tomographies of 34 patients at the chronic stage of acute carbon monoxide poisoning. *Arch Psychiatr Nervenkv* 233:271–278, 1983.

KOVANEN J, ERKINJUNTTI T, LIVANAINEN M, et al: Cerebral MR and CT imaging in Creutzfeldt-Jacob disease. *J Comput Assist Tomogr* 9:125–128, 1985.

KRETZSCHMAR K, NIX W, ZSCHIEDRICH H, et al: Morphologic cerebral changes in patients undergoing dialysis for renal failure. *AJNR* 4:439–441, 1983.

KUHN MJ, JOHNSON KA, DAVIS KR: Wallerian degeneration: Evaluation with MR imaging. *Radiology* 168:199–202, 1988.

KVICALA V, VYMAZAL J, NEVSIMALOVA S: Computed tomography of Wilson's disease. *AJNR* 4(3):429–430, 1983.

LAFFEY PA, PEYSTER RG, NATHAN R, et al: Computed tomography and aging: Results in normal aging population. *Neuroradiology* 26:273–278, 1984.

LAWLER GA, PENNOCK JM, STEINER RE, et al: Nuclear magnetic resonance (NMR) imaging in Wilson's disease. *J Comput Assist Tomogr* 7:1–8, 1983.

LEMAY M, NEW PFJ: Radiological diagnosis of occult normal pressure hydrocephalus. *Radiology* 96:347–358, 1970.

LEMAY M: Radiologic changes of aging brain and skull. *AJR* 143:383–389, 1984.

LEMAY M: CT changes in dementing diseases: A review. *AJNR* 7:841–853, 1986.

LENNOX G, JONES R: Gaze distractability in Wilson's disease. *Ann Neurol* 25:415–417, 1989.

LORENZO AV, BRESNAN MJ, BARLOW CF: Cerebrospinal fluid absorption deficit in normal pressure hydrocephalus. *Arch Neurol* 30:387–394, 1974.

LOTZ PR, BALLINGER WE Jr, QUISLING RG: Subcortical arteriosclerotic encephalopathy: CT spectrum and pathologic correlation. *AJNR* 7:817–822, 1986.

MACCHI G, ABBAMONDI AL, DI TRAPANI G, et al: On the white matter lesions of the Cruetzfeldt-Jacob disease. *Can J Neurol Sci* 63:197–206, 1984.

MALKO JA, HOFFMAN JC Jr, MCCLEESE EC, et al: A phantom study of intracranial CSF signal loss due to pulsatile motion. *AJNR* 9:83–89, 1988.

MARMAROU A, SHULMAN K, LAMORGESE J: Compartmental analysis of compliance and outflow resistance of the cerebrospinal fluid system. *J Neurosurg* 43:523–534, 1975.

MARSHALL VG, BRADLEY WG Jr, MARSHALL CE, et al: Deep

white matter infarction: Correlation of MR imaging and histopathologic findings. *Radiology* 167:517–522, 1988.

MASTERS CL, RICHARDSON EP Jr: Subacute spongiform encephalopathy (Creutzfeldt-Jacob disease): The nature and progression of spongiform change. *Brain* 101:333–344, 1978.

MAYTAL J, ALVAREZ LA, ELKIN CM, et al: External hydrocephalus: Radiologic spectrum and differentiation from cerebral atrophy. *AJNR* 8:271, 1987.

MCCREA ES, RAO KCVG, DIACONIS JN: Roentgenographic changes during long term diphenylehydantoin therapy. *South Med J* 73:310–311, 1980.

MCGEACHI RE, FLEMING JO, SHARER LR, et al: Diagnosis of Pick's disease by computed tomography. *J Comput Assist Tomogr* 3:113–115, 1979.

MEDINA L, CHI TL, DEVIVO DC, et al: MR findings in patients with subacute necrotizing encephalomyelopathy (Leigh's syndrome): Correlation with biochemical defect. *AJNR* 11: 379–384, 1990.

MILHORAT TH: The third circulation revisited. *J Neurosurg* 42:629–645, 1975.

MILLS CM, BRANT-ZAWADZKI M, CROOKS LE, et al: Nuclear magnetic resonance: Principles of blood flow imaging. *AJNR* 4:1161–1166, 1983.

MIROWITZ S, SARTOR K, GADO MG, et al: Focal signal intensity variations in the posterior internal capsule: Normal MR findings and distinction from pathologic findings. *Radiology* 172:535–539, 1989.

MOODY DM, BELL MA, CHALLA VR: The corpus callosum, a unique white matter tract: Anatomic features that may explain sparing in Binswanger's disease and resistance to flow of fluid masses. *AJNR* 9:1051–1059, 1988.

MORI K, HANDA T, MURATA T, et al: Periventricular lucency in computed tomography of hydrocephalus and cerebral atrophy. *J Comput Assist Tomogr* 4:204–209, 1980.

MOSELEY ME, COHEN Y, MINTOROVICH J, et al: Diffusion weighted MR imaging in experimental brain research: Syllabus: special course (presented at the 76th annual meeting of Radiological Society of North America), 1990, pp 63–67.

NABATAME H, FUKUYAMA H, AKIGUCHI I, et al: Spinocerebellar degeneration: qualitative and quantitative MR analysis of atrophy. *J Comput Assist Tomogr* 12:298–306, 1988.

NAESER MA, GEBHARDT C, LEVINE HC: Decreased computerised tomography numbers in patients with presenile dementia. *Arch Neurol* 37:401–418, 1980.

NARDIZZI LR: Computerized tomographic correlate of carbon monoxide poisoning. *Arch Neurol* 36:38–39, 1979.

OHARA S, NAGAI H, MATSUMOTO T, et al: MR imaging of CSF pulsatory flow and its relation to intracranial pressure. *J Neurosurg* 69:675–682, 1988.

OKUNO T, MASATOSHI I, KONISHI Y, et al: Cerebral atrophy following ACTH therapy. *J Comput Assist Tomogr* 4:20–23, 1980.

PARKINSON J: *An Essay on the Shaking Palsy.* London, Sherwood, Neely and Jones, 1817.

PASTAKIA B, POLINSKY R, DICHIRO G, et al: Multiple system atrophy (Shy-Drager syndrome): MR imaging. *Radiology* 159:499–502, 1986.

PATEL DV, HIER DB, THOMAS CM, et al: Intracerebral hemorrhage secondary to cerebral amyloid angiopathy. *Radiology* 151:397–400, 1984.

PEARL GS, ANDERSON RE: Creutzfeldt-Jacob disease: High caudate signal on magnetic resonance imaging. *South Med J* 82:1177–1180, 1989.

PEDERSEN HM, GYLDENSTED M, GYLDENSTED C: Measurement of the normal ventricular system and supratentorial subarachnoid space in children with computed tomography. *Neuroradiology* 17:231–237, 1979.

PENNER MW, LI KC, GEBARSKI SS, et al: MR imaging of Pelizaeus-Merzbacher disease. *J Comput Assist Tomogr* 11:591–593, 1987.

PICK A: Ueber die Benziehungen der senilen hirnatrophie zur Aphasie. *Prager Med Wochenschr* 17:165–167, 1892.

PORTNOY HD, BHOPP M, BRANCH C, et al: Cerebrospinal fluid pulse waveform as an indicator of cerebral autoregulation. *J Neurosurg* 56:666–678, 1982.

POST MJD, BERGER JR, QUENCER RM: Asymptomatic and neurologically symptomatic HIV-seropositive individuals: Prospective evaluation with cranial MR imaging. *Radiology* 178:131–139, 1990.

RAMOS A, QUINTANA F, DIEZ C, et al: CT findings in spinocerebellar degeneration. *AJNR* 8:635, 1987.

RAMSAY RG, HUCKMAN MS: Computed tomography of porencephaly and other cerebrospinal fluid-containing lesions. *Radiology* 123:211–215, 1977.

RAO KCVG, BRENNAN TG, GARCIA JH: Computed tomography in the diagnosis of Creutzfeldt-Jacob disease. *J Comput Assist Tomogr* 1:211–215, 1977.

RICHTER GW: The iron-loaded cell—the cytopathology of iron storage: A review. *Am J Pathol* 91:361–404, 1978.

ROMÁN GC: White matter lesions and normal pressure hydrocephalus: Binswanger disease or Hakim syndrome? *AJNR* 12:40–41, 1991.

ROPPER AH, HATTEN HP, DAVIS KR: Computed tomography of Wilson's disease: Report of two cases. *Ann Neurol* 5:102–103, 1979.

ROSEN WG, TERRY RD, FULD PA, et al: Pathologic verification of the ischemic score in the differentiation of dementias. *Ann Neurol* 7:486–488, 1980.

ROSENBERG GA, KORNFIELD M, STOVRING J, BICKNELL JM: Subcortical arteriosclerotic encephalopathy (Binswanger) and computerized tomography. *Neurology* 29:1102–1106, 1979.

RUSINEK H, DE LEON MJ, GEORGE AE, et al: Alzheimer disease:

Measuring loss of cerebral gray matter with MR imaging. *Radiology* 178:109–114, 1991.

RUTLEDGE JN, HILAL SK, SILVER AJ, et al: Study of movement disorders and brain iron by MR. *AJNR* 8:397–411, 1987.

SALAMON A, TEATES AE, BURGER PC, et al: Subcortical arteriosclerotic encephalopathy: Brain stem findings with MR imaging. *Radiology* 165:625–629, 1987.

SANDOR T, ALBERT M, STAFFORD J, et al: Use of computerised CT analysis to discriminate between Alzheimer patients and normal control subjects. *AJNR* 9:1181–1187, 1988.

SAVAZZI FGM: Cerebral CT in uremic and hemodyalized patients. *J Comput Assist Tomogr* 10:567–570, 1986.

SAVOIARDO M, BRACCHI M, PASSERINI A, et al: Computed tomography of olivopontocerebellar degeneration. *AJNR* 4(3): 509–512, 1983.

SAVOIARDO M, STRADA L, GIROTTI F, et al: MR imaging in progressive supranuclear palsy and Shy-Drager syndrome. *J Comput Assist Tomogr* 13:555–560, 1989.

SAVOIARDO M, STRADA L, GIROTTI F, et al: Olivopontocerebellar atrophy: MR diagnosis and relationship to multisystem atrophy. *Radiology* 174:693–696, 1990.

SAWA G, WATSON C, TERBRUGGE K, et al: Delayed encephalopathy following carbon monoxide intoxication. *Can J Neurol Sci* 8:77–79, 1981.

SCHEIBEL ME, et al: Progressive dendritic changes in aging human cortex. *Exp Neurol* 47:392–403, 1975.

SCHELAHAS KP, SIEBERT RC, HEITHOFF KB, et al: Congenital choroid plexus papilloma of the third ventricle: Diagnosis with real time sonography and MR imaging. *AJNR* 9:797–801, 1988.

SCHOENE WC: Degenerative diseases of the central nervous system, in Davis RL, Robertson DM (eds): *Textbook of Neuropathology*. Baltimore, Williams & Wilkins, 1985, pp 788–823.

SCHROTH G, NAEGELE T, KLOS U, et al: Reversible brain shrinkage in abstinent alcoholics, measured by MRI. *Neuroradiology* 30:385–389, 1988.

SCHUTZ H, TERBRUGGE K, CHUI M, et al: Determination of CSF shunt patency with a lumbar infusion test. *Neurosurgery* 58:553–556, 1983.

SHERMAN JL, CITRIN CM, GANGAROSA RE, et al: The MR appearance of CSF flow in patients with ventriculomegaly. *AJNR* 7:1025–1031, 1986*a*.

SHERMAN JL, CITRIN CM: Magnetic resonance demonstration of normal CSF flow. *AJNR* 7:3–6, 1986*b*.

SHERMAN JL, CITRIN CM, BOWEN BJ, et al: MR demonstration of altered cerebrospinal fluid flow by obstructive lesions. *AJNR* 7:571–579, 1986*c*.

SHERMAN JL, CITRIN CM, BARKOVICH AJ, et al: MR imaging of the mesencephalic tectum: normal and pathologic variations. *AJNR* 8:59–64, 1987*a*.

SHERMAN JL, CLAWSON LL, CITRIN CH, et al: MR evaluation of amyotrophic lateral sclerosis (ALS). *AJNR* 8:941–946, 1987*b*.

SIMMONS JT, PASTAKIA B, CHASE TN, et al: Magnetic resonance imaging in Huntington disease. *AJNR* 7:25–28, 1986.

SJAASTAD O, SKALPE IO, ENGESET A: The width of the temporal horn in the differential diagnosis between pressure hydrocephalus and hydrocephalus ex vacuo. *Neurology* 19: 1087–1093, 1969.

SMITH CB: Aging and changes in cerebral energy metabolism. *Trends Neurosci* 7:203–208, 1984.

SPECTOR R, JOHANSON CE: The mammalian choroid plexus. *Sci Amer* 261:68–74, 1989.

STERN MB, BRAFFMAN BH, SKOLNICK BE, et al: Magnetic resonance imaging in Parkinson's disease and parkinsonian syndromes. *Neurology* 39:1524–1526, 1989.

SYMON J, HINZ R, PETER T: Enigma of normal pressure hydrocephalus. *Clin Neurosurg* 24:285–315, 1977.

SZE G, DEARMOND SJ, BRANT-ZAWADZKI M, et al: Foci of MRI signal (pseudolesions) anterior to the frontal horns: Histologic correlation of a normal finding. *AJNR* 7:381–387, 1986.

TAKEDA S, MATSUZAWA T: Brain atrophy during aging: A quantitative study using computed tomography. *J Am Geriatr Soc* 32:520–524, 1984.

TANNA NK, KOHN MI, HORWICH DN, et al: Analysis of brain and cerebrospinal fluid volumes with MR imaging: Impact on PET data correction for atrophy. *Radiology* 178:123–130, 1991.

TERBRUGGE KG, SCHUTZ H, CHIU MC, et al: CSF dynamics in adults with hydrocephalus (presented at the 18th annual meeting of the ASNR, 1980, Los Angeles).

TOMLINSON BE, BLESSED G, ROTH M: Observations on the brains of nondemented old people. *J Neurol Sci* 7:331–356, 1968.

TOMLINSON BE, BLESSED G, ROTH M: Observations on the brains of demented old people. *J Neurol Sci* 11:204–242, 1970.

TOMLINSON BE, CROSELLIS JAN: Aging and the dementias, in Adams JH, Crosellis JAN, Duchen LW (eds): *Greenfield's Neuropathology*. New York: Wiley, 1984.

WAGLE WA, SMITH TW, WEINER M: Intracerebral hemorrhage caused by cerebral amyloid angiopathy: Radiographic-pathologic correlation. *AJNR* 5:171–176, 1984.

WESCHLER D: *The Measurement of Adult Intelligence,* 3d ed. Baltimore, Williams & Wilkins, 1944.

WILLIAMS JB, WALSHE JM: Wilson's disease: An analysis of the cranial computerized tomographic appearances found in 60 patients and the changes in response to treatment with chelating agents. *Brain* 104:735–752, 1981.

WIPPOLD FJ, GADO MH, MORRIS JC, et al: Senile dementia and healthy aging: A longitudinal CT study. *Radiology* 179:215–219, 1991.

WOLFSON BJ, FAEVLEER EN, TRUEX RC Jr: The "keyhole": A sign of herniation of a trapped fourth ventricle and other posterior fossa cysts. *AJNR* 8:473–478, 1987.

WOLPERT S: The ventricular size on computed tomography. *J Comput Assist Tomogr* 1:222–226, 1977.

WWIKKELSO C, ANDERSSON H, BLOMSTRAND C, et al: Computed tomography of the brain in the diagnosis of and prognosis in normal pressure hydrocephalus. *Neuroradiology* 31:160–165, 1989.

YAMADA H, NAKAMURA S, TATIMA M, et al: Neurological manifestation of pediatric achondroplasia. *J Neurosurg* 54:49–57, 1981.

YAMARU H, ITO M, KUBOTA K, et al: Brain atrophy during aging. A quantitative study with computer tomography. *J Gerentol* 35:492–497, 1980.

ZEISS J, BRINKER RA: MR imaging of cerebral hemiatrophy. *J Comput Assist Tomogr* 12:640–644, 1988.

ZEUMER H, SCHONSKY B, STRUM KW: Predominant white matter involvement in subcortical arteriosclerotic encephalopathy (Binswanger disease). *J Comput Assist Tomogr* 4:14–19, 1980.

ZILKHA A: CT of cerebral hemiatrophy. *AJR* 135:263–267, 1980.

ZIMMERMAN RA, BILANIUK LT: Computed tomography of choroid plexus lesions. *CT* 3:93–102, 1979.

ZIMMERMAN RD, FLEMING CA, LEE BCP, et al: Periventricular hyperintensity as seen by magnetic resonance: Prevalence and significance. *AJNR* 7:13–20, 1986.

8 PRIMARY TUMORS IN ADULTS

James G. Smirniotopoulos
S. Howard Lee

GENERAL CONSIDERATIONS

Eighty percent of CNS tumors occur intracranially: the remainder are found within the spinal canal. When assessing either CT or MR images for neoplasms, the following should be ascertained: (1) tumor location and extent, (2) tumor characterization, (3) mass effect and edema, and (4) brain herniation.

Frequently, tumor is initially detected by the associated presence of peritumoral edema. Often, peritumoral edema is a more conspicuous and directly attributable finding than tumor itself, notably in metastasis, malignant glioma, and brain abscess. The amount of mass effect depends to a large degree upon the amount of surrounding edema. The mass effect, rather than tumor size per se, may lead to brain herniation and severe neurologic dysfunction. However, a lack of apparent mass effect does not exclude the diagnosis of neoplasm.

Brain Edema

Brain edema can be classified into three types: vasogenic, cytotoxic, and interstitial (Fishman 1975).

Vasogenic edema results from a breakdown of the blood-brain barrier (BBB) (Fig. 8-1), which allows excessive fluid to pass from the capillaries into the extracellular space (Fig.8-2). Macromolecules may also pass through the disrupted BBB, setting up an osmotic gradient that further attracts water molecules. There is more extracellular space between the cells in white matter than in gray matter, so that vasogenic edema occurs more readily in white matter. Thus peritumoral edema is most prominent in white matter, extending along the white matter fiber tracts and generally sparing the cortical gray matter. Tumor vessels also have an abnormal BBB. Vasogenic edema is produced by a variety of pathologic processes, including primary and metastatic tumors, vasoocclusive disease, hemorrhage, contusion, and inflammation (Bradley 1984). On CT, hypodensity in the white matter extends like fingers along white matter tracts. On MR, the same areas are iso- to hypointense on T_1WI and hyperintense on T_2WI.

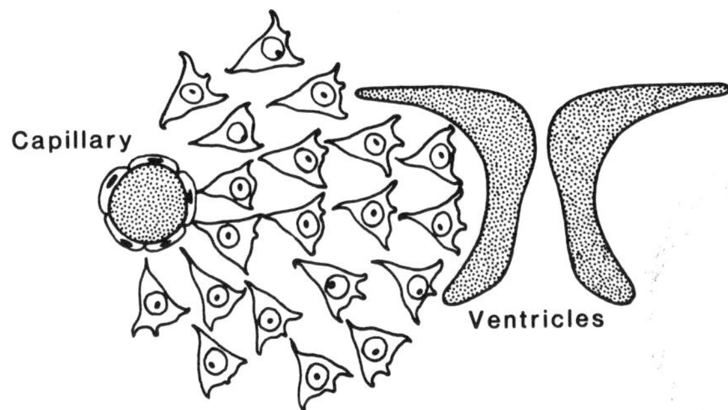

Figure 8-1 Schematic representation of normal blood-brain barrier, cells, and extracellular space. (*From Bradley, 1984.*)

Cytotoxic (cellular) edema begins as intracellular swelling secondary to any type of insult to the cell membrane and is most often due to ischemia (Latchaw 1991) (Fig. 8-3). When the blood supply to a cell is decreased

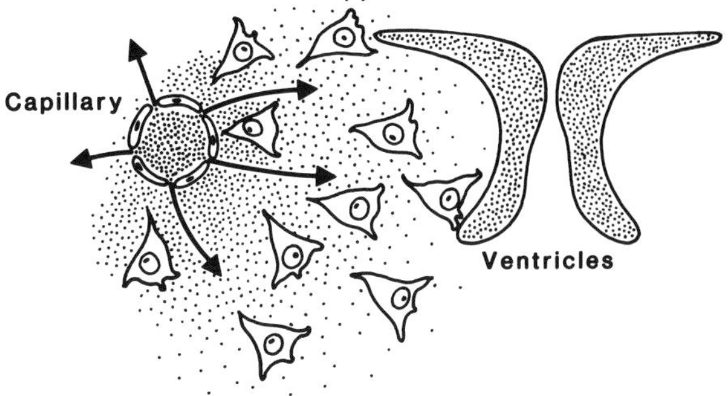

Figure 8-2 Schematic representation of vasogenic edema demonstrating breakdown of the blood-brain barrier and increased fluid in the extracellular space. (*From Bradley, 1984.*)

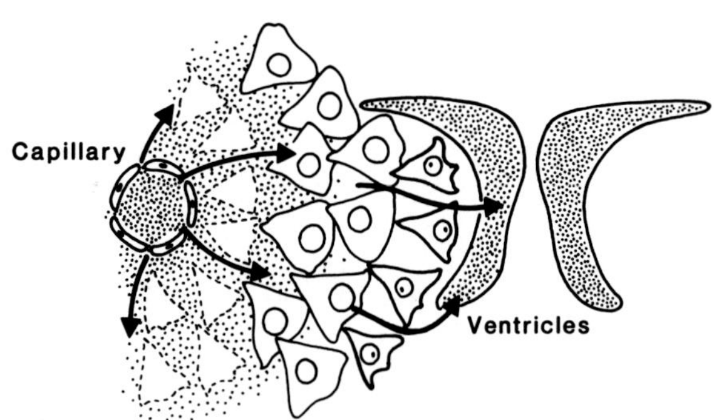

Figure 8-3 Schematic representation of cytotoxic edema. Cells at periphery of infarct are swollen, decreasing extracellular space and limiting diffusion of vasogenic edema produced centrally by breakdown of the blood-brain barrier. (*From Bradley, 1984.*)

and oxidative phosphorylation ceases, leading to a reduction of ATP and failure of the Na/K pump, intracellular influx of Na and water results in cellular swelling and concomitant decrease in the volume of the extracellular space (Klatzo 1967). This results in loss of basic cellular function. Such an insult may be reversible if the oxygen supply to the cell is reestablished early (Shaller 1980). Cytotoxic edema tends to involve both gray and white matter, preferentially more gray than the subjacent white matter, as typically seen in ischemic infarction. But if damage to the BBB follows, vasogenic edema may ensue in addition to cytotoxic edema.

Interstitial edema results from transependymal migration of CSF under a pressure gradient from the ventricles into the periventricular white matter (Fishman 1975) (Fig. 8-4). This results in diffuse periventricular hypodensity on CT and hyperintensity on MR along the lateral ventricles (Bradley 1984). It is observed in the various acute forms of obstructive and communicating hydrocephalus. It is also reported in patients with normal-pressure hydrocephalus (Bradley 1988).

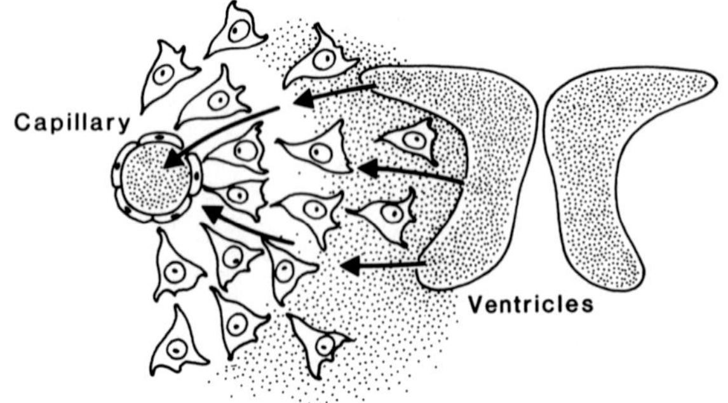

Figure 8-4 Schematic representation of interstitial edema. Increased intraventricular pressure forces the CSF transependymally into the periventricular tissues. (*From Bradley, 1984.*)

Brain Herniation

The intracranial contents have the ability to buffer the pressure effects of an expanding mass, but this ability is limited because of subdivision by inelastic dura into several compartments within the rigid bony calvarium. An expanding mass is compensated for at the expense of CSF and vascular spaces, resulting in compression and displacement of brain tissue. Persistent increased intracranial pressure may result in brain herniation. Recognition of brain herniation on CT and MR is important because it is more commonly the cause of death than is the tumor itself. Internal brain herniations can be divided into four groups: occipital (foramen magnum, tonsillar), tentorial (ascending and descending), sphenoidal (ascending and descending), and lateral (subfalcine, cingulate). Among them, subfalcine, transtentorial, and cerebellar tonsilar herniations are well known and clinically significant (Fig.8-5). Another type is external transcalvarial herniation, where swollen brain herniates through an opening in the calvarium due to trauma or surgical procedure.

In *subfalcine herniation,* the cingulate gyrus is pushed under the falx (Fig. 8-6), which may displace or compress the internal cerebral vein and the anterior cerebral artery. Infarction of the anterior cerebral artery territory can occur. *Transtentorial herniations* can be described

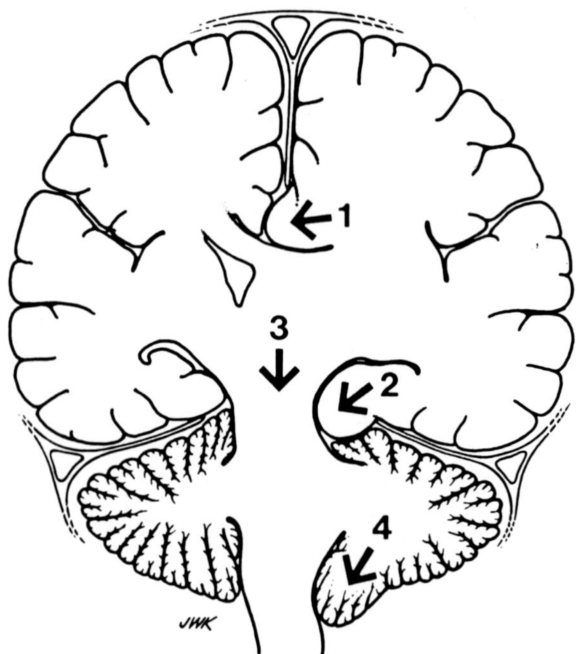

Figure 8-5 Patterns of brain herniation. (1) Cingulate herniation under the falx. (2) Uncal herniation through the tentorial incisura. (3) Central transtentorial herniation through the incisural notch. (4) Cerebellar tonsillar herniation through the foramen magnum.

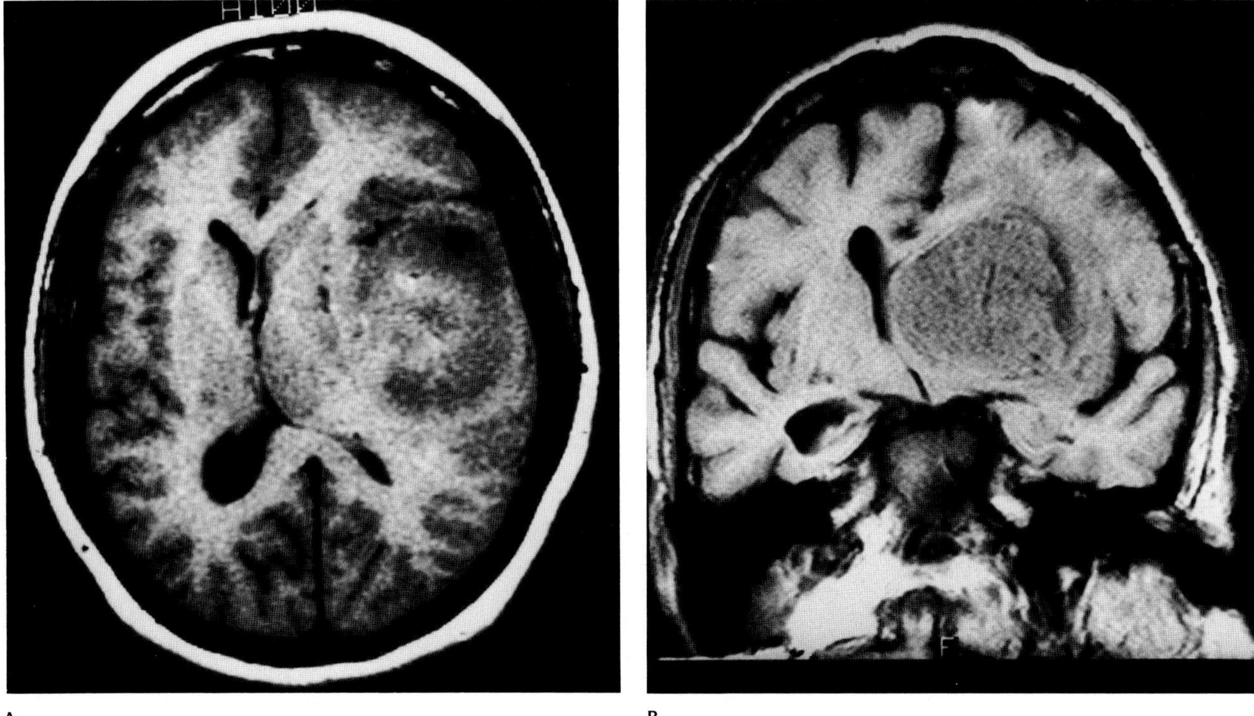

A B

Figure 8-6 Subfalcine herniation. Axial (**A**) and coronal (**B**) MR demonstrate displacement of the corpus callosum and cingulate gyrus.

as descending (lateral or central) or ascending. In descending herniations, displacement of the uncus of the temporal lobe medially toward the suprasellar cistern and inferiorly over the edge of tentorium is called uncal herniation (Fig. 8-7). Medial displacement of the hippocampal gyrus over the more posterior edge of the tentorium is called hippocampal herniation (Fig. 8-7), a type frequently seen with a unilateral supratentorial mass. In

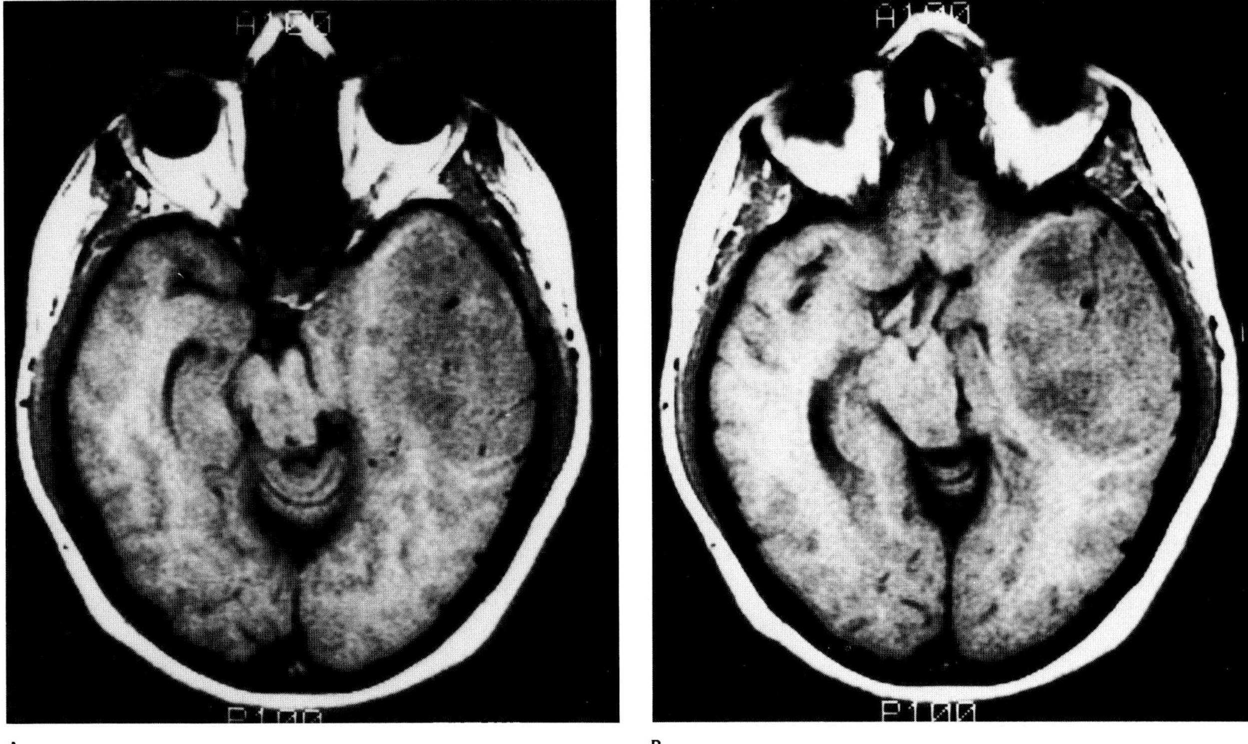

A B

Figure 8-7 Transtentorial herniation, descending. **A.** Uncal herniation and medial displacement of the uncus to the suprasellar cistern. **B.** Uncal and hyppocampal herniation resulting in compression of the hypothalamus and midbrain.

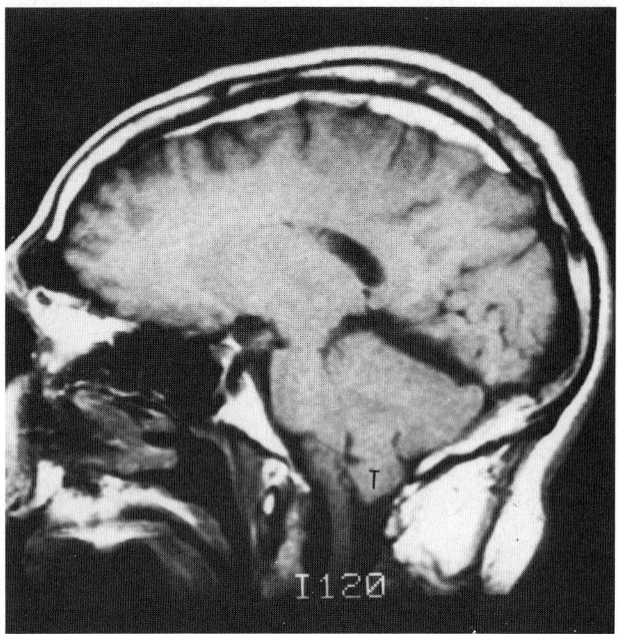

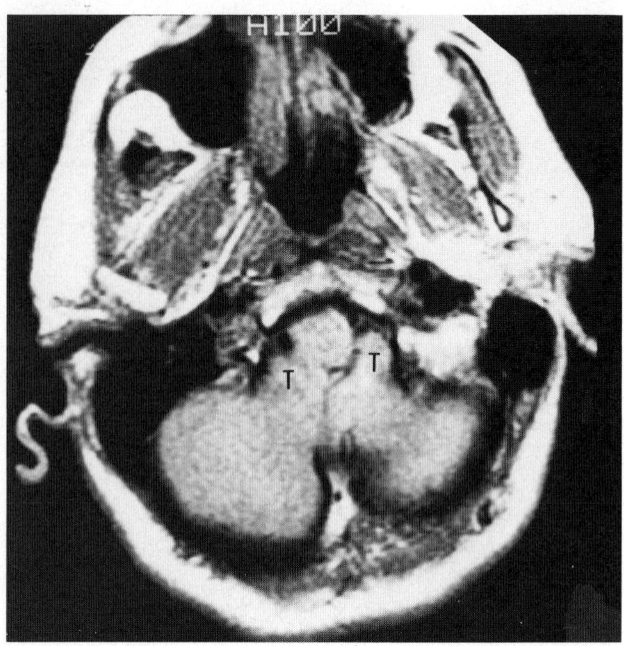

A B

Figure 8-8 Tonsillar herniation. Sagittal MR shows tonsils (T) below the foramen magnum by more than 5 mm. Note forward compression of the brainstem and cervicomedullary junction.

hippocampal herniation the brainstem can be displaced and compressed, resulting in hemorrhage. Often, oculomotor (III) nerve involvement is the earliest sign of transtentorial herniation. Bilateral cerebral masses can cause bilateral hippocampal herniation, also known as central transtentorial herniation. Ascending transtentorial herniation represents the upward herniation of the vermis and adjacent portions of the cerebellar hemispheres through the incisura due to infratentorial mass (Fig. 8-8). Compression of the midbrain, cerebral peduncle, or aqueduct can result in hemorrhage, necrosis, or hydrocephalus. Infarctions in the distribution of posterior cerebral, superior cerebellar, and anterior choroidal arteries may occur, as well as oculomotor nerve dysfunction. *Cerebellar tonsillar herniation* consists of downward displacement of the inferior mesial parts of the cerebellar hemisphere through the foramen magnum, behind the cervical spinal cord (Fig. 8-8). The displacement may be bilateral or unilateral. The lethal effects of this herniation are the results of medullary compression (Adams and Victor 1985). The mean position of normal tonsils is 1 mm above the foramen magnum, with a range from 8 mm above to 5 mm below. Patients with tonsillar ectopia of more than 3 mm tend to be significant clinically. (Barkovich 1986).

Intraaxial and Extraaxial Localization

Following identification of the lesion and its secondary edema, determining the mass effect, and evaluating for herniation, the first step in differential diagnosis should be to determine whether the site of origin of the neoplasm is intraaxial or extraaxial. Primary intraaxial tumors are usually of glial origin, most commonly astrocytomas, while the most common extraaxial tumors are meningiomas. The prognoses and surgical approaches for the two types are significantly different. Most extraaxial tumors are benign. The extraaxial mass is separated from the brain surface by an anatomic boundary consisting of CSF, pial blood vessels, and frequently the dura (Goldberg 1991). Frequently, tissue contrast between an extraaxial mass and the brain parenchyma can be of help in demonstrating the cleavage plane. Most extraaxial tumors exhibit early and intense contrast enhancement on CT and MR. Frequently, contrast enhancement can contribute to increasing tissue contrast between the brain parenchyma and extraaxial lesions (Fig. 8-9).

CONTRAST ENHANCEMENT

CT Contrast Enhancement

When CT first became available, Ambrose (1975*b*) observed that intravenous iodinated contrast media (CM) enhanced the visualization of brain tumors. Contrast enhancement can be attributed to two mechanisms: (1) extravascular and (2) intravascular concentration of contrast material (Gado 1975). Contrast enhancement in tumors depends to a significant extent on the CM accumulation

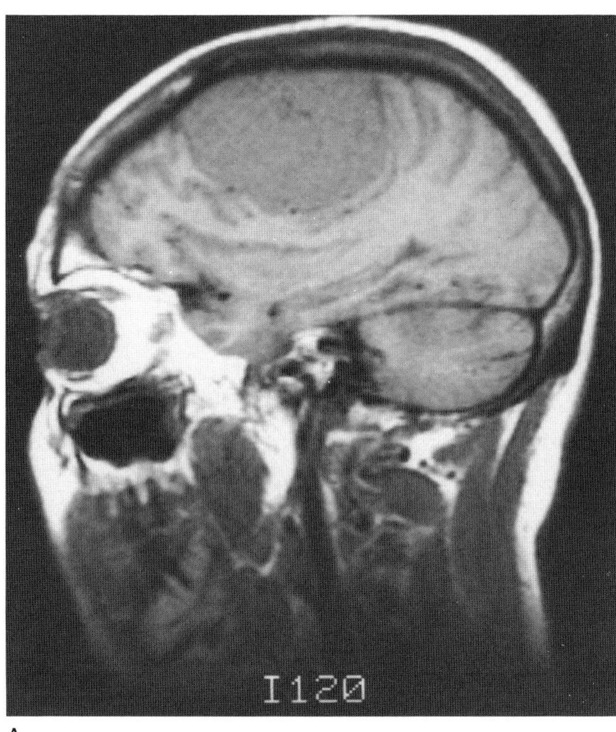

A

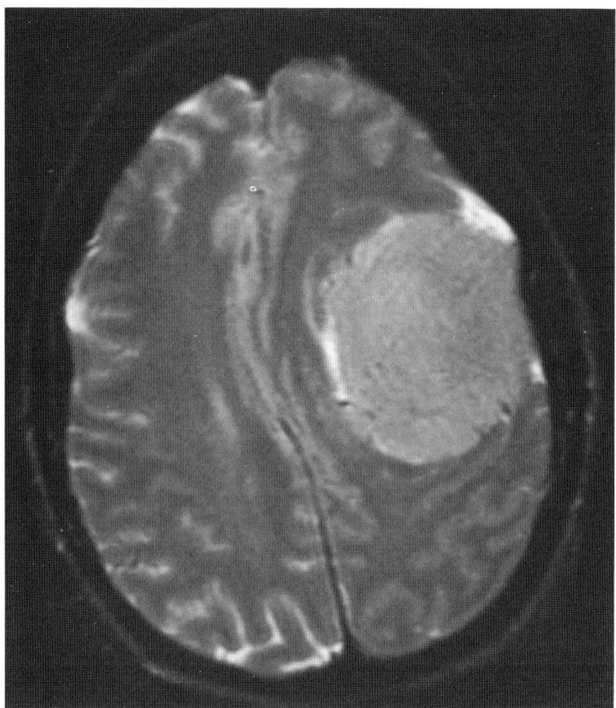

B

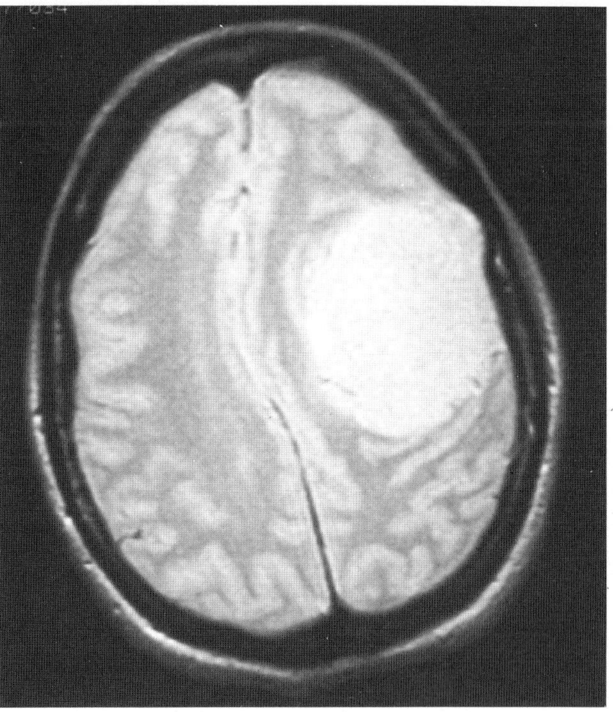

C

Figure 8-9 Extra- versus intraaxial mass. Meningioma shows pial vessel displacement as peripheral signal void (**A**), CSF cleft (**B**), and buckled gray and white matter (**C**).

in an extravascular compartment due to the leakage of CM across an abnormal BBB, analogous to that of radionuclide leakage (Gado 1975). The portion contributed by increased intravascular accumulation of CM in tumors may not be as significant as in cerebrovascular anomalies.

In the early period of CT utilization, there were significant differences of opinion regarding the necessity of, and indications for, contrast enhancement (New 1975; Paxton 1974). The total dosage of iodine, its concentration, and the mode of administration (bolus, infusion, or both) were set arbitrarily by different groups. At present, the consensus is to use the dose which provides about 30 to 40 g of intravenous iodine (100 to 150 ml of 60% iodinated CM), given intravenously as a bolus, or else 300 ml of 30% solution as a drip infusion for an adult patient of average weight. Larger amounts, up to 80 g of iodine ("double dose"), have been utilized (Kramer 1975; Butler 1978; Hayman 1979) and have been useful in detecting very small neoplasms. As a guideline, properties of iodine-containing CM (both ionic and nonionic) in current use are presented in Table 8-1.

The time interval between administration of intravenous iodinated CM and CT has also been debated. In general, CECT, when performed immediately following injection of CM, demonstrates enhancement of the lesion unless the patient is on large doses of steroids. Delayed CT studies may occasionally be helpful in demonstrating smaller lesions or in patients who are on high doses of steroids. Although the exact mechanism is not clearly

Table 8-1(A) Properties of Contrast Media

I) Ionic CM

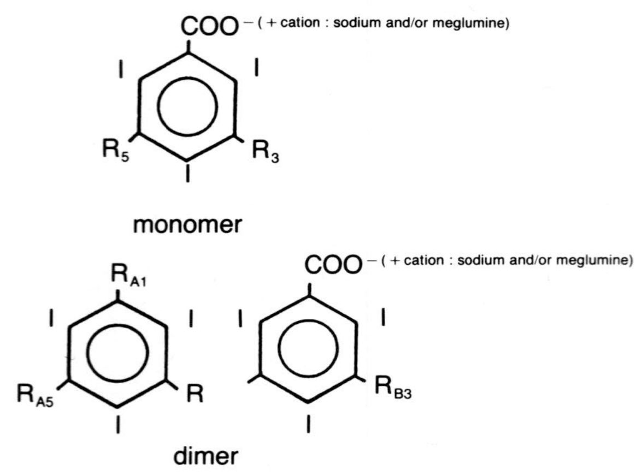

COO − (+ cation : sodium and/or meglumine)

I I R_5 R_3 I

monomer

R_{A1} COO − (+ cation : sodium and/or meglumine)

I I I I R_{A5} R R_{B3} I I

dimer

II) Nonionic CM

R_1

I I R_5 R_3 I

monomer

R_{A1} R_{B1}

I I I I R_{A5} R R_{B3} I I

dimer

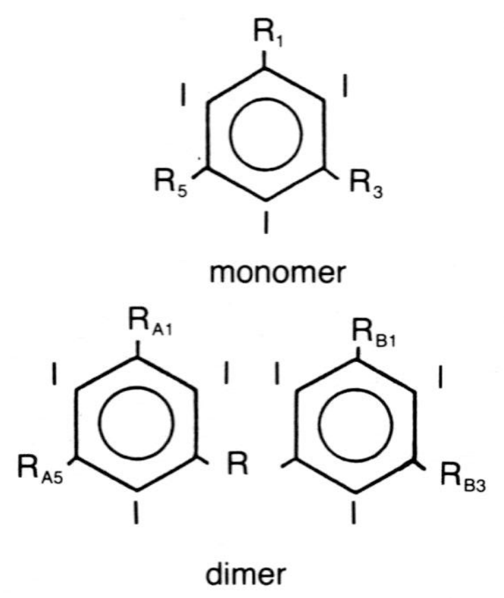

Source: Modified from Skucas 1989.

Table 8-1(B) Contrast Comparison Chart: Ionic and Non-Ionic Contrast Media

(I) Ionic Contrast Media

PRODUCT	MANUFACTURER	% CONC.	ANION	CATION	IODINE, MG/ML	OSMOLALITY, MOSM/KG	VISCOSITY, 37°C CPS	PACKAGING (ML) V/B	IODINE, G/UNIT
Vascoray® (Iothalamate Meglumine 52% and Iothalamate Sodium 26% Injection USP)	Mallinckrodt	78	Iothalamate	Meglumine 52% Sodium 26%	400	2,400	9.0	25V 50V 100B 200B	10.00 20.00 40.00 80.00
Renografin ® 76 (Diatrizoate Meglumine and Diatrizoate Sodium Injection USP)	Squibb	76	Diatrizoate	Meglumine 66% Sodium 10%	370	1,940	8.4	20V 50V 100B 200B	7.40 18.50 37.00 74.00
Hypaque ® 76 (Diatrizoate Meglumine and Diatrizoate Sodium Injection USP [66%/10%])	Winthrop	76	Diatrizoate	Meglumine 66% Sodium 10%	370	2,016	8.32	30V 50V 100V 100 in 200B 150 in 200B 200B	11.10 18.50 37.00 37.00 55.50 74.00

MD-76® (Diatrizoate Meglumine and Diatrizoate Sodium Injection USP [66%/10%])	Mallinckrodt	76	Diatrizoate	Meglumine 66% Sodium 10%	370	2,179	9.0	50V 100B 150B 200B	18.50 37.00 55.50 74.00
Angiovist® 370 (Diatrizoate Meglumine and Diatrizoate Sodium Injection [66%/10%])	Berlex	76	Diatrizoate	Meglumine 66% Sodium 10%	370	2,100	9.0	50V 100V 150B 200B 500B	18.50 37.00 55.50 74.00
Conray® 400 (Iothalamate Sodium Injection USP 66.8%)	Mallinckrodt	66.8	Iothalamate	Sodium	400	2,348	4.49	25V 50V	10.00 20.00
Renovist® (Diatrizoate Meglumine and Diatrizoate Sodium Injection USP)	Squibb	69.3	Diatrizoate	Meglumine 34.3% Sodium 35%	371	1,900	5.7	50V	18.55
Conray® 325 (Iothalamate Sodium Injection USP 54.3%)	Mallinckrodt	54.3	Iothalamate	Sodium	325	1,797	2.8	30V 50V	9.75 16.25
Hexabrix® (Ioxaglate Meglumine Injection 39.3% and Ioxaglate Sodium Injection 19.6%)	Mallinckrodt	58.9	Ioxaglate	Meglumine 39.3% Sodium 19.6%	320	600	7.5	20V 30V 50V 100B 150B 200B	6.4 9.6 16.0 32.0 48.0 64.0
MD 50® (Diatrizoate Sodium Injection USP 50%)	Mallinckrodt	50	Diatrizoate	Sodium	300	1,546	2.4	30V 50V	9.00 15.00
Hypaque® 50 (Diatrizoate Sodium Injection USP)	Winthrop	50	Diatrizoate	Sodium	300	1,515	2.34	20V 30V 50V 150 in 200B 200B	6.00 9.00 15.00 45.00 60.00
Urovist® (Diatrizoate Sodium Injection 50%)	Berlex	50	Diatrizoate	Sodium	300	1,550	2.4	50V	15.00
Renografin® 60 (Diatrizoate Meglumine and Diatrizoate Sodium Injection USP)	Squibb	60	Diatrizoate	Meglumine 52% Sodium 8%	292	1,450	4.0	10V 30V 50V 100V 100B	2.92 8.76 14.60 29.20 29.20

(continued on next page)

Table 8-1(B) *continued*

(I) Ionic Contrast Media

PRODUCT	MANUFACTURER	% CONC.	ANION	CATION	IODINE, MG/ML	OSMOLALITY, MOSM/KG	VISCOSITY, 37°C CPS	PACKAGING (ML) V/B	IODINE, G/UNIT
MD-60® (Diatrizoate Meglumine and Diatrizoate Sodium Injection USP [52%/8%])	Mallinckrodt	60	Diatrizoate	Meglumine 52% Sodium 8%	292	1,557	4.1	30V	8.76
								50V	14.60
Angiovist® 292 (Diatrizoate Meglumine and Diatrizoate Sodium Injection [52%/8%])	Berlex	60	Diatrizoate	Meglumine 52% Sodium 8%	292	1,500	4.0	30V	8.76
								50V	14.60
								100V	29.20
Reno-M-60® (Diatrizoate Meglumine Injection USP 60%)	Squibb	60	Diatrizoate	Meglumine	282	1,404	4.0	10V	2.82
								30V	8.46
								50V	14.10
								100V	28.20
								100B	28.20
								150B	42.30
Hypaque® 60 (Diatrizoate Meglumine Injection USP)	Winthrop	60	Diatrizoate	Meglumine	282	1,415	4.1	20V	5.64
								30V	8.64
								50V	14.10
								100V	28.20
								100 in 200B	28.20
								150 in 200B	42.30
								200B	56.40
Angiovist® 282 (Diatrizoate Meglumine Injection 60%)	Berlex	60	Diatrizoate	Meglumine	282	1,400	4.1	50V	14.10
								100V	28.20
								150V	42.30
								500V	141.00
								1000V	282.00
Conray® 60 (Iothalamate Meglumine Injection USP 60%)	Mallinckrodt	60	Iothalamate	Meglumine	282	1,539	4.13	20V	5.64
								30V	8.46
								50V	14.10
								100V	28.20
								100B	28.20
								150B	42.30
								200B	56.40

Conray® 43 (Iothalamate Meglumine Injection USP 43%)	Mallinckrodt	43	Iothalamate	Meglumine	202	1,025	2.24	50V 100V 150B 200B 250B 300B	10.10 20.20 30.30 40.40 50.50 42.30
Reno-M-DIP® (Diatrizoate Meglumine Injection USP 30%)	Squibb	30	Diatrizoate	Meglumine	141	566	1.4	300B	42.30
Hypaque ® 30 (Diatrizoate Meglumine Injection USP)	Winthrop	30	Diatrizoate	Meglumine	141	633	1.43	100B 300B	14.10 42.30
Urovist® DIU/CT (Diatrizoate Meglumine Injection 30%)	Berlex	30	Diatrizoate	Meglumine	141	640	1.4	300B	42.30
Conray® 30 (Iothalamate Meglumine Injection USP 30%)	Mallinckrodt	30	Iothalamate	Meglumine	141	681	1.43	50V 150V 300B	7.05 21.15 42.30

Note: V = vial CPS = centipose
B = bottle mL = milliliters
G = grams mg = milligrams

(II) Nonionic Contrast Media

PRODUCT	MANUFACTURER	% CONC.	ANION	CATION	IODINE, MG/ML	OSMOLALITY, MOSM/KG	VISCOSITY, 37°C CPS	PACKAGING (ML) V/B	IODINE, G/UNIT
Isovue®-370 (Iopamidol Injection 76%)	Squibb	76	None	None	370	796	9.4	20V 30V 50V 75B 100B 150B 175B 200B	7.4 11.1 18.5 27.75 37.0 55.5 64.75 74.0

(continued on next page)

Table 8-1(B) *continued*

(II) Nonionic Contrast Media

PRODUCT	MANUFACTURER	% CONC.	ANION	CATION	IODINE, MG/ML	OSMOLALITY, MOSM/KG	VISCOSITY, 37°C CPS	PACKAGING (ML) V/B	IODINE, G/UNIT
Omnipaque® 350 (Iohexol Injection)	Winthrop	N/A	None	None	350	844	10.4	50V	17.5
								50B	17.5
								75B	26.25
								100B	35.0
								125B	43.75
								150B	52.5
								175B	61.25
								200B	70.0
Optiray® 320 (Ioversol Injection 68%)	Mallinckrodt	68	None	None	320	702	5.8	20V	6.4
								30V	9.6
								50V	16.0
								100B	32.0
								150B	48.0
								200B	64.0
								50S	16.0
								95S	30.4
								125S	40.0
Isovue®-300 (Iopamidol Injection 61%)	Squibb	61	None	None	300	616	4.7	30V	9.0
								50V	15.0
								75B	22.5
								100B	30.0
								150B	45.0
Isovue-M® 300 (Iopamidol Injection 61%)	Squibb	61	None	None	300	616	4.7	15V	4.5
Omnipaque® 300 (Iohexol Injection)	Winthrop	N/A	None	None	300	672	6.3	10V	3.0
								30V	9.0
								50V	15.0
								50B	15.0
								100B	30.0
								150B	45.0

Omnipaque® 240 (Iohexol Injection)	Winthrop	N/A	None	None	240	520	3.4	10V	2.4
								20V	4.8
								50V	12.0
								50B	12.0
								100B	24.0
								150B	36.0
								200B	48.0
Omnipaque® 210 (Iohexol Injection)	Winthrop	N/A	None	None	210	466	2.5	15V	3.15
Optiray® 240 (Ioversol Injection 51%)	Mallinckrodt	51	None	None	240	502	3.0	50V	12.0
								100B	24.0
								200B	48.0
								50S	12.0
Isovue®-200 (Iopamidol Injection 41%)	Squibb	41	None	None	200	413	2.0	50V	10.0
								100B	20.0
								200B	
Isovue-M® 200 (Iopamidol Injection 41%)	Squibb	41	None	None	200	413	2.0	20V	4.0
Omnipaque® 180 (Iohexol Injection)	Winthrop	N/A	None	None	180	408	2.0	10V	1.8
								20V	3.6
Optiray® 160 (Ioversol Injection 34%)	Mallinckrodt	34	None	None	160	355	1.9	50V	8.0
								100B	16.0
								125S	20.0
								95S	15.2
Omnipaque® 140 (Iohexol Injection)	Winthrop	N/A	None	None	140	322	1.5	50V	7.0
Isovue®-128 (Iopamidol Injection 26%)	Squibb	26	None	None	128	290	1.4	50V	6.4

Note: V = vial; B = bottle; G = grams; S = syringe; CPS = centipose; mL = milliliters; mg = milligrams

Modified from Fischer 1986 with permission.

understood, it is presumed that steroids restore the normal BBB and reverse the abnormal capillary permeability associated with metastatic and primary brain tumors. Hayman (1980) has shown that in patients on heavy doses of steroids, the smaller metastases can be demonstrated by CT immediately following large doses of intravenous contrast infusion (80 g of iodine), suggesting that visualization of certain neoplasms, regardless of their size or histology, may be related to the volume of CM. The authors believe that both the disruption of the BBB and the volume of CM influence detection of the lesion. CECT may also show varying degrees of enhancement of the cisternal spaces in leptomeningeal carcinomatosis (Enzmann 1979). Enhancement of epidural and subdural metastases is common on CECT. Delayed examination is useful in determining whether a lesion is truly cystic, forming contrast/fluid levels, or solid and necrotic (Afra 1980).

The limited value of NCCT prior to CECT has been debated (Latchaw 1978*a*; Butler 1978). Its omission will decrease radiation exposure and result in time and cost savings to the patient. Eliminating NCCT, however, may cause difficulty in differentiating acute hemorrhage and calcification/ossification, which can be of clinical significance. We believe each case should be individually assessed in deciding whether to omit NCCT or CECT.

MR Contrast Enhancement

Pathologic intracranial processes are recognized on CT and MR by virtue of alterations of normal anatomy and tissue attenuation (CT) and signal intensity (MR).

Proton MRI provides excellent inherent contrast and spatial resolution between most biologic tissues. Contrast in proton MRI is a direct result of inherent differences in the observed signals from body tissues (Wehrle 1983). Tissue contrast is a multifaceted variable dependent upon physiochemical tissue properties and upon operator-chosen variables for MRI signal acquisition.

MR contrast is determined by (1) intrinsic tissue factors, such as proton density, blood flow, and the T_1 and T_2 relaxation times, and (2) external factors, such as the strength of the external magnetic field and operator-chosen pulse sequences (Wehrle 1990). Modification of relaxation times (T_1 and T_2) is more effective in increasing contrast enhancement in MR than modification of proton density. Proton density influences the signal intensity linearly, while relaxation times do so exponentially (Paajanen 1989). Exogeneous MR contrast agents can basically be classified into the paramagnetics (T_1 contrast agent) and the ferromagnetics (T_2 contrast agent).

Ferromagnetic agents provide a simple monophasic effect of progressive signal loss (T_2 effect) with increasing dose. Although virtually all biologic iron is paramagnetic, the clusters of iron ions create the collective domain with a magnetic moment 10 to 100 times greater than the sum of the paramagnetic iron ions (Cullity 1972). In the clustered form iron is either ferromagnetic or supermagnetic. Particulate iron less than 30 nm in size is superparamagnetic; larger particles are ferromagnetic. The fundamental difference between paramagnetics and ferromagnetics in regard to MR imaging is that the former enhance the proton signal, whereas the latter tend to destroy the signal, thus inducing the negative contrast (Saini 1987; Mendonca 1986; Olsson 1986; Renshaw 1986). No clinical CNS application has been proposed so far with this agent.

Paramagnetic substances have a permanent magnetism that is due to spin moment in random alignment. Upon exposure to an external magnetic field, the magnetic moments align with the field and generate strong local magnetic fields that shorten both the T_1 and T_2 of neighboring protons. When paramagnetic ions are added to water, the relaxation process of water molecules is more enhanced in the vicinity of the paramagnetic centers through dipole-dipole interactions between the unpaired electrons of the paramagnetic species and the water protons. This results in a reduction in T_1 and T_2 that is called *proton relaxation enhancement* (Burton 1979). A short TE is the most important pulse parameter in paramagnetic contrast enhancement.

The tissue response to paramagnetics is a complex biphasic curve; at low doses there is signal enhancement (T_1 effect), but at higher doses signal loss occurs (T_2 effect). However, there is evidence that slightly higher dosage, such as 0.2 or 0.3 mmol/kg of Gd-D03A, will result in increase in the area of enhancement, signal intensity, and/or the number of lesions (Yuh 1991).

At present, the only paramagnetic agent available commercially is gadolinium-labeled diethylenetriamine pentaacetic acid (Gd-DTPA), which is also known as gadopentetate dimeglumine (Magnevist, Schering AG/Berlex Corp.) The recommended dose (0.1 mmol/kg) is 1/100 of the 50 percent lethal dose (Ld_{50}) in rats (10 mmol/kg). This safety index of 100 is far greater than the 10 to 20 safety index of iodinated CM. Gd-DTPA is eliminated unmetabolized by glomerular filtration, with a half-life of 1.6 ± 0.13 hours; 83 ± 14 percent is excreted in 6 hours, and 91 ± 1.3 percent in 24 hours (Goldstein 1984; Weinmann 1984).

Unlike iodinated CM, which affects the CT image directly by its own attenuation of the x-ray beam, Gd-DTPA appears indirectly on MR image due to its influence upon the relaxation properties of adjacent protons. However, the pattern of contrast enhancement on MR is very similar to that of CT. Contrast accumulation in the extracellular space, crossing of disrupted blood-brain-barrier (Runge 1985; Frank 1986), and normal physiologic enhancement in the pituitary gland, infundibulum, cavernous sinus, cranial nerves, dura, choroid plexus and nasal mucosa (Kilgore 1986; Berry 1986) are noted on CEMR. In addition, veins will normally increase in signal intensity while arteries will not.

Contrast enhancement in MR has been of particular value in defining the relationship of brain tumors and perifocal edema (Carr 1984; Claussen 1985; Felix 1985; Curati 1986), although histological tumor margins cannot be defined with certainty on both CECT and CEMR (Earnest 1988). Tumors of high malignancy grades generally show more enhancement than low-grade tumors (Graif 1985; Felix 1985; Claussen 1985), but the intensity of enhancement does not necessarily correlate with the grade of the tumor. Most extraaxial tumors exhibit consistent and intense enhancement on CT/MR because of lack of BBB and the presence of neovascularity, while with NCCT/NCMR they can be difficult to detect (Goldberg 1991).

The time-intensity profile with MR is similar to that observed in CT (Felix 1985; Schöfner 1986). Except for pituitary microadenomas, metastatic disease, and low-grade neoplasms, delayed CEMR is of limited value and should, in our opinion, be discouraged in view of time constraints, logistical problems, and poor yields. The overall superiority of T_2WI in the detection of intraaxial brain disease when compared with Gd-DTPA-enhanced T_1WI has been observed (Brandt-Zawadzki 1986). This is based on the fact that water accumulation may predate the more severe BBB disruption needed for leakage of larger large molecules such as iodinated CT or MR contrast agents, across the barrier. Water is an inherent contrast-enhancing substance for T_2WI; this accounts for MR's superior sensitivity to increased tissue water.

The atomic number of Gd-DTPA is 64, which compares favorably with that of the x-ray CM, iodine-53. Therefore, high attenuation by concentrated Gd-DTPA on CT is expected. This observation may warrant further research into the potential of Gd-DTPA as a CT CM (Bloem 1989).

SPECIFICITY AND SENSITIVITY

The literature is replete with descriptions of the higher sensitivity of MR in comparison to CT (Bydder 1982; Weinstein 1984; Brant-Zawadzki 1983, 1984; Daniels 1984). MR is far superior to CT in detecting and localizing tumors, but its characterization is somewhat disappointing. In other words, the specificity of MR lags behind its sensitivity. Quantitative analysis of MR tissue parameters measured in a three-dimensional T_1/T_2/proton density space has limited value in characterizing brain tumors or increasing the specificity of MR imaging (Just 1988). The vast majority of neoplasms have elevated proton density, i.e., prolonged T_1 and T_2 on spin-echo sequences, so that most tumors demonstrate hypointensity on T_1WI and hyperintensity on T_2WI. Calcification is of diagnostic importance in the differential diagnosis of brain tumors. CT is superior to MR in the detection of calcification. The signal intensity of calcified regions on spin-echo images is varied and nonspecific (Holland 1985; Oot 1986). Rapid gradient-echo techniques can help in characterization of the lesion by documenting flow as hyperintensity and intratumoral calcification or hemorrhage as hypointensity (Atlas 1991). Contrast-enhanced MR allows better definition of the boundaries of a tumor by distinguishing edema from tumor, and improves tumor characterization. It is well known, however, that the actual histologic tumor boundary does not correlate with the margin of the tumor as demonstrated by contrast enhancement. Also, the lack of contrast enhancement does not necessarily indicate lack of tumor.

In general, T_2WI series have more contrast resolution and better detect pathologic changes, while T_1WI series have better spatial resolution and better delineate morphology. Therefore it is wise to investigate T_2WI series first to localize the lesion and then to study T_1WI series to characterize it better. Analysis of the basic intensity pattern is an essential step to achieve specific diagnosis. Hyperintense signal on T_1WI can be seen in subacute or chronic hemorrhage (methemoglobin), melanin, fat, high protein concentration, slow-flowing blood, iodinated or paramagnetic IV contrast enhancement, and paramagnetic cations such as manganese, iron, and copper. Hypointense signal on T_2WI can be seen in low proton density (calcification, scant cytoplasm, dense cellularity, and fibrocartilagenous stroma), paramagnetic effect (iron, ferritin or hemosiderin, deoxyhemoglobin, intracellular methemoglobin, melanin, or other free radicals), macromolecular content (very high protein concentration, fibrocollagenous stroma), and signal void from rapid blood flow (Atlas 1991). Combined analysis of the signal intensity and morphologic characteristics of a lesion, together with clinical data and history, can lead to maximum specificity in the MR imaging of brain tumors.

CLASSIFICATION OF ADULT PRIMARY INTRACRANIAL TUMORS

Intracranial neoplasms can be grouped for practical purposes into three broad categories: primary neoplasms; secondary neoplasms; and cysts and tumorlike masses (such as arachnoid cysts, craniopharyngiomas, dermoids and epidermoids, etc.) (Table 8-2). The most common intracranial neoplasms are primary tumors. Primary tumors may arise either from the brain itself (e.g., gliomas) and from its coverings (the meninges, skull, and nerve sheaths) or from other sites, such as the anterior pituitary (pituitary adenoma). In most published series the primary tumors of the central nervous system exceed metastatic intracranial deposits by a factor of 2 to 1 (Zulch 1986; Baker 1980; Robbins 1983; Okazaki 1989) (Tables 8-3 and 8-4).

Table 8-2 Classification of Intracranial Neoplasms

Primary neoplasms
- Glia, neurons, pineocytes
- Meninges, Schwann, pituitary
- Craniopharyngioma, chordoma,
- Chondroma, paraganglioma, etc.
- Germ cell, lymphoma

Secondary neoplasms
- Hematogenous metastases
- CSF dissemination
- Regional extension

Cysts and tumorlike lesions

Table 8-3 Intracranial Neoplasms: CT
NCI Study: 2,928 pts./1,071 Neoplasms

HISTOLOGY	NUMBER (%)
Primary	728 (68%)
Glioma	366 (34%)
Meningioma	164 (15%)
Schwannoma	49 (5%)
Pituitary Adenoma	42 (4%)
Lymphoma	18
Craniopharyngioma	12
Hemangioblastoma	10
Medulloblastoma	7
Pinealoma	6
Secondary (mets.)	343 (32%)

Source: Baker 1980.

Table 8-4 Intracranial Neoplasms

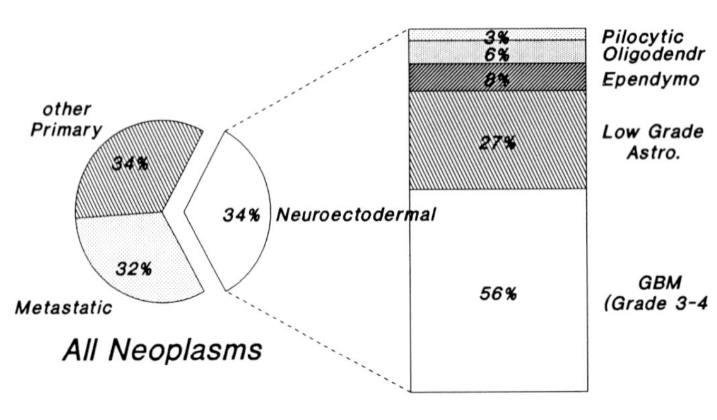

Source: Zulch 1986.

Glial Tumors

GLIOMAS

Gliomas are the most common tumors of the central nervous system. In most series, they represent about one-third of *all* intracranial tumors, and about one-half of all *primary* intracranial neoplasms. The male to female ratio varies from 2 to 1 to about 3 to 2. Although gliomas may present at any age, a disproportionately large number are noted in childhood, especially in the posterior fossa and diencephalic (optic nerve, chiasm, hypothalamus and thalamus) regions. The glia are the supporting cells for the CNS, and there are three basic types of glial cells: astrocytic, oligondendrocytic, and ependymal. In addition, the epithelial lining of the choroid plexus, which is derived from the ependyma, may be considered a fourth type of glial cell (Table 8-5). There are a variety of systems for categorizing neoplasms of glial origin. Some classification systems are based on the proposed genealogy (or cell of origin) of glial tumors. However, most of the practical classification systems in common use are based on certain histologic features and attempt to define a grading system that predicts neoplasm behavior and prognosis (Table 8-6). The Kernohan (Kernohan and Sayre 1952) grading system for the gliomas and its many modified versions are the most widely used. When limited to dif-

Table 8-5 Neuroectodermal Cell Lines

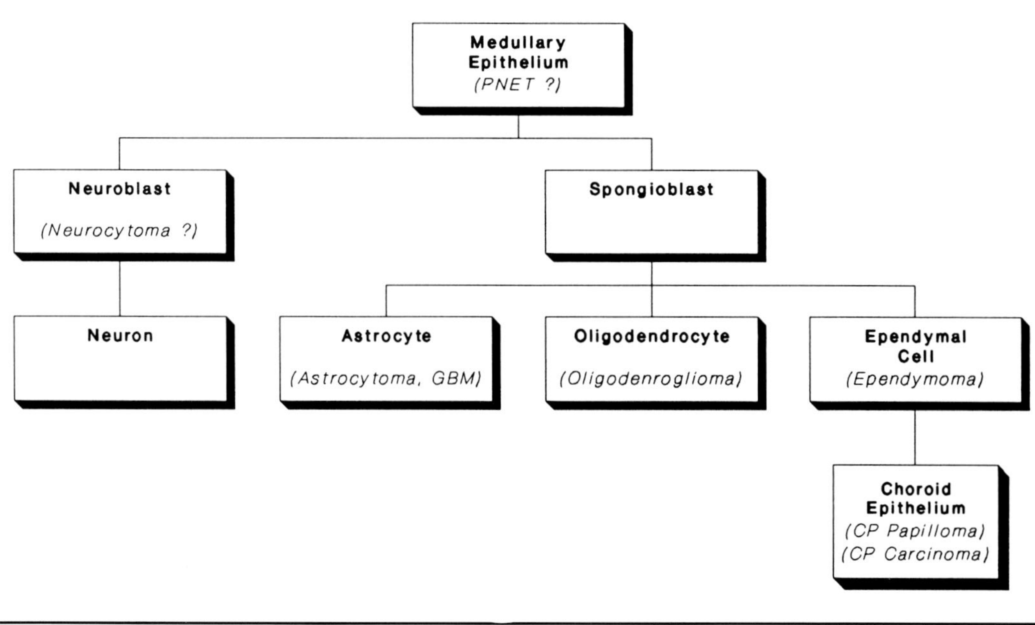

Table 8-6 Grading System for Astrocytomas from Kernohan and Sayre

CONSTITUENT CELLS	GRADE 1	GRADE 2	GRADE 3	GRADE 4
Cellularity	N1 to slight	Increased	1.5	Markedly increased
Anaplasia	Rare	Slight in half of cells	Moderate in half	Pronounced in most cells
Mitoses	None	None	1/HPF	4 to 5/HPF
Giant cells	None	None	Occasional	Frequent
Necrosis	None	None	Increased	Markedly increased
Blood Vessels	N1	N1	Increased	Markedly increased
Endothelial/ Adventitial Proliferation	None	Minimal	Quite prominent	Markedly increased

Source: Modified from Cokazaki 1989.

fuse and fibrillary astrocytomas the Kernohan grading scheme has shown good correlation with patient prognosis (Mahaley 1989) (Table 8-7). However, when applied across the board to all astrocytic tumors, the Kernohan system has some prognostic shortcomings. Quite often prognosis is more dependent on the nature of the glial cell subtype than on the Kernohan histologic grade. One notable example of this variance in prognosis is the pilocytic astrocytoma ("cystic cerebellar astrocytoma"). Histologically this is a low-grade (Kernohan 1 to 2) astrocytoma. However, this particular astrocytic subtype has a 5-year survival of 78 percent, which is more than twice the survival of low-grade astrocytomas (33 percent) composed of fibrillary astrocytes (Table 8-7) (Mahaley 1989). This has prompted the division of astrocytomas into two broad categories: "diffuse" and "circumscribed" (Table

Table 8-7 CNS Primary Tumors
(Five-Year Survival)

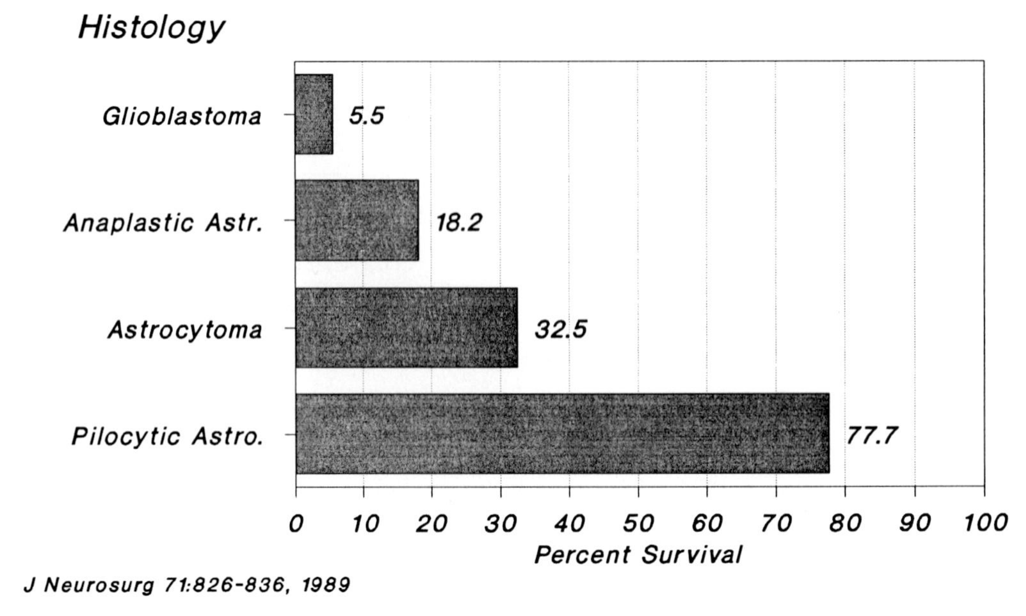

Source: J Neurosurg 71:826–836, 1989.

Table 8-8 Pattern Analysis
Neoplasm

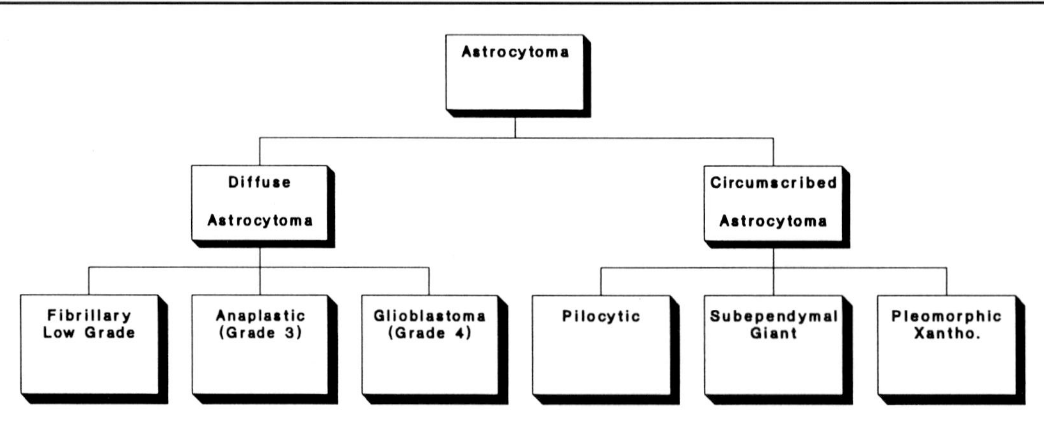

8-8). Whenever possible the radiologist should not only narrow the differential diagnosis to the type of glioma, but also should suggest the probable glial subtype and histologic grade of the glioma. These considerations often have a great impact on the therapeutic options, and may indicate a need for additional preoperative procedures to accurately stage the patient's disease.

The treatment of gliomas includes various degrees of cytoreduction surgery (to diminish tumor volume); radiation therapy to the tumor bed; radiation of the entire neuraxis, in the case of neoplasms that disseminate via CSF; and possible adjunctive chemotherapy. Many factors in addition to cell type and grade of neoplasm determine the overall prognosis. Tumor location, age of patient at the time of diagnosis, presence or absence of CSF or other dissemination, and various other factors affect the morbidity and mortality due to intracranial neoplasms.

Astrocytomas on CT

Astrocytomas constitute the largest category of the gliomas, usually representing about one-third to one-half. Here we present a somewhat condensed, yet practical and clinically useful, classification system that offers a good correlation between imaging characteristics and tumor biology. Astrocytomas are commonly graded on an ascending scale of malignancy, ranging from grade 1 (low-grade or benign) to grade 4 (high-grade or malignant). Virtually all grade 4 astrocytomas can be labeled by the time-honored term *glioblastoma multiforme*. Almost all glioblastomas are recognizable as poorly differentiated astrocytic tumors. Rarely, a glioblastoma may arise from ependymal cells or oligodendrocytes.

The histologic criteria for the classic Mayo Clinic (Kernohan and Sayre) grading system is summarized in Table 8-6. However, in addition to considering the histologic grade, we must discuss the important cell subtypes of astrocytoma: fibrillary and protoplasmic astrocytes (commonly forming a diffusely infiltrating neoplasm or "diffuse astrocytoma"), gemistocytic astrocytoma, subependymal giant cell astrocytoma (the intraventricular tumor of tuberous sclerosis), pilocytic astrocytoma (juvenile pilocytic, cystic cerebellar astrocytoma), and pleomorphic xanthoastrocytoma. All cell types and grades of astrocytoma are infiltrating, nonencapsulated neoplasms. However, there is a tendency for some of them to show extensive infiltration, and for others to remain remarkably well localized (even though microscopically invasive). This marked dichotomy in the potential for infiltration and spread along the white matter tracts has a great influence on overall patient prognosis. Thus, a third classification of astrocytomas is suggested: a division into diffuse astrocytoma and circumscribed astrocytoma. This latter scheme is extremely useful, and is more accurate than the simple Kernohan system in correlating the imaging of astrocytomas with both their pathology and their prognosis (Table 8-8).

Low-grade astrocytomas (fibrillary astrocytoma, Kernohan grades 1 and 2) may present on NCCT as irregular, homogeneous hypodense lesions (20 HU), which may appear less well demarcated than high-grade tumors (Fig. 8-10). However, many low-grade astrocytomas present as relatively well-defined hypodense lesions which are regular in shape (Fig. 8-11). On MR, they appear as well-defined regions of increased water content, i.e., hypointense on T_1WI and hyperintense on T_2WI. Calcification may be present on CT, probably much more often than the reported incidence of 13 percent on plain skull roentgenograms (Gilbertson 1956). MR is relatively insensitive

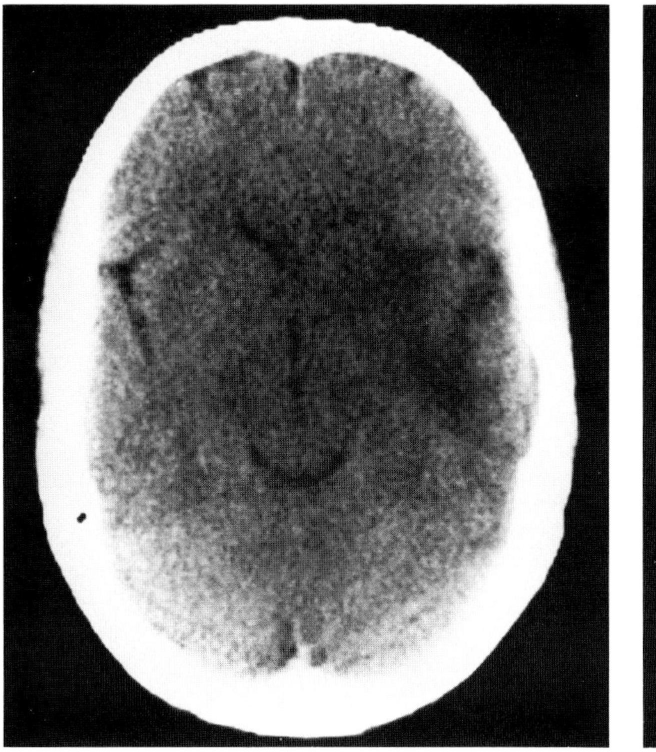

A

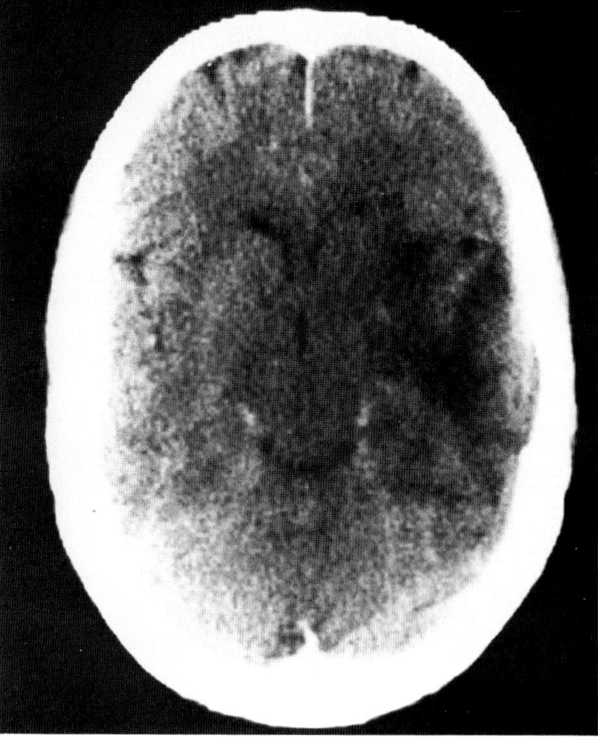

B

Figure 8-10 Low-grade astrocytoma. NCCT (**A**) shows a left frontotemporal lobe lesion with homogeneous low attenuation and mild mass effect. CECT (**B**) shows minimal enhancement. (*Continued on p. 312.*)

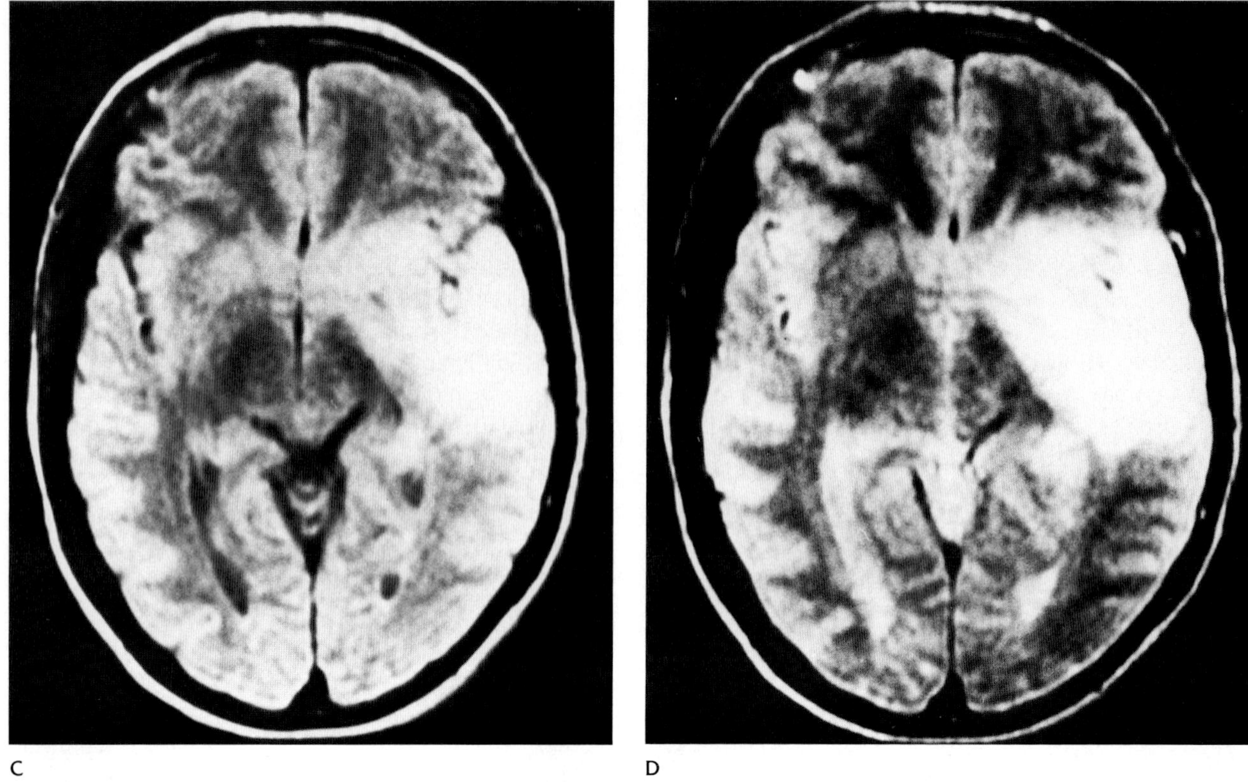

C D

Figure 8-10 (continued) MR scans with PDWI (**C**) and T_2WI (**D**) show a homogeneous lesion with increased signal intensity.

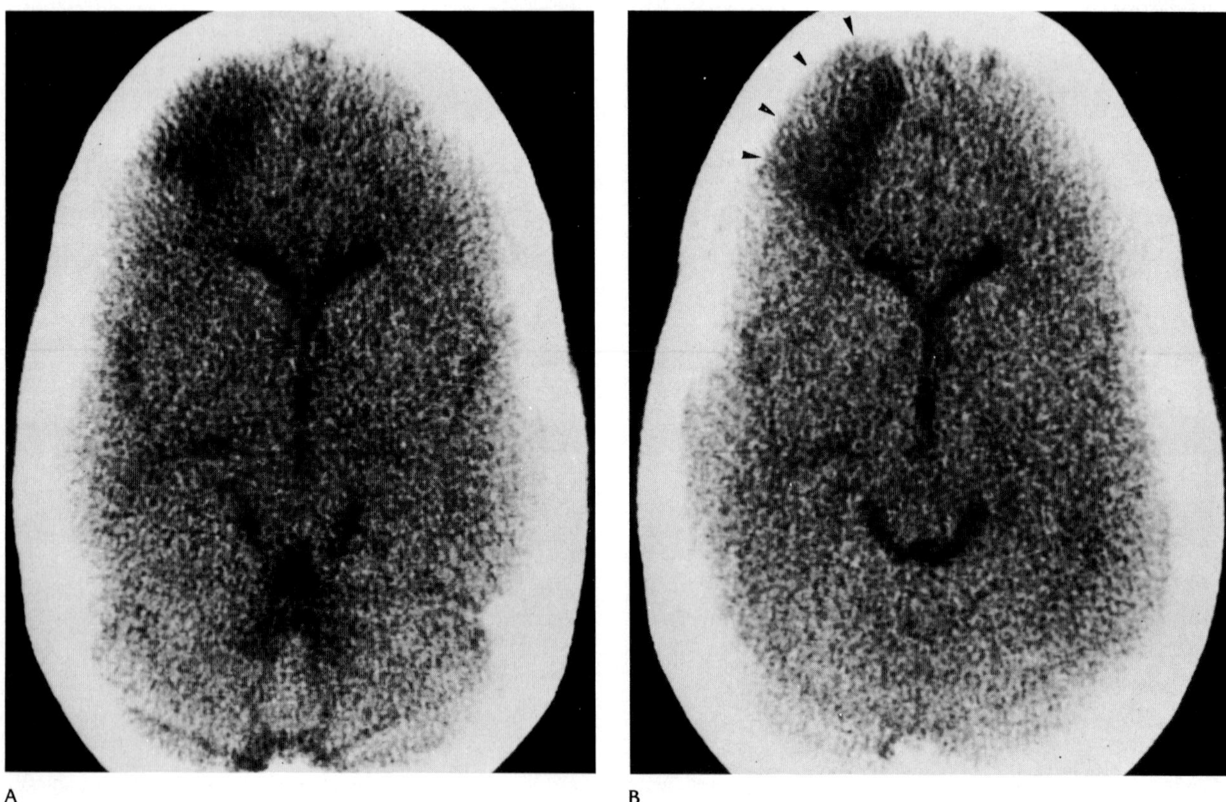

A B

Figure 8-11 Low-grade astrocytomas (grade II). **A.** NCCT shows a fairly well marginated, hypodense lesion in the right frontal lobe with no mass effect on the frontal horn. **B.** CECT shows minimal contrast enhancement within the lesion (arrowheads). Cerebral angiogram (not shown) demonstrates slight tumor blush. At surgery, a solid low-grade astrocytoma was found.

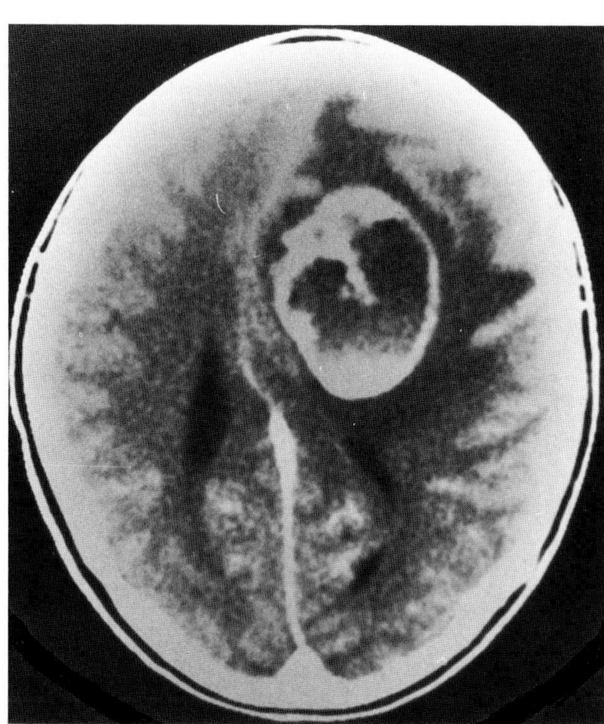

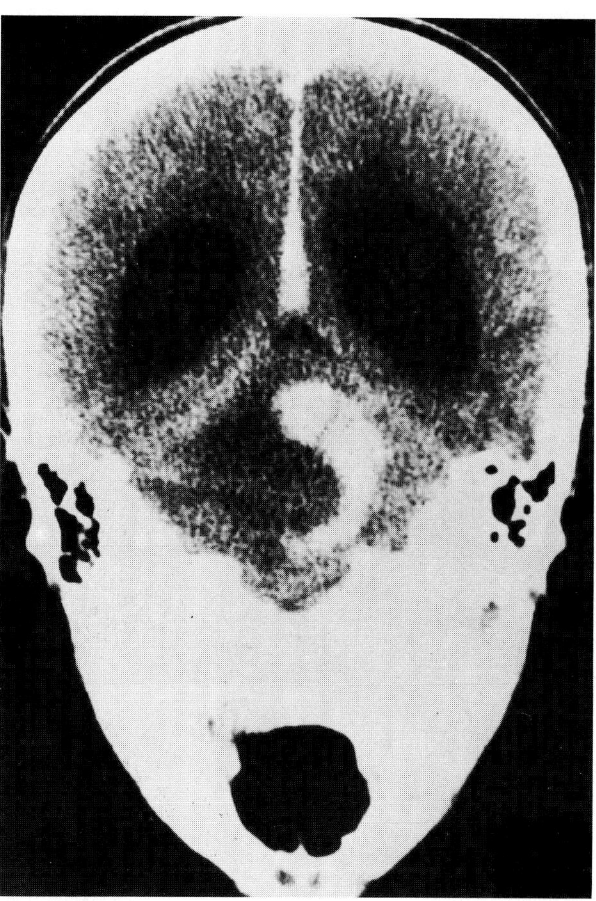

A B

Figure 8-12 Cystic astrocytoma: juvenile pilocytic astrocytoma. CECT (**A**) shows a large mass in the left frontal lobe with vasogenic edema and prominent contrast enhancement. The hypodense center is not necrotic but cystic, as evidenced by dependent layering of contrast with fluid-contrast level. **B.** CECT shows a large cerebellar cystic astrocytoma with mural tumor nodules. The remainder of the cyst wall, devoid of tumor tissue, shows no contrast enhancement.

to the presence of small areas of calcification, unless GRE scans are obtained. Vasogenic edema around low-grade (fibrillary) astrocytomas is minimal or absent (Tchang 1977). However, in low-grade *circumscribed* astrocytomas, both contrast enhancement and vasogenic edema may be noted, especially when these tumors occur in the supratentorial hemispheric white matter (Fig. 8-12). Although on CT some low-grade tumors may be isodense, it would be exceptional for the same tumor also to be isointense on MR. However, the margins of the tumor may appear to blend into the surrounding tissue, making it difficult to distinguish the edge from the surrounding edema or adjacent normal brain. These observations are expected, since *all* gliomas are unencapsulated and may be poorly demarcated from the surrounding parenchyma, especially in low-grade fibrillary astrocytomas. This is true on both imaging and histologic examination. Very hypodense areas on CT may represent a cystic fluid component (Fig. 8-13); however, even a solid astrocytoma may also present with near water density, as in microcystic fibrillary astrocytoma.

On CECT, 45 to 50 percent of low-grade astrocytomas will enhance, with a wide range of absorption values (Oi 1979). However, enhancement in low-grade astrocytomas is almost invariably in the circumscribed types (e.g., pilocytic astrocytoma) rather than the diffuse fibrillary astrocytomas. Grade 1 tumors may show minimal enhancement (Steinhoff 1978) (Fig. 8-10). Steinhoff (1977) reported contrast enhancement in grade 2 neoplasms in as many as 89 percent of cases and ring enhancement in 26 percent but did not distinguish between diffuse fibrillary astrocytomas and circumscribed astrocytomas such as pilocytic astrocytoma.

High-grade astrocytomas (Kernohan grades 3 and 4) are heterogeneous on gross pathology as well as on both CT and MR. On NCCT, high-grade astrocytomas may have heterogeneous moderately decreased (Fig. 8-14), mixed, or, rarely, increased (Fig. 8-15) densities. Occasionally,

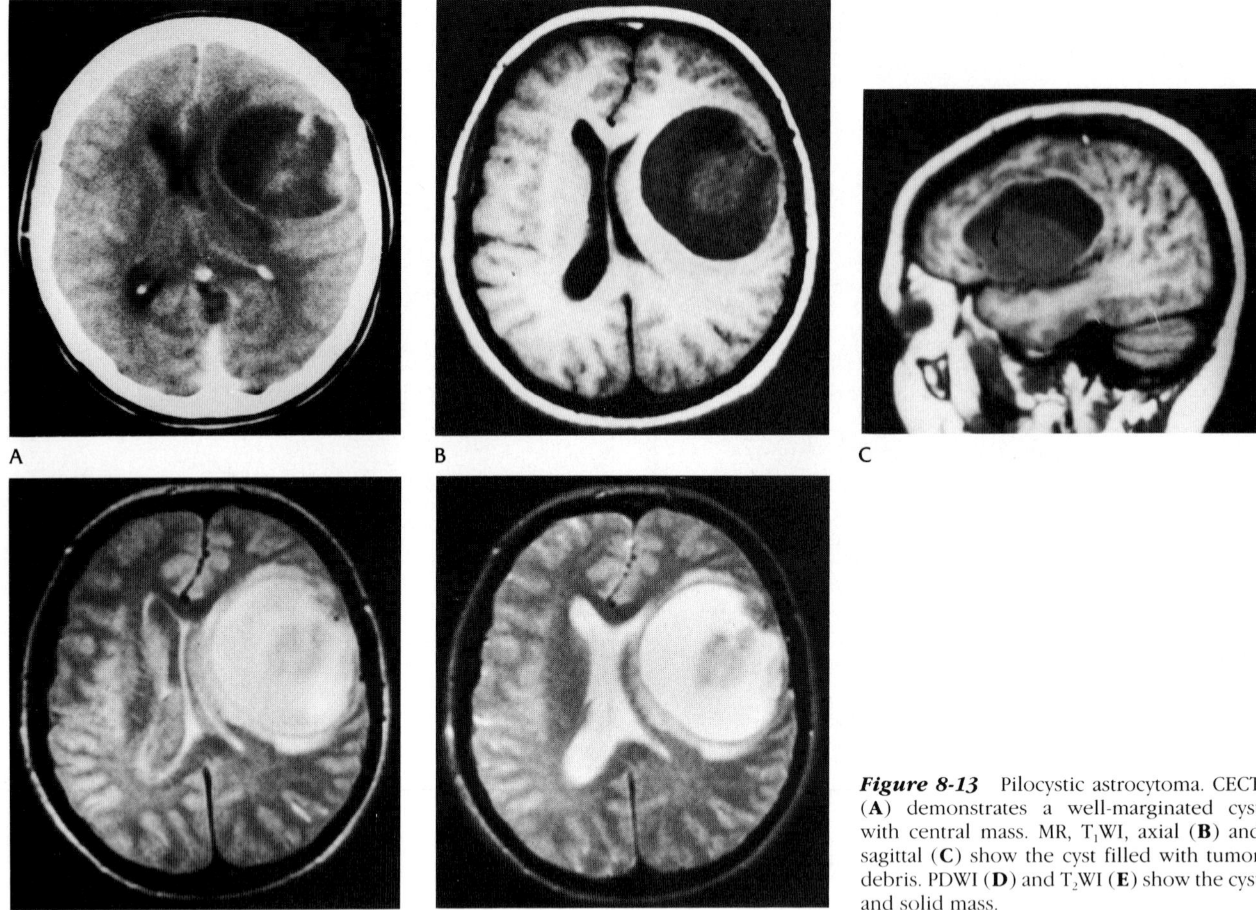

Figure 8-13 Pilocystic astrocytoma. CECT (**A**) demonstrates a well-marginated cyst with central mass. MR, T_1WI, axial (**B**) and sagittal (**C**) show the cyst filled with tumor debris. PDWI (**D**) and T_2WI (**E**) show the cyst and solid mass.

differentiation between cystic and necrotic components may not be possible by density measurements or intensity patterns. True tumor cysts usually have a relatively thin enhancing rim with very smooth inner margins on both CT and MR (Fig. 8-13). Tumor necrosis, which is usually central, typically has very shaggy and irregular inner margins with relatively thick walls on CT (Figs. 8-15 and 8-16). The differentiation of neoplastic cyst (a benign feature) from tumor necrosis (a malignant sign) may be made using delayed CECT: the formation of contrast/fluid levels may be demonstrated in cystic areas but not in necrotic centers (Afra 1980) (Fig. 8-12).

Tans and Jongh (1978) described three types of CECT appearance of astrocytomas: (1) the ring lesion, characterized by an irregular wall of varying thickness surrounding a region of central necrosis; (2) the nodular type, marked by the presence of one or more rounded nodules with fairly sharp margins and homogeneous solid enhancement; and (3) the mixed type, with heterogeneous enhancement distributed irregularly in a low-density lesion. Some high-grade astrocytomas are of the nodular type, with irregular, indistinct margins (Fig. 8-14). Others form multiple irregular rings (Fig. 8-17). In general, the degree of contrast enhancement on both CT (Tans 1978) and MR correlates well with the amount of histologic neovascularity (Fig. 8-18). However, there is less correlation between contrast enhancement noted on CT and MR and neovascularity seen on angiograms (Fig. 8-16). In the annular type, a faintly visible isodense or slightly hyperdense ring may surround the tumor, demarcating it from edema (Fig. 8-15). In the fibrillary astrocytomas the incidence and intensity of enhancement tend to increase with the grade of malignancy. The degree and extent of peritumoral vasogenic edema, ventricular distortion, and mass effect tend to increase with tumor grade. Thomson (1976) suggested that heterogeneous lesions or those with hypodensity are more likely to be rapidly growing tumors of high malignancy, whereas slow-growing tumors may have a hyperdensity pattern, especially one that is homogeneous. However, the usefulness of these distinctions without considering other features is extremely limited.

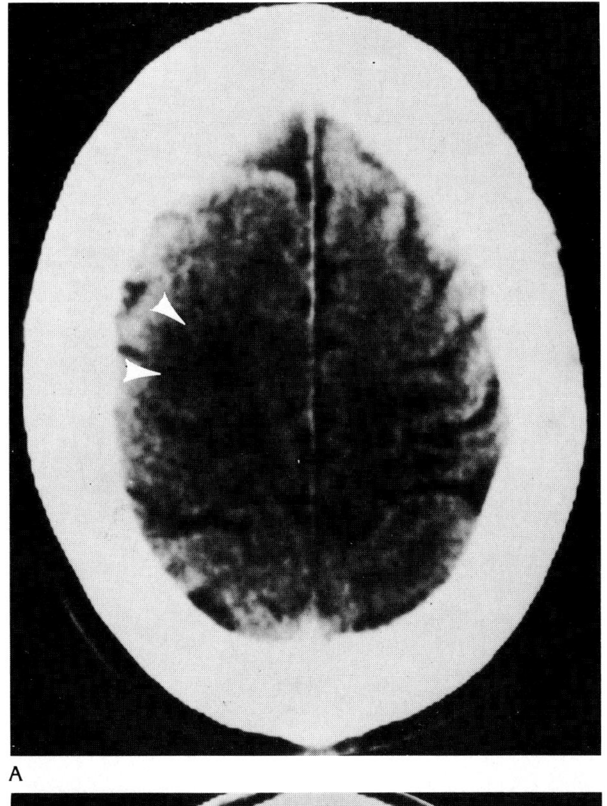
A

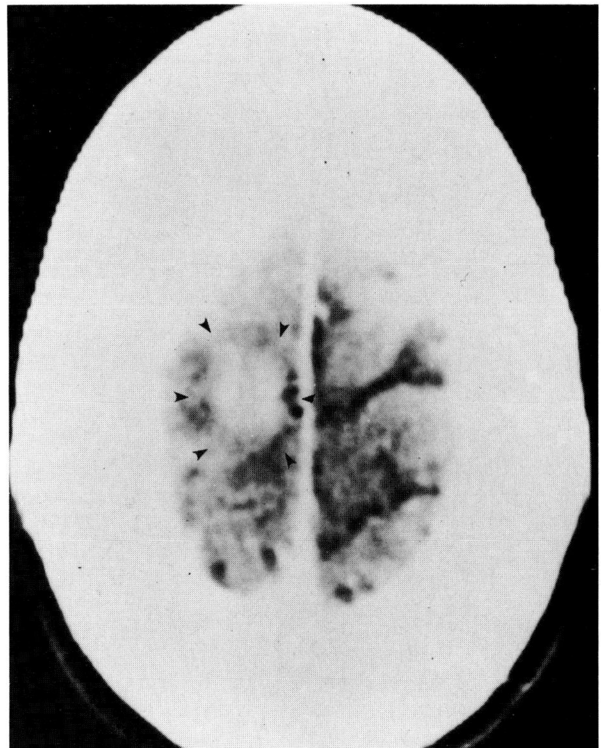
B

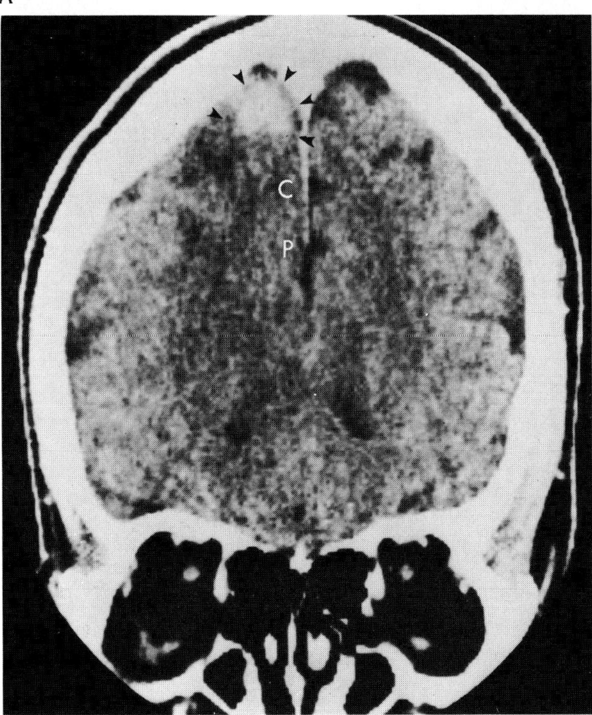

C

Figure 8-14 High-grade astrocytoma: hypodensity with nodular contrast enhancement. **A.** NCCT shows a focal area of hypodensity in the frontoparietal white matter (arrowheads). Effacement of convexity cortical sulci reflects mass effect. **B.** CECT displays a nodular enhancement in the superior border of the tumor (arrowheads). **C.** Coronal CECT exhibits nodular contrast enhancement in the cortex, with irregular hypodense areas underneath indicating deep white-matter involvement. Note effacement of the ipsilateral pericallosal (*P*) and cingulate (*C*) sulci.

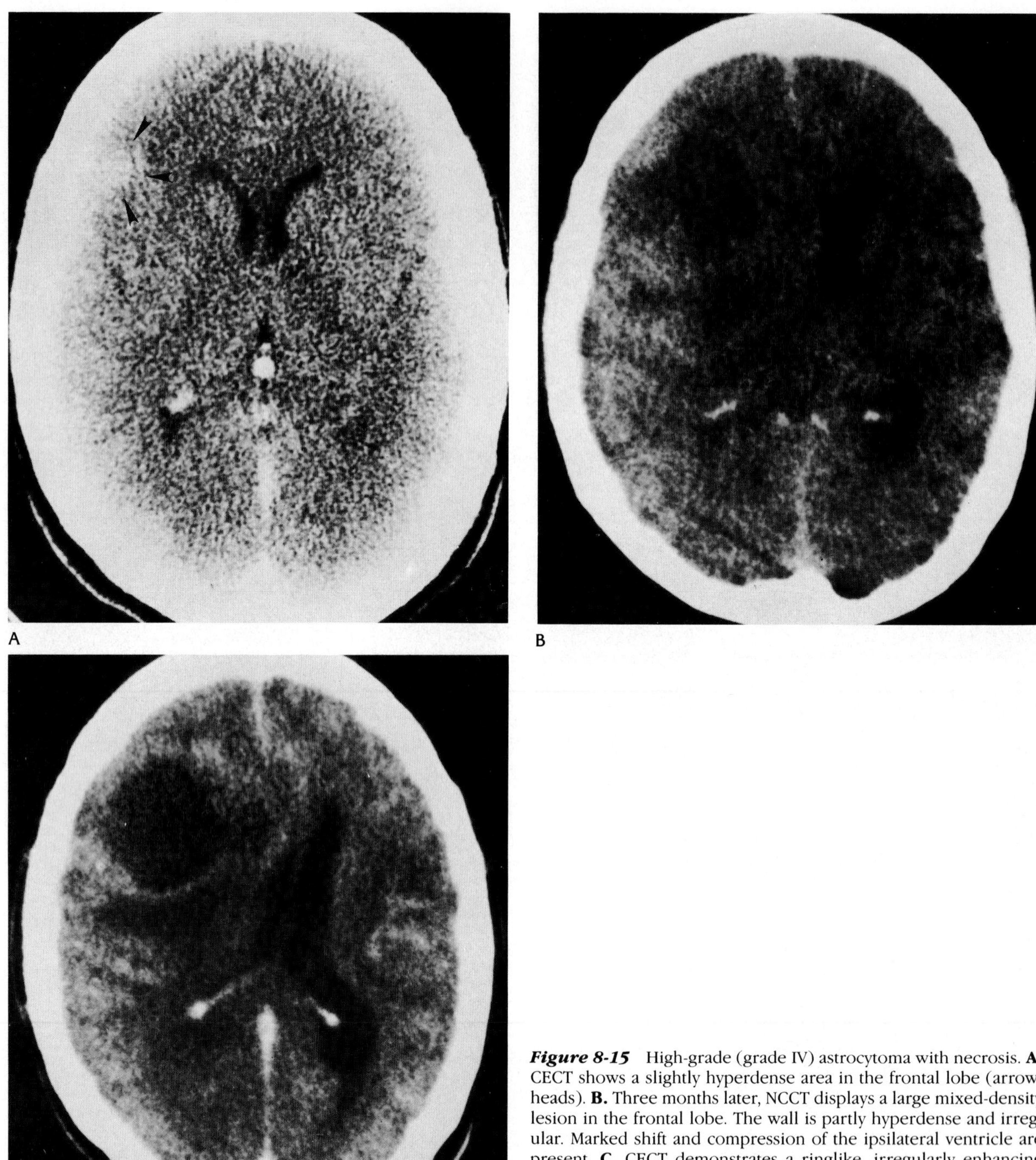

Figure 8-15 High-grade (grade IV) astrocytoma with necrosis. **A.** CECT shows a slightly hyperdense area in the frontal lobe (arrowheads). **B.** Three months later, NCCT displays a large mixed-density lesion in the frontal lobe. The wall is partly hyperdense and irregular. Marked shift and compression of the ipsilateral ventricle are present. **C.** CECT demonstrates a ringlike, irregularly enhancing wall of varying thickness at the periphery of the tumor. The central hypodense area represents necrosis. Minimal surrounding edema is present in the white matter.

Glioblastoma multiforme is rare in persons under the age of 30, and its peak incidence is at about 50 years of age, with males predominating. They constitute 50 percent of all gliomas. At least half of all glioblastomas are thought to arise out of preexisting lower-grade neoplasm. Overwhelmingly, glioblastomas have histologic evidence of astrocytic derivation, and they are considered to be highly malignant (Kernohan grade 4) astrocytomas. Average survival after diagnosis and surgery is 8 to 12 months (Reeves 1979). The anaplastic astrocytoma (Kernohan grade 3) is less common, but has a better prognosis, with a median survival of 28 months. The white matter is usually affected, although the tumor may extend to and through the gray matter, with the most common

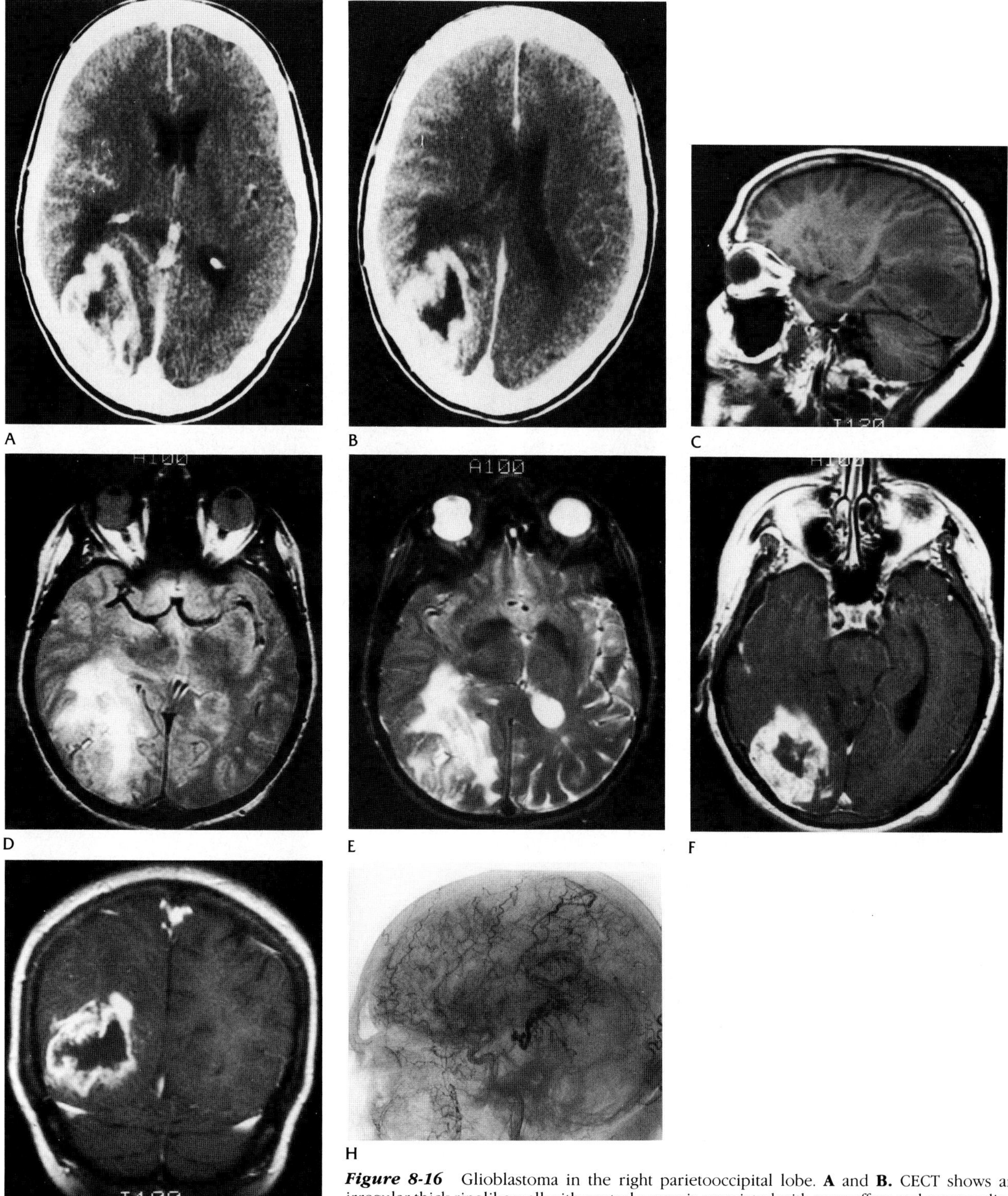

Figure 8-16 Glioblastoma in the right parietooccipital lobe. **A** and **B.** CECT shows an irregular thick ringlike wall with central necrosis associated with mass effect and surrounding edema. **C.** NCMR, T_1WI (sagittal view) shows a slightly hypointense lesion with poorly defined margins. **D.** NCMR, PDWI (axial view) shows an isointense mass. On T_2WI (**E**) the tumor exhibits slight hyperintensity in relation to gray matter. Surrounding edema and mass effect are evident. Axial (**F**) and coronal (**G**) CEMR demonstrate a thick irregular wall with indistinct margination and central hypointensity representing necrosis. **H.** Cerebral angiogram, lateral view, shows tumor vascularity, staining, and early-draining veins.

site being in the frontal lobes. Next in order of frequency are the temporal lobe and basal ganglia or thalamus. The tumor may extend from one area or lobe to another by spreading along the white matter tracts. When the corpus callosum is infiltrated by the tumor, a bihemispheric "butterfly" pattern may be seen in coronal sections and, if the genu or splenium is involved, on axial sections. It should be emphasized that almost three-fourths of all "butterfly" masses are gliomas, with high-grade astrocytomas the most frequent type. Grossly, a high-grade astro-

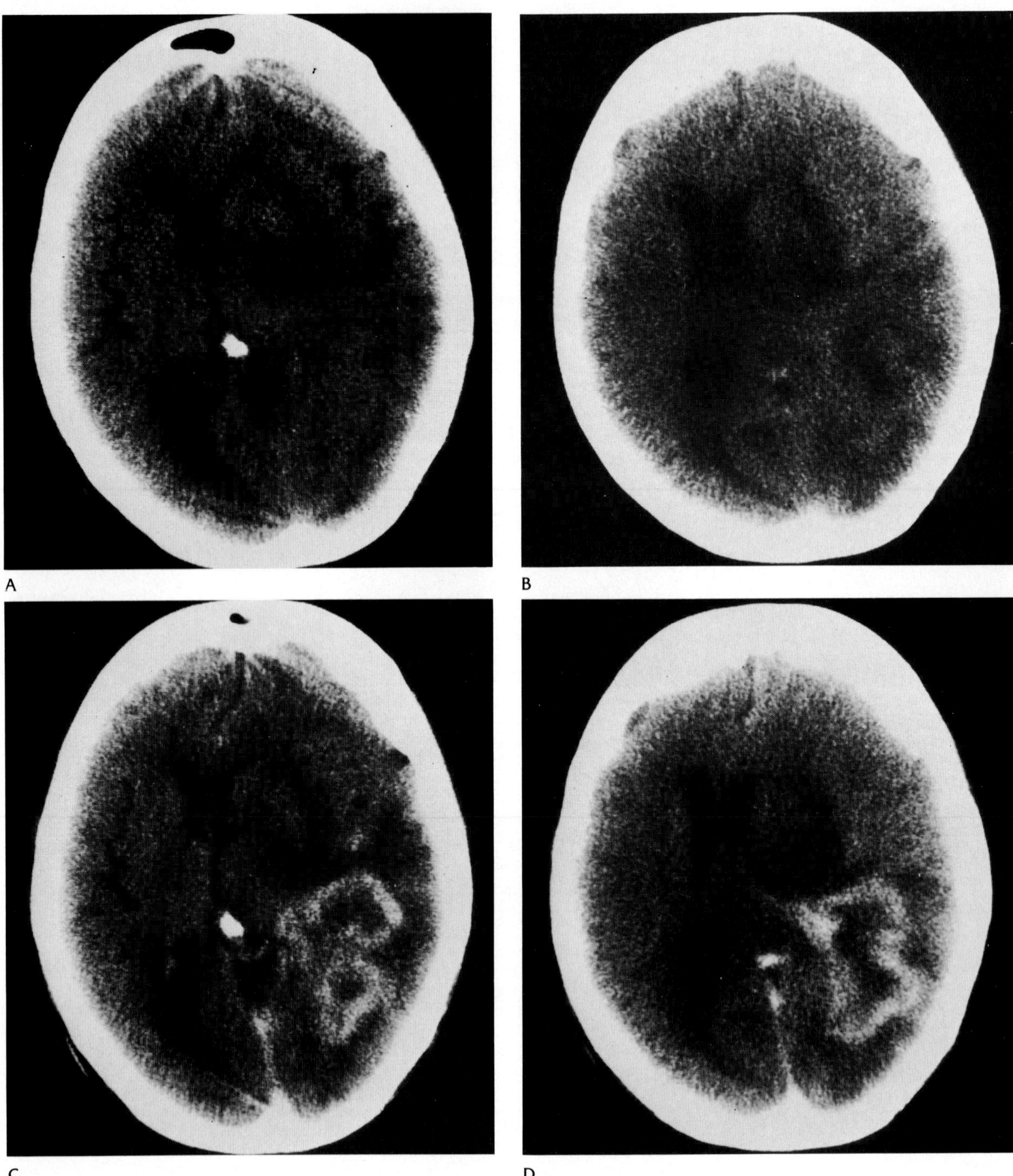

Figure 8-17 Glioblastoma multiforme in the temporooccipital lobe. **A.** and **B.** NCCT demonstrates ventricular compression and shift of the midline structures. A large mixed-density (isodense and hypodense) area is noted in the left temporooccipital lobe (**C** and **D**). On CECT, the central necrotic area is surrounded by a thick, irregular wall of ameboid appearance. Note the involvement of the ventricular wall and extension into the choroid plexus. (*Continued on p. 319.*)

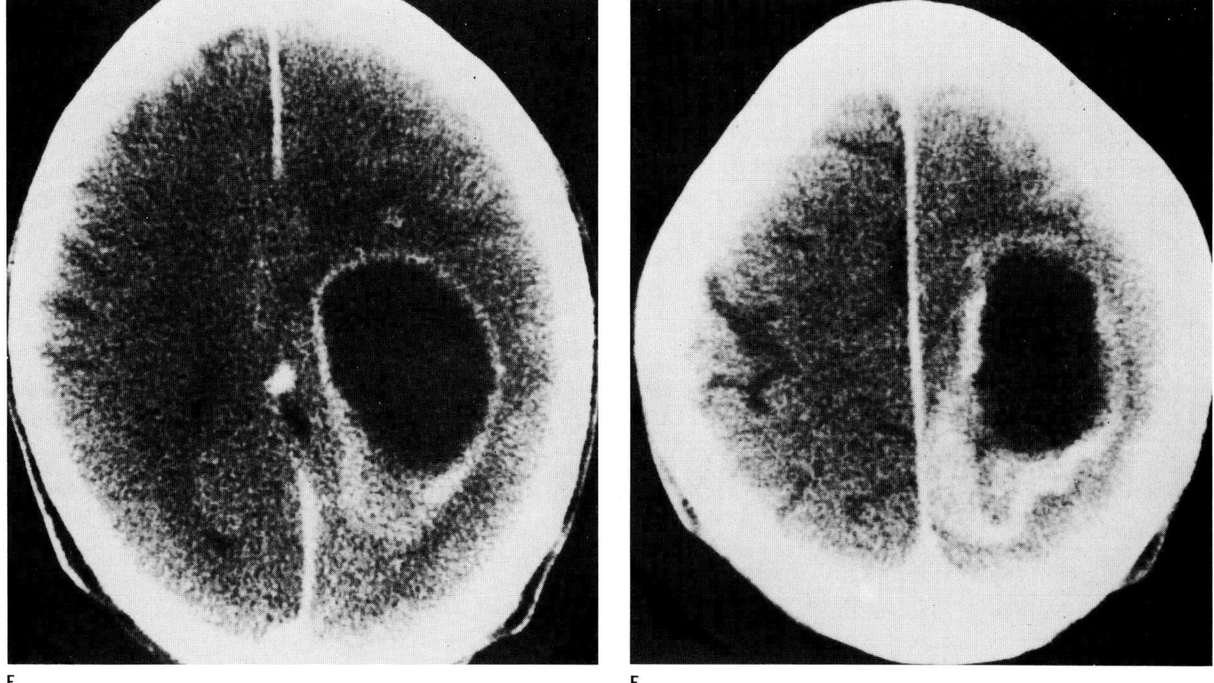

E F

Figure 8-17 ***(continued)*** **E** and **F.** Glioblastoma with central cystic cavity. CECT (**E**) demonstrates a large oval lesion with a relatively thin enhancing rim and a large central hypodense area. Posteriorly the rim shows an irregular thick wall. At a higher level (**F**), an irregular thick wall is well shown. Surgery revealed a large cyst of a clear yellowish fluid within the tumor.

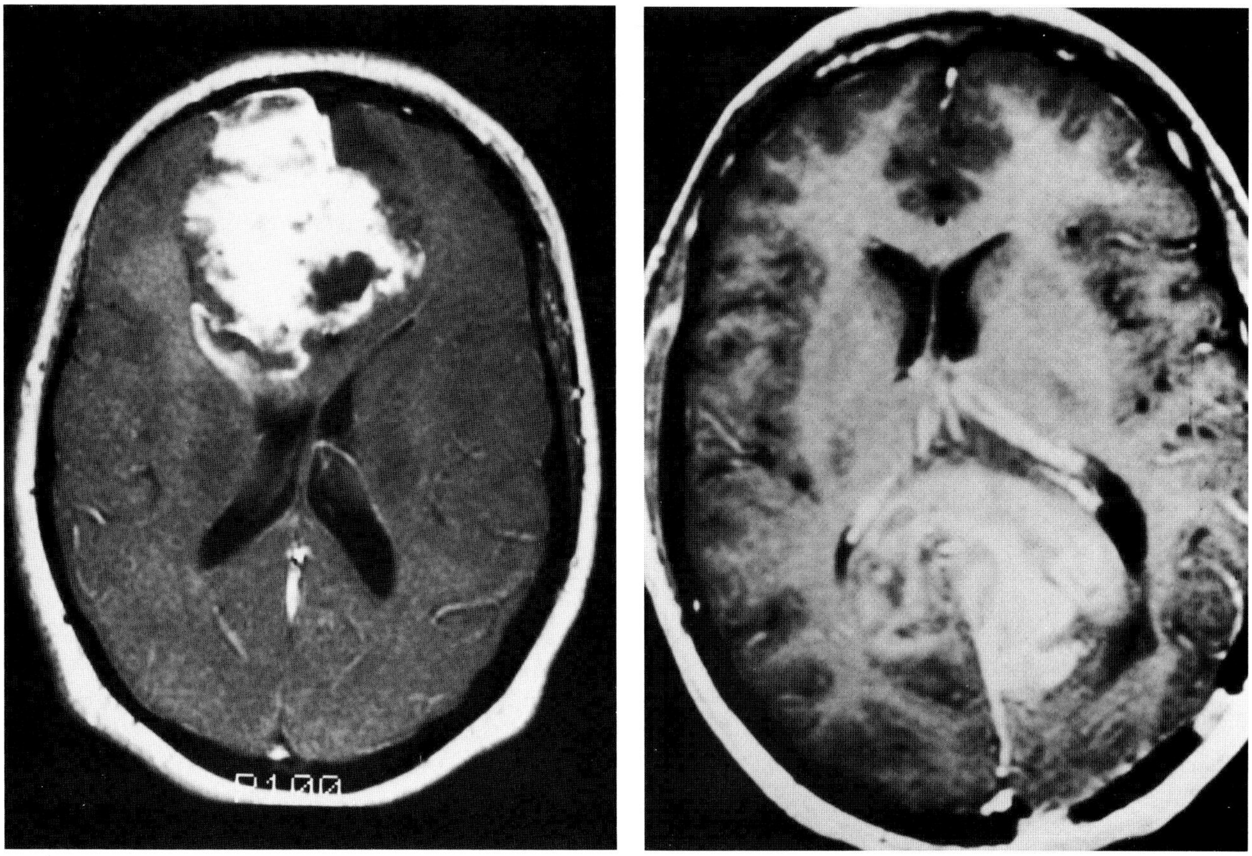

A B

Figure 8-18 Glioma of the corpus callosum (butterfly glioma). CEMR: involvement of the genu extending into the ventricle (**A**) and involvement of the splenium in another patient (**B**).

cytoma is heterogeneous. It often has a creamy yellow center of necrosis with a variegated surface, surrounded by the more solid and viable portions of the neoplasm. On gross inspection at surgery or autopsy, rapidly growing glioblastomas (grade 4) and anaplastic astrocytomas (grade 3) may appear to be well demarcated from the surrounding brain parenchyma. However, careful microscopic analysis of both types invariably reveals islands of neoplastic cells remote from the perceived gross margins. Because of tumor heterogeneity and sampling error, a clear histologic distinction between glioblastoma and anaplastic astrocytoma may not always be possible—a fact that compounds the difficulty of imaging correlation.

Compared to the brain, the glioblastoma density on NCCT may be increased (8.5 to 18 percent), decreased (11.8 to 27 percent), isodense (14.4 to 16.5 percent), or mixed (38.5 to 65.3 percent) (Steinhoff 1977, 1978). Heterogenous mixed density is the most frequent CT appearance prior to contrast injection (Fig. 8-17). Calcification is not a common feature in glioblastoma, but it can occur, either as a dystrophic process or because the tumor arose out of a preexisting benign glioma. Almost all glioblastomas will enhance on imaging studies. The frequency of contrast enhancement on CT varies from 91 percent (Tchang 1977) to 100 percent (Steinhoff 1978). However, in the early years of CT, a few hypodense and nonenhancing glioblastomas were reported (Tchang 1977; Steinhoff 1977). According to Steinhoff (1978), the annular type with central hypodensity is the most frequent pattern (55 percent) (Figs. 8-16 and 8-17). The annular zone of hyperdensity represents the hypercellular, solid, and well-vascularized portion of the neoplasm, while the central zone of hypodensity usually corresponds to an avascular area of tumor necrosis, or, less commonly, intramural cyst (Fig. 8-17). The enhanced rim of a glioblastoma is usually thick (more than 5 mm) and irregular, with a shaggy inner margin (Fig. 8-17). This can be a differential feature of neoplasm compared with abscess; the latter usually has a thin, uniform rim of enhancement with a smooth inner wall. The mixed type of enhancement, the second most frequent manifestation (27 percent), is characterized by zones of variable density and heterogeneous enhancement of the glioblastoma (Fig. 8-17). The pathologic substrate of this type consists of an intermingling of solid and necrotic parts. The nodular pattern of enhancement (18 percent) represents a homogeneous solid tumor without cavitation, which can easily be differentiated from surrounding edema on CECT. This pattern, without cavitation or necrosis, is suggestive of an anaplastic (grade 3) astrocytoma rather than a grade 4 glioblastoma, but can be seen in smaller glioblastomas (under 3 cm in diameter).

Perifocal vasogenic edema occurs because of the abnormally increased permeability of the tumor's neovascularity. The vasogenic edema expands the subcortical white matter, typically creating a "digital," "pseudopod," or "garland" configuration (Figs. 8-16 and 8-17). Although this pattern is common from any cause of neovascularity, it is especially frequent around malignant gliomas and metastases. A pattern of perifocal vasogenic edema is seen in 88 percent of glioblastomas on CT (Steinhoff 1978), and is virtually universal on long TR (PD or T_2-weighted) MR scans. Grading the extent of edema has been considered to be helpful: grade 1 when its margin has a width of 2 cm or less, grade 2 when it includes up to half of the hemisphere, and grade 3 when it is larger than half of the hemisphere. In glioblastomas, grade 1 and 2 edemas predominate, but no correlation between the frequency or grade of edema and the specific histology of intracranial neoplasms has been found (Tchang 1977).

Astrocytomas on MR

MRI has improved the detection and localization of intrinsic primary glial tumors, but has not yet been proven to add specificity beyond what can be obtained with CT. Generally speaking, MR in suspected CNS gliomas is obtained in at least two planes (usually axial and coronal) and is almost invariably augmented with contrast enhancement (Gd-DPTA). The signal abnormalities produced by glial neoplasms can be subdivided into five types: intrinsic neoplasm; neoplasm-associated cysts; necrotic neoplasm; neoplasm-induced neovascularity with BBB breakdown and contrast enhancement; and neoplasm-produced edema, usually vasogenic. Most of these are associated with an increase in brain water and a corresponding prolongation of both T_1 and T_2 relaxation times, which typically produces slight decreases in signal intensity on T_1WI and pronounced increased signal intensity on T_2WI. Investigators from the Mayo Clinic (Kelly 1988) have described three different patterns on MR of brain gliomas, roughly corresponding to low-grade (benign) glioma, anaplastic glioma, and glioblastoma multiforme.

Low-grade (benign) gliomas (Kernohan grade 1–2) are usually seen as nonenhancing homogeneous areas of T_2 prolongation (Kelly 1988) (Fig. 8-20). Dean (1990) described low-grade astrocytoma as a nonhemorrhagic well-defined mass, usually with little mass effect. MR appears more sensitive than CT in that it may demonstrate signal abnormalities in regions of microscopic infiltrations (beyond the boundaries of the solid neoplasm) that are normal on CT (Figs. 8-19 and 8-20). However, tumor infiltration even beyond the MR signal abnormalities is often present. Scott (1991) stated that solid low-grade tumors generally demonstrate hyperintensity on PD-WI, but cystic or necrotic zones usually do not. However, without identifying a fluid-fluid level, the distinction between "cyst" and "solid" could be extremely difficult on both CT and MR (Abrahms 1989). Abrahms classified fluid levels as fluid-precipitate level, air-fluid level, and fat-fluid

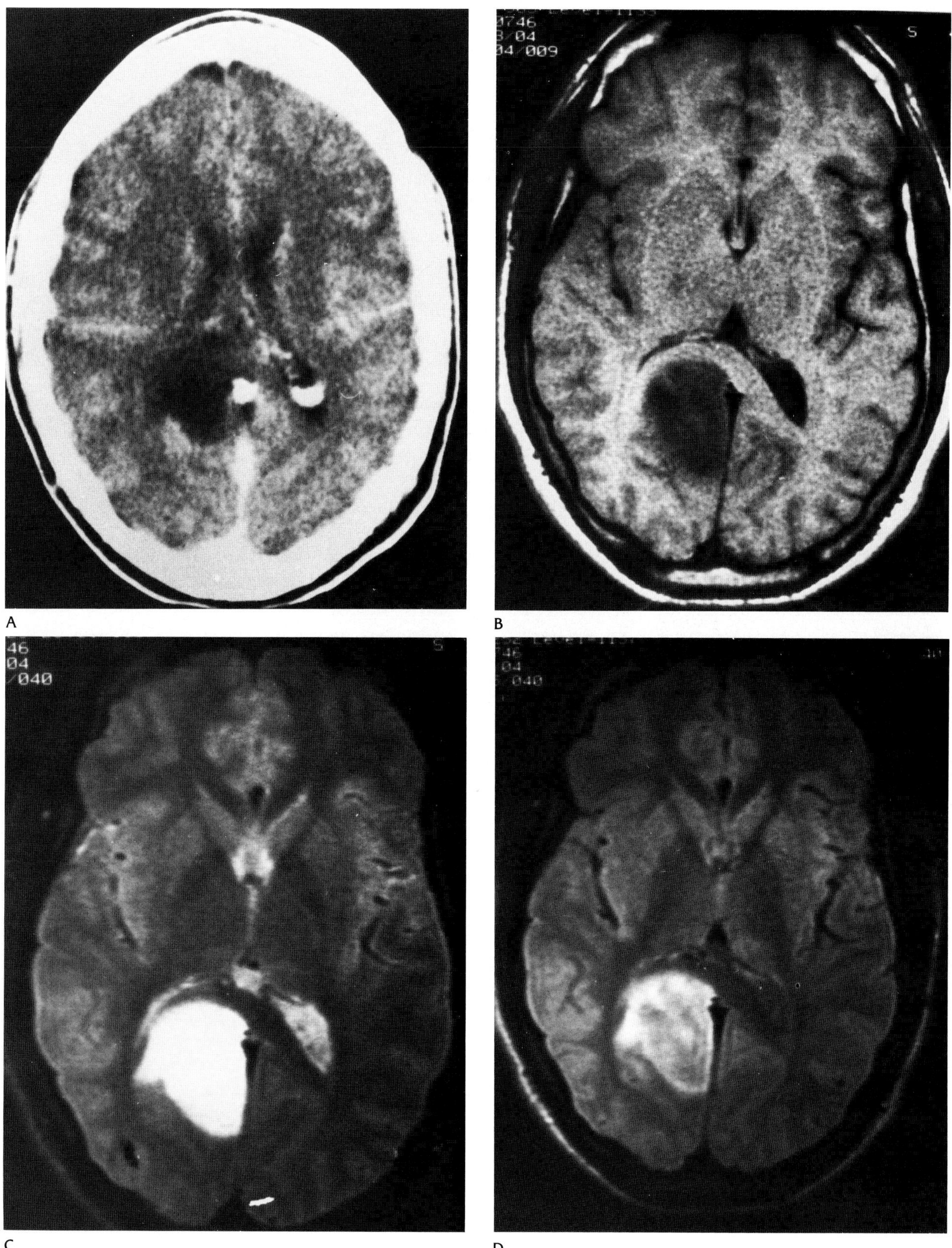

Figure 8-19 Low-grade astrocytoma. **A.** CECT shows a well-marginated hypodense lesion in the right parietal lobe with minimal contrast enhancement at the periphery. On NCMR (**B**) the hypointense lesion increases in intensity on T_2WI (**C**). PDWI (**D**) shows nonhomogeneity of the tumor.

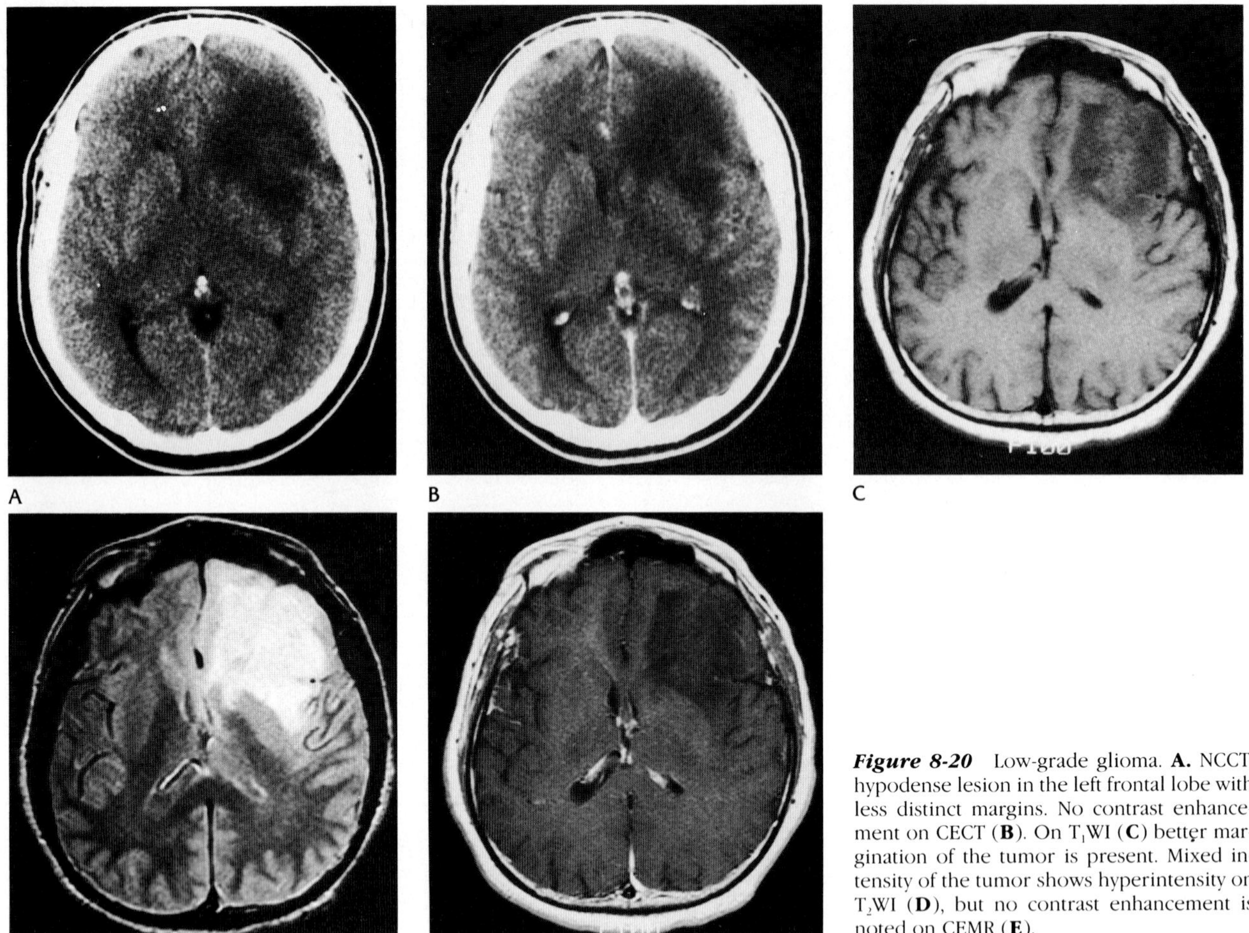

Figure 8-20 Low-grade glioma. **A.** NCCT: hypodense lesion in the left frontal lobe with less distinct margins. No contrast enhancement on CECT (**B**). On T_1WI (**C**) better margination of the tumor is present. Mixed intensity of the tumor shows hyperintensity on T_2WI (**D**), but no contrast enhancement is noted on CEMR (**E**).

level on MR. The appearance of fluid levels on MR varies with their composition, the ratio of the components, the sequence parameters, and the position of the patient.

Anaplastic gliomas (Kernohan grade 3) are usually homogeneous areas of increased signal on T_2WI (Kelly 1987). However, Dean (1990) indicates that these tend to be more often heterogeneous and less well defined than low-grade astrocytomas, and have more mass effect and vasogenic edema. Contrast enhancement with Gd-DTPA is common, but variable (Fig. 8-21). Although MR is more sensitive than CT for neoplastic infiltration, tumors may also extend beyond the limits of the lesion as defined on MR (Ernest 1988).

Glioblastoma multiforme (Kernohan grade 4) is usually identified on MR as a heterogeneous lesion that can be divided into four zones (Kelly 1987). The innermost region, central necrosis, is hypodense on CT and shows prolongation of both T_1 and T_2 relaxation times (more hypointense than brain on T_1WI and more hyperintense on T_2WI). The second zone is the solid, viable, fleshy, and hypercellular portion of the neoplasm. This is also the area of greatest tumor-induced neovascularity. This region shows contrast enhancement forming an irregular ring on both CT and MR (Fig. 8-22) and is often hypervascular on angiography (Fig. 8-16). Ring enhancement in glioblastomas usually has thick walls of varying width and a very shaggy inner margin—the interface between living tumor and necrotic debris. The solid ring of neoplastic tissue occasionally shows slight hyperdensity on NCCT and may display a corresponding decreased signal intensity on both PD- and T_2WI. The exact mechanism for these changes is not established, but potential causes include the increased tissue density of the glial cells as well as the blood, connective tissue, and dense vascular proliferations characteristic of glioblastoma. Dean (1990) emphasized that one of the MR features that distinguishes the anaplastic (grade 3) astrocytoma from the glioblastoma (grade 4) is hemosiderin or other evidence of prior hemorrhage. It must be emphasized that routine MR, even with contrast enhancement, depicts only the gross macroscopic boundaries of the tumor. Neoplastic infiltration of malignant glial cells commonly extends well beyond the limits of any MR-detected abnormality (Kelly 1987; Earnest 1988).

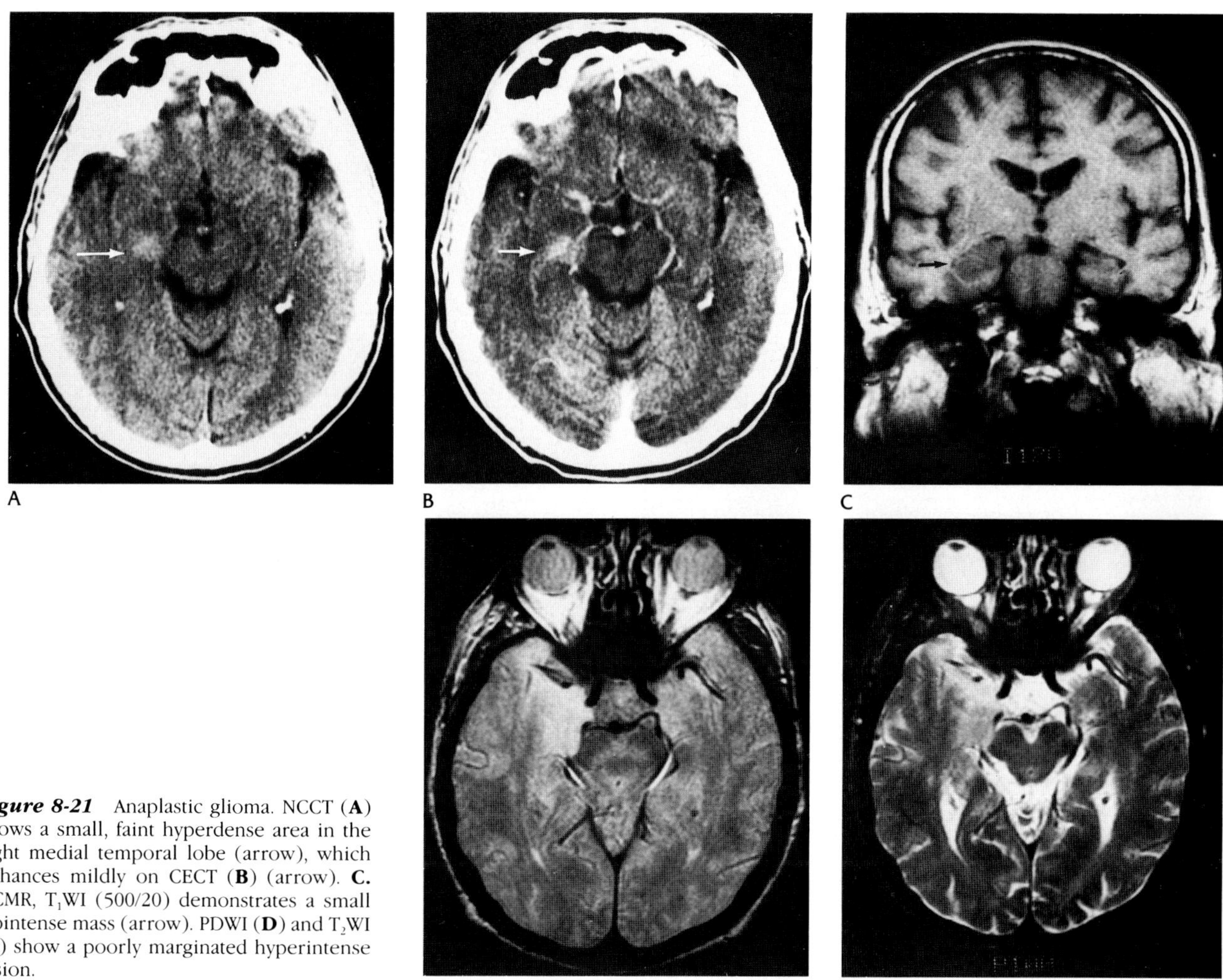

Figure 8-21 Anaplastic glioma. NCCT (**A**) shows a small, faint hyperdense area in the right medial temporal lobe (arrow), which enhances mildly on CECT (**B**) (arrow). **C.** NCMR, T_1WI (500/20) demonstrates a small isointense mass (arrow). PDWI (**D**) and T_2WI (**E**) show a poorly marginated hyperintense lesion.

Beyond the signal intensity abnormalities, which are quite nonspecific, it is the morphology and location of astrocytomas that frequently suggest the correct diagnosis. Spread across the corpus callosum (Fig. 8-18) strongly suggests an astrocytic glioma, although a similar pattern of spread can be seen in primary CNS lymphoma.

OLIGODENDROGLIOMA

Oligodendroglioma is a relatively uncommon neoplasm that arises from the oligodendrocytes of the CNS. The oligodendrocytes are supportive cells that make the central myelin; in the peripheral nervous system myelin is made by the Schwann cells. Oligodendrogliomas constitute 1 to 9 percent of all intracranial gliomas. They can present at almost any age, but they are most commonly identified in adults, especially in the fourth and fifth decades (35 to 45 years old). There is a slight male predominance of 5 to 4. They are very slowly growing tumors, and can attain remarkable size before making the patient sufficiently symptomatic to initiate medical evaluation. The clinical symptoms in these patients may be years or even decades in duration. Undoubtedly, with the proliferation of noninvasive imaging, smaller and smaller lesions will be found. Despite their slow growth rate and prolonged clinical history, survival after diagnosis and treatment is less than 50 percent at 5 years.

Oligodendrogliomas are distributed throughout the CNS in rough approximation to the volume of neural tissue. Thus the frontal lobes, which are the largest, are the most common site of origin for oligodendroglioma (38 percent). The temporal lobe is a close second, containing slightly more than one-third of all oligodendrogliomas, followed by the parietal lobe. They are uncommon in the cerebellum and distinctly rare in the brainstem. Oligodendrogliomas are, like all other gliomas, unencapsulated and infiltrating neoplasms (Russell 1989). However, they tend to grow by expansion and are not as likely to spread along the white matter tracts as the astrocytomas.

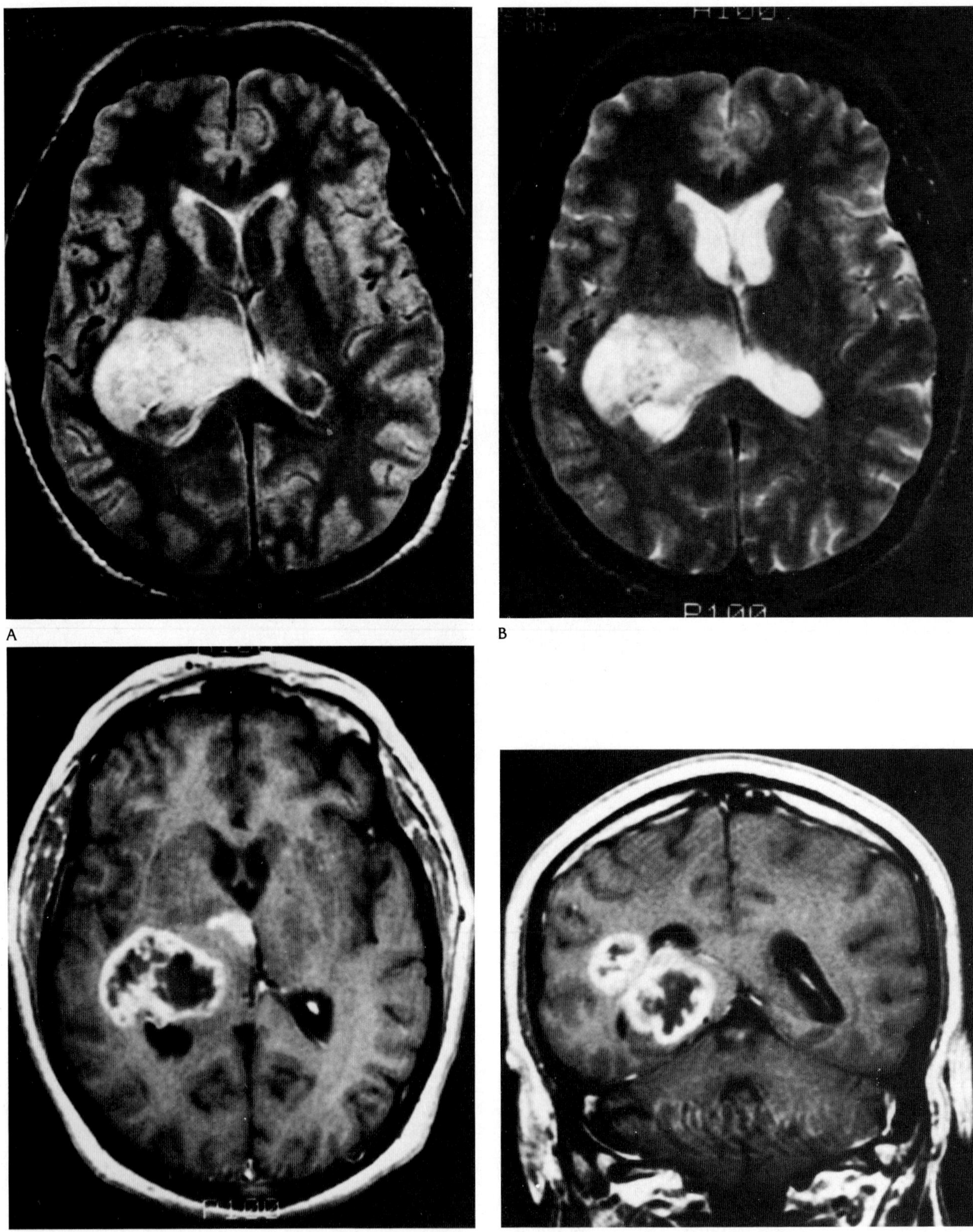

Figure 8-22 Glioblastoma multiforme. NCMR: On PDWI (**A**) and T_2WI (**B**) the tumor shows sharp margination and is relatively homogeneous. CEMR: On axial (**C**) and coronal (**D**) views, multiple contiguous foci of irregular ring enhancement with central necrosis are present.

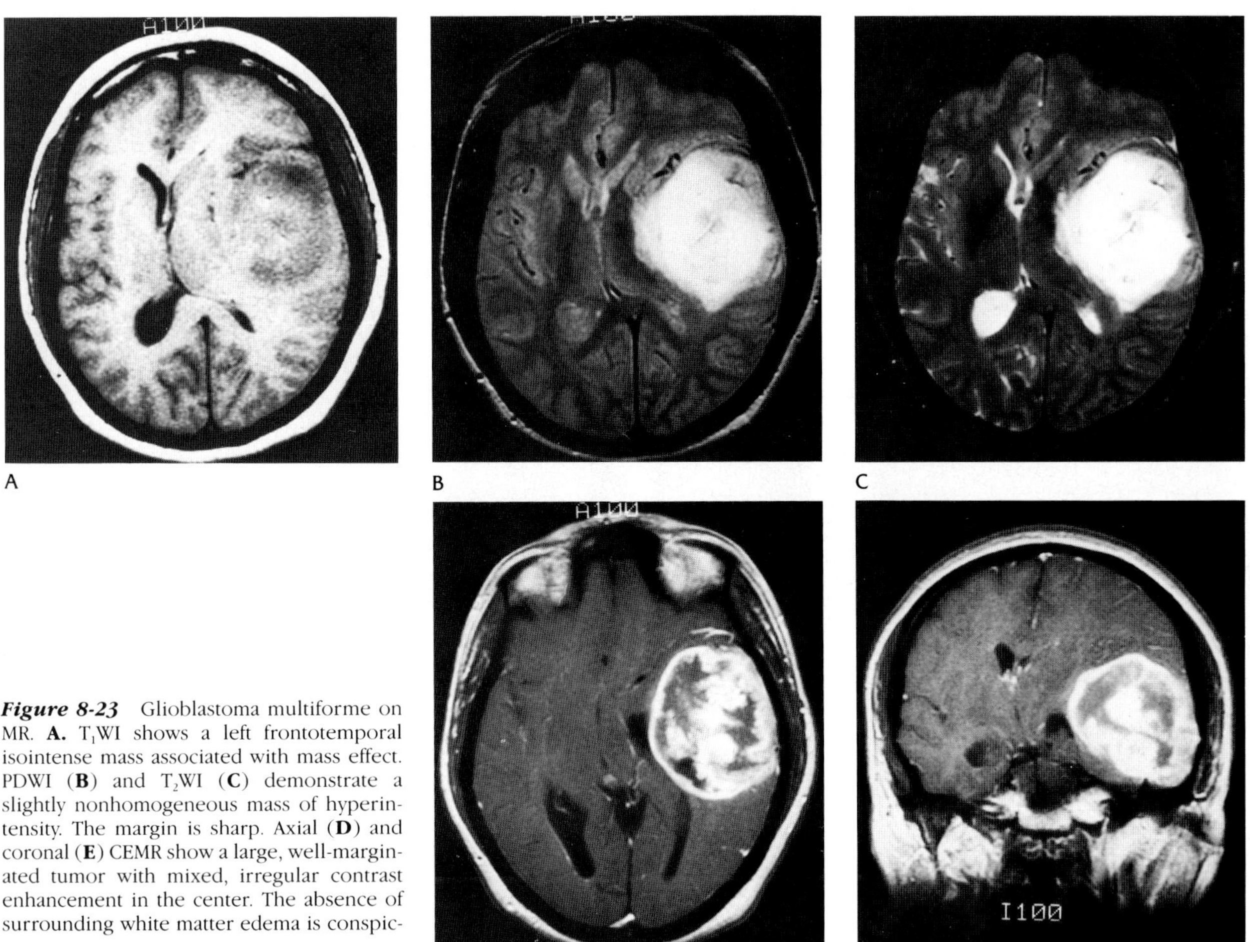

Figure 8-23 Glioblastoma multiforme on MR. **A.** T_1WI shows a left frontotemporal isointense mass associated with mass effect. PDWI (**B**) and T_2WI (**C**) demonstrate a slightly nonhomogeneous mass of hyperintensity. The margin is sharp. Axial (**D**) and coronal (**E**) CEMR show a large, well-marginated tumor with mixed, irregular contrast enhancement in the center. The absence of surrounding white matter edema is conspicuous.

Oligodendrogliomas are rarely seen as pure tumors. Most commonly there is an associated component of astrocytic proliferation as well, which is usually benign. It is also common for a neoplasm which is largely astrocytic to have areas of oligodendrocytic proliferation. The components that are characteristic of other glial cell types may be either reactive or neoplastic. When more than 75 percent of a tumor is composed of neoplastic oligodendrocytes, the tumor is an oligodendroglioma. When the majority cell type is less than 75 percent, the tumor is called a "mixed glioma." It should be mentioned that a somewhat histologically similar tumor often seen in the midline of the cerebral hemispheres, arising near the septum pellucidum or the third ventricle, is commonly mistaken for an oligodendroglioma. This "mimic" is properly known as a *central neurocytoma*—a tumor of mature neurons, not a glioma at all. Although most oligodendrogliomas arise in the white matter, they have a marked tendency to extend to, and through, the cerebral cortex. There they may spread along the surface of the cerebrum in a subpial location, or, less commonly, into the subarachnoid space.

There have been many attempts to grade oligodendrogliomas like the astrocytomas; however, the only generally accepted differentiation is between the histologically benign oligodendrogliomas and the more aggressive or malignant "anaplastic" oligodendrogliomas.

Grossly, oligodendrogliomas are heterogeneous masses, regardless of their histologic grade. In addition to the solid cellular portions of the tumor, areas of mucoid or myxoid accumulation are often formed. These myxoid lakes make the tumor appear partially cystic. Oligodendrogliomas have a fine capillary meshwork of neovascularity. These vessels are usually too small to be seen angiographically or as signal voids on MR; however, they may produce spontaneous hemorrhage, which is a common feature of oligodendroglioma. Multiple hemorrhages of various sizes and ages may be present, adding to the heterogeneity of these neoplasms. Calcification within the neoplasm is the hallmark of oligodendrogliomas, and the reported frequency varies with the sensitivity of the imaging technique. On skull radiograph almost 47 percent of oligodendrogliomas have discernible calcification (Kalan 1962). The detection frequency for

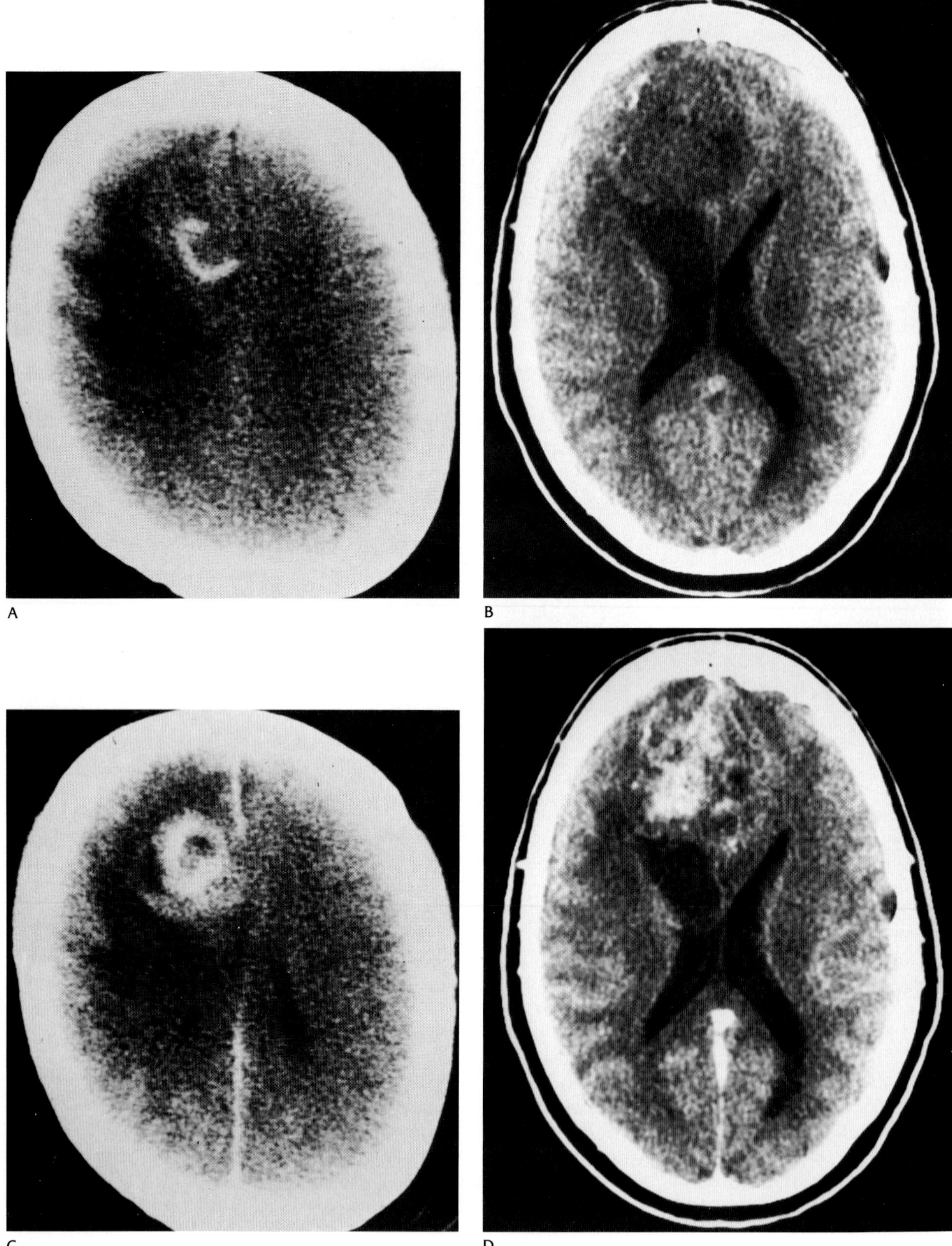

Figure 8-24 Different calcification patterns of oligodendroglioma on CT. NCCT: **A** and **B** show a nonhomogeneous region with calcification. CECT: **C** and **D** show mixed contrast enhancement.

calcification rises to 91 percent on CT (Vonofakos 1979), and is an almost universal finding on histologic examination. Calcification may be in the form of calcospherites or of deposits within the microvasculature of the neoplasm. Calcification can occur anywhere within the neoplasm, but is especially common where the tumor has infiltrated into the cortical gray matter, where it may form an irregular gyriform ribbon.

In contrast to low-grade astrocytomas, which are usually homogeneous, even benign oligodendrogliomas are heterogeneous masses on imaging. On NCCT, they are commonly seen as mixtures of hypodensity, isodensity, calcification, and occasionally hemorrhage. The hypodensity is produced by the areas of mucoid or myxoid change mentioned above. Mass effect may be appropriate for the size of the lesion, but can be less than expected, and edema may be only slight to moderate. Calcification is often nodular and can be massive and central within the tumor; however, curvilinear peripheral (gyral) "dot-dash" patterns are also reported (Vonofakos 1979) (Figs. 8-24 and 8-25). Calcification, especially if it is finely stippled or diffuse, can be difficult to detect on MR. Although oligodendrogliomas are the most commonly calcified of all gliomas, because of their relative rarity, other gliomas should be considered when a calcified neoplasm is identified on NCCT. Astrocytoma and ependymoma should always be included in the discussion of any mineralizing parenchymal neoplasm, as well as metastatic adenocarcinoma and sarcomas. Another distinguishing feature of oligodendroglioma is the presence of scalloped erosion of the inner table of the calvarium (Fig. 8-25). Calvarial erosion may be noted in at least one-third of oligodendrogliomas, and is related to two intrinsic features: (1) chronicity from a slow rate of growth without symptomatic neurologic dysfunction and (2) proximity of the neoplasm to the inner table from a pronounced tendency to extend out toward and through the cerebral cortex (Lee 1989). However, these features are not pathognomonic for oligodendroglioma and are also observed in slow-growing benign astrocytomas, as well as in gangliogliomas and other neoplasms.

On CECT, there is heterogeneous enhancement, which may be in a thick and irregular ring, often at the periphery, which is sometimes described as "connecting the

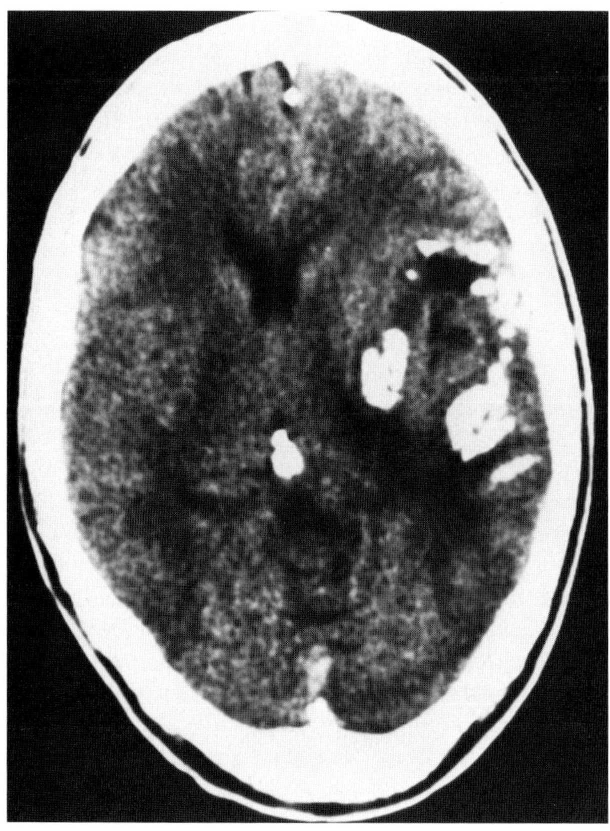

A

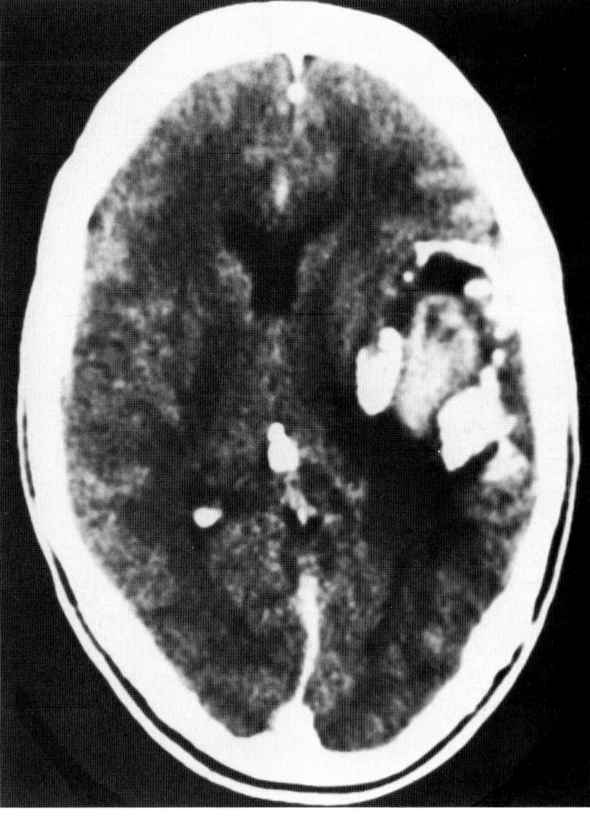

B

Figure 8-25 Oligodendroglioma (benign) of the parietal lobe. **A.** NCCT shows large chunks of calcification, "cystic" areas, and some regions isodense to brain, all in a mass that extends to the cortical surface. **B.** On CECT the previously isodense areas enhance; the "cystic" areas do not. (*Continued on p. 328.*)

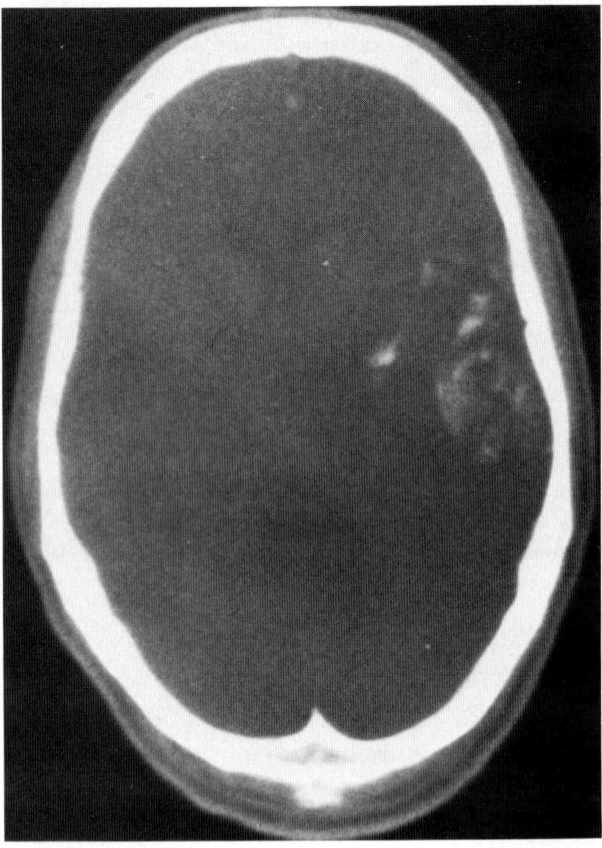

C

Figure 8-25 (continued) **C.** Bone windows reveal the expansile nature of the mass with slight enlargement of the hemicrania and erosion of the inner table, features that suggest chronicity in the mass. Calcification is evident.

dots" between areas of calcification noted on the preinfusion images. The nonenhancing areas may represent the myxoid regions or cystic degeneration (Figs. 8-24 and 8-25). Occasionally a fluid-fluid level or a blood-fluid level may be noted within the substance of the tumor. Vonofakos et al. (1979) reported that all cases with contrast enhancement and a cystic component (fluid-fluid level) noted on CT were malignant histologically. However, this might be accepted with caution, since the histologic grading system is not as clearly established in oligodendrogliomas as in astrocytomas. In our experience, benign oligodendrogliomas may also enhance. In addition to spontaneous hemorrhage, oligodendrogliomas may be complicated by CSF metastasis.

On MR, the oligodendroglioma presents as a mass that is usually heterogeneous on all pulse sequences (Lee 1989). The lesion is typically in the frontal lobe and may extend to the cortical surface. Hyperintensity from previous hemorrhage may be noted on T_1WI. In some cases there may be one or several large chunks of calcification that are hypointense on all spin-echo sequences (Fig. 8-26). However, it may be necessary to use a gradient-echo technique to identify small calcifications or diffuse fine calcifications. The gradient-echo technique may also enhance the detection of hemosiderin, which is indicative of subacute or chronic hemorrhage. It may be difficult to recognize the erosive calvarial changes produced by an oligodendroglioma on MR.

CHOROID PLEXUS TUMORS

Choroid plexus tumors usually have a papillary appearance under the microscope and may be histologically benign (choroid plexus papilloma) or malignant (choroid plexus carcinoma). They arise from the choroid epithelium, and are therefore sometimes considered to be variants or subcategories of ependymoma. The male predominance varies from as high as 2 to 1 to 3 to 2 or less. Choroid plexus tumors account for less than 1 percent of all intracranial gliomas. However, they represent about 4 percent of those that present in childhood, and 10 to 20 percent of all intracranial neoplasms seen in the first year of life. Eighty-five percent present below the age of 10, and a significant number are noted in infancy, at birth, or even in utero. They are uncommon in adults. Overall, the lateral ventricle, especially the trigone, is the most common location (38 percent) for choroid plexus papillomas (Zulch 1986). In addition, almost half of all intraventricular masses in this location are papillomas, and virtually all trigonal masses in childhood are either papillomas or carcinomas (Jelinek 1990). In adults, however, the fourth and third ventricles are the predominant locations, in that order (Fig. 8-27). It should be remembered that papillomas in the posterior fossa may occur anywhere along the course of the normal choroid, including its extension along the lateral recesses, and even through the foramina of Luschka and Magendie into the cerebellopontine angle and cisterna magna, respectively. Grossly the tumor is usually globular, sometimes rounded and smooth and sometimes lobulated. Despite the gross appearance, close inspection reveals an irregular surface. Occasionally the tumor may macroscopically or microscopically invade the adjacent brain.

On NCCT the tumor usually presents as a well-demarcated smooth or lobulated mass of relatively homogeneous increased density. Mechanical effects of the tumor may cause local expansion of the surrounding ventricle. However, papillomas can produce hydrocephalus with panventricular enlargement. There are two mechanisms. First, papillomas may produce excessive quantities of CSF, duplicating the normal function of the choroid plexus. Second, these extremely vascular tumors are somewhat friable and thus prone to hemorrhage. Previous episodes of hemorrhage can lead to arachnoiditis in the skull base or plugging of the reabsorption pathway through the arachnoid granulations—both of which result in a communicating hydrocephalus. Following con-

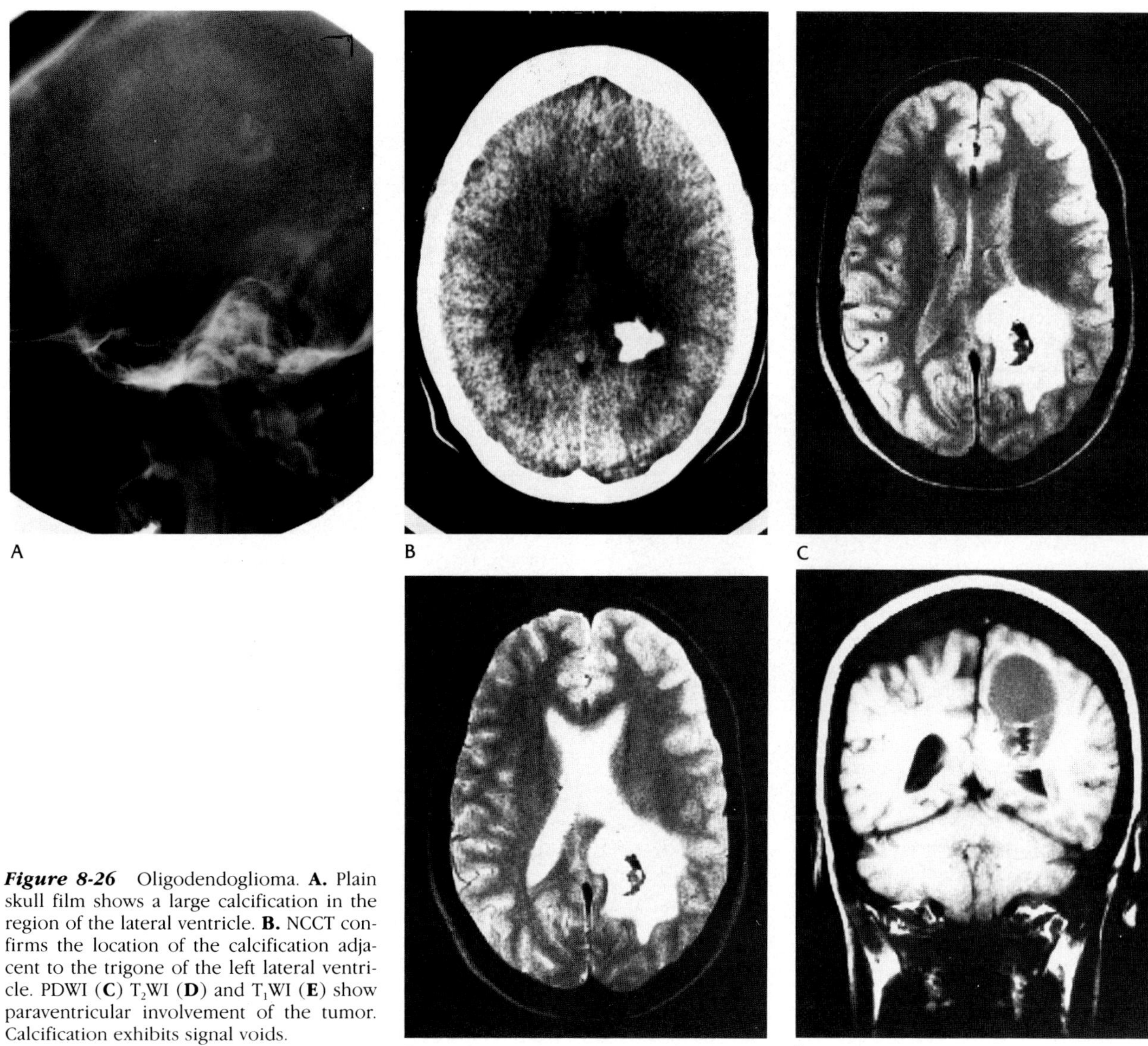

Figure 8-26 Oligodendoglioma. **A.** Plain skull film shows a large calcification in the region of the lateral ventricle. **B.** NCCT confirms the location of the calcification adjacent to the trigone of the left lateral ventricle. PDWI (**C**) T_2WI (**D**) and T_1WI (**E**) show paraventricular involvement of the tumor. Calcification exhibits signal voids.

trast infusion there is dense and usually homogeneous enhancement (Figs. 8-27 and 8-28). Occasionally, nonenhancing lucencies are present, either adjacent to the tumor or, occasionally, inside it (Zimmerman 1979*c*). These lucencies may represent degenerative changes in the tumor, but they are often caused by entrapped lakes of CSF.

In children, choroid plexus papilloma is most often diagnosed based on its characteristic location within the trigone of the lateral ventricle (Fig.8-28). Choroid plexus papillomas are commonly hypo- to isointense to brain at most pulse sequences; however, they are occasionally hyperintense on T_2WI. The hypointensity observed may be due to a combination of microscopic calcifications, as well as the presence of vascular signal voids from the innumerable small vessels in these highly vascular tumors. Recognizable serpentine signal voids from the large feeding and draining vessels are uncommon but may be present. On MR, the sequela of hydrostatic edema is easily recognized as a region of hyperintensity in the periventricular white matter on T_2WI.

Other masses can be noted within the choroid plexus. Vascular malformations, including both the arteriovenous type and cavernous hemangiomas, can occur. Because of its high vascularity, the choroid plexus can also be a site of intracranial metastasis in adults. The embryologic development of the choroid plexus involves invagination of the meningeal coverings into the developing ventricular system. This occasionally results in the incorporation of arachnoid tissue or dermal elements within the choroid tissue. In adults, the most common neoplasm in the lateral trigone is an intraventricular meningioma

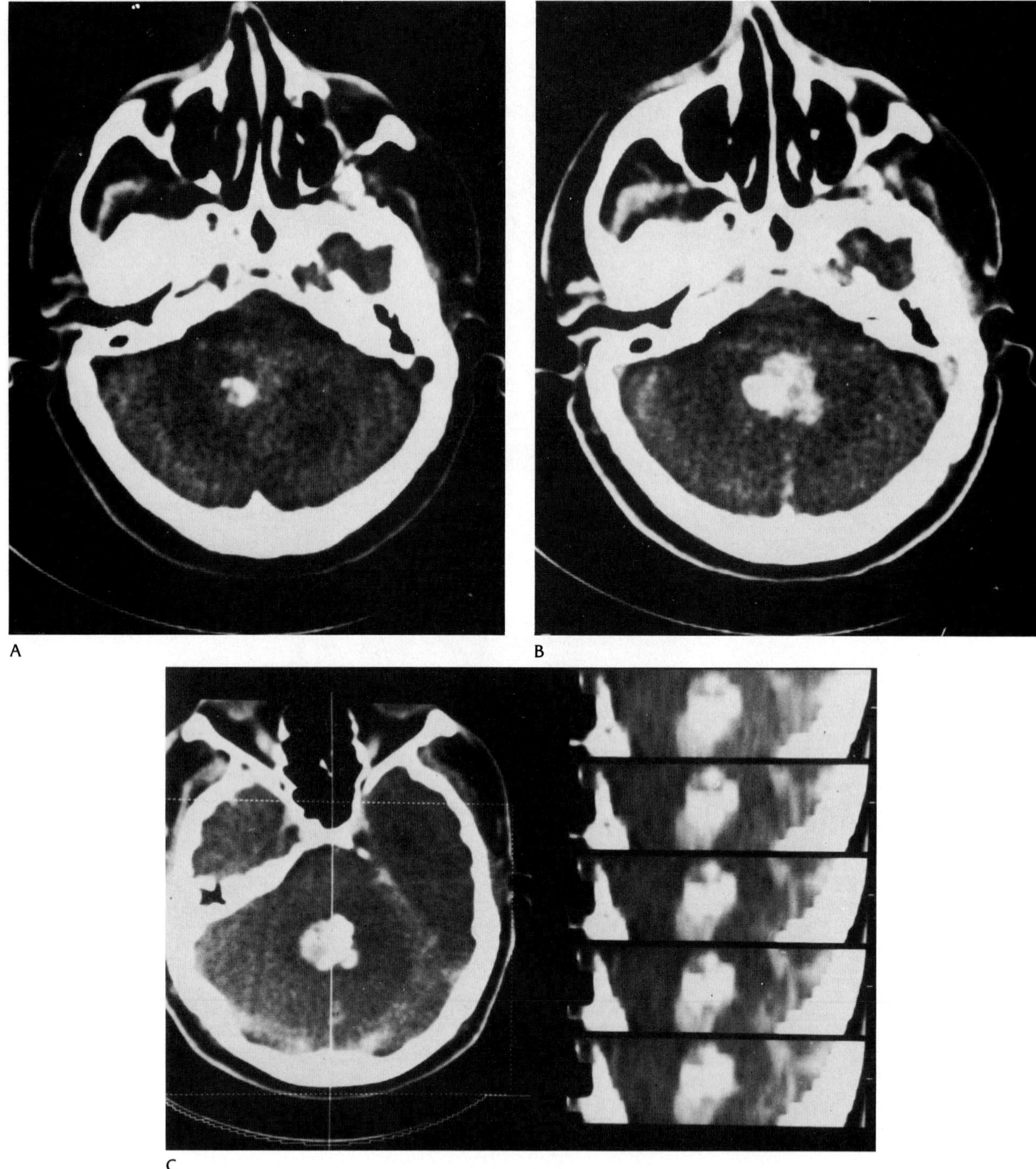

Figure 8-27 Choroid plexus papilloma of the fourth ventricle. **A.** NCCT: A slightly hyperdense lesion with poor demarcation is noted in the region of the fourth ventricle. Multiple calcifications are eccentrically located within the lesion. **B.** CECT: Intense contrast enhancement of the tumor manifests as a mottled appearance with sharp, irregular margins. **C.** Sagittal reformation images confirm the tumor within the fourth ventricle.

(Jelinek 1990). Intraventricular dermoids and epidermoids may also present within the choroid plexus. The choroid plexus is also affected in some of the neurocutaneous syndromes ("phakomatoses"). There is an association of large globular calcification in the choroid plexus in patients with neurofibromatosis. Intraventricular meningiomas have been reported in patients with neurofibromatosis. In Sturge-Weber syndrome (enceph-

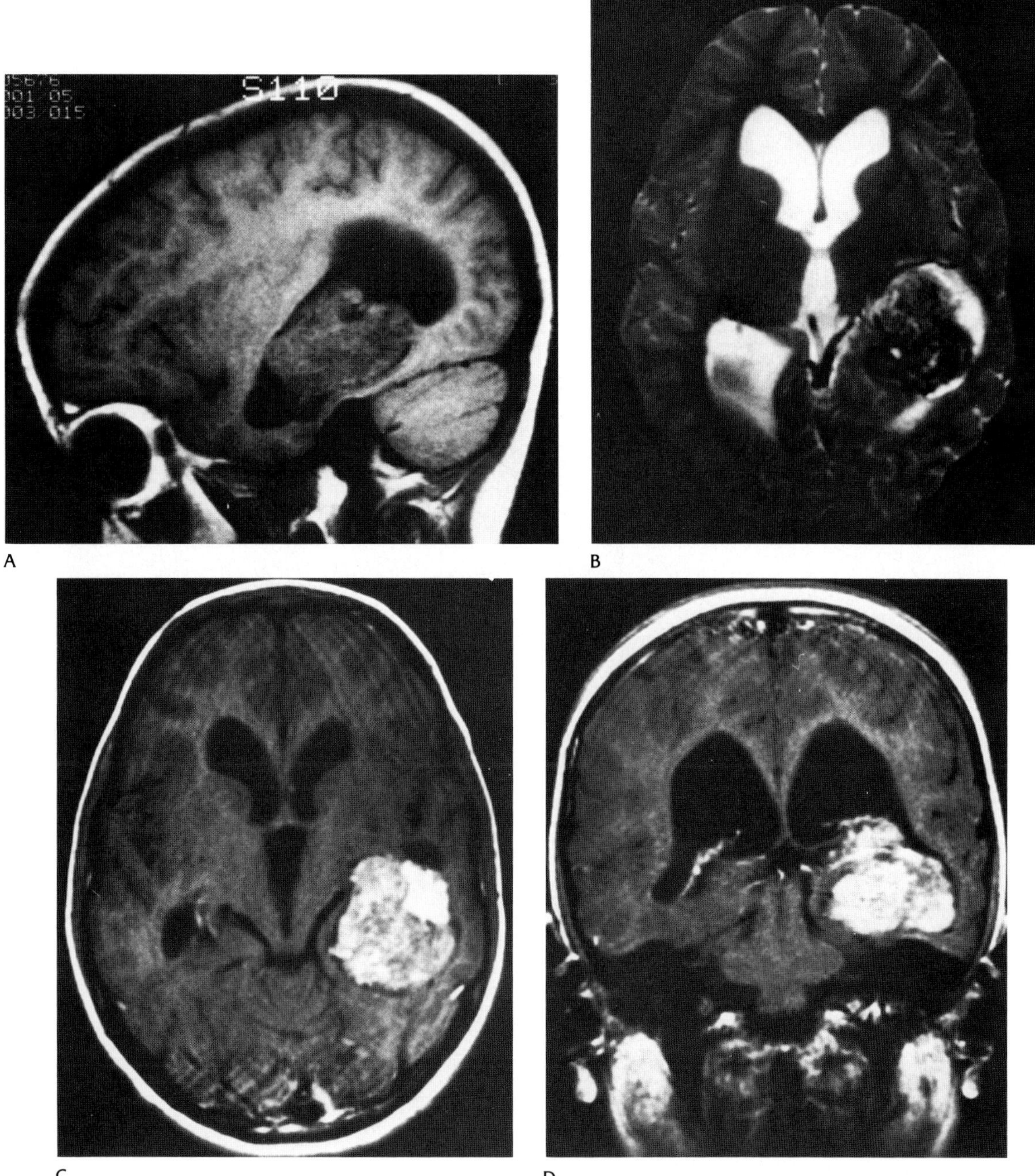

Figure 8-28 Choroid plexus papilloma on MR. **A.** Sagittal T_1WI shows an isointense intraventricular mass with mixed, granular texture in the trigone of the lateral ventricle. **B.** Axial T_1WI shows irregular hypointensity representing calcification in the left lateral ventricle. Note hydrocephalus. Axial (**C**) and coronal (**D**) CEMR shows irregular punctate contrast enhancement.

alotrigeminal angiomatosis), the choroid of the lateral ventricles may develop a spongiform enlargement, probably from an associated "angioma." These vascular changes in Sturge-Weber syndrome may develop because of the abnormal venous drainage of the cerebral cortex and secondary development of collateral circulation through the medullary and choroidal veins.

GANGLIOGLIOMAS

Gangliogliomas are uncommon tumors that exhibit both glial and neuronal proliferations. These lesions present most commonly in children and young adults; 60 percent of patients are under the age of 30 (Anderson 1942; Garrido 1978). Gangliogliomas are slow-growing tumors, and it is not uncommon for patients to have a prolonged

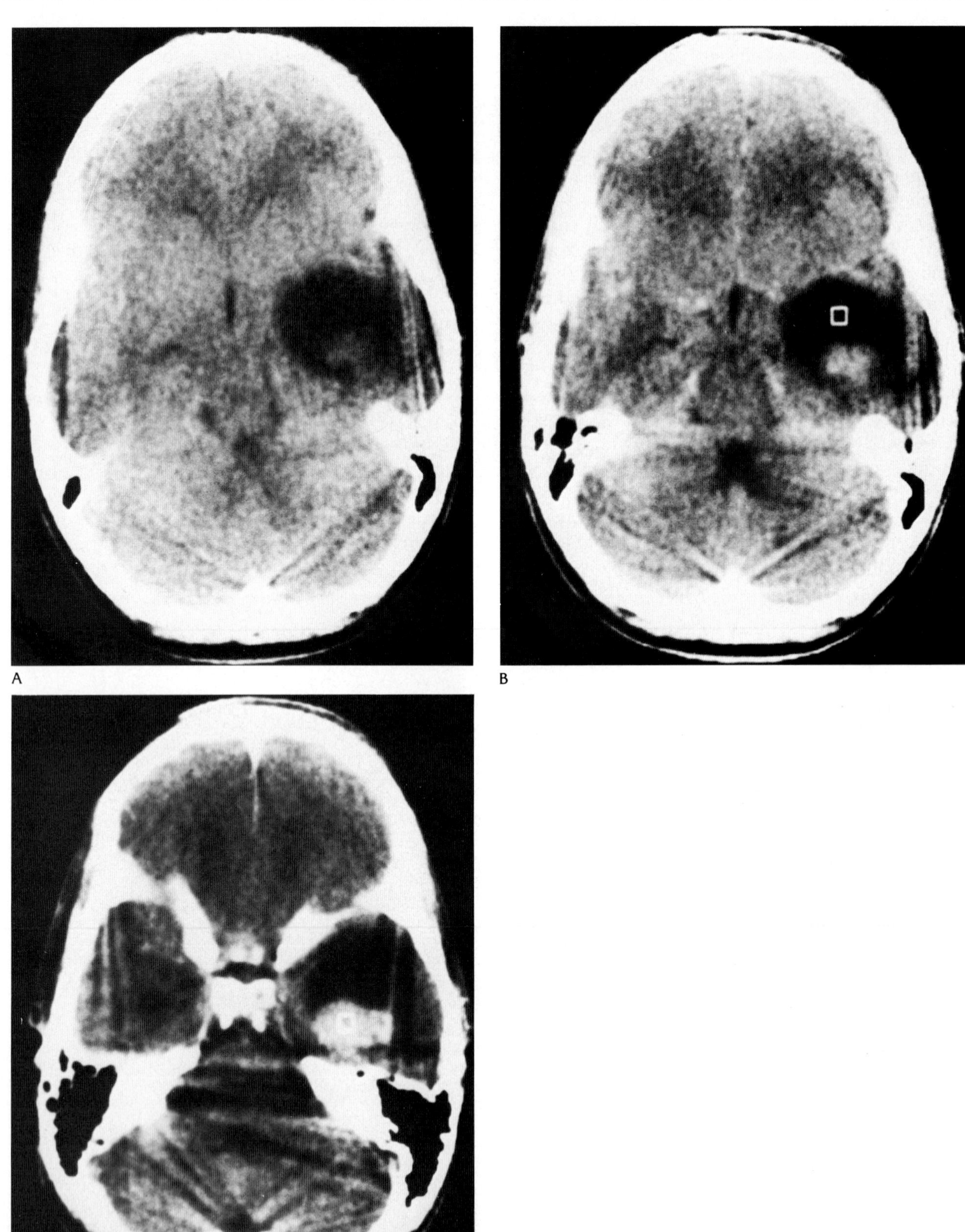

Figure 8-29 Ganglioglioma. NCCT (**A**) demonstrates a mass in the left temporal lobe that is partially cystic and has a mural nodule. CECT (**B** and **C**) demonstrates enhancement in the nodule alone; the cyst lining does not enhance. This is usual for ganglioglioma but also occurs in other benign gliomas, especially pilocytic astrocytoma.

clinical history. Many patients have a long history of seizures or headaches beginning in childhood. Gangliogliomas are usually cerebral hemispheric masses, with an overwhelming predilection for the temporal lobes; less often they are seen in the parietal lobe, brainstem, cerebellum, thalamus, or even in the pineal region (Dorne 1986). Although rarely there may be multiple gangliogliomas, they are usually solitary masses.

Grossly, this neoplasm is firm and very well circumscribed, without significant infiltration into the surrounding brain. This sharp margination facilitates surgical cure. Calcification and cyst formation are common, and gangliogliomas may mimic the appearance of a pilocytic astrocytoma exactly by forming a cystic mass with a mural nodule containing a focus of calcification.

CT demonstrates a well-circumscribed hypodense or isodense mass. This is punctuated by foci of calcification in at least one-third of cases (Fig. 8-29) (Dorne 1986). Following contrast infusion there may be one or more enhancing areas or there will be nodules of mural enhancement within a cystic mass. Contrast enhancement is an almost universal finding (Fig. 8-29). It should be apparent that these radiologic findings are nonspecific. However, a long clinical history and a temporal lobe mass in a young adult or older child should prompt consideration of ganglioglioma. These patients respond well to surgical extirpation.

MR will often show the classic appearance of a partially cystic temporal lobe mass with a mural nodule (Fig. 8-30). The cystic portion of the lesion is usually slightly higher in signal than CSF on T_1WI and PD-WI, and almost isointense to CSF on the T_2WI. The solid portions, or mural nodules, tend to be slightly hypointense on T_1WI and hyperintense on T_2WI. Gangliogliomas almost always enhance with MR contrast agent.

Nonglial Tumors

MENINGIOMAS

Meningiomas are the most common of all extraaxial neoplasms occurring within the cranial cavity. They are also the most common nonglial primary tumor of the CNS, and represent about 15 to 18 percent of all intracranial tumors and about 25 percent of all spinal neoplasms (Zulch 1986; Okazaki 1989). Although common in adults, they are much less frequent in childhood, representing less than 5 percent of CNS neoplasms in the pediatric population. However, childhood meningiomas can be

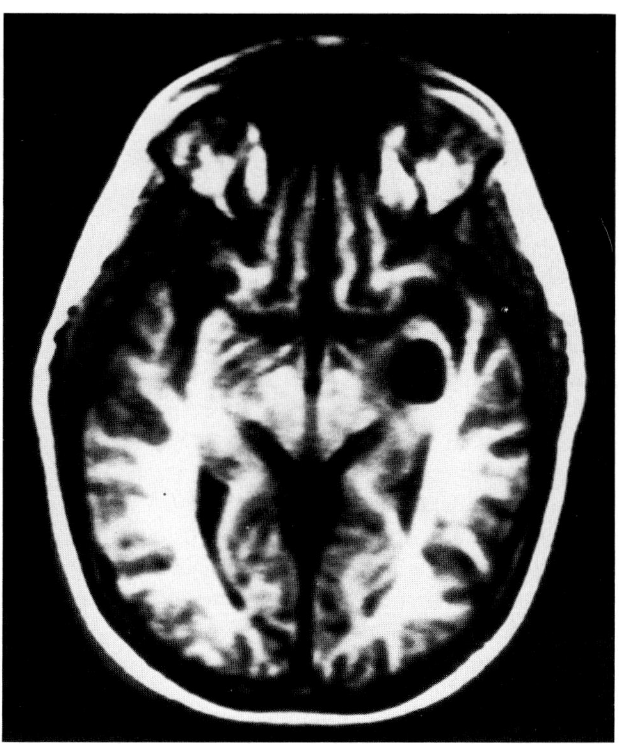

A

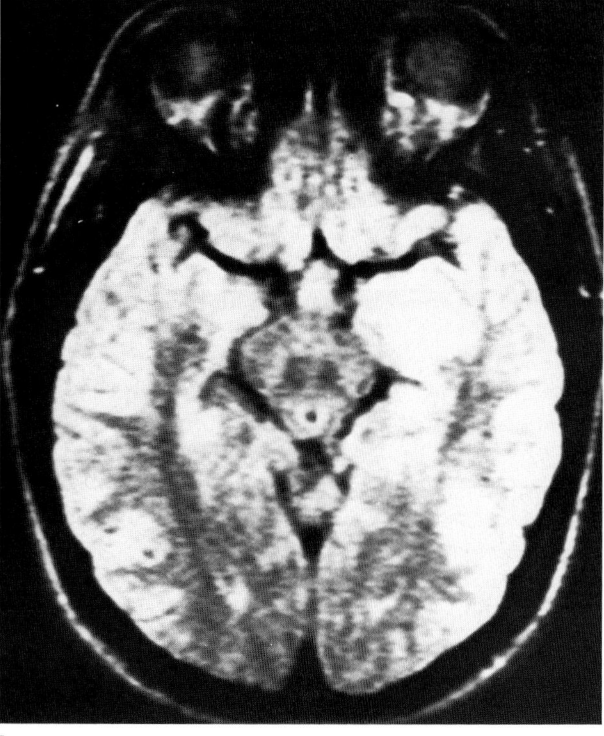

B

Figure 8-30 Ganglioglioma. Axial MR (**A**) shows inversion recovery and T_2WI (**B**) demonstrates a sharply marginated, partially cystic mass involving the medial left temporal lobe. Focal edema is present. (*Continued on p. 334.*)

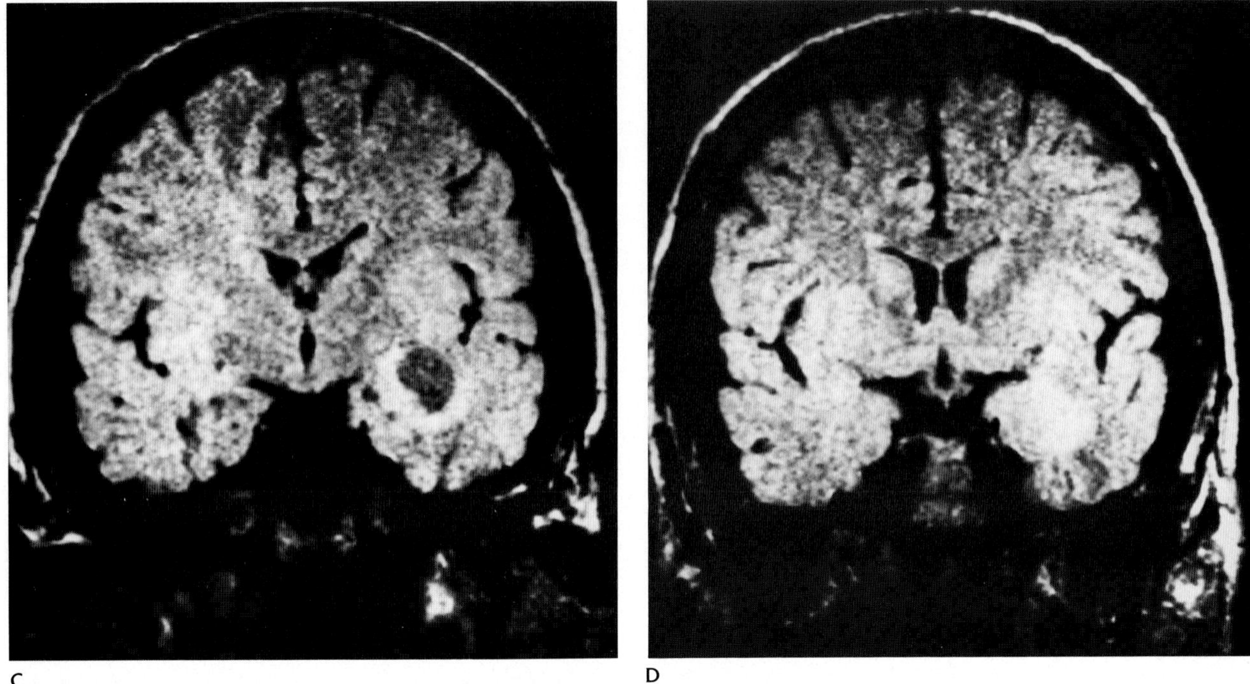

Figure 8-30 (continued) Coronal PDWI (**C** and **D**) again demonstrates a well-circumscribed temporal lobe mass. Because of its protein content, the cyst fluid has a higher signal than does CSF.

more aggressive and are often associated with type 2 neurofibromatosis, or "central" neurofibromatosis. Overall, intracranial meningiomas manifest a clear female predominance, ranging from 2 to 1 to 4 to 1 (Zulch 1986; Rohringer 1989). The female predominance reflects the hormonal sensitivity of meningiomas. There is no female predilection prior to puberty, and little female predominance after menopause. It is well known that meningiomas often grow and/or present clinically during pregnancy; they are also associated with both pituitary adenoma and breast carcinoma. The average incidence of meningioma is 2.3 per 100,000 population per year; however, the incidence is strongly age-related, rising from almost nothing in childhood (less than 1/100,000) to a high of 8.4 per 100,000 per year in the seventh decade (Rohringer 1989). Most meningiomas are detected during an incidence peak near midlife, in the age range from 40 to 55 (Zulch 1986).

Macroscopically, meningiomas are usually spherical or globular but may also be flat or platelike thickenings (en plaque). Occasionally, meningiomas of the falx or tentorium form bilobed dumbbell or "butterfly" shapes. They are usually very well circumscribed, sharply demarcated, and readily separated by inspection or surgery from the adjacent brain tissue. The proposed cell of origin for meningiomas has been debated over the years, and dural cells, including fibroblasts, have been suggested. However, most neuropathologists now agree that these tumors arise from meningoendothelial arachnoid "cap" cells, which are most numerous in the arachnoid granulations. This may account for the high frequency of meningiomas found in and around the large dural sinuses, which also have most of the arachnoid villi. Rests of arachnoidal cells are also occasionally found within the tissue of the choroid plexus of the ventricular system, presumably accounting for the occurrence of intraventricular meningiomas. Many different histologic subtypes of meningioma are recognized. Microscopically, they may be classified as syncytial, transitional, fibroblastic, angioblastic, or sarcomatous. The diversity of types of meningioma reflects the adaptive potential of these cells (Russell 1989). Although such microscopic characterization may explain differences in imaging characteristics (Elster 1989), it may not offer any significant prognostic advantage (Okazaki 1988). However, classifying meningiomas into broad categories such as typical, atypical, and malignant is clinically useful for prognosis. "Typical" meningiomas include the subcategories listed in Table 8-9. Meningiomas are considered "atypical" when they have features of infiltration into the brain, necrosis, and excessive numbers of mitoses. Further complicating the classification of meningiomas is the category of "malignant" meningioma, which often includes nonmeningotheliomatous tumors such as hemangiopericytoma arising in the CNS, as well as the malignant and metastatic variants of "true" meningioma. Hemangiopericytomas that arise in the meninges are histologically similar to other mesothelial and soft-tissue hemangiopericytomas, and are not

Table 8-9 Neoplasms of the Meninges

I. Meningioma
  A. Meningioma (typical)
    1. Syncytial
    2. Transitional/mixed
    3. Fibrous (fibroblastic)
    4. Psammomatous
    5. Metaplastic variants (myxoid, xanthomatous, etc.)
  B. Atypical meningioma
  C. Anaplastic (malignant) meningioma
    1. Variants of typical meningioma
    2. Papillary meningioma
II. Mesenchymal neoplasms
  A. Benign: osteoma, lipoma, fibrous histiocytoma
  B. Malignant: malignant fibrous histiocytoma, etc.
III. Neoplasms of uncertain origin
  A. Hemangiopericytoma
  B. Hemangioblastoma (capillary hemangioblastoma)

related to typical meningiomas in terms of cell of origin, histology, or prognosis. Nonetheless, hemangiopericytomas are the most common neoplasms reported to be "malignant" meningiomas, and they are also often included under the category of "angioblastic" meningioma. Superficial hemangioblastomas (whether intraaxial or extraaxial) are also often mistaken for meningioma. This error is understandable since hemangioblastomas are usually near the leptomeninges and can have an angiographic pattern similar to that of meningioma, with a pronounced and prolonged capillary blush.

In addition to the subtypes listed above, true meningiomas may develop other connective tissue elements, including myxoid material, fat, true bone, and cartilage. Further complicating classification are other neoplasms which arise from the dura itself, and not the arachnoid, as well as the primary mesodermal calvarial masses that may mimic meningioma by location and gross appearance. Lymphoma, metastasis, myeloma, and other lesions extending from the calvarium may also simulate meningioma on radiologic studies. Meningiomas are well known to stimulate changes in the adjacent bones, with or without microscopic invasion, and alkaline phosphatase may be elevated within some meningiomas, although the serum levels are usually normal (Okazaki 1988).

Both CT and MR make detection and evaluation of meningiomas far simpler than earlier techniques of plain film and angiography. The common sites for intracranial meningiomas are as follows: supratentorial—overlying the lateral hemispheric convexity (34 percent); parasagittal or falcine (22 percent); sphenoid ridge (17 percent); olfactory groove (3 to 10 percent); suprasellar region or tuberculum (3 to 8 percent); posterior fossa (7 to 10 percent—cerebellar convexity 5 percent, tentorium 4 percent, cerebellopontine angle 2 percent, and foramen magnum 1 percent); inside the lateral ventricle (5 percent); and, rarely, intracerebral, intraorbital, and pineal region locations (Rohringer 1989; Baker 1973; New 1980).

CT Findings of Meningiomas

NCCT of meningioma characteristically demonstrates a sharply delineated oval, rounded, or hemispherical isodense or, most frequently, hyperdense mass (16 to 50 HU) adjacent to a dural surface (inner table, falx, or tentorium) (New 1980). On CECT, there is intense and homogeneous contrast enhancement in 72 percent of benign meningiomas (Rohringer 1989). Mass effect is an almost universal CT feature of meningiomas; they displace the CSF away from themselves as they grow toward the brain, and squeeze the CSF out of the sulci. At the time of clinical presentation, many are large enough to completely obliterate the adjacent subarachnoid space and cisterns and can distort the underlying brain to alter the shape of the ventricular system (Claveria 1977*a*). A useful feature in confirming the extraaxial location of the suspected meningioma is the compressive phenomenon on CT recognized by the inward "buckling" of the white matter (George 1980). Because of its superior tissue contrast and multiplanar sectioning, MR has advantages over CT in demonstrating both the white matter buckling and the inward displacement of the cortical gray matter, which helps localize the mass to the extraaxial compartment. Other useful imaging characteristics which help to suggest meningioma include demonstration of a broad base of the tumor abutting the dura and finding the bone changes (whether hyperostotic or destructive) produced by the meningioma. In one large study, hyperostosis of the adjacent calvarium was noted in only 18 percent of benign meningiomas. The same study associated malignant meningiomas with hyperostosis at the even lower incidence of 7 percent (Rohringer 1989). En plaque meningiomas have a greater association with hyperostosis seen on CT (Kim 1983).

The hyperdensity on NCCT has been attributed to (1) the dense compactness of the tumor cells, (2) associated connective tissue with collagen, (3) the hypervascularity of the tumor (blood at 40 HU is more dense than brain), and (4) the presence of psammoma bodies (calcification) within the tumor (Fig. 8-31). *Calcifications* are usually microscopic or punctate, but may be large, conglomerate, peripheral, or central. Calcifications are present on CT in 20 to 27 percent of meningiomas (Claveria 1977*a*; Rohringer 1989) (Fig. 8-31). Among the histologic sub-

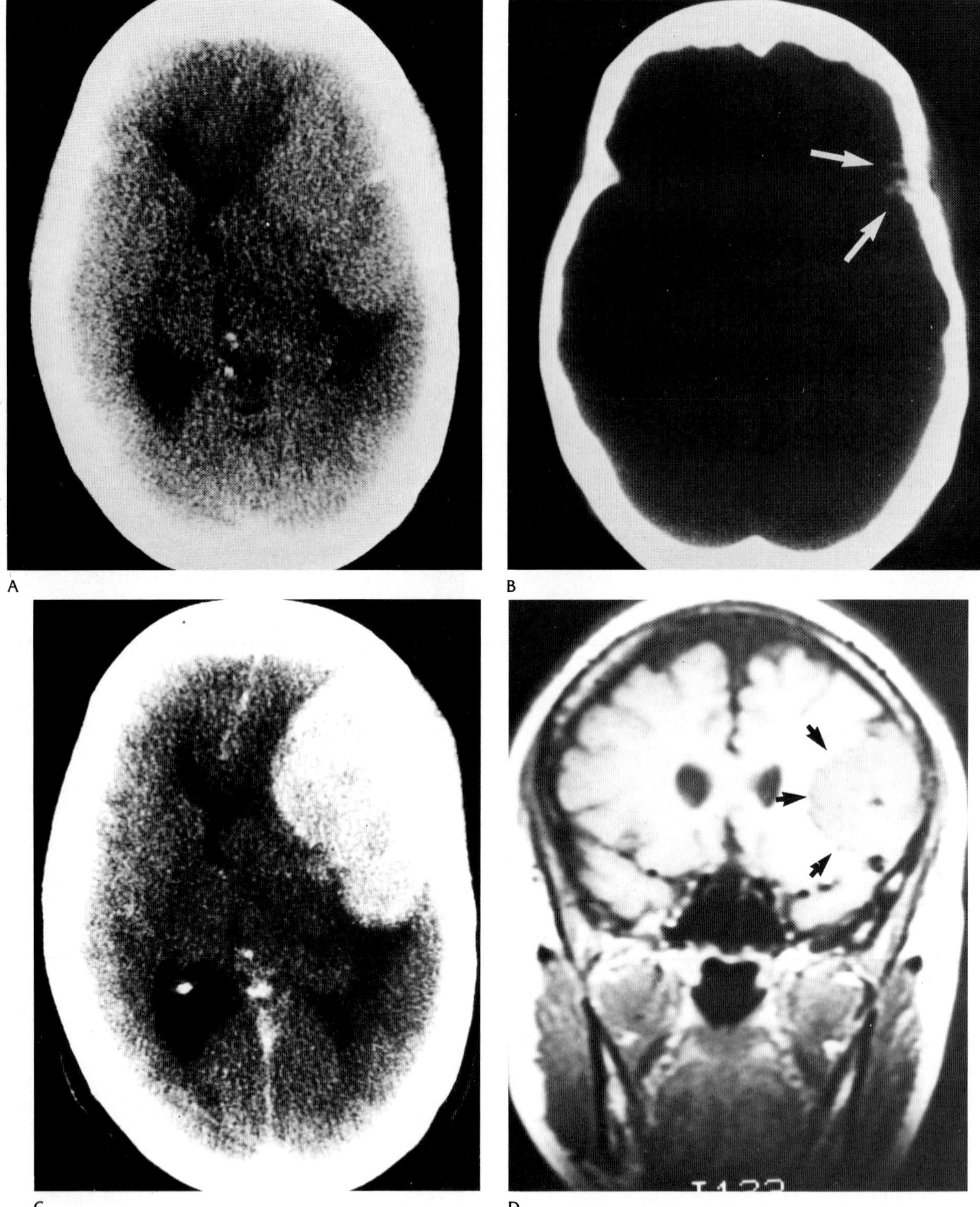

Figure 8-31 Pterional meningioma. **A.** NCCT shows a large, well-demarcated, lobulated hyperdense mass with compression and displacemnt of the adjacent brain tissue and the ventricle. **B.** On bone settings, hyperostosis of the pterion, involvement of the calvarium, and extension into the scalp are well demonstrated (arrows). **C.** CECT delineates the well-marginated, homogeneously enhancing tumor abutting the inner table of the skull. **D** and **E.** MRI: **D** (T_1-coronal image) and (*Continued on p. 337.*)

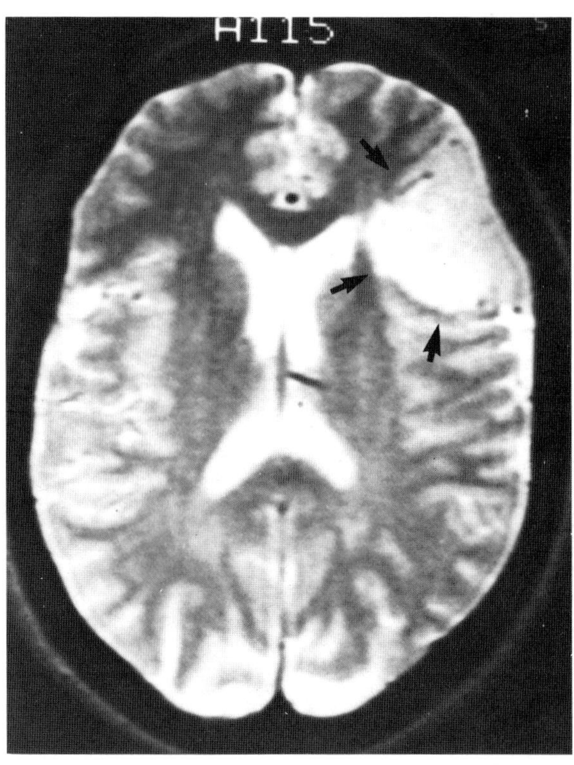

E

Figure 8-31 (continued) **E** (T_2-axial image) demonstrate a meningioma (arrows) with mild signal intensity change and minimal mass effect in another patient.

types, transitional and fibroblastic meningiomas are most frequently seen with visible calcium aggregates (39 percent), a feature that suggests their slowly progressive benign nature (Vassilouthis 1979; Ambrose 1975*a*). Malignant meningiomas are rarely calcified. There are isodense meningiomas, which may be difficult to distinguish from the surrounding normal brain tissue on NCCT (Mani 1978; Amundensen 1978); however, with the use of contrast, the usual intense enhancement renders them obvious. Occasionally a hyperdense area within a largely isodense mass is present, which may represent subacute hemorrhage within the tumor (Fig. 8-32). However, frank hypodensity within the tumor on NCCT is a rare (and somewhat atypical) finding and may represent tumor necrosis, much older hemorrhage, cystic change, myxoid material, or lipomatous transformation (Russell 1980; Vassilouthis 1979). Areas of hypodensity in meningioma may exhibit minimal or no contrast enhancement. True cyst formation may be located centrally or peripherally within the tumor, or rarely within the adjacent brain parenchyma outside of the tumor (peritumoral arachnoid cyst), and may be difficult to differentiate from adjacent edematous brain (Rengachary 1979).

Although true *lipomatous change* in a meningioma is extremely unusual, it is a benign feature. Despite the ominous sound of the name "lipoblastic meningioma," there is no alteration in prognosis related to the presence of fat (Kepes 1982). Lipomatous meningiomas are markedly hypodense on CT (negative HU, much lower than CSF) and may have minimal to slight enhancement within the fat-bearing regions; and, on MR, T_1WI shows a characteristically hyperintense signal (LeRoux 1989; Salibi 1989). Often the lipoblastic meningioma has solid components

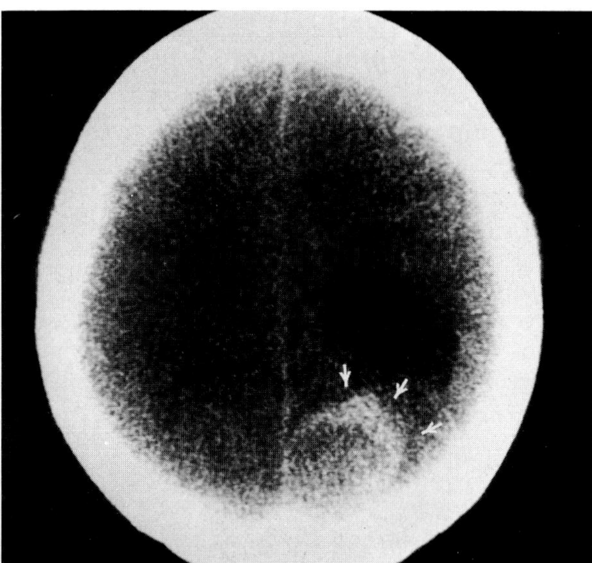

A

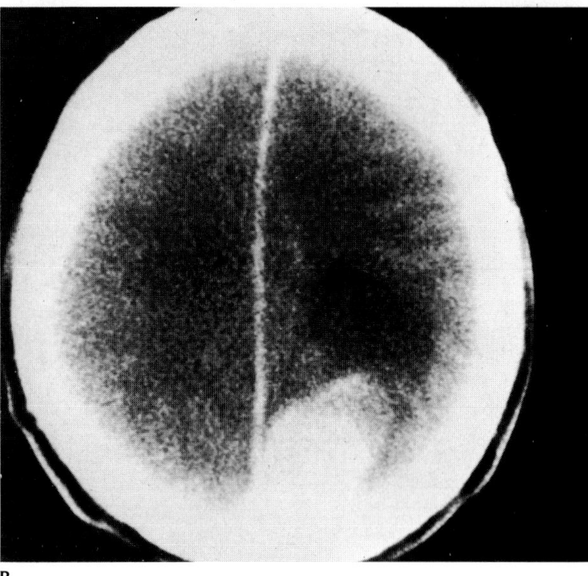

B

Figure 8-32 Meningioma with intratumoral hemorrhage. **A.** NCCT demonstrates an area of hyperdensity on the anterolateral portion of the tumor (arrowheads) with a mass effect. Increased density in the interhemispheric fissures represents subarachnoid hemorrhage. **B.** On CECT, an eccentric intense enhancement of the posteromedial portion of the meningioma is seen. At surgery, the hyperdensity in the anterolateral portion was found to be due to hemorrhage within the tumor.

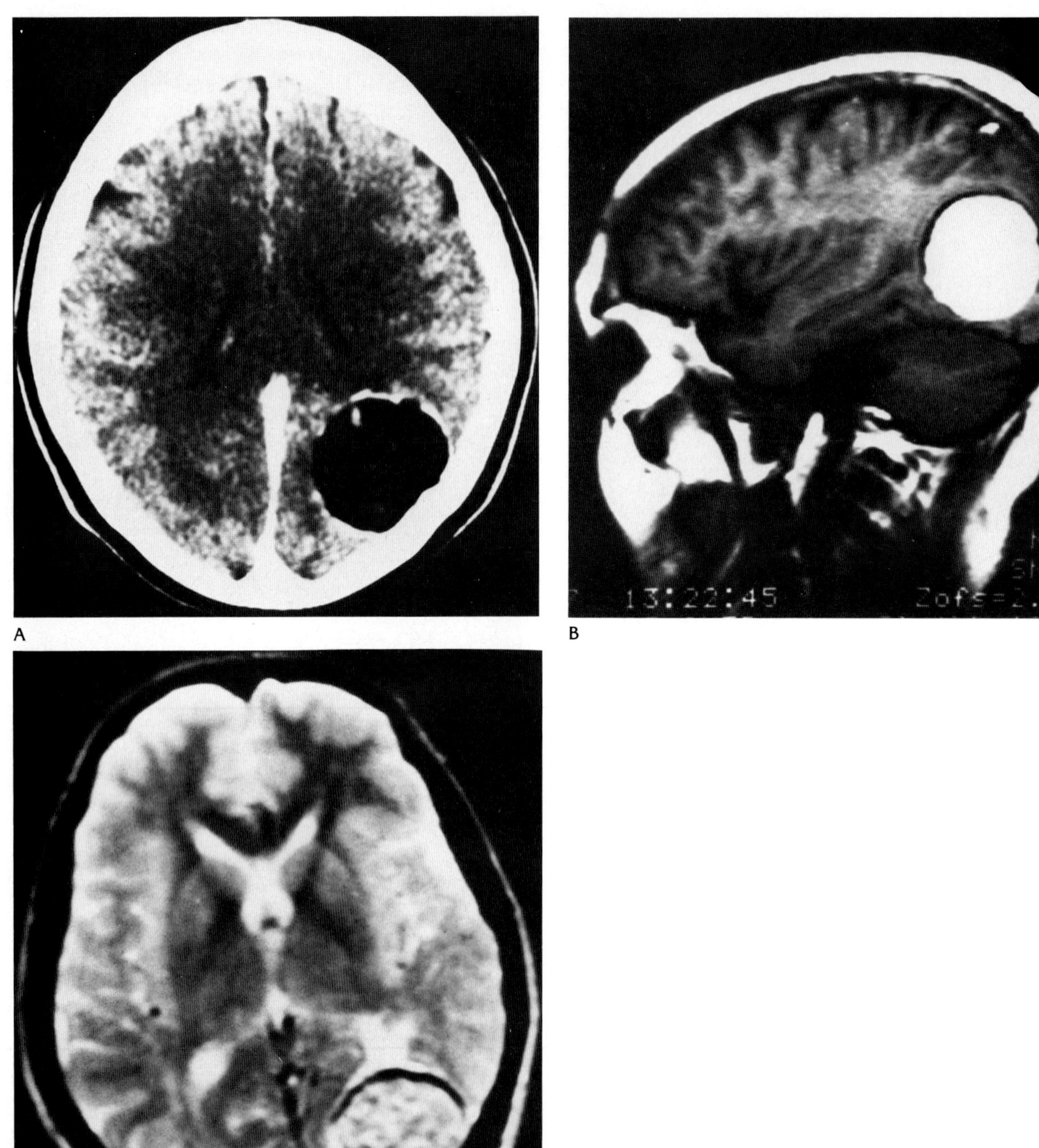

Figure 8-33 Lipoblastic meningioma. **A.** CECT shows a well marginated tumor with a fatty center and a fleck of calcification. **B.** NCMR: Sagittal T_1WI demonstrates a hyperintensity lesion with no significant change in intensity on T_2WI (**C**). (*Case courtesy of Dr. Micheal P. Buetow.*)

in addition to the fat which show a more typical CT hyperdensity, MR signal, and enhancement characteristics (Fig. 8-33).

Intratumoral hemorrhage within meningioma is rare and, when acute, presents on CT as a focal area of high density (Vassilouthis 1979) (Fig. 8-32). Intratumoral hemorrhage in meningioma will also produce characteristic findings on MR, including hyperintensities on both T_1WI and T_2WI in the subacute phase and hemosiderin deposition with decreased signal on T_2WI in the chronic phase. Intratumoral hemorrhage may occur in fibroblastic and meningoendotheliomatous meningiomas, as well as in the angioblastic variants (Russell 1989). Its exact mechanism is not known, although a constant association of hemorrhage with large and small thin-walled endothelial channels has been noted (Modesti 1976), and the onset of bleeding has been attributed to acute pressure changes (Vassilouthis 1979). The extremely rare coexistence of hemorrhage and necrosis within a tumor may present as a more complex lesion on CT and MR. Rarely, bleeding into subarachnoid or subdural spaces occurs.

The consistency of meningiomas may be of surgical importance when the tumors are in close proximity to vital structures. According to Kendall (1979), 90 percent of "hard" meningiomas, excluding those showing diffuse calcification, are hyperdense, and the other 10 percent are of the same density as brain. Of the "soft" meningiomas, 49 percent, excluding those showing marked cystic or necrotic changes, are hyperdense, but compared to the brain 35 percent are isodense and 16 percent are hypodense. Lipomatous and lipoblastic meningiomas may also have a soft consistency (Salibi 1989). The Kendall (1979) study, however, found no relationship between the degree of contrast enhancement and either the consistency or the vascularity of the tumor as estimated by the surgeon or histologist.

CT features have been considered helpful in predicting the histology and aggressiveness of meningiomas (Vassilouthis 1979). Less aggressive types, such as transitional tumors, are well defined, with more or less regular shapes, and contain visible calcium aggregates. Most meningiomas (up to 92 percent) are surrounded by intraaxial vasogenic edema of varying degrees, and the presence of edema is not considered a specific feature except in the fibroblastic type, where it is almost invariably mild to moderate. Tumor density on NCCT has not been considered specific in predicting histologic types, but homogeneous density on CECT may suggest the transitional type (Fig. 8-34). Marked edema, absence of visible calcium aggregates, heterogeneous contrast enhancement, nonenhancing central low-density components, and poorly defined irregular borders all point to aggressive or invasive characteristics that are more commonly found in malignant meningiomas or the angioblastic and syncytial variants (Shapir 1985; Rohringer 1989). Another morphologic feature which suggests malignancy in meningioma is "mushrooming," a pattern where the lesion has an intracranial diameter of incursion that is much larger than its base of dural attachment, which was re-

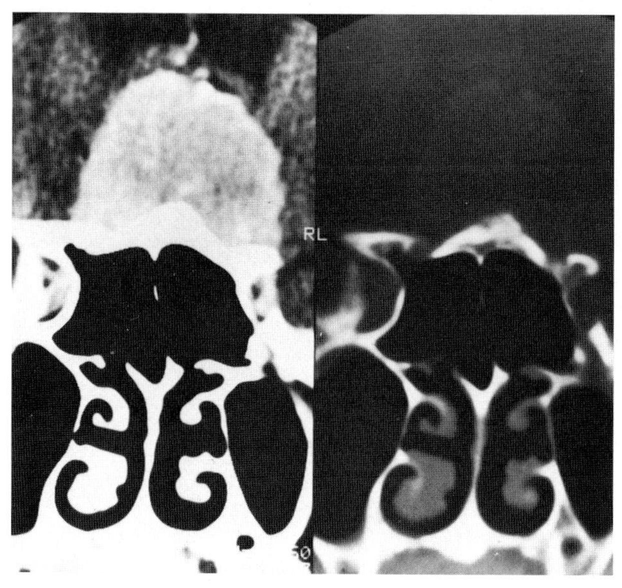

A

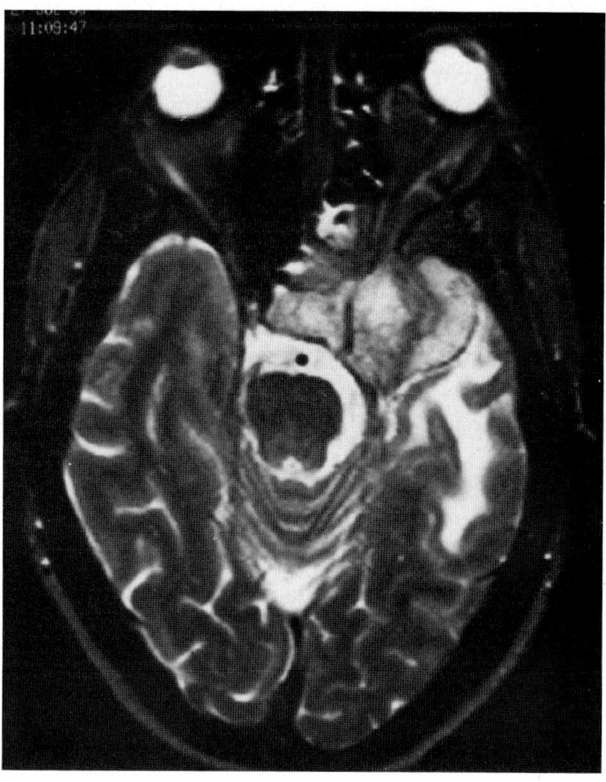

B

Figure 8-34 Meningioma at the planum sphenoidale. **A.** CECT shows a homogeneous enhancing mass with "blistering" of the planum sphenoidale. **B.** T_2WI MR shows an isointense (to gray matter), well-marginated mass surrounded by CSF and pial vessels, indicative of extraaxial mass. Tumor extends into the left chiasmatic groove. (*Continued on p. 340.*)

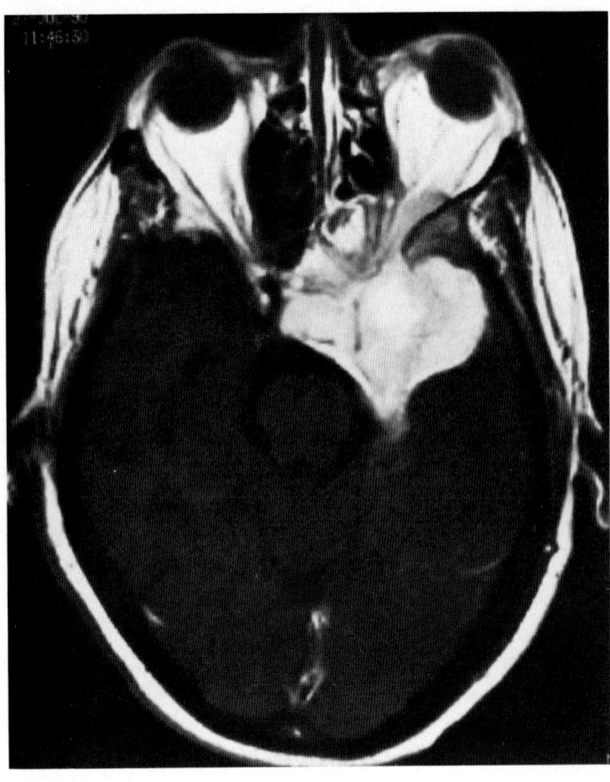

C

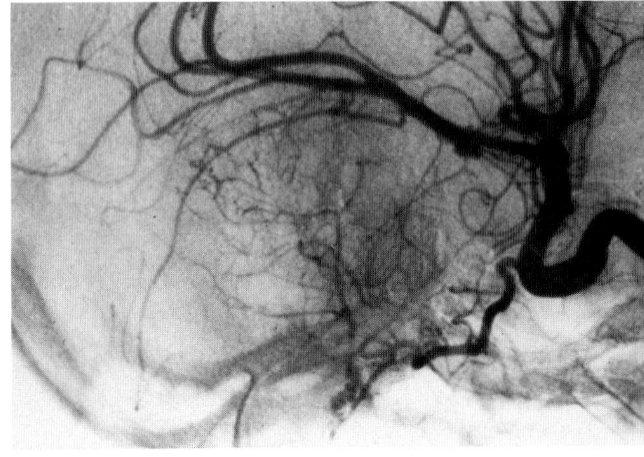

D

Figure 8-34 (continued) **C.** CEMR shows the mass extending into the orbital apex and the medial temporal lobe. **D.** Lateral cerebral angiogram demonstrates tumor blush supplied by branches from the ophthalmic artery.

ported by Rohringer et al. (1989). One additional feature that may suggest a more aggressive histology is marked lobulation of the tumor contour. Benign meningiomas are usually smooth masses with a single radius, whereas malignant meningiomas, such as hemangiopericytoma of the meninges, can be bosselated, with multiple protrusions. Necrosis can be suggestive of a more aggressive histologic variant. However, even benign and typical forms of meningioma may undergo necrosis, either from intrinsic local vascular causes or from systemic hemodynamic deficiency, such as a hypotensive episode (Pullicino 1983).

Intraventricular meningiomas arise in either the choroid plexus or the tela choroidea, probably from congenital rests of arachnoidal cap cells. They represent 17 percent of meningiomas in children and 1.6 percent in adults. An association between intraventricular meningioma and neurofibromatosis is well known. CT demonstrates a homogeneous, isodense or slightly hyperdense mass, with well-defined margins, in the ventricle, particularly in the region of the choroid plexus and most often within the atrium of the lateral ventricle. Intense, homogeneous contrast enhancement is almost always present on CECT, as well as ipsilateral or bilateral ventricular dilatation (Fig. 8-35). MR shows isointensity on both T_1WI and T_2WI with intense enhancement in CEMR (Fig. 8-36). Differentiation from other intraventricular lesions such as choroid plexus papilloma or carcinoma, vascular malformation, cavernous angioma, hemangioma, and astrocytoma may be possible on the basis of age, location, density differences with contrast enhancement, and associated systemic mesenchymal abnormalities (Zimmerman 1979c).

The occurrence of *multiple meningiomas* is uncommon and is usually seen in association with neurofibromatosis (type 2) (Fig. 8-37). Association of meningioma with other types of primary neoplasm such as glioblastoma multiforme or pituitary adenoma (Brenner 1977) is probably coincidental. However, meningiomas in women have been associated with breast cancer (Knuckey 1989), and meningiomas can be recipients of systemic metastasis (Tally 1988).

MR Findings of Meningiomas

Meningiomas are commonly described as being difficult to detect on MR and more than half the time are more obvious on CT (Zimmerman 1985). However, with careful observation, visualization of subtle abnormalities allows MR to approach the same accuracy as CT in the detection and categorization of these tumors. The primary difficulty in the identification of meningiomas on MR stems from their low tissue contrast characteristics

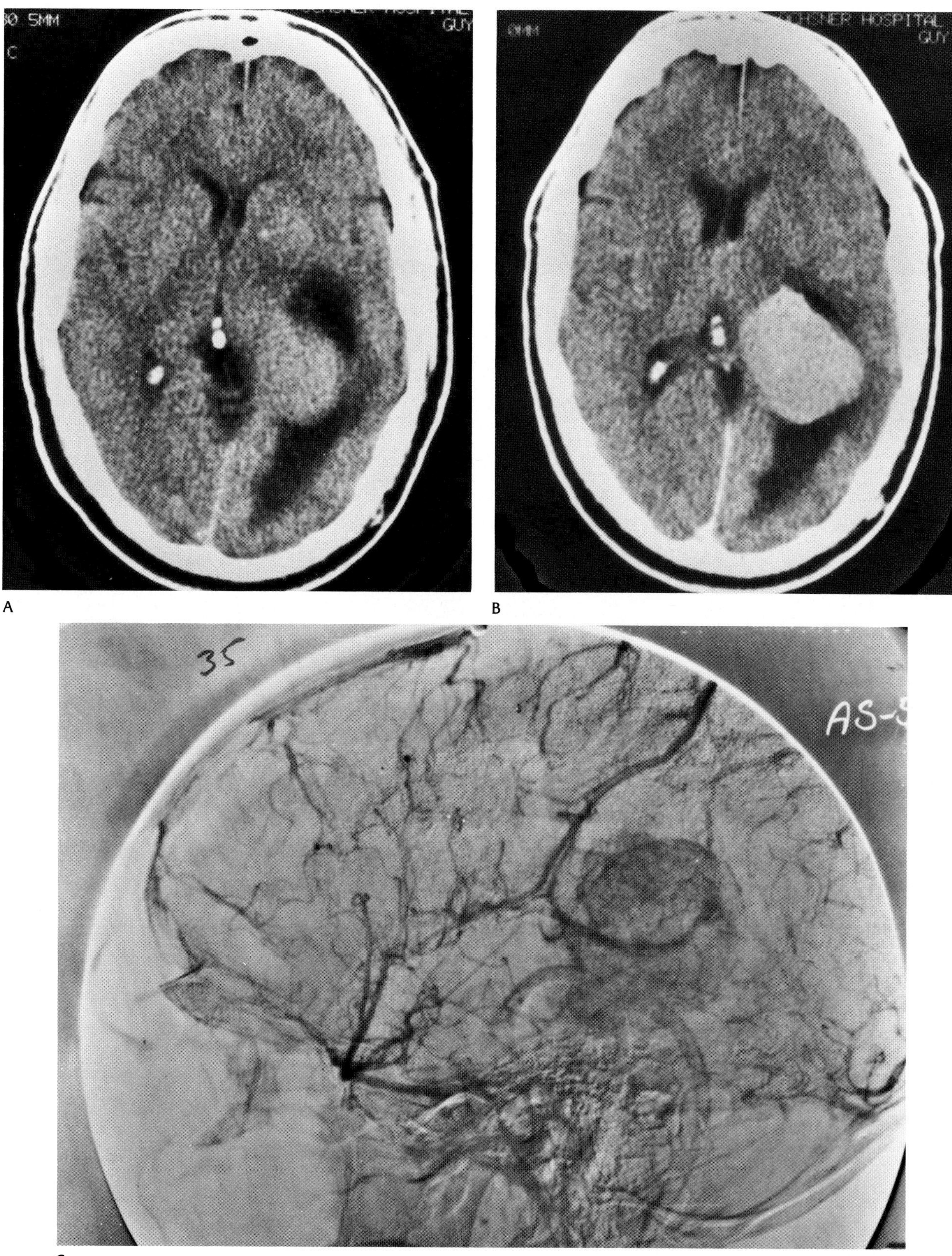

Figure 8-35 Intraventricular meningioma on CT. **A.** NCCT shows an isodense mass in the left lateral ventricle. **B.** CECT demonstrates homogeneous intense contrast enhancement. Note the trapped occipital horn. Faint tumor blush is present on the cerebral angiogram (**C**).

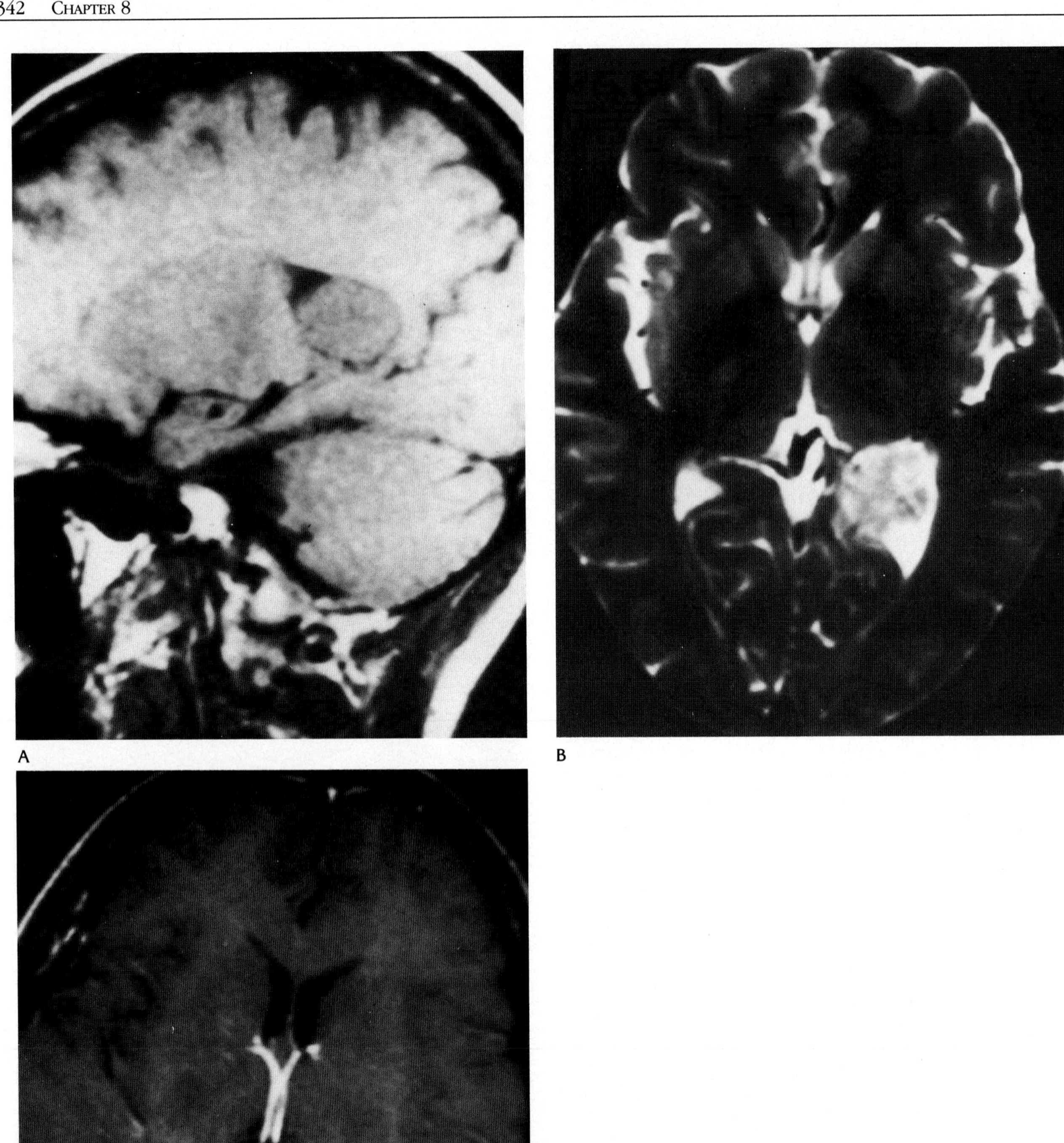

Figure 8-36 Intraventricular meningioma on MR. Sagittal T_1WI (**A**) shows a round isointense mass in the trigone of the lateral ventricle. Axial T_2WI (**B**) demonstrates a minimal increase in intensity in comparison to the surrounding CSF. Intense homogeneous contrast enhancement is noted on CEMR (**C**).

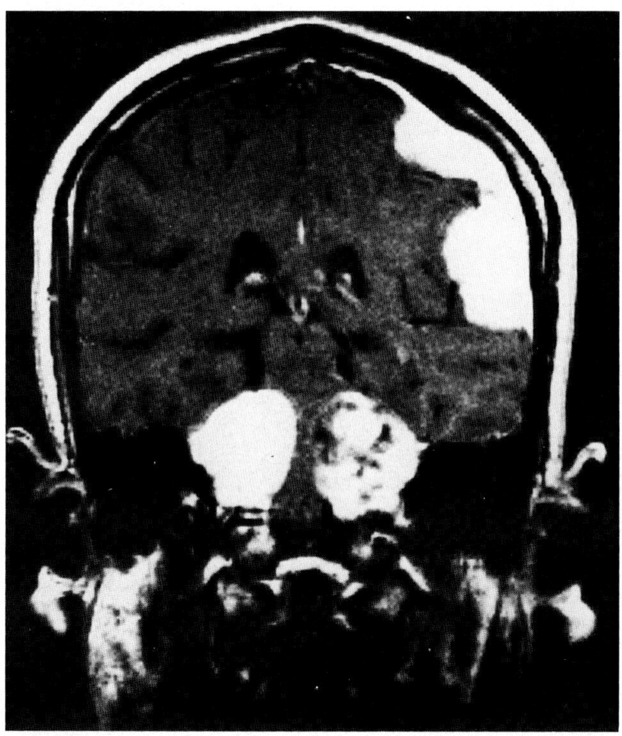

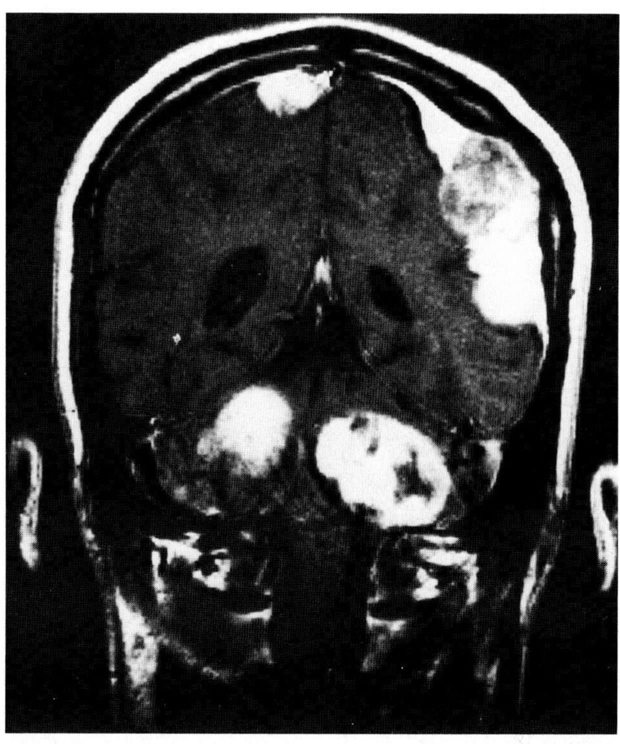

A B

Figure 8-37 Multiple meningiomas in neurofibromatosis type 2. CEMR (**A**) and (**B**) shows multiple contrast-enhancing masses over the convexities and cebellopontine angle cisterns. Note the "tail" sign of the convexity meningiomas.

(Zimmerman 1985). Unlike the situation with CT, where they are grossly, more dense than normal brain, meningiomas are commonly almost isointense to the adjacent cerebral cortex (Chakeres 1989). Isointensity is more common on T_1WI but may be noted on multiple and varied pulse sequences (Spagnoli 1986; Elster 1989). Some authors advocate inversion recovery pulse sequences for suspected meningioma (Zimmerman 1985; Bydder 1985). The problem of relative inconspicuousness is readily solved by the administration of MR contrast, since almost all meningiomas show contrast enhancement. Despite their frequent isointensity, they can nonetheless be identified by their local effects on the adjacent brain (Zimmerman 1985). In fact, their relative isointensity is often of differential value in distinguishing them from other dura-based or extraaxial masses, such as hemorrhage, metastasis, and schwannoma, which are less commonly isointense. The most useful MR characteristics for identifying meningioma include inward displacement of cortical gray matter (cortical buckling), broad base against the dural surface, pseudocapsule of displaced vessels or CSF (Zimmerman 1985; Spagnoli 1986) (Fig. 8-38), and secondary intraaxial vasogenic edema.

Early reports of MR in meningioma found no correlation between histology and signal characteristics (Spagnoli 1986). However, Elster et al. (1989) suggested that combining signal characteristics of the tumor with observations of secondary effects (such as edema) improved the ability of MR to predict histology. In their experience, syncytial and angioblastic meningiomas were markedly hyperintense on T_2WI compared to fibroblastic and transitional meningiomas, which could be hypointense (Elster 1989). This may be a somewhat moot point, since within the group of typical meningiomas (Table 8-9), which includes syncytial meningioma, there is no prognostic implication connected with any particular microscopic pattern. In contrast, the differentiation or identification of hemangiopericytomas and both papillary and angioblastic meningiomas will be of value, because of their clearly poorer prognosis. Recently, Demaerel (1991) investigated the histologic basis of varying signal intensities on T_1WI, T_2WI, and PD-WI of MR and found great difficulty in differentiating among various meningioma subtypes.

Several authors have disagreed about the etiology of the enhancing meningeal "tail sign" seen adjacent to some meningiomas on CEMR (Figs. 8-38 and 8-39). This dural tail sign is nonspecific and has been described in a wide variety of conditions such as postsurgery, radiation, sarcoidosis, lymphoma, chloroma, aspergillosis, metastasis, and schwannoma (Tien 1991). It is seen in 60 percent of meningiomas (Goldsher 1990). The enhancing tail seen with confirmed meningioma has been reported to represent a reactive (nonspecific) process in the meninges (Aoki 1990; Tokumaru 1990), but it can also be caused by extension of neoplasm through dural infiltration (Wilms 1989; Tokumaru 1990; Goldsher 1990).

SCHWANNOMAS

(Refer to Chap. 11.)

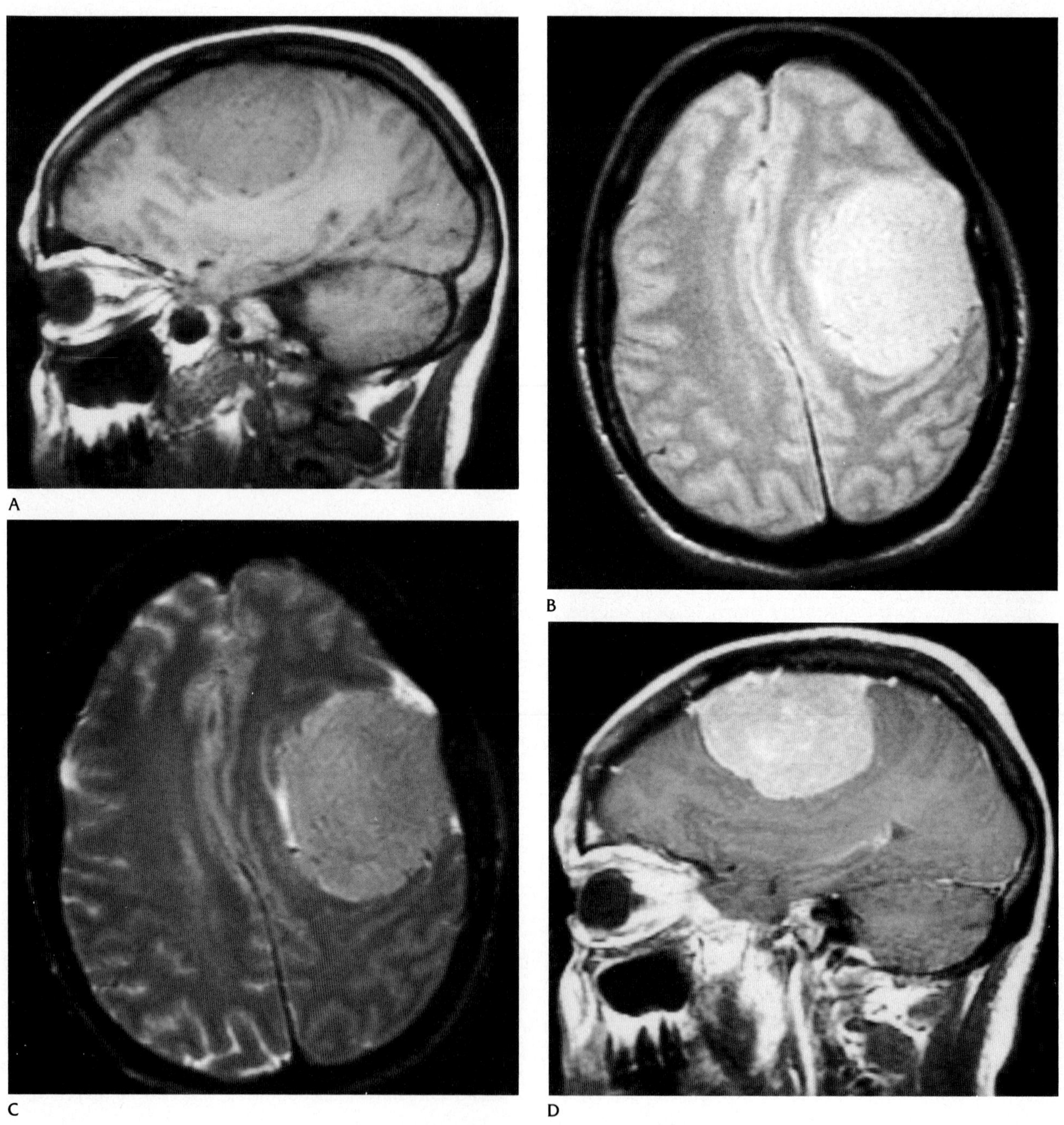

Figure 8-38 Meningioma on MR. **A.** Sagittal T_1WI. A frontoparietal meningioma exhibits isointensity surrounded by adjacent compressed brain tissue, mimicking an "onion peel" appearance. Note displaced pial vessels at the periphery. Axial PDWI (**B**) and T_2WI (**C**) show a mild increase in intensity. Sagittal (**D**) and (*Continued on p. 345.*)

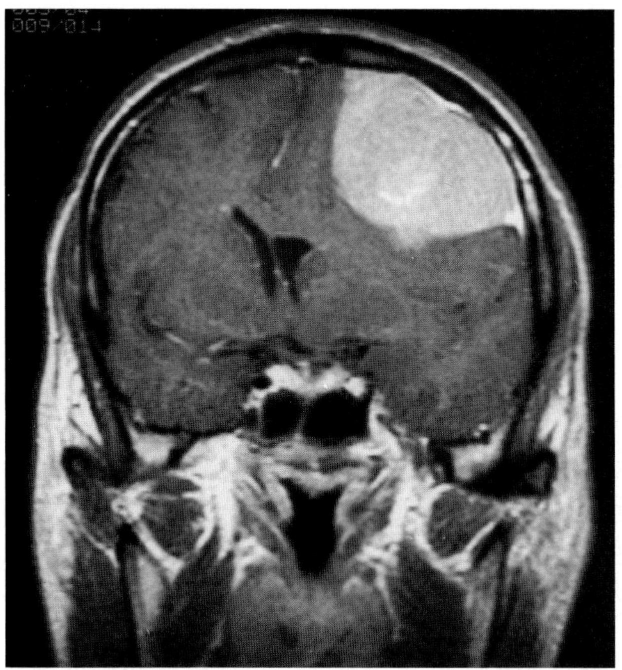

E

Figure 8-38 (continued) axial (**E**) CEMR display intense homogeneous contrast enhancement. Note dural attachment and the "tail sign" at the margins of the tumor.

Congenital Intracranial Tumors

This group of tumors makes up less than 5 percent of all intracranial masses. Epidermoids are the most common within the group, followed closely by lipomas, dermoids, and teratomas (Russell 1989). Embryologically, these tumors arise from incorporation of one or more of the three germ layers (ectoderm, mesoderm, and endoderm) into the neural tube during its closure. This closure occurs at 3 to 5 weeks' gestation. The stage of fetal development during which the incorporation takes place determines the location of the tumor. If inclusion is early (3 weeks), the lesion is usually midline. Later inclusions place the tumor farther from the midline, and if extremely late, the lesion becomes intradiploic (Toglia 1965).

EPIDERMOIDS

The incidence of this tumor ranges from 0.2 to 1.8 percent of all intracranial neoplasms. The age of presentation is 25 to 60, and the male to female ratio is 2 to 1. Ectodermal inclusion during closure of the neural tube gives rise to this lesion, which occurs in the midline or, more commonly, laterally.

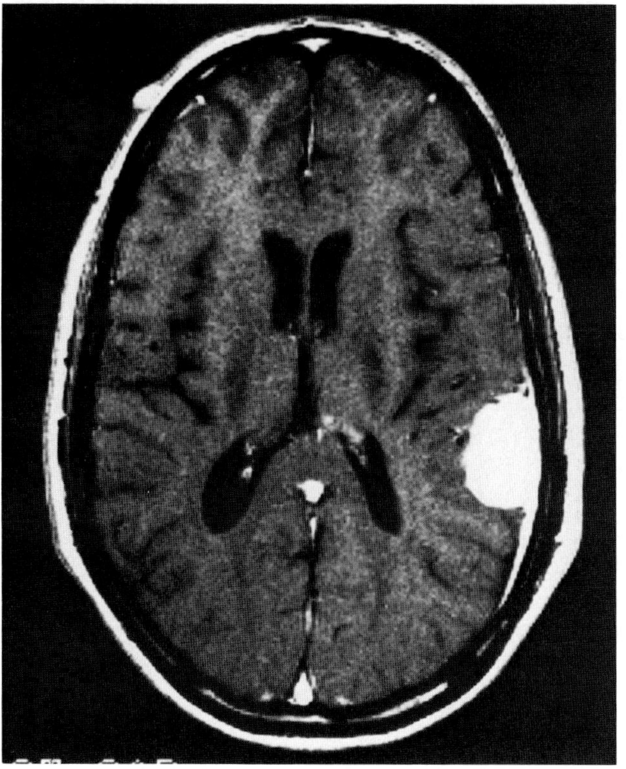

A

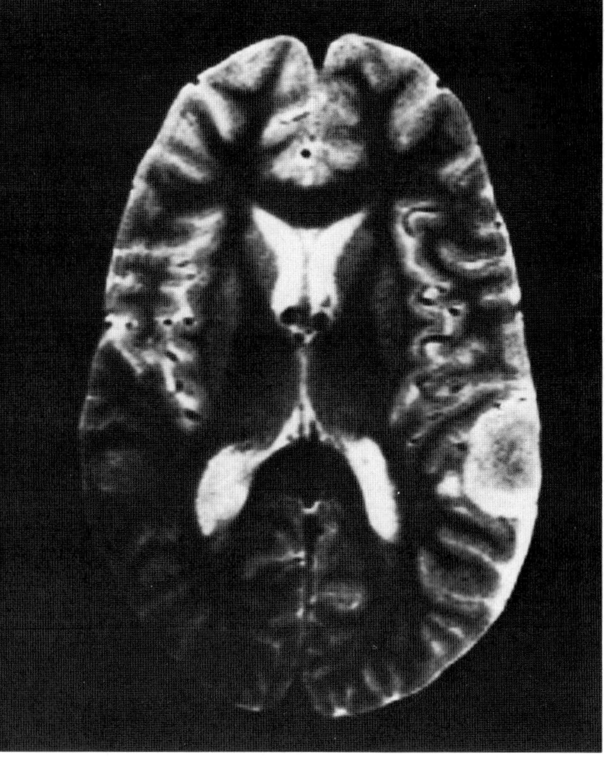

B

Figure 8-39 Meningioma. **A.** CEMR demonstrates a typical appearance for meningioma with an extraaxial hemispheric mass, homogeneous enhancement, and a "dural tail" sign representing abnormal thickened and enhancing dura extending posteriorly from the mass. **B.** T_2WI at the same level, without contrast, shows an isointense mass.

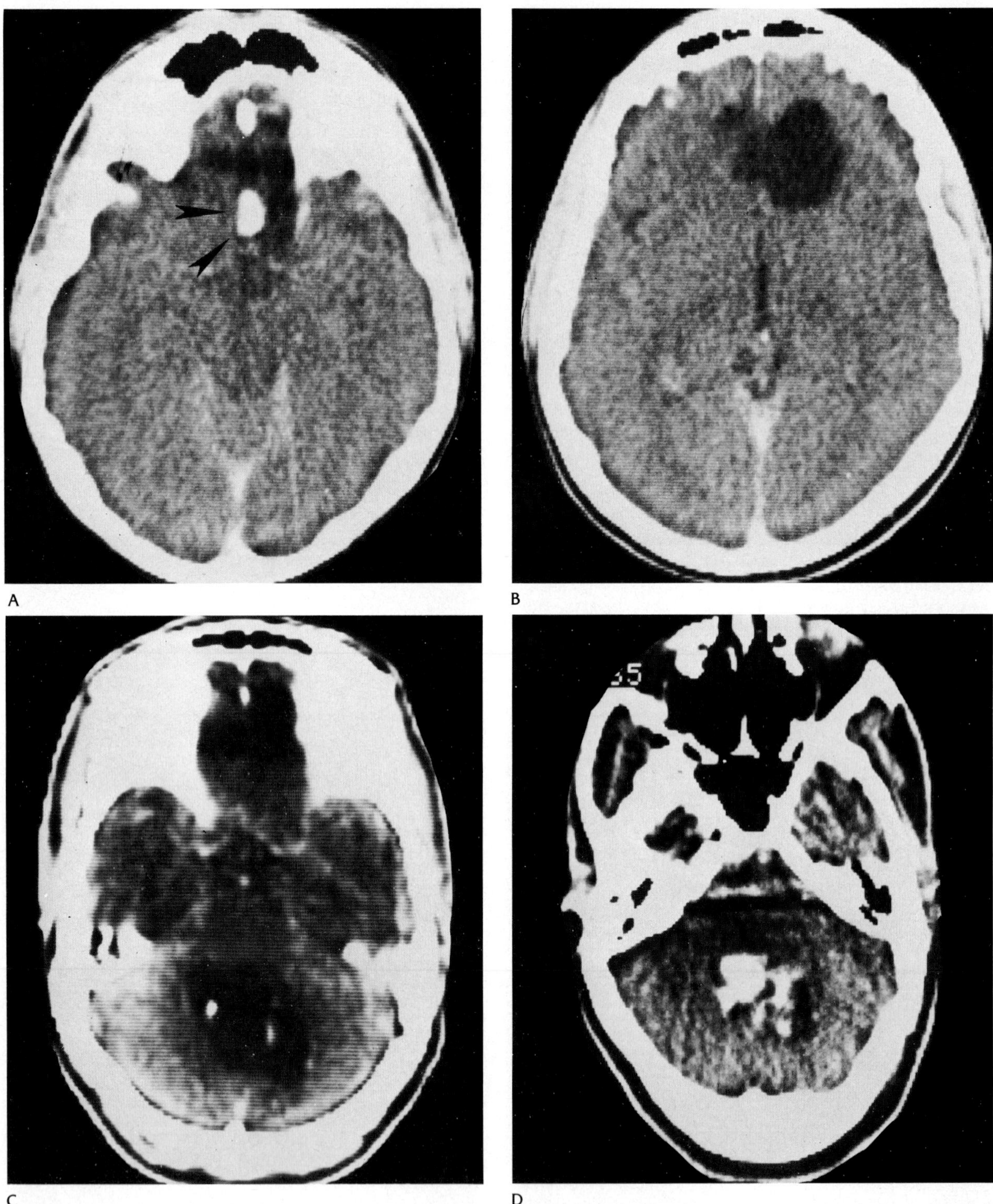

Figure 8-40 Epidermoid calcifiction on CT. Epidermoid tumors. **A** and **B.** Multiple areas of hypodensity in the basal frontal area, with the crista galli anteriorly and a calcification posteriorly (arrowheads) within the tumor. Lobulated epidermoid crosses the midline. The absence of contrast enhancement of the wall and the absence of mass effect are noteworthy. Intraventricular epidermoid. **C.** The fourth ventricle is enlarged and deformed, with flecks of calcification within and at the periphery of the hypodense lesion. The lateral and third ventricles are normal on a higher level. **D.** CT after intrathecal metrizamide. The metrizamide fills the interstices of the epidermoid within the fourth ventricle.

Epidermoids may have a multilobulated, grayish-white appearance suggesting a pearl. They may be intradural, extradural, or intraventricular but are predominantly intradural and occur most commonly at the cerebellopontine angle. Other sites, in order of frequency, include the parasellar region and midposterior cranial fossa. Intradural lesions rarely calcify and were difficult to diagnose in the past because of minimal neurologic findings and normal skull radiographs. Extradural masses, which make up 25 percent of all epidermoids, are easier to recognize on plain films because of well-defined radiolucent defects and bone erosion of the adjacent skull. Their edges are sclerotic and may be scalloped (Chambers 1977). This radiographic appearance is not specific and should be differentiated from slowly erosive lesions such as schwannoma, meningioma, aneurysm, chordoma, and, rarely, metastatic lesions (Tadmor 1977). Some epidermoids are found in the ventricles. The fourth ventricle is the most common location, followed by the temporal horn of the lateral ventricles (Chambers 1977). Epidermoids may also rupture into the ventricular system, producing a fat-CSF fluid level (Laster 1977; Zimmerman 1979*a*).

On CT, epidermoids most frequently show a low density that is similar to that of the CSF (Fig. 8-40). The tumor density reflects the composition of the two major components, keratin cellular debris and cholesterin (Davis 1976*b*; Zimmerman 1979*a*). Most frequently, the density on CT is greater than the negative value of lipids, which is accounted for by the presence of a large amount of nonlipid material (keratin) compared to the chief lipid, cholesterin. Less often, the cholesterin is present in greater proportion than the keratin, so that the tumor density falls into the minus range (-16 to -80 HU) (Cornell 1977; Laster 1977). Epidermoid calcification is generally an inconstant finding. However, occasional increased density ($+80$ to $+120$ HU) and mural calcification (Fig. 8-40) are thought to be due to calcification of the keratinized debris, with saponification to calcium salts (Fawcitt 1976; Braun 1977). The absence of enhancement on CECT is a constant finding. This reflects the structureless, avascular nature of the contents of these tumors and their thin, avascular wall (Davis 1976; Chambers 1977). Cerebral angiography merely confirms the avascular nature of this tumor. Rare occurrence of contrast enhancement at the periphery of the lesion is considered to be a result of the surrounding vascular connective tissue and dura mater (Tadmor 1977), the presence of gliosis (Mikhael 1978), and cerebral vessels stretched around the mass (Chambers 1977). Nosaka (1979) reported that primary epidermoid carcinoma presents as an isodense or slightly increased density which enhances homogeneously throughout the lesion on CECT.

Absence of hydrocephalus, relative absence of a mass effect, and lack of surrounding edema in spite of the size and site of these lesions are noteworthy, and are due to the soft consistency, the slow rate of growth, and the expansion of tumor into the available spaces (Mikhael 1978). Rupture of the capsule further reduces the mass effect. Because the density of intraventricular epidermoids is similar to that of CSF, they may not be readily detected. Rarely, intraventricular epidermoids are accompanied by focal ventricular dilatation or noncommunicating hydrocephalus.

The appearance of intracranial epidermoid tumors is quite variable on MR images, and very different from their appearance on CT. Although epidermoids are commonly homogeneous on CT, they are usually heterogeneous on MR, often having a lamellated or onionskin appearance (Steffey 1988). They also tend to have more irregular margins on MR than on CT. Horowitz et al. (1990) describe two types of epidermoids on MR, both of which are hypodense on CT. So-called "black epidermoids" are relatively solid tumors, of the pearly keratin type described earlier; chemically they lack triglycerides. These are usually of water density on CT (rather than fat) and are hypointense on T_1WI (Fig. 8-41). The second type, "white epidermoids," can have a low attenuation on CT, are usually cystic, and are hyperintense on T_1WI. This type of epidermoid contains mixed triglycerides, which probably accounts for both the T_1 shortening (increased signal intensity on T_1WI) as well as the lower attenuation on CT. Epidermoids are usually hyperintense on T_2WI (Steffey 1988). Rupture of the tumor, with escape of keratin and cholesterin into the ventricular system, allows the less dense cholesterin to float, while the heavier keratin sinks (Laster 1977). As a result, a lipid-CSF level is present in the ventricles, which can be clearly detected by CT and MRI. Rupture of the tumor into the subarachnoid space may deposit cholesterin droplets in the adjoining cisterns and sulci.

Early diagnosis may permit curative surgery. Satisfactory treatment consists of surgical removal of the mass with its capsule. Iatrogenic liberation of its contents into the CSF compartments during surgery can initiate a chemical granulomatous meningitis and facilitate meningeal implantation, producing a "metastatic epidermoid."

DERMOIDS

Dermoids are less common than epidermoids, representing roughly 1 percent of all intracranial tumors. Although they are of congenital origin, like epidermoids, their slow rate of growth often leads to a delay in clinical presentation until the third or fourth decade. Dermoids are derived entirely from ectoderm (Robbins 1979). The name *dermoid* merely means "skinlike," and the ectodermal derivatives that form the lining of a dermoid (and skin itself) include squamous epithelium, sebaceous glands, apocrine sweat glands, and hair follicles. Even

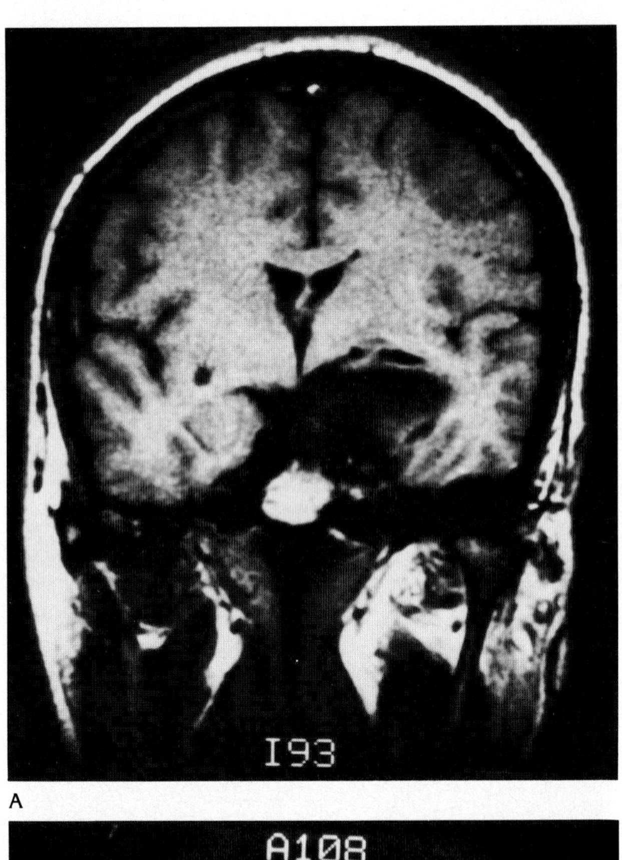

A

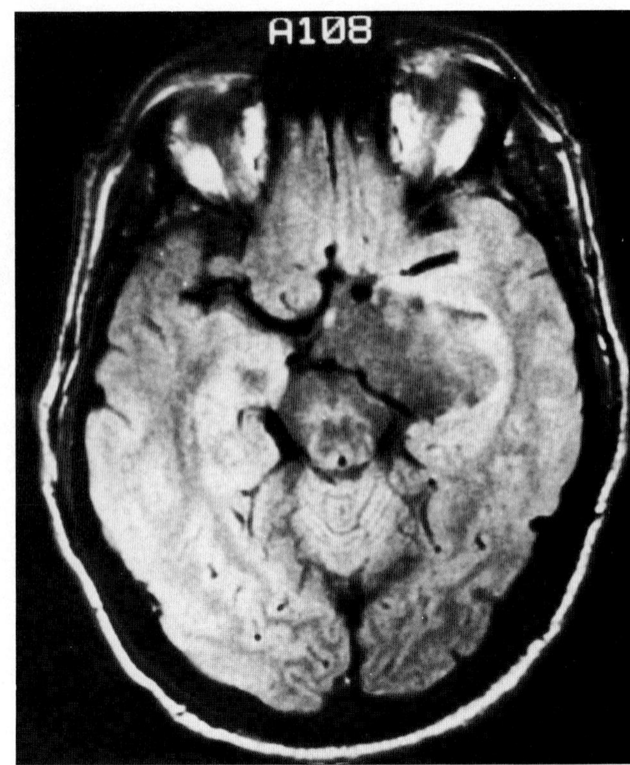

B

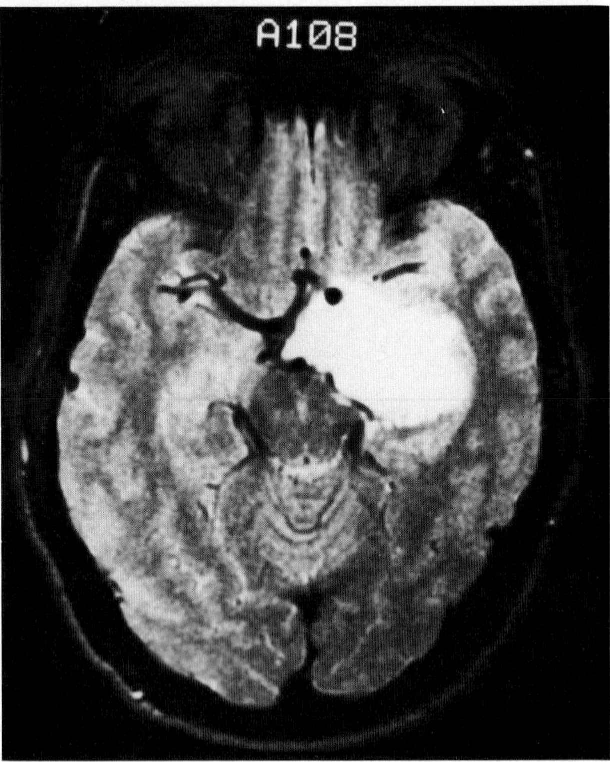

C

Figure 8-41 Epidermoid in the suprasellar and parasellar region. **A.** Coronal MR, T_1WI (800/200) demonstrates a hypointense mass in the left suprasellar region with minimal mass effect on the medial temporal lobe. **B.** Axial MR: PDWI (2000/20) shows an isointense lesion encasing the patent internal carotid artery. **C.** Axial MR: T_2WI (2000/20) exhibits a hyperintense lesion with minimal mass effect on the brainstem. (*Case courtesy of Dr. John Hesselink, University of California, San Diego.*)

teeth, which are exceptional in intracranial dermoids, are ectodermal derivatives and have been reported in craniopharyngiomas (Burger 1982). True adipose tissue is not seen in a dermoid, and its presence may indicate another type of congenital tumor, such as teratoma or intracranial lipoma. (It should be noted here that most "dermoids" found outside of the CNS are in reality benign cystic teratomas, where the primary direction of differentiation has been into ectodermal tissues. The old medical school dogma about one, two, and three germ layers for epidermoid, dermoid, and teratoma, respectively, is fallacious.) Dermoids have a more complex histologic makeup than epidermoids. Dermoids have a thicker wall, and are more likely to show calcification and recognizable contrast enhancement than epidermoids. In addition, the contents of the dermoid cyst are almost invariably heterogeneous, with the light lipid-containing debris forming a supernatant layer over the heavier proteinaceous keratin material.

Dermoids are much more likely than epidermoids to present as midline masses. It has been suggested that the midline location is related to an embryologically earlier incorporation of ectodermal tissue into the neuraxis, which is consistent with the more complex nature of the dermoid. Also distinct from epidermoids is the common association of more complex malformations with dermoids, such as a dorsal or ventral dysraphia or a persistent cutaneous sinus tract—either open or a fibrous strand. Dermoids usually occur at the base of the brain, either in the posterior fossa (where they may invade the fourth ventricle) or in the suprasellar cistern. Peripheral ringlike or eggshell calcification is occasionally seen on plain films (Gross 1945; Lee 1977). Skull films may also reveal a bony defect from an associated dysraphism or an intradiploic component of the dermoid. Dermoids are usually avascular masses on angiography.

CT of dermoids usually demonstrates a hypodense mass that is less dense than an epidermoid, often in the range of attenuation for true fat (−20 to −120 HU) (Amendola 1978; Handa 1979) (Fig. 8-42). The very negative absorption coefficients are not true fat, but rather the lipid material that accumulates from the sebaceous and apocrine sweat glands, as well as cholesterol from the breakdown of squamous epithelium. In vitro dermoid cyst fluid has been measured as low as −80 HU (Handa 1979). The thicker and more complex wall of a dermoid often develops dystrophic peripheral calcifications around the outside of the cyst (Fig. 8-42). In some cases, with appropriate windowing techniques, a Rokitansky nodule, or "hairball," can be identified floating between the lipid-protein interface (Lee 1977) (Fig. 8-43). The tissue contrast of modern third- and fourth-generation

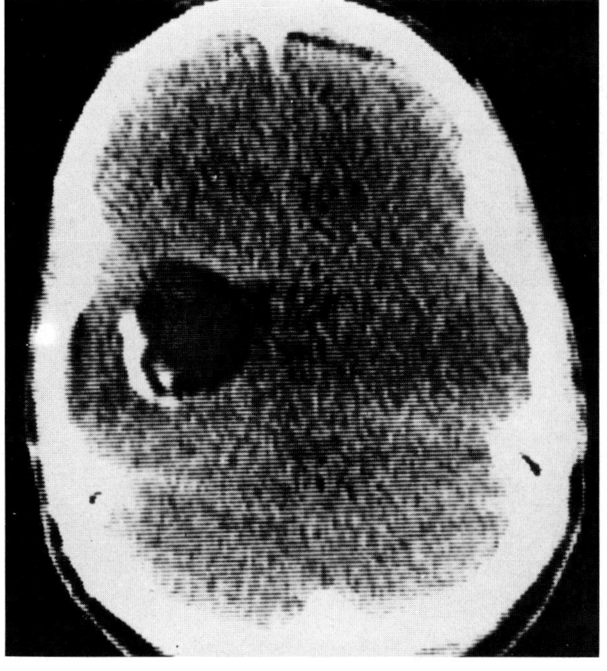
A

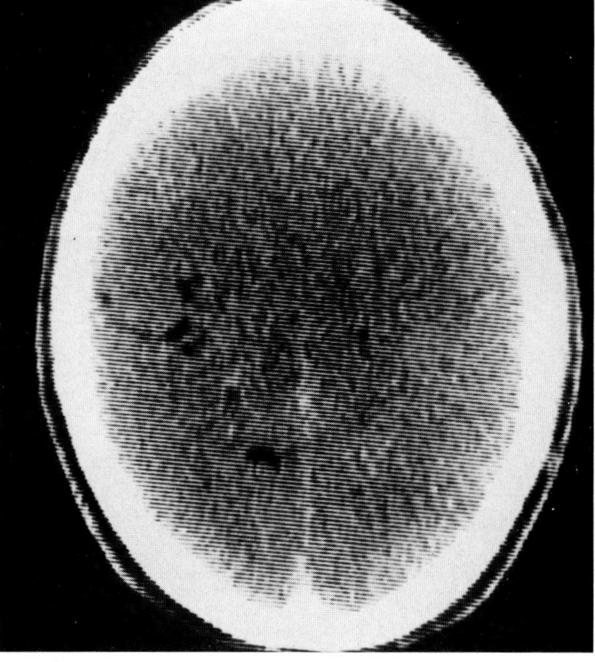
B

Figure 8-42 Dermoid tumor in the temporal lobe. **A.** Temporal lobe hypodense mass (−70 HU) with mural calcification. Soft tissue mass within the cavity is faintly visible. **B.** Multiple small fat densities (lipomatosis) are noted in the sylvian cisterns and convexity sulci. (*Continued on p. 350.*)

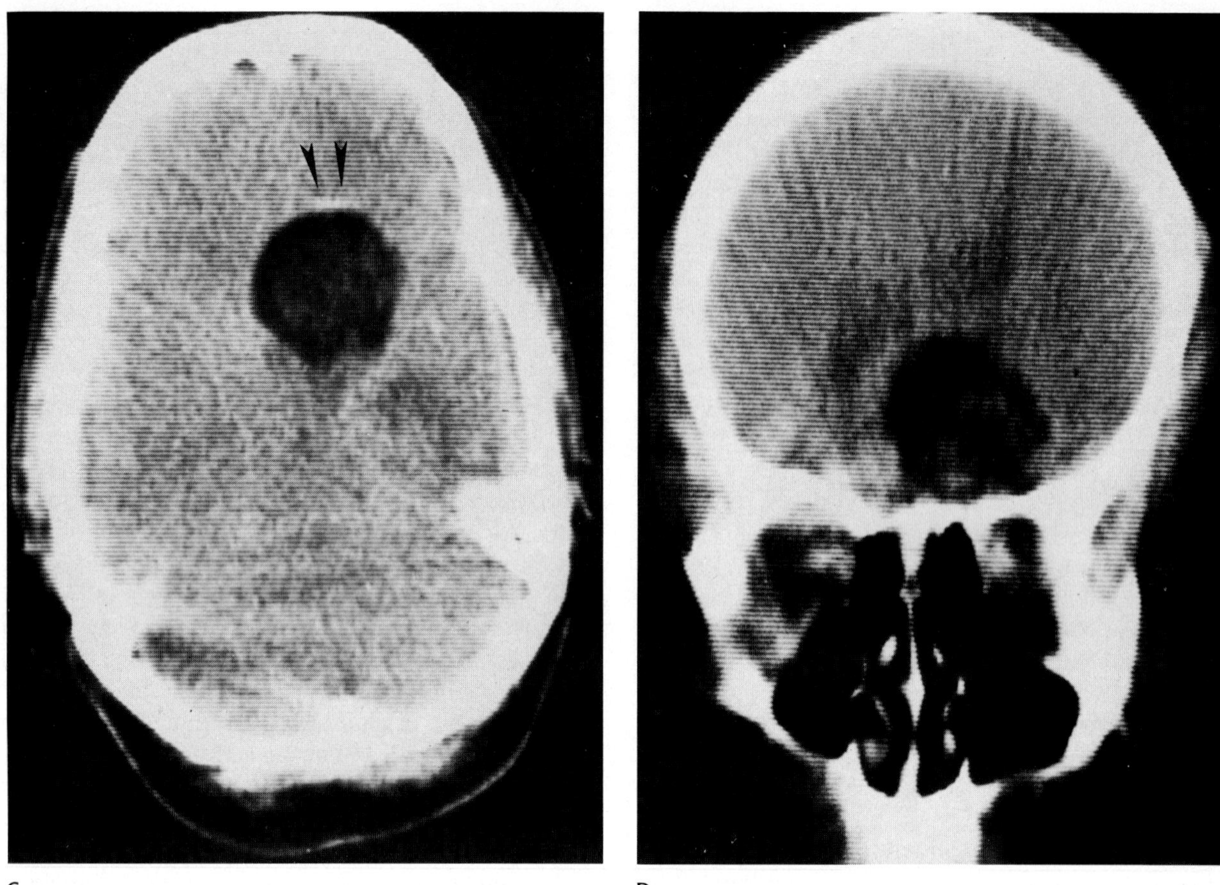

C D

Figure 8-42 (continued) **C.** Dermoid. A large, hypodense, round lesion (−80 HU) with minimal mural calcification (arrowheads) and a soft tissue mass inside, which turned out at surgery to be a hair ball. **D.** Coronal view shows a large soft tissue mass within.

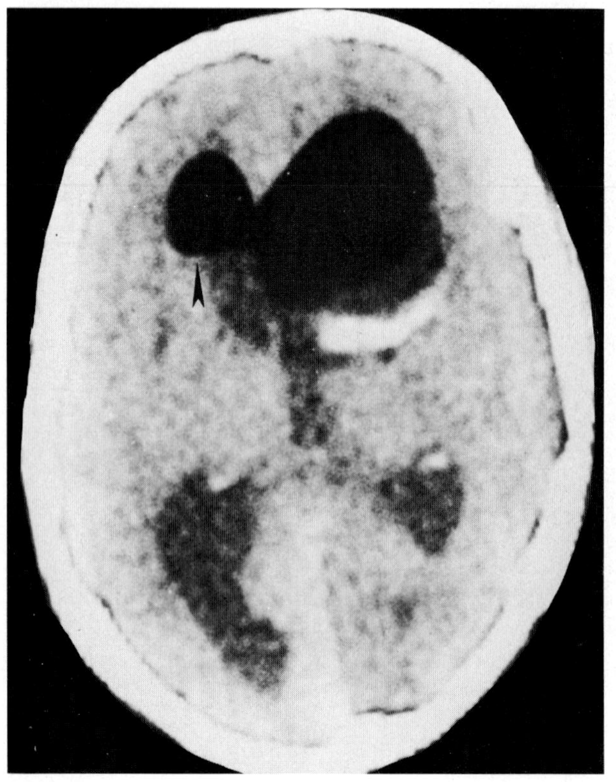

A

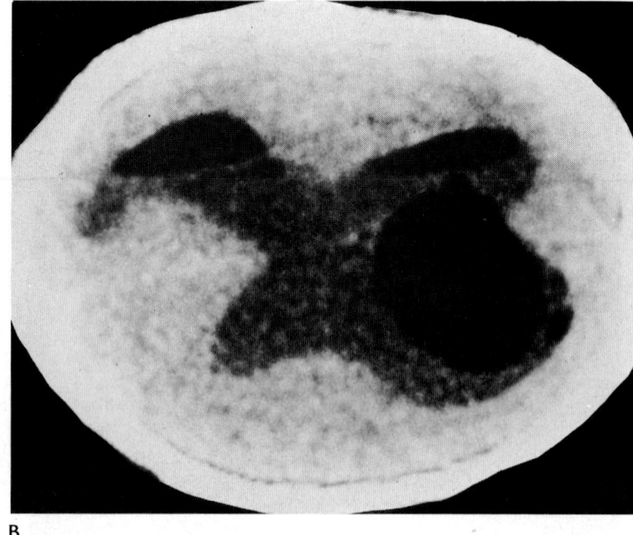

B

Figure 8-43 Frontal dermoid with intraventricular rupture. **A.** Axial CT in supine position demonstrates a large fat-containing mass projecting into the right frontal horn of the lateral ventricle. Calcification is present in the inferior wall of the mass. A fat-CSF level is present in the left front horn (arrowhead). **B.** Right lateral decubitus axial CT demonstrates multiple fat-CSF levels in the left lateral ventricle. Hydrocephalus and the right frontal dermoid are well visualized (*Zimmerman, 1979a*).

scanners often allows visualization of contrast enhancement in the wall of a dermoid. These tumors can be quite soft and pliable, and tend to mold themselves around the contour of adjacent structures.

Spontaneous or iatrogenic rupture of dermoids may allow the cyst contents to spread into the subarachnoid spaces or into the ventricular system—often with catastrophic consequences. Spillage of dermoid material initiates an acute and chronic reaction in the meninges. Acutely, there is a chemical meningitis, which may lead to severe vasospasm and even infarction. Later sequelae include granulomatous changes in the meninges, and the potential for implantation of debris causing "metastatic" dermoid tumors. CT and MR can clearly demonstrate the spread of lipid material into the subarachnoid spaces or even the ventricular system, producing lipid-CSF levels (Zimmerman 1979*a*; Fawcitt 1976; Laster 1977; Amendola 1978; Smith 1991) (Figs. 8-43 and 8-44). Delayed hydrocephalus may accompany rupture of a dermoid cyst. Surgery should be carefully performed to avoid spilling the cyst contents and to effect complete and total removal. These tumors are not truly invasive, but, like craniopharyngiomas, they are often adherent to the adjacent brain, which can make complete resection difficult.

MR of dermoids demonstrates a sharply demarcated heterogeneous extraaxial mass, typically in a midline location. Although expansile, the mass appears "soft," seemingly conforming to the shape of the structures around it. The mass is almost invariably heterogeneous, often demonstrating a characteristic fluid-fluid level. On T_1-WI the dependent portion tends to be dark, but slightly higher in signal than CSF. The supernatant usually has a short T_1, and is quite hyperintense on T_1WI. On T_2WI the entire lesion may become hyperintense. If rupture has occurred, there may be multiple lipid droplets spread throughout the subarachnoid spaces exhibiting conspicuous hyperintensity on T_1WI (Fig. 8-44). This can be pathognomonic when associated with a midline mass. However, residual droplets of the old oily myelographic contrast material, Pantopaque, can also appear as bright droplets on T_1WI.

LIPOMAS

Intracranial lipomas are rare tumors of developmental origin. Recent research (Truwit 1990) suggests that intracranial lipomas may arise from an abnormal persistence of the meninx primativa with subsequent differentiation of that tissue into fat, rather than through an aberrant mesodermal inclusion. About one-half of all intracranial lipomas are asymptomatic, and they are often found in the midsagittal plane in or near the corpus callosum or quadrigeminal plate cistern. Other sites of occurrence

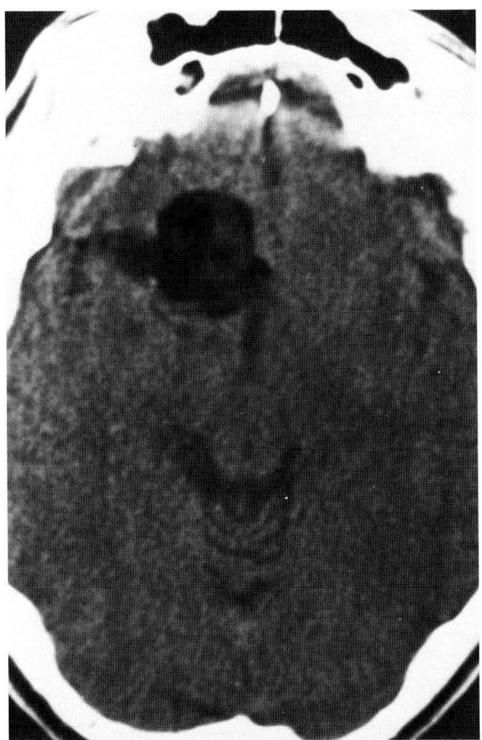

A

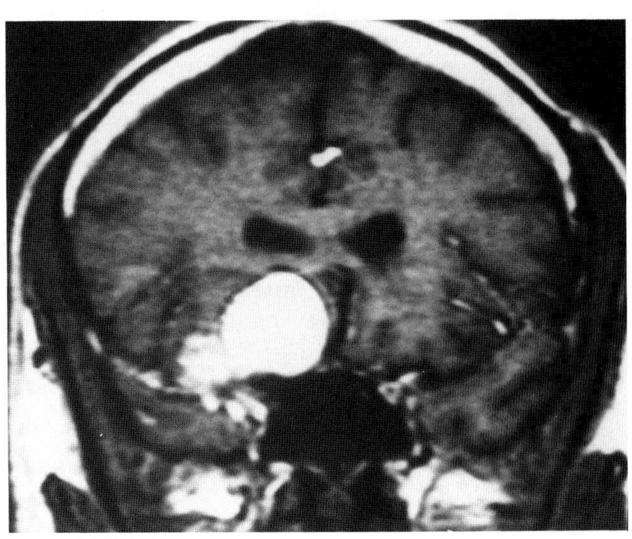

B

Figure 8-44 Ruptured dermoid. On NCCT (**A**) a hypointense mass at the right basal frontal region extends into the sylvian fissure. MR, T_1WI (**B**) shows hyperintensity fatty tumor with multiple CSF seedings. (*Continued on p. 352.*)

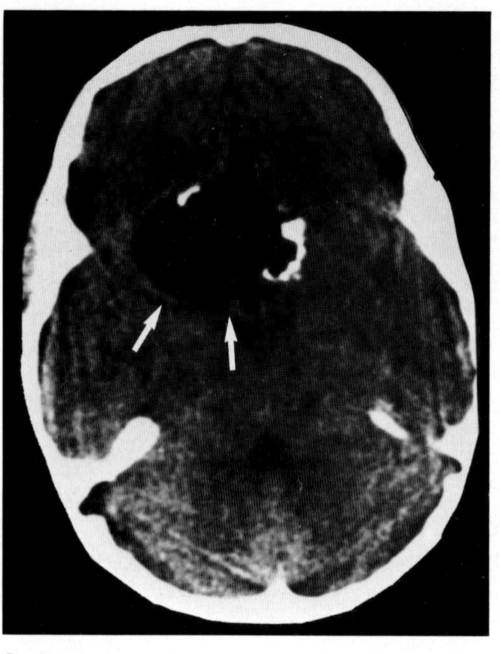

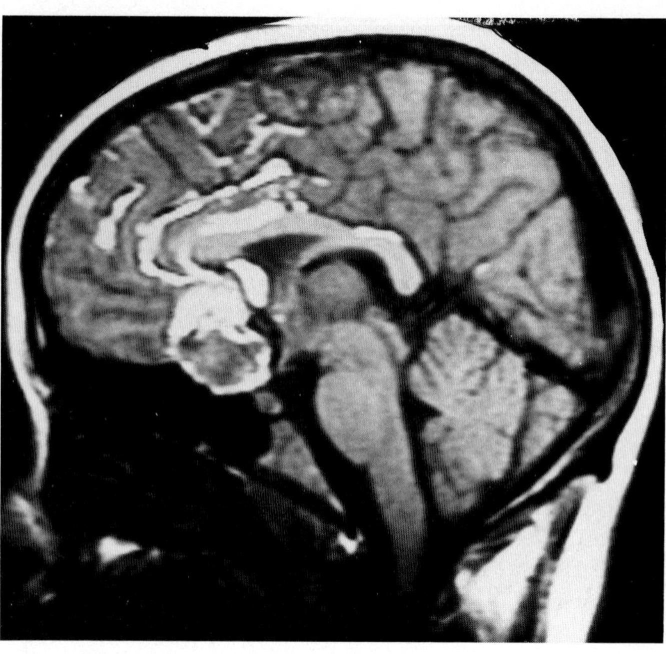

C D

Figure 8-44 ***(continued)*** **C.** and **D.** Rupture of a dermoid into the subarachnoid space. Axial NCCT (**C**) demonstrates a parasellar fatty mass (arrows) with peripheral calcifications. A sagittal MRI, T_1-weighted (**D**) discloses a hyperintense parasellar mass (dermoid) with hyperintense frontal sulci representing fatty tissue in the adjacent and distant sulci. Sulcal widening by fat is a characteristic MR finding in a ruptured intracranial dermoid. (*Courtesy of Dr. Francis J. Hahn, University of Nebraska Medical Center, Omaha, Nebraska.*)

are at the base of the skull, including the cerebellopontine angle cistern. Some lipomas develop other elements, including calcification, or are part of a more complex malformation such as lipomeningocele, agenesis of the vermis, and cranium bifidum (Zettner 1960; Kushnet 1978).

Lipoma of the corpus callosum is associated with agenesis of the corpus callosum in almost half of the cases (Zettner 1960). Skull radiographs may show midline curvilinear or "eggshell" mural calcifications in the rim of the callosal lipoma surrounding the radiolucent fat. These findings are usually anterior, within the genu of the corpus callosum. Imaging studies, including pneumoencephalography and axial cross-sectional scans, will demonstrate a symmetrical separation of the frontal horns of the lateral ventricles where they are spread apart by the lipoma. This alteration is clearly depicted on CT (see Chap. 4). An almost definitive diagnosis of lipoma can be made on CT in the presence of hypodensity of very low attenuation (e.g., less than −90 HU); and on MR, definitive diagnosis is made on the basis of the characteristic signal intensity of fat: marked T_1 and T_2 shortening with hyperintensity on T_1WI and iso- or hypointensity on T_2WI (Fig. 8-45).

GERM CELL TUMORS

Germ cell tumor is the most common neoplasm found in the pineal region, and the majority of intracranial germ neoplasms are related to the pineal. However, all types of germ cell neoplasms may also be seen, although less commonly, in the suprasellar or parasellar regions. There are two prevailing theories which may explain the unusual origin of germ cell neoplasms deep within the CNS. One theory suggests that the fetal tissues of an aborted twin become absorbed into the viable fetus at the early stage of neural tube closure, 3 to 5 weeks. The second theory, more plausible, suggests that during the time that the germ cells normally migrate to form the urogenital ridge, some cells become abnormally implanted within other tissues in other regions, almost invariably in a midline location. These germ cell rests may later develop into a variety of germ cell neoplasms, including tumors of fetal-type tissues.

CNS *germinomas* are histologically almost identical to testicular seminomas. Tumors with the same histology occurring in the mediastinum or the ovary are often called *dysgerminomas.* These tumors have a "two cell" pattern—lobules of primitive germ cells embedded in a matrix of lymphocytes (or lymphocyte-like cells). In addition to the typical germinoma histologic types, other germ-cell tumors can occur: benign teratoma (mature), malignant teratoma (teratocarcinoma, immature teratoma, teratoma with malignant change), embryonal carcinoma, choriocarcinoma, and endodermal sinus tumor (yolk-sac tumor) (Table 8-10). The immature teratomas are composed of embryonic or fetal-type tissue; mature

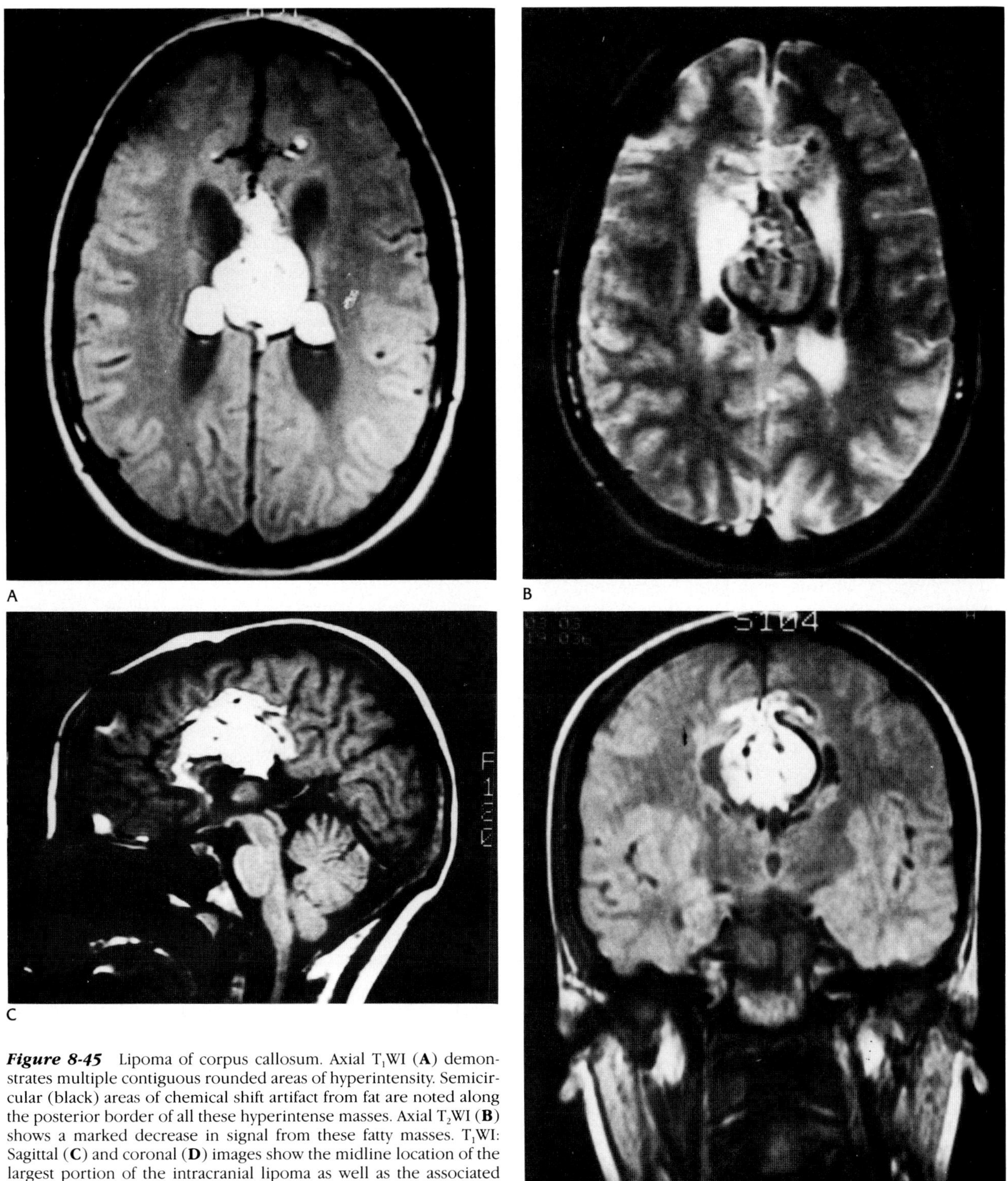

Figure 8-45 Lipoma of corpus callosum. Axial T_1WI (**A**) demonstrates multiple contiguous rounded areas of hyperintensity. Semicircular (black) areas of chemical shift artifact from fat are noted along the posterior border of all these hyperintense masses. Axial T_2WI (**B**) shows a marked decrease in signal from these fatty masses. T_1WI: Sagittal (**C**) and coronal (**D**) images show the midline location of the largest portion of the intracranial lipoma as well as the associated maldevelopment of the corpus callosum.

teratomas have adult-type tissues. In both types there is a combination of tissues derived from more than one germ layer.

Germinomas tend to be isointense to gray matter on T_1WI and isointense or slightly hyperintense on T_2WI. Choriocarcinoma is prone to hemorrhage; dermoid, epidermoid, and teratoma may contain lipid (cholesterol) or true fat. Thus, any of these four tumors may have hyperintense regions on T_1WI, and teratomas (Fig. 8-46) and epidermoids can also be hypointense (Tien 1990). Re-

Table 8-10 Germ Cell Neoplasms

I. Germinoma (dysgerminoma, seminoma)
II. Embryonal carcinoma
  A. Extraembryonic type
    1. Endodermal sinus (yolk sac) tumor
    2. Choriocarcinoma
  B. Embryonic type
    1. Immature teratoma
    2. Mature teratoma
III. Mixed types
  A. Teratocarcinoma (teratoma and embryonal carcinoma)
  B. Other mixtures

gions of T_1 shortening in a dermoid may show less intensity on the T_2WI sequence when that signal is due mostly to lipid. However, the hyperintense regions of an epidermoid on T_1WI may become even more hyperintense on T_2WI because they have proteinaceous fluid in addition to cholesterol.

Pineal-Region Tumors

Tumors in the region of the pineal gland, which represent 1 to 3 percent of all intracranial neoplasms, are of various histologic types. Tumors in this region have been generically referred to as "pinealomas," after the predominant neoplasm in this location. However, the vast majority of the tumors that are called pinealoma are not derived from pineal tissue but instead arise from embryologic rests of germ cells. Approximately 59 percent of pineal-region masses are of such germ cell derivation, with the largest group, 39 percent, being typical germinomas. Many different lesions may present in the pineal region, and within the germ cell group, chemotherapeutic regimens are often quite specific for particular histologies. It is frequently not possible to accurately predict the actual tumor histology based on CT or MR alone, and therefore biopsy is usually required. Also, because of the high frequency of mixed germ cell tumors, the neurosurgeon must be careful to obtain an adequate sample. The identification of serum markers may also suggest a particular histology (see Table 8-11).

PINEAL GERMININOMAS

Germinomas may spread readily through the subarachnoid space and can infiltrate into the posterior third ventricle and thalamus. However, in some cases they are surprisingly well localized and demarcated. Eighty percent of intracranial germinomas will be found in the pineal region; the other 20 percent are usually suprasellar.

Germinomas tend to be very homogeneous masses on both CT and MR and are almost always slightly more dense than normal brain on NCCT (Chang 1989). On MR, germinomas tend to be isointense to gray matter on T_1WI, and may be isointense (Zee 1991) or slightly hyperintense on T_2WI (Tien 1990). The lesions may be rounded or slightly lobulated, and can conform to the shape of the CSF-containing spaces that they fill, including anterior extension along the cistern of the velum interpositum (Fig. 8-47). However, they are also capable of CSF spread and direct invasion into the third ventricle and/or the adjacent thalamus and brainstem tissues. The germinoma itself is usually not calcified; however, there is a strong association between the presence of a germinoma and early dense calcification within the pineal gland itself (Chang 1989). As with many other masses that involve the subarachnoid space, occasionally the tumor may pinch off a "lake" of CSF, and thus appear to be partially cystic. Since these tumors (and the normal pineal gland) lack a blood-brain barrier, contrast-infused CT and MR invariably demonstrate some degree of enhancement, which is usually very uniform (Chang 1989). CEMR will demonstrate homogeneous enhancement and may reveal CSF seeding (Tien 1990) (Fig. 8-47).

PINEOCYTOMAS AND PINEOBLASTOMAS

These are the true intrinsic tumors of the pineal gland. The malignant pineoblastoma is a subtype of primitive neuroectodermal tumors (PNET), and is about six times more common than the benign pineocytoma; these neoplasms account for 12 and 2 percent of all pineal-region masses, respectively. One distinguishing characteristic of potential differential value is that these tumors usually contain intrinsic calcification and are *inside* rather than *around* the pineal gland (unlike the germ cell tumors). Most intrinsic pineal neoplasms are similar in radiologic appearance: partially calcified and slightly hyperdense on NCCT, with contrast enhancement on CECT. These tumors may be slightly hypointense to white matter on

Table 8-11 Laboratory Tests for Pineal Neoplasms

NEOPLASM	HCG	AFP
Germinoma	—*	—
Yolk sac	—	Increased
Choriocancer	Increased	—
Embryonal cancer	Increased	Increased

**Occasionally positive.*

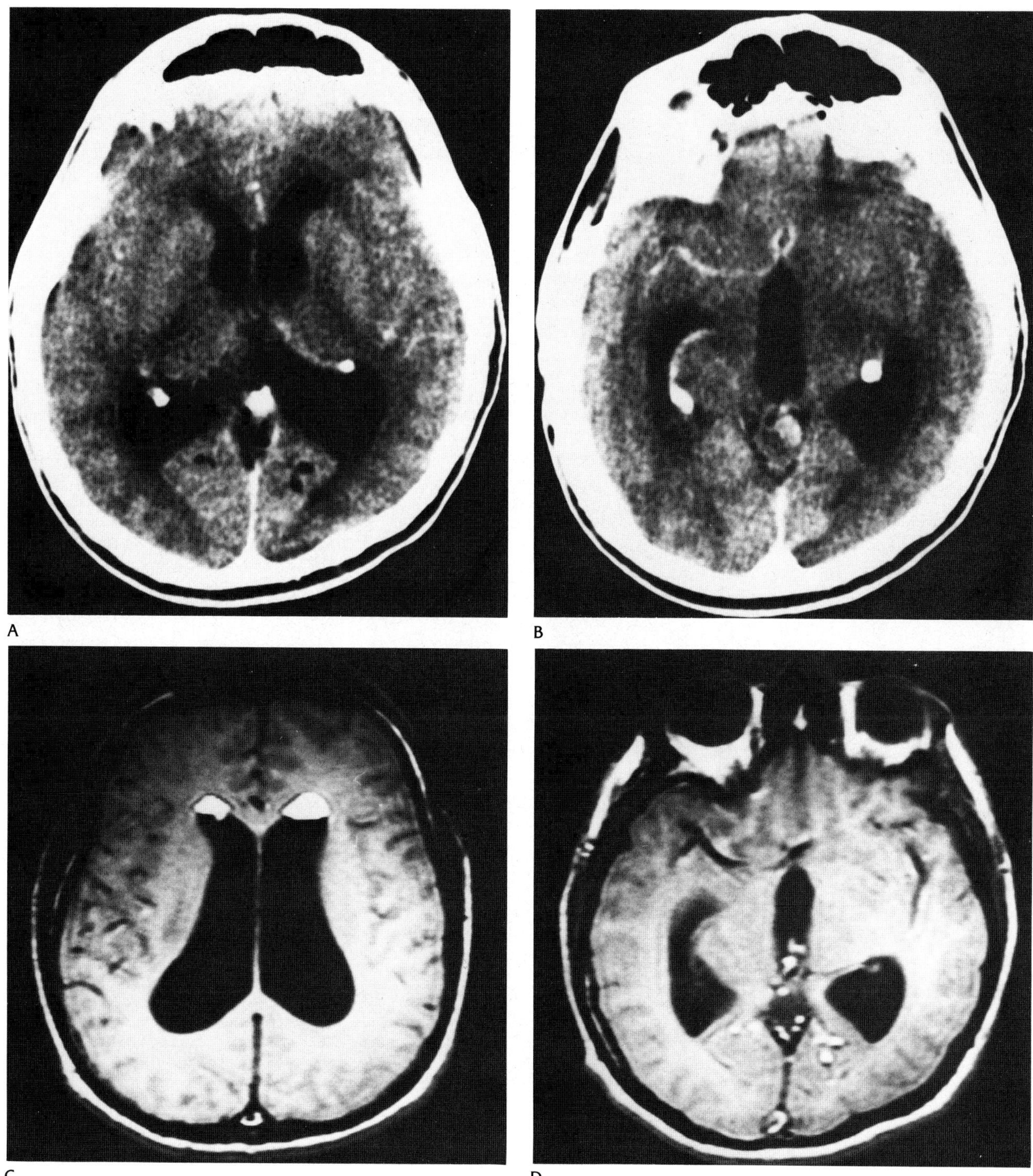

Figure 8-46 Ruptured teratoma. CECT (**A** and **B**) shows a complex pineal region mass consisting of hyperdense foci of calcification and hypodense droplets of lipid. Because of rupture, lipid droplets are found in the subarachnoid spaces of the medial occipital sulci (**B**). T_1WI (**C**) shows the high intensity of the fat droplets in the sulci and in the ruptured teratoma itself. There is a fat-CSF level in the lateral ventricles on the adjacent section (**D**).

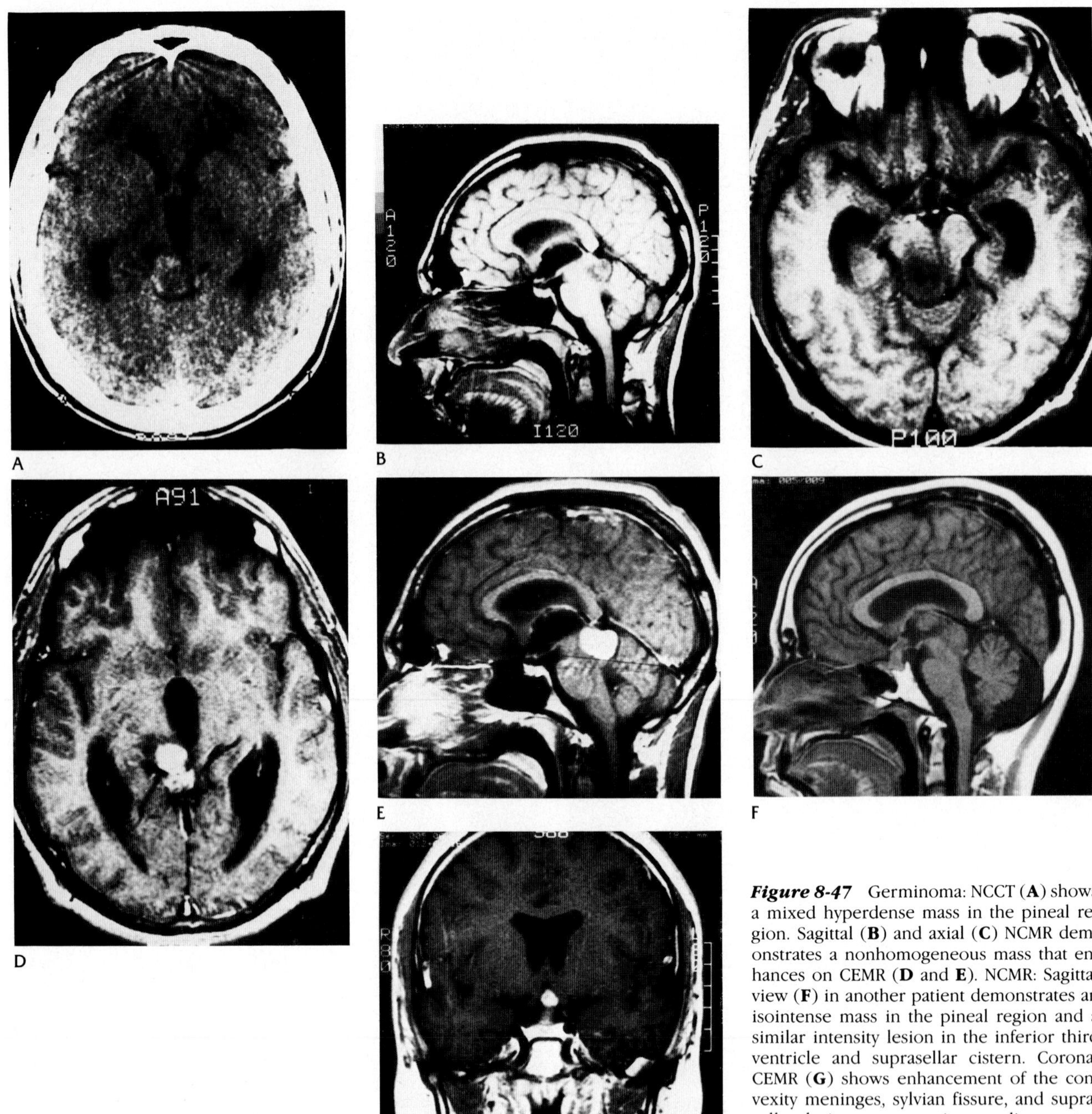

Figure 8-47 Germinoma: NCCT (**A**) shows a mixed hyperdense mass in the pineal region. Sagittal (**B**) and axial (**C**) NCMR demonstrates a nonhomogeneous mass that enhances on CEMR (**D** and **E**). NCMR: Sagittal view (**F**) in another patient demonstrates an isointense mass in the pineal region and a similar intensity lesion in the inferior third ventricle and suprasellar cistern. Coronal CEMR (**G**) shows enhancement of the convexity meninges, sylvian fissure, and suprasellar lesion, representing seeding metastasis from the pineal germinoma.

T_1WI (Fig. 8-48) and have variable characteristics ranging from isointensity to hyperintensity on PD-WI and T_2WI. The pineal gland may also harbor another PNET, a *retinoblastoma,* in patients with inherited (or somatic mutation) multifocal retinoblastoma. This condition with bilateral occular lesions and a third focus in the pineal gland is called *trilateral retinoblastoma.*

In addition to the germ cell tumors and true tumors of the pineal parenchyma—the malignant pineoblastoma and the benign pineocytoma—there is a wide variety of other tumors that may present in the pineal region, which includes the tectal plate of the mesencephalon and the adjacent quadrigeminal plate cistern. These include gliomas of the tectum and splenium of the corpus callosum; benign pineal cysts; dermoid, epidermoid, and arachnoid cysts; lipomas; and meingiomas. Rarely, gliomas can arise from the pineal gland itself since the normal pineal gland includes fibrillary astrocytes. This cannot be differentiated from other pineal region tumors (Fig. 8-49).

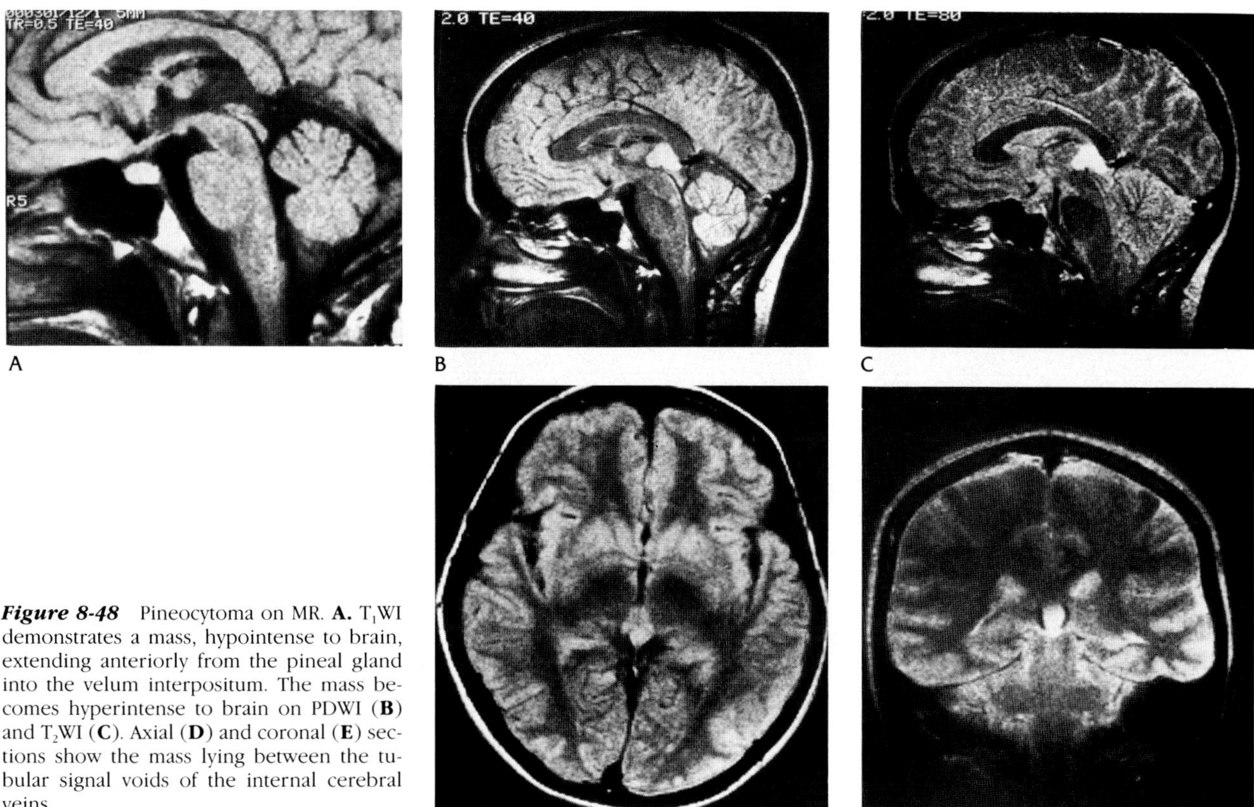

Figure 8-48 Pineocytoma on MR. **A.** T_1WI demonstrates a mass, hypointense to brain, extending anteriorly from the pineal gland into the velum interpositum. The mass becomes hyperintense to brain on PDWI (**B**) and T_2WI (**C**). Axial (**D**) and coronal (**E**) sections show the mass lying between the tubular signal voids of the internal cerebral veins.

PINEAL CYSTS

Pineal cysts have been recognized with increased frequency on MR, with an incidence approaching about 5 percent. They may represent a residual ependymal-lined space of the pineal diverticulum from the third ventricle but also can be a degenerative process. Benign pineal cysts are sharply demarcated intraparenchymal homogeneous masses which are hypointense to brain but hyperintense to CSF on T_1WI. Because they may contain proteinaceous fluid, they are often more hyperintense than CSF on PD-WI and T_2WI. The cyst itself will not enhance; however, normal enhancement in the pineal gland tissue, which is compressed into a rim around the cyst, may give an erroneous impression of a ring-shaped enhancing neoplasm. This latter finding is uncommon on CT, but may be more easily detected on CEMR (Fig. 8-50).

Tumors in the pineal region may be differentiated by careful analysis of their characteristic features. The germinomas tend to be homogeneous masses surrounding a prematurely calcified pineal gland. The other lesions tend to be heterogeneous, complicated by hemorrhage (choriocarcinoma), fat (teratoma), cholesterol (dermoid and epidermoid), and calcification within the tumor itself (teratoma), not the gland. The pineal parenchymal tumors enlarge the pineal gland from inside, and may displace preexisting calcification of the gland. The pineal cyst is homogeneous and nearly iosintense to CSF; the pineocytoma is homogeneous and nearly isointense to brain; and the pineoblastoma is often heterogeneous and hyperintense on T_2WI. Both pineal parenchymal neoplasms enhance; this is not surprising, since the normal gland also enhances. CEMR increases the specificity of pineal neoplasms by providing better delineation of the tumor margin and demonstrating cystic components of the neoplasm (Zee 1991).

COLLOID CYSTS

This entity accounts for 0.5 to 1 percent of all intracranial tumors (Guner 1976). Very few colloid cysts are seen in infancy and childhood, with most being found in early adult life. Males and females are about equally affected. It is thought that most colloid cysts are generated from the ependymal pouches (Ariens-Kappers 1955). Mucoid or dense hyaline material is surrounded by a smooth, spherical, fibrous wall, and the cyst is attached to the collagenous stroma of the choroid plexus. Within the third ventricle the cyst is notorious for obstructing the foramen of Monro and can be as large as 3 cm. If the mass is somewhat pendulous and movable, intermittent obstruction becomes a possibility (Guner 1976).

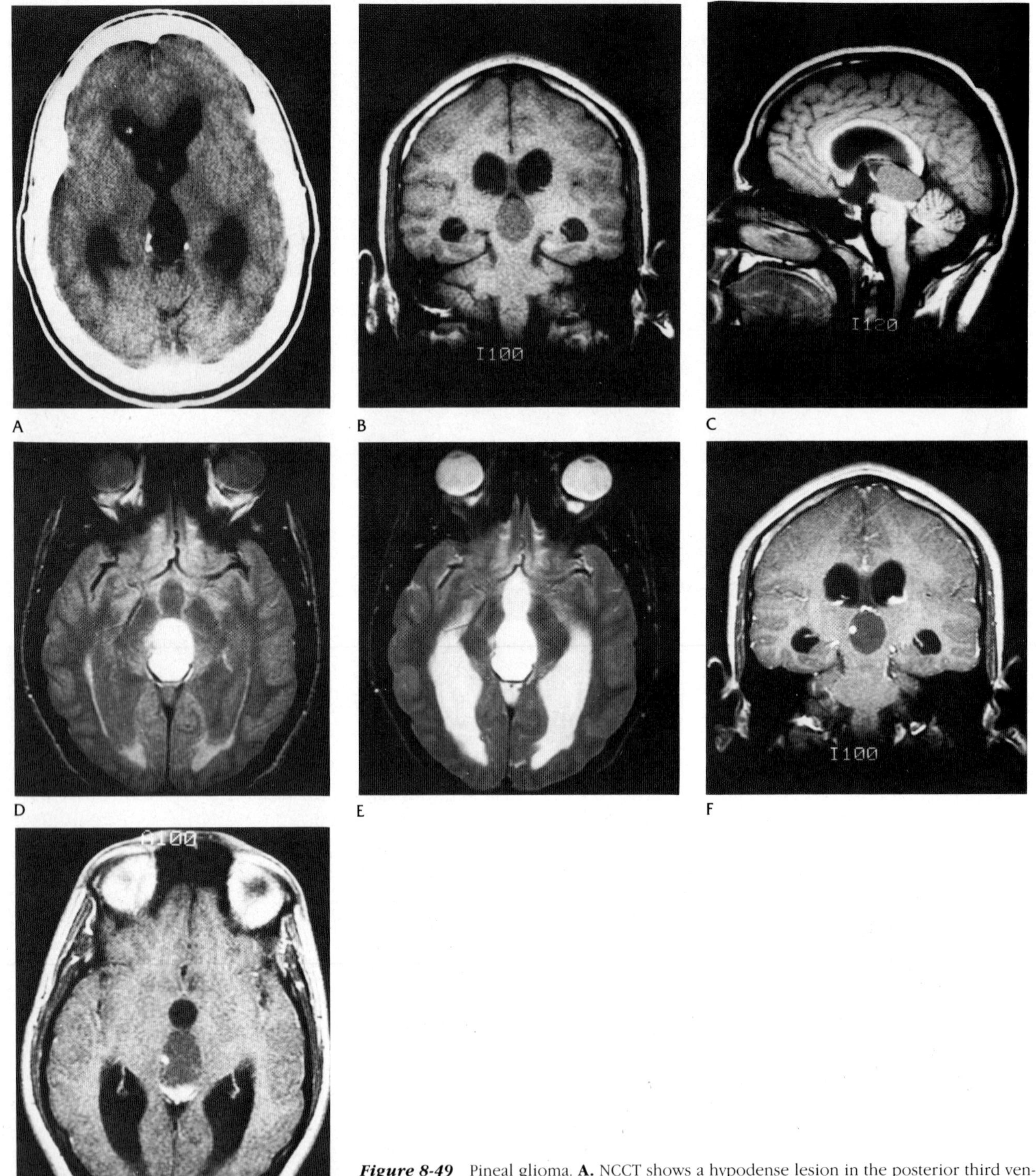

Figure 8-49 Pineal glioma. **A.** NCCT shows a hypodense lesion in the posterior third ventricular region with calcification. T_1WI: Coronal (**B**) and sagittal (**C**) views exhibit isointensity that increases in intensity on T_2WI, coronal (**D**) and sagittal (**E**). CEMR: coronal (**F**) and axial (**G**) views show marginal enhancement.

Common symptoms and physical findings are headache, gait disturbance, and papilledema (Little 1974). Although these tumors are benign and can be completely removed early in their course, Guner et al. (1976) report a postoperative mortality as high as 53 percent. It is presumed that this figure is high because of the difficult surgical approach and the complex regional anatomy.

NCCT shows a sharply marginated spherical or ovoid lesion of homogeneously high density (45 to 75 HU) in the anterior third ventricle, in front of or behind the fo-

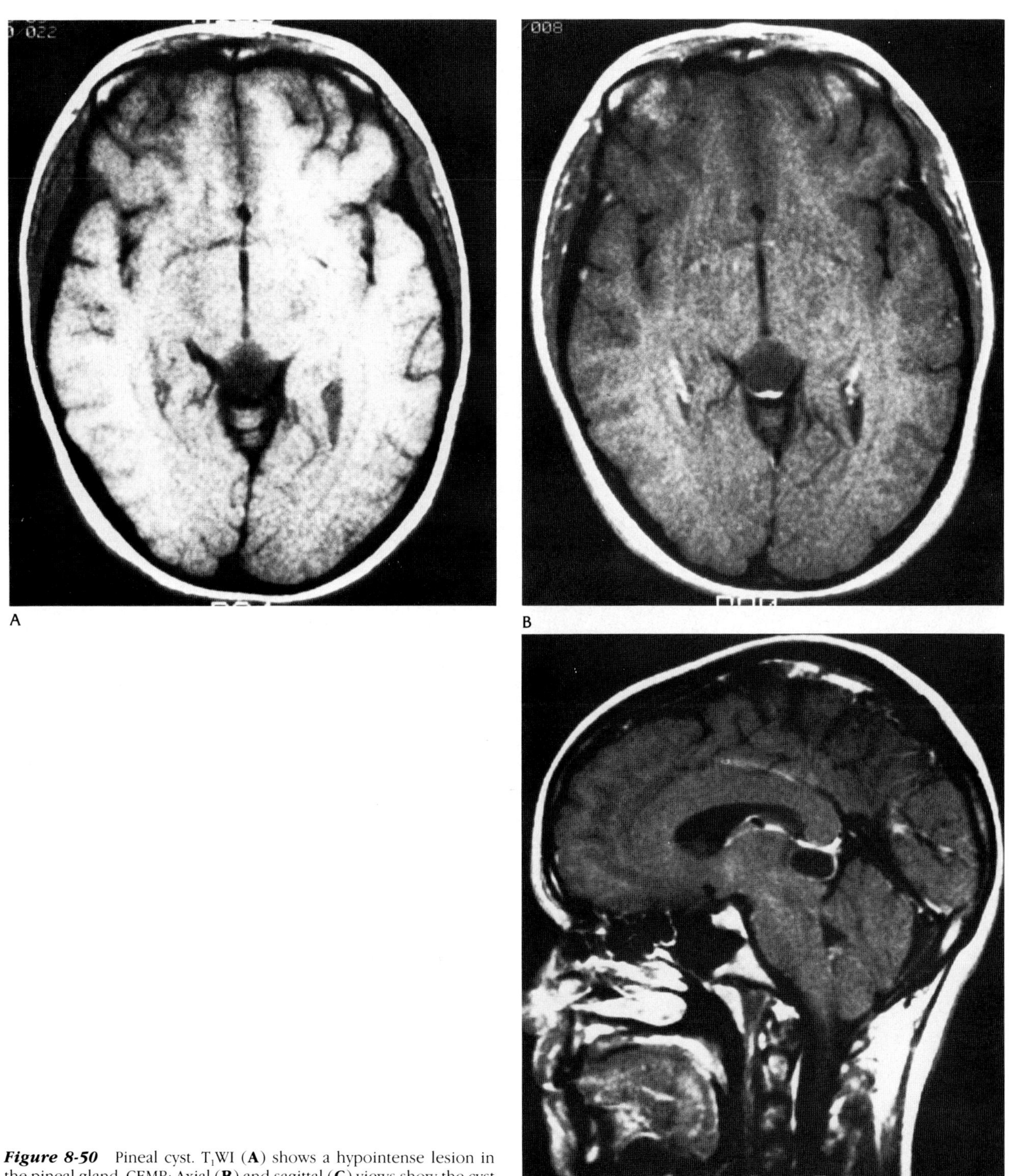

Figure 8-50 Pineal cyst. T_1WI (**A**) shows a hypointense lesion in the pineal gland. CEMR: Axial (**B**) and sagittal (**C**) views show the cyst clearly.

ramen of Monro (Fig. 8-51). Uncommonly, the lesion is isodense, and, rarely, a central hypodensity within the lesion is noted (Ganti 1981). The high density on NCCT is probably due to desquamative secretory products from the cyst wall, hemosiderin, and possibly microscopic foci of calcification, although the latter are not apparent on CT. Only mild enhancement has been shown on CECT (Osborn 1977; Ganti 1981) (Fig. 8-51), but absence of contrast enhancement is not unusual. The presence of blood vessels in the wall or even inside the cyst, as well as diffusion of contrast media into the cavity, may account for the enhancement. Hemorrhage is rare (Malik 1980).

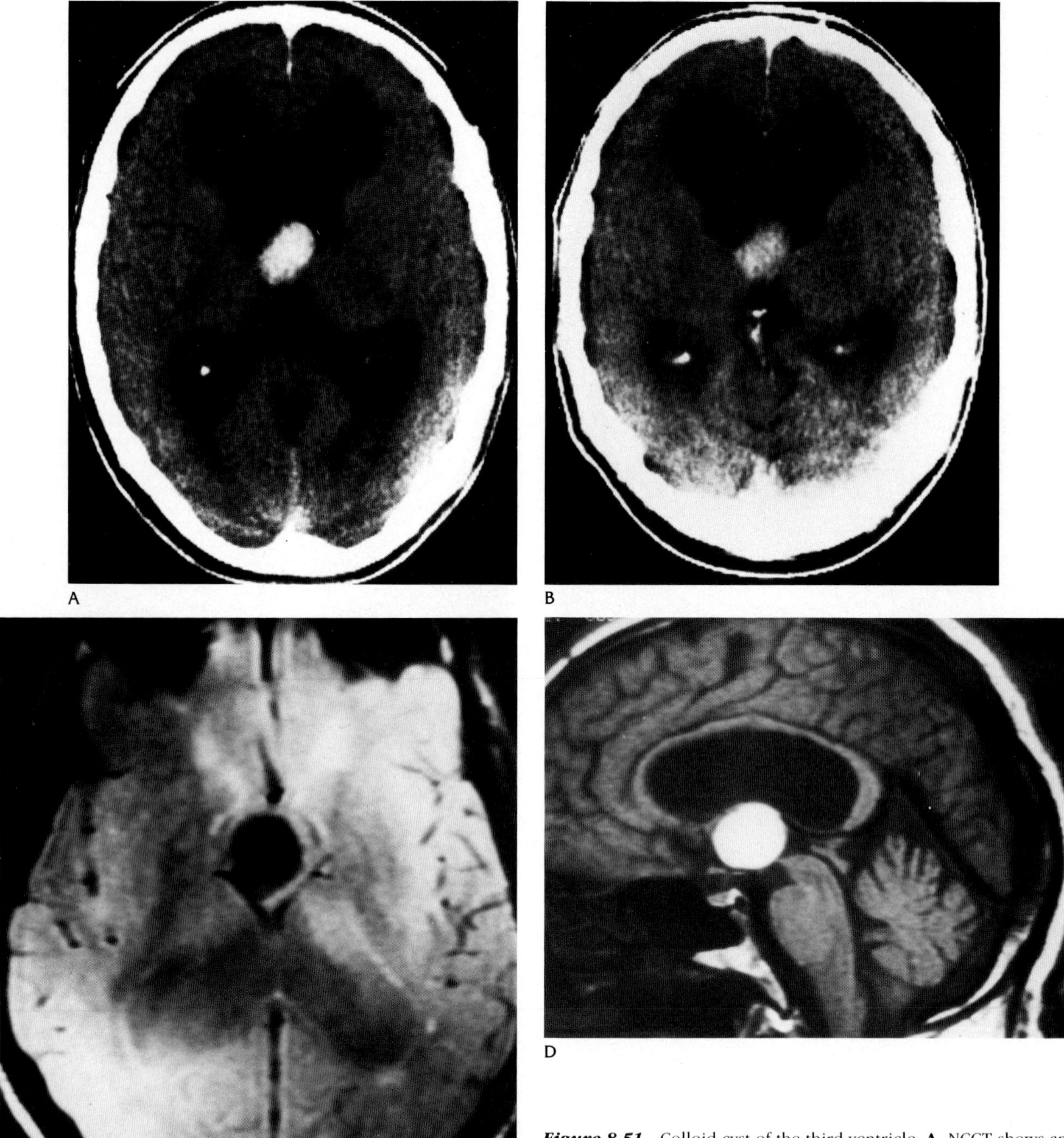

Figure 8-51 Colloid cyst of the third ventricle. **A.** NCCT shows an oval hyperdense lesion in the region of the third ventricle with separation of the posteromedial sides of the frontal horns. **B.** Axial CECT demonstrates mild CE. Noncommunicating hydrocephalus is apparent. Angiogram prior to surgical intervention is necessary to rule out aneurysm. **C.** PDWI shows hypointensity. **D.** T_1WI shows hyperintensity.

Although minimal to moderately severe hydrocephalus is present in most cases, its degree is not always proportional to the size of the cyst. Frequently, the anterior portion of the third ventricle is not well visualized, and the posterior third ventricle is usually collapsed. Widening of the septum pellucidum and the separation of the posteromedial aspects of the frontal horns are demonstrated in most cases on axial and coronal sections (Ganti 1981) (Fig. 8-51). Intraventricular ependymoma, glioma, meningioma, choroid plexus papilloma, arteriovenous malformation, craniopharyngioma, teratomatous tumors, tuberous sclerosis, and cysticercosis should be considered in the differential diagnosis. Occasionally, contrast ventriculography or cisternography may be necessary to localize the lesion within the third ventricle. However, the need for additional invasive study has greatly diminished since the availability of high-resolution CT scanners and, especially, the multiplanor capability of MRI. However, when atypical and unusual contrast enhancement is present, the possibility of aneurysm or ectatic vessels should be strongly considered and investigated by cerebral angiography.

The appearance of colloid cysts on MR images is quite variable (Maeder 1990; Wilms 1990; Roosen 1987). Their appearance on MR is similar to their gross appearance on CT; they are sharply circumscribed lesions of the anterior superior third ventricle, usually in or near the foramen of Monro in symptomatic patients (Fig. 8-52). If the foramen is obstructed by the colloid cyst, MR may demonstrate periventricular signal abnormalities related to hydrostatic interstitial edema, as well as altered CSF flow dynamics within the ventricular system itself. Although usually homogeneous on CT, colloid cysts are heterogeneous on MR in the majority of cases (Maeder 1990). The signal intensity of colloid cysts is an unreliable diagnostic criterion, since they may vary from hypointense to hyperintense on both T_1WI and T_2WI. (Maeder 1990; Wilms 1990; Roosen 1987) (Figs. 8-51 and 8-52). One unex-

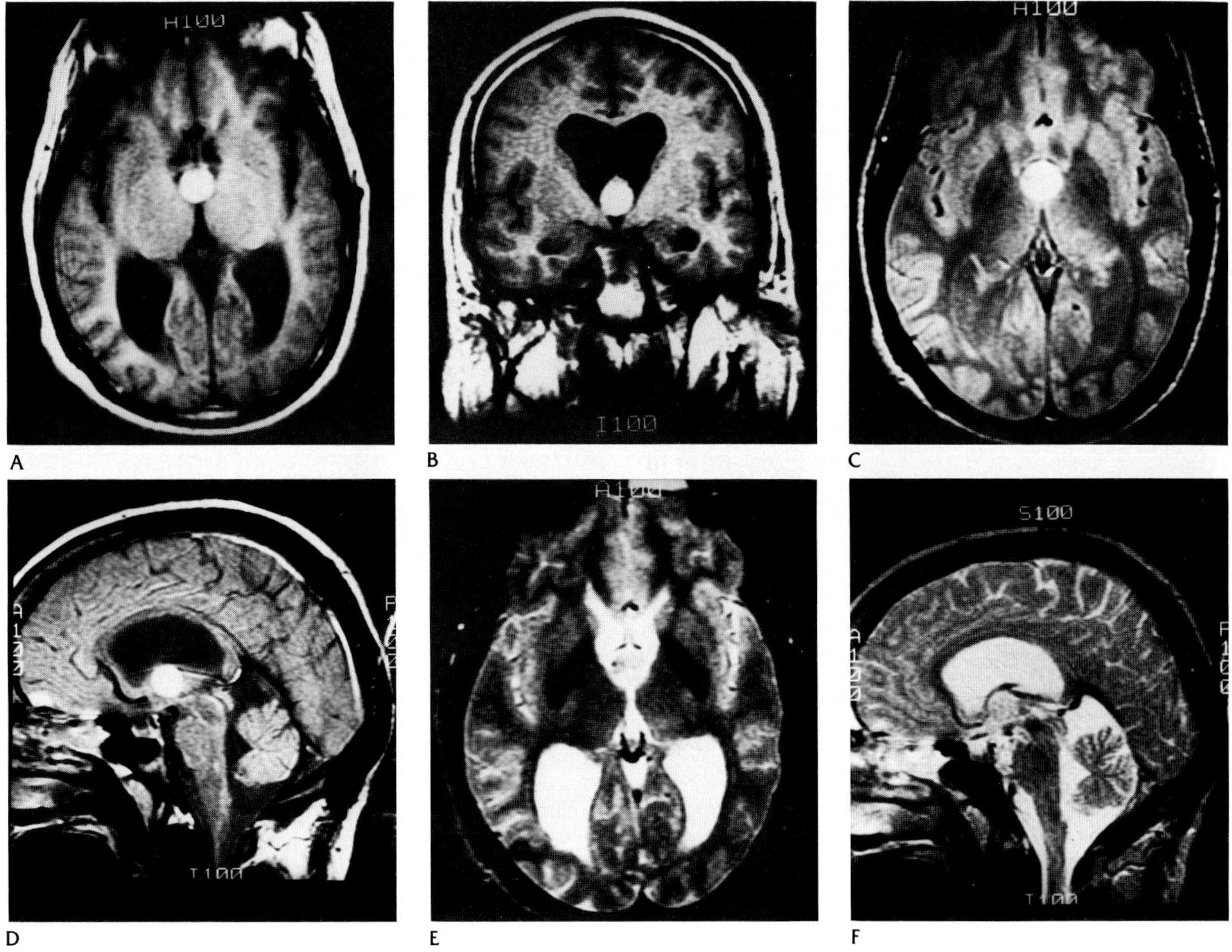

Figure 8-52 Colloid cyst. T_1WI: **A** and **B** show a hyperintense lesion in the anterior third. PDWI: **C** and **D** show hyperintensity, which slightly decreases on T_2WI (**E**) and (**F**).

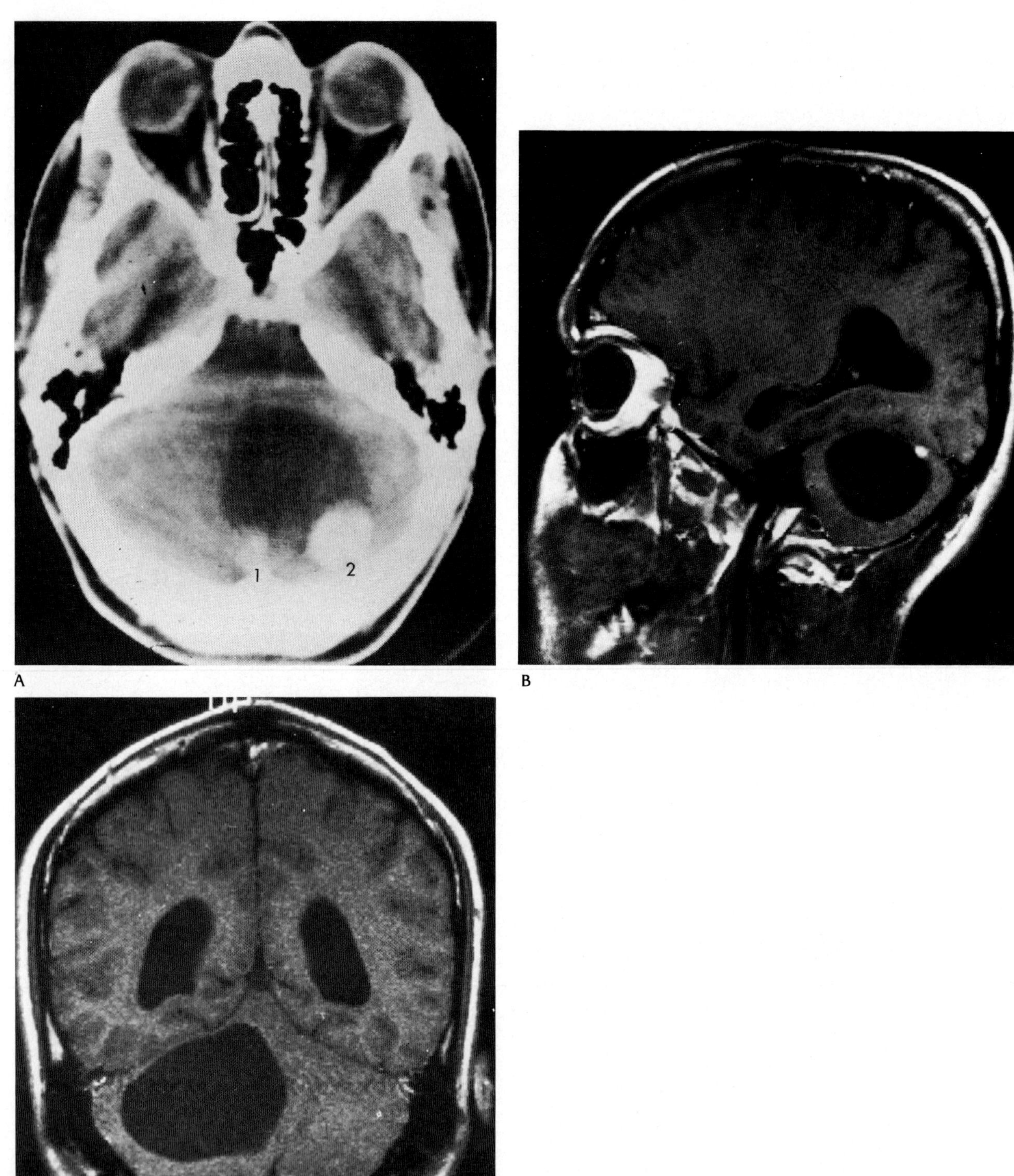

Figure 8-53 Hemangioblastoma. **A.** On CECT, a large cystic posterior fossa tumor is noted in the left cerebellum. Two round, homogeneously enhancing tumor nodules (1, 2) are present at the posterolateral wall of the cyst. Absence of enhancement of the cyst wall itself is characteristic. **B** and **C.** A cystic lesion with a mural nodule.

pected MR finding, seen on T_2WI, is the presence of a hyperintense peripheral rim surrounding a hypo- to isointense center—a target lesion (Fig. 8-52) (Maeder 1990; Wilms 1990). This finding remains unexplained; it is not due to any pathologically visible process (Wilms 1990), nor has it been clarified by chemical analysis (Maeder 1990). Therefore, the most characteristic and suggestive features of colloid cyst remain its sharp delineation and characteristic location within the third ventricle near the foramen of Monro.

Miscellaneous Tumors

HEMANGIOBLASTOMAS

These are histologically benign true neoplasms of vascular origin and composition. They constitute from 1.1 to 2.5 percent of all intracranial tumors; approximately 35 to 60 percent are cystic, with a mural nodule. The tumor may be associated with erythrocytosis and is the primary feature of Hippel-Lindau disease (Russell 1989). They are the most common primary intraaxial neoplasms of the posterior fossa in adults. CT may demonstrate a solid homogeneous isodense mass with distinctive contrast enhancement after intravenous contrast injection. More characteristically, a cystic tumor with one or more solid mural nodules is demonstrated (Fig. 8-53). The mural nodules are enhanced homogeneously and may be solitary or multiple (Adair 1978). The central hypodense areas of the cyst fluid range from 4 to 23 HU and show no contrast enhancement (Fig. 8-53). An isodense cyst margin with no demonstrable contrast enhancement represents gliosis and compressed cerebellum and is not neoplastic. In contrast, areas that are hyperdense on NCCT and that show contrast enhancement correspond to the richly vascular neoplastic tissue. Rarely, central hypodensity suggestive of a cyst may prove to be solid tumor tissue. Angiography not only confirms the presence of the hypervascular mural nodules but also increases the detection rate for multiple lesions (Seeger 1981). Rare cases of supratentorial hemangioblastoma have been recorded (Wylie 1973; Bachmann 1978).

MR of hemangioblastoma reveals the same gross characteristics noted on CT. The tumor may be solid, in which case differential diagnosis can be difficult (Fig. 8-53). However, MR may also reveal only a cyst or the classic cyst with mural nodule appearance (Fig. 8-52). Three additional features of hemangioblastoma have been identified on MR (Lee 1989; Katz 1989). First, the T_1WI may show foci of signal hyperintensity within the solid portions of a hemangioblastoma (Fig. 8-54). These foci may contain blood breakdown products from previous hemorrhage; alternatively, the T_1 shortening may come from the lipid-containing "stromal" cells that are an essential component of hemangioblastoma. Second, previous hemorrhage may deposit hemosiderin within or around the hemangioblastoma, which can cause hypointense curvilinear bands. The third unique MR feature of hemangioblastoma is a curvilinear or serpentine signal void representing the larger sinusoids within the tumor or the larger vessels supplying or draining the tumor. Thus there are two causes of arcs of hypointensity for hemangioblastoma, and either may be noted around or leading

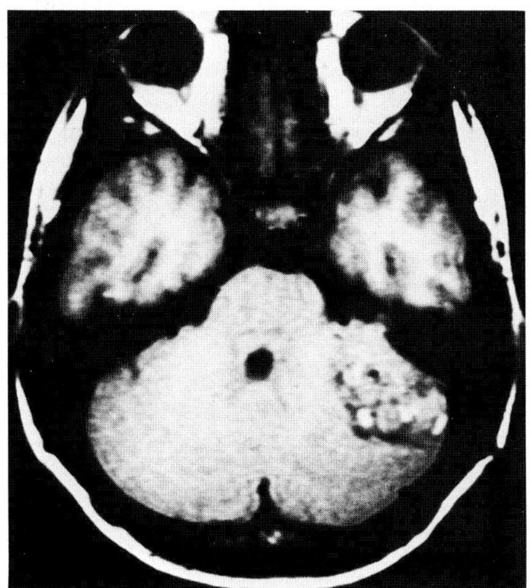
A

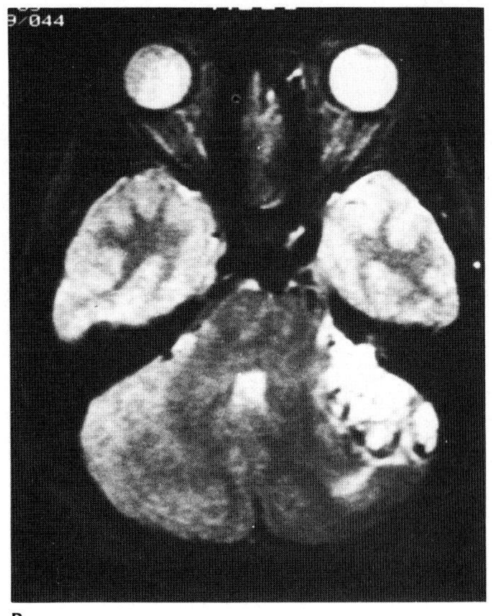
B

Figure 8-54 Solid hemangioblastoma. **A.** T_1WI demonstrates multiple hyperintense foci in the left cerebellopontine angle. This can be caused by lipid-laden stromal cells and/or subacute hemorrhage. **B.** T_2WI shows an overall increase in signal intensity but with persistence of the peripheral curvilinear dark bands, representing either previous hemorrhage or large sinusoids or vessels around the tumor.

to the tumor, as well as within it (Fig. 8-54). The presence of a serpentine signal void related to a cystic mass, especially with a mural nodule, may be pathognomonic for hemangioblastoma (Lee 1989). The nodule or nodules in hemangioblastoma will enhance after MR contrast injection.

PRIMARY INTRACRANIAL LYMPHOMA

CNS lymphoma has always been a confusing and controversial neoplasm. There have been numerous classifications of lymphoreticular proliferations in general and CNS lymphoma in particular. CNS lymphoma has been called by a variety of terms (Tadmor 1978; Kazner 1978; Hochberg 1988), including recticulum cell sarcoma, microglioma, histiocytic lymphoma, perithelial sarcoma, and lymphosarcoma.

Tumors of the lymphoreticular system may be primary brain lesions or metastatic lesions that are part of a disseminated systemic lymphoma. In the past, primary malignant lymphoma of the brain was a relatively rare tumor, with an incidence ranging from 0.8 percent (Jellinger 1975) to 1.5 percent (Zimmerman 1975) of all intracranial tumors. However, over the last decade its incidence has increased significantly. Although the incidence of CNS lymphoma is higher in the immunosuppressed population, the overall increase is not entirely related to the immunosuppressed transplant population or the AIDS epidemic.

The clinical presentation of these tumors is varied and nonspecific; in most cases they run a fulminating course if left untreated, with 3 to 5 months' survival after appearance of the initial symptoms. Ocular involvement (anterior chamber and vitreous) has been reported to occur in more than 80 percent of cases, often preceding the brain lesions (Hochberg 1988). A much higher incidence of primary CNS lymphoma is noted in patients with AIDS as well as in patients with inherited and iatrogenic causes of immunosuppression. The course may be slightly altered by radiotherapy, and early diagnosis assumes major importance. Chemotherapy trials have reported better success rates, with some patients showing complete response to combination therapy and radiation (Hochberg 1988). Grossly, no single uniform pattern of involvement by primary cerebral lymphoma is recognizable; patterns range from solitary or multiple circumscribed nodules to diffuse infiltration or widespread distribution. A mixed pattern is rather frequent. There is a distinct predilection for the deeper portions of the cerebral hemispheres, including the basal ganglia, thalamus, periventricular white matter, and corpus callosum. However, primary intracranial lymphomas may occur elsewhere, involving the cerebellar hemispheres, vermis, brainstem, and meninges. It should be noted that CNS lymphomas in patients with AIDS may be of uncommon and highly unusual histologic types.

The hallmark of CNS lymphoma is its hyperdensity on NCCT, its periventricular localization and its "fluffy" pattern of contrast enhancement. A "soft" mass crossing the corpus callosum is also very suggestive, especially if it is slightly hyperdense on NCCT. Jack (1985) reviewed 28 cases and summarized CT findings as follows: hyperdensity on NCCT, 63 percent; contrast enhancement, 100 percent (homogeneous enhancement, 71 percent); and prominent peritumoral edema zone, 87 percent (Fig. 8-55 and 8-56). Almost all primary and secondary lymphomas are in contact with either the ventricular ependyma or the superficial subarachnoid space (Holtas 1984). Occasionally a heterogeneous area with mixed enhancement is noted, particularly in the diffuse infiltrating type. Tadmor (1978) emphasized the absence of conspicuous mass effect or ventricular enlargement (Fig. 8-55). The tumor margins are often poorly defined and irregular, probably because of the characteristic perivascular infiltration pattern of the tumor cells. This has been seen in as many as 50 percent of cases, and was thought to be an important diagnostic clue (Kazner 1978). In one study, however, well-defined tumor margins were noted in 85 percent of 27 lesions (Jack 1985). Multicentricity (43 percent) and infiltration into the adjoining tissue and across the midline (through the commissures) unconstrained by the normal anatomic boundaries, are frequently observed (Fig. 8-55). Contrast enhancement of the subarachnoid space due to leptomeningeal involvement occurs but is often not detected on CT (Enzmann 1979). Cerebral angiography may demonstrate a meningioma-like pattern, i.e., homogeneous vascular stain in the late arterial or early venous phase.

On MR, primary CNS non-Hodgkins lymphomas exhibit slight hypointensity on T_1WI and hypointensity to slight hyperintensity on PD-WI and T_2WI, relative to gray matter (Fig. 8-55). They induce mild edema and little mass effect, considering the size of the mass (Schwaighofer 1989). In a series of non-AIDS patients, 75 percent of the lesions were larger than 2 cm in diameter, were mostly solitary, and were primarily found in the deep parietal lobe (Schwaighofer 1989). Intense homogeneous contrast enhancement is the most common presentation on CEMR, similar to enhancement noted on CT (Fig. 8-56).

In AIDS patients in the same series, 82 percent of the lesions were smaller than 2 cm in diameter and were frequently located in the temporal lobes and basal ganglia (Schwaighofer 1989). They were often multiple, in contrast to those reported by Jack et al. (1988), where single, larger lesions were noted in the corpus callosum. In the AIDS population CNS lymphoma is frequently indistinguishable from other lesions, including opportunistic infection. The situation is further complicated by the frequent presence of lesions due to combined pathology, e.g., toxoplasmosis and lymphoma coexisting in the same mass. Because CNS lymphoma in AIDS is often atypical

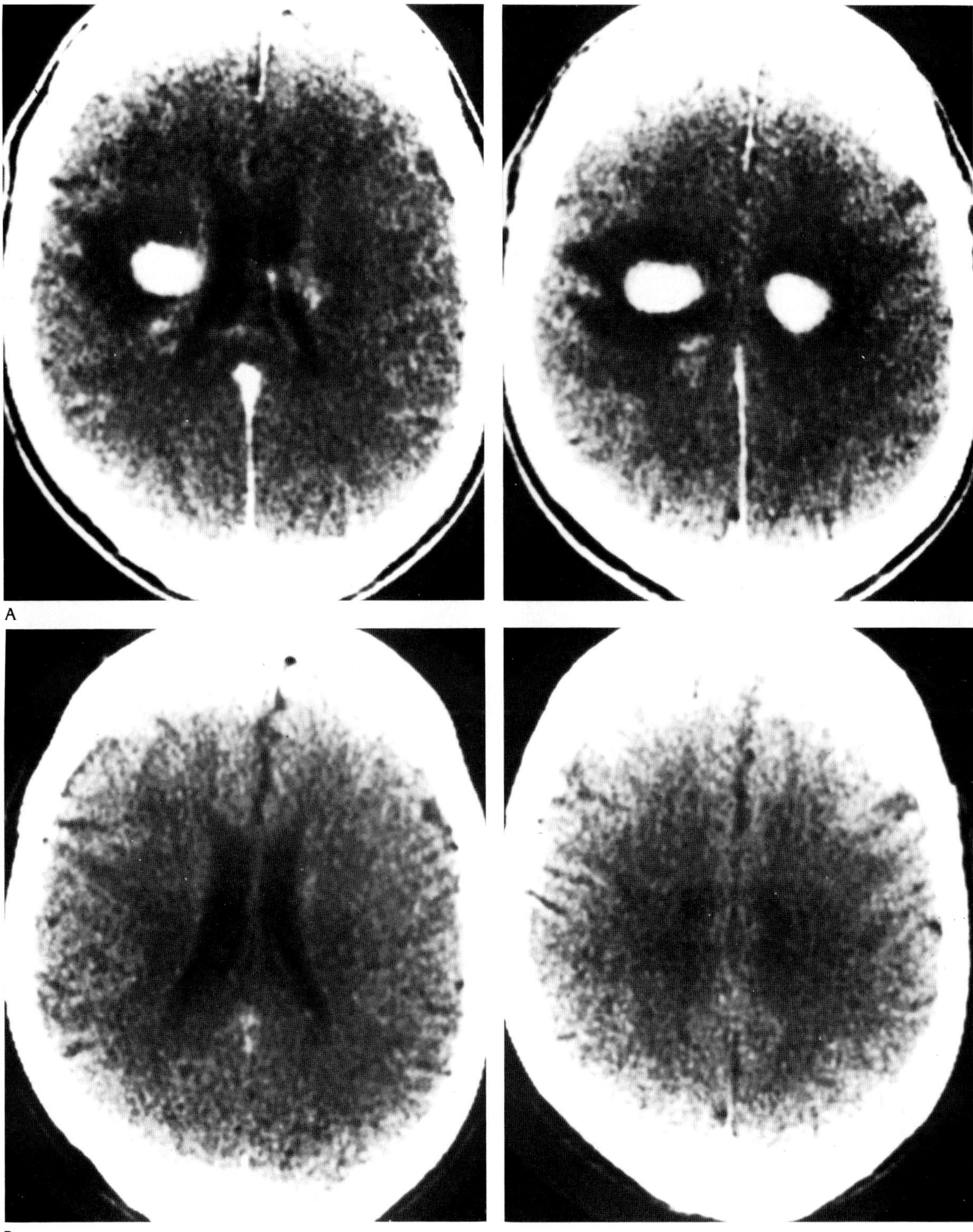

Figure 8-55 Primary CNS lymphoma in an AIDS patient. **A.** Another case with involvement of the basal ganglia and deep white matter and surrounding edema. Intense, homogeneous CE is characteristic. **B.** The same patient as in **A** exhibits almost complete disappearance of tumors after x-ray therapy. (*Continued on p. 366.*)

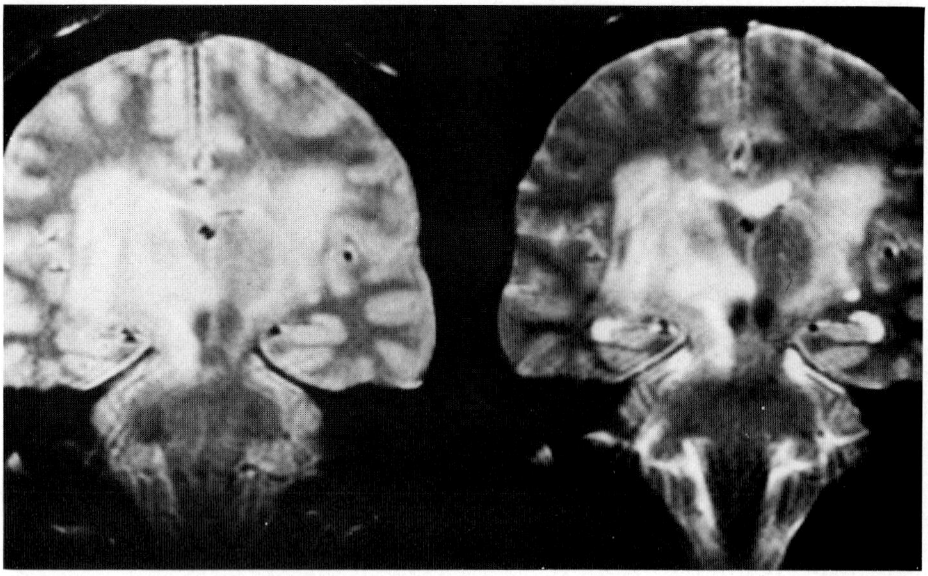

C

Figure 8-55 (continued) **C.** NCMR show nonspecific hyperintense lesions in the basal ganglia in another patient.

histologically, commonly with hemorrhage and necrosis, it is frequent for the lesions to present as ring enhancement (Fig. 8-54). These do not have any unique features, and may be mistaken for high-grade glioma or abscess. A high index of clinical suspicion may be the only factor promoting the correct diagnosis of lymphoma in these cases. Because of the foregoing problems, histologic confirmation of CNS lymphoma in AIDS may be considered.

The most common site for *secondary* lymphoma involvement is the cerebral meninges; these tumors are rarely detectable by CT (Brant-Zawadzki 1978; Pagani 1981). Cases of parenchymal involvement of the brain

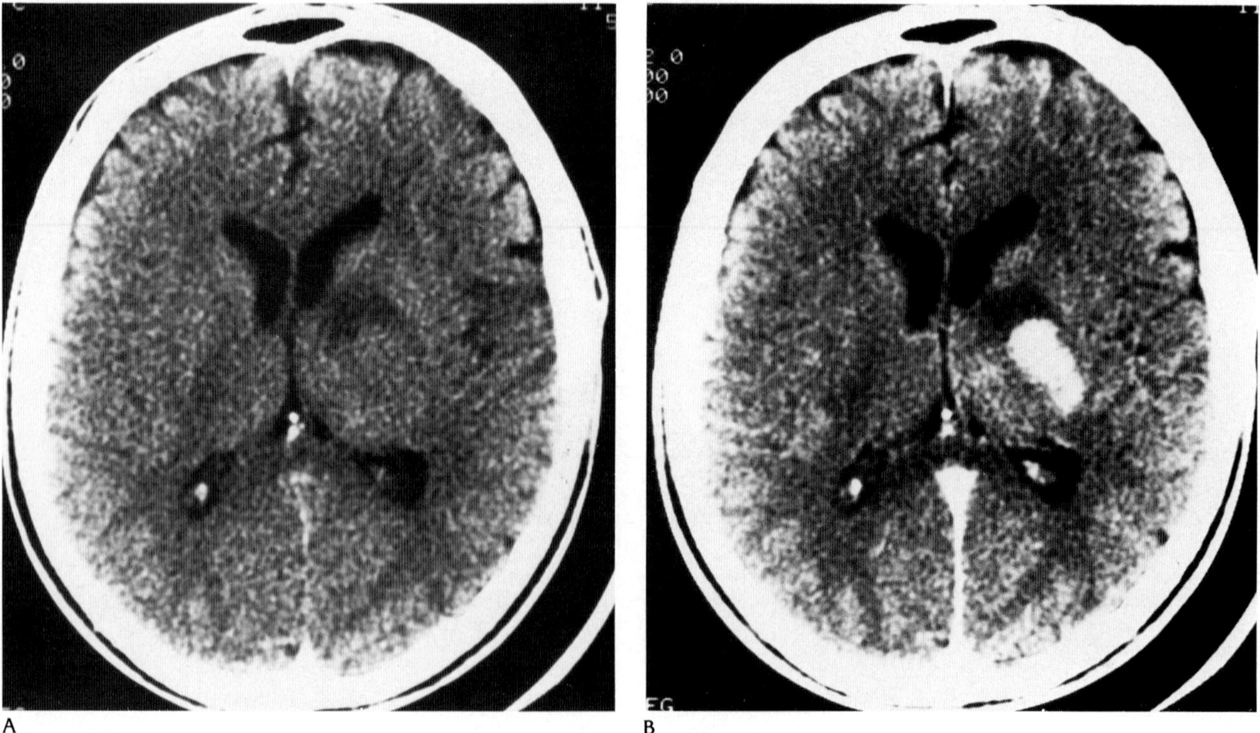

A B

Figure 8-56 Primary lymphoma. (**A**) NCCT shows a mixed-density lesion in the left basal ganglia that enhances markedly on CECT (**B**). (*Continued on p. 367.*)

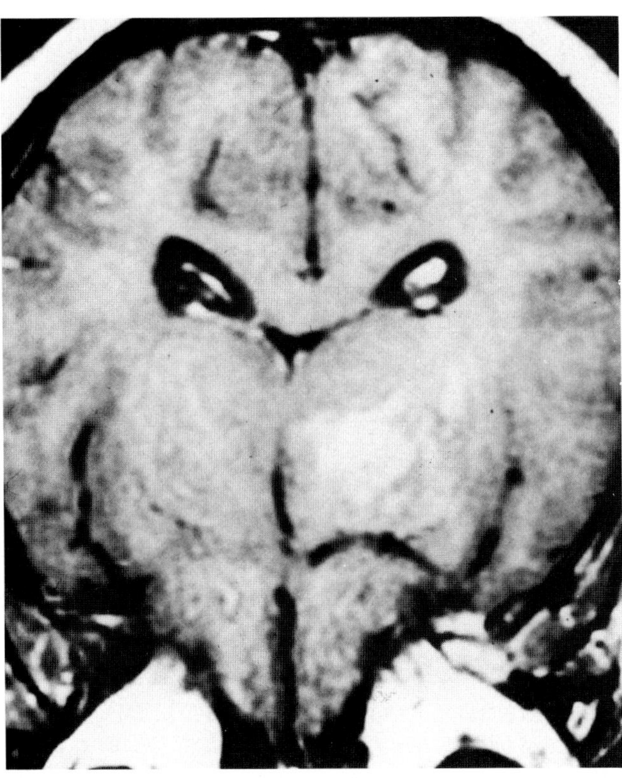

C
Figure 8-56 ***(continued)*** Coronal CEMR (**C**) shows irregular contrast enhancement.

from systemic lymphoma are indistinguishable on CT from cases of parenchymal involvement of the brain by primary malignant lymphoma (Brant-Zawadzki 1978). Differentiation from glioma, metastasis, melanoma, meningioma, or progressive multifocal leukoencephalopathy may be difficult on CT. MR has much greater sensitivity than CT in detecting leptomeningeal pathology, but lacks specificity (Phillips 1990; Paakko 1990).

UNUSUAL FEATURES

Hemorrhage

A variety of vascular changes can occur within a tumor, resulting in infarction, necrosis, and hemorrhage. Massive hemorrhage into a brain tumor may cause rapidly deteriorating neurologic function and death. Hemorrhage occurs in less than 5 percent of all gliomas (Russell 1989). The overall incidence is 3.6 percent of all intracranial tumors as detected by CT (Zimmerman 1980*a*). It occurs in a variety of primary cerebral neoplasms, such as glioblastoma multiforme, chromophobe adenoma (pituitary apoplexy; see Chap. 10), grade I astrocytoma, medulloblastoma, central neuroblastoma, histiocytic lymphoma, oligodendroglioma, and hemangiopericytoma (Little 1979; Zimmerman 1980*a*; Post 1980). Less frequently, ependymoma, choroid plexus papilloma, and hemangioblastoma have been associated with intratumoral hemorrhage and, rarely, meningioma (Modesti 1976; Russell 1980). High-grade malignancy and extensive, abnormal vascularity have been considered to be predisposing factors. Analysis of the CT appearance of tumoral hemorrhage led Zimmerman (1980*a*) to establish a classification of various patterns: Central hemorrhage was most commonly observed in glioblastomas and astrocytomas, and other patterns, such as solid hemorrhage and hemorrhagic infarction, were found most frequently in patients with metastasis. Little (1979) noted CT findings in 13 patients, including a neoplastic core (high or low density); small multifocal hemorrhage, usually at the margin of the tumor (Fig. 8-32); and surrounding, often extensive edema (Fig. 8-57). Enhancement of tumor tissue on CECT may have a peripheral distribution in proximity to the site of the hemorrhage (Fig. 8-57). Intramural hemorrhage may dissect into the adjacent compressed and edematous brain (peritumoral hematoma) and extend through the cortex into the subarachnoid space (subarachnoid hemorrhage) (Fig. 8-32) or deep through the white matter and ependyma into the ventricle (intracerebral and intraventricular hematoma) (Mandybur 1977). Differentiation from atypical intracranial hemorrhage from various causes, such as aneurysm, vascular malformation, trauma, and hypertension, is frequently difficult since most of these lesions demonstrate a mass consisting of a hematoma and concentric or eccentric contrast enhancement on CT; this pattern is almost indistinguishable from intratumoral hemorrhage. Angiography is helpful when tumor vascularity is demonstrated.

MR patterns of intratumoral hemorrhage differ from those of nonneoplastic hemorrhage. These patterns include more heterogeneous and complex signal intensity, atypical evolution of hemorrhage resulting in multiple concomitant stages of hematoma, lack of a complete hemosiderin rim at the periphery, and persistent perilesional edema (Atlas 1987; Destian 1989) (Fig. 8-58).

The diagnosis of intratumoral hemorrhage should be considered whenever patients with certain types of tumor with a propensity for hemorrhage exhibit an intracerebral hematoma that is atypical in relation to the clinical history, age of the patient, location, or CT and/or MR appearance.

Rapid growth or morphological alteration of gliomas can occur and may present as false-negative CT scans initially, presumably because of the infiltrating nature of the lesions. They can become positive as early as 14 to 17 days after initial CT (Tenfler 1977; Rao 1979) and present as mass lesions, probably because of sudden vascular changes, hemorrhage, and necrosis, or the rapid growth of the mass (Fig. 8-59).

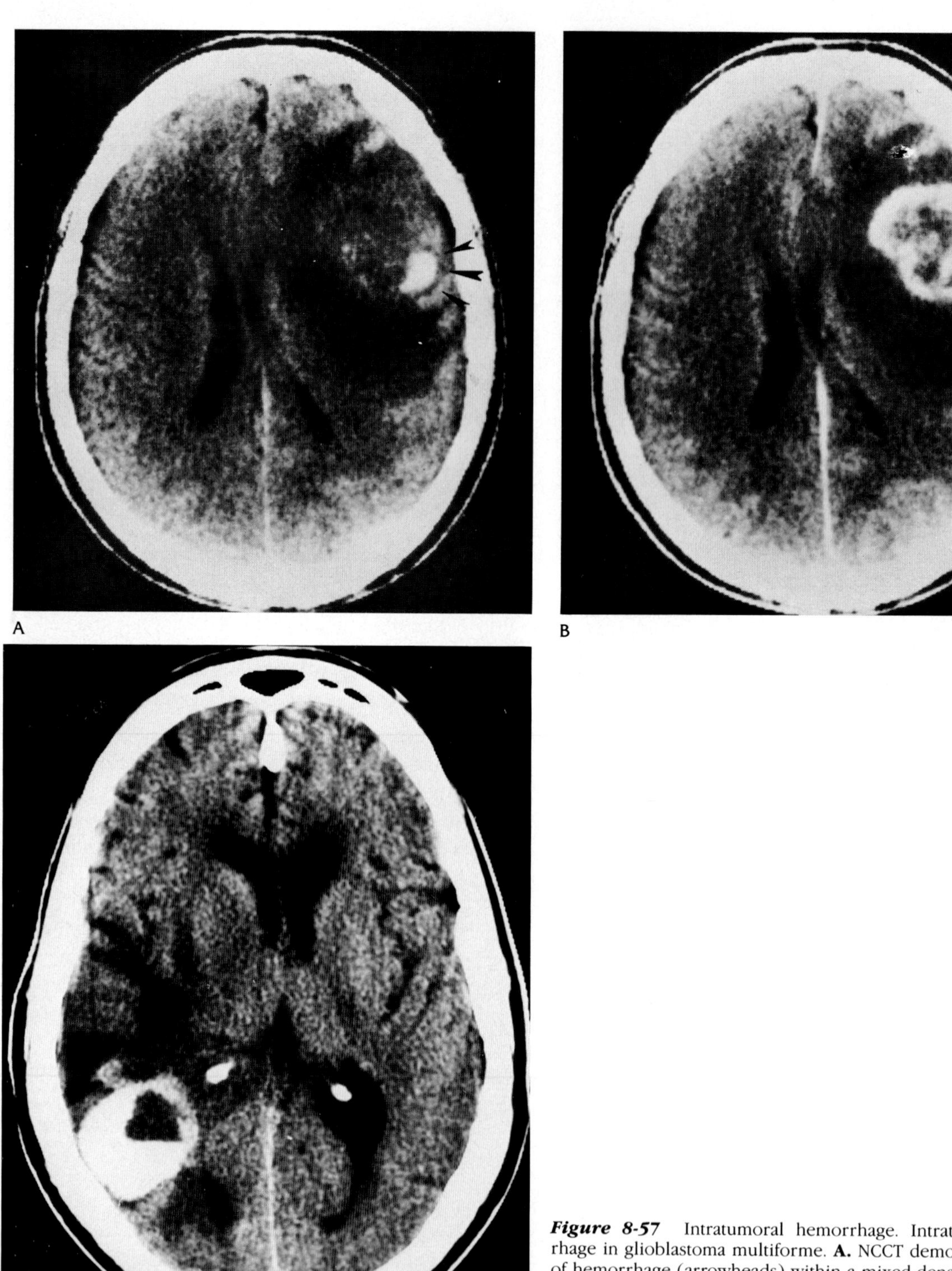

Figure 8-57 Intratumoral hemorrhage. Intratumoral hemorrhage in glioblastoma multiforme. **A.** NCCT demonstrates an area of hemorrhage (arrowheads) within a mixed-density tumor in the frontoparietal lobe. Note the surrounding edema. **B.** CECT shows nonhomogeneous enhancement of the entire tumor with central necrosis. The intratumoral hemorrhage is completely obscured by contrast enhancement. **C.** Tumoral hemorrhage with a fluid level.

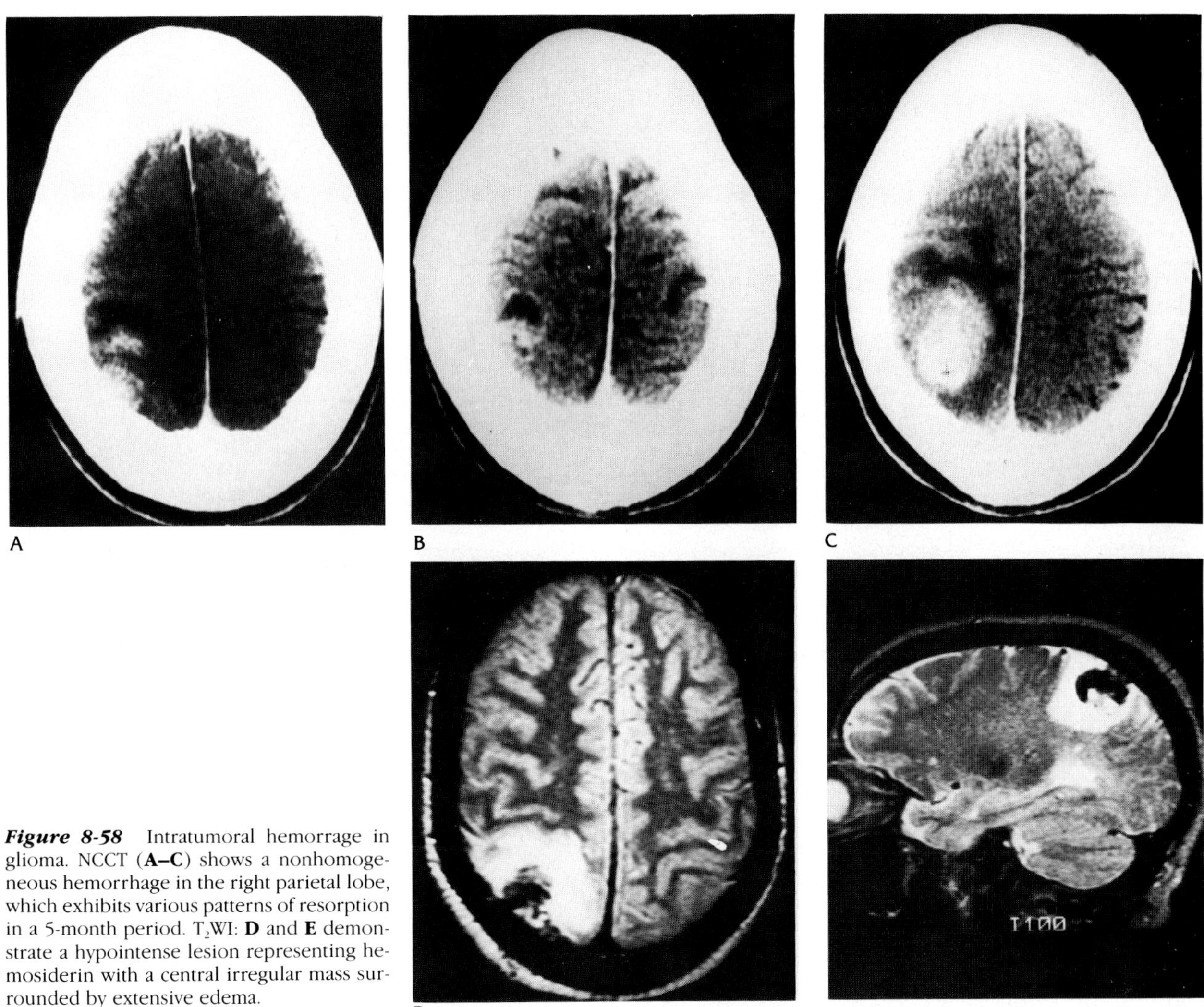

Figure 8-58 Intratumoral hemorrage in glioma. NCCT (**A–C**) shows a nonhomogeneous hemorrhage in the right parietal lobe, which exhibits various patterns of resorption in a 5-month period. T_2WI: **D** and **E** demonstrate a hypointense lesion representing hemosiderin with a central irregular mass surrounded by extensive edema.

Multicentric Tumors

Multicentric tumors are uncommon and account for only 4 to 6 percent of all gliomas (Russell 1989). The multicentricity, when present, is most frequently seen in glioblastomas. It is also demonstrated in primary malignant lymphoma and rarely in anaplastic astrocytoma. Multicentricity usually takes the form of grossly separate lesions with one or more small and distinct foci a short distance away from the main tumor. However, the tumors may be widely separated, occupying different lobes of the same hemisphere or opposite hemispheres. Although a diagnosis of multicentric tumors is usually obtained at autopsy because of the nonspecific clinical presentation, in vivo recognition significantly improves the management of the patient. CT, with its high sensitivity, can visualize multicentric patterns such as bihemispheric involvement (Fig. 8-60) and satellite foci of a tumor (Fig. 8-61). However, differentiation from infiltrating primary tumors with microscopic continuity or multiple metastatic foci may be extremely difficult to achieve on the basis of CT findings alone (Rao 1980). MR, especially with contrast, improves the detection of these lesions significantly (Fig. 8-61). The synchronous and metachronous patterns are most often seen in multifocal tumors (Van Tussel 1988). Mixed different grades of glioma may exist in these tumors.

Gliomatosis cerebri is a rare, extreme form of diffusely infiltrating tumor that involves large areas and sometimes the major part of the brain (Russell 1989). This tumor represents a diffuse cerebral astrocytoma (Chap. 9).

Concurrent Tumors

The concurrence of histologically different intracranial tumors has been well documented in dysgenic syndromes such as tuberous sclerosis, von Hippel-Lindau syndrome, neurocutaneous melanosis, and neurofibromatosis. other associations of multiple tumors, such as

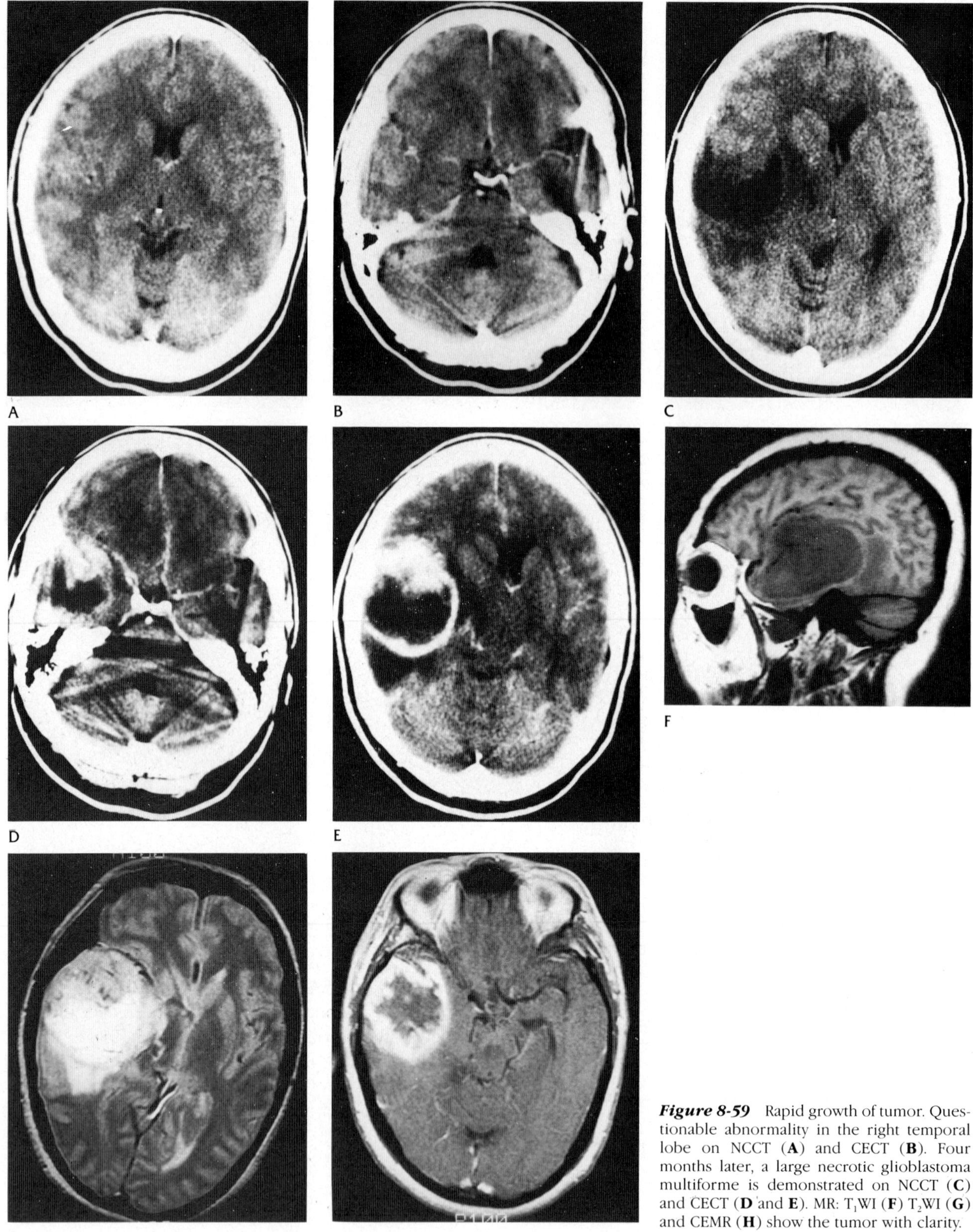

Figure 8-59 Rapid growth of tumor. Questionable abnormality in the right temporal lobe on NCCT (**A**) and CECT (**B**). Four months later, a large necrotic glioblastoma multiforme is demonstrated on NCCT (**C**) and CECT (**D** and **E**). MR: T_1WI (**F**) T_2WI (**G**) and CEMR (**H**) show the tumor with clarity.

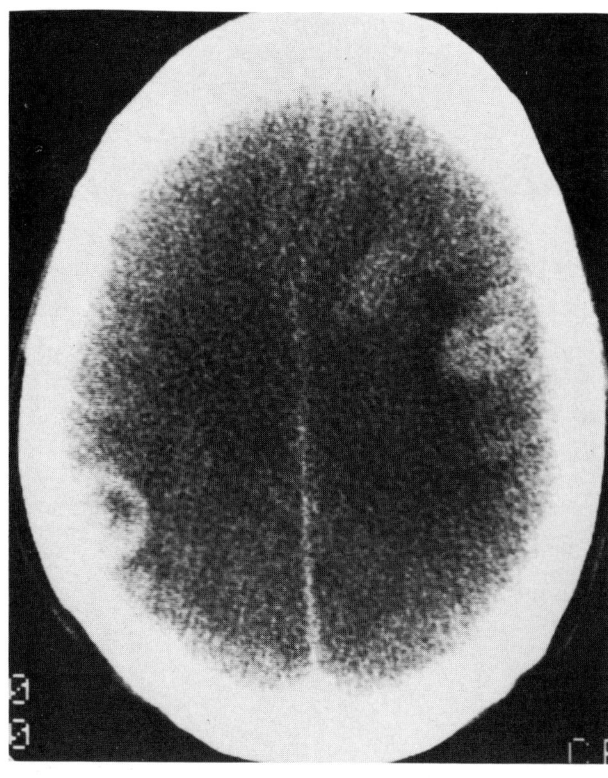

Figure 8-60 Multicentric glioblastoma multiforme. CECT demonstrates multiple enhancing lesions involving both hemispheres. Relative absence of edema is conspicuous. A differential diagnosis from metastic lesions may be extremely difficult.

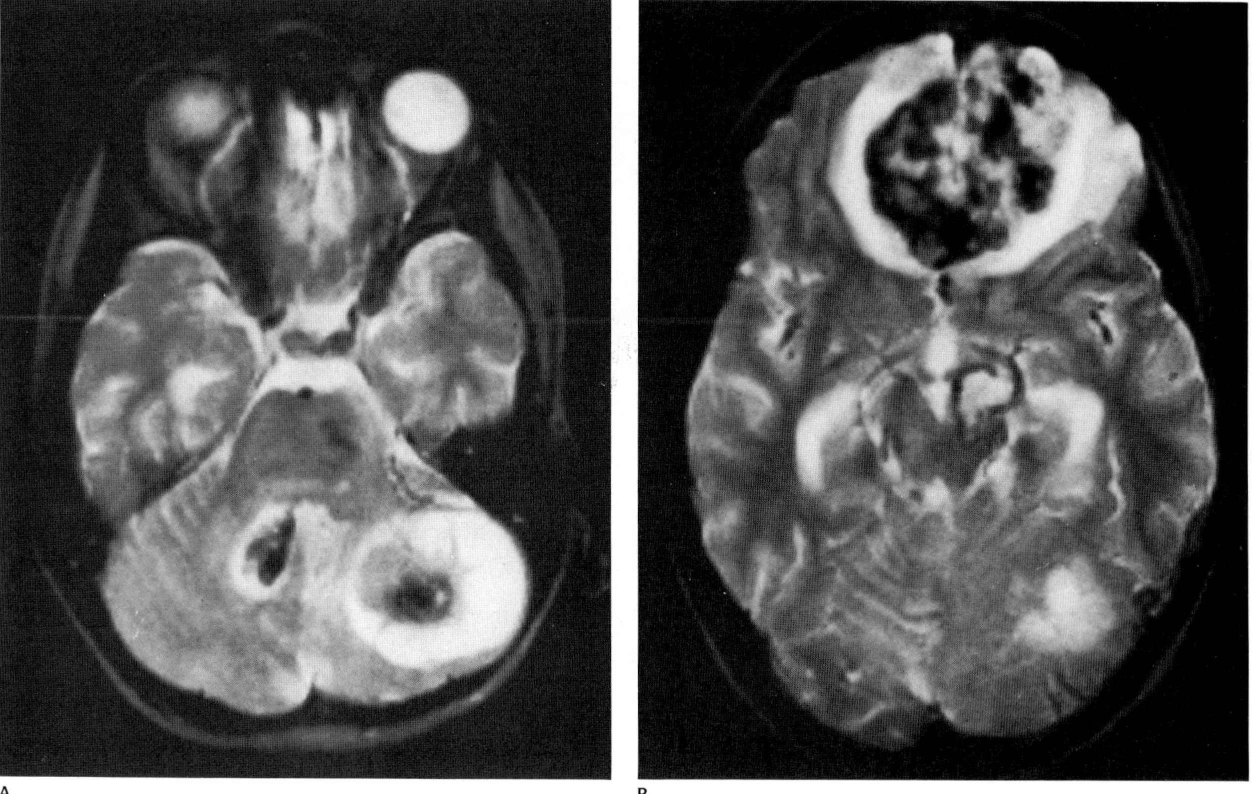

A B

Figure 8-61 Multicentric glioma. Lesions are demonstrated in the cerebellum, vermis, left brainstem, right frontal lobe, and left frontoparietal lobe. (*Continued on p. 372*)

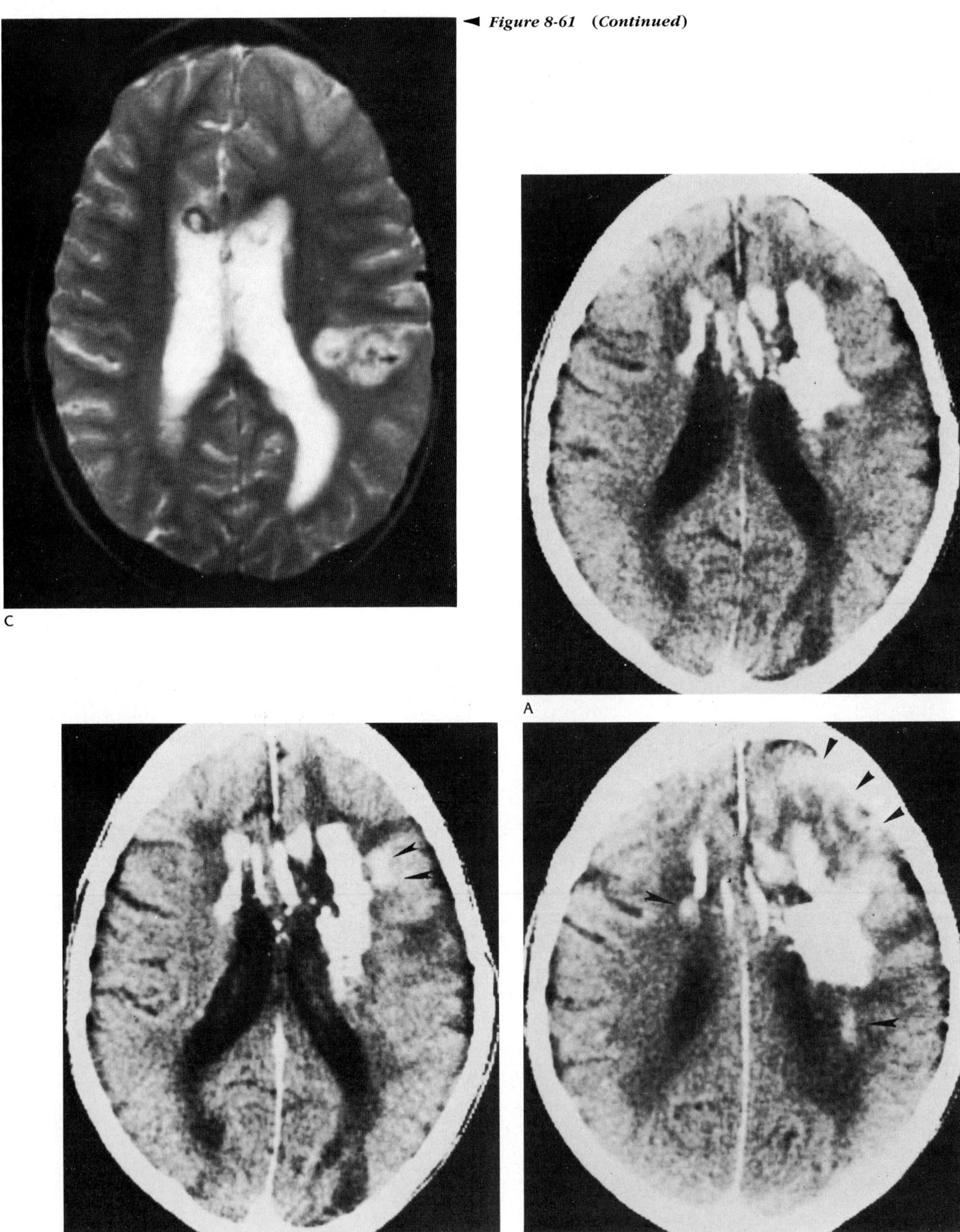

◄ ***Figure 8-61*** **(*Continued*)**

Figure 8-62 Mixed glioma (oligodendroglioma and astrocytoma). **A.** NCCT exhibits multiple thick, bandlike calcifications in both frontal lobes. The frontal horns are compressed. **B** and **C.** On CECT, multiple small scattered areas of contrast enhancement (arrowheads) are intermixed with calcifications. On histologic examination, mixed glioma (oligodendroglioma and astrocytoma) was found.

meningioma, glioblastoma, acoustic neurinoma, and gliosarcoma, may be coincidental. In these collision or tandem tumors, CT or MR may demonstrate a multiplicity of lesions (Fig. 8-37), but histologic diagnosis should rely on the CT or MR characteristics and location of each tumor. The rare occurrence of mixed gliomas may render CT or MR differential diagnosis difficult. Unfortunately in mixed tumors, CT and MR distinction between the two histologically different tumor components may not be possible, although the characteristic CT and MR features of one tumor component may predominate (Fig. 8-62).

The synchronous and metachronous patterns most often represent multifocal tumors (Van Tussel 1988). Mixed different grades of glioma may exist in these tumors.

Metastasis

Local spread beyond the confines of a primary tumor by direct infiltration into the immediately adjacent meninges and ependymal surface has been observed, although this feature bears little relation to the intrinsic malignancy of the tumor. Of great concern is the manner in which ependymal infiltration leads to metastasis via the CSF. Dissemination has been noted in glioblastoma multiforme, medulloblastoma, ependymoma, pineoblastoma, teratoma, and other germ cell neoplasms. Diffuse or nodular metastases via CSF pathways are easily detectable in the ependymal and subependymal layers of the ventricles on CECT (Osborn 1978*a*) (Fig. 8-63). Meningeal spread is difficult to detect on CT (Enzmann 1978; Pagani 1981; Onda 1990). MR, especially with contrast enhancement, significantly improves the detection of leptomeningeal metastasis (Chap. 11).

Remote metastasis of a primary tumor may occur when the tumor cells obtain access to the lymphatics or to veins outside the CNS. Such metastases have been recorded in glioblastoma, medulloblastoma, ependymoma, and oligodendroglioma, in decreasing order of frequency. Most patients had had one or more previous operations; this mechanical violation of the hematolymphatic system must play a decisive role in the process (Tratting 1990; Myers 1990).

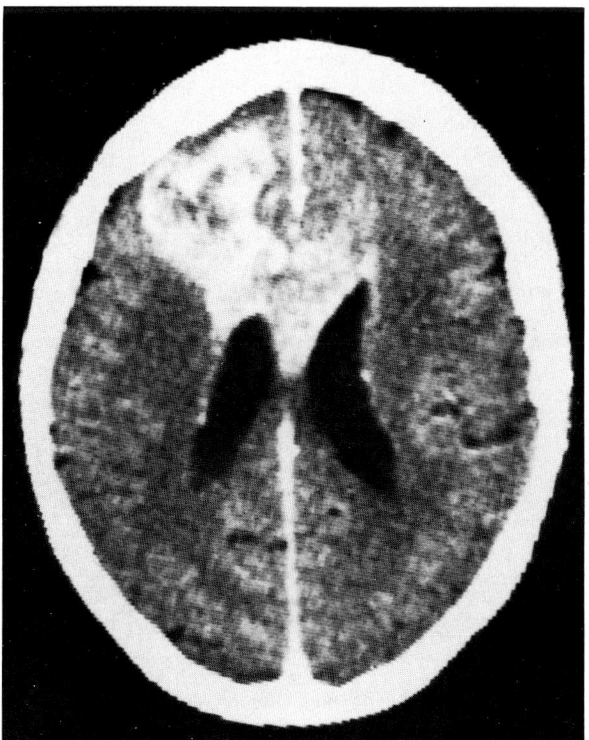
A

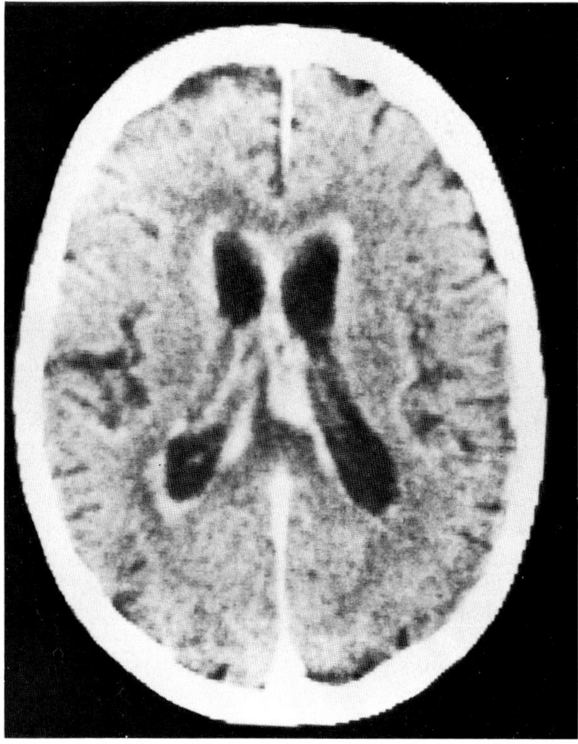
B

Figure 8-63 Local and distant metastasis. **A.** Frontal glioblastoma with direct ventricular invasion with ependymal infiltration. **B.** Subependymal dissemination of high-grade glioma presents as contrast enhancement along the ventricular margins. (*Courtesy of Dr. Douglas Yock, Minneapolis, Minnesota.*)

References

ABRAHMS JJ, LINDOR L, ARTILES C: A fluid level. *AJNR* 10:895–902, 1989.

ADAIR LB, ROPPER AH, DAVIS KR: Cerebellar hemangioblastoma: CT, angiographic and clinical condition in seven cases. *J Comput Tomogr* 2:281–294, 1978.

ADAMS RD, VICTOR M: *Principles of Neurology.* New York, McGraw-Hill, 1985.

AFRA D, NORMAN D, LEVIN CA: Cysts in malignant glioma identification by CT. *J Neurosurg* 53:821–825, 1980.

AIZPURU RN, QUENCER RM, NORENBERG M, ALTMAN N, SMIRNIOTOPOULOS JG: Meningioangiomatosis: Clinical, radiologic, and histopathologic correlation. *Radiology* 179(3): 819–821, 1991.

ALDERSON PO et al: Optimal utilization of computerized cranial tomography and radionuclide brain imaging. *Neurology* 26:803–807, 1976.

ALDERSON PO, GADO MH, SIEGAL BA: CCT and RN imaging in the detection of intercranial mass lesions. *Semin Nucl Med* VII:161–174, 1977.

ALTEMUS LR, RADVANY J: Multifocal glioma visualized by contrast enhanced computed tomography: Report of a case with pathologic correlation. *J Maine Med Assoc* 68:324–327, 1977.

AMBROSE JU, GOODING MB, RICHARDSON AE: An assessment of the acuracy of computerized transverse axial scanning (EMI scanners) in the diagnosis of intracranial tumor: A review of 366 patients. *Brain* 98:569–582, 1975*a*.

AMBROSE JU, GOODING MB, RICHARDSON AE: Sodium iothalamate as an aid to diagnosis of intracranial lesions by computerized transverse axial scanning. *Lancet* 669–674, 1975*b*.

AMENDOLA MA et al: Preoperative diagnosis of a ruptured intracranial dermoid cyst by computed tomography: Case report. *J Neurosurg* 48:1035–1037, 1978.

AMUNDSEN P, DUGSTAD G, SYVERTSEN AH: The reliability of computer tomography for the diagnosis and differential diagnosis of meningiomas, gliomas, and brain metastasis. *Acta Neurochir* 41:177–190, 1978.

ANDERSON FM, ADELSTEIN LJ: Ganglion cell tumor in the third ventricle. *Arch Surg* 45:129, 1942.

AOKI S, SASAKI T, MACHIDA T, et al: Contrast-enhanced MR images in patients with meningioma: Importance of enhancement of the dura adjacent to the tumor. *AJNR* 11:935–938, 1990.

ARIENS-KAPPERS J: The development of the paraphysis cerebri in man with comments on its relationship to the intercolumnar tubercle and its significance for the origin of cystic tumors in the third ventricle. *J Comp Neurol* 102:425, 1955.

ATLAS SW: *Magnetic Resonance Imaging of the Brain and Spine.* New York: Raven Press, 1991.

ATLAS SW, GROSSMAN RI, GOMORI JM, et al: Hemorrhagic intracranial malignant neoplasms: Spin-echo MR imaging. *Radiology* 164:71–77, 1987.

BACHMANN K, MARKWALDER R, SEILER RW: Supratentorial hemangioblastoma: Case report. *Acta Neurochir* 44:173–177, 1978.

BAKER HL, HOUSER OW, CAMPBELL JK: National Cancer Institute Study: Evaluation of CT in the diagnosis of intracranial neoplasms: I. Overall results. *Radiology* 136:91–96, 1980.

BAKER AB, BAKER LH: *Clinical Neurorology.* Hagerstown, Md, Harper & Row, 1973.

BANERJEE T, KRIGMAN MR: Intracranial epidermoid tumor: Discussion of four cases. *South Med* 7:1977.

BARKOVICH AJ, WIPPOLD FJ, SHERMAN JR, et al: Significance of cerebellar tonsillar position on MR. *AJNR* 7:795–799, 1986.

BATZDORF U, MALMUD N: The problem of multicentric gliomas. *J Neurosurg* 20:122–136, 1963.

BECKER D, NORMAN D, WILSON CB: Computerized tomography and pathological correlation in cystic meningiomas: Report of two cases. *J Neurosurg* 50:103–105, 1979.

BENTSON JR, WILSON GN, NEWTON TH: Cerebral venous drainage pattern of the Sturge Weber syndrome. *Radiology* 101:11–118, 1971.

BERRY I, BRANT-ZAWADZKI M, OSAKI L, et al: Gd-DTPA in clinical MR of the brain. 2. Extraaxial lesions and normal structures. *AJR* 147:1231–1235, 1986.

BLOEM J, WANDERGEM J: Gd-DTPA as a contrast agent in CT. *Radiology* 11:578–579, 1989.

BODIAN M, LAWSON D: The intracranial neoplastic diseases of childhood. *Brit J Surg* 40:368, 1953.

BRADAC GB, FERSZT R, BENDER A, et al: Peritumoral edema in meningiomas; A radiological and histological study. *Neuroradiology* 28:304–312, 1986.

BRADLEY WG Jr: NMR imaging of the central nervous system. *Neurol Res* 6:91–106, 1984

BRADLEY WG Jr: *Magnetic Resonance Imaging,* Stark DD, Bradley WG Jr (eds). St. Louis, Mosby, 1988.

BRANT-ZAWADZKI M, ENZMANN DR: Computed tomographic brain scanning in patients with lymphoma. *Radiology* 129:67–71, 1978.

BRANT-ZAWADZKI M, BADAMI JP, MILLS CM, et al: Primary intracranial tumor imaging: A comparison of magnetic resonance and CT. *Radiology* 150:435–440, 1984.

BRANT-ZAWADZKI M, DAVIS PL, CROOKS LE, et al: NMR demonstration of cerebral abnormalities: Comparison with CT. *AJNR* 4:117–124, 1983.

BRAUN IE et al: Dense intracranial epidermoid tumors. *Radiology* 122:717–719, 1977.

BRENNER TG, RAO KCVG, ROBINSON W, et al: Tandem lesions: Chromophobe adenoma and meningioma. *J Comput Tomogr* 1:517–520, 1977.

BUELL U, NIENDORF HP, KAZNER E, et al: CAT and cerebral serial scintigraphy in intracranial tumors: Rates of detection and tumor-type identification. *J Nucl Med* 19:476–479, 1977.

BUETOW PC, SMIRNIOTOPOULOS JG, DONE S: Congenital brain tumors: A review of 45 cases. *AJNR* 11:793–799, 1990.

BURGER PC, VOGEL FS: *Surgical Pathology of the Nervous System and Its Coverings.* New York, Churchill Livingstone, 1982.

BURTON DR, FORSEN S, KARLSTROM G: Proton relaxation enhancement (PRE) in biochemistry: a critical survey. *Progr NMR Spectroscopy* 13:1–45, 1979.

BUTLER AR, HORRI SC, KRICHEFF II, et al: Computed tomography in astrocytomas: A statistical analysis of the parameters of malignancy and positive contrast-enhanced CT scan. *Radiology* 129:433–439, 1978.

BYDDER GM, KINGSLEY PE, BROWN W, et al: MR imaging of meningiomas including studies with and without gadolinium-DTPA. *J Comput Assist Tomogr* 9:690–697, 1985.

BYDDER GM, STEINER RE, YOUNG IR, et al: Clinical MR imaging of the brain: *AJR* 139:215–236, 1982.

CAMINS MB, TAKEUCHI J: Normotopic plus heterotopic atypical teratomas. *Childs Brain* 4:151–160, 1978.

CARR DH: The use of iron and gadolinium chelates as NMR contrast agents: animal and human studies. *Physiol Chem Phys Med NMR* 16:137–143, 1984.

CASTILLO M, DAVIS PC, TAKEI TD, et al: Intracranial ganglioma—MR, CT, and clinical findings in 18 patients. *AJNR* 11:109–114, 1990.

CHAKERES DW, CURTIN A, FORD G: Magnetic resonance imaging of pituitary and parasellar abnormalities. *RSNA* 27:265–281, 1989.

CHAMBERS AA et al: Cranial epidermoid tumors: Diagnosis by computed tomography. *Neurosurgery* 1:276–280, 1977.

CHANG T, TENG M, GUO W, SHENG W: CT of pineal tumors and intracranial germ-cell tumors. *AJNR* 10:1039–1044, 1989.

CLAVERIA LE, SUTTON D, TRESS BM: The radiological diagnosis of meningiomas, the impact of EMI scanning. *Br J Radiol* 50:15–22, 1977*a*.

CLAVERIA LE, KENDALL BE, DUBOULAY GH: CAT in supratentorial gliomas and metastasis, in DuBoulay GH, Moseley IF (eds): *CAT in Clinical Practice.* Heidelberg, Springer-Verlag, 1977*b*, p 85.

CLIFFORD JR, CONNOLLY ES, VOORHIES RM: Comparison of radionuclide scan with computer assisted tomography in diagnosis of intracranial disease. *Neurology* 26:119–1123, 1976.

CORNELL SH, GRAF CJ, DOLAN KD: Fat-fluid level in intracranial epidermoid cyst. *Am J Roentgenol* 128:502–503, 1977.

COWLEY AR: Influence of fiber tracts on the CT appearance of cerebral edema: Anatomic-pathologic correlation. *AJNR* 4: 915–925, 1983.

CULLITY BD: *Introduction to Magnetic Materials.* Reading, MA, Addison-Wesley, 1972.

DANIELS DL, HERPKINS R, KOEHLER PR, et al: MRI of the internal auditory canal. *Radiology* 151:105–108, 1984.

DAVIS KR et al: Theoretical considerations in the use of contrast media for computed cranial tomography. *Neurosurgery* 1:9–12, 1976*a*.

DAVIS KR, TAVERAS JM: Diagnosis of epidermoid tumor by computed tomography. *Radiology* 119:347–353, 1976.

DAVIS JM, DAVIS KR, NEWHOUSE J, et al: Expanded high iodine dose in computed cranial tomography: A preliminary report. *Radiology* 131:373–387, 1979.

DEAN BL, DRAYER BP, BIRD RC, et al: Gliomas: Classification with MR imaging. *Radiology* 174:411–415, 1990.

DECK MDF, MESSINA AV, SACKETT JP: Computerized tomography in metastatic disease of the brain. *Radiology* 119:115–120, 1976.

DEMAEREL P, WILMS G, LAMMENS M, et al: Intracranial meningiomas: Correlation between MRI and histology in fifty patients. *J Comput Assist Tomogr* 15(1):45–51, 1991.

DESTIAN S, SZE G, KROL G, et al: MR imaging of hemorrhagic intracranial neoplasms. *AJR* 152:137–144, 1989.

DORNE HL, O'GORMAN AM, MELANSON D: CT of intracranial gangliomas. *Am J Neuroradiol* 7:281–285, 1986.

DORSCH JA, WADSENHEIM A: Density of intracranial masses in computed tomography. *J Belge Radiol* 61:292–296, 1978.

EARNEST F, KELLY PJ, SCHEITHAUER BW, et al: Cerebral Astrocytomas: Histopathologic correlation of MR and CT contrast enhancement with stereotactic biopsy. *Radiology* 166:823–827, 1988.

ELSTER AD, CHALLA VR, GILBERT TH, et al: Meningiomas: MR and histopathologic features. *Radiology* 170:857–862, 1989.

ENZMANN DR et al: CT in primary reticulum cell sarcoma of the brain. *Radiology* 130:165–170, 1979.

ENZMANN DR, TOKYE KC, HAYWARD R: CT in leptomeningeal spread of tumor. *J Comput Assist Tomogr* 2:448–455, 1978 (abstract).

EVANS RG, JOST RG: The clinical efficacy and cost analysis of cranial computed tomography and the radionuclide brain scan. *Semin Nucl Med* VII:129–136, 1977.

FAWCITT RA, ISHERWOOD I: Radiodiagnosis of intracranial pearly tumors with particular reference to the value of CT. *Neuroradiology* 11:1234–242, 1976.

FELIX R, SCHÖRNER W, LINIADO M, et al: Brain tumors: MR imaging with gadolinium-DTPA. *Radiology* 156:681, 1985.

FILLING-KATZ MR, CHOYKE PL, PATRONAS NJ, et al: Radiologic screening for von Hippel-Lindau disease: The role of Gd-DTPA-enhanced MR imaging of the CNS. *J Comput Assist Tomogr* 13:745–755, 1989.

FISHMAN RA: Brain edema. *N Engl J Med* 293:706–711, 1975.

FRANK JA, DWYER AJ, GIRTON M, et al: Opening of blood-ocular barrier demonstrated by contrast-enhanced MR imaging. *J Comput Assist Tomogr* 10:912–916, 1986.

FUTRELL NN, OSOBRNE AQ, CHESON BD: Pineal region tumors: CT-pathologic spectrum. *Am J Neuroradiol* 2:415–420, 1981.

GADO MH, PHELPS ME, COLEMAN RE: An extravascular component of contrast enhancement in cranial computed tomography. *Radiology* 177:589–593, and 595–597, 1975.

GANTI SR, ANTUNES JL, LOUIS KM, et al: CT in the diagnosis of colloid cysts of the third ventricle. *Radiology* 138:385–391, 1981.

GANTI SR, HILAL SK, STEIN BM, et al: CT of pineal region tumors: *Am J Neuroradiol* 7:97–104, 1986.

GARDEUR D, SABLAYROLLES JL, KLAUSZ R, et al: Histographic studies in computed tomography of contrast enhanced cerebral and orbital tumors. *J Comput Assist Tomogr* 1:231–240, 1977.

GARRIDO E, BECKER LF, HOFFMAN HJ, et al: Gangliogliomas in children. *Childs Brain* 4:339–346, 1978.

GAWLER J et al: Computer assisted tomography (EMI scanner): Its place in investigation of suspected intracranial tumors. *Lancet* 2:419–423, 1979.

GEORGE AE, RUSSEL EJ, KRICHEFF II: White matter buckling: CT sign of extra-axial intracranial mass. *Am J Neuroradiol* 1:425–430, 1980.

GHOSHHAJRA K, BHAGAI-NAINI P, HAHN HS: Spontaneous rupture of a pineal teratoma. *Am J Neuroradiol* 17:215–217, 1979.

GILBERTSON EL, GOODING CA: Roentgenographic signs of tumors of the brain. *Am J Roentgenol* 76:226, 1956.

GOLDBERG HI: *Extraaxial Brain Tumors in MRI of the Brain & Spine.* New York, Raven Press, 1991.

GOLDSHER D, LITT AW, PINTO RS, et al: Dural "tail" associated with meningiomas on Gd-DTPA-enhanced images. *Radiology* 176:447–450, 1990.

GOLDSTEIN EJ, BURNETT KR, HANSELL JR, et al: Gadolinium DTPA (an NMR proton imaging contrast agent): Chemical structure, paramagnetic properties, and pharmakokinetics. *Physiol Chem Phys Med NMR* 16:97–104, 1984.

GRAIF M, BYDDER GM, STEINER RE, et al: Contrast-enhanced MR imaging of malignant brain tumors. *AJNR* 6:855–862, 1985.

GROSS SW: Radiographic visualization of an intracranial dermoid cyst. *J Neurosurg* 2:72–75, 1945.

GUNER M, SHAW M: Computed tomography in the diagnosis of colloid cyst. *J Neurosurg* 2:72–75, 1976.

HANDA J, HANDA H: Radiolucent intracranial dermoid cyst, case report. *Neuroradiology* 17:211–214, 1979.

HAYMAN LA, EVANS RA, HINCK V: Rapid high dose cranial CT: A concise review of normal anatomy. *J Comput Assist Tomogr* 3:147–154, 1979.

HAYMAN LA, EVANS RA, HINCK V: Delayed high iodine dose contrast computed tomography: Cranial neoplasms. *Radiology* 136:677–684, 1980.

HILAL SK, CHANG CH: Specificity of computed tomography in the diagnosis of supratentorial neoplasms: Consideration of metastasis and meningiomas. *Neuroradiology* 16:537–539, 1978.

HILAL SK, CHANG CH: Sensitivity and specificity of CT in supratentorial tumors. *J Comput Assist Tomogr* 2:511, 1978.

HOCHBERG FH, MILLER DC: Primary central nervous system lymphoma. *J Neurosurg* 68:835–853, 1988.

HOLLAND BA, KUCHARCZYK W, BRANT-ZAWADZKI M, et al: MR imaging of calcified intracranial lesions. *Radiology* 157:353–356, 1985.

HOLTAS S, NYMAN U, CRONQUIST S: CT of malignant lymphoma of the brain. *Neuroradiology* 26:33–38, 1984.

HOROWITZ BL, CHARI MV, JAMES R, et al: MR of intracranial epidermoid tumors: Correlation of in vivo imaging with in vitro C spectroscopy. *AJNR* 11:299–302, 1990.

HUCKMAN MS: Clinical experience with the intravenous infusion of the iodinated contrast material as an adjunct to CT. *Surg Neurol* 4:297–318, 1975.

HUCKMAN M, ACKERMAN L: Use of automated measurements of mean density as an adjunct to computed tomography. *J Comput Assist Tomogr* 1:37–42, 1977.

IKEZAKI K, FUJII K, KISHIKAWA T: Magnetic resonance imaging of an intraventricular craniopharyngioma. *Neuroradiology* 32:247–249, 1990.

JACK CR, O'NEILL B, BANKS PM, et al: CNS lymphoma: Histologic types and CT appearance. *Radiology* 167:211–215, 1988.

JACK CR, REESE DF, SCHEITHAUER BW: Radiographic findings in 32 cases of primary CNS lymphoma. *AJNR* 6:899–904, 1985.

JELINEK J, SMIRNIOTOPOULOS JG, PARISI JE, KANZER M: Lateral ventricular neoplasms: Differential diagnosis with clinical, CT, and MR imaging. *AJNR* 11:567–574, 1990.

JELLINGER K, RADSKIEWICZ T, SLOWIK F: Primary malignant lymphomas of the central nervous system in man. *Acta Neuropath,* suppl VI: 95–102, 1975.

JUST M, THELEN M: Tissue characterization with T_1, T_2, and proton density values: Results in 160 patients with brain tumors. *Radiology* 169:779–785, 1988.

KALAN C, BURROWS EH: Calcification in intracranial gliomata. *Br J Radiol* 35:589–602, 1962.

KAZNER E, WILSKE J, STEINHOFF H, et al: Computer assisted tomography in primary malignant lymphomas of the brain. *J Comput Assist Tomogr* 2:125–134, 1978.

KELLY PJ, DAUMAS-DUPORT C, KISPERT DB, et al: Imaging-based stereotaxic serial biopsies in untreated intracranial glial neoplasms. *J Neurosurg* 66:865–874, 1988.

KENDALL B, PULLICINO P: Comparison of consistency of meningiomas and CT appearance. *Neuroradiology* 18:173–176, 1979.

KENDALL BE: Difficulties in diagnosis of supratentorial gliomas by CAT scan. *J Neurol Neurosurg Psychiatr* 42:485–492, 1975.

KEPES JJ: *Meningiomas: Biology, Pathology and Differential Diagnosis.* New York, Masson, 1982.

KERNOHAN JW, SAYRE GP: Tumors of the central nervous system. Fascicle 35, *Atlas of Tumor Pathology.* Washington, Armed Forces Institute of Pathology, 1952.

KILGORE DP, STROTHER CM, STARSHAK RJ, et al: Pineal germinoma: MR imaging. *Radiology* 158:435–438, 1986.

KIM KS, ROGERS LF, LEE C: The dural lucent line: Characteristic sign of hyperostosing meningioma en plaque. *AJR* 141:1217–1221, 1983.

KLATZO I, SEITELBERGER F (eds): *Brain Edema.* New York, Springer Verlag, 1967.

KNUCKLEY NW, STOLL J, EPSTEIN MH: Intracranial and spinal meningiomas in patients with breast carcinoma: Case reports. *Neurosurgery* 25:112–117, 1989.

KRAMER RA, JANETOS GP, PERLSTEIN G: An approach to contrast enhancement in computed tomography of the brain. *Radiology* 16:641–647, 1975.

KUSHNET MW, GOLDMAN RL: Lipoma of the corpus callosum associated with a frontal bone defect. *Am J Roentgenol* 131:517–518, 1978.

LASTER DW, MOODY DM: Epidermoid tumors of with intraventricular and subarachnoid fat: Report of two cases. *Am J Roentgenol* 128:504–507, 1977.

LATACK JT, KARTUSH JM, KEMINK JL, et al: Epidermoidomas of the cerebellopontine angle and temporal bone: CT and MR aspects. *Radiology* 157:361–366, 1985.

LATCHAW RE: *MR and CT Imaging of the Head, Neck, and Spine,* 2d ed. St. Louis, Mosby Year Book, 1991.

LATCHAW RE, GOLD LHA, TORRIJE EJ: A protocol for the use of contrast enhancement in cranial computed tomography. *Radiology* 126:681–687, 1978*a*.

LATCHAW RE, PAYNE JT, GOLD LH: Effective atomic number and electron density as measured with a computed tomography scanner: Computation and correlation with brain tumor histology. *J Comput Assist Tomogr* 2:199–208, 1978*b*.

LATCHAW R, PAYNE JT, LOEWENSON RB: Predicting brain tumor histology: Change of effect atomic number with contrast enhancement. *Am J Neuroradiol* 1:289–294, 1980.

LEE DH, NORMAN D, NEWTON TH: MR imaging of pineal cysts. *J Comput Assist Tomogr* 11:586–590, 1987.

LEE Y, TASSEL PV: Intracranial oligodendrogliomas: Imaging findings in 35 untreated cases. *AJNR* 10:119–127, 1989.

LEE SH, DELGADO TE, BUCHEIT WA: Intracranial dermoid tumor: Diagnosis by computed tomography, a case report. *Neurosurgery* 1:281–283, 1977.

LEE SR, SANCHES J, MARK AS, et al: Posterior fossa hemangioblastomas: MR imaging. *Radiology* 171:463–468, 1989.

LEROUX P, HOPE A, LOFTON S, et al: Lipomatous meningioma: An uncommon tumor with distinct radiographic findings. *Surg Neurol* 32:360–365, 1989.

LEWANDER R, BERGSTROM M, BERVALL U: Contrast enhancement of cranial lesions in computed tomography. *Acta Radiolog* 19:529–553, 1978.

LITTLE JR et al: Brain hemorrhage from intracranial tumor. *Stroke* 10:283–288, 1979.

LITTLE JR, MACCARTY CS: Colloid cysts of the third ventricle. *J Neurosurg* 40:230–235, 1974.

MAEDER PP, HOLTAS SL, BASIBUYUK LN, et al: Colloid cysts of the third ventricle: Correlation of MR and CT findings with histology and chemical analysis. *AJNR* 11:575–581, 1990.

MAHALEY M et al: National survey of patterns of care for brain-tumor patients. *J Neurosurg* 71:826–836, 1989.

MALIK GM et al: Colloid cysts. *Surg Neurol* 13:73–77, 1980.

MAMOURIAN AC, TOWFIGHT J: Pineal cysts: MR imaging. *AJNR* 7:1081–1086, 1986.

MANCES P, BABIN E, WACKENHEIM SA: Contribution of histograms to the computer tomographic study for brain tumors. *J Belge Radiol* 61:297–312, 1978.

MANDYBUR TI: Intracranial hemorrhage caused by metastatic tumors. *Neurology* 27:650–655, 1977.

MANI RL et al: Radiographic diagnosis of meningioma of the lateral ventricle: Review of 22 cases. *J Neurosurg* 49:249–255, 1978.

MAUERSBERGER W, CUEVAS-SOLORZANO JA: Spontaneous intracerebellar hematoma during childhood caused by spongioblastoma of the fourth ventricle. *Neuropadiatrie* 8:443–450, 1977.

MCCORMACK TJ, PLASSCHE WM, LIN SR: Ruptured teratoid tumors in the pineal region. *J Comput Assist Tomogr* 2:449–501, 1978.

MENDONCA-DIAS MH, LAUTERBUR PC: Ferromagnetic particles as contrast agents for magnetic resonance imaging of liver and spleen. *Magn Reson Med* 3:328–330, 1986.

MIKHAEL MA, MATTAR AG: Intracranial pearly tumors: the role of CT, angiography and pneumoencephalography. *J Comput Assist Tomogr* 2:421–429, 1978.

MODESTI LM, BINET EF, COLLINS GH: Meningiomas causing spontaneous intracranial hematomas. *J Neurosurg* 45:437–441, 1976.

MONAJATI A, HEGGENESS L: Patterns of edema in tumors vs. infarcts: Visualization of white matter pathways. *AJNR* 3:251–255, 1982.

MONJIATI A, HEGGENESS L: Patterns of edema in tumors vs infarcts: Visualization of white matter pathways. *AJNR* 3:251–255, 1982.

MULLER-FORELL W, SCHROTH G, EGAN PJ: MR imaging in tumors of the pineal region. *Neuroradiology* 30:224–231, 1988.

MYERS T, EGELHOFF J, MYERS M: Glioblastoma multiforme presenting as osteoblastic metastatic disease: Case report and review of the literature. *AJNR* 11:802, 1990.

NAIDICH TP, PINTO RS, KUSHNER MJ, et al: Evaluation of sellar and parasellar masses by computed tomography. *Radiology* 120:91–99, 1976.

NAKAGAWA H, IWASAKI S, KICHIKAWA K, et al: *AJNR* 11:195–198, 1990.

NAUTA HJW et al: Xanthochromic cysts associated with meningioma. *J Neurol Neurosurg Psychiatr* 42:529–535, 1979.

NEUWELT EA et al: Malignant pineal region tumors. *J Neurosurg* 51:597–607, 1979.

NEW PFJ, SCOTT WR, SCHNUR JA, et al: Computed tomography with the EMI scanner in the diagnosis of primary and metastatic intracranial neoplasms. *Radiology* 114:75–87, 1975.

NEW PFJ, ARONOW S, HESSELINK JR: National Cancer Institute Study: Evaluation of computed tomography in the diagnosis of intra-cranial neoplasms. IV: Meningiomas. *Radiology* 136:665–675, 1980.

NORMAN D et al: Quantitative aspects of contrast enhancement in cranial computed tomography. *Radiology* 129:683–688, 1978.

NOSAKA Y et al: Primary intracranial epidermoid carcinoma. *J Neurosurg* 50:830–833, 1979.

OI S, WETZEL N: Gliomas in computerized axial tomography, correlation with tumor malignancy in 100 cases. *Neurosurgery (Japan)* 7:759–763, 1979.

OKAZAKI H: *Fundamentals of Neuropathology.* New York, Igaku-Shoin, 1989.

OKAZAKI H, SCHEITHAUER BW: Neoplasms and related lesions, in *Atlas of Neuropathology.* New York, Gower, 1988, chap 3, pp 59–218.

OLIVERCRONIA H: The cerebellar angioreticulomas. *J Neurosurg* 9:317–330, 1952.

OLSSON MBE, PERSSON BRB, SALFORD LG, et al: Ferromagnetic particles as contrast agent in T2 NMR imaging. *Magn Reson Imaging* 4:437–440, 1986.

OOT RF, NEW PFJ, PILLE-SPELLMANN JT, et al: Detection of intracranial calcification by MR. *AJNR* 7:801–809, 1986.

OSBORN AG: Diagnosis of descending transtentorial herniation by cranial computed tomography. *Radiology* 123:93–96, 1977.

OSBORN AG, HEASTON DK, WING SD: Diagnosis of ascending transtentorial herniation by cranial computed tomography. *A JR* 130:755–760, 1978*a*.

OSBORN AG et al: The evaluation of ependymal and subependymal lesions by cranial computed tomography. *Radiology* 127:397–401, 1978*b*.

PAAKKO E, PATRONAS NJ, SCHELLINGER D: Meningeal Gd-DTPA enhancement in patients with malignancies. *J Comput Assist Tomogr* 14:542–546, 1990.

PAGANI JJ et al: Cranial nervous system leukemia of lymphoma: CT manifestations. *Am J Neuroradiol* 2:397–403, 1981.

PATEL AN: Lipoma of the corpus callosum: A nonsurgical entity. *NC Med J* 26:328–335, 1965.

PAXTON R, AMBROSE J: The EMI scanner: A brief review of the first 650 patients. *Br J Radiol* 47:530–565, 1974.

PENDERGRASS HP, MCKUSICK KA, NEW PFJ: Relative efficacy of radionuclide imaging and computed tomography of the brain. *Radiology* 116:363–366, 1975.

PENMAN J, SMITH MC: Intracranial gliomata, Spec Rep Series, No. 284, Med Res Council, HM Stationary Office, London 1954.

PHILLIPS ME, RYALS TJ, KAMBHU SA, et al: Neoplastic vs. inflammatory meningeal enhancement with Gd-DTPA. *J Comput Assist Tomogr* 14:536–541, 1990.

POST JD, NOBLE JD, GLASER JS, et al: Pituitary apoplexy: Diagnosis by CT. *Radiology* 134:665–670, 1980.

PUSEY E, KORTMAN KE, FLANNIGAN BD, et al: MR of craniopharyngiomas: Tumor delineation and characterization. *AJNR* 8:439–444, 1987.

PULLICINO P, WILBUR DC, LEVY RJ, et al: Infarction in a meningioma after cardiac arrest. *Arch Neurol* 40:456–457, 1983.

RAO KCVG, GOVINDAN S: CAT in rapidly growing brain tumors. *Comput Tomogr* 3:9–13, 1979.

RAO KCVG, LEVINE H, ITANI A, et al: CT findings in multicentric glioblastoma: Diagnostic-pathologic correlation. *J Comput Tomogr* 4:187–192, 1980.

REEVES GI, MARKS JE: Prognostic significance of lesion size for glioblastoma multiforme. *Radiology* 132:469–471, 1979.

RENGACHARY S et al: Cystic lesions associated with intracranial meningiomas. *Neurosurgery* 4:107–114, 1979.

RENSHAW PF, OWEN CS, McLAUGHLIN AC, et al: Ferromagnetic contrast agents: a new approach. *Magn Reson Med* 3:217–225, 1986.

ROBBINS SL, COTRAN RS: *Pathologic Basis of Disease.* Philadelphia, Saunders, 1979.

ROHRINGER M, SUTHERLAND GR, LOUW DF, et al: Incidence and clinicopathological features of meningioma. *J Neurosurg* 71:665–672, 1989.

ROOSEN N, GAHLEN D, STORK W, et al: Magnetic resonance imaging of colloid cysts of the third ventricle. *Neuroradiology* 29:10–14, 1987.

RUNGE VM, PRICE AC, WEHR CJ, et al: Contrast enhanced MRI: evaluation of a canine model of osmotic blood-brain barrier disruption. *Invest Radiol* 20:830–844, 1985.

RUNGE VM, WOOD ML, OSBORNE MA, et al: Flash/Fisp—applications with Gd DTPA. *Magn Reson Imaging* 5:95–96, 1987.

RUSSELL DS: Meningeal tumors: A review. *J Clin Pathol* 3:191, 1950.

RUSSELL DS, RUBINSTEIN LJ: *Pathology of Tumors of the Nervous System,* ed 4. Baltimore, Williams and Wilkins, 1989.

RUSSELL EG, GEORGE AJ, KRICHEFF II, et al: Atypical CT features of intracranial meningioma: Radiological-pathological correlation in a series of 131 consecutive cases. *Radiology* 134:409–414, 1980.

SAINI S, STARK DD, HAHN PF, et al: Ferrite particles: A superparamagnetic MR contrast agent for the reticuloendothelial system. *Radiology* 162:211–216, 1987.

SALIBI SS, NAUTA HJW, BREM H, et al: Lipomeningioma: Report of three cases and review of the literature. *Neurosurg* 25:122–126, 1989.

SCHÖFNER W, LINIADO M, HIENDORF HP, et al: Time-dependent changes in image contrast in brain tumors after gadolinium-DTPA. *AJNR* 7:1013, 1986.

SCHWAIGHOFER BW, HESSELINK JR, PRESS GA, et al: Primary intracranial CNS lymphoma: MR manifestations. *Am J Neuroradiol* 10:725–729, 1989.

SEEGER JF et al: CT and angiographic evaluation of hemangioblastomas. *Radiology* 138:65–73, 1981.

SHAFFER KA, HAUGTON VM, WILSON CR: High resolution CT of the temporal bone. *Radiology* 134:409–414, 1980.

SHALLER CA, JACQUES DB, SHELDEN CH: The pathophysiology of stroke: a review with molecular considerations. *Surg Neurol* 14:433–443, 1980.

SHAPIR J, COBLENTZ C, MALANSON D, et al: New CT findings in aggressive meningioma. *Am J Neuroradiol* 6:101–102, 1985.

SMITH AS, BENSON JE, BLASER SI, et al: Diagnosis of ruptured intracranial dermoid cyst: Value of MR over CT. *AJNR* 12:175–180, 1991.

SPAGNOLI MV, GOLDBERG HI, GROSSMAN RI, et al: Intracranial meningiomas: High-field MR imaging. *Radiology* 161:369–375, 1986.

STEFFEY DJ, FILIPP GJ, SPERA T, et al: MR Imaging of primary epidermoid tumors. *J Comput Assist Tomogr* 12:438–440, 1988.

STEINHOFF H, AVILES C: Contrast enhancement response of intracranial neoplasms: Its validity for the differential diagnosis of tumors in CT, in Lanksch W, Kazner E (eds): *Cranial Computerized Tomography.* New York, Springer-Verlag, 1976, pp 151–161.

STEINHOFF H, KAZNER E, LANKSCH W, et al: The limitations of the computerized axial tomography in the detection and differential diagnosis of intranial tumors: A study based on 1304 neoplasms, in Bories J (ed): *The Diagnostic Limitations of Computerized Axial Tomography.* New York, Springer-Verlag, 1978, pp 40–49.

STEINHOFF H et al: CT in the diagnosis and differential diagnosis of glioblastomas. *Neuroradiology* 14:193–200, 1977.

STOVRING J: Contralateral temporal horn widening in unilateral supratentorial mass lesions: A diagnostic sign indicating tentorial herniation. *J Comput Assist Tomogr* 1:319–323, 1977.

SZE G, KROL G, OLSEN WL, et al: Hemmorrhagic neoplasms: MR mimics of occult vascular malformation. *AJR* 8:795, 1987.

TADMOR R, DAVIS K, ROBERSON G, et al: Computed tomography in primary malignant lymphoma of the brain. *J Comput Assist Tomogr* 2:135–140, 1978.

TADMOR R, TAVERAS JM: Computed tomography in extradural epidermoid and xanthoma. *Surg Neurol* 7:371–375, 1977.

TAKEUCHI J, HANDA H, NAGAT I: Suprasellar germinoma. *J Neurosurg* 49:41–48, 1978.

TAKEUCHI J et al: Neuroradiological aspects of supratentorial astrocytoma. *Clin Neurol Neurosurg* 80:156–168, 1978.

TALLY PW, LAWS ER Jr, SCHEITHAUER BW: Metastases of central nervous system neoplasms: Case report. *J Neurosurg* 68:811–816, 1988.

TANS J, DE JONGH IE: Computed tomography of supratentorial astrocytoma. *Clin Neurol, Neurosurg* 80:156–168, 1978.

TCHANG S et al: Computerized tomography as a possible aid to histological grading of supratentorial gliomas. *J Neurosurg* 46:735–739, 1977.

TENFLER RL, PALACIOS E: False negative CT in brain tumor. *JAMA* 238:339–340, 1977.

THOMSON JLG: Computerized axial tomography and the diagnosis of glioma: A study of 100 consecutive histologically proven cases. *Clin Radiol* 27:431–441, 1976.

TIEN RD, BARKOVICH AJ, EDWARDS MSB: MR imaging of pineal tumors *AJNR* 11:557–565, 1990.

TIEN RD, YANG PJ, CHU PK: "Dural tail sign": A specific MR sign for meningioma? *J Comput Assist Tomogr* 15:64–66, 1991.

TOGLIA JU et al: Epithelial tumors of the cranium: Their common nature and pathogenesis. *J Neurosurg* 23:384–393, 1965.

TOKUMARU A, O'UCHI T, EGUCHI T, et al: Prominent meningeal enhancement adjacent to meningioma on Gd-DTPA-enhanced MR images: Histopathologic correlation. *Radiology* 175:431–433, 1990.

TRATTING S, SCHINDLER E, UNGERSBÖCK, et al: Extra-CNS metastasis of glioblastoma: CT and MR studies. *J Comput Assist Tomogr* 14:294, 1990.

TRUWIT CL, BARKOVICH AJ: Pathogenesis of intracranial lipoma: An MR study in 42 patients. *AJNR* 11:665–674, 1990.

VAN TASSEL P, LEE YY, BRUNER JM: Synchronous and metachronous malignant gliomas: CT findings. *AJNR* 9:725–732, 1988.

VASSILOUTHIS J, AMBROSE J: Computerized tomography scanning appearance of intracranial meningiomas. *J Neurosurg* 50:320–327, 1979.

VONOFAKOS D, HACKER H: CT histogram in the pathologic definition of supratentorial brain tumors. *Neuroradiology* 16:552–555, 1978.

VONOFAKOS D, MARCU H, HACKER H: Oligodendrogliomas: CT patterns with emphasis on features indicating malignancy. *J Comput Assist Tomogr* 3:783–788, 1979.

WEHRLI FW, MacFALL JR, NEWTON TH: Parameters determining the appearance of NMR images, in Newton TH, Potts DG (eds): *Modern Neuroradiology, vol 2, Advanced Imaging Techniques.* San Anselmo, Clavadel Press, 1983, pp 81–117.

WEINMANN HJ, BRASCH RC, PRESS WR, et al: Characteristics of gadolinium-DTPA complex: A potential NMR contrast agent. *AJR* 142:619–629, 1984.

WEINMANN HJ, LANIADO M, MUTZEL W: Pharmacokinetics of Gd-DTPA/dimeglumine after intravenous injection into healthy volunteers. *Physiol Chem Phys Med NMR* 16:167–172, 1984.

WEINSTEIN MA, MODIC MT, PAVLICEK W, et al: Nuclear magnetic resonance for the examination of brain tumors. *Semin Roentgenol* 19:139–147, 1984.

WENDE S et al: A German multicentric study of intracranial tumors, in duBoulay GH, Moseley IF (eds): *Computerized Axial Tomography in Clinical Practice.* Heidelberg, Springer-Verlag, 1977.

WILMS G, LAMMENS M, MARCHAL G, et al: Thickening of dura surrounding meningiomas: MR features. *J Comput Assist Tomogr* 13:763–768, 1989.

WILMS G, MARCHAL G, VAN HECKE P, et al: Colloid cysts of the third ventricle: MR findings. *J Comput Assist Tomogr.* 14:527–531, 1990.

WYLIE IG, JEFFREYS R, MACLAINE GN: Cerebral hemangioblastoma. *Br J Radiol* 46:472–476, 1973.

YUH WTC: MRI with Gd-DO3A, presented at the Society of Magnetic Resonance in Medicine, New York, 1991.

YUH WTC, BARLOON TJ, JACOBY OG, et al: MR of fourth-ventricular epidermoid tumors. *AJNR* 9:794–796, 1988.

YUH WTC, FISHER DJ, ENGELKEN JD, et al: MR evaluation of CNS tumors: Dose comparison study with gadopentetate dimeglumine and gadoteridol. *Radiology* 180:485–491, 1991.

ZEE CS, SEGALL H, APUZZO M, et al: MR imaging of pineal region neoplasms. *J Comput Assist Tomogr* 15:56–63, 1991.

ZETTNER A, NETSKY MG: Lipoma of the corpus callosum. *J Neuropathol Exp Neurol* 19:305–319, 1960.

ZIMMERMAN HM: Malignant lymphomas of the nervous system. *Acta Neuropathol* suppl VI: 69–74, 1975.

ZIMMERMAN RA, BILANIUK LT: Age-related incidence of pineal calcification detected by computed tomography. *Radiology* 142:659–662, 1982.

ZIMMERMAN RA, BILANIUK LT: Cranial computed tomography of epidermoid and congenital fatty tumors of maldevelopment origin. *J Comput Assist Tomogr* 3:40–50, 1979*a*.

ZIMMERMAN RA, BILANIUK LT: CT of intracerebral gangliogliomas. *J Comput Assist Tomogr* 3:24–29, 1979*b*.

ZIMMERMAN RA, BILANIUK LT: Computed tomography of choroid plexus lesions. *J Comput Assist Tomogr* 3:93–102, 1979*c*.

ZIMMERMAN RA, BILANIUK LT: Computed tomography of acute intratumoral hemorrhage. *Radiology* 135:355–359, 1980*a*.

ZIMMERMAN RA et al: CT of pineal, parapineal and histologically related tumors. *Radiology* 137:669–677, 1980*b*.

ZIMMERMAN RD, FLOEMING CA, SAINT-LOUIS LA, et al: Magnetic resonance imaging of meningiomas. *AJNR* 6:149–157, 1985.

ZULCH KJ: *Brain Tumors: Their Biology and Pathology.* New York, Springer-Verlag, 1986.

PEDIATRIC BRAIN TUMORS

Robert A. Zimmerman

INTRODUCTION

The most common site for the occurrence of solid tumors in childhood is the central nervous system (CNS) (Heideman 1989). Almost one-half of the 2.5 brain tumors per 100,000 children that occur annually are found in the posterior fossa (Young 1975; Segall 1985); the remainder arise in the supratentorial space. In childhood, primary neoplasms represent the vast majority of brain tumors, with metastatic lesions to the brain parenchyma being uncommon (Gusnard 1990).

The differential diagnosis of a brain tumor in a child is based on anatomic localization, clinical symptomatology, age, and changes in density with CT and signal intensity with MR (Zimmerman 1990*b*). Pediatric tumors in the CNS are of diverse histological origin and include tumors arising from primitive stem cells of the germinal matrix (e.g., primitive neuroectodermal tumors), from the supporting cell structure of the brain (e.g., astrocytomas and gliomas), from the choroid plexus (e.g., choroid plexus papillomas and carcinomas), from the ependymal lining of the ventricles or ependymal rests within the white matter (e.g., ependymomas), and from embryological rests within the pineal gland (e.g., germinomas) as well as tumors arising as inclusions (e.g., lipomas, dermoids, and teratomas) and tumors arising from malformative processes (e.g., hamartomas) (Zimmerman 1990*b*). Some of these tumors are highly aggressive in nature, with a propensity to spread into the subarachnoid and intraventricular spaces (Heideman 1989). The evaluation and treatment of these patients are made more difficult by their young age; in the infant, the brain is still undergoing active myelination and neuronal organization.

The purpose of an imaging evaluation is to determine if a tumor is present and, if this proves to be the case, to localize it and suggest the most likely histological diagnosis. After treatment, the goal is to detect response, persistence of tumor, regrowth of tumor, and tumor dissemination as well as to detect possible postoperative or posttherapeutic complications.

The two primary methods of evaluation are computed tomography (CT) and magnetic resonance imaging (MRI). The choice of technique first depends on availability and the patient's clinical stability (Zimmerman 1989). CT is relatively rapid but somewhat insensitive to small tumors characterized by increased water content. MR is sensitive to tumors with increased water content, shows more obvious tumor enhancement, is more sensitive to the presence of old blood products, and is less sensitive to calcification. MR scans take longer than CT scans do, and so motion can be a problem; thus, sedation is generally required during the first 6 years of life and in older retarded or otherwise uncooperative patients (Zimmerman 1986). With MR, the use of a magnetic field requires special considerations. Unstable patients who require monitoring and support are more difficult to examine with MR than with CT. In general, the increased sensitivity of MR to the presence of a cerebral neoplasm justifies the greater difficulty in acquiring an MR study.

POSTERIOR FOSSA TUMORS

The three most common tumors of the pediatric posterior fossa are brainstem gliomas, cerebellar astrocytomas, and primitive neuroectodermal tumors (medulloblastoma) (Heideman 1989). Ependymomas, choroid plexus papillomas, dermoids, epidural neuroblastoma metastases, and other neoplasms are much less common.

Brainstem Gliomas

The peak age for the onset of symptoms of brainstem gliomas is around 5 years, with males slightly more frequently affected than females (Bilaniuk 1980; Mantravadi 1982). In up to 90 percent of patients, cranial nerve palsies are a significant form of presentation (Albright 1983). These palsies are most often bilateral and multiple, with the sixth and seventh nerves most often affected (Albright

1983). Long track signs, ataxia, paraparesis, sensory deficits, and gaze disorders also may be present. Hydrocephalus usually is not present at diagnosis but develops after later growth of the mass. In patients with midbrain tectal lesions, hydrocephalus may be the initial form of presentation. Hydrocephalus has been reported to be present at the time of diagnosis in up to 30 percent of these patients (Bilaniuk 1980). Brainstem gliomas most commonly arise within the pons, from which they may extend superiorly into the midbrain and thalamus, laterally into the cerebellar peduncle and cerebellum, and inferiorly into the medulla and upper cervical spinal cord. Subarachnoid spread is not present at the time of diagnosis but can be found in up to 20 percent of patients with malignant gliomas before death (Mantravadi 1982; Packer 1983*a*). Exophytic extension commonly occurs into the basilar subarachnoid space, often partially encompassing the basilar artery; less frequently, it impinges on the internal auditory canal.

Histologically, most pontine gliomas are fibrillary astrocytomas, a type of neoplasm that has a tendency to develop foci of anaplasia that undergo malignant degeneration, giving rise to an aggressive tumor that results in the patient's ultimate demise (Russell 1989). It is these foci of malignant degeneration that undergo cystic necrosis, hemorrhage, and contrast enhancement. Histologically, a fibrillary astrocytoma has little edema but enough interstitial fluid to appear high in signal intensity on proton density and T_2-weighted images (T_2WI). Fibrillary astrocytomas usually lack the microvasculature necessary for contrast enhancement. A smaller percentage of brainstem gliomas are pilocytic in nature, arising chiefly in the medulla and midbrain, often as exophytic masses (Smith 1990). These tumors usually do not undergo malignant degeneration but may be associated with cysts, as is often seen with cystic cerebellar astrocytomas. These tumors have a microvasculature that usually produces contrast enhancement. Their slow growth rate appears to be responsible for the small incidence of long-term survivors with brainstem tumors.

Most brainstem gliomas are low in signal intensity on T_1-weighted images (T_1WI) (Fig. 9-1*A*) and high in signal intensity on long TR images (Fig. 9-2). On plain CT they are low in density, are isodense, or have a mixture of low-density and isodense components (Fig. 9-3). Calcification and hemorrhage in a brainstem glioma are unusual at diagnosis, but both may be seen in patients who have been treated with radiation. Hemorrhage seen on MR is not an uncommon finding with tumor progression (Fig. 9-4). With CT and MR, contrast enhancement is infrequent in malignant tumors at the time of diagnosis but occurs with increasing frequency with tumor progression (Fig. 9-5). Contrast enhancement is common on both CT and MR in low-grade pilocytic astrocytomas of the medulla and midbrain (Fig. 9-6).

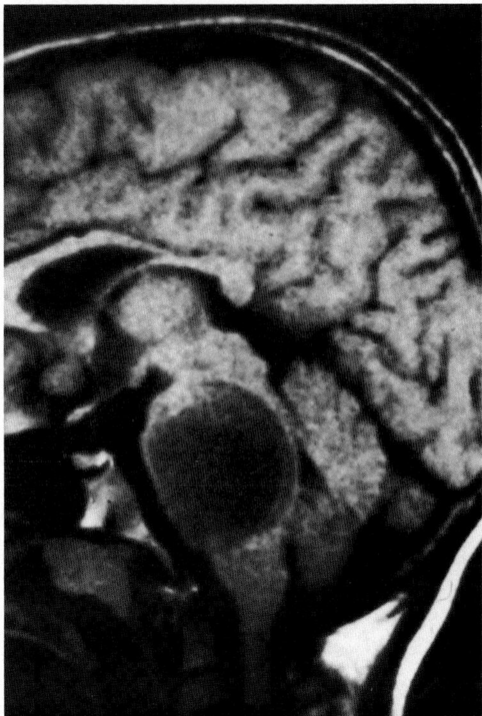

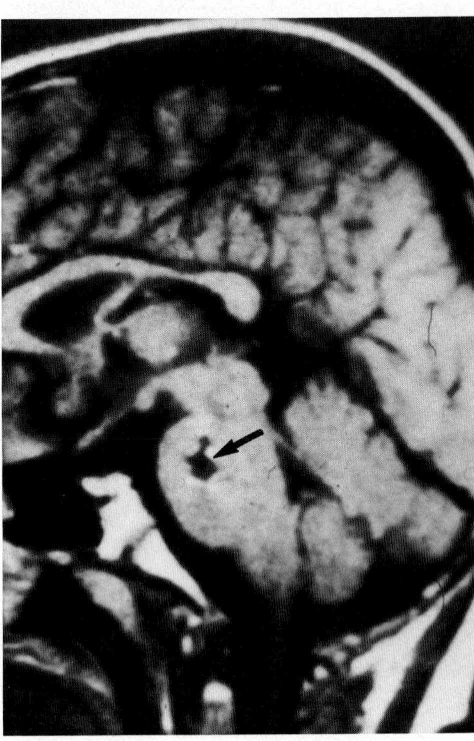

Figure 9-1 Pontine glioma before and after hyperfractionation. **A.** Sagittal T_1WI shows a hypointense mass expanding the pons and displacing and compressing the fourth ventricle. This examination was done before hyperfractionation radiotherapy. **B.** Sagittal T_1WI after hyperfractionation radiotherapy shows marked reduction in the size of the tumor. There is a focal area of low signal intensity (arrow) within the upper pons. Note that the fourth ventricle is no longer as compressed.

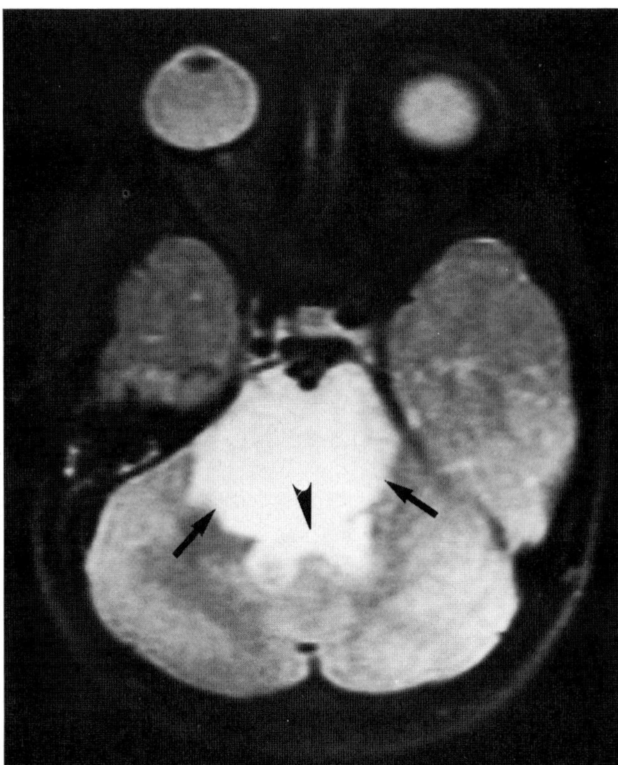

Figure 9-2 Pontine glioma. Axial T_2WI shows a high-signal-intensity mass (arrows) expanding the pons and compressing the fourth ventricle (arrowhead).

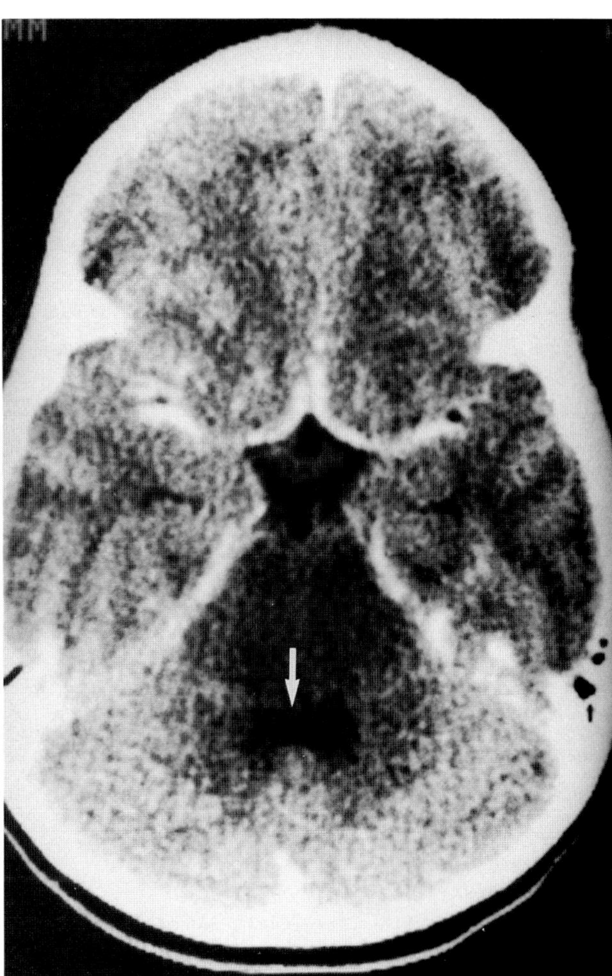

Figure 9-3 Pontine glioma. Axial CT after contrast injection shows a hypodense mass expanding the pons and compressing the fourth ventricle (arrow). The mass does not contrast-enhance.

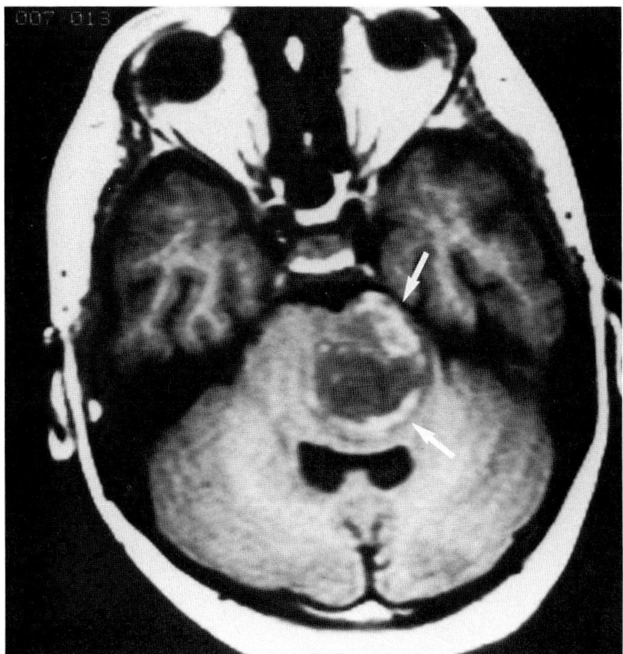

Figure 9-4 Pontine glioma. Axial T_1WI shows a hyperintense methemoglobin hemorrhage within portions of a pontine mass. The fourth ventricle is deformed, and most of the mass is of low signal intensity.

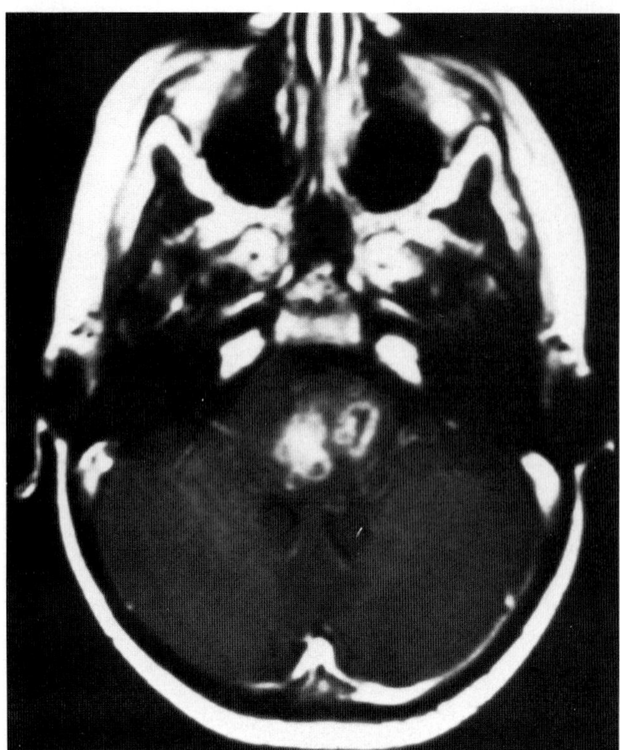

Figure 9-5 Progressive pontine glioma. Axial T_1WI after MR contrast injection shows enhancement of the inferior portion of the pontine mass.

Intrinsic pontine gliomas that are diagnosed by imaging methods when the clinical findings are consistent are not subjected to biopsy. Surgery is still performed when the tumor is largely exophytic, so that debulking and a histological diagnosis can be made; when the tumor is largely cystic, so that the cyst can be decompressed; and when the diagnosis of tumor is in doubt, so that therapy will not be instituted for a nonneoplastic disease process. Radiation is the only effective temporary therapy at present. Conventional doses up to 5400 cGy have been reported to result in a 5-year survival rate between 10 and 30 percent (Farwell 1977). Hyperfractionation radiotherapy with a twice-daily application of 100 cGy in doses of 6800 to 8200 cGy have led to some increase in survival, but the results so far are only preliminary (Packer 1987). The adjunctive use of chemotherapy has not resulted in improved survival. Follow-up studies of brainstem gliomas after hyperfractionation radiotherapy in some patients have indicated a significant reduction in tumor size (Fig. 9-1*B*). However, the course over the next 6 to 12 months is usually one of progressive growth and extension of the tumor from the pons through the cerebral peduncles into the cerebellum and from the pons superiorly and inferiorly into the adjacent brainstem structures (Smith 1990).

The main differential diagnosis of brainstem gliomas includes the occult vascular malformation, other causes of brainstem bleeding, and other causes of brainstem lesions that appear hypodense on CT and hyperintense on T_2-weighted MR images. Such hyperintense lesions on T_2-weighted MR include multiple sclerosis, acute disseminated encephalomyelitis (Fig. 9-7), dysmyelinating disease, and central pontine myelinolysis (Smith 1990). The occult vascular malformation may be of increased density on CT, shows some contrast enhancement, and on MR

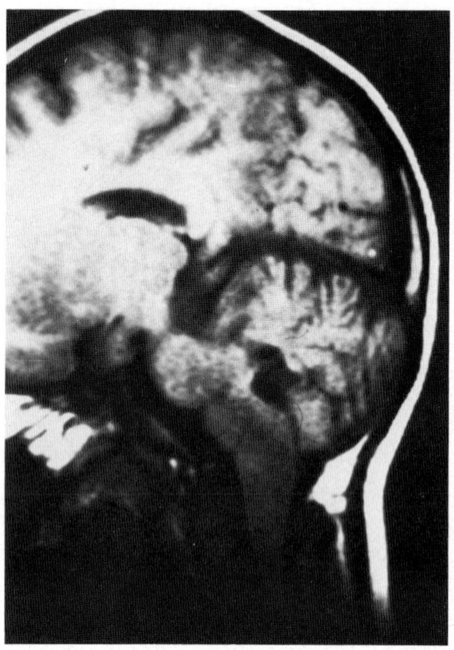

A

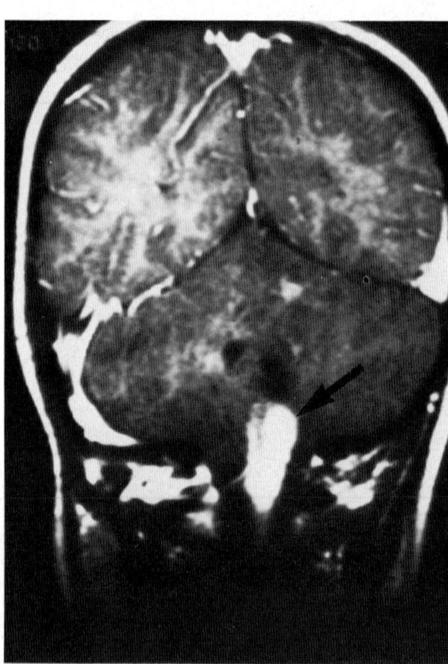

B

Figure 9-6 Pilocytic astrocytoma in the medulla and upper cervical cord. **A.** Sagittal T_1WI without contrast shows expansion of the medulla and upper cervical cord. **B.** Coronal T_1WI after MR contrast injection shows enhancement of the tumor (arrow).

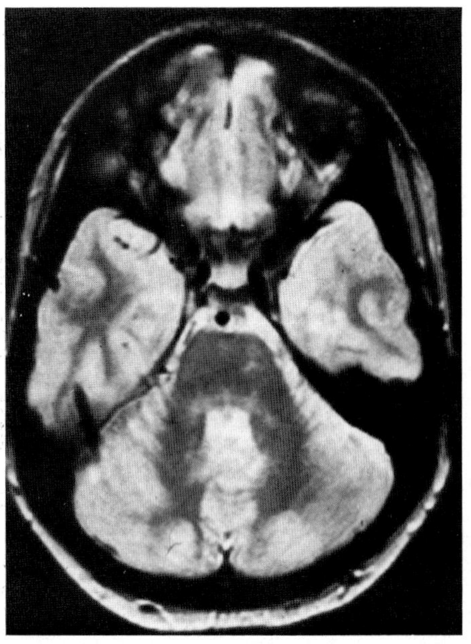

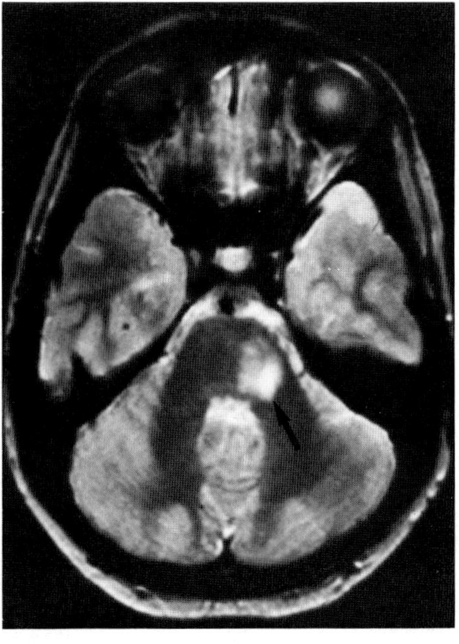

Figure 9-7 Acute multiple sclerosis involving the pons. **A.** Axial PDWI shows no abnormality in the pons. **B.** Repeat axial PDWI 29 days after the first examination shows high-signal-intensity demyelination (arrow) within the left side of the pons.

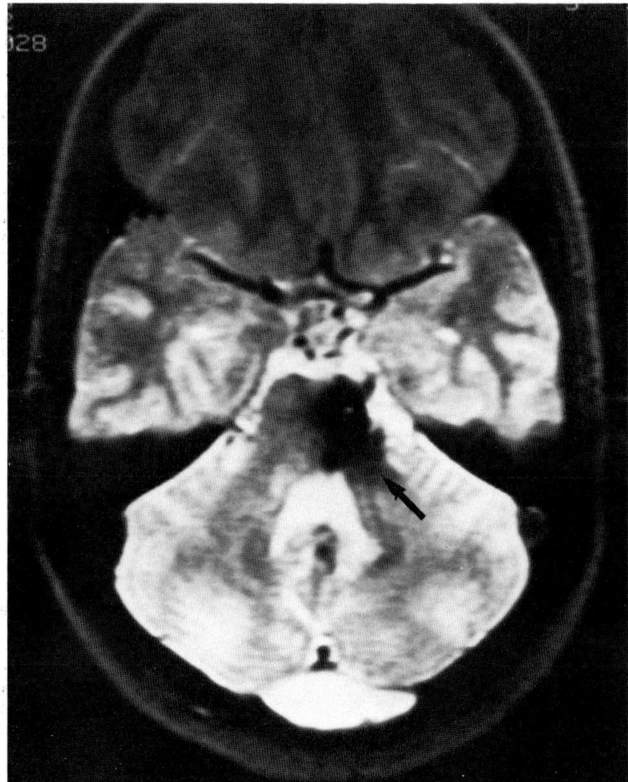

Figure 9-8 Occult vascular malformation in the pons. Axial T_2WI shows hypointense hemosiderin (arrow) in the left side of the pons at the site of an old occult vascular malformation that had hemorrhaged 8 years before.

shows mixed signal intensity on both T_1WI and T_2WI (Savoiardo 1978; Gomori 1986). The presence of subacute blood products, including methemoglobin and hemosiderin, is suggestive (Fig. 9-8). Arteriovenous malformations may appear to be quite similar. Acute disseminated encephalomyelitis arising after vaccination or a viral infection affects not only the brainstem but the white matter of the supratentorial space and cerebellum (Dunn 1986; Atlas 1986). The multiplicity of lesions and the relationship to the inciting event help in making the differential diagnosis. Dysmyelinating disease is characterized by its clinical onset, symmetry, and supratentorial components. Central pontine myelinolysis is unusual in infants and children and more common in adults and is associated with episodes of hyponatremia, such as those in ethanol abuse (Koch 1989).

Cerebellar Astrocytoma

Cerebellar astrocytomas are one of the most common posterior fossa tumors of childhood, often listed as second to primitive neuroectodermal tumors (medulloblastoma). Histologically, two types occur most frequently: juvenile pilocytic astrocytomas (75 to 85 percent) and more diffuse fibrillary astrocytomas (15 to 20 percent) (Russell 1989; Lee 1989; Steinberg 1985). A small percentage of cerebellar astrocytomas are malignant, either anaplastic astrocytomas or glioblastomas, and a still smaller percentage are oligodendrogliomas. Pilocytic astrocytomas are characterized by long-term survival of 90 percent or better, whereas fibrillary astrocytomas have a much less favorable outcome (Winston 1977; Auer 1981). Anaplastic astrocytomas and glioblastomas are usually fatal. The pre-

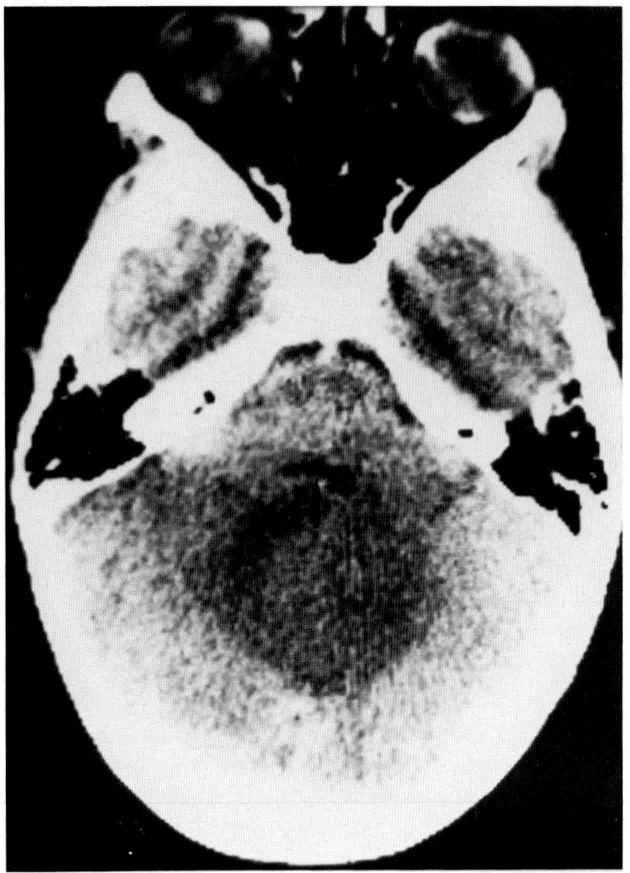

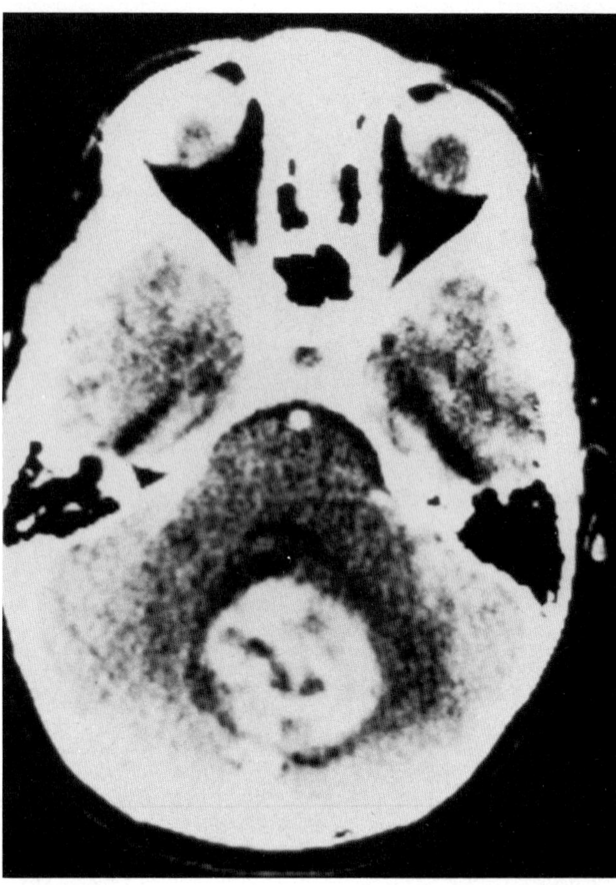

A B

Figure 9-9 Cerebellar astrocytoma. **A.** Axial NC CT injection shows a hypodense mass in the vermis, displacing the fourth ventricle (arrow) forward. **B.** Axial CE CT shows enhancement of a cerebellar astrocytoma.

sentation in patients with cerebellar astrocytomas usually takes the form of signs of increased intracranial pressure (headache, nausea, vomiting), with the symptoms lasting weeks to years before diagnosis (Geissinger 1971). Cerebellar signs may or may not be evident at the time of diagnosis. Cerebellar astrocytomas tend to be large at diagnosis. Approximately half of these tumors are solid masses. In cystic tumors, the cyst walls are often made up of compressed nonneoplastic cerebellar tissue, with the tumor being a mural nodule (Gol 1959). However, some of these tumors are actually solid tumors that have undergone cystlike central necrosis, so that tumor surrounds the necrotic center. Tumors arise both in the vermis and in the cerebellar hemispheres.

In most instances hydrocephalus is present at the time of diagnosis. On CT and MR, the lateral and third ventricles are markedly dilated and the fourth ventricle is displaced anteriorly by a vermian mass or contralaterally by a cerebellar hemispheric mass. On CT, the tumor mass is lower in density than is the uninvolved cerebellar tissue (Fig. 9-9*A*) (Zimmerman 1978*a*). The solid portion of the tumor is usually slightly more dense than the cystic portion is (Fig. 9-10). Fluid within the cyst is proteinaceous and usually is slightly denser than cerebrospinal fluid (CSF) (Zimmerman 1978*a*). Calcification is uncommon, between 13 and 20 percent (Gusnard 1990; Zimmerman 1978*a*). Contrast enhancement is common with both CT (Fig. 9-9*B*) and MR (Fig. 9-11*B*) (Gusnard 1990). Both the cystic and solid components appear hypointense on T_1WI (Fig. 9-11*A*). Both components appear hyperintense on proton density weighted images (PDWI) and T_2WI (Figs. 9-12 and 9-13). Hemorrhage is uncommon in the solid portion of the tumor on MR, but the presence of hemosiderin within the cyst cavity wall, which is seen on long TR MR as a rim of hypointensity (Fig. 9-13), is not uncommon. This arises from repeated episodes of bleeding into the cystic cavity. Such episodes of bleeding contribute to the high protein content that frequently makes the cystic cavity higher in signal intensity on PDWI than is the solid tumor. While pilocytic astrocytomas show marked enhancement after MR contrast injection (Fig. 9-11*B*), fibrillary astrocytomas may show none. Subarachnoid dissemination of primary cerebellar astrocytomas is uncommon but can be found late in the disease process.

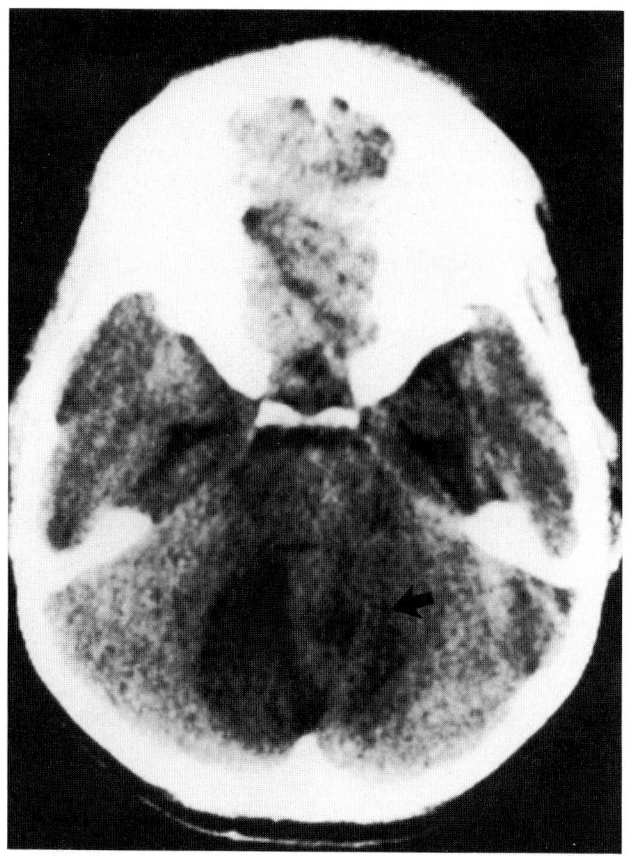

Figure 9-10 Cystic cerebellar astrocytoma. Axial NC CT shows a cystic mass in the cerebellar vermis, containing a denser mural nodule (arrow).

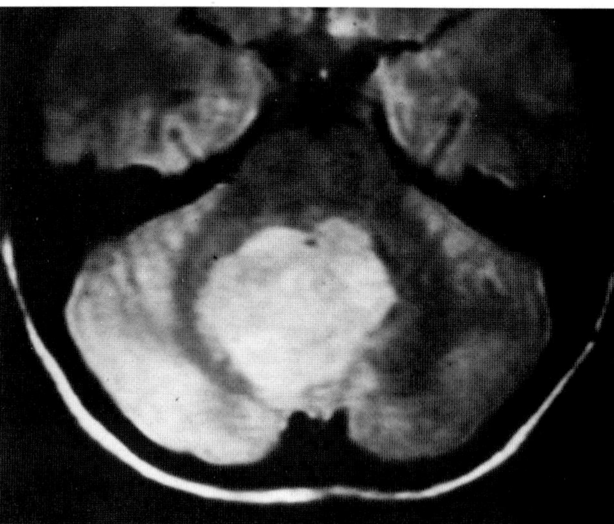

Figure 9-12 Solid vermian astrocytoma. Axial PDWI shows a high-signal-intensity vermian mass.

Figure 9-11 Cystic cerebellar astrocytoma. **A.** Axial T_1WI shows a hypointense mass in the right cerebellar hemisphere, displacing the fourth ventricle forward and to the left. **B.** Axial T_1WI after MR contrast injection shows enhancement of the tumor in the wall of the cystic cerebellar astrocytoma.

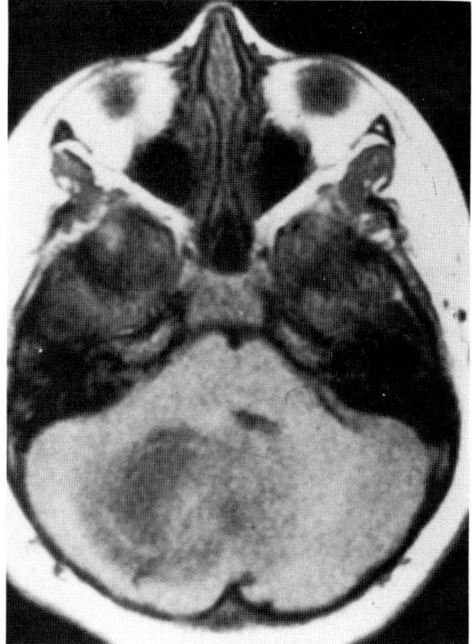

A

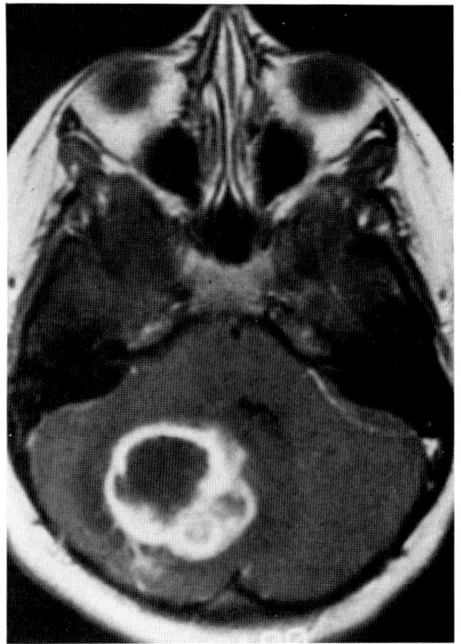

B

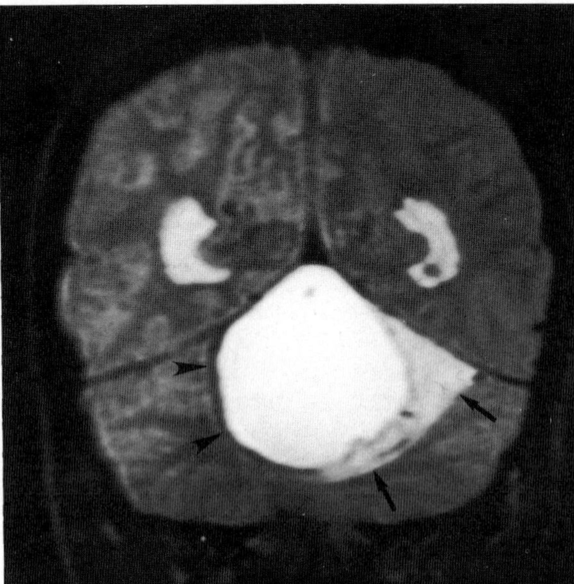

Figure 9-13 Cystic cerebellar astrocytoma. Coronal T_2WI shows a high-signal-intensity cyst cavity with a margin of low-signal-intensity hemosiderin (arrowheads) and a left lateral mass of astrocytoma (arrows) that is less intense than the cystic fluid.

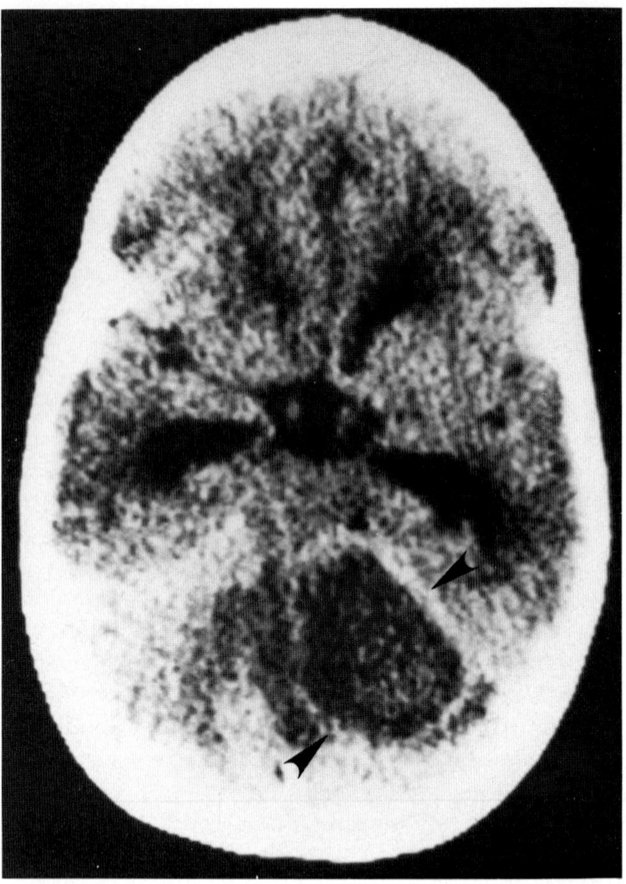

Figure 9-14 Cerebellar abscess. Axial NC CT shows the high-density rim (arrowheads) of a left cerebellar abscess wall.

In general, the long-term survival of patients with a cerebellar astrocytoma stems from the relatively benign nature of these tumors. Even patients with a tumor that is subtotally resected often have a survival measured in decades. This is true for pilocytic astrocytomas but not for the more aggressive fibrillary, anaplastic, and malignant ones. Successful treatment depends on surgical resection. If tumor is evident on follow-up examination after an initial surgery and reresection is feasible, that is the subsequent therapeutic course. Radiation therapy has proved to be of little value in the management of benign cerebellar astrocytomas. Radiation therapy and chemotherapy have been utilized in treating malignant cerebellar astrocytomas, with results no better than those seen with brainstem gliomas. The differential diagnosis of a cerebellar astrocytoma in childhood includes the occult vascular malformation, dysmyelinating disease, Lhermitte-Duclos disease, and other dysplastic diseases of cerebellar tissue. Occult vascular malformations of the cerebellar hemisphere and vermis as well as arteriovenous malformations (AVMs) are diagnosed by the presence of mixed blood products and, in the case of AVMs, by feeding arteries, the vascular nidus, and the draining veins. Dysmyelinating diseases such as Alexander's disease can affect the cerebellum and may be differentiable only on the basis of biopsy. Infectious diseases of the cerebellum such as abscesses can cause diagnostic problems. In the preantibiotic era, cerebellar abscesses were not uncommon, usually secondary to mastoiditis. Even in the antibiotic era, cerebellar abscesses occasionally present and require diagnostic consideration.

In general, the solid component that constitutes the wall of a cystic cerebellar astrocytoma is relatively hypodense, whereas the solid component that makes up the enhancing wall of a cerebellar abscess is often isodense to slightly hyperdense (Fig. 9-14) before the injection of iodinated contrast material (Zimmerman 1987*b*). On MR, cerebellar abscesses are often slightly hyperintense on T_1WI, whereas cerebellar astrocytomas are usually hypointense (Gusnard 1990; Zimmerman 1987*b*). Both abscesses and cerebellar astrocytomas may produce surrounding vasogenic edema in the cerebellar white matter. Tuberculomas are more common in underdeveloped countries and can mimic cerebellar astrocytomas. Parasitic cysts within the fourth ventricle, such as those found with cysticercosis, can produce a mass with a parenchymal reactive change.

Primitive Neuroectodermal Tumors (Medulloblastoma)

Depending on the series, medulloblastoma or cerebellar astrocytoma is the most common primary neoplasm of the pediatric posterior fossa. Primitive neuroectodermal tumors of both the supratentorial and infratentorial spaces are the most common primary malignant CNS tumors in the pediatric population (Arseni 1982). Three of four patients with medulloblastoma present within the first decade (Farwell 1977; Chou 1983). These are rapidly growing tumors characterized by a short duration of symptoms, often on the order of weeks to months (Hoffman 1983). The signs are those of a posterior fossa mass, most often associated with obstructive hydrocephalus. Compression or occlusion of the fourth ventricle is responsible for the hydrocephalus. Histologically, these tumors are highly cellular, consisting of cells with scant cytoplasm and large nuclei, and frequently undergo mitosis (Russell 1989). These tumors tend to have a rich vascular supply. Tumors that occur in patients under 3 years of age, those that tend to disseminate early, those that are so large or difficult in location that they are not candidates for gross total resection, and those that show features of histological differentiation along more mature cell lines have a significantly worse prognosis (Rorke 1983; Packer 1985–1986).

On CT and MR, the common findings are a posterior fossa mass, arising in the vermis or cerebellar hemispheres, that compresses and obstructs the fourth ventricle, producing enlargement of the third and lateral ventricles (hydrocephalus) (Figs. 9-15 and 9-16) (Gusnard 1990; Zimmerman 1978*b*). On CT, the mass is usually isodense to hyperdense before contrast injection (Fig. 9-16*A*) (Zimmerman 1978*b*). The mass is most often solid, relatively homogeneous, and diffusely enhancing (Fig. 9-16*B*) (Ramondi 1979). Occasionally small cystic or necrotic areas and even larger ones may be present. Calcification is uncommon, on the order of 10 to 15 percent (Gusnard 1990; Ramondi 1979). On MR, the mass is hypointense on T_1WI (Fig. 9-15*A*), often slightly hyperintense on proton density weighted images (PDWI) (Fig. 9-17*A*), and most often hypointense to isointense on T_2WI (Fig. 9-17*B*) (Gusnard 1990). This is different from a cerebellar astrocytoma, which is high in signal intensity on T_2WI (Fig. 9-13). The etiology of the hypointensity to isointensity on T_2WI is most likely the highly cellular nature of the tumor and its relatively low interstitial water content. After contrast injection, enhancement occurs on both CT and MR. Subarachnoid dissemination of tumor has been reported at the time of diagnosis (Heideman 1989). This may occur both intracranially and intraspinally.

Treatment of medulloblastoma is performed with gross total resection (Ramondi 1979) with radiation therapy to the craniospinal axis (Heideman 1989). Adjunctive chemotherapy has been shown to improve survival (Pendergrass 1987). After gross total resection and before the institution of radiotherapy to the craniospinal axis, myelography with water-soluble dye is carried out in the entire spinal canal to prove or rule out subarachnoid drop metastases. Tumor may be found adherent to the pial surface of the cord, the arachnoid lining the thecal sac, or the nerve roots. In the postoperative period, false-positive myelographic findings can be due to the presence of operative debris or clot within the subarachnoid

A

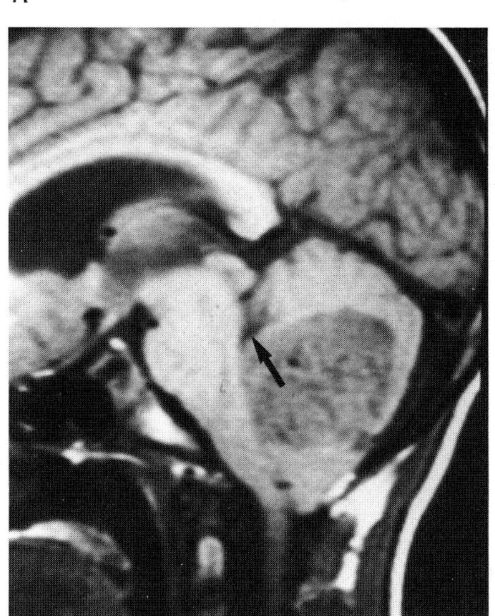

B

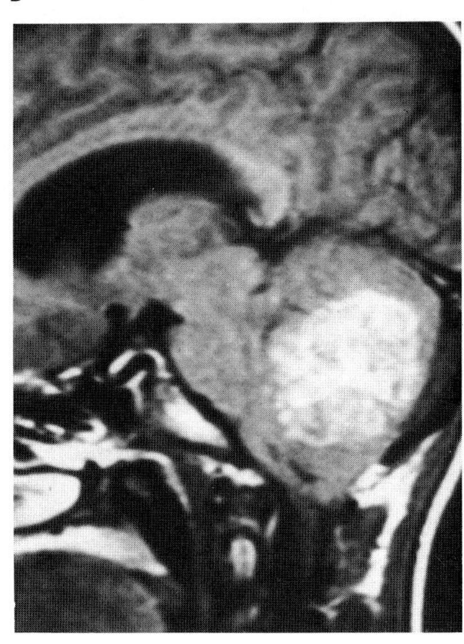

Figure 9-15 Primitive neuroectodermal tumor (medulloblastoma type). **A.** Sagittal T_1WI shows a slightly hypointense mass within the vermis, compressing the brainstem and fourth ventricle (arrow) and producing hydrocephalus. **B.** Sagittal T_1WI after MR contrast injection shows enhancement of the tumor.

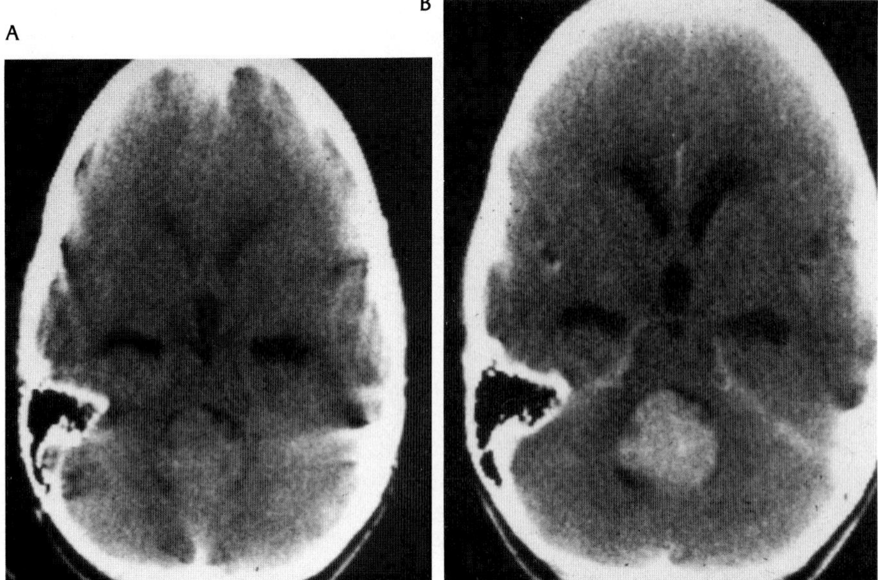

Figure 9-16 Primitive neuroectodermal tumor (medulloblastoma type). **A.** Axial NC CT shows an isodense to slightly hyperdense mass in the vermis, filling the fourth ventricle. There is early hydrocephalus with dilatation of the temporal horns and third ventricle. **B.** Axial CE CT shows homogeneous enhancement of the mass.

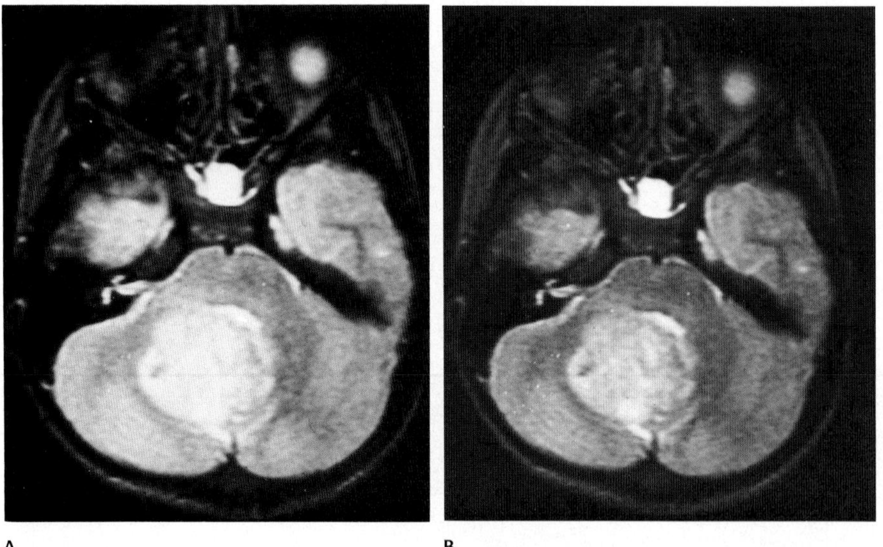

Figure 9-17 Primitive neuroectodermal tumor (medulloblastoma type). **A.** Axial PDWI shows a hyperintensity mass in the vermis, compressing the brainstem. **B.** Axial T_2WI shows that the mass becomes more hypointense on T_2WI.

space (Kramer 1991). Contrast-enhanced T_1-weighted MR is able to show enhancement of tumor on the pial surface of the cord (Fig. 9-18*B*), which is not easily detected on myelography (Kramer 1991). MR contrast also can demonstrate tumor adherent to nerve roots. Nonenhanced MR has been unsatisfactory in the evaluation of subarachnoid dissemination.

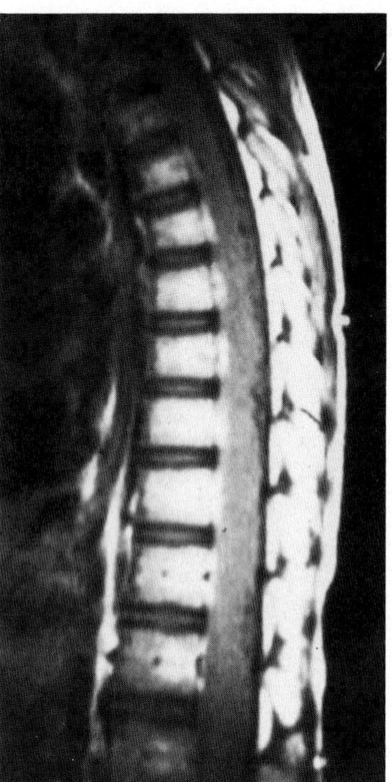

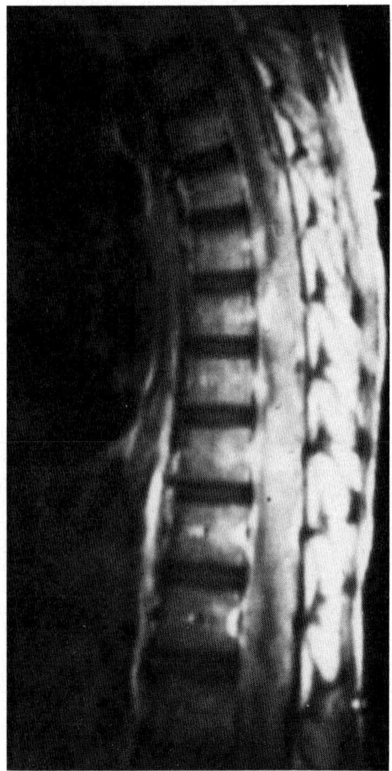

Figure 9-18 Spinal subarachnoid dissemination of a primitive neuroectodermal tumor (medulloblastoma type). **A.** Axial T_1WI before contrast injection shows loss of subarachnoid space in the thoracic spinal canal. **B.** Sagittal T_1WI after contrast injection shows an enhanced tumor coating the surface of the thoracic cord.

Ependymomas

Over two-thirds of ependymomas are infratentorial in location, occurring predominantly in children usually less than 5 years of age, with a later but smaller peak in the third decade in adults (Kun 1988; Swartz 1982). Supratentorial and infratentorial ependymomas constitute under 10 percent of all primary CNS tumors of childhood. In the posterior fossa, ependymomas arise from the ependymal lining of the fourth ventricle or along the course of the tela choroidea, which extends through the lateral recesses of the fourth ventricle into the cerebellopontine angle cisterns (Russell 1989). In the supratentorial space, ependymomas arise both intraventricularly and from ependymal rests in the white matter (Russell 1989).

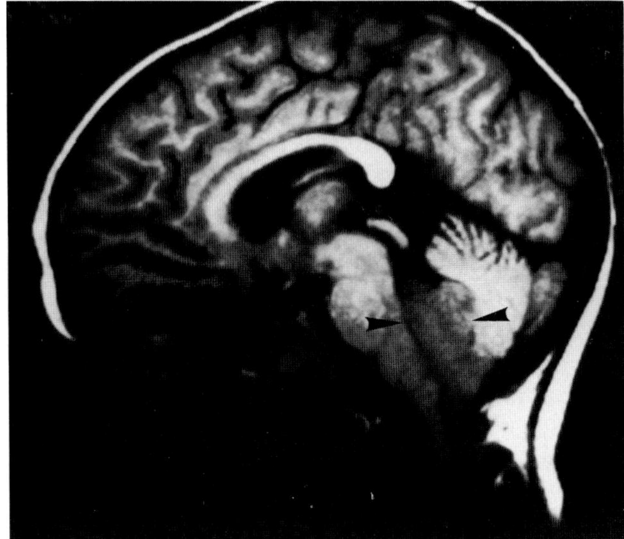

Figure 9-19 Ependymoma. Sagittal T_1WI shows an intra-fourth-ventricular slightly hypointense mass (arrowheads) extending into the cisterna magna.

Ependymomas are classified as benign or malignant (Rorke 1987). Ependymoblastoma has been recategorized as one form of primitive neuroectodermal tumor (Rorke 1985). The tumor tends to expand within the fourth ventricle (Fig. 9-19), extending in a plasticlike fashion through the lateral recesses (Fig. 9-20) and through the foramen of Magendie into the adjacent cisterns. The tumor tends to wrap around the blood vessels and cranial nerves, making total surgical resection difficult. Hypervascularity, evidence of previous hemorrhage, and calcification are common features of ependymomas (Russell 1989). In general, histological features, benign versus more malignant, have not been major factors in survival (Liu 1976). Survival has been equally dismal in patients with both the benign and malignant forms. Despite treatment, both types have tended to recur locally and to disseminate with time.

Ependymomas are most often isointense on plain CT and frequently, but not always, show contrast enhancement (Fig. 9-21) (Swartz 1982). Calcification in the form

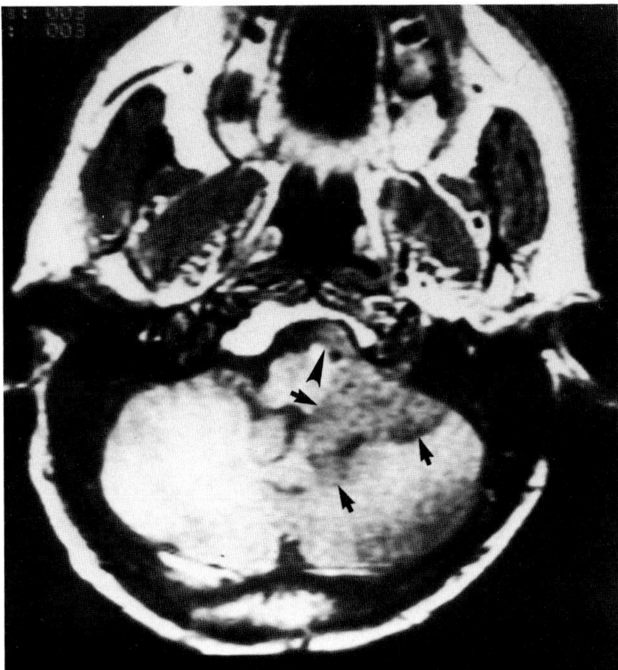

Figure 9-20 Axial T_1WI shows a hypointense mass (arrows) in the lateral recess of the fourth ventricle extending anterior to the medulla (arrowhead).

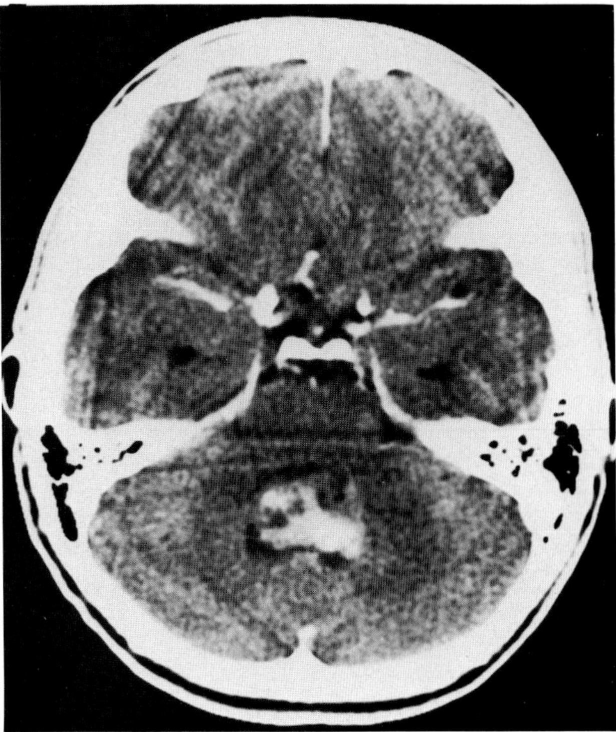

Figure 9-21 Ependymoma. Axial CE CT shows an intra-fourth-ventricular enhanced tumor.

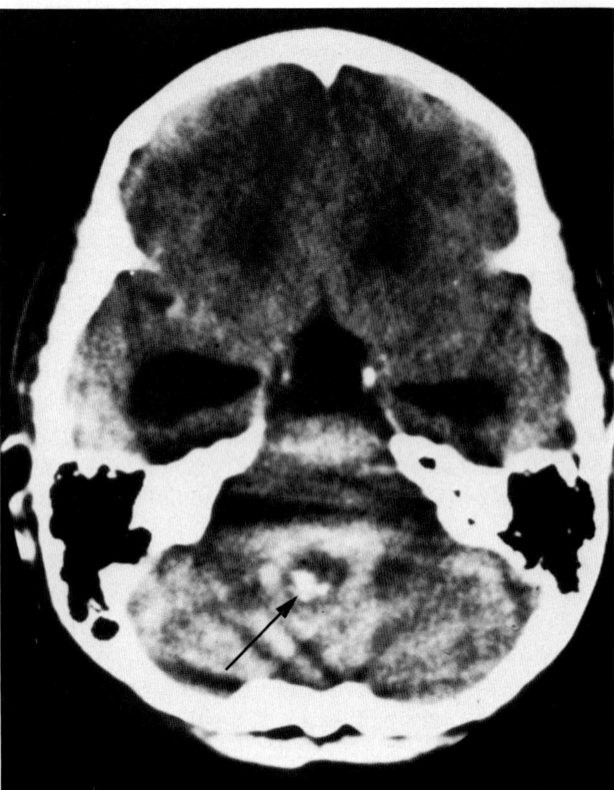

Figure 9-22 Ependymoma. Axial NC CT shows focal calcification (arrow) in an ill-defined mass in the region of the fourth ventricle. Note that there is marked dilatation of the third ventricle and temporal horns, consistent with hydrocephalus.

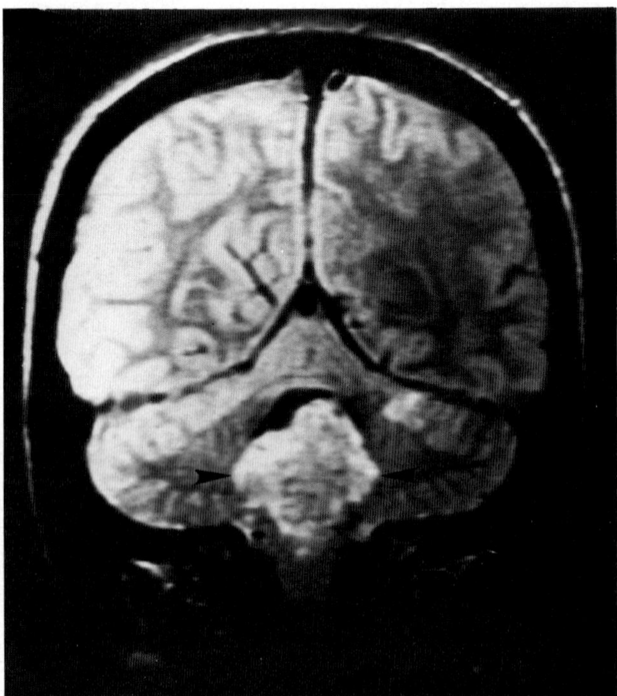

Figure 9-23 Ependymoma. Coronal PDWI shows a hyperintensity mass (arrowheads) filling the fourth ventricle.

of small round flecks occurs in approximately 50 percent of these patients (Fig. 9-22), making this one of the most common posterior fossa tumors to show calcium deposits (Swartz 1982). The incidence of calcification is similar in the supratentorial ependymoma. On MR, the tumor is usually low in signal intensity on T_1WI (Figs. 9-19 and 9-20) and high in signal intensity on T_2WI but often has mixed interspersed signals because of prior hemorrhage, calcification, or tumor blood vessels (Fig. 9-23) (Gusnard 1990). Even with contrast-enhanced MR, the tumor may not enhance in a small percentage of patients. Not infrequently, small seedings of the tumor to the ventricular ependyma, subarachnoid space, or spinal canal do not show contrast enhancement until the tumor reaches a certain degree of enlargement. Thus, recognition of the dissemination of an ependymoma may be difficult in the early stages. Ependymomas are one type of tumor in which water-soluble myelography may remain an important adjunct in staging tumor dissemination.

In general, most patients with posterior fossa ependymomas are young and develop signs and symptoms of increased intracranial pressure due to hydrocephalus from obstruction of the CSF outlets, with the onset of symptoms occurring over a variable period of time (Coulon 1977). Invasion of the cerebellum may lead to cerebellar signs, while cranial nerve palsies may be due to tumor encasing the nerves (Heideman 1989).

The treatment of a posterior fossa ependymoma consists of gross total resection and radiation therapy either by local portals or, if there is a question of dissemination, to the craniospinal axis by craniospinal irradiation. Adjunctive chemotherapy has been used without great success (Heideman 1989). With recurrent ependymoma, chemotherapy is a mainstay but does not appear to alter the ultimate course. Both benign and malignant ependymomas tend to evolve over several years, with local recurrence followed by dissemination.

Choroid Plexus Papilloma and Carcinoma

Tumors of the choroid plexus represent less than 1 percent of all intracranial tumors, but when they occur, they are found in childhood (Zimmerman 1979*c*). Most occur within the first decade of life, primarily within the first 2 years (Laurence 1979). The lateral and third ventricles are affected more frequently in those under age 2, while the fourth ventricle is more often affected in adolescents (Laurence 1979). Choroid plexus carcinomas are even less common and are found in infancy (Zimmerman 1979*b*). Invasion of adjacent neural tissue and loss of the papillary architecture of the tumor are two signs of malignancy. Both choroid plexus papilloma and carcinoma may seed the subarachnoid space and ventricles. Seeding is more common and occurs earlier with carcinoma.

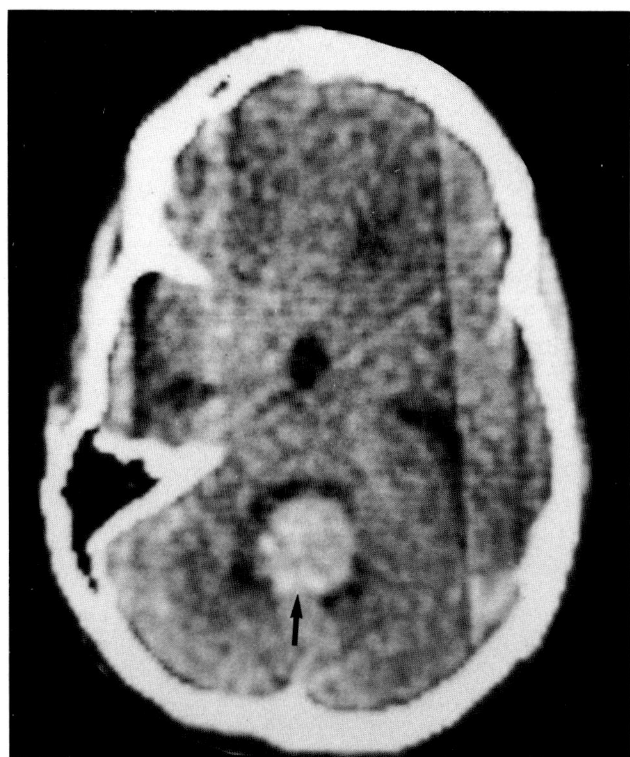

Figure 9-24 Choroid plexus papilloma. Axial NC CT shows a high-density mass filling the fourth ventricle, attached posteriorly (arrow) at the site of the choroid plexus.

Papillomas appear as reddish cauliflowerlike masses that expand the ventricle within which they grow (Russell 1989). The production of CSF by the tumor can produce a generalized hydrocephalus when CSF production exceeds the reabsorptive capacity of the arachnoid villi (Milhorat 1976). Hydrocephalus can also result from obstruction of the outlets of the fourth ventricle by tumor or occur when a subarachnoid hemorrhage produces adhesions and scarring that prevent CSF flow.

The CT appearance of a choroid plexus papilloma is that of a radiographically dense, often calcified frondlike mass arising at the site of the choroid within the fourth ventricle (Fig. 9-24) and sometimes extending through the lateral recess into the cerebellopontine angle (Zimmerman 1979*c*). Some tumors arise purely within the cerebellopontine angle. The fourth ventricle is expanded, and if obstruction or overproduction of CSF occurs the aqueduct, third ventricle, and lateral ventricles are dilated. After contrast injection, the tumor enhances markedly, usually homogeneously (Fig. 9-25*B*). Vertebral angiography shows dilatation of the posterior inferior cerebellar arteries and their choroidal branches. Dense tumor stain begins in the arterial phase and lasts into the venous phase. Choroid plexus carcinomas show a contrast-enhancing mass that extends into the cerebellum, the brainstem, or the walls of the fourth ventricle (Fig. 9-26). On MR, a choroid plexus papilloma appears an isointense to hypointense frondlike mass (Fig. 9-25*A*) on T_1WI. On PDWI and T_2WI, the tumor tends to be relatively hypointense to CSF (Fig. 9-25*C*). This most likely reflects both calcification and rich blood flow within the tumor mass. After MR contrast injection, the tumor enhances intensely. Contrast enhancement is an ideal method of demonstrating cerebellar and brainstem invasion as well as spread of a carcinoma to distal sites.

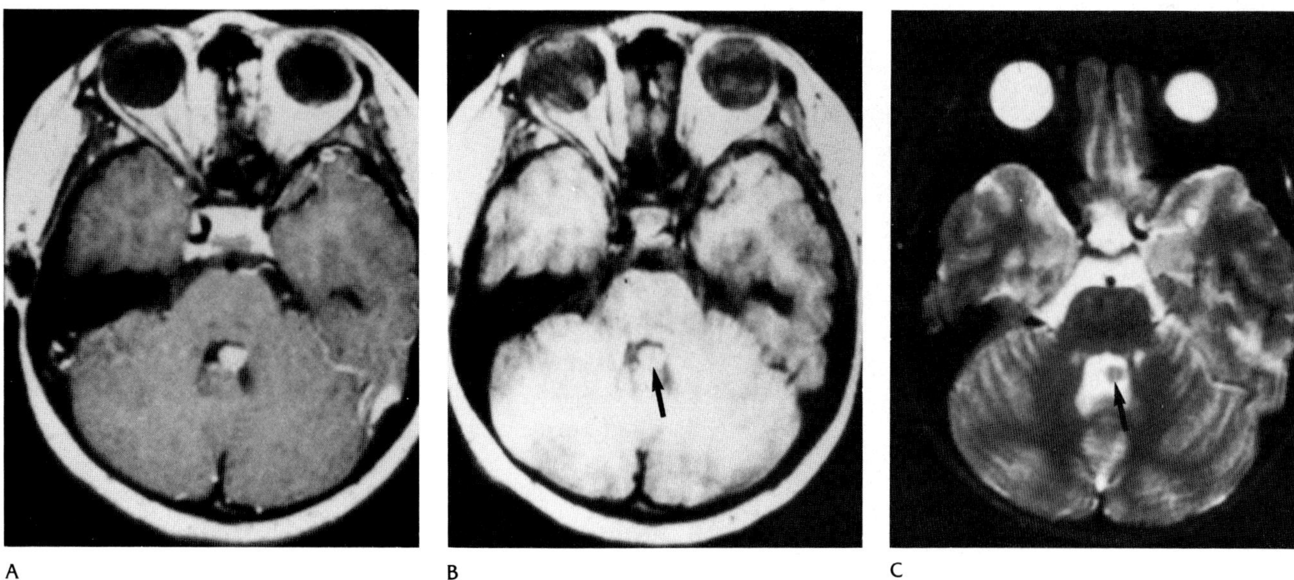

Figure 9-25 Choroid plexus papilloma. **A.** Axial T_1WI shows an isointense mass (arrow) within the fourth ventricle. **B.** Axial T_1WI after MR contrast injection shows enhancement of the intra-fourth-ventricular mass. **C.** Axial T_2WI shows that the mass (arrow) is isointense to brain.

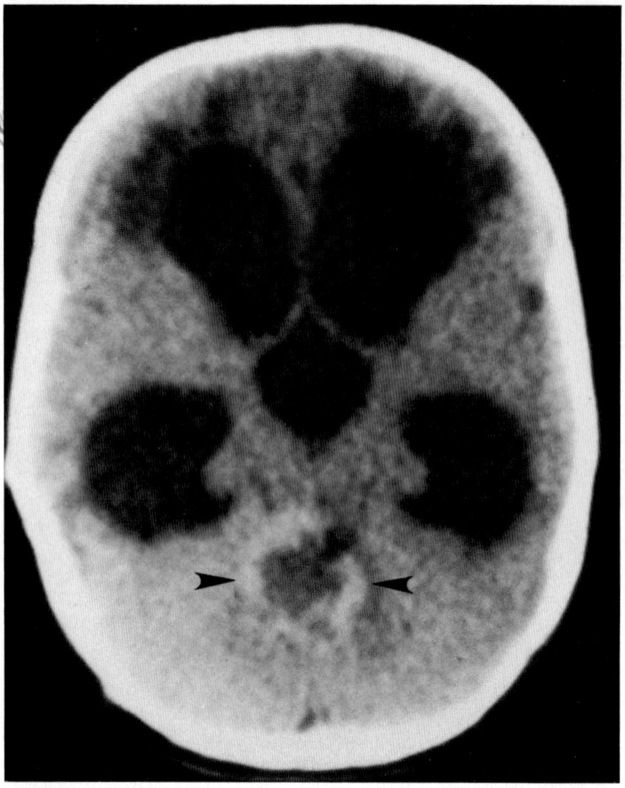

Figure 9-26 Choroid plexus carcinoma. Axial CE CT shows increased density within an ill-defined, irregular mass (arrowheads) in the vicinity of the fourth ventricle. There is marked hydrocephalus with dilatation of the lateral ventricles, the third ventricle, and the temporal horns of the lateral ventricles.

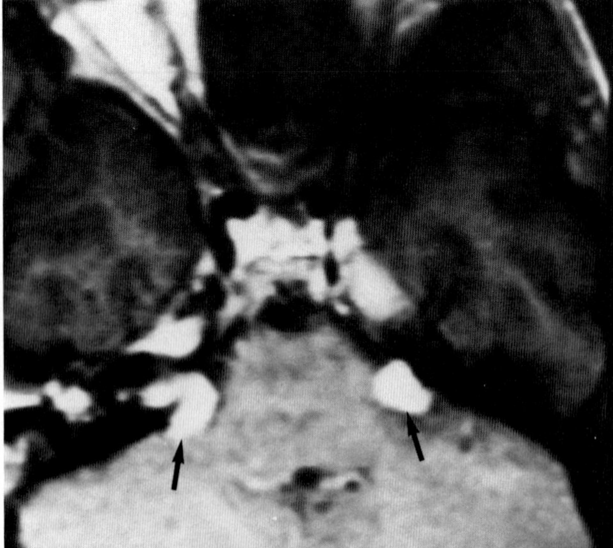

Figure 9-27 Neurofibromatosis type 2 with bilateral acoustic neurinomas. Axial T_1WI after MR contrast injection shows a bilateral enhanced (arrows) acoustic neurinoma.

Treatment consists of gross total resection of the papilloma or carcinoma (Heideman 1989). A papilloma is often totally resectable, while a carcinoma, because of invasion, is not. A postoperative papilloma patient is reexamined by CT or MR to determine whether residual disease is present. Residual disease, if symptomatic, may require reoperation at a future date. Choroid plexus carcinomas are rarely cured by means of surgical resection. Postoperatively, radiation therapy and chemotherapy are utilized. The treatment of choroid plexus carcinomas is complicated by the often young age of the patients, immature myelination, and the dangers that are entailed when radiation is given to an immature brain. Long-term survival of patients with choroid plexus papillomas is excellent, whereas even short-term survival of patients with choroid plexus carcinomas is limited (Heideman 1989).

OTHER POSTERIOR FOSSA TUMORS OF CHILDHOOD

Congenital inclusion masses such as lipomas, dermoids, and teratomas may be found in the posterior fossa (Zimmerman 1979*b*). Dermoids may be associated with a sinus track that leads through the calvarium, in the midline, from an orifice in the skin. As a result, infection of an intracranial dermoid with abscess formation is possible. Lipomas in the vicinity of the tectum of the midbrain are an incidental finding (Zimmerman 1979*b*). Lipomas involving the pars acoustica are less frequent but, with stretching of the seventh and eighth nerves, may become symptomatic. Acoustic neurinomas are found in childhood, almost exclusively in the circumstance of a patient with neurofibromatosis type 2 (Zimmerman 1990*c*). In these circumstances, the acoustic neurinomas will eventually be bilateral. Their synchrony, the rate at which they grow, and therefore the ease with which the first entity and then the second is recognized, is variable. CT with contrast enhancement and bone windows is less effective, whereas MR with contrast is the best diagnostic method for demonstrating findings consistent with a bilateral acoustic neurinoma (Fig. 9-27). In addition, neurinomas of other cranial nerves, meningiomas, and spinal cord ependymomas may be demonstrated in these patients (Zimmerman 1990*c*).

In childhood, tumors that involve the bony wall of the posterior cranial fossa are most often metastatic, either neuroblastomas (Fig. 9-28) (Zimmerman 1980*a*) or Ewing's sarcomas. Rare primary bone tumors, such as angiosarcomas and osteogenic sarcomas, may present as posterior fossa cranial masses. Tumors of the bony vault are best evaluated on CT with or without contrast, utilizing soft tissue and bone windows. MR is complementary and adds the ability to evaluate blood flow in the dural

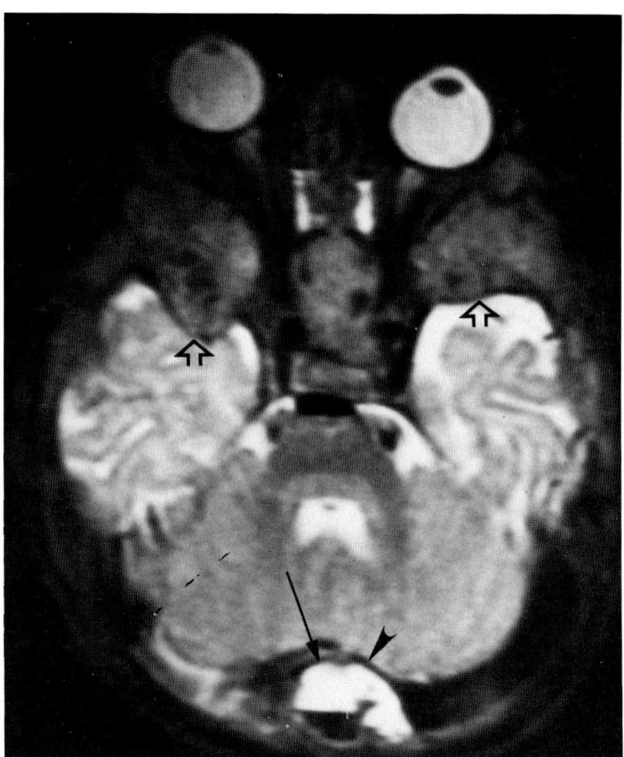

Figure 9-28 Metastatic neuroblastoma to the calvarium. Axial T_2WI shows a mixed-signal-intensity mass (arrow) in the vicinity of the torcular Herophili (arrowhead), consistent with hemorrhagic neuroblastoma. The torcula and left transverse sinus are compressed by the mass. The walls of both orbits (open arrows) are markedly expanded by the tumor.

venous sinuses. Compromise of the dural venous sinuses by calvarial vault tumor masses can produce venous hypertension, increased intracranial pressure, and papilledema (Zimmerman 1980*a*). Eosinophilic granuloma is an inflammatory osseous vault mass lesion that can produce a tumorlike mass effect. This is usually recognized because of beveled edges at the site of involvement of the cranial vault and intense homogeneous enhancement. Rhabdomyosarcomas of the ear produce destruction of the temporal bone and invasion of the posterior cranial fossa (Zimmerman 1978*c*).

Supratentorial Tumors

The classic concept that most pediatric brain tumors are infratentorial in location was changed first by CT and then by MR. MR, with its ability to detect small low-grade astrocytomas and gangliogliomas because of their increased water content, has made it possible to detect tumors earlier and altered the ratio of supratentorial to infratentorial tumors. Today, at least 50 percent of pediatric brain tumors are found in the supratentorial space (Zimmerman 1990*b*).

Once a mass has been identified, the differential diagnosis depends primarily on its anatomic localization. In the pediatric supratentorial space, tumors have been categorized as those that are intrasellar and/or suprasellar, those that arise within the parenchyma of the cerebral hemisphere or basal ganglia, those that are intraventricular, those that arise in the region of the pineal gland, and those that arise superficially from the meninges, pia, or cortex.

Intrasellar and Suprasellar Tumors

Neoplasms in and around the sella are more common in adults than in children because of the increasing frequency of pituitary adenomas, metastases, and meningiomas with age. Neoplasms and other masses with a predilection for the pediatric population include craniopharyngioma and visual pathway glioma–hypothalamic astrocytoma. Less frequently neurinoma, arachnoid cyst, germinoma, epidermoid, Rathke's cleft cyst, hamartoma, teratoma, histiocytosis, and basilar meningitis produce an intrasellar, suprasellar, or parasellar mass (Zimmerman 1990*a,b*).

CRANIOPHARYNGIOMA

Two-thirds of all craniopharyngiomas present before the age of 20. Overall, craniopharyngiomas constitute 6 to 9 percent of all primary CNS tumors (Farwell 1977; Cohen 1983). Craniopharyngiomas arise from epithelial cell rests along the involuted pathway of the hypophysis—Rathke's duct (Russell 1989). These tumors, while smooth, may be solid, cystic, or mixed. The content of the cysts varies from a cholesterol-rich fluid to a gelatinous mass (Russell 1989). Calcification is common within the solid portion. Most craniopharyngiomas are suprasellar, attached to the hypothalamus; a smaller proportion project into the sella turcica from the hypothalamus; and a very small proportion are purely intrasellar in location.

The visual field abnormalities are due to compression of the optic chiasm and tract, and the endocrinological disturbances (hypogonadism) are due to involvement of the hypothalamus and infundibular stalk (Thomsett 1980). The growth of the mass is slow, and the symptoms are insidious in their onset.

Plain skull radiographs may show suprasellar calcification, expansion of the sella, and/or erosion of the dorsum sellae. Such findings in a child are highly suggestive of a craniopharyngioma. On CT, the mass is usually less dense than the adjacent brain but of greater density than CSF (Fig. 9-29) (Rao 1977). Calcification occurs frequently in the wall or solid portion (Fig. 9-30). After contrast injection, there is enhancement of the cyst wall and solid portion (Fig. 9-29) (Rao 1977). The cystic component does not enhance. A tumor may be lobulated and may even extend through adjacent CSF spaces such as

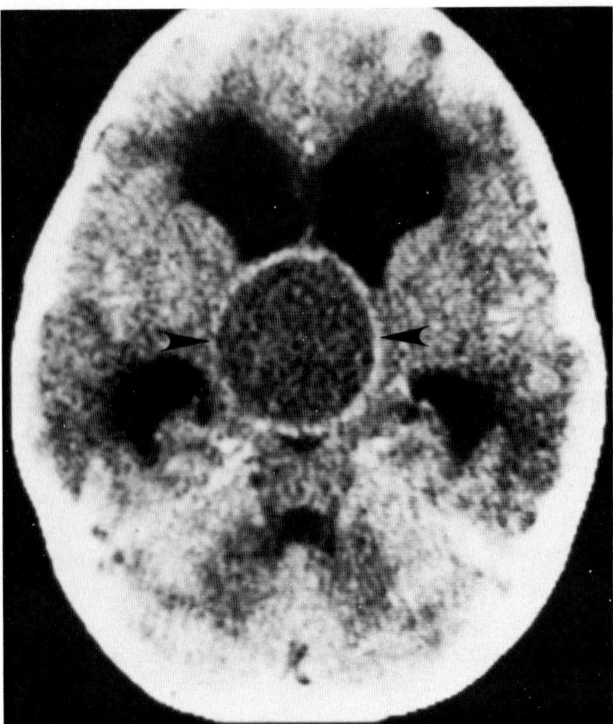

Figure 9-29 Craniopharyngioma. Axial CE CT shows a cystic mass with a contrast-enhanced thin wall (arrowheads) and a hypodense cavity that is denser than CSF. There is hydrocephalus with dilatation of the frontal and temporal horns in the lateral ventricle.

under the frontal lobe, up against the temporal lobe, down along the clivus, or even into the cerebellopontine angle cistern. Coronal CT sections often complement the axial study. Infrequently, the craniopharyngioma may be hyperdense on NC CT and may be solid. On MR with T_1WI, the cystic contents are of variable signal intensity, most often hypointense but occasionally hyperintense (Fig. 9-31) (Young 1987). On PDWI and T_2WI, the cystic contents may be slightly to markedly hyperintense (Fig. 9-32) (Pusey 1987). On T_1WI after contrast injection, the solid portion and the wall enhance (Fig. 9-33) (Zimmerman 1990*a*). Sagittal and coronal MR studies with thin sections give an anatomic depiction of the relationship between the craniopharyngioma and the optic chiasm, optic tracks, and pituitary gland. Differentiation from other suprasellar masses is usually not difficult, except in rare hypothalamic astrocytomas that contain significant calcification or are located inferiorly with exophytic cyst formation. Differentiation is also difficult when one is attempting to distinguish a purely intrasellar craniopharyngioma from an intrasellar Rathke's cleft cyst.

RATHKE'S CLEFT CYST

Epithelial rests from remnants of Rathke's cleft may persist and form cysts between the anterior and intermediate pituitary lobes. Goblet cells line Rathke's cleft and secrete a mucinous or serous fluid (Fairburn 1964). Often these

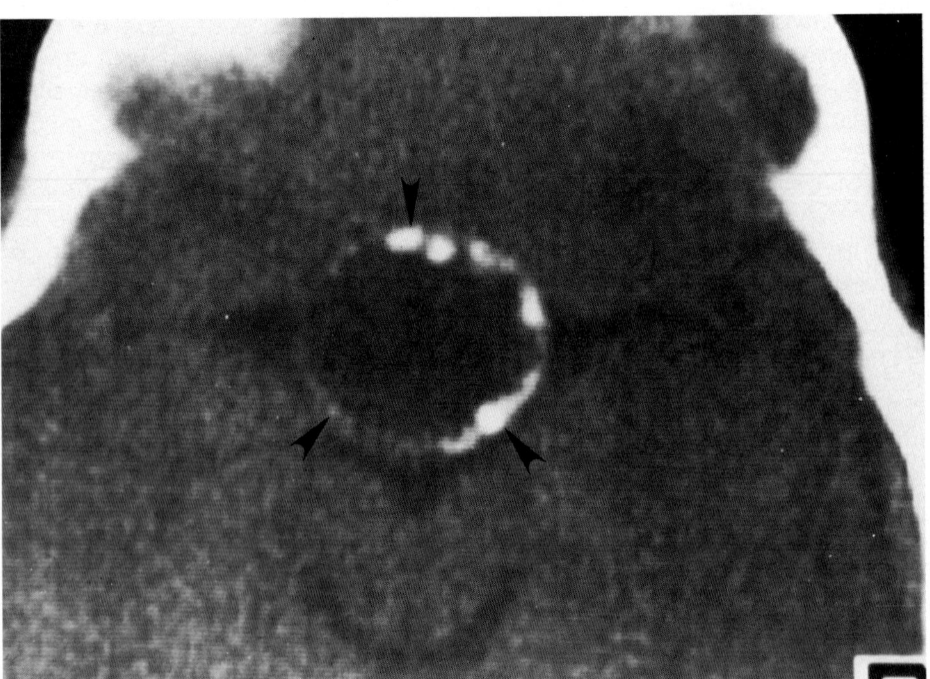

Figure 9-30 Craniopharyngioma. Axial NC CT shows the partially calcified wall (arrowheads) of a cystic suprasellar mass, consistent with craniopharyngioma.

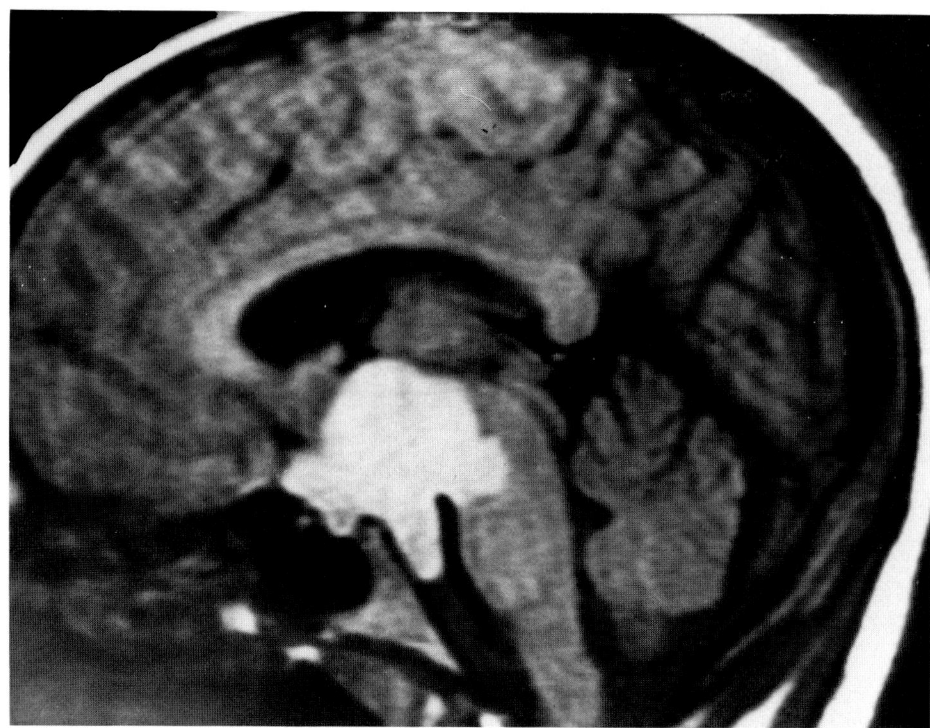

Figure 9-31 Craniopharyngioma. Sagittal T_1WI shows an intrasellar, suprasellar, and retrosellar high-signal-intensity mass compressing the midbrain and hypothalamus.

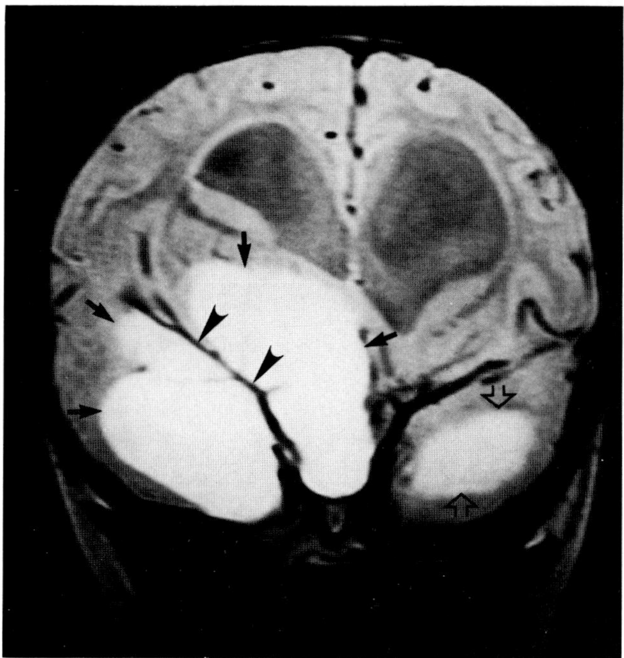

Figure 9-32 Craniopharyngioma. Coronal PDWI shows a mass of high signal intensity (arrows) encasing the distal internal carotid and middle cerebral arteries (arrowheads) on the right, involving the sella and the suprasellar and parasellar regions and producing hydrocephalus with marked dilatation of both frontal horns of the lateral ventricles. Tumor (open arrows) is present in the left temporal horn of the lateral ventricle.

cysts are found incidentally, but occasionally they are associated with pituitary dysfunction.

The CT appearance of a Rathke's cleft cyst is that of a low-density mass, usually intrasellar, in or near the pars intermedia. It is not calcified and does not enhance. Surrounding normal pituitary tissue does enhance. The MR findings in a Rathke's cleft cyst usually consist of increased signal intensity on T_1WI and T_2WI (Fig. 9-34) (Zimmerman 1990*a*). This is thought to be related to the high protein and/or starch contents of the mucoid material. They may be hypointense on T_1WI. The main differential diagnosis is between Rathke's cleft cyst and craniopharyngioma.

VISUAL PATHWAY AND HYPOTHALAMIC ASTROCYTOMA

Visual pathway gliomas (VPGs) include gliomas found within the optic nerves, chiasm, and optic tracts. Together these tumors constitute 5 percent of all primary CNS tumors of childhood (Oxenhandler 1978). They tend to present in the first decade of life. It has been reported that 6 to 58 percent of patients with VPGs have neurofibromatosis type 1 (NF 1) (Hope 1981). The exact incidence and interrelationship between VPG and neurofibromatosis are uncertain, as a VPG may present years before the clinical stigmata of NF 1 are present (Packer 1988).

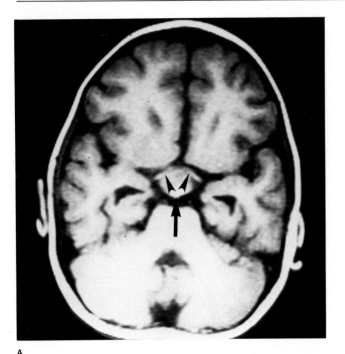

A

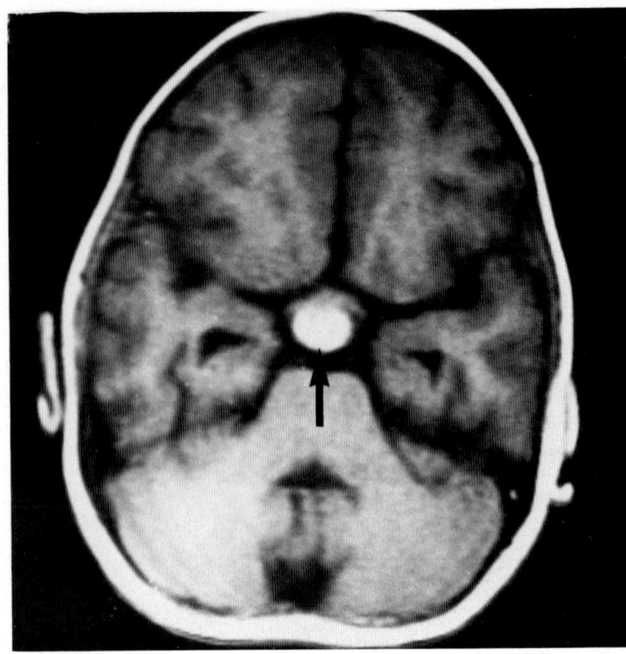

B

Figure 9-33 Craniopharnygioma. **A.** Axial T_1WI shows the optic chiasm pushed forward (arrowheads) by an isointense retrochiasmal mass (arrow). **B.** Axial T_1WI after contrast injection shows enhancement of the mass (arrow).

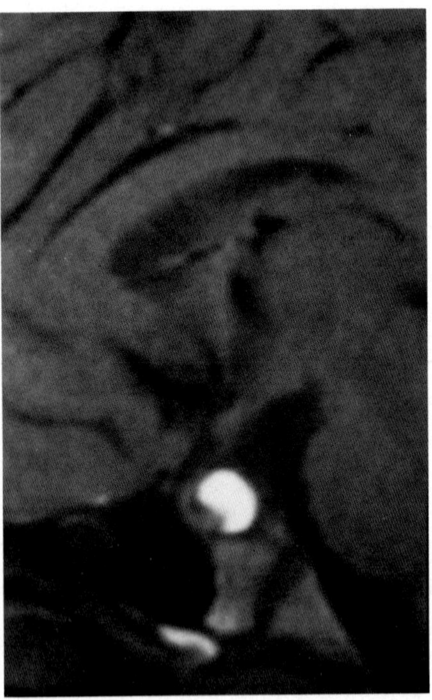

A

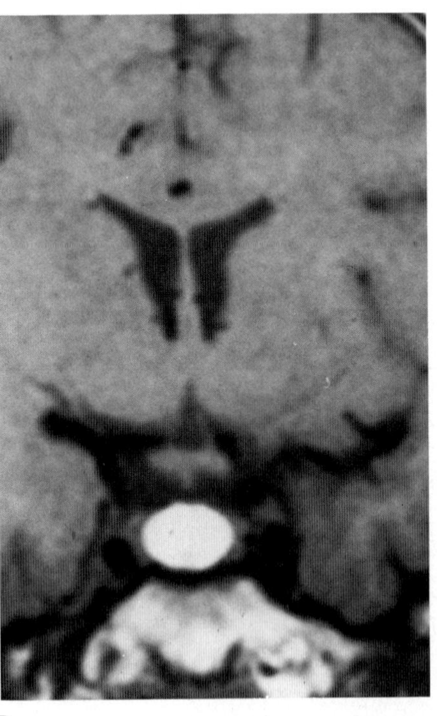

B

Figure 9-34 Cyst of Rathke's pouch. **A.** Sagittal T_1WI shows a hyperintense intrasellar mass. **B.** Coronal T_1WI of the same hyperintense mass.

Histologically, these tumors are either piloid astrocytomas or fibrillary astrocytomas (Braffman 1990). In our experience, more are pilocytic, and these tend to be the ones that involve more of the extent of the visual pathway. Thus far, despite the use of CT and MR, we have not demonstrated that the tumors grow by further extension along the visual pathway; rather, they expand areas that are involved as the tumors slowly grow. Tumor growth is slow, with survival often exceeding a decade (Packer 1983*b*).

The signs and symptoms of VPGs relate to the location of the tumor and the age at presentation (Heideman 1989). Developmental difficulties, strabismus and/or nystagmus, and signs of hydrocephalus are the modes of presentation in infants and young children. In older children, proptosis and reduced visual acuity as well as growth disturbances, along with signs of hydrocephalus, are the forms of presentation (Packer 1983*b*).

When only the optic nerve is involved, a differential diagnosis is necessary. In older children, adolescents, and young adults, the differential diagnosis includes perioptic meningioma. Differentiation with MR may be difficult because both optic nerve gliomas and perioptic meningiomas can produce peripheral signal-intensity changes and contrast enhancement around the optic nerve. Calcification is more common in meningiomas, which tend to extend out onto the dural surface surrounding the intracranial portion of the optic nerve canal. When both optic nerves, the optic nerve and chiasm, or the chiasm and optic tracts are involved, the tumor differential is limited to the VPG. The nontumor portion of the differential diagnosis at that point also includes inflammatory conditions that expand the visual pathway, such as demyelinating disease, and diseases that encase the surface of the visual pathway, such as sarcoid, meningitis, arachnoiditis,

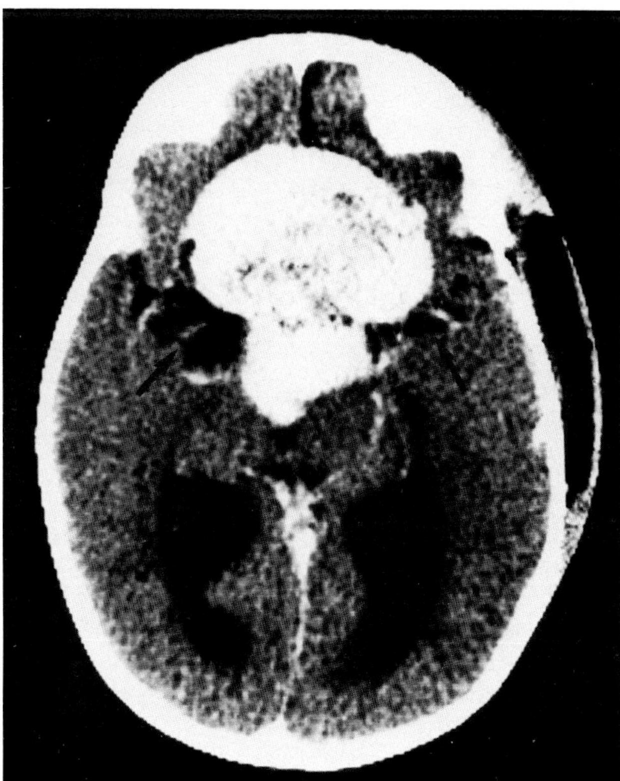

Figure 9-35 Visual pathway glioma with hypothalamic involvement. Axial CE CT shows a large suprasellar mass contrast-enhancing with posterolateral arachnoid cysts (arrows). Previous surgical changes are present in the left temporal region.

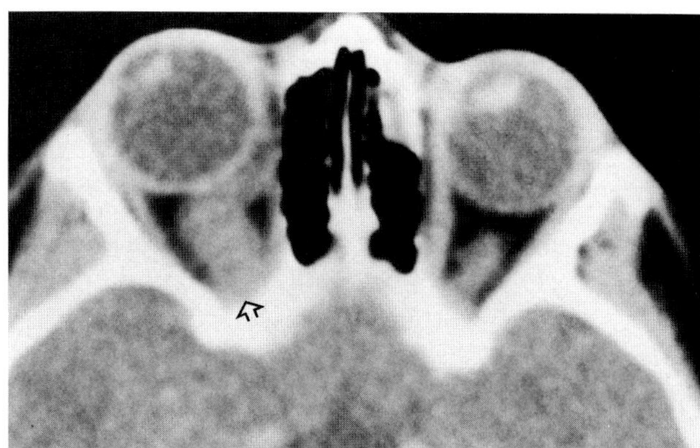

Figure 9-36 Unilateral optic glioma. Axial CE CT shows marked enhancement of the enlarged right optic nerve (open arrow).

and an occasional rare vascular malformation (Armington 1990). In a patient with NF 1, other stigmata of this condition must be looked for, including high-signal-intensity lesions in the globus pallidus, thalamus, brainstem, and cerebellum (Braffman 1990). Brainstem gliomas, cerebellar astrocytomas, and other glial neoplasms also may be present. Neurinomas of the cranial nerves, spinal neurofibromas, and bony dysplasia involving the walls of the orbit, the internal auditory canals, or the spinal canal may be present.

On CT, a VPG appears as an expansile mass involving the optic nerve, chiasm, and tract and/or a mass that infiltrates and expands the hypothalamus (Fig. 9-35) (Zimmerman 1990*a*). They are isodense to hypodense before contrast and usually show enhancement (Fig. 9-35) (Fletcher 1986). The optic nerve may be fusiformly dilated with peripheral enhancement (Fig. 9-36). On MR, these tumors are hypointense on T_1-WI (Fig. 9-37*A*) and hyperintense on PDW and T_2-WI (Fig. 9-38) (Zimmerman 1987*a*). Enhancement characteristics are quite variable on CE MR: Some tumors do not enhance, some show peripheral enhancement, and others enhance throughout (Fig. 9-37*B*) (Zimmerman 1990*a*).

The role of CT and MR is in making the diagnosis of a VPG. In a patient with NF 1 and a VPG, follow-up may be done every 6 months to ascertain whether the tumor is growing. At the time of growth, with obstruction of the foramen of Monro and the production of hydrocephalus, shunting and further treatment may be required. Biopsy is often carried out during the early course to establish the histology. If the mass is progressive and the patient is a young child, chemotherapy may be utilized (Rosenstock 1985). In older children with tumor progression, radiation therapy has been the treatment of choice (Danoff 1980). Among children with only optic nerve involvement and no evidence of neurofibromatosis, some of these tumors are resected for cosmetic reasons (Tenny 1982).

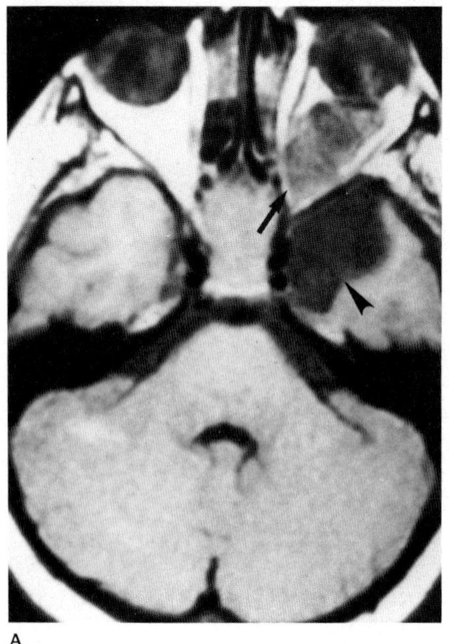

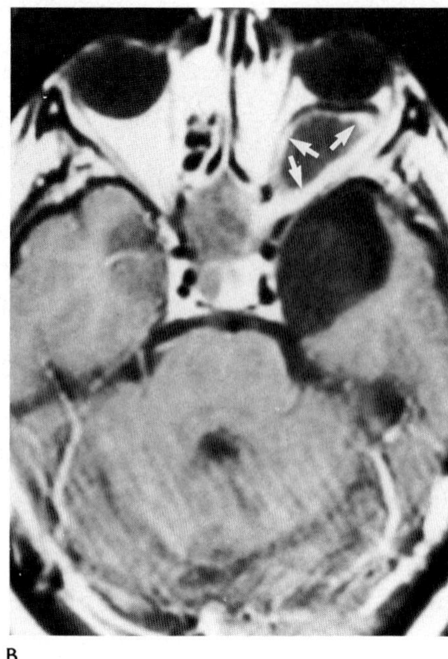

A B

Figure 9-37 Optic glioma. **A.** Axial T_1WI without contrast shows expansion of the left optic nerve (arrow) and an arachnoid cyst in the left middle cranial fossa (arrowhead). **B.** Axial T_1WI after contrast injection shows enhancement of the periphery (arrows) of the expanded left optic nerve.

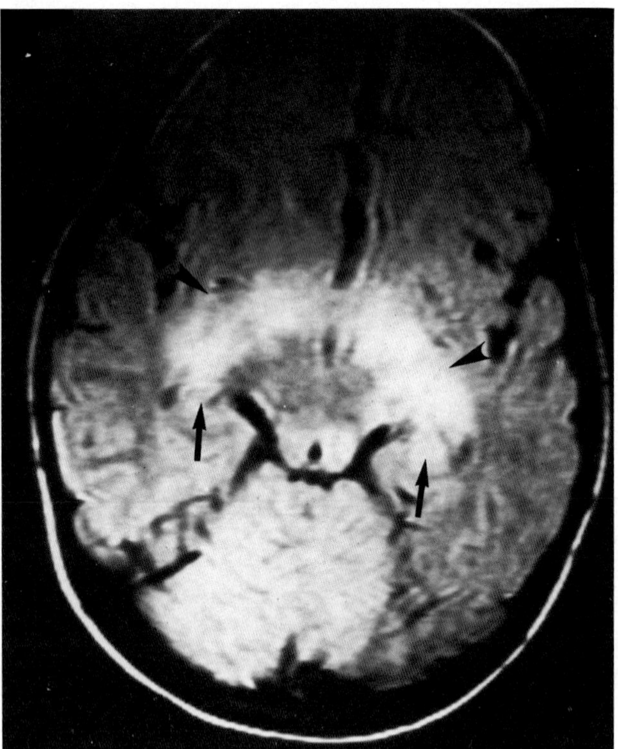

Figure 9-38 Visual pathway glioma. Axial PDWI shows an increased-signal-intensity mass involving the optic chiasm and hypothalamus and extending posteriorly in both optic tracks (arrowheads) to the lateral geniculate nuclei (arrows).

GERMINOMAS

The most frequent type of germ cell tumor originating in the suprasellar area is the germinoma (Jenkin 1978). In the suprasellar area, the male predominance seen in the pineal gland is reversed, so that more often the patient is female. The tumor typically presents as a disturbance of growth or hypothalamic-sexual development. On CT, the mass is isointense to slightly hyperdense before contrast and enhances (Fig. 9-39) (Zimmerman 1980*b*). On MR the mass is usually isointense to slightly hypointense on T_1WI (Fig. 9-40*A*) and enhances markedly after gadolinium injection (Fig. 9-40*B*). On PDWI the mass may be isointense or slightly hyperintense, while on T_2WI it is often hypointense or isointense (Fig. 9-40*C*)

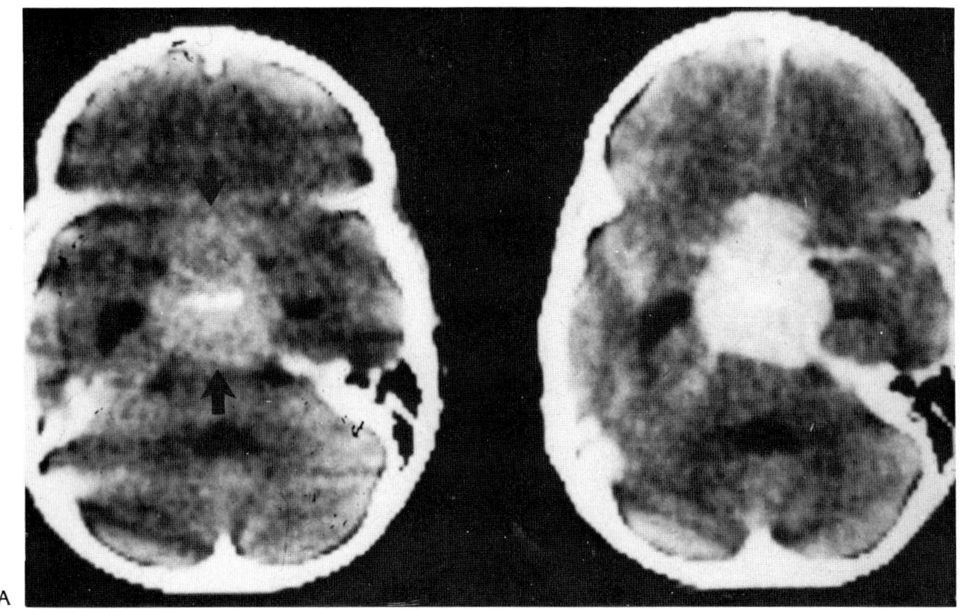

Figure 9-39 Suprasellar germinoma. **A.** Axial NC CT shows a suprasellar mass of increased density (arrows). **B.** Axial CE CT shows uniform enhancement of the suprasellar mass.

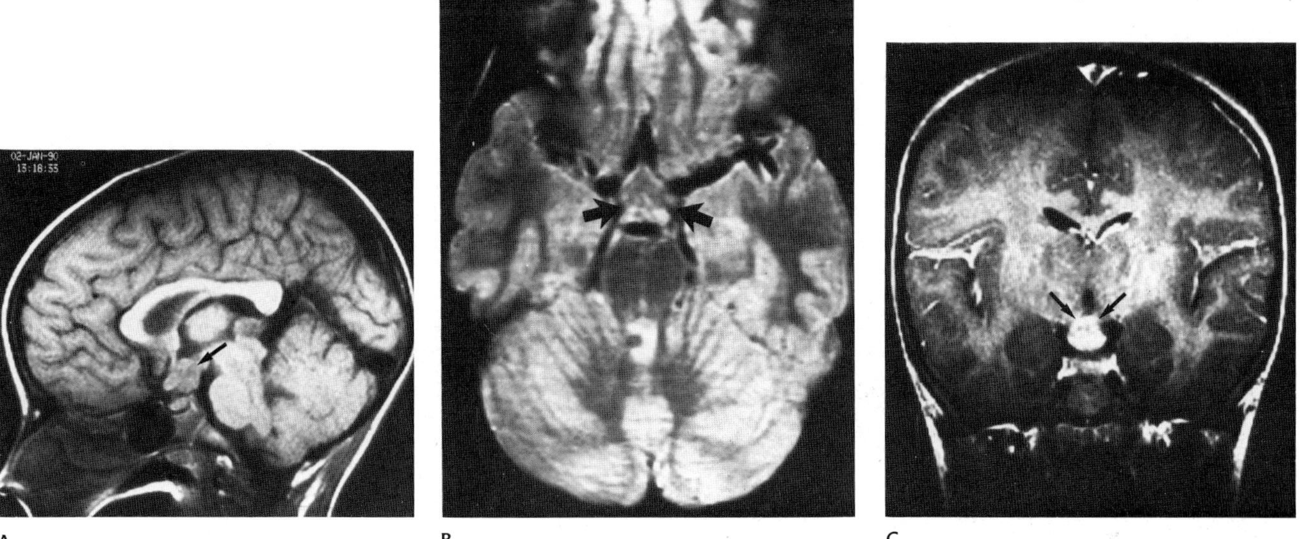

Figure 9-40 Suprasellar germinoma, MRI. **A.** Sagittal T_1WI shows an isointense suprasellar mass (arrow) involving the hypothalamus and chiasm. **B.** Axial PDWI (long TR, short TE) shows the mass (arrows) to be isointense. **C.** Coronal T_1WI after contrast injection shows the mass (arrows) to be enhanced.

(Zimmerman 1990*a*). The change in signal intensity is thought to be related to the highly cellular nature of the tumor. Treatment consists of biopsy for tissue and then radiation therapy with or without adjuvant chemotherapy (Rustin 1986). The tumor is highly radiosensitive, and in Japan, where there is a high incidence of germinomas, patients have been treated without biopsy and have received radiation doses up to 3000 rad in order to see whether the tumor responds (Onoyama 1979). If it disappears, it is thought to have been a germinoma.

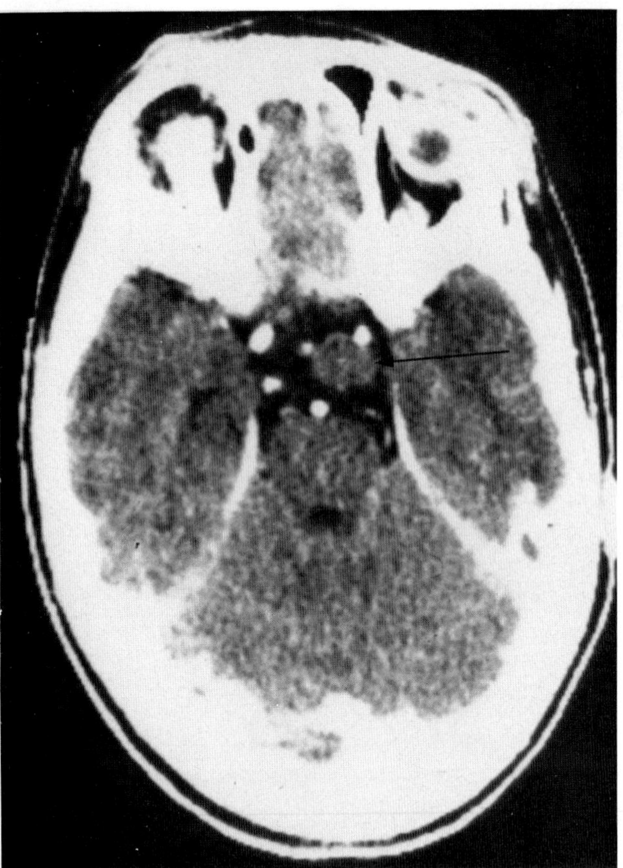

Figure 9-41 Hypothalamic hamartoma. Axial CE CT shows no enhancement of an isodense suprasellar mass (arrow).

Hamartomas of the Tuber Cinereum

These are well-defined masses composed of mature ganglionic tissue attached to the tuber cinereum or the mammillary bodies (Russell 1989). They occur in both men and women and are associated with precocious puberty (Wolman 1963). Seizures, described as gelastic in nature, consisting of episodes of laughing, may also be seen. Because the tissue is made up of mature cerebral gray matter, the CT appearance is that of a mass isodense to cortex that does not enhance (Fig. 9-41) (Diebler 1983). On MR, the mass is isointense to gray matter on T_1WI and typically isointense on PDW and T_2WI (Fig. 9-42*A*). Occasionally it is slightly hyperintense on PDW and T_2WI (Fig. 9-42*B*). After MR contrast injection, there is no enhancement (Boyko 1991). When the diagnosis is in doubt, a biopsy can be performed.

Other Suprasellar Tumors of Childhood

A broad array of conditions, both neoplastic and nonneoplastic, produce masses in the suprasellar region during childhood. These include benign conditions such as arachnoid cysts, inflammatory conditions such as sarcoid and eosinophilic granuloma, and neoplastic conditions such as subarachnoid dissemination of a malignant tumor arising from the brain or orbit (retinoblastoma) (Zimmerman 1990*a*).

A

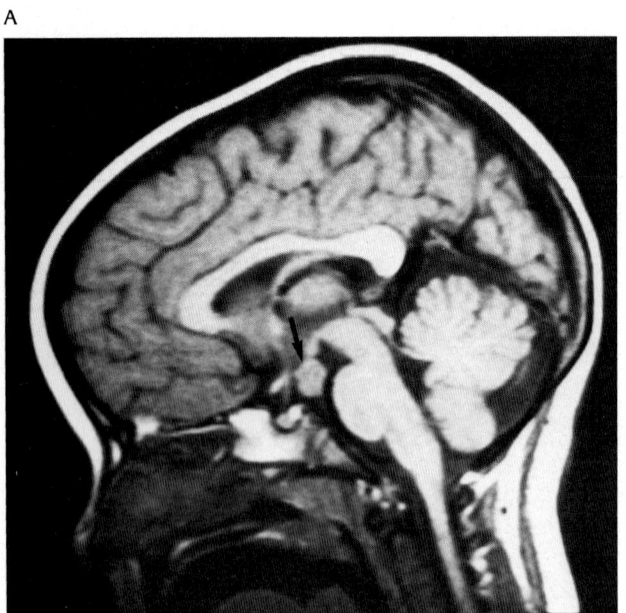

B

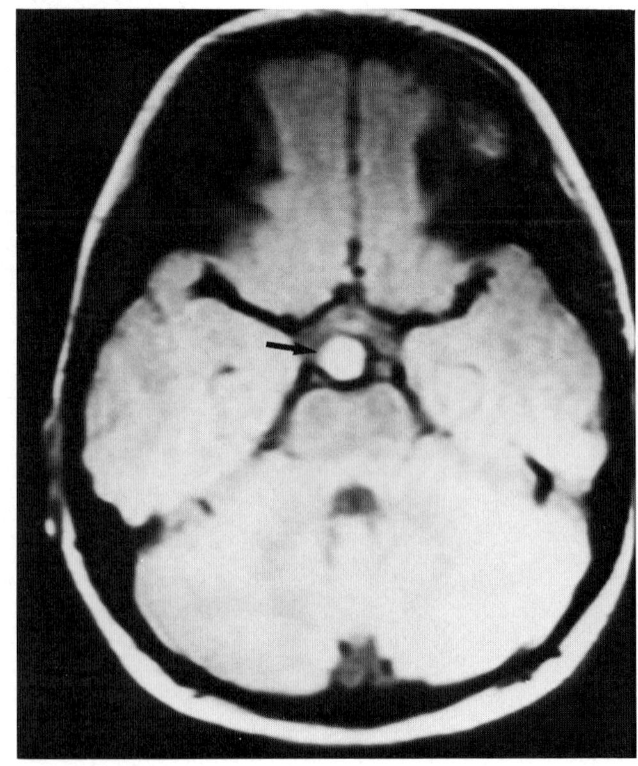

Figure 9-42 Hypothalamic hamartoma. **A.** Sagittal T_1WI shows an isointense mass (arrow) at the site of the mammillary body. **B.** Axial PDWI shows a slightly intense hypothalamic mass (arrow) projecting into the chiasmatic cistern.

PARENCHYMAL TUMORS OF THE CEREBRAL HEMISPHERES AND BASAL GANGLIA

Supratentorial astrocytic tumors represent one-third of pediatric brain tumors when VPGs are included (Heideman 1989). More than half occur in the cerebral hemispheres or basal ganglia outside the VPG. Males are affected more frequently; the age peak occurs between 2 and 4 years with a VPG and occurs in adolescence usually with more hemispheric tumors (Heideman 1989). These tumors are classified as fibrillary, pilocytic, or anaplastic, or as glioblastoma multiforme (Russell 1989). Subcategories are recognized, such as the oligodendroglioma and gliomatosis cerebri, and there are less common types. In general, pilocytic astrocytomas are more frequently diencephalic and have histological features analogous to those of cerebellar astrocytomas. Fibrillary astrocytomas are densely cellular, tend not to be cystic, and infiltrate (Russell 1989). Within the cerebral hemispheres, fibrillary astrocytomas are more common; this tumor has been implicated in malignant degeneration. So-called malignant or high-grade astrocytomas are labeled as anaplastic and as glioblastoma multiforme. They are highly cellular, undifferentiated tumors with frequent mitosis, areas of necrosis, and hemorrhage. They are widely invasive, grow rapidly, and spread into the subarachnoid pathways over time (Russell 1989).

The clinical presentation of a patient with a cerebral hemispheric astrocytoma is that of increased intracranial pressure (50 to 75 percent) or seizures (25 to 50 percent) (Heideman 1989). The incidence of seizures as a form of presentation is higher with low-grade tumors than it is with high-grade tumors. The location of a tumor is an important factor in determining the type of symptoms with which it presents.

On CT, low-grade astrocytomas are variable in appearance (Naidich 1984). A fibrillary astrocytoma is found within the white matter of the cerebral hemisphere as a low-density infiltrating lesion on CT (Fig. 9-43*A*) (Zimmerman 1990*b*). These tumors usually do not enhance after contrast administration. Pilocytic astrocytomas are more often cystic or present as a mural tumor nodule on the margin of a cyst, are of decreased density without contrast, and enhance after contrast injection (Fig. 9-44) (Zimmerman 1990*b*). The solid portion of the tumor tends to be slightly higher in density than is the fluid-filled cystic portion. Calcification can be present but is not as frequent or as marked as it is in oligodendroglioma or ependymoma. On MR, the appearance of both pilocytic and fibrillary astrocytomas is that of a hypointense mass on T_1WI and a hyperintense mass on PDW and T_2WI (Figs. 9-43*B*, 9-45*A*). After MR contrast injection

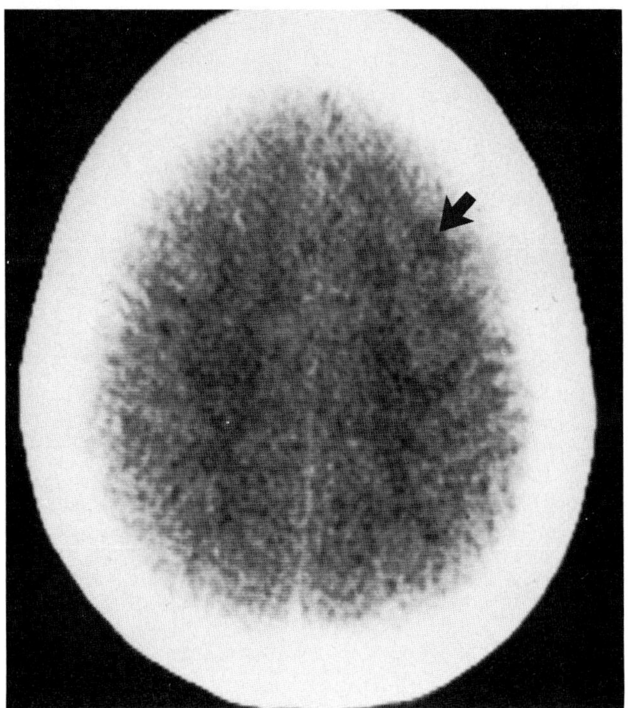

A

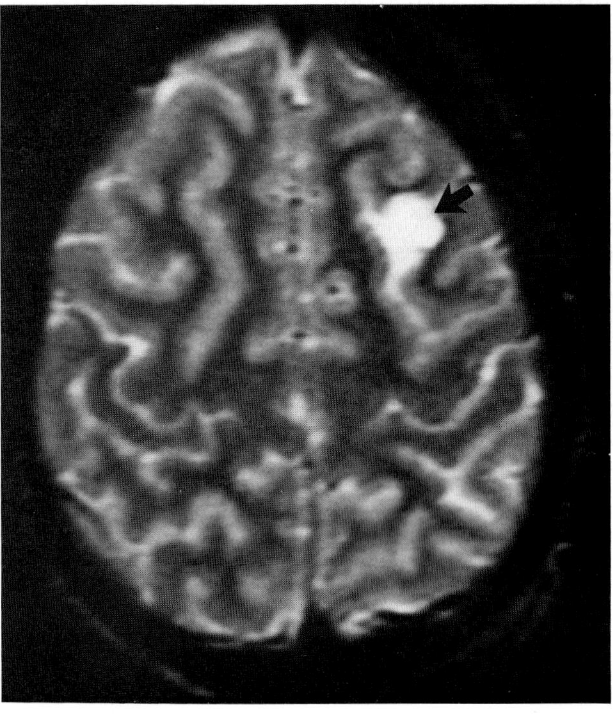

B

Figure 9-43 Low-grade fibrillary astrocytoma. **A.** Axial NC CT shows a faint hypodensity (arrow) in the left frontal lobe. **B.** Axial T_2WI shows a hyperintensity lesion in the left frontal lobe (arrow).

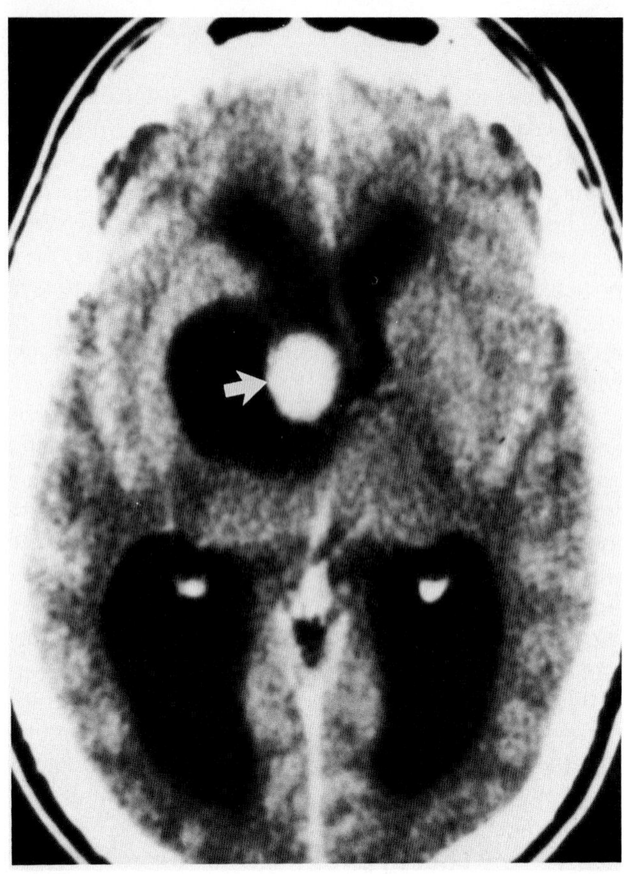

Figure 9-44 Cystic pilocytic astrocytoma in the basal ganglia. Axial CE CT shows a mural enhancing tumor nodule (arrow). The mural tumor nodule lies in the wall of a nonenhancing cyst. The mass produces hydrocephalus with dilatation of both lateral ventricles by compression of the foramen of Monro.

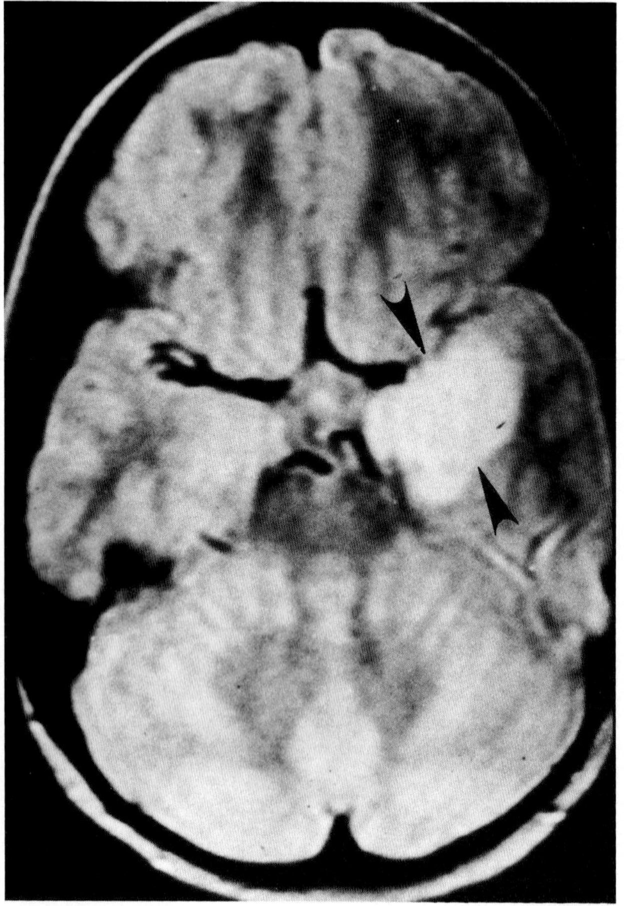

A

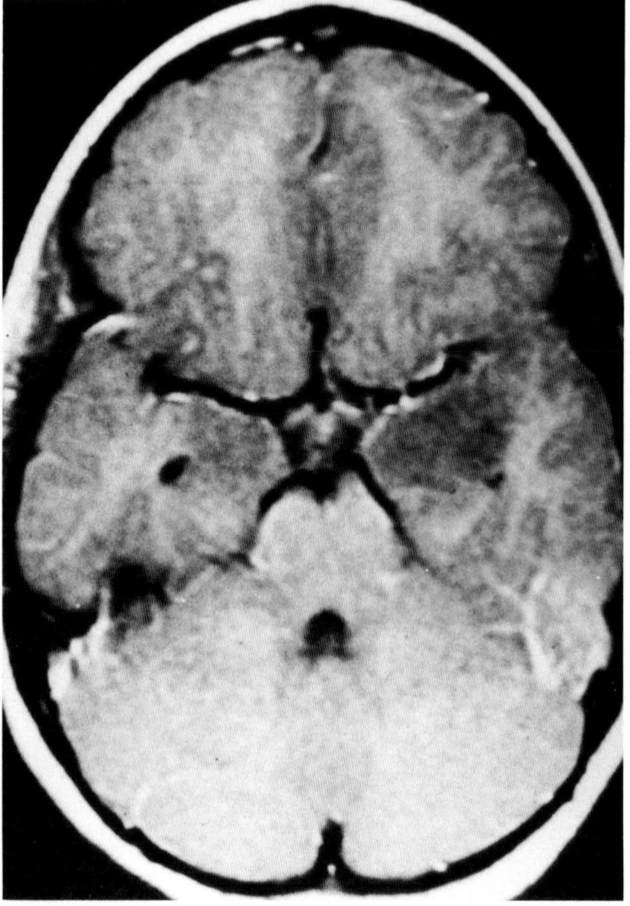

B

Figure 9-45 Fibrillary astrocytoma in the left temporal lobe. **A.** Axial PDWI shows a high-signal-intensity mass (arrowheads) in the medial aspect of the left temporal lobe. **B.** Axial T_1WI after MR contrast shows no evidence of enhancement.

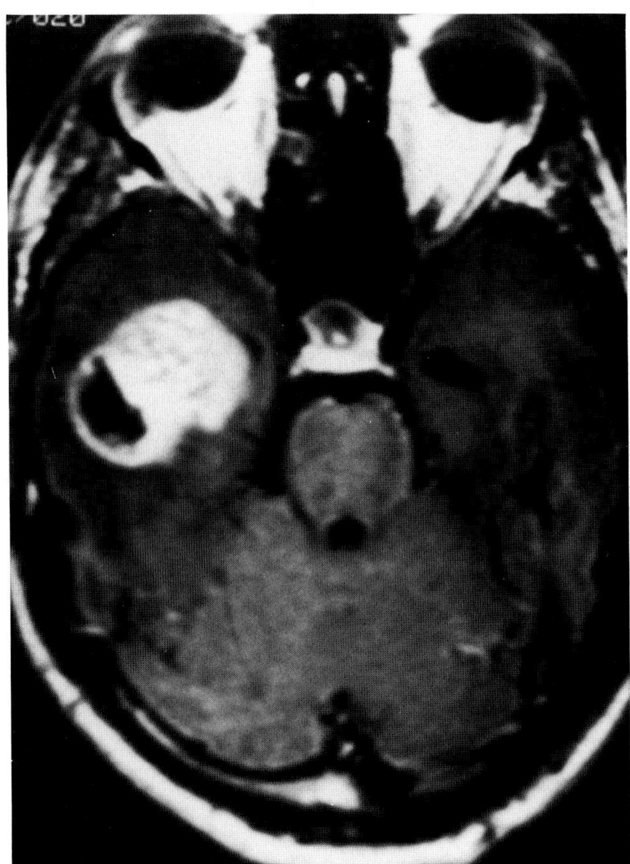

Figure 9-46 Low-grade pilocytic astrocytoma in the right temporal lobe. Axial T_1WI after MR contrast injection shows a partially cystic contrast-enhancing mass in the right temporal lobe.

there is more frequent enhancement with a pilocytic astrocytoma (Fig. 9-46) than with a fibrillary astrocytoma (Fig. 9-45*B*), but both may enhance (Zimmerman 1989*b*). Tumor dissemination is not usually present at diagnosis but may be found in a small percentage of cases years after treatment. This is more often a complication of fibrillary astrocytomas (Zimmerman 1990*b*).

With the more aggressive astrocytoma and glioblastoma multiforme there are generally rapidly proliferating, poorly formed tumor blood vessels that result in a disturbance of the blood-brain barrier (BBB) that leads to the formation of surrounding vasogenic edema and permits contrast enhancement of the core of the viable tumor (Zimmerman 1990*b*). These tumors tend to be more widely invasive, producing significant mass effect, and are frequently necrotic. On CT, The tumor masses are low in density, enhance after contrast injection, have irregular margins, and are surrounded by vasogenic edema (Zimmerman 1989). On T_1WI, the lesions are usually hypointense unless a subacute hemorrhage is present in the form of methemoglobin (high in signal intensity). On PDW and T_2WI, these tumors are hyperintense (Fig. 9-47*A*). After MR contrast injection, the solid portions of the tumor contrast-enhance (Fig. 9-47*B*). Vasogenic edema surrounding the tumor may have the same signal intensity that the tumor has on PDW and T_2WI. Hypointense flow voids within tumor blood vessels may be due to increased tumor vascularity.

In benign pilocytic and fibrillary astrocytomas, survival is measured in years to decades, whereas in anaplastic astrocytoma and glioblastoma multiforme it is measured in months to years (Heideman 1989). Treatment begins with surgical excision of as much of the tumor as is possible, with the realization that in an invasive anaplastic astrocytoma and glioblastoma multiforme, gross total resection is usually impossible (Heideman 1989). Small, noninvasive low-grade tumors can be totally resected provided that they lie in a favorable site such as the anterior temporal lobe. At present, the major form of therapy is radiation therapy, but this has not been effective in providing long-term survival in patients with the more aggressive tumors (Sheline 1977). Chemotherapy has been used in children under 3 years of age and as an adjuvant in older children (Pendergrass 1987).

Ganglioglioma

This is a common (4.5 percent) pediatric low-grade tumor of the supratentorial white matter and the adjacent gray matter (Zimmerman 1979*a*). The tumors are composed of a mixture of ganglion cells and glial elements (Russell 1989). Eighty percent of gangliogliomas are found in children and young adults. The most frequent site is the temporal lobe, but no area of the CNS is spared. These tumors are of considerable variability in appearance (Zimmerman 1979*a*). They are usually not hemorrhagic and have a variable contrast-enhancement pattern. Calcification and/or cystic changes may be found. The tumors are usually not necrotic. On CT, they are usually hypodense and may or may not contrast-enhance (Zimmerman 1979*a*). On MR, they are hypointense on T_1WI and hyperintense on PDW and T_2WI (Fig. 9-48) (Thomsett 1980). Contrast enhancement after MR contrast injection is variable (Fig. 9-48*B*) (Zimmerman 1991). They should be suspected in a patient who presents with the symptoms of a seizure in whom a cortical or subcortical tumor is found. The differential diagnosis is that of other astrocytic tumors.

Gliomatosis Cerebri

This is a rare form of a diffusely infiltrating low-grade tumor that often involves major portions of the cerebral hemispheres and most commonly presents in the first or second decade of life. Typically, there is involvement of the internal capsules and adjacent white matter pathways with inferior extension into the brainstem. The tumor also is found in the corpus callosum and to some extent in the white matter of the frontoparietal lobes. Usually both hemispheres are involved. These tumors tend not

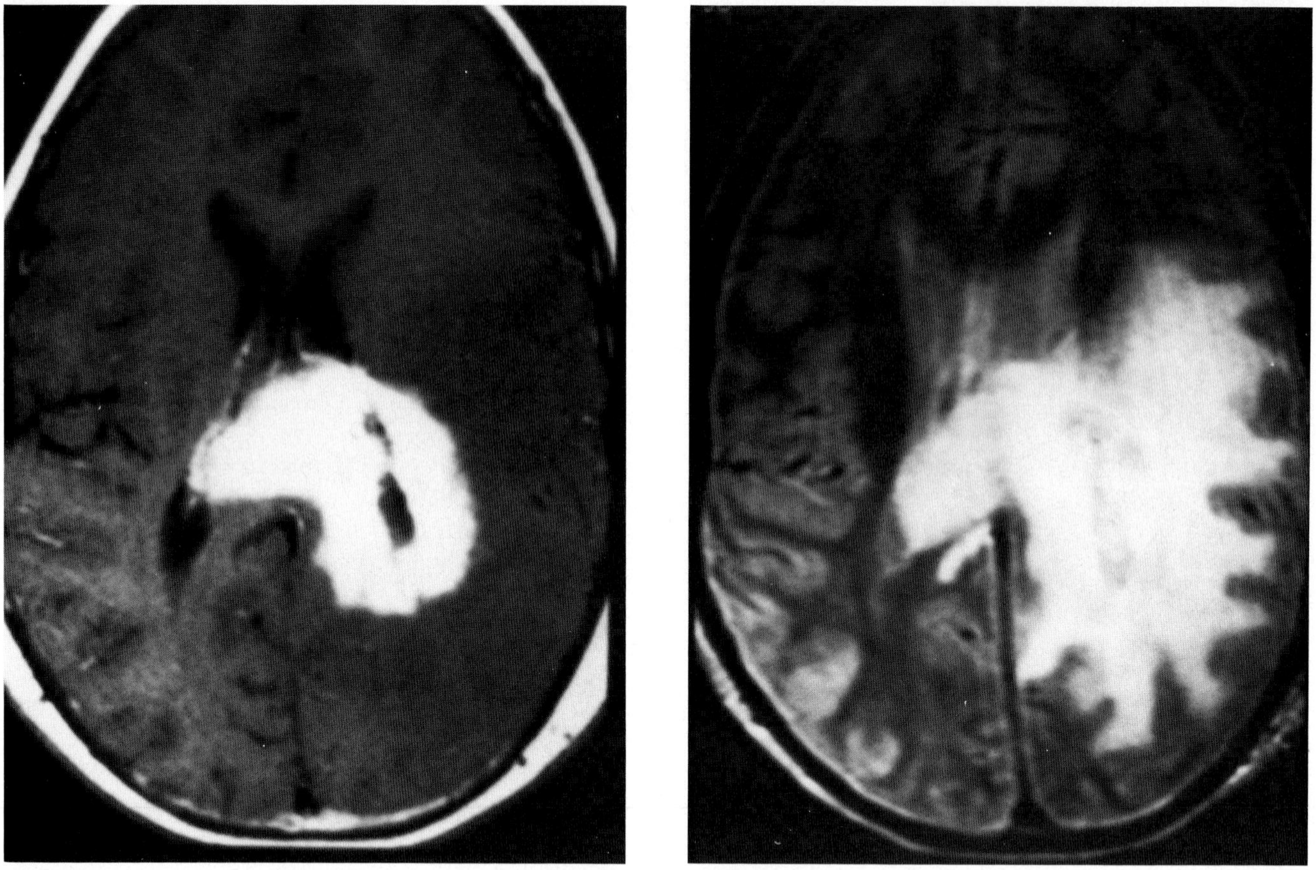

A B

Figure 9-47 Malignant glioma in the corpus callosum. **A.** Axial T_1WI after MR contrast injection shows a contrast-enhanced mass extending from the left cerebral hemisphere through the splenium of the corpus callosum. **B.** Axial PDWI shows high-signal-intensity edema and tumor involving extensive portions of the left posterior frontal and parietal lobes, with crossing of the splenium of the corpus callosum.

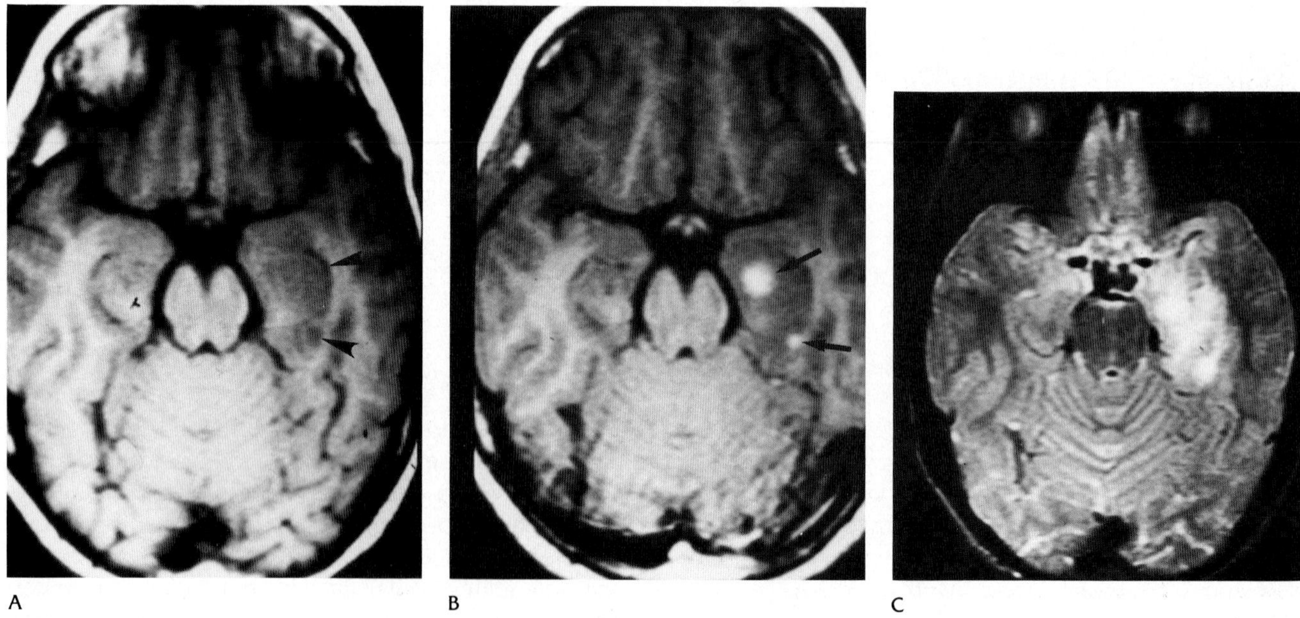

Figure 9-48 Ganglioglioma. **A.** Axial T_1WI shows hypointense expansion of the hippocampal gyrus (arrowheads). **B.** Axial T_1WI after MR contrast injection shows two areas of enhancement (arrows). **C.** Axial T_2WI shows a high-signal-intensity mass involving the medial aspect of the left temporal lobe.

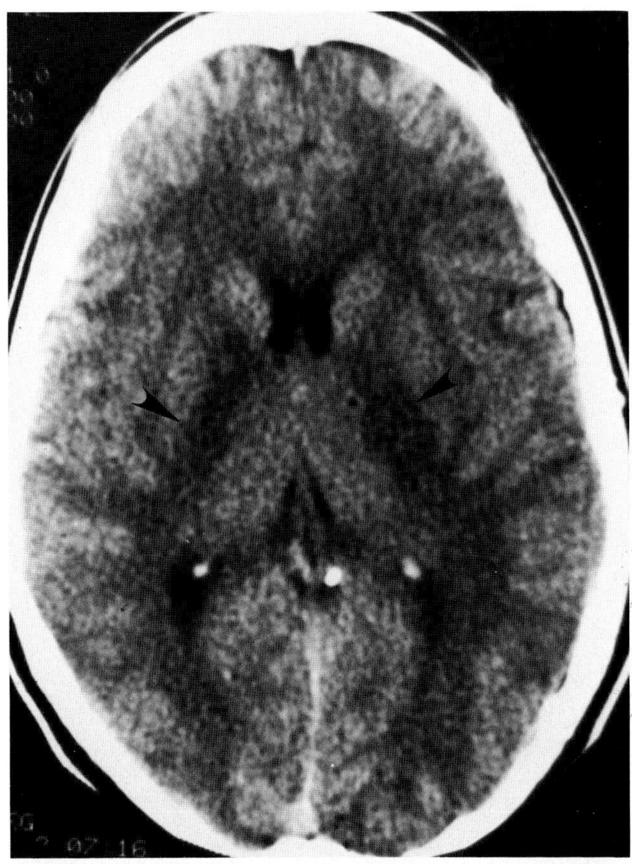

A

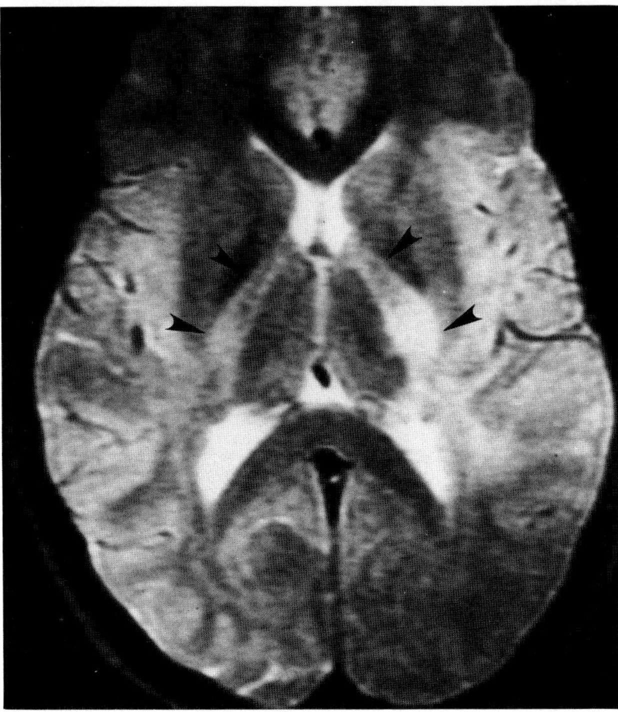

B

Figure 9-49 Gliomatosis cerebri. **A.** Axial CE CT shows slight fullness in the white matter of both internal capsules (arrowheads). There is no evidence of contrast enhancement and no mass effect. **B.** Axial T_2WI shows high signal intensity involving both internal capsules (arrowheads).

to be hemorrhagic, tend not to enhance, and rarely show calcification (Zimmerman 1990*b*). On CT, the finding is that of expansion of the white matter, usually not different in density from the white matter (Fig. 9-49*A*). On MR with T_1WI, the tumor may not be recognizable, as it blends in with the white matter. On PDW and T_2WI, the signal intensity of the white matter appears to be high and is abnormal (Fig. 9-49*B*) (Spagnoli 1987). The characteristic expansion of the white matter by the tumor mass usually helps differentiate it from demyelinating diseases.

Ependymomas

One-third of all ependymomas occur in the supratentorial space (Heideman 1989). Within this space they arise from ependymal rests in the white matter or within or adjacent to the ependymal lining of the ventricular system (Russell 1989). They tend to occur early in life, although they are found throughout childhood (Kun 1988; Swartz 1982). They tend to be well demarcated and partially encapsulated and are frequently hemorrhagic and cystic. They vary in grade from those that are "benign" to those that are malignant. Their clinical presentation in the supratentorial space relates to their location and size and the age of the patient. If ependymomas obstruct the CSF pathways, they can produce hydrocephalus, whereas if they occur within the white matter, they present predominantly by mass effect and increased intracranial pressure. More peripheral ependymomas may produce seizures. On CT, calcification is common (50 percent), with the tumor tissue usually being hypodense on plain CT (Fig. 9-50*A*) (Swartz 1982). Enhancement occurs frequently, and the tumor is often centrally necrotic (Fig. 9-50*B*). On T_1WI the signal intensity is low, whereas on PDWI and T_2WI signal intensity is quite variable (Fig. 9-51) (Zimmerman 1990*b*). Tumor dissemination is usually not present at the time of diagnosis but occurs with some frequency after local recurrence (Packer 1985). Treatment consists of surgical resection when possible. Radiation therapy is used, but the overall results suggest that it is not very effective. Chemotherapy has been used, but again, the results have not been promising.

Intraventricular Tumors

In addition to ependymomas, the two major intraventricular tumors seen in childhood are choroid plexus papillomas and choroid plexus carcinomas (Zimmerman 1990*b*). In other children, intraventricular meningiomas may be found in association with neurofibromatosis (Fletcher 1986). Glial tumors arising within the brain parenchyma can extend into the ventricle, appearing as primary intraventricular masses.

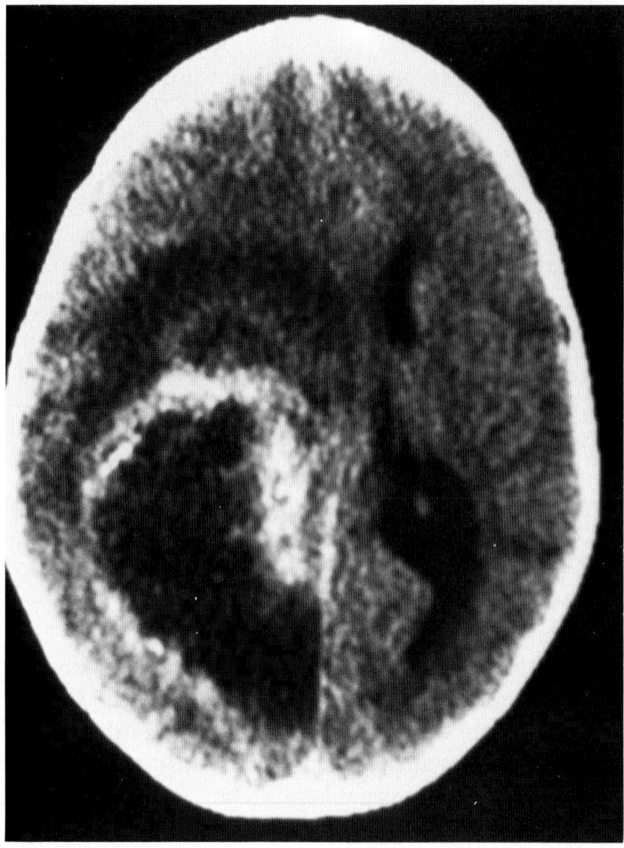

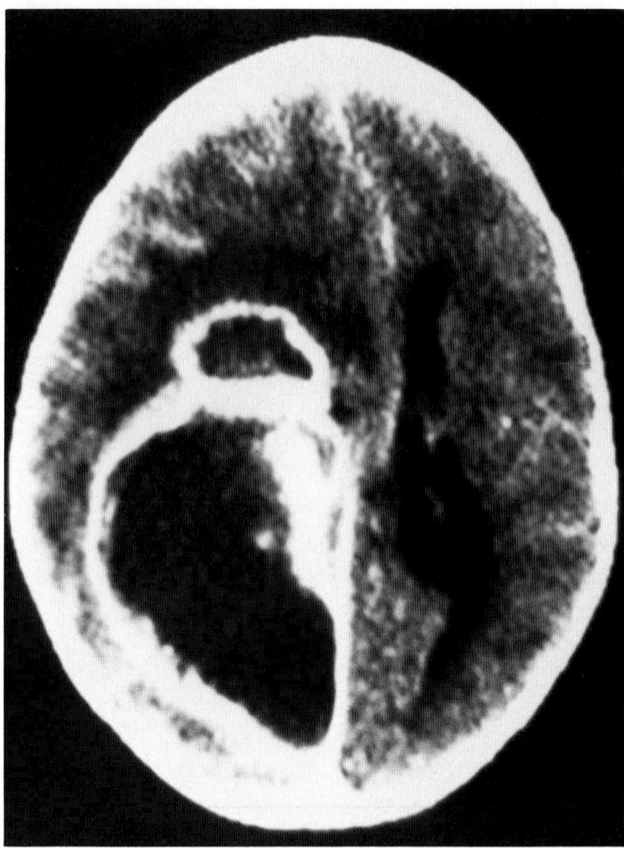

A B

Figure 9-50 Ependymoma. **A.** Axial NC CT shows a large right parietal occipital mass that is centrally necrotic and contains multiple small calcifications within its walls. **B.** Axial CE CT shows enhancement of the necrotic tumor wall.

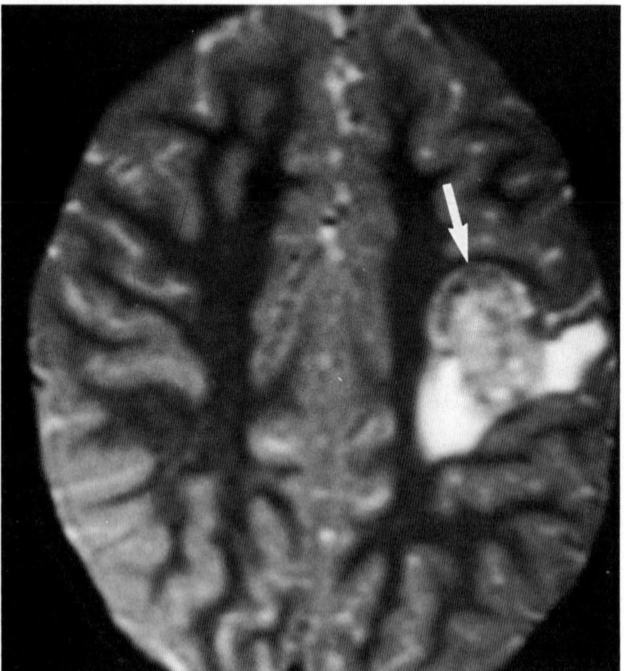

Figure 9-51 Ependymoma. Axial T_2WI shows a mass (arrow) that is isointense to gray matter and is partially surrounded by vasogenic edema.

CHOROID PLEXUS TUMORS

Tumors of the choroid plexus account for up to 10 to 20 percent of brain tumors occurring during the first year of life but represent only 3 percent of all pediatric brain tumors (Zimmerman 1979*c*; Laurence 1979). Choroid plexus papillomas occurring during the first year of life are found within the lateral ventricle (Laurence 1979). Most of these papillomas are benign, and some are capable of CSF production (Milhorat 1976). Only 10 to 20 percent of choroid plexus tumors are carcinomas (Carpenter 1982). Choroid plexus carcinomas have a tendency to invade the margin of the ventricle and involve the subependymal white matter, producing vasogenic edema. They also have a tendency to disseminate within the ventricular system and the subarachnoid spaces (Carpenter 1982).

Choroid plexus papillomas are often calcified or hyperdense on plain CT (Fig. 9-52) and enhance homogeneously after contrast administration (Fig. 9-53) (Zimmerman 1979*c*). Hydrocephalus is a frequent finding that possibly is caused by overproduction of CSF (Milhorat 1976) or episodes of subarachnoid hemorrhage with resultant hydrocephalus (Zimmerman 1990*b*). On MR, they are hypointense to isointense on T_1WI and of hypoin-

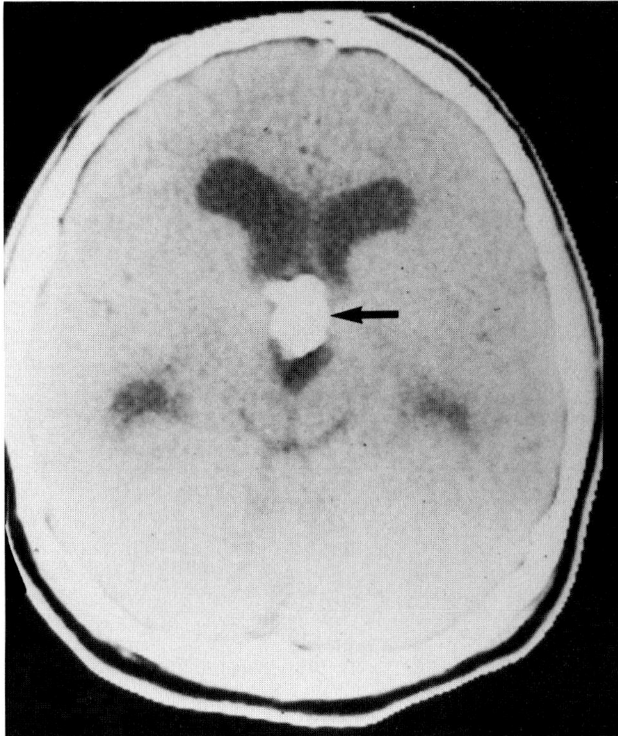

Figure 9-52 Choroid plexus papilloma in the third ventricle. Axial NC CT shows a calcified mass (arrow) in the anterior third ventricle; hydrocephalus is present.

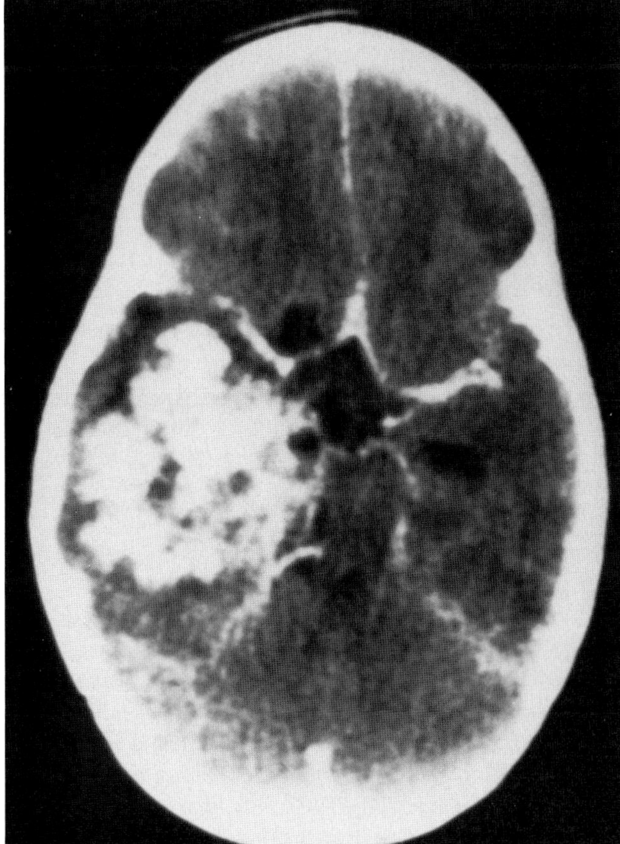

Figure 9-53 Choroid plexus papilloma. Axial CE CT shows an enhanced frondlike mass in the anterior aspect of the right temporal lobe.

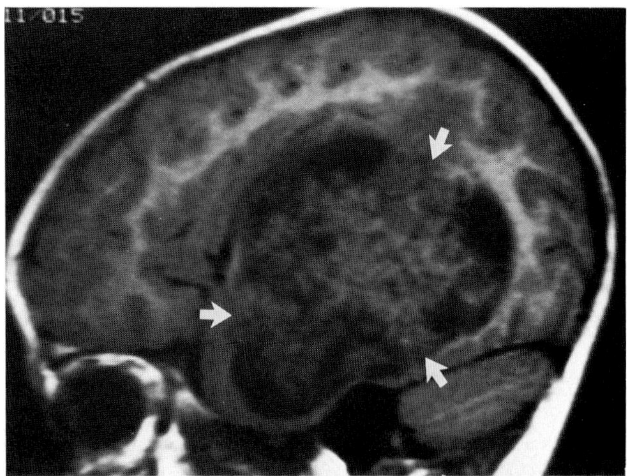

A

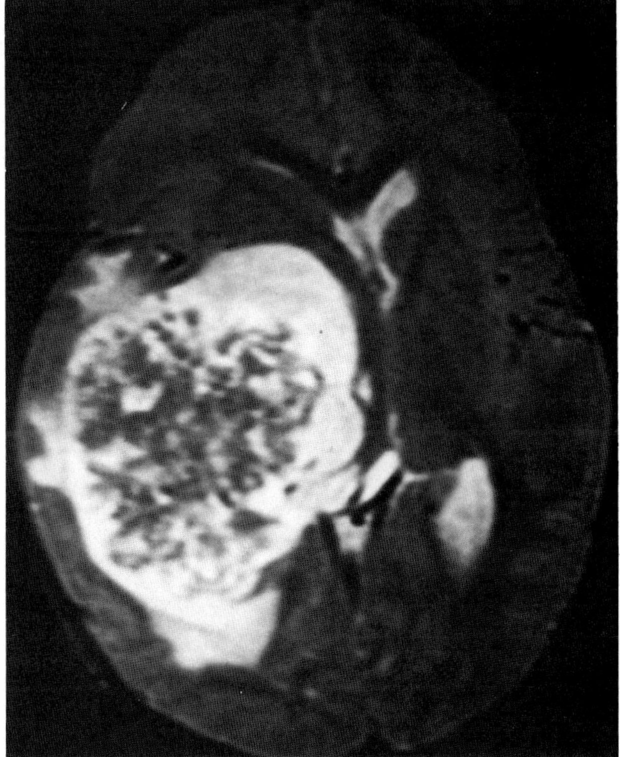

B

Figure 9-54 Choroid plexus papilloma. ***A.*** Sagittal T_1WI shows that the right temporal horn is expanded and is filled with a papillary-appearing isointense mass (arrows). ***B.*** Axial T_2WI shows marked dilatation of the temporal horn, which is filled with a hypointense frondlike or papillarylike mass.

tensity on PDW and T_2WI (Fig. 9-54) (Zimmerman 1990*b*). They enhance intensely after contrast injection (Fig. 9-55).

INTRAVENTRICULAR MENINGIOMAS

In childhood, these meningiomas are most often found in association with neurofibromatosis (Braffman 1990). An intraventricular meningioma appears as a mass of increased density (Fig. 9-56), with or without calcification, that enhances on CT and is usually located within the atrium of the lateral ventricle. Hydrocephalus is due to compression of the third ventricle or trapping of the atria

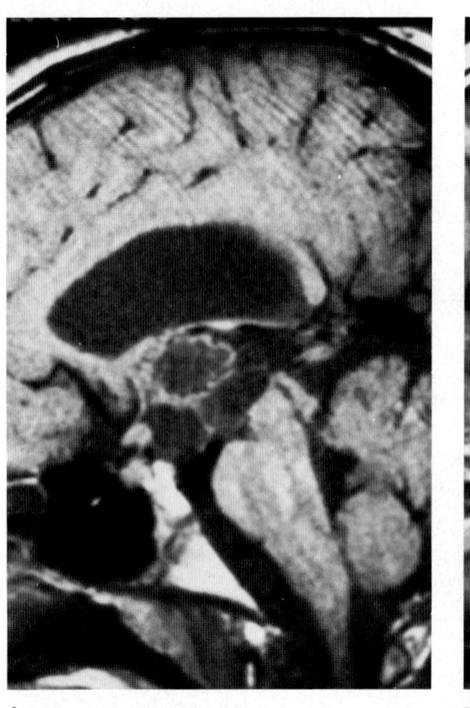

A

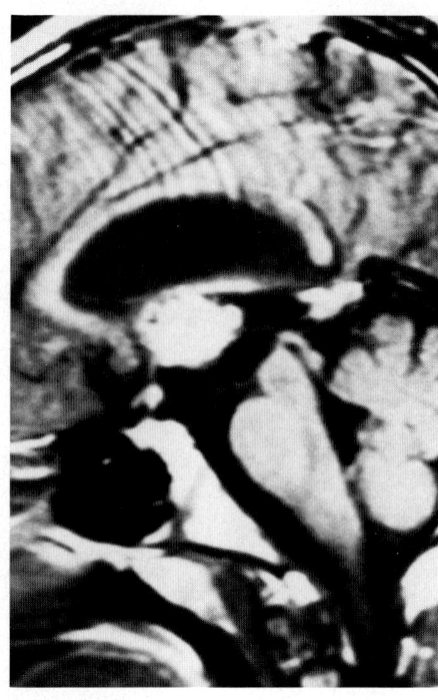

B

Figure 9-55 Third ventricular choroid plexus papilloma. **A.** Sagittal T_1WI without contrast shows a multilobulated mass in the third ventricle and hydrocephalic dilatation of the lateral ventricles. **B.** Sagittal T_1WI after MR contrast injection shows enhancement of the third ventricular mass.

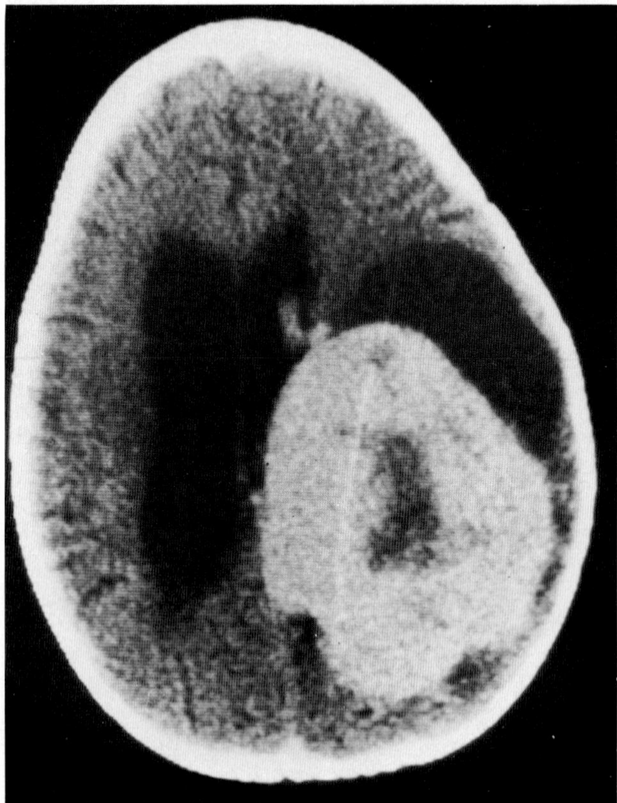

Figure 9-56 Intraventricular meningioma. Axial NC CT shows a high-density mass in an atrium of the left lateral ventricle capped by CSF trapped in the obstructed and markedly expanded temporal horn.

of the lateral ventricle, producing the signs and symptoms of increased intracranial pressure. Compression of the visual pathway and the optic radiations produces a homonymous hemianopsia. On MR, a meningioma is isointense on T_1WI, may be slightly hyperintense on PDWI, and is usually isointense to hypointense on T_2WI (Spagnoli 1986). These entities enhance intensely after MR contrast injection.

PINEAL TUMORS

Tumors of the pineal region are a heterogeneous group representing 0.5 to 2 percent of all childhood CNS tumors (Zimmerman 1980*b*). Tumors of the pineal parenchyma, pineoblastomas (a primitive neuroectodermal tumor), and pineocytomas represent one major group. Germ cell tumors, including germinomas, embryonal cell carcinomas, teratomas (benign and malignant), and choriocarcinomas represent the other major group (Zimmerman 1980*b*). Germ cell tumors are found more frequently in men and tend to occur in the second decade of life, whereas pineal parenchymal tumors occur more frequently in the first decade of life and are more equally distributed between the sexes (Packer 1984). The third category includes tumors that arise from the supporting structures of the pineal gland and are of an astrocytic nature. Tumors of adjacent structures can arise and simulate tumors of the pineal region. From the adjacent meninges, meningiomas can involve the pineal region, while enlargement of the vein of Galen as a result of an arteriovenous malformation can simulate a pineal tumor. The

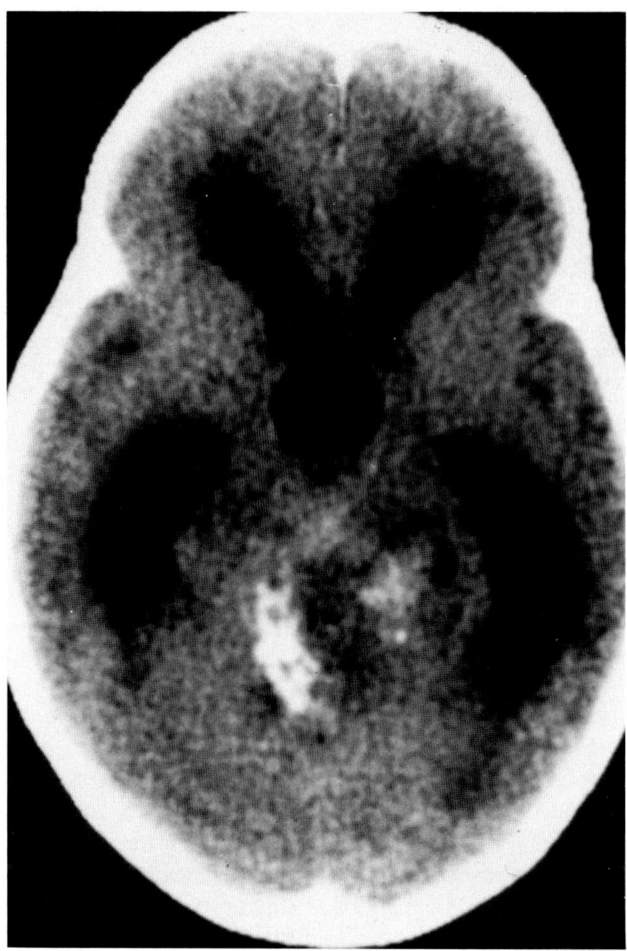
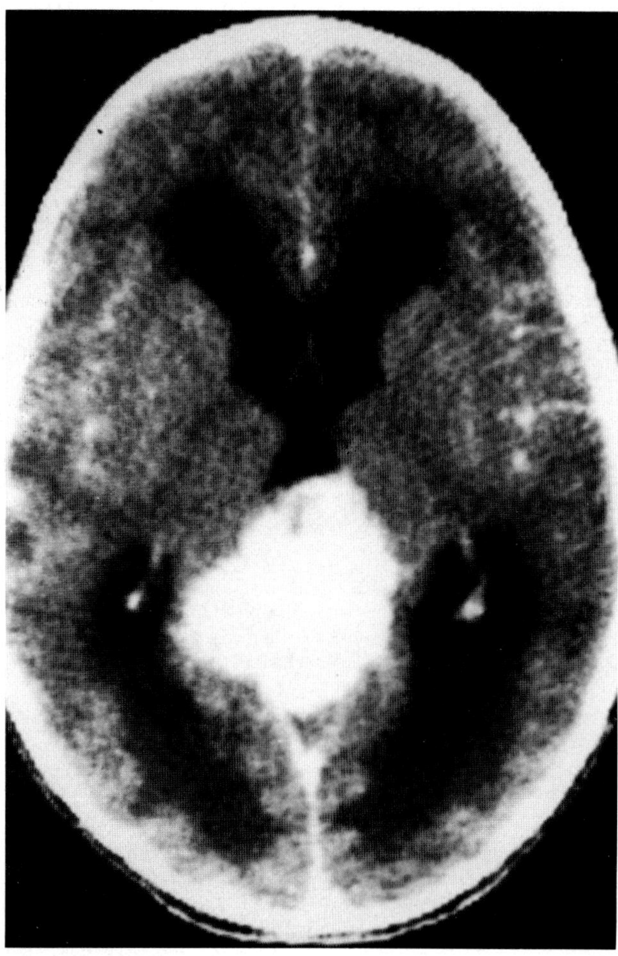

A B

Figure 9-57 Primitive neuroectodermal tumor (pineoblastoma type). **A.** Axial non-contrast-enhanced CT shows a poorly marginated, isodense, partially calcified pineal gland mass. There is hydrocephalus with dilatation of the third and lateral ventricles. **B.** Axial CT after contrast shows that the mass enhances.

most common difficulty encountered with CT in which the cuts are done in the axial plane occurs when a tumor in the tectum of the midbrain projects superiorly into the pineal region, mimicking a pineal neoplasm. This differentiation can be made on sagittal and coronal MR images.

The signs and symptoms of tumors in the pineal area are often nonspecific and nonlocalizing (Packer 1984). They arise primarily from obstruction of the outlet of the third ventricle, with the production of hydrocephalus. Compression of the collicular plate may produce vertical gaze paresis (Parinaud's syndrome).

Pineocytomas and pineoblastomas appear on CT as tumors of slightly increased density, often with calcification, and contrast-enhance (Fig. 9-57) (Zimmerman 1980*b*). They infiltrate the surrounding structures, and hydrocephalus is found frequently. On MR, these tumors are usually low in signal intensity on T_1WI (Fig. 9-58*A*) and frequently have mixed signal intensity on PDW and T_2WI (Zimmerman 1990*b*). On PDWI they may be slightly increased in signal intensity, but they are usually lower in signal intensity on T_2WI. This is thought to reflect the highly cellular nature of these tumors. They enhance intensely with MR contrast (Fig. 9-58*B*) (Zimmerman 1991). The best method of evaluating these tumors is with thin T_1WI sagittal and coronal sections before and after MR contrast injection. Subarachnoid dissemination should be looked for, as it is not uncommon and in fact may be the presenting manifestation of a pineoblastoma or germinoma (Fig. 9-59). There is an increased incidence of pineoblastoma in association with congenital bilateral retinoblastoma (Bader 1982). Given the history of bilateral retinoblastoma, any early calcification in the pineal gland (before age 6) should be looked at on CT as the initial manifestation of a pineoblastoma (Zimmerman 1982). This combination of retinoblastoma and pineoblastoma has been labeled *trilateral retinoblastoma* (Fig. 9-58) (Bader 1982).

On CT, germ cell tumors are usually of increased density, contrast-enhance, and may have calcifications (Zimmerman 1980*b*). In a germinoma the calcifications are

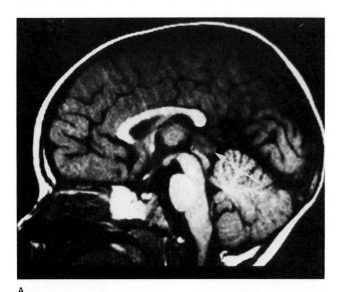

A

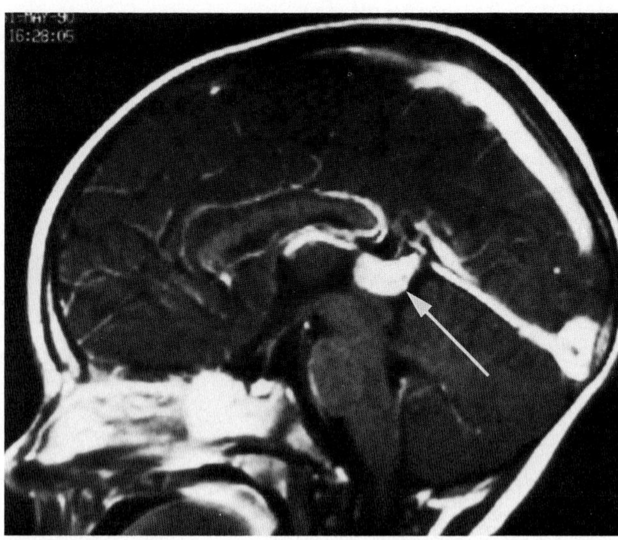

B

Figure 9-58 Primitive neuroectodermal tumor (pineoblastoma type) associated with bilateral congenital retinoblastoma (trilateral retinoblastoma). **A.** Sagittal T_1WI without contrast enhancement shows a large pineal gland, consistent with a small tumor mass (arrow). **B.** Sagittal T_1WI after MR contrast injection shows an enhanced pineal mass (arrow).

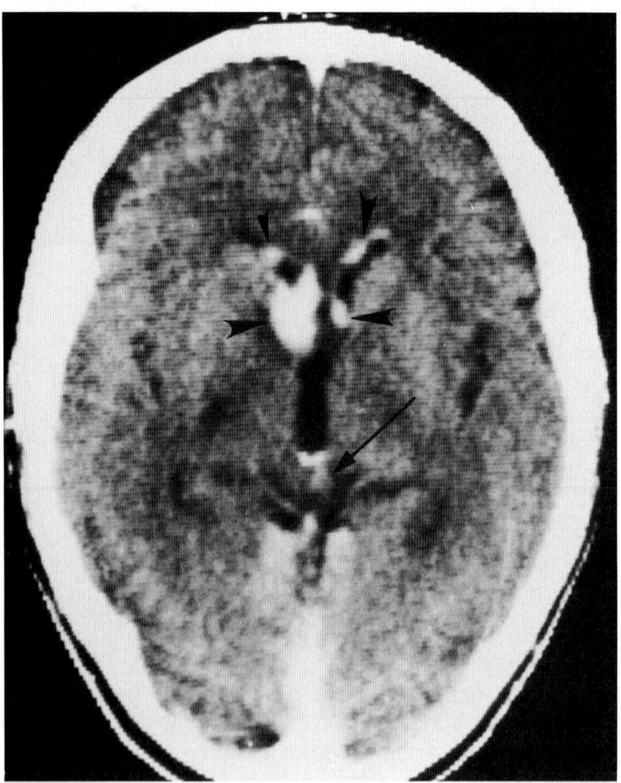

Figure 9-59 Intraventricular dissemination of pineal germinoma. Axial CT after contrast shows an enhanced tumor (arrowheads) disseminated within the frontal horns of the lateral ventricle. The upper portion of the pineal mass is just seen (arrow). The pineal mass was better shown on a lower section.

usually found in the invaded pineal gland but may occur throughout the tumor matrix after treatment. In an embryonal cell carcinoma, calcifications are seen frequently throughout the tumor matrix. Benign or malignant teratomas frequently have calcification or ossification, such as in teeth. Embryonal carcinomas tend to undergo necrosis. All malignant germ cell tumors are invasive and have a potential for CSF dissemination (Packer 1984).

Surgical resection is recommended; when surgery is not feasible, biopsy is performed so that treatment can be appropriate to the type of lesion (Packer 1984). Radiotherapy is curative in germinomas (Onoyama 1979). Chemotherapy may also be curative in some germinomas (Rustin 1986). The response to therapy of pineoblastomas, pineocytomas, and embryonal cell carcinomas has generally been disappointing (Packer 1984). Cysts of the pineal gland are common, appearing on CT as low-density, sometimes partially calcified ringlike lesions. Contrast enhancement occurs in the adjacent veins and the residual portion of the pineal gland. On MR, pineal cysts are hypointense on T_1WI (Fig. 9-60) and hyperintense on PDWI; they are isointense to CSF on T_2WI. Pineal cysts may get larger than the normal upper limits of the pineal gland (1 cm in diameter) but do not appear to produce hydrocephalus or compression of the collicular plate and cerebral aqueduct. Pineal cysts are thought to arise as a degeneration of the pineal gland and contain slightly proteinaceous fluid.

SUPERFICIAL TUMORS OF THE MENINGES, PIA, OR CORTEX

There is a small but real incidence of meningiomas in childhood. Their appearance is usually not different from that in adults (Spagnoli 1986); even in the young, the tu-

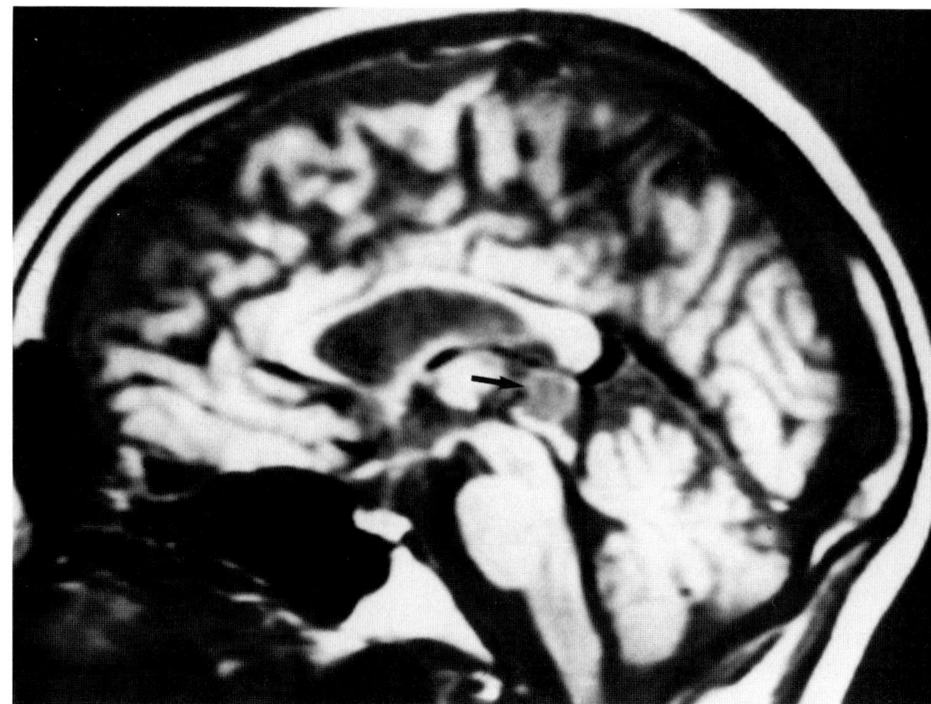

Figure 9-60 Pineal cyst. Sagittal T_1WI shows cystic expansion of the pineal gland (arrow) without hydrocephalus or compression of the aqueduct or tectum of the midbrain.

mor can be large. There is an increased incidence in childhood of meningiomas that are more aggressive ("malignant"), and some of these tumors burrow within the brain parenchyma. Identification of large meningiomas is not a problem, as they can be recognized by their mass effect. Small meningiomas may not be seen on CT or MR unless contrast is given. Meningiomas have an increased incidence in patients with either type of neurofibromatosis and should be looked for in that clinical setting (Braffman 1990). Other tumors that arise from the calvarium or dura in children include chondrosarcomas, metastases due to neuroblastoma and Ewing's sarcoma, metastatic rhabdomyosarcomas, and rhabdomyosarcomas invading extracranial to intracranial through the bone or along the neural foramina and the nerves they contain. Superficial cortical astrocytomas are uncommon but can be found in childhood. An uncommon mass that is probably related to the phacomatoses is referred to as *meningoencephaloangiomatosis* (MEAN) (Duhaime 1985). Subarachnoid tumor dissemination should also be considered, as should meningitis and sarcoid, when there is enhancement of the pial surface of the brain.

References

ALBRIGHT AL, PRICE RA, GUTHKELCH AN: Brain stem gliomas of children: A clinicopathologic study. *Cancer* 52:2313–2319, 1983.

ARMINGTON WG, ZIMMERMAN RA, BILANIUK LT: Imaging of the retroorbital visual pathway, in Som PM, Bergeron RT (eds), *Head and Neck Imaging,* St. Louis, CV Mosby, 1990, pp 829–873.

ARSENI C, CIURZA AV: Statistical survey of 276 cases of medulloblastomas (1935–1978). *Acta Neurochir (Wien)* 57:159–162, 1982.

ATLAS SW, GROSSMAN RI, GOLDBERG HI, et al: MR diagnosis of acute disseminated encephalomyelitis. *J Comput Assist Tomogr* 10(5):798–801, 1986.

AUER R, RICE JG, HINTON G, et al: Cerebellar astrocytoma with benign histology and malignant clinical course. *J Neurosurg* 54:128–132, 1981.

BADER JL, MEADOWS AT, ZIMMERMAN LE, et al: Bilateral retinoblastoma with ectopic intracranial retinoblastoma: Trilateral retinoblastoma. *Cancer Genet Cytogenet* 5:203–213, 1982.

BILANIUK L, ZIMMERMAN R, LITTMAN P, et al: Computed tomography of brain stem gliomas in children. *Neuroradiology* 134:89–95, 1980.

BOYKO OB, CURNES JT, OAKES WH, et al: Hamartomas of in tuber cinereum: CT, MR, and pathologic findings. *AJNR* 12: 309–314, 1991.

BRAFFMAN BH, BILANIUK LT, ZIMMERMAN RA: MR of central nervous system neoplasia of the phakomatoses. *Semin Roentgenol* 25(2):198–217, 1990.

CARPENTER DB, MICHELSON WG, HAYS AP: Carcinoma of the choroid plexus. *J Neurosurg* 56:722–727, 1982.

CHOU M, LENA G, HASSOUN J: Prognosis and long term followup in patients with medulloblastoma. *Clin Neurosurg* 30:246–277, 1983.

COHEN ME, DUFFNER PK: Craniopharyngiomas, in *Brain Tumors in Children,* New York, Raven Press, 1983, pp 193–210.

COULON RA, TILL K: Intracranial ependymomas in children: A review of 43 cases. *Childs Brain* 3:154–168, 1977.

DANOFF BF, KRAMER S, THOMPSON N: The radiotherapeutic management of optic gliomas of children. *Int J Radiat Oncol Biol Phys* 6:45–50, 1980.

DIEBLER C, PONSOT G: Hamartomas of the tuber cinereum. *Neuroradiology* 25:93–101, 1983.

DUHAIME AC, SCHUT L, RORKE LB, et al: The MEAN disease. *Concepts Pediatr Neurosurg* 5:154–164, 1985.

DUNN V, BALE JF, ZIMMERMAN RA, et al: MRI in children with postinfectious disseminated encephalomyelitis. *Magn Reson Imaging* 4:25–32, 1986.

FAIRBURN B, LARKIN IM: A cyst of Rathke's cleft. *J Neurosurg* 21:223–225, 1964.

FARWELL JR, DOHRMANN GJ, FLANNERY JT: Central nervous system tumors in children. *Cancer* 40:3123–3132, 1977.

FLETCHER WA, IMES RK, HOYT WF: Chiasmal gliomas: Appearance and long-term changes demonstrated by computerized tomography. *J Neurosurg* 65:154–159, 1986.

GEISSINGER J, BUCY P: Astrocytomas of the cerebellum in children: Long term study. *Arch Neurol* 29:125–135, 1971.

GOL A, MCKISSACK W: The cerebellar astrocytomas: A report on 98 verified cases. *J Neurosurg* 16:287–296, 1959.

GOMORI JM, GROSSMAN RI, GOLDBERG HI, et al: Occult cerebral vascular malformations: High field MR imaging. *Radiology* 158:707–713, 1986.

GUSNARD DA: Cerebellar neoplasms in children. *Semin Roentgenol* 25(3):263–278, 1990.

HEIDEMAN RL, PACKER RJ, ALBRIGHT LA, et al: Tumors of the central nervous system, in Pizzo PA, Poplack DG (eds), *Principles and Practice of Pediatric Oncology,* Philadelphia, Lippincott, 1989, pp 505–553.

HOFFMAN HJ, HENDRICK EB, HUMPHREYS RP: Management of medulloblastoma. *Clin Neurosurg* 30:226–245, 1983.

HOPE DG, MULVIHILL JJ: Malignancy in neurofibromatosis, in Riccardi VM, Mulvihill JJ (eds), *Neurofibromatosis.* Advances in Neurology, vol 29, New York, Raven Press, 1981, pp 33–35.

JENKIN RDT, SIMPSON WJK, KEEN CW: Pineal and suprasellar germinomas. *J Neurosurg* 48:99–107, 1978.

KOCH KJ, SMITH RR: Gd-DTPA enhancement in MR imaging of central pontine myelinolysis. *AJNR* 10(suppl):558, 1989.

KRAMER ED, RAFTO S, PACKER RJ, et al: Comparison of myelography with computed tomography follow-up vs. gadolinium magnetic resonance imaging for subarachnoid metastatic disease in children. *Neurology* 41:46–50, 1991.

KUN LE, KOVNER EH, SANFORD RA: Ependymomas in children. *Pediatr Neurosci* 14:57–63, 1988.

LAURENCE KM: The biology of choroid plexus papilloma in infancy and childhood. *Acta Neurochir (Wien)* 50:79–90, 1979.

LEE Y, VAN TASSEL P, BRUNER JM, et al: Juvenile pilocytic astrocytomas: CT and MR characteristics. *AJNR* 10:363–370, 1989.

LIU HM, BOGGS J, KIDD J: Ependymomas of childhood: I. Histological survey and clinicopathological correlation. *Childs Brain* 2:92–110, 1976.

MANTRAVADI R, PHATAK R, BELLUR S, et al: Brain stem gliomas: An autopsy study of 25 cases. *Cancer* 49:1294–1296, 1982.

MILHORAT TH, HAMMOCK MK, DAVIS DA, et al: Choroid plexus papilloma: Proof of cerebrospinal fluid overproduction. *Childs Brain* 2:273–289, 1976.

NAIDICH TP, ZIMMERMAN RA: Primary brain tumors in children. *Semin Roentgenol* 19:100–114, 1984.

ONOYAMA Y, ONO K, NAKAJIMA T, et al: Radiation therapy of pineal tumors. *Radiology* 130:757–760, 1979.

OXENHANDLER DC, SAYERS MP: The dilemma of childhood optic gliomas. *J Neurosurg* 48:34–41, 1978.

PACKER R, ALLEN J, NIELSON S, et al: Brainstem glioma: Clinical manifestations of meningeal gliomatosis. *Ann Neurol* 14:177–182, 1983*a*.

PACKER RJ, SAVINO PJ, BILANIUK L, et al: Chiasmatic gliomas of childhood: A reappraisal of natural history and effectiveness of cranial irradiation. *Childs Brain* 10:393–403, 1983*b*.

PACKER RJ, SUTTON LN, ROSENSTOCK JG, et al: Pineal region tumors of childhood. *Pediatrics* 74:97–103, 1984.

PACKER RJ, SIEGEL KR, SUTTON LN, et al: Leptomeningeal dissemination of primary central nervous system tumors of childhood. *Ann Neurol* 18:217–227, 1985.

PACKER RJ, SUTTON LN, D'ANGIO G, et al: Management of children with primitive neuroectodermal tumors of the posterior fossa/medulloblastoma. *Pediatr Neurosci* 12:272–282, 1985–1986.

PACKER RJ, LITTMAN PA, SPOSTO RM, et al: Results of a pilot study of hyperfractionated radiation therapy for children with brain stem gliomas. *Int J Radiat Oncol Biol Phys* 13:1647–1651, 1987.

PACKER RJ, BILANIUK LT, COHEN BH, et al: Intracranial visual pathway gliomas in children with neurofibromatosis. *Neurofibromatosis* 1:212–222, 1988.

PENDERGRASS TW, MILSTEIN JM, GEYER RJ, et al: Eight drugs in one-day chemotherapy for brain tumors: Experience in 107 children and rationale for preradiation chemotherapy. *J Clin Oncol* 5:1221–1231, 1987.

PUSEY E, KORTMAN KE, FLANNIGAN BD, et al: MR of craniopharyngiomas: Tumor delineating and characterization. *AJNR* 8:439–444, 1987.

RAMONDI A, TOMITA T: Medulloblastoma in childhood: Comparative results of partial and total resection. *Childs Brain* 5:310–328, 1979.

RAO KCVG, FITZ CR, HARWOOD-NACH DC: Craniopharyngiomas in children: Neuroradiological evaluation. *Rev Interam Radiol* 2:149–157, 1977.

RORKE LB: The cerebellar medulloblastoma and its relationship to primitive neuroectodermal tumors. *J Neuropathol Exp Neurol* 42:1–15, 1983.

RORKE LB, GILLES FH, DAVIS RL, et al: Revision of the World Health Organization classification of brain tumors for childhood brain tumors. *Cancer* 56:1869–1886, 1985.

RORKE LB: Relationship of morphology of ependymoma in children to prognosis. *Prog Exp Tumor Res* 30:170–174, 1987.

ROSENSTOCK JG, PACKER RJ, BILANIUK LT, et al: Chiasmatic optic glioma treated with chemotherapy: A preliminary report. *J Neurosurg* 63:862–866, 1985.

RUSSELL DS, RUBINSTEIN LJ: *Pathology of Tumours of the Nervous System,* Baltimore, Williams & Wilkins, 1989.

RUSTIN GJ, NEWLAND ES, BAGSHAWE KD, et al: Successful management of metastatic and primary germ cell tumors of the brain. *Cancer* 57:2108–2113, 1986.

SAVOIARDO M, PASSERINI A: CT, angiography and RN scans in intracranial cavernous hemangiomas. *Neuroradiology* 16:256–260, 1978.

SEGALL HD, BATNITZKY S, ZEE C, et al: Computed tomography in the diagnosis of intracranial neoplasms in children. *Cancer* 56:1748–1755, 1985.

SHELINE GE: Radiation therapy of brain tumors. *Cancer* 39:873–881, 1977.

SMITH RR: Brain stem tumors. *Semin Roentgenol* 25(3):249–262, 1990.

SMITH RR, ZIMMERMAN RA, PACKER RJ, et al: Pediatric brainstem glioma: Post-radiation MR follow-up. *Neuroradiology* 32:265–271, 1990.

SPAGNOLI MV, GOLDBERG HI, GROSSMAN RI, et al: High-field MRI of intracranial meningiomas. *Radiology* 161:369–375, 1986.

SPAGNOLI MV, GROSSMAN RI, PACKER RJ, et al: Magnetic resonance imaging determination of gliomatosis cerebri. *Neuroradiology* 29:15–18, 1987.

STEINBERG GK, SHUER LM, CONLEY FK, et al: Evolution and outcome in malignant astroglial neoplasms of the cerebellum. *J Neurosurg* 62:9–17, 1985.

SWARTZ JD, ZIMMERMAN RA, BILANIUK LT: Computed tomography of intracranial ependymomas. *Radiology* 143:97–101, 1982.

TENNY RT, LAWS ER, YOUNGE BR, et al: The neurosurgical management of optic glioma. *J Neurosurg* 57:452–458, 1982.

THOMSETT MJ, CONTE FA, KAPLAN SL, et al: Endocrine and neurologic outcome in children with craniopharyngioma: Review of effect of treatment in 42 patients. *J Pediatr* 97:728–738, 1980.

WINSTON K, GILLES FH, LEVITON A, et al: Cerebellar gliomas in children. *JNCI* 58:833–838, 1977.

WOLMAN L, BALMFORTH CG: Precocious puberty due to a hypothalamic hamartoma in a patient surviving to late middle age. *J Neurol Neurosurg Psychiatry* 26:275, 1963.

YOUNG J, MILLER R: Incidence of malignant tumors in U.S. children. *J Pediatr* 86:254–258, 1975.

YOUNG SC, ZIMMERMAN RA, NOWELL MA, et al: Giant cystic craniopharyngiomas. *Neuroradiology* 29:468–473, 1987.

ZIMMERMAN RA, BILANIUK LT, BRUNO L, et al: Computed tomography of cerebellar astrocytoma. *AJR* 130:170–174, 1978*a*.

ZIMMERMAN RA, BILANIUK LT, PAHLAJANI H: Spectrum of medulloblastomas demonstrated by computed tomography. *Radiology* 126:137–141, 1978*b*.

ZIMMERMAN RA, BILANIUK LT, LITTMAN P, et al: Computed tomography of pediatric craniofacial sarcoma. *CT: J Comput Tomogr* 2:113–121, 1978*c*.

ZIMMERMAN RA, BILANIUK LT: Computed tomography of intracerebral gangliogliomas. *CT: J Comput Tomogr* 3:24–30, 1979*a*.

ZIMMERMAN RA, BILANIUK LT: Cranial CT of epidermoid and congenital fatty tumors of maldevelopmental origin. *CT: J Comput Tomogr* 3:40–50, 1979*b*.

ZIMMERMAN RA, BILANIUK LT: Computed tomography of choroid plexus lesions. *CT: J Comput Tomogr* 3(2):93–103, 1979*c*.

ZIMMERMAN RA, BILANIUK LT: Computed tomography of primary and secondary craniocerebral neuroblastoma. *AJNR* 1:431–434, 1980*a*.

ZIMMERMAN RA, BILANIUK LT, WOOD JH, et al: Computed tomography of pineal, parapineal and histologically related tumors. *Radiology* 137:669–677, 1980*b*.

ZIMMERMAN RA, BILANIUK LT: Age related incidence of pineal calcification detected by CT. *Radiology* 142:659–662, 1982.

ZIMMERMAN RA, BILANIUK LT, HACKNEY DB: Applications of magnetic resonance imaging in diseases of the pediatric central nervous system. *Magnet Reson Imaging* 4:11–24, 1986.

ZIMMERMAN RA, BILANIUK LT, SCHUT L, et al: Medical imaging of pediatric brain tumors. *Prog Exp Tumor Res* 30:61–80, 1987*a*.

ZIMMERMAN RA, BILANIUK LT, SZE G: Intracranial infection, in Brant-Zawadski M, Norman D (eds), *Magnetic Resonance Imaging of the Central Nervous System,* New York, Raven Press, 1987*b,* pp 235–257.

ZIMMERMAN RA, BILANIUK LT: CT and MR: Diagnosis and evolution of head injury, stroke, and brain tumors. *Neuropsychology* 3:191–230, 1989*a*.

ZIMMERMAN RA: Imaging of intrasellar, suprasellar, and parasellar tumors. *Semin Roentgenol* 25(2):174–197, 1990*a*.

ZIMMERMAN RA: Pediatric supratentorial tumors. *Semin Roentgenol* 25(3):225–248, 1990*b*.

ZIMMERMAN A: The phakomatoses, In Ishibashi Y, Hori Y (eds), *Tuberous Sclerosis and Neurofibromatosis: Epidemiology, Pathophysiology, Biology and Management,* Amsterdam, Elsevier, 1990*c,* pp 249–280.

ZIMMERMAN RA, GUSNARD DA, BILANIUK LT: Gadolinium DTPA enhanced MR evaluation of pediatric brain tumors. *Am J Pediatr Hematol Oncol,* 1991.

10 INTRACRANIAL METASTATIC DISEASES

Carl E. Johnson
Gordon Sze

Metastasis to the central nervous system (CNS) is a relatively common occurrence in patients with systemic cancer. Approximately 15 percent of patients with a systemic malignancy can be expected to develop neurological signs or symptoms during the course of illness (Posner 1978). Among these patients intracranial metastatic disease is one of the most common causes of the neurological disorder. Headache is the most frequent presenting symptom, occurring in about 50 percent of patients (Posner 1979). Motor signs are more common than are mental and personality changes. Extrapyramidal signs are uncommon even with metastases to the basal ganglia (Lesse 1954). In approximately 15 percent of patients a seizure is the presenting event (Posner 1979). Seizures are more common in children younger than 15 years, constituting an initial symptom in about 50 percent (Graus 1983).

Intracranial metastases have been found in 11 to 35 percent of patients with systemic malignancies in various autopsy series (Posner 1978; Abrahms 1950; Lesse 1954; Earle 1954). The incidence of intracranial metastases may be considerably higher, however, when specific tumor types are considered. For example, melanoma and lung carcinoma commonly metastasize to the brain, while brain metastases are an infrequent occurrence in patients with ovarian carcinoma. Consequently, a patient with malignant melanoma who presents with neurological symptoms is likely to have brain metastases, while the opposite is true for a patient with ovarian carcinoma (Posner 1978).

The site and type of intracranial metastasis also vary in accordance with the primary tumor type. For instance, lung carcinoma most often metastasizes to the brain parenchyma, while lymphoma and leukemia most frequently involve the leptomeninges. Intracranial prostate metastases are commonly dural in location, with parenchymal metastases being rare (Posner 1978; Lynes 1986; Castaldo 1983).

Although series differ in regard to the most frequently encountered metastatic lesions, in adults common systemic neoplasms that metastasize intracranially are, in decreasing order of frequency, lung, breast, melanoma, genitourinary tract, lymphoma or leukemia, gastrointestinal tract, and head and neck (Posner 1978; Potts 1980; Lesse 1954; Vieth 1965). In children, solid tumors that metastasize intracranially include sarcomas (especially osteogenic), germ cell tumors, Wilms's tumors, and uncommonly neuroblastoma (Graus 1983). Pulmonary metastases usually precede brain metastases in children (Graus 1983; Chee 1987). The rarity of pulmonary metastases in patients with neuroblastoma probably explains the infrequent occurrence of brain metastases in this disease.

Metastatic lesions arise through a number of routes. The most common is hematogenous spread of a tumor to the brain and meninges through the arterial circulation. Dissemination of malignant cells in the cerebrospinal fluid (CSF), secondary invasion of the meninges and brain by metastatic disease involving the calvarium and skull base, and direct or perineural intracranial extension of head and neck neoplasms are alternative routes.

Until recently, computed tomography (CT) was the primary imaging method for the evaluation of patients with suspected intracranial metastatic disease. However, magnetic resonance imaging (MRI) has now assumed a central role. Contrast-enhanced MR (CEMR) is the most sensitive imaging method for the detection of intracranial metastases and is at least as specific as contrast-enhanced CT (CECT).

CT and MR have replaced angiography in the evaluation of metastases. However, angiography may still be used in a few selected cases when surgical resection of a highly vascular metastasis, such as one arising from renal cell carcinoma, is contemplated. Angiography may also be useful in distinguishing hemorrhagic metastases from hemorrhages with other causes. In addition to mass effect, the angiogram may demonstrate abnormal medullary arteries or veins, tumor neovascularity, and tumor stain. It may exclude another etiology for hemorrhage, such as an arteriovenous malformation or a ruptured aneurysm (Rosenbaum 1975; Scatliff 1971; Sole-Llenas 1977).

HEMATOGENOUS METASTASES TO THE BRAIN

Metastases to the brain may occur anywhere within the parenchyma, though they are most frequently located at the corticomedullary junction in the anatomic watershed areas of the main cerebral arteries, in keeping with arterial tumor microemboli (Delattre 1988). Overall, single parenchymal metastases are nearly as common as multiple lesions are (Posner 1978; Delattre 1988). Certain tumors tend to have a single metastasis, while others have a propensity to present with multiple lesions. Renal cell carcinoma metastases and metastases arising from tumors of the pelvis and abdomen are much more likely to be single lesions, while those of lung carcinoma and melanoma are usually multiple. Breast carcinoma metastases are evenly divided between single and multiple lesions.

In general, metastases are evenly distributed between the supratentorial and infratentorial compartments when the respective proportion of the brain in each of these structures is considered (Posner 1978; Pechova'-Peterova' 1986). However, single metastases of renal cell carcinoma and of pelvic or abdominal tumors are very often infratentorial (Posner 1978; Delattre 1988). The reasons for this phenomenon are unknown. Batson's vertebral venous plexus is not a probable source of tumor spread, since there is not an increased incidence of spine or skull base lesions in patients with pelvic and abdominal tumors. These tumors may have an affinity for different parts of the brain and meninges because of unique biological and surface properties (Delattre 1988; Brunson 1978). Another reason for this phenomenon may be related to the "fertile-soil" hypothesis, which states that circulating tumor cells arrest in a variety of regions but that metastases occur only in certain locations (Delattre 1988; Cairncross 1983). In addition to lesions occurring within the brain parenchyma, metastases may arise within the pineal gland, the pituitary gland, and the ventricles (Fig. 10-1) (Schreiber 1982; Morrison 1984; Kart 1986; Jelinek 1990).

Metastases can appear hypodense, isodense, or hyperdense relative to cerebral white matter on non-contrast-enhanced CT (NCCT). Low-density lesions are often encountered with metastases arising from lung, breast, kidney, and head and neck carcinomas (Potts 1980; Deck 1976; Tarver 1984). There is usually associated surrounding white matter edema, which is also of decreased density. Often the tumor margin may be difficult if not impossible to separate from surrounding edema.

Metastatic lesions of higher attenuation than the brain parenchyma are frequently seen on NCCT in the gastrointestinal tract and in patients with choriocarcinoma or melanoma (Fig. 10-2) (Potts 1980; Deck 1976; Ruelle 1987). The increased density of these lesions is usually related to hemorrhage. Calcification rarely causes this increased attenuation, since, with the exception of osteogenic sarcoma metastases, calcification is rare in untreated metastases. Although secondary lymphoma usually metastasizes to the leptomeninges, parenchymal lesions occur that are often isodense to mildly hyperdense (Yang 1985; Bennett 1983; Brant-Zawadzki 1978; Holtas 1984). Similarly, leukemic parenchymal metastases (chloromas), though rare, are usually hyperdense (Barnett 1986). The higher attentuation of lymphoma, leukemia, and other metastases in which neither calcification nor hemorrhage is found on pathological examination may be caused by a more compact cellular density.

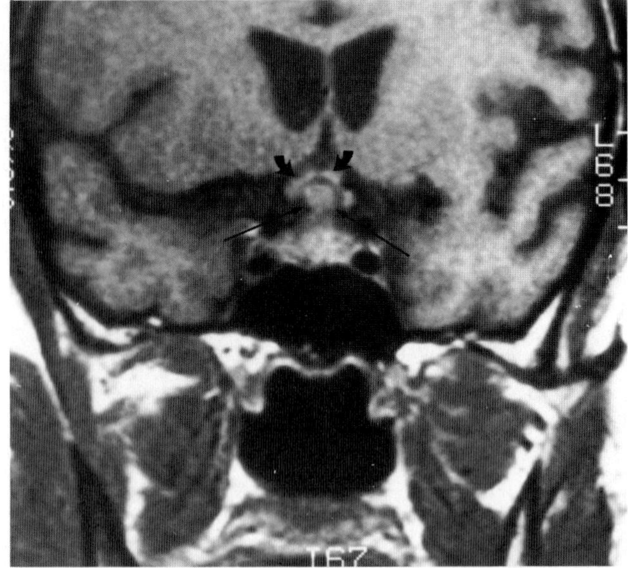

A

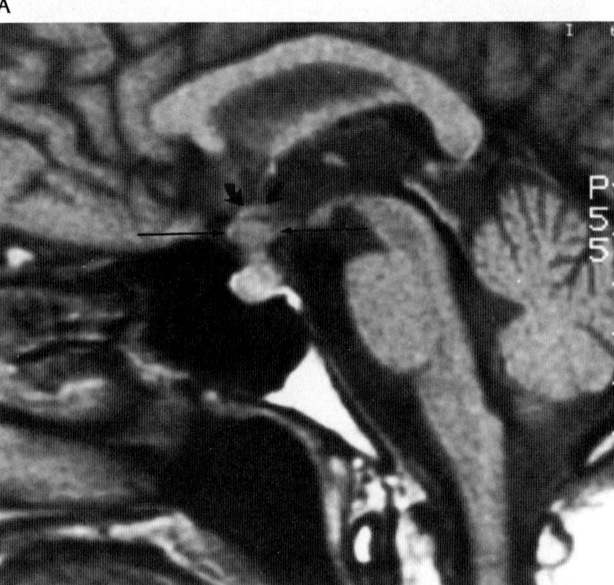

B

Figure 10-1 Lung carcinoma metastasis to the pituitary stalk. **A** and **B.** Coronal and sagittal MRI. T_1WI (SE 600/20) show a mass involving the pituitary stalk (long arrows). The optic chiasm is seen above the pituitary stalk mass (curved arrows). The patient presented clinically with diabetes insipidus.

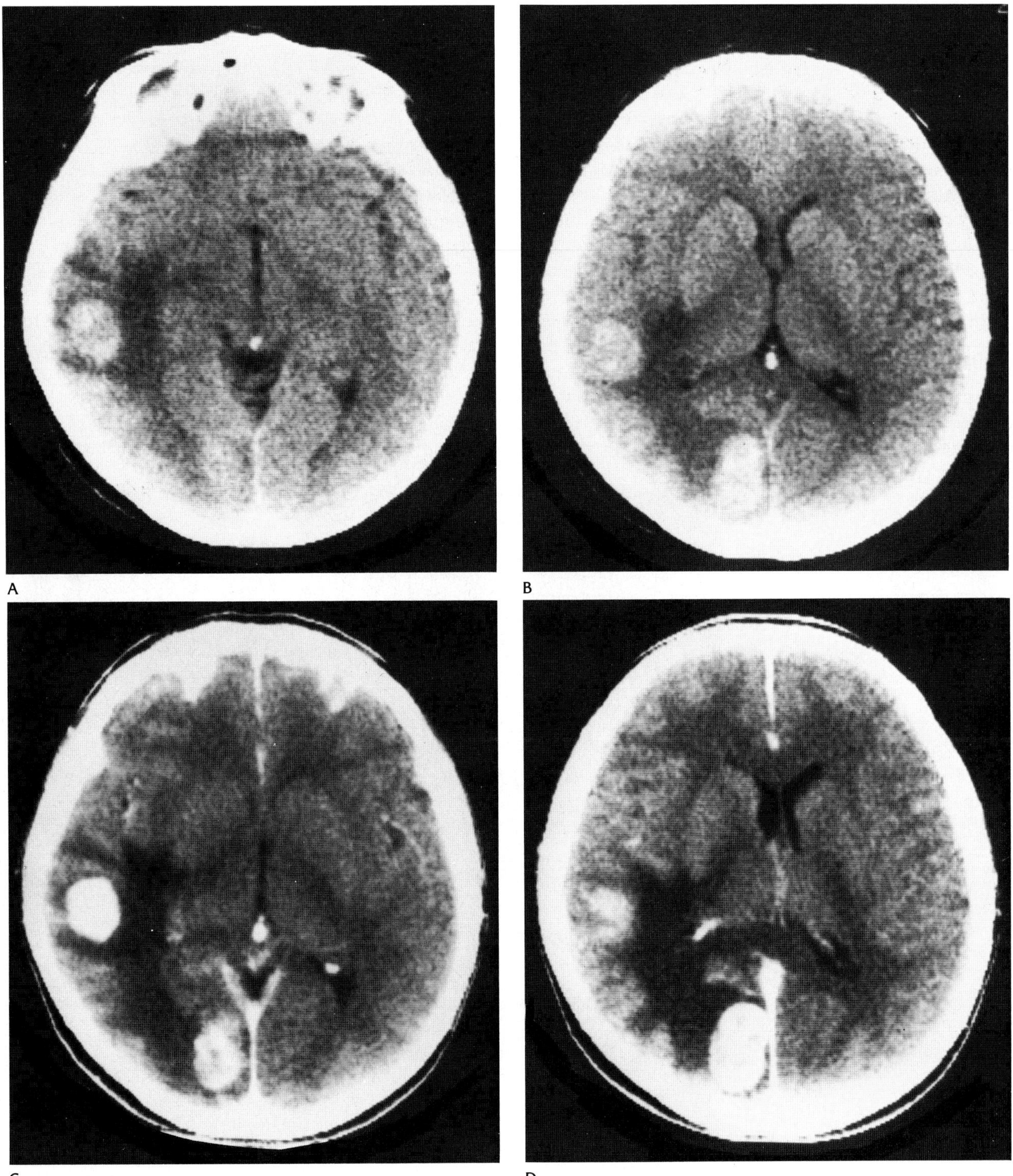

Figure 10-2 Colon carcinoma metastases. **A** and **B.** NCCT shows two hyperdense masses in the right posterior temporal and occipital lobes. There is surrounding hypodense white matter edema. **C** and **D.** CECT demonstrates that the lesions enhance homogeneously. White matter edema and mass effect with a slight midline shift to the left are apparent.

Different lesions from a single primary source may have both increased and decreased attentuation as a result of tumoral hemorrhage in some but not all of the lesions. This is frequently the case with melanoma. Variable densities may also be found in metastases from renal cell and lung carcinomas.

Finally, metastases may be isodense on NCCT. In these instances, their presence must be inferred from associated mass effect and edema. Lesions without a significant amount of surrounding edema can be extremely difficult to visualize without the use of contrast material. In addition, multiple bilateral lesions may exert equal "balanced" pressure, obscuring any apparent focal mass effect. Consequently, it is necessary to obtain a CECT study when one is searching for metastases, both to define the borders of the neoplasm from surrounding edema better and to detect lesions that are inapparent on NCCT.

Most metastases enhance after a standard dose of intravenous contrast (approximately 40 g of iodine), though in a number of cases additional lesions may be identified with delayed scans obtained about 1 hour to 1.5 hours after a high-dose contrast infusion (80 to 85 g of iodine) (Hayman 1980; Shalen 1981). Contrast enhancement occurs secondary to breakdown of the blood-brain barrier. (See Chap. 8.)

After contrast infusion, a metastasis may show diffuse, nodular, or ringlike enhancement. The ringlike enhancement is frequently thick, as opposed to the thin rim of enhancement more often seen surrounding an abscess. However, it is not always possible to differentiate a ring-enhancing metastasis from an abscess or a resolving hematoma on CT. Occasionally, delayed scans show permeation of contrast throughout the lesion in the case of a tumor but not in an abscess or hematoma. Regions of metastases that fail to enhance are related to central necrosis. Contrast may accumulate within a necrotic cystic cavity and produce a fluid-fluid level. Some metastases may have true nonnecrotic cystic components. These components typically are more sharply marginated than are regions of necrosis. Hemorrhagic fluid levels have been described in cystic renal cell carcinoma and other metastases (Kaiser 1983).

With its superior anatomic detail, multiplanar capability, and sensitivity for both intraparenchymal and extraax-

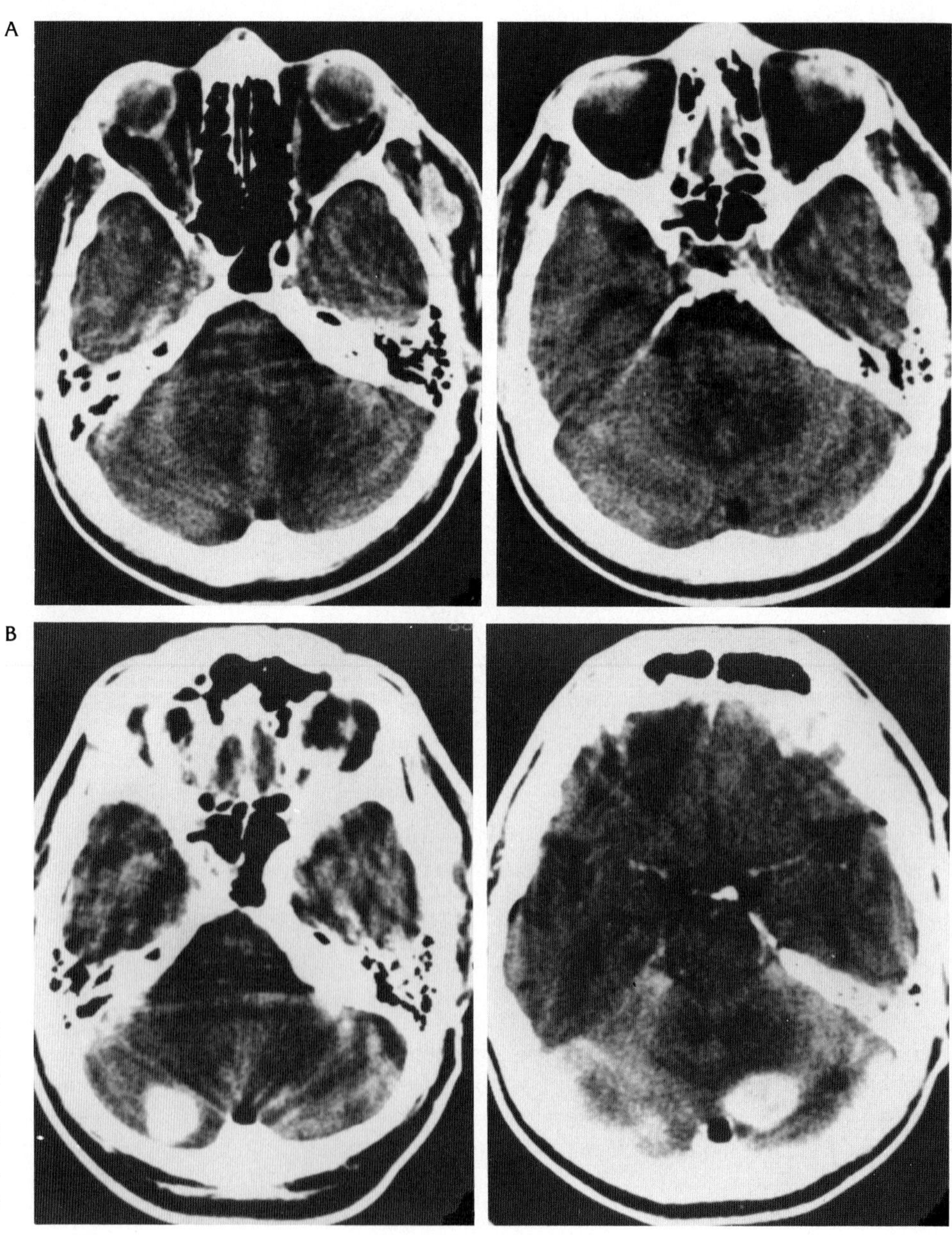

Figure 10-3 Melanoma metastases. **A** and **B.** CT without (**A**) and with (**B**) contrast shows two enhancing masses within the right and left cerebellar hemispheres, respectively. The metastases are isodense on the preinfusion scan. Notice that the masses "balance" each other so that there is no apparent mass effect. (*Continued on page 421.*)

ial lesions, MR is the procedure of choice for the detection and evaluation of intracranial metastases (Brant-Zawadzki 1984; Bradley 1984; Haughton 1986). Noncontrast MR (NCMR) can demonstrate tumors either directly or indirectly by anatomic distortion caused by the mass effect. Cystic components of tumors are readily detected and characterized on MR (Kjos 1985). Nonhemorrhagic metastatic lesions typically appear as masses that are subtly hypointense to isointense compared with white matter on spin-echo images obtained with a short repetition time (TR) (T_1WI). On long TR images (T_2WI), metastases are usually hyperintense. Surrounding perifocal edema may also be seen as regions of subtle hypointensity within the white matter on T_1WI and as regions of increased signal intensity on T_2WI. Lesions on NCMR are best detected on T_2WI, because these are most sensitive to subtle changes in brain water concentration.

While MR is very sensitive in detecting lesions, it is not always possible to distinguish metastatic deposits from regions of ischemic change, edema, and demyelination or from other benign lesions that have similar characteristics. A recent prospective blinded study of 75 patients with known systemic tumors showed that neither NCMR nor CECT was consistently superior in the detection of metastases (Sze 1988). While MR was superior to CT in demonstrating lesions in the posterior fossa or adjacent to the calvarium and in showing small punctate metastatic lesions, CECT occasionally demonstrated lesions that were difficult to detect on MR because they were nearly isointense to the adjacent brain parenchyma (Fig. 10-3).

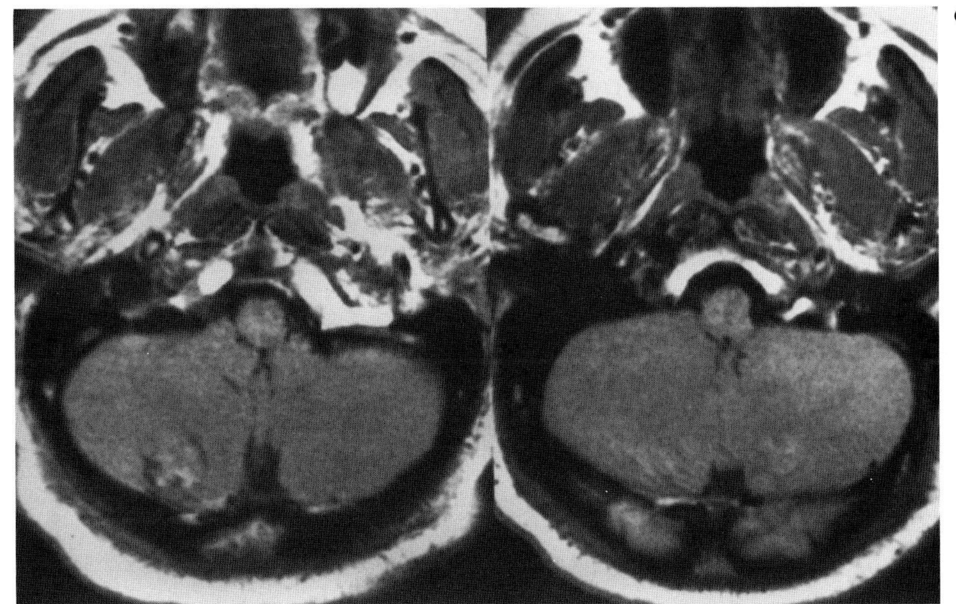
C

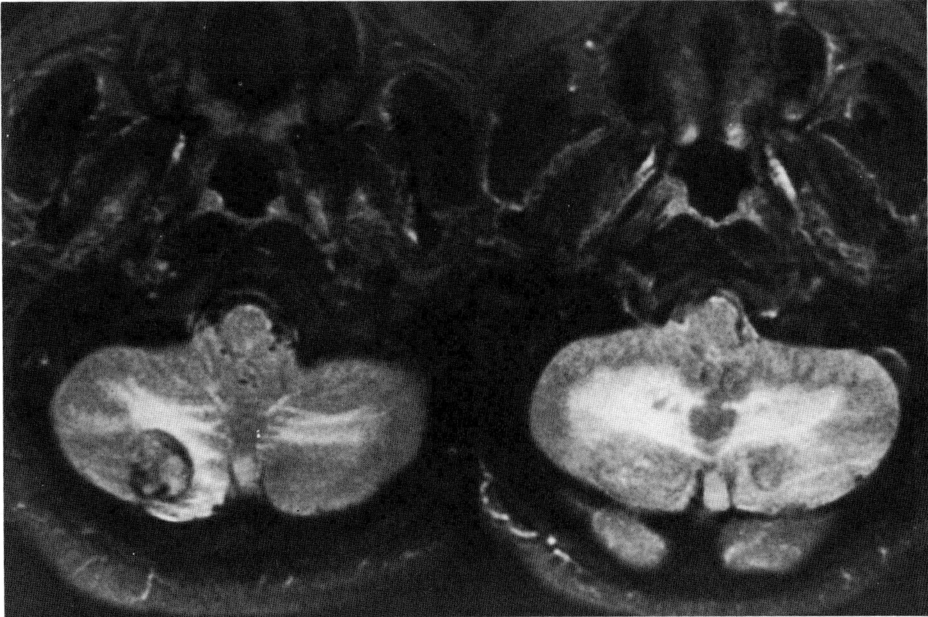
D

Figure 10-3 (continued) **C** and **D.** MRI. T_1WI (SE 600/20) (**C**) and T_2WI (SE 2000/70) (**D**) show that the right cerebellar lesion contains regions of hemorrhage that are not apparent on CT. There is surrounding hyperintense white matter edema on T_2WI. Only subtle heterogeneous signal intensity can be seen in the region of the left cerebellar metastasis that is easily identified on the CECT. (*Reprinted with permission from G Sze, Radiology 1988.*)

In addition, CECT better delineated lesions that were close to confluent surrounding edema and was superior to MR in differentiating infarct from neoplasm.

The use of the intravenous paramagnetic contrast agent gadopentetate dimeglumine (Gd-DTPA) combines the greater sensitivity of MR for lesion detection with the specificity for lesion characterization provided by CECT. For example, differentiation of tumor from adjacent tissues on NCMR is not always possible since tumor often cannot be clearly separated from edema on T_2WI (Graif 1985; Bydder 1984). Definition of the metastasis-edema margin is consistently possible, however, following Gd-DTPA administration (Felix 1985; Claussen 1985; Graif 1985). CEMR also improves the conspicuity of cerebral metastases (Russell 1987; Healy 1987), particularly in lesions that are nearly isointense to the brain parenchyma and in which there is little or no associated edema and in lesions that remain undetected on NCMR because of edema from adjacent lesions (Fig. 10-4). In addition, CEMR is superior to double-dose delayed CECT in detection of cerebral metastases (Davis 1991).

Surgical resection of a solitary brain metastasis often results in improvement in length of survival and functional independence (MacGee 1971; Sundaresan 1985; Magilligan 1986; Mandell 1986; Patchell 1986, 1990a). It is desirable to perform CEMR before undertaking surgical resection of a presumed solitary lesion to ensure that there are not small lesions that are not apparent on CT or NCMR. Care must be taken in interpreting punctate foci of enhancement in the basal ganglia or white matter in elderly patients as metastases, since these foci may represent subacute enhancing lacunar infarcts (Sze 1990*a*). If there is doubt about whether a punctate region of enhancement is a metastasis or a subacute lacunar infarct, a follow-up scan can help differentiate the two.

CEMR with short TR scans (T_1WI) is superior to NCMR with short TR (T_1WI) or long TR images (T_2WI) for lesion detection, particularly in metastases that are located in the posterior fossa or cortex (Sze 1990*c*). Delayed images obtained 20 to 30 minutes after contrast injection do not show a consistent advantage over those obtained immediately after contrast infusion, though in some cases me-

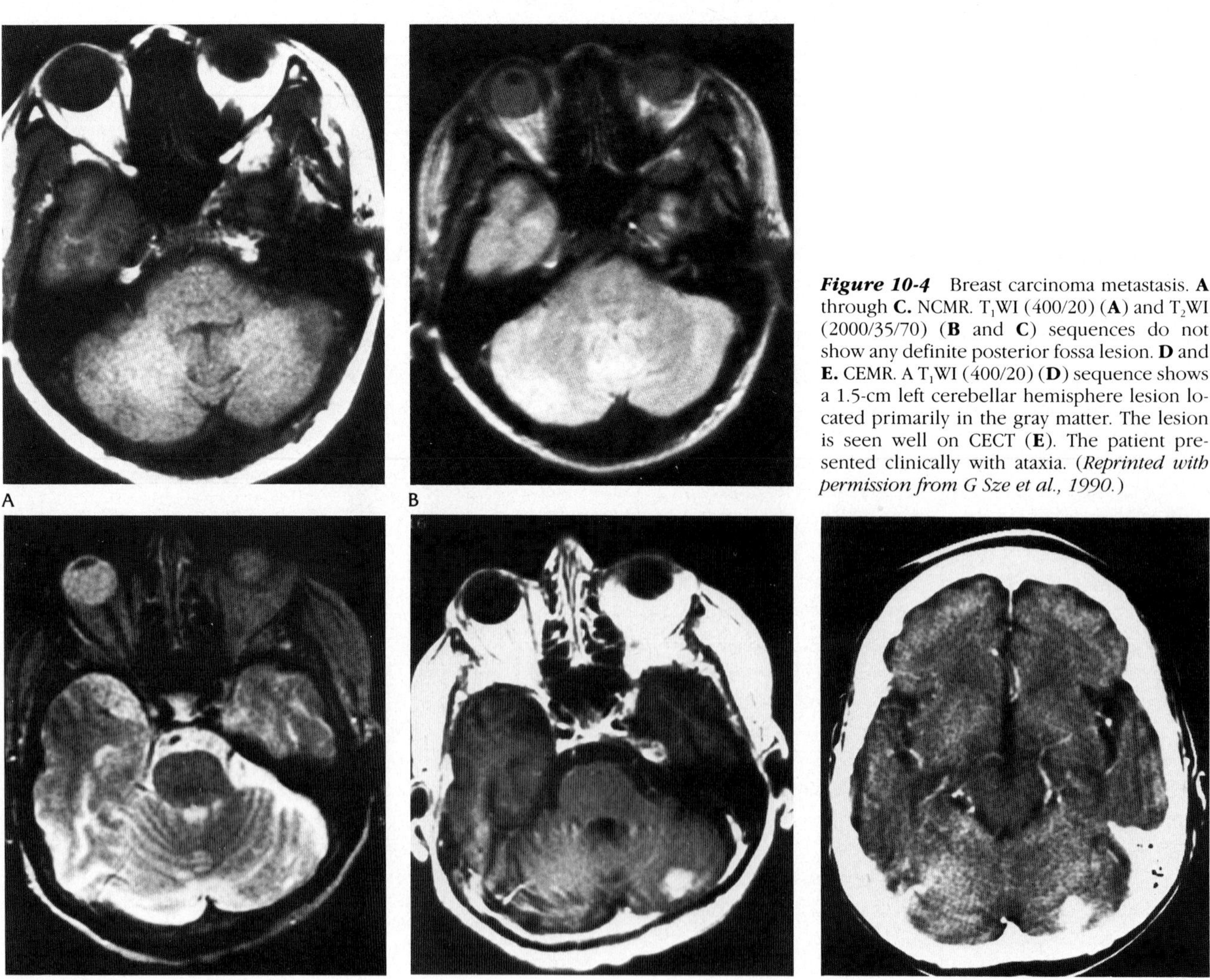

Figure 10-4 Breast carcinoma metastasis. **A** through **C.** NCMR. T_1WI (400/20) (**A**) and T_2WI (2000/35/70) (**B** and **C**) sequences do not show any definite posterior fossa lesion. **D** and **E.** CEMR. A T_1WI (400/20) (**D**) sequence shows a 1.5-cm left cerebellar hemisphere lesion located primarily in the gray matter. The lesion is seen well on CECT (**E**). The patient presented clinically with ataxia. (*Reprinted with permission from G Sze et al., 1990.*)

tastases are better seen on delayed postcontrast MR scans (Sze 1990*a,b*). Delayed CEMR may also help to better define the lesions (Sze 1990*a*). Consequently, in the workup of metastatic disease an examination might start with a noncontrast T_1WI. Afetr contrast injection, obtaining a long TR double echo (proton density and T_2-weighted) sequence followed by a short TR (T_1-weighted) sequence is suggested to provide a delay time. As with CT, MR contrast enhancement occurs in regions of breakdown of the blood-brain barrier. Unlike iodinated contrast, in which enhancement is related to attenuation of the x-ray beam by iodine, Gd-DTPA contrast enhancement is related to shortening of the T_1 relaxation time. The size of the Gd-DTPA molecule is similar to that of the iodinated contrast molecule. Consequently, patterns of enhancement after Gd-DTPA injection are similar to those observed on CT. While the usual dose of Gd-DTPA is 0.1 mmol/kg, in some selected cases a higher dose (0.2 mmol/kg) may improve tumor visualization (Niendorf 1987) (See Chap. 8.). Also, delayed double-dose CEMR has been suggested to enhance detection of tumors (Haustein 1990).

Two subcategories of intraparenchymal metastases deserve special attention. Both hemorrhagic metastases and melanoma in the absence of hemorrhage can have a characteristic MR appearance. A number of metastatic lesions have a tendency to hemorrhage; these lesions include metastases from melanoma, renal cell carcinoma, choriocarcinoma, and thyroid carcinoma (Fig. 10-5) (Weisberg 1985*b*; Mandybur 1977). While metastases from bronchogenic carcinoma do not have a high propensity to hemorrhage, hemorrhagic lesions may be seen because lung carcinoma metastases are so frequently encountered.

Hemorrhagic metastases may present clinically with the sudden onset of a neurological deficit caused by acute hemorrhage (Gildersleeve 1977; Mandybur 1977; Weir 1978; Little 1979; Bitoh 1984; van den Doel 1985; Weisberg 1985). CT typically shows a hyperdense lesion secondary to hemorrhage. A hypodense rim of vasogenic edema usually surrounds the hemorrhagic metastasis. After contrast injection, there may be nodular, ringlike, or diffuse enhancement. CT features that aid in distinguishing hemorrhagic metastatic lesions from simple hemorrhage include (1) hemorrhage in association with a mass of lower density, (2) atypical location of a hemorrhage, (3) ring enhancement around a lesion at a time when interval enhancement around a hematoma would not be expected, and (4) a multiplicity of hemorrhagic lesions (Gildersleeve 1977).

MR is uniquely suited for the evaluation of hemorrhagic metastases because of its sensitivity for detecting hemorrhage and evaluating hemoglobin breakdown products. Simple intracerebral hemorrhage normally follows a complex but orderly progression of evolutionary

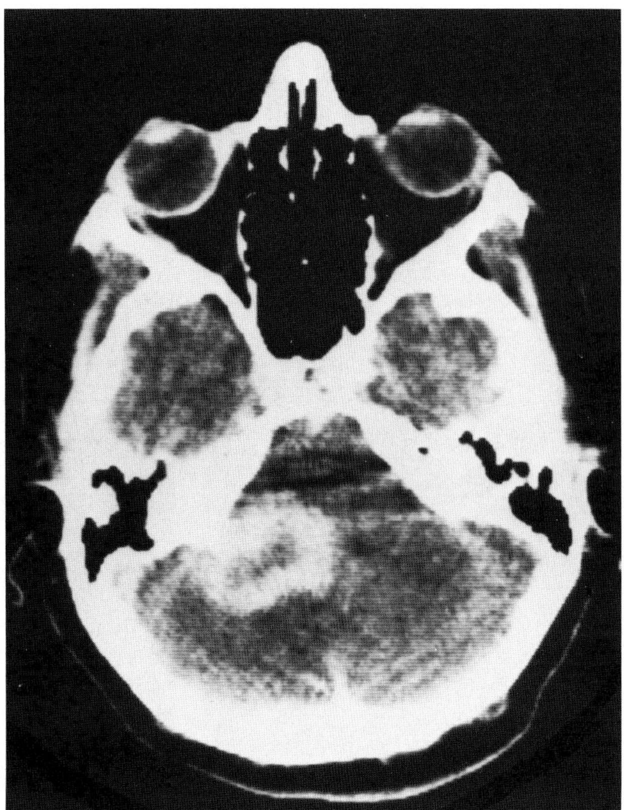
A

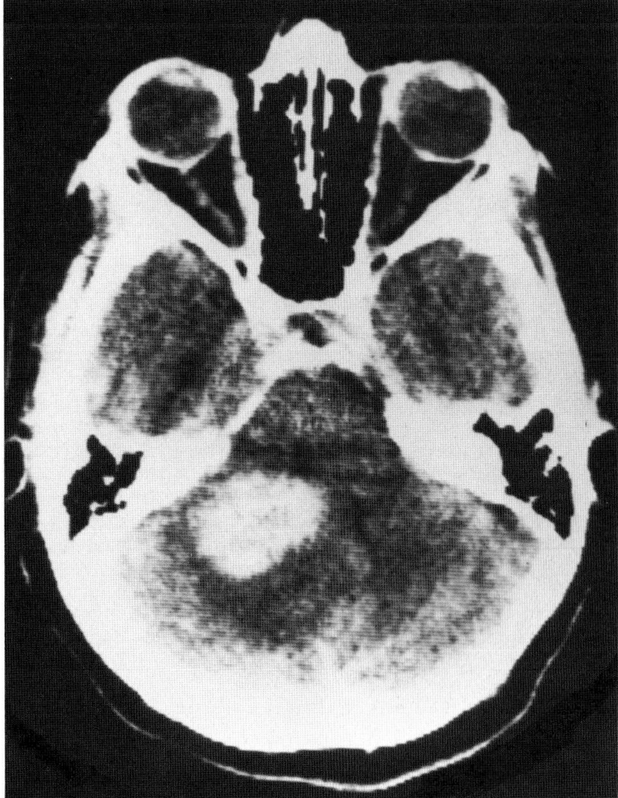
B

Figure 10-5 Renal cell carcinoma metastasis. **A** and **B.** NCCT shows a hyperdense mass within the right cerebellar hemisphere. There is a small amount of surrounding hypodensity representing edema. The mass proved to be grossly hemorrhagic at pathology.

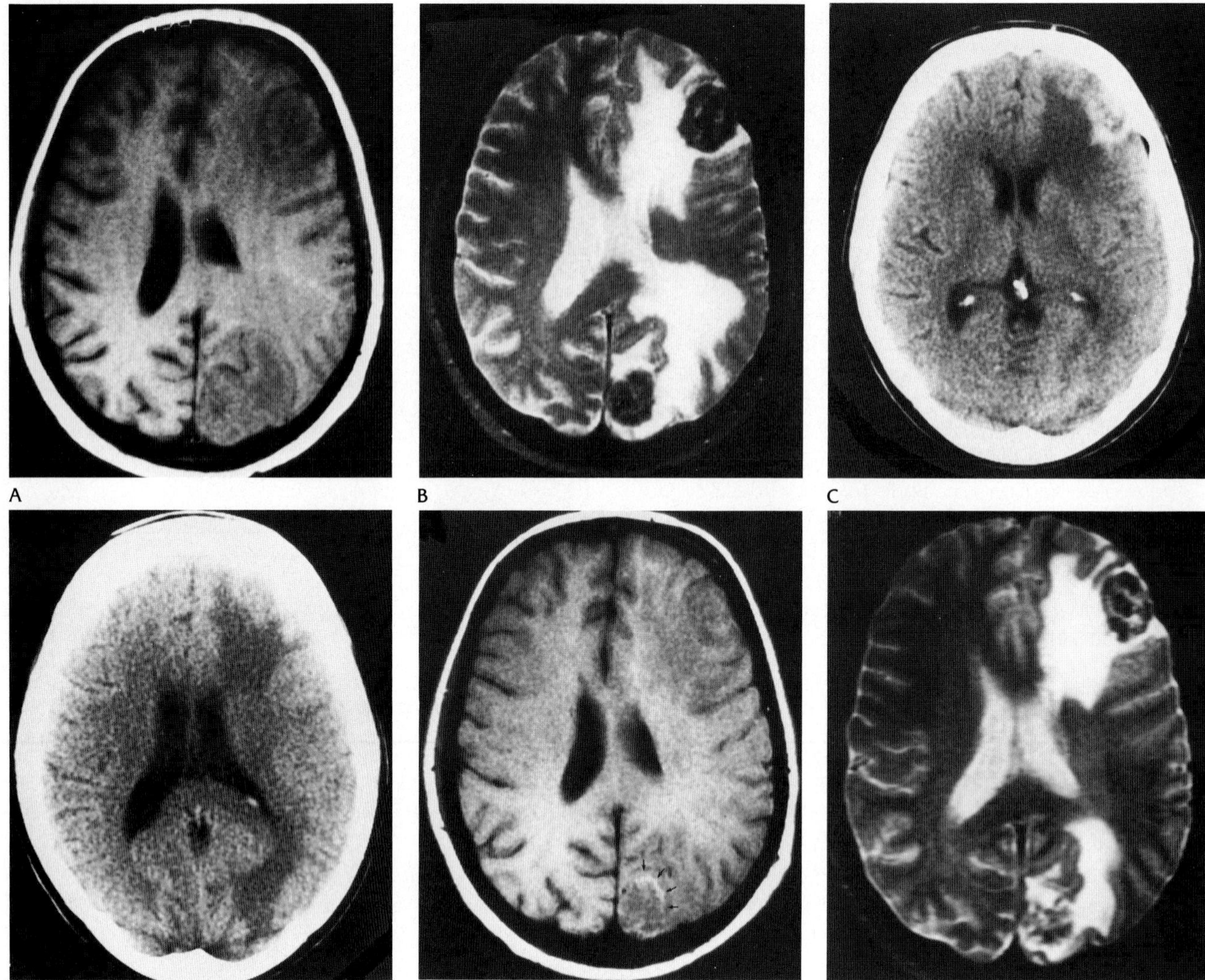

Figure 10-6 Hemorrhagic metastases from colon carcinoma showing delayed evolution of hemorrhage. **A** and **B.** The initial MR examination demonstrates mildly hypointense lesions within the left frontal and left occipital lobes on T_1WI (SE 600/20) (**A**) that become markedly hypointense on T_2WI (SE 2000) (**B**). Note the extensive surrounding hyperintense white matter edema on T_2WI (**B**). A portion of what appeared to be the left occipital mass on T_1WI (**A**) was actually due to edema within the adjacent white matter. **C** and **D.** CT without contrast obtained approximately 1 month after the initial MR study shows a nonhomogeneous hyperdense left frontal lesion consistent with hemorrhage. There is surrounding hypodensity representing edema. The left occipital lesion is essentially isodense compared with the brain parenchyma, but mass effect with surrounding edema is present. The hemorrhagic nature of these metastases is more easily recognized on MR. **E** and **F.** Five months after the initial MR examination, T_1WI (SE 800/20) (**E**) again shows subtle hypointense masses within the left frontal and occipital lobes. There is minimal hyperintensity at the peripheral aspect of the left occipital lesion (arrows). On T_2WI (SE 2000/70) (**F**), the metastases are still predominantly hypointense but now contain irregular central regions of hyperintensity. Hyperintense white matter edema is again apparent.

changes in signal intensity on MR that are related to the metabolism of hemoglobin, clot retraction, changes in protein concentration, red cell lysis, and the accumulation of water in a hematoma (Bradley 1985; Gomori 1985, 1987; Di Chiro 1986; Zimmerman 1988; Hayman 1989*a,b*). A simple intracerebral hemorrhage less than 24 hours old may have subtle increased signal intensity on T_1WI and moderate to marked increased signal intensity on T_2WI. In hematomas between 1 and 3 days old, the metabolism of oxyhemoglobin into deoxyhemoglobin within intact red blood cells and clot retraction cause decreased signal intensity; this is particularly notable on T_2WI because of the shortening of the T_2 relaxation time. This decreased signal intensity is due to the heterogeneous distribution of paramagnetic substances (deoxyhemoglobin and methemoglobin) that are concentrated within red blood cells but absent in the extracellular space, causing local variations in the magnetic field (mag-

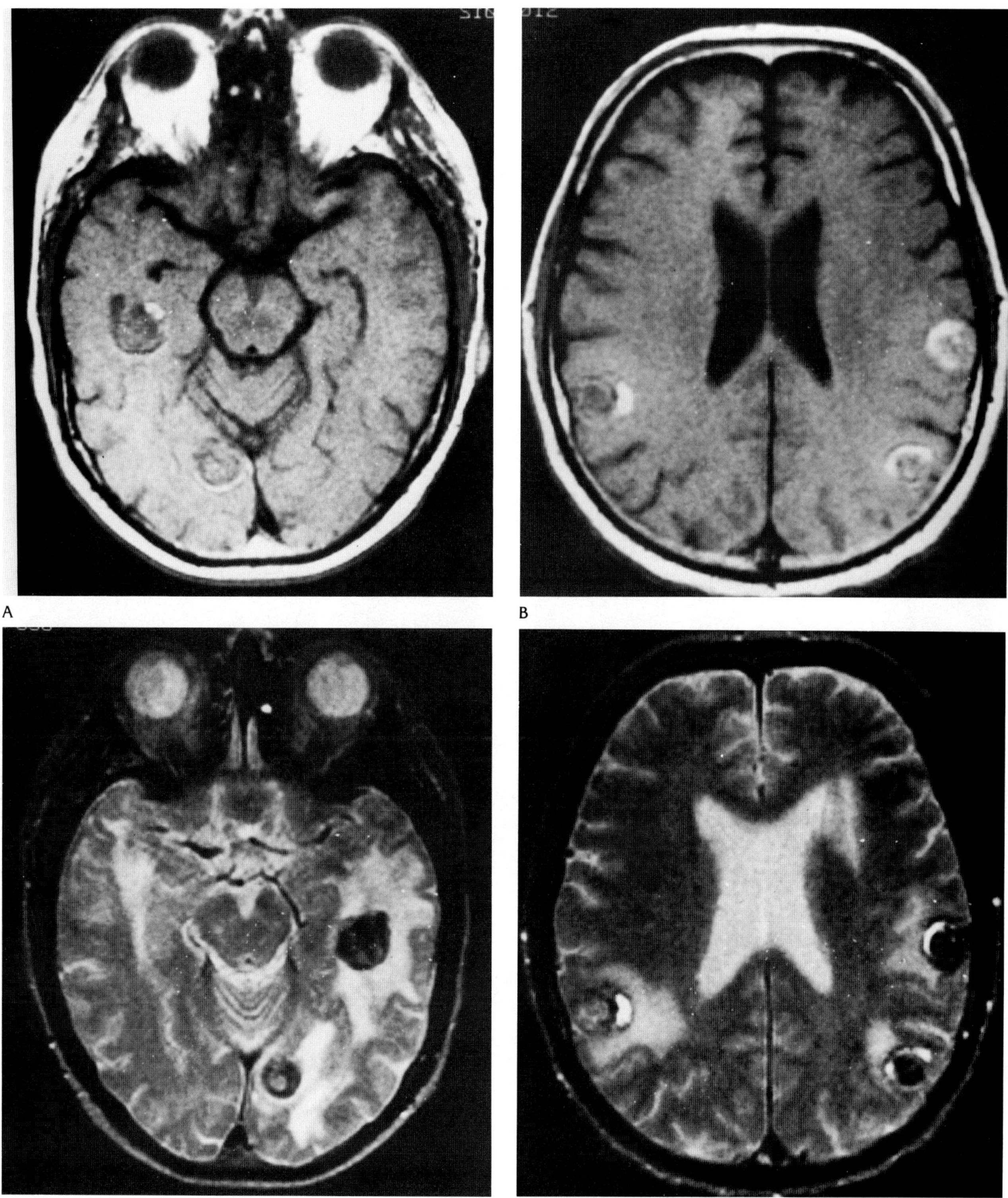

Figure 10-7 Melanoma metastases. **A** and **B.** T_1WI (SE 600/20) show multiple heterogeneous metastases with regions of decreased and increased signal intensity. **C** and **D.** On comparable T_2WI (SE 2000/80), the lesions become predominantly markedly hypointense. Small regions of hyperintensity are seen, especially at the peripheral aspect of the lesions. The appearance is consistent with multiple hemorrhagic metastases with hemorrhage of variable age. Hyperintense white matter edema is seen surrounding the metastases.

netic susceptibility effects), and an increase in protein concentration with decreased free water that occurs with clot retraction. Methemoglobin, which forms after approximately 3 to 4 days, causes selective shortening of the T_1 relaxation time and hence increased signal intensity on T_1WI. This increased signal intensity on T_1WI typically lasts for months. As red cell lysis occurs and water accumulates in the hematoma, increased signal intensity also develops on T_2WI. The final hemoglobin breakdown product—hemosiderin—is deposited in macrophages and typically appears as a ring of decreased signal intensity on both T_1WI and T_2WI, again as a result of magnetic susceptibility effects.

A number of MR features of hemorrhagic metastases distinguish these metastases from simple hematomas (Atlas 1987*a*). On spin-echo MR imaging tumors may have a prolonged phase of decreased signal intensity on T_2WI (Fig. 10-6). This is secondary to the persistent presence of deoxyhemoglobin, perhaps related to continued oozing of blood from the lesion or rapid reabsorption of hemoglobin breakdown products before methemoglobin can form (Atlas 1987*a*; Destian 1988). Unlike nonneoplastic bleeds, hemorrhagic tumors can demonstrate persistent hypointensity for weeks or even months. In addition, because of multiple episodes of bleeding, a heterogeneous appearance of a tumor hemorrhage is also common, with the simultaneous occurrence of multiple hemoglobin breakdown products from hemorrhages of different ages in the same lesion (Fig. 10-7). Thus, a metastatic lesion may have regions of fairly acute hypointense blood superimposed on regions of subacute hyperintense blood and chronic hypointense rims of hemosiderin deposition (Destian 1988). The complete hemosiderin rim that is characteristic of chronic nonneoplastic hematomas may be seen with metastatic lesions but is often diminished. Areas of abnormal soft tissue signal are sometimes seen corresponding to nonhemorrhagic tumor tissue. CEMR may be expected to show regions of nodular or ringlike enhancement, as are found on CECT. If the lesions are predominantly hypointense, contrast can enhance the nodules of a tumor in a very diagnostic fashion, although enhancement is not always visible in a hemorrhagic metastasis. Gradient-recalled echo acquisition techniques may be used adjunctively

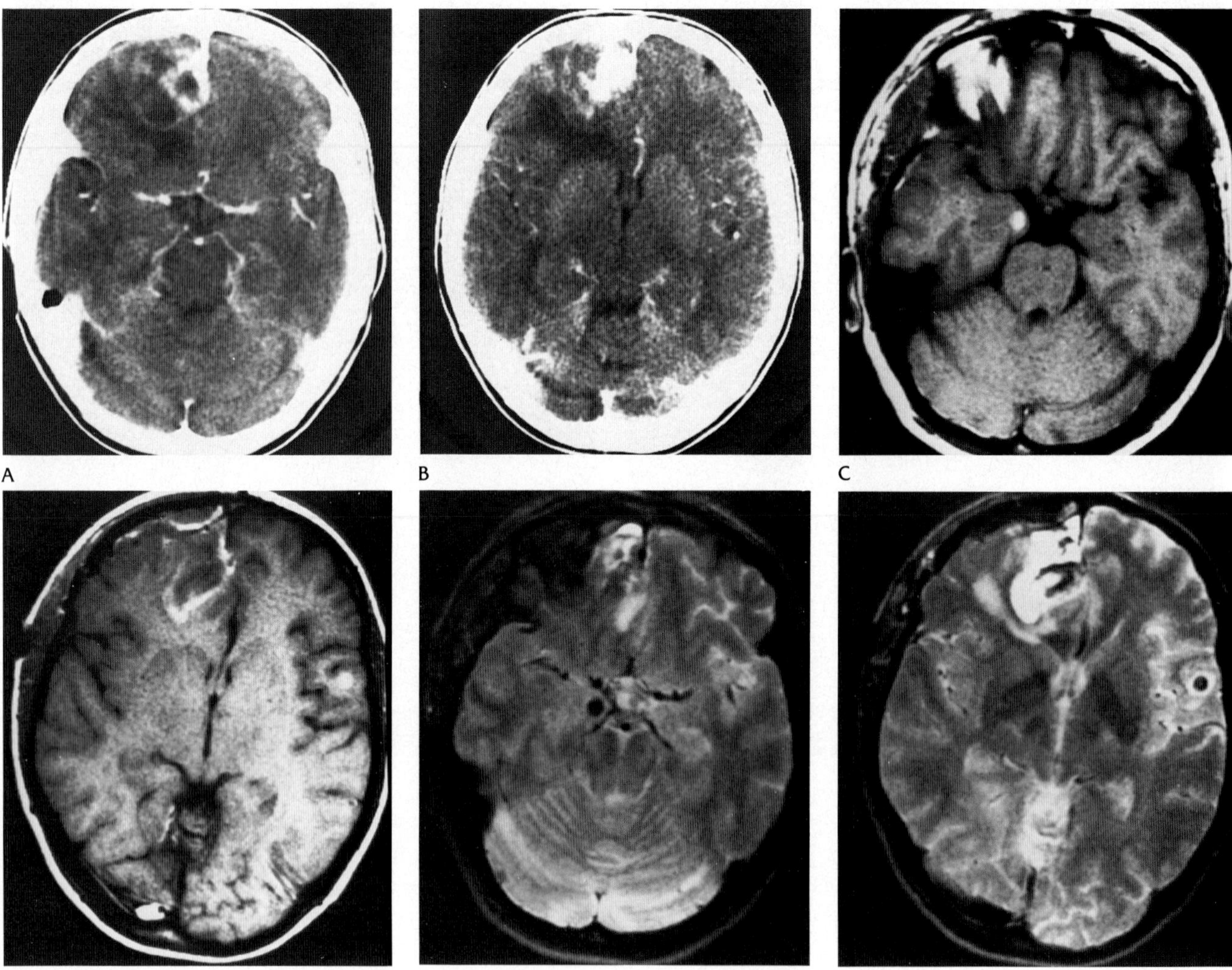

Figure 10-8 Metastatic melanoma. **A** and **B.** CECT scans are normal, except for very recent postoperative changes in the right frontal lobe for removal of a large metastasis. **C** through **F.** NCMR. T_1WI (SE 600/20) (**C** and **D**) and T_2WI (SE 2000/70) (**E** and **F**) reveal multiple small hemorrhagic metastases in addition to the region of recent operation. (*Reprinted with permission from G Sze, Radiology 1988.*)

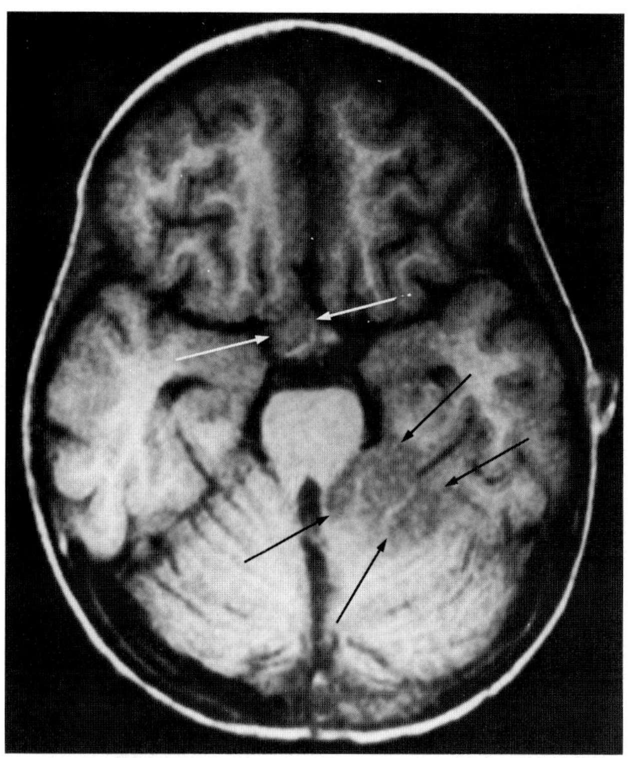

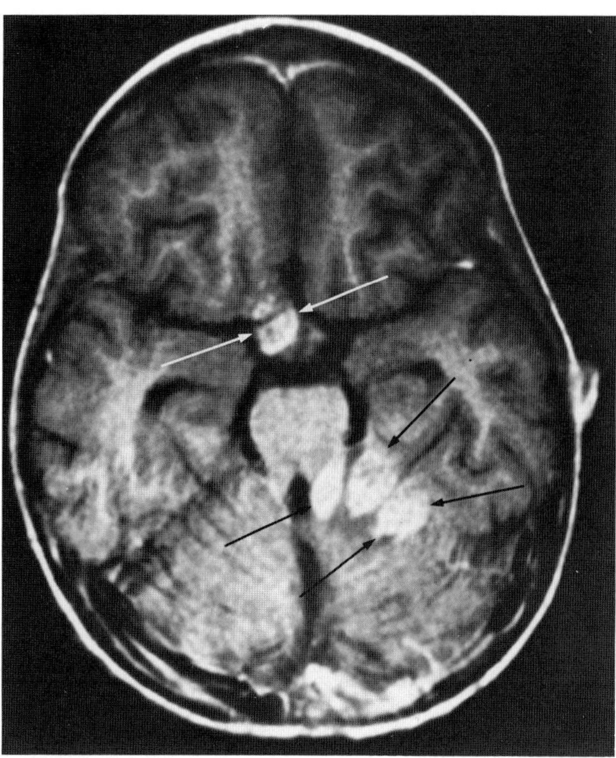

A B

Figure 10-9 **A.** Medulloblastoma with subarachnoid seeding NCMR. T_1WI (SE 600/20) shows a mass within the suprasellar cistern (white arrows). Subtle hypointense subarachnoid deposits are also seen along the left tentorial edge (black arrows). **B.** CEMR. T_2WI (SE 600/20) shows enhancement of the subarachnoid metastases within the suprasellar cistern and left cerebellar sulci (arrows).

with routine spin-echo MR imaging in evaluating hemorrhagic metastases as a result of the increased sensitivity of gradient-echo imaging in detecting hemorrhage (Atlas 1988).

Malignant melanoma metastases may also be uniquely characterized by MR; this is related not only to the propensity of a melanoma to hemorrhage but also to the inherent paramagnetic effects of melanin, which may be related to stable free radicals (Woodruff 1987; Atlas 1987*b*). On NCCT melanoma has a variable appearance that depends on the presence or absence of hemorrhage, with decreased, mixed, or increased density (Enzmann 1978; Ginaldi 1981; Holtas 1981). Contrast enhancement is usually homogeneous, though ringlike enhancement does occur (Weisberg 1985*a*). While the signal characteristics of melanoma on NCMR are also predominantly related to the presence or absence of hemorrhage (Fig. 10-8), one may be able to differentiate nonhemorrhagic melanotic melanoma, nonhemorrhagic amelanotic melanoma, and hemorrhagic melanoma on the basis of signal intensity patterns (Atlas 1987*b*). Nonhemorrhagic melanotic melanoma is hyperintense on T_1-WI and mildly hypointense or isointense on T_2WI. Nonhemorrhagic amelanotic melanoma is mildly hypointense or isointense on T_1WI and mildly hyperintense or isointense on T_2WI. The signal intensity of hemorrhagic melanoma depends on the age of the hemorrhage. As with CT, homogeneous enhancement is usually seen after MR contrast administration.

Another tumor that may have an unusual MR appearance is gastrointestinal carcinoma. Gastrointestinal adenocarcinoma metastatic to the brain may be hypointense and/or isointense on T_1WI and hypointensity on T_2WI. These are mucinous adenocarcinomas without blood or increased iron deposition histologically. This low signal intensity on T_2WI may be related to the high protein content within the lesion (Egelhoff 1990).

LEPTOMENINGEAL METASTASES

Leptomeningeal metastases have been estimated to account for 8 to 10 percent of intracranial metastatic disease (Posner 1978; Lee 1984). A patient with leptomeningeal carcinomatosis often has neurological symptoms more widespread than can be accounted for by the presence of a single lesion (Posner 1979). Furthermore, signs demonstrable on neurological examination are often more numerous than the patient's symptomatology would indicate (Wasserstrom 1982). This results from the widespread distribution of tumor cells throughout the CSF. Focal symptoms occur as a result of cell proliferation at multiple locations.

Tumor most often spreads to the leptomeninges through thin-walled meningeal vessels, with subsequent

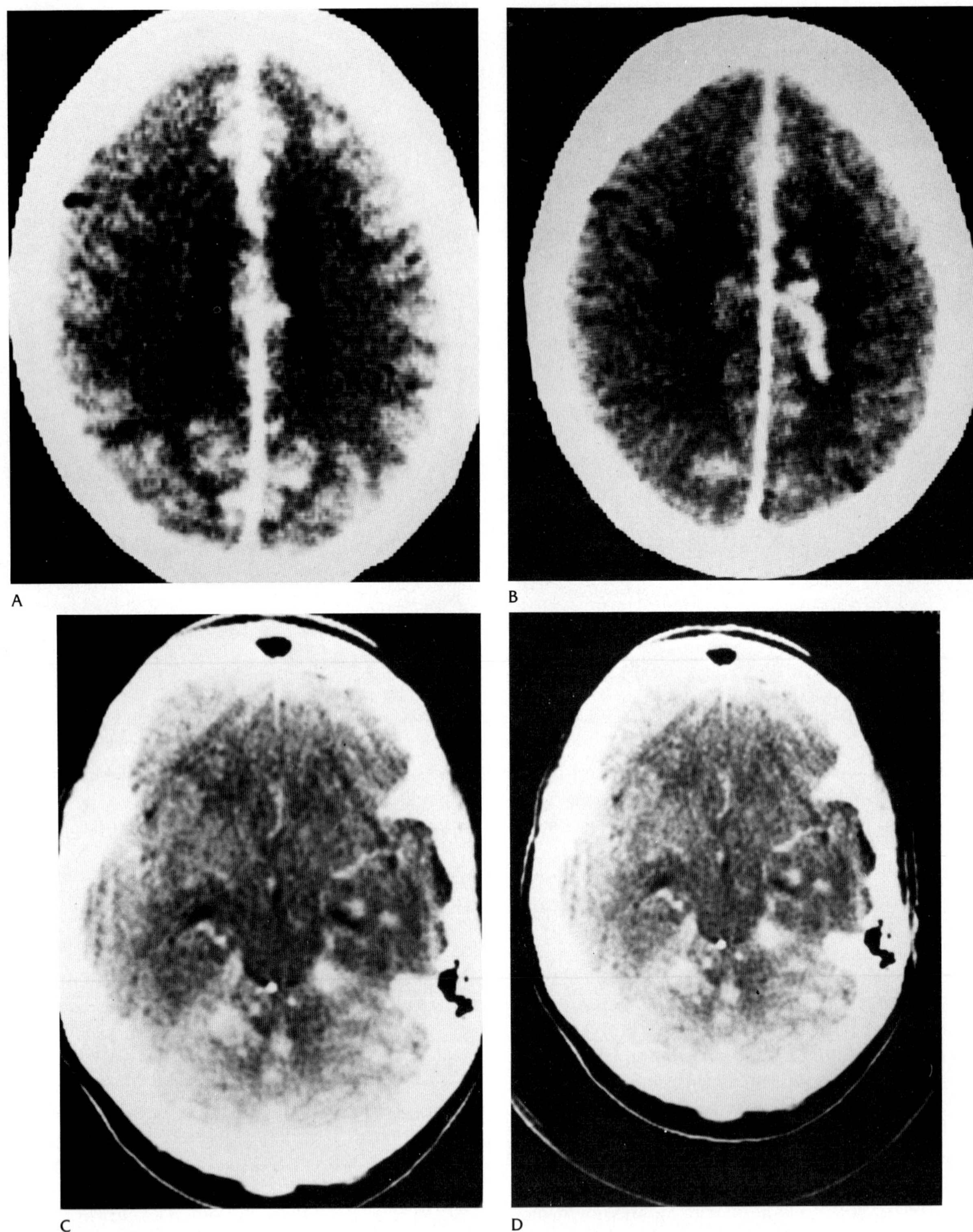

Figure 10-10 Leptomeningeal carcinomatosis. **A** and **B.** CECT from primary lung carcinoma. Intense irregular enhancement over the convexity is not as well appreciated as the interhemispheric fissure CE. **C** and **D.** CECT. Multiple irregular nodular lesions along the tentorium cerebelli represent widespread metastases.

dissemination into the subarachnoid space (Wasserstrom 1982; Fischer-Williams 1955). Direct leptomeningeal invasion of tumor from adjacent structures can occur, as in a superficially placed parenchymal tumor, but is less common owing to a fibrotic meningeal reaction that walls off tumor, preventing its dissemination within the subarachnoid space.

Primary CNS tumors associated with leptomeningeal

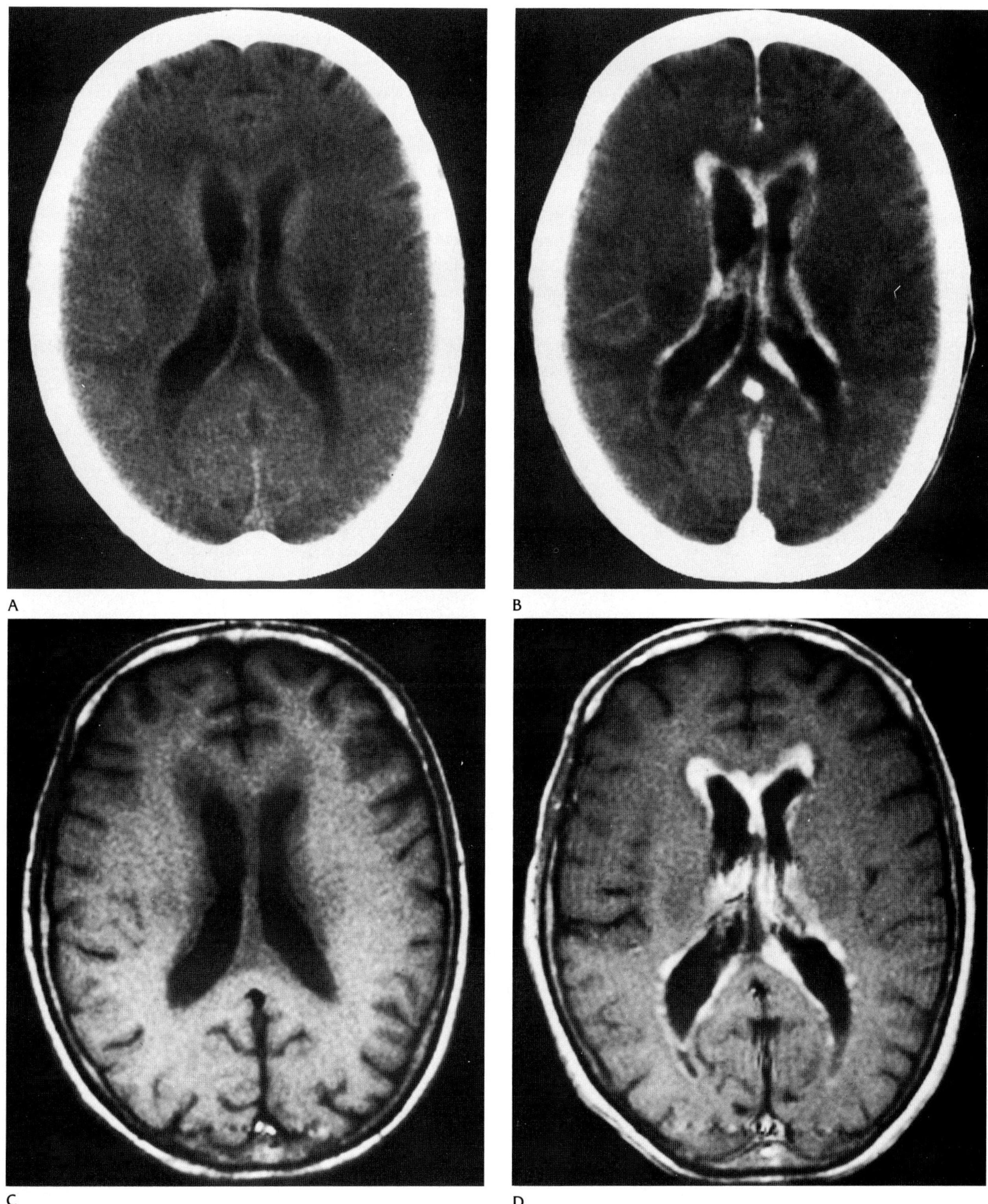

Figure 10-11 Lymphoma leptomeningeal metastases. **A** and **B.** CT obtained without (**A**) and with (**B**) contrast demonstrates slightly irregular diffuse enhancing subependymal metastases along the ventricular margins. **C** and **D.** MR. T_1WI (SE 600/20) obtained before (**C**) and after (**D**) the injection of Gd-DTPA also demonstrate enhancing subependymal lymphoma.

tumor spread include medulloblastoma, ependymoma, pineoblastoma, and retinoblastoma (Fig. 10-9) (Nadich 1984; Rippe 1990; Mackay 1984). Spread occurs through dissemination of cells in the subarachnoid space. Glioblastomas may infrequently disseminate in the subarachnoid space. Among systemic tumors, carcinomatous meningitis most commonly arises from lymphoma, leukemia, and melanoma, followed by breast and lung carcinoma (Lee 1984). In a patient with lymphoma, leptomeningeal tumor spread usually is from non-Hodgkin's lymphoma; intracranial Hodgkin's disease is rare (Sapozink 1983).

With leptomeningeal metastases NCCT may demonstrate obliteration of the subarachnoid space, basal cisterns, and sulci. After contrast infusion there may be sulcal-cisternal enhancement (Lee 1984; Ito 1986), especially in the basal cisterns, in the sylvian fissures, and along the high-convexity cortical sulci (Fig. 10-10). Tentorial enhancement can also occur. The enhancement can be diffuse or localized. Since the tentorium normally enhances, enhancement should be considered significant only if it occurs over a widened area or is irregular in configuration (Fig. 10-10). Within the ventricles, there may be ependymal or subependymal enhancement in a diffuse or a nodular pattern. This appearance is particularly characteristic of lymphoma (Fig. 10-11) (Dubois 1978). Leptomeningeal enhancement is not specific for meningeal carcinomatosis, and infectious and inflammatory processes or ischemic change may mimic meningeal metastases. Enhancement due to periventricular tumor spread must be differentiated clinically from ventriculitis.

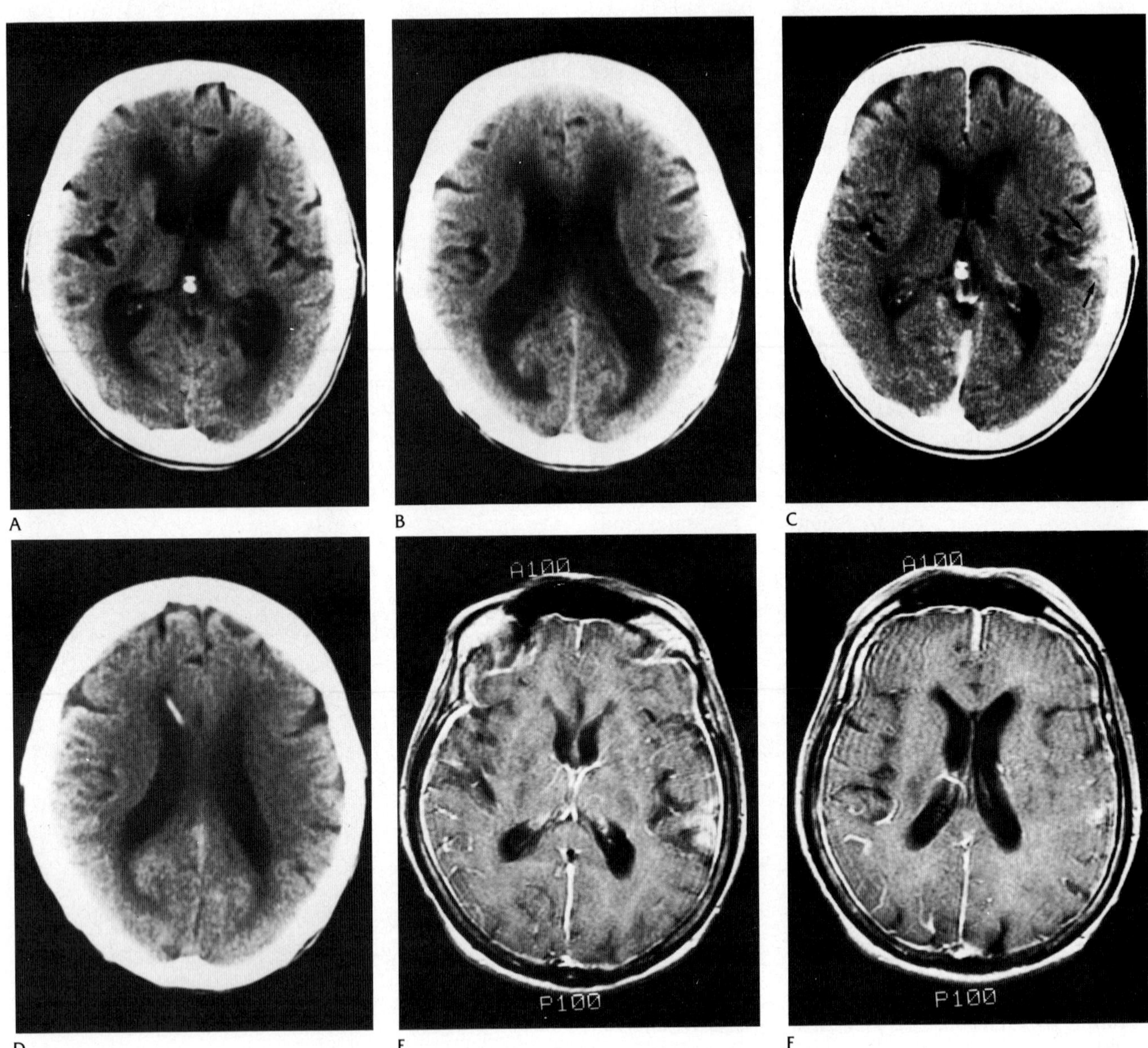

Figure 10-12 Leptomeningeal carcinomatosis from breast carcinoma. **A** and **B.** NCCT demonstrate moderate ventriculomegaly with paraventricular hypodensity suggestive of communicating hydrocephalus. **C.** CECT at slightly lower level shows gyral enhancement in the left frontoparietal cortex (arrows). **D.** NCCT after shunting reveals normal-sized ventricles with decreased periventricular CSF transgression. **E** and **F.** CEMR sho extensive leptominengeal CE and focal gyral involvement (arrows). Ventricles are normal in size after shunting.

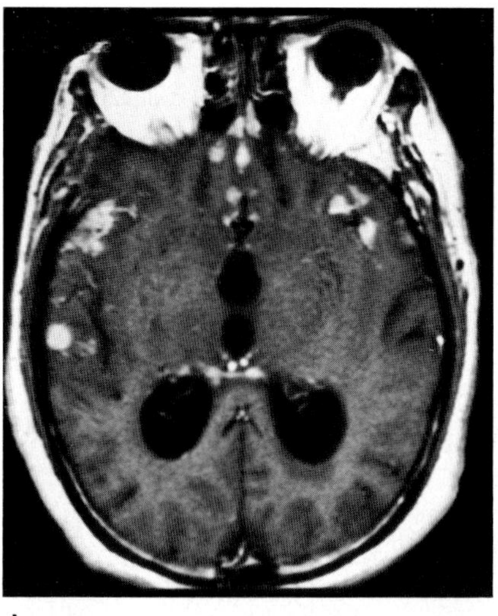
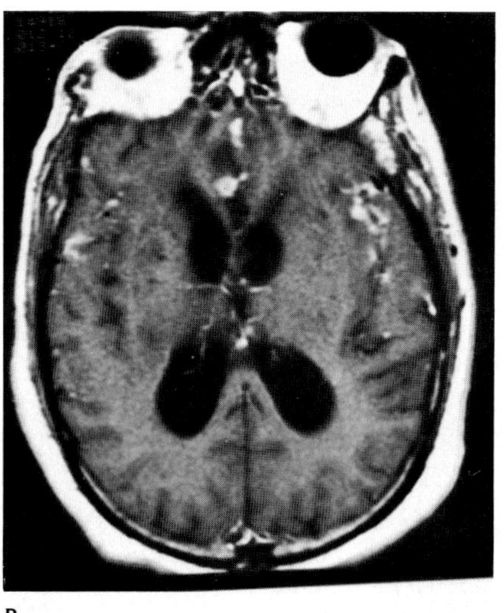
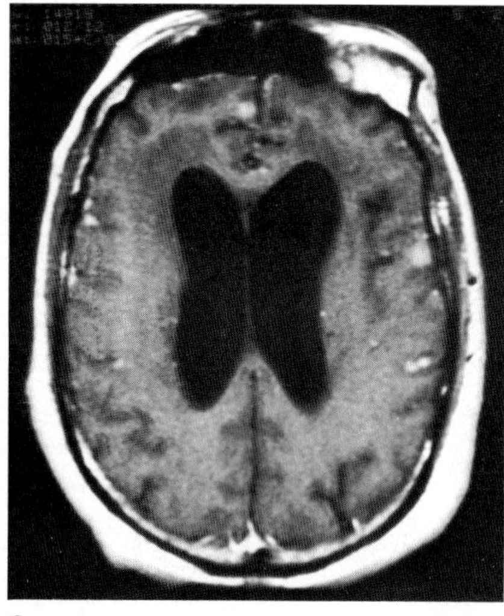

A B C

Figure 10-13 Leptomeningeal metastases from melanoma. **A, B,** and **C.** CEMR demonstrate multiple nodular lesions of varying sizes in the subarachnoid cisterns. Note mild hydrocephalus also. NCMR (not shown) revealed no discernible nodules on both T_1WI and T_2WI obscured by CSF intensity.

Communicating hydrocephalus with or without leptomeningeal enhancement is the second most common abnormality found on CT after sulcal-cisternal enhancement (Lee 1984). Leptomeningeal disease impairs the reabsorption of CSF, resulting in mild to moderate symmetrical dilatation of the ventricular system with the subsequent development of increased intracranial pressure. Leptomeningeal metastases should be strongly considered in any patient with a systemic neoplasm who has communicating hydrocephalus on CT and MRI (Fig. 10-12). Lumbar puncture may be required in making the diagnosis; repeated CSF examinations may be necessary.

NCMR is relatively insensitive in detecting leptomeningeal metastases, though leptomeningeal disease is sometimes found on unenhanced scans. Regions of sulcal, cisternal, or subependymal enhancement found on CECT may remain undetected on NCMR (Krol 1988; Davis 1987). Abnormal leptomeningeal enhancement is, however, found after contrast injection. CEMR is more sensitive than CECT is for the detection of leptomeningeal metastases (Fig. 10-12) (Sze 1989; Rippe 1990; Frank 1988). On MR, as on CT, meningeal enhancement is often seen within the basal cisterns, sylvian fissures, and cortical sulci, and along the tentorium (Fig. 10-12). Meningeal enhancement in carcinomatosis tends to show a nodular pattern (Fig. 10-13), whereas a diffuse linear pattern is commonly present with inflammatory conditions (Phillips 1990). Less frequently, leptomeningeal metastases present as loculated and isolated lesions (Lee 1990). Enhancing subependymal metastases may also be found. Diffuse meningeal enhancement applied to the inner table of the skull, while not apparent on CECT, is frequently seen (Fig. 10-12) (Sze 1989). However, the presence of contrast enhancement does not necessarily indicate the presence of tumor, because reactive meningeal enhancement related to other causes, such as prior craniotomy, shunt placement, extraaxial fluid collections, and prior intrathecal chemotherapy, or radiotherapy, may appear identical to meningeal tumor spread. Conversely, the absence of contrast enhancement does not exclude the possibility of leptomeningeal metastases. In some cases of recurrent medulloblastoma, subependymal metastases that do not enhance may be shown on T_2WI but not on CEMR (Rollins, 1990).

CALVARIAL, SKULL BASE, AND DURAL METASTASES

Metastases to the skull or dura may occur from a variety of tumors. In adults, metastases from carcinoma of the lung, breast, and prostate are common. In the pediatric age group, neuroblastoma or sarcomas are more often seen (Posner 1978; Healy 1981).

Unless they are very aggressive, metastatic tumors generally do not transgress dural boundaries. Consequently, calvarial and epidural metastases do not usually involve the brain parenchyma (Posner 1978). Similarly, metastases generally do not cross the falx to invade the contralateral hemisphere.

Dural-based metastases, as can be found in prostate carcinoma, are easily recognized on CECT or MR (Fig. 10-14). Metastatic disease to the dura must be differentiated from the normal enhancement of the falx and tentorium seen on both CT and MR. Normal linear enhancement of sections of the dura, more pronounced in the parasagittal regions near the Pacchionian granulations, is present on MR (Sze 1989; West 1990).

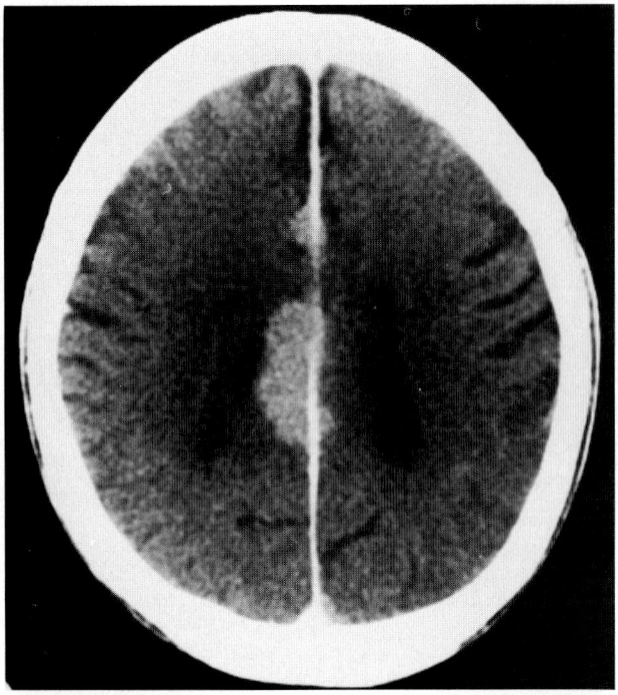

A

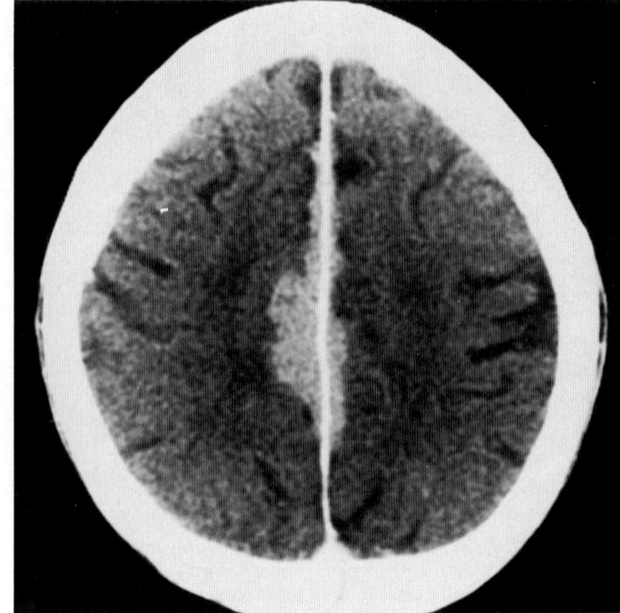

B

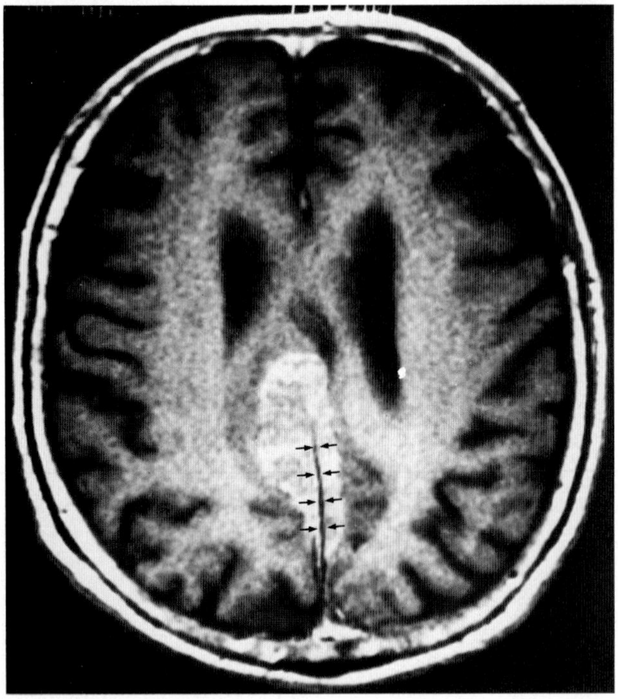

C

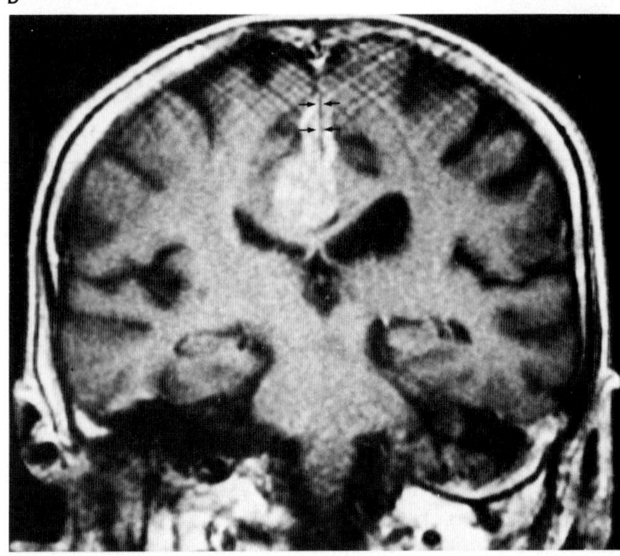

D

Figure 10-14 Prostate carcinoma metastasis to the dura. **A** and **B.** CECT shows enhancing dural-based metastasis to the falx. **C** and **D.** CEMR. Axial and coronal T_1WI (SE 600/20) demonstrate the enhancing metastasis to the falx. MR better demonstrates that the lesion has grown around the undersurface of the falx rather than transgressing the boundaries of the falx, which can be seen as a thin hypointense line (arrows). Coronal MR better demonstrates the relationship of the mass to the corpus callosum and lateral ventricles as well as the intact boundary of the dura.

In adults, metastases to the calvarium are usually lytic. However, prostate carcinoma can produce either a mixed lytic and blastic or a purely osteoblastic response. Differentiation from meningioma may be difficult. In the pediatric age group, rhabdomyosarcoma, neuroblastoma, lymphoma, and Langerhans giant cell granulomatosis (histiocytosis X) may produce bone destruction with intracranial extension of mass (Scotti 1982). In neuroblastoma there may be a mixed osteolytic and blastic response.

CT readily shows lytic calvarial and skull base lesions. Intracranial extension of the mass is also well shown. Sclerotic metastases to the calvarium can be somewhat more subtle.

On NCMR, recognition of skull metastases requires recognition of the asymmetry of the normal diploic space

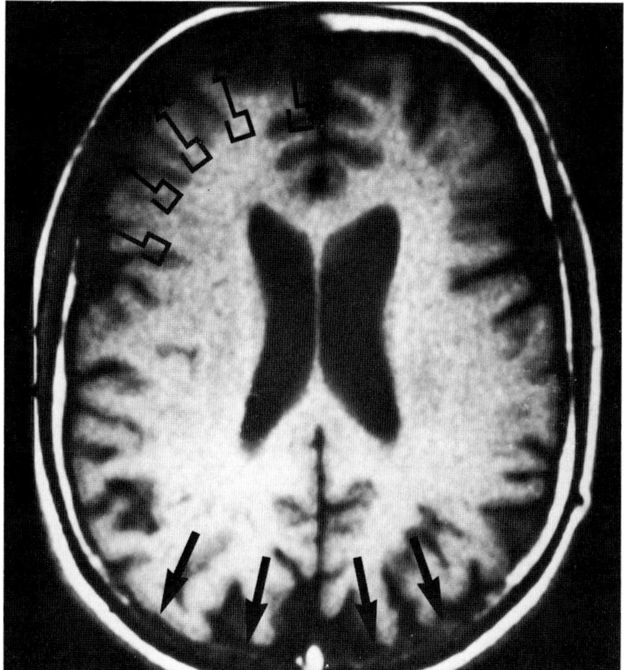

A

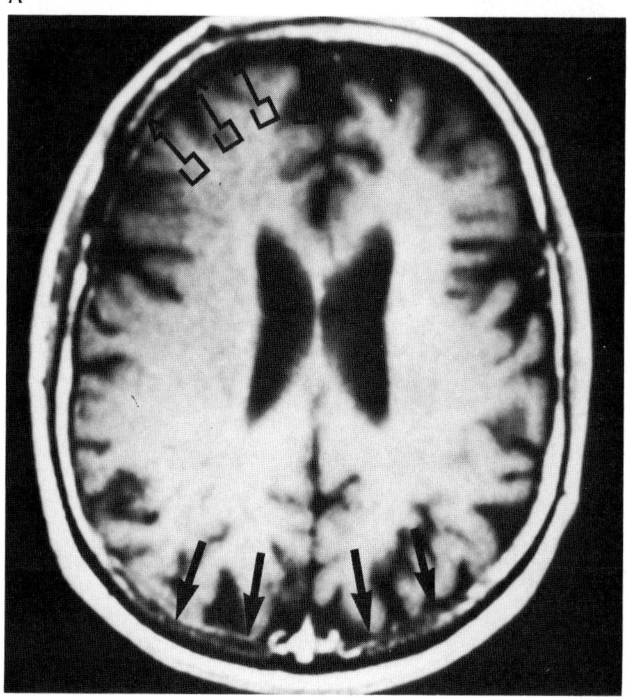

B

Figure 10-15 Calvarial metastases from bladder carcinoma. **A.** NCMR. T_1WI (600/20) reveals markedly abnormal asymmetrical distribution of the frontal intradiploic hyperintense marrow. Decreased right frontal signal intensity indicates diploic infiltration by tumor (open arrows). There is also less obvious bioccipital hypointensity (closed arrows). **B.** CEMR shows enhancement in the right frontal diploic space (open arrows) and subtler abnormal bioccipital enhancement (closed arrows), indicating the presence of bone metastases. Although NCMR showed the frontal metastases, the full extent of the disease is best seen with close comparison of both NCMR and CEMR. (*Reprinted with permission from G Sze, Neuroradiology 1990a.*)

marrow signal (West 1990). The normal diploic space may have several appearances, including (1) uniform high signal intensity on T_1WI owing to fatty marrow, (2) patchy nonuniform areas of hypointensity within hyperintense fatty marrow, or (3) predominantly low signal intensity (West 1990). The distribution of the diploic marrow signal, however, is usually uniform from side to side. Metastatic lesions are seen on NCMR as regions of hypointense tumor replacing the normal hyperintense marrow signal in an asymmetrical fashion (West 1990; Daffner 1986). This is most easily recognized in regions of high fat concentration, such as the skull base. If the diploic space is of predominantly low signal intensity, metastases can be difficult to recognize on NCMR.

After contrast injection, the normal diploic space in adults does not enhance except in occasional diploic venous channels or at the site of previous surgical intervention, such as the region of a previous burr hole placement. Metastatic calvarial lesions, however, enhance after contrast administration, allowing detection (Fig. 10-15). CEMR is more sensitive than is NCMR in detecting calvarial metastases (West 1990), though careful comparison of both images is required for the evaluation of the calvarium and skull base to ensure that lesions are not masked by enhancing to isointensity with normal adjacent fatty marrow. Intracranial extension of mass is easily recognized on MR (Fig. 10-16). In general, CEMR is more sensitive than is NCMR in detecting intracranial extension. However, NCMR is superior in demonstrating tumor extension into fat-containing regions such as the orbits (West 1990).

DIRECT OR PERINEURAL EXTENSION OF EXTRACRANIAL TUMORS

Malignancies of the head and neck may erode through the skull base with direct intracranial extension or may extend along neural pathways to gain intracranial access (Lee 1985; Laine 1990). Tumor extends in a retrograde fashion along the perineural or endoneural spaces, entering the intracranial compartment through the basal foramina (Ballantyne 1963; Laine 1990). Multiple tumors of the head and neck, including squamous cell carcinoma, basal cell carcinoma, melanoma, adenoid cystic carcinoma, lymphoma, and neurofibroma, may enter the intracranial cavity in this manner (Laine 1990; Dodd 1970; Woodruff 1986). Among these tumors, adenoid cystic carcinoma, though less common than head and neck carcinomas arising from the skin and mucous membranes, has a predilection for perineural extension (Spiro 1974; Lee 1985; Laine 1990). Entrance along the mandibular division of the trigeminal nerve through the foramen ovale is a relatively common pathway for intracranial tumor extension. Intracranial metastases arising from a perineural tumor extension are often noncontiguous with "skip" metastases, producing the appearance of a distinct intra-

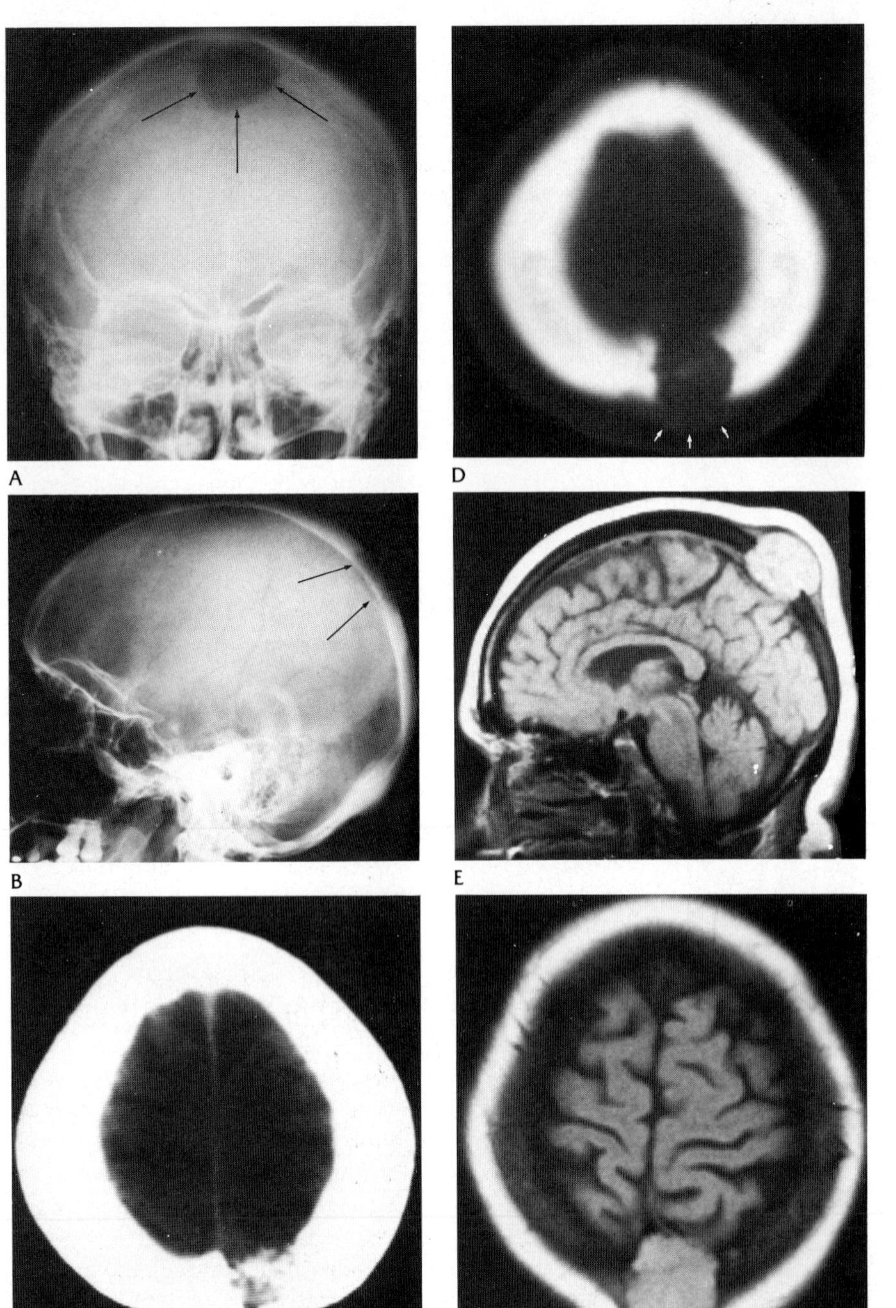

Figure 10-16 Thyroid carcinoma metastasis to the calvarium. **A** and **B.** AP and lateral skull radiographs show a lytic lesion in the parietal region (arrows). **C** and **D.** CECT (**C**) shows a nonhomogeneously enhancing lytic lesion involving the left parietal bone with intracranial extension of mass. The wide window setting (**D**) better demonstrates the extent of calvarial destruction and the extracranial component of the mass (white arrows). **E** and **F.** NCMR. T_1WI (SE 750/33) sagittal and axial images clearly demonstrate the calvarial lesion and its intracranial and extracranial components. Note that while there is intracranial extension of mass, the dura has not been transgressed and the underlying brain parenchyma has been spared.

cranial extraaxial mass (Lee 1985; Laine 1990; Curtin 1984). Consequently, a mass with the appearance of meningioma in a patient with a head and neck neoplasm should be considered a metastasis until proved otherwise (Lee 1985).

The extracranial mass and intracranial extension of head and neck neoplasms can be demonstrated on CT. These lesions typically demonstrate homogeneous contrast enhancement. Associated findings of perineural tumor extension include widening of the basal foramina and muscle denervation atrophy. MR has several advantages, including superior contrast resolution, absence of beam-hardening artifact related to scanning through the skull base, and ease of obtaining multiple planes. MR findings of perineural tumor extension include isointense thickening of the involved nerve and enlargement of the basal foramen, lateral bulging of the cavernous sinus, and, in perineural tumor extension along the man-

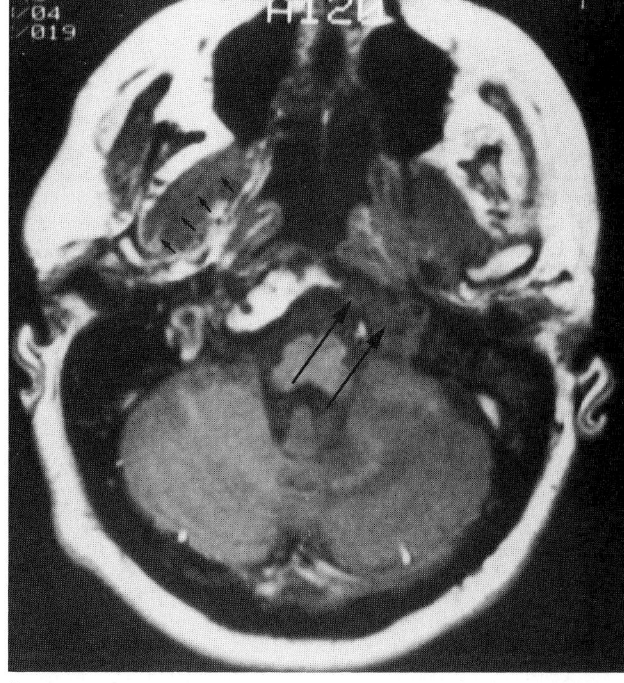
A

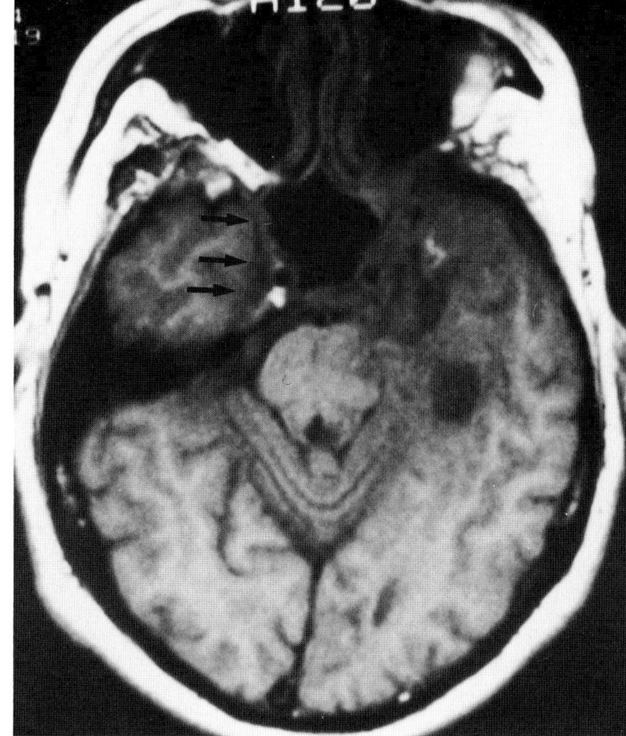
B

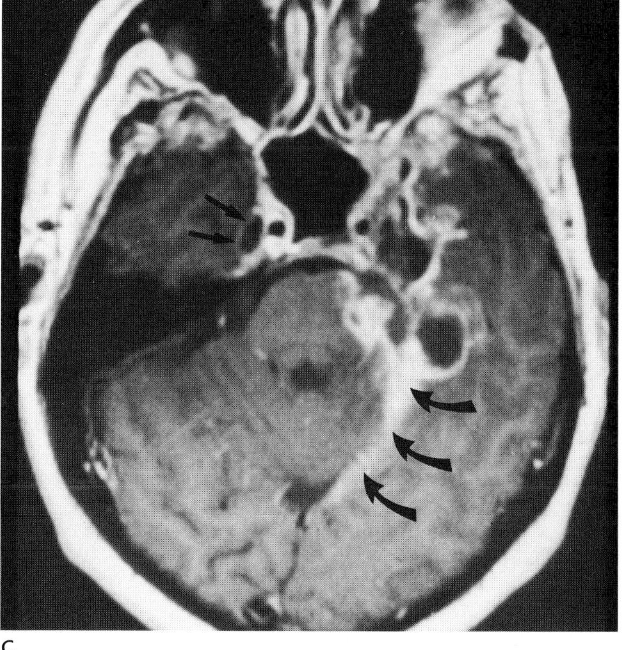
C

Figure 10-17 Squamous cell carcinoma of the mouth with perineural metastases. **A.** The patient presented with left cranial nerve deficits. T_1WI (SE 400/20) shows tumor infiltration of the left nasopharynx. Note that the hyperintensity of fat separating the normal medial and lateral pterygoid muscles and within the parapharyngeal space on the right (small arrows) is not clearly seen on the left because of tumor infiltration. In addition, note the hypointensity in the left side of the clivus (long arrows), indicating tumor extension into the clivus, replacing normal fat-containing marrow. **B** and **C.** NCMR. T_1WI (SE 400/20) (**B**) at a higher level reveals that the normal cavernous sinus structures seen on the right are not present on the left. Note that the lateral border of the right cavernous sinus is clearly identified (arrows) but is indistinct on the left. On CEMR (**C**), marked tumor enhancement is seen in the region of the left cavernous sinus. Compare this appearance with the normal Meckel's cave on the right (straight arrows). In addition, the tumor extends posteriorly via the cranial nerves to involve the brainstem. Enhancing tumor is also seen extending along the edge of the tentorium posteriorly (curved arrows). (*Reprinted with permission from G Sze 1990b.*)

dibular nerve, replacement of the normal hypointensity of the trigeminal ganglion cistern by an isointense mass on T_1WI (Fig. 10-17) (Laine 1990). Homogeneous tumor enhancement is typically seen after MR contrast injection. However, it is necessary to obtain NCMR images first; if only CEMR images are obtained, the extracranial component of the tumor may remain undetected because of the similar signal intensities of fat and enhancing tumor (Laine 1990).

References

ABRAHMS HL, SPIRO R, GOLDSTEIN N: Metastases in carcinoma: Analysis of 1000 autopsied cases. *Cancer* 3:74–85, 1950.

ATLAS SW, GROSSMAN RI, GOMORI JM: Hemorrhagic intracranial malignant neoplasms: Spin-echo MR imaging. *Radiology* 164:71–77, 1987*a*.

ATLAS SW, GROSSMAN RI, GOMORI JM: MR imaging of intracranial metastatic melanoma. *J Comput Assist Tomogr* 11: 577–582, 1987*b*.

ATLAS SW, MARK AS, GROSSMAN RI, et al: Intracranial hemorrhage: Gradient-echo MR imaging at 1.5T: Comparison with spin-echo imaging and clinical applications. *Radiology* 168: 803–807, 1988.

BALLANTYNE AJ, MCCARTEN AB, IBANEZ ML: The extension of cancer of the head and neck through peripheral nerves. *Am J Surg* 106:651–657, 1963.

BARNETT MJ, ZUSSMAN WV: Granulocytic sarcoma of the brain: A case report and review of the literature. *Radiology* 160:223–225, 1986.

BENNETT RH, ROBY DS, GARFINKLE W: Computed tomographic appearance of systemic malignant lymphoma involving brain. *Arch Neurol* 40:187–188, 1983.

BITOH S, HASEGAWA H, OHTSUKI H, et al: Cerebral neoplasms initially presenting with massive intracerebral hemorrhage. *Surg Neurol* 22:57–62, 1984.

BRADLEY WG Jr, WALUCH V, YADLEY RA, et al: Comparison of CT and MR in 400 patients with suspected disease of the brain and cervical spinal cord. *Radiology* 152:695–702, 1984.

BRADLEY WG Jr, SCHMIDT PG: Effect of methemoglobin formation on the MR appearance of subarachnoid hemorrhage. *Radiology* 156:99–103, 1985.

BRANT-ZAWADZKI M, ENZMANN DR: Computed tomographic brain scanning in patients with lymphoma. *Radiology* 129: 67–71, 1978.

BRANT-ZAWADZKI M, BADAMI JP, MILLS CM, et al: Primary intracranial tumor imaging: A comparison of magnetic resonance and CT. *Radiology* 150:435–440, 1984.

BRUNSUN KW, BEATTIE G, NICOLSON GL: Selection and altered properties of brain-colonizing metastatic melanoma. *Nature* 272:543–544, 1978.

BYDDER GM, PENNOCK JM, STEIN RE, et al: The NMR diagnosis of cerebral tumors. *Magnet Reson Med* 1:5–29, 1984.

CAIRNCROSS JG, POSNER JB: The management of brain metastases, in Walker MD (ed), *Oncology of the Nervous System*, Hingham, Mass., Martinus-Nijhoff, 1983, pp 341–378.

CASTALDO JE, BERNAT JL, MEIER FA, et al: Intracranial metastases due to prostate carcinoma. *Cancer* 52:1739–1747, 1983.

CHEE CP: Solitary cerebral metastasis from Wilms' tumor without pulmonary involvement. *Surg Neurol* 27:154–156, 1987.

CLAUSSEN C, LANIADO M, SCHÖRNER W, et al: Gadolinium-DTPA in MR imaging of gliobastomas and intracranial metastases. *AJNR* 6:669–674, 1985.

CURTIN HD, WILLIAMS R, JOHNSON J: CT of perineural tumor extension: Pterygopolatine fossa. *AJNR* 5:731–737, 1984; 144:163–169, 1985.

DAFFNER RH, LUPETIN AR, DASH N, et al: MRI detection of malignant infiltration of bone marrow. *AJR* 146:353–358, 1986.

DAVIS PC, FRIEDMAN NC, FRY SM, et al: Leptomeningeal metastasis: MR imaging. *Radiology* 163:449–454, 1987.

DAVIS PC, HUDGINS PA, PETERMAN SB, et al: Diagnosis of cerebral metastases: Double-dose delayed CT vs. contrast-enhanced MR imaging. *AJNR* 12:293–300, 1991.

DECK MDF, MESSINA AV, SACKETT JF: Computed tomography in metastatic disease of the brain. *Radiology* 119:115–120, 1976.

DELATTRE JY, KROL G, THALER HT, et al: Distribution of brain metastases. *Arch Neurol* 45:741–744, 1988.

DESTIAN S, SZE G, KROL G, et al: MR imaging of hemorrhagic intracranial neoplasms. *AJNR* 9:1115–1122, 1988; 152:137–144, 1989.

DI CHIRO G, BROOKS RA, GIRTON ME, et al: Sequential MR studies of intracerebral hematomas in monkeys. *AJNR* 7:193–199, 1986.

DODD GD, DOLON PA, BALLANTYNE AJ, et al: The dissemination of tumors of the head and neck via the cranial nerves. *Radiol Clin North Am* 8:445–461, 1970.

DUBOIS PJ, MARTINEZ AJ, MEYEROWITZ RL, et al: Subependymal and leptomeningeal spread of systemic malignant lymphoma demonstrated by cranial computed tomography. *J Comput Assist Tomogr* 2:218–221, 1978.

EARLE KM: Metastatic and primary tumors of the adult male. *J Neuropathol Exp Neurol* 13:448–454, 1954.

EGELHOFF J, ROSS JS, MODIC MT, et al: Findings at MR imaging of adenocarcinoma metastatic to the brain. Presented at the Radiological Society of North America (RSNA) annual meeting, Chicago, November 25–30, 1990.

ENZMANN D, KRAMER R, NORMAN D: Malignant melanoma metastatic to the central nervous system. *Radiology* 127:177–180, 1978.

FELIX R, SCHORNER W, LANIADO M, et al: Brain tumors: MR imaging with gadolinium-DTPA. *Radiology* 156:681–688, 1985.

FISCHER-WILLIAMS M, BOSANQUET FD, DANIEL PM: Carcinomatosis of the meninges: A report of 3 cases. *Brain* 78:42–58, 1955.

FRANK JA, GIRTON RT, DWYER AJ, et al: Meningeal carcinomatosis in the VX2 rabbit tumor model: Detection with Gd-DTPA-enhanced MR imaging. *Radiology* 164:825–829, 1988.

GILDERSLEEVE N JR, KOO AH, MCDONALD CJ: Metastatic tumor presenting as intracerebral hemorrhage: Report of 6 cases examined by computed tomography. *Radiology* 124: 109–112, 1977.

GINALDI S, WALLACE S, SHALEN P, et al: Cranial computed tomography of malignant melanoma. *AJR* 136:145–149, 1981.

GOMORI JM, GROSSMAN RI, GOLDBERG HI, et al: Intracranial hematomas: Imaging by high-field MR. *Radiology* 157:87–93, 1985.

GOMORI JM, GROSSMAN RI, YU-IP C, et al: NMR relaxation times of blood: Dependence on field strength, oxidation state, and cell integrity. *J Comput Assist Tomogr* 11:684–690, 1987.

GRAIF M, BYDDER GM, STEINER RE, et al: Contrast-enhanced MR imaging of malignant brain tumors. *AJNR* 6:855–862, 1985.

GRAUS F, WALKER RW, ALLEN JC: Brain metastases in children. *J Pediatr* 103:558–561, 1983.

HAUGHTON VM, RIMM AA, SOBOCINSKI KA, et al: A blinded clinical comparison of MR imaging and CT in neuroradiology. *Radiology* 160:751–755, 1986.

HAUSTEIN J, BAUR W, HILBERTZ T, et al: Double-dose of Gd-DTPA in MR imaging of intracranial tumors: Presented at Radiological Society of North America (RSNA) annual meeting, Chicago, November 25–30, 1990.

HAYMAN LA, EVANS RA, HINCK VC: Delayed high iodine dose contrast computed tomography: Cranial neoplasms. *Radiology* 136:677–681, 1980.

HAYMAN LA, MCARDLE CB, TABER KH, et al: MR of hyperacute intracranial hemorrhage in the cat. *AJNR* 10:681–686, 1989*a*.

HAYMAN LA, TABER KH, FORD JJ, et al: Effect of clot formation and retraction on spin-echo MR images of blood: An in vitro study. *AJNR* 10:1155–1158, 1989*b*.

HEALY JF, MARSHALL WH, BRAHME PJ, et al: CT of intracranial metastases with skull and scalp involvement. *AJNR* 2:335–338, 1981.

HEALY ME, HESSELINK JR, PRESS GA, et al: Increased detection of intracranial metastases with intravenous GD-DTPA. *Radiology* 165:619–624, 1987.

HOLTAS S, CRONQVIST S: Cranial computed tomography of patients with malignant melanoma. *Neuroradiology* 22:123–127, 1981.

HOLTAS S, NYMAN V, CRONQVIST S: Computed tomography of malignant lymphoma of the brain. *Neuroradiology* 26:33–38, 1984.

ITO U, TOMITA H, YAMAZAKI S, et al: CT findings of leptomeningeal and periventricular dissemination of tumors: Report of four cases. *Clin Neurol Neurosurg* 88:115–120, 1986.

JELINEK J, SMIRNIOTOPOULOS JG, PARIS JE, et al: Lateral ventricular neoplasms of the brain: Differential diagnosis based on clinical, CT, and MR findings. *AJNR* 11:567–574, 1990.

KAISER MC, RODESCH G, CAPESIUS P: Blood-fluid levels in multiloculated cystic brain metastases of a hypernephroma: A case report. *Neuroradiology* 25:339–341, 1983.

KART BH, REDDY SC, RAO GR, et al: Choroid plexus metastasis: CT appearance. *J Comput Assist Tomogr* 10:537, 1986.

KJOS BO, BRANT-ZAWADZKI M, KUCHARCZYK W, et al: Cystic intracranial lesions: Magnetic resonance imaging. *Radiology* 155:363–369, 1985.

KROL G, SZE G, MALKIN M, et al: MR of cranial and spinal meningeal carcinomatosis: Comparison with CT and myelography. *AJNR* 9:709–714, 1988; *AJR* 151:583–588, 1988.

LAINE FJ, BRAUN IF, JENSEN ME, et al: Perineural tumor extension through the foramen ovale: Evaluation with MR imaging. *Radiology* 174:65–71, 1990.

LEE YY, GLASS JP, GEOFFRAY A, et al: Cranial computed tomographic abnormalities in leptomeningeal metastasis. *AJNR* 5:559–563, 1984; *AJR* 143:1035–1039, 1984.

LEE YY, CASTILLO M, NAUERT C: Intracranial perineural metastases of adenoid cystic carcinoma of the head and neck. *J Comput Assist Tomogr* 9:219–223, 1985.

LEE YY, TIEN RD, BRUNS JM, et al: Lobulated intracranial leptomeningeal metastasis: CT and MR characteristics. *AJNR* 10:1171–1179, 1989.

LESSE S, NETSKY MG: Metastasis of neoplasms to the central nervous system and meninges. *Arch Neurol Psych* 77:133–153, 1954.

LITTLE JR, DIAL B, BELANGER G, et al: Brain hemorrhage from intracranial tumor. *Stroke* 10:283–288, 1979.

LYNES WL, BOSTWICK DG, FREIHA FS, et al: Parenchymal brain metastases from adenocarcinoma of prostate. *Urology* 28: 280–287, 1986.

MACGEE EE: Surgical treatment of cerebral metastases from lung cancer: The effect on quality and duration of survival. *J Neurosurg* 35:416–420, 1971.

MACKAY CJ, ABRAMSON DH, ELLSWORTH RM: Metastatic patterns of retinoblastoma. *Arch Ophthalmol* 102:391–396, 1984.

MAGILLIGAN DJ JR, DUVERNOY C, MALIK G, et al: Surgical approach to lung cancer with solitary cerebral metastasis: Twenty-five years experience. *Ann Thorac Surg* 42:360–364, 1986.

MANDELL L, HILARIS B, SULLIVAN M, et al: The treatment of single brain metastases from non-oat cell lung carcinoma:

Surgery and radiation versus radiation therapy alone. *Cancer* 58:641–649, 1986.

MANDYBUR TI: Intracranial hemorrhage caused by metastatic tumors. *Neurology* 27:650–655, 1977.

MORRISON D, SOBEL DF, KELLY WM, et al: Intraventricular mass lesions. *Radiology* 153:435–442, 1984.

NADICH TP, ZIMMERMAN RA: Primary brain tumors in children. *Semin Roentgenol* 19:100–114, 1984.

NIENDORF HP, LANIADO M, SEMMLER W, et al: Dose administration of gadolinium-DTPA in MR imaging of intracranial tumors. *AJNR* 8:803–815, 1987.

PATCHELL RA, CIRRINCIONE C, THALER HT, et al: Single brain metastases: Surgery plus radiation or radiation alone. *Neurology* 36:447–453, 1986.

PATCHELL RA, TIBBS PA, WALSH JW, et al: Randomized trial of surgery in the treatment of single metastases to the brain. *N Engl J Med* 332:494–500, 1990.

PECHOVA'-PETEROVA' V, KALVACH P: CT findings in cerebral metastases. *Neuroradiology* 28:254–258, 1986.

PHILLIPS ME, RYALS TJ, KAMBHU S, et al: Neoplastic vs. inflammatory meningeal enhancement with Gd-DTPA. *J Comput Assist Tomogr* 14(4):536–541, 1990.

POSNER JB, CHERNIK NL: Intracranial metastases from systemic cancer. *Adv Neurol* 19:579–591, 1978.

POSNER JB: Neurologic complications of systemic cancer. *Med Clin North Am* 63:783–800, 1979.

POTTS DG, ABBOTT GF, VON SNEIDERN JV: National Cancer Institute study: Evaluation of computed tomography in the diagnosis of intracranial neoplasms: III. Metastatic tumors. *Radiology* 136:657–664, 1980.

RIPPE DJ, BOYKO OB, FRIEDMAN HS, et al: Gd-DTPA-enhanced MR imaging of leptomeningeal spread of primary intracranial CNS tumor in children. *AJNR* 11:329–332, 1990.

ROLLINS N, MENDELSOHN D, MULNE A, et al: Recurrent medulloblastoma: Frequency of tumor enhancement on Gd-DTPA-MR imaging. *AJNR* 11:583–587, 1990; *AJR* 155:153–158, 1990.

ROSENBAUM AE, BAKER RA, SCHOENE WC: Medullary arteries in cerebral neoplasms. *Acta Radiol [Suppl] (Stockh)* 347:209–215, 1975.

RUELLE A, BAMBINI C, MACCHIA G, et al: Brain metastasis from colon cancer: Case report showing a clinical and CT unusual appearance. *J Neurosurg Sci* 31:31–36, 1987.

RUSSELL EJ, GEREMIA GK, JOHNSON CE, et al: Multiple cerebral metastases: Detectability with Gd-DTPA-enhanced MR imaging. *Radiology* 165:609–617, 1987.

SAPOZINK MD, KAPLAN HS: Intracranial Hodgkins disease: A report of 12 cases and review of the literature. *Cancer* 52:1301–1307, 1983.

SCATLIFF JH, GUINTO FC JR, RADCLIFFE WM: Vascular patterns in cerebral neoplasms and their differential diagnosis. *Semin Roentgenol* 6:59–69, 1971.

SCHREIBER D, BERNSTEIN K, SCHNEIDER J: Metastases of the central nervous system: A prospective study. 3rd communication: Metastases in the pituitary gland, pineal gland, and choroid plexus. *Zentralbl Allg Pathol* 126:64–73, 1982.

SCOTTI G, HARWOOD-NASH DC: Computed tomography of rhabdomyosarcomas of the skull base in children. *J Comput Assist Tomogr* 6:33–39, 1982.

SHALEN PR, HAYMAN LA, WALLACE S, et al: Protocol for delayed contrast enhancement in computed tomography of cerebral neoplasia. *Radiology* 139:397–402, 1981.

SOLE-LLENAS J, MERCADER JM, PONS-TORTELLA E: Morphologic aspects of the vessels of brain tumors. *Neuroradiology* 13:51–54, 1977.

SPIRO RH, HUVOS AG, STRONG EW: Adenoid cystic carcinoma of salivary origin: A clinicopathologic study of 242 cases. *Am J Surg* 128:512–520, 1974.

SUNDARESAN N, GALICICH JH: Surgical treatment of brain metastases: Clinical and computerized tomography evaluation of the results of treatment. *Cancer* 55:1382–1388, 1985.

SZE G: New applications of MR contrast agents in neuroradiology. *Neuroradiology* 32:1–18, 1990*a*.

SZE G: Magnetic resonance imaging of the brain in oncology, in Breit A (ed), *Magnetic Resonance in Oncology,* Berlin, Springer-Verlag, 1990*b*.

SZE G, SHIN J, KROL G, et al: Intraparenchymal brain metastases: MR imaging vs. contrast-enhanced CT. *Radiology* 168:187–194, 1988.

SZE G, SOLETSKY S, BRONEN R, et al: MR imaging of the cranial meninges with emphasis on contrast enhancement and meningeal carcinomatosis. *AJNR* 10:965–975, 1989; *AJR* 153:1039–1049, 1989.

SZE G, MILANO E, JOHNSON C, et al: Detection of brain metastases: Comparison of contrast-enhanced MR with unenhanced MR and enhanced CT. *AJNR* 11:785–791, 1990*c*.

TARVER RD, RICHMOND BD, KLATTE EC: Cerebral metastases from lung carcinoma: Neurologic and CT correlation. *Radiology* 153:689–692, 1984.

VAN DEN DOEL EM, VAN MERRIENBOER FJ, TULLEKEN CA: Cerebral hemorrhage from unsuspected choriocarcinoma. *Clin Neurol Neurosurg* 87:287–290, 1985.

VIETH RG, ODOM GL: Intracranial metastases and their neurosurgical treatment. *J Neurosurg* 23:375–383, 1965.

WASSERSTROM WR, GLASS JP, POSNER JB: Diagnosis and treatment of leptomeningeal metastases from solid tumors: Experience with 90 patients. *Cancer* 49:759–772, 1982.

WEIR B, MACDONALD N, MIELKE B: Intracranial vascular complications of choriocarcinoma. *Neurosurgery* 2:138–142, 1978.

WEISBERG LA: Computerized tomographic findings in intracranial metastatic malignant melanoma. *Comput Radiol* 9:365–372, 1985*a*.

WEISBERG LA: Hemorrhagic metastatic intracranial neoplasms: Clinical computed tomographic correlations. *J Comput Assist Tomogr* 9:105–114, 1985*b*.

WEST M, RUSSELL EJ, BREIT R, et al: Calvarial and skull base metastases: Comparison of nonenhanced and Gd-DTPA enhanced MR images. *Radiology* 175:85–91, 1990.

WOODRUFF WW Jr, YEATES AE, MCLENDON RE: Perineural tumor extension to the cavernous sinus from superficial facial carcinoma: CT manifestations. *Radiology* 161:395–399, 1986.

WOODRUFF WW Jr, DJANG WT, MCLENDON RE, et al: Intracerebral malignant melanoma: High-field-strength MR imaging. *Radiology* 165:209–213, 1987.

YANG PJ, KNAKE JE, GABRIELSEN TO, et al: Primary and secondary histocytic lymphoma of the brain: CT features. *Radiology* 154:683–686, 1985.

ZIMMERMAN RD, HEIER LA, SNOW RB, et al: Acute intracranial hemorrhage: Intensity changes on sequential MR scans at 0.5 T. *AJNR* 9:47–57, 1988.

THE BASE OF THE SKULL: SELLA AND TEMPORAL BONE

David L. Daniels
Katherine A. Shaffer
Victor M. Haughton

The skull base consists of membranous bone and cartilage perforated by nerves, the spinal cord, arteries, and veins. The complex anatomic relationships, especially within the sella and temporal bone, can be effectively evaluated with CT or MR. CT is optimal for demonstrating osseous structures and abnormal calcification, whereas MR is best used for soft tissues, vessels, and nerves. The multitude and complexity of abnormalities at the base of the skull will be discussed in regard to the sella and the temporal bones.

SECTION A: THE SELLA

When the appropriate techniques are used, CT effectively demonstrates the pituitary fossa and its adjacent structures (Reich 1976; Gyldenstein 1977; Belloni 1978; Wolpert 1979; Gardeur 1981). To achieve a high degree of diagnostic accuracy, one must use coronal imaging, thin sections, a high radiation flux, and an effective dose of intravenous contrast agent. With these techniques, CT is sensitive and accurate in the differential diagnosis.

The role of MR in studying the sella has been well documented (Mark 1984; Pojunas 1986; Daniels 1984*a*, 1986*a*; Lee 1985; Oot 1984; Bilaniuk 1984; Daniels 1987*a*, *b*, 1988*b*; Sartor 1987). When used with thin sections, appropriate imaging parameters, and intravenous contrast agents, MR can demonstrate pituitary adenomas and most microadenomas noninvasively and without ionizing radiation and probably exceeds the sensitivity of CT in detecting microadenomas. The effectiveness of MR in distinguishing actively secreting and inactive adenomas requires evaluation. MR can be used as a primary screening test for sellar and parasellar lesions (Chakeres 1989).

TECHNICAL ASPECTS

Direct coronal CT images of the sella permit more accurate demonstration of sellar abnormalities and a lower radiation dose to the lens than is possible with axial images (Earnest 1981; Taylor 1982). High-quality coronal images with minimal movement can be obtained if the patient is placed supine or prone on the scanning table with the neck extended in a specially designed head holder. A digital localizer image is used to select a plane of section nearly perpendicular to the sellar floor to avoid artifacts from dental fillings (Fig. 11-1). Technical factors related to CT imaging include a high radiation flux, long scan times to maximize contrast resolution (4 to 10 seconds), and thin (1.5 mm or less) sections to maximize spatial resolution. If the sella is enlarged, 5-mm-thick sections are more practical. If direct coronal sections are not feasible because the patient cannot extend the neck sufficiently, coronal images can be obtained by reformatting multiple, contiguous 1.5-mm axial sections at 1- or 1.5-mm intervals.

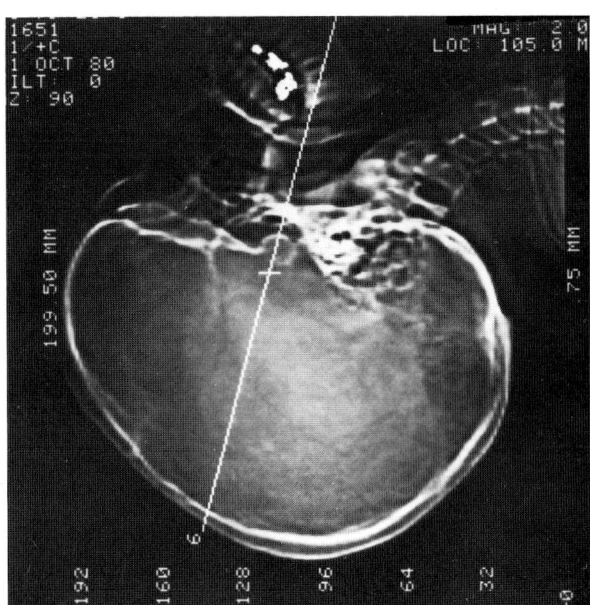

Figure 11-1 Lateral localizer image demonstrating the optimal CT gantry angle (white line) perpendicular to the sellar floor for CT imaging of the sella. (*From Daniels 1985a.*)

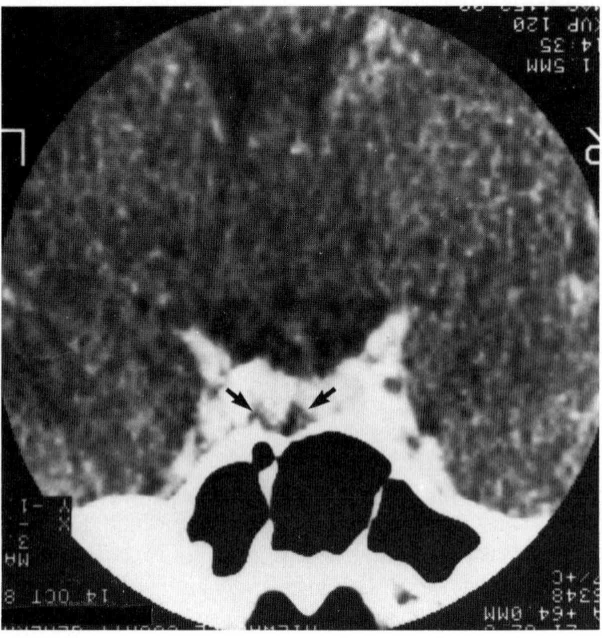

A

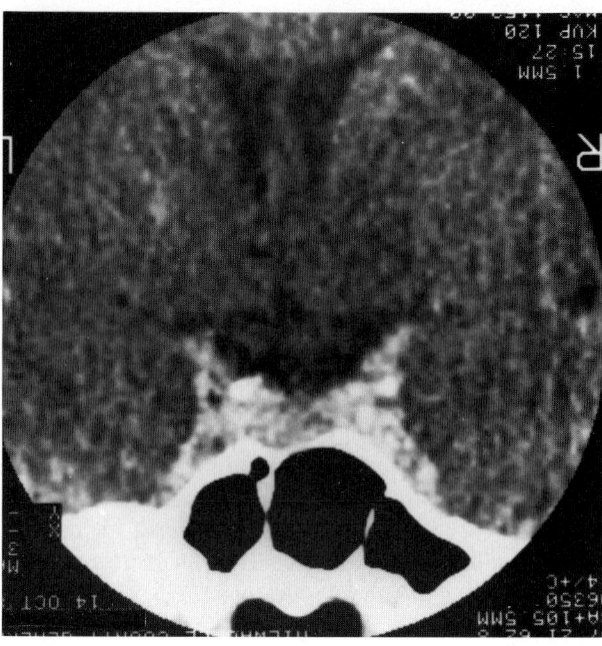

B

Figure 11-2 Coronal CT scans of a prolactinoma. After intravenous contrast administration, the tumor (arrows, **A**) appears as a hypodense area, and (**B**) 15 minutes later it is nearly isodense with normal pituitary tissue. (*From Hemminghytt 1983.*)

Because of their incomplete blood-brain barrier, the cavernous sinuses, pituitary gland, and pituitary stalk increase substantially in density on CT after the administration of iodinated intravenous contrast medium. This increase in density, or "contrast enhancement," may be helpful in characterizing intrasellar and juxtasellar masses. To achieve optimal contrast enhancement, a high plasma concentration of iodinated contrast medium is obtained by infusing 200 ml of 30 percent iodinated contrast medium rapidly into an antecubital vein immediately before scanning. To maintain a high plasma iodine concentration during scanning, an additional 100 ml of 30 percent contrast medium is infused during the scanning procedure. Contrast enhancement facilitates the detection of microadenomas, which enhance to a lesser degree than do the normal pituitary gland and the vascular structures in the sella. If scanning is delayed more than 20 minutes after the intravenous injection of contrast medium, the detection of microadenomas may be impaired because the adenoma increases progressively in density while the gland and cavernous sinuses gradually diminish in density (Hemminghytt 1983) (Fig. 11-2).

Dynamic scanning, which refers to sequential CT sections obtained at a single level every few seconds after a bolus injection of contrast medium, can be used to evaluate the sella (Cohen 1982; Pinto 1982; Wing 1980). On these studies, vascular, glandular, and neoplastic tissues, which have different density versus time curves, can be effectively differentiated (Fig. 11-3). Aneurysms and normal vessels have a rapid increase and then a decrease in density after the bolus injection. Venous structures have a rapid increase and then decrease in density, which follows the arterial peak by several seconds. Solid tumors within or near the sella, such as pituitary adenomas, have a slow increase and an even slower decrease in density. Cystic, avascular, or densely calcified tumors, such as cranipharyngiomas, have little change in density with time.

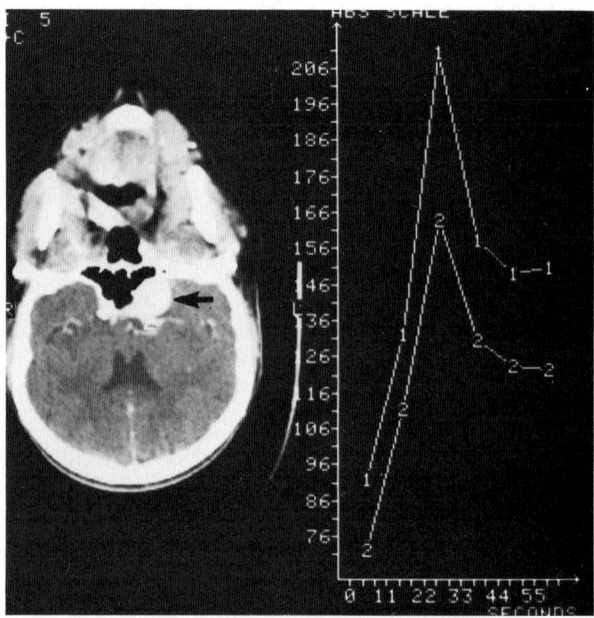

Figure 11-3 Dynamic CT scanning in a parasellar aneurysm (arrow). The aneurysm has almost the same time-density curve (1) as an adjacent artery (2). (*From Daniels 1985a.*)

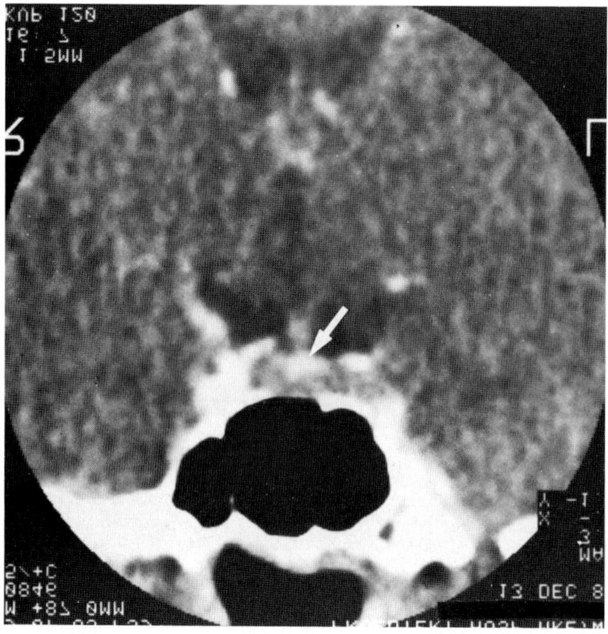

A

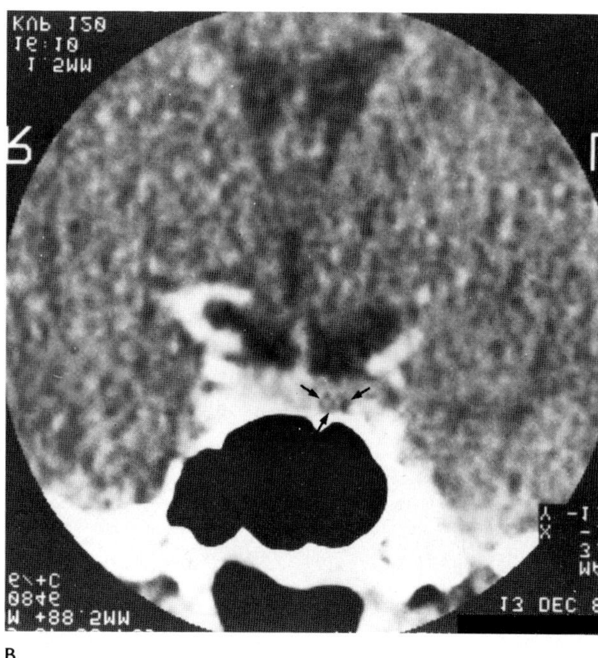

B

Figure 11-4 Arterial phase of coronal dynamic CT sequence showing a normal capillary "tuft" (arrow, **A**) below the surface of a pituitary gland. The tuft is not displaced by a hypodense basophilic adenoma (small black arrows, **B**) that is demonstrated in a nondynamic coronal CECT study. (*From Daniels 1985a.*)

With dynamic scanning, a small capillary bed ("tuft") in the midline below the upper margin of the pituitary gland can be demonstrated during the arterial phase of dynamic scanning (Fig. 11-4) (Bonneville 1983). Displacement of the capillary bed indicates an expanding intrasellar process such as a pituitary adenoma.

Intrathecal contrast agent has few applications in CT study of the sella. It has been used to verify an empty sella when the intravenously enhanced images have been suboptimal or not diagnostic (Fig. 11-5). Intrathecal enhancement is accomplished by performing a lumbar puncture, injecting 5 ml of an intrathecal water-soluble

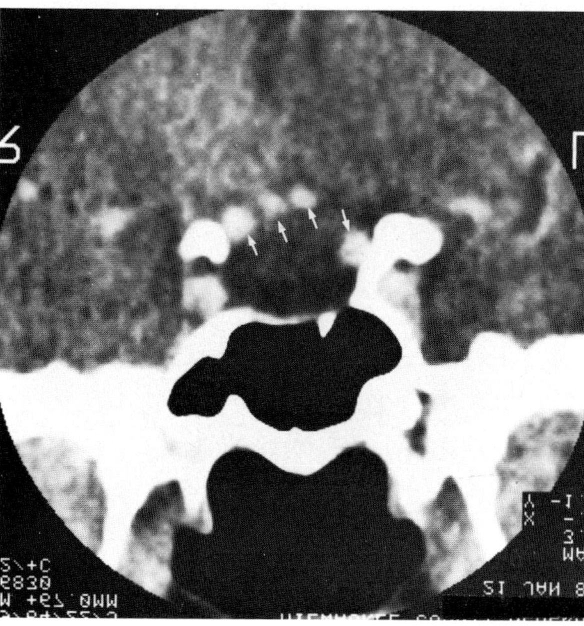

A

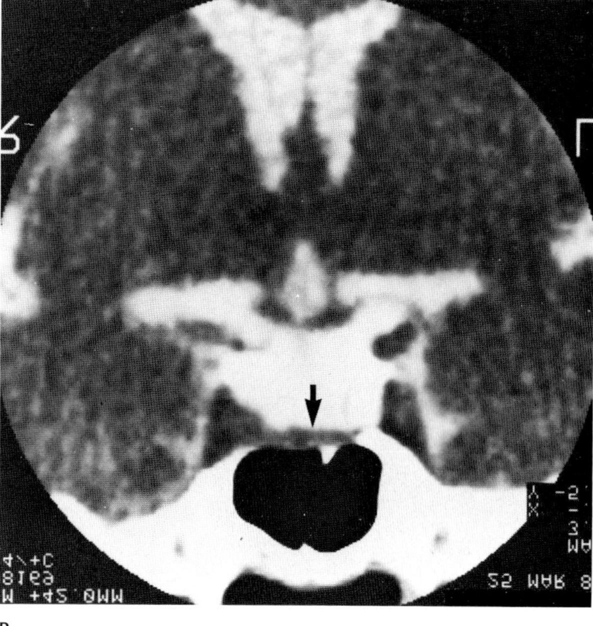

B

Figure 11-5 Empty sella. In intravenously enhanced coronal CT (**A**) it appears as a region of hypodensity in the sella. Enhancing round structures (small white arrows) represent suprasellar blood vessels. In **B**, after opacification of the pituitary fossa with an intrathecal contrast agent, a small gland (black arrow) is demonstrated. (*From Daniels 1985a.*)

contrast medium such as iohexol or iopamidol (170 to 200 mg I/ml), tilting the patient prone and head down on a fluoroscopic table for 2 minutes, and then scanning with the patient supine.

MR study of the pituitary gland requires a high-resolution imager, a slice thickness of 1 to 3 mm, a high-resolution (256 × 256) matrix, and good patient cooperation. The study is initiated with a sagittal spin echo (SE) T_1-weighted image (T_1WI) with a TR of 800 msec and a TE of 20 msec. A series of coronal T_1WI is obtained in which the pituitary gland, the upper contour of the gland, and the cavernous sinuses are demonstrated. Coronal T_1-weighted gradient echo images obtained with a single-slice acquisition technique, 1- to 3-mm-thick sections, a 256 × 256 matrix, four excitations, a TR of 100 msec, a TE of 15 msec, a 90° flip angle, and flow compensation can be used to define cavernous venous spaces, which have a distinctive high signal intensity with this technique. If a large mass is identified, T_1-weighted sagittal and axial images may be useful. If a cystic tumor is suspected, T_2-weighted images (T_2WI) (TR 2500, TE 80) may be useful in characterizing the fluid within the tumor. T_1WI, because of greater spatial resolution, are best for screening the sella; T_2WI are useful in differentiating blood, glandular tissue, and fluid.

Unless non-contrast-enhanced MR (NCMR) images are

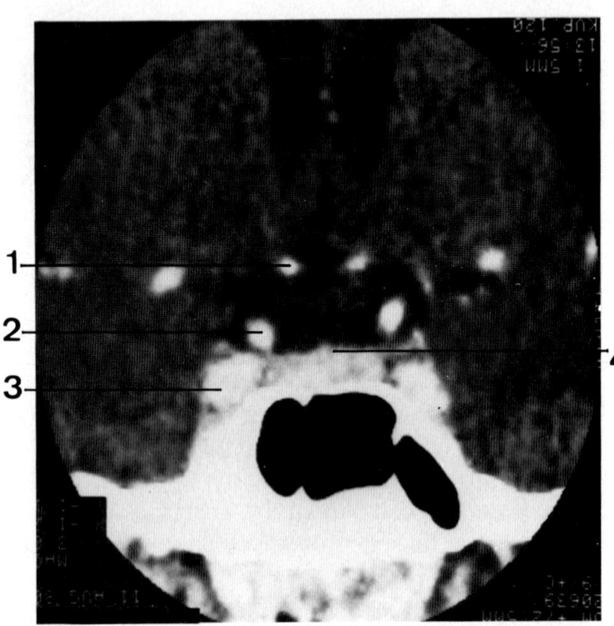

1. anterior cerebral artery 2. supraclinoid internal carotid artery 3. intracavenous internal carotid artery 4. pituitary gland

A

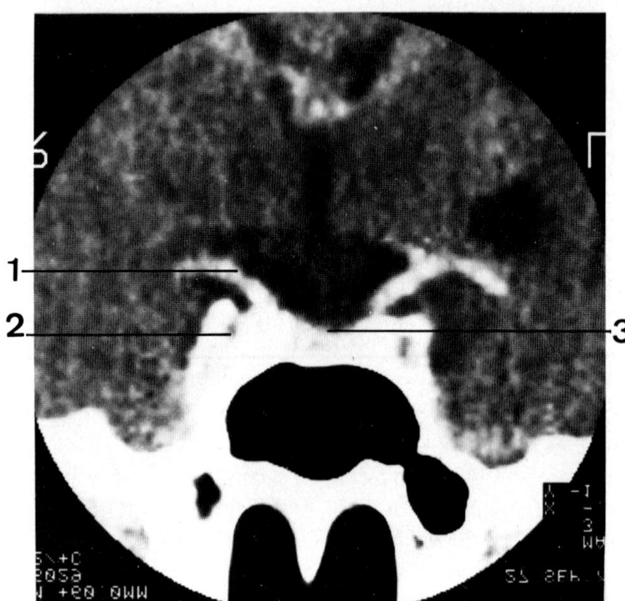

1. supraclinoid internal carotid artery 2. oculomotor nerve 3. pituitary gland

B

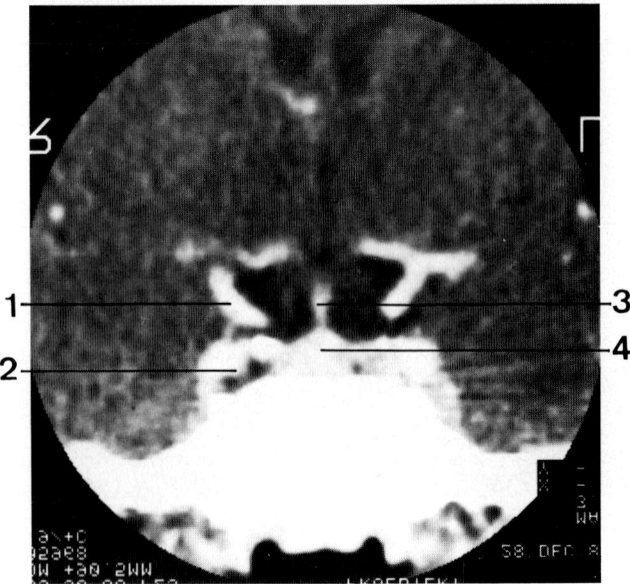

1. supraclinoid internal carotid artery 2. intracavernous internal carotid artery 3. infundibulum 4. pituitary gland

C

Figure 11-6 Examples of normal pituitary glands in coronal CECT images. The glands homogeneously enhance and have straight (**A**), concave (**B**), or, at the attachment point of the infundibulum, a midline convex upper contour (**C**). (*From Daniels 1985a.*)

considered diagnostic of an intrasellar or parasellar mass, a paramagnetic contrast medium (e.g., Gd-DTPA) is administered intravenously, and the T_1-weighted coronal images are repeated immediately. Paramagnetic contrast medium shortens the relaxation times of the tissues in which it accumulates, increasing the signal intensity of the normal pituitary gland, the infundibulum, and the cavernous venous spaces in T_1WI (Kilgore 1986). The risks and side effects are minimal. The conventional dose is 0.1 mmol/kg.

Pituitary Fossa

The sella is a saddle-shaped osseous structure with the following landmarks: anteriorly the tuberculum sellae, inferiorly the lamina dura, and posteriorly the dorsum sellae. The pituitary gland is within the sella. Its upper surface is usually straight or very mildly concave or, especially in adolescents or menstruous women, slightly convex (Fig. 11-6) (Wolpert 1984; Gardeur 1982). Its height normally is 2 to 9 mm, with an average height of 3.5 mm in men and 4.8 mm in women (Mark 1984; Syvertsen 1979). It appears nearly homogeneous and isodense with the cavernous sinuses in CT images with or without the use of intravenous contrast enhancement. It may have a mild degree of nonhomogeneity, especially in adolescents and menstruous women, but without discrete and well-demarcated low-attenuation regions (Swartz 1983; Roppolo 1983*a,b*). The areas of greater density or enhancement may represent more compact glandular or vascular tissue. Tiny colloid cysts in the pars intermedia that have a lower density can also cause nonhomogeneity.

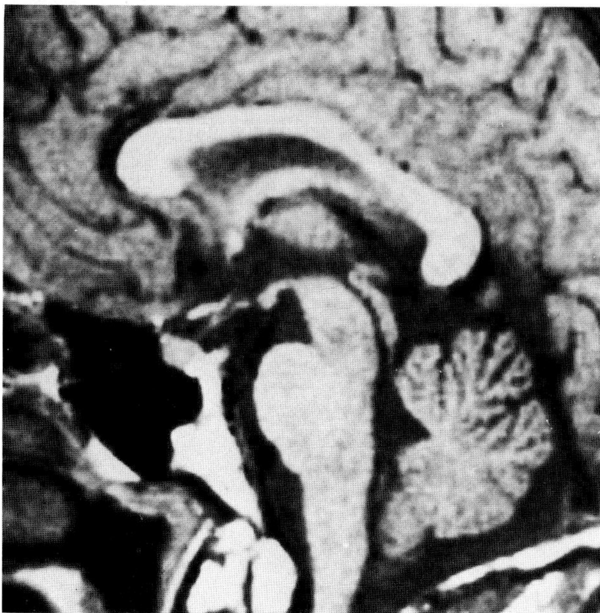

Figure 11-7 Sagittal T_1-weighted MRI in which a normal pituitary gland has a nearly straight upper contour and a homogeneous signal that contrasts with the negligible signal (black) from cerebrospinal fluid and cortical bone and the high-intensity signal (white) from fat in the dorsum sellae.

The appearance of the pituitary gland in MR images has been analyzed in a series of reports (Colombo 1987; Fujisawa 1987*a,b*; Mark 1984, 1989; Brooks 1989; Wolpert 1988; Kucharczyk 1988; Shapiro 1987; Sze 1987; Elster 1990). In short TR and TE (T_1-weighted) SE images, the anterior part of the pituitary gland has a nearly homogeneous signal intensity with or without intravenous contrast medium, in contrast to the negligible signal (black) from the cortical bone in the sella and the cerebrospinal fluid in the suprasellar cistern (Fig. 11-7). The posterior

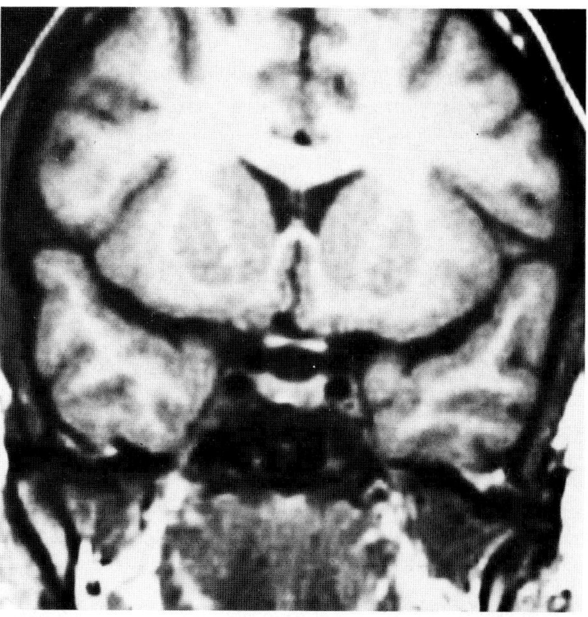

A

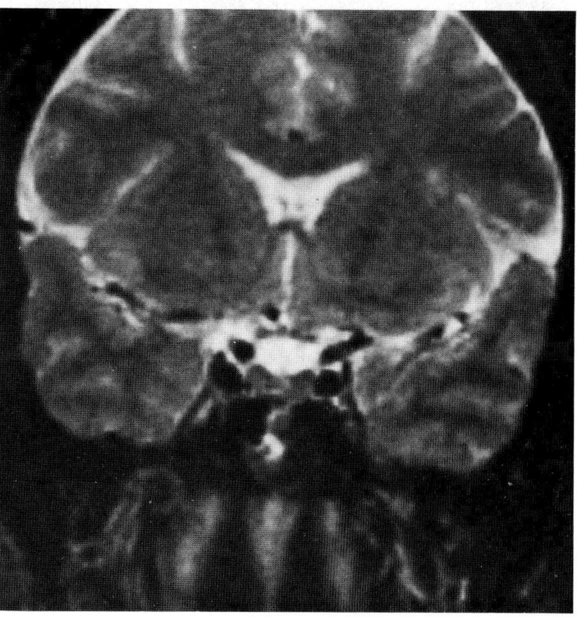

B

Figure 11-8 Coronal T_1-weighted (**A**) and T_2-weighted (**B**) MR images of a normal pituitary gland. The gland has a mildly concave upper contour; the cavernous internal carotid arteries have a negligible signal in **A** and **B.** In **B,** the lateral wall of the cavernous sinus has a negligible signal in contrast to the high signal intensity (white) of the adjacent CSF.

lobe of a normal pituitary gland characteristically has a higher signal intensity than does the anterior lobe. Evidence is accumulating that this heightened signal intensity is due to phospholipids in neurosecretory granule membranes that have a function in hormone secretion (Kucharczyk 1990). Fat in the marrow of the dorsum sellae and within the posteroinferior pituitary fossa also appears as a region of hyperintense signal in MR images. Small venous channels, which have a negligible signal because of flowing blood, are prominent at the lateral part of the pituitary gland. In long TR and TE (T_2-weighted) images, the gland's signal is nearly homogeneous and is less intense than that of CSF, which appears white (Fig. 11-8). The diaphragma sellae, a thin membrane rostral to the gland through which the infundibulum courses, is demonstrated in coronal, long TR, and short TE images as a transversely oriented thin band with a negligible signal (Daniels 1986).

Cavernous Sinuses

The cavernous sinuses on either side of the pituitary fossa appear nearly triangular in coronal CT and MR sections, with a straight or slightly concave lateral wall (Figs. 11-9 and 11-10). The lateral wall is formed by a layer of dura that is underlain by a fenestrated membrane that contains cranial nerves III (oculomotor), IV (trochlear), and V_1, V_2 (trigeminal, first and second divisions) (Umansky 1982). Cranial nerve VI (the abducens) is contained within the lumen of the cavernous sinus. The important anatomic landmarks related to the back of the cavernous sinus are the gasserian ganglion and Meckel's cave, an oval dural invagination containing CSF and trigeminal rootlets (Daniels 1986*b*) (Figs. 11-11 and 11-12). A portion of the internal carotid artery lies within the cavernous sinus. The cranial nerves, Meckel's cave, portions of the internal carotid artery, and the venous spaces can be identified within the enhanced cavernous sinuses on CT, especially when dynamic scanning is used (Kline 1981; Bonneville 1989).

In MR, the anatomy of the cavernous sinus is effectively shown (Daniels 1985*b*, 1986*b*; Braffman 1987; Hutchins 1989). Flowing blood in the cavernous venous sinuses and the carotid artery usually has intermediate and negligible signal intensity in T_1- and T_2-weighted SE sequences, respectively (Fig. 11-8). Meckel's cave is nearly isointense with CSF; that is, it shows hypointensity in T_1WI and hyperintensity in T_2WI (Fig. 11-12). The dural margin of the sinus has a low-intensity signal in both T_1WI and T_2WI. The cavernous portions of cranial nerves III through VI and the cavernous venous spaces usually have a similar signal intensity in T_1-weighted SE images. After intravenous paramagnetic contrast medium injection, the signal intensity in the cavernous venous spaces and gland increases in T_1WI (Kilgore 1986). Cavernous cranial nerves appear as small filling defects in the enhanced cavernous sinuses (Fig. 11-10). In T_1-weighted gradient echo images, the cavernous venous spaces and carotid arteries have a high signal intensity that differentiates them from the pituitary gland and cavernous cranial nerves and connective tissue (Daniels 1988*a*).

The suprasellar cistern contains the hypothalamus, op-

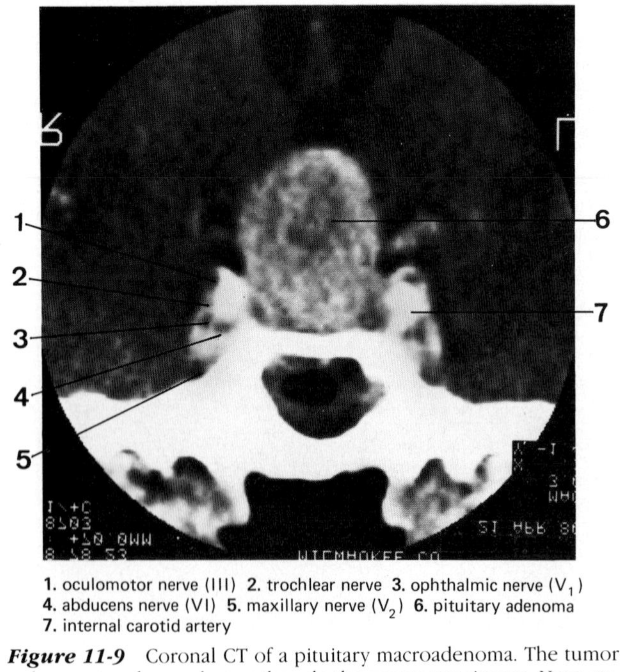

1. oculomotor nerve (III) 2. trochlear nerve 3. ophthalmic nerve (V_1) 4. abducens nerve (VI) 5. maxillary nerve (V_2) 6. pituitary adenoma 7. internal carotid artery

Figure 11-9 Coronal CT of a pituitary macroadenoma. The tumor enhances to a lesser degree than do the cavernous sinuses. Note cranial nerves III through VI, which appear as filling defects in the enhanced cavernous sinuses. (*From Daniels 1985a.*)

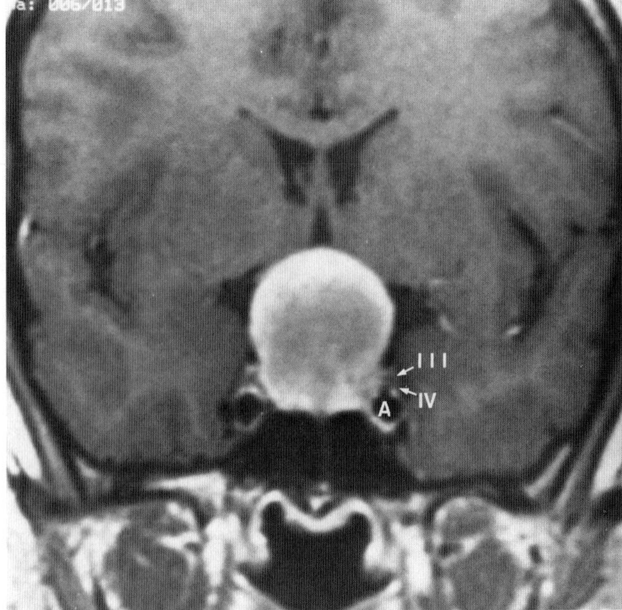

Figure 11-10 Coronal MRI with intravenous Gd-DTPA of a pituitary macroadenoma. Cranial nerves III and IV appear as small filling defects in the enhanced cavernous sinuses. (A = cavernous carotid artery.)

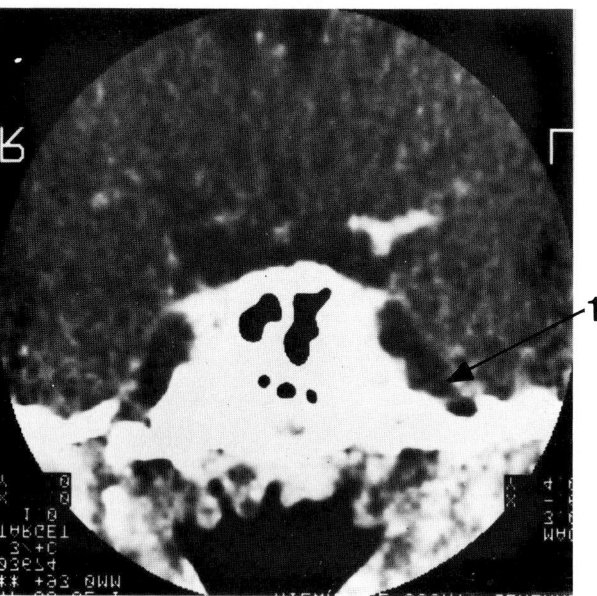

1. Meckel's cave

Figure 11-11 Meckel's cave in a coronal CECT through the posterior aspect of the cavernous sinuses. The cave (arrow) has the density of CSF. (*From Daniels 1985a.*)

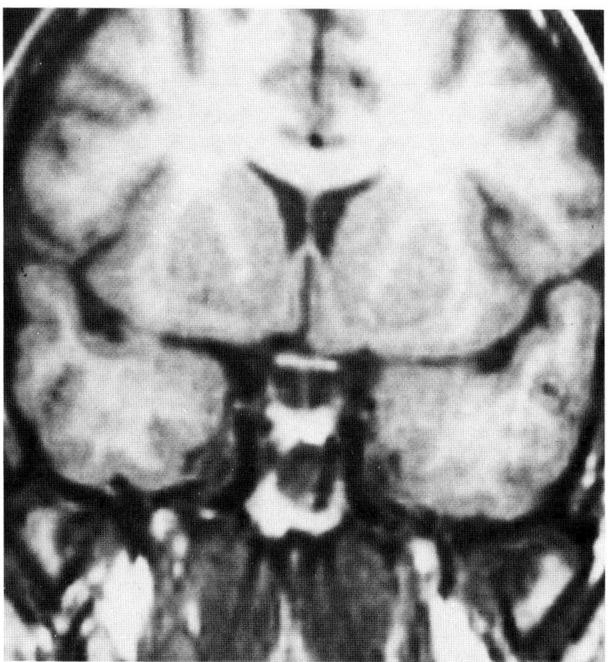

Figure 11-12 Coronal T_1-weighted MRI through the posterior aspect of the sella. Meckel's cave, containing neural structures and CSF, has a slightly greater signal intensity than does CSF. The cavernous internal carotid arteries have a negligible signal.

tic chiasm, infundibulum, and mammillary bodies (Peyster 1984*a*; Daniels 1980, 1984*b*). Because of the surrounding cerebrospinal fluid, the optic chiasm can be demonstrated effectively in axial or coronal CT or MR images (Fig. 11-13). In axial images through the lower part of the chiasm and the adjacent optic nerves a U-shaped structure can be identified. Slightly more rostral sections show the chiasm and proximal optic tracts as a boomerang-shaped structure. In a slice intermediate between these two levels, the chiasm has a butterfly shape. In coronal images, the optic chiasm and the adjacent hypothalamus appear as a U-shaped structure just below the teardrop-shaped optic recess (Fig. 11-13). Coronal sections slightly anterior to this level demonstrate a dumbbell-shaped structure representing the junction of the optic nerves and optic chiasm. Immediately posterior to the chiasm in axial images, the infundibulum can be identified as a round structure that enhances with intravenous contrast medium in both CT and MR. Behind the infundibulum are the mammillary bodies. In coronal images the infundibular recess of the third ventricle appears slit-like and is pointed inferiorly immediately above the infundibulum. In axial sections the suprasellar cistern appears either pentagonal or hexagonal, depending on whether the section is at the level of the pons or that of the mesencephalon. On sagittal MR, the optic chiasm lies on a line at roughly 45° posterosuperior to the tuberculum. An average chiasm-tuberculum distance is 3.8 mm (2.6 mm for women, 4.3 mm for men). The prefixed chiasm closely abuts the tuberculum, and the postfixed chiasm overlies the dorsum sellae. These findings are of surgical concern and are readily visible on MRI (Doyle 1990).

PATHOLOGY

Pituitary Adenomas

The most common intrasellar tumors are pituitary adenomas. They are classified as macroadenomas, when they are larger than 1 cm in diameter, or as microadenomas. Macroadenomas usually present because of pituitary insufficiency or bitemporal visual field impairment or are found in the evaluation of an incidentally discovered enlarged sella. Microadenomas present because of amenorrhea and/or galactorrhea due to excessive secretion of prolactin, Cushing's disease due to hypersecretion of ACTH, or gigantism or acromegaly due to hypersecretion of human growth hormone (HGH) (Merritt 1969; Chason 1971; Post 1980). Pituitary macroadenomas are usually solid encapsulated tumors that may have necrotic, cystic, hemorrhagic, or, rarely, calcified regions. The pituitary adenomas that cause hypersecretion are usually diagnosed very accurately in serum assays. However, medications (e.g., α-methyldopa, reserpine, phenothiazines, butyrophenones, tricyclic antidepressants, and oral contraceptives) or diseases that involve the hypothalamus or pituitary gland (e.g., sarcoidosis, histiocytosis, neoplasm, hypothyroidism, renal failure, and severe stress) may cause false-positive elevated serum prolactin levels.

CT or MR diagnosis of microadenomas is sensitive and

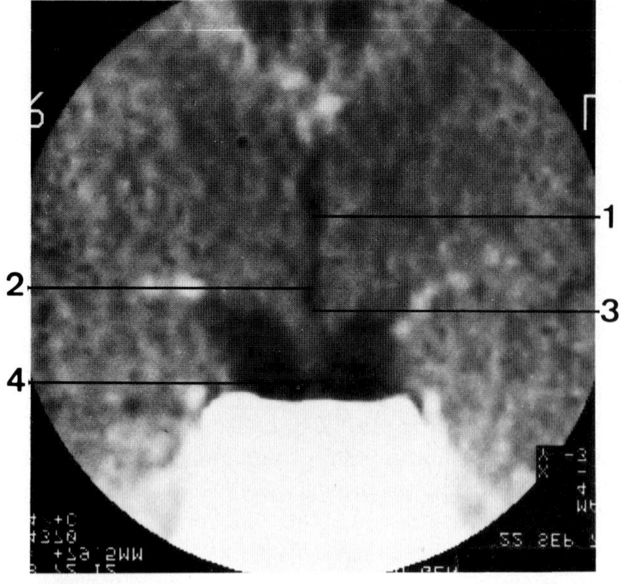

1. third ventricle **2.** infundibular recess **3.** tuber cinereum **4.** infundibulum

A

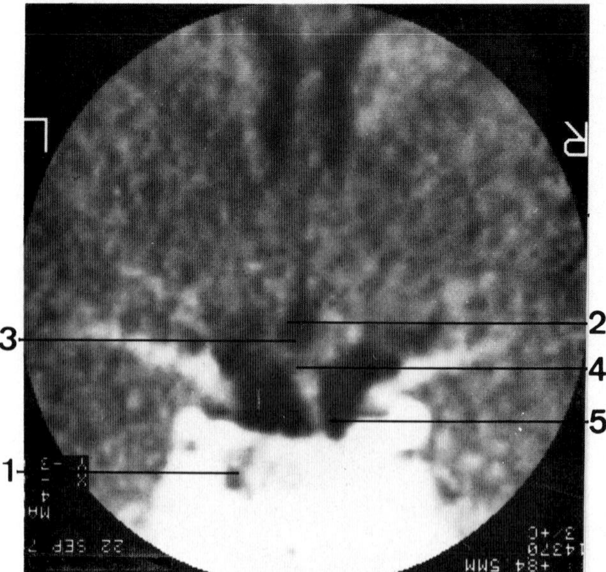

1. pituitary microadenoma **2.** optic recess **3.** hypothalamus **4.** optic chaism **5.** infundibulum

B

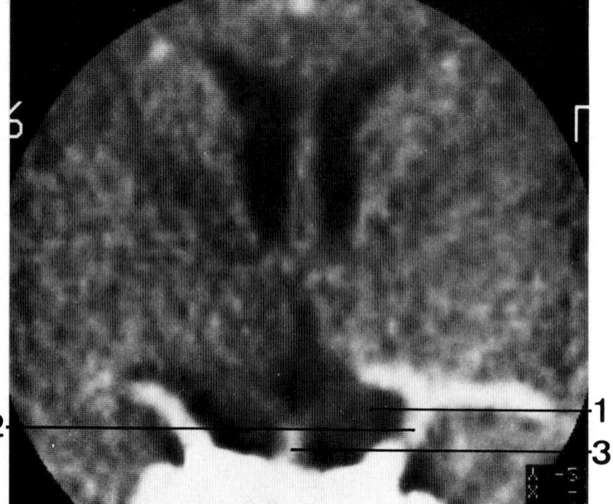

1. optic chaism **2.** internal carotid artery **3.** infundibulum

C

Figure 11-13 Coronal CECT from posterior to anterior through the optic chiasm and hypothalamus in which (**A**) the tuber cinereum appears conical and the infundibular recess of the third ventricle is thin and inferiorly pointed, (**B**) the optic chiasm and adjacent hypothalamus together appear U-shaped and the optic recess of the third ventricle has a teardrop shape, and (**C**) the optic chiasm appears dumbbell-shaped near its attachment point with the optic nerves. Note that the infundibulum is deviated from the midline in **B** as a result of a low-density pituitary microadenoma. (*From Daniels 1980.*)

precise if the patients are appropriately selected and the images and clinical findings are correlated. In CT, the most common microadenoma, the prolactin-secreting adenoma, typically produces some enlargement of the pituitary gland and a discrete hypodense region within the enhanced gland (Fig. 11-14) (Hemminghytt 1983; Syvertsen 1979; Marcovitz 1988*a*). In MR, most microadenomas have less signal intensity than does the normal gland in nonenhanced T_1WI, with variable signals on T_2WI and decreased signal intensity in enhanced images (Figs. 11-15 and 11-16) (Kucharczyk 1986; Pojunas 1986; Newton 1989; Kulkarni 1988). Rarely they may be isointense with the gland. Usually, the upper surface of the gland is convex and the height of the gland is greater than 9 mm. However, a gland may have a normal size and contour and still contain a small prolactinoma. Imaging findings which are often present but not specific for intrasellar tumor include thinning or asymmetry of the sellar floor, displacement of the infundibulum from the midline (Ahmadi 1990), and displacement of the "capillary tuft"

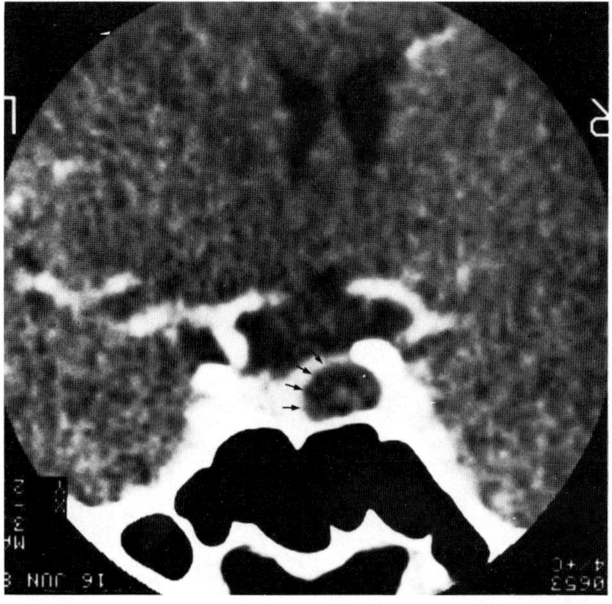
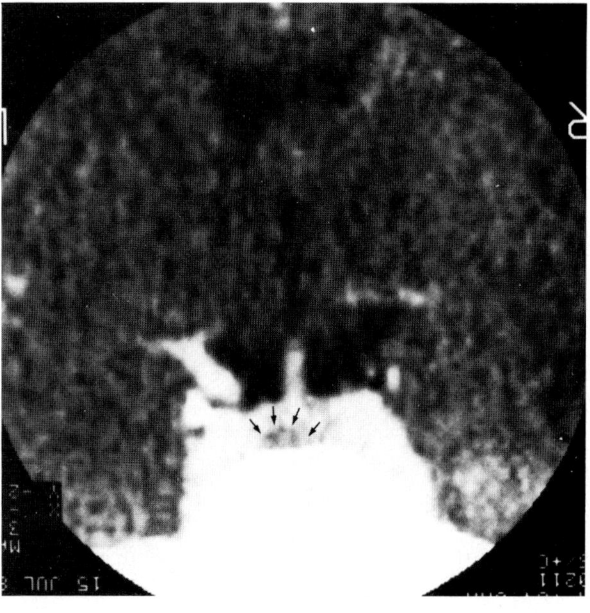

A B

Figure 11-14 Two examples of prolactinomas (arrows) that appear in coronal CECT as hypodense regions in the gland. The pituitary gland is enlarged in one case (**A**) but not in the other (**B**). (*From Hemminghytt 1983.*)

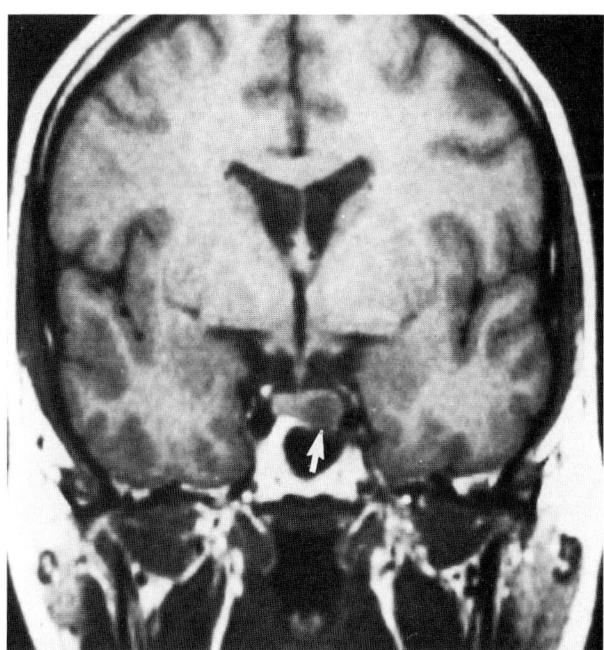

Figure 11-15 Prolactin-producing microadenoma in coronal T_1-weighted MRI. The tumor (arrow) has a signal intensity slightly less than that of a normal pituitary gland. The infundibulum is slightly deviated from the midline, and the gland is mildly enlarged.

(Bonneville 1983; Syvertsen 1979; Roppolo 1983*b*). Small cysts may simulate prolactin-secreting adenomas; therefore, the diagnosis of prolactinoma should not be made in a patient with no evidence of hyperprolactinemia. In adolescents and menstruous women with normal prolactin levels, nonhomogeneity or slight enlargement of the gland should not be interpreted as evidence of a prolactinoma (Wolpert 1984; Gardeur 1982; Swartz 1983; Elster 1990). Serial imaging may be useful in patients receiving bromocriptine treatment to demonstrate shrinkage of an adenoma (Fig. 11-17).

HGH- and ACTH-secreting microadenomas produce less distinctive CT and MR findings (Figs. 11-18 and 11-19) (Hemminghytt 1983; Marcovitz 1988*b*; Saris 1987;

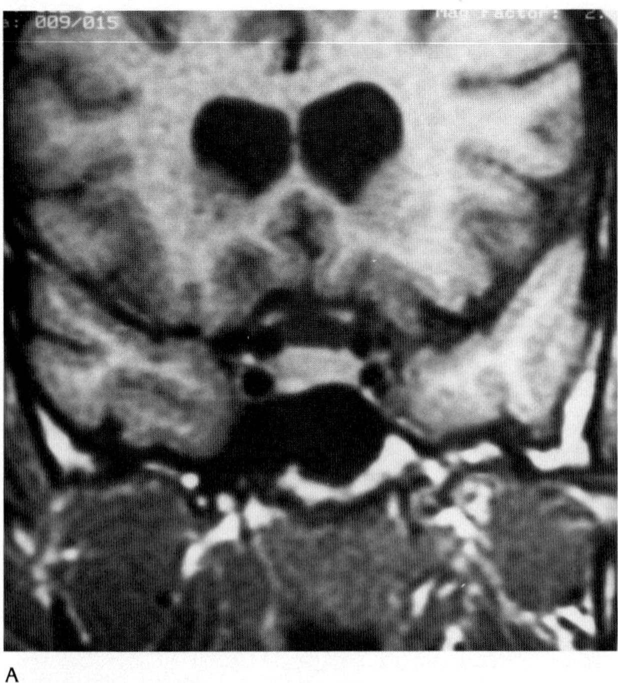

A

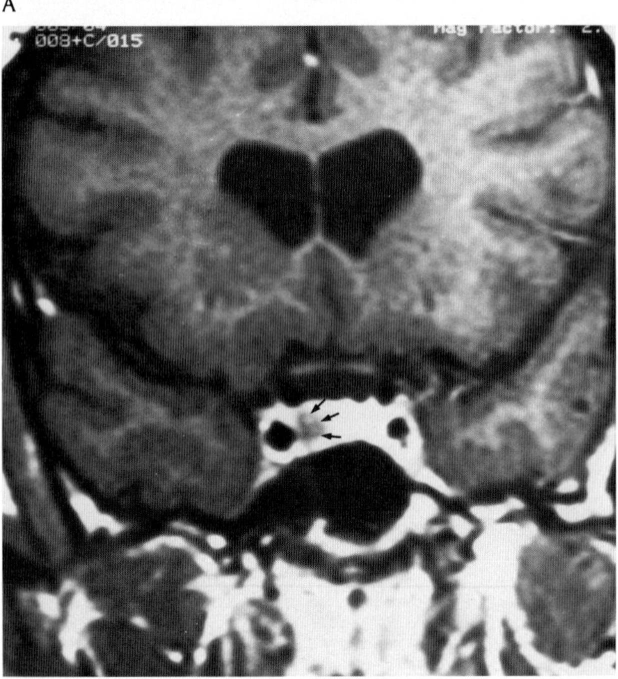

B

Figure 11-16 Prolactin-secreting microadenoma in coronal T_1WI without (**A**) and with (**B**) IV MR contrast (Gd-DTPA). The tumor is difficult to identify in **A** but not in **B,** where it (arrows) enhances less than the normal glandular tissue does.

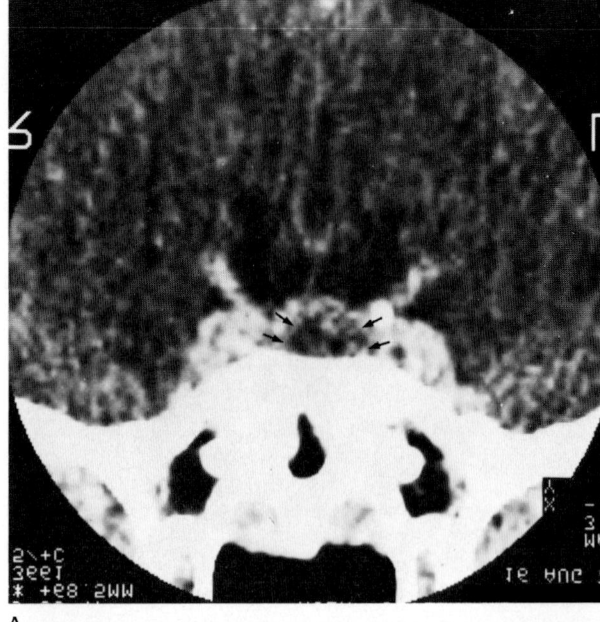

A

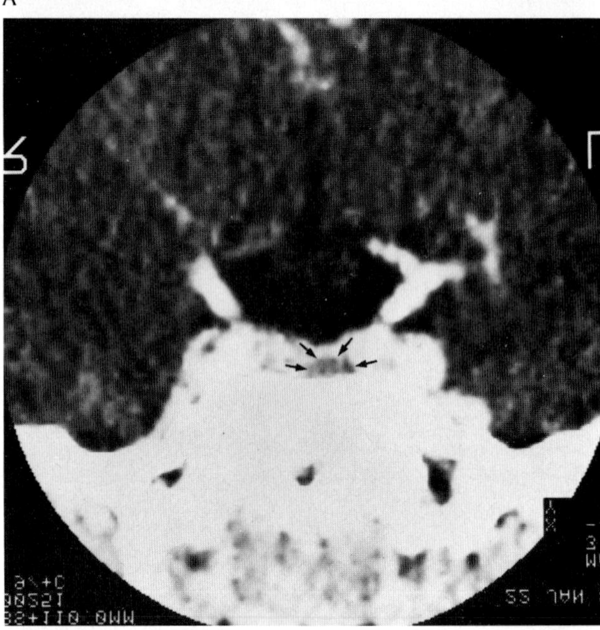

B

Figure 11-17 Effect of bromocriptine on a pituitary microadenoma. Coronal CECT shows a hypodense region (arrows, **A**) that decreases in size during bromocriptine therapy (arrows, **B**). (*From Daniels 1985a.*)

Davis 1987*a*). Because the tumors are less well encapsulated and less discrete, abnormal regions within the gland are identified less regularly. Furthermore, the gland may have minimal enlargement. MR, especially with intravenous contrast, is more effective than is CECT in detecting ACTH-secreting microadenomas (Peck 1988; Dwyer 1987; Doppman 1988). In a patient with the appropriate clinical symptomatology and chemical findings, the demonstration of a normal-sized and homogeneously enhancing pituitary gland does not exclude the diagnosis of adenoma. Conversely, asymptomatic pituitary adenomas are a common incidental finding at the time of autopsy (4.8 to 27 percent). These subclinical "incidentalomas" mostly represent slowly growing pituitary microadenomas and macroadenomas and do not necessarily require neurosurgical intervention, especially in the absence of abnormal visual fields or an abnormal pituitary function test (Reincke 1990).

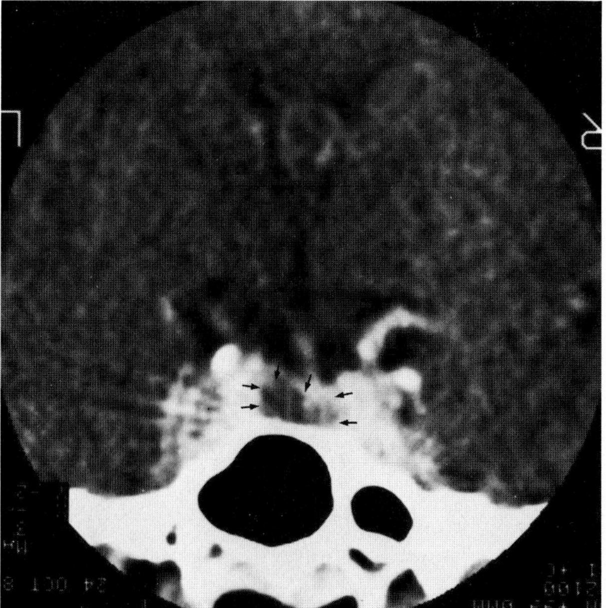

Figure 11-18 ACTH-secreting microadenoma in coronal CECT. The tumor (small black arrows) appears as a hypodense region that displaces the infundibulum. (*From Hemminghytt 1983.*)

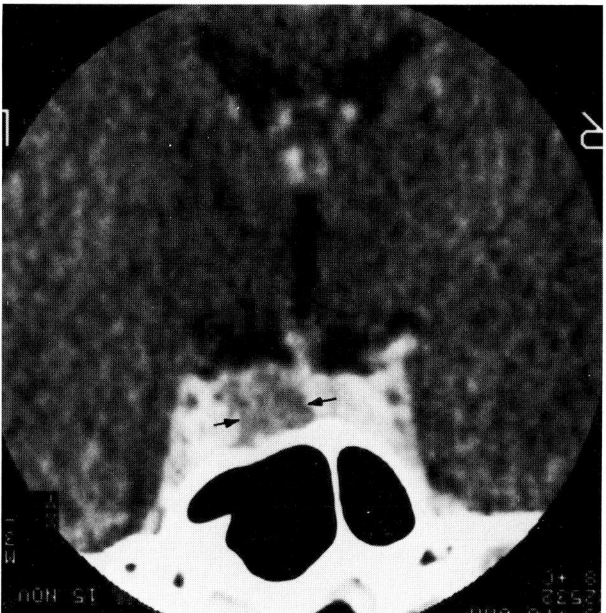

Figure 11-19 HGH-secreting microadenoma. Coronal CECT shows a hypodense region (small black arrows) associated with mild gland enlargement. (*From Hemminghytt 1983.*)

Macroadenomas can be reliably and accurately identified with CT (Fig. 11-20). Macroadenomas are isodense or slightly less dense than are the cavernous sinuses in CECT (Daniels 1981). A macroadenoma usually enlarges the sella, compresses the sphenoid sinus, or encroaches on the suprasellar cistern and may displace the chiasm or temporal lobes. A solid adenoma enhances homogeneously; cystic or necrotic regions appear as zones of hypodense areas within it. In some cases calcification is identified in the rim of the tumor or, even less commonly, homogeneously throughout the tumor matrix (Fig. 11-21) (Gyldenstein 1977; Critin 1977). Rarely, pituitary adenomas destroy the skull base or degenerate to carcinoma (Fig. 11-22).

MR also can be used to effectively evaluate pituitary adenomas (Kucharczyk 1986; Davis 1987*b*). Large solid pituitary adenomas appear as masses that are nearly isointense with brain in both T_1WI and T_2WI and that en-

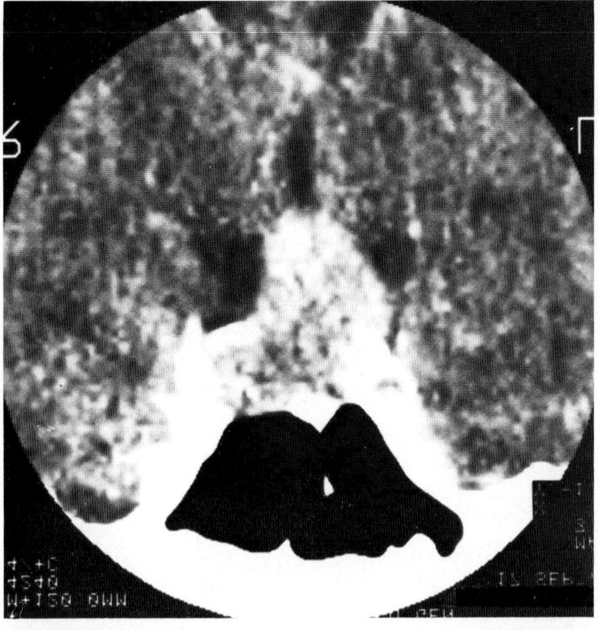
A

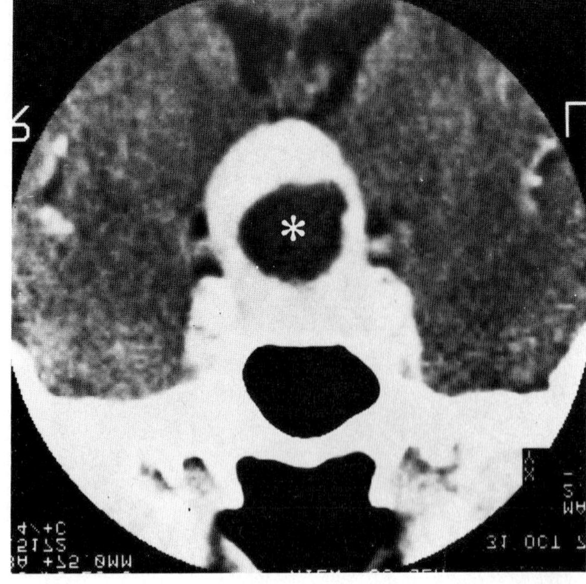
B

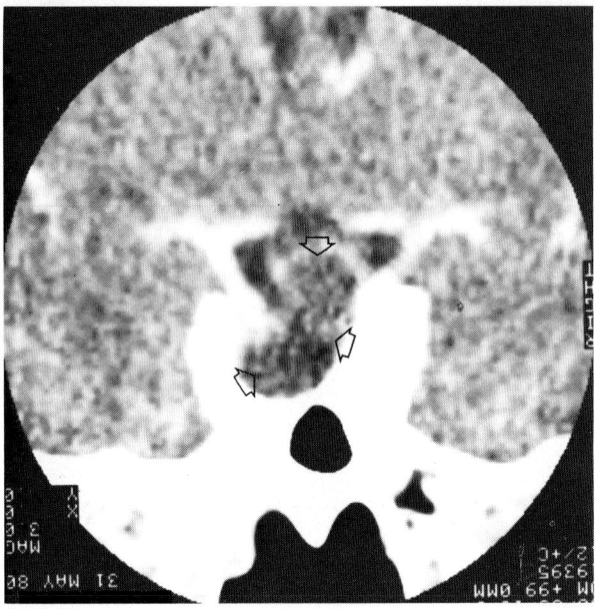
C

Figure 11-20 Examples of pituitary adenomas with solid (**A**), partially necrotic (asterisk * in **B**), and cystic (open arrows in **C**) regions. Necrotic tissue and fluid are not distinguishable on CT. (*From Hemminghytt 1983.*)

hance moderately with intravenous gadolinium (Figs. 11-23 through 11-25) (Lee 1985; Oot 1984; Bilaniuk 1984; Hawkes 1983; Davis 1987*a,b*). Pituitary adenomas reach a peak of contrast enhancement later than a normal pituitary gland does (Sakamoto 1991), and the best imaging contrast between them was achieved within 3 minutes after a bolus injection of MR contrast agent (Miki 1990). Cystic or necrotic components within the tumor have a signal intensity intermediate between that of CSF and that of tumor in T_1WI and have high signal intensity in T_2WI (Chakeres 1989). Coronal MR images effectively demonstrate adenomas which extend upward to the optic chiasm or laterally to obliterate the cavernous sinus (Figs. 11-23 through 11-25). The chiasm displaced by an adenoma can be identified more effectively with MR than it can be with CT (Bilaniuk 1984). Sagittal MR images are

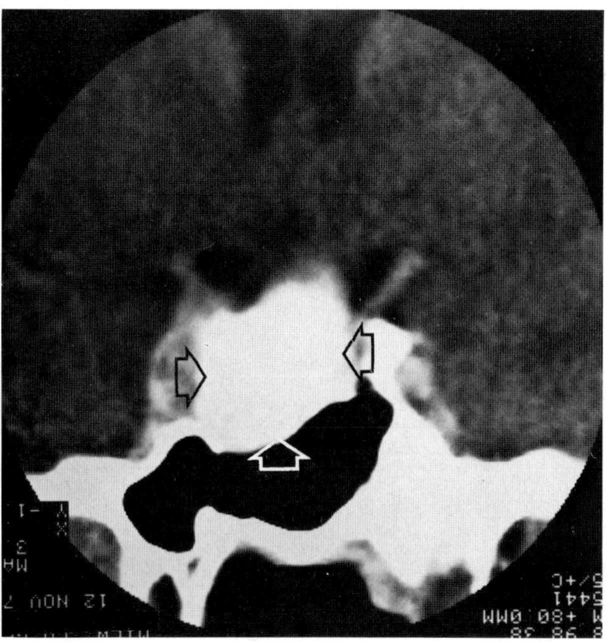

Figure 11-21 Atypical pituitary adenoma that is densely calcified (open arrows) on coronal CT. (*From Daniels 1981.*)

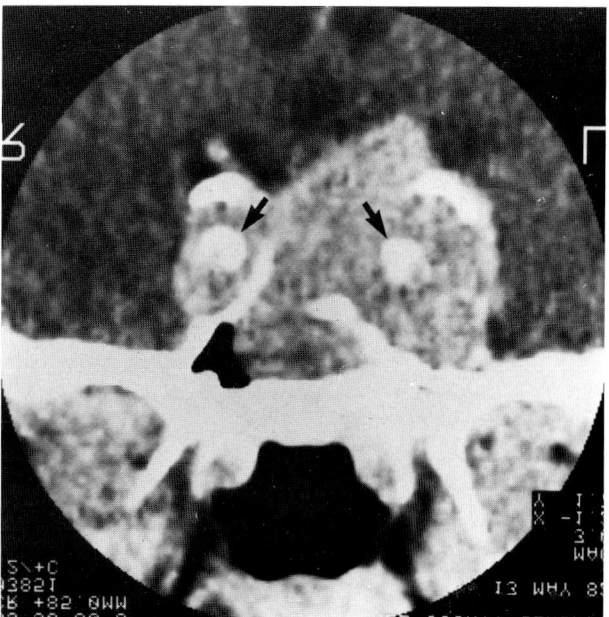

Figure 11-22 Aggressive benign pituitary macroadenoma on coronal CECT. The tumor destroys bone and extends into both cavernous sinuses, where it enhances less than the internal carotid arteries (black arrows) do. (*From Daniels 1985a.*)

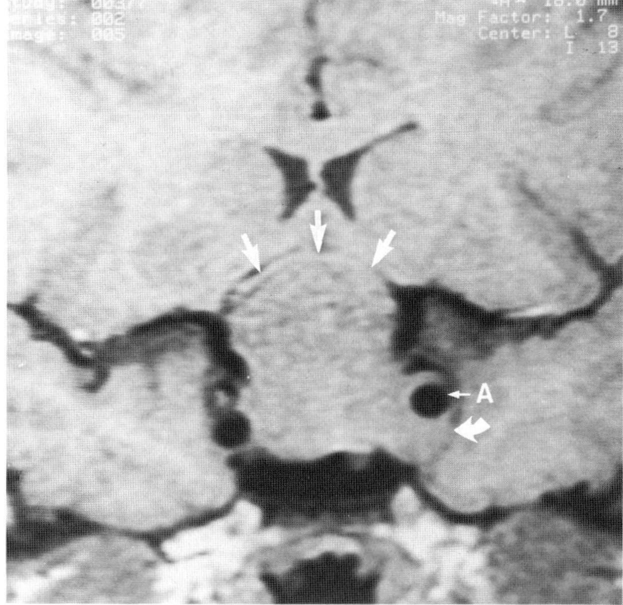

Figure 11-23 Pituitary adenoma extending upward to compress the optic chiasm (straight arrows) and laterally to invade and enlarge the left cavernous sinus (curved arrow) and displace the cavernous internal carotid artery (A) is demonstrated in coronal T_1-weighted MRI (*From Daniels 1987b.*)

especially useful in demonstrating chiasmal compression and posterior extension of the tumor. Extension of a tumor into the cavernous sinus is characterized by tissue with an intermediate signal intensity that displaces the cavernous sinus wall and encases and/or deforms the carotid artery (Daniels 1986*a*; Young 1988; Scotti 1988; Hirsch 1988). At present, MR with or without contrast agent does not reliably show subtle cavernous sinus invasion by a pituitary tumor (Scotti 1988). Identification of a venous space medial or inferomedial to the cavernous carotid artery in T_1-weighted gradient echo images excludes significant invasion of tumor into the sinus (Fig. 11-26). The absence of this venous space is a nonspecific finding that cannot be used to differentiate normal anatomic variation from cavernous sinus compression or invasion by a pituitary tumor. Tumor may

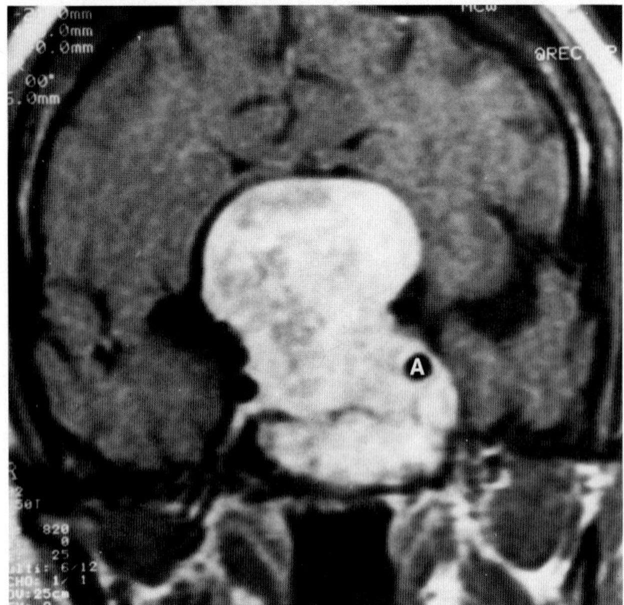

A

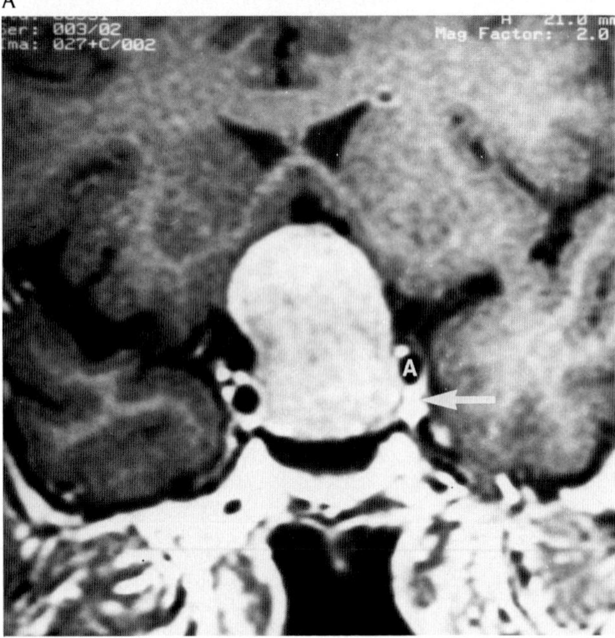

B

Figure 11-24 Examples of pituitary adenomas that enhance nearly homogeneously in coronal T_1-weighted MRI (**A** and **B**) with intravenous Gd-DTPA. In **A,** the tumor invades the sphenoid and left cavernous sinuses and displaces the cavernous internal carotid artery (A). In **B,** the adenoma compresses the left cavernous sinus and carotid artery (A) and enhances less than do the cavernous venous spaces (arrow).

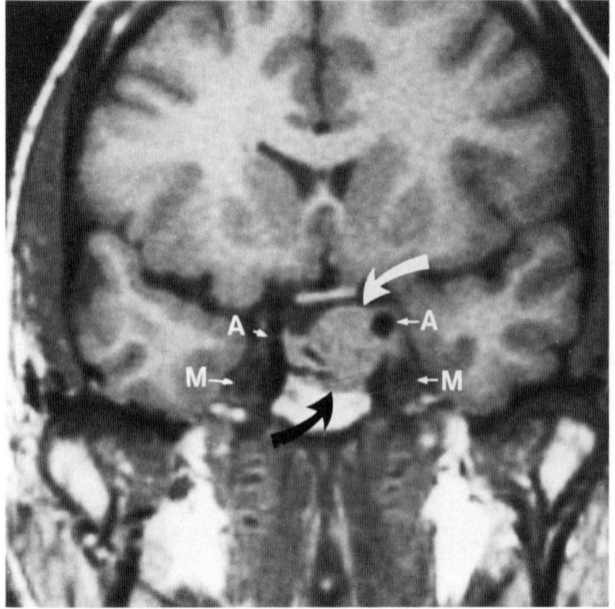

Figure 11-25 A pituitary macroadenoma in coronal T_1-weighted MRI. The tumor (curved arrows) extends to the left cavernous sinus, encases the internal carotid artery (A), and deforms Meckel's cave (M).

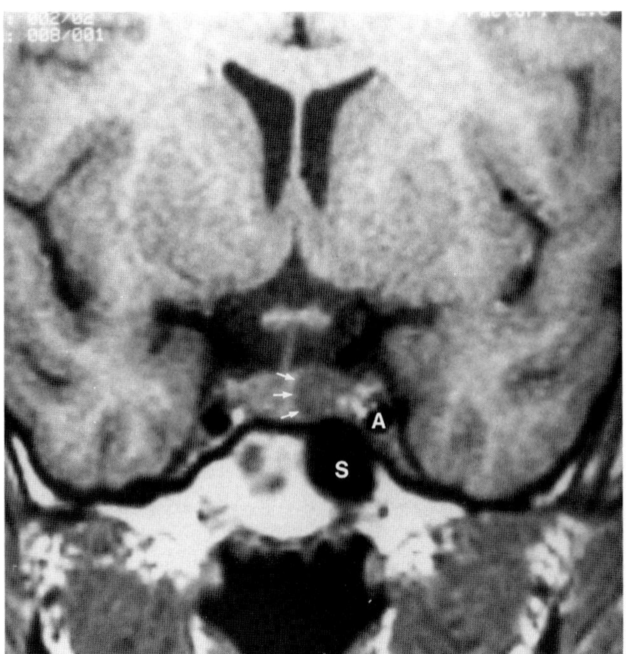

A

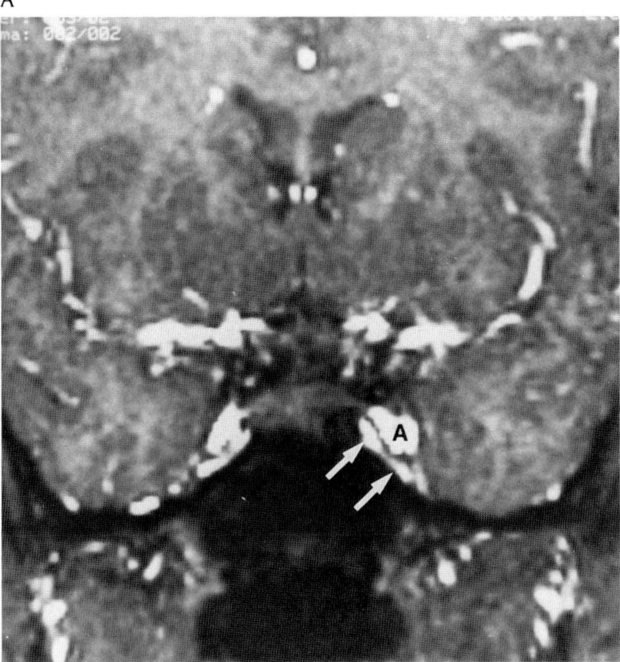

B

Figure 11-26 In coronal T_1-weighted SE MRI (**A**), a pituitary microadenoma (small arrows) appears hypointense to normal glandular tissue. In a corresponding coronal T_1-weighted gradient echo image (**B**), identification of an ipsilateral cavernous venous space with high signal intensity (large arrows) excludes significant cavernous sinus invasion. In **B,** a low-intensity area at the left side of the pituitary gland represents a magnetic susceptibility artifact due to asymmetrical aeration of the sphenoid sinus (S).

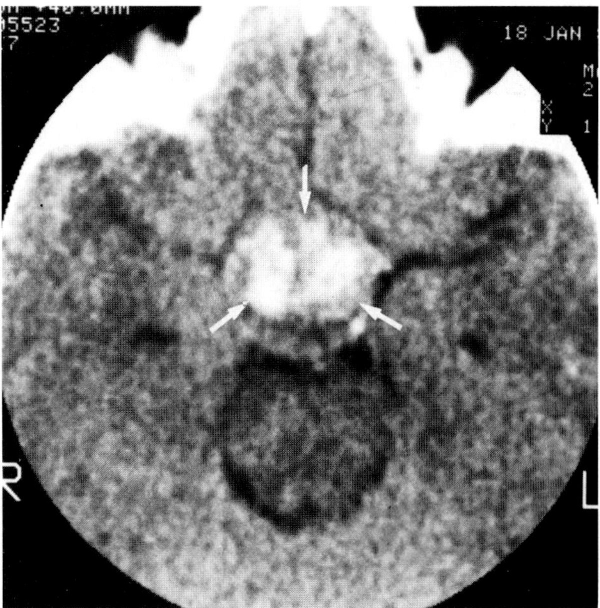

Figure 11-27 Pituitary apoplexy: Hemorrhage (arrows) in a pituitary adenoma is demonstrated on axial NCCT of a patient who suddenly developed right eye blinders. (*From Daniels 1981.*)

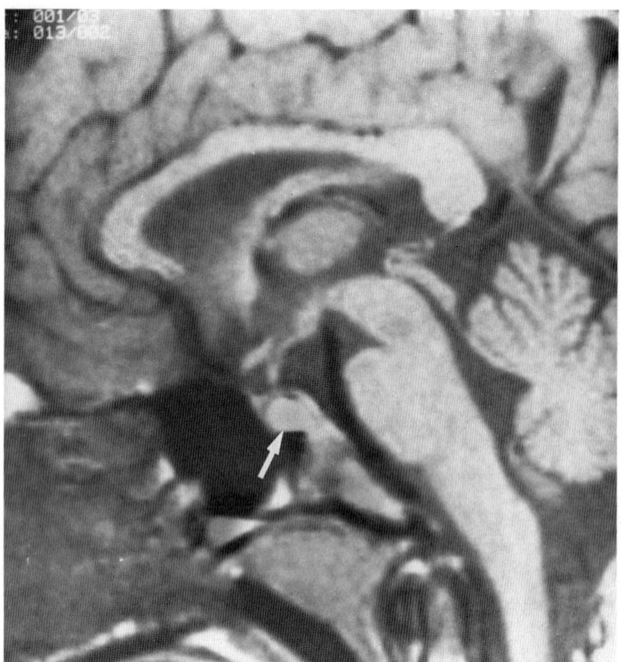
A

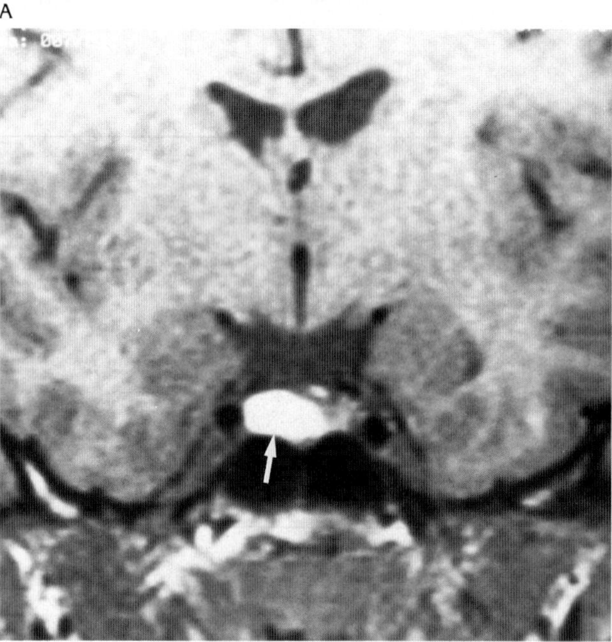
B

Figure 11-28 Hemorrhage (arrow) in a pituitary adenoma has a high signal intensity on sagittal (**A**) and coronal (**B**) T_1-weighted MRI.

spread along the dura without invading the cavernous sinus spaces.

Pituitary tumors occasionally undergo ischemic necrosis and hemorrhage if the blood supply to the tumor is impaired. Bromocriptine therapy can result in intratumoral hemorrhage in some cases (Pojunas 1986; Weissbuch 1986; Yousem 1989). With hemorrhage, the patient may show evidence of a rapidly expanding sellar mass; compression of the third, fourth, or sixth cranial nerve; diplopia; optic nerve compression with visual impairment; headache; and occasionally signs of meningeal irritation (Banna 1976). Rapid expansion of a pituitary tumor has been termed *pituitary apoplexy.* The choice of medical or surgical management depends almost exclusively on the status and impending threat to the visual apparatus (Rovit 1985). Pituitary apoplexy can occur spontaneously or after radiotherapy. In pituitary apoplexy CT may show hyperdensity due to hemorrhage (Fig. 11-27) or may show only hypodensity in the sella with a rim of enhancement (Post 1980). MR is more sensitive than CT in detecting hemorrhage in pituitary tumors. Incidental pituitary hemorrhage has been seen with MR (Ostrov 1989). In MR, a subacute hemorrhage (i.e., more than 1 week old) in the pituitary gland has hyperintensity in T_1WI and T_2WI because of methemoglobin formation (Fig. 11-28) (Gomori 1985; Kyle 1990).

Craniopharyngioma

Craniopharyngiomas are the second most common intrasellar tumor. They are encapsulated cystic tumors of the sella or the suprasellar region which originate from remnants of Rathke's pouch (Chason 1971). The contents of the cystic components are variable. Fluid within a cyst may appear similar to CSF or to "motor oil." Blood, protein, or cholesterol may be present in the cyst fluid (Pusey 1987; Chakeres 1989). The clinical manifestations of the tumor usually include hypopituitarism, diabetes insipidus, and hypothalamic or visual symptoms. Although these tumors may occur at any age, there are two incidence peaks: the second and fifth decades of life.

The characteristic CT findings of craniopharyngioma are a combination of hypodense areas representing cysts and focal hyperdense areas representing calcifications (Figs. 11-29 and 11-30) (Daniels 1981). The cystic components can be extensive, reaching even into the posterior fossa. Calcification, which is effectively demonstrated with CT, is less common and extensive in adults than it is in children. Except when the tumors are completely solid and lack calcification or cystic areas, they are usually easily distinguished from pituitary adenomas (Fig. 11-31).

In MR, solid and cystic portions of the craniopharyngioma can be shown (Fig. 11-32) (Karnaze 1986; Pusey 1987; Lee 1985; Sartor 1987). The solid component appears nearly isointense with brain in all pulse sequences. Tumor calcification, when detected, appears as a region of negligible signal intensity. The appearance of the cysts varies. Some are isointense with CSF in T_1WI and T_2WI; those with a high protein content are slightly hyperintense with respect to CSF. Hemorrhagic cysts containing subacute blood have high signal intensity in T_1WI or T_2WI (Chakeres 1989). In some cases sagittal MR images complement the study by defining some anatomic relationships effectively.

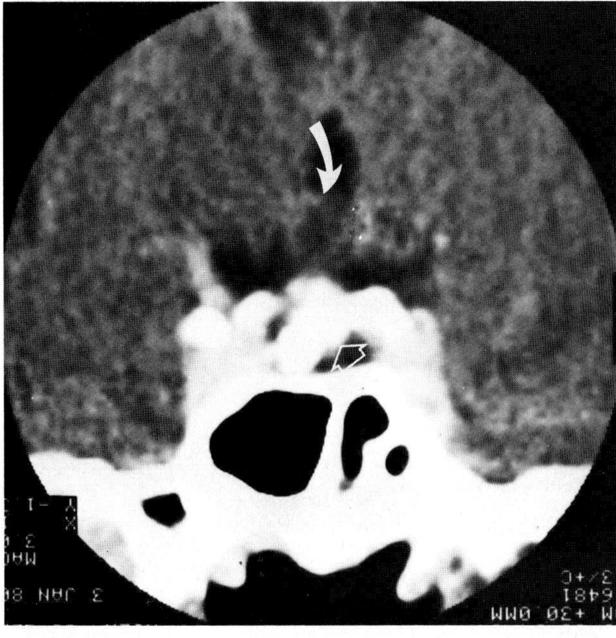

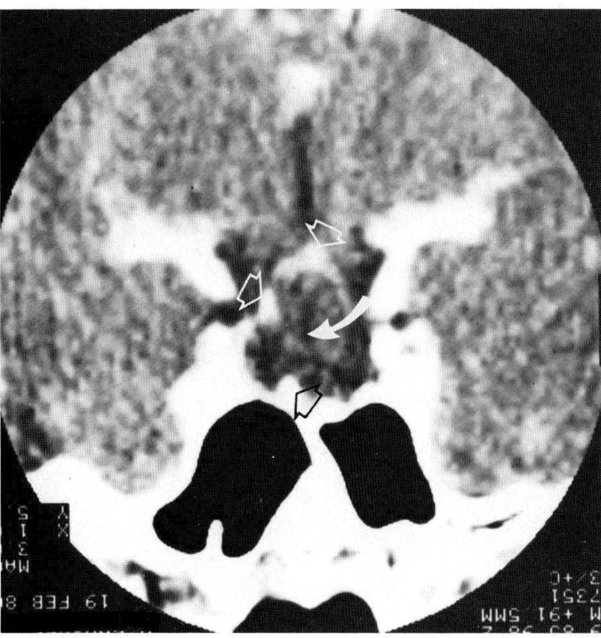

A B

Figure 11-29 Two examples (**A** and **B**) of intrasellar and suprasellar craniopharyngiomas on coronal enhanced CT. Dense globular calcification (open arrows) and cystic regions (curved arrows) are common. (*From Daniels 1985a.*)

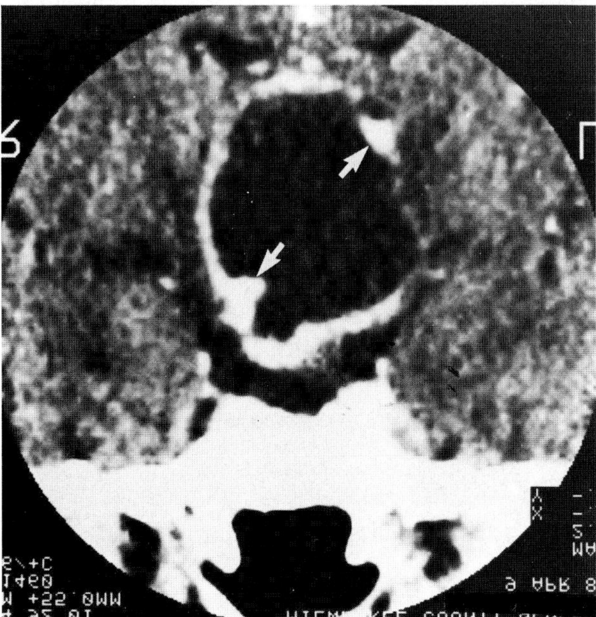

Figure 11-30 Cystic craniopharyngioma on coronal CECT. Rim enhancement and focal rim calcification (straight arrows) are detected. (*From Daniels 1981.*)

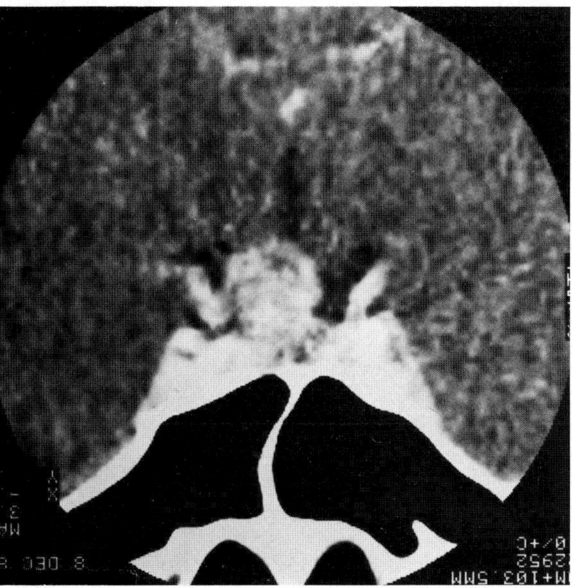

Figure 11-31 Atypical craniopharyngioma on coronal CECT. The tumor homogeneously enhances without calcification or a significant cystic component. (*From Daniels 1985a.*)

Meningioma

Meningiomas arise on the dural surface of the anterior clinoid processes, the diaphragma sellae, tuberculum, or dorsum sellae or cavernous sinuses. Many suprasellar and parasellar meningiomas have characteristic features which permit a specific diagnosis on CT. Globular calcification, which is less common in parasellar meningiomas than it is in meningiomas elsewhere, and hyperostotic bone adjacent to the tumor are more characteristic of meningiomas than they are of other parasellar neoplasms (Figs. 11-33 through 11-35) (Lee 1976).

The matrix of a meningioma is usually homogeneous

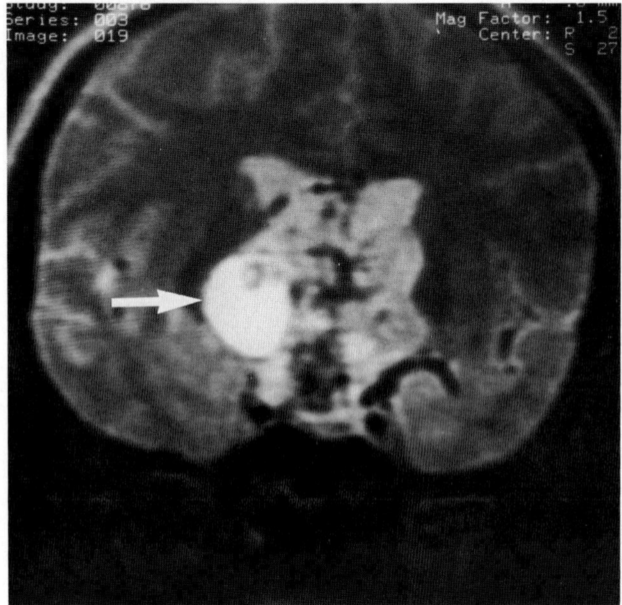

A

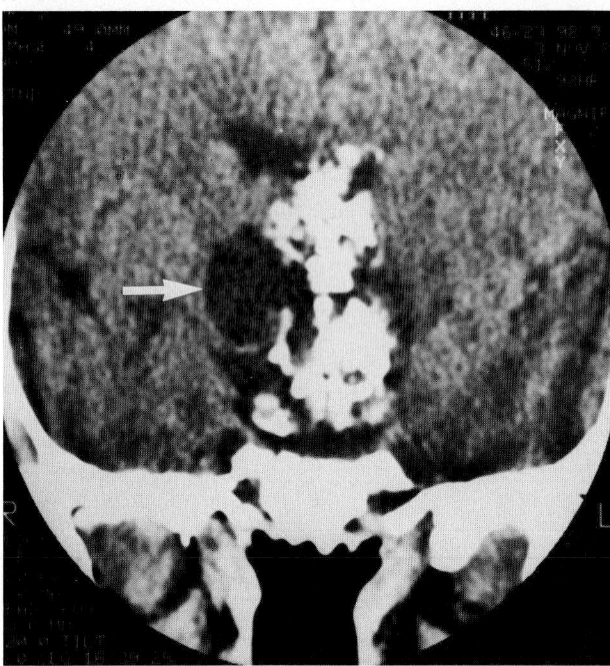

B

Figure 11-32 Suprasellar craniopharyngioma on coronal T_2-weighted MR (**A**) and nonenhanced CT (**B**) sections. The tumor contains a hemorrhagic cyst (arrow) and dense globular calcification, which are easier to demonstrate in **A** and **B,** respectively.

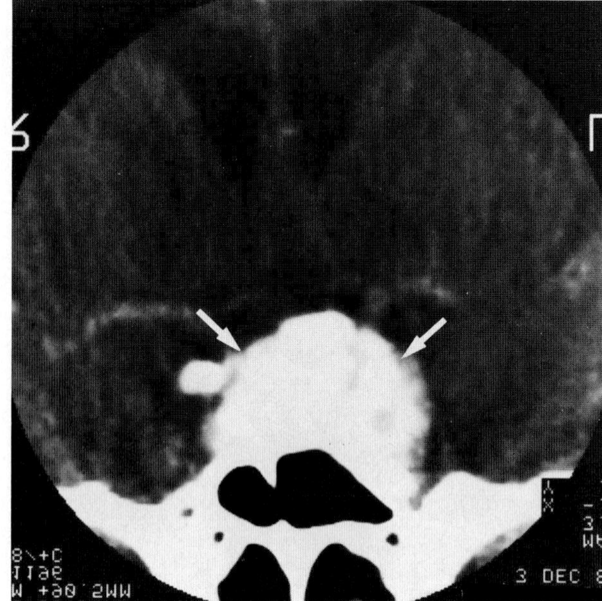

Figure 11-33 Densely calcified meningioma (arrows) on coronal CECT.

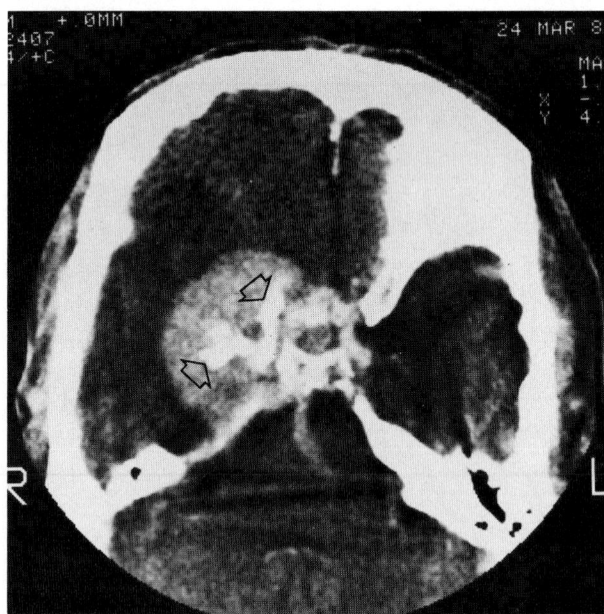

Figure 11-34 Axial CECT demonstrates a parasellar meningioma that contains dense globular calcifications (open arrows). (*From Daniels 1985a.*)

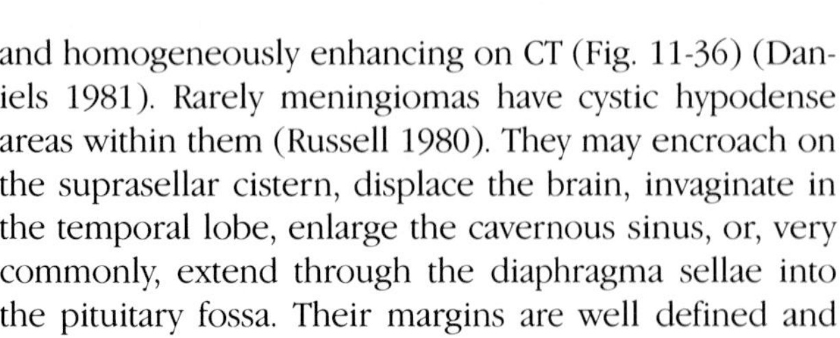

and homogeneously enhancing on CT (Fig. 11-36) (Daniels 1981). Rarely meningiomas have cystic hypodense areas within them (Russell 1980). They may encroach on the suprasellar cistern, displace the brain, invaginate in the temporal lobe, enlarge the cavernous sinus, or, very commonly, extend through the diaphragma sellae into the pituitary fossa. Their margins are well defined and smoothly marginated. Cerebral edema may be present when the brain is compressed. The attachment of the meningioma to the dural surface is usually broad, sessile, and eccentrically located with respect to the sella. Therefore, reformatted sagittal images can help distinguish adenomas from meningiomas (Fig. 11-37). Angiography may be necessary in questionable cases to distinguish the

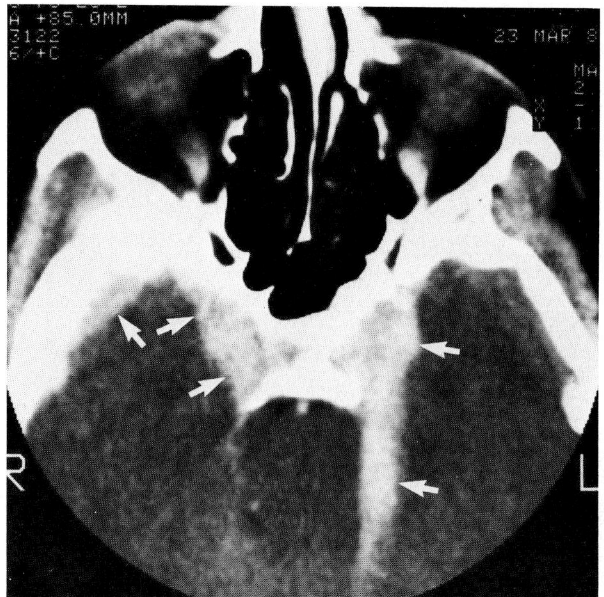

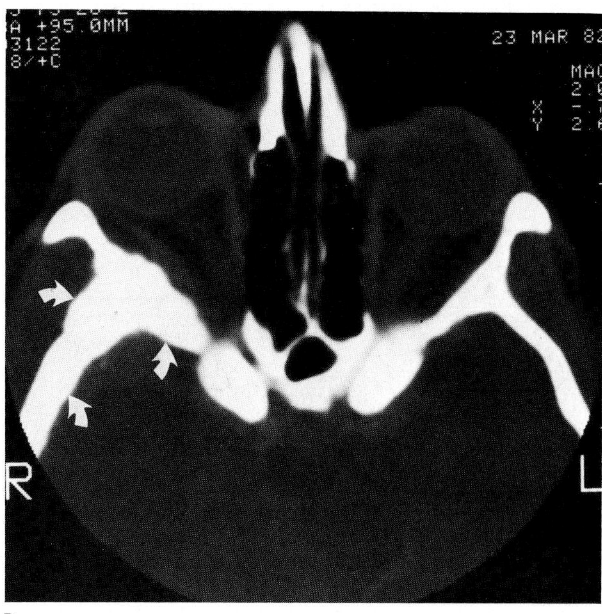

A B

Figure 11-35 Parasellar meningioma on axial CT; soft tissue (**A**) and bone (**B**) windows. It spreads along the tentorial reflections and the right sphenoid bone (short arrows in **A**) and has associated sphenoid hyperostosis (curved arrows in **B**). (*From Daniels 1981.*)

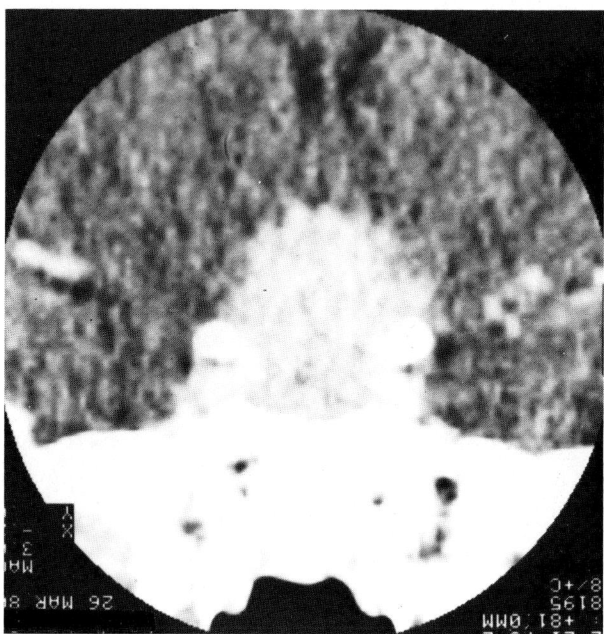

Figure 11-36 Meningioma on coronal CT. Homogeneously enhancing without calcification, the tumor could be mistaken for a pituitary adenoma. (*From Daniels 1985a.*)

characteristic dense stain and dural arterial supply of a meningioma from the late faint venous blush and capsular arterial supply of a pituitary adenoma. Meningiomas that lack calcification and hyperostosis are more difficult to distinguish from adenomas and other parasellar tumors (Fig. 11-29).

Juxtasellar meningiomas also can be evaluated with MR (Yeakley 1988). Because most meningiomas are approximately isointense with brain in T_1WI or T_2WI, they are more conspicuous with MR if contrast medium is used. After intravenous administration of Gd-DTPA, meningiomas have hyperintensity in T_1WI (Fig. 11-38) (Breger 1987). The globular or psammomatous calcifications in meningiomas may produce focal regions of hypointensity

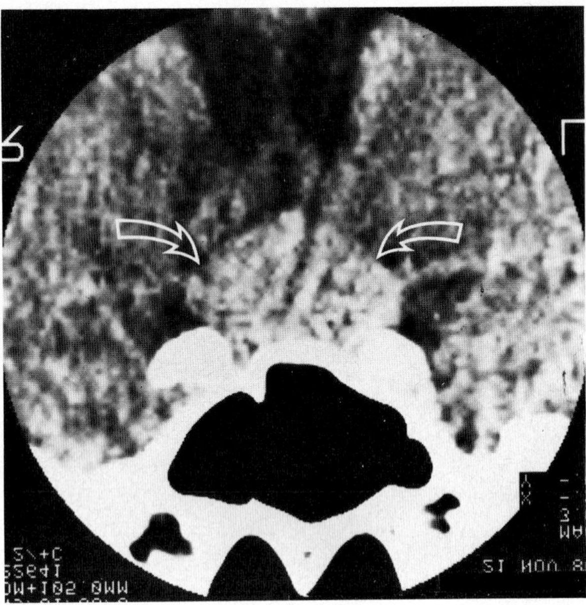

A

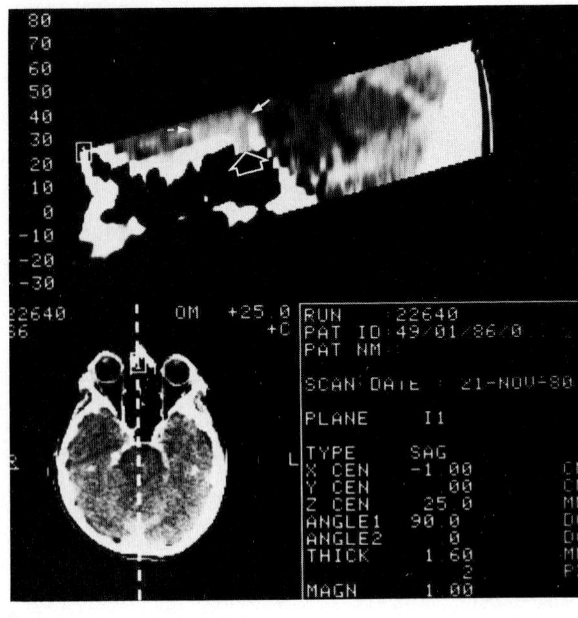

B

Figure 11-37 Example of tuberculum sellae meningioma. The tumor (open curved arrows, **A**) homogeneously enhances and appears somewhat diamond-shaped on coronal CECT. In a sagittal reformatted image (**B**), the tumor (small arrows) is broad-based and centered anterior to a normal-sized sella (open arrow). (*From Daniels 1985a.*)

or may not be recognized in MR images. A pituitary macroadenoma that extends upward and through the diaphragma sellae may simulate a miningioma. However, in sagittal images a meningioma has a broader base and is usually not entered above the pituitary fossa.

Aneurysm

Aneurysms are included in the differential diagnosis of intrasellar and parasellar masses (Daniels 1981). Internal carotid artery aneurysms which erode into the sella represent a greater differential diagnostic problem than do

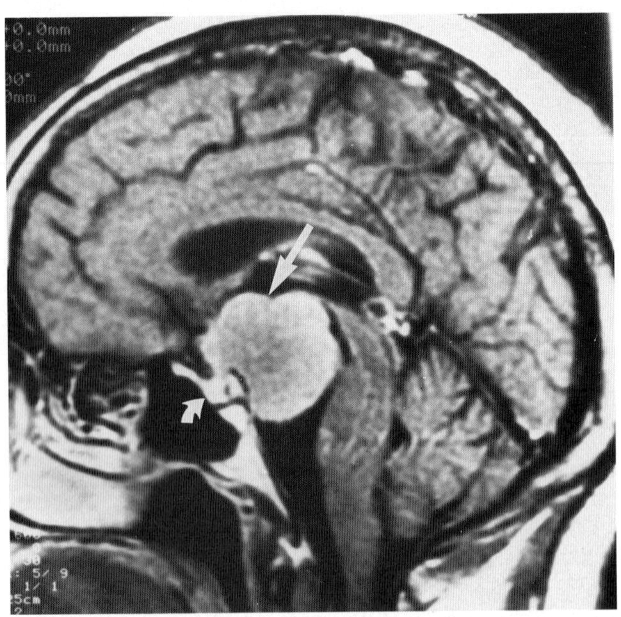

A

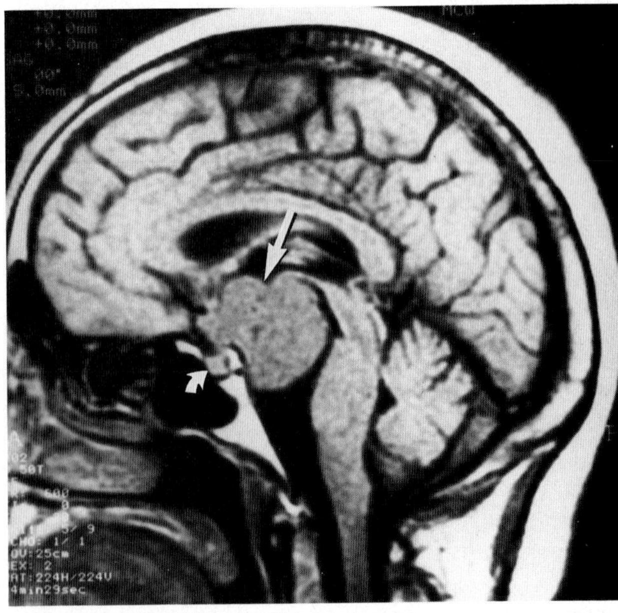

B

Figure 11-38 Juxtasellar meningioma (straight arrow) intensely enhances in sagittal T_1-weighted MRI without (**A**) and with (**B**) intravenous gadolinium. The tumor is centered posterior to a normal-sized pituitary fossa (curved arrow).

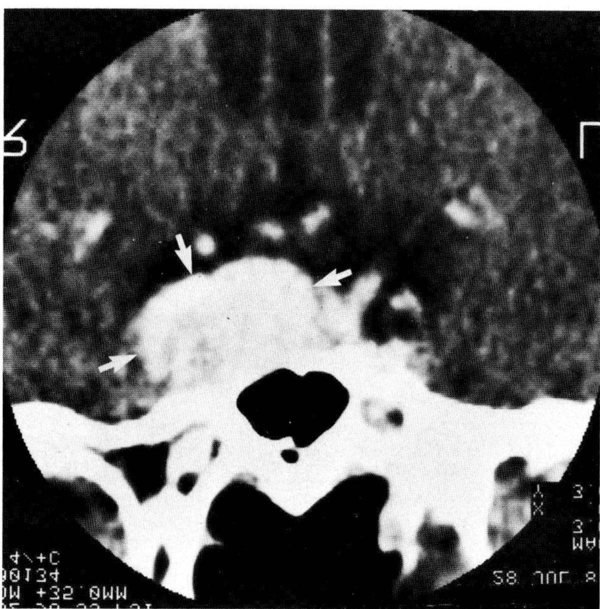

Figure 11-39 Giant aneurysm of the cavernous internal carotid artery (white arrows) with an intrasellar component is demonstrated. Coronal CECT shows intense homogeneous enhancement. (*From Daniels 1985a.*).

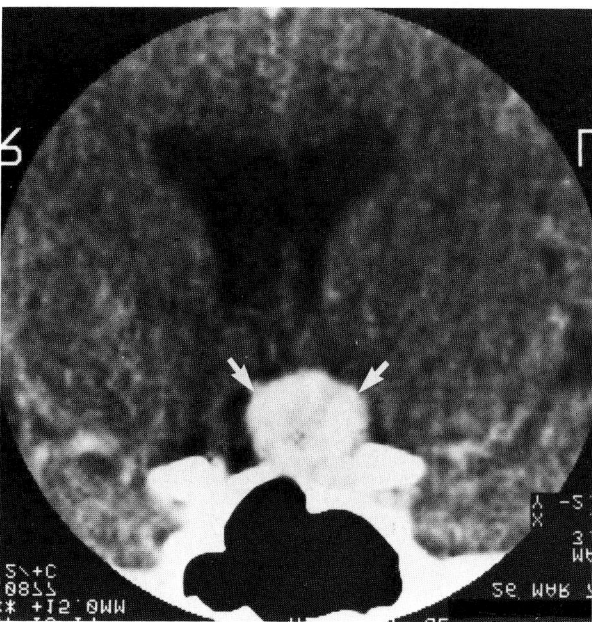

Figure 11-40 Supraclinoid internal carotid artery aneurysm (arrows) on coronal CECT. It has dense homogeneous enhancement. (*From Daniels 1985a.*)

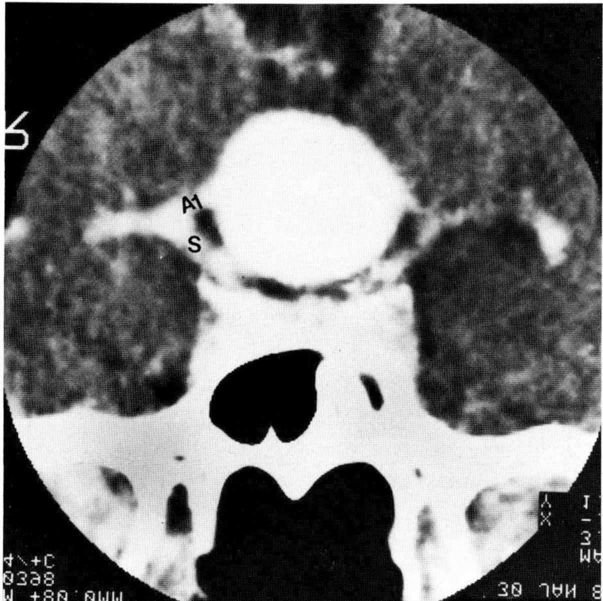

Figure 11-41 Anterior communicating artery aneurysm markedly enhances and appears oval on coronal CECT. S = supraclinoid internal carotid artery; A_1 = A_1 segment of internal carotid artery. (*From Daniels 1985b.*)

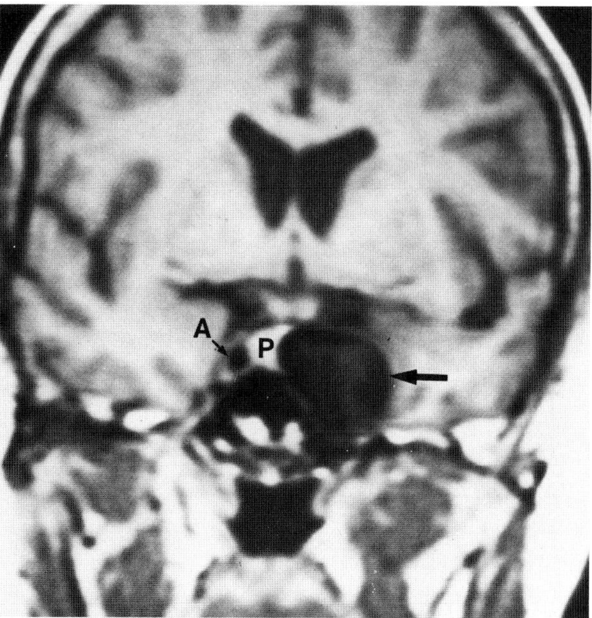

Figure 11-42 Giant aneurysm (arrow) of the cavernous internal carotid artery distorting the pituitary gland (P) on coronal T_1-weighted MRI. The aneurysm has a hypointense signal with some inhomogeneity, probably as a result of turbulent blood flow. (A = internal carotid artery). (*From Daniels 1985b.*)

those which occur in the circle of Willis. Aneurysms at the anterior communicating, posterior communicating, internal carotid, and middle cerebral arteries have a characteristic anatomic relationship to the cerebral vessels, especially in coronal CT images. In CT intracavernous and paracavernous aneurysms may appear as homogeneously enhancing rounded or lobulated masses (Figs. 11-39 through 11-41). They may have calcification, especially in the rim. When an organized thrombus is present, the aneurysm appears nonhomogeneous in CECT images because the thrombus enhances less than do the lumen and the vessel wall.

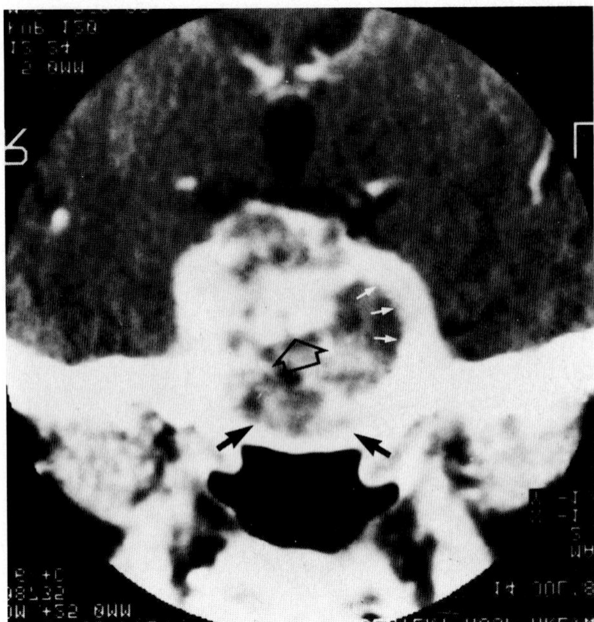

Figure 11-43 Chordoma, which nonhomogeneously enhances, has central calcification (open arrow), destroys the skull base (black arrows), and displaces the left cavernous sinus (small white arrows) on coronal CECT.

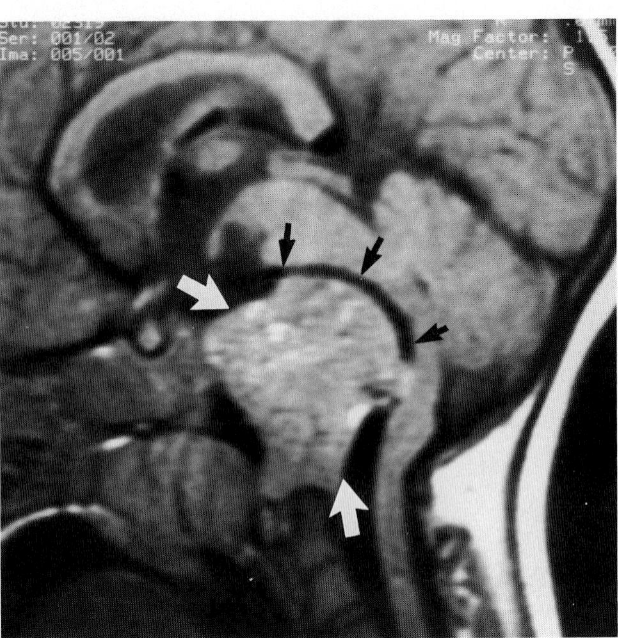

Figure 11-44 Chordoma (white arrows) destroying the clivus, containing hemorrhagic foci with a high signal intensity, and displacing the brainstem and basilar artery (black arrows) is shown on sagittal T_1-weighted MRI. (*From Daniels 1988b.*)

MR may help characterize juxtasellar aneurysms (Fig. 11-42) (Daniels 1985*b*). In T_1- and T_2-weighted SE images, flowing blood within the aneurysm may have very low signal intensity. Turbulent flow may produce a nonhomogeneous signal. A thrombus within an aneurysm usually has a signal intensity higher than that of the blood. In T_1-weighted gradient echo images, the lumen of an aneurysm typically has high signal intensity.

Aneurysms present in a number of different ways. They may cause a cranial nerve palsy if they compress the cavernous sinus, visual impairment if the chiasm is compressed, and severe headache and meningismus if they bleed.

Chordoma

Chordomas—neoplasms of primitive notochord remnants—are locally invasive, slowly growing neoplasms that occur in the clivus and the sphenoid bone. Characteristic CT features are destruction of bone in the skull base and a soft tissue mass which is often calcified (Fig. 11-43) (Daniels 1985*a*). They usually occur in the sixth and seventh decades of life but can occur earlier. The degree of CT enhancement and nonhomogeneity is variable. In MR, a chordoma usually appears as a soft tissue mass that replaces fatty marrow in the clivus and appears hypointense or isointense to cerebral tissue in T_1WI and hyperintense in T_2WI (Sze 1988). A chordoma may contain areas of hemorrhage that have hyperintensity in T_1WI and T_2WI (Fig. 11-44). Chordomas are therefore distinctive from most other sellar or parasellar masses except for metastasis. An aggressive pituitary adenoma may simulate a chordoma.

Metastasis

Metastases to the sellar region most commonly arise from lung, breast, kidney, GI tract, or nasopharyngeal tumors (Figs. 11-45 and 11-46) (Taveras 1976). In CT, metastases to the bone sella or the pituitary gland produce a permeative destructive pattern in the sphenoid bone characterized by irregular, indistinct margins. These tumors show a varying degree of enhancement and rarely calcification (Daniels 1981). Differentiation from an aggressive pituitary adenoma or a chordoma may be difficult. MR effectively demonstrates the mass which may be invading the pituitary fossa, cavernous sinus, sphenoid sinus, and sellar cortex (Fig. 11-47). Bone destruction is, however, difficult to demonstrate. Hemorrhagic areas within malignant tumors may appear as hyperintense regions in both T_1WI and T_2WI (Gomeri 1985).

Empty Sella

The empty sella usually is an incidental finding most commonly seen in women with an incomplete diaphragma sellae (Taveras 1976). Either an involved pituitary tumor or a congenital weakness of the diaphragma sellae has been suggested as a cause for empty sella (Taylor 1982). Intrasellar herniation of the optic chiasm has been found with empty sella.

The diagnosis can be made in coronal CT or MR images (Figs. 11-48 and 11-49). The sella is usually enlarged.

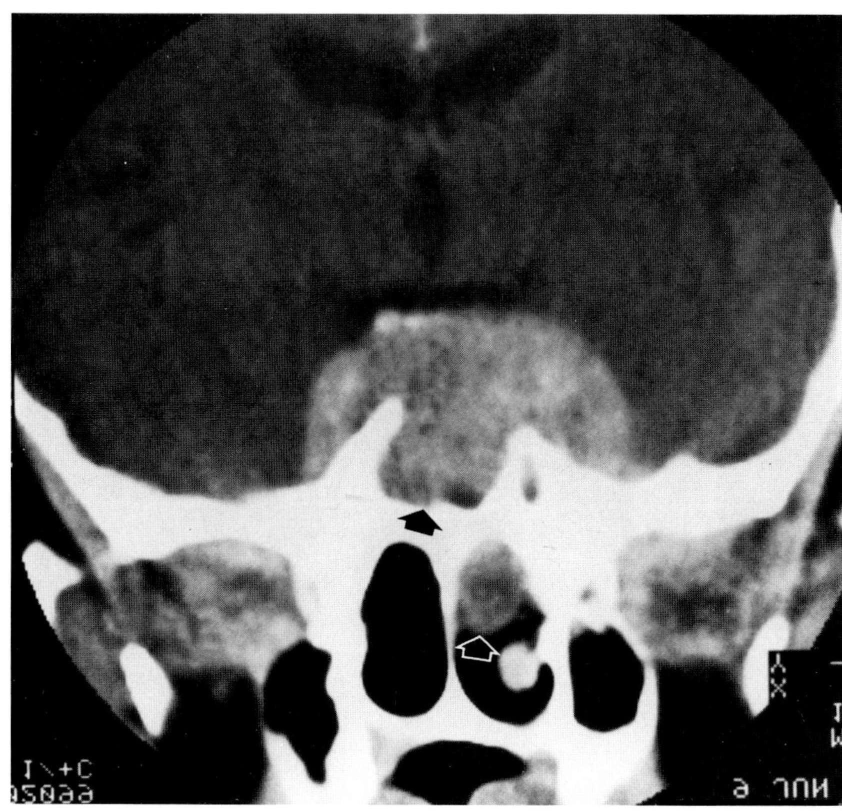

Figure 11-45 Nasopharyngeal carcinoma (open arrow) invades the sphenoid sinus (closed arrow) and sellar region on coronal CECT. (*From Daniels 1985a.*)

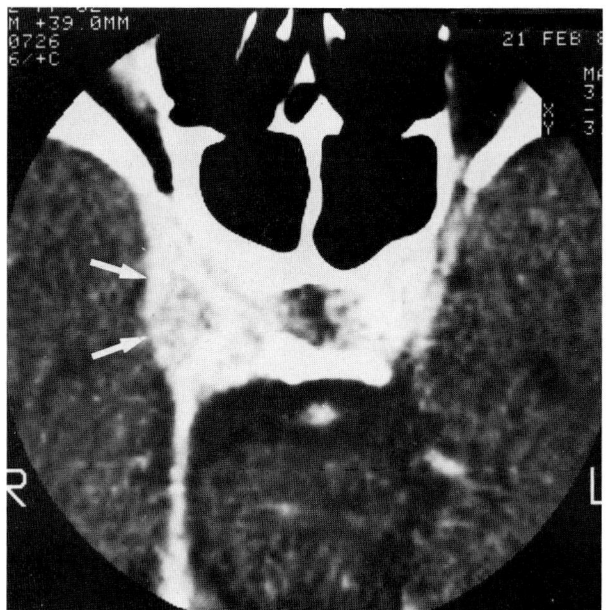

Figure 11-46 Squamosal carcinoma metastatic to the right cavernous sinus is shown by abnormal bulging of the right lateral cavernous sinus margin (long arrows). (*From Daniels 1985a.*)

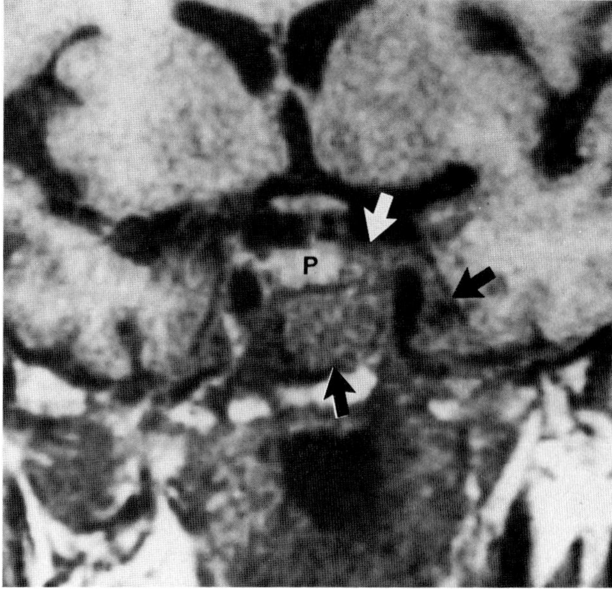

Figure 11-47 Squamous cell carcinoma (arrows) that is invading the sphenoid and left cavernous sinuses and has slightly lower signal intensity than the deformed pituitary gland (P) is demonstrated on coronal T_1-weighted MRI. (*From Daniels 1988b.*)

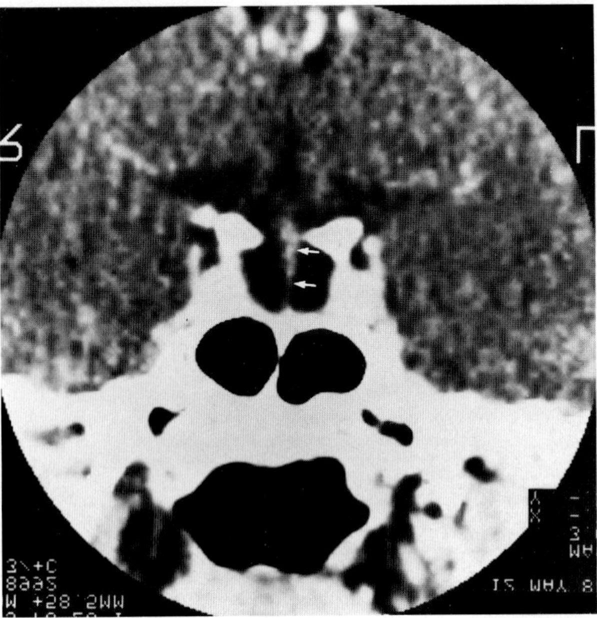

Figure 11-48 Coronal CECT of an empty sella. The infundibulum (arrows) extends to the sellar floor. (*From Daniels 1985a.*)

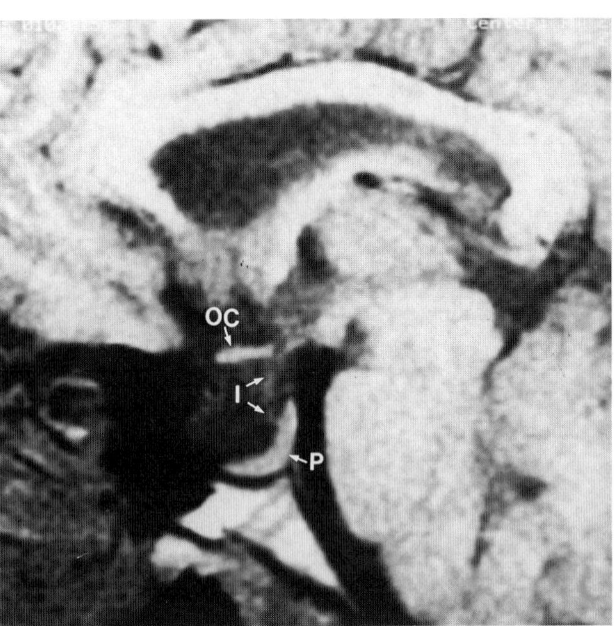

Figure 11-49 Empty sella in sagittal T_1-weighted MRI. The infundibulum (I) can be seen extending to the small pituitary gland (P). (OC = optic chiasm.) (*From Daniels 1988b.*)

A normal or elongated infundibulum connects the tuber cinereum with the small pituitary gland in the sella. Identification of the infundibulum by means of CT is facilitated by intravenous contrast administration and thin high-resolution coronal sections (Fig. 11-48) (Haughton 1980). The "infundibulum sign" can be used to differentiate an empty sella from other low-density processes, such as a cystic tumor or an intrasellar third ventricle, which displace the infundibulum. In rare cases when the infundibulum cannot be identified in CT and MR is not available, intrathecally enhanced CT can be used to diagnose empty sella.

Neurinoma

Parasellar neurinomas may arise from cranial nerves III, IV, V, or VI in the cavernous sinus. A neurinoma of cranial nerve V involving the gasserian ganglion characteristically erodes bone near the foramen ovale and the tip of the petrous pyramid (Fig. 11-50) (Escourolle 1978). Neurinomas of cranial nerves III, IV, or V are less common. CT or MR shows a neurinoma as a mass in the cavernous sinus which homogeneously enhances with intravenous contrast medium (Breger 1987; Watabe 1989). In NCMR, trigeminal neurinomas typically have hypointensity in T_1-WI and hyperintensity in T_2-WI (Yuh 1988). Calcification and necrosis are uncommon findings in these tumors.

Epidermoid and Dermoid

Epidermoids and dermoids are included in the differential diagnosis of suprasellar cystic lesions. Epidermoids have a thin epithelial cyst wall and fluid contents; dermoids have hair, complex dermal elements, calcification,

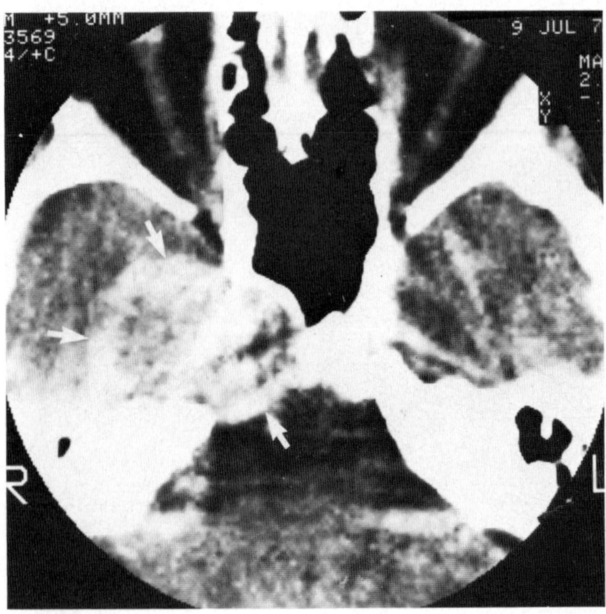

Figure 11-50 Axial CECT of a neurinoma of cranial nerve V (arrows) effaces the skull base by the right petrous apex. It enhances nonhomogeneously.

or fat in addition to epithelium (Paul 1972). On CT images, a dermoid or epidermoid, like an arachnoid cyst, may be isodense with CSF (5 to 15 HU). The presence of calcification or fat in a predominantly cystic lesion suggests a dermoid rather than an epidermoid. Intrathecal contrast agents may be required to define the margins of a dermoid or epidermoid that is isodense with CSF. Enlargement of the suprasellar cistern and displacement of the normal cisternal structures such as the chiasm suggest the presence of a cystic suprasellar mass. In MR, an epidermoid typically has hypointensity in T_1WI and hyperintensity in T_2WI (Tampieri 1989). Fat within a dermoid has high and low signal intensity in T_1WI and T_2WI respectively.

Chiasmal Glioma

The most common presentation of a chiasmal glioma is in adolescent girls with bilateral visual abnormalities and optic atrophy (Merritt 1969; Miller 1980). Some chiasmal gliomas are associated with neurofibromatosis. In CT or MR, they appear as sharply defined globular suprasellar masses (Figs. 11-51 and 11-52). In CT, a chiasmal glioma may have slightly increased density and slight contrast enhancement (Daniels 1980). MR shows optic gliomas ef-

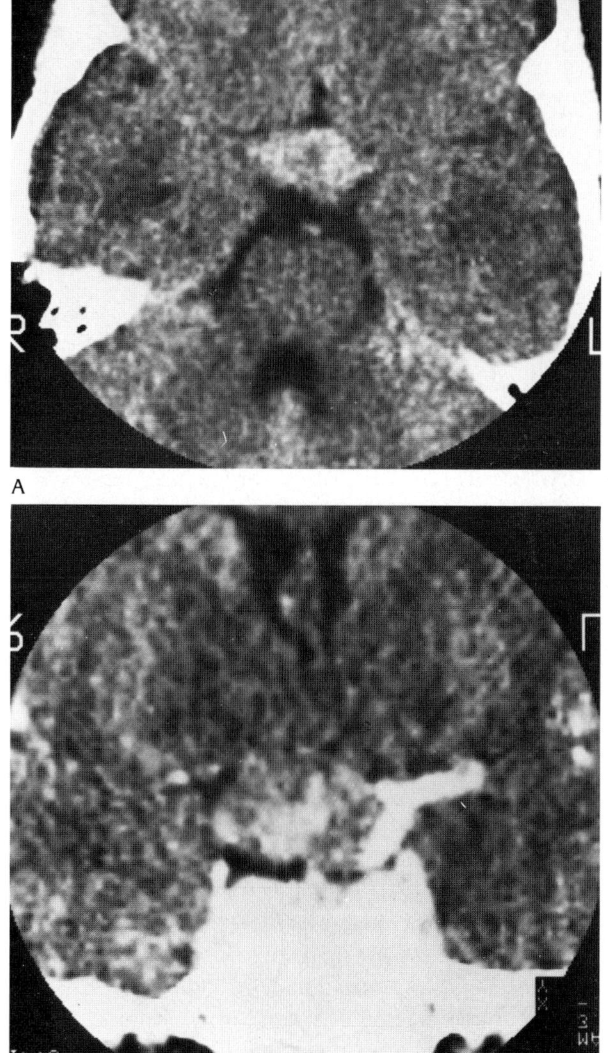

A

C

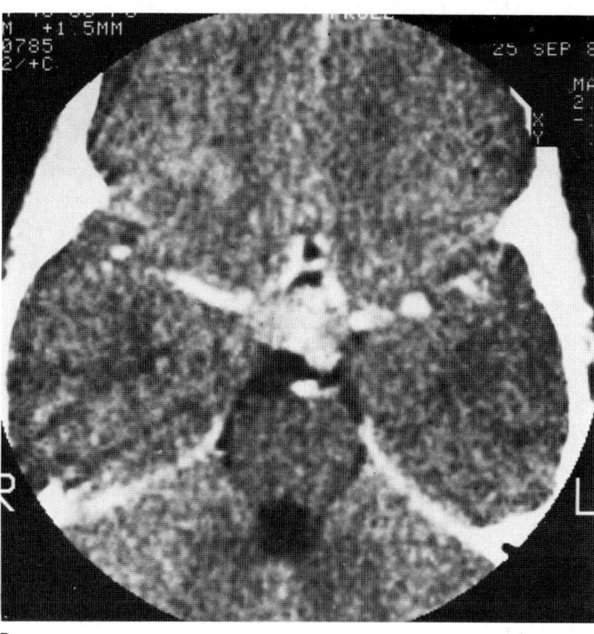

B

Figure 11-51 Chiasmal glioma hyperdense on axial NCCT (**A**), axial CECT (**B**), and coronal CECT (**C**).

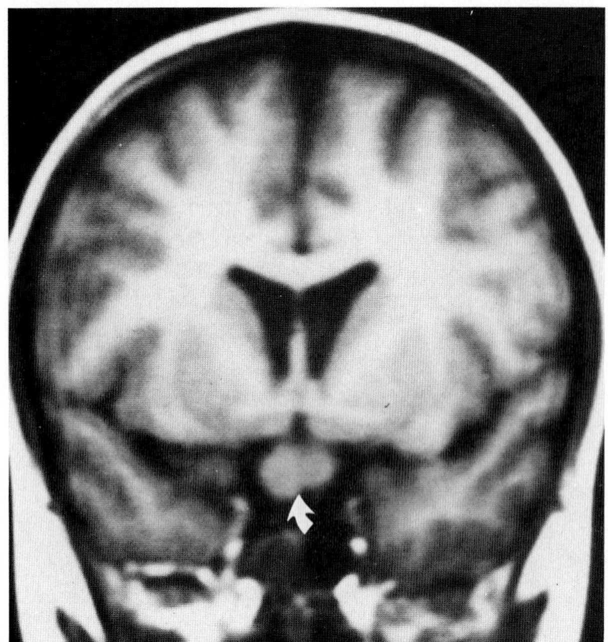

Figure 11-52 Chiasmal glioma (curved arrow) on coronal T_1-weighted MRI. (*From Daniels 1985a.*)

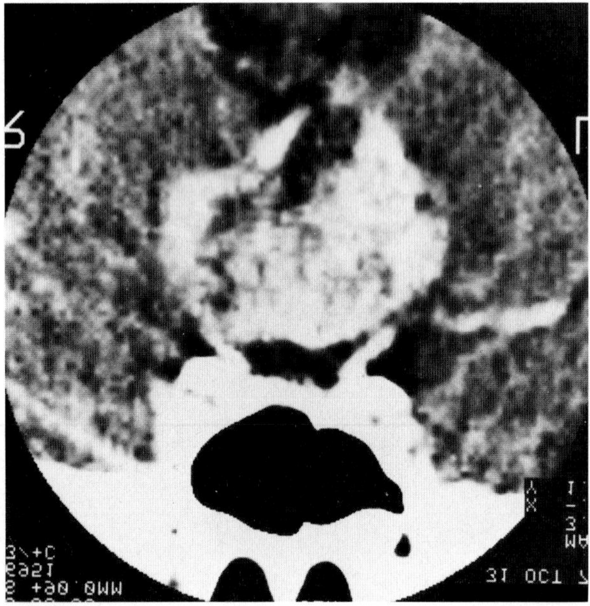

Figure 11-53 Hypothalamic glioma on coronal CECT. It enhances nonhomogeneously. (*From Daniels 1985a.*)

fectively and in many cases shows alterations of the posterior optic pathway caused by the tumor. MR shows hyperintensity in optic tracts, radiations, etc., in T_2-WI in many cases (Albert 1986; Pomeranz 1987; Brown 1987). To detect a chiasmal glioma, the vertical diameter of the chiasm may be measured: A diameter greater than 6 mm indicates a tumor. The CT or MR appearance of chiasmal gliomas is usually characteristic: sharply defined contours, globular shape, position below the hypothalamus, and lack of a cystic component and calcification.

Optic gliomas must be distinguished from chiasmal neuritis, which has a characteristic clinical picture consisting of the acute onset and rapid progression of visual loss in a young woman. In these cases the chiasm is min-

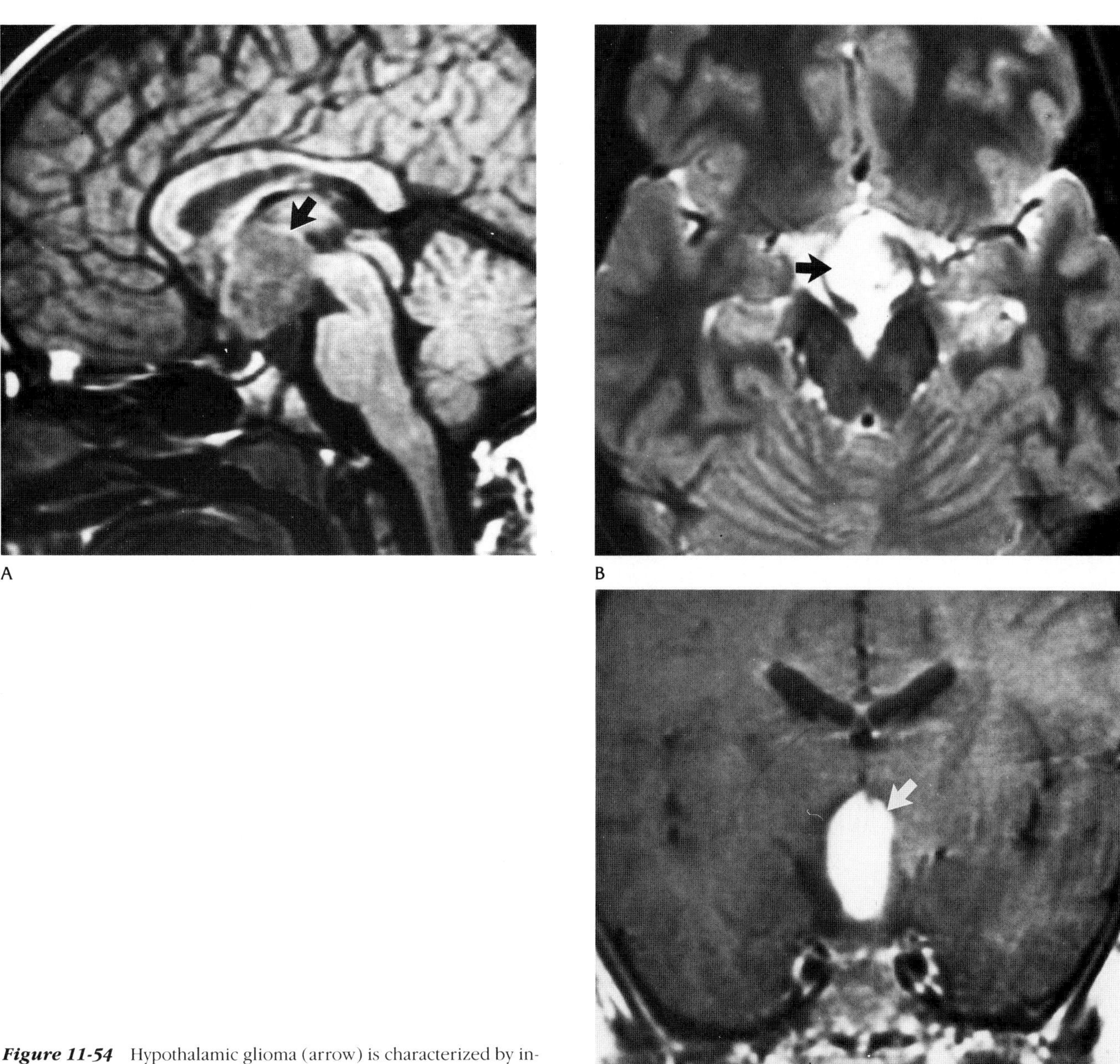

Figure 11-54 Hypothalamic glioma (arrow) is characterized by intermediate and high-intensity signals on sagittal T_1-weighted MRI (**A**) and axial T_2-weighted MRI (**B**), respectively, and intense enhancement on coronal T_1-weighted MRI with intravenous gadolinium (**C**).

imally enlarged. It may show contrast enhancement. In cases of optic neuritis, vision usually improves after steroid therapy.

Hypothalamic Glioma

Hypothalamic gliomas have a variety of clinical presentations. A hypothalamic astrocytoma in an infant typically produces a syndrome of failure to thrive in spite of adequate caloric intake, unusual alertness, and hyperactivity (Merritt 1969). In a young adult, a hypothalamic glioma usually produces visual symptoms, fever, and an altered level of consciousness.

Hypothalamic gliomas typically are large and irregularly contoured masses that enhance nonhomogeneously in CT and MR (Figs. 11-53 and 11-54). Tumor calcification may be present but is difficult to detect with MR. The

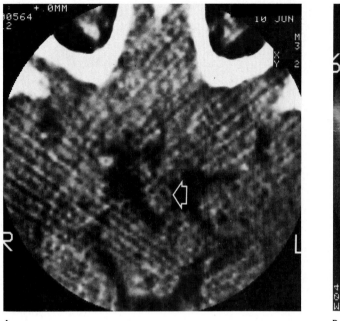

A

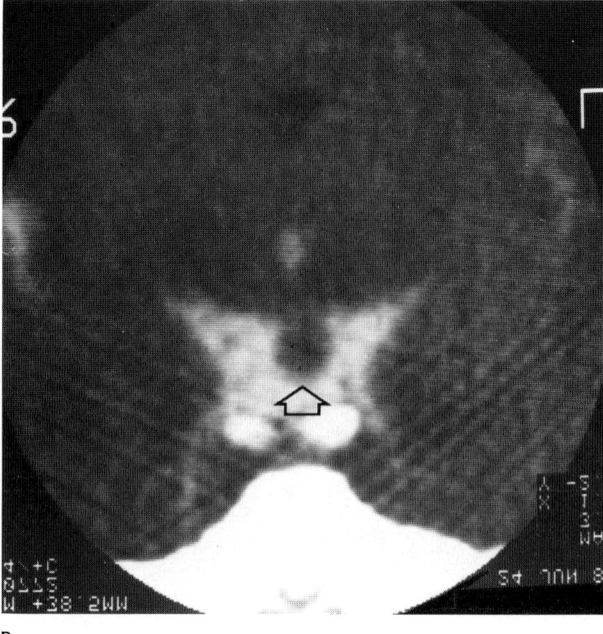

B

Figure 11-55 Hamartoma (open arrow) of the tuber cinereum on (**A**) axial NCCT and (**B**) coronal intrathecally enhanced CT.

cystic components are usually not as large as those associated with craniopharyngiomas. The nonhomogeneity of a hypothalamic glioma differentiates it from a chiasmal glioma.

Hamartoma of the Tuber Cinereum

A hamartoma of the tuber cinereum is a rare benign distinctive lesion with nerve cells similar to those normally present in the tuber cinereum. The tumor presents with precocious puberty, seizures, behavior disorders, or intellectual deterioration (Lin 1978).

On CT it appears as a small mass that is isodense with respect to brain, nonenhancing, sharply defined, smoothly contoured, and attached to the posterior aspect of the hypothalamus between the tuber cinereum and the pons (Fig. 11-55) (Lin 1978). Uncommonly, the mass may be large and densely calcified, resembling a craniopharyngioma. On MR, the mass is easily identified in sagittal

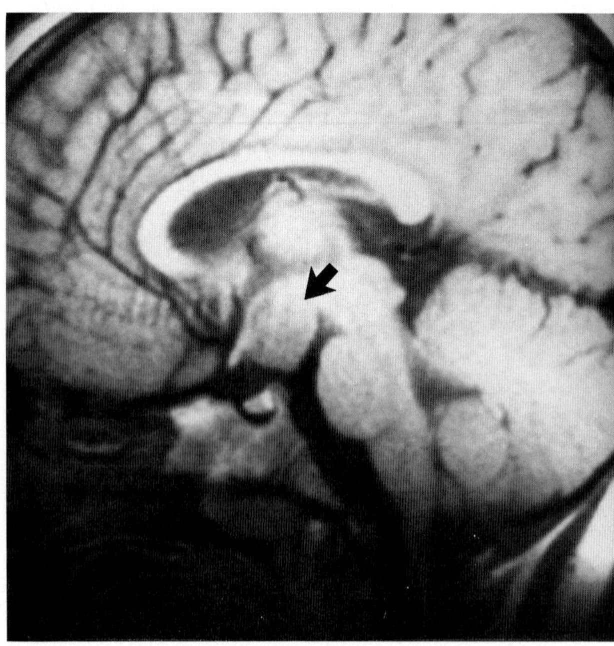

A

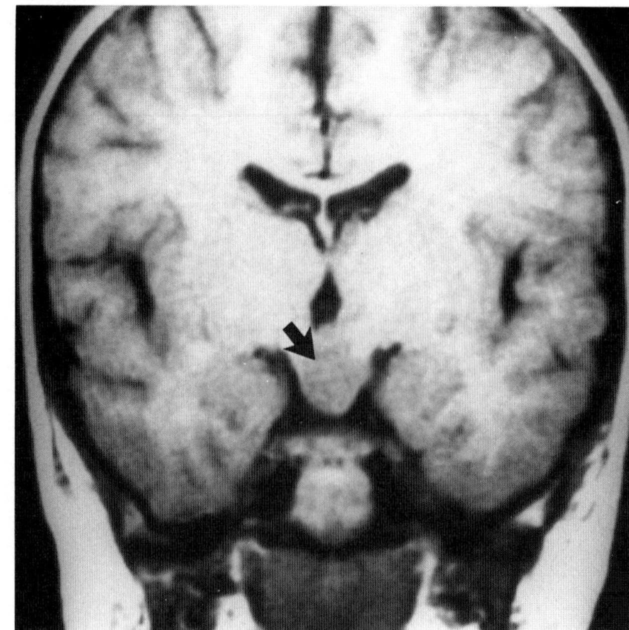

B

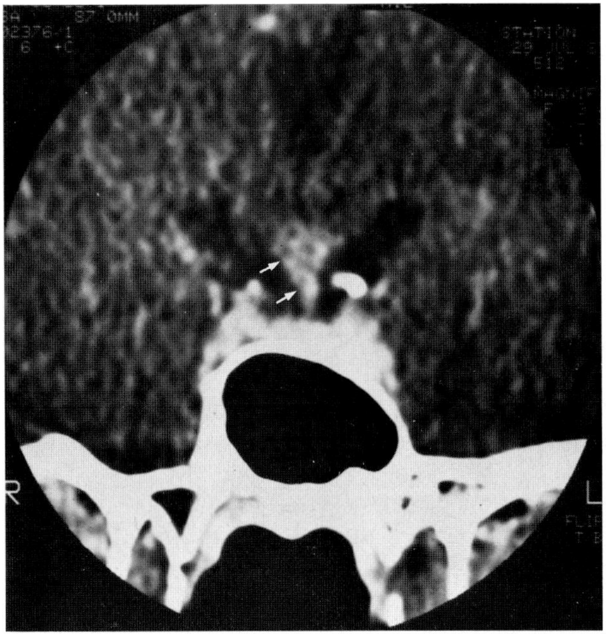

A

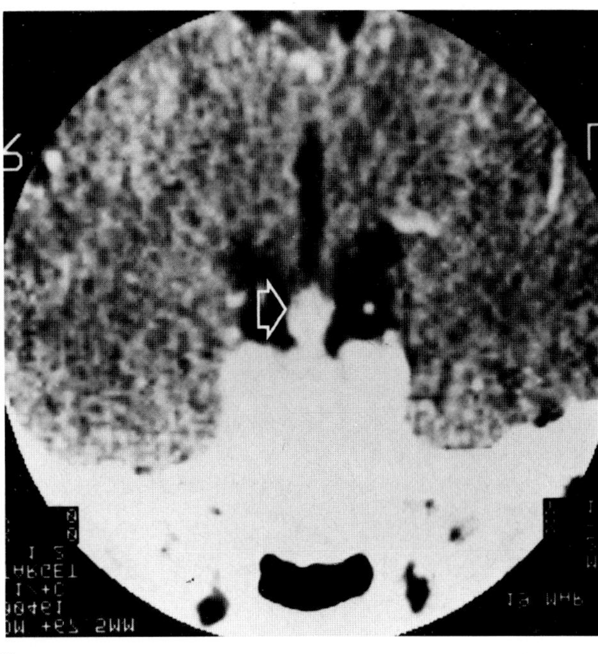

B

Figure 11-57 Examples of abnormal infundibula in (**A**) a patient with sarcoidosis, and (**B**) a patient with histiocytosis X. The infundibula are enlarged and enhanced. (**A** *from Daniels 1985a;* **B** *courtesy of Anne M. Hubbard, M.D., Philadelphia.*)

images and is typically isointense with normal gray matter in T_1WI and hyperintense in T_2WI (Fig. 11-56) (Hahn 1988; Burton 1989; Boyko 1991).

Infundibular Tumor

Infundibular masses include tumors (metastatic carcinoma, especially breast; glioma; lymphoma), histiocytosis X, and sarcoid (O'Sullivan 1991). Diabetes insipidus is common with infundibular masses (Chason 1971; Manelfe 1979; Peyster 1984*b*; Brooks 1982). Involvement of the infundibulum with one of these processes usually enlarges it to a diameter greater than 4.5 mm or greater than that of the basilar artery. An infundibulum with a mass usually has a cone shape in coronal CT or MR images (Fig. 11-57) (Peyster 1984*a*). CT or MR shows an enhancing, usually homogeneous mass. With sarcoid, CT or MR

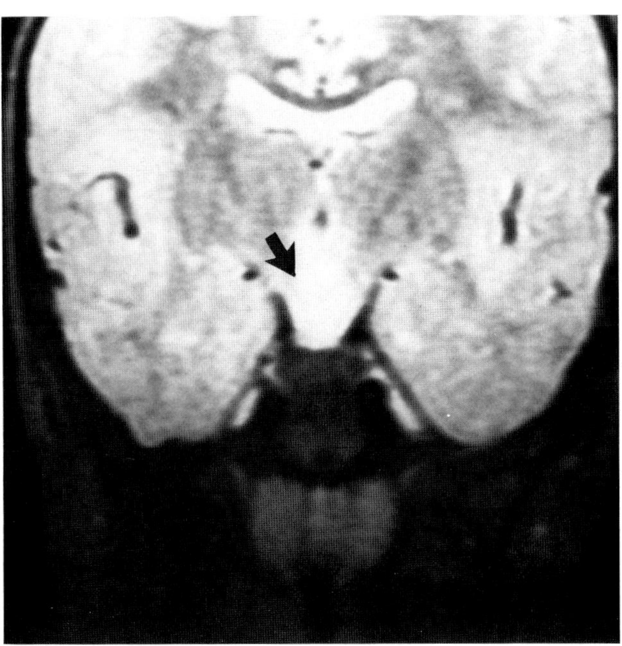

C

Figure 11-56 Hamartoma of the tuber cinereum (arrow) appears isointense to gray matter on sagittal (**A**) and coronal (**B**) T_1-weighted MRI and hyperintense on coronal T_2-weighted MRI (**C**).

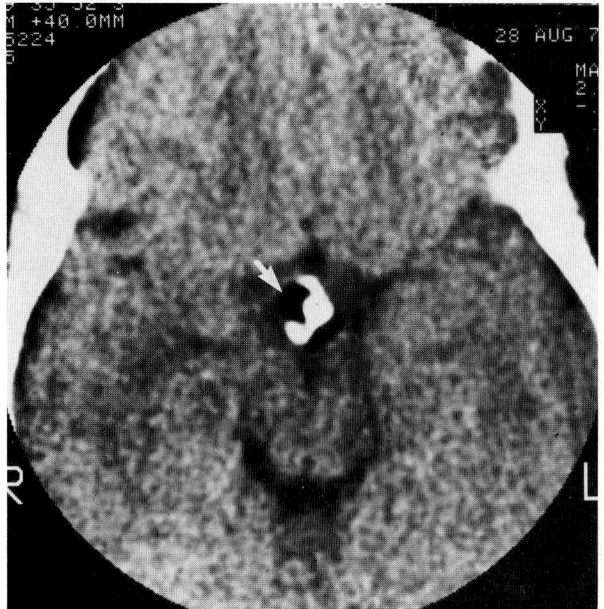

Figure 11-58 Suprasellar teratoma. Axial CT shows fat (arrow) and dense calcification in the tumor. (*From Daniels 1985a.*)

may show enhancement of meningeal granulomas and infiltration of the basal cisterns and leptomeninges, and also often shows hydrocephalus (Hayes 1987).

Germ Cell Tumor

Germ cell tumors such as germinomas (atypical teratomas), teratomas, and teratocarcinomas sometimes occur as isolated suprasellar masses (Futrell 1981). In CT, suprasellar germ cell tumors may be hypodense or hyperdense with respect to brain, homogeneous or nonhomogeneous, enhancing or nonenhancing, and frequently calcified (Figs. 11-58 and 11-59) (Futrell 1981). Solid suprasellar germ cell tumors may resemble glial tumors on CT: a teratoma containing fat or globular calcification may resemble a dermoid or epidermoid.

In MR, germinomas are typically isointense with brain in T_1WI and sometimes hyperintense in T_2WI. Fat within teratomas has high and low signal intensity in T_1WI and T_2WI, respectively (Karnaze 1986).

Arachnoid and Rathke's Cleft Cysts

Suprasellar arachnoid cysts may present with hydrocephalus, visual impairment, or endocrine dysfunction (Armstrong 1983). The characteristic CT appearance of these cysts is a mass with CSF density (5 to 15 HU) and no solid or enhancing structures (Gentry 1986*a*) (Fig. 11-60). Because the capsule is thin, a suprasellar arachnoid cyst cannot be reliably demonstrated on CT unless intrathecal enhancement is used (Fig. 11-61). CT cisternography with intrathecal contrast medium can be valuable in selecting the optimal method of treatment (Gentry 1986*b*). The most important clue to the presence of an arachnoid cyst may be an enlarged suprasellar cistern or pituitary fossa in which no solid tissue is present and normal structures such as the infundibulum and optic chiasm are displaced or are not identified. Large arachnoid cysts may be difficult to differentiate from an enlarged third ventricle; small intrasellar arachnoid cysts may suggest an empty sella. An arachnoid cyst can be distinguished from an in-

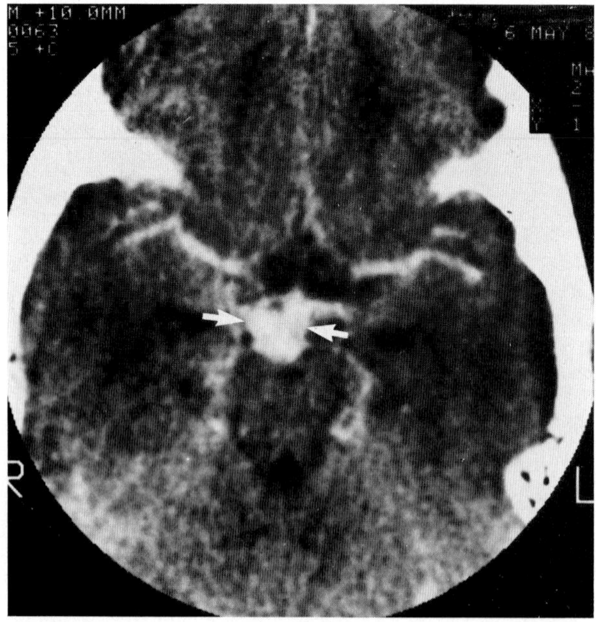

A

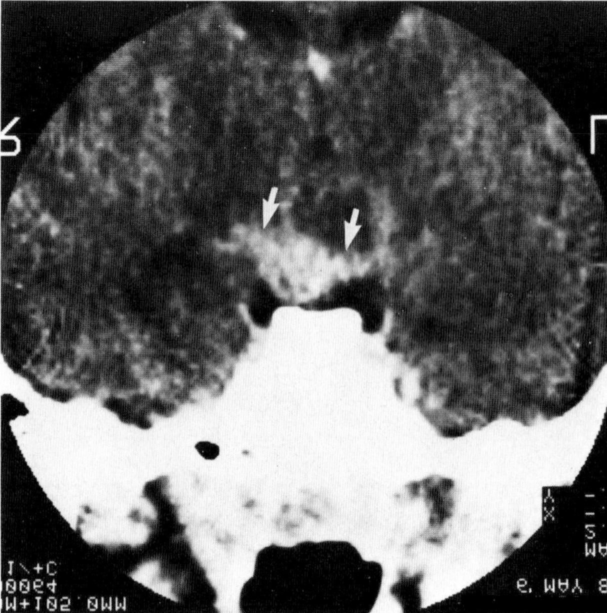

B

Figure 11-59 Dysgerminoma (arrows) on (**A**) axial and (**B**) coronal CECT. The tumor enhances homogeneously. (*From Daniels 1985a.*)

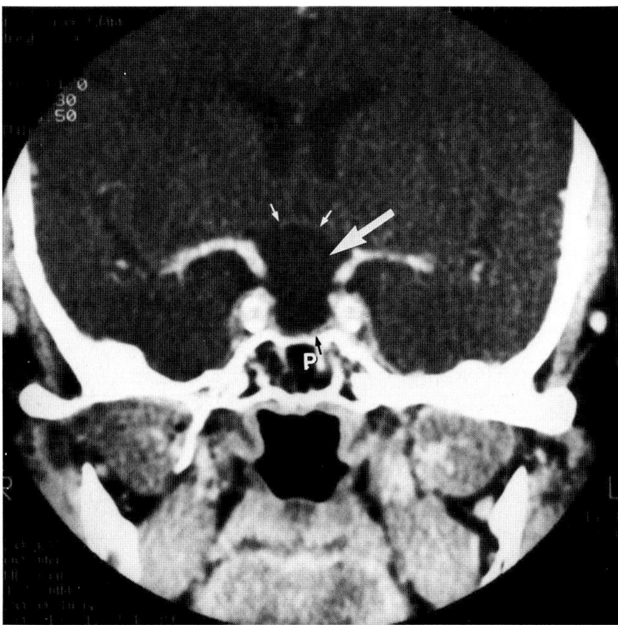

A

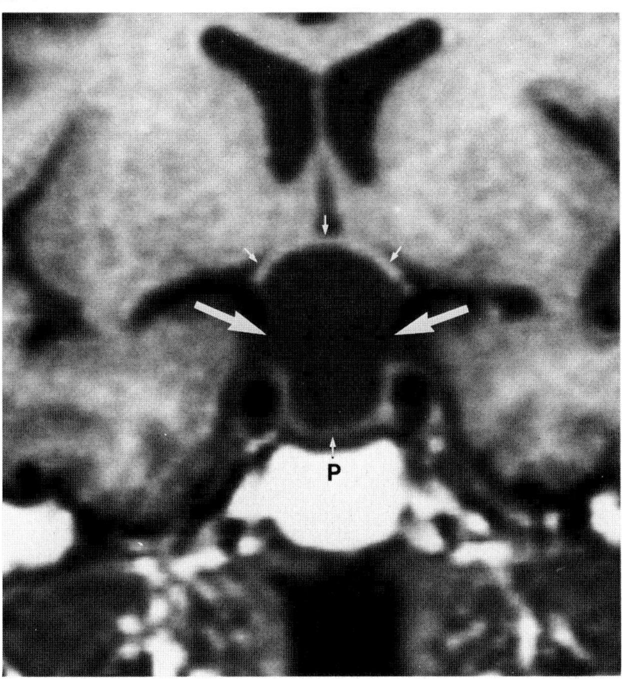

B

Figure 11-60 Intrasellar and suprasellar arachnoid cyst (large arrows) displaces the pituitary gland (P) downward and the optic chiasm (small arrows) upward on coronal CT (**A**) and T_1-weighted MRI (**B**). The infundibulum could not be identified using either CT or MRI.

traventricular cyst by its location and from a suprasellar epidermoid, cystic glioma, or craniopharyngioma by the lack of enhancing or solid or calcified components. Suprasellar epidermoids are rare in infants, while arachnoid cysts are not. With intrathecal contrast medium, CT shows an arachnoid cyst as a mass within the suprasellar cistern that has sharply defined and curvilinear margins

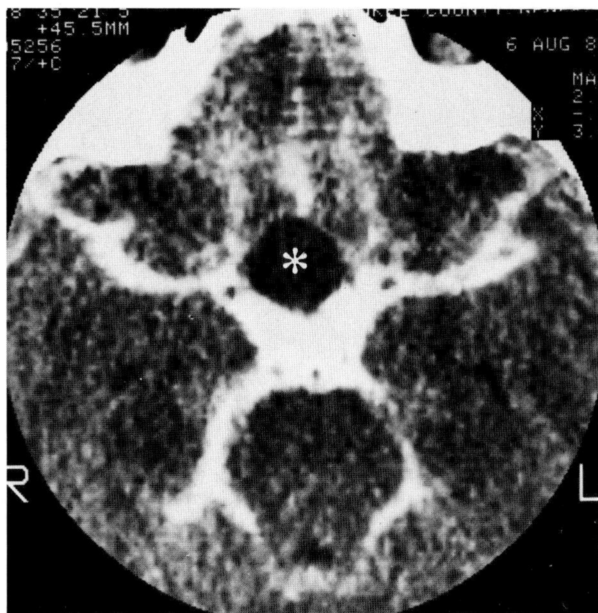

Figure 11-61 Suprasellar epidermoid tumor (asterisk) with hypodensity and a sharply defined contour is shown on axial intrathecally enhanced CT. Preoperatively, the differential diagnosis included arachnoid cyst. (*From Daniels 1985a.*)

and that fails to opacify (Fig. 11-61). In MR, a Rathke's cleft cyst usually has a signal intensity similar to that of CSF in all pulse sequences (Kucharczyk 1987*b*).

Diabetes Insipidus

Diabetes insipidus (DI) occurs as a result of deficient secretion of the antidiuretic hormone arginine vasopressin from the hypothalamus (neurogenic DI) or from an inadequate response to this peptide at the level of the renal tubules (nephrogenic DI). Arginine vaspressin is synthesized in the hypothalamus, linked to the specific carrier protein neurophysin, and then transported to the posterior lobe of the pituitary gland. Subsequently, the hormone is released into the perivascular spaces of the posterior pituitary gland.

Hyperintensity of the posterior pituitary lobe was not seen on T_1WI in all patients with DI of central origin (Fujisawa 1987*b*; Tien 1991). Similarly, the hyperintensive signal was not observed in the posterior lobe or hypothalamus of patients with histiocytosis and DI. All of these patients also had a thickened pituitary stalk on MR (Tien 1990).

Lymphoid Hypophysitis

Lymphoid hypophysitis is an autoimmune disorder in which lymphocytes infiltrate the pituitary gland. The condition usually presents postpartum with thyrotoxicosis and hypopituitarism.

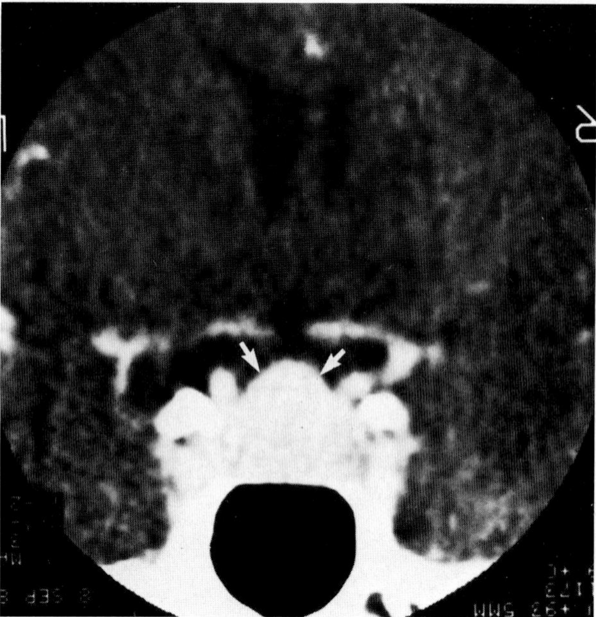

Figure 11-62 Coronal CT study of lymphoid hypophysitis appearing as an enlarged homogeneously enhancing pituitary gland (arrows). The postpartum woman with thyrotoxicosis subsequently had a normal CT study of the pituitary gland. (*From Daniels 1985a.*)

CT demonstrates an enlarged and homogeneously enhancing pituitary gland, which with treatment undergoes spontaneous regression (Fig. 11-62) (Hungerford 1982; Quencer 1980; Zeller 1982). The sella is usually of a normal size. MR shows a symmetrically enlarged gland with high signal intensity in T_2WI (Kucharczyk 1987*a*). The CT and MR appearance can simulate that of a solid pituitary tumor with a suprasellar extension.

Pituitary Abscess

Pituitary abscesses are a rare complication of meningitis or sphenoid sinusitis. In the few CT studies of pituitary abscess reported, the abscess has appeared as a hypodense intrasellar and suprasellar mass with a thin rim of enhancement (Chambers 1982; Enzmann 1983). With radiographic or CT findings alone, an abscess cannot be differentiated from other cystic pituitary masses.

Postoperative Sella

The bony defect in the sellar floor and the soft tissue in the sphenoid sinus after transsphenoidal surgery are usually identified with CT and MR. CT better demonstrates the osseous detail of the postoperative site. The muscle or other tissue placed surgically in the sella may also be identified.

CT (Taylor 1982) and MR can be used to detect a residual or recurrent tumor (Fig. 11-63). Fibrotic tissue, muscle (placed in the sella at surgery), and tumor have similar degrees of enhancement (Fig. 11-64). Only tumor is usually associated with an upwardly convex gland contour and contralateral displacement of the infundibulum. Intrasellar fat is distinctive because of its high and low

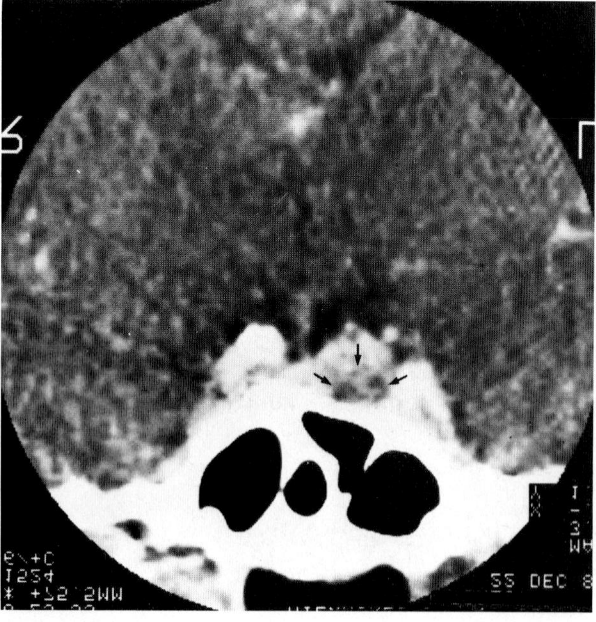

A

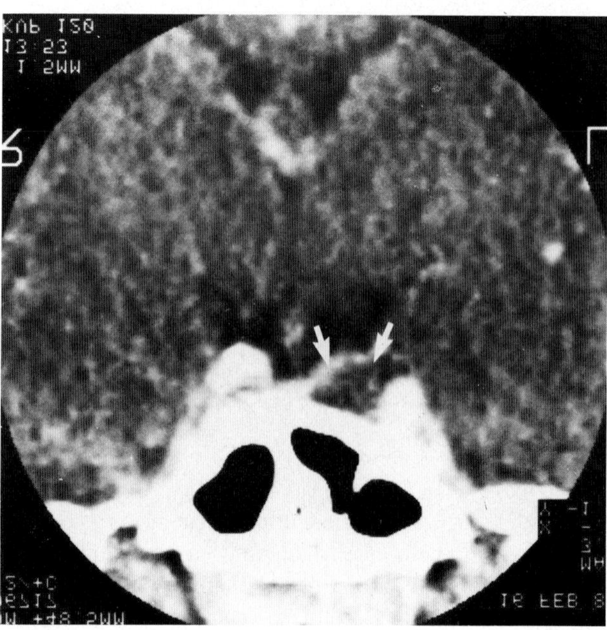

B

Figure 11-63 CECT demonstrates a recurrent prolactinoma. A hypodense region (black arrows in **A**) was proved by transsphenoidal surgery to be a prolactinoma. It recurred (white arrows in **B**).

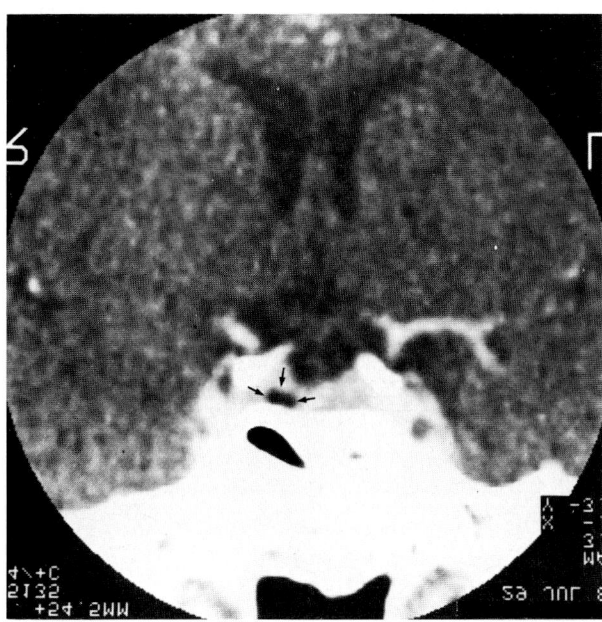

Figure 11-64 Postoperative sella. Fat (black arrows) placed in the sella transsphenoidally after removal of a pituitary tumor can be confused with a microadenoma if postoperative changes are not recognized.

signal intensity in T_1WI and T_2WI, respectively. The best means of identifying tumor is by showing increasing amounts of enhancing intrasellar tissue in sequential CT and MR studies (Waller 1983). Imaging findings should be correlated with hormonal assays if a hormone-secreting tumor is present.

References

AHMADI H, LARSON EM, JINKINS JR: Normal pituitary gland: Coronal MR imaging of infundibular tilt. *Radiology* 177:389–392, 1990.

ALBERT A, LEE BCP, SAINT-LOUIS L, et al: MRI of optic chiasm and optic pathways. *AJNR* 7:255–258, 1986.

ARMSTRONG EA, HARWOOD-NASH DCF, HOFFMAN H, et al: Benign suprasellar cysts: The CT approach. *AJNR* 4:163–166, 1983.

BANNA M: Radiology, in Hankinson J, Banna M (eds), *Pituitary and Parapituitary Tumors,* Philadelphia, Saunders, 1976, pp 135–149.

BELLONI G, BACIOCCO A, BURELLI P, et al: The value of CT for the diagnosis of pituitary microadenomas in children. *Neuroradiology* 15:179–181, 1978.

BILANIUK LT, ZIMMERMAN RA, WEHRLI FW, et al: Magnetic resonance imaging of pituitary lesions using 1.0 to 1.5 T field strength. *Radiology* 153:415, 1984.

BONNEVILLE JF, CATTIN F, MOUSSA-BACHA K, et al: Dynamic computed tomography of the pituitary gland: The "tuft sign." *Radiology* 149:145–148, 1983.

BONNEVILLE JF, CATTIN F, RACLE A, et al: Dynamic CT of the laterosellar extradural venous spaces. *AJNR* 10:535–542, 1989.

BOYKO OB, CURNES JT, OAKES WJ, et al: Hamartomas of the tuber cinereum: CT, MR, and pathologic findings. *AJNR* 12:309–314, 1991.

BRAFFMAN DH, ZIMMERMAN RA, RABISCHONG P: Cranial nerves III, IV, and VI: A clinical approach to the evaluation of their dysfunction, in Harnsberger R (ed), *Seminars in Ultrasound, CT and MR,* Philadelphia, Grune & Stratton, 1987, pp. 185–213.

BREGER RK, PAPKE RA, POJUNAS KW, et al: Benign extraaxial tumors: Contrast enhancement with Gd-DTPA. *Radiology* 163:427–429, 1987.

BROOKS BS, EL GAMMAL TE, HUNGERFORD GD, et al: Radiologic evaluation of neurosarcoidosis: Role of computed tomography. *AJNR* 3:513–521, 1982.

BROOKS BS, EL GAMMAL TE, ALLISON JD, et al: Frequency and variation of the posterior pituitary bright signal on MR images. *AJNR* 10:943–948, 1989.

BROWN EW, RICCARDI VM, MAWAD M, et al: MR imaging of optic pathways in patients with neurofibromatosis. *AJNR* 8:1031–1036, 1987.

BURTON EM, BALL WS Jr, CRONE K, et al: Hamartoma of the tuber cinereum: A comparison of MR and CT findings in four cases. *AJNR* 10:497–501, 1989.

CHAKERES DW, CURTIN A, FORD G: Magnetic resonance imaging of pituitary and parasellar abnormalities. *Radiol Clin North Am* 27(2):265–281, 1989.

CHAMBERS EF, TURSKI PA, LAMASTERS D, et al: Regions of low density in the contrast-enhanced pituitary gland: Normal and pathologic processes. *Radiology* 144:109–113, 1982.

CHASON JL: Nervous system and skeletal muscle, in Anderson WAD (ed), *Pathology,* St.Louis, Mosby, 1971, pp 1403–1428, 1796–1799, 1838–1842.

COHEN WA, PINTO RS, KRICHEFF II, et al: Dynamic CT scanning for visualization of the parasellar carotid arteries. *AJNR* 3:185–189, 1982.

COLOMBO N, BERRY I, KUCHARCZYK J, et al: Posterior pituitary gland: Appearance on MR images in normal and pathologic states. *Radiology* 165:481–485, 1987.

CRITIN CM, DAVIS DO: Computed tomography in the evaluation of pituitary adenomas. *Invest Radiol* 12:27–35, 1977.

DANIELS DL, HAUGHTON VM, WILLIAMS AL, et al: Computed tomography of the optic chiasm. *Radiology* 137:123–127, 1980.

DANIELS DL, WILLIAMS AL, THORNTON RS, et al: Differential diagnosis of intrasellar tumors by computed tomography. *Radiology* 141:697–701, 1981.

DANIELS DL, POJUNAS KW, PECH P, et al: *Magnetic Resonance Imaging of the Sella and Juxtasella Region,* Milwaukee, General Electric Company, 1984*a*.

DANIELS DL, HERFKINS R, GAGER WE, et al: Magnetic resonance imaging of the optic nerves and chiasm. *Radiology* 152:79–83, 1984*b*.

DANIELS DL: The sella and juxtasellar region, in Williams AL, Haughton VM (eds), *Cranial Computed Tomography: A Comprehensive Text,* St. Louis, Mosby, 1985*a*, pp. 444–511.

DANIELS DL, PECH P, MARK L, et al: Magnetic resonance imaging of the cavernous sinus. *AJNR* 6:187–192, 1985*b*.

DANIELS DL, POJUNAS KW, KILGORE DP, et al: MR imaging of the diaphragma sellae. *AJNR* 7:765–769, 1986*a*.

DANIELS DL, PECH P, POJUNAS KW, et al: Trigeminal nerve: Anatomic correlation with MR imaging. *Radiology* 159:577–583, 1986*b*.

DANIELS DL, HAUGHTON VM, NAIDICH T: *Cranial and Spinal Magnetic Resonance Imaging: Atlas and Guide,* New York, Raven Press, 1987*a*.

DANIELS DL, HAUGHTON VM: Magnetic resonance imaging of the sella and temporal bone, in Kressel HY (ed), *Magnetic Resonance Annual 1987,* New York, Raven Press, 1987*b*, pp. 121–158.

DANIELS DL, CZERVIONKE LF, BONNEVILLE JF, et al: MR imaging of the cavernous sinus: Value of spin echo and gradient recalled echo images. *AJNR* 9:947–952, 1988*a*.

DANIELS DL, HAUGHTON VM, CZERVIONKE LF: MR of the skull base, in Bradley WG, Stark D (eds), Magnetic Resonance Imaging, St. Louis, Mosby, 1988*b*.

DAVIS PC, HOFFMAN JC Jr, SPENCER T, et al: MR imaging of pituitary adenoma: CT, clinical, and surgical correlation. *AJNR* 8:107–112, 1987*a*.

DAVIS PC, HOFFMAN JC Jr, MALKO JA, et al: Gadolinium-DTPA and MR imaging of pituitary adenoma: A preliminary report. *AJNR* 8:817–823, 1987*b*.

DOPPMAN JL, FRANK JA, DWYER AJ, et al: Gd-DTPA enhanced MR imaging of ACTH-secreting microadenomas of the pituitary gland. *J Comput Assist Tomogr* 12(5):728–735, 1988.

DOYLE AJ: Optic chiasm position on MR images. *AJNR* 11:553–555, 1990.

DWYER AJ, FRANK JA, DOPPMAN JL, et al: Pituitary adenomas in patients with Cushing disease: Initial experience with Gd-DTPA-enhanced MR imaging. *Radiology* 163:421–426, 1987.

EARNEST F IV, MCCULLOUGH EC, FRANK DA: Fact or artifact: An analysis of artifact in high-resolution computed tomographic scanning of the sella. *Radiology* 140:109–114, 1981.

ELSTER AD, CHEN MY, WILLIAMS DW, et al: Pituitary gland: MR imaging of physiologic hypertrophy in adolescence. *Radiology* 174:681–685, 1990.

ENZMANN DR, SIELING RS: CT of pituitary abscess. *AJNR* 4:79–80, 1983.

ESCOUROLLE R, POIRIER J: *Manual of Basic neuropathology,* Philadelphia, Saunders, 1978.

FUJISAWA I, ASATO R, NISHIMURA K, et al: Anterior and posterior lobes of the pituitary gland: Assessment by 1.5 T MR imaging. *J Comput Assist Tomogr* 11:214–220, 1987*a*.

FUJISAWA I, NISHIMURA K, ASATO R, et al: Posterior lobe of the pituitary in diabetes insipidus: MR findings. *J Comput Assist Tomogr* 11:221–225, 1987*b*.

FUTRELL NN, OSBORN AG, CHASON BD: Pineal region tumors: Computed tomographic-pathologic spectrum. *AJNR* 2:415–420, 1981.

GARDEUR D, NAIDICH TP, METZGER J: CT analysis of intrasellar pituitary adenomas with emphasis on patterns of contrast enhancement. *Neuroradiology* 20:241–247, 1981.

GARDEUR D, METZGER J: *Pathologie sellaire,* Paris, France, *Ellipses,* 1982, p. 10.

GENTRY LR, SMOKER WR, TURSKI PA, et al: Suprasellar arachnoid cysts: I. CT recognition. *AJNR* 7:79–86, 1986*a*.

GENTRY LR, MENEZES AH, TURSKI PA, et al: Suprasellar arachnoid cysts: II. Evaluation of CSF dynamics. *AJNR* 7:87–96, 1986*b*.

GOMORI JM, GROSSMAN RI, GOLDBERG HI, et al: Intracranial hematomas: Imaging by high-field MR. *Radiology* 157:87–93, 1985.

GYLDENSTEIN C, KARLE A: Computed tomography of infra- and juxta-sellar lesions: A radiological study of 108 cases. *Neuroradiology* 14:5–13, 1977.

HAHN FJ, LEIBROCK LG, HUSEMAN CA, et al: The MR appearance of hypothalamic hamartoma. *Neuroradiology* 30:65–68, 1988.

HAUGHTON VM, ROSENBAUM AE, WILLIAMS AL, et al: Recognizing the empty sella by CT: The infundibulum sign. *AJNR* 1:527–529, 1980.

HAWKES RC, HOLLAND GN, MOORE WS, et al: The application of NMR imaging to the evaluation of pituitary and juxtasellar tumors. *AJNR* 4:221–222, 1983.

HAYES WS, SHERMAN JL, STERN BJ, et al: MR and CT evaluation of intracranial sarcoidosis. *AJNR* 8:841–847, 1987.

HEMMINGHYTT S, KALKHOFF RK, DANIELS DL, et al: Computed tomographic study of hormone-secreting microadenomas. *Radiology* 146:65–69, 1983.

HIRSCH WL, HRYSHKO FG, SEKHAR LN, et al: Comparison of MR imaging, CT, and angiography in the evaluation of the enlarged cavernous sinus. *AJNR* 9:907–915, 1988.

HUNGERFORD GD, BIGGS J, LEVINE JH, et al: Lymphoid adenohypophysitis with radiologic and clinical findings resembling a pituitary tumor. *AJNR* 3:444–446, 1982.

HUTCHINS LG, HARNSBERGER HR, HARDIN CW, et al: The radiologic assessment of trigeminal neuropathy. *AJNR* 10: 1031–1038, 1989.

KARNAZE MG, SARTOR K, WINTHROP JD, et al: Suprasellar lesions: Evaluation with MR imaging. *Radiology* 161:77–82, 1986.

KILGORE DP, BREGER RK, DANIELS DL, et al: Normal MR appearance of cranial tissues after intravenous gadolinium-DTPA injection. *Radiology* 160:757–761, 1986.

KLINE LB, ACKER JD, POST MJD, et al: The cavernous sinus: A computed tomographic study. *AJNR* 2:229–305, 1981.

KUCHARCZYK W, DAVIS DO, KELLY W, et al: Pituitary adenomas: High-resolution MR imaging at 1.5 T. *Radiology* 161:761–765, 1986.

KUCHARCZYK W: The pituitary gland and sella turcica, in Brant-Zawadzki M, Normal D (eds), *Magnetic Resonance Imaging of the Central Nervous System,* New York, Raven Press, 1987*a*, pp 187–208.

KUCHARCZYK W, PECK WW, KELLY WM, et al: Rathke cleft cysts: CT, MR imaging and pathologic features. *Radiology* 165:491–495, 1987*b*.

KUCHARCZYK J, KUCHARCZYK W, BERRY I, et al: Histochemical characterization and functional significance of the hyperintense signal on MR images of the posterior pituitary. *AJNR* 9:1079–1083, 1988.

KUCHARCZYK W, LENKINSKI RE, KUCHARCZYK J, et al: The effect of phospholipid vesicles on the NMR relaxation of water: An explanation for the MR appearance of the hemohypophysiology. *AJNR* 11:693–700, 1990.

KULKARNI MV, LEE KF, MCARDLE CB, et al: 1.5 T MR imaging of pituitary microadenomas: Technical considerations and CT correlation. *AJNR* 9:5–11, 1988.

KYLE CL, LASTER RA, BURTON EM, et al: Subacute pituitary apoplexy: MR and CT appearance. *J Comput Assist Tomogr* 14(1):40–44, 1990.

LEE BCP, DECK MDF: Sellar and juxtasellar lesion detection with MR. *Radiology* 157:143–147, 1985.

LEE KF: The diagnostic value of hyperostosis in midline subfrontal meningioma. *Radiology* 119:121–130, 1976.

LIN S-R, BRYSON MM, GOBLEN RP, et al: Radiologic findings of hamartomas of the tuber cinereum and hypothalamus. *Radiology* 127:697–703, 1978.

MANELFE C, LONVEY JP: Computed tomography in diabetes insipidus. *J Comput Assist Tomogr* 3:309–316, 1979.

MARCOVITZ S, WEE R, CHAN J, et al: Diagnostic accuracy of preoperative CT scanning of pituitary prolactinomas. *AJNR* 9:13–17, 1988*a*.

MARCOVITZ S, WEE R, CHAN J, et al: Diagnostic accuracy of preoperative CT scanning of pituitary somatotrophy adenomas. *AJNR* 9:19–22, 1988*b*.

MARK L, PECH P, DANIELS D, et al: The pituitary fossa: A correlative anatomic and MR study. *Radiology* 153:453–457, 1984.

MARK LP, HAUGHTON V, HENDRIX L, et al: Sources of high intensity signals within the posterior pituitary fossa studied with fat suppression techniques. Presented at the 27th annual ASNR meeting, Orlando, Florida, March 1989.

MERRITT HH: *A Textbook of Neurology,* Philadelphia, Lea & Febiger, 1969, pp 243–254, 269–279, 281–282.

MIKI Y, MATSUO M, NISHIZAWA S, et al: Pituitary adenomas and normal pituitary tissue: Enhancement patterns on gadopentetate-enhanced MR imaging. *Radiology* 177:35–38, 1990.

MILLER JH, PENA AM, SEGALL HD: Radiological investigation of sellar region masses in children. *Radiology* 134:81–87, 1980.

NEWTON DR, DILLON WP, NORMAN D, et al: Gd-DTPA-enhanced MR imaging of pituitary adenomas. *AJNR* 10:949–954, 1989.

OOT R, NEW PFJ, BUONANNO FS, et al: MR imaging of pituitary adenomas using a prototype resistive magnet: Preliminary assessment. *AJNR* 5:131–137, 1984.

OSTROV SG, QUENCER RM, HOFFMAN JC, et al: Hemorrhage within pituitary adenomas: How often associated with pituitary apoplexy syndrome? *AJNR* 10:503–510, 1989.

O'SULLIVAN RM, SHEEHAN M, POSKITT KJ, et al: Langerhans cell histocytosis of hypothalamus and optic chiasm: CT and MR studies. *J Comput Assist Tomogr* 15(1):52–55, 1991.

PAUL LW, JUHL H: *The Essentials of Roentgen Interpretation,* Hagerstown, Md., Harper & Row, 1972, pp 366–372, 375.

PECK WW, DILLON WP, NORMAN D, et al: High-resolution MR imaging of microadenomas at 1.5 T: Experience with Cushing disease. *AJNR* 9:1085–1091, 1988.

PEYSTER RG, HOOVER ED, ADLER LP: CT of the normal pituitary stalk. *AJNR* 5:45–47, 1984*a*.

PEYSTER RG, HOOVER ED: CT of the abnormal pituitary stalk. *AJNR* 5:49–52, 1984*b*.

PINTO RS, COHEN WA, KRICHEFF II, et al: Giant intracranial aneurysms: Rapid sequential computed tomography. *AJNR* 3:495–499, 1982.

POJUNAS K, DANIELS D, WILLIAMS A, et al: MR imaging of prolactin-secreting microadenomas. *AJNR* 7:209–213, 1986.

POMERANZ SJ, SHELTON JJ, TOBIAS J, et al: MR of visual pathways in patients with neurofibromatosis. *AJNR* 8:831–836, 1987.

POST MJD, DAVID NJ, GLASEN JS, et al: Pituitary apoplexy: Diagnosis by computed tomography. *Radiology* 134:665–670, 1980.

PUSEY E, KORTMAN KE, FLANNIGAN BD, et al: MR of craniopharyngiomas: Tumor delineation and characterization. *AJNR* 8:439–444, 1987.

QUENCER RM: Lymphocytic adenohypophysis: Autoimmune disorder of the pituitary gland. *AJNR* 1:343–345, 1980.

REICH NE, ZELCH JV, et al: Computed tomography in the detection of juxtasellar lesions. *Radiology* 118:333–335, 1976.

REINCKE M, ALLOLIO B, SAEGER W, et al: The "incidentaloma" of the pituitary gland: Is neurosurgery required? *JAMA* 263(20):2772–2776, 1990.

ROPPOLO HMN, LATCHAW RE: Normal pituitary gland: II. Microscopic anatomy–CT correlation. *AJNR* 4:937–944, 1983*a*.

ROPPOLO HMN, LATCHAW RE, MEYER JD, et al: Normal pituitary gland: I. Macroscopic anatomy–CT correlation. *AJNR* 4:927–935, 1983*b*.

ROVIT RL: Pituitary apoplexy, in Wilkins RH, Rengachary SS (eds), *Neurosurgery,* vol. 1, New York, McGraw-Hill, 1985, pp 879–883.

RUSSELL EJ, GEORGE AE, KRICHEFF II, et al: Atypical computed tomographic features of intracranial meningioma: Radiological-pathological correlation in a series of 131 consecutive cases. *Radiology* 135:673–682, 1980.

SAKAMOTO Y, TAKAHASHI M, KOROGI Y, et al: Normal and abnormal pituitary glands: Gd-DTPA-enhanced MRI. *Radiology* 178:441–445, 1991.

SARIS SC, PATRONAS NJ, DOPPMAN JL, et al: Cushing syndrome: Pituitary CT scanning. *Radiology* 162:775–777, 1987.

SARTOR K, KARNAZE MG, WINTHROP JD, et al: MR imaging in infra-, para- and retrosellar mass lesions. *Neuroradiology* 29:19–29, 1987.

SCOTTI G, YU CY, DILLON WP, et al: MR imaging of cavernous sinus involvement by pituitary adenomas. *AJNR* 9:657–664, 1988.

SHAPIRO MD, SOSTMAN HD, PEYSTER RG: The source of pituitary "high signal": An anatomical-MR correlation. *AJNR* 8:957, 1987.

SWARTZ JD, RUSSELL KB, BASILE BA, et al: High resolution computed tomographic appearance of the intrasellar contents in women of child-bearing age. *Radiology* 147:115–117. 1983.

SYVERTSEN A, HAUGHTON VM, WILLIAMS AL, et al: The computed tomographic appearance of the normal pituitary gland and pituitary microadenomas. *Radiology* 133:385–391, 1979.

SZE G, PARDI F, DE GROOT J: The posterior pituitary gland: MR correlation with function and anatomy. *AJNR* 8:935, 1987.

SZE G, UICHANCO LS, BRANT-ZAWADZKI MN, et al: Chordomas: MR imaging. *Radiology* 166:187–191, 1988.

TAMPIERI D, MALANSON D, ETHIER R: MR imaging of epidermoid cysts. *AJNR* 10:351–356, 1989.

TAVERAS JM, WOOD EH: *Diagnostic Neuroradiology,* Baltimore, Williams & Wilkins, 1976, pp 70, 519–537, 736–749.

TAYLOR S: High resolution computed tomography of the sella, in Leeds NE (ed), *Radiologic Clinics of North America,* vol. 20, no. 1, Philadelphia, Saunders, 1982, pp 207–236.

TIEN RD, NEWTON TH, MCDERMOTT MW, et al: Thickened pituitary stalk on MR images in patients with diabetes insipidus and Langerhans cell histocytosis. *AJNR* 11:703–708, 1990.

TIEN RD, KUCHARCZYK J, KUCHARCZYK W: MR imaging of the brain in patients with diabetes insipidus. *AJNR* 12:553–542, 1991.

UMANSKY F, NATHAN H: The lateral wall of the cavernous sinus with special references to the nerves related to it. *J Neurosurg* 56:228–234, 1982.

WALLER RM, HOFFMAN JC, TINDALL GT: CT of the sellar and parasellar regions following transsphenoidal surgery. Scientific exhibit presented at annual meeting of the Radiological Society of North America, Chicago, 1983.

WATABE T, AZUMA T: T_1 and T_2 measurements of meningiomas and neuromas before and after Gd-DTPA. *AJNR* 10:463–470, 1989.

WEISSBUCH SS: Explanation and implications of MR signal changes after bromocriptine therapy. *AJNR* 7:214–216, 1986.

WING SD, ANDERSON RE, OSBORN AG: Dynamic cranial computed tomography: Preliminary results. *AJNR* 1:135–139, 1980.

WOLPERT SM, POOL KD, BILLER BJ, et al: The value of computed tomography in evaluating patients with prolactinomas. *Radiology* 131:117–119, 1979.

WOLPERT SM, MOLITCH ME, GOLDMAN JA, et al: Size, shape and appearance of the normal female pituitary gland. *AJNR* 5:263–267, 1984.

WOLPERT SM, OSBORNE M, ANDERSON M, et al: The bright pituitary gland—a normal MR appearance in infancy. *AJNR* 9:1–3, 1988.

YEAKLEY JW, KULKARNI MV, MCARDLE CT, et al: High-resolution MR imaging of juxtasellar meningiomas with CT and angiographic correlation. *AJNR* 9:279–285, 1988.

YOUNG SC, GROSSMAN RI, GOLDBERG HI, et al: MR of vascular encasement in parasellar masses: Comparison with angiography and CT. *AJNR* 9:35–38, 1988.

YOUSEM DM, ARRINGTON, JA, ZINREICH SJ: Pituitary adenomas: Possible role of bromocriptine in intratumoral hemorrhage. *Radiology* 170:239–243, 1989.

YUH WTC, WRIGHT DC, BARLOON TJ, et al: MR imaging of primary tumors of trigeminal nerve and Meckel's cave. *AJNR* 9:665–670, 1988.

ZELLER JR, CERLETTY JM, RABINOVITCH RA, et al: Spontaneous regression of a post-partum pituitary mass demonstrated by computed tomography. *Arch Intern Med* 142:373–374, 1982.

SECTION B: THE TEMPORAL BONE

CT with submillimeter spatial resolution, a slice thickness of 2 mm or less, a wide CT number range, "bone detail" reconstruction programs, target reconstruction, and high-quality image reformations is effective in evaluating temporal bone pathology (Shaffer 1980, 1985; Turski 1982). Compared with pluridirectional tomography, CT has superior low-contrast resolution which permits visualization of middle ear muscles, ligaments, and the tympanic membrane; inflammatory disease; and neoplasms (Lufkin 1982; Shaffer 1982; Mafee 1983*a*). There is nearly equivalent bony resolution, resulting in precise evaluation of the ossicles, otic capsule, fractures, and otodystrophies. Conventional pluridirectional tomograms can be substituted for CT coronal reformatted scans when direct coronal scans cannot be obtained.

Magnetic resonance (MR) imaging with any intravenous contrast agent is superior to CT in evaluating cerebellopontine angle cisterns and internal auditory canals (Valvassori 1988; Swartz 1989). Because bone produces a negligible MR signal, MR images of the internal auditory canal are minimally affected by partial volume averaging and other artifacts. Therefore, MR can demonstrate the cranial nerves within the internal auditory and facial nerve canals (Daniels 1984*a,b,* 1985; Reese 1984). MR is excellent for imaging acoustic neurinomas (Bydder 1982; Young 1983; New 1985; Kingsley 1985). Intravenous contrast agent increases the sensitivity of MR for cerebellopontine angle and intracanalicular tumors because most of these tumors enhance intensely (Curati 1986; Daniels 1987*c*; Swartz 1989).

TECHNICAL ASPECTS

Temporal Bone CT Scanning

Scanning in two planes, usually axial and coronal, is required for optimal demonstration of temporal bone structures. The axial scan plane is kept parallel to the infraorbitomeatal line to avoid scanning the eyes, and the coronal plane is kept nearly perpendicular to the axial plane with the patient supine in a hanging head position or prone with the neck extended. Other gantry angulations for axial and coronal scans have been suggested for evaluating specific intratemporal structures (Zonneveld 1983; Chakeres 1983). Specialized views, such as semiaxial, sagittal, and Stenvers, must be obtained separately for each ear, and patient positioning is difficult, particularly if an angling table is not available.

The technical factors utilized in obtaining CT images depend on the clinical indications for a particular study. For an acoustic neurinoma and other intracranial abnormalities that lack contrast with adjacent tissues, a high photon flux is necessary, and so high mAs, a reconstruction algorithm for soft tissue, and narrow windows are used. For osseous pathology or high-contrast structures such as bone and air in the middle ear, low mAs, a reconstruction algorithm for bone detail, and very wide windows are used. If reformatted images are planned because a patient cannot assume the position for coronal scans or because other image planes are needed, 1.5-mm axial sections at 1-mm intervals provide optimal image detail.

CT Cisternography

CT gas cisternography has replaced Pantopaque cisternography for the diagnosis of small acoustic neurinomas (Fig. 11-65) (Sortland 1979; Anderson 1981). Gas CT cisternography is performed to diagnose an intracanalicular tumor when MR imaging with intravenous contrast agent is unavailable or contraindicated and when intravenously enhanced CT appears normal or equivocal despite strong clinical evidence of a tumor. Gas cisternography is not indicated, and is not safe, in patients with a large cerebellopontine angle or intracranial masses.

Several techniques for gas CT cisternography have been described (Pinto 1982; Anderson 1982). Gas CT cisternography can be performed on outpatients. The only significant side effect reported has been headache, usually mild to moderate, which nearly all patients experience. This side effect can be minimized by using CO_2, which is more rapidly reabsorbed from the cisternal spaces. Disabling "spinal headaches," which can be treated with epidural blood patch therapy, are rare if large-gauge needles are avoided (Anderson 1982; Johnson 1984*a*). Bilateral studies can be obtained without the injection of more gas by turning the patient to the opposite decubitus position after images have been obtained on one side (Lee 1981; Johnson1984*a*).

Temporal Bone MR Imaging

In evaluating the internal auditory canals with a commercial 1.5-T MR system, 3-mm-thick contiguous axial and coronal images through the temporal bones are obtained. An SE pulse sequence with a short repetition time (TR) of 600 to 800 msec and a short echo time (TE) of 20 to 25 msec, a 256 × 256 matrix, and two excitations provides excellent contrast and detail, especially if an intravenous contrast agent is used. An SE sequence with a long TR (2000 to 2500 msec) and long TE (75 to 100 msec) is sometimes used if gadolinium is not injected, although the signal-to-noise ratio is poorer. Head coils are usually used to permit side-to-side comparison. Surface coils provide images with higher spatial resolution of one side. For contrast enhancement, Gd-DTPA (0.1 mmol/kg) is intravenously injected. Acoustic neurinomas, cerebellopontine angle meningiomas, and other benign tumors intensely enhance in T_1WI (e.g., acoustic neuromas enhance as much as 60 percent). T_1-weighted gradient echo images are excellent for defining the neural and vascular structures in the jugular foramen. Such images are obtained with a single-slice acquisition technique, 3-mm-thick sections, a 256 × 256 matrix, four excitations, a TR of 100, a TE of 15, a 90° flip angle, and flow compensation (Daniels 1988*a*).

The cranial nerves in the internal auditory canal are best demonstrated with T_1-weighted MR images (Daniels 1984*a,* 1987*d,* 1988*b;* Enzmann 1987). In short TR and TE MR images (T_1WI), the cranial nerves are almost isointense with brain, in contrast to the hypointense signal from the temporal bone or CSF (Fig. 11-66). In long TR and TE MR images (T_2WI), the nerves may be demon-

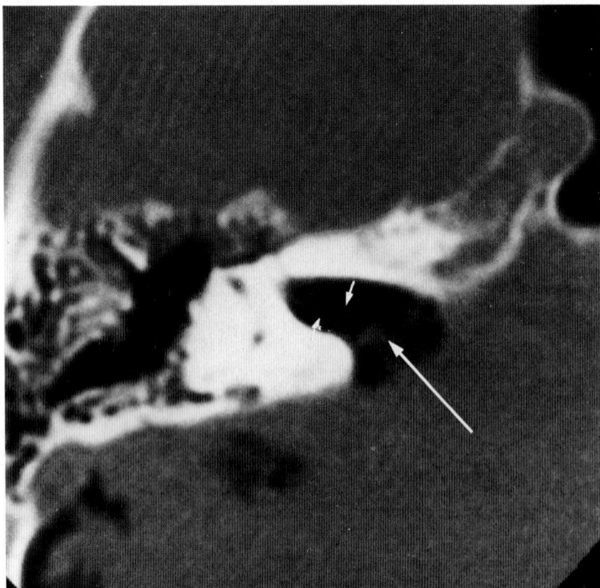

Figure 11-65 Axial scan from a normal air CT cisternogram (oriented similarly to a standard axial scan) with bone detail reconstruction viewed at a 4000-HU window. Individual nerves (small arrows) and a probable vascular loop (long arrow) are demonstrated in a mildly widened internal auditory canal. (*From Shaffer 1985.*)

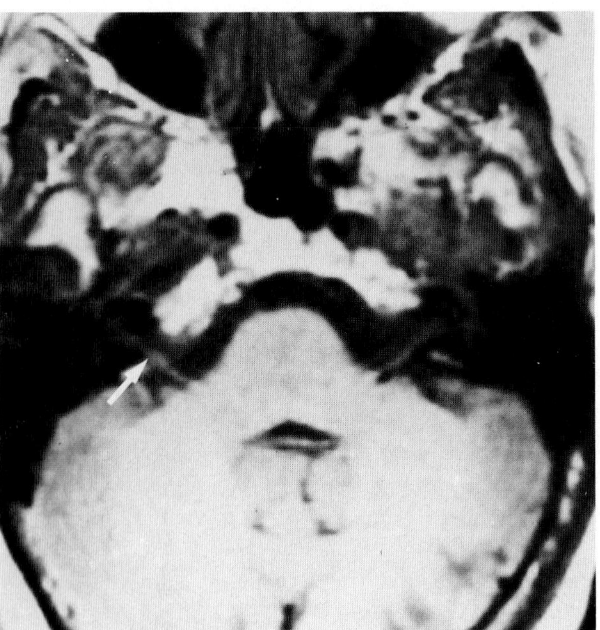

Figure 11-66 The cisternal and intracanalicular segments of cranial nerves VII and VIII (arrow) shown in a T_1-weighted axial MR image.

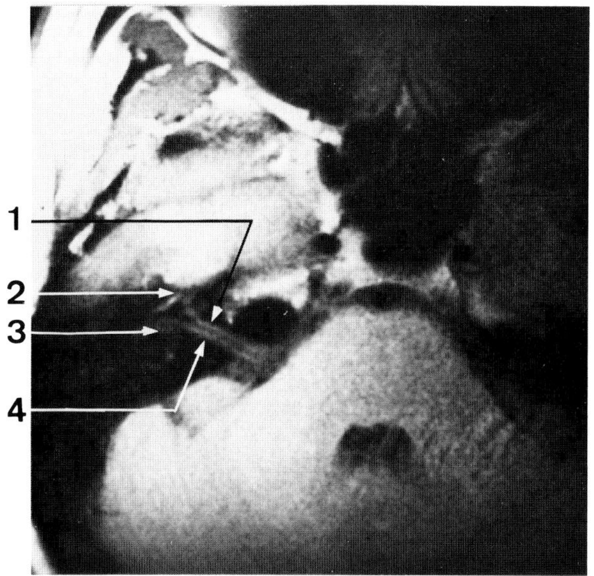

1. facial nerve 2. geniculate ganglion 3. vestibule 4. superior vestibular nerve

A

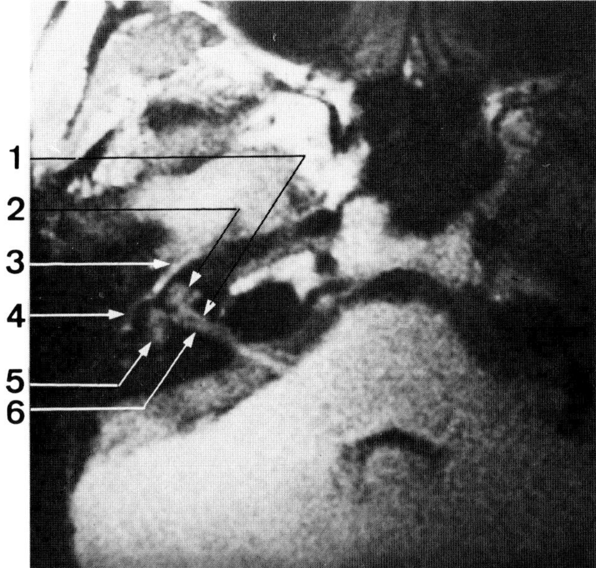

1. cochlear nerve 2. cochlea 3. greater superficial petrosal nerve 4. horizontal segment of facial nerve 5. vestibule 6. inferior vestibular nerve

B

Figure 11-67 Cranial nerves in the internal auditory canal demonstrated on surface coil MRI. Axial short T_1WI identify nerves in the upper (**A**) and lower (**B**) parts of the canal.

strated, in contrast to the hyperintense signal from CSF (the fluid appears white). The increased resolution provided by surface coil imaging improves the visualization of the individual cranial nerves (Fig. 11-67) (Daniels 1985).

NORMAL ANATOMY

Several articles have described the CT and MR anatomy of the temporal bone in detail (Zonneveld 1983; Chakeres 1983; Swartz 1983*a;* Brogan 1989). In this chapter, the key landmarks of the temporal bone are emphasized (Figs. 11-68 and 11-69).

The temporal bone is composed of the styloid process and the tympanic, mastoid, squamous, and petrous portions. The tympanic portion forms the anterior and inferior walls of the bony external auditory canal. The mastoid portion forms the posterior wall of the external canal and the middle ear and contains the mastoid air cells and mastoid antrum. The squamous portion superiorly is part of the calvarium, and the petrous portion is a wedge-shaped bone which contains the inner ear.

External Auditory Canal

The shape of the external auditory canal is variable (Virapongse 1983). Its medial two-thirds is bony, while the rest is cartilaginous. The tympanic membrane forms the sloping medial end of the canal.

Middle Ear

The middle ear is an air-filled chamber which can be subdivided into the epitympanic recess (attic) above the tympanic annulus, the hypotympanum below it, and the mesotympanum medial to it. The eustachian tube provides a communication between the widest (anterior) part of the hypotympanum and the nasopharynx. The epitympanic recess communicates with the mastoid antrum posteriorly through the aditus ad antrum. The mastoid is variably pneumatized depending on hereditary factors and childhood middle ear infections.

The ossicles transmit sound from the tympanic membrane through the middle ear to the oval window. The malleus handle attaches to the tympanic membrane, and the head articulates with the body of the incus, which is immediately behind it in the epitympanum. The incus has a long process, which articulates with the stapes, and a short process. The malleus and incus appear as an ice-cream cone on axial CT scans, with the malleus head representing the ice cream ball and the short process of the incus representing the cone (Mancuso 1982). The stapes is the smallest of the ossicles. Its two crura and a footplate in the oval window resemble a stirrup. CT shows the stapedial crura but seldom the obliquely oriented footplate, which is only 0.05 to 0.1 mm thick centrally.

The complex posterior wall of the middle ear, including the round window niche, sinus tympani, pyramidal eminence, and facial recess, is best visualized in axial CT sections (Swartz 1983*a*). The tensor tympani muscle, the stapedius muscle, and ligaments in the posterior middle ear also can often be identified on high-resolution CT scans.

Labyrinth

The bony labyrinth is located in the inner ear. The membranous labyrinth, which contains primarily perilymph and an endolymphatic space surrounded by perilymph in the cochlea, is inside the bony labyrinth. Sound waves transmitted through the ossicular chain are transferred through the oval window to the perilymph and the organ

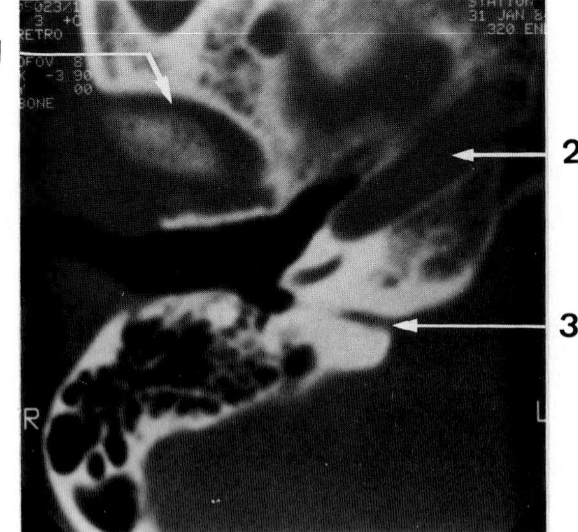

1. temporomandibular joint **2.** carotid canal **3.** cochlear aqueduct

A

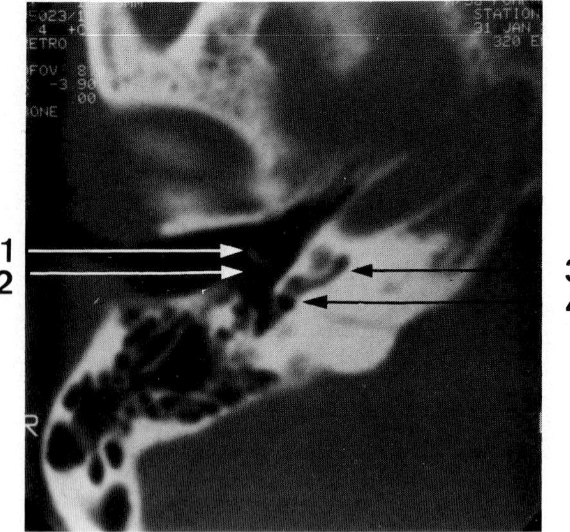

1. malleus handle **2.** long process of incus **3.** cochlea **4.** round window niche

B

1. stapes **2.** vestibule **3.** sinus tympani

C

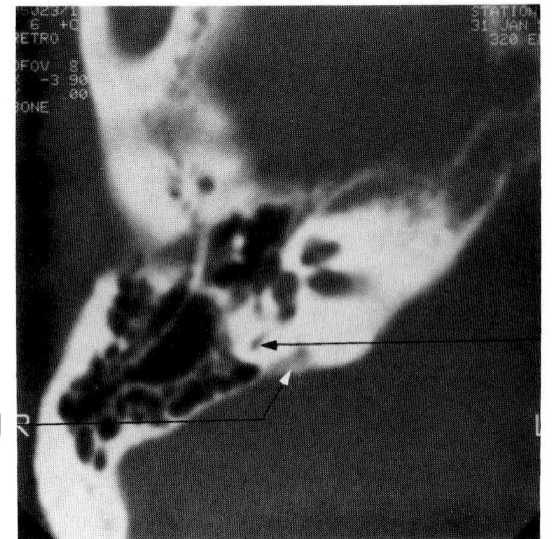

1. endolymphatic fossa and vestibular aqueduct **2.** posterior semicircular canal

D

Figure 11-68 Normal axial 1.5-mm-thick contiguous CT scans of the right ear from posterior to anterior (**A** to **G**).

of Corti in the endolymphatic space to produce the sensation of sound. The cochlea resembles a snail with 2½ to 2¾ turns. The basal turn of the cochlea in the medial wall of the tympanic cavity forms the cochlear promontory in the middle ear. The round window is an opening in the basal turn of the cochlea and is covered by a membrane. The cochlear aqueduct, which is parallel to and below the internal auditory canal, connects the cochlea and the posteromedial surface of the petrous pyramid to equilibrate perilymph with the CSF. Posterior and slightly superior to the cochlea, the bony inner ear contains lateral, posterior, and superior semicircular canals, which are connected to the vestibule. The semicircular canals are perpendicular to each other. The posterior semicircular canal is parallel to the posterior surface of the petrous pyramid, which is oriented at approximately 45° to the coronal plane.

Internal Auditory Canal

The internal auditory canal is usually oriented in a nearly coronal plane. The porus acousticus is the medial end of the internal auditory canal. The posterior lip of the porus is well defined, while the anterior wall blends with the petrous apex. The internal canal contains the facial (VII) and cochlear (VIII) nerves anteriorly, separated by the falciform crest, and the superior and inferior divisions of the vestibular (VIII) nerve posteriorly.

The vestibular aqueduct, which is the bony canal for the endolymphatic duct, originates in the vestibule and curves superiorly, posteriorly, and then inferiorly to the posterior surface of the temporal bone.

The facial (VII) nerve has a complex course through the temporal bone. It enters into the anterosuperior portion of the internal auditory canal, exits from the anterolateral end of the canal, and extends anteriorly to the ge-

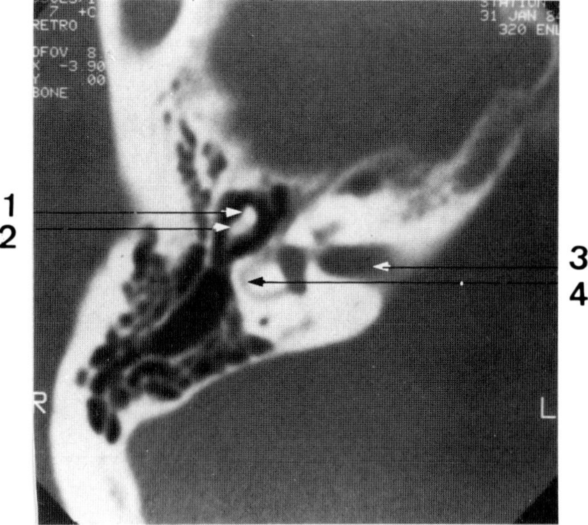

1. malleus head 2. body and short process of the incus
3. internal auditory canal 4. lateral semicircular canal
E

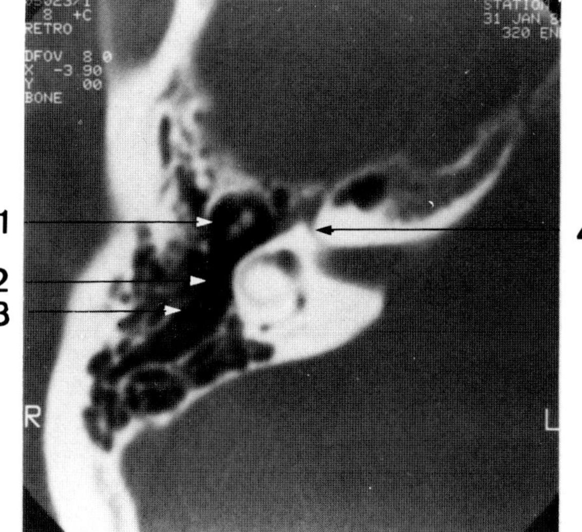

1. attic 2. aditus ad antrium 3. antrum
4. labyrinthine segment of facial nerve canal
F

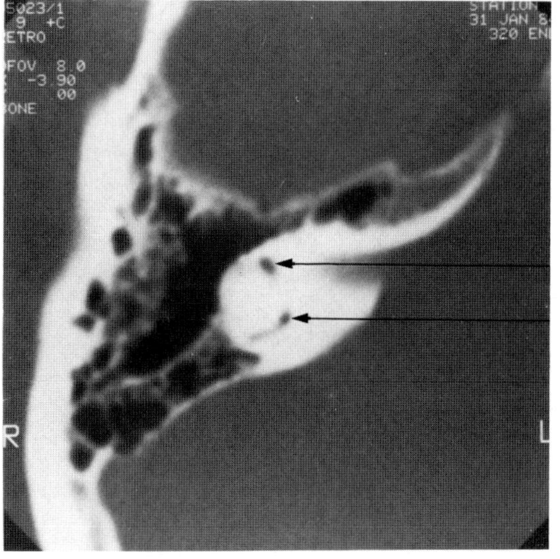

1. superior semicircular canal 2. common crus between superior and posterior semicircular canals
G

Figure 11-68 (continued)

niculate ganglion, which is above the cochlea and is the site where the greater superficial petrosal nerve originates. The facial nerve then reverses its course, passing along the medial wall of the middle ear under the lateral semicircular canal. Posterior to the middle ear at the level of the sinus tympani, the nerve turns approximately 90° to exit inferiorly at the stylomastoid foramen and then continues into the parotid gland. The locations of the geniculate ganglion and of the horizontal and vertical portions of the facial nerve are easily identified on CT. MR can demonstrate the facial nerve within its canal (Reese 1984; Teresi 1987*a,b*).

Jugular Foramen

The jugular foramen, which is posterior to the temporal bone, is divided into a small anteromedial pars nervosa containing the glossopharyngeal (IX) nerve and the inferior petrosal sinus and a large posterolateral pars vascularis containing the jugular bulb and the vagus (X) and spinal accessory (XI) nerves. The right jugular foramen is often larger than the left, because the right jugular vein and sigmoid sinus are larger. CT is superior to MR in demonstrating the osseous margin of the jugular foramen. MR (especially with T_1-weighted gradient echo images) is superior to CT in demonstrating cranial nerves IX through XI in the jugular foramen, the inferior petrosal sinus, and the jugular bulb, with the vascular structures having high signal intensity (Fig. 11-70) (Daniels 1985, 1988*a*).

CONGENITAL ANOMALIES

Congenital malformations of the ear usually affect the inner ear or the middle and external ear but not usually

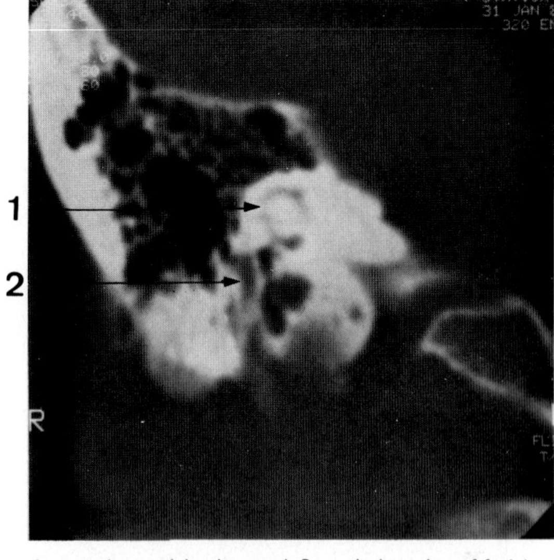

1. posterior semicircular canal **2.** vertical portion of facial nerve canal

A

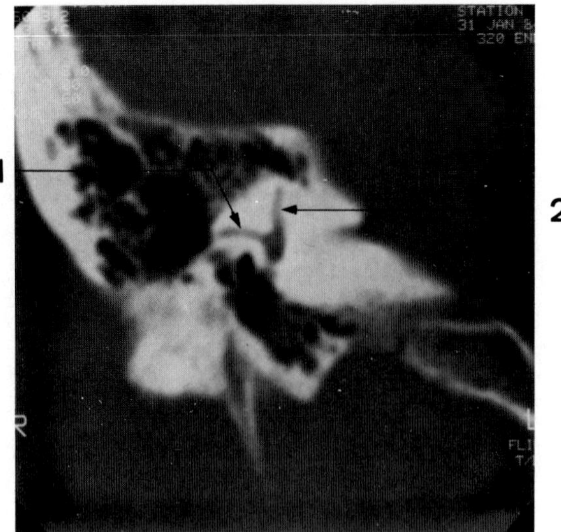

1. lateral semicircular canal **2.** superior semicircular canal

B

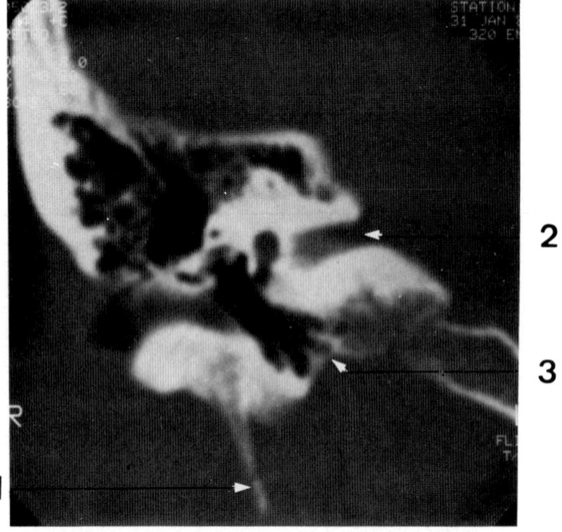

1. styloid process **2.** internal auditory canal **3.** shallow jugular fossa

C

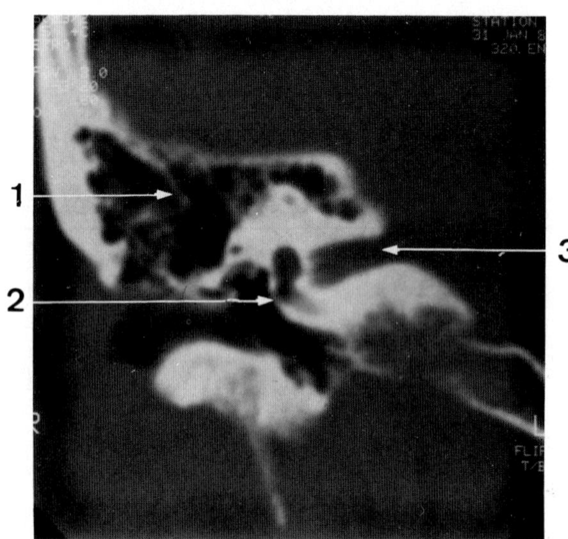

1. Koerner's septum **2.** round window **3.** internal auditory canal

D

Figure 11-69 Normal coronal 1.5-mm-thick contiguous CT scans of the right ear from posterior to anterior (**A** to **G**).

both, except in a few specific conditions such as maternal ingestion of thalidomide, chromosomal abnormalities, and craniofacial dysplasias (Hanafee 1980). The inner ear forms during the second and third months from the otocyst, which arises from ectodermal thickening on the side of the head. The auricle, ossicles, and external auditory canal develop from the first and second branchial arches and the first branchial groove. The endoderm-lined first pharyngeal pouch forms the tympanic cavity and eustachian tube. Pneumatization of the mastoid begins in the seventh to eighth fetal month and may continue into adulthood. The cartilaginous otic capsule ossifies in the fifth fetal month.

External and Middle Ear

Except for isolated minor soft tissue malformations of the pinna and external auditory canal, bony anomalies usually coexist in the external canal and middle ear. The bony external auditory canal may be partially filled with soft tissue, hypoplastic, or nonexistent (Fig. 11-71). The degree of hypoplasia correlates with mastoid pneumatization; normal pneumatization generally indicates a less severe anomaly. When the external canal is atretic, the length of the atretic segment correlates with the severity of ossicular malformation. The temporomandibular joint is usually deformed in patients with congenital anomalies of the external ear. The glenoid fossa may be flattened, and the distance from the condyle to the tympanic bone may be markedly increased (Wright 1981). Other middle ear anomalies that occur with external canal atresia include a deformed fused incus and malleus, complete or partial absence of the ossicles, and aplasia of the middle ear (Bergstrom 1980).

A common CT finding in these anomalies is a bony plate replacing the tympanic membrane. The middle ear cavity is usually smaller than normal and often is not

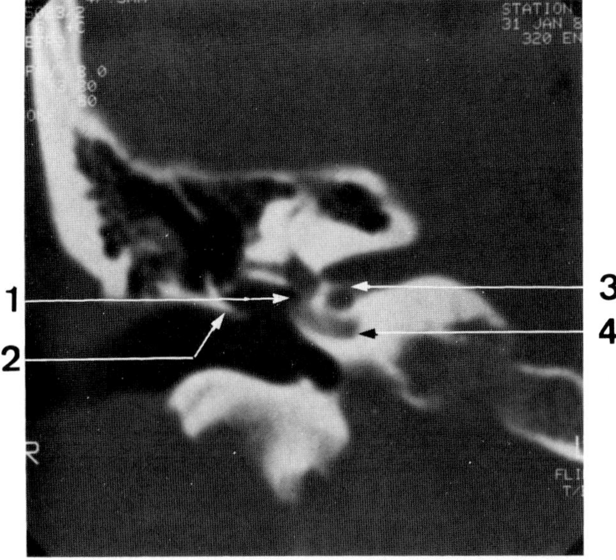

1. oval window **2.** drum spur **3.** falciform crest **4.** basal turn of cochlea
E

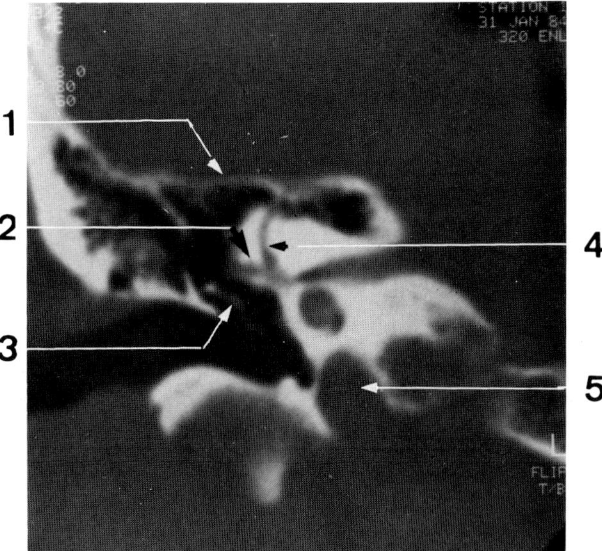

1. tegmen **2.** lateral semicircular canal **3.** incus **4.** superior semicircular canal **5.** carotid canal
F

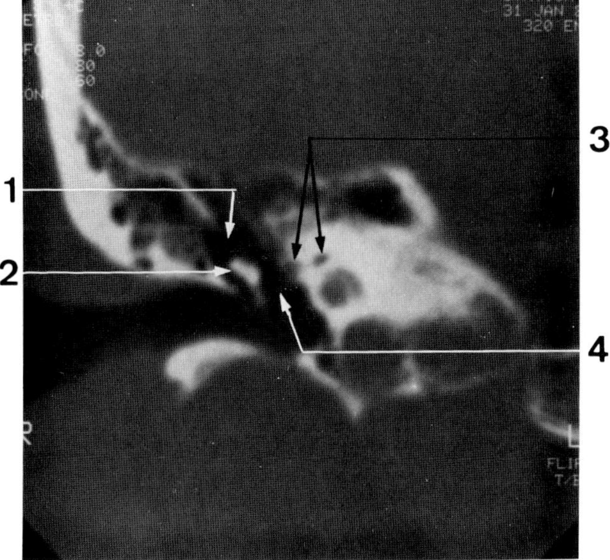

1. attic **2.** malleus **3.** limbs of facial nerve canal **4.** tensor tympani muscle
G

Figure 11-69 (continued)

pneumatized. CT may show a misshapen bony mass instead of normal ossicles, fusion of the malleus handle to the atresia plate, no osseous covering over the facial nerve in the middle ear, partial absence of the ossicles, or variable mastoid development and pneumatization. The tympanic portion of the temporal bone may be hypoplastic. In less severe anomalies, abnormal soft tissue may be demonstrated in an otherwise normal canal. In more severe malformations, CT shows an abnormal course of the nerve or a bifid canal through the middle ear. The descending portion of the nerve is frequently positioned anteriorly in patients with a contracted tympanic cavity and a hypoplastic tympanic bone (Fig. 11-72) (Phelps 1981*a*; Wright 1982; Eelkema 1989). A surgeon must know the position of the facial nerve, particularly the vertical portion, before attempting to reconstruct the external auditory canal in a patient with atresia.

Inner Ear

Several malformations of the inner ear, each associated with an eponym, have been described. The rare Michel deformity refers to total aplasia of the inner ear. The Mondini malformation designates a decreased number of cochlear turns that results because the apical and intermediate coils are combined as a single cavity, while the Mondini-Alexander malformation includes vestibular abnormalities as well as the cochlear malformation (Fig. 11-73). The Scheibe and Siebenmann-Bing malformations involve the membranous labyrinth only and have no specific CT findings. Another anomaly without an eponym is an abnormally short and broad lateral semicircular canal, which is an incidental finding. Clinical manifestations of severe vestibular and semicircular canal malformations include hearing loss, CSF leakage into the middle ear, and recurrent episodes of meningitis. CT findings include enlarged semicircular canals and a sac-

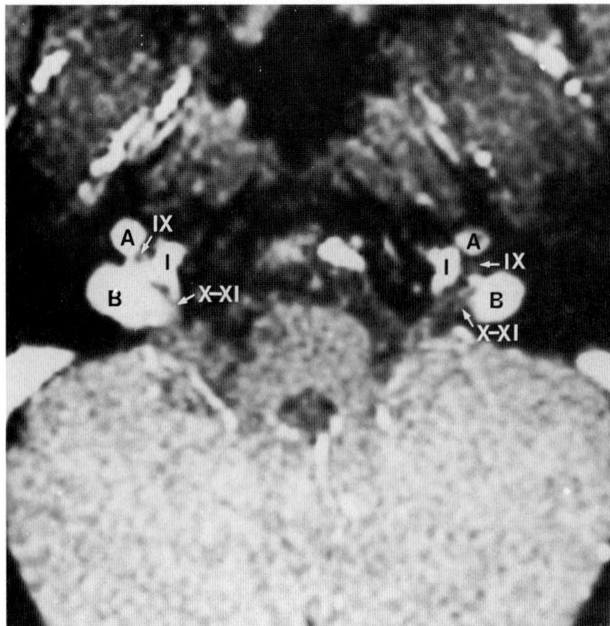

Figure 11-70 Normal jugular foramina are demonstrated in an axial T_1-weighted gradient echo image. Vascular structures have a high signal intensity. (A = petrous internal carotid artery, I = inferior petrosal sinus in anterior part of jugular foramen, B = jugular bulb, IX = cranial nerve IX, X–XI = cranial nerves X and XI together.) (*From Daniels 1988a.*)

shaped cochlea. If CT shows a small internal auditory canal (2 mm or less), atresia of the eighth nerve should be suspected (Fig.11-74). Progressive sensorineural hearing loss may be seen in patients, including children, with the isolated anomaly of a large vestibular aqueduct (Fig. 11-75) (Swartz 1986*a*; Levenson 1989).

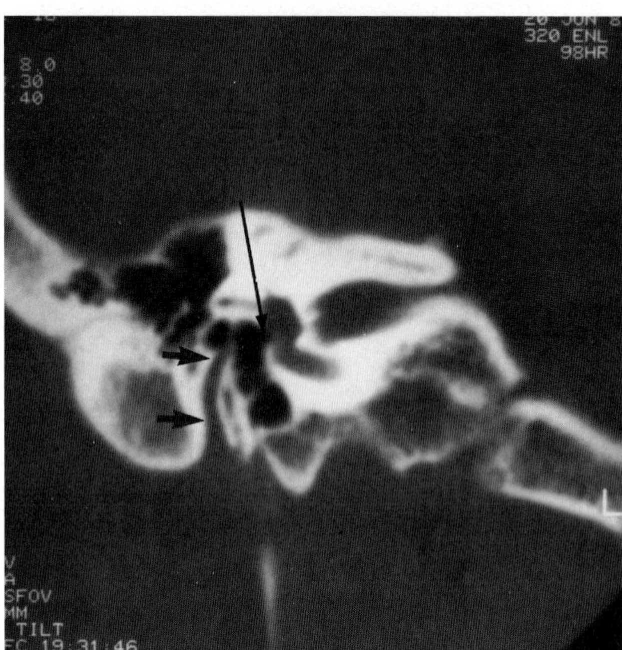

Figure 11-72 Anterior displacement of the descending facial nerve canal (short arrows) to the level of the oval window (long arrow) in a patient with a hypoplastic tympanic bone and absent external auditory canal.

Miscellaneous

A high jugular bulb or aberrant carotid artery may produce a mass in the middle ear (Fig. 11-76). The clinical manifestations include pulsatile tinnitus and hearing loss. The aberrant internal carotid artery is a rare anatomic variant that if not recognized can lead to an injudicious

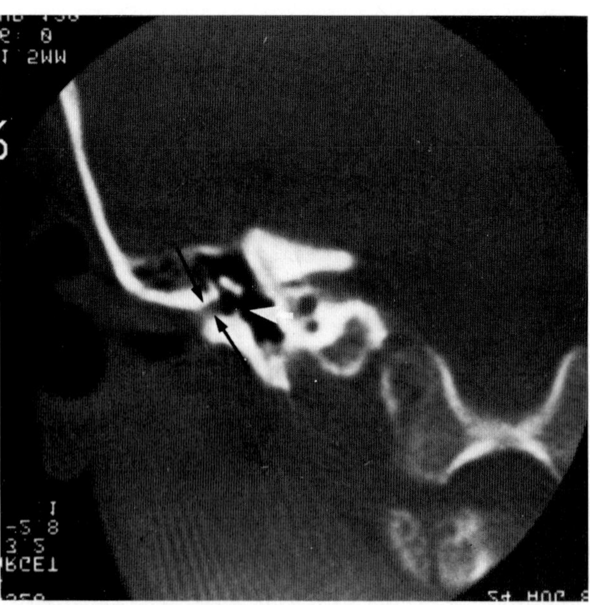

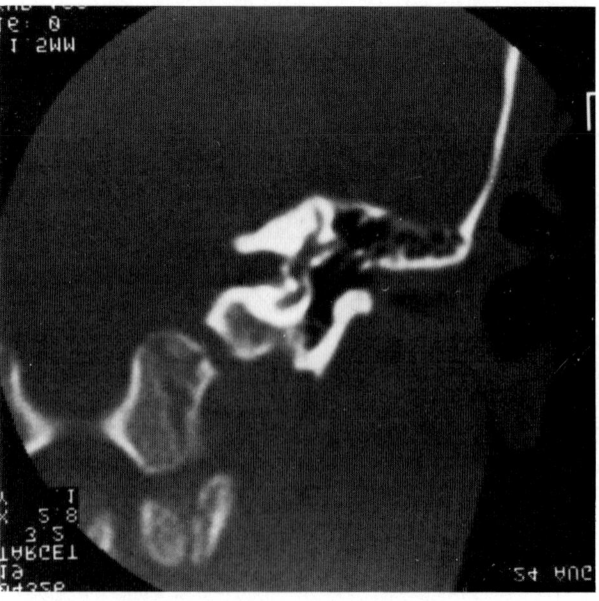

A B

Figure 11-71 Congenital atresia of the external auditory canal in coronal CT. In the right ear (**A**), soft tissue (black arrows) is demonstrated in the narrow bony external auditory canal and the malleus handle may be fused to the atresia plate (white arrow). In the left ear (**B**), the middle ear and ossicles appear normal but a similar external canal malformation is present. (*From Shaffer 1985.*)

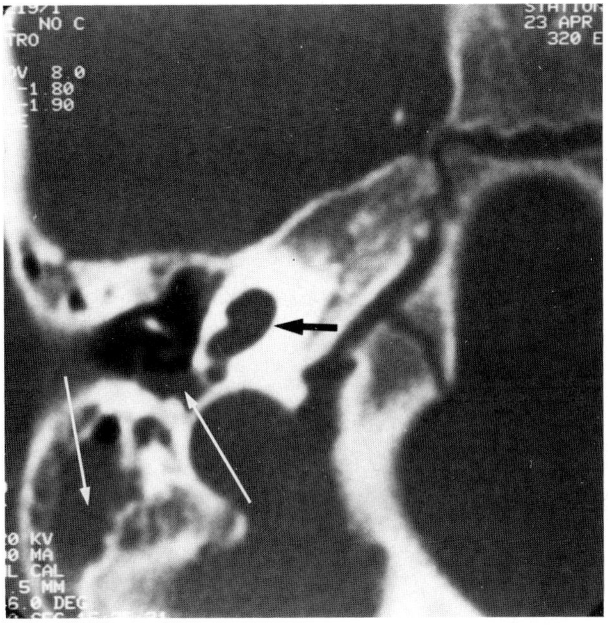

A

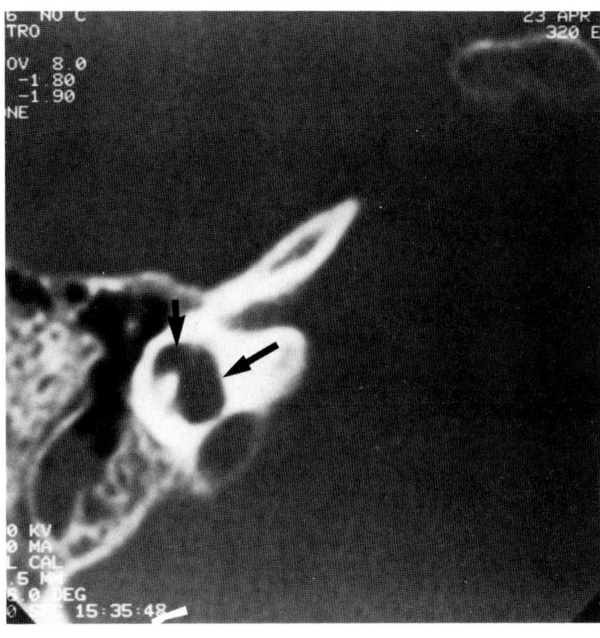

B

Figure 11-73 Mondini-Alexander malformation of the cochlea and vestibule on axial CT. The lower section (**A**) demonstrates fewer cochlear turns than normal (black arrow) and fluid in the middle ear and mastoid (white arrows). In **B** the enlarged vestibule (long arrow) and dilated lateral semicircular canal (short arrow) are identified. (*From Shaffer 1985.*)

attempt at biopsy. The persistence of a primitive vessel lateral to the normal location of the carotid artery results in the carotid artery's lying within the middle ear. Other anatomic variations, such as a persistent stapedial artery or an aberrant middle meningeal artery, may be associated with these vascular anomalies (Guinto 1972; Damsma 1984; Lo 1985). CT shows a defect in the normal bony covering of the carotid canal or jugular vein. The tissue within the dehiscence and the mass in the middle ear have enhancement similar to that of the carotid artery or jugular vein on dynamic CT scans. If CECT is not confirmatory, conventional or MR angiography can be used to verify the anomaly.

Axial CT demonstrates the osseous and soft tissue findings in congenital anomalies of the ear as well as or better than pluridirectional tomography can. Coronal CT im-

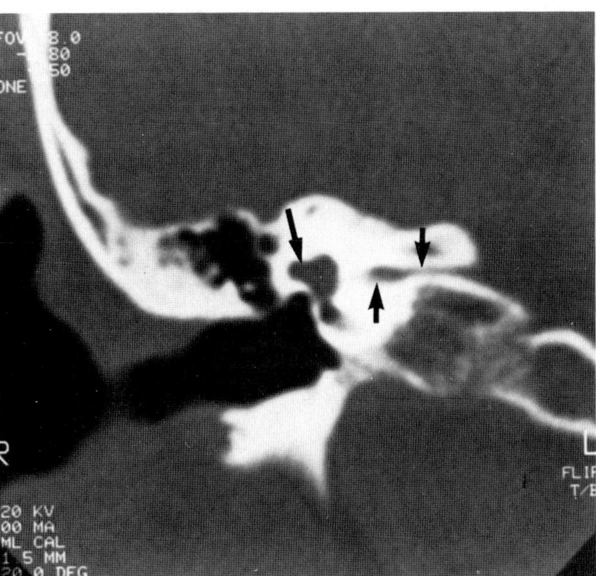

Figure 11-74 Hypoplastic internal auditory canal (short arrows) in a deaf child. Coronal CT also demonstrates a bulbous lateral semicircular canal (long arrow).

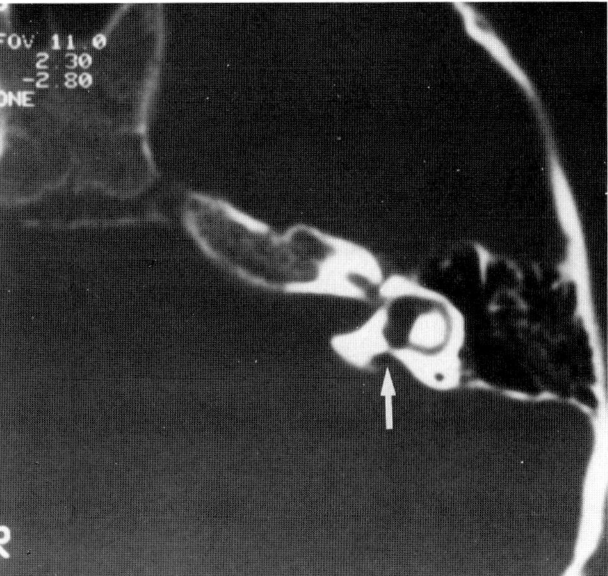

Figure 11-75 Large vestibular aqueduct (arrow) as an isolated anomaly in a child with increasing left sensorineural hearing loss.

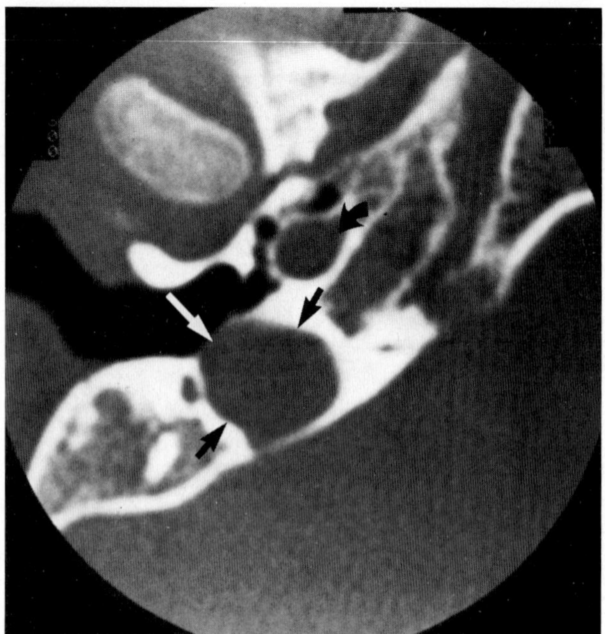

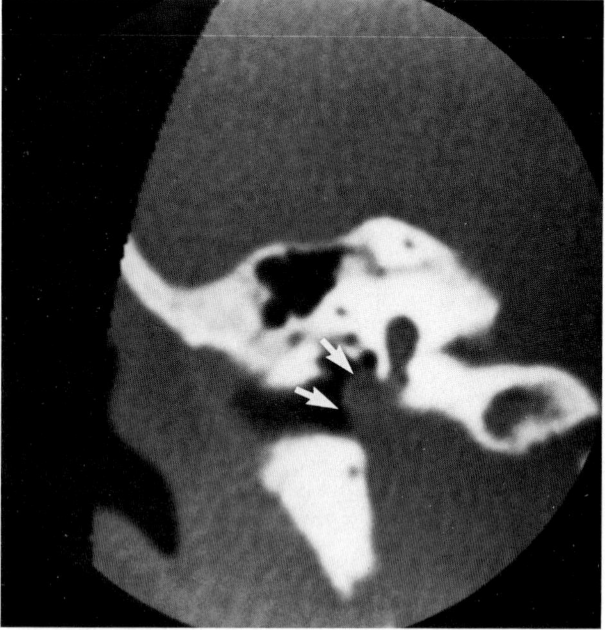

A B

Figure 11-76 High jugular bulb (straight arrows) demonstrated in axial (**A**) and coronal (**B**) CT [curved arrow = carotid canal; straight arrows = large jugular bulb with dehiscent bone (white arrow)]. In **B,** the bulb lacking a bony covering protrudes into the middle ear. Clinically, it appeared as a bluish mass in the hypotympanum. (*From Shaffer 1985.*)

ages are necessary to evaluate the bony walls covering the carotid artery and jugular bulb and the vertical portion of the facial (VII) nerve canal.

TRAUMA

Fractures

Thin-section CT is effective in evaluating temporal bone fractures. These fractures are classified as longitudinal or transverse according to the direction of the major fracture line with respect to the long axis of the petrous pyramid (Kaseff 1969). Fractures may have both longitudinal and transverse components or may fit neither classification. The thick (10-mm) CT sections done routinely in nearly all patients with significant head injuries usually fail to detect temporal bone fractures (Holland 1984). To evaluate patients with fractures, more than one scan plane, obtained directly or by reformation, is essential (Johnson 1984*b*). Understanding the normal linear lucencies in the temporal bone is important in distinguishing them from fractures (Dolanik 1989). While MR can detect blood or fluid in the mastoid, CT remains the method of choice for diagnosing fractures (Zimmerman 1987).

LONGITUDINAL FRACTURES

Three-quarters of temporal bone fractures are longitudinal, produced by direct trauma to the temporoparietal region (Fig. 11-77). The longitudinal fracture lines usually pass from the squamous portion of the temporal bone anteriorly and inferiorly through the tegmen tympani, external auditory canal, middle ear, and foramen lacerum. The clinical signs of longitudinal fracture in-

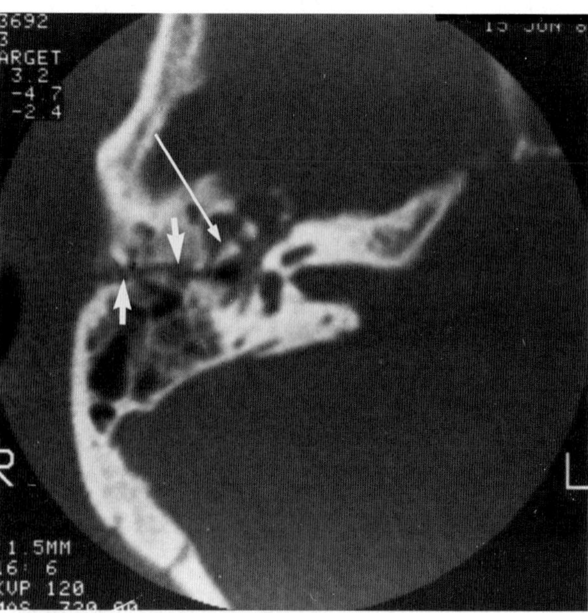

Figure 11-77 Axial CT scan showing a longitudinal fracture (short arrows) through the right mastoid. Also shown is dislocation of the incus (long arrow) from the malleus, appearing as an ice cream cone separated from its scoop. (*From Shaffer 1985.*)

clude blood in the external auditory canal, conductive hearing loss, and tearing of the tympanic membrane. The facial nerve is injured in one-quarter of cases. Facial weakness or paralysis occurring with some delay after trauma and resolving spontaneously is probably due to edema of the nerve. Paralysis that occurs immediately after trauma suggests a bone fragment in the facial nerve canal or nerve disruption. Temporal bone fractures can also cause pneumocephalus, CSF leak manifested as otorrhea, and temporal lobe herniation into the temporal bone if a large defect is produced in the tegmen.

Longitudinal temporal bone fractures may cause ossicular dislocation or fractures. Because of its relatively loose attachments to the malleus and stapes, the incus is dislocated more frequently than is the malleus, which is anchored to the tympanic membrane, or the stapes, which is fixed in the oval window. When the malleus or stapes is fractured or dislocated, the incus usually is involved as well (Wright 1974).

Longitudinal fractures can be identified accurately on axial CT scans. The tegmen, drum spur, and facial nerve canal are best evaluated on coronal images. CT findings in longitudinal fractures include fracture lines in the mastoid and fluid or air-fluid levels in the air cells (Fig. 11-77). If the incus is subluxed or dislocated or if the ossicular chain is more severely disrupted, the ice cream cone shape of the malleus and incus is distorted. The malleus and incus, which are normally equidistant from the medial and lateral attic walls, may be displaced. The stapes is usually obscured in CT sections when blood is present in the middle ear. When facial nerve paralysis is present, the course of the nerve should be inspected. Longitudinal fractures commonly injure the facial nerve near the geniculate ganglion (Holland 1984).

TRANSVERSE FRACTURES

Although transverse fractures of the temporal bone are less common than longitudinal ones and are not usually produced by trauma directly to the temporal bone, the clinical manifestations are usually more severe. Transverse fractures crossing the long axis of the petrous pyramid usually injure the bony labyrinth and may extend laterally to the middle ear (Fig. 11-78). The clinical findings include vertigo, sensorineural hearing loss, and facial nerve paralysis (approximately 50 percent of patients). Dural tears with CSF leakage (as in rhinorrhea when the tympanic membrane is intact), blood and fluid in the middle ear, and facial nerve paralysis which seldom recovers spontaneously are common findings.

Transverse fractures are seen equally well on axial and coronal scans which are perpendicular to the fracture planes. CT findings include fracture lines through the internal auditory canal, cochlea, vestibule, and semicircular or facial nerve canals and occasional opacification of the middle ear or mastoid.

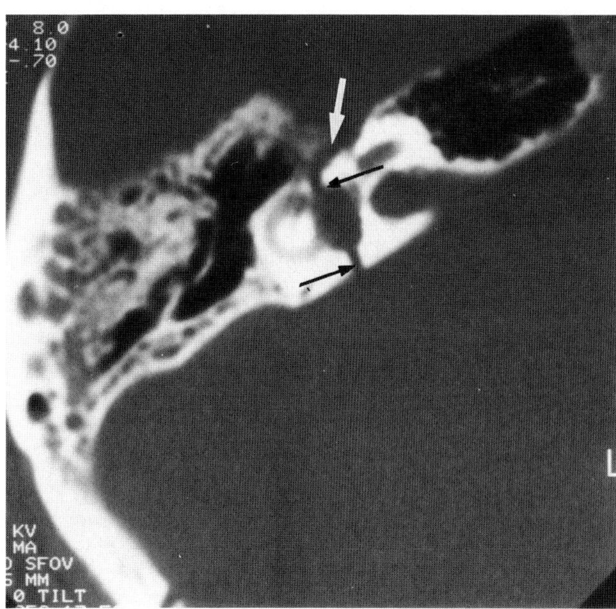

Figure 11-78 Transverse fracture through the vestibule (black arrows) also involving the geniculate ganglion area (white arrow). Mastoid air cells are opacified. The patient had "dead ear" and facial paralysis.

OTHER FRACTURES

Trauma to the mandible may fracture the anterior wall of the external auditory canal. This injury usually does not involve the middle ear or inner ear. Bleeding and deformity of the external canal are evident otoscopically. These fractures can be identified on axial and sagittal reformatted CT scans or lateral pleuridirectional tomograms. Microfractures in the region of the oval and round windows which are not visible on radiographs may cause hearing loss. Occasionally, a direct blow to the mastoid produces a localized fracture which does not extend into the remainder of the temporal bone. Isolated fractures of the styloid process may occur, causing facial nerve paresis.

Foreign Bodies

Foreign bodies such as bullets, slag, and shrapnel are easily seen on CT (Fig. 11-79). Nonopaque foreign bodies may not be detected by CT unless they are associated with other abnormalities. CT is useful in detecting ossicular dislocation by an ear swab or identifying displacement of a stapes prosthesis causing sudden hearing loss or vertigo.

NEOPLASMS

External Ear and Mastoid

BENIGN TUMOR

Exostoses occur in the external auditory canal, especially in people who swim frequently in cold water. Although

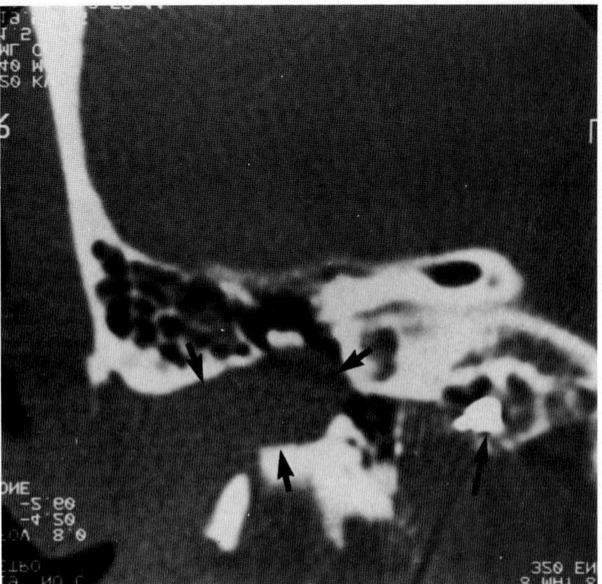

Figure 11-79 Cholesteatoma (short arrows) in the external auditory canal and middle ear on coronal CT. The mass developed after a gunshot wound; one fragment (long arrow) is still present near the carotid canal. (*From Shaffer 1985.*)

these bony projections are often multiple and bilateral, they do not extend into the adjacent mastoid (Fig. 11-80). Exostoses become significant when they narrow the canal, hindering examination of the tympanic membrane and occasionally obstructing the egress of squamous debris from the canal. CT shows multiple uniformly dense ovoid masses blending with the external canal walls. They resemble osteomas, which are, however, usually single. Osteomas, unlike exostoses, are neoplasms which increase in size and invade adjacent bone. In the external auditory canal they occur at the junction of the bony and cartilaginous portions of the canal. They are also common in the mastoid. CT shows an osteoma as a solitary uniformly dense bony mass of variable size.

Gland cell tumors arise rarely from eccrine, modified apocrine (ceruminous), and sebaceous glands within the skin of the external auditory canal. Apocrine adenomas (ceruminomas) constitute the majority of gland cell tumors (Batsakis 1979). CT shows a ceruminoma as a soft tissue mass in the external auditory canal (Fig. 11-81). If bone destruction is associated with the tumor, malignancy should be suspected.

PRIMARY MALIGNANT TUMOR

The most frequently occurring primary malignancies of the external ear are squamous carcinoma, basal cell carcinoma or less frequently adenocarcinoma, adenoid cystic carcinoma, and melanoma of the pinna. Tumors in the external auditory canal are not usually detected as early as are pinna malignancies. Patients who develop external auditory canal carcinomas often have chronic suppurative otitis media, which delays the diagnosis of tumor (Phelps 1981*b*). Malignant tumors usually produce otorrhea, pain, hearing loss, or facial nerve palsy. CT may show only permeative bone destruction which is not easily distinguished from an aggressive infection (Fig. 11-82). Resectability and survival can be predicted by the staging of a malignancy of the external auditory canal. Bone destruction and the soft tissue extent of disease can be identified only with a combination of axial and coronal CT scans (Bird 1983). Coronal scans are necessary to evaluate the tegmen, the floor of the middle ear, the superior and inferior walls of the external auditory canal,

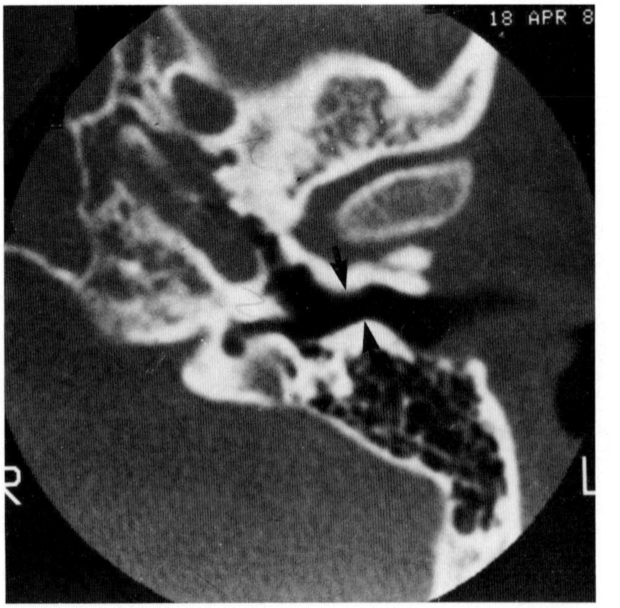

Figure 11-80 Exostoses (arrows) narrow the inferior aspect of the external auditory canal on axial CT. (*From Shaffer 1985.*)

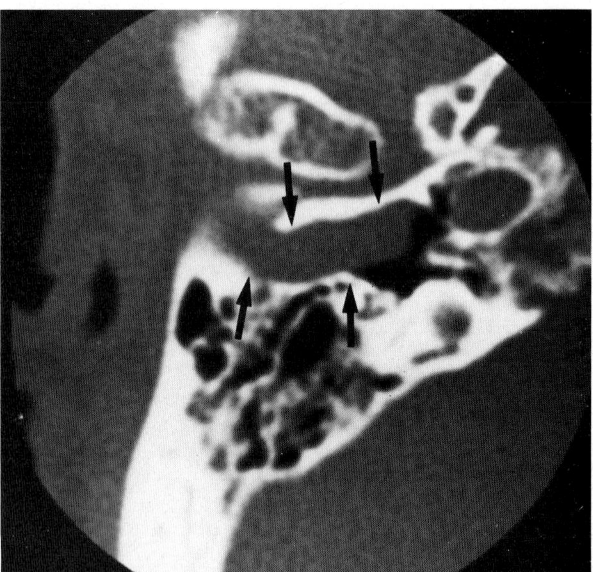

Figure 11-81 Ceruminoma (arrows) on axial CT. A soft tissue mass filling the right external auditory canal does not erode bone. (*From Shaffer 1985.*)

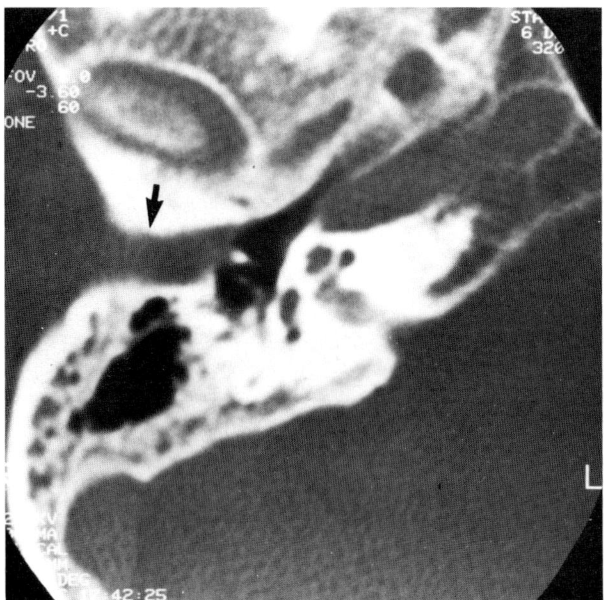

Figure 11-82 Squamous carcinoma on axial CT. A tumor fills the right external canal and minimally erodes bone (arrow) but does not invade the middle ear. (*From Shaffer 1985.*)

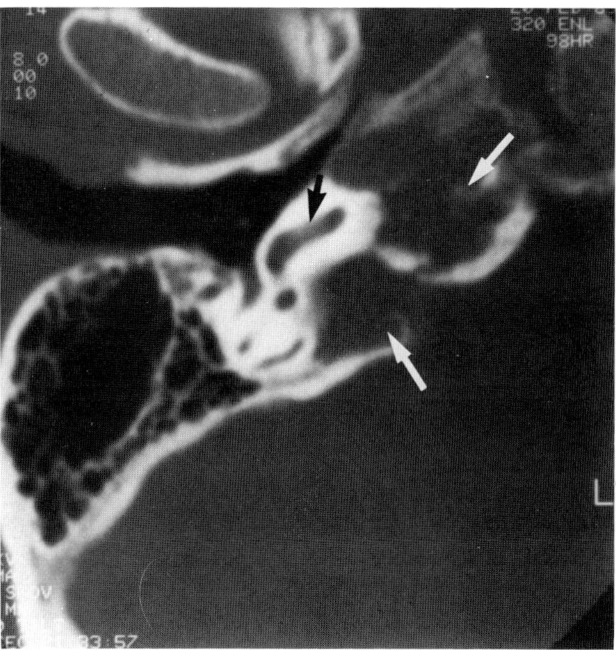

Figure 11-83 Woman with right cranial nerve palsies and a history of renal cell carcinoma. Large destructive metastasis (white arrows) anterior and posterior to the cochlea (black arrow).

and the carotid and jugular canal roofs. CECT or MR is needed if extension into the brain is suspected. The preferred treatment is surgical extirpation followed by radical irradiation.

METASTASIS

Temporal bone metastases are of two types: from hematogenous spread, usually to the marrow spaces, and from direct extension of a local lesion. Neoplasms which commonly metastasize to the temporal bone include carcinomas of the breast, prostate, lung, kidney, and thyroid. Temporal bone metastases usually occur late in the course of malignant disease, and so they may not be evaluated radiographically. Neoplasms arising in the skin, parotid gland, nasopharynx, brain, and meninges may invade the temporal bone through foramina and along nerves and fascial planes. Systemic malignancies such as leukemia, lymphoma, and myeloma occasionally affect the temporal bone (Berlinger 1980).

CT shows temporal bone metastases as bone destruction and soft tissue masses (Fig. 11-83). The differential diagnosis includes primary tumor, histiocytosis X, malignant external otitis, and large cholesteatoma. The CT appearance of metastatic disease is not specific.

HISTIOCYTOSIS X

Idiopathic proliferation of histiocytes characterizes three syndromes called *histiocytosis* or *histiocytosis X.* The three, in order of increasing age at onset and decreasing severity, are Letterer-Siwe disease, Hand-Schüller-Christian syndrome, and eosinophilic granuloma. Eosiniphilic granuloma usually involves bone, whereas Letterer-Siwe disease and Hand-Schüller-Christian syndrome involve viscera. In approximately 15 percent of cases of histiocytosis X, the ear is involved. Ear drainage, external otitis, and swelling over the temporal bone are common symptoms (McCaffrey 1979). In patients with histiocytosis of the temporal bone, CT shows a soft tissue mass and irregular bone destruction which may be indistinguishable from infection, metastatic disease, or cholesteatoma.

Middle Ear

GLOMUS TUMOR

Glomus tumors, also known as *chemodectomas* or *nonchromaffin paragangliomas,* arise from chemoreceptor cells at several sites in the head and neck. Masses that arise primarily on the cochlear promontory are called glomus tympanicum tumors (Fig. 11-84). Glomus jugulare tumors arise in the jugular fossa and may invade the middle ear from below. The symptoms of glomus tumors are usually pulsatile tinnitus and hearing loss. A glomus tumor is often visible behind the tympanic membrane. Chemodectomas, although usually benign, are sometimes multiple and are histologically malignant in about 10 percent of patients (Som 1983). Chemodectomas are more common in women than they are in men.

A glomus jugulare tumor appears as a soft tissue mass in the jugular fossa that rarely extends intracranially (Fig. 11-85). On MR, small areas of signal void representing blood vessels can be identified in glomus tumors but usually not in neurofibromas (Fig. 11-86) (Olsen 1986).

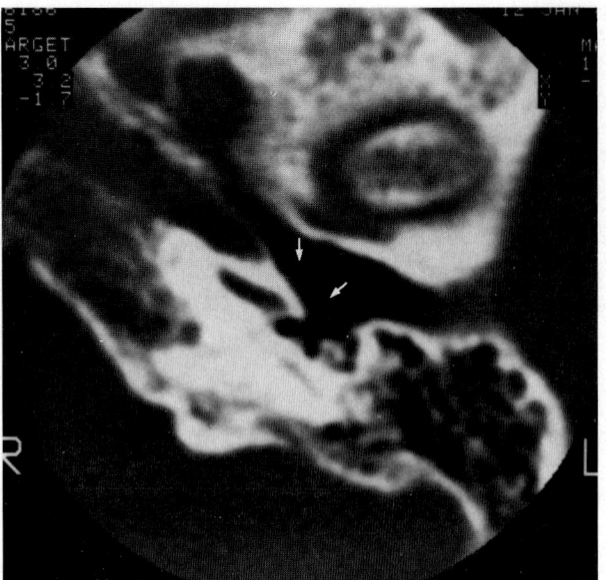

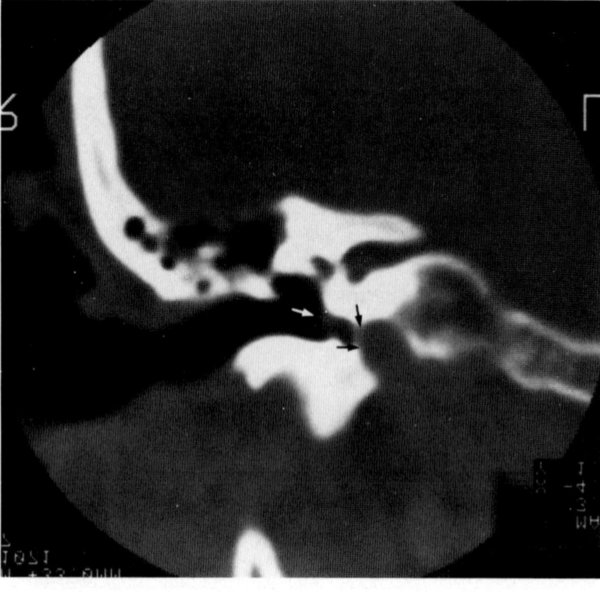

A B

Figure 11-84 Two examples of glomus tympanicum tumors (white arrows). In one case, axial CT (**A**) demonstrates a mass adjacent to the cochlear promontory. In the second case, coronal CT (**B**) shows the normal carotid canal (black arrows) below a tumor (white arrow) in the middle ear. (*From Shaffer 1985.*)

Glomus tumors enhance intensely with intravenous Gd-DTPA and typically occlude the ipsilateral jugular bulb, a finding best evaluated with T_1-weighted gradient echo images (Fig. 11-86) (Breger 1987; Haughton 1988; Daniels 1988*a*). On CT, glomus tumors also enhance after intravenous contrast administration. The margins of osseous destruction are better defined with CT than with MR.

The small soft tissue mass produced by a glomus tympanicum tumor is identified on CT scans, although it may be missed on pluridirectional tomograms (Larson 1987). Dynamic CT scans show that the maximal enhancement of the tumor occurs later than that of the carotid artery and earlier than that of the jugular vein (Mafee 1983*b*). Seldom in glomus tympanicum tumors and commonly in

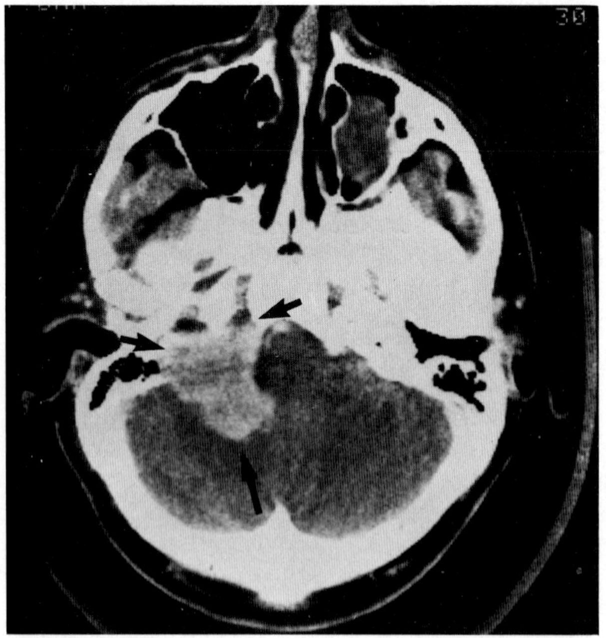

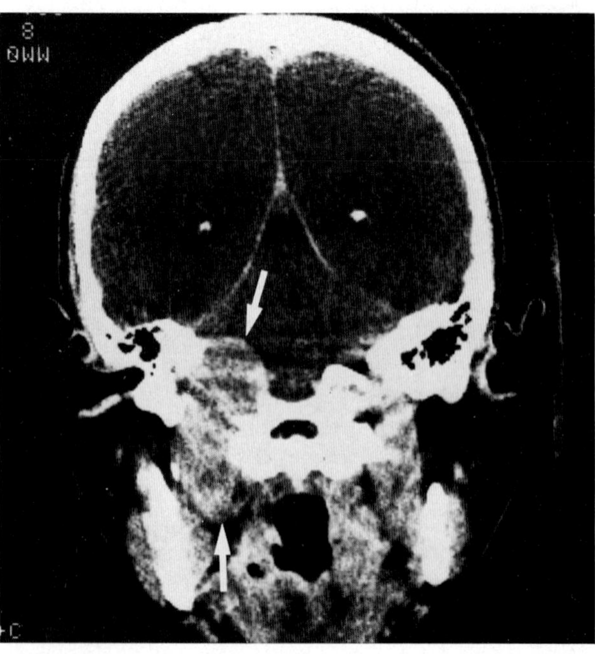

A B

Figure 11-85 Large glomus jugulare tumor (long arrow) that erodes the jugular fossa (short arrows) and extends into the right cerebellar hemisphere on axial CT (**A**). On coronal CT (**B**), the tumor's extension below the skull base is demonstrated. (*From Shaffer 1985.*)

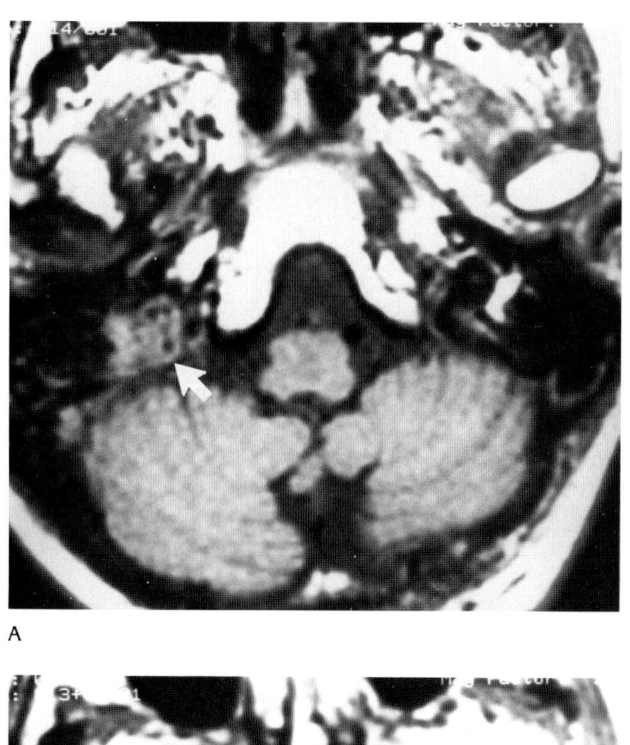

A

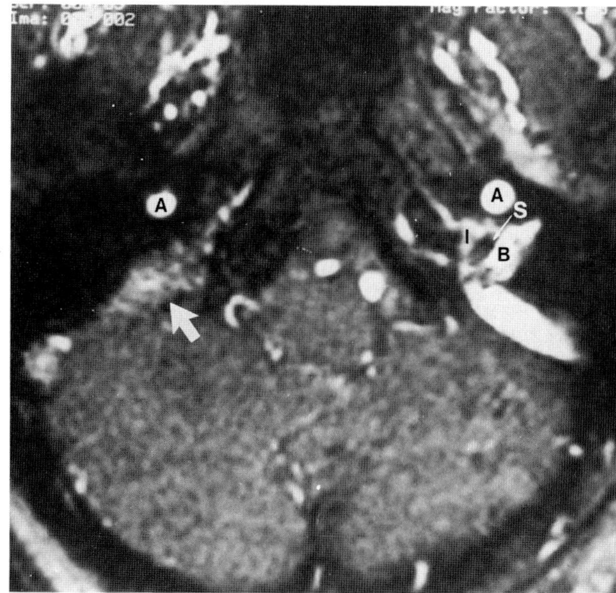

B

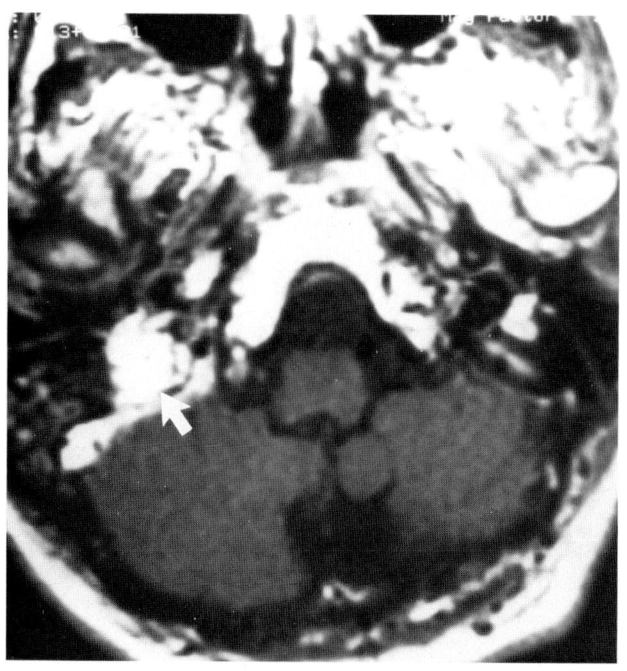

C

Figure 11-86 Glomus jugulare tumor (arrow) on axial T_1-weighted SE (**A**, and **C** with intravenous Gd-DTPA) and gradient echo MRI (**B**). The tumor is characterized by blood vessels with negligible and high signal intensity in **A** and **B,** respectively, and by intense enhancement in **C.** In **B,** contralateral normal vascular structures have high signal intensity. (A = petrous internal carotid artery, I = inferior petrosal sinus in anterior part of jugular foramen, B = jugular bulb, S = jugular spine.) (**B** *From Daniels 1988a.*)

glomus jugulare tumors, CT shows bone erosion in the roof of the jugular bulb and the septum between the carotid artery and the jugular vein. On MR, glomus tympanicum tumors demonstrate intense enhancement with IV contrast administration (Vogl 1989).

The differential diagnosis of a middle ear mass with pulsatile tinnitus includes an aberrant carotid artery and dehiscence of the bone covering the jugular vein. The key CT finding in vascular anomalies is loss of the osseous margin of the carotid or jugular canal on coronal CT scans. Angiography may be needed to verify the vascular origin of the middle ear mass. The correct diagnosis is needed prior to surgery to prevent serious complications.

FACIAL NERVE NEURINOMA

In approximately 5 percent of cases of persistent Bell's palsy, a facial nerve neurinoma or another tumor is the cause. Neurinomas occur along the intracranial, intratemporal, or extratemporal portion of the facial nerve. A facial nerve neurinoma in the internal auditory canal is indistinguishable from the more common intracanalicular acoustic neurinoma. Elsewhere in the temporal bone, the tumor is identified primarily by means of its expansion of the facial canal. The detection of an abnormality in the vertical portion of the facial nerve canal requires high-quality direct coronal CT scans or reformatted sagittal images. The identification of extratemporal tumors depends on the recognition of tumor enhancement and displacement of normal soft tissue planes (Curtin 1983).

CT shows a uniformly enhancing homogeneous mass which, if located in the facial nerve canal or internal auditory canal, causes pressure erosion. The middle ear may be completely filled with soft tissue. A correct diagnosis depends on recognizing that the mass or bone erosion is related to the course of the facial nerve. On MR, facial nerve tumors appear as soft tissue masses which follow the course of the facial nerve and show intense enhancement with intravenous gadolinium (Figs. 11-87 and 11-88) (Daniels 1987*b*). This enhancement is nonspecific because facial nerve inflammation in, for example, Bell's palsy is associated with facial nerve enhancement (Daniels 1989). However, in Bell's palsy the abnormal facial nerve is normal-sized (Fig. 11-89). In differentiating enhancing facial nerve tumors from high-signal-intensity fatty marrow and fat below the skull base, it is helpful to compare T_1-weighted SE images with and without Gd-DTPA.

MALIGNANT TUMOR

When squamous cell carcinoma occurs in the middle ear, it usually results from spread from the external auditory canal (Chen 1978). Adenocarcinomas and their variants

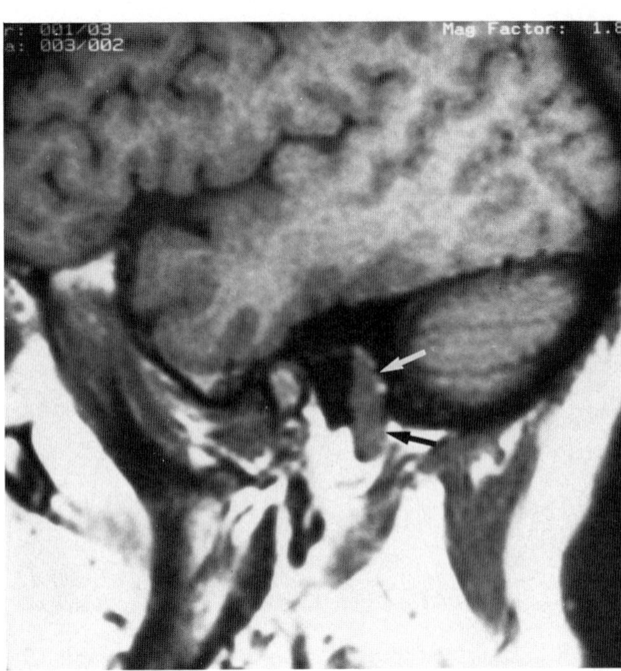

Figure 11-88 A facial nerve tumor (arrows) involving the vertical portion of the facial nerve is shown on sagittal T_1-weighted MRI.

are also rare in the middle ear (Adam 1982). The diagnosis of malignant tumor is often delayed, since the tumor may masquerade as chronic inflammatory disease. Rhabdomyosarcoma, usually of the embryonal type, is the most common soft tissue sarcoma in children, and the ear is the most common site after the orbit and nasopharynx (Fig. 11-90) (Schwartz 1980).

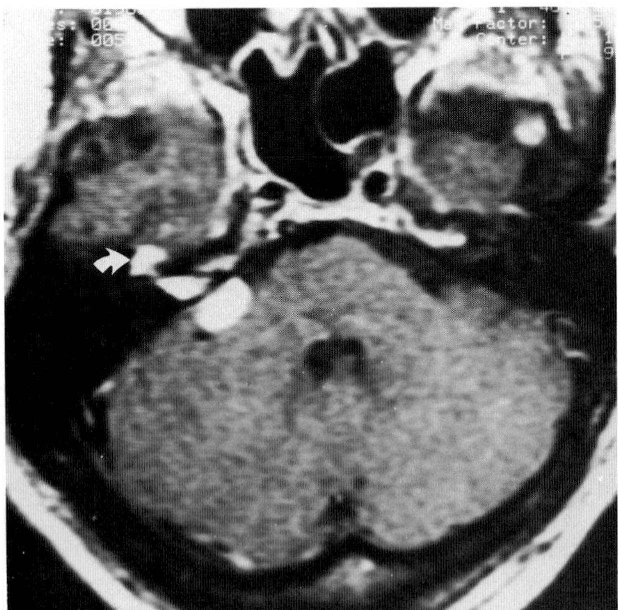

Figure 11-87 Facial nerve tumor on axial T_1-weighted MRI with intravenous Gd-DTPA. Note the tumor's intensely enhancing extracanalicular and intracanalicular components and a tumor involving the geniculate ganglion (curved arrow). (*From Daniels 1988b.*)

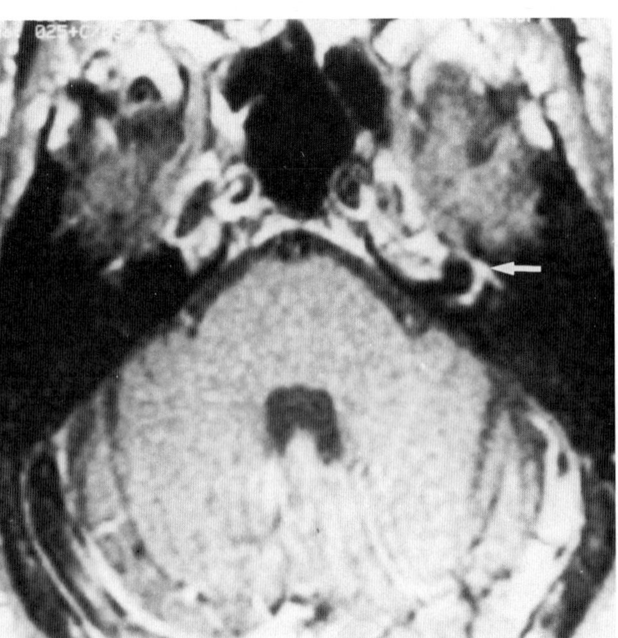

Figure 11-89 Abnormally enhancing but normal-sized facial nerve (arrow) in a patient with ipsilateral Bell's palsy is demonstrated on axial T_1-weighted MRI with intravenous Gd-DTPA.

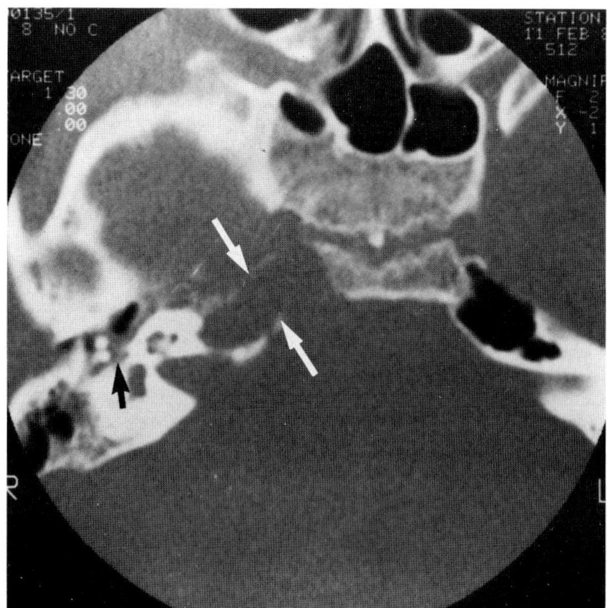

Figure 11-90 Rhabdomyosarcoma in a 12-year-old boy with right-sided hearing loss. Axial CT demonstrates petrous apex destruction (white arrows) and a tumor in the middle ear (black arrow). (*From Shaffer 1985.*)

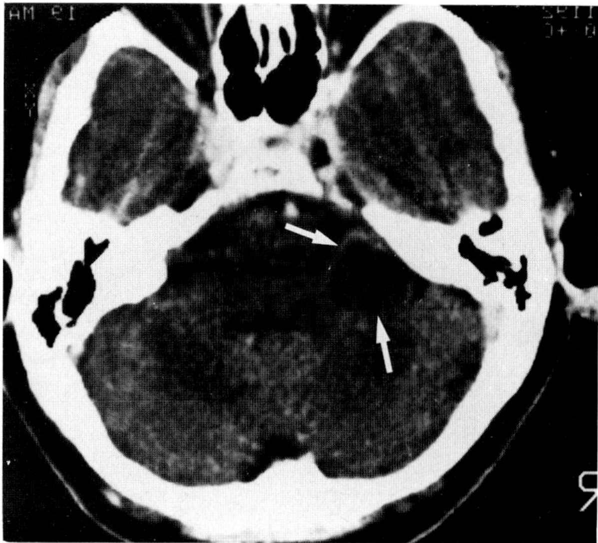

Figure 11-91 Necrotic acoustic neurinoma (arrows) on axial enhanced CT. The central low density with rim enhancement is atypical of an acoustic neurinoma. (*From Shaffer 1985.*)

A soft tissue mass in the middle ear that destroys bone characterizes most primary middle ear malignancies and aggressive benign processes such as infection. The primary role of CT in malignant tumors of the temporal bone is in staging rather than in the differential diagnosis.

Inner Ear

ACOUSTIC NEURINOMA

These benign tumors arise from Schwann cells, especially those near Scarpa's ganglion of the superior vestibular nerve. The tumors frequently arise in the internal auditory canal and grow medially into the cistern. Expansion of the bony canal, particularly its medial end, is a common feature of most acoustic neurinomas. They are slow in growth, and most have a cerebellopontine angle mass by the time of diagnosis. Patients with acoustic neurinomas present with a variety of symptoms, including sensorineural hearing loss with poor discrimination, dizziness or true vertigo, tinnitus, facial nerve paralysis, pain, decreased corneal sensation, and brainstem signs.

The sensitivity of CT in detecting acoustic neurinomas is high, especially when newer scanners with improved resolution and thin sections are used. CT shows acoustic neurinomas as enhancing masses in the internal auditory canal or cerebellopontine angle (Valvassori 1982; Wu 1986). Contrast enhancement is characteristic of acoustic neurinomas because there is no restriction of capillary permeability (blood-brain barrier), although there may be hypodense areas in the tumor (Fig. 11-91). Patients can be scanned immediately after the iodinated contrast agent (42 g iodine) has been administered or while the last 10 g is being infused. Enhanced thin-section CT scans must be reconstructed with a standard algorithm for brain and viewed at a soft tissue window to see subtle tumors. If only bone detail reconstruction and filming are done, the contrast administration is of no value since only the indirect bony changes of the tumor will be detected.

Completely intracanalicular acoustic neurinomas without enlargement of the canal are difficult to detect on CT scans through contrast enhancement alone, but identification is easier if the canal is expanded by the tumor (Fig. 11-92). The normal canal contains nerves and CSF which together have a density intermediate between the density of brain and that of CSF; after enhancement, a tumor has a substantially higher density. A comparison of one side with the other usually reveals the tumor. However, a negative CT study in a patient with strong clinical evidence of an acoustic neurinoma should be followed by MR. Thick slices cannot be used to identify intracanalicular tumors because of partial volume averaging, which obscures the intracanalicular enhancement.

Although rarely performed when MR is available, CT gas cisternography is a reliable test for diagnosing intracanalicular tumors (Robertson 1983; Solti-Bohman 1984). CT demonstration of an internal auditory canal not filled with gas provides evidence of an intracanalicular acoustic neuroma if a convex surface of the tumor is projecting into the cerebellopontine angle (Fig. 11-92). A canal filled with gas excludes the possibility of a tumor. Surface tension between gas and CSF in the cistern may prevent gas from entering the internal auditory canal; therefore, the patient's head should be shaken gently to dislodge fluid from the canal if gas fails to fill the canal. When the interface between the gas and the contents of the canal is con-

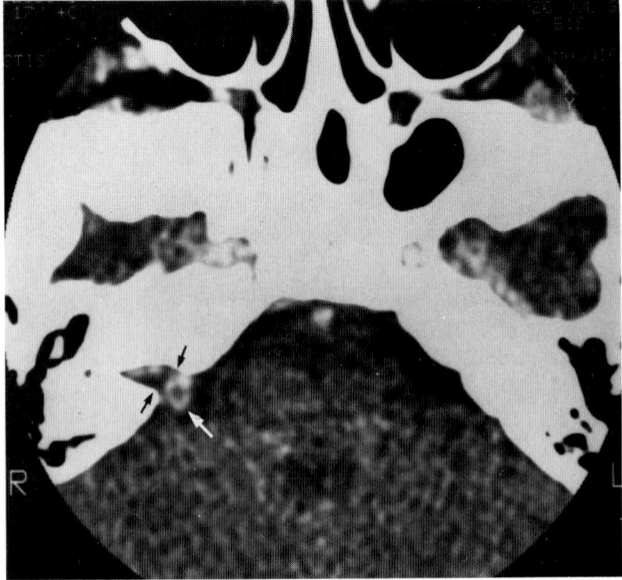

A

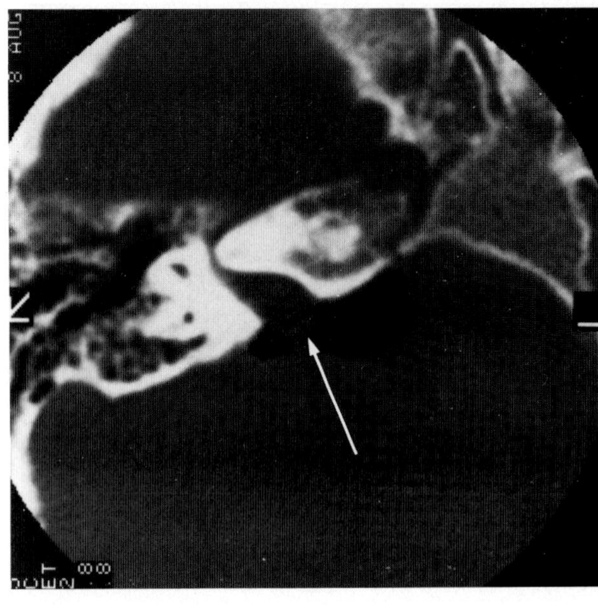

B

Figure 11-92 Acoustic neurinoma with a small extracanalicular component (arrows). The tumor enhances on axial CT (**A**) and displaces air from the right internal auditory canal on an air CT cisternogram (**B**). (*From Shaffer 1985.*)

cave, a technical cause for obstruction to gas, rather than a neoplasm, should be considered. A loop of anterior inferior cerebellar artery (AICA) in the internal auditory canal or thickened nerves may mimic tiny acoustic neurinomas by preventing gas from entering the canal. In these cases, imaging the contralateral ear with gas can be helpful. Intracanalicular tumors as small as 3 mm have been diagnosed with gas CT cisternography (Johnson 1984*a*).

Because MR demonstrates even small intracanalicular acoustic neurinomas effectively, it can replace CT cisternography and contrast-enhanced CT in studying patients with sensorineural hearing loss (Figs. 11-93 and 11-94) (Gentry 1987; Mafee 1987; Armington 1988; Press 1988; Valvassori 1988; Swartz 1989). With intravenous Gd-DTPA, relatively fast T_1-weighted imaging sequences can be used to identify acoustic neurinomas, which typically enhance intensely (Figs. 11-95 and 11-96) (Breger 1987; Haughton 1988). The MR exam is therefore effective, fast, and safe. CT should be reserved for cases in which visualization of osseous structures is crucial, such as congenital anomalies, trauma, otodystrophies, inflammatory disease, and some tumors that primarily affect the temporal bone.

MENINGIOMA

Meningiomas, which arise along the posterior surface of the petrous portion of the temporal bone, must be differentiated from the more common acoustic neurinomas (Valavanis 1981). Less commonly, meningiomas arise from ectopic arachnoid granulations in the temporal bone (Guzowski 1976).

On CT, a meningioma appears as a uniformly enhancing mass in the cerebellopontine angle cistern. Meningiomas resemble acoustic neurinomas only superficially. A meningioma has a sessile broad-based attachment to the petrous bone, which is atypical of acoustic neurinoma, and rarely enlarges the internal auditory canal. Frequently, meningiomas cause hyperostosis or have dense focal calcifications that can be better shown with CT than with MR (Fig. 11-97). On MR, meningiomas have

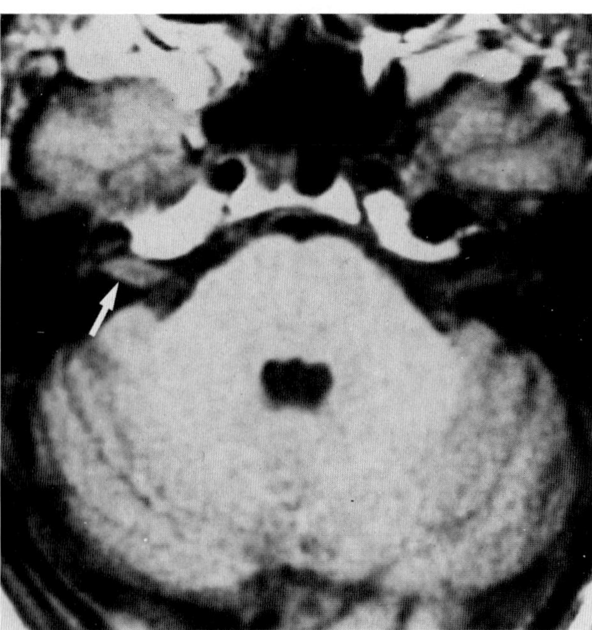

Figure 11-93 Intracanalicular acoustic neurinoma (arrow) on axial T_1-weighted MRI. The tumor has a nonhomogeneous signal (darker center) as a result of a truncation artifact (Daniels 1987*a*). (*From Daniels 1984a.*)

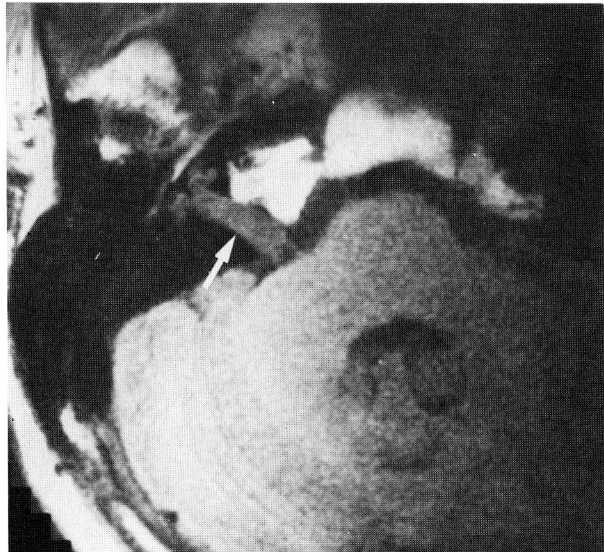

Figure 11-94 Surface coil MR image of a predominantly intracanalicular acoustic neurinoma (arrow) obscuring the nerves in the right internal auditory canal. (Axial short TR/TE scan.) (*From Daniels 1985.*)

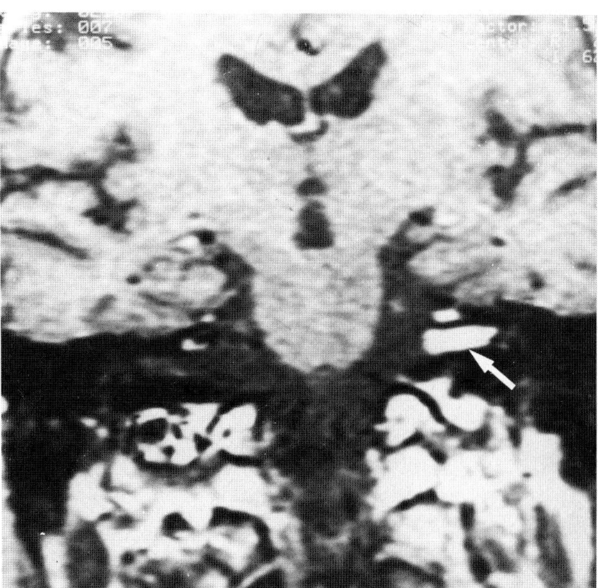

Figure 11-96 Intense enhancement of an intracanalicular acoustic neurinoma (arrow) is demonstrated on coronal T_1-weighted MRI after Gd-DTPA injection.

a signal intensity similar to that of brain in T_1WI and variable in T_2WI (Fig. 11-98) (Gentry 1987). Meningiomas enhance intensely with intravenous Gd-DTPA (Breger 1987; Haughton 1988). The identification of a small amount of enhancing tissue that extends from the meningioma along a dural surface and is due to either dural reaction or tumor extension helps differentiate meningioma from acoustic neurinoma, since the latter is not associated with the "tail sign" (Fig. 11-99) (Goldsher 1990). In cases which are not easily differentiated by CT or MR, angiography is indicated to distinguish the characteristic blush and dural blood supply of a meningioma from the more subtle changes of an acoustic neurinoma.

EPIDERMOID TUMOR

Epidermoid tumors, also called *congenital* or *primary cholesteatomas,* arise from ectodermal rests at multiple intracranial sites, including the cerebellopontine angle

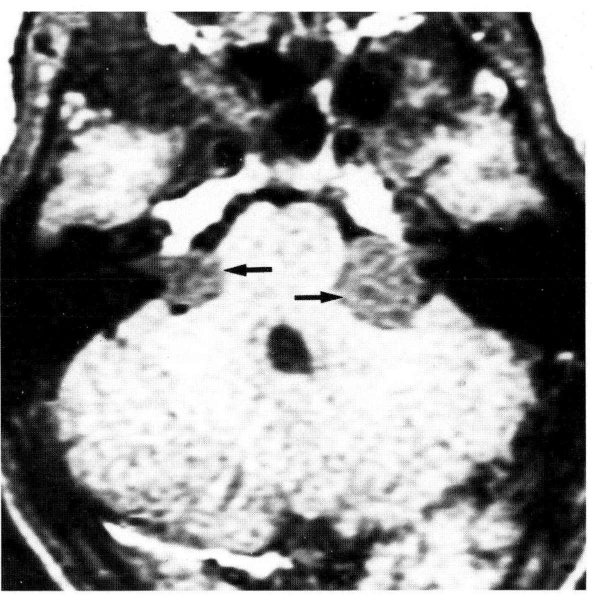

A

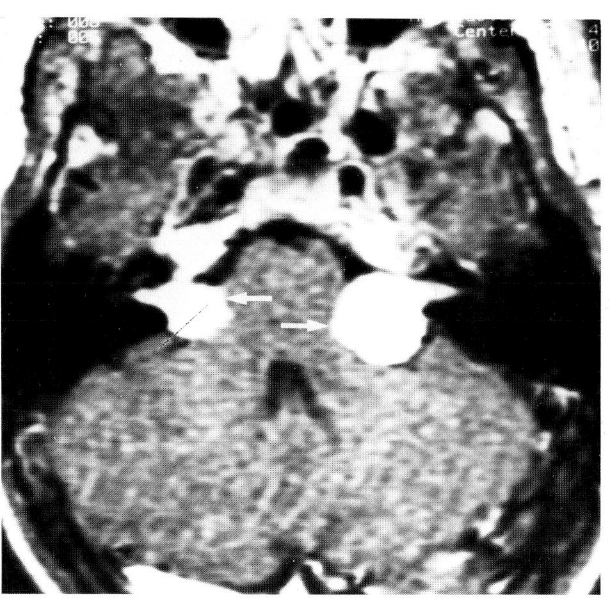

B

Figure 11-95 Bilateral large acoustic neurinomas (arrows) without (**A**) and with (**B**) intravenous gadolinium in a patient with neurofibromatosis. Axial T_1WI demonstrates that the tumors are slightly less intense than the normal brainstem (**A**) and are markedly enhancing (**B**).

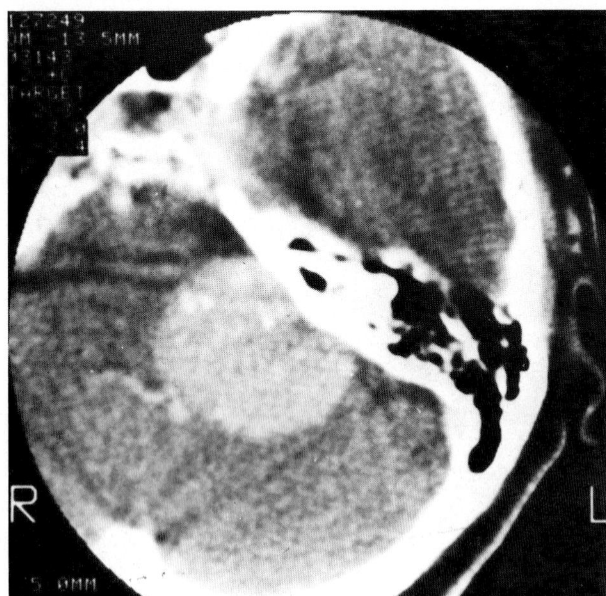

Figure 11-97 A meningioma presents as a homogeneously enhancing round mass with punctate calcifications in the cerebellopontine angle cistern on CECT.

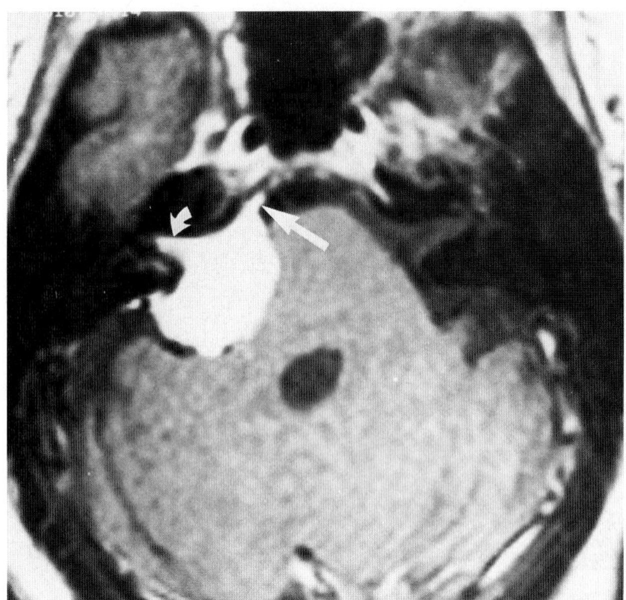

Figure 11-99 Enhancing cerebellopontine angle meningioma on axial T_1-weighted MRI with intravenous Gd-DTPA. The tumor extending into the internal auditory canal (curved arrow) and along the dura (straight arrow) is evident.

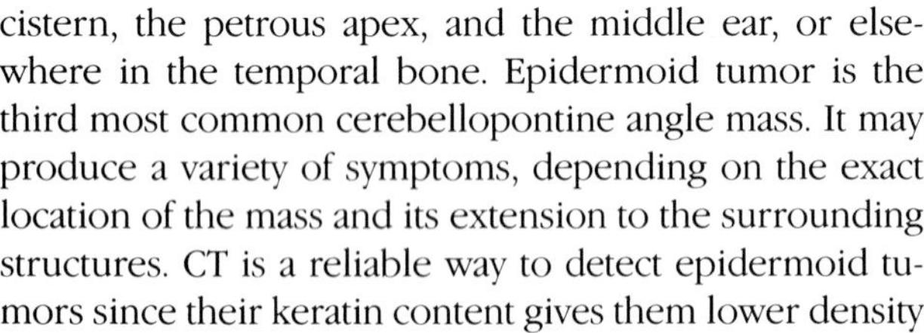

cistern, the petrous apex, and the middle ear, or elsewhere in the temporal bone. Epidermoid tumor is the third most common cerebellopontine angle mass. It may produce a variety of symptoms, depending on the exact location of the mass and its extension to the surrounding structures. CT is a reliable way to detect epidermoid tumors since their keratin content gives them lower density than brain has on NCCT and CECT. Smooth or scalloped borders are typical (Latack 1985) (Fig. 11-100). In MR, epidermoids have negligible or low-intensity signals in T_1WI and high-intensity signals in T_2WI (Fig. 11-101) (Gentry 1987; Griffin 1987). Typically, epidermoids do not enhance with IV Gd-DTPA. A cerebellopontine angle epidermoid may be difficult to differentiate from an

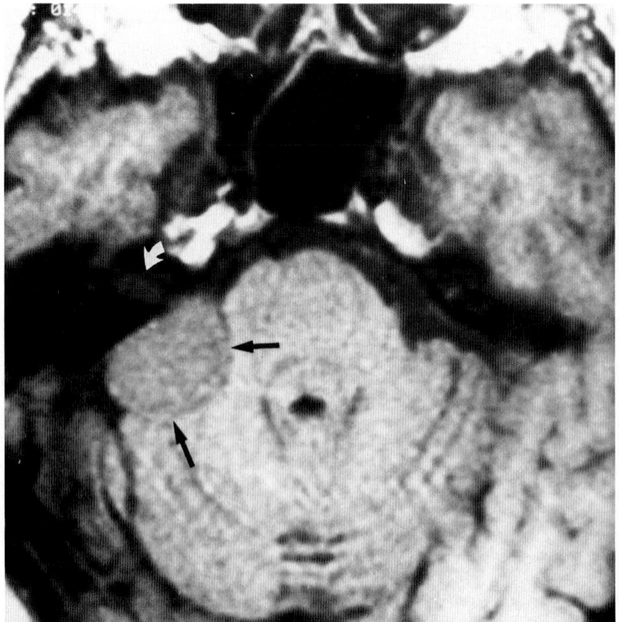

A

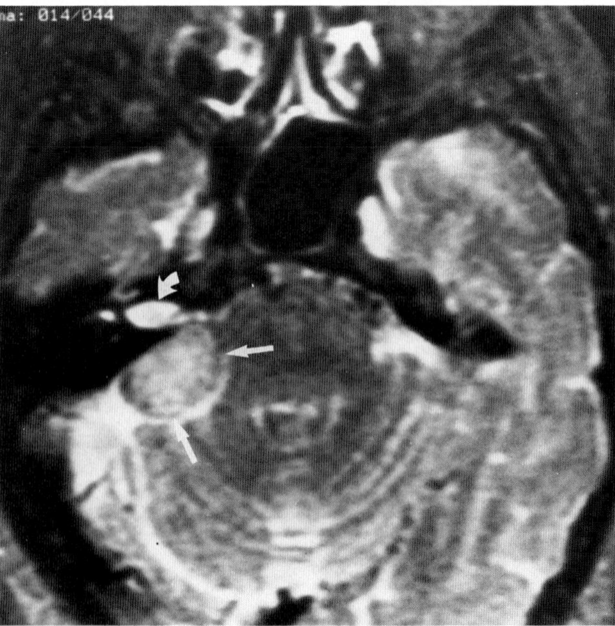

B

Figure 11-98 Cerebellopontine angle meningioma (straight arrows) that is less intense than the brainstem and CSF on axial T_1-weighted (**A**) and T_2-weighted (**B**) MRI is shown. The tumor is centered posterior to the internal auditory canal (curved arrow) containing cranial nerves VII and VIII and CSF.

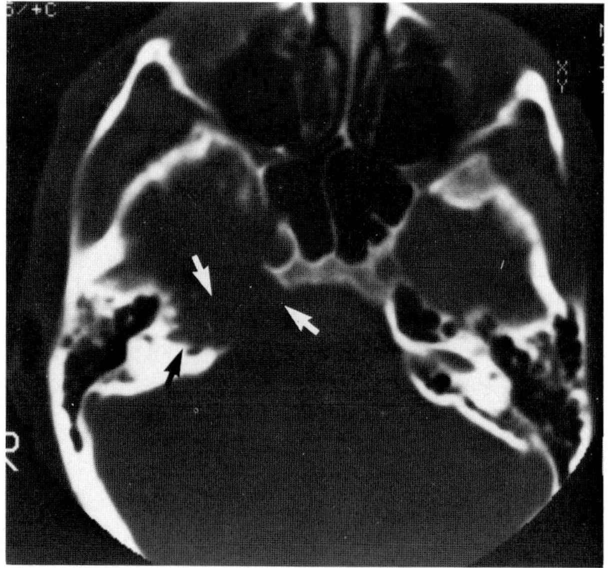

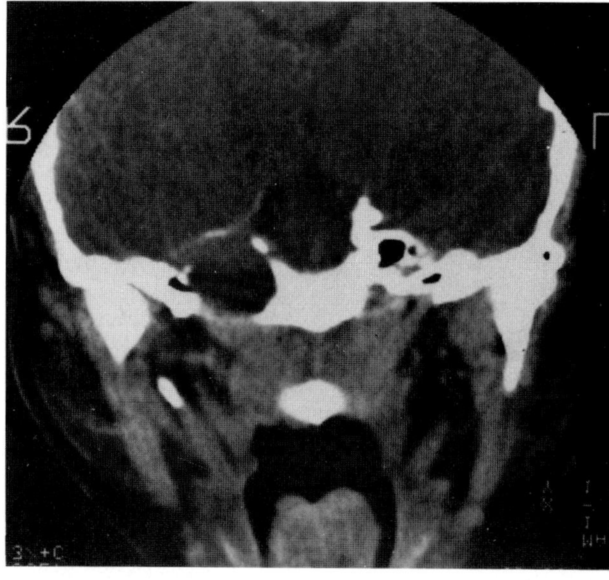

A B

Figure 11-100 Epidermoid in the petrous apex erodes the apex and skull base on axial CT (**A**) and does not enhance on coronal CECT (**B**). (*From Shaffer 1985.*)

arachnoid cyst because of its similar signal intensities in T_1WI and T_2WI (Fig. 11-102).

The differential diagnosis of a petrous apex epidermoid includes schwannoma, meningioma, glomus tumor, metastasis, petrositis, histiocytosis, cholesterol granuloma, and mucocele (Gacek 1980). With CT, the smooth bone erosion and lack of enhancement differentiate epidermoid tumors from most other masses except mucocele and cholesterol granuloma. With MR, epidermoids at the petrous apex can be differentiated from cholesterol granulomas, which typically have high signal intensity in T_1WI and T_2WI as a result of old hemorrhage (Fig. 11-103) (Gomori 1985; Gentry 1987; Griffin 1987; Greenberg 1988).

OTHER TUMORS

Neurinomas of the fifth, seventh, ninth, tenth, eleventh, or twelfth cranial nerves may erode bone in the inner ear. Neurinomas of the fifth cranial nerve characteristically can amputate the petrous apex. Neurinomas of the

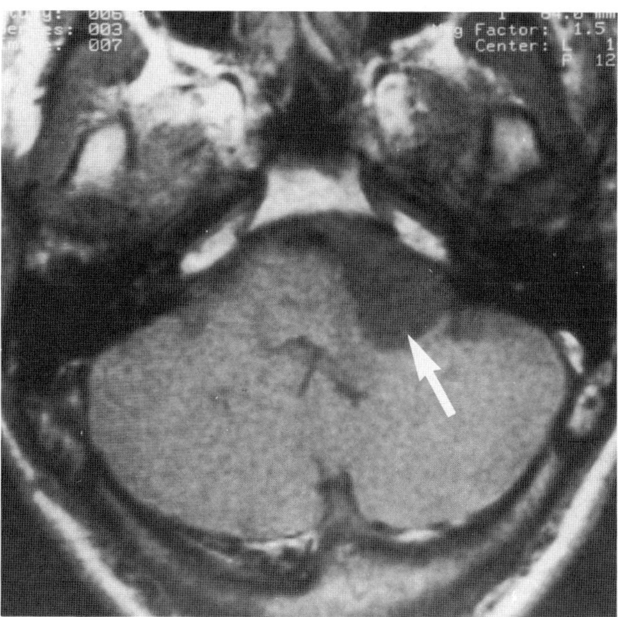

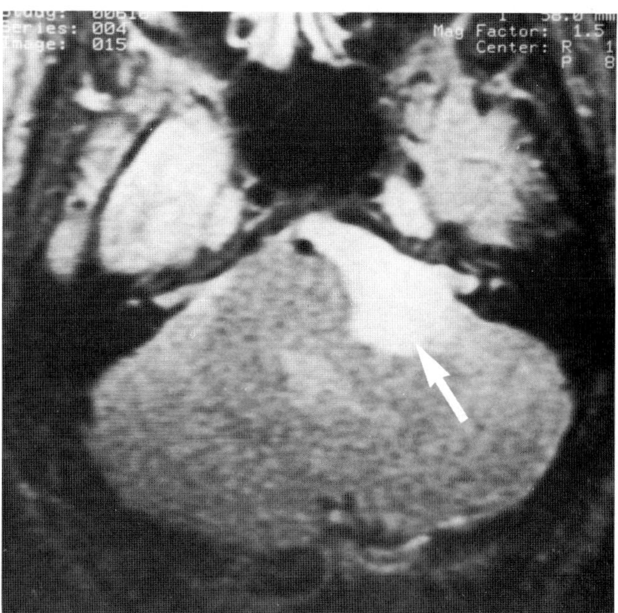

A B

Figure 11-101 Cerebellopontine angle epidermoid (arrow) isointense with CSF and displacing the brainstem is demonstrated on axial T_1-weighted (**A**) and T_2-weighted (**B**) MRI. (*From Daniels 1988b.*)

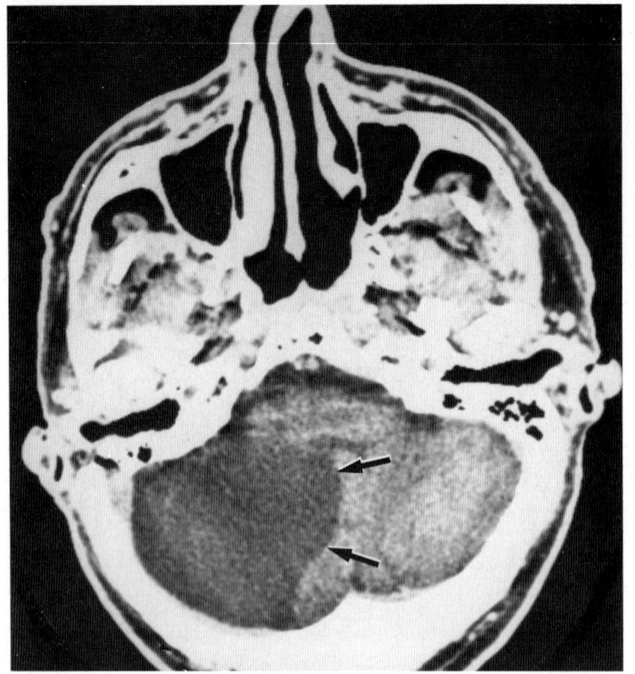

A

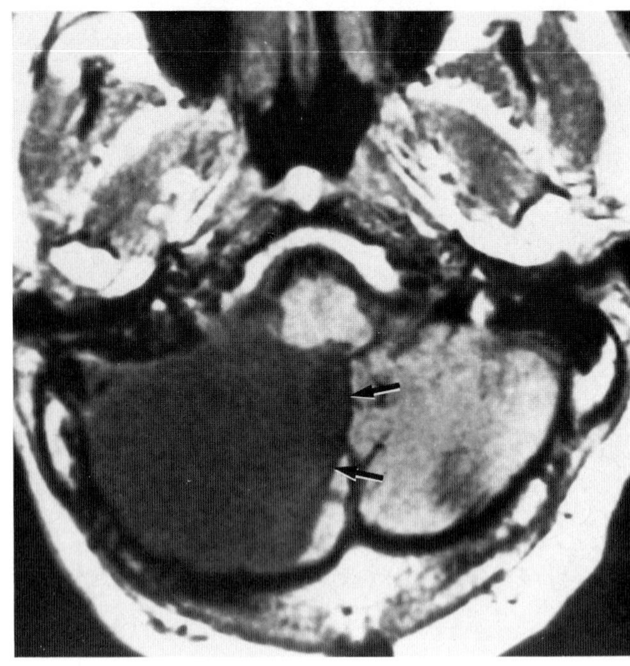

B

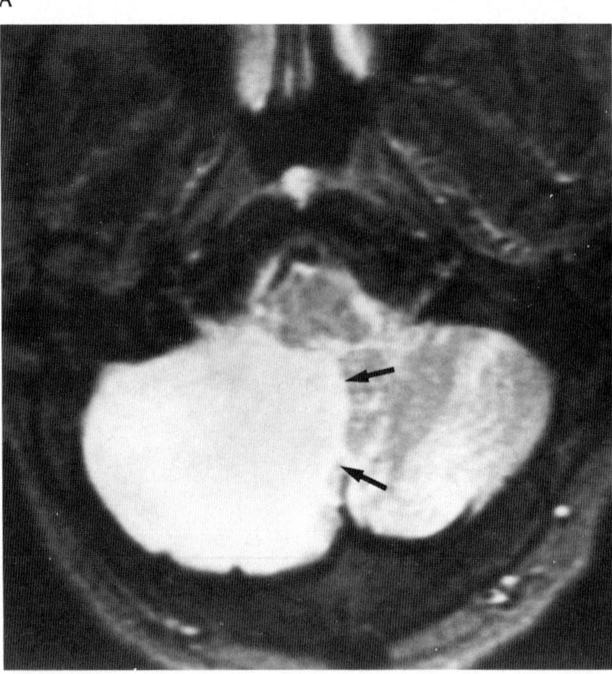

C

Figure 11-102 Large posterior fossa arachnoid cyst (arrows) with mass effect appearing isodense and isointense with CSF is identified on axial CT (**A**) and T_1- and T_2-weighted MRI (**B** and **C**).

seventh cranial nerve arising in the intracanalicular segment of the nerve expand the internal canal exactly as an acoustic neurinoma does. Neurinomas of the ninth, tenth, and eleventh cranial nerves enlarge the jugular fossa in the manner of a glomus tumor, but without irregular margins. On CT and MR, neurinomas enhance homogeneously and less than glomus tumors, which are extremely vascular (Breger 1987; Daniels 1987*b*).

A cholesterol granuloma may be mistaken for an epidermoid tumor in the petrous apex, middle ear, or mastoid. It may be caused by obstructed ventilation, poor drainage, or hemorrhage. Cholesterol granulomas, unlike epidermoid tumors, contain cholesterol crystals, giant cells, and dark or yellow material, while epidermoids contain pale and flaky material. CT shows a mass that smoothly erodes bone and has a density nearly isodense to the brain and therefore higher than that of an epidermoid (Lo 1984).

MR often shows a cholesterol granuloma with high-intensity signals in T_1WI and T_2WI from old hemorrhage and methemoglobin formation (Gomori 1985; Gentry 1987; Griffin 1987; Greenberg 1988).

Mucocele is another process which, like a cholesterol granuloma or epidermoid, destroys bone in the petrous apex. Since a mucocele arises in an apex air cell, CT usually shows a pneumatized air cell on the opposite side.

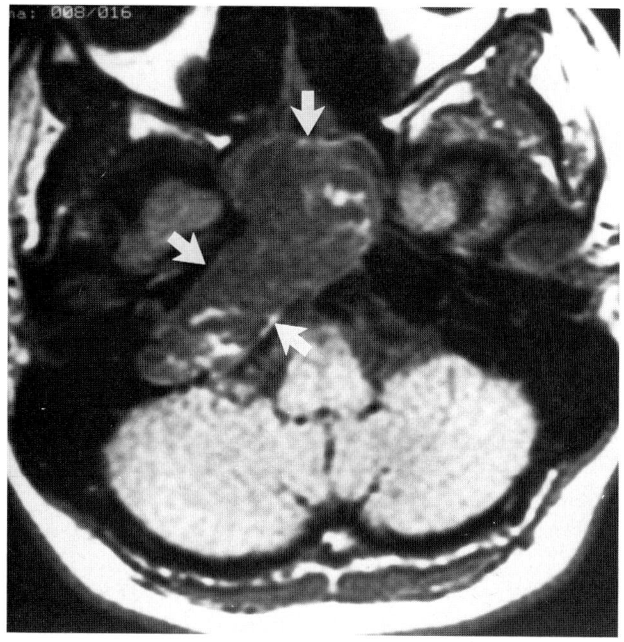

A

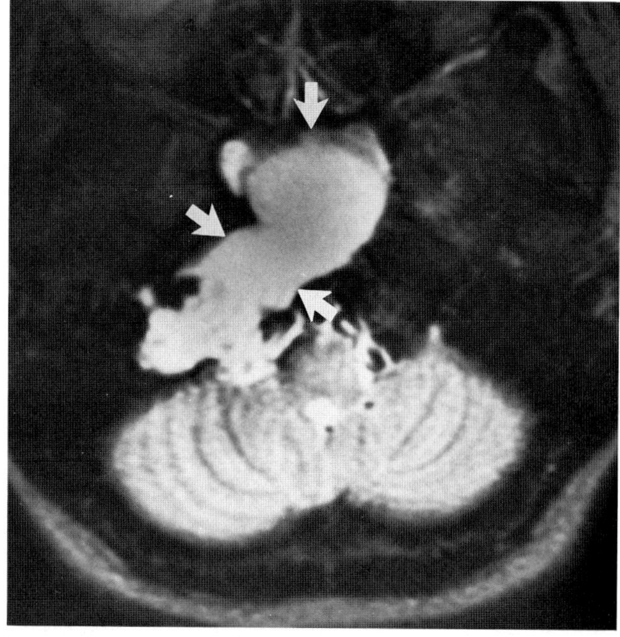

B

Figure 11-103 Petrous apex and sphenoid epidermoid (arrows) are characterized by predominantly low-intensity and high-intensity signals on T_1- weighted (**A**) and T_2-weighted (**B**) MRI.

Ipsilaterally, the mastoid air cells may be fluid-filled (Osborn 1979).

Hemangiomas are rare tumors which occur in the internal auditory canal or any portion of the temporal bone. Characteristic features, including spokelike trabeculations or phleboliths, can be demonstrated with CT in some cases (Lo 1984; Curtin 1987).

Fibroosseous tumors, including chondroma and osteoma, affect the inner ear as well as other portions of the temporal bone.

Metastatic involvement of the inner ear occurs through direct extension or hematogenous spread of tumor. A tumor can extend directly to the inner ear from a nasopharyngeal carcinoma, a meningeal carcinomatosis, or an adjacent intracranial malignancy. Hematogenous metastasis to the temporal bone usually occurs late in the course of disease. Most cases arise from tumors which commonly metastasize to bone, such as carcinomas of the breast, prostate, lung, and kidney. The petrous apex contains marrow spaces which may trap circulating tumor cells, but the otic capsule and well-pneumatized bone are not often involved (Schuknecht 1968).

INFLAMMATORY DISEASE

External Ear

Except for the so-called malignant form, otitis externa is seldom evaluated radiographically. The *malignant* appellation refers to the aggressive course of *Pseudomonas aeruginosa* infection in elderly diabetics and immunosuppressed patients. Malignant external otitis is divided into an early stage characterized by soft tissue changes without bone destruction and an advanced stage with spread of infection and bone destruction (Mendez 1979). Pain, drainage from the ear, impaired hearing, and granulation tissue in the external auditory canal occur in both stages. Facial nerve paralysis, other cranial nerve palsies, and temporomandibular joint involvement occur late. Long-term systemic antibiotic therapy and local surgical debridement are used to treat this condition.

CT findings in malignant external otitis include abnormal soft tissue in the external auditory canal, middle ear, and mastoid; destruction of bone in the external canal and skull base; and a mass in the nasopharynx and subtemporal space (Fig. 11-104). CT findings of malignant external otitis are not specific. The nasopharyngeal inflammatory mass may be mistaken radiographically for malignant tumor since the infection crosses fascial planes. The CT abnormalities are easily interpreted only with the typical clinical findings. In these patients, CT is effective in evaluating bone destruction as well as soft tissue spread in the ear and subtemporal space. Nuclear scanning more effectively defines the extent of active infection in patients who are being treated for malignant external otitis. Technetium 99m bone scanning is more sensitive than CT in detecting bony involvement. Gallium 67 citrate scans can determine the activity of an infection under treatment (Strashun 1984).

Middle Ear

Temporal bone cholesteatoma, an epithelium-lined cyst filled with keratin debris, is usually a complication of inflammatory disease but rarely is a congenital neoplasm arising from epithelial rests. Congenital cholesteatoma in

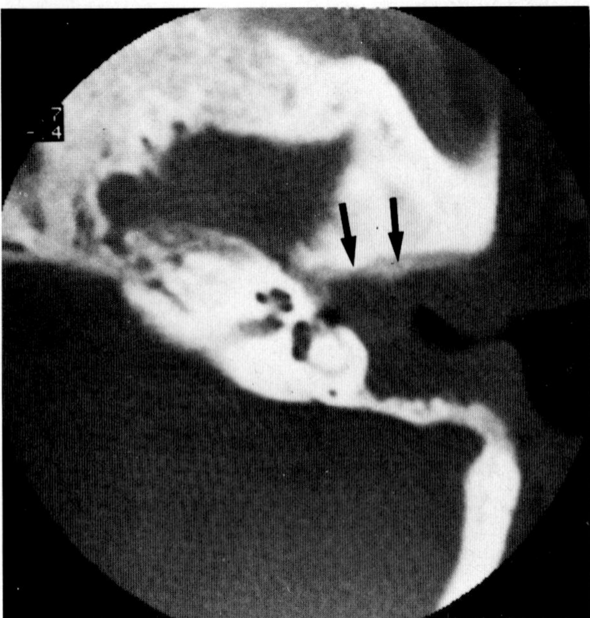

Figure 11-104 Malignant external otitis in a diabetic woman with a history of a left mastoidectomy. On axial CT, soft tissue filling the surgical defect destroys bone anteriorly (arrows). *Pseudomonas aeruginosa* was cultured from the ear. (*From Shaffer 1985.*)

the middle ear appears as a pearly mass behind an intact tympanic membrane in a patient with no history of middle ear inflammatory disease.

Acquired cholesteatomas usually occur in patients with a history of otitis media. Retraction of the pars flaccida portion of the tympanic membrane, tympanic membrane perforation, and migration of epithelial cells into the middle ear cause most acquired cholesteatomas (Nager 1977; Swartz 1984*a*). Dysfunction of the eustachian tube, poor pneumatization of the mastoid, and hereditary factors are contributory. The epithelial cells produce a cyst which accumulates keratin debris. Bone destruction results in most cases because of collagenase activity of the cholesteatoma or associated inflammatory disease.

CT is the most accurate means of determining the extent of disease before surgical treatment is planned. CT demonstrates the soft tissue mass in the middle ear, air-fluid levels, erosion of the tegmen and lateral semicircular canal, and the posterior wall of the middle ear more accurately than pluridirectional tomography can (Fig. 11-105) (Shaffer 1984). Characteristically, CT shows bone erosion, particularly involving the drum spur (scutum) and the long process of the incus. In an extensive cholesteatoma there may be erosion of the lateral semicircular canal, the lateral attic wall, and occasionally the tegmen tympani. In a partially opacified middle ear and mastoid, movement of fluid between axial and coronal scans and air-fluid levels help distinguish fluid from mass. Granulation tissue from chronic infection, which often coexists with cholesteatoma, cannot be differentiated reliably from cholesteatoma by means of CT numbers. CT may show calcification (tympanosclerosis) or retraction of the tympanic membrane (Swartz 1983*b*, 1984*a*, 1986*a*).

In a patient previously operated on for cholesteatoma, it is difficult to determine which abnormalities resulted from disease, which were due to surgery, and which developed afterward. In a modified radical mastoidectomy, a mastoidectomy cavity is created with or without an intact canal wall. CT in a postoperative patient is useful in identifying recurrent cholesteatoma or granulation tissue and evaluating ossicular reconstruction. Baseline axial CT scans 3 to 6 months after surgery may be helpful in patients who have residual cholesteatoma or an intact canal wall mastoidectomy and who therefore have a higher risk of developing a recurrent cholesteatoma (Johnson 1984*c*).

Acute otomastoiditis is seldom studied radiographically, but when there is evidence of complication, such as coalescent mastoiditis or intracranial spread of infection, CT or MR is indicated (Mafee 1985*c*; Holliday 1989). CT is also useful in studying patients who have chronic middle ear infections without clinical evidence of cholesteatoma (Mafee 1986).

Inner Ear

Labyrinthitis ossificans, or bone filling the inner ear, is most commonly due to suppurative labyrinthitis but may result from trauma, severe otosclerosis, surgery, or tumors (Hoffman 1979). Labyrinthitis ossificans has a characteristic appearance with a decreased luminal size and sclerosis of the affected ear structures (Fig. 11-106). The affected ear usually has no auditory or vestibular function ("dead ear"). Acute labyrinthitis is a clinical diagnosis without radiographic findings.

Petrositis is an infection of petrous apex air cells secondary to middle ear and mastoid infection. The majority of individuals, without air cells in the petrous apices, do not develop petrositis. The classical clinical presentation of petrositis is pain along the fifth cranial nerve distribution and sixth cranial nerve palsy (Gradenigo's syndrome). Air cell opacification, middle ear disease, and bone destruction are important CT findings in patients with petrositis. Infection in any portion of the temporal bone can cause meningitis, lateral sinus thrombosis, and epidural, subdural, or brain abscess.

OTODYSTROPHIES

Otosclerosis

Otosclerosis, a disease of unknown etiology, is responsible for hearing loss and tinnitus, particularly in young white women. The dense endochondral layer of the bony labyrinth is replaced by foci of thick vascular bone. Oto-

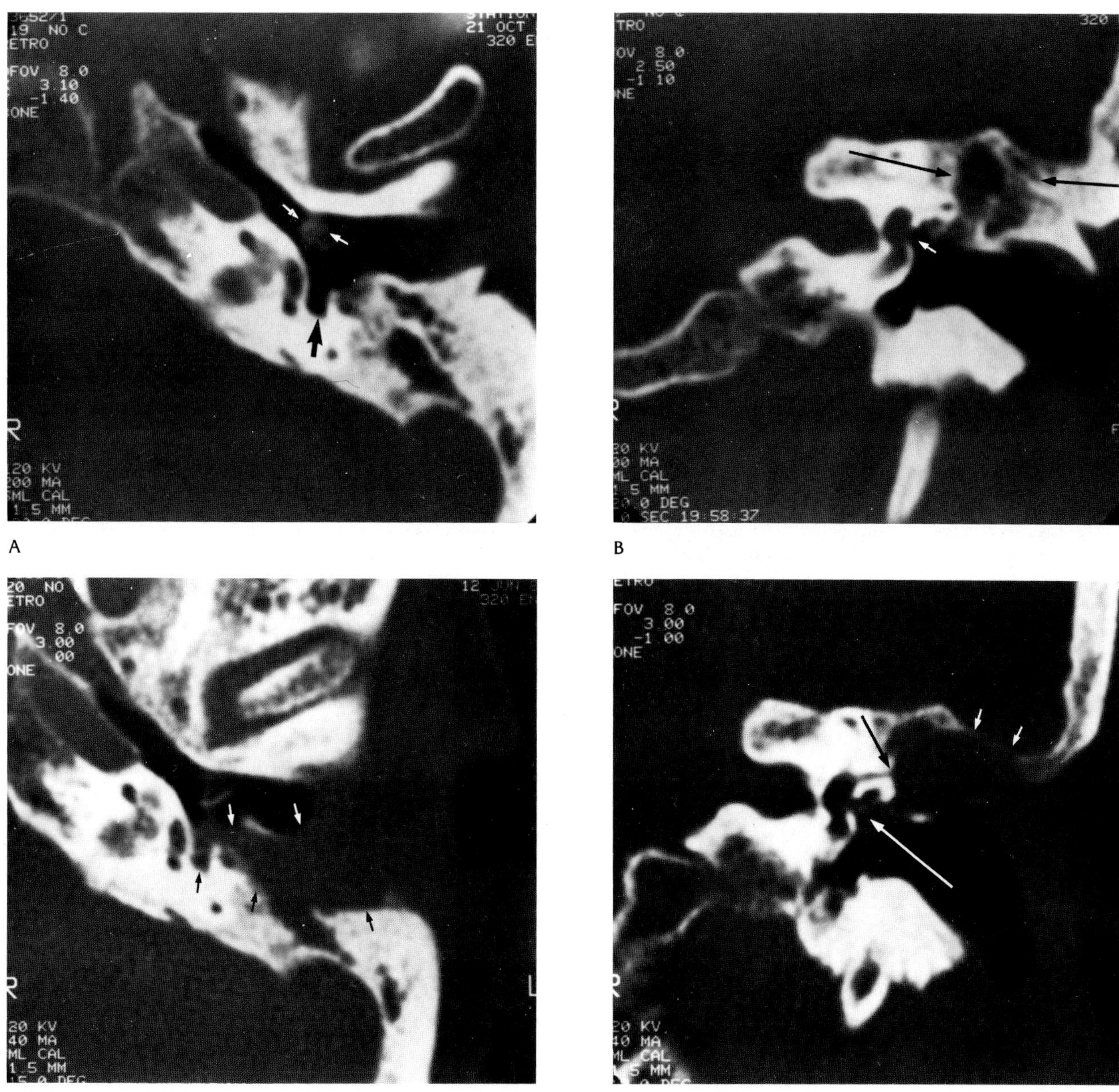

Figure 11-105 Cholesteatoma on axial (**A**) and coronal (**B**) CT scans. The soft tissue mass (white arrows) is small in **A**, sparing the sinus tympani (black arrow). Mastoid antrum opacification (long black arrows) and a clear oval window (white arrow) are shown in **B.** In follow-up study 7 months after a modified radical mastoidectomy, the increase in the size of the cholesteatoma is demonstrated on axial (**C**) and coronal (**D**) CT. A cholesteatoma (arrows, **C**) is present in the surgical cavity, extending into the sinus tympani. In **D,** a cholesteatoma that erodes the bone over the lateral semicircular canal (black arrow) and fills the oval window niche (long white arrow) is identified. Thinning of the tegmen (small white arrows) was probably secondary to surgery. (*From Shaffer 1985.*)

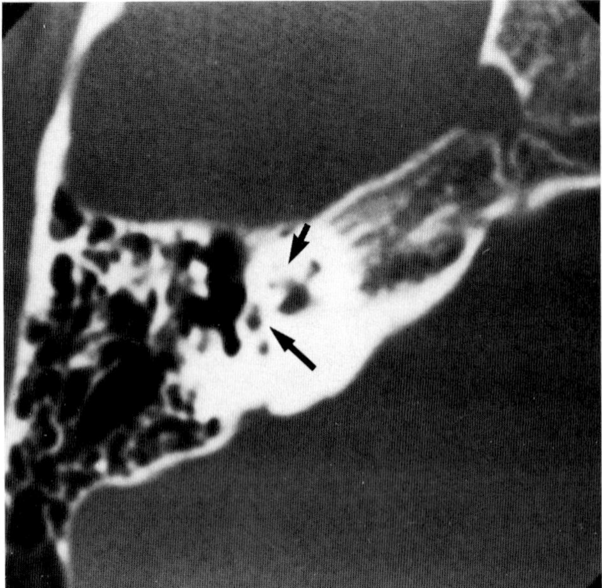

A

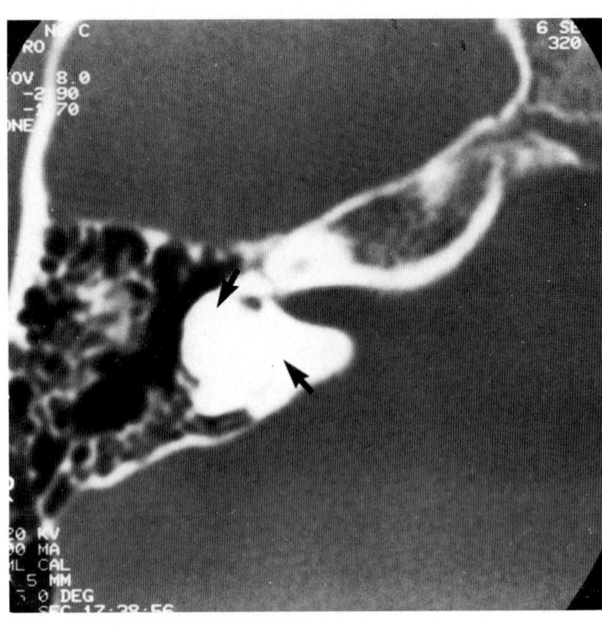

B

Figure 11-106 Postinfectious labyrinthitis ossificans in a deaf 8-year-old boy. Axial CT (**A** and **B**) demonstrates bone that obliterates most of the cochlear turns (short arrow, **A**), vestibule (long arrow, **A**), and semicircular canals (arrows, **B**). (*From Shaffer 1985.*)

sclerosis may be hereditary and is frequently bilateral. Stapedial otosclerosis, the more common form, fixes the stapes footplate in the oval window, causing conductive hearing loss. CT shows lytic (spongiotic) changes early and sclerotic reparative changes later. CT may show bone obliterating the oval window niche (Fig. 11-107) (Swartz 1984*b*; Mafee 1985*a*). Small otosclerotic foci can produce hearing loss without radiographic abnormalities. When otosclerosis involves the otic capsule and cochlea in addition to the stapes, sensorineural as well as conductive hearing loss (mixed hearing loss) may be present.

The CT diagnosis of otosclerosis is not precise. The semiaxial projection perpendicular to the plane of the oval window provides the best view of the stapes footplate. However, with this projection, each ear must be scanned separately. CT demonstrates replacement of the

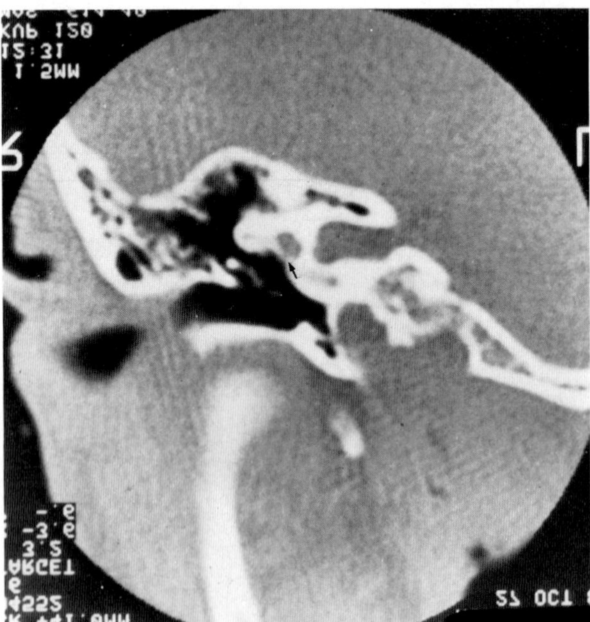

Figure 11-107 Otosclerotic reclosure of the oval window (arrow) on coronal CT. The patient had a history of stapedectomy and a wire loop prosthesis. (*Courtesy of Kedar N. Chintapalli, M.D., San Antonio.*)

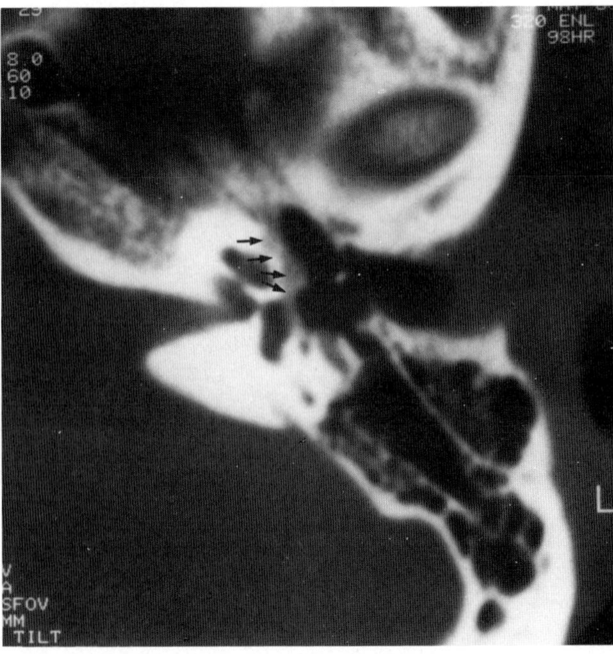

Figure 11-108 Young woman with left-sided mixed hearing loss and a history of otosclerosis. Demineralized areas of the cochlear capsule are seen with cochlear otosclerosis (arrows).

oval or round windows with bone in moderately advanced cases. The improved contrast resolution of CT compared with pluridirectional tomography allows more accurate identification of the lytic foci in the otic capsule. Advanced cochlear otosclerosis has been demonstrated on CT as a lucent halo of small demineralized foci around the cochlea (Fig. 11-108). The CT appearance of cochlear otosclerosis is quite specific, except for differentiation from osteogenesis imperfecta (Mafee 1985*b*). Other processes, such as tumor, infection, and Paget's disease, produce lucent areas in the petrous portion of the temporal bone but do not affect the otic capsule primarily.

CT is also useful in studying the poststapedectomy ear when there has been sudden or progressive hearing loss (Swartz 1986*b*). Ankylosis of the prosthesis in the oval window or posttraumatic dislocation can be identified. Dislocation is demonstrated as a displacement of the prosthesis away from the oval window or protrusion into the vestibule, producing vertigo (Fig. 11-109).

Paget's Disease

Paget's disease produces chronic progressive changes in the skeletons of middle-aged and elderly adults. A lytic phase characterized by loss of bone is followed by a sclerotic phase characterized by coarse thickened trabeculae. The skull and, less frequently, the temporal bones may be affected. Temporal bone involvement usually causes conductive hearing loss if the stapes becomes fixed in the oval window or sensorineural hearing loss if the cochlea is involved. Paget's disease of the temporal bone usually is accompanied by severe skull involvement.

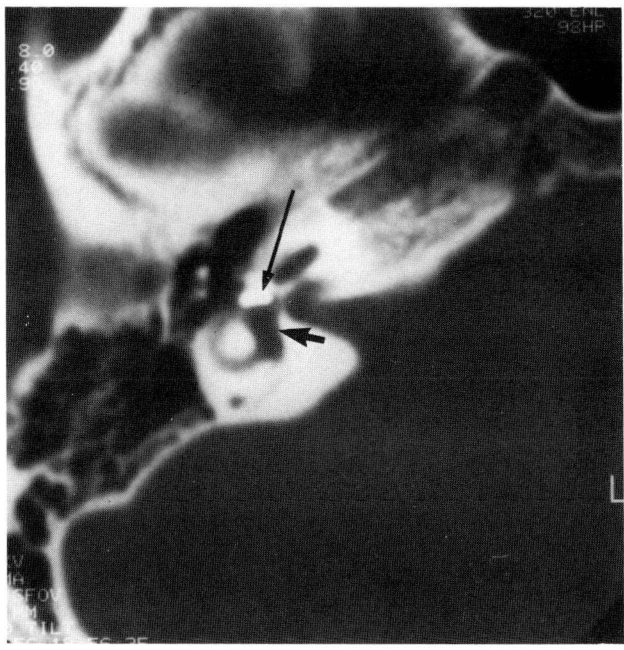

Figure 11-109 Patient dizzy after placement of a stapes prosthesis. The metal prosthesis (long arrow) is positioned too far into the anterior vestibule (short arrow).

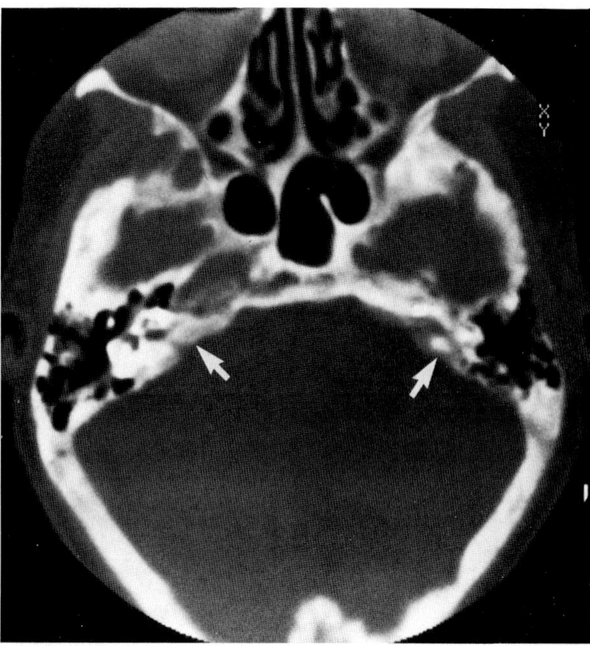

Figure 11-110 Paget's disease causing bilateral mixed hearing loss in a middle-aged woman. Demineralized petrous apices (arrows) and normal otic capsule density are shown on axial CT. (*From Shaffer 1985.*)

In Paget's disease, temporal bone changes are usually lytic (Petasnick 1969). Demineralization begins medially in the petrous pyramid and progresses laterally. The dense otic capsule bone is the last to be affected (Fig. 11-110). The diagnosis of Paget's disease is made by identifying calvarial changes in association with the lytic changes in the temporal bone. By themselves, the lytic areas in the temporal bone cannot be distinguished from otosclerosis, metastases, or luetic osteitis.

Fibrous Dysplasia

Fibrous dysplasia is a congenital osseous disorder of unknown etiology in which cancellous bone is replaced by fibrous tissue that erodes and expands normal cortical bone from within. There are monostotic and polyostotic types. There is a variable amount of metaplastic bone formation, and so fibrous dysplasia can have a cystic, a dense, or a "ground glass" appearance, depending on the proportion of bony and soft tissue elements. The temporal bone is involved less frequently than is the skull (Nager 1982). When fibrous dysplasia occurs in the sinuses or temporal bones, the lesion usually is osteomatoid, appearing as a uniformly dense region of expanded bone. Patients often present with mastoid prominence and hearing loss caused by narrowing of the external auditory canal or middle ear.

On CT, fibrous dysplasia of the temporal bone is usually characterized by homogeneous dense thickened

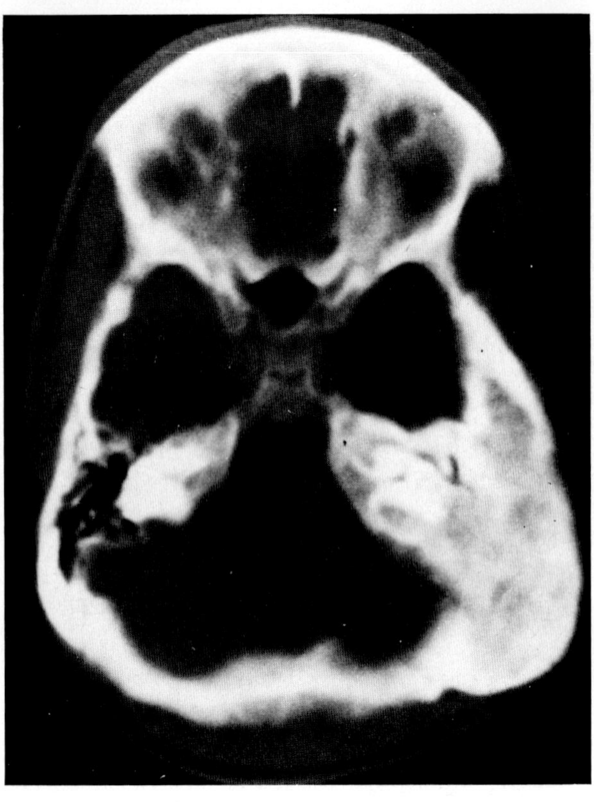

Figure 11-111 Fibrous dysplasia markedly enlarging the left temporal bone on axial CT. (*From Shaffer 1985.*)

bone which may narrow the external auditory canal and middle ear (Fig. 11-111). The uncommon lucent foci caused by fibrosis have an expanded cortex. The differential diagnosis includes metastasis, meningioma, Paget's disease, osteosarcoma, ossifying fibroma, and osteopetrosis.

References

ADAM W, JOHNSON JD, PAUL DJ, et al: Primary adenocarcinoma of the middle ear. *AJNR* 3:674–676, 1982.

ANDERSON R, DIEHL J, MARAVILLA K, et al: Computerized axial tomography with air contrast of the cerebellopontine angle and internal auditory canal. *Laryngoscope* 91:1083–1097, 1981.

ANDERSON R, OLSON J, DORWART R, et al: CT air-contrast scanning of the internal auditory canal. *Ann Otol Rhinol Laryngol* 91:501–504, 1982.

ARMINGTON WG, HARNSBERGER HR, SMOKER WRK, et al: Normal and diseased acoustic pathway: Evaluation with MR imaging. *Radiology* 167:509–515, 1988.

BATSAKIS JG: *Tumors of the Head and Neck,* 2d ed., Baltimore, Williams & Wilkins, 1979.

BERGSTROM L: Pathology of congenital deafness—present status and future priorities. *Ann Otol Rhinol Laryngol* 89(Suppl 74):31–42, 1980.

BERLINGER NT, KOUTROUPAS S, ADAM S, et al: Patterns of involvement of the temporal bone in metastatic and systemic malignancy. *Laryngoscope* 90:619–627, 1980.

BIRD CR, HASSO AN, STEWART EC, et al: Malignant primary neoplasms of the ear and temporal bone studied by high-resolution computed tomography. *Radiology* 149:171–174, 1983.

BREGER RK, PAPKE RA, POJUNAS KW, et al: Benign extraaxial tumors: Contrast enhancement with Gd-DTPA. *Radiology* 163:427–429, 1987.

BROGAN M, CHAKERES DW: Computed tomography and magnetic resonance imaging of the normal anatomy of the temporal bone. *Semin Ultrasound CT MR* 10:179–194, 1989.

BYDDER GM, STEINER RE, YOUNG IR, et al: Clinical NMR imaging of the brain: 140 cases. *AJNR* 3:459–480, 1982; *AJR* 139:215–236, 1982.

CHAKERES DW, SPIEGEL PK: A systematic technique for comprehensive evaluation of the temporal bone by computed tomography. *Radiology* 146:97–106, 1983.

CHEN KTK, DEHNER LP: Primary tumors of the external and middle ear: I. Introduction and clinicopathologic study of squamous cell carcinoma. *Arch Otolaryngol* 104:247–252, 1978.

CURATI WL, GRAIF M, KINGSLEY DPE, et al: Acoustic neuromas: Gd-DTPA enhancement in MR imaging. *Radiology* 158:447–451, 1986.

CURTIN HD, WOLFE P, SNYDERMAN N: The facial nerve between the stylomastoid foramen and the parotid: Computed tomographic imaging. *Radiology* 149:165–169, 1983.

CURTIN HD, JENSEN JE, BARNES L Jr, et al: "Ossifying" hemangiomas of the temporal bone: Evaluation with CT. *Radiology* 164:831–835, 1987.

DAMSMA H, MALI WPTM, ZONNEVELD FW: CT diagnosis of an aberrant internal carotid artery in the middle ear. *J Comput Assist Tomogr* 8:317–319, 1984.

DANIELS DL, HERFKINS R, KOEHLER PR, et al: Magnetic resonance imaging of the internal auditory canal. *Radiology* 151:105–108, 1984*a*.

DANIELS DL, PECH P, HAUGHTON VM: *Magnetic Resonance Imaging of the Temporal Bone,* Milwaukee, General Electric Systems Group, 1984*b*.

DANIELS DL, SCHENCK JF, FOSTER T, et al: Surface-coil magnetic resonance imaging of the internal auditory canal. *AJNR* 6:487–490, 1985.

DANIELS DL, BREGER RK, STRANDT JA, et al: "Truncation" artifact in MR images of the internal auditory canal. *AJNR* 8:793–794, 1987*a*.

DANIELS DL, CZERVIONKE LF, POJUNAS KW, et al: Facial nerve enhancement in MR imaging. *AJNR* 8:605–607, 1987*b*.

DANIELS DL, MILLEN SJ, MEYER GA, et al: MR detection of tumor in the internal auditory canal. *AJNR* 8:249–252, 1987*c*.

DANIELS DL, HAUGHTON VM, NAIDICH T: *Cranial and Spinal Magnetic Resonance Imaging: Atlas and Guide,* New York, Raven Press, 1987*d*.

DANIELS DL, CZERVIONKE LF, PECH P, et al: Gradient recalled echo MR imaging of the jugular foramen. *AJNR* 9:675–678, 1988*a*.

DANIELS DL, HAUGHTON VM, CZERVIONKE LF: MR of the skull base, in Bradley WG, Stark D (eds), *Magnetic Resonance Imaging,* St. Louis, Mosby, 1988*b*.

DANIELS DL, CZERVIONKE LF, MILLEN SJ, et al: MR imaging of facial nerve enhancement in Bell palsy or after temporal bone surgery. *Radiology* 171:807–809, 1989.

DOLANIK D: Temporal bone fractures. *Semin Ultrasound CT MR* 10:262–279, 1989.

EELKEMA E, CURTIN HD: Congenital anomalies of the temporal bone. *Semin Ultrasound CT MR* 10:195–212, 1989.

ENZMANN DR, O'DONOHUE J: Optimizing MR imaging for detecting small tumors in the cerebellopontine angle and internal auditory canal. *AJNR* 8:99–106, 1987.

GACEK RR: Evaluation and management of primary petrous apex cholesteatoma. *Otolaryngol Head Neck Surg* 88:519–523, 1980.

GENTRY LR, JACOBY CG, TURSKI PA, et al: Cerebellopontine angle–petromastoid mass lesions: Comparative study of diagnosis with MR imaging and CT. *Radiology* 162:513–520, 1987.

GOLDSHER D, LITT AW, PINTO RS, et al: Dural "tail" associated with meningiomas on Gd-DTPA-enhanced MR images. *Radiology* 176:447–450, 1990.

GOMORI JM, GROSSMAN RI, GOLDBERG HI, et al: Intracranial hematomas imaging by high-field MR. *Radiology* 157:87–93, 1985.

GREENBERG JJ, OOT RF, WISMER GL, et al: Cholesterol granuloma of the petrous apex: MR and CT evaluation. *AJNR* 9:1205–1214, 1988.

GRIFFIN C, DELAPAZ R, ENZMANN E: MR and CT correlation of cholesterol cysts of the petrous bone. *AJNR* 8:825–829, 1987.

GUINTO FC Jr, GARRABRANT EC, RADCLIFFE WB: Radiology of the persistent stapedial artery. *Radiology* 105:365–369, 1972.

GUZOWSKI J, PAPARELLA MM, RAO KN, et al: Meningiomas of the temporal bone. *Laryngoscope* 84:1141–1146, 1976.

HANAFEE WN, BERGSTROM L: Radiology of congenital deformities of the ear. *Head Neck Surg* 2:213–221, 1980.

HAUGHTON VM, RIMM AA, CZERVIONKE LF, et al: Sensitivity of Gd-DTPA-enhanced MR imaging of benign extraaxial tumors. *Radiology* 166:829–833, 1988.

HOFFMAN RA, BROOKLER KH, BERGERON RT: Radiologic diagnosis of labyrinthitis ossificans. *Ann Otol Rhinol Laryngol* 88:253–257, 1979.

HOLLAND B, BRANT-ZAWADZKI M: High-resolution CT of temporal bone trauma. *AJNR* 5:291–295, 1984; *AJR* 143:391–395, 1984.

HOLLIDAY RA, REEDE DL: MRI of mastoid and middle ear disease. *Radiol Clin North Am* 27:283–299, 1989.

JOHNSON DW: Air cisternography of the cerbellopontine angle using high-resolution computed tomography. *Radiology* 151: 401–403, 1984*a*.

JOHNSON DW, HASSO AW, STEWART CE, et al: Temporal bone trauma: High-resolution computed tomographic evaluation. *Radiology* 151:411–415, 1984*b*.

JOHNSON DW: CT of the postsurgical ear. *Radiol Clin North Am* 22:67–76, 1984*c*.

KASEFF LG: Tomographic evaluation of trauma to the temporal bone. *Radiology* 93:321–327, 1969.

KINGSLEY DPE, BROOKS GB, LEUNG AW-L, et al: Acoustic neuromas: Evaluation by magnetic resonance imaging. *AJNR* 6:1–5, 1985.

LARSON TC, REESE DF, BAKER HL, et al: Glomus tympanicum chemodectomas: Radiographic and clinical characteristics. *Radiology* 163:801–806, 1987.

LATACK JT, KARTUSH JM, KEMINK JL, et al: Epidermoidomas of the cerebellopontine angle and temporal bone: CT and MR aspects. *Radiology* 157:361–366, 1985.

LEE SH, LEWIS E, MONTOYA JH, et al: Bilateral cerebellopontine angle air-CT cisternography. *AJNR* 2:105–106, 1981.

LEVENSON MJ, PARISIER SC, JACOBS M, et al: The large vestibular aqueduct syndrome in children. *Arch Otolaryngol Heaa Neck Surg* 115:54–58, 1989.

LO WWM, SOLTI-BOHMAN LG, BRACKMANN DE, et al: Cholesterol granuloma of the petrous apex: CT diagnosis. *Radiology* 153:705–711, 1984.

LO WEM, SOLTI-BOHMAN L, MCELVEEN JT Jr: Aberrant carotid artery: Radiologic diagnosis with emphasis on high-resolution computed tomography. *Radiographics* 5:985–993, 1985.

LUFKIN R, BARNI JJ, GLEN W, et al: Comparison of computed tomography and pluridirectional tomography of the temporal bone. *Radiology* 143:715–718, 1982.

MCCAFFREY TV, MCDONALD TJ: Histiocytosis X of the ear and temporal bone: Review of 22 cases. *Laryngoscope* 89: 1735–1742, 1979.

MAFEE MF, KIMAR A, YANNIAS DA, et al: Computed tomography of the middle ear in the evaluation of cholesteatomas and other soft tissue masses: Comparison with pluridirectional tomography. *Radiology* 148:465–472, 1983*a*.

MAFEE MF, VALVASSORI GE, SHUGAR MA, et al: High resolution and dynamic sequential computed tomography: Use in the evaluation of glomus complex tumors. *Arch Otolaryngol* 109:691–696, 1983*b*.

MAFEE MF, HENDRICKSON GC, DEITCH RL, et al: Use of CT in stapedial otosclerosis. *Radiology* 156:709–714, 1985*a*.

MAFEE MF, VALVASSORI GE, DEITCH RL, et al: Use of CT in the evaluation of cochlear otosclerosis. *Radiology* 156:703–708, 1985*b*.

MAFEE MF, SINGLETON EL, VALVASSORI GE, et al: Acute otomastoiditis and its complications: Role of CT. *Radiology* 155:391–397, 1985*c*.

MAFEE MF, AIMI K, KAHEN H, et al: Chronic otomastoiditis: A conceptual understanding of CT findings. *Radiology* 160: 193–200, 1986.

MAFEE MF: Acoustic neuroma and other acoustic nerve disorders: Role of MRI and CT—an analysis of 238 cases. *Semin Ultrasound CT MR* 8:256–283, 1987.

MANCUSO AA, HANAFEE WN: *Computed Tomography of the Head and Neck,* Baltimore, Williams & Wilkins, 1982, pp 244–287.

MENDEZ G Jr, QUENCER RM, POST MJD, et al: Malignant external otitis: A radiographic-clinical correlation. *AJR* 132:957–961, 1979.

NAGER GT: Cholesteatoma of the middle ear: Pathogenesis and surgical indication, in McCabe BF, Sade J, Abramson M (eds), *Cholesteatoma First International Conference,* Birmingham, Ala., Aesculapius, 1977, pp 193–203.

NAGER GT, KENNEDY DW, KIPSTEIN E: Fibrous dysplasia: A review of the disease and its manifestations in the temporal bone. *Ann Otol Rhinol Laryngol [Suppl]* 92:5–52, 1982.

NEW PFJ, BACHOW TB, WISMER GL, et al: MR imaging of acoustic nerves and small acoustic neuromas at .6T: Prospective study. *AJNR* 6:165–170, 1985.

OLSEN WL, DILLON WP, KELLY WM, et al: MR imaging of paragangliomas. *AJNR* 7:1039–1042, 1986.

OSBORN AG, PARKIN JL: Mucocele of the petrous temporal bone. *AJR* 132:680–681, 1979.

PETASNICK JP: Tomography of the temporal bone in Paget's disease. *AJR* 105:838–843, 1969.

PHELPS PD, LLOYD GAS: Course of the facial nerve in congenital ear deformities. *Acta Radiologica Diagn* 22(fasc. 4): 475–583, 1981*a*.

PHELPS PD, LLOYD GAS: The radiology of carcinoma of the ear. *Br J Radiol* 54:103–109, 1981*b*.

PINTO RS, KRICHEFF II, BERGERON RT, et al: Small acoustic neuromas: Detection by high resolution gas CT cisternography. *AJR* 139:129–132, 1982.

PRESS GA, HESSELINK JR: MR imaging of cerebellopontine angle and internal auditory canal lesions at 1.5 T. *AJNR* 9: 241–251, 1988.

REESE DF, HARNER SG, KIPENT DB, et al: Magnetic resonance display of the internal auditory canal, cochlea, vestibular apparatus, and facial nerve. Presented at the annual meeting of the American Society of Neuroradiology, Boston, June 1984.

ROBERTSON HJ, HATTEN HP Jr, KEATING JW: False-positive CT gas cisternogram. *AJNR* 4:474–477, 1983.

SCHUKNECHT HF, ALLAM AF, MURAKAMI Y: Pathology of secondary malignant tumors of the temporal bone. *Ann Otol Rhinol Laryngol* 77:5–22, 1968.

SCHWARTZ RH, MOROSSAGHI N, MARION ED: Rhabdomyosarcoma of the middle ear: A wolf in sheep's clothing. *Pediatrics* 65:1131–1132, 1980.

SHAFFER KA, VOLZ DJ, HAUGHTON VM: Manipulation of CT data for temporal-bone imaging. *Radiology* 137:825–829, 1980.

SHAFFER KA, LITTLETON JT, DURIZCH ML, et al: Temporal bone anatomy: Comparison of computed tomography and complex motion tomography. *Head Neck Surg* 4:296–300, 1982.

SHAFFER KA: Comparison of computed tomography and complex motion tomography in the evaluation of cholesteatoma. *AJNR* 5:303–306, 1984; *AJR* 143:397–400, 1984.

SHAFFER KA: The temporal bone, in Williams AL, Haughton WM (eds), *Cranial Computed Tomography: A Comprehensive Text,* St. Louis, CV Mosby, 1985.

SOLTI-BOHMAN LG, MAGARAM DL, LO WWM, et al: Gas-CT cisternography for detection of small acoustic nerve tumors. *Radiology* 150:403–407, 1984.

SOM PM, REEDE DL, BERGERON RT, et al: Computed tomography of glomus tympanicum tumors. *J Comput Assist Tomogr* 7:14–17, 1983.

SORTLAND O: Computed tomography combined with gas cisternography for the diagnosis of expanding lesions in the cerebellopontine angle. *Neuroradiology* 18:19–22, 1979.

STRASHUN AM, NEGATHEIM M, GOLDSMITH SJ: Malignant external otitis: Early scintigraphic detection. *Radiology* 150: 541–545, 1984.

SWARTZ JD: High resolution computed tomography of the middle ear and mastoid: I. Normal radioanatomy including normal variations. *Radiology* 148:449–454, 1983*a*.

SWARTZ JD, GOODMAN RS, RUSSELL KB, et al: High resolution computed tomography of the middle ear and mastoid: II. Tubotympanic disease. *Radiology* 148:455–459, 1983*b*.

SWARTZ JD: Cholesteatomas of the middle ear: Diagnosis, etiology and complications. *Radiol Clin North Am* 22:15–36, 1984*a*.

SWARTZ JD, FAERBER EN, WOLFSON RJ, et al: Fenestral otosclerosis: Significance of preoperative CT evaluation. *Radiology* 151:703–707, 1984*b*.

SWARTZ JD: *Imaging of the Temporal Bone,* New York, Thieme, 1986*a*.

SWARTZ JD, LANSMAN AK, BERGER AS, et al: Stapes prosthesis: Evaluation with CT. *Radiology* 158:179–182, 1986*b*.

SWARTZ JD: Current imaging approach to the temporal bone. *Radiology* 171:309–317, 1989.

TERESI L, LUFKIN R, WORTHAM D, et al: MR imaging of the intratemporal facial nerve using surface coils. *AJNR* 8:49–54, 1987*a*.

TERESI L, LUFKIN R, NITTA K, et al: MRI of the facial nerve: Normal anatomy and pathology. *Semin Ultrasound CT MR* 8:240–255, 1987*b*.

TURSKI P, NORMAN D, DEGROOT J, et al: High-resolution CT of the petrous bone: Direct vs. reformatted images. *AJNR* 3:391–394, 1982.

VALAVANIS A, SCHUBIGER O, HAYEK J, et al: CT of meningiomas on the posterior surface of the petrous bone. *Neuroradiology* 22:111–121, 1981.

VALVASSORI GE, MAFEE MF, DOBBEN GD: Computerized tomography of the temporal bone. *Laryngoscope* 92:562–565, 1982.

VALVASSORI GE, MORALES FG, PALACIOS E, et al: MR of the normal and abnormal internal auditory canal. *AJNR* 9:115–119, 1988.

VIRAPONGSE C, SARWAR M, SASAKI C, et al: High resolution computed tomography of the osseous external canal: I. Normal anatomy. *J Comput Assist Tomogr* 7:486–492, 1983.

VOGL T, BRUNING R, SCHEIDEL H, et al: Paragangliomas of the jugular bulb and carotid body: MR imaging with short sequences and Gd-DTPA enhancement. *AJR* 153:583–587, 1989.

WRIGHT JW Jr: Trauma of the ear. *Radiol Clin North Am* 12:527–532, 1974.

WRIGHT JW Jr: Polytomography and congenital external and middle ear anomalies. *Laryngoscope* 91:1806–1811, 1981.

WRIGHT JW Jr, WRIGHT JW III, HICKS G: Polytomography and congenital anomalies of the ear. *Ann Otol Rhinol Laryngol* 91:480–484, 1982.

WU E-R, TANG Y-S, ZANG Y-T, et al: CT in the diagnosis of acoustic neuromas. *Am J Neuroradiol* 7:645–650, 1986.

YOUNG IR, BYDDER GM, HALL AS, et al: The role of NMR imaging in the diagnosis and management of acoustic neuroma. *AJNR* 4:223–224, 1983.

ZIMMERMAN RA, BILANIUK LT, HACKNEY DB, et al: Magnetic resonance imaging in temporal bone fracture. *Neuroradiology* 29:246–251, 1987.

ZONNEVELD FW, VAN WAES PFGM, DAMSMA H, et al: Direct multiplanar computed tomography of the petrous bone. *Radiographics* 3:400–449, 1983.

12 CRANIOCEREBRAL TRAUMA

Robert A. Zimmerman

INTRODUCTION

Head injuries are responsible for 200 to 300 hospital admissions per 100,000 population per year in the United States (Bakay 1980). Most admissions are brief, with the patient discharged within 48 hours, and most of the patients are men. Serious head trauma occurs in only 3 percent of nonvehicular and 15 percent of vehicular injuries (Caveness 1979). However, craniocerebral trauma still constitutes the major cause of accidental death in the United States and represents more than 50 percent of deaths between ages 15 and 24 (Caveness 1979). Nine deaths per 100,000 population per year result from head injuries in the United Kingdom (Jennett 1981); this constitutes 1 percent of all deaths, 25 percent of traumatic deaths, and 50 percent of deaths due to road accidents. Thus, in the United States and other economically developed countries, head injury represents not only a serious cause of loss of life but also a significant source of financial burden, resulting in a prolonged loss of earnings and a financial loss in terms of the health care resources expended in treating and caring for these patients.

When a patient has a head injury, there is an urgent need to understand the nature, extent, and rapidity of its progression (Zimmerman 1978*a*). If this can be accomplished, it may be possible to correct certain problems and institute measures that protect the brain from greater or irreversible damage.

A variety of factors contribute to the way in which a head injury occurs, and other factors act to mitigate this process (Zimmerman 1984). It is the interplay between the factors that produce the traumatic event and those that protect a person from it that produces the end result. Physical factors include the thickness of the scalp and hair, the density of ossification, and the dimensions and thickness of the calvarium. The position of the head at the time of injury, the protection afforded by objects surrounding the head, and the direction and nature of the force that produces the injury are variables that affect the traumatic outcome.

Newborns, infants, and young children with open sutures and a thin calvarium have an advantage in that a greater impact can be absorbed by a more flexible skull (Zimmerman 1981). Also, the lack of myelination in younger persons contributes to greater plasticity of the cerebral hemispheres. Calvarial flexibility and cerebral plasticity, however, permit more severe distortion between the skull and the dura relative to the cerebral hemispheres and their superficial vessels. When they are severe, such forces produce posterior fossa subdural hematomas, tentorial dura venous sinus tears, and other lesions rarely seen in older children and adults (Zimmerman 1981). Posttraumatic swelling appears to be a more rapid and more diffuse problem in a young child (Zimmerman 1978*b*); a similar degree of swelling is rarely seen in an adult. The patterns of brain injury change as a child ages; the sutures fuse, the calvarium thickens, myelination progresses, and cerebrovascular responsiveness matures (Zimmerman 1978*b*). Cerebral injury patterns in adults are different from those in children.

Not only are there differences in head injuries between infants and adults, there is also a difference in the nature of the cervical spinal injuries that occur as a component of the overall traumatic episode. Weakness of the neck muscles, a proportionately larger head mass relative to that of the body, open ossification centers, and ligamentous elasticity are all present in an infant and permit greater motion between the occiput, C1, and C2 (Melzak 1969). This elasticity results in a variety of subluxations, dislocations, and fractures that are found less frequently in older children and adults. With further maturation, adult proportions between the head and the body are reached, the epiphyses fuse, muscular development takes place, ligamentous elasticity decreases, and cervical spine injuries become analogous to those in adults (Ogden 1982). There is also a significant difference in the incidence of cervical spine injury in young children (1 in 230) as opposed to adults (1 in 20) (Henrys 1977). Thus, it is important for physicians who perform posttraumatic brain and spine imaging studies to recognize the limitations of these studies caused by differences in biomechanical factors in an infant or a young child.

IMAGING TECHNIQUES

Plain skull radiographs, CT, arteriography, and MR can be used to assess skull and brain injury. With a cervical spine injury, plain spine radiographs, CT, myelography, and MR are utilized. The choice of technique depends on several factors, including availability, speed of performance, diagnostic information desired, information derived, limitations of the technology, clinical circumstances, and cost (Zimmerman 1984). For example, the demonstration of an operable intracranial hematoma with a technology that takes more time (MR) rather than with one that is faster but less elegant (CT) delays the removal of the hematoma, perhaps resulting in increased disability or the death of the patient. An imaging procedure that is more rapid but insensitive, such as a skull radiograph, when one is attempting to determine whether there has been parenchymal brain damage only delays the diagnosis and the treatment of the patient (Zimmerman 1983).

In the emergency room, after the institution of support and monitoring and after the patient has been stabilized, the immediate radiographic question is stability of the spine to ensure that cord injury does not occur as a result of movement. This requires a good-quality lateral radiograph of the cervical spine that shows the relationship between the skull, C1, and the cervical vertebrae through C7. Such alignment on a lateral radiograph does not assure that ligamentous injury has not occurred or demonstrate with clarity the presence of fractures and epiphyseal separations that require a more complete cervical spine radiographic examination or CT study. However, at this point the patient usually can be moved with a physician and nurse in attendance so that a CT study can be performed. The CT examination is done to evaluate the brain and/or spine.

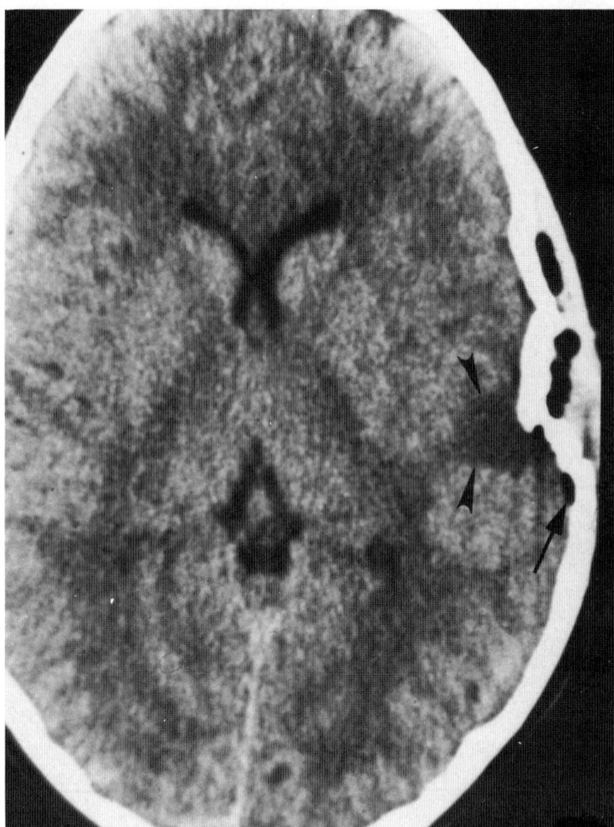

Figure 12-1 Depressed fracture with an underlying contusion in a 10-year-old male hit on the left side of the head. Axial CT shows gas within the subgaleal region, intracranial air (arrow) in the subdural space, and a depressed fracture. There is an underlying area of hypodensity (arrowheads) consistent with nonhemorrhagic contusion.

Computed Tomography

Current CT scanners have data acquisition times of 1 to 3 seconds per slice (Gibbey in press). Because of interscan delay, tube cooling, and reconstruction, the total examination time for a brain study is between 10 and 25 minutes. A more detailed examination that requires thin sections for the evaluation of facial injury or cervical spine trauma requires a longer period of time. Patient motion during data acquisition degrades or destroys the image quality of a scan done while the motion occurred. When the motion stops, the scans will again be of good quality. With CT, it is easy to rescan sections that were made useless by motion. This should be done routinely by the technician unless the patient's clinical condition is deteriorating. Monitoring and support equipment function in the CT scanner room but do not pose a management problem. Anesthesiologists accompanying the patient are shielded from the scatter radiation because they wear lead aprons. The CT scan that is generated is photographed onto x-ray film to make a hard copy.

In a typical head injury, windows and window levels are optimized for the brain (brain window) (Fig. 12-1), used to assess the presence or absence of blood adjacent to the inner table of the skull, as is seen in a subdural or epidural hematoma (intermediate windows) (Fig. 12-2), and used to determine the presence or absence of a bony fracture (bone windows) (Fig. 12-3). In the spine, usually one set of windows is used for the spinal cord and one for the bony anatomy. If a spinal subdural or epidural hematoma is suspected, intermediate windows can be useful. If intermediate windows are not used in the head, small but significant life-threatening extracerebral hematomas may be missed. The studies can always be rephotographed, but it is important to have the critical information early so that an appropriate management decision can be made prospectively.

Magnetic Resonance Imaging

Data acquisition periods for a T_1-weighted set of images are on the order of several minutes, while those for a set

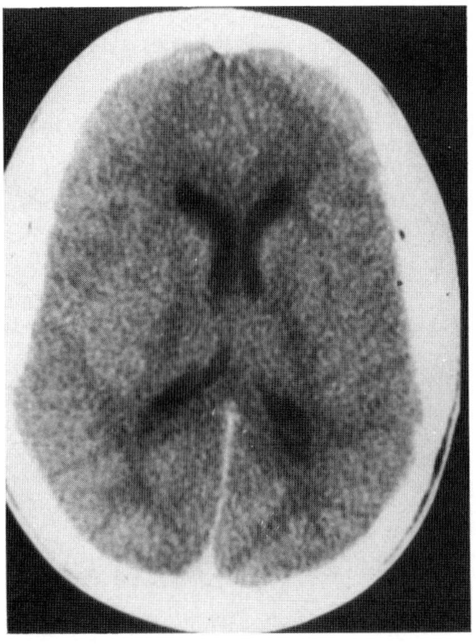
A

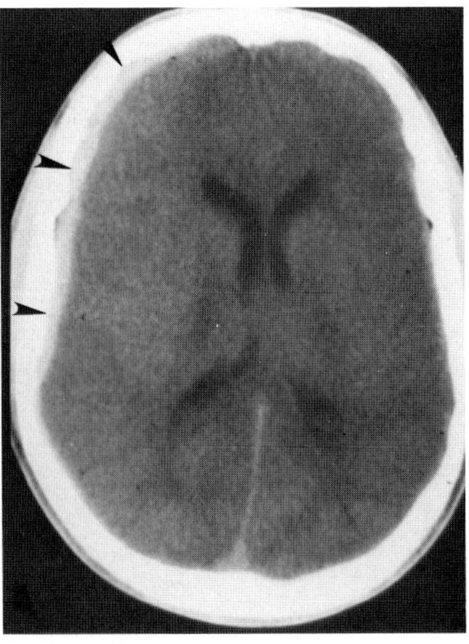
B

Figure 12-2 Acute subdural hematoma in a 17-year-old man rendered comatose in a motor vehicle accident. **A.** Axial CT with brain windows shows no definite extracerebral collection of blood. **B.** Same section displayed with intermediate windows demonstrates a small, peripheral acute subdural hematoma (arrowheads) encompassing the anterior two-thirds of the right cerebral hemisphere.

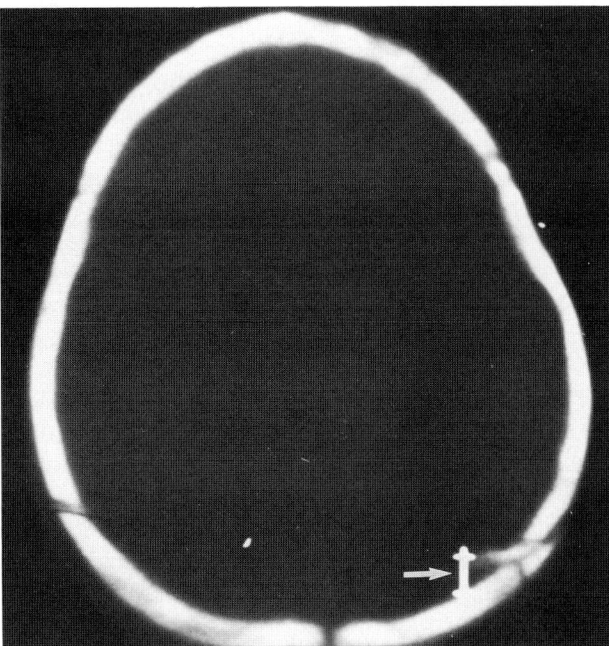

Figure 12-3 A 5-year-old male with a depressed skull fracture. Axial CT displayed at bone windows shows a comminuted depressed fracture of the left parietal region. The measurement device of the CT scanner (arrow) equals a 1-cm depression of the fracture.

of proton and T_2-weighted multiecho images require 8 or more minutes (Zimmerman 1989). Long acquisition times can cause problems in regard to motion. Image quality is degraded by motion, and the scans may be uninterpretable. Motion can be controlled by means of sedation, but sedation eliminates one's ability to evaluate a patient's neurological signs. However, many seriously injured comatose patients are intubated and paralyzed; these patients can be examined in the acute situation when support, the monitoring equipment, and the intubation devices utilized are compatible with the requirements of the MR room (Zimmerman 1989). Nonferromagnetic equipment must be used because it cannot be pulled into the magnetic field of the MR magnet. Ultra-low-field MR systems and some permanent magnets are exceptions. The fields generated by these units are so low that it may be possible to use ferromagnetic equipment. However, plastic intubation devices and subarachnoid bolts are a standard part of the neuroanesthesiologist's and neurosurgeon's armamentarium today. Electronic monitoring equipment becomes a matter of concern in the MR room if it generates a radiofrequency (RF) signal that interferes with the signals of the scanner. An extraneous RF source degrades the image quality. The magnetic field can interfere with the readout or the functioning of monitoring devices. For instance, strong magnetic fields deflect the output of the electron gun on an ECG monitor, making the readout uninterpretable. At present, nonferromagnetic respirators, shielded cables for ECGs, pulse oximeters that work in the magnetic field, and a variety of other monitoring and support devices allow MR examination of emergency head injury patients. With experience, the setup times have decreased, and studies have been done in as little as 1 hour.

Two investigational aspects of head injury are worth noting here. MR scanners can generate MR angiographic (MRA) images of blood vessels with fast flow by utilizing the three-dimensional (3D) time of flight techniques with gradient-echo T_1-weighted images (T_1WI) processed by means of a maximum-intensity projection (Masaryk 1989). At present a total of 6.4 cm of brain can be examined. MRA can show the integrity of the circle of Willis and its branches. The potential of this technique will be realized in the demonstration of traumatic vascular injury resulting in obstruction of a major vessel or the production of a pseudoaneurysm. Magnetic resonance spectroscopy (MRS) is another technique that has research applications in the evaluation of head injury patients (Schnall 1987). Acquisition times for spectroscopic data are long. Proton spectra can be acquired for a region of interest measuring 3 by 3 by 3 cm in 20 minutes, following a 10-minute period of shimming. A proton spectrum can show whether lactates are elevated in the brain (Detre 1990) secondary to a hypoxic-ischemic insult. A longer data acquisition time displays the relative concentration of phosphorous metabolites in the brain (Sutton 1990). The relationship between inorganic phosphorous and phosphocreatine gives a relative measure of brain pH.

Cerebral Angiography

Prior to the availability of CT, cerebral angiography was routinely used to assess the presence or absence of intracranial mass lesions. Today it is reserved for the demonstration of vascular injury in the form of dissections, ruptures, pseudoaneurysms, and fistulas (Davis 1983). Invasive cerebral angiography is time-consuming, requiring several hours, and necessitates control of patient motion during the injection of dye and filming. Support and monitoring equipment are not a problem.

Myelography

Prior to the availability of CT and spinal MR, myelography was widely used to demonstrate posttraumatic cord compression. Myelographic procedures are invasive, requiring puncture of the subarachnoid space and the introduction of radiographic dye. These studies take an hour or more and necessitate patient compliance or motion control. Support and monitoring equipment are not a problem.

SKULL FRACTURE

A calvarial or even a vertebral fracture provides evidence of bone injury from trauma. However, a fracture does not mean that the brain or spinal cord has been injured. In general, in cases of trauma, what has happened to the brain and/or spinal cord tissue is the most important factor. Osseous injury is significant not only as a sign of injury but often as a pathway for the spread of infection when the fracture is associated with disruption of the overlying soft tissues. A finding of cranial nerve palsy in association with trauma indicates the necessity of identifying a fracture through the foramen or canal in which that nerve passes. The two most effective ways of demonstrating calvarial injury are skull radiographs (Fig. 12-4) and CT (Fig. 12-3). Both studies show bone as a high density and the fracture within it as a lucency.

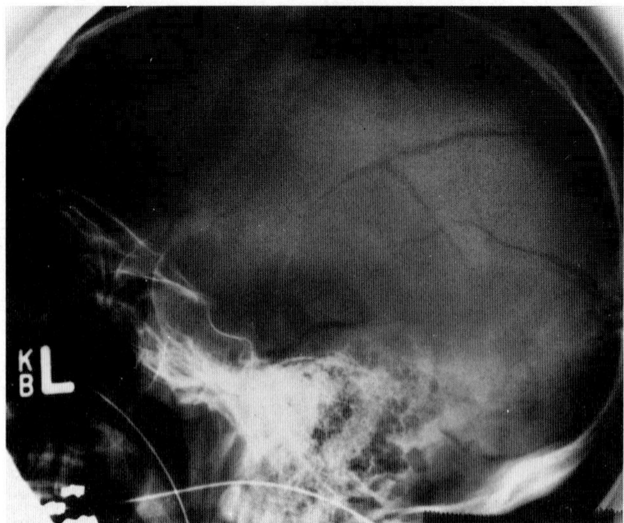

Figure 12-4 Multiple calvarial fractures. Lateral skull radiograph shows multiple irregular lucent fracture lines within the temporoparietal region.

MR does not usually show fractures, because the protons of cortical bone are nonmobile; as a result, the cortical bone appears as a linear hypointensity or blackness that is not discernible from air or cerebrospinal fluid (CSF). When the cortical bone lies in apposition to a tissue with higher signal intensity, such as fat within the scalp, the bone may be visualized in contrast as a structure with low signal intensity. The intradiploic marrow may be seen in older patients because of its fatty nature. On T_2-weighted images (T_2WI) when the CSF is made high in signal intensity, it outlines the inner table, with the skull appearing as a hypointense line. In some instances fractures can be recognized on MR if the observer knows how to look for them. Zimmerman and coworkers (Zimmerman 1987) evaluated seven patients with temporal bone fractures and found that six of eight fractures were visible with MR. Fractures were recognized by (1) interposition between the fracture fragments of higher-signal-intensity posttraumatic tissue (CSF, hemorrhage, or brain), (2) disruption of the hypointense black line of cortical bone, (3) displacement of the hypointense line of cortical bone, and (4) orbital fat displaced through a fractured defect (Fig. 12-5).

With an increase in the severity of brain injury, there is an increase in the incidence of fractures. Eighty-one percent of 151 fatal injuries examined at autopsy had associated skull fractures (Adams 1975). The converse—that 19 percent of those fatal injuries did not include a skull fracture—is also of interest. The yield of fractures varies from a high of 15 percent to a low of 2.7 percent in general urban hospital emergency rooms (St. John 1968; Balasubramaniam 1981; Strong 1978). Significant fractures—those associated with the presence of intracranial air or

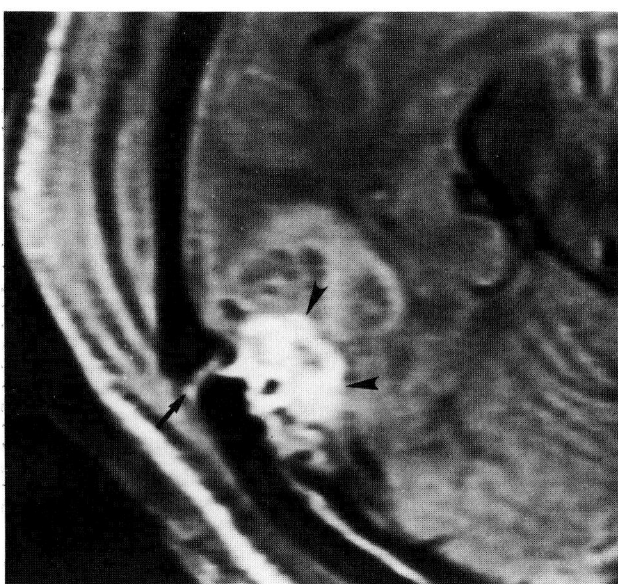

Figure 12-5 Calvarial fracture underlying hemorrhagic contusion. Axial proton density image shows a disruption of the hypointense line of cortical bone (arrow). A high-signal-intensity cortical hemorrhagic contusion (arrowheads) underlies the fracture site.

a foreign body, those in which the fracture passes through an air-containing space such as the paranasal sinus and mastoid air cells, a fracture that is associated with laceration of the overlying scalp, and a depressed fracture over the motor strip or major dural venous sinus—are rare. Among 570 children with 49 fractures, only 2 fractures were significant (Roberts 1972). In this series the overall incidence of fractures was 8.25 percent, while the incidence of significant fractures was only 0.35 percent.

Since most patients seen in the emergency room with head injuries do not have fractures, it is easy to guess right in predicting their absence. Among 7970 patients, the physician was correct in predicting the absence of a skull fracture in 96.6 to 99 percent (Balasubramaniam 1981; Royal College of Radiologists 1980). It is more difficult to predict a positive examination. Among 2102 patients, the correct positive diagnosis of fracture was made by means of clinical examination in only 17.4 percent (Balasubramaniam 1981). It should be noted that among patients in whom the physician correctly predicted a fracture, the incidence of brain injury was higher (24 percent) (Balasubramaniam 1981). When the physician predicted a skull fracture but it was absent, brain injury was less frequent (7.5 percent) (Balasubramaniam 1981). High-yield criteria (Bell 1971) exist for obtaining a trauma emergency skull radiograph; adherence to these criteria decreases the number of skull radiographs performed in the emergency room. However, the current practice in emergency medicine in the United States is to obtain a CT scan for most of these indications. Today the skull radiograph is complementary to CT in demonstrating depressed fractures, in localizing foreign bodies, and as another method for assessing and following craniofacial fractures (Zimmerman 1986*a*). Skull radiographs may be useful in an emergency situation by demonstrating a calvarial fracture in a comatose patient when a history is lacking and CT is negative. This situation is relatively uncommon.

When a patient has minimal evidence of head injury, it must be decided whether a skull radiograph should be done if a CT scan is not performed. A very small percentage of these patients may have acute subdural or epidural hematomas, and some of them would be observed more closely if a skull fracture were demonstrated. Even with the use of the high-yield criteria for the ordering of skull radiographs, it has been noted that a proportion of patients who might benefit from the information derived from the skull radiographs would not be examined. It has been pointed out that 50 percent of patients with compound depressed fractures do not suffer loss of consciousness and that 40 percent of patients with intracranial hematomas do not have an initial loss of consciousness (Jennett 1981). Thus, there is a small ill-defined population of patients who fall through the high-yield criteria. Some of these patients represent a potential catastrophe. Finally, if a fracture is present, there is a possibility of an associated intracranial hematoma. If there is scalp laceration and a fracture, there is a possibility of infection (Jennett 1980). Ultimately, if skull radiographs are performed, they should be adequate in their projections and well penetrated, and the person interpreting the study should be trained in the recognition of these abnormalities.

Linear Skull Fractures

These fractures appear more lucent than do vascular grooves and closed cranial sutures (Fig. 12-4). Linear fractures are wider in the midportion and narrower at either end (Zimmerman 1986*a*). Typically, they are less than 3 mm in overall width. A young child with a thin calvarium or an adult with a thin temporal squama may present problems, as the fracture line in these areas may be more difficult to identify. Linear fractures are most common in the temporoparietal, frontal, and occipital regions. These fractures tend to extend from the calvarium toward the cranial base. The fractures should be able to be identified on more than one projection, but it is not uncommon to have difficulty identifying a fracture on all views. As a fracture heals, the line becomes less distinct and the fracture becomes more difficult to distinguish from normal structures such as vascular grooves and sutures (Zimmerman 1986*a*). A linear fracture in a young patient such as an infant heals in less than 3 to 6 months, whereas in an adult this often takes 2 to 3 years (Zimmerman 1986*a*). If

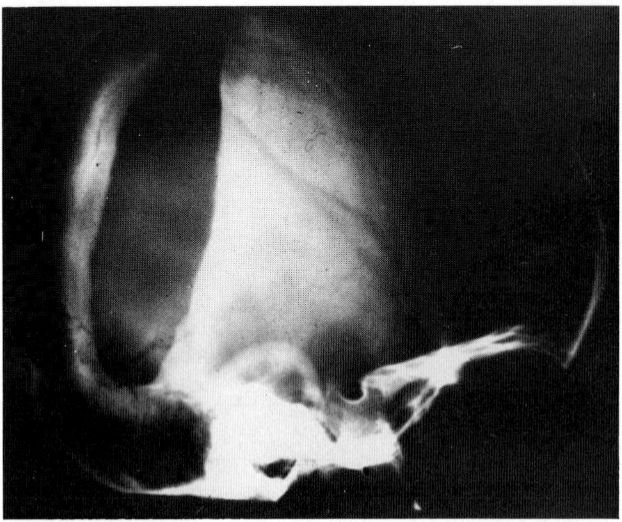

Figure 12-6 Leptomeningeal cyst. Lateral skull radiograph shows a widened fracture line with beveled edges that has increased in size over the course of the year. The etiology was a leptomeningeal cyst.

a fracture line does not heal but continues to enlarge (Fig. 12-6), the presence of a leptomeningeal cyst or brain hernia should be considered (Taveras 1953). Both conditions occur as a result of a compound fracture that rends the dura mater so that either brain tissue or arachnoid is interposed between the dura and the fracture fragments. As a result, brain pulsations are transmitted to the CSF at the fracture edges, preventing healing and eventually leading to widening of the defect (Fig. 12-6) (Taveras 1953). Leptomeningeal cysts occur most often in pediatric patients under age 2, with an incidence estimated to be less than 1 percent. They are more common in the frontal and parietal regions.

Sutural Diastasis

The coronal and lambdoid sutures are no wider than 2 mm (Zimmerman 1986*a*). Traumatic separation (diastasis) of the sutures is recognized when the width of the suture is more than 3 mm. This occurs when a fracture extends into the suture. Sutural diastasis occurs most often in a suture that has not undergone bony union. The coronal suture fuses at around age 30, while the lambdoid suture does not fuse until after age 60. In the adult population, diastasis of the lambdoid suture is most common. Sutural diastasis can be bilateral.

Depressed Fracture

Locking of a fracture edge under the intact adjacent calvarium or failure of bone to rebound produces a depressed fracture (Figs. 12-1 and 12-3). There is a high incidence of underlying cerebral parenchymal injury (Fig. 12-1) and tearing of the dura with these fractures. They occur most often in the parietal and frontal regions and occur frequently in young adults and adolescents. A depressed fracture is considered clinically significant when the fracture fragment is depressed below the edge of the intact adjacent inner table of the skull or the fracture overlies a major dural venous sinus or the motor cortex (Zimmerman 1986*a*). These fractures are also significant if they are associated with dural tears, penetration of the cerebral parenchyma by a foreign object, or the presence of an underlying parenchymal injury. Compound depressed fractures (Fig. 12-1) are important because they carry the additional risk of intracranial infection (Jennett 1980).

The zone of increased density identified at the fracture site on skull radiographs is due to the overlapping of fracture fragments beneath the adjacent calvarium or the rotation of a fracture fragment onto its side so that it projects a greater radiographic thickness than does the adjacent skull (Fig. 12-7). On a skull radiograph, the examiner looks for the site from which the bone has been depressed, the fracture hole, and the bone that is de-

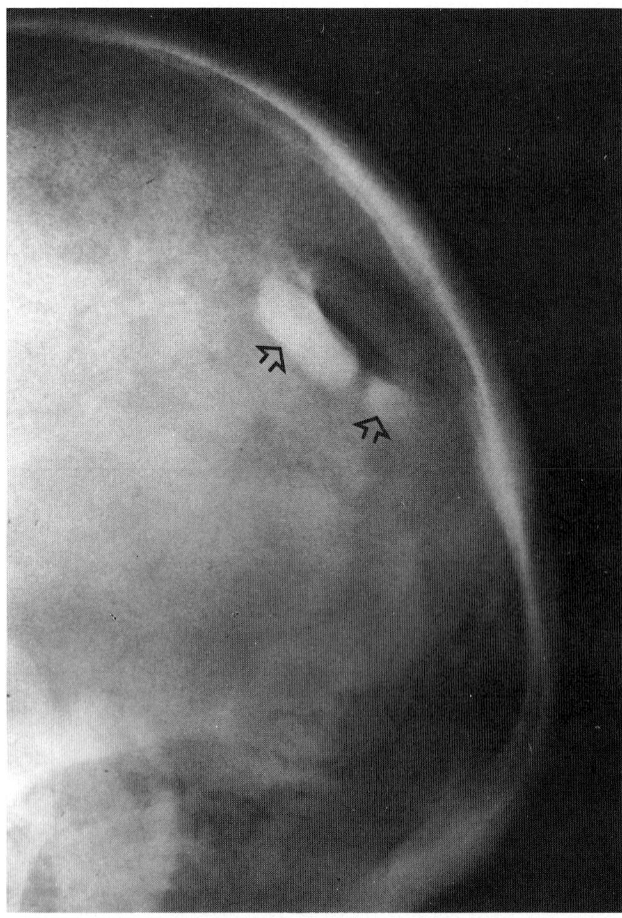

Figure 12-7 Depressed fracture. Tangential skull radiograph shows a lucency at the site from which the fracture fragment is depressed. The zone of increased density (open arrows) is a superimposition of the fracture fragment on the adjacent bone.

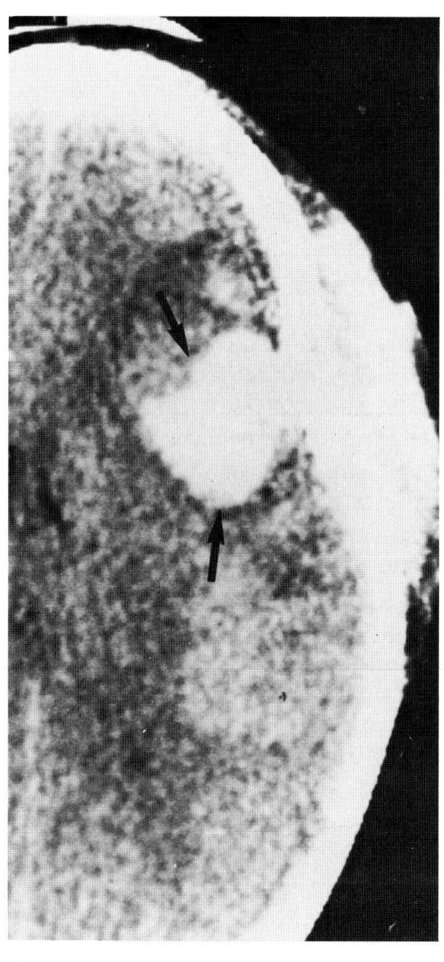

A

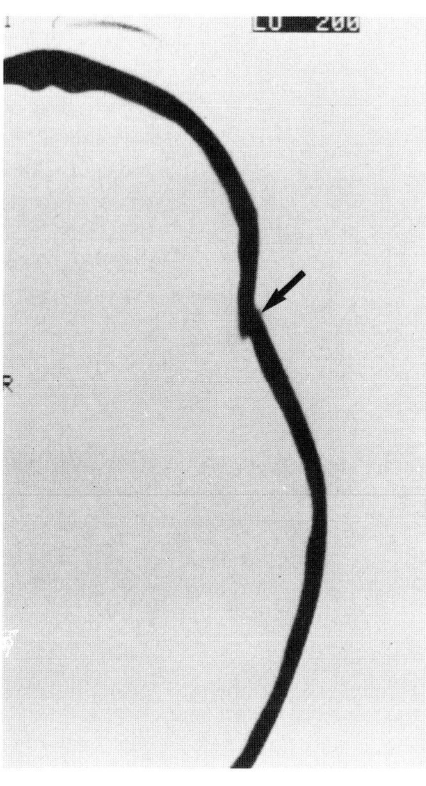

B

Figure 12-8 Depressed fracture with underlying contusional hematoma. **A.** Axial CT with brain windows shows a high-density hematoma (arrows) and a subgaleal hematoma. **B.** Bone windows at the same slice level show that the calvarium is depressed with a fracture (arrow). Note that the contrast has been reversed so that the bone window is displayed with the bone black instead of white.

pressed (Fig. 12-7). Tangential views of the fracture site are useful. CT can show not only the depressed fracture but an adjacent parenchymal brain injury (Figs. 12-1 and 12-8) (Zimmerman 1984).

FRACTURES OF THE SKULL BASE

When blood is present behind the tympanic membrane without direct ear trauma, when there is evidence of otorrhea or rhinorrhea or a subcutaneous hematoma surrounds the mastoid process (battle sign), or when ecchymoses surround the orbits without direct orbital trauma (raccoon sign), evidence of a basilar skull fracture should be sought. Skull radiographs have generally been suboptimal in demonstrating these fractures (Harwood-Nash 1970). High-resolution cranial CT with thin sections is the best modality for demonstrating such fractures (Figs. 12-9 and 12-10) (Zimmerman 1986*a*).

Both otorrhea and rhinorrhea occur in 0.5 to 2 percent of hospitalized head trauma patients (Zimmerman 1986*a*). Basilar skull fractures become compound fractures when a communication exists between the intracranial compartment and the outside. A fracture through the cranium and dura that extends into the paranasal sinuses, nasal cavity, or mastoid air cells is a compound fracture. Patients with compound basilar skull fractures are at risk

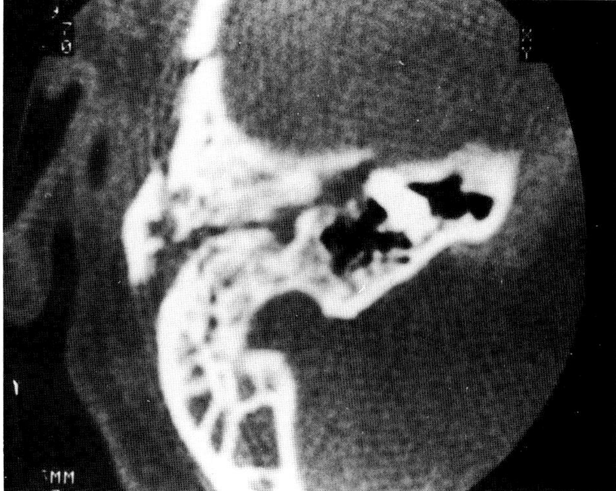

Figure 12-9 Comminuted basilar skull fracture involving the temporal bone. Axial CT shows multiple fracture fragments involving the right temporal bone, extending in a longitudinal fashion.

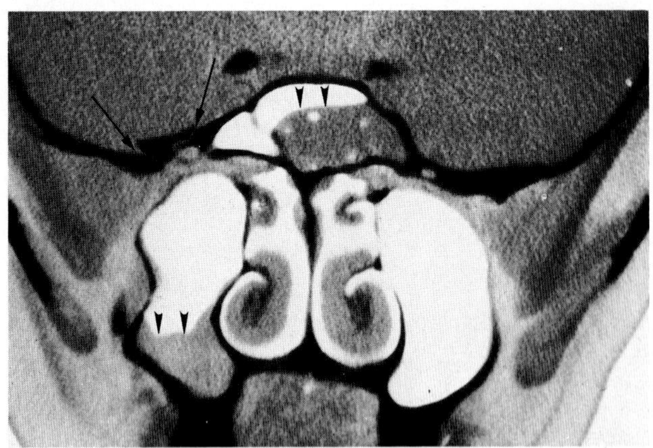

Figure 12-10 Basilar skull fractures. Coronal CT with reverse contrast shows a comminuted fracture (arrows) of the right cranial base involving the lateral wall of the sphenoid sinus. Note that there is an air-fluid level (arrowheads) in the left sphenoid sinus air cell and in the right maxillary sinus.

for developing pneumocephalus and its complications (osteomyelitis, meningitis, and abscess formation).

Basilar skull fractures may result in compression and entrapment of the cranial nerves that pass through basal foramina. The ossicular chain can be dislocated with fractures of the petrous bone. Fractures of the optic canal can be associated with loss of vision. Fracture of the sphenoid bone can be associated with injury to the cranial nerves that pass through the cavernous sinus (third, fourth, sixth, and the first and second divisions of the fifth cranial nerves). Sphenoidal fractures can also be associated with disruption of the intracavernous internal carotid artery, leading to pseudoaneurysms or a carotid cavernous fistula. Fractures of the internal auditory canal, middle ear, or otic capsule can injure the seventh and eighth cranial nerves. The ninth, tenth, and eleventh cranial nerves can be injured when fractures pass through the jugular canal, as can the twelfth cranial nerve when a fracture passes through the hypoglossal canal. All these cranial nerve injuries associated with fracture of the cranial base are best demonstrated with high-resolution CT (Figs. 12-9 and 12-10). The indirect signs of a basilar skull fracture are the presence of intracranial air and air-fluid (blood or CSF) levels in basilar sinuses (Robinson 1967).

CEREBROSPINAL FLUID LEAKS AND PNEUMOCEPHALUS

Pneumocephalus is found in approximately 20 percent of patients with active CSF rhinorrhea (Zimmerman 1986*a*); it also occurs without clinical evidence of CSF leakage. In the initial day or two after trauma, CSF leakage is not common. Blood clot fills the traumatic fracture, and the focally swollen and injured brain compresses the subarachnoid space, preventing CSF leakage. Days later, with necrosis of the injured brain and lysis of the blood clot within the fracture, CSF leakage occurs (Lantz 1980). In 70 percent of patients, the CSF leak stops within the first week; in 99 percent, it stops within 6 weeks (Lantz 1980). The risk of a CSF leak lies in the development of meningitis. Treatment of a posttraumatic CSF leak is a matter of watchful waiting, reduction of paranasal sinus fractures, and antibiotics. If the leak persists for a prolonged period, the risk of developing CSF meningitis increases and may be higher than 50 percent.

The problem in evaluating a patient with a CSF leak radiographically lies in the difficulty of identifying the site of the leak. Posttraumatic CSF leaks most often involve the frontal sinuses, ethmoid sinuses, and cribriform plate (Yoshiharu 1980). Less frequently, the sphenoid sinus, the petrous bone, and other calvarial sites are the source. Plain radiographs, while useful as a survey, usually do not identify the site of the leak. Thin axial CT sections after the intrathecal installation of water-soluble nonionic contrast media (used for myelography) are the current method of choice. Several milliliters of Isovue or Omnipaque in a concentration of 200 mg/ml is injected into the lumbar subarachnoid space, using a 22-gauge needle. The patient is placed in a prone head down position for 1 or 2 minutes at an angle of 75°, utilizing the fluoroscopic table. The patient is then taken to the CT scanner and examined in a prone coronal position with thin 1- or 2-mm sections taken through the frontal sinuses, ethmoid sinuses, and cribriform plate (Manelfe 1982). If necessary, the examination can be carried out through the sphenoid sinus and temporal bone. The study is positive when the leak is demonstrated as contrast entering the nasal cavity or paranasal sinuses and when the defect in the bone through which the leak has occurred is identified (Fig. 12-11).

It should be kept in mind that patients with trauma may have multiple fractures and that a bony defect does not have to be the source; another bony defect that has not been shown may have caused the condition. The study may be helped by the installation of 1.5 ml/min of saline or artificial CSF through a lumbar needle into the subarachnoid space, increasing CSF pressure to 600 ml H_2O for 15 minutes (Naidich 1980). When this technique is used, an equivocal CSF CT examination can be turned into a positive one. However, this maneuver carries the risk of opening the CSF leak and the attendant risk of an infection. Alternative methods include the installation of radioactive isotopes into the lumbar CSF with measurement of activity on cotton pledgets placed within the nasal cavity.

Coughing, the Valsalva maneuver, and other methods of increasing pressure in the upper respiratory tract can force air into the intracranial cavity when a fracture is present. The air can lie within the epidural, subdural, subarachnoid, or intraparenchymal space. Only large

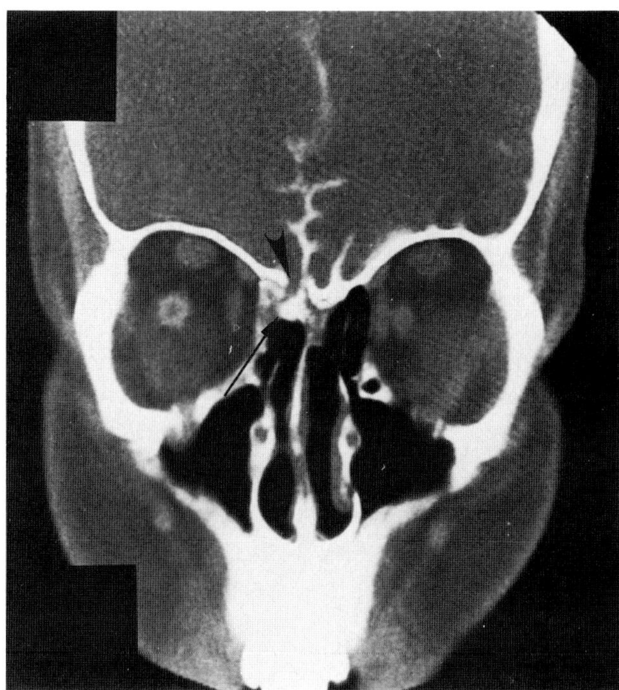

Figure 12-11 CSF rhinorrhea through a bony defect in right cribriform plate secondary to trauma. Coronal thin CT section after installation of water-soluble dye shows contrast (arrow) extending through the defect (arrowhead) in the cribriform plate.

amounts of air are seen on skull radiographs, whereas small amounts can be demonstrated on CT (Fig. 12-12) (Osborn 1978). Air within the epidural space is bound down by the attachments of the dura at the sutures. Air within the subdural space gravitates to the most superior extent of that space overlying the frontal lobes (Fig. 12-13). When the patient is placed brow down, the air moves to the region of the occipital lobe. Subdural air does not fill sulci, but subarachnoid air does. Intraventricular air gravitates to the most superior portion of the ventricular system, usually the frontal horns. Intraparenchymal air gains access to the tissue at the site of contusional necrosis (Fig. 12-14*A*). Often the fracture, torn dura, arachnoid, and contused brain are adherent to each other so that as the hemorrhagic contusion necroses, air can enter the cavity that has been formed (Fig. 12-14*B*). Posttraumatic intraparenchymal pneumatoceles are found weeks to months after the injury, often with subtle clinical manifestations. As with CSF leaks, the risk with pneumocephalus is the development of infection.

A calvarial fracture that communicates to a paranasal sinus or one in which a scalp laceration overlies the fracture can easily lead to intracranial infection. The infection may involve the meninges, the subdural or epidural spaces, or the brain. Persistent pneumocephalus, the development of unexplained areas of infarction, the development of new areas of mass effect at nontraumatic sites, the persistence of mass effect at sites of trauma for too

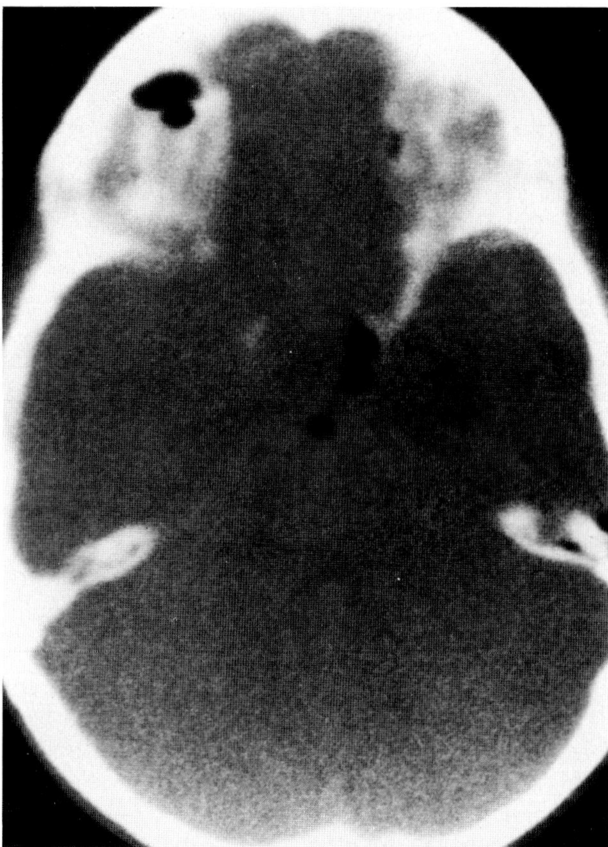

Figure 12-12 Subarachnoid pneumocephalus. Axial CT shows air in the suprasellar cistern and the subarachnoid space just above the orbit. Air entered through basilar skull fractures.

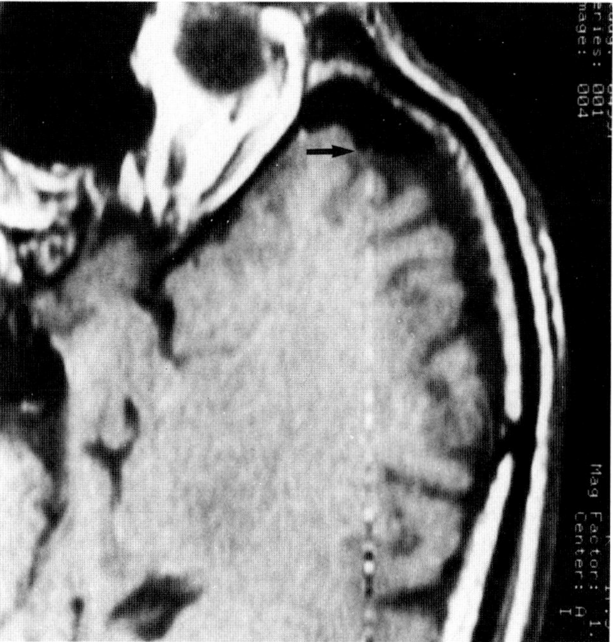

Figure 12-13 Subdural pneumocephalus. Sagittal brow-up T_1-weighted MR scan shows subdural air as a hypointense collection overlying the frontal lobe, with an air-fluid level (arrow) between air and CSF.

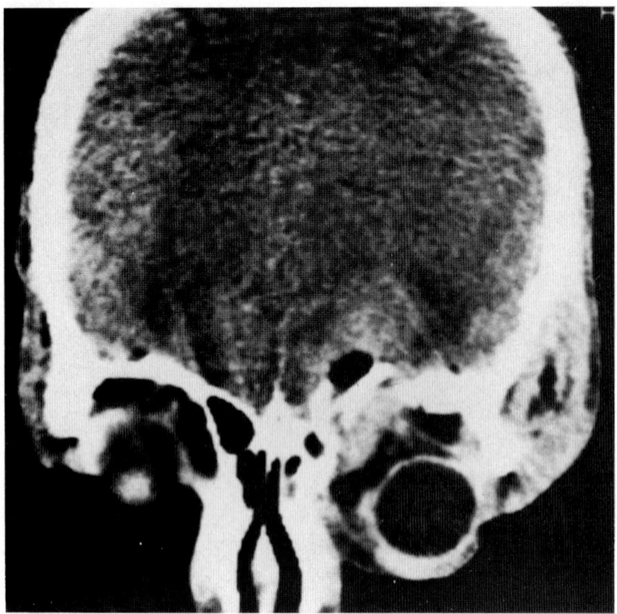

A

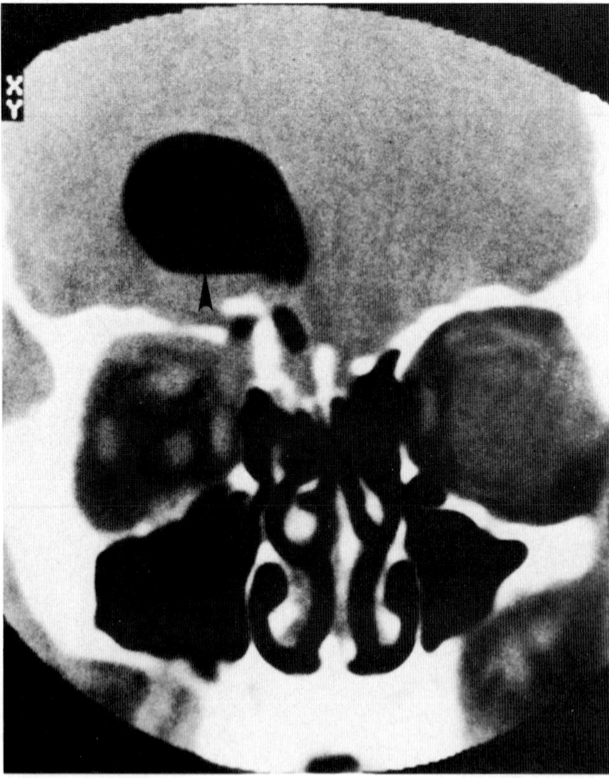

B

Figure 12-14 Development of posttraumatic pneumatocele. **A.** Coronal CT shows fracture of the roof of the orbit with contusion of the frontal lobe, intracranial pneumocephalus, and an intraorbital subperiosteal hematoma. **B.** Coronal CT 6 weeks later shows air extending through the fracture site into an intraparenchymal cavity at the site of the contused brain. An air-fluid level (arrowhead) is present within the cavity.

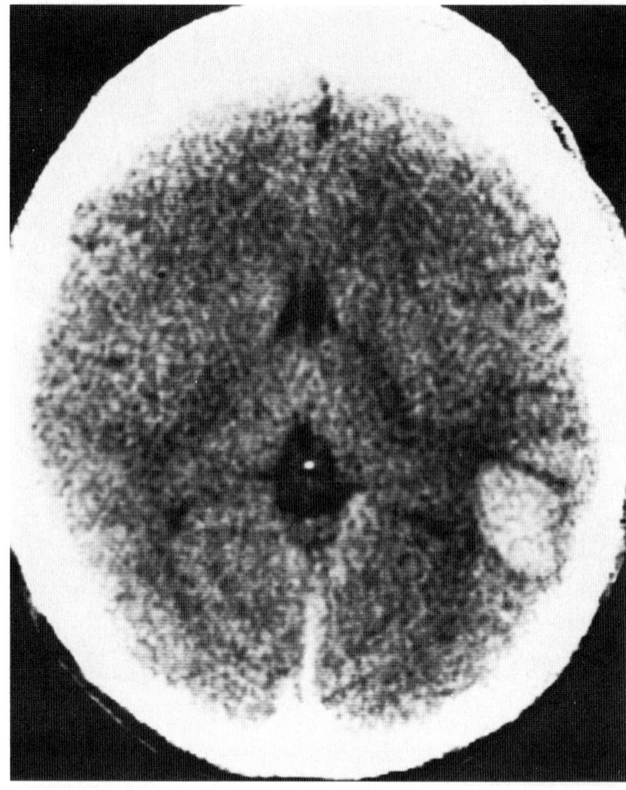

A

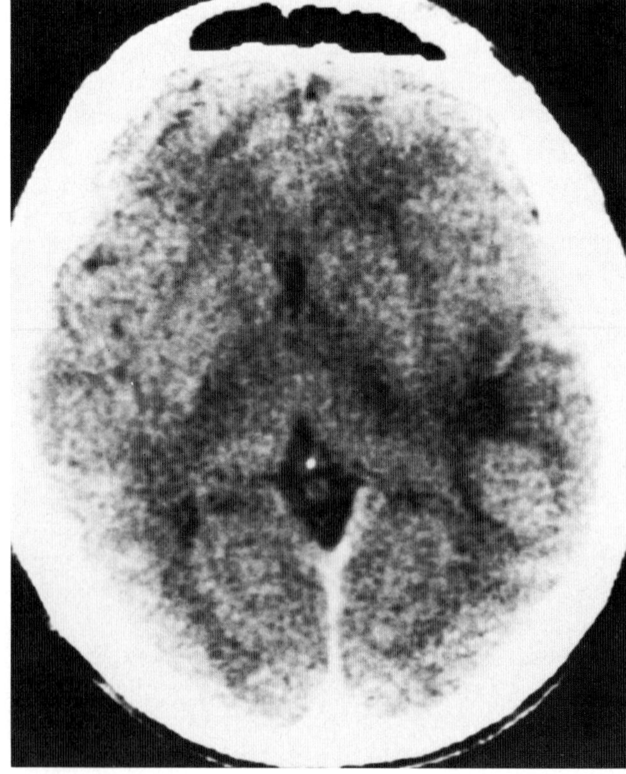

B

Figure 12-15 Progressive changes in clot density with time. **A.** High-density acute left temporal lobe intracerebral hematoma. **B.** Follow-up CT 3 weeks later shows that the hematoma is isodense. A small amount of focal edema helps outline the anterior margin of the resorbing hematoma.

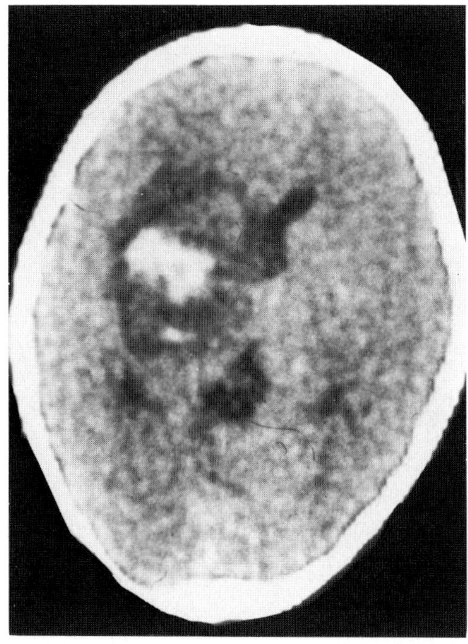

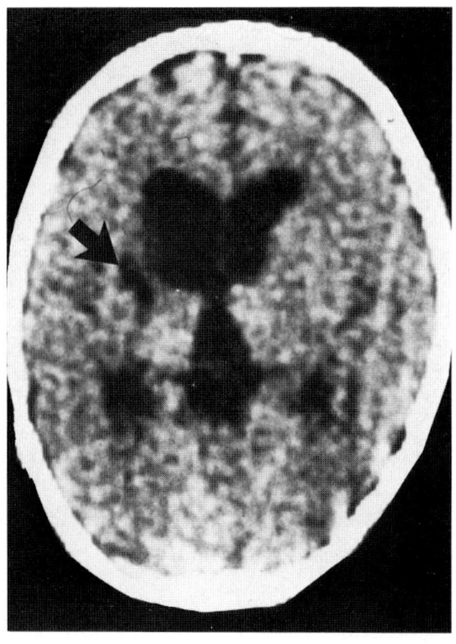

Figure 12-16 Resolution of traumatic intracerebral hematoma. **A.** Axial CT on the day of injury shows an acute basal ganglionic hematoma with surrounding edema. **B.** Axial CT 10 months later shows resolution of the hematoma into a slitlike cavity (arrow) along with atrophic dilatation of the ventricular system.

long a period, the development of a slowing expanding extracerebral mass, and the development of a new extracerebral mass that was not present immediately after a head injury are findings that raise concern regarding the development of a posttraumatic infection (Zimmerman 1986*a*). They indicate a need for a diagnostic workup to determine the source of infection and the nature of the infecting organism so that appropriate treatment can be instituted.

SEQUENTIAL CHANGES OF BLOOD PRODUCTS ON CT AND MR

To understand the interpretation of CT and MR images relative to posttraumatic bleeding, it is necessary to understand the evolution of such hematomas as they are depicted with medical imaging. On CT, a hematoma has high density as a result of the relative density of the globin molecule in stopping the x-ray beam (Dolinskas 1977). Clot retraction occurs over the hours following hematoma formation, and serum is extruded. The hematoma becomes higher in density after clot retraction (Fig. 12-15*A*). Clots typically measure 60 to 100 Hounsfield units. As the globin molecule breaks down, the density of the clot is progressively lost (Fig.12-15*B*). Clot density decreases from the periphery and progresses centrally. A 2.5-cm clot becomes isodense in 25 days (Dolinskas 1977). The clot is not gone, but it is no longer visible on CT. With enough time, the clot is completely reabsorbed by macrophages that digest the blood products. A small or larger cavity will typically be the residuum of an old hematoma (Fig. 12-16).

Blood within the vascular system is in the oxyhemoglobin state. When it is extruded into a clot, deoxygenation changes it to deoxyhemoglobin (Gomori 1986). With MR, on T_1WI the deoxyhemoglobin is hypointense to isointense (Fig. 12-17), while on T_2WI it is markedly hypointense (a susceptibility effect) (Fig. 12-18) (Gomori 1985*b*). *Susceptibility* refers to the inherent magnetic fields within the different tissues that constitute the brain. Intact red blood cells containing deoxyhemoglobin have a susceptibility different from that of the surrounding extracellular fluid. A proton that is exposed to the varying local fields, one due to intracellular deoxyhemoglobin, or one due to surrounding extracellular fluid has its spin thrown out of phase so that it does not give back a signal. This susceptibility effect appears as an area of blackness on the MR study. Deoxyhemoglobin is subsequently oxidized to methemoglobin. Evidence of this is seen about 3 days after the formation of the hematoma. It appears as a high signal intensity on T_1WI (Fig. 12-19), first at the periphery of the hematoma. Unpaired electrons in methemoglobin produce a paramagnetic T_1 shortening effect (Schnall 1987). At this point the red blood cell membrane is still intact, containing intracellular methemoglobin within it. Because the inherent fields within the cell differ from the field surrounding it, the susceptibility effect is found on T_2WI. Thus, the hematoma appears black on T_2WI. Subsequently, the red blood cell membrane dies as a result of failure of nutrient supply. With the rupture of the red blood cell membranes, a solution of methemoglobin is formed which is bright on both T_1WI and T_2WI (Zimmerman 1986*b*).

Intracellular methemoglobin is found first around 3 days after the formation of a hematoma. The formation

A

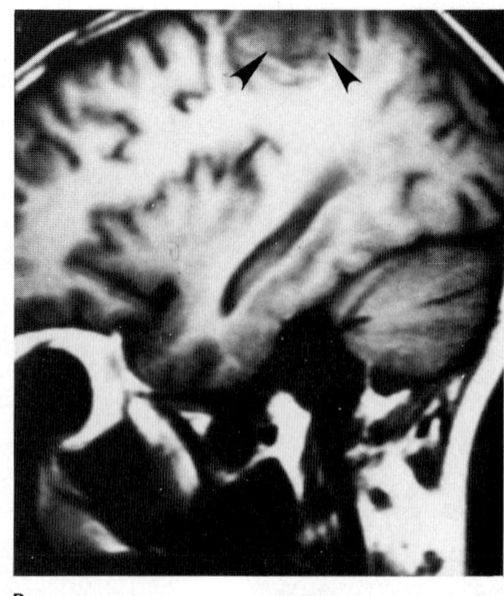

B

Figure 12-17 Acute intracerebral hematoma. **A.** Axial CT shows a high-density parietal hematoma (arrowheads). **B.** Sagittal T_1-weighted image shows a slightly hypointense hematoma (arrowheads) composed of deoxyhemoglobin.

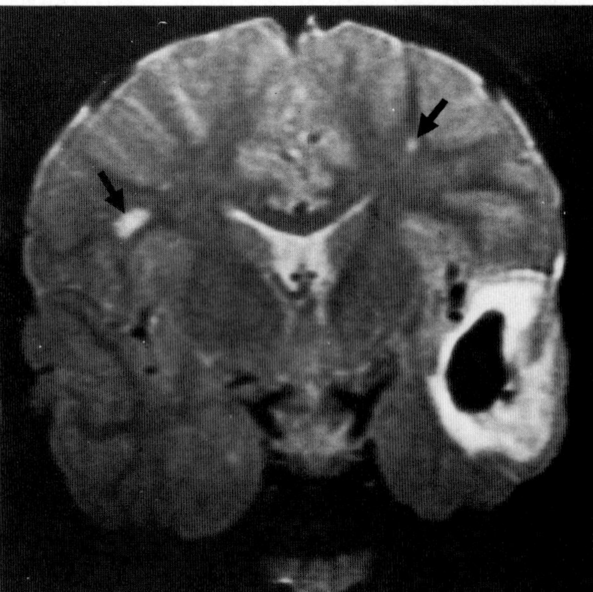

Figure 12-18 A 5-year-old male involved in a motor vehicle accident, suffering from intracerebral hematoma and diffuse axonal injury. Coronal T_2-weighted image shows a left temporal lobe hematoma that is markedly hypointense, surrounded by high-signal-intensity edema. The hypointense hematoma consists of deoxyhemoglobin, methemoglobin, or both. A T_1-weighted image is needed to determine whether it is deoxyhemoglobin or methemoglobin. Two areas of high signal intensity (arrows) are present in the frontal white matter and are consistent with areas of diffuse axonal injury.

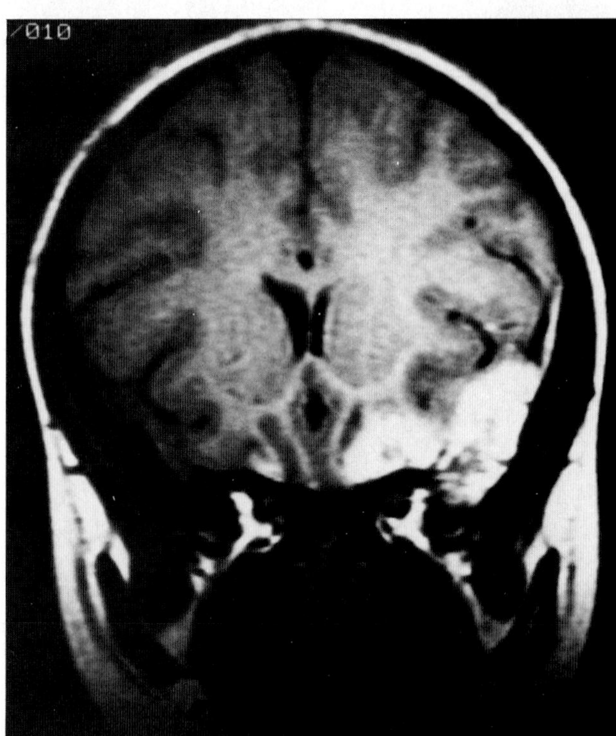

Figure 12-19 Contrecoup hemorrhagic contusions in the methemoglobin state. Coronal T_1-weighted image shows a predominantly left-sided subfrontal and anterior temporal high-signal-intensity peripheral cortical hemorrhagic contusion. A small contusion is present in the right inferior frontal lobe.

of intracellular methemoglobin progresses from the periphery of the hematoma centrally (Zimmerman 1985). Extracellular methemoglobin is found about the end of the first week. Deoxyhemoglobin within the center of the hematoma may persist for weeks. Macrophages are mobilized and move in to digest the hematoma. As a result of the ingestion of the blood products, hemosiderin is found within the lysosomes of the macrophage (Gomori 1985*a*). Hemosiderin within the lysosome again creates a susceptibility effect that makes the area of hemosiderin black on T_2WI (Fig. 12-20). It is found within the brain tissue at sites of traumatic bleeding, perhaps for the rest of the patient's life. Extracellular methemoglobin has been found months to years after an injury but is eventually reabsorbed. MR can demonstrate subacute and old bleeding when CT is no longer able to show such blood products (Zimmerman 1989).

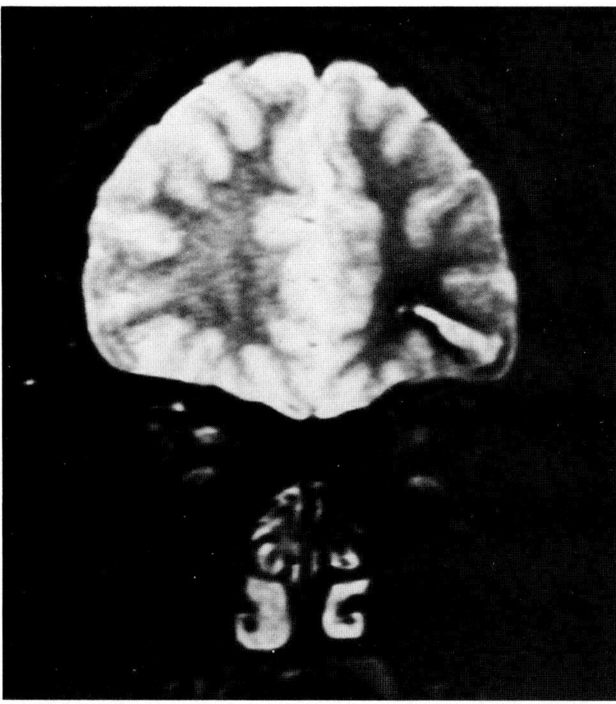

Figure 12-20 Old hematoma cavity lined by hemosiderin and filled with high-signal-density fluid. Coronal T_2-weighted image shows a left inferior frontal hematoma cavity that is old, with the hematoma having been reabsorbed. The cavity is lined by hemosiderin which is markedly hypointense. Hemosiderin and ferritin extend into the surrounding white matter, producing hypointensity. The cavity is filled with high-signal-intensity fluid.

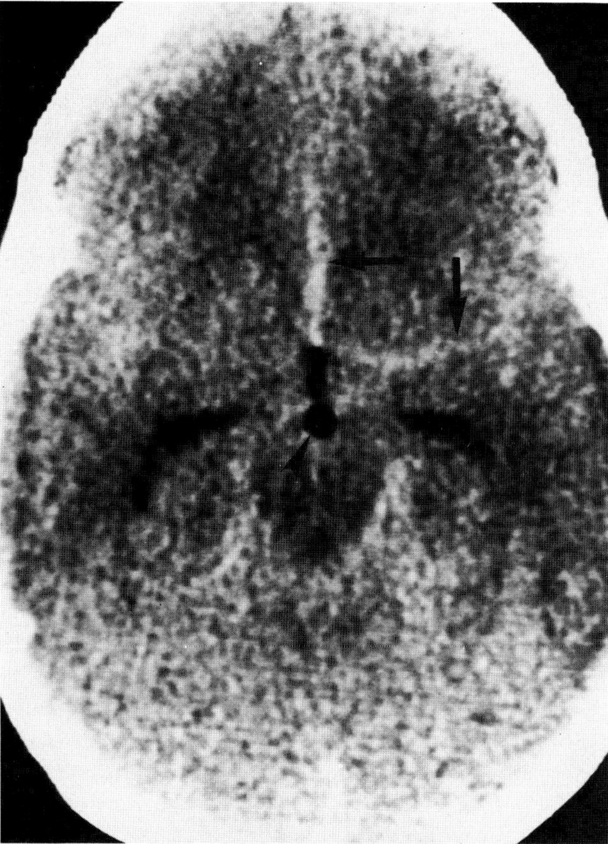

Figure 12-21 Subarachnoid hemorrhage. Axial non-contrast-enhanced CT shows increased density (arrows) in the interhemispheric fissure between the frontal lobes. Note that there is a drop of subarachnoid air (arrowhead) in the intrapeduncular cistern. The temporal horns are slightly enlarged, consistent with early hydrocephalus.

SUBARACHNOID HEMORRHAGE

Subarachnoid hemorrhage occurs as a result of injury to surface vessels, veins, and arteries on the pia or the arachnoidal meninges and as a result of cerebral laceration associated with contusion (Zimmerman 1986*a*). Rupture of an intracerebral hematoma into the ventricular system with dissemination of blood through the intraventricular fluid to the fourth ventricle, exiting through the foramina of Magendie and Luschka, is another source of subarachnoid hemorrhage (Zimmerman 1986*a*). Hemorrhage within the subarachnoid space may be focal or diffuse, with the diffuse form being more common in rupture of an aneurysm than it is in head injury. In our experience, after injury subarachnoid blood has often been focal, overlying the area of contusion or found in the interhemispheric fissure along the falx cerebri (Dolinskas 1978).

CT is the procedure of choice in identifying the radiographic findings of a subarachnoid hemorrhage because blood that occupies the full thickness of a CT slice shows the increased density as a distinct area of brightness (Fig. 12-21). When the blood lies parallel to the plane of the slice, it occupies only a part of the volume. Thus, there is volume averaging of the blood with brain, a process that tends to obscure the presence of a subarachnoid hemorrhage. The normal falx may be slightly dense and may be even calcified or ossified, and so it may be mistaken for a parafalcine subarachnoid hemorrhage (Osborn 1980). The increased density of the falx and its calcification and ossification are normal findings in older adolescents and adults. When a subarachnoid hemorrhage is present along the falx, it typically disappears over the ensuing week (Dolinskas 1978). In our experience with children, the incidence of subarachnoid hemorrhage as seen on CT increases with the increasing severity of a head injury.

When the patient is examined long after the initial trauma, blood in the subarachnoid space may have decreased in density to isodense so that the subarachnoid spaces appear obliterated (but are not), or it may have decreased to a point where the sulci and cisterns appear to be of CSF density. Thus, subarachnoid hemorrhage is difficult to appreciate when the CT study is done more than several days after a trauma. A complication of subarachnoid hemorrhage—fibroblastic proliferation within the subarachnoid space and the arachnoid villi—may lead to the production of communicating hydrocephalus.

Intraventricular blood can produce ependymitis, which can obstruct the aqueduct of Sylvius or the outlets of the fourth ventricle, leading to obstructive hydrocephalus.

Subarachnoid hemorrhage is poorly demonstrated or not shown at all on MR. Oxyhemoglobin is not paramagnetic and does not produce a change in signal intensity. Blood in the subarachnoid space may remain in the oxyhemoglobin state for a longer period than it does in the brain parenchyma. This is thought to occur because of higher oxygen tension in CSF (Kemp 1986). Flowing blood that is not clotted is not seen. Blood that is clotted and has undergone clot retraction may be seen subacutely as an area of high-signal-intensity methemoglobin on T_1WI (Bradley 1984).

CONTUSIONS

A contusion is a bruise of the surface of the brain. The apex of the gyrus is damaged from its outer surface inward to its junction with the white matter and beyond. The degree of involvement of subcortical white matter is variable. The mechanism of contusion has been classically subdivided into two types: coup and contrecoup (Gurdjian 1976). A coup contusion occurs when an object impacts on the stationary head so that the overlying calvarium moves inward, physically distorting the contiguous brain tissue (Fig. 12-1). As a result, petechial hemorrhages and torn capillaries, along with evidence of mechanical damage to adjacent neurons, are found. Contrecoup contusions are produced at a site remote from the point of initial impact. For this to occur, the brain has to be set in motion relative to the calvarium. Thus, the site of the contusion occurs at a point remote from the site of the initial impact. With a blow to one temporal region, a contrecoup contusion of the opposite temporal lobe may occur (Fig. 12-22*C*). With a fall on the occiput, contrecoup contusions are often found in the anterior temporal lobes and inferior frontal lobes (Fig. 12-22*D* and *E*). It is possible to have a mixture of coup and contrecoup lesions in the same patient. Coup contusions occur most frequently in the frontal and temporal regions, and contrecoup lesions occur most often in the inferior frontal, anterior temporal, and lateral temporal lobes.

Contusions are examined by means of two diagnostic radiological methods: CT and MR. With CT, contusions may produce a high-density (hemorrhagic) or low-density (nonhemorrhagic or hemorrhagic with partial voluming of hemorrhagic elements with necrotic or edematous brain) area of mass effect (Figs. 12-1, 12-8*A*, and 12-14*A*). Depressed fractures, which frequently accompany a coup contusion, are usually well seen on CT, especially when bone windows are done (Fig. 12-8*B*). The problem with CT is in recognizing small superficial contusions when a thin stripe of high-density cortical blood lies next to high-density bone. Beam-hardening artifacts may obscure blood on the surface of the brain adjacent to bone. Contusions of the parietal vertex and inferior temporal lobe may be partially volumed with contiguous bone on the axial slice, resulting in an overall bony density that obscures the presence of the contusion (Fig. 12-22*A*). Unless coronal images are obtained, such contusions are frequently missed. Wider windows than are customary for examination of brain tissue are also effective in separating blood from adjacent bone and should be utilized when there is a possibility of superficial hemorrhagic contusions.

The single most frequent traumatic hemorrhagic parenchymal lesion seen on CT is a hemorrhagic contusion (Zimmerman 1978*a*). In a series of 286 head injuries, hemorrhagic contusions were present in 21.3 percent and multiple in 29 percent (Koo 1977). Thirty-nine percent of these patients with contusions had other significant focal mass effects, such as subdural hematomas.

MR is an ideal way of examining the brain for the presence or absence of hemorrhagic contusions (Zimmerman 1986*b*). Acutely, hemorrhagic contusions consist of swollen necrotic cortical tissue that contains blood elements in the deoxyhemoglobin state. An acute hemorrhagic contusion is not easily recognized on T_1WI, but on T_2WI the hypointensity of the deoxyhemoglobin and the surrounding high signal intensity of the vasogenic edema characterize the lesion (Fig. 12-18) (Zimmerman 1986*b*). Subacutely, several days after injury, hemorrhagic contusions are even more easily identified on MR (Figs. 12-19 and 12-22*B*) because of oxidation of deoxyhemoglobin to methemoglobin (Zimmerman 1986*b*). Intracellular methemoglobin is high in signal intensity on T_1WI and low in signal intensity on T_2WI. The T_1WI appearance makes identification easy. Differentiating the hemorrhagic areas from the surrounding edema is not possible on T_1WI but is obvious on T_2WI because of the contrast between the hyperintense signal of the surrounding edema and the hypointense signal of the intracellular methemoglobin. When the red blood cell membrane breaks down, a solution of extracellular methemoglobin is formed that is uniformly high in signal intensity on both T_1WI and T_2WI. At this point it is no longer possible to differentiate the edema from the methemoglobin on T_2WI. By comparing T_1WI and T_2WI, one can still evaluate the extent of the surrounding edema.

The neuropathological changes that occur in a hemorrhagic contusion as it undergoes resolution can be correlated with imaging studies (Koo 1977). Four distinct phases occur, the first of which is the acute damage. The second phase is liquefaction of the contusion with the development of edema. The softening and swelling that result from edema formation occur between the third

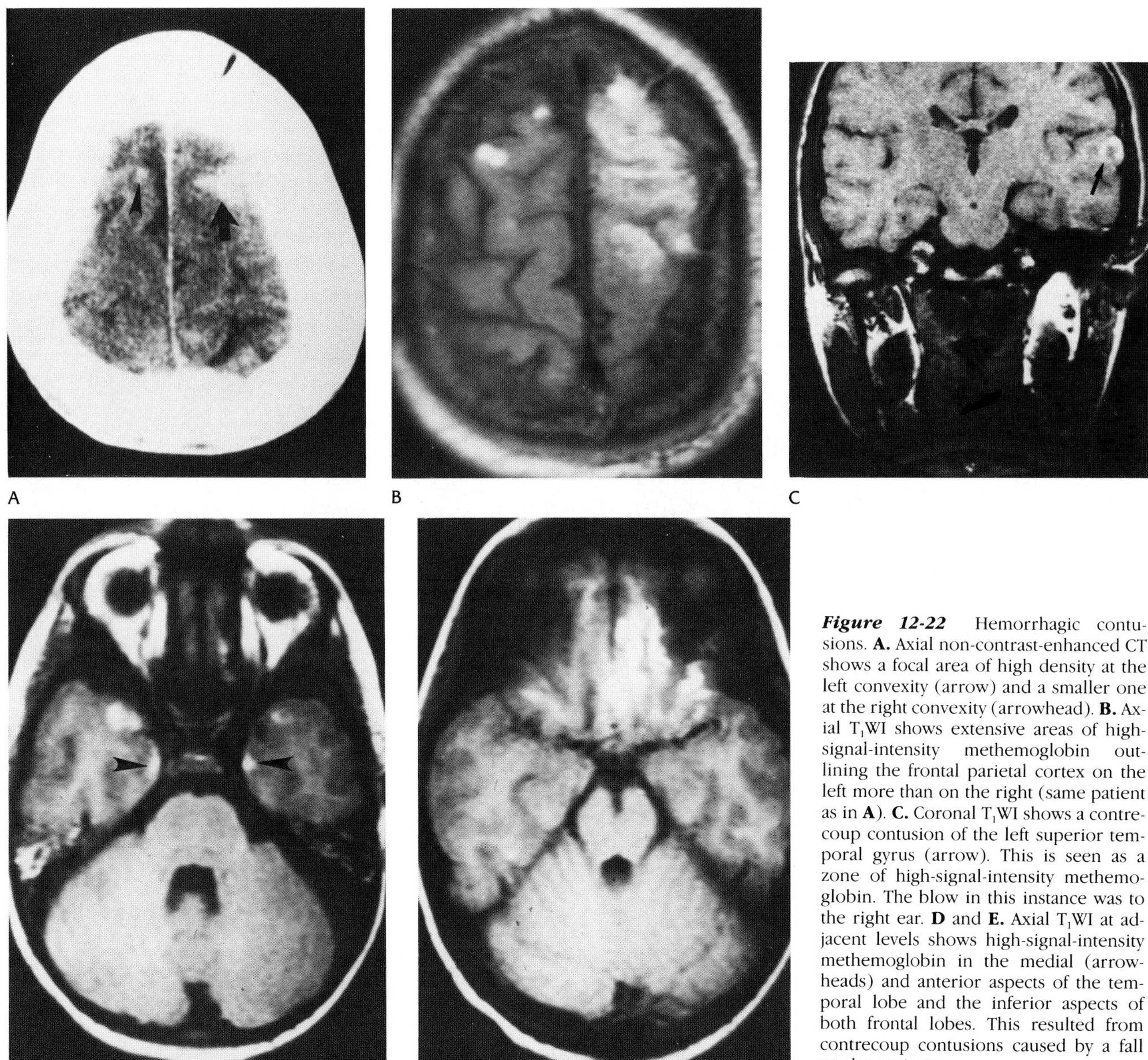

Figure 12-22 Hemorrhagic contusions. **A.** Axial non-contrast-enhanced CT shows a focal area of high density at the left convexity (arrow) and a smaller one at the right convexity (arrowhead). **B.** Axial T_1WI shows extensive areas of high-signal-intensity methemoglobin outlining the frontal parietal cortex on the left more than on the right (same patient as in **A**). **C.** Coronal T_1WI shows a contrecoup contusion of the left superior temporal gyrus (arrow). This is seen as a zone of high-signal-intensity methemoglobin. The blow in this instance was to the right ear. **D** and **E.** Axial T_1WI at adjacent levels shows high-signal-intensity methemoglobin in the medial (arrowheads) and anterior aspects of the temporal lobe and the inferior aspects of both frontal lobes. This resulted from contrecoup contusions caused by a fall on the occiput.

and seventh days after injury. It is at this time that the hemorrhagic components are converted from deoxyhemoglobin to methemoglobin and the T_1WI MR signal intensity changes. Also at this time, the admixture of edema with hemorrhage produces on CT a volume averaging that may appear as an area of decreased density at the site of contusion (Koo 1977). This depends on the relative proportions of globin and water within the tissue. At this point in time the swelling and edema that are produced result in increased mass effect, and thus there is danger of developing cerebral herniation.

The third phase is repair, during which macrophages remove the blood elements and the damaged tissue and new blood vessels proliferate around the area of healing. The new vessels lack tight endothelial junctures, and so a blood-brain barrier (BBB) disturbance is present. At this point the mass effect is decreasing, as is the edema. With both CT and MR, if a contrast agent is given, enhancement analogous to that seen with a cerebral infarct occurs at the margin of the contusion (Fig. 12-23) (Koo 1977). On CT, the area of contusion continues to decrease in density and the mass effect lessens. On MR, the high signal intensity of the methemoglobin persists but the surrounding edema may decrease. The presence of hemosiderin within the lysosomes of the macrophages and the susceptibility effect that it produces on T_2WI are seen as a rim of hypointensity outlining portions of the hemorrhagic contusion (Fig. 12-24*C*).

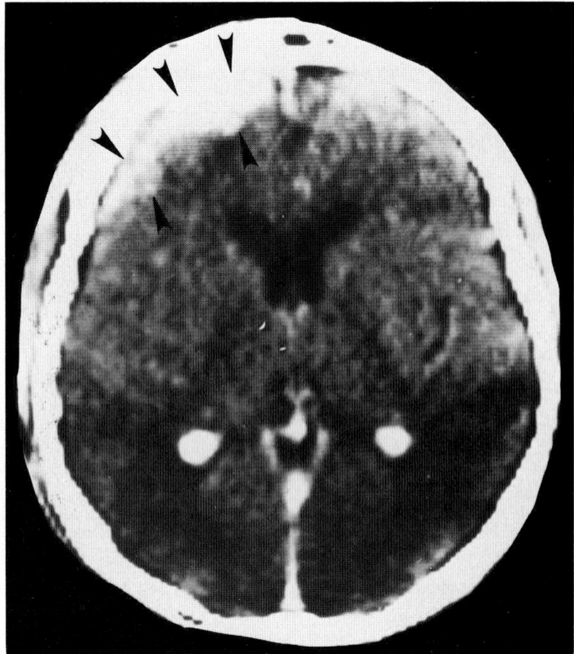

Figure 12-23 Contrast-enhancing contusion. Axial postcontrast CT shows enhancement (arrowheads) in the right frontal lobe. The patient had been involved in an accident 3 weeks before and at surgery was found to have a subacute contusion of the frontal lobe.

A fourth stage of neuropathological evolution takes place in which the necrotic tissue is sloughed and cystic cavities are formed. This takes place over the ensuing 6 to 12 months. The superficially contused brain may be sloughed into the CSF pathways so that an irregular surface of the contused portions of the hemisphere results. CT shows an area of decreased density within the brain parenchyma, often with enlargement of the overlying CSF spaces (Fig. 12-24*B*), a decrease in size of the cortical gyri, and an enlargement of the adjacent underlying ventricle (Koo 1977). MR shows the encephalomalacia as an irregular surface with hypointense cortex on T_1WI; this surface becomes higher in signal intensity than a normal brain is on T_2WI (Fig. 12-24*B* and *C*). Ultimately, dense fibroglial scars are formed and involve the surface of the gyri, possibly extending quite deep into the white matter. The walls of cystic cavities contain gliosis and scarring with hemosiderin.

Intracerebral Hematoma

Large intracerebral hematomas occur in a distribution similar to that of contusions in that they are mostly frontal and temporal. They may be related to hemorrhagic contusions into which bleeding has occurred with clot formation, with the clot dissecting through the white matter, or may arise from the rupture of a penetrating vessel deep within the white matter (Zimmerman 1984). Once bleeding begins, blood dissects between the white matter axons and the hematoma is formed, subsequently undergoing clot formation and retraction. During the active phase of dissection of blood through the white matter, the blood may rupture through the ependyma into the ventricle (Zimmerman 1978*a*). The frequency of intracerebral hematomas is lower than that of hemorrhagic contusions. It has been reported to be relatively low (5 percent) (Koo 1977), but when it is present, there is an associated high incidence of other traumatic lesions, such

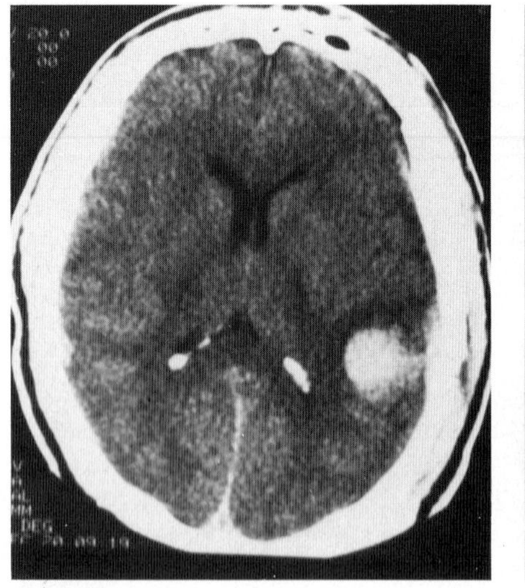

A

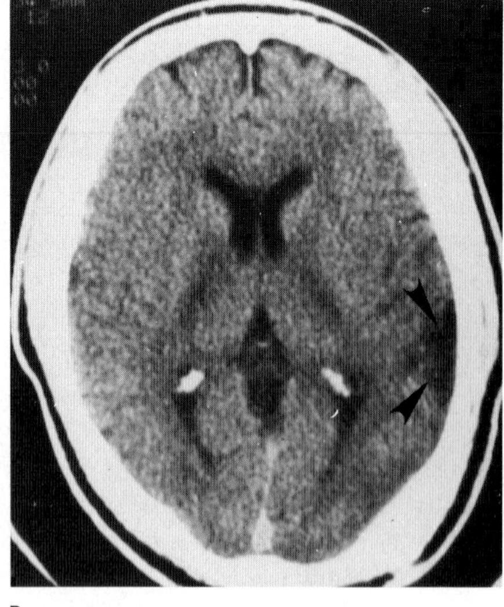

B

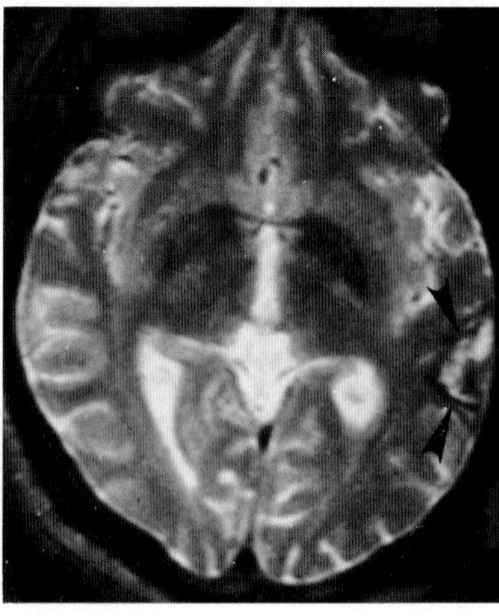

C

Figure 12-24 Resolving hemorrhagic contusion in the left posterior temporal lobe. **A.** Axial CT at the time of an acute injury shows a high-density hematoma at the site of a coup contusion. **B.** Follow-up CT examination 1 year later shows a loss of cortical tissue (arrowheads) at the site of the contusion and reabsorption of the blood products. **C.** T_2-weighted image at the same slice location shows encephalomalacia and hemosiderin (arrowheads).

as subdural hematomas and/or epidural hematomas (56 percent) (Zimmerman 1978*a*). Traumatic intracerebral hematomas appear to occur more frequently in adults than they do in children. Intraventricular extension was found in a CT series of traumatic cases in one-third of the intracerebral hematomas studied (Zimmerman 1978*a*).

Most intracerebral hematomas are visible on CT immediately after trauma. They are hyperdense, measuring from 50 to 100 Hounsfield units (Dolinskas 1977), and may be found to have a surrounding rim of hypodensity caused by extravasated serum from a retracting clot. Subsequently, during the week after the formation of the hematoma, edema develops around the hematoma, extending through the white matter pathways and increasing the mass effect. While most intracerebral hematomas are demonstrated on the initial day of injury, a small percentage develop in a delayed fashion, appearing 1 to 7 days after the injury (Dolinskas 1977). These hematomas occur most often at the site of contusion or the site of parenchymal ischemia. They are found most often in the frontotemporal and temporal regions. A factor in the formation of delayed intracerebral hematoma may be the removal by surgery of an intracranial mass such as a subdural hematoma. It has been hypothesized that in these instances the removed hematoma produced a tamponade effect on a torn vessel and the removal of the tamponading mass allowed the vessel to rebleed. Vascular necrosis may also result from tissue lactate acidosis or ischemia of a blood vessel wall as a result of spasm. A delayed intracerebral hematoma is an important and treatable cause of secondary deterioration after head injury (Zimmerman 1986*a*).

In the weeks after hematoma formation, the hematoma decreases in size and density because of chemical breakdown of the globin molecule (Dolinskas 1977). At some point the density of the hematoma on CT will approximate that of the adjacent brain. Usually the decrease in mass effect does not correspond to the decrease in density (Dolinskas 1977). Thus, while the hematoma may not be apparent as a density difference, the mass effect persists (Fig. 12-15*B*). New vessel formation occurs in the tissue surrounding the hematoma; new vessels lack a tight endothelial juncture, and as a result, when a contrast agent is injected, there is enhancement of a rim of tissue surrounding the hematoma (Zimmerman 1986*a*). With CT, when a previous study is not available or the history is not helpful, this may be useful in identifying a subacute hematoma that is isodense. On MR, an intracerebral hematoma has the same signal intensity characteristics that are described in the section on hemorrhagic contusion.

Thus, when the clot is no longer visible on CT, it is highly visible on MR. Exactly how long the clot will remain visible on MR is uncertain, but we have followed a patient for over 4 years, during which time we have seen residual high-signal-intensity methemoglobin on T_1WI. Macrophages that carry off blood breakdown products produce hemosiderin, giving the rim of the hematoma cavity a hypointense signal intensity on T_2WI. Follow-up MR studies show that the hematoma cavity decreases in size with time, just as follow-up CT studies show a subsequent CSF density residuum. Frequently, with both techniques there is a demonstration of overlying cortical sulcal enlargement and adjacent ventricular dilatation, changes that correlate with parenchymal brain damage from injury.

Diffuse Axonal Injury or Shearing Injury

When one cerebral hemisphere is put in motion relative to the other, shearing stresses are produced along the courses of the white matter axons that connect the two hemispheres. As a result of these stresses, disruption of axons occurs, along with the rupture of the small accompanying blood vessels (Zimmerman 1978*c*). This type of injury occurs most often among drivers and passengers in high-speed motor vehicle accidents. Often the patient is rendered comatose at the time of the accident, undergoes emergency imaging evaluation, and is hospitalized for a prolonged period, not infrequently in a persistent vegetative state that may last months or years and often necessitates institutionalization (Zimmerman 1978*c*). A CT examination may be unremarkable, may show some degree of cerebral swelling, or may show small focal

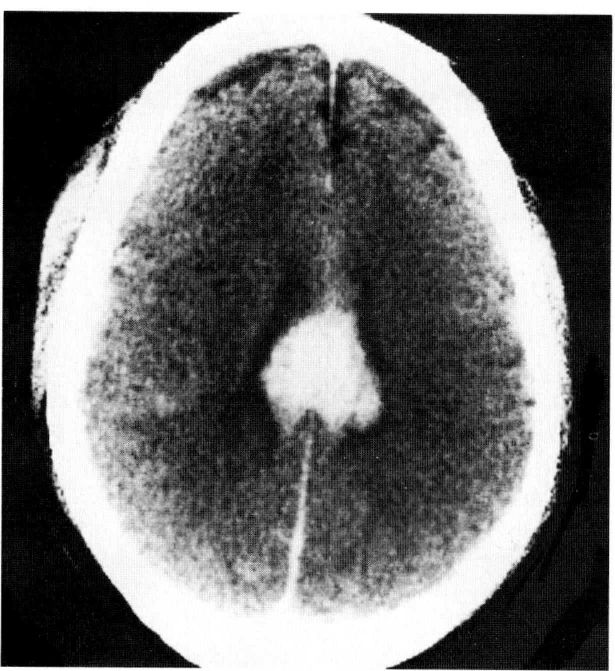

Figure 12-25 Shearing injury with corpus callosal hemorrhage. Axial non-contrast-enhanced CT shows a high-density hemorrhage within the posterior portion of the corpus callosum.

hemorrhages (Fig. 12-26) or even more extensive injury (Zimmerman 1978*c*). Characteristically, the lesions in diffuse axonal injury (DAI) occur in four sites: (1) corpus callosum (Figs. 12-25 and 12-26*C*), (2) corticomedullary junctures, (3) upper brainstem (Fig. 12-26*B*), and (4) basal ganglia (Strich 1961). Axonal tears occur not only where the hemorrhages are found but throughout the white matter as well (Gentry 1988). CT can show only the hemorrhagic component and the brain swelling that may accompany it. The presence of a small amount of intraventricular blood in the occipital horn of one or both ventricles should arouse suspicion that there has been a tear of the corpus callosum with transependymal extension of the bleeding. Often it is not possible to see small hemorrhages in the corpus callosum on CT.

MR has proved to be superior to CT in demonstrating findings consistent with DAI. The sites of disrupted axonal bundles that are unaccompanied by hemorrhage are shown by MR as zones of high-signal-intensity edema on T_2WI (Fig. 12-27) (Zimmerman 1986*b*; Gentry 1988). Depending on their chemical state, hemorrhages are shown at the classic locations in the corpus callosum, corticomedullary junctures, dorsal midbrain, and basal ganglia (Zimmerman 1988). The course of brain injury after DAI is one of secondary wallerian degeneration of torn axons (Zimmerman 1978*c*). As a result, brain atrophy occurs over months to years, with enlargement of the sulci and ventricles (Fig. 12-28). The white matter may be seen to undergo a loss of volume with scattered areas of high signal intensity on T_2WI at sites of wallerian degenera-

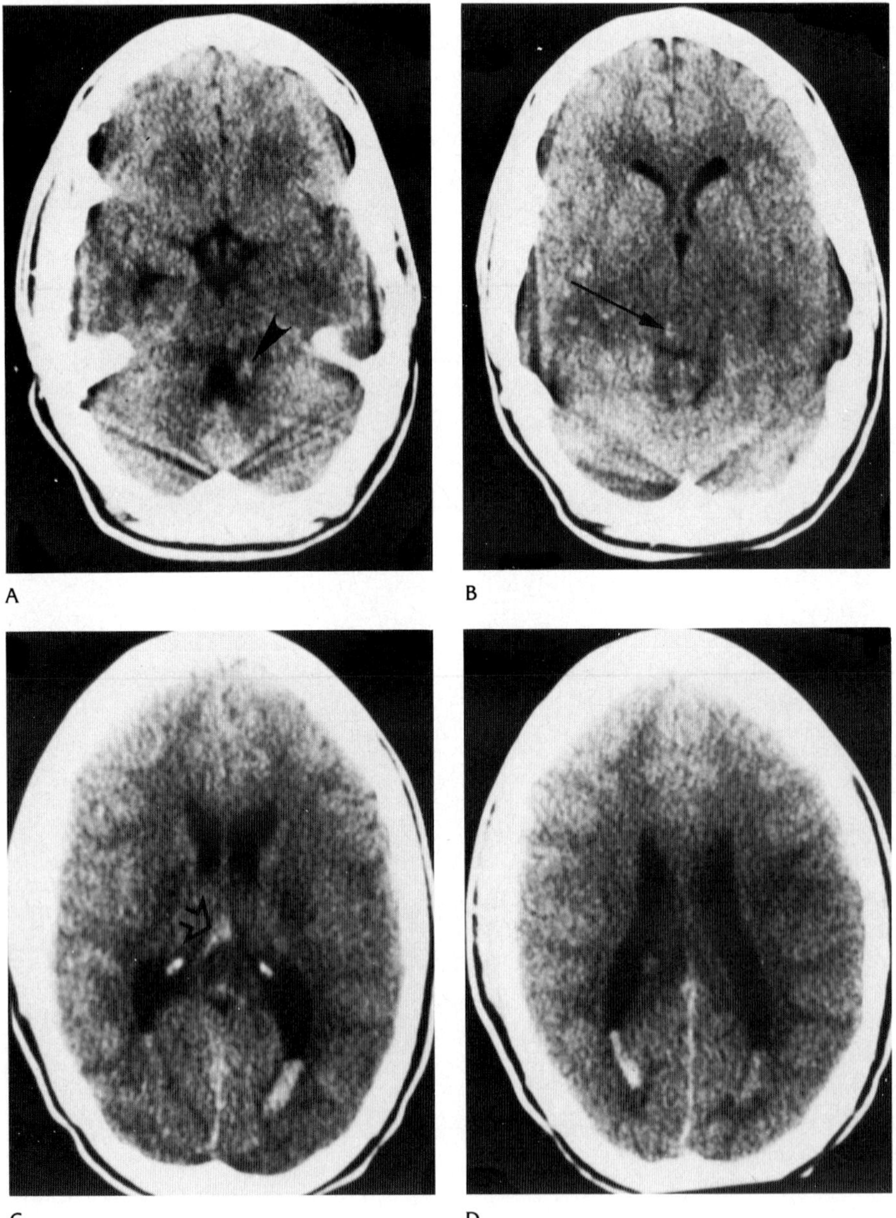

Figure 12-26 Shearing injury. **A–D.** Multiple axial CT scans show small focal areas of hemorrhage in the pons (arrowhead), midbrain (arrow), corpus callosum (open arrow), and both occipital horns of the lateral ventricles.

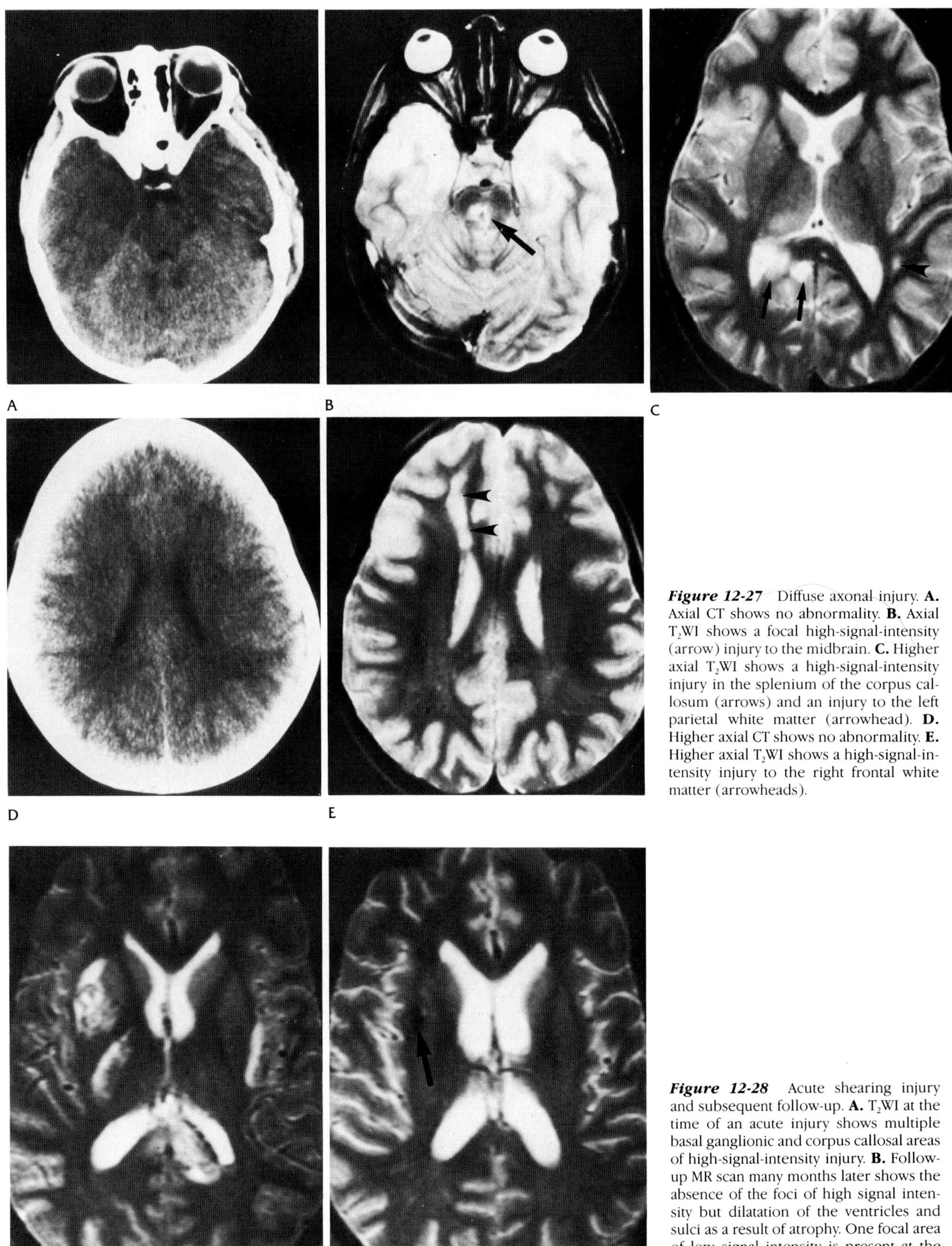

Figure 12-27 Diffuse axonal injury. **A.** Axial CT shows no abnormality. **B.** Axial T_2WI shows a focal high-signal-intensity (arrow) injury to the midbrain. **C.** Higher axial T_2WI shows a high-signal-intensity injury in the splenium of the corpus callosum (arrows) and an injury to the left parietal white matter (arrowhead). **D.** Higher axial CT shows no abnormality. **E.** Higher axial T_2WI shows a high-signal-intensity injury to the right frontal white matter (arrowheads).

Figure 12-28 Acute shearing injury and subsequent follow-up. **A.** T_2WI at the time of an acute injury shows multiple basal ganglionic and corpus callosal areas of high-signal-intensity injury. **B.** Follow-up MR scan many months later shows the absence of the foci of high signal intensity but dilatation of the ventricles and sulci as a result of atrophy. One focal area of low signal intensity is present at the site of an old hemorrhage (arrow).

tion. MR is particularly successful in examining a mystery patient who has been rendered comatose by a prior DAI. The atrophy, tears in the corpus callosum, and the presence of old blood products in the form of hemosiderin at characteristic sites help in making a diagnosis of a prior DAI (Fig. 12-28*B*).

Subdural Hematoma

The subdural space is a potential space that lies between the dura and the arachnoid. With trauma, tearing, and separation of the arachnoid from the dura, there may be associated bleeding and hematoma formation. Hematomas within the subdural space are classified as either acute or chronic. Posttraumatic subdural collections may be filled with CSF when there is a tear in the arachnoid so that CSF dissects between the arachnoid and dura. A CSF-filled collection of this type is called a *subdural hygroma.* In general, acute and chronic subdural hematomas and subdural hygromas differ in their history, their significance, and often their pattern of resolution (Zimmerman 1986*a*).

ACUTE SUBDURAL HEMATOMAS

Acute subdural hematomas follow acute trauma, becoming manifest within hours after injury. They are often associated with an underlying brain injury. The damage to the cerebral substance results not only from the mass effect produced by the clot in the subdural space but also from the brain injury and swelling that accompany it. Despite modern methods of treatment, acute subdural hematomas associated with parenchymal brain injury, most often in the form of an intracerebral hematoma or contusion, continue to carry significant morbidity and mortality (Fobben 1989). On CT, an acute subdural hematoma is seen as a peripheral collection of blood-density clot lying between the inner table and the cerebral hemisphere (Figs. 12-2 and 12-29). Subdural hematomas tend to extend around the hemisphere from front to back and frequently extend around the occipital pole or frontal pole into the inner hemispheric fissure, under the temporal lobe to the floor of the middle cranial fossa, or under the occipital lobe onto the tentorium (Fig. 12-30) (Zimmerman 1986*a*). The full extent of the clot and the space that it occupies intracranially reduce the amount of space available for the brain within the cranial vault. In addition, there is a further decrease in intracranial volume as a result of the associated brain injury (Fig. 12-29) and swelling, which also raise the intracranial pressure, leading to herniation or impaired cerebral perfusion. Surgery is utilized to decrease the size of an acute subdural hematoma. However, the degree of mass effect postoperatively may be larger than it is preoperatively because parenchymal injury has become more manifest (Zimmerman 1978*a*). Residual blood left after the evacuation of an acute subdural hematoma is usually reabsorbed gradually. With reabsorption of the hematoma and resolution of the sites of parenchymal brain injury, evidence of focal ventricular and sulcal enlargement is commonly seen (Zimmerman 1978*a*).

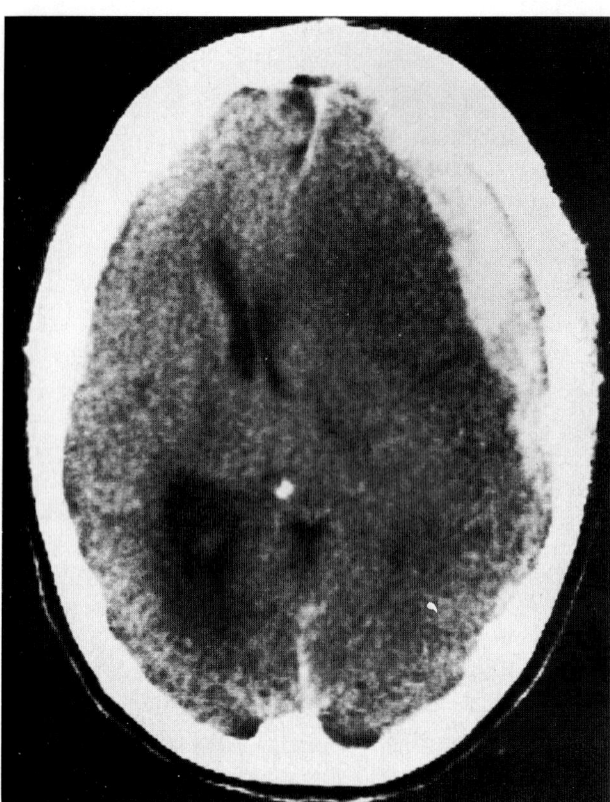

Figure 12-29 Acute subdural hematoma. Axial non-contrast-enhanced CT shows a peripheral high-density extracerebral collection within the subdural space that compresses and displaces the left cerebral hemisphere. There is a subfallaceal midline shift. The falx is bent to the right. The pineal gland, which is calcified, is shifted. There is hypodensity in the underlying left cerebral hemisphere, notably below the region of the subdural hematoma.

Acute subdural hematomas may be found primarily within the interhemispheric fissure (Fig. 12-31). While these hematomas may extend peripherally onto the convexity, they are frequently kept localized by the binding down of the subdural space by the arachnoid granulations that parallel the superior sagittal sinus. It is thought that a proportion of these interhemispheric subdural hematomas are derived from the rupture of bridging veins. This is in contradistinction to more lateral acute subdural hematomas, which are more often due to arterial injury, or brain contusion and laceration. In our experience, interhemispheric subdural hematomas are seen in two situations: an older adult who undergoes a whiplash-type injury and an infant who undergoes a similar injury as a manifestation of child abuse. In both of these patient populations it is thought that the enlarged subarachnoid space contributes to excessive mobility of the brain

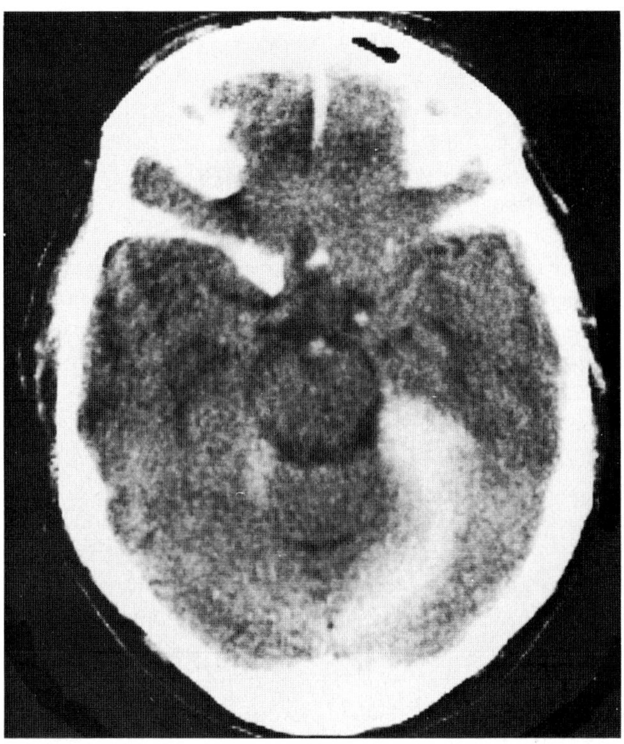
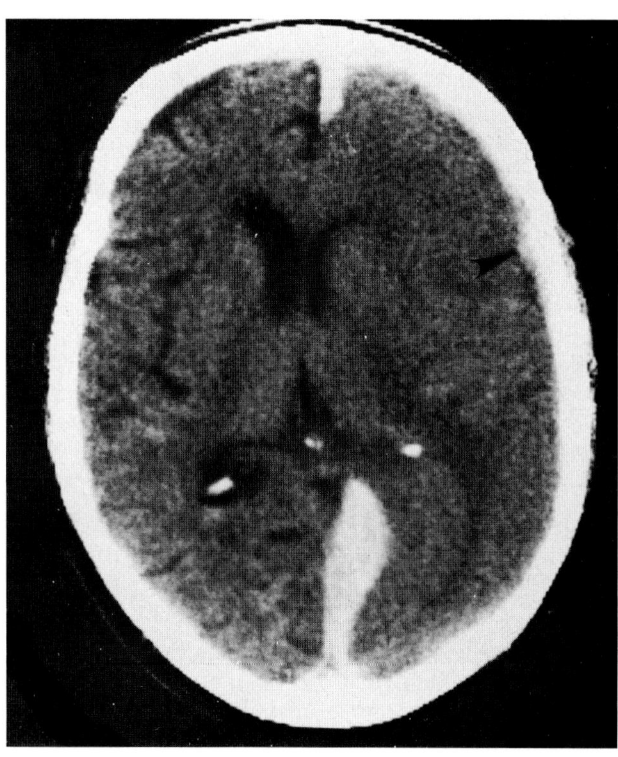

A B

Figure 12-30 Acute subdural hematoma. **A.** Axial CT at the level of the tentorium shows high-density blood conforming to the medial aspect of the tentorium, representing an infratemporal and infraoccipital extension of a subdural hematoma. **B.** A higher section shows a subdural hematoma in the interhemispheric fissure between the left occipital lobe and the falx as well as in the interhemispheric fissure between the left frontal lobe and the falx. There is a smear of subdural hematoma adjacent to the inner table of the skull (arrowhead).

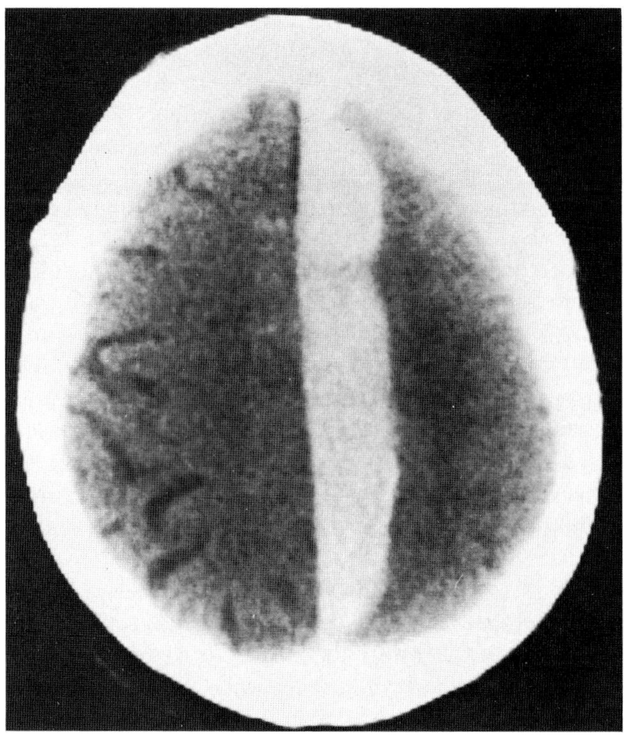

within the calvarium. When the brain moves at a rate of speed different from that of the calvarium and falx, its attachment by bridging cortical veins is disrupted (Zimmerman 1979), leading to interhemispheric subdural bleeding.

CT has limitations in showing thin subdural collections of blood that are against the inner table of the skull because of (1) beam-hardening artifacts that tend to obscure them, (2) brain windows in which the hematoma blends into the adjacent bone density (avoided by using intermediate windows) (Figs. 12-2 and 12-30*B*), and (3) extracerebral hematomas under the temporal and occipital lobes and those below the tentorium, as well as small subdurals over the convexity that are often obscured by volume averaging with adjacent bone (Zimmerman 1986*a*).

Figure 12-31 Parasagittal acute subdural hematoma. Axial noncontrast-enhanced CT shows a left parafalcine high-density collection of blood displacing the medial aspect of the left hemisphere laterally.

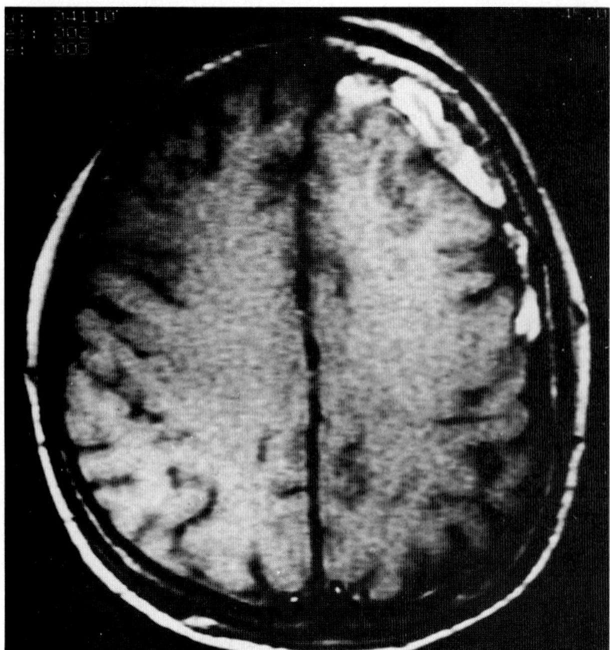

Figure 12-32 Acute subdural hematoma. Axial T_1WI shows high-signal-intensity methemoglobin in the left anterior subdural space, compressing the frontal gyri.

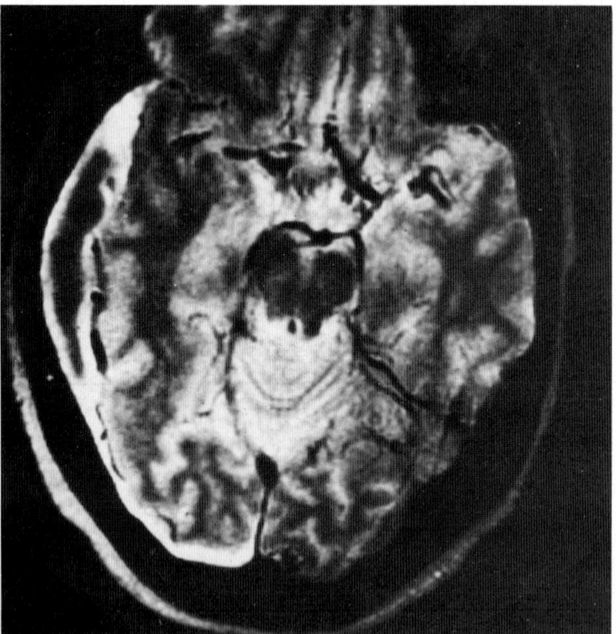

Figure 12-33 Acute subdural hematoma—MR findings. Axial T_2WI shows low-signal-intensity deoxyhemoglobin surrounded by high-signal-intensity extruded serum within the subdural space on the right side. Note that the temporal lobe is displaced medially.

MR has an advantage over CT in that direct multiplanar imaging is easily accomplished. This, together with the ability to show a subacute hemorrhage as high-signal-intensity methemoglobin, has distinct advantages in demonstrating subacute subdural hematomas. This occurs in part because the cortical bone does not produce a signal, so that the methemoglobin is seen unimpeded by bone (Fig. 12-32) (Zimmerman 1988). However, in the very acute phase, when the blood is in the deoxyhemoglobin state, recognition of a subdural hematoma is more difficult (Zimmerman 1986*b*). At that stage, displacement of the brain and extrusion of serum from the subdural hematoma become important criteria in identifying the subdural hematoma. Extruded serum comes to lie laterally between the clot and the inner table of the skull and medially next to the compressed arachnoid. The serum is high in signal intensity on T_2WI, while the deoxyhemoglobin is low in signal intensity (Fig. 12-33) (Zimmerman 1986*b*). With MR, there is a potential for differentiating the subdural hematoma from a subarachnoid hemorrhage and an epidural hematoma. This is predicated on the facts that subdural blood does not extend into the sulci and that the dura can be seen on MR as a thin hypointense stripe separating subdural from epidural blood (Zimmerman 1986*b*).

CHRONIC SUBDURAL HEMATOMA

The origin of a chronic subdural hematoma appears to be different from that of an acute one (Zimmerman 1984). It is thought that a chronic subdural hematoma is caused by a slow effusion of venous blood into the subdural space. As such, parenchymal brain injury is not found in association with chronic subdural hematomas (Dolinskas 1979). As a result of bleeding into the subdural space, a thick membrane develops on the dural side of the clot and a thinner membrane develops on the arachnoidal side. The dural component is usually vascular, and the vessels are fragile, making it a source of repeated episodes of rebleeding at the time of a relatively minor head injury. Often a patient with a chronic subdural hematoma does not give a history of trauma, and when it is recounted, the injury may be described as minor.

The CT appearance of a chronic subdural hematoma depends on the interval between the last major episode of bleeding and the current examination (Dolinskas 1979). Most often, blood within a chronic subdural hematoma has broken down to a point where the fluid appears to be low in density relative to the brain (Fig. 12-33). The high protein content of the fluid makes the density higher than that of CSF. When the patient is reexamined after an episode of rebleeding, the fluid collection may be increased in density in toto or in part (Fig. 12-34). Fresh blood elements within the hematoma tend to gravitate to the more dependent portions (Zimmerman 1986*a*). Fluid collections tend to conform to the configuration of the brain. Compartmentalization can occur within the hematoma with the formation of fibrous

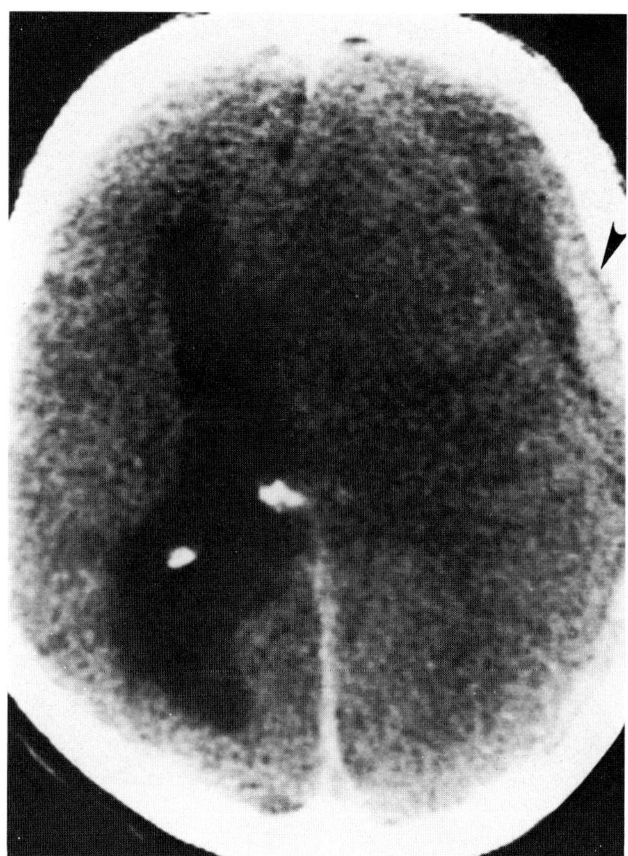

Figure 12-34 Chronic subdural hematoma. Axial non-contrast-enhanced CT shows a peripheral left frontal hypodense collection within the subdural space, consistent with a chronic subdural hematoma. Inferiorly and laterally within the collection there is a higher-density collection of acute rebleeding (arrowhead) within a loculation. There is a marked mass effect with subfallaceal shift of the ventricle.

septa. Rebleeding can occur into one compartment but not the other (Fig. 12-34).

Thus, a chronic subdural hematoma can be of low density, high density, isodensity, or mixed density. In isodense subdural hematomas, the breakdown of blood products has reached a stage where there is essentially no difference in the density of the hematoma and that of the adjacent brain (Naidich 1979). When they are unilateral and of sufficient size, isodense subdural hematomas, because of their displacement of the brain and ventricular system, do not present diagnostic problems. Bilateral chronic subdural hematomas may compress the brain and ventricular system so that the ventricles, while smaller than normal, remain in the midline (Fig. 12-35) (Naidich 1979). This type of chronic subdural hematoma can present diagnostic difficulties. Recognition of such a bilateral chronic subdural hematoma may be made via the observation that the ventricles and sulci are too small for a patient of that age (Fig. 12-36*A*) and that the cerebral white matter is displaced inward away from the inner table of the skull more than it should be (Fig. 12-36*A*), via contrast enhancement of a subdural membrane (Fig. 12-36*B*), or via recognition that enhanced cortical blood vessels are displaced inward away from the inner table of the skull (Fig. 12-35*B*) (Naidich 1979). Contrast media can be found layered in some chronic subdural hematomas hours after injection.

MR has revolutionized our ability to identify chronic subdural hematomas because with coronal imaging, the relationship between the brain and the inner table of the skull can be exquisitely demonstrated (Zimmerman 1988). When the brain is displaced from the inner table, the signal intensity of the item producing the displacement becomes critical. Chronic subdural hematomas may be seen as high-signal-intensity methemoglobin, as lower-signal-intensity proteinaceous fluid on T_1WI, or as being higher-than-CSF-in-signal-intensity proteinaceous fluid on proton density weighted images (PDWI) (Fig. 12-37*B*) (Fobben 1989). Gd-DTPA can be used to bring out subdural membranes as an area of increased contrast enhancement on T_1WI (Fig. 12-38). In fact, contrast may leak

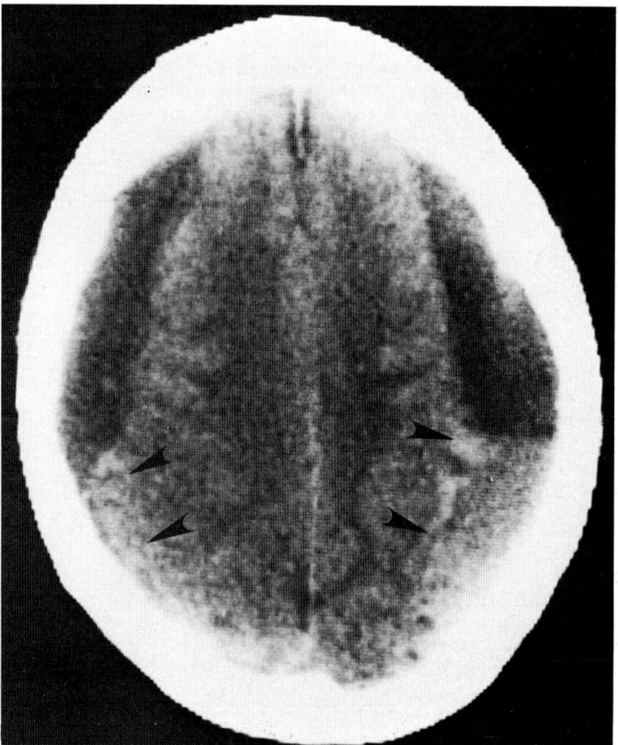

Figure 12-35 Bilateral chronic subdural hematomas. Axial CT without contrast shows bilateral peripheral extracerebral low-density collections displacing the brain inward. On both sides the lower portion of the collection (arrowheads) is of higher density than is the superior portion. This represents gravitational settling of blood breakdown products in the inferior aspect of the collection. Note that the gray matter and white matter are medially displaced and that there is no midline shift.

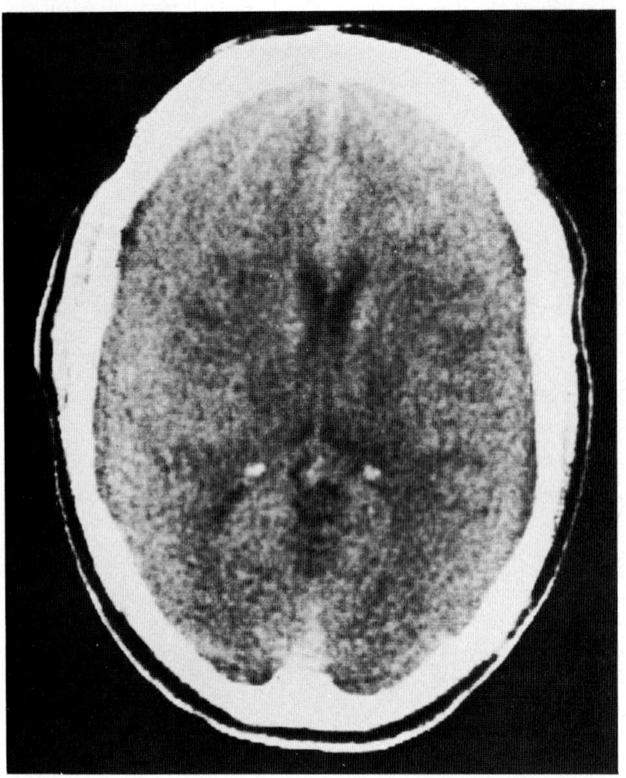

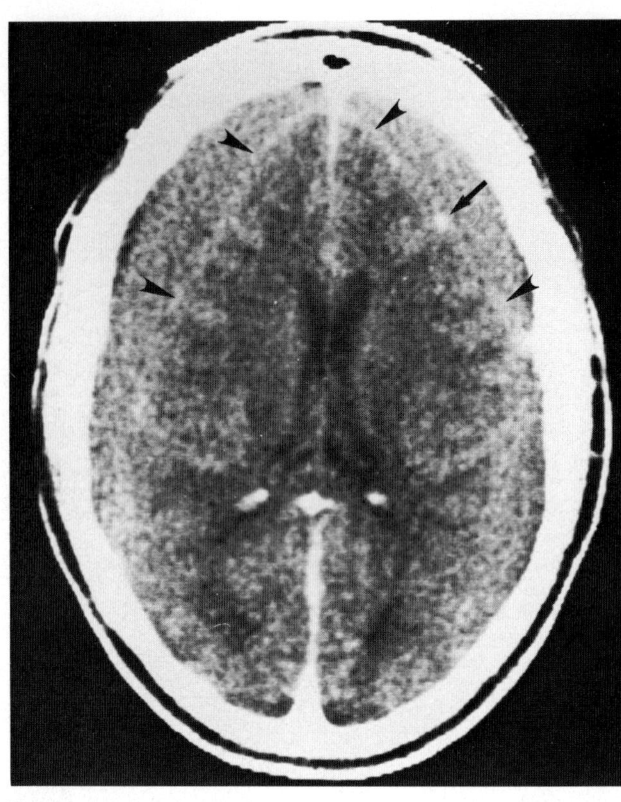

A B

Figure 12-36 Isodense chronic subdural hematomas. **A.** Axial CT without contrast enhancement shows bilateral isodense collections displacing the brain parenchyma inward. Note that the lateral ventricles are quite small for a 75-year-old patient. Note that the white matter is medially displaced. **B.** Axial CT after contrast enhancement shows a thin rim of enhancement of the subdural membrane (arrowheads) and inward displacement of a cortical vessel (arrow).

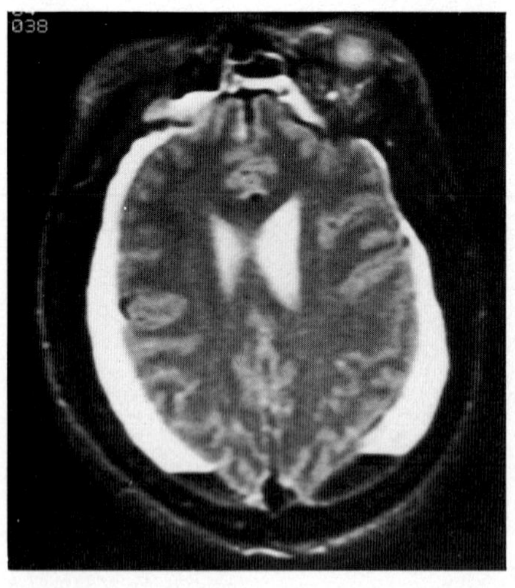

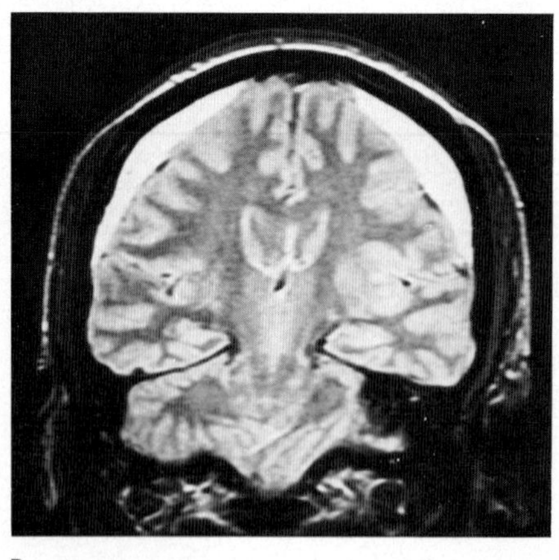

A B

Figure 12-37 MR of bilateral chronic subdural hematomas. **A.** Axial T_2WI shows high-signal-intensity peripheral collections displacing the brain inward. The inferior aspect of both collections has a hypointense or dependent fluid collection, creating an interface between the higher-signal-intensity proteinaceous fluid above and the lower-signal-intensity blood breakdown products below. **B.** Coronal PDWI shows that the fluid in the bilateral chronic subdurals is higher in signal intensity than is the CSF within the lateral ventricles.

into a subdural hematoma, increasing its overall signal intensity on T_1WI (Fig. 12-38*B*). Thus far, subdural hygromas have not shown membrane formation and have not enhanced with gadolinium. Subdural hygromas have behaved in the manner of a CSF-filled subdural space on CT and on T_1WI, PDWI, and T_2WI (Fig. 12-39).

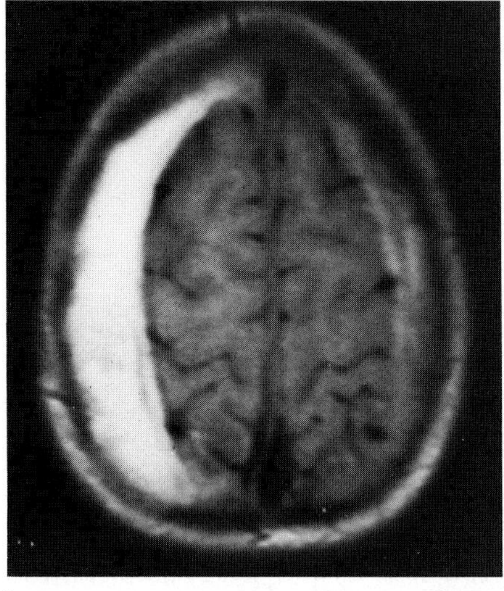
A

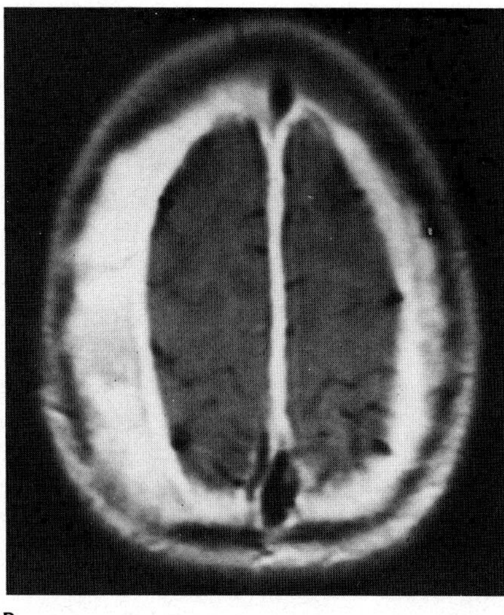
B

Figure 12-38 Bilateral chronic subdural hematomas. **A.** Axial T_1WI shows that the right subdural collection is higher in signal intensity (methemoglobin) than is the left subdural collection (proteinaceous fluid). **B.** Axial T_1WI after gadolinium injection shows enhancement of subdural membranes and higher signal intensity in the right and left subdural collections. This examination was done 1.5 minutes after the intravenous injection of gadolinium.

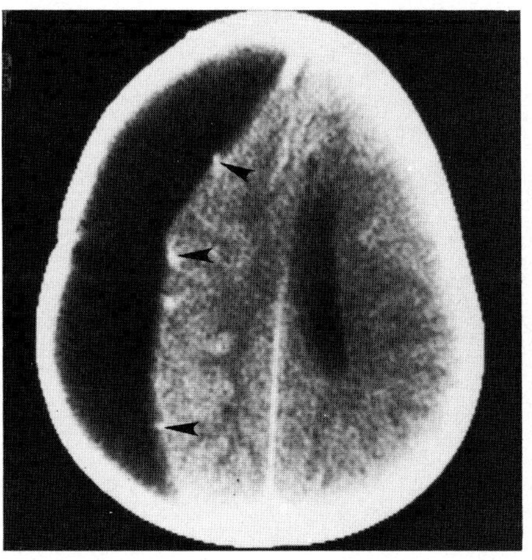
A

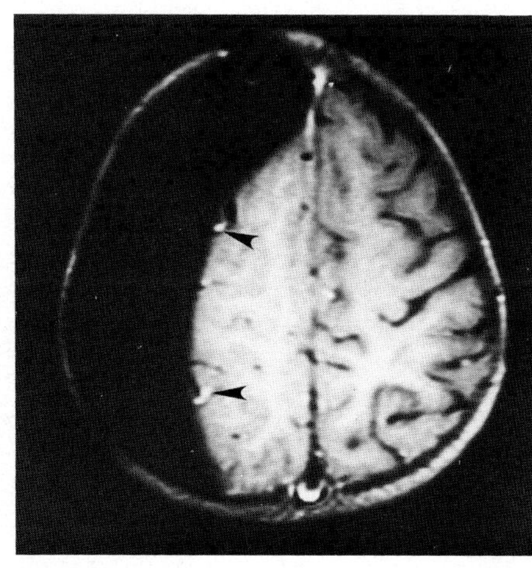
B

Figure 12-39 Right-sided subdural hygroma. **A.** Axial contrast-enhanced CT shows a hypodense CSF density collection displacing the brain tissue inward. Enhanced cortical vessels are identified (arrowheads). There is no membrane enhancement. **B.** Axial T_1WI after gadolinium injection shows no increase in signal intensity in the subdural hygroma. Enhanced cortical vessels (arrowheads) are displaced inward by the collection.

Epidural Hematomas

The epidural space is a potential space between the cranial periosteum and the inner table (Lindenberg 1977). The dura and the periosteum are inseparable. The potential epidural space is bound down at the sutural margins. The dural blood supply lies on the inner table of the skull between the skull and the dura, so that with fracture of the inner table, laceration of a meningeal artery is possible. Not all epidural hematomas are arterial in nature. Some are venous in origin and arise because of a disruption of a major dural venous sinus. Dural venous sinuses are contained within the dura, and with fracture of the skull and laceration of the venous sinus, bleeding between the calvarium and the sinus leads to displacement of the dura and its contained sinus by an epidural hematoma. However, most epidural hematomas are of meningeal vascular origin, are acute, and occur in the temporoparietal region. Fractures were associated with epidural hematomas in 91 percent of patients in a series of Zimmerman and coworkers (Zimmerman 1982). The rate of growth of the hematoma depends on whether a vein or artery is involved, the transsected artery goes into spasm, the collection of blood is walled off to create an aneurysm, the epidural collection is drained into the diploic veins by the meningeal veins, and the hematoma decompresses through the fracture into the scalp (Zimmerman 1982). Epidural hematomas of venous origin are usually slow to form and are found either incidentally or because they produce delayed findings, such as chronic venous epidural hematomas of the posterior fossa producing displacement of the cerebellum and hydrocephalus (Zimmerman 1982).

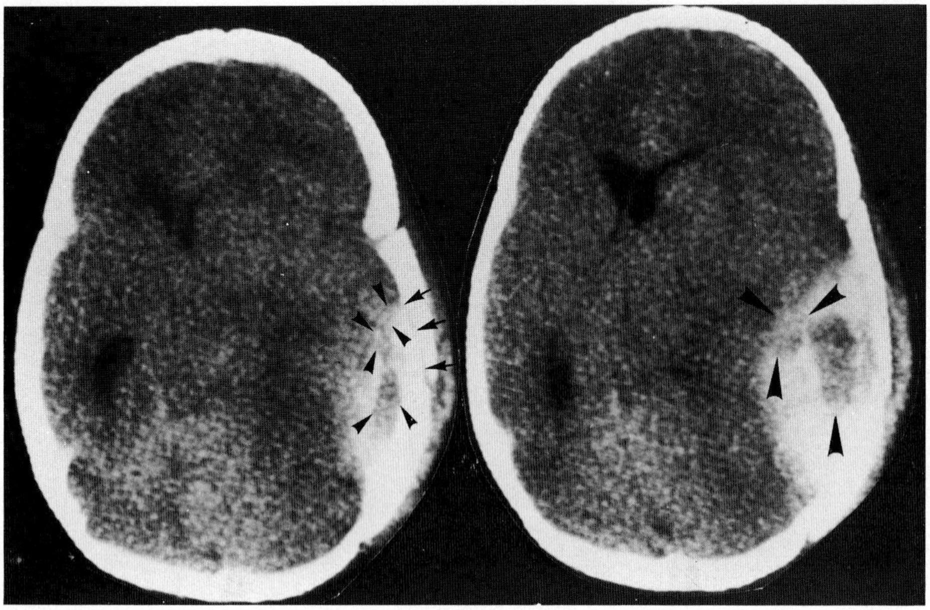

A B

Figure 12-40 Acute epidural hematoma. **A** and **B.** Axial non-contrast-enhanced CT sections at adjacent levels, demonstrating a peripheral high-density extracerebral collection of blood consistent with an epidural hematoma lying in the left middle cranial fossa, contiguous with the inner table of the skull. A fracture line (arrows) leads to the collection, which contains within it a hypointense irregular collection of nonopaque blood that is not clotted (arrowheads). This is indicative of acute active bleeding.

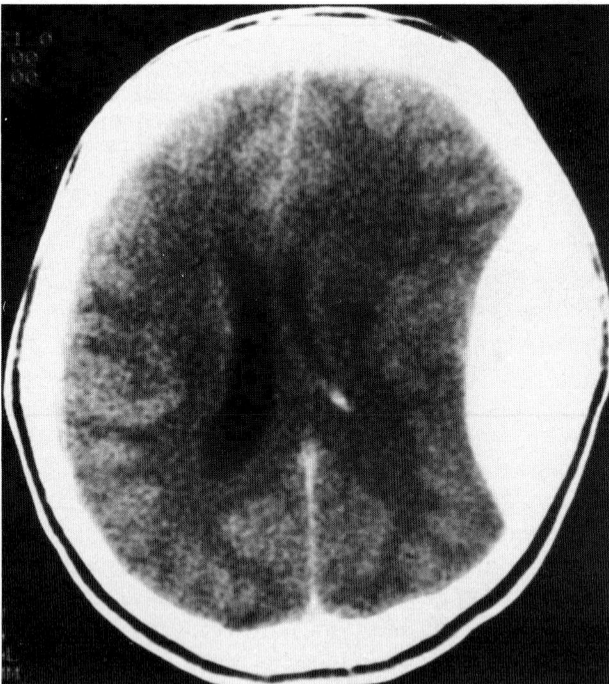

Figure 12-41 Subacute epidural hematoma. Axial non-contrast-enhanced CT shows a peripheral high-density biconvex blood collection bound down by the frontal and lambdoid sutures.

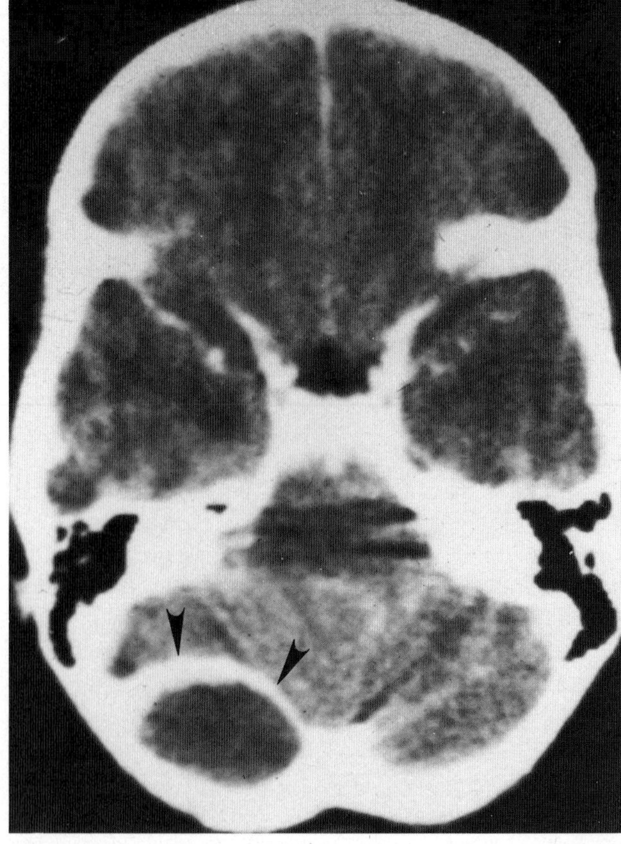

Figure 12-42 Chronic posterior fossa venous epidural hematoma. Axial CT after contrast enhancement shows a high-density peripheral rim of a biconvex collection in the right posterior fossa. Preinjection studies showed some blood products adjacent to the rim, which then enhanced (arrowheads).

Zimmerman and associates staged traumatic epidural bleeding into three types based on the age of the hematoma (Zimmerman 1982). Type 1 represents an acute epidural hematoma (Fig. 12-40); type 2, a subacute epidural hematoma (Fig. 12-41); and type 3, a chronic epidural hematoma (Fig. 12-42). The CT appearance of an epidural hematoma depends on the source of bleeding, the interval between injury and CT, the severity of the hemorrhage, and the degree of clot organization or breakdown. Rapid arterial epidural bleeding frequently produces a large hematoma that displaces the adjacent brain tissue, leading to herniation and death. The vast majority of epidural hematomas are biconvex in appearance. An acute epidural hematoma shows high blood density and often a swirllike lucency within a portion of the clot (Fig. 12-39) (Zimmerman 1982). It is thought that the lucency represents an admixture between serum that is extruded from the retracting clot and active bleeding (unclotted blood is less dense than clotted blood is). As the pressure within the epidural hematoma rises, eventually a tamponade at the bleeding site is produced. A subacute epidural hematoma is one in which the hematoma has become clotted and organized, producing a homogeneous, hyperdense collection (Fig. 12-40). Resorption is carried out by the perivascular elements derived from the dural vessels, forming a membrane similar to that found in a subdural hematoma. Contrast injection demonstrates enhancement of the displaced dura because of neovascularity and granulation tissue (Fig. 12-42). With breakdown of the blood products, the hematoma becomes partly or totally lucent. In the series of Zimmerman and associates (Zimmerman 1982), type 1 epidural hematomas were found in 58 percent of patients, type 2 subacute hematomas in 31 percent, and type 3 chronic hematomas in 11 percent. Venous bleeding was a source of the epidural hematoma most often in chronic hematomas and second most often in subacute hematomas. After surgical evacuation of an acute epidural hematoma, the ventricles often return to the midline; if there is no associated traumatic lesion of the brain parenchyma, the brain appears normal. In instances in which there is associated traumatic injury to the brain or in which the brain has been compressed to the point where the underlying arteries have been occluded, mass effect may be present as a result of injury or infarction. Epidural hematomas are rarely bilateral.

Acute epidural hematomas are examined by means of CT and managed with surgical evacuation. In a stable patient, MR shows a biconvex mass separated from the overlying dura by a thin stripe of high-signal-intensity extruded serum lying between the clot and the dura on T_2WI (Zimmerman 1988). Subacutely, MR shows the epidural hematoma as a biconvex high-signal-intensity mass on T_1WI. The dura is often visible as a thin hypointense stripe displaced inward by the clot (Fig. 12-43).

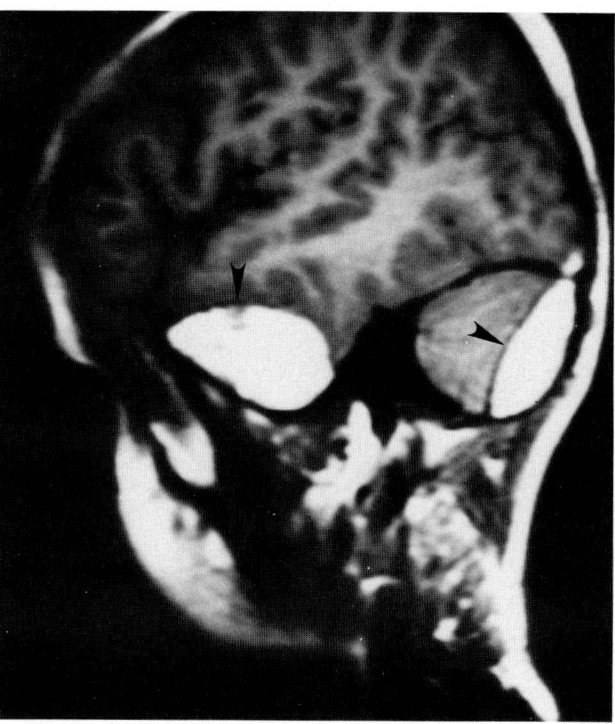

Figure 12-43 Subacute epidural hematoma. Sagittal T_1WI shows two epidural collections, one in the anterior aspect of the middle cranial fossa floor and one in the posterior fossa. Note the hypointense line of dura displaced inward (arrowheads) by the epidural collections. Both collections were in continuity, having arisen from a tear in the transverse dural venous sinus in the tentorial edge.

The relationship between the dural venous sinuses and the hematoma is particularly well shown with coronal and sagittal MR (Zimmerman 1986*b*). Venous epidural hematomas occurring at the convexity of the brain as a result of laceration of the superior sagittal sinus are difficult to demonstrate on CT because of partial voluming of the epidural hematoma with the inner table of the skull. Sagittal and coronal MR show the blood interposed between the inner table of the skull and the venous sinus (Fig. 12-44).

CONCLUSION

CT remains the first diagnostic step in the definitive evaluation of an emergency patient with craniocerebral trauma. It is used in determining whether surgical evacuation of a hematoma or medical management is indicated. However, it can no longer be said that CT is the most accurate noninvasive imaging modality for showing the morphological manifestations of brain injury. MR in many instances is more accurate though more difficult to obtain. The advent of MR angiography and spectroscopy will add important aspects to our understanding of brain injury.

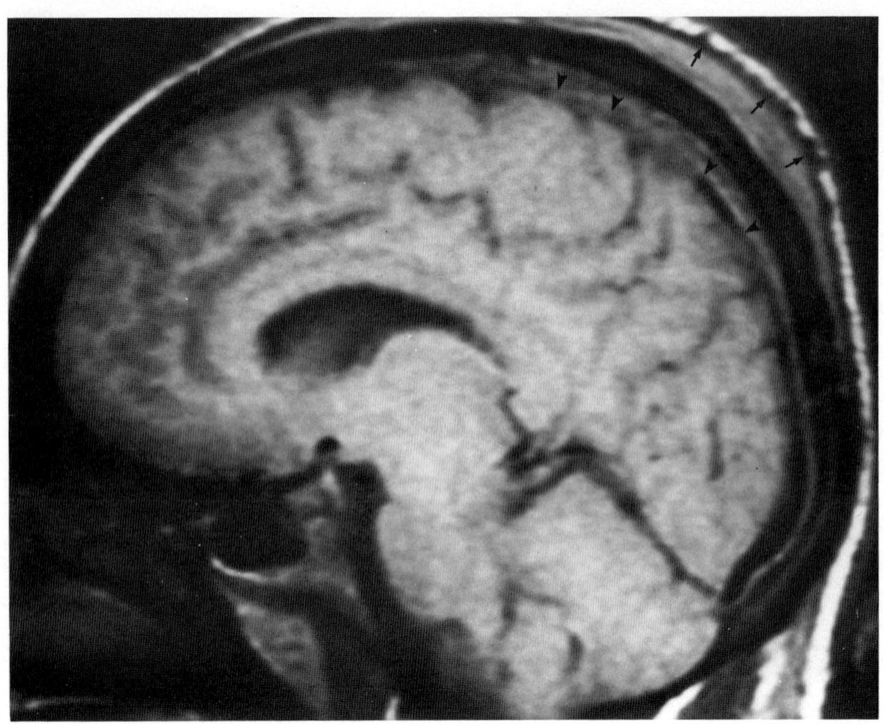

Figure 12-44 Acute venous epidural hematoma. Sagittal T_1WI shows downward displacement of the superior sagittal sinus (arrowheads) by an isodense mass of deoxyhemoglobin within the epidural space lying between the superior sagittal sinus and the inner table of the skull. Note the subperiosteal collection of deoxyhemoglobin displacing the periosteum (arrows) and subcutaneous fat peripherally. The patient had a biparietal fracture crossing the superior sagittal sinus, which was lacerated.

References

ADAMS JH: The neuropathology of head injury, in Vinken PJV, Bruyn GW (eds), *Handbook of Clinical Neurology,* vol 23, New York, American Elsevier, 1975, pp 35–65.

BAKAY L, GLASAUER FE: *Head Injury,* Boston, Little, Brown, 1980.

BALASUBRAMANIAM S, KADAPIA T, CAMPBELL JS, et al: Efficacy of skull radiography. *Am J Surg* 142:366, 1981.

BELL R, LOOP JW: The utility and futility of radiographic skull examinations in trauma. *N Engl J Med* 284:236, 1971.

BRADLEY WG, SCHMIDT PG: Effect of methemoglobin formation on the MR appearance of subarachnoid hemorrhage. *Radiology* 156:99–103, 1984.

CAVENESS WF: Incidence of cranio-cerebral trauma in 1976 with trend from 1970 to 1975, in Thompson RA, Green JRG (eds), *Advances in Neurology,* vol 22, New York, Raven Press, 1979, pp 1–3.

DAVIS JM, ZIMMERMAN RA: Injury of the carotid and vertebral arteries. *Neuroradiology* 25:55–69, 1983.

DETRE JA, WANG Z, BOGDAN AR, et al: Regional variation in brain lactate in Leigh syndrome by localized ^{1}H magnetic resonance spectroscopy. *Ann Neurol* 29:218–221, 1991.

DOLINSKAS C, BILANIUK LT, ZIMMERMAN RA, et al: Computed tomography of intracerebral hematomas: I. Transmission CT observations of hematoma resolution. *AJR* 129:681–688, 1977.

DOLINSKAS C, ZIMMERMAN RA, BILANIUK LT: A sign of subarachnoid bleeding on cranial computed tomograms of pediatric head trauma patients. *Radiology* 126:409, 1978.

DOLINSKAS CA, ZIMMERMAN RA, BILANIUK LT, et al: Computed tomography of post-traumatic extracerebral hematomas: Comparison to pathophysiology and responses to therapy. *J Trauma* 19:163, 1979.

FOBBEN ES, GROSSMAN RI, ATLAS SW, et al: MR characteristics of subdural hematomas and hygromas at 1.5 T. *AJNR* 10:687–693, 1989.

GENTRY LR, GODERSKY JC, THOMPSON B: MR imaging of head trauma: Review of the distribution and radiopathologic features of traumatic lesions. *AJNR* 9:101, 1988.

GIBBY WA, ZIMMERMAN RA: *X-Ray Computed Tomography,* in Mazziotta and Gilman (eds), Contemporary Anatomy Series, Philadelphia, Davis (in press).

GOMORI JM, GROSSMAN RI, BILANIUK LT, et al: High-field MR imaging of superficial siderosis of the central nervous system. *J Comput Assist Tomogr* 9(5):972–975, 1985*a*.

GOMORI M, GROSSMAN RI, GOLDBERG HI, et al: High field magnetic resonance imaging of intracranial hematomas. *Radiology* 157:87–93, 1985*b*.

GOMORI JM, GROSSMAN RI: Mechanisms responsible for the MR appearance and evolution of intracranial hemorrhage. *Radiology* 161(P):364, 1986.

GURDJIAN ES: Cerebral contusions: Reevaluation of the mechanism of their development. *J Trauma* 16:35, 1976.

HARWOOD-NASH DC: Fractures of the petrous and tympanic parts of the temporal bone in children: A tomographic study of 35 cases. *AJR* 110:598, 1970.

HENRYS P, LYNE ED, LIFTON C, et al: Clinical review of cervical spine injuries in children. *Clin Orthop* 129:172, 1977.

JENNETT B: Skull x-rays after recent head injury. *Clin Radiol* 31:463, 1980.

JENNETT B, TEASDALE G: *Management of Injuries,* Philadelphia, Davis, 1981.

KEMP SS, GROSSMAN RI: The importance of oxygenation in the appearance of acute subarachnoid hemorrhage on high field magnetic resonance imaging (abst). XIII Symposium Neuroradiologicum, Stockholm, June 1986.

KOO AH, LA ROQUE RL: Evaluation of head trauma by computed tomography. *Radiology* 123:345, 1977.

LANTZ EJ, FORBES GS, BROWN ML, et al: Radiology of cerebrospinal fluid rhinorrhea. *AJR* 135:1023, 1980.

LINDENBERG R: Pathology of craniocerebral injuries, in Newton TH, Potts DS (eds), *Radiology of the Skull and Brain: Anatomy and Pathology,* vol 3, St. Louis, CV Mosby, 1977.

MANELFE C, CELLERIER P, SOBEL D, et al: Cerebrospinal fluid rhinorrhea: Evaluation with metrizamide cisternography. *AJR* 138:471, 1982.

MASARYK TJ, MODIC MT, RUGGIERI PM, et al: Three-dimensional (volume) gradient-echo imaging of the carotid bifurcation: Preliminary clinical experience. *Radiology* 171:801, 1989.

MELZAK J: Paraplegia among children. *Lancet* ii:45, 1969.

NAIDICH TP, MORAN CJ, PUDLOWSKI RM, et al: CT diagnosis of the isodense subdural hematoma, in Thompson RA, Green JR (eds), *Advances in Neurology,* vol 22, New York, Raven Press, 1979.

NAIDICH TP, MORAN CJ: Precise anatomic localization of atraumatic sphenoethmoidal cerebrospinal fluid rhinorrhea by metrizamide CT cisternography. *J Neurosurg* 53:222, 1980.

OGDEN JA: *Skeletal Injury in the Child,* Philadelphia, Lea & Febiger, 1982.

OSBORN AG, DAINES JH, WING SD, et al: Intracranial air on computerized tomography. *J Neurosurg* 48:355, 1978.

OSBORN AG, ANDERSON RE, WING SD: The false falx sign. *Radiology* 134:421, 1980.

ROBERTS F, SHOPFNER CE: Plain skull roentgenograms in children with head trauma. *AJR* 114:230, 1972.

ROBINSON AE, MEARES BM, GOREE JA: Traumatic sphenoid sinus effusion: An analysis of 50 cases. *Am J Radium Ther Nucl Med* 101:795, 1967.

ROYAL COLLEGE OF RADIOLOGISTS: A study of the utilization of skull radiography in nine accidents and emergency units in the UK. *Lancet* i:1234, 1980.

SCHNALL MD, BOLINGER L, RENSHAW PF, et al: Multinuclear MR imaging: Technique for combined anatomic and physiologic studies. *Radiology* 162:863, 1987.

ST. JOHN EG: The role of the emergency skull roentgenogram in head trauma. *AJR* 76:315, 1968.

STRICH SJ: Shearing of nerve fibers as a cause of brain damage due to head injury: A pathological study of twenty cases. *Lancet* ii:443, 1961.

STRONG I, MACMILLAN R, JENNETT B: Head injuries in accident and emergency departments at Scottish hospitals. *Injury* 10:154, 1978.

SUTTON LN, LENKINSKI RE, COHEN BH, et al: Localized ^{31}P magnetic resonance spectroscopy of large pediatric brain tumors. *J Neurosurg* 72:65–70, 1990.

TAVERAS JM, RANSOHOFF J: Leptomeningeal cysts of the brain following trauma, with erosion of the skull. *J Neurosurg* 10:223, 1953.

YOSHIHARU T, HANAFEE WN: Cerebrospinal fluid rhinorrhea: The significance of an air-fluid level in the sphenoid sinus. *Radiology* 135:101, 1980.

ZIMMERMAN RA, BILANIUK LT, DOLINSKAS C, et al: Computed tomography of acute intracerebral hemorrhagic contusion. *J Comput Tomogr* 1:271–280, 1977.

ZIMMERMAN RA, BILANIUK LT, GENNARELLI T, et al: Cranial computed tomography in diagnosis and management of acute head trauma. *AJR* 131:27, 1978*a*.

ZIMMERMAN RA, BILANIUK LT, BRUCE D, et al: Computed tomography of pediatric head trauma: Acute general cerebral swelling. *Radiology* 126:403, 1978*b*.

ZIMMERMAN RA, BILANIUK LT, GENNARELLI T: Computed tomography of shearing injuries of the cerebral white matter. *Radiology* 127:393–396, 1978*c*.

ZIMMERMAN RA, BILANIUK LT, BRUCE D, et al: Computed tomography of craniocerebral injury in the abused child. *Radiology* 10:687, 1979.

ZIMMERMAN RA, BILANIUK LT: Computed tomography in pediatric head trauma. *J Neuroradiol* 8:257, 1981.

ZIMMERMAN RA, BILANIUK LT: Computed tomographic staging of traumatic epidural bleeding. *Radiology* 144:809, 1982.

ZIMMERMAN RA: The effectiveness of skull plain films in the evaluation of traumatic coma. *J Neuroradiol* 10:145, 1983.

ZIMMERMAN RA, BILANIUK LT: Head trauma, in RN Rosenberg (ed), *The Clinical Neurosciences,* Edinburgh, Churchill Livingstone, 1984, p 483.

ZIMMERMAN RA, BILANIUK LT, GROSSMAN RI, et al: Resistive NMR of intracranial hematomas. *Neuroradiology* 27:16–20, 1985.

ZIMMERMAN RA: Evaluation of head injury: Supratentorial, in Taveras J, Ferrucci E (eds), Philadelphia, Lippincott, 1986*a*.

ZIMMERMAN RA, BILANIUK LT, HACKNEY DB, et al: Head injury: Early results of comparing CT and high-field MR. *AJNR* 7:757–764, 1986*b*.

ZIMMERMAN RA, BILANIUK LT, HACKNEY DB, et al: Magnetic resonance imaging in temporal bone fracture. *Neuroradiology* 29:246–257, 1987.

ZIMMERMAN RA: Magnetic resonance of head injury, in Taveras J, Ferrucci E (eds), *Radiology: Diagnosis-Imaging-Intervention,* Philadelphia, Lippincott, 1988, pp 1–12.

ZIMMERMAN RA, BILANIUK LT: CT and MR: Diagnosis and evolution of head injury, stroke, and brain tumors. *Neuropsychology* 3:191–230, 1989.

13 INFECTIOUS DISEASES

Gordon Sze
S. Howard Lee

GENERAL CONSIDERATIONS

Central nervous system (CNS) infections are a group of life-threatening diseases that present a formidable challenge to physicians. Despite the development of effective antimicrobial agents and modern surgical techniques, significant mortality and morbidity persist among patients with CNS infections. Since the introduction of cross-sectional imaging, earlier diagnosis has become possible, and this has led to a decrease in both morbidity and mortality. For example, the use of CT has brought a marked decrease in mortality among patients with brain abscesses (Rosenbaum 1978), and the advent of MR has accelerated this trend (Brant-Zawadzki 1983; Schroth 1987).

The brain and spinal cord are well protected from direct spread of infectious disease processes by osseous and membranous coverings, including the pachymeninges (dura) and leptomeninges (pia-arachnoid) (Adams 1985), and by the blood-brain and blood-CSF barriers at a microscopic level (Harriman 1984). Possible reasons for the peculiar CNS response to microorganisms include certain structural peculiarities of the brain and its coverings, such as the absence of true lymphatics; differences in vascular supply in gray and white matter; the absence of capillaries in the subarachnoid space; direct intercommunication between intra- and extracranial venous systems via diploic and emissary veins; and the presence of a perivascular arachnoid space around the veins as well as the large vessels (Virchow-Robin spaces) and the perivascular glial membrane. Cerebrospinal fluid (CSF) also is an excellent culture medium for bacterial growth.

Infections reach the brain or meninges predominantly by two routes: (1) hematogenous dissemination from a distant infective focus to the meninges, corticomedullary junction, and choroid plexus and (2) direct extension by bony erosion from an adjacent focus of suppuration (otitis, mastoiditis, sinusitis) or by transmission along cranial nerves after neurosurgery or a traumatic craniocerebral wound. An infectious process varies with time and the intrinsic ability of the host to react and with the nature of the infectious agent. Infectious agents are considered pathogenic when a normal individual is infected by an adequate inoculum and opportunistic when the host is compromised (Parker 1985). In this chapter the various groups of organisms—bacterial, granulomatous, viral, and parasitic—that affect the brain will be discussed. In addition, a final section will be devoted to acquired immune deficiency syndrome (AIDS), because many of its manifestations form a characteristic constellation and because it is almost certainly the most common cause of infections of the CNS today.

BACTERIAL INFECTION

Subdural Empyema

Subdural infection accounts for about 13 to 20 percent of all cases of intracranial bacterial infection and 5.1 percent of all space-occupying lesions in the subdural space (Weinman 1972; Galbraith 1974; Danziger 1980; Blaquiere 1983). It is frequently associated with epidural abscess (Kaufmann 1975; Zimmerman 1984) and usually presents a fulminating clinical course and an emergent neurosurgical condition. Before the era of CT, subdural empyema was associated with a mortality rate as high as 40 percent; since the advent of CT (Bhardari 1970; Weinman 1972; LaBeau 1973), mortality has dropped significantly (Schroth 1987), but it remains considerable. The high morbidity and mortality are related more to the response of the cerebral vasculature and brain to the inflammatory process than to the mass effect of the extraaxial collection (Sadhu 1980; Zimmerman 1984). Whenever progressive neurological deterioration coexists with a systemic manifestation of infection, this diagnosis should be strongly considered.

The most common cause of subdural empyema is paranasal sinusitis (Kaufmann 1975; Carter 1983). In Zimmerman's (1984) series of 49 patients, frontal sinusitis was the most common cause of empyema; more than 40 percent of these patients had preceding frontal sinusitis. Less frequently, subdural empyema may be secondary to otitic infection, a penetrating wound of the skull, craniectomy, or osteomyelitis of the skull.

The mechanism of subdural infection may be twofold: progressive retrograde thrombophlebitis or (less likely) direct spread after penetration of the dura. The most common location of a subdural empyema is over the convexity of one or both hemispheres (80 percent). The interhemispheric fissure is the next most frequent location (12 percent). In this space, subdural empyema may occur as an extension of the convexity collection (Stephanov 1979). Convexities or combined convexities–interhemispheric empyemas have a predilection for the anterior aspects of the cranial cavity near the frontal lobes, while an isolated interhemispheric empyema may occur at the base of the brain or beneath the tentorium (Weinman 1972; Grinelli 1977).

CT findings of acute subdural empyema may be subtle and not apparent initially. Noncontrast CT (NCCT) demonstrates a crescentic or, more frequently, lentiform-shaped area of low density (0 to 16 HU) adjacent to the inner border of the skull, representing pus. Frequently, mass effect of the underlying brain may be more prominent than the subtle extracerebral collection (Fig. 13-1). The white matter may appear hypodense as a result of edema, cerebritis, or infarction (Enzmann 1984). On contrast-enhanced CT (CECT), a zone of enhancement separates the hypodense extracerebral collection from the brain surface (Fig. 13-1). This curvilinear enhancement is due to granulation tissue formation at the boundary of the empyema on its leptomeningeal surface and perhaps inflammation or ischemia in the subjacent cerebral cortex (Grinelli 1977; Weisberg 1986) (Fig. 13-1). The margins of the enhanced zone may show varying degrees of irregularity and thickness (Stephanov 1979; Sadhu 1980; Zimmerman 1984).

Currently, MR has become the modality of choice in the evaluation of suspected subdural empyema (Weingarten 1989). MR offers several advantages over CT. First, it is considerably more sensitive in the detection of extracerebral fluid collections. While fluid collections may be obscured on CT because of the adjacent skull, on MR even small crescentic empyemas are readily visible since the bony inner table appears as a signal void. This is more evident in paratentorial and subtemporal locations on coronal MR images. Second, MR can often differentiate subdural from epidural empyemas (Fig. 13-2). The dura itself can be detected in an epidural empyema as a hypointense medial rim separating the fluid collection from the underlying subarachnoid space and brain paren-

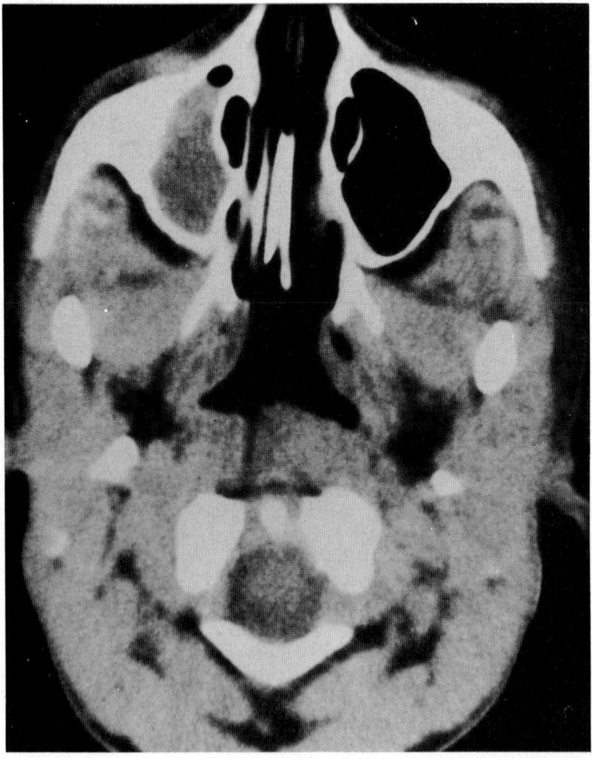
A

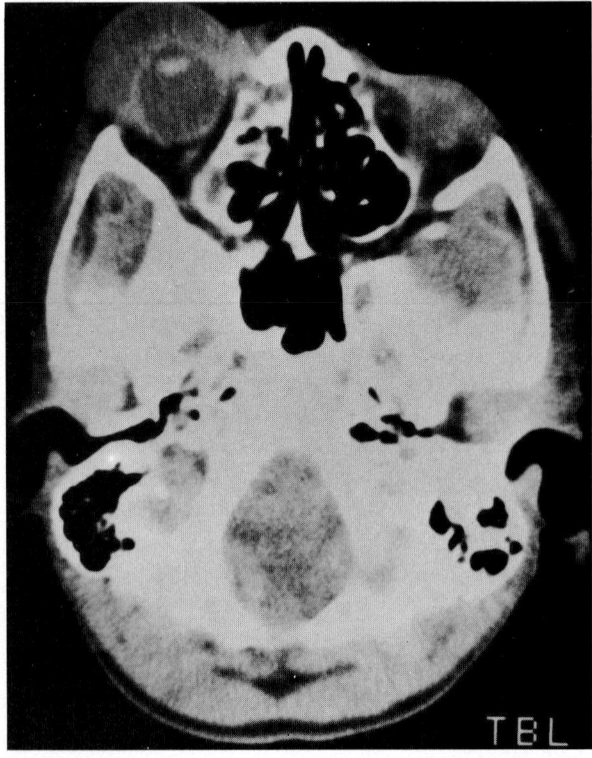

B

Figure 13-1 Subdural empyema associated with leptomeningitis and cerebritis. Right maxillary sinusitis (**A**) extends into the right orbit (**B**). (*Continued on p. 541.*)

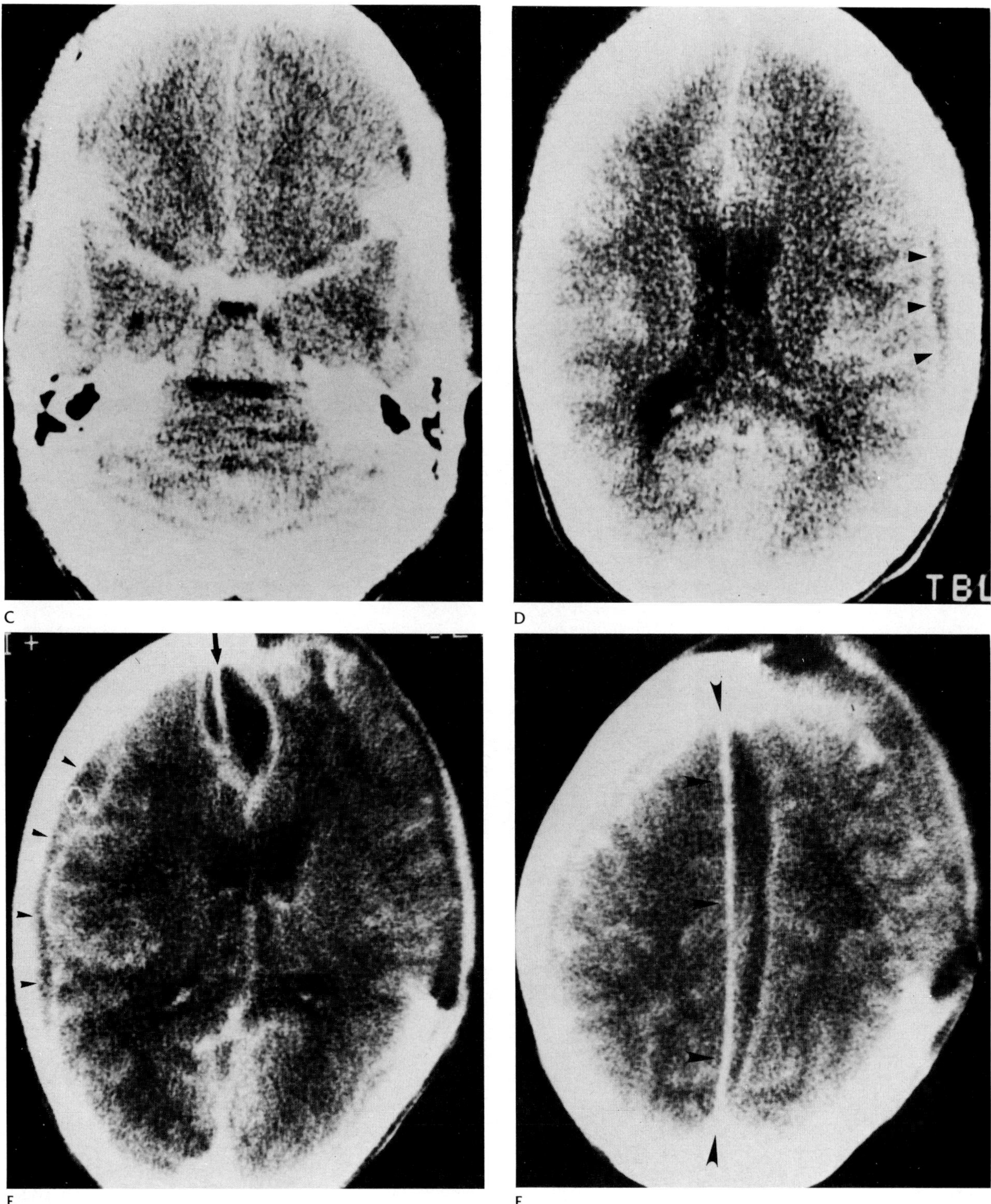

Figure 13-1 (continued) CECT at the base (**C**) shows marked contrast enhancement at the basal cistern representing extensive leptomeningitis. **D.** A thin, crescentic, left hemispheric subdural empyema (arrowheads) with marked contrast enhancement of the underlying gyri and of the interhemispheric fissure (leptomeningitis, cerebritis, and/or venous thrombosis). **E.** CECT following surgical evacuation of the left subdural empyema demonstrates occurrence of the right subdural empyema with underlying cerebritis (arrowheads). Frontal interhemispheric subdural empyema can be seen on both sides of the falx cerebri (arrow). **F.** On CECT, convexity level shows a large interhemispheric subdural empyema delineated by a thick falx cerebri on the medial side (arrowheads) and an early membrane formation on the lateral side. Note also gyral contrast enhancement on both hemipheres.

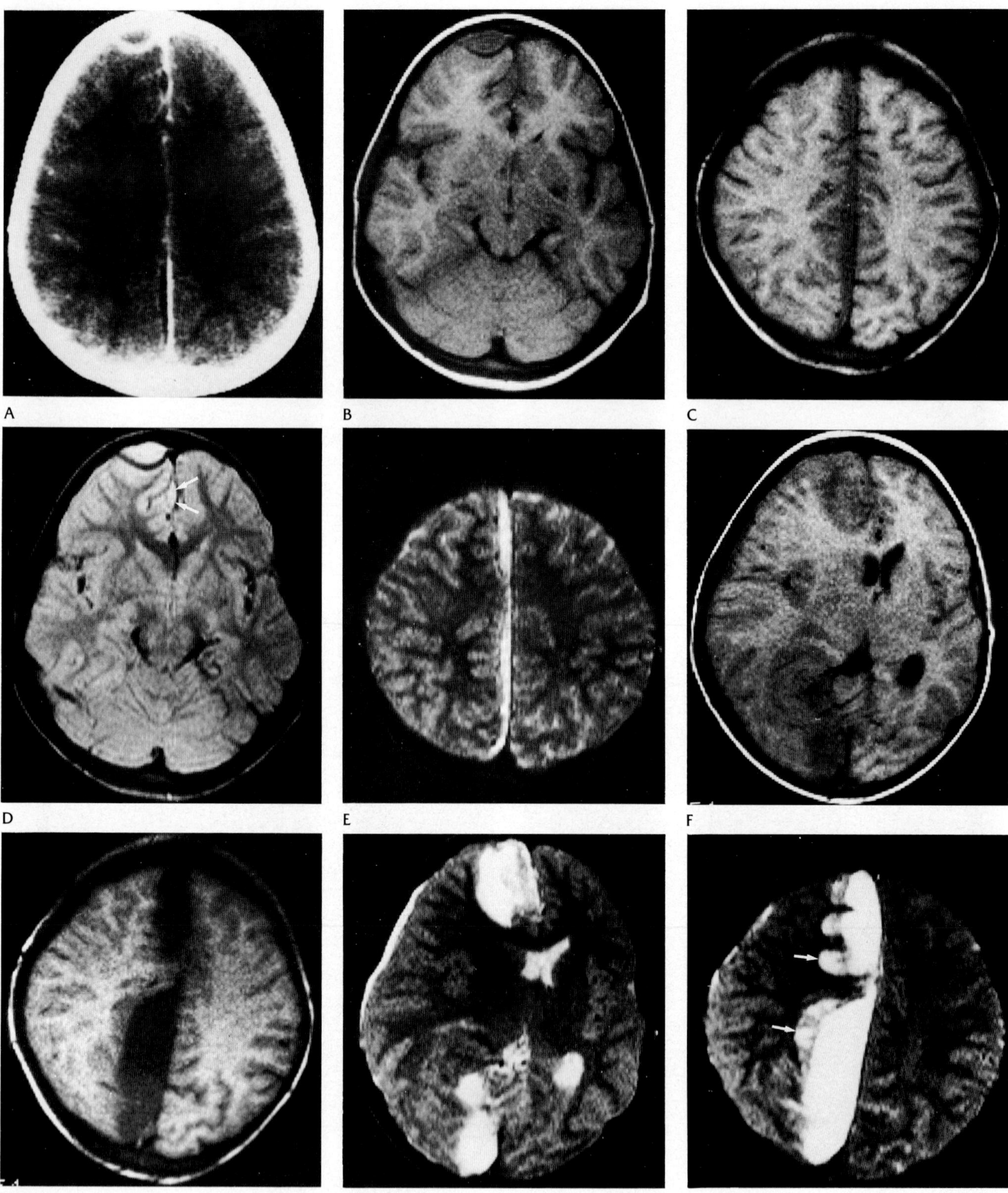

Figure 13-2 Subdural and epidural empyemas in a 9-year-old boy with postsinusitis. **A.** Contrast-enhanced CT shows extraaxial collections in posterior interhemispheric fissure and anterior to right frontal lobe. Note thickening of falx and marginal enhancement of right frontal collection. **B–E.** MR images the same day. Axial T_1WI (500/30) and T_2WI (2150/60, 120) scans show collections seen on CT. Note superior delineation of anterior interhemispheric collection (arrows), hyperintensity of collections relative to CSF, and presence of hypointense rim between right frontal collection and underlying cortex. **F–I.** MR images 2 weeks after craniotomy. Axial T_1WI (500/30) and T_2WI (2150/120) show loculated interhemispheric subdural empyemas and parenchymal abnormalities. In particular, note excellent visualization of right convexity collection, cortical hyperintensity of right convexity collection, cortical hyperintensity in right parasagittal gray matter (arrows), and absence of hypointense rim surrounding all subdural loculations. (*Reprinted with permission from Weingarten, 1989.*)

chyma. Third, MR can provide better characterization of the contents of extraaxial fluid (Brant-Zawadzki 1985). Very purulent collections have decreased T_1 and T_2 relaxation times and are hyperintense on T_1- and T_2WI compared with pure CSF using routine parameters. While both chronic hematoma and empyema appear as hypodense collections on CT, MR is able to differentiate the two easily (Weingarten 1989). Subacute to chronic hematomas have a markedly increased signal on both T_1- and T_2WI as a result of products of hemoglobin degradation, unlike pure empyemas, which exhibit signal characteristics similar to those of a proteinaceous fluid. Fourth, MR is superior in the detection of concomitant parenchymal alterations and venous thrombosis (Figs. 13-2 and 13-3). Edema in underlying parenchyma and secondary infarcts resulting from vasculitis or thrombosis are easily seen.

Sulcal alterations such as effacement and reversible cortical hyperintensities on T_2WI are also more readily assessed with MR than with CT. These cortical hyperintensities were thought to represent cortical hyperemia or edema resulting from ischemia induced by inflammatory vasospasm (Weingarten 1989; Sze 1988*b*).

After administration of contrast, enhancement on MR can be seen on both the inner and outer surfaces of a subdural empyema, unlike in CT (Sze 1989). Since the inner table of the skull is not visualized, contrast enhancement of the inflamed dura stands out. Often the outer aspect of the subdural fluid collection enhances more significantly and evenly than does the inner aspect adjacent to the brain parenchyma.

Epidural Empyema

Extension of infection from the paranasal sinuses or mastoids is the most frequent route of infection of the skull and epidural space (Sharif 1982). The infectious process is localized outside the dural membrane and beneath the inner table of the skull. The frontal region is most frequently affected, probably because of its close relation-

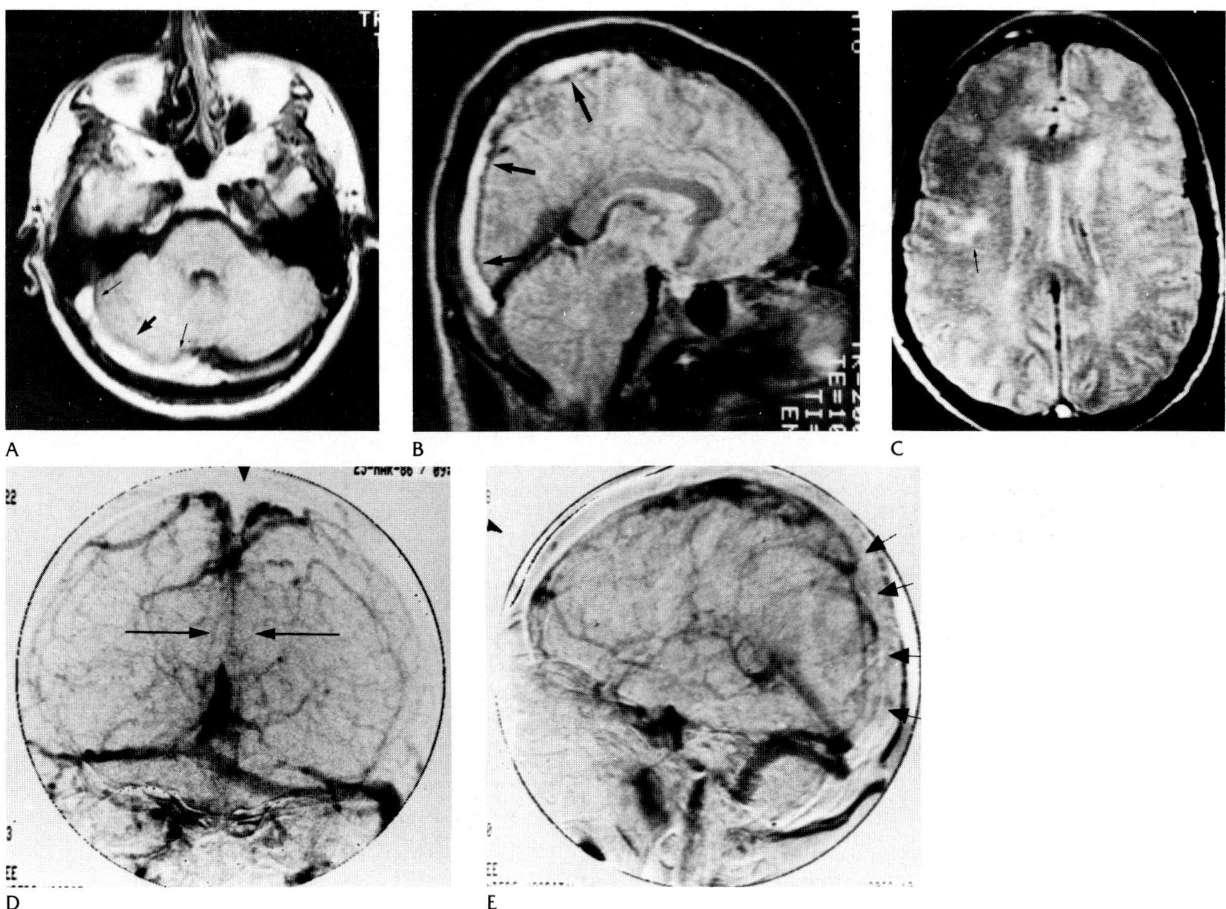

Figure 13-3 Sagittal sinus thrombosis due to sinusitis: **A.** Axial MRI (T_1WI). **B.** Sagittal MRI (T_2WI) shows hyperintense sagittal and right transverse sinuses (arrows). **C.** Axial MRI (T_2WI) demonstrates white matter infarct (arrow). Note thrombosed hyperintense posterior sagittal sinus. **E.** AP and lateral carotid DSA confirm the diagnosis of thrombosis of sinuses (arrows). (*Case courtesy of Drs. Y. Oh and C. Salvati, Edison, N.J.*)

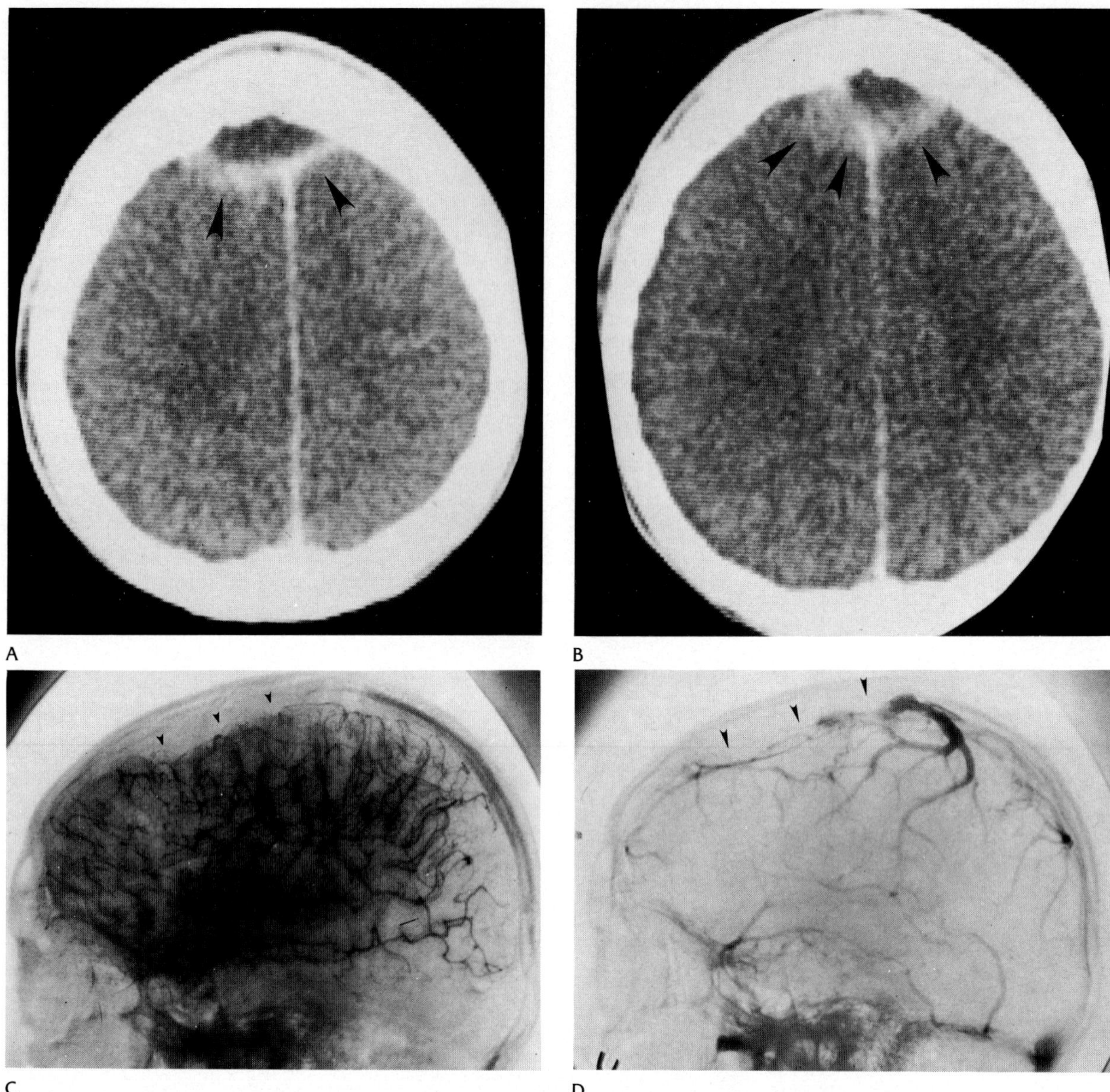

Figure 13-4 Epidural abscess. **A.** Biconvex hypodense lesion with contrast-enhanced dural margin (arrowheads) crosses the falx on CECT. **B.** Thick, irregular, nonhomogeneous membrane displaces the falx away from the inner table of the skull (arrowheads). **C.** Lateral cerebral angiogram, arterial phase, demonstrates avascular mass compressing the brain tissue (arrowheads). **D.** On venous phase, detachment of the superior sagittal sinus from the inner table of the skull (arrowheads) confirms its extradural location. Also note sinus thrombosis.

ship to the frontal sinuses and the ease with which the dura can be stripped from the bone. Epidural abscess can also arise from infection of the diploë (osteomyelitis), which may spread through the inner table of the skull. It can also occur as a result of surgery or trauma (Sze 1988*b*).

Clinically, epidural abscess is often silent if it occurs alone. Focal seizures or neurological deficits, however, may result from compression or irritation of the underlying cerebral cortex when they occur in combination with the simultaneous or subsequent development of other infections such as subdural empyema. At surgery, the integrity of the dura usually is preserved because of its prophylactic role as a relatively impermeable barrier protecting the underlying brain.

On NCCT, epidural infection appears as a poorly defined area of hypodensity adjacent to the inner table of the skull. On CECT, the hypodense lentiform collection displaces the dura inward; if the collection lies in the midline, the attachment of the interhemispheric falx is

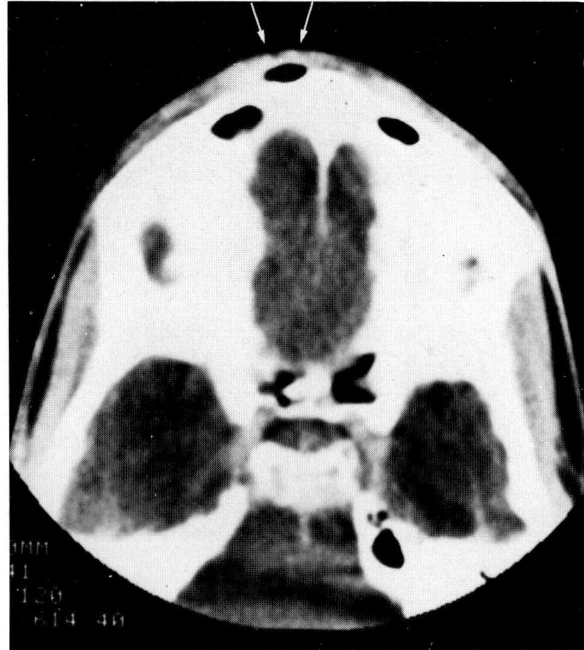

A

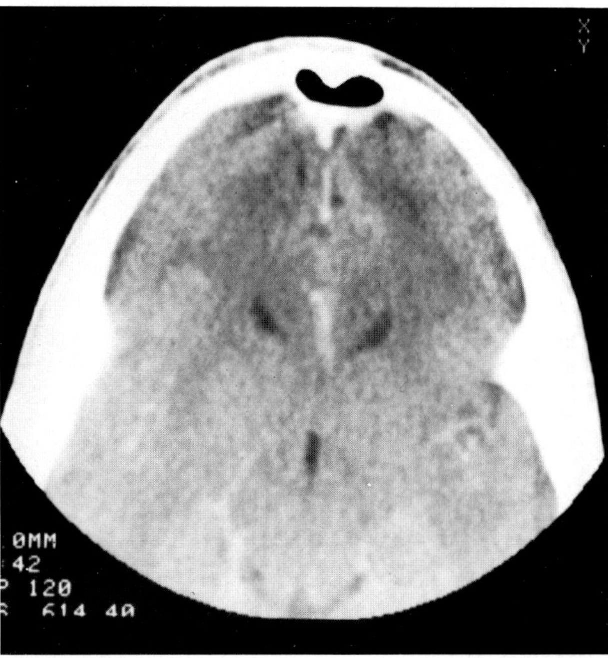

B

Figure 13-5 Epidural abscess in an 11-year-old with painsinusitis on CT. **A.** Frontal soft-tissue swelling with air collection (arrows). **B.** Frontal epidural collection with air-fluid level. **C.** Slightly higher level than **B,** a thick membrane crossing the anterior interhemispheric dura is characteristic of epidural abscess which was confirmed at surgery. Of interest was absence of bony dehiscence at surgery.

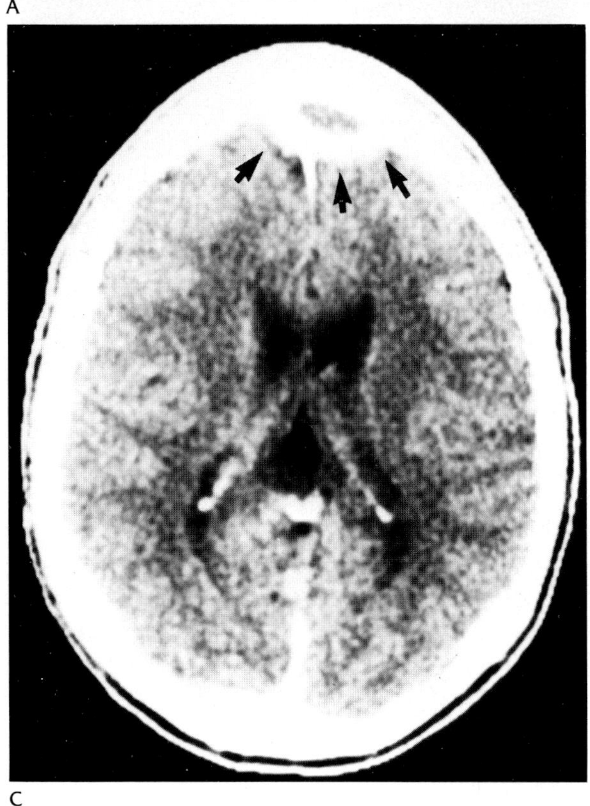

C

displaced inward and separated from the adjacent skull, identifying its extradural location (Lott 1977; Kaufmann 1977). Thick smooth-walled enhancement on the convex inner side represents an inflamed dural membrane. The membrane enhancement is often thicker in epidural abscesses than it is in subdural abscesses (Figs. 13-4 and 13-5). The underlying brain tissue appears normal (unless concomitant cerebritis is present), but there may be significant displacement of brain parenchyma if the epidural abscess is large. When the epidural abscess is situated on the convexity of one hemisphere, differentiation from a subdural empyema may be difficult on the basis of CT appearance alone. Associated findings such as underlying bone destruction, subgaleal soft tissue mass, and air collection may provide a clue (Fig. 13-5). In addition, CT may demonstrate evidence of paranasal sinus or mastoid infection (fluid, soft tissue thickening) (Carter 1983) and may complement skull radiography in demonstrating associated osteomyelitis. It is also important to know that no epidural collection has occurred in the interhemispheric space and along the tentorium cerebelli because anatomically two layers of the dura converge and become one layer at these locations. Any collection in these spaces is either subdural or subarachnoid in nature.

As with subdural empyema, MR is more sensitive than CT in the evaluation of epidural empyema (Sze 1988*b;* Weingarten 1989). Even small extraaxial fluid collections can be easily identified as a result of the signal void of the inner table of the skull. The signal characteristics of the fluid in epidural empyemas resemble those of subdural empyemas and are increased on both T_1WI and T_2WI compared with pure CSF. MR also facilitates the differentiation of epidural empyemas from subdural empye-

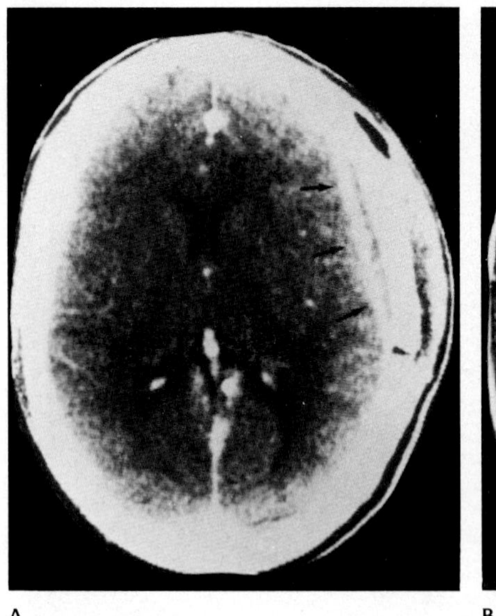
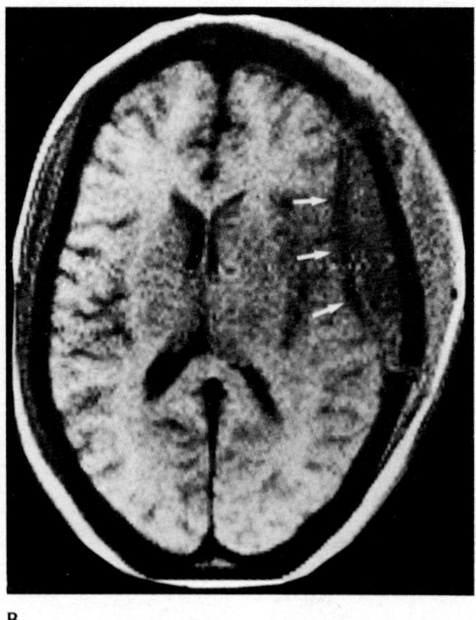
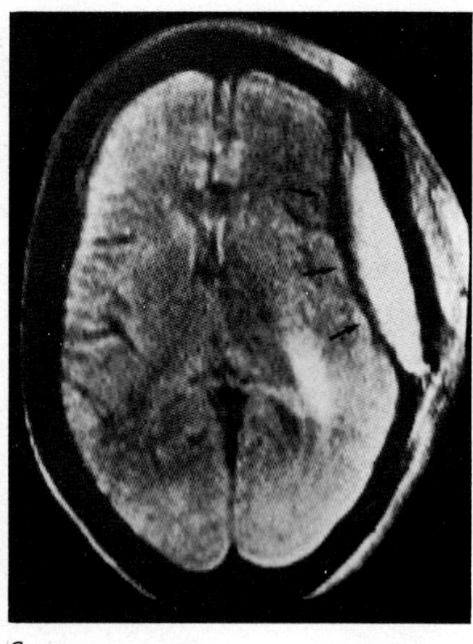

A B C

Figure 13-6 Postoperative epidural empyema in a 24-year-old woman (craniotomy 1 year before for epidural metastatic disease). **A.** CECT shows extraaxial mass underlying left frontotemporal craniotomy defect indistinguishable from tumor recurrence. Thick-walled medial rim enhancement suggests an inflammatory cause. NCMR: Axial T_1WI (500/30) (**B**) and T_2WI (1250/60) (**C**) the same day show extraaxial fluid collection, which is hyperintense relative to CSF and has hypointense medial rim (arrows). (*Reprinted with permission from Weingarten 1989.*)

mas. Visualization of the hypointense dura is the most obvious definitive method for distinguishing between subdural and epidural empyemas (Figs. 13-2 and 13-6). Other criteria follow from CT, although MR is less accurate in the determination of osteomyelitis in the adjacent skull or air in the lesion itself. In an isolated epidural empyema, often only mass effect on the subjacent brain is seen without actual involvement of the parenchyma because of the protective nature of the tough dura. However, it is more common to have epidural empyema in combination with subdural empyema simultaneously or subsequently as a result of spread from retrograde venous thrombosis or, less frequently, direct extension.

After the administration of MR contrast, enhancement of the inflamed dural membrane can be seen on the medial border of the epidural empyema. Additional enhancement can be seen on the lateral border.

Cerebritis and Abscess

Cerebritis and abscess formation constitute a continuum. Cerebritis results from the initial infection of the brain parenchyma. Areas of vascular congestion, petechial hemorrhage, and edema are seen pathologically. The center of cerebral softening in cerebritis may undergo necrosis and liquefaction, resulting in a central cavitation abscess. The body attempts to wall off the infection by forming a fibrous capsule. Pathologically, the abscess capsule consists of three layers: an inner layer of granulation tissue, a relatively thick middle layer of collagen, and an outer layer of reactive glial tissue (Harriman 1984). The collagen layer plays a major role in encapsulating the infected brain tissue and is derived from fibroblasts that can be found in the meninges and in the walls of neophyte vessels (Waggener 1974; Moore 1974).

Brain cerebritis and abscesses typically occur as a result of preceding extracerebral infection. They can be produced by direct extension from adjacent infectious foci, such as otitis, mastoiditis, paranasal sinusitis, facial cutaneous infection, dental abscess, and penetrating skull injury. Alternatively, they can be due to osteomyelitis and congenital cyanotic heart disease with a right-to-left shunt. Most venous-blood-borne infections are situated in subcortical white matter and appear on gross inspection as ill-defined areas of infected encephalomalacia (suppurative cerebritis). Arterial-blood-borne infections often commence in gray matter rather than in white matter and are located in the distribution of the anterior and middle cerebral arteries, with a strong tendency toward multiplicity (disseminated microabscesses). Very rarely an abscess is secondary to meningitis. In about one-quarter of cases of brain cerebritis and abscess, the source of the infection is uncertain (Kerr 1958), and sterile abscesses on smear and culture are not uncommon. Anaerobic organisms are isolated in the majority of abscesses, but multiple organisms are frequently found. Overall, the most commonly cultured organisms from a brain abscess are staphylococci and streptococci in individuals with a normal immune system.

On CT, cerebritis is initially manifested by an area of

hypodensity in the white matter with poorly defined borders and regional or widespread mass effect reflecting vascular congestion and edema. There may be little or no contrast enhancement at this early stage. Further progression of the inflammatory process leads to cerebral softening and petechial hemorrhage, reflecting progressive damage to the blood-brain barrier. At this stage, CECT reveals mottled irregular areas of enhancement, mostly in the regional gray matter (New 1976, 1980) (Fig. 13-1). The appearance of contrast enhancement often simulates the gyral patterns of cerebral infarction. Patchy, irregular enhancement of the white matter may also be noted (Fig. 13-7). Experimental studies of the evolution of brain abscess after direct inoculation of organisms have demonstrated ring enhancement as early as the cerebritis stage (Enzmann 1979).

MR is more accurate than CT in the evaluation of the early stages of cerebritis (Davidson 1985; Schroth 1987). Because of its sensitivity to altered water content, MR can detect changes of early infection sooner. T_1WI may show mild hypointensity and mass effect (Fig. 13-8). Sulcal effacement is common. T_2WI discloses hyperintensity in both the central inflammatory zone and the surrounding edematous brain. As with CT, contrast enhancement on MR may be absent at this early stage. If the infection progresses, however, enhancement may develop, often in a gyral or irregular pattern similar to that seen with CT.

With necrosis of the center and formation of the fibrous capsule, an abscess evolves. Thinning of the medial margin of the capsule is frequently observed and is thought to be due to the relatively poor vascular supply of the white matter. This may account for the tendency of abscesses to rupture into the ventricular system and form daughter abscesses in the white matter. Delay in capsule formation on the deep medial side of the abscess makes the wall less firm than it is on the side adjacent to the gray matter. Although medial thinning of the abscess wall has been reported in 48 percent of cerebral abscesses (Stevens 1978), increased thickness of the medial wall of the capsule has also been found. Although the innermost layer of the wall is irregular in pathological specimens because of uneven layers of necrotic debris and inflammatory granulation tissue (Harriman 1984), it may appear smooth on either CT or MR, a finding which is thought to be strongly suggestive of abscess (Stevens 1978).

On CT, mass effect on the ventricular system or the midline structures is noted in more than 80 percent of brain absecesses (Nielsen 1977). On NCCT, an ill-defined hypodense area is almost always seen (Claveria 1976; Nielsen 1977; Stevens 1978). Frequently a ring of slightly

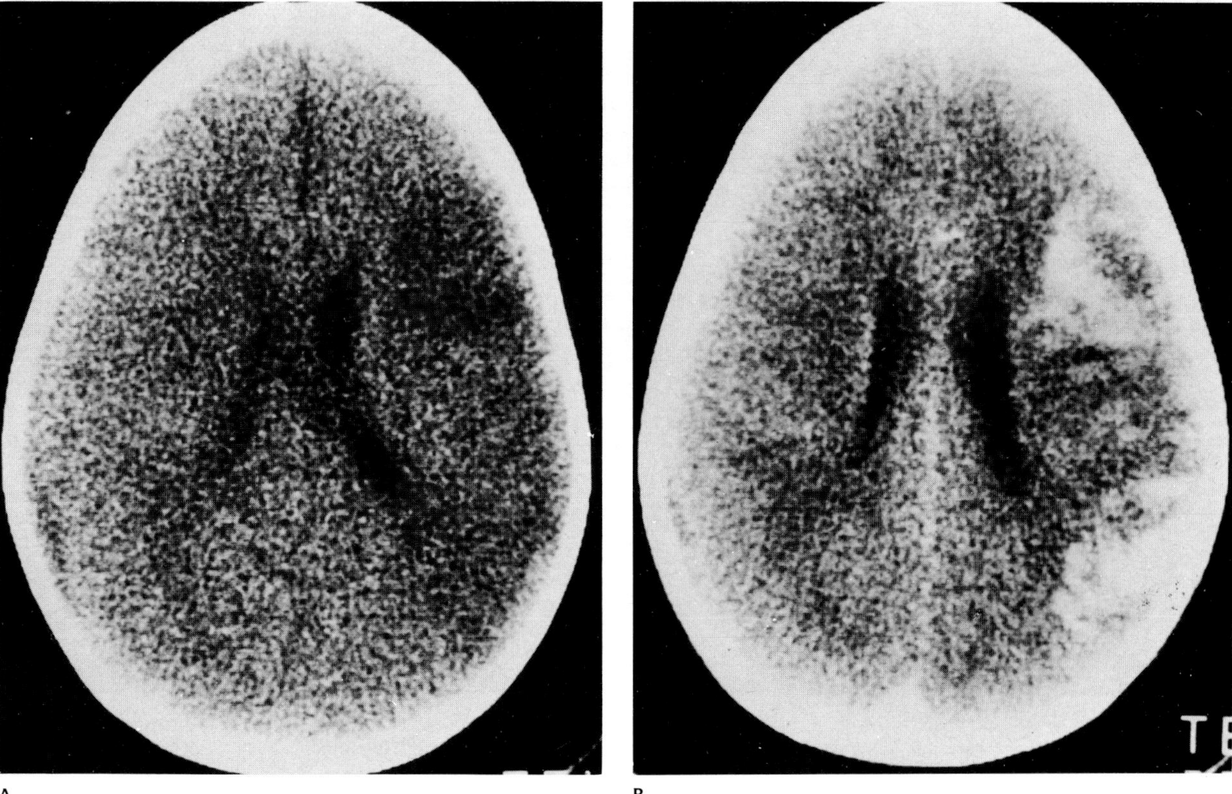

A B

Figure 13-7 Cerebritis involving both gray and white matter. **A.** NCCT shows poorly defined reginal hypodense areas in the left frontal arc parietal lobes. **B.** CECT exhibits intense patchy enhancement in the white matter of the frontal lobe and gyral enhacement in the parietal lobe.

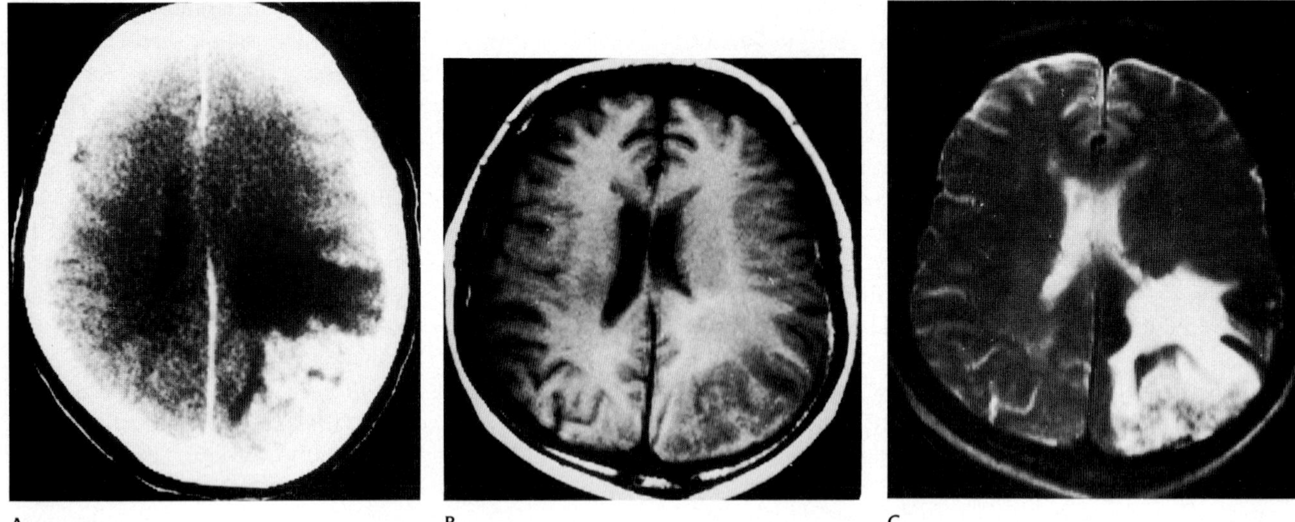

Figure 13-8 Tuberculous cerebritis in a 52-year-old man with right-sided weakness. **A.** CECT demonstrates heterogeneous enhancement in the left parietooccipital region, with surrounding edema. **B.** T_1WI (600/25) discloses effacement of sulci and mass effect in left parietooccipital region. **C.** T_2WI (2000/70) shows increased intensity in the region of the cerebritis. Surrounding hyperintensity due to edema is also noted. No evidence of frank abscess formation is visible. (*Courtesy J. Barkovich, University of California, San Francisco.*)

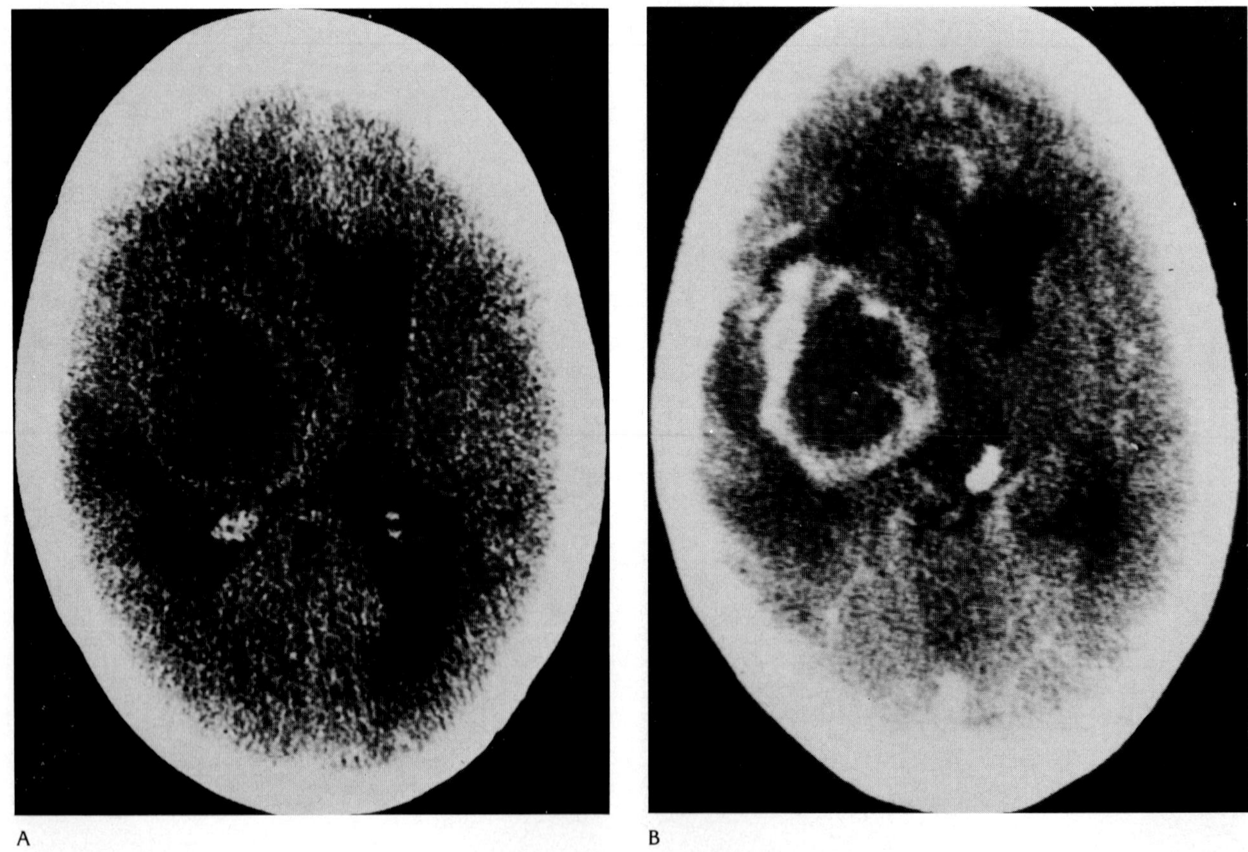

Figure 13-9 Temporal lobe abscess with thick, irregular capsule. **A.** NCCT shows a round, ringlike, hyperdense capsule differentiated from central low density (pus) and marked surrounding edema in the white matter. The compressed ipsilateral ventricle has shifted. **B.** On CECT, densely enhanced abscess capsule is evident. The irregular, thick wall of the capsule is not usual in pyogenic abscess. Central low density represents pus collection and does not change after IV contrast injection. The differentiation from glioblastoma may be extremely difficult in this case.

high density surrounding a central area of hypodensity is noted (Paxton 1974; Joubert 1977; Stevens 1978; Whelan 1980). Attenuation values within the central hypodense area may vary between 4 and 28 HU. The presence of gas collections within the brain with no antecedent history of penetrating craniocerebral trauma or surgical intervention may permit a specific diagnosis of abscess.

On CECT, the central hypodense area in the cavity does not change in appearance or CT number. Oval or circular peripheral ringlike contrast enhancement is an almost constant finding, delineating the formation of an abscess capsule (Kaufmann 1977). The wall is usually thin (3 to 6 mm) and of uniform thickness, although some abscesses display an irregularly thick wall which may mimic the wall of a glioblastoma (Figs. 13-9 and 13-10). A ringlike pattern on contrast study does not necessarily predict a firm capsule at surgery. Firmness of the capsule is a time-dependent phenomenon (Whelan 1980).

On MR, as the abscess core becomes necrotic, its T_1 and T_2 relaxation times lengthen (Haimes 1989). Hence, on T_1WI the central contents become of low signal intensity, while on T_2WI they appear to be of high signal intensity (Fig. 13-11). The appearance of the core provides information regarding its contents. Very liquefied abscesses have long T_1 and T_2 relaxation times and appear more hypointense on T_1WI and more hyperintense on T_2WI than do abscesses which are filled with gelatinous or necrotic debris. In all cases, however, the abscess core appears to be of higher signal intensity than CSF on all parameters.

The abscess rim displays changes in signal intensity very different from those of the necrotic core (Haimes 1989). Against the hypointense center, it often appears as isointense to normal brain parenchyma or, occasionally, hyperintense on T_1WI. The hyperintensity may be related to hemorrhage. While hemorrhage is usually not associated with abscess formation on CT, MR is able to detect very small amounts of blood. On T_2-WI, the rim may appear isointense or become hypointense. The etiology of the hypointense rim surrounding many abscesses has been the subject of speculation. It may be due to the presence of hemoglobin breakdown products, such as deoxyhemoglobin, or other aspects of clot formation. Alternatively, it has been suggested that the presence of free radicals produced by actively phagocytosing macrophages is responsible for the marked hypointensity of some abscess capsules (Haimes 1989). As on CT, after the administration of contrast, the abscess capsule can be seen to enhance on MR (Grossman 1984). Other features of the enhancing wall, such as thinness and evenness, are known from CT.

Surrounding the abscess capsule, prominent edema is seen in 80 to 90 percent of patients (Paxton 1974; Nielsen 1977; Haimes 1989). The volume of the surrounding

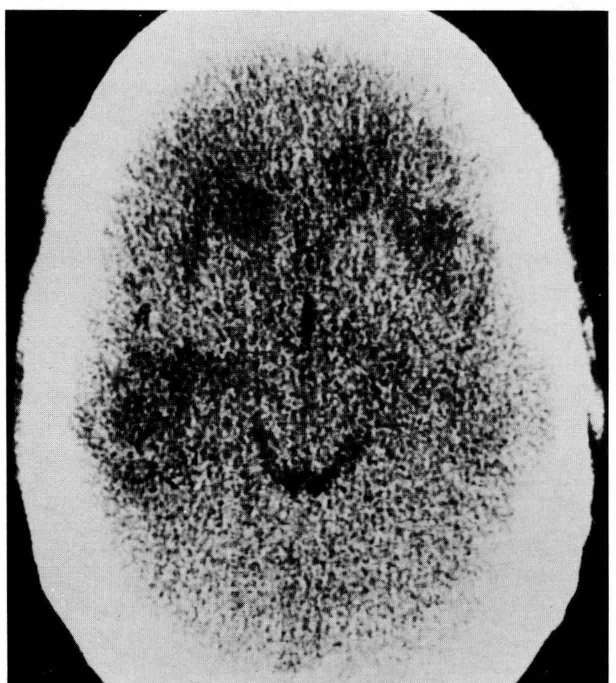

A

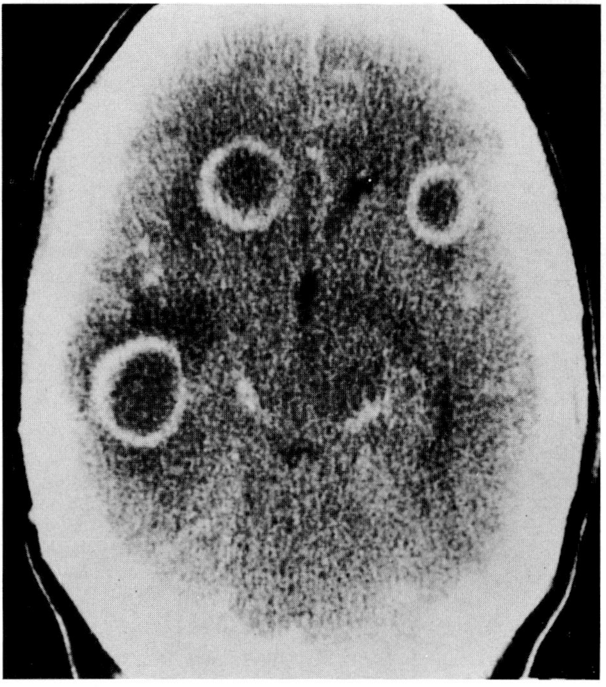

B

Figure 13-10 Multiple abscesses (staphylococcal) of unknown origin in a 25-year-old man. **A.** NCCT shows multiple round, hypodense areas in both hemispheres. Faint ringlike hyperdense capsules are visible. **B.** CECT reveals multiple abscesses in the white matter. (*Continued on p. 550.*)

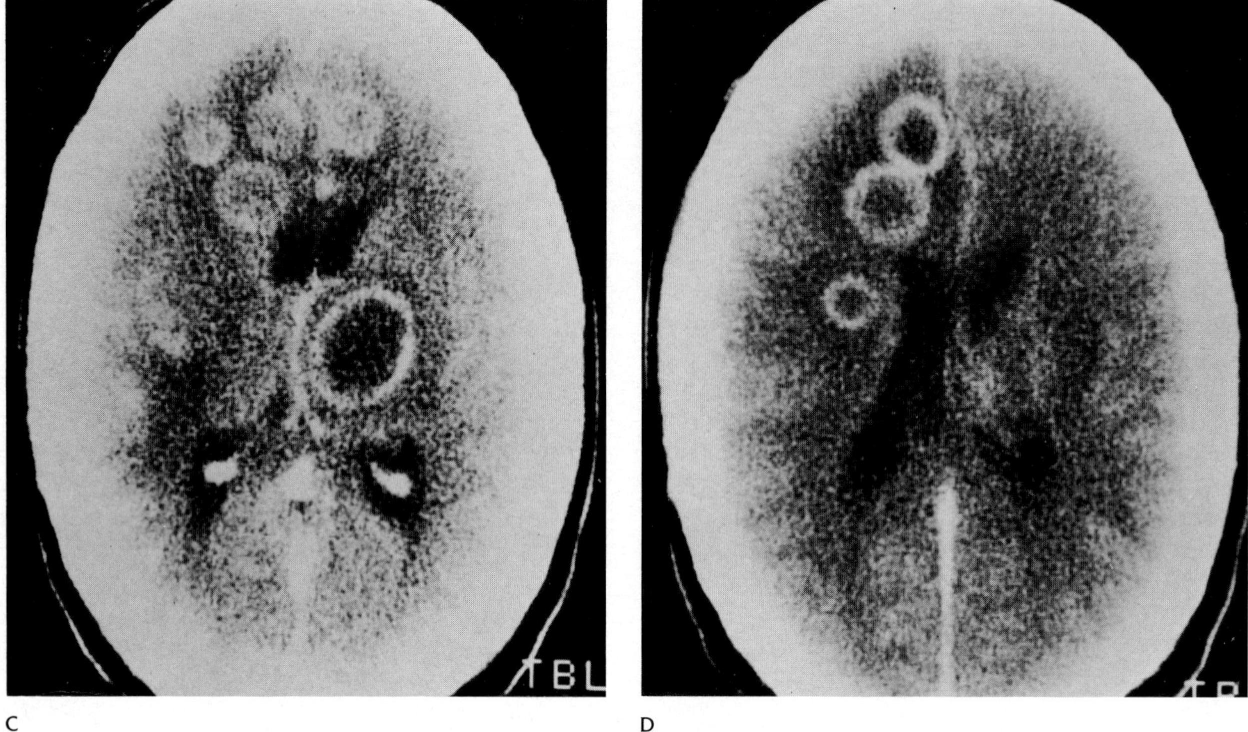

C D

Figure 13-10 ***(continued)*** **C** and **D.** At the higher level, numerous cavities in the white matter, corticomedullary junction of both frontal lobes, and deep gray matter are present.

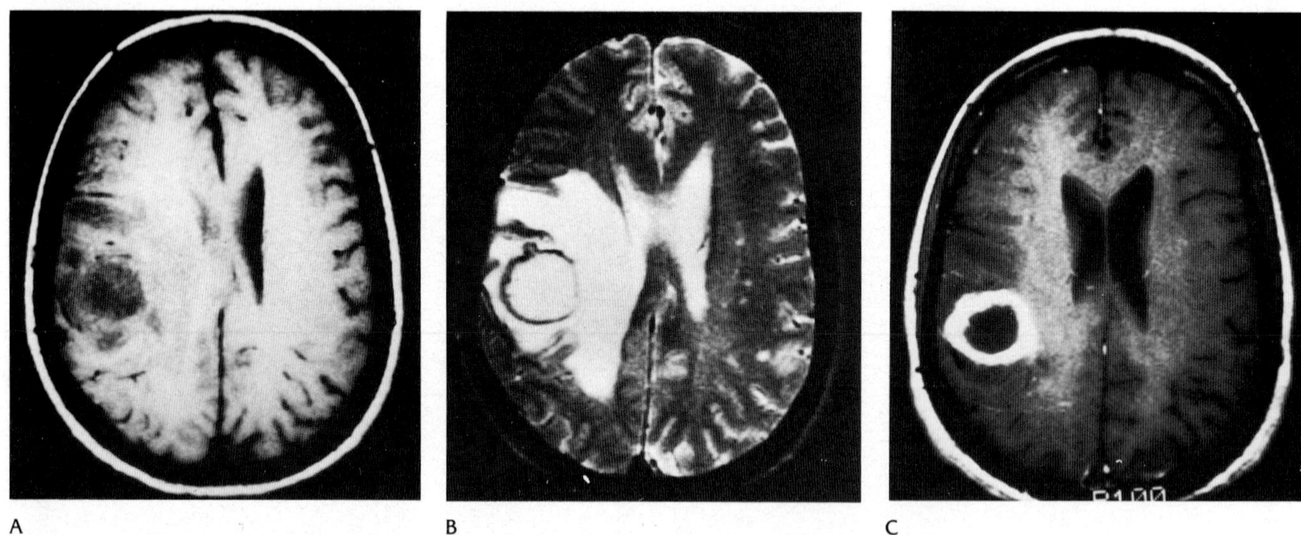

A B C

Figure 13-11 *H. influenzae* abscess; NG and CEMRI. A 36-year-old woman with tetralogy of Fallot and left-sided weakness. **A** and **B.** T_1WI after the administration of Gd-DTPA (CEMR) shows the enhancing capsule surrounding the nectrotic central core. (*Courtesy A. Haimes and R. D. Zimmerman, The New York Hospital–Cornell Medical Center, New York.*)

edematous white matter is often greater than that of the abscess and is therefore responsible for much of the mass effect (Figs. 13-9 and 13-10). On T_1WI the edematous regions appear to be of slightly low intensity; on T_2WI they become high-intensity. Fingers of vasogenic edema often follow white matter tracts.

The majority of abscesses are supratentorial. Two special circumstances—cerebellar abscesses and intrasellar abscesses—deserve mention. Cerebellar abscesses constitute 2 to 18 percent of all brain abscesses (Fig. 13-12). They are less likely to be encapsulated but have a better prognosis than do supratentorial abscesses if they are

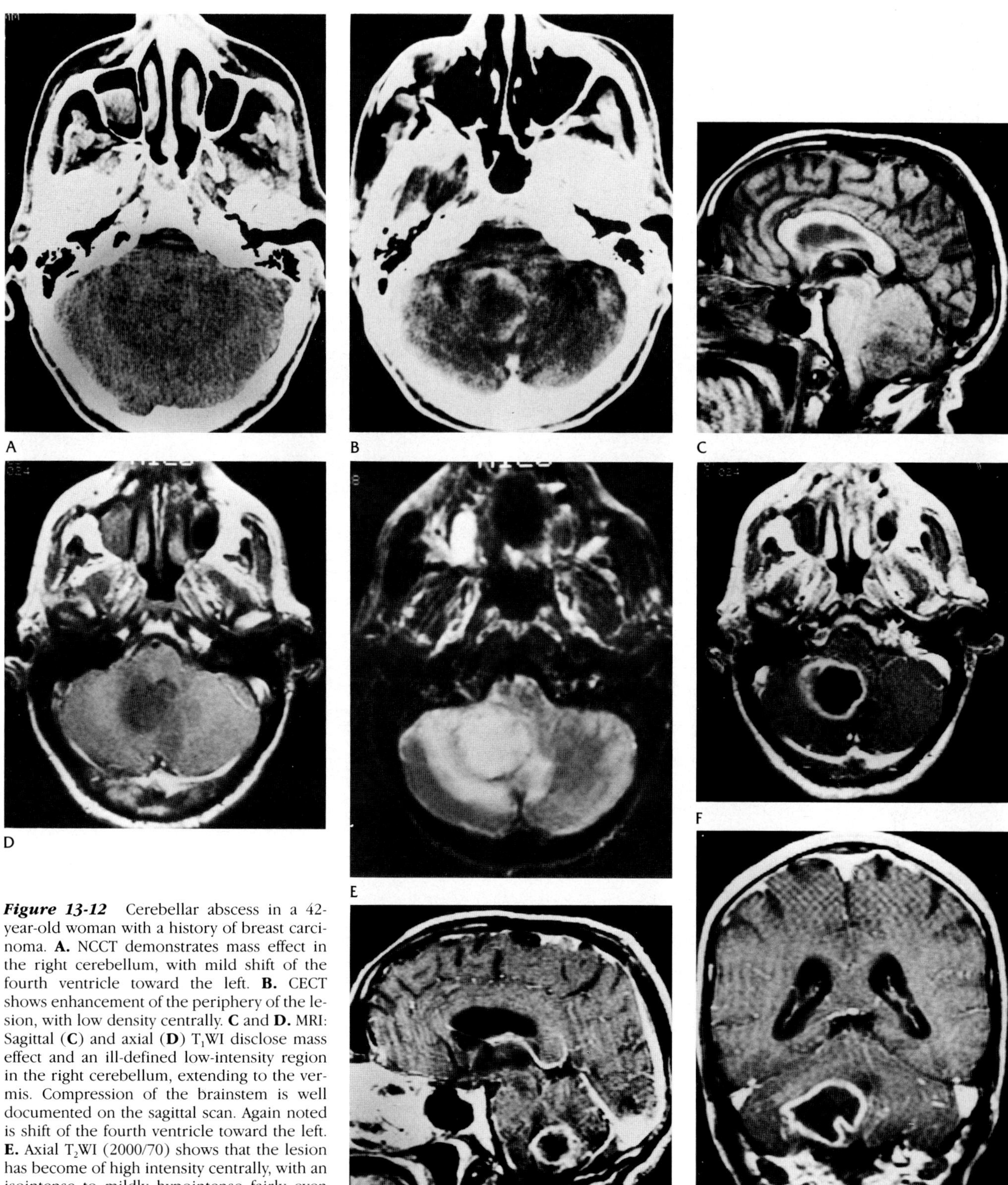

Figure 13-12 Cerebellar abscess in a 42-year-old woman with a history of breast carcinoma. **A.** NCCT demonstrates mass effect in the right cerebellum, with mild shift of the fourth ventricle toward the left. **B.** CECT shows enhancement of the periphery of the lesion, with low density centrally. **C** and **D.** MRI: Sagittal (**C**) and axial (**D**) T_1WI disclose mass effect and an ill-defined low-intensity region in the right cerebellum, extending to the vermis. Compression of the brainstem is well documented on the sagittal scan. Again noted is shift of the fourth ventricle toward the left. **E.** Axial T_2WI (2000/70) shows that the lesion has become of high intensity centrally, with an isointense to mildly hypointense fairly even rim. Surrounding high intensity caused by edema is also noted. **F–.** T_1WI (600/12) axial, sagittal, and coronal MR scans demonstrate enhancement of the rim of the lesion, with hypointensity centrally. At surgery this proved to be a cerebellar abscess caused by mixed gram-negative bacilli.

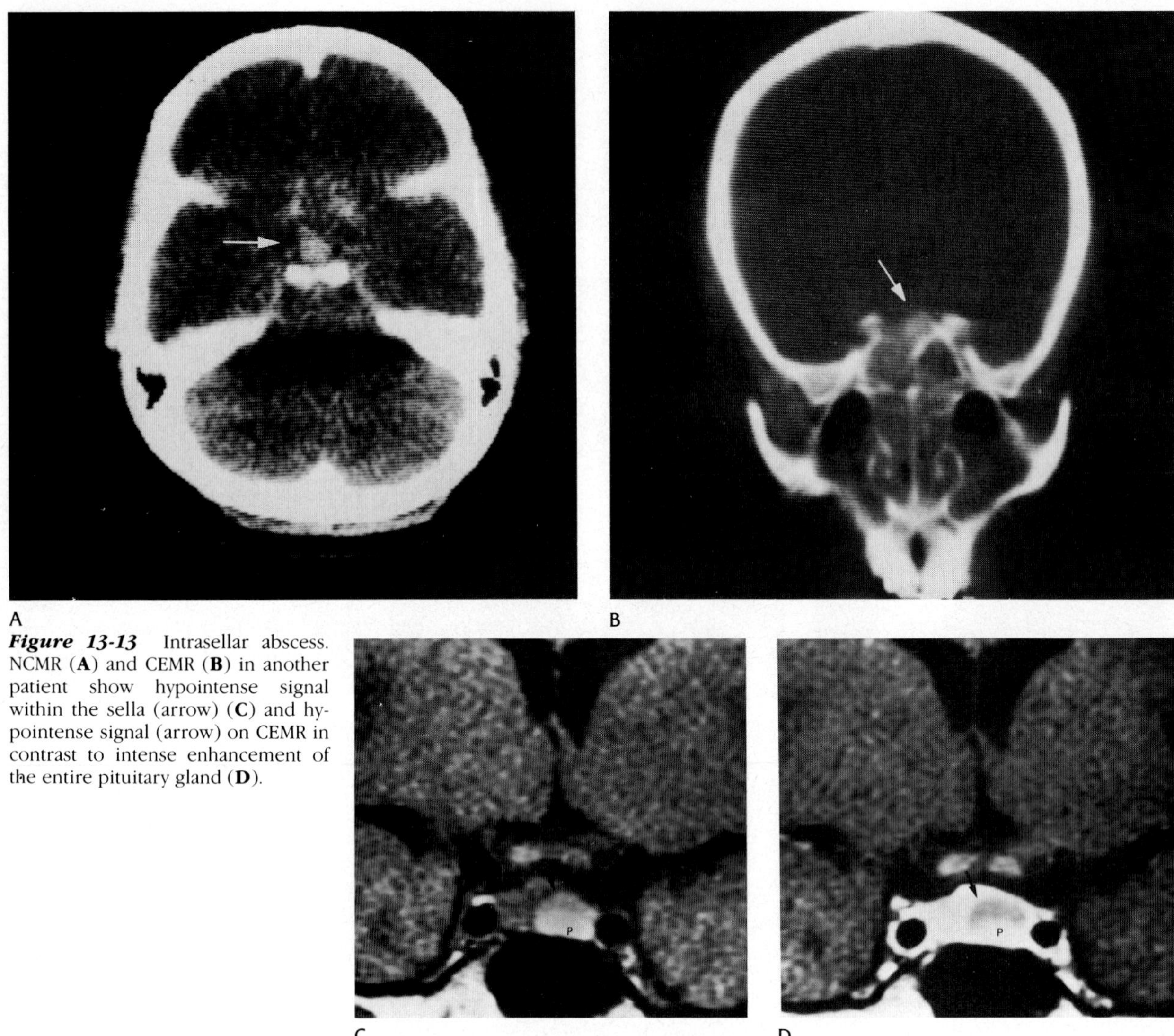

Figure 13-13 Intrasellar abscess. NCMR (**A**) and CEMR (**B**) in another patient show hypointense signal within the sella (arrow) (**C**) and hypointense signal (arrow) on CEMR in contrast to intense enhancement of the entire pituitary gland (**D**).

recognized early and treated surgically prior to the onset of irreversible brainstem damage (Morgan 1975). Pituitary or intrasellar abscesses should be suspected if a rapidly expanding mass in the sella is seen in a patient with a history of recurrent episodes of meningitis and rhinorrhea. CECT can demonstrate focal contrast enhancement or ring enhancement within the sella (Fig. 13-13). MR discloses a pituitary mass with enhancement (Fig. 13-13). Differentiation from tumor may be difficult. In some cases, hemoglobin breakdown products may produce hyperintensity on T_1WI.

In patients with abscesses, clinical improvement with medical therapy has been correlated with a decrease in both the degree of contrast enhancement of the ring and the amount of surrounding edema (Robertheram 1979; Kamin 1981). Delayed postsurgical contrast enhancement may be due to vascular granulation tissue present about the circumference of the previous abscess and may not represent persistence of the abscess capsule. Steroids may reduce the inflammatory edema associated with brain abscesses (Wallenfang 1981) but can also suppress the contrast enhancement of the capsule completely. Also, withdrawal of steroids may result in a rebound increase in the degree of enhancement (Robertheram 1979).

Complications of abscess formation include raised intracranial pressure with the potential risk of cerebral herniation and rupture of the abscess into the ventricle. It is thus extremely important to determine the severity of the associated edema and to determine the size of an abscess accurately. The multiplanar capability of MR is particularly useful. In addition, demonstration of an abscess associated with contrast enhancement of an adjacent ventricular wall indicates rupture of an abscess into the ventricle with secondary ependymitis. The prognosis in this situation is usually poor.

Mycotic Aneurysms

Aneurysms of inflammatory origin may be bacterial, syphilitic, or mycotic. Although the term *mycotic* is used in the general sense of microorganisms, a bacterial etiology is the most common. These aneurysms originate mainly as an embolic complication of bacterial endocarditis; less commonly, they form as a complication of cardiac surgery, meningitis, cavernous sinus thrombophlebitis, or osteomyelitis. The most frequent location is the peripheral branches of the middle cerebral artery, followed by the anterior cerebral artery, the internal carotid artery, and the basilar artery, where abscesses are often

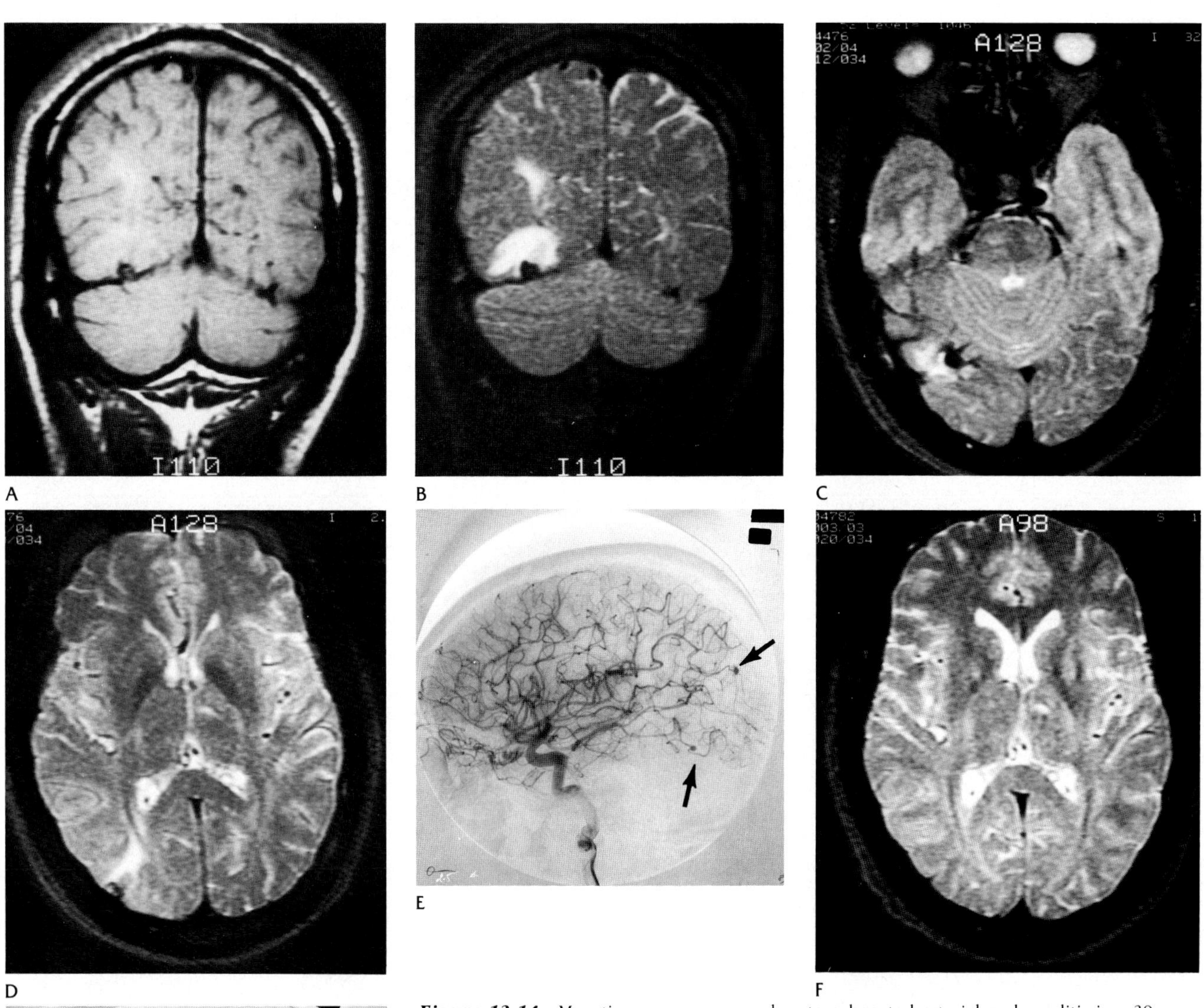

Figure 13-14 Mycotic aneurysm secondary to subacute bacterial endocarditis in a 39-year-old man. MRI: Coronal T_1WI (**A**), T_2WI (**B**), and axial T_2WI (**C**) show a round signal void region in the right occipital lobe. Axial T_2WI (**D**) demonstrates another lesion in the right posterior parietal lobe near the cortex. Cerebral angiogram (**E**) demonstrates two aneurysms (arrows). After vigorous antibiotic treatment, they have resolved completely, as confirmed by MRI (T_2WI) (**F**) and repeat angiogram (**G**). (*Case courtesy of Dr. Joseph Robbins, Piscataway, NJ.*)

multiple. Progressive weakening of the elastica and the media of the aneurysm wall may result in enlargement and rupture, with hemorrhage into the adjacent cortex or the subarachnoid or subdural spaces, or may cause multiple coalescent infarcts (Harriman 1984).

CT and MR clearly demonstrate the complications of septic emboli as well as "mycotic" aneurysms at the peripheral branches near the cortex. On CECT, a small enhancing focus may be noted in the parenchyma. An enhancing vessel leading to the focus is strongly suggestive of an aneurysm but is not always seen because of its small size. On MR, a small area of signal void is visualized associated with adjacent parenchymal alteration (Fig. 13-14). Angiography may confirm the presence of the aneurysm itself. Complications of mycotic aneurysms include meningitis, cerebral abscess, and cerebral infarction in addition to hemorrhage.

Meningitis

Haemophilus influenzae and *Escherichia coli* in neonates and young children and meningococci and pneumococci in adolescents and adults account for most instances of suppurative meningitis. Organisms may spread to the meninges hematogenously or by direct extension. The subarachnoid space offers little resistance to infection, and the CSF facilitates its spread over the brain and spinal canal and into the ventricles. In other words, meningitis is always cerebrospinal (Adams 1985). The common initial response to these invading organisms is meningeal vascular congestion, edema, and minute hemorrhages. The underlying brain and its ependymal surfaces remain intact. Once infection progresses, however, the subpial cortex of the brain and the ependymal lining of the ventricles also show evidence of an inflammatory reaction.

In early or mild meningitis, CT may be normal (Claveria 1976; Zimmerman 1976), and it may continue to be normal if treatment is instituted promptly and adequately. If infection continues, slightly increased density in the basal cisterns, interhemispheric fissure, and choroid plexuses can be seen on NCCT and may simulate contrast enhancement, probably because of a combination of hypervascularity in the acutely inflamed leptomeninges and

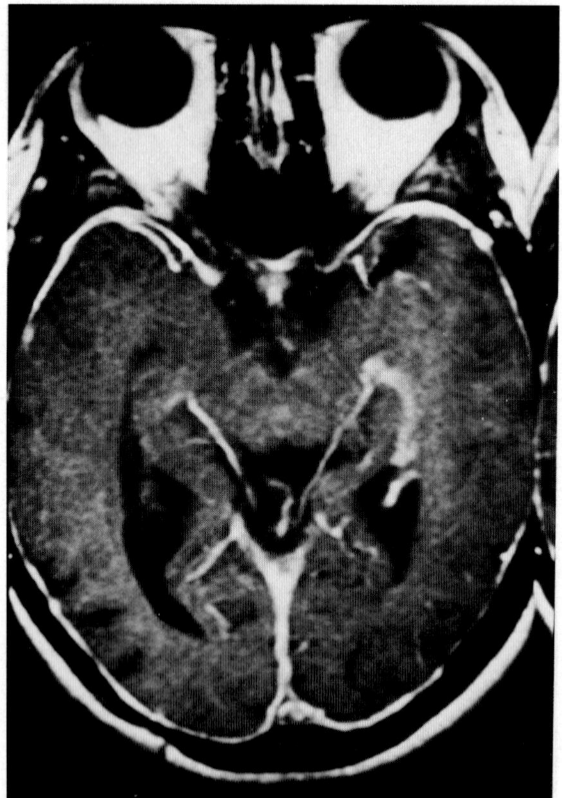

A

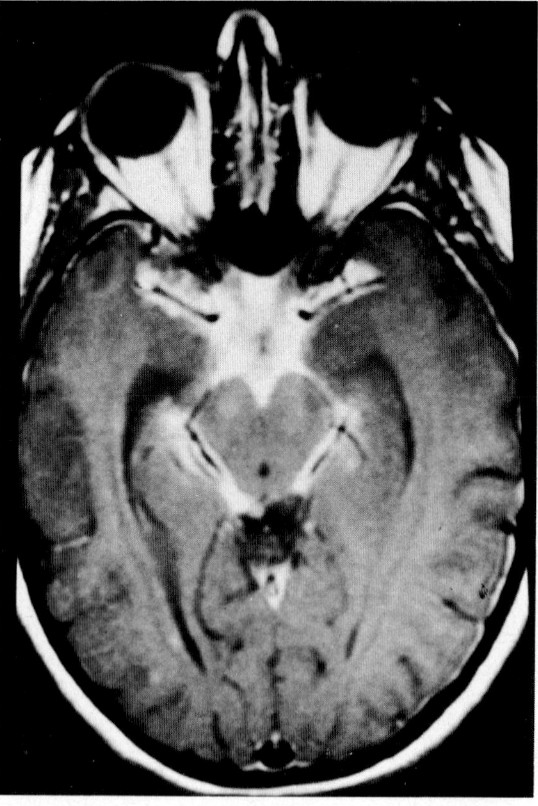

B

Figure 13-15 Tuberculous meningitis. **A.** CEMR scan demonstrates diffuse enhancement of all the meninges surrounding the brain parenchyma. Also noted is enhancement extending along the falx. Enhancement of the falx is too prominent to be normal. **B.** On a higher section, enhancing tuberculous granulation tissue is seen to fill all the basal cisterns. On both images, note the slight prominence of the lateral ventricles, suggestive of communicating hydrocephalus.

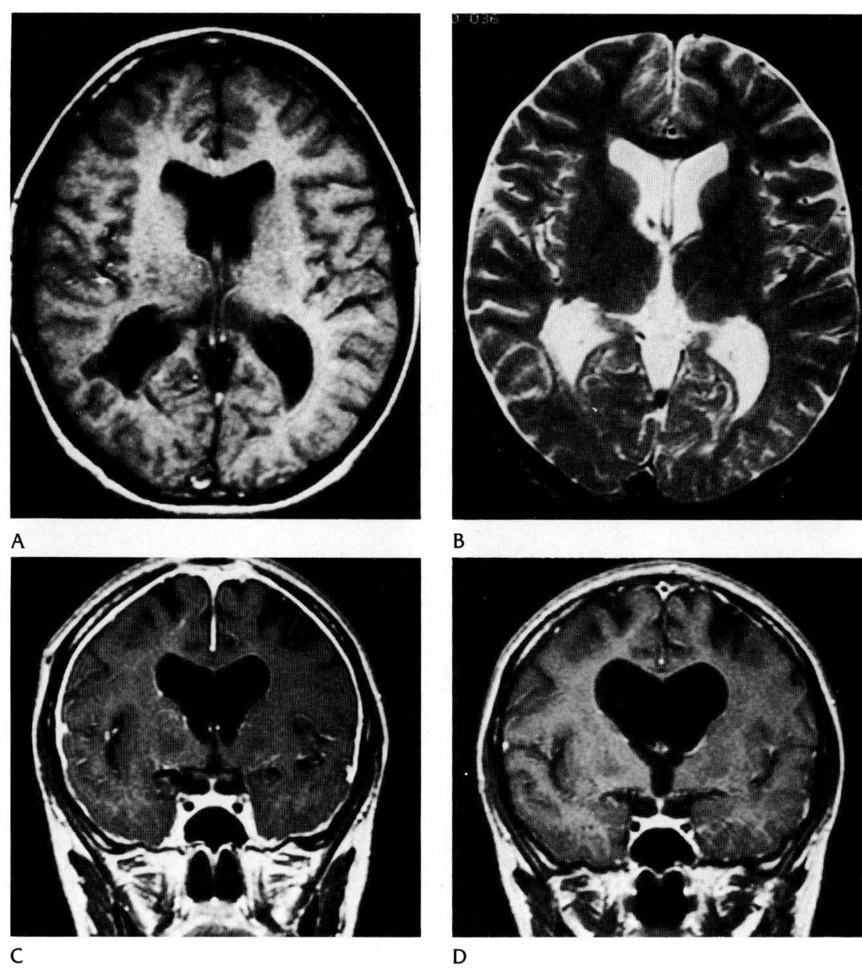

Figure 13-16 Bacterial meningitis. A 32-year-old woman with headache and stiff neck. Cause: *Propionibacterium acnes* meningitis. NCMR (**A** and **B**): Axial T_1WI (600/20) and T_2WI (2000/70) images do not disclose a meningeal abnormality, although mild prominence of the ventricle is present. A shunt trace is seen entering the right occipital horn. **C.** CEMR: T_1WI (600/20) demonstrates marked enhancement of the meninges surrounding the entire brain. Enhancement of the falx may be a normal finding, although in this case the enhancement is pathological. **D.** After treatment with antibiotics, follow-up CEMR coronal scan shows resolution of previously ntoed meningeal enhancement. If fibrous change occurs in the meninges, however, enhancement after meningitis or other meningeal pathology may be permanent. (*Reprinted with permission from* Bronen R 1990.)

choroid plexuses and fibrinous or hemorrhagic exudate in the subarachnoid space in the interhemispheric fissure and the basal cisterns. The lateral and third ventricles are symmetrically compressed and extremely small (Auh 1980), and the subarachnoid spaces are effaced, probably because of diffuse brain swelling representing both cortical congestion and edematous white matter. The cortical congestion is often less severe than it is in encephalitis. Focal areas of hypodensity representing edema may be seen on CT. Abnormal contrast enhancement in a bandlike or gyral configuration in the leptomeningeal and cortical zones may be observed, resulting from the vascular congestion of the meninges and disruption of the blood-brain barrier (Fig. 13-1).

Changes in MR resemble those in CT. In early or mild disease, both NCMR and CEMR are negative. In more severe cases of meningitis, increased signal intensity can be seen on NCMR in the basal cisterns or interhemispheric fissure because of the purulent exudate (Sze 1989). Close comparison with the intensity of CSF in other regions—for example, in the ventricles—is necessary because the findings are usually subtle. In addition, since CSF flow artifacts can produce changes in signal intensity, caution must be used. The intensity of the subarachnoid spaces should not be compared with areas of pulsatile CSF flow, such as the aqueduct of Sylvius, which may exhibit signal void.

Verification of changes suspected on NCMR can be obtained by the administration of contrast (Fig. 13-15). Enhancement of the meninges may be seen and can take several patterns on CEMR (Sze 1989). Enhancement can be peripheral and diffuse, surrounding the entire brain, or peripheral and focal, located, for example, only in basal cisterns or over one lobe (Figs. 13-15 and 13-16). Alternatively, enhancement can also be nodular when infectious agents are localized in the subarachnoid space and grow (Fig. 13-17).

CEMR is more sensitive than CECT in the evaluation of suspected meningitis (Sze 1989). Enhancement of the meninges is often obscured on CT as a result of the high density of the adjacent inner table. On MR, however, these changes are easily detected (Bronen 1990). Experimental studies utilizing an animal model have demonstrated that abnormal meningeal enhancement can be

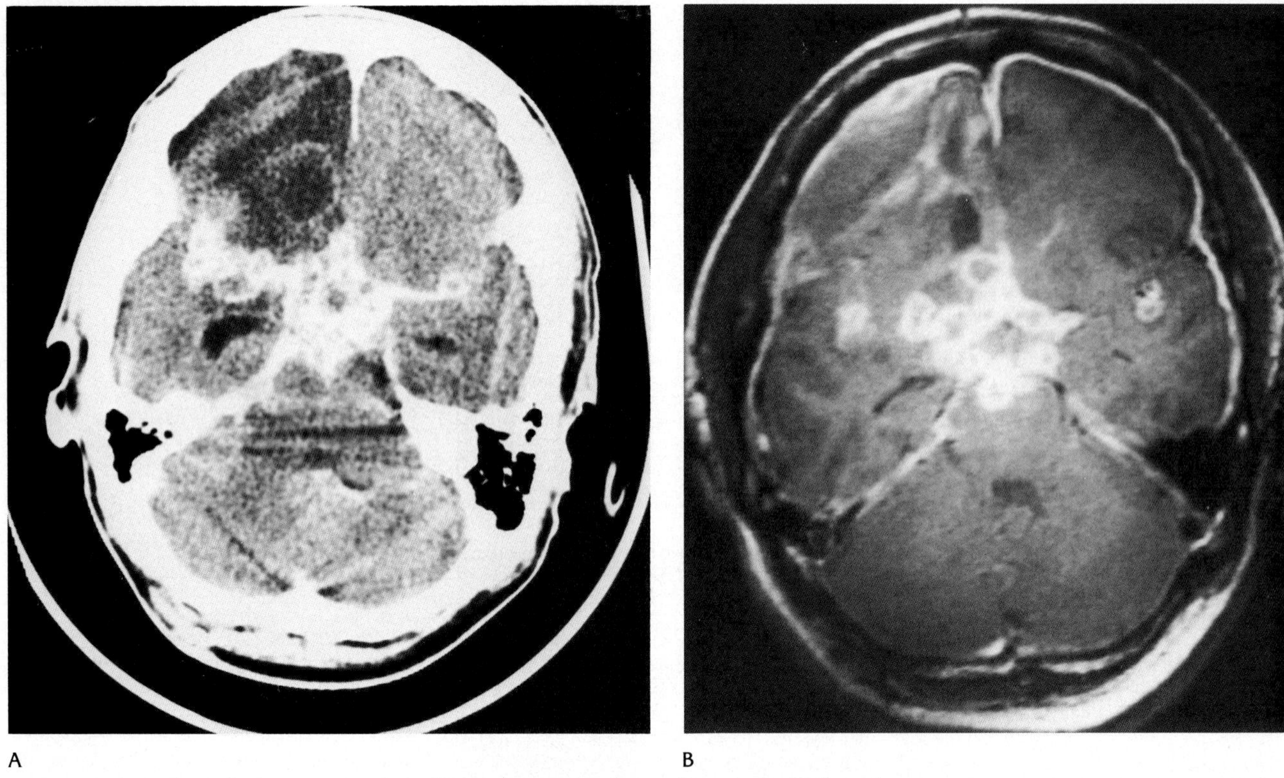

Figure 13-17 Tuberculosis meningitis. **A.** CECT demonstrates exuberant linear and nodular enhancement at the basal cisterns and leptomeninges. **B.** CEMR reveals the contrast-enhancing lesions to better advantage, especially at the peripheral leptomeningeal coverings. (*Reprinted with permission from Chang 1990.*)

detected in bacterial meningitis as early as 4 hours after infection (Mathews 1988).

Both CT and MR can be used to detect complications of meningitis, although MR is more sensitive to early changes such as thrombosis of the draining sinuses (Fig. 13-3). On spin-echo images, signal void in the course of the sinuses should be present on multiple planes or sequences. Flow-related enhancement may cause artifactually increased signal and misinterpretation if only a single plane or sequence is examined. Gradient-echo sequences exhibit a lack of high signal intensity in the course of the sinus if thrombosis is present. Arterial or venous thrombosis may lead to areas of cerebral infarction. In such cases diffuse or localized areas of involvement can be seen within the brain parenchyma, usually conforming to the distribution of the involved vessels (Brant-Zawadzki 1983). Hyperintensity in the ischemic regions can be seen on T_2WI (Chap. 15).

Hydrocephalus is another complication of meningitis and can result from impaired absorption of CSF from the subarachnoid space (Fig. 13-15). Extension of infection to the ependyma may result in hydrocephalus from obstruction of the fourth ventricle. Both communicating and obstructive hydrocephalus can be evaluated adequately with CT and MR (Chap. 7).

The development of subdural effusion can also complicate meningitis. Loculations of fluid between the thickened meninges occur over the base of the brain and on the surfaces of the cerebral hemispheres. In general, these effusions resolve spontaneously, although they rarely may develop into subdural empyemas. Occasionally, calcification can develop in the walls of a postmeningitis subdural effusion (Nelson 1969; Claveria 1976). Differentiation between subdural effusion and empyema can be made on MR (Weingarten 1989). Effusion exhibits a CSF-like intensity pattern, while empyema has a high protein content in general.

Ependymitis

Ependymitis may occur secondary to leptomeningitis in retrograde extension of an infection or spontaneous or iatrogenic rupture of an abscess cavity directly into the ventricles. Alternatively, ependymitis is often associated with foreign bodies, particularly shunts within the ventricles.

On CECT, acute bacterial ependymitis shows distinct thin contrast enhancement along the ventricular wall either locally or diffusely (Zimmerman 1976; Nielsen 1977) (Fig. 13-18). On MR, changes may be very subtle in

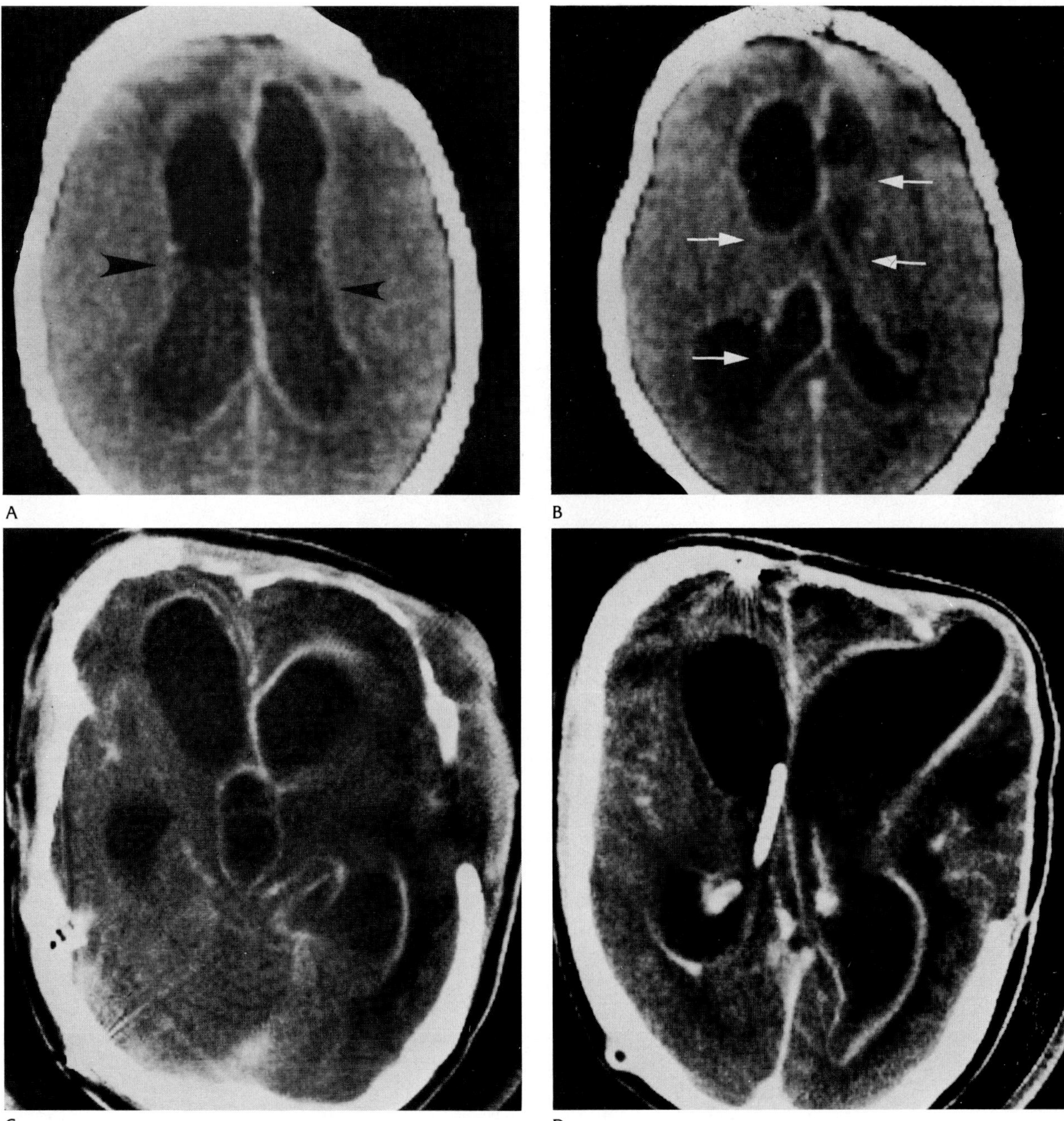

Figure 13-18 **A** and **B.** Ependymitis with septations following surgery for frontal sinusitis and abscess. On CECT (**A**) extensive ependymitis shows as a thin contrast enhancement along the ventricular wall. CSF levels in the ventricles (arrowheads) are due to layering of pus in the dependent posterior halves of the bodies of dilated lateral ventricles. Frontal craniotomy defect is the result of surgery for frontal abscess secondary to frontal sinusitis. CECT at lower level (**B**) demonstrates intraventricular septations (arrows) resulting in multiple compartmentalization. Note again extensive enhancement of the inflamed ventricular wall. **C** and **D.** A young man sustained multiple craniofacial fractures following a gas-tank explosion. Postsurgical evacuation of the extracerebral collection was complicated by the wound infection and drainage of pus in the shunt tube. CECT demonstrates intense linear contrast enhancement along the walls of the ventricular system. Pus-CSF fluid levels are also noted in the lateral ventricles. Noncommunicating hydrocephalus is evident.

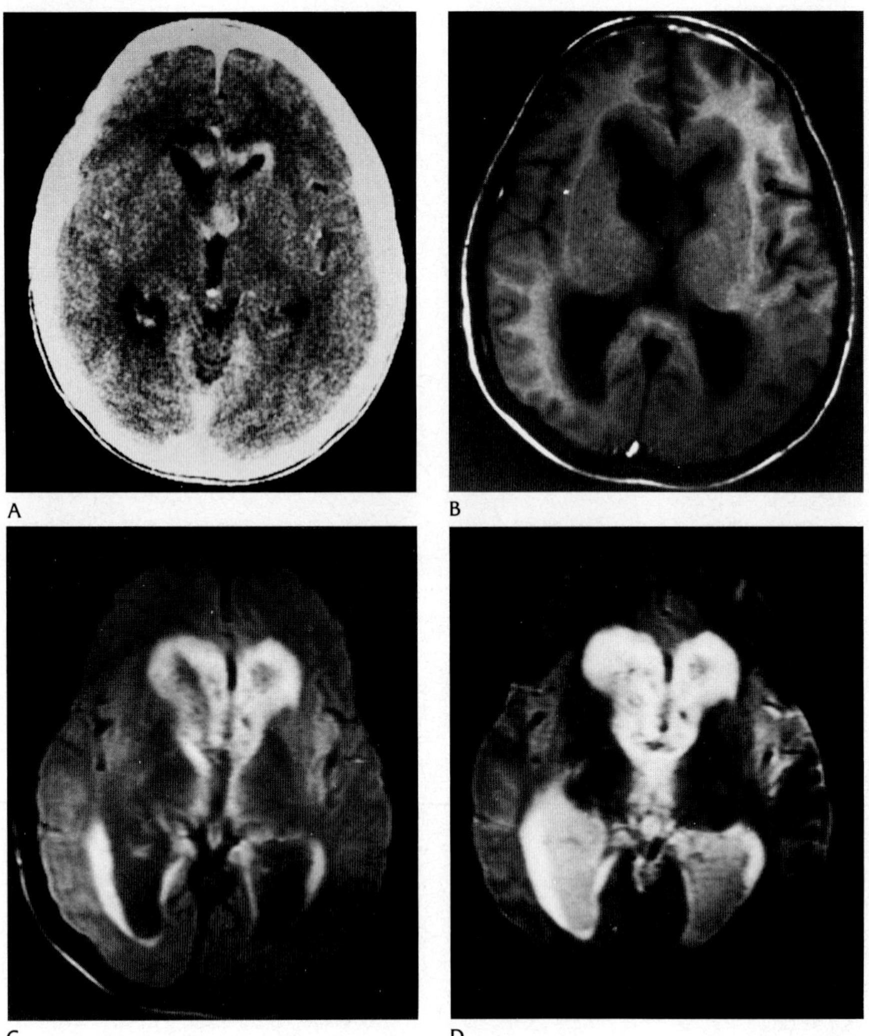

Figure 13-19 Cytomegalovirus ependymitis. **A.** CECT discloses mild enlargement of the ventricles associated with mild enhancement of the ependyma. **B.** MR: T_1WI (600/20) demonstrates a thick irregular ring surrounding the ventricles. **C** and **D.** MR: T_2WI (2000/35, 70) show hyperintensity surrounding all the ventricles. Note that the high signal intensity appears to be uneven and nodular, in contrast to the thin linear appearance that is more typical of hydrocephalus.

cases of mild ependymitis. However, in more severe cases T_1WI disclose irregular hypointensity in a periventricular pattern. On T_2WI, irregular hyperintensity surrounds the ventricles (Barloon 1990). In severe cases, the periventricular signal is often more nodular and uneven than one sees in hydrocephalus (Fig. 13-19). In addition, while transependymal exudate caused by hydrocephalus frequently spares the corpus callosum, which is composed of tightly packed white matter fibers, in ependymitis, involvement of the corpus callosum is often present. As in CECT, contrast enhancement can often be seen in the ventricular wall. If purulent debris fills the ventricles, increased signal on both T_1WI and T_2WI will be detected in the CSF; comparison with the vitreous of the globe may be useful since concomitant meningitis may prevent comparison with CSF in the basal cisterns (Barloon 1990). A CSF-debris layer may also be demonstrated within the ventricles.

Intraventricular septations and compartmentalization resulting from organization of exudate and debris blockage of intraventricular formamina by purulent exudate lead to obstructive hydrocephalus. The loculated infection of the ventricles can become a reservoir of infected material. Trapping of the fourth ventricle can act as an expanding mass in the posterior fossa and may require shunting (Zimmerman 1978) (Fig. 13-20). Both CT and MR not only precisely depict the size and shape of the ventricles but also may suggest the presence of intraventricular septations and compartmentalization (Fig. 13-18). MR is probably slightly more sensitive than is CT in showing septations. In addition, loculations can be assessed on MR since they are often of higher signal than the surrounding CSF as a result of either proteinaceous exudate or the lack of CSF pulsations within them (Fig. 13-18).

GRANULOMATOUS INFECTION

Tuberculous Infection

Tuberculosis may involve the CNS either as meningitis or as parenchymal granulomas or abscesses. Tuberculous

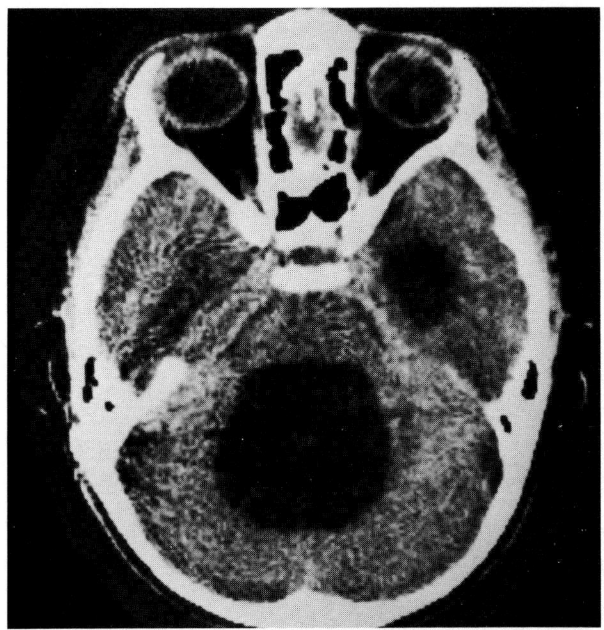

A

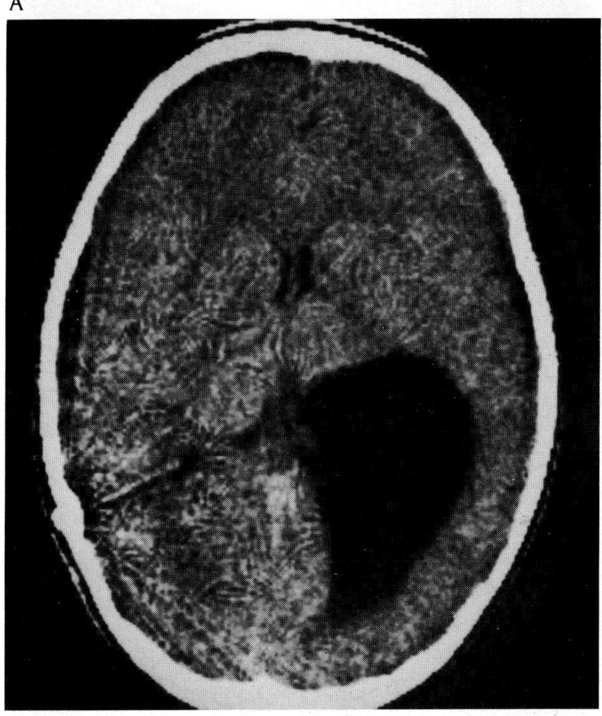

B

Figure 13-20 Trapped ventricles. A four-year-old child with a history of tuberculosis meningitis. A shunt was placed for hyrocephalus. **A.** The trapped fourth ventricle shows a rounded appearance and may present as an expanding mass. Dilated temporal horn is noted. **B.** In this CT, taken at a higher level, the trapped trigone of the lateral ventricle is also seen.

meningitis results from the hematogenous dissemination of bacilli from a primary lesion in the thorax, abdomen, or genitourinary tract. Bacilli may enter the CSF in regions of absent blood-brain barrier such as the choroid plexus. Alternatively, they may spread to the CSF if small granulomas in the cerebral cortex or the meninges rupture into the subarachnoid space, initiating a widespread meningeal infectious process. Tuberculous meningitis occurs primarily in the pediatric population and in the elderly; an increasing association with AIDS has been reported (Bishburg 1986; Sellwyn 1989).

Pathologically, tuberculous meningitis manifests as a fibrinous pachymeningitis, associated with a purulent exudate and the formation of granulation tissue. Communicating hydrocephalus can result from obstruction at the level of the basal cisterns. Constriction of the major vessels at the base of the brain and in the sylvian fissure is seen in response to direct insult by the infecting organism (vasculitis) and as a result of the surrounding meningeal inflammation. Secondary infarcts may occur (Chang 1990).

On NCCT, the basal cisterns are often difficult to visualize since they may be partially obscured by the presence of inflammatory tissue and exudate. On CECT, the involved cisterns enhance uniformly and intensely; the appearance may resemble the NCCT appearance of the head after subarachnoid hemorrhage or after the instillation of intrathecal contrast (Enzmann 1976). The basal cisterns are most frequently affected, although often the sylvian cisterns and other subarachnoid spaces are involved (Armitsu 1979; Casselman 1980) (Figs. 13-15 and 13-17). Communicating hydrocephalus is usually persistent and often does not improve even if antituberculous therapy is given (Price 1978; Stevens 1978). In 48 percent of cases calcification of the meninges at the base of the brain may be demonstrated 18 months to 3 years after the onset of the disease (Lorber 1958).

On MR, exudate in the basal cisterns often appears hyperintense compared with normal CSF. On T_1WI and proton-density images, signal increase may be seen when the cisterns are compared with ventricular CSF (Chang 1990). On T_2WI, the differentiation may be difficult since both the purulent exudate and the CSF appear as high signal intensity (Sze 1989). After IV administration of MR contrast agent, marked enhancement of the basal cisterns is often seen (Fig. 13-15).

As with bacterial meningitis, MR is more sensitive than CT to subtle enhancement along the bony inner table of the skull (Mathews 1988, 1989) (Fig. 13-15). However, MR is markedly insensitive to the presence of calcifications, which are a late sequela of tuberculous meningitis (Holland 1985).

Tuberculosis can also occur intraparenchymally. Granuloma formation is far more common than tuberculous abscess. Although cerebral tuberculoma is a rare manifestation of tuberculosis in the United States, it is very common in developing countries and is frequently the most common cause of a brain mass. The infrequency of the disease in this country often results in diagnosis oversight, since 42 percent of patients with intracranial tuberculomas have no evidence of extracranial disease

(Mayers 1978). The clinical features of intracerebral tuberculoma are rarely distinguishable from those of other space-occupying intracranial lesions (Anderson 1975).

Pathologically, a tuberculoma is composed of a caseous center surrounded by a ring of granulomatous tissue; it may be spherical or multiloculated and single or multiple. Tuberculomas are found in any part of the cerebral or cerebellar tissue; they are usually located in the cortical-subcortical location and may also occur in the meninges. Multiple tubercules may be found within the brain at the corticomedullary junction and in the paraventricular regions in patients with extensive hematogenous spread, usually from miliary tuberculosis of the lungs. For practical purposes, tuberculoma and tuberculous abscesses are variants of a similar pathological process, with the abscess being a tuberculoma with a necrosed and completely liquefied center (Vegasarkar 1986).

On NCCT, varying image patterns have been reported:

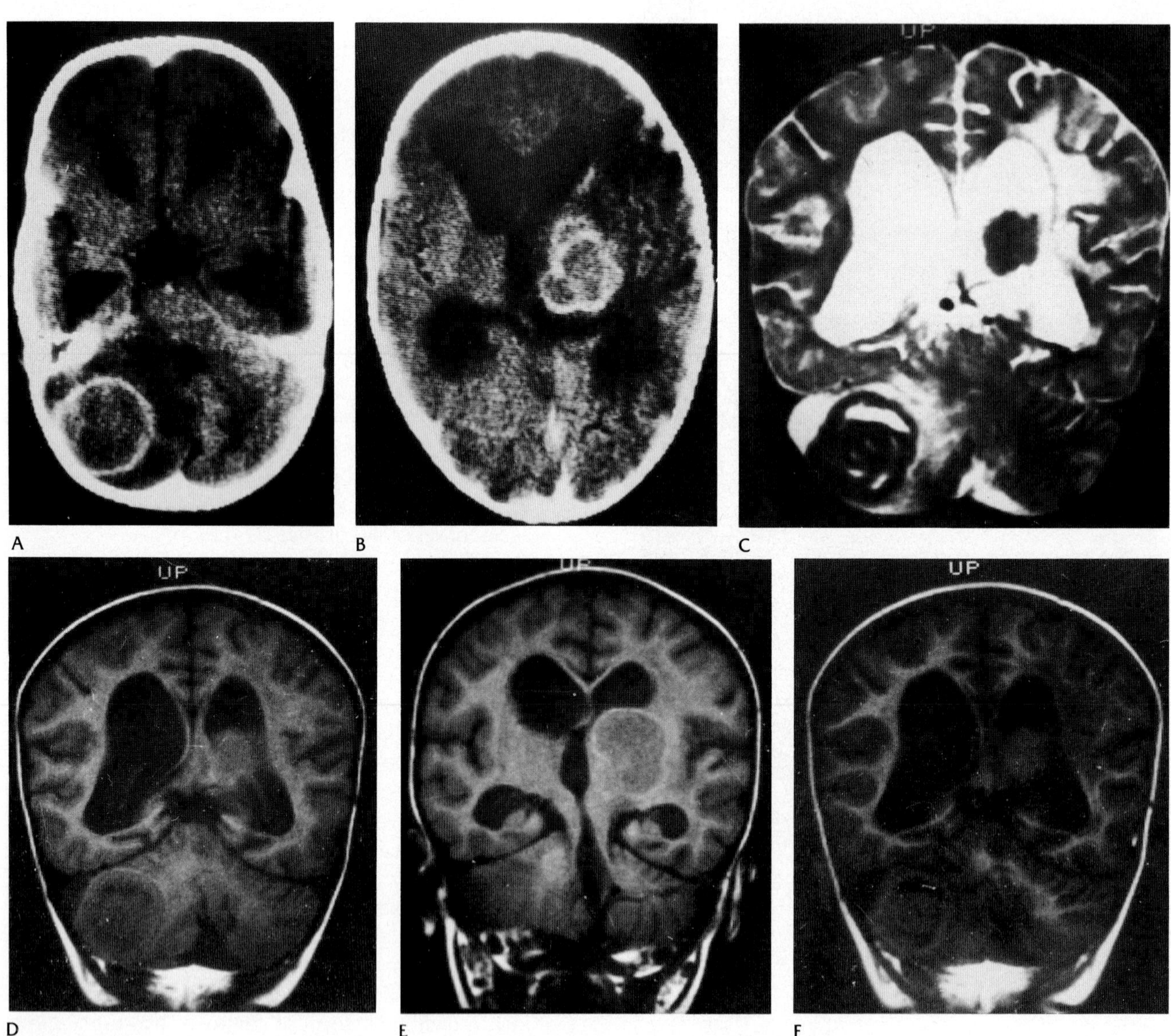

Figure 13-21 Tuberculoma. **A** and **B.** CECT scans show hypodense mass in the right cerebellum (**A**) with ring enhancement and an isodense mass with ring enhancement in the left periventricular region (**B**). An association with ventriculomegaly is present. **C.** Coronal T_2WI (3.2/112) shows a low-intensity, well-defined mass in the right cerebellum with edema surrounding the lesion. Note the hyperintense lines in the mass corresponding to verified areas of necrosis. Another low-intensity mass is seen in left periventricular region with associated hydrocephalus. **D** and **E.** Coronal T_1WI (0.7/28) show isointense lesions in right cerebellum and left periventricular region with ventriculomegaly. Note the low-intensity lines in the cerebellar lesion. **F.** Coronal IR (TI 600, TR 1800) scan shows the hypointense lines in right cerebellar lesion more clearly. (*Reprinted with permission from Gupta 1988.*)

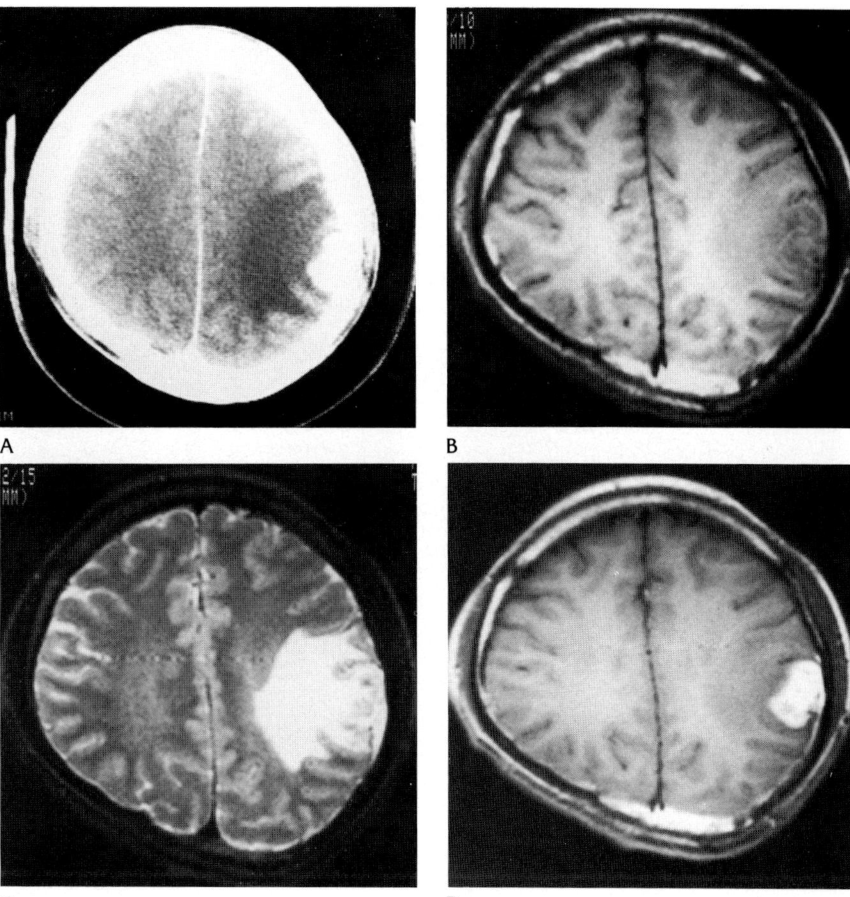

Figure 13-22 Tuberculoma. CECT **A** demonstrates an enhancing mass in the cortex at the left parietal lobe, associated with extensive edema exhibiting mass effect. MR. T_1WI (**B**) shows irregular hypointensity similar to the cortex. MR. T_2WI (**C**) shows a nonhomogeneous mass of hyperintensity surrounded by edema. CEMR (**D**) demonstrates the lesion to better advantage, almost identical to CECT (**A**). (*Case courtesy of Dr. Kee-Hyun Chang, Seoul, Korea.*)

A tuberculoma may be isodense (Welchman 1979), hyperdense, or occasionally of mixed density (Lee 1979). Calcification within a tuberculoma is not common; it is seen in 1 to 13 percent of cases (Lorber 1958). After contrast injection, ringlike enhancement of the capsule is often visualized (Welchman 1979), but homogeneous enhancement (Claveria 1976; Peatfield 1979), irregular heterogeneous enhancement (Price 1978; Lee 1979), and absence of enhancement have also been described. The ringlike enhancement, usually in larger tuberculomas, tends to be unbroken and is usually of uniform thickness (Hirsh 1978; Draouat 1987). It may be smooth or irregularly outlined (Draouat 1987). The density of the tissue within the ring is usually similar to that of surrounding brain (Welchman 1979) but can be variable, depending on the degree of necrosis liquefaction.

The rare "target sign" (Welchman 1979) represents a central nidus of calcification or contrast enhancement surrounded by a ring of enhancement and is strongly suggestive of tuberculoma. Extensive surrounding edema and mass effect are usually seen in the acute inflammatory stage but are not as prominent in chronic tuberculomas.

On MR, tuberculomas may vary in appearance. Lesions with central necrosis tend to be of central hyperintensity on T_2WI and to have a peripheral hypointensity rim (Gupta 1988, 1990). However, more organized solid lesions often appear strikingly hypointense on T_2WI as a result of the granulation tissue and compressed glial tissue in the central core (Fig. 13-21). Occasionally, alternating rings of hypointense and hyperintense signal form as a result of layers of granulation tissue deposition. In all cases, lesions appear to be of gray matter intensity on T_1WI (Fig. 13-22).

When antituberculous therapy is given, edema diminishes and central caseous liquefaction often occurs, resulting in decreasing hyperintensity surrounding the lesion but increasing hyperintensity in the center of the tuberculoma on T_2WI (Gupta 1990). The lesions then gradually decrease in size. In occasional cases, release of tuberculous proteins can result in a temporary paradoxical increase in edema when treatment is started and apparent enlargement of the lesion. These changes may occur in the first 18 months.

Tuberculomas can also be predominantly extracerebral in location and attached to the dura (Welchman 1979). These en plaque tuberculomas closely resemble meningiomas both clinically and operatively (Fig. 13-23).

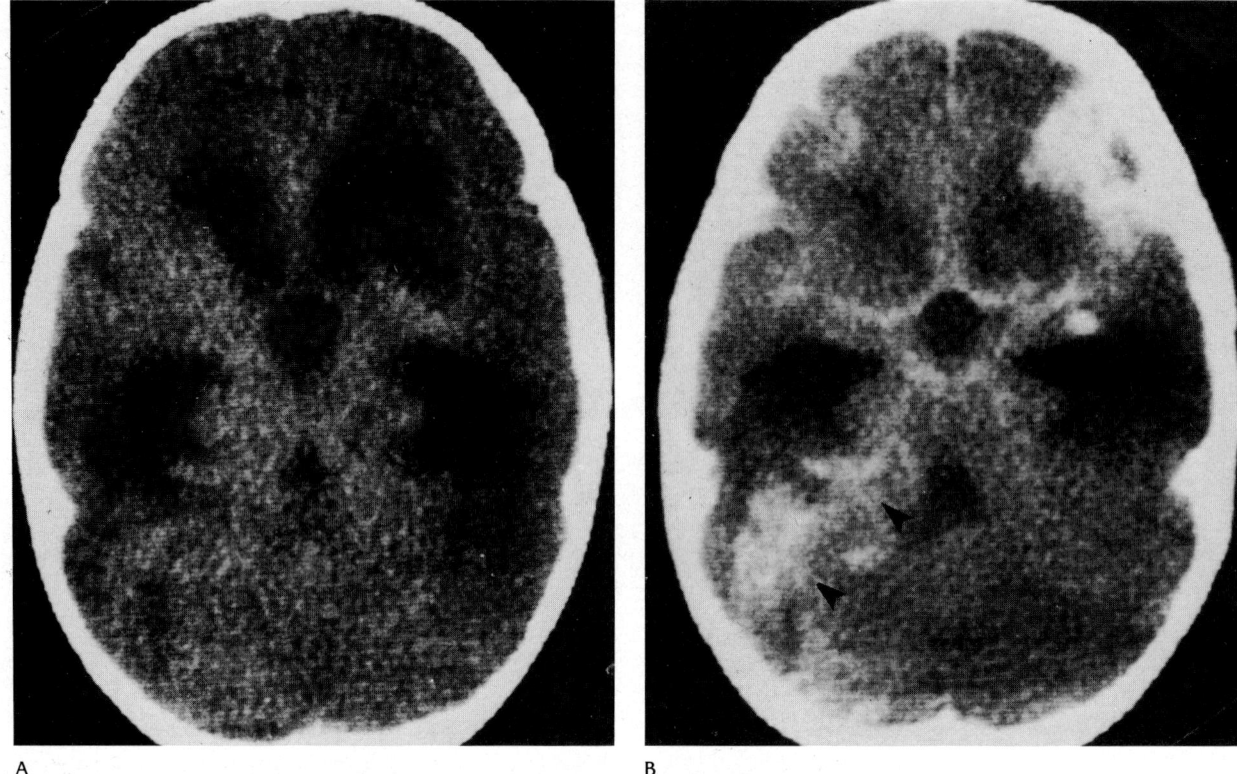

Figure 13-23 Tuberculomas, intracerebral and extracerebral. **A.** NCCT shows obliteration of the basal cistern and slightly increased density along the tentorial margins. Noncommunicating hydrocephalus (third and lateral ventricles) is due to obstruction at the level of the basal cistern. **B.** CECT demonstrates extradural granulomas (en plaque tuberculomas) along the right tentorial margin (arrowheads) and in the basal subarachnoid cistern. Irregular, mixed contrast-enhancing lesion in the left frontal lobe represents intracerebral tuberculoma.

They may undergo complete resolution after antituberculosis therapy. CT and/or MR are essential both in establishing the diagnosis of tuberculous meningitis and tuberculomas and in monitoring the response of tuberculous lesions and the associated hydrocephalus to therapy.

Sarcoidosis

Involvement of the CNS is a rare occurrence in systemic sarcoidosis. Approximately 4 to 7 percent of patients with sarcoidosis present with neurological manifestations; approximately 2 to 15 percent of patients with known sarcoidosis have CNS involvement (Silverstein 1965). Rarely, CNS involvement may be the only manifestation of this disease (Cahill 1981; Griggs 1973). Sarcoid may present at any age but is most common in the third and fourth decades and usually occurs in women. Two patterns of intracranial involvement have been identified: (1) granulomatous leptomeningitis and (2) intracerebral mass. Granulomatous leptomeningitis may occur diffusely or as a circumscribed process at the skull base involving the optic chiasm, the pituitary gland, the floor of the third ventricle, and the hypothalamus. Communicating hydrocephalus is a common result. The second pattern of CNS sarcoid, which is less commonly seen, consists of noncaseating granulomas scattered diffusely in the brain parenchyma or occurring as a single large mass which mimics a brain neoplasm (Saltzman 1958; Silverstein 1965; Robert 1948; Griggs 1973).

On CT, patients with neurosarcoidosis may have normal scans, as was seen in 60 percent of cases in a review of 32 patients (Ketonen 1986). Leptomeningeal sarcoid can appear similar to bacterial meningitis, with enhancement of the meninges along the inner table of the skull (Fig. 13-24). It can also present initially as hydrocephalus (Morehouse 1981). Hydrocephalus may occur as a result of an obstructing mass lesion (Bahgr 1978; Kendall 1978; Kumpe 1979). Differentiation from other causes of communicating hydrocephalus may be difficult unless the patient has proven pulmonary sarcoidosis. Parenchymal sarcoid is seen as a hyperdense area on NCCT, with further homogeneous enhancement on CECT (Fig. 13-24). Another common abnormality that involves the parenchyma is the occurrence of hydrodense white matter lesions attributed to small vessel involvement. Finally, linear or nodular meningeal contrast enhancement extending deep into the parenchyma is highly suggestive of a men-

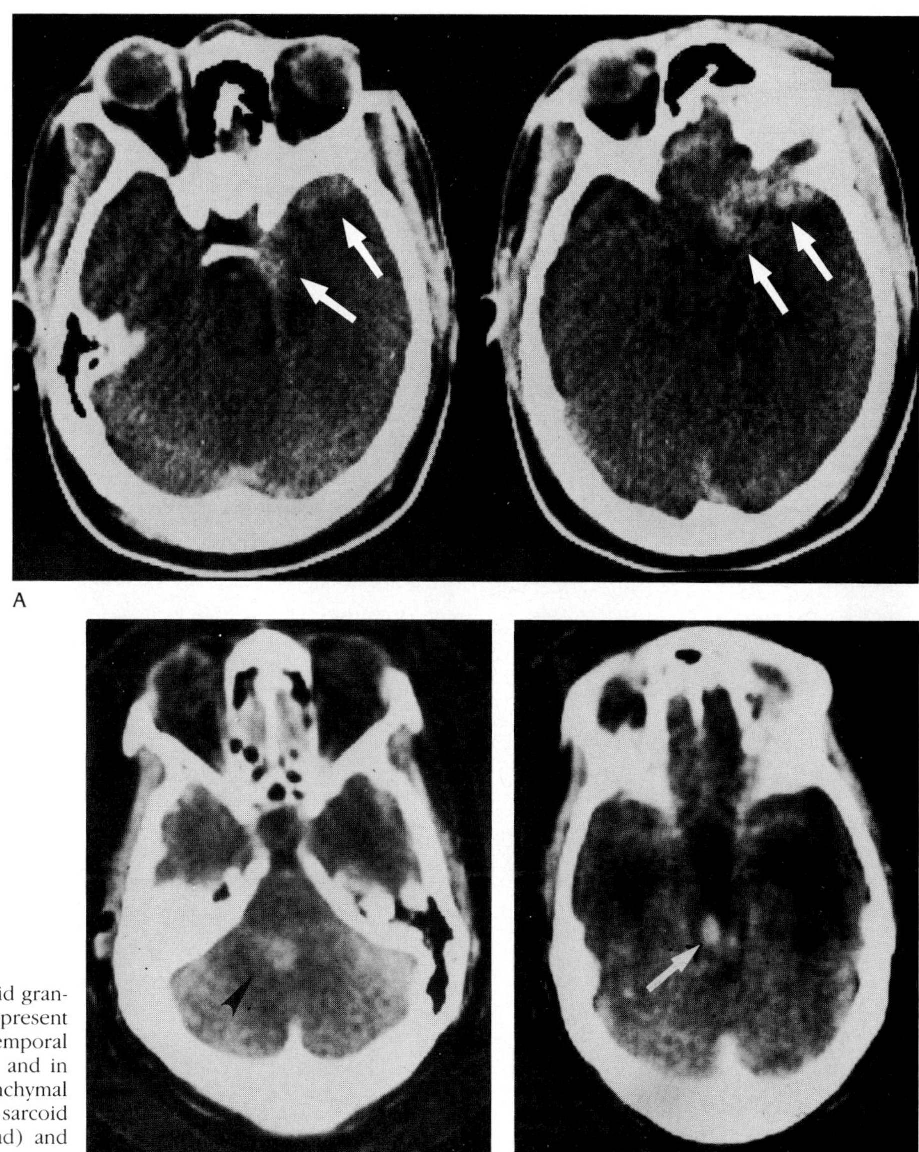

Figure 13-24 **A.** Leptomeningeal sarcoid granulomas. On CECT, extensive granulomas present as nonhomogeneous densities in the temporal fossa along the sphenoid bone (arrows) and in the parasellar region (arrows). **B.** Parenchymal sarcoid granulomas. CECT demonstrates sarcoid granulomas in the brainstem (arrowhead) and midbrain (arrow).

ingeal infiltrative process with secondary parenchymal extension through the Virchow-Robin spaces, another path of spread in neurosarcoidosis (Mirfakharee 1986).

On MR, sarcoid involvement of the leptomeninges is difficult to detect without contrast, although large deposits may be seen as masses compressing the underlying brain parenchyma (Fig. 13-25). In addition, obliteration of CSF spaces, for example, in the suprasellar cistern, may also be detected, as it is with other types of meningitis (Sze 1989). After the administration of MR contrast agent, marked enhancement of the sarcoid granulation tissue occurs. Enhancement can be seen throughout the meninges or may be very localized, especially in the suprasellar cistern. Compared with bacterial meningitis, meningeal sarcoid often, although not always, appears more focal and nodular. Contrast MR is the most accurate modality for documenting disease. As with CT, linear or nodular enhancement extending into the parenchyma can represent infiltration of disease into the sulci and Virchow-Robin spaces. Again, white matter involvement resulting from small vessel disease may occur and is seen as areas of high signal intensity on T_2WI (Fig. 13-25).

On MR, sarcoid granulomas are generally isointense or hypointense relative to cerebral cortex on T_1WI and hyperintense on T_2WI (Hayes 1987) (Fig. 13-26). They enhance homogeneously with contrast. When there is no evidence of peripheral sarcoidosis, differentiation from neoplasm or multiple sclerosis may be difficult unless a

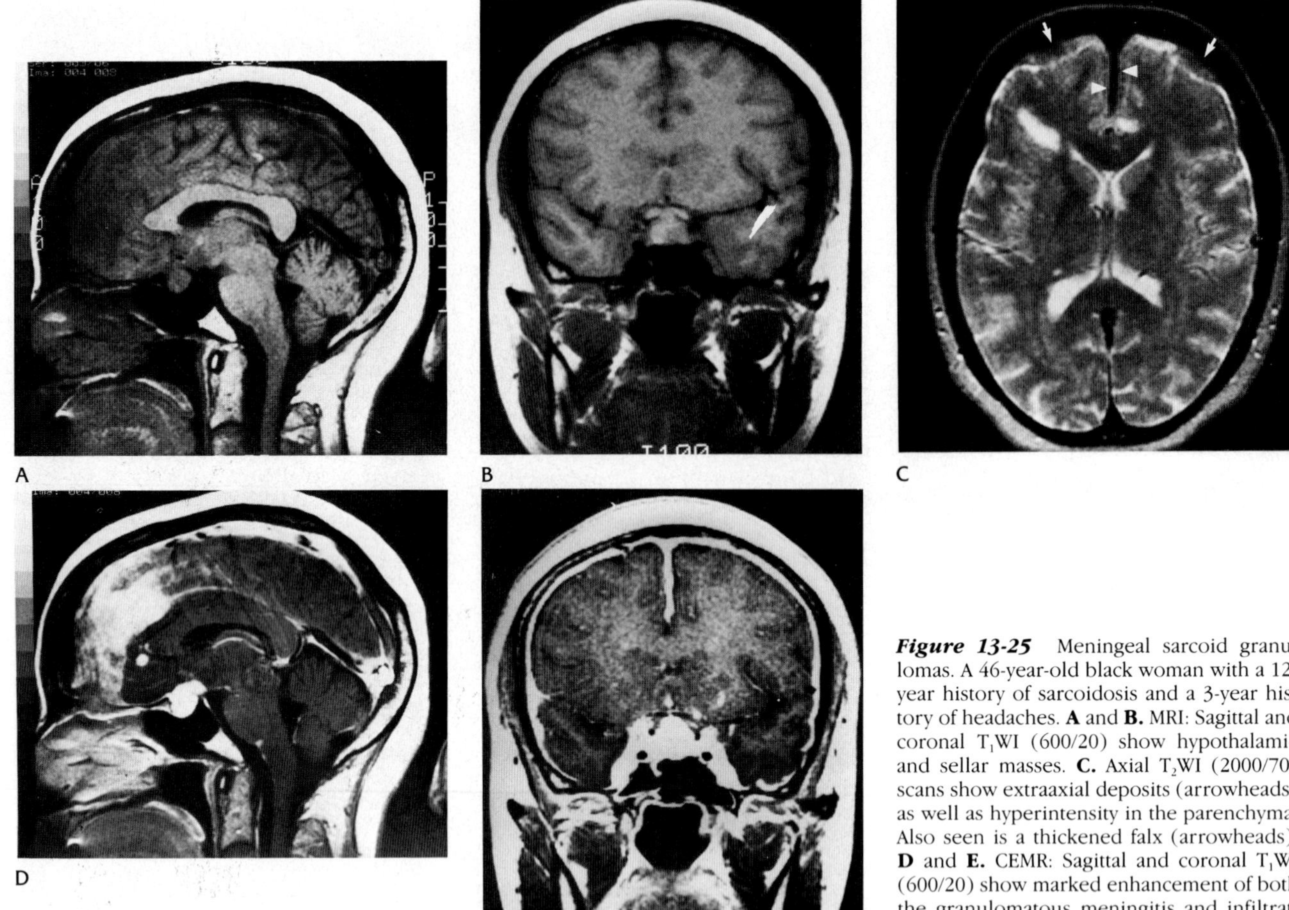

Figure 13-25 Meningeal sarcoid granulomas. A 46-year-old black woman with a 12-year history of sarcoidosis and a 3-year history of headaches. **A** and **B.** MRI: Sagittal and coronal T_1WI (600/20) show hypothalamic and sellar masses. **C.** Axial T_2WI (2000/70) scans show extraaxial deposits (arrowheads) as well as hyperintensity in the parenchyma. Also seen is a thickened falx (arrowheads). **D** and **E.** CEMR: Sagittal and coronal T_1WI (600/20) show marked enhancement of both the granulomatous meningitis and infiltrating granulomas of the pituitary-hypothalamus. (*Reprinted with permission from Sze 1988.*)

biopsy is performed (Smith 1989). Of note, sarcoid granulomatous masses within the parenchyma rarely demonstrate significant surrounding edema. In addition, they decrease in size dramatically after treatment with steroids.

FUNGAL INFECTION

Fungal infections generally affect the CNS as opportunistic granulomatous disese which may be acute and fulminant or chronic and indolent. Infection may be meningeal, parenchymal (fungal "abscess"), or both (Riccio 1989; Mikhael 1985). In most instances the primary portal of entry is the lungs, but fungal osteomyelitis or lymphadenitis may also precede brain involvement. The frequency of CNS fungal infection has increased significantly in recent years because of the growing numbers of immunosuppressed patients (Britt 1981).

Although a variety of opportunistic organisms may involve the CNS, few of these entities have a characteristic pattern that suggests the diagnosis purely on the basis of imaging findings. Most often CT and MR are used to demonstrate and localize the parenchymal or meningeal involvement; confirmation of the specific fungus involved is based on a variety of CSF studies, especially CSF culture. CT and MR features of fungal infection are varied and nonspecific (Enzmann 1980; Mikhael 1985; Riccio 1989). In general, ringlike contrast enhancement on CT and MR probably reflects the host's ability to wall off the organisms.

Cryptococcus neoformans infection of the CNS can occur in immunocompetent individuals as a manifestation of disseminated pulmonary cryptococcosis. In AIDS patients, CNS cryptococcosis is the most common fungal infection (Riccio 1989). As in *Listeria* infection, meningitis is more prevalent than parenchymal involvement in cryptococcosis. MR and CT findings can be grouped into four patterns (Tien 1991): (1) parenchymal cryptococcoma (toruloma), (2) multiple miliary parenchymal and leptomeningeal nodules, (3) symmetrical perivascular spread in the basal ganglia and midbrain, and (4) a mixed

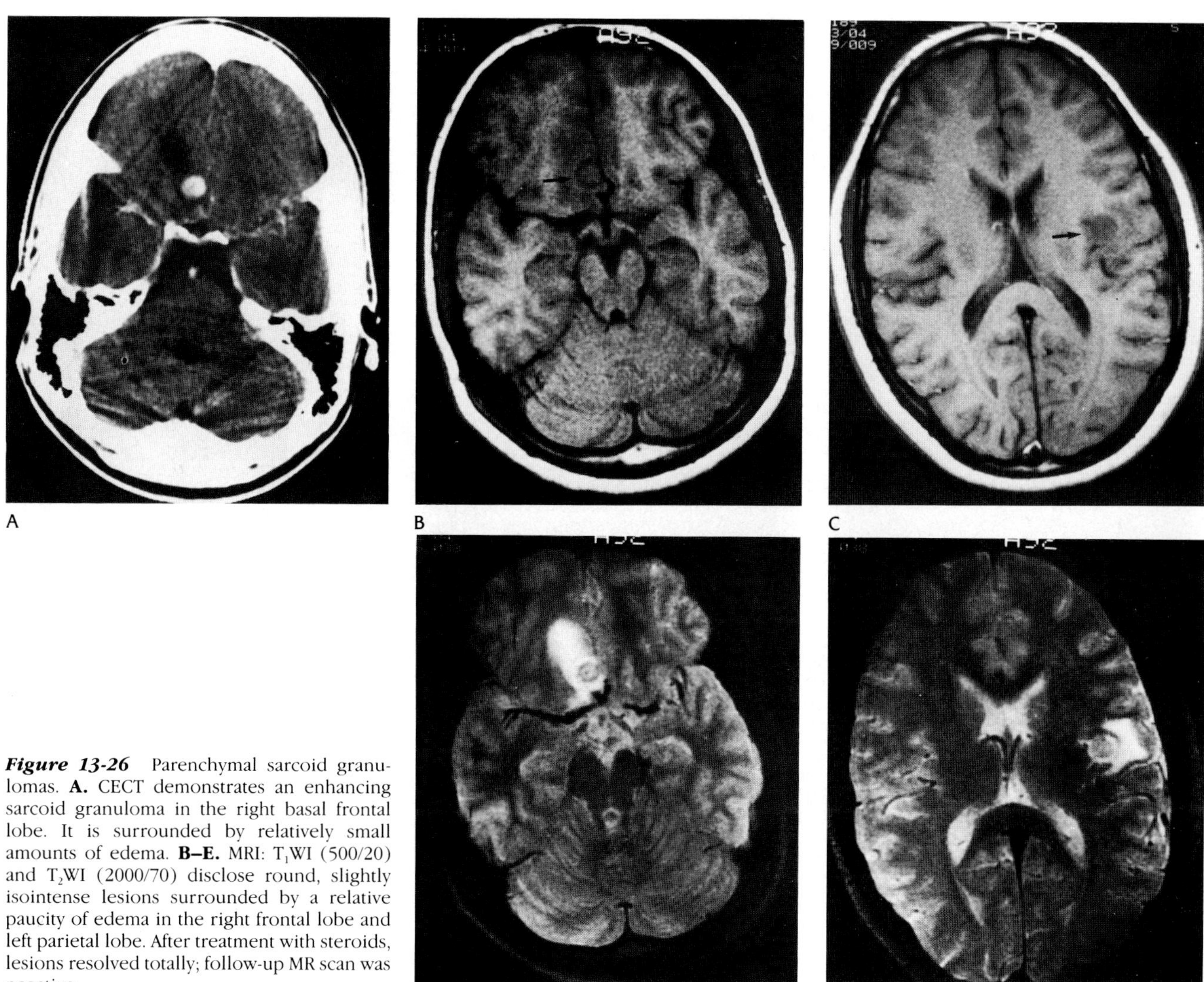

Figure 13-26 Parenchymal sarcoid granulomas. **A.** CECT demonstrates an enhancing sarcoid granuloma in the right basal frontal lobe. It is surrounded by relatively small amounts of edema. **B–E.** MRI: T_1WI (500/20) and T_2WI (2000/70) disclose round, slightly isointense lesions surrounded by a relative paucity of edema in the right frontal lobe and left parietal lobe. After treatment with steroids, lesions resolved totally; follow-up MR scan was negative.

pattern. Types 1 and 2 are different presentations of hematogenous dissemination of the fungi. Intracranial torulomas may exhibit ringlike contrast enhancement (Long 1980; Arrington 1984) or focal homogeneous nodules with or without circumferential edema on CT (Fujita 1981). Tan (1987) and Popovich (1990) reported a variety of CT changes such as hydrocephalus, diffuse cortical atrophy, nonspecific white matter changes, and basal meningeal enhancement. Forty-three to 50 percent of the patients in their series showed normal CT scans.

MR findings demonstrate hypointense lesions on T_1WI and hyperintense lesions on T_2WI. Postcontrast T_1WI can clearly demonstrate the lesions and are essential, especially for miliary nodules in the leptomeninges and parenchyma (Riccio 1989). Fungal invasion of the perivascular spaces (Virchow-Robin spaces) in the basal ganglia is better seen on MR than on CT (Tien 1991). This presents as symmetrical, bilateral hypointensity or isointensity relative to gray matter on T_1WI and SDWI and as hyperintensity on T_2WI (Fig. 13-27). Very little edema is associated with these lesions; this is most likely due to the intact blood-brain barrier and the extraaxial location. Extension into the midbrain can also be detected on MR.

Coccidioides imitis is a dust-borne fungus endemic to the southwestern part of the United States, especially the San Joaquin Valley of California, as well as portions of Mexico and central South America (Fraser 1978). It is spread by inhalation of the spore, which is present in soil. Only 0.02 to 0.2 percent of cases progress to the disseminated form involving the brain, meninges, and other systemic organs (Einstein 1974). Pathologically, CNS coccidiodomycosis is characterized by thickened, congested leptomeninges with multiple granulomas, which are especially prominent in the basal cisterns. Complications include communicating hydrocephalus, vasculitis, ependymitis, and periventricular lesions (focal granulomas without calcification) (McGahan 1981). The most common CT and MR findings are hydrocephalus (86 percent),

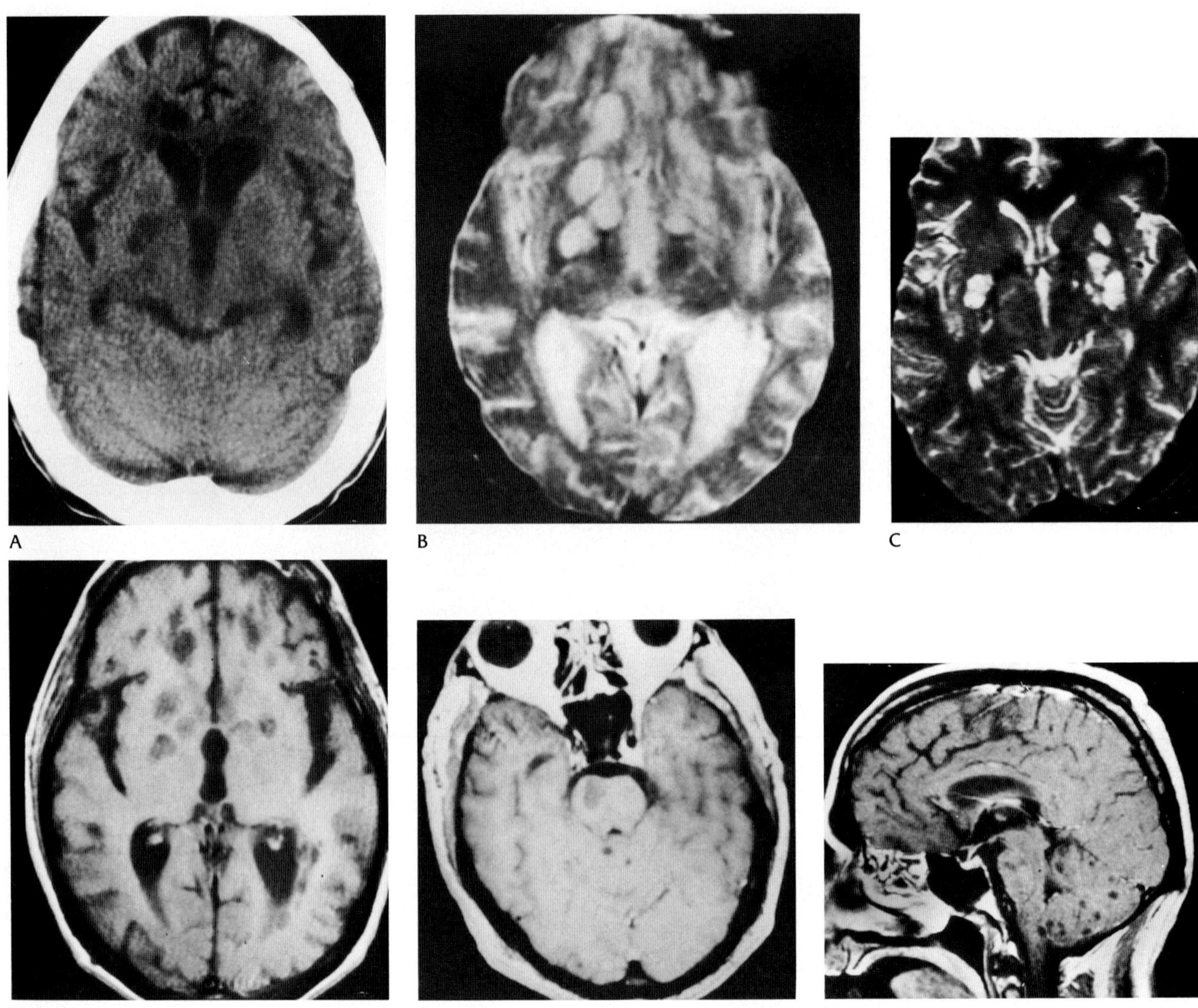

Figure 13-27 Cryptococcosis in an AIDS patient. **A.** NCCT demonstrates multiple hypodense lesions in the basal ganglia and frontal lobes. Also seen is prominence in the ventricles and sulci consistent with atrophy. **B** and **C.** T_2WI MR scan demonstrates hyperintense lesions in the basal ganglia, with minimal surrounding edema and very little mass effect. T_1WI axial image (**D**) demonstrates multiple low-intensity lesions scattered throughout the cerebrum, cerebellum, and brainstem. No evidence of contrast enhancement is seen on CEMR (**E** and **F**). These lesions have a typical appearance for collections of cryptococcus expanding the Virchow-Robin spaces. (*Courtesy of Dr. Robert Stoud, Baltimore, Maryland.*)

abnormal basal or convexity cisternal contrast enhancement (71 percent), and entrapment of the ventricles as a result of ependymitis (Enzmann 1976; Dublin 1980; Rodriguez-Carbajal 1986).

Candida albicans has been increasingly associated with CNS infection, particularly in patients with diabetes mellitus and those with an altered immune status (Lipton 1984). Candidiasis of the CNS is characterized by scattered granulomas, microabscesses, leptomeningitis, and numerous thrombosed vessels. CT demonstrates areas of poorly circumscribed hypodensity without contrast enhancement in immunosuppressed patients (Enzmann 1980). Cavity formation of various thicknesses and with a hypodense or isodense center may be seen in immunocompetent patients (Fig. 13-28). On MR, these areas have high signal intensity on T_2WI (Fig. 13-29) and resemble those of other granulomatous processes (Sze 1988*a*).

Aspergillus fumigatus usually appears as an opportunistic infection and reaches the brain by hematogenous dissemination from a primary focus in the lungs or by direct extension from the ear, nose, or paranasal sinuses (Parker 1985). It may manifest as a solitary brain abscess; alternatively, vascular involvement may occur and result in thrombosis with hemorrhagic necrosis and/or massive

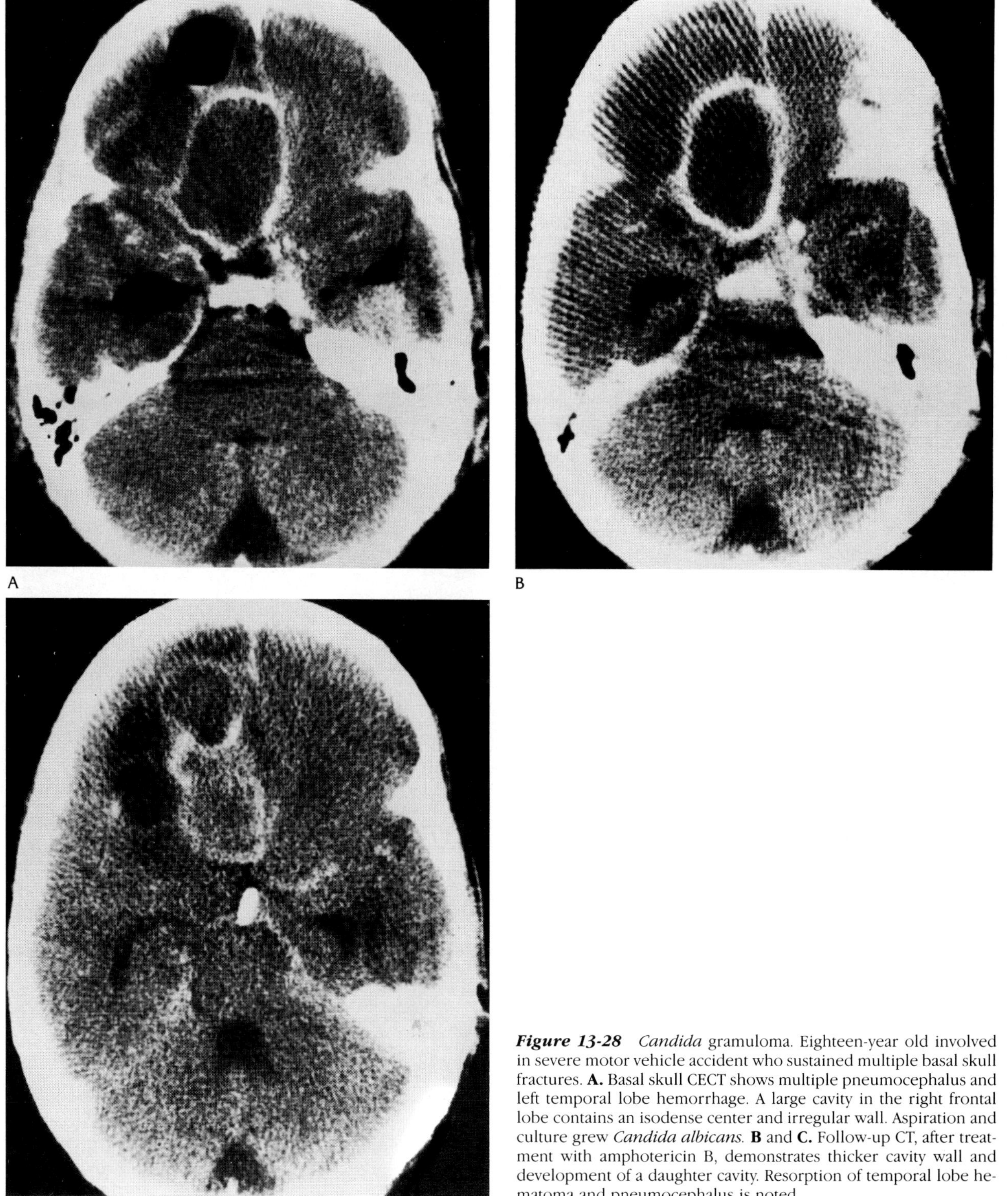

Figure 13-28 *Candida* gramuloma. Eighteen-year old involved in severe motor vehicle accident who sustained multiple basal skull fractures. **A.** Basal skull CECT shows multiple pneumocephalus and left temporal lobe hemorrhage. A large cavity in the right frontal lobe contains an isodense center and irregular wall. Aspiration and culture grew *Candida albicans.* **B** and **C.** Follow-up CT, after treatment with amphotericin B, demonstrates thicker cavity wall and development of a daughter cavity. Resorption of temporal lobe hematoma and pneumocephalus is noted.

subarachnoid and intracranial hemorrhage (Visudhiphan 1973). On CT, nonspecific, poorly circumscribed areas of subtle hypodensity are seen. There may be little or no contrast enhancement and mass effect (Enzmann 1980; Grossman 1981), or a ring configuration representing a well-formed, thick, and regular abscess capsule may be noted (Claveria 1976). Compared wih the neuropathological findings, the CT findings generally underestimate

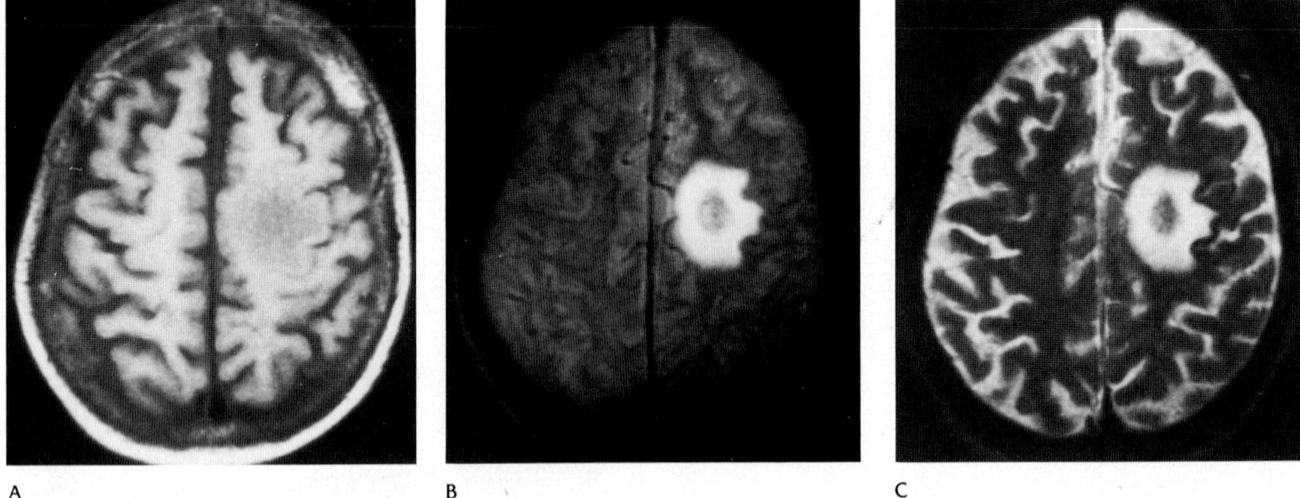

Figure 13-29 Candida abscess. MRI: **A.** T_1WI (600/20) shows an area of hypointensity and mass effect in the superior aspect of the left parietal lobe. **B** and **C.** Proton density and T_2WI (2000/20, 70) NCMR show a central focus of mild hyperintensity surrounded by a more extensive area of hyperintensity. As with bacterial abscess formation, the central portion of the abscess appears of mildly increased signality compared with the markedly increased signal of the surrounding edema.

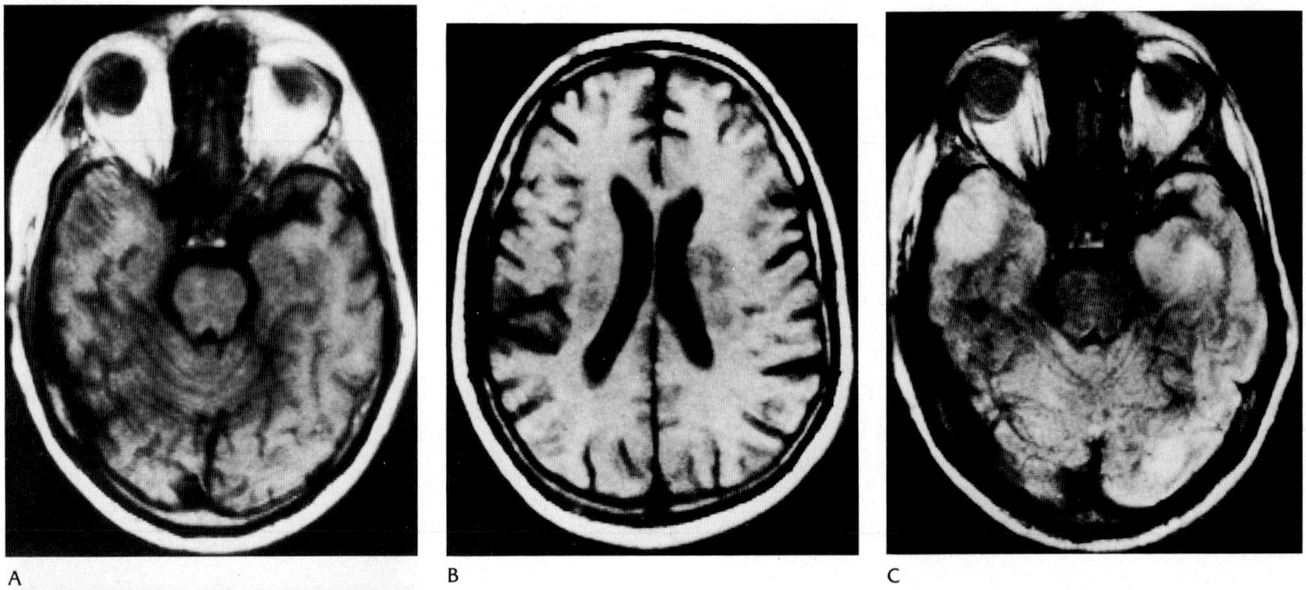

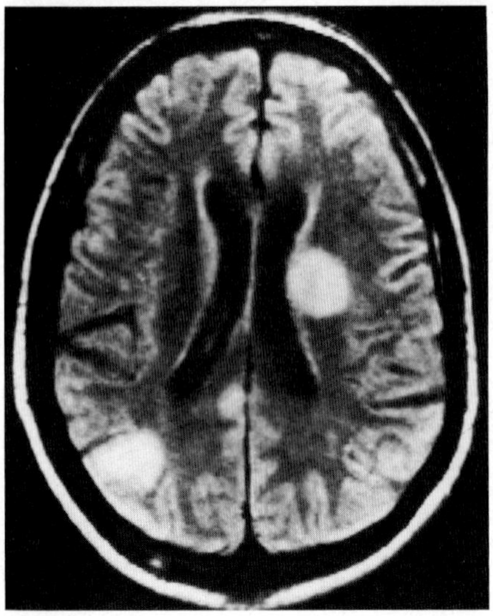

Figure 13-30 Nocardial "abscess." **A** and **B.** NCMR: T_1WI (500/20) demonstrate several ill-defined and poorly seen areas of mild hypointensity. **C** and **D.** Proton density (2000/35) NCMR disclose multiple foci of high signal intensity. Biopsy of the temporal lesion revealed nocardia.

the extent of involvement. On MR, *Aspergillus* infections may appear nonspecific compared with other fungal processes; however, because of the propensity of *Aspergillus* to involve vessels and cause hemorrhage, lesions may have varying signal intensities depending on the age of the bleed.

Nocardia asteroides infection may demonstrate multiple extensive hydrodense lesions on NCCT, with ringlike appearance on CECT. On MR, these lesions appear hypointense on T_1WI and hyperintense on T_2WI (Fig. 13-30). Irregular contrast enhancement may be seen.

VIRAL INFECTION

Acquired

Manifestations of viral diseases of the CNS differ from those of bacterial or fungal diseases in their tendency toward diffuse parenchymal involvement and the frequent absence of distinctive gross alterations in the involved parenchyma. Most of the encephalitides therefore resemble each other and have few identifying imaging characteristics. Areas of involvement show edema, mass effect, hyperintensity on T_2WI, and perhaps petechial hemorrhage. The few encephalitides that have typical features include herpes simplex type I, encephalitis, progressive multifocal leukoencephalopathy (PML), and AIDS encephalopathy. The latter two entities are discussed in the section on AIDS. In addition, varicella encephalitis may particularly affect the cerebellum, even when panencephalitis is seen (Hurst 1988).

Herpes simplex virus (HSV) type I is the most common cause of sporadic viral encephalitis in the United States. HSV encephalitis is characterized by a fulminant necrotizing encephalitis with petechial hemorrhages and early involvement of the subfrontal and medial temporal regions. Mortality is high, approaching 70 percent. The success of treatment depends on early diagnosis and prompt institution of therapy.

The primary role of cross-sectional imaging in the evaluation of HSV encephalitis is to confirm the clinical diagnosis and indicate the best site for biopsy as well as to exclude the presence of an abscess or tumor. Early definitive diagnosis is essential before treatment because of the known toxicity of antiviral agents.

The most commonly noted CT findings in HSV infections are a poorly marginated hypodense area (63 to 64 percent), mass effect (50 to 52 percent), and nonhomogeneous contrast enhancement (50 to 57 percent) (Davis 1978; Leo 1978). Low density is usually centered in the temporal and frontal lobes, which are also the characteristic sites of involvement in gross pathological specimens (Davis 1978; Leo 1978) (Fig. 13-31). The hypodense area may later extend to involve the deep frontal or occipital

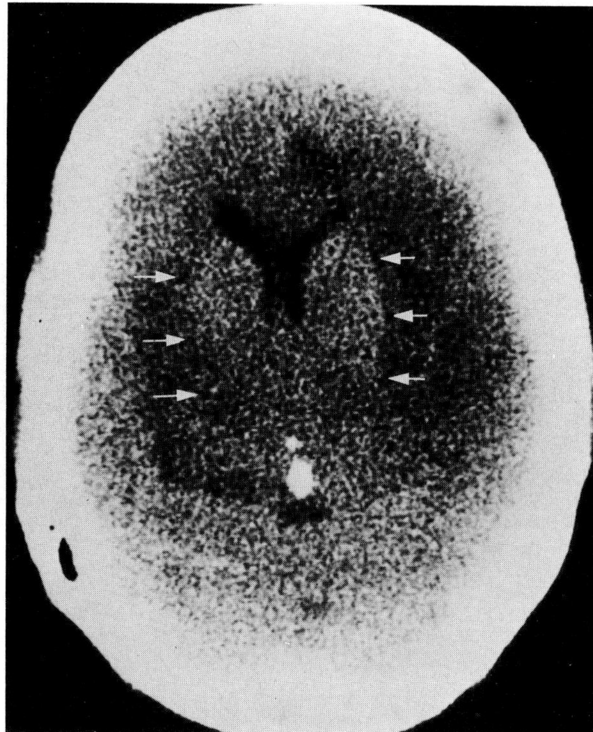

A

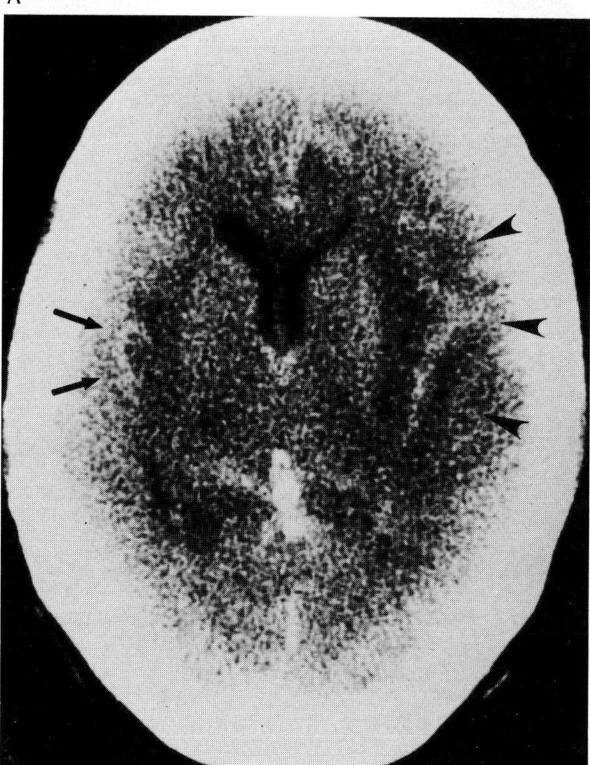

B

Figure 13-31 Herpes simplex (type 1) encephalitis. **A.** On NCCT, extensive low-density lesions in both temporal lobes, more on the left than the right, are clearly demarcated by the lateral margin of the basal ganglia (arrowheads). **B.** CECT show different patterns of contrast enhancement: linear streaks (arrowheads) on the left and ringlike figures (arrows) on the right. Absence of midline shift is due to bilateral, balanced involvement.

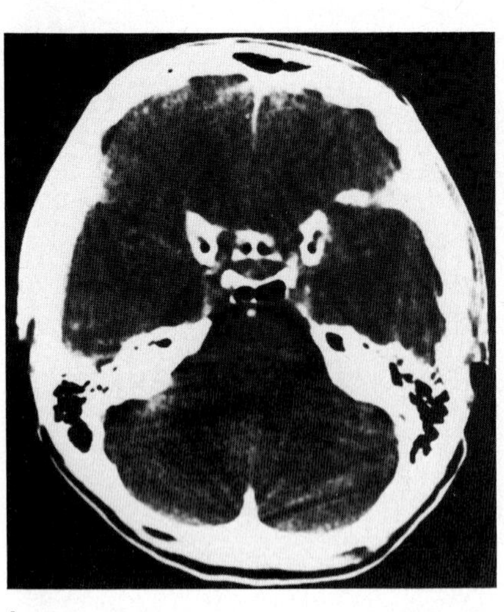

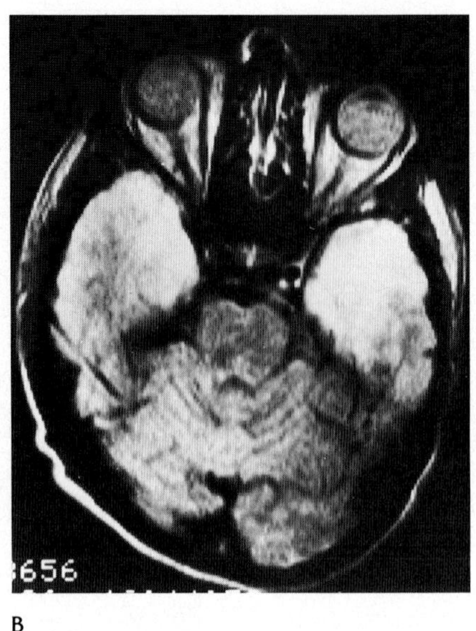

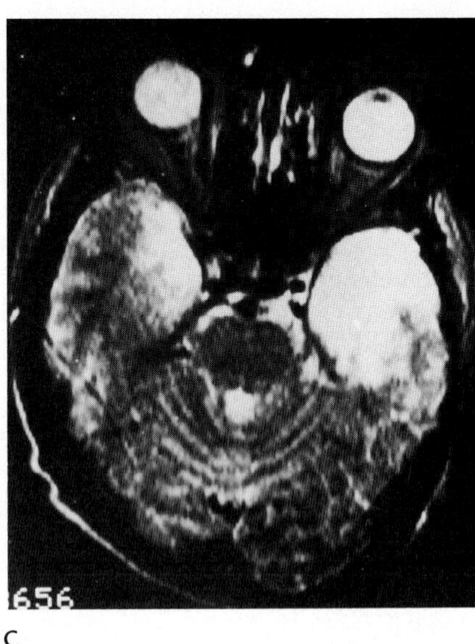

A B C

Figure 13-32 Herpes simplex (type 1) encephalitis. A 28-year-old woman with acute mental status changes. **A.** CECT suggests subtle low density and mass effect in left temporal lobe. MRI: Proton density (**B**) and T_2WI (**C**) show high-intensity signal in both temporal lobes, strongly suggestive of herpes simplex encephalitis. (*Case courtesy of C. Elkin, Montefiore Medical Center, New York.*)

lobes, but isolated frontal or occipital lobe involvement is uncommon (Ketonen 1980). An abrupt transition to normal density at the lateral margin of the lenticular nucleus, sparing the putamen, has been characteristic on CT (Zimmerman 1980) and MR (Sze 1988*b*) (Fig. 13-31). The pattern of contrast enhancement in HSV encephalitis on CT is varied. It may be gyral (Davis 1978), patchy, or multiple ringlike (Ketonen 1980) or may consist of linear streaks at the periphery of the hypodense lesion (Enzmann 1978) (Fig. 13-31). CT abnormalities are usually not seen in the initial 5 to 7 days after the onset of illness (Zimmerman 1980; Greenberg 1981).

MR is the modality of choice in the detection of the early changes of HSV encephalitis (Lester 1988). Because of the surrounding bony structures at the base of the skull, the temporal lobe is often not well imaged on CT. On MR, the temporal lobe is easily assessed (Fig. 13-32) (Sze 1988*b*). Subtle gyral effacement can be detected. Because encephalitis leads to a rapid increase in water content, the involved brain parenchyma appears mildly hypointense on T_1WI and markedly hyperintense on T_2WI (Guilleux 1986; Mark 1989). Bilateral temporal lobe involvement, which is almost pathognomonic of HSV encephalitis, is easily detected with MR. The mass effect is manifested as either a midline shift or a focal mass causing compression of the ventricles or sylvian cisterns. Occasionally there may not be a midline shift, owing to bilateral balanced involvement (Fig. 13-31).

Subarachnoid enhancement suggestive of meningeal involvement is unusual but can be seen on MR earlier than on CECT. Parenchymal petechial hemorrhage in the subacute phase is consistently seen on pathological specimens. This is rarely seen on CT (Enzmann 1978; Zegers 1980) but may be more readily detected on MR.

Late follow-up CT or MR can demonstrate widespread encephalomalacia involving the temporal and frontal lobes, indicating extensive involvement of the brain. HSV infection in AIDS patients may not have the typical CT and MR appearance, may progress rapidly, and may be involved more extensively (Post 1986*a*).

Congenital

A large number of infectious agents may involve the CNS while an infant is still in utero. The most common of these are "torch" agents, an acronym for toxoplasmosis, other, rubella, cytomegalovirus, and herpes. Unlike HSV type I encephalitis, HSV type II encephalitis is a panencephalitis. Infection with HSV type II in a newborn infant may be acquired transplacentally or during delivery, presumably secondary to genital and perineal infection in the mother. Early intrauterine infection with type II virus is known to have marked neurotrophic teratogenic potential and has been associated with microcephaly, microencephaly, intracranial calcification, microophthalmia, and retinal dysplasia (South 1969; Whitley 1980). Disseminated encephalitis in infants may produce widespread calcifications conforming to an atrophic cerebral hemisphere.

On initial NCCT (2 to 30 days), a gyral pattern of cortical hyperdensity which may represent hemorrhage is noted. These findings are usually accentuated by a diffuse

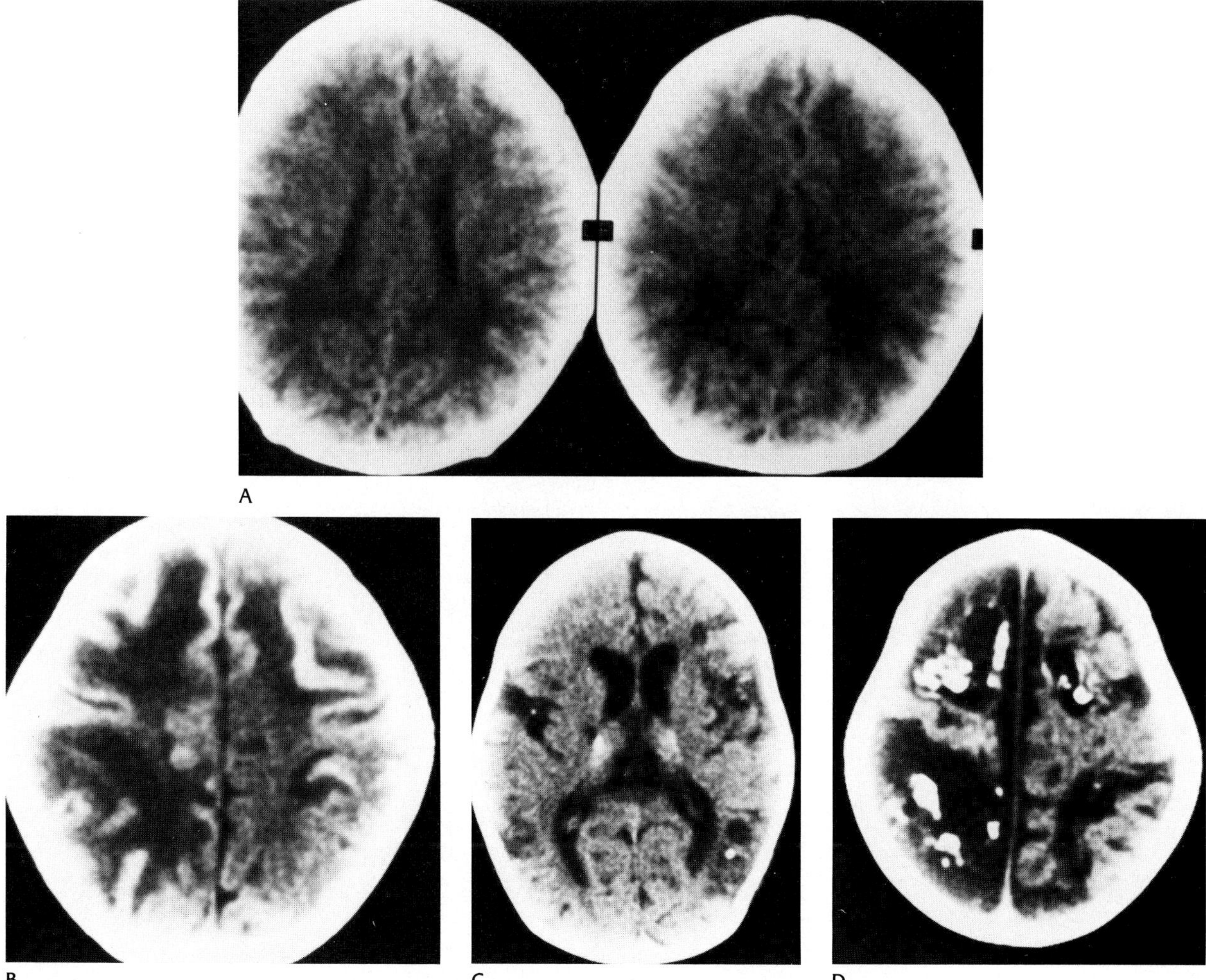

Figure 13-33 Herpes simplex (type II) encephalitis. **A.** NCCT, 2 months old, shows multiple areas of hypodensity in fronto-parietal regions. **B.** NCCT, 10 days later, reveals extensive white matter involvement with parenchymal thinning. Gyral hyperdensity is evident. **C** and **D.** NCCT, 6 months later, demonstrates multiple, focal areas of encephalomalacia, punctate calcifications in the basal ganglia, and the parenchymal remnants. Ventriculomegaly is apparent. (*Courtesy of Dr. Douglas Yock, Abotte-Northwestern Hospital, Minneapolis, Minnesota.*)

decrease in white matter density (Sage 1981; Herman 1985). Subsequently (after more than 30 days), extensive cerebral destruction, multicystic encephalomalacia, and calcifications are seen, manifested by diffuse hypodense cystic areas interspersed with scattered calcifications (Herman 1985) (Fig. 13-33). Microcephaly with grossly dilated ventricles and a thin cortical mantle are also noted.

MR is much less capable of detecting the scattered calcifications of congenital infections (Holland 1985; Boesch 1989) (Fig. 13-34). However, it can document areas of continuing encephalitis, which are seen as hyperintense on T_2WI. Occasionally, hypointensity due to magnetic susceptibility of undetermined origin, not necessarily hemorrhage, occupies a cortical distribution (Enzmann 1990). Gyral or meningeal enhancement may be present. In addition, congenital infections often lead to delayed development of normal parenchymal structures (Martin 1990). MR accurately depicts myelination of white matter tracts and can indicate patients with retarded maturation (Holland 1986).

Other causes of congenital calcification of the brain include toxoplasmosis, rubella, and cytomegalovirus (Boesch 1989). Toxoplasmosis and rubella calcifications are evenly distributed in necrotic brain substance but may be compressed by hydrocephalus and thus mimic the periventricular subependymal calcifications of cytomegalovirus. Occasionally, cortical and subcortical white matter calcification is found in cytomegalovirus infection (Harwood-Nash 1970; Malloy 1963).

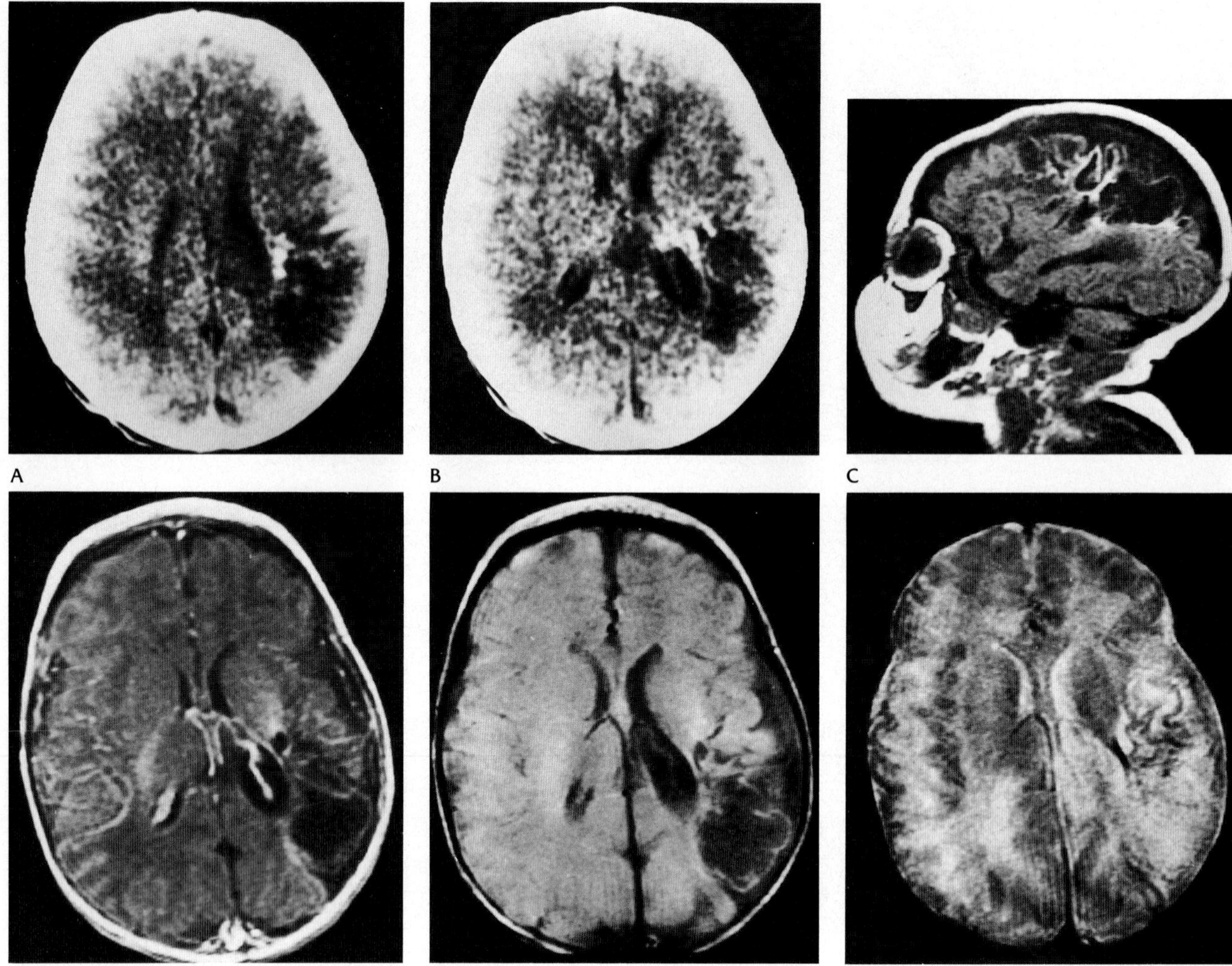

Figure 13-34 Herpes simplex (type II) encephalitis. A 3-week-old infant with difficulty feeding and respiratory distress. Diagnosis by Tzanck prep and viral cultures. NCCT (**A** and **B**) shows areas of brain destruction and cystic change in the left parietal and parietooccipital regions. In addition, focal areas of calcification are visible. **C.** Sagittal MR: T_1WI (500/20) confirms the marked encephalomalacia and destruction of brain tissue. High intensity seen at the periphery of the disrupted regions may represent petechial hemorrhage. **D.** CEMR: Axial T_1WI (500/30) shows very little enhancement. Hyperintensity seen in the regions of the internal capsules is secondary to early myelination. Also seen is a focal area of hypointensity with some surrounding high signal near the left basal ganglia, secondary to the calcification visualized on CT. **E** and **F.** Spin-density and T_2WI (2500/20, 100) disclose hyperintensity in other areas, particularly in the white matter in the frontal lobes and the right parietooccipital lobe. This appearance is caused by increased water content resulting from lack of myelination at this age.

PARASITIC INFECTIONS

Cysticercosis

Cysticercosis is one of the most common parasitic diseases that affect the brain. Humans serve as the intermediate hosts of *Taenia solium,* the pork tapeworm, in this disease, which is prevalent in parts of Asia, India, Africa, Europe, and Latin America. There appears to have been a recent increase in the incidence of cysticercosis in the United States because of the growing numbers of immigrants. The CNS is the most frequently affected organ system, involved in up to 92 percent of cases (Dixon 1961). Anatomically, cysticercosis may be meningeal (subarachnoid) or intraventricular (parenchymal, mixed, or intraspinal), with the meningeal and parenchymal forms being the most common (Carbajal 1977; Byrd 1982; Suss 1986; Lotz 1988).

Meningeal involvement is manifested by extracerebral cysts, arachnoiditis, and vasculitis. Since the walls of the

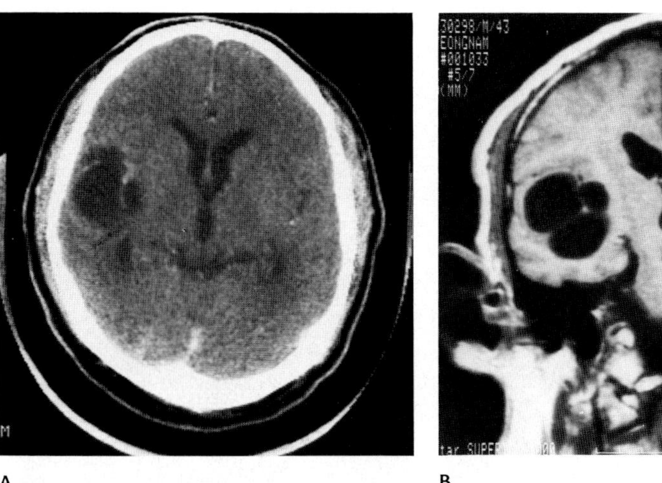

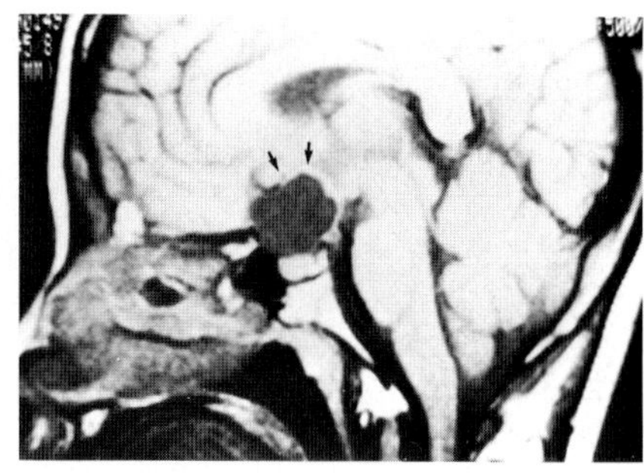

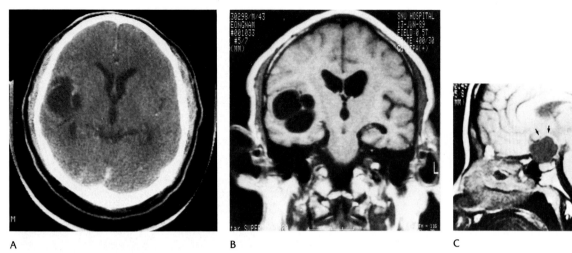

A B C

Figure 13-35 Meningeal ("racemose") cysticercosis: CECT **A** shows multilobular cysts in the right Sylvian fissure isodense to CSF. No contrast enhancement is evident. CEMR: **B.** Coronal T_1WI shows multiple cysts of CSF intensity in the right Sylvian fissure with mild mass effect but no edema. **C.** Sagittal T_1WI (600/20) shows a cystic suprasellar mass elevating the floor of the third ventricle and pushing the hypothalamus and infundibulum posteriorly. Note the CSF-like intensity of this lesion. (*Reprinted with permission from Suh 1989.*)

cysts are not visible on CT and the density of the fluid contents is identical to that of CSF, the detection of these cysts is based on focal areas of apparent enlargement of the subarachnoid spaces. On MR, however, the cyst walls are more often detected (Martinez 1989; Suss 1986) (Fig. 13-35). In addition, multiplanar visualization of the basal cisterns free from bony artifact particularly facilitates MR visualization of these cysts (Chang 1990). Breakdown of the cyst walls can provoke arachnoiditis. The occurrence of one or more cysts in the basal cisterns can obstruct CSF pathways, with resultant communicating hydrocephalus. Vasculitis associated with a meningeal cysticercal infestation may cause arterial narrowing, with thrombosis and secondary cerebral infarction. The differential diagnosis includes arachnoid cyst and epidermoid and can be extremely difficult without the appropriate clinical information.

Solitary or multiple intraventricular cysts may be attached to the ventricular walls or may be free-floating (Martinez 1989). Larger cysts may cause focal expansile deformities of the affected ventricle. A large cyst or cluster of cysts within the fourth ventricle may simulate dilatation of that ventricle (Figs. 13-36 and 13-37). Noncommunicating hydrocephalus due to obstruction of the foramen of Monro, unilateral or bilateral, or of the fourth ventricle is a common finding (Zee 1980) (Fig. 13-37). On CT, intraventricular cysts may not be identified because of their thin walls, approximately CSF-equivalent contents, and lack of contrast enhancement (Carbajal 1977; Benson 1977). MR is more sensitive than CT in the evaluation of suspected intraventricular cysts (Martinez 1989). Not only are the cyst walls often visible, but the scolices themselves can frequently be seen (Fig. 13-36). Visualization of the scolex is pathognomonic of cysticercosis (Rhee 1987; Zee 1988): otherwise, ependymal cysts, intraventricular epidermoids, and even colloid cysts must be considered in the differential diagnosis.

In parenchymal cysticercosis, rounded cystic structures of CSF-equivalent density (Fig. 13-38) up to 2 or 3 cm in diameter are seen within the substance of the brain, often in the cortex (Rodriguez-Carbajal 1983). As with intraventricular cysts, MR often reveals a scolex within a cyst that is of CSF intensity (Fig. 13-39). When the larvae are alive, there is little reaction in the surrounding brain. Consequently, contrast enhancement or focal edema around the cysts is rarely observed in association with living cysticerci. This lack of inflammatory reaction is a striking feature of the disease and is probably due to the poor antigenicity of the cyst walls (Biagi 1974).

When the larvae die, however, the cysts incite an inflammatory response. Ringlike or nodular contrast enhancement occurs, often accompanied by surrounding focal edema (Martinez 1989) (Fig. 13-40). Often the cyst fluid becomes turbid. Cysts can appear isodense to CSF on CT and isointense to CSF on MR sequences. Pericystic hyperintensity surrounding lesions of various ages on PD- or T_2WI represents gliosis, edema, and inflammation (Teitelbaum 1989). Contrast enhancement on MR usually occurs in patients in whom precontrast MR findings have shown an active inflammatory reaction in the degenerating stage of the worm (Chang 1991).

Calcifications are a manifestation of dead larvae. They can appear as early as 8 months after the acute phase (Rodriguez-Carbajal 1983) or may require 10 years or

A

Figure 13-36 Intraventricular cysticercosis. **A.** MR: T_1WI (600/20) demonstrates the cystic lesion filling the fourth ventricle. Note signal void in the aqueduct superiorly, indicating patency of CSF flow (arrows). Also note the mass effect of the cyst, with the brainstem pushed anteriorly. **B.** T_1WI (500/30) in another patient shows the fourth ventricle filled completely with the cyst. Punctate hyperdense scolex (arrows) is noted.

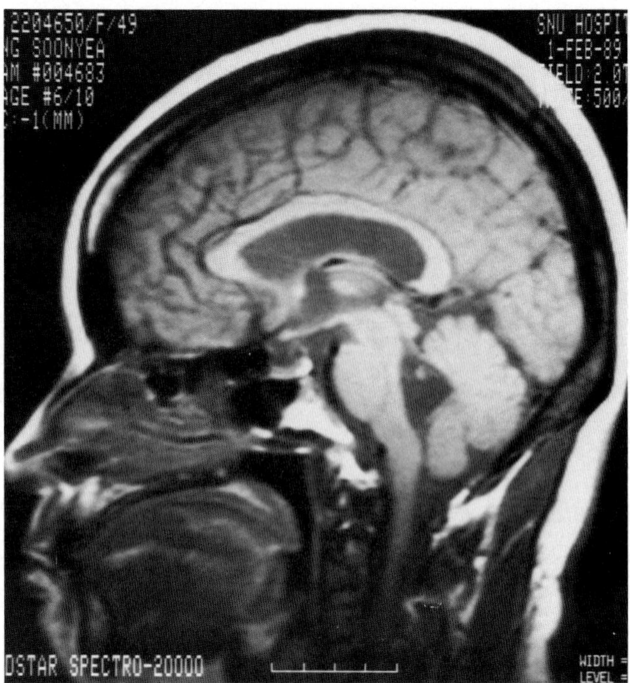

B

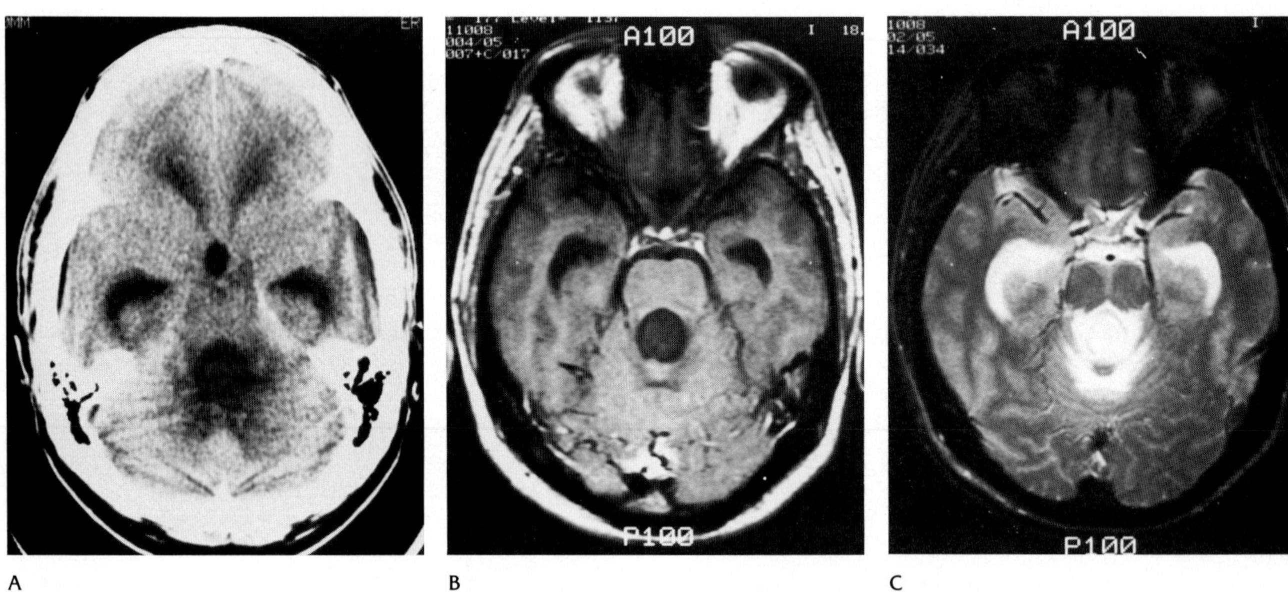

A B C

Figure 13-37 Intraventricular cysticercosis. **A.** NCCT shows fourth ventricular mass with symmetrical dilatation of temporal horns and third ventricle representing obstructive hydrocephalus. **B.** MR: Axial T_1WI (600/30) shows fourth ventricular mass. **C.** MR: Axial T_2WI (2600/80) shows hyperintensity of the fourth ventricle and associated surrounding hyperintense regions, representing pericystic inflammation.

more to develop (Dixon 1961). Calcifications are seen only in the parenchymal form, not in ventricular or cisternal cysts. Usually they are located in the gray matter or the gray-white matter junction, but they are sometimes seen in the basal ganglia or the deep white matter (Santin 1966). Calcifications may involve both the wall and contents of the cyst. They typically appear round and slightly oval and range from 7 to 16 mm in size (Carbajal 1977). These wholly or partially calcified spheres frequently contain an eccentric small nodular calcification measuring 1 to 2 mm in diameter that represents the scolex of the erupted larva (Jankowski 1979). Both dead larvae with calcifications and living larvae may coexist in cases of reinfestation (Fig. 13-39). Vasculitis may develop in the vicinity of these lesions and lead to cortical arterial occlusion and infarction.

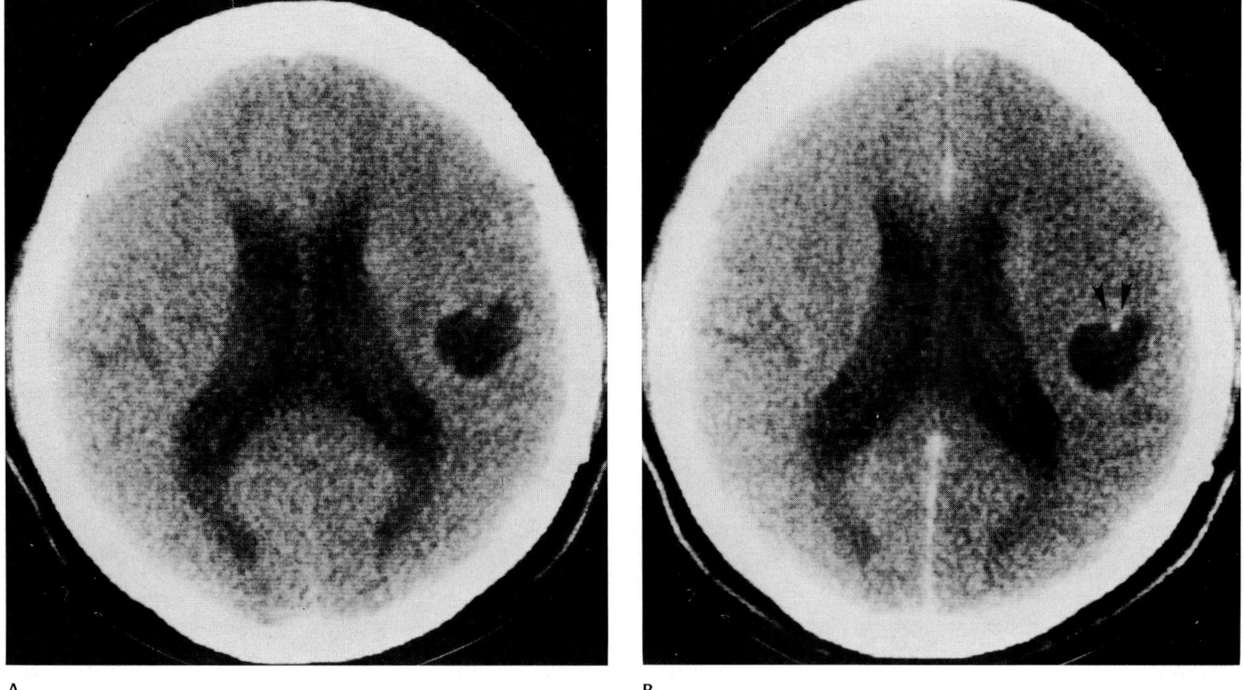

Figure 13-38 Living intraparenchymal cysticercus. **A.** NCCT demonstrates a rounded cystic structure of CSF-equivalent density in the white matter of the parietal lobe. No surrounding edema is present. **B.** CECT shows no contrast enhancement around the cyst, but the scolex (arrowheads) is slightly enhanced, indicating the living cysticercus. Note also the absence of adjacent edema or mass effect. (*Courtesy of Dr. S. Y. Kim, Seoul, Korea.*)

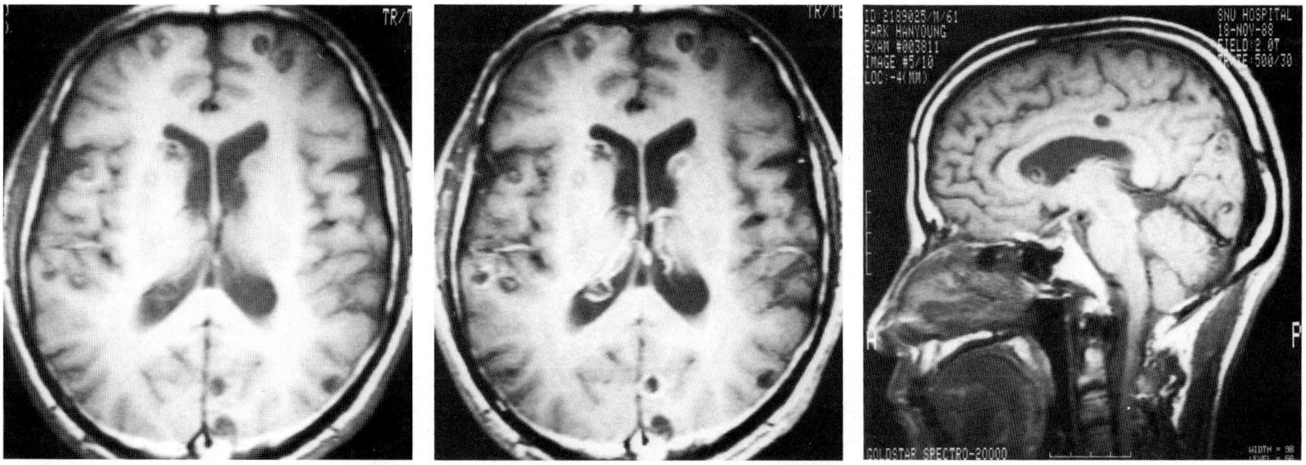

Figure 13-39 Mixed pattern of cysticercosis with coexistence of dead and living larvae. **A** MR: Axial T_1WI (500/30) demonstrates multiple cortical and paraventricular hypodense lesions, the majority with scolices within. Left parietooccipital lesions show signal void representing calcifications. **B.** CEMR: Axial T_1WI (500/30) shows mild peripheral enhancement except for left parietooccipital lesions representing calcified dead larvae. Note clear visualization of intraventricular cysts. **C** and **D.** Sagittal T_1WI (500/30) demonstrate the mixed pattern to better advantage. **E.** T_2WI (2600/80) demonstrates hyperintensity of cysts isointense to CSF. (*Reprinted with permission from Chang 1990.*)

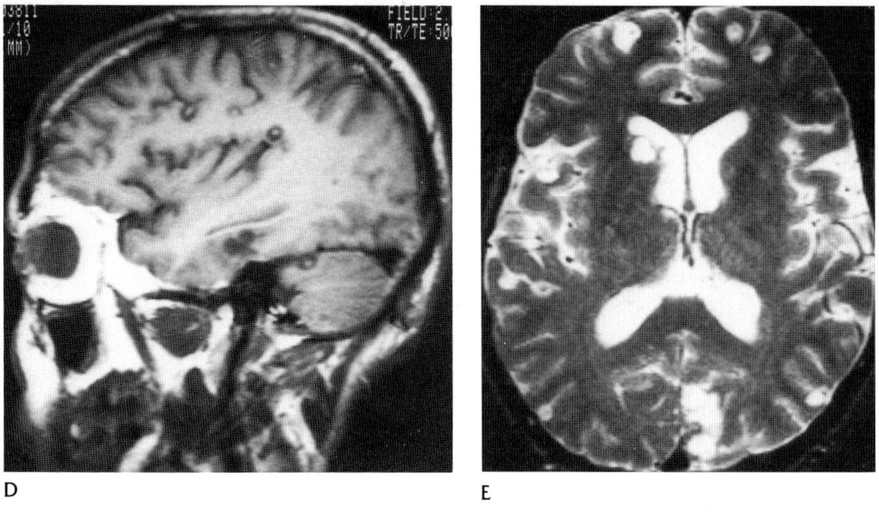

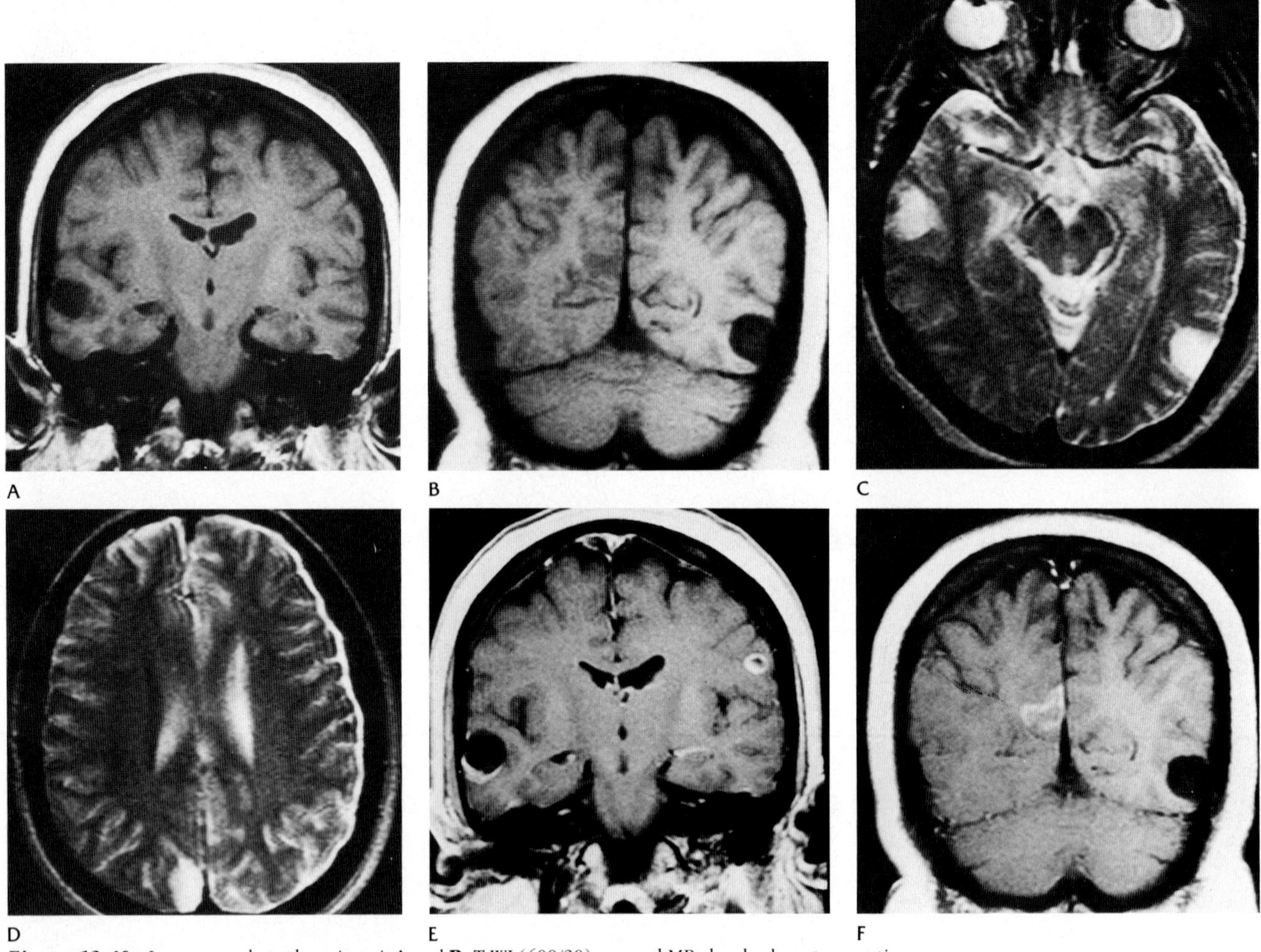

Figure 13-40 Intraparenchymal cysticerci. **A** and **B.** T_1WI (600/20) coronal MR clearly show two cystic lesions. The signal intensity of the lesions is slightly higher than that of CSF in the ventricles. No definite scolices can be determined **C** and **D.** T_2WI (2000, 70) show hyperintensity of the cystic lesions. **E** and **F.** T_1WI (600/20): Coronal CEMR show a small amount of enhancement surrounding the two cystic lesions. Additional enhancing lesions can be seen in the left parietal lobe and right occipital lobe. In this case, CEMR was able to detect lesions poorly seen on NCMR. (*Courtesy of C. S. Zee, University of Southern California, Los Angeles.*)

MR is more sensitive than CT in the recognition of parenchymal, intraventricular, and subarachnoid cysts; perifocal edema; and internal changes indicative of cyst death (Suss 1986; Martinez 1989; Suh 1989). CT is far superior in the demonstration of calcification (Teitelbaum 1989). Therefore, if parenchymal cysticercosis is suspected, CT is the preferred initial screening modality.

Hydatid Disease

Hydatid disease due to *Echinococcus granulosus* is usually manifested by cysts in the liver and lungs. Only 2 percent of hydatid infestations involve the CNS (Dew 1934). Hydatid cysts of the brain are usually large and solitary, lying just a few millimeters below the cortex. Extradural cysts have been reported (Ozgen 1979). Multiple cysts are rare, but daughter cysts are not uncommon after inadvertent rupture or intentional puncture of a solitary cyst (Adams 1984).

On CT and MR, a hydatid cyst appears as a large intraparenchymal cystic lesion, spherical in shape, with sharply defined borders. The appearance of the cyst contents is similar to that of water on CT (Ozgen 1979; Rudwan 1988) and that of CSF on MR (Coates 1990) (Figs. 13-41 and 13-42). Calcification is rare. Severe distortion of the brain parenchyma and shift of the ventricular system often result. Hydrocephalus due to partial obstruction of CSF pathways is common. The lack of contrast enhancement at the periphery of the cyst and hypodense/hypointense thin cyst wall serve to differentiate this lesion from cerebral abscess on CT and MR (Abbassioun 1978; Coates 1990). A primary extradural hydatid cyst resembles an arachnoid cyst (Ba'assiri 1984).

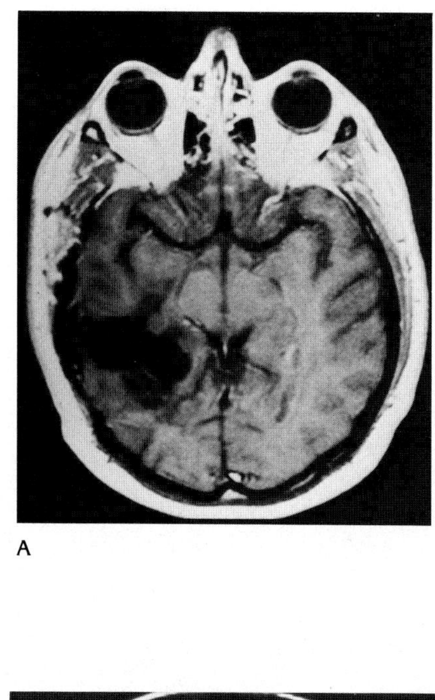
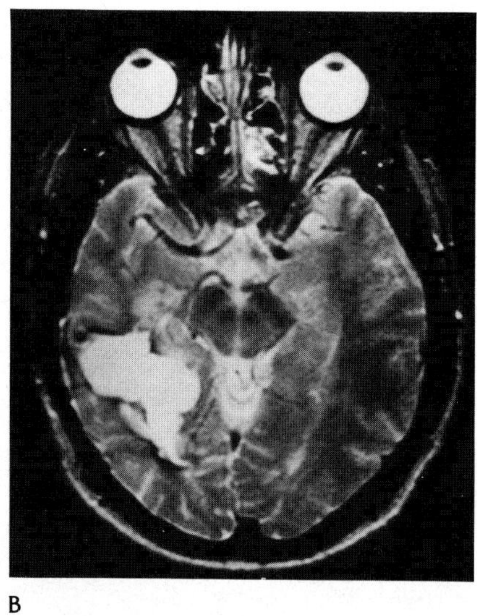

A B

Figure 13-41 Hydatid cysts. **A.** T_1WI CEMR discloses multiloculated cystic lesions in the right temporal-occipital region. No enhancement of the cysts is seen. The cyst fluid appears to be of low signal intensity but is probably slightly hyperintense compared with CSF. **B.** T_2WI NCMR demonstrates high intensity of internal components of the lesion. In addition, a hypointense rim is seen in portions of the cysts. (*Courtesy of C. S. Zee, University of Southern California, Los Angeles.*)

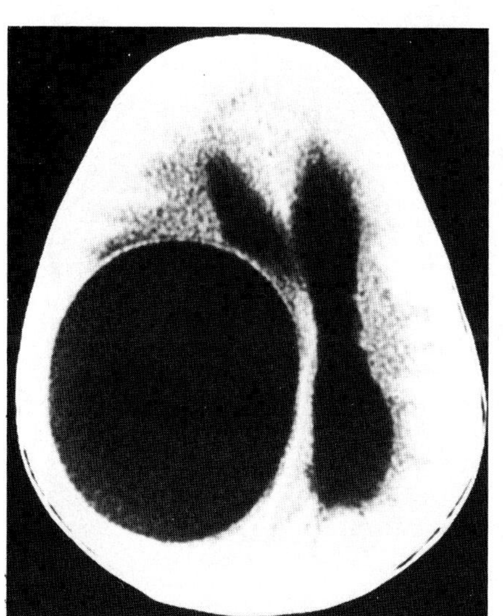
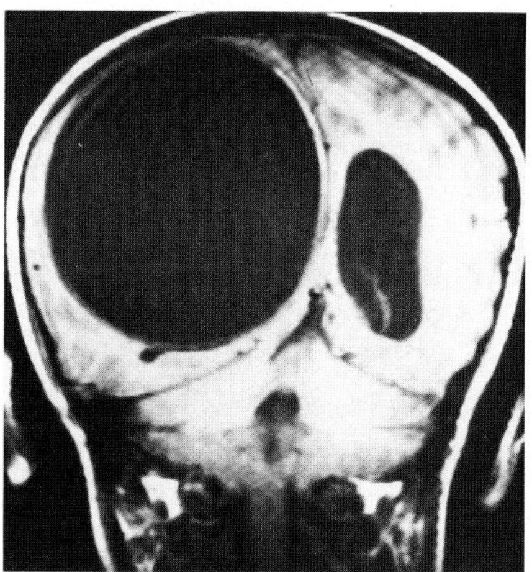
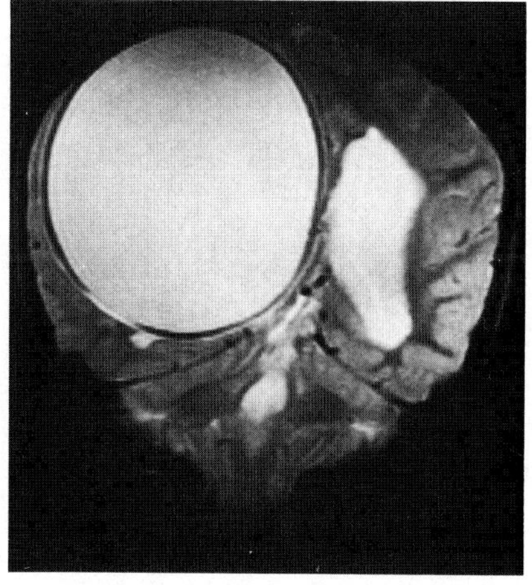

A B C

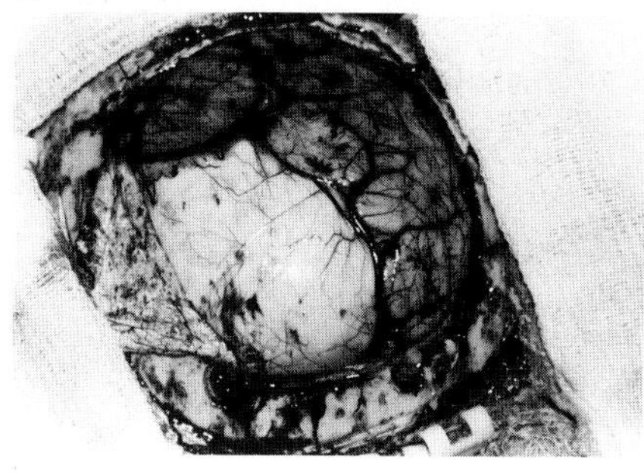

D

Figure 13-42 **A.** Axial CT scan of right parietal spherical hydatid cyst. **B.** Coronal MR image (600/20) of spherical right parietal hydatid cyst; signal intensity of contents is identical to that of CSF. **C.** Coronal MR image (2000/80) of right parietal hydatid cyst with peripheral rim of low signal intensity. **D.** Intraoperative photograph of typical pearly white hydatid cyst. (*Reprinted with permission from Coates 1990.*)

ACQUIRED IMMUNE DEFICIENCY SYDROME

The acquired immune deficiency syndrome (AIDS) is due to the group of retroviruses known as the human immunodeficiency viruses (HIV). HIV primarily disrupt normal T-cell lymphocyte numbers and functions, resulting in an alteration of cell-mediated immunity. Homosexual men and intravenous drug abusers are most frequently affected, and the mortality rate approaches 100 percent, although new antiviral agents have shown considerable promise.

Neurological signs and symptoms occur in 30 to 70 percent of cases and can be attributed to the following: (1) opportunistic infections such as toxoplasmosis, cryptococcosis, papovavirus, candidiasis, cytomegalovirus,

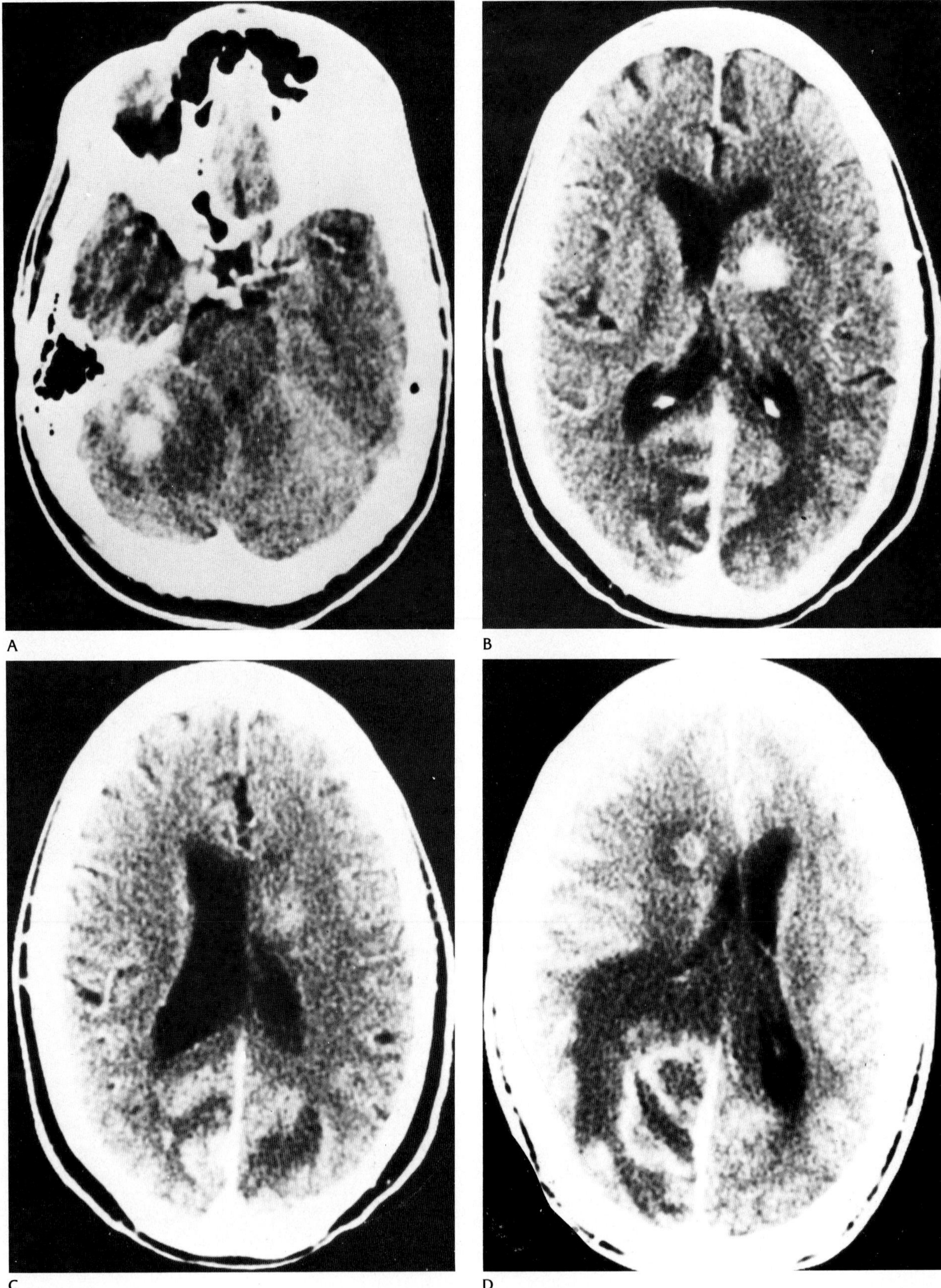

Figure 13-43 AIDS patients with toxoplasmosis: CECT of the posterior fossa (**A**) shows multiple nodular enhancing lesions in the right cerebellum. Mild edema is present. Left basal ganglia mass and abnormal gyral enhancement of the occipital lobes are noted (**B**). At higher level (**C**), irregular hypodense lesions of the parieto-occipital lobes are associated with irregular nodular enhancing lesions. (**D.**) Another patient with peripheral enhancement in right frontal and occipital lobes.

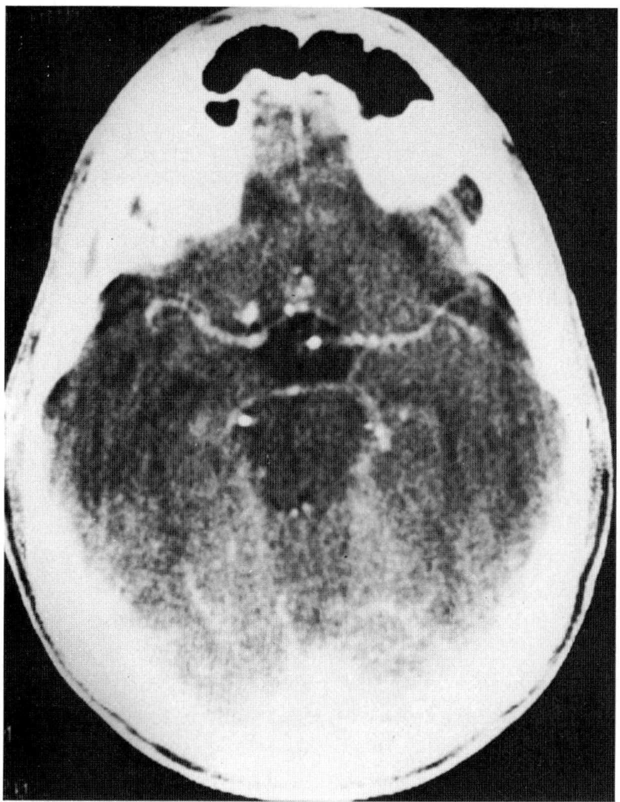

A

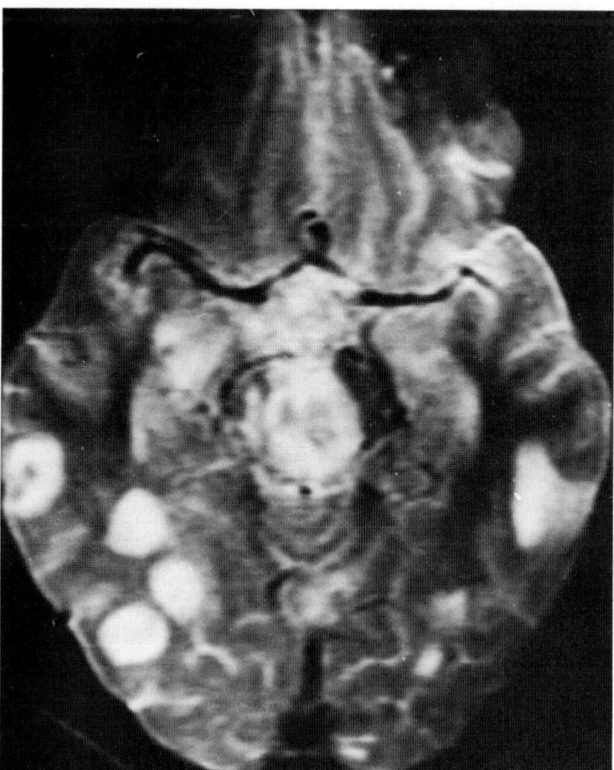

B

Figure 13-44 Toxoplasmosis. **A.** CECT scan does not show any definitive lesions. **B.** T_2WI (2000/70) shows multiple high-intensity foci involving both temporal lobes and the brainstem. This appearance in a patient with AIDS is consistent with but not diagnostic of toxoplasmosis.

Mycobacterium tuberculosis and *M. avium-intracellulare,* and aspergillosis, (2) neoplasms, especially primary and secondary lymphoma, and (3) an actual neurotrophic effect of HIV itself (Sze 1987).

The response of the brain to pathogens in AIDS patients differs from that in individuals with normal cell-mediated immune systems. Because of the atypical reaction, the usual imaging criteria for intracranial lesions may be altered and are not diagnostically pathognomonic.

Toxoplasmosis is by far the most common infection of the brain parenchyma in AIDS patients (Whelan 1983; Post 1985; Levy 1986, 1990; Ramsey 1988). Patients present with the symptoms of a mass lesion, with focal neurological abnormalities, seizures, or decreased mental status.

CT findings consist of multiple intraparenchymal lesions with ring or nodular contrast enhancement and hypodense areas. The basal ganglia are affected in up to 75 percent of cases (Post 1983; Whelan 1983; Elkin 1985; Bursztyn 1984) (Fig. 13-43). Involvement of the corticomedullary junction is common, but the cerebellum and brainstem are less frequently involved (Post 1985, 1986*a*).

MR is more sensitive than CT to early infections (Davidson 1985; Schroth 1987). Frequently, spin-density MRI is more sensitive in the detection of lesions than is CECT (Levy 1986). For this reason, it is the modality of choice in AIDS patients with neurological symptoms or signs (Levy 1990). As with cerebritis from other causes, toxoplasmosis creates areas of mild hypointensity on T_1WI and hyperintensity on T_2WI (Post 1986*b*) (Fig. 13-44). Occasionally lesions may appear somewhat hypointense on T_2WI, surrounded by higher-intensity edema (Kupfer 1990). On CECT and CEMR, smooth ringlike or nodular enhancements are surrounded by a variable degree of white matter edema (Post 1986*bc;* Levy 1990). Actual abscess formation, with development of the fibrous capsule, often does not take place because of the altered immune status of these patients and their inability to mount a sufficient immune response. Necrosis of the central regions occurs but is generally irregular in shape and poorly defined. In this situation, contrast enhancement can be heterogeneous or uneven. Toxoplasmosis lesions generally do not contain hemorrhage, although bleeding can occur (Levy 1990). MR is excellent for follow-up after medical treatment.

Cryptococcus neoformans is an opportunistic infection that affects the CNS in AIDS patients at least as frequently as does *Toxoplasma;* however, it generally manifests as subacute meningitis rather than a mass in the brain parenchyma. Headache is the most common symptom, but patients may also present with fever, meningeal signs, confusion, seizures, and rarely focal deficits. While patients with normal immune status often develop thick basilar exudate in cases of cryptococcal meningitis, pa-

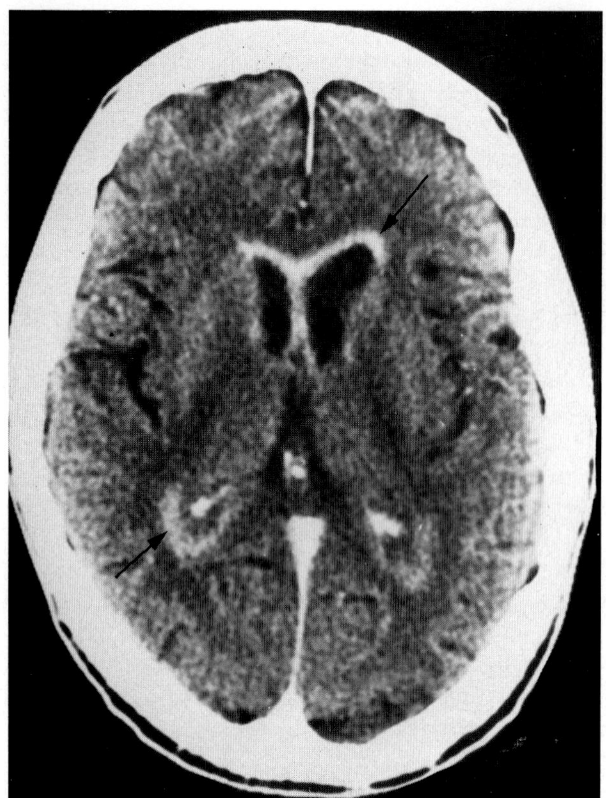

Figure 13-45 AIDS with cytomegalovirus (CMV). CECT shows marked, diffuse periventricular enhancement denoting ependymal and subependymal involvement (arrows). [*From Post (1985) with permission.*]

tients with AIDS may not. Therefore, the CT and MR findings are usually normal. Even CEMR rarely shows significant enhancement of the meninges. Associated findings such as communicating hydrocephalus may be seen. Occasionally patients with cryptococcal meningitis can develop basal ganglia lesions as a result of collections of cryptococcus in the Virchow-Robin spaces, as described earlier (Wehn 1989) (Fig. 13-27).

Cytomegalovirus (CMV) is a common infection in the general population. In AIDS patients, however, CMV can become more active. Its most common manifestations are encephalitis and ependymitis. Widespread white matter disease with diffuse subependymal contrast enhancement, often irregular in outline around the lateral ventricles, can be present (Figs. 13-19 and 13-45). CT is less sensitive than MR in detecting CMV encephalitis (Post 1986*a*). The changes of ependymitis are often superimposed on those of hydrocephalus. On MR, CMV ependymitis is often demonstrated by periventricular hyperintensity on T_2WI that is often nodular and invasive and often involves the corpus callosum. Both changes are less frequently seen in hydrocephalus.

Progressive multifocal leukoencephalopathy (PML) is a progressive disease of the central nervous system that predominantly involves the white matter (Post 1985; Levy 1986). While it can occur in any immunosuppressed patient, it is particularly common in AIDS patients (Mark 1989). Papovavirus (JC, SV 40) is acquired in childhood asymptomatically and becomes reactivated when the host's immune system declines. Thus, the virus can be isolated from lesions of PML. The usual clinical course is one of progression to coma, leading to death in 3 to 6 months after the onset of symptoms. The final diagnosis of PML depends on biopsy or postmortem examination. Drug therapy has had little success.

Pathological examination in PML demonstrates multifocal areas of demyelination with relative sparing of neurons (Olsen 1988*a*). The mechanism for demyelination is considered by some to be a result of the death of oligodendroglia, the cells responsible for sheath formation (Sze 1988*b*). The demyelinating lesions of PML appear to have a predilection for the subcortical white matter. Atrophy is a late occurrence.

Imaging plays an important role in the diagnosis of PML. On CT, characteristic hypodense foci in the subcortical white matter are seen (Whelan 1983; Post 1985). The lesions are sharply marginated with a scalloped outer border (Fig. 13-45). There appears to be a predilection for the parietooccipital region (Post 1985). Follow-up examinations may show progressive enlargement of the demyelinating areas (Sze 1988*b*). Although rare, mass effect may be present, as may contrast enhancement (Mark 1989).

MR is more sensitive than CT in detecting white matter abnormalities caused by PML (Sze 1988*b*). While the findings may be nonspecific, the detection of an optimal biopsy site can be facilitated. Again, areas of white matter hyperintensity are usually seen. These lesions are initially focal (Olsen 1988*b*) but later coalesce (Mark 1989) and become larger (Fig. 13-46). Although PML classically affects the parietooccipital region, in patients with AIDS, other regions may also be affected (Fig. 13-47). Therefore, in patients with AIDS, PML must be suspected if any lesion of hyperintensity on T_2WI, without mass effect or contrast enhancement, is documented. Lesions may occur even in the deep gray matter or the cortex (Sze 1988*b;* Mark 1989) (Fig. 13-47).

Navia (1986) established *AIDS dementia complex* as a distinct clinical and pathological entity which is caused by direct brain infection by HIV. Both CT and MR are relatively insensitive to the diffuse microglial nodules with multinucleated giant cells which are the primary changes seen in HIV infection of the brain (Post 1988). However, they do show the sequelae of the infection. CT and MR demonstrate a variable degree of cortical atrophy, frequently accompanied by ventricular dilatation (Levin 1990) (Fig. 13-48). Cerebellar and brainstem atrophy are also noted (Flowers 1990). Diffuse white matter abnormalities may be prominent, with relative sparing of the

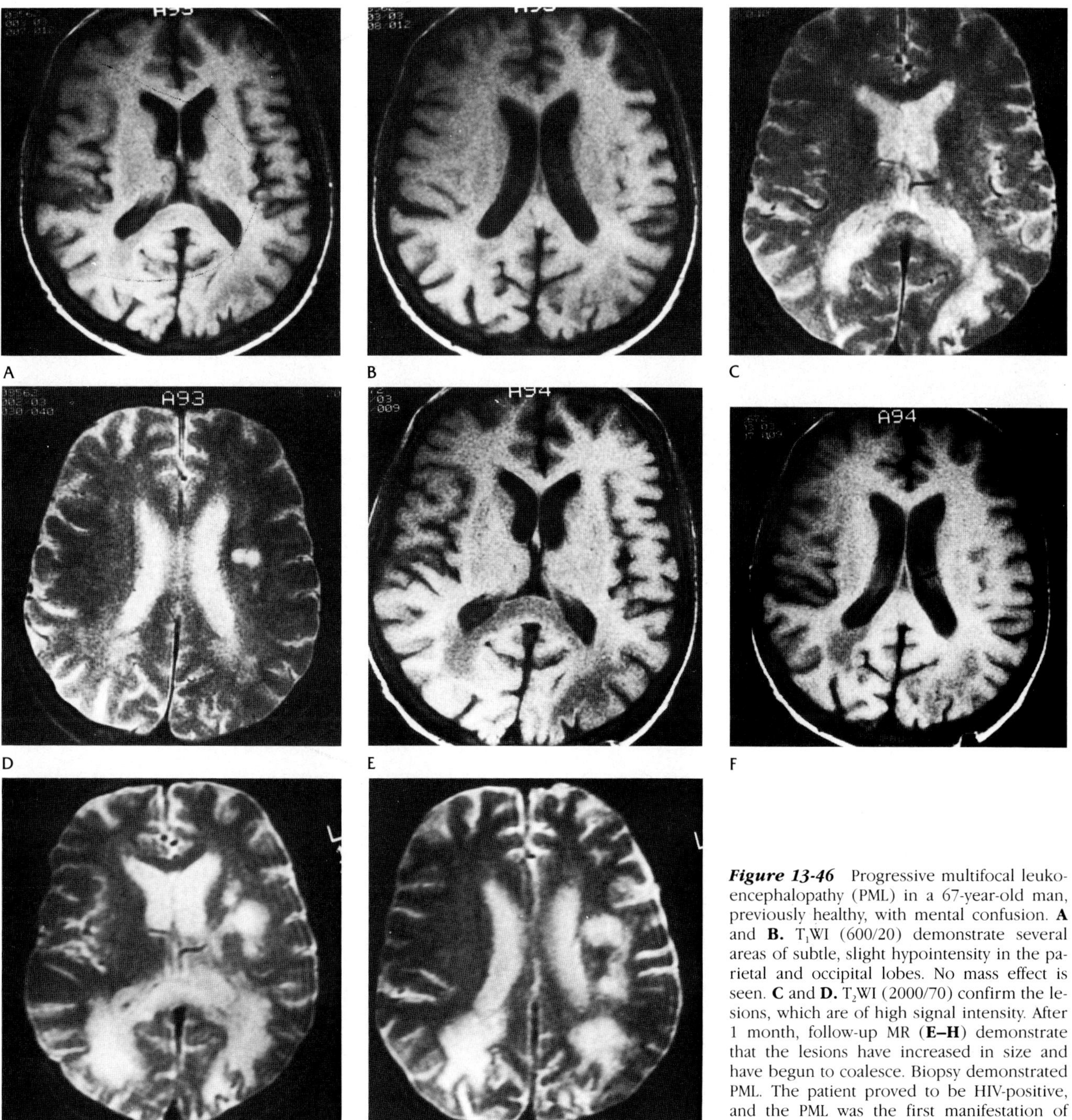

Figure 13-46 Progressive multifocal leukoencephalopathy (PML) in a 67-year-old man, previously healthy, with mental confusion. **A** and **B.** T_1WI (600/20) demonstrate several areas of subtle, slight hypointensity in the parietal and occipital lobes. No mass effect is seen. **C** and **D.** T_2WI (2000/70) confirm the lesions, which are of high signal intensity. After 1 month, follow-up MR (**E–H**) demonstrate that the lesions have increased in size and have begun to coalesce. Biopsy demonstrated PML. The patient proved to be HIV-positive, and the PML was the first manifestation of AIDS. Despite treatment, the patient died.

cortex and gray matter (Chrysikopoulos 1990; Flowers 1990). MR is particularly sensitive to the white matter changes (Olsen 1988*a,b*). On T_2WI, hyperintensity is seen in the white matter as a result of demyelination (Figs. 13-48 and 13-49). These changes may initially be focal, but they later coalesce and become diffuse. Typically, they lack mass effect or contrast enhancement and closely resemble changes in PML.

Initially it was hoped that MR would be able to predict which patients who were HIV-positive might go on to develop AIDS or which patients who had AIDS might progress to develop dementia. However, in general, MR has not proved to be a good predictor (Freund-Levi 1989; McArthur 1990). White matter changes often follow rather than precede clinical dementia, although early cognitive impairment has been reported to be associated

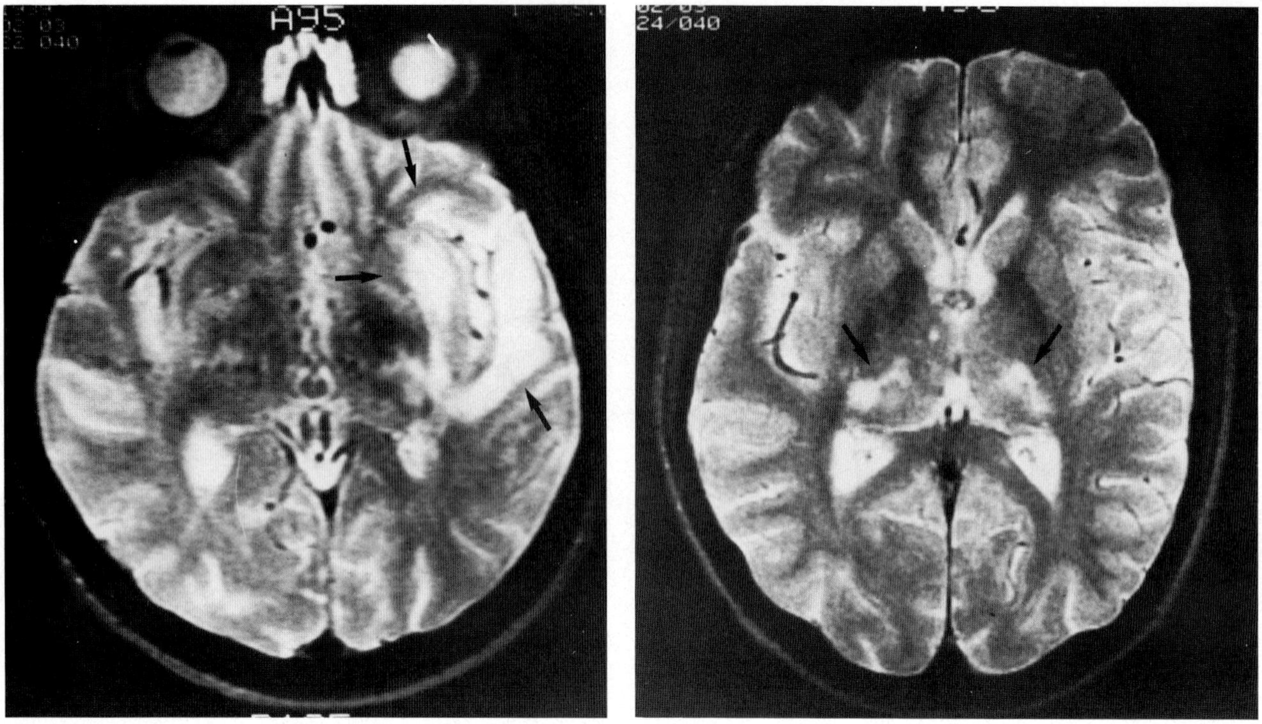

A

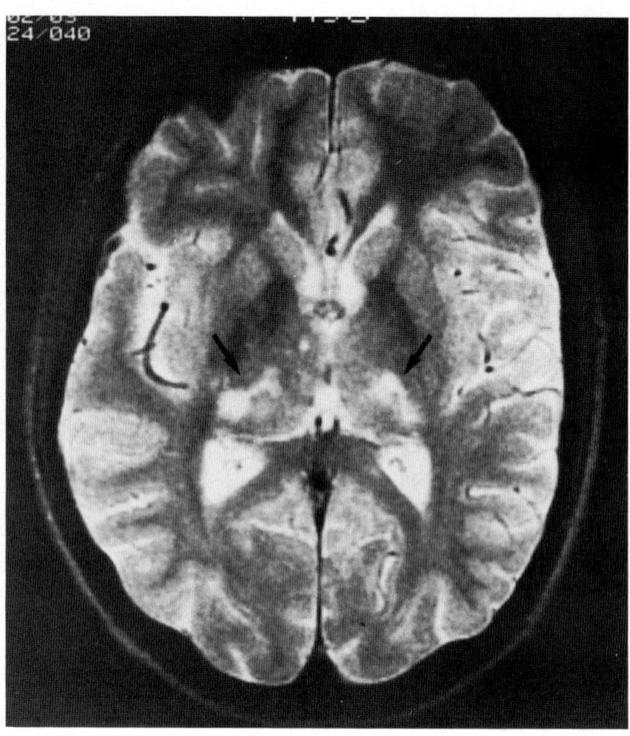

B

Figure 13-47 Progressive multifocal leukoencephalopathy (PML), biopsy proved in two patients with AIDS. **A** and **B.** MRI: T_2WI (2000/70) disclose lesions in **A**) both temporal lobes and in the left insular white matter (arrows) and the basal ganglia (arrows) in **B**), both unusual distributions in typical PML.

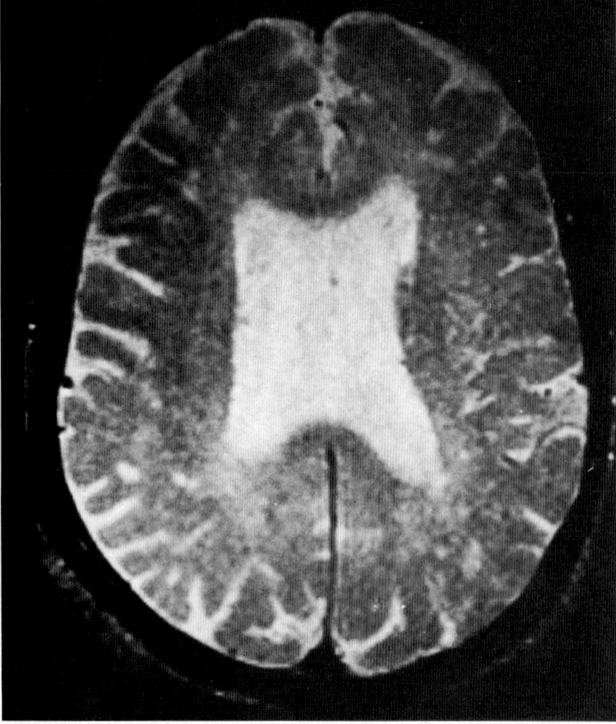

with high signal intensity in the splenium of the corpus callosum and the crura of the fornices on T_2WI (Kieburtz 1990).

CT and MR observations in other infections and neoplasms associated with AIDS are described in other sections. All AIDS patients should be studied with CT or, preferably, MR when they develop altered mental status, fever associated with seizures, and/or focal neurological deficits (Post 1986*a*).

Figure 13-48 HIV encephalopathy. T_2WI (2000/70) shows diffuse scattered foci of hyperintensity in this patient with mild to moderate atrophy.

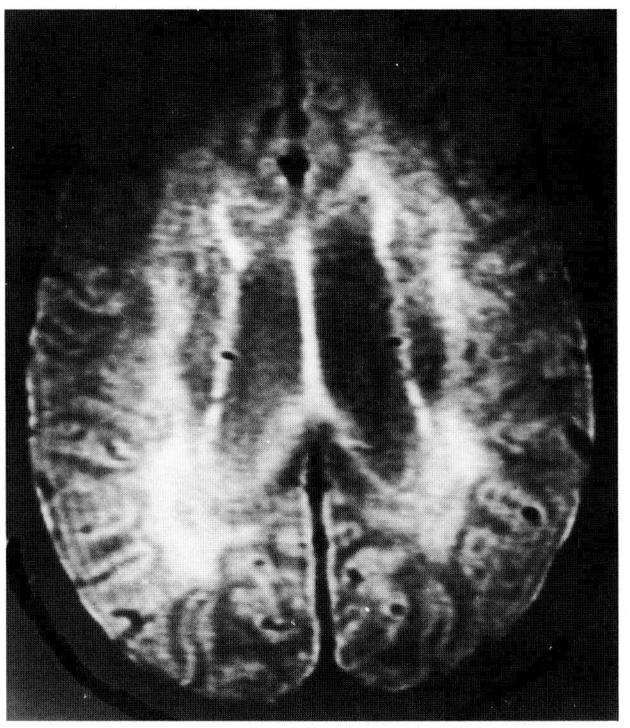

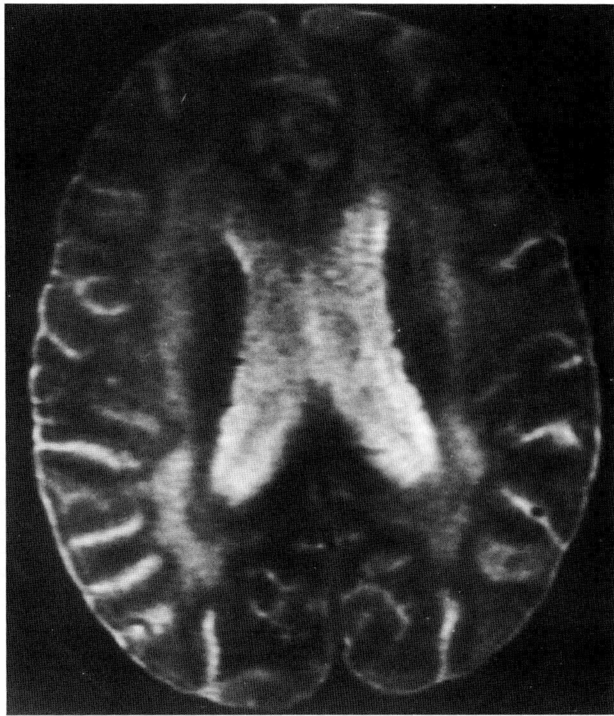

A B

Figure 13-49 HIV encephalopathy. A 26-year-old man with AIDS and severe dementia. **A** and **B.** T_2WI (2000/35, 70) disclose hyperintensity in the white matter bilaterally. The pattern of involvement is diffuse and confluent as a result of widespread involvement and demyelination. On pathological examination the extent of involvement exceeded that seen on MR.

REFERENCES

ABBASSIOUN K et al: CT in hydatid cyst of the brain. *J Neurosurg* 49:408–411, 1978.

ADAMS H: *Greenfield's Neuropathy.* Chicago, Year Book, 1984, p 317.

ADAMS RD, VICTOR M: *Principles of Neurology,* 3d ed. New York, McGraw-Hill, 1985, pp 510–534.

ANDERSON JM, MACMILLAN JJ: Intracranial tuberculoma: An increasing problem in Britain. *J Neurol Neurosurg Psychiatry* 38:194–201, 1975.

ARMITSU T et al: CT in verified cases of tuberculous meningitis. *Neurology* 29:384–386, 1979.

ARRINGTON JA, MURTAGH FR, MARTINEZ CR, et al: CT of multiple intracranial cryptococcoma. *AJNR* 5:472–473, 1984.

AUH YH, LEE SH, TOGLIA JU: Excessively small ventricles on cranial CT: Clinical correlation in 75 patients. *J Comput Assist Tomogr* 4:325–329, 1980.

BA'ASSIRI A, HADDAD F: Primary extradural intracranial hydatid disease: CT appearance. *AJNR* 5:474–475, 1984.

BAHGR AL, KRUMBHOLZ A, KRISTT D, HODGES FJ: Neuroradiological manifestations of intracranial sarcoidosis. *Radiology* 127:713–717, 1978.

BARLOON TJ, YUH WT, KNEPPER LE, BILLER J, RYALS TJ, SATO Y. Cerebral ventriculitis: MR findings. *J Comput Assist Tomogr* 14:272–275, 1990.

BENSON JR et al: CT in intracranial cysticercosis. *J Comput Assist Tomogr* 1(4):464–471, 1977.

BHARDARI T, SARKAN N: Subdural empyema: A review of 37 cases. *J Neurosurg* 32:35–39, 1970.

BIAGI F, WILLIAMS K: Immunologic problems in the diagnosis of human cysticercosis. *Am Parasitol Hum Comp* 49:509–513, 1974.

BISHBURG E, SUNDERAM G, REICHMAN LB, et al: CNS tuberculosis with AIDS and its related complex. *Ann Intern Med* 105:210–213, 1986.

BLAQUIERE RM: The computed tomographic appearances on intra- and extracerebral abscesses. *Br J Radiol* 56:171–181, 1983.

BOESCH C, ISSAKAINEN J, KEWITZ G, KIKINIS R, MARTIN E, BOLTSHAUSER E: Magnetic resonance imaging of the brain in congenital cytomegalovirus infection. *Pediatr Radiol* 19:91–93, 1989.

BRANT-ZAWADZKI M, DAVIS PL, CROOKS LE, et al: NMR demonstration of cerebral abnormalities: Comparison with CT. *AJNR* 4:117–124, 1983*b*.

BRANT-ZAWADZKI M et al: NMR imaging of experimental brain abscess: Comparison with CT. *AJNR* 4:250–253, 1983*a*.

BRANT-ZAWADZKI M, KELLY W, KJOS B, et al: Magnetic resonance imaging and characterization of normal and abnormal intracranial cerebrospinal fluid (CSF) spaces: Initial observations. *Neuroradiology* 27:3–8, 1985.

BRITT RH, ENZMANN DR, REMINGTON JS: Intracranial infection in cardiac transplant recipients. *Ann Neurol* 9:107–119, 1981.

BRONEN R, SZE G: Magnetic resonance imaging contrast agents: Theory and application to the central nervous system. *J Neurosurg* 73:820–839, 1990.

BURSZTYN EM, LEE BC, BAUMAN J: CT of AIDS. *AJNR* 5:711–714, 1984.

BYRD SE, LOCKE GE, BIGGERS S, PERCY AK: The computed tomographic appearance of cerebral cysticercosis in adults and children. *Radiology* 144:819–823, 1982.

CAHILL DW, SALCUMAN M: Neurosarcoidosis—A review of the rare manifestation. *Surg Neurol* 15(3):204–211, 1981.

CARBAJAL JR et al: Radiology of cysticercosis of the CNS, including CT. *Radiology* 125:127–131, 1977.

CARTER BL, BANKOF MS, FISK JD: CT detection of sinusitis responsible for intracranial and extracranial infections. *Radiology* 147:739–742, 1983.

CASSELMAN ES et al: CT of tuberculous meningitis in infants and children. *J Comput Assist Tomogr* 4(2):211–216, 1980.

CHANG KH, HAN MH, ROH JK, KIM IO, HAN MC, KIM CW: Gd-DTPA-enhanced MR imaging of the brain in patients with meningitis: Comparison with CT. *AJR* 154:809–816, 1990.

CHANG KH, LEE JH, HAN MH, et al: The role of contrast-enhanced MR imaging in the diagnosis of neurocysticercosis. *AJNR* 12:509–512, 1991.

CHRYSIKOPOULOS HS, PRESS GA, GRAFE MR, HESSELINK JR, WILEY CA: Encephalitis caused by human immunodeficiency virus: CT and MR imaging manifestations with clinical and pathologic correlation. *Radiology* 175:185–191, 1990.

CLAVERIA LE, DUBOULAY GH, MOSELEY IF: Intracranial infections: Investigations by C.A.T. *Neuroradiology* 12:59–71, 1976.

COATES R, VON SINNER W, RAHM R: MR imaging of an intracerebral hydatid cyst. *AJNR* 11:1249–1250, 1990.

DANZIGER A, PRICE H, SCHECHTER MM: An analysis of 113 intracranial infections. *Neuroradiology* 19:31–34, 1980.

DAVIDSON HD, STEINER RE: Magnetic resonance imaging in infections of the central nervous system. *AJR* 6:499–504, 1985.

DAVIS JM, et al: CT of herpes simplex encephalitis with clinicopathological correlation. *Radiology* 129:409–417, 1978.

DEW HR: Hydatid disease of the brain. *Surg Gynecol Obstet* 59:312–319, 1934.

DIXON HBF, LIPSCOMB FM: Cysticercosis: An analysis and followup of 450 Cases. Privy Council, Medical Research Council Report, No. 339. London, Her Majesty's Stationery Office, 1961, pp 1–57.

DRAOUAT S, ABDENABI B, COHANEM, et al: CT of cerebral tuberculosis. *J Comput Assist Tomogr* 11(4):594–597, 1987.

DUBLIN AB, PHILLIPS HE: CT of disseminated cerebral coccidioidomycosis. *Radiology* 135:361–368, 1980.

EINSTEIN HE: Coccidioidomycosis of the CNS. *Adv Neurol* 6:101–105, 1974.

ELKIN CM, LEON E, GRENELL SL, LEEDS NE: Intracranial lesions in AIDS: Radiologic (CT) features. *JAMA* 253(3):393–396, 1985.

ENZMANN DR, NORMAN D, MAIN J, NEWTON TH: CT of granulomatous basal arachnoiditis. *Radiology* 120:341–344, 1976.

ENZMANN DR et al: CT of herpes simplex encephalitis. *Radiology* 129:419–425, 1978.

ENZMANN DR, BRITT RH, YEAGER AS: Experimental brain abscess evolution: Computed tomographic and neuropathologic correlation. *Radiology* 133:113–122, 1979.

ENZMANN DR, BRANT-ZAWADZKI M, BRITT RH: Computed tomography of central nervous system infections in immunosuppressed patients. *AJNR* 1:239–243, 1980.

ENZMANN DR: *Imaging of Infections and Inflammations of the Central Nervous System: CT, US and MRI.* New York, Raven Press, 1984, pp 234–249.

ENZMANN D, CHANG Y, AUGUSTYN G: MR findings in neonatal herpes simplex encephalitis type II. *J Comput Assist Tomogr* 14:453–457, 1990.

FLOWERS CH, MAFEE MF, CROWELL R, et al: Encephalopathy in AIDS patients: Evaluation with MR Imaging. *AJNR* 11:1235–1245, 1990.

FRASER RG, PARE JAP: *Diagnosis of Diseases of the Chest,* 2d ed. Philadelphia, Saunders, 1978, vol 2, pp 778–787.

FREUND-LEVI Y, SAFF J, WAHLUND LO, WETTERBERG L: Ultra low field brain MRI in HIV transfusion infected patients. *Magn Reson Imaging* 7:225–230, 1989.

FUJITA NK, et al: Cryptococcal intracerebral mass lesions: The role of CT and non-surgical management. *Ann Intern Med* 94:382–388, 1981.

GALBRAITH JG, VARR VW: Epidural abscess and subdural empyema. *Adv Neurol* 6:257–267, 1974.

GREENBERG SB et al: CT in brain biopsy-proven herpes simplex encephalitis: Early normal results. *Arch Neurol* 38:58–59, 1981.

GRIGGS RC, MANESBERRY WR, CONDEMI JJ: Cerebral mass due to sarcoidosis: Regression during corticosteroid therapy. *Neurology* 23:981–989, 1973.

GRINELLI VS, BENTSON JR, HELMER E, WINTER J: Diagnosis of interhemispheric subdural empyema by CT. *J Comput Assist Tomogr* 1(2):99–105, 1977.

GROSSMAN RI et al: CT of intracranial aspergillosis. *J Comput Assist Tomogr* 5(5):646–650, 1981.

GROSSMAN RI, WOLF G, BIERY D, et al: Gadolinium enhanced nuclear magnetic resonance images of experimental brain abscess. *J Comput Assist Tomogr* 8:204–207, 1984.

GUILLEUX M-H, STEINER RE, YOUNG IR: MR imaging in progressive multifocal leukoencephalopathy. *AJNR* 7:1033–1035, 1986.

GUPTA RK, JENA A, SHARMA A, GUHA DK, KHUSHU S, GUPTA AK: MR imaging of intracranial tuberculomas. *J Comput Assist Tomogr* 12:280–285, 1988.

GUPTA R, SINGH AK, BISHNU P, MALHOTRA V: Intracranial aspergillus granuloma simulating meningioma on MR imaging. *J Comput Assist Tomogr* 14:467–469, 1990.

HAIMES AB, ZIMMERMAN RD, MORGELLO S, et al: MR imaging of brain abscesses. *AJNR* 10:279–291, 1989.

HARRIMAN DGE: *Greenfield's Neuropatholoy.* Chicago, Year Book, 1984, pp 236–259.

HARWOOD-NASH DC, et al: Massive calcification of the brain in a newborn infant. *AJR* 108:528–532, 1970.

HAYES WS, SHERMAN GL, STERN BJ, et al: MR and CT evaluation of intracranial sarcoidosis. *AJR* 149:1043–1049, 1987.

HERMAN PE, CLEVELAND RH, KUSHNER DC, TAVERAS JM: CT of neonatal herpes encephalitis. *AJNR* 6:773–775, 1985.

HIRSH LF, LEE SH, SILBERSTEIN SD: Intracranial tuberculomas and the CAT scan. *Acta Neurochir (Wien)* 45:155–161, 1978.

HOLLAND BA, KURCHARCZYK W, BRANT-ZAWADZKI M, et al: MR imaging of calcified intracranial lesions. *Radiology* 157:353–356, 1985.

HOLLAND BA, PERRETT LV, MILLS CM: Meningovascular syphilis: CT and MR findings. *Radiology* 158:439–442, 1986.

HURST DL, MEHTA S: Acute cerebellar swelling in varicella encephalitis. *Pediatr Neurol* 4:122–123, 1988.

JANKOWSKI R, ZIMMERMAN RD, LEEDS NE: Cysticercosis presenting as a mass lesion at the foramen of Monro. *J Comput Assist Tomogr* 3(5):694–696, 1979.

JOUBERT MD, STEPHANOV S: CT and surgical treatment in intracranial suppuration. *J Neurosurg* 47:73–78, 1977.

KAMIN M, BIDDLE D: Conservative management of focal intracerebral infection. *Neurology* 31:103–106, 1981.

KAUFMANN DM, MILLER MH, STEIGBIGEL NH: Subdural empyema: Analysis of 17 recent cases and review of the literature. *Medicine (Baltimore)* 54(6):485–498, 1975.

KAUFMANN DM, LEEDS NE: CT in the diagnosis of intracranial abscesses. *Neurology* 27:1069–1073, 1977.

KENDALL BE, TATELER GLV: Radiological findings in neurosarcoidosis. *Br J Radiol* 51:81–92, 1978.

KERR FWL, KING RB, MEAGHER JN: Brain abscess: A study of 47 consecutive cases. *JAMA* 168:868–872, 1958.

KETONEN L, KOSKINIEMI ML: CT appearance of herpes simplex encephalitis. *Clin Radiol* 31:161–165, 1980.

KETONEN L, OKSANEN V, KUULIALA I, et al: Hypodense white matter lesions in computed tomography of neurosarcoidosis. *J Comput Assist Tomogr* 10(2):181–183, 1986.

KIEBURTZ KD, KETONEN L, ZETTELMAIER AE, KIDO D, CAINE ED, SIMON JH: Magnetic resonance imaging findings in HIV cognitive impairment. *Arch Neurol* 47:643–645, 1990.

KUMPE DA, RAO KCVE, GARCIA JH, HECK AF: Intracranial neurosarcoidosis. *J Comput Assist Tomogr* 3(3):324–330, 1979.

KUPFER MC, ZEE CS, COLLETTI PM, BOSWELL WD, RHODES R: MRI evaluation of AIDS-related encephalopathy: Toxoplasmosis vs. lymphoma. *Magn Reson Imaging* 8:51–57, 1990.

LABEAU J et al: Surgical treatment of brain abscess and subdural empyema. *J Neurosurg* 38:198–199, 1973.

LEE SH, KUMAR ARV, LORBER B: Tuberculosis of the CNS presenting as mass lesions: Diagnostic dilema. *Pa Med* 82:36–38, 1979.

LEO JS et al: CT in herpes simplex encephalitis. *Surg Neurol* 10:313–317, 1978.

LESTER JW JR, CARTER MP, REYNOLDS TL: Herpes encephalitis: MR monitoring of response to acyclovir therapy. *J Comput Assist Tomogr* 12:941–943, 1988.

LEVIN HS, WILLIAMS DH, BORUCKE MJ, et al: MR imaging and neuropsychological findings in human immunodeficiency virus infection. *J Acquir Immune Defic Syndr* 3:757–762, 1990.

LEVY RM, ROSENBLOOM S, PERRETT LV: Neuroradiological findings in AIDS: A review of 200 cases. *AJNR* 7:833–839, 1986.

LEVY RM, MILLS CM, POSIN JP, MOORE SG, ROSENBLUM ML, BREDESEN DE: The efficacy and clinical impact of brain imaging in neurologically symptomatic AIDS patients: A prospective CT/MRI study. *J Acquir Immune Defic Syndr* 3:461–471, 1990.

LIPTON SA, HICKEY WF, MORRIS JH, LOSCALZO J: Candidal infection in the CNS. *Am J Med* 76:101–108, 1984.

LONG JA et al: Cerebral mass lesion in torculosis demonstrated by CT. *J Comput Assist Tomogr* 4(6):766–769, 1980.

LORBER J: Intracranial calcification following tuberculous meningitis in children. *Acta Radiol* 50:204–210, 1958.

LOTT T et al: Evaluation of brain and epidural abscess by CT. *Radiology* 122:371–374, 1977.

LOTZ J, HEWLETT R, ALHEIT B, BOWEN R: Neurocysticercosis: Correlative pathomorphology and MR imaging. *Neuroradiology* 30:35–41, 1988.

MALLOY PM, NEYMAN RM: The lack of specificity of neonatal paraventricular calcification. *Radiology* 80:98–102, 1963.

MARK AS, ATLAS SW: Progressive multifocal leukoencephalopathy in patients with AIDS: Appearance on MR images. *Radiology* 173:517–522, 1989.

MARTIN E, BOESCH C, ZUERRER M, KIKNIS R, MOLINARI L, KAELIN P, BOLTSHAUSER E, DUC G: MR imaging of brain maturation in normal and developmentally handicapped children. *J Comput Assist Tomogr* 14:685–692, 1990.

MARTINEZ HR, RANGEL-GUERRA R, ELIZONDO G, et al: MR imaging in neurocysticercosis: A study of 56 cases. *AJNR* 10:1011–1017, 1989.

MATHEWS VEP, KUHARIK MA, EDWARDS ME, et al: Gd-DTPA-enhanced MR imaging of experimental bacterial meningitis: Evaluation and comparison with CT. *AJNR* 9:1045–1050, 1988.

MATHEWS VP, SMITH PR, BOGNAMO JR, et al: Gd-DTPA-enhanced MR of meningiomas: Initial clinical experience. *AJNR* 10:1290–1294, 1989.

MAYERS MM, KAUFMANN DF, MILLER MM: Recent cases of intracranial tuberculomas. *Neurology* 28:256–260, 1978.

MCARTHUR JC, KUMAR AJ, JOHNSON DW, SELNES OA, BECKER JT, HERMAN C, COHEN BA, SAAH A: Incidental white matter hyperintensities on MRI in HIV-1 infection: Multicenter AIDS Cohort Study. *J Acquir Immune Defic Syndr* 3:252–259, 1990.

MCGAHAN JP: Classic and temporary imaging of coccidioidomycosis. *AJR* 136:393–404, 1981.

MIKHAEL MA, CIRIC IS, WOLFF AP: Differentiation of cerebellopontine angle neuromas and meningiomas with MR imaging. *J Comput Assist Tomogr* 9(5):852–856, 1985.

MIRFAKHAREE M, CROFFORD M, GUINTO FC, et al: Virchow-Robin space: A path of spread in neurosarcoidosis. *Radiology* 158:715–720, 1986.

MOORE GA, THOMAS LA: Infections including abscesses of the brain, spinal cord, intraspinal and intracranial lesions. *Surg Annu* 6:413–417, 1974.

MOREHOUSE H, DANZINGER A: CT findings in intracranial neurosarcoid. *Comput Tomogr* 4:267–270, 1981.

MORGAN H, HOOD MW: Cerebellar abscesses: A review of 7 cases. *Surg Neurol* 3:93–96, 1975.

NAVIA BA, JORDAN BA, PRICE RW: The AIDS dementia complex: I. Clinical features. *Ann Neurol* 19:517–524, 1986.

NELSON JD, WATTS CC: Calcified subdural effusion following bacterial meningitis. *Am J Dis Child* 117:730–733, 1969.

NEW PFJ, DAVID KR, BALLANTINE HT: Computed tomography in cerebral abscess. *Radiology* 121:641–646, 1976.

NEW P, DAVID KR: The role of CT scanning in the diagnosis of infections of the central nervous system, in Remington J, Swartz M (eds): *Current Clinical Topics in Infectious Diseases.* New York, McGraw-Hill, 1980, pp 1–33.

NIELSEN H, GLYDENSTADT C: CT in the diagnosis of cerebral abscess. *Neuroradiology* 12:207–217, 1977.

OLSEN WL, LONGO FM, MILLS CM, NORMAN D: White matter disease in AIDS: Findings at MR imaging. *Radiology* 169:445–448, 1988*a*.

OLSEN WL, JEFFREY RB, TOLENTINO CS: Closed system for arterial puncture in patients at risk for AIDS. *Radiology* 166:551–552, 1988*b*.

OZGEN T, et al: The use of CT in the diagnosis of cerebral hydatid cysts. *J Neurosurg* 50:339–342, 1979.

PARKER JC, DYER ML: Neurologic infections due to bacteria, fungi and parasites, in David RL, Robertson DM (eds): *Textbook on Neuropathology.* Baltimore, Williams & Wilkins, 1985, pp 632–703.

PAXTON R, AMBROSE J: The EMI scanner: A brief review of the first 600 patients. *Br J Radiol* 47:530–565, 1974.

PEATFIELD RC, SHADOWDON HH: Five cases of intracranial tuberculoma followed by serial CT. *J Neurol Neurosurg Psychiatry* 42:373–379, 1979.

POPOVICH MJ, ARTHUR RH, HELMER E: CT of intracranial cryptococcosis. *AJNR* 11:139–142, 1990.

POST MJD, CHAN JC, HENSLEY G, et al: Toxoplasma encephalitis in Haitian adults with AIDS. A clinical-pathologic-CT correlation. *AJNR* 4:155–162, 1983.

POST MJD, KURSUNOGLU SJ, HENSLEY GT, et al: Cranial CT in acquired immunodeficiency syndromes: Spectrum of diseases and optimal contrast enhancement technique. *AJNR* 6:743–754, 1985.

POST MJD, HENSLEY GT, MOSKOWITZ LB, FISCHL M: Cytomegalic inclusion virus encephalitis in patients with AIDS: CT, clinical, and pathological correlation. *AJNR* 7:275–280, 1986*a*.

POST MJD, SHELDON JJ, HENSLEY GT, et al: CNS disease in AIDS: Prospective correlation using CT, MRI and pathologic studies. *Radiology* 158:141–148, 1986*b*.

POST MJD, BERGER JR, HENSLEY GT: The radiology of the CNS in AIDS, in Taveras JM, Ferrucci JT (eds): *Radiology: Diagnosis, Imaging, Intervention.* Philadelphia, Lippincott, 1986*c*, pp 1–26.

POST MJD, TATE LG, QUENCER RM, et al: CT, MR, and pathology in HIV encephalitis and meningitis. *AJNR* 9:469–476, 1988.

PRICE HI, DANZIGER A: CT in cranial tuberculosis. *AJR* 130:769–771, 1978.

RAMSEY RG, GEREMIA GK: CNS complications of AIDS: CT and MR findings. *AJR* 151:449–454, 1988.

RHEE RS, KUMASAKI DY, SARWAR M, et al: MR imaging of intraventricular cysticercosis. *J Comput Assist Tomogr* 11:598–601, 1987.

RICCIO TJ, HESSELINK JR: Gd-DTPA-Enhanced MR of multiple cryptococcal brain abscesses. *AJNR* 10:565–566, 1989.

ROBERT F: Sarcoidosis of the central nervous system. *Brain* 71:451–474, 1948.

ROBERTHERAM EB, KESSLER LA: Use of computerized tomography in nonsurgical management of brain abscess. *Arch Neurol* 36:25–26, 1979.

RODRIGUEZ-CARBAJAL J, SALGADO P, GUTIERREZ-ALVARADO R, ESCOBAR-IZQUIERDO A, ARUFFO C, PALACIOS E: The acute encephalitic phase of neurocysticercosis: Computed tomographic manifestations. *AJNR* 4:51–55, 1983.

RODRIGUEZ-CARBAJAL J, PALACIOS E, NADICH TA: Infections and parasitic disorders—supratentorial, in Taveras JM, Ferrucci JT (eds): *Radiology: Diagnosis Imaging Intervention,* vol 3. Philadelphia, Lippincott 1986, pp 1–22.

ROSENBAUM ML et al: Decreased mortality from brain abscesses since advent of CT. *J Neurosurg* 49:659–668, 1978.

RUDWAN MA, KHAFFAJI S: CT of cerebral hydatid disease. *Neuroradiology* 30:496–499, 1988.

SADHU VK, HANDEL SF, PINTO RS, GLASS TF: Neuroradiologic diagnosis of subdural empyema and CT limitation. *AJNR* 1:39–44, 1980.

SAGE R, DUBOIE J, OAKS S, et al: Rapid development of cerebral atrophy due to perinatal herpes simplex encephalitis. *J Comput Assist Tomogr* 5:763–766, 1981.

SALTZMAN GD: Roentgenologic changes in cerebral sarcoidosis. *Acta Radiol [Diagn] (Stockh)* 50:235–241, 1958.

SANTIN G, VARGAS J: Roentgen study of cysticercosis of CNS. *Radiology* 86:520–528, 1966.

SCHROTH G, KRETZSCHMAR K, GAWEHN J, et al: Advantage of magnetic resonance imaging in the diagnosis of cerebral infections. *Neuroradiology* 29:120–126, 1987.

SELLWYN PA, HARTED D, LEWIS UA, et al: A prospective study of the risk of tuberculosis among intravenous drug users with human immunodeficiency virus infection. *N Engl J Med* 320:545–550, 1989.

SHARIF HA, IBRAHIM A: Intracranial epidural abscess. *Br J Radiol* 55:81–84, 1982.

SILVERSTEIN A, FEUER MM, SILTZBACH LE: Neurologic sarcoidosis: Study of 18 cases. *Arch Neurol* 12:1–11, 1965.

SMITH AS, MEISLER DM, WEINSTEIN MA, et al: High signal periventricular lesions in patients with sarcoidosis: Neurosarcoidosis or multiple sclerosis. *AJNR* 153:147–152, 1989.

SOUTH MA et al: Congenital malformation of the CNS associated with genital type (type 2) herpes virus. *J Pediatr* 75:13–18, 1969.

STEPHANOV S et al: Combined convexity and parafalx subdural empyema. *Surg Neurol* 11:147–151, 1979.

STEVENS EA et al: CT brain scanning in intraparenchymal pyogenic abscesses. *AJR* 130:111–114, 1978.

SUH DC, CHANG KH, HAN MH, LEE SR, HAN MC, KIM CW: Unusual MR manifestations of neurocysticercosis. *Neuroradiology* 31:396–402, 1989.

SUSS RA, MARAVILLA KR, THOMPSON J: MR imaging of intracranial cysticercosis: Comparison with CT and anatomicopathologic features. *AJNR* 7:235–242, 1986.

SZE G, NEWTON TH, BRANT-ZAWADZKI M. Neuroradiology of acquired immunodeficiency syndrome. *Semin Roentgenol* 22:42–53, 1987.

SZE G: Infections and inflammatory diseases, in Stark DD, Bradley WG Jr (eds): *Magnetic Resonance Imaging.* St. Louis, Mosby, 1988*a,* pp 317–355.

SZE G, ZIMMERMAN RD: MRI of infections and inflammatory diseases. *Radiol Clin North Am* 26:839–859, 1988*b*.

SZE G, SOLETSKY S, BRONEN R, KROL G: MR imaging of cranial meninges with emphasis on contrast enhancement and meningeal carcinomatosis. *AJNR* 10:965–975, 1989.

TAN CT, KUAN BB: Cryptococcus meningitis, clinical-CT scan considerations. *Neuroradiology* 29:43–46, 1987.

TEITELBAUM GP, OTTO RJ, LIN M, et al: MR imaging of neurocysticercosis. *AJNR* 10:709–718, 1989.

TIEN RD, CHU PK, HESSELINK JR, DUBERG A, WILEY C: Intracranial cryptococcosis in immunocompromised patients: CT and MR findings in 29 cases. *AJNR* 12:283–289, 1991.

VEGASARKAR US, PISPATY RP, PAREKLY B, et al: Intracranial tuberculoma and the CT scan. *J Neurosurg* 64:568–574, 1986.

VISUDHIPHAN P et al: Cerebral aspergillosis: Report of 3 cases. *J Neurosurg* 38:472–476, 1973.

WAGGENER JD: The pathophysiology of bacterial meningitis and cerebral abscesses: An anatomical interpretation. *Adv Neurol* 6:1974.

WALLENFANG TH, REULEN JG, SCHURMANN K: Therapy of brain abscess. *Adv Neurosurg* 9:41–47, 1981.

WEHN SM, HEINZ ER, BURGER PC, OBYKO OB: Dilated Virchow-Robin spaces in cryptococcal meningitis associated with AIDS: CT and MR findings. *J Comput Assist Tomogr* 13:756–762, 1989.

WEINGARTEN K, ZIMMERMAN RD, BECKER RD, HEIER LA, HAIMES AB, DECK MDF: Subdural and epidural empyemas: MR imaging. *AJNR* 10:81–87, 1989.

WEINMAN D, SAMARASHINGHE HHG: Subdural empyema. *Aust N Z J Surg* 41:324–328, 1972.

WEISBERG L: Subdural empyema—clinical and computed tomograph relations. *Arch Neurol* 43:497–500, 1986.

WELCHMAN JM: CT of intracranial tuberculomata. *Clin Radiol* 30:567–573, 1979.

WHELAN MA, HILAL SK: Computed tomography as a guide in the diagnosis and followup of brain abscesses. *Radiology* 135:663–671, 1980.

WHELAN MA, KRICHEFF II, HANDLER M, et al: Acquired immunodeficiency syndrome: Cerebral CT manifestations. *Radiology* 149:477–484, 1983.

WHITLEY RJ, NAHMIAS AJ, VISTINE AM, FLEMING CL, CLIFFORD CA: The natural history of herpes simplex virus infection of mother and newborn. *Pediatrics* 66:489–494, 1980.

ZEE CS, SEGALL HD, MILLER C, et al: Unusual features of intracranial cysticercosis. *Radiology* 137:397–407, 1980.

ZEE CS, SEGALL HD, BOSWELL W, et al: MR imaging of neurocysticercosis. *J Comput Assist Tomogr* 12:927–934, 1988.

ZEGERS DE, BEYL D, NOTERMAN J, MARTELART A, FLAMENT-DURAND J, BALERIAUX D: Multiple cerebral hematoma and viral encephalitis. *Neuroradiology* 20:47–48, 1980.

ZIMMERMAN RA, PATEL S, BILANIUK LT: Demonstration of purulent bacterial intracranial infections by computed tomography. *AJR* 127:155–165, 1976.

ZIMMERMAN RA, BILANIUK LT, GALLO E: CT of the trapped fourth ventricle. *AJR* 130:503–506, 1978.

ZIMMERMAN RD, et al: CT in the early diagnosis of herpes simplex encephalitis. *AJR* 134:61–66, 1980.

ZIMMERMAN RD, LEEDS NE, DANZIGER A: Subdural empyema: CT findings. *Radiology* 150:417–422, 1984.

14 CEREBRAL VASCULAR ANOMALIES

Karel G. TerBrugge
Krishna C.V.G. Rao

Cerebral vascular anomalies, which include aneurysms and vascular malformations, commonly present with a history of intracranial hemorrhage. With aneurysms, there often are a variety of clinical findings, such as transient ischemic attacks and signs of cranial nerve involvement. By contrast, with vascular malformations, seizures may be the presenting clinical symptom. CT is the first modality of examination that provides an approach to selecting patients who need further investigation. MRI can be performed to further characterize the lesion, but angiography is often necessary for the definitive examination before treatment planning. CT, MRI, and angiography have been shown to be complementary, with each modality playing a role in the diagnosis and treatment planning of patients with cerebral vascular anomalies.

INTRACRANIAL ANEURYSMS AND SUBARACHNOID HEMORRHAGE

An *aneurysm* is an abnormal focal enlargement of an artery. Aneurysms can be classified according to their appearance as saccular or fusiform. The etiologic classification of aneurysms includes congenital, arteriosclerotic, mycotic, and dissecting. The traditional concept is that most aneurysms are congenital and are caused by a defect in the tunica media (Crawford 1959; Crompton 1966). With advancing age, arteriosclerotic changes are thought to cause further weakening of an already defective tunica media, and this may result in enlargement or rupture of the aneurysm (Crompton 1966; Nystrom 1963; DuBoulay 1965; Sarwar 1976*a*). Recently, this concept has been questioned (Stehbens 1989). Aneurysms are most likely acquired degenerative lesions which result from hemodynamic stress. Hypertension and connective tissue disorders may be aggravating factors. No congenital, developmental, or inherited weakness of the vessel wall may be identified (Stehbens 1989).

The incidence of intracranial aneurysms in the general population is approximately 3 percent (Chason 1958; Housepian 1958). The aneurysm involves the carotid system in 96 percent of cases (Locksley 1966). The anterior communicating artery is the single most common site (30 percent), followed by the posterior communicating artery (25 percent) and the middle cerebral artery (20 percent) (Locksley 1966). Approximately 20 percent of patients with an intracranial aneurysm have more than one aneurysm demonstrated at angiography (McKissock 1964; Locksley 1966; Kendall 1976*b*). The great majority of aneurysms are small in size (diameter less than 1 cm) and present with a subarachnoid hemorrhage (DuBoulay 1965; Locksley 1966). Large (diameter between 1 and 2.5 cm) and giant (diameter greater than 2.5 cm) aneurysms usually do not present with subarachnoid hemorrhage but rather with clinical symptoms related to their localized mass effect and pressure on the adjacent brain and cranial nerves (Bull 1969; Morley 1969; Sarwar 1976*a,b;* Scotti 1977; Nadjmi 1978; Deeb 1979; Pinto 1979; Thron 1979).

Computed Tomography

The CT appearance of intracranial aneurysms depends on whether the entire lumen is patent or whether there is partial or complete thrombosis. If the entire lumen of the aneurysm is patent, the lesion can be seen on CT as a rounded or elongated area of slightly increased density (Fig. 14-1) (Scotti 1977; Handa 1978; Pinto 1979). After intravenous injection of contrast material, the lumen shows homogeneous enhancement and the margin of the lesion is well defined (Scotti 1977; Handa 1978; Pinto 1979; Yock 1980). This appearance can be explained on the basis of a hyperdense blood pool which is subsequently opacified by circulating iodine contrast material (Pressman 1975*b;* Pinto 1979; Yock 1980).

Partially thrombosed aneurysms have a different appearance, which is related to the presence of the thrombus and the degree of patency of the lumen within the aneurysm. On NCCT they show as a central eccentric hyperdense region within an isodense or calcific area. The

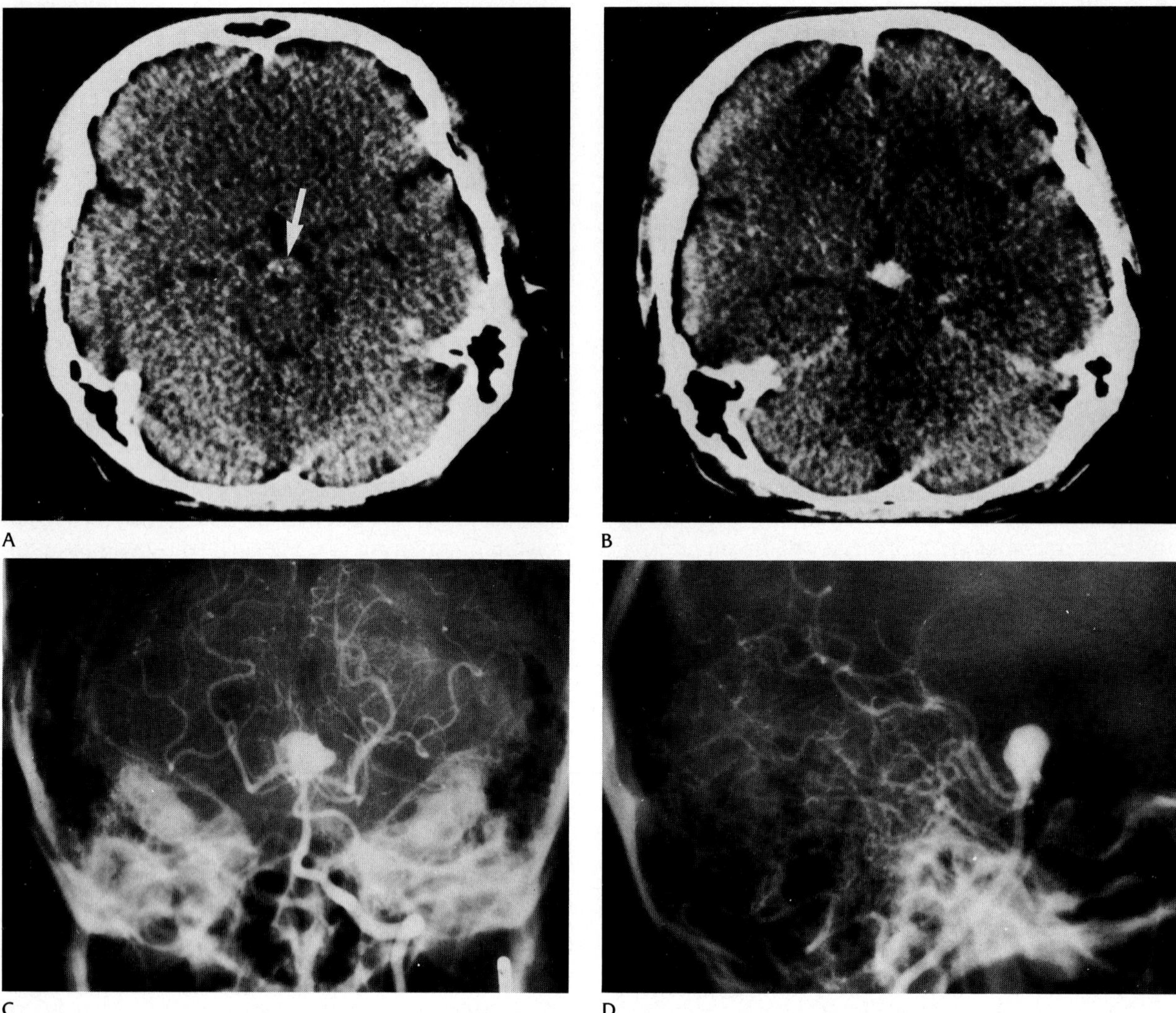

Figure 14-1 Basilar artery aneurysm. **A.** NCCT shows a rounded area of slightly increased density at the level of the interpeduncular cistern (arrow). **B.** Enhancement occurs on CECT. **C, D.** Angiograms disclose a large aneurysm arising from the tip of the basilar artery.

lesions are rounded or lobulated in appearance, and the margins are well defined. The central and peripheral zones are enhanced by contrast material, while the isodense zone is not (Fig. 14-2) (Lukin 1975; Sarwar 1976*a;* Scotti 1977; Perrett 1977; Handa 1978; Nadjmi 1978; Babu 1979; Pinto 1979; Thron 1979; Schubiger 1980). The CT appearance of a partially thrombosed aneurysm is due to a central eccentric patent lumen of the aneurysm which enhances after contrast infusion. The lumen is surrounded by thrombotic material which is isodense on CT. The peripheral wall of the aneurysm consists of fibrous tissue which is hyperdense on CT and is often calcified. This rim of tissue contains increased vascularity; this is thought to be a meningeal response to the enlarging aneurysm, and enhancement of this tissue may be a phenomenon similar to dural enhancement in other locations (Pinto 1979).

A *completely thrombosed aneurysm* exhibits a central area of isodensity or slightly decreased density and a peripheral rim of increased and often calcific density (Fig. 14-3). The peripheral rim of increased density may show enhancement after contrast infusion (Nadjmi 1978; Pinto 1979). The central area of isodensity represents a thrombus within the aneurysm, while the peripheral ring enhancement is thought to be due to increased microvascularity within the tissue along the wall of the aneurysm, similar to dural enhancement (Pinto 1979). Recent formation of a blood clot in the acute stage of a thrombosing aneurysm will show as an area of increased density on NCCT (Fig. 14-3). A meningioma or malignant glioma

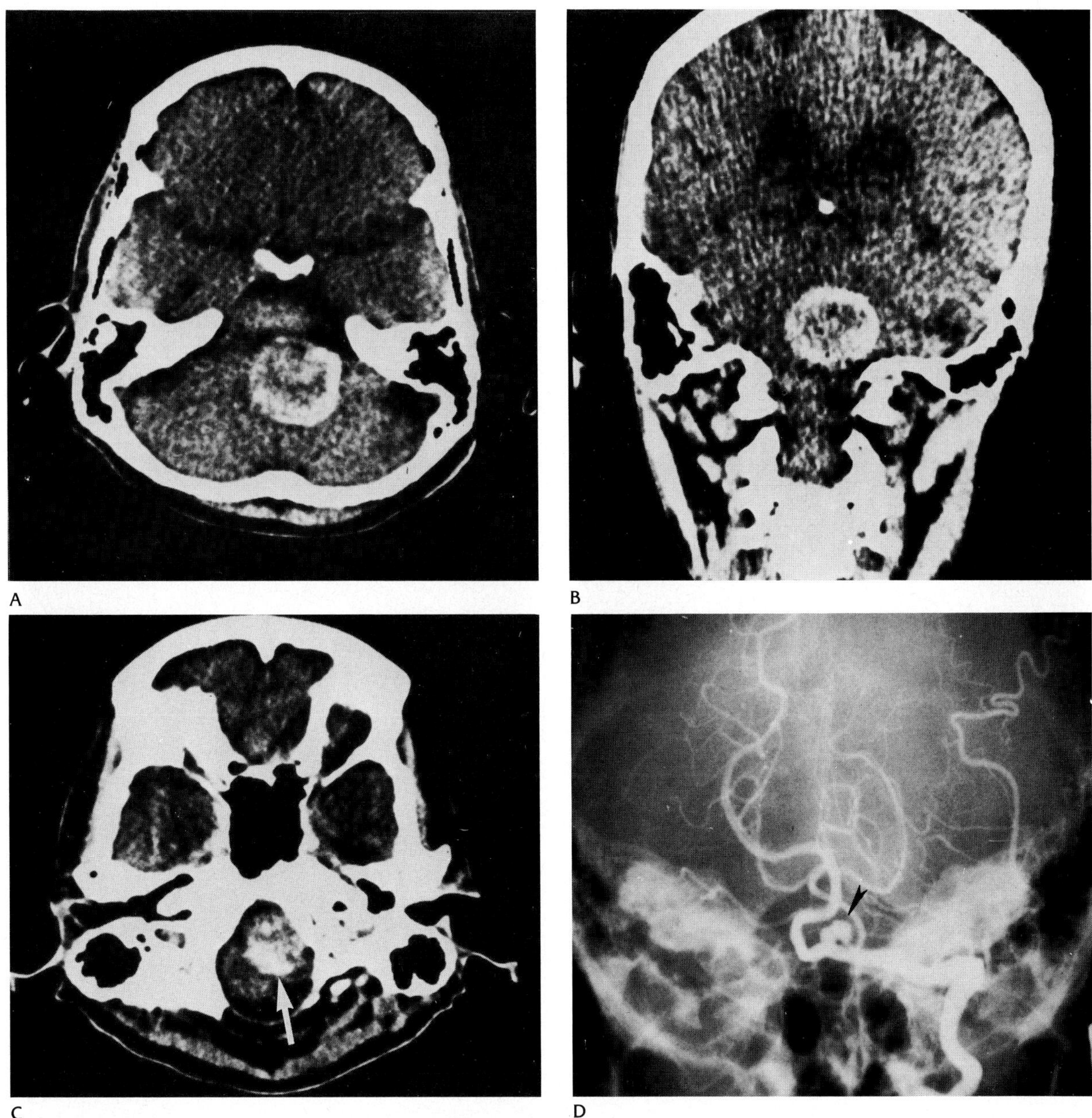

Figure 14-2 Posterior inferior cerebellar artery (PICA) aneurysm. **A.** NCCT shows a rounded lesion adjacent to the left cerebellopontine angle cistern with a peripheral rim of calcification. **B.** Coronal CT shows a lesion to the left of the midline, superior to the foramen magnum. A central hypodense area is present with a rim of calcification. **C.** CECT at the level of the foramen magnum shows that the lesion is extraaxial in location, and there is eccentric enhacenemnt in part of the lesion (arrow). **D.** Angiogram shows the PICA aneurysm on the left side, consisting of a large thrombosed part and a small patent lumen.

may mimic a giant aneurysm (larger than 1 cm), but the lack of edema in an aneurysm should rule out these tumors (Pinto 1979).

Ectasia of the intracranial arteries, in particular the basilar artery, can be diagnosed on CT (Peterson 1977; Scotti 1978; Deeb 1979; Smoker 1986). An ectatic basilar artery may be seen crossing the prepontine cistern toward a cerebellopontine angle cistern as an elongated bandlike structure of increased density on NCCT. Homogeneous enhancement occurs after contrast infusion (Fig. 14-4). Tortuous vertebrobasilar arteries may be associated with cranial nerve syndromes and may result in

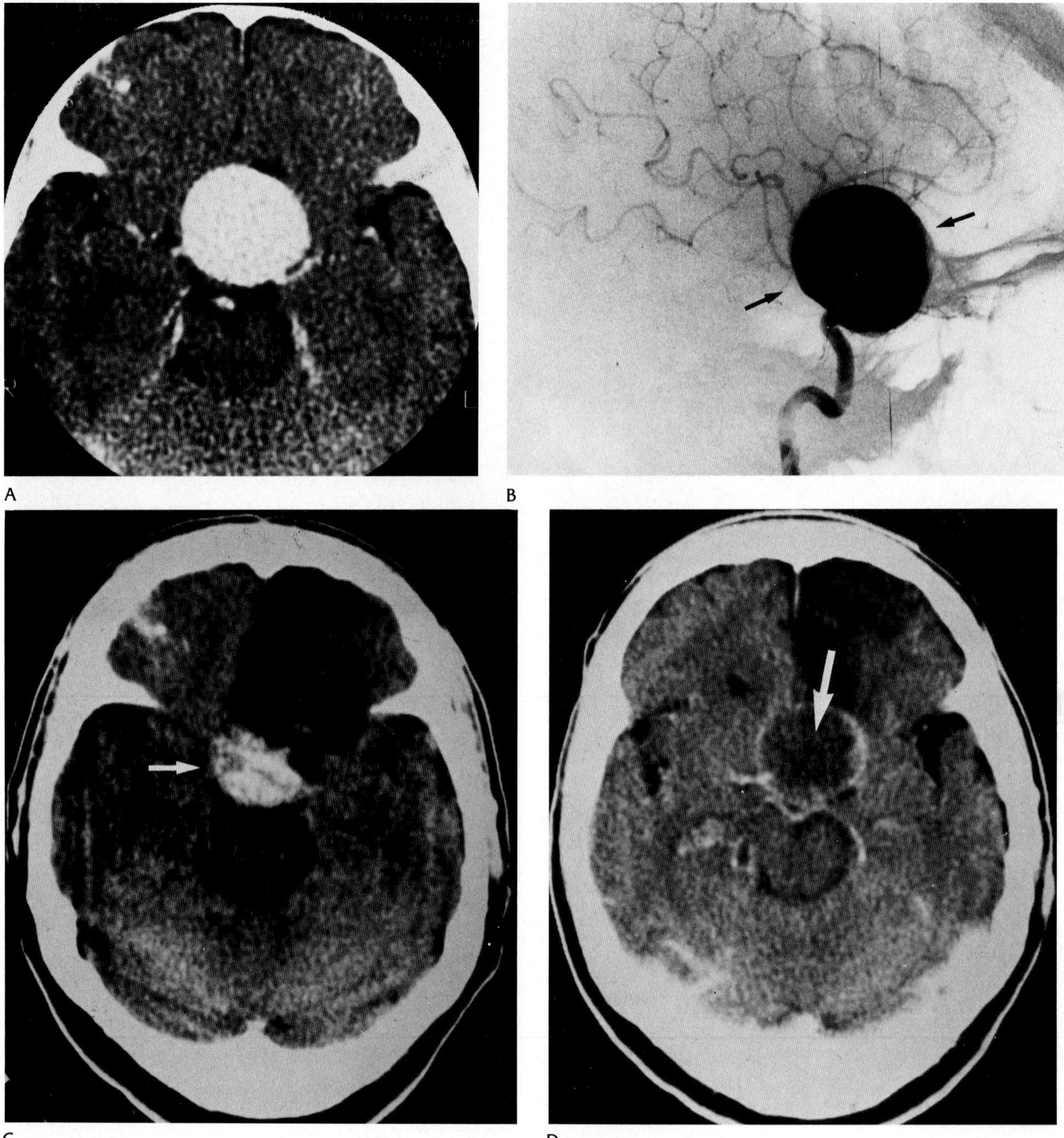

Figure 14-3 Giant patent internal carotid artery aneurysm with acute thrombosis after balloon detachment. **A.** Transaxial CECT shows a large rounded suprasellar lesion with homogeneous enhancement. **B.** Carotid angiogram shows a giant-size aneurysm of the cavernous segment of the internal carotid artery (arrows). **C.** NCCT 2 days after balloon detachment in the internal carotid artery (ICA) shows acute clot formation with the aneurysm as an area of increased density (arrow). **D.** CECT 2 months after sacrifice of the ICA shows complete thrombosis of the aneurysm (arrow) and enhancement along its wall.

hydrocephalus from transmitted pulsation of an ectatic fusiform dilatated vertebral basilar artery. CT has proved excellent in screening such cases, sometimes obviating angiography (Deeb 1979); if angiography is necessary, the digital subtraction technique is preferred to conventional methods to minimize possible complications (Smoker 1986) (Fig. 14-4).

The *differential diagnosis* of lesions that may mimic a small aneurysm consists mainly of variations from the normal vascular anatomy, such as looping of vessels and

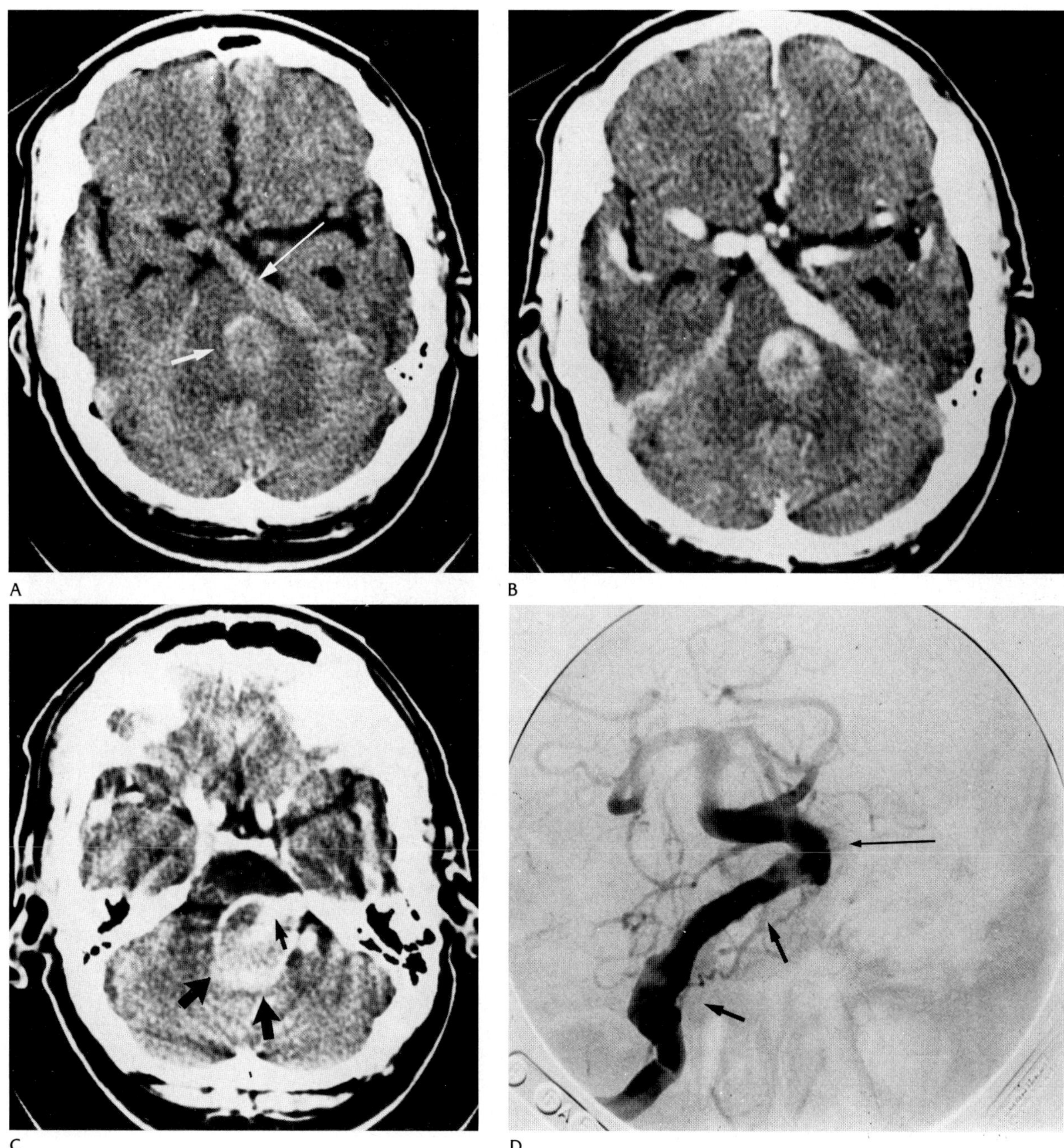

Figure 14-4 Fusiform aneurysmal dilatation of the basilar artery. **A.** NCCT shows an elongated band of increased density at the level of the ambient and suprasellar cisterns (large arrow) as well as a rounded density representing the dome of the aneurysm (small arrow). **B.** CECT shows enhancement of the basilar artery as well as the distal internal carotid and proximal middle cerebral arteries. **C.** CECT at the level of the posterior fossa shows a partially thrombosed aneurysm (arrows) with an eccentric patent lumen (small arrow). **D.** Angiogram shows an elongated and ectatic basilar artery (large arrows) and the irregular outline of the opacified lumen (small arrow) at the site of the aneurysm shown on CT.

prominent veins. Depending on the clinical situation, angiography is often necessary to sort out these diagnostic problems. The CT appearance of large and giant aneurysms may be mimicked by a number of disease processes and depends to a certain degree on the location of the lesion. In the posterior fossa, large aneurysms may simulate intraaxial and extraaxial lesions (Handa 1978; Thron 1979). The extraaxial lesions which most often mimic an aneurysm are acoustic neuromas and meningiomas. Epidermoid tumors and chordomas may occa-

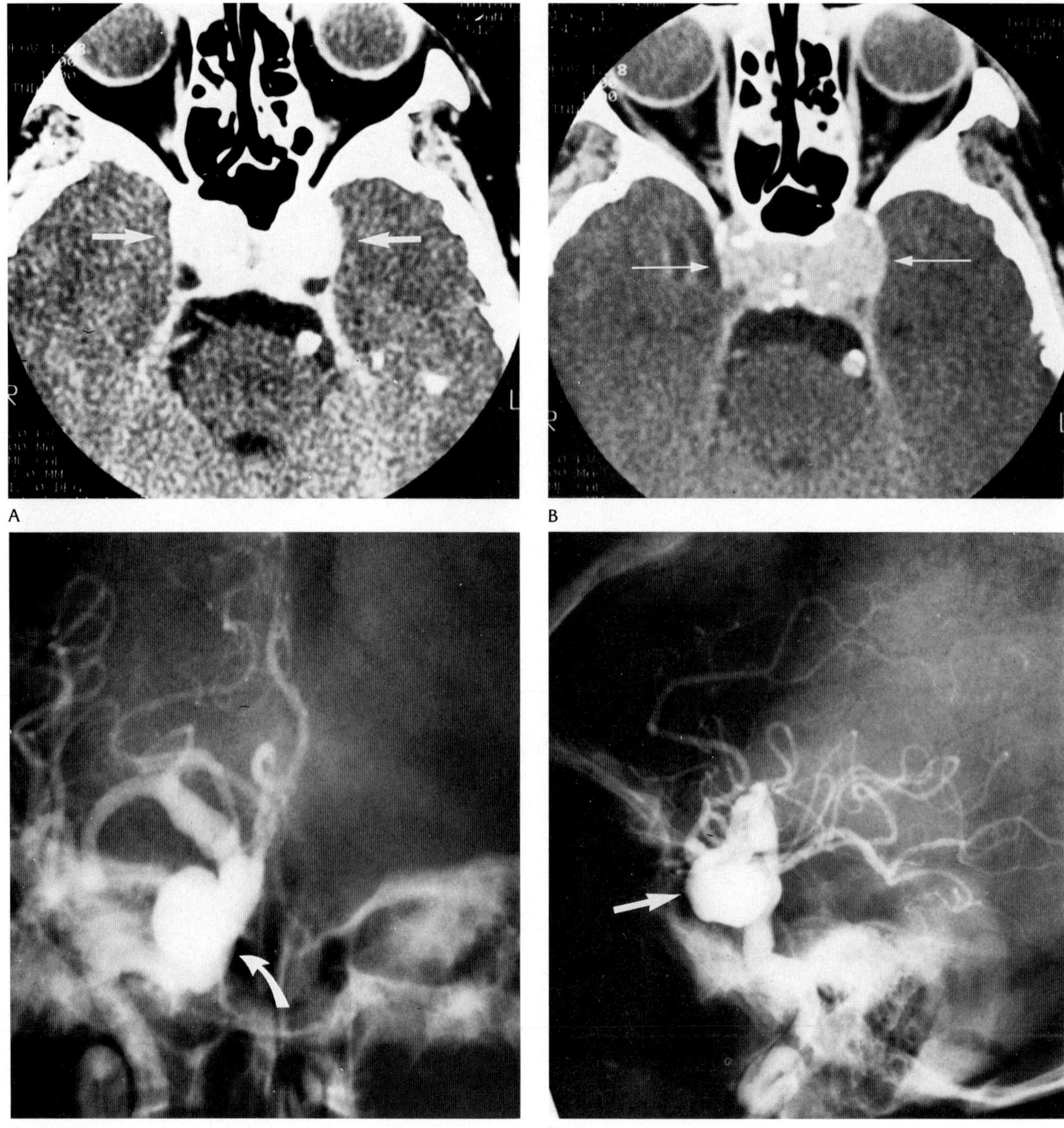

Figure 14-5 Bilateral internal carotid artery aneurysms. **A.** CECT at the level of the floor of the sella shows homogeneous enhancement of two rounded lesions (arrows) just anterior to the location of the trigeminal ganglia. **B.** CECT at the level of the pituitary fossa shows obliteration of the parasellar cisterns by enhancing mass lesions (arrows) which may simulate pituitary adenoma or meningioma. **C, D.** Angiograms reveal evidence of bilateral aneurysms at the level of the cavernous segment of the internal carotid artery (arrow).

sionally exhibit a CT pattern similar to that of large aneurysms. Intraaxial tumors which sometimes have a CT appearance mimicking large aneurysms include gliomas, medulloblastomas, ependymomas, choroid plexus papillomas, and metastatic disease (Byrd 1978). Parasellar and suprasellar lesions which may have a CT appearance similar to that of large aneurysms include pituitary adenomas, meningiomas, craniopharyngiomas, third ventricular tumors, and metastatic disease (Fig. 14-5) (Perrett 1977; Handa 1978; Babu 1979). Important features of

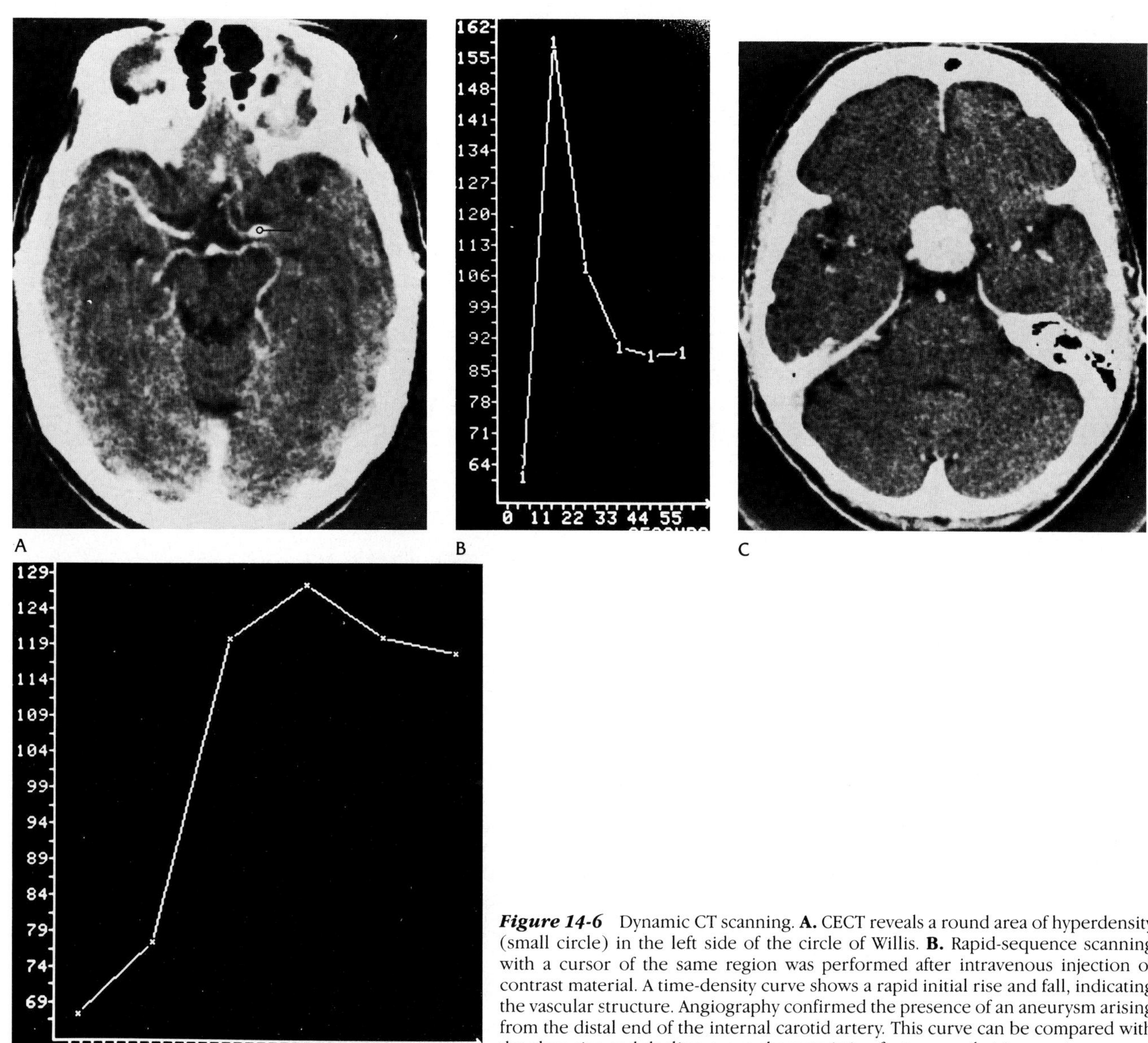

Figure 14-6 Dynamic CT scanning. **A.** CECT reveals a round area of hyperdensity (small circle) in the left side of the circle of Willis. **B.** Rapid-sequence scanning with a cursor of the same region was performed after intravenous injection of contrast material. A time-density curve shows a rapid initial rise and fall, indicating the vascular structure. Angiography confirmed the presence of an aneurysm arising from the distal end of the internal carotid artery. This curve can be compared with the slow rise-and-decline curve characteristic of a tumour that is seen in a case of tuberculumsellae meningioma (**C, D**).

large aneurysms on CT include the absence of surrounding edema and the presence of curvilinear peripheral calcifications. These characteristics are extremely uncommon in neoplastic disease, with the exception of craniopharyngiomas. In such cases, rapid-sequence (dynamic) CT scanning after intravenous bolus injection may help distinguish an aneurysm from a tumor (Fig. 14-6).

The advent of CT has led to the postponement of invasive neuroradiological methods such as angiography. Past experience has indicated that many large and giant aneurysms were diagnosed on CT as a neoplastic disease, and the possibility of a vascular abnormality was often not considered (Lukin 1975; Perrett 1977; Handa 1978; Nadjmi 1978; Babu 1979; Pinto 1979; Thron 1979). Therefore, awareness of the CT appearance of large aneurysms is important, and angiography is indicated if the possibility of such an aneurysm cannot be excluded on CT. *Angiography* generally establishes the diagnosis but demonstrates only the part of the aneurysm with circulating blood. The mass effect related to the thrombus in a partially thrombotic aneurysm is often much better appreciated on CT. Angiography can be frankly misleading in a totally thrombosed aneurysm, which may show only as a nonvascular mass lesion (Fig. 14-7) (Nadjmi 1978; Pinto 1979; Thron 1979). Aneurysms may increase in size, and this further growth can be correctly diagnosed by means

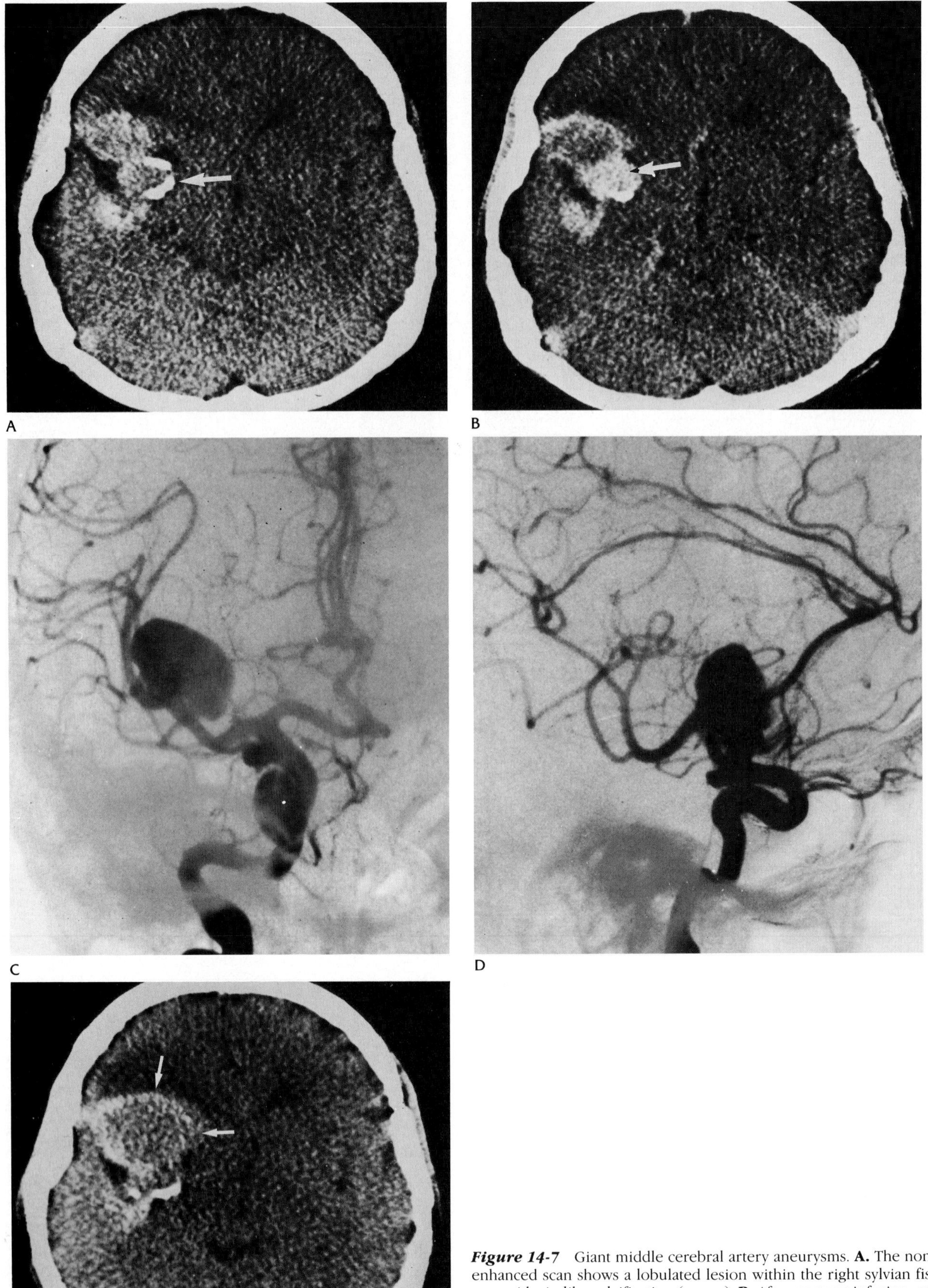

Figure 14-7 Giant middle cerebral artery aneurysms. **A.** The nonenhanced scan shows a lobulated lesion within the right sylvian fissure with rimlike calcification (arrow). **B.** After contrast infusion, eccentric enhancement is present (arrow). **C, D.** Angiogram in frontal and lateral projections show a giant middle cerebral artery aneurysm. **E.** One-year follow-up without specific treatment shows an increase in the size of the thrombosed aneurysm (arrows). (*Continued on p. 597)*

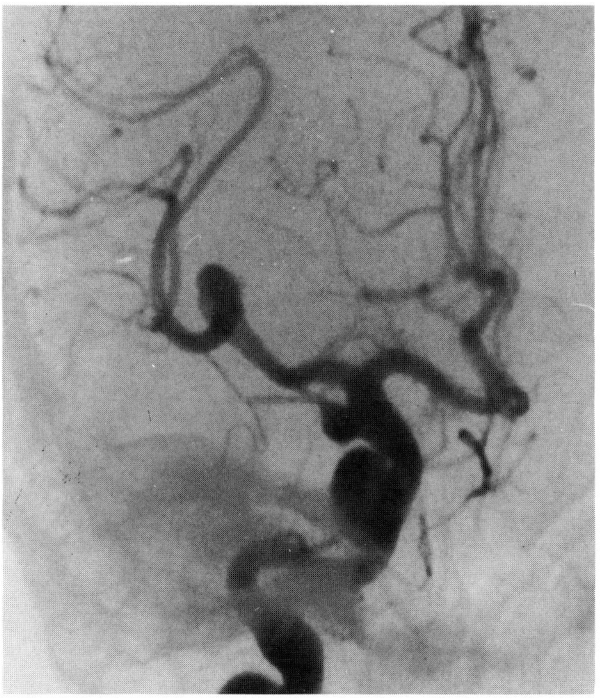

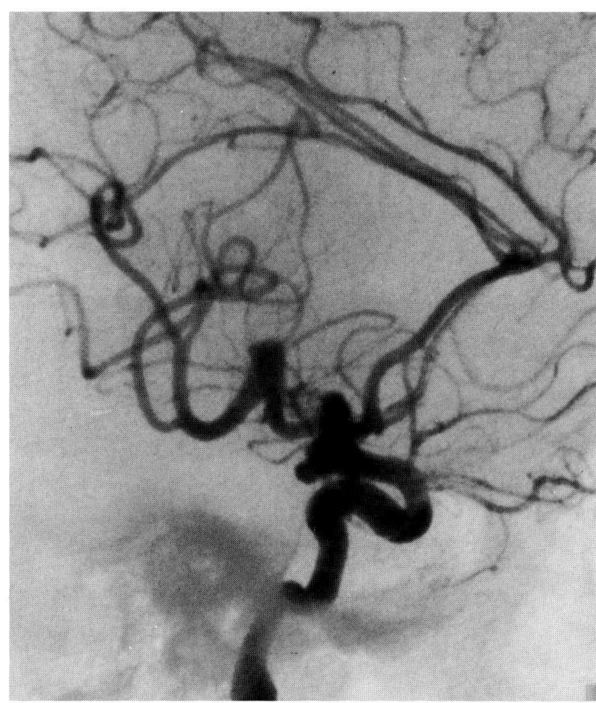

F G

Figure 14-7 (continued) **F, G.** Angiogram shows that the patent lumen of the aneurysm has diminished dramatically since the initial examination.

of CT, while a change in the patent lumen of an aneurysm is better demonstrated with angiography (Fig. 14-7). CT also can be used to assess the postoperative status of an aneurysm, and it is the method of choice for investigating the status of the remaining lumen of a giant unclippable aneurysm which has been treated by balloon detachment or proximal ligation of the parent vessel (Fig. 14-3) (Handa 1978).

CT significantly changed the method of investigation and management of patients with *subarachnoid hemorrhage* (Kendall 1976*b;* Liliequist 1977; Scotti 1977; Weir 1977; Modesti 1978; Adams 1983). The mortality of patients with a subarachnoid hemorrhage is high in the first few days after the ictus (40 to 60 percent) and is related to the mass effect of an intracranial hematoma (Weir 1977; Weisberg 1978, 1981).

CT continues to be the imaging modality of choice in the demonstration of acute subdural, subarachnoid (Fig. 14-8), and intracerebral or intraventricular hemorrhages (Hayward 1977). Approximately 75 percent of patients with a subarachnoid hemorrhage have a ruptured aneurysm, and 5 percent have an arteriovenous malformation; in 15 percent no cause for bleeding is identified on angiography (Bjorkesten 1965).

In the first few days after an ictus, CT identifies blood in the subarachnoid space in approximately 80 percent of cases. The accuracy of detection of recently extravasated blood in the subarachnoid space declines with time, and generally no blood can be demonstrated 1 week after the ictus (Scotti 1977; Weir 1977; Modesti 1978). A false-negative CT scan is not uncommon in patients with good neurological grades and therefore probably indicates a relatively small amount of blood in the subarachnoid space. This phenomenon is, however, not necessarily associated with a better clinical outcome (Weir 1977).

Various patterns can be recognized on CT in patients with subarachnoid hemorrhage, depending on the location of the ruptured aneurysm (Scotti 1977; Modesti 1978; Yock 1980). Anterior communicating artery aneurysms tend to bleed into the interhemispheric fissure and suprasellar cistern. The cingulate and callosal gyri are often outlined by blood. Frequently blood is also present around the brainstem and in the sylvian fissure (Fig. 14-9). The asymmetrical presence of blood in the sylvian fissure has been shown to occur with ruptured anterior communicating artery aneurysms and thus does not exclude that possibility (Yock 1980). Internal carotid and posterior communicating artery aneurysms tend to bleed into the suprasellar cistern and the adjacent sylvian fissure. Blood is less frequently present within the interhemispheric fissure. Middle cerebral artery aneurysms

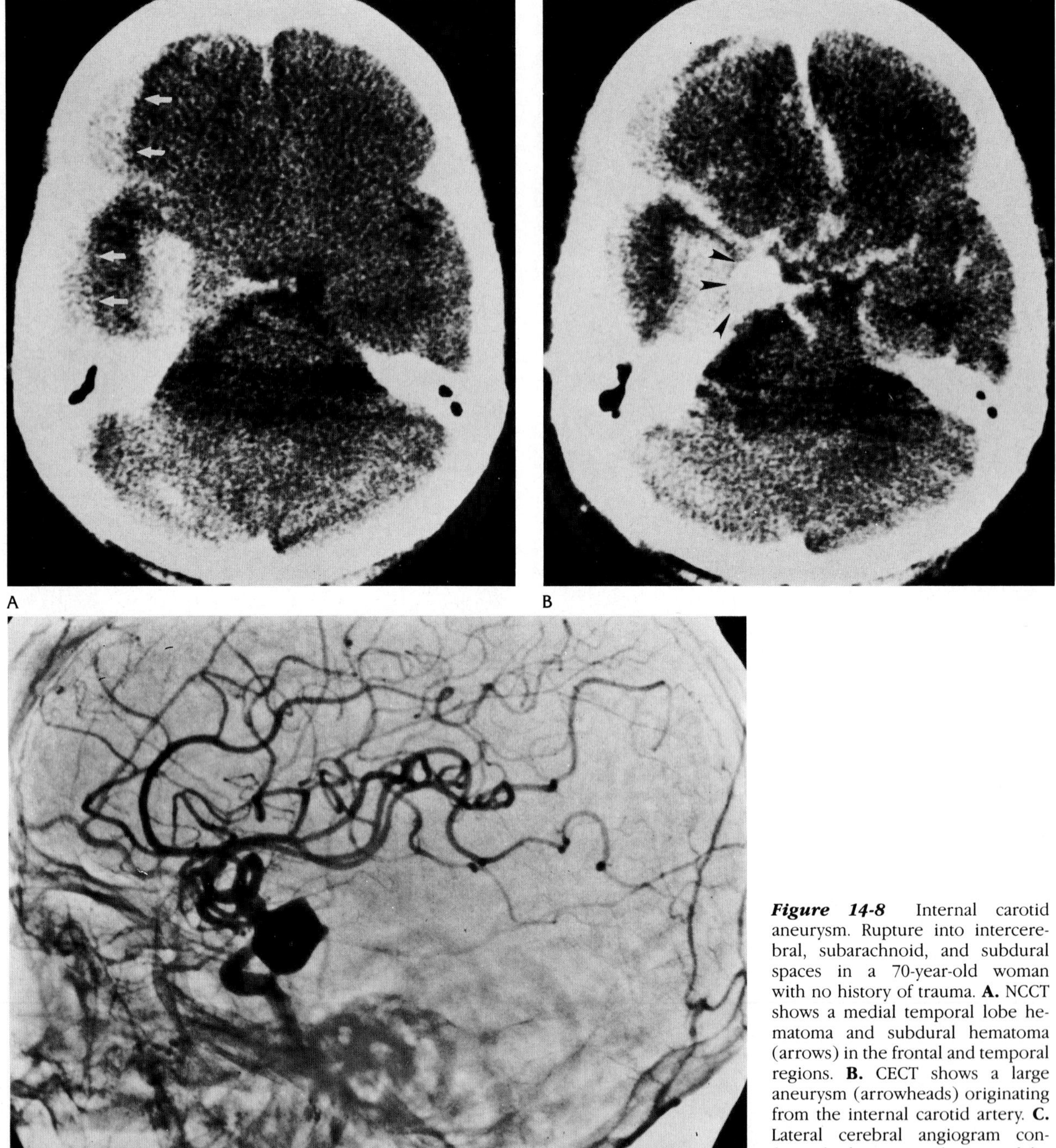

Figure 14-8 Internal carotid aneurysm. Rupture into intercerebral, subarachnoid, and subdural spaces in a 70-year-old woman with no history of trauma. **A.** NCCT shows a medial temporal lobe hematoma and subdural hematoma (arrows) in the frontal and temporal regions. **B.** CECT shows a large aneurysm (arrowheads) originating from the internal carotid artery. **C.** Lateral cerebral angiogram confirms the location and origin of the bleeding aneurysm.

invariably bleed into the sylvian fissure and the adjacent suprasellar cistern. Aneurysms arising from the tip of the basilar artery bleed into the interpeduncular cistern around the brainstem and the suprasellar cistern, while bleeding into the sylvian and interhemispheric fissures is uncommon. Ruptured aneurysms arising from the posterior inferior cerebellar artery are often associated with false-negative findings on CT unless the bleeding is massive. In most cases, blood can be seen outlining the brainstem.

Care should be taken to distinguish a *normal falx* from blood that has recently extravasated into the interhemispheric fissure (Lim 1977). The posterior or retrocallosal aspect of the falx can be visualized in 88 percent of normal patients, while the anterior aspect is visualized on CT in 38 percent of patients without subarachnoid hemor-

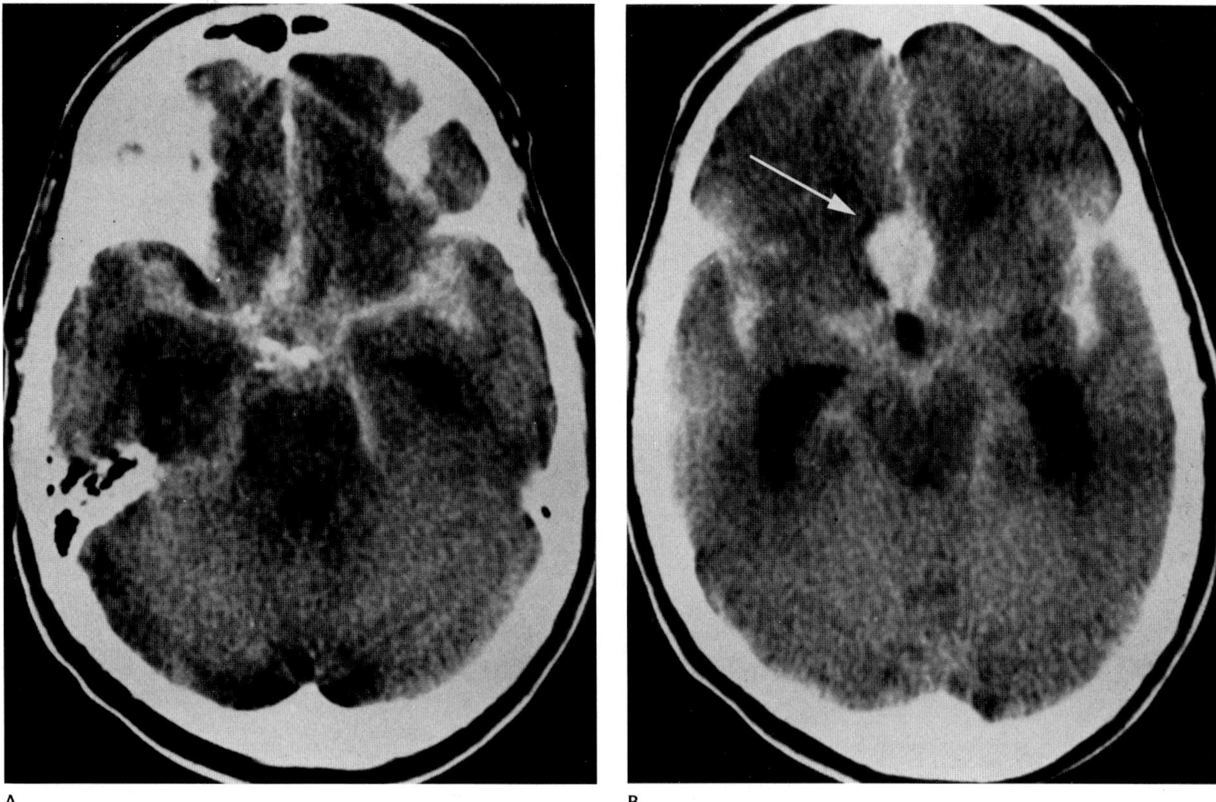

Figure 14-9 Subarachnoid hemorrhage after rupture of the anterior communicating artery aneurysm. **A.** The hyperdense recently extravasated blood outlines the prepontine and suprasellar cisterns, the first segment of the sylvian fissures, and the interhemispheric fissure. **B.** NCCT shows a hemorrhage in the interpeduncular cistern, the ambient and suprasellar cisterns, and the sylvian fissure. A localized hematoma is present at the level of the interhemispheric fissure (arrow). Note ventricular enlargement.

rhage (Zimmerman 1982). When the increased density in the interhemispheric fissure does not extend into the paramedian sulci or does not show any change from previous CT, the diagnosis of a normal falx is established (Osborn 1980).

The ability to localize a ruptured aneurysm by means of CT is greatly improved if a localized *hematoma* is present. Aneurysms arising from the anterior cerebral arterial complex tend to bleed into the adjacent frontal lobes and the septum pellucidum. A septal hematoma is present in 30 percent of ruptured anterior communicating artery aneurysms and invariably indicates the particular location of the aneurysm (Fig. 14-10) (Hayward 1976; Scotti 1977; Yock 1980), although the authors have seen such a hematoma arising from a ruptured pericallosal artery

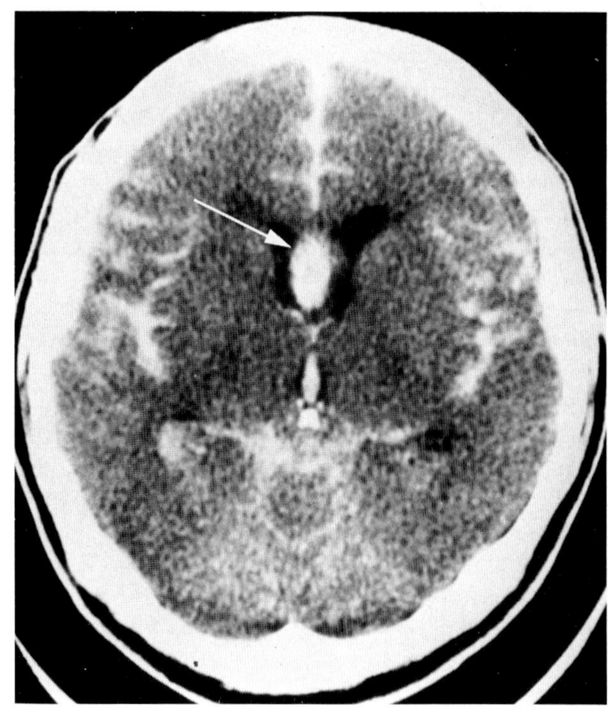

Figure 14-10 Septal hematoma caused by rupture of an anterior communicating artery aneurysm. On NCCT, a recent subarachnoid hemorrhage is noted at the level of both sylvian fissures and the interhemispheric fissure and a localized hematoma is noted at the level of the septum pellucidum (arrow).

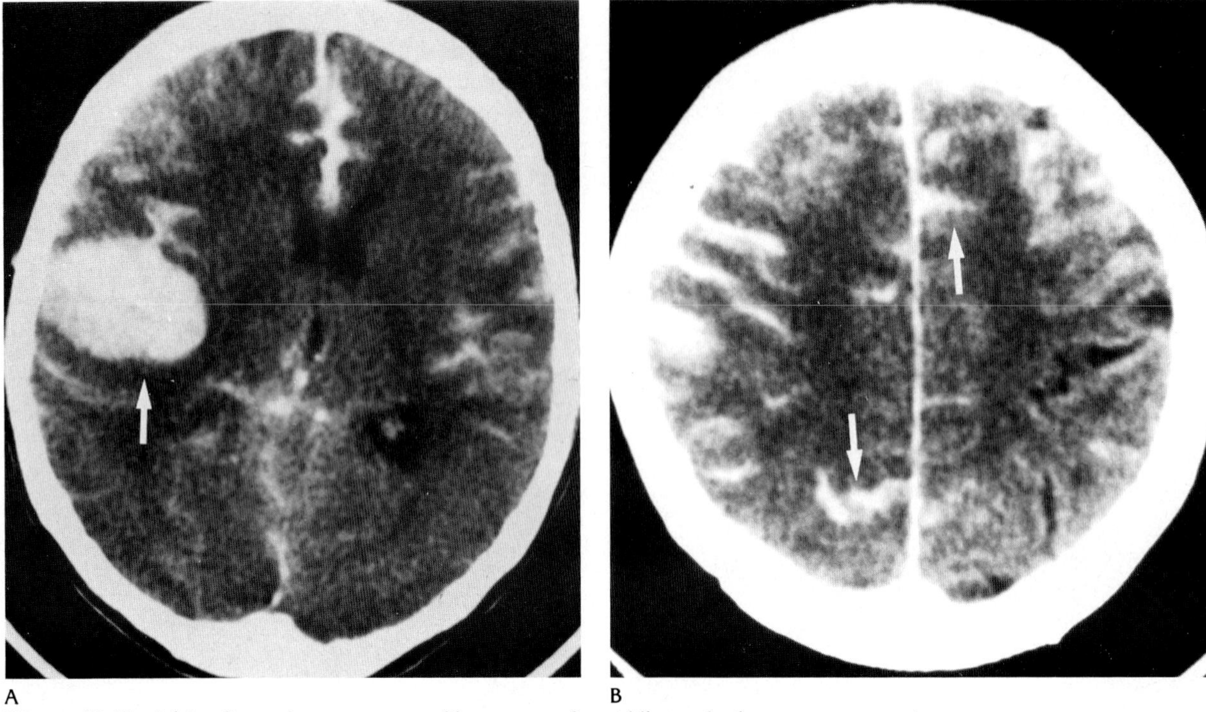

Figure 14-11 Sylvian fissure hematoma caused by rupture of a middle cerebral artery aneurysm. **A.** NCCT shows a recent subarachnoid hemorrhage at the level of the interhemispheric fissure and a localized hematoma expanding the right sylvian fissure (arrow). **B.** Extravasated blood is also noted within the cortical sulci over the convexity of the brain and adjacent to the falx (arrows).

aneurysm and a posterior communicating artery aneurysm. Temporal lobe and basal ganglia hematomas occur with middle cerebral, posterior communicating, and internal carotid artery aneurysms (Fig. 14-8). Comma-shaped sylvian fissure hematomas are characteristic of ruptured middle cerebral artery aneurysms and are easily distinguishable from the external capsule hematomas which occur in primary intracerebral hemorrhage in patients with hypertension (Fig. 14-11). Hayward (1976) reported 90 percent accuracy in the ability of CT to distinguish primary intracerebral hemorrhage from intracerebral hematoma caused by a ruptured intracranial aneurysm.

In cases of *multiple intracranial aneurysms,* CT is of limited value in identifying which one has bled if a nonspecific CT pattern is encountered. However, when localized hematoma is present in addition to the subarachnoid hemorrhage, the accuracy of CT can approach 100 percent (Aalmaani 1978). MRI also can be used to indicate the site of a rupture in patients with multiple intracranial aneurysms (Nehls 1985; Hackney 1986).

Depending on the location of an aneurysm, contrast enhancement allows direct visualization of the aneurysm in 30 to 76 percent of cases of subarachnoid hemorrhage and is therefore recommended (Ghoshhajra 1979; Yock 1980). When a subarachnoid hemorrhage is associated with an intracerebral or *subdural hematoma* without a history of trauma, a subdural hematoma of arterial origin (aneurysm or arteriovenous malformation) should be considered (Rengachary 1981). In such cases CECT is indicated to elicit the source of bleeding (Fig. 14-8).

The advent of CT has greatly changed the role of angiography in the investigation and follow-up of patients with a subarachnoid hemorrhage. The need for emergency angiography for diagnostic purposes has diminished. However, depending on the clinical situation (good neurological grade or life-threatening hematoma), most neurosurgical teams want to proceed with surgery and therefore require presurgical angiography. In cases where immediate surgery is not warranted, angiography may be postponed until the patient's condition stabilizes. Angiography should be directed primarily toward a detailed demonstration of vessels adjacent to the abnormality shown on CT.

The frequency of neurological deterioration among patients with a subarachnoid hemorrhage is well known. CT has a definite role in the follow-up of these patients. Rebleeding of the aneurysm and ventricular enlargement are readily shown on CT. The development of *ventricular enlargement* appears to be a much more common phenomenon than was previously realized and occurs in the first few days after the ictus in up to 60 percent of patients with a subarachnoid hemorrhage (Modesti 1978). However, in contrast to the preliminary study by Davis (1980), CT findings in patients with *vasospasm* are not as impressive in the author's experience. Although CT may show cerebral edema and infarction, it often fails to show any change in patients with angiographic evidence of severe vasospasm (Liliequist 1977; Ghoshhajra 1979; Saito 1979; Fisher 1980). A negative CT may be useful in such cases, since it can exclude rebleeding and ventricular enlargement and therefore may indirectly indicate vasospasm in a patient who is clinically deteriorating; however, consistent correlation between vasospasm and clinical deterioration has not been proved.

CT should be the first investigative procedure for patients with possible subarachnoid hemorrhage. The study should be done as early as possible after the ictus and, if clinically indicated, should be performed as an emergency procedure. In addition to the subarachnoid hemorrhage, CT can accurately diagnose a significant intracranial hemorrhage or ventricular enlargement which may require immediate neurosurgical intervention. In cases where in addition to the subarachnoid hemorrhage a small localized hematoma is present, cerebral angiography should be carried out to allow for immediate treatment planning. A negative CT scan does not exclude the possibility of a recent subarachnoid hemorrhage, and in these circumstances a lumbar puncture is warranted. If the puncture reveals evidence of a subarachnoid hemorrhage, either digital subtraction or conventional angiography must be performed to search for the cause of bleeding.

Magnetic Resonance Imaging

The role of MRI in the evaluation of patients with intracranial aneurysms is still evolving. Although MR angiography holds promise for demonstrating small aneurysms (less than 1 cm) utilizing a 3D (volume) acquisition technique with gradient-echo sequences (Fig. 14-12A), existing software and pulse sequences do not demonstrate such aneurysms reliably. Large and giant-size aneurysms are eloquently visualized with MR (Alvarez 1986; Hahn 1986; Atlas 1987; Olsen 1987; Tsuruda 1988). The MR techniques being developed will improve the angiographic capabilities of this modality (Tsuruda 1988; Keller 1989; Masaryk 1989; Ruggieri 1989), possibly resulting in a noninvasive screening study to detect even the smaller aneurysms. Aneurysms have decreased signal (flow void) intensity on both T_1WI and T_2WI, whereas intraluminal and mural thrombosis of the aneurysm, when present, is shown as an isointense to hyperintense signal component on both T_1- and T_2-weighted sequences (Fig. 14-12) (Worthington 1983; Hahn 1986; Olsen 1987; Biondi 1988*a*). A thin rim of low signal outlining the aneurysm may represent evidence of hemosiderin deposition or calcification (Hahn 1986; Atlas 1987). Flow within a larger aneurysm can sometimes be extremely slow, and MR angiographic techniques may not reveal the expected high-intensity signal associated with fast-flowing blood. The role of MRI in the investigation of patients with a recent subarachnoid hemorrhage is still under evaluation (Chakeras 1986). In patients with multiple aneurysms, MRI may demonstrate the bleeding site more conclusively than either CT or angiography can (Hackney 1986; Satoh 1988), although this has not been the experience of the author. CT is still the modality of choice in most institutions for the emergency evaluation of patients suspected of having a subarachnoid hemorrhage.

INTRACRANIAL VASCULAR MALFORMATION

Vascular malformations are developmental malformations of the vascular bed. They are traditionally classified into four groups: capillary telangiectasis, cavernous hemangioma, arteriovenous malformation, and venous angioma (Russell 1977). This pathological classification has been questioned as recent radiological and clinical experience has significantly improved our understanding of these entities (Wakai 1985; Lasjaunias 1986*c;* Valavanis 1986; Lobato 1988; Willinsky 1991). Venous angiomas in fact represent a variation of the norm and therefore should be classified as developmental anomalies rather than malformations (Lasjaunias 1986*c*). An intracerebral cavernous hemangioma is not a neoplasm and should therefore be identified as a cavernoma or cavernous malformation. An increase in the size of the malformation may occasionally be demonstrated and progressive destruction of the adjacent brain tissue may occur, but there is no evidence of neural tissue proliferation and therefore no evidence of neoplastic disease (Russell 1977).

Capillary Telangiectasis

These lesions are composed of dilated capillary blood vessels which vary greatly in caliber; the vessels are separated by normal neural tissue. These lesions are a relatively common incidental finding at autopsy but are rarely symptomatic. They are uncommonly associated with hemorrhage. In the hereditary form, called Rendu-Osler-Weber disease, multiple cutaneous and mucosal lesions are present. This form is often symptomatic and may be associated with other vascular anomalies, such as cavernous angiomas and arteriovenous malformations of the brain (Sobel 1984). The lesions of telangiectasis are most often located in the pons but may be seen in the cerebral cortex and subcortical white matter. Angiographically, a blush may be demonstrated in the capillary phase within the malformation, but most often the angio-

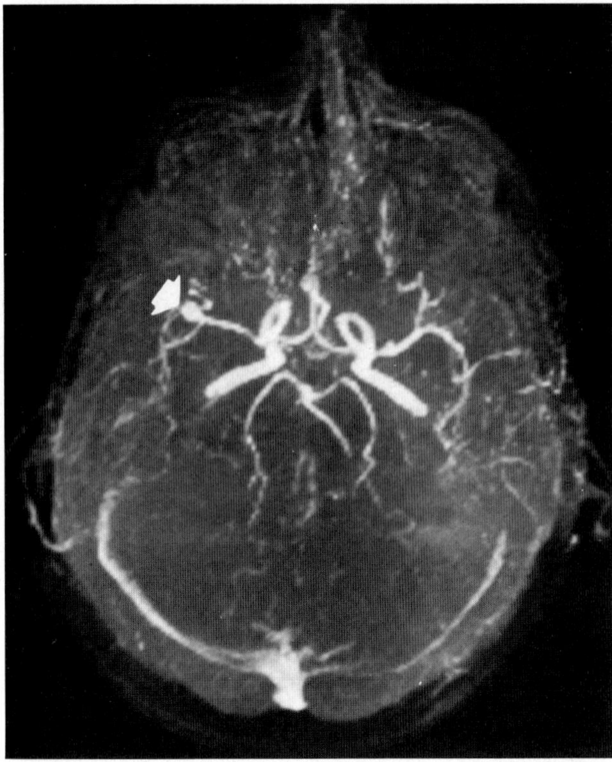

A

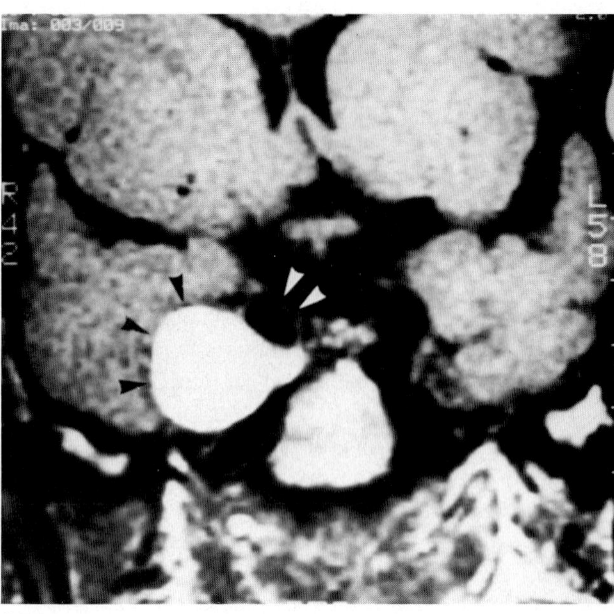

B

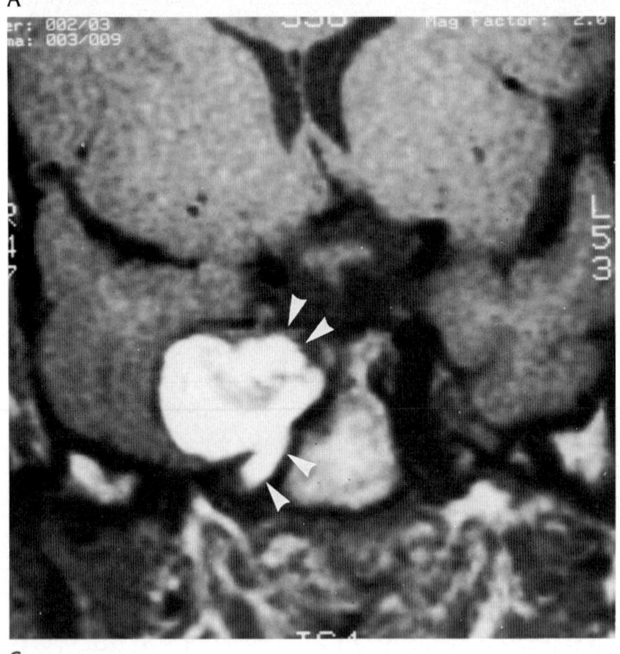

C

Figure 14-12 **A.** MR with gradient-echo technique, demonstrating an aneurysm (arrow) of middle cerebral artery. **B.** On MRI, a giant partially thrombosed internal carotid aneurysm shows decreased signal (white arrowheads) on T_1WI (flow void) and an increased signal within the thrombosed part (black arrowheads). **C.** After embolization, the lumen of the aneurysm and the internal carotid artery show an increased signal, indicating recent thrombosis (white arrowheads).

gram is negative (Poser 1957; Roberson 1974). CT may demonstrate cerebellar atrophy in capillary telangiectasis (Assencio-Ferreira 1981), although actual CT demonstration of the lesion itself has, to the author's knowledge, not been reported.

The MRI appearance of capillary telangiectasis has not been described; it appears, therefore, that this condition is mostly CT, MRI, and angiographically occult.

Cavernous Malformations

Cavernous malformations are composed of large sinusoidal vascular spaces which are closely clustered together; the vessels are not separated by normal neural tissue. Cavernomas represent the rarest form of vascular malformation but are clinically important because they are often symptomatic, causing seizures and intracerebral hemorrhage. They are often located within the intracerebral hemispheres, particularly in the subcortical region. Calcification is present in 30 percent of cases. Angiography is invariably normal (Savoiardo 1983), although prolonged injection angiography may demonstrate an abnormal capillary blush (Numaguchi 1979). CT findings consist of a hyperdense and often partially calcified lesion which shows fairly homogeneous enhancement of a minimal degree (Fig. 14-13) or no appreciable enhancement, depending on whether the lesions are partially or completely thrombosed. The lesion is not associated with mass effect or surrounding edema except when recent hemorrhage is present (Fig. 14-14) (Bartlett 1977; Ito 1978; Numaguchi 1979; Ramina 1980). Rarely, cavernous malformations may coexist with other types of vascular malformation within the lesion. These complex malformations show histological evidence of recent or old hemorrhage but do not have any specific CT characteristics (Ahmadi 1985). Occasionally the CT appearance

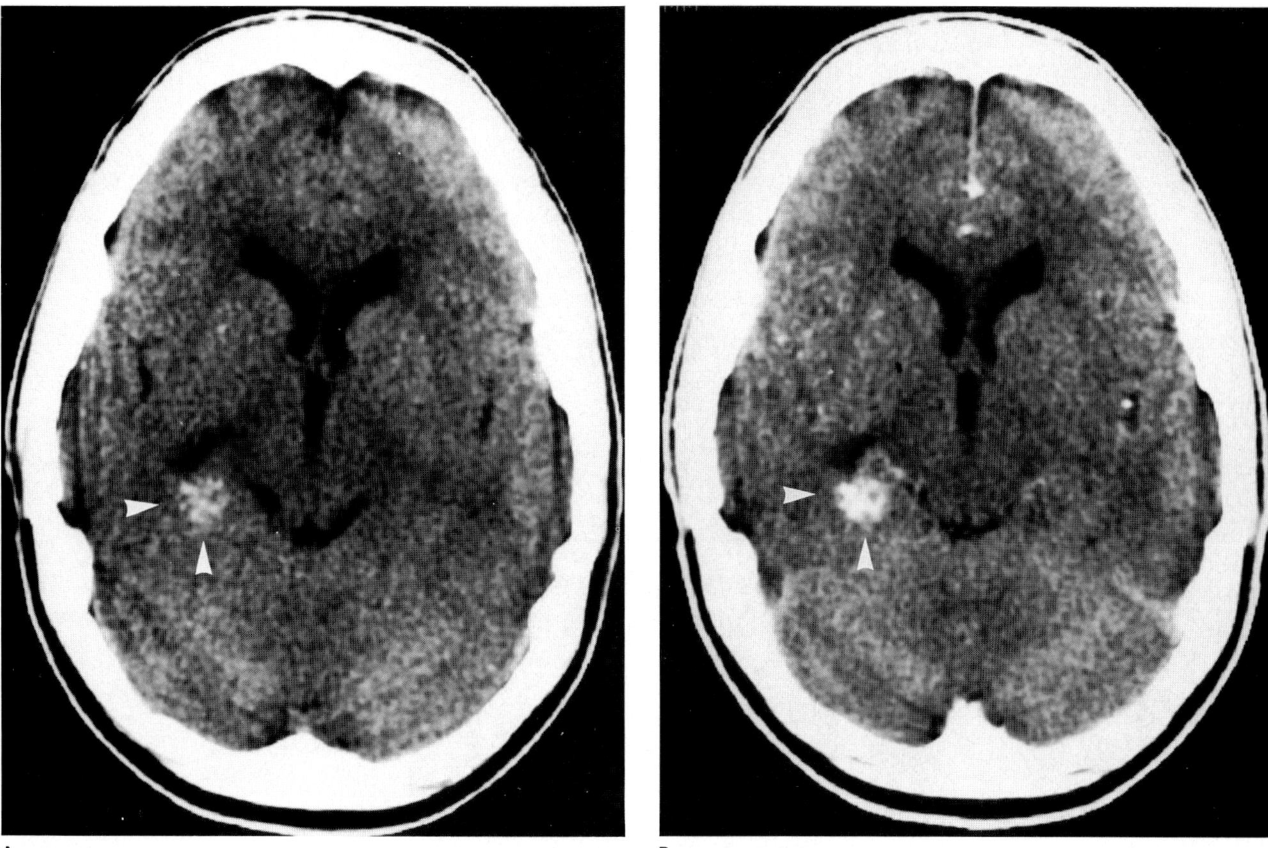

Figure 14-13 Cavernous malformation. **A.** A slightly hyperdense lesion (arrowheads) is shown on NCCT. **B.** Nonhomogeneous enhancement is noted on CECT is a surgically proven cavernoma in which angiography was normal.

may be indistinguishable from that of a meningioma (Ishikawa 1980); however, most cavernous malformations are intracerebral in location.

The MRI appearance of cavernous malformations has been well described (Savoiardo 1983; Augustin 1985; Lee 1985; Biondi 1988*b;* Imakita 1989; Rapacki 1990). Cavernomas appear as a well-defined area of mixed but predominantly increased signal intensity surrounded by a hypointense rim on T_1WI and T_2WI (Fig. 14-14). The central area of bright signal is caused by the presence of methemoglobin, the mixed densities by subacute and chronic hemorrhage, and the hypointense rim by hemosiderin deposition. Although initially the MR findings were thought to be pathognomonic, further experience has shown that other conditions, such as thrombosed arteriovenous malformations and hemorrhagic metastases, may have a similar appearance (Griffin 1987; Rigamonti 1987; Sze 1987; Biondi 1988*b;* Rapacki 1990). Multiple cavernomas may be identified (Fig. 14-14), and a familial occurrence is occasionally present (Rigamonti 1988).

MRI and CT can both be used to follow patients with known intracerebral cavernomas. Angiography is utilized primarily to exclude meningiomas from cavernomas that are peripherally located adjacent to the calvarium or the falx.

Arteriovenous Malformations

In vascular malformation there is an intimate topographic admixture of arteries and veins. It represents the most common form of vascular malformation and is clinically important because it is often symptomatic (Crawford 1986; Brown 1988). According to LeBlanc (1979), 55 percent of arteriovenous malformations (AVMs) present with intracranial hemorrhage, 36 percent with a seizure disorder, and 9 percent with headaches and a progressive neurological deficit. Approximately 12 percent of patients with a subarachnoid hemorrhage were found to have an underlying AVM (Hayward 1976). Patients with an unruptured brain AVM have a 2 to 4 percent risk per year of bleeding from the malformation. After the first bleed, the risk of subsequent hemorrhage increases to 25 percent per 4-year period and to 25 percent per year once the second hemorrhage has occurred. The lesions may occur

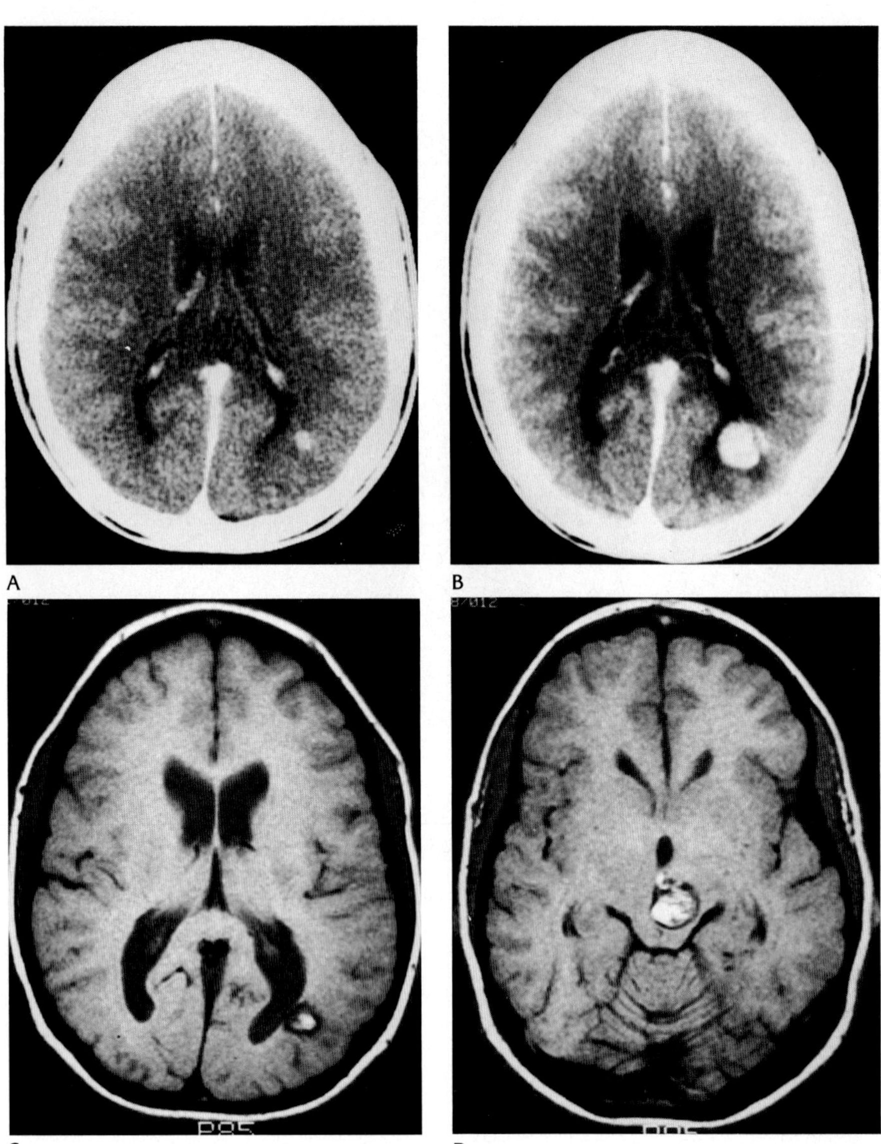

Figure 14-14 Cavernous malformations. **A.** CECT showed a hyperdense lesion adjacent to the occipital horn. **B.** Repeat CECT (3-year interval) showed an increase in the size of the lesion after the recent onset of acute headaches. NECT showed similar findings (associated hemorrhage). **C.** Follow-up MRI (2-year interval) showed on T_1 a lesion of mixed signal with a rim of decreased signal, indicating a resolved hematoma effect. **D.** Second lesion is noted at the midbrain level, revealing the characteristic MRI pattern of a cavernoma. Angiography had been normal, while CT showed that the midbrain lesion was unchanged in size during the interval.

in all parts of the central nervous system but are commonly located in the distribution of the middle cerebral artery along the cortex of the brain. The brain parenchyma adjacent to an AVM shows destructive and atrophic changes (Terbrugge 1977; Russell 1977). Calcifications are often present within the vascular channels as well as in the adjacent brain parenchyma (Fig. 14-15).

The angiographic appearance of an AVM is one of abnormally dilated and tortuous feeding arteries and a racemose tangle of increased vascularity, which drains into tortuous and elongated veins. Cerebral microarteriovenous malformations (micro AVMs) have been identified as lesions with a nidus less than 1 cm, fed by normal-size arteries with rapid shunting into normal-size veins (Willinsky 1988*b*). Occasionally the malformation becomes partially or completely thrombosed, and angiography may fail to show any evidence of it (angiographically occult).

The CT appearance of an intracranial AVM that is not associated with a recent hemorrhage is fairly characteristic (Pressman 1975*a;* Kendall 1976*a,* Terbrugge 1977; Brunelle 1983; Kumar 1984). The lesion most commonly presents on NCCT as an area of mixed density in which focal areas of hyperdensity are interspersed with areas of decreased density. The margins of the lesions are poorly defined and irregular in outline. After contrast infusion, the lesion shows heterogeneous enhancement (Figs. 14-15, 14-16, and 14-19). Feeding arteries and draining veins may be recognized on CT. The lesion may be associated with focal atrophy (Fig. 14-15) and localized mass effect (Fig. 14-17), but surrounding edema is extremely uncommon (TerBrugge 1977; LeBlanc 1979; Kumar 1985).

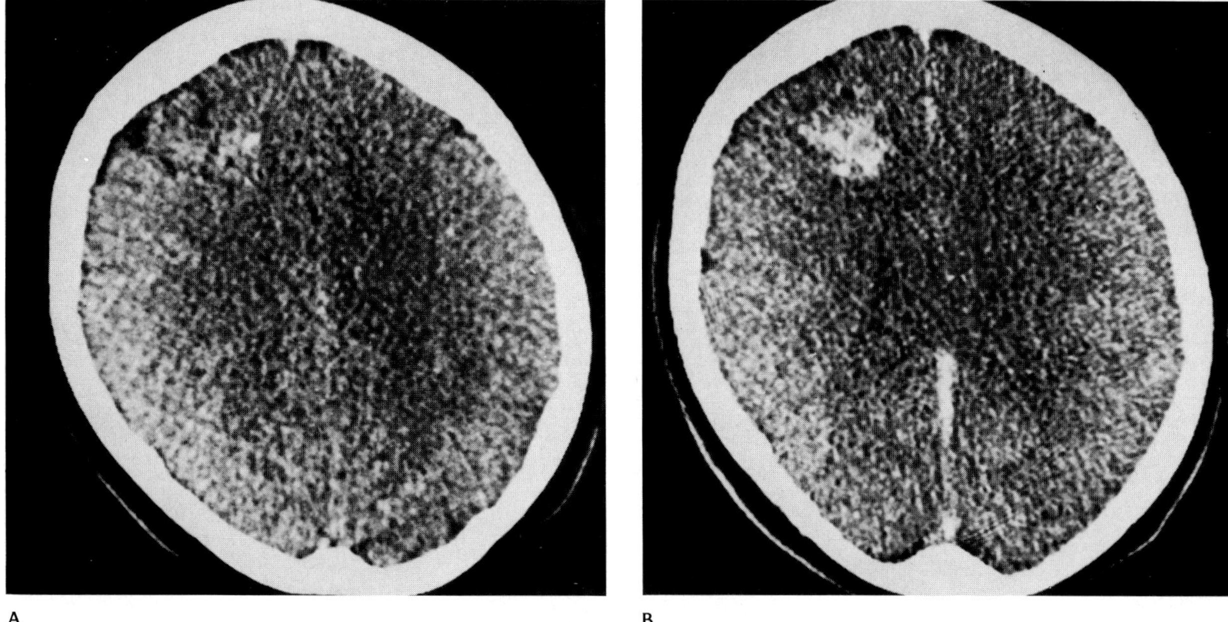

A B

Figure 14-15 Arteriovenous malformation (AVM). **A.** A focal area of cortical atrophy is noted on NCCT, with minute calcifications. **B.** Nonhomogeneous enhancement is present on CECT. The margins are poorly defined, without evidence of edema, in the angiographically proven AVM.

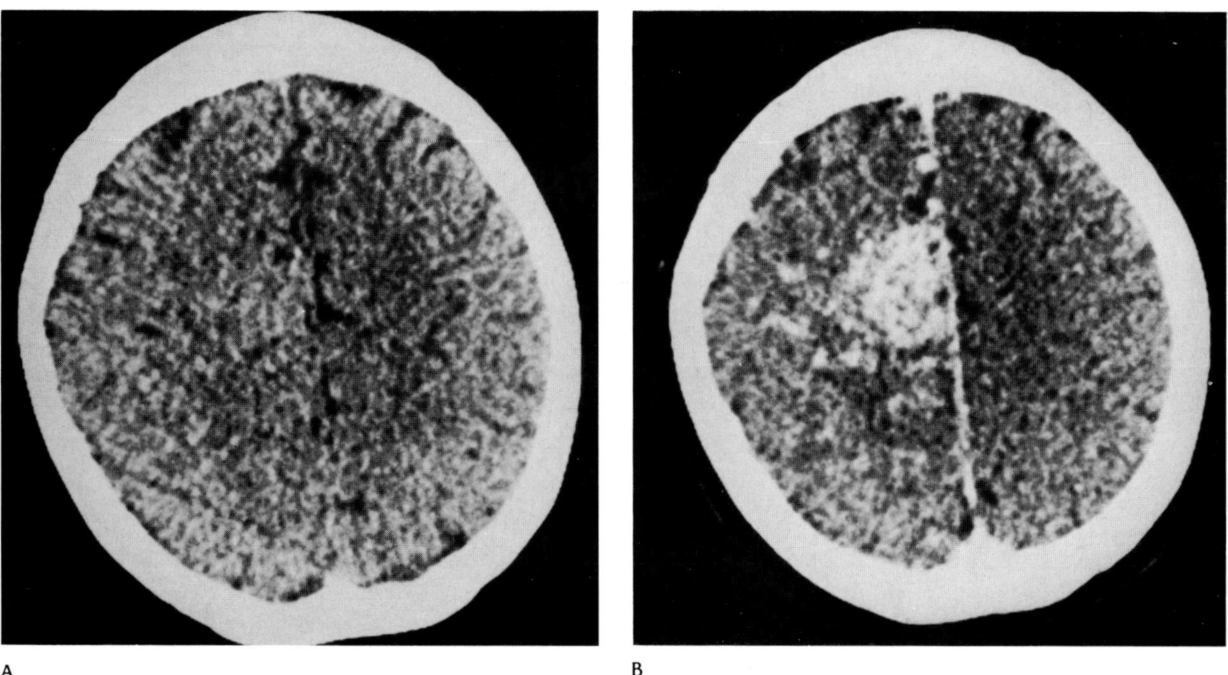

A B

Figure 14-16 Arteriovenous malformation. **A.** NCCT shows slightly increased density. **B.** On CECT there is nonhomogeneous enhancement of the lesion with poorly defined margins representing a central angiomatous mass. Multiple peripheral dotlike enhancement sites represent adjacent enlarged vessels.

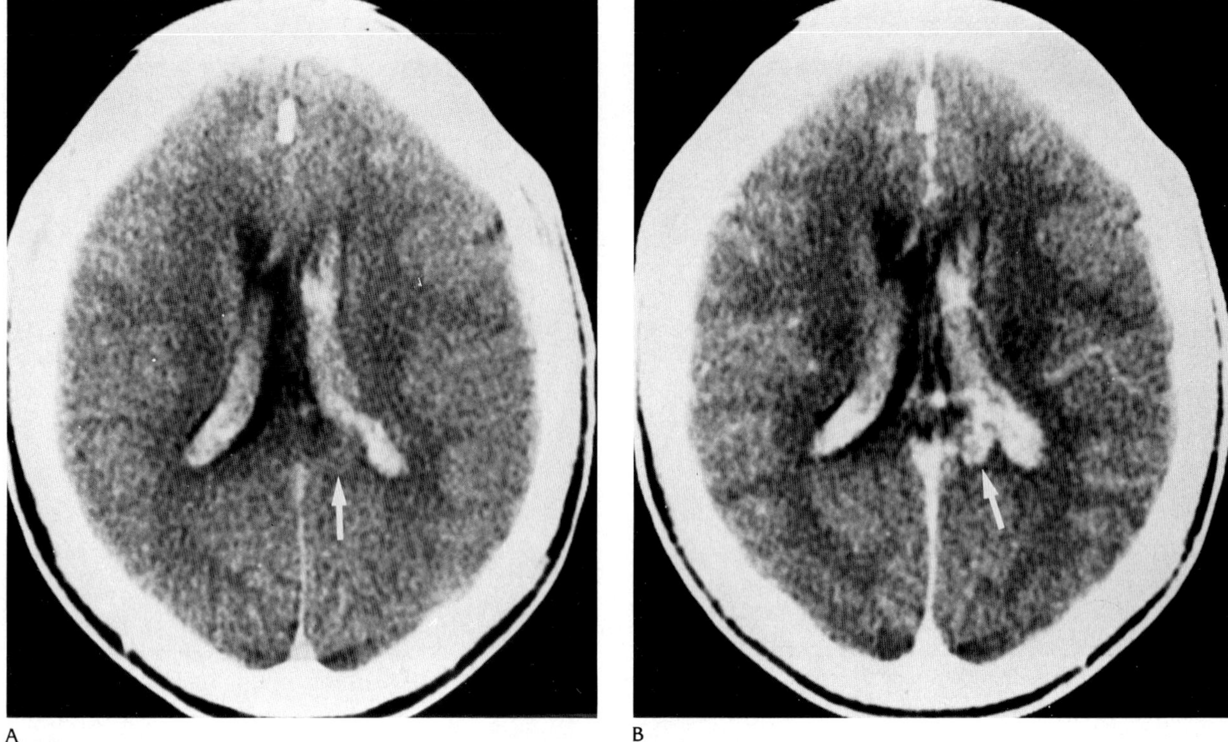

A B

Figure 14-17 Arteriovenous malformation with interventricular hemorrhage. **A.** NCCT shows a recent intraventricular hemorrhage and a small isodense mass lesion (arrow) indenting the left lateral ventricle. **B.** CECT shows evidence of enhancement of this lesion (arrow), which at angiography proved to be a small arteriovenous malformation in that location.

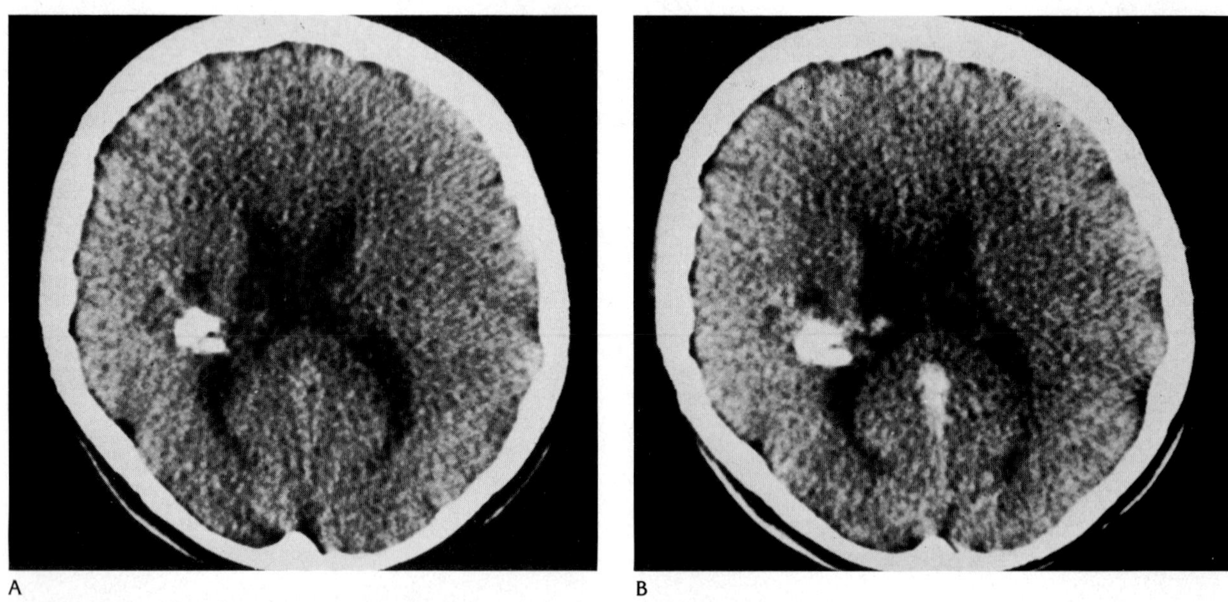

A B

Figure 14-18 Thrombosed arteriovenous malformation (AVM). **A.** NCCT shows a small, predominantly calcified lesion adjacent to the trigone of the right lateral ventricle. **B.** CECT shows subtle enhancement detectable only by means of CT number measurements. The angiogram proved to be normal. A thrombosed AVM was proved at surgery.

A significant number of AVMs do not show as an abnormality on NCCT and become apparent only after contrast infusion, which is therefore a mandatory part of the examination (TerBrugge 1977). CECT often shows heterogeneous enhancement and poorly defined margins of the lesion (Fig. 14-16).

One may observe areas of increased density, usually in the range of 40 to 50 HU, on NCCT. Postulated explanations for this baseline increased density imply the presence of local gliosis and hemosiderosis (New 1975), mural thrombus or calcification, or an increased blood pool (Pressman 1975*a*). CECT demonstrates enhancement of the central angiomatous mass and visualizes the adjacent vessels (Figs. 14-16 and 14-17).

A small number of AVMs exhibit a predominantly hyperdense appearance and are heavily calcified (Fig. 14-18). Enhancement may be difficult to detect in these angiographically occult malformations with high CT number measurements (Kramer 1977; Golden 1978; Sartor 1978; Bell 1978; Teraco 1979; LeBlanc 1981; Chin 1983; Yeates 1983). Delayed high-dose CT scanning is of little value in the evaluation of patients with angiographically occult thrombosed AVMs (Hayman 1981). Contrast enhancement of these calcified thrombosed malformations, as mentioned in the section on cavernous malformations, probably depends on the degree and extent of thrombosis.

Unusual patterns of AVM on CT have been described in which a well-defined area of decreased density is a prominent feature (Fig. 14-19). These cases frequently involve patients who have had previous episodes of hemorrhage associated with the AVM, with subsequent resolving hematoma and "cyst" formation (Daniels 1979; Britt 1980). On careful inspection, a partial curvilinear en-

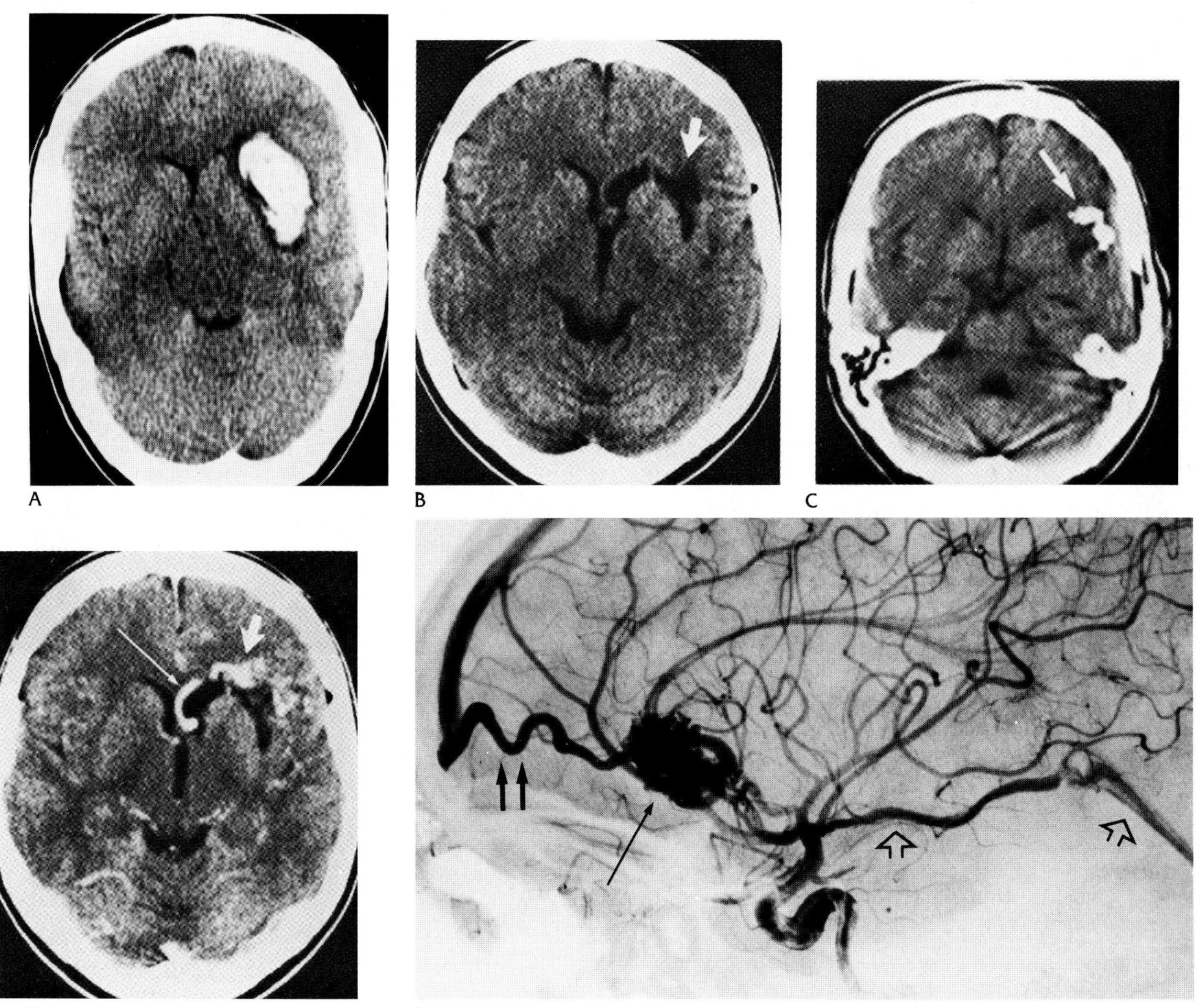

Figure 14-19 Arteriovenous malformation associated with intracerebral hemorrhage. **A.** Acute intracerebral hemorrhage deep within the left frontal lobe. **B.** NCCT 6 weeks later shows a resolved hematoma cavity. **C.** NCCT shows an area of mixed density (arrow) adjacent to the inferior aspect of the cavity. **D.** CECT shows nonhomogeneous enhancement of a lesion along the anterior aspect of the insular cortex (arrow). **E.** Angiogram done at the time of the initial hemorrhage shows a moderate-size AVM (arrow) fed by branches of the MCA with early superficial (double arrows) and deep venous (open arrow) drainage.

hancement of the margin of the cystlike lesion, without surrounding edema or mass effect, may give a clue to the presence of underlying AVM (Fig. 14-19). Occasionally, in rupture of AVMs, extravasation of blood into the preexisting cystic cavities presents as intraparenchymal blood-fluid levels (Richmond 1981). Spontaneous closure of an AVM of the basal ganglia may be demonstrated on CT as a nonenhancing, well-demarcated hypodensity with focal dilatation of the adjacent lateral ventricle (Sartor 1978).

A characteristic but rare form of AVM has been described in the midbrain, associated with ipsilateral angiomatosis of the retina and the presence of a cutaneous nevus in the distribution of the trigeminal nerve; it is called *Wyburn-Mason syndrome* (Wyburn-Mason 1943). CECT usually demonstrates a nonhomogeneous density of varying size, most commonly in the midbrain (Fig. 14-20). The orbital component of a vascular malformation around the optic nerve, which is always on the same side

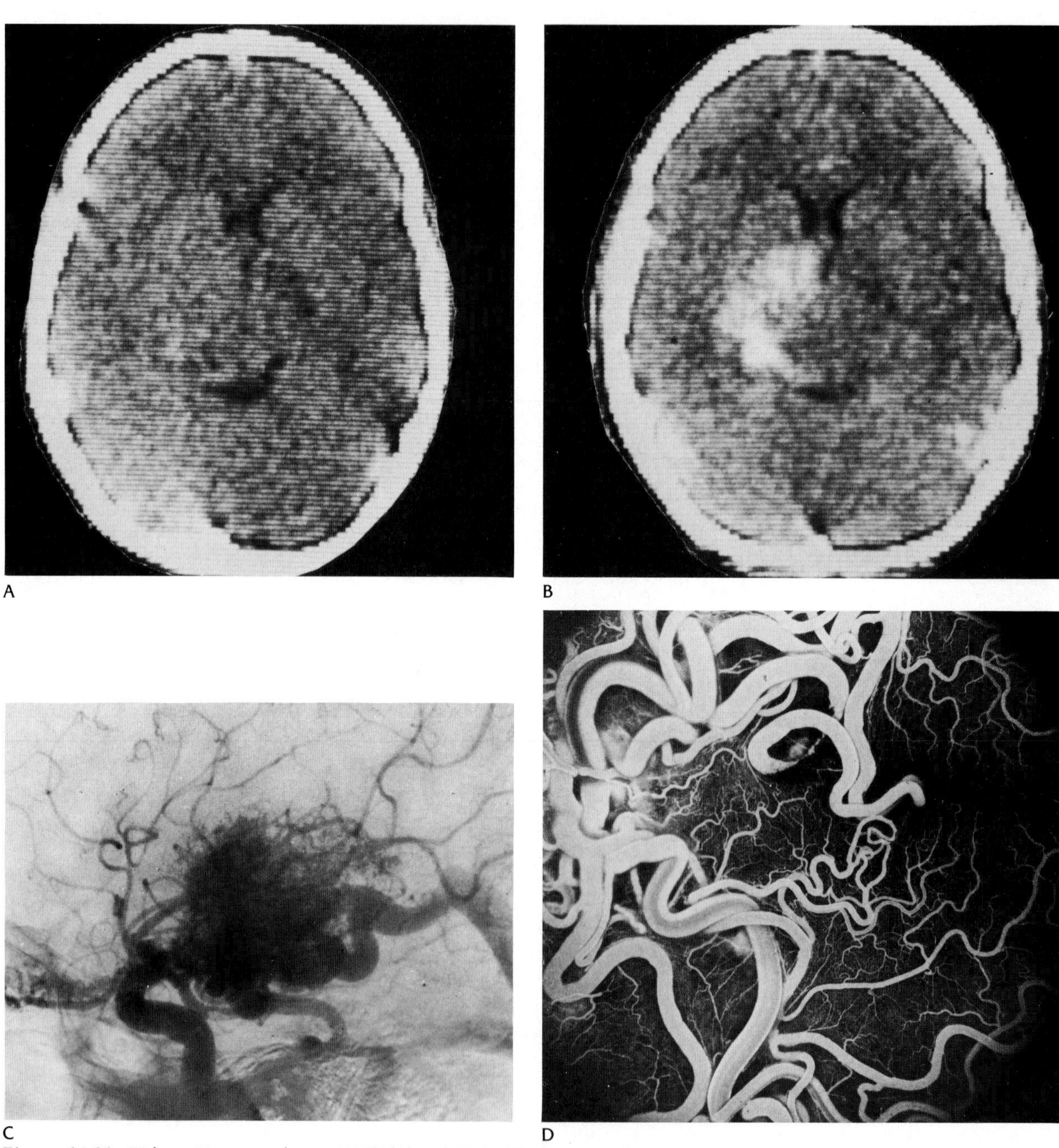

Figure 14-20 Wyburn-Mason syndrome. NCCT (**A**) and CECT (**B**) show a nonhomogeneous enhancing lesion in the midbrain and thalamus. **C.** Angiogram demonstrates the vascular malformation, with extension of the vascular anomaly along the optic nerve into the orbit. **D.** Racemose retinal angiomatosis shown by fluorescein angiography.

as the retinal angioma and the intracranial AVM, may not be detected by means of CT unless high-resolution thin sections are obtained or the orbital vascular component is very large. The extent of the orbital as well as the intracranial vascular anomaly can be confirmed with angiography.

Another variant of an AVM is the so-called *aneurysm of the vein of Galen.* The venous ectasia seen in this condition is usually caused by increased flow through a deep-seated arteriovenous shunt in the presence of a dural venous obstacle downstream from the vein of Galen aneurysm (Lasjaunias 1987*a*). Aneurysmal dilatation of the vein of Galen may cause compression of the midbrain and aqueduct. CT findings in patients with this aneurysm are fairly characteristic (MacPherson 1979; Spalline 1979). A well-defined, hyperdense rounded or triangular mass lesion in the region of the vein of Galen is noted on NCCT. Homogeneous enhancement occurs after contrast infusion (Fig. 14-21). Hydrocephalus is invariably present. CT is of great value in the postoperative assessment of these patients; ventricular size and possible subdural effusions can be demonstrated readily (Diebler 1981). Advances in therapeutic angiography have permitted endovascular treatment of these lesions (Lasjaunias 1986*a,* 1987*b,* 1989). CT may be helpful in showing the presence of embolic material within the shunt and the development of a thrombosis within the varix (Lasjaunias 1989).

Approximately 50 percent of patients with an AVM present with intracranial hemorrhage (LeBlanc 1979; Willinsky 1988*a*). Bleeding often occurs into the subarachnoid space or into the ventricular system and often into the brain parenchyma (Figs. 14-18 and 14-19). They rarely bleed into the subdural space (Rengachary 1981). Intracranial hemorrhage may occasionally obscure an AVM on initial CT. Therefore, follow-up CT subsequent to resorption of the hemorrhage may be necessary to demonstrate the underlying AVM. Furthermore, when a cortical hematoma is identified in a young patient who is normotensive, an underlying vascular malformation should be strongly suspected and angiography should be done (Solis 1977; Cone 1979). A normal angiogram in the acute phase does not exclude an AVM, and the author recommends a repeat cerebral angiogram 2 months after the ictus; the angiogram may at this time reveal the source of hemorrhage (micro AVM). An MRI should also be obtained in order to exclude cavernous malformation as the cause of the bleeding. Only vascular malformations which cannot be demonstrated on repeat MRI and angiography should be called occult to present imaging methods. The term *cryptic vascular malformation* should probably be abolished as it denotes a clinical suspicion that cannot be substantiated by means of imaging, surgery, or autopsy.

A rare complication associated with cerebral AVMs is vascular occlusive disease (Mawad 1984; Kayama 1986;

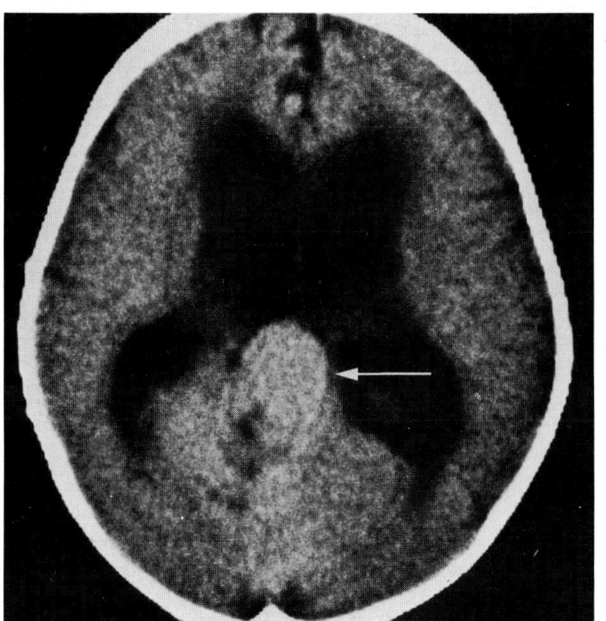

A

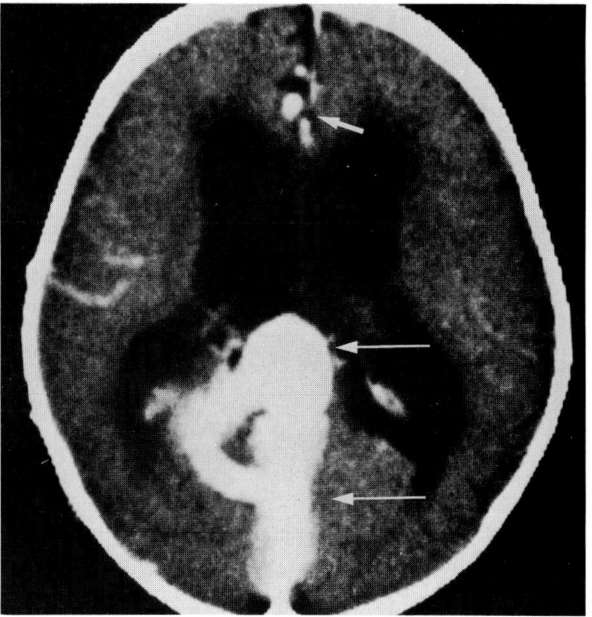

B

Figure 14-21 Midline arteriovenous malformation (AVM) with aneurysmal dilatation of the inferior longitudinal sinus and vein of Galen. **A.** An elongated area of slightly increased density is present at the level of the vein of Galen (arrow). **B.** CECT. Enhancement outlines the enlarged anterior cerebral arteries (small arrow) and the engorged vein of Galen and straight sinus (large arrows). (*Continued on p. 610.*)

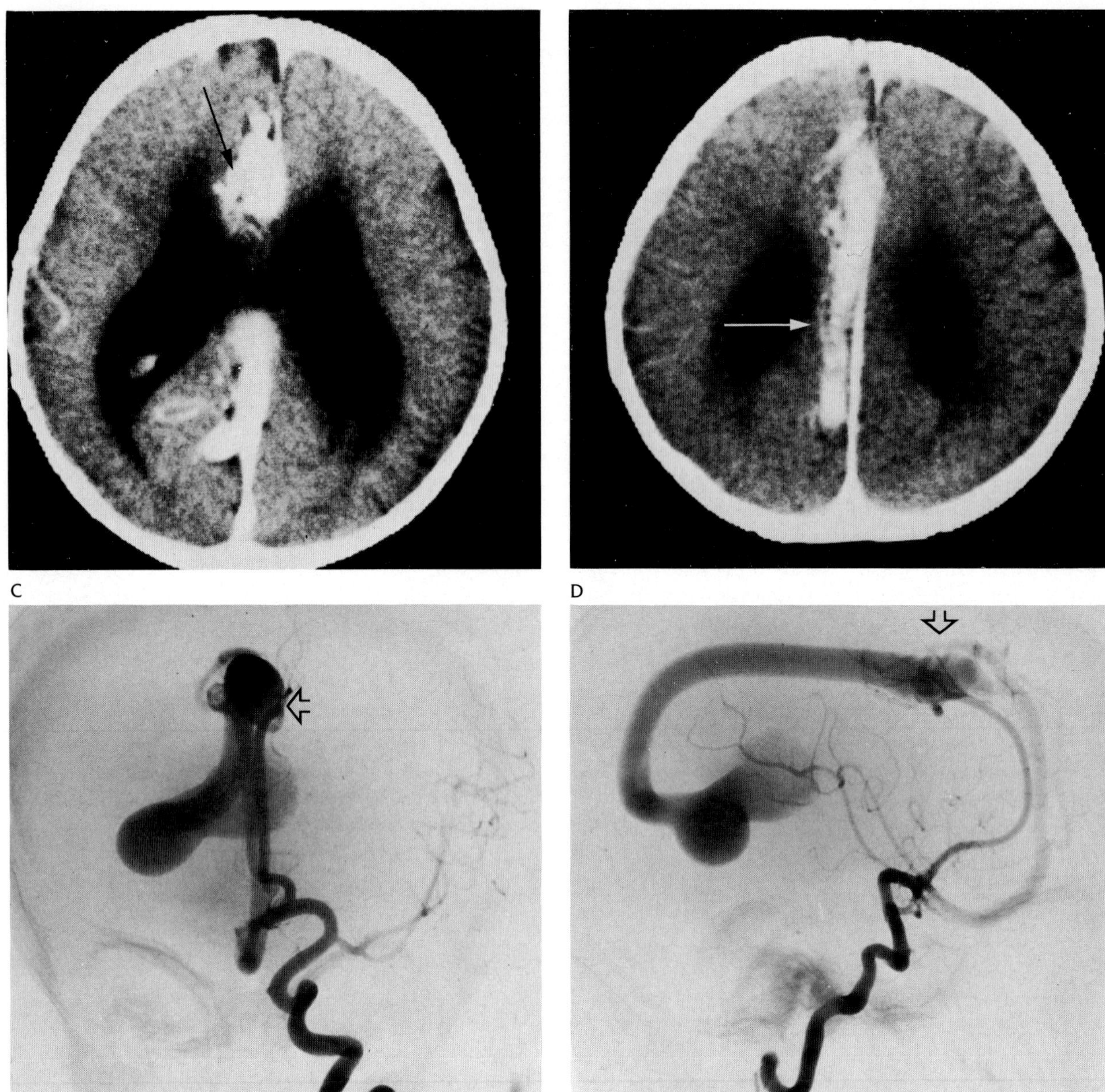

Figure 14-21 (continued) **C, D.** Enhancement of the vascular malformation along the anterior-superior aspect of the corpus callosum (black arrow) and the ectatic inferior longitudinal sinus (white arrow). **E, F.** Angiogram in the frontal and lateral projections show a midline AVM (arrow) with secondary enlargement of the inferior longitudinal sinus and vein of Galen. (*Courtesy of Dr. D. Harwood-Nash, Toronto Hospital for Sick Children.*)

Lichtor 1987; Montanera 1990). Presumably the high flow induced by an AVM produces in certain patients a vasculopathy in the feeding arteries with progressive stenosis that eventually leads to the development of collateral flow (moya-moya phenomenon), which sometimes can be recognized on CT and MRI but is clearly best shown on angiography.

The MRI appearance of an intracerebral AVM has been extensively described (Lee 1985; Kucharczyk 1985; LeBlanc 1987; Biondi 1988*b;* Smith 1988; Edelman 1989). A low-intensity signal (flow void) on both T_1WI and T_2WI has been noted to involve the nidus as well as the feeding arteries and draining veins (Fig. 14-22). Slow flow within the lesion may result in increased signal on T_1 and T_2, while previous hemorrhage may also be revealed as a bright signal on both T_1 and T_2. In order to distinguish between blood flow, calcification, and hemorrhage, special gradient-echo imaging techniques can be used. When

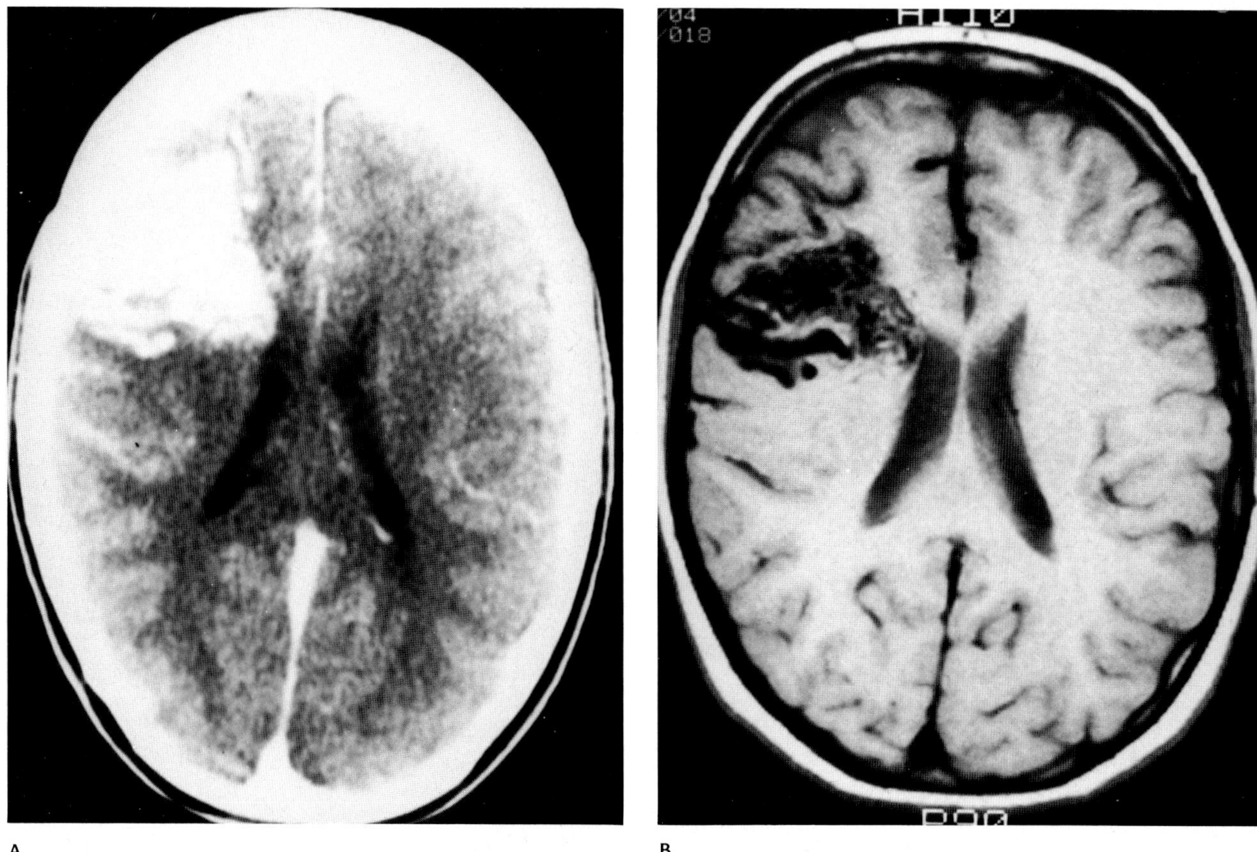

A B

Figure 14-22 Corticoventricular arteriovenous malformation showing nonhomogeneous enhancement of CECT (**A**). MRI delineates the nidus and feeding arteries as an area of decreased signal (flow void) on T_1WI (**B**).

one uses sequential acquisition, gradient refocused, limited flip-angle techniques, flowing blood is shown as a high signal intensity. Calcification or embolic material from previous endovascular treatment is often better shown on CT (Fig. 14-23). CT has also proved to be more sensitive than MRI in delineating small calcified AVMs (New 1986; Gomori 1986; Lemme-Plaghos 1986). MRI is superior to CT and angiography in demonstrating the exact anatomic relationships between the nidus, the feeding and draining vessels, and the adjacent structures (Noorbehesht 1987). Angiography is still mandatory in the treatment planning for intracerebral AVMs (endovascular, surgical, or radiotherapy) and is the only method for reliably demonstrating a micro AVM (Willinsky 1988*b*).

CT and MRI are equally efficient in demonstrating complications after treatment, but MRI is more accurate in assessing residual nidus after partial embolization or radiotherapy (Fig. 14-24) (Marks 1988; Smith 1988).

Pure *dural arteriovenous malformations* differ from brain AVMs in that they represent an acquired condition. Although they occasionally occur in neonates and infants, they most frequently present in adults with a previous history of head injury or inflammatory disease. Venous drainage may be into the dural sinuses or into the cortical veins. The presence of cortical venous drainage may account for central venous system symptomatology and indicates a higher incidence of associated intracranial hemorrhage (Lasjaunias 1986*b*). Dural AVMs along the anterior cranial fossa and tentorium are frequently associated with subarachnoid and intracerebral hemorrhage (Fig. 14-25). Although the nidus of the lesion is rarely shown on CT, abnormally prominent venous drainage channels may provide secondary evidence of such a lesion (Fig. 14-26). False-negative CT results in pure dural AVM are therefore common, and frequently only the associated complications are apparent on CT.

MRI of dural AVMs has so far been unrewarding and has been limited to the demonstration of complications of dural AVMs with cortical venous drainage, such as hemorrhage, venous congestion, and enlarged draining veins (DeMarco 1990). The actual dural nidus is rarely identified prospectively on MRI. Angiography remains the only method for demonstrating the nidus of a dural AVM. It should include selective visualization of the middle meningeal, ascending pharyngeal, and occipital branches of the external carotid system (Lasjaunias 1987*c*).

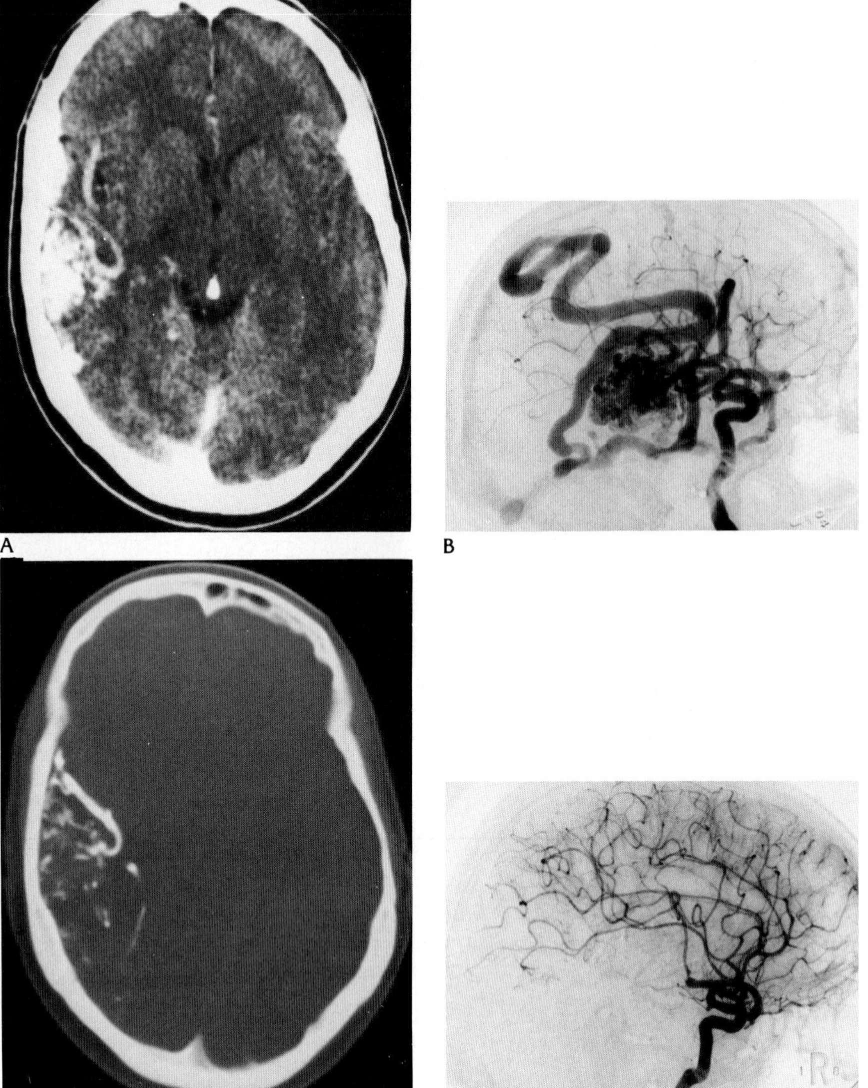

Figure 14-23 Temporabl lobe arteriovenous malformation. **A.** CECT reveals nonhomogeneous enhancement, while no evidence of calcification was noted on NECT. **B.** Carotid angiogram shows the angioarchitecture of the malformation. **C.** Embolic material (NBCA) is clearly demonstrated within the nidus of the lesion. **D.** Follow-up angiogram (2-year interval) revealed stable and compelte obliteration of the lesion after endovascular treatment.

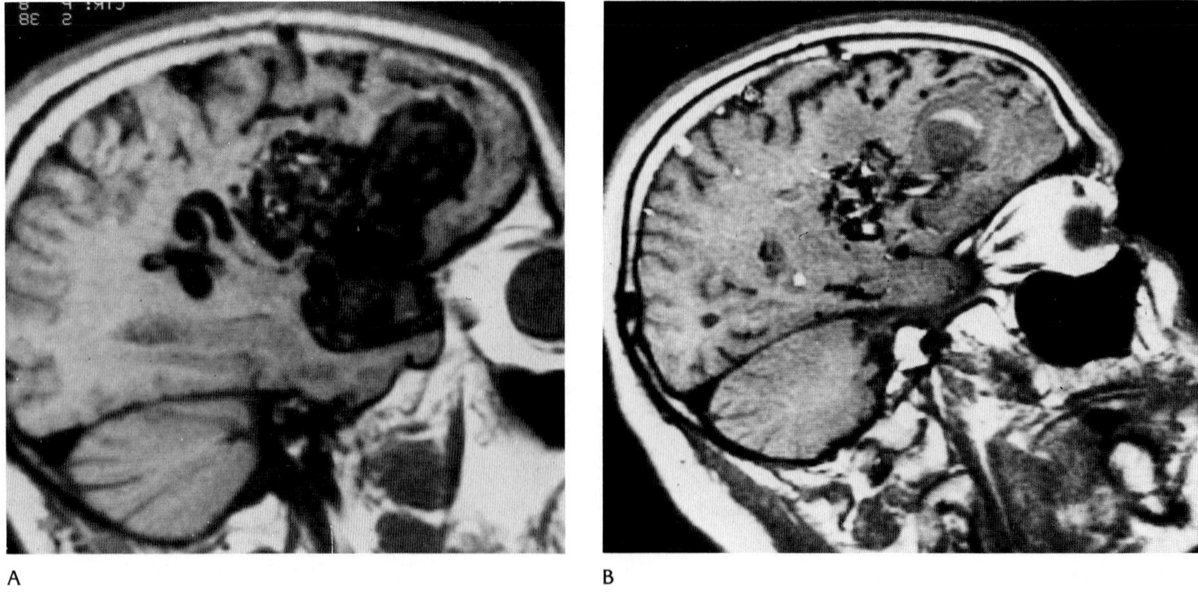

Figure 14-24 T_1-weighted MRI of a frontal lobe AVM before (**A**) and after (**B**) endovascular treatment with NBCA shows a change in the size and patency of the nidus of the malformation.

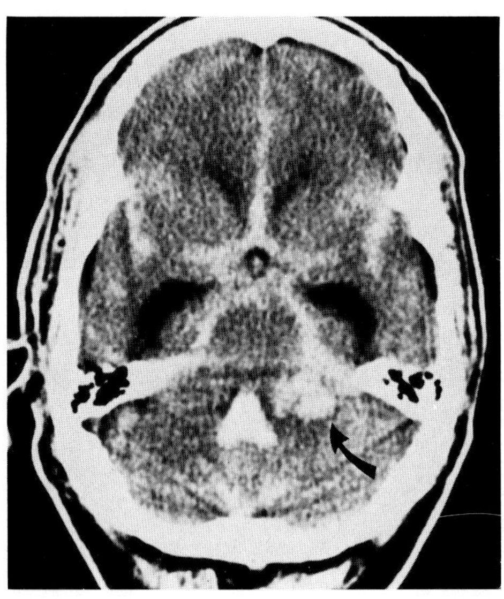

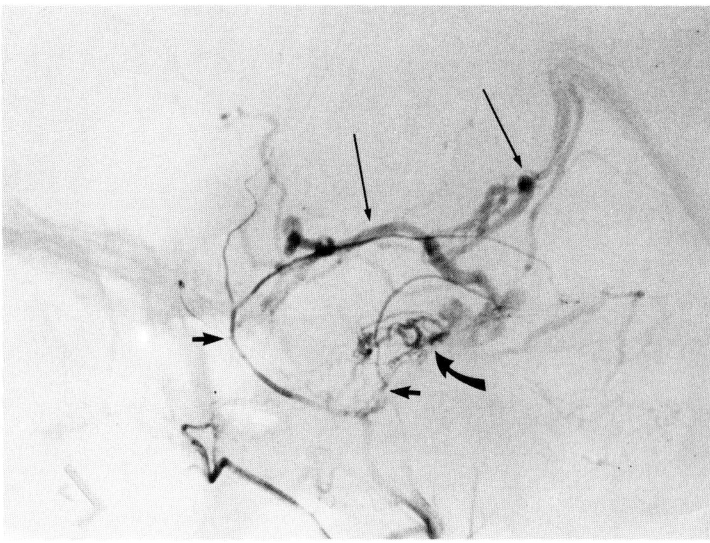

A B

Figure 14-25 Dural arteriovenous malformation (AVM) with subarachnoid hemorrhage (SAH) and interventricular hemorrhage (IVH). **A.** NCCT shows evidence of recent SAH and IVH with a localized hematoma at the cerebellopontine junction (arrow). **B.** Selective angiography revealed evidence of supply from the midline meningeal artery (small arrows) toward a tentorial dural AVM (curved arrow), which drained into the deep venous system (large arrows).

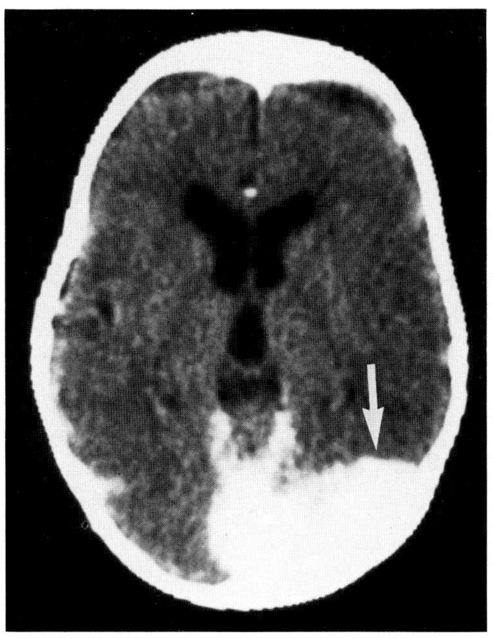

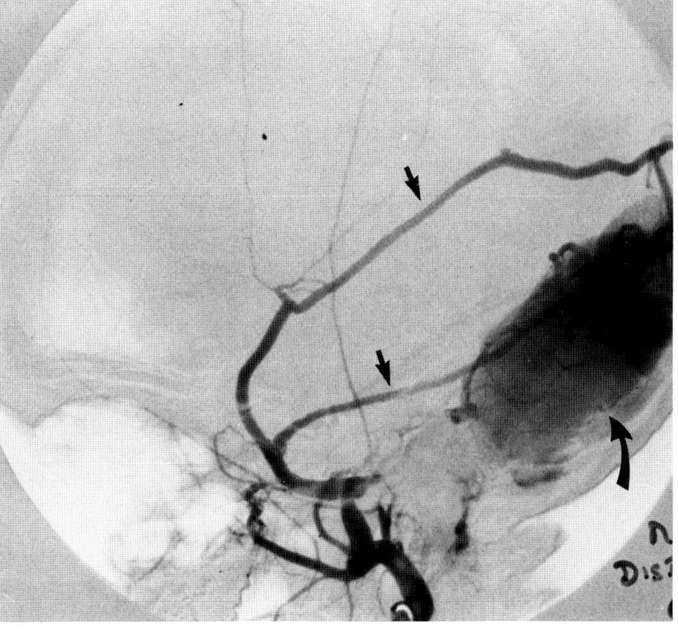

A B

Figure 14-26 Dural arteriovenous malformation. **A.** CECT shows an elongated area of enhancement at the level of the transverse sinus (arrow). **B.** Selective angiography shows branches of the middle meningeal artery (arrows) supplying a dural AVM which drains into an enlarged transverse sinus (curved arrow). Its outflow farther downstream showed a partial block. (*Courtesy of D. P. Lasjaunias, Paris, France.*)

Developmental Venous Anomalies (Venous Angioma)

Although traditionally included as one of the vascular malformations, venous angioma has recently been understood to represent an extreme variation of the normal venous drainage pattern. The superficial and deep venous drainage systems are normally in equilibrium, but depending on developmental circumstances, one or the other may become dominant (Lasjaunias 1986c; Jimenez 1989). Therefore, either system may extend toward the other territory and develop tributaries which drain into

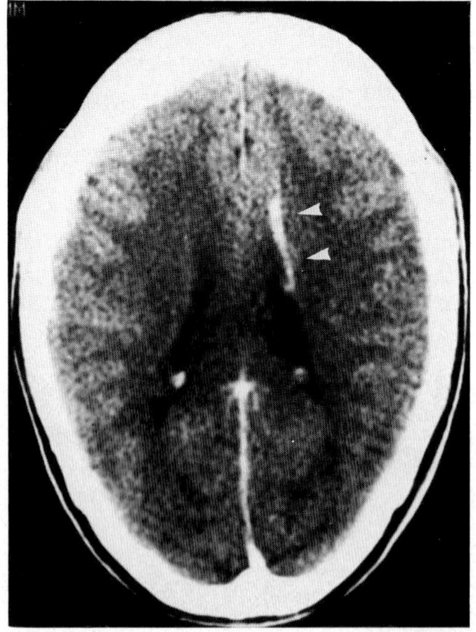

A

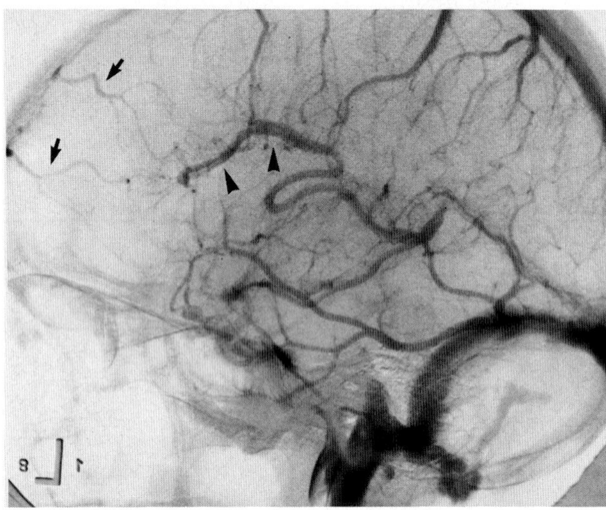

B

Figure 14-27 Developmental venous anomaly (DVA) in the frontal lobe. **A.** CECT shows a linear area of enhancement adjacent to the lateral ventricle (arrowheads). **B.** Venous phase of the angiogram showed poorly developed superficial cortical veins (arrows) and dominant drainage toward the deep venous system (arrowheads).

an enlarged venous channel that is often perpendicular to either the cortex or the ventricular wall. They are often clinically asymptomatic but may be associated with a subarachnoid or intracerebral hemorrhage or with seizures (Wendling 1976; Saito 1981; Rothfus 1984). Cerebellar venous angiomas are more prone to bleed, resulting in spontaneous subacute recurrent hemorrhage (Rothfus 1984).

The angiogram shows a normal arterial and capillary phase with multiple venules draining in an umbrella or stellate pattern toward an engorged draining vein, which is often positioned perpendicular to the cortex or ventricle (Figs. 14-27 and 14-28) (Wendling 1976; Valavanis 1983). NCCT is normal in the majority of cases, although sometimes a rounded hyperdense area is noted. Venous

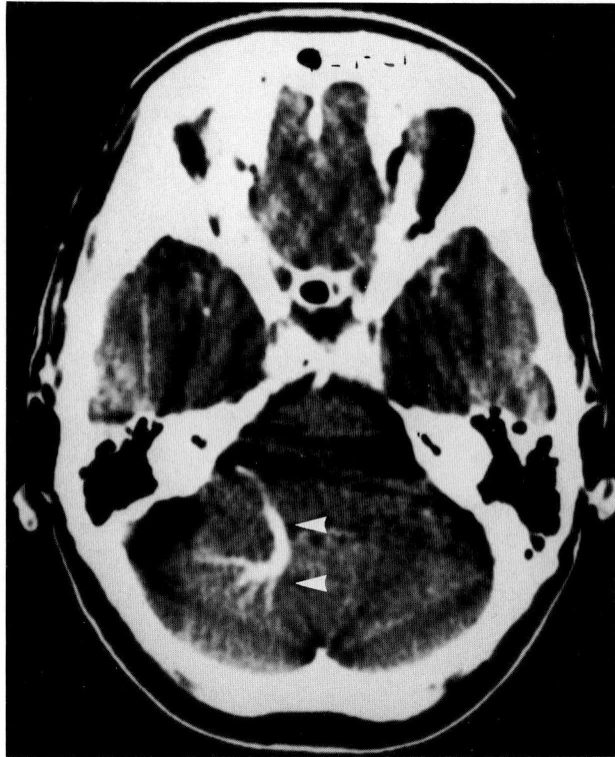

A

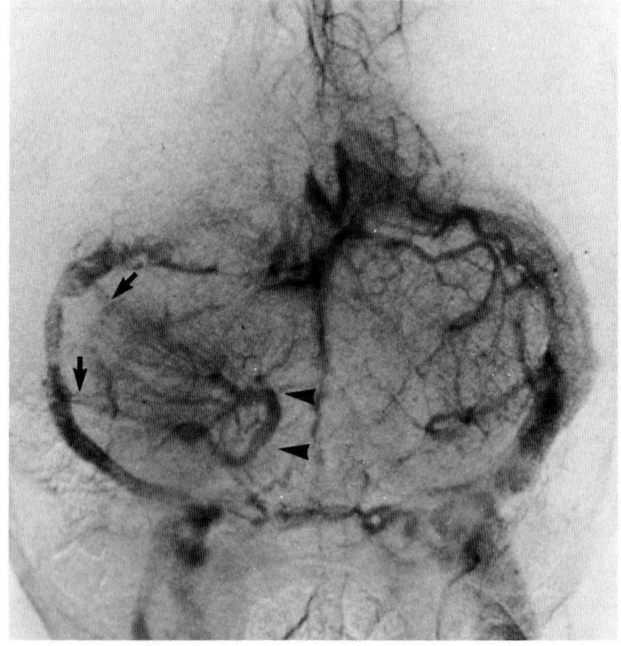

B

Figure 14-28 Developmental venous anomaly of the posterior fossa. **A.** CECT shows linear enhancement with an umbrella-type pattern toward the deep cerebellar hemisphere (arrowheads). **B.** Venous phase angiogram reveals a dominant deep venous drainage pattern (arrowheads), while the superficial cortical veins are poorly developed (arrows).

angiomas on CECT show a rounded, linear, or stellate area of enhancement that is not associated with mass effect or surrounding edema (Figs. 14-27 and 14-28) (Michels 1977; Fierstein 1979). Dynamic rapid-sequence CT scanning can be a suitable method for the evaluation of venous angioma (Lotz 1983). MRI is ideal imaging modality in demonstrating venous angiomas. It usually has a stellate pattern of hypointense signal in both T_1 and T_2WI due to the increased venous flow, often located within the brain parenchyma (Fig. 14-29). There is usually no mass effect, unless associated with bleeding without mass effect (Olson 1984; Scott 1985; Lee 1985; Augustin 1985; Cammarata 1985; Fontaine 1987; Biondi 1988*b*).

A variant of venous malformation is encephalofacial angiomatosis of *Sturge-Weber disease*. This rare condition is characterized by the association of an extensive capil-

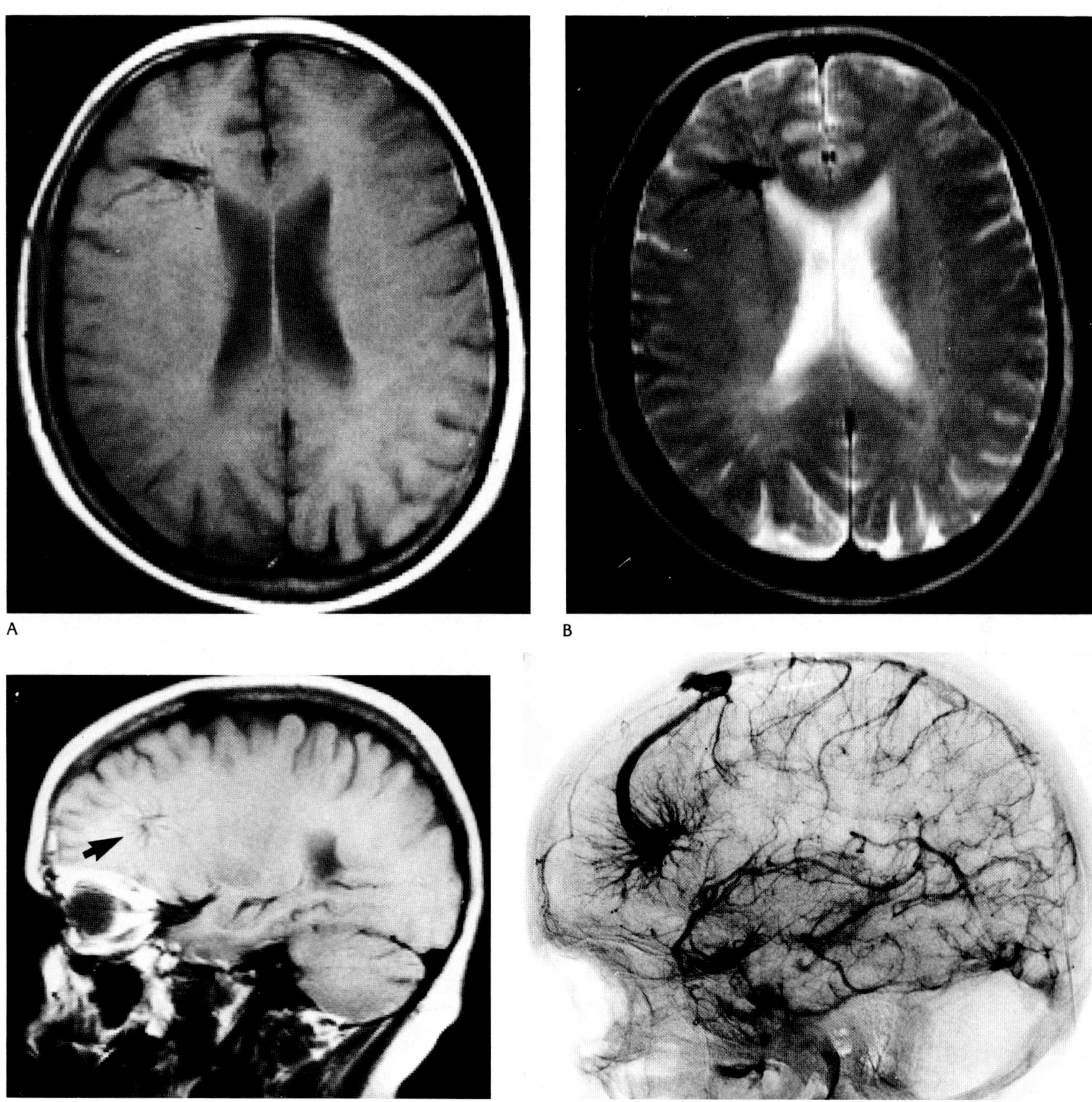

Figure 14-29 Venous angioma. Stellate hypointense (flow void) signal lesion in the right frontal lobe in (**A**) axial, (**B**) T_2WI axial MR studies, and (**C**) sagittal T_1WI. CT not shown demonstrated an enhancing lesion in this area. (**D**) Sagittal venous phase of the angiogram demonstrating the typical confluence of venous channels draining into a large cortical vein.

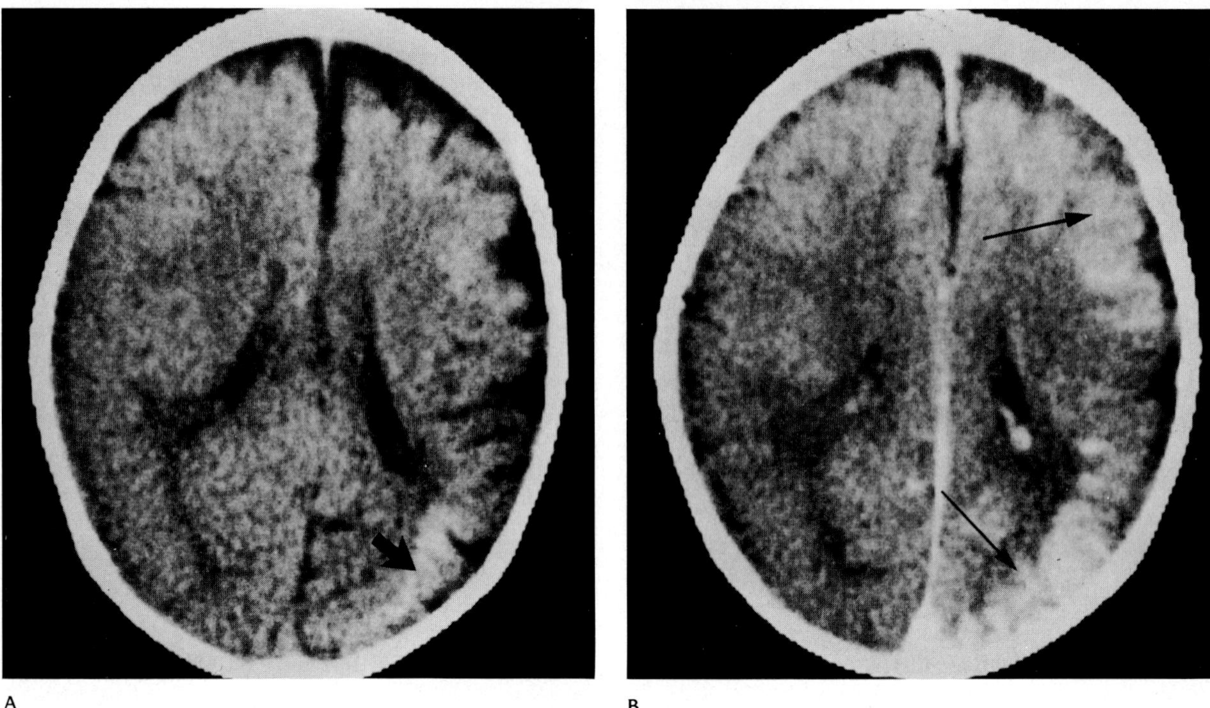

Figure 14-30 Sturge-Weber syndrome. **A.** NCCT shows cortical atrophy with calcification along the cortex (arrow) in a 1-year-old child. **B.** Enhancement after contrast infusion along the cortex of the left frontal and parietal lobes (arrow). (*Courtesy of Dr. D. Harwood-Nash, Toronto Hospital for Sick Children.*)

lary venous malformation that affects the leptomeninges of one cerebral hemisphere with a homolateral cutaneous nevus or port-wine stain in the trigeminal nerve distribution, together with contralateral hemiparesis and Jacksonian epilepsy. Plain skull films may show characteristic "tram line" calcification along the cortical gyri. The affected brain is atrophied, and the overlying leptomeninges are thickened. The angiogram shows a decrease in the number of, or a complete absence of, cortical superficial veins and enlargement of the deep cerebral venous system (Bentson 1971). On NCCT there is cortical atrophy with superficial cortical calcification (Welch 1980). Enhancement of the involved cortex occurs after contrast infusion (Fig. 14-30). The ipsilateral cranial vault is thickened, and the hemicranium is most often smaller than the normal opposite side. Ipsilateral enlargement of the hemicranium is uncommon (Enzmann 1977).

CT, MRI, and angiography are complementary in the evaluation and follow-up of patients with intracranial vascular malformations. Because of its accuracy and efficiency, CT is often the modality of choice in the acute situation. MRI is probably the preferred modality in the follow-up of vascular malformations. Angiography remains the gold standard in treatment planning for cerebral and dural AVMs, while its role with regard to cavernomas and developmental venous anomalies has been reduced to confirming a diagnosis already suspected on the basis of CT and MRI.

References

AALMAANI WS, RICHARDSON AE: Multiple intracranial aneurysms: Identifying the ruptured lesion. *Surg Neurol* 9:303–305, 1978.

ADAMS HP, KASSELL MF, TORNER JC, et al: CT and clinical correlation in recent aneurysmal subarachnoid hemorrhage: A preliminary report of the cooperative aneurysm study. *Neurology* 33:981–988, 1983.

AHMADI J, MILLER CA, SEGALL HD, et al: CT patterns in histologically complex cavernous hemangiomas. *AJNR* 6:389–393, 1985.

ALVAREZ O, HYMAN RA: Even echo MR rephasing in diagnosis of giant intracranial aneurysm. *J Comput Assist Tomogr* 10(4):699–701, 1986.

ASSENCIO-FERREIRA VJ, et al: Computed tomography in ataxia-telangiectasia. *J Comput Assist Tomogr* 5(5):660–661, 1981.

ATLAS SW, GROSSMAN RI, GOLDBERG HI, et al: Partially thrombosed giant intracranial aneurysms: Correlation of MR and pathologic findings. *Radiology* 162:111–114, 1987.

AUGUSTIN GT, SCOTT JA, OLSON E, et al: Cerebral venous angiomas: MR imaging. *Radiology* 156:391–395, 1985.

BABU VS, EISEN H: Giant aneurysm of anterior communicating artery simulating third ventricular tumour. *Comput Tomogr* 3:159–163, 1979.

BARTLETT JE, KISHORE PRS: Intracranial cavernous angioma. *Am J Roentgenol Radium Ther Nucl Med* 128:653–656, 1977.

BELL BA, KENDALL BE, SYMON L: Angiographically occult A-V malformations of the brain. *J Neurol Neurosurg Psychiatry* 41:1057–1064, 1978.

BENTSON JR, WILSON GH, NEWTON TH: Cerebral venous drainage pattern of Sturge-Weber syndrome. *Radiology* 101:111–118, 1971.

BIONDI A, SCIALFA G, SCOTTI G: Intracranial aneurysms: MR imaging. *Neuroradiology* 30:214–318, 1988*a*.

BIONDI A, SCIALFA G: Morphological and blood flow MR findings in cerebral vascular malformations. *J Neuroradiol* 15:253–265, 1988*b*.

BJORKESTEN G, HALONEN V: Incidence of intracranial vascular lesions in patients with subarachnoid hemorrhage investigated by four-vessel angiography. *J Neurosurg* 23:29–32, 1965.

BRITT RH, SILVERBERG GD, ENZMANN DR, et al: Third ventricular choroid plexus arteriovenous malformation simulating a colloid cyst. *J Neurosurg* 52:246–250, 1980.

BROWN RD, WIEBERS DO, FORBES G, et al: The natural history of unruptured intracranial arteriovenous malformations. *J Neurosurg* 68:352–357, 1988.

BRUNELLE FOS, HARWOOD-NASH DCF, FITZ CR, et al: Intracranial vascular malformations in children: Computed tomographic and angiographic evaluation. *Radiology* 149:455–461, 1983.

BULL JWD: Massive aneurysm at the base of the brain. *Brain* 92:535–570, 1969.

BYRD SE, BENTSON JR, WINTER J, et al: Giant intracranial aneurysms simulating brain neoplasms on computed tomography. *J Comput Assist Tomogr* 2:303–307, 1978.

CAMMARATA C, HAN JS, HAAGA JR, et al: Cerebral venous angiomas imaged by MR. *Radiology* 155:639–643, 1985.

CHAKERAS DW, NICK BR: Acute subarachnoid hemorrhage: In vitro comparison of magnetic resonance and computed tomography. *AJNR* 7:223–228, 1986.

CHASON JL, HINDMAN WM: Berry aneurysms of the circle of Willis: Results of a planned autopsy study. *Neurology* 8:41–44, 1958.

CHIN D, HARPER C: Angiographically occult cerebral vascular malformations with abnormal computed tomography. *Surg Neurol* 20(2):138–142, 1983.

CONE JD, MARAVILLA KR, COOPER PR, et al: Computed tomography findings in ruptured arteriovenus malformation of corpus callosum. *J Comput Assist Tomogr* 3:478–482, 1979.

CRAWFORD T: Some observations on the pathogenesis and natural history of intracranial aneurysm. *J Neurol Neurosurg Psychiatry* 22:259–266, 1959.

CRAWFORD PM, WEST CR, CHADWICK DW, et al: Arteriovenous malformations of the brain: Natural history in unoperated patients. *J Neurol Neurosurg Psychiatry* 49:1–10, 1986.

CROMPTON MR: Mechanism of growth and rupture in cerebral berry aneurysm. *Br Med J* 1:1138–1142, 1966.

DANIELS DL, HAUGHTON WM, WILLIAMS AL, et al: Arteriovenous malformation simulating a cyst on computed tomography. *Radiology* 133:393–394, 1979.

DAVIS JM, DAVIS KR, CROWELL RM: Subarachnoid hemorrhage secondary to ruptured intracranial aneurysm: Prognostic significance of cranial CT. *AJNR* 1:17–21, 1980.

DEEB ZL, JANETTA PJ, ROSENBAUM AE, et al: Tortuous vertebro-basilar arteries causing cranial nerve syndromes: Screening by computed tomography. *J Comput Assist Tomogr* 3:774–778, 1979.

DEMARCO JK, DILLON WP, HALBACH VV, et al: Dural arteriovenous fistulas: Evaluation with MR imaging. *Radiology* 175:193–199, 1990.

DIEBLER C, DULAC O, RENIER D, et al: Aneurysms of the vein of Galen in infants aged 2 to 15 months: Diagnosis and natural evolution. *Neuroradiology* 21:185–197, 1981.

DUBOULAY GH: Some observations on the natural history of intracranial aneurysms. *Br J Radiol* 38:721–757, 1965.

EDELMAN RR, WENTZ KU, MATTLE HP, et al: Intracerebral arteriovenous malformations: Evaluation and selective MR angiography and venography. *Radiology* 173:831–837, 1989.

ENZMANN DR, HAYWARD RW, NORMAN D, et al: Cranial computed tomographic scan appearance of Sturge-Weber disease: Unusual presentation. *Radiology* 122:721–724, 1977.

FIERSTEIN SB, PRIBRAM HW, HIESHIMA G: Angiography and computed tomography in the evaluation of cerebral venous malformations. *Neuroradiology* 52:246–250, 1979.

FISHER CM, KISTLER JP, DAVIS JM: Relation of cerebral vasospasm to subarachnoid hemorrhage visualized by computed tomography scanning. *Neurosurgery* 6:1–9, 1980.

FONTAINE S, DE LA SAYETTE V, GIANFELICE D, et al: CT, MRI and angiography of venous angiomas: A comparative study. *J Can Assoc Radiol* 38:259–263, 1987.

GHOSHHAJRA K, SCOTTI L, MARASCO J, et al: CT detection of intracranial aneurysms in subarachnoid hemorrhage. *Am J Roentgenol Radium Ther Nucl Med* 132:613–616, 1979.

GOLDEN JB, KRAMER RA: The angiographically occult cerebrovascular malformation. *J Neurosurg* 48:292–296, 1978.

GOMORI JM, GROSSMAN RI, GOLDBERG HI, et al: Occult cerebral vascular malformations: High-field MR imaging. *Radiology* 158:707–713, 1986.

GRIFFIN C, DELAPAZ R, ENZMANN D: Magnetic resonance appearance of slow flow vascular malformations of the brainstem. *Neuroradiology* 29:506–511, 1987.

HACKNEY DB, LESNICK JE, ZIMMERMAN RA, et al: MR identification of bleeding site in subarachnoid hemorrhage with multiple intracranial aneurysms. *J Comput Assist Tomogr* 10(5):878–880, 1986.

HAHN FJ, ONG E, MCCOMB R, et al: Peripheral signal void ring in giant vertebral aneurysm: MR and pathology findings. *J Comput Assist Tomogr* 10(6):1036–1038, 1986.

HANDA J, NAKANO Y, AII J, et ak Computed tomography with giant intracranial aneurysms. *Surg Neurol* 9:257–263, 1978.

HAYMAN LA, FOX AJ, EVANS RA: Effectiveness of contrast regimens in CT detection of vascular malformations of the brain. *AJNR* 2:421–425, 1981.

HAYWARD RD: Intracranial arteriovenous malformations. *J Neurol Neurosurg Psychiatry* 39:1027–1033, 1976.

HAYWARD RD, O'REILLY GVA: Intracerebral hemorrhage. *Lancet* i:1–4, 1977.

HOUSEPIAN EM, POOL JL: A systemic analysis of intracranial aneurysms from the autopsy file of the Presbyterian Hospital, 1914–1956. *J Neuropathol Exp Neurol* 17:409–423, 1958.

IMAKITA S, NISHIMURI T, YAMADA N, et al: Cerebral vascular malformations: Applications of magnetic resonance imaging to differential diagnosis. *Neuroradiology* 31:320–325, 1989.

ISHIKAWA M, et al: Computed tomography of cerebral cavernous hemangiomas. *J Comput Assist Tomogr* 4(5):587–591, 1980.

ITO J, SATO I, TANIMURA K: Angiographic and computed tomography findings of a convexity cavernous hemangioma. *Jpn J Clin Radiol* 23:204–205, 1978.

JIMENEZ JL, LASJAUNIAS P, TERBRUGGE K, et al: The trans-cerebral veins: Normal and nonpathologic angiographic aspects. *Surg Radiol Anat* 11:63–72, 1989.

KAYAMA T, SUZUKI S, SAKURAI Y, et al: A case of moya-moya disease accompanied by an arteriovenous malformation. *Neurosurgery* 18:464–468, 1986.

KELLER PJ, DRAYER BP, FRAM EK, et al: MR angiography with two-dimensional acquisition and three dimensional display. *Radiology* 173:527–532, 1989.

KENDALL BE, CLAVERIA LE: The use of computed axial tomography for the diagnosis and management of intracranial angiomas. *Neuroradiology* 12:141–160, 1976*a*.

KENDALL BE, LEE BCP, CLAVERIA E: Computerized tomography and angiography in subarachnoid hemorrhage. *Br J Radiol* 49:483–501, 1976*b*.

KRAMER RA, WING SD: Computed tomography of angiographically occult cerebral vascular malformations. *Radiology* 123:649–652, 1977.

KUCHARCZYK W, LEMME-PLAGHOS L, USKE A, et al: Intracranial vascular malformations: MR and CT imaging. *Radiology* 156:383–389, 1985.

KUMAR AJ, FOX AJ, VINUELA F, et al: Revisited old and new CT findings in unruptured larger arteriovenous malformations of the brain. *J Comput Assist Tomogr* 8(4):648–655, 1984.

KUMAR AJ, VINUELA F, FOX AJ, et al: Unruptured intracranial arteriovenous malformations do cause mass effect. *AJNR* 6(1):29–32, 1985.

LASJAUNIAS P, TERBRUGGE K, CHIU M: A coaxial balloon-catheter device for endovascular treatment of newborns and infants. *Radiology* 159:269–271, 1986*a*.

LASJAUNIAS P, CHIU M, TERBRUGGE K, et al: Spontaneous intracranial dural arteriovenous malformations (D AVM): Neurological manifestations. *J Neurosurg* 64:724–730, 1986*b*.

LASJAUNIAS P, BURROWS P, PLANET C: Developmental venous anomalies (DVA): The so-called venous angioma. *Neurosurg Rev* 9:233–244, 1986*c*.

LASJAUNIAS P, TERBRUGGE K, LOPEZ IBOR L, et al: The role of dural anomalies in vein of Galen aneurysms: Report of six cases and review of the literature. *AJNR* 8:185–192, 1987*a*.

LASJAUNIAS P, TERBRUGGE K, PISKE R, et al: Dilatation de la veine de galien formes anatomo-cliniques et traitement endovasculaire a propos de 14 cas explores et/ou traites entre 1983 et 1986. *Neurochirurgie* 33:315–333, 1987*b*.

LASJAUNIAS P, BERENSTEIN A: Endovascular treatment of craniofacial lesions. *Surg Neuroangiog* 2:273–313, 1987*c*.

LASJAUNIAS P, RODESCH G, TERBRUGGE K, et al: Vein of Galen aneurysmal malformations: Report of 36 cases managed between 1982 and 1988. *Acta Neurochir (Wien)* 99:26–37, 1989.

LEBLANC R, ETHIER R, LITTLE JR: Computerized tomography findings in arteriovenous malformations of the brain. *J Neurosurg* 51:765–772, 1979.

LEBLANC R, ETHIER R: The CT appearance of angiographically occult arterio-venous malformation of the brain. *Can J Neurosci* 8:7–13, 1981.

LEBLANC R, LEVESQUE M, COMAIR Y, et al: Magnetic resonance imaging of cerebral arteriovenous malformations. *Neurosurgery* 21:15–20, 1987.

LEE BCP, HERZBERG L, ZIMMERMAN RD, et al: MR imaging of cerebral vascular malformations. *AJNR* 6:863–870, 1985.

LEMME-PLAGHOS L, KUCHARCZYK W, BRANT-ZAWADZKI M, et al: MR imaging of angiographically occult vascular malformation. *AJNR* 7:217–222, 1986.

LICHTOR T, MULLAN S: Arteriovenous malformation in moyamoya syndrome: Report of three cases. *J Neurosurg* 67:603–608, 1987.

LILIEQUIST B, LINDQUIST M, VALDIMARSSON E: Computed tomography and subarachnoid hemorrhage. *Neuroradiology* 14:21–26, 1977.

LIM ST, SAGE DJ: Detection of subarachnoid blood clot and other thin flat structures by computed tomography. *Radiology* 123:79–84, 1977.

LOBATO RD, PEREZ C, RIVAS JJ, et al: Clinical, radiological, and pathological spectrum of angiographically occult intracranial vascular malformations. *J Neurosurg* 68:518–531, 1988.

LOCKSLEY HB: Report on the cooperative study of intracranial aneurysms and subarachnoid hemorrhage. *J Neurosurg* 25:219–239, 1966.

LOTZ PR, QUISLING RG: CT of venous angiomas of the brain. *AJNR* 4:1124–1126, 1983.

LUKIN RR, CHABERS AA, MCLAURIN R, et al: Thrombosed giant middle cerebral aneurysms. *Neuroradiology* 10:125–129, 1975.

MACPHERSON P, TEASDALE GM, LINDSAY KW: Computed tomography in diagnosis and management of aneurysm of the vein of Galen. *J Neurol Neurosurg Psychiatry* 42:786–789, 1979.

MARKS MP, DELAPAZ RL, FABRIKANT JI, et al: Intracranial vascular malformations: Imaging of charged-particle radiosurgery. *Radiology* 168:447–455, 1988.

MASARYK TJ, MODIC MT, ROSS JS, et al: Intracranial circulation: Preliminary clinical results with three-dimensional (volume) MR angiography. *Radiology* 171:793–799, 1989.

MAWAD ME, HILAL SK, MICHELSEN WJ, et al: Occlusive vascular disease associated with cerebral arteriovenous malformations. *Radiology* 153:301–408, 1984.

MCKISSOCK W, RICHARDSON A, WALSH L, et al: Multiple intracranial aneurysms. *Lancet* i:623–626, 1964.

MICHELS LG, BEAVERSON JR, WINTER J: Computed tomography of cerebral venous angiomas. *J Comput Assist Tomogr* 1:149–154, 1977.

MODESTI LM, BINET EF: Value of computed tomography in the diagnosis and management of subarachnoid hemorrhage. *Neurosurgery* 3:151–156, 1978.

MONTANERA W, MAROTTA TR, TERBRUGGE KG, et al: Cerebral arteriovenous malformations associated with moya-moya phenomenon. *AJNR* 11:1153–1156, 1990.

MORLEY TP, BARR HWK: Giant intracranial aneurysms: Diagnosis, course and management. *Clin Neurosurg* 16:73–94, 1969.

NADJMI M, RATZKA M, WODARZ M: Giant aneurysms in CT and angiography. *Neuroradiology* 16:284–286, 1978.

NEHLS DG, FLOM RA, CARTER LP, et al: Multiple intracranial aneurysms: Determining the site of rupture: *J Neurosurg* 63:342–348, 1985.

NEW PFJ, SCOTT WR: *Computed Tomography of the Brain and Orbit (EMI Scanning)*, Baltimore, Williams & Wilkins, 1975.

NEW PJ, OJEMANN RG, DAVIS KR, et al: MR and CT of occult vascular malformations of the brain. *AJNR* 7:771–779, 1986.

NOORBEHESHT B, FABRIKANT JI, ENZMANN DR: Size determination of supratentorial arteriovenous malformations by MR, CT and angio. *Neuroradiology* 29:512–518, 1987.

NUMAGUCHI Y, KISHIKAWA T, FUKUI M, et al: Prolonged injection angiography for diagnosis of intracranial cavernous hemangiomas. *Radiology* 131:137–138, 1979.

NYSTROM SHM: Development of intracranial aneurysms as revealed by electron microscopy. *J Neurosurg* 20:329–337, 1963.

OLSEN WL, BRANT-ZAWADZKI M, HODES J, et al: Giant intracranial aneurysms: MR imaging. *Radiology* 163:431–435, 1987.

OLSON E, GILMOR RL, RICHMOND B: Cerebral venous angiomas. *Radiology* 151:97–104, 1984.

OSBORN AG, ANDERSON RE, WING SD: The false falx sign. *Radiology* 134:421–425, 1980.

PERRETT LV, SAGE MR: Computerized tomography and giant intracranial aneurysms. *Aust Radiol* 21:308–312, 1977.

PETERSON NT, DUCHESNEAU PM, WESTBROOK EL, et al: Basilar artery ectasia demonstrated by computed tomography. *Radiology* 122:713–715, 1977.

PINTO RS, KRICHEFF II, BUTLER AR, et al: Correlation of computed tomographic angiographic and neuropathological changes in giant cerebral aneurysms. *Radiology* 132:85–92, 1979.

POSER CM, TAVERAS JM: Cerebral angiography in encephalotrigeminal angiomatosis. *Radiology* 68:327–336, 1957.

PRESSMAN BD, KIRKWOOD JR, DAVIS DO: Computerized transverse tomography of vascular lesions of the brain: I. Arteriovenous malformations. *Am J Roentgenol Radium Ther Nucl Med* 124:208–215, 1975*a*.

PRESSMAN BD, GILBERT GE, DAVIS DO: Computerized transverse tomography of vascular lesions of the brain: II. Aneurysms. *Am J Roentgenol Radium Ther Nucl Med* 124:215–219, 1975*b*.

RAMINA R, INGUNZA W, VONOFAKOS D: Cystic cerebral cavernous angioma with dense calcification. *J Neurosurg* 52: 259–262, 1980.

RAPACKI TFX, BRANTLEY MJ, FURLOW TW, et al: Heterogeneity of cerebral cavernous hemangiomas diagnosed by MR imaging. *J Comput Assist Tomogr* 14(1):18–25, 1990.

RENGACHARY SS, SZYMANSKI DC: Subdural hematomas of arterial origin. *Neurosurgery* 8(2):166–172, 1981.

RICHMOND T, VIRAPONGSE C, SARWAR M, et al: Intraparenchymal blood fluid levels: New CT sign of arteriovenous malformation: rupture. *AJNR* 2:577–579, 1981.

RIGAMONTI D, DRAYER BP, JOHNSON PC, et al: The MRI appearance of cavernous malformations (angiomas). *J Neurosurg* 67:518–524, 1987.

RIGAMONTI D, HADLEY MN, DRAYER BP, et al: Cerebral cavernous malformations: Incidence and familial occurrence. *N Engl J Med* 319:343–347, 1988.

ROBERSON GH, KASE CS, WOLPOW ER: Telangiectases and cavernous angiomas of the brain stem: "Cryptic" vascular malformations. *Neuroradiology* 8:83–89, 1974.

ROTHFUS WE, ALBRIGHT AL, CASEY EF, et al: Cerebellar venous angioma: "Benign" entity? *AJNR* 5:61–66, 1984.

RUGGIERI PM, LAUB GA, MASARYK TJ, et al: Intracranial circulation: Pulse-sequence considerations in three-dimensional (volume) MR angiography. *Radiology* 171:785–791, 1989.

RUSSELL DS, RUBINSTEIN LJ: *Pathology of Tumours of the Nervous System,* 4th ed, Edinburgh, E. Arnold, 1977.

SAITO I, SHIGENU T, ARITAKE K, et al: Vasospasm assessed by angiography and computerized tomography. *J Neurosurg* 51:466–475, 1979.

SAITO Y, KOBAYASHI N: Cerebral venous angiomas: Clinical evaluation and possible etiology. *Radiology* 139:87–94, 1981.

SARTOR K: Spontaneous closure of cerebral arteriovenous malformation demonstrated by angiography and computed tomography. *Neuroradiology* 15:95–98, 1978.

SARWAR M, BATNITZKY S, SCHECHTER MM: Tumorous aneurysm. *Neuroradiology* 12:79–97, 1976*a*.

SARWAR M, BATNITZKY S, SCHECHTER MM, et al: Growing intracranial aneurysms. *Radiology* 120:603–607, 1976*b*.

SATOH S, KADOYA S: Magnetic resonance imaging of subarachnoid hemorrhage. *Neuroradiology* 30:361–366, 1988.

SAVOIARDO M, STRADA L, PASSERINI A: Intracranial cavernous hemangiomas: Neuroradiologic review of 36 operated cases. *AJNR* 4:945–950, 1983.

SCHUBIGER O, VALAVANIS A, HAYEK J: Computed tomography in cerebral aneurysms with special emphasis on giant intracranial aneurysms. *J Comput Assist Tomogr* 4:24–32, 1980.

SCOTT JA, AUGUSTYN GT, GILMOR RL, et al: Magnetic resonance imaging of a venous angioma. *AJNR* 6:284–286, 1985.

SCOTTI G, ETHIER R, MELANCON D, et al: Computed tomography in the evaluation of intracranial aneurysms and subarachnoid hemorrhage. *Radiology* 123:85–90, 1977.

SCOTTI G, DEGRAND C, COLOMBO A: Ectasis of the intracranial arteries diagnosed by computed tomography. *Neuroradiology* 15:183–184, 1978.

SMITH HJ, STROTHER CM, KIKUCHI Y, et al: MR imaging in the management of supratentorial intracranial AVMs. *AJNR* 9: 225–235, 1988.

SMOKER WRK, CORBETT JJ, GENTRY LR, et al: High-resolution CT of the basilar artery: Vertebrobasilar dolichoectasia: Clinicopathologic correlation and review. *AJNR* 7:61–72, 1986.

SOBEL D, NORMAN D: CNS manifestations of hereditary hemorrhagic telangiectasia. *AJNR* 5(5):569–573, 1984.

SOLIS OJ, DAVIS KR, ELLIS GT: Dural arteriovenous malformation associated with subdural and intracerebral hematoma: A CT scan and angiographic correlation. *Comput Tomogr* 1:145–150, 1977.

SPALLINE A: Computed tomography in aneurysms of the vein of Galen. *J Comput Assist Tomogr* 3:779–782, 1979.

STEHBENS WE: Etiology of intracranial berry aneurysms. *J Neurosurg* 70:823–831, 1989.

SZE G, KROL G, OLSEN WL, et al: Hemorrhagic neoplasms: MR mimics of occult vascular malformations. *AJNR* 8:795–802, 1987.

TERACO H, HOZI T, MATSUTANI M, et al: Detection of cryptic vascular malformation by computerized tomography. *J Neurosurg* 51:546–551, 1979.

TERBRUGGE KG, SCOTTI G, ETHIER R, et al: Computed tomography in intracranial arteriovenous malformations. *Radiology* 122:703–705, 1977.

THRON A, BOCKENHEIMER S: Giant aneurysms of the posterior fossa suspected as neoplasms on computed tomography. *Neuroradiology* 18:93–97, 1979.

TSURUDA JS, HALBACH VV, HIGASHIDA RT, et al: MR evaluation of large intracranial aneurysms using cine low flip angle gradient-refocused imaging. *AJR* 151:153–162, 1988.

VALAVANIS A, WELLAUER J, YASARGIL MG: The radiological diagnosis of cerebral venous angioma: Cerebral angiography and computed tomography. *Neuroradiology* 24:193–199, 1983.

VALAVANIS A, SCHUBINGER D, WICHMANN W: Classification of brain arteriovenous malformation nidus by magnetic resonance imaging. *Acta Radiol* 369:86–89, 1986.

WAKAI S, UEDA Y, INOH S, et al: Angiographically occult angiomas: A report of thirteen cases with an analysis of the cases documented in the literature. *Neurosurgery* 17:549–556, 1985.

WEIR B, MILLER J, RUSSELL D: Intracranial aneurysms: A clinical, angiographic and computerized tomographic study. *Can J Neurol Sci* 4:99–105, 1977.

WEISBERG LA, NICE C, KATZ M: *Cerebral Computed Tomography: A Text-Like Atlas,* Philadelphia, Saunders, 1978.

WEISBERG L: Direct visualization of intracranial aneurysms by computed tomography. *J Comput Assist Tomogr* 5:191–199, 1981.

WELCH K, NAHEEDY MH, ABROMS IF, et al: Computed tomography of Sturge-Weber syndrome in infants. *J Comput Assist Tomogr* 4:33–36, 1980.

WENDLING LR, MOORE JS, KIEFFER SA, et al: Intracerebral venous angioma. *Radiology* 119:141–147, 1976.

WILLINSKY R, LASJAUNIAS P, TERBRUGGE K, et al: Brain arteriovenous malformations: Analysis of angio-architecture in relationship to hemorrhage. *J Neuroradiol* 15:225–237, 1988*a*.

WILLINSKY R, LASJAUNIAS P, COMOY J, et al: Cerebral microarteriovenous malformations (mAVMs). *Acta Neurochir (Wien)* 91:37–41, 1988*b*.

WILLINSKY RA, TERBRUGGE KG, LASJAUNIAS P: Cerebral vascular malformations: A clinical-morphological analysis. *Can J Neurol Sci* 1991 (in press).

WORTHINGTON BS, KEAN DM, HAWKES RC, et al: NMR imaging in the recognition of giant intracranial aneurysms. *AJNR* 4:835–836, 1983.

WYBURN-MASON R: *The Vascular Abnormalities and Tumours of the Spinal Cord and Its Membranes,* London, Kingston, 1943.

YEATES A, ENZMANN D: Cryptic vascular malformations involving the brainstem. *Radiology* 146:71–75, 1983.

YOCK DH, LARSON DA: Computed tomography of hemorrhage from anterior communicating artery aneurysms, with angiographic correlation. *Radiology* 1234:399–407, 1980.

ZIMMERMAN RD, YURBERG E, LEEDS NE: The falx and interhemispheric fissure on axial computed tomography: I. Normal anatomy. *AJNR* 3:175–180, 1982.

15 STROKE

Herbert I. Goldberg
S. Howard Lee

Stroke is the third leading cause of death in the United States, exceeded only by heart disease and cancer (*Report to the President* 1964–65). It kills over 200,000 people a year in this country (Kurtzke 1980) and affects close to 400,000 (Whisnant 1971). The incidence rate and death rate from stroke increase dramatically with age (Eisenberg 1964). About 15 to 35 percent of patients die with each episode of cerebral infarction (Eisenberg 1964; Matsumoto 1973); a much higher mortality—60 to 80 percent—occurs with cerebral hemorrhage (Whisnant 1971). Those who survive are usually left with permanent disability. With the increasing mean age in this country, stroke will become an even greater medical and social problem. Accurate and early diagnosis may improve the morbidity and mortality rates in the future as newer and more effective therapies are instituted.

The advent of computed tomography (CT) in the early 1970s greatly facilitated the diagnosis and management of stroke and added significantly to our understanding of the pathophysiological brain alterations it causes in humans. With CT, it became possible for the first time to noninvasively and reliably diagnose and distinguish between stroke caused by cerebral infarction and stroke caused by cerebral hemorrhage. In addition, other brain lesions that could present clinically as strokelike syndromes, such as primary or metastatic brain tumor, brain abscess, and subdural hematoma, could usually be clearly differentiated by CT examination. In most instances it was no longer necessary to perform cerebral angiography to exclude a possible surgical lesion in patients in whom the clinical diagnosis of stroke was in doubt.

Despite the introduction of MR imaging in 1984 and its many recent advances, CT continues to be the initial imaging modality for acute stroke patients. The major consideration for obtaining a brain imaging examination in a patient with an acute stroke is to evaluate for an intracerebral hemorrhage that CT can detect with great sensitivity and specificity. With MRI, while acute hemorrhage can be readily demonstrated with T_2-weighted images (T_2WI) on high-field-strength units and with susceptibility-weighted gradient-echo images at almost all field strengths, the employment of MR for the initial evaluation of stroke patients is frequently limited. MRI demands much greater patient cooperation than does CT because of its longer imaging times. This is not always possible with acute stroke patients, who are frequently confused and uncooperative. In addition, acute stroke patients frequently require critical monitoring with equipment that is usually incompatible with MRI. In addition, MRI is not as universally available as CT within acute care facilities. In certain situations in which the patient's clinical condition cannot be fully explained by CT, MRI may be of great value. MRI can more readily detect small amounts of petechial hemorrhage and is more definitive in the evaluation and detection of venous sinus occlusion. MR is also much more sensitive and accurate in the detection of brainstem and cerebellar infarctions.

The high spatial and contrast resolution capabilities of both CT and MRI allow accurate identification and localization of cerebral infarction in its acute and chronic phases. Ischemic infarction, hemorrhagic infarction, and intracerebral hemorrhage are usually readily distinguished. MRI, however, has a higher sensitivity for detecting brain edema of ischemic infarction as well as the presence of small amounts of blood products associated with hemorrhagic infarction and intracerebral hematoma and can more readily determine the relative age of these events than CT can.

In the evaluation of stroke, additional and frequently valuable information may be gained when scans are performed both before and after the intravenous administration of contrast material. Contrast enhancement greatly aids in the recognition of other types of brain lesions that may present clinically as stroke. Up to 13 percent of infarcts on CT become visible only after contrast enhancement (Masdeu 1977; Wing 1976). Although the underlying nature of the vascular pathology causing an infarction is usually not directly demonstrated on CT or MRI, distinguishing pathophysiological alterations frequently will be evident with contrast enhancement, which, in combination with the alterations evident on the non-contrast-enhanced images, will suggest the correct etiology for the infarction; this may be important in patient management. The infarction could be related to a primary intracerebral large vessel occlusion, an embolus to a major cerebral artery, or a perfusional deficit in a watershed region of the brain from a transitory hemodynamic event or from small penetrating artery occlusive disease. In this differentiation, follow-up noncontrast and contrast-enhanced scans are frequently valuable during the first 2 to 3 weeks, as distinctive differences in the temporal evolution of these conditions may be revealed. The differentiation of these varieties of infarction has important therapeutic implications.

Besides diagnosing large artery, atherosclerotic, and embolic occlusive disease, CT and MR may reveal alterations that suggest the involvement of smaller arteries and other etiologies for a stroke. Hypertensive vascular disease, which primarily affects small penetrating arteries (arteriolosclerosis), usually shows ischemic change in the deep gray masses and the periventricular white matter. In some cases of primary and secondary arteritis, the imaging patterns of ischemia, in conjunction with other imaging alterations and the patient's age, sex, and clinical history, will suggest the correct diagnosis. Cerebral sinovenous thrombosis frequently demonstrates unique CT and MRI changes.

Although intracerebral hematomas all appear relatively similar on CT and MRI regardless of etiology, their various causes may be suggested by the location of the hemorrhage and associated changes that may be revealed on pre- or postcontrast scans. This frequently permits differentiation of hematomas caused by hypertension, trauma, tumor, venous thrombosis, arteriovenous malformation, and aneurysm.

Stroke may be classified as being caused by decreased circulation to the brain (infarction) or by intracerebral hemorrhage. The former produces brain injury from ischemic necrosis, while the latter causes brain damage by compression necrosis and vascular disruption. The incidence of the major causes of stroke, based on a communitywide survey of diagnoses in Rochester, Minnesota, during the years 1955–1969, before the introduction of CT, was as follows: cerebral infarction, 79 percent, with embolism representing 8 percent of this group; intracerebral hemorrhage, 10 percent; subarachnoid hemorrhage, 6 percent; and ill-defined causes, 5 percent (Matsumoto 1973). Utilizing CT, Kinkel (1976) found a much higher incidence of intracerebral hemorrhage as a cause of supratentorial stroke (26 percent). In this series, a large percentage of cases were clinically misdiagnosed as to the type of stroke. Forty-three percent with cerebral hemorrhage were clinically thought to have cerebral infarction, and 14 percent with cerebral infarction were diagnosed as having cerebral hemorrhage. A clinical survey by Mohr (1980), using the records of the Harvard Cooperative Stroke Registry, in which all appropriate laboratory aids were employed, including CT, four-vessel cerebral angiography, and CSF examination, found that cerebral embolism accounted for 31 percent of all strokes, atherosclerotic thrombosis accounted for 33 percent, and lacunar infarcts accounted for 18 percent. Hypertensive intracerebral hemorrhage caused 11 percent of the strokes, and hemorrhage from ruptured aneurysm and vascular malformation caused 7 percent. The high incidence of cerebral embolism (31 percent) in this clinical series is in agreement with an autopsy study of Fisher and Adams (1951) (Mohr 1980), in which cerebral embolism was found to cause 32 percent of the strokes.

Transient ischemic attacks (TIAs) are acute neurological deficits that clear completely within 24 h. These attacks are caused by a short period of reduced blood flow to the eye or brain that does not result in permanent tissue damage. The reduced circulation may result from either small emboli or severe cerebrovascular occlusive disease, the latter usually in association with a transient reduction in arterial pressure (Ruff 1981).

Recovery from a TIA occurs because of the rapid return of normal arterial perfusion pressure to the affected brain tissue. When the TIA is related to a severe vascular stenosis, either a rise in blood pressure or a return to a normal cardiac rate and rhythm, depending on the inciting cause, reestablishes normal perfusion pressure. When the TIA is caused by emboli, either rapid clot lysis or the immediate development of adequate collateral blood flow probably accounts for complete clearing of the ischemic symptom. A TIA is an important warning sign of a possible subsequent major stroke. The CT scan is usually normal after a TIA (Kinkel 1976; Bradac 1980). MRI is also usually normal. There have, however, been reports of CT abnormalities with TIAs, such as focal low densities, in up to 20 percent of cases (Buell 1979; Ladurner 1979; Perrone 1979). These abnormalities may be related to previous small silent infarcts, not to the current TIA episodes (Bradac 1980).

Tables 15-1 and 15-2 list the major causes of cerebral infarction and nontraumatic intracerebral hemorrhage.

Although cerebral angiography is the only technique short of pathological examination that may specifically localize and indicate the nature of the vascular disease in some of the categories listed in Tables 15-1 and 15-2, CT and more frequently MRI alterations often are indicative and strongly suggestive of many of these etiologies. The use of intravenous contrast material after non-contrast-enhanced imaging and the obtaining of follow-up studies in many instances significantly aid in the determination

Table 15-1 Causes of Cerebral Infarction

Arterial occlusive disease
- Atherosclerotic occlusion
- Embolism
- Hemodynamic ischemia
- Arteriolosclerosis (lacunar disease)
- Vasculitis
- Moyamoya disease

Anoxic ischemia
Venous thrombosis

Table 15-2 Causes of Intracerebral Hemorrhage

Hypertensive vascular disease (arteriolosclerosis)
Aneurysm
Vascular malformation
Hemorrhagic arterial and venous infarction
Mycotic aneurysm
Amyloid angiopathy
Premature neonatal germinal matrix
Hemorrhagic hematologic disorders

of the correct vascular etiology of a stroke, as does correlation of the imaging changes with the patient's age, sex, history, and neurological findings.

CEREBRAL INFARCTION

CT is positive in ischemic stroke in 66 to 98 percent of cases (Bradac 1980; Buell 1979; Campbell 1978; Kinkel 1976). The percentage of cases with positive scans is highest when follow-up CT studies are obtained (Campbell 1978; Inoue 1980) and when CT is performed both before and after intravenous contrast (Norton 1978; Weisberg 1980; Wing 1976). CT may be faintly positive as early as 3 h after the onset of symptoms, but usually a low-density abnormality first becomes evident at 18 to 24 h (Inoue 1980). The size and location of the infarct, along with the degree of patient motion, significantly influence the time at which the lesion will first be detected. Small lesions that are usually not associated with significant edema may not become evident until very late, when necrotic tissue absorption has produced a well-demarcated, hypodense cystic lesion. Infratentorial infarcts (cerebellum and brainstem) have a lower incidence of detection, with focal abnormality apparent in 31 to 44 percent of cases (Campbell 1978; Kingsley 1980). Brainstem infarcts are rarely identified because they are frequently very small and because of the usual presence of prominent spatial artifacts in this region produced by the dense petrous ridges.

Third- and fourth-generation fast CT scanners have increased the early detection of cerebral infarction because of the improved spatial and contrast resolution. Detection rates of only 40 to 50 percent were found for ischemic strokes within 48 h utilizing the early-generation scanners (Davis 1975). Inoue (1980) reported that approximately 90 percent of supratentorial infarcts that eventually became positive on sequential CT scanning were evident by 24 h. All scans obtained between 25 and 35 days after the ictus revealed a focal abnormality in this series. Wall (1981) demonstrated subtle mass effects and/or focal areas of hypodensity within gray matter corresponding to regions of clinical deficit in 79 percent of cases. Of particular note is the fact that among all the positive scans, 65 percent were obtained at or less than 12 h after infarction. Early CT evaluation of suspected cerebral infarction is clinically important not only in establishing a specific diagnosis but also in excluding hemorrhage, neoplasm, and other significant pathological entities. Infarcts in the first 24 h are more frequently visible on MRI than on CT (Levy 1989). Acute infarcts were visualized in 81 percent of patients with MRI, compared with 20 percent on CT. T_1-weighted scans were more sensitive than CT in detecting the presence of hemorrhage.

Whereas CT will frequently reveal abnormality during the first week after an infarction, the radionuclide scan usually does not become positive until the second week (Bland 1971; Di Chiro 1974). The detection rates for both types of studies are approximately equal during the second week for both supra- and infratentorial infarctions, but CT provides much greater specificity (Campbell 1978; Masdeu 1977; Lewis 1978; Chiu 1977).

The CT alterations that develop and evolve over time with ischemic infarction reflect the pathological changes that are occurring in the brain tissue (Brierly 1976). In the first few hours after a large cerebral artery occlusion, widespread tissue damage can be recognized microscopically, involving the gray and white matter. In the central regions of the infarct, coagulation necrosis may develop in all tissue elements. At the periphery of the infarction, where damage is less severe, there is disintegration of nerve cells, myelin sheaths, and oligodendroglia, along with varying lesser degrees of damage to the astrocytes; the microglia and blood vessels are preserved. The small blood vessels and tissues are infiltrated with polymorphocytic leukocytes, which reach their maximum concentration at 3 days and then begin to decline. They are replaced by phagocytic mononuclear cells, which become evident by the fifth day. These cells continue to increase through the fourth week, removing the products of enzymatic digestion of neuronal and myelin disintegration. Beginning around day 5, proliferation of capillary endothelial cells becomes evident at the margins of the infarct. During the next several weeks, these new capillaries greatly increase in number. They grow first into the cortex and deep gray areas of infarction and later into the white matter regions. As the process of tissue breakdown continues, the phagocytes become fat-laden and then degenerate, leaving cystic spaces filled with yellowish fluid. Astrocytes also undergo hypertrophy and hyperplasia, laying down collagen fibers that contribute to tissue repair at the infarct margins. After several months, the necrotic tissue has been replaced by cystic spaces containing fluid and a variable number of fat-filled phagocytes. The margin between the infarct and the adjacent normal brain tissue is sharply defined during all stages of infarct evolution.

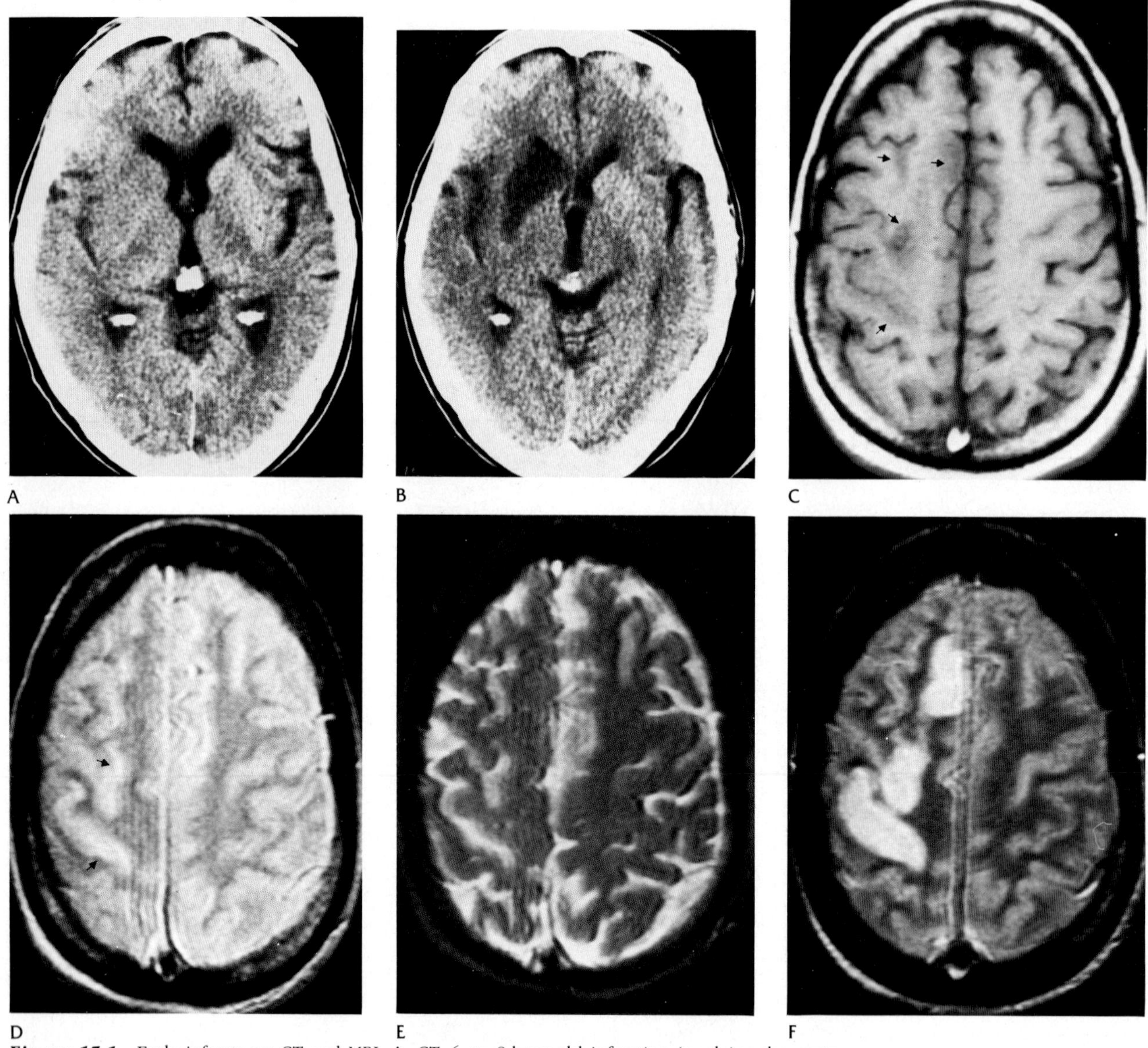

Figure 15-1 Early infarcts on CT and MRI. **A.** CT, 6- to 8-hour-old infarction involving the cortex proximal to the right middle cerebral artery territory. A slight hypodensity is present, involving the head of the right caudate nucleus, putamen, and insula cortex. This is best appreciated by comparing with the normal densities of these structures on the left. **B.** Follow-up CT at 3 days demonstrates well-defined and more marked hypodensity in the same regions as in **A** on the right side. **C–E.** MRI of a 6- to 8-hour-old infarct in the distal right anterior cerebral artery territory. **C.** Axial T_1WI through superior convexity region. Mild hypointense thickening of cortex along multiple right-sided convolutions (arrows). **D.** PDWI (TR 2500, TE 30) reveals mild hyperintensity and thickening of the cortex in the same convolutions as shown in **C** (arrows). **E.** T_2WI (TR 2500, TE 90) at the same level as **D** fails to demonstrate cortical thickening and hyperintensity. **F.** Follow-up PDWI 3 days later reveals very prominent cortical thickening and hyperintensity in the same cortical regions as **C** and **D.**

Arterial Occlusive Diseases

LARGE-ARTERY THROMBOTIC INFARCTION (ATHEROSCLEROTIC OCCLUSION)

Between 8 and 24 h after the onset of ischemic symptoms, non-contrast-enhanced computed tomography (NCCT) frequently reveals a subtle loss of gray-white matter differentiation in the area of the infarction, reflecting a mild hypodensity involving mainly the deep gray matter and the cortex and, to a lesser extent, the underlying white matter down to the ventricular surface (a fogging effect on the normal slightly hyperdense gray matter) (Figs. 15-1 and 15-4*A*) (Baker 1975; Davis 1975; Yock 1975). This hypodensity becomes more distinct after a few days and assumes a triangular or wedge-shaped configuration, with its base on the brain surface. The hypodensity is confined within the vascular territory of the occluded artery (Figs. 15-2 and 15-3). When the proximal segment of the middle cerebral artery is occluded, the hypodensity may involve the basal ganglia and the internal capsule region either alone or with a convexity region (Figs. 15-3, 15-4, and 15-20). This initial low-density pattern represents tissue necrosis with intracellular edema (cytotoxic edema) (Alcala 1978). Little or no mass effect may be evident during the first 24 h of the infarct. Detection of infarct changes during the first 24 h is dependent on the size of the infarct, the degree of the ischemic insult, and the availability of scans of high contrast resolution with minimal artifacts from patient motion. MR is more sensitive than CT in the detection of acute infarcts within the first 24 h (Levy 1989). Proton-density-weighted images (PDWI) and T_1WI usually demonstrate the alterations most conspicuously. T_2WI may also reveal alterations, but the usual high CSF intensity of the subarachnoid spaces frequently makes it difficult to differentiate these alterations from the early infarct changes. Alterations in the intensity and architecture of the cerebral cortex are usually the first MRI alterations seen. On PDWI, there is a slight increase of the signal intensity and thickness of the involved cortex. This is related to early neuronal swelling with cytotoxic intracellular edema. The same cortical thickening and cortical hypointensity with loss of sulci may be observed on T_1WI (Fig. 15-1). T_2WI are less sensitive in detecting early infarct changes.

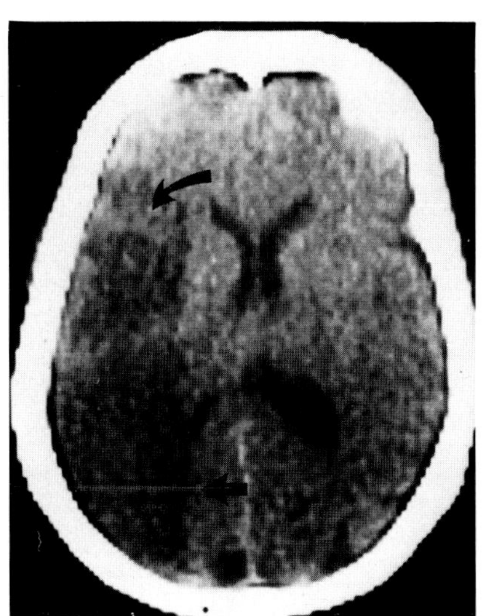

A

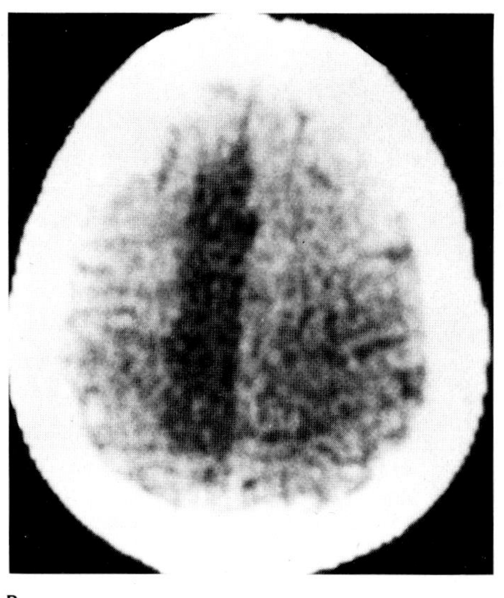

B

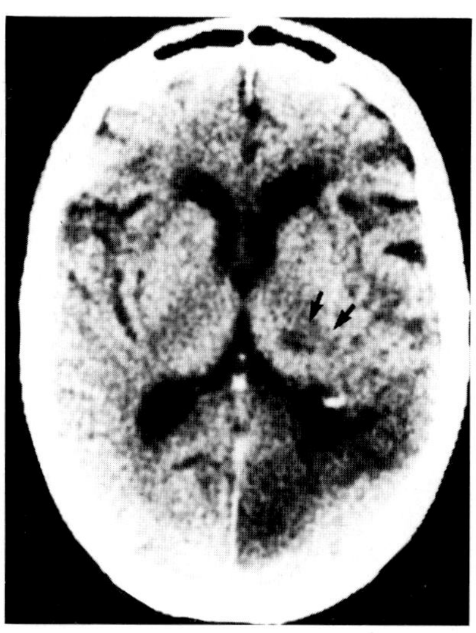

C

Figure 15-2 CT and MRI of 3- to 5-day-old infarcts in major cerebral artery territories. **A–C.** CT images. **A.** Peripheral middle cerebral artery territory infarct: well-defined homogeneous hypodensity involving cortex and underlying white matter in right posterior temporal and lateral occipital region. The basal ganglia region is normal, indicating that the proximal middle cerebral artery segment from which the lenticulostriate supply arises is not occluded. Linear demarcation at watershed between infarct hypodensity in middle cerebral artery territory and normal tissue density of posterior cerebral artery territory (straight arrow). Hypodensity of cortex and white matter in anterior temporal region is nonhomogeneous, suggesting incomplete infarction in this region (curved arrow). Right lateral ventricle is compressed and shifted slightly to left of midline. **B.** Anterior cerebral artery territory infarct: rectangular well-defined, homogeneous hypodensity involving the cortex and underlying white matter in the superior medial aspect of the right hemisphere. There is sharp margination of the hypodensity at the watershed region with the middle cerebral artery territory laterally and the posterior cerebral artery territory posteriorly. The hypodensity extends inferiorly on lower sections to the level of the roof of the lateral ventricle. **C.** Posterior cerebral artery territory infarct. Hypodensity involving posterior thalamus on the left (arrow) along with sharply defined cortical and white matter lesion in the medial posterior occipital region. (*Continued on p. 628.*)

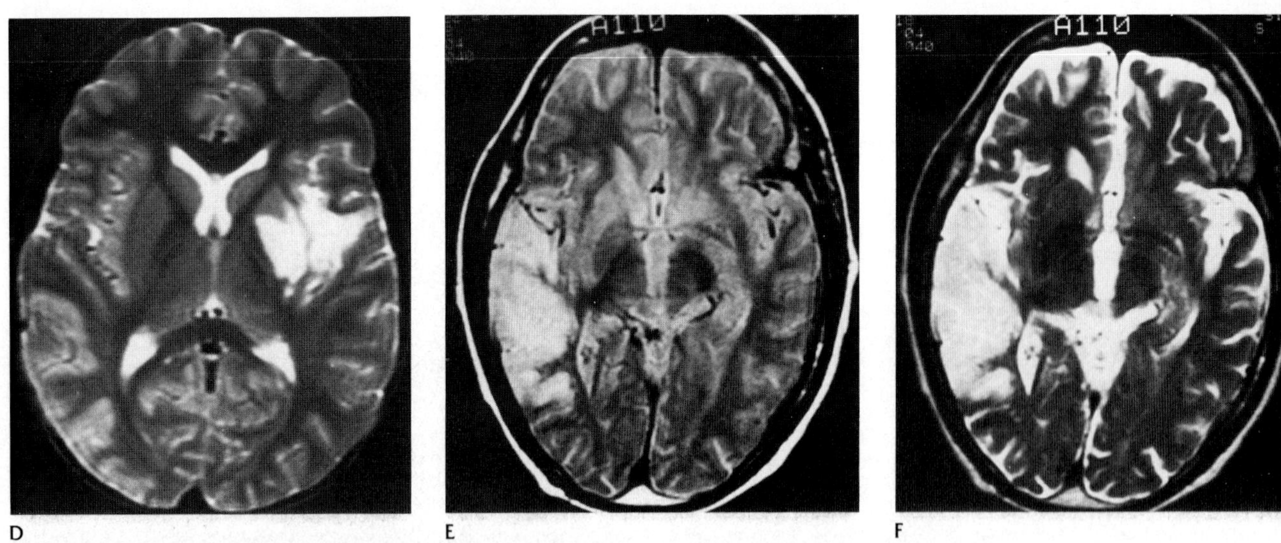

Figure 15-2 ***(continued)*** **D.** MRI of the proximal middle cerebral artery territory infarct. T_2WI reveals hyperintensity involving the posterior two-thirds of the left putamen, the insula-sylvian cortex, and the adjacent subcortical white matter. **E, F.** MRI of a right middle cerebral infarction in the territory of the posterior temporal artery branch. **E.** PDWI demonstrates sharply demarcated hyperintensity involving the right superior temporal cortex and underlying white matter. **F.** T_2WI at same level as **E** demonstrates greater hyperintensity in the right superior temporal region with obliteration of overlying cortical sulci and compression of the underlying insula cistern.

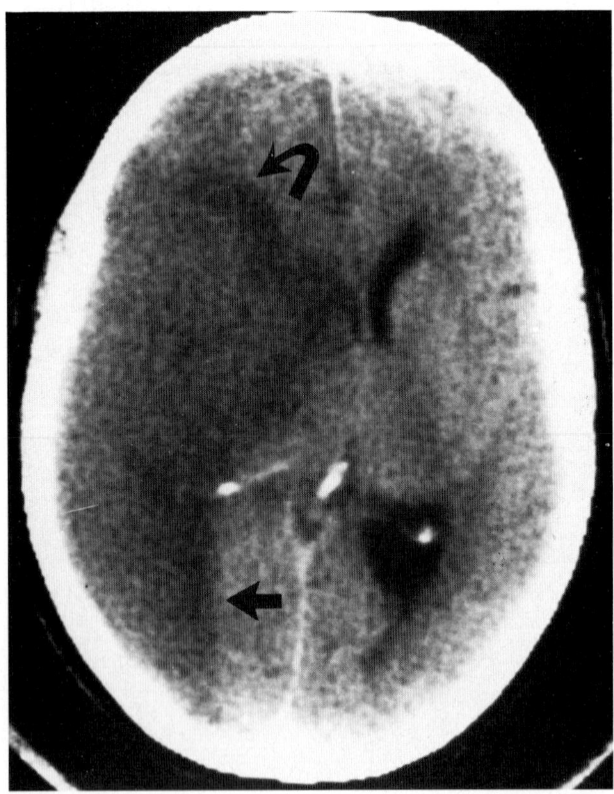

Figure 15-3 Four-day-old complete right middle cerebral artery territory infarction. Obliteration of right lateral ventricle and marked midline shift to the left. Homogeneous hypodensity involving lateral basal ganglia and all cortical white matter regions of peripheral middle cerebral artery distribution. Sharp linear margination anteriorly at junction with anterior cerebral artery territory (curved arrow) and posteriorly with posterior cerebral artery territory (straight arrow).

Between the third and fifth days, the region of infarction becomes a more hypodense and homogeneous area with sharper margins (Figs. 15-2*A* and 15-4*B*) (Davis 1975; Inoue 1980). Pathologically, tissue necrosis and intracellular edema reach a maximum at this time. This results in a variable degree of mass effect that depends on the size and degree of infarction. Swelling may be mild to severe, with CT revealing focal or diffuse compression of the ventricular system and midline shift (Figs. 15-2*B*, 15-3, and 15-4*B*). With large infarcts, early signs of tissue swelling may become evident before 24 h. At this time there may be obliteration or effacement of surface sulci and the sylvian fissure on the side of the infarct, and the ipsilateral ventricle may be slightly smaller and compressed (Fig. 15-4). Mass effect of some degree is reported in 21 to 70 percent of infarcts (Masdeu 1977; Wing 1976; Yock 1975) and is most marked between the third and fifth days. With large hemispheric infarctions, brain swelling may be considerable, with the development of a considerable midline shift. This may result in posterior cerebral artery occlusion from transtentorial herniation with occipital lobe infarction. With small infarcts there may be no mass effect or only slight focal ventricular distortion. Brain swelling begins to decrease after the first week and usually resolves completely in 12 to 21 days.

With embolic infarcts, greater brain swelling may develop that is partially vasogenic in nature. This results from antegrade circulation being reestablished after clot lysis, which usually develops between the second and fourteenth days after the infarction. It results in increased

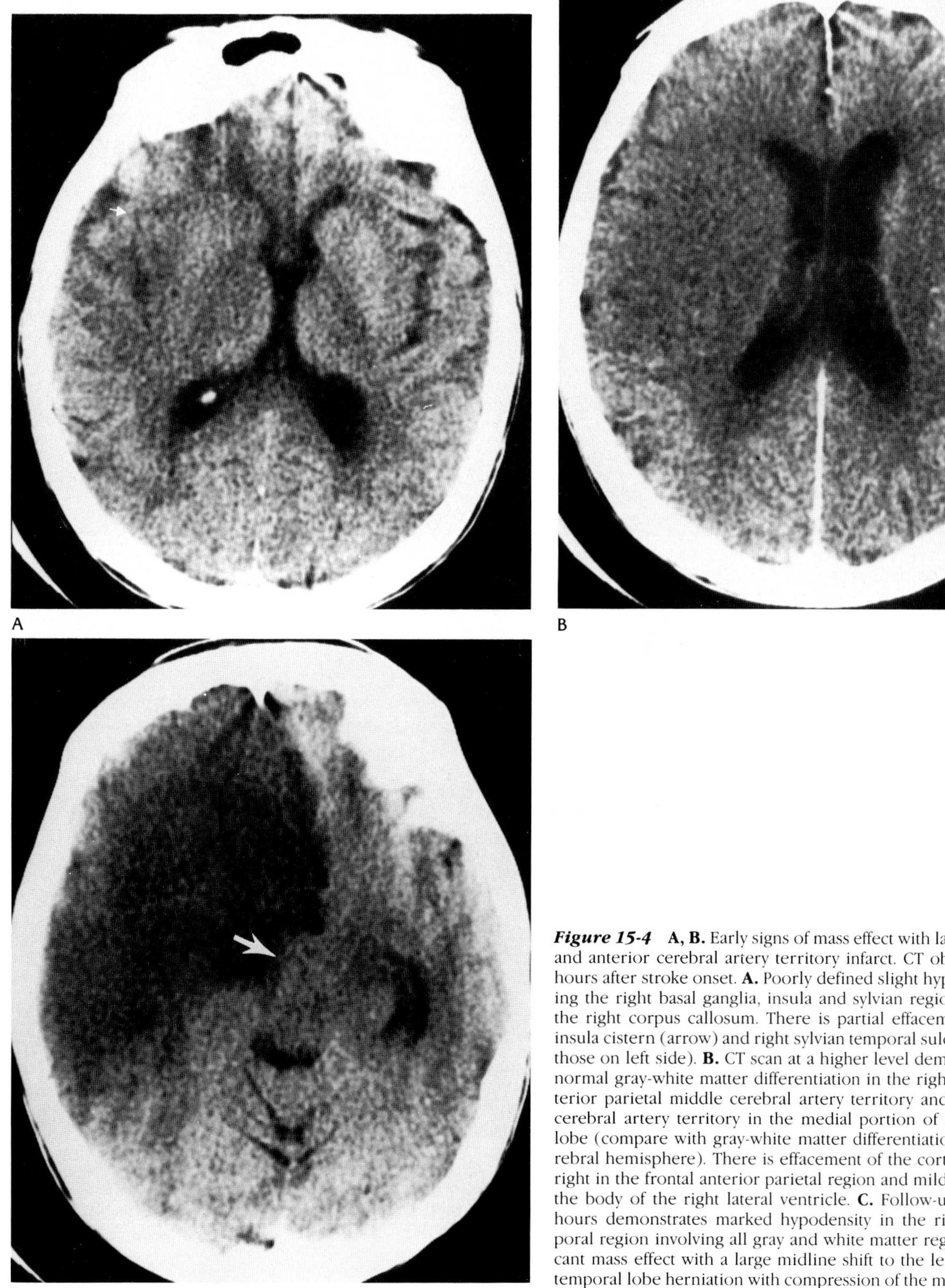

Figure 15-4 **A, B.** Early signs of mass effect with large right middle and anterior cerebral artery territory infarct. CT obtained about 12 hours after stroke onset. **A.** Poorly defined slight hypodensity involving the right basal ganglia, insula and sylvian regions, and genu of the right corpus callosum. There is partial effacement of the right insula cistern (arrow) and right sylvian temporal sulci (compare with those on left side). **B.** CT scan at a higher level demonstrates loss of normal gray-white matter differentiation in the right frontal and anterior parietal middle cerebral artery territory and in the anterior cerebral artery territory in the medial portion of the right frontal lobe (compare with gray-white matter differentiation in the left cerebral hemisphere). There is effacement of the cortical sulci on the right in the frontal anterior parietal region and mild compression of the body of the right lateral ventricle. **C.** Follow-up CT scan at 48 hours demonstrates marked hypodensity in the right frontal temporal region involving all gray and white matter regions and significant mass effect with a large midline shift to the left. There is right temporal lobe herniation with compression of the midbrain (arrow).

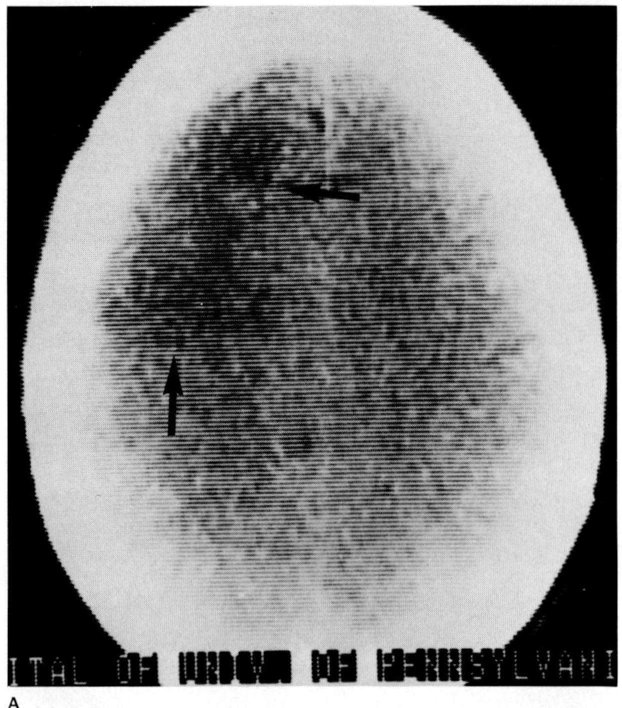

A

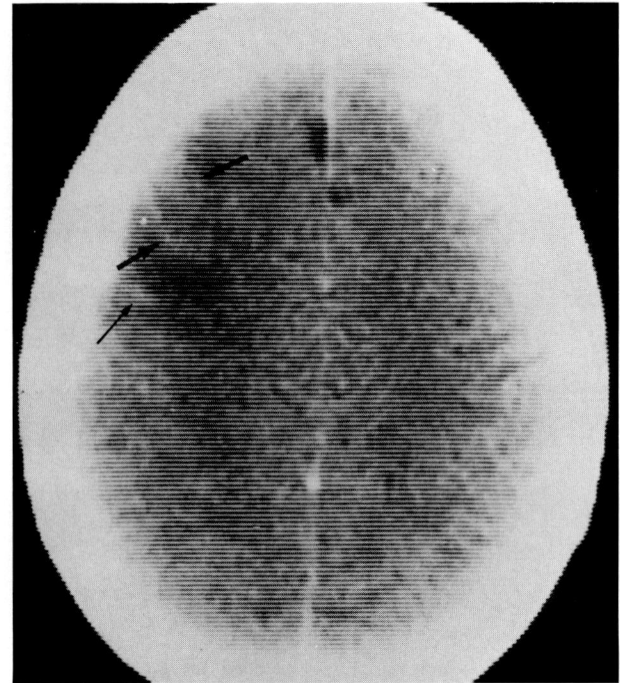

B

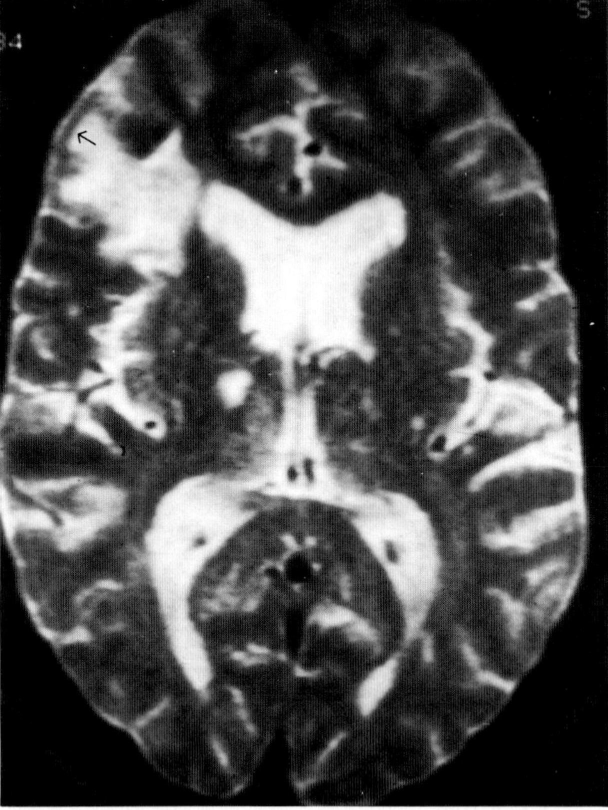

C

Figure 15-5 Development of isodense cortical bands on NCCT in right middle cerebral territory infarct. **A.** Relatively homogeneous hypodensity involving the cortical gray and underlying white matter at day 3 (arrows). **B.** At day 12 isodense bands representing the infolded cortical ribbon (arrows) extend down into white matter hypodensity. Infarct appears smaller with indistinct margins because cortex at periphery of infarct has become isodense. **C.** MRI of a 10-day-old right frontal middle cerebral artery territory infarct with reversion of the cortex to isointensity on T_2WI. Hyperintensity in the right fontal white matter extends from the subcortical region down to the frontal horn. The overlying cortical ribbon is isointense at this time (arrow). Incidentally noted are punctate and focal hyperintensities of lacunar infarcts bilaterally in the basal ganglia and thalamic regions.

leakage of fluid from the ischemically damaged capillary bed when it is exposed to the higher intravascular pressure of reperfusion.

On CT, the hypodensity of infarction remains strictly confined to the distribution of the arterial system involved. MRI, PDWI, and T_2WI reveal hyperintensity in a similar distribution (Fig. 15-2). This sharp localization is due to cellular necrosis and edema, which are mainly intracellular (cytotoxic), in contrast to the vasogenic form of edema, which is extracellular, spreads along white matter tracts, and is commonly associated with brain tumor and inflammatory disease.

The pattern of hypodensity on CT and hyperintensity on T_2-weighted MRI associated with infarction can usually be differentiated from that seen with tumor and inflammatory disease. With infarction, the region of change usually involves both the gray matter and the white matter, while with tumor and inflammation, it is situated mainly within the white matter, although it may extend to the cortex. With arterial infarction, the pattern has sharply demarcated margins, assumes a square or wedge-shaped configuration, and is located within or between arterial distributions. In contrast to tumor and abscess, the density impurity spreads diffusely within the white matter in a pseudopodlike manner, has ill-defined and rounded margins, and is usually not limited to an arterial division or a watershed distribution.

During the second and third weeks on CT, isodense to slightly hyperdense curvilinear bands and nodular regions frequently develop within the hypodensity of the infarct (Inoue 1980). With MRI, these changes are reflected on PDWI and T_2WI as a loss of the hyperintensity that had previously involved the cortex and deep gray masses of the brain. On T_1WI, isointense bands appear within the region of overall infarct hypointensity (Fig. 15-5). These changes are located mainly in gray matter regions and result from hyperemia related to new capillary ingrowth and improved collateral circulation in thrombotic infarcts. Some of the density-intensity changes may be caused by petechial hemorrhage, particularly in an embolic infarct. The density changes appear most commonly as curvilinear bands in the expected location of the cortical ribbon that are most prominent at the margins of the infarct (Fig. 15-5). They may also occur in the deep cortical regions of the infarct and in the deep gray masses. They tend to produce a mottled appearance at the margins of the infarct, which is then less sharply defined than it was on earlier poststroke scans. The infarcted white matter usually does not show any density-intensity changes.

Starting at about 4 to 5 weeks and continuing for the next 2 to 3 months, the infarct region becomes more sharply outlined as a result of phagocytes removing necrotic tissue. The CT and MRI density changes become more homogeneous, approaching the density of cerebrospinal fluid (Davis 1975; Inoue 1980). The isodense cortical bands usually convert to the same density as the rest of the infarct. Pathologically, there is cystic cavitation of the necrotic infarcted brain tissue, prominent lipid content, and gliosis. The cystic change predominantly affects the white matter and the region of the basal ganglia, where tissue necrosis is generally most severe. The infarct appears smaller because of absorption of necrotic tissue and contraction from gliosis (McCall 1975). The adjacent portion of the lateral ventricle dilates and extends toward the region of infarction. A shift of the brain midline to the side of the infarct may also develop with large lesions. The overlying cortex reveals atrophic change, with enlargement of the adjacent sulci and cisterns (Fig. 15-6). With cortical infarcts, sulcal enlargement may be the only long-term abnormality (Fig. 15-7). The brain changes usually become stable by the end of the third month.

Contrast Enhancement

Contrast-enhanced computed tomography (CECT) has been of great value in the diagnosis and characterization of infarcts. A significant percentage of infarcts reveal contrast enhancement, which usually first appears during the second week after the onset of symptoms (Fig. 15-8). Early studies reported contrast enhancement on CT in only about 60 percent of cerebral infarcts (Wing 1976;. Masdeu 1977); recent studies have observed enhancement in up to 82 to 88 percent of infarcts evaluated between the second and fourth weeks (Pullicino 1980; Lee 1978). In a study of supratentorial infarcts with serial CT examinations, 93 percent of those which developed an abnormality showed contrast enhancement between the second and third weeks (Inoue 1980). There has been a wide range in the reported incidence of enhancement occurring during the first week of the infarct, from 0 to 62 percent (Weisberg 1980; Lee 1978). This large variation probably reflects differences in infarct etiology in these series. Series that have a high percentage of embolic and hemodynamic infarcts (see next section) reveal a high incidence of early enhancement because these infarcts are reperfused early at systemic arterial pressure levels. Blood-brain barrier abnormalities that are not evident in persistently anemic infarcts may then be revealed. Hayman (1981), employing high-dose contrast infusion (80 g iodine) along with immediate and delayed (3 h) CT scans, found a 72 percent incidence of enhancement (13 of 18) within the first 28 h. Most of the patients with early enhancement had embolic infarcts. In addition, these authors found that enhancement that occurred predominantly on the 3-h-delayed scans had a grave prognostic implication: Four of seven patients with this type of enhancement subsequently developed hemor-

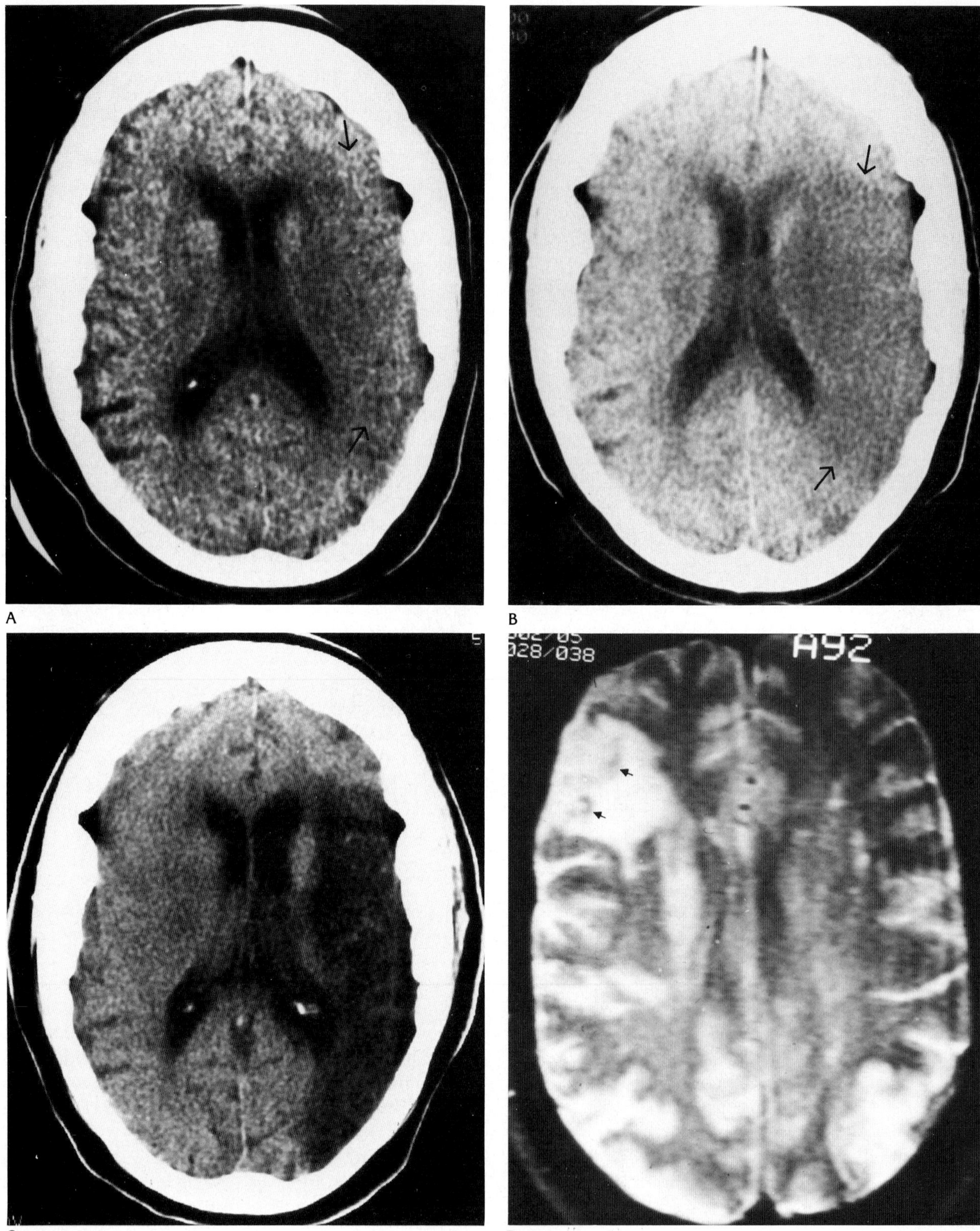

Figure 15-6 Infarct evolution from the acute to the chronic phase. **A–C.** Evolution on CT. **A.** Infarct at 6 hours demonstrates slight loss of normal gray-white differentiation in the left middle cerebral artery territory (arrows) and mild sulcal effacement. **B.** Infarct at 24 hours demonstrates a well-defined and more uniform hypodensity involving the cortex and underlying white matter in the left middle cerebral artery territory (arrows). There is mild compression of the left lateral ventricle. **C.** Infarct at 6 months. Marked hypodensity in the left middle cerebral artery territory approximating that of CSF. There is dilatation of the left lateral ventricle and a slight midline shift to the left. **D.** Acute and chronic MR infarct changes. T_2WI demonstrates high intensity in the cortex and underlying white matter in the left posterior parietal region with effacement of the overlying sulci, indicative of acute stroke changes. Chronic infarct in the right frontal region reveals marked sulcal dilatation with a thin hypointense underlying cortex (arrows). The subajacent white matter down to the ventricle is uniformly hyperintense.

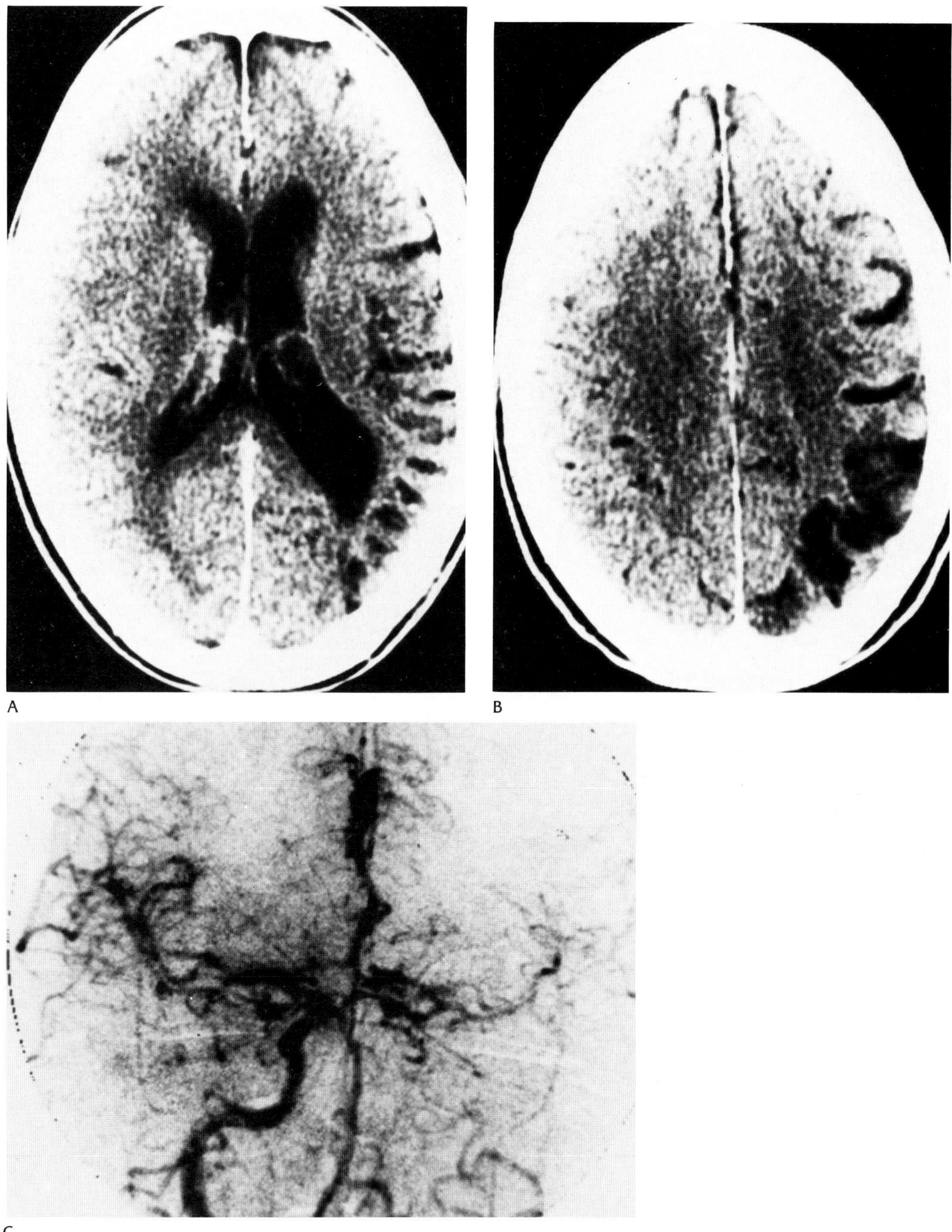

Figure 15-7 Dilated cortical sulci from an old cortical infarct. Axial CECTs (**A, B**) show dilated left parietal sulci with normal white matter density. On lower sections (not shown) the ipsilateral sylvian fissure is dilated. Ap digital subtraction angiogram (**C**) discloses complete occlusion of left internal carotid artery with spontaneous interhemispheric cross filling. (*Continued on p. 634.*)

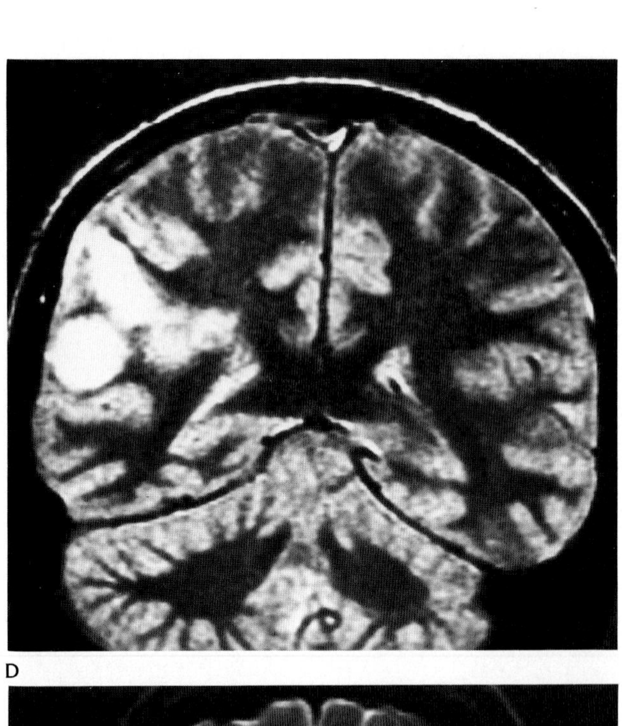

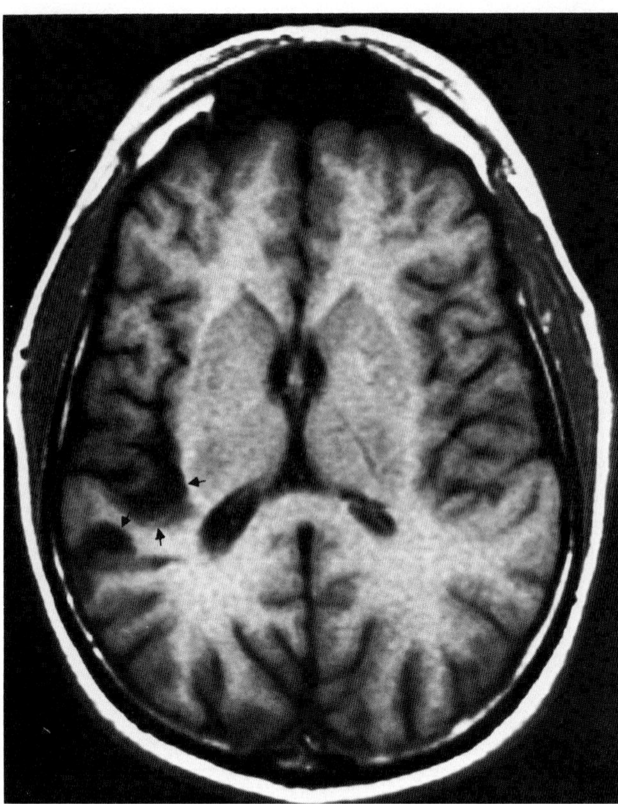

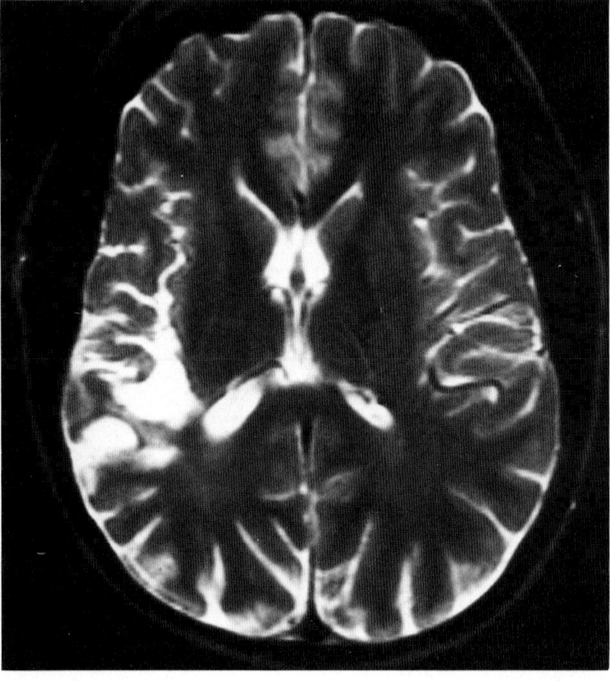

Figure 15-7 (continued) **D.** MRI of an acute stroke in the right inferior parietal region. Coronal projection demonstrates cortical thickening and hyperintensity with patchy hyperintensity in the underlying white matter. **E.** Axial T_1WI 2 years after **D.** Marked dilatation of the sulci present in the posterior portion of the right sylvian fissure and inferior parietal region (arrows). The cortical ribbon cannot be defined in the brain adjacent to these dilated sulci. The right atrium is mildly dilated. **F.** T_2WI at same level and time as **E.** Hyperintensity of the dilated sylvian and inferior parietal sulci are evident. On PDWI (not shown) no hyperintensity was present in the right sylvian and inferior parietal region, confirming the presence of dilated CSF spaces in these areas.

rhagic infarcts and died. None of the patients with only immediate enhancement on high-dose scans had this sequela.

Contrast administration either at a high dose (Hayman 1981) or by rapid injection (Heinz 1979; Norman 1981) during the first 24 h of an infarct or later may reveal characteristic nonenhancing abnormalities in an otherwise normal CT scan. With both of these techniques, the cortical gyri and deep gray matter in the infarct region may demonstrate a deficiency in the normal contrast blush of

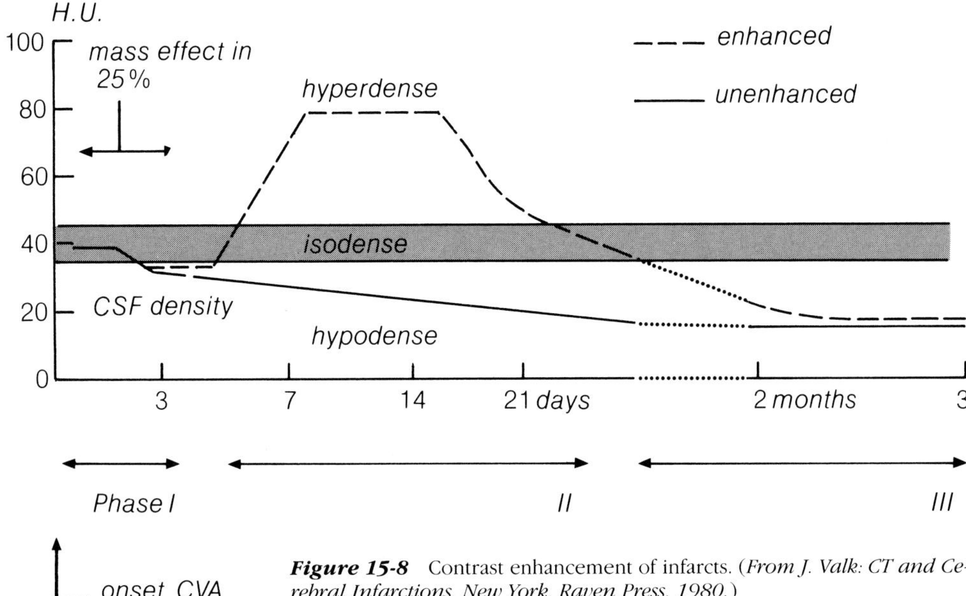

Figure 15-8 Contrast enhancement of infarcts. (*From J. Valk: CT and Cerebral Infarctions, New York, Raven Press, 1980.*)

the capillary bed. The blush will be evident in the surrounding uninvolved gray matter and in homologous regions of the opposite hemisphere. With the high-dose technique advocated by Hayman (1981), routine scanning methods that may utilize slow scanning times will demonstrate this change. With the rapid-injection technique (dynamic CT), however, 40 to 50 ml of contrast must be injected in about 5 sec and four to six fast scans (5 sec or less) must be obtained in rapid sequence, that is, 2 to 3 sec apart (Fig. 15-9) (Norman 1981). This technique requires CT equipment with these special capabilities.

The intensity of enhancement begins to decline after the third week. It will usually persist for 6 to 7 weeks and, with large infarcts, up to 12 weeks (Weisberg 1980; Pullicino 1980). It may rarely last as long as 9 months (Norton 1978).

The amount of radiographic contrast injected greatly influences the intensity of enhancement. Weisberg (1980) observed that only 5 percent of 100 patients with infarction demonstrated contrast enhancement after the injection of a 50-ml bolus of a 60 percent iodinated contrast agent (14 g of iodine), whereas enhancement occurred in 65 percent of 100 patients after a drip infusion of 300 ml of a 30 percent contrast agent (42 g of iodine).

The mechanism of CT contrast enhancement appears to be identical to that producing delayed uptake in a radionuclide brain scan and is related to abnormality in the blood-brain barrier. Using a cat stroke model, Anderson (1980) found a strong positive correlation between tissue concentrations of ^{99m}Tc, sodium pertechnetate, and methylglucamine iothalamate in the area of infarct and the surrounding brain tissues at all time intervals, indicating a similarity in the temporal profile in these two studies. The radionuclide, however, revealed a consistently higher brain-blood ratio than did the iodinated contrast material. This probably accounts for the slightly higher incidence of positive nuclide scans compared with standard-dose CECT scans. Depending on the dose of contrast given, at some time periods the brain-blood ratio may be below the level of tissue concentration that can be resolved on CT. Masdeu (1977), in a study in humans, found a slightly higher incidence of positive radionuclide brain scans with infarction compared with CECT at 2 weeks (72 percent versus 63 percent), using a standard contrast dose. Gado (1975) showed in human studies that CT contrast enhancement primarily results from contrast material in the extracellular space. Only a small degree of contrast enhancement can be explained by tissue hypervascularity, except perhaps when large blood pools are present, as in an arteriovenous malformation.

The pathophysiological abnormality that permits the passage of contrast material into the extravascular space is a breakdown in the blood-brain barrier mechanisms of the capillary endothelium (Fishman 1975; Anderson 1980). Brain capillaries, unlike those in other parts of the body, restrict the passage of most large molecules through their walls because of tight endothelial cell junctions. Ischemic insult to the brain damages the blood-brain barrier, permitting large molecules to leak into the extravascular space. Although animal studies have shown that after infarction produced by a permanent arterial occlusion, capillary leakage may become evident at about 4 h (O'Brien 1974), a CECT or isotope brain scan will usually not become positive until after the first week (Bland 1971; Inoue 1980). This appears to be related to

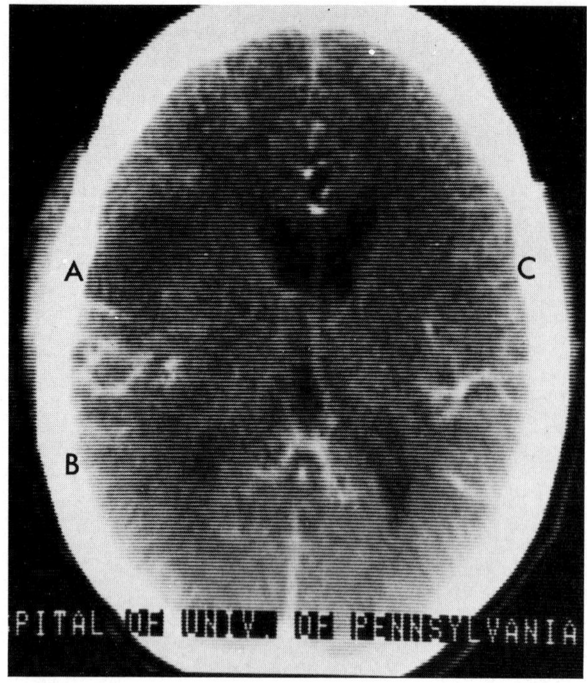

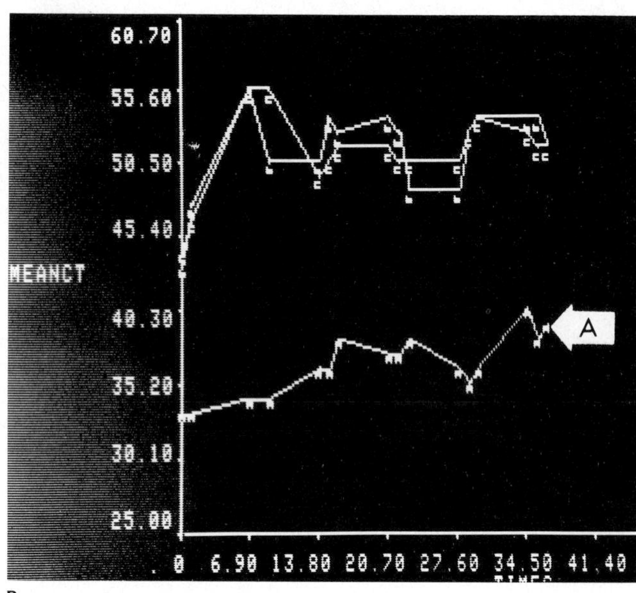

A B

Figure 15-9 Ischemic changes on rapid-sequence CT: 2-day-old right middle cerebral territory infarct. **A.** High-speed CT scan (2.4- second scan time) 12 seconds after rapid intravenous injection of 40 ml contrast. Absence of surface vessels and cortical gyral blush in right posterior frontal region (*A*; normal cortical blush in regions *B* and *C*). **B.** Time-density curves following bolus contrast injection in region *A* (area of infarct) and regions *B* and *C* (normal cortical regions) in **A.** Time in seconds displayed on horizontal axis, and CT density (H units) on vertical axis. Curves *B* and *C* (upper) display a rapid rise and decline of contrast density, reflecting normal initial circulation of the contrast bolus through the brain. The subsequent fluctuations in the curves reflect to a large extent recirculation of the bolus. Curve *Z* over the infarct indicates a slow circulation, probably in association with a defective blood-brain barrier. It seems likely that some of the slow density increase of the infarct results from leakage of contrast from poorly filled, damaged capillaries.

persistent severe ischemia of the infarct region during the first week, caused by limited collateral or antegrade circulation. As a result of this low flow, insufficient contrast is delivered to the infarct for enhancement to be demonstrated even in the presence of a severely disturbed blood-brain barrier. By 7 to 10 days brain swelling is less, and this improves collateral circulation and results in sufficient leakage of contrast from infarct capillaries to allow visualization. Concomitantly, considerable neovascular capillary proliferation is occurring around areas of necrosis, and these vessels have an incompetent blood-brain barrier (Dudley 1970; Yamaguchi 1971; Hayman 1980; Anderson 1980). This neovascularity is responsible for the persistence of contrast enhancement during the next 4 to 8 weeks as the reparative process is completed. On MRI, contrast enhancement is currently achieved mainly with gadolinium (Gd-DTPA) administered intravenously. CEMR demonstrates enhancement patterns similar to those seen on CT but develops at an earlier time and with greater conspicuity. MRI is able to detect smaller amounts of contrast leakage through a damaged blood-brain barrier than CT can with iodinated agents. A higher contrast dose and the use of delayed imaging at 20 to 40 min after injection facilitates visualization of the more minimally damaged blood-brain barrier regions that occur with infarcts. Contrast enhancement of ischemic infarcts may be visualized as early as 4 to 6 h on MRI. Enhancement is seen on T_1WI as a thin band of hyperintensity within the region of the cortical ribbon, frequently in the depth of a sulcus (Fig. 15-10). Some of the cortical hyperintensity seen after gadolinium administration may be related to stagnated blood flow in small pial arteries and veins in the region of infarction.

Contrast enhancement on CT may develop before the usual 7 to 10 days if perfusion at the infarct increases significantly (Hayman 1980). Large molecule leakage at a disturbed blood-brain barrier varies directly with the systemic blood pressure level (Klatzo 1972). Contrast enhancement tends to occur early with embolic infarcts (after clot lysis) and with hemodynamic infarcts.

Contrast enhancement develops primarily in the cortex and deep gray masses (Inoue 1980). The gray matter is considerably more vascular than is the white matter. The cortex at the margins of the infarct tends to show

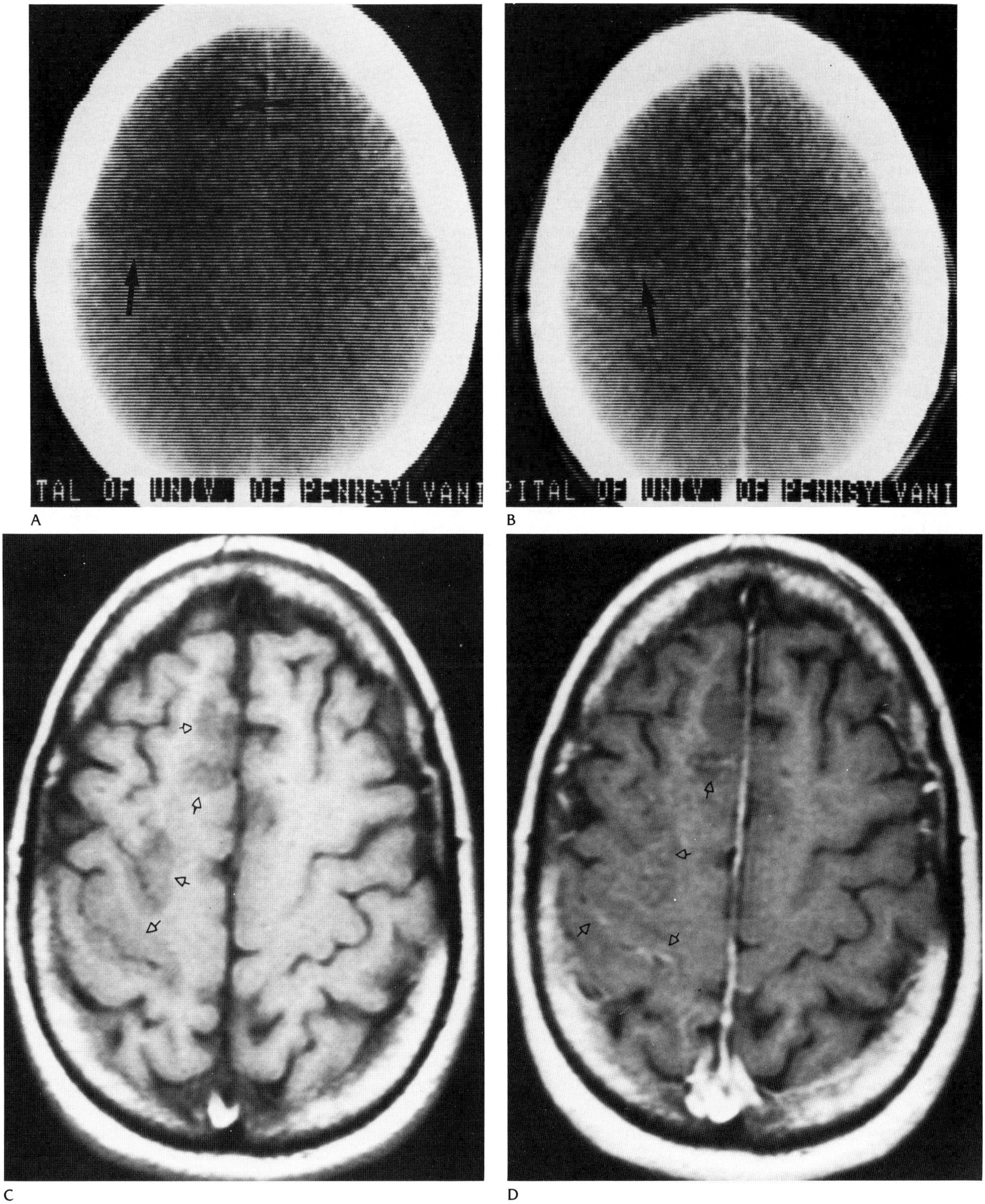

A

B

C

D

Figure 15-10 Marginal enhancement in 3-day-old infarct. **A.** NCCT demonstrating wedge-shaped hypodensity involving the cortex and white matter within the right middle cerebral artery territory (arrows). **B.** CECT reveals slight linear enhancement at posterior margin of the infarct (arrow), most probably in the cortex of the infolded convolution. (See Fig. 15-12 for progression of enhancement at day 12.) **C, D.** MRI demonstrating perisulcal enhancement in a 3-day-old infarct. **C.** NCMR T_1WI reveals thickening and mild increased hypointensity of the cortex in the right parasagittal region (arrows). **D.** Gd-DTPA T_1WI demonstrates mild intra- and perisulcal enhancement (arrows) along the same convolutions which demonstrated cortical thickening and hypointensity in **C.**

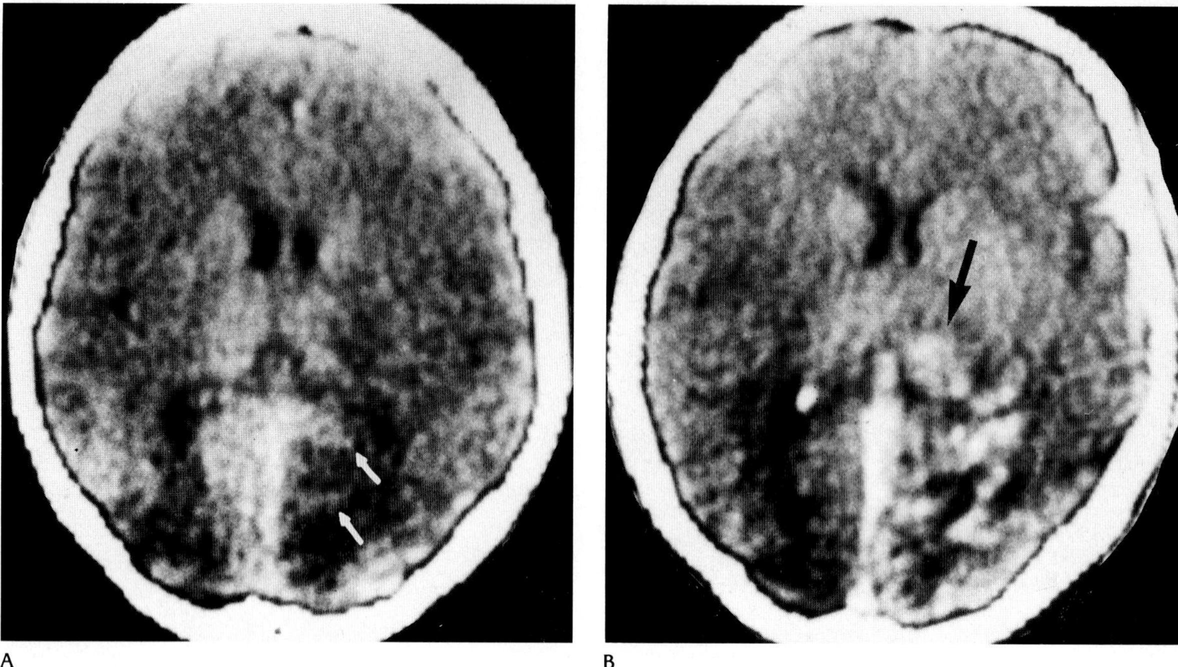

Figure 15-11 Heterogeneous enhancement of posterior cerebral artery territory infarct at day 10. **A.** NCCT reveals poorly defined hypodensity in left occipital and posterior thalamic region which contains bands and nodules of isodensity (arrows). **B.** CECT reveals linear and nodular regions of enhancement roughly corresponding in location to the isodense areas within the infarct in **A.** Homogeneous region of enhancement in posterior thalamus (arrows).

enhancement earliest, since collateral circulation to this region is initially more adequate (Fig. 15-10). Delayed scans may demonstrate enhancement extending into the underlying white matter. This may be caused either by diffusion of contrast material leaked from the more numerous cortical capillaries or by the slower edema buildup related to lower blood flow in white matter. Vasogenic edema fluid accumulates primarily in white matter, and this may decrease its circulation further (Klatzo 1972).

The pattern of infarct enhancement on CT usually has a heterogeneous appearance, which may be related to avascular regions of coagulation necrosis or to variability in the degree of collateral recirculation to different portions of the infarct (Fig. 15-11). At times the enhancing pattern is homogeneous, suggesting incomplete tissue necrosis and more uniform reperfusion of the infarct (Fig. 15-6). With both of these patterns, the cortical ribbon and basal ganglia are the regions that predominantly enhance when immediate scans are obtained; with delayed scans after contrast (30 min to 3 h), both homogeneous and heterogeneous enhancement may also develop in the white matter (Fig. 15-12). Norton (1978) reported that the patterns of enhancement are homogeneous in 22 percent and heterogeneous in 59 percent of infarcts.

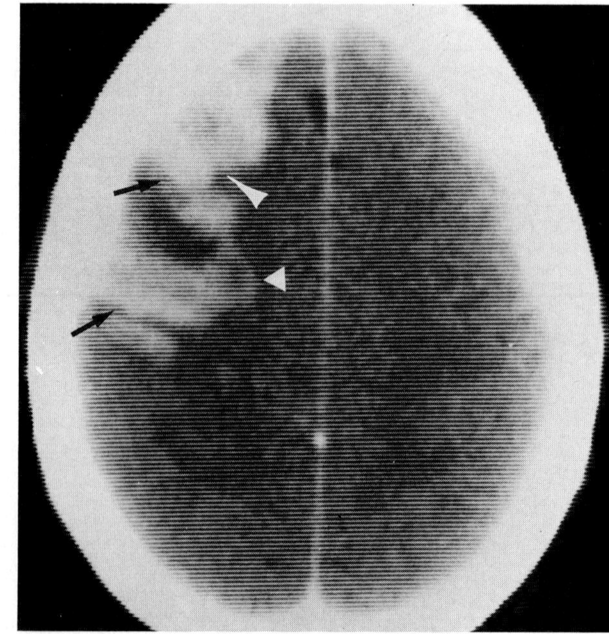

Figure 15-12 CECT: cortical ribbon (gyriform) enhancement (arrows) right middle cerebral artery territory at day 12. Some enhancement of white matter (arrowheads) on delayed CECT at 45 min. See NCCT in Figure 15-5 for isodense bands corresponding to the regions of cortical ribbon enhancement.

Infarct enhancement may also show a multifocal linear, bandlike configuration or central, peripheral, or ring patterns (Norton 1978; Pullicino 1980). The linear bandlike and central patterns usually represent different regions of enhancement in the cortical ribbon within and surrounding the area of infarction (Fig. 15-12). Since the cortical ribbon extends into the depth of the brain a variable distance around the sulci, a region of cortical enhancement may appear at times to be situated within the white matter. The central pattern may also represent enhancement in the deep gray masses (Fig. 15-6). Differences in these enhancement patterns probably occur because of variations in collateral reperfusion and in the degree of necrosis in different regions of the infarct.

The peripheral enhancing pattern appears as a rim of enhancement that assumes a roughly hemispheric configuration about the lateral gray matter and deep white matter margins of the infarct. This pattern would tend to develop about areas of hemispheric infarction when there is necrosis in both gray and white matter as indicated by homogeneous hypodensity in both of these regions on NCCT.

The ringlike enhancing pattern is most commonly seen around necrotic infarcts in the basal ganglia (Fig. 15-13) but may also develop around necrotic tissue in the white matter portion of a hemispheric infarct when there is incomplete nonnecrotic involvement of the overlying cortex. Basal ganglia infarcts may be small, resulting from a single lenticulostriate artery occlusion (Fig. 15-13), or large, as occurs when multiple lenticulostriate arteries are blocked secondary to proximal middle cerebral artery occlusion. In the latter case, associated infarction may be present in the territory of the peripheral middle cerebral artery (Fig. 15-14). Central coagulation necrosis commonly develops with basal ganglia infarcts because of inadequate collateral channels to this territory. Ring enhancement develops from the rich neovascular ingrowth in surrounding unaffected portions of the basal ganglia. When the ring pattern surrounds a necrotic white matter infarct, the ring results from a combination of overlying cortical and peripheral deep white matter neovascular ingrowth.

In most cases, contrast enhancement on CT will elevate a low-density region to one of higher-than-normal tissue density. Occasionally a zone of hypodensity becomes isodense with the surrounding brain (Fig. 15-15), and the infarction may not be recognized if only CECT is obtained. Wing (1976) noted this postcontrast normalization phenomenon in about 5 percent of recent infarcts. Conversely, these authors also observed that in 11 percent of infarcts that enhanced, NCCT was normal (Fig. 15-16).

The central, peripheral, and ring enhancement patterns present an appearance that may strongly resemble

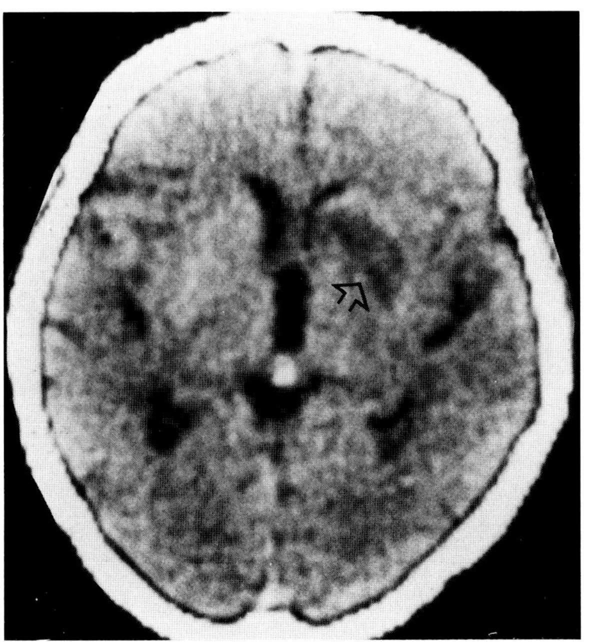
A

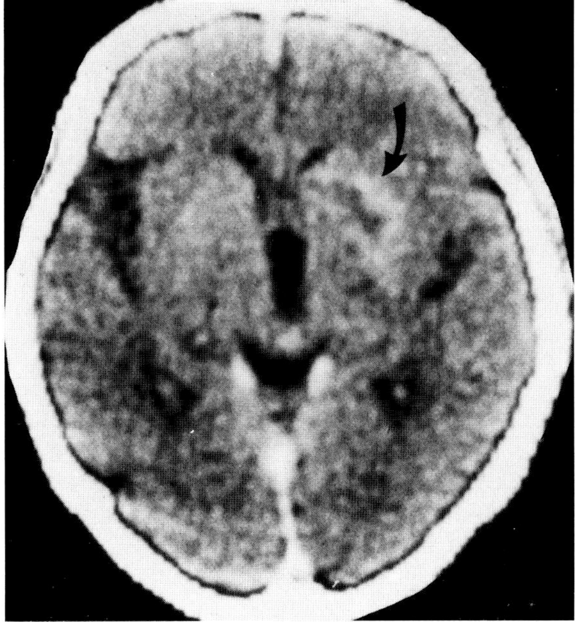
B

Figure 15-13 Ring enhancement in a 9-day-old infarct in the basal ganglia-anterior capsule region. **A.** NCCT reveals hypodensity involving left anterior capsule-basal ganglia region (arrow) with compression of adjacent frontal horn. CT was normal 7 days before. **B.** CECT demonstrates ring enhancement within outer margin of hypodensity (arrow).

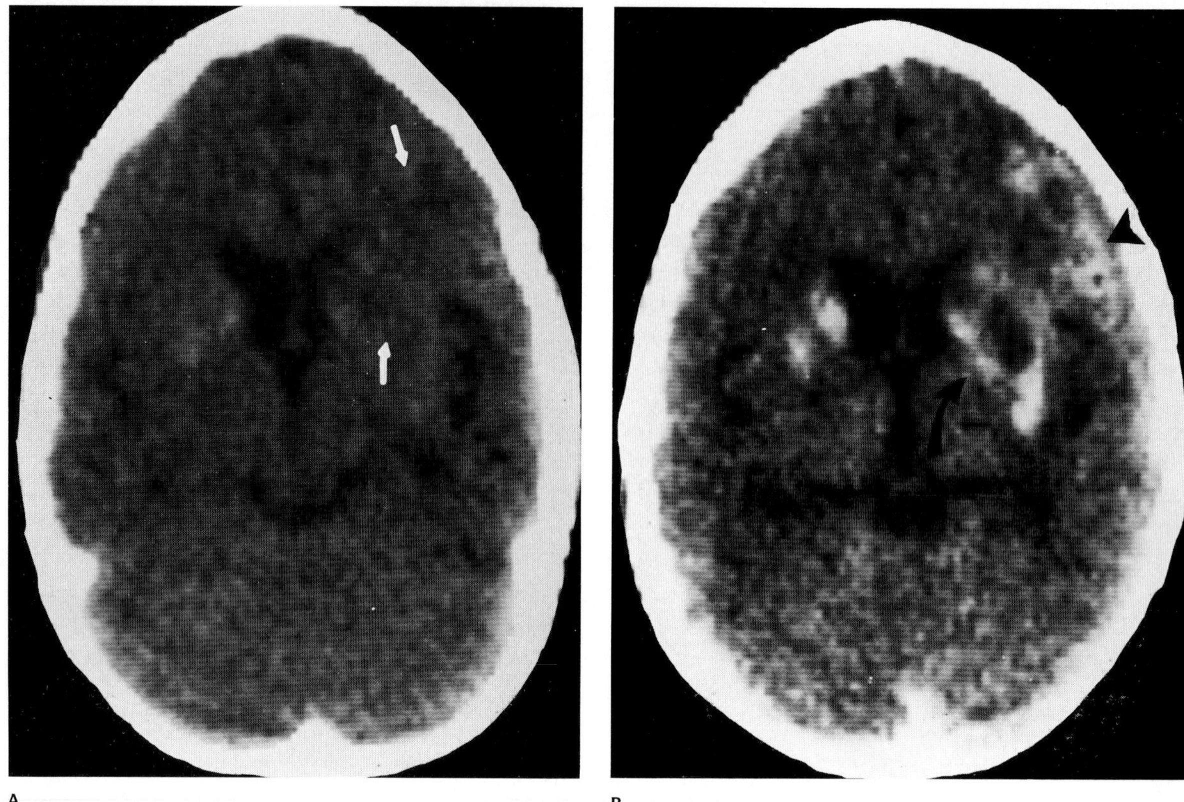

A B

Figure 15-14 Left basal ganglionic, middle cerebral artery, and right anterior ganglionic infarct at day 16, secondary to bilateral middle cerebral artery emboli from cardiomyopathy (subsequent autopsy confirmation). **A.** NCCT: hypodensity of left basal ganglionic and presylvian region (arrows) with compression of frontal horn. **B.** CECT demonstrates irregular ring enhancement of left basal ganglia (arrow) along with patchy enhancement in the left cortex (arrowhead) and in the right anterior basal ganglia.

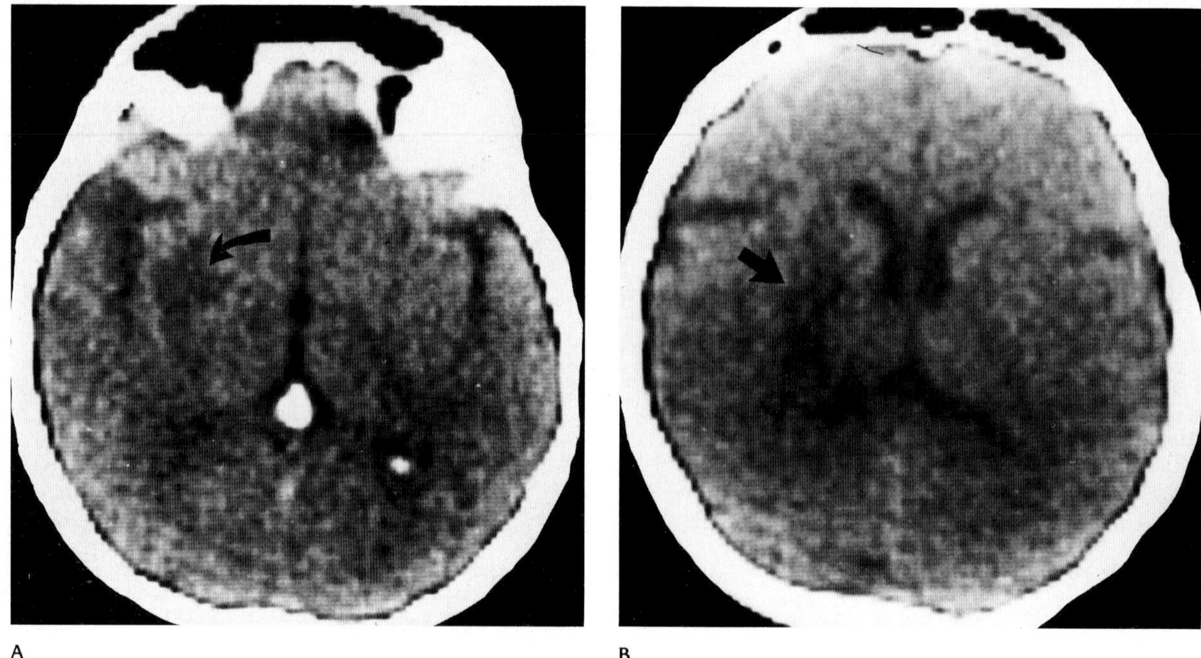

A B

Figure 15-15 Masking of recent infarct with enhancement. **A** and **B.** NCCT, contiguous sections: large right basal ganglia-capsular hypodensity (arrows). (*Continued on p. 641.*)

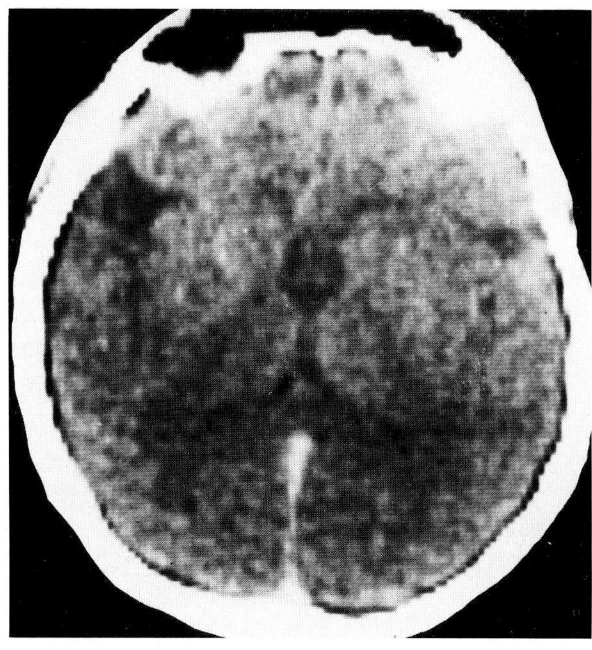

C

Figure 15-15 (continued) **C.** CECT: region of infarct hypodensity in **A** and **B** isodense after enhancement. Similar change was noted on adjacent sections.

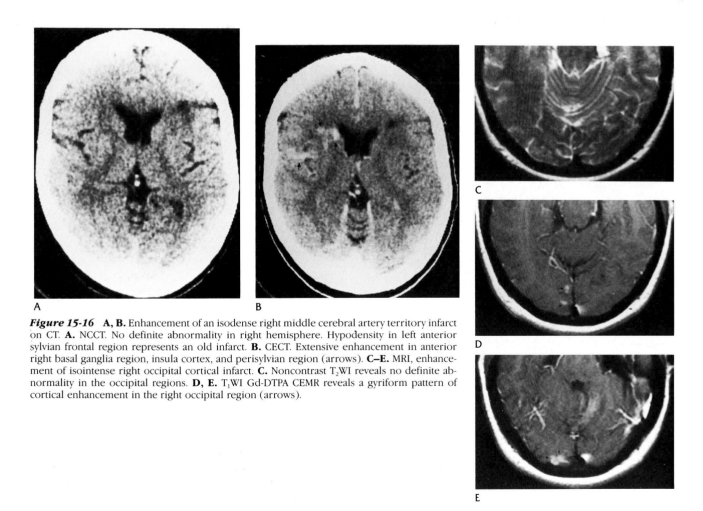

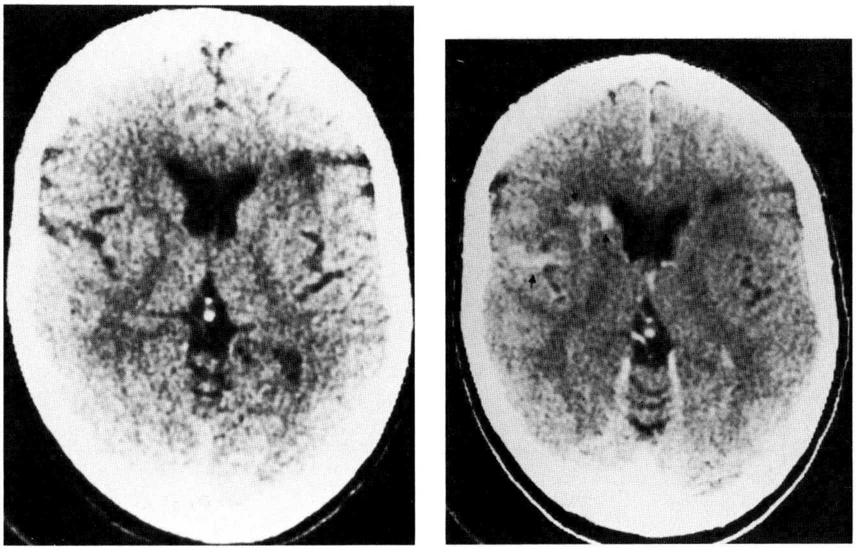

A B 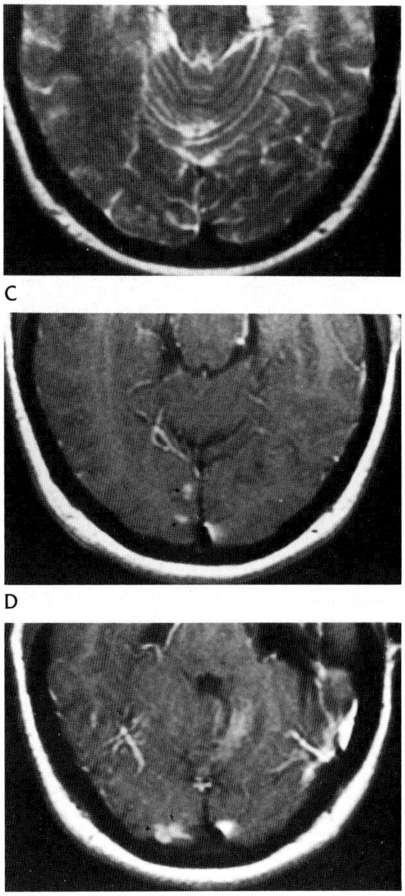 C D E

Figure 15-16 **A, B.** Enhancement of an isodense right middle cerebral artery territory infarct on CT. **A.** NCCT. No definite abnormality in right hemisphere. Hypodensity in left anterior sylvian frontal region represents an old infarct. **B.** CECT. Extensive enhancement in anterior right basal ganglia region, insula cortex, and perisylvian region (arrows). **C–E.** MRI, enhancement of isointense right occipital cortical infarct. **C.** Noncontrast T_2WI reveals no definite abnormality in the occipital regions. **D, E.** T_1WI Gd-DTPA CEMR reveals a gyriform pattern of cortical enhancement in the right occipital region (arrows).

that of a tumor or abscess. With infarction, however, most of the mass effect has usually resolved by the time enhancement appears, and the entire lesion (low density and area of enhancement) is confined to the territory of one vascular distribution in a wedge-shaped or rectangular pattern. There is usually also involvement of cortex. The combination of these changes, which are generally not present with tumor or inflammatory disease, should in most cases reliably differentiate these conditions. If the diagnosis remains uncertain, a follow-up CT study should clearly differentiate infarction from the other conditions. With infarction, the enhancement usually disappears or decreases markedly in 3 to 4 weeks and atrophic changes develop over the next 1 to 3 months, as evidenced by focal ventricular dilatation and enlargement of overlying cortical sulci.

On MR, contrast enhancement demonstrates similar patterns of infarct enhancement as with CECT. T_1WI (short TR, short TE) are utilized to demonstrate this enhancement. Subacute infarcts which involve only gray matter are frequently normal on NCMR and on both T_1WI and T_2WI. These infarcts usually become evident on CEMR as a prominent gyriform enhancing pattern involving the surface of the brain and also as regional enhancement of the basal ganglia. The ability of MR to readily image in the coronal plane permits very reliable determination of the anatomic regions of contrast enhancement (Fig. 15-16).

Weisberg (1980) observed that patients in whom an infarct showed enhancement on CT had a better prognosis than did those without enhancement: There were no deaths in a group of 50 patients who had enhancement, whereas 5 of 35 patients without enhancement died after the cerebral infarction. Functional recovery from motor, sensory, visual, and language disturbances was better for patients who showed enhancement and whose follow-up scans showed no residual hypodensity area, indicating an absence of brain necrosis. These findings are in contrast to those of Pullicino (1980), who reported that enhancing infarcts in their series had a significantly *poorer* prognosis than did those without enhancement. They also found that enhancement was more common with larger infarcts and in infarcts that had mass effect. These two factors probably explain the more adverse prognosis associated with enhancement in their series.

EMBOLIC INFARCTION

Embolic infarction is probably much more frequent than is concluded on clinical grounds. Adams (1953) indicated that it is responsible for 50 percent of infarcts. Lhermitte (1970) found in an autopsy study that 68 percent of middle cerebral artery occlusions are embolic in origin. Cerebral emboli frequently originate from heart disease and from atheromatous disease in the aorta or the carotid or vertebral arteries.

Yock (1981) and others (Tomsick 1990) identified emboli on NCCT in the middle and anterior cerebral arteries. They appear as focal hyperdensity at the usual location near major bifurcations in these vessels. The emboli have peak attenuation values of 84 to 214 HU, indicating that most consist of calcific material with or without thrombus. Those with a density less than 90 HU may represent only dense clot.

With embolic infarction, the temporal evolution of early CT and MR changes is different from the changes seen with atherosclerotic thrombotic infarcts. Whereas atherosclerotic occlusion usually results in a relatively permanent arterial obstruction, an embolic occlusion frequently fragments and undergoes lysis between the first and fifth days, resulting in reestablishment of normal antegrade circulation. This exposes the infarcted brain tissue to a much higher perfusion pressure than was present before clot lysis, when circulation depended on the adequacy of collateral channels. The hemodynamic consequences of clot lysis are responsible for the differences in the CT and MRI alterations that accompany embolic infarction. A scan performed prior to lysis of an embolus will be similar to that present with an atherosclerotic occlusion, except that there may be infarcts in more than one vascular distribution of approximately the same age (Fig. 15-17). After fragmentation and dissolution of the embolus, the rise in perfusion pressure results in a marked increase in blood flow in and around the infarcted tissue, which frequently becomes higher than normal, and also in an increased breakdown of the blood-brain barrier. This hyperemia develops from the loss of normal autoregulatory control of blood flow in the infarct region.

Autoregulation is a unique intrinsic property of normal cerebral vasculature that maintains blood flow at a constant level over a wide range of arterial pressures. This control is located mainly in the arterioles, which constrict with rising pressure and dilate with falling pressure. In a normal person, the limits of autoregulation extend over a mean arterial pressure ranging from about 50 mmHg to 140 mmHg. The control of this mechanism appears to be mediated through an intrinsic myotonic stretch reflex in the arteriolar wall. In addition, changes in blood and tissue chemical factors such as carbon dioxide, lactic acid, and molecular oxygen concentrations may alter arteriolar diameter and affect autoregulation. Increased carbon dioxide and lactic acid concentrations and decreased oxygen tension cause vasodilatation. Vessels with a loss of autoregulation may lose their response to these chemical regulators. Infarction, as well as other conditions that cause brain injury, such as trauma, infection, subarachnoid hemorrhage, and tumors, results in a

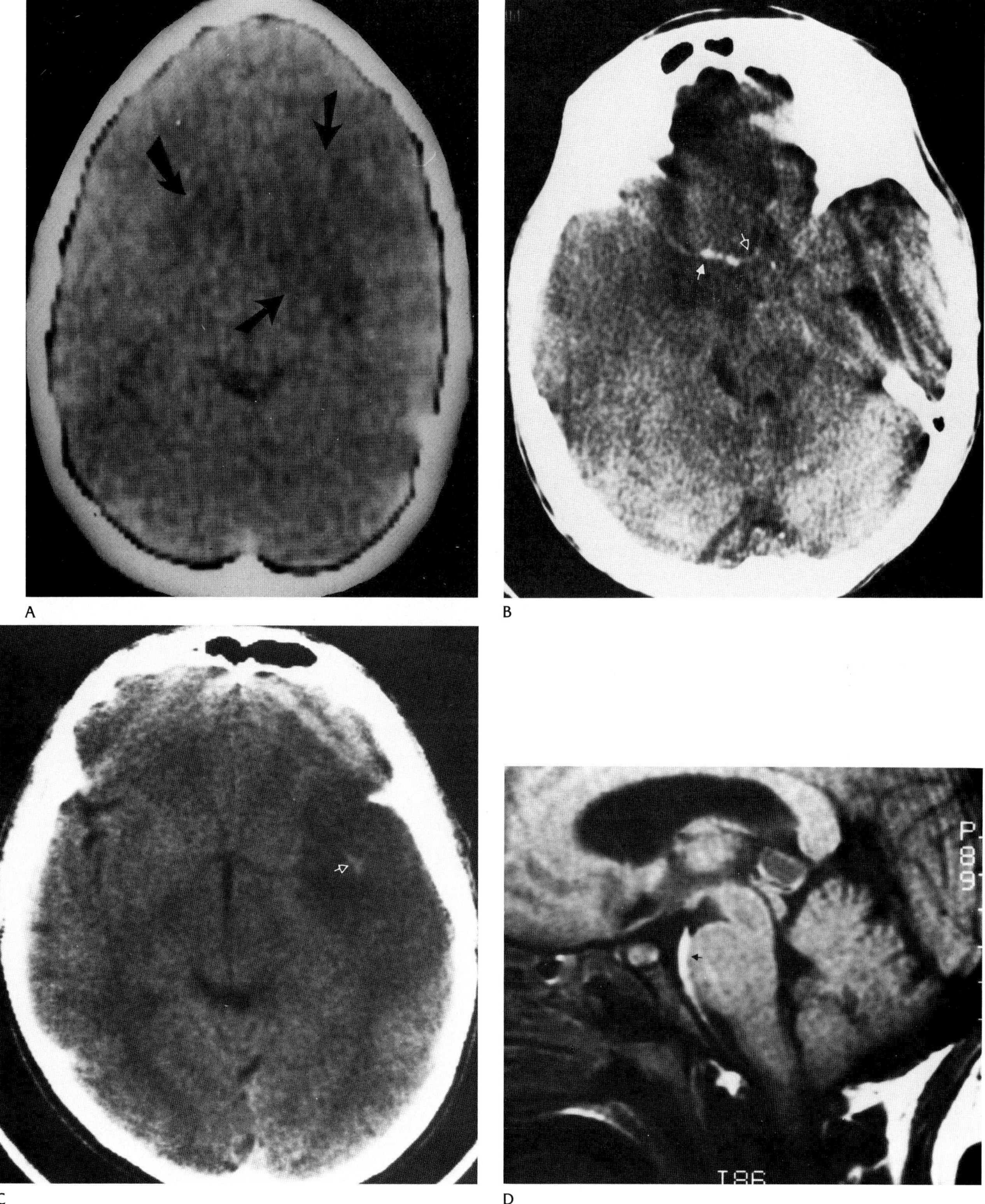

Figure 15-17 Bilateral embolic middle cerebral artery territory infarctions at 36 hours (same patient as in Figure 15-14). Large, poorly defined hypodensity involving basal ganglia and posterior frontal region on left (arrows). Similar but smaller area of hypodensity on right (arrowhead). **B.** CT demonstrating a hyperdense embolic clot in proximal middle cerebral and proximal anterior cerebral arteries with distal acute infarction. Linear hyperdensity extending from the region of internal carotid artery bifurcation into the proximal middle cerebral artery (solid arrow) and the proximal anterior cerebral artery (open arrow). There is marked hypodensity of the brain in the inferior frontal and anterior temporal regions with considerable mass effect. **C.** CT demonstrating a hyperdense embolic clot in the distal middle cerebral artery and surrounding acute infarct. Curvilinear hyperdensity evident in left insula cistern (arrow). There is surrounding hypodensity involving the cortex and white matter in the temporal and inferior frontal lobes and lateral basal ganglia region. **D.** MRI. Basilar artery embolus from a vertebral artery dissection. Sagittal T_1WI demonstrates hyperintensity within the basilar artery (arrow). A large acute pontine infarct is present (see Figure 15-36).

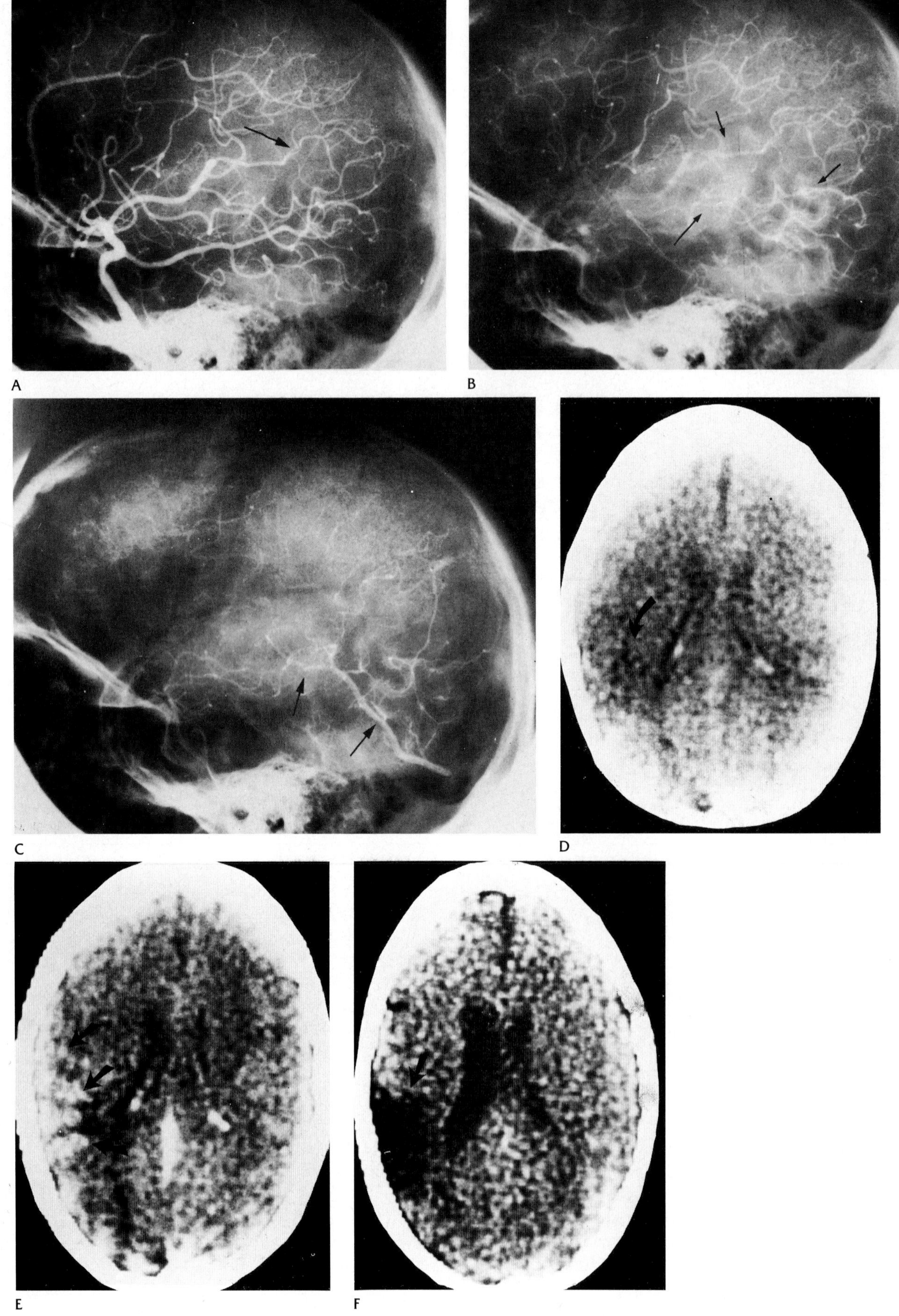
A
B
C
D
E
F

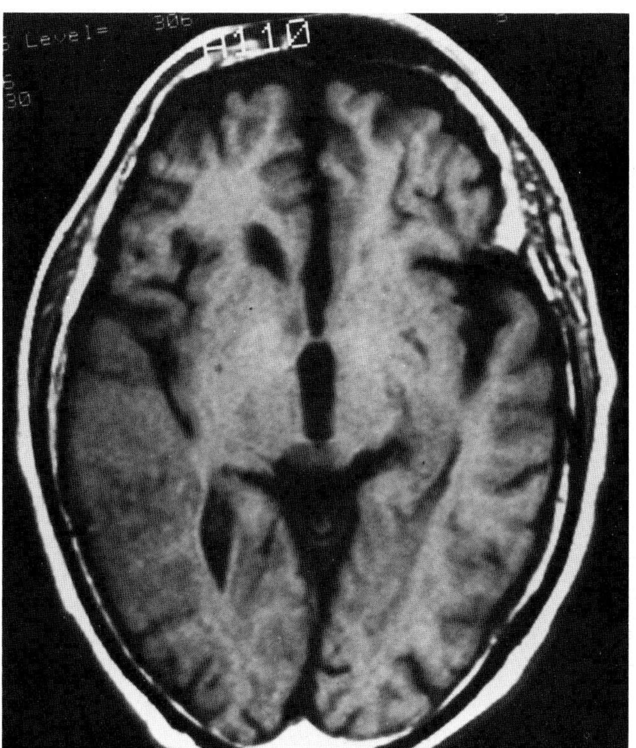

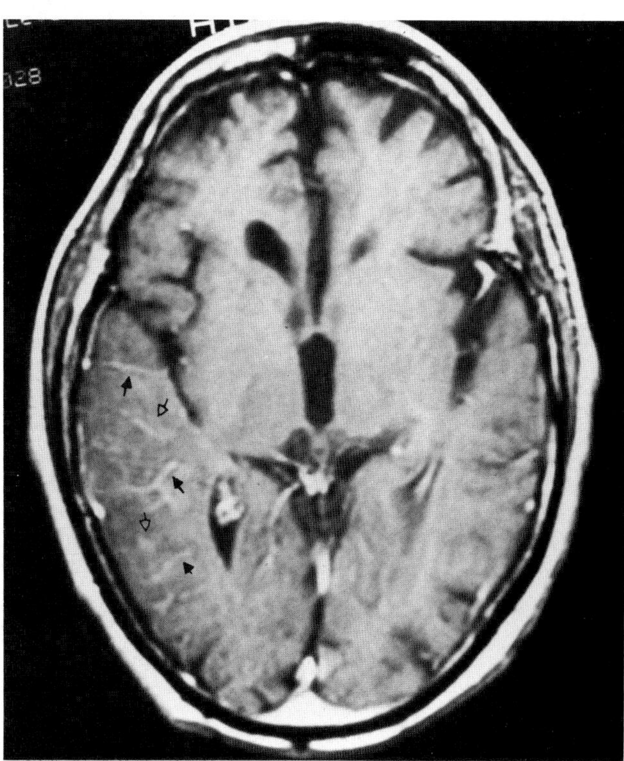

G H

Figure 15-18 Embolic infarction reactive hypermia (luxury perfusion) at day 5 following major clot lysis and reestablishment of antegrade circulation. **A.** Lateral right carotid angiogram, midarterial phase, revealing small embolic fragment partially occluding the angular gyrus artery distally (arrow). **B.** Lateral right carotid angiogram, late arterial phase, revealing early appearance of a prominent gyriform capillary blush (reactive hyperemia) in the posterior temporal-inferior parietal region (arrows). **C.** Lateral right carotid angiogram, capillary phase, revealing early venous filling (luxury perfusion) in the posterior temporal-inferior parietal region (arrows). **D.** NCCT at time of angiogram. Suggestion of ill-defined slight hypodensity in right posterior temporal-parietal region (arrow). **E.** CECT: gyriform enhancement in right posterior temporal-parietal region (arrows). **F.** NCCT 4 months after stroke. Well-defined region of marked hypodensity involving cortex and underlying white matter (arrow) in the right posterior temporal-parietal region, associated with ventricular dilatation. **G, H.** Luxury perfusion on MRI after an embolic right middle cerebral artery territory infarct. **G.** NCMR T_1WI reveals nonhomogeneous slight hypointensity in the mid- and posterior temporal lobe on the right with an effacement of adjacent sulci. **H.** Gd-DTPA CEMR reveals dilated sulcal veins (solid arrows) and patchy cortical enhancement (open arrows) in the right mid and posterior temporal region.

loss of normal autoregulation and varying degrees of vasoparalysis in the vascular bed of the affected region.

Loss of autoregulation may persist for several weeks after an infarction; its duration is dependent on the severity of the ischemic injury. During this time, circulation in these regions passively follows changes in perfusion pressure, as the arterioles no longer have the capacity to dilate or constrict in response to changes in blood pressure. The local tissue acidosis that develops within the area of infarction as a result of the buildup of acid metabolites causes vasoparalysis (Myer 1957; Lassen 1966; Kassik 1968). This results in arteriolar dilatation, with blood flow becoming markedly increased with the reestablishment of normal perfusion pressure. Lassen (1966) characterized this hyperemia as "luxury perfusion," because blood flow to the tissues is above the normal metabolic requirements. The *hyperemic (luxury perfusion) reaction* associated with loss of autoregulation becomes evident only after the return of normal perfusion pressure to the region of infarction, as occurs after lysis of an embolic occlusion. With persistent arterial occlusion this reaction is not seen, except possibly at the margins of the infarct, which could be supplied by antegrade flow through nonoccluded vessels. Not infrequently, some degree of hypertension develops after infarction, producing further arteriolar dilatation and resulting in a higher rate of blood flow. Cerebral angiography in the first few weeks after the dissolution of an embolus usually reveals dilated cortical arterioles and gyral hyperemia associated with early filling of regional draining veins (Fig. 15-18) (Cronqvist 1967, 1968; Ferris 1966; Irino 1977*a, b*; Leeds 1973; Pitts 1964). Concomitantly, the radionuclide brain scan will demonstrate a region of high activity in the dynamic flow sequence (Yarnell 1975; Soin 1976). Focal el-

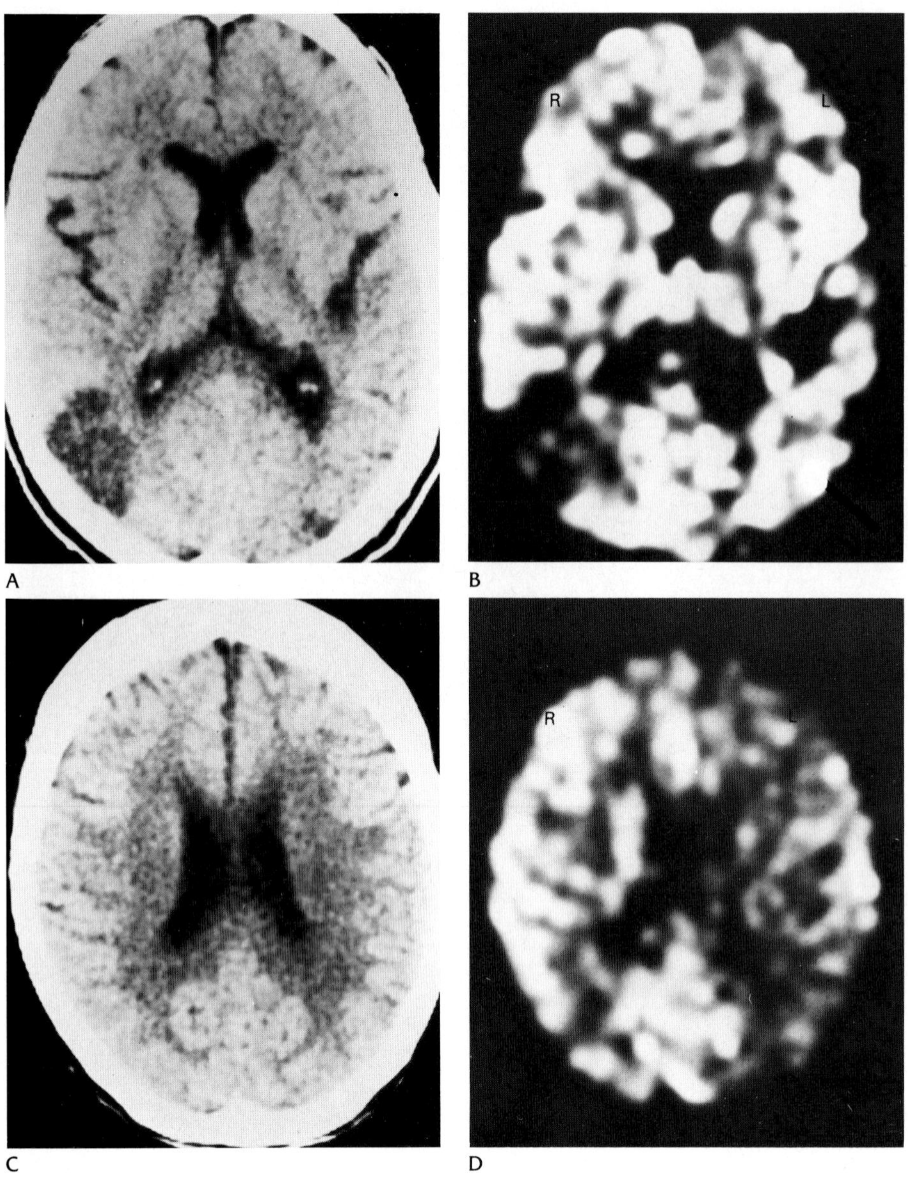

Figure 15-19 Xe/CT cerebral blood flow: **A** (NCCT) and **B** (Xe/CT) show an old right occipital infarct and hyperperfusion on the left frontotemporal lobe representing "luxury perfusion" for recent infarct. **C** (NCCT) and **D** (Xe/CT) demonstrate normal CT and decreased left hemispheric blood flow due to vasospasm and vasculitis. (*Courtesy of GE Co. Medical Systems, Milwaukee, Wisconsin.*)

evation of cerebral blood flow may also be revealed with the ^{133}Xe technique (Cronqvist 1967, 1968; Hoedt-Rasmussen 1967; Paulson 1970).

Continued development and recent refinement of the stable xenon inhalation method utilizing CT since its introduction in 1978 have made this technique an advanced and clinically useful method for measuring cerebral blood flow. It has been utilized in ischemia from cerebrovascular diseases, from vasoregulatory alterations, and secondary to aneurysm bleed (Fig. 15-19). It also is useful in the coma state, brain death, closed head injury or seizure disorders, and degenerative syndromes such as acute progressive dementia, Alzheimer's disease, and multiple sclerosis (Wolfson 1985). This technique, although limited, holds promise of widespread clinical application because of its relatively high anatomic resolution, low cost, and ease of administration.

Infarct hyperemia (luxury perfusion) generally causes some regions that were hypodense on CT obtained before revascularization to become isodense or slightly hyperdense on NCCT (Fig. 15-20). On MRI, some regions that were hyperintense on T_2WI and hypointense on T_1WI became isointense after the development of hyperemia (Fig. 15-20). This change develops mainly in the cortex and deep gray matter because these regions have a large capillary bed that passively dilates after reperfusion. Rapid-sequence CT scanning after bolus contrast injection may demonstrate the luxury perfusion reaction (Fig. 15-21). Besides the elevation in blood volume, some of the increase in cortical density may result from the petechial hemorrhages (Inoue 1980). Because of the great sensitivity of MRI to the demonstration of both acute and subacute blood product (Gomori 1985), it more readily detects small amounts of petechial hemorrhage than

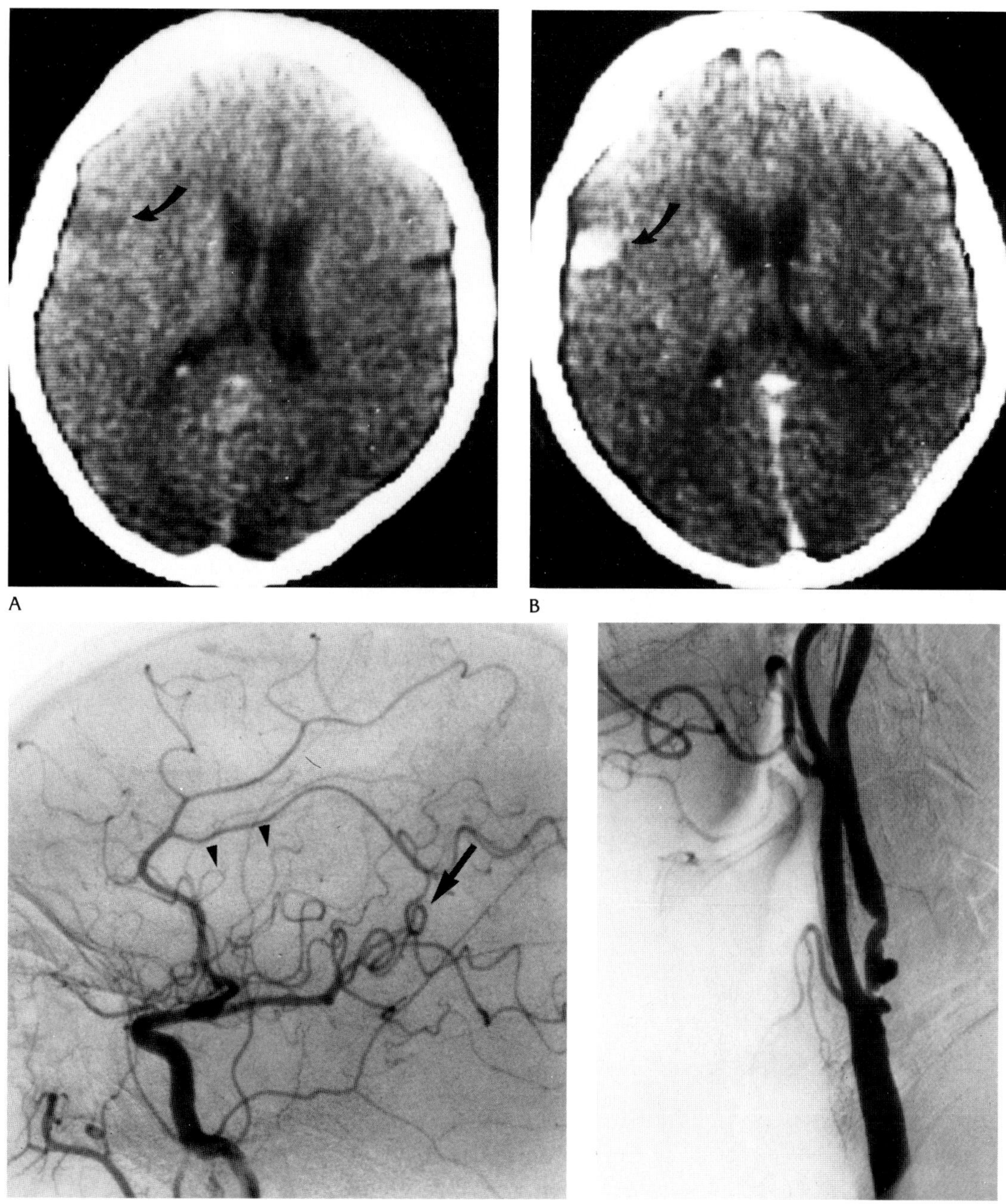

Figure 15-20 Embolic infarction, conversion on NCCT of hypodense tissue to isodensity after reestablishment of antegrade circulation. **A.** NCCT on day 3 reveals cortical hypodensity in the posterior frontal region (arrow). NCCT on day 8 fails to demonstrate hypodensity. **B.** CECT on day 8 reveals cortical enhancement (arrow) in region of hypodensity in **A. C.** Lateral carotid angiogram on day 9 demonstrates embolic occlusion of posterior inferior (arrow) and parietal branches (arrowheads) of middle cerebral artery tributary. Avascular parietal region fills well on subsequent films from distal anterior cerebral artery branches. There is relatively normal antegrade circulation into the region of CT abnormality in posterior frontal area (arrowheads), suggesting previous lysis of embolic fragment. Large ulcerated plaque at origin of internal carotid artery is probable source of emboli (**D**).

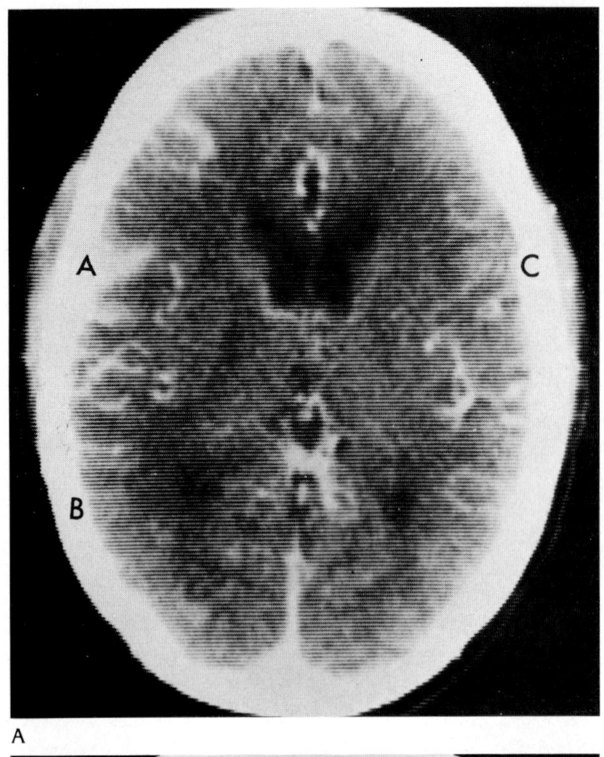

A

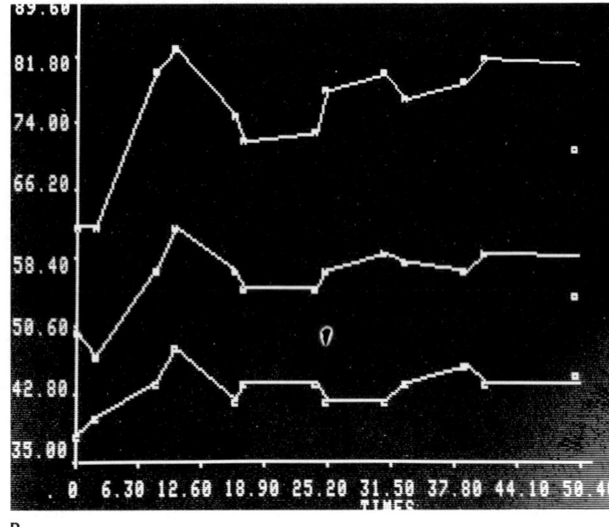

B

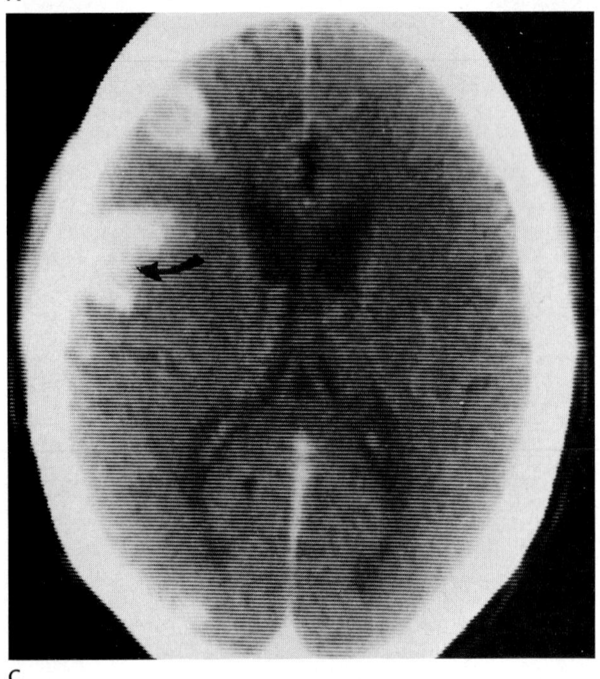

C

Figure 15-21 Hyperemic changes on rapid-sequence bolus injection CT. Probable embolic infarction at day 10. **A.** Rapid-sequence CT approximately 6 seconds after contrast bolus arrival at brain. Maximum vascular phase contrast density at this time. Highest cortical contrast density at location *A*, site of ischemic circulatory changes at day 2 (Fig. 15-9). Locations *B* and *C* over uninvolved cortical regions on previous CT. **B.** Time-density curves of locations, *A, B,* and *C* in **A.** Graph parameters are the same as in Fig. 15-9*B*. Curve *A* (upper) demonstrates a more rapid and greater rise and a fall of contrast density than curves *B* (middle) and *C* (lower) during their first passage through the brain. Secondary density increase of curve *A* reflects tissue enhancement due to a defective blood-brain barrier and high tissue perfusion pressure. **C.** CT 30 minutes after **A.** Increased cortical enhancement (arrow) with spread of enhancement into adjacent white matter as evidenced by thickening of the cortical ribbon (compare with **A**) and obliteration of the intergyral white matter hypodensity.

does CT. In the acute phase (initial 3 to 5 days after reperfusion), hemoglobin in the red blood cells is in the deoxyhemoglobin state. T_2WI and gradient-echo images utilizing a short flip angle and a long TE will demonstrate hypointensity in the regions of a petechial hemorrhage, which appears as a gyriform cortical pattern. After 3 to 5 days, subacute phase methemoglobin is formed within the red blood cells. T_1WI will then demonstrate a hyperintense gyral enhancing pattern. (Hecht-Leavitt 1986). Because of its much lower capillary volume, the white matter does not contribute appreciably to the hyperemic reaction. The density increase in the cortex is usually diffuse but may be spotty, depending on the degree of fragmentation and lysis of the embolus. NCCT may have a normal appearance, but the underlying white matter usually remains hypodense (Fig. 15-18).

Prominent enhancement develops after lysis of the embolus, usually appearing as a cortical gyral pattern (Fig. 15-18) with frequent involvement of the basal ganglia. The high reperfusion pressure potentiates the spread of enhancement into the adjacent white matter (Fig. 15-21). Enhancement appears in most cases by the fifth day and frequently develops earlier, depending on the time it takes for clot lysis to occur. Enhancement is related to a disturbance in the blood-brain barrier and, to a lesser extent, hyperemia. Kohlmeyer (1978), evaluating the relationships between CT and cerebral blood flow, found that enhancement is usually not associated with luxury perfusion unless the enhancement develops during the first 3 to 5 days after the stroke. These observations suggest that early enhancement, since it is associated with increased cerebral blood flow, may indicate embolic infarction after clot lysis. Enhancement and luxury perfusion are potentiated by high reperfusion pressure. Hayman (1981) described an ominous enhancement pattern in infarcts 9 to 28 h old that were mainly embolic in origin. The enhancement appeared 1 to 3 h after the intravenous infusion of 80 g of iodine. The enhancement pattern consisted of a large, frequently wedge-shaped nonhomogeneous zone of hyperdensity that involved the cortex and extended down through the white matter to the ventricle (Fig. 15-22). Over half the patients with this pattern (four of seven) subsequently developed hemorrhagic infarcts and died. No other "double-dose" CECT pattern could be associated with the development of hemorrhagic infarction.

Brain swelling is frequently present when enhancement develops with embolic infarcts. This occurs because enhancement usually becomes evident between the second and fifth days, a period when infarct brain swelling is maximal. This is in contrast to the general lack of mass effect at the time when enhancement appears with atherosclerotic thrombotic infarcts at 10 to 14 days. Brain swelling with embolic infarcts may further increase after the appearance of enhancement, because the increased perfusion pressure resulting from clot lysis potentiates the formation of vasogenic edema (Olsson 1971). In the extreme case, hemorrhagic infarction may develop and further increase the degree of mass effect.

Hemorrhagic Infarction

This is in most instances an adverse sequela of embolic infarction related to the effects of high-pressure reperfusion of severely ischemic brain. Fisher (1951) found that of 66 hemorrhagic infarcts, only 3 were not clearly caused by embolism. Jorgensen (1969) observed that 80 percent of embolic infarcts were found at autopsy to be hemorrhagic. Angiography in combination with CT has

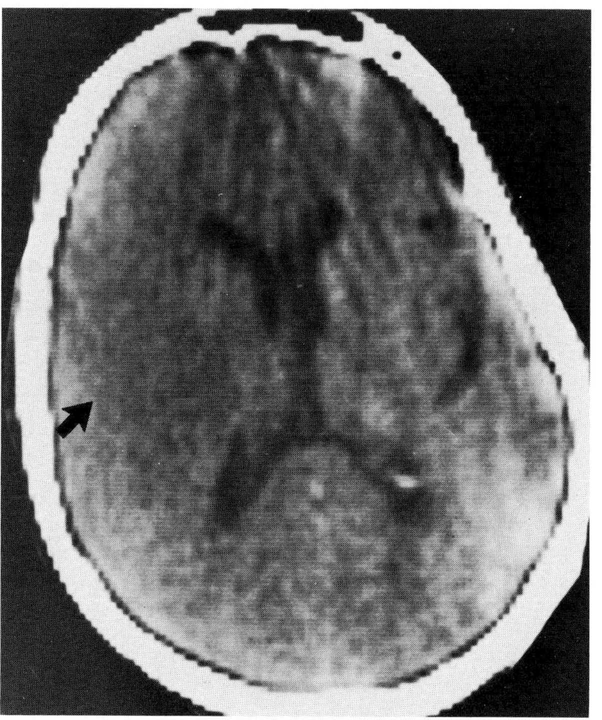

A

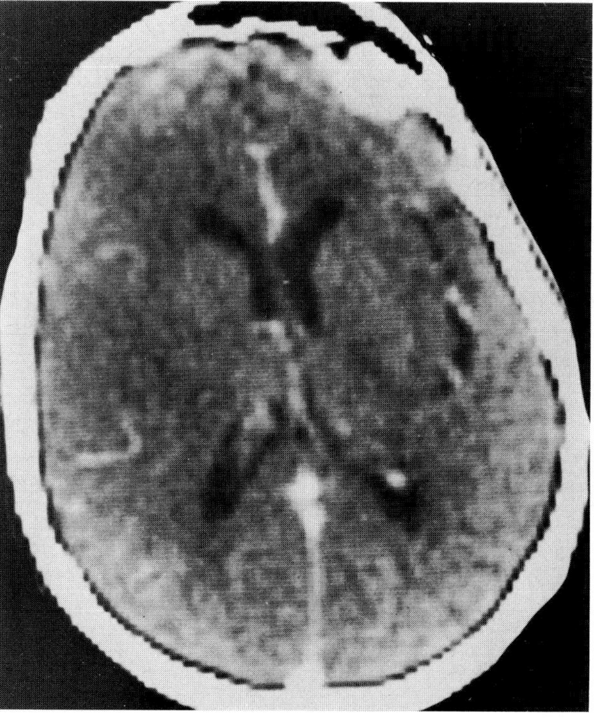

B

Figure 15-22 Enhancement on delayed high-contrast dose CT during the first day after the infarct. **A.** NCCT 20 hours after infarct reveals obliteration of the right sylvian fissure and ill-defined slight hypodensity in right posterior frontal region (arrow). **B.** Immediate high-contrast dose CT demonstrates absence of enhancement. (*Continued on p. 650.*)

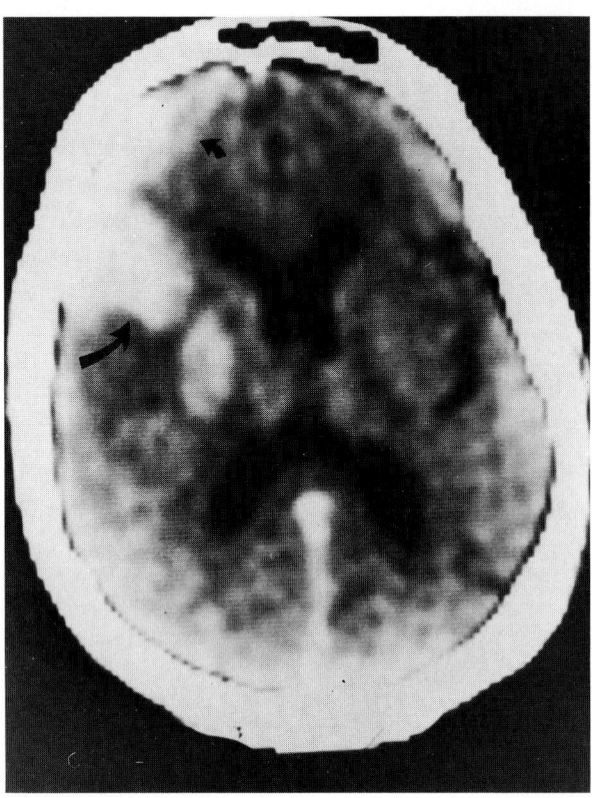

C

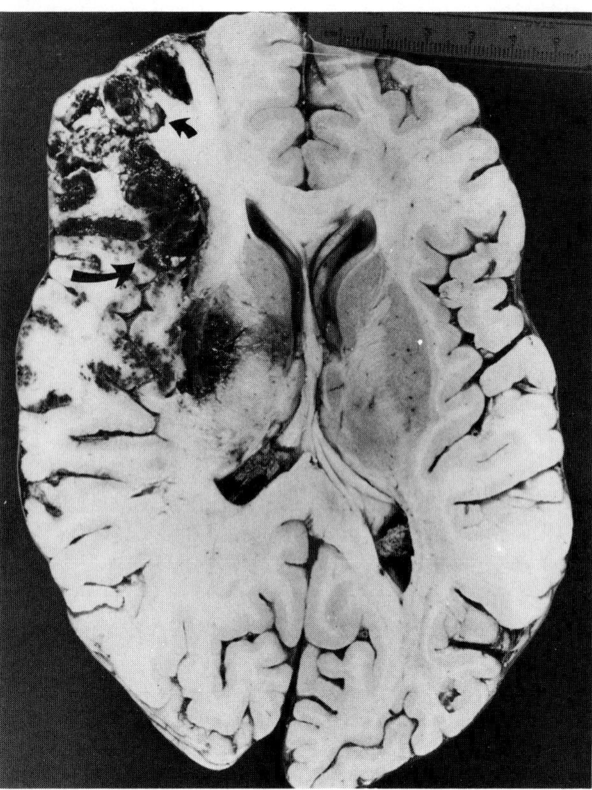

D

Figure 15-22 (continued) **C.** Delayed high-dose CT 3 hours after **B.** Marked enhancement of the cortex in the right frontal region (short arrow) extending in a wedge-shaped fashion deep into the white matter in the middle and posterior-frontal region (large arrow). There is in addition enhancement in the region of the right basal ganglia. **D.** Autopsy section of brain 8 days later at same level as CT scans. There is hemorrhagic infarction in region of enhancement on delayed CT in **C** (arrows) and anemic infarction with small cortical petechial hemorrhage in nonenhanced region of adjacent middle cerebral artery territory. (*From Hayman LA et al. 1981.*)

confirmed the relationship between fragmentation and lysis of the embolus and hemorrhagic infarction (Irino 1977*b*; Davis 1975, 1977). In the report of Davis (1977), three patients with hemorrhagic infarction all had clinical evidence of an embolic stroke, and in two, cerebral angiography documented the embolic occlusion before there was clinical or CT evidence of the hemorrhagic infarct. In one patient, a repeat cerebral angiogram at the time of neurological deterioration and the appearance of the hemorrhagic infarct on CT revealed lysis of a previously demonstrated embolic occlusion. Hemorrhagic infarction may also occur with atherosclerotic thrombotic infarcts in patients with coagulation disorders and in those on antithrombotic therapy (Wood 1958). The incidence of hemorrhagic infarction has been reported to range between 18 and 23 percent (Fisher 1951; Davis 1977; Hayman 1981).

Small areas of petechial hemorrhage are identified pathologically on the periphery of many otherwise bland infarcts, but in hemorrhagic infarcts, the petechial hemorrhage is more marked and spreads diffusely throughout, though predominantly in the cortex and deep gray matter (Adams 1968). It may involve only areas of cortex located in the depth of sulci. On occasion an area of frank hemorrhage develops from leakage of blood out of small arteries and capillaries into the perivascular spaces. Microscopically, vessels may not show evidence of ischemic damage, which is usually very severe in the surrounding brain parenchyma.

Hemorrhagic infarct is more likely to develop when tissue necrosis is marked. In animal studies, prolonging the initial period of ischemia from 6 to 24 h before reperfusion increases the incidence of hemorrhagic infarction from 40 to 60 percent (Kamijyo 1977). Increasing blood pressure (Laurent 1976) and the use of heparin (Wood 1958) have also been shown to result in hemorrhagic transformation of some infarcts produced by permanent arterial occlusions. Clinical experience with carotid endarterectomy has similarly shown that reestablishing increased perfusion pressure by means of surgical removal of the obstructing atheromatous plaque during the first several weeks after a recent infarct may cause conversion of an anemic infarct into a hemorrhagic infarct.

In a serial CT study by Cronqvist (1976), the initial CT scan obtained during the first 5 days revealed only a low-density lesion within the brain in six of seven patients who developed hemorrhagic infarcts. In one patient, the initial scan at 2 days demonstrated hemorrhage infarction. In the six with initial low-density lesions, hemorrhagic infarction became evident between 5 and 21 days after the onset of the stroke. In another study, Davis (1977) reported that 10 of 12 stroke patients who developed secondary abrupt neurological deterioration revealed hemorrhagic infarct on CT within 5 days of the initial stroke. Two of these patients had had earlier scans that showed no evidence of hemorrhage. Four developed the hemorrhagic infarct after 1 day, three after 2 days, one after 4 days, and two at 5 days.

A hemorrhagic infarct will in most instances reveal a very characteristic CT and MRI appearance, which can usually be readily differentiated from that of an intracerebral hematoma (Davis 1975; Hecht-Leavitt 1986). The hemorrhage primarily involves the cortex (Figs. 15-23 and 15-24) alone, as confluent petechiae, or with occasional secondary extension into the underlying white matter (Davis 1977). It may also involve the deep gray matter if the embolus initially arrests in the middle cerebral artery proximal to or at the origins of the lenticulostriate arteries. Cortical hemorrhage generally appears as a ribbon or bandlike region of slightly to moderately increased density on CT. It has unsharp margins and assumes the wavy configuration of the cortical gyri. The surrounding white matter is hypodense, and its involvement is limited to the same vascular distribution as the region of hemorrhage. This pattern may be diffuse over a large region of the cortex or may be more localized to the depth of one or more sulci. The hemorrhage may be nonhomogeneous or speckled in appearance (Fig. 15-25). At times the petechial hemorrhage is mild and, because of volume averaging, may elevate the hypodensity only up to the isodense range (Alcala 1978). If the hemorrhage extends into the white matter, it may resemble an intracerebral hematoma, and differentiation may be difficult. An intracerebral hematoma is usually homogeneously dense, with a rounded to oval configuration and sharp, distinct borders. White matter extension of a hemorrhagic infarct, in contrast, may be wedge-shaped to rectangular and is not usually homogeneously dense; its border may be somewhat indistinct.

On MRI in the first few days after clot lysis, during the time when the cortical hemorrhage is hyperdense on CT, it appears isointense to slightly hypointense on T_1WI and marketedly hypointense on T_2WI and low-flip-angle gradient-echo images (Fig. 15-23). After 5 to 7 days, at which time CT usually no longer reveals the hyperdensity of hemorrhage, T_1WI demonstrate marked hyperintensity as a gyriform pattern along the cortical ribbon (Fig. 15-24). On T_2WI, there is conversion of the cortical hypointensity to hyperintensity at this same time or within a few days (Hecht-Leavitt 1986).

On CECT and MRI, hemorrhagic infarction will usually develop contrast enhancement in the already dense cortical and basal ganglia and, to a variable degree, in the

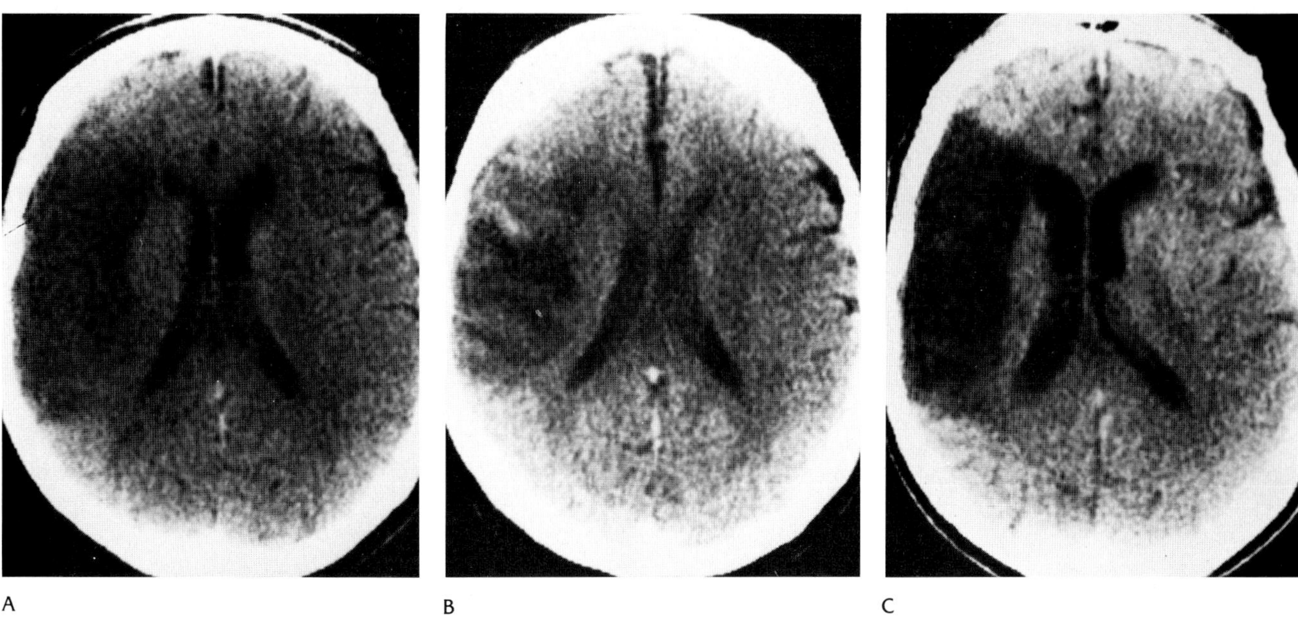

Figure 15-23 Evolution of cortical hemorrhagic infarct in 73-year-old female. **A.** NCCT 2 days after onset of stroke demonstrates well-defined hypodensity in right frontoparietal cortex. **B.** NCCT 10 days later shows mild cortical hemorrhage. **C.** NCCT 5 months later reveals encephalomalacia with ipsilateral ventriculography. DSA study disclosed right ICA occlusion and severe stenosis of left ICA. (*Continued on p. 652.*)

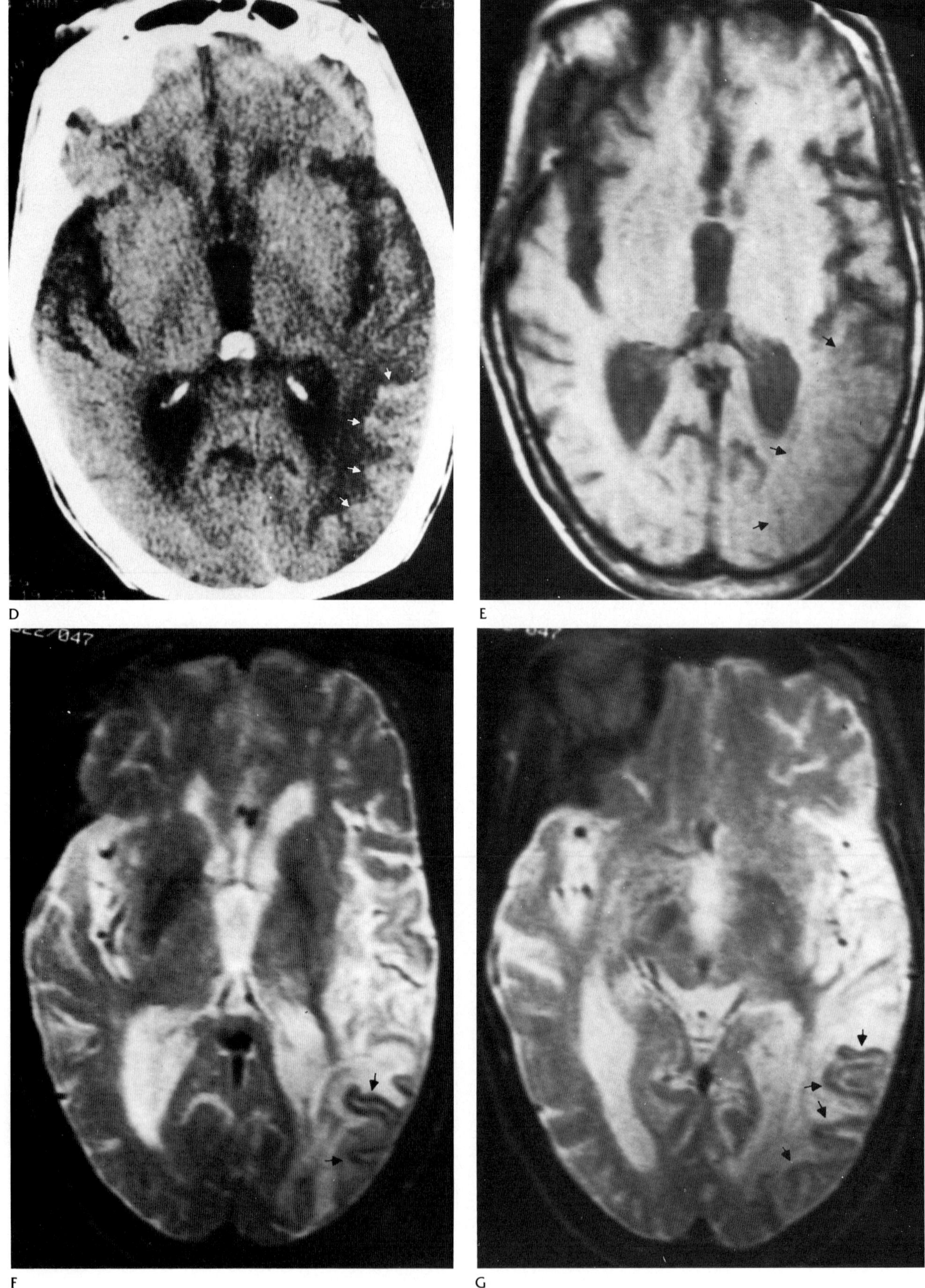

D E F G

Figure 15-23 (continued) **D–G.** MRI of acute hemorrhagic infarct left middle cerebral artery territory. **D.** NCCT reveals gyriform hyperdensity (arrows) and underlying white matter hypodensity in the left posterior temporal region, indicative of acute hemorrhagic infarct. **E.** T_1WI at the same level and at the same time as **D.** Diffuse hypointensity involving the cortex and underlying white matter is present in the left posterior temporal region (arrows). **F, G.** T_2WI reveal hypointensity along the cortical ribbon in the left posterior temporal region (arrows), indicating the presence of acute blood products at high field strength (deoxyhemoglobin). Hyperintensity is present in the underlying white matter. The hyperintensity more anteriorly in the temporal lobe reflects a dilated left sylvian fissure and dilated sulci from old ischemia.

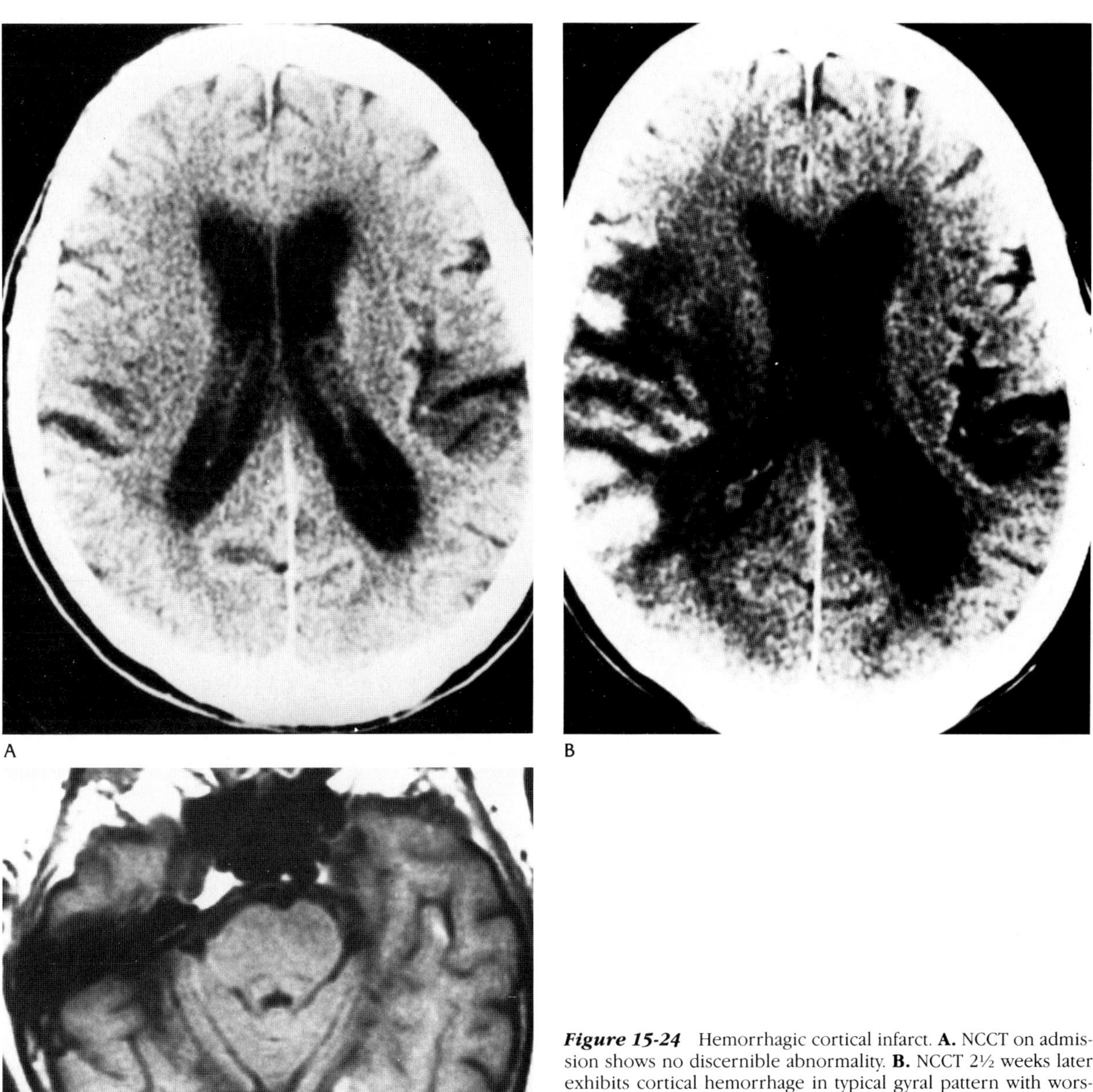

Figure 15-24 Hemorrhagic cortical infarct. **A.** NCCT on admission shows no discernible abnormality. **B.** NCCT 2½ weeks later exhibits cortical hemorrhage in typical gyral pattern with worsening of clinical status; 6 months and 18 months following, CTs (not shown) revealed an area of encephalomalacia with ipsilateral ventriculomegaly. **C.** Subacute hemorrhagic infarct in occipital lobes on MR. T_1WI NCMR demonstrates a cortical gyriform pattern of hyperintensity along the medial aspect of the left occipital lobe and to a lesser extent along the medial aspect of the right occipital lobe. This appearance indicates blood in the methemoglobin phase, signifying a cortical hemorrhage which is about 5 days old. (*Continued on p. 654.*)

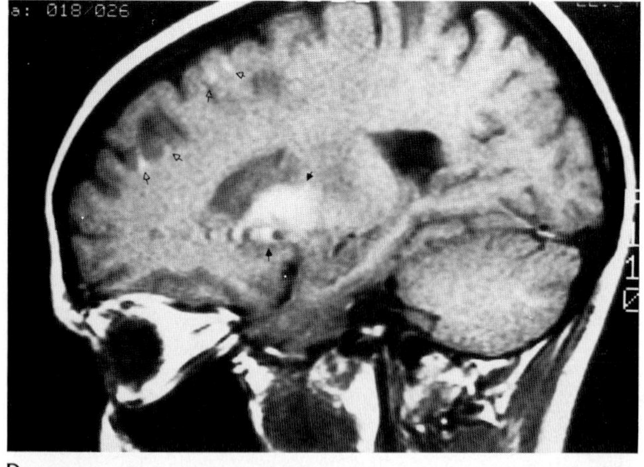

D

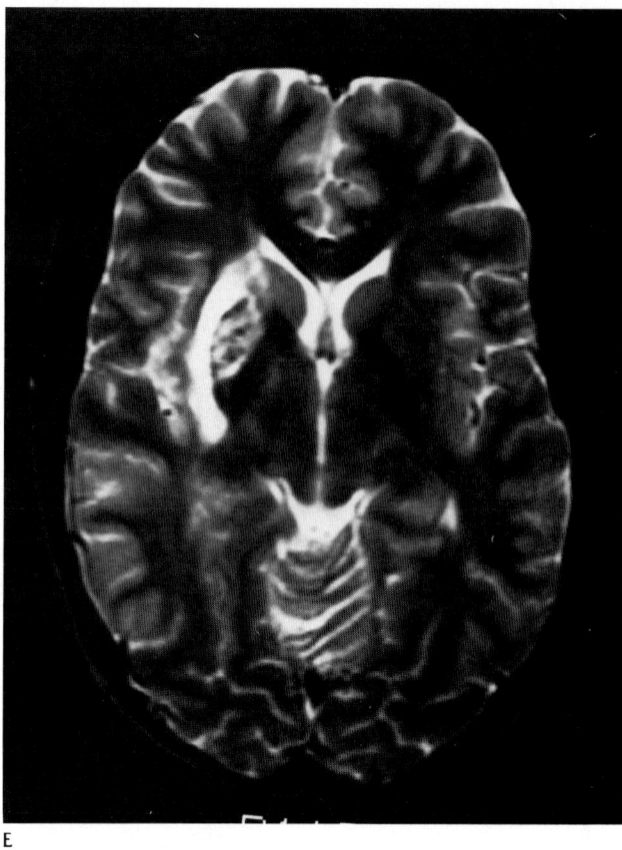

E

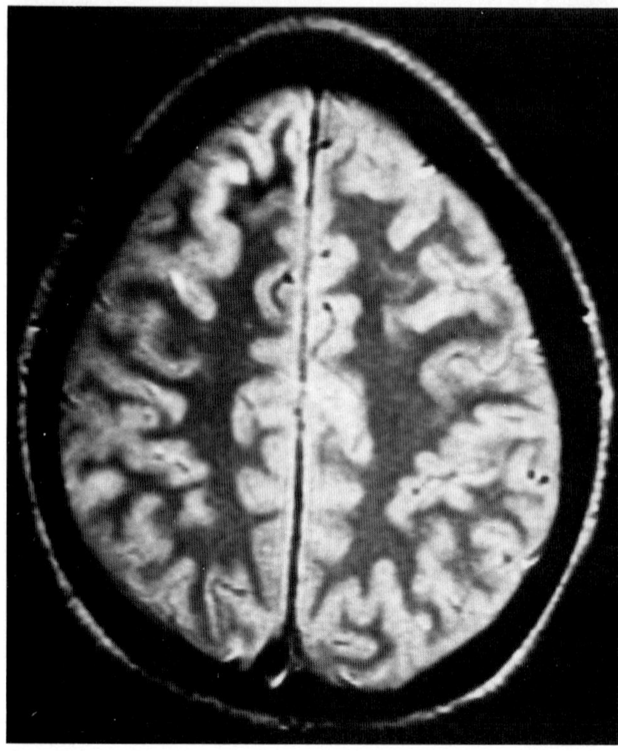

F

Figure 15-24 (continued) **D–F.** MRI of a subacute embolic hemorrhagic infarct in the right middle cerebral and anterior cerebral artery territories. **D.** Sagittal T_1WI NCMR through the midportion of the right cerebral hemisphere reveals a region of high intensity in the basal ganglia area (solid arrow) and foci of high intensity within the cortical ribbon superiorly in the front lobe (open arrows). T_2WI demonstrates high intensity involving the right basal ganglia. **F.** PDWI through a high-convexity region demonstrates high intensity within the cortical ribbon on the right in the distribution of an anterior cerebral artery branch (arrows). This high intensity is in the same region of high intensity demonstrated on the T_1WI in **D.**

surrounding nonhemorrhagic cortex (Fig. 15-25). The intracerebral hematoma does not show enhancement in the area of hemorrhage.

Clinical deterioration and increased mass effect usually occur when significant hemorrhagic infarction develops; they are related to the extravasated blood in the brain and the increase in vasogenic edema resulting from the higher perfusion pressure at the infarct after clot lysis. Minor petechial hemorrhage is usually not clinically apparent.

HEMODYNAMIC INFARCTION

Cerebral ischemic episodes may develop in patients with vasoocclusive disease when there are temporary alterations in circulatory dynamics (Denny-Brown 1960; Brierley 1976). This occurs primarily in older patients with hypertension or cardiac arrhythmias who have a fixed vascular lesion in an extra- or intracranial artery (Ruff 1981). The vascular lesion can be either a severe stenosis or an occlusion of long standing.

Cerebral blood flow studies have demonstrated disturbed autoregulation in this group of patients (Kindt 1967); any decrease in perfusion pressure may therefore cause a proportional decrease in cerebral blood flow either focally or diffusely. Depending on the length of time the perfusion pressure is reduced and its severity, the patient may incur a TIA, a reversible ischemic neurological deficit, or an infarction. In many of these patients, the stroke occurs while they are asleep at night,

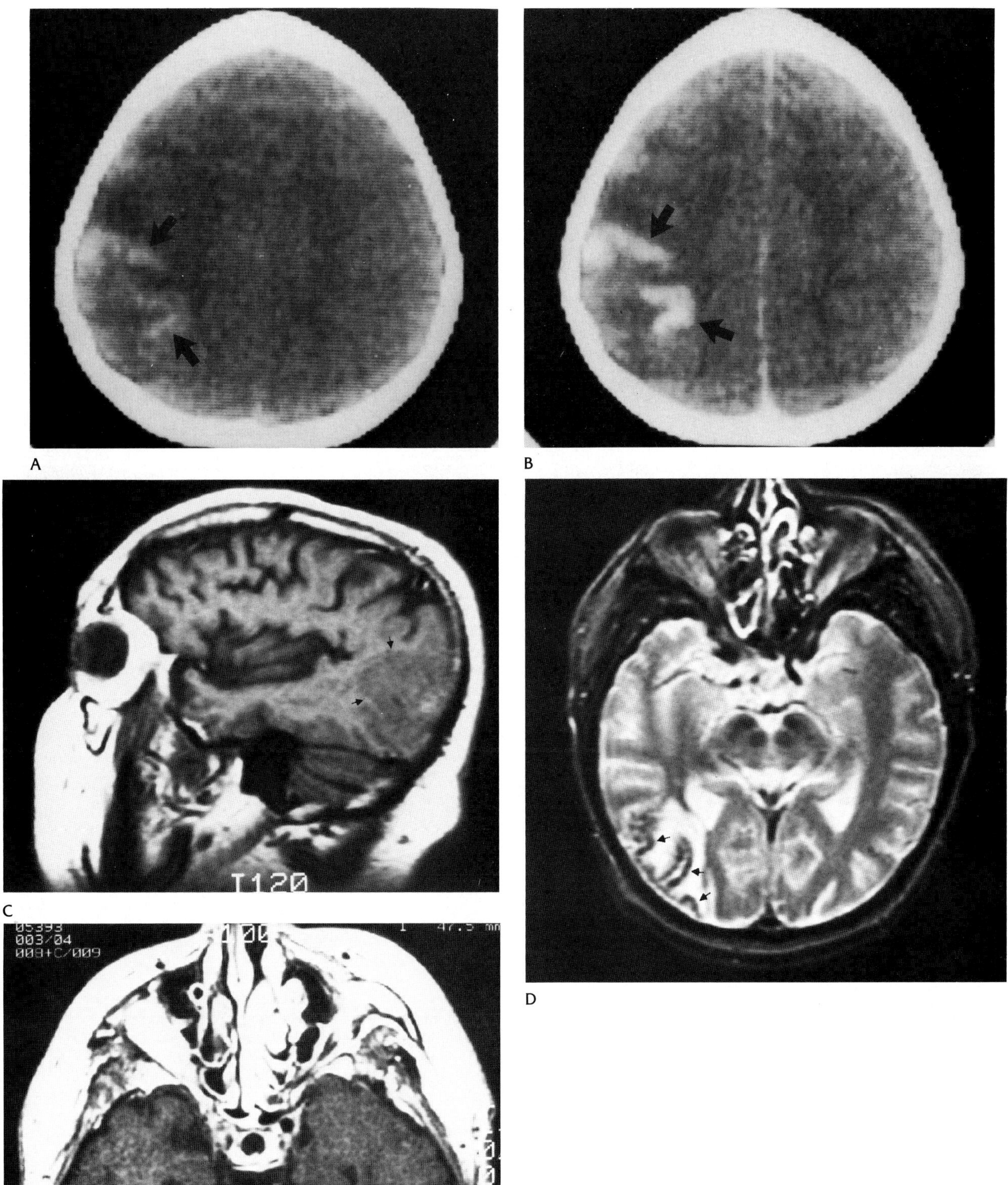

Figure 15-25 Contrast enhancement of cortical hemorrhagic infarct. **A.** NCCT: patchy gyriform cortical hemorrhagic involvement in the right superior posterior parietal region (arrows). Ischemic infarct hypodensity involving adjacent cortex and underlying white matter. **B.** CECT: enhancement in region of hemorrhagic cortical ribbon (arrows). **C–E.** Contrast enhancement of hemorrhagic infarct on MRI. **C.** Sagittal T_1WI NCMR through mid portion of right cerebral hemisphere demonstrates hypointense lesion in posterior temporal occipital area (arrows). **D.** Axial T_2WI reveals right posterior temporal white matter hyperintensity with an overlying hypointense cortical ribbon (arrows) signifying the presence of acute blood products. **E.** Gd-DTPA T_1WI CEMR reveals diffuse gyriform cortical enhancement within the region of hemorrhagic infarction in the right posterior temporal lobe.

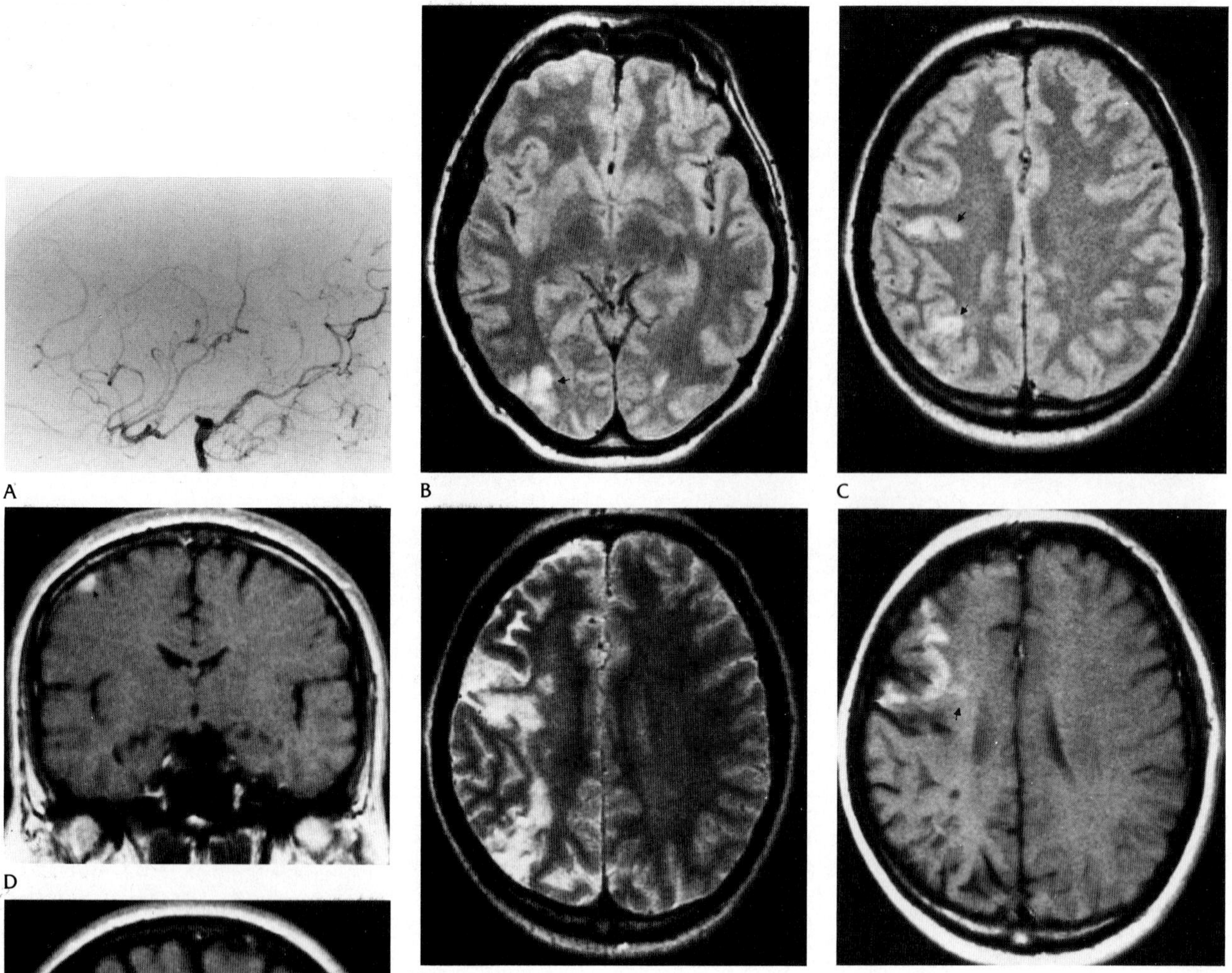

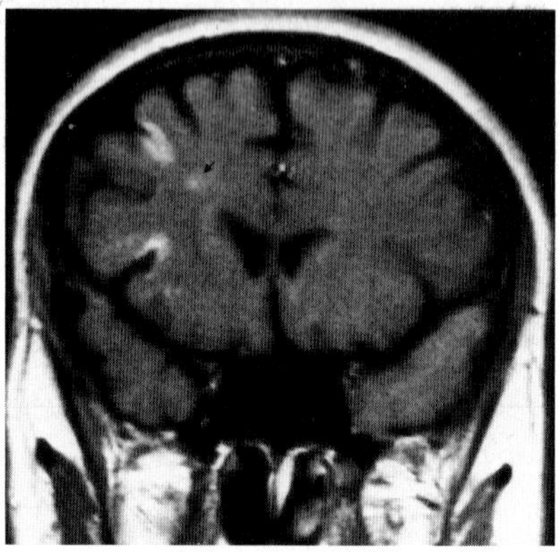

A B C D E F G

Figure 15-26 Progressive watershed infarction in the right internal carotid artery territory involving predominantly the cortex. **A.** Lateral vertebral angiogram demonstrates retrograde flow through the posterior communicating artery into a proximally occluded right internal carotid artery. There is slow intracranial filling into the right middle and anterior cerebral artery branches. **B, C.** PDWI reveal hyperintensity involving predominantly the cortical ribbon (arrows) in the posterior and superior watershed regions of the right cerebral hemisphere. **D.** Gd-DTPA T_1WI CEMR reveals a small region of cortical enhancement in the right frontal parietal watershed zone (arrow). **E–G.** Follow-up MRI at about 1 year. **E.** T_2WI reveals a larger region of superficial cortical hyperintensity in the watershed zone of the right cerebral hemisphere, extending into the subcortical white matter. **F, G.** Gd-DTPA T_1WI CEMR in the axial and coronal planes demonstrates extensive contrast enhancement of the cortex in the watershed regions of the right cerebral hemisphere with some enhancement extending into the underlying white matter watershed territory (arrows).

probably brought about by a nocturnal reduction of blood pressure. In some hypertensive persons, a reduction in blood pressure, even to only a normotensive level, can result in severe focal cerebral ischemia in the brain already perfused through a stenosed artery or collateral circulation. Cardiac arrhythmias, which can reduce both cardiac output and blood pressure, may cause hemodynamic infarction. Not infrequently, when a patient is first examined after a stroke, blood pressure has returned to its usual level and the cardiac arrhythmia has cleared. Correction of the hemodynamic alteration reestablishes brain perfusion pressure at its normal level and accounts for the early appearance of luxury perfusion on angiography and abnormalities in the blood-brain barrier on CT and MRI (Fig. 15-26).

The regions of the brain most severely affected by hemodynamic infarction are the border zones, or watershed areas (Romanul 1964; Brierley 1976), which are located at the junctions of the anterior, middle, and posterior cerebral artery circulations. Border zones are most vulnerable to ischemic injury from a generalized reduction in perfusion pressure because they are the terminal areas of supply of each major artery and therefore have the lowest perfusion pressure in these vascular distributions. If significant occlusive disease develops in the large arteries at the base of the brain or extracranially, ischemic damage in the watershed region may develop from even a mild reduction in blood pressure, because the occlusive disease reduces distal perfusion pressure to a level at which autoregulation produces maximum vasodilatation. At this point no further compensation for additional pressure reduction is possible, particularly in the watershed zone, and ischemic injury occurs. The watershed region tends to shift into the territory of the involved vascular system. The parietal occipital border zone is the region most susceptible to hemodynamic ischemic injury, as it is the most peripheral region of the anterior, middle, and posterior cerebral arterial circulations to the cerebral hemispheres.

On CT and MRI, the cortical luxury perfusion pattern in hemodynamic infarction is similar to that seen with embolic infarction after clot lysis but occurs earlier and in a different distribution. It is usually present when the patient is first seen during the initial 24 h. NCCT and MRI will in most instances appear normal but may show a slight reduction in density in the white matter on CT and hyperintensity on T_2-weighted MRI. This may become evident only in later scans or may not develop at all. The ischemic injury frequently remains localized to the cortex, which histologically reveals incomplete infarction, with the damage limited to neurons in the third or the fifth and sixth cortical layers or both. This variety of infarction is frequently referred to as *laminar necrosis.* If the ischemic insult is severe, all the layers of the cortex will be involved, along with the underlying white matter (Brierley 1976). On CECT and CEMR, a cortical gyral blush develops, predominantly in the parietooccipital watershed region (Fig. 15-26). Enhancement may persist for only a few days or may last for several weeks, depending on the severity of the initial ischemic damage. On MRI, contrast enhancement in deep white matter may develop.

Hemodynamic watershed infarction may on occasion be hemorrhagic in nature (Brierley 1976). This may occur if the initial ischemia is very severe or the reperfusion pressure is high, as may occur with hyperintensive disease.

The chronic change of incomplete (laminary) cortical infarction is sulcal dilatation (Fig. 15-7). It generally becomes evident after 2 to 3 months in the region where the gyral enhancement pattern was demonstrated. In patients with more profound ischemia resulting in complete cortical infarction and white matter involvement on CT, the affected cortex, which is initially isodense, becomes hypodense during the next 4 to 6 weeks; the underlying white matter, which may originally have been slightly hypodense, becomes a more sharply demarcated region of hypodensity. The adjacent portion of the lateral ventricle usually dilates. Some surrounding sulci may also enlarge because of incomplete infarction in the bordering cortex.

Another CT and MRI pattern associated with hemodynamic infarction is hypodensity on CT and hyperintensity on T_2-weighted MRI, involving mainly the deep periventricular white matter. This alteration tends to occur when there is a long-standing carotid occlusion and chronic ischemia in the hemisphere as a result of poor collateral circulation (Fig. 15-27). It is not entirely clear why the white matter is preferentially involved in these circumstances. It is possible that with chronic ischemia there is a change in the blood flow relationship between the cortex and the white matter, with greater flow going to cortical areas. This may occur because of a more pronounced effect of autoregulatory vasodilatation in the cortical vascular bed, which is about four times greater than that in the white matter, and the potentially higher perfusion pressure in the cortical arterioles, which are closer to the supplying vessels on the brain surface. The combination of these two factors would tend to result in shunting of circulation away from the white matter. A reduction in arterial perfusion pressure might then cause significant ischemia only in the white matter and not in the cortex. With MRI, contrast enhancement will frequently develop in the deep white matter and cortical regions of a watershed infarct and may persist for 4 to 6 weeks or longer.

This white matter involvement is primarily located adjacent to the superior lateral border of the lateral ventricle, in the region of the body and trigone (Fig. 15-27). This area not only is a terminal field of supply for the penetrating (ventriculopetal) transmedullary white matter arteries originating on the brain surface but also is a deep watershed zone between these arteries and the short arterial branches radiating outward from the lateral ventricle (ventriculofugal tributaries) (De Reuck 1971*a,b*). The ventriculofugal arteries originate from two sources. They are the terminal tributaries of the lenticulostriate artery branches that supply the lateral aspect of the caudate nucleus as well as tributaries of branches from the anterior choroidal and posterior lateral choroidal arteries that supply the ventricular wall.

A severe episode of hypotension or reduction in cardiac output, such as may occur after myocardial infarction or during surgery, can result in extensive bilateral cortical infarction with accentuation in the watershed distribution even in patients without preexisting vascular disease (Brierley 1976). White matter involvement is not common but may occur in patients with severe circulatory deficiency or, more commonly, if there is associated hypoxia (De Reuck 1978). In addition, the terminal ter-

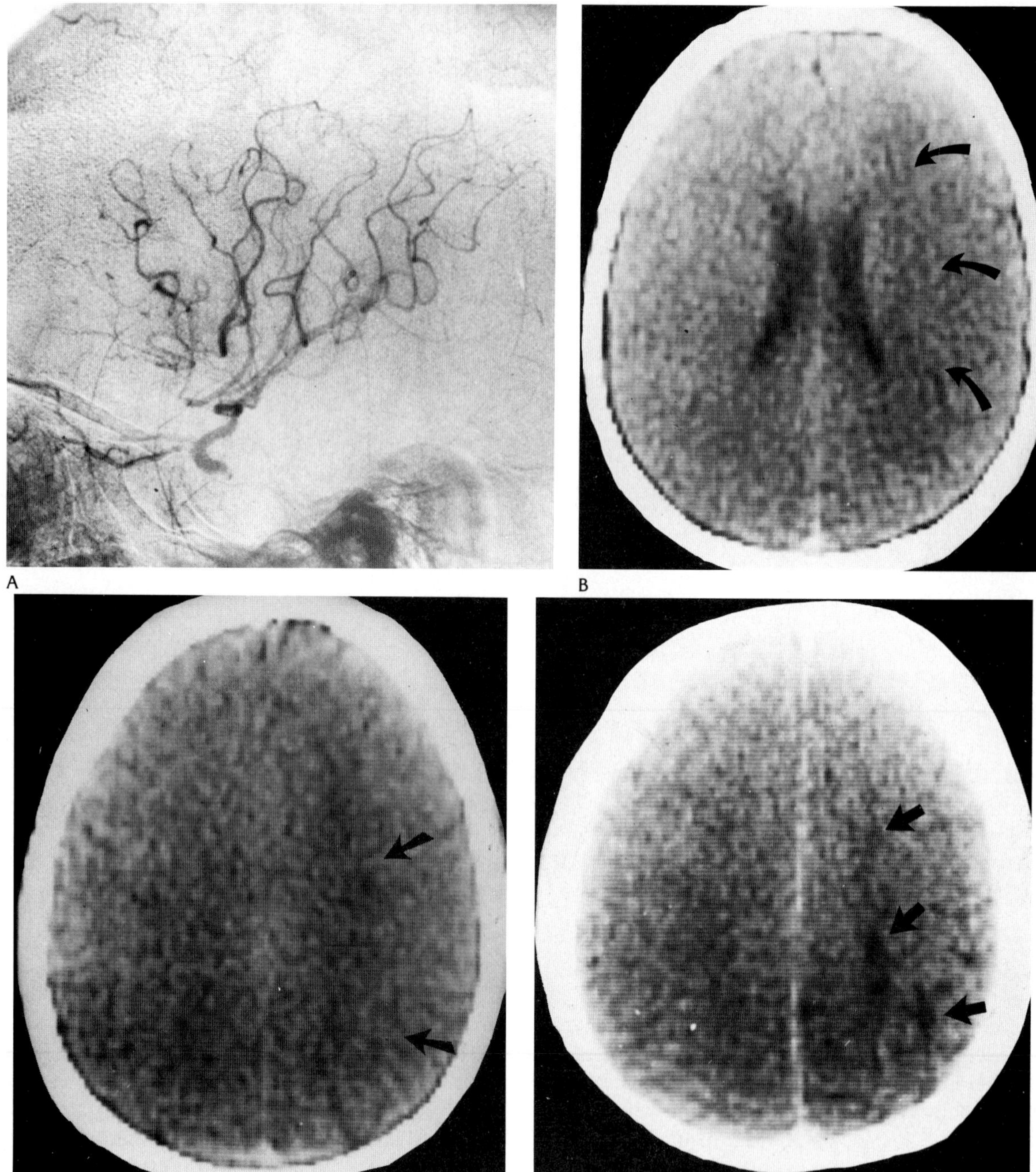

Figure 15-27 Deep watershed infarct. **A.** Lateral carotid angiogram, midarterial phase. Internal carotid artery completely occluded in neck at origin (not shown). Retrograde ophthalmic artery flow to intracranial carotid and middle cerebral arteries. Very slow filling and washout of middle cerebral artery branches. **B.** NCCT 3 days after stroke: poorly defined diffuse slight hypodensity in left periventricular white matter (arrows). **C.** NCCT, day 3, at supraventricular level: slight white-matter hypodensity on the left extends more superficially in parietal-occipital watershed region (arrows). **D.** NCCT at 4 months: well-defined, more hypodense region in left central white matter extending superficially in parietal-occipital watershed region (arrows). (*Continued on p. 659.*)

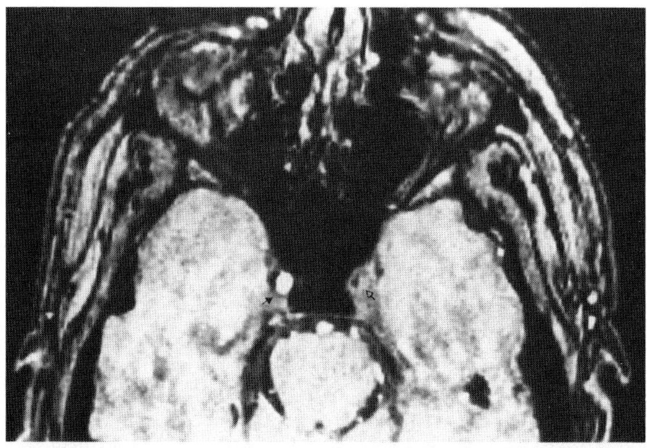

E

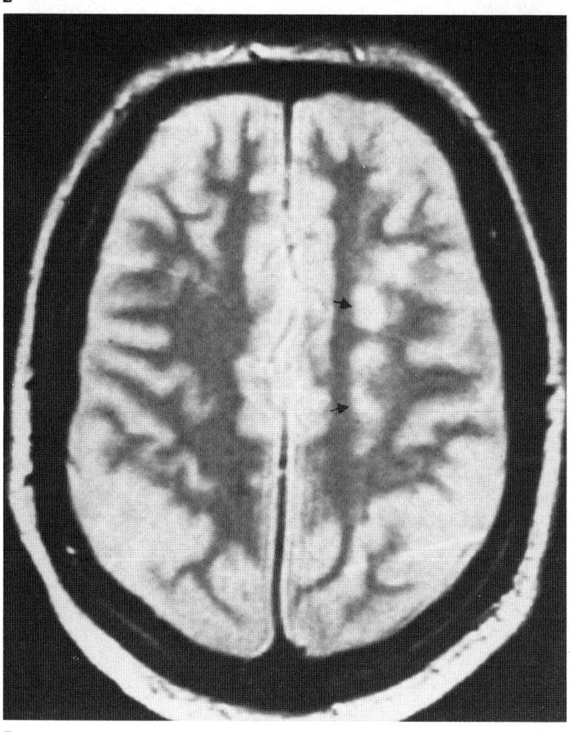

F

Figure 15-27 (continued) **E, F.** Deep left hemisphere watershed infarct on MRI. **E.** Flow-sensitive gradient-echo MRI at the level of the cavernous sinus. Normal high-intensity flow signal present in the right internal carotid artery (solid arrow) and basilar artery. No flow signal is present in the region of the left internal carotid artery (open arrow), indicating its occlusion. **F.** PDWI at supraventricular level demonstrates patchy high intensity within the deep white matter of the left cerebral hemisphere in the watershed territory (arrows).

ritories of the lenticulostriate supply to the basal ganglia may be affected. The main areas of basal ganglia involvement are the inferomedial portion of the head of the caudate nucleus, the upper and outer border of the head and body of the caudate nucleus, and the upper part of the anterior third of the putamen (Brierley 1976). The thalamus is usually not significantly affected. Watershed infarction may also occur in the cerebellum, in the boundary between the areas supplied by the superior cerebellar and posterior inferior cerebellar arteries. In the acute phase, the gray matter regions may be isodense on NCCT and show enhancement on CECT. In the chronic stage, depending on the severity of the initial oligemia, the gray matter may demonstrate hypodense necrotic areas or diffuse atrophic change. White matter may become hypodense, particularly in the periventricular regions.

INTRACEREBRAL ARTERIOLAR DISEASE

Occlusive disease of the intraparenchymal arterioles may be the sole or major vascular involvement in several disease entities. *Arteriolosclerosis* is the pathological process encountered most frequently in patients with long-standing hypertension. The long, penetrating lenticulostriate arteries and arterioles supplying the internal capsule and basal ganglia region are the ones most commonly involved with this disease process (Prineas 1966; Fisher 1979). To a lesser extent, the penetrating arteries to the brainstem and cerebral white matter are affected. Pathologically, arteriolosclerosis resembles atherosclerosis of the larger arteries in that there may be fibroblastic intimal proliferation with increased collagen fibers, but wall thickening and stenosis from hyalin deposition in the subintimal, medial, and outer layers of the arteries also occur. Microaneurysms develop from wall weakening as a result of the hyalin degeneration (Russell 1963; Cole 1967) and may lead to thrombosis of the vessel or intracerebral hemorrhage, both of which are prevalent in hypertensive persons.

Amyloid or *congophilic angiopathy* is another type of small vessel disease that occurs with increasing incidence in the elderly. It has been reported to be present in 46 percent of persons over 70 years of age (Vinters 1981). The disease, unlike arteriolosclerosis, affects only the intracortical arterioles and does not involve the penetrating arteries to the white matter, basal ganglia nuclei, brainstem, and cerebellum. The occipital and parietal cortex is most commonly involved. The disease is associated with Alzheimer's plaques in patients without a familial history of Alzheimer's disease. Dementia is commonly associated with amyloid angiopathy. Occasionally, intracerebral hemorrhage situated mainly in the cortex and superficial white matter and frequently associated with subarachnoid hemorrhage occurs, in contrast to hypertensive intracerebral hemorrhages, which are usually centered more deeply in the white matter and rarely involve the cortex or extend into the subarachnoid space (Wagle 1984; Gilles 1985).

Several varieties of collagen arteritis may affect the small intracerebral arteries, including polyarteritis nodosa, lupus erythematosus, and Wegener's granulomatosis. Granulomatous arteritis, infectious or allergic, primarily involves the intracerebral arterioles but may affect the larger surface arteries. Some forms of central nervous system (CNS) infection, including viral meningoencephalitis, purulent meningitis, mucormycosis meningitis, and syphilitic angiitis, may have prominent intraparenchymal arterial involvement.

Lacunar Infarcts

The arteriolosclerotic vascular disease process associated with chronically hypertensive patients frequently produces small lacunar infarcts, most commonly in the basal ganglia–internal capsule territory. These infarcts are in the distribution of the 6 to 12 lenticulostriate penetrating arteries that arise from the proximal anterior and middle cerebral arteries. Other arteries to this territory arise from the anterior choroidal artery. A severe neurological deficit may develop from occlusion or significant stenosis of even one of these small penetrating vessels (Fisher 1965), which range in size at their origin from about 0.2 to 0.8 mm in diameter. The lacunar infarcts may be as small as 0.5 cm or as large as 2.5 cm in maximum diameter. The variation in infarct size is determined by the site of lenticulostriate artery occlusion (origin or peripheral branch) and the caliber of the individual artery at its origin (Fisher 1979).

Lacunar infarcts assume a cylindrical to conical configuration and extend through a portion of the basal ganglia and internal capsule, often terminating in the periventricular white matter (Fig. 15-28). The location of the infarct in the basal ganglia depends on which striate artery is occluded (Manelfe 1981). When a middle cerebral artery lenticulostriate branch is occluded, the infarct may involve a greater or lesser portion of either the putamen, along with the superior and periventricular part of the knee and posterior limb of the internal capsule and body of the caudate nucleus (Fig. 15-15), or the lateral aspects of the head of the caudate nucleus and anterior limb of the internal capsule. When the anterior cerebral striate artery (recurrent artery of Heubner) is involved, the medial inferior portion of both the head of the caudate nucleus and the anterior limb of the internal capsule are affected. When anterior choroidal striate arteries are occluded, the infarct involves the globus pallidus (Fig. 15-28), the inferior part of the knee and posterior limb of the internal capsule, and the retrolenticular capsular fibers. Less frequently, lacunar infarcts involve the thalamus. Brainstem lacunar infarcts are commonly observed pathologically but may escape detection on CT, especially

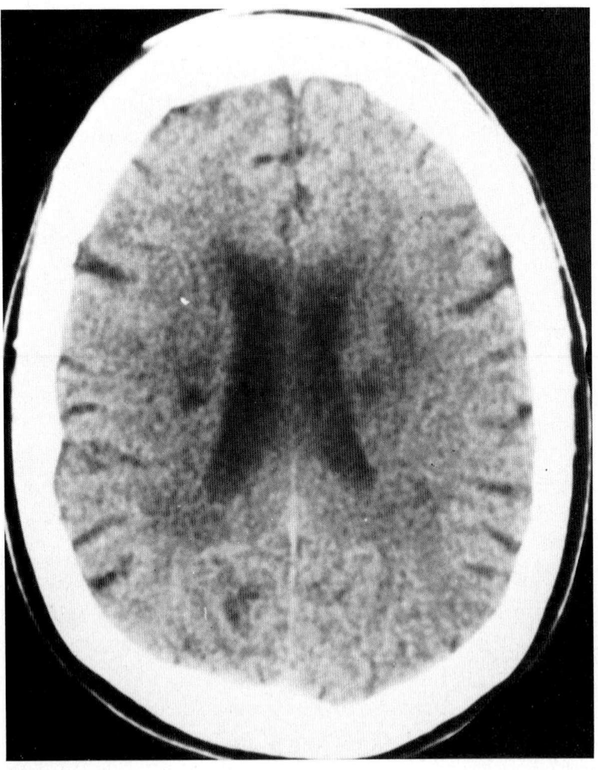
A

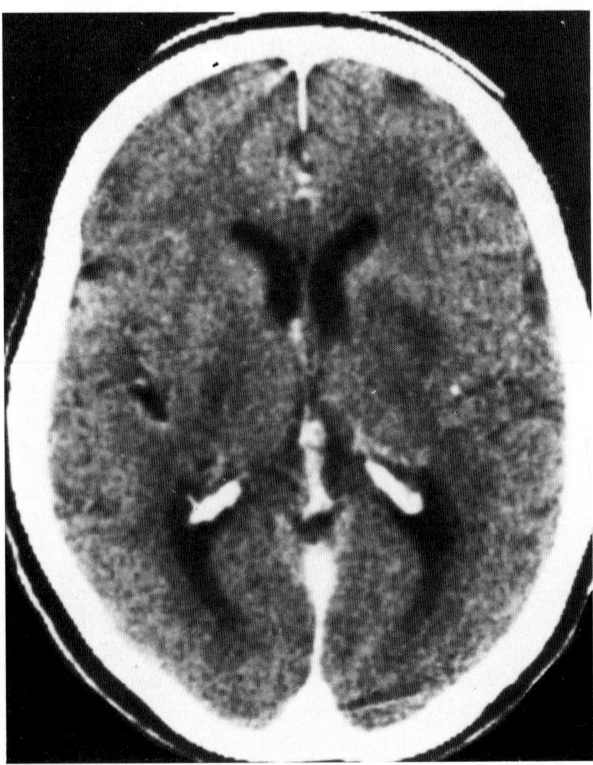
B

Figure 15-28 **A, B.** CT manifestations of intracerebral arteriolar disease. **A.** Old right paraventricular white matter infarct presents as a well-demarcated discrete hypodense lesion. Recent left infarcts show slightly less hypodense and relatively poorly marginated lesions with mild mass effect. **B.** Acute infarction of left basal ganglia involving the globus pallidus and left frontal white matter. (*Continued on p. 661.*)

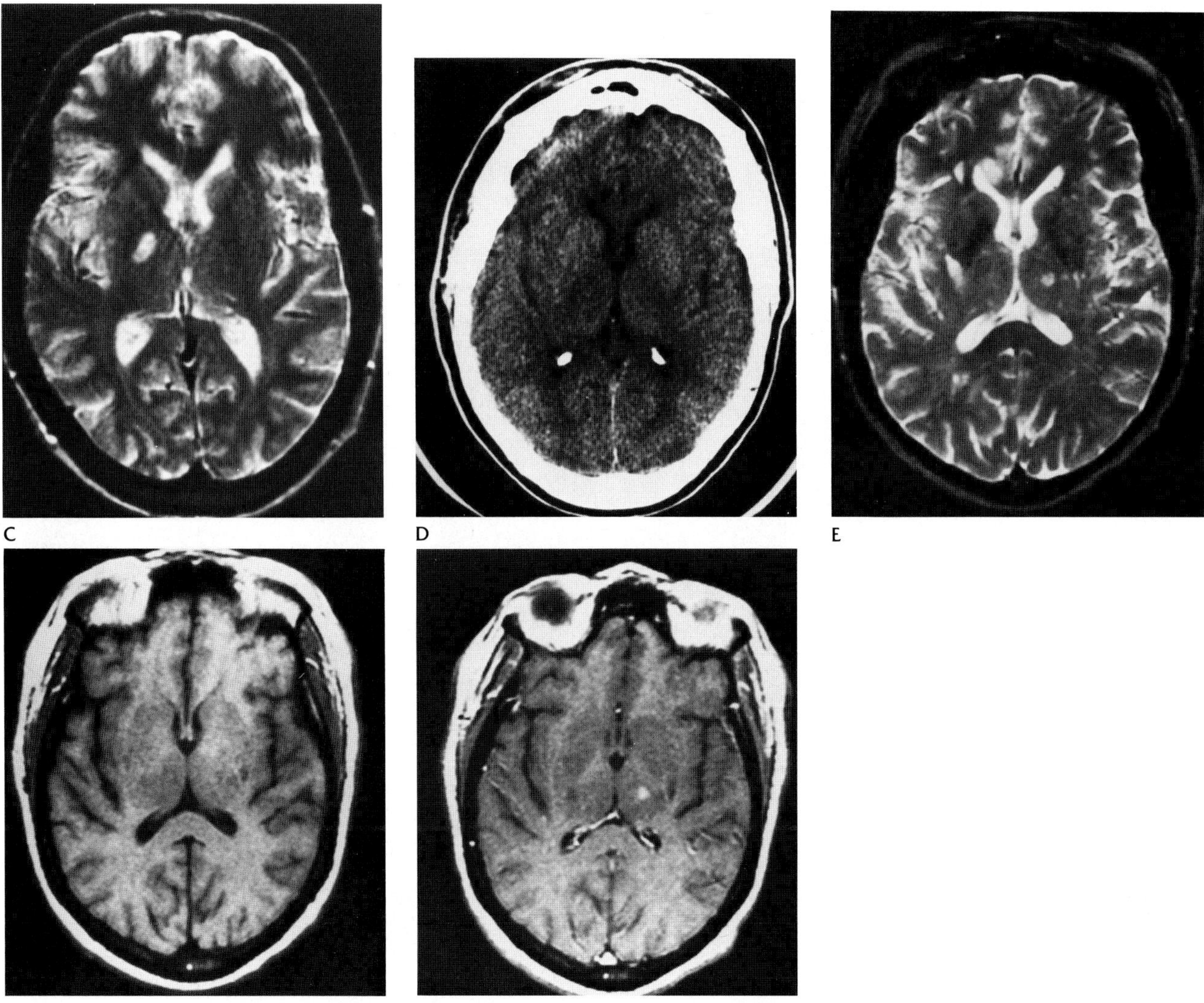

Figure 15-28 (continued) **C–G.** MR manifestations of intracerebral arteriolar disease. **C.** T_2WI reveals an oval region of hyperintensity in the right medial basal ganglia region, representing an infarction in the anterior choroidal artery distribution. **D–G.** Comparison of CT with MR in the detection of small vessel intracerebral arterial disease. **D.** CT section fails to clearly define any basal ganglia–capsular infarcts. A small hypodense old infarction is noted in the anterior right corpus callosum. **E.** T_2WI at the same level as **D** clearly defines multiple foci of hyperintensity in the basal ganglia region bilaterally, left thalamus, right anterior subinsula region, and anterior right corpus callosum. **F.** T_1WI through basal ganglia region poorly and incompletely demonstrates the basal ganglia lacunar infarcts. There are several foci of slight to moderate hypointensity scattered throughout the basal ganglia area. No definite lesion in the left thalamus can be identified. **G.** Gd-DTPA T_1WI CEMR through the basal ganglia region demonstrates contrast enhancement of left thalamic lacunar infarct, indicating its subacute nature.

in the early stage of small infarcts; however, they are readily detected on MRI (Fig. 15-29) as linear and patchy regions of hyperintensity on T_2WI. Larger lesions can be identified on CT (Fig. 15-29). MRI clearly depicts anatomic details in the basal ganglia region and the brainstem (Figs. 15-28 through 15-30).

Depending on the size of the occluded lenticulostriate artery, a basal ganglia lacunar infarct may or may not be revealed in the acute phase by CT (Nelson 1980). Those less than 1 cm in size are usually not defined during the first week after the infarct but may become evident after 3 to 4 weeks, when cystic encephalomalacic change has developed. Larger lesions are usually demonstrated by 48 h, appearing as ill-defined oval regions of hypodensity with their longest dimension in the anterior posterior direction (Fig. 15-15). They lie within the confines of the basal ganglia and adjacent internal capsule. Comparison with the tissue density in the contralateral homologous

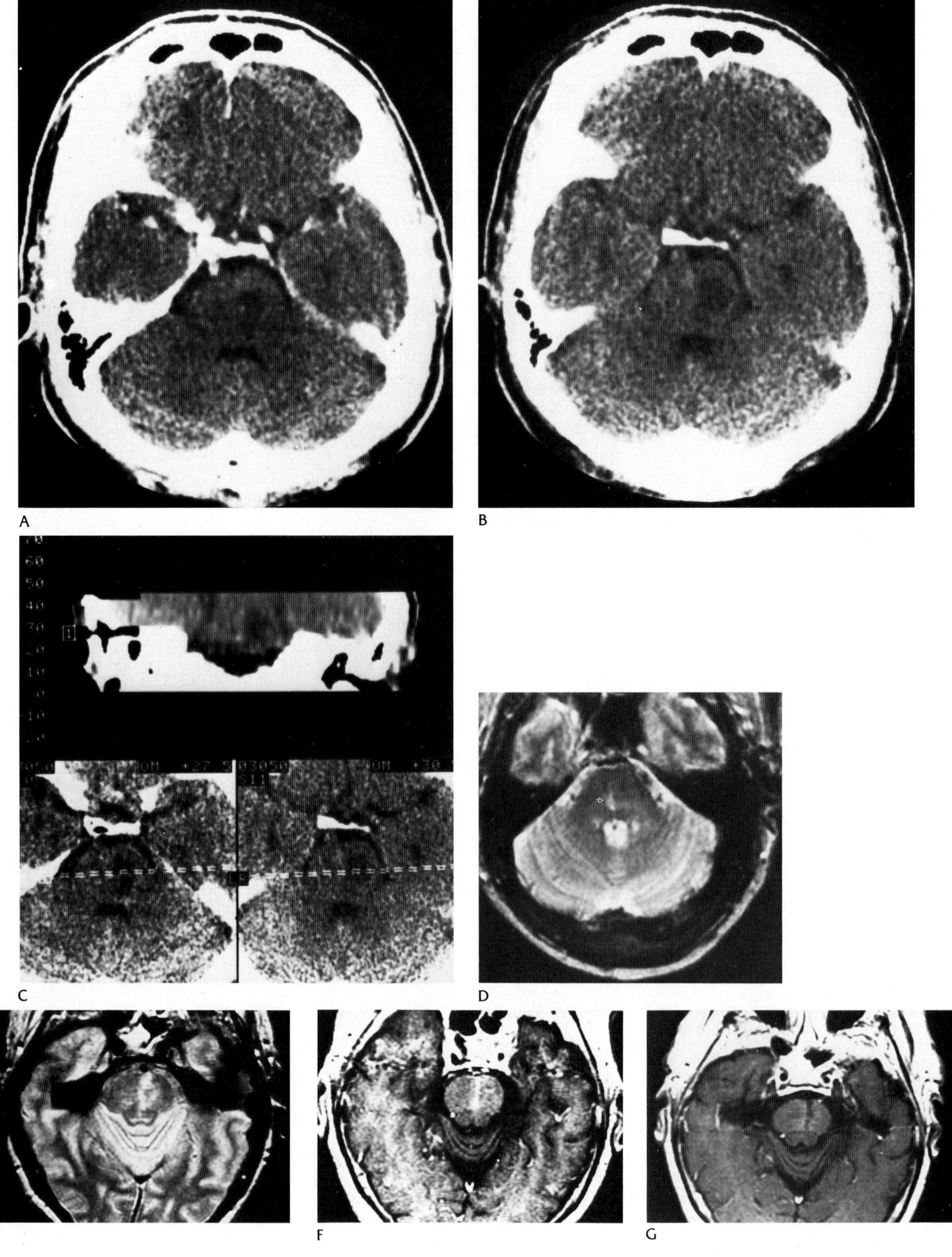
A
B
C
D
E
F
G

Figure 15-29 CT of acute brainstem infarct. Acute left brainstem infarct with mild compression of the fourth ventricle (**A** and **B**). Coronal re-formation image (**C**) clarifies the exact location. **D.** MRI of small pontine lacune in distribution of paramedian penetrating artery. T_2WI demonstrates a small right paramedian high-intensity focus (arrow) which has a sharp medial midline border. **E–G.** Evolution of acute left pontine infarct. **E.** T_2WI demonstrates patchy high intensity in the medial half of the left pons. The infarct does not cross the midline, although there is a small transverse band of high intensity in the posterior aspect of the right pons which appears to represent a separate lesion. **F.** Gd-DTPA T_1WI CEMR 5 weeks after **E** reveals contrast enhancement which is intense in the left paramedian region of the pons but extends in a nonhomogeneous pattern to the outer third of the left pons. T_2WI (not shown) revealed similar high intensity as in **E** within the left pons. **G.** Gd-DTPA T_1WI CEMR 6 months after **F** reveals an irregular bandlike area of hypodensity in the left paramedian region of the pons, representing cystic malacia. There is minimal marginal enhancement about this region.

basal ganglia region aids in appreciating early, minimal low-density change. Not infrequently the hypodense region involves only the most superior portion of the putamen and the white matter adjacent to the outer angle of the lateral ventricle (Fig. 15-28). Slight mass effect and contrast enhancement may develop at the appropriate times, that is, 3 to 5 days for mass effect and 7 to 10 days for enhancement (Figs. 15-13, 15-28, and 15-29). After 3 to 4 weeks a more sharply defined lesion of lower density becomes evident. Small lacunes not previously identified may be revealed, confined to a single CT section. Naturally, the thinner the CT section, the more likely that small lesions will be identified.

Binswanger's Disease (Subcortical Arteriosclerotic Encephalopathy)

At times the arteriolosclerotic vasculopathy of hypertension may predominantly involve the long, penetrating transmedullary arterioles that extend from the brain surface into the deep frontal and parietal white matter. The arteries to the basal ganglia usually are also affected. Progressive dementia is the cardinal clinical feature of this peculiar variety of hypertensive vascular disease. There is usually also a history, physical findings, and CT and MRI evidence of previous lacunar stroke.

The neuropathological changes in Binswanger's disease consist of diffuse demyelination or focal areas of

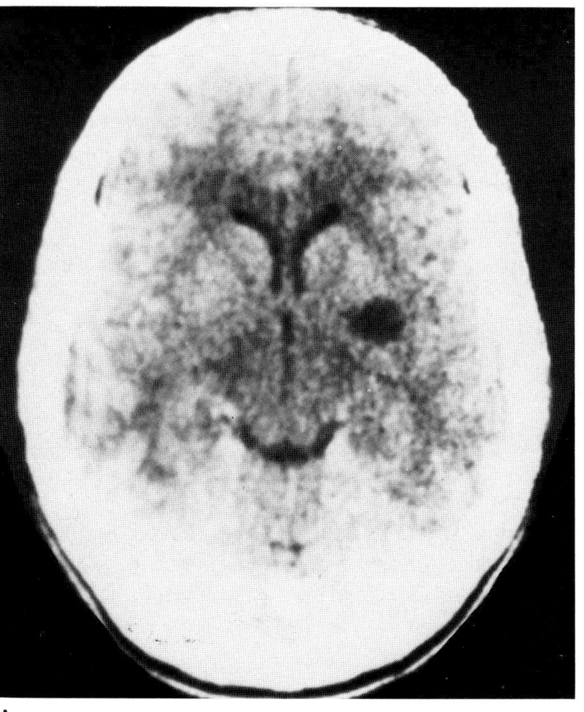

A

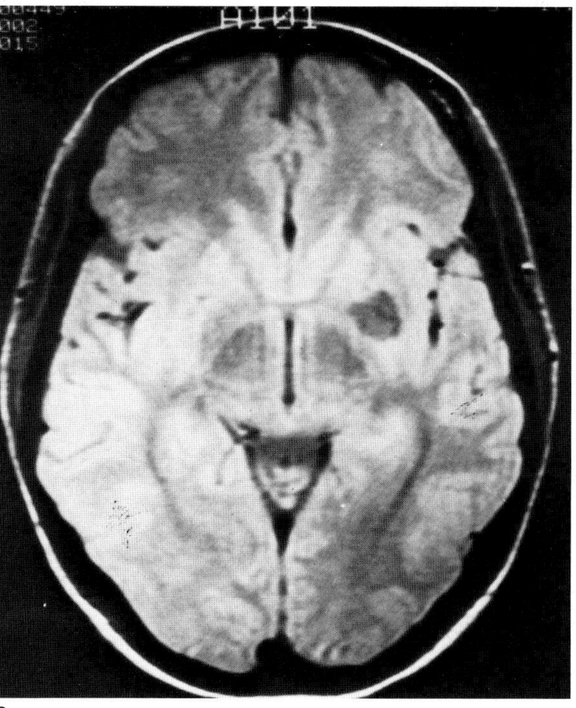

B

Figure 15-30 Large left basal ganglia in the Virchow-Robin space (dilated perivascular subarachnoid fluid compartment) mimicking a lacunar infart. **A.** Axial CT demonstrates a well-demarcated hypodense rounded lesion within the inferior portion of the left putamen. MRI: **B** (axial PDWI). (*Continued on p. 664.*)

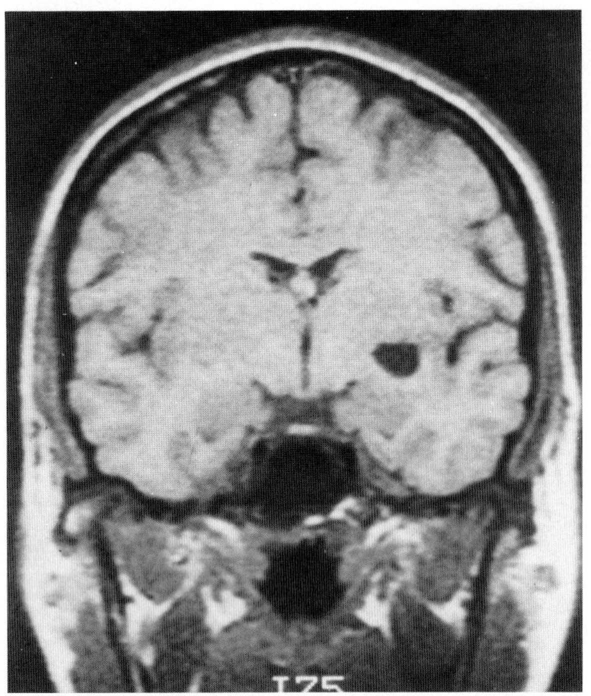

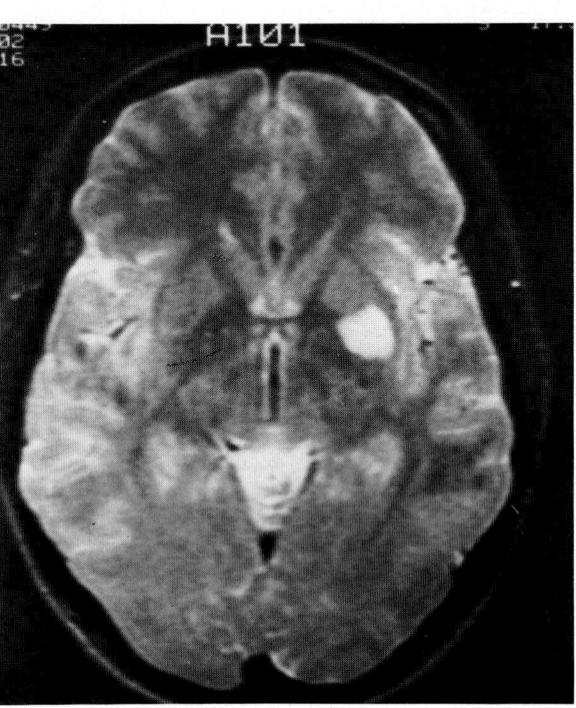

C D

Figure 15-30 (continued) **C** (coronal T_1WI), and **D** (axial T_2WI) demonstrates the lesion to be in the most inferior aspect of the left putamen and below the level of the anterior commissure. It is hypointense on PDWI and T_1WI (**B, C**) and hyperintense on T_2WI (**D**). On all these sequences, the intensity of the lesions follows exactly that of the cerebrospinal fluid. These characteristics indicate that the lesion is not a large lacunar infarct but a cystic dilatation of a CSF space. A lacunar infarct would have high intensity on PDWI and would not be large and localized only to the inferior aspect of the basal ganglia capsular region.

partial necrosis in the cerebral white matter (or both), mainly in the frontal and occipital lobes. Lacunar infarcts in the basal ganglia are frequently present. The white matter and basal ganglia arterioles are affected by arteriolosclerosis.

On CT, Binswanger's disease demonstrates either diffuse or patchy low-density areas in the white matter of the centrum semiovale and the frontal and occipital regions with prominent involvement of the periventricular area. The changes occur bilaterally but not always in a symmetrical pattern. MRI demonstrates extensive patchy and confluent high-intensity regions in the deep white matter on PDWI and T_2WI. The MR alterations are usually more extensive than are those revealed on CT. One or more lacunar infarcts are usually evident in the basal ganglia–internal capsule region or thalamus (Fig. 15-31) (Rosenberg 1979; Zeumer 1980; Lotz 1986). MR findings are described in Chap. 16.

ARTERITIS

Cerebral arteritis may involve the large arteries at the base of the brain, the convexity branches, the smaller intracerebral arterioles, or a combination of the three (Sole-Llenas 1978). Many of the disease processes that cause arteritis characteristically involve arteries of only one size. Cranial arteritis may be primary or secondary. When it is primary, the disease process primarily involves the arteries; when secondary, the disease primarily affects the meninges or brain parenchyma and involves the arteries secondarily.

With *primary arteritis,* the cerebral involvement may be only one of many manifestations of a systemic disorder, such as collagen disease, giant cell arteritis, sarcoidosis, or tertiary syphilis. Occasionally the intracranial arteritis is the sole manifestation at the time of one of these disease processes. Alternatively, primary arteritis may be caused by a disease process that affects mainly the brain arteries, such as granulomatous and/or chemical arteritis. Cerebral chemical arteritis may be caused by amphetamine and heroin abuse (Rumbaugh 1971), ergotamine, and anovulatory medication. There are undoubtedly other drugs and chemical agents that produce cerebral arteritis. In many cases the exact cause of primary arteritis cannot be identified.

The CT and MRI alterations caused by primary cerebral arteritis are nonspecific and quite varied but may suggest the disease. Correlation of the imaging findings with the

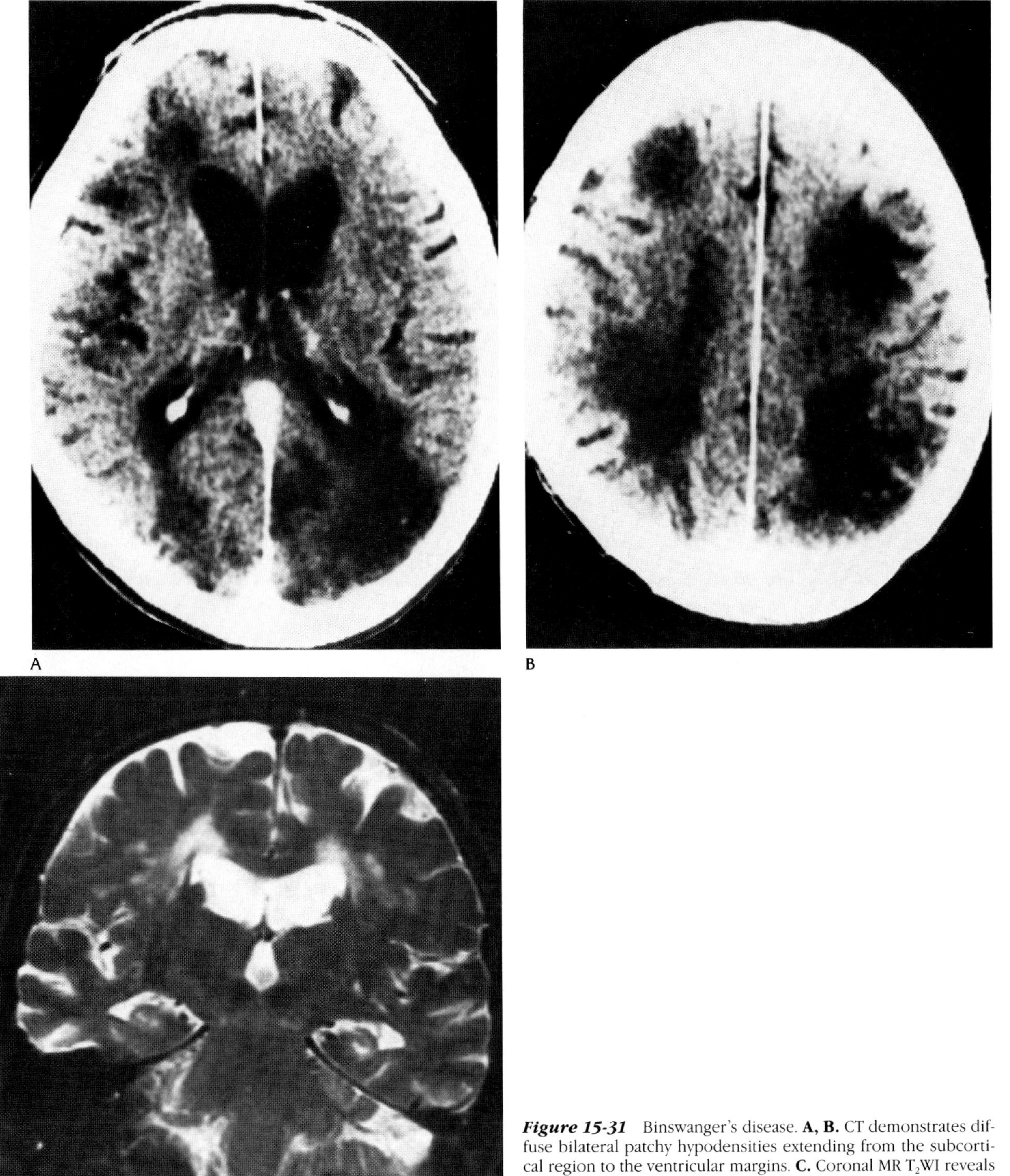

Figure 15-31 Binswanger's disease. **A, B.** CT demonstrates diffuse bilateral patchy hypodensities extending from the subcortical region to the ventricular margins. **C.** Coronal MR T_2WI reveals patchy bilateral subcortical and periventricular high intensities and small basal ganglia high intensities.

clinical history, physical examination, age, and sex of the patient will greatly aid in arriving at the appropriate diagnosis.

Cerebral arteritis develops with systemic lupus erythematosus (SLE) and occurs mainly in young women, who may manifest psychosis, mental alterations, seizures, or focal neurological deficits (Johnson 1968; Glaser 1952, 1955; Bilaniuk 1977). Nervous system involvement in SLE has been reported in 25 to 75 percent of cases (Johnson 1968), but arteritis is not common, being present in 6 to

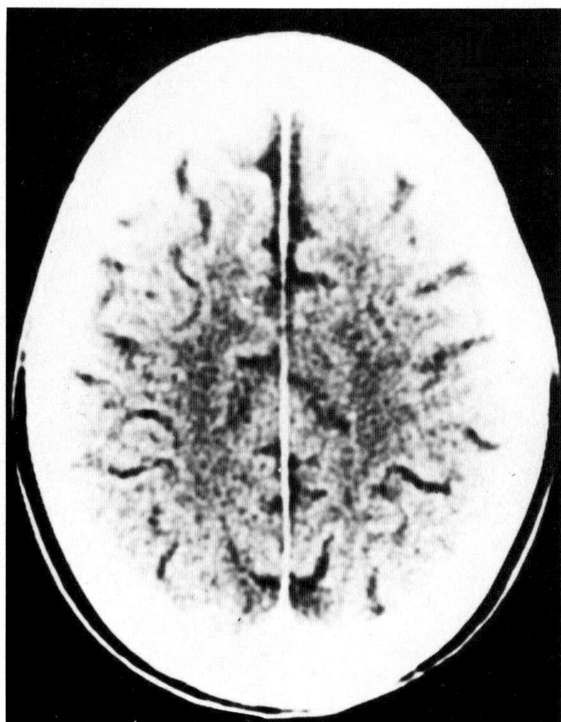

Figure 15-32 Systemic lupus erythematosus in an 18-year-old female. Progressive mental deterioration with enlarged sulci for age.

13 percent of cases (Ellis 1979). It primarily involves the small cerebral arteries. On CT, the most frequent abnormality is enlargement of cortical sulci (Fig. 15-32) (Bilaniuk 1977). This change reflects arteritic involvement of the cortical arterioles, resulting in microinfarcts in this region (Johnson 1968). The small arteries supplying the basal ganglia–internal capsule region may also be involved, causing either lacunar infarcts or intracerebral hemorrhage (Bilaniuk 1977; Ellis 1979). Arteritis involvement of the large arteries at the base of the brain and the medium-sized arteries in the sylvian fissures and over the convexity is rare and may cause more typical cerebral hemispheric infarcts (Trevor 1972). Aeisen (1985) reported three patterns of MR findings of SLE: large white matter infarctions, microinfarctions of white matter, and gray matter hyperintensity.

Granulomatous arteritis predominantly involves the small leptomeningeal and penetrating arteries and veins of less than 200 μm in diameter to the white matter. Occasionally the larger cerebral arteries are affected (Cravioto 1959; Nurick 1972; Rosenblum 1972). The CT manifestation of this involvement is a diffuse edematouslike, bilateral, white matter low-density pattern (Fig. 15-33) (Faer 1977). Contrast enhancement is generally not seen with white matter involvement (Faer 1977). There may also be focal low-density regions of the cortex and

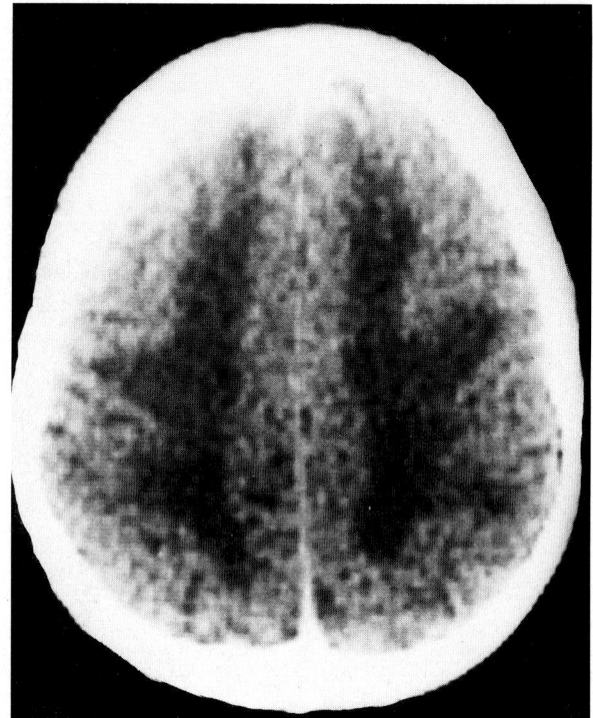

A

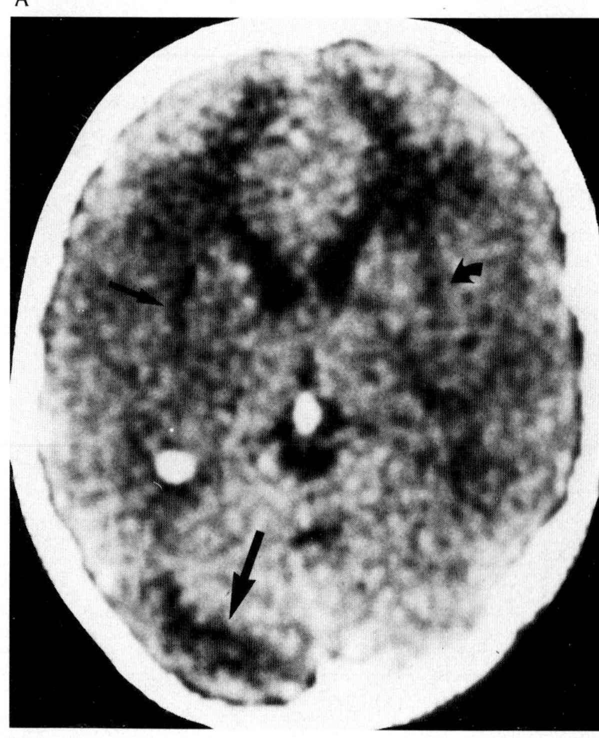

B

Figure 15-33 Granulomatous arteritis in a 38-year-old male (biopsy confirmation). **A.** Diffuse bilateral white matter hypodensity. **B.** Diffuse bilateral anterior frontal white matter hypodensity. Focal infarct hypodensities at left posterior putamen (curved arrow), right occipital region (large arrow), and right occipital region (large arrow). (*Continued on p. 667.*)

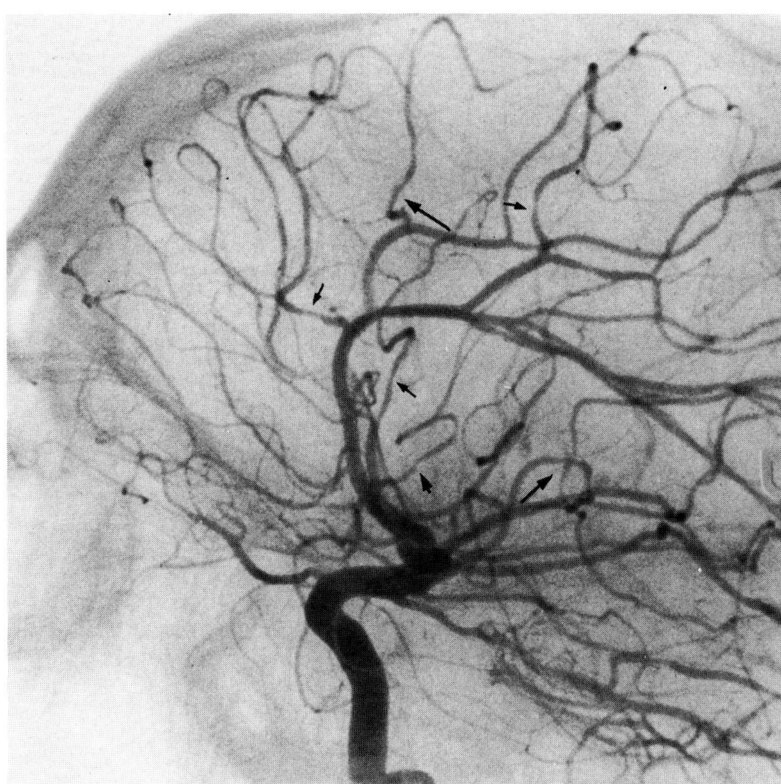

C

Figure 15-33 (continued) **C.** Lateral carotid angiogram: multiple focal regions of peripheral arterial branch narrowing (arrows). **D.** MRI of a 33-year-old female with granulomatous arteritis. Cerebral angiography demonstrated stenosis in the multiple cerebral arteries and occlusion of the branches to the left parietal region (not shown). T_2WI reveals hyperintensity involving the cortex predominantly in the left parietal region but also a small cortical area in the left posterior frontal region. In addition, there are multiple patchy areas of high intensity within the white matter bilaterally (arrows), indicating arteriolar disease not evident on the cerebral angiogram.

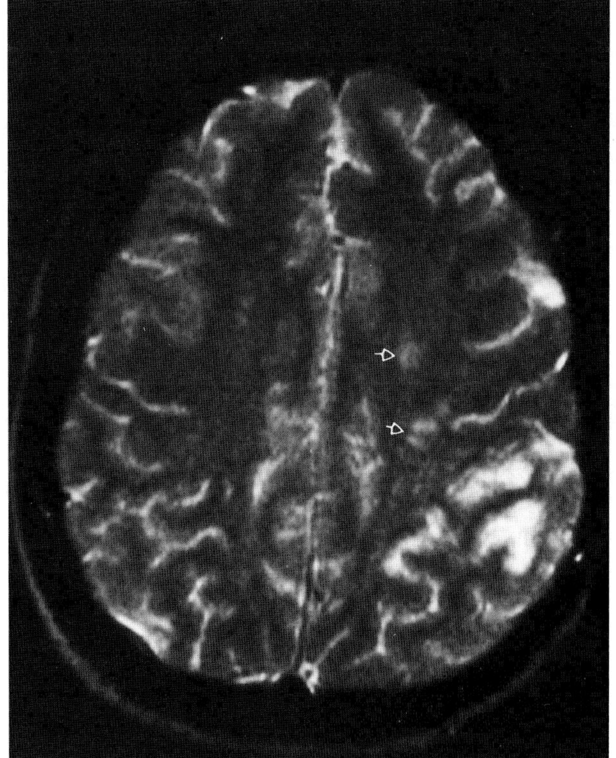

D

white matter representing more typical infarcts and reflecting arteritic involvement of large and medium-sized branches (Fig. 15-33). Contrast enhancement and mass effect develop with lesions in this location (Valvanis 1979). On MRI, hemispheric and multiple penetrating artery lacunar infarcts in the basal ganglia and subcortical white matter may be seen either together or by themselves (Fig. 15-33). When only subcortical and deep white matter infarcts are present with arteritis, the MR appearance strongly resembles that of multiple sclerosis.

In most cases of primary arteritis, there is bilateral involvement, with multiple areas of infarction similar to those seen with emboli. Angiography is usually required to substantiate the diagnosis and will demonstrate multiple segmental regions of irregular narrowing in the secondary and tertiary peripheral branches of the main cerebral arteries (Fig. 15-33).

Secondary cerebral arteritis is caused by CNS inflammatory disease. Although the diagnosis can usually be readily established clinically and by CSF examination, occasionally the appropriate clinical manifestations are not apparent and only the manifestations caused by the arteritis are evident. In these instances, CT and MR may reveal alterations that suggest the correct diagnosis. This situation may occur with the more indolent types of meningitis, such as tuberculous and fungal.

Besides revealing alterations of ischemic disease, secondary arteritis frequently reveals other abnormalities related to the subarachnoid inflammatory disease that are suggestive of this diagnosis. CECT and CEMR may show enhancement of the subarachnoid spaces around the basal cisterns, in the sylvian fissure, over the convexity, or in a combination of these locations (Enzmann 1976; Bilaniuk 1978; Chu 1980). Hydrocephalus may develop from obstruction of the subarachnoid pathways, the ventricular outflow at the exit foramina of the fourth ventricle, or the aqueduct of Sylvius by inflammatory exudate and fibrosis (Sole-Llenas 1978).

Purulent meningitis causes a heavy inflammatory exudate that accumulates mainly around the base of the brain. In this location it may produce arteritic involvement of the supraclinoid carotid (Leeds 1971), the proximal segments of the anterior and middle cerebral arteries, or the penetrating arteries to the basal ganglia and thalamic region (Cairns 1946). Bilateral or unilateral infarctions may develop in the basal ganglia, cerebral hemisphere, or both.

With *Haemophilus influenzae* meningitis, the purulent exudate may be around the base but is also located more peripherally over the brain surface, causing arteritis in the insula and convexity arteries (Leeds 1971). This may produce multiple small or large regions of infarction, which are more frequently located anteriorly in the frontal lobes (Cockrill 1978).

Tuberculous meningitis may involve both the basal and convexity subarachnoid spaces and can affect the arteries at either location or both (Daster 1966; Lehrer 1966; Leeds 1971). Depending on which region is primarily involved, CT and MRI may reveal either a large infarct in one vascular territory or one or more small infarcts in several vascular territories (Chu 1980). Hydrocephalus may be a prominent feature of tuberculous meningitis (Chap. 13).

MOYAMOYA DISEASE

Moyamoya disease is a condition of unknown etiology resulting in progressive occlusion of the terminal segment of the supraclinoid portion of the internal carotid artery and the proximal portions of the anterior and middle cerebral arteries. The proximal posterior cerebral arteries may also be affected. The disease usually develops in childhood and is most prevalent in the Japanese (Kudo 1968), but it has been reported in other groups as well (Taveras 1969).

In children, the initial manifestations are usually related to cerebral ischemia and include motor and sensory disturbance, involuntary movements, convulsions, headaches, and mental deterioration. In adults, the disease usually presents with subarachnoid or intracerebral hemorrhage.

Angiography and pathological examination reveal tapered partial to complete occlusions of the vessels about the internal carotid artery bifurcation bilaterally. Marked dilatation develops in the intraparenchymal arteries in the basal ganglia, upper brainstem, and thalamus, which provide collateral circulation to the middle and anterior cerebral arteries distal to their occlusions. This vascular dilatation is the so-called moyamoya blush (Fig. 15-34*A*) (*moyamoya* means "puff of smoke" in Japanese). The collateral vessels arise from the internal carotid artery proximal to its occlusion and from the anterior choroidal, posterior communicating, and terminal basilar artery bifurcations (Nishimoto 1968; Suzuki 1969; Taveras 1969; Pecker 1973).

CT and MR may reveal nonspecific abnormalities related to focal and diffuse ischemia, such as multiple small areas of parenchymal hypodensity on CT and hyperintensity on T_2-weighted MRI, along with evidence of cerebral atrophy consisting of dilatation of sulci, interhemispheric and sylvian fissures, and ventricles (Handa 1977). In adults and occasionally in children, hemorrhage occurs that may be subarachnoid, basal ganglionic (Fig. 15-34*C*), or intraventricular. The hemorrhage is caused by the rupture of a dilated collateral vessel that may develop pseudoaneurysms (Kodama 1978). Takahashi (1980) reported a more characteristic abnormality consisting of irregular interrupted or tortuous curvilinear densities in the basal ganglia on CECT. Similar high intensities are seen with CEMR. On NCMR, numerous punctate and curvilinear hypointensities representing flow voids may be evident in the deep gray masses (Fig. 14-34*D*). Flow-sensitive gradient-echo sequences will reveal punctate and curvilinear high intensities within the basal ganglia region. The supraclinoid carotid artery and the proximal middle and anterior cerebral arteries will appear very hypoplastic or be absent. These densities correspond to the locations of the most prominent parenchymal collaterals on carotid angiography (Fig. 15-34*B*).

COMPLICATED MIGRAINE

The majority of patients with classical migraine have EEG abnormalities during the attack, usually most marked in the occipital region, and many of these patients develop focal neurological changes at this time. It is postulated that during the prodromal phase vasospasm develops in some intracranial arteries, resulting in localized cerebral ischemia. This is supported by angiographic and cerebral blood flow studies, which have shown vasospasm and decreased flow during such an attack.

Abnormal CT scans have been noted during and sometimes shortly after the migraine attack in one-third to one-half of patients (Mathew 1976; Hungerford 1976). CT reveals focal hypodense regions that do not enhance or cause mass effect. They are more commonly located pos-

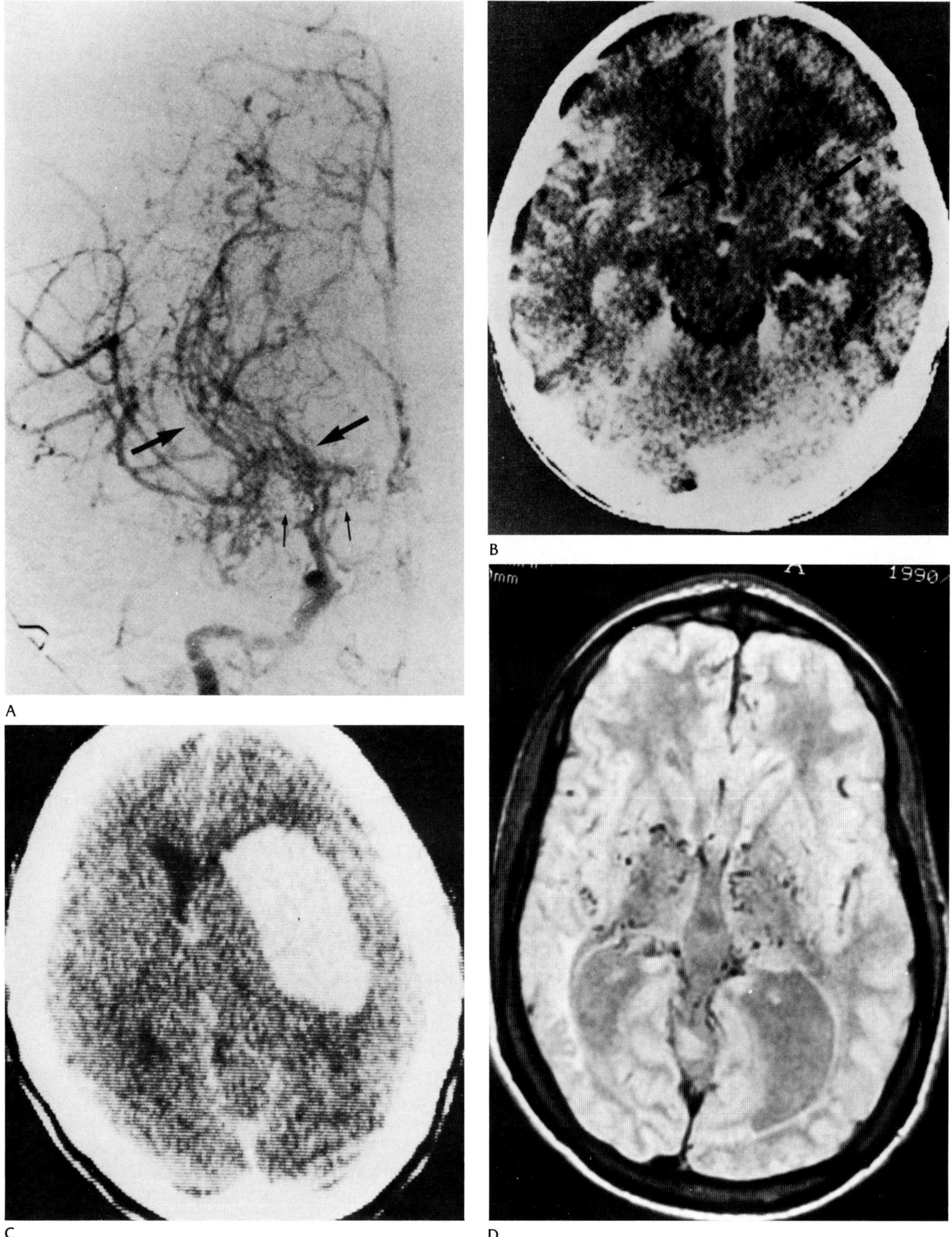

Figure 15-34 Moyamoya disease. **A.** Frontal carotid angiogram: tapered occlusion of proximal segments of anterior and middle cerebral arteries (small arrows). Marked dilatation of lenticulostriate arteries, representing the moyamoya blush (large arrows). **B.** CECT: prominent curvilinear and punctate vascularlike densities in lenticulostriate artery distribution (arrows). (*From Takahashi M, et al. 1980.*) **C.** Moyamoya disease with large hematoma in basal ganglia on left. (*Courtesy of J. H. Suh, M.D., Severance Hospital, Seoul, Korea.*) **D.** MRI: Axial PDWI at basal ganglia level demonstrates multiple punctate and curvilinear hypointensities within the basal ganglia, internal capsule and thalamus. These represent flow voids of dilated intracerebral arteries which were present on a cerebral angiogram (not shown).

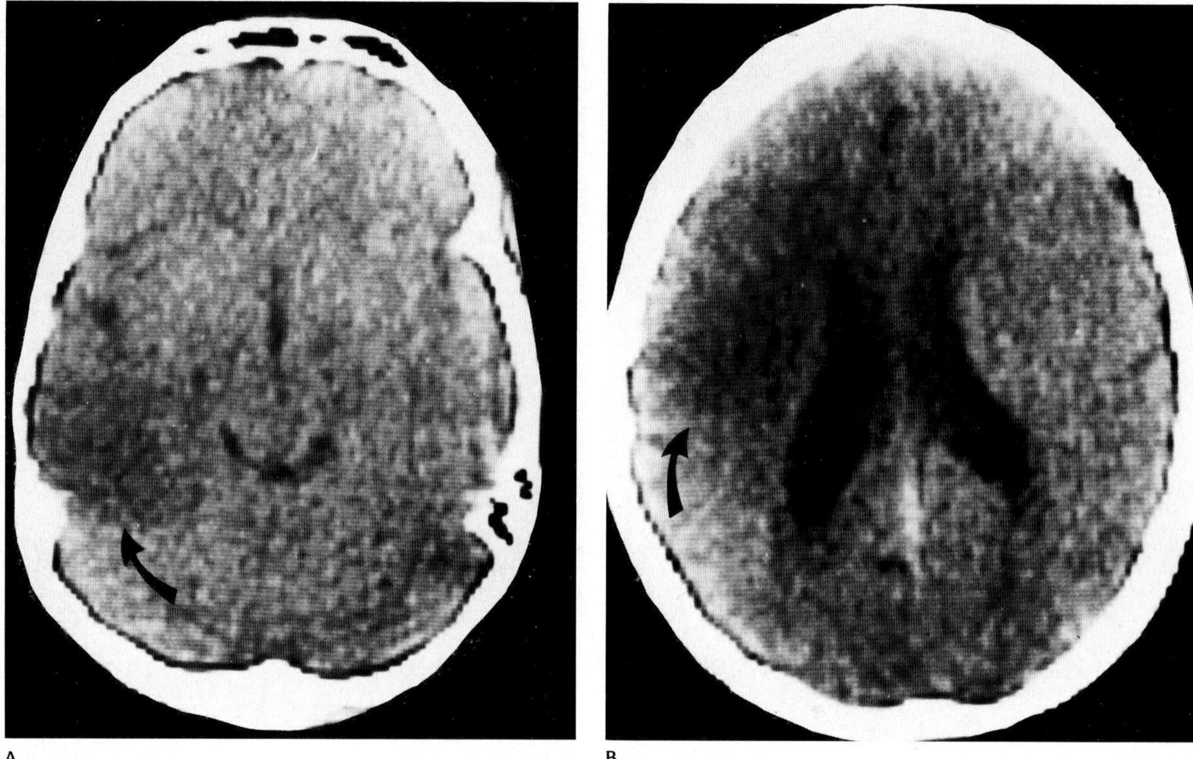

Figure 15-35 Complicated migraine: recurrent neurological deficits associated with headaches. **A.** Diffuse mild hypodensity in right posterior temporal region (arrow). **B.** Diffuse hypodensity in right parietal and posterior frontal region (arrow). Moderate ventricular dilatation.

teriorly in the cerebral hemispheres (Fig. 15-35). The hypodensities may resolve completely on follow-up scans obtained after several weeks if the neurological deficit clears.

BRAINSTEM AND CEREBELLAR INFARCTION

Fewer infarcts are detected by CT in the posterior fossa (Campbell 1978; Kingsley 1980), in part because of inherent computer artifacts in this region caused by the dense petrous ridges and occipital bony crest that degrade the images. In addition, a significant neurological deficit may result from very small, critically located infarcts in the brainstem. These small lesions are frequently below the resolution capability of the CT scanner, especially during the acute phase of the infarct. MRI can be of help in this situation (Fox 1986). With MRI, there are no bone artifacts to obscure visualization of the brainstem and cerebellum. Small ischemic lesions are therefore usually well defined along the anatomic distributions of the central penetrating and circumflex branches of the basilar artery. They appear as linear and patchy regions of hyperintensity on PDWI and T_2WI (Figs. 15-29 and 15-36). Follow-up CT scans at 3 months may reveal a higher percentage of infarcts because of the sharper demarcation and greater hypodensity of residual small cystic areas of necrosis. The fourth ventricle and brainstem cisterns may dilate in the chronic phase. In patients with a diffuse ischemic insult, degeneration in the cerebellar cortex may be a prominent abnormality (Brierley 1976). Large brainstem infarctions are more readily identifiable on CT and MRI, usually by 48 h (Fig. 15-36).

Infarcts in the anterior and inferior portions of the cerebellum may be difficult to define, particularly in the acute phase on CT, because of their proximity to the regions where bone artifacts are maximal. Superior cerebellar infarcts are more readily identified, but care must be taken to distinguish them from infarcts in the adjacent inferior occipital lobe on the opposite side of the tentorium (Fig. 15-36). In this situation, CECT will usually aid in determining the correct location by identifying the enhancing tentorium, especially in coronal views.

With a large cerebellar infarct, severe secondary neurological deficits may develop from brainstem compression secondary to cerebellar swelling and tonsillar herniation. The infarct edema usually becomes maximum between the third and fifth days. It may be difficult to distinguish between infarction and tumor at this time; the fourth ventricle will be displaced and the brainstem cisterns will be compressed in both situations. With infarction, however, the low density tends to remain localized

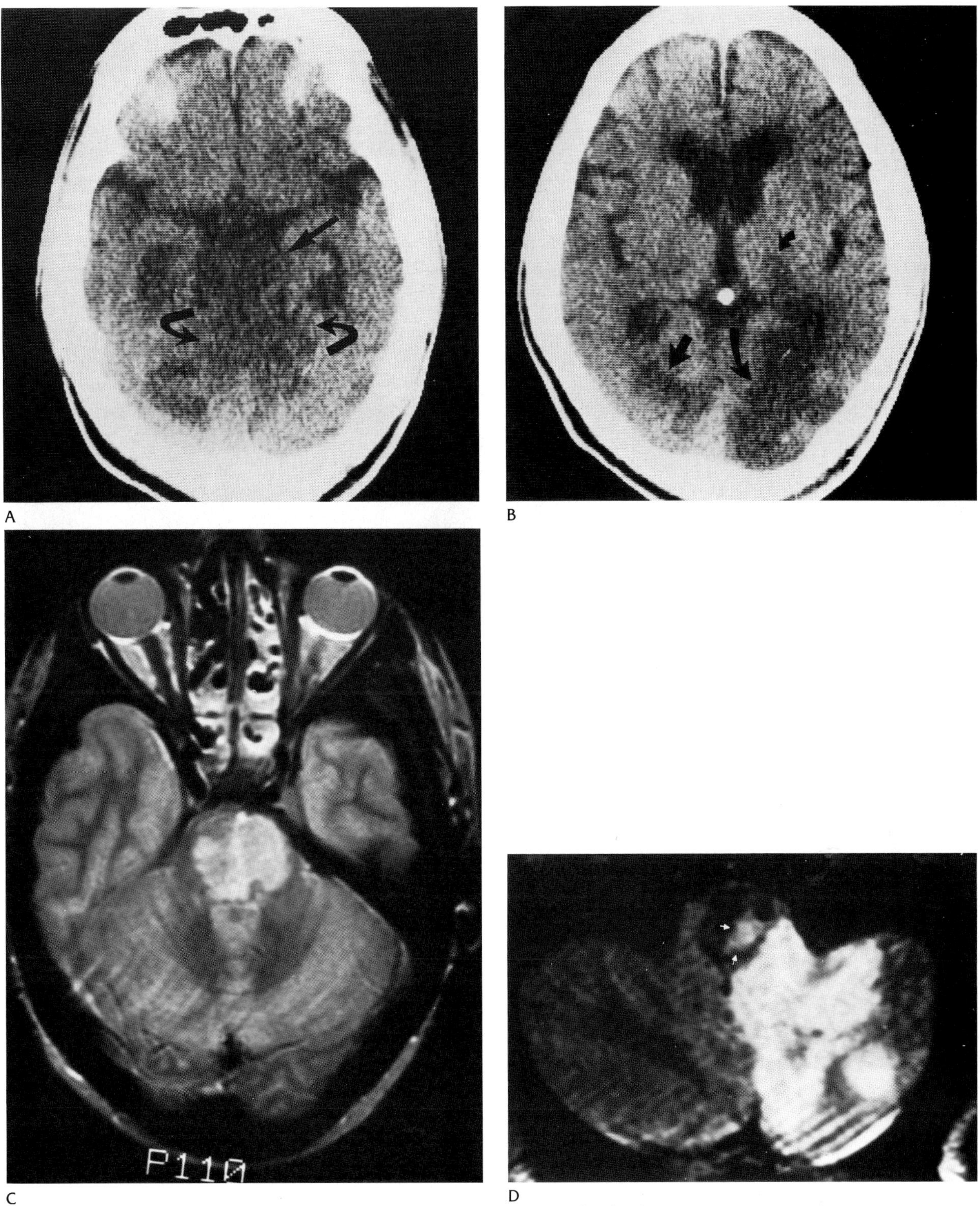

Figure 15-36 Basilar occlusion with large infarcts of the brainstem, superior cerebellus, and occipital lobe. **A.** CT through upper brainstem: diffuse hypodensity of midbrain (arrow) and superior cerebellum (curved arrows). **B.** CT through occipital lobes: large posterior cerebral artery territory occipital (large curved arrow) and posterior thalamic hypodensity (small curved arrow) on left with smaller occipital hypodensity on right (straight arrow). **C.** MRI of bilateral acute pontine infarct from basilar occlusion Axial PDWI reveals diffuse bilateral pontine hyperintensity and swelling. There is obliteration of the pontine cistern anteriorly. Hyperintensity present within basilar artery anterior to midpons, representing subacute thrombus (see also T_1WI in Fig. 15-17*D*). **D.** Infarct in the posterior lateral medulla and inferior cerebellum in the distribution of the posterior inferior cerebellar artery. Axial T_2WI demonstrates a triangular region of high intensity in the posterior lateral aspect of the medulla (arrows) on the left side and diffuse high intensity within the inferior medial two-thirds of the left cerebellum. The medial aspect of the cerebellar hyperintensity stops sharply at the midline. There is slight midline displacement of the cerebellum to the right.

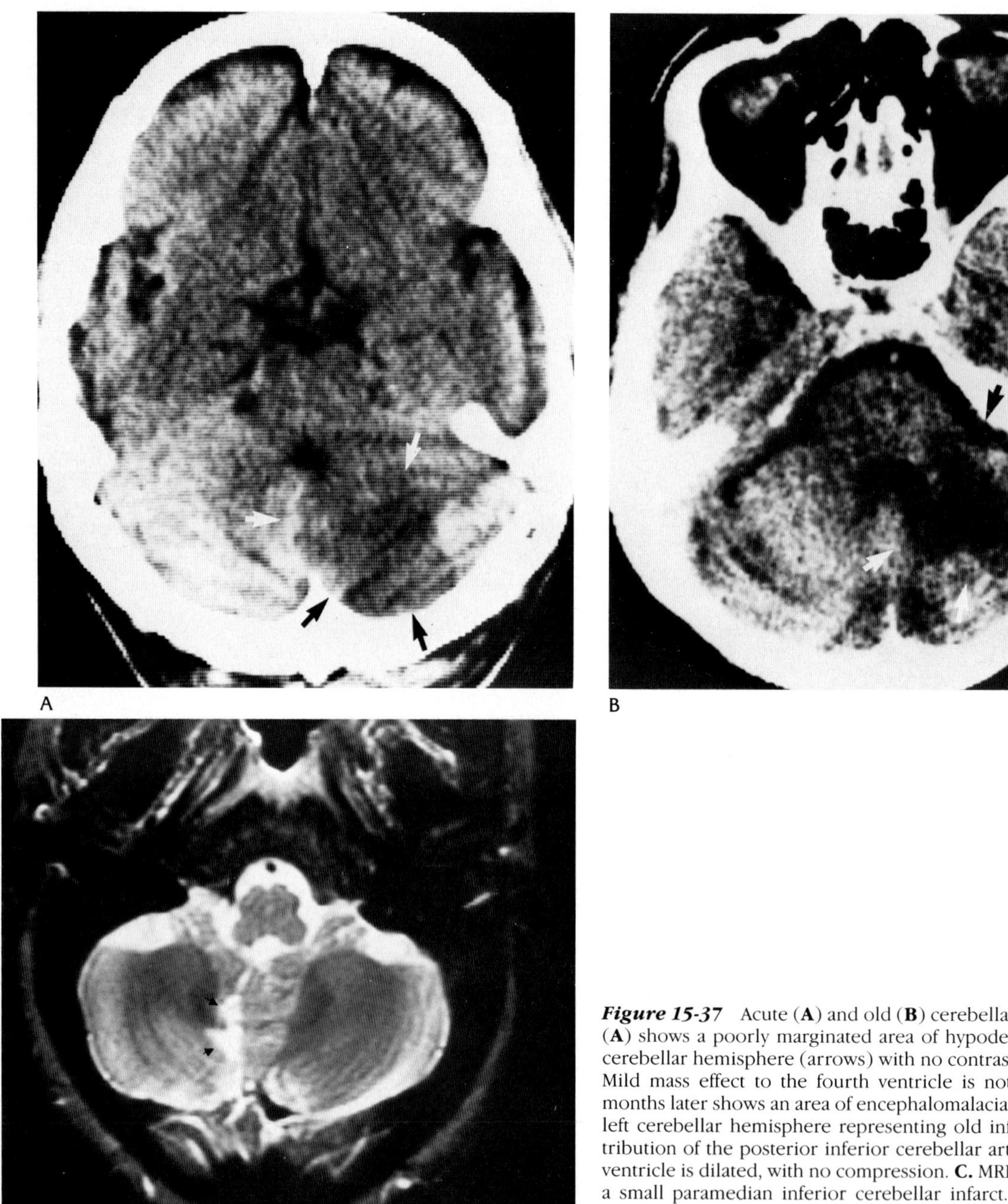

Figure 15-37 Acute (**A**) and old (**B**) cerebellar infarcts. CECT (**A**) shows a poorly marginated area of hypodensity in the left cerebellar hemisphere (arrows) with no contrast enhancement. Mild mass effect to the fourth ventricle is noted. CCT (**B**) 6 months later shows an area of encephalomalacia (arrows) in the left cerebellar hemisphere representing old infarct in the distribution of the posterior inferior cerebellar artery. The fourth ventricle is dilated, with no compression. **C.** MRI demonstrating a small paramedian inferior cerebellar infarct. Axial T_2WI reveals an irregular region of high intensity involving the medial aspect of the right cerebellar hemisphere and the lateral margin of the adjacent inferior vermis (arrows).

within a vascular distribution and usually does not cross the vermis to the opposite side of the midline (Fig. 15-37). In addition, contrast enhancement is not present at this time with most infarctions but is frequently present with tumor. It is important to evaluate carefully for any early evidence of swelling caused by infarction in order to alert clinicians to the possibility of later severe developments; the prognosis might then be favorably affected by early surgical decompression and removal of necrotic cerebellar tissue.

Follow-up scans after the first week that show contrast enhancement in the cerebellar folia suggest infarction in one or more branches of the vertebral and basilar arteries. After several months, a sharply demarcated low-density region will usually become evident on CT, involving the cerebellar surface and extending into the white matter. Focal dilatation of the ipsilateral side of the fourth ventricle may also develop (Fig. 15-37).

MRI detects cerebellar infarcts with much greater sensitivity than does CT (Figs. 15-36 and 15-37).

Anoxic Ischemic Encephalopathy and Carbon Monoxide Poisoning

Individuals who suffer acute respiratory insufficiency such as may occur with allergic reaction, primary central respiratory failure, or overdose from central respiratory depressant drugs such as alcohol, narcotics, or barbiturates may develop either acute or delayed-onset brain damage. Carbon monoxide intoxication may cause similar clinical manifestations and pathological alterations in the brain (Brucher 1967; Lapresle 1967; Ginsberg 1974, 1979). Anoxia or prolonged hypoxia usually results in hypotension and cardiac failure, adding cerebral ischemic insult to the hypoxemia, as may be seen in drowning victims (Murray 1984). Conversely, acute cardiac failure or hypotension may lead to respiratory failure (De Reuck 1978), possibly as a result of brainstem ischemia.

Clinically, most patients with anoxic ischemia present with coma (De Reuck 1978; Ginsberg 1979). Some never demonstrate significant recovery, while others awaken and initially improve, only to have a delayed onset of progressive neurological deterioration after a period of several weeks (Plum 1962; Ginsberg 1976, 1979). Pathologically, patients with irreversible acute brain injury reveal necrosis, which may affect predominantly either the gray matter or the white matter. The watershed region, particularly the periventricular white matter, is usually the most severely affected area (Brierley 1976; De Reuck 1978). The deep parts of the basal ganglia, which can also be considered a terminal field of supply, are also commonly involved (De Reuck 1971*a,b*; Brierley 1976). The pathological change that develops in patients with delayed onset of hypoxic ischemic symptoms is progressive demyelination, with or without zones of focal necrosis that is most severe in the periventricular region (Plum 1962; Ginsberg 1976, 1979). Rarely, the neuropathological alterations are confined to the basal ganglia in patients with the delayed-onset hypoxic ischemic syndrome (Ginsberg 1979).

CT in patients with unremitting neurological deficits demonstrates by 24 to 48 h low-density regions that may be situated in the basal ganglia, the watershed cortex and white matter, or the periventricular white matter (Fig. 15-38). MRI demonstrates with greater sensitivity than CT, on T_2WI and PDWI, hyperintensity in these same regions (Fig. 15-38). The involved gray matter may be isodense during the acute phase, since reperfusion hyperemia during this period can counterbalance the basic hypoxic ischemic low-density tissue change. On CECT, diffuse enhancement in the watershed cortex may appear, probably indicating hyperemia with blood-brain barrier abnormality (Fig. 15-39). If the patient survives the acute phase, marked enlargement of the lateral ventricular system and cortical sulci will develop during the next few months, and previously isodense enhancing regions will become hypodense (Fig. 15-40).

In the most severe cases of anoxic ischemic insult, all the cortical, basal ganglia, and white matter regions of the cerebrum may be involved and reveal diffuse hypodensity after a few days. Initially there is preservation of normal tissue density in the posterior fossa region. The lateral ventricles and basal cisterns are obliterated, reflecting the development of marked brain swelling and increased supratentorial intracranial pressure, which causes further ischemic insult by reducing perfusion pressure. Eventually this vicious circle causes cessation of blood flow in the supratentorial region. The vertebrobasilar circulation to the posterior fossa is similarly affected because the increased intracranial pressure is transmitted transtentorially. A state of cerebral death exists when circulation ceases both supra- and infratentorially. If the patient is kept alive by artificial measures, hypodensity develops in all posterior fossa tissues. Once cerebral death occurs, the large arteries at the base of the brain (internal carotid, proximal anterior, and middle cerebral and basilar) and the large cerebral veins and sinuses (vein of Galen and the superior sagittal, straight, and transverse sinuses) are not visualized on CECT (Rangel 1978; Rappaport 1978). Rapid bolus contrast injection (40 ml in 5 sec) or large bolus infusion (80 g iodine) more dramatically indicates the lack of vascular contrast filling. Al-

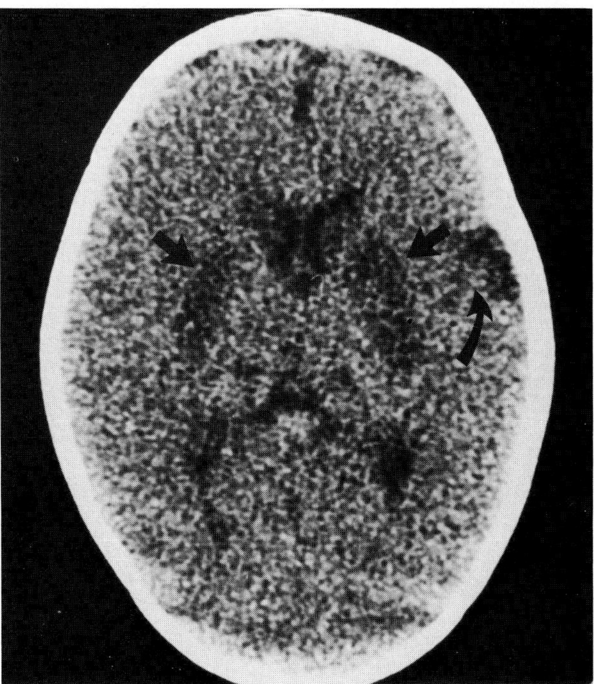

A

Figure 15-38 **A.** Respiratory arrest in a 4-month-old child (crib anoxia), at 2 weeks. Hypodensity involving caudate and putamen bilaterally (arrows) and left anterior temporal (curved arrow) and frontal pole regions of the cortex. (*Continued on p. 674.*)

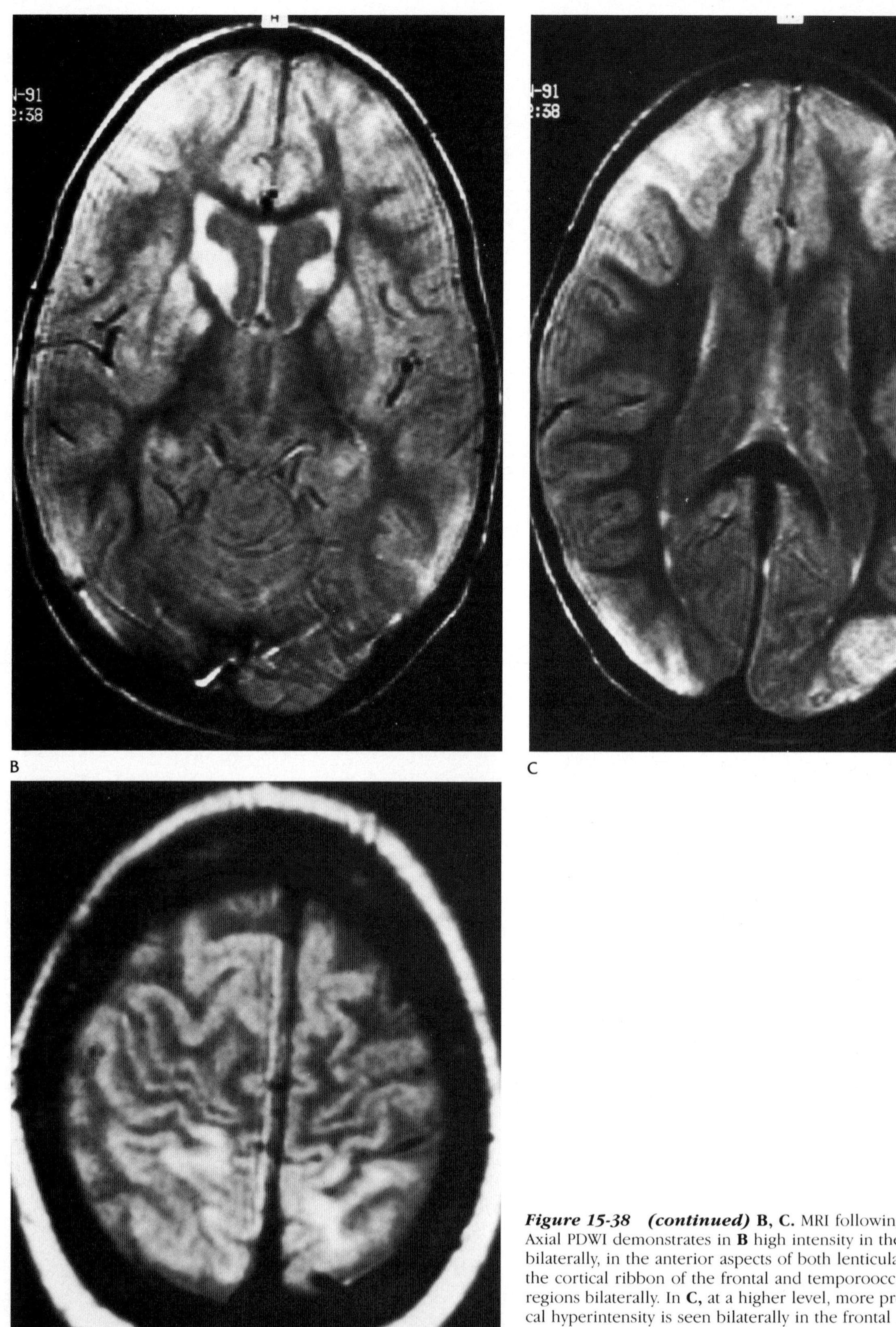

Figure 15-38 (continued) **B, C.** MRI following cardiac arrest. Axial PDWI demonstrates in **B** high intensity in the caudate nuclei bilaterally, in the anterior aspects of both lenticular nuclei, and in the cortical ribbon of the frontal and temporooccipital watershed regions bilaterally. In **C,** at a higher level, more pronounced cortical hyperintensity is seen bilaterally in the frontal and temporooccipital watershed regions. **D.** Another patient with cardiac arrest demonstrates on PDWI a very limited region of cortical hyperintensity bilaterally in the posterior superior watershed zone as the only area of involvement.

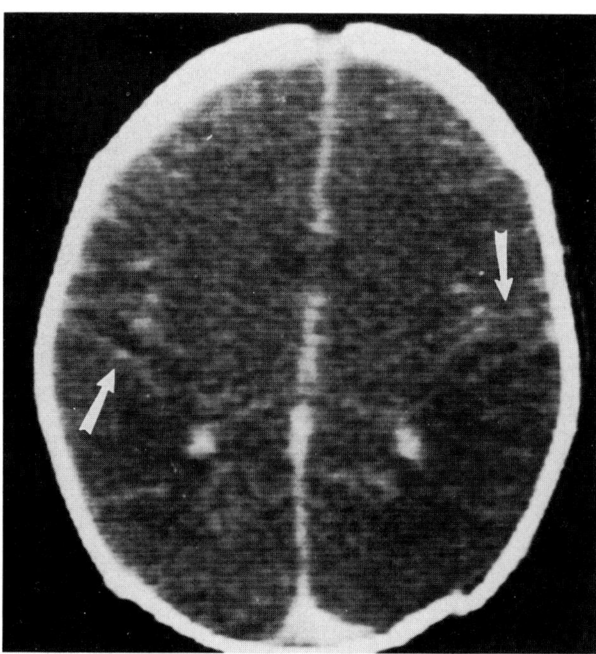

Figure 15-39 CECT: postanoxic cortical enhancement (arrows). Cortical ribbon isodense on NCCT. Diffuse white matter hypodensity.

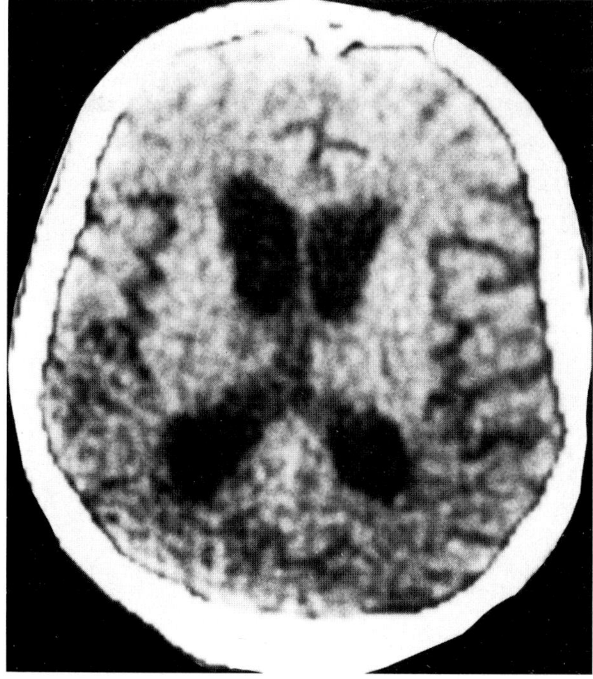

Figure 15-40 Chronic post-anoxic-ischemic changes. Six months after anoxic-ischemic insult: diffuse cortical and ventricular enlargement. Normal CT before episode of respiratory arrest.

though the CT findings may strongly indicate an absence of cerebral circulation, angiography is still needed for confirmation.

In patients who manifest the biphasic clinical response to hypoxic ischemic insult with a delayed onset of secondary neurological deterioration, CT obtained during the first 1 to 2 weeks may be entirely normal. With the onset of neurological deterioration after 3 to 5 weeks, a mild, diffuse low density will appear in the white matter. Over the next 3 to 4 weeks the hypodensity becomes progressively more marked (Yagnik 1980). The hypodensity is most severe in the deep white matter regions but extends in a pseudopodlike manner outward in the white matter tracts between the involved cortical convolutions.

With acute *carbon monoxide* poisoning (a form of anemic hypoxia caused by a reduction in the amount of circulating oxyhemoglobin), the prevalent CT abnormality appears to be bilateral hypodensity in the basal ganglia, most conspicuous in the region of the globus pallidus (Fig. 15-41). This was present in all nine patients reported by Kim (1980). It was observed in four of five patients examined during the first week, being present as early as the first day in two. Five of five patients examined after 6 weeks had bilateral basal ganglia involvement. Diffuse bilateral white matter hypodensity developed in three of the nine patients. Only one of those patients had a relapsing clinical course with delayed onset of neurological deterioration after recovery from initial coma. All the rest had a severe original deficit that showed little, if any, improvement.

In Miura's series (1985), the most common finding was symmetric and diffuse white matter hypodensity (23 of 60 patients), followed by a symmetric, bilateral, round hypodense lesion in the globus pallidus (18 of 60) with frequent extension to the internal capsules (Fig. 15-41). Miura stated that the prognosis depended on the severity of the cerebral white matter changes and not on that of hypodense globus pallidus lesions.

MRI demonstrates with great sensitivity, on PDWI and T_2WI, hyperintensity developing in the globus pallidus and central white matter. The alterations in the globus pallidus may appear early and then clear, with the white matter changes developing more slowly and persisting (Fig. 15-41).

HYPERTENSIVE ENCEPHALOPATHY

Persons, particularly normotensive individuals, who experience a rapid and sustained elevation in blood pressure may develop hypertensive encephalopathy (Ziegler 1965). This is manifested by severe headache, vomiting, convulsions, focal neurological signs, and drowsiness or coma. Pathologically, the brain demonstrates generalized edema, petechial hemorrhages, and patchy vessel wall necrosis. These changes are believed to occur because the normal limit of autoregulatory vasoconstriction has been exceeded (Lassen 1972). This breakthrough in the

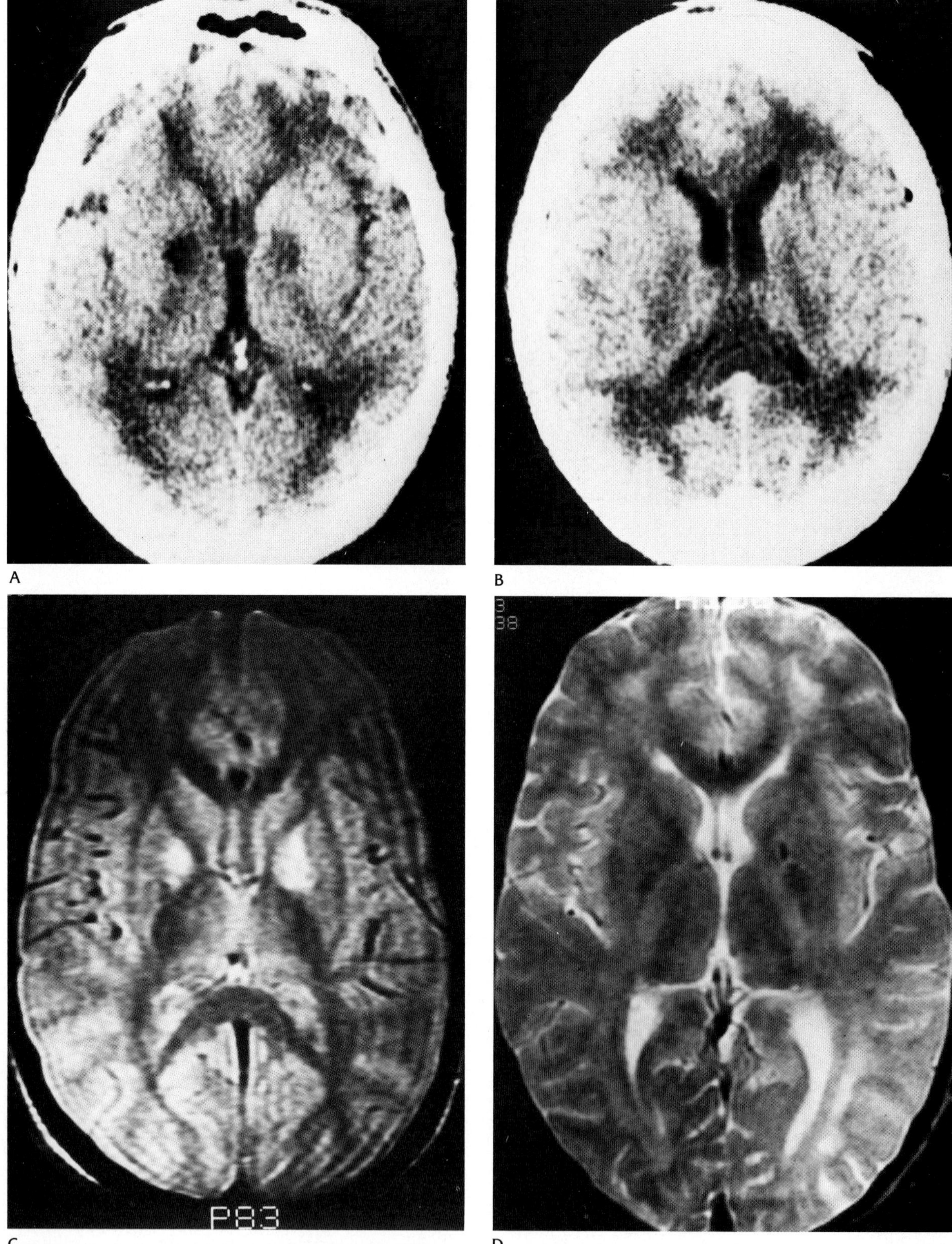

Figure 15-41 Acute carbon monoxide insult. **A.** Bilateral, symmetrical globus pallidus and diffuse white matter hypodense lesions. **B.** Extension to the internal capsules and symmetricity of white matter hypodensity are more apparent at a higher level. **C–E.** Evolution on MRI of carbon monoxide poisoning. **C.** Axial PDWI 2 days after carbon monoxide poisoning. Hyperintensity involves the globus pallidus bilaterally. At a slightly higher level there was very mild hyperintensity in the periatrial region (not shown). **D, E.** Follow-up T_2WI at 6 weeks. **D.** Section at same level as **C** demonstrates clearing of the bilateral globus pallidus hyperintensity. Considerable white matter hyperintensity has developed bilaterally in the anterior frontal regions and in the left posterior temporal region. (*Continued on p. 677.*)

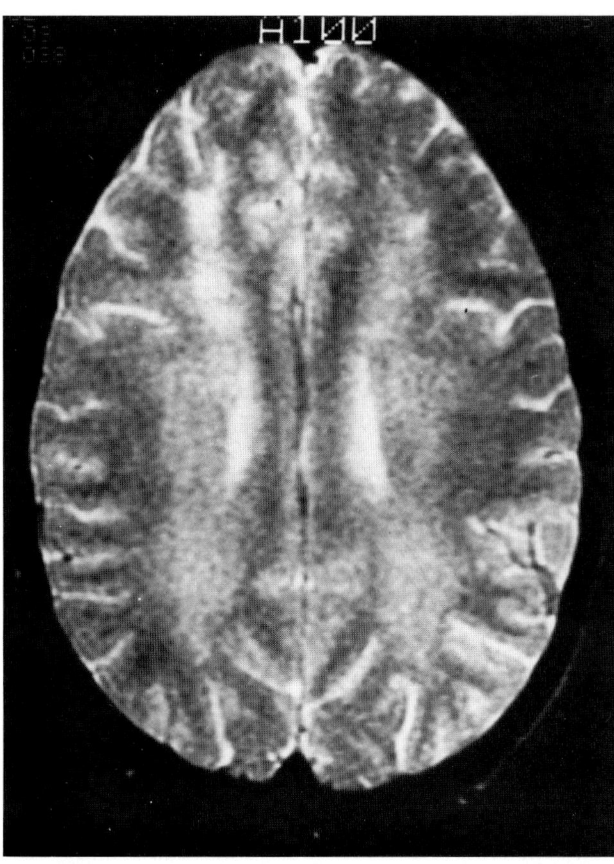

E

Figure 15-41 ***(continued)*** **E.** Axial section through higher portion of brain reveals more extensive diffuse white matter hyperintensity bilaterally. Moderate sulcal dilatation is now evident.

upper limits of autoregulation leads to increased cerebral blood flow and capillary perfusion pressure, and these hemodynamic alterations result in the pathological abnormalities.

The CT and MRI appearance reflects the main pathological change: diffuse edema. Generalized, well-demarcated symmetrical hypodensity is present in the cerebral white matter (Kendall 1977; Gibby 1989), which may be more marked in the upper posterior parts of the cerebral hemispheres (Fig. 15-42) (Rail 1980), and is also noted in the posterior fossa (Weingarten 1985). Varying degrees of mass effect on the ventricles and subarachnoid spaces are present. The degree and duration of blood pressure elevation correlate well with the severity of edema (Weingarten 1985). Follow-up scans demonstrate resolution of the hypodensity after the blood pressure has been reduced for a period of time.

Cerebral Venous Thrombosis

Venous thrombosis in the brain may involve the major venous sinuses, superficial cortical veins, or deep venous system, or two or more of these regions may be affected simultaneously. There is a high incidence of grave mor-

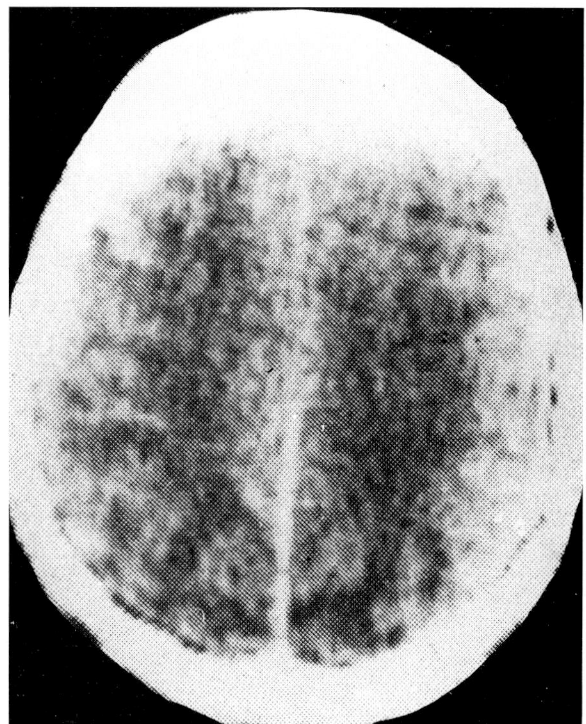

A

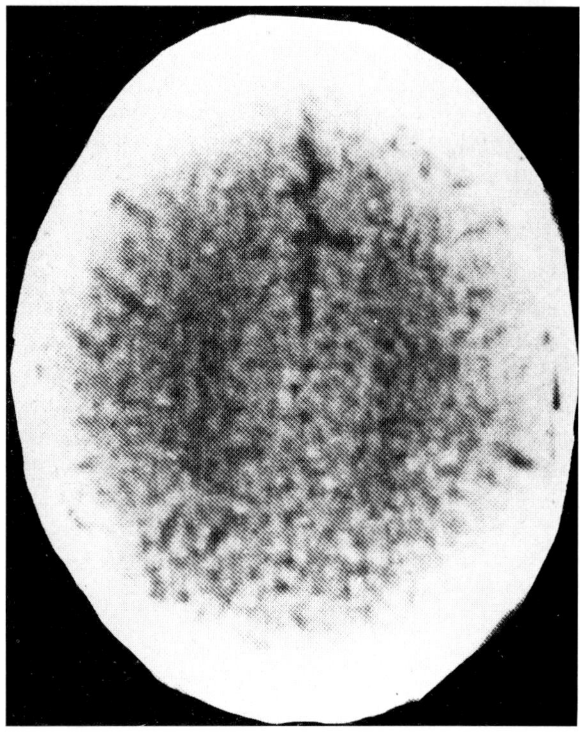

B

Figure 15-42 Hypertensive encephalopathy. **A.** CT at time of severe hypertension and symptoms: hypodensity throughout white matter most marked in the upper posterior portions of the cerebral hemispheres. **B.** CT 2 months after control of hypertension, with mild residual mental function deficits: resolution of white matter hypodensity, moderate prominence of cortical sulci. (*From Rail DL 1980.*)

bidity and mortality with cerebral sinovenous occlusion (Kalbag 1967). To improve survival and reduce debilitating complications, early recognition and institution of appropriate therapy are essential.

The causes of cerebral venous thrombosis fall into two main categories: septic and aseptic. Septic sinovenous occlusion results from inflammatory vasculitis, which may be caused either by direct involvement of the cerebral veins from intracranial infections such as meningitis, encephalitis, and subdural and epidural empyema or by the intracranial spread of paracranial infections along emissary and communicating veins from inflammatory disease in such areas as the mastoids, paranasal sinuses, face, and scalp (Rao 1981; Eick 1981).

The aseptic causes of venous sinus thrombosis are numerous (Buonanno 1978). They include pregnancy in the prepartum and postpartum periods, use of oral contraceptives, dehydration, rapid diuresis, polycythemia vera, sickle cell disease, sickle cell trait, leukemia, thrombocytopenia, disseminated intravascular coagulation, cryofibrinogenemia, malnutrition, acquired and congenital heart disease, head trauma, diabetes mellitus, collagen vascular disease, cerebral arterial occlusion, cerebral and dural arteriovenous malformations, carotid cavernous fistula, compression or invasion by intracranial tumor, and the indirect effects of extracranial neoplasms and chronic inflammatory diseases (Merritt 1979). Many cases are idiopathic.

The clinical manifestations are nonspecific and include headache, increased intracranial pressure, stroke, seizures, personality change, hallucinations, decreased mental function, diplopia, blurred vision, and coma (Merritt 1979). Patients with this disorder not infrequently are initially diagnosed as having "functional" problems or benign pseudotumor cerebri. The clinical symptomatology may develop over a relatively long period or be fulminant, with rapid progression to coma and death. The mortality rate has been reported to range from 40 percent to as high as 88 percent (Krayenbuhl 1954; Buonanno 1978).

CT and MRI reveal a wide spectrum of abnormalities, which may change over the course of the disease. Some of the CT and MRI abnormalities are diagnostic for sinovenous occlusion, while others may be either strongly suggestive or nonspecific. The abnormalities may be present singly or in combination. If subsequent scans are obtained, additional abnormalities may be identified. Occasionally no CT abnormality is present. Buonanno (1978) reported that only 1 patient of 11 with sinovenous occlusion had a normal-appearing CT.

A diagnostic CT abnormality that may be present during the first 1 to 2 weeks after the development of sinovenous occlusion is increased density on NCCT within the region of a dural sinus or a superficial or deep vein (Wendling 1978; Buonanno 1978; Eick 1981). This hyper-

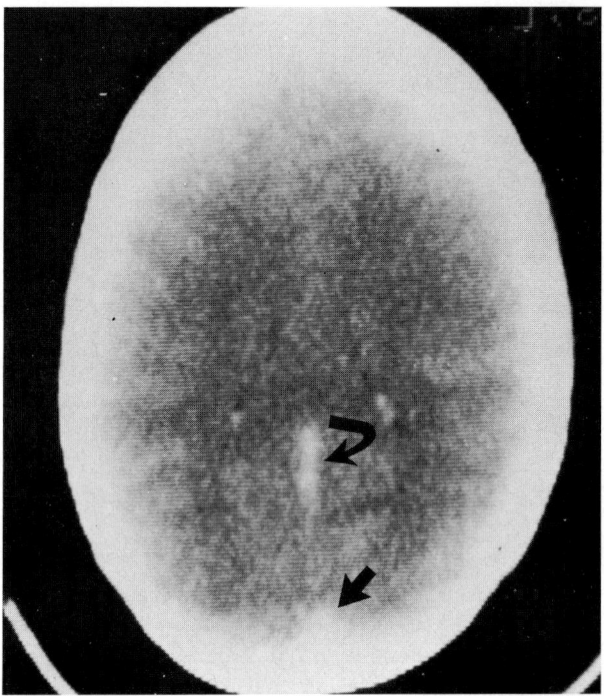

A

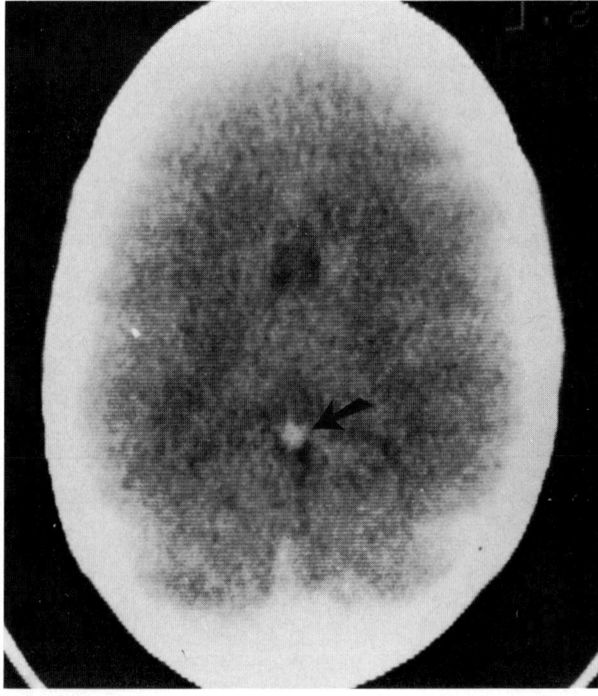

B

Figure 15-43 Venous thrombosis 3 days after onset of symptoms. Dense thrombus in straight sinus, superior sagittal sinus, and vein of Galen; diffuse brain swelling. **A.** NCCT: band of increased density along course of straight sinus (curved arrow) and posterior aspect of superior sagittal sinus (straight arrow). Diffuse increased hypodensity throughout white matter with compressed lateral ventricles. **B.** NCCT, section 1 cm below **A:** increased density of vein of Galen (arrow). Diffuse white matter hypodensity with ventricular compression.

density on CT is due to a recent blood clot in the vein and measures between 50 and 90 HU. It is best seen when the scan plane is perpendicular to the long axis of the thrombosed sinus or vein. Small thrombosed convexity veins situated immediately adjacent to the calvarium may be obscured by the overlying bony density. Fresh thrombus in the straight sinus region can usually be readily appreciated, since it is sufficiently removed from the skull table. Here it appears as an elongated oval or a bandlike density that follows the expected course of the straight sinus (Fig. 15-43). Likewise, recent thrombosis of the vein of Galen, which is just anterior and inferior to the beginning of the straight sinus, should be visualized (Fig. 15-43). Care must be taken not to confuse the thrombosed vein of Galen with a partially calcified pineal gland; the latter is slightly anterior and inferior to the vein of Galen and immediately adjacent to the posterior third ventricle. A fresh thrombus within the superior sagittal sinus may be identified by its density on axial scans if the occlusion is in its posterior vertical portion. In this location the scan plane is relatively perpendicular to the sinus and, because of the large size of the sinus at this location, should not be obscured by the overlying bone (Fig. 15-44). For occlusions more anteriorly situated in the horizontal portion of the superior sagittal sinus, coronal scans made perpendicular to its long axis are necessary. Occasionally the increased density of small thrombosed surface veins is evident if they are not located close to the calvarium—for example, those in sulci or the sylvian cistern (Fig. 15-44).

Another diagnostic CT abnormality of venous sinus occlusion may appear on CECT, usually not becoming evident for at least a week or more after the development of sinus thrombosis, since it follows the breakdown of hemoglobin molecules in the clotted blood of the sinus, which then becomes isodense. The superior sagittal sinus, which normally is demonstrable on CECT as a homogeneous region of increased density, reveals only enhancement of its outer triangular margin; its central luminal area remains relatively hypodense—the "empty triangle" or "delta" sign (Fig. 15-45) (Buonanno 1978).

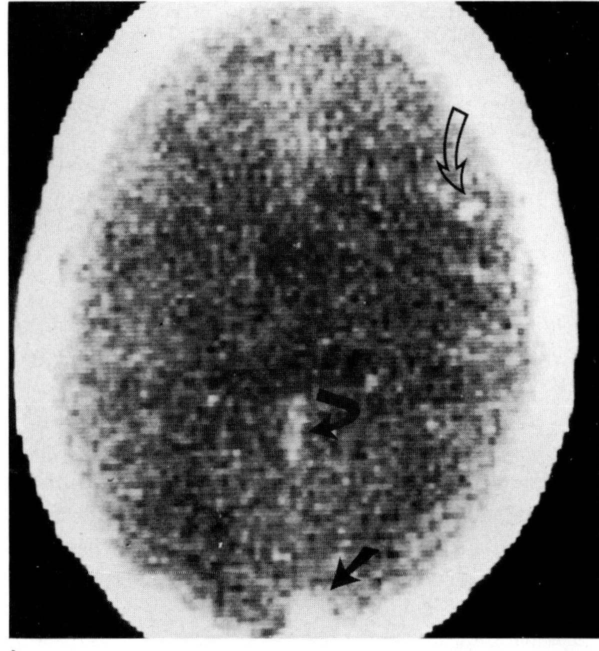

A

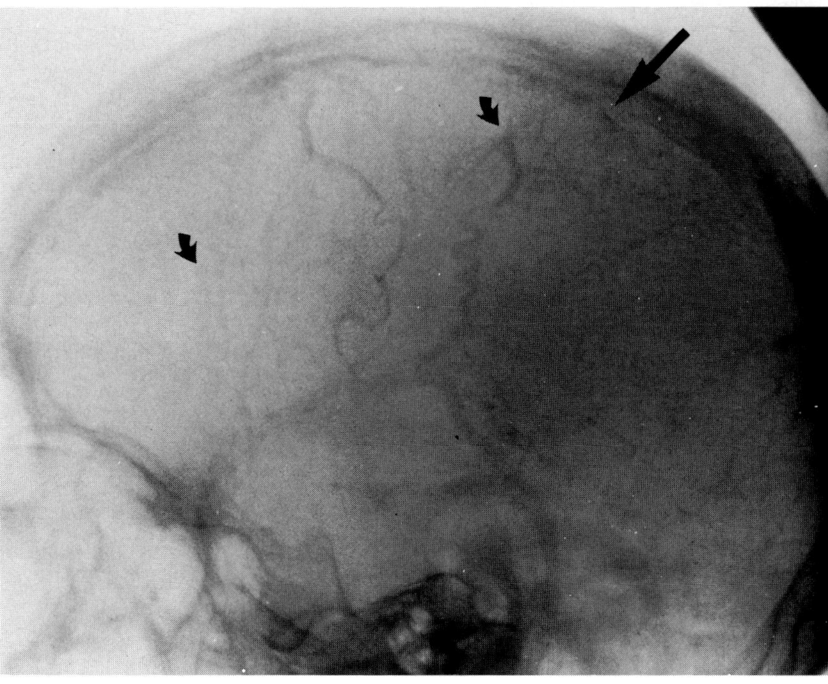

B

Figure 15-44 Venous thrombosis. Development of dense thrombus in cortical vein. **A** NCCT: same patient as in Fig. 15-43 four days later. Persistent hyperdensity of superior sagittal sinus (straight arrow) and straight sinus (curved arrow). Nodular hyperdensity has appeared near brain surface on left (open arrow). **B.** Lateral carotid angiogram, late venous phase: occlusion of superior sagittal sinus (straight arrow), vein of Galen, straight sinus (not filled), and cortical veins (curved arrows). Tortuous convexity veins provide collateral drainage inferiorly for the superior aspect of the brain.

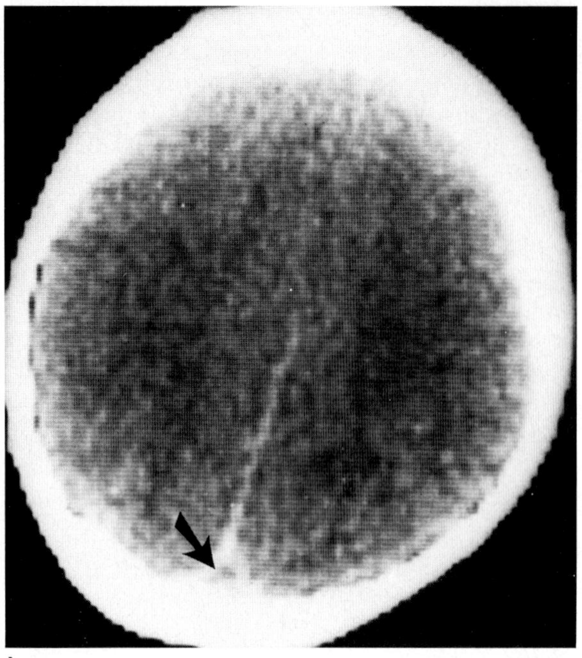

A

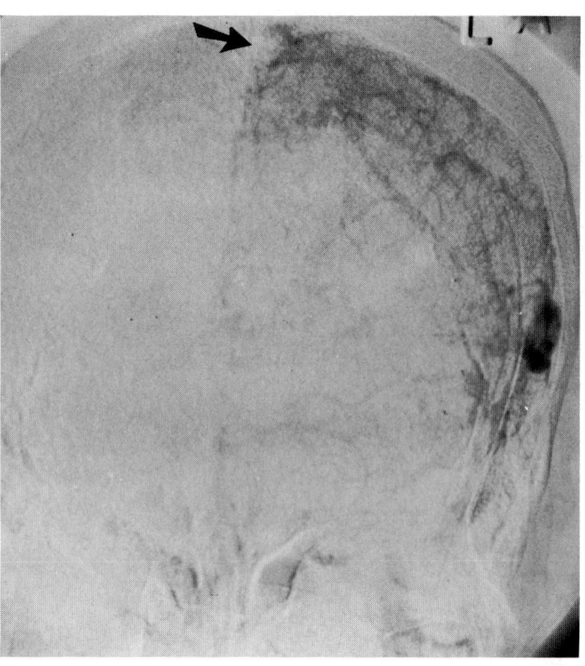

B

Figure 15-45 Venous thrombosis "delta" sign **A.** CECT: no contrast density in central lumen of posterior aspect of superior sagittal sinus with thick enhancement of its walls (arrow). **B.** Frontal carotid angiogram, venous phase: no contrast filling of superior sagittal sinus (arrow).

This appearance represents absence of contrast flow into the sinus (the nonenhanced center) in that region. The enhancing outer triangle represents the normal enhancement of the dural walls of the sinus in combination with the added increased density from the collateral venous channels that develop in the dura (Vines 1971) and from the neovascularity that is probably appearing in the outer portion of the thrombus secondary to its organization. Both processes may cause the sinus wall to appear thickened and encroach on the lumen.

On a standard axial scan, the delta sign is identified mainly in cases in which the sinus thrombosis involves the posterior third of the superior sagittal sinus, since this is the region where the scan plane is most perpendicular to the sinus. It may be necessary to utilize a high window setting to identify the delta sign, since the thickened enhanced wall of the sinus may obscure the central hypodensity when viewed at normal brain window settings (Zilkha 1980). On an axial scan, the anterior third of the superior sagittal sinus is also perpendicular to the scan plane, and the delta sign may be seen with thrombosis in this location (Rao 1981). It may not be evident, however, because of the small size of the sinus in this region. To identify the delta sign in occlusion of the middle portion of the superior sagittal sinus, coronal scans are needed for perpendicular sections of this region. Buonanno (1978) observed the delta sign in only 2 of 11 patients (18 percent) with sinovenous occlusion, whereas Rao (1981) identified it in 8 of 11 patients (72 percent). In addition, Rao observed the delta sign outside the usual location in the superior sagittal sinus in two cases. It was demonstrated as a filling defect in the transverse sinus in one patient and in the straight sinus in a second.

Another highly probable pathognomonic finding of venous thrombosis on CECT is visualization of punctate and streaklike hyperdensities within the deep white matter of the brain (Fig. 15-46) (Banna 1979). These hyperdensities have been postulated to represent engorgement and dilatation of transcerebral medullary veins, which serve as collateral channels between the cortical and deep venous systems. Angiographically, dilated medullary veins may be observed with occlusion of either the deep or the superficial venous systems (Gabrielsen 1969). To identify these dilated medullary veins on CT, scans with very high spatial resolution are needed.

Venous infarctions with CT abnormalities similar to those of arterial infarction frequently develop with sinovenuos occlusion but usually have characteristics that distinguish them from arterial infarction. Since the major cerebral veins generally drain more than one arterial distribution, venous infarcts usually are not confined, as with arterial infarcts, to the territory of a single artery or to the watershed zone (Fig. 15-47). The involvement, particularly in the white matter, may extend asymmetrically, usually between the three main arterial regions. On NCCT, the white matter is hypodense as a result of congestive edema and necrosis. The pattern of white matter low density in venous infarcts usually appears differ-

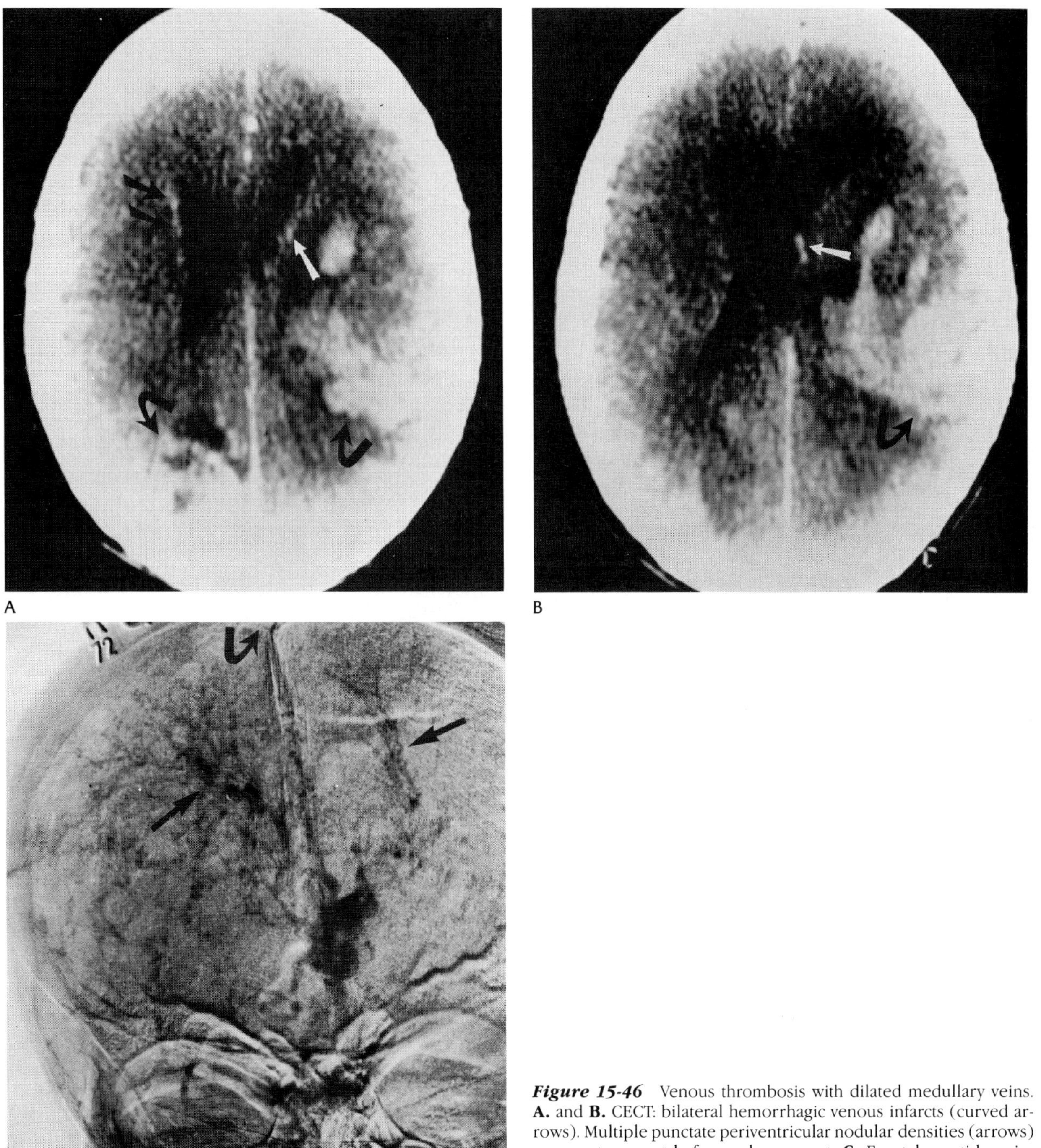

Figure 15-46 Venous thrombosis with dilated medullary veins. **A.** and **B.** CECT: bilateral hemorrhagic venous infarcts (curved arrows). Multiple punctate periventricular nodular densities (arrows) were not present before enhancement. **C.** Frontal carotid angiogram, venous phase: nonfilling of superior sagittal sinus (curved arrow) and superficial veins. Marked dilatation of medullary veins (arrows) draining into deep venous system.

ent from that in arterial infarcts (Fig. 15-47). In venous infarction, the white matter hypodensity tends to have a rounded, ill-defined border, compared with the more sharply marginated wedge or rectangular shape of an arterial infarct. These differences are probably related to a greater degree of vasogenic edema in venous infarction caused by the high capillary pressure from back-pressure congestion. This factor also results in a greater mass effect on venous infarction for a lesion of comparable size.

With venous infarcts, the cortex is usually isodense to slightly hyperdense on NCCT because of congestive dilatation of the capillaries and petechial hemorrhages. On CECT, a frequent cortical abnormality is an intense gyral enhancement pattern over and around the region of the

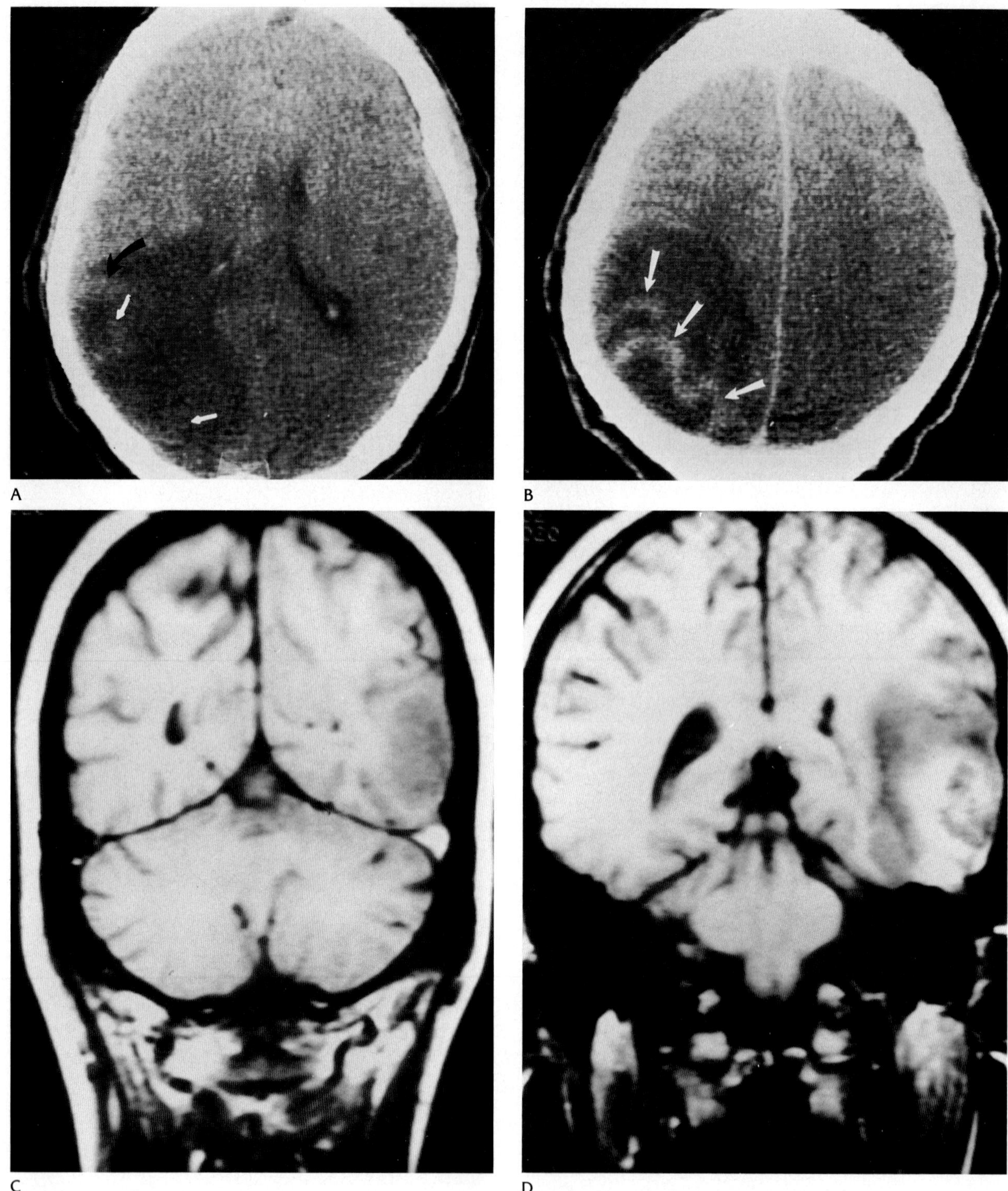

Figure 15-47 Venous infarct, mass effect, and enhancement. **A.** NCCT: large hypodensity involving right posterior temporal, parietal, and occipital regions. Hypodensity not confined to an arterial territory. Cortical density within infarct territory, although reduced, is more isodense than the white matter (arrows). Considerable compression of ipsilateral ventricle. **B.** CECT at higher level: enhancement of cortical ribbon (arrows) centrally in posterior part of infarct. **C, D.** MRI of hemorrhagic venous infarct. **C.** Coronal T_1WI demonstrates a hyperintense signal of subacute thrombus within left transverse sinus and an isointense signal in straight sinus (normal flow void in right transverse sinus). Hypointensity present on left in lateral aspect of temporal lobe. **D.** Coronal T_1WI anterior to **C.** Nonhomogeneous hyperintensity present within inferior and lateral aspect of left temporal lobe, representing subacute cortical and brain hemorrhage. Surrounding hypointensity involving the cortex and white matter superiorly and inferior medially in the temporal lobe represents ischemic venous infarct which is within both the middle cerebral artery and posterior cerebral artery distributions.

venous infarction (Fig. 15-47). Prominent gyral enhancement may also occur in the absence of other evidence of venous infarction. The gyral enhancement is caused by capillary engorgement and breakdown of the blood-brain barrier related to high venous back pressure and its associated ischemic effects. Rao (1981) observed gyral enhancement in 7 of 11 patients with venous infarcts. This is a considerably higher frequency than Rao found in a review of the literature, in which only 4 of 14 patients having CECT demonstrated gyral enhancement.

Intense enhancement, considerably greater than normal, may develop in the tentorium and falx. This probably reflects enlargement of dural venous collateral channels (Vines 1971) and increased dural capillary pressure, leading to a greater leakage of contrast into the dura. This enhancement has been observed most commonly in the tentorium and is associated with thrombosis of the straight sinus (Buonanno 1978; Rao 1981).

Hemorrhage is also frequently associated with venous infarcts. The hemorrhage most commonly involves the cortex but may affect the white matter in the central and deep portions of the infarct (Figs. 15-46 and 15-47). Extensive low density in the white matter when the hemorrhage is first observed is related to the necrosis and edema caused by the venous infarction. The venous infarction hemorrhage may assume a dense gyral pattern similar in appearance to that of an arterial hemorrhagic infarction. Venous hemorrhages tend to be more bulky and less strictly confined to the cortical ribbon. In addition, the white matter hypodensity and the hemorrhagic region may not be located within the territory of a single major cerebral artery as with an arterial hemorrhagic infarction. At times the venous hemorrhage is very bulky and extends deeply into the white matter, strongly resembling an arterial intracerebral hematoma. The venous hemorrhage may, however, reveal changes different from those occurring with an arterial hemispheric hematoma. With venous infarction the hematoma is not sharply demarcated, and its density may be slightly nonhomogeneous. It is also more superficially located and is surrounded by a greater degree of hypodensity in the white matter, especially in its early stage.

Not infrequently, multiple separate regions of venous infarction may develop. A common pattern seen with multiple venous infarcts is bilateral involvement in the parasagittal high-convexity region of the brain. This may reveal bilateral hypodensities in the anterior cerebral territory, frequently extending beyond the watershed zone into the middle cerebral artery territory. Occasionally multiple venous hemorrhagic infarcts develop in this same distribution.

Nonspecific alterations that may develop with sinovenous thrombosis include small ventricles, mild diffuse white matter hypodensity that may be unilateral or bilateral, and obliteration of the basal cisterns (Fig. 15-43). These alterations reflect increased intracranial pressure from vasogenic edema caused by the increasing outflow resistance from venous obstruction.

CT may demonstrate nonfilling of a variable segment of the superior sagittal, straight, transverse, or sigmoid sinuses and/or obstruction of superficial convexity or deep veins (Figs. 15-44 and 15-45). Thrombi may be identified within occluded or partially obstructed venous sinuses and cerebral veins. Enlargement and frequently corkscrew tortuosity of anastomotic collateral veins (Fig. 15-44) and medullary veins (Fig. 15-46) may be observed. Although the characteristic and highly specific CT findings frequently strongly suggest a diagnosis of sinovenous thrombosis, cerebral angiography is the definitive method for diagnosis and is indicated in questionable cases for confirmation (Krayenbuhl 1954; Gabrielsen 1969, 1981; Vines 1971).

MRI has been extremely sensitive in detecting sinovenous thrombosis and underlying parenchymal alterations in the authors' experience (Figs. 15-47 and 15-48). In the acute phase, usually up to about 7 days, T_1WI reveal an isointense signal within the venous sinus instead of the normal flow void. T_2WI at high field strength demonstrate at this time a marked hypointense signal within the venous sinus that simulates that of the normal flow void. Gradient-echo flow images fail to demonstrate a flow enhancement, that is, a high-intensity signal within the sinus region. After about 7 days T_1WI and usually T_2WI demonstrate a hyperintense signal of the venous sinus blood clot and adjacently clotted cerebral veins (Macchi 1986). The conversion of the venous blood clots to hyperintensity at this time results from the formation of methemoglobin within the thrombus. The ability of MR to obtain images readily in various planes facilitates optimal visualization of the various venous sinuses. Hemorrhagic and nonhemorrhagic venous infarcts in both the acute and subacute phases are usually very well seen with MRI. After about 2 to 3 weeks, partial to complete recanalization of the venous sinus occlusions may be demonstrated with MRI as a return of flow voids within these areas. Enlarged venous collateral channels may be identified similarly as flow voids within the brain parenchyma or on its surface.

INTRACEREBRAL HEMORRHAGE

CT is an accurate and very highly reliable method for diagnosing an acute intracerebral hematoma. The true incidence of this diagnosis has increased since the advent of CT. The density of freshly clotted blood on CT (55 to 90 HU) is significantly greater than that of brain tissue, permitting ready identification of even very small intracerebral hematomas. Hemorrhages down to 5 mm in diameter can usually be diagnosed if technically good scans are obtained (Fig. 15-49). Intracerebral hematomas may extend to the brain surface, resulting in secondary sub-

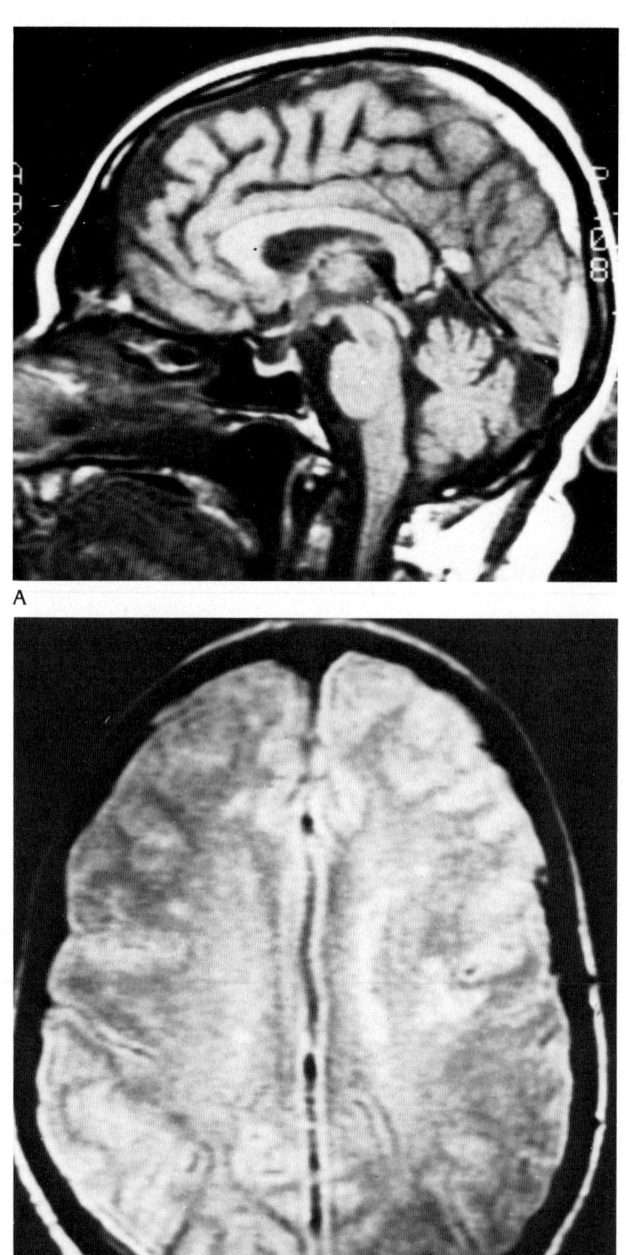

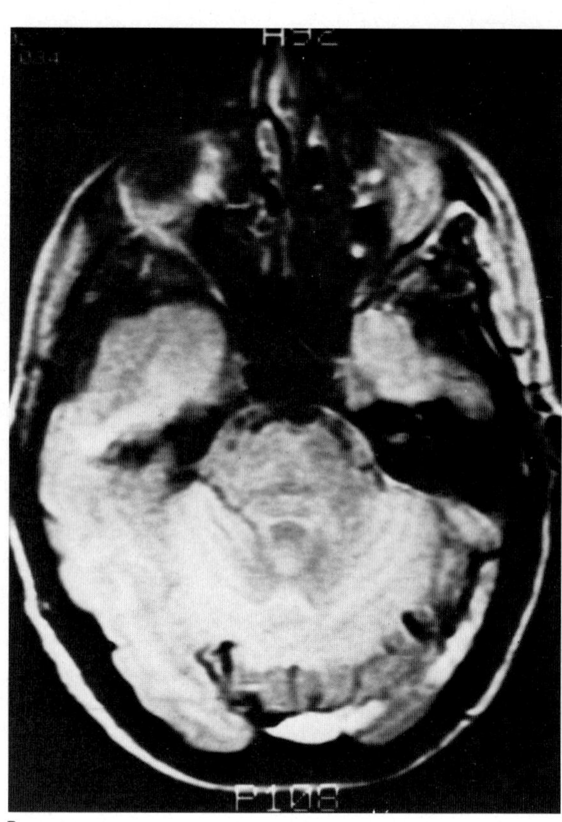

Figure 15-48 Venous thrombosis. MRI: **A** (sagittal T_1) and **B** (axial T_1) show hyperintense lesions along the sagittal, straight, and transverse sinuses. **C** (Axial T_2) shows thrombosed sagittal sinus as hyperintense lesion on T_2 weighted image. Abnormal signal lesions are noted in the white matter of both hemispheres. (*Continued on p. 685.*)

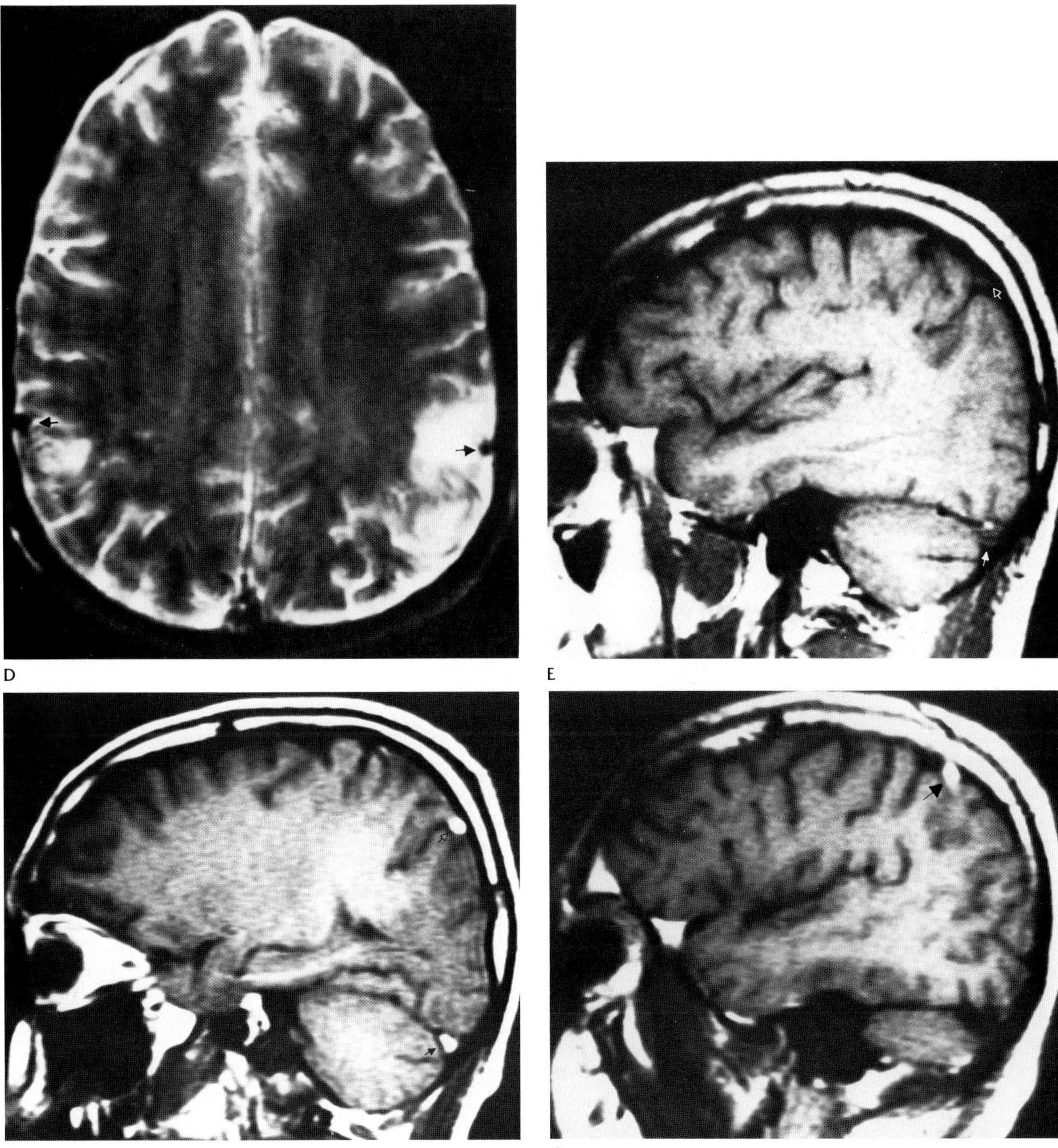

Figure 15-48 (continued) **D–G.** Temporal evolution on MRI of bilateral superficial vein thrombosis and venous sinus thrombosis. **D.** Axial T_2WI demonstrates hyperintensity bilaterally in the parietal regions involving the cortex and underlying white matter. On the surface overlying each parietal lesion is a prominent rounded signal void within the CSF (arrows). These represent the signal loss on T_2WI at high field strength from acute clots which here are in superficial veins. **E.** Sagittal T_1WI through midportion of the left cerebral hemisphere. Isointense signal present within the transverse sinus (solid arrow) and high parietal vein (open arrow). Parietal vein same as hypointense vein on left in **C.** The right transverse sinus demonstrated a normal flow void (not shown). **F, G.** Follow-up sagittal T_1WI at 2 weeks. **F.** Sagittal image through midportion of left cerebral hemisphere now demonstrates a high-intensity signal representing a subacute clot in the left transverse sinus (solid arrow) and in the high parietal vein (open arrow). **G.** Sagittal image through right cerebral hemisphere reveals a normal flow void in right transverse sinus and a high-intensity signal of subacute clot in the right high parietal vein (arrow).

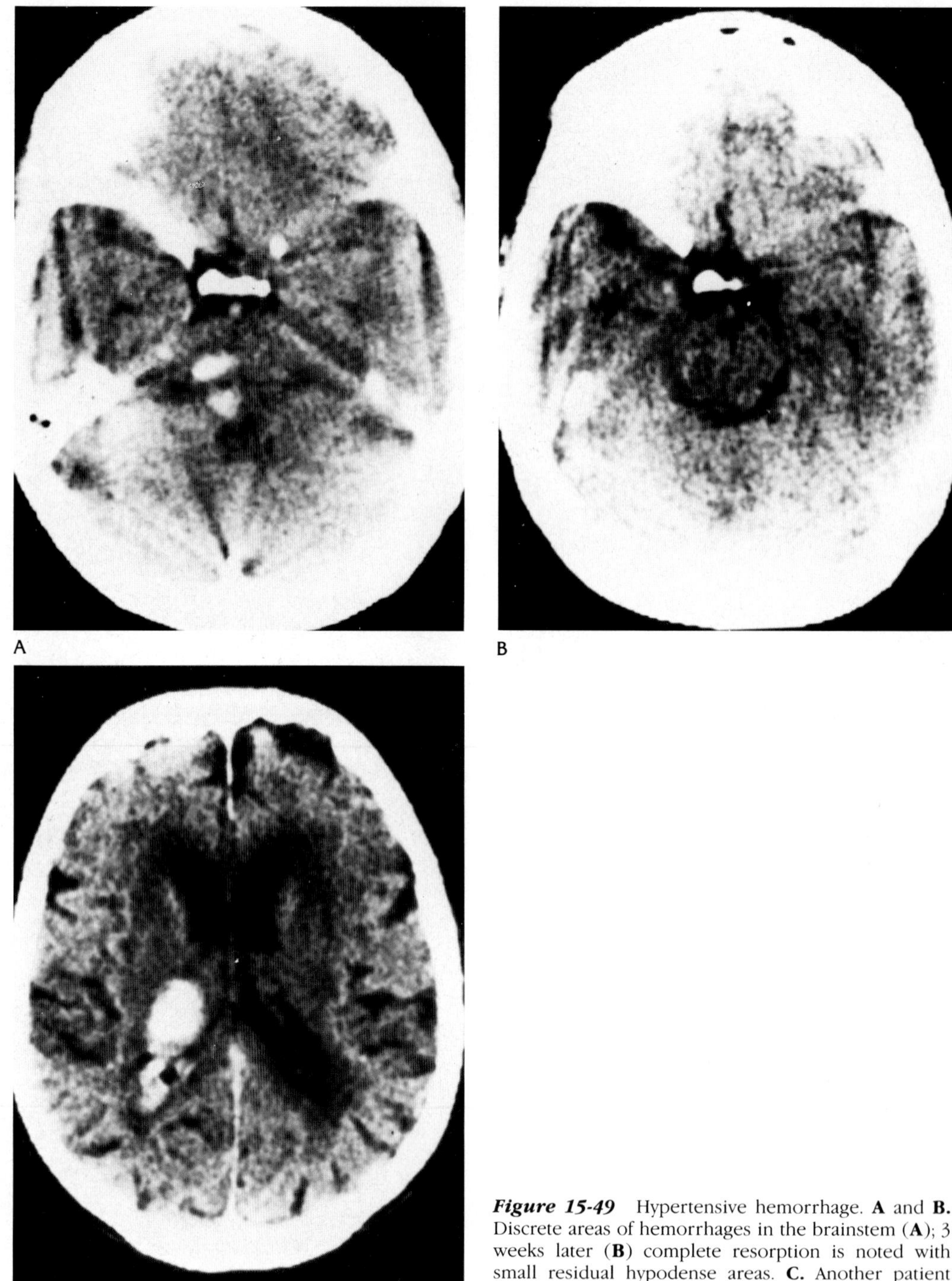

Figure 15-49 Hypertensive hemorrhage. **A** and **B.** Discrete areas of hemorrhages in the brainstem (**A**); 3 weeks later (**B**) complete resorption is noted with small residual hypodense areas. **C.** Another patient with hypertensive thalamic hemorrhage.

arachnoid hemorrhage or rupture intraventricularly. MRI has the unique ability to detect not only acute hemorrhage but also subacute and chronic blood products in the brain (Gomori 1987). CT usually cannot detect any specific characteristics that indicate the presence of subacute and chronic hemorrhage.

Aside from head trauma, the principal cause of intracerebral hematoma is hypertensive vascular disease. Rupture of a berry aneurysm and arteriovenous malformation are less frequent causes. Other etiologies include venous thrombosis, amyloid angiopathy in patients over 70 years of age, collagen vascular disease, anticoagulation therapy, primary and metastatic brain tumor, and prematurity in neonates. Although hematomas from various causes may present a similar CT appearance, the correct etiology is frequently suggested by consideration of the patient's age, the clinical history, and the location of the hematoma. The use of contrast may reveal associated specific enhancement characteristics that indicate the diagnosis (Weisberg 1979). Hematomas caused by venous infarction were discussed earlier in this chapter; those associated with trauma, aneurysm, arteriovenous malformation, and tumor are presented in Chaps. 2 and 14.

Hypertensive Hematoma

Intracerebral hematomas caused by hypertensive vascular disease tend to occur in older patients, usually those in the seventh decade. These hematomas are most commonly situated in the basal ganglia and internal capsule region. They predominantly involve the lateral portion of the putamen but also occur in the head of the caudate nucleus and the thalamus, brainstem, and cerebellum (Figs. 15-49 and 15-50). They occasionally develop in the deep cerebral white matter in the parietal and posterior temporal occipital area (Cole 1967). Small hematomas may present clinically as a vasoocclusive stroke (Kinkel 1976). CT and MRI are then needed for appropriate diagnosis and management.

Larger basal ganglia–capsular hematomas not infrequently rupture into the lateral ventricle. Since the advent of CT, intraventricular rupture has been recognized as being much more common than was previously believed. Small amounts of intraventricular bleeding do not significantly increase mortality. With a large intraventricular rupture, the prognosis becomes very grave (Fig. 15-50) (Weisberg 1979). Once it becomes intraventricular, a hemorrhage from any region can spread throughout the entire ventricular system and into the subarachnoid space.

An intracerebral hemorrhage frequently extends away from its site of origin into adjacent regions along white matter tracts. Occasionally, the degree of spread may be so great that determining the primary site of hemorrhage will be difficult. A basal ganglia–capsular hemorrhage may extend superiorly into the deep frontoparietal white matter via the internal capsule or inferiorly into the temporal lobe via the external capsule (Fig. 15-50*C*). Intraventricular rupture into the body of the lateral ventricle from this location occurs frequently. Thalamic hematomas may dissect inferiorly into the brainstem, laterally into the posterior limb of the internal capsule, or medially into the third ventricle. Superior extension into the lateral ventricle is not usual, probably because of the intervening subarachnoid space of the velum interpositum. Brainstem hematomas may extend superiorly into the thalamus or posteriorly either into the cerebellum through the cerebellar peduncles or directly into the fourth ventricle. Conversely, cerebellar hematomas can dissect anteriorly into the pons. Large cerebellar hematomas cause significant brainstem compression and tonsillar herniation and frequently require urgent surgical evacuation.

Hypertensive hematoma is believed by many researchers to be caused by the rupture of microaneurysms on the penetrating arteries. These aneurysms were first described by Charcot and Bouchard (1868) and are often called *Charcot-Bouchard aneurysms*. Recent elegant microradiographic and histopathological studies have reconfirmed their presence, their strong association with hypertension, and their prevalence at the usual sites of intracerebral hemorrhage; they are most frequent in the basal ganglia–internal capsule region (Russell 1963; Cole 1967). They result from hyalin degeneration in the walls of the penetrating arteries, with loss of elastic fibers and smooth muscle in the intima and media. These microaneurysms are most often located at points of branching and are either fusiform or saccular dilatations ranging in size from 50 to 1000 μm (Kido 1978). They may occasionally be demonstrated with high-detail-magnification angiography and angiotomography (Goldberg 1973).

A fresh hematoma on NCCT appears as a homogeneously dense (55 to 90 HU), well-defined lesion with a rounded to oval configuration. The hemorrhage separates brain tissue rather than intermixing with it. A thin, well-defined low-density zone surrounding the hematoma can be observed as early as a few hours after the hemorrhage (Fig. 15-51). This early hypodense rim is probably caused by the clotting of the liquid hemorrhage with extrusion of the low-density plasma at the periphery of the hematoma. A fresh hemorrhage on MRI demonstrates iso- to slight hypointensity (to gray matter) on T_1-WI and marked hypointensity on T_2WI at high field strength (Fig. 15-51) or on susceptibility-weighted gradient-echo images (Gomori 1987). This appearance is due to the conversion of red cell oxyhemoglobin to deoxyhemoglobin during the first 3 to 5 h after the hemorrhage. After 3 to 4 days, additional low density on CT and high signal on T_2-weighted MRI appears around the hematoma, spreading peripherally in the white matter. This is caused by compression ischemic necrosis of surrounding tissue and the development of edema related to clot lysis, with breakdown of the blood-brain barrier (Fig. 15-51) (Stephens 1972; Grubb 1974; Laster 1978). Hematomas produce ventricular compression and, when large, considerable midline shift and brain herniation. Mass effect may increase during the third to seventh day from the development of edema. Steroid treatment, especially in nontraumatic hematomas, will usually control edema formation and therefore eliminate or considerably reduce the secondary increased mass effect both clinically and on brain imaging.

A hematoma that is nonhomogeneously dense should lead the physician to consider hemorrhage occurring with tumor, inflammation, contusion, or arterial and ve-

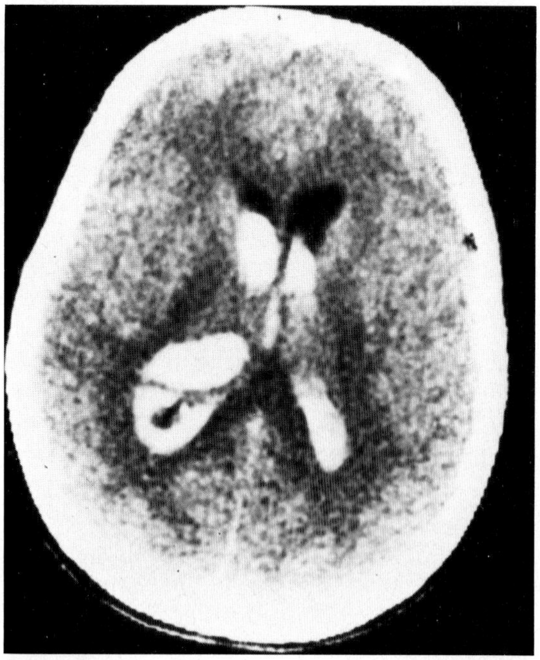

A

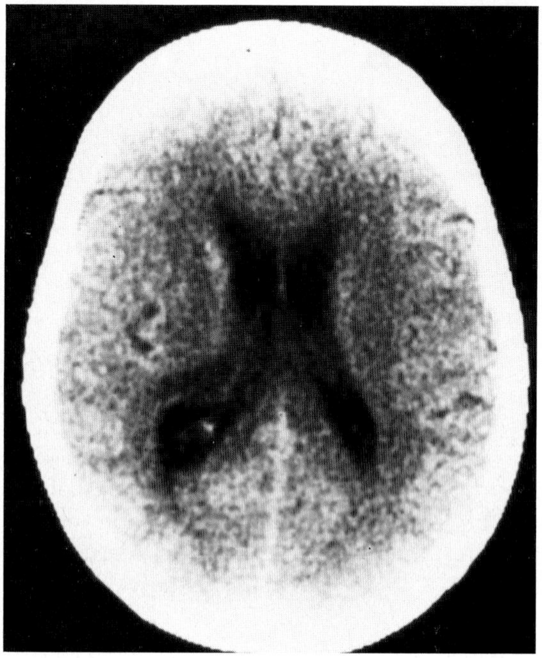

B

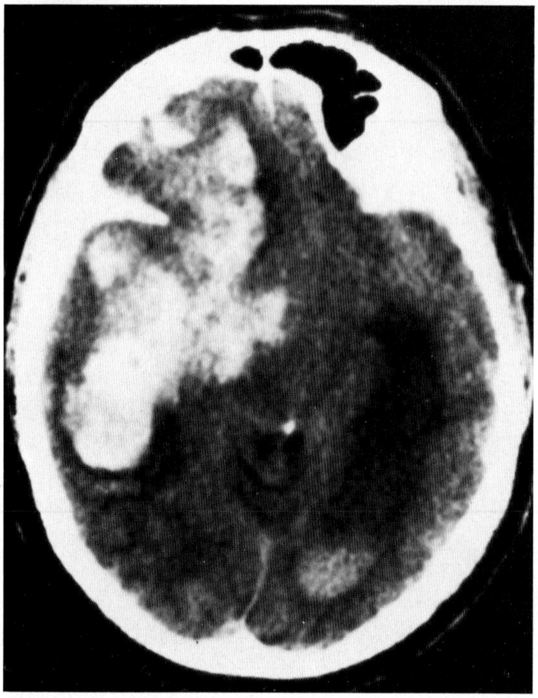

C

Figure 15-50 Hypertensive hemorrhage. **A** and **B.** Right thalamic hemorrhage (arrows) with rupture into the lateral ventricles (**A**). Six months later (**B**) complete resorption of hemorrhage is noted with a small area of encephalomalacia. **C.** Right basal ganglia hemorrhage extends into the frontal and temporal lobes as well as the ventricles and upper midbrain.

nous infarction. In these situations, the hemorrhage usually develops within the abnormal and necrotic tissue and, depending on the etiology, may appear as a poorly marginated and patchy region of increased density, a nonhomogeneous region of hyperdensity centrally located in an area of hypodensity, or a complete or incomplete irregular ring of increased density around a low-density or isodense center with surrounding edema. CECT and MRI frequently reveal abnormal enhancement within the hemorrhages and about them, aiding in their differentiation from vascular disease hemorrhage.

Dolinskas et al. (1977*a*) reported that hematomas show a decreasing peak density averaging 0.7 ± 0.31 EMI units per day (these values would be approximately double in Hounsfield units). In this study, small hematomas tended to lose their density faster than did the larger ones; hematomas of 2 cm or less reached isodensity on or before the nineteenth day after the bleeding, while larger hematomas frequently took 4 to 6 weeks to become isodense. The decreasing density of a hematoma is due to lysis of the red blood cells. Hematomas lose their density from the periphery inward and therefore show a progressive decrease in apparent size on CT (Fig. 15-51). Dolinskas (1977*a*) found a reduction in the visualized size of the hematoma, averaging 0.65 ± 0.32 mm per day. Small hematomas showed this size reduction sooner than did large ones. Although the visualized portion of the hematoma becomes smaller on CT, the actual size of the clot does not change significantly at this time; it merely becomes isodense, and this is reflected in a delay in the reduction of its mass effect. Mass effect may be prominent for as long as 4 weeks with a large hematoma. These au-

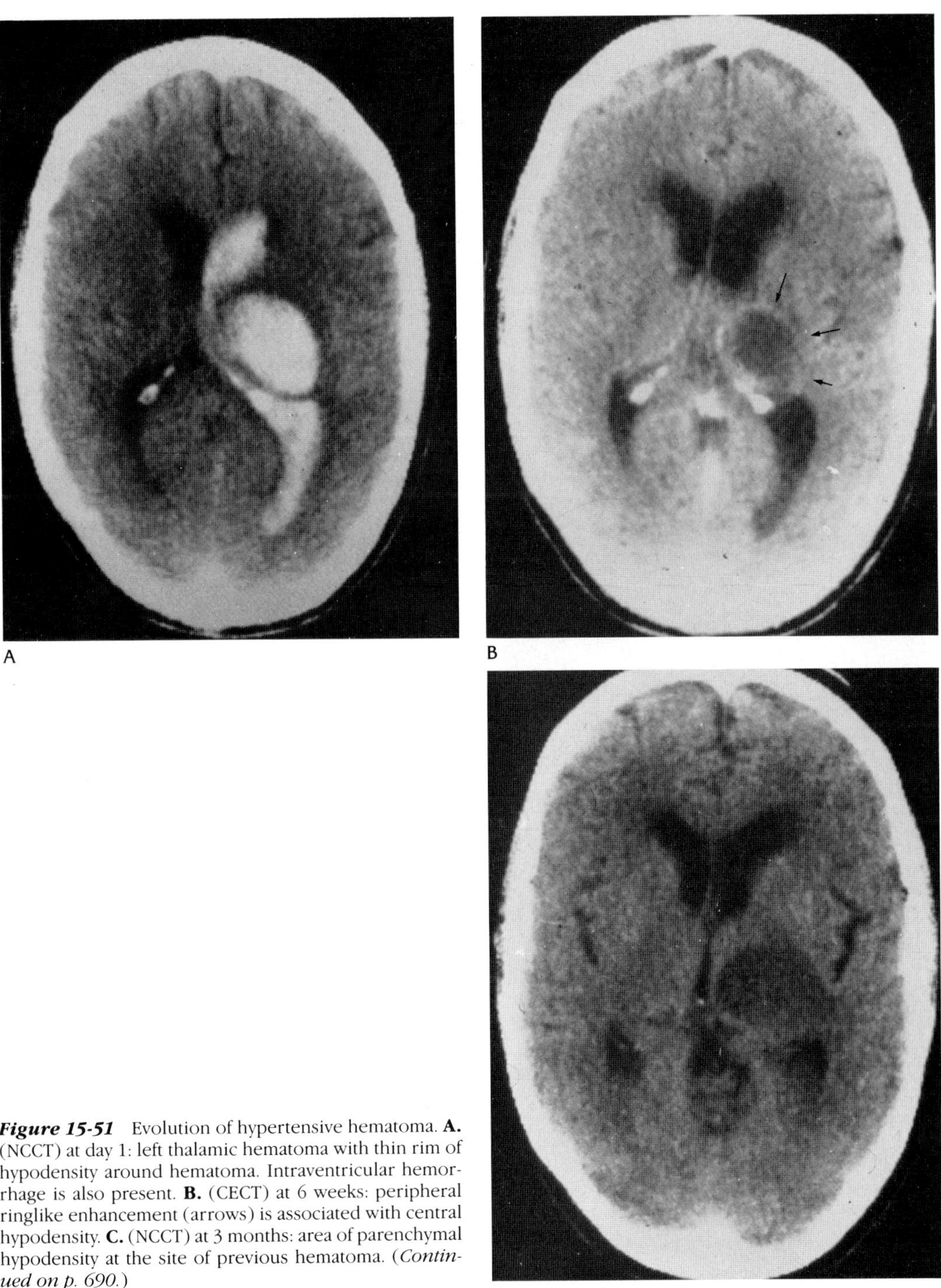

Figure 15-51 Evolution of hypertensive hematoma. **A.** (NCCT) at day 1: left thalamic hematoma with thin rim of hypodensity around hematoma. Intraventricular hemorrhage is also present. **B.** (CECT) at 6 weeks: peripheral ringlike enhancement (arrows) is associated with central hypodensity. **C.** (NCCT) at 3 months: area of parenchymal hypodensity at the site of previous hematoma. (*Continued on p. 690.*)

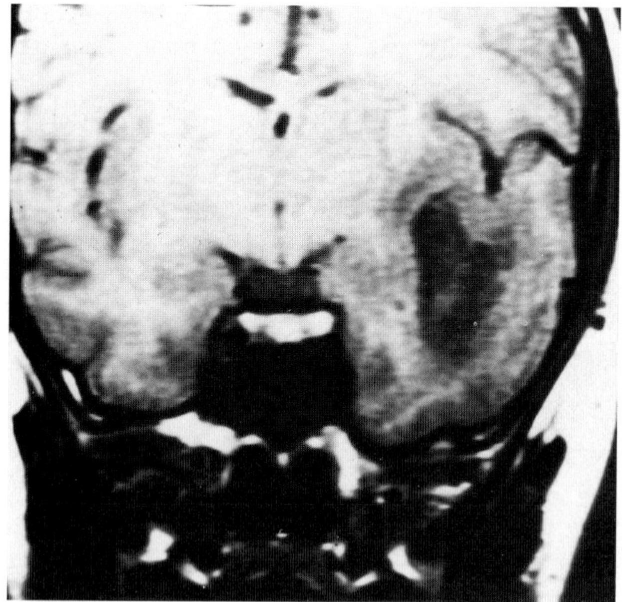

D

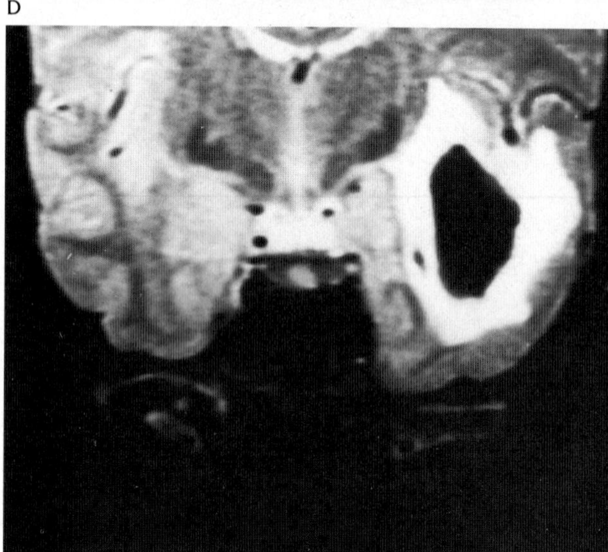

E

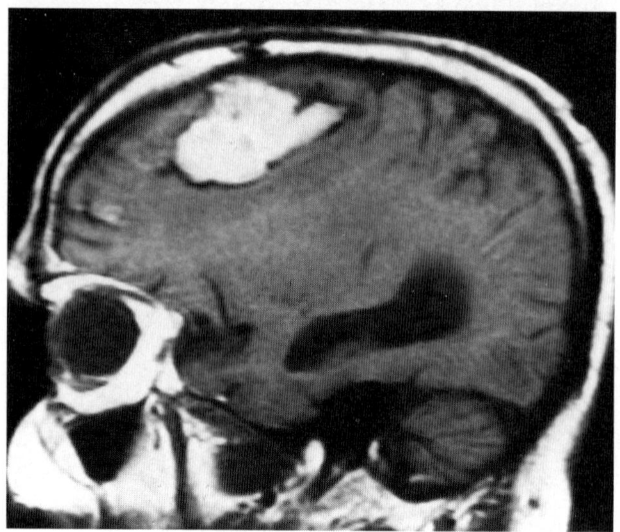

F

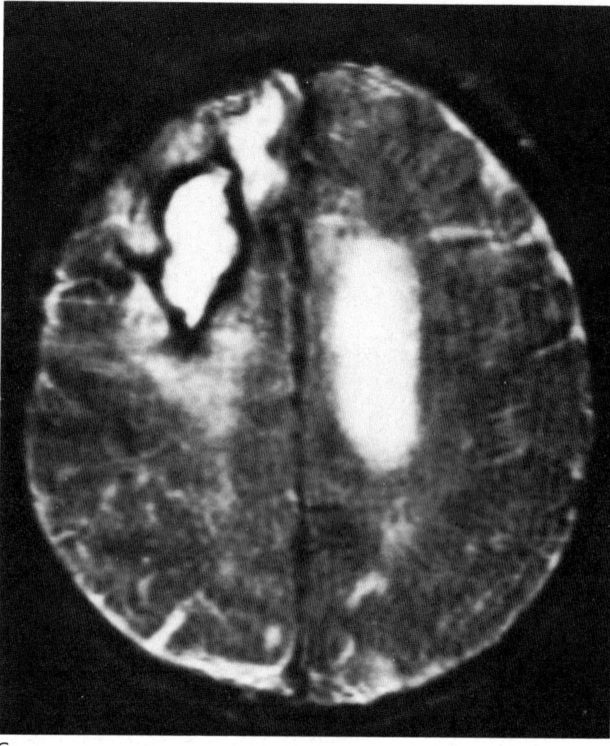

G

Figure 15-51 (continued) **D–G.** Evolution of intracerebral hematoma on MRI. **D, E.** Temporal lobe hematoma at 2 days. **D.** Coronal T_1WI demonstrates a hypointense lesion in deep left temporal lobe. **E.** Coronal T_2WI reveals greater hypointensity of lesion in left temporal lobe which is surrounded by a broad rim of hyperintensity representing edema. The marked central hypointensity on T_2WI reflects signal loss from susceptibility effects at high field strength from the paramagnetic deoxyhemoglobin associated with acute blood clots. **F, G.** Subacute intracerebral hematoma at 14 days in another patient. **F.** Sagittal T_1WI through the midportion of the right cerebral hemisphere demonstrates a high-intensity lesion within the superior aspect of the right frontal lobe. **G.** Axial T_2WI through a right frontal lobe hematoma demonstrates the high intensity of the hematoma with a surrounding thin rim of marked hypointensity which represents the accumulation of hemosiderin particles within macrophages. There is hyperintensity surrounding the hemosiderin rim, indicating the persistence of brain edema with subacute hematoma. High-intensity lesion in left cerebral hemisphere is of uncertain etiology.

thors also noted that the earliest visualized decrease in mass effect for hematomas of all sizes averaged 16.7 days after bleeding. Smaller hematomas lost their mass effect faster than did larger ones. In addition, it was found that mass effect did not increase unless an operation was performed or the hematoma was secondary to trauma. On MRI, as CT density of the clot is being lost, on T_1WI the clot begins to develop hyperintensity in comparable regions that first become evident about 5 to 7 days after the hemorrhage (Fig. 15-51). This results from the conversion by oxidation of the deoxyhemoglobin of the early clot to methemoglobin, which has a strong paramagnetic effect on T_1WI. Shortly after the conversion to methemoglobin, red cells begin to lyse. This event results in hyperintensity developing on T_2WI in regions that were previously markedly hypointense (Gomori 1985). The MR intensity changes, as with the evolution of the density changes on CT, begin at the periphery of the hematoma and progress centrally.

Over the next 2 to 3 months on CT, the density of a hematoma is completely lost. After passing through the isodense stage (Fig. 15-51), the hematoma becomes hypodense (Dolinskas 1977*a*; Laster 1978). At its end stage, which may vary between 3 and 6 months depending on the initial size, a well-defined low-density region, which may be considerably smaller than the original lesion, is present at the site of the original hematoma. With small hematomas, a slitlike cystic area may be the residual change. Atrophic dilatation of the adjacent portion of the ventricular system occurs, as well as sulcal enlargement (Fig. 15-51). Rarely, calcification develops at the hematoma site. The residual low density and the focal atrophic changes are pathologically related to the formation of a cystic encephalomalacic cavity containing a yellowish, high-protein fluid with vascular trabeculations. This region is surrounded by a variable degree of gliosis (Stephens 1972). On MRI, after conversion to methemoglobin and the beginning of lysis of the clotted red blood cells, a marked hypointense rim develops around the periphery of the hematoma on T_2WI at high field strength (Fig. 15-51) and on susceptibility-weighted gradient-echo images. This occurs as a result of brain macrophages taking up and converting the methemoglobin to hemosiderin. The hemosiderin latent macrophages remain entrapped with in the surrounding brain parenchyma as a result of the presence of an intact blood-brain barrier, which they are not able to penetrate. This change is not evident on T_1WI, as hemosiderin has no effect on T_1 shortening. Over the next 3 to 6 months or longer, all the methemoglobin is removed from the clot and a residual collapsed oval to rounded solid region of marked hypointensity remains at the site of the hematoma on T_2WI and gradient-echo images. A region of central hyperintensity secondary to cystic encephalomalacia may be evident on T_2WI. These chronic changes persist in the brain for many years and possibly forever and are a reliable indicator of the occurrence of a previous hemorrhage. T_1WI will usually not reveal any significant abnormal parenchymal signal intensity alterations, as it is usually not affected by hemosiderin. Occasionally, if calcification occurs within the hemosiderin region, hypointensity may be evident on T_1WI.

Contrast enhancement usually develops around the periphery of a hematoma after 7 to 9 days (Zimmerman 1977; Laster 1978). The appearance of contrast enhancement corresponds to the time at which radionuclide studies become positive (Dolinskas 1977*b*). Pathologically, there is ingrowth of capillary neovascularity at the margin of the hematoma by the end of the first week (Sugitani 1973; Zimmerman 1977). These newly formed capillaries, as in infarctions, have an abnormal blood-brain barrier, resulting in extravasation of contrast material around the hematoma (Molinari 1967; Di Chiro 1974).

The contrast enhancement on CT appears as a ringlike density near the inner margin of the surrounding low-density zone, separated from the hematoma density by a thin isodense or hypodense zone (Fig. 15-51) (Dolinskas 1977*b*; Laster 1978). At the time when the hematoma is passing through its isodense stage, NCCT may show little abnormality except for possibly a slight residual mass effect. However, the ring contrast enhancement on CECT persists through the isodense period and into the first few months of the hypodense state (Fig. 15-51). The surrounding edema is clearing during the third to fourth week, and the ring enhancement then appears to surround an isodense or hypodense core, with normal surrounding brain tissue and no mass effect (Zimmerman 1977). The enhancing capsule becomes more intense and thicker over the next 4 to 6 weeks before beginning to fade. Pathologically, at this stage there is a well-developed glial vascular capsule (Stephens 1972; Laster 1978) that may be identified angiographically (Leeds 1973). The diameter of the enhancing ring decreases during the final hypodense stage as the gliotic capsule constricts around the absorbed hematoma. The CT appearance of the enhancing ring may easily be confused with that of a tumor or abscess. The lack of enhancement of the central region when the hematoma is isodense and the lack of surrounding edema and mass effect, particularly during the hypodense phase, tends to strongly favor a diagnosis of a resolving hematoma. In addition, with hemorrhagic tumors, the enhancing rim is usually present on the initial scan during the first day and is thicker and irregular in shape (Gildersleve 1977).

Amyloid Angiopathy

Amyloid angiopathy is an infrequent cause of nonhypertensive massive spontaneous intracerebral hemorrhage in older persons. Among subjects over the age of 70, more than 40 percent of the brains surveyed in one autopsy series demonstrated the presence of amyloid in the cerebral parenchymal blood vessels. In subjects between the ages of 60 and 70, only about 12 percent of the brains demonstrated amyloid change in the blood vessels. The disease affects only the arterioles of the cortex. This vascular disease has not been found in the white matter, basal ganglia, brainstem, or cerebellum. The cortical arterioles are most frequently involved in the parietal region (Vinters 1981).

These patients commonly have dementia, and pathologically Alzheimer's plaques may be found in association with the vascular lesions. The angiopathy, however, is

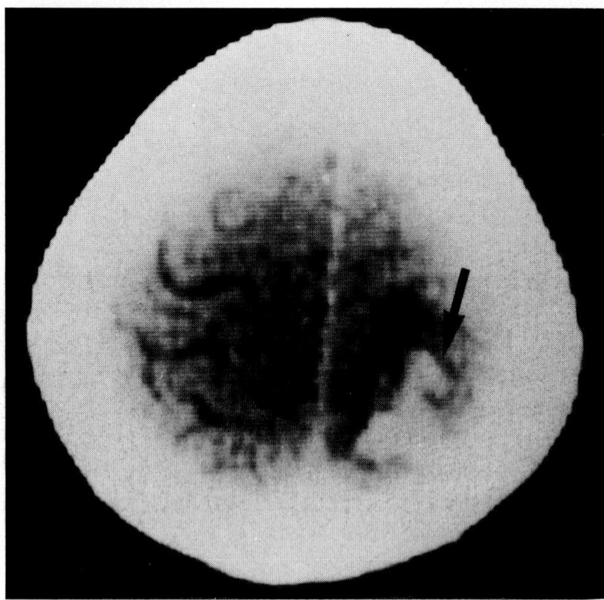

Figure 15-52 Superficial brain hemorrhage (arrow) in an elderly individual with dementia suggesting amyloid angiopathy with hemorrhage.

often present without Alzheimer's changes or clinical dementia. Probably the amyloid change is not related to a specific disease entity but instead is due to age-related change in the blood vessels.

The hemorrhage associated with amyloid angiopathy primarily involves the cortex with irregular borders, surrounding edema, and frequent extension into the adjacent portion of the brain (Wagle 1984) (Fig. 15-52). This is in contrast to the usual deep location of hypertensive hemorrhages, which only on occasion extend to the brain surface. As might be expected from its superficial origin, a subarachnoid hemorrhage is commonly associated with an amyloid vasculopathy hemorrhage.

Hemorrhage in Premature Neonates

Intracerebral hemorrhage develops in 40 to 70 percent of neonates weighing less than 1500 g (Burstein 1979; Lee 1979). The hemorrhage is mild in about 25 percent of cases. Intraventricular hemorrhage of varying degree develops in over 75 percent of such cases (Albright 1981). The hemorrhage is clinically unsuspected in the majority of these infants. Burstein (1979) reported that 68 percent of surviving premature infants had unsuspected hemorrhage found on CT.

These neonatal hemorrhages originate in the germinal matrix, a loose meshwork of highly vascular tissue with little supporting stroma that contains primitive nerve cells (De Reuck 1977) and is located beneath the ependyma lining the lateral wall of the lateral ventricle. The germinal matrix is largest in the region of the head of the caudate nucleus. Its size is greatest between the twenty-fourth and thirty-second weeks of gestation, after which involution occurs. It is the source of nerve cells that migrate to the surface cortex during fetal development (Friede 1976). The exact cause of germinal-matrix hemorrhage is uncertain, but cerebral hypoxia related to neonatal respiratory distress, which is frequently associated with cardiac and vasomotor instability, is thought to predispose to this hemorrhage (Lou 1980). The hemorrhage usually develops during the first 4 days of life and is frequently not present at birth (Lee 1979).

These hemorrhages may range in degree from mild to very severe. They may be localized in one or several regions of the germinal matrix. The head of the caudate nucleus adjacent to the frontal horn is the site most frequently involved (Fig. 15-53) with hemorrhages, which may also originate from the region of the body and trigone of the lateral ventricle (Lee 1979). Varying degrees of intraventricular rupture occur in the majority of cases; they are mild in about 25 percent (Fig. 15-53). Large brain hemorrhage or ventricular hemorrhage develops in about 25 percent of the cases and carries a grave prognosis (Burstein 1979).

Small intraventricular hemorrhages clear by 7 to 9 days; large ones take up to 2 weeks (Albright 1981), and parenchymal hemorrhages may take up to 3 weeks to resolve. Parenchymal hemorrhages frequently lead to porencephalic ventricular dilatation. Intraventricular hemorrhage results in hydrocephalus about one-third of the time. Burstein (1979) reported that small intraventricular hemorrhages did not cause hydrocephalus, whereas 90 percent of large ones did. In contrast, Albright (1981) observed that the size of the intraventricular hemorrhage did not correlate well with the subsequent development of the hydrocephalus. In that series, hydrocephalus was closely related to ventricular size at the time of the initial hemorrhage; the larger the initial size of the ventricles, the greater the probability for development of progressive hydrocephalus requiring shunting. Symptomatic hydrocephalus usually becomes evident between the first and third weeks after birth.

PERIVENTRICULAR LEUKOMALACIA

Periventricular hypodensity greater than would be expected with prematurity alone (Robinson 1966) has been observed in about 95 percent of premature neonates with intracerebral hemorrhage (Albright 1981). Serial CT scans on these infants have shown worsening of the periventricular hypodensity in 54 percent on scans obtained during the following several weeks. The areas of white matter hypodensity become larger, with a progressively lower attenuation value. Subsequently, atrophic mild-to-severe ventricular and sulcal dilatation develops, depending on the maximum severity of periventricular hypo-

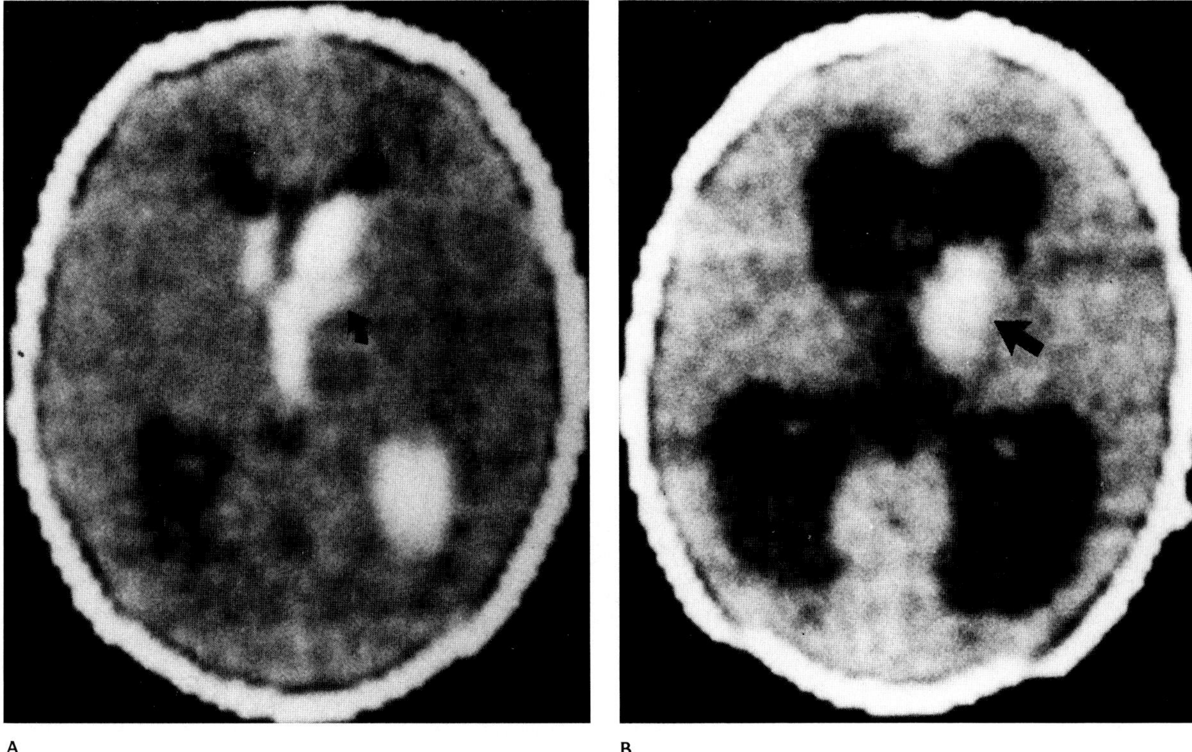

Figure 15-53 Large intraventricular rupture of germinal matrix hemorrhage with development of hydrocephalus. **A.** Extensive hemorrhage filling left lateral and third ventricles with small extension into right frontal horn. Site of hemorrhage appears to be subependymal in the posterior portion of caudate nucleus head (arrow). **B.** Two weeks after **A:** Marked hydrocephalus has developed. Residual localized hematoma remains against the lateral wall at the posterior aspect of left frontal horn.

density (Volpe 1976). The parenchymal hypodensity becomes less evident with the ventricular enlargement, although there may be some persistence of hypodensity in the white matter. Pathological studies have shown leukomalacia and white matter coagulation necrosis, indicating that an anoxic ischemic insult to the brain is the most probable cause (De Reuck 1972). The hypodensity involves the frontal white matter alone in 45 percent, the frontal and parietooccipital white matter together in 33 percent, the parietooccipital white matter alone in 8 percent, and the white matter diffusely in 15 percent of cases (Albright 1981). Its bilateral distribution in the white matter is frequently asymmetric.

Abnormal and progressive periventricular low density also develops in premature infants who have respiratory distress without intracerebral hemorrhage (Di Chiro 1978); a majority of these premature neonates develop this hypodensity (Albright 1981). Its distribution is similar to that seen in those infants with germinal-matrix hemorrhage. Caution must be exercised when calling periventricular hypodensity "abnormal" during the first 1 to 2 weeks postpartum in premature infants, in whom the white matter is normally less dense than that in full-term infants because of less developed myelinization (Estrada 1980). In order to accurately evaluate these infants for possible periventricular leukomalacia, follow-up scans should be obtained in 4 to 6 weeks. The ultimate prognosis for surviving premature infants, both those with and those without intracerebral hemorrhage, appears most closely related to the degree and persistence of periventricular hypodensity and its subsequent atrophic consequences.

References

ADAMS RD, VANDER EECKEN HM: Vascular diseases of brain. *Ann Rev Med* 4:213, 1953.

ADAMS RD, SIDMAN RL: *Introduction to Neuropathology*. New York, McGraw-Hill, 1968.

AEISEN AL, GABRIELSEN TO, MCCUNE WJ: MR imaging of systemic lupus erythematosus involving the brain. *AJNR* 6:197–201, 1985.

ALBRIGHT L, FELLOWS R: Sequential CT scanning after neonatal intracerebral hemorrhage. *AJNR* 2:133–137, 1981.

ALCALA H, GADO M, TORACK RM: The effect of size, histologic elements, and water content on the visualization of cerebral infarcts. *Arch Neurol* 35:1–7, 1978.

ANDERSON DC, COSS DT, JACOBSON RL, MEYER MW: Tissue pertechnetate and iodinated contrast material in ischemic stroke. *Stroke* 11:617–622, 1980.

BAKER HL Jr, CAMPBELL JK, HOUSER OW et al: Early experience with the EMI scanner for study of the brain. *Radiology* 116:327–333, 1975.

BANNA M, GROVES JT: Deep vascular congestion in dural venous thrombosis on computed tomography. *J Comput Assist Tomogr* 3:539–541, 1979.

BILANIUK LT, PATEL S, ZIMMERMAN RA: Computed tomography of systemic lupus erythematosus. *Radiology* 124:119–121, 1977.

BILANIUK LT, ZIMMERMAN RA, BROWN L, YOO HJ, GOLDBERG H: Computed tomography in meningitis. *Neuroradiology* 16:13–14, 1978.

BLAND WH: *Nuclear Medicine*. New York, McGraw-Hill, 1971, pp 262–267.

BRADAC GM, OBERSON R: CT and angiography in cases with occlusive disease of supratentorial cerebral vessels. *Neuroradiology* 19:193–200, 1980.

BRIERLEY JB: Cerebral hypoxia, in Blackwood W, Corsellis JAN (eds): *Greenfield's Neuropathology*. London, Edward Arnold, 1976, pp 43–85.

BRUCHER JM: Neuropathological problems posed by carbonmonoxide poisoning and anoxia. *Prog Brain Res* 24:75–100, 1967.

BUELL V, KAZNER E, RATH M, STEINHOFF H, KLEINHANS E, LANKSCH W: Sensitivity of computed tomography and serial scintigraphy in cerebrovascular disease. *Radiology* 131:393, 1979.

BUONANNO FS, MOODY DM, BALL MR, LASTER DW: Computed cranial tomographic findings in cerebral sinovenous occlusion. *J Comput Assist Tomogr* 2:281–290, 1978.

BURSTEIN J, PAPILE LA, BURSTEIN R: Intraventricular hemorrhage and hydrocephalus in premature newborns: A prospective study with CT. *AJR* 132:631–635, 1979.

CAIRNS H, RUSSELL DS: Cerebral arteritis and phlebitis in pneumococcal meningitis. *J Pathol Bacteriol* 58:649–665, 1946.

CAMPBELL JK, HOUSER OWN, STEVENS JC, WAHNER HW, BAKER HL, FOLGER WN: Computed tomography and radionuclide imaging in the evaluation of ischemic stroke. *Radiology* 126:695–702, 1978.

CHARCOT JD, BOUCHARD C: Nouvelles recherches sur la pathogénie de l'hemorrhagie cérébrale. *Arch Physiol Norm Path (Paris)* 1:110–127, 1868.

CHIU LC, CHRISTIE JH, SCHAPIRO RL: Nuclide imaging and computed tomography in cerebral vascular disease. *Semin Nucl Med* 7:175–195, 1977.

CHU NS: Tuberculous meningitis: Computerized tomographic manifestations. *Arch Neurol* 37:458–460, 1980.

COLE FM, TAYES PO: The occurrence and significance of intracerebral microaneurysms. *J Pathol Bacteriol* 93:393–411, 1967.

COCKRILL HH Jr, DREISBACH J, LOWE B, YAM AUCHI T: Computed tomography in leptomeningeal infections. *AJR* 130: 511–515, 1978.

CRAVIOTO H, FEIGIN I: Noninfectious granulomatous angiitis with a predilection for the nervous system *Neurology* 9:599–609, 1959.

CRONQVIST S, LAROCHE F: Transient hyperaemia in focal cerebral vascular lesions studied by angiography and regional cerebral blood flow measurements. *Br J Radiol* 40:270–274, 1967.

CRONQVIST S: Regional cerebral blood flow and angiography in apoplexy. *Acta Radiol [Diagn] (Stockholm)* 7:521–534, 1968.

CRONQVIST S, BRISMAR J, KJELLIN K, SODERSTROM CE: Computer assisted axial tomography in cerebrovascular lesions. *Radiology* 118:498, 1976.

DASTER DK, UDANI PM: The pathology and pathogenesis of tuberculous encephalopathy. *Acta Neuropathol (Berl)* 6:311–326, 1966.

DAVIS KR, TAVERAS JM, NEW PFJ, SCHNUR A, ROBERSON GH: Cerebral infarction diagnosis by computerized tomography: Analysis and evaluation of findings. *AJR* 124:643–660, 1975.

DAVIS KR, ACKERMAN RH, KISTLER JP, MOHR JP: Computed tomography of cerebral infarction: Hemorrhagic, contrast enhancement, and time of appearance. *Comput Tomogr* 1:71–86, 1977.

DENNY-BROWN D: Recurrent cerebrovascular episodes. *Arch Neurol* 2:194–210, 1960.

DE REUCK J: Arterial vascularisation and angioarchitecture of the nucleus caudatus in human brain. *Eur Neurol* 5:130–136, 1971*a*.

DE REUCK J: The human periventricular arterial blood supply and the anatomy of cerebral infarctions. *Eur Neurol* 5:321–334, 1971*b*.

DE REUCK J, CHATTA AS, RICHARDSON EP: Pathogenesis and evolution of periventricular leukomalacia in infancy. *Arch Neurol* 27:229–236, 1972.

DE REUCK JL: The significance of the arterial angioarchitecture in perinatal cerebral damage. *Acta Neurol Belg* 77:65–94, 1977.

DE REUCK JL, VANDER EECKEN HM: Periventricular leukomalacia in adults. *Arch Neurol* 35:517–521, 1978.

DI CHIRO G, TIMINS EL, JONES AE, JOHNSTON GS, HAMMOCK MK, SWANN SJ: Radionuclide scanning and microangiography of evolving and completed brain infarction: A correlative study in monkeys. *Neurology* 24:418–423, 1974.

DI CHIRO G, ARIMITSU T, PELLOCK JM, LANDES RD: Periventricular leukomalacia related to neonatal anoxia: Recognition by computed tomography. *J Comput Assist Tomogr* 2:352–355, 1978.

DOKINSKAS CA, BILANIUK LT, ZIMMERMAN RA, KUHL DE: Computed tomography of intracerebral hematomas: I. Transmission CT observations on hematoma resolution. *AJR* 129:681–688, 1977*a*.

DOKINSKAS CA, BILANIUK LT, ZIMMERMAN RA, KUHL DE, ALAVI A: Computed tomography of intracerebral hematomas: II. Radionuclide and transmission CT studies of the perihematoma region. *AJR* 129:689–692, 1977*b*.

DUDLEY AW Jr, LUNZER S, HEYMAN A: Localization of radioisotope (chlormerodrin He-203) in experimental cerebral infarction. *Stroke* 1:143–148, 1970.

EICK JJ, MILLER KD, BELL KA, TUTTON RH: Computed tomography of deep cerebral venous thrombosis in children. *Radiology* 140:399–402, 1981.

EISENBERG H, MORRISON JT, SULLIVAN P, FOOTE FM: Cerebrovascular accidents. *JAMA* 189:883–888, 1964.

ELLIS GG, VERITY MA: Central nervous system involvement in systemic lupus erythematosus: A review of neuropathologic findings in 57 cases, 1955–1977. *Semin Arthritis Rheum* 8:212–221, 1979.

ENZMANN DR, NORMAN D, MANI J, NEWTON H: Computed tomography of granulomatous basal arachnoiditis. *Radiology* 120:341–344, 1976.

ESTRADA M, GAMMA TE, DYKEN PR: Periventricular low attenuations: A normal finding in computerized tomographic scans of neonates? *Arch Neurol* 37:754–756, 1980.

FAER MJ, MEAD JH, LYNCH RD: Cerebral granulomatous angiitis: Case report and literature review. *AJR* 129:463–467, 1977.

FERRIS EJ, SHAPIRO JH, SIMEONE FA: Arteriovenous shunting in cerebrovascular occlusive disease. *Am J Roentgenol Radium Ther Nucl Med* 98:631–636, 1966.

FISHER CM, ADAMS RD: Observations on brain embolism with special reference to the mechanism of hemorrhagic infarction. *J Neuropathol Exp Neurol* 10:92–94, 1951.

FISHER CM, CURRY HB: Pure motor hemiplegia of vascular origin. *Arch Neurol* 13:30–44, 1965.

FISHER CM: Capsular infarcts: The underlying vascular lesion. *Arch Neurol* 36:65–73, 1979.

FISHMAN RA: Brain edema. *N Engl J Med* 293:706–711, 1975.

FOX AJ, BOGOUSSLAVSKY J, CAREY LS, et al: MRI of small medullary infarctions. *AJNR* 7:229–233, 1986.

FRIEDE RL: *Developmental Neuropathology*. New York, Springer, 1976, pp 1–37.

GABRIELSEN TO, HEINZ ER: Spontaneous aseptic thrombosis of the superior sagittal sinus and cerebral veins. *Am J Roentgenol Radium Ther Nucl Med* 107:579–588, 1969.

GABRIELSEN TO, SEEGER JF, KNAKE JE, STILWILL EW: Radiology of cerebral vein occlusion without dural sinus occlusion. *Radiology* 140:403–408, 1981.

GADO MH, PHELPS ME, COLEMAN RE: An extravascular component of contrast enhancement in cranial computed tomography. *Radiology* 117:595–597, 1975.

GIBBY WA, STECKER MM, GOLDBERG HI, et al: Reversal of white matter edema in hypertensive encephalopathy. *AJNR* 10:78, 1989.

GILDERSLEVE N, KOO AH, MCDONALD CJ: Metastatic tumor presenting as intracerebral hemorrhage. *Radiology* 124:109–112, 1977.

GILLES C et al: Cerebral amyloid angiopathy as a cause of multiple cerebral hemorrhage. *Neurology* 34:730–735, 1985.

GINSBERG MD, MYERS RE, MCDONAGH BF: Experimental carbon-monoxide encephalopathy in the primate: II. Clinical aspects, neuropathology, and physiological correlation. *Arch Neurol* 30:209–216, 1974.

GINSBERG MD, HEDLEY-WHYTE TE, RICHARDSON EP Jr: Hypoxic ischemic leukoencephalopathy in man. *Arch Neurol* 33:5–14, 1976.

GINSBERG MD: Delayed neurological deterioration following hypoxia, in Fahn S et al (eds): *Advances in Neurology*. New York, Raven Press, 1979, pp 21–47.

GLASER GH: Lesions of CNS in disseminated lupus erythematosus. *Arch Neurol Psychiatr* 67:745–753, 1952.

GLASER GH: Neurologic manifestation in collagen diseases. *Neurology* 5:751–766, 1955.

GOLDBERG HI: Clinical cerebral microangiography—magnification angiography and angiotomography, in Hilal S (ed): *Symposium on Small Vessel Angiography.* St. Louis, Mosby, 1973, pp 219–237.

GOMORI JM, GROSSMAN RI, GOLDBERG HI, et al: Intracranial hematomas: Imaging by high-field MR. *Radiology* 157:87–93, 1985.

GOMORI JM, GROSSMAN RI, GOLDBERG HI, et al: Variable appearances of subacute intracranial hematomas on high-field spin-echo MR. *AJNR* 8:1019–1026, 1987.

GRUBB RL, COXE WS: Central nervous system trauma: Cranial, in Eliasson SG, Prensky AL, Hardin WB (eds): *Neurological Pathophysiology.* New York, Oxford University Press, 1974, pp 292–309.

HANDA J, HANDA H, NAKANO Y, OKUNO T: Computed tomography in moyamoya: Analysis of 16 cases. *Comput Axial Tomogr* 1:165–174, 1977.

HAYMAN LA, SAKAI F, MEYER JS, ARMSTRONG D, HINCK VC: Iodine-enhanced CT patterns after cerebral arterial embolization in baboons. *AJNR* 1:233–238, 1980.

HAYMAN LA, EVANS RA, BASTION FO, HINCK, VC: Delayed high dose contrast CT; Identifying patients at risk of massive hemorrhagic infarction. *AJNR* 2:139–147, 1981.

HECHT-LEAVITT C, GOMORI JM, GROSSMAN RI, et al: High field MRI of hemorrhagic cortical infarction. *AJNR* 7:581–585, 1986.

HEINZ ER, DUBOIS P, OSBORNE D, et al: Dynamic computed tomography study of the brain. *J Comput Assist Tomogr* 3:641–649, 1979.

HOEDT-RASMUSSEN K, SKINHOJ E, PAULSON O, et al: Regional cerebral blood flow in acute apoplexy: The "luxury perfusion syndrome" of brain tissue. *Arch Neurol* 17:271–281, 1967.

HUNGERFORD GD, DUBOULAY GH: CT in patients with severe migraine. *Neurol Neurosurg Psychiatr* 39:990, 1976.

INOUE Y, TAKEMOTA K, MIYAMOTO T, YOSHIKAWA N, TANIGUCHI S, SAIWAI S, NISHIMURA Y, KOMATSU T: Sequential computed tomography scans in acute cerebral infarction. *Radiology* 135:655–662, 1980.

IRINO T, MINAMI T, TANEDA M, HARA K: Brain edema and angiographical hyperemia in postrecanalized cerebral infarction. *Acta Neurol Scand* [Suppl] 64:134–135, 1977*a*.

IRINO T, TANEDA M, MINAMI T: Angiographic manifestations in postrecanalized cerebral infarction. *Neurology* 17:471–475, 1977*b*.

JOHNSON RT, RICHARDSON EP: The neurological manifestations of systemic lupus erythematosus: A clinical pathological study of 24 cases and review of literature. *Medicine* 47:337–367, 1968.

JORGENSEN L, TORBIK A: Ischaemic cerebrovascular diseases in an autopsy series: II. Prevalency, location, pathogenesis and clinical course of cerebral infarcts. *J Neurol Sci* 9:285–320, 1969.

KALBAG RM, WOOLF AL: *Cerebral Venous Thrombosis,* with Special Reference to Primary Aseptic Thrombosis. London, Oxford University Press, 1967, p. 237.

KAMIJYO Y, GARCIA JH, COOPER J: Temporary regional cerebral ischemia in the cat. *J Neuropathol Exp Neurol* 36:338–350, 1977.

KASSIK AE, NILSSON L, SIESJO BK: Acid-base and lactate-pyruvate changes in brain and CSF in asphyxia and stagnant hypoxia. *Scand J Clin Lab Invest* 22 (suppl 102) 3:6, 1968.

KENDALL BE, CLAVERIA LE, QUIROGA W: CAT in leukodystrophy and neuronal degeneration, in du Boulay GH, Moseley IF (eds): *Computerized Axial Tomography in Medical Practice.* New York, Springer-Verlag, 1977.

KIDO DK, GOMEZ DG, SANTOS-BUCH CA, CASTON TV, POTTS DG: Microradiographic study of cerebral and ocular aneurysms in hypertensive rabbits. *Neuroradiology* 15:21–26, 1978.

KIMS KS, WEINBERG PE, SUH JH, HO SU: Acute carbon monoxide poisoning: Computed tomography of the brain. *AJNR* 1:399–402, 1980.

KINDT GW, YOUMANS JR, ALBRANDO O: Factors influencing the autoregulation of cerebral blood flow during hypotension and hypertension. *J Neurosurg* 26:299–305, 1967.

KINGSLEY DPE, WRADUE E, DUBOULAY EPGH: Evaluation of computed tomography in vascular lesions of the vertebrobasilar territory. *J Neurol Neurosurg Psychiatry* 43:193–197, 1980.

KINKEL WR, JACOBS L: Computerized axial transverse tomography in cerebrovascular disease. *Neurology* 26:924–930, 1976.

KLATZO J: Pathophysiological aspects of brain edema, in Reulen HJ, Schurmann K (eds): *Steroids and Brain Edema.* New York, Springer-Verlag, 1972, pp 1–8.

KODAMA N, SUZUKI J: Moyamoya disease associated with aneurysm. *J Neurosurg* 58:565–569, 1978.

KOHLMEYER K, GRASER C: Comparative studies of computed tomography and measurements of regional cerebral blood flow in stroke patients. *Neuroradiology* 16:233–237, 1978.

KRAYENBUHL H: Cerebral venous thrombosis: The diagnostic value of cerebral angiography. *Schweiz Arch Neurol Psychiatr* 74:261–287, 1954.

KUDO T: Spontaneous occlusion of the circle of Willis: A disease apparently confined to Japanese. *Neurology* 18:485–496, 1968.

KURTZKE JF: Epidemiology of cerebrovascular disease, in *Cerebrovascular Survey Report.* National Institute of Neurological and Communicative Disorders and Stroke and National Heart and Lung Institute, Joint Council Subcommittee on Cerebrovascular Disease, 1980, pp 135–176.

LADURNER G, SAGER WD, ILIFF LD, LECHNER H: A correlation of clinical findings and CT in ischaemic cerebrovascular disease. *Eur Neurol* 18:281–288, 1979.

LAPRESLE J, FARDEAU M: The central nervous system and carbonmonoxide poisoning: II. Anatomical study of brain lesions following intoxication with carbonmonoxide (22 cases). *Prog Brain Res* 24:31–75, 1967.

LASSEN NA: The luxury-perfusion syndrome and its possible relation to acute metabolic acidosis localized within the brain. *Lancet* ii:1113–1115, 1966.

LASSEN NA, AGNOLI A: The upper limit of autoregulationof cerebral blood flow in the pathogenesis of hypertensive encephalopathy. *Scand J Clin Lab Invest* 30:113–115, 1972.

LASTER DW, MOODY DM, BALL MR: Resolving intracerebral hematoma: Alteration of the "ring sign" with steroids. *AJR* 130:935–939, 1978.

LAURENT JP, MOLINARI GF, OAKLEY JC: Primate model of cerebral hematoma. *J Neuropathol Exp Neurol* 35:560–568, 1976.

LEE KF, CHAMBERS RA, DIAMOND C, PARK CH, THOMPSON NL, SCHNAPF D, PRIPSTEIN S: Evaluation of cerebral infarction by computed tomography with special emphasis on microinfarction. *Neuroradiology* 16:156–158, 1978.

LEE BCP, GRASSI AE, SCHECHNER S, AULD PAM: Neonatal intraventricular hemorrhage: A serial computed tomography study. *J Comput Assist Tomogr* 3:483–490, 1979.

LEEDS NE, GOLDBERG HI: Angiographic manifestations in cerebral inflammatory disease. *Radiology* 98:595–604, 1971.

LEEDS NE, GOLDBERG HI: Abnormal vascular patterns in benign intracranial lesions: Pseudotumors of the brain. *AJR* 118:567–575, 1973.

LEHRER H: The angiographic triad in tuberculous meningitis. *Radiology* 87:829–835, 1966.

LEVY LM, KILLIAN JM, MAWAD M, et al: Acute cerebral infarction: early diagnosis with MR. *AJNR* 10:872, 1989.

LEWIS SE, HICKEY DC, PARKEY RW: Radionuclide brain imaging: Its role and relation to CT scanning. *Comput Tomogr* 2:155–172, 1978.

LHERMITTE F, GAUTIER JC, DEROUSNE C: Nature of occlusion of the middle cerebral artery. *Neurology* 20:82, 1970.

LOTZ PR, BALLINGER WE Jr, QUISLING RG: Subcortical arteriosclerotic encephalopathy: CT spectrum and pathologic correlation. *AJNR* 7:817–822, 1986.

LOU HC: Perinatal hypoxic-ischemic brain damage and intraventricular hemorrhage: A pathogenic model. *Arch Neurol* 37:585–587, 1980.

MACCHI PJ, GROSSMAN RI, GOLDBERG HI, et al: Occult cerebral vascular malformations: High-field MR imaging. *Radiology* 158:707–713, 1986.

MANELFE C, CLANET M, GIGUAD M, BONAFE A, GUIRAUD B, RASCOL A: Internal capsule: Normal anatomy and ischemic changes demonstrated by computed tomography. *AJNR* 2:149–155, 1981.

MASDEU JC, BERHOOZ A-K, RUBINA FA: Evaluation of recent cerebral infarction by computerized tomography. *Arch Neurol* 34:417–421, 1977.

MATHEW NT, MEYERS JS: Abnormal CT scans in migraine. *Headache* 16:272, 1976.

MATSUMOTO N, WHISNANT JP, KURLAND LT, OKAZAKI H: Natural history of stroke in Rochester, Minn., 1955 through 1969: An extension of a previous study, 1945 through 1954. *Stroke* 4:20–29, 1973.

MCCALL AJ, FLETCHER PJH: Pathology, in KutchinsonEC, Ackason EJ (eds): *Strokes: Natural History, Pathology and Surgical Treatment.* Philadelphia, Saunders, 1975, pp 36–105.

MERRITT HH: *A Textbook of Neurology,* 6th ed. Philadelphia, Lea & Febiger, 1979, pp 40–45.

MIURA T, MITOMO M, KAWAI R, HARADA K: CT of the brain in acute carbon monoxide intoxication: characteristic features and prognosis. *AJNR* 6:739–742, 1985.

MOHR JP, FISHER CM, ADAMS RD: Cerebrovascular diseases, in Isselbacher KJ, Adams RD, Braunwald E, Petersdorf RG, Wilson JD (eds): *Harrison's Principles of Internal Medicine,* 9th ed. McGraw-Hill, 1980, pp 1911–1942.

MOLINARI GF, PIRCHER F, HEYMAN A: Serial brain scanning using technetium 99m in patients with cerebral infarction. *Neurology* 17:627, 1967.

MURRAY RR, KAPILA A, et al: Cerebral CT in drowning victims. *AJNR* 5:177–179, 1984.

MYERS JS, DENNY-BROWN D: The cerebral collateral circulation: I. Factors influencing collateral blood flow. *Neurology* 7:447–458, 1957.

NELSON RF, PULLICINO P, KENDALL BE, MARSHALL J: Computed tomography in patients presenting with lacunar syndromes. *Stroke* 11:256–261, 1980.

NISHIMOTO A, TAKEUCHI S: Abnormal cerebrovascular network related to the internal carotid arteries. *J Neurosurg* 29:255–260, 1968.

NORMAN D, AXEL L, BERNINGER WH, EDWARDS MS, CANN C, REDINGTON RW, COX E: Dynamic computed tomography of the brain: Techniques, data analysis, and applications. *AJNR* 2:1–12, 1981.

NORTON GA, KISHORE PRS, LIN J: CT contrast enhancement in cerebral infarction. *AJR* 131:881–885, 1978.

NURICK S, BLACKWOOD W, MAIR WGP: Giant cell granulomatous angiitis of the central nervous system. *Brain* 95:133–142, 1972.

O'BRIEN MD, JORDAN MM, WALTZ AG: Ischemic cerebral edema and the blood-brain barrier: Distribution of pertechnetate, albumin, sodium, and antipyrine in brains of cats after occlusion of the middle cerebral artery. *Arch Neurol* 30:461–465, 1974.

OLSSON Y, CROWELL RM, KLATZO I: The blood brain barrier to protein tracers in focal cerebral ischemia and infarction caused by occlusion of the middle cerebral artery. *Acta Neuropathol* 18:89–102, 1971.

PAULSON OB, LASSEN NA, SKINHOJ E: Regional cerebral blood flow in apoplexy without arterial occlusion. *Neurology* 20:125–138, 1970.

PECKER J, SIMON J, GUY G, HERRY JF: Nishimoto's disease: Significance of its angiographic appearances. *Neuroradiology* 5:223–230, 1973.

PERRONE P, CANDELISE L, SCOTTI G, DE GRANDI C, SCIALFA G: CT evaluation in patients with transient ischemic attack: Correlation between clinical and angiographic findings. *Eur Neurol* 18:217–221, 1979.

PITTS FW, HASKIN ME, RIGGS HE, GROFF RA: Tumor-strain in cerebrovascular disease. *J Neurosurg* 21:298–300, 1964.

PLUM F, POSNER JB, HAIN RF: Delayed neurological deterioration after anoxia. *Arch Intern Med* 110:18–25, 1962.

PRINEAS J, MARSHALL J: Hypertension and cerebral infarction. *Br Med J* 1:14–17, 1966.

PULLICINO P, KENDALL BE: Contrast enhancement in ischemic lesions: I. Relationship to prognosis. *Neuroradiology* 19:235–239, 1980.

RAIL DL, PERKIN GD: Computerized tomographic appearance of hypertensive encephalopathy. *Arch Neurol* 37:310–311, 1980.

RANGEL RA: Computerized axial tomography in brain death. *Stroke* 9:597–598, 1978.

RAO KCVG, KNIPP HC, WAGNER EJ: Computed tomographic findings in cerebral sinus and venous thrombosis. *Radiology* 140:391–398, 1981.

RAPPAPORT ZH, BRINKER RA, ROVIT RL: Evaluation of brain death with contrast enhanced computerized cranial tomography. *Neurosurgery* 2:230–232, 1978.

Report to the President: A National Program to Conquer Heart Disease, Cancer and Stroke. Washington, President's Commission on Heart Disease, Cancer and Stroke, 1964, 1965.

ROBINSON MA, TIZARD MA: The cerebral nervous system in the newborn. *Br Med Bull* 22:49–55, 1966.

ROMANUL FCA, ABRAMOWICZ A: Changes in brain and pial vessels in arterial border zones. *Arch Neurol* 11:40–65, 1964.

ROSENBLUM WI, HADFIELD MG: Granulomatous angiitis of the nervous system in cases of herpes zoster and lymphosarcoma. *Neurology* 22:348–354, 1972.

ROSENBERG GA, KORNFELD M, STOVRING J, BICKNELL JM: Subcortical arteriosclerotic encephalopathy (Binswanger): Computerized tomography. *Neurology* 29:1102–1106, 1979.

RUFF RL, TALMAN WT, PETITO F: Transient ischemic attacks associated with hypotension in hypertensive patients with carotid artery stenosis. *Stroke* 12:353–355, 1981.

RUMBAUGH CL, BERGERON RT, FANG HCH, MCCORMICK R: Cerebral angiographic changes in drug abuse patients. *Radiology* 101:335–344, 1971.

RUSSELL RWR: Observations on intracerebral aneurysms. *Brain* 86:425–442, 1963.

SOIN JS, BURDINE JA: Acute cerebral vascular accident associated with hyperfusion. *Radiology* 118:109–112, 1976.

SOLE-LLENAS J, PONS-TORTELLA E: Cerebral angiitis. *Neuroradiology* 15:1–11, 1978.

STEPHENS WE: *Pathology of the Cerebral Blood Vessels.* St. Louis, Mosby, 1972, pp 291–323.

SUGITANI Y, NAKAMA M, YAMAGUCHI Y, IMAIZUMI M, NAKADA T, ABE H: Neovascularization and increased uptake of ^{99}m Tc in experimentally produced cerebral hematoma. *J Nucl Med* 14:912–916, 1973.

SUZUKI J, TAKAKU A: Cerebrovascular "moyamoya" disease: Disease showing abnormal net-like vessels in base of brain. *Arch Neurol* 20:88–299, 1969.

TAKAHASHI M, SAITO Y, KONNO K: Intraventricular hemorrhage in childhood moyamoya disease. *J Comput Assist Tomogr* 4:117–120, 1980.

TAVERAS JM: Multiple progressive intracranial arterial occlusion: A syndrome of children and young adults. *Am J Roentgenol Radium Ther Nucl Med* 106:235–268, 1969.

TOMSICK TA, BROTT TG, CHAMBERS AA, et al: Hyperdense middle cerebral artery sign on CT: Efficacy in detecting middle cerebral artery thrombosis. *AJNR* 11:473–477, 1990.

TREVOR RP, SONDHEINER FK, FESSEL WJ, et al: Angiographic demonstrations of major cerebral vessel occlusion in systemic lupus erythematosus. *Neuroradiology* 4:202–207, 1972.

VALAVANIS A, FRIEDE R, SCHUBIGER O, HAYEK J: Cerebral granulomatous angiitis simulating brain tumor. *J Comput Assist Tomgr* 3:536–538, 1979.

VALK J: *Computed Tomography and Cerebral Infarction.* New York, Raven Press, 1980, p. 56.

VINES FS, DAVIS DO: Clinical-radiological correlation in cerebral venous occlusive disease. *Radiology* 98:9–22, 1971.

VINTERS HV, GILBERT JJ: Amyloid angiopathy: Its incidence and complications in the aging brain. *Stroke* 12:118, 1981.

VOLPE JJ: Perinatal hypoxic ischemic brain injury. *Pediatr Clin North Am* 23:383–397, 1976.

WAGLE WA, SMITH TW, WEINER M: Intracerebral hemorrhage caused by cerebral amyloid angiopathy—pathologic correlation. *AJNR* 5:171–176, 1984.

WALL SD, BRANDT-ZAWADZKI M, JEFFREY RB, BARNES B: High frequency CT findings within 24 hours after cerebral infarction. *AJNR* 2:553–557, 1981.

WEINGARTEN KL, ZIMMERMAN RD, PINTO RS, WHELAN MA: CT changes of hypertensive encephalopathy. *AJNR* 6:395–398, 1985.

WEISBERG LA: Computerized tomography in intracranial hemorrhage. *Arch Neurol* 36:422–426, 1979.

WEISBERG LA: Computerized tomographic enhancement patterns in cerebral infarction. *Arch Neurol* 37:21, 1980.

WENDLING LR: Intracranial venous sinus thrombosis: Diagnosis suggested by computed tomography. *AJR* 130:978–980, 1978.

WHISNANT JP, FITZGIBBONS JP, KURLAND LT, SAYRE GP: Natural history of stroke in Rochester, Minnesota, 1945 through 1954. *Stroke* 2:11–21, 1971.

WING SD, NORMAN D, POLLOCK JA, NEWTON TH: Contrast enhancement of cerebral infarcts in computed tomography. *Radiology* 121:89–92, 1976.

WOLFSON SK Jr, GUR D, YONAS H: Latchaw RE (ed): Cerebral blood flow determination, in CT of the Head, Neck and Spine. Chicago, Year Book, 1985, pp 27–52.

WOOD MW, WAKIM KG, SAYRE, GP, MILLIKAN CH, WHISNANT JP: Relationship between anticoagulants and hemorrhagic cerebral infarction in experimental animals. *Arch Neurol Psychiatry* 79:390–396, 1958.

YAGNIK P, GONZALEZ C: White matter involvement in anoxic encephalopathy in adults. *J Comput Assist Tomogr* 4:788–790, 1980.

YAMAGUCHI T, WALTZ AG, OKAZAKI H: Hyperemia and ischemia in experimental cerebral infarction: Correlation of histopathology and regional blood flow. *Neurology* 21:565–578, 1971.

YARNELL PR, EARNEST MP, SANDERS B, BURDICK D: The "hot stroke" and transient vascular occlusions. *Stroke* 6:517–520, 1975.

YOCK DH Jr, MARSHALL WH Jr: Recent ischemic brain infarcts at computed tomography: Appearances pre- and postcontrast infusion. *Radiology* 117:599–608, 1975.

YOCK DH Jr: CT demonstration of cerebral emboli. *J Comput Assist Tomogr* 5:190–196, 1981.

ZEUMER H, SCHONSKY B, STRUM KW: Predominant white matter involvement in subcortical arteriosclerotic encephalopathy (Binswanger disease). *J Comput Assist Tomogr* 4:14–19, 1980.

ZIEGLER DK, ZOSA A, ZILELI T: Hypertensive encephalopathy. *Arch Neurol* 12:472–478, 1965.

ZILKHA A, DAIZ AS: Computed tomography in the diagnosis of superior sagittal sinus thrombosis. *J Comput Assist Tomogr* 4:124–126, 1980.

ZIMMERMAN RD, LEEDS NE, NAIDICH TP: Ring blush with intracerebral hematoma. *Radiology* 122:707–711, 1977.

16 WHITE MATTER DISEASE

T. Linda Chi
Jacqueline A. Bello

INTRODUCTION

White matter disorders of the central nervous system (CNS) constitute a complex group of diseases. Only recently, with advances in imaging technology, have we begun to understand these diseases. To clarify this topic, many classification schemes have evolved, based on clinical, pathological, genetic, and biochemical criteria. For the purpose of clarity, imaging analysis of this large group of disorders will be limited to the more common diseases that primarily affect the white matter, specifically the myelin metabolism, of the CNS.

Primary white matter diseases can be categorized into two main groups: hereditary and acquired (Valk 1989). The pathogenesis of diseases in the hereditary category (Table 16-1) has been attributed to dysmyelination. By definition, *dysmyelination* results from abnormalities of myelin production, maintenance, and breakdown. Classically, all inherited leukodystrophies fall into this category. In contrast, *demyelination* refers to the destruction of preformed normal myelin. Multiple sclerosis is the prototype of demyelinating disorders. The differentiation of demyelination and dysmyelination has been a source of great confusion in the literature, because of a lack of understanding of the pathogenesis of certain disease processes. Through new advances in biochemistry, cell biology, and genetics, the defective enzyme systems responsible for the metabolism and catabolism of myelin are being elucidated.

The acquired group of leukodystrophies mainly represents demyelinating diseases, which include disorders of inflammatory, infectious, toxic, vascular, and traumatic etiologies (Table 16-2). The precise etiology is often nonspecific.

CT manifestations of white matter disease have been described extensively in the literature. The limited diagnostic utility of CT is due to the narrow range of attenuation values for white matter. MR has been invaluable in increasing our detection and understanding of white matter diseases as a result of its superior anatomic resolution and greater sensitivity to even subtle changes associated with white matter disease. Many disorders affecting the white matter present in neonates or during infancy; the changes in signal characteristics during this period in normal individuals may mask abnormal changes in white matter. It is conceivable that with greater clinical application of MR spectroscopy (Barany 1988; Boesch 1989) and with intravoxel incoherent motion MR imaging (LeBihan 1988), separation of normal and abnormal myelin will be possible.

Table 16-1 Hereditary Leukodystrophies

Hereditary Leukodystrophies
Lysosomal disorders
Metachromatic leukodystrophy
Krabbe's (globoid) leukodystrophy
Peroxisomal disorders
Adrenoleukodystrophy
Zellweger cerebrohepatorenal syndrome
Mitochondrial dysfunction (predominantly gray matter involvement)
Leigh's disease
MELAS (mitochondrial myopathy, encephalopathy, lactic acidosis, and strokelike episodes)
MERRF (myoclonus epilepsy with ragged red fibers)
Alpers' disease
Kearns-Sayre syndrome
Amino acid and organic acid metabolic disorders
Canavan's disease
Maple syrup urine disease
White matter disease of unknown metabolic defect
Pelizaeus-Merzbacher disease
Alexander's disease
Congenital muscular dystrophy

Adapted from Valk 1989.

Table 16-2 Acquired Leukodystrophies

Inflammatory
- Multiple sclerosis and variants
- Acute disseminated encephalomyelitis
- Acute hemorrhagic encephalomyelitis

Infectious
- Progressive multifocal leukoencephalopathy (PML)
- Lyme disease
- AIDS encephalopathy
- Subacute sclerosing panencephalitis
- Creutzfeldt-Jakob disease
- Other infections

Metabolic
- Central pontine myelinolysis
- Marchiafava-Bignami syndrome
- Malnutrition
- Vitamin B_{12} deficiency

Vascular
- Aging changes that affect white matter
- Hypertensive encephalopathy
- Hypoxic-ischemic edema

Trauma
- Radiation and/or chemotherapy
- Hydrocephalus
- Diffuse axonal injury

Adapted from Valk 1989.

INHERITED LEUKODYSTROPHIES (DYSMYELINATING DISEASES)

Metachromatic Leukodystrophy

This was one of the first lipidoses to be associated with an enzyme deficiency. The term *metachromatic leukodystrophy* is derived from the marked staining properties of the stored sulphatides. *Metachromatic leukodystrophy* refers to several disorders caused by deficient hydrolase activity of the enzyme arylsulfatase A (Austin 1989; Diebler 1987), which results in an accumulation of sulfated lipids. The membranes of the myelin sheath break down in both the central and peripheral nervous systems. Prenatal diagnosis can be achieved by assaying the activity of the enzyme in cultured amniotic fluid cells (Austin 1989).

Several forms of this disease have been described according to age at onset and clinical presentation. The most common type is the late infantile variant, which is transmitted as an autosomal recessive trait. The onset of symptoms usually occurs before 2 years of age. The infant is normal at birth and becomes unsteady with a gait disorder between 12 and 18 months of age (Austin 1989; Menkes 1985). The neurological examination reveals weakness and hypotonia with decreased to absent reflexes, especially in the lower extremities, with progression to the upper extremities. Speech becomes indistinct, swallowing is impaired, and dementia and optic atrophy become apparent. The juvenile form is slightly more rare, with onset between 4 and 21 years of age by definition. Most patients in this category present from 6 to 10 years of age. Early presenting signs and symptoms include impaired school performance and emotional lability. The neurological examination reveals cerebellar incoordination, pyramidal tract signs, and decreased reflexes in the lower extremities (Austin 1989; Lake 1984). In the more uncommon adult form, patients tend to present with dementia and progress to develop motor signs (Lake 1984).

Laboratory abnormalities include abnormal nerve conduction and frequently elevated cerebrospinal fluid (CSF) protein in the infantile form, while the CSF protein may be normal in the juvenile or adult form (Austin 1989; Wright 1988). A definitive diagnosis is made by documenting a deficiency of arylsulphatase A in urine, leukocytes, and fibroblasts as well as in tissue samples (Lake 1984; MacFaul 1982).

Pathologically, the gross brain may appear slightly atrophic. Marked loss of myelin is seen throughout the cerebral white matter, with preservation of the subcortical arcuate fibers (Lake 1984). The affected white matter is replaced by macrophages that stain PAS-positive and contain cerebroside sulphate, which is responsible for the metachromasia. As with Krabbe's leukodystrophy, the peripheral nervous system shows decreased normal myelination.

CT studies of patients with metachromatic leukodystrophy demonstrate nonspecific progressive atrophy with ventricular enlargement and diffuse low attenuation of the white matter (Fig. 16-1). No contrast enhancement or mass effect is seen (Barkovich 1990*a*). The areas of low attenuation on CT are manifested as areas of increased T_2 and T_1 relaxation times on long TR/TE sequences (Barkovich 1990*a*). The distinguishing MR feature of this disease entity is the sparing of the subcortical arcuate fibers (Fig. 16-2), as is seen in Krabbe's leukodystrophy and perhaps in adrenoleukodystrophy but not in Canavan's disease or Alexander's disease.

Krabbe's Leukodystrophy

Globoid cell leukodystrophy and Krabbe's disease are synonyms that often are used to describe this rare genetic disease transmitted as an autosomal recessive trait. The hallmarks of the diagnosis are a deficiency of the lysosomal enzyme B-galactocerebrosidase in serum, leukocytes, and cultured skin fibroblasts and the aggregation of globoid cells around small blood vessels in demyelinated areas of the white matter of the brain with relative

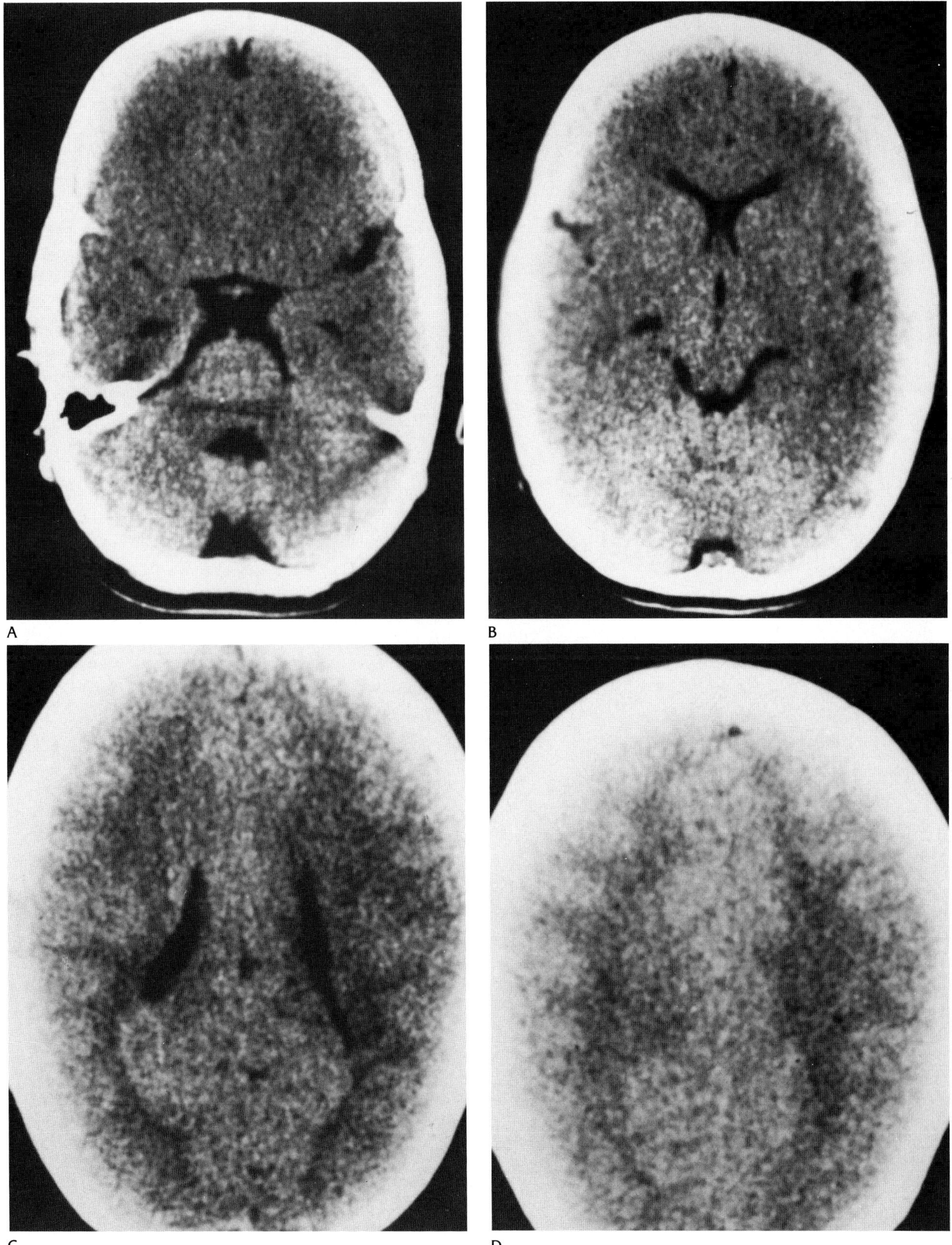

Figure 16-1 Metachromatic leukodystrophy. Noncontrast axial CT images (**A–D**) of a 3-year-old boy show mild ventricular enlargement and nonspecific, poorly defined low attenuation in the parietal white matter.

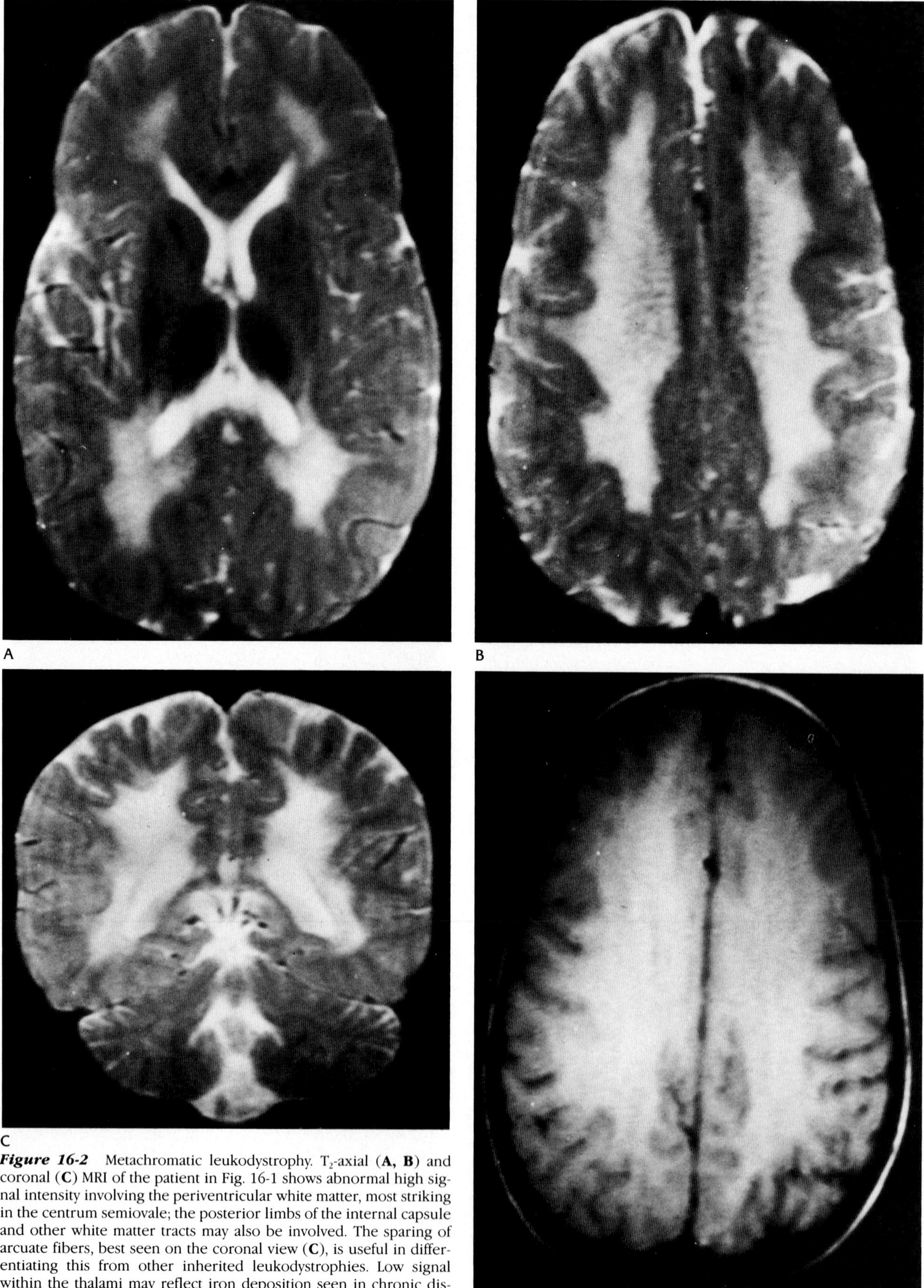

Figure 16-2 Metachromatic leukodystrophy. T_2-axial (**A, B**) and coronal (**C**) MRI of the patient in Fig. 16-1 shows abnormal high signal intensity involving the periventricular white matter, most striking in the centrum semiovale; the posterior limbs of the internal capsule and other white matter tracts may also be involved. The sparing of arcuate fibers, best seen on the coronal view (**C**), is useful in differentiating this from other inherited leukodystrophies. Low signal within the thalami may reflect iron deposition seen in chronic disease or may be secondary to the disease itself. In the T_1-weighted MR image (**D**), the white matter changes are not readily visualized.

sparing of the subcortical arcuate fibers (Allen 1984; Johnson 1989*b*; Diebler 1987). Demyelination is also present in the peripheral nerves (Matsuyama 1963). Prenatal diagnosis is possible because B-galactocerebrosidase can be assayed from fibroblasts and cultured amniotic fluid cells.

Affected infants are normal at birth. Classically, the onset of symptoms begins early, between 3 and 6 months, with inexplicable crying and irritability, fever, feeding difficulty, vomiting, opisthotonic posturing, seizures, and slowing of mental and motor development. Optic atrophy and blindness may follow; the patients may become decerebrate and usually die by age 2 years secondary to intercurrent respiratory infection or bulbar paralysis. A later onset of symptoms has been described in a few patients diagnosed by means of galactocerebrosidase deficiency who demonstrate slower progression of dementia, optic atrophy, and pyramidal tract signs without neuropathy (Johnson 1989*b*; Crome 1973). Pathological diagnosis of globoid cell leukodystrophy has also been described in an adult-onset disorder without biochemical correlation.

Diagnostic parameters include elevated CSF protein and decreased nerve conduction velocity. The most reliable diagnostic clue is decreased activity of B-galactocerebrosidase in leukocytes or skin fibroblasts. Both galactosylcerebroside and galactosylsphingosine (psychosine) are substrates for the deficient enzyme. Psychosine is markedly increased in the brains of patients with Krabbe's leukodystrophy, and its accumulation is probably the cause of the disease. Injection of this compound into the white matter of a rat brain causes greater globoid cell reaction than occurs with galactocerebroside alone (Suzuki 1978). Psychosine poisons oligodendrocytes, resulting in cessation of myelin production and subsequent demyelination (Johnson 1989*a*; Allen 1984); this is considered to represent dysmyelination by Barkovich (1990*a*). Although this disease is considered demyelinating by Lake (1984), there is no increase in white matter cholesterol esters, and lipid-laden macrophages are not usually present, unlike most other demyelinating diseases.

The gross pathology usually consists of a small brain with atrophy. There is gross loss of myelin without cystic degeneration in the white matter and astrocytic gliosis, especially along the periventricular region and the centrum semiovale, with sparing of the subcortical arcuate fibers. Gray matter is also involved, including the pons, dentate nucleus, and thalamus more often than the cortex (Baram 1986; Allen 1984). In the brainstem, atrophy of the cerebral peduncles and pyramids is seen.

The CT findings in Krabbe's disease in the early stage consist of symmetric high density in the thalami, caudate, and corona radiata (Barkovich 1990*a*; Ieshima 1983). With progression, low-attenuation regions develop in the white matter. Compared with the other leukodystrophies, the low density within the white matter seen in Krabbe's leukodystrophy is less striking (Ieshima 1983). The CT findings of end-stage disease may be very similar to those of other white matter diseases of metabolic origin.

Baram (1986) described the MR findings in a case of Krabbe's leukodystrophy. Using a TR of 2000 msec and a TE of 56 msec, he noted generalized hyperintensity on T_2WI and hypointensity on T_1WI in the white matter, especially in the centrum semiovale and corona radiata. The thalami were hypointense on T_1WI. The cerebellum and the brainstem were described as mottled, with scattered areas of hyperintensity on T_2WI. In our experience, the long TR/TE sequence is the most striking feature, with increased signal intensity involving the white matter diffusely and symmetrically, best seen in the centrum semiovale. As predicted by the pathological descriptions (Ieshima 1983; Allen 1984), the subcortical arcuate fibers are not involved (Fig. 16-3). Both the corpus callosum and the posterior limb of the internal capsule may also show abnormal high signal intensity. The deep nuclei and the cerebellum do not seem to be affected as much. Cerebral atrophy may be apparent.

Adrenoleukodystrophy

Classified under the larger category of sudanophilic leukodystrophy, this disorder has several clinical forms. The classic X-linked recessive form is seen exclusively in men. The responsible gene has been mapped to the distal end of the long arm of the X chromosome (Johnson 1989*a*). Although a specific enzyme defect has not been identified, a defective enzyme in the peroxisomal fatty acid B-oxidation pathway is suspected, leading to an accumulation of very long chain fatty acids (VLCFAs) in the plasma and tissue (Johnson 1989*a*; Igarashi 1976). The mechanism that leads to demyelination secondary to the accumulation of VLCFAs is unknown. Prenatal diagnosis can be achieved by assaying amniotic fluid cells or by chorionic villi sampling (Johnson 1989*a*).

Symptoms usually occur after a normal early development. The average age of onset is around 8 years, with a range between 3 and 12 years of age (Johnson 1989*a*). The neurological manifestations usually precede symptoms of adrenal involvement. Some patients develop overt adrenal insufficiency; in others, the adrenal insufficiency is latent. Behavioral change is the most common presenting feature. Visual loss in the form of cortical blindness, progressive gait disturbance, and pyramidal tract signs may also occur early. Dysarthria, dysphagia, and deafness are often seen. Seizures may be either a presenting sign or a late event. Death occurs 1 to 10 years after the onset of symptoms as a result of an adrenal crisis or other intercurrent infection. In typical cases there is

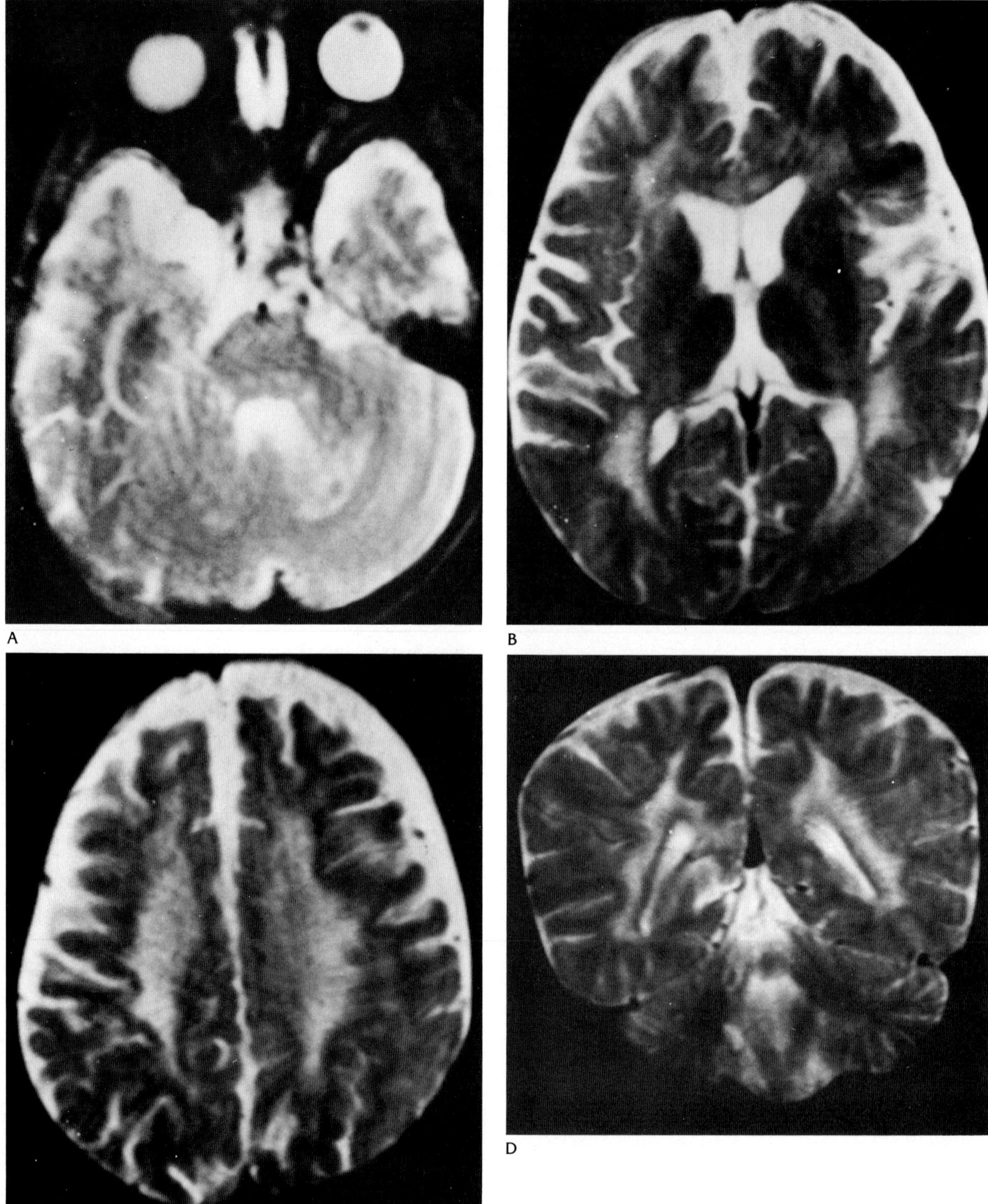

Figure 16-3 Krabbe's leukodystrophy. T_2 axial (**A–C**) and coronal (**D**) MRI of a 14-month-old boy demonstrates abnormal high signal in periventricular white matter, which does not involve the arcuate fibers, similar to metachromatic leukodystrophy (Fig. 16-2). White matter tracts including the posterior limb of the internal capsule and corpus callosum are also affected. Very low signal is again noted in the thalami. Marked atrophy is present with ventriculomegaly.

no clinical involvement of the peripheral nerves; however, electron microscopy demonstrates lamellar cytoplasmic inclusions in Schwann cells, which seem specific for the disease (Arsenio Nunes 1981; Martin 1980). There are also cases in which there is predominant spinal cord and peripheral nerve involvement without cerebral involvement; these cases are grouped under the term *adrenomyeloneuropathy*.

The diagnosis is suggested by the clinical history and characteristic findings on imaging studies. The CSF protein is elevated. Assay of plasma or cultured skin fibroblasts for the presence of elevated VLCFAs establishes the diagnosis. Fractionation of the abnormal white matter in the brain shows markedly decreased myelin (Kishimoto 1985) and an increase in abnormal cholesterol esters (Brown 1983).

Pathologically, widespread demyelination of the cerebral white matter is seen, most pronounced in the parietal, occipital, and posterior temporal lobes. The demyelination process extends across the splenium of the corpus callosum to the contralateral side. Schaumburg (1975) described three histological zones; the first two zones contain macrophages and correspond to the active demyelination zone. It is the anterior advancing border of the demyelinating area that enhances with contrast on CT. The third zone is the area of reactive glial fibrosis. The arcuate fibers show partial sparing. The optic nerves and tract, fornix, hippocampal commissure, posterior cingulum, and corpus callosum are severely affected (Allen 1984).

The typical CT finding early in the course of the disease is bilateral and symmetric decreased attenuation of the posterior cerebral white matter, extending across the midline via the splenium of the corpus callosum (Fig. 16-4). Enhancement may be seen at the anterior border of the advancing demyelination on contrast-enhanced computed tomography (CECT). On CT, the caudorostral progression of the disease can be demonstrated; later in the course, there is frontal involvement, which is sometimes asymmetric. Cerebellar involvement is not consistent. Cerebral atrophy is a late manifestation of the disease (Barkovich 1990*a*; Kumar 1987; Diebler 1987).

The areas of involvement are better defined on MR. On long TR/TE sequences, involvement of the visual system

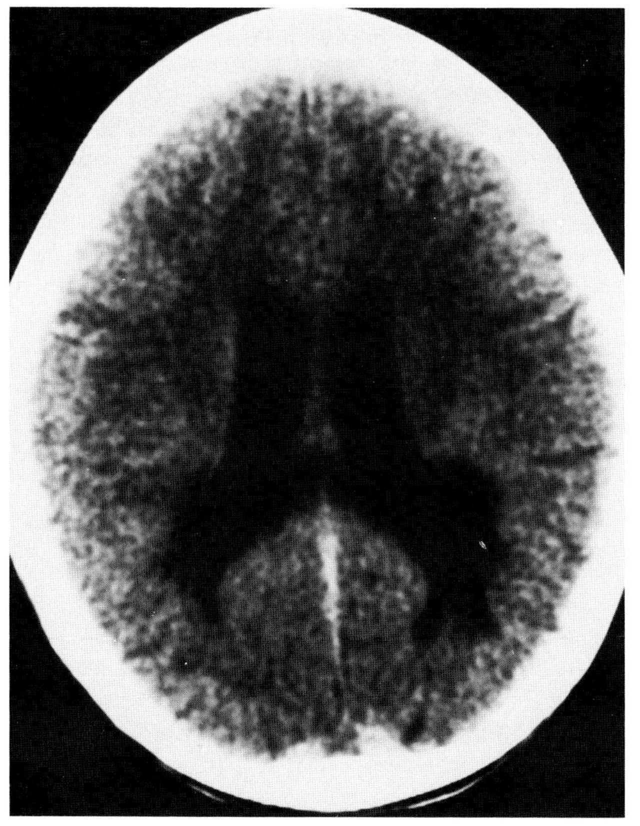

A

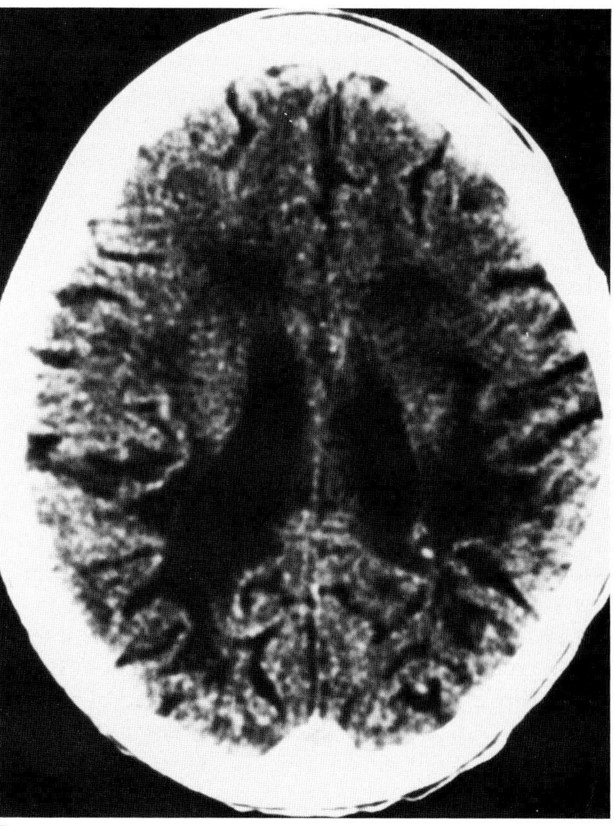

B

Figure 16-4 Adrenoleukodystrophy. Axial NC CT (**A**), initial (**B**), over a 15-month interval demonstrate cortical atrophy and caudorostral progression of white matter hypodensity. In the earlier CT (**A**), the parietal white matter change extends across the midline via the corpus callosum.

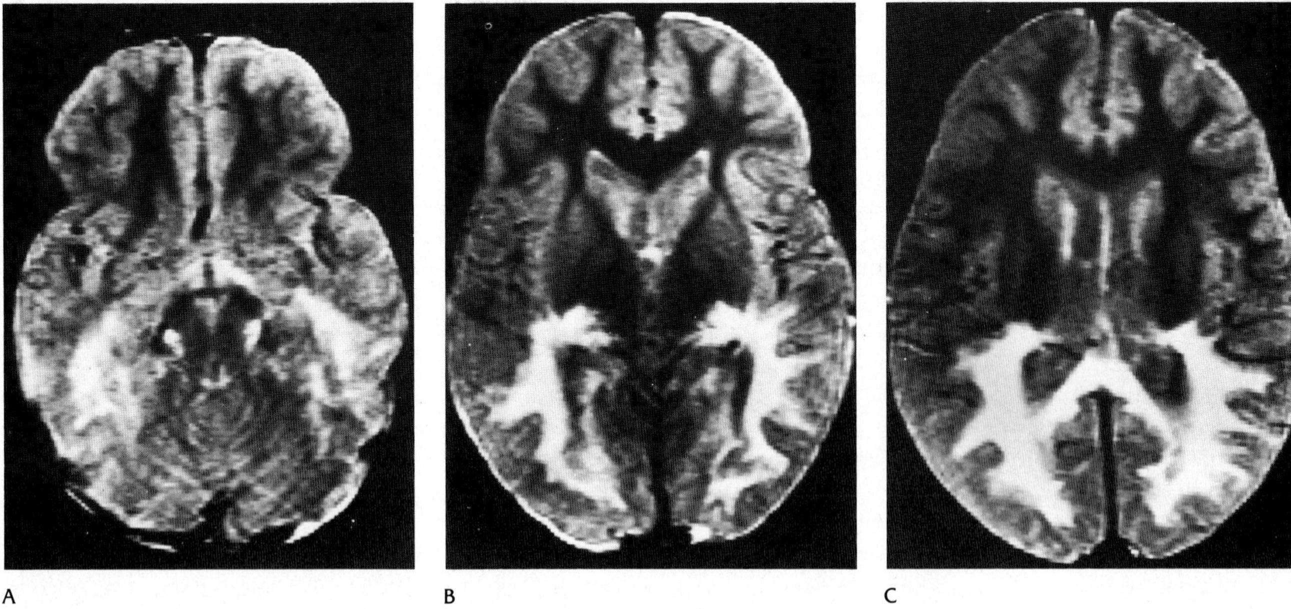

Figure 16-5 Adrenoleukodystrophy. Long TR MR (axial images **A–C**) is more sensitive to the abnormal white matter changes in the patient shown in Fig. 16-4, and shows early involvement of the parietal, occipital, and posterior temporal lobes. Typically, the pattern of involvement includes the visual and auditory systems and the pyramidal tracts of the brainstem. The lesions typically progress from the parietal lobes anteriorly.

(the lateral geniculate bodies and the optic radiations), the auditory system (lateral lemniscus, brachium of inferior colliculi, acoustic radiations, transverse temporal gyrus of Heschl), and the pyramidal tracts within the brainstem can be exquisitely defined as areas of high signal (Kumar 1987). Marked prolongation of the T_1 and T_2 relaxation times of the splenium of the corpus callosum and the parietooccipital white matter is seen (Fig. 16-5). The pattern of involvement may be asymmetric in a third of the cases (Barkovich 1990*a*). Enhancement of the anterior leading edge of the lesion corresponding to the zone of active demyelination with gadolinium-DTPA, similar to that seen with CECT, has been described (Jenson 1990).

Canavan's Disease

Canavan's disease, also known as spongiform leukodystrophy (Allen 1984), spongy degeneration of the cerebral white matter, and van Bogaert-Canavan disease, is transmitted as an autosomal recessive trait. Deficiency of the enzyme aspartoacylase has only recently been described in this disease, resulting in an accumulation of N-acetylaspartic acid in the urine and plasma (Matalon 1988). Three forms have been described: congenital, infantile, and juvenile (Allen 1984). There is a predilection for the infantile form in northern Ashkenazi Jews. These infants tend to be normal at birth. The onset of symptoms usually occurs by age 4 months, and the accelerated head growth, an important clinical feature in distinguishing the various leukodystrophies, is usually evident by age 6 months. Initially, hypotonia predominates, followed by psychomotor regression and spasticity. An opisthotonic crisis may develop in response to auditory, visual, and tactile stimuli. Blindness and optic atrophy may be present. Late in the disease seizures develop, and paroxysmal episodes of vomiting, sweating, hypotension, and hyperthermia can occur. Choreoathetoid movements have also been reported, correlating well with the pathological finding of basal ganglia involvement. Death usually occurs by age 2 years (Rapin 1989*b*).

In the past, the definitive diagnosis could be made only from a brain biopsy. With the discovery of aspartoacylase deficiency associated with Canavan's disease, enzyme activity can be assayed from cultured skin fibroblasts, cultured amniotic cells, and chorionic villi, making prenatal diagnosis of this disorder possible (Matalon 1988). Late in the disease, both the EEG and brainstem auditory evoked potentials are abnormal. The CSF is usually normal, but the CSF protein may be elevated (Allen 1984).

Pathological findings include spongiform degeneration of the white matter, often extending into deeper layers of the cortex. In our experience, the subcortical arcuate fibers are not spared, in contrast to Krabbe's disease and metachromatic leukodystrophy. The white matter most affected is the centrum semiovale, where the "white matter may be converted into a loose meshwork of bare glial and axonal fibers" (Allen 1984). With progression of the disease, the cerebellum, brainstem, spinal cord, and basal ganglia become involved. Vacuolation

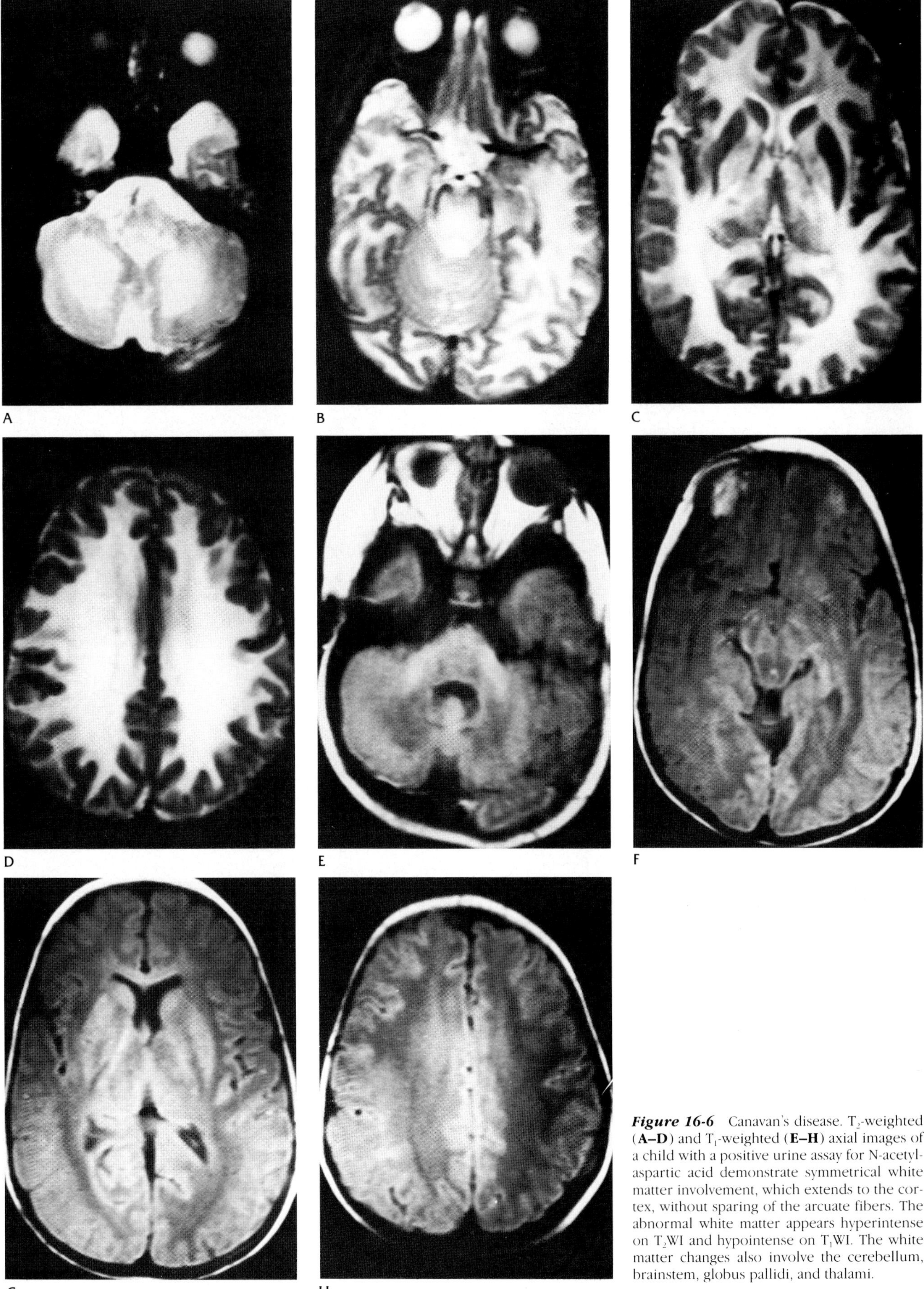

Figure 16-6 Canavan's disease. T_2-weighted (**A–D**) and T_1-weighted (**E–H**) axial images of a child with a positive urine assay for N-acetyl-aspartic acid demonstrate symmetrical white matter involvement, which extends to the cortex, without sparing of the arcuate fibers. The abnormal white matter appears hyperintense on T_2WI and hypointense on T_1WI. The white matter changes also involve the cerebellum, brainstem, globus pallidi, and thalami.

spreads, and cystlike structures of CSF density replace the white matter. In advanced stages there is severe myelin destruction, gliosis, and cerebral atrophy.

CT and MR findings have been described in Canavan's disease (Barkovich 1990*a*; Andriola 1982; Bolthauser 1978). The hallmark is symmetric involvement of the white matter, especially the centrum semiovale. This manifests as hypointense regions on CT and as hyperintense regions on long TR/TE and a hypointense signal on short TR/TE MRI sequences. The extensive involvement of the white matter from the central area to the corticomedullary gray-white junction, including the arcuate fibers, is best appreciated on MRI (Fig. 16-6). In our experience, the corpus callosum appears to be spared. However, the long tracts are involved, including the internal capsules, and this may represent Wallerian degeneration. The globi pallidi and the anterior thalami show increased signal intensity on long TR/TE sequences, corresponding to the clinical and pathological changes.

Other than Canavan's disease, there are several enzyme deficiency disorders that affect the developing brain (Table 16-3). In all these enzyme deficiency disorders there is arrested or delayed myelination rather than dysmyelination. These disorders result in varying degrees of severe neonatal atrophy. Early detection may help in correcting the metabolic end result on the brain tissue, with clinical improvement.

In nonketotic hyperglycemia caused by dysfunction of the glycine-clearing enzyme system, there is defective metabolism of glycine. In neonates this results in delayed or arrested myelination. Affected children present with seizures and abnormal muscle tone and reflexes. Without treatment, there is developmental delay, and death follows within 5 years of onset. On both CT and MR, atrophy is found in addition to decreased or absent myelination and apparent thinning of the corpus callosum.

Defective myelination is also seen in maple syrup urine disease, galactosemia, and phenylketonuria. The accumulation of polypeptides results in defective myelin formation and spongy degeneration. The CT and MR findings may mimic those of Canavan's disease.

Table 16-3 Enzyme Deficiencies and Neonatal Atrophy

Nonketotic hyperglycemia
Methylmalonic acidemia
Propionic acidemia
Maple syrup urine disease
Tyrosinemia
Phenylketonuria
Hyper-β-alanemia

Pelizaeus-Merzbacher Disease

On the basis of pathological studies and staining characteristics, Pelizaeus-Merzbacher disease (PMD) has been classified in the group of sudanophilic leukodystrophies. This is based on the staining characteristics of myelin breakdown products, which are seen as sudanophilic lipid droplets consisting of cholesterol esters. In reality, the presence of sudanophilic products of myelin degradation in this disease entity is scarce on histological examination. Lipid analysis shows that the more distinctive feature of the disease is actually myelin aplasia or hypoplasia, perhaps caused by an inability to synthesize cerebrosides as a result of an inactive enzyme system for fatty acid chain elongation in the CNS (Witter 1980). Koepper (1987) reported a lack of proteolipid protein in the CNS of patients with PMD, resulting in defective production of myelin. A specific enzyme defect has not been identified.

Six subtypes of PMD were identified by Seitelberger in 1970, of which the classic form is the original description by Pelizaeus in 1885 and Merzbacher in 1910. The clinical presentations are similar, but the age of onset, rate of progression, and inheritance pattern are different. In general, the earlier the onset of disease, the more rapid the rate of deterioration. The two most common forms are the classical form and the connatal form. In the classic form, the onset of symptoms occurs in infancy. The inheritance pattern is an X-linked recessive trait. The most striking feature is bizarre pendular nystagmus associated with head tremor. Slow psychomotor development is seen; independent ambulation is not achieved. Dementia may be present but is difficult to assess. Optic atrophy is not severe, and hearing is preserved. The course is typically one of progressive deterioration with increasing ataxia, spasticity with hyperreflexia, and development of choreathetotic movements (Rapin 1989*c*). Severe growth failure is seen, and death usually ensues in late adolescence or early adulthood. The connatal form presents in the first months of life and has a more severe clinical course. The pattern of inheritance is controversial, but this is probably an autosomal recessive trait.

The diagnosis is made by means of brain biopsy. Pathologically, the most frequently used adjective is the *tigroid* appearance of the white matter on the myelin stain, reflecting the residual islands of preserved myelin against a background of "nonmyelin." Axons and nerve cells are well preserved (Allen 1984). Total lipids in the brain are decreased. There is no sparing of the subcortical arcuate fibers.

The CT appearance of PMD varies widely from normal to diffuse decreased density in the white matter and atrophy with ventricular dilatation (Journel 1987). MR findings are more striking; the brain of an affected child has the appearance of that of a newborn with persistent reversal of the gray to white signal characteristics on long TR/TE sequences (Barkovich 1990*a*; Journel 1987). A

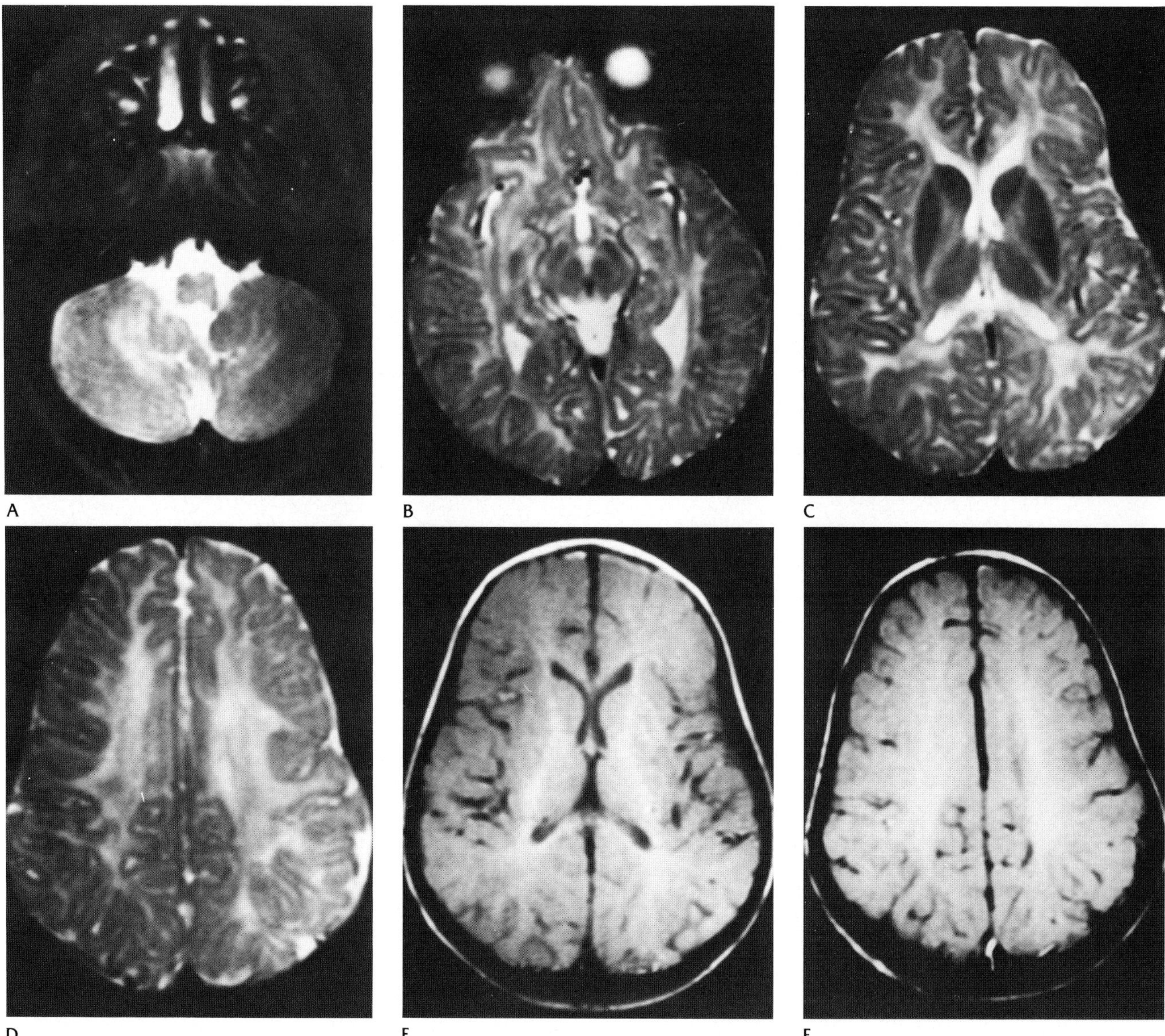

Figure 16-7 Pelizaeus-Merzbacher disease. MRI in a 5-year-old child shows an immature-appearing brain. There is persistence of white matter high signal on T_2WI (**A–D**). T_1WI (**E–F**) are less sensitive to the extent of hypomyelination of the white matter.

high signal on short TR/TE sequences in the internal capsule, optic radiations, and proximal corona radiata may be seen as the only areas of myelination (Barkovich 1990*a*). Mild to moderate atrophy is seen as cortical sulcal prominence. Additionally, we have noted a relatively decreased signal in the caudate, putamen, and thalamus on long TR/TE sequences; this may be due to increased iron deposition, as seen in other degenerative diseases of the brain (Drayer 1986). We have also noted that in addition to the "immature" appearance of the brain (Fig. 16-7), the gyral pattern is abnormal with polymicrogyria; this has been recognized in the gross pathology of PMD (Rapin 1989*c*).

Alexander's Disease

This disease was first described by Alexander in 1949. The pathogenesis is unknown, and most cases occur sporadically without a known genetic basis or inheritance pattern. It is considered a disease that primarily affects the astrocytes. The onset may occur at any age. The earlier the onset, the more rapid the neurological deterioration. In the infantile variant, in which the onset predates the union of the cranial sutures, patients usually present with megalencephaly, which may be due to an enlarged brain or hydrocephalus secondary to obstruction of the aqueduct of Sylvius by Rosenthal fibers. Other

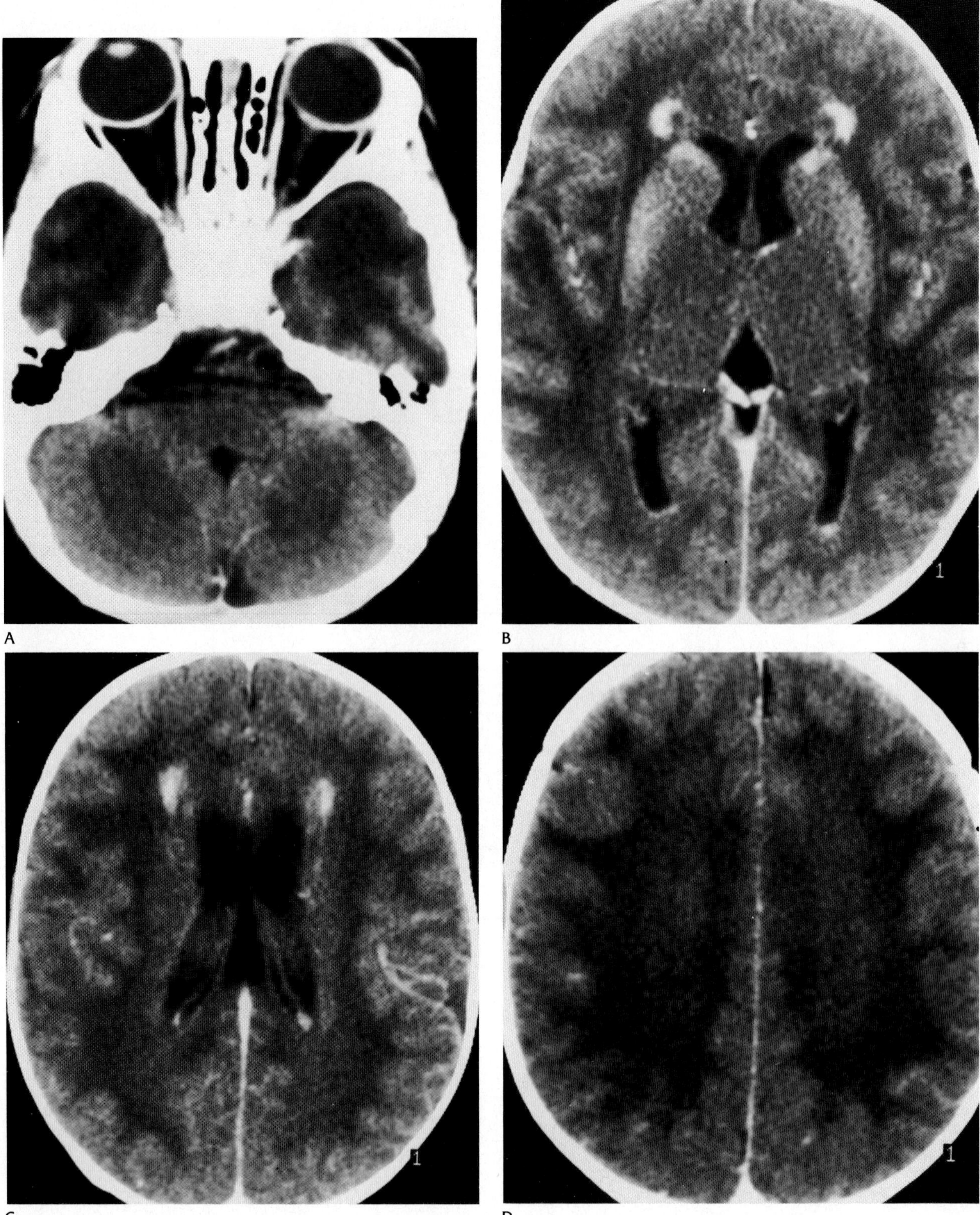

Figure 16-8 Alexander's disease. Contrast-enhanced axial CT (**A–D**) in a 1-year-old male shows extensive white matter hypodensity and characteristic enhancement of the frontal periventricular white matter as well as enhancement of the caudate nucleus and putamen.

presenting symptoms and signs include progressive motor and developmental deficits, seizures, and spasticity. The peripheral nervous system is not involved. Unlike Canavan's disease, which constitutes the major differential diagnosis, optic atrophy is atypical in Alexander's disease. Most patients die in a vegetative state during infancy or during the preschool years (Rapin 1989*a*; Allen 1984; Diebler 1987). Prenatal diagnosis is not currently possible. A definitive diagnosis can be made only by means of a brain biopsy in correlation with the clinical history and imaging studies. CSF and nerve conduction velocity remain normal (Diebler 1987).

Pathologically, the brain is usually enlarged. Histological studies show little stainable myelin. The presence of large numbers of Rosenthal fibers throughout the CNS is characteristic of this disease. These fibers are most densely concentrated around the blood vessels (Holland 1980) and also lie free in the footplates of the astrocytes in the subpial and subependymal regions of the brain. Demyelination with loss of oligodendrocytes and sparing of the axons and neurons occurs in regions rich in Rosenthal fibers (Rapin 1989*a*). Demyelination of the centrum semiovale may be so severe that it leads to cavitation. There is little or no sparing of the subcortical arcuate fibers. The loss of myelin is most severe frontally.

The CT features of this disease have been described (Farrell 1984; Trommer 1983; Diebler 1987; Holland 1980; Bolthauser 1978). Decreased attenuation of the cerebral white matter is usually very extensive (Fig. 16-8). Some authors have reported contrast enhancement of the caudate, the anterior columns of the fornices, and the periventricular white matter when areas of low density abutted these structures. The low density in the white matter tends to involve the frontal lobes first, with gradual extension posteriorly into the parietal region. On MR studies, prolonged T_1 and T_2 relaxation times are seen involving the white matter, first in the frontal lobes and then extending posteriorly to the internal and external capsules and to the parietal lobes (Barkovich 1988). In late disease, frank cystic changes may develop in the frontal lobes, along with marked atrophy of the corpus callosum, especially the genu and the body. Our experience has shown that the MR findings in Alexander's disease are similar to those seen in Canavan's disease. In both diseases, the subcortical arcuate fibers are involved, in contrast to Krabbe's leukodystrophy and metachromatic leukodystrophy, in which they are spared. We have also observed that the white matter within the frontal and temporal lobes has very prolonged T_2 values and T_1 values, suggesting cystic degeneration (Fig. 16-9). The white matter long tracts and the brainstem appear to be less involved. The deep nuclear masses show variable involvement, which requires more analysis.

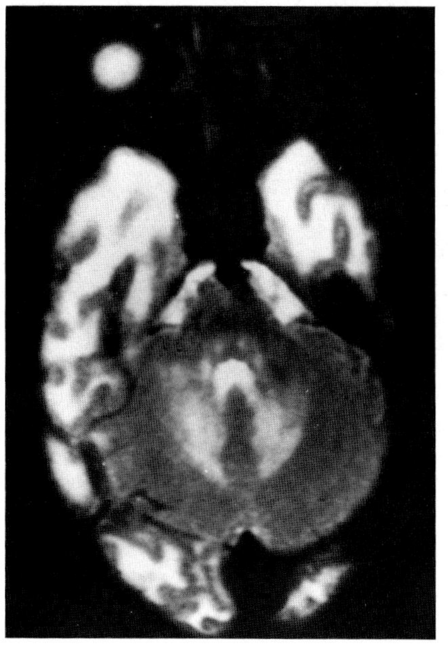

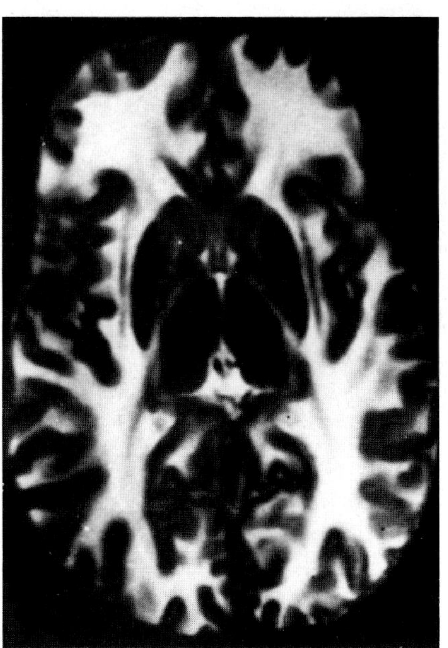

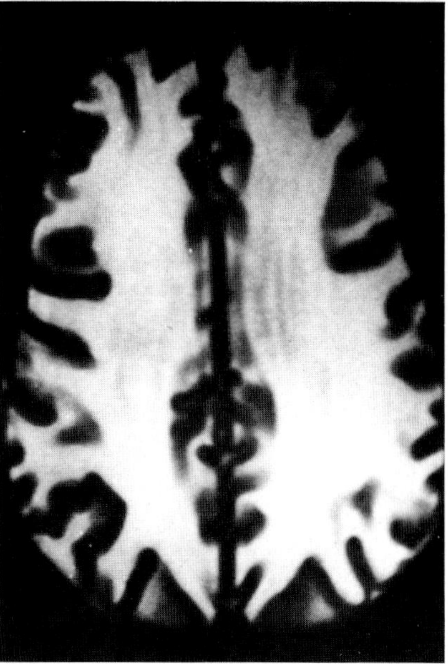

Figure 16-9 Alexander's disease. (**A–C**). T_2-weighted axial MR images of a 2-year-old demonstrate abnormal white matter signal hyperintensity that extends peripherally and involves the subcortical arcuate fibers. The signal from deep nuclei appears extremely hypointense, the significance of which is unknown. On T_1-weighted MR images (not shown), the abnormal white matter signal appears hypointense and may contain areas of cystic change in the frontal and temporal lobes.

ACQUIRED LEUKODYSTROPHIES (DEMYELINATING DISEASES)

Multiple Sclerosis

Multiple sclerosis (MS) includes a clinical and pathological spectrum of several subtypes. The classic Charcot type is characteristically a disease of young adults, presenting between ages 20 and 40 years. It typically has a chronic course of relapsing and remitting neurological signs and symptoms, separated in time and space. In contrast, the Marburg variant, which also affects young adults, has a more acute and fulminant course, resulting in deterioration and death within a few months of onset. Balo concentric sclerosis, as the name implies, is a pathological variant. This rare subtype of MS is clinically similar to the Marburg type but occurs in patients in the second and third decades of life. The characteristic pathological finding is alternating bands of demyelination and normal myelination. Finally, the Devic type (neuromyelitis optica) is a clinical variant in which the optic nerves and spinal cord are primarily affected (Allen 1984).

The cause of MS is unknown, and its pathogenesis is poorly understood. A currently held theory is altered immunity, probably genetically determined. Environmental factors play an unknown yet important role. In general, the disease increases in frequency with increasing latitude in both the northern and southern hemispheres, and there is a lower incidence of disease in Asians at every latitude. The female-to-male ratio is about 1.4:1 and has been higher in some series (Sibley 1978, 1984, 1989; Uhlenbrock 1988). Clinical manifestations vary depending on the areas of the nervous system involved. There is no specific test for MS. The diagnosis is based on history, neurological examination, and laboratory tests including CSF analysis and functional testing such as evoked potentials.

Pathologically, MS is a disease of oligodendrocytes and myelin sheaths. In the acute phase, an inflammatory re-

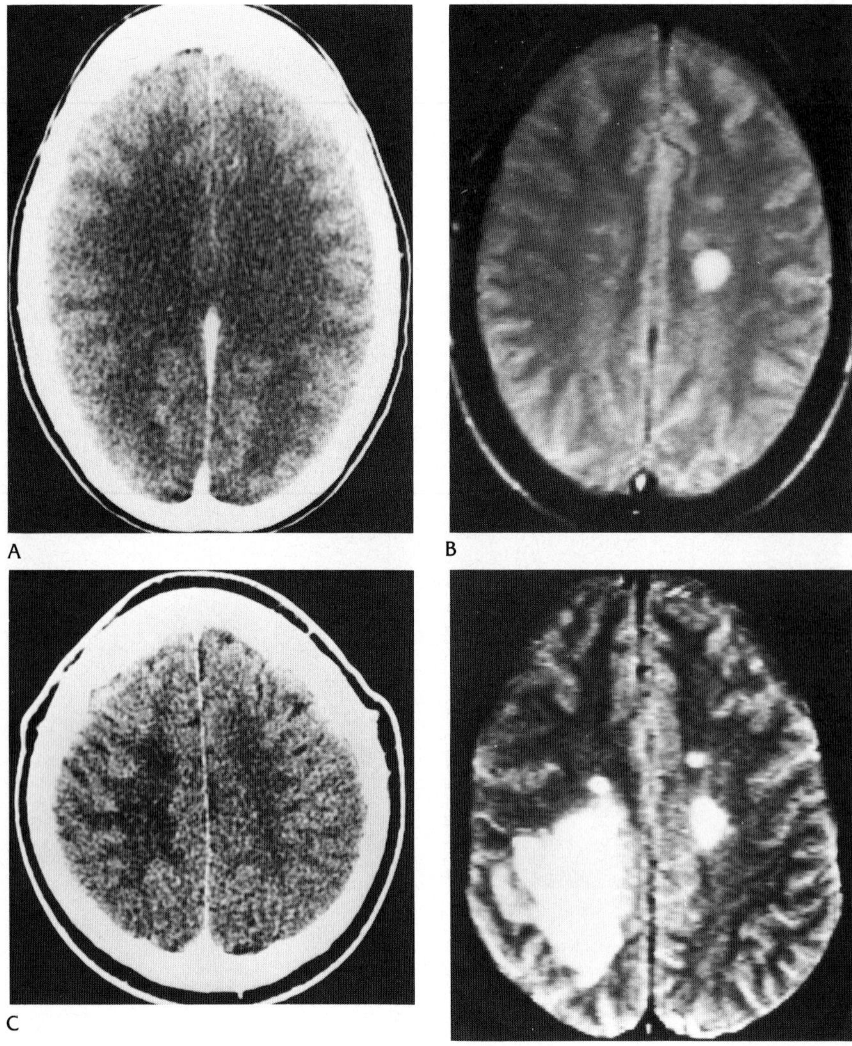

Figure 16-10 Multiple sclerosis. Contrast-enhanced axial CT (**A**) and proton density axial MR (**B**) in a patient with multiple sclerosis demonstrate increased lesion conspicuity by MRI. Technically similar CT (**C**) and MR (**D**) images of a different patient show that multiple sclerosis lesions appear hypodense when detected by CT. On MRI, multiple sclerosis plaques may coalesce and present as "mass lesions."

action with infiltration by macrophages, lymphocytes, and plasma cells is seen, accompanied by edema and a variable degree of demyelination. It is important to note that edema surrounding an acute lesion may not be accompanied by demyelination and that remyelination may occur to a certain degree (Grossman 1986, 1988; Allen 1984; Brownell 1962).

The role of imaging in MS is both to support the clinical diagnosis and to exclude other mass lesions simulating the clinical diagnosis of MS. When CT was the only imaging modality of choice, even with a double dose of intravenous contrast, the sensitivity of CT in the detection of MS lesions varied widely, from 9 to 80 percent (Hershey 1979; Weinstein 1984; Maravilla 1988). The usual findings on CT are areas of low density with or without contrast enhancement and diffuse atrophy (Fig. 16-10). Enhancement of a lesion differentiates an active plaque from a gliotic scar. Lesions less than 7 mm in size are missed on CT (Maravilla 1985). Larger low-density lesions in the periventricular region may not be apparent because of volume averaging with CSF.

Without doubt, MR is superior to CT in the detection of MS lesions. Uhlenbrock (1988) reported that the sensitivity of MR in the diagnosis of MS is 96 percent, which agrees with the results of other studies (Gerbarski 1985; Kirshner 1985; Mandler 1985; Siddharthan 1985). Typically, MS lesions on MRI are manifested as small well-circumscribed plaques, which may become confluent, most commonly located in the periventricular white matter (Fig. 16-11). Although MS lesions are most commonly seen in the periventricular white matter, 5 percent of these lesions can be found in gray matter (Fog 1965). Other common sites include the more peripheral cerebral white matter, corpus callosum, middle cerebral peduncle, brainstem, and internal capsule. These lesions characteristically have prolonged T_1 and T_2 relaxation times (Fig. 16-12). Active lesions, which are perivascular in distribution, have been given the eponym *Dawson's fingers* (Hallpike 1983). This is the pathological basis of Horowitz's explanation of the ovoid lesions commonly seen in the periventricular white matter on proton density and T_2-weighted MR images in MS patients (Horowitz 1989). In Horowitz's study, 86 percent of the patients with clinically documented MS and a positive MR scan had at least one ovoid lesion. The long axis of these demyelinating lesions is oriented perpendicular to the ventricular surface, in the same orientation as vessels in the periventricular white matter. Plaques may be microscopic and may not be detected by MRI. In the small percentage of MS patients with the spinal form of the disease, MRI of the head is negative.

MS lesions are best demonstrated on T_2-weighted pulse sequences. Proton-weighted images are useful in delineating lesions close to the ventricular surface, brainstem, and cerebellum. T_1-weighted pulse sequences may offer a way to distinguish scar from acute inflammation.

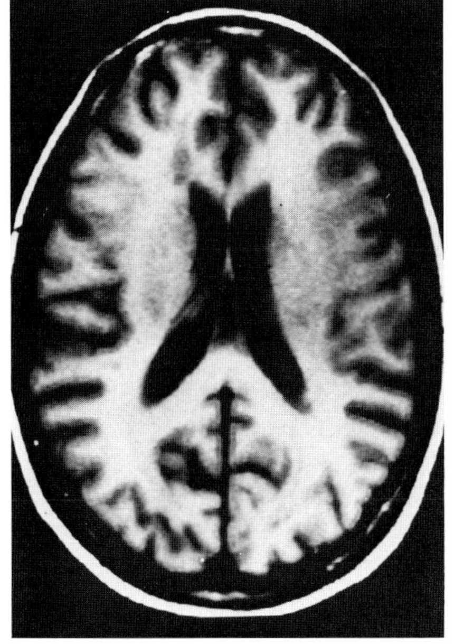
A

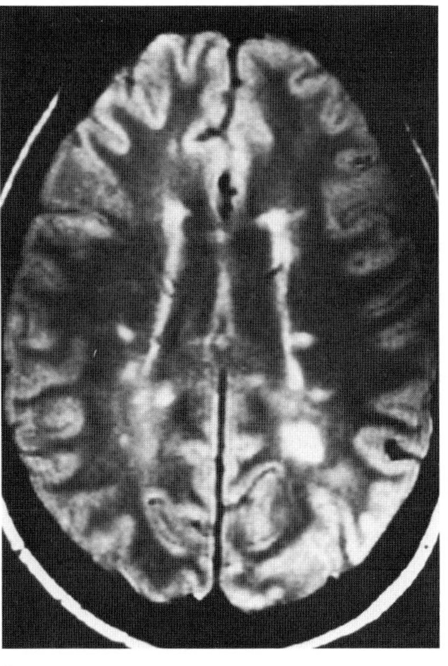
B

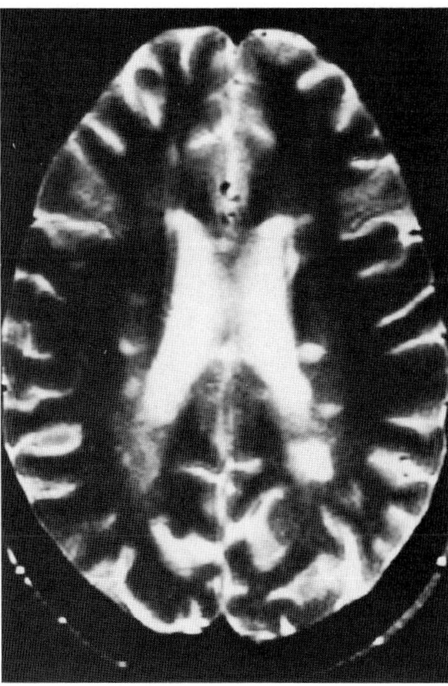
C

Figure 16-11 Multiple sclerosis. T_1-weighted (**A**), proton density (**B**), and T_2-weighted (**C**) images show characteristic periventricular lesions. The T_1WI may be helpful in differentiating chronic from active plaque. Chronic plaques may have lower signal intensity than active lesions on T_1WI; active plaques typically enhance with gadolinium (not shown). The proton density image (**B**) better demonstrates lesions adjacent to the ventricle than does the T_2WI (**C**).

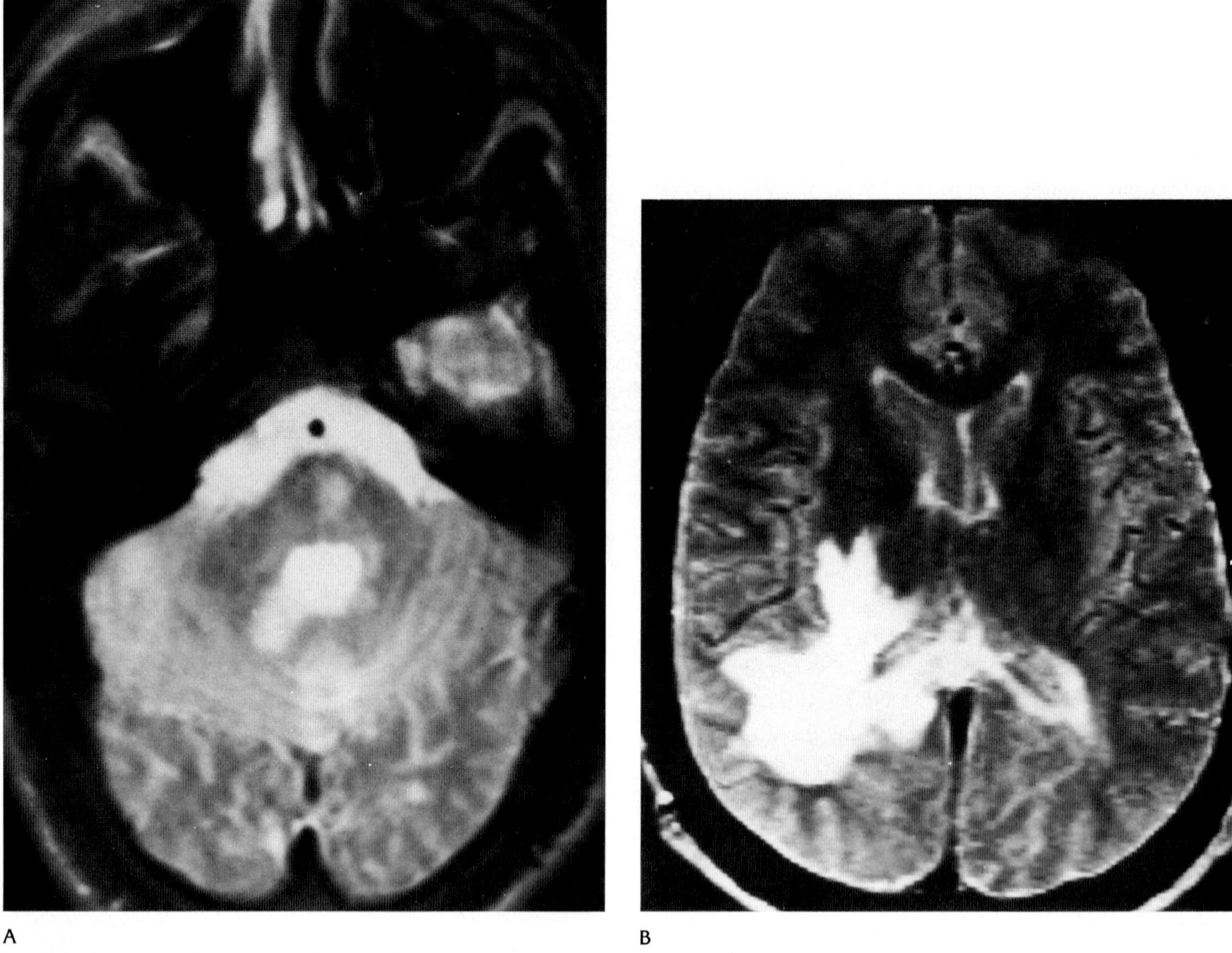

Figure 16-12 Multiple sclerosis. T_2-weighted (**A**) and proton density (**B**) images show brainstem and internal capsule involvement; these are common locations for MS plaques.

Scars tend to appear as a very low signal on T_1WI. Because of the prolonged T_1 relaxation time, there are proponents of the use of the inversion recovery technique to visualize plaques. The disadvantages of this technique include the tendency for the periventricular plaques to be volume-averaged with the CSF in ventricles. Gadolinium is useful in demonstrating acute demyelinating lesions, as are CECT exams, based on the same principle of blood-brain barrier breakdown. Gadolinium-enhanced MR imaging is more sensitive in detecting acute plaques than is high-dose CECT (Grossman 1986, 1988) and is more sensitive than clinical examination alone. The most efficient time to scan for MS lesions is within 3 minutes after Gd-DTPA injection (Grossman 1988). It has also been noted that MS lesions are dynamic and that both enhancing and nonenhancing lesions can show change on serial MR images. Not all enhancing lesions remain hyperintense on long TR pulse sequences; some actually revert back to isointensity, and this implies that the active lesions have remyelinated or that edema and inflammation may occur without demyelination.

MR findings in MS do not always correspond to clinical activity (Uhlenbrock 1988). When CSF studies are negative, it is worth obtaining MRI in clinically suspected cases of MS. MRI tends to be positive in patients who are scanned during acute relapse rather than in patients who are scanned during remission (Sheldon 1985; Uhlenbrock 1988). There is no correlation between the number of lesions and the Kurtzke score, which is based on clinical data and not on the morphological pattern (Crisp 1985; Kirshner 1985; Uhlenbrock 1988).

MS is rare in children and adolescents. Based on CT and MRI studies, apparent differences between adult and pediatric populations with MS have been described (Osborn 1990). In children with MS, the female-to-male ratio is approximately 5:1. Lesions involving the cerebellum and brainstem were described in 33 percent and 14 percent of patients, respectively, in the adult group. In contrast, a higher incidence of brainstem and cerebellar involvement, in the range of 70 to 80 percent, has been reported in adolescents (Osborn 1990). Although less common, hypointense lesions in the thalamus or putamen on T_2WI have been reported in adult patients with MS (Drayer 1987). These lesions most likely do not represent demyelinating plaques and may be due to iron deposition.

The radiological differential diagnosis of MS is wide and varied. Mention should be made of cerebrovascular disease, which is often indistinguishable from MS on the basis of the MRI pattern alone. Cerebrovascular lesions are often more subcortical than periventricular in distribution and occur in older populations. However, 10 percent of adults with MS present after age 50 years (Maravilla 1988). Other processes which can simulate MS include Lyme disease, vasculitis, and acute disseminated encephalomyelitis (Zimmerman 1986; Fernandez 1990).

Viral Encephalitides

In the following sections the acute and subacute forms of viral encephalitides will be discussed. The acute encephalitides may be secondary to a known causative agent or may be an autoimmune response to a nonspecific viral illness or vaccination. The subacute encephalitides include infections of the brain by a diversified group of viral agents: subacute sclerosing panencephalitis caused by the measles virus, Lyme disease, PML resulting from opportunistic infection by papovavirus, kuru, and Creutzfeldt-Jakob disease. These entities are characterized by a long incubation period and spongiform degeneration of the brain.

ACUTE VIRAL ENCEPHALITIDES

Acute Infective Necrotizing Encephalitis

This form of acute encephalitis is caused by the intracellular growth of virus in the brain accompanied by an inflammatory reaction. Invariably, the infective viral agent can be isolated. In humans the viruses frequently implicated include herpes, rabies, arthropod-born adenovirus, and enterovirus. Clinically, acute infective necrotizing encephalitis is difficult to distinguish from acute disseminated encephalitis, which is an immune complex–mediated disease without a known causative agent.

Acute Disseminated Encephalitis

Acute disseminated encephalitis (ADE, ADEM) is a disease of widespread perivenous demyelination, most conspicuously involving the white matter of the cerebrum, cerebellum, and brainstem. It typically follows measles, chickenpox, rubella, mumps, or nonspecific viral upper respiratory infections; the latter is probably the most common cause (Jubelt 1989). It may also be seen after vaccination against smallpox or rabies. Isolation of the infective agent is usually not achieved. The current theory of the pathogenesis of this disease is immune-mediated meylin destruction as a response to viral infection rather then direct viral invasion of the CNS (Brownell 1984; Schumacher 1965; Adams 1985; Jubelt 1989; Dunn 1986). According to some authors, acute hemorrhagic leukoencephalitis is a more fulminant form of ADE.

The onset of neurological symptoms usually occurs between 4 and 21 days after a viral illness or vaccination. Fever, headaches, and meningeal signs may progress to seizures, ataxia, cranial nerve palsies, choreoathetosis, stupor, and even coma and death. The onset of symptoms is usually abrupt. The monophasic course of ADEM is important in differentiating it from other white matter lesions. Mortality is high in the acute phase (10 to 30 percent) (Jubelt 1989; Atlas 1986, 1987). In patients who survive, the neurological signs usually improve considerably; approximately 90 percent of patients have a complete recovery (Jubelt 1989).

The diagnosis is made clinically, often in retrospect, and may be a diagnosis of exclusion. Laboratory analysis is usually nonspecific. The CSF pressure is usually normal, with a mild to moderate increase in the white cell count. The protein content may be normal or slightly elevated; CSF glucose is normal. CSF myelin basic protein is usually increased. The EEG is usually abnormal. Pathologically, the distinguishing feature is multifocal perivenous demyelination and an inflammatory infiltrate consisting predominantly of lymphocytes and monocytes (Brownell 1984).

Early in the disease process, CT has been reported to be negative. With the progression of disease, CT may become abnormal with poorly defined areas of hypodensity, particularly in the centrum semiovale (Atlas 1986, 1987). MRI is more sensitive than CT in detecting demyelination but is not more specific. Typically, ADE lesions are relatively few in number, nonhemorrhagic, and asymmetric and correlate well with the clinical symptoms and signs. The white matter of the cerebrum, cerebellum, and brainstem is most often involved, with less consistent involvement of the spinal cord. Follow-up MRI after treatment shows resolution of lesions, corresponding to clinical improvement (Atlas 1986, 1987). The radiological differential diagnosis includes all the acute and subacute infective encephalitides, acute multiple sclerosis of the Marburg type, and cerebrovascular disease, which would have a vascular distribution. The treatment for ADE consists of corticosteroids, to which patients usually have a dramatic response (Jubelt 1989; Dunn 1986).

Progressive Multifocal Leukoencephalopathy

Progressive multifocal leukoencephalopathy (PML) was initially described by Astrom (1958). It is known to be a progressive demyelinating disease of the CNS secondary to an opportunistic viral infection, which has been attributed to the papovavirus family, specifically the JC virus and perhaps simian virus 40 as well (Berger 1987; Marks 1989; Smith 1982; Weiner 1972). Patients with altered cell-mediated immunity are at increased risk for this viral infection (Marks 1989; Berger 1987). Historically, the patients at highest risk were patients with lymphoproliferative disorders, such as lymphoma and leukemia. PML was also reported in patients with chronic diseases such as sarcoidosis, tuberculosis, autoimmune disorders, Whipple disease, and nontropical sprue and in renal transplant recipients treated with immunosuppressive drugs (Walker 1985). Increasingly, PML has been recognized in patients with AIDS, in which a profound defect in cell-mediated immunity results from infection with the HTLV-III virus. The estimated incidence of PML in AIDS patients ranges from 1 to 3.8 percent (Krupp 1985).

Clinically, the most common presenting complaint is weakness (Berger 1987), followed in frequency by altered mental status, visual disturbances such as homonymous hemianopia, and gait abnormalities. The clinical presentation varies depending on the distribution of lesions. Krupp (1985) reported a CT-clinical dissociation in which the clinical symptoms and signs were far more prominent than were the CT findings. This is probably a reflection of the relatively low sensitivity of CT in detecting these white matter lesions.

Pathologically, PML lesions in the brain are manifested as areas of focal or confluent demyelination predominantly involving the subcortical white matter. Radiographically, early lesions may appear round or oval, progressing to a more confluent configuration with scalloped borders. PML may be differentiated from other diseases of the white matter on the basis of the distribution of lesions that originate near the gray-white junction. Only with disease progression do the lesions extend to involve the deeper white matter. Although historically the incidence of gray matter involvement has been reported to be less frequent, MR studies have demonstrated gray matter involvement in 50 percent of AIDS patients with PML (Marks 1989). This may reflect the greater sensitivity of MR imaging or a more aggressive course of this disease in patients with AIDS (Levy 1986). The gray matter involvement includes the basal ganglia and thalamus as well as the cortical gray matter (Marks 1989; Levy 1986).

Microscopically, PML is characterized by multifocal demyelination, basophilic swollen oligodendroglial nuclei, and enlarged astrocytes. The most significant finding is the presence of intranuclear inclusion bodies, which on electron microscopy are viral particles characteristic of papovavirus. Absence of perivenous inflammatory response has been reported (Marks 1989; Brooks 1984). Virus particles have been found within myelin lamellae; it is not clear what role viral particles within the myelin sheaths play in the destruction of myelin. It is postulated that myelin destruction is probably secondary to the inability of infected oligodendroglial cells to manufacture, support, and maintain the integrity of the myelin, leading to its destruction (Brooks 1984). PML lesions are typically characterized by different zones of cell activity. The peripheral zone contains swollen oligodendroglial cells with virus particles in their nuclei. Toward the center of the lesion, there are fewer oligodendroglial cells but more abnormal astrocytes as well as macrophages. Viral-specific nucleic acid has been found within the vascular endothelial cells of the brain in patients with PML, suggesting that these cells may play a role in the entry of the papovavirus into the brain (Dorries 1983).

The diagnosis of PML is made definitely only by means of a brain biopsy or at necropsy. CSF findings and the EEG are nonspecific. CT findings have shown focal nonenhancing regions of low attenuation on the white matter that have no mass effect and do not enhance with contrast. The reported predilection for the parietooccipital area has not been substantiated by all authors (Marks 1989; Berger 1987).

MR is more sensitive than CT in detecting white matter disease (Levy 1986; Guilleux 1986; Berger 1987). PML lesions are characteristically described as focal high signal white matter lesions seen on long TR/TE sequences (Fig. 16-13). Apart from a high percentage of gray matter involvement in AIDS patients with PML, other atypical features include edema crossing the corpus callosum, which in the general population is more characteristic of tumors than of PML, and hemorrhagic foci within the PML lesions (Marks 1989). This suggests that the PML lesions seen in the AIDS population may be more aggressive than the lesions seen in other associated diseases.

Although MR imaging may be more sensitive, it is not more specific than CT in diagnosing PML. The radiological differential diagnosis of white matter lesions is enormous. However, clues such as the subcortical distribution typical of PML lesions make diagnoses of MS and vascular ischemic lesions secondary to aging less likely. In the AIDS population, the specific diagnosis of PML is more difficult to make. Demyelination resulting from infections other than papovavirus has been described, such as cytomegalovirus. Perivascular demyelination has been described with HIV encephalopathy (Nielsen 1984; Moskowitz 1984; Horten 1981; Marks 1989). Because of the many look-alike lesions, some researchers have recommended early brain biopsy to exclude treatable disease, since the prognosis for PML patients is dismal (Krupp 1985; Smith 1982; Berger 1987). Scattered reports of long-term survival are available, but PML is more often associated with rapid progression and death.

Lyme Disease of the CNS

Lyme disease is a multisystem inflammatory reaction secondary to spirochetal infection caused by *Borrelia burgdorferi.* It is a disease that occurs in deer, mice, raccoons,

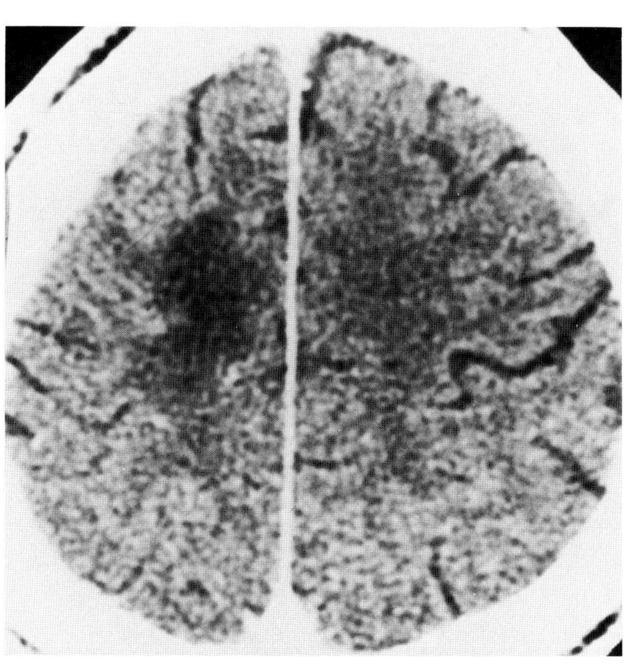

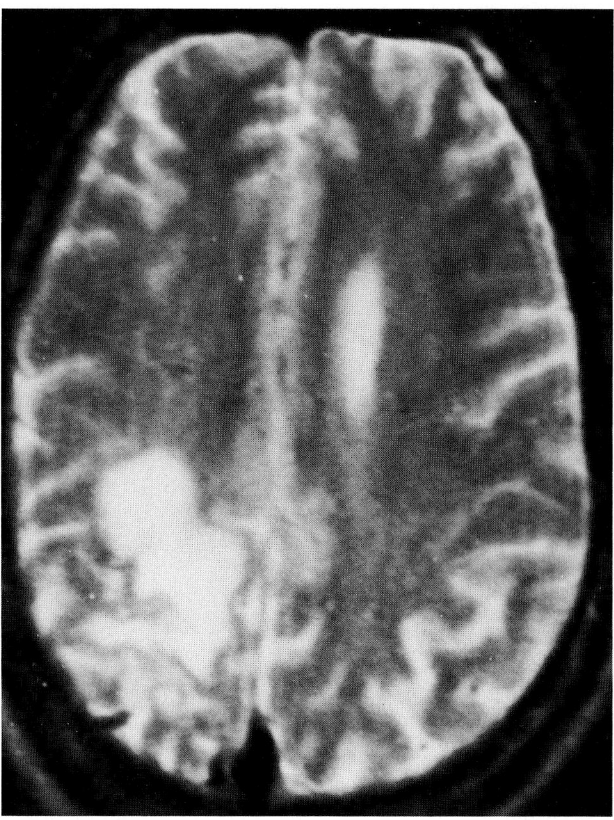

A B

Figure 16-13 Progressive multifocal leukoencephalopathy. Axial CECT (**A**) in a patient with AIDS and biopsy-proven PML shows a right parietal subcortical white matter hypodense lesion without mass effect or enhancement. Axial T_2-weighted MRI (**B**) demonstrates high signal intensity within the subcortical lesion.

and birds, with incidental transmission to humans by infected ixodid ticks (Fernandez 1990; Rafto 1990). Three clinical stages have been recognized; they may occur separately or overlap. Stage I includes a characteristic expanding skin rash, erythema chronicum migrans, and flulike symptoms. Stage II consists of cardiac and neurological symptoms. Stage III is characterized by arthritis and chronic neurological symptoms. The incidence of neurological symptoms varies from rare occurrence to 15 percent (Rafto 1990; Fernandez 1990). The neurological syndromes include peripheral neuropathies, radiculopathies, myelopathies, encephalitides, meningitides, pain syndromes, cognitive disorders, and movement disorders (Pachner 1985; Steere 1978; Finkel 1988; Goldings 1986). The mechanism for CNS manifestations of Lyme disease is not known. It has been postulated that direct brain invasion or vasculopathy may be involved in the pathogenesis of this disease in the CNS.

Multiple areas of the brain may be affected, including the subcortical and periventricular white matter as well as white matter tracts such as the corpus callosum and tracts in the pons and thalami (Reik 1985; Krohler 1986). There have been CT reports of contrast enhancement of CNS lesions. MRI demonstrates high signal regions on long TR/TE sequences. The white matter lesions on MR average 2 to 3 mm in size, lack mass effect, and simulate MS plaques. The basal ganglia and thalami may also be involved. The differential diagnosis includes other demyelinating processes (acute disseminated encephalomyelitis), vasculitis, and inflammatory or infectious processes.

CNS Involvement in AIDS: White Matter Disease

Acquired immune deficiency syndrome (AIDS) is characterized by a deficiency in cellular immunity without a known cause. Predisposing risk factors for this disease in the general population include homosexuality, intravenous drug abuse, blood transfusions, Haitian heritage, and, for children, fetal transmission across the placenta.

The affected population is not insignificant in number, with reported new cases doubling in 6-month intervals and more than 50,000 new cases reported every year, according to Armed Forces Institute of Pathology (AFIP) sta-

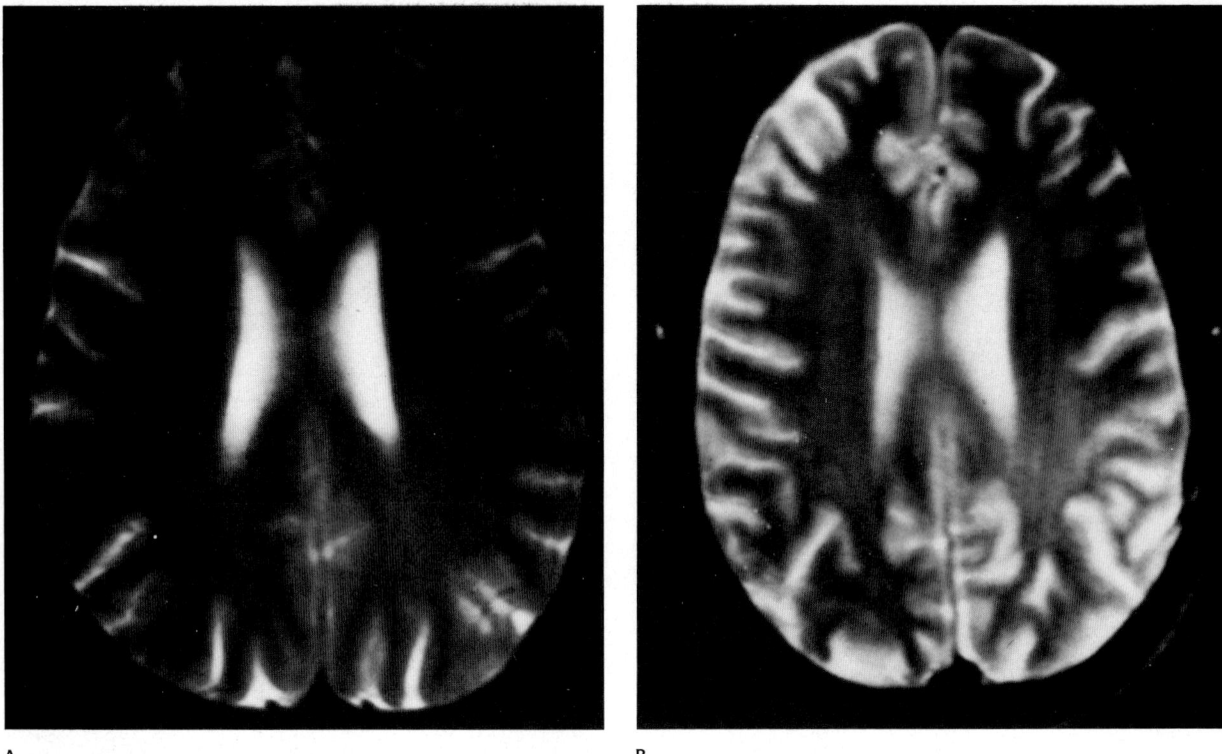

Figure 16-14 AIDS. Axial T_2-weighted MR images in a 33-year-old normal volunteer (**A**) compared with a 33-year-old HIV-positive patient (**B**). Note the atrophy with ventriculomegaly and cortical sulcal prominence in the AIDS patient.

tistics. The causative agent, the human immunodeficiency virus (HIV), also known as the human T-lymphotropic virus type III (HTLV-III), is a neurotropic lentivirus, a subtype of the retrovirus family (Gabuzda 1986, 1987). CNS involvement in AIDS is manifest clinically in 30 to 73 percent of patients (Levy 1985, 1990; Jarvik 1988; Post 1988; Berger 1984; Snider 1983). Neurological symptoms may be the presenting symptoms in 10 to 25 percent of patients with AIDS (Levy 1990). CNS involvement at autopsy, reported in 73 to 87 percent of cases (Levy 1985; Post 1988; Ho 1985; Nielsen 1984), is even higher than is clinically apparent.

CNS involvement in AIDS includes acute encephalopathy, subacute encephalitis, acute and chronic meningitis, vacuolar myelopathy, and peripheral neuropathy (Levy 1985; Gabuzda 1987; Post 1988; Snider 1983; Ho 1985). Among these various forms of CNS involvement, subacute encephalitis is most frequently associated with cerebral white matter disease (Jarvik 1988; Post 1988; Chrysikopoulos 1990; Shabas 1987; Olsen 1988; Grafe 1990). The typically diffuse, symmetric white matter disease that occurs in HIV encephalitis is not always detected by neuroimaging studies (Chrysikopoulos 1990). In this regard, MRI is more sensitive than CT in defining the extent of lesions and in detecting additional lesions (Chrysikopoulos 1990). The most common neuroimaging finding, however, is atrophy, which is reported in 75 to 80 percent of patients, with a predominantly central distribution (Chrysikopoulos 1990; Grafe 1990) (Fig. 16-14). Progression of atrophy has been reported in 63 percent of patients studied serially over 2 to 12 months (Chrysikopoulos 1990). White matter disease, which is detected by MRI in 31 percent of patients with AIDS, may be categorized according to various patterns on T_2 and proton density weighted images (Olsen 1988). These patterns include punctate foci of signal hyperintensity, larger focal and diffuse areas of hyperintensity, and less-well-defined patchy areas of hyperintensity. On these long TR sequences, patchy subcortical hyperintense lesions, asymmetrically located primarily in the parietooccipital regions or seen as isolated lesions in the posterior fossa, are suggestive of progressive multifocal leukoencephalopathy (PML). The more symmetric, diffuse lesions in the periventricular white matter and within the centrum semiovale suggest underlying HIV infection (Chrysikopoulos 1990). However, correlative studies of MRI and pathological findings have demonstrated that the white matter changes seen in HIV encephalitis represent associated regions of myelin pallor or demyelination, gliosis, and vacuolation of the white matter rather than the primary CNS lesion (Post 1988; Chrysikopoulos 1990). The primary HIV lesions, which are not visible by neuroimaging modalities, have been described as microglial nodules, with perivascular multinucleated giant cells harboring virus particles (Post 1988; Chrysikopoulos 1990). These primary lesions are microscopic and are not apparent on gross examination (Chrysikopoulos 1990). HIV infection most commonly affects the deep white matter, followed in frequency by the subcortical white matter, and less commonly involves gray matter (Chrysikopoulos 1990). The implication of HIV as a causative factor in the pathogenesis of CNS disease has been made by means of direct evidence, based on detecting the virus itself in neural tissue and HIV-specific nucleic acids, antibodies, and antigens within the CSF (Chrysikopoulos 1990). Routine CSF evaluation may be normal or may demonstrate mild to marked elevation of total protein, with or without pleocytosis (Chrysikopoulos 1990).

Progressive cognitive and motor dysfunctions have been reported as part of the AIDS dementia complex (Kieburtz 1990). From 36 to 75 percent of patients in different series manifest a progressive encephalopathy, with altered mental status, decreased short-term memory, and difficulty in concentrating and word finding in addition to slowed speech, thought processes, and reaction times (Chrysikopoulos 1990; Kieburtz 1990; Levin 1990).

Reports vary concerning pathological, clinical, and neuroimaging correlation in HIV encephalitis (Post 1988; Chrysikopoulos 1990; Grafe 1990; Kieburtz 1990; Levin 1990).

While some authors have reported that the severity of dementia correlates with the severity of HIV encephalitis (Chrysikopoulos 1990) and others have correlated progressive cognitive demise with increased atrophy and white matter changes (Kerburtz 1990), there are discrepant reports of discordance among serostatus, neuropsychological abnormalities, and focal signal hyperintensity seen within the cerebral white matter on MRI (McArthur 1990). Additional reports correlate clinical neurobehavioral dysfunction with atrophy but not with focal white matter lesions (Levin 1990). The reversibility of MRI abnormalities has also been addressed in patients treated with AZT, who show a clinical response with improved cognition as well as partial or complete resolution of white matter lesions on MRI (Olsen 1988).

In autopsy studies of HIV encephalitis, coexisting disease has been reported in 71 percent of patients (Chrysikopoulos 1990; Olsen 1988; Post 1985). Most commonly, cytomegalovirus (CMV) is found in conjunction with HIV. Imaging studies with pathological correlation have demonstrated central atrophy and multifocal white matter infarcts in these patients (Grafe 1990). With toxoplasmosis added to HIV and CMV, contrast-enhancing mass lesions, often with surrounding edema and mass effect, are seen in addition to the atrophy and diffuse white matter disease typical of HIV infection alone. Coexistent lymphoma may also present with single or multiple contrast-enhancing mass lesions, often with subependymal and meningeal seeding. Patients with HIV encephalitis and PML demonstrate bilateral asymmetric foci of white matter hyperintensity on MRI and hypodensity on CT, without mass effect or contrast enhancement. Crypotococcal coinfection, usually meningitis, adds little to the imaging findings.

In the pediatric population, HIV affects 30 to 50 percent of children with AIDS as a progressive encephalopathy, usually presenting from 2 months to 5 years after exposure, with an episodic course and a fatal outcome (Epstein 1988). Loss of developmental milestones and intellectual ability, as well as progressive motor decline, are the key clinical features. In addition to atrophy and diffuse white matter abnormal signal on MRI and density on CT, basal ganglia and frontal periventricular white matter calcifications have been reported.

In patients who have no obvious risk factors and whose serum status is not known, underlying HIV encephalitis should be considered in the differential diagnosis of a diffuse hyperintense signal in the white matter, especially in the setting of prominent central atrophy. As discussed above, these are secondary white matter changes rather than the primary CNS lesion of HIV encephalitis; coexisting disease processes may introduce mass lesions and/or alter the pattern of white matter involvement.

Central Pontine Myelinolysis

Central pontine myelinolysis (CPM) was first described by Adams (1959), based on case materials consisting of chronic alcoholics. Although characterized by focal areas of demyelination throughout the brain, the changes were most prominent in the pons. Since then, this entity has been described in all age groups. The common denominator appears to be electrolyte imbalance, most notably hyponatremia that has been corrected rapidly (Miller 1988). Some evidence suggests that the rapid increase in serum sodium concentration in a patient with chronic hyponatremia is more important in producing this phenomenon than are other factors, including the hyponatremia itself. CPM has been seen in patients who have mild hypo-, hyper-, or normonatremia (Miller 1988). The exact pathogenesis is unclear, although the temporal relationship between CPM and the rapid correction of hyponatremia appears to have been established.

Clinically, these patients may present with quadriparesis, pseudobulbar palsy, and acute change in mental status, which may progress to coma or death. This disease is not uniformly fatal, as was once thought. There are survivors who have residual neurological deficits (Miller 1988; Messert 1979; Rosenbloom 1984; Yufe 1980; Sztencel 1983). The diagnosis can be made by having the appropriate history and the finding of pontine abnormality on CT and/or MR. Electrophysiological data such as brain-

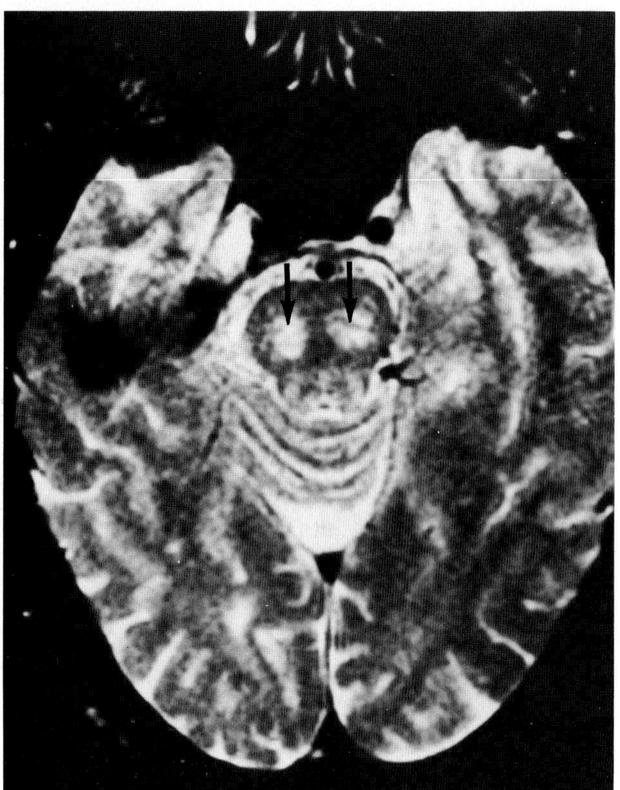

Figure 16-15 Central pontine myelinolysis. Axial T_2-weighted MR image shows the classic appearance of bilateral high signal within the pons (arrows).

stem auditory-evoked potentials (BAEP) that reflect the conduction velocity in the pons are useful in supporting the diagnosis (Sztencel 1983).

The imaging modality of choice is MR. It is often difficult to demonstrate on CT the pontine lesions because of the inherent limitations of beam-hardening artifacts from the surrounding bone. If CT is positive, low attenuation areas will be seen in the pons.

The MR appearance of CPM (Fig. 16-15) consists of a symmetric round or oval area of prolonged T_1 and T_2 relaxation within the base of the pons (Miller 1988; Rippe 1987; Price 1987*a*). Price (1987*b*) suggested that the characteristic lesion in CPM is a trident-shaped lesion as a result of sparing of the corticospinal tracts in the ventrolateral aspect of the pons. Extrapontine sites of CPM have been reported (Miller 1988; Price 1987*b*; Rippe 1987) involving the lateral basal ganglia, the thalamus, and the subcortical white matter. The development of the lesion in CPM has been likened to that of an infarct, with the initial study often being negative. After 1 to 2 weeks the lesion in the pons may be quite large, probably as a result of demyelination and edema. Follow-up studies may show no change, a reduction in size of the lesion, or complete resolution of the lesion, depending on the size at onset (Ingram 1986).

The MR findings in CPM are not specific. The radiological differential diagnosis of CPM includes demyelination on an inflammatory or infectious basis such as Lyme disease (Fernandez 1990), age-related leukoencephalopathy, cerebrovascular disease, chemotherapy and radiation therapy changes, and, less likely, neoplasm.

White Matter Lesions in the General Population

Deep white matter regions of low attenuation/hypodensity have been noted on CT scans of elderly patients. However, it was not until the availability of MRI with its increased sensitivity that it became apparent how common white matter lesions are in the general population. The gamut of periventricular hyperintensity on long TR/TE MRI pulse sequences ranges from a simple thin rim of high signal outlining the ependyma of the ventricle to almost sheetlike areas of high signal extending to the corticomedullary junction. On CT, similar patterns are seen as areas of hypodensity/low attenuation.

There is poor correlation between neurological function and the extent of such periventricular white matter disease (Salomon 1987; George 1986*a,b*). A progressive increase in periventricular white matter disease is seen with increasing age; in patients with normal mental status; in the absence of hypertension, diabetes, or cardiac disease; and in cognitively impaired patients (George 1986*a,b*). Thirty percent of patients over age 60 show periventricular high signal foci or lesions on MRI (Marshall 1988). Although this finding is more common in demented patients, the difference between patients with normal mental status and demented patients is not statistically significant (George 1986*a,b*). The severity of periventricular white matter disease is reportedly not related to the clinical severity of dementia (George 1986*a,b*).

The clinical significance of periventricular white matter disease is unclear. Findings on imaging studies are nonspecific, and there is no consensus on the pathophysiology of such periventricular white disease. The clinical correlate of these lesions was thought to represent Binswanger disease or subcortical arteriosclerotic encephalopathy. When this entity was first described, in 1894, the clinical syndrome included hypertension, strokes, and dementia (Goto 1981; Tomonaga 1982). The pathology described resulted from arteriosclerosis of the long penetrating end arteries (lenticulostriates, thalamoperforators, pontine perforators, and medullary arteries). George (1986*a,b*) described a large number of patients with white matter disease on CT who were neither demented nor hypertensive. Histopathological studies of postmortem specimens revealed that the white matter lesions may represent myelin pallor that may be related to ischemia close to the ventricular surface. Lesions distant from the immediate ependymal surface may be focal infarcts (Marshall 1988) with surrounding areas of demyelination and astrogliosis oriented along degenerated axons up to several centimeters from the center of the infarct. This has been referred to as *isomorphic gliosis* with increased water and protein content in the reactive astrocytes resulting in increased intensity on T_2WI that increases the apparent size of the lesion (Marshall 1988).

Periventricular white matter disease changes on MR have been reported in demyelinating disease (Zimmerman 1986), hydrocephalus, and chronic communicating hydrocephalus (Bradley 1990). According to Young (1981, 1983), periventricular hyperintensity on MRI associated with a demyelinating disease is a result of the destruction of hydrophobic myelin. The high intensity around the ventricles in cases of hydrocephalus is due to transependymal reabsorption of CSF. In patients with normal-pressure hydrocephalus (chronic communicating hydrocephalus), there may be an increased incidence of deep white matter ischemia and infarction (Bradley 1990).

It is clear that all hyperintense white matter lesions on T_2-weighted MRI do not represent ischemia or infarction (Fig. 16-16). Depending on the underlying etiology, these white matter changes may be reversible. On both CT and MRI, white matter changes in hypertensive encephalopathy, chronic renal failure (Anlar 1989), and eclampsia have been described as reversible (Fig. 16-17). These changes probably represent white matter edema without infarction, which resolves when the underlying problem resolves.

In addition to the more diffuse and confluent white matter changes discussed above, more focal hyperintensities can be seen in the centrum semiovale, the low basal ganglia region around the anterior commissure (Hier 1989), and the midbrain (Elster 1990) as a result of dilated perivascular spaces (*état criblé*). Finally, the ependymal lining may be discontinuous at the anterolateral angle of the frontal horns (ependymitis granularis) (Sze 1985), resulting in focal hyperintensities that represent normal variants.

Periventricular Leukomalacia

The determining factor for different patterns of perinatal ischemia in the CNS as seen on imaging studies is the time of anoxic insult. The theoretical correlate is based

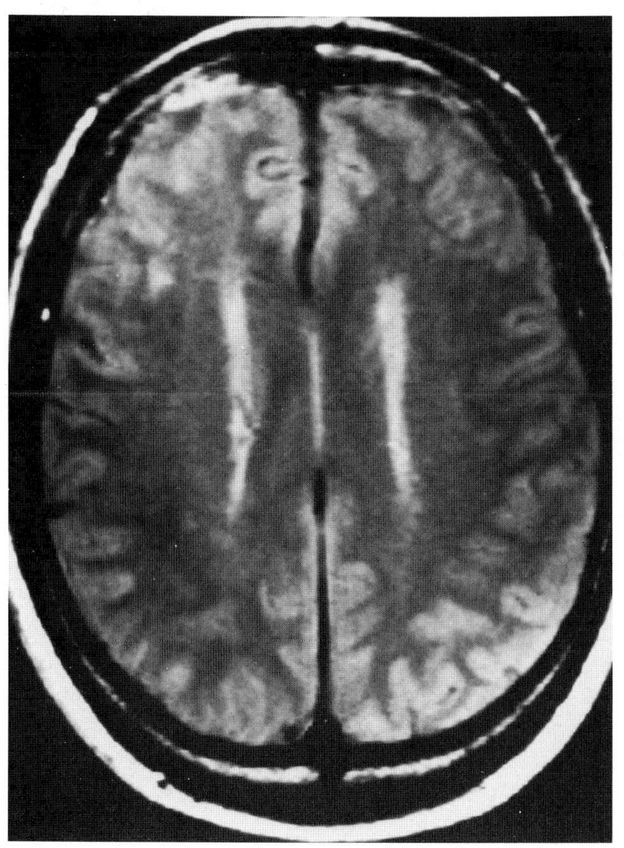

A

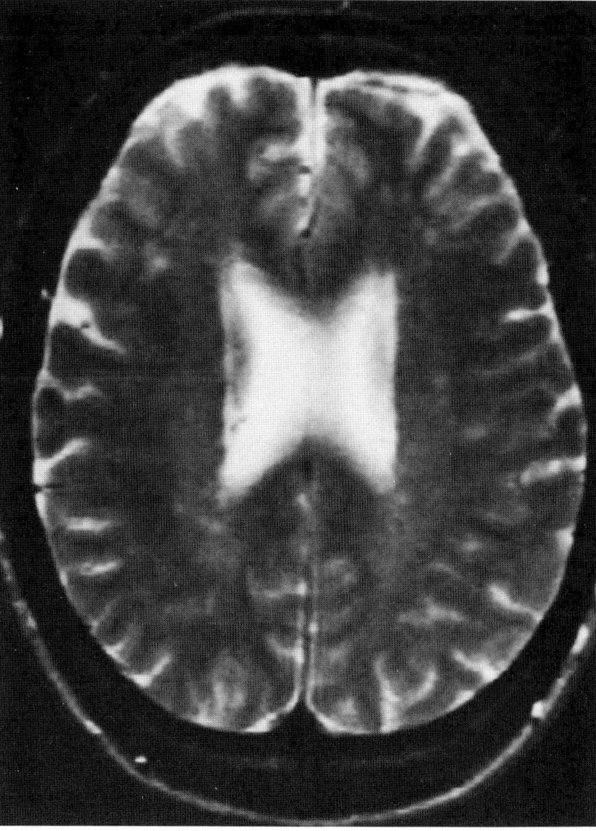

B

Figure 16-16 White matter changes and aging. Proton density and T_2-weighted axial MR images in an elderly patient (**A, B**) show a thin rim of high signal adjacent to the ventricles. (*Continued on p. 724.*)

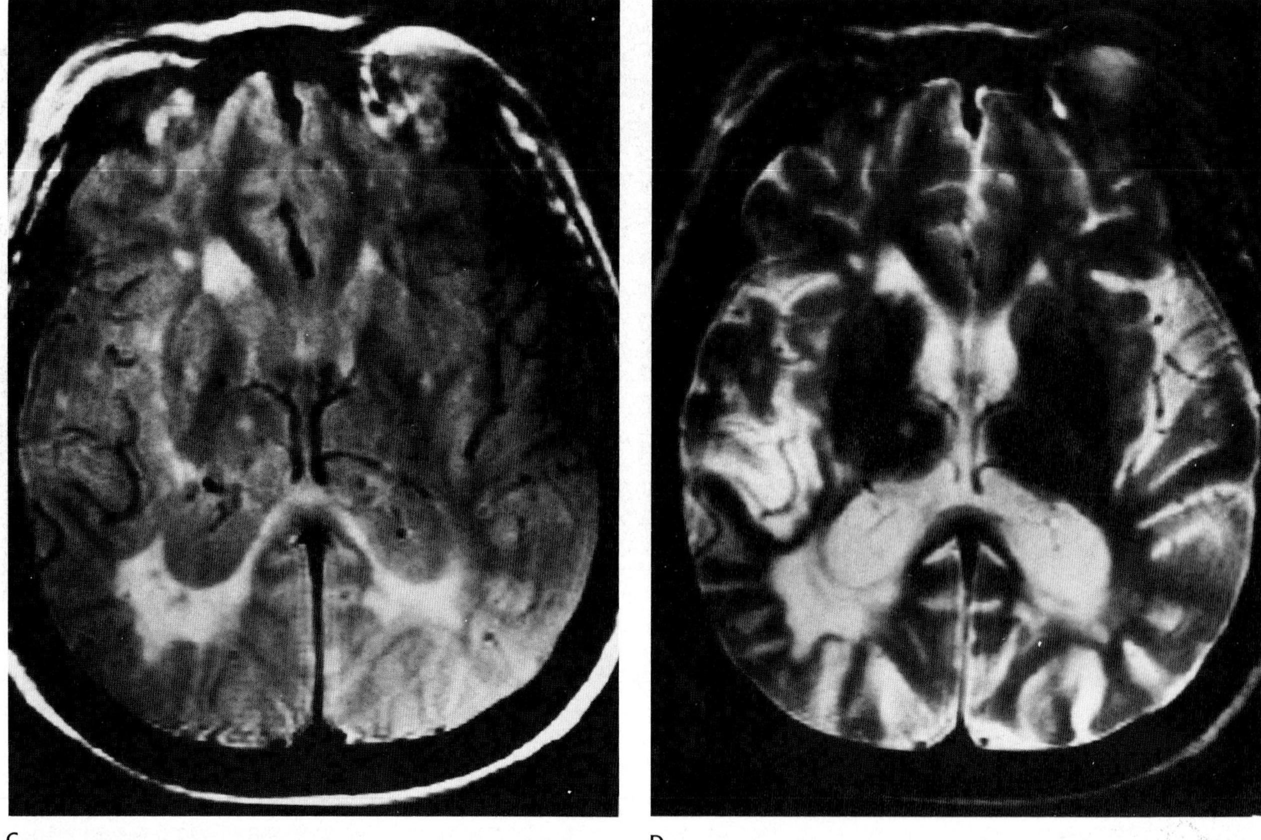

C D

Figure 16-16 (continued) In another patient, proton density (**C**) and T_2-weighted (**D**) images show more extensive periventricular white matter changes, cortical atrophy, basal ganglia, and right thalamic lacunar infarcts.

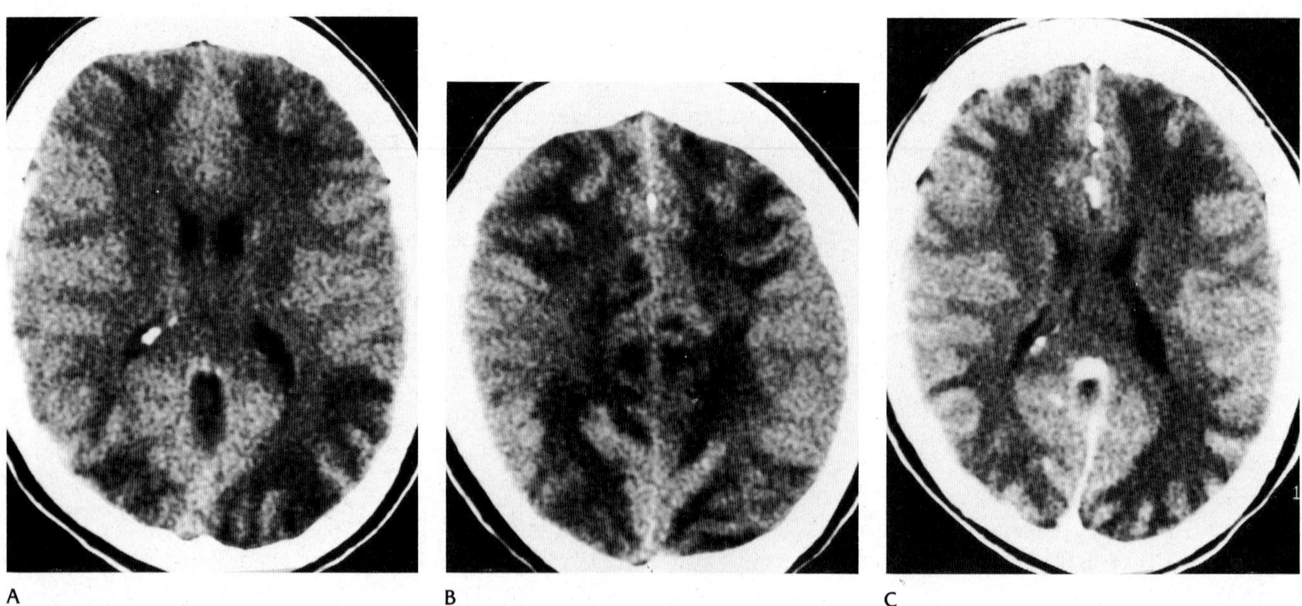

A B C

Figure 16-17 White matter changes in eclampsia. NCCT (**A, B**) and CECT (**C, D**) in a patient with eclampsia demonstrate diffuse and symmetric low-density white matter, without enhancement of mass effect. (*Continued on p. 725.*)

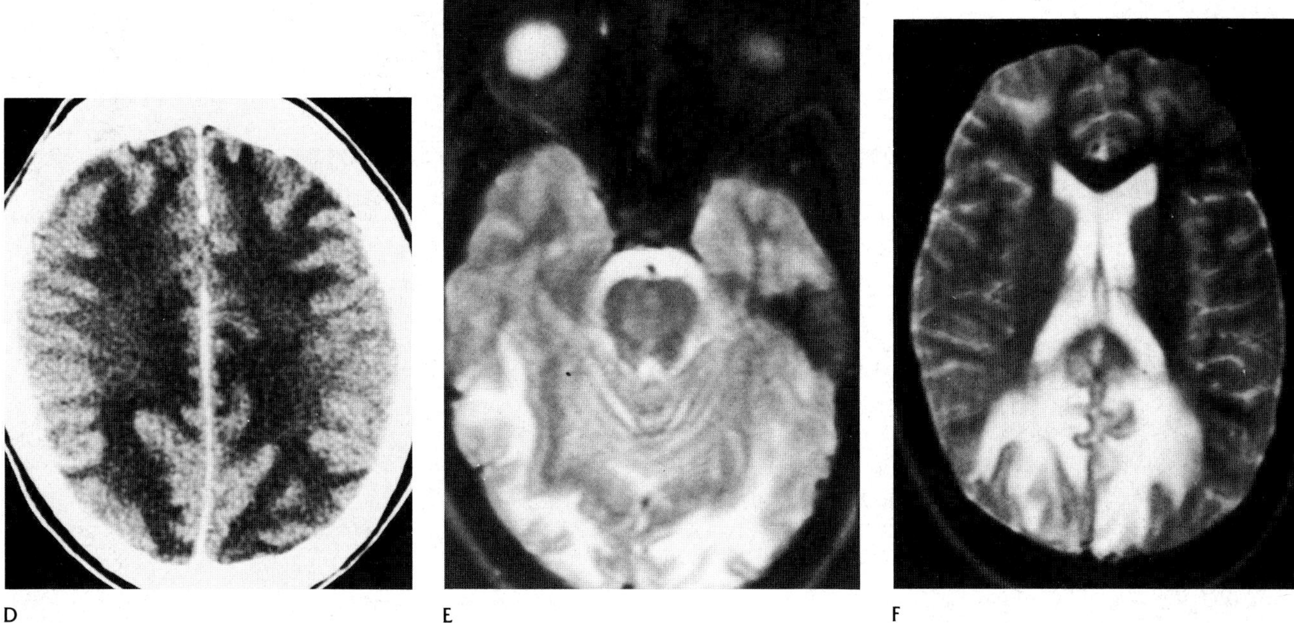

Figure 16-17 (continued) Follow-up T_2-weighted axial MR images (**E, F**) after clinical resolution of symptoms demonstrate residual white matter changes only in the temporal and parietal lobes.

on vascular maturation studies of the CNS (Takashima 1978). The deep periventricular white matter is thought to be at highest risk for ischemic insult before maturation of centrifugal arteries since the vascular supply to this area is tenuous, solely dependent on the medullary arteries arising from the cortical surface (Takashima 1978; DeReuk 1972). It has been postulated that when the ischemic insult occurs approximately at 28 to 34 gestational weeks, the "watershed" area is periventricular. With increasing age, as the centrifugal arteries mature, the watershed zone moves more peripherally; therefore, the ischemic changes are located in the subcortical and cortical regions (Barkovich 1990*b*). An injury during the period of 28 to 34 gestational weeks results in leukoencephalopathy in the form of periventricular leukomalacia (PVL) and encephalomalacia (Schellinger 1985; Dunn 1987; Baker 1988). These changes may be seen in premature as well as full-term infants who suffered perinatal cerebral ischemia during the critical time period of 24 to 26 gestational weeks.

Pathologically, the most severely involved areas in PVL include the occipital radiation at the trigone of the lateral ventricles and the frontal periventricular white matter, dorsal to the internal capsule, at the level of the foramen of Monro (Baker 1988). In the acute stage of PVL, white matter undergoes congestion and coagulative necrosis, which progress to cavitation within the necrotic regions and cyst formation. End-stage PVL is characterized by involution of the cysts, periventricular gliosis, demyelination, and loss of periventricular white matter (Baker 1988; Schellinger 1985). Hemorrhagic PVL is a variant of PVL that represents hemorrhagic white matter infarction. *Encephalomalacia* refers to more extensive brain damage.

In the realm of imaging, ultrasound and CT are useful in the detection of acute and subacute stages of PVL. MRI is thought to be better in the evaluation of end-stage PVL because an abnormality in the areas of white matter loss is better appreciated on MRI than on CT. Ultrasound is of limited value once the cranial sutures fuse. The characteristic findings of PVL on T_2-weighted MRI include abnormal high signal intensity in the trigone area bilaterally, marked loss of periventricular white matter in regions of abnormal white matter signal, and compensatory focal ventricular enlargement adjacent to the areas of abnormal signal (Baker 1988; Schellinger 1985). These changes persist into later life.

The mild to moderately increased signal intensity seen on T_2 images, which represents normal unmyelinated white matter in infants, can be distinguished by its separation from the ventricular wall by a thin band of normally myelinated white matter (Barkovich 1988). In contrast, the abnormal white matter signal seen in PVL directly abuts the ventricular surface and is best appreciated on coronal T_2 images. White matter changes secondary to obstructive hydrocephalus are also in the differential diagnosis. The hyperintense rim around the ventricles in obstructive hydrocephalus is usually diffuse and the ventriculomegaly is symmetric, whereas in PVL the ventricles are not usually symmetrically dilated and the abnormal high signal is not as diffuse. The white matter lesions seen in MS are less confluent and involve other favored sites, such as the brainstem and the cerebellum. The abnormal white matter signal seen in patients after radiation and chemotherapy extends more peripherally, away from the periventricular zone.

Adverse Intracranial Effects of Radiation and/or Chemotherapy

The adverse effects on the CNS secondary to therapeutic irradiation for vascular malformations and intracranial neoplasms, with or without the synergistic effect of chemotherapy, have been studied at length (Davis 1986; Deck 1989; Di Chiro 1987), utilizing both CT and MR (Curnes 1986; Tsuruda 1987; Marks 1988; Dooms 1986). The changes that have been described as being attributable to the radiation effect include atrophy, calcification, white matter disease including radiation necrosis, and vasculopathy. It is beyond the scope of this chapter to include in detail all the abnormalities that can be encountered in a previously treated patient; therefore, only the white matter changes resulting from radiation and/or chemotherapy will be discussed, with only a listing of the other effects.

The adverse effects of irradiation on the brain can be classified into categories according to the time of the onset of the reaction (Marks 1981, 1988; Sheline 1980; Liebel 1987). Acute reactions occur during the course of therapy and are probably due to endothelial capillary damage, breakdown of the blood-brain barrier (BBB), and resultant vasogenic edema, which is responsive to corticosteroid therapy. Within a few weeks to months after therapy, the onset of symptoms classified as early-delayed reactions may occur, thought to be related to demyelination (Tsuruda 1987; Sheline 1980*a,b*). These reactions are generally transient but may be progressive. The late-delayed reactions, including radiation necrosis and disseminated necrotizing leukoencephalopathy, are generally irreversible and are dose-related. The onset of symptoms usually occurs months to years after therapy. The response to corticosteroids is nonconstant. Pathological studies demonstrate white matter coagulation necrosis.

Although not as sensitive as MR in detecting diffuse white matter lesions, CT has often detected white matter changes after radiation therapy (Safadari 1985; Fukamachi 1982; Tsuruda 1987). The spectrum of white matter findings has ranged from atrophy and diffuse decreased attenuation of the deep cerebral white matter to focal lesions known as radiation necrosis or late-delayed reaction. In children as well as adults, atrophy is frequently noted on CT (Davis 1986; Tsuruda 1987). The true incidence of radiation-induced lesions is unknown. In children, CT findings and pathology of methotrexate combined with low doses of radiation have been well documented (Davis 1986). The incidence of radiation necrosis after radiation therapy remains low (Curnes 1986). When this stage is reached, CT may show an enhancing mass with mass effect, which is difficult to distinguish from recurrent and/or residual tumor (Sheline 1980*a,b*; Safadari 1985; Tsuruda 1987) or radiation-induced tumor.

With the advent of MR, radiation-related CNS changes have been well recognized. In patients receiving 2400 to 6000 rad (24 to 60 Gy) to the brain, MR demonstrates abnormalities of the periventricular white matter in the majority of patients (Curnes 1986). These abnormalities are best demonstrated on coronal long T_2-weighted sequences. A characteristic scalloped appearance of the high signal abnormality extending to the corticomedullary junction has been described in the more severe cases. These changes are presumably due to vascular damage and are most apparent in the deep white matter adjacent to the ventricles, where the blood supply is most tenuous (Curnes 1986; Tsuruda 1987). All the white matter fiber tracts are potentially involved, with the exception of the corpus callosum, which is supplied directly by short perforators from pial arteries (Fig. 16-18).

Although the symmetric high signal foci in the periventricular white matter may parallel the age-related ischemic changes, they are more prevalent and severe in the irradiated group, with advancing age or longer survival (Tsuruda 1987).

The differential diagnosis of white matter lesions related to therapeutic radiation includes white matter disease seen in the normal aging process, cerebrovascular disease, and MS. The lesions of MS and small infarcts are not as symmetric as the radiation-related lesions. However, on MRI, the lesions in the periventricular white matter seen in the elderly population are indistinguishable from radiation-related white matter lesions except in prevalence and severity.

Like CT, MR is not specific in differentiating radiation necrosis from residual tumor and/or recurrence. The initial enthusiasm for conventional MR imaging, even utilizing contrast (Gadopentate), in differentiating residual or recurrent tumor has not been useful in the majority of cases. Other MR imaging techniques, such as perfusion imaging and sodium imaging, as well as spectral analysis of other biochemical products are being utilized. Their clinical application has not been confirmed. In perfusion imaging the hypothesis is based on the residual tumor's demonstrating greater perfusion than necrotic tissue does. Hilal (1987) proposed the utility of sodium imaging to differentiate normal tissue from pathological tissue by potentially separating a short T_2 fraction from a long T_2 fraction, representing intracellular and extracellular sodium, respectively. This hypothesis suggests that the in-

Figure 16-18 Chemotherapy effects on white matter. NCCT images (**A, B**) in a child who has received intrathecal methotrexate (MTX) show low attenuation of periventricular white matter as well as cortical atrophy and ventriculomegaly. T_1WI, T_2WI, and proton density MR images (**C–E**) at the level of the lateral ventricles in another patient who has received MTX demonstrate the characteristic changes in the white matter in a periventricular distribution and scalloped edges. Note the atrophy with ventriculomegaly.

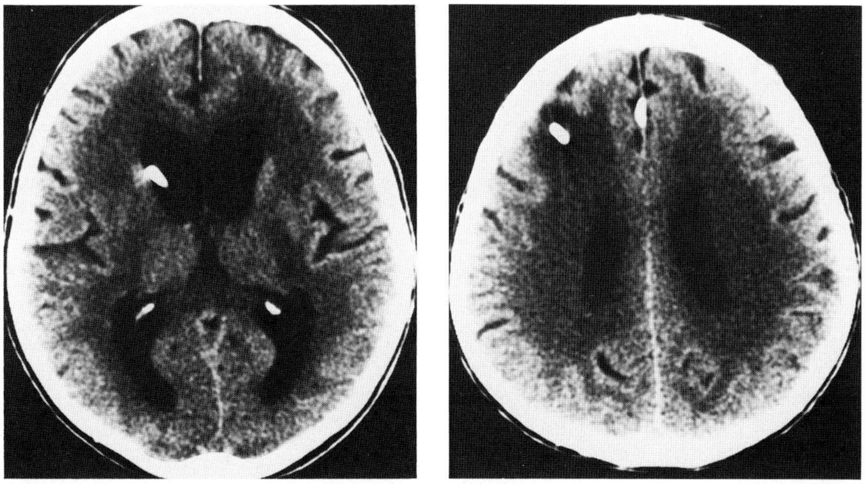

A

B

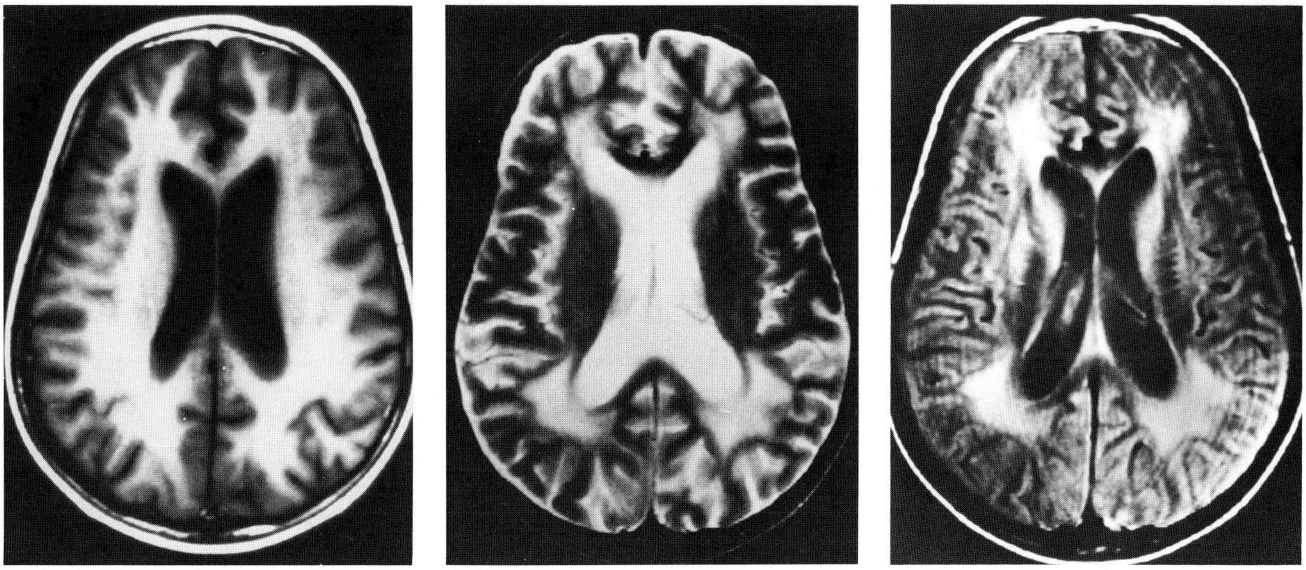

C

D

E

tracellular sodium is increased in malignant processes and that the short T_2 fraction, which can be measured, should therefore be increased in the case of tumor recurrence as opposed to radiation necrosis.

Other imaging techniques currently being investigated include positron emission tomography (PET) utilizing F18-deoxyglucose (FDG) to differentiate recurrent tumor from radiation-induced changes (DiChiro 1987; Doyle 1987). Differentiation is based on the theory that the tumor is hypermetabolic and that areas of necrosis are hypometabolic.

Other CNS changes secondary to radiation have been described, including calcifications, most frequently at the corticomedullary junction and basal ganglia (Davis 1986). Premature atherosclerotic and vascular occlusive disease in large vessels within the field of radiation exposure have been described (Marks 1988; Brant-Zawadzki 1980). Small vessels are more commonly affected than are medium-size or larger arteries. Arterial occlusion occurs secondary to intimal proliferation. Damage to the larger vessels occurs as a result of radiation effects on the walls of the vasa vasorum, causing infarction. The latent period for vascular injury varies widely from 4 months to 23 years (Marks 1988; Brant-Zawadzki 1980).

References

ADAMS RD, VICTOR M (eds): *Principles of Neurology,* 3d ed. New York, McGraw Hill, 1985.

ADAMS RD, VICTOR M, MANCALL EL: Central pontine myelinolysis: A hitherto undescribed disease occurring in alcoholic and malnurished patients. *Arch Neurol Neurosurg Psychiatry* 81:154–172, 1959.

ALLEN IV: Demyelinating diseases, in Adams JH, Corsellis JAN, Duchen LW (eds): *Greenfield's Neuropathology,* 4th ed. New York, Wiley, 1984, pp 338–384.

ALVES D, PIROS MM, GUIMARAES A, MIRANDA MD: Four cases of late onset metachromatic leukodystrophy in a family: Clinical, biochemical, and neuropathological studies. *J Neurol Neurosurg Psychiatry* 49:1417–1422, 1986.

ANDRIOLA MR: Computed tomography in the diagnosis of Canavan's disease. *Ann Neurol* 11:323–324, 1982.

ANLAR B, ERZEN C, SAATCI U: Patchy cerebral white matter edema in chronic renal failure. *Pediatr Radiol* 19:444–445, 1989.

ARSENIO NUNES ML, GOUTIERES F, AICARDI J: An ultramicroscopic study of skin and conjunctival biopsies in chronic neurological disorder of childhood. *Ann Neurol* 9:163–173, 1981.

ASTROM KE, MANCALL EL, RICHARDSON EP Jr: Progressive multifocal leukoencephalopathy: A hitherto unrecognized complication of chronic lymphatic leukemia and Hodgkin's disease. *Brain* 81:93–111, 1958.

ATLAS SW, GROSSMAN RI, GOLDBERG HI, et al: MR diagnosis of acute disseminated encephalomyelitis. *J Comput Assist Tomogr* 10(5):798–801, 1986.

ATLAS SW, GROSSMAN RI, PACKER RJ: Magnetic resonance imaging diagnosis of disseminated necrotizing leukoencephalopathy. *CT: J Comput Tomogr* 11:39–43, 1987.

AUSTIN JH: Metachromatic leukodystrophy, in Rowland LP (ed): *Merritt's Textbook of Neurology,* 8th ed. Philadelphia, Lea & Febiger, 1989, pp 527–530.

BAKER LL, STEVENSON DK, ENZMANN DR: End-stage periventricular leukomalacia: MR evaluation. *Radiology* 168:809–815, 1988.

BARAM TZ, GOLDMAN AM, PERCY AK: Krabbe disease: Specific MRI and CT findings. *Neurology* 36:111–115, 1986.

BARANY M, LANGER BG, GLICK RP, et al: In vivo spectroscopy in humans at 1.5T. *Radiology* 167:839–844, 1988.

BARKOVICH AJ, KJOS BO, JACKSON DE Jr, NORMAN D: Normal maturation of the neonatal and infant brain: MR imaging at 1.5T. *Radiology* 166:173–180, 1988.

BARKOVICH AJ: Metabolic and destructive brain disorders, in Norman D (ed): *Contemporary Neuroimaging:* Vol. 1: *Pediatric Neuroimaging.* New York, Raven Press, 1990*a*, pp 35–75.

BARKOVICH AJ, TRUWIT CL: Brain damage from perinatal asphyxia: Correlation of MR findings with gestational age. *AJNR* 11:1087–1096, 1990*b*.

BARNES DM, ENZMANN D: The evolution of white matter diseases as seen on computed tomography. *Radiology* 168:809–815, 1988.

BERGER JR, MOSKOWITZ L, FISCHL M, et al: Neurological complications in the adult immune deficiency syndrome: Often the initial manifestation. *Neurology* 34 (Suppl 1): 134–135, 1984.

BERGER JR, KASZOVITZ B, DONOVAN POST MJ, DICKINSON G: Progressive multifocal leukoencephalopathy associated with human immunodeficiency virus infection. *Ann Intern Med* 107:78–87, 1987.

BOESCH C, GRUETTER R, MARTIN E, et al: Variations in the in vivo p-31 MR spectra of the developing human brain during post natal life. *Radiology* 172:197–199, 1989.

BOLTHAUSER E, SPEISS H, ISLER W: Computed tomography in neurodegenerative disorders in childhood. *Neuroradiology* 16:41–43, 1978.

BRADLEY WG Jr: *White matter disease in the elderly* (presented at the 76th Scientific Assembly and Annual Meeting of the RSNA, November 25–30, 1990).

BRANT-ZAWADZKI M, ANDERSON M, DeARMOND SJ, et al: Radiation-induced large intracranial vessel occlusive vasculopathy. *AJR* 134:51–55, 1980.

BROOKS BR, WALKER DL: Progressive multifocal leukoencephalopathy. *Neurol Clin North Am* 2(2):299–312, 1984.

BROWN FR III, CHEN WW, KIRSCHNER DA, et al: Myelin membrane from adrenoleukodystrophy brain white matter: Biochemical properties. *J Neurochem* 41:341–348, 1983.

BROWNELL B, HUGHES JT: The distribution of plaques in cerebrum in multiple sclerosis. *J Neurol Neurosurg Psychiatry* 25:315–320, 1962.

BROWNELL B, TOMLINSON AH: In Adams JH, Corsellis JAN, Duchen LW (eds): *Greenfield's Neuropathology,* 4th ed. New York, Wiley, 1984, pp 260–303.

CAVENES WF: Experimental observations: Delayed necrosis in normal monkey brain, in Gilbert HA, Kagan AR (eds): *Radiation Damage to the Nervous System.* New York, Raven Press, 1980, pp 1–38.

CHRYSIKOPOULOS H, PRESS G, GRAFE M, et al: Encephalitis caused by human immunodeficiency virus: CT and MR imaging manifestations with clinical and pathologic correlation. *Radiology* 175:185–191, 1990.

COURVILLE CB, MEYERS RO: The process of demyelination in the central nervous system: II. Mechanism of demyelination and necrosis of the cerebral centrum incident to X-radiation. *J Neuropathol Exp Neurol* 17:158–181, 1958.

CRISP DT, KLEINER JE, DE FILLIP GJ, et al: Clinical correlations with magnetic resonance imaging in multiple sclerosis. *Neurology* 35(Suppl 1): 137, 1985.

CROME L, HANEFELD F, PATRICK D, WILSON J: Late onset globoid cell leukodystrophy. *Brain* 96:841–848, 1973.

CURNES JT, LASTER DW, BALL MR, et al: Magnetic resonance imaging of radiation injury to the brain. *AJNR* 7:389–394, 1986.

DAVIS PC, HOFFMAN JC Jr, PEARL GS: CT evaluation of effects of cranial radiation therapy in children. *AJNR* 7:639–644, 1986.

DECK MDF: *Postoperative and Radiation Changes of the Skull and Brain* (postgraduate course on neuroradiology, Neurological Institute of New York, Columbia-Presbyterian Medical Center, Sadek K. Hilal, program director, April 11–15, 1989).

DeREUK J, CHATTAH AS, RICHARDSON EP: Pathogenesis and evolution of periventricular leukomalacia in infancy. *Arch Neurol* 27:229–236, 1972.

Di CHIRO G, OLDFIELD E, WRIGHT DC, et al: Cerebral necrosis after radiotherapy and/or intraarterial chemotherapy for brain tumors: PET and neuropathologic studies. *AJNR* 8:1083–1091, 1987.

DIEBLER C, DULAC O: Inherited metabolic diseases, in *Pediatric Neurology and Neuroradiology: Cerebral and Cranial Diseases.* New York, Springer-Verlag, 1987, pp 112–137.

DOOMS GC, HECHT S, BRANT-ZAWADZKI M, et al: Brain radiation lesions: MR imaging. *Radiology* 158:149–155, 1986.

DORRIES K, TER MEULEN V: Progressive multifocal leukoencephalopathy: Detection of papovavirus JC. *J Med Virol* 11:307–317, 1983.

DOYLE WK, BUDINGER TF, VALK PE, et al: Differentiation of cerebral radiation necrosis from tumor recurrence by F-18-FDg and Rb-82 positron emission tomography. *J Comput Assist Tomogr* 11:563–570, 1987.

DRAYER BP, OLANOW W, BURGER P, et al: Parkinson plus syndrome: Diagnosis using high field MR imaging of brain iron. *Radiology* 159:493–498, 1986.

DRAYER B, BURGER P, HURWITZ B, et al: Reduced signal intensity on MR images of thalamus and putamen in multiple sclerosis: Increased iron content? *AJR* 149:357–363, 1987.

DUNN V, BALE JF Jr, ZIMMERMAN RA, et al: MRI in children with postinfectious disseminated encephalomyelitis. *Magn Reson Imaging* 14:25–32, 1986.

DUNN D, WEISBERG L: Computed tomography of the brain in asphyxiated infants. *Comput Radiol* 3(3):147–150, 1987.

EICHENFIELD AH: Diagnosis and management of Lyme disease. *Pediatr Ann* 15:583–594, 1986.

ELSTER AD, RICHARDSON DN: Focal high signal on MR scans of the midbrain caused by enlarged perivascular spaces: MR-pathologic correlation. *AJNR* 11:1119–1122, 1990.

EPSTEIN L, SHARER L, GOUDSMIT J, et al: Neurological and neuropathological features of human immunodeficiency virus infection in children. *Ann Neurol* 23(Suppl):S19–S23, 1988.

FALCO RC, FISH D: Prevalence of Ixodes dammini near the homes of Lyme disease patients in Westchester County, New York. *Am J Epidemiol* 127:826–830, 1988.

FARRELL K, CHUANG S, BECKER LE: Computed tomography in Alexander's disease. *Ann Neurol* 15:605–609, 1984.

FERNANDEZ RE, ROTHBERG M, FERENCZ G, et al: Lyme disease of the CNS: MR imaging findings in 14 cases. *AJNR* 11:479–481, 1990.

FINKEL MF: Lyme disease and its neurologic complications. *Arch Neurol* 45:99–104, 1988.

FOG T: The topography of plaques in multiple sclerosis with special reference to cerebral plaques. *Acta Neurol Scand* 41(Suppl 15):1–161, 1965.

FUKAMACHI A, WAKAO T, AKAI J: Brain stem necrosis after irradiation of pituitary adenoma. *Surg Neurol* 8:343–350, 1982.

GABUZDA DH, HO DD, DE LA MONTE SM, et al: Immunohistochemical identification of HTLV-III antigen in brains of patients with AIDS. *Ann Neurol* 20:289–295, 1986.

GABUZDA D, HIRSCH M: Neurologic manifestations of infection with human immunodeficiency virus. *Ann Intern Med* 107:383–391, 1987.

GALL JC, HAYLES AB, SIEKERT RG, KEITH HM: Multiple sclerosis in children: A clinical study of 40 cases with onset in childhood. *Pediatrics* 21:703–709, 1958.

GEORGE AE, DE LEON MJ, KALNIN A, et al: Leukoencephalopathy in normal and pathologic aging: I. MRI of brain lucencies. *AJNR* 7:561–566, 1986*a*.

GEORGE AE, DE LEON MJ, GENTES CI, et al: Leukoencephalopathy in normal and pathologic aging: II. CT brain lucencies. *AJNR* 7:567–570, 1986*b*.

GERBARSKI SS, GABRIELSEN TO, GILMAN S: The initial diagnosis of multiple sclerosis: Clinical impact of magnetic resonance imaging. *Ann Neurol* 17:469–474, 1985.

GOLDEN GS,WOODY RC: The role of nuclear magnetic resonance imaging in the diagnosis of MS in childhood. *Neurology* 37:689–693, 1987.

GOLDINGS EA, JERICHO J: Lyme disease. *Clin Rheum Dis* 12:343–367, 1986.

GOTO K, ISHIL N, FUKASAWA H: Diffuse white matter disease in the geriatric population. *Radiology* 141:687–695, 1981.

GRAFE M, PRESS G, BERTHOTY D, et al: Abnormalities of the brain in AIDS patients: Correlation of postmortem MR findings with neuropathology. *AJNR* 11:905–911, 1990.

GROSSMAN RI, GONZALEZ-SCARANO F, ATLAS S, et al: Multiple sclerosis: Gadolinium enhancement in MR imaging. *Radiology* 161:721–725, 1986.

GROSSMAN RI, BRAFFMAN BH, BORSON JR, et al: Multiple sclerosis: Serial study of gadolinium-enhanced MR imaging. *Radiology* 169:117–122, 1988.

GUILLEUX MH, STEINER RE, YOUNG IR: MR imaging in progressive multifocal leukoencephalopathy. *AJNR* 7:1033–1035, 1986.

HALLPIKE JF, ADAMS CWM, TOURTELOTTE WW (eds): *Multiple Sclerosis: Pathology, Diagnosis and Management.* Baltimore: Williams & Wilkins, 1983.

HERSHEY LA, GADO MH, TROTTER JL: Computerized tomography in the diagnostic evaluation of multiple sclerosis. *Ann Neurol* 5:32–39, 1979.

HIER LA, BAUER CJ, SCHWARTZ L, et al: Large Virchow-Robin spaces: MR-clinical correlation. *AJNR* 10:929–936, 1989.

HILAL SK: *Current Status of Sodium Imaging in Neuroradiology: MRI & CT of the Brain & Spine* (postgraduate course, Neurological Institute of New York, Columbia-Presbyterian Medical Center, Sadek K. Hilal, program director, March 31–April 4, 1987).

HO DD, ROTD TR, SCHOOLEY RT: Isolation of HTLV-III from cerebrospinal fluid and neural tissue of patients with neurologic syndromes related to the acquired immunodeficiency syndrome. *N Engl J Med* 313:1493–1499, 1985.

HOLLAND IM, KENDALL BE: Computed tomography in Alexander's disease. *Neuroradiology* 20:103–106, 1980.

HOROWITZ AL, KAPLAN RD, GREWE G: The ovoid lesion: A new MR observation in patients with multiple sclerosis. *AJNR* 10:303–305, 1989.

HORTEN B, PRICE RW, JIMENEZ D: Multifocal varicella-zoster virus leukoencephalitis temporally remote from herpes zoster. *Ann Neurol* 9:251–266, 1981.

IESHIMA A, EDA I, MATSUI A, et al: Computed tomography in Krabbe's disease: Comparison with neuropathology. *Neuroradiology* 25:323–327, 1983.

IGARASHI M, SCHAUMBURG HH, POWERS JM, et al: Fatty acid abnormality in adrenoleukodystrophy. *J Neurochem* 26:851–860, 1976.

INGRAM DA, TAUB M, KOPELMAN PG, et al: Brain-stem auditory evoked responses in diagnosis of central pontine myelinolysis. *J Neurol* 233:23–24, 1986.

JACKSON JA, LEAKE DR, SCHNEIDERS NJ, et al: Magnetic resonance imaging in multiple sclerosis; results in 32 cases. *AJNR* 6:171–176, 1985.

JARVIK J, HESSELINK J, KENNEDY C, et al: Acquired immunodeficiency syndrome magnetic resonance patterns of brain involvement with pathologic correlation. *Arch Neurol* 45:731–736, 1988.

JENSON ME, SAWYER RW, BRAUN IF, RIZZO WB: MRI imaging appearance of childhood adrenoleukodystrophy with auditory, visual, and motor pathway involvement. *Radiographics* 10:53–66, 1990.

JOHNSON WG: Adrenoleukodystrophy, in Rowland LP (ed): *Merritt's Textbook of Neurology,* 8th ed. Philadelphia, Lea & Febiger, 1989*a,* pp 536–538.

JOHNSON WG: Lysosomal diseases and other storage diseases, in Rowland LP (ed): *Merritt's Textbook of Neurology,* 8th ed. Philadelphia, Lea & Febiger, 1989*b,* pp 501–527.

JOURNEL H, ROUSSEY M, GANDON Y, et al: Magnetic resonance imaging of Pelizaeus-Merzbacher disease. *Neuroradiology* 29:403–405, 1987.

JUBELT B, MILLER JR: Viral infections, in Rowland LP (ed): *Merritt's Textbook of Neurology,* 8th ed. Philadelphia, Lea & Febiger, 1989, pp 96–136.

KIEBURTZ D, KETONEN L, ZETTELMAIER A, et al: Magnetic resonance imaging findings in HIV cognitive impairment. *Arch Neurol* 47:643–645, 1990.

KIRSHNER HS, TSAI SI, RUNGE VM, PRICE AC: Magnetic resonance imaging and other techniques in the diagnosis of multiple sclerosis. *Arch Neurol* 42:859–863, 1985.

KISHIMOTO Y, MOSER HW, SUZUKE K: Adrenoleukodystrophy, in Lathga A (ed): *Handbook of Neurochemistry.* New York, Plenum, 1985, pp 125–151.

KOEPPER AH, RONCA NA, GREENFIELD EA, HANS MB: Defective biosynthesis of proteolipid protein in Pelizaeus Merzbacher disease. *Ann Neurol* 21:159–10, 1987.

KROHLER J, KASPER J, KERN U, et al: Borrelia encephalomyelitis (letter). *Lancet* ii:35, 1986.

KRUPP LB, LIPTON R, SWERDLOW ML, et al: Progressive multifocal leukoencephalopathy: Clinical and radiologic features. *Ann Neurol* 17:344–349, 1985.

KUMAR AJ, ROSENBAUM AE, NAIDU S, et al: Adrenoleukodystrophy: Correlating MR imaging with CT. *Radiology* 165:497–504, 1987.

LAKE BD: Lysosomal enzyme deficiencies, in Adams JH, Corsellis JAN, Duchen LW (eds): *Greenfield's Neuropathology,* 4th ed. New York, J Wiley, 1984, pp 491–572.

LeBIHAN D, BRETON E, LALLEMAND D, et al: Separation of diffusion and perfusion intravoxel incoherent motion MR imaging. *Radiology* 168:497–501, 1988.

LEVIN H, WILLIAMS D, BORUCKI M, et al: Magnetic resonance imaging and neuropsychological findings in human immunodeficiency virus infection. *J Acq Immune Deficiency Synd* 3:757–762, 1990.

LEVY R, BREDESEN D, ROSENBLUM M: Neuroradiological manifestations of the acquired immunodeficiency syndrome (AIDS): Experience at UCSF and review of the literature. *Neurosurgery* 62:475–495, 1985.

LEVY JD, COTTINGHAM KL, CAMPBELL RJ, et al: Progressive multifocal leukoencephalopathy and magnetic resonance. *Ann Neurol* 19:399–401, 1986.

LEVY R, MILLS C, POSIN J, et al: The efficacy and clinical impact of brain imaging in neurologically symptomatic AIDS patients: A prospective CT/MRI study. *J Acq Immune Deficiency Synd* 3:461–471, 1990.

LIEBEL SA, SHELINE GE: Radiation therapy for neoplasms of the brain. *J Neurosurg* 66:1–22, 1987.

MacFAUL R, CAVANAGH N, LAKE BD, et al: Metachromatic leucodystrophy: Review of 38 cases. *Arch Dis Child* 57:168–175, 1982.

MANDLER RN, PATRONAS N, PAPADOPOULOS N, McFARLAND HF: Nuclear magnetic resonance imaging in multiple sclerosis. *Neurology* 35(Suppl 1):252, 1985.

MARAVILLA KR, WEINREB JC, SUSS R, NUNNALLY RL: Magnetic resonance demonstration of multiple sclerosis plaques in the cervical cord. *AJR* 144:381–385, 1985.

MARAVILLA KR: Multiple sclerosis, in Stark DD, Bradley WG (eds): *Magnetic Resonance Imaging*. St. Louis, Mosby 1988, pp 344–356.

MARKS AS, ATLAS SW: Progressive multifocal leukoencephalopathy in patients with AIDS: Appearance on MR images. *Radiology* 173:517–520, 1989.

MARKS JE, BAGLAN RJ, PRASSAD SC: Cerebral radionecrosis: Incidence and risk in relation to dose, time, fractionation, and volume. *Int J Radiat Oncol Biol Phys* 7:243–252, 1981.

MARKS MP, DELAPAZ RL, FABRIKANT JI: Intracranial vascular malformations: Imaging of charged particle radiosurgery: II. Complications. *Radiology* 168:457–462, 1988.

MARSHALL VG, BRADLEY WG Jr, MARSHALL CE, et al: Deep white matter infarction: Correlation of MR imaging and histopathologic findings. *Radiology* 167:517–522, 1988.

MARTIN JJ, CEUTERIK C, LIBERT J: Skin and conjunctival nerve biopsies in adrenoleukodystrophy and its variants. *Ann Neurol* 8:291–295, 1980.

MATALON R, MICHALS K, SEBESTA D, et al: Aspartoacylase deficiency and N-acetylaspartic aciduria in patients with canavan disease. *Am J Med Genet* 29:463–471, 1988.

MATSUYAMA H, MINOSHIMA I, WATAMABE I: An autopsy case of leukodystrophy of Krabbe type. *Acta Pathol Jpn* 13:195–199, 1963.

McARTHUR J, KUMAR A, JOHNSON D, et al: Incidental white matter hyperintensities on magnetic resonance imaging in HIV-1 infection. *J Acq Immune Deficiency Synd* 3:252–259, 1990.

McFARLIN DE, McFARLAND HF: Multiple sclerosis. *N Engl J Med* 307:1183–1188, 1982.

MENKES JH: *Textbook of Child Neurology*. Philadelphia, Lea & Febiger, 1985.

MESSERT B, ORRISON WW, HAWKINS MJ, QUAGLIERI CE: Central pontine myelinolysis: Consideration on etiology, diagnosis, and treatment. *Neurology* 29:147–160, 1979.

MILLER GM, BAKER HL, OKAZAKI H, WHISNANT JP: Central pontine myelinolysis and its imitators: MR findings. *Radiology* 168:794–802, 1988.

MORARIU MA, WILKINKS DE, PATEL S: Multiple sclerosis and serial computerized tomography—delayed contrast enhancement of acute and early lesions. *Arch Neurol* 37:189–190, 1980.

MOSKOWITZ LB, GREGORIOS JB, HENSLEY GT, BERGER JR: Cytomegalovirus: Induced demyelination associated with acquired immune deficiency syndrome. *Arch Pathol Lab Med* 108:873–877, 1984.

NIELSEN SL, PETITIO CK, UMACHER CD, et al: Subacute encephalitis in adult immune deficiency syndrome: A postmortem study. *Am J Clin Pathol* 82:678–682, 1984.

OLSEN W, LONGO F, MILLS C, et al: White matter disease in AIDS: Findings at MR imaging. *Radiology* 169:445–448, 1988.

ORMEROD IE, BRONSTEIN A, RUDGE P, et al: Magnetic resonance imaging in clinically isolated lesions of the brain stem. *J Neurol Neurosurg Psychiatry* 49(7):737–743, 1986.

OSBORN AG, HARNSBERGER HR, SMOKER WRK, BOYER RS: Multiple sclerosis in adolescents: CT and MR findings. *AJNR* 11:489–494, 1990.

PACHNER AP, STEERE AC: The triad of neurologic manifestations of Lyme disease: Meningitis, cranial neuritis and radiculoneuritis. *Neurology* 35:47–53, 1985.

PAMPHLETT R, SILBERSTEIN P: Pelizaeus-Merzbacher disease in a brother and sister. *Acta Neuropathol (Berl)* 69:343–346, 1986.

PATY DW, OGER JJF, KASTRUKOFF LF, et al: MRI in the diagnosis of MS: A prospective study with comparison of clinical evaluation, evoked potentials, oligoclonal banding, and CT. *Neurology* 38:180–185, 1988.

PENNER MW, LI KC, GEBARSKI SS, ALLEN RJ: MR imaging of Pelizaeus-Merzbacher disease. *J Comput Assist Tomogr* 11(4):591–593, 1987.

POSER C, PATTY DW, SCHEINBERG L, et al: New diagnostic criteria for multiple sclerosis: Guidelines for research protocols. *Ann Neurol* 13:227–231, 1983.

POST M, KURSUNOGLU S, HENSLEY G, et al: Cranial CT in acquired immunodeficiency syndrome: Spectrum of disease and optimal contrast enhancement technique. *AJR* 145:929–940, 1985.

POST M, TATE L, QUENCER R, et al: CT, MR, and pathology in HIV encephalitis and meningitis. *AJR* 151:373–380. 1988.

PRICE BH, MESULAM MM: Behavior manifestations of central pontine myelinolysis. *Arch Neurol* 44:671–673, 1987*a*.

PRICE DB, KRAMER J, HOTSON GC, LOH JP: Central pontine myelinolysis: Report of a case with distinctive appearance in MR imaging (letter). *AJNR* 8:576–577, 1987*b*.

RAFTO SE, MILTON WJ, GALETTA SL, et al: Biopsy-confirmed CNS Lyme disease: MR appearance at 1.5T. *AJNR* 11:482–484, 1990.

RAINE CS: Demyelinating diseases, in Davis RL, Robertson DM (eds): *Textbook of Neuropathology.* Baltimore: Williams & Wilkins, 1985, pp 568–547.

RAPIN I: Alexander disease, in Rowland LP (ed): *Merritt's Textbook of Neurology,* 8th ed. Philadephia, Lea & Febiger, 1989*a,* pp 558–559.

RAPIN I: Spongy degeneration of the nervous system, in Rowland LP (ed): *Merritt's Textbook of Neurology,* 8th ed. Philadelphia, Lea & Febiger, 1989*b,* pp 553–555.

RAPIN I: Pelizaeus-Merzbacher disease, in Rowland LP (ed): *Merritt's Textbook of Neurology,* 8th ed. Philadelphia, Lea & Febiger, 1989*c,* pp 557–558.

REESE L, CARR TJ, NICHOLSON RL, LEPP EK: Magnetic resonance imaging for detecting lesions of multiple sclerosis: Comparison with computed tomography and clinical assessment. *Can Med Assoc J* 15:639–643, 1986.

REIK L, SMITH L, KHAN A, et al: Demyelinating encephalopathy in Lyme disease. *Neurology* 35:267–269, 1985.

RESNICK L, DIMARZO VERONESE F, SCHIPBACH J, et al: Intra blood-brain-barrier synthesis of HTLV-III specific IgG in patients with neurologic symptoms associated with AIDS or AIDS-related complex. *N Engl J Med* 313:1498–1504, 1985.

RIPPE DJ, EDWARDS MK, D'AMOUR PG, et al: MR imaging of central pontine myelinolysis. *J Comput Assist Tomogr* 11:724–726, 1987.

ROSENBLOOM S, BUCHHOLZ D, KUMAR AJ, et al: Evolution of central pontine myelinolysis on CT. *AJNR* 5:110–112, 1984.

RUNGE VM, PRICE AC, KIRSHNER HS, ALLEN JH, PARTAIN CL, JAMES AE: The evaluation of multiple sclerosis by magnetic resonance imaging. *Radiographics* 6(2):203–212, 1986.

SAFADARI GH, FUENTES JM, DUBOIS JB: Radiation necrosis of the brain: Time of onset and incidence related to total dose and fractionation of radiation. *Neuroradiology* 27:44–47, 1985.

SALOMON A, YEATES AE, BURGER PC, HEINTZ ER: Subcortical arteriosclerotic encephalopathy: Brain stem findings with MR imaging. *Radiology* 165:624–529, 1987.

SCHAUMBURG HH, POWERS JM, RAINE CS, SUZUKI K, RICHARDSON EP: Adrenoleukodystrophy: A clinical and pathological study of 17 cases. *Arch Neurol* 32:577–591, 1975.

SCHELLINGER D, GRANT EG, RICHARDSON JD: Neonatal leukoencephalopathy: A common form of cerebral ischemia. *Radiographics* 5(2):221–242, 1985.

SCHUMACHER GA: The demyelinating diseases, in Baker AB (ed): *Clinical Neurology.* New York, Harper Row, 1965, pp 1226–1284.

SEARS SE, McCAMMON A, BIGELOW R, HAYMAN LA: Maximizing the harvest of contrast-enhancing lesions in multiple sclerosis. *Neurology* 32:815–820, 1982.

SEITELBERGER F: Pelizaeus-Merzbacher disease, in Vinken PJ, Bruyn GW (eds): *Handbook of Clinical Neurology, vol X.* New York, Elsevier-North Holland, 1970, pp 150–202.

SHABAS D, GERARD G, CUNHA B, et al: MRI appearance of AIDS subacute encephalopathy. *Comput Radiol* 11(2):69–73, 1987.

SHAW AM, HARPER ME, HAHN BH, et al: HTLV-III infection in brains of children and adults with AIDS encephalopathy. *Science* 27:177–181, 1985.

SHELDON J, SIDDHARTHAN R, TOBIAS J, et al: MR imaging of multiple sclerosis: Comparison with clinical and CT examinations in 74 patients. *AJR* 145:957–964, 1985.

SHELINE GE, WARA WM, SMITH V: Therapeutic irradiation and brain injury. *Int J Radiat Oncol Biol Phys* 6:1215–1228, 1980*a.*

SHELINE GE: Irradiation injury of the human brain: A review of clinical experience, in Gilbert HA, Kagan AR (eds): *Radiation Damage to the Nervous System.* New York, Raven Press, 1980*b,* pp 39–58.

SHIPPER HIU, SEIDEL D: CT in late onset metachromatic leukodystrophy. *Neuroradiology* 26:398–404, 1984.

SIBLEY WA, BAMFORD CR, LAGUNDA JF: Anamnestic studies in multiple sclerosis: A relationship between familial multiple sclerosis and neoplasia. *Neurology* 28:125–132, 1978.

SIBLEY WA, BAMFORD CR, CLARK K: Triggering factors in multiple sclerosis, in Poser CM (ed): *The Diagnosis of Multiple Sclerosis.* New York, Thieme Stratton, 1984, pp 14–24.

SIBLEY WA, POSER CM, ALTER M: Demyelinating diseases, in Rowland LP (ed): *Merritt's Textbook of Neurology,* 8th ed. Philadelphia, Lea & Febiger, 1989, pp 741–765.

SIDDHARTHAN R, SHEREMATA WA, DEFORTUNA S, SAZANT A, SHELDON J: Multiple sclerosis (M.S.): Correlation of magnetic resonance imaging with cerebrospinal fluid findings. *Neurology* 35(Suppl 1):104, 1985.

SMITH CR, SIMA AAF, SALIT IE, GENTILI F: Progressive multifocal leukoencephalopathy: Failure of cytarabine therapy. *Neurology* 32:200–203, 1982.

SNIDER WD, SIMPSON DM, NIELSEN S, et al: Neurological complications of adult immune deficiency syndrome: Analysis of 50 patients. *Ann Neurol* 14:403–418, 1983.

STEERE AC, BRODERICK TF, MALAWISTA SE: Erythema chronicum migrans and Lyme arthritis: Epidemiology evidence for a tick vector. *Am J Epidemiol* 108:312–321, 1978.

STERNS RH, RIGGS JE, SCHOCHET SS Jr: Osmotic demyelination syndrome following correction of hyponatremia. *N Engl J Med* 314:1535–1542, 1986.

STEWART JM, HOUSER OW, BAKER HL, et al: Magnetic resonance imaging and clinical relationships in multiple sclerosis. *Mayo Clin Proc* 62:174–184, 1987.

SUZUKI K, SUZUKI Y: Galactosylceramide lipidosis: Globoid cell leukodystrophy (Krabbe's disease), in Stanbury JB, Wyngaarden JB, Fredrikson DS, Goldstein JL, Brown MS (eds): *The Metabolic Basis of Inherited Diseases.* New York, McGraw-Hill, 1978, pp 747–769.

SZE G, DeARMOND S, BRANT-ZAWADZKI M, et al: "Abnormal" MR foci anterior to the frontal horn. *AJNR* 6:467–468, 1985.

SZTENCEL J, BALERIAUX D, BORENSTEIN S, et al: Central pontine myelinolysis: Correlation between CT and electrophysiologic data. *AJNR* 4:529–530, 1983.

TAKASHIMA S, TANAKA K: Development of cerebrovascular architecture and its relationship to periventricular leukomalacia. *Arch Neurol* 35:11–16, 1978.

TOMONAGA BM, YAMAMOUCHI H, TOHGI H, KAMEYAMA M: Clinical pathologic study of progressive subcortical vascular encephalopathy (Binswanger type) of the elderly. *J Am Geriatr Soc* 30(8):524–529, 1982.

TROIANO R, HAFSTEIN M, RUDERMAN M, DOWLING P, COOK S: Effect of high-dose intravenous steroid administration on contrast-enhancing computed tomographic scan lesions in multiple sclerosis. *Ann Neurol* 15:257–263, 1984.

TROMMER BL, NAIDICH TP, DEL CENTO MC, et al: Noninvasive CT diagnosis of infantile Alexander's disease: Pathologic correlation. *J Comput Assist Tomogr* 7:509–512, 1983.

TSURUDA JS, KORTMAN KE, BRADLEY WG: Radiation effects on cerebral white matter: MR evaluation. *AJNR* 8:431–437, 1987.

UHLENBROCK D, SEIDEL D, GEHLEN W, et al: MR imaging in multiple sclerosis: Comparison with clinical, CSF, and visual evoked potential findings. *AJNR* 9:59–67, 1988.

VALK J, VAN DER KNAAP MS: *Magnetic Resonance of Myelin, Meylination, and Myelin Disorders.* New York, Springer-Verlag, 1989.

VAN DER KNAPP MS, VALK J: The reflection of histology in MR imaging of Pelizaeus-Merzbacher disease. *AJNR* 10:99–103, 1989.

WALKER DL: Progressive multifocal leukoencephalopathy, in Vinken J, Bruyn GW, Klawans HL (eds): *Handbook of Clinical Neurology,* vol 7. New York, Elsevier, 1985, pp 503–524.

WEINER LP, HERNDON RM, NARAYAN O, et al: Isolation of virus related to SV40 from patients with progressive multifocal leukoencephalopathy. *N Engl J Med* 286(8):385–390, 1972.

WEINSTEIN MA, LEDERMAN RJ, ROTHNER AD, DUCHESNEAU PM, NORMAN D: Interval computed tomography in multiple sclerosis. *Radiology* 129:689–694, 1978.

WEINSTEIN MA: CT and MR of demyelinating and degenerative disease, in *Basic Review and Recent Advances in Neuroradiology* (syllabus). Boston: Department of Radiology, Harvard Medical School, and Eye and Ear Infirmary, Massachusetts General Hospital, October 3, 1984, pp 1–11.

WITTER B, DEBUCH H, KLEIN H: Lipid investigation of central and peripheral nervous system myelin in connatal Pelizaeus Merzbacher disease. *J Neurochem* 34:957–962, 1980.

WRIGHT GDS, PATEL MK, MIKEL J: An adult onset metachromatic leukodystrophy with dominant inheritance and normal arysulphatase A levels. *J Neurol Sci* 87:153–166, 1988.

YOUNG IR, HALL AS, PALLIS CA, et al: Nuclear magnetic resonance imaging of the brain in multiple sclerosis. *Lancet* ii:1063–1066, 1981.

YOUNG IR, RANDELL CP, KAPLAN PW, JAMES A, BYDDER GM, STEINER RE: Nuclear magnetic resonance (NMR) imaging in white matter disease of the brain using spin-echo sequences. *J Comput Assist Tomogr* 7:290–294, 1983.

YUFE RS, HYDE ML, TERBRUGGE K: Auditory evoked responses and computerized tomography in central pontine myelinolysis. *Can J Neurol Sci* 7:297–300, 1980.

ZIMMERMAN RD, FLEMING CA, LEE BCP, et al: Perventricular hyperintensity as seen by magnetic resonance: Prevalence and significance. *AJNR* 7:13–20, 1986.

INDEX

Page numbers in *italics* indicate material in figures and tables.